MW00563015

# INTERNATIONAL LAW

## CASES AND MATERIALS

## Third Edition

By

**Louis Henkin**
*University Professor Emeritus,*
*Columbia University, School of Law*

**Richard Crawford Pugh**
*Distinguished Professor of Law,*
*University of San Diego, School of Law*

**Oscar Schachter**
*Hamilton Fish Professor Emeritus of*
*International Law and Diplomacy,*
*Columbia University, School of Law*

**Hans Smit**
*Stanley H. Fuld Professor of Law, Director,*
*Parker School of Foreign and Comparative Law,*
*Columbia University, School of Law*

AMERICAN CASEBOOK SERIES®

WEST PUBLISHING CO.
ST. PAUL, MINN., 1993

610 Opperman Drive
P.O. Box 64526
St. Paul, MN 55164-0526
1-800-328-9352



**Library of Congress Cataloging-in-Publication Data**

International law : cases and materials. — 3rd ed. / by Louis Henkin ... [et al.]
p. cm. — (American casebook series)
Includes index.
ISBN 0-314-02272-4
1. International law—Cases. I. Henkin, Louis. II. Series.
JX68.I498 1993
341'.0268—dc20 93-11981
CIP

**ISBN** 0-314-02272-4

(H. P. S. & S.) Int'l Law, 3rd Ed. ACB
1st Reprint-1994

# Preface to the Third Edition

This edition renews and enriches our "classical" casebook.

The years since the previous edition was published have witnessed radical transformations in the international political system, with corresponding change—of course—in international law and institutions. It seems timely, therefore, to make explicit the political character and context of international law and to place it up front: Chapter One, page one. The demise of international Communism has mooted the significance of Marxist–Leninist ideology and of ideological conflict for international law; the dissolution of the Soviet Empire and the dismemberment of the Soviet Union itself have required rethinking the significance of the U.S.S.R.'s contribution, and that of its scholars, to international law. Time has also relegated the end of colonialism to history and has rendered the first wave of "the new states" less new. (A new group of states took their seats in the United Nations during 1992: Armenia, Azerbaijan, Bosnia-Herzegovina, Croatia, Georgia, Kazakhstan, Kyrgyzstan, Moldova, San Marino, Slovenia, Tajikistan, Turkmenistan and Uzbekistan). We have had to ponder and to reflect the changed significance, with the end of bipolarism, of the "Third World" and of "non-alignment" for the international system and therefore for international law and institutions.

The changed world order has persuaded us to reexamine and to reconstruct. Notably, the Chapter on the Law of Force has been reconceived and updated to attend to the implications of the Gulf War and United Nations involvement in Somalia, and in Yugoslavia, including the rebirth of collective security and the revival of the United Nations Security Council.

The Third Edition also reflects other, less dramatic but no less important developments in and because of the changed world order—other transformative developments that have prompted us to reorder, replace and update. A heightened sense of danger for the world environment has energized the pursuit of stronger international and regional norms and institutions. The international system for trade and finance is in trouble and in flux. There have been new developments in the law of human rights and some further thoughts on the 1982 Convention on the Law of the Sea. Collective bodies, such as the North Atlantic Treaty Organization (NATO) and the enlarged Conference on Security and Cooperation in Europe (the CSCE, deriving from the 1975 Helsinki Accords), have been pursuing new roles; the European Community is changing and continues its uncertain quest for greater political integration. The Foreign Relations Law of the United States now includes cases on international crime control, materials on treaty interpretation, and more on Presidential War Powers.

The Third Edition continues to reflect our aspiration to enable teaching international law in the "grand" classical tradition, seeking to reflect, as does international law, essential continuity with fresh appreciation and even some radical change. In pursuing that aim we profited from our own experience in teaching from the previous editions, and from suggestions by colleagues. The result we believe is a casebook tailored and fit for the changed world order at the end of the Twentieth Century.

L.H.
R.C.P.
O.S.
H.S.

# Documents

The editors of this book have compiled a collection of documents under the title "International Law, Basic Documents," published by the same publisher, for use in connection with this book.

In most cases when this book refers to an instrument, such as a treaty or United Nations resolution, or to specific articles or parts thereof, the reader will find the original text in "International Law, Basic Documents."

Of course, the reader may also find such instruments in original sources or in other collections of documents.

*

# Abbreviations

| | |
|---|---|
| A.F.D.I. or Ann. Français | Annuaire Français de Droit International |
| A.J.I.L. | American Journal of International Law |
| Ann. de l'Institut de Droit Int. | Annuaire de l'Institut de Droit International |
| Ann. Dig. | Annual Digest |
| A.S.I.L. Proc. | American Society of International Law Proceedings |
| Brit. Y.B.I.L. or Brit. Y.B. Int'l Law | British Yearbook of International Law |
| E.S.C. Res. | Economic and Social Council Resolution |
| E.S.C.O.R. | United Nations Economic and Social Council Official Records |
| G.A.O.R. | United Nations General Assembly Official Records |
| G.A. Res. | United Nations General Assembly Resolution |
| Gr. Brit. T.S. | Great Britain Treaty Series |
| Hackworth | Hackworth, Digest of International Law (1940–44) |
| Hyde | Hyde, International Law Chiefly as Interpreted and Applied by the United States (2nd ed. 1945) |
| Hudson | Hudson, International Legislation |
| I.C.A.O. Doc. | International Civil Aviation Organization Document |
| I.L.C.Rep. | International Law Commission Reports |
| I.C.J. | International Court of Justice Reports |
| I.C.L.Q. | International and Comparative Law Quarterly |
| I.L.R. | International Law Reports |
| I.L.M. or Int'l Leg. Mat'ls | International Legal Materials |
| L.N.T.S. | League of Nations Treaty Series |
| Malloy | Malloy, Treaties, Conventions, International Acts, Protocols and Agreements Between the United States of America and Other Powers (1910–38) |

| | |
|---|---|
| O'Connell | O'Connell, International Law (2nd ed. 1970) |
| Oppenheim | Oppenheim, International Law, vol. 1 (9th ed. Jennings and Watts 1992), vol. 2 (7th ed. Lauterpacht 1952) |
| P.C.I.J. | Permanent Court of International Justice Reports |
| Rec. des Cours | Recueil des Cours Academie de Droit International |
| Restatement (Revised) | Restatement of the Foreign Relations Law of the United States (Revised) (1986) |
| Restatement (Second) 1965 | Restatement, Second, Foreign Relations Law of the United States (1965) |
| S.C.O.R. | United Nations Security Council Official Records |
| S.C. Res. | United Nations Security Council Resolution |
| State Dept. Bull. | State Department Bulletin |
| Stat. | Statutes at Large, United States |
| T.D.O.R. | United Nations Trade and Development Board Official Records |
| T.I.A.S. | Treaty and Other International Act Series |
| U.N.C.I.O. | United Nations Conference on International Organization |
| U.N.Doc. | United Nations Document |
| U.N.R.I.A.A. or U.N. Rep. Int'l Arb. Awards | United Nations Reports of International Arbitration Awards |
| U.N.T.S. | United Nations Treaty Series |
| U.S.C.A. | United States Code Annotated |
| U.S.G.A.O. | United States General Accounting Office |
| U.S.T. | United States Treaties and Other International Agreements |
| Whiteman | Whiteman, Digest of International Law (1963–73) |
| Yb.I.L.C. | Yearbook of the International Law Commission |

# Acknowledgements

We acknowledge and are indebted to a large number of individuals who generously contributed their time and effort to make our Third Edition possible. We naturally include those people who assisted in the previous editions.

In the preparation of this edition we would like to extend special thanks and appreciation to Donald K. Anton, Esq. and Alexander L. W. Snyder, Columbia Law School Class of 1994, for their exceptional dedication and untiring efforts in conceptualizing, researching, and drafting, as well as coordinating the compilation of the manuscript of the new edition.

We would also like to extend our appreciation to the following present and former students at Columbia Law School for their research assistance: Wayne K. Morgan, LL.M. Class of 1992; Penelope E. Mathew, LL.M. Class of 1993 and J.S.D. Candidate; Laura W. Brill, J.D. Class of 1994; Mark N. Mazda, J.D. Class of 1995; Mark D. Selwyn, J.D. Class of 1993; and Gretchen Kindel and Nancy Poirier at the University of San Diego School of Law, J.D. Class of 1993.

We would like to thank Anna Brailovsky, Liz Martin, Lynn Elliott, Brenda Fox, Tracy Brooks and Julie Ebreck for their dedication and assistance with the manuscript.

We extend our warm thanks, for reference assistance readily and frequently given by James L. Hoover, Professor of Law and Law Librarian; Kent McKeever, Associate Librarian; Marilyn Johnson Raisch, Foreign and Comparative Law Librarian; and Antonio Ramírez, Assistant Foreign and Comparative Law Librarian. We also single out for thanks the following members of the library staff: Alan Kennis, Hamid Mubarak, Monté Pagan, and Richard Markwald.

Finally, we acknowledge our indebtedness to the following authors and publishers who granted us permission to reprint copyrighted material:

Allanheld, Osumun & Co., and the American Society of International Law, for permission to reprint from Buergenthal, ed., Human Rights, International Law and the Helsinki Accord (1977).

George Allen and Unwin, Ltd., for permission to reprint from Akehurst, A Modern Introduction to International Law (4th ed. 1984).

The American Assembly, for permission to reprint from Gullion, ed., The Uses of The Seas (1968).

The American Law Institute, for permission to reprint from the Model Penal Code (Proposed Official Draft, 1962), copyrighted © 1962; Pugh, Legal Protection of International Transactions Against Non-Commercial Risks, in Surrey and Shaw, A Lawyer's Guide to International Business Transactions 301, copyrighted © 1963; and The Restatement of the Law, Second, Foreign Relations Law of the United States (1965), copyrighted © 1965 and The Restatement of the Foreign Relations Law of the United States (Revised), copyrighted © 1986; Restatement of the Foreign Relations Law of the United States (Third), copyrighted © 1987.

The American Society of International Law, for permission to reprint from the following articles appearing in the American Journal of International Law: Acheson Remarks, A.J.I.L. Proceedings (1963) Vol. 57; Briggs, Unilateral Denunciation of Treaties: The Vienna Convention and the International Court of Justice, 68 A.J.I.L. 51 (1974); Charlesworth, Chinkin & Wright, Feminist Approaches to International Law, 85 A.J.I.L. 613 (1991); Friedmann, United States Policy and the Crisis of International Law, 59 A.J.I.L. 857 (1965); International Military Tribunal (Nuremberg) Judgement and Sentences, 41 A.J.I.L. 172 (1946); Joyner, Reflections on the Lawfulness of Invasion, 78 A.J.I.L. 131 (1984); Kearney and Dalton, The Treaty on Treaties, 64 A.J.I.L. 495 (1970); McDougal, The Soviet-Cuban Quarantine and Self-Defense, 57 A.J.I.L. 597 (1963); Meeker, Defensive Quarantine and the Law, 57 A.J.I.L. 515 (1963); Moore, Grenada and the International Double Standard, 78 A.J.I.L. 145 (1984); Mullerson, Sources of International Law: New Tendencies in Soviet Thinking, 83 A.J.I.L. 494 (1989); Opinions 9 and 10 of the Yugoslavia Arbitration Commission, from 31 I.L.M. 1523–26; Bilateral Investment Treaty Between United States and Turkey, from 25 I.L.M. 92–95; Peterson, Recognition of Governments Should Not Be Abolished, 77 A.J.I.L. 32 (1983); Reisman, Coercion and Self-Determination: Constructing Charter Article 2(4), 78 A.J.I.L. 642 (1984); Reisman, International Law after the Cold War, 84 A.J.I.L. 859 (1990); Rush, Statement, 68 A.J.I.L. 736 (1974); Schachter, The Twilight Existence of Nonbinding International Agreements, 71 A.J.I.L. 296 (1977); Schachter, The Legality of Pro-Democratic Invasion, 78 A.J.I.L. 645 (1984); Schachter, United Nations Law in the Gulf Conflict, 85 A.J.I.L. 542 (1991); Sohn, The Security Council's Role in the Settlement of International Disputes, 78 A.J.I.L. 402 (1984); Sohn & Baxter, Responsibility of States for Injuries to the Economic Interests of Aliens, 55 A.J.I.L. 545 (1961); and for permission to reprint from International Legal Materials: Indonesian Oil Decrees, 4 Int'l Leg. Mat'ls 440 (1965); Texaco Overseas Petroleum, et al. v. Libyan Arab Republic, Int'l Arbitral Award, 17 Int'l Leg. Mat'ls 1 (1978); Weil, Toward Relative Normativity in International Law, 77 A.J.I.L. 413 (1983).

The American Society of International Law, for permission to reprint from the following articles from Law and Force in the New International Order (Damrosch & Scheffer, eds. 1991): Chayes, The Use of Force in the Persian Gulf; Gardner, Commentary on the Law of Self-Defense; Schachter, Authorized Uses of Force by the United Nations and Regional Organizations; Scheffer, Commentary on Collective Security.

Boston University International Law Journal, for permission to reprint from Davis, International Management of Cetaceans Under the New Law of the Sea Convention, 3 Bost. U.Int'l L.J. 484–88 (1985).

The British Institute of International and Comparative Law, for permission to reprint from the following articles in the International and Comparative Law Quarterly: Seyersted, Jurisdiction over Organs and Officials of States, The Holy See and Intergovernmental Organizations, 14 I.C.L.Q. 31 (1965); Toth, The Individual & European Law, 24 I.C.L.Q. 659 (1975).

Buttersworth & Company (Publishers) Ltd., for permission to reprint from the following materials from the International Law Reports: ARAMCO Arbitration Award, 27 Int'l L.Rep. 117 (1958); and Dralle v. Republic of Czechoslovakia, [1950] Int'l L.Rep. 155.

The University of California Press, for permission to reprint from Kelsen, Pure Theory of Law (Knight trans. 1967).

The Cambridge University Press, for permission to reprint from Lauterpacht, International Law: Collected Papers, Vol. 1 (1970); Lauterpacht, Recognition in International Law (1947).

The Canadian Institute of International Affairs, for permission to reprint from Friedmann, The Role of International Law in the Conduct of International Affairs, 20 International Journal 158 (1965).

The Cardozo Law Review, for permission to reprint from Henkin, International Human Rights as "Rights," 1 Cardozo L.Rev. 446 (1979).

The Carnegie Endowment for International Peace, for permission to reprint from Lissitzyn, The International Court of Justice (1951); Sorensen, ed., The Manual of Public International Law (1968).

Chinese Yearbook of International Law, for permission to reprint from Chui, Some Problems Concerning the Delimitation of the Maritime Boundary Between the Republic of China and the Philippines, 3 Chinese Y.B. Int'l L. 10–12 (1983).

The Clarendon Press, Oxford, England, for permission to reprint from Brierly, The Law of Nations (6th ed. Waldock, 1963); Brownlie, International Law and the Use of Force by States (1963); Brownlie, Principles of Public International Law (2d ed. 1973); Intervention in World Politics (1984); Hart, The Concept of Law (Bull, ed. 1961); Mann, International Delinquencies Before Municipal Courts in Studies in International Law (1973).

The Columbia Journal of Transnational Law, for permission to reprint from Henkin, Act of State Today: Recollections In Tranquility, 6 Colum.J. Transnat'l L. 175 (1967).

The Columbia University General Education Seminar, for permission to reprint from Henkin, The Internationalization of Human Rights, Proceedings of General Education Seminar, Vol. 6, No. 1 (Fall, 1977).

The Columbia University Press, for permission to reprint from Carlston, The Process of International Arbitration (1946); Fatouros, Government Guarantees to Foreign Investors (1962); Friedmann, The Changing Structure of International Law (1964); Goodrich, Hambro & Simons, Charter of the United Nations 49 (3rd ed. 1969); Henkin, How Nations Behave (2d ed. 1979); Henkin, The Age of Rights (1991); The International Bill of Rights: The Covenant on Civil and Political Rights (Henkin, ed. 1981).

The Council of Europe, for permission to reprint from What is the Council of Europe Doing to Protect Human Rights? (1977).

Council on Foreign Relations Press, for permission to reprint from Boutros-Ghali, Empowering the United Nations, 71 Foreign Affairs 89 (Winter 1992–93); Henkin, The Use of Force: Law and U.S. Policy 37, in Right v. Might: International Law and the Use of Force (2nd ed. 1991).

Duke Law Journal, for permission to reprint from Charney, Transnational Corporations and Developing Public International Law, 48 Duke L.J. 748 (1985).

The Foundation Press, for permission to reprint from Henkin, Foreign Affairs and the Constitution (2d ed. 1972).

Gower Publishing Company, for permission to reprint from McCoubrey, International Humanitarian Law: The Regulation of Armed Conflicts 1–4 (1990).

Greenwood Press, for permission to reprint from Vasak, International Dimensions of Human Rights (1982).

Harvard International Law Journal Association, for permission to reprint from Norton, Between the Ideology and the Reality, Vol. 17 (1976).

Harvard Law Review Association, for permission to reprint from Henkin, The Constitution and United States Sovereignty: A Century of *Chinese Exclusion* and its Progeny, 100 Harv.L.Rev. 853 (1987).

The Harvard University Press, for permission to reprint from Tunkin, Theory of International Law (Butler trans., 1974).

The International Finance Corporation, for permission to reprint from International Finance Corporation 1992 Annual Report.

The International Law Association, for permission to reprint from The Helsinki Rules on the Uses of the Waters of International Rivers, in International Law Association, Report of the Fifty-Second Conference, Helsinki, 1966.

The International Lawyer, for permission to reprint from Shihata, The Multilateral Investment Guarantee Agency, Vol. 20 (1986).

The Journal of Air Law and Commerce (Northwestern University School of Law), for special permission to reprint from Lissitzyn, The Legal Status of Executive Agreements on Air Transportation, 17 Journal of Air Law and Commerce 436 (1950).

Journal of International Affairs, for permission to reprint from Schachter, The Emergence of International Environmental Law, [1990] Journal of International Affairs 457.

Kansinoikeus Ius Gentium, for permission to reprint from Koskenniemi, Sovereignty: Prolegomena to a Study of International Law as Discourse, 4 Kansinoikeus Ius Gentium 71 (nos. 1–2, 1987).

Kluwer Academic Publishers and Académie de Droit International, for permission to reprint from, Dupuy & Rémond-Gouilloud, The Preservation of the Marine Environment, in 2 A Handbook on the New Law of the Sea 1151–52 (Dupuy, ed. 1991).

Alfred A. Knopf, Inc., for permission to reprint from Morgenthau, Politics among Nations (4th ed. 1967); and Morgenthau & Thompson, Politics among Nations (6th ed. 1985).

Min-Chuan Ku, for permission to reprint from Ku, A Comprehensive Handbook of the United Nations, Vol. 1 (1978), Vol. 2 (1979).

Little, Brown and Company, for permission to reprint from Hyde, International Law Chiefly as Interpreted and Applied by the United States (2d ed. revised 1945).

Longman Group UK Ltd., for permission to reprint from Oppenheim's International Law (Jennings & Watts, eds. 1992).

Pierre Lortie, for permission to reprint from Lortie, Economic Integration and the Law of GATT (1975).

The David McKay Company, Inc., for permission to reprint from Oppenheim, International Law, Vol. 1 (8th ed. Lauterpacht 1955), Vol. 2 (7th ed. Lauterpacht 1952).

The Macmillan Company, for permission to reprint from Jessup, A Modern Law of Nations (1948); Manning, The Nature of International Society (1962).

The Maitland Publications Proprietary, Ltd., for permission to reprint from Stone, Legal Controls of International Conflict (1959). U.S. edition out of print. Copies available from Maitland Publications Pty. Ltd., 65 York Street, Sydney, N.S.W. 2000, Australia.

The Manchester University Press, and Oceana Publications, Inc., for permission to reprint from The Vienna Convention on the Law of Treaties (1973).

The Michigan Law Review, for permission to reprint from Henkin, International Law as Law in the United States, 82 Mich.L.Rev. 1555 (1984); Schachter, The Right of States to Use Armed Force, 82 Mich.L.Rev. 1620 (1984).

Michigan Yearbook of International Law, for permission to reprint from Wolf, Humanitarian Intervention, IX Michigan Yearbook of International Legal Studies 339 (1988).

The Modern Law Review, for permission to reprint from Fitzmaurice, The Foundations of the Authority of International Law and the Problem of Enforcement, 19 Modern Law Review 1 (1956).

Martinus Nihoff, The Hague, The Netherlands, for permission to reprint from Cot & Boniface, Disarmament and Arms Control, in International Law: Achievements and Prospects 811 (Bedjaoi, ed. 1991); Henkin, International Law: Politics, Values and Functions—General Course on Public International Law, 216 Recueil des Cours 9 (1989–IV); Macdonald & Johnson, eds., The Structure and Process of International Law (1984); Schachter, International Law in Theory and Practice (1991); Schachter, International Law in Theory and Practice: General Course in Public International Law, 178 Recueil des Cours 9 (1982–V).

Nomos Verlagsgesellschaft, for permission to reprint from Kennedy, International Legal Structures (1987).

Oceana Publications, Inc., for permission to reprint from Lissitzyn, International Law Today and Tomorrow (1965); Raman, ed., Dispute Settlement Through the United Nations (1977); Oceana Publications, Inc., and the Association of the Bar of the City of New York, for permission to reprint from Henkin, Disarmament: The Lawyer's Interest in Disarmament, Proceedings of the Fourth Hammarskjöld Forum (1964).

The Oxford University Press, for permission to reprint from Allot, A New Order for a New World (1990); Brownlie, Principles of Public International Law (4th ed. 1990); Franck, The Power of Legitimacy Among Nations (1990).

The Oxford University Press, for permission to reprint the following articles published in the British Yearbook of International Law for the Royal

Institute of International Affairs: Akehurst, Custom as a Source of International Law, [1974–1975] Brit. Y.B.I.L. 31 (Vol. 47); Akehurst, The Hierarchy of Sources of International Law, [1974–1975] Brit. Y.B.I.L. 273 (Vol. 47); Bowett, Reservations to Non-Restricted Multilateral Treaties, [1976–1977] Brit. Y.B.I.L. 67 (Vol. 48); Fawcett, Security Council Resolutions on Rhodesia, [1965–1966] Brit. Y.B.I.L. 120 (Vol. 41); Lauterpacht, Sovereignty over Submarine Areas, [1950] Brit. Y.B.I.L. 376 (Vol. 27); Mann, Reflections on a Commercial Law of Nations, [1957] Brit. Y.B.I.L. 20 (Vol. 33); Rama-Montaldo, International Legal Personality and Implied Powers of International Organizations, [1970] Brit. Y.B.I.L. 123 (Vol. 44).

Max Planck Institut für Ausländisches Öffentliches Recht und Völkerrecht, for permission to reprint from Henkin, The International Bill of Rights; The Universal Declaration and the Covenants 6–9, in International Enforcement of Human Rights (Bernhardt & Jolowicz, eds. 1987).

The Political Science Quarterly, for permission to reprint from Henkin, Politics and the Changing Law of the Sea, 89 Pol.Sci.Q. 46 (1974).

Prentice-Hall, Inc., for permission to reprint from Ball, ed., Global Economies: The Political Economy of World Business, copyrighted © 1975, The American Assembly, Columbia University.

The Procedural Aspects of International Law Institute, Inc., for permission to reprint from Brownlie, Humanitarian Intervention; and Lillich, Humanitarian Intervention: A Reply to Dr. Brownlie and a Plea for Constructive Alternatives, both in Law and Civil War in the Modern World (Moore, ed. 1974); and the Institute and the American University Law Review, for permission to reprint from Lillich and Paxman, State Responsibility for Injuries to Aliens Caused by Terrorist Activity, 26 Am.L.Rev. 217 (1976–1977).

Quadrangle Press, for permission to reprint from Taylor, Nuremberg & Vietnam: An American Tragedy (1970).

The Rand Corporation, for permission to reprint from Builder & Graubard, The International Law of Armed Conflict: Implications for the Concept of Assured Destruction (Series in International Security and Arms Control, 1982).

A.W. Sijthoff and Noordhoff Publishing Co., Leyden, The Netherlands, and the Hague Academy of International Law, for permission to reprint the following from Académie de Droit International, Recueil des Cours: Baxter, Treaties and Custom, 129 Rec. des Cours 31 (1970–I); De Arechaga, International Law in the Past Third of a Century, 159 Rec. des Cours 9 (1978–I); Henkin, International Law: Politics, Values and Functions, 216 Rec. des Cours 9 (1989–IV); Lissitzyn, Territorial Entities Other Than Independent States in the Law of Treaties, 125 Rec. des Cours 5 (1968–III); Schachter, International Law in Theory and Practice, 178 Rec. des Cours 21 (1982–V); Waldock, General Course on International Law, 106 Rec. des Cours 5 (1962–II); and A.W. Sijthoff, for permission to reprint from Rosenne, The Law and Practice of the International Court (1965).

Southern Methodist University Press, for permission to reprint from Thomas and Thomas, The Concept of Aggression in International Law (1972).

St. Martin's Press, for permission to reprint from Skubiszewski, Use of Force by States. Collective Security. Law of War and Neutrality, in Manual of Public International Law 739 (Sorensen, ed. 1968).

Stanford University Press, for permission to reprint from Triska and Slusser, The Theory, Law and Policy of Soviet Treaties (1962).

Stevens & Sons, for permission to reprint from Bowett, The Law of International Institutions (4th ed. 1982); O'Connell, International Law (2d ed. 1970); Friedmann, The Changing Structure of International Law (1964).

Taylor & Francis, for permission to reprint from Oxman, Environmental Warfare, 22 Ocean Development and International Law 433 (1991).

Temple University Press, for permission to reprint from Falk, Explorations at the Edge of Time: The Prospects for World Order (1992).

UNESCO, for permission to reprint from Cot & Boniface, Disarmament and Arms Control, in International Law: Achievements and Prospects 811–12 (Bedjaoi, ed. 1991).

Virginia Journal of International Law, for permission to reprint from Schachter, Towards a Theory of International Obligation, 8 Virginia Journal of International Law 300 (1968).

The Virginia Law Review Association, for permission to reprint from Falk, The Adequacy of Contemporary Theories of International Law—Gaps in Legal Thinking, 50 Va.L.Rev. 23 (1964); Fatouros, International Law and the Third World, 50 Va.L.Rev. 783 (1964).

University Press of Virginia, for permission to reprint from Lillich, The Valuation of Nationalized Property in International Law Vol. 3 (1976).

West Publishing Co., for permission to reprint from Jackson, International Economic Relations (1977); Jackson & Davey, Legal Problems of International Economic Relations (2d ed. 1986); Berman, Goebel, Davey & Fox, Cases and Materials on European Community Law 142 (1993).

Westview Press, Inc., for permission to reprint from Law and Force in the New International Order (Damrosch & Scheffer, eds. 1991), Chayes, The Use of Force in the Persian Gulf 3–7; Gardner, Commentary on the Law of Self-Defense; Schachter, Authorized Uses of Force by the United Nations and Regional Organizations 86–88; Scheffer, Commentary on Collective Security 107–08.

Board of Regents of the University of Wisconsin system, for permission to reprint from Goodrich, The Maintenance of International Peace and Security, 19 Int'l Org. 429 (1965).

The World Bank, for permission to reprint from The World Bank and the International Finance Corporation (1985); World Bank 1992 Annual Report.

The Yale Law Journal and Fred B. Rothman & Co., for permission to reprint the following articles from the Yale Law Journal: Falk, International Law and the United States Role in the Vietnam War, 75 Yale Law Journal 1122 (1966).

The Yale University Press, for permission to reprint from McDougal and Feliciano, Law and Minimum World Public Order (1961); and Reisman, Nullity and Revision (1971).

Zeitschrift für Ausländisches Öffentliches Recht und Völkerrecht, for permission to reprint from Wildhaber & Breitenmoser, Law and Municipal Law in Western European Countries, 49 Zeitschrift für Ausländisches Öffentliches Recht und Völkerrecht 163 (1988).

# Introduction to the Study of International Law

Traditionally, international law is seen as the law of the international community of states, principally governing relations among states, the basic units in the world political system for more than 300 years. For more than half a century, however, international law has increasingly dealt with also other entities, including, notably, the individual human rights.

That international law is law made by states to govern relations among them implies important limitations. *Unless states have made them the subject of law between them,* non-governmental international organizations—the Catholic Church, the League of Red Cross Societies, the International Chamber of Commerce, the World Federation of Trade Unions—are not governed by international law. Furthermore, international law does not deal directly with multi-national corporations, conglomerates, or other companies. It does not address other domestic matters that may be of international interest. International law is to be distinguished from national law that governs foreign and other transnational transactions and relations.

From some perspectives, no doubt, these exclusions are artificial. Some have insisted that contemporary international relations, surely, consist of much more than official relations between states or their governments; that even these relations cannot be understood in isolation from other relations involving other actors; and that the law of inter-governmental relations cannot be seen independently of other law governing other transnational relations. For these reasons, some prefer a more comprehensive perspective that would include all the law—national, international or mixed—that applies to all actors whose activities or influences cross state lines.

Certainly, for more than half a century, international law has governed relations between states and other entities and the status, rights, and duties of such entities. Ever-growing numbers of intergovernmental organizations have acquired existence and personality, rights and duties. The end of the Twentieth Century has also witnessed sustained efforts to subject states to the authority of particular intergovernmental organizations, such as the European Economic Community. In addition, international law now protects human rights, and even accords individual human beings independent status and standing before some international bodies. International law also imposes duties on individuals and may bring them to international trial and punishment.

Nevertheless, as the Secretary-General of the United Nations said of the international order in 1992, "the foundation stone . . . is and must remain the state." * For purposes of study and analysis, there are good reasons for maintaining the traditional focus on interstate relations and institutions, even

* Agenda for Peace, U.N. Doc. A/47/277, S/24111 (June 17, 1992), reprinted in, XXXI Int'l Legal Materials 959 (1992).

while recognizing that one must attend to all the other rings in the world circus as well. International law is a conceptually distinct and self-contained system of law, independent of the national systems with which it interacts. It deals with relations which individual states do not effectively govern. (The relation of international law to national law is a question with which each of them must struggle, in different ways for their different purposes. See Chapter 3.) The study of international law in the United States (and this volume too) admix some constitutional and other national laws governing the conduct of foreign relations. For example, the treaty-making powers of the President-and-Senate, and limitations on those powers in favor of States' rights or individual rights, are questions of "Foreign Relations Law of the United States" that may have important international interest and even some international legal relevance. But they are not questions of international law.

International law is a discrete, comprehensive, legal system and the law of an international political order. While international law is therefore best studied with a minimum of confusing excursions into other, related legal domains, in other respects the study of international law might profit from a broader perspective. The governance and the law of the international political order would repay study with the care and the insights devoted to national law and how national societies are governed. Students of law and jurisprudence, of politics, of sociology, or of ideas, would do well to keep ever in mind that—*mutatis mutandis*—one can, and should, ask the same questions, from the same variety of perspectives, about international law as about domestic law or law generally, though the answers might be very different and even the questions themselves might have different significance. (Feminist analysis and "critical legal studies," too, have not overlooked international law).

International law is not a "course"; it is a curriculum. Whether studied under one embracing rubric or spread over many, international law is a comprehensive, many-sided legal system. One can find in it the basic concepts of any legal system—property and tort, injury and remedy, status and contract. It has its own law-making and law-applying procedures. There is international commercial law and anti-trust law, and a law of organizations and corporate bodies. There is law governing "public lands" and common environments, as in outer-space and the deep sea. The "public law" of the international legal system is not yet vast, as was true of the national law of even developed states only a few decades ago; nonetheless, it might well fill several courses in any comprehensive curriculum of international law, including international counterparts of constitutional law, administrative law, legislation, and judicial process. International trade law, the international law of intellectual property, international human rights law, and international environmental law have already earned study in independent courses and in courses combining national and international cases and materials.

Philosophers and other scholars of law can also impose their perspectives and ask their questions about the international legal system. There is a jurisprudence and a sociology of international law, and the beginnings of a criminology. The student of political science can—and should—consider the character of the international political system, its premises and assumptions, and how it is governed; he or she might ask whether there are legislative, executive, and judicial functions, and how they are exercised. He (she) might ask why law is made, and how it is made; whether law is enforced and what mechanisms are used to induce compliance with it; by what institutions is law interpreted, applied, developed; how are disputes settled; what is its system of administration, administrative regulation, law and procedure.

Analogies, and nomenclature, from domestic law are, of course, deceptive, for there are profound differences between domestic societies and international society (itself a metaphor), and between national and international law. But the concepts, the perspectives, even the nomenclature of domestic law, when used with caution and with awareness of the differences, can be directed at the international system as well. A comprehensive perspective on international law like that which is commonly applied to domestic law would help explain international law and render defensive, apologetic justifications for studying it supererogatory.

*

# Historical Introduction*

---

Human history has long known tribes and peoples, inhabiting defined territories, governed by chiefs or princes, and interacting with each other in a manner requiring primitive forms of diplomatic relations and covenants of peace or alliances for war. These relations between peoples or princes, however, were not governed by any agreed, authoritative principles or rules. At various times, moreover, most of the peoples of the known world were part of large empires and relations between them were subject to an imperial, "domestic" government and law. Empire, actual or potential, was also sometimes supported by an ideology that claimed universal authority over all peoples, or otherwise rejected the independence and equality of nations or any principles governing relations between them other than imperial law.

Thus, classical Chinese philosophy, as formulated by Confucius in the 6th Century B.C., regarded the ruler of China as the "Son of Heaven," who governs the universe as a righteous ruler. From this conception—often greatly at variance with the division of China into many rival kingdoms and factions—developed a notion that frequently shaped Chinese attitudes toward international relations: that Chinese rulers were culturally superior "fathers" or "elder brothers" of other nations or states. This notion served to legitimate Chinese conquest and subjugation of others.

Similarly, Islam, like Christianity in its formative phase, was a crusading religion and therefore hostile to recognizing the equality and respecting the integrity of non-Islamic nations. For the Moslem jurists, the world was divided into countries under Moslem rule (*dar al Islam*) and the rest of the world (*dar al Harb*).

In medieval Christianity, the Holy Roman Empire claimed universal authority for the Pope as the spiritual, and for the Emperor as the temporal, head of the Christian nations of Europe. Thus, religious and political goals coalesced to legitimatize European efforts to conquer—and then convert—non-Christian peoples around the world. Even among the nations of Europe, as long as the concept of universal authority was ascendant, there was little need to develop rules concerning diplomatic intercourse between sovereign states, principles of territorial sovereignty, jurisdiction, treaty-making, state responsibility, and other aspects of interstate relations that form the bulk of the modern law of nations.

Ancient Judaism, ideologically committed to monotheism, did not in principle accept the equality of polytheistic nations. But Judaism has not been the ideology of a politically independent people for 2000 years until our own day, and Judaism did not develop a universalist political ideology comparable to that of Christianity or Islam.

* See generally Nussbaum, A Concise History of the Law of Nations (rev. ed. 1954); Verzijl, et al., International Law in Historical Perspective, 11 vols. (1968–1992); History of the Law of Nations, 7 Encyclopedia of Public International Law 126–273 (1984).

Universalist ideologies and approaches to international relations were modified in recent centuries. Nation-states of different religions increasingly came into contact with each other and were compelled to deal with each other on a basis of equality and mutual respect for sovereignty. The structure and development of the modern law of nations is intimately connected with the era of sovereign national states dealing with each other as independent units. In a strict sense, therefore, the history of the modern law of nations begins with the emergence of independent nation-states from the ruins of the medieval Holy Roman Empire, and is commonly dated from the Peace of Westphalia (1648).

*Origins of International Law in the Western World before Grotius*

Before the Macedonian conquest, the Greek states never achieved unity; they alternated between peace and war. As a result, the Greeks, in their classical period, developed rules governing relations between the various Greek city-states, rules that more closely parallel the modern system of international law than those of any other early civilization. Any reader of Thucydides' *History of the Peloponnesian War* will detect a modern ring in the reasoning and techniques used by the Greek city-states in diplomatic practices, in treaties of alliance and in certain elementary rules of war. Disputes were sometimes submitted to arbitration. However, relations between Greeks and non-Greeks were not regulated in the same way; the latter were regarded by the Greeks as barbarians, and not as moral or legal equals.

The Roman Empire, which at its height comprised hundreds of different races, tribes and religions, could not acknowledge an international legal system in the modern sense, within the borders of an empire that comprised almost the entire civilized world. Although there were always wars at the borders of the Roman Empire, they gave rise to very few rules or usages. The significance of the Roman contribution to international law lies not in the development of any modern system of interstate legal relations, but rather in the development of *jus gentium*, a system of legal rules governing the relations between Roman citizens and foreigners. The *jus gentium* contained many principles of general equity and "natural law," some of which are similar to certain "general principles of law recognized by civilized nations"—one of the sources of contemporary international law listed in Article 38 of the Statute of the International Court of Justice. But the *jus gentium* was strictly a municipal system of law administered by a Roman magistrate, the *Praetor peregrinus*, as a system parallel to the *jus civile* applicable to relations between Roman citizens.

*The Rise of the National State and the Evolution of International Law*

As the medieval Holy Roman Empire disintegrated, the void was filled by a growing number of separate states, ranging from large nation-states such as England and France to hundreds of smaller kingdoms, dukedoms, principalities and city republics, especially in Germany and Italy. This multiplicity of independent political units spurred the development of a system of interstate relations.

Frederick III, German emperor from 1440 to 1493, was the last of the emperors crowned in Rome by the Pope, but at that time Europe was already divided into a large number of independent states. The collapse of the political, legal and moral authority of the emperors, and the weakening of the ecclesiastical authority of the Pope—greatly accelerated by the Reformation—made it necessary for the newly emerging independent states to develop a system of rules that could govern their mutual relations. For these legal relations, they drew predominantly upon Roman law and canon law. The professional clerks who ran the chancelleries of the newly emerging states and city republics received their training largely in universities such as Bologna, Padua or Paris, where the Renaissance had revived the study of classical civilization and, in particular, the study of Roman law. The system of the Roman law, as codified in Justinian's *Corpus Juris*, dominated the teaching of the so-called "Glossators" at these universities. Justinian's code thus spread its influence over the entire European continent, except for the Scandinavian countries. England remained largely free from the influence of Roman law both in the structure and in the substantive principles of its legal system. Although the legal systems of most of the states of continental Europe were progressively codified and modernized during the 19th and 20th centuries, they are still heavily influenced by Roman law. Some concepts of Roman law have strongly influenced international legal rules, such as those governing the acquisition of title over territory.

However, the division between the civil law world—comprising most of continental Europe, and a large number of non-European states—and the English-speaking, common law world is of relatively little significance in international legal relations. In the first place, canon law, with its essentially Romanistic conceptual framework, had an important influence on many aspects of English law. Second, the growth of international trade from the 8th century onwards led to the development of an international law merchant and, in particular, to various compilations of maritime law which gained increasing international recognition. The most famous of these are the Rhodian laws, a collection of maritime laws probably compiled between the 7th and 9th centuries, and the *Consolato del Mare*, a private collection of rules and customs of maritime law published in Barcelona during the 14th century.

*The Foundations of the Modern Law of Nations*

The several centuries that preceded the Thirty Years' War (1618–1648) were marked in Europe by an intensification of international trade, improvements in navigation and military techniques, and the discovery of many distant lands. These events stimulated the further development of international practices and the emergence of modern conceptions of a law of nations. In northern Europe, the Hanseatic League, founded in the 13th century by certain German city-states and comprising at its height in the early 15th century over 150 trading cities and centers, established a network of commercial and diplomatic relations which contributed substantially to the growth of international usages and customs. In Italy, city-republics, such as Venice, Genoa and Florence, developed the practice of sending resident ambassadors to the capitals of other states, thus giving rise to legal principles governing diplomatic relations and, in particular, the immunities of ambassadors and their staffs. The growth of trade led to an increasing number of commercial treaties. The discovery and subjugation of distant lands and peoples by European explorers and conquerors produced conflicting claims of sovereignty, jurisdiction and rights of trade and navigation, as well as problems of relations with indigenous populations. These difficulties stimulated juristic thought, encouraged resort to Roman law for helpful norms or analogies, and ultimately led to new practices and principles.

By the beginning of the 17th century, the growing complexity of international customs and treaties had given rise to a need for compilation and systematization. At the same time, the growing disorders and sufferings of war, especially of the Thirty Years' War, which laid waste hundreds of towns and villages and inflicted great suffering and privation on peasants and city dwellers, urgently called for some further rules governing the conduct of war. The preoccupation with war is demonstrated by the titles of the two most important treatises of the period: the De Jure Belli Libri Tres *(De Jure Belli)* (1598) by Alberico Gentili (1552–1608), the Italian-born Professor of Civil Law at Oxford, and the classic treatise of Hugo Grotius, De Jure Belli, Ac Pacis Libri Tres *(De Jure Belli Ac Pacis)* (1623–1624), which is generally regarded as the foundation of modern international law.

Although the relative importance of the laws of war and the laws of peace has greatly shifted since the time of Grotius, the latter being by far the more important part of the contemporary law of nations, the importance of these classical treatises, and others, lay in their attempts to systematize the growing number of customs, usages and state practices that had developed over the previous centuries. The details of their systems are not of much contemporary importance, except for the history of international law. However, it is of interest and not without importance or reward to survey the basic ideas underlying the evolution of international law, and of the principal phases of development from the time of Grotius to the present.

*Natural Law Philosophy and the Principles of International Law*

Hugo Grotius (1583–1645), a Dutch jurist, historian, theologian and diplomat, who for the last ten years of his life was the ambassador of Sweden in Paris, is the best known of an important school of international jurists guided by the philosophy of natural law. Among his predecessors in this approach are the Spanish theologians Francisco de Vitoria (probably 1486–1546) and Francisco Suárez (1548–1617). The most important of the later natural law philosophers in international law is the German, Samuel Pufendorf (1632–1694), who occupied a chair for the law of nature and nations at the University of Heidelberg and whose most important work is *De Jure Naturae et Gentium* (1672). Vitoria and Suárez closely follow the natural law philosophy of St. Thomas Aquinas (1225–1274). Aquinas believed that all human laws derive from, and are subordinate to, the law of God. This law is partly reflected in the law of nature, a body of permanent principles grounded in the Divine Order, and partly revealed in the Scripture. By contrast, Grotius is a rationalist who derives the principles of the law of nature from universal reason rather than from divine authority.

Natural law adherents have been divided, throughout the ages, over the positive meaning of the laws of nature in the world of human institutions and actions. Two of the most important principles of the law of nature in Grotius' system of the law of nations are (1) that restitution must be made for a harm done by one party to another and, (2) that promises given, through signature to treaties or otherwise, must be kept (*pacta sunt servanda*). These two principles have been preserved and developed—though with many variations and modifications—throughout subsequent phases of international law, even without the doctrinal support of natural law philosophy. Another basic principle of natural law for Grotius is the freedom of the seas, a thesis expounded in an early work published in 1609, *Mare Liberum*. On this issue, he was strongly opposed by the Englishman John Selden (1584–1645), who in 1635 published a defense of the closed sea Mare Clausum Sive De Dominio Maris *(Mare Clausum)*. The opposing theses illustrates the difficulties of agreement on the concrete applications of natural law where opposing political, economic or social interests are involved. The rejection of the freedom of the seas by Selden corresponded to the interests of England, at that time navally inferior to Holland. The work of Grotius served to vindicate the interests of the Netherlands as a rising maritime and colonial power not only against England, but also against Spain and Portugal, states which claimed the right to control navigation on distant oceans and trade with the East Indies. Later, when England became dominant at sea, it also became an ardent champion of the freedom of the seas—at least in times of peace.[1]

*The Turn to Positivism*

No less important than the emphasis on the law of nature as a basis of the law of nations, is the distinction made by Grotius between the *jus naturale*—to which Grotius devotes his main attention—and the *jus gentium*, the customary law of nations (also called *jus voluntarium, i.e.,* a body of law formed by the conduct and will of nations).

This latter aspect of the law of nations gained increasing significance as adherence to natural law philosophy declined and positivist philosophy gained. Although positivism has a number of different meanings and nuances,[2] its essential meaning in the theory and development of international law is reliance on the practice of states and the conduct of international relations as evidenced by customs or treaties, as against the derivation of norms from basic metaphysical principles. The rise of positivism in Western political and legal theory, especially from the latter part of the 18th century to the early part of the 20th century, corresponds to the steady rise of the national state and its increasingly absolute claims to legal and political supremacy. In the theory of the law of nations the shift from natural law to positivism came gradually, through increasing emphasis on the voluntary law of nations built up by state practice and custom. The most influential exponents of this turn toward positivism were the Englishman Richard Zouche (1590–1660), Professor of Civil Law at Oxford and a Judge of the Admiralty Court, and the Swiss lawyer Emerich de Vattel (1714–1767). Zouche's work, *Juris et Iudicii Fecialis, sive Juris inter Gentes* (1650), has been called the first manual of international law. Without denying the existence of the law of nature, it emphasizes the customary law of nations which he calls *jus inter gentes*. The relegation of natural law to a secondary position is made explicit by Vattel, whose treatise dominated the philosophy of international law from the middle of the 18th century to the end of the First World War. Vattel's treatise, *Le Droit des Gens, ou Principes de la Loi Naturelle, appliqués á la Conduite et aux Affairs des Nations et des Souverains* (1758), although including the *principes de la*

1. In times of war, belligerent naval powers—like Britain in the two world wars of this century—sought to restrict the freedom of the seas, especially neutral trade, to the utmost. Neutral powers stressed the freedom of the seas.

2. See Friedmann, Legal Theory, ch. 21 (5th ed. 1967).

*loi naturelle* in the title, distinguishes between the internal law of nations (law of conscience) and the external law (law of action). While Vattel acknowledges natural law with the assertion that "the law of nations is originally no other than the law of nature applied to nations," he considers all effective international law to have been derived from the will of nations, a presumed consent expressing itself in treaties or customs.

There is an interesting parallel between this theory and Hindu doctrine which distinguishes between *dharmasastras* (principles of right conduct) and *arthasastras* (manuals of international politics). The former corresponds to Vattel's "law of conscience" and the latter to his "law of action." As an Indian scholar has observed, "Hindu conditions presented a comparable picture to that of modern international law." [3] This approach to international law, in part foreshadowed by the German philosopher, Christian Wolff (1679–1754), in effect expresses the philosophy of the modern national state, which recognizes no international obligations other than those to which it has voluntarily agreed through practice hardening into custom, or through specific written consent expressed in treaties or other international agreements.[4]

The period between the publication of Vattel's treatise and the outbreak of the first World War in 1914 was one of phenomenal growth of international law as the diplomatic and commercial relations between nations—almost all of which were Western—multiplied and intensified. The physical volume of international law increased through a continuous growth of custom and treaties, and very few writers continued to assert the supremacy of the law of nature. The bulk of legal and political theory discussed the sovereignty of the state. It was impossible to justify international law under the state sovereignty theory, except as norms voluntarily accepted by sovereign states. Among the best known treatises reconciling the validity of international law with the concept of sovereignty are those of Georg Jellinek (1851–1911), *Allgemeine Rechtslehre* (1905), Heinrich Triepel (1868–1946), *Volkerrecht und Landesrecht* (1899), and Giorgio del Vecchio (1878–1970), *Lezioni di Filosofia del Diritto* (1929). These writers of the early 20th century sought to reconcile the sovereignty of the state with the binding nature of international law in a number of ways: by developing a doctrine of "self-limitation" of the state (Jellinek); by merging agreements made by states into an objective body of conventions which then becomes binding upon states (Triepel); or by half-heartedly reviving the natural law principle that reason demands the mutual recognition of states as equals (del Vecchio). Other positivists rejected this compromise. The English jurist, John Austin (1790–1859), whose *Province of Jurisprudence Determined* (1832) dominated jurisprudential thinking in the common law world in the 19th century, regarded a command emanating from a definite superior and punitive sanction enforcing the command as indispensable elements of law. He therefore relegated international law to the status of "positive morality." On the other hand, ideological approaches to international law were dominated by nationalist philosophy. The most influential of

3. Chacko, India's Contribution to the Field of International Law Concepts, [1958] 93 Rec. des Cours. 122.

4. Among other eighteenth century exponents of the positivist philosophy of international law are the Dutch jurist, Cornelius van Bynkershoek (1673–1743), the German jurist, Johann Jakob Moser (1701–1785), and George Friedrich von Martens (1756–1821).

the nationalist philosophers, the German Georg Wilhelm Friedrich Hegel (1770–1831), in his *Philosophy of Law and State*, constructed an elaborate dialectic system, culminating in the glorification of the national (monarchic) state and denying the validity of international law (for which he substituted "The Passing of the State into World History").

From a different point of departure, Marxist doctrine challenged the national state and its legal system as an instrument of exploitation of the working class by the capitalist bourgeoisie, and called for revolution by the working classes of the world. This, of course, was incompatible with the structure of the law of nations, built on a system of sovereign national states. This philosophy influenced Soviet Communism and was proclaimed by Maoist China, but ceased to be heard in the last half of the 20th century, long before the demise of Soviet Communism.

*The League of Nations and the Evolution of International Law*

The most important aspect of the era of positivism and the supremacy of the national state was the freedom of the state to choose between war and peace. The Hague and Geneva Conventions of the 20th century formulated a number of rules of conduct in warfare, as distinct from principles governing the rightness or wrongness of war. Any state had the legal right to pursue its aims by means of war. This freedom meant the denial of any legally relevant distinction between just and unjust wars. A major break in this orientation came with the establishment of the League of Nations following the First World War.

In condemning "external aggression" against "the territorial integrity and existing political independence" of League members, and in providing for economic and even military sanctions to be imposed by the international community against a state violating its obligations, the League Covenant limited the legal freedom of the sovereign state to pursue war as the ultimate instrument of national policy.

The era of the League of Nations, *i.e.,* the interwar period, was marked by another significant departure in the development of international law. The constitution of the International Labour Organisation, (ILO), in association with the League of Nations, signals the end of an era in which international law was, with few exceptions, confined to the regulation of relations between the states. The ILO was the first permanent international organization concerned with the improvement of labor conditions and social welfare on a world-wide scale. At the same time the establishment of the Permanent Court of International Justice—a counterpart to the limitation on the unrestricted right of states to seek solutions to international disputes by force—was a major attempt to substitute organic methods of peaceful and legal settlement of disputes for the use of force in international affairs. Parallel to the establishment of the Permanent Court, there was a significant growth in the number of bilateral treaties requiring arbitration and other methods of peaceful settlement for disputes between states.

The noble attempt to substitute international authority for national use of force collapsed because of inadequate support from the major nations in times of crisis—notably on the occasion of the Italian invasion of Abyssinia (Ethiopia) in 1935. The efforts of the ILO to achieve international standards for labor and social welfare remained severely limited by continuing divergencies in national standards. The Permanent Court of International Justice played only a marginal role in the affairs of the nations. But the world did not return to the pre-1914 state of affairs after the Second World War. It did not return to a system in which international law included no control in the use of force; nor did it abandon its halting efforts to develop an international organization of mankind for purposes of cooperation. The interwar period also brought the first major threat to the universality of the system of international law, as it had gradually developed since the time of Grotius. The original family of nations, consisting of the older European states, was, at the end of the 18th century, enlarged by the accession of the United States and, a few decades later, by the newly independent states of Latin America. Only a small number of relatively impotent non-Western states joined the family of nations. With the success of the Bolshevik Revolution and the establishment of the Soviet Union, differences of political and social ideology began to challenge the universality of the system in international law. The Soviet Union established itself essentially within the confines of the old Russia as a single major state with a radically different political and social philosophy, but it was compelled to co-exist with other states. To that extent, the Soviet challenge to the traditional system of international law was mitigated. In fact, it was the aggression-minded, fascist states of Germany, Italy and Japan that left the League of Nations and challenged the whole system of international law more immediately than did the Soviet Union.

The impact of ideological and other structural divergencies between states on the universality of the law of nations was to become a matter of major importance in the reorganization and development of international law following the end of World War II.

*International Law since the Second World War*

The creation of the United Nations Organization was a major development in the international political system, although the attempt in the United Nations Charter to reintroduce a system of collective security against aggression was, historically and ideologically, essentially a resumption of the League of Nations effort. However, three major developments following the end of the Second World War signaled a new departure in the evolution of international law. The first was the massive expansion of international organization for cooperative purposes, of which the ILO had been a forerunner. The United Nations, its specialized agencies and other international organizations, some on a universal and others on a regional level, marked the transition of international law from the traditional system of formal rules of mutual respect and abstention to an incipient system of organized, cooperative efforts. Organizations were formed to address a broad range of ills plaguing the world community. Most of these organizations lack executive powers and make only limited encroachments upon the traditional prerogatives of national sovereignty, but their creation confirmed a new pattern of international conduct. Their concerns include international peace and security; monetary control; international development aid; food production and distribution; universal standards of health; international communication and transport; protection of the environment; outer space and the ocean bed; and the international promotion and protection of human rights. This new phase has reflected the needs of an international society where ready communication and increased interdependence, the threat of nuclear annihilation, the growth of population and the increasing threat of exhaustion of the resources of the earth no longer permit an international attitude of laissez-faire. Consequently, international law is no longer predominantly a system of interstate diplomatic norms. It has deeply penetrated the economic and social fabrics of national life.

A second development has been the growing importance of states representing non-Western civilizations as members of the family of nations. This second major development raised the question of the compatibility of the basic cultural values and institutions of these non-Western societies with the system of international law developed by a relatively small group of Western nations. The experience with the new states of Asia and Africa has shown that this development did not fundamentally affect the system of interstate relations. Since their accession to United Nations membership, states such as India (with a long Hindu cultural tradition), Indonesia (with a Moslem background) and the new African nations (most of them emerging from tribal societies), have not adopted attitudes toward interstate relations that differ basically from the traditional attitudes of Western countries. The new states have generally accepted the traditional norms of customary law, participated in international treaties and joined a variety of international organizations. For new states, the necessity of collaboration—to face the problems of statehood and sovereignty in a divided world, the issues of war and peace, the conflicts of political and economic aspirations and the tensions between competition and cooperation in the affairs of mankind—prevailed over the diversity of cultural traditions.

The third development has been the growing gap between the economically developed and the economically less developed countries. It resulted in the creation of new types of international organization specifically designed to deal with the problems arising from the co-existence of rich and poor nations. Included among such bodies are the International Bank for Reconstruction and Development, the International Monetary Fund, and the United Nations Conference on Trade and Development (UNCTAD). The division between developed and less-developed states intensified challenges to certain norms of international law developed by the economically advanced and capital-exporting states of the West, notably for the protection of the economic interests of foreign investors. It created the demands for a New International Economic Order. It led to new arrangements in international law favored by Third World States—such as key elements in a new law of the sea; and for some forms of cooperation for economic development. But the Third World has not succeeded in obtaining significant steps towards a new international economic order. Insufficient commitment by the states of the Third World, and the competition for their favor by East and West, have had the unhappy effect of politicizing and hampering various international programs—as in the protection of human rights. They have given to some Third World states some protection for violations of international law, such as acts of aggression against neighbors, or harboring hijackers or other terrorists.

Even in a divided world living in the ever-present shadow of possible nuclear destruction, the dramatic increase in the number of new states and the appearance of many problems in the economic and the social spheres have accounted for many important new developments in international law, and greatly increased both its scope and complexity. But in a larger historical context this is the continuation and intensification of an evolution that has accompanied the entire history of international law. Many norms of international law, such as the freedom of the seas, the extent of territorial waters and the principles of state responsibility, have always been the product of an adjustment between conflicting national interests.

Perhaps the most significant development of the post-war period, the addition of a new field of international cooperation and organization to the traditional system of the law of nations, has not fulfilled all its promises. But the law of nations has passed from the phase in which it was primarily an international law of co-existence—which characterized it from its birth in the early 17th century to mid-twentieth century—to a phase in which the nations of the world must develop new forms of cooperation and organization to supplement the traditional rules of interstate relations.

*International Law after the Cold War*

During more than four decades following the end of the Second World War, international law reflected and was shaped by ideological conflict and Cold War between nuclear superpowers, as well as the end of colonialism, the multiplication of new nations, and the emergence of the "Third World." Ideological conflict, together with divergent interests between developed and developing states ("North and South"), hampered the growth of international law and frustrated the development of international institutions—notably the United Nations Security Council and the International Court of Justice. Traditional approaches to international law were maintained, uncomfortably, along side special attitudes of the Soviet Union, Communist China, and groupings of the "new states." New developments in the law, such as the birth of the law of human rights, had to "paper over" fundamental differences; institutions to induce compliance with the law were reduced to a very low common denominator. The effort to codify a new law of the sea was frustrated after more than a decade of hard bargaining; that, as of 1993, it remains frustrated is evidence that the end of the Cold War has not eliminated all differences.

However, the end of the Cold War, the demise of international Communism, the dissolution of the Soviet Empire and the fragmentation of the Soviet Union itself, have led to a radically changed world order with new opportunities and challenges for international law. Recent times have seen the law of collective security and the authority of the U.N. Security Council revisited, revived and extended. Civil wars and ethnic hostilities in the wake of political change in Europe, the plight of the Kurds and Somalis, and the attempt to find a Cambodian solution, suggest the need to reexamine the traditional conceptions of state sovereignty and to enlarge the scope of permissible collective intervention for humanitarian assistance and protection of human rights. Political change has revived aspirations for the International Court of Justice and given impetus to proposals to extend its jurisdiction and to modernize its procedures. New needs and new perceptions have enhanced efforts to develop new norms and new institutions to protect the global environment and to reorder economic relations. Regional arrangements that once responded in part to East-West rivalry have broadened their membership and created new functions, as seen in the Conference on Security and Cooperation in Europe (CSCE) and the North Atlantic Treaty Organization (NATO). The European Community continues its quest for political integration.

As the twenty-first century approaches, the problems facing the international community are many and acute. If there is political will, if cooperation among states is pursued, new international law will surely be made in the decades ahead, as an essential tool to give effect to new solutions to new and old human problems.

*

# Summary of Contents

# Table of Contents

*

# Table of Cases

---

**The principal cases are in bold type. Cases cited or discussed in the text are roman type. References are to pages. Cases cited in principal cases and within other quoted materials are not included.**

---

*

# INTERNATIONAL LAW

## CASES AND MATERIALS

## Third Edition

*

# Chapter 1

# THE NATURE OF INTERNATIONAL LAW

## SECTION 1. THE LAW OF THE INTERNATIONAL STATE SYSTEM

### LAW AND POLITICS

*HENKIN, INTERNATIONAL LAW: POLITICS, VALUES AND FUNCTIONS*

216 Rec. des Cours 22 (1989–IV) (footnotes omitted).

First, law is politics. Students of law as well as students of politics are taught to distinguish law from politics. Law is normative, and failure to abide by legal obligations invites legal remedies and brings other legal responses; politics suggests freedom of choice, diplomacy, bargaining, accommodation. In fact, however, the distinction between law and politics is only a part-truth. In a larger, deeper sense, law is politics. Law is made by political actors (not by lawyers), through political procedures, for political ends. The law that emerges is the resultant of political forces; the influences of law on State behaviour are also determined by political forces.

Second, also obvious, is the normative expression of a political system. To appreciate the character of international law and its relation to the international political system, it is helpful to invoke (though with caution) domestic law as an analogue. Domestic (national) law, such as the law of the Netherlands or of Nigeria, is an expression of a domestic political system in a domestic (national) society. A domestic society consists of people, human beings, though in developed societies law has also created artificial juristic persons (e.g., companies, associations). Domestic law is a construct of norms, standards, principles, institutions and procedures that serve the purposes of the society. Law serves, notably, to establish and maintain order and enhance the reliability of expectations; to protect persons, their property and other interests; to promote the welfare of individuals (or of some of them), and to further other societal values—justice, the good life, the good society.

Similarly, analogously, international law is the product of its particular "society", its political system. International law, too, is a construct of norms, standards, principles, institutions and procedures. The purposes of international law, like those of domestic law, are to establish and maintain order and enhance reliable expectations, to protect "persons", their property and other interests, to further other values. But the constituency of the international society is different. The "persons" constituting international society are not individual human beings but political entities, "States", and the society is an inter-State system, a system of States.

### *Notes*

1. In the international system of states, as in its domestic counterpart, politics turn to law to achieve their desired ends and to promote the values of members. One value common to international and domestic political systems is maintaining orderly relations among members. International law fosters the security and autonomy of states, paramount values in a "liberal" system of states; to that end, the law prohibits the threat or use of force by any state against the territorial integrity or political independence of any other state. Increasingly, the law pursues those values through intergovernmental organizations and collective action. International institutions and collective action are instruments also for enhancing cooperation in areas of interdependence such as international environmental protection and in economic matters. For more than a half of a century, the international system has shown commitment to values that transcend purely "state values," notably to human rights, and has developed an impressive corpus of human rights law. Changing values and new means for promoting them cannot help but influence the traditional axioms and assumptions of the state system.

2. Professor Schachter has queried whether we can "propose an ordered framework to help us discuss and comprehend the many factors affecting development of international law." He suggests:

> One possibility is to seek a universal and overriding interest ("value") under which other interests could be subsumed. In the present society of sovereign states, the most promising candidate for that supreme interest would be self-preservation of the state. * * * Self-preservation implies not only security but also a degree of autonomy (that is, freedom of action in regard to its territory and people). It also implies a sufficiency of material means to give the state the capability to meet its need for self-preservation and autonomy. There is no difficulty in seeing how these postulated interests give rise to normative principles that have been formulated as fundamental rights and duties. These duties and rights, focused on the concept of sovereignty, define the basic structure of international society and provide, one might say, the centre of political gravity in a continuously changing social environment. As postulates of the existing international order, they provide a measure of coherence to the multifarious changes of international law. It is important to recognize that their generality—which is essential to their universal and basic character—means that they must have a variable empirical content. Even the "rock-bottom" interest in self-preservation of a state will have a diversity of expression influenced by external events. The "self" that it seeks to preserve is a changing "self." One might say (to

paraphrase a remark of Santayana) that what a state strives to preserve, in preserving itself, is something which it never has been at any particular moment. If a state can be said to have a centre of gravity ("the soul of a nation"), it is almost surely a moving centre, buffeted by outside forces and shifted by internal transformations. Hence the postulates of self-preservation and sovereignty, though they define to some degree our international legal order, are not in themselves sufficient to lead us through the "incorrigibly plural" world of international legal development.

Schachter, The Nature and Process of Legal Development in International Society, in The Structure and Process of International Law: Essays in Legal Philosophy Doctrine and Theory 745, 748 (Macdonald & Johnston, eds. 1983) (footnote omitted).

## LAW AND THE CHANGING INTERNATIONAL ORDER

The commitment of states to the rule of law in international relations, the norms of international law that the system has developed, and the measure of compliance with those norms at different periods and in different contexts, all reflect the major political forces in the system and respond to periodic change in that system. See Henkin, How Nations Behave: Law and Foreign Policy, chapters 1–4 (2d ed. 1979).

International law divides meaningfully between the law before and the law after the Second World War. In 1945, the Allied victory introduced a new order with important changes in international law, represented by the Charter of the United Nations and by the United Nations Organization. Article 1 of the Charter sets forth the major purposes of the United Nations:

1. To maintain international peace and security * * *
2. To develop friendly relations among nations * * *
3. To achieve international co-operation in solving international problems of an economic, social, cultural, or humanitarian character, and in promoting and encouraging respect for human rights and for fundamental freedom for all * * *.

Charter of the United Nations, done San Francisco, June 26, 1945. The Charter established the U.N. Organization with organs empowered to carry out those purposes, principally the General Assembly, the Security Council, the Secretary General, and the International Court of Justice. See Chapters 11, 17 & 18 infra.

Progress towards the realization of U.N. goals was frustrated early. For its first 40 years under the Charter, the international system suffered ideological conflict between two super-powers and their respective allies, armed with increasingly destructive nuclear weapons, and the Cold War, punctuated by only brief periods of détente, put into serious question whether there was any common bona fide commitment to U.N. purposes. The Cold War also underscored ideological differences in attitude towards international law generally, preventing or curtailing the development of new norms, institutions and procedures, and rendering others the subject of only specious agreement or of minimal value.

The decades after the Second World War also saw the transformation of the international system by the end of colonialism and the proliferation of new, mostly poor, less-developed nations, soon emerging as "the Third World." In general, these new states declared themselves ideologically "unaligned" in the Cold War between East and West, but many of them frequently joined with the Communist bloc, both in pressing for normative change that the West resisted and in resisting developments pursued by the West. These new states also pressed their own agenda to establish principles of "economic self-determination," economic and social development, and a new international economic order. See Chapter 17.

In the late 1980's the political cast of the international system changed dramatically. The end of the Cold War, the collapse of the Soviet Empire, the splintering of the U.S.S.R., the demise of international Communism, and a spreading commitment to democracy and to the market economy, have relaxed large international tensions and reordered political and economic alignments. These developments have brought and promise further important changes in international law and institutions. An early example is the renaissance of the United Nations Security Council and the extension of its authority that apparently occurred during the Gulf War in 1991 and in Somalia in 1992. See Chapter 11.

Fragmentation of the U.S.S.R. and Yugoslavia, and realignment of multi-ethnic states, also fueled rivalries leading to repression and irrupting into civil wars, revealing inadequacies in the laws of war, in humanitarian law and the law of human rights, especially in the protection of the rights of minorities. Resulting disorder has challenged established legal norms and the traditional commitment to state autonomy. The desperate plight of the populations in war torn Somalia and Bosnia–Herczegovina evoked clamor for new forms of collective action for humanitarian assistance requiring new interpretations of the U.N. Charter to enlarge the authority of the Security Council and of regional bodies.

Political transformations have freed nations to attend to crying needs—the urgency of controlling the proliferation of weapons of mass destruction and trade in weapons generally; the threat of environmental catastrophe, such as climate change and related causes; the causes of incessant flows of refugees and the rights of refugees; the continuing population explosion; chaos in financial and economic relations; regulation of the movement of people, goods, capital and ideas; and control of drug smuggling, terrorism and other transnational crimes. Political change with important implications for international law continues in different regions, notably in the development and extent of the European Community, the role of NATO and of the Conference on Security and Cooperation in Europe.

### *REISMAN, INTERNATIONAL LAW AFTER THE COLD WAR*

84 A.J.I.L. 859, 860–64 (1990) (footnotes omitted).*

The Cold War deformed the traditional international law that had developed over centuries to facilitate and regulate political, economic and other human relationships across national boundaries. It could hardly have

* Reprinted with permission from the American Sociey of International Law.

been otherwise. For almost half a century, the world lived in a state of neither war nor peace. The independence and rights of choice of smaller states were restricted by larger neighbors in their own interest and, it was often avowed, in the interest of systemic security. The slow effort to centralize authoritative coercive force and to restrict the freedom of unilateral action, the hallmark of civilized political arrangements and the major acknowledged defect of international law, was impeded by an international security system that accorded a veto power to each of the major protagonists. That insured its ineffectiveness. Even the freedom of the oceans, one of the most venerable struts of the international system, which had reserved five-sevenths of the planet as a public highway for exchange, was attenuated to facilitate weapons development. As soon as outer space became accessible, it, too, became part of the military arena.

* * *

Some of the traditional norms and practices of international law that were suppressed during the Cold War can now be revived. As between the two blocs, the distinction between war and peace, each with its own legal regime, will be reinstated. As a consequence, there should be reduced tolerance for, hence conduct of, covert activities. There should be less international tolerance, but not necessarily less national public support, for interventions in so-called critical defense zones under rubrics such as the Brezhnev and Reagan Doctrines. * * * Nevertheless, in terms of a pre-Cold War baseline, one should expect some revival of the norm of national political autonomy.

But national political autonomy will not mean a revival of the older notion of sovereignty in its entirety. Radical changes in conceptions of the legitimacy of national authority, deriving from the international human rights program, have supplanted the older absolute notions. There is much more room for the operation of human rights norms, for the global communications system means that all of the inhabitants of the globe live in a state of electronic simultaneity, if not physical proximity. Instantaneous communication has extended the basis for symbolic, and perhaps physical, interventions into domestic processes in which gross violations of international norms are occurring. But because such humanitarian interventions, as exercises of power, are perforce reflections of the world power process, the arena of their operation will continue to be the internal affairs of smaller and weaker states.

* * *

* * * The international political system is at the threshold of a time of hope. The ending of the Cold War is a major achievement * * *. The need for international law after the Cold War will be more urgent than it was during the conflict. In many ways, what is expected of international law will be greater.

* * * The Challenge to international lawyers and scholars must be to clarify continuously the common interests of this ever-changing community, drawing on historic policies but bearing in mind that the constitutive and institutional arrangements that were devised to achieve them may be no longer pertinent or effective.

### *Notes*

1. The Cold War and "Third World non-alignment" did not prevent significant development of international law. Some new areas of law and new norms that developed during the past 50 years are now firmly established; for example, international human rights law, the fundamentals of international environmental law and the law governing outer space. But the norms and institutions developed during this period often reflected only the lowest common denominator of agreement or concealed differences with minimal success. The "New Economic Order" has not come, but a new economic order is continually in process, an order made up of discrete steps, some small, some larger—some preferences in trade, some debt relief, some financial assistance—within the present liberal free-market system. See Chapter 17. Ten years of negotiation produced a new draft Convention on the Law of the Sea in 1982, though as of 1993 its fate as conventional international law remains uncertain. See Chapter 14.

2. Four decades of Cold War, the end of colonialism and the emergence of the "Third World" left marks on the literature of international law as well as on the law itself and its international institutions. See Lissitzyn, International Law Today and Tomorrow, 4–5, 102–104 (1965). The attitudes of the U.S.S.R., and to a lesser extent of Communist China, influenced the theory and content of international law, and Soviet scholars and writers, notably Professor Grigory Tunkin, were prominent in legal literature. See, e.g., Tunkin, Theory of International Law (Butler, trans. 1974). They were particularly influential in the theory of international law and coexistence and on several sharply controversial issues, such as the meaning of "general principles of law" as a source of international Law. See Chapter 2, p. 104 infra.

For the attitude of the Soviet Union toward international law during the Cold War, see Grzybowski, Soviet Public International Law: Doctrines and Diplomatic Practice (1970); The Soviet Impact on International Law (Baade, ed. 1965); Kulski, The Soviet Interpretation of International Law, 49 A.J.I.L. 518 (1955); Lapenna, The Legal Aspects and Political Significance of the Soviet Concept of Co-existence, 12 I.C.L.Q. 737 (1963); Osakwe, Contemporary Soviet Doctrine on the Juridical Nature of Universal International Organizations, 65 A.J.I.L. 502 (1971); Pechota, The Contemporary Marxist Theory of International Law, 75 A.S.I.L. Proc. 149 (1981); Tunkin, The Contemporary Soviet Theory of International Law, 31 Current Legal Probs. 177 (1978).

Since the end of the Cold War, writers of the former U.S.S.R. have been stressing the need for cooperation in international law. R.A. Mullerson, then Head of the Department of International Law, Institute of State and Law of the Academy of Sciences of the U.S.S.R., wrote in 1989:

> In spite of different class approaches to social problems and different schools of thought, there is only one worldwide science of international law. New global problems challenging humanity—the threat of nuclear holocaust, environmental crises, economic difficulties of the "Third World"—can be solved only by all states acting together, by the common efforts of all nations. In the contemporary world, interests and values common to all mankind must prevail over the interests of single nations, parties or social classes. Moreover, I think that nowadays values and interests common to all mankind cannot be contrary to the interests of individual states. Avoidance of nuclear holocaust, disarmament, the resolution of environmental problems and mutually beneficial cooperation between nations in all fields

of human activity are in the interest of all. Too often, when statesmen or politicians speak of the national interest and justify their actions by the notion of national interest, they are not talking about genuine national interest but, rather, about the self-interest of certain influential groups.

Hence, it is necessary for specialists in international law from different countries to cooperate, to coordinate their opinions so as to help to align the initiatives of their respective governments as they seek to define and implement principles and norms of international law * * *.

Mullerson, Sources of International Law: New Tendencies in Soviet Thinking, 83 A.J.I.L. 494, 495 (1989). Gorbachev's policy of Perestroika also influenced the Soviet attitude to international law. See, e.g., Perestroika and the Rule of Law: Anglo–American and Soviet Perspectives (Butler, ed. 1991); Perestroika and International Law: Current Anglo–Soviet Approaches to International Law (Carty & Danilenko, eds. 1990); Perestroika and Law (U.S.S.R. Academy of Sciences, 1989); Quigley, Perestroika and International Law, 82 A.J.I.L. 788 (1988).

On new Soviet thinking about international law generally, see Green, Socialist Internationalism: Theoria and Praxis in Soviet International Law, 13 Yale J.Int'l L. 306 (1988); Agora: New Thinking by Soviet Scholars, 83 A.J.I.L. 494 (1989); McWhinney, The "New Thinking" in Soviet International Law: Soviet Doctrines and Practice in the Post–Tunkin Era, 28 Can.Y.B.Int'l L. 309 (1990). For an historical account, see Grabar, The History of International Law in Russia, 1647–1917 (Butler, trans. 1990).

3. The early dismissive attitudes of the People's Republic of China toward international law were reflected in Chiu, Communist China's Attitude Toward International Law, 60 A.J.I.L. 245 (1966); Chiu & Edwards, Communist China's Attitude Toward the United Nations, 62 A.J.I.L. 20 (1968); Cohen & Chiu, People's China and International Law (1974). Following the removal of the "Gang of Four" in the late 1970's, the People's Republic of China displayed renewed interest in international law. See Selected Articles from Chinese Yearbook of International Law (Chinese Society of Int'l Law, ed. 1983). See also Chen, The People's Republic of China and Public International Law, 8 Dalhousie L.J. 3 (1984); Wang, Teaching and Research of International Law in Present Day China, 22 Colum. J. Transnat'l L. 77 (1983).

It is unclear what effect the demise of international Communism and of the U.S.S.R. will have on the Chinese attitudes to international law. For recent reflections of Chinese attitudes, see Chiu, Chinese Attitudes Towards International Law in the Post–Mao Era, 1978–1987, 21 Int'l Lawyer 1127 (1987); Chiu, Chinese Views on the Sources of International Law, 28 Harv.Int'l L.J. 289 (1987); Kim, The Development of International Law in Post–Mao China: Change and Continuity, 1 J.Chinese L. 117 (1987); Chiu, The International Law of Recognition and the Status of the Republic of China, 3 J. Chinese L. 193 (1989); Wang, International Law in China, 221 Rec. des Cours 195 (1990–II).

4. The expansion of the international system after the Second World War with the addition of "new states" has had important consequences for international law. The law lost its Europe-based homogeneity, but contrary to fears expressed during the early years of decolonization, international law has not been discarded and, instead, its universalism has been established. See Henkin, How Nations Behave 121–27 (2d ed. 1979).

The recent literature exploring the influence of "new states" on international law includes: Anand, International Law and the Developing Countries: Confrontation or Cooperation? (1987); Caribbean Perspectives on International Law and Organizations (Ramcharan & Francis, eds. 1989); Elias, Africa and the Development of International Law (2d ed. 1988); Elias, New Horizons in the Development of International Law (1980); Makonnen, International Law and the New States of Africa (1983); Third World Attitudes Toward International Law: An Introduction (Snyder & Sathirathai, eds. 1989); Norchi, Methods for Evaluating the Transcultural Applications of International Legal Prescription, 86 A.S.I.L.Proc. 570 (1992); Garcia–Amador, Current Attempts to Revise International Law—A Comparative Analysis, 77 A.J.I.L. 286 (1983); Krasner, Transforming International Regimes: What the Third World Wants and Why, 25 Int'l Studies Q. 119 (1981); Park, The Third World as an International Legal System, 7 Bost. Coll. Third World L.J. 37 (1987); Sathirathai, An Understanding of the Relationship Between International Legal Discourse and Third World States, 25 Harv. Int'l L.Rev. 395 (1984), reprinted in, International Law 445 (Koskenniemi, ed. 1992); Wang, The Third World and International Law, in The Structure and Process of International Law: Essays in Legal Philosophy Doctrine and Theory 955 (Macdonald & Johnston, eds. 1983).

For earlier discussion, see Anand, New States and International Law (1972); Asian States and the Development of Universal International Law (Anand, ed. 1979); Sinha, New Nations and the Law of Nations (1967); Syatauw, Some Newly Established Asian States and International Law (1961); Abi–Saab, The Newly Independent States and the Rules of International Law: An Outline, 8 Howard L.J. 95 (1962); de Arechaga, International Law in the Past Third Century, 159 Rec. des Cours 1 (1978–I); El–Erian, International Law and the Developing Countries, in Transnational Law in a Changing Society 84 (Friedmann, Henkin & Lissitzyn, eds. 1979); Falk, The New States and International Legal Order, 118 Rec. des Cours 1 (1966); Merillat, Law and Developing Countries, 60 A.J.I.L. 71 (1966); Sinha, Perspectives of the Newly Independent States on the Binding Quality of International Law, 14 I.C.L.Q. 121 (1965); Udokang, The Role of the New States in International Law, 15 Archiv des Volkerrechts 145 (1973).

5. For the interplay of East–West conflict during the Cold War with the interests of the Third World, see generally Lissitzyn, International Law Today and Tomorrow (1965); Henkin, How Nations Behave, chapters 5–6 & 9 (2d ed. 1979). For a notable illustration, Henkin suggests how the interplay of interests contributed to shape the development of the Law of the Sea in the U.N. General Assembly and at the U.N. Conference on the Law of the Sea:

> Since about 1960, changes in international society have modified the prevailing political forces, beating against several pillars of the international system and of its law. Decolonization (and other "self-determination") has increased to more than one hundred and forty the number of states, the units of the political system which have authority to make and to change law. The mass of new states share with older states in Latin America, the Middle East, Asia and Africa, bonds of poverty and underdevelopment, and some resentment against the Western, developed states which have long dominated the international political scene. This "Third World" has developed loose forms of political and economic cooperation including "bloc" voting in international organizations. With varying success they have cooperated to complete decolonization and end white racism in Southern Africa, to begin their own economic development, to change the laws and

> patterns of international trade, to assert national sovereignty and control over their natural resources against the claims of foreign investors, and in other ways to resist "economic imperialism."
>
> In these efforts they have had some support from the USSR (when her own interests would not be jeopardized, of course); and recently Communist China has sought to emerge as their champion. The United States and other Western powers, often the principal targets of proposed changes, have supported some efforts and resisted others; but even resistance has not been as wholehearted as it might have been in the past. This attitude comes perhaps from some guilt over past imperialism and present wealth, from some sympathy for the aspirations of the underdeveloped, and from some reluctance to allow these many states to identify their interests with those of Communist powers. Even when smaller nations challenged cherished principles of traditional law, even when they attacked important Western interests—as when they expropriated (without meaningful compensation) major American investments—resistance and retaliation were restrained. Certainly there have been no ready uses of force or of "gunboat diplomacy" for they would violate the United Nations Charter and are otherwise impolitic. The threshold of national interest that will support them is very high; in particular, only very big stakes will cause larger states to use force against smaller ones, and economic interests are usually not big enough.

Henkin, Politics and the Changing Law of the Sea, 89 Pol.Sci.Q. 46, 51–52 (1974).

6. In the Preamble to the U.N. Charter the peoples of the United Nations, apparently in recognition of the world's diversity among states and cultures, dedicate themselves "to practice tolerance and live together with one another as good neighbors." There have been differences among writers as to the significance of cultural diversity for international law. Bozeman notes that international society is characterized by diverse cultures, political systems, and ideologies, and declares that there is no universal acceptance of Western notions of sovereignty and moral law. In fact, she notes, the word law does not translate easily into a number of foreign idea systems. Bozeman argues that Western ideals of international law can never create more than a false sense of world unity. Bozeman, The Future of International Law in a Multicultural World xii–xiii, 180–86 (1971). In contrast, others argue that a universal culture or ideology is not a prerequisite for the existence or growth of international law, since in its essentials international law responds to interests and needs common to states generally. See, e.g., Higgins, Conflict of Interests: International Law in a Divided World (1965); Jenks, The Common Law of Mankind (1958); Jessup, Diversity and Uniformity in the Law of Nations, 58 A.J.I.L. 341–358 (1964); Kunz, Pluralism of Legal Systems and Value Systems in International Law, 49 A.J.I.L. 370 (1955); Lissitzyn, International Law in a Divided World, International Conciliation, No. 542 (March 1963).

An effort to take account of different legal cultures can be seen in the provisions for the selection of judges for the International Court of Justice. In Article 9 of the Court's Statute, electors of judges are reminded to take into account when choosing among nominees that in the Court "as a whole the representation of the main forms of civilization and of the principal legal systems of the world should be assured." According to the final report of the Committee of Jurists that drafted the Statute for the Permanent Court of International Justice (on which Article 9 of the I.C.J. Statute is based), the Article is a specific attempt to accommodate "distinct systems of legal education.

* * * The intention is to try and ensure that, no matter what points of national law may be involved in an international suit, all shall be equally comprehended; and further, since it is always possible to appoint a judge *ad hoc* [I.C.J. Statute, Article 31], chosen by any party which does not already possess one of its nationality, whenever a particular legal system is involved in a case, to enable the other systems of law to be brought into line with it, so that the Bench may really and permanently represent the legal conceptions of all nations." League of Nations Doc. V.1920.2, at 710. See McWhinney, 'Internationalizing' the International Court: The Quest for Ethno-cultural and Legal–Systemic Representativeness, in Essays in Honor of Judge Taslim Olawale Elias 277 (Bello & Ajibola, eds. 1992). For the present composition of the Court, see Chapter 10 infra.

For recent writing on cultural diversity and international law, see Cassese, International Law in a Divided World (1986); The Future of International Law in a Multicultural World (Dupuy, ed. 1984); McWhinney, United Nations Law Making[:] Cultural and Ideological Relativism and International Law Making for and Era of Transition (1984); Schachter, International Law in Theory and Practice, chapter 2 (1991); Bozeman, The International Order in a Multicultural World, in The Expansion of International Society (Bull & Weston, eds. 1984); Dore, Universality and Diversity in World Culture, in The Expansion of International Society 408 (Bull & Weston, eds. 1984); Herczegh, International Law in a Multicultural World, in 3 Questions of International Law[:] Hungarian Perspectives (Bokor–Szego, ed. 1986); Jennings, Universal International Law in a Multicultural World, in Liber Amicorum for Lord Wilberforce (Bos & Brownlie, eds. 1987); Joyner, Bridging the Cultural Chasm: Cultural Relativism and the Future of International Law, 20 Cal.W.Int'l L.J. 275 (1989–90); Vereshchetin & Danilenko, Cultural and Ideological Pluralism and International Law, 29 German Y.B Int'l L. (1986).

7. Nineteenth century positivism stressed law as science and played down the original affinity between religion and international law. The diversity of cultures and ideologies in the international system of the twentieth century has also led to reluctance to consider continuing connections between international law and religion. See generally The Influence of Religion on the Development of International Law (Janis, ed. 1991); Falk, Explorations at the Edge of Time: The Prospects for World Order 24–36 (1992).

## SECTION 2. INTERNATIONAL LAW AS LAW

### A. IS IT LAW?

International law has had to justify its legitimacy and reality. Its title to law has been challenged on the ground that by hypothesis and definition there can be no law governing sovereign states. Skeptics have argued that there can be no international law since there is no international legislature to make it, no international executive to enforce it, and no effective international judiciary to develop it or to resolve disputes about it. International law has been said not to be "real law" since it is commonly disregarded, states obeying it only when they wish to, when it is in their interest to do so.

The jurisprudence of international law, however, has rejected the narrow definitions and unfounded assumptions implied in these challenges.

The sociology of international law has denied the allegations as to how nations behave in regard to law.

## LAW AS COMMANDS ENFORCED BY SANCTIONS

*AUSTIN, THE PROVINCE OF JURISPRUDENCE DETERMINED (1832)*

133, 201 (1954 ed. Berlin, Hampshire & Wollheim, eds.).

Laws properly so called are a species of *commands.* But, being a *command,* every law properly so called flows from a *determinate source* * * *. * * * [W]henever a *command* is expressed or intimated, one party signifies a wish that another shall do or forbear: and the latter is obnoxious to an evil which the former intends to inflict in case the wish be disregarded. * * * Every sanction properly so called is an eventual evil *annexed to a command.* * * *

And hence it inevitably follows, that the law obtaining between nations is not positive law: for every positive law is set by a given sovereign to a person or persons in a state of subjection to its author. As I have already intimated, the law obtaining between nations is law (improperly so called) set by general opinion. The duties which it imposes are enforced by moral sanctions: by fear on the part of nations, or by fear on the part of sovereigns, of provoking general hostility, and incurring its probable evils, in case they shall violate maxims generally received and respected.

## INTERNATIONAL LAW AND INTERNATIONAL MORALITY

*HART, THE CONCEPT OF LAW*

222–225 (1961).*

Sometimes insistence that the rules governing the relations between states are only moral rules, is inspired by the old dogmatism, that any form of social structure that is not reducible to orders backed by threats can only be a form of "morality". It is, of course, possible to use the word "morality" in this very comprehensive way; so used, it provides a conceptual wastepaper basket into which will go the rules of games, clubs, etiquette, the fundamental provisions of constitutional law and international law, together with rules and principles which we ordinarily think of as moral ones, such as the common prohibitions of cruelty, dishonesty, or lying. The objection to this procedure is that between what is thus classed together as "morality" there are such important differences of both form and social function, that no conceivable purpose, practical or theoretical, could be served by so crude a classification. Within the category of morality thus artificially widened, we should have to mark out afresh the old distinctions which it blurs.

In the particular case of international law there are a number of different reasons for resisting the classification of its rules as "morality". The first is that states often reproach each other for immoral conduct or praise themselves or others for living up to the standard of international morality. No doubt *one* of the virtues which states may show or fail to show is that of abiding by international law, but that does not mean that that law is morality. In fact the appraisal of states' conduct in terms of morality is recognizably different from the formulation of claims, demands, and the acknowledgements of rights and obligations under the rules of international law. * * * [C]ertain features * * * might be taken as defining characteristics of social morality: among them * * * the distinctive form of moral pressure by which moral rules are primarily supported. This consists not of appeals to fear or threats of retaliation or demands for compensation, but of appeals to conscience, made in the expectation that once the person addressed is reminded of the moral principle at stake, he may be led by guilt or shame to respect it and make amends.

Claims under international law are not couched in such terms though of course, as in municipal law, they may be joined with a moral appeal. What predominate in the arguments, often technical, which states address to each other over disputed matters of international law, are references to precedents, treaties and juristic writings; often no mention is made of moral right or wrong, good or bad. Hence the claim that the Peking Government has or has not a right under international law to expel the Nationalist forces from Formosa is very different from the question whether this is fair, just, or a morally good or bad thing to do, and is backed by characteristically different arguments. No doubt in the relations between states there are halfway houses between what is clearly law and what is clearly morality, analogous to the standards of politeness and courtesy recognized in private life. Such is the sphere of international "comity" exemplified in the privilege extended to diplomatic envoys of receiving goods intended for personal use free of duty.

A more important ground of distinction is the following. The rules of international law, like those of municipal law, are often morally quite indifferent. A rule may exist because it is convenient or necessary to have some clear fixed rule about the subjects with which it is concerned, but not because any moral importance is attached to the particular rule. It may well be but one of a larger number of possible rules, any one of which would have done equally well. Hence legal rules, municipal and international, commonly contain much specific detail, and draw arbitrary distinctions, which would be unintelligible as elements in moral rules or principles. * * * Law, however, though it also contains much that is of moral importance, can and does contain just such rules, and the arbitrary distinctions, formalities, and highly specific detail which would be most difficult to understand as part of morality, are consequently natural and easily comprehensible features of law. For one of the typical functions of law, unlike morality, is to introduce just these elements in order to maximize certainty and predictability and to facilitate the proof or assessments of claims. Regard for forms and detail carried to excess, has earned for law the reproaches of "formalism" and "legalism"; yet it is important to remember that these vices are exaggerations of some of the law's distinctive qualities.

It is for this reason that just as we expect a municipal legal system, but not morality, to tell us how many witnesses a validly executed will must have, so we expect international law, but not morality, to tell us such things as the number of days a belligerent vessel may stay for refueling or repairs in a neutral port; the width of territorial waters; the methods to be used in their measurement. All these things are necessary and desirable provisions for *legal rules* to make, but so long as the sense is retained that such rules may equally well take any of several forms, or are important only as one among many possible means to specific ends, they remain distinct from rules which have the status in individual or social life characteristic of morality. Of course not all the rules of international law are of this formal, or arbitrary, or morally neutral kind. The point is only that legal rules *can* and moral rules *cannot* be of this kind.

The difference in character between international law and anything which we naturally think of as morality has another aspect. Though the effect of a law requiring or proscribing certain practices might ultimately be to bring about changes in the morality of a group, the notion of a legislature making or repealing moral rules is * * * an absurd one. A legislature cannot introduce a new rule and give it the status of a moral rule by its *fiat*, just as it cannot, by the same means, give a rule the status of a tradition, though the reasons why this is so may not be the same in the two cases. Accordingly morality does not merely lack or happen not to have a legislature; the very idea of change by human legislative *fiat* is repugnant to the idea of morality. This is so because we conceive of morality as the ultimate standard by which human actions (legislative or otherwise) are evaluated. The contrast with international law is clear. There is nothing in the nature or function of international law which is similarly inconsistent with the idea that the rules might be subject to legislative change; the lack of a legislature is just a lack which many think of as a defect one day to be repaired.

### *Notes*

1. Glanville Williams insists that jurisprudential debate over the reality of international law is merely a debate about words. Williams, International Law and the Controversy Concerning the Word "Law," 22 Brit.Y.B.I.L. 146, 159–62 (1945). See also Ian Brownlie's criticism of Austin and Hart in The Reality and Efficacy of International Law, 52 Brit.Y.B.I.L. 1 (1981).

2. The relation of international law and morality has been addressed from other perspectives. There is an old but recurrent controversy as to the applicability of moral principles to the behavior of states and governments. For a rejection of the "legalistic—moralistic approach to international relations," see Kennan, American Diplomacy, 1900–1950, 95–99 (1951); see also Kennan, Morality and Foreign Policy, 64 Foreign Affairs 205 (Winter 1985–86). For a different view see Henkin, How Nations Behave 335–37 (2d ed. 1979).

## INTERNATIONAL LAW AND STATE SOVEREIGNTY

*BRIERLY, THE LAW OF NATIONS*

54–55 (6th ed., Waldock, 1963).*

The notion that the validity of international law raises some peculiar problem arises from the confusion which the doctrine of sovereignty has introduced into international legal theory. Even when we do not believe in the absoluteness of state sovereignty we have allowed ourselves to be persuaded that the fact of their sovereignty makes it necessary to look for some specific quality, not to be found in other kinds of law, in the law to which states are subject. We have accepted a false idea of the state as a personality with a life and a will of its own, still living in a "state of nature", and we contrast this with the "political" state in which individual men have come to live. But this assumed condition of states is the very negation of law, and no ingenuity can explain how the two can exist together. It is a notion as false analytically as it admittedly is historically. The truth is that states are not persons, however convenient it may often be to personify them; they are merely *institutions,* that is to say, organizations which men establish among themselves for securing certain objects, of which the most fundamental is a system of order within which the activities of their common life can be carried on. They have no wills except the wills of the individual human beings who direct their affairs; and they exist not in a political vacuum but in continuous political relations with one another. Their subjection to law is as yet imperfect, though it is real as far as it goes; the problem of extending it is one of great practical difficulty, but it is not one of intrinsic impossibility. There are important differences between international law and the law under which individuals live in a state, but those differences do not lie in metaphysics or in any mystical qualities of the entity called state sovereignty.

## CORFU CHANNEL CASE

## (UNITED KINGDOM v. ALBANIA)

*(INDIVIDUAL OPINION BY JUDGE ALVAREZ)*

International Court of Justice, 1949.

1949 I.C.J. 39, 43.

* * *

By sovereignty, we understand the whole body of rights and attributes which a State possesses in its territory, to the exclusion of all other States, and also in its relations with other States.

Sovereignty confers rights upon States and imposes obligations on them.

* * *

Some jurists have proposed to abolish the notion of the sovereignty of States, considering it obsolete. That is an error. This notion has its foundation in national sentiment and in the psychology of the peoples, in fact it is very deeply rooted. The constituent instrument of the International Organization has especially recognized the sovereignty of States and has endeavoured to bring it into harmony with the objects of that Organization (No. 1 of Art. 2).

This notion has evolved, and we must now adopt a conception of it which will be in harmony with the new conditions of social life. We can no longer regard sovereignty as an absolute and individual right of every State, as used to be done under the old law founded on the individualist régime, according to which States were only bound by the rules which they had accepted. To-day, owing to social interdependence and to the predominance of the general interest, the States are bound by many rules which have not been ordered by their will. The sovereignty of States has now become an *institution,* an *international social function* of a psychological character, which has to be exercised in accordance with the new international law.

### *Notes*

1. In its first contentious case, the Permanent Court of International Justice said: "The Court declines to see in the conclusion of any treaty by which a State undertakes to perform or refrain from performing a particular act an abandonment of its sovereignty. No doubt any convention creating an obligation of this kind places a restriction upon the exercise of the sovereign rights of the State, in the sense that it requires them to be exercised in a certain way. But the right of entering into international engagements is an attribute of State sovereignty." S.S. Wimbledon Case, P.C.I.J., Series A, No. 1, at 25 (1923).

2. In the Matter of an Arbitration Between the Osaka Shosen Kaisha and the Owners of the S.S. Prometheus, 2 Hong Kong L.Rpts. 207, 225 (1904):

> It was contended on behalf of the owners of the *Prometheus* that the term "law" as applied to this recognised system of principles and rules known as international law is an inexact expression, that there is, in other words, no such thing as international law; that there can be no such law binding upon all nations inasmuch as there is no sanction for such law, that is to say that there is no means by which obedience to such law can be imposed upon any given nation refusing obedience thereto. I do not concur in that contention. In my opinion a law may be established and become international, that is to say binding upon all nations, by the agreement of such nations to be bound thereby, although it may be impossible to enforce obedience thereto by any given nation party to the agreement. The resistance of a nation to a law to which it has agreed does not derogate from the authority of the law because that resistance cannot, perhaps, be overcome. Such resistance merely makes the resisting nation a breaker of the law to which it has given its adherence, but it leaves the law, to the establishment of which the resisting nation was a party, still subsisting. Could it be successfully contended that because any given person or body of persons possessed for the time being power to resist an established municipal law such law had no existence? The answer to such a contention would be that the law still existed, though it might not for the time being be possible to enforce obedience to it.

### *HENKIN, INTERNATIONAL LAW: POLITICS, VALUES AND FUNCTIONS*

216 Rec. des Cours 24–28 (1989–IV) (some footnotes omitted).

States are commonly described as "sovereign", and "sovereignty" is commonly noted as an implicit, axiomatic characteristic of Statehood. The pervasiveness of that term is unfortunate, rooted in mistake, unfortunate mistake. Sovereignty is a bad word, not only because it has served terrible national mythologies; in international relations, and even in international law, it is often a catchword, a substitute for thinking and precision. It means many things, some essential, some insignificant; some agreed, some controversial; some that are not warranted and should not be accepted. Once there was serious debate as to whether there is, or should be, a law of nations since, it was argued, a sovereign State cannot be subject to any other authority, even to agreements of its own making or to law which it helped make or to which it consented. If today such arguments are no longer heard, States continue to argue that certain kinds of law or agreements, certain kinds of institutions, are impossible or inappropriate for "sovereign States", inconsistent with their sovereignty.*

* * *

For legal purposes at least, we might do well to relegate the term to the shelf of history as a relic from an earlier era. To this end, it is necessary to analyse, "decompose", the concept; to identify the elements that have been deemed to be inherent in, or to derive from, "sovereignty"; and to determine which of them are appropriate and desirable for a "State" in a system of States at the end of the twentieth century. As applied to a State, elements long identified with "sovereignty" are inevitably only metaphors, fictions, fictions upon fictions; some of them, however, do constitute essential characteristics and indicia of Statehood today. I consider these to include principally: independence, equality, autonomy, "personhood", territorial authority, integrity and inviolability, impermeability and "privacy".

* * *

The essential quality of Statehood in a State system is the autonomy of each State. State autonomy suggests that a State is not subject to any external authority unless it has voluntarily consented to such authority. The State has a "will", moral authority, the power to consent, to enter into relations, to conclude agreements, to form associations. By their ability to consent, to have relations and conclude agreements, States have in effect created the international political system, by a kind of "social contract". By their ability to consent to external authority and to conclude agreements, they have created norms and institutions to govern these relations, the international law of the system. Only States can make law for the system but nothing suggests that they can make law only for themselves. States can make law for entities they create (e.g. international organizations), for entities created by individual states (e.g. companies), and for human individuals.

### *ALLOTT, EUNOMIA: NEW ORDER FOR A NEW WORLD*

416–419 (1990).

**20.18** Through the idea and ideal of democracy and through actual experience in the reality-forming of actual societies, sovereignty was socialized. It became possible to recognize that society, including its legal sub-

* States sometimes dare even to invoke their "sovereignty" to preclude scrutiny and judgment when they are charged with violating international law and their international obligations, notably in respect of human rights. * * *

The banner of "sovereignty" also continues to frustrate the system in smaller but significant ways. For example, the International Court of Justice continues to struggle with inadequate * * * procedures because to modernize them even in modest respects, such as imposing limitations on the number of pages in a memorial or on the number of hours of oral argument, would be unthinkable since the parties are "sovereign States".

system, was a self-willed ordering, in which the self-creating of the members of society and the self-creating of society could be reconciled.

* * *

**20.20** International Society had to find its own theory. It chose to see itself as a collection of state-societies turned inside-out, like a glove. It chose to be an unsocial society creating itself separately from the development of its subordinate societies, ignoring the idea and the ideal of democracy, depriving itself of the possibility of using social power, especially legal relations, to bring about the survival and prospering of the whole human race.

* * *

**20.21** There is no reason why international society should not reconceive itself as a society, using social power, and especially legal relations, to bring about the survival and prospering of the whole human race.

* * *

**20.22** * * * International society is a self-ordering of the whole human race and of all subordinate societies. In the non-social, undemocratized and unsocialized, international society, self-ordering has taken aberrant forms. Force and the threat of force have been used as substitutes for self-ordering. The social process has been a stunted process of interaction between the public realms of state-societies, so-called international relations conducted through a vestigial will-forming system called diplomacy.

* * *

**20.24** International law has been the primitive law of an unsocial international society. Itself a by-product of that unsocialization, it has contributed to holding back the development of international society as society. Failing to recognize itself as a society, international society has not known that it has a constitution. Not knowing its own constitution, it has ignored the generic principles of a constitution.

**20.25** In an international society which knows itself as a society, state-societies have no natural and inherent and unlimited powers. Like any other of the myriad societies of international society, they have only the legal relations, including powers and obligations, conferred by the international constitution and by international law. Their particular status is as constitutional organs of international society, having special responsibility for the organization of its public realms, including the public realms of their own societies.

**20.26** State-societies, like all other members of international society, have social power, including legal power, to serve the purposes of international society, to will and act for its survival and prospering, that is to say, for the survival and prospering of the whole human race. They are socially and legally accountable for the exercise of their powers and the carrying out of their obligations. Non-statal societies, including industrial and commercial and financial enterprises of all kinds, exercise social power and carry out obligations on the same conditions.

**20.27** The new international law will be as dynamic and as rich as the law of any subordinate society, organizing human willing and acting in every field which concerns the survival and prospering of the society of which it is the law.

### *Notes*

1. At the end of 1992 the Secretary–General of the United Nations writing about the nature of sovereignty suggested:

> While respect for the fundamental sovereignty and integrity of the state remains central, it is undeniable that the centuries-old doctrine of absolute and exclusive sovereignty no longer stands, and was in fact never so absolute as it was conceived to be in theory. A major intellectual requirement of our time is to rethink the question of sovereignty—not to weaken its essence, which is crucial to international security and cooperation, but to recognize that it may take more than one form and perform more than one function. This perception could help solve problems both within and among states. And underlying the rights of the individual and the rights of peoples is a dimension of universal sovereignty that resides in all humanity and provides all peoples with legitimate involvement in issues affecting the world as a whole. It is a sense that increasingly finds expression in the gradual expansion of international law.
>
> Related to this is the widening recognition that states and their governments cannot face or solve today's problems alone. International cooperation is unavoidable and indispensable. The quality, extent and timeliness of such cooperation will make the difference between advancement or frustration and despair. * * *

Boutros–Ghali, Empowering the United Nations, 71 For.Aff. 89, 98–99 (Winter 1992/93). The Secretary–General's predecessor expressed similar views on sovereignty. See Pérez de Cuéllar, Address to the University of Florence, Nov. 21, 1991, reprinted in Int'l Commission of Jurists Review 24, 24–27 (No. 47, Dec. 1991).

2. In the exercise of their "sovereignty" states have accepted international law and submitted to the authority of international institutions. States have accepted norms that govern their treatment of their own inhabitants and monitoring and investigation that intrude upon their territory. See Chapter 8 infra. States have submitted to the authority of the U.N. Security Council to issue mandatory, binding orders under Chapter VII of the U.N. Charter. See Chapter 11 infra. To maintain international peace and security the Security Council has ordered measures that impose upon territorial integrity and political independence. New departures by the Security Council, seen by many as new derogations from state sovereignty, have occurred in the former Yugoslavia to overcome obstacles preventing the delivery of humanitarian assistance. Other innovations have been witnessed in the U.N. authorization of a military presence in Somalia to provide a secure environment for the distribution of relief, as well as in developments in other countries in Africa (Liberia, Ethiopia, Togo, the Sudan) and Asia (Cambodia). In 1991, the U.N. General Assembly reasserted respect for state sovereignty, while opening avenues to collective intervention to impose humanitarian assistance even on unwilling governments. See Report on the Work of the Organization, U.N. Doc. A/46/1, at 10–11 (Sept. 1991). See Chapter 11 infra.

3. Henkin, in a paper entitled "The Mythology of Sovereignty," concludes that "sovereignty" in itself is not a normative principle of international law. He declares "that it is time to bring "sovereignty" down to earth, cut it down to size, discard its overblown rhetoric; to examine, analyze, reconceive the concept and break out its normative content; to repackage it, even rename it, and slowly ease the term out of polite language in international relations, surely in law." [1992] Can.Council Int'l L.Proc. (forthcoming).

Professor Lillich has suggested "that the concept of sovereignty in international law is an idea whose time has come and gone." In assessing the limits of the "tyrannical" concept of sovereignty, Lillich advances three major premises: (1) " 'humanity'—is the *raison d'être* of any legal system. It goes without saying, one would think, but it needs saying nevertheless;" (2) "the international system for over 300 years, since the Peace of Westphalia, has not been fulfilling what should be its primary function, namely, the protection and development of the human dignity of the individual;" (3) "any proposed 'new world order' should be structured so as to maximize benefits not for States but for individuals living within States, all the way from freedom of speech and elections, on the one hand, to freedom from hunger and the right to education on the other hand." Lillich, Sovereignty and Humanity: Can they Converge?, in The Spirit of Uppsala 406, 406–07 (Grahl–Madsen & Toman, eds. 1984).

4. What implications for traditional notions of sovereignty are raised by the increasing interdependence of states in solving problems that are international and regional in scope? Professor Falk writes:

> [A]n emergent global ethos suggests the reality of a shared destiny for the human species and a fundamental unity across space and through time, built around the bioethical impulse of all human groups to *survive* and *flourish*. Such an ethos has implications for the assessment of problems, the provision of solutions, and the overall orientation of action and actors. For most people and leaders, this sense of shared destiny does not displace a persisting primary attachment to the state as a vehicle for aspiration and as an absolute, unconditional bastion of security.
>
> * * *
>
> As interdependence grows more salient, the competence and confidence of the state tends to be eroded unless it can facilitate the development of innovative and imaginative formats for problem-solving. In a sense, the state must learn to get out of its own way if over time it is to retain, and regain the full plenum of its legitimacy. But the cumulative consequence of such adaptation is likely to be a far less state-centric global political system. Paradoxically, in order to remain potent the state must give way to a variety of alternative ordering frameworks; the more willingly and forcefully it does so, the better its legitimate sphere of authority can be eventually sustained. * * *
>
> The state has demonstrated a remarkable degree of resilience over the several centuries of its existence, but whether it can significantly reorient its sense of sovereign prerogative from space (protecting territory) to time (contributing to a viable and desirable future) is uncertain in the extreme. * * * Only if specific persons, acting on behalf of the state, can develop the sort of understanding and backing needed can states be led away from their boundary-obsessed territorialism to a more formless contouring of authority that responds to the bewildering array of dangers and opportunities in the

world today. To make this shift at all viable requires an active civil society that gives its citizens "the space" to explore "adjustments," including transnational initiatives, and depends on the secure establishment of human rights and democracy, including on the international accountability of leaders for violation of international law. * * * The natural flow of political life in response to the agenda of global concerns is to encourage evasions [of sovereignty] as a matter of deliberate tactics. Is the state flexible enough to preside over its own partial dissolution, circumvention, and reconstruction?

Falk, Explorations at the Edge of Time: The Prospects for World Order 198–213 (1992).

## B. THE BINDING CHARACTER OF INTERNATIONAL LAW

### PACTA SUNT SERVANDA

#### *KELSEN, PURE THEORY OF LAW*

215–17 (Knight trans. 1967).*

[G]eneral international law is regarded as [a] set of objectively valid norms that regulate the mutual behavior of states. These norms are created by custom, constituted by the actual behavior of the "states," that is, of those individuals who act as governments according to national legal orders. These norms are interpreted as legal norms binding the states, because a basic norm is presupposed which establishes custom among states as a law-creating fact. The basic norm runs as follows: "States—that is, the governments of the states—in their mutual relations ought to behave in such a way"; or: "Coercion of state against state ought to be exercised under the conditions and in the manner, that conforms with the custom constituted by the actual behavior of the states." This is the "constitution" of international law in a transcendental-logical sense.

One of the norms of international law created by custom authorizes the states to regulate their mutual relations by treaty. The reason for the validity of the legal norms of international law created by treaty is this custom-created norm. It is usually formulated in the sentence: *pacta sunt servanda.*

The presupposed basic norm of international law, which institutes custom constituted by the states as a law-creating fact, expresses a principle that is the basic presupposition of all customary law: the individual ought to behave in such a manner as the others usually behave (believing that they ought to behave that way), applied to the mutual behavior of states, that is, the behavior of the individuals qualified by the national legal orders as government organs.[80]

No affirmation of a value transcending positive law is inherent in the basic norm of international law, not even of the value of peace guaranteed by the general international law created by custom and the particular

* Reprinted by permission of the Regents of the University of California. Some footnotes omitted.

**80.** The theory held by many authors (and at one time also by myself) that the norm of *pacta sunt servanda* is the basis of international law is to be rejected because it can be maintained only with the aid of the fiction that the custom established by the conduct of states is a tacit treaty.

international law created by treaty. International law and—if its primacy is assumed—the subordinated national legal orders are not valid "because" and "insofar as" they realize the value that consists in peace; they may realize this value if and so far as they are valid; and they are valid if a basic norm is presupposed that institutes custom among states as a law-creating fact regardless of the content of the norms thus created. If the reason for the validity of national legal orders is found in a norm of international law, then the latter is understood as a legal order superior to the former and therefore as the highest sovereign legal order. If the states—that is, the national legal orders—are nevertheless referred to as "sovereign," then this "sovereignty" can only mean that the national legal orders are subordinated *only* to the international legal order.

## THE QUEST FOR ORIGINAL PRINCIPLES

### *FITZMAURICE, THE FOUNDATIONS OF THE AUTHORITY OF INTERNATIONAL LAW AND THE PROBLEM OF ENFORCEMENT*

19 Mod.L.Rev. 1, 8–9 (1956).*

The real foundation of the authority of international law resides similarly in the fact that the States making up the international society recognize it as binding upon them, and, moreover, as a system that *ipso facto* binds them *as* members of that society, irrespective of their individual wills. * * *

* * * As Verdross, Brierly and others have conclusively shown, it is not consent, as such, that creates the obligation, though it may be the occasion of it. It is a *method* of creating rules, but it is not, in the last resort, the element that makes the rules binding, when created. In short, consent could not, in itself create obligations unless there were already in existence a rule of law according to which consent had just that effect. Another way of putting it is to say that it is because international law already makes consent a source of obligation that obligations can arise from consent. Others have put it in the following way: "There is a customary rule of international law that the consent of the States to a rule makes that rule binding upon them." Be it so; but then, of course, the difficulty is merely removed a stage further back, and the inquirer will have to ask what is the juridical foundation for this customary rule itself, and what is it that makes *that* rule binding. To this question it is very difficult to give an answer, or at any rate a final answer. It can be said, with Kelsen, that the reason why a customary rule is binding is that there is an antecedent and still more fundamental legal principle to the effect that "States have a duty to go on behaving as they have customarily behaved"—but then what is the source of *that* duty? Or it can be held, with Lauterpacht, that the antecedent principle that confers binding force on customary rules is one according to which the general will of the community must prevail, and there is a duty to conform to that will as expressed in customary rules of law—but here again a duty is postulated that has itself, in the legal sense, to be accounted for. The point is that, however the matter is put, finality can, in the nature of

the case, never be attained. The discussion merely enters what is known to the mathematicians as an infinite regress—a series in which each proposition is explicable in terms of the previous one, and derives its validity from it; but this antecedent proposition itself requires to be accounted for by a similar process.

### *Notes*

1. Brierly adds:

> The international lawyer then is under no special obligation to explain why the law with which he is concerned should be binding upon its subjects. If it were true that the essence of all law is a command, and that what makes the law of the state binding is that for some reason, for which no satisfactory explanation can ever be given, the will of the person issuing a command is superior to that of the person receiving it, then indeed it would be necessary to look for some special explanation of the binding force of international law. But that view of the nature of law has been long discredited. If we are to explain why any kind of law is binding, we cannot avoid some such assumption as that which the Middle Ages made, and which Greece and Rome had made before them, when they spoke of natural law. The ultimate explanation of the binding force of all law is that man, whether he is a single individual or whether he is associated with other men in a state, is constrained, in so far as he is a reasonable being, to believe that order and not chaos is the governing principle of the world in which he has to live.

Brierly, The Law of Nations 55–56 (6th ed. 1963).*

2. Compare:

> Law is a factor in the social scheme of things, consisting of a set of ideas in principle belonging together as elements in a logically coherent system—a system deriving its character as law not from the quality of its component ideas but from its status as a factor in the social scheme. For law is not simply a set of ideas, it is a social institution, not even conceivable—as law—in separation from the social milieu in which it has the status which is the very essence of its "law-ness". And, as law—that is as being, by status, law—it is, by status, *binding* law—for as little can one conceive of a law that is not binding law as one can conceive of a circle that is not circular. It is of the very nature of a circle to be circular, and of law to be binding. The imputation to it by the society it serves of its status as law is by the same token an imputation to it of binding character. Not naturally, but in point of status, it is binding. So far from the members of the society having rendered it binding upon them by any virtual equivalent of a formal consent, the membership to which they lay claim in the society in question is a membership in subjection to the law of that society, for such is the nature of that society. It is a society which has, historically, taken shape as a society of members subject to that law. Their subjection to it is no more detachable from their membership than is its binding force from its character as law. And to ask for evidence of their subjection, or of its binding character, or indeed of the existence of such a society—if this means asking for evidence of a *fact*—is, as it happens, a category mistake.

Manning, The Nature of International Society 106–107 (1962).**

## THE REALITY OF INTERNATIONAL LAW

*HENKIN, HOW NATIONS BEHAVE*

25–26, 320–21 (2d ed. 1979).*

[T]o many an observer, governments seem largely free to decide whether to agree to new law, whether to accept another nation's view of existing law, whether to comply with agreed law. International law, then, is voluntary and only hortatory. It must always yield to national interest. Surely, no nation will submit to law any questions involving its security or independence, even its power, prestige, influence. Inevitably, a diplomat holding these views will be reluctant to build policy on law he deems ineffective. He will think it unrealistic and dangerous to enact laws which will not be observed, to build institutions which will not be used, to base his government's policy on the expectation that other governments will observe law or agreement. Since other nations do not attend to law except when it is in their interest, the diplomat might not see why his government should do so at the sacrifice of important interests. He might be impatient with his lawyers who tell him that the government may not do what he would like to see done.

These depreciations of international law challenge much of what the international lawyer does. Indeed, some lawyers seem to despair for international law until there is world government or at least effective international organization. But most international lawyers are not dismayed. Unable to deny the limitations of international law, they insist that these are not critical, and they deny many of the alleged implications of these limitations. If they must admit that the cup of law is half-empty, they stress that it is half-full. They point to similar deficiencies in many domestic legal systems. They reject definitions (commonly associated with the legal philosopher John Austin) that deny the title of law to any but the command of a sovereign, enforceable and enforced as such. They insist that despite inadequacies in legislative method, international law has grown and developed and changed. If international law is difficult to make, yet it is made; if its growth is slow, yet it grows. If there is no judiciary as effective as in some developed national systems, there is an International Court of Justice whose judgments and opinions, while few, are respected. The inadequacies of the judicial system are in some measure supplied by other bodies: international disputes are resolved and law is developed through a network of arbitrations by continuing or *ad hoc* tribunals. National courts help importantly to determine, clarify, develop international law. Political bodies like the Security Council and the General Assembly of the United Nations also apply law, their actions and resolutions interpret and develop the law, their judgments serve to deter violations in some measure. If there is no international executive to enforce international law, the United Nations has some enforcement powers and there is "horizontal enforcement" in the reactions

* Reprinted by permission of Columbia University Press. Footnotes omitted.

of other nations. The gaps in substantive law are real and many and require continuing effort to fill them, but they do not vitiate the force and effect of the law that exists, in the international society that is.

Above all, the lawyer will insist, critics of international law ask and answer the wrong questions. What matters is not whether the international system has legislative, judicial, or executive branches, corresponding to those we have become accustomed to seek in a domestic society; what matters is whether international law is reflected in the policies of nations and in relations between nations. The question is not whether there is an effective legislature; it is whether there is law that responds and corresponds to the changing needs of a changing society. The question is not whether there is an effective judiciary, but whether disputes are resolved in an orderly fashion in accordance with international law. Most important, the question is not whether law is enforceable or even effectively enforced; rather, whether law is observed, whether it governs or influences behavior, whether international behavior reflects stability and order. The fact is, lawyers insist, that nations have accepted important limitations on their sovereignty, that they have observed these norms and undertakings, that the result has been substantial order in international relations.

* * *

[International] law works. Although there is no one to determine and adjudge the law with authoritative infallibility, there is wide agreement on the content and meaning of law and agreements, even in a world variously divided. Although there is little that is comparable to executive law enforcement in a domestic society, there are effective forces, internal and external, to induce general compliance. Nations recognize that the observance of law is in their interest, and that every violation may also bring particular undesirable consequences. It is the unusual case in which policy-makers believe that the advantages of violation outweigh those of law observance, or where domestic pressures compel a government to violation even against the perceived national interest. The important violations are of political law and agreements, where basic interests of national security or independence are involved, engaging passions, prides, and prejudices, and where rational calculation of cost and advantage is less likely to occur and difficult to make. Yet, as we have seen, the most important principle of law today is commonly observed: nations have not been going to war, unilateral uses of force have been only occasional, brief, limited. Even the uncertain law against intervention, seriously breached in several instances, has undoubtedly deterred intervention in many other instances. Where political law has not deterred action it has often postponed or limited action or determined a choice among alternative actions.

None of this argument is intended to suggest that attention to law is the paramount or determinant motivation in national behavior, or even that it is always a dominant factor. A norm or obligation brings no guarantee of performance; it does add an important increment of interest in performing the obligation. Because of the requirements of law or of some prior agreement, nations modify their conduct in significant respects and in substantial degrees. It takes an extraordinary and substantially more important interest to persuade a nation to violate its obligations. Foreign policy, we know, is far from free; even the most powerful nations have learned that there are forces within their society and, even more, in the society of nations that limit their freedom of choice. When a contemplated action would violate international law or a treaty, there is additional, substantial limitation on the freedom to act.

### *Notes*

1. Since Henkin wrote How Nations Behave, instances of unilateral use of force appear to have increased. Does that fact seriously undermine Henkin's point that international law works? See Chapter 11.

2. Brownlie writes that we cannot use the existence of wars to disprove the reality of international law unless we are willing to admit that civil wars disprove the existence of domestic law:

> * * * on empirical grounds, given the number of civil wars, wars of secession and *coups d'état* since—let us say—1945, a good case can be made out for saying that public international law is *more* efficacious than *public* law within States. At any rate, whether or not such a judgment is sustainable, those who would judge international law would do well, on grounds of logical consistency, to start out by taking a hard look at the performance of *national* legal systems. It is a striking fact that in discussion of the efficacy of sanctions directed at the Smith regime in Rhodesia after U.D.I. it was common for reference to be made to the 'ineffectiveness' of United Nations resolutions. In this context it was unusual to hear reference to the efficacy of the Southern Rhodesia Act of 1965 and the law of treason as applicable in Rhodesia. Logically the Westminster *grundnorm* was as much in issue as the New York *grundnorm*.
>
> Indeed, within States a fair degree of common sense prevails in assessing the performance of law. It does not seem sensible to say, for example, that because the rule of law is weak in Northern Ireland, and murders occur continuously, we can conclude that the law of the United Kingdom is not a reality. That kind of logic involves saying that if an ideal score of one hundred is not achieved any other lesser score is not to be counted.

Brownlie, The Reality and Efficacy of International Law, 52 Brit.Y.B.I.L. 1, 2–3 (1981).

3. The Restatement (Third), Part I, Chapter 1, Introductory Note, states:

> *International law as law.* The absence of central legislative and executive institutions has led to skepticism about the legal quality of international law. Many observers consider international law to be only a series of precepts of morality or etiquette, of cautions and admonitions lacking in both specificity and binding quality. Governments, it is sometimes assumed, commonly disregard international law and observe it only when they deem it to be in their interest to do so.
>
> These impressions are mistaken. International law is law like other law, promoting order, guiding, restraining, regulating behavior. States, the principal addressees of international law, treat it as law, consider themselves bound by it, attend to it with a sense of legal obligation and with concern for the consequences of violation. Some states refer to international law in their constitutions; many incorporate it into their domestic legal systems; all take account of it in their governmental institutional arrangements and in their international relations. There is reference to the "Law

of Nations" in the Constitution of the United States (Article 1, section 8). It is part of the law of the United States, respected by Presidents and Congresses, and by the States, and given effect by the courts.*

## C. ENFORCEMENT AND COMPLIANCE

### IDENTIFYING VIOLATIONS IN A DECENTRALIZED SYSTEM

#### *FALK, THE ADEQUACY OF CONTEMPORARY THEORIES OF INTERNATIONAL LAW—GAPS IN LEGAL THINKING*

50 Va.L.Rev. 231, 249–50 (1964).**

Among the most serious deficiencies in international law is the frequent absence of an assured procedure for the identification of a violation. Theoretical inquiry can clarify the problem and provide some insight into the solution. The status of controverted behavior as legal or illegal is quite problematical, in the first instance, because no central institutions exist to make judgments that will be treated as authoritative by states. This is the familiar weakness of international law that results from reliance upon self-interpretation to discern the scope of permissible behavior. How is a violation of law to be identified in a decentralized social system? National officials may help shape behavior so that it minimizes conflict with legal rules, but once behavior is undertaken, then national officials elaborate a legal argument to support the challenged action rather than attempt to reach a balanced or impartial judgment on its legality. Furthermore, the strength of psychological allegiance to one's national sovereign often seems to render non-governmental specialists incapable of divorcing their role as citizen from their role as expert. The consequence is that the international system frequently lacks the means to determine definitely that certain behavior constitutes a violation of law. This inability to identify violations is especially prominent when the action is performed by a leading international actor who is able to block censure resolutions in the political organs of the United Nations. In such event, scholars in third states might be capable of providing the most objective account, but their relative obscurity and the special interests that might underlie their outlooks act to restrict the influence of their judgment. Existing theory does not take into sufficient account this difficulty of establishing a violation of international law.

This problem has deep, as well as obvious, consequences. The obvious consequence is a conclusion that, since there is no assured way to identify what is forbidden, everything is permitted. For how can international law claim to be a system of restraint if it lacks a means to identify transgressions? This question, far from suggesting the irrelevance of international law, points toward a better understanding of its function and purpose. For, although rules of restraint are the core of the system, their influence is often realized by a combination of self-restraint and reconciliation. A state bureaucracy refrains, under routine circumstances, from violating rules and approaches them in a spirit of impartiality. Once it is alleged that restraints have been broken, the extent of adherence to applicable rules has a great bearing upon the response of the complaining party. Therefore, the

* The numerous quotations of the Restatement are all reprinted by permission of American Law Institute.

** Reprinted by permission of the Virginia Law Review. Footnotes omitted.

degree and manner of violation may be more crucial than the fact of violation. The possibility of degrees of violation must be introduced explicitly into international legal theory. There is a need for an image of compliance and violation that draws inspiration from the idea of a spectrum or a prism, rather than insists upon a rigid dichotomy between legal or illegal conduct.

### *Notes*

1. The need to improve procedures to deter or remedy violations of international law has placed increased emphasis on the development of international courts, quasi-judicial commissions, and "alternative means of dispute resolution." See Chapter 10. The development of new norms often depends on accompanying arrangement for dispute resolution: states are more likely to agree to a norm or a particular expression of a norm only if there is put in place a means for resolving disputes as to its meaning or application, but even this is no guarantee. See, e.g., the 1982 Convention on the Law of the Sea, Part XV, Arts. 279–299.

2. States may decide to violate international law in an attempt to work a change of custom or treaty interpretation. As Henkin explains, these violations are dangerous:

> Customary international law, and even the interpretation of a treaty, may * * * change in response to new needs and new insights. A state might knowingly deviate from what had been established law (or established interpretation of a treaty) in the hope of changing the law. But that state does so at its peril. It does so at the peril that it will not succeed in changing the law and will be adjudged to have violated the law. It does so at the peril that it may succeed in destroying or eroding established law, to its later deep regret.

Henkin, The Invasion of Panama Under International Law: A Gross Violation, 29 Colum.J.Intl.L. 293, 311 (1991). On the question whether customary law remains law despite frequent violations, see Military and Paramilitary Activities in and Against Nicaragua (Merits), 1986 I.C.J. 14, 98.

## POWER AS ENFORCER OF LAW

### *MORGENTHAU & THOMPSON, POLITICS AMONG NATIONS*

312 (6th ed. 1985).*

[W]hether or not an attempt will be made to enforce international law and whether or not the attempt will be successful do not depend primarily upon legal considerations and the disinterested operation of law-enforcing mechanisms. Both attempt and success depend upon political considerations and the actual distribution of power in a particular case. The protection of the rights of a weak nation that is threatened by a strong one is then determined by the balance of power as it operates in that particular situation. Thus the rights of Belgium were safeguarded in 1914 against their violation by Germany, for it so happened that the protection of those rights seemed to be required by the national interests of powerful neighbors. Similarly, when in 1950 South Korea was attacked by North Korea, their concern with the maintenance of the balance of power in the Far East and of territorial stability throughout Asia prompted the United States and some of its allies, such as France and Great Britain, to come to the aid of South Korea. On the other hand, the rights of Colombia, when the United States supported the revolution in 1903 which led to the establishment of the Republic of Panama, and the rights of Finland, when attacked by the Soviet Union in 1939, were violated either with impunity or, as in the case of Finland, without the intervention of effective sanctions. There was no balance of power which could have protected these nations.

## ENFORCEMENT WITHOUT CENTRALIZED SANCTIONS

*BRIERLY, THE LAW OF NATIONS*

100–02 (6th ed., Waldock, 1963).*

The international system has no central organ for the enforcement of international legal rights as such, and the creation of any such general scheme of sanctions is for the present a very distant prospect. But the most urgent part of the problem of enforcement is the subjection to law of the use of force by states, and in modern times two notable experiments, in the Covenant of the League of Nations and the Charter of the United Nations, have been made with this end in view. These two experiments have followed different lines. The system of the Covenant relied on the fulfilment by the members of undertakings which they had severally given to take certain prescribed measures against an aggressor, but it did not set up a supra-national authority; the organs of the League could be used for coordinating the actions of the individual members, but they could not issue directions as to the action these members were to take. On the other hand, the Charter has created for the first time an authority which, at least according to the letter of its constitution, is to exercise a power of this supra-national kind * * *.

This absence of an executive power means that each state remains free, subject to the limitations on the use of force to be discussed later, to take such action as it thinks fit to enforce its own rights. This does not mean that international law has no sanctions, if that word is used in its proper sense of means for securing the observance of the law; but it is true that the sanctions which it possesses are not systematic or centrally directed, and that accordingly they are precarious in their operation. This lack of system is obviously unsatisfactory, particularly to those states which are less able than others to assert their own rights effectively.

But the difficulties of introducing any radical change into the present means of enforcing international law are extremely formidable. The problem has little analogy with that of the enforcement of law within the state, and the popular use of such phrases as an "international police force" tends to make it appear much simpler than it really is. Police action suggests the bringing to bear of the overwhelming force of the community against a comparatively feeble individual lawbreaker, but no action of that sort is possible in the international sphere, where the potential law-breakers are

* Reprinted by permission of Clarendon Press, Oxford. Footnotes omitted.

states, and the preponderance of force may even be on the law-breaking side. Even in a federation, as the experience of the United States has shown, the problem of enforcing the law against a member state has not been easy to solve.

## THE UNITED NATIONS AND LAW ENFORCEMENT

### *FITZMAURICE, THE FOUNDATIONS OF THE AUTHORITY OF INTERNATIONAL LAW AND THE PROBLEM OF ENFORCEMENT*

19 Mod.L.Rev. 1, 5–6 (1956).*

[I]t must be asked how far the international society has, in respect of breaches of international law *generally,* provided any new sanction to take the place of the former sanctions which, however crude and unsatisfactory their operation, did in some sort exist. It is sometimes thought that the Charter of the United Nations provides such a substitute, or at any rate the beginnings of one, particularly by means of those provisions which enable collective action of a forcible kind to be taken against aggression or breach of the peace. But this involves a misconception as to the scope of these Charter provisions. It is not against law-breaking as such that they are directed, but against that particular type of law-breaking that takes the form of an act of aggression or of committing a breach of the peace. Now it is possible to violate a large part of international law in all sorts of different ways, and to commit breaches of treaties right and left, without ever having recourse to aggression or breaking the peace, or even threatening a breach of the peace.

[There follows a brief survey of the enforcement powers of the Security Council and the General Assembly under the United Nations Charter.]

It must, therefore, be concluded that, as things are at present, neither of the main political organs of the United Nations can, in any but the most qualified sense, be regarded as an instrument for the enforcement of the legal rights of States, or the redress of legal wrongs *generally.*

### *Notes*

1. Fitzmaurice emphasizes that the Security Council's enforcement powers are limited to situations involving an act of aggression or breach of the peace. The Council has called for the use of force pursuant to these powers only twice; during the Korean war in the early 1950s and during the Gulf war in 1990. In the 1990s, however, the Security Council has begun to interpret its authority under the Charter broadly. In 1992, the Security Council, acting under Chapter VII of the Charter, authorized the Secretary–General and member states to use "all necessary means" to establish "a secure environment for humanitarian relief operations in Somalia." See Chapter 11 infra. On several occasions the Council has imposed economic sanctions for unlawful actions that it found to be threats to the peace; earlier against Rhodesia and South Africa, more recently against Serbia and Libya. See Chapter 11 infra. The Organization of American States has also used sanctions, recently against Haiti to press military authorities who had seized power in a 1991 coup to restore the democratically elected president.

Both the Security Council and the General Assembly have sometimes censured states for violating Charter principles. The General Assembly has rejected the credentials of South African delegations and refused to seat them because South Africa was practicing apartheid in violation of Security Council resolutions and principles of international law. In 1992, the General Assembly denied Serbia the former Yugoslavian seat in the Assembly because Serbia failed to comply with Security Council resolutions. See Blum, UN Membership of the "New" Yugoslavia: Continuity or Break?, 86 A.J.I.L. 830 (1992). On the rejection of credentials as a "sanction," see Halberstam, Excluding Israel from the United Nations be a Rejection of Its Credentials, 78 A.J.I.L. 179 (1984).

2. Many of the specialized agencies of the United Nations have deprived South Africa of privileges of membership on the ground that its apartheid practices violate basic principles of human rights. Should an offending state be excluded from a technical or economic convention or from a specialized agency because that state has violated a basic rule of international law? Or should the autonomy of the treaty regime prevail over the interest in enforcement of legal norms? Is the exclusion of defaulters from joint activities of the international community an effective sanction?

3. Do you agree that "despite * * * deficiencies resulting from the decentralized character of the legislative function, a legal system might still be capable of holding in check the power aspirations of its subjects if there existed judicial agencies that could speak with authority whenever a dissension occurred with regard to the existence or the import of a legal rule"? Morgenthau & Thompson, Politics Among Nations 302 (6th ed. 1985).* In the absence of compulsory jurisdiction by any international tribunal, can it be said that there exists a rule of law in international relations? Compare the following statement by Judge Dillard of the International Court of Justice:

> Law and what is legally permitted may be determined by what a court decides, but they are not only what a court decides. Law "goes on" every day without adjudication of any kind. In answer to a question put by a judge in the oral proceedings (C.R. 71/19, p. 23), Counsel for the United States, in a written reply received in the Registry on 18 March 1971, declared:
>
> > "The fact that in the international as opposed to a municipal legal system the other party cannot be assured of bringing a case involving material breach before an international tribunal except where both parties have accepted the compulsory jurisdiction of an international tribunal is a problem relating to the efficacy of international law and institutions generally and not especially to the problem of the material breach doctrine."
>
> It is part of the weakness of the international legal order that compulsory jurisdiction to decide legal issues is not part of the system. To say this is not to say that decisions taken by States in conformity with their good faith understanding of what international law either requires or permits are outside a legal frame of reference even if another State objects and despite the absence of adjudication.

Separate Opinion of Judge Dillard, Legal Consequences for States of the Continued Presence of South Africa in Namibia (South West Africa) notwithstanding

* Reprinted by permission of Clarendon Press, Oxford. Footnotes omitted.

S.C.Res. 276 (1970), 1971 I.C.J. 138, 156. See also The International Court of Justice at a Crossroads (Damrosch, ed. 1987).

4. Does the absence of a legislature encourage compliance with or contribute to the violation of international law? Consider the following observation of one British writer: "All legal systems correspond to some extent to the prevailing climate of opinion in the society in which they operate, but in national legal systems the concentration of legislative power in the hands of a small number of individuals may result in the enactment of rules which most people do not want and are reluctant to obey. In international law the absence of a legislature means that states very largely create law for themselves, and it is unlikely that they will create law which is not in their interests or which they will be tempted to break." Akehurst, A Modern Introduction to International Law 8 (5th ed. 1984).*

5. In the changed world order of the 1990s, groups of states have attempted to enforce international law by collective action, e.g., by sanctions against Serbia to induce it to desist from hostilities and to permit access to territory under its control for humanitarian assistance. Some suggested that the Conference on Security and Cooperation in Europe (CSCE) establish such a permanent role for itself. See generally Krylov, International Peacekeeping and Enforcement Actions After the Cold War, in Law and Force in the New International Order 94 (Damrosch & Scheffer, eds. 1991).

## HORIZONTAL ENFORCEMENT

### *LISSITZYN, THE INTERNATIONAL COURT OF JUSTICE*

5–6 (1951).**

In the absence of organized authority superior to the independent state, the principal sanctions of international law, aside from unilateral use of force the effectiveness of which depends on the power relationship between the contestants, are the disadvantages incurred by its breach, including the termination of the relations regulated by it and retaliation. Rational appreciation of the advantages of a relationship acts as a restraint upon the temptations to disregard the standards governing the relationship. For example, a state which persistently fails to respect the privileges and immunities of foreign diplomatic representatives may find itself excluded from diplomatic intercourse with the rest of the world. Furthermore, since the stronger nations have a preponderant influence in the development of some rules of international law, they often find it advantageous to support the observance of such rules. These sanctions are reinforced by the principles of moral obligation and good faith, the influence of public opinion, the advantages of a reputation for integrity and fair dealing, and the force of habit.

### *Notes*

1. The law against the use or threat of force may be enforced by collective action through the United Nations, but it is subject also to "horizontal enforce-

ment" by the victim acting in self-defense or with others in collective self-defense. See Chapter 11 infra.

2. Measures that are in themselves unlawful might be permissible when taken by a state in response to a violation of law by another state. See Restatement (Third) § 905; Zoller, Peacetime Unilateral Remedies: An Analysis of Countermeasures (1984). Is the use of force ever justified as a means of enforcing international law (except as indicated in note 1)? A reprisal, often including the use of force, by one state to exact compliance with an international duty on the part of another state, was traditionally subject to the requirement that the aggrieved state first seek peaceful vindication of its asserted rights. Compare Kelsen, Pure Theory of Law 321–22 (1967). On the present status of forcible reprisals in international law, see Chapter 11. On non-forcible measures to induce compliance or "punish" violations, see Chapter 7.

3. Reciprocity of obligations may function on a bilateral or multilateral level to encourage compliance. The use of the most-favored nation clause is an example of the extension of obligations on the basis of reciprocity, each state agreeing to treat the other contracting party as well as it treats the most-favored nation. See p. 1396 infra. Where nations undertake different obligations, asymmetry may contribute to antagonism. Before the issue was essentially resolved at the Third Law of the Sea Conference, the difference between states claiming 3–mile limits to their territorial waters and those claiming 12–mile limits led to friction. Following the seizure of the Pueblo, an American intelligence vessel, off the coast of North Korea in 1968, there was a demand that the United States extend its own 3–mile limit to a 12–mile limit with respect to those states adhering to the second formula. See Henkin, How Nations Behave, Chapter 3 (2d ed. 1979).

4. Who are the participants in the international sanctioning process? McDougal and Feliciano object to the fact that these participants "are customarily and summarily described as the attacking and target states and their respective allies." They argue that "[f]or purposes of precision in description * * * as well as for the application of certain sanctioning procedures such as those providing for criminal liability, one must frequently go behind the institutional abstraction 'state' and refer to the effective decision-makers * * *." McDougal & Feliciano, Law and Minimum World Public Order 12–13 (1961). The authors identify the decision-makers in the international "process of coercion":

> The authoritative decision-makers established by the public order of the world community for resolving controversies about international coercion are substantially the same as those established for other—"peacetime"—problems. Reflecting the decentralized structure of decision-making in the international community, they include not only the officials of international governmental organizations and judges of international courts and military and arbitration tribunals but also the officials of nation-states, whether participant or nonparticipant in the coercion process. Such authorized nation-state officials who respond to claims to exercise coercion may of course be the same officials who, at other times and in another capacity, assert claims to apply coercion; they may alternately be claimants making claims on their own behalf and decision-makers assessing the claims of others. This dualism in role and function, in a decentralized and primitively organized arena, permits reciprocity to operate as a sanctioning procedure and promotes recognition of the common interest in self-restraint. Conspicuous among decision-makers is, of course, the military commander who must

> on occasion, and at least in the first instance, pass upon the lawfulness both of his own proposed measures and of measures being taken against him.

Id. at 39–40.*

On the dual function of officials of states, as organs of both their national communities and of the international community, see Scelle, Le phénomène juridique de dédoublement fonctionnel, in Rechtsfragen der Internationalen Organisation, Festschrift für Hans Wehberg 324 (Schätzel ed. 1956); cf. Kelsen, General Theory of Law and State 327, 351 (1945).

5. Falk has observed that "the decentralized quality of international law places a special burden upon all legal institutions at the national level," not least domestic courts. See Falk, The Role of Domestic Courts in the International Legal Order 65–66 (1964). See also Mann, The Consequences of an International Wrong in International Law, 48 Brit.Y.B.I.L. 1 (1976–1977). Friedmann noted the "great temptation for national courts—to which they have yielded mostly—to arrive at and justify a decision that favors their own nationals." Friedmann, National Courts and the International Legal Order: Projections on the Implications of the Sabbatino Case, 34 Geo.Wash.L.Rev. 443, 453 (1966). Compare the majority and dissenting opinions in Banco Nacional de Cuba v. Sabbatino, 376 U.S. 398, 84 S.Ct. 923, 11 L.Ed.2d 804 (1964), p. 181 infra.

6. It has been suggested that what a state says about its own questionable actions, and the temptation to distort a principle of international law to justify a violation, may be more deleterious for international law than the particular violation itself. See, e.g., Henkin, The Invasion of Panama Under International Law: A Gross Violation, 29 Colum.J.Transnat'l L. 293, 314 (1991). See generally Henkin, How Nations Behave 39–87 (2d ed. 1979).

## WHY STATES OBSERVE INTERNATIONAL LAW

### *HENKIN, HOW NATIONS BEHAVE*

89–90, 92–95, 97–98 (2d ed. 1979).**

Much of international law resembles the civil law of domestic society (torts, contracts, property); some of it is analogous to "white collar crimes" (violations of antitrust or other regulatory laws, tax evasion) sometimes committed by "respectable" elements. Like such domestic law, international law too has authority recognized by all. No nation considers international law as "voluntary."

* * *

In arguments that international law is voluntary there lies also a common confusion about the relation of law to "policy." The two are often contrasted, suggesting that law is obligatory while policy is voluntary. In fact, law and policy are not in meaningful contrast, and their relation is not simple, whether in domestic or international society. All law is an instrument of policy, broadly conceived. Law is not an end in itself: even in the most enlightened domestic society it is a means—to order, stability, liberty,

* Footnotes omitted. Reprinted by permission of Yale University Press. Copyright© 1961 by Yale University.

** Footnotes omitted. Reprinted by permission of the Foundation Press.

security, justice, welfare. The policies served by law are sometimes articulated—in a constitution, in statutory preambles, in legislative pronouncements, in the opinions of the courts; often these policies are tacit, and commonly assumed. International law, too, serves policy, and the policies are not too different from the domestic: order and stability, peace, independence, justice, welfare.

* * *

Much is made of the fact that, in international society, there is no one to compel nations to obey the law. But physical coercion is not the sole or even principal force ensuring compliance with law. Important law is observed by the most powerful, even in domestic societies, although there is no one to compel them. In the United States, the President, Congress, and the mighty armed forces obey orders of a Supreme Court whose single marshal is unarmed.

Too much is made of the fact that nations act not out of "respect for law" but from fear of the consequences of breaking it. And too much is made of the fact that the consequences are not "punishment" by "superior," legally constituted authority, but are the response of the victim and his friends and the unhappy results for friendly relations, prestige, credit, international stability, and other interests which in domestic society would be considered "extra-legal." The fact is that, in domestic society, individuals observe law principally from fear of consequences, and there are "extra-legal" consequences that are often enough to deter violation, even were official punishment lacking. * * * In international society, law observance must depend more heavily on these extra-legal sanctions, which means that law observance will depend more closely on the law's current acceptability and on the community's—especially the victim's—current interest in vindicating it. It does not mean that law is not law, or that its observance is less law observance.

There are several mistakes in the related impression that nations do pursuant to law only what they would do anyhow. In part, the criticism misconceives the purpose of law. Law is generally not designed to keep individuals from doing what they are eager to do. Much of law, and the most successful part, is a codification of existing mores, of how people behave and feel they ought to behave. To that extent law reflects, rather than imposes, existing order. * * * To say that nations act pursuant to law only as they would act anyhow may indicate not that the law is irrelevant, but rather that it is sound and viable, reflecting the true interests and attitudes of nations, and that it is likely to be maintained.

At the same time much law (particularly tort law and "white collar crimes") is observed because it is law and because its violation would have undesirable consequences. The effective legal system, it should be clear, is not the one which punishes the most violators, but rather that which has few violations to punish because the law deters potential violators. He who does violate is punished, principally, to reaffirm the standard of behavior and to deter others. This suggests that the law does not concern itself principally with "criminal elements" on the one hand or with "saints" on the other. * * * In international society, too, law is not effective against the Hitlers, and is not needed for that nation which is content with its lot and has few temptations. International law aims at nations which are in principle law-abiding but which might be tempted to commit a violation if there were no threat of undesirable consequences. In international society, too, the reactions to a violation—as in Korea in 1950 or at Suez in 1956—reaffirm the law and strengthen its deterrent effect for the future.

In many respects, the suggestion that nations would act the same way if there were no law is a superficial impression. The deterrent influence of law is there, though it is not always apparent, even to the actor himself. The criticism overlooks also the educative roles of law, which causes persons and nations to feel that what is unlawful is wrong and should not be done. The government which does not even consider certain actions because they are "not done" or because they are not its "style" may be reflecting attitudes acquired because law has forbidden these actions.

In large part, however, the argument that nations do pursuant to law only what they would do anyhow is plain error. The fact that particular behavior is required by law brings into play those ultimate advantages in law observance that suppress temptations and override the apparent immediate advantages from acting otherwise. In many areas, the law at least achieves a common standard or rule and clarity as to what is agreed. * * *

The most common deprecation of international law, finally, insists that no government will observe international law "in the crunch, when it really hurts." If the implication is that nations observe law only when it does not matter, it is grossly mistaken. Indeed, one might as well urge the very opposite: violations in "small matters" sometimes occur because the actor knows that the victim's response will be slight; serious violations are avoided because they might bring serious reactions. The most serious violation—the resort to war—generally does not occur, although it is only when major interests are at stake that nations would even be tempted to this violation. On the other hand, if the suggestion is that when it costs too much to observe international law nations will violate it, the charge is no doubt true. But the implications are less devastating than might appear, since a nation's perception of "when it really hurts" to observe law must take into account its interests in law and in its observance, and the costs of violation. * * *

Whether, in the total, there is an effective "international order" is a question of perspective and definition. Order is not measurable, and no purpose is served by attempts to "grade" it in a rough impressionistic way. How much of that order is attributable to law is a question that cannot be answered in theory or in general, only in time and context. Law is one force—an important one among the forces that govern international relations at any time; the deficiencies of international society make law more dependent on other forces to render the advantages of observance high, the costs of violation prohibitive. In our times the influence of law must be seen in the light of the forces that have shaped international relations since the Second World War.

## *Notes*

1. Henkin declares: "It is probably the case that *almost all nations observe almost all principles of international law and almost all of their obligations almost all of the time.*" Henkin, How Nations Behave 47 (2d ed. 1979).

2. Professor Thomas Franck suggests that states are likely to obey norms of international law that have a high degree of "legitimacy." Franck defines legitimacy as "a property of a rule or rulemaking institution which itself exerts a pull toward compliance on those addressed normatively because those addressed believe that the rule or institution has come into being and operates in accordance with generally accepted principles of right process." Franck, The Power of Legitimacy Among Nations 24 (1990) (emphasis omitted). He identifies four indicators of legitimacy: "determinacy"—the ability of a rule to convey a clear message; "symbolic validation"—a ritual or signal of "pedigree" that induces compliance by communicating the authority of the rule or of its originator; "coherence"—the extent to which application of a rule is consistent and also justifiable in principled terms; "adherence"—the nexus between a "primary rule of obligation" and a "hierarchy of secondary rules" that defines how rules are to be made, interpreted and applied. Franck concludes that "to the extent a rule, or rule process, exhibits these four properties it will exert a strong pull on states to comply. To the extent these properties are not present, the institution will be easier to ignore and the rule easier to avoid by a state tempted to pursue its short-term self-interest." Id., at 49. In context, "[i]t is the community which invests legitimacy with meaning; it is in the community that legitimacy exerts its pull to rule compliance. It is because states constitute a community that legitimacy has the power to influence their conduct." Id., at 205. See also Franck's earlier article, Legitimacy in the International System, 82 A.J.I.L. 705 (1988). For a critique of Franck's concept of "legitimacy" in international law, see Alvarez, The Quest for Legitimacy: An Examination of The Power of Legitimacy Among Nations by Thomas M. Franck, 24 N.Y.U.J.Int'l L. & Pol. 199 (1991). See generally Hyde, The Concept of Legitimation in the Sociology of the Law, [1983] Wisc.L.Rev. 387.

3. It has been suggested that states are less likely to comply with "soft" international law. Professor Weil writes:

> [A]longside "hard law," made up of the norms creating precise legal rights and obligations, the normative system of international law comprises * * * more and more norms whose substance is so vague, so uncompelling, that A's obligation and B's right all but elude the mind. One does not have to look far for examples of this "fragile," "weak," or "soft law," as it is dubbed at times: * * * the purely hortatory or exhortatory provisions whereby [states] undertake to "seek to," "make efforts to," "promote," "avoid," "examine with understanding," "take all due steps with a view to," etc. * * * Whether a rule is "hard" or "soft" does not, of course, affect its normative character. A rule of treaty or customary law may be vague, "soft"; but * * * it does not thereby cease to be a legal norm. In contrast, however definite the substance of a non-normative provision—certain clauses of the Helsinki Final Act, say, or of the Charter of Economic Rights and Duties of States—that will not turn it in to a legal norm.[7]

7. The term "soft law" is not used solely to express the vague and therefore, in practice, uncompelling character of a legal norm but is also used at times to convey the sublegal value of some non-normative acts, such as certain resolutions of international organizations * * *. It would seem better to reserve the term "soft law" for rules that are imprecise and not really compelling, since sublegal obligations are neither "soft law" nor "hard law": they are simply not law at all. Two basically different categories are involved here; for while there are, on one hand, legal norms that are not in practice compelling, because too vague, there are also, on the other hand, provisions that are precise, yet remain at the pre- or subnormative stage. To discuss both of these categories in terms of "soft law" or "hard law" is to foster confusion.

Weil, Towards Relative Normativity in International Law?, 77 A.J.I.L. 413, 414–15 (1983).

Weil argues that the proliferation of "soft law" weakens the international legal system by blurring the line between law and nonlaw. However, states do in fact respect and rely on "soft law" norms. Much of international environmental law, for example, is "soft law" commonly respected by states, and may be, moreover, a step towards the formulation of more precise conventional rules or customary law. See Dupuy, Soft Law and the International Law of the Environment, 12 Mich.J.Int'l L. 420 (1991); Palmer, New Ways to Make International Environmental Law, 86 A.J.I.L. 259 (1992); Chapter 16 infra. Can "soft law" meet Franck's definition of "determinacy?"

On "soft law" generally, see A Hard Look at "Soft Law," 82 A.S.I.L.Proc. 371 (1988); Bierzanek, Some Remarks on "Soft" Law, 17 Polish Y.B. Int'l L. 21 (1988); Chinkin, The Challenge of Soft Law: Development and Change in International Law, 38 I.L.C.Q. 850 (1989); Dupuy, Declaratory Law and Programmatory Law: From Revolutionary Custom to "Soft Law," in Liber Röling: Declaration on Principles—A Quest for Universal Peace 247 (Akkermans, et al., eds. 1977); Gruchalla-Wesierki, A Framework for Understanding Soft Law, 30 McGill L.J. 37 (1984); Riphagen, From Soft Law to Ius Cogens and Back, 17 Vic.U.Wellington L.Rev. 81 (1987); Sztucki, Reflections on International "Soft Law," in Festskrift till Lars Hjerner: Studies in International Law 549 (1990).

For the legal character of various forms of "soft law," see Chapter 2, pp. 126–48.

4. For attempts to explain the sense of obligation in international law, see, e.g., 1 Oppenheim's International Law 8–13 (9th ed., Jennings & Watts, eds. 1992); Trimble, International Law, World Order and Critical Legal Studies, 42 Stan.L.Rev. 811 (1990); Brierly, The Basis of Obligation in International Law (Lauterpacht & Waldock, eds. 1958). Professor Schachter states:

> As a subject, the "foundation of obligation" is as old as international law itself; it had a prominent place in the seminal treatises of the founding fathers—Suarez, Vittoria, Grotius, Pufendorf et al—and it remained a central issue in the great controversies of the nineteenth century. In our century it has had a lesser place; it was largely overtaken by the discussion of "sources" and evidence, centered around Article 38 of the Statute of the International Court. Although subordinated, it was not neglected and each of the leading scholars of the twentieth century found himself impelled to advance a fresh analysis. No single theory has received general agreement and sometimes it seems as though there are as many theories or at least formulations as there are scholars. We can list at least a baker's dozen of "candidates" which have been put forward as the basis (or as one of the bases) of obligation in international law:
>
> (i) Consent of states
> (ii) Customary practice
> (iii) A sense of "rightness"—the juridical conscience
> (iv) Natural law or natural reason
> (v) Social necessity
> (vi) The will of the international community (the "consensus" of the international community)
> (vii) Direct (or "stigmatic") intuition
> (viii) Common purposes of the participants

(ix) Effectiveness
(x) Sanctions
(xi) "Systemic" goals
(xii) Shared expectations as to authority
(xiii) Rules of recognition

* * *

* * * [C]onceptions as to the basis of obligation arise time and again, and not only in theoretical discussion about the binding force of international law. They come up in concrete controversies as to whether a rule of law has emerged or has been terminated; whether an event is a violation or a precedent; and whether practice under a treaty is accepted as law. * * * The peculiar features of contemporary international society have generated considerable normative activity without at the same time involving commensurate use of the formal procedures for international "legislation" and adjudication.

* * *

But when we examine the arguments and the grounds for decision, we find more frequently than not that the test of whether a "binding" rule exists or should be applied will involve basic jurisprudential assumptions. Even the International Court of Justice, which is governed expressly by Article 38 of its Statute as to the sources of law, has demonstrated time and again that in their deliberative process the judges have had to look to theory to evaluate practice.

Schachter, Towards a Theory of International Obligation, 8 Virg.J.Int'l L. 300, 300–04 (1968).

5. What is the proper and practical role for international law in the creation of a better-ordered world community? According to James, some confusion in this regard may be attributed to the phrase "law and order:"

> [T]he smoothness with which it comes off the tongue can suggest that virtually all that is needed for order is the right kind of law, and in the inter-war period something of this kind was often assumed. In time the fallacy of this approach was eagerly exploded by "realistic" students of affairs, a task which was particularly easy as the word "order" was generally used in this connection to mean security. However, in their enthusiasm they threw the baby out with the bath water, and ever since students of international relations have had little time for international law. In consequence there has been a wide failure in this quarter to note that even with regard to security law can perform very useful services; that it is often a necessary means of changing and improving international society, and can sometimes make a small independent contribution towards these ends; and, above all, that the creation and maintenance of an ongoing and involved system of relationships, such as exists internationally, requires law. When, therefore, order is used to refer to such a system of relationships, it can truly be said that order is dependent on law. For order cannot exist without understandings about permissible behaviour, and the most fundamental as well as the most numerous of these understandings are unavoidably legal in character. Thus the significance of international law is enduring and vital. It does not control the ebb and flow of international politics, but it does provide an indispensable framework for the political process. Without it

relations, if not minimal, could not be other than anarchical in the most drastic meaning of the word. Internationally, as elsewhere, law is a concomitant of ordered relations. *Ubi societas, ibi ius.*

James, Law and Order in International Society, in The Bases of International Order 60, 83–84 (James ed. 1973).

6. See Restatement (Third), Part I, Chapter 1, Introductory Note.

## INTERNATIONAL LAW AND NATIONAL INTEREST

### *FRIEDMANN, THE ROLE OF INTERNATIONAL LAW IN THE CONDUCT OF INTERNATIONAL AFFAIRS*

20 Int'l J. 158, 159–62, 164–65, 168–69 (1965).*

* * * [T]he present state of international society tends to weaken the fabric and function of international law in certain respects, and to strengthen it in others. The weakening factors are the continuing supremacy of national policy objectives over the restraints of international law with regard to the use of force, where national policy and international order conflict. This implies a narrow definition of "national interest." It excludes the question whether the "national interest" in contemporary conditions does not require the strengthening of international law and authority. The strengthening factor is the gradual emergence of an international law of cooperation, implemented by an increasing number of international organizations, pursuing the common interests of mankind in the fields of economic and social development, health, communications and other matters of human welfare. Which of these two trends will prevail remains an open question, fateful for the future of mankind.

* * *

The philosophy of the supremacy of national interest over international law was recently expressed by Dean Acheson [3] in the following terms:

> "* * * those involved in the Cuban crisis of October 1962, will remember the irrelevance of the supposed moral considerations brought out in the discussions. Judgment centered about the appraisal of dangers and risks, the weighing of the need for decisive and effective actions against considerations of prudence; the need to do enough, against the consequence of doing too much."

* * *

The attitude outlined [by Mr. Acheson] expresses the prevailing instincts of most people. When the chips are down, the average Russian, Chinese, American, Frenchman, Indian or Indonesian will rally around the flag; he will respond to patriotic appeals even if it means a defiance of international legal prohibitions. Is this a simple matter of "realism" versus "wishful

* Some footnotes omitted. Reprinted by permission of the Canadian Institute of International Affairs. The author has made minor changes in the text of the article as it originally appeared.

3. In an address given at Amherst College, as reported in The New York Times, December 10, 1964.

thinking"? It is submitted that the role of international law in our time is a more complex issue.

* * * It is the *meaning* of "national interest" which has shifted and today includes universally binding rules against aggression as an aspect of national survival. * * *

* * *

The basic defect of the Acheson thesis does not so much lie in its analysis of the present situation as in the implication that the present state of affairs should be recognized as the only "realistic" approach to the conduct of international relations. A similar argument would have appeared persuasive to the majority of contemporaries over the last eight centuries, while in one country after another central authority and law gradually established their supremacy over warring kingdoms, dukes, archbishops and city republics. * * *

What distinguishes the contemporary problem from that of previous centuries is the desperate urgency of the human condition. Just as the jet plane and the long-range missile move at speeds hundreds or thousands of times greater than that of the horse and buggy, so the need to create organized alternatives to mutual destruction * * * cannot be met with the means of earlier ages. "Co-operate or perish" is a stark fact, not an evangelistic aspiration.

### *Notes*

1. Acheson also said about the Cuban missile crisis:

I must conclude that the propriety of the Cuban quarantine is not a legal issue. The power, position and prestige of the United States had been challenged by another state; and law simply does not deal with such questions of ultimate power—power that comes close to the sources of sovereignty. I cannot believe that there are principles of law that say we must accept destruction of our way of life. One would be surprised if practical men, trained in legal history and thought, had devised and brought to a state of general acceptance a principle condemnatory of an action so essential to the continuation of preeminent power as that taken by the United States last October. Such a principle would be as harmful to the development of restraining procedures as it would be futile. No law can destroy the state creating the law. The survival of states is not a matter of law.

However, in the action taken in the Cuban quarantine, one can see the influence of accepted legal principles. These principles are procedural devices designed to reduce the severity of a possible clash. Those devices cause wise delay before drastic action, create a "cooling off" period, permit the consideration of others' views. The importance of the Organization of American States was also procedural, and emphasized the desirability of collective action, thus creating a common denominator of action. Some of these desirable consequences are familiar to us in the domestic industrial area.

In October the United States was faced with grave problems of policy and procedure in relation to its own and outside interests. The action taken was the right action. "Right" means more than legally justifiable, or even successful. The United States resolved very grave issues of policy in a way consonant with ethical restraint.

The Cuban Quarantine, Remarks by the Honorable Dean Acheson, 57 A.S.I.L.Proc. 9, 14 (1963).*

In contrast to Acheson's view of the irrelevance of international law in the Cuban Missile Crisis, Henkin has argued that persons conversant with the constrictions of international law influenced the final decision to implement a quarantine rather than resorting to bombing of Cuban territory. See Henkin, How Nations Behave 286–90 (2d ed. 1979).

Regardless of the influence of international law on the decision-making process, would it be wise, from the point of view of the integrity of international law, to recognize certain areas as immune from the prescriptions of international law? Where policy issues are likely to be of decisive importance in determining the behavior of nations, should international law recognize sovereign prerogatives? Is aggression between states, especially when factual issues perform a major role in assessing legal implications, an area where international law should remain silent? See Chapter 11.

2. On the common view that there is continuing tension between international law and national interest:

> It is perhaps this circumscribed view of the law which has caused Professor Morgenthau to take also a narrow view of "national interest." There follows "that iron law of international politics, that legal obligations must yield to the national interest." [Morgenthau, In Defense of the National Interest 144 (1951)]. Of course, that statement may suggest merely the truism that nations, like individuals, balance the advantages and disadvantages of law observance and may decide to violate the law and accept the consequences. But the implications of Mr. Morgenthau's "iron law" are broader. It seems to set up a dichotomy between law observance and national interest, to treat their concurrence as coincidental and their opposition as common. If so, it seems to see immediate tangible advantage—the gain from a violation—as the only national interest. It does not seem to consider that the law of nations may be in the interest of all nations, as the law of an enlightened society is in the interest of all its citizens. It does not see national interest in law observance—in order and stability, in reliable expectations, in confidence and credit, in the support of other nations and peoples, in friendly relations, in living up to a nation's aspirations and self image, in satisfying the "morality" of its own officials and of its own citizens. It tends to discount the national interest in avoiding other, immediate "concrete" responses to violation. The issue of law observance, I would suggest, is never a clear choice between legal obligation and national interest; a nation that observes law, even when it "hurts," is not sacrificing national interest to law; it is choosing between competing national interests; when it commits a violation it is also sacrificing one national interest to another.

Henkin, How Nations Behave 331 (2d ed. 1979).** On the various national interests served by the observance of international law, see, e.g., Weston, The Logic and Utility of a Lawful United States Foreign Policy, 1 Transnat'l L. & Contemp.Probs. 1 (1991).

3. The view that international law must bow to national interest was again prominent in public discussion after international lawyers criticized the United States invasion of Grenada in 1983 and United States actions in Central America, particularly in relation to Nicaragua and Panama. See Chapter 11.

## SECTION 3. CONTEMPORARY PERSPECTIVES ON INTERNATIONAL LAW

### *MACDONALD & JOHNSTON, INTERNATIONAL LEGAL THEORY: NEW FRONTIERS OF THE DISCIPLINE,*

in The Structure and Process of International Law: Essays in Legal Philosophy Doctrine and Theory 6–8 (Macdonald & Johnston, eds. 1983).

In the context of international law it seems evident that theory has taken on an expanded meaning in modern times. Traditionally, the theorist was a scholar immersed in philosophy or theology who approached the discipline of international law within the tradition of preexisting schools of thought, focussing on metaphysical and ethical aspects of the 'science' of international law. Virtually all of the 'classical' theorists of international law regarded themselves more or less consciously as exponents of a particular philosophical view point with an intellectual and moral responsibility to develop the discipline within the selected tradition. Essentially, the philosophical theorist's approach was that of linear development from philosophical premises of his own choosing. Even today, many of the philosophical theorists in international law tend to be associated, directly or indirectly, with the tradition of natural law, and this has tended to produce a more or less explicitly ethical approach to the discipline.

By the nineteenth century, positivism had become prevalent in the legal thinking of many Western nations, and the particular result of this in international law was a trend toward what might be termed the development of the 'systematic anatomy' of the body of international law. The philosophic disposition to break down the field of international law into fundamental elements, concepts and doctrines, was easily reconciled with contemporary trends in municipal law, and with the pedagogical need to prepare systematic treatises suitable for introducing students to the science of international law. The benefit of this kind of 'dissectionist,' doctrinal scholarship was to provide a clarification and even development of rules, which nation-states by the late nineteenth century recognized as necessary for the orderly exercise of state-craft in world affairs. Today, most *doctrinal theorists* are influenced, more or less overtly, by the positivist school of jurisprudence. They are rarely concerned with the kinds of metaphysical questions that challenged the early classicists. By and large they are content to regard international law as an emerging system of rules and procedures generally accepted in state practice and consent as the most fundamental element in the process of legal development.

* * *

The prominence, even pre-eminence, of the arena in contemporary international law seems to have created the need for a different kind of legal theorist, one essentially concerned with problem-solving in modern trans-national society, or more properly, with the 'problem of problem-solving.' For this kind of 'scientific' theorist, theoretical concerns focus on questions related to the gathering of information, the comparison of insights from different disciplines, and the choice of analogies and techniques from all areas of knowledge relevant to the problem to be solved. This kind of interest is, of course, of special appeal to academics involved in methodological issues and those responsive to the latest information technologies in the ivory tower. But the problem-solving approach of the scientific theorist also brings him into frequent contact with international lawyers in the arena, who have official responsibility for producing 'solutions' to difficult problems in the organized world community. Accordingly, the scientific theorist, unlike his philosophical and doctrinal counterparts, tends to be drawn into collaborative undertakings with colleagues both of the tower and of the arena. What seems to be happening in the late twentieth century is that these collaborative undertakings sometimes have the effect of extracting theoretical contributions from international lawyers of the arena as well as from international lawyers of the tower.

There is also a constituency of international lawyers associated with the market place of private service: that is, the *forum*. International lawyers have always contributed to the development and maintenance of international trade, but practitioners of this kind have had virtually no opportunity to make theoretical contributions to the discipline. This may soon change, as specialists in the legal aspects of trans-national corporate and commercial affairs are required to forge increasingly sophisticated linkages with lawyers of the arena, in conformity with modern views regarding the need for inter-governmental regulation over such matters.

---

The continuing development of international law has attracted critical attention from intellectual movements of the latter decades of the Twentieth Century, notably from feminist writers and proponents of "critical legal studies."

## A. FEMINIST PERSPECTIVES ON INTERNATIONAL LAW

### *CHARLESWORTH, CHINKIN & WRIGHT, FEMINIST APPROACHES TO INTERNATIONAL LAW*

85 A.J.I.L. 613, 615–629 (1991) (footnotes omitted).*

By challenging the nature and operation of international law and its context, feminist legal theory can contribute to the progressive development of international law. A feminist account of international law suggests that we inhabit a world in which men of all nations have used the statist system to establish economic and nationalist priorities to serve male elites, while basic human, social and economic needs are not met. International institutions echo these same priorities. By taking women seriously and describing the silences and fundamentally skewed nature of international law, feminist theory can identify possibilities for change.

* * *

## III. The Masculine World of International Law

In this section we argue that the international legal order is virtually impervious to the voices of women and propose two related explanations for this: the organizational and normative structures of international law.

### *The Organizational Structure of International Law*

The structure of the international legal order reflects a male perspective and ensures its continued dominance. The primary subjects of international law are states and, increasingly, international organizations. In both states and international organizations the invisibility of women is striking. Power structures within governments are overwhelmingly masculine: women have significant positions of power in very few states, and in those where they do, their numbers are minuscule. Women are either unrepresented or under represented in the national and global decision-making processes.

States are patriarchal structures not only because they exclude women from elite positions and decision-making roles, but also because they are based on the concentration of power in, and control by, an elite and the domestic legitimation of a monopoly over the use of force to maintain that control. This foundation is reinforced by international legal principles of sovereign equality, political independence and territorial integrity and the legitimation of force to defend those attributes.

International organizations are functional extensions of states that allow them to act collectively to achieve their objectives. Not surprisingly, their structures replicate those of states, restricting women to insignificant and subordinate roles. Thus, in the United Nations itself, where the achievement of nearly universal membership is regarded as a major success of the international community, this universality does not apply to women.

* * *

Women are excluded from all major decision making by international institutions on global policies and guidelines, despite the often disparate impact of those decisions on women. Since 1985, there has been some improvement in the representation of women in the United Nations and its specialized agencies. It has been estimated, however, that "at the present rate of change it will take almost 4 more decades (until 2021) to reach equality (i.e. 50% of professional jobs held by women). * * *"

The silence and invisibility of women also characterizes those bodies with special functions regarding the creation and progressive development of international law. Only one woman has sat as a judge on the International Court of Justice and no woman has ever been a member of the International Law Commission. Critics have frequently pointed out that the distribution of judges on the Court does not reflect the makeup of the international community, a concern that peaked after the decision in the *South West Africa* cases in 1966. Steps have since been taken to improve "the representation of the main forms of civilization and of the principal legal systems of the world" on the Court, but not in the direction of representing women, half of the world's population.

* * *

Why is it significant that all the major institutions of the international legal order are peopled by men? Long-term domination of all bodies wielding political power nationally and internationally means that issues traditionally of concern to men become seen as human concerns, while "women's concerns" are relegated to a special, limited category. * * * The orthodox face of international law and politics would change dramatically if their institutions were truly human in composition: their horizons would widen to include issues previously regarded as domestic—in the two senses of the word. * * *

*The Normative Structure of International Law*

* * * International jurisprudence assumes that international law norms directed at individuals within states are universally applicable and neutral. It is not recognized, however, that such principles may impinge differently on men and women; consequently, women's experiences of the operation of these laws tend to be silenced or discounted.

The normative structure of international law has allowed issues of particular concern to women to be either ignored or undermined. For example, modern international law rests on and reproduces various dichotomies between the public and private spheres, and the "public" sphere is regarded as the province of international law. One such distinction is between public international law, the law governing the relations between nation-states, and private international law, the rules about conflicts between national legal systems. Another is the distinction between matters of international "public" concern and matters "private" to states that are considered within their domestic jurisdiction, in which the international community has no recognized legal interest. Yet another is the line drawn between law and other forms of "private" knowledge such as morality.

At a deeper level one finds a public/private dichotomy based on gender. One explanation feminist scholars offer for the dominance of men and the male voice in all areas of power and authority in the western liberal tradition is that a dichotomy is drawn between the public sphere and the private or domestic one. The public realm of the work place, the law, economics, politics and intellectual and cultural life, where power and authority are exercised, is regarded as the natural province of men; while the private world of the home, the hearth and children is seen as the appropriate domain of women. The public/private distinction has a normative, as well as a descriptive, dimension. Traditionally, the two spheres are accorded asymmetrical value: greater significance is attached to the public, male world than to the private, female one. * * * Its reproduction and acceptance in all areas of knowledge have conferred primacy on the male world and supported the dominance of men.

* * *

In one sense, the public/private distinction is the fundamental basis of the modern state's function of separating and concentrating juridical forms of power that emanate from the state. The distinction implies that the private world is uncontrolled. In fact, the regulation of taxation, social security, education, health and welfare has immediate effects on the private sphere. The myth that state power is not exercised in the "private" realm allocated to women masks its control.

What force does the feminist critique of the public/private dichotomy in the foundation of domestic legal systems have for the international legal order? Traditionally, of course, international law was regarded as operating only in the most public of public spheres: the relations between nation-states. We argue, however, that the definition of certain principles in international law rests on and reproduces the public/private distinction. It thus privileges the male world view and supports male dominance in the international legal order.

The grip that the public/private distinction has on international law, and the consequent banishment of women's voices and concerns from the discipline, can be seen in the international prohibition on torture. The right to freedom from torture and other forms of cruel, inhuman or degrading treatment is generally accepted as a paradigmatic civil and political right. It is included in all international catalogs of civil and political rights and is the focus of specialized United Nations and regional treaties. The right to be free from torture is also regarded as a norm of customary international law—indeed, like the prohibition on slavery, as a norm of *jus cogens*. The basis for the right is traced to "the inherent dignity of the human person." Behavior constituting torture is defined in the Convention against Torture as

> any act by which severe pain or suffering, whether physical or mental, is intentionally inflicted on a person for such purposes as obtaining from him or a third person information or a confession, punishing him for an act he or a third person has committed or is suspected of having committed, or intimidating or coercing him or a third person, or for any reason based on discrimination of any kind, when such pain or suffering is inflicted by or at the instigation of or with the consent or acquiescence of a public official or other person acting in an official capacity.

This definition has been considered broad because it covers mental suffering and behavior "at the instigation of" a public official. However, despite the use of the term "human person" in the Preamble, the use of the masculine pronoun alone in the definition of the proscribed behavior immediately gives the definition a male, rather than a truly human, context. More importantly, the description of the prohibited conduct relies on a distinction between public and private actions that obscures injuries to their dignity usually sustained by women. The traditional canon of human rights law does not deal in categories that fit the experiences of women. It is cast in terms of discrete violations of rights and offers little redress in cases where there is a pervasive, structural denial of rights.

The international definition of torture requires not only the intention to inflict suffering, but also the secondary intention that the infliction of suffering will fulfill a purpose. Recent evidence suggests that women and children, in particular, are victims of widespread and apparently random terror campaigns by both governmental and guerrilla groups in times of civil unrest or armed conflict. Such suffering is not clearly included in the international definition of torture.

A crucial aspect of torture and cruel, inhuman or degrading conduct, as defined, is that they take place in the public realm: a public official or a person acting officially must be implicated in the pain and suffering. The rationale for this limitation is that "private acts (of brutality) would usually be ordinary criminal offenses which national law enforcement is expected to repress. *International* concern with torture arises only when the State itself abandons its function of protecting its citizenry by sanctioning criminal action by law enforcement personnel." Many women suffer from torture in this limited sense. The international jurisprudence on the notion of torture arguably extends to sexual violence and psychological coercion if the perpetrator has official standing. However, severe pain and suffering that is inflicted outside the most public context of the state—for example, within the home or by private persons, which is the most pervasive and significant violence sustained by women—does not qualify as torture despite its impact on the inherent dignity of the human person. Indeed, some forms of violence are attributed to cultural tradition. * * *

States are held responsible for torture only when their designated agents have direct responsibility for such acts and that responsibility is imputed to the state. States are not considered responsible if they have maintained a legal and social system in which violations of physical and mental integrity are endemic. * * * A feminist perspective on human rights would require a rethinking of the notions of immutability and state responsibility and in this sense would challenge the most basic assumptions of international law. If violence against women were considered by the international legal system to be as shocking as violence against people for their political ideas, women would have considerable support in their struggle.

## *Notes*

1. Feminist analysis of international law is a recent phenomenon. The implications of the public/private distinction in international law have been explored in greater detail in connection with issues of development. See Charlesworth, The Public/Private Distinction and the Right to Development in International Law, 12 Australian Y.B.Int'l L. 190 (1992). On feminist critiques of the use of force, international humanitarian law, and international human rights, see the Symposium, in 12 Australian Y.B.Int'l L. (1992), especially, Chinkin, A Gendered Perspective to the International Use of Force, at 279; Gardam, A Feminist Appraisal of Certain Aspects of International Humanitarian Law, at 265; Wright, Economic Rights and Social Justice: A Feminist Analysis of Some International Human Rights Conventions, at 242.

On international law and women's rights generally, see the bibliographies in Peace and World Order Studies: A Curriculum Guide, Chapter XVII, Women and World Order (Thomas & Klare, eds., 1989); Cook, Women's International Human Rights: A Bibliography, 24 N.Y.U.J.Int'l L. & Pol. 857 (1992). See also Ahooja–Patel, Women's Rights, in International Law: Achievements and Prospects 1105 (M. Bedjaoui, ed. 1991); Byrnes, Women, Feminism and International Human Rights—Methodological Myopia, Fundamental Flaws or Meaningful Marginalisation? Some Current Issues, 12 Australian Y.B.Int'l L. 205 (1992); Holt, Women's Rights and International Law: The Struggle for Recognition and Enforcement, 1 Column.J. Gender & L. 117 (1991). On Human Rights generally see Chapter 8.

2. It has been suggested that international refugee law is ripe for feminist analysis because women seeking asylum from sexual violence or from laws that

punish the victims of sexual violence may not fit within the definition of "refugee" contained in the Convention and subsequent Protocol Relating to the Status of Refugees. See Castel, Rape, Sexual Assault and the Meaning of Persecution, 4 Int'l J. Refugee L. 39 (1992); Note, Obtaining Political Asylum: Classifying Rape As A Well-Founded Fear of Persecution on Account of Political Opinion, 10 Bost.Coll.Third World L.J. 355 (1990). It was not until 1990 that the United Nations High Commissioner for Refugees adopted a policy on the particular needs of women refugees in response to growing concerns that those needs were not being met. See UNHCR Policy on Refugee Women, U.N. Doc. A/AC.96/754 (1990).

## B. INTERNATIONAL LAW AND THE CRITICAL LEGAL STUDIES MOVEMENT

Critical Legal Studies have drawn attention to the "discourse" of international law, and to the legitimizing power of language, examining the effect of language upon ideas of rights and obligations in international relations. For example, Professor David Kennedy writes about the discourse on the sources of international law:

> Discourse about sources searches abstractly to delimit the norms which bind sovereigns in a way which relies neither on the interests of sovereigns nor on some vision of the good which is independent of state interests. The search is for a decisive discourse—not for a persuasive justification—which can continually distinguish binding from nonbinding norms while remaining open to expressions of sovereign will. The argumentative moves made by those engaged in sources discourse reflect this central goal.
>
> The result is a discourse of evasion which constantly combines that which it cannot differentiate and emphasizes that which it can express only by hyperbolic exclusion. Pursued in this fashion, sources doctrine moves us forward from theory towards other doctrines which it supplements, remaining both authoritatively independent and parasitic. This paradoxical position between theoretical discourse and doctrines of substance and process is maintained by endlessly embracing and managing a set of ephemeral rhetorical differences. The turn to sources doctrine thus seems to provide an escape from fruitless theoretical argument, moving us towards legal order, precisely by opening up an endlessly proliferating field of legal argumentation.

Kennedy, International Legal Structures 107 (1987).

Martti Koskenniemi uses the concept of "state sovereignty" to suggest that "the use of sovereignty within international legal discourse follows from a set of contradictory assumptions which control the production of arguments within it and render it ultimately incapable of providing determinate answers to legal problems." He continues:

> Within international legal discourse "State sovereignty" is interpreted from the perspective of two conflicting assumptions. Sometimes sovereignty is taken to mean the completeness of State power within its territory which is inherent in the concept of statehood and precedes the international normative order. At other times, sovereignty is conceptualized as a "systemic" concept, determined from within the international

normative system which in this sense precedes it. These two assumptions contradict each other. The former legitimizes the international normative order from the given legitimacy of State power. The latter legitimizes State power from the assumed legitimacy of the normative order. * * *

International legal discourse does not establish priority between these conflicting models of legitimation. It works with a fluid conception of sovereignty which contains both simultaneously. Therefore, it is unable to produce coherent or convincing solutions to legal problems. Each disputing State's position can be expressed so as to manifest either of the legitimation models. By taking one or other model as one's starting-point it is possible to support whatever position one needs to support. As dispute solution cannot prefer either, it will remain materially uncontrolling. What look like solutions determined by the law emerge as facade legitimation, following from adopting interpretations about the parties positions which are undetermined by the legal arguments themselves.

* * *

The idea of sovereignty is incoherent inasmuch as it expresses the State's subjective freedom as well as its objective submission to an international normative order. The structure of international legal discourse follows from this basic ambiguity. The dynamics of the discourse is provided by the constantly renewed effort to solve the contradiction between the two incompatible perspectives towards sovereignty. As the contradiction remains unsolved, however, the discourse remains open-ended. No certainty about correct norms or correct patterns of behavior can be attained within it.

Koskenniemi, Sovereignty[:] Prolegomena to a Study of the Structure of International Law as Discourse, 4 Kansainoikeus Ius Gentium 71, 71–72, 106 (Nos. 1/2, 1987).

### *Notes*

1. Critical legal scholars have argued that much, if not all of international law, is merely an ideological construct intended to secure the observance of international norms by convincing states and people that the law is politically neutral and just. See Purvis, Critical Legal Studies in Public International Law, 32 Harv.Int'l L.J. 81 (1991).

2. Critical perspectives on international law include: Carty, The Decay of International Law: A Reappraisal of the Limits of Legal Imagination in International Affairs (1986); Franck, The Power of Legitimacy Among Nations (1990); Koskenniemi, From Apology to Utopia: The Structure of International Legal Argument (1989); International Law (Koskenniemi, ed. 1992); Allott, Language, Method and the Nature of International Law, 45 Brit.Y.B.Int'l L. 79 (1971); Boyle, Ideals and Things: International Legal Scholarship and the Prison–House of Language, 26 Harv.Int'l L.J. 327 (1985); Carty, Critical International Law: Recent Trends in the Theory of International Law, 2 Eur.J.Int'l L. 66 (1991); Franck, Legitimacy in the International System, 82 A.J.I.L. 705 (1988); Kennedy, Theses About International Legal Discourse, 23 German Y.B.Int'l L. 353 (1980); Kennedy, A New Stream of International Legal Scholarship, 7 Wis.Int'l

L.J. 1 (1988); Trimble, International Law, World Order and Critical Legal Studies, 42 Stan.L.Rev. 811 (1990); Sathirathai, An Understanding of the Relationship Between International Legal Discourse and Third World States, 25 Harv.Int'l L.Rev. 395 (1984); Scobbie, Towards the Elimination of International Law: Some Radical Scepticism about Sceptical Radicalism, 61 Brit.Y.B. Int'l L. 339 (1990).

# Chapter 2

# SOURCES AND EVIDENCE OF INTERNATIONAL LAW

## SECTION 1. SOURCES

*Restatement (Third) § 102* *

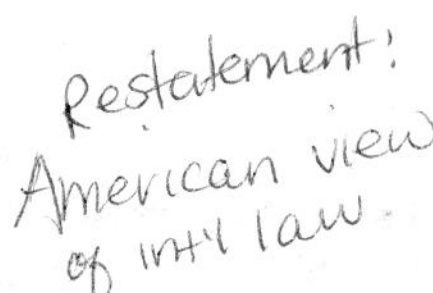
Restatement:
American view
of int'l law.

**Sources of International Law**

(1) A rule of international law is one that has been accepted as such by the international community of states

(a) in the form of customary law;

(b) by international agreement; or

(c) by derivation from general principles common to the major legal systems of the world.

(2) Customary international law results from a general and consistent practice of states followed by them from a sense of legal obligation.

(3) International agreements create law for the states parties thereto and may lead to the creation of customary international law when such agreements are intended for adherence by states generally and are in fact widely accepted.

(4) General principles common to the major legal systems, even if not incorporated or reflected in customary law or international agreement, may be invoked as supplementary rules of international law where appropriate.

*Statute of the International Court of Justice*

ARTICLE 38

1. The Court, whose function is to decide in accordance with international law such disputes as are submitted to it, shall apply:

a. international conventions, whether general or particular, establishing rules expressly recognized by the contesting states;

* Reprinted with permission of the American Law Institute.

b. international custom, as evidence of a general practice accepted as law;

c. the general principles of law recognized by civilized nations;

d. subject to the provisions of Article 59, judicial decisions and the teachings of the most highly qualified publicists of the various nations, as subsidiary means for the determination of rules of law.

2. This provision shall not prejudice the power of the Court to decide a case *ex aequo et bono,* if the parties agree thereto.

## THE DOCTRINE OF SOURCES AND THE INDUCTIVE SCIENCE OF LAW

*SCHACHTER, INTERNATIONAL LAW IN THEORY AND PRACTICE*

35–36 (1991).

The principal intellectual instrument in the last century for providing objective standards of legal validation has been the doctrine of sources. That doctrine which became dominant in the nineteenth century and continues to prevail today lays down verifiable conditions for ascertaining and validating legal prescriptions. The conditions are the observable manifestations of the "wills" of States as revealed in the *processes* by which norms are formed—namely, treaty and State practice accepted as law. (These are the principal processes; Article 38 of the Statute of the Court expands them to include general principles of law.) The emphasis in this doctrine on criteria of law applied solely on the basis of observable "positive" facts can be linked to those intellectual currents of the nineteenth century that extolled inductive science. It has been suggested that the sociological positivism of Comte was especially influential on juristic thinking. Not surprisingly, the conception of a positive science of law had a strong attraction in the prevailing intellectual climate.

Moreover, within the field of international law itself, the competing ideas of natural law based on moral and philosophic conceptions were increasingly perceived as irrelevant to the political order of sovereign States. It had become evident to international lawyers as it had to others that States, which made and applied law, were not governed by morality or "natural reason;" they acted for reasons of power and interest. It followed that law could only be ascertained and determined through the actual methods used by States to give effect to their "political wills". In this way, the powerful ideas of positive science and State sovereignty were harnessed to create a doctrine for removing subjectivism and morality from the "science" of international law. It was intended to make international law realistic and definite. It satisfied those concerned with the realities of State power and the importance of sovereignty. It also met the intellectual requirements of the analytical theorists of law who sought to place jurisprudence on scientific foundations. Interestingly, the doctrine of sources became acceptable to the Marxist–Leninist legal theorists despite Marxist objections to philosophical positivism. From their standpoint, the doctrine of sources properly recognized the will of sovereign States as decisive. The Soviet jurists saw international law as the product of the "coordination of wills" of the sovereign States manifested in treaties and practice *accepted* by them as law.

The doctrine of sources was more than a grand theoretical conception. It also provided the stimulus for a methodology of international law that called for detailed "inductive" methods for ascertaining and validating law. If sources were to be used objectively and scientifically, it was necessary to examine in full detail the practice and related legal convictions (*opinio juris*) of States. * * *. The favored instruments of the positivist methodology were the national digests of State practice prepared by, or in close association with the government of the State concerned. * * * They were mainly systematic collections of legal conclusions and relevant facts expressed in diplomatic correspondence and in governmental officials' legal opinions * * *. It would be possible for an arbiter to conclude whether a particular decision came within the rule evidenced by the precedents in the digest. * * * However, a closer look * * * indicates that these were significant deviations from the doctrine and its methodology. These deviations suggest that the idea of an inductive, factual positive science of international law may be characterized more as myth than reality.

## VOLUNTARISM AND POSITIVISM

These two terms are often used in the writings on international law relating to sources. They conceptualize theories of international law that have been widely accepted and also strongly criticized. Their significance goes beyond legal theory; they reflect conceptions of international order that influence political and legal decisions.

"Voluntarism" is the classic doctrine of state sovereignty applied to the formation of international law. It holds that international legal rules emanate exclusively from the free will of states as expressed in conventions or by usages generally accepted as law. (See the Lotus Case decision on p. 63.) "Positivism" as used in this context emphasizes the obligatory nature of legal norms and the fixed authoritative character of the formal sources. It also tends to consider that to be "law," the international norm must be capable, in principle, of application by a judicial body.

The political significance of "positivist voluntarism" is brought out in the following comment by a contemporary proponent:

> This means that states are at once the creators and addressees of the norms of international law and that there can be no question today, any more than yesterday, of some 'international democracy' in which a majority or representative proportion of states is considered to speak in the name of all and thus be entitled to impose its will on other states. Absent voluntarism, international law would no longer be performing its function.

Prosper Weil, Towards Relative Normativity in International Law?, 77 Am.J.Int.L. 413, 420 (1983).*

Supporters of "voluntarism" emphasize its necessity for a heterogeneous, pluralistic world society. Moreover, they stress the importance of maintaining a clear distinction between existing law (*lex lata*) and law in formation (*lex ferenda*). In Weil's words, the legal system must be "perceived as a self-contained, self-sufficient world." Id. at 421. Legal normativity cannot be a matter of more or less.

The material in this chapter will present various questions that bear on this thesis. Is it realistic to consider that actual legal rules are the product of state "will" or consent in a meaningful sense? Are there not basic and axiomatic norms that are recognized as such independently of consent? Does "general acceptance" of *new* law require verifiable expressions of "will" by all states? What are the advantages and disadvantages of considering the international legal system as a "self-contained, self-sufficient world" of "positive" rules? What legal significance should be given to various types of norms and standards that do not meet the criteria of article 38 but influence state conduct and accountability (sometimes called "soft law")?

Is international law moving toward gradations in the legal force of its rules? Do recent tendencies give greater importance to the "general will of the international community" and less to the "sovereign equality" of states in the formation law? Do such tendencies result in increased power for a "de facto oligarchy"? What processes for determining the community "will" would support legal development in the common interest? All of these questions are implicitly raised by recent trends relating to "sources". They are not easily answered, but they merit reflection in studying the material that follows.

## SOURCES AND EVIDENCE

Note that Article 38 of the Statute refers to judicial decisions and to teachings of the most highly qualified publicists as "subsidiary means for the determination of rules of law." The Restatement (Third) § 103 characterizes judicial decisions and the "writings of scholars" as "evidence" of whether a rule has become international law. It also includes as evidence the pronouncements by states that undertake to state a rule of international law when such pronouncements are not seriously challenged by other states. The Restatement notes in Comment *c* to § 103 that such pronouncements include declaratory resolutions of international organizations. See Section 6 infra.

The present chapter deals separately with each of the categories referred to §§ 102 and 103 of the Restatement and in Article 38 of the Statute of the Court. It also includes a brief section on political declarations of states that bear on rules of law. (Section 6B)

## SECTION 2. CUSTOM

Article 38(1)(b) refers to "international custom, as evidence of a general practice accepted as law." Some writers have found this formulation curious, since it is the practice which is evidence of the emergence of a custom.

However, the order of words makes little difference. What is clear is that the definition of custom comprises two distinct elements (1) "general practice" and (2) its acceptance as law.

Clear as it may seem to be, this definition gives rise to a number of questions, many of which are highly controversial. In reading the material that follows, you should bear in mind the following questions, which are divided into several groups.

(1) What constitutes state practice?

(a) Are claims or assertions of states in themselves practice or must they be accompanied by physical acts? Would assertions *in abstracto* constitute practice or must they be made in the context of particular situations? Are votes for general declarations of law in international bodies manifestations of practice?

(b) Is state practice made only by organs competent to bind or speak for states in international affairs? May national laws, municipal court judgments, executive acts of an internal character constitute practice? Are there circumstances in which actions of non-official entities may be regarded as state practice? Are omissions and absence of action a form of practice?

(2) How much practice is required?

(a) Is repetition required or may a single act be sufficient to constitute general practice? What if a large number of states participate in a single act (e.g., a decision of a conference)? What if there is no practice contradicting the rule asserted in regard to a single act?

(b) How much time is required? What if no precedents can be found against the rule? Are there special circumstances which affect the requirement of time?

(c) How many states are needed? Is it necessary that there be "a very widespread and representative participation in the practice"? (International Court of Justice in *North Sea Continental Shelf Cases,* p. 78 infra). Must it include states specially affected? Is there a significant difference in the numbers required when there is conflicting practice or the absence of conflict? Is a greater number required to overturn an existing rule of law?

(d) Is the practice of some states more important than the practice of others? How much weight should be given to the non-participation of states with special interests?

(3) How much consistency is required?

(a) Are minor inconsistencies sufficient to negate a custom?

(b) Can one resolve apparent inconsistencies on the basis of new conditions and attitudes? Can 19th century precedents be considered as inconsistent with 20th century practice, when conditions are substantially different?

(4) Are dissenting and non-participating States bound by custom?

(a) May a state be bound if it has no practice and if the precedents did not involve it? Can a state prevent a rule of customary law from becoming binding on it? At what time must it express opposition?

(b) Are new states bound by established custom in which they had no opportunity to participate? How may they change rules to which they are opposed?

(5) Do regional and special customs involve different requirements? May a special custom (i.e., one which conflicts with general custom) bind a state which has not supported the special custom?

Is a more rigorous standard of proof required to show the existence of a special custom? Are special customs essentially similar to tacit international agreements?

(6) What evidence is required for *opinio juris,* the requirement that practice be accepted as law?

(a) Must states "believe" that something is law before it can become law?

(b) Is *opinio juris* necessary to distinguish usage from custom, legal from non-legal obligations? Can one presume *opinio juris* from consistent practice when there are no negative statements (or disclaimers) as to legal obligations?

(c) Can the requirement of *opinio juris* be met by a finding that the practice was socially necessary or suited to international needs?

(d) Is it necessary that the belief as to legal requirement be accompanied by statements that the conduct in question is obligatory? May the context provide evidence of belief in the absence of such statements?

Are such statements or positive indication required to prove an obligation to act, but not required to support a permissive rule (the freedom to act)?

(e) What significance do protests and acquiescence have for *opinio juris*?

Are isolated protests enough to prevent customary law on the basis of substantial practice? Would protest by a single state carry decisive weight if that state was the only one seriously affected?

Is failure to protest against an abstract assertion of law less significant than failure to protest concrete application of the purported rule? May protests override practice arising from physical acts (e.g., seizures) by states?

(7) May treaties be invoked as evidence of customary law? May they create customary law?

(a) Should decisive weight be given to statements in a treaty or in preparatory work to the effect that some or all provisions are declaratory of existing law?

(b) May one infer that a treaty is not declaratory of international law from the fact that it provides for withdrawal, revision, or reservations?

(c) Under what circumstances are treaty rules which are not declaratory initially likely to become part of customary law by subsequent practice?

(d) Would bilateral treaties which have similar rules and are widely adhered to constitute evidence of state practice accepted as law or of custom?

(e) What effect would a resolution of the General Assembly or of an unofficial expert body (such as the *Institut de droit international*) have on the recognition of a treaty or the draft of a treaty as customary law?

(f) Are there circumstances in which the negotiation of a treaty and drafts of treaties will substantially affect the positions of states and the *opinio juris* as to new rules?

(g) May tacit international agreements be treated as local or special custom? Does it make any difference whether treaty or custom is the basis of the obligation?

8. Is there a normative hierarchy in customary law?

(a) Are some general principles accepted implicitly irrespective of consent as postulates of the state system (e.g., territorial integrity of a state, *pacta sunt servanda,* autonomy)?

(b) Does this mean that current state practice and *opinio juris* are no longer relevant in defining their application?

9. Would declarations of law adopted without dissent by the UN General Assembly constitute presumptive evidence of accepted international law, irrespective of actual state practice?

(a) Would the rules stated in a General Assembly declaration be binding on a state that claimed it voted for the declaration on the understanding that the General Assembly had only the authority to make recommendations?

(b) Would a declaration adopted by a substantial majority that asserts the existence of a particular legal principle have evidentiary value as a statement of customary law in litigation before an international or national judicial tribunal?

10. Would the adoption of recommended standards of conduct by the UN General Assembly or another representative international assembly give rise to customary law if they are generally followed by states? Would such compliance constitute state practice for purposes of establishing customary law? What factors would be relevant to showing *opinio juris* in respect of such practice?

All of the questions stated above have arisen in cases or in exchanges of views among states. They have often given rise to controversy. The material that follows will provide the answers to, or at least throw further light on, these questions.

## THE PAQUETE HABANA

Supreme Court of the United States, 1900.
175 U.S. 677, 20 S.Ct. 290, 44 L.Ed. 320.

Mr. Justice Gray delivered the opinion of the court:

These are two appeals from decrees of the district court of the United States for the southern district of Florida condemning two fishing vessels and their cargoes as prize of war.

Each vessel was a fishing smack, running in and out of Havana, and regularly engaged in fishing on the coast of Cuba; sailed under the Spanish flag; was owned by a Spanish subject of Cuban birth, living in the city of Havana; was commanded by a subject of Spain, also residing in Havana. * * * Her cargo consisted of fresh fish, caught by her crew from the sea, put on board as they were caught, and kept and sold alive. Until stopped by the blockading squadron she had no knowledge of the existence of the war or of any blockade. She had no arms or ammunition on board, and made no attempt to run the blockade after she knew of its existence, nor any resistance at the time of the capture. * * *

We are then brought to the consideration of the question whether, upon the facts appearing in these records, the fishing smacks were subject to capture by the armed vessels of the United States during the recent war with Spain.

By an ancient usage among civilized nations, beginning centuries ago, and gradually ripening into a rule of international law, coast fishing vessels, pursuing their vocation of catching and bringing in fresh fish, have been recognized as exempt, with their cargoes and crews, from capture as prize of war. * * *

[The Court then describes the earliest known acts protecting foreign fishermen in time of war. In 1403 and 1406, Henry IV of England issued orders protecting fishermen of foreign states. The order of 1406 placed all fishermen of France, Flanders and Brittany, with their fishing vessels and boats and equipment, everywhere on the sea, under his special protection. As long as they were coming or going from fishing activities in good conduct, they were not to be hindered by His Majesty's officers. This practice, based upon prior agreement with the French King for reciprocal treatment, was followed in a treaty made October 2, 1521 between the Emperor Charles V and Francis I of France. In 1536, Dutch edicts permitted herring fishing in time of war. Early French practice even permitted admirals to accord fishing truces in time of war. In ordinances passed in 1681 and 1692, France curtailed this practice, apparently because of the failure of her enemies to accord reciprocal treatment.]

The doctrine which exempts coast fishermen, with their vessels and cargoes, from capture as prize of war, has been familiar to the United States from the time of the War of Independence.

On June 5, 1779, Louis XVI, our ally in that war, addressed a letter to his admiral, informing him that the wish he had always had of alleviating, as far as he could, the hardships of war, had directed his attention to that class of his subjects which devoted itself to the trade of fishing, and had no other means of livelihood; that he had thought that the example which he should give to his enemies * * * would determine them to allow to fishermen the same facilities which he should consent to grant; and that he had therefore given orders to the commanders of all his ships not to disturb English fishermen, nor to arrest their vessels laden with fresh fish * * *; provided they had no offensive arms, and were not proved to have made any signals creating a suspicion of intelligence with the enemy; and the admiral was directed to communicate the King's intentions to all officers under his control. By a royal order in council of November 6, 1780, the former orders were confirmed; and the capture and ransom, by a French cruiser, of *The John and Sarah,* an English vessel, coming from Holland, laden with fresh fish, were pronounced to be illegal. 2 Code des Prises (ed. 1784) 721, 901, 903.

Among the standing orders made by Sir James Marriott, Judge of the English High Court of Admiralty, was one of April 11, 1780, by which it was "ordered that all causes of prize of fishing boats or vessels taken from the enemy may be consolidated in one monition, and one sentence or interlocutory, if under 50 tons burthen, and not more than 6 in number." Marriott's Formulary, 4. But by the statements of his successor, and of both French and English writers, it appears that England, as well as France, during the American Revolutionary War, abstained from interfering with the coast fisheries. The Young Jacob and Johanna, 1 C.Rob. 20; 2 Ortolan, 53; Hall, § 148.

In the treaty of 1785 between the United States and Prussia, article 23 (which was proposed by the American Commissioners, John Adams, Benjamin Franklin, and Thomas Jefferson, and is said to have been drawn up by Franklin), provided that, if war should arise between the contracting parties, "all women and children, scholars of every faculty, cultivators of the earth, artisans, manufacturers, and fishermen, unarmed and inhabiting unfortified towns, villages, or places, and in general all others whose occupations are for the common subsistence and benefit of mankind, shall be allowed to continue their respective employments, and shall not be molested in their persons, nor shall their houses or goods be burnt or otherwise destroyed, nor their fields waisted by the armed force of the enemy, into whose power, by the events of war, they may happen to fall; but if anything is necessary to be taken from them for the use of such armed force, the same shall be paid for at a reasonable price." 8 Stat. at L. 96; 1 Kent, Com. 91, note; Wheaton, History of the Law of Nations, 306, 308. Here was the clearest exemption from hostile molestation or seizure of the persons, occupations, houses, and goods of unarmed fishermen inhabiting unfortified places. The article was repeated in the later treaties between the United States and Prussia of 1799 and 1828. 8 Stat. at L. 174, 384. And Dana, in a note to his edition of Wheaton's International Laws, says: "In many treaties and decrees, fishermen catching fish as an article of food are added to the class of persons whose occupation is not to be disturbed in war." Wheaton, International Law (8th ed.) § 345, note 168.

Since the United States became a nation, the only serious interruptions, so far as we are informed, of the general recognition of the exemption of coast fishing vessels from hostile capture, arose out of the mutual suspicions and recriminations of England and France during the wars of the French Revolution.

[The Court then surveys the measures and countermeasures taken by both governments.

[On May 23, 1806, the British government "ordered in council, that all fishing vessels under Prussian and other colors, and engaged for the purpose of catching fish * * * shall not be molested * * *." An order in council of May 2, 1810 directing the capture of certain vessels, specifically excepted "vessels employed in catching and conveying fish fresh to market * * *."]

In the war with Mexico, in 1846, the United States recognized the exemption of coast fishing boats from capture. * * *

[I]t appears that Commodore Conner, commanding the Home Squadron blockading the east coast of Mexico, on May 14, 1846, wrote a letter * * * to Mr. Bancroft, the Secretary of the Navy, inclosing a copy of the commodore's "instructions to the commanders of the vessels of the Home Squadron, showing the principles to be observed in the blockade of the Mexican ports," one of which was that "Mexican boats engaged in fishing on any part of the coast will be allowed to pursue their labors unmolested;" and that on June 10, 1846, those instructions were approved by the Navy Department. * * *

In the treaty of peace between the United States and Mexico, in 1848, were inserted the very words of the earlier treaties with Prussia, already quoted, forbidding the hostile molestation or seizure in time of war of the persons, occupations, houses, or goods of fishermen. 9 Stat. at L. 939, 940. * * *

[The Court then notes that France had forbidden the molestation of enemy coastal fisheries during the Crimean, Italian and Prussian wars, and that England had justified destruction by her cruisers of fisheries on the Sea of Azof during the Crimean War on the ground that these were on a large scale and intended directly for the support of the Russian army.]

Since the English orders in council of 1806 and 1810, before quoted, in favor of fishing vessels employed in catching and bringing to market fresh fish, no instance has been found in which the exemption from capture of private coast fishing vessels honestly pursuing their peaceful industry has been denied by England or by any other nation. And the Empire of Japan (the last state admitted into the rank of civilized nations), by an ordinance promulgated at the beginning of its war with China in August, 1894, established prize courts, and ordained that "the following enemy's vessels are exempt from detention," including in the exemption "boats engaged in coast fisheries," as well as "ships engaged exclusively on a voyage of scientific discovery, philanthropy, or religious mission." Takahashi, International Law, 11, 178.

International law is part of our law, and must be ascertained and administered by the courts of justice of appropriate jurisdiction as often as questions of right depending upon it are duly presented for their determination. For this purpose, where there is no treaty and no controlling executive or legislative act or judicial decision, resort must be had to the customs and usages of civilized nations, and, as evidence of these, to the works of jurists and commentators who by years of labor, research, and experience have made themselves peculiarly well acquainted with the subjects of which they treat. Such works are resorted to by judicial tribunals, not for the speculations of their authors concerning what the law ought to be, but for trustworthy evidence of what the law really is. Hilton v. Guyot, 159 U.S. 113, 163, 164, 214, 215, 16 S.Ct. 139, 40 L.Ed. 95, 108, 125, 126.

Wheaton places among the principal sources international law "text-writers of authority, showing what is the approved usage of nations, or the general opinion respecting their mutual conduct, with the definitions and modifications introduced by general consent." As to these he forcibly observes: "Without wishing to exaggerate the importance of these writers, or to substitute, in any case, their authority for the principles of reason, it may be affirmed that they are generally impartial in their judgment. They are witnesses of the sentiments and usages of civilized nations, and the weight of their testimony increases every time that their authority is invoked by statesmen, and every year that passes without the rules laid down in their works being impugned by the avowal of contrary principles." Wheaton, International Law (8th ed.), § 15.

Chancellor Kent says: "In the absence of higher and more authoritative sanctions, the ordinances of foreign states, the opinions of eminent statesmen, and the writings of distinguished jurists, are regarded as of great consideration on questions not settled by conventional law. In cases where the principal jurists agree, the presumption will be very great in favor of the solidity of their maxims; and no civilized nation that does not arrogantly set all ordinary law and justice at defiance will venture to disregard the uniform sense of the established writers on international law." 1 Kent, Com. 18.

[The Court then discusses the views of French, Argentine, German, Dutch, English, Austrian, Spanish, Portuguese, and Italian writers on international law, and concludes:]

This review of the precedents and authorities on the subject appears to us abundantly to demonstrate that at the present day, by the general consent of the civilized nations of the world, and independently of any express treaty or other public act, it is an established rule of international law, founded on considerations of humanity to a poor and industrious order of men, and of the mutual convenience of belligerent states, that coast fishing vessels, with their implements and supplies, cargoes and crews, unarmed and honestly pursuing their peaceful calling of catching and bringing in fresh fish, are exempt from capture as prize of war. * * *

This rule of international law is one which prize courts administering the law of nations are bound to take judicial notice of, and to give effect to, in the absence of any treaty or other public act of their own government in relation to the matter. * * *

[Finding no express intention on the part of the United States to enforce the 1898 blockade of Cuba against coastal fishermen peacefully pursuing their calling, the Court ordered the reversal of the District Court decree and the payment to the claimants of the proceeds of the sale of the vessels and cargo, together with damages and costs.

[Chief Justice Fuller argued in a dissenting opinion, in which Harlan and McKenna, JJ., concurred, that the captured vessels were of such size and range as not to fall within the exemption, and that the exemption in any case had not become a customary rule of international law but was only "an act of grace" that had not been authorized by the President.]

### *Notes*

1. Did not the Supreme Court find inconsistencies in the practice of states in respect of the alleged rule? How many states did it refer to in support of the practice? Consider the rather small number of states in the world during the time covered. Would such support meet the requirement of a "very widespread and representative participation" as required by the International Court of Justice in the *North Sea Continental Shelf Cases* (see p. 78 infra)? Does the case show that a small number of states create a rule of customary law, if there is no practice which conflicts with the rule and no protests? Is it necessary (and realistic) to assume the acquiescence of the large majority of non-participating and silent states? Would the inconsistent conduct of one or two states be sufficient to prevent the creation of a general custom; if so, in what circumstances? See discussion of Non-Consenting States infra pp. 87–89.

2. Note the wide range of evidence of custom considered by the Court. It includes national law, executive decrees, acts of military commanders as well as judgments of national tribunals. Does this mean that states may create customary law by their unilateral acts? Does it mean that the conduct of military officers and other subordinate officials may constitute state practice? Is every official act of a state official an element of state practice? For examples, see Akehurst, Custom as a Source of International Law, 47 Brit.Y.B.I.L. 8–10 (1974–75); Wolfke, Custom in Present International Law (1964).

3. What evidence did the Court consider in arriving at its conclusions concerning the alleged "ancient usage among civilized nations"? Are executive pronouncements, legislative acts, and municipal court decisions of equal weight in "committing" a state to a given practice? What significance should be attached to the acts of military commanders, acting independently in the field? See generally Wolfke, Custom in Present International Law *passim* (1964); Waldock, General Course on Public International Law, 106 Rec. des Cours, 1, 42–43 (1962–II) and sources cited. It has been stated that "there is * * * no doubt that every document demonstrating the conduct of States in certain situations can serve as evidence of the element of practice." Wolfke at 122. See *The Case of the S.S. "Lotus,"* infra.

4. Note the weight given by the Supreme Court to the writers on international law and the quotation from Chancellor Kent that "no civilized nation will venture to disregard the uniform sense of the established writers on international law". How objective are the leading writers? Schachter suggests that "the selective tendency of the writers to quote the generalities of other writers, meant that their statements were steps removed from the ideal of an inductive approach." International Law in Theory and Practice 38 (1991). For further comment on the role of international law scholars, see pp. 123–26 below.

5. Myres S. McDougal has described customary law "as a process of continuous interaction, of continuous demand and response, in which the decision-makers of particular nation-states unilaterally put forward claims of the most diverse and conflicting character * * * and in which other decision-makers, external to the demanding state * * * weigh and appraise these competing claims * * * and ultimately accept or reject them." In this process, McDougal observes, state officials honor each other's unilateral claims "by mutual tolerances—expressed in countless decisions in foreign offices, national courts, and

national legislatures—which create expectations that effective power will be restrained and exercised in certain uniformities of pattern." In a footnote, he adds that it is "the reciprocal tolerances of the external decision-makers which create the expectations of pattern and uniformity in decision, of practice in accord with rule, commonly regarded as law." McDougal emphasizes that states are influenced by "reasonableness" in their claims and reactions and he considers that the process is one in which values are clarified and "perceptions of common interest" realized. McDougal, The Hydrogen Bomb Tests, 49 A.J.I.L. 357–58 (1955). See also McDougal, Studies in World Order (1960).

6. Would states be more likely to realize common interests by negotiating multilateral law-making treaties to meet perceived needs than by relying on the case-by-case gradualism of customary law? Is customary law more responsive to disparities in power and interest and therefore more realistic than law-making by international conferences in which all States take part on an equal footing? See comments on Treaty and Custom.

## THE CASE OF THE S.S. LOTUS (FRANCE v. TURKEY)

Permanent Court of International Justice (1927).
P.C.I.J. Ser. A No. 10.
2 Hudson, World Ct. Rep. 20.

[A collision on the high seas between a French steamer, the Lotus, and a Turkish steamer, the Boz–Kourt in 1926 resulted in the sinking of the Turkish vessel and the death of eight Turkish nationals. When the French ship reached Constantinople (Istanbul) the Turkish authorities instituted criminal proceedings against the French officer on watch-duty at the time of the collision (Lieutenant Demons). The Turkish Court overruled Demons' objection that Turkey had no jurisdiction and after a trial sentenced him to 80 days imprisonment and a fine of 22 pounds. The French Government challenged Turkey's action as violation of international law and demanded reparation. Following negotiations, the two states by special agreement submitted the question of jurisdiction to the Permanent Court of International Justice. The arguments put forward by the two parties related exclusively to whether according to principles of international law Turkey has or has not jurisdiction to prosecute the case. Both parties recognized the applicability of the Convention of Lausanne of 1923 which provided in Article 15: "Subject to the provisions of Article 16, all questions of jurisdiction as between Turkey and the other contracting parties shall be decided in accordance with the principles of international law."]

The Court, having to consider whether there are any rules of international law which may have been violated by the prosecution in pursuance of Turkish law of Lieutenant Demons, is confronted in the first place by a question of principle which, in the written and oral arguments of the two Parties, has proved to be a fundamental one. The French Government contends that the Turkish Courts, in order to have jurisdiction, should be able to point to some title to jurisdiction recognized by international law in favour of Turkey. On the other hand, the Turkish Government takes the view that Article 15 allows Turkey jurisdiction whenever such jurisdiction does not come into conflict with a principle of international law.

The latter view seems to be in conformity with the special agreement itself, No. 1 of which asks the Court to say whether Turkey has acted contrary to the principles of international law and, if so, what principles. According to the special agreement, therefore, it is not a question of stating principles which would permit Turkey to take criminal proceedings, but of formulating the principles, if any, which might have been violated by such proceedings.

This way of stating the question is also dictated by the very nature and existing conditions of international law.

International law governs relations between independent States. The rules of law binding upon States therefore emanate from their own free will as expressed in conventions or by usages generally accepted as expressing principles of law and established in order to regulate the relations between these co-existing independent communities or with a view to the achievement of common aims. Restrictions upon the independence of States cannot therefore be presumed.

Now the first and foremost restriction imposed by international law upon a State is that—failing the existence of a permissive rule to the contrary—it may not exercise its power in any form in the territory of another State. In this sense jurisdiction is certainly territorial; it cannot be exercised by a State outside its territory except by virtue of a permissive rule derived from international custom or from a convention.

It does not, however, follow that international law prohibits a State from exercising jurisdiction in its own territory, in respect of any case which relates to acts which have taken place abroad, and in which it cannot rely on some permissive rule of international law. Such a view would only be tenable if international law contained a general prohibition to States to extend the application of their laws and the jurisdiction of their courts to persons, property and acts outside their territory, and if, as an exception to this general prohibition, it allowed States to do so in certain specific cases. But this is certainly not the case under international law as it stands at present. Far from laying down a general prohibition to the effect that States may not extend the application of their laws and the jurisdiction of their courts to persons, property and acts outside their territory, it leaves them in this respect a wide measure of discretion which is only limited in certain cases by prohibitive rules; as regards other cases, every State remains free to adopt the principles which it regards as best and most suitable.

* * *

In these circumstances, all that can be required of a State is that it should not overstep the limits which international law places upon its jurisdiction; within these limits, its title to exercise jurisdiction rests in its sovereignty.

It follows from the foregoing that the contention of the French Government to the effect that Turkey must in each case be able to cite a rule of international law authorizing her to exercise jurisdiction, is opposed to the generally accepted international law to which Article 15 of the Convention of Lausanne refers. Having regard to the terms of Article 15 and to the construction which the Court has just placed upon it, this contention would apply in regard to civil as well as to criminal cases, and would be applicable on conditions of absolute reciprocity as between Turkey and the other contracting Parties; in practice, it would therefore in many cases result in paralyzing the action of the courts, owing to the impossibility of citing a universally accepted rule on which to support the exercise of their jurisdiction.

*

Nevertheless, it has to be seen whether the foregoing considerations really apply as regards criminal jurisdiction, or whether this jurisdiction is governed by a different principle: this might be the outcome of the close connection which for a long time existed between the conception of supreme criminal jurisdiction and that of a State, and also by the especial importance of criminal jurisdiction from the point of view of the individual.

Though it is true that in all systems of law the principle of the territorial character of criminal law is fundamental, it is equally true that all or nearly all these systems of law extend their action to offences committed outside the territory of the State which adopts them, and they do so in ways which vary from State to State. The territoriality of criminal law, therefore, is not an absolute principle of international law and by no means coincides with territorial sovereignty.

* * *

The Court therefore must, in any event, ascertain whether or not there exists a rule of international law limiting the freedom of States to extend the criminal jurisdiction of their courts to a situation uniting the circumstances of the present case.

* * *

The arguments advanced by the French Government, other than those considered above, are, in substance, the three following:

(1) International law does not allow a State to take proceedings with regard to offences committed by foreigners abroad, simply by reason of the nationality of the victim; and such is the situation in the present case because the offence must be regarded as having been committed on board the French vessel.

(2) International law recognizes the exclusive jurisdiction of the State whose flag is flown as regards everything which occurs on board a ship on the high seas.

(3) Lastly, this principle is especially applicable in a collision case.

* * *

As has already been observed, the characteristic features of the situation of fact are as follows: there has been a collision on the high seas between two vessels flying different flags, on one of which was one of the persons alleged to be guilty of the offence, whilst the victims were on board the other.

This being so, the Court does not think it necessary to consider the contention that a State cannot punish offences committed abroad by a foreigner simply by reason of the nationality of the victim. For this contention only relates to the case where the nationality of the victim is the only criterion on which the criminal jurisdiction of the State is based. Even if that argument were correct generally speaking—and in regard to this the

Court reserves its opinion—it could only be used in the present case if international law forbade Turkey to take into consideration the fact that the offence produced its effects on the Turkish vessel and consequently in a place assimilated to Turkish territory in which the application of Turkish criminal law cannot be challenged, even in regard to offences committed there by foreigners. But no such rule of international law exists. No argument has come to the knowledge of the Court from which it could be deduced that States recognize themselves to be under an obligation towards each other only to have regard to the place where the author of the offence happens to be at the time of the offence. On the contrary, it is certain that the courts of many countries, even of countries which have given their criminal legislation a strictly territorial character, interpret criminal law in the sense that offences, the authors of which at the moment of commission are in the territory of another State, are nevertheless to be regarded as having been committed in the national territory, if one of the constituent elements of the offence, and more especially its effects, have taken place there. French courts have, in regard to a variety of situations, given decisions sanctioning this way of interpreting the territorial principle. Again, the Court does not know of any cases in which governments have protested against the fact that the criminal law of some country contained a rule to this effect or that the courts of a country construed their criminal law in this sense. Consequently, once it is admitted that the effects of the offence were produced on the Turkish vessel, it becomes impossible to hold that there is a rule of international law which prohibits Turkey from prosecuting Lieutenant Demons because of the fact that the author of the offence was on board the French ship. Since, as has already been observed, the special agreement does not deal with the provision of Turkish law under which the prosecution was instituted, but only with the question whether the prosecution should be regarded as contrary to the principles of international law, there is no reason preventing the Court from confining itself to observing that, in this case, a prosecution may also be justified from the point of view of the so-called territorial principle.

* * *

The second argument put forward by the French Government is the principle that the State whose flag is flown has exclusive jurisdiction over everything which occurs on board a merchant ship on the high seas.

It is certainly true that—apart from certain special cases which are defined by international law—vessels on the high seas are subject to no authority except that of the State whose flag they fly. In virtue of the principle of the freedom of the seas, that is to say, the absence of any territorial sovereignty upon the high seas, no State may exercise any kind of jurisdiction over foreign vessels upon them. Thus, if a war vessel, happening to be at the spot where a collision occurs between a vessel flying its flag and a foreign vessel, were to send on board the latter an officer to make investigations or to take evidence, such an act would undoubtedly be contrary to international law.

But it by no means follows that a State can never in its own territory exercise jurisdiction over acts which have occurred on board a foreign ship on the high seas. A corollary of the principle of the freedom of the seas is that a ship on the high seas is assimilated to the territory of the State the flag of which it flies, for, just as in its own territory, that State exercises its authority upon it, and no other State may do so. All that can be said is that by virtue of the principle of the freedom of the seas, a ship is placed in the same position as national territory; but there is nothing to support the claim according to which the rights of the State under whose flag the vessel sails may go farther than the rights which it exercises within its territory properly so called. It follows that what occurs on board a vessel on the high seas must be regarded as if it occurred on the territory of the State whose flag the ship flies. If, therefore, a guilty act committed on the high seas produces its effects on a vessel flying another flag or in foreign territory, the same principles must be applied as if the territories of two different States were concerned, and the conclusion must therefore be drawn that there is no rule of international law prohibiting the State to which the ship on which the effects of the offence have taken place belongs, from regarding the offence as having been committed in its territory and prosecuting, accordingly, the delinquent.

This conclusion could only be overcome if it were shown that there was a rule of customary international law which, going further than the principle stated above, established the exclusive jurisdiction of the State whose flag was flown. The French Government has endeavoured to prove the existence of such a rule, having recourse for this purpose to the teachings of publicists, to decisions of municipal and international tribunals, and especially to conventions which, whilst creating exceptions to the principle of the freedom of the seas by permitting the war and police vessels of a State to exercise a more or less extensive control over the merchant vessels of another State, reserve jurisdiction to the courts of the country whose flag is flown by the vessel proceeded against.

In the Court's opinion, the existence of such a rule has not been conclusively proved.

In the first place, as regards teachings of publicists, and apart from the question as to what their value may be from the point of view of establishing the existence of a rule of customary law, it is no doubt true that all or nearly all writers teach that ships on the high seas are subject exclusively to the jurisdiction of the State whose flag they fly. But the important point is the significance attached by them to this principle; now it does not appear that in general, writers bestow upon this principle a scope differing from or wider than that explained above and which is equivalent to saying that the jurisdiction of a State over vessels on the high seas is the same in extent as its jurisdiction in its own territory. On the other hand, there is no lack of writers who, upon a close study of the special question whether a State can prosecute for offences committed on board a foreign ship on the high seas, definitely come to the conclusion that such offences must be regarded as if they had been committed in the territory of the State whose flag the ship flies, and that consequently the general rules of each legal system in regard to offences committed abroad are applicable.

In regard to precedents, it should first be observed that, leaving aside the collision cases which will be alluded to later, none of them relates to offences affecting two ships flying the flags of two different countries, and that consequently they are not of much importance in the case before the Court. The case of the *Costa Rica Packet* is no exception, for the prauw on which the alleged depredations took place was adrift without flag or crew, and this circumstance certainly influenced, perhaps decisively, the conclusion arrived at by the arbitrator.

On the other hand, there is no lack of cases in which the State has claimed a right to prosecute for an offence, committed on board a foreign ship, which it regarded as punishable under its legislation. Thus Great Britain refused the request of the United States for the extradition of John Anderson, a British seaman who had committed homicide on board an American vessel, stating that she did not dispute the jurisdiction of the United States but that she was entitled to exercise hers concurrently. This case, to which others might be added, is relevant in spite of Anderson's British nationality, in order to show that the principle of the exclusive jurisdiction of the country whose flag the vessel flies is not universally accepted.

The cases in which the exclusive jurisdiction of the State whose flag was flown has been recognized would seem rather to have been cases in which the foreign State was interested only by reason of the nationality of the victim, and in which, according to the legislation of that State itself or the practice of its courts, that ground was not regarded as sufficient to authorize prosecution for an offence committed abroad by a foreigner.

Finally, as regards conventions expressly reserving jurisdiction exclusively to the State whose flag is flown, it is not absolutely certain that this stipulation is to be regarded as expressing a general principle of law rather than as corresponding to the extraordinary jurisdiction which these conventions confer on the state-owned ships of a particular country in respect of ships of another country on the high seas. Apart from that, it should be observed that these conventions relate to matters of a particular kind, closely connected with the policing of the seas, such as the slave trade, damage to submarine cables, fisheries, etc., and not to common-law offences. Above all it should be pointed out that the offences contemplated by the conventions in question only concern a single ship; it is impossible therefore to make any deduction from them in regard to matters which concern two ships and consequently the jurisdiction to two different States.

The Court therefore has arrived at the conclusion that the second argument put forward by the French Government does not, any more than the first, establish the existence of a rule of international law prohibiting Turkey from prosecuting Lieutenant Demons.

[The Court then addressed itself to the third argument advanced by the French Government, that according to international law criminal proceedings arising from collision cases are within the exclusive jurisdiction of the state whose flag is flown. In offering this view, the French Agent pointed out that questions of jurisdiction in collision cases, which frequently arise before civil courts, rarely are presented to criminal courts. This fact led him to conclude that prosecutions only occur before the courts of the state whose flag is flown, which was proof of a tacit adherence by states to the rule of positive international law barring prosecutions by other states.

[The Court rejected this argument, explaining that even if the facts alleged were true, they would merely show that states had often abstained from instituting criminal proceedings, not that they felt obligated to do so. The Court observed that there were no decisions of international tribunals in the matter and that, of the four municipal court decisions cited by the parties, two supported the exclusive jurisdiction of the flag state and two supported the opposite contention. The Court pointed out that "as municipal jurisprudence is thus divided, it is hardly possible to see in it an indication of the existence of the restrictive rule of international law which alone could serve as a basis for the contention of the French Government." On the other hand, the Court stressed the fact that the French and German governments had failed to protest against the exercise of criminal jurisdiction by states whose flag was not being flown in the two cases cited by Turkey, and observed that the French and German governments would hardly have failed to protest if they "had really thought that this was a violation of international law."]

The conclusion at which the Court has therefore arrived is that there is no rule of international law in regard to collision cases to the effect that criminal proceedings are exclusively within the jurisdiction of the State whose flag is flown.

* * *

* * * Neither the exclusive jurisdiction of either State, nor the limitations of the jurisdiction of each to the occurrences which took place on the respective ships would appear calculated to satisfy the requirements of justice and effectively to protect the interests of the two States. It is only natural that each should be able to exercise jurisdiction and to do so in respect of the incident as a whole. It is therefore a case of concurrent jurisdiction.

* * *

FOR THESE REASONS, the Court, having heard both Parties, gives, by the President's casting vote—the votes being equally divided—judgment to the effect

(1) that, following the collision which occurred on August 2nd, 1926, on the high seas between the French steamship *Lotus* and the Turkish steamship *Boz-Kourt,* and upon the arrival of the French ship at Stamboul, and in consequence of the loss of the *Boz-Kourt* having involved the death of eight Turkish nationals, Turkey, by instituting criminal proceedings in pursuance of Turkish law against Lieutenant Demons, officer of the watch on board the *Lotus* at the time of the collision, has not acted in conflict with the principles of international law, contrary to Article 15 of the Convention of Lausanne of July 24th, 1923, respecting conditions of residence and business and jurisdiction;

(2) that, consequently, there is no occasion to give judgment on the question of the pecuniary reparation which might have been due to Lieutenant Demons if Turkey, by prosecuting him as above stated, had acted in a manner contrary to the principles of international law.

[The six dissenting judges disagreed with the proposition that France had the burden of showing a customary law rule that prohibited Turkey's exercise of jurisdiction. They took issue with the basic premise of the judgment that "restrictions upon the freedom of states cannot be presumed" and its implicit corollary that international law permits all that it does not forbid. In their view, the question was whether international law authorized Turkey to exercise jurisdiction in the particular circumstances and they concluded that customary law did not authorize a state to exercise criminal jurisdiction over a foreigner for an act committed in a foreign country or in a vessel of another state on the high seas.]

### *Notes*

1. The *Lotus Case* has been strongly criticized for its "extreme positivism" and especially for asserting that restrictions on the freedom of states cannot be presumed. Was this principle necessary for the Court to rule on the French contention that Turkey was not permitted under customary law to prosecute the French officer? Note that the Court's jurisdiction rested on a special agreement of the parties that asked it to decide whether Turkey acted contrary to principles of international law. Did this formulation make it reasonable for the Court to impose the burden of proof on France to show that Turkey's action violated international law rather than requiring Turkey to prove its legal right to do so?

2. If the Court found no specific customary law that either permitted or prohibited criminal jurisdiction in the given circumstances, should it have declined to decide the case? Is it necessary to assume the formal completeness of the international legal system so that there is no gap in the system? Kelsen wrote: "If there is no norm of conventional or customary international law imposing * * * the obligation to behave in a certain way, the subject is, under international law, legally free to behave as it pleases; and by a decision to this effect existing international law is applied." Kelsen, Principles of International Law 438–39 (R. Tucker ed. 1966). Some writers who agree that international law must be formally complete (i.e., every dispute must be capable of legal determination) reject the residual principle of state freedom expressed in the *Lotus Case*. They consider that every case can be decided by either existing legal rules or by deriving such rules from general principles and concepts within the legal system. See Oppenheim's International Law 12–13 (9th ed. R. Jennings & A. Watts 1992). This position expressed most influentially by Sir Hersch Lauterpacht (as a scholar and when a judge in the International Court) relies heavily on general principles and analogy to solve hard cases in order to ensure the coherence and effectiveness of the international legal system. On that view judges cannot evade decisions by *non liquet* (refusal to decide) or by residual principles such as sovereignty; for them (if not for states) the system must be seen as materially (and not only formally) complete. Other writers move beyond decisions limited to legal rules and principles. They would turn to "purposes" and "policies" of the international community (sometimes expressed as "equity" or "natural justice") for determining criteria in a balancing process. See O. Schachter, Theory and Practice in International Law 18–31 (1991); M. McDougal and M. Reisman, International Law in Policy–Oriented Perspective, in The Structure and Process of International Law 103–29 (Macdonald–Johnston eds. 1983). Can a good argument be made that an international court should decline to decide a case if the law is not clear enough (*non liquet* )? For that view, see J. Stone, Non Liquet and the Function of Law in the International Community, 35 Brit.Y.B.I.L. 124 (1959).

3. Notwithstanding the criticism of the *Lotus* principle, the International Court and other tribunals may still consider first whether an act that has been challenged is prohibited by existing law and, if not, to sustain its validity. In effect, the presumption of freedom is then applied. See, for example, Nicaragua v. U.S. (1986), North Sea Continental Shelf Cases (1969), Nuclear Test Cases

(1974). However, in some cases, especially those involving maritime delimitation, the tribunals have tended to view the conflicting legal claims in terms of balancing equities. This is probably a consequence of the substantive rules that require maritime delimitation to be determined by equitable principles. But it also has been applied in cases involving territorial disputes. (See, e.g., the Island of Palmas decision p. 309 referring to the relative strengths of the claims in regard to shared resources such as international waterways.) The freedom to use natural resources within a state—presumably a sovereign prerogative—is increasingly viewed as limited by the state's duty to take account of trans-border environmental damage. Such balancing of equities or "constructivist" solutions to conflicting claims are sometimes seen as departing from law. Judge Oda commented in a delimitation case that the ICJ was adopting "[t]he principle of non-principle." Oda, Diss.Op. in Tunisia–Libya Case, 1982 I.C.J. 157. Actually the I.C.J. and other international tribunals regard such decisions taken on equitable grounds as within the law, that is, as equity *infra legem* not as *ex aequo et bono*). (See p. 115 below.) For a discussion of judicial reasoning sympathetic to "constructivist approaches" but critical of the claim of judicial objectivity in such cases, see M. Koskenniemi, From Apology to Utopia 220–36 (1989).

4. Referring again to the *Lotus Case*, does it seem unreasonable or unjust that Turkey should have the right to try a French captain of a French vessel for his acts outside of Turkish jurisdiction because Turkish nationals were injured in a collision between the French and Turkish vessels? Is it significant that the national courts in many countries apply their criminal law to acts committed outside the country if such acts have effects in the country? Do such municipal law cases constitute state practice? Can it be shown that they are accompanied by a belief that their acts are permissible under international law when that question does *not* arise? Is the absence of protests in such cases supportive of customary law? Suppose, as the Court says, most countries recognize the exclusive jurisdiction of the flag state even if the victims of an accident are non-nationals but a few states (for example, the United States) do not? Should exceptions weigh decisively against a customary rule of exclusive jurisdiction?

5. Why did France fail in its argument that abstention of states from exercising jurisdiction over foreign vessels or nationals involved in high seas collisions showed that there was a rule of international law restricting such jurisdiction to the flag state? What would satisfy the Court that such abstention was followed because of a conviction that it was required by international law? When does practice give rise to *opinio juris?* See section below re *opinio juris.*

6. In the *Fisheries Jurisdiction Case* between Iceland and United Kingdom (Judgment on Merits 1974), several judges of the International Court emphasized the existence of protests as refuting the claim of Iceland to an exclusive fishing zone exceeding twelve miles; other judges disagreed by noting that many interested states had not protested. How much weight is to be given isolated protests or the failure to protest? Judge Dillard's separate opinion in the *Fisheries Jurisdiction Case,* Merits, notes the importance of protest by states specially affected. Conversely, the lack of protests by non-interested states does not imply that they necessarily acquiesce in the claims. See Dillard, Separate Opinion, 1974 I.C.J. 58.

7. As the *Lotus Case* indicates, protests and acquiescence are critical factors in the formation of customary law. In that case, the Court envisaged verbal protests such as those made in diplomatic correspondence or in international conferences. They have often been regarded as effective expressions of a

state's objection to an asserted rule. See, for example, *North Sea Continental Shelf Case* (infra) and *Fisheries Jurisdiction Case,* 1974 I.C.J. 47, 58, 161. Yet states sometimes consider it necessary to back their protests by physical action, as by seizing allegedly trespassing ships or sending their vessels into waters claimed by other states. For example, the U.S. rejection of the Canadian claim of competence to exclude vessels from certain Asiatic waters has been emphasized by sending in a U.S. vessel without Canadian authorization. Are there good reasons to require physical acts to demonstrate the "seriousness" of the protest? Judge Read said: "The only convincing evidence of state practice is to be found in seizures where the coastal state asserts its sovereignty over trespassing foreign ships." Would such requirement increase the danger of armed conflict and give advantages to great powers? See conflicting views in Akehurst, Custom as a Source of International Law, 47 Brit.Y.B.I.L. 1, 39–42 (1974–75), and D'Amato, The Concept of Custom in International Law 88–89 (1971).

## ASYLUM CASE
## (COLOMBIA v. PERU)

International Court of Justice, 1950.
1950 I.C.J. 266.

[The case concerns the institution of diplomatic asylum in Latin America. In 1949, a Peruvian political leader, Victor Raul Haya de la Torre was given asylum in the Colombian Embassy in Lima, Peru. The Colombian Ambassador requested the government of Peru to allow Haya de la Torre to leave the country on the ground that the Colombian government qualified him as a political refugee. Peru refused to accept the right of Colombia to define unilaterally the nature of Haya de la Torre's offense. After diplomatic correspondence, the case was referred to the International Court.

In its submission, Colombia claimed the right to qualify (i.e., characterize) the nature of the offense by unilateral decision that would be binding on Peru. It based this claim on certain international agreements among Latin-American states and in addition on "American international law." With respect to this latter contention, the Court said:]

The Colombian Government has finally invoked "American international law in general". In addition to the rules arising from agreements which have already been considered, it has relied on an alleged regional or local custom peculiar to Latin-American States.

The Party which relies on a custom of this kind must prove that this custom is established in such a manner that it has become binding on the other Party. The Colombian Government must prove that the rule invoked by it is in accordance with a constant and uniform usage practised by the States in question, and that this usage is the expression of a right appertaining to the State granting asylum and a duty incumbent on the territorial State. This follows from Article 38 of the Statute of the Court, which refers to international custom "as evidence of a general practice accepted as law".

* * *

It is particularly the Montevideo Convention of 1933 which Counsel for the Colombian Government has also relied on in this connexion. It is contended that this Convention has merely codified principles which were already recognized by Latin-American custom, and that it is valid against Peru as a proof of customary law. The limited number of States which have ratified this Convention reveals the weakness of this argument, and furthermore, it is invalidated by the preamble which states that this Convention modifies the Havana Convention.

Finally, the Colombian Government has referred to a large number of particular cases in which diplomatic asylum was in fact granted and respected. But it has not shown that the alleged rule of unilateral and definitive qualification was invoked or—if in some cases it was in fact invoked—that it was, apart from conventional stipulations, exercised by the States granting asylum as a right appertaining to them and respected by the territorial States as a duty incumbent on them and not merely for reasons of political expediency. The facts brought to the knowledge of the Court disclose so much uncertainty and contradiction, so much fluctuation and discrepancy in the exercise of diplomatic asylum and in the official views expressed on various occasions, there has been so much inconsistency in the rapid succession of conventions on asylum, ratified by some States and rejected by others, and the practice has been so much influenced by considerations of political expediency in the various cases, that it is not possible to discern in all this any constant and uniform usage, accepted as law, with regard to the alleged rule of unilateral and definitive qualification of the offence.

The Court cannot therefore find that the Colombian Government has proved the existence of such a custom. But even if it could be supposed that such a custom existed between certain Latin-American States only, it could not be invoked against Peru which, far from having by its attitude adhered to it, has, on the contrary, repudiated it by refraining from ratifying the Montevideo Conventions of 1933 and 1939, which were the first to include a rule concerning the qualification of the offence in matters of diplomatic asylum.

* * *

### *Notes*

1. The *Asylum Case* deals with "American international law"—that is, regional customary law. May states of a region adopt customary law rules that derogate from general international law with respect to conduct and events within the region? Would such regional law be effective as against states outside the region? For example, may a regional group extend exclusive national jurisdiction over adjacent high seas beyond the limits established by international law? Or may they follow regional custom that gives foreign nationals doing business in the region no more than national treatment irrespective of customary law rights? See discussion of Calvo doctrine in Chapter 9.

2. Does the *Asylum Case* indicate that a state within a region is not bound by a regional custom unless it expressly agrees to be bound? Should a regional custom be treated within the regional group in the same way, as general customary law—namely, binding all states that have not opposed it? Objections to regional customary law point to the difficulty of dividing the world into

regions and to potential conflicts between regional and international norms. See S. Prakash Sinha, Identifying a Principle of International Law Today, 11 Can.Y.B.I.L. 106 (1973).

3. May the concept of regional custom be extended to cover special customary rules for particular groups of states? For example, could there be a rule of restrictive sovereign immunity for one group of states and a rule of absolute immunity for another group?

4. Note the distinction drawn by the Court between practice followed for reasons of expediency and practice accepted by law. What evidence is cited for finding that the practice of diplomatic asylum lacked acceptance as law? Does the Court base its inference on subjective elements or on "objective" facts such as inconsistency, fluctuation and contradictions on practice and in statements? Under what circumstances might a uniform and general practice be sufficient to show the requisite psychological factor, the *opinio juris?* See below for further discussion of *opinio juris* and practice.

5. Charles de Visscher, a former President of the International Court, has written that "mere uniformity or external regularity never justifies a conclusion of normativity." "Governments [he wrote] attach importance to distinguishing between custom by which they hold themselves bound and the mere practices often dictated by consideration of expediency and therefore devoid of definite legal meaning. * * * The inductive reasoning that establishes the existence of custom is a tied reasoning: the matter is not only one of counting the observed regularities but of weighing them in terms of social ends deemed desirable." de Visscher, Theory and Reality in Public International Law 156–57 (Corbett trans. 1968). Does this comment imply that a state may withhold recognizing an established customary rule as law because it does not agree with its social end? Or does it mean only that, in the nascent period of a rule when a state considers it desirable (from its own standpoint), that certain conduct be recognized as in accordance with law, *de lege ferenda,* it would claim that it is law? If such recognition becomes widespread, then "this is sufficient to distinguish the emerging legal rule from the usage, or potential usage, of courtesy or convenience". Thirlway, International Customary Law and Codification 55 (1972). On this view of *opinio juris,* there is "a qualitative difference between the psychological accompaniment of the first examples of a given practice and that of subsequent repeated instances". Id. at 56.

6. The Soviet position on *opinio juris* was expressed by Tunkin, as follows: "*Opinio juris* signifies that a state regards a particular customary rule as a norm of international law, as a rule legally binding on the international plane. This is an expression of the will of a state, in a way a proposal to other states. When other states also express their will in the same direction, a tacit agreement is formed with regard to recognizing a customary rule as an international legal norm." Tunkin, Theory of International Law 133 (Butler trans. 1974). This implies that a dissenting state would not be bound. However, Tunkin and other Soviet writers did *not* claim that a customary norm once recognized by a state may be rejected by it because it now disagreed with it.

7. Schachter points out the difference between recognizing a norm as authoritative and agreeing to it. "Opinio juris involves the former but not necessarily the latter element."

See also Schachter, Towards a Theory of International Obligation, 8 Va. J.I.L. 300 (1968), also in The Effectiveness of International Decisions 1, 21 (S. Schwebel ed.).

## SPECIAL CUSTOM

# CASE CONCERNING RIGHT OF PASSAGE OVER INDIAN TERRITORY (MERITS) (PORTUGAL v. INDIA)

International Court of Justice, 1960.
1960 I.C.J. 6.

[In an application referring its dispute with India to the International Court of Justice under Article 36(2) of the Statute, the Portuguese government charged that India was unlawfully obstructing the right of passage claimed by Portugal through the Indian territory that surrounded certain Portuguese enclaves in the Indian peninsula. The Indian action, it was alleged, was in furtherance of Indian efforts to annex the Portuguese territories in India, and had made it impossible for Portugal to exercise her rights of sovereignty in the affected areas.

[The Court first pointed out that the right claimed by Portugal was a limited one, in that it was not alleged to be accompanied by any immunity in favor of those exercising the right, i.e., passage was to remain subject to Indian regulation and control, exercised in good faith. Six preliminary objections interposed by India and going to the Court's jurisdiction were then overruled.

[Turning to the merits of the Portuguese claim, the Court concluded from an examination of the Treaty of Poona, concluded in 1779 between Portugal and the Maratha ruler, and subsequent decrees of the latter, that the Portuguese rights at that time did not amount to sovereignty over the enclaves with respect to which a right of passage was now claimed, but only to a "revenue grant." The Court then directed its attention to the subsequent history of the Portuguese presence in India.]

It is clear from a study of the material placed before the Court that the situation underwent a change with the advent of the British as sovereign of that part of the country in place of the Marathas. The British found the Portuguese in occupation of the villages and exercising full and exclusive administrative authority over them. They accepted the situation as they found it and left the Portuguese in occupation of, and in exercise of exclusive authority over, the villages. The Portuguese held themselves out as sovereign over the villages. The British did not, as successors of the Marathas, themselves claim sovereignty, nor did they accord express recognition of Portuguese sovereignty, over them. The exclusive authority of the Portuguese over the villages was never brought in question. Thus Portuguese sovereignty over the villages was recognized by the British in fact and by implication and was subsequently tacitly recognized by India. As a consequence the villages comprised in the Maratha grant acquired the character of Portuguese enclaves within Indian territory.

For the purpose of determining whether Portugal has established the right of passage claimed by it, the court must have regard to what happened during the British and post-British periods. During these periods, there had developed between the Portuguese and the territorial sovereign with regard to passage to the enclaves a practice upon which Portugal relies for the purpose of establishing the right of passage claimed by it.

[The Court then rejected the argument that a local custom could not have been established between only two states, and proceeded to examine whether the right of passage asserted by Portugal was established on the basis of the prevailing practice between the parties during the British and post-British periods. The Court observed that all merchandise other than arms and ammunition passed freely between Daman (a Portuguese port) and the enclaves during the periods in question, subject only to such regulation and control as were necessitated by security or revenue.]

The Court, therefore, concludes that, with regard to private persons, civil officials and goods in general there existed during the British and post-British periods a constant and uniform practice allowing free passage between Daman and the enclaves. This practice having continued over a period extending beyond a century and a quarter unaffected by the change of regime in respect of the intervening territory which occurred when India became independent, the Court is, in view of all the circumstances of the case satisfied that that practice was accepted as law by the Parties and has given rise to a right and a correlative obligation.

The Court therefore holds that Portugal had in 1954 a right of passage over intervening Indian territory between coastal Daman and the enclaves and between the enclaves, in respect of private persons, civil officials and goods in general, to the extent necessary, as claimed by Portugal, for the exercise of its sovereignty over the enclaves, and subject to the regulation and control of India.

As regards armed forces, armed police and arms and ammunition, the position is different.

[The Court then discussed an incident concerning Paragraph 3 of Article 18 of the Treaty of Commerce and Extradition of December 26, 1878 between Great Britain and Portugal which provided that the armed forces of the two governments should not enter the India dominions of the other, except for specified purposes. The Governor–General of Portuguese India stated that, following the practice of centuries of respecting treaties and according due deference to British authorities, "Portuguese troops never cross British territory without previous permission."]

It would thus appear that, during the British and post-British periods, Portuguese armed forces and armed police did not pass between Daman and the enclaves as of right and that, after 1878, such passage could only take place with previous authorization by the British and later by India, accorded either under a reciprocal arrangement already agreed to, or in individual cases. Having regard to the special circumstances of the case, this necessity for authorization before passage could take place constitutes, in the view of the Court, a negation of passage as of right. The practice predicates that the territorial sovereign had the discretionary power to withdraw or to refuse permission. It is argued that permission was always granted, but this does not, in the opinion of the Court, affect the legal position. There is nothing in the record to show that grant of permission was incumbent on the British or on India as an obligation.

As regards arms and ammunition, paragraph 4 of Article XVIII of the Treaty of 1878 provided that the exportation of arms, ammunition or military stores from the territories of one party to those of the other "shall not be permitted, except with the consent of, and under rules approved of by, the latter."

* * *

There was thus established a clear distinction between the practice permitting free passage of private persons, civil officials and goods in general, and the practice requiring previous authorization, as in the case of armed forces, armed police, and arms and ammunition.

The Court is, therefore, of the view that no right of passage in favour of Portugal involving a correlative obligation on India has been established in respect of armed forces, armed police, and arms and ammunition. The course of dealings established between the Portuguese and the British authorities with respect to the passage of these categories excludes the existence of any such right. The practice that was established shows that, with regard to these categories, it was well understood that passage could take place only by permission of the British authorities. This situation continued during the post-British period.

Portugal also invokes general international custom, as well as the general principles of law recognized by civilized nations, in support of its claim of a right of passage as formulated by it. Having arrived at the conclusion that the course of dealings between the British and Indian authorities on the one hand and the Portuguese on the other established a practice, well understood between the Parties, by virtue of which Portugal had acquired a right of passage in respect of private persons, civil officials and goods in general, the Court does consider it necessary to examine whether general international custom or the general principles of law recognized by civilized nations may lead to the same result.

As regards armed forces, armed police and arms and ammunition, the finding of the Court that the practice established between the Parties required for passage in respect of these categories the permission of the British or Indian authorities, renders it unnecessary for the Court to determine whether or not, in the absence of the practice that actually prevailed, general international custom or the general principles of law recognized by civilized nations could have been relied upon by Portugal in support of its claim to a right of passage in respect of these categories. * * *

[Having found that Portugal had in 1954 a right of passage over intervening Indian territory between Daman and the enclaves in respect of private persons, civil officials, and goods in general, the Court nevertheless then concluded that India had lawfully exercised its power of regulation and control of the Portuguese rights when it "suspended" all passage in July 1954 because of "tension" created by the overthrow of Portugal's rule in the enclaves.]

[Dissenting and separate opinions omitted.]

### *Notes*

1. Why did the Court regard it as unnecessary to consider whether Portugal had a right of passage for its armed forces and arms on the basis of general international custom and general principles of law (as Portugal contended)?

Should the finding that a particular custom was not established preclude the possibility of applying a general custom? How would you justify the Court's decision on this point?

2. Does the case support the argument that special or particular custom requires a higher degree of proof than general custom? Does it amount to showing tacit agreement and would that make a difference in proof?

3. As Portugal's sovereignty over the enclaves was not in question, could it be maintained that the necessity for passage of armed forces was implicit in the idea of sovereignty? This view was taken by Judge Spender in a dissenting opinion. Would a similar judgment have been reached 50 years earlier when colonialism was accepted?

## OPINIO JURIS

## NORTH SEA CONTINENTAL CASES (FEDERAL REPUBLIC OF GERMANY v. DENMARK) (FEDERAL REPUBLIC OF GERMANY v. NETHERLANDS)

International Court of Justice, 1969.
1969 I.C.J. 3.

[The cases involved a dispute over the delimitation of the Continental Shelf shared by Denmark, Netherlands and the Federal Republic of Germany. Denmark and Netherlands claimed that the dispute should be decided in accordance with the principle of equidistance under Article 6 of the Geneva Convention of 1958 on the Continental Shelf. The Court rejected the application of the Convention to which Germany was not a party. However, Denmark and Netherlands also maintained that the principle in Article 6 of the Convention is part of the corpus of general international law, and in particular of customary law. The Court rejected this contention by a vote of 11 to 6 for the reasons given below.]

70. * * * [Denmark and the Netherlands argue] that even if there was at the date of the Geneva Convention no rule of customary international law in favour of the equidistance principle, and no such rule was crystallized in Article 6 of the Convention, nevertheless such a rule has come into being since the Convention, partly because of its own impact, partly on the basis of subsequent State practice * * *.

71. In so far as this contention is based on the view that Article 6 of the Convention has had the influence, and has produced the effect described, it clearly involves treating that Article as a norm-creating provision which has constituted the foundation of, or has generated a rule which, while only conventional or contractual in its origin, has since passed into the general *corpus* of international law, and is now accepted as such by the *opinio juris*, so as to have become binding even for countries which have never, and do not, become parties to the Convention. There is no doubt that this process is a perfectly possible one and does from time to time occur: it constitutes indeed one of the recognized methods by which new rules of customary international law may be formed. At the same time this result is not lightly to be regarded as having been attained.

72. It would in the first place be necessary that the provision concerned should, at all events potentially, be of a fundamentally norm-creating character such as could be regarded as forming the basis of a general rule of law. Considered *in abstracto* the equidistance principle might be said to fulfill this requirement. Yet in the particular form in which it is embodied in

Article 6 of the Geneva Convention, and having regard to the relationship of that Article to other provisions of the Convention, this must be open to some doubt. In the first place, Article 6 is so framed as to put second the obligation to make use of the equidistance method, causing it to come after a primary obligation to effect delimitation by agreement. Such a primary obligation constitutes an unusual preface to what is claimed to be a potential general rule of law. * * * Secondly the part played by the notion of special circumstances relative to the principle of equidistance as embodied in Article 6, and the very considerable, still unresolved controversies as to the exact meaning and scope of this notion, must raise further doubts as to the potentially norm-creating character of the rule. Finally, the faculty of making reservations to Article 6, while it might not of itself prevent the equidistance principle being eventually received as general law, does add considerably to the difficulty of regarding this result as having been brought about (or being potentially possible) on the basis of the Convention: for so long as this faculty continues to exist, * * * it is the Convention itself which would, for the reasons already indicated, seem to deny to the provisions of Article 6 the same norm-creating character as, for instance, Articles 1 and 2 possess.

73. With respect to the other elements usually regarded as necessary before a conventional rule can be considered to have become a general rule of international law, it might be that, even without the passage of any considerable period of time, a very widespread and representative participation in the convention might suffice of itself, provided it included that of States whose interests were specially affected. In the present case however, the Court notes that, even if allowance is made for the existence of a number of States to whom participation in the Geneva Convention is not open, or which, by reason for instance of being land-locked States, would have no interest in becoming parties to it, the number of ratifications and accessions so far secured is, though respectable, hardly sufficient. That nonratification may sometimes be due to factors other than active disapproval of the convention concerned can hardly constitute a basis on which positive acceptance of its principles can be implied. The reasons are speculative, but the facts remain.

74. As regards the time element, the Court notes that it is over ten years since the Convention was signed, but that it is even now less than five since it came into force in June 1964 * * *. Although the passage of only a short period of time is not necessarily, or of itself, a bar to the formation of a new rule of customary international law on the basis of what was originally a purely conventional rule, an indispensable requirement would be that within the period in question, short though it might be, State practice, including that of States whose interests are specially affected, should have been both extensive and virtually uniform in the sense of the provision invoked;—and should moreover have occurred in such a way as to show a general recognition that a rule of law or legal obligation is involved.

75. The Court must now consider whether State practice in the matter of continental shelf delimitation has, subsequent to the Geneva Convention, been of such a kind as to satisfy this requirement. * * * [S]ome fifteen cases have been cited in the course of the present proceedings, occurring mostly since the signature of the 1958 Geneva Convention, in which continental

shelf boundaries have been delimited according to the equidistance principle—in the majority of the cases by agreement, in a few others unilaterally—or else the delimitation was foreshadowed but has not yet been carried out. But even if these various cases constituted more than a very small proportion of those potentially calling for delimitation in the world as a whole, the Court would not think it necessary to enumerate or evaluate them separately, since there are, *a priori,* several grounds which deprive them of weight as precedents in the present context.

* * *

77. The essential point in this connection—and it seems necessary to stress it—is that even if these instances of action by nonparties to the Convention were much more numerous than they in fact are, they would not, even in the aggregate, suffice in themselves to constitute the *opinio juris;*—for, in order to achieve this result, two conditions must be fulfilled. Not only must the acts concerned amount to a settled practice, but they must also be such, or be carried out in such a way, as to be evidence of a belief that this practice is rendered obligatory by the existence of a rule of law requiring it. The need for such a belief, i.e., the existence of a subjective element, is implicit in the very notion of the *opinio juris sive necessitatis.* The States concerned must therefore feel that they are conforming to what amounts to a legal obligation. The frequency, or even habitual character of the acts is not in itself enough. There are many international acts, e.g., in the field of ceremonial and protocol, which are performed almost invariably, but which are motivated only by considerations of courtesy, convenience or tradition, and not by any sense of legal duty.

78. In this respect the Court follows the view adopted by the Permanent Court of International Justice in the *Lotus* case * * *. [T]he position is simply that in certain cases—not a great number—the States concerned agreed to draw or did draw the boundaries concerned according to the principle of equidistance. There is no evidence that they so acted because they felt legally compelled to draw them in this way by reason of a rule of customary law obliging them to do so—especially considering that they might have been motivated by other obvious factors.

[In a dissenting opinion, Judge Lachs took issue with the Court's conclusion regarding *opinio juris.* He said, in part:]

All this leads to the conclusion that the principles and rules enshrined in the Convention, and in particular the equidistance rule, have been accepted not only by those States which are parties to the Convention on the Continental Shelf, but also by those which have subsequently followed it in agreements, or in their legislation, or have acquiesced in it when faced with legislative acts of other States affecting them. This can be viewed as evidence of a practice widespread enough to satisfy the criteria for a general rule of law.

* * *

Can the practice above summarized be considered as having been accepted as law, having regard to the subjective element required? The process leading to this effect is necessarily complex. There are certain areas of State activity and international law which by their very character may only with great difficulty engender general law, but there are others, both old and new, which may do so with greater ease. Where Continental Shelf law is concerned, some States have at first probably accepted the rules in question, as States usually do, because they found them convenient and useful, the best possible solution for the problems involved. Others may also have been convinced that the instrument elaborated within the framework of the United Nations was intended to become and would in due course become general law (the teleological element is of no small importance in the formation of law). Many States have followed suit under the conviction that it was law.

Thus at the successive stages in the development of the rule the motives which have prompted States to accept it have varied from case to case. It could not be otherwise. At all events, to postulate that all States, even those which initiate a given practice, believe themselves to be acting under a legal obligation is to resort to a fiction—and in fact to deny the possibility of developing such rules. For the path may indeed start from voluntary, unilateral acts relying on the confident expectation that they will find acquiescence or be emulated; alternatively the starting-point may consist of a treaty to which more and more States accede and which is followed by unilateral acceptance. It is only at a later stage that, by the combined effect of individual or joint action, response and interaction in the field concerned, i.e., of that reciprocity so essential in international legal relations, there develops the chain-reaction productive of international consensus.

* * *

In sum, the general practice of States should be recognized as prima facie evidence that it is accepted as law. Such evidence may, of course, be controverted—even on the test of practice itself, if it shows 'much uncertainty and contradiction' (Asylum, Judgment, I.C.J. Reports 1950, p. 277). It may also be controverted on the test of *opinio juris* with regard to "the States in question" or the parties to the case."

### *Notes*

1. What evidence would satisfy the requirement of *opinio juris* under the majority opinion in the North Sea Case? Some writers maintain that an inference of *opinio juris* can only be supported by their statements as to legal right or obligation. On the other hand, as Judge Lachs points out, individual governments often act for convenience or utility even though their legal right to do so is unclear or non-existent. If other governments do not object and take similar actions, the general practice is recognized as a legal rule. Thus, a nascent period of formation of a rule would not exhibit the *opinio juris generalis* but with repeated instances, states come to treat the practice as law. A much cited example is the way in which the Truman Proclamation in 1945 of exclusive jurisdiction over the adjacent continental shelf—a novel position unsupported by existing law—became recognized as general customary law when other coastal states followed the U.S. action and none objected to it.

2. Kelsen points out that "in practice it appears that the *opinio juris* is commonly inferred from the constancy and uniformity of state conduct. But to the extent that it is so inferred, it is this conduct and not the state of mind that is decisive." He notes that in a period of stability, this creates no great concern.

However, at a time of pervasive and rapid change, and "the equivocal nature of much state practice today," the uncertainties of law-creation through custom are much greater than in the past. H. Kelsen, Principles of International Law 450–52 (2d ed. R. Tucker 1966).

3. Has custom become less important in this time of pervasive change (as Kelsen suggests) or has its character changed in response to rapidly changing demands? Today some writers refer to "instant custom" or to "custom on demand." Instead of emphasis on uniformities of conduct (the material element), more importance is accorded to the psychological element, the "*opinio juris*" particularly when declared by states collectively with reasonable expectation of future conduct conforming to the new principle. Henkin comments: "Such efforts to create new customary law by purposeful activity have included * * * resolutions adopted by international organizations * * * to promote, declare or confirm principles of law by overwhelming majorities or by consensus resolutions which discourage dissent." Henkin, International Law: Politics, Values and Functions, 216 Rec. des Cours 58 (1989–IV). (See material below on the effect of UN Resolutions and Declarations.)

4. Some years ago, Sir Robert Jennings wrote that what many commentators characterize as custom "is not only not custom; it does not faintly resemble a customary law." The Identification of International Law, in International Law, Teaching and Practice 5 (Bin Cheng ed. 1982). The tendency to "find" new customary law based mainly on *opinio juris* (i.e., statements that a legal rule has now been recognized) without demonstrating uniform conduct among states in general is especially evident in regard to human rights, environmental protection, and economic development. Is this attempt to put new wine into old bottles legitimized by the felt necessity to extend law to meet social objectives, when neither treaties nor uniform practice serve that function? For varied views, see following articles in Australian Y.B.I.L. vol. 12 (1992); O. Schachter, Recent Trends in International Law–Making, pp. 1–15; A. Pellet, The Normative Dilemma: Will and Consent in International Law–Making, pp. 22–53; B. Simma and P. Alston, The Sources of Human Rights Law: Customs, Jus Cogens and General Principles, pp. 82–108.

See also M. McDougal, H. Lasswell, L.C. Chen, Human Rights and World Public Order 223–74, 325–27 (1980); T. Meron, Human Rights and Humanitarian Norms as Customary Law 92–97, 134 (1989). The contradictory tendencies are emphasized by M. Koskenniemi, From Apology to Utopia 342–421 (1989).

## CASE CONCERNING MILITARY AND PARAMILITARY ACTIVITIES IN AND AGAINST NICARAGUA

## (NICARAGUA v. UNITED STATES (MERITS))

International Court of Justice (1986).

1986 I.C.J. 14.

[In 1984 Nicaragua instituted proceedings against the United States in the International Court of Justice, alleging unlawful military and paramilitary acts by the United States in Nicaragua (for the substance see p. 911 below). The United States contested the jurisdiction of the Court on several grounds including a reservation it had made in accepting the Court's jurisdiction that its acceptance would not apply to a dispute concerning the application of a treaty—in this case, the U.N. Charter. Nicaragua responded that its claim was based not only on the Charter but also under rules of customary law which were similar in content to the Charter and applicable to these facts. The Court accepted the Nicaraguan contention for the reasons given below.]

182. The Court concludes that it should exercise the jurisdiction conferred upon it by the United States declaration of acceptance under Article 36, paragraph 2, of the Statute, to determine the claims of Nicaragua based upon customary international law notwithstanding the exclusion from its jurisdiction of disputes "arising under" the United Nations and Organization of American States Charters.

* * *

183. In view of this conclusion, the Court has next to consider what are the rules of customary international law applicable to the present dispute. For this purpose, it has to direct its attention to the practice and *opinio juris* of States; as the Court recently observed,

> "It is of course axiomatic that the material of customary international law is to be looked for primarily in the actual practice and *opinio juris* of States, even though multilateral conventions may have an important role to play in recording and defining rules deriving from custom, or indeed in developing them." (*Continental Shelf (Libyan Arab Jamahiriya/Malta), I.C.J. Reports 1985,* pp. 29–30, para. 27.)

In this respect the Court must not lose sight of the Charter of the United Nations and that of the Organization of American States, notwithstanding the operation of the multilateral treaty reservation. Although the Court has no jurisdiction to determine whether the conduct of the United States constitutes a breach of those conventions, it can and must take them into account in ascertaining the content of the customary international law which the United States is also alleged to have infringed.

184. The Court notes that there is in fact evidence, to be examined below, of a considerable degree of agreement between the Parties as to the content of the customary international law relating to the non-use of force and non-intervention. This concurrence of their views does not however dispense the Court from having itself to ascertain what rules of customary international law are applicable. The mere fact that States declare their recognition of certain rules is not sufficient for the Court to consider these as being part of customary international law, and as applicable as such to those States. Bound as it is by Article 38 of its Statute to apply, *inter alia,* international custom "as evidence of a general practice accepted as law", the Court may not disregard the essential role played by general practice. Where two States agree to incorporate a particular rule in a treaty, their agreement suffices to make that rule a legal one, binding upon them; but in the field of customary international law, the shared view of the Parties as to the content of what they regard as the rule is not enough. The Court must satisfy itself that the existence of the rule in the *opinio juris* of States is confirmed by practice.

185. In the present dispute, the Court, while exercising its jurisdiction only in respect of the application of the customary rules of non-use of force and non-intervention, cannot disregard the fact that the Parties are bound by these rules as a matter of treaty law and of customary international law.

Furthermore, in the present case, apart from the treaty commitments binding the Parties to the rules in question, there are various instances of their having expressed recognition of the validity thereof as customary international law in other ways. It is therefore in the light of this "subjective element"—the expression used by the Court in its 1969 Judgment in the *North Sea Continental Shelf* cases (*I.C.J. Reports 1969,* p. 44)—that the Court has to appraise the relevant practice.

186. It is not to be expected that in the practice of States the application of the rules in question should have been perfect, in the sense that States should have refrained, with complete consistency, from the use of force or from intervention in each other's internal affairs. The Court does not consider that, for a rule to be established as customary, the corresponding practice must be in absolutely rigorous conformity with the rule. In order to deduce the existence of customary rules, the Court deems it sufficient that the conduct of States should, in general, be consistent with such rules, and that instances of State conduct inconsistent with a given rule should generally have been treated as breaches of that rule, not as indications of the recognition of a new rule. If a State acts in a way prima facie incompatible with a recognized rule, but defends its conduct by appealing to exceptions or justifications contained within the rule itself, then whether or not the State's conduct is in fact justifiable on that basis, the significance of that attitude is to confirm rather than to weaken the rule.

* * *

187. The Court must therefore determine, first, the substance of the customary rules relating to the use of force in international relations, applicable to the dispute submitted to it. The United States has argued that, on this crucial question of the lawfulness of the use of force in inter-State relations, the rules of general and customary international law, and those of the United Nations Charter, are in fact identical. In its view this identity is so complete that, as explained above (paragraph 173), it constitutes an argument to prevent the Court from applying this customary law, because it is indistinguishable from the multilateral treaty law which it may not apply. In its Counter–Memorial on jurisdiction and admissibility the United States asserts that "Article 2(4) of the Charter *is* customary and general international law". It quotes with approval an observation by the International Law Commission to the effect that

> "the great majority of international lawyers today unhesitatingly hold that Article 2, paragraph 4, together with other provisions of the Charter, authoritatively declares the modern customary law regarding the threat or use of force" (*ILC Yearbook,* 1966, Vol. II, p. 247).

The United States points out that Nicaragua has endorsed this view, since one of its counsel asserted that "indeed it is generally considered by publicists that Article 2, paragraph 4, of the United Nations Charter is in this respect an embodiment of existing general principles of international law". And the United States concludes:

> "In sum, the provisions of Article 2(4) with respect to the lawfulness of the use of force *are* 'modern customary law' (International Law Commission, *loc. cit.*) and the 'embodiment of general principles of

international law' (counsel for Nicaragua, Hearing of 25 April 1984, morning, *loc. cit.*). There is no other 'customary and general international law' on which Nicaragua can rest its claims."

"It is, in short, inconceivable that this Court could consider the lawfulness of an alleged use of armed force without referring to the principal source of the relevant international law—Article 2(4) of the United Nations Charter."

As for Nicaragua, the only noteworthy shade of difference in its view lies in Nicaragua's belief that

"in certain cases the rule of customary law will not necessarily be identical in content and mode of application to the conventional rule".

188. The Court thus finds that both Parties take the view that the principles as to the use of force incorporated in the United Nations Charter correspond, in essentials, to those found in customary international law. The Parties thus both take the view that the fundamental principle in this area is expressed in the terms employed in Article 2, paragraph 4, of the United Nations Charter. They therefore accept a treaty-law obligation to refrain in their international relations from the threat or use of force against the territorial integrity or political independence of any State, or in any other manner inconsistent with the purposes of the United Nations. The Court has however to be satisfied that there exists in customary international law an *opinio juris* as to the binding character of such abstention. This *opinio juris* may, though with all due caution, be deduced from, *inter alia,* the attitude of the Parties and the attitude of States towards certain General Assembly resolutions, and particularly resolution 2625 (XXV) entitled "Declaration on Principles of International Law concerning Friendly Relations and Co-operation among States in accordance with the Charter of the United Nations". The effect of consent to the text of such resolutions cannot be understood as merely that of a "reiteration or elucidation" of the treaty commitment undertaken in the Charter. On the contrary, it may be understood as an acceptance of the validity of the rule or set of rules declared by the resolution by themselves. The principle of non-use of force, for example, may thus be regarded as a principle of customary international law, not as such conditioned by provisions relating to collective security, or to the facilities or armed contingents to be provided under Article 43 of the Charter. It would therefore seem apparent that the attitude referred to expresses an *opinio juris* respecting such rule (or set of rules), to be thenceforth treated separately from the provisions, especially those of an institutional kind, to which it is subject on the treaty-law plane of the Charter.

## *Notes*

1. Note how the Court related *opinio juris* to evidence of practice. It found (in para. 184) "a considerable degree of agreement between the parties as to the content of the customary international law relating to the non-use of force and non-intervention." In this light, the Court referred only generally to the relevant practice. A Dutch scholar concludes from this judgment that "if there exist concordant views as to the existence of an applicable rule, less stringent proof is required to establish existence of a settled practice and *opinio juris.* * * * Where concordant views exist, the dispute will not concern the question

whether a particular rule exists or whether the parties are bound by that rule but will above all concern * * * the facts, particularly * * * whether certain acts are prohibited or permitted by the rule." P. Rijpkema, Customary International Law in the Nicaragua Case, XX Netherlands Y.B.I.L. 91, 96–97 (1989). Compare this conclusion to the Court's decision in both the Lotus and the North Sea Continental Shelf Cases where one of the parties denied the existence of an applicable customary law norm. In those cases the Court looked to see if practice was accepted as law (i.e., *opinio juris*). In the Nicaragua Case, *opinio juris* (the subjective element) was not disputed and the Court states in para. 185 that it will "appraise the relevant practice" in the light of the "subjective element." Thus, *opinio juris* is established prior to appraising practice in contrast to the Lotus and North Sea judgments.

2. Is the question of state practice of less importance when the norms in question are recognized as "fundamental" and universal? The Court refers to the fact that the non-use of force, as expressed in article 2(4), is frequently referred to as a fundamental or cardinal principle and as a principle *jus cogens* (peremptory norm). Is this a good reason for the Court to be less stringent in requiring proof of a general practice in conformity with the norm? See Schachter, Entangled Treaty and Custom, in International Law at a Time of Perplexity 717 (Dinstein, ed. 1989) cit. supra at pp. 733–34, noting that the "higher normativity" of the rule against aggression justifies maintaining the rule even in the face of inconsistent practice.

3. After the invasion of Panama in 1990, the State Department Legal Adviser, in justifying the legality of the U.S. action, argued for a "common law approach to use of force rules" that "would take account of the circumstance of each case and avoid a mechanical application of the rules." A. Sofaer, The Legality of the United States Invasion of Panama, 29 Colum.J.Transnat'l Law 281, 282 n. 10. Henkin, in response, wrote:

> Customary international law indeed has important similarities to the common law but there are essential differences between them * * *. Customary international law, and even the interpretation of a treaty, may also change in response to new needs or new insights. A state might knowingly deviate from what had been established law (or established interpretation of a treaty) in the hope of changing the law. But that state does so at its peril. It does so at the peril that it will not succeed in changing the law and will be adjudged to have violated the law. It does so at the peril that it may succeed in destroying or eroding established law, to its later deep regret.
>
> If the invasion of Panama, and the legal arguments to justify it, were designed to erode or modify established law, they have been rejected by the large majority of the states and of the legal communities—"the judges" of the "international common law." Indeed, the history of the common law rejects its use as an analogy to justify the U.S. invasion of Panama. When the common law proved inadequate, when society could not tolerate the law's ambiguities and uncertainties and its dependence on imperfect institutions, the law was codified, made more clear, more firm, leaving less room for violators and for reliance on an imperfect judiciary * * *. Because the "common law" on the use of force failed, the law was codified, establishing clearer, firmer prohibitions, designed to leave few loopholes and little room for distortion.

Henkin, The Invasion of Panama and International Law: A Gross Violation, 29 Colum.J.Transnat'l L. 311–12 (1991).

## THE POSITION OF "NON-CONSENTING" STATES

*WALDOCK, GENERAL COURSE ON PUBLIC INTERNATIONAL LAW*

106 Rec. des Cours 1, 49–53 (1962–II) *

* * * The view of most international lawyers is that customary law is not a form of tacit treaty but an independent form of law; and that, when a custom satisfying the definition in Article 38 is established, it constitutes a general rule of international law which, subject to one reservation, applies to every State. The reservation concerns the case of a State which, while the custom is in process of formation, unambiguously and persistently registers its objection to the recognition of the practice as law. Thus, in the *Anglo-Norwegian Fisheries* case [26] the Court, having rejected the so-called ten-mile rule for bays, said:

> "In any event, the ten-mile rule would appear to be inapplicable as against Norway, inasmuch as she has always opposed any attempt to apply it to the Norwegian coast."

Similarly, in the *Asylum* [27] case it said:

> "Even if it could be supposed that such a custom existed between certain Latin-American States only, it could not be invoked against Peru, which, far from having by its attitude adhered to it, has on the contrary repudiated it."

These pronouncements seem clearly to indicate that a customary rule may arise notwithstanding the opposition of one State, or even perhaps a few States, provided that otherwise the necessary degree of generality is reached. But they also seem to lay down that the rule so created will not bind the objectors; in other words, that in international law there is no majority rule even with respect to the formation of customary law.

On the other hand, it is no less clear that, if a custom becomes established as a general rule of international law, it binds all States which have not opposed it, whether or not they themselves played an active part in its formation. This means that in order to invoke a custom against a State it is not necessary to show specifically the acceptance of the custom as law by that State; its acceptance of the custom will be presumed so that it will be bound unless it can adduce evidence of its actual opposition to the practice in question. The Court in applying a general custom may well refer to the practice, if any, of the parties to the litigation in regard to the custom; but it has never yet treated evidence of their acceptance of the practice as a *sine qua non* of applying the custom to them. The position is, of course, quite different in regard to a particular custom between two or three States, as in the *Right of Passage* case, because that is a derogation from the general law and the acceptance of the custom by the parties to the litigation themselves is the whole basis of the exceptional rule.[29] Here an interesting point suggests itself as to whether a regional custom is to be viewed as a

* Some footnotes omitted. Reprinted by permission of A.W. Sijthoff & Noordhoff International.

**26.** I.C.J. Reports, 1951, at p. 131.

**27.** I.C.J. Reports, 1950, at p. 211.

**29.** I.C.J. Reports, 1960, at pp. 39–43.

"general" or a "particular" custom for this purpose. In the context of general international law, a regional custom is, of course, a particular rule to be proved specially, as the Court emphasized in both the *Asylum* and the *U.S. Nationals in Morocco* cases. But within the regional group the custom may appear as a general law, to which there may also be exceptions between particular States; at any rate, that is how the Court seems to have viewed the matter when confronted with the problem of custom in the Organisation of American States. * * *

An aspect of this question of the legal basis of custom which is of particular importance to-day is the position of the new-born State with regard to existing general rules of customary law. We know that, generally speaking, a new State begins with a clean slate in regard to treaties, although often of its own choice it takes over many of the treaty obligations formerly applicable to the territory. Logically enough on the treaty theory of custom, Communist writers maintain that the same is true for customary law; and they have strong things to say about "European" or "Western" States trying to impose norms of general international law upon the new States of Asia and Africa.

This doctrine has not been without its attraction for new States emerging from colonial régimes. But, quite apart from any theoretical difficulty about the nature of customary law, the fundamental objection to it is that it really denies the existence of a general international legal order and the new States have at least as much to lose as anyone else from a denial of the validity of existing international law. If consent is so far the basis of customary law that a new State may reject any customary rule it chooses, how can it be said that an older State is not free, vis-à-vis the new State, to reject any customary rule that it may choose? Either there is an international legal order or there is not. * * *

* * * The new States have every right to a full and equal voice both in resolving the existing controversies and in shaping the new customary law; but surely that right will itself be meaningless if it is not founded upon and given expression through a stable legal order. At any rate, it is an encouraging sign that, when controversial points in customary law are debated in the [U.N.] International Law Commission and the Sixth [Legal] Committee [of the U.N. General Assembly], a large measure of common agreement is often reached and the divisions of opinion when they occur are on other lines than the differences between new and old States.

### Notes

1. The Restatement (Third) agrees that "in principle a dissenting state which indicates its dissent from a practice while the law is still in a state of development is not bound by that rule of law even after it matures" (§ 102, Comment *d*). Presumably, a state that is silent during the period of formation would be bound by the rule when it comes into force as would a new state. Is it reasonable to apply this principle to states that had no interest in or knowledge of the conduct that developed the rule?

2. The only judicial expression of the rule is found in the two I.C.J. cases mentioned by Waldock. Both cases arguably concern regional (or special) custom. States have rarely claimed or granted an exemption on the basis of the dissenting state principle (sometimes described as the principle of the persistent

objector). See T. Stein, The Approach of the Different Drummer: The Principle of the Persistent Objector in International Law, 26 Harv.Int'l L.J. 457, 459–60 (1985); J. Charney, The Persistent Objector Rule and the Development of Customary International Law, 56 Brit.Y.B.I.L. 1–24 (1985). Notwithstanding the paucity of practice, Stein concludes that the principle of the persistent dissenter will be increasingly used to claim exemption from new principles of customary law developed by the majority of states. He points to the trend toward formation of new principles of customary law as a consequence of majority positions adopted in international conferences and in United Nations organs. He anticipates that the states opposing such rules will increasingly have recourse to the persistent objector principle to claim exemption. Id. at 463–69.

3. Should South Africa be exempt from the generally accepted customary law rule prohibiting systematic racial discrimination such as apartheid because it persistently dissented from that rule during the time the rule was being developed? The United Kingdom, in its pleadings in the *Anglo–Norwegian Fisheries Case,* questioned the right of a persistent dissenter to an exemption from a rule of law of fundamental importance. 1951 I.C.J. *Fisheries Case,* II Pleadings, Oral Arguments, 428–30. The Restatement (Revised) § 702 suggests that the persistent objector rule would not apply to peremptory norms (*jus cogens*) that permit no derogation—and it indicates that the rule against apartheid falls into the class of peremptory norms. On peremptory norms, see below.

4. The Restatement (Third) gives only one example of the application of the "persistent dissenter" principle. It states that the United States would not be bound by a customary law rule that prohibited deep seabed mining outside the regime established by the 1982 Convention on the Law of the Sea. It notes in § 523 that the U.S. rejected those principles as binding on states not parties to the Convention (see Chapter 14). Charney, in contrast, observes that "[n]o case is cited in which the objector effectively maintained its status after the rule became well accepted in international law. * * * This is certainly the plight that befell the U.S., UK and Japan in the law of the sea. Their objections to expanded coastal state jurisdiction were ultimately to no avail, and they have been forced to accede to 12–mile territorial seas and 200–mile exclusive economic zones" (loc. cit. p. 24). Does this mean that the persistent objector "rule" is of no significance? Charney suggests that it gives an objecting state "a tool it may use over the short term with direct and indirect negotiations with the proponents of a new rule. * * * As a particularly affected state, it will have leverage in determining the evolution of the applicable rule of law and will have the theoretical advantage of invoking the persistent objector rule. * * * When the rule does settle, * * * a few states may continue to maintain their objection to a new rule of law. If they are few, they will not be able to block a finding that the new rule represents international law" (loc. cit. pp. 23–24).

5. Is the "persistent objector" rule likely to be asserted more often because of declarations by international conferences or UN bodies that purport to state international legal rules? Henkin comments that "efforts to make new law purposefully by custom (in effect, circumventing the multilateral treaty which requires individual consent) has given the persistent objector principle new vitality, perhaps its first real life" (216 Rec. des Cours 59 (1989–IV)). Would this new "vitality" be significantly different from the traditional requirement of "*opinio juris*" required of states generally and especially of those particularly affected by the rule in question? Is the critical factor the effective power of the objecting state vis-à-vis the majority of states? Does an exception for "perempto-

ry norms," as in the case of apartheid, open up a large exception to the persistent objector rule? See below on creation of peremptory norms.

6. Does the problem of the dissenting state suggest the desirability of more individualized customary rules that make exceptions for special geographical features or other particular needs?

In the Anglo–Norwegian Fisheries Case, 1951 I.C.J. 128, the Court found that Norway's practice in departing from the general rule of customary law had been condoned or acquiesced in by other states having knowledge of Norway's practice or being in a position where such knowledge was attributed to them. In this way, a state departing from a rule—in effect, violating it—may build up what is described as a historic or prescriptive right. This is not the same as a "local custom" since it comes into being not by consent of two or three states but by conduct at variance with a rule that is acquiesced in by other states. Judge Fitzmaurice wrote:

> If other States are in fact willing to acquiesce in this way and in effect to condone what are violations of the law, this can only be because they recognize that the circumstances are indeed unusual or exceptional.

Fitzmaurice, General Principles of International Law, 92 Rec. des Cours 111–12 (1957–II).

See also Schachter, The Nature and Process of Legal Development in International Society, in Structure and Process of International Law 745, 779 (Macdonald and Johnston eds., 1983).

7. What is the consequence of a large number of states departing from an existing rule of law? Such "departures" are, in their inception, clearly violations of law. However, such violations carried out by a number of states may—and often has—resulted in new customary law. This development occurred dramatically in recent years as states by practice eroded the existing principle of the freedom of the seas by extending their jurisdiction over adjacent waters up to 200 miles and over the continental shelf. See Chapter 14. To determine when such new law has repealed the old rule, it is necessary to consider the same elements that are involved in creating customary law—namely, (1) the extent, consistency and frequency of the departures from old law, (2) the relation of the states concerned (both those departing and those adhering) to the subject matter of the rule, and (3) the time of the process. *Opinio juris* must also be considered. At some point, a large number of "representative states" may conclude that their infringements have become new law, and that they will not be charged with violating existing law. Presumably, the new rule will not be opposable to states that have openly manifested their opposition to it from the start. But such states, if few, cannot prevent the adoption of a new rule. In this regard, Judge Fitzmaurice commented * * * "although such opposition may for a time, perhaps for a considerable time, prevent the rule from being opposable to themselves, it is liable in the long run to be overborne". 92 Rec. des Cours at 115.

8. May a state that was not in existence at the time a customary rule was formed object to the rule when it emerges as an independent state? In fact, many new states have objected to particular rules of international law. Their objections were made mainly in regard to state responsibility, some rules of treaty law (in particular, relating to unequal treaties), and some aspects of the law of the sea. See Anand, New States and International Law 62 (1972); Abi–Saab, The Newly–Independent States and the Rules of International Law, 8 Howard L.J. 95 (1962); Guha Roy, Is the Law of Responsibility of States a Part of

Universal International Law, 55 A.J.I.L. 866 (1961); Bokor–Szego, New States and International Law (1970). These states did not reject existing customary law in its entirety. Nor did they maintain that their consent was required for every rule to be binding upon them. Their basic position was that a rule of customary law should no longer be considered as a general rule valid for all states when most (or many) states rejected it as law. Thus the question was not whether a new state may reject a rule it did not like but rather whether the objection by a large number of states (often a majority) to a general rule must mean that that rule is no longer valid (if it ever was) for the entire international community.

## RELATIVE NORMATIVITY IN INTERNATIONAL CUSTOMARY LAW

*PROSPER WEIL, TOWARDS RELATIVE NORMATIVITY IN INTERNATIONAL LAW*

77 Am.J.Int.L. 413, 421 (1983).*

There is now a trend towards the replacement of the monolithically conceived normativity of the past by graduated normativity. While it has always been difficult to locate the threshold beyond which a legal norm existed, at least there used to be no problem once the threshold could be pronounced crossed: the norm created legal rights and obligations; it was binding, its violation sanctioned with international responsibility. There was no distinction on that score to be made between one legal norm and another. But the theory of *jus cogens,* with its distinction between peremptory and merely binding norms, and the theory of international crimes and delicts, with its distinction between norms creating obligations essential for the preservation of fundamental interests and norms creating obligations of a less essential kind, are both leading to the fission of this unity. Normativity is becoming a question of "more or less": some norms are now held to be of greater specific gravity than others, to be more binding than others. Thus, the scale of normativity is reemerging in a new guise, its gradations no longer plotted merely between norms and non-norms, but also among those norms most undeniably situated on the positive side of the normativity threshold. Having taken its rise in the subnormative domain, the scale of normativity has now been projected and protracted into the normative domain itself, so that, henceforth, there are "norms and norms."

## JUS COGENS (PEREMPTORY NORMS)

*OPPENHEIM'S INTERNATIONAL LAW*

7–8 (9th ed., R.Y. Jennings and A. Watts eds. 1992).

§ 2 *Ius cogens* States may, by and within the limits of agreement between themselves, vary or even dispense altogether with most rules of international law. There are, however, a few rules from which no derogation is permissible. The latter—rules of *ius cogens,* or peremptory norms of general international law—have been defined in Article 53 of the Vienna Convention on the Law of Treaties 1969 (and for the purpose of that Convention) as norms 'accepted and recognised by the international community of states as a whole as a norm from which no derogation is permitted and which can be modified only by a subsequent norm of general international law having the same character'; and Article 64 contemplates the emergence of new rules of *ius cogens* in the future.

Such a category of rules of *ius cogens* is a comparatively recent development and there is no general agreement as to which rules have this character. The International Law Commission regarded the law of the Charter concerning the prohibition of the use of force as a conspicuous example of such a rule. Although the Commission refrained from giving in its draft Articles on the Law of Treaties any examples of rules of *ius cogens,* it did record that in this context mention had additionally been made of the prohibition of criminal acts under international law, and of acts such as trade in slaves, piracy or genocide, in the suppression of which every state is called upon to cooperate; the observance of human rights, the equality of states and the principle of self-determination. The full content of the category of *ius cogens* remains to be worked out in the practice of states and in the jurisprudence of international tribunals. * * *

The operation and effect of rules of *ius cogens* in areas other than that of treaties are similarly unclear. Presumably no act done contrary to such a rule can be legitimated by means of consent, acquiescence or recognition; nor is a protest necessary to preserve rights affected by such an act; nor can such an act be justified as a reprisal against a prior illegal act; nor can a rule of customary international law which conflicts with a rule of *ius cogens* continue to exist or subsequently be created (unless it has the character of *ius cogens,* a possibility which raises questions—to which no firm answer can yet be given—of the relationship between rules of *ius cogens,* and of the legitimacy of an act done in reliance on one rule of *ius cogens* but resulting in a violation of another such rule).

### *Notes*

1. In its 1986 Judgment in the Nicaragua Case (supra), the I.C.J. referred to the rule against the use of force as "a conspicuous example of a rule of international law having the character of jus cogens." I.C.J. Reports 1986, p. 100 [para. 190].

2. The peremptory norms mentioned above in Oppenheim are examples of rules to which no state would claim exceptions—e.g., the prohibition of genocide, slavery, aggression. Would the "international community as a whole" be likely to determine that past acts which some states have engaged in by mutual consent or without objection (e.g., environmental pollution) have now become illegal under newly created *jus cogens*?

3. Should the expression "the international community as a whole" meet a qualitative as well as a quantitative standard? Some suggest a "very large majority" is sufficient; others would require that the large majority include "essential" or "important" states. Would the latter rule (asserted by the United States and other major powers) mean that peremptory rules would not be recognized unless accepted as such by all major powers and countries from all regions of the world? During the conference on the Law of the Sea Convention, a large majority of states declared that a peremptory norm of customary law had evolved to the effect that the sea bed beyond national jurisdiction was the

common heritage of mankind and not open to exploitation by individual states except when carried out under the international regime contemplated by the 1982 Convention. The fact that important industrial states including the United States opposed this position was not considered by its proponents as sufficient to negate the new principle. A similar effort has also been made in United Nations bodies to establish the principle of "permanent sovereignty over resources" as part of *jus cogens,* in spite of the opposition of several large industrial states. Neither of these efforts have thus far resulted in acceptance of the new rules by dissenting states. Considering these examples a recent study by a Russian scholar concludes that "the emergence of effective international peremptory norms obviously requires the achievement of a genuine consensus among all essential components of the modern international community * * * opposition to a proposed norm on the part of at least one important element of the international community, whatever its numerical strength, would undermine any claim that such norm is a general peremptory rule * * *" G. Danilenko, International Jus Cogens, 2 Eur.J.Int.L. 42, 65 (1991).

4. Macdonald has suggested that it is inherent in the conception of peremptory norm that it applies against states that have not accepted the norm. See R.St.J. Macdonald, Fundamental Norms in Contemporary International Law, 25 Can.Y.B.I.L. 115, 131 (1987). To same effect, L. Alexidze, Legal Nature of Jus Cogens in Contemporary International Law, 172 Rec. des Cours 219, 246–47, 258 (1981–III). See also Restatement (Third) Comment *d* that the persistent objector rule does not apply to peremptory norms, citing the generally accepted view that apartheid was now prohibited, notwithstanding the objection of South Africa during the evolution of the rule (though South Africa was most clearly the "important" state).

## "FUNDAMENTAL" AND SUPERIOR NORMS OF GENERAL INTERNATIONAL LAW

Neither article 38 of the Statute nor positivist doctrine draws hierarchical distinctions among customary norms. However, international tribunals and writers have done so under various headings. The International Court of Justice has referred to "fundamental principles" as a category differentiated from ordinary custom or treaty norms. See Case Concerning U.S. Hostages in Tehran (infra p. 823) and Nicaragua v. U.S. (supra). Some writers have described principles such as sovereign equality, political independence, and territorial integrity as axiomatic or constitutional in character. Henkin, for example, refers to assumptions and conceptions of axiomatic "constitutional" character as including concepts of state autonomy, *pacta sunt servanda,* and the concept of nationality. Such constitutional law, he suggests, "did not result from practice * * * they were implicit, inherent in Statehood in a State System" (Henkin, General Course, 216 Rec. des Cours 52 (1989–IV)). Schachter refers to these principles as "authoritative by virtue of the inherent necessities of a pluralist society." Such "rules of necessity" are considered as akin to "entrenched" constitutional rules that cannot be set aside by majorities whether through practice or agreements. Their emphasis on autonomy and equality as basic rights is not unlike the declarations of individual rights that reflect Western political thought. See Schachter, International Law in Theory and Practice 30–31 (1991). Although described as "implicit" and "unwritten," they have been expressed in various declarations of basic rights of states prepared by international legal bodies and in UN declarations (as well as in the Principles of the UN Charter). See, for example, the Declaration of Rights and Duties of States, prepared by the U.N. International Law Commission and adopted by the General Assembly in 1949 Res. 375 (IV). The much cited Declaration of Principles of International Law adopted by the UN General Assembly in 1970 (without dissent) is also a statement of basic principles that are mostly postulates of the state system. (See Document Supp.) Although they may be described as higher law and as axiomatic, this does not mean that their content is fixed, beyond influence of state practice and agreements.

Another category of "higher norms" is found in article 103 of the UN Charter which declares that

> In the event of a conflict between the obligations of Members of the United Nations under the present Charter and their obligations under any other international agreement, their obligations under the present Charter shall prevail.

The International Court of Justice referred to article 103 in its 1984 Judgment on Jurisdiction in Nicaragua v. U.S. pointing out that "all regional, bilateral and even unilateral arrangements that the parties have made * * * must be made always subject to the provisions of article 103." I.C.J. Reports 1984, p. 440 para. 107. Some commentators consider that treaties contrary to the Charter are null and void. A.D. McNair, The Law of Treaties 222 (1961). Others maintain that article 103 only requires suspension or modification of treaty obligations—that it is in effect "a compatibility clause" rather than superior law comparable to peremptory norms. See W. Czaplinski and G. Danilenko, Conflicts of Norms in International Law 21 Neth.Y.B.I.L. 14–15 (1990).

Does this position mean that a number of new states may terminate any rule of customary international law they do not like? May they do this by resolution adopted by majority votes in the General Assembly? May they accomplish that goal by collectively disregarding the old rule and asserting that it is no longer law? Would they have to establish a new customary rule by general and consistent practice accompanied by *opinio juris* which other states would recognize? Would a minority of the older states be able to prevent such changes?

## SECTION 3. TREATIES AS A SOURCE OF LAW

### A. THE ROLE OF TREATIES

Article 38 of the Statute of the International Court, in its list of "sources" according to which disputes are to be decided, gives first place to "international conventions, whether general or particular, establishing rules expressly recognized by the contracting States." Although Article 38 does not provide for a hierarchy among sources, the priority of position given to treaties reflects the understanding of states and of international lawyers that, in Lauterpacht's words:

> * * * The rights and duties of States are determined in the first instance, by their agreement as expressed in treaties—just as in the case of individuals their rights are specifically determined by any contract

> which is binding upon them. When a controversy arises between two or more States with regard to a matter regulated by a treaty, it is natural that the parties should invoke and that the adjudicating agency should apply, in the first instance, the provisions of the treaty in question.

1 Lauterpacht, International Law: Collected Papers, 86–87 (1970).

That it may be "natural" to apply a treaty in the first instance should not be taken to mean that a treaty provision necessarily prevails over a customary rule. The maxim, *lex specialis derogat generali,* the specific prevails over the general, is an accepted guide; it may give priority either to treaty or custom. The intentions of the parties are of paramount importance. They may show a common intent to replace a treaty with a customary rule; a treaty may become a dead-letter terminated by desuetude. When neither specificity nor intentions provide sufficient guidance, treaty and custom have equal weight with priority to the later in time, subject however to certain presumptions of interpretation. These presumptions operate in both directions. It is presumed that a treaty is not terminated or altered by subsequent custom in the absence of evidence that the parties had that intention. On the other hand, there is support for a general presumption that treaties are not intended to derogate from general custom. The complex interaction of treaty and custom is dealt with below and also in the chapter on the law of international agreements.

Whether treaties should logically be regarded as a source of law has been questioned by some jurists. Fitzmaurice, for example, has written that "treaties are no more a source of law than an ordinary private law contract that creates rights and obligations * * * In itself, the treaty and 'the law' it contains only applies to the parties to it. True, where it reflects (e.g., codifies) existing law, non-parties may conform to the same rules but they do so by virtue of rule of general law thus reflected in the treaty, not by virtue of the treaty itself." Fitzmaurice, Some Problems Regarding the Formal Sources of International Law, in Symbolae Verzijl 153, 157–58 (Von Asbeck, et al., eds., 1958). A distinction between treaties and "international law" (or the law of nations) is often made in popular usage and sometimes in U.S. statutes. See, for example, the Alien Tort Statute, 28 U.S.C.A. § 1350 (1982), p. 126 infra. The U.S. Constitution also refers separately to "Treaties" (Article II and VI) and to the "Law of Nations" (Article I, § 8).

While it is true, as Fitzmaurice insists, that treaties have a contractual character binding only the parties to it, their provisions create legal obligations for the parties and may prevail over general law. Moreover many treaties especially multilateral treaties lay down broad rules of conduct for states generally and are in that respect more like legislation than contracts. In international usage, treaties are generally considered as part of international law and in accordance with Article 38 of the Statute of the Court as a source of "law." When appropriate, a distinction is made between customary international law and "conventional" (i.e., treaty) international law.

That treaties govern much of international relations is evidenced by the member of such treaties and their wide scope. International agreements—the *lex scripta* of the society of states—have proliferated since the end of World War Two. More than 30,000 treaties have been registered with the United Nations since 1945. Most are bilateral agreements or agreements among a small number of states. Over 2000, it may be estimated, are multilateral. Virtually every aspect of social life affecting transnational relations and intercourse is dealt with in treaties. Nearly all treaties that have entered into force since 1946 are published in the United Nations Treaty Series. Agreements that have been adopted but have not yet come into force (pending the requisite acts of acceptance) are not available in any one collection. Many may be found in national publications such as the United States Treaties and Other International Agreements (TOIA) or International Legal Materials (published by the American Society of International Law).

Three classes of treaties may be distinguished from the standpoint of their relevance as sources of law. First is the general multilateral treaty open to all states of the world or to all members of a large regional group. Such treaties lay down rules of behavior which in the words used by the International Court of Justice are of a fundamentally norm-creating character such as could be regarded as forming the basis of a general rule of law (*North Sea Continental Shelf Case*). These treaties may be codification treaties; they may be "law-making" or a combination of both.

A second category comprises treaties that establish a collaborative mechanism for States to regulate or manage a particular area of activity. They may be designed for universal adherence (for example, regulating allocation of radio frequencies) or for regional or functional groups (e.g. fishing or commodity agreements). Such treaties normally include purposes and principles and they operate through decisions by their organs (such decisions may take the form of concrete rules, orders, or recommendations). In that respect they are distinct from the "legislative type" of treaty that lays down general law. The institutional and administrative character of this group of treaties has led them to be characterized as international regimes or sometimes as international administrative law. Some comprehensive international conventions include both the first and second types of provisions. A notable example is the 1982 U.N. Convention on the Law of the Sea which contains the *corpus juris* pertaining to the seas generally and a mechanism for exploitation of seabed mineral resources. See Chapter 14.

A third category of treaties—by far the largest in number—includes bilateral agreements and, for some purposes agreements by three or four states. Such treaties are drafted in contractual terms of mutual exchange of rights and obligations and in that respect are different from the multilateral treaties that have a more legislative form. The bilateral treaties differ widely in scope and subject matter. Many are detailed, specific and for a fixed period. Others lay down general norms and express intentions as, for example, treaties of alliance and some treaties of friendship. It is not uncommon to find standardized provisions for particular subjects, and establishing similar rights and duties for a large group of states. Many such agreements on extradition, air transport, rivers and foreign investment may create networks of obligation that are virtually general international law. However, whether they may be considered as evidence of custom and therefore binding for non-parties is another matter. On this aspect see the section on treaties and custom.

### *Notes and Questions*

1. Are treaties superior to custom for international law-making? Richard Baxter wrote in 1970:

> As one looks at the present state of international law and attempts to see into the future, it should be quite clear that treaty law will increasingly gain paramountcy over customary international law. The treaty-making process is a rational and orderly one, permitting participation in the creation of law by all States on a basis of equity. Newly independent States, otherwise subject to a body of customary international law in the making of which they played no part, can influence the progressive development of the law or help to "codify" it in such a way as to make it more responsive to their needs and ideals. For the more established States, the codification process provides a welcome opportunity to secure widespread agreement upon norms which have hitherto been the subject of doubt or controversy or have been rejected by other States.
>
> Even in those cases in which customary international law is already clear and generally agreed upon, the treaty will strengthen that rule and simplify its application. Article 1 of the Chicago Convention confirms what is already agreed to be a State's sovereign right to exclude foreign aircraft from its airspace. The presence in bilateral treaties of a requirement of exhaustion of local remedies reminds us that the well-understood rule of customary international law has not lost its validity.

Baxter, Treaties and Custom, 129 Rec. des Cours 25, 101 (1970–I) (footnotes omitted). Tunkin maintains that treaties are the dominant and "basic source" of international law, Theory of International Law 133–36 (Butler trans. 1974).

2. What are the advantages of custom over treaty for developing law to meet new needs? Is custom more responsive to concrete situations and more malleable than multilateral treaties? Does it give more weight to power? For comment on "competition" between treaty and custom, see Schachter, Entangled Treaty and Custom, in International Law at a Time of Perplexity, 717, 720–22 (Dinstein ed. 1989).

3. Regional law-making may be preferred to global conventions as for example, in regard to trade, economic integration, migration, cultural exchange. Would such regional conventions always prevail over general international law under the *lex specialis* rule of interpretation? Could they diminish rights of non-regional states vis-à-vis the regional members?

## B. TREATIES OF CODIFICATION AND PROGRESSIVE DEVELOPMENT

### SCIENTIFIC AND POLITICAL CODIFICATION

*SCHACHTER, INTERNATIONAL LAW IN THEORY AND PRACTICE*

66–69, 71–72 (1991).

The rationalist belief in the development of law through deliberate, carefully considered and well designed instruments finds expression in two closely related processes: codification and "progressive development" through multilateral law-making treaties. Both aim at achieving an international *lex scripta* through the international equivalent of a legislative process. It is easy to see advantages of that process. In place of the uncertain and slow process of custom, built upon instances that are necessarily contingent and limited, governments negotiate and collaborate in formulating rules and principles to meet perceived needs of the entire community of states. The texts bring clarity and precision where there had been obscurity and doubt. Moreover, all governments have the opportunity to take part in the legislative process and to express their consent or objection in accordance with their constitutional procedures. Neither of these opportunities was clearly available to all states in the creation of customary law.

* * *

Codification is distinct, in principle, from the so-called law-making treaty that comes within "progressive development." The Statute of the U.N. International Law Commission defined codification as "the more precise formulation and systematization of rules of international law in fields where there already has been extensive state practice, precedent and doctrine." There is almost a deceptive simplicity about this definition, as indeed there is about the act of codification.

* * *

Before the United Nations began its work in the early nineteen-fifties, sharp differences had been expressed on whether codification should be a scientific or political task. The debate on this issue reflected, in some degree, the differences concerning positivism, voluntarism, and state sovereignty. Those who saw codification as essentially scientific considered as Cecil Hurst did that its task was to "ascertain" and "declare the existing rule of international law, irrespective of any question as to whether the rule is satisfactory or unsatisfactory, obsolete or still adequate to modern conditions, just or unjust in the eyes of those who formulate it." That task could be carried out, it was assumed, solely on the basis of state practice and precedent. It was in its essence an inductive process that could and should be entrusted to independent jurists, not governments. Indeed, Cecil Hurst argued that governments could not achieve scientific codification * * *.

* * *

The idea of a truly scientific, non-governmental restatement of international law did not find the requisite support in the United Nations. Nor was it generally supported by international lawyers, though there were notable exceptions. The objection to scientific, non-official codification had several grounds. There was a basic difficulty with the idea implicit in the I.L.C. definition (referred to earlier) that "extensive state practice, precedent and doctrine" would yield a rule of law. Hersch Lauterpacht commented that the absence of state practice could show the non-existence of a rule but that the converse did not hold because, in his view, the area of agreement that would be revealed by state practice "is small in the extreme." Others went further, pointing out that any attempt to formulate an explicit and clear rule, or systematizing rules based on precedent, involved elements of novelty. It assumes agreement where none may exist.

* * *

The experience of the last 25 years showed that the skepticism about the practicality of universal codification * * * was excessive. For one thing, the governments in the United Nations and the International Law Commission quickly recognized that codification involved "new law" to some degree but that it was possible and desirable to distinguish codification that had a substantial foundation in customary law from treaties that sought to formulate new principles and rules for matters previously unregulated by international law. In the former category, the drafts prepared by the Commission were mainly based on practice and precedent but often filled in lacunae and removed inconsistencies found in State practice. These elements of "progressive development" were identified in the reports of the Commission and in the *travaux préparatoires* leading to adoption by the conference of States. Since such new law generally did not involve significant conflicts of interest between States, it was regarded as essentially technical ("lawyers' law") and therefore appropriate in a codification. The fact that the codifications were drafted as treaties and passed upon in detail by conferences which included nearly all States was perceived as "settling" rather than unsettling customary law (except for the few provisions that were identified as new law in the *travaux* ).

* * *

The anticipated difficulties proved less of an obstacle than had been predicted. Governments were not deterred by the fact that in reducing the unwritten law of precedents to written, generalized rules they were performing a "legislative" act that was in some measure "progressive development." They realized (as did the I.L.C.) that the customary law that they were ostensibly declaring was also being supplemented and, in a degree, modified in the light of present conditions and attitudes. Inevitably this reflected current political views and some bargaining in the negotiations at the conference. But the apprehension that codification would not be acceptable to the States "wedded to uncompromising maintenance of sovereignty" was not borne out. A considerable measure of support by all groups of States was in fact achieved in the two-stage procedure of Commission and conference. In the Commission, the draft conventions were adopted by consensus. The Commission was informed of the governmental views in the course of its work through written comments and the discussions in the Legal Committee of the General Assembly. In the conferences, most decisions were taken by consensus and compromises were reached to avoid any significant defections.

What is noteworthy is that although these texts were in the form of conventions requiring ratification or accession, they have been widely accepted as generally declaratory of existing law and therefore actually given legal effect even prior to their formal entry into force, and, when in force, applied by non-parties as well as by parties to the treaties. In this way, the old issue of "restatement" versus convention was rendered academic since the conventions were in fact regarded and used as if they were restatements except where there was persuasive evidence that a particular provision was intended to be *de lege ferenda* * * *.

* * *

There is a practical side to this conclusion that merits mention here. This relates to what might be called the bureaucratic factor in the codification process. The legal advisers and other government officials concerned with the application of law play a major part in codification. They do so mainly by way of comments on the drafts in the preparatory stages and at the conference of plenipotentiaries at which the final text is adopted. Officials who subsequently have to ascertain and involve law naturally look to the product of the process in which they or their colleagues took part. The text is, so to speak, "their" law. Moreover, the adopted text has the great advantage for busy officials of providing "black letter" law in an instrument that has been adopted by nearly all States of the world. The law is declared in a concise and definitive form that is highly convenient for lawyers and officials. In most cases there is little reason for them to search for the precedents that might underlie the rule; it is in any case difficult to challenge the validity of a rule that had received the support of their own government as well as of others. These practical and bureaucratic factors help to increase the use made of the adopted texts (whether or not the instrument has entered into force or has been ratified by the state invoking its authority). The consequences over time are two-fold: (1) the instrument generally accumulates more authority as declaratory of customary law and (2), in cases where the declaratory nature of a particular provision is shown to be contrary to the understanding of the drafters (as in the *North Sea Continental Shelf Cases* ), the tendency to apply that provision will in time result in custom "grafted" upon the treaty. This latter process was described by the Court in the *North Sea Continental Shelf Cases* although the majority did not find that a customary rule had actually developed.

In suggesting that the generally accepted codification conventions tend to prevail over competing customary law I do not mean to suggest that they entirely replace customary law in the field covered. Custom may still apply to fill in the gaps that always occur or the treaty itself may recognize that exceptions to its rules are permissible in accordance with special custom. * * * In other words, a codification convention, authoritative as it may seem because of its universal (or nearly universal) acceptance, cannot entirely freeze the development of law. Changing conditions and new perceptions of interests and aims continue to operate. The existence of written codified law may impede the pace of change but it cannot prevent it.

## RECENT MULTILATERAL CONVENTIONS

By 1985 a substantial part of customary international law had been codified in multilateral conventions prepared by the International Law Commission approved by the General Assembly and adopted by international plenipotentiary conferences. Among the most notable of these conventions were those on the law of treaties (see Chapter 6) on diplomatic and consular immunities (see Chapter 13) and on the law of the sea. (see Chapter 14). The 1982 Convention on the Law of the Sea was adopted by the Third United Nations Conference on the Law of the Sea after discussion and negotiation by the Conference over a 10–year period (see Chapter 14.)

A large number of general multilateral treaties are appropriately considered as "development" or "law-making" rather than as codification of existing customary law. These treaties may be based to some degree on prior practice but by and large they are perceived as expressing new law required by states for political, social or technical reasons. They include a large number open to all states (potentially universal) and others open to all states in a major region of the globe. The United Nations alone is a depository of over 300 such multilateral treaties. Most of them were prepared and negotiated by United Nations bodies, generally expert or specialized committees broadly representative of the main political and geographical groups in the United Nations. The subject matter of the treaties is diverse; it includes matters such as outer space, dispute settlement, narcotics, status of women, refugees, human rights of various kinds, arms control, transportation, maintenance obligations, environmental protection and telecommunication. Other related United Nations bodies have also produced hundreds of treaties. There are for example, dozens of such treaties relating to intellectual property, many on education, some 150 conventions on labor and social welfare, and numerous treaties on civil aviation, shipping and broadcasting. As indicated above, many of these treaties provide for regulation of activities covered through international bodies or procedures. Others are primarily statements of rules of conduct for the states that have adhered to the instrument. Regional and functional organizations have also generated numerous treaties in their respective fields. These treaties comprise the main corpus of international law for the special subjects they deal with. They are the product, together with the more general codification treaties, of an "international legislative process" that operates through many different organizations and conferences. That process has resulted in a dense, intricate body of rules and practices followed by governments.

## ENTANGLED TREATY AND CUSTOM

As already indicated, treaty rules may be accepted as customary law and therefore be binding on states not parties to the treaty in question. The International Court of Justice has noted that this would occur when one of the following conditions existed:

1. Where the treaty rule is declaratory of pre-existing custom
2. Where the treaty rule is found to have crystallized customary law in process of formation
3. Where the treaty rule is found to have generated new customary law subsequent to its adoption

The leading I.C.J. case that enunciated these conditions is the 1969 Judgment in the North Sea Shelf Cases (supra). The conditions were affirmed in the 1986 Judgment of the I.C.J. in the Nicaragua Case (supra).

The Court recognized the first condition particularly in regard to certain provisions of the Vienna Convention of the Law of Treaties (see infra chap. 6). See Advisory Opinion on Namibia, I.C.J.Rep.1971, p. 47; Iceland Fisheries Cases (Jurisdiction) I.C.J.Rep.1973, pp. 18, 63.

The second condition was recognized in the North Sea Continental Shelf Cases in respect of articles 1 to 3 of the 1982 Convention on the Law of the Sea. I.C.J.Rep.1969, p. 35.

In the same case the Court dealt with the third condition. It declared that a provision in the Convention on the Law of the Sea, which was of a norm-creating character, "generated a rule which, while only conventional or contractual in its origin, has since passed into the general corpus of international law and is now accepted as such by the *opinio juris,* so as to become binding even for countries which have never and do not, become parties to the Convention." (Ibid.; p. 41.)

In its Nicaragua Judgment of 1986, the Court used a different justification to support its conclusion that articles 2(4) and 51 of UN Charter were customary law. It declared

> The Charter gave expression in this field to principles already present in customary international law and that law has in the subsequent four decades developed under the influence of the Charter to such an extent that a number of rules have acquired a status independent of it * * * even if two norms belonging to two sources of international law appear identical in content, and even if the States in question are bound by these rules both on the level of treaty-law and on that of customary law, those norms retain a separate existence.

Finding customary law identical with the Charter provisions enabled the Court to avoid the effect of a US reservation that excluded from its acceptance of compulsory jurisdiction all cases involving multilateral treaties unless all treaty parties agreed to jurisdiction. Judge Jennings, in a dissent, observed that the Court did not reveal how it determined that practice since 1945 by UN Members was "customary" rather than treaty. It appeared to him as if the Court, unable to take jurisdiction in regard to the Charter applied its rules anyway by calling them customary law (see I.C.J.Rep. 1986, Jennings Diss.Op. at 532).

### *Notes*

1. If virtually all states are parties to a treaty—as is the case for the UN Charter and the Geneva Conventions on the Law of Armed Conflict—does it make any difference whether the rules are also customary as well as treaty law? Theodor Meron suggests some advantages of recognizing customary law parallel to treaty law: (1) states are not free to withdraw from customary law obligations as they might be under treaty law; (2) in many states, customary law is part of domestic law whereas treaty rules do not become domestic law unless the legislature so decides; (3) customary law—or general international law—has more weight than contractual obligations and may be a basis for the "*erga omnes*" character of the rules, allowing all states to have a legal interest in their compliance. T. Meron, Human Rights and Humanitarian Norms as Customary Law 3–10, 114–35, 192–95 (1989).

2. In the North Sea Judgment, the Court suggests that a treaty rule might be considered a customary rule of international law if the treaty has a "widespread and representative participation * * * including states where interests were specially affected." I.C.J.Rep.1969, p. 43 (para. 73). Would this conclusion, if applied, mean that non-parties would be subject to obligations of a treaty whenever many states have become parties? Would it not be necessary to show practice and *opinio juris* on the part of non-parties as well as parties to conclude that the non-parties are subject to the treaty rules in question? Is a convention

designed to codify existing custom presumptive evidence that its rules are customary, hence applicable to all states?

3. If states not parties to a general multilateral treaty declare that some but not all of its provisions are accepted as customary law (even if of recent origin), can they claim such rights vis-à-vis parties to the treaty? The United States, which was not a party to the comprehensive 1982 UN Convention on the Law of the Sea, declared in a Presidential Proclamation of March 1983 that it regards the provisions of the convention as existing customary law with the exception of provisions on the seabed beyond national jurisdiction and provisions concerned with dispute settlement and administration. It announced it will assert its rights based on the customary law provisions and reciprocally recognize such rights of others. However, other states (and commentators) question the right of non-parties to pick the provisions they like and disregard what they do not like inasmuch as the Convention, contains interlinked provisions, involving a "package deal" of compromises. Should this preclude non-parties from relying on prior custom reflected in the treaty or on new rules accepted as customary during the period the treaty was negotiated? See Caminos and Molitor, Progressive Development of International Law and the Package Deal, 79 A.J.I.L. 871 (1985).

4. Consider the difference between multilateral conventions that proclaim a rule of law that virtually all states accept in principle even if they do not become parties to the treaty (for example, a treaty against torture or air highjacking) and a treaty that involves bargained-for compromise solutions such as a trade treaty or the law of the sea treaty. It has been suggested that in the former case, an inference of *opinio juris* may be made, based on statements of the governments even if actual practice is slight. However, in the latter case, an attempt to transport into customary law the substantive rules, disregarding the "deals" and compromises, may be difficult to justify. See Schachter, Recent Trends in International Law–Making, 12 Australia Y.B.I.L. 1, 7 (1992).

5. May a treaty be changed by custom? May the parties to a treaty alter its obligations by practical interpretation accepted as law? The 1958 Conventions on the Continental Shelf and on The High Seas were changed in important ways by the extension of jurisdiction by coastal states without any formal change in those treaties. Did President Reagan breach the U.S. obligations under those treaties (to which it was a party) when he proclaimed that the United States accepted as customary law many of the provisions of the 1982 Convention which the U.S. did not sign or ratify? (See chapter 14.)

6. Many bilateral treaties include common provisions on legal rights and obligations. Examples are found in treaties on extradition, air transport, rivers, compensation for expropriation, and commercial trade. As the treaties constitute state practice, can one infer that the common provisions in many treaties are evidence of customary law? May one distinguish between those bilateral treaties which deal with matters which are clearly recognized as within the discretion of the states and those which deal with matters generally regulated by international law? In the first category, one would include extradition and aviation on the premises that states are under no customary duty to grant the rights given in the bilateral treaties. In such cases, the successive treaties, numerous as they may be, would not have the *opinio juris* necessary to establish customary law. In the other category, an example would be treaties on riparian rights as there are requirements of international customary law about riparian states' duties toward others. May one therefore conclude that such bilateral

treaties are accompanied by *opinio juris* because they are in implementation of customary law? On riparian treaties, see Garretson, Hayton and Olmstead, The Law of International Drainage Basins 861–84 (1967). A more controversial issue is whether agreements for lump-sum compensation are evidence of the state of customary law. See Lillich & Weston, International Claims: Their Settlement by Lump–Sum Agreements 34–43 (1975); Barcelona Traction Case, 1970 I.C.J. 3, Chapter 9, Section 2D infra.

# SECTION 4. GENERAL PRINCIPLES OF LAW AND EQUITY

## A. THE BROAD EXPANSE OF GENERAL PRINCIPLES OF LAW

### *SCHACHTER, INTERNATIONAL LAW IN THEORY AND PRACTICE*

50–55 (1991).

We can distinguish five categories of general principles that have been invoked and applied in international law discourse and cases. Each has a different basis for its authority and validity as law. They are

(1) The principles of municipal law "recognized by civilized nations".

(2) General principles of law "derived from the specific nature of the international community".

(3) Principles "intrinsic to the idea of law and basic to all legal systems".

(4) Principles "valid through all kinds of societies in relationships of hierarchy and co-ordination".

(5) Principles of justice founded on "the very nature of man as a rational and social being".

Although these five categories are analytically distinct, it is not unusual for a particular general principle to fall into more than one of the categories. For example, the principle that no one shall be a judge in his own cause or that a victim of a legal wrong is entitled to reparation are considered part of most, if not all, systems of municipal law and as intrinsic to the basic idea of law.

Our first category, general principles of municipal law, has given rise to a considerable body of writing and much controversy. Article 38(1)*(c)* of the Statute of the Court does not expressly refer to principles of national law but rather general principles "recognized by civilized nations". The travaux préparatoires reveal an interesting variety of views about this subparagraph during the drafting stage. Some of the participants had in mind equity and principles recognized "by the legal conscience of civilized nations". (The notion of "legal conscience" was a familiar concept to European international lawyers in the nineteenth and early part of the twentieth century.) Elihu Root, the American member of the drafting committee, prepared the text finally adopted and it seemed clear that his amendment was intended to refer to principles "actually recognized and applied in national legal systems". The fact that the subparagraph was distinct from those on treaty and custom indicated an intent to treat general principles as an independent source of law, and not as a subsidiary source. As an independent source, it did not appear to require any separate proof that such principles of national law had been "received" into international law.

However, a significant minority of jurists holds that national law principles, even if generally found in most legal systems, cannot *ipso facto* be international law. One view is that they must receive the *imprimatur* of State consent through custom or treaty in order to become international law. The strict positivist school adheres to that view. A somewhat modified version is adopted by others to the effect that rules of municipal law cannot be considered as recognized by civilized nations unless there is evidence of the concurrence of States on their status as international law. Such concurrence may occur through treaty, custom or other evidence of recognition. This would allow for some principles, such as *res judicata,* which are not customary law but are generally accepted in international law. The Soviet scholars and some Third World jurists tend to follow this line. One of their arguments is that as legal systems reflect the class nature of society, there can be no truly "common" national law principles between socialist and capitalist societies. However, as already indicated, they are prepared to treat certain juridical notions or concepts common to municipal law as general principles (or postulates) of international law.

Several influential international legal scholars have considered municipal law an important means for developing international law and extending it into new areas of international concern. For example, Wilfred Jenks and Wolfgang Friedmann have looked to a "common law of mankind" to meet problems raised by humanitarian concerns, environmental threats and economic relations. In this respect they followed the lead of Hersch Lauterpacht suggested in his classic work, *Private Law Sources and Analogies of International Law.* The growth of transnational commercial and financial transactions has also been perceived as a fruitful area for the application of national law rules to create a "commercial law of nations", referred to as a "vast *terra incognita* ".

Despite the eloquent arguments made for using national law principles as an independent source of international law, it cannot be said that either courts or the political organs of States have significantly drawn on municipal law principles as an autonomous and distinct ground for binding rules of conduct. It is true that the International Court and its predecessor the Permanent Court of International Justice have made reference on a number of occasions to "generally accepted practice" or "all systems of law" as a basis for its approval of a legal rule. (But curiously the Court has done so without explicit reference to its own statutory authority in Article 38(I)*(c).*) Those references to national law have most often been to highly general ideas of legal liability or precepts of judicial administration. In the former category, we find the much-quoted principles of the *Chorzów Factory* case that "every violation of an engagement involves an obligation to make reparation" and that "a party cannot take advantage of his own wrong". These maxims and certain maxims of legal interpretation, as for example, *lex specialis derogat generalis,* and "no one may transfer more than he has", are also regarded as notions intrinsic to the idea of law and legal reasoning.

As such they can be (and have been) accepted not as municipal law, but as general postulates of international law, even if not customary law in the specific sense of that concept.

The use of municipal law rules for international judicial and arbitral procedure has been more common and more specific than any other type of application. For example, the International Court has accepted *res judicata* as applicable to international litigation; it has allowed recourse to indirect evidence (i.e., inferences of fact and circumstantial evidence) and it has approved the principle that legal remedies against a judgment are equally open to either party. Arbitral tribunals have applied the principle of prescription (or laches) to international litigation relying on analogies from municipal law. Lauterpacht's *Private Law Sources and Analogies of International Law,* written in 1927, still remains a valuable repository of examples, as does Bin Cheng's later work on *General Principles as Applied by International Courts and Tribunals.*

But considerable caution is still required in inferring international law from municipal law, even where the principles of national law are found in many "representative" legal systems. The international cases show such use in a limited degree, nearly always as a supplement to fill in gaps left by the primary sources of treaty and custom. Waldock's conclusions expressed in 1962 at this Academy still largely hold. Referring to the corpus of "common law" applied by the International Court, he says:

> "In this corpus customary law enormously predominates and most of the law applied by the Court falls within it. But paragraph *(c)* adds to this corpus—very much in the way actually intended by its authors—a flexible element which enables the Court to give greater completeness to customary law and in some limited degree to extend it".

The most important limitation on the use of municipal law principles arises from the requirement that the principle be appropriate for application on the international level. Thus, the universally accepted common crimes—murder, theft, assault, incest—that apply to individuals are not crimes under international law by virtue of their ubiquity. In the *Right of Passage over Indian Territory* case (India v. Portugal), the Court rejected arguments that the municipal law of easements found in most legal systems were appropriate principles for determining rights of transit over State territory. Similarly, a contention that the law of trusts could be used to interpret the mandate of South Africa over South West Africa (Namibia) did not win approval as international law but it may possibly have had an indirect influence on the Court's reasoning in its advisory opinions. Lord McNair, in an individual opinion, in the 1950 Advisory Opinion on the *International Status of South West Africa,* expressed a balanced conclusion on the subject of analogies from private law that merits quotation here.

> "International law has recruited and continues to recruit many of its rules and institutions from private systems of law * * *. The way in which international law borrows from the source is not by means of importing private law institutions 'lock, stock and barrel', ready-made and fully equipped with a set of rules * * *. In my opinion the true view of the duty of international tribunals in this matter is to regard any features or terminology which are reminiscent of the rules and

institutions of private law as an indication of policy and principles rather than as directly importing these rules and institutions".

I would subscribe to this general formulation and stress the requirement that the use of municipal law must be appropriate for international relations.

At the same time, I would suggest a somewhat more positive approach for the emergent international law concerned with the individual, business companies, environmental dangers and shared resources. Inasmuch as these areas have become the concern of international law, national law principles will often be suitable for international application. This does not mean importing municipal rules "lock, stock and barrel", but it suggests that domestic law rules applicable to such matters as individual rights, contractual remedies, liability for extra-hazardous activities, or restraints on use of common property, have now become pertinent for recruitment into international law. In these areas, we may look to representative legal systems not only for the highly abstract principles of the kind referred to earlier but to more specific rules that are sufficiently widespread as to be considered "recognized by civilized nations". It is likely that such rules will enter into international law largely through international treaties or particular arrangements accepted by the parties. But such treaties and arrangements still require supplementing their general provisions and such filling-in can often be achieved by recourse to commonly accepted national law rules. The case-law under the European Convention on Human Rights exemplifies this process. The fact that treaties and customary law now pervade most of the fields mentioned above means that the use of municipal law for specific application will normally fall within an existing frame of established international law. It would be rare that an international tribunal or organ or States themselves would be faced with the necessity of finding a specific rule in an area unregulated by international law. But there still may be such areas where injury and claims of redress by States occur in fields hitherto untouched by international regulation. Weather modification, acid rain, resource-satellites are possible examples. In these cases, municipal law analogies may provide acceptable solutions for the States concerned or for a tribunal empowered to settle a dispute.

The second category of general principles included in our list comprises principles derived from the specific character of the international community. The most obvious candidates for this category of principles are those mentioned in the last section of Chapter II as the necessary principles of co-existence. They include the principles of *pacta sunt servanda,* non-intervention, territorial integrity, self-defence and the legal equality of States. Some of these principles are in the United Nations Charter and therefore part of treaty law, but others might appropriately be treated as principles required by the specific character of a society of sovereign independent members.

Our third category is even more abstract but not infrequently cited: principles "intrinsic to the idea of law and basic to all legal systems". As stated it includes an empirical element—namely, the ascertainment of principles found in "all" legal systems. It also includes a conceptual criterion—"intrinsic to the idea of law". Most of the principles cited in World Court and arbitral decisions as common in municipal law are also referred to as "basic" to all law. In this way, the tribunals move from a purely empirical municipal law basis to "necessary" principles based on the logic of the law. They thus afford a reason for acceptance by those who hesitate to accept municipal law *per se* as international law but are prepared to adopt juridical notions that are seen as intrinsic to the idea of law. Some of the examples that fall under this heading would seem to be analytical (or tautologous) propositions. *Pacta sunt servanda,* and *nemo plus iuris transfere potest quam ipse habet* (no one can transfer more rights than he possesses) are good examples. (Expressing tautologies in Latin apparently adds to their weight in judicial reasoning.) Several other maxims (also commonly expressed in Latin phrases), considered as intrinsic to all representative legal systems, are sometimes described as juridical "postulates", or as essential elements of legal reasoning. Some principles of interpretation fall in this category: for example, the *lex specialis* rule and the maxim *lex posterior derogat priori* (the later supersedes the earlier law, if both have the same source). These are not tautologies, but can be considered as "legal logic". A similar sense of lawyers' logic supports certain postulates of judicial proceedings: for example, *res judicata* and the equality of parties before a tribunal. The latter suggests that reciprocity on a more general basis may be considered as an intrinsic element of legal relations among members of a community considered equal under the law.

These various examples lend support to the theory that the general principles of law form a kind of substratum of legal postulates. In Bin Cheng's words, "They belong to no particular system of law but are common to them all * * *. Their existence bears witness to the fundamental unity of law". In actual practice those postulates are established by "logic" or a process of reasoning, with illustrative examples added. The underlying and sometimes unstated premise is that they are generally accepted. They may be used "against" a State in a case because they are established law. However, if a particular principle or postulate becomes a subject of dispute regarding its general acceptance, it is likely to lose its persuasive force as an intrinsic principle. Hence, in the last analysis, these principles, however "intrinsic" they seem to be to the idea of law, rest on an implied consensus of the relevant community.

The foregoing comments are also pertinent to the next two categories of general principles. The idea of principles "*jus rationale*" "valid through all kinds of human societies" (in Judge Tanaka's words) is associated with traditional natural law doctrine. At the present time its theological links are mainly historical as far as international law is concerned, but its principal justification does not depart too far from the classic natural law emphasis on the nature of "man", that is, on the human person as a rational and social creature.

The universalist implication of this theory—the idea of the unity of the human species—has had a powerful impetus in the present era. This is evidenced in at least three significant political and legal developments. The first is the global movements against discrimination on grounds of race, colour and sex. The second is the move toward general acceptance of human rights. The third is the increased fear of nuclear annihilation. These three developments strongly reinforce the universalistic values inherent in natural law doctrine. They have found expression in numerous international and constitutional law instruments as well as in popular movements throughout the world directed to humanitarian ends. Clearly, they are a "material source" of much of the new international law manifested in treaties and customary rules.

In so far as they are recognized as general principles of law, many tend to fall within our fifth category—the principles of natural justice. This concept is well known in many municipal law systems (although identified in diverse ways). "Natural justice" in its international legal manifestation has two aspects. One refers to the minimal standards of decency and respect for the individual human being that are largely spelled out in the human rights instruments. We can say that in this aspect, "natural justice" has been largely subsumed as a source of general principles by the human rights instruments. The second aspect of "natural justice" tends to be absorbed into the related concept of equity which includes such elements of "natural justice" as fairness, reciprocity, and consideration of the particular circumstances of a case. The fact that equity and human rights have come to the forefront in contemporary international law has tended to minimize reference to "natural justice" as an operative concept, but much of its substantive content continues to influence international decisions under those other headings. Judge Sir Gerald Fitzmaurice was not far from the mark when he concluded in 1973 that there was a "strong current of opinion holding that international law must give effect to principles of natural justice" and "that this is a requirement that natural law in the international field imposes *a priori* upon States, irrespective of their individual wills or consents".

## *Notes*

1. If "general principles of law" are a distinct and independent source of law, why would the Court tend to treat such general principles and customary law "very much as a single corpus of law" (as Waldock suggests)? Does blurring the distinction between the two sources enable the Court to imply that the "general and well-recognized principles" derived from national law have been "received into" international law?

2. Is it necessary to show that many states have recognized a principle of municipal law as appropriate to inter-state relations in order to apply it in international law? Tunkin, a leading Soviet authority, argued that this was a requirement that could only be met by showing that the rule in question had been accepted by custom or treaty. G. Tunkin, op. cit. 200–01. However, Henkin suggests that "principles of law common to every developed legal system, for example, principles of property, tort and contract were in the international system from the very beginning, whenever that was." Henkin, General Course, 216 Rec. des Cours at 52. Would this mean that a principle of contract law common to "developed" countries would apply as a rule to treaty law? Compare Schachter's comment that the rule must be appropriate for inter-state relations and Judge McNair's even more cautious view that private law rules may be regarded as "indications of policy and principles rather than directly importing them into international law." I.C.J.Rep. 1950, p. 148.

3. In the *Right of Passage Case* (p. 75 supra), the Court rejected arguments that private law easements and servitude were appropriate principles for determining rights of transit over state territory. The fact that a rule of municipal law—whether private or public law—is common to many legal systems would not in itself be enough to qualify that rule as suitable for inter-state relations.

4. International tribunals and scholars have tended to favor analogies drawn from private law to fill in gaps in international law. For example, is the concept of analogy helpful for drawing on private law sources? The use of analogies drawn from municipal legal systems to develop or supplement international law is as old as international law itself. International tribunals have frequently employed such analogies in deciding disputes between states. For example, tribunals have found support in municipal law principles of laches and statutes of limitation for rejecting international claims on the ground that they had not been presented or pressed for a long time. For many other examples, see Lauterpacht, Private Law Sources and Analogies of International Law (1927); Cheng, General Principles of Law as Applied by International Courts and Tribunals (1953).

5. Some legal scholars and judges look upon certain "general principles of law" as a primary source of international law because they have the "character of *jus rationale* " and are "valid through all kinds of human societies." (Judge Tanaka in his dissenting opinion in the 1966 South West Africa Case, 1966 I.C.J. 296). O'Connell holds that certain principles are part of international law because they are "basic to legal systems generally" and hence part of the *jus gentium.* These principles, he believes, are established by a process of reasoning based on the common identity of all legal systems. If there should be doubt or disagreement, one must look to state practice and determine whether the municipal law principle provides a just and acceptable solution. It might then be applied on the basis of paragraph (c) of Article 38(1), but it would not have the cogency of the first category of "basic" principles. O'Connell, Int'l Law 12–13 (2d ed. 1970).

6. Is the fact that customary law is part of national law (see Ex Parte Habana, supra) a practical reason for characterizing a general principle common to municipal law as custom? Filartiga v. Pena–Irala, 630 F.2d 876 (2d Cir. 1980) infra. Would recognition of human rights as customary law provide a stronger ground than general principles for holding states legally bound even when they were not parties to the human rights treaties? However some writers consider custom a weaker ground for human rights in view of violations and lack of uniform practice. They contend that "general principles" is the more appropriate source based on the support of human rights in international declarations and national constitutions. B. Simma and P. Alston, The Sources of Human Rights Law: Custom, Jus Cogens and General Principles, 12 Australia Y.B.I.L. 82 (1992).

### *MANN, REFLECTIONS ON A COMMERCIAL LAW OF NATIONS*

33 Brit.Y.B.I.L. 20, 34–39 (1957).*

The general principles as a whole and the commercial law of nations in particular are determined and defined by comparative law, i.e., by the process of comparing municipal systems of law. Although publicists rarely refer in terms to comparative law as a "source" of international law, the great majority is likely to agree. This is so for the obvious reason that since the elimination of the direct influence of Roman law there does not exist any system or branch of law, other than comparative law, which could develop general principles. * * *

* * * In a sense it is quite true that all law and all legal systems incorporate and are based upon some such maxims as find expression in the maxims of English equity, in Article 1134 of the French or in s. 242 of the German Civil Code or in similar provisions of codified law. Many, if not most, of the specific rules and provisions accepted in the systems of municipal law can be said to be manifestations or applications of such maxims. Yet "general clauses," as they have been called, have been proved to be an unsatisfactory guide and dangerous to legal development. While no legal system has found it possible to do without them none has found it possible to work with them alone. They leave much room for a subjective approach by the court. They leave the result unpredictable. They lack that minimum degree of precision without which every legal decision would be wholly uncertain. They may, on occasions, be useful to fill a gap but in essence they are too elementary, too obvious and even too platitudinous to permit detached evaluation of conflicting interests, the specifically legal appreciation of the implications of a given situation. In short they are frequently apt to let discretion prevail over justice. For these reasons they cannot be the sole source of a sound and workable commercial law of nations. * * *

A principle of law is a general one if it is being applied by the most representative systems of municipal law.

That universality of application is not a prerequisite of a general principle of law is emphasized by almost all authors. It should be equally clear that a single system of municipal law cannot provide a general principle within the meaning of Article 38. What is usually required is that the principle pervades the municipal law of nations in general. It is believed, however, that a more specific formula ought to be found.

Where a rule of customary international law or a treaty between States having heterogeneous legal systems is in issue a wide field of application is normally both necessary and sufficient to establish a general principle. * * *

The process of comparison should be different where the issue arises from a treaty between States having related legal systems. In this case a principle common to the law of the countries in question may be treated as a general one and may even prevail over a different principle accepted by all or most other countries of the world. * * *

A principle of law is a general one even though the constituent rules of the representative systems of law are similar rather than identical. * * *

## Notes

1. Disputes between states and foreign companies involving concession agreements or development contracts have involved references to principles of law common to the national legal systems of the countries involved or in a more general way to principles of law generally recognized. In at least one well known arbitration, involving nationalization of an oil company, the sole arbitrator considered that a provision of that kind in a concession agreement brought that agreement within the domain of international law and required reference to the rules of international law, more particularly the international law of contracts. Arbitration between Libya and Texaco Overseas Petroleum Company

et al. (TOPCO), Award of January 19, 1977, 17 I.L.M. 1 (1978), especially paragraphs 46–51. For further discussion of this point see Chapter 9.

2. In another arbitration involving the nationalization and termination of an oil concession, the relevant agreements indicated that the applicable law included both the law common to the territorial state and the home state of the company and principles of law prevailing in the modern world. The arbitral tribunal noted that the law of the territorial state (Kuwait) also incorporated international law. However, instead of declaring that the applicable law was international law, the tribunal concluded that the three sources of law—municipal law of the state concerned general principles and international public law—should be considered as a common body of law. See Kuwait and American Independent Oil Company (Aminoil) Award of Sept. 26, 1977, 21 I.L.M. 976, especially paras. 6–10.

3. The tribunals that have applied "general principles" have not considered it necessary to carry out a detailed examination of the main (or "representative") systems of national law to determine whether the principles pervade "the municipal law of nations in general" (Mann, supra). They have at most referred to highly general concepts such as *pacta sunt servanda,* good faith, legitimate expectations of the parties, the equilibrium of the contract. Occasionally reference has been made to a provision of the Vienna Convention on the Law of Treaties. Query whether much would be gained by tribunals seeking to distill specific rules from several diverse legal systems in order to ascertain "general principles recognized by civilized nations." See Schlesinger, Research on the General Principles of Law Recognized by Civilized Nations, 51 A.J.I.L. 734 (1957); Friedmann, The Uses of "General Principles" in the Development of International Law, 57 A.J.I.L. 279 (1963).

4. General principles of municipal law have also been relied on by the administrative tribunals established by the United Nations and other international organizations to adjudicate disputes between the organization and members of its staff. In some cases such general principles of law have been held to limit the power of the governing bodies of the international organization to alter the conditions of employment of staff members. See de Merode et al. v. The World Bank, World Bank Administrative Tribunal Reports 1981 Decision No. 1. For commentary see C.F. Amerasinghe, in The Law of the International Civil Service 151–58 (1988). The body of law applied and developed by the various administrative tribunals is sometimes described as "international administrative law" or the law of the international civil service. It is not law that applies directly to states. However, since the international organizations are "international persons" (see Chapter 5), the law governing their relation to their staff has been considered by some writers as a part of international law, although quite distinct from the law governing inter-state relations. See W. Friedmann, The Changing Structure of International Law 159–162 (1964). One eminent international law scholar, Suzanne Bastid, for many years the President of the United Nations Administrative Tribunal, has referred to the principles applied by Administrative Tribunals as a type of customary law. She wrote:

> These rules are undoubtedly inspired by the internal law of certain states, but it does not appear that they are being applied as general principles of law. "Here again one may consider that a custom is being established, which has not been contested, notably by the organs which could have recourse to the International Court of Justice against the judgments which apply the custom."

Bastid, Have the U.N. Administrative Tribunals Contributed to the Development of International Law, in Transnational Law in a Changing Society 298, 311 (Friedmann, Henkin and Lissitzyn eds., 1972).

Why would Professor Bastid prefer to regard the "general principles" as custom? Is it significant that she refers to the "internal law of certain states"? If a principle is invoked for the first time in a tribunal, and has only had application as a rule of national law, could the tribunal justifiably adopt it as "custom"?

The complexities of the law and politics applicable to international officials are well brought out in Meron, The United Nations Secretariat, The Rules and Practice (1977). For a thorough scholarly treatise, see C.F. Amerasinghe, The Law of the International Civil Service, 2 vols. (1988).

## B. CONSIDERATIONS OF EQUITY AND HUMANITY

### *FRIEDMANN, THE CHANGING STRUCTURE OF INTERNATIONAL LAW*

197 (1964).*

Probably the most widely used and cited "principle" of international law is the principle of general equity in the interpretation of legal documents and relations. There has been considerable discussion on the question of whether equity is part of the law to be applied, or whether it is an antithesis to law, in the sense in which "*ex aequo et bono*" is used in Article 38, paragraph 2, of the Statute of the International Court of Justice. A strict distinction must of course be made between, on the one hand, the Roman *aequitas* and the English equity, both separate systems of judicial administration designed to correct the insufficiencies and rigidities of the existing civil or common law, and, on the other hand, the function of equity as a principle of interpretation. In the latter sense, it is beyond doubt an essential and all-pervading principle of interpretation in all modern civil codifications, and it is equally important in the modern common law systems, under a variety of terminologies such as "reasonable," "fair" or occasionally even in the guise of "natural justice." There is thus overwhelming justification for the view developed by Lauterpacht,[20] Manley Hudson,[21] De Visscher,[22] and Dahm,[23] that equity is part and parcel of any modern system of administration of justice. * * *

* Reprinted by permission of Columbia University Press and Stevens and Sons, Ltd. Some footnotes omitted.

**20.** Private Law Sources and Analogies of International Law (1927), para. 28.

**21.** The Permanent Court of International Justice (1943), p. 617, where the task of equity is described as being "to liberalize and to temper the application of law, to prevent extreme injustice in particular cases, to lead into new directions for which received materials point the way."

**22.** "Contribution à L'Etude des Sources du Droit International," 60 Revue de Droit International et Législation Comparée (1933), 325, 414 et seq.

**23.** 1 Völkerrecht (1958), p. 40 et seq.

## THE DIVERSION OF WATER FROM THE MEUSE (NETHERLANDS v. BELGIUM)

Permanent Court of International Justice, 1937.
P.C.I.J., Ser. A/B, No. 70, 76–78.
4 Hudson, World Ct.Rep. 172, 231–33.

[The case concerned a complaint by the Netherlands that construction of certain canals by Belgium was in violation of an agreement of 1863 in that the construction would alter the water level and rate of flow of the Meuse River. The Court rejected the Netherlands claim and a Belgian counter-claim based on the construction of a lock by the Netherlands at an earlier time. Judge Hudson, in an individual concurring opinion said:]

The Court has not been expressly authorized by its Statute to apply equity as distinguished from law. Nor, indeed, does the Statute expressly direct its application of international law, though as has been said on several occasions the Court is "a tribunal of international law". Series A, No. 7, p. 19; Series A, Nos. 20/21, p. 124. Article 38 of the Statute expressly directs the application of "general principles of law recognized by civilized nations", and in more than one nation principles of equity have an established place in the legal system. The Court's recognition of equity as a part of international law is in no way restricted by the special power conferred upon it "to decide a case *ex aequo et bono,* if the parties agree thereto". [Citations omitted.] It must be concluded, therefore, that under Article 38 of the Statute, if not independently of that Article, the Court has some freedom to consider principles of equity as part of the international law which it must apply.

It would seem to be an important principle of equity that where two parties have assumed an identical or a reciprocal obligation, one party which is engaged in a continuing non-performance of that obligation should not be permitted to take advantage of a similar non-performance of that obligation by the other party. The principle finds expression in the so-called maxims of equity which exercised great influence in the creative period of the development of the Anglo–American law. Some of these maxims are, "Equality is equity"; "He who seeks equity must do equity". It is in line with such maxims that "a court of equity refuses relief to a plaintiff whose conduct in regard to the subject-matter of the litigation has been improper". 13 Halsbury's Laws of England (2nd ed., 1934), p. 87. A very similar principle was received into Roman Law. The obligations of a vendor and a vendee being concurrent, "neither could compel the other to perform unless he had done, or tendered, his own part".

### *Notes*

1. While Friedmann and Hudson refer to equity as "a principle" of law, the concept of equity is used in such diverse ways by tribunals and governments that it is difficult to regard it as a single principle. Consider, for example, the following five uses of equity distinguished by Schachter:

(1) Equity as a basis for "individualized" justice tempering the rigours of strict law.

(2) Equity as consideration of fairness, reasonableness and good faith.

(3) Equity as a basis for certain specific principles of legal reasoning associated with fairness and reasonableness: to wit, estoppel, unjust enrichment, and abuse of rights.

(4) Equitable standards for the allocation and sharing of resources and benefits (notably, in boundary delimitation).

(5) Equity as a broad synonym for distributive justice used to justify demands for economic and social arrangements and redistribution of wealth.

Schachter, International Law in Theory and Practice 55–56 (1991).

2. The use of equity to "individualize" decisions and to escape the rigors of rules is akin (as Schachter notes) to the practice of tribunals and legal advisers to distinguish prior cases in terms of the particular facts. In doing this they attribute weight to individual circumstances and thereby allow for exceptions to general rules. Treaty clauses that refer to equitable principles similarly permit exceptions on grounds of the particular facts. As Judge Jimenez de Aréchaga remarked in the 1982 *Tunisia–Libya Case* in the International Court:

> * * * the judicial application of equitable principles means that a court should render justice in the concrete case, by means of a decision shaped by and adjusted to the "relevant factual matrix of that case".

1982 I.C.J. 100, para. 4.

3. In discussing exceptions to rules on equitable grounds, international lawyers (especially in Europe) often refer to decisions *infra legem* (within the law), *praeter legem* (outside the law) and *contra legem* (against the law). A decision on equitable grounds that is *infra legem* typically occurs when a rule leaves a margin of discretion to a state or law applying organ. Exercising such discretion on equitable grounds is clearly within the law. A decision that is *contra legem* would not normally be justifiable on grounds of equity, unless the tribunal had been authorized to act *ex aequo et bono.* See Judgment of International Court of Justice in Tunisia–Libya Case, 1982 I.C.J. 100, para. 71. In very exceptional circumstances, a tribunal may feel it necessary to disregard a rule of law on grounds that it is unreasonable or unfair in the circumstances. Governments may consider themselves more free than tribunals to make such exceptions. The question of whether equity may be used to support a decision *praeter legem* arises when an issue is not covered by a relevant rule and the law appears to have a lacuna in that situation. In one view, a tribunal should hold, in that event, that it cannot decide the issue in accordance with law and therefore refrain from judgment. This distinction is designated as *non liquet* (the law is not clear enough for a decision). A contrary view maintains that no court may refrain from judgment because the law is silent or obscure. Lauterpacht has argued that the principle prohibiting *non liquet* is itself a general principle of law recognized by civilized nations. Lauterpacht, The Function of Law in the International Community 67 (1933). If that position is adopted, a tribunal may be allowed to use equitable principles as a basis for decisions *praeter legem.*

4. Substantive concepts of equity such as estoppel, unjust enrichment and abuse of rights have been treated as general principles of law. On estoppel, see Temple of Preah Vihear, 1962 I.C.J. 31, 32, 39–51, 61–65; Case on Arbitral Award of King of Spain (Honduras v. Nicaragua) 1960 I.C.J. 192. On unjust enrichment, see Friedmann, The Changing Structure of International Law 206–210 (1964). On abuse of rights, see B. Cheng, General Principles of Law Applied by International Courts 121–36 (1953). See also Schwarzenberger, "Equity in International Law" 26 Yb. of World Affs. 362 (1972).

5. Equity and "equitable doctrine" are also invoked in cases of international claims for breach of contract or taking of property by a government. The Iran–U.S. Claims Tribunal has had occasion to refer to equity as a basis for a general principle of law and also in some cases as a ground for departing from law. It declared, for example, that the concept of "unjust enrichment" has been recognized in the great majority of municipal legal systems and "assimilated into the catalogue of general principles available to be applied by international tribunals * * *. Its equitable foundation makes it necessary to take into account all the circumstances of each specific situation." Sea-land Services v. Iran, 6 Iran–U.S. C.T.R. 149, 168 (1984).

In another case, the Claims Tribunal was faced with a claim of a U.S. company that shares in an Iranian company, belonged to the claimant although they were registered in the name of a third party. Iran, the respondent, argued that under Iranian law the nominal registration was conclusive as to ownership. However, the tribunal majority did not accept the Iranian argument, noting that the nominal owner had acted on the basis that the shares belonged to the claimant. The tribunal concluded that a contrary result would "be both illogical and inequitable." Foremost Tehran v. Iran, 10 Iran–US C.T.R. 228, 240 (1986). Was this a use of equity *contra legem?* Would the tribunal have been able to rely on a generally accepted principle such as beneficial ownership or estoppel to reach the same result?

6. Is "equity" an appropriate basis to recognize that non-performance of a contract was caused by external political events not contemplated by the parties? The dissenting opinion of an Iranian member of the Claims Tribunal called for an "equitable settlement" that would take into account such "external" events and "human factors". Gould Marketing v. Ministry of Defence, 6 Iran–U.S. C.T.R. 293–94 (1984). Is this a legitimate reason to apply equity *contra legem* as a basis for departing from strict contractual law on grounds of fairness?

7. Are there situations in which equity *contra legem* would be appropriate to allow a tribunal (or the governments concerned) to take account of circumstances that would not be germane in a purely legal adjudication? It has been suggested that this might be the case where new international law is emerging as, for example, in regard to transborder environmental damage or access to common resources. See V. Lowe, The Role of Equity in International Law, 12 Australia Y.B.I.L. 54, 69 (1992). As an alternative, would it be more acceptable to rely on concepts that have been accepted as general principles of law as, for example, the obligation of a state "not to allow knowingly its territory to be used for acts contrary to the rights of other states" (Corfu Channel Case, I.C.J. Rep. 1949, p. 22). The Latin version of this "*sic utere tuo ut alienum non laedas* " (i.e., use your own so as not to injure another) is often mentioned in international legal writing and judicial decisions. (See chapter 16 on Environmental Law.)

## EQUITABLE PRINCIPLES AND SOLUTIONS FOR BOUNDARY DELIMITATION: THE RELATION OF LAW AND EQUITY

1. Equitable principles and equitable solutions have become key concepts in the law governing the delimitation of maritime boundaries between states. The International Court of Justice and ad hoc arbitral tribunals have adjudicated a number of delimitation disputes based on the principle

enunciated by the Court in the North Sea Continental Shelf Cases (supra) that "it is precisely a rule of law that calls for an application of equitable principles." The opinion added, "there is no legal limit to the considerations which states may take account of for the purpose of making sure that they apply equitable procedures and more often than not it is the balancing-up of all such considerations that will produce this result rather than reliance on one to the exclusion of others." I.C.J.Rep. 1969, p. 50.

2. In the 1982 case between Tunisia and Libya, the International Court emphasized "equitable solutions" and the "particular circumstances," declaring

> "Each continental shelf case in dispute should be considered and judged on its own merits, having regard to its peculiar circumstances * * * therefore no attempt should be made to over conceptualize the application of the principles and rules." Similar emphasis on the specific circumstance can be found in the judgment of a Chamber of the Court in the Gulf of Maine Case between Canada and the United States

(I.C.J.Rep. 1984, para. 110, 114).

3. Criticism of such "individualization" by dissenting judges Gros, Oda, and Evensen and by commentators may have influenced the International Court to adopt a more "legal" view of equity. In 1985, it declared "Even though [equity] looks with particularity to the peculiar circumstances of an instant case, it also looks beyond it to principles of more general application * * * having a more general validity and hence expressible in general terms." Libya–Malta Case, I.C.J.Rep.1985, p. 39. As examples of such equitable principles the opinion referred to the "principle that there is to be no question of refashioning geography or compensating for the inequalities of nature; and the related principles of non-encroachment by one party on the natural prolongation of the other" (ibid.).

4. The idea of "proportionality" has often been referred to as an "equitable criterion." It has been called "the touchstone of equitableness." In delimitation cases, proportionality has been generally construed to refer to the ratio between the lengths of the coasts of each state that border the marine area to be delimited. The state with the longer coast-line would get the proportionally larger share of the area delimited. (The size of the area behind the coast would not be relevant at all.) The case-law has distinguished between proportionality as an "operative" criterion and its application as a test (or corrective) of a solution reached by other criteria. The latter position was adopted by the International Court in the Libya–Malta Case of 1985. It was followed in the Gulf of Maine Case between Canada and the United States and in the 1992 decision of the Court of Arbitration established by Canada and France to delimit the marine areas between the French islands of St. Pierre and Miquelon and the opposite and adjacent coasts of Canada (31 I.L.M. 1145–1219, Sept.1992). In the latter case, the international tribunal declared that geographical features are at the heart of delimitation and that certain equitable criteria are prescribed by international law. It noted that the maritime rights of a territory did not depend on its political status and that a key principle of equity under established jurisprudence was "non-encroachment," i.e. the avoidance of "cut-off." Hence a delimitation would assure each party of "space" sufficient for

maritime use and providing protection against undue interference. The tribunal took account of the disparity in the coastal lengths of the respective territories (which was considerable) but it applied "proportionality" only as a check on the solution reached on the basis of other criteria particularly, avoidance of encroachment. In fact, the result reached by the tribunal largely reflected the disparity in the coastal lengths of the parties. A dissenting Canadian judge argued that the decision did not fully reflect that disparity while the dissenting French judge considered that "proportionality" was wrongly applied as the main criterion (ibid.).

5. Should equity take account of the economic and social factors and needs in delimiting boundaries? The cases, beginning with the North Sea Shelf Cases, have all declared that delimitation should not involve "refashioning" geography and should not "compensate for the inequalities of nature". Thus in principle economic factors or needs would not be appropriate equitable criteria. However, in two recent cases this principle was somewhat attenuated. In the Gulf of Maine Case between Canada and the U.S., the judgment declared that human and economic factors were not considered as criteria to be "applied in the delimitation process itself". But it then stated that it had to assure itself that the result reached was "not radically inequitable * * * that is to say, as likely to entail catastrophic repercussions for the livelihood and well-being of the population of the countries concerned." (I.C.J.Rep.1984, para. 237.) The Court found no such consequence in that case. A similar approach was followed in the decision of the tribunal in the Canadian–French delimitation. In that case, the tribunal recognized the importance of fisheries to the parties. It found that the "full reciprocity" accorded by a treaty in force between the two states indicated that the proposed demarcation would not have a "radical impact" on the existing pattern of fishing in the area. (31 I.L.M. at 1173–74.) The tribunal also referred to possible hydrocarbon resources but concluded that it had no reason to consider potential mineral resources as relevant to the delimitation (id. at 1175). A leading expert has asked: if there is really any difference between taking account of geographical and economic factors successively and "doing it altogether at once"? P. Weil, The Law of Maritime Delimitation–Reflections 262 (1989). Would the answer not depend essentially on the weight accorded to economic repercussions?

6. Equitable principles have also been considered as part of the law applicable to land frontier disputes. The tribunal in the Ram of Kutch arbitration between India and Pakistan held that the parties were free to rely on principles of equity in their arguments. 50 Int.L.Rep.1968, p. 2. However, some arbitral tribunals have considered that they could not apply equity where the *compromis* (the special agreement setting up the arbitration) required a decision based on law. See Carlston, The Process of International Arbitration 158 (1946); Feller, The Mexican Claims Commissions 223 ff. (1935). For general discussion, see deVisscher, De L'Equité dans le Reglement Arbitral ou Judiciaire de Litiges de Droit International Public (1972); R. Lapidoth, Equity in International Law, 81 Proc.Am.Soc.I.L. 138–47 (1987).

## CORFU CHANNEL CASE (UNITED KINGDOM v. ALBANIA)

International Court of Justice, 1949.
1949 I.C.J. 4, 22.

[The case involved the explosion of mines in Albanian waters which damaged British warships and caused loss of life of British naval personnel on those vessels. The United Kingdom claimed Albania was internationally responsible and under a duty to pay damages. In regard to the obligations of Albania, the Court stated:]

> The obligations incumbent upon the Albanian authorities consisted in notifying, for the benefit of shipping in general, the existence of a minefield in Albanian territorial waters and in warning the approaching British warships of the imminent danger to which the minefields exposed them. Such obligations are based, not on the Hague Convention of 1907, No. VIII which is applicable in time of war, but on certain general and well-recognized principles, namely: elementary considerations of humanity, even more exacting in peace than in war; the principle of the freedom of maritime communication and every State's obligation not to allow knowingly its territory to be used for acts contrary to the rights of other States.

### *Notes*

1. "Elementary considerations of humanity" may also be based today on the provisions of the United Nations Charter on human rights, the Universal Declaration of Human Rights, and the various Human Rights Conventions. See the Advisory Opinion of the International Court in the Namibia Case, 1971 I.C.J. 57, also discussed in note 5, p. 1088 infra. In its earlier decision in the 1966 *Southwest Africa Case* (2d Phase), the majority of the court declared that humanitarian considerations were not decisive and that moral principles could be considered only insofar as they are given "a sufficient expression in legal form" (1966 I.C.J. at 34).

2. For a Soviet writer's view that humanitarian considerations and principles of morality have a necessary role in forming international law, see Lukashuk, Morality and International Law, 14 Indian J.Int'l L. 321–331 (1974). The article is strongly critical of Western positivists who seek to exclude moral considerations from international law. Contemporary Western jurists who have placed high value on the role of humanitarian and moral factors in international law include such representative scholars as Hersch Lauterpacht, Myres McDougal, H. Mosler, and G. Schwarzenberger.

## SECTION 5. EVIDENCE OF INTERNATIONAL LAW AND SUBSIDIARY MEANS FOR DETERMINATION OF RULES OF LAW

### A. JUDICIAL DECISIONS

#### *1. International Court of Justice*

Article 38 of the Statute in its paragraph 1(d) directs the Court to apply judicial decisions as "subsidiary means for the determination of rules of law." It is expressly made subject to Article 59 which states that "the decision of the Court has no binding force except between the parties and in respect of that particular case." Hence the principle of *stare decisis* is not meant to apply to decisions of the International Court. That qualification and the relegation of judicial decisions generally to a "subsidiary status" reflect the reluctance of states to accord courts—and the International Court in particular—a law-making role. The Court's decisions are supposed to be declaratory of the law laid down by the states in conventions and customary rules. In addition, the stated objection to *stare decisis* reflects a perception of international disputes as especially individual, each distinguished by particular features and circumstances.

Despite these qualifications, the decisions of the International Court of Justice are, on the whole, regarded by international lawyers as highly persuasive authority of existing international law. The very fact that state practices are often divergent or unclear adds to the authority of the Court. Its decisions often produce a degree of certainty where previously confusion and obscurity existed. A much-quoted dictum of Justice Cardozo reflects the attraction of judicial authority, especially to lawyers in the common law tradition:

> International law or the law that governs between States, has at times, like the common law within States, a twilight existence during which it is hardly distinguishable from morality or justice, till at length the imprimatur of a court attests to its jural quality.

New Jersey v. Delaware, 291 U.S. 361, 54 S.Ct. 407, 78 L.Ed. 847 (1934).

A decision of the International Court is generally accepted as the "imprimatur of jural quality" when the Court speaks with one voice or with the support of most judges. However judgments and advisory opinions by a significantly divided court have diminished authority. This is especially true when the issues are perceived as highly political and the judges seem to reflect the positions of the states from which they come. Notable examples are the 1966 decision of the Court in the *Case Concerning South West Africa* (infra p. 1088) and the 1984 decision on jurisdiction and admissibility in the case brought by Nicaragua against the United States. Not infrequently, the separate opinions of dissenting judges or other individual opinions contain cogent reasoning that influences subsequent doctrine more than the decision of the majority. Judgments and advisory opinions are not always compelling to states. Governments respond in various ways to decisions they consider unfounded or unwise. For example, after the *Lotus Case* (supra), many governments adopted a treaty provision which reversed the Court's ruling and prohibited a state other than the flag state from exercising criminal jurisdiction against a non-national in case of a collision or accident on the high seas. Individual states have also reacted to unfavorable decisions by altering or withdrawing their consent to jurisdiction (see Chapter 10).

Notwithstanding these reactions the Court's pronouncements, especially in non-political matters, are a primary source for international lawyers. Every judgment or advisory opinion is closely examined, dissected, quoted and pondered for its implications. They are generally lengthy and learned analyses of relevant principles and practices and particular cases include opinions often amounting to more than 200–300 pages. After more than 70 years the case-law and associated opinions of the two "World Courts" constitute a substantial *corpus juris* relevant to many of the questions facing states in their international relations.

The fact that the Statute excludes *stare decisis* (Article 59) has not meant that the Court's case-law ignores precedent. The Court cites its earlier decisions and often incorporates their reasoning by reference. When the Court seems to depart from precedent, it generally distinguishes the cases and explains the reasons for the different views. See cases cited in Rosenne, 2 The Law and Practice of the International Court 611–613 (1965). However, Article 59 still has an effect. In excluding *stare decisis,* it must mean that the Court's prior decisions are not to be treated as conclusive evidence of the law. Hence there is no strict rule of precedent as there is in many municipal law jurisdictions. In Waldock's words, "the authority of the jurisprudence of international tribunals depends more directly on its subsequent recognition by states as acceptable than is the case with municipal decisions." Waldock, General Course, at 95.

A more complex problem concerns the role of the Court in "developing" international law and reaching decisions that go beyond declarations of existing law. It is clear that states, by and large, do not expect or wish the Court to "create" new law. Yet as Brierly observed some years ago "the act of the Court is a creative act in spite of our conspiracy to represent it as something else." The Basis of Obligation in International Law 98 (Waldock ed., 1958). Both states and judges are aware "of the discretionary elements in the art of judging: the selection of 'relevant' facts, the need to give specific meaning to broad undefined concepts, the subtle process of generalizing from past cases, the uses of analogy and metaphor, the inevitable choices between competing rules and principles." Schachter, International Law in Theory and Practice 41 (1991). These discretionary elements are more evident in international law than in most areas of domestic law. The fragmentary character of much international law and the generality of its concepts and principles leave ample room for "creative" judicial application. On the other hand, the judges are well aware of the dangers of appearing to be "legislating" and of their precarious consensual jurisdiction (See Chapter 10). One way to meet the problem is to place emphasis on the particular facts of the case to avoid the appearance of creating new law. But there is also a pull in the opposite direction. The Court needs to show that its decisions are principled and in accord with the agreed basic concepts of international law. This requirement leads to reliance on broad doctrinal concepts and precepts taken from treatises and prior case-law. When applied to new situations, the abstractions of basic doctrine create new law. Though many governments hesitate to accept or recognize this, international lawyers acknowledge the formative role of the Court while recognizing the political necessity for the Court to appear solely as an organ for declaring and clarifying the existing law.

### *Notes*

1. The 15 judges of the International Court are elected for 9–year terms by majority votes of political bodies, namely the Security Council and the General Assembly of the United Nations. (Statute of the Court, Articles 3–18). They are required to have the qualifications required in their respective countries for appointment to the highest judicial office or to be "jurisconsults of recognized

competence in international law." (Id. Art. 2). They are supposed to represent the "main forms of civilization and of the principal legal systems of the world." This requirement is considered to be met by a geographical and political distribution of seats among the main regions of the world. Many of the judges have been well known legal scholars. In recent years, most have had prior service in their national governments, as legal advisors to the foreign office or as representatives to international bodies.

2. Does the fact that the judges are elected by political bodies and are considered likely to reflect the views of their own governments impugn or reduce "the jural quality" of their decisions? Is it legally justifiable to minimize a judicial decision as a source of law because many of the judges have taken the same position as their own governments? How can states parties to cases before the Court seek to reduce the effect of ideological or national bias, assuming they wish to do so? Former Judge Mosler (Federal Republic of Germany) has written:

> Where there is no common agreement as to the substantive rules and especially where there is no complete agreement as to the sources of general international law, the subjective views of the individual judges assume increased importance.

The International Society as a Legal Community, 140 Rec. des Cours 293 (1974–IV). See also Suh, Voting Behaviors of National Judges in International Courts, 63 A.J.I.L. 224 (1969); S. Rosenne, The Composition of the Court, in The Future of the International Court of Justice 377 (L. Gross ed., 1976); Schachter at 69–73 (1991).

### 2. *Decisions of International Arbitral Tribunals and Other International Courts*

International judicial decisions also embrace the numerous decisions of arbitral tribunals established by international agreement for individual disputes or for categories of disputes. Though they are not in a strict sense judicial bodies, they are generally required to decide in accordance with law and their decisions are considered an appropriate subsidiary means of determining international law. Governments and tribunals refer to such decisions as persuasive evidence of law. The International Court has only occasionally identified specific arbitral awards as precedents but it has also referred generally to the jurisprudence and consistent practice of arbitral tribunals. Governments do not hesitate to cite international arbitral decisions in support of their legal positions. Such decisions may be distinguished on the basis of the agreements establishing the tribunal or other special circumstances but in many cases they have been accepted as declaratory of existing international law.

The decisions of arbitral tribunals are published by the United Nations in Reports of International Arbitral Awards (U.N.R.I.A.A.). Other publications containing texts of arbitral decisions include the International Law Reports, an annual publication (E. Lauterpacht ed.), and International Legal Materials (published by the American Society of International Law 7 times each year). For further discussion of arbitration as a means of dispute settlement see Chapter 10.

Two European courts—the Court for the European Economic Community (located in Luxembourg) and the European Court of Human Rights (in Strasbourg) also hand down many decisions that express or interpret principles and rules of international law relevant to their special areas of competence. The Inter–American Court of Human Rights has had only a few cases (including advisory opinions) but they too may be regarded as part of international case-law.

### *3. Decisions of Municipal Courts*

The Paquete Habana and the Lotus Case (supra) opinions cite municipal court decisions as evidence of customary law. Such decisions are indicative of state practice and *opinio juris* of the state in question. However, inasmuch as national courts in many countries also apply principles and rules of international law, their decisions may be treated as a subsidiary source independently of their relation to state practice. While the authority of a national court would as a rule be less than that of an international court or arbitral body, particular decisions of the higher national courts may be the only case-law on a subject or the reasoning and learning in the decisions may be particularly persuasive. Decisions of the United States Supreme Court have been relied on by arbitral bodies and have been cited by states in support of their claims. In some areas of law such as state responsibility and sovereign immunity, national court decisions have had a prominent role. See Chapters 1 and 8.

## B. THE TEACHINGS OF THE MOST HIGHLY QUALIFIED PUBLICISTS OF THE VARIOUS NATIONS

The place of the writer in international law has always been more important than in municipal legal systems. The basic systematization of international law is largely the work of publicists, from Grotius and Gentilis onwards. In many cases of first impression only the opinions of writers can be referred to in support of one or the other of the opposing contentions of the parties. The extent to which writers are referred to as "subsidiary" authorities differs often according to the tradition of the court and the individual judge. Here the practice of national as well as of international courts is relevant. As a corollary to the position of precedent in common law jurisdictions, there has traditionally been judicial reluctance, more marked in the British jurisdictions than in the United States, to refer to writers. In the civilian systems reference to textbook writers and commentators is a normal practice, as the perusal of any collection of decisions of the German, Swiss or other European Supreme Courts will show. In France the notes appended by jurists to important decisions published in the *Recueil Dalloz* and *Recueil Sirey* enjoy high authority and often influence later decisions. A prominent example of reliance on writers in a common law court is the decision of the U.S. Supreme Court in the *Paquete Habana* case (see p. 58 supra).

The practice of the International Court of Justice and of its predecessor has generally been to refer to doctrine, i.e., teachings, only in very general terms. Lauterpacht, The Development of International Law by the International Court 24 (1958). Lauterpacht suggests as a reason for the Court's reluctance to refer to writers: "There is no doubt that the availability of official records of the practice of States and of collections of treaties has substantially reduced the necessity for recourse to writings of publicists as evidence of custom. Moreover, the divergence of view among writers on many subjects as well as apparent national bias may often render citations from them unhelpful. On the other hand, in cases—admittedly rare—in which it is possible to establish the existence of a unanimous or practically unanimous interpretation, on the part of writers, of governmental or judicial practice, reliance on such evidence may add to the weight of the Judgments and Opinions of the Court." Id.

Although the Court itself has been reluctant to identify writers in its judgments and advisory opinions, it is evident from the pleadings and from the references in the separate and dissenting opinions of the judges that the opinions of authorities on international law have been brought to the attention of the Court and have often been taken into account by some of the judges. For a broad historical survey of the role and influence of "teachings" in the development of international law, see lectures by Judge Manfred Lachs, Teachings and Teaching of International Law, 151 Rec. des Cours 163–252 (1976–III).

The major treatises of international law usually cited by states and tribunals were generally produced by jurists of Western Europe. The citations in those treatises referred to state practice and judicial decisions in only a few countries. Most writers also relied heavily on quotations and paraphrases of statements by earlier writers. These highly selective tendencies, presented in support of broad conclusions of law were far from consistent with the prevailing doctrine of sources based on state practice accepted by law by states generally. Moreover, many of the well known treatises were written from the standpoint of national concerns and perceptions. Schachter has commented that

> many of the legal scholars had close links with their official communities and there were often pressures on them, sometimes obvious and sometimes subtle to conform to the official point of view. Even apart from such pressures, we recognize that social perspectives and values are generally shared by those in the same political and cultural community * * *. That a degree of bias is inescapable is recognized by the common assumption that more credible judgments on controversial issues of international law were more likely if made by a broadly representative body than by persons (however expert) from a single country or a particular political outlook.

Schachter at 38–39 (1991).

International bodies of "publicists" include the International Law Commission, an organ of the United Nations composed of 34 individuals elected by the U.N. General Assembly on the basis of government nominations and criteria of wide geographical representation. See Article 2 of the Statute of the I.L.C. They are concerned, as indicated above (section 3) with the preparation of codification conventions and other draft treaties. However, in the course of their work, and in their reports, positions are expressed by the Commission as a whole on existing rules of law.

A non-official body, the Institut de Droit International, established in 1873, is composed of about 120 members and associate members elected by the Institut on the basis of individual merit and published works. Its resolutions setting forth principles and rules of existing law and, on occasion, proposed rules, have often been cited by tribunals, states and writers. The biennial Annuaire of the Institut contains its resolutions and the lengthy reports and records of discussion that preceded the resolution. For an account of its contribution from 1873 to 1973, see its centenary volume, Livre du Centenaire, Annuaire de l'Institut de Droit International (1973), particularly articles by Charles de Visscher and H. Battifol.

Another unofficial body, the International Law Association, (also founded in 1873) has about a thousand members, organized in national branches in many countries. Resolutions adopted by majority votes at conferences of the Association are based on reports and studies of international committees. The multinational character of the Association adds weight to those of its resolutions that are adopted by general consensus or large majorities representative of different regions and political systems. The biennial reports of the I.L.A. contain the resolutions and committee reports.

Another category of the writings of publicists is the Restatement of the Foreign Relations Law of the United States, prepared by recognized legal scholars and adopted after discussion by the American Law Institute, a non-official professional body. The first restatement appeared in 1965 designated curiously as the Restatement Second. A revised restatement was adopted in 1986 (Restatement Third). The restatement contains rules of international law as it applies to the United States in its relations with other states and also rules of U.S. domestic law that have substantial significance for the foreign relations of the United States. Although this is a restatement of existing rules by a United States professional association, it does not purport to state the rules that the U.S. government would put forward or support in all cases. As stated in its introduction, "the Restatement in stating rules of international law represents the opinion of the American Law Institute as to the rules that an international tribunal would apply if charged with deciding a controversy in accordance with international law." In considering what a hypothetical international court would decide is an applicable rule, the American Law Institute adopts a standard that aims at an objective international determination of general international law.

Writings of authoritative international law scholars are published annually by the Hague Academy of International Law in its Collected Courses, generally referred to by its French title, Recueil des Cours. The scholars are selected by the international curatorium of the Academy on a broad geographical basis. Although Western European contributors tend to predominate, there is increasingly representation of scholars and practitioners from other areas and with diverse points of view. In addition to discussion of particular topics, the Recueil includes an annual comprehensive work by a well-known publicist under the heading of General Course. As of 1993, the Recueil includes over 230 published volumes.

### *Notes and Questions*

1. If "the most highly qualified publicists" are generally influenced by the interest and policies of their own states (and by their legal cultures), is their authority open to question on that ground? Would a tribunal look for majority opinions, "representative" views or "objective" data? Nardin, a political theorist, concluded that international law is founded not only on the customs of the community of states but on those of the community of international lawyers. T. Nardin, Law, Morality and the Relations of States 173 (1983). Schachter has described the "invisible college of international lawyers" as engaged in a continuous process of communication and collaboration across national lines. Schacht-

er, The Invisible College of International Lawyers, 72 Northwestern Univ.L.Rev. 217 (1977).

2. Since the "leading" publicists are often engaged or consulted by their own governments, they influence state conduct and are in turn influenced by their governments. What advantages and drawbacks are likely in this dual role? Can the legal advisers of foreign offices meet the sometimes conflicting demands of their "clients" and the obligation to ascertain the law objective? Do they have the double function of applying the law in the national interest and supporting international legal system? See Report of a Joint Committee on The Role of the Legal Adviser of the State Department, 85 Am.J.Int.L. 358–71 (1991).

3. The vast increase in international law has naturally led to specialization. It is no longer possible for international lawyers to claim expertise on the subject as a whole. Many find it difficult to keep abreast of developments in any one of the main specialized areas. (In 1992, the American Society of International Law had more than 30 "interest groups.") Has this reduced the role of general international law? See D. Vagts, Are There No International Lawyers Anymore? 75 Am.J.Int.L. 134–37 (1981). Schachter argues for maintaining international law as a unified discipline. "The Invisible College of International Lawyers" loc. cit. supra at 221–23. See also T. Franck, Review Essay—The Case of the Vanishing Treatises, 81 Am.J.Int.L. 763 (1987).

## SECTION 6. DECLARATIONS AND RESOLUTIONS—"SOFT LAW"

### A. GENERAL ASSEMBLY RESOLUTIONS

#### FILARTIGA v. PENA–IRALA

United States Court of Appeals, Second Circuit, 1980.
630 F.2d 876.

[This was a wrongful death action which was brought in the federal district court (Eastern District, N.Y.) by two nationals of Paraguay, the father and sister of a 17–year old Paraguayan, who, it was alleged, was tortured to death in Paraguay by the defendant Pena–Irala who at the time was Inspector–General of the police. Jurisdiction was claimed principally on the basis of the Alien Tort Statute (28 U.S.C. § 1350) which provides:

> "The district courts shall have original jurisdiction of any civil action by an alien for a tort only, committed in violation of the law of nations or a treaty of the United States."

The plaintiffs claimed that the conduct resulting in the wrongful death constituted torture which they contended violated the "law of nations" that is, international customary law. The District Court dismissed the complaint on jurisdictional grounds, the district judge considering himself bound by higher court decisions to construe "the law of nations" as used in the Alien Tort Law, as excluding that law which governs a states treatment of its own citizens. On appeal, the Second Circuit Court of Appeals reversed the district court and ruled that the Alien Tort Law provides federal jurisdiction. The Court held that deliberate torture under the color of official authority violated the universal rules of international law regardless of the nationality of the parties. In reaching the conclusion that the prohibition of torture has become part of customary international law, the Court referred as evidence to the Universal Declaration of Human Rights and as particularly relevant, the 1975 Declaration on the Protection of all Persons from Torture.

The relevant portions of the Court's opinion read as follows:]

The Declaration goes on to provide that "[w]here it is proved that an act of torture or other cruel, inhuman or degrading treatment or punishment has been committed by or at the instigation of a public official, the victim shall be afforded redress and compensation, in accordance with national law." This Declaration, like the Declaration of Human Rights before it, was adopted without dissent by the General Assembly.

These U.N. declarations are significant because they specify with great precision the obligations of member nations under the Charter. Since their adoption, "[m]embers can no longer contend that they do not know what human rights they promised in the Charter to promote." Moreover, a U.N. Declaration is, according to one authoritative definition, "a formal and solemn instrument, suitable for rare occasions when principles of great and lasting importance are being enunciated." 34 U.N. ESCOR, Supp. (No. 8) 15, U.N.Doc. E/cn. 4/1/610 (1962) (memorandum of Office of Legal Affairs, U.N. Secretariat). Accordingly, it has been observed that the Universal Declaration of Human Rights "no longer fits into the dichotomy of 'binding treaty' against 'non-binding pronouncement,' but is rather an authoritative statement of the international community." E. Schwelb, Human Rights and the International Community 70 (1964). Thus, a Declaration creates an expectation of adherence, and "insofar as the expectation is gradually justified by State practice, a declaration may by custom become recognized as laying down rules binding upon the States." 34 U.N. ESCOR, supra. Indeed, several commentators have concluded that the Universal Declaration has become, *in toto,* a part of binding, customary international law.

Turning to the act of torture, we have little difficulty discerning its universal renunciation in the modern usage and practice of nations. Smith, supra, 18 U.S. (5 Wheat.) at 160–61, 5 L.Ed. 57. The international consensus surrounding torture has found expression in numerous international treaties and accords. E.g., American Convention on Human Rights, Art. 5, OAS Treaty Series No. 36 at 1, OAS Off.Rec. OEA/Ser 4 v/II 23, doc. 21, rev. 2 (English ed., 1975) ("No one shall be subjected to torture or to cruel, inhuman or degrading punishment or treatment"); International Covenant on Civil and Political Rights, U.N. General Assembly Res. 2200 (XXI)A, U.N. Doc. A/6316 (Dec. 16, 1966) (identical language); European Convention for the Protection of Human Rights and Fundamental Freedoms, Art. 3, Council of Europe, European Treaty Series No. 5 (1968), 213 U.N.T.S. 211 (*semble*). The substance of these international agreements is reflected in modern municipal—i.e. national—law as well. Although torture was once a routine concomitant of criminal interrogations in many nations, during the modern and hopefully more enlightened era it has been universally renounced. According to one survey, torture is prohibited, expressly or implicitly, by the constitutions of over fifty-five nations, including both the United States and

Paraguay. Our State Department reports a general recognition of this principle:

> There now exists an international consensus that recognizes basic human rights and obligations owed by all governments to their citizens * * *. There is no doubt that these rights are often violated; but virtually all governments acknowledge their validity.

### *Notes and Questions*

1. After the *Filartiga* case was remanded to the district court, defendants took no part in the action (having been deported to Paraguay). A default was granted and damages assessed by the U.S. district court to cover the expenses of the plaintiffs plus punitive damages of $5,000,000 to each plaintiff. Filartiga v. Pena–Irala, 577 F.Supp. 860 (E.D.N.Y.1984). These damage awards were not enforced. The district court also cited the General Assembly Declaration, particularly noting that it declared that the victim shall be afforded redress and compensation "in accordance with national law." Id.

2. Did the Court's reliance on the General Assembly Declaration as evidence of a binding rule against torture have the effect of conferring on the Assembly a degree of law-making authority inconsistent with the UN Charter? Does a "declaration" of a legal principle by the General Assembly have more weight than a resolution of a recommendatory character?

3. Does the Court's reference to the Universal Declaration as an "authoritative statement of the international community" imply a new "source" of international law other than treaty or custom? Would a declaration have obligatory force because it specified "with great precision" the obligations of member states under the Charter? If so, is there any reason to declare that the Declaration is customary law?

4. The Court refers to the "universal renunciation" of torture in usage and practice. However, reports of Amnesty International regularly show that torture is employed in many countries under color of official authority. Does that rebut a finding of "state practice" sufficiently consistent and general to support a finding of custom? Is "state practice" the laws prohibiting torture or the acts of torture by state officials?

5. Would the problem of inconsistent practice be avoided by treating the prohibition of torture as a general principle of law recognized in the law of all countries? Should a declaration by the General Assembly of a general principle of law be regarded as a definitive finding if adopted without dissent? Would it be subject to rebuttal if invoked in a particular case? See comments and notes below.

6. The Filartiga Case has been widely cited in the United States for the proposition that certain human rights principles are customary law and therefore part of the law of the United States. See infra chapter 8. Resolutions of the General Assembly have also been cited by national courts in many countries as evidence (or definitive proof) that a proposition of law expressed or implied by the resolution is binding international law. See C. Schreuer, Decisions of International Institutions before Domestic Courts (1981); L. Henkin, Resolutions of International Organizations in American Courts, in Essays on the Development of the International Legal Order (Kalshoren, Kuyper & Lammers, eds. 1980).

## THE LEGAL EFFECT OF GENERAL ASSEMBLY RESOLUTIONS AND DECISIONS

The legal effect of General Assembly resolutions and other decisions has been a subject of much scholarly discussion and diverse views of governments. Article 38 of the Statute of the International Court (supra) does not mention resolutions or decisions of international organs as either a principal "source" or subsidiary means of determining applicable international law. Moreover, the UN Charter does not confer on the General Assembly power to enact rules for the conduct of its members except for certain internal organizational matters. In contrast to the Security Council it does not have authority to adopt mandatory decisions in specific cases except for certain organizational actions such as admission of members and credentials. Many such decisions have "dispositive force and effect," as the International Court noted in its Opinion in the Expenses Case (I.C.J.Rep. 1962, p. 163).

The more general problem of legal effect is raised by General Assembly resolutions and decisions that express or clearly imply legal principles or specific rules of law. The General Assembly has adopted nearly 8000 resolutions and numerous other decisions from 1946 to 1993. Some—perhaps 70 or 80—express general rules of conduct for states (as the Declaration against Torture in the Filartiga Case). They are usually formulated as "declarations" or "affirmations" of law. In many cases, they were the product of study and debate over many years and were adopted by consensus (without a vote) or by near-unanimity. Two other types of resolutions raise questions of legal effect:

1. resolutions dealing with specific situations and expressing or implying a general legal prescription for states, and

2. resolutions addressed to a particular state or states and implying that the conduct required of that state or states would be required of all states.

These resolutions, declarations or decisions may be considered by governments and by courts or arbitral tribunals as evidence of international custom or as expressing (and evidencing) a general principle of law. They may also serve to set forth principles for a future treaty (this has been the case for the Declaration against Torture and a number of other Declarations in the field of human rights). The fact that a law-declaring resolution has been adopted without a negative vote or abstention is usually regarded as strong presumptive evidence that it contains a correct statement of law. A resolution that has less than unanimous support is more questionable. The size and composition of the majority, the intent and expectations of states, the political factors and other contextual elements are pertinent in judging the effect.

### *Notes and Questions*

1. The International Court of Justice has referred particularly to the General Assembly declarations of self-determination and independence of peoples in territories that have not yet attained independent as having legal effect,

and as "enriching the corpus juris gentium." Adv.Op. on Namibia I.C.J.Rep. 1971, p. 31. See also Adv.Op. on Western Sahara I.C.J.Rep. 1975. May these "declarations" be regarded as "authentic" interpretation of the principles of the Charter that already bind the member states and therefore as obligatory or legally authoritative for all members?

2. Could it be plausibly argued that when such broad principles as self-determination and human rights are given more specific meaning in General Assembly declarations, they would go beyond "recommendations" and have a legislative effect beyond that authorized by the Charter? Can one assume that the governments voting in favor of such law-declaring resolutions intend to accept them as binding, rather than recommendatory? If they do not all have that intention, can the declaration be properly regarded as a binding interpretation of the Charter? Suppose it is necessary that the governments voting for a resolution that expresses a rule of conduct do not all understand that the resolution would be binding. Does that mean it could not be regarded as a generally accepted interpretation of a Charter obligation?

3. Does the General Assembly have law-making power when it makes a determination in specific cases? Note that the International Court, in its 1971 *Advisory Opinion on Namibia* (see infra), commented on the authority of the General Assembly to assume functions under the Mandate for South West Africa as follows: "For it would not be correct to assume that because the General Assembly is in principle vested with recommendatory powers, it is debarred from adopting in specific cases within the framework of its competence, resolutions which make determinations or have operative design" 1971 I.C.J. 50. Does this not mean that if an international body is given authority (i.e., competence to make decisions) such decisions when made by the requisite majority are binding? Would this include resolutions which recognize particular entities as states for purposes of participation in that body? Would it also include resolutions that treat items as within the competence of that body and as outside the exclusively domestic jurisdiction of a State. See Schachter, id., on these issues.

4. It should be noted that "even those who are the most opposed to attributing any direct legislative effect to Assembly resolutions will usually concede that they are capable, like many other things, of *contributing* to the formation of rules of *lex communis,* and can in that sense constitute material influencing the content of law, but not creating it," G. Fitzmaurice, Special Report to the Institut de Droit International in Livre du Centenaire 1873–1973, 269 (1973).

### *SCHACHTER, INTERNATIONAL LAW IN THEORY AND PRACTICE*

178 Rec. des Cours 114–21 (1982–V) (footnotes omitted).

We come now to the declaratory resolution that purports to state the law independently of any Charter rule. Let us assume—as in the previous case of Charter construction—that the resolution is unanimously adopted (as was the case, for example, of the resolution declaring genocide an international crime). One may say (and governments have said) that the resolution, notwithstanding its formulation as a declaration, can only be regarded, in legal effect, as a recommendation to member States to accept the asserted rule of principle as legally binding. That it can be no more than a recommendation is said to follow from the fundamental constitutional tenet of the Charter governing the legal authority of the General Assembly. However, can we stop with this analysis? When all the States in the United Nations declare that a State norm is legally binding, it is difficult to dismiss that determination as ultra vires—or reduce it to a recommendation—because it was made in the General Assembly. The fact is that the declaration purports to express the *opinio juris communis,* not a recommendation. In considering whether that *opinio juris communis* should be given legal effect, we face two questions. The first is whether the States actually "mean" to express that conviction. * * *

The second question is whether the assertion in good faith by all States that a norm is legally binding is sufficient to validate the norm as law even though State practice is negligible or inconclusive. International lawyers differ on the answer. Some maintain that at least in some matters the *opinio juris communis,* articulated in a declaration, is sufficient to qualify the norm as a customary law. Others consider that the *opinio juris* must relate to State practice as an essential element of a conclusion that the norm constitutes law. The point is important for our problem. If *opinio juris*—as expressed in resolutions—is itself sufficient, new law may be created by agreement of States manifested in their approval of a law-declaring resolution. This has been called "instant custom", an unfortunate phrase which sounds self-contradictory and may be misleading. The fact remains that several resolutions have asserted rules or principles of general international law when practice was negligible or inconclusive and these resolutions have been regarded as sufficient evidence of the legal character of the norm asserted. An example already noted is the 1946 resolution declaring genocide a crime. A more recent example is the General Assembly Declaration of Principles on the Sea-bed Beyond National Jurisdiction of 1971. The Declaration adopted unanimously characterized the sea-bed as "common heritage" and forbade national appropriation of any part of it. * * *

Let us take a closer look at the assumption that if all or nearly all States agree on what is the law, that is enough to constitute conclusive evidence that the declared rule or principle is law. Are there good reasons to question that assumption? One plausible reason is that a vote for a resolution may not be intended to signify agreement on the legal validity of the asserted norm. There is evidence that governments do not always have that intent when they vote for a resolution or fail to object to it. They may assume that since resolutions generally have no more than recommendatory effect, their vote should mean no more than that. They may cast their vote solely on political grounds in the belief that a resolution of the General Assembly is entirely a political matter without legal effect. Moreover, the difficulties of determining the intent of States with respect to declaratory resolutions are compounded by the equivocal language used in many resolutions. For example, many resolutions affirm or declare "principles" without specifying that they are principles of law. In some cases these principles include some that are clearly legal whereas the legal character of others may be more debatable. These considerations obviously raise questions as to the nature and extent of the agreement manifested in votes on resolutions and therefore cast doubt on whether such votes should generally be given a decisive role in endowing resolutions with legal effect.

The right of a United Nations representative to "commit" his government through a vote in the United Nations merits some comment. Since governments generally do not expect or intend to be bound by Assembly resolutions, it is reasonable to assume their representatives lack authority to bind their government by their votes. * * * A somewhat different question is whether the government is sufficiently aware of the legal significance of a resolution that "merely" interprets or applies a provision of the Charter or customary law rule. If the government assumes that a resolution would not have legal significance, does that mean that the position taken by the representative on the declaration of law cannot be regarded as his government's position? * * *

It still remains important to clarify the legal force of the declaration and determinations of law. Much of the debate has focused on the choice between two polar categories: "binding" and "hortatory" (i.e., without legal force *et al.*). That categorization—however clear it may appear—seems much less appropriate than treating the law-declaring resolutions as evidence for the asserted proposition of law. This would be compatible with the basic principle that such resolutions are not binding in the sense that treaties or judicial judgments are legally binding on the parties. However, it recognizes that interpretations and declarations of law by the Assembly are official expressions of the governments concerned and consequently are relevant and entitled to be given weight in determinations of the law in question. By characterizing them as "evidentiary" we invite an assessment of the pertinent data. We would assess the degree and character of support received in the United Nations and the relation if any of the asserted rule to an underlying Charter or customary law principle. Moreover, relevant State practice and *opinio juris* manifested outside of the United Nations would be considered.

This analysis assumes that the intent of States to express a rule of law in a declaratory resolution is an important factor in determining the legal effect of the resolution. * * * Generally the intention to express a rule of law would be a necessary (though not sufficient) element in attributing weight to the assertion. If it is clear that the States voting for the resolution did not intend to express a requirement of law, it is unlikely that their assertion will be treated as a legal rule. It is however conceivable, if improbable, that a formal declaration of a principle of conduct, even if not intended as a legal rule, will be treated in the light of practice as a legal requirement. The absence of an intent at the time of adoption will not be decisive if other factors create expectations that the principle should be considered a legal norm. If the intent to declare law exists, it should be made clear in the resolution and in related committee proceedings that the norm expressed in the resolution is regarded as a Charter obligation or as a customary law rule. This may of course lead to reservations or dissents by States which do not accept the rule as *lex lata*. But such clarification would help to ensure genuine agreement. There will no doubt be instances of divergent positions on whether a norm correctly constitutes a principle or rule of law. * * *

In many cases, it would be pertinent to determine whether State practice both before and after the adoption of the resolution varies so significantly from the norm asserted as to deprive it of validity as custom or agreed interpretation. This determination—namely, whether inconsistent practice should vitiate an asserted principle—may involve drawing distinctions among norms based on value judgments of their significance. For example, a norm considered essential to peace (such as the principle of non-intervention) or one that expresses a basic universally held moral principle (such as that against torture) would retain its validity despite inconsistent practice. On the other hand, a norm relating to demarcation of jurisdiction or States' rights in areas beyond national territory (for example, the declarations on sea-bed mining or outer space) should probably not be maintained as valid in the face of substantial inconsistent State conduct. I believe we cannot escape such judgments of value in appraising the effect of State practice on declared norms.

## WESTERN SAHARA CASE

International Court of Justice, Advisory Opinion, 1975.
1975 I.C.J. 12.

[In 1974, the General Assembly of the United Nations after considering the decolonization of the Western (formerly Spanish) Sahara and claims to its territorial sovereignty made by Morocco and Mauritania, requested the International Court of Justice to render an advisory opinion on two questions:

1. Was Western Sahara at the time of colonization by Spain a territory belonging to no one (*terra nullius* )? If the answer to this question is in the negative,
2. What were the legal ties between this territory and the Kingdom of Morocco and the Mauritanian entity?

General Assembly Resolution 3292 (XXIX), 29 GAOR, Supp. 31 (A/9631) at 103 (13 December 1974). The Court answered the first question in the negative. In response to the second question, it concluded that there were legal ties, but that there was no tie of territorial sovereignty between the territory and Morocco or Mauritania.

In its advisory opinion, the Court found it necessary to consider the legal effect of the resolutions of the General Assembly on decolonization and self-determination.

On the basis of these resolutions, it concluded that the right of self-determination for non-selfgoverning territories had become a norm of international law. The following extracts pertain to this issue:]

52. Extensive argument and divergent views have been presented to the Court as to how, and in what form, the principles of decolonization apply in this instance, in the light of the various General Assembly resolutions on decolonization in general and on decolonization of the territory of Western Sahara in particular. This matter is not directly the subject of the questions put to the Court, but it is raised as a basis for an objection to the Court's replying to the request. In any event, the applicable principles of decoloni-

zation call for examination by the Court, in that they are an essential part of the framework of the questions contained in the request. The reference in those questions to a historical period cannot be understood to fetter or hamper the Court in the discharge of its judicial functions. That would not be consistent with the Court's judicial character; for in the exercise of its functions it is necessarily called upon to take into account existing rules of international law which are directly connected with the terms of the request and indispensable for the proper interpretation and understanding of its Opinion (cf. I.C.J.Reports 1962, p. 157).

53. The proposition that those questions are academic and legally irrelevant is intimately connected with their object, the determination of which requires the Court to consider, not only the whole text of resolution 3292 (XXIX), but also the general background and the circumstances which led to its adoption. This is so because resolution 3292 (XXIX) is the latest of a long series of General Assembly resolutions dealing with Western Sahara. All these resolutions, including resolution 3292 (XXIX), were drawn up in the general context of the policies of the General Assembly regarding the decolonization of non-self-governing territories. Consequently, in order to appraise the correctness or otherwise of Spain's view as to the object of the questions posed, it is necessary to recall briefly the basic principles governing the decolonization policy of the General Assembly, the general lines of previous General Assembly resolutions on the question of Western Sahara, and the preparatory work and context of resolution 3292 (XXIX).

* * *

56. The Court had occasion to refer to this resolution in the abovementioned Advisory Opinion of 21 June 1971. Speaking of the development of international law in regard to non-self-governing territories, the Court there stated:

> "A further important stage in this development was the Declaration on the Granting of Independence to Colonial Countries and Peoples (General Assembly resolution 1514 (XV) of 14 December 1960), which embraces all peoples and territories which 'have not yet attained independence'." (I.C.J.Reports 1971, p. 31.)

It went on to state:

> "* * * the Court must take into consideration the changes which have occurred in the supervening half-century, and its interpretation cannot remain unaffected by the subsequent development of law, through the Charter of the United Nations and by way of customary law" (ibid.).

The Court then concluded:

> "In the domain to which the present proceedings relate, the last fifty years, as indicated above, have brought important developments. These developments leave little doubt that the ultimate objective of the sacred trust was the self-determination and independence of the peoples concerned. In this domain, as elsewhere, the *corpus iuris gentium* has

been considerably enriched, and this the Court, if it is faithfully to discharge its functions, may not ignore." (Ibid., pp. 31 f.)

57. General Assembly resolution 1514 (XV) provided the basis for the process of decolonization which has resulted since 1960 in the creation of many States which are today Members of the United Nations. It is complemented in certain of its aspects by General Assembly resolution 1541 (XV), which has been invoked in the present proceedings. The latter resolution contemplates for non-self-governing territories more than one possibility, namely:

*(a)* emergence as a sovereign independent State;

*(b)* free association with an independent State; or

*(c)* integration with an independent State.'

At the same time, certain of its provisions give effect to the essential feature of the right of self-determination as established in resolution 1514 (XV). Thus principle VII of resolution 1541 (XV) declares that: "Free association should be the result of a free and voluntary choice by the peoples of the territory concerned expressed through informed and democratic processes."

### *Notes*

1. As the International Court indicated, the declarations of the General Assembly on decolonization and self-determination implement the Charter provisions in Articles 1, 55, 56 and Chapter XI (on non-self governing territories). Is it legally significant that the declarations are an interpretation of the Charter provisions? If the resolutions were adopted by consensus (i.e., without a negative vote) are the declarations to be regarded as an "authentic interpretation" of already binding principles to which all the parties have agreed? See Article 31(3)(a) of the Vienna Convention on the Law of Treaties concerning agreement of the parties on interpretation of a treaty. See also Schachter, The Relation of Law, Politics and Action in the United Nations, 109 Rec. des Cours 165, 183–88 (1963–II).

2. At the San Francisco Conference of 1945 at which the Charter was drafted, a committee report noted that the General Assembly was competent to interpret the Charter. Such competence, they said, is "inherent in the functioning of any body which operates under an instrument defining its functions and powers." It then added that an interpretation of the Charter by the General Assembly would be binding on the member states if that interpretation "was generally accepted." Does this mean that the adoption of an interpretive resolution by unanimous vote (or near-unanimity) would be legally binding on the members? Would the question arise whether the Charter was being interpreted or in effect amended? If such resolutions involve a significant modification of the rights and duties of members, should they not be required to follow the amendment procedure which involves ratification? When such broad principles as self-determination, equality of states, human rights, and political independence are construed and given more specific meaning, is there not inevitably a "legislative" component inherent in the interpretation? Nonetheless, even member States which are opposed to extending the authority of the General Assembly are prepared to regard unanimous resolutions interpreting the Charter principles as legally authoritative resolutions. See statement of U.S. repre-

sentative at Legal Committee of the U.N. General Assembly in 1974 in regard to the Declaration of Principles of International Law in Digest of United States Practice in International Law 18–20 (1974). The Soviet Union and many other states are prepared to replace the requirement of unanimity by the more flexible condition "generally accepted". The latter standard is said to call for support from the "main groupings of states," i.e., socialist, capitalist, and non-aligned. See Tunkin, Theory of International Law 165, 170, 172 (Butler trans., 1974). For a contrary view, see Arango Ruiz, The Normative Role of The General Assembly and the Declaration of Principles of Friendly Relations, 137 Rec. des Cours, 419, 513–518 (1972–III). Other writings on this subject include Castañeda, Legal Effects of United Nations Resolutions (1969); Higgins, The Development of International Law Through the Political Organs of the United Nations (1963); Lachs, The Law in and of the United Nations in 1 Indian J. Int'l L., 429, 439 (1960–61); Schachter, The Crisis of Legitimation in the United Nations, 50 Nordisk Tidsskrift for Int'l Ret 3–19 (1981), Schachter, International Law in Theory and Practice, 178 Rec. des Cours 111–123 (1978–V).

3. Does the General Assembly have law-making power when it makes a determination in specific cases? Note that the International Court, in its 1971 *Advisory Opinion on Namibia* (see infra), commented on the authority of the General Assembly to assume functions under the Mandate for South West Africa as follows: "For it would not be correct to assume that because the General Assembly is in principle vested with recommendatory powers, it is debarred from adopting in specific cases within the framework of its competence, resolutions which make determinations or have operative design" 1971 I.C.J. 50. Does this not mean that if an international body is given authority (i.e., competence to make decisions) such decisions when made by the requisite majority are binding? Would this include resolutions which recognize particular entities as states for purposes of participation in that body? Would it also include resolutions that treat items as within the competence of that body and as outside the exclusively domestic jurisdiction of a State. See Schachter, id., on these issues.

4. It should be noted that "even those who are the most opposed to attributing any direct legislative effect to Assembly resolutions will usually concede that they are capable, like many other things, of *contributing* to the formation of rules of *lex communis,* and can in that sense constitute material influencing the content of law, but not creating it," G. Fitzmaurice, Special Report to the Institut de Droit International in Livre du Centenaire 1873–1973, 269 (1973).

## TEXACO OVERSEAS PETROLEUM ET AL. v. LIBYAN ARAB REPUBLIC

International Arbitral Award Jan. 19, 1977.

17 I.L.M. 1 (1978).*

[In 1973 and 1974, Libya promulgated decrees purporting to nationalize all of the rights, interests and property of two international oil companies in Libya. The companies claimed such action by the Libyan Government violated the deeds of concession granted to them jointly by the Government. Under the arbitration clause of the concessions, the companies requested the President of the International Court of Justice to appoint a sole arbitrator to

* Reprinted with permission of the American Society of International Law.

hear and determine the dispute. The Libyan Government opposed the request and filed a memorandum with the President of the Court contending, *inter alia,* that the disputes were not subject to arbitration because the nationalizations were acts of sovereignty. The President, after considering the Libyan memorandum, appointed a sole arbitrator, Professor Rene–Jean Dupuy. Libya did not take part in the subsequent proceedings, but the arbitrator specifically considered the points raised by Libya in its memorandum to the President of the Court. The companies submitted memorials. On January 19, 1977, the Sole Arbitrator delivered an Award on the Merits in favor of the companies. He held that the deeds of concession were binding on the parties, that the Government by adopting the nationalization decrees breached its obligations under the deeds of concession, and that the Government was bound to give the deeds full force and effect.

In his decision, the Arbitrator considered the contention of Libya that the U.N. resolutions on permanent sovereignty over natural wealth and resources confirmed the sovereign rights to nationalize its natural resources and that the resolutions provide that any dispute related to nationalization or its consequences should be settled in accordance with the domestic law of the State concerned. In view of this contention, the Arbitrator considered the legal force of U.N. resolutions generally and specifically in respect of the resolutions on sovereignty over natural wealth and resources, including the Charter of Economic Rights and Duties of States. The text of his decision on these issues follows in unofficial English translation:]

Refusal to recognize any legal validity of United Nations Resolutions must, however, be qualified according to the various texts enacted by the United Nations. These are very different and have varying legal value, but it is impossible to deny that the United Nations' activities have had a significant influence on the content of contemporary international law. In appraising the legal validity of the above-mentioned Resolutions, this Tribunal will take account of the criteria usually taken into consideration, i.e., the examination of voting conditions and the analysis of the provisions concerned.

84. (1) With respect to the first point, Resolution 1803 (XVII) of 14 December 1962 was passed by the General Assembly by 87 votes to 2, with 12 abstentions. It is particularly important to note that the majority voted for this text, including many States of the Third World, but also several Western developed countries with market economies, including the most important one, the United States.

The principles stated in this Resolution were therefore assented to by a great many States representing not only all geographical areas but also all economic systems.

From this point of view, this Tribunal notes that the affirmative vote of several developed countries with a market economy was made possible in particular by the inclusion in the Resolution of two references to international law, and one passage relating to the importance of international cooperation for economic development. According to the representative of Tunisia:

> "* * * the result of the debate on this question was that the balance of the original draft resolution was improved—a balance be-

tween, on the one hand, the unequivocal affirmation of the inalienable right of States to exercise sovereignty over their natural resources and, on the other hand, the reconciliation or adaptation of this sovereignty to international law, equity and the principles of international cooperation." (17 U.N. GAOR 1122, U.N. Doc. A/PV. 1193 (1962).)

The reference to international law, in particular in the field of nationalization, was therefore an essential factor in the support given by several Western countries to Resolution 1803 (XVII).

85. On the contrary, it appears to this Tribunal that the conditions under which Resolutions 3171 (XXVII), 3201 (S–VI) and 3281 (XXIX) (Charter of the Economic Rights and Duties of States) were notably different:

— Resolution 3171 (XXVII) was adopted by a recorded vote of 108 votes to 1, with 16 abstentions, but this Tribunal notes that a separate vote was requested with respect to the paragraph in the operative part mentioned in the Libyan Government's Memorandum whereby the General Assembly stated that the application of the principle according to which nationalizations effected by States as the expression of their sovereignty implied that it is within the right of each State to determine the amount of possible compensation and the means of their payment, and that any dispute which might arise should be settled in conformity with the national law of each State instituting measures of this kind. As a consequence of a roll-call, this paragraph was adopted by 86 votes to 11 (Federal Republic of Germany, Belgium, Spain, United States, France, Israel, Italy, Japan, The Netherlands, Portugal, United Kingdom), with 28 abstentions (South Africa, Australia, Austria, Barbados, Canada, Ivory Coast, Denmark, Finland, Ghana, Greece, Haiti, India, Indonesia, Ireland, Luxembourg, Malawi, Malaysia, Nepal, Nicaragua, Norway, New Zealand, Philippines, Rwanda, Singapore, Sri Lanka, Sweden, Thailand, Turkey).

This specific paragraph concerning nationalizations, disregarding the role of international law, not only was not consented to by the most important Western countries, but caused a number of the developing countries to abstain.

— Resolution 3201 (S–VI) was adopted without a vote by the General Assembly, but the statements made by 38 delegates showed clearly and explicitly what was the position of each main group of countries. The Tribunal should therefore note that the most important Western countries were opposed to abandoning the compromise solution contained in Resolution 1803 (XVII).

— The conditions under which Resolution 3281 (XXIX), proclaiming the Charter of Economic Rights and Duties of States, was adopted also show unambiguously that there was no general consensus of the States with respect to the most important provisions and in particular those concerning nationalization. Having been the subject matter of a roll-call vote, the Charter was adopted by 118 votes to 6, with 10 abstentions. The analysis of votes on specific sections on the Charter is most significant insofar as the present case is concerned. From this point of view, paragraph 2(c) of Article 2 of the Charter, which limits consideration of the characteristics of compensation to the State and does not refer to international law, was voted by 104 to 16, with 6 abstentions, all of the industrialized countries with market economies having abstained or having voted against it.

86. Taking into account the various circumstances of the votes with respect to these Resolutions, this Tribunal must specify the legal scope of the provisions of each of these Resolutions for the instant case.

A first general indication of the intent of the drafters of the Charter of Economic Rights and Duties of States is afforded by the discussions which took place within the Working Group concerning the mandatory force of the future text. As early as the first session of the Working Group, differences of opinion as to the nature of the Charter envisaged gave rise to a very clear division between developed and developing countries. Thus, representatives of Iraq, Sri Lanka, Egypt, Kenya, Morocco, Nigeria, Zaire, Brazil, Chile, Guatemala, Jamaica, Mexico, Peru and Rumania held the view that the draft Charter should be a legal instrument of a binding nature and not merely a declaration of intention.

On the contrary, representatives of developed countries, such as Australia, France, Federal Republic of Germany, Italy, Japan, United Kingdom and United States expressed doubt that it was advisable, possible or even realistic to make the rights and duties set forth in a draft Charter binding upon States (Report of the Working Party on its 1st Session, U.N.Doc. TD/B/AC.12/1 (1973), at 6).

The form of resolution adopted did not provide for the binding application of the text to those to which it applied, but the problem of the legal validity to be attached to the Charter is not thereby solved. In fact, while it is now possible to recognize that resolutions of the United Nations have a certain legal value, this legal value differs considerably, depending on the type of resolution and the conditions attached to its adoption and its provisions. Even under the assumption that they are resolutions of a declaratory nature, which is the case of the Charter of Economic Rights and Duties of States, the legal value is variable. Ambassador Castañeda, who was Chairman of the Working Group entrusted with the task of preparing this Charter, admitted that 'it is extremely difficult to determine with certainty the legal force of declaratory resolutions', that it is 'impossible to lay down a general rule in this respect', and that 'the legal value of the declaratory resolutions therefore includes an immense gamut of nuances' ('La Valeur Juridique des Résolutions des Nations Unies', 129 R.C.A.D.I. 204 (1970), at 319–320).

As this Tribunal has already indicated, the legal value of the resolutions which are relevant to the present case can be determined on the basis of circumstances under which they were adopted and by analysis of the principles which they stated:

— With respect to the first point, the absence of any binding force of the resolutions of the General Assembly of the United Nations implies that such resolutions must be accepted by the members of the United Nations in order to be legally binding. In this respect, the Tribunal notes that only Resolution 1803 (XVII) of 14 December 1962 was supported by a majority of Member States representing all of the various groups. By contrast, the other Resolutions mentioned above, and in particular those referred to in the Libyan Memorandum, were supported by a majority of States but not by any of the developed countries with market economies which carry on the largest part of international trade.

87. (2) With respect to the second point, to wit the appraisal of the legal value on the basis of the principles stated, it appears essential to this Tribunal to distinguish between those provisions stating the existence of a right on which the generality of the States has expressed agreement and those provisions introducing new principles which were rejected by certain representative groups of States and having nothing more than a *de lege ferenda* value only in the eyes of the States which have adopted them; as far as the others are concerned, the rejection of these same principles implies that they consider them as being *contra legem.* With respect to the former, which proclaim rules recognized by the community of nations, they do not create a custom but confirm one by formulating it and specifying its scope, thereby making it possible to determine whether or not one is confronted with a legal rule. As has been noted by Ambassador Casteñeda, "[such resolutions] do not create the law; they have a declaratory nature of noting what does exist" (129 R.C.A.D.I. 204 (1970), at 315).

On the basis of the circumstances of adoption mentioned above and by expressing an *opinio juris communis,* Resolution 1803 (XVII) seems to this Tribunal to reflect the state of customary law existing in this field. Indeed, on the occasion of the vote on a resolution finding the existence of a customary rule, the States concerned clearly express their views. The consensus by a majority of States belonging to the various representative groups indicates without the slightest doubt universal recognition of the rules therein incorporated, i.e., with respect to nationalization and compensation the use of the rules in force in the nationalizing State, but all this in conformity with international law.

88. While Resolution 1803 (XVII) appears to a large extent as the expression of a real general will, this is not at all the case with respect to the other Resolutions mentioned above, which has been demonstrated previously by analysis of the circumstances of adoption. In particular, as regards the Charter of Economic Rights and Duties of States, several factors contribute to denying legal value to those provisions of the document which are of interest in the instant case.

— In the first place, Article 2 of this Charter must be analyzed as a political rather than as a legal declaration concerned with the ideological strategy of development and, as such, supported only by non-industrialized States.

— In the second place, this Tribunal notes that in the draft submitted by the Group of 77 to the Second Commission (U.N. Doc. A/C.2/L. 1386 (1974), at 2), the General Assembly was invited to adopt the Charter "as a first measure of codification and progressive development" within the field of the international law of development. However, because of the opposition of several States, this description was deleted from the text submitted to the vote of the Assembly. This important modification led Professor Virally to declare:

"It is therefore clear that the Charter is not a first step to codification and progressive development of international law, within the meaning of Article 13, para. 1(a) of the Charter of the United Nations, that is to say an instrument purporting to formulate in writing the rules of customary law and intended to better adjust its content to the requirements of international relations. The persisting difference of opinions in respect to some of its articles prevented reaching this goal and it is healthy that people have become aware of this." (La Charte des Droits et Devoirs Economiques des Etats. Notes de Lecture, 20 A.F.D.I. 57 (1974), at 59.)

The absence of any connection between the procedure of compensation and international law and the subjection of this procedure solely to municipal law cannot be regarded by this Tribunal except as a *de lege ferenda* formulation, which even appears *contra legem* in the eyes of many developed countries. Similarly, several developing countries, although having voted favorably on the Charter of Economic Rights and Duties of States as a whole, in explaining their votes regretted the absence of any reference to international law.

89. Such an attitude is further reinforced by an examination of the general practice of relations between States with respect to investments. This practice is in conformity, not with the provisions of Article 2(c) of the above-mentioned Charter conferring exclusive jurisdiction on domestic legislation and courts, but with the exception, stated at the end of this paragraph. Thus a great many investment agreements entered into between industrial States or their nationals, on the one hand, and developing countries, on the other, state, in an objective way, the standards of compensation and further provide, in case of dispute regarding the level of such compensation, the possibility of resorting to an international tribunal. In this respect, it is particularly significant in the eyes of this Tribunal that no fewer than 65 States, as of 31 October 1974, had ratified the Convention on the Settlement of Investment Disputes between States and Nationals of other States, dated March 18, 1965.

90. The argument of the Libyan Government, based on the relevant resolutions enacted by the General Assembly of the United Nations, that any dispute relating to nationalization or its consequences should be decided in conformity with the provisions of the municipal law of the nationalizing State and only in its courts, is also negated by a complete analysis of the whole text of the Charter of Economic Rights and Duties of States.

From this point of view, even though Article 2 of the Charter does not explicitly refer to international law, this Tribunal concludes that the provisions referred to in this Article do not escape all norms of international law. Article 33, paragraph 2, of this Resolution states as follows: "2. In their interpretation and application, the provisions of the present Charter are interrelated and each provision should be construed in the context of the other provisions." Now, among the fundamental elements of international economic relations quoted in the Charter, principle (j) is headed as follows: "Fulfillment in good faith of international obligations".

Analyzing the scope of these various provisions, Ambassador Castañeda, who chaired the Working Group charged with drawing up the Charter of Economic Rights and Duties of States, formally stated that the principle of performance in good faith of international obligations laid down in Chapter I(j) of the Charter applies to all matters governed by it, including, in particular, matters referred to in Article 2. Following his analysis, this particularly competent and eminent scholar concluded as follows:

> "The Charter accepts that international law may operate as a factor limiting the freedom of the State should foreign interests be affected, even though Article 2 does not state this explicitly. This stems legally from the provisions included in other Articles of the Charter which should be interpreted and applied jointly with those of Article 2." (La Charte des Droits et Devoirs Economiques des Etats. Note sur son Processus d'Elaboration, 20 A.F.D.I. 31 (1974), at 54.)

91. Therefore, one should note that the principle of good faith, which had already been mentioned in Resolution 1803 (XVII), has an important place even in Resolution 3281 (XXIX) called "The Charter of Economic Rights and Duties of States". One should conclude that a sovereign State which nationalizes cannot disregard the commitments undertaken by the contracting State: to decide otherwise would in fact recognize that all contractual commitments undertaken by a State have been undertaken under a purely permissive condition on its part and are therefore lacking of any legal force and any binding effect. From the point of view of its advisability, such a solution would gravely harm the credibility of States since it would mean that contracts signed by them did not bind them; it would introduce in such contracts a fundamental imbalance because in these contracts only one party—the party contracting with the State—would be bound. In law, such an outcome would go directly against the most elementary principle of good faith and for this reason it cannot be accepted.

## *Notes*

1. Even if the General Assembly resolutions of 1974 referred to in the arbitral award cannot be considered as declaratory of international law (because of lack of general consensus), are they significant evidence of a *lack* of consensus in support of principles previously adopted in 1962? Does the disappearance of a prior consensus erode a rule once part of customary law? May one conclude from the division of opinion (and of *opinio juris*) expressed in 1974 and prior

thereto that there is no generally agreed customary law rule on the issue of the law applicable to compensation for taking of alien property? (See U.S. Supreme Court decision in *Sabbatino Case* infra). Should the Arbitrator have considered this question in the above case?

2. Are the bilateral investment treaties and the Convention on Investment Disputes (referred to by the Arbitrator), which provide for the possibility of international adjudication of disputes, evidence of a customary law obligation to pursue such international procedures or, on the contrary, are they evidence that such international adjudication may be undertaken only when the states concerned so agree (as envisaged in Article 2 of the Charter of Economic Rights and Duties)? For further analysis of this problem, see Baxter, Treaties and Custom, at 75–91, and Schachter, The Evolving International Law of Development, at 8–9.

### *SCHACHTER, INTERNATIONAL LAW IN THEORY AND PRACTICE*

178 Rec. des Cours 120 (1982–V) (footnotes omitted).

An interesting question is presented by a majority resolution that on its face expresses a clear belief that an alleged rule has not been or is no longer existing law. Examples of this can be seen in the several recent resolutions which are meant to deny the international legal validity of certain requirements for compensation in cases of nationalization and to assert that questions of compensation are matters exclusively of the domestic law of the nationalizing State. Can such majority decisions be taken as a decisive indication that the supposed rule of international responsibility now lacks sufficient *opinio juris* to enable it to be regarded as a rule of customary law? Would the resolution have "delegitimized" what may have been an existing rule? Two points need to be made here. One is that the views of a majority of States must be considered as relevant evidence of *opinio juris*. The fact that those views have been formally expressed in a resolution does not *deprive* them of evidentiary value. At the same time, they should not foreclose the possibility of challenging the evidentiary value of a majority decision on grounds of contrary practice and contrary *opinio juris* manifested in other contexts. * * *

## B. VOLUNTARY CODES AND GUIDELINES

International organizations have adopted a variety of texts, called "codes of conduct" or "guide-lines," which prescribe norms for state conduct and, in some cases, for conduct of non-state entities. Such texts are recognized as "non-binding". They are usually drafted in hortatory rather than obligatory language. However, it is clear that the states voting for such non-binding codes or guide-lines intend them to be followed in practice. In many cases, the texts provide for reports by governments and for periodic renew by an international organ. In some cases, specific cases of non-compliance may be brought to the attention of the competent international organ.

Examples of such codes or guide-lines are mainly found in economic and social fields. Foreign investment and transnational corporations have the subject of several such texts: UN Code on Restrictive Business Practices 19 I.L.M. 813 (1981); World Bank Guidelines on the Treatment of Foreign Direct Investment 31 I.L.M. 1363 (1992). The United Nations also been engaged for many years in the preparation of a comprehensive code of conduct for transnational corporations. See chapters 9 and 17.

The specialized agencies of the United Nations have relied on voluntary codes for important areas of international regulation. For example, the World Health Organization has adopted an International Code for the Marketing of Breast Milk Substitutes, 20 I.L.M. 1004 (1981), and the Food and Agriculture Organization jointly with the World Health Organization has promulgated the Codex Alimentarius. See infra pp. 144–45.

### *Notes and Questions*

1. Does the notion of estoppel bar a state that voted in favor of a code of conduct from asserting that an action taken by another state consistent with the voluntary code is illegal?

## *THE WHO INTERNATIONAL CODE OF MARKETING BREAST-MILK SUBSTITUTES*

This Code was adopted by the World Health Assembly in 1981 with near-unanimity, the only dissenting vote cast by the United States. The Code is concerned with a single product, infant milk substitutes. Its main object is to prohibit certain marketing and promotional activities that foster inappropriate and dangerous use of the milk substitutes in poor countries especially those with inadequate sanitation and clean water. The Code was legally a WHO recommendation, not a binding set of rules. It is addressed to governments, to private firms, to institutions (such as hospitals), and to the medical and nursing professions. A few countries enacted the Code as a whole into domestic law; a considerable number gave legal effect to major parts of the Code. Some of the principal producers of the milk-substitutes at first resisted the Code, most notably Nestlés, by far the largest producer. In reaction, a group of non-governmental organizations instituted an international boycott of Nestlés which resulted in major changes by the company in its marketing and promotional activities.

Some practices were still regarded as violations of the Code and remain the grounds for continued boycott (as of 1993). See N.E. Zelman, The Nestle Infant Formula Controversy: Restricting the Marketing Practices of Multinational Corporation in the Third World, 3 Transnational Lawyer 697 (1990).

### *Note and Questions*

What are the positive and negative aspects of consumer boycotts to induce compliance with a code that is legally a recommendation? Should the international body provide recourse to a target of the boycott?

## *THE FAO/WHO CODEX ALIMENTARIUS*

A joint project of the Food and Agriculture Organization and the World Health Organization, the Codex Alimentarius provides an institutional framework for the codification of food standards that are necessary for "protecting the health of consumers and ensuring fair practices in the food trade." Statutes, Article 1. Codex Alimentarius Commission Procedural Manual 5 (7th ed. 1989). Established in 1962, the Codex covers "all principal foods, whether processed, semi-processed or raw, for distribution to the consumer. * * * It also includes provisions of an advisory nature in the form of codes of practice, guidelines and other recommended measures." Id. at 23. Governments may respond to new standards proposed by the Codex Alimentarius Commission in one of four ways: full acceptance, target acceptance, acceptance with specific deviations, or no acceptance. Governments that refuse to accept a standard, or that prefer target acceptance, must provide an explanation of the way its own food requirements differ from the proposed ones, and must indicate whether they will allow the free distribution within their own borders of a product complying with the standard. The success of the Codex is not only to be measured by the number of acceptances for the standards, as the Codex also has exerted a powerful influence on non-accepting states, as well as food growers, packagers, transporters, and preparers. In 1979 the Codex Alimentarius Commission enacted a Code of Ethics for International Trade in Food, which recommends that "all those engaging in the international trade in food commit themselves morally to this Code and undertake voluntarily to support its implementation in the larger interest of the world community." Document CAC/RCP 20–1979, Rev. 1 (1985).

## C. GENERALLY ACCEPTED INTERNATIONAL STANDARDS

The conception of "generally accepted international standards" has emerged in the treaties on the law of the sea and has been extended by some authorities to other fields, particularly the law of the environment. Such standards may be adopted in a treaty or by international organizations pursuant to a treaty. With respect to standards relating to marine safety and related matters, the Restatement (Third) has taken the position that "once a standard has been generally accepted, a state is obligated in particular to apply it to all ships flying its flag and to adopt any necessary laws or regulations" (section 502, Comment *c*). This obligation is said to apply to all states whether or not parties to the convention by virtue of customary law. The Restatement also declares that a similar principle requires all states to conform to international rules or standards derived form international conventions or adopted by international organizations pursuant to such conventions. Restatement (Third) section 601 and Comment *b*.

Oxman writes:

> The duty entails a legally binding obligation to observe generally accepted standards. This obligation, however, is created by general acceptance of a standard in fact, rather than by the procedure by which the standard was articulated. Thus, it creates a useful bridge between so-called "soft law" and "hard law." This, indeed, was part of its original function. Where appropriate, standards (or guidelines) can be developed in a somewhat more relaxed procedural environment which is not specifically designed to generate legally binding obligations as such;

yet those same standards can become legally binding if they become generally accepted.

The effect of the duty under discussion is to impose a legal obligation on a state to respect a standard which it would not otherwise be legally bound to respect. The consensual requirements of international law for the imposition of legal obligations are not offended by this proposition; those requirements have previously been satisfied through acceptance of the general duty either by treaty or by customary international law. It is unnecessary to restrict the scope of the duty itself to conform to such requirements.

B. Oxman, The Duty to Respect Generally Accepted International Standards, 24 N.Y.U.J.Int.L. & Pol. 143–44 (1991).

### *Notes and Questions*

1. Why differentiate between generally accepted standards and customary law? Would such standards be regarded as binding all states without extensive state practice and recognition that a rule of law is involved (i.e. *opinio juris*)?

2. Should non-consenting states be required to apply technical standards that are meant to provide new detailed regulation for particular activities, which are in large part, private?

3. Oxman observes "like many legal duties it will function best where its existence encourages voluntary compliance" and he concludes "the less said, the better" (id. p. 159). Do you agree?

## D. INTERNATIONAL RULES OF NON-GOVERNMENTAL BODIES

1. International non-governmental organization in various fields adopt rules and standards in their respective fields of activity, many of which are given effect by official agencies, courts, and international organizations. Technical and scientific bodies in particular are authoritative sources of norms that are incorporated by reference or explicitly into rules observed by states and public agencies. Examples include the International Organization for Standardization of Weights and Measures and the International Air Transportation Association.

2. A more striking example of an international non-governmental legal regime is the Olympic Movement. The Olympic Charter vests "supreme authority in the International Olympic Committee (IOC)" and provides that "any person or organization belonging in any capacity to the Olympic Movement is bound by the provisions of the Charter and shall abide by the decisions of the IOC." The rules, by-laws and decisions of the IOC constitute an autonomous regime governing the relevant sports world and given effect as such by governments. A study by a European scholar in 1988 noted that "the sui generis law of the Olympic Movement is accepted, respected and applied as a State-independent body of legal rules in a growing number of municipal court decisions." Bruno Simma, quoted in J. Nafziger, International Sports Law, 86 Am.J.I.L. 489, 492 (1992). When Olympic arrangements were challenged in the U.S., the Ninth Circuit declared that "[t]he Olympic Games are organized and conducted under the terms of an international agreement—the Olympic Charter. We are extremely hesitant * * * to alter an event that is staged * * * under the terms of that agreement."

Martin v. IOC, 740 F.2d 670, 677 (9th Cir.1984). See also Behagen v. Amateur Basketball Ass'n of U.S., 884 F.2d 524, 527 (10th Cir.1989) (noting the centrality of the IOC in "governing structures for * * * American involvement in international amateur sports"). The decision of the IOC to exclude South African athletes from international competition between 1964 and 1991 for violating its rule against apartheid laws was effectively observed. IOC rules on substance abuse and "doping" have been accepted as binding on all, though in practice supervision has been inconsistent and some times haphazard (Nafziger id. 503).

## E. CONCERTED ACTS OF GOVERNMENTS AND POLITICAL DECLARATIONS

Governments engage in concerted acts of various kinds that express common understandings and positions but which are not recognized as treaties or customary law. Such acts may be expressed in exchanges of communication or in a communiqué after an exchange of views. On occasion they are expressed in formal instruments such as the Final Act of a conference as for example the Final Act of the Helsinki Conference at Helsinki in 1975. "Gentlemen's Agreements" are not uncommon. They are not binding but they may be strictly observed as long as the parties consider them useful. For a further discussion of non-binding agreements, see Chapter 6.

Political declarations have been used instead of treaties in processes of settling major disputes. For example, at the end of the Second World War, the most important understandings relating to territorial disposition and post-war organization were expressed in Declarations at the Yalta, Potsdam and Cairo Conferences.

It has been suggested in recent writings that the so-called purely political instruments may have legal consequences. Schachter considers that as such instruments are official acts of states, they are evidence of the positions taken by states and "it is appropriate to draw inferences that the States concerned have recognized the principles, rules, status and rights acknowledged. This does not mean that 'new law' or a new obligation is created. However, where the points of law are not entirely clear and are disputed the evidence of official positions drawn from these instruments can be significant." Schachter, International Law in Theory and Practice at 129. A non-legal text may also over time become customary law on the basis of state practice and *opinio juris*. That consequence does not depend on the original intent of the parties to the instrument.

What are the implications of non-compliance with a non-legal declaration? Schachter suggests:

> * * * States entering into a non-legal commitment generally view it as a political (or moral) obligation and intend to carry it out in good faith. Other parties and other States concerned have reason to expect such compliance and to rely on it. What we must deduce from this, I submit, is that the political texts which express commitments and positions of one kind or another are governed by the general principle of good faith. Moreover, since good faith is an accepted general principle

of international law, it is appropriate and even necessary to apply it in its legal sense. Id. at 130.

A significant practical consequence of the "good faith" principle is that a party which committed itself in good faith to a course of conduct or to recognition of a legal situation would be estopped from acting inconsistently with its commitment or adopted position when the circumstances showed that other parties reasonably relied on that undertaking or position.

These problems were considered by the Institut de droit international in 1983. See reports of 7th Commission (Virally, rapporteur) and comments of members. 60–I Ann. de l'Institut de droit int'l 166–374 (1983) and 60–II id. 117–54. (1984). See also Schachter, "Non-Conventional Concerted Acts" in M. Bedjaoui (ed.) International Law, Achievements and Prospects 265–269 (1991).

# Chapter 3

# THE RELATION OF INTERNATIONAL LAW TO MUNICIPAL LAW

## SECTION 1. MUNICIPAL LAW IN INTERNATIONAL LAW

International law is binding on all states, and every state is obliged to give effect to it. The international obligation is upon the state, not upon any particular branch, institution, or individual member of its government, but the state is responsible for violations by any branch or subdivision of its government or by any official (and in some contexts also for acts and omissions by private individuals). The state is responsible to assure that its constitution and its laws enable its government to carry out its international obligations.

The principle that a state cannot plead its own law as an excuse for non-compliance with international law has been long established and generally recognized. In 1887, for example, Secretary of State Bayard declared:

> "[I]t is only necessary to say, that if a Government could set up its own municipal laws as the final test of its international rights and obligations, then the rules of international law would be but the shadow of a name and would afford no protection either to States or to individuals. It has been constantly maintained and also admitted by the Government of the United States that a government can not appeal to its municipal regulations as an answer to demands for the fulfillment of international duties. Such regulations may either exceed or fall short of the requirements of international law, and in either case that law furnishes the test of the nation's liability and not its own municipal rules. * * * " [1887] U.S. Foreign Rel. 751, 753.

Article 13 of the Draft Declaration of Rights and Duties of States adopted by the International Law Commission in 1949 provides: "Every State has the duty to carry out in good faith its obligations arising from treaties and other sources of international law, and it may not invoke provisions in its constitution or its laws as an excuse for failure to perform this duty." See Vienna

Convention on the Law of Treaties, art. 46; Restatement (Third) § 311(3). There is an abundance of decisions of international courts and tribunals recognizing this principle. See, e.g., Case Concerning Certain German Interests in Polish Upper Silesia (Merits), P.C.I.J., Ser. A, No. 7, at 19, 22, 42 (1926); Case Concerning the Factory at Chorzow (Merits), P.C.I.J., Ser. A, No. 17, at 33–34 (1928); Free Zones Case, P.C.I.J., Ser. A/B, No. 46, at 167 (1932); The Greco–Bulgarian "Communities," Advisory Opinion, P.C.I.J., Ser. A, No. 17, at 32 (1930); Treatment of Polish Nationals and Other Persons of Polish Origin or Speech in Danzig Territory, Advisory Opinion, P.C.I.J., Ser. A/B, No. 44, at 24 (1932); Case Concerning Rights of Nationals of the United States of America in Morocco (France v. U.S.), 1952 I.C.J. 176; Norwegian Shipowners' Claims (Norway v. U.S.), 1922, 1 U.N.Rep.Int'l Arb. Awards 307; Shufeldt Claim (U.S. v. Guatemala), 1930, 2 U.N.Rep. Int'l Arb. Awards 1079. The principle was also recognized by jurists of the U.S.S.R. See Academy of Sciences of the U.S.S.R., Institute of State and Law, International Law 15 (Ogden trans. 1961).

The United States has never doubted the supremacy of international law in principle, but neither the President, Congress, nor the courts will give effect to a norm of customary international law or to a treaty provision that is inconsistent with the U.S. Constitution. See 161 infra. On several occasions, in becoming a party to human rights treaties, the United States has entered reservations to assure that it would not be undertaking international obligations that it would be unable to carry out because to do so would violate the U.S. Constitution. See Chapter 8 infra.

International tribunals have sometimes declared municipal legislation to be subject to international obligations. In 1987, for example, the U.S. Congress enacted the Anti–Terrorism Act containing provisions that the U.N. Secretary General believed to be inconsistent with the U.N. Headquarters Agreement. The Secretary General declared that a dispute existed between the U.S. and the U.N. regarding the interpretation and application of the Agreement and requested arbitration to resolve the dispute as provided in the Agreement. In an advisory opinion, the International Court of Justice concluded that a dispute existed and that the United States was obliged to enter into arbitration. Applicability of the Obligation to Arbitrate under Section 21 of the United Nations Headquarters Agreement of 26 June 1947, [1988] I.C.J. 12 (advisory opinion). International human rights tribunals have declared invalid municipal legislation as inconsistent with a state's obligations under international human rights conventions.

In many cases international tribunals have awarded damages because a state's courts have disregarded or misapplied international law. For example, an arbitral tribunal awarded damages to Great Britain for the detention or condemnation in the United States of six British vessels as prize during the Civil War, holding that in these cases the condemnation or detention was contrary to international law, although it had been upheld by the Supreme Court as lawful. 3 Moore, International Arbitrations 3209–10 (1898); 4 id. 3902, 3911, 3928, 3935, 3950 (1898). In such cases the international tribunal normally has no power to reverse or set aside the judgment of the municipal court, which may continue to have legal effect (e.g., to pass title to property); but the international tribunal will award damages to the aggrieved state.

Questions of municipal law may arise in disputes between states and international tribunals may find it necessary to interpret such law. This may happen, for example, in disputes arising out of alleged breaches of state contracts. In the *Serbian Loans* and *Brazilian Loans* cases, the Permanent Court of International Justice had to determine the meaning and effect of French legislation governing payments of debts in gold or at gold value. P.C.I.J., Ser. A, Nos. 20/21, at 5, 40–47, 93, 120–125 (1929). In construing this legislation, the Court attached controlling weight to the manner in which it had been applied by the French courts, saying in the latter case:

> Though bound to apply municipal law when circumstances so require, the Court, which is a tribunal of international law, and which, in this capacity, is deemed itself to know what this law is, is not obliged also to know the municipal law of the various countries. All that can be said in this respect is that the Court may possibly be obliged to obtain knowledge regarding the municipal law which has to be applied. And this it must do, either by means of evidence furnished it by the Parties or by means of any researches which the Court may think fit to undertake or to cause to be undertaken.
>
> Once the Court has arrived at the conclusion that it is necessary to apply the municipal law of a particular country, there seems no doubt that it must seek to apply it as it would be applied in that country. It would not be applying the municipal law of a country if it were to apply it in a manner different from that in which that law would be applied in the country in which it is in force.
>
> It follows that the Court must pay the utmost regard to the decisions of the municipal courts of a country, for it is with the aid of their jurisprudence that it will be enabled to decide what are the rules which, in actual fact, are applied in the country the law of which is recognized as applicable in a given case. If the Court were obliged to disregard the decisions of municipal courts, the result would be that it might in certain circumstances apply rules other than those actually applied; this would seem to be contrary to the whole theory on which the application of municipal law is based.
>
> Of course, the Court will endeavour to make a just appreciation of the jurisprudence of municipal courts. If this is uncertain or divided, it will rest with the Court to select the interpretation which it considers most in conformity with the law. But to compel the Court to disregard that jurisprudence would not be in conformity with its function when applying municipal law. As the Court has already observed in the judgment in the case of the Serbian loans, it would be a most delicate matter to do so, in a case concerning public policy—a conception the definition of which in any particular country is largely dependent on the opinion prevailing at any given time in such country itself—and in a case where no relevant provisions directly relate to the question at issue. Such are the reasons according to which the Court considers that it must construe Article VI of the Special Agreement to mean that, while the Court is authorized to depart from the jurisprudence of the municipal courts, it remains entirely free to decide that there is no ground for

attributing to the municipal law a meaning other than that attributed to it by that jurisprudence."

Id. at 124–25.

Where international law requires exhaustion of local remedies as a condition of pursuing international relief, see p. 693 infra, an international tribunal may consider the adequacy of a state's judicial and administrative procedures and even the judgments of its courts. In 1989, a chamber of the International Court of Justice considered Italian judicial and administrative procedures, decisions of its courts and administrative tribunals, and the weight to be given to their interpretation of Italian law. See Case Concerning Elettronica Sicula S.p.A. (ELSI) (U.S. v. Italy), [1989] I.C.J. 15. The *Elettronica* case involved a dispute arising out of the "requisition" by the Mayor of Palermo, Italy, of a plant and assets of Raytheon–Elsi S.p.A, an Italian company based in Sicily but wholly owned by two U.S. corporations. The U.S. claimed that the requisition had caused the bankruptcy of the company, thereby violating a Supplemental Agreement to a bilateral Treaty of Friendship, Commerce and Navigation (FCN), which provided that nationals of each country would "not be subjected to arbitrary or discriminatory measures within" the territory of the other. Italy objected to the admissibility of the case, claiming that the Italian Civil Code permits private actions for the breach of self-executing treaties, that the FCN was such a treaty, and that the U.S. corporations had failed to exhaust their domestic remedies by litigating their treaty rights in the Italian courts. The International Court of Justice rejected this argument holding that Italy had not met the burden of showing that the corporations could have obtained redress for the treaty violations in Italian courts. The Court then addressed domestic interpretations of domestic law in determining the parties' obligations under international law. The U.S. claimed that the requisition of the plant and assets was a violation of the FCN treaty because it was "arbitrary" and unlawful under Italian law. The U.S. pointed to a decision of the Prefect of Palermo which called the requisition order "destitute of any juridical cause which may justify it or make it enforceable," and which was affirmed by the Court of Appeal of Palermo. The International Court of Justice disagreed:

> Yet it must be borne in mind that the fact that an act of a public authority may have been unlawful in municipal law does not necessarily mean that that act was unlawful in international law, as a breach of treaty or otherwise. A finding of the local courts that an act was unlawful may well be relevant to an argument that it was also arbitrary; but by itself, and without more, unlawfulness cannot be said to amount to arbitrariness. * * * To identify arbitrariness with mere unlawfulness would be to deprive it of any useful meaning in its own right. Nor does it follow from a finding by a municipal court that an act was unjustified, or unreasonable, or arbitrary, that that act is necessarily to be classed as arbitrary in international law, though the qualification given to the impugned act by a municipal authority may be a valuable indication.

[1989] I.C.J. at 74. The Court held that under international law "[a]rbitrariness is not so much something opposed to *a* rule of law, as something opposed to *the* rule of law. * * * It is a wilful disregard of due process of law, an act which shocks, or at least surprises, a sense of juridical propriety. Nothing in the decision of the Prefect, or in the judgment of the Court of Appeal of Palermo, conveys any indication that the requisition ordered * * * was to be regarded in that light." Id., at 76. See generally Dixon, Case Concerning Elettronica Sicula S.p.A (ELSI) (United States v. Italy), 41 Int'l & Comp.L.Q. 701 (1992).

Exceptionally, an international tribunal may reject an interpretation of a state's law by a court of that state if it is obviously fraudulent or erroneous. See, in general, Freeman, The International Responsibility of States for Denial of Justice 342–54 (1938); Jenks, The Prospects of International Adjudication 547–603 (1964).

For a general discussion, see Ferrari–Bravo, International and Municipal Law: The Complementarity of Legal Systems, in The Structure and Process of International Law (Macdonald & Johnston eds. 1983).

## SECTION 2. INTERNATIONAL LAW IN MUNICIPAL LAW

International law requires a state to carry out its international obligations but, in general, how a state accomplishes this result is not of concern to international law. In some instances, however, states may undertake to carry out their obligations by particular means, for example, by enacting legislation or by taking specified executive or judicial measures. See, e.g., the 1966 Covenant on Civil and Political Rights, Article 2, 999 U.N.T.S. 171. The 1948 Genocide Convention requires states party to make genocide a crime under domestic law. Convention on the Prevention and Punishment of the Crime of Genocide, Articles V & VI, 78 U.N.T.S. 277. See Chapter 8.

Since a state's responsibility to give effect to international obligations does not fall upon any particular institution of its government, international law does not require that domestic courts apply and give effect to international obligations. (Of course, insofar as international law accords immunity from the jurisdiction of courts, say to foreign state or to its diplomats, the exercise of jurisdiction by a domestic court contrary to the limitations of international law would constitute a violation by the state.) States differ as to whether international law is incorporated into domestic law and forms a part of "the law of the land," and whether the executive or the courts will give effect to norms of international law or to treaty provisions in the absence of their implementation by domestic legislation.

*The Monist–Dualist Debate.* The relation of international law to municipal law has long troubled analytical jurisprudence. The fact that municipal courts apply international law challenged assertions that the two systems of law were independent and discrete. The notion once extant that only states, and not individuals, are "subjects of international law" was distasteful particularly to jurists who sought the vindication and protection of human rights in international law.

Two principal "schools" see the relation of international law to municipal law differently. Dualists (or pluralists) regard international law and municipal law as separate legal systems which operate on different levels.

International law can be applied by municipal courts only when it has been "transformed" or "incorporated" into municipal law. Further, international law as incorporated into municipal law is subject to constitutional limitations applicable to all domestic law, and may be repealed or superseded by act of parliament for purposes of domestic law. Dualists also emphasize the international legal personality of states, rather than of individuals or other entities. The monists, on the other hand, regard international law and municipal law as parts of a single legal system. In a traditional version of monism, municipal law is seen as ultimately deriving its validity from international law, which stands "higher" in a hierarchy of legal norms. Therefore, international law cannot be subject to domestic law, not even to constitutional limitations. Monists thus find it easier to maintain that individuals have international legal personality. There have been efforts to surmount the dichotomy between dualism and monism and to develop other approaches. See Borchard, The Relation Between International Law and Municipal Law, 27 Va.L.Rev. 137 (1940).

A related but different question is whether, even in a state committed to a dualist conception, international law is considered to be incorporated into domestic law, and, if so, whether such incorporation resulted from an act of parliament or other political act, or was assumed and given effect by the courts even without a political act of incorporation. For the position of the United States, see p. 161 below.

## A. INTERNATIONAL LAW IN THE MUNICIPAL LAW OF OTHER STATES

### *WILDHABER & BREITENMOSER, THE RELATIONSHIP BETWEEN CUSTOMARY INTERNATIONAL LAW AND MUNICIPAL LAW IN WESTERN EUROPEAN COUNTRIES*

48 Zeitschrift für Ausländisches Öffentliches Recht und Völkerrecht 163, 179–204 (1988) (footnotes omitted).

3.1 Constitutions with an explicit reference to customary international law

3.1.1 The Federal Republic of Germany (FGR)

* * *

Today, Art. 25 of the Basic Law (GG) is among the most favourable provisions in Western Europe with regard to customary international law:

> "The general rules of public international law shall be an integral part of federal law. They shall take precedence over the laws and shall directly create rights and duties for the inhabitants of the federal territory."

According to the practice of the Federal Constitutional Court and the predominant doctrine, the general rules of international law are norms which are recognized as binding by a predominant majority of countries (but not necessarily by the FRG itself). They include—among others—customary law (but not regional customary law) and the principles generally recognized by civilized countries. Treaty Law, on the contrary, acquires municipal validity only after a special transformation act; indeed, according to Art. 59(2) GG, "treaties which regulate the political relations of the Federation or relate to matters of federal legislation shall require the consent or participation, in the form of a federal law, of the bodies competent in any specific case for such federal legislation. Contrary to customary international law, treaty law is not superior to municipal law; likewise, however, it may be overruled by a *lex posterior.*

* * *

The constitutional principle of an interpretation and application of the municipal law in conformity with international law requests that German courts refrain from recognizing either foreign laws which violate general international law or the general reservation of the international *ordre public,* even where international law itself does not proscribe such an application.

### 3.1.2 Italy

Art. 10(1) of the Italian Constitution of 1948 provides that "Italy's legal system conforms with the generally recognized principles of international law."

Already three years after this provision had been adopted, the Court of Cassation said:

> "There thus exist overriding principles based upon the need to secure mutual existence among civilised States, and between the latter in relation to their nationals and to nationals of [other] States * * * These principles applied already before they were embodied in Article 10 * * * They require that Italian municipal law must conform to customary international law * * *"

* * * In Italy * * * the generally recognized principles of international law become an integral part of the Italian legal system only after what is called a procedure of "automatic conformance", i.e. after having been transformed into parallel Italian customary law. But this * * * position "has only the effect of a *petitio principi,* since it does not have any influence upon the practical value of the norms concerned."

* * *

* * * [T]he general principles of law, as stated in Art. 38(1) *lit.* (c) of the Statute of the ICJ are held not to fall within the scope of Art. 10(1) of the Italian Constitution. The same is true, incidentally, of international treaty law. According to * * * doctrine, there is no indirect constitutional recognition of treaties by means of the general principle of *pacta sunt servanda.* Therefore, only customary international law is within the scope of application of Art. 10(1).

The Italian Constitution does not regulate the rank of customary international law in the hierarchy of the municipal legal order. Nevertheless, according to the predominant doctrine, Art. 10(1) "implies that in the Italian legal system rules of general international law are superior to ordinary legislation, although according to most authorities they do not possess the same status as provisions of the Constitution".

### 3.1.3 Austria

* * * [I]n Austria customary international law may display an effect within the sphere of municipal law. Art. 9 of the Austrian Federal Constitution * * * reads: "The generally recognized principles of International Law are valid parts of the Federal Law". * * *

According to Austrian doctrine and practice, "a rule of international law does not have to be recognized unanimously by all states in order to be considered a 'generally recognized rule of international law' under Art. 9 of the Constitution". This provision is interpreted extensively as comprising the generally recognized rules of private and of administrative international law.

* * *

It is controversial whether the "generally recognized principles of international law" may be overridden by ordinary statutes. In a decision more than thirty years old, the Constitutional Court explicitly—but without any substantiation—declared that these rules ranked equally with ordinary statutes but were not on the same level as the Constitution * * *

### 3.1.4 Greece

In the new Greek Constitution of 1975 * * * Art. 28(1) is worded thus:

> "The generally acknowledged rules of international law, as well as international conventions as of the time they are sanctioned by law and become operative according to the conditions therein, shall be an integral part of domestic Greek law and shall prevail over any contrary provision of the law. * * *"

* * *

* * * [I]nternational agreements will only acquire internal validity after having been sanctioned by an act of Parliament. * * * During the drafting of the new Constitution, a controversy arose concerning the legal effect of treaties:

> "The issue was resolved in the same manner as to both customary and conventional international law. They were given enhanced formal validity, so that they supersede both prior and subsequent acts of Parliament. * * * "

### 3.1.5 France

In France, * * * the fourteenth paragraph of the preamble of the Constitution of the Fourth Republic of October 27, 1946 [provides]:

> "The French Republic, faithful to its tradition, abides by the rules of international law".

In several decisions, the Supreme Administrative Court [Conseil d'Etat] applied general principles of international law by way of interpretation of this preamble. According to this merely declaratory provision, which represented no modification of prior practice concerning the relationship between international law and municipal law, international law was applied *per se:*

> " * * * the French tribunals have regarded the rules of customary international law as directly applicable whenever they are relevant to

the adjudication of an issue of which they have jurisdiction, and concerning which there is no controlling legislative or executive act. They * * * have developed no coherent doctrine of 'adoption' or 'incorporation' * * *. [But] they have not been influenced by the doctrines of dogmatic dualism, which would require the specific 'transformation' of a rule of international law into one of internal law as a prerequisite to its judicial application".

In the new preamble of the Constitution of the Fifth Republic of 1958 it is now stated, that "the French people hereby solemnly proclaims its attachment to the Rights of Man and the principles of national sovereignty as defined by the Declaration of 1789, reaffirmed and complemented by the Preamble of the Constitution of 1946".

Notwithstanding some doubts as to whether that preamble constituted a source of law, French courts do not hesitate to apply rules of customary international law. Indeed it is argued that an explicit reference to these rules of international law would not be necessary, "as it would merely be the expression of what is in any event a general conviction" * * *.

The predominant doctrine in France * * * regards the reference of the Constitution of 1958 to the Preamble of the Constitution of 1946 as sufficient legal basis for applying international law.

* * *

3.2 Constitutions with no explicit reference to customary international law

3.2.1 Switzerland

In the Swiss Federal Constitution, there is no explicit provision concerning the relationship between international law and municipal law. But according to unanimous doctrine, there is an unwritten rule, implicit in the Constitution, that customary international law and the general principles of international law are valid immediately and without any special procedure, i.e., that they become municipally applicable upon their international entry into force: * * *

* * *

The Federal Tribunal repeatedly confirmed this view. It held that international law had to be considered as Swiss federal law, "because its nature requires general municipal applicability, so that it has to be equated with the uniform domestic law".

In the context of judicial proceedings, the Federal Tribunal also equated the violation of customary international law with that of treaty law: * * *

* * *

Rules of customary international law have only to be completed and implemented by Swiss federal law, if they are not clear enough and therefore unfit for immediate application and execution.

With respect to treaties, no formal transformation into a federal statute is required. Treaties become municipally applicable upon their international entry into force * * *.

* * *

Although the question of the rank of international law [in relation to Swiss constitutional and statutory law] continues to be disputed in doctrine and practice, there is a strong tendency to grant both customary and conventional international law a rank above federal statutes or even the same rank as the Constitution.

* * *

### 3.2.3 The Netherlands

[I]n the Dutch Constitution, there has never been any provision concerning the applicability and the rank of customary international law. On the other hand, international treaties have long ago been given a most favourable position in the text of the Constitution. The previous Constitution (adopted in 1953 and revised in 1956) went even as far as to permit international treaties to modify and lawfully overrule provisions of the Constitution itself.

In the next text, passed in 1983, however, it is not quite clear whether the primacy of international law is only proclaimed with respect to statutory law, while the Constitution remains unaffected. Unquestionably, according to Art. 94 of the new Constitution, international treaties override at least statutory rules * * *.

* * *

According to their monistic legal system, the Netherlands courts apply customary international law directly and immediately as such, and not by virtue of a transformation into municipal law.

Regarding the question of the rank of customary international law in cases of conflicts with statutory law, some old decisions of domestic tribunals held that statutes which violated rules of customary international law, nevertheless had a legal validity, because an examination of their constitutionality was not provided for by the constitution. On the other hand, the domestic courts applied the traditional principle of an interpretation of municipal law in conformity with international law. Also they recognized the presumption, according to which the legislature did not intend to violate rules of customary international law, until such an intention was not explicitly and clearly proved. * * *.

### *Notes*

1. *International law in the municipal systems of other states.* Wildhaber and Breitenmoser address also the jurisprudence of Belgium, the principality of Liechtenstein, Portugal and Spain.

The constitutional and jurisprudential problems faced by European states arise also in the domestic law of other countries around the world. See, e.g., *Australia*—International Law in Australia, (Ryan, ed. 1984); Byrnes & Charlesworth, Federalism and the International Legal Order: Recent Developments in Australia, 79 A.J.I.L. 622 (1985); McGinley, The Status of Treaties in Australian Municipal Law, 12 Adel.L.Rev. 367 (1990). *Canada*—International Law[:] Chiefly as Interpreted and Applied in Canada, Chap. 4 (4th ed., Kindred, gen. ed., 1987); Campbell, Federalism and International Relations: The Canadian Experience, 85 A.S.I.L. Proc. 125 (1991); Schwartz, The Charter and the Domestic Enforcement of International Law, 16 Man.L.J. 149 (1986). *China*—Wang,

International Law in China, 221 Rec. des Cours 195 (1990–II). *Indonesia*—Hartano, The Interaction Between National Law and International Law in Indonesia, in International Law and Development (de Waart, ed. 1988). *Israel*—Lapidoth, International Law Within the Israel Legal System, 24 Israel L.Rev. 451 (1990). *Japan*—Oda, The Practice of Japan in International Law, 1961–1970 (1982); *Nigeria*—Okeke, The Theory and Practice of International Law in Nigeria (1986). *South Africa*—Roodt, National Law and Treaties: An Overview, 13 S.Afr.Ybk.Int'l L. 72 (1987–88).

See also Tunkin, International Law 90–100 (1986); International Law and Municipal Law (Tunkin & Wolfrum, eds. 1988); International Law 49–64 (Mullerson & Tunkin, eds. 1990); The Effects of Treaties in Domestic Law (Jacobs & Roberts, eds. 1987); du Droit International au Droit de L'integration (Capotorti, et al., eds. 1987); Rights, Institutions and Impact of International Law According to the German Basic Law (Starck, ed. 1987); Mann, Foreign Affairs in English Courts (1986).

Under the law of the European Community, the Treaty of Rome has a constitutional character and has supremacy over national laws, whether adopted earlier or later. See Chapter 19, Section 2 infra.

2. English courts have applied customary international law since before the American revolution, saying that the law of nations was "part of the law of England." See Lord Mansfield in Triquet and Others v. Bath, 97 Eng.Rep. 936, 938, 3 Burr. 1478, 1481 (K.B. 1764). In 1938, the Privy Council said: "The Courts acknowledge the existence of a body of rules which nations accept amongst themselves. On any judicial issue they seek to ascertain what the relevant rule is, and, having found it, they will treat it as incorporated into the domestic law, so far as it is not inconsistent with rules enacted by statutes or finally declared by their tribunals." Chung Chi Cheung v. The King, [1939] A.C. 160, 168 (Hong Kong) (1938). In Mortensen v. Peters, 8 Sess.Cas. (5th ser.) 93 (1906), the Scottish Court of Justiciary upheld the conviction of a Danish national, master of a Norwegian ship, for fishing in violation of a statute regulating fishing in a part of Moray Firth more than three miles from the nearest land. Appellant argued that the application of British law to foreign nationals in this place would be a violation of international law and that the statute must be presumed not to extend to foreign nationals outside of British territory. The Court expressed doubt whether it was contrary to international law to treat Moray Firth, a bay, as British territory; the following statement was made by Lord Dunedin: "In this Court we have nothing to do with the question of whether the Legislature has or has not done what foreign powers may consider a usurpation in a question with them. Neither are we a tribunal sitting to decide whether an Act of the Legislature is ultra vires as in contravention of generally acknowledged principles of international law. For us an Act of Parliament duly passed by Lords and Commons and assented to by the King, is supreme, and we are bound to give effect to its terms." After this decision, several masters of Norwegian ships were convicted, but eventually released upon Norwegian protest. In Parliament, it was stated on behalf of the British Foreign Office that the Act, as interpreted by the court, was "in conflict with international law." 170 Parl.Deb. (4th ser.) 472 (1907). Subsequently, an Act of Parliament prohibited the landing or selling in the United Kingdom of fish caught by the forbidden methods within the areas specified. 9 Edw. VIII, c. 8 (1909). For the status of international law in British law generally, see Brownlie, Principles of Public International Law 42–50 (4th ed. 1990); Mann, Foreign Affairs in English

Courts (1986). Britain's entry into the European Community has had a significant effect on its legal system. See Note 3.

3. The European Court of Justice has established that European Community law not only is the law of all member states, to be directly applied by all the national courts, but that it is the higher law of the member states, prevailing over conflicting national legislation. See Chapter 19, Section 2. An eminent British jurist, Lord Denning, notes that the body of community legislation penetrates the British legal system "like an incoming tide. It flows into the estuaries and up the rivers. It cannot be held back * * *. Parliament has decreed that [community law] is * * * to be part of our law." Bulmer v. Bollinger, [1974] 2 All E.R. 1226. But the Constitutional Court of the Federal Republic of Germany has held that Orders of the European Community are not enforceable if they violate individual rights under the German Constitution. Bundesgerschtshof, Order of 18 Oct. 1967, B. VerG.E. 223 (1967). See also the discussion of the Italian Corte Constituzionale, Judgement of 27 Dec. 1973, n. 183, in Giureisprudenza Constitutionale. Compare the U.S. jurisprudence, pp. 163–67 infra.

4. Under Article 25 of the German Constitution, quoted by Wildhaber & Breitenmoser, treaty provisions would take precedence over domestic law only to the extent that they embody "general rules of international law." Contrast the Netherlands Constitution:

> Article 94. Statutory regulations in force within the Kingdom shall not be applicable if such application is in conflict with provisions of treaties that are binding on all persons or of resolutions by international institutions.

XI Blaustein & Flanz, Constitutions of the Countries of the World, Netherlands 23–24 (1990). Compare those distinctions between customary international law and international agreements with United States jurisprudence. See pp. 167–71 infra.

5. In most countries municipal courts will give effect to customary international law in appropriate cases unless there is controlling municipal law. See, e.g., Masters, International Law in National Courts (1932); Erades & Gould, The Relation Between International Law and Municipal Law in the Netherlands and in the United States (1961). For Italy, see De Meeus v. Forzano, [1940] Foro Ital. I 336, [1938–40] Ann.Dig. 423 (Corte di Cassazione, United Sections, 1940). The situation in the Soviet Union was not clear. See Ginsburgs, The Validity of Treaties in the Municipal Law of the "Socialist" States, 59 A.J.I.L. 523 (1965), and sources there cited. See also International Law 49–62 (Tunkin & Mullerson, eds. 1990). International agreements are sometimes treated differently, as Wildhaber and Breitenmoser indicate.

6. See in general, 1 Oppenheim's International Law 52–86 (5th ed., Jennings & Watts, eds. 1992); Brownlie, Principles of Public International Law 50–55 (4th ed. 1990); Starke, An Introduction to International Law 71–95 (10th ed. 1989); International Law and Municipal Law (Tunkin & Wolfrum, eds. 1988); The Effect of Treaties in Domestic Law (Jacobs & Roberts, eds. 1987); Kelsen, Principles of International Law 551 (2nd ed., Tucker, ed. 1966); Jessup, Transnational Law (1956); Churchill & Foster, European Community Law and Prior Treaty Obligations of Member States: The Spanish Fisherman's Cases, 36 I.C.L.Q. 504 (1987); Ferrari–Bravo, International Law and Municipal Law: The Complementarity of Legal Systems, in The Structure and Process of International Law: Essays in Legal Philosophy Doctrine and Theory 715 (Macdonald & Johnston, eds. 1983); Cassese, Modern Constitutions and International Law, 192

Rec. des Cours 331 (1985–III); Sasse, The Common Market: Between International and Municipal Law, 75 Yale L.J. 695 (1966); Ginsburgs, The Validity of Treaties in the Municipal Law of the "Socialist" States, 59 A.J.I.L. 523 (1965). See also Rights, Institutions and Impact of International Law According to the German Basic Law (Starck, ed. 1987); du Droit International au Droit de L'integration (Capotorti, et al., eds. 1987); La Pergola & Del Duca, Community Law, International Law and the Italian Constitution, 79 A.J.I.L. 598 (1985).

## B. INTERNATIONAL LAW IN THE LAW OF THE UNITED STATES

### 1. *Reception of International Law Into United States Law*

#### *HENKIN, INTERNATIONAL LAW AS LAW IN THE UNITED STATES*

82 Mich.L.Rev. 1555 (1984).*

"International law is part of our law." Justice Gray's much-quoted pronouncement in *The Paquete Habana* was neither new nor controversial when made in 1900, since he was merely restating what had been established principle for the fathers of American jurisprudence and for their British legal ancestors. And Gray's dictum remains unquestioned today. But, after more than two hundred years in our jurisprudence, the import of that principle is still uncertain and disputed. How did, and how does, international law become part of our law?

* * *

*When* international law—"the law of nations"—first became part of our law can be readily stated: *how* it became our Law has been a conceptual issue not without jurisprudential implications. That it is part of federal, not state, law has been recognized only recently.

International law became part of "our law" with independence in 1776. One view has it that the law of nations came into our law as part of the common law. In the eighteenth century, the law of nations was part of the law of England, and English law, including the law of nations, applied in her colonies. With American independence, the law of England in the colonies (including the law of nations) was "received" as common law in the United States.

A different conception sees the law of nations as coming into our law not by "inheritance" but by implication from our independence, by virtue of international statehood. An entity that becomes a State in the international system is *ipso facto* subject to international law. While the obligations of international law are upon the State as an entity, a State ordinarily finds it necessary or convenient to incorporate international law into its municipal law to be applied by its courts. In the United States, neither state constitutions nor the federal Constitution, nor state or federal legislation, have expressly incorporated international law; from our beginnings, however, following the English tradition, courts have treated international law as incorporated and applied it as domestic law.

* Reprinted with the permission of University of Michigan Law Review. Footnotes omitted.

The two conceptions, and variations upon them, may bear different consequences. If international law was part of the common law that each state received from England, international law was state law. It would cease to be state law and become federal law only if the U.S. Constitution, or an act of Congress pursuant to the Constitution, so provided. On the other hand, if international law became domestic law by virtue of independence, its status as state or federal law may turn on the international character of our independence and the status of the states between 1776 and 1789. Some have insisted that during those years the states were thirteen independent states (in the international sense), each equal in status to England, France and other nations of the time, each subject to international law. Each state decided for itself whether to incorporate international law, but all of them did so, in the tradition inherited from England. On this view, as on the "common law" view, international law was state law between 1776 and 1789 and remained state law unless the federal Constitution or later federal law pursuant to the Constitution rendered it federal law.

A different view, however, concludes that the thirteen states were never independent States; that for international purposes we were from independence one nation, not thirteen. By virtue of independence and statehood, international law became binding on the United States, not on the individual states. Between 1776 and 1789, there being no national domestic law, international law could not be incorporated into national law, but the national obligations of the United States could be carried out through state law and institutions. In 1789, the obligations of the United States to give effect to international law became effectively the responsibility of the new federal government, to be carried out through federal institutions (including federal courts), through state institutions (including state courts), or both.

Between 1776 and 1789, then, international law was the law of each of the thirteen states, either as state common law, or by incorporation pursuant to the state's international obligations or those of the United States. Whatever the basis, the status of international law as state law could have been changed, or confirmed, in 1789 when the states united into "a more perfect union"—but the new Constitution did not expressly address the matter. The Constitution recognized that the United States was subject to the law of nations and gave Congress the power to define offenses against the law of nations. The judicial power of the United States was extended to cases arising under treaties, cases affecting ambassadors, cases within admiralty or maritime jurisdiction, and controversies to which foreign states or citizens are party.

But neither the constitutional grants to Congress and the federal courts, nor any act of Congress, declared or necessarily implied that the law of nations was incorporated as self-executing domestic law, or that it had the status of law of the United States rather than of the states. Nevertheless, from our national beginnings both state and federal courts have treated customary international law as incorporated and have applied it to cases before them without express constitutional or legislative sanction.

## THE INTERPLAY OF U.S. AND INTERNATIONAL LAW
## *RESTATEMENT (THIRD) PART I, CHAPTER 2, INTRODUCTORY NOTE*

International law and the domestic law of the United States are two different and discrete bodies of law, but often they impinge on the same conduct, relations, and interests. The relation between international law and United States law raises complex conceptual issues that have important legal consequences.

The obligations of the United States under international law do not rest on the international plane alone: International law is, and is given effect as, law in the United States. But, like the strictly domestic law of the United States, international law as law of the United States is subject to the Constitution, and is also subject to "repeal" by other law of the United States. See § 111, Comment *a,* and § 115. When international law is not given effect in the United States because of constitutional limitations or supervening domestic law, the international obligations of the United States remain and the United States may be in default. See § 115, Comment *b.*

*International law as United States law.* International law was part of the law of England and, as such, of the American colonies. With independence, it became part of the law of each of the thirteen States. When the United States became a state it became subject to international law. See § 206. From the beginning, the law of nations, later referred to as international law, was considered to be incorporated into the law of the United States without the need for any action by Congress or the President, and the courts, State and federal, have applied it and given it effect as the courts of England had done. Customary international law as developed to that time was law of the United States when it became a state. Customary law that has developed since the United States became a state is incorporated into United States law as of the time it matures into international law. Under the Supremacy Clause, self-executing treaties concluded by the United States become law of the United States as of the time they come into force for the United States. See § 111(3) and § 115, Comment *c.* As to non-self-executing treaties, see § 111(4) and Comment *h* to that section.

The Constitution declares treaties of the United States (as well as the Constitution itself and the laws of the United States) to be "the supreme Law of the Land" (Article VI), and provides that cases arising under treaties are within the Judicial Power of the United States (Article III, Section 2). The status of other international agreements and of customary international law is not clearly indicated. During the reign of Swift v. Tyson, 41 U.S. (16 Pet.) 1, 10 L.Ed. 865 (1842), State and federal courts respectively determined international law for themselves as they did common law, and questions of international law could be determined differently by the courts of various States and by the federal courts. From the beginning, the interpretation or application of United States treaties by State courts was subject to review by the Supreme Court of the United States under Section 25 of the Judiciary Act of 1789, but the Court originally thought that it could not review State court determinations or applications of customary international law. See § 111, Reporters' Note 3. Similarly, after Congress gave the inferior federal courts "federal question" jurisdiction (Section 1 of the Judiciary Act of 1875, 18 Stat. 470), issues arising under customary international law, unlike those arising under treaties, apparently were not considered federal questions, and therefore did not provide a basis for such jurisdiction. Claims based on customary international law in State courts (unlike those based on treaties) did not provide a basis for removal to the federal courts.

Erie R.R. Co. v. Tompkins, 304 U.S. 64, 58 S.Ct. 817, 82 L.Ed. 1188 (1938), held that, in suits based on diversity of citizenship jurisdiction, a federal court was bound to apply the common law as determined by the courts of the State in which the federal court sat. On that basis, some thought that the federal courts must also follow State court determinations of customary international law. However, a different view has prevailed. It is now established that customary international law in the United States is a kind of federal law, and like treaties and other international agreements, it is accorded supremacy over State law by Article VI of the Constitution. Hence, determinations of international law by the Supreme Court of the United States, like its interpretations of international agreements, are binding on the States. See § 111, Comment *d*, § 112(2) and Comment *a* to that section, § 326, Comment *d*. Also, cases "arising under" customary international law arise under "the laws" of the United States. They are within the Judicial Power of the United States (Article III, Section 2) and the jurisdiction of the federal courts (28 U.S.C. §§ 1257, 1331). See § 111(2) and Comment *e* to that section. See, generally, Henkin, "International Law as Law in the United States," 82 Mich.L.Rev. 1555 (1984).

### 2. *International Law as "Law of the Land"*

## THE LAW OF NATIONS AS UNITED STATES LAW

### *MEEKER, THE LAW OF NATIONS IN THE NATIONAL GOVERNMENT*

1 Whiteman 106.

In looking at the function and place of the law of nations in the national government, we are bound to begin asking how, and in what ways, the United States becomes concerned with the body of international law. * * * The Constitutional provision is familiar which gives Congress the power "To define and punish * * * Offenses against the Law of Nations;". (Art. I, sec. 8, cl. 10).

Before the Constitution, it is interesting to note, the Chief Justice of Pennsylvania stated, in Respublica v. de Longchamps, that that case was "one of the first impression in the United States. It must be determined on the principles of the laws of nations, which form a part of the municipal law of Pennsylvania;". 1 Dall. 120, 123 (Pa. Oyer and Terminer, 1784). Interestingly enough, the case was a criminal prosecution for a non-statutory and uncodified offense against international law: assault upon the representative of a foreign country, France. The defendant was convicted, and sentenced to a fine, two years' imprisonment, and the posting of heavy bond for seven years to secure good behavior. The Chief Justice repeated his statement on international law, saying:

> "The first crime in the indictment is an infraction of the law of nations. This law, in its full extent, is a part of the law of this state,

and is to be collected from the practice of different nations, and the authority of writers."

The Constitutional provision mentioned earlier may have brought to an end the common law of crimes against the law of nations in this country, but for purposes of civil suit the rules of international law continued applicable. The United States Supreme Court in 1815 decided in favor of private claims in a prize case by reason of the law of nations. The Nereide, 9 Cr. 388 (U.S. 1815). In the Court's opinion, Chief Justice Marshall said that in the absence of an act of Congress "the Court is bound by the law of nations which is a part of the law of the land."

### *Notes*

1. The United States Constitution, Article VI, provides that U.S. treaties "shall be the supreme Law of the Land." See p. 198 infra. The only reference to international law generally is that in Article I, section 8 giving Congress power to "define and punish * * * Offences against the Law of Nations." Nonetheless, in the often-quoted language of The Paquete Habana, 175 U.S. 677, 700, 20 S.Ct. 290, 299, 44 L.Ed. 320, 328–29 (1900) (p. 58 supra): "International law is part of our law, and must be ascertained and administered by the courts of justice of appropriate jurisdiction as often as questions of right depending upon it are duly presented for their determination." American courts frequently apply customary international law.

2. On the "define and punish clause" of the U.S. Constitution, Note 1, Henkin writes:

> The law of nations and the rule of law at sea loomed large in the minds of the Constitutional Framers, hence the explicit grant to Congress of the power to define and punish piracies, felonies on the high seas and offenses against the law of nations. Congress has made it a federal crime to commit piracy as defined by international law and has prescribed punishment for offenses committed at sea, as on American vessels, and more recently in the air, as on American airplanes.
>
> The power to define and punish offenses against the law of nations has been little used and its purport is not wholly clear. Since, in general, traditional international law imposes duties only upon states, not upon individuals, it is not obvious how an individual can commit an offense against the law of nations. Presumably the clause would permit punishment of officials for acts or omissions that constitute violations of international law by the United States, e.g., when they deny fundamental "justice" to an alien, arrest a diplomat, violate an embassy, or fail to carry out a treaty obligation. The clause would also authorize Congress to enact into national law any international rules designed to govern individual behavior, for example, the laws of war relating to the treatment of prisoners-of-war. If international law or a treaty of the United States applied directly to individuals, as perhaps happened in the Nuremberg Charter, as might happen some future day pursuant to the Genocide Convention or to human rights covenants, Congress could implement that law by providing for punishment under this clause, though it could also do so amply under other powers * * *.
>
> But Congress apparently, and the Supreme Court explicitly, gave the clause a broader meaning. In upholding a statute that made it a crime to counterfeit foreign currency, the Supreme Court said:

> "* * * A right secured by the law of nations to a nation, or its people, is one the United States as the representatives of this nation are bound to protect. Consequently, a law which is necessary and proper to afford this protection is one that Congress may enact, because it is one that is needed to carry into execution a power conferred by the Constitution on the Government of the United States exclusively. * * *
>
> "* * * This statute defines the offence, and if the thing made punishable is one which the United States are required by their international obligations to use due diligence to prevent, it is an offence against the law of nations." [United States v. Arjona, 120 U.S. 479, 487–88, 7 S.Ct. 628, 30 L.Ed. 728 (1887)]

> It is perhaps under such an interpretation of the Offences clause that Congress long ago made it a crime to harass diplomats, to impersonate them, to damage the property of foreign governments, or to initiate activities directed against the peace and security of foreign nations. That power, then, would enable Congress also to enforce by criminal penalties any new international law or obligation the United States might accept, say that American companies shall abide by a new international regime for the sea.

Foreign Affairs and the Constitution at 72–74 (footnotes omitted).

3. It has been suggested that the power of Congress to define offenses against the law of nations authorizes Congress to provide remedies in tort for such offenses instead of, or in addition to, criminal penalties. For the suggestion that Congress could legislate to that effect under its powers deriving from the sovereignty of the United States, see Henkin, The Treaty Makers and the Law Makers: The Law of the Land and Foreign Relations, 107 U.Pa.L.Rev. 903, 919–20 (1959). Cf. United States v. Curtiss-Wright Export Corp., 299 U.S. 304, 57 S.Ct. 216, 81 L.Ed. 255 (1936).

In 1791 Congress gave to U.S. district courts "original jurisdiction of any civil action by an alien for a tort only, committed in violation of the law of nations or a treaty of the United States." See 28 U.S.C.A. § 1350. There has been disagreement as to whether that statute a) provided a domestic, federal forum for suits where international law itself establishes a tort with a private right of recovery; b) created a federal tort and provided a federal forum for an action that constitutes a violation of international law even though international law does not itself create the tort and the private right; or c) created a federal forum for adjudication of such claims under the law of torts (common law or statutory) of the State in which the federal court sits. Compare Filartiga v. Pena-Irala, 630 F.2d 876 (2d Cir.1980), with Tel-Oren v. Libyan Arab Republic, 726 F.2d 774 (D.C.Cir.1984), cert. denied, 470 U.S. 1003, 105 S.Ct. 1354, 84 L.Ed.2d 377 (1985). Filartiga was accepted as more persuasive in Forti v. Suarez-Mason, 672 F.Supp. 1531 (N.D.Cal.1987), reconsideration granted in part, 694 F.Supp. 707 (1988). All three cases were cited to the Supreme Court in Argentine Republic v. Amerada Hess Shipping Corp., 488 U.S. 428, 109 S.Ct. 683, 102 L.Ed.2d 818 (1989), but the Court did not address the purport or proper construction of the Alien Tort Statute. See Chapter 8 infra.

4. Citing Kansas v. Colorado, 185 U.S. 125, 146, 22 S.Ct. 552, 560, 46 L.Ed. 838, 846 (1901), two states have recognized that "international law controls the states of the United States in their relations one with the other except as modified by the federal constitution." Sinclair Pipe Line Co. v. State Com'n of Revenue and Tax, 184 Kan. 713, 718, 339 P.2d 341, 346 (1959) (looking to international law to determine the tax status of a Delaware corporation doing

business in Kansas); State v. Miller, 157 Ariz. 129, 755 P.2d 434 (App.1988) (applying international law to determine jurisdiction over extraterritorial conduct in Colorado and Nevada).

5. On the proposition that international law is the law of the land in the United States, see Henkin, International Law as Law in the United States, 82 Mich.L.Rev. 1555 (1984). See also Maier, Preemption of State Law: A Recommended Analysis, 83 A.J.I.L. 832 (1989). For earlier writings, see Jessup, The Uses of International Law (1959); Dickinson, The Law of Nations as Part of the National Law of the United States, 101 U.Pa.L.Rev. 26 (1952); Sprout, Theories as to the Applicability of International Law in the Federal Courts of the United States, 26 A.J.I.L. 280 (1932).

### *a. International Law as Federal "Common Law"*

## CUSTOMARY INTERNATIONAL LAW IN THE UNITED STATES

### *HENKIN, THE CONSTITUTION AND UNITED STATES SOVEREIGNTY: A CENTURY OF CHINESE EXCLUSION AND ITS PROGENY*

100 Harv.L.Rev. 853, 867–78 (1987) (footnotes omitted).*

The Constitution * * * explicitly addresses the place of treaties in our jurisprudence. It says little, however, about customary international law. It does not declare expressly whether, and if so how, customary international law is part of our law; it says nothing about how such law relates to the Constitution and to our political institutions; whether customary international law is federal or state law; whether it is supreme over state law; or whether the federal courts have jurisdiction over cases or controversies arising under international law. The Constitution expressly establishes neither the relation of treaties and customary law to each other nor that of either to the Constitution or to laws enacted by Congress. It provides no explicit direction to the courts as to what law should govern a case involving an act of Congress or an action of the President that is inconsistent with a provision in a treaty or with a principle of international law. Nor does it expressly declare that the President is obligated to respect treaties or customary law and to take care that they be faithfully executed.

* * *

The [Supreme] Court has yet to declare that the Constitution is * * * supreme over the law of nations and principles of customary law. Arguably, the fact that treaties are subject to constitutional limitations does not conclude the issue with respect to customary law. Customary law is general law binding on all nations, and no country should be able to derogate from it because of that country's particular constitutional dispositions. The law of nations antedated the Constitution, and the framers evinced no disposition to subordinate that law to the new Constitution. Nevertheless, it is unlikely that the Court would subordinate the Constitution to the law of nations and give effect to a principle of international law without regard to constitutional constraints. The Court's jurisprudence about treaties inevitably reflects assumptions about the relation between international and United States law and, at least by implication, places the United States outside the strict monist camp. Thus we can assume that, like treaties, customary international law is inferior to the United States Constitution in the hierarchy of our domestic law.

* * *

* * * During the Spanish American War, the United States Navy seized fishing vessels belonging to private Spanish citizens and condemned them as prize of war. In *The Paquete Habana,* the owners of those vessels challenged the seizure and sought recovery of the ships, asserting that under international law private fishing vessels, even if belonging to enemy aliens, were not subject to seizure as war prize. The Supreme Court examined the state of international law, found that it indeed exempted such fishing vessels from seizure, and ordered that the proceeds of the sale of these vessels be paid to the original owners.

In supporting its conclusion, the Court made two oft-quoted statements:

> International law is part of our law, and must be ascertained and administered by the courts of justice of appropriate jurisdiction as often as questions of right depending upon it are duly presented for their determination. For this purpose, where there is no treaty and no controlling executive or legislative act or judicial decision, resort must be had to the customs and usages of civilized nations * * *.

And a few pages later:

> This rule of international law is one which prize courts administering the law of nations are bound to take judicial notice of, and to give effect to, in the absence of any treaty or other public act of their own government in relation to the matter.

The statement that international law is law of the land was essential to support the judgment. The qualifying clause "where there is no treaty and no controlling executive or legislative act or judicial decision" was dictum: neither party in the case claimed that there was any relevant treaty, any "controlling executive or legislative act or judicial decision," or any "other public act of their own government" requiring a different result. In the eighty-seven years since *The Paquete Habana,* the Court repeatedly has emphasized that international law is the law of the land, and it has given effect to principles of customary international law as the law of the United States. * * *

* * *

Some * * * would construe the *The Paquete Habana* dictum as asserting that customary international law is not equal but rather is inferior to federal law. They argue that unlike treaties, which the Court has held to be equal to acts of Congress, customary international law is subject to "repeal" by subsequent acts of Congress; indeed, it cannot be given effect in the face of even an earlier act of Congress. For support, this view relies on repeated references in legal literature to customary law as "common law" which, it is argued, is inherently inferior to legislation.

I think that this argument is misconceived. * * *

* * *

Of course, customary international law resembles common law: both are United States law that has not been enacted by Congress, and neither appears in a formal act or instrument. And when relevant to a judicial proceeding, international law is determined by the court, not by construction of an authoritative text. For the purposes that are relevant here, however, international law differs from the common law in important respects. First, international law is the law of an international political system, not solely of the United States. Although courts in the United States sometimes apply international law to decide domestic cases, the principal applications of that law are in the international arena. Second, however one views the role of the courts in relation to the common law, courts do not *create* but rather find international law, generally by examining the practices and attitudes of foreign states. Even the practices and attitudes of the United States that contribute to international law do not emanate from and respond to life in this society, as does the common law. Rather, they are external, relating to other nations, to persons, things, acts, and events outside the United States.

Above all, the reasons that the common law bows to legislation are inapplicable to international law. Common law is "inferior" to legislation because, under prevailing theories of government—parliamentary supremacy in England, republican democratic principles here—the legislature is the principal lawmaking body; the courts, if they are to make law at all, do so only temporarily and interstitially. But when courts determine international law, they do not act as surrogates for the national legislature. Indeed, the legislature's role in determining international law is marginal, whereas determining international law, for purposes of adjudication in a decentralized, international system, is inherently the role of domestic courts.

* * * In fact, one could advance persuasive arguments that customary international law supersedes any United States law and should be given effect even when it conflicts with a subsequent act of Congress. The law of nations, including both treaties and customary international law, is binding on the United States. The framers of the Constitution respected the law of nations, and it is plausible that they expected the political branches as well as the courts to give effect to that law. Other countries have accepted the supremacy of international law: their courts give effect to international law over domestic legislation. Our legal system subordinates treaties to subsequent congressional acts, because the Court has determined that the supremacy clause imposes that hierarchy. But no similar textual basis exists for subordinating customary international law. Customary international law is universal and lasting and has better claim to supremacy than do treaties, which govern only the parties and can be readily terminated or replaced by those parties.

Despite these arguments, it is unlikely that the Supreme Court will now distinguish customary international law from treaties and declare the former supreme over federal statutory law. I see no basis, however—either in principle, in text, in history, or in contemporary practice—for interpreting *The Paquete Habana* dictum as meaning that customary international law has a status lower than that of treaties. Both treaties and customary law are law of the United States because they constitute binding international obligations of the United States. Like treaties, customary law has now been declared to be United States law within the meaning of both article III and the supremacy clause. If an act of Congress can modify customary law for domestic purposes, it is not because customary law is like federal common law but rather because, like treaties, customary law is equal in status to legislation, and the more recent of the two governs.

### *Notes*

1. Professor Henkin also writes:

> To some extent, the view that customary international law is inferior to treaties and to acts of Congress relies on the differences in their creation. Treaties are made by the President-and-Senate, but the Senate has no role in making customary law. There is reluctance to give status as law to practices of a single individual, the President, in which Congress did not have any part. But law is made by the President alone when he makes an executive agreement under his constitutional authority. In any event, our jurisprudence from the beginning accepted customary law as law although it had been "legislated" before there was a Congress or a President, content to rely on the authority and the safeguards of the complex multinational process by which such law is made.
>
> Much is made also of the fact that, unlike treaties, customary law is not mentioned expressly in the Supremacy Clause or in the constitutional listing of U.S. law in article III. I do not consider that omission significant for our purposes. The Supremacy Clause was addressed to the states, and was designed to assure federal supremacy. The federal law whose binding quality was mentioned in the Supremacy Clause included the Constitution and the laws and treaties made under the authority of the United States—acts taken under the authority of the new United States Government, authority which had to be impressed on the states and on state courts. The law of nations of the time was not seen as something imposed on the states by the new U.S. government; it had been binding on and accepted by the states before the U.S. government was even established. It was "supreme" over federal as well as state laws, and binding on federal as well as state courts. There was no fear that the states would flout it, and therefore no need to stress its supremacy.

Henkin, International Law as Law in the United States, 82 Mich.L.Rev. 1555, 1565–66 (1984) (footnotes omitted).

For a view that customary international law is inferior to federal statute, see Goldklang, Back on Board The Paquete Habana: Resolving the Conflict Between Statutes and Customary International Law, 25 Va.J.Int'l L. 143 (1984). Compare Trimble, A Revisionist View of Customary International Law, 33 U.C.L.A.L.Rev. 665 (1986). The Circuit Court of Appeals for the District of Columbia has held that later statutes supersede customary international law. See Committee of U.S. Citizens Living in Nicaragua v. Reagan, 859 F.2d 929, 939 (D.C.Cir.1988); United States v. Yunis, 924 F.2d 1086, 1091 (D.C.Cir.1991). There has been no judicial discussion of whether a new rule of customary international law supersedes an earlier federal statute.

For the view that some international law cannot be superseded by an act of Congress, see Paust, Rediscovering the Relationship Between Congressional Power and International Law: Exceptions to the Last in Time Rule and the Primacy of Custom, 28 Va.J.Int'l L. 393 (1988); Paust, Customary International Law: Its Nature, Sources and Status as Law of the United States, 12 Mich.J.Int'l L. 59 (1990).

2. Customary international law is treated in the United States as automatically "incorporated" from the time that the norm is deemed to have come into existence, without the need of any formal act of incorporation by Congress or the President. See Restatement (Third) § 111(3) and Part I, Chapter I, Introductory Note. Compare the distinction between "self-executing" and "non-self-executing" treaties, p. 212 below.

3. The Restatement (Third) § 115, Comment *d* states:

> *Conflict between successive international agreements or principles of customary law.* In principle, a treaty of the United States or a Congressional-Executive agreement would supersede any prior international agreement or pre-existing rule of customary law as the law of the United States. Similarly, a later principle of customary law would supersede an earlier one. However, there have apparently been no judicial decisions to that effect. A sole executive agreement that is within the President's constitutional authority (§ 303(4)) would supersede a prior sole executive agreement and probably a pre-existing rule of customary law as United States law. Whether it would supersede an earlier treaty or Congressional–Executive agreement is uncertain. It has also not been authoritatively determined whether a rule of customary international law that developed after, and is inconsistent with, an earlier statute or international agreement of the United States should be given effect as the law of the United States. In regard to the law of the sea, the United States has accepted customary law that modifies earlier treaties as well as United States statutes. See Introductory Note to Part V. Compare § 102, Comment *j*.

Compare Restatement (Third) § 102, Comment *j*. For a discussion of executive agreements, see p. 230 below.

### *b. Judicial Application of International Law*

## INTERNATIONAL LAW AND AGREEMENTS AS LAW OF THE UNITED STATES

### *RESTATEMENT (THIRD) § 111*

(1) International law and international agreements of the United States are law of the United States and supreme over the law of the several States.

(2) Cases arising under international law or international agreements of the United States are within the Judicial Power of the United States and, subject to Constitutional and statutory limitations and requirements of justiciability, are within the jurisdiction of the federal courts.

(3) Courts in the United States are bound to give effect to international law and to international agreements of the United States, except that a "non-self-executing" agreement will not be given effect as law in the absence of necessary implementation.

* * *

## DETERMINATION OF INTERNATIONAL LAW

### *RESTATEMENT (THIRD) § 112*

* * *

(2) The determination and interpretation of international law present federal questions and their disposition by the United States Supreme Court is conclusive for other courts in the United States.

### *Notes*

1. Henkin writes: "Determination and application of international law are integral to the conduct of foreign relations and are the responsibility of the federal government. In the absence of federal statute, treaty, or authoritative Executive action, international law is determined, "made," by the federal courts as though it were federal law, and their views bind the state courts. Issues of international law that arise in the state courts, then, are federal questions and can be appealed to the Supreme Court; and the Supreme Court can determine and establish a single, uniform rule of customary international law for state as well as federal courts." Foreign Affairs and the Constitution 223 (1972).

2. The Restatement (Third) accepts as established several principles that in the past had been uncertain or debated: that issues of customary law, like those arising under treaties, are matters of federal, not state, law; that matters arising under customary law "arise under the laws of the United States" for purposes of the jurisdiction of the federal courts, U.S. Constitution, Article II, and 28 U.S.C.A. § 1331, and are part of the "laws" of the United States which are supreme to State law under Article VI, clause 2 of the Constitution. See § 111, Comments *c, d* and *e* and Reporters' Notes 2–4.

The Restatement (Third) indicates that "customary international law is considered to be like common law in the United States, but it is federal law." § 111, Comment *d*. Compare Henkin's view, p. 169 supra.

In Bergman v. De Sieyes, 170 F.2d 360 (2d Cir.1948), removed to the federal district court from the New York state courts on the ground of diversity of citizenship, the defendant pleaded diplomatic immunity and the complaint was dismissed. In affirming, Judge Learned Hand said: "[S]ince the defendant was served while the cause was in the state court, the law of New York determines [the service's] validity, and, although the courts of that state look to international law as a source of New York law, their interpretation of international law is controlling upon us, and we are to follow them so far as they have declared themselves. Whether an avowed refusal to accept a well-established doctrine of international law, or a plain misapprehension of it, would present a federal question we need not consider, for neither is present here." Id. at 361. Judge Hand apparently thought he was following the dictates of Erie R. Co. v. Tompkins, 304 U.S. 64, 58 S.Ct. 817, 82 L.Ed. 1188 (1938), requiring a federal court in a diversity case to follow New York law as determined by New York courts.

However, in Banco Nacional de Cuba v. Sabbatino, 376 U.S. 398, 83 S.Ct. 923, 11 L.Ed.2d 804 (1964), the Supreme Court said:

> We could perhaps in this diversity action avoid the question of deciding whether federal or state law is applicable to this aspect of the litigation. * * * Thus our conclusions might well be the same whether we dealt with this problem as one of state law * * * or federal law.

> However, we are constrained to make clear that an issue concerned with a basic choice regarding the competence and function of the Judiciary and the National Executive in ordering our relationships with other members of the international community must be treated exclusively as an aspect of federal law. It seems fair to assume that the Court did not have rules like the act of state doctrine in mind when it decided Erie R. Co. v. Tompkins. Soon thereafter, Professor Philip C. Jessup, now a judge of the International Court of Justice, recognized the potential dangers were Erie extended to legal problems affecting international relations. He cautioned that rules of international law should not be left to divergent and perhaps parochial state interpretations. His basic rationale is equally applicable to the act of state doctrine.

Id. at 424–25, 83 S.Ct. 938–39, 11 L.Ed.2d at 821–22.

Consider Judge Friendly's view that "by leaving to the states what ought to be left to them, *Erie* led to the emergence of a federal decisional law in areas of national concern that is truly uniform because, under the supremacy clause, it is binding in every forum * * *. The clarion yet careful pronouncement of *Erie* 'there is no federal common law,' opened the way to what, for want of a better term, we may call a specialized federal common law." Friendly, In Praise of Erie—and of the New Federal Common Law, 39 N.Y.U.L.Rev. 381, 405 (1964). See Restatement (Third), Part I, Chapter 2, Introductory Note. See generally Hill, The Law–Making Power of the Federal Courts: Constitutional Preemption, 67 Colum.L.Rev. 1024, 1042–81 (1967); Moore, Federalism and Foreign Relations, [1965] Duke L.J. 248; Henkin, The Foreign Affairs Power of the Federal Courts: Sabbatino, 64 Colum.L.Rev. 805 (1964); Jessup, The Doctrine of Erie R.R. v. Tompkins Applied to International Law, 33 A.J.I.L. 740 (1939).

3. The Restatement (Third) § 133, Comment *e* states:

> *Federal jurisdiction over cases "arising under" international law and agreements.* Cases arising under treaties to which the United States is a party, as well as cases arising under customary international law, or under international agreements of the United States other than treaties, are "Cases * * * arising under * * * the Laws of the United States, and Treaties made * * * under their Authority," and therefore within the Judicial Power of the United States under Article III, Section 2 of the Constitution. Civil actions arising under international law or under a treaty or other international agreement of the United States are within the jurisdiction of the United States district courts. 28 U.S.C. § 1331 (quoted in Reporters' Note 4). For the purpose of Section 1331, all valid international agreements of the United States, whatever their designation and whatever the form by which they are concluded (see § 303), are "treaties of the United States." Customary international law, like other federal law, is part of the "laws * * * of the United States."
>
> The jurisprudence implied in the phrase "arising under" is extensive and complex. (See generally Hart and Wechsler, The Federal Courts and the Federal System, Comment *d,* Chapter 7.) Some of its implications are clear. An action arises under an international agreement of the United States, or under customary international law as part of the law of the United States, if the plaintiff's complaint properly asserts a justiciable claim based upon such international law or agreement. An action does not arise under international law or agreement if the rule of international law or the provision of the agreement enters the case only by way of defense. Louis-

ville & Nashville R.R. Co. v. Mottley, 211 U.S. 149, 29 S.Ct. 42, 53 L.Ed. 126 (1908); Wright, Miller and Cooper, Federal Practice and Procedure: Jurisdiction § 3566 (2d ed. 1984). In the latter situation, a federal court does not have jurisdiction under 28 U.S.C. § 1331; it might have jurisdiction if the action arises under some other law of the United States, for example, the Foreign Sovereign Immunities Act. See § 457, Reporters' Note 5.

4. In Zschernig v. Miller, 389 U.S. 429, 88 S.Ct. 664, 19 L.Ed.2d 683 (1968), the Supreme Court invalidated an Oregon statute which had been applied by the state courts to deny an inheritance to the heir of an Oregon resident, living in East Germany. The statute provided that non-resident aliens could inherit only if (a) there was a reciprocal right for a United States citizen to take property in the foreign country; (b) American citizens in the United States could receive payment from an estate in the foreign country and (c) foreign heirs would receive the proceeds of the Oregon estate "without confiscation." The Supreme Court held the Oregon statute invalid as "an intrusion by the State into the field of foreign affairs which the Constitution entrusts to the President and the Congress." The Court purported to distinguish Clark v. Allen, 331 U.S. 503, 67 S.Ct. 1431, 91 L.Ed. 1633 (1947).

In his opinion concurring in the result Justice Harlan expressed disagreement with the majority's view that the Oregon statute was unconstitutional, stating in part, 389 U.S. 429, 461, 88 S.Ct. 664, 681, 19 L.Ed.2d 683, 703–04:

> If the flaw in the statute is said to be that it requires state courts to inquire into the administration of foreign law, I would suggest that that characteristic is shared by other legal rules which I cannot believe the Court wishes to invalidate. For example, the Uniform Foreign Money–Judgments Recognition Act provides that a foreign-country money judgment shall not be recognized if "it was rendered under a system which does not provide impartial tribunals or procedures compatible with the requirements of due process of law." When there is a dispute as to the content of foreign law, the court is required under the common law to treat the question as one of fact and to consider any evidence presented as to the actual administration of the foreign legal system.

For discussion of this unique case, see Henkin, Foreign Affairs and the Constitution 61–63, 238–41 (1972). For cases that apparently did not consider the Zschernig principle applicable, see, e.g., Clark v. Allen, 331 U.S. 503, 67 S.Ct. 1431, 91 L.Ed. 1633 (1947); Gorun v. Fall, 393 U.S. 398, 89 S.Ct. 678, 21 L.Ed.2d 628 (1969); De Canas v. Bica, 424 U.S. 351, 96 S.Ct. 933, 47 L.Ed.2d 43 (1976).

Despite the broad language in *Zschernig,* state and local regulation often affects foreign states, persons and property; for example, state and local measures directed against investment in South Africa, were upheld in Board of Trustees of Employees' Retirement System of City of Baltimore v. Mayor and City Council of Baltimore City, 317 Md. 72, 562 A.2d 720 (1989), cert. denied sub nom., Lubman v. Mayor and City Council of Baltimore City, 493 U.S. 1093, 110 S.Ct. 1167, 107 L.Ed.2d 1069 (1990). But see, Springfield Rare Coin Galleries v. Johnson, 115 Ill.2d 221, 104 Ill.Dec. 743, 503 N.E.2d 300 (1986) (exclusion of South African coinage from tax exempt status "is an impermissible encroachment upon a national prerogative—the authority of the Federal government to conduct foreign affairs."). See generally Lewis, Dealing with South Africa: The Constitutionality of State and Local Divestment Legislation, 61 Tulane L.Rev. 469 (1987).

State and local "buy American" laws that mandate the purchase by public authorities of goods made in the United States have been upheld as having only an "incidental or indirect effect" on foreign relations. See, e.g., Trojan Technologies, Inc. v. Commonwealth of Pennsylvania, 916 F.2d 903, 913–14 (3d Cir.1990), cert. denied, ___ U.S. ___, 111 S.Ct. 2814, 115 L.Ed.2d 986 (1991).

Compare the established constitutional doctrine that the states may not burden commerce with foreign nations, and the cases holding particular state actions involving U.S. foreign affairs to have been preempted by federal action and therefore invalid under "the Supremacy Clause," Article VI, clause 2 of the Constitution. See, e.g., Hines v. Davidowitz, 312 U.S. 52, 61 S.Ct. 399, 85 L.Ed. 581 (1941). See generally Henkin, Foreign Affairs and the Constitution, Chapter IX (1972).

5. Henkin writes: "Like treaties, customary international law is law for the Executive and the courts to apply, but the Constitution does not forbid the President (or the Congress) to violate international law, and the courts will give effect to acts within the constitutional powers of the political branches without regard to international law. On the other hand, the courts have enforced international law against lower federal officials not directed by the President to disregard international law." Foreign Affairs and the Constitution at 221–22. Did Henkin's statement require additional qualification? The Restatement (Third) § 111, Comment *c* provides:

> That international law and agreements of the United States are law of the United States means also that the President has the obligation and the necessary authority to take care that they be faithfully executed. United States Constitution, Article II, Section 2. But under the President's Constitutional authority, as "sole organ of the nation in its external relations" or as Commander in Chief (§ 1, Reporters' Note 2), the President has the power to take various measures including some that might constitute violations of international law by the United States. * * *.

The Restatement (Third) § 115, Reporters' Note 3 explains:

> *President's power to supersede international law or agreement.* There is authority for the view that the President has the power, when acting within his constitutional authority, to disregard a rule of international law or an agreement of the United States, notwithstanding that international law and agreements are law of the United States and that it is the President's duty under the Constitution to "take care that the Laws be faithfully executed." Article II, Section 3. Compare the authority of the President to terminate international agreements on behalf of the United States, § 339. That the courts will not compel the President to honor international law may be implied in Supreme Court statements that courts will give effect to international law "where there is no treaty, and no controlling executive or legislative act or judicial decision," and "in the absence of any treaty or other public act of their own government in relation to the matter." The Paquete Habana, 175 U.S. 677, 700, 708, 20 S.Ct. 290, 299, 302, 44 L.Ed. 320 (1900); compare Brown v. United States, 12 U.S. (8 Cranch) 110, 128, 3 L.Ed. 504 (1814). Tag v. Rogers, 267 F.2d 664 (D.C.Cir.1959), certiorari denied, 362 U.S. 904, 80 S.Ct. 615, 4 L.Ed.2d 555 (1960); and The Over the Top, 5 F.2d 838 (D.Conn.1925) are sometimes cited, but those cases addressed the power of Congress to act contrary to international law, not the powers of the President.

In 1986, in Garcia–Mir v. Meese, 788 F.2d 1446 (11th Cir.1986), certiorari denied, ___ U.S. ___, 107 S.Ct. 289, 93 L.Ed.2d 263 (1986), the court, relying on The Paquete Habana, gave effect to an action of the Attorney General authorizing detention of aliens although it accepted that such detention was in violation of international law. Citing this Reporters' Note (as it appeared in Tentative Draft No. 6 of this Restatement, § 135, Reporters' Note 3), the court concluded that "the power of the President to disregard international law in service of domestic needs is reaffirmed." However, the President may have power to act in disregard of international law "when acting within his constitutional authority," but the Court of Appeals failed to find any constitutional authority in the President to detain the aliens in question. See Henkin, "The Constitution and United States Sovereignty: A Century of *Chinese Exclusion* and its Progeny," 100 Harv. L.Rev. 853, 878–86 (1987).

Some courts may be disposed to treat a claim that the President was violating international law as raising a "political question" and not justiciable. See, e.g., United States v. Berrigan, 283 F.Supp. 336, 342 (D.Md.1968) affirmed, 417 F.2d 1009 (4th Cir.1969), certiorari denied, 397 U.S. 909, 90 S.Ct. 907, 25 L.Ed.2d 90 (1970). See § 1, Reporters' Note 4.

What are the sources and the scope of the President's independent constitutional authority? Are acts by the President under that authority the law of the land, equal in status and authority to acts of Congress? Could the President, acting under that authority, disregard an act of Congress or violate a treaty of the United States? Can such Presidential constitutional authority provide authority for executive officials other than the President that violate international law?

See generally the discussion in, The Authority of the United States Executive to Interpret, Articulate or Violate Customary International Law, 80 A.S.I.L. Proc. 297 (1986); Agora: May the President Violate Customary International Law, 80 A.J.I.L. 913 (1986); Agora: May the President Violate Customary International Law (Cont'd), 81 A.J.I.L. 371 (1987). See also, Lobel, The Limits of Constitutional Power: Conflicts Between Foreign Policy and International Law, 71 Va.L.Rev. 1071 (1985); Glennon, Raising the *Paquete Habana:* Is Violation of Customary International Law by the Executive Unconstitutional?, 80 Nw. U.L.Rev. 322 (1985); Leigh, Editorial Comment, Is the President Above Customary International Law?, 86 A.J.I.L. 757 (1992). See also Glennon, Constitutional Diplomacy 232–48 (1990).

Compare the presidential power to make sole executive agreements, p. 233 below.

In Garcia–Mir v. Meese, supra, the district court had found that the long detention of a large number of undocumented aliens from Cuba was arbitrary, and a violation of customary international law. See Chapter 8 below. The court held, however, that the decision of the Attorney General was a "controlling executive act" binding on the courts. (The phrase derives from the Supreme Court's opinion in *The Paquete Habana,* p. 58 above.) The Court of Appeals affirmed, and a petition for certiorari was denied, 479 U.S. 889, 107 S.Ct. 289, 93 L.Ed.2d 263 (1986).

If international law is the law of the land and it is the President's duty to "take care that the law be faithfully executed," (U.S. Constitution Article II, section 3), should the court refuse to give effect to international law because of a "controlling executive act"? What executive act is "controlling" for this purpose? See Henkin, International Law as Law in the United States, 82 Mich. L.Rev. 1555, 1567–69 (1984); 80 A.S.I.L. Proc. 297 (1986).

The continued detention in *Garcia–Mir* was held to be a violation of international law, though not remediable in the circumstances by the courts. Are other remedies available? In the early 1990s, courts in the United States had occasion to decide whether a federal court could exercise criminal jurisdiction over an accused who had been kidnapped from foreign territory by agents of the Drug Enforcement Agency. The Court of Appeals for the Ninth Circuit held that such abduction violated an extradition treaty with Mexico and consequently deprived the U.S. courts of jurisdiction. See United States v. Verdugo–Urquidez, 939 F.2d 1341 (9th Cir.1991), and United States v. Alvarez–Machain, 946 F.2d 1466 (9th Cir.1991). The U.S. Supreme Court reversed in Alvarez–Machain, ___ U.S. ___, 112 S.Ct. 2188, 119 L.Ed.2d 441 (1992), and vacated the judgment in Verdugo–Urquidez, ___ U.S. ___, 112 S.Ct. 2986, 120 L.Ed.2d 864 (1992). The majority of the Court found that the abduction did not violate the extradition treaty, and held that the manner in which the defendant had come before the trial court was immaterial, relying on Ker v. Illinois, 119 U.S. 436, 7 S.Ct. 225, 30 L.Ed. 421 (1886). On remand, the defendant argued that, the extradition treaty aside, the abduction nevertheless was a violation of international law and that *Ker,* therefore, did not control. See United States v. Alvarez–Machain, 971 F.2d 310 (9th Cir.1992). The Court of Appeals, however, ruled that the Supreme Court's decision and its reliance on *Ker* were controlling. For differing views on *Alvarez–Machain,* see Agora: International Kidnaping, 86 A.J.I.L. 736, 746 (1992); Henkin, Correspondence, 87 A.J.I.L. 100 (1993). See also Schneebaum, The Supreme Court Sanctions Transborder Kidnapping in *United States v. Alvarez–Machain:* Does International Law Still Matter?, 18 Brooklyn J.Int'l L. 303 (1992). For international reactions, see Extradition, 8 Int'l Enforcement L. Rept. 444–51 (1992). See also the compilation of documents by the Mexican Secretaria de Relaciones Exteriores, Limits to National Jurisdiction: Documents and Judicial Resolutions on the Alvarez Machain Case (1992). On the abduction of individuals under international law generally, see Mann, Reflections on the Prosecutions of Persons Abducted in Breach of International Law, in Further Studies in International Law, chap. 14 (1990). See also p. 610 below.

On November 17, 1992, twenty-one Latin American countries proposed that the United Nations General Assembly request from the International Court of Justice an advisory opinion regarding actions "involving the extraterritorial exercise of the coercive power of a state and the subsequent exercise of its criminal jurisdiction."

6. The Restatement (Third) § 112, Comment *c* states:

> *Weight given to views of Executive Branch.* Courts give particular weight to the position taken by the United States Government on questions of international law because it is deemed desirable that so far as possible the United States speak with one voice on such matters. Compare Baker v. Carr, 369 U.S. 186, 217, 82 S.Ct. 691, 710, 7 L.Ed.2d 663 (192), quoted in § 1, Reporters' Note 4. The views of the United States Government, moreover, are also state practice, creating or modifying international law. See § 102 and Comment *b* thereto. Even views expressed by the Executive Branch as a party before the court or as *amicus curiae* will be given substantial respect since the Executive Branch will have to answer to a foreign state for any alleged violation of international law resulting from the action of a court. The degree of respect or deference to Executive Branch views is described

variously—"particular weight," "substantial respect," "great weight"—but these various expressions are not used with precision and do not necessarily imply different degrees of deference. Compare the principle that courts will give "great weight" to interpretations by the Executive Branch of international agreements of the United States, § 326 and Reporters' Note 4 thereto.

See also Restatement (Third) § 112, Reporters' Note 1:

*Judicial and Executive determinations.* Since, in deciding cases, the Supreme Court is the final arbiter of United States law (Cooper v. Aaron, 358 U.S. 1, 17–19, 78 S.Ct. 1401, 1409–1410, 3 L.Ed.2d 5 (195[8]); United States v. Nixon, 418 U.S. 683, 703, 94 S.Ct. 3090, 3105, 41 L.Ed.2d 1039 (1974)), a determination or interpretation of international law by the Supreme Court would also bind the Executive Branch in a case to which the United States is a party for purposes of that case, and effectively for other purposes of domestic law. The President may, however, be free to take a different view of the law vis-á-vis other nations. See § 326.

7. The Restatement (Third) § 113, Comment *b* states:

*Judicial notice of international law.* The determination of international law or the interpretation of an agreement is a question of law for the court, not a question of fact for a jury. As was stated in The Paquete Habana, 175 U.S. 677, 708, 20 S.Ct. 290, 302, 44 L.Ed. 320 (1900):

> This rule of international law is one which prize courts, administering the law of nations, are bound to take judicial notice of, and to give effect to, in the absence of any treaty or other public act of their own government in relation to the matter.

State courts take judicial notice of federal law and will therefore take judicial notice of international law as law of the United States. Since it is a question of law, it need neither be pleaded nor proved. But see Comment *c*.

8. *Political Questions.* The Executive Branch has sometimes resisted the adjudication of issues involving international law (or the foreign affairs power of the President) on the ground that these issues are nonjusticiable political questions.

The political question doctrine was restated and guidelines for its application were laid down in Baker v. Carr, 369 U.S. 186, 211–12, 82 S.Ct. 691, 706–07, 7 L.Ed.2d 663, 682–83 (1962). The Court stated:

> There are sweeping statements to the effect that all questions touching foreign relations are political questions. Not only does resolution of such issues frequently turn on standards that defy judicial application, or involve the exercise of a discretion demonstratably committed to the executive or legislature; but many such questions uniquely demand single-voiced statements of the Government's views. Yet it is error to suppose that every case or controversy which touches foreign relations lies beyond judicial cognizance.

369 U.S. at 211. Many "foreign affairs" issues are decided by the courts, and since *Baker* no foreign affairs issue has been held to be non-justiciable by the Supreme Court. In 1986, the Supreme Court held that the judicial interpretation of a statute of the United States, even if it involves foreign relations, is not a political question that precludes justiciability. Japan Whaling Ass'n v. American Cetacean Soc'y, 478 U.S. 221, 106 S.Ct. 2860, 92 L.Ed.2d 166 (1986). In

Goldwater v. Carter, 444 U.S. 996, 100 S.Ct. 533, 62 L.Ed.2d 428 (1979), four justices thought the courts should not adjudicate an issue between the President and the Congress as to who has the authority to terminate treaties, but that was not the majority view.

In November 1990, following Iraq's invasion of Kuwait, a number of members of Congress sought to enjoin the President from initiating an armed attack against Iraq without a declaration of war or other explicit Congressional approval. Dellums v. Bush, 752 F.Supp. 1141 (D.D.C.1990). The Department of Justice, representing the President, opposed the injunction, maintaining, *inter alia,* that the complaint presented a nonjusticiable political question. The Justice Department argued "that by their very nature the determination whether certain types of military actions require a declaration of war is not justiciable, but depends instead upon delicate judgments" by the executive branch. Id. at 1145. Relying on Mitchell v. Laird, 488 F.2d 611, 614 (D.C.Cir.1973), the district court held that it had the power to make the legal determination of whether the nation's military actions constituted a "war" for the purposes of the "war clause." U.S. Const., Article I, § 8. But see Crockett v. Reagan, 558 F.Supp. 893 (D.D.C.1982), aff'd, 720 F.2d 1355 (D.C.Cir.1983), cert. denied, 467 U.S. 1251, 104 S.Ct. 3533, 82 L.Ed.2d 839 (1984); Greenham Women Against Cruise Missiles v. Reagan, 591 F.Supp. 1332 (S.D.N.Y.1984), aff'd, 755 F.2d 34 (2d Cir.1985); Sanchez-Espinoza v. Reagan, 770 F.2d 202 (D.C.Cir.1985), where the lower courts applied the political question doctrine or decided that in the circumstances equitable relief was inappropriate.

Compare United States v. Sisson, 294 F.Supp. 515 (D.Mass.1968), in which the defendant urged, as a defense to the charge of refusing induction in the armed forces of the United States, that U.S. operations in Vietnam violated international law. The court, Wyzanski, C.J., commented: "Because a domestic tribunal is incapable of eliciting the facts during a war, and because it is probably incapable of exercising a disinterested judgment which would command the confidence of sound judicial opinion, this court holds that the defendant has tendered an issue which involves a so-called political question not within the jurisdiction of this court." 294 F.Supp. at 517–18.

The courts have long refused to review some Presidential decisions (e.g., the determination of foreign political boundaries or the recognition of foreign governments) on the ground that they were political questions. Williams v. Suffolk Ins. Co., 38 U.S. (13 Pet.) 415, 420, 10 L.Ed. 226 (1839); Jones v. United States, 137 U.S. 202, 212 (1890). See also Occidental of Umm Al Qaywayn, Inc. v. A Certain Cargo of Petroleum, 577 F.2d 1196, 1201–05 (5th Cir.1978), cert. denied, 442 U.S. 928, 99 S.Ct. 2857, 61 L.Ed.2d 296 (1979); Antolok v. United States, 873 F.2d 369, 379–384 (1988). Henkin suggests that the courts did not say—or need not have said—that the issues were not justiciable, but rather that the decisions were within the President's Constitutional authority to make, and therefore should be given effect by the courts. See Henkin, Is There a "Political Question Doctrine?", 85 Yale L.J. 597 (1976).

On the political question doctrine generally, see Henkin, Foreign Affairs and the Constitution 208–16 (1972); Charney, Judicial Deference in Foreign Relations, 83 A.J.I.L. 805 (1989); Glennon, Foreign Affairs and the Political Question Doctrine, 83 A.J.I.L. 814 (1989); Horlick, Political Questions in International Trade: A Review of Section 301?, 10 Mich.J.Int'l L. 735 (1989); Champlin & Schwarz, Political Question Doctrine and Allocation of the Foreign Affairs Power, 13 Hofstra L.Rev. 215 (1985).

### *3. The Act of State Doctrine: Judicial Application of International Law to Acts of Foreign States*

That international law is part of the law of the United States means it will be given effect as United States law by the Executive Branch and by the courts. Generally, it means that international law will be applied to give effect to limitations that international law imposes upon the United States Government, as in *The Paquete Habana* and in innumerable cases recognizing sovereign or diplomatic immunity. See Note 1, p. 193 below. Compare the cases where the courts give effect to treaty obligations assumed by the United States, p. 212 below.

In a series of cases, the issue arose whether courts in the United States should consider the validity of acts of a foreign state under international law. The act of state doctrine developed in those cases is not a rule of international law, but a domestic rule established by the United States Supreme Court. It is a rule of judicial self-restraint, not unlike other prudential rules of judicial self-restraint. It may apply to foreign acts of state that raise no issues under international law. See pp. 193–95 below. The doctrine became a subject of controversy when it was applied to preclude scrutiny by United States courts of acts of foreign states alleged to be in violation of international law.

#### *HENKIN, INTERNATIONAL LAW: POLITICS, VALUES AND FUNCTIONS*

216 Rec. des Cours 101–102 (1989–IV) (footnotes omitted).

A spirit of dualism tends not only to promote independence from international law for the State's own legal system, but also to foster acquiescence in such independence for other States. States are reluctant to use their institutions, particularly their courts, to compel other States to comply with international law. Compare, for example, the Act of State doctrine, which flourishes notably—but not only—in the United States. In its common formulation the doctrine declares: "The courts of one country will not sit in judgment on the acts of the government of another done within its own territory." The Act of State doctrine emerged in the United States as an expression of respect for other States, but it has been applied to give effect even to an act of a foreign State that violates international law.

There is much to be said for respect by a State for the autonomy of another State within its own territory (except where human rights are implicated). The Act of State doctrine was doubtless inspired by judicial judgment that the resolution of a dispute involving a foreign State should be left to diplomacy rather than to public adversary adjudication in national courts. But as applied where the act of a foreign State is alleged to be in violation of international law, the doctrine is one additional concession to Statehood and State autonomy, one fewer weapon for inducing compliance with international law. The Act of State doctrine reminds us that behind each State are particular interests and parochial institutions. Every State can—should—do more about policing its own international obligations and maximizing the likelihood that they will be honoured; but can a State and

State institutions, even courts that strive to maintain independence and impartiality, be trusted to enforce international law against another State when (as often) the forum State's own interests or those of its nationals are at issue? Political bodies, ministries, diplomats cannot avoid the tensions of the *dédoublement fonctionnel,* an inevitable consequence of applying inter-State law in a State system without a comprehensive impartial, neutral judiciary. Is a national judiciary, dressed in the mantle of justice, more trustworthy than are political bodies? Even if a particular national judiciary is trustworthy, is it in fact trusted by other States?

## BANCO NACIONAL DE CUBA v. SABBATINO

Supreme Court of the United States, 1964.
376 U.S. 398, 84 S.Ct. 923, 11 L.Ed.2d 804.

[In retaliation for an American reduction in the import quota for Cuban sugar, the Cuban Government nationalized many companies in which Americans held interests, including Compañia Azucarera Vertientes—Camaguey de Cuba (CAV). Farr, Whitlock, an American commodities broker, had contracted to buy a shipload of CAV sugar. To obtain the now-nationalized sugar, Farr, Whitlock entered into a new agreement to buy the shipload from the Cuban Government, which assigned the bills of lading to its shipping agent, Banco Nacional. Farr, Whitlock gained possession of the shipping documents and negotiated them to its customers, but protected by CAV's promise of indemnification, Farr, Whitlock turned the proceeds over to CAV instead of Cuba. Banco Nacional sued Farr, Whitlock for conversion of the bills of lading and also sought to enjoin Sabbatino, the temporary receiver of CAV's New York assets, from disposing of the proceeds. Farr, Whitlock defended on the ground that title to the sugar never passed to Cuba because the expropriation violated international law.]

MR. JUSTICE HARLAN delivered the opinion of the Court.

* * *

* * * While acknowledging the continuing vitality of the act of state doctrine, the court [i.e., the District Court] believed it inapplicable when the questioned foreign act is in violation of international law. Proceeding on the basis that a taking invalid under international law does not convey good title, the District Court found the Cuban expropriation decree to violate such law in three separate respects: It was motivated by a retaliatory and not a public purpose; it discriminated against American nationals; and it failed to provide adequate compensation. Summary judgment against petitioner was accordingly granted.

The Court of Appeals, 307 F.2d 845, affirming the decision on similar grounds, relied on two letters (not before the District Court) written by State Department officers which it took as evidence that the Executive Branch had no objection to a judicial testing of the Cuban decree's validity. The court was unwilling to declare that any one of the infirmities found by the District Court rendered the taking invalid under international law, but was satisfied that in combination they had that effect. We granted certiorari because the issues involved bear importantly on the conduct of the country's foreign relations and more particularly on the proper role of the Judicial Branch in this sensitive area. * * * For reasons to follow we decide that the judgment below must be reversed.

* * *

The classic American statement of the act of state doctrine * * * is found in Underhill v. Hernandez, 168 U.S. 250, where Chief Justice Fuller said for a unanimous Court (p. 252):

> "Every sovereign state is bound to respect the independence of every other sovereign state, and the courts of one country will not sit in judgment on the acts of the government of another, done within its own territory. Redress of grievances by reason of such acts must be obtained through the means open to be availed of by sovereign powers as between themselves."

Following this precept the Court in that case refused to inquire into acts of Hernandez, a revolutionary Venezuelan military commander whose government had been later recognized by the United States, which were made the basis of a damage action in this country by Underhill, an American citizen, who claimed that he had been unlawfully assaulted, coerced, and detained in Venezuela by Hernandez.

None of this Court's subsequent cases in which the act of state doctrine was directly or peripherally involved manifest any retreat from Underhill. See American Banana Co. v. United Fruit Co., 213 U.S. 347, 29 S.Ct. 511, 53 L.Ed. 826; Oetjen v. Central Leather Co., 246 U.S. 297, 38 S.Ct. 309, 62 L.Ed. 726; Ricaud v. American Metal Co., 246 U.S. 304, 38 S.Ct. 312, 62 L.Ed. 733; Shapleigh v. Mier, 299 U.S. 468, 57 S.Ct. 261, 81 L.Ed. 355; United States v. Belmont, 301 U.S. 324, 57 S.Ct. 758, 81 L.Ed. 1134; United States v. Pink, 315 U.S. 203, 62 S.Ct. 552, 86 L.Ed. 796. On the contrary in two of these cases, Oetjen and Ricaud, the doctrine as announced in Underhill was reaffirmed in unequivocal terms.

* * *

In deciding the present case the Court of Appeals relied in part upon an exception to the unqualified teachings of Underhill, Oetjen, and Ricaud which that court had earlier indicated. In Bernstein v. Van Heyghen Freres Societe Anonyme, 2 Cir., 163 F.2d 246, suit was brought to recover from an assignee property allegedly taken, in effect, by the Nazi Government because plaintiff was Jewish. Recognizing the odious nature of this act of state, the court, through Judge Learned Hand, nonetheless refused to consider it invalid on that ground. Rather, it looked to see if the Executive had acted in any manner that would indicate that United States Courts should refuse to give effect to such a foreign decree. Finding no such evidence, the court sustained dismissal of the complaint. In a later case involving similar facts the same court again assumed examination of the German acts improper, Bernstein v. N.V. Nederlandsche–Amerikaansche Stoomvaart–Maatschappij, 2 Cir., 173 F.2d 71, but, quite evidently following the implications of Judge Hand's opinion in the earlier case, amended its mandate to permit evidence of alleged invalidity, 2 Cir., 210 F.2d 375, subsequent to receipt by plaintiff's attorney of a letter from the Acting Legal Adviser to the State Department written for the purpose of relieving the court from any constraint upon the exercise of its jurisdiction to pass on that question.

This Court has never had occasion to pass upon the so-called Bernstein exception, nor need it do so now. For whatever ambiguity may be thought to exist in the two letters from State Department officials on which the Court of Appeals relied, 307 F.2d at 858, is now removed by the position which the Executive has taken in this Court on the act of state claim; respondents do not indeed contest the view that these letters were intended to reflect no more than the Department's then wish not to make any statement bearing on this litigation.

The outcome of this case, therefore, turns upon whether any of the contentions urged by respondents against the application of the act of state doctrine in the premises is acceptable: (1) that the doctrine does not apply to acts of state which violate international law, as is claimed to be the case here; (2) that the doctrine is inapplicable unless the Executive specifically interposes it in a particular case; and (3) that, in any event, the doctrine may not be invoked by a foreign government plaintiff in our courts.

Preliminarily, we discuss the foundations on which we deem the act of state doctrine to rest, and more particularly the question of whether state or federal law governs its application in a federal diversity case.

We do not believe that this doctrine is compelled either by the inherent nature of sovereign authority, as some of the earlier decisions seem to imply, see Underhill, supra; American Banana, supra; Oetjen, supra, 246 U.S. at 303, 38 S.Ct. at 311, 62 L.Ed. 726, or by some principle of international law. If a transaction takes place in one jurisdiction and the forum is in another, the forum does not by dismissing an action or by applying its own law purport to divest the first jurisdiction of its territorial sovereignty; it merely declines to adjudicate or makes applicable its own law to parties or property before it. The refusal of one country to enforce the penal laws of another * * * is a typical example of an instance when a court will not entertain a cause of action arising in another jurisdiction. While historic notions of sovereign authority do bear upon the wisdom of employing the act of state doctrine, they do not dictate its existence.

That international law does not require application of the doctrine is evidenced by the practice of nations. Most of the countries rendering decisions on the subject fail to follow the rule rigidly. No international arbitral or judicial decision discovered suggests that international law prescribes recognition of sovereign acts of foreign governments, see 1 Oppenheim's International Law, § 115aa (Lauterpacht, 8th ed. 1955), and apparently no claim has ever been raised before an international tribunal that failure to apply the act of state doctrine constitutes a breach of international obligation. If international law does not prescribe use of the doctrine, neither does it forbid application of the rule even if it is claimed that the act of state in question violated international law. The traditional view of international law is that it establishes substantive principles for determining whether one country has wronged another. Because of its peculiar nation-to-nation character the usual method for an individual to seek relief is to exhaust local remedies and then repair to the executive authorities of his own state to persuade them to champion his claim in diplomacy or before an international tribunal. * * * Although it is, of course, true that United States courts apply international law as a part of our own in appropriate circumstances, * * * the public law of nations can hardly dictate to a country which is in theory wronged how to treat that wrong within its domestic borders.

Despite the broad statement in Oetjen that "The conduct of the foreign relations of our government is committed by the Constitution to the executive and legislative * * * departments," 246 U.S. at 302, 38 S.Ct. at 311, 62 L.Ed. 726, it cannot of course be thought that "every case or controversy which touches foreign relations lies beyond judicial cognizance." Baker v. Carr, 369 U.S. 186, 211, 82 S.Ct. 691, 707, 7 L.Ed.2d 663. The text of the Constitution does not require the act of state doctrine; it does not irrevocably remove from the judiciary the capacity to review the validity of foreign acts of state.

The act of state doctrine does, however, have "constitutional" underpinnings. It arises out of the basic relationships between branches of government in a system of separation of powers. It concerns the competency of dissimilar institutions to make and implement particular kinds of decision in the area of international relations. The doctrine as formulated in past decisions expresses the strong sense of the Judicial Branch that its engagement in the task of passing on the validity of foreign acts of state may hinder rather than further this country's pursuit of goals both for itself and for the community of nations as a whole in the international sphere. Many commentators disagree with this view; they have striven by means of distinguishing and limiting past decisions and by advancing various considerations of policy to stimulate a narrowing of the apparent scope of the rule. Whatever considerations are thought to predominate, it is plain that the problems involved are uniquely federal in nature. If federal authority, in this instance this Court, orders the field of judicial competence in this area for the federal courts, and the state courts are left free to formulate their own rules, the purposes behind the doctrine could be as effectively undermined as if there had been no federal pronouncement on the subject.

* * *

If the act of state doctrine is a principle of decision binding on federal and state courts alike but compelled by neither international law nor the Constitution, its continuing vitality depends on its capacity to reflect the proper distribution of functions between the judicial and political branches of the Government on matters bearing upon foreign affairs. It should be apparent that the greater the degree of codification or consensus concerning a particular area of international law, the more appropriate it is for the judiciary to render decisions regarding it, since the courts can then focus on the application of an agreed principle to circumstances of fact rather than on the sensitive task of establishing a principle not inconsistent with the national interest or with international justice. It is also evidence that some aspects of international law touch much more sharply on national nerves than do others; the less important the implications of an issue are for our foreign relations, the weaker the justification for exclusivity in the political branches. The balance of relevant considerations may also be shifted if the government which perpetrated the challenged act of state is no longer in existence, as in the Bernstein case, for the political interest of this country may, as a result, be measurably altered. Therefore, rather than laying down or reaffirming an inflexible and all-encompassing rule in this case, we decide only that the Judicial Branch will not examine the validity of a taking of property within its own territory by a foreign sovereign government, extant and recognized by this country at the time of suit, in the absence of a treaty or other unambiguous agreement regarding controlling legal principles, even if the complaint alleges that the taking violates customary international law.

* * *

The possible adverse consequences of a conclusion to the contrary of that implicit in these cases is highlighted by contrasting the practices of the political branch with the limitations of the judicial process in matters of this kind. Following an expropriation of any significance, the Executive engages in diplomacy aimed to assure that United States citizens who are harmed are compensated fairly. Representing all claimants of this country, it will often be able, either by bilateral or multilateral talks, by submission to the United Nations, or by the employment of economic and political sanctions, to achieve some degree of general redress. Judicial determinations of invalidity of title can, on the other hand, have only an occasional impact, since they depend on the fortuitous circumstance of the property in question being brought into this country. * * *

* * * If the Executive Branch has undertaken negotiations with an expropriating country, but has refrained from claims of violation of the law of nations, a determination to that effect by a court might be regarded as a serious insult, while a finding of compliance with international law would greatly strengthen the bargaining hand of the other state with consequent detriment to American interests.

Even if the State Department has proclaimed the impropriety of the expropriation, the stamp of approval of its view by a judicial tribunal, however impartial, might increase any affront and the judicial decision might occur at a time, almost always well after the taking, when such an impact would be contrary to our national interest. Considerably more serious and far-reaching consequences would flow from a judicial finding that international law standards had been met if that determination flew in the face of a State Department proclamation to the contrary. When articulating principles of international law in its relations with other states, the Executive Branch speaks not only as an interpreter of generally accepted and traditional rules, as would the courts, but also as an advocate of standards it believes desirable for the community of nations and protective of national concerns. In short, whatever way the matter is cut, the possibility of conflict between the Judicial and Executive Branches could hardly be avoided.

* * *

[A] serious consequence of the exception pressed by respondents would be to render uncertain titles in foreign commerce, with the possible consequence of altering the flow of international trade. If the attitude of the United States courts were unclear, one buying expropriated goods would not know if he could safely import them into this country. Even were takings known to be invalid, one would have difficulty determining after goods had changed hands several times whether the particular articles in question were the product of an ineffective state act.

Against the force of such considerations, we find respondents' countervailing arguments quite unpersuasive. Their basic contention is that United States courts could make a significant contribution to the growth of international law, a contribution whose importance, it is said, would be magnified by the relative paucity of decisional law by international bodies. But given the fluidity of present world conditions, the effectiveness of such a patchwork approach toward the formulation of an acceptable body of law concerning state responsibility for expropriations is, to say the least, highly conjectural. Moreover, it rests upon the sanguine presupposition that the decisions of the courts of the world's major capital exporting country and principal exponent of the free enterprise system would be accepted as disinterested expressions of sound legal principle by those adhering to widely different ideologies.

* * *

It is suggested that if the act of state doctrine is applicable to violations of international law, it should only be so when the Executive Branch expressly stipulates that it does not wish the courts to pass on the question of validity. See Association of the Bar of the City of New York, Committee on International Law, A Reconsideration of the Act of State Doctrine in United States Courts (1959). We should be slow to reject the representations of the Government that such a reversal of the Bernstein principle would work serious inroads on the maximum effectiveness of United States diplomacy. Often the State Department will wish to refrain from taking an official position, particularly at a moment that would be dictated by the development of private litigation but might be inopportune diplomatically. Adverse domestic consequences might flow from an official stand which could be assuaged, if at all, only by revealing matters best kept secret. Of course, a relevant consideration for the State Department would be the position contemplated in the court to hear the case. It is highly questionable whether the examination of validity by the judiciary should depend on an educated guess by the Executive as to probable result and, at any rate, should a prediction be wrong, the Executive might be embarrassed in its dealings with other countries. We do not now pass on the Bernstein exception, but even if it were deemed valid, its suggested extension is unwarranted.

However offensive to the public policy of this country and its constituent States an expropriation of this kind may be, we conclude that both the national interest and progress toward the goal of establishing the rule of law among nations are best served by maintaining intact the act of state doctrine in this realm of its application.

* * *

The judgment of the Court of Appeals is reversed and the case is remanded to the District Court for proceedings consistent with this opinion. It is so ordered.

MR. JUSTICE WHITE, dissenting.

I am dismayed that the Court has, with one broad stroke, declared the ascertainment and application of international law beyond the competence of the courts of the United States in a large and important category of cases. I am also disappointed in the Court's declaration that the acts of a sovereign state with regard to the property of aliens within its borders are beyond the reach of international law in the courts of this country. However clearly established that law may be, a sovereign may violate it with impunity, except insofar as the political branches of the government may provide a remedy. This backward-looking doctrine, never before declared in this Court, is carried a disconcerting step further: not only are the courts powerless to question acts of state proscribed by international law but they are likewise powerless to refuse to adjudicate the claim founded upon a foreign law; they must render judgment and thereby validate the lawless act. Since the Court expressly extends its ruling to all acts of state expropriating property, however clearly inconsistent with the international community, all discriminatory expropriations of the property of aliens, as for example the taking of properties of persons belonging to certain races, religions or nationalities, are entitled to automatic validation in the courts of the United States. No other civilized country has found such a rigid rule necessary for the survival of the executive branch of its government; the executive of no other government seems to require such insulation from international law adjudications in its courts; and no other judiciary is apparently so incompetent to ascertain and apply international law.

I do not believe that the act of state doctrine, as judicially fashioned in this Court, and the reasons underlying it, require American courts to decide cases in disregard of international law and of the rights of litigants to a full determination on the merits.

* * *

The reasons for nonreview, based as they are on traditional concepts of territorial sovereignty, lose much of their force when the foreign act of state is shown to be a violation of international law. All legitimate exercises of sovereign power, whether territorial or otherwise, should be exercised consistently with rules of international law, including those rules which mark the bounds of lawful state action against aliens or their property located within the territorial confines of the foreign state. * * * Contrariwise, to refuse inquiry into the question of whether norms of the international community have been contravened by the act of state under review would seem to deny the existence or purport of such norms, a view that seems inconsistent with the role of international law in ordering the relations between nations. Finally, the impartial application of international law would not only be an affirmation of the existence and binding effect of international rules of order, but also a refutation of the notion that this body of law consists of no more than the divergent and parochial views of the capital importing and exporting nations, the socialist and free-enterprise nations.

* * *

Obviously there are cases where an examination of the foreign act and declaration of invalidity or validity might undermine the foreign policy of the Executive Branch and its attempts at negotiating a settlement for a

nationalization of the property of Americans. The respect ordinarily due to a foreign state, as reflected in the decisions of this Court, rests upon a desire not to disturb the relations between countries and on a view that other means, more effective than piecemeal adjudications of claims arising out of a large-scale nationalization program of settling the dispute, may be available. Precisely because these considerations are more or less present, or absent, in any given situation and because the Department of our Government primarily responsible for the formulation of foreign policy and settling these matters on a state-to-state basis is more competent than courts to determine the extent to which they are involved, a blanket presumption of nonreview in each case is inappropriate and a requirement that the State Department render a determination after reasonable notice, in each case, is necessary.
* * *

## *Notes*

1. The act of state doctrine as reaffirmed in *Sabbatino* was limited by act of Congress in "The Second Hickenlooper Amendment," and the ruling in the *Sabbatino* case itself, remanded to the district court, was thereby effectively reversed. See p. 193 below.

On the background, the litigation and aftermath of *Sabbatino,* see Association of the Bar of the City of New York, Background Papers and Proceedings of the Seventh Hammarskjold Forum, The Aftermath of Sabbatino (1965). The international legal principles concerning the duty of a state to pay compensation for the taking of alien-owned property are discussed at p. 725 infra.

2. Restatement (Third) § 443, Comment *b* states:

> *Scope of act of state doctrine and exceptions.* In the principal contemporary formulation of the doctrine, Banco Nacional de Cuba v. Sabbatino, 376 U.S. 398, 84 S.Ct. 923, 11 L.Ed.2d 804 (1964), Justice Harlan wrote:
>
>> [R]ather than laying down or reaffirming an inflexible and all-encompassing rule in this case, we decide only that the Judicial Branch will not examine the validity of a taking of property within its own territory by a foreign sovereign government, extant and recognized by this country at the time of suit, in the absence of a treaty or other unambiguous agreement regarding controlling legal principles, even if the complaint alleges that the taking violates customary international law.
>
> 376 U.S. at 428, 84 S.Ct. at 940, 11 L.Ed.2d at 823–24. The *Sabbatino* case involved property taken by the government of a recognized state within its own territory, and the legal challenge to the taking was founded on a principle of customary international law as to which there was substantial controversy, not on a treaty or other unambiguous agreement. The Court said "we decide only * * *" the kind of case before it, and it is not clear whether it intended to limit application of the act of state doctrine to situations in which all of the conditions listed are present. The applicability of the doctrine where one or more of those conditions is not present should be determined in the light of the reasons for the doctrine. See Comment *a.*
>
> As of 1987, the Supreme Court had not passed on the applicability of the doctrine to an act of a foreign government in respect of property outside that state's territory, to an act of a government not recognized by the United States, to an act alleged to violate a provision of a treaty or other unambiguous agreement, or a principle of customary law not in dispute. Since

*Sabbatino,* the Supreme Court has not had occasion to apply the doctrine to a case not involving the taking of property, as it had done in *Underhill.*

Lower courts have been unanimous in holding that the act of state doctrine does not apply to a taking by a foreign state of property outside of its territory at the time of taking, but have been divided as to how the territorial limitations should be applied to intangible property. See Reporters' Note 4. The doctrine has been held inapplicable in the context of a challenge to a taking by a foreign state alleged to be in violation of a treaty between the United States and that state. See Reporters' Note 5. In *Sabbatino,* the Court stressed that the principles of international law on which the challenge to the foreign state's act was based were in sharp dispute, 376 U.S. at 428–30, 84 S.Ct. at 940–941, 11 L.Ed.2d at 824–25, see § 712, Reporters' Note 1; it has been argued that the doctrine was not intended to preclude review of an act of a foreign state challenged under principles of international law not in dispute, but as of 1986 no such case had been decided. No post-*Sabbatino* case has considered application of the doctrine to acts by an unrecognized state or government. A divided Supreme Court has held that the doctrine would not preclude a counterclaim against the foreign state in certain circumstances. See Reporters' Notes 2 and 9.

It is accepted that the act of state doctrine should not apply to a taking by a state of property located outside its territory at the time of the taking. Republic of Iraq v. First National City Bank, 353 F.2d 47 (2d Cir.1965), cert. denied, 382 U.S. 1027, 86 S.Ct. 648, 15 L.Ed.2d 540 (1966). Several cases have attempted to apply that exception to takings of intangibles. In various transnational financial transactions courts have sought to determine whether there has been a taking and what was the situs of the debt at the time of the taking. To determine the situs of the debt, courts have considered factors such as whether the state had jurisdiction over the debtor, the intent of the parties as to what law should govern the transaction, the currency in which the debt was denominated. See, e.g., Libra Bank Ltd. v. Banco Nacional De Costa Rica, S.A., 570 F.Supp. 870 (S.D.N.Y.1983); Callejo v. Bancomer, S.A., 764 F.2d 1101 (5th Cir.1985). See generally Restatement (Third) § 443, Reporters' Note 4; Note, The Act of State Doctrine: Resolving Debt Situs Confusion, 86 Colum.L.Rev. 594 (1986). The Restatement Reporters suggest: "In principle, it might be preferable to approach the question of the applicability of the act of state doctrine to intangible assets not by searching for an imaginary situs for property that has no real situs, but by determining how the act of the foreign state in the particular circumstances fits within the reasons for the act of state doctrine and for the territorial limitation." Is that suggestion helpful?

Lower courts have applied the act of state doctrine to cases not involving a taking of property. Several involved suits alleging conspiracies in violation of United States antitrust laws by foreign governments or by a government in conspiracy with private companies. International Association of Machinists and Aerospace Workers (IAM) v. Organization of Petroleum Exporting Countries (OPEC), 649 F.2d 1354 (9th Cir.1981), cert. denied, 454 U.S. 1163, 102 S.Ct. 1036, 71 L.Ed.2d 319 (1982); Clayco Petroleum Corp. v. Occidental Petroleum Corp., 712 F.2d 404 (9th Cir.1983). See Restatement (Third) § 443, Reporter's Notes 3 and 7.

The act of state doctrine was held not to apply in the case of a claim based on an act alleged to be in violation of a treaty between the United States and

Ethiopia. Kalamazoo Spice Extraction Co. v. Government of Socialist Ethiopia, 729 F.2d 422 (6th Cir.1984). Does the rationale of the doctrine support such a treaty exception? Should it apply where the treaty is one to which the United States is not a party? Compare Occidental of Umm Al Qaywayn, Inc. v. A Certain Cargo of Petroleum, 577 F.2d 1196 (5th Cir.1978), cert. denied 442 U.S. 928, 99 S.Ct. 2857, 61 L.Ed.2d 296 (1982).

3. In Alfred Dunhill of London, Inc. v. Republic of Cuba, 425 U.S. 682, 96 S.Ct. 1854, 48 L.Ed.2d 301 (1976), a majority of the Supreme Court found that the mere refusal of a commercial agency of a foreign government to repay funds mistakenly paid to it did not constitute an act of state, since there was no reason to suppose that the agency possessed governmental as distinguished from commercial authority. Four Justices also expressed the view that repudiation by a foreign government of a commercial debt is not entitled to respect as an act of state. "[T]he mere assertion of sovereignty as a defense to a claim arising out of purely commercial acts by a foreign sovereign is no more effective if given the label 'Act of State' than if it is given the label 'sovereign immunity.'" 425 U.S. at 705, 96 S.Ct. at 1866, 48 L.Ed.2d at 318.

In W.S. Kirkpatrick & Co., Inc. v. Environmental Tectonics Corp., Int'l, 493 U.S. 400, 110 S.Ct. 701, 107 L.Ed.2d 816 (1990), the plaintiff, an unsuccessful bidder for a Nigerian military contract, alleged that the defendants had violated federal antitrust and racketeering statutes by bribing Nigerian officials in order to secure the contract. In holding that the act of state doctrine did not bar the plaintiff's claim, the Supreme Court distinguished between cases that require a court to "declare invalid the official act of a foreign sovereign performed within its own territory," and cases that require a court only to impute an "unlawful motivation" to foreign officials in the performance of official duties. Because the central issue in the case was whether the bribes had occurred, and not whether the Nigerian Government's contracts were valid, the Court ruled the act of state doctrine had no application. See generally, Act of State—A Bribery Exception to the Act of State Doctrine? Act of State Doctrine Bars Judicial Inquiry Into the Validity of Foreign Acts, but not Into the Motivations Behind the Acts. W.S. Kirkpatrick, Inc. v. Environmental Tectonics, 22 Vand.J.Transnat'l L. 1231 (1989).

4. *Human rights violations.* A restrictive view of the act of state doctrine has also been invoked in connection with human rights violations. In Forti v. Suarez–Mason, 672 F.Supp. 1531 (N.D.Cal.1987), the court held that the act of state doctrine did not bar an action for torture under the Alien Tort Statute, 28 U.S.C.A. § 1350. Id. at 1544–47. The Torture Victim Protection Act, Pub.L. 102–256, 106 Stat. 73 (Mar. 12, 1992), provides that "[a]n individual who, under actual or apparent authority or under color of law of any foreign nation, subjects another individual to torture or extrajudicial killing shall be liable for damages in a civil action * * *." Id., § 2(a). In reporting on the legislation, the Senate Committee on the Judiciary said:

> [T]he committee does not intend the "act of state" doctrine to provide a shield from lawsuit for [individuals]. In Banco Nacional de Cuba v. Sabbatino, 376 U.S. 398 (1964), the Supreme Court held that the "act of state" doctrine is meant to prevent U.S. courts from sitting in judgment of the official public acts of a sovereign foreign government. Since this doctrine applies only to "public" acts, and no state commits torture as a matter of public policy, this doctrine cannot shield [individuals] from liability under this legislation.

S.Rep. No. 249, 102nd Cong. 1st Sess. 8 (1991). See 138 Cong.Rec. S2667, S2668–69 (March 3, 1992).

See also Filartiga v. Pena–Irala, 630 F.2d 876, 889 (2d Cir.1980) (unauthorized torture by a state official, in violation of the law of the foreign state, could not properly be characterized as an act of state); Sharon v. Time, Inc., 599 F.Supp. 538, 544–45 (S.D.N.Y.1984) (alleged unauthorized approval of massacre by general is not an act of state). In an unreported Ninth Circuit decision, the plaintiffs had alleged various acts of kidnapping, torture, beatings, and murder carried out by the former President of the Philippines while in office and others. The district court dismissed the action on the basis of the act of state doctrine. Emphasizing that the former dictator was no longer in power, the Court of Appeals reversed and remanded for trial on the various human rights violations. Trajano v. Marcos, 878 F.2d 1439 (9th Cir.1989), disposition tabled, 878 F.2d 1439 (9th Cir.1989). cf. Liu v. Republic of China, 892 F.2d 1419 (9th Cir.1989), cert. dismissed, 497 U.S. 1058, 111 S.Ct. 27, 111 L.Ed.2d 840 (1990) (act of state doctrine did not bar action against Chinese officials for allegedly ordering the assassination of an American citizen in the U.S.). See generally, Bazyler, Litigating the International Law of Human Rights: A "How To" Approach, 7 Whittier L.Rev. 713, 734–35 (1985); Steinhardt, Human Rights Litigation and the "One Voice" Orthodoxy in Foreign Affairs, in World Justice? U.S. Courts and International Human Rights 23 (Gibney, ed., 1991).

Would the act of state doctrine apply in a case where the law of a foreign state clearly authorized torture? Would, for example, the act of state doctrine apply to officials who applied the "five techniques" of officially sanctioned interrogation of criminal suspects described in Ireland v. United Kingdom, 25 Eur.Ct.H.R. (ser.A) (1978), reprinted in 58 Int'l L.Rep. 190 (1978) (the five techniques consisted of: (1) wall-standing, (2) hooding, (3) prolonged exposure to loud noise, (4) sleep deprivation, (5) sustenance deprivation). During the debates on the 1992 Torture Victim Protection Act it was asserted that "if any sovereign acknowledges that it engaged in torture or extrajudicial killing as a matter of official policy, then the act of state doctrine might bar the suit under this act." 103 Cong.Rec. S2667, S2669 (March 3, 1992). The Restatement (Third) § 443, Comment *c* states:

> [a] claim arising out of an alleged violation of fundamental human rights—for instance, a claim on behalf of a victim of torture or genocide—would (if otherwise sustainable) probably not be defeated by the act of state doctrine, since the accepted international law of human rights is well established and contemplates external scrutiny of such acts.

See also Id., § 443, Reporter's Note 3.

When suit for a violation of human rights is brought against a foreign state, the doctrine of sovereign immunity may preclude the action (unless immunity is waived). See, e.g., Siderman de Blake v. Republic of Argentina, 965 F.2d 699 (9th Cir.1992), petition for cert. filed, 61 U.S.L.W. 3156 (1992). On the immunity of foreign states from the jurisdiction of domestic courts, see Chapter 13 infra.

5. *Private acts of heads of state.* Republic of Philippines v. Marcos, 806 F.2d 344 (2d Cir.1986), concluded that the act of state doctrine does not apply to "purely private acts" of the head of government as distinguished from his or her "public acts." Id., at 358–59. In a related case, the Ninth Circuit reached the same conclusion. Republic of Philippines v. Marcos, 862 F.2d 1355 (9th Cir.1988) (en banc). The Second Circuit noted that the complaint alleged both public and private acts, and ruled that the defendants seeking to invoke the act of state

doctrine had the burden of demonstrating that the relevant acts were public and entitled to protection from judicial scrutiny under the act of state doctrine. Can one readily distinguish between public and private acts? See, Jimenez v. Aristeguieta, 311 F.2d 547 (5th Cir.1962) (act of state doctrine did not apply to private acts of embezzlement, fraud and receipt of unlawfully obtained money by former Venezuelan dictator); DeRoburt v. Gannett Co., Inc., 733 F.2d 701 (9th Cir.1984) (doctrine did not shield privately motivated, illegal loans by the former President of Nauru). See generally, Note, Defining the "Public Act" Requirement in the Act of State Doctrine, 58 U.Chi.L.Rev. 1151 (1991). cf. W.S. Kirkpatrick & Co., Inc. v. Environmental Tectonics Corp. Int'l, 493 U.S. 400, 110 S.Ct. 701, 107 L.Ed.2d 816 (1990), note 3, p. 190 supra.

6. Can the act of state doctrine be effectively waived? By the foreign state? By private parties? The Restatement (Third) § 443, Comment *e*, states that "the doctrine cannot be 'waived' by the foreign state." It also notes that when a sovereign state has consented to adjudication in the courts of another state, the justification for applying the doctrine is "significantly weaker." Are these statements consistent?

Waiver may be asserted in a number of situations. It may be explicit or it may be inferred from a failure to plead the doctrine. Does selection of an American forum or of American law as the applicable law imply waiver of the act of state doctrine? Or does it include selection of the American act of state doctrine? The party that has allegedly waived application of the doctrine may be the state whose act is challenged or a private litigant. To the extent that the doctrine reflects judicial limitation of judicial power, should waiver be possible? To the extent that the doctrine seeks to avoid disturbing the relations of the United States with the foreign state, should a private litigant be able to waive its application?

7. In First Nat. City Bank v. Banco Nacional de Cuba, 406 U.S. 759, 92 S.Ct. 1808, 32 L.Ed.2d 466 (1972), a majority of the Supreme Court held that the act of state doctrine should not apply to bar a counter-claim. There was no opinion of the Court. Three Justices reached the result on the ground that the Executive Branch, by a letter to the Court, had suggested that the act of state doctrine should not apply in such cases and urged that the courts should follow the Executive Branch. Mr. Justice Powell, who had joined the Court after *Sabbatino,* concurred in the judgment because he questioned the decision in that case. Justice Douglas took the view that the act of state doctrine should not be applied to counterclaims, citing National City Bank v. Republic of China, 348 U.S. 356, 75 S.Ct. 423, 99 L.Ed. 389 (1955). Justices Brennan, Stewart, Marshall and Blackmun dissented, on the ground that *Sabbatino* applied; like the concurring justices they rejected the "*Bernstein*" exception, i.e., the view that the courts had to follow direction by the Executive Branch in such cases. See 406 U.S. at 776–77, 92 S.Ct. at 1817–18, 32 L.Ed.2d at 487–88.

8. Although the Court in *Sabbatino* disclaims any intimation that the courts of the United States "are broadly foreclosed from considering questions of international law" (376 U.S. at 430 n. 34, 84 S.Ct. at 941 n. 34, 11 L.Ed.2d at 824 n. 34), does its approach to the act of state issue suggest that certain issues involving aspects of international law that are unsettled and that affect sensitive national interests should be regarded as non-justiciable? Would the justiciability of the issue be influenced by whether the Executive Branch has taken a position?

On the Act of State doctrine generally, see 1 Oppenheim's International Law 365–71 (9th ed., Jennings & Watts, eds. 1992); Born & Westin, International Civil Litigation in United States Courts (1989); Dellapenna, Suing Foreign Governments and Their Corporations, Chap. 8 (1988); Franck & Glennon, Foreign Relations and National Security Law (1987); Brilmayer, International Law in American Courts: A Modest Proposal, 100 Yale L.J. 2277 (1991); Kirgis, Understanding the Act of State Doctrine's Effect, 82 A.J.I.L. 58 (1988); Koh, Transnational Public Law Litigation, 100 Yale L.J. 2347 (1991).

### *THE SECOND HICKENLOOPER AMENDMENT*

Pub.L. 89–171, 79 Stat. 653 (1964), 22 U.S.C. § 2370(e)(2).

Notwithstanding any other provision of law, no court in the United States shall decline on the ground of the federal act of state doctrine to make a determination on the merits giving effect to the principles of international law in a case in which a claim of title or other right to property is asserted by any party including a foreign state (or a party claiming through such state) based upon (or traced through) a confiscation or other taking after January 1, 1959, by an act of that state in violation of the principles of international law including the principles of compensation and the other standards set out in this subsection: *Provided,* That this subparagraph shall not be applicable (1) in any case in which an act of a foreign state is not contrary to international law or with respect to a claim of title or other right to property acquired pursuant to an irrevocable letter of credit of not more than 180 days duration issued in good faith prior to the time of the confiscation or other taking, or (2) in any case with respect to which the President determines that application of the act of state doctrine is required in that particular case by the foreign policy interests of the United States and a suggestion to this effect is filed on his behalf in that case with the court.

### *Notes*

1. The Senate Foreign Relations Committee's Report on the Hickenlooper Amendment stated in part:

> The amendment is intended to reverse in part the recent decision of the Supreme Court in Banco de [sic] Nacional de Cuba v. Sabbatino. The act-of-state doctrine has been applied by U.S. courts to determine that the actions of a foreign sovereign cannot be challenged in private litigation. The Supreme Court extended this doctrine in the *Sabbatino* decision so as to preclude U.S. courts from inquiring into acts of foreign states, even though these acts had been denounced by the State Department as contrary to international law. * * *
>
> The effect of the amendment is to achieve a reversal of presumptions. Under the *Sabbatino* decision, the courts would presume that any adjudication as to the lawfulness under international law of the act of a foreign state would embarrass the conduct of foreign policy unless the President says it would not. Under the amendment, the Court would presume that it may proceed with an adjudication on the merits unless the President states officially that such an adjudication in the particular case would embarrass the conduct of foreign policy.

S.Rep. No. 1188, pt. I, 88th Cong., 2d Sess. 24 (1964).

2. Henkin has commented:

Act of state is a special rule modifying the ordinary rules of conflict of laws. If there were no act of state doctrine, a domestic court in a case like *Sabbatino* would decide it on "conflicts" principles. It would first decide what law "governed" the issues. If under accepted choice of law principles the foreign law should govern, the court could still refuse to apply that law if it were found to be contrary to the public policy of the forum. The act of state doctrine, however, says that the foreign "law" (i.e., the act of state) must govern certain transactions and that no public policy of the forum may stand in the way. * * *

* * * [Under the Supreme Court's decision, as] a substantive federal rule, [the act of state doctrine] supersedes any conflicts principle, state or federal, that might otherwise prevail. There is no room for any public policy conflicting with the policy of act of state as applied by the courts.

* * * [B]ecause the draftsmen of the Amendment did not have a clear idea of the act of state doctrine and its relation to general conflicts principles, the statute does not give a clear idea as to what is left after the Supreme Court is overruled. Did the statute intend to remove act of state from these cases? If so, are the courts left to traditional conflicts principles, and Erie R.R. v. Tompkins? Did Congress, instead, intend to prescribe new federal substantive law to govern these cases? If so, what exactly is the new law? And may Congress properly prescribe law for these transactions?

* * * The Amendment directs the courts not to "decline on the ground of the federal act of state doctrine to make a determination on the merits giving effect to the principles of international law * * *." But, first, when the courts apply act of state, they are not declining to make a "determination on the merits." There is a determination on the merits whether act of state is applied or not. The only question is which principle of conflicts and consequently which substantive law is to be applied to determine the merits. Second, act of state does not require courts to decline to give effect to international law: were there no such doctrine, courts would not "give effect to international law" in these cases. They would give effect to domestic principles of conflicts and the substantive law to which those principles point. International law might become relevant only if, somehow, the governing substantive law made it relevant, or if the public policy of the forum invoked it.

Perhaps the statute also sought to build on the proposition that "international law is part of the law of the United States." This proposition is established and unexceptionable; it is also irrelevant. Effectively, it means that the courts will apply international law in an appropriate case *against the United States,* the one government which is subject to the law of the United States. In a case like *Sabbatino,* however, the Government of Cuba, acting in Cuba, obviously was not subject to the laws of the United States. Of what relevance, then, is the fact that international law is part of the law of the United States? International law might have been relevant if it required the United States to respond to Cuba's violation in a particular way; for example, if international law forbade the United States to give effect to Cuba's confiscations, American courts would carry out that obligation and refuse to give them effect. But international law does not tell the United States how to react to Cuban acts that violate international law. The United States is free to condone, acquiesce in, implement, or even applaud them.

> International law could become relevant to a case like *Sabbatino* in the courts of the United States (as distinguished from an appropriate international tribunal) only if governing law made it relevant. For example, international law could come in through the "side-door" of public policy. Congress could declare that regardless of any principles of conflicts, or of the act of state doctrine, it is the policy of the United States not to allow its courts to apply foreign law that contravenes international law. Or Congress could pass a statute providing that in *Sabbatino*-type cases, courts shall not apply the substantive law designated either by act of state or by traditional conflicts principles, but shall apply instead a new federal substantive law, which incorporates by reference the principles of international law as Congress saw them. The courts in *Farr,* in effect, treated the Second Hickenlooper Amendment as though it were one of these two possible Congressional enactments. * * *

Henkin, Act of State Today: Recollections in Tranquility, 6 Colum.J.Transnat'l L. 175, 178–82 (1967). See also Henkin, Foreign Affairs and the Constitution 223–24 (1972).

Is, as Henkin suggests, international law applicable to acts of a foreign state before a United States court only insofar as United States law makes international law applicable in the case? It has been argued that United States courts should consider international law applicable in its own right, as a kind of superior law to which the foreign act is subject; a foreign act should not be applied by a domestic court if that law is invalid under international law. Compare:

> [w]hen dealing with international delinquencies committed by a foreign State a municipal court ought to be bound by international law in the sense that this overrides the foreign law which, though applicable to a given set of facts, is objectionable. In other words, foreign law, *prima facie* applicable to a case, should be refused effect by a municipal court if and to such extent as public international law so requires. * * *
>
> A principle on these lines has much to commend it. In the first place it is consonant with the dignity, moral force and inherent vitality of public international law to enforce it as such, by means of direct application rather than in an oblique fashion by using public policy as a back door. If "we admit unreservedly the supremacy of international law" it would not be fitting if it had to be harnessed to the unruly horse of public policy. Secondly, the relative objectivity and uniformity of its standards, as compared with the varying notions of public policy, makes public international law a more attractive guide to judicial decision. To invoke public policy means a condemnation on grounds which are liable to create the impression of special pleading and which thus conceal, behind the interests involved in the case, the peculiarly legal quality of the issue. Thirdly, the judicial application of international law is, and ought to be, a matter of duty, not, as Zitelmann suggested, of mere right. In other words the requirements of public international law are absolute and leave no room for the relativity of public policy. Foreign measures which do not affect the forum are not contrary to its public policy. Yet a judge who, in a case involving an international delinquency committed by State A against State B, applies the law of the former, may assist in the consummations of that delinquency and thus engage his own Sovereign's international responsibility.

Mann, International Delinquencies Before Municipal Courts, in Studies in International Law 378–80 (1973) (footnotes omitted). See also his later article, The Consequences of an International Wrong in International Law, in Further Studies in International Law, Chapter 4 (1990); The Rose Mary, [1953] 1 W.L.R. 246.

3. In applying the Hickenlooper Amendment, is a court required to adopt the view of international law or expropriation apparently adopted by Congress, or should it make an independent determination as to what the applicable international law provides? See Restatement (Third) § 444, Comments *b* and *d*. On expropriation at international law generally, see Norton, A Law of the Future or a Law of the Past: Modern Tribunals and the International Law of Expropriation, 85 A.J.I.L. 474 (1991); Christie, What Constitutes a Taking of Property Under International Law?, 38 Brit.Y.B.Int'l L. 307 (1964).

4. The Second Hickenlooper Amendment was applied by the district court in *Sabbatino* itself on remand and the complaint was dismissed. Banco Nacional de Cuba v. Farr, 243 F.Supp. 957 (S.D.N.Y.1965), aff'd, 383 F.2d 166 (2d Cir.1967), cert. denied, 390 U.S. 956, 88 S.Ct. 1038, 19 L.Ed.2d 1151 (1968).

5. In French v. Banco Nacional de Cuba, 23 N.Y.2d 46, 295 N.Y.S.2d 433, 242 N.E.2d 704 (1968), the New York Court of Appeals applied the act of state doctrine in rejecting a claim based on breach of contract by a foreign government. The court held that the Hickenlooper Amendment did not apply. "It is plain enough upon the face of the statute—and absolutely clear from its legislative history—the Congress was not attempting to assure a remedy in American courts for every kind of monetary loss resulting from actions, even unjust actions, of foreign governments. The law is restricted, manifestly, to the kind of problem exemplified by the *Sabbatino* case itself, a claim of title or other right to specific property which had been expropriated abroad." 23 N.Y.2d at 57–58, 295 N.Y.S.2d at 444–45, 242 N.E.2d at 712. See Restatement (Third) § 444, Comment *e* and Reporters' Note 4.

In West v. Multibanco Comermex, 807 F.2d 820 (9th Cir.1987), cert. denied, 482 U.S. 906, 107 S.Ct. 2483, 96 L.Ed.2d 375 (1987), the court rejected the reasoning of *French* as overly formalistic and contrary to the policies underlying the Hickenlooper Amendment. The defendants argued that ownership interests in certificates of deposit are "contractual," and thus not "tangible property" that could be expropriated within the meaning of the Amendment. The court, however, concluded that the "tangibleness" of property was not a dispositive factor and that certificates of deposits were property capable of being expropriated within the meaning of the Hickenlooper Amendment. See generally, Vandevelde, Reassessing the Hickenlooper Amendment, 29 Va.J.Int'l L. 115 (1988–89). Compare p. 189 on the "situs" of intangibles.

The reference to "property" in the Second Hickenlooper Amendment was inserted in 1965, when the Amendment was reenacted, to assure that the act of state doctrine might still be available and the courts would give effect to foreign acts that do not involve the taking of property.

6. Henkin, Note 2 above, describes the act of state doctrine as "a special rule modifying the ordinary rules of conflict of laws." Professor Anne–Marie Burley takes the position that the Supreme Court in *Sabbatino* made "a more fundamental statement that the act of state doctrine could not function as a conflicts rule on the particular facts of the case." Burley, Law Among Liberal States: Liberal Internationalism and the Act of State Doctrine, 92 Colum.L.Rev. 1907, 1950 (1992). Burley concludes that the act of state doctrine operates not as

a special conflicts rule, but as a rule required by constitutional separation of powers. Are these two views inconsistent? Can the act of state doctrine be characterized as "a special rule of conflicts deriving from concerns for the constitutional separation of powers?" Are there practical consequences to the different characterizations? Burley suggests that the courts should apply the act of state doctrine differently in regard to "liberal" and "nonliberal" states. Is that feasible? Is it desirable?

7. *The Act of State doctrine in the courts of other states.* Restatement (Third) § 443, Reporter's Note 12, surveys the judicial application of the act of state doctrine in countries other than the United States:

> As the Supreme Court stated in *Sabbatino,* no rule of international law requires application of the act of state doctrine. Nevertheless, the courts of most states have exercised judicial restraint in adjudicating challenges to expropriation by foreign states, whether by application of the act of state doctrine, A.M. Luther v. James Sagor & Co. (U.K.), [1921] 3 K.B. 532 (C.A.); by narrow construction of the responsibility of states to alien investors, Anglo–Iranian Oil Co. Ltd. v. S.U.P.O.R. Co. (Italy), [1955] Int'l L.Rep. 23 (Civil Ct.Rome, Sept. 13, 1954); or by application of local public policy (*ordre public*) to oust normal rules of conflict of laws, Reporters' Note 1, in actions by local plaintiffs only. Soc. Minera El Teniente, S.A. v. A.G. Norddeutsche Affinerie (German Fed.Republic), 12 Int'l Leg.Mat. 251 (Hamburg, Landgericht Jan. 22, 1973). Contra: Anglo–Iranian Oil Co., Ltd. v. Jaffrate, [1953] W.L.R. 246, [1953] Int'l L.Rep. 316 (Aden Sup.Ct.); Senembah Maatschappij N.V. v. Republiek Indonesie Bank Indonesia, Ned. Jurisprudentsie 1959, No. 73, p. 218 (Amsterdam Ct.App.). For a survey of cases to 1965, see Reeves, "The Act of State—Foreign Decisions cited in *Sabbatino* Case: A Rebuttal and Memorandum of Law," 33 Fordham L.Rev. 599, 618–70 (1965). After many years of uncertainty, see Singer, "The Act of State Doctrine in the United Kingdom: An Analysis with Comparison to United States Practice," 75 Am.J.Int'l L. 283 (1981), the House of Lords decided in 1981 to adopt the United States view of the act of state doctrine, on the basis of a shared view of the nature and limits of the judicial function. Buttes Gas & Oil Co. v. Hammer, [1982] A.C. 888, 936–38 (H.L.(E.)), the House of Lords reaffirmed that "an English court will recognise the compulsory acquisition of a foreign state and will recognise the change of title to property which has come under the control of the foreign state and * * * the consequences of that change of title. The English court will decline to consider the merits of compulsory acquisition * * * [or to entertain an attack on the motives of the friendly sovereign state]."

For a discussion of the Act of State doctrine in the jurisprudence of other states generally, see 1 Oppenheim's International Law 365–71 (9th ed., Jennings & Watts, eds. 1992).

8. Attacks on the Act of State Doctrine continue. See Leigh, *Sabbatino's* Silver Anniversary and the Restatement: No Cause for Celebration, 24 Int'l Lawyer 1 (1990); Chow, Rethinking the Act of State Doctrine: An Analysis in Terms of Jurisdiction to Prescribe, 62 Wash.L.Rev. 397 (1987); Bazyler, Abolishing the Act of State Doctrine, 134 U.Pa.L.Rev. 325 (1986). See also Halberstam, Sabbatino Resurrected: The Act of State Doctrine in the Revised Restatement of U.S. Foreign Relations Law, 79 A.J.I.L. 68, and the reply by Henkin & Lowenfeld, Act of State and the Restatement, 79 A.J.I.L. 717 (1985). A bill to limit the

doctrine was introduced and hearings held in 1986, but the measure was not enacted.

## C. INTERNATIONAL AGREEMENTS IN THE LAW OF THE UNITED STATES: TREATIES

### *1. The Treaty Power*

#### UNITED STATES CONSTITUTION

ARTICLE II, SECTION 2

He [the President] shall have Power, by and with the Advice and Consent of the Senate, to make Treaties, provided two-thirds of the Senators present concur. * * *

ARTICLE VI

This Constitution, and the Laws of the United States which shall be made in Pursuance thereof; and all Treaties made, or which shall be made, under the Authority of the United States, shall be the supreme Law of the Land; and the Judges in every State shall be bound thereby, any Thing in the Constitution or Laws of any State to the Contrary notwithstanding.

#### *Notes*

1. Under international practice, a treaty is often signed subject to later ratification; or, especially in multilateral treaties, a state may accede to a treaty without having signed it. "Ratification" of treaties is not mentioned in the Constitution. In practice, treaties are ratified (or acceded to) by the President after the Senate has given its advice and consent. It is incorrect therefore to refer to the action of the Senate as "ratification." The President is under no duty to proceed with ratification, exchange of ratifications, or other accession to a treaty after the Senate has given its advice and consent. A number of treaties have remained unratified after favorable action by the Senate.

The Senate may impose conditions to its consent. It may insist that obligations under the treaty be modified. In such cases the Senate sometimes enters a "reservation" or "amendment"; technically, the Senate can neither amend the treaty nor enter a reservation to it; it can consent to the treaty on condition that the United States (through the President) enter a reservation to it. The Senate has sometimes imposed conditions that sought to control the effect of a treaty in the United States: for example, that it shall not take effect in the United States until implemented by Congress. See the discussion on self-executing treaties p. 212 below.

2. Article I, section 10 of the Constitution provides:

> "No State shall enter into any Treaty, Alliance, or Confederation * * *.
>
> "No State shall, without the Consent of the Congress, * * * enter into any Agreement or Compact with * * * a foreign Power * * *."

3. The Senate may express its understanding of a treaty provision that is arguably ambiguous. If the Senate indicates its interpretation of such a provision, the President must honor it: the treaty as so understood is the treaty to which the Senate consents. See Rainbow Navigation, Inc. v. Department of the Navy, 699 F.Supp. 339, 343–44 (D.D.C.1988), rev'd on other grounds, 911 F.2d 797 (D.C.Cir.1990) ("Any other rule would undermine the authority of the Senate under Article 2 section 2 of the Constitution to concur or to fail to concur in

treaties made by the Chief Executive."); United States v. Stuart, 489 U.S. 353, 374, 109 S.Ct. 1183, 1195–96, 103 L.Ed.2d 388, 410 (1989) (Scalia, J. concurring) ("Of course the Senate has unquestioned power to enforce its understanding of treaties."). See also ABM Treaty and the Constitution: Joint Hearings Before the Senate Comm. on Foreign Relations and Comm. on the Judiciary, 100th Cong., 1st Sess. (1987) (particularly the statements of Sen. Sam Nunn, id. at 54, L. Henkin, id. at 81, and L. Tribe, id. at 83); Review of ABM Treaty Interpretation Dispute and SDI: Hearing Before the Subcomm. on Arms Control, Int'l Security and Science of the House Comm. on Foreign Relations, 100th Cong. 1st Sess. (1987).

In 1985, controversy erupted when the Reagan Administration sought to give to the Anti-Ballistic Missile (ABM) Treaty an interpretation that was contrary to the Senate's understanding when it gave consent. As a result, when the Intermediate–Range Missiles (INF) Treaty came up for advice and consent in 1988, the Senate attached a condition declaring that "the United States shall interpret the Treaty in accordance with the common understanding of the Treaty shared by the President and the Senate at the time the Senate gave its advice and consent to ratification." See 134 Cong.Rec. S7277–01 (1988). See also Garthoff, Policy Versus the Law: The Reinterpretation of the ABM Treaty (1987); Kennedy, Treaty Interpretation by the Executive Branch: The ABM Treaty and "Star Wars" Testing and Development, 80 A.J.I.L. 854 (1986); Henkin, Constitutionalism, Democracy and Foreign Affairs 51–57 (1990); Glennon, Interpreting "Interpretation:" The President, the Senate, and When Treaty Interpretation Becomes Treaty Making," 20 U.C.D.L.Rev. 913 (1987).

4. Over sharp disagreement by Justice Scalia, the Supreme Court has looked to Senate pre-ratification materials for guidance in the interpretation of treaties. See United States v. Stuart, 489 U.S. 353, 109 S.Ct. 1183, 103 L.Ed.2d 388 (1989). See also, Vagts, Senate Materials and Treaty Interpretation: Some Research Hints for the Supreme Court, 83 A.J.I.L. 546 (1989).

### 2. *Restraints on the Treaty Power*

#### a. *Applicability of Constitutional Restraints*

## TREATIES AND THE SUPREMACY CLAUSE

*HENKIN, FOREIGN AFFAIRS AND THE CONSTITUTION*

137–40 (1972) (some footnotes omitted).*

The Constitution does not expressly impose prohibitions or prescribe limits on the Treaty Power, nor does it patently imply that there are any. No provision in any treaty has been held unconstitutional by the Supreme Court and few have been seriously challenged there. It is now settled, however, that treaties are subject to the constitutional limitations that apply to all exercises of federal power, principally the prohibitions of the Bill of Rights; numerous statements also assert limitations on the reach and compass of the Treaty Power.

Once, indeed, there was extant a myth that treaties are equal in authority to the Constitution and not subject to its limitations. The doctrine, propagated even by eminent authority, found its origins, no doubt, in the language of the Supremacy Clause (Article VI, section 2):

> "This Constitution, and the Laws of the United States which shall be made in Pursuance thereof; and all Treaties made, or which shall be made, under the Authority of the United States, shall be the supreme Law of the Land * * *."

Reading that language, Mr. Justice Holmes said:

> "Acts of Congress are the supreme law of the land when made in pursuance of the Constitution, while treaties are declared to be so when made under the authority of the United States. It is open to question whether the authority of the United States means more than the formal acts prescribed to make the convention." [Missouri v. Holland, p. 206 infra]

Holmes read "in pursuance of" the Constitution to mean "consistent with its substantive prohibitions" and that phrase has been generally so interpreted; if so, the language does indeed lend itself to his dictum. Long before he wrote, however, that curious language of the Supremacy Clause had been explained otherwise: to the Framers, "in pursuance of" the Constitution meant—or meant also—"following its adoption," and they wished to provide that treaties made before the adoption of the Constitution (principally the treaties with France and Great Britain that were being resisted in some States) should also be the law of the land and binding on the States.

* * *

In 1957, Mr. Justice Black laid the issue to rest:

> "* * * no agreement with a foreign nation can confer power on the Congress, or on any other branch of Government, which is free from the restraints of the Constitution.
>
> "* * * The prohibitions of the Constitution were designed to apply to all branches of the National Government and they cannot be nullified by the Executive or by the Executive and the Senate combined." [Reid v. Covert, 354 U.S. 1, 16–17, 77 S.Ct. 1222, 1 L.Ed.2d 1148 (1957)]

The prohibitions set forth in Article 1, section 9, then, though contained in the article devoted principally to Congress and following immediately upon the catalogue of its powers, would doubtless be held to apply to treaties as well: a treaty cannot grant a title of nobility, or lay a duty on articles exported from any State, or give preference to the ports of one State over those of another. Treaties, surely, are also subject to more important prohibitions, notably in the Bill of Rights, protecting individual rights.*

---

See Restatement (Third) §§ 302(2) and 721.

* Even the First Amendment expressly addressed to Congress, and the prohibitions implied elsewhere, e.g., in the citizenship clause of the Fourteenth Amendment. * * *

An argument might be made that these prohibitions do not limit the power to make treaties, but only forbid giving them effect as law of the United States; that conceptual distinction will generally have no consequence in fact, since Presidents will not make treaties that would be unenforceable. * * *

### b. *The Bill of Rights*

## INDIVIDUAL RIGHTS IN FOREIGN RELATIONS

*HENKIN, FOREIGN AFFAIRS AND THE CONSTITUTION*
254 (1972) (footnotes omitted).*

In principle * * * the Bill of Rights limits foreign policy and the conduct of foreign relations as it does other federal activities. The President, for example, would not make a treaty that forbids teaching or advocating racial superiority because it would probably violate the First Amendment. Largely on the basis of that Amendment, the Supreme Court refused the Executive Branch an injunction against press-publication of the classified "Pentagon Papers." The constitutional provisions that afford fair criminal procedures apply also to persons charged with violating foreign affairs statutes, even to foreign nationals accused of espionage. The United States could not adhere to an international criminal court without considering the relevance of the rights assured to those accused of crime in the Fourth, Fifth, Sixth and Eighth Amendments. Since the Bill of Rights generally protects aliens equally with citizens, it satisfies (and probably exceeds) standards of "justice" required by international law, or special protections promised in treaties, e.g., the "bill of rights" for the accused under the NATO Status of Forces Agreement. But, by that token, the United States could not abridge these basic alien rights, say in retaliation for mistreatment or to promote better treatment of Americans abroad. Foreign governments, however, and probably foreign diplomats in their official capacity, have no constitutional rights, and there are no constitutional obstacles, say, to tapping wires of foreign embassies.

Even the "preferred freedoms" of the First Amendment, moreover, are not absolute but are "balanced" against, and might be outweighed by, important public interests. One may expect that the national interest in war and peace and even lesser concerns of foreign relations would have important weight in any balance. So, for example, courts have upheld prohibitions on picketing foreign embassies. Hypothetically, it is far from obvious that they would bar, say, a statute or treaty that forbids publication of matter inciting to war or seriously exacerbating international relations, or private research related to nuclear or biological weapons. Similarly, the Fourth Amendment affords important protection to the "right of the people to be secure in their persons, houses, papers, and effects," but only "against unreasonable searches and seizures"; the national interest in maintaining an important disarmament system and in gaining required inspection rights in other countries might render "reasonable" some intrusive inspections of private establishments and records.

### *Notes*

1. The Restatement (Third) § 721 sets forth protections provided to individuals by the Constitution in matters relating to foreign relations. See, e.g., Comments *f, g* and *i:*

> *f. Due process of law and equal protection of the laws.* The due process clause requires fair procedure in matters relating to foreign relations, in civil as in criminal matters, for aliens as for citizens. See § 722. What process is due, however, differs with the circumstances. Presidential deci-

* Reprinted with permission of the Foundation Press.

sions generally, even when they affect private interests, are not judicial in character and do not require judicial kinds of procedures. Thus, for example, a hearing is not required as of constitutional right before the President exercises his constitutional authority, or authority delegated to him by Congress, to suggest immunity from suit (see Introductory Note to Part IV, Chapter 5, Subchapter A), to impose a tariff, to invoke the act of state doctrine (§ 444 and Comment *f* thereto), to extradite an individual for trial by a foreign country (§ 478), or to settle an international claim (§ 713, Comment *a,* and this section, Comment *g*).

The due process clause also gives some substantive protection to life, liberty, or property affected, for example, by a regulation of foreign commerce or of the right to travel. Comment *i.* To date, the due process clause has not been held to prevent deportation of an alien, even one long resident in the United States, for whatever reason Congress chooses, so long as notice, hearing, and fair procedures are provided. See § 722, Comment *i* and Reporters' Note 12.

The due process clause of the Fifth Amendment also incorporates the requirement that the federal government afford the equal protection of the laws. For equal protection of the laws as applied to aliens, see § 722, Comments *c* and *d.*

*g. Taking of private property.* In matters affecting foreign relations as in domestic matters, it is not always easy to distinguish a regulation that is within the police power of the United States from a taking of private property requiring just compensation under the Fifth Amendment. See § 712, Comment *g* and Reporters' Note 6. In foreign relations, the distinction must take account of the conceptions and traditions of international law. For example, under international law and practice, claims between a national or resident of the United States and a foreign state, its national or resident, are seen as claims between the United States and the other state which they can settle by international agreement. See § 713, Comment *a* and Reporters' Note 9, and § 902, Comment *i* and Reporters' Note 8. Usually, the Executive Branch consults with representatives of claimants, and Congress has generally made monies received in settlement available for distribution to the private claimants. In general, a settlement by treaty or executive agreement of foreign claims of United States nationals or residents neither deprives them of their property without due process of law (see Comment *f*) nor constitutes a taking of their property requiring compensation. In special circumstances, however, a sacrifice of private claims for a national purpose may constitute a taking requiring compensation. See Reporters' Note 8.

* * *

*i. Right to travel.* "The right to travel abroad is part of the 'liberty' of which the citizen cannot be deprived without due process of law * * *. Freedom of movement is basic in our scheme of values." Kent v. Dulles, 357 U.S. 116, 125–26, 78 S.Ct. 1113, 1122, 2 L.Ed.2d 1204 (1958). As a fundamental right, it may not be curtailed lightly and the Executive may limit such travel only if clearly authorized by Congress. The right to travel may not be denied or limited on grounds that would infringe First Amendment rights, *e.g.,* because of a person's political opinions. But in Haig v. Agee, 453 U.S. 280, 306–307, 101 S.Ct. 2766, 2781, 69 L.Ed.2d 640 (1981), the Court distinguished "the *freedom* to travel outside the United States" from "the *right* to travel within the United States," the former being "no more than an aspect of the 'liberty' protected by the Due Process Clause of the Fifth Amendment." The Secretary of State may revoke a passport when he determines that the individual's activities abroad are causing or are likely to cause serious damage to the national security or foreign policy of the United States. The Secretary may also forbid the use of the passport for travel to designated countries and, upon appropriate findings of fact, may confiscate the passport if it is abused; under 22 U.S.C. § 211a, enacted in 1978, the Secretary can impose such restrictions in respect of a country with which the United States is at war, where armed hostilities are in progress, or where there is imminent danger to the health or safety of United States travelers.

Reporters' Note 13 addresses remedies:

*Remedies for violation of individual rights.* The United States Civil Rights Acts may have some application in cases with significance for United States foreign relations. 18 U.S.C. §§ 242–43, and 42 U.S.C. §§ 1981 *et seq.*, which provide criminal and civil remedies for violations by State officials or persons conspiring with them, apply to violations of rights of "persons," therefore including aliens. 18 U.S.C. § 242 has also been held to apply to federal officials acting under color of federal law who deprive aliens of federal rights. United States v. Otherson, 637 F.2d 1276 (9th Cir.1980), certiorari denied, 454 U.S. 840, 102 S.Ct. 149, 70 L.Ed.2d 123 (1981) (upholding conviction of United States border patrol agents for assaulting illegal aliens). See Screws v. United States, 325 U.S. 91, 108, 65 S.Ct. 1031, 1038, 89 L.Ed. 1495 (1945), and cases in 325 U.S. at 97, n. 2. There are some judicially created remedies against federal officials for violations of constitutional rights which might be applied or extended to circumstances significant for United States foreign relations. See Bivens v. Six Unknown Named Agents, 403 U.S. 388, 91 S.Ct. 1999, 29 L.Ed.2d 619 (1971) (remedy for unlawful search and seizure); Carlson v. Green, 446 U.S. 14, 100 S.Ct. 1468, 64 L.Ed.2d 15 (1980) (remedy for violation of Eighth Amendment).

Some United States civil rights legislation protects United States nationals outside the United States. See, *e.g.*, Bryant v. International Schools Services, Inc., 502 F.Supp. 472 (D.N.J.1980) (Title VII of United States Civil Rights Act forbidding discrimination in employment on basis of gender applies to employment of United States citizens in school operated by United States nationals in Iran), reversed on other grounds, 675 F.2d 562 (3d Cir.1982) (findings of fact failed to substantiate discrimination charge).

2. Aliens also enjoy broad Constitutional protections. See Restatement (Third) § 722, Comments *a* and *c*, and Reporters' Note 14:

*a. Constitutional rights of aliens.* The Bill of Rights of the United States Constitution (Amendments I–X) declares the rights of persons, not of citizens only. Aliens in the United States therefore enjoy, notably, the freedoms of speech, press, religion, and assembly (Amendment I), the rights of privacy and freedom from unreasonable arrest and search or seizure (Amendment IV), the safeguards for fair trial in criminal process (Amendments V, VI, and VIII), the due process protections for life, liberty, and property (Amendment V), the right to jury trial in civil cases (Amendment VII). Aliens are also protected from slavery (Amendment XIII). Unlike citizens, however, aliens may be subject to deportation, and aliens admitted other than for permanent residence are subject to the conditions of their entry. See Comments *i* and *j*.

The principal provisions of the Fourteenth Amendment safeguarding individual rights against violation by the States also prescribe rights of persons, not only of citizens: "nor shall any State deprive any person of life, liberty, or property, without due process of the law; nor deny to any person within its jurisdiction the equal protection of the laws." Since the Fourteenth Amendment has been held to make most provisions of the Bill of Rights applicable to the States, aliens enjoy those protections against the States as well. Aliens are protected also against State impairment of the obligation of contracts, bills of attainder, and *ex post facto* laws. Article I, Section 10; see § 721, Comment *k*. Aliens need not, however, be accorded those rights implied in the citizenship clause of the Fourteenth Amendment, the privileges and immunities of citizens of the United States (Amendment XIV, Section 1), or the privileges and immunities of citizens of the several States (Article IV, Section 2). The Constitution reserves for citizens the office of President and Vice President (Article I, Sections 2, 3) and membership in the House of Representatives and the Senate (Article II, Section 2; Amendment XII). The Constitution does not limit voting to citizens, but leaves qualifications for voting to be determined by the States, subject to regulation by Congress. See Comment *c* and Reporters' Note 3. Apparently, however, the Constitution assumes that only citizens would be allowed to vote: several Amendments bar denial of the right of "citizens of the United States" to vote, on account of race, sex, nonpayment of a tax, or age (for persons 18 or older). Amendments XV, XIX, XXIV, XXVI.

In general, this section applies to all aliens in the United States, including those admitted for limited purposes and those present in the United States unlawfully. See Comments *j* and *k*. As regards aliens subject to United States authority outside the United States, see Comment *m*.

This section addresses the rights of aliens under United States constitutional law. For the rights of aliens under international law, see §§ 711–13.

* * *

*c. Equal protection for resident aliens by States of the United States.* The equal protection of the laws does not forbid all classifications or distinctions, only those that are unreasonable. Discriminations against resident aliens by the States, however, are generally suspect and will be subject to strict scrutiny and upheld only if they serve a compelling State interest. (Considerations of cost and "fiscal integrity" are not compelling interests.) Therefore, States cannot deny resident aliens the right to practice a profession, to be employed in the classified civil service, or to have access to welfare programs. However, strict scrutiny will not be applied and a compelling state interest not required where the State deals "with matters firmly within a state's constitutional prerogative" and seeks "to preserve the basic conception of a political community." Foley v. Connelie, 435 U.S. 291, 295–96, 98 S.Ct. 1067, 1070, 55 L.Ed.2d 287 (1978). States may, therefore, deny aliens the right to vote and to hold public office, Comment *a*, and apparently all States do. Since "the right to govern belongs to citizens," a State may also deny aliens access to public employment that "fulfills a most fundamental obligation of government to its constituency" (*id.*, 435 U.S. at 297, 98 S.Ct. at 1071), including employment as teachers in the public schools or as members of the police force. A State may probably deny to aliens what it may deny to citizens of other States, *e.g.,* access to its public parks and lands, publicly owned game, and other natural resources. For State distinctions between resident and nonresident aliens, see Comment *j.*

* * *

14. *Illegal or undocumented aliens.* Aliens unlawfully in the United States are also entitled to constitutional protections. Such an alien is protected by the due process clause, Matthews v. Diaz, Reporters' Note 6, 426 U.S. at 77, 96 S.Ct. at 1890; also Shaughnessy v. United States *ex rel.* Mezei, Reporters' Note 12; Leng May Ma v. Barber, 357 U.S. 185, 187, 78 S.Ct. 1072, 1073, 2 L.Ed.2d 1246 (1958); and the equal protection clause, Plyler v. Doe, 457 U.S. 202, 102 S.Ct. 2382, 72 L.Ed.2d 786 (1982) (State may not deny undocumented school-age children free public education provided for citizen or resident alien children, where such discrimination does not further substantial State interest); *cf.* Holley v. Lavine, 529 F.2d 1294 (2d Cir.), certiorari denied, 426 U.S. 954, 96 S.Ct. 3181, 49 L.Ed.2d 1193 (1976) (equal protection claims of illegal alien who was denied welfare benefits for minor children cannot be dismissed out of hand). See Bolanos v. Kiley, 509 F.2d 1023, 1025 (2d Cir.1975).

Undocumented aliens were also held to be within the protection of the Civil Rights Act, 18 U.S.C. § 242. United States v. Otherson, 637 F.2d 1276 (9th Cir.1980), certiorari denied, 454 U.S. 840, 102 S.Ct. 149, 70 L.Ed.2d 123 (1981) (affirming conviction of United States border patrol agents for assaulting aliens who had entered United States illegally).

For the special protection of refugees, by United States treaty and act of Congress, against deportation to a country where their life or freedom would be threatened, see § 711, Reporters' Note 7.

The Restatement (Third) § 721, Comment *l* addresses the rights of foreign government officials:

*Rights of foreign governments and officials under the United States Constitution and laws.* Subject to international agreements and to immunities and other principles of international law (Part IV, Chapter 5), a foreign state or international organization, engaged in activities or party to any suit in the United States, is generally treated as a person for purposes of United States law. A foreign state or an international organization is not a "person" enjoying rights under the United States Constitution generally, but foreign states are accorded procedural due process and may claim also the minimum due process requirements for the exercise of *in personam* jurisdiction by courts in the United States. See § 453, Reporters' Note 3. Their status under international law apart, accredited diplomatic representatives and officials of foreign governments or of international organizations have status and rights under the Constitution similar to those of other aliens admitted to the United States temporarily for special purposes (see § 722, Comment *j*), but are subject to different procedures in respect of entry to and departure from the United States.

3. *Constitutional rights beyond U.S. borders.* In United States v. Verdugo–Urquidez, 494 U.S. 259, 110 S.Ct. 1056, 108 L.Ed.2d 222 (1990), rehearing denied, 494 U.S. 1092, 110 S.Ct. 1839, 108 L.Ed.2d 968 (1990), the U.S. Supreme Court held that the Fourth Amendment did not apply to a search and seizure by United States agents of property owned by a non-resident alien and located in a foreign country. The majority relied in part on the particular language of the

Fourth Amendment, but statements in the Court's opinion may suggest the view that other provisions of the Constitution, and the Constitution generally, have no application outside the United States, at least in respect of individuals who are not citizens of the United States. If so, the Court has rejected implications to the contrary in earlier cases. See, e.g., Reid v. Covert, 354 U.S. 1, 77 S.Ct. 1222, 1 L.Ed.2d 1148 (1957). See generally, Henkin, The Constitution as Compact and as Conscience: Individual Rights Abroad and at Our Gates, 27 Wm. & Mary L.Rev. 11 (1985). Compare United States v. Alvarez–Machain, ___ U.S. ___, 112 S.Ct. 2188, 119 L.Ed.2d 441 (1992), discussed p. 177 above.

### c. *Other Suggested Limitations*

## FEDERALISM

## MISSOURI v. HOLLAND

Supreme Court of the United States, 1920.
252 U.S. 416, 40 S.Ct. 382, 64 L.Ed. 641.

MR. JUSTICE HOLMES delivered the opinion of the Court.

This is a bill in equity brought by the State of Missouri to prevent a game warden of the United States from attempting to enforce the Migratory Bird Treaty Act of July 3, 1918, c. 128, 40 Stat. 755, and the regulations made by the Secretary of Agriculture in pursuance of the same. The ground of the bill is that the statute is an unconstitutional interference with the rights reserved to the States by the Tenth Amendment, and that the acts of the defendant done and threatened under that authority invade the sovereign right of the State and contravene its will manifested in statutes. The State also alleges a pecuniary interest, as owner of the wild birds within its borders and otherwise, admitted by the Government to be sufficient, but it is enough that the bill is a reasonable and proper means to assert the alleged quasi sovereign rights of a State. * * * A motion to dismiss was sustained by the District Court on the ground that the Act of Congress is constitutional. 258 Fed. 479. * * * The State appeals.

On December 8, 1916, a treaty between the United States and Great Britain was proclaimed by the President. It recited that many species of birds in their annual migrations traversed many parts of the United States and of Canada, that they were of great value as a source of food and in destroying insects injurious to vegetation, but were in danger of extermination through lack of adequate protection. It therefore provided for specified closed seasons and protection in other forms, and agreed that the two powers would take or propose to their lawmaking bodies the necessary measures for carrying the treaty out. 39 Stat. 1702. The above mentioned act of July 3, 1918, entitled an act to give effect to the convention, prohibited the killing, capturing or selling any of the migratory birds included in the terms of the treaty except as permitted by regulations compatible with those terms, to be made by the Secretary of Agriculture. Regulations were proclaimed on July 31, and October 25, 1918. 40 Stat. 1812, 1863. * * * [T]he question raised is the general one whether the treaty and statute are void as an interference with the rights reserved to the States.

To answer this question it is not enough to refer to the Tenth Amendment, reserving the powers not delegated to the United States, because by Article 2, Section 2, the power to make treaties is delegated expressly, and by Article 6 treaties made under the authority of the United States, along with the Constitution and laws of the United States made in pursuance thereof, are declared the supreme law of the land. If the treaty is valid there can be no dispute about the validity of the statute under Article 1, Section 8, as a necessary and proper means to execute the powers of the Government. The language of the Constitution as to the supremacy of treaties being general, the question before us is narrowed to an inquiry into the ground upon which the present supposed exception is placed.

It is said that a treaty cannot be valid if it infringes the Constitution, that there are limits, therefore, to the treaty-making power, and that one such limit is that what an act of Congress could not do unaided, in derogation of the powers reserved to the States, a treaty cannot do. An earlier act of Congress that attempted by itself and not in pursuance of a treaty to regulate the killing of migratory birds within the States had been held bad in the District Court. United States v. Shauver, 214 F. 154. United States v. McCullagh, 221 F. 288. Those decisions were supported by arguments that migratory birds were owned by the States in their sovereign capacity for the benefit of their people, and that under cases like Geer v. Connecticut, 161 U.S. 519, [16 S.Ct. 600, 40 L.Ed. 793,] this control was one that Congress had no power to displace. The same argument is supposed to apply now with equal force.

Whether the two cases cited were decided rightly or not they cannot be accepted as a test of the treaty power. Acts of Congress are the supreme law of the land only when made in pursuance of the Constitution, while treaties are declared to be so when made under the authority of the United States. It is open to question whether the authority of the United States means more than the formal acts prescribed to make the convention. We do not mean to imply that there are no qualifications to the treaty-making power; but they must be ascertained in a different way. It is obvious that there may be matters of the sharpest exigency for the national well being that an act of Congress could not deal with but that a treaty followed by such an act could, and it is not lightly to be assumed that, in matters requiring national action, "a power which must belong to and somewhere reside in every civilized government" is not to be found. * * * [W]hen we are dealing with words that also are a constituent act, like the Constitution of the United States, we must realize that they have called into life a being the development of which could not have been foreseen completely by the most gifted of its begetters. It was enough for them to realize or to hope that they had created an organism; it has taken a century and has cost their successors much sweat and blood to prove that they created a nation. The case before us must be considered in the light of our whole experience and not merely in that of what was said a hundred years ago. The treaty in question does not contravene any prohibitory words to be found in the Constitution. The only question is whether it is forbidden by some invisible radiation from the general terms of the Tenth Amendment. We must consider what this country has become in deciding what that amendment has reserved.

The State as we have intimated founds its claim of exclusive authority upon an assertion of title to migratory birds, an assertion that is embodied in statute. * * * If we are to be accurate we cannot put the case of the State upon higher ground than that the treaty deals with creatures that for the moment are within the state borders, that it must be carried out by officers of the United States within the same territory, and that but for the treaty the State would be free to regulate this subject itself.

As most of the laws of the United States are carried out within the States and as many of them deal with matters which in the silence of such laws the State might regulate, such general grounds are not enough to support Missouri's claim. * * * No doubt the great body of private relations usually fall within the control of the State, but a treaty may override its power. We do not have to invoke the later developments of constitutional law for this proposition; it was recognized as early as Hopkirk v. Bell, 3 Cranch 454, 2 L.Ed. 497 with regard to statutes of limitation, and even earlier, as to confiscation, in Ware v. Hylton, 3 Dall. 199, 1 L.Ed. 568. * * *

Here a national interest of very nearly the first magnitude is involved. It can be protected only by national action in concert with that of another power. The subject matter is only transitorily within the State and has no permanent habitat therein. But for the treaty and the statute there soon might be no birds for any powers to deal with. We see nothing in the Constitution that compels the Government to sit by while a food supply is cut off and the protectors of our forests and our crops are destroyed. It is not sufficient to rely upon the States. The reliance is vain, and were it otherwise, the question is whether the United States is forbidden to act. We are of opinion that the treaty and statute must be upheld. * * *

Decree affirmed.

MR. JUSTICE VAN DEVANTER and MR. JUSTICE PITNEY dissent.

### *Notes*

1. Justice Holmes's suggestion that treaties may not be subject to Constitutional restraints was laid to rest in Reid v. Covert. See p. 200 above.

2. Between 1950 and 1955, Senator Bricker of Ohio led a campaign to amend the Constitution so as to "reverse" *Missouri v. Holland.* A principal section would have provided that a treaty could not become law in the United States except by act of Congress which would have been valid in the absence of the treaty. See S.J.Res. 1, 83d Cong. 1st Sess., 99 Cong.Rec. 6777 (1953); Treaties and Executive Agreements, Hearings before a Subcommittee on S.J.Res. 1 and S.J.Res. 43, 83d Cong., 1st Sess. (1953); S.Rep. No. 412, 83d Cong., 1st Sess. (1953).

See Whitton and Fowler, Bricker Amendment—Fallacies and Dangers, 48 A.J.I.L. 23 (1954) and Finch, The Need to Restrain the Treaty-Making Power of the U.S. Within Constitutional Limits, 48 A.J.I.L. 57 (1954). For an extensive bibliography on the proposed amendment, see Bishop, International Law 112 n. 39 (3d ed. 1971).

3. Henkin writes:

Whatever the States retain in regard to foreign affairs as a matter of constitutional right must be found in * * * doctrines [other than the Tenth Amendment]. There are dicta by Justices and by writers asserting hypothetical limitations on federal power, including its foreign affairs powers, in specific constitutional guarantees to the States and in implied state sovereignty and inviolability. Justices have said that a treaty cannot cede State territory without its consent; presumably, the United States could not, by treaty or by statute for international purposes, modify the republican character of state governments or, perhaps, abolish all state militia. Under the Eleventh Amendment foreign governments and their nationals cannot sue a State in the courts of the United States without its consent. There is also something more left, too—how much cannot be said with confidence—of the sovereign immunity of the States, that would presumably limit federal regulation under foreign affairs powers as well. State immunities have shrunk radically and state activities are generally subject to federal regulation. But Mr. Justice Frankfurter said:

> * * * There are, of course, State activities and State-owned property that partake of uniqueness from the point of view of intergovernmental relations. These inherently constitute a class by themselves. Only a State can own a Statehouse; only a State can get income by taxing. These could not be included for purposes of federal taxation in any abstract category of taxpayers without taxing the State as a State.

* * *

* * * The States do not conduct foreign relations, but the extent to which they can influence them is also limited by constitutional safeguards for individual rights. Increasingly, the rights of the individual against infringement by the States have become virtually identical with those protected against the Federal Government. The original Constitution forbids the States *ex post facto* laws, bills of attainder, and laws impairing the obligation of contracts (Article I, section 10, clause 1). And while the Bill of Rights did not apply to the States, virtually all of its provisions now do, having been "incorporated" in the Fourteenth Amendment. The due process clause of that Amendment, in particular, affords procedural and substantive protections identical to those that by the same clause in the Fifth Amendment govern the Federal Government.

It is particularly important to the conduct of foreign relations that the Fourteenth Amendment forbids the States to deny to any person the equal protection of the laws, and discriminations and distinctions which might be reasonable if made by the Federal Government might yet constitute denials of equal protection if established by a State. The Equal Protection Clause has long protected aliens against state discriminations denying them equal right to common employment. New doctrine giving new vitality to the equal protection clause has rendered alienage a "suspect classification" and requires a "compelling state interest" to support discrimination against aliens.

Foreign Affairs and the Constitution 246, 269 (1972) (Footnotes omitted).* See discussion of Bill of Rights safeguards, p. 201 above.

## CONGRESSIONAL POWER AND THE TREATY POWER

*HENKIN, FOREIGN AFFAIRS AND THE CONSTITUTION*

148–50 (1972) (footnotes omitted).*

Because the President and the Congress compete for power in the conduct of foreign relations, because the treaty-makers are the President and one house of Congress but not the other, because treaties, * * * often have effect as law like acts of Congress, it was inevitable that questions should arise about the relations between this "Fourth Branch of Government" and the Congress, and not surprising that these relations might suggest limitations on the scope of the Treaty Power. Early in our history members of the House of Representatives [and Thomas Jefferson] argued that treaties could regulate only that which could not be otherwise regulated * * *; and they could not deal with matters that were in the domain of Congress since that would exclude the House from its rightful legislative role * * *.

* * * [These limits] would virtually wipe out the Treaty Power, as Jefferson himself recognized: under contemporary views of the powers of Congress there is little—or nothing—that is dealt with by treaty that could not also be the subject of legislation by Congress.

Even in Jefferson's day, as he noted, this limitation was hardly accepted by all; it has now been long dead. * * * The House of Representatives has frequently bristled, but its exclusion from the treaty process was the clear constitutional plan, and the House could not command the cooperation of the Senate and the President to accept modifications of their privileged prerogatives. The House had to find consolation in that the treaty-makers voluntarily left some subjects to regulation by Congress (e.g., international tariffs and trade), and that it has some say also when, as often, the President must come to Congress as a whole to seek appropriation of funds or other implementation of a treaty. Presidents have also learned to take account of House sensibilities informally by consulting its leaders about major treaties.

While the Treaty Power is not limited by the powers of Congress, it is assumed to be subject to other radiations from the separation of powers. It has been stated that a treaty cannot increase, diminish, or redistribute the constitutional powers of the branches of the federal government or delegate them to others—say, the power of Congress to declare war, or the President's command of American forces, or a court's exercise of judicial power, or indeed the power of the treaty-makers to make international agreements for the United States. These examples are almost wholly hypothetical, but such issues have been raised, particularly in regard to United States participation in international organizations * * *.

### *Notes*

1. During 200 years Congress, and the House of Representatives in particular, sought to offset its exclusion from treaty-making in various ways. Sometimes it was content to support the treaty-makers, often purporting to "authorize" the negotiation of a treaty that would come to the Senate. For an early example see Act of March 3, 1815, 13th Cong., 3d Sess., 3 Stat. 224, authorizing conventions to provide for reciprocal termination of alien discriminations. Compare ch. 1079, § 4, 32 Stat. 373 (1902); ch. 3621, § 4, 34 Stat. 628 (1906); Wright 281–82. In 1925 the House of Representatives resolved that it "desires to

express its cordial approval of the [World Court] and an earnest desire that the United States give early adherence" to it with certain reservations. The House also expressed "its readiness to participate in the enactment of such legislation as will necessarily follow such approval." H.R.Res. 426, 68 Cong., 2d Sess., 66 Cong.Rec. 5404–05 (1925). Sometimes it sought to forestall a treaty by legislating: to preserve its authority over commerce it sought to enact the provisions of a treaty with Great Britain. See 5 Moore, Digest at 223. On occasion it purported to prescribe that international agreements should go to Congress for approval rather than as a treaty to the Senate alone for its consent. Compare the United Nations Participation Act of 1945, 22 U.S.C. § 287d (1988), in regard to agreements under Article 43 of the UN Charter.

Compare the argument that the Panama Canal Treaty was invalid because it disposed of "Territory or other property belonging to the United States," a power expressly granted to Congress. (U.S. Const. Art. IV, § 3, cl. 2). The argument was rejected in Edwards v. Carter, 580 F.2d 1055 (D.C.Cir.1978), cert. denied, 436 U.S. 907, 98 S.Ct. 2240, 56 L.Ed.2d 406 (1978).

On treaties and the legislative powers of Congress, see Restatement (Third) § 303, Comment *c*.

2. It has been suggested that giving the House of Representatives a role in treaty-making would make the treaty power more democratic. See Henkin, Treaties in a Constitutional Democracy, 10 Mich.J.Int'l L. 406, 412–23 (1989), reprinted in, Henkin, Constitutionalism, Democracy and Foreign Affairs 58–68 (1990). For the distribution of power between Congress and the President in foreign affairs generally, see Special Issue, The United States Constitution in its Third Century: Foreign Affairs, 83 A.J.I.L. (October, 1989), published also as Foreign Affairs and the U.S. Constitution (Henkin, Glennon & Rogers, eds., 1990).

## SUBJECT MATTER OF "INTERNATIONAL CONCERN"

For some years there existed the impression that in order to pass constitutional muster, a treaty had to deal with matters of "international concern," a view attributable to a 1929 address by Charles Evans Hughes to the American Society of International Law. See 23 A.S.I.L.Proc. 194–96 (1929); Restatement (Second) Foreign Relations Law of the United States § 117. This address had been invoked to suggest that the United States could not constitutionally adhere to human rights treaties because they involved matters of purely domestic concern. This view has long since been abandoned. See Restatement (Third) § 302, Reporter's Note 2. Henkin writes:

> If there are reasons in foreign policy why the United States seeks an agreement with a foreign country, it does not matter that the subject is otherwise "internal," that the treaty "makes laws for the people of the United States," or that—apart from the treaty—the matter is "normally and appropriately * * * within the local jurisdiction of states." Any treaty that has effect within the United States, including traditional treaties of friendship and commerce, are specifically designed to change the laws of the United States that might otherwise apply, e.g., the rights of aliens here. As other laws of the United States become of interest to

other countries they are equally subject to modification by treaty if the United States has foreign policy reasons for negotiating them.

If there is any basis for the Hughes doctrine, and if it bars some hypothetical agreement on some hypothetical subject, surely it is not relevant where it has been invoked—to prevent adherence by the United States to international human rights conventions. Human rights have long been of international concern and the subject of international agreements * * *

Henkin, Foreign Affairs and the Constitution 154 (1972) (footnotes omitted).* See also, Henkin, The Age of Rights 74–80 (1990).

As of 1993, the United States had adhered to several human rights treaties. Presidents have also sought the consent of the Senate to several covenants and conventions (see p. 627 below) and the constitutional propriety of United States adherence to such treaties is no longer challenged.

The Restatement (Third) has abandoned the requirement of "international concern." See § 302, Comment *c* and Reporters' Note 2.

The Foreign Affairs Manual of the Department of State (§ 311) provides: "Treaties are designed to promote United States interests by securing actions by foreign governments in a way deemed advantageous to the United States." Circular No. 175, as revised. Is that a complete statement of United States interests, particularly in multilateral treaties?

### 3. *Treaties as Law of the Land*

### "SELF-EXECUTING" AND "NON-SELF-EXECUTING" AGREEMENTS

## FOSTER AND ELAM v. NEILSON

Supreme Court of the United States, 1829.
27 U.S. (2 Pet.) 253, 7 L.Ed. 415.

[Appellants sued to recover a tract of land in Louisiana which they claimed under a grant made by the Spanish governor. The possessor of the land argued that the grant on which appellants relied was void because it was made subsequent to the transfer to France and the United States of the territory in which the land was situated. The district court upheld the defense, and the case was brought to the Supreme Court by a writ of error. The Court held that it was obliged to conform its decision on the question of sovereignty to that already reached by the executive and legislative branches of government, and that the territory had to be considered as having been part of the United States at the time of the grant. Appellants relied further, however, on Article 8 of a treaty concluded in 1819 between the United States and Spain (8 Stat. 252), which provided that "all the grants of land made before the 24th of January 1818, by his Catholic majesty, or by his lawful authorities, in the said territories ceded by his majesty to the United States, shall be ratified and confirmed to the persons in possession of the lands, to the same extent that the same grants would be valid if the territories had remained under the dominion of his Catholic majesty," arguing that the land in question formed part of the specified ceded territo-

* Reprinted with permission of Foundation Press.

ries. The Court found it unnecessary to decide the latter question, holding that the treaty did not operate in itself to ratify or confirm appellants' title.]

MARSHALL, C.J.: * * * Do these words [of Article 8] act directly on the grants, so as to give validity to those not otherwise valid; or do they pledge the faith of the United States to pass acts which shall ratify and confirm them?

A treaty is in its nature a contract between two nations, not a legislative act. It does not generally effect, of itself, the object to be accomplished, especially so far as its operation is infra-territorial; but is carried into execution by the sovereign power of the respective parties to the instrument.

In the United States a different principle is established. Our constitution declares a treaty to be the law of the land. It is, consequently, to be regarded in courts of justice as equivalent to an act of the legislature, whenever it operates of itself without the aid of any legislative provision. But when the terms of the stipulation import a contract, when either of the parties engages to perform a particular act, the treaty addresses itself to the political, not the judicial department; and the legislature must execute the contract before it can become a rule for the Court.

The article under consideration does not declare that all the grants made by his Catholic majesty before the 24th of January 1818, shall be valid to the same extent as if the ceded territories had remained under his dominion. It does not say that those grants are hereby confirmed. Had such been its language, it would have acted directly on the subject, and would have repealed those acts of Congress which were repugnant to it; but its language is that those grants shall be ratified and confirmed to the persons in possession, & c. By whom shall they be ratified and confirmed? This seems to be the language of contract; and if it is, the ratification and confirmation which are promised must be the act of the legislature. Until such act shall be passed, the Court is not at liberty to disregard the existing laws on the subject. Congress appears to have understood this article as it is understood by the Court. * * * [The Court then cited legislation which it construed as inconsistent with an intention on the part of Congress to preserve grants of land made by Spanish authorities.]

[Judgment of the district court affirmed.]

### *Notes*

1. The Restatement (Third) § 111, Comment *i* states:

*Constitutional restraints on self-executing character of international agreement.* An international agreement cannot take effect as domestic law without implementation by Congress if the agreement would achieve what lies within the exclusive law-making power of Congress under the Constitution. Thus, an international agreement providing for the payment of money by the United States requires an appropriation of funds by Congress in order to effect the payment required by the agreement. It has been commonly assumed that an international agreement cannot itself bring the United States into a state of war. Similarly, it has been assumed that an international agreement creating an international crime (*e.g.,* genocide) or requiring states parties to punish certain actions (*e.g.,* hijacking) could not itself become part of the criminal law of the United States, but would require

Congress to enact an appropriate statute before an individual could be tried or punished for the offense. It has also been suggested that a treaty cannot "raise revenue" by itself imposing a new tax or a new tariff, in view of the provision in Article I, Section 7: "All Bills for raising Revenue shall originate in the House of Representatives." Treaties of friendship, commerce and navigation, however, frequently affect tariffs and trade by "most-favored-nation," "national treatment," and analogous clauses. Compare § 801.

2. The Restatement (Third) § 111, Comment *h* states:

*Self-executing and non-self-executing international agreements.* In the absence of special agreement, it is ordinarily for the United States to decide how it will carry out its international obligations. Accordingly, the intention of the United States determines whether an agreement is to be self-executing in the United States or should await implementation by legislation or appropriate executive or administrative action. If the international agreement is silent as to its self-executing character and the intention of the United States is unclear, account must be taken of any statement by the President in concluding the agreement or in submitting it to the Senate for consent or to the Congress as a whole for approval, and of any expression by the Senate or by Congress in dealing with the agreement. See § 314, Comments *b* and *d;* § 303, Comment *d.* After the agreement is concluded, often the President must decide in the first instance whether the agreement is self-executing, *i.e.,* whether existing law is adequate to enable the United States to carry out its obligations, or whether further legislation is required. Congress may also consider whether new legislation is necessary and, if so, what it should provide. Whether an agreement is to be given effect without further legislation is an issue that a court must decide when a party seeks to invoke the agreement as law. Whether an agreement is or is not self-executing in the law of another state party to the agreement is not controlling for the United States.

Some provisions of an international agreement may be self-executing and others non-self-executing. If an international agreement or one of its provisions is non-self-executing, the United States is under an international obligation to adjust its laws and institutions as may be necessary to give effect to the agreement. The United States would have a reasonable time to do so before it could be deemed in default. There can, of course, be instances in which the United States Constitution, or previously enacted legislation, will be fully adequate to give effect to an apparently non-self-executing international agreement, thus obviating the need of adopting new legislation to implement it.

Under Subsection (3), strictly, it is the implementing legislation, rather than the agreement itself, that is given effect as law in the United States. That is true even when a non-self-executing agreement is "enacted" by, or incorporated in, implementing legislation.

Whether a treaty is self-executing is a question distinct from whether the treaty creates private rights or remedies. See Comment *g.*

3. In United States v. Percheman, 32 U.S. (7 Pet.) 51, 8 L.Ed. 604 (1833), Marshall relied in part on the Spanish text of Article 8 of the 1819 treaty to support the Court's conclusion that an adverse decision by a board of land commissioners did not foreclose claimant from pursuing judicial remedies to confirm his title to land claimed under a Spanish grant. Emphasizing that "the

modern usage of nations, which has become law," demanded that private rights and property be respected upon a transfer of sovereignty over territory, Marshall held that Article 8 merely restated this principle and needed no implementing legislation.

> The Spanish has been translated, and we now understand that the article, as expressed in that language, is, that the grants "shall remain ratified and confirmed to the persons in possession of them, & c.,"—thus conforming exactly to the universally received doctrine of the law of nations. * * * No violence is done to the language of the treaty by a construction which conforms the English and Spanish to each other. Although the words "shall be ratified and confirmed" are properly the words of contract, stipulating for some future legislative act; they are not necessarily so. They may import that they "shall be ratified and confirmed" by force of the instrument itself. When we observe that in the counterpart of the same treaty, executed at the same time by the same parties, they are used in this sense, we think the construction proper, if not unavoidable.
>
> In the case of Foster v. Elam [*sic* ] 2 Peters 253, this court considered these words as importing contract. The Spanish part of the treaty was not then brought to our view, and we then supposed that there was no variance between them. We did not suppose that there was even a formal difference of expression in the same instrument, drawn up in the language of each party. Had this circumstance been known, we believe it would have produced the construction which we now give to the article.

Id. at 88–89.

4. Treaties that create obligations to refrain from acting are generally self-executing. In an opinion characterized by the Supreme Court as "very able" (United States v. Rauscher, 119 U.S. 407, 427–28, 7 S.Ct. 234, 244–45, 30 L.Ed. 425 (1886)), the Court of Appeals of Kentucky said:

> When it is provided by treaty that certain acts shall not be done, or that certain limitations or restrictions shall not be disregarded or exceeded by the contracting parties, the compact does not need to be supplemented by legislative or executive action, to authorize the courts of justice to decline to override those limitations or to exceed the prescribed restrictions, for the palpable and all-sufficient reason, that to do so would be not only to violate the public faith, but to transgress the "supreme law of the land."

Commonwealth v. Hawes, 76 Ky. (13 Bush) 697, 702–03 (1878).

5. It has been suggested that there should be a strong presumption that a treaty is self-executing unless the contrary is clearly indicated. Since ordinarily a treaty creates international obligations for the United States from the date it comes into force for the United States, if a treaty is not self-executing the United States is obligated to act promptly to implement it. If a treaty has been in effect for some time and the Executive has not sought and Congress has not enacted implementing legislation, it is reasonable to assume that the Executive Branch and Congress had concluded that no implementation was necessary. As to a treaty that has been in effect for some time, a finding that it is not self-executing in effect puts the United States in default on its international obligations. See Restatement (Third) § 111, Reporters' Note 5. See also Iwasawa, The Doctrine of Self-Executing Treaties in the United States: A Critical Analysis, 26 Va. J.Int'l L. 627 (1986); Paust, Self-Executing Treaties, 82 A.J.I.L. 760 (1988); Jackson, Status of Treaties in Domestic Legal Systems: A Policy Analysis, 86

A.J.I.L. 310 (1992). In Cannon v. U.S. Justice Dep't, 973 F.2d 1190, 1197 (5th Cir.1992), reh'g denied, 979 F.2d 211, the court stated that "[p]rocedural legislation which makes operation of a treaty more convenient cannot amend or abrogate a self-executing treaty."

It would appear that the Constitution intended treaties to be law of the land without requiring implementing legislation (contrary to English jurisprudence and practice, which reflects a different division of power between the Executive and the Legislature). That would seem to be implied by the language of Article VI. It may be implied also by the exclusion of the House of Representatives from the treaty-making process. Marshall's suggestion that some treaties, by their nature, are not self-executing was in effect a construction of the Supremacy Clause: since by their nature some treaties are not legislative in character but imply rather a promise by the United States to take action, Article VI could not have intended to give character as law to that which does not have such character.

Recently, cases seem to have increasingly held treaties to be non-self-executing. Examples include:

a. *Non-self-executing treaties*

* Hague Convention Respecting the Law and Customs of War on Land, 1907, Art. 3, 36 Stat. 2277, 2290. See Goldstar (Panama) v. United States, 967 F.2d 965 (4th Cir.1992), cert. denied, ___ U.S. ___, 113 S.Ct. 411, 121 L.Ed.2d 335 (1992).

* United Nations Protocol Relating to the Status of Refugees, 1967, 19 UST 6223; T.I.A.S. No. 6577. See United States v. Aguilar, 883 F.2d 662 (9th Cir.1989), cert. denied, 498 U.S. 1046, 111 S.Ct. 751, 112 L.Ed.2d 771 (1991).

* Geneva Convention Relative to the Protection of Civilian Persons in Time of War, 1949, 6 UST 3516; T.I.A.S. No. 3365; Geneva Convention Relative to the Treatment of Prisoners of War, 1949, 6 UST 3316; T.I.A.S. No. 8413; Convention to Prevent and Punish the Acts of Terrorism Taking the Forms of Crime Against Persons and Related Extortion That Are of International Significance, 1971, 27 UST 3949; T.I.A.S. No. 8413. See Tel–Oren v. Libyan Arab Republic, 726 F.2d 774, 808–09 (D.C.Cir.1984) (Bork, J., concurring), cert. denied, 470 U.S. 1003, 105 S.Ct. 1354, 84 L.Ed.2d 377 (1985).

* Geneva Convention on the High Seas, 1958, 13 UST 2312; T.I.A.S. No. 5200. See United States v. Peterson, 812 F.2d 486 (9th Cir.1987).

* Geneva Convention on Territorial Sea and Contiguous Zone, 1958, 15 UST 1606, T.I.A.S. No. 5639. See United States v. Thompson, 928 F.2d 1060 (11th Cir.1991), cert. denied, ___ U.S. ___, 112 S.Ct. 270, 116 L.Ed.2d 222 (1991).

* Basel Convention on the Control of Transboundary Movements of Hazardous Wastes, 1989, reprinted in, 28 Int'l Legal Materials 657 (1989). See Greenpeace USA v. Stone, 748 F.Supp. 749 (D.Hawaii 1990), appeal dismissed, 924 F.2d 175 (9th Cir.1991).

*b. Treaties held to be self-executing*

* Convention for the Unification of Certain Rules Relating to International Transportation by Air, 1929, T.S. 876 (1934), reprinted at, 49 U.S.C.A. § 1502 note. See Trans World Airlines, Inc. v. Franklin Mint Corp., 466 U.S. 243, 104 S.Ct. 1776, 80 L.Ed.2d 273 (1984).

* Treaty on the Execution of Penal Sentences, 1976, 20 UST 7399; T.I.A.S. No. 8718. See Cannon v. U.S. Dep't of Justice, 973 F.2d 1190 (5th Cir.1992). See also note 7 below.

6. The United Nations Charter and in particular its human rights provisions have been held to be non-self-executing. See Sei Fujii v. California, 217 P.2d 481 (Cal.App.1950) rehearing denied, 218 P.2d 595 (1950), in which the California District Court of Appeal held invalid a state statute forbidding aliens ineligible for citizenship to "acquire, possess, enjoy, use, cultivate, occupy, and transfer" real property, on the ground that the statute conflicted with the United Nations Charter. On appeal, the California Supreme Court held the statute invalid under the Fourteenth Amendment, expressly rejecting the lower court's view that the Charter provisions on human rights had become the "supreme law of the land." 38 Cal.2d 718, 242 P.2d 617 (1952). Gibson, C.J., stated in part: "The fundamental provisions in the charter pledging cooperation in promoting observance of fundamental freedoms lack the mandatory quality and definiteness which would indicate an intent to create justiciable rights in private persons immediately upon ratification. Instead, they are framed as a promise of future action by the member nations." 38 Cal.2d at 724, 242 P.2d at 621–22. What legal obligations, whether or not self-executing, are actually imposed by Articles 1(3), 55 and 56 of the Charter? For comments on the *Sei Fujii* litigation, see Hudson, Charter Provisions on Human Rights in American Law, 44 A.J.I.L. 543 (1950); Wright, National Courts and Human Rights—The Fujii Case, 45 A.J.I.L. 62 (1951); Fairman, Finis to Fujii, 46 A.J.I.L. 682 (1952). See also Frolova v. Union of Soviet Socialist Republics, 761 F.2d 370 (7th Cir.1985); Spiess v. C. Itoh & Co. (America), Inc., 643 F.2d 353, 363 (5th Cir.1981), vacated, 457 U.S. 1128, 102 S.Ct. 2951, 73 L.Ed.2d 1344 (1982); Hitai v. Immigration and Naturalization Service, 343 F.2d 466 (2d Cir.1965), cert. denied, 382 U.S. 816, 86 S.Ct. 36, 15 L.Ed.2d 63 (1965); Vlissidis v. Anadell, 262 F.2d 398 (7th Cir.1959); Rice v. Sioux City Memorial Park Cemetery, Inc., 245 Iowa 147, 60 N.W.2d 110 (1953), aff'd, 348 U.S. 880, 75 S.Ct. 122, 99 L.Ed. 693 (1954), cert. dismissed on rehearing, 349 U.S. 70, 75 S.Ct. 614, 99 L.Ed. 897 (1955); Sipes v. McGhee, 316 Mich. 614, 25 N.W.2d 638 (1947), reversed on other grounds, 334 U.S. 1, 68 S.Ct. 836, 92 L.Ed. 1161 (1948). See generally Lockwood, The United Nations Charter and United States Civil Rights Litigation: 1946–1955, 69 Iowa L.Rev. 901 (1984); see also Chapter 8, p. 600 below; see also pp. 203–04, supra.

In Weir v. Broadnax, 56 Empl.Prac.Dec. (CCH) 40, 684 (S.D.N.Y.1990), the plaintiff's statement of claim alleging the breach of Articles 55 and 56 of the U.N. Charter, based on a pattern of systematic racial discrimination, was struck on defendant's motion; the court rejected plaintiff's argument that the articles reflect customary law and are sufficient to support a private cause of action. See also United States v. Caro–Quintero, 745 F.Supp. 599 (C.D.Cal.1990), aff'd sub nom. United States v. Alvarez–Machain, 946 F.2d 1466 (9th Cir.1990), rev'd, ___ U.S. ___, 112 S.Ct. 2188, 119 L.Ed.2d 441 (1992) (neither the U.N. Charter nor the Charter of the Organization of American States reflects customary law); United States v. Noriega, 746 F.Supp. 1506 (S.D.Fla.1990); Helms v. Secretary of Treasury, 721 F.Supp. 1354 (D.D.C.1989).

7. Marshall did not suggest that treaties (or treaty provisions) of a self-executing nature could be rendered non-self-executing by Presidential or Senatorial declaration. That practice developed largely after World War II in special circumstances, on the basis of arguments for cooperation between the "treaty makers and the law makers."

For example, following the Second World War the United States and Canada concluded a treaty concerning the Niagara River which provided for the allocation as between the two countries of the hydro-electric power produced. The United States Senate in its resolution of advice and consent included a "reservation" that the United States reserves the right to provide by legislation for the use of the United States share of electric power and that no project for the use of that share should be undertaken until specifically authorized by Congress. Canada did not express any objection to the reservation, saying it was none of its concern. The New York Power Authority requested a license for a project to use the United States share of the power, but it was refused by the Federal Power Commission on the ground that Congress had not legislated and therefore the project was contrary to the reservation incorporated into the treaty. What legal objection could be made to this opinion? See Power Authority of New York v. Federal Power Commission, 247 F.2d 538 (App.D.C.1957) (vacated on remand) which held that the "reservation" had not the effect of law. What is the basis for that decision? For critical comment, see Henkin, The Treaty Makers and the Law Makers: The Niagara Power Reservation, 56 Colum.L.Rev. 1151 (1956).

Henkin later wrote:

> Some who wished to see the treaty come into effect without the Senate's limitation argued that the reservation had no legal effect: it was not a proper treaty provision since it contained no element of international obligation. That objection, of course, does not relate to the Senate's part in the treaty-making process; it would apply as well if the same provision had been inserted by the negotiators in the original treaty. (I discuss that objection below). But the arguments failed to consider the effect of the Senate proviso as a condition to its consent. If the Senate gave its consent only on condition that the United States share of the waters should await disposition by Congress, the treaty could take effect only subject to that condition. If the Senate's condition did not operate to prevent the treaty from coming into effect, it is questionable whether the President had authority to ratify the treaty until Congress adopted the implementing legislation called for by the Senate, and whether his ratification in disregard of the Senate's condition was constitutionally effective.

Foreign Affairs and the Constitution at 135.* See also id. at 160–61.

The practice has been extended beyond the special circumstances of the Niagara River Treaty and has become more common towards the end of the 20th century, particularly in ratifying human rights agreements. For example, in 1986, the Senate gave its consent to ratification of the Genocide Convention subject to a proviso that the President was not to deposit the instrument of ratification until after Congress had enacted implementing legislation. See 132 Cong.Rec. S12297–02 (1986). See also the declarations by the Senate in connection with its consent to the United Nations Convention against Torture and Other Cruel, Inhuman or Degrading Treatment or Punishment, G.A.Res. 39/46 (1984), reprinted in 23 I.L.M. 1027 (1984), and the International Covenant on Civil and Political Rights, 999 U.N.T.S. 171, reprinted in, 6 I.L.M. 368 (1967). See Chapter 8 infra.

Declaring a treaty non-self-executing is sometimes justified on the ground that it gives a role in the treaty-making process to the House of Representatives and make the process more "democratic" insofar as the House is a more representative body than the Senate. It sometimes appears that the President and the Senate may have declared treaties to be non-self-executing from resistance to "law making by treaty," particularly by multilateral treaties because they are made largely by other countries, or in order to delay or even frustrate U.S. implementation of its undertakings. It has been suggested that since other states may have to adopt legislation to give effect to treaties, the U.S. too, should not enforce its obligations immediately. Compare United States v. Postal, 589 F.2d 862 (5th Cir.1979), cert. denied, 444 U.S. 832, 100 S.Ct. 61, 62 L.Ed.2d 40 (1979). But see Restatement (Third) § 111, Reporters' Note 5, declaring that view to be "misconceived."

The practice of the Senate (or the President) to declare non-self-executing a treaty that would otherwise be self-executing is being increasingly questioned. See, e.g., Damrosch, The Role of the United States Senate Concerning "Self–Executing" and "Non–Self–Executing" Treaties, 67 Chi.–Kent L.Rev. 515, 516–18 (1991); Riesenfeld & Abbott, The Scope of U.S. Senate Control Over the Conclusion and Operations of Treaties, 67 Chi.–Kent L.Rev. 571, 631 (1991); Vasquez, Treaty–Based Rights and Remedies of Individuals, 92 Colum.L.Rev. 1082 (1992). Is it implausible to argue that for the President or the Senate to declare non-self-executing a treaty that could be executed without implementing legislation is contrary to both the letter and spirit of the Constitution, and to the distribution of power between the Senate and the House intended by the Framers?

8. In Attorney–General for Canada v. Attorney–General for Ontario, [1937] A.C. 326, the Privy Council was asked to decide whether certain Canadian statutes, enacted in order to fulfill Canada's obligations under a number of International Labor Conventions, were constitutionally effective without the consent of the Canadian provinces to bring the law of those provinces into conformity with the provisions of the conventions. In the course of his opinion holding that the statutes were *ultra vires* of the Parliament of Canada under the British North America Act of 1867, Lord Atkin made the following general observations on the internal effect of treaties under the British system:

> * * * It will be essential to keep in mind the distinction between (1.) the formation, and (2.) the performance, of the obligations constituted by a treaty, using that word as comprising any agreement between two or more sovereign States. Within the British Empire there is a well-established rule that the making of a treaty is an executive act, while the performance of its obligations, if they entail alteration of the existing domestic law, requires legislative action. Unlike some other countries, the stipulations of a treaty duly ratified do not within the Empire, by virtue of the treaty alone, have the force of law. If the national executive, the government of the day, decide to incur the obligations of a treaty which involve alteration of law they have to run the risk of obtaining the assent of Parliament to the necessary statute or statutes. To make themselves as secure as possible they will often in such cases before final ratification seek to obtain from Parliament an expression of approval. But it has never been suggested, and it is not the law, that such an expression of approval operates as law, or that in law it precludes the assenting Parliament, or any subsequent Parliament, from refusing to give its sanction to any legislative proposals that may subsequently be brought before it. Parliament, no doubt, as the Chief Justice points out, has a constitutional control over the executive: but it cannot be disputed that the creation of the obligations undertaken in treaties and the assent to their form and quality are the function of the executive alone. Once they are created, while they bind the State as against the other contracting parties, Parliament may refuse to perform them and so leave the State in default. In a unitary State whose Legislature possesses

unlimited powers the problem is simple. Parliament will either fulfil or not treaty obligations imposed upon the State by its executive. The nature of the obligations does not affect the complete authority of the Legislature to make them law if it so chooses. But in a State where the Legislature does not possess absolute authority, in a federal State where legislative authority is limited by a constitutional document, or is divided up between different Legislatures in accordance with the classes of subject-matter submitted for legislation, the problem is complex. The obligations imposed by treaty may have to be performed, if at all, by several Legislatures; and the executive have the task of obtaining the legislative assent not of the one Parliament to whom they may be responsible, but possibly of several Parliaments to whom they stand in no direct relation. The question is not how is the obligation formed, that is the function of the executive; but how is the obligation to be performed, and that depends upon the authority of the competent Legislature or Legislatures.

[1937] A.C. at 347–48. See the symposium on this case in 15 Canadian Bar Rev. 393 (1937), and see generally McNair, The Law of Treaties 81–110 (1961). If difficulties are expected in the process of implementing the provisions of an international agreement, what precautions might the executive of a state take in order to avoid international responsibility for defaulting on the obligations imposed by the agreement?

9. Section 34 of the Convention on the Privileges and Immunities of the United Nations, 1946, 1 U.N.T.S. 15, provides: "It is understood that, when an instrument of accession is deposited on behalf of any Member, the Member will be in a position under its own law to give effect to the terms of this convention." Article X(1) of the Interim Convention on Conservation of North Pacific Fur Seals, 1957, 8 U.S.T. 2283, 314 U.N.T.S. 105, provides: "Each Party agrees to enact and enforce such legislation as may be necessary to guarantee the observance of this Convention and to make effective its provisions with appropriate penalties for violation thereof." Article III(5) of the Treaty between the French Republic and the Federal Republic of Germany on French–German Cooperation, 2 I.L.M. 229 (1963), provides: "The present Treaty will enter into force as soon as each of the two Governments will have made known to the other that, on the domestic level, the necessary conditions for its implementation have been fulfilled." Section 15 of the Tracking Stations Agreement between the United States and Spain, 1964, 15 U.S.T. 153, 511 U.N.T.S. 61, provides: "It is understood that, to the extent the implementation of this agreement will depend on funds appropriated by the Congress of the United States, it is subject to the availability of such funds." Even a treaty that is self-executing may sometimes include obligations on the parties to adopt implementing legislation. See, for example, Article 2(2) of the International Covenant on Civil and Political Rights, discussed pp. 610 and 619 below; Schachter, The Obligation to Implement the Covenant in Domestic Law, in The International Bill of Rights: the Covenant on Civil and Political Rights (Henkin ed. 1981).

10. For the different—but important—question whether an individual (in contrast to a state party to a treaty) has rights under a treaty, see Dreyfus v. Von Finck, 534 F.2d 24, 30 (2d Cir.1976). Dreyfus was a Swiss citizen who sued West German citizens in a United States court for unlawful confiscation of his property in Nazi Germany in 1938. He based his private right of action on four treaties to which the United States was a party. In concluding that Dreyfus could not sue under any of the treaties, the court said that they were not self-executing and that, in any event, it is only when a treaty "prescribes rules by

which private rights may be determined, that it may be relied upon for the enforcement of such rights * * * [N]one of these [treaties] dealt with the expropriations by Germans of the property of German citizens and none conferred any private rights which were enforceable in American courts." Id. at 30. See Restatement (Third) § 111, Comment *g*.

In Committee of United States Citizens Living in Nicaragua v. Reagan, 859 F.2d 929 (1988), the Court of Appeals for the D.C. Circuit held that provisions of the United Nations Charter requiring compliance with International Court of Justice decisions do not create rights that are enforceable by individuals in United States Courts.

## CONFLICT OF TREATY WITH UNITED STATES STATUTE

### WHITNEY v. ROBERTSON

Supreme Court of the United States, 1888.
124 U.S. 190, 8 S.Ct. 456, 31 L.Ed. 386.

[Plaintiff sued to recover amounts paid under protest to the Collector of Customs at New York in satisfaction of duties assessed upon plaintiff's shipments of sugar from the Dominican Republic. Plaintiff alleged that sugar from the Hawaiian Islands was admitted free of duty into the United States, and claimed that a clause of the treaty between the United States and the Dominican Republic guaranteed that no higher duty would be assessed upon goods imported into the United States from the Dominican Republic than was assessed upon goods imported from any other foreign country. Judgment was entered for the Collector of Customs upon the latter's demurrer, and plaintiff appealed. The Supreme Court, in an opinion by Mr. Justice Field, first held that the treaty could not be interpreted to foreclose the extension by the United States of special privileges to countries such as the Hawaiian Islands which were willing in return to extend special privileges to the United States.]

FIELD, J.: * * * But, independently of considerations of this nature, there is another and complete answer to the pretensions of the plaintiffs. The act of Congress under which the duties were collected, authorized their exaction. It is of general application, making no exception in favor of goods of any country. It was passed after the treaty with the Dominican Republic, and, if there be any conflict between the stipulations of the treaty and the requirements of the law, the latter must control. A treaty is primarily a contract between two or more independent nations, and is so regarded by writers on public law. For the infraction of its provisions a remedy must be sought by the injured party through reclamations upon the other. When the stipulations are not self-executing, they can only be enforced pursuant to legislation to carry them into effect, and such legislation is as much subject to modification and repeal by Congress as legislation upon any other subject. If the treaty contains stipulations which are self-executing, that is, require no legislation to make them operative, to that extent they have the force and effect of a legislative enactment. Congress may modify such provisions, so far as they bind the United States, or supersede them altogether. By the Constitution, a treaty is placed on the same footing, and made of like obligation, with an act of legislation. Both are declared by that instrument to be the supreme law of the land, and no superior efficacy is given to either over the other. When the two relate to the same subject, the courts will always endeavor to construe them so as to give effect to both, if that can be done without violating the language of either; but, if the two are inconsistent, the one last in date will control the other: provided, always, the stipulation of the treaty on the subject is self-executing. If the country with which the treaty is made is dissatisfied with the action of the legislative department, it may present its complaint to the executive head of the government, and take such other measures as it may deem essential for the protection of its interests. The courts can afford no redress. Whether the complaining nation has just cause of complaint, or our country was justified in its legislation, are not matters for judicial cognizance. * * *

Judgment affirmed.

### *Notes*

1. The Restatement (Third) § 115 states:

*Inconsistency Between International Law or Agreements and Domestic Law: Law of the United States*

(1)(a) An act of Congress supersedes an earlier rule of international law or a provision of an international agreement as law of the United States if the purpose of the act to supersede the earlier rule or provision is clear or if the act and the earlier rule or provision cannot be fairly reconciled.

(b) That a rule of international law or a provision of an international agreement is superseded as domestic law does not relieve the United States of its international obligation or of the consequences of a violation of that obligation.

(2) A provision of a treaty of the United States that becomes effective as law of the United States supersedes as domestic law any inconsistent preexisting provision of a law or treaty of the United States.

* * *

As to conflict between statutes and customary international law, see p. 167 above. For the principle of interpretation to avoid conflict between a federal statute and international obligation, see p. 224 below.

The Restatement here states rules of United States law. For the applicable rules of international law, see Chapter 6.

2. In a Memorandum prepared for President Harding, October 8, 1921, Secretary of State Charles Evans Hughes stated, "Congress [by passing inconsistent legislation] has the power to violate treaties, but if they are violated, the Nation will be none the less exposed to all the international consequences of such a violation because the action is taken by the legislative branch of the Government." 5 Hackworth at 324–25. "Where a treaty and an act of Congress are wholly inconsistent with each other and the two cannot be reconciled, the courts have held that the one later in point of time must prevail. While this is necessarily true as a matter of municipal law, it does not follow, as has sometimes been said, that a treaty is repealed or abrogated by a later inconsistent statute. The treaty still subsists as an international obligation although it may not be enforceable by the courts or administrative authorities." Id. at 185–86. See, also The Cherokee Tobacco, 78 U.S. (11 Wall.) 616, 20 L.Ed. 227 (1871); Chae Chan Ping v. United States, 130 U.S. 581, 9 S.Ct. 623, 32 L.Ed. 1068 (1889);

Rainey v. United States, 232 U.S. 310, 316, 34 S.Ct. 429, 58 L.Ed. 617 (1914); and other cases cited in 5 Hackworth at 185–98. For a discussion of the jurisprudence of the Supreme Court on the hierarchy between statutes and treaties, see Henkin, The Constitution and United States Sovereignty: A Century of Chinese Exclusion and Its Progeny, 100 Harv.L.Rev. 853 (1987); Westen, The Place of Foreign Treaties in the Courts of the United States: A Reply to Louis Henkin, 101 Harv.L.Rev. 511 (1987); Henkin, Lexical Priority or "Political Question:" A Response, 101 Harv.L.Rev. 524 (1987).

The interplay between the treaty obligations of the United States and apparently inconsistent legislation was raised in 1987 by the Anti–Terrorism Act (22 U.S.C.A. §§ 5201–5203). The Act was construed by the Attorney General to require the closure of the P.L.O.'s Permanent Observer Mission to the United Nations. Such closure, it was assumed, would have violated U.S. obligations under the United Nations Headquarters Agreement. The dispute led to an advisory opinion of the International Court of Justice, as well as to proceedings in the U.S. federal courts. It was resolved when the District Court ruled that the Act did not require closure of the Mission, thus avoiding conflict with the treaty. See Applicability of the Obligation to Arbitrate Under Section 21 of the U.N. Headquarters Agreement of 26 June 1947, 1988 I.C.J. 12; United States v. Palestine Liberation Organization, 695 F.Supp. 1456 (S.D.N.Y.1988). See also Quigley, Congress and the P.L.O. and Conflicts between Statutes and Treaties, 35 Wayne L.Rev. 83 (1988).

Note that "a treaty will not be deemed to have been abrogated or modified by a later statute unless such purpose on the part of Congress has been clearly expressed." Cook v. United States, 288 U.S. 102, 120, 53 S.Ct. 305, 311, 77 L.Ed. 641 (1933) (Brandeis, J.). See also Steinhardt, The Role of International Law as a Canon of Domestic Statutory Construction, 43 Vand.L.Rev. 1103 (1990). Do the foregoing principles apply equally to executive agreements? See Restatement (Third) § 114, p. 224 below. See also p. 236 below.

Sohn has suggested that the United States should adopt the rule of the Netherlands and give effect to a multilateral law-codifying treaty even in the face of a later inconsistent statute. Sohn, 63 A.S.I.L.Proc. 180 (1969). Can such a principle be supported by constitutional doctrine? See Henkin, Foreign Affairs and the Constitution 163–64 (1972), suggesting that contrary to what the Supreme Court may have implied, the rule announced by Whitney v. Robertson is not compelled by the language of the Supremacy Clause. U.S. Const., Art. VI.

4. In Tag v. Rogers, 267 F.2d 664 (D.C.Cir.1959), cert. denied, 362 U.S. 904, 80 S.Ct. 615, 4 L.Ed.2d 555 (1960), the appellant argued that international practice, formalized in a rule of law, forbids the seizure or confiscation of the property of enemy nationals during time of war, at least where that property had been acquired by enemy nationals before the war and in reliance upon international agreements. In rejecting this argument the court said in part: "Once a policy has been declared in a treaty or statute, it is the duty of the federal courts to accept as law the latest expression of policy made by the constitutionally authorized policy-making authority. If Congress adopts a policy that conflicts with the Constitution of the United States, Congress is then acting beyond its authority and the courts must declare the resulting statute to be null and void. When, however, a constitutional agency adopts a policy contrary to a trend in international law or to a treaty or prior statute, the courts must accept the latest act of that agency." 267 F.2d at 668. See also The Over the Top, 5 F.2d 838 (D.Conn.1925); Committee of United States Citizens Living in Nicara-

gua v. Reagan, 859 F.2d 929 (D.C.Cir.1988). As to whether the courts will give effect to Executive acts that violate international law, see pp. 175–76.

In *The Paquete Habana,* p. 58 supra, the Supreme Court said: "This rule of international law is one which prize courts, administering the law of nations, are bound to take judicial notice of, and to give effect to, *in the absence of any treaty or other public act of their own government in relation to the matter.*" (Emphasis supplied). 175 U.S. 677, 708, 20 S.Ct. 290, 302, 44 L.Ed. 320, 332; see also 175 U.S. at 700, 20 S.Ct. at 299, 44 L.Ed. at 328. In that case the Court found that the seizure of fishing boats as prize in violation of international law had not been authorized by the President, and that the President had clearly manifested a policy that the war should be conducted in accordance with international law. 175 U.S. at 712, 20 S.Ct. at 304, 44 L.Ed. at 333.

Will the courts give effect to a newly developed principle of customary law in the face of an earlier inconsistent statute, treaty, or executive action? See Restatement (Third) § 115, Reporters' Note 4.

5. "Most-favored-nation" clauses such as that relied upon by plaintiff in the principal case were included in commercial treaties by the United States until 1923 on either a "conditional" basis or on an "unconditional" basis, i.e., without regard to reciprocal tariff and other concessions. In 1923, the United States adopted the policy of negotiating such treaties on an unconditional most-favored-nation basis. Secretary of State Hughes explained that "[w]hen the conditional most-favored-nation policy was first formulated, discrimination in commercial matters was the general rule among nations, and it was deemed advisable for the United States to adopt a policy of making concessions only to such states as granted in each case some definite and equivalent compensation. Since that time, however, the principle of equality of treatment has made great progress, and it is now considered to be in the interest of the trade of the United States, in competing with the trade of other countries in the markets of the world, to endeavor to extend the acceptance of that principle." 5 Hackworth at 272; see generally id. at 269–96. The General Agreement on Tariffs and Trade, see T.I.A.S. No. 1700 (1947), is based upon the unconditional most-favored-nation clause.

## INTERPRETATION OF FEDERAL STATUTE IN LIGHT OF INTERNATIONAL LAW OR AGREEMENT

### *RESTATEMENT (THIRD) § 114*

Where fairly possible, a United States statute is to be construed so as not to conflict with international law or with an international agreement of the United States.

* * *

### REPORTERS' NOTES

1. *Interpretation to avoid violation of international obligation.* Chief Justice Marshall stated that "an Act of Congress ought never to be construed to violate the law of nations if any other possible construction remains * * *." Murray v. Schooner Charming Betsy, 6 U.S. (2 Cranch) 64, 118, 2 L.Ed. 208 (1804). See also Lauritzen v. Larsen, 345 U.S. 571, 578, 73 S.Ct.

921, 926, 97 L.Ed. 1254 (1953). On several occasions the Supreme Court has interpreted acts of Congress so as to avoid conflict with earlier treaty provisions. Chew Heong v. United States, 112 U.S. 536, 539–40, 5 S.Ct. 255, 255–56, 28 L.Ed. 770 (1884) (later immigration law did not affect treaty right of resident Chinese alien to reenter); Weinberger v. Rossi, 456 U.S. 25, 33, 102 S.Ct. 1510, 1516, 71 L.Ed.2d 715 (1982); *cf.* Clark v. Allen, 331 U.S. 503, 67 S.Ct. 1431, 91 L.Ed. 1633 (1947) (Trading with the Enemy Act not incompatible with treaty rights of German aliens to inherit realty which were succeeded to by the United States). See also Cook v. United States, 288 U.S. 102, 53 S.Ct. 305, 77 L.Ed. 641 (1933), in which the Supreme Court found that reenactment, after a series of "liquor treaties" with Great Britain, of prior statutory provisions for boarding vessels did not reflect a purpose of Congress to supersede the effect of the treaties as domestic law. Construing an international agreement to avoid conflict with a statute is more difficult since the proper interpretation of a treaty is an international question as to which courts of the United States have less leeway. The disposition to seek to construe a treaty to avoid conflict with a State statute is less clear. Compare Nielsen v. Johnson, 279 U.S. 47, 52, 49 U.S. 223, 224, 73 L.Ed. 607 (1929), with Guaranty Trust Co. v. United States, 304 U.S. 126, 143, 58 S.Ct. 785, 794, 82 L.Ed. 1224 (1938).

---

Other national legal systems generally also accept the principle that, where fairly possible, domestic law should be interpreted to avoid inconsistency with international obligations. See Sorensen, Report Concerning Obligations of a State Party to a Treaty, in Human Rights in National and International Law 13 (Robertson ed. 1968).

### 4. *Suspension or Termination of Treaties*

## THE POWER TO "UNMAKE" TREATIES

*HENKIN, FOREIGN AFFAIRS AND THE CONSTITUTION*

167–71 (1972) (footnotes omitted).*

The United States sometimes has the right to terminate a treaty by its own terms, at some prescribed time after giving notice of its intention to do so (e.g., the Nuclear Test Ban of 1963). Treaties can be terminated by more or less formal agreement of the parties. The international law of treaties permits termination for important breach by the other side, or because of a fundamental change in circumstances (the principle of *rebus sic stantibus*). International law also recognizes the power—though not the right—to break a treaty and abide the international consequences.

No doubt, the Federal Government has the constitutional power to terminate treaties on behalf of the United States in all these ways and circumstances: neither the declaration in the Supremacy Clause that treaties are law of the land, nor anything else in the Constitution, denies the United States these powers inherent in its sovereignty. But while the Constitution tells us who can make treaties, it does not say who can unmake them.

* Reprinted with permission of Foundation Press.

At various times the power to terminate treaties has been claimed for the President, the President-and-Senate, the Congress. Presidents have claimed authority, presumably under their foreign affairs power, to act for the United States to terminate treaties, whether in accordance with their terms, or in accordance with or in violation of international law. Franklin Roosevelt, for example, denounced an extradition treaty with Greece in 1933 because Greece had refused to extradite the celebrated Mr. Insull; in 1939 he denounced the Treaty of Commerce, Friendship and Navigation with Japan. Without formal termination, Presidents in conducting foreign relations have acted contrary to treaty obligations, even where the treaty had domestic effect as law of the land, sometimes inviting the other party to terminate the treaty.

In principle, one might argue, if the Framers required the President to obtain the Senate's consent for making a treaty, its consent ought to be required also for terminating it, and there is eminent dictum to support that view. But perhaps the Framers were concerned only to check the President in "entangling" the United States; "disentangling" is less risky and may have to be done quickly, and is often done piecemeal, or *ad hoc,* by various means or acts. In any event, since the President acts for the United States internationally he can effectively terminate or violate treaties, and the Senate has not established its authority to join or veto him.

Congress, we know, has some power effectively to breach treaties. While it is probably required to pass legislation necessary and proper to implement treaty obligations, it could refuse to do so, put the United States in default, perhaps compel the President to terminate the treaty or induce the other party to do so; often it can achieve these ends too later, by enacting legislation inconsistent with treaty obligations. Congress can also declare war and terminate or suspend treaty relations with the other belligerent.

In the past, Congress purported also to denounce or abrogate treaties for the United States or to direct the President to do so. Those instances, no doubt, reflect the recurrent claims of Congress to general powers to make foreign policy, as well as particular arguments that the maintenance or termination of treaties is intimately related to war-or-peace for which Congress has sole responsibility. But Congressional resolutions have no effect internationally unless the President adopts and communicates them, and while some Presidents have chosen to comply with Congressional wishes, others have disregarded them.

* * *

If issues as to who has power to terminate treaties arise again, however, it seems unlikely that Congress will successfully assert the power. Especially with the changed character of war and its place in international relations, Congress will probably be unable to claim plausibly that the maintenance or termination of treaties is intimately related to war-or-peace; a President who wishes to maintain a treaty will doubtless treat a Congressional denunciation or directive to terminate as only a hortatory "sense resolution." (Politically of course, the President could not lightly disregard the sense of Congress especially if both houses have joined, claimed constitutional power, and publicly proclaimed a call for radical action.)

The power to terminate a treaty is a political power: courts do not terminate treaties, though they may interpret political acts or even political silences to determine whether they implied or intended termination. If there is a breach of a treaty by the other party, it is the President not the courts who will decide whether the United States will denounce the treaty, consider itself liberated from its obligations, or seek other relief or none at all.

Nor do courts sit in judgment on the political branches to prevent them from terminating or breaching a treaty. Where fairly possible, the courts will interpret actions of the President or of Congress to render them consistent with international obligations, but both President and Congress can exercise their respective constitutional powers regardless of treaty obligations, and the courts will give effect to acts within their powers even if they violate treaty obligations or other international law.

### *Note*

See also Henkin, Foreign Affairs and the Constitution at 136:

> Once the Senate has consented, the President is free to make (or not to make) the treaty and the Senate has no further authority in respect of it. Attempts by the Senate to withdraw, modify or interpret its consent after a treaty is ratified have no legal weight; nor has the Senate any authoritative voice in interpreting a treaty or in terminating it. Of course, in its legislative capacity as one of the two houses of Congress (as distinguished from its executive role as treaty-maker) the Senate participates in whatever Congress can do about treaties.*

In 1979, several U.S. Senators challenged the authority of the President to terminate the Mutual Defense Treaty of 1954 with the Republic of China (Taiwan). The District Court held that the power to terminate the treaty was shared between the Congress and the President, but the Court of Appeals, *en banc,* reversed, four judges holding that the President had authority to terminate the treaty in question on his own authority. The Supreme Court vacated the judgment with instructions to dismiss, four of the Justices reaching that result on the ground that the case presented a political question. (See p. 178 above on political questions.) Only one justice, dissenting, reached the substantive issue and upheld the power of the President to terminate the treaty in this case as incidental to his power to recognize governments. Goldwater v. Carter (D.D.C. June 6, 1979) (Memorandum–Order), reprinted in 125 Cong.Rec. S7050 (daily ed. June 6, 1979), altered and amended, 481 F.Supp. 949 (D.D.C.1979) (granting injunctive and declaratory relief), rev'd, 617 F.2d 697 (D.C.Cir.), vacated and remanded with instructions to dismiss, 444 U.S. 996, 100 S.Ct. 533, 62 L.Ed.2d 428 (1979).

The United States Senate voted an amendment to a pending resolution in which the Senate would declare that it is the sense of the Senate that the President may not terminate any mutual defense treaty without the consent of the Senate. See 125 Cong.Rec. S7015, S7038 (daily ed. June 6, 1979). The resolution was not finally adopted.

The Senate Foreign Relations Committee had suggested instead a resolution expressing the sense of the Senate that the President should not terminate treaties on his own authority except in certain circumstances, and that the

Senate may prescribe terms for termination of a particular treaty as a condition of Senate consent to its ratification. See S.Rep. No. 96–119, 96th Cong., 1st Sess. 1 (1979).

The Restatement (Third) § 339, Comment *a* states: "If the United States Senate, in giving consent to a treaty declares that it does so on condition that the President shall not terminate the treaty without the consent of the Congress or of the Senate, or that he shall do so only in accordance with some other procedure, that condition presumably would be binding on the President if he proceeded to make the treaty."

## TERMINATION FOR BREACH OF AGREEMENT

## CHARLTON v. KELLY

Supreme Court of the United States, 1913.
229 U.S. 447, 33 S.Ct. 945, 57 L.Ed. 1274.

[Petitioner brought a writ of habeas corpus to prevent his extradition as a fugitive from justice in Italy. He argued, *inter alia,* that as a U.S. citizen he was not extraditable under the treaty since Italy had refused to extradite Italian nationals to the United States. On appeal from dismissal of the petition, the Supreme Court affirmed.]

* * *

LURTON, J.:

* * *

4. We come now to the contention that by the refusal of Italy to deliver up fugitives of Italian nationality, the treaty has thereby ceased to be of obligation on the United States. The attitude of Italy is indicated by its Penal Code of 1900 which forbids the extradition of citizens, and by the denial in two or more instances to recognize this obligation of the treaty as extending to its citizens.

* * *

* * * If the attitude of Italy was, as contended, a violation of the obligation of the treaty, which, in international law, would have justified the United States in denouncing the treaty as no longer obligatory, it did not automatically have that effect. If the United States elected not to declare its abrogation, or come to a rupture, the treaty would remain in force. It was only voidable, not void; and if the United States should prefer, it might waive any breach which in its judgment had occurred and conform to its own obligation as if there had been no such breach. * * *

* * *

That the political branch of the Government recognizes the treaty obligation as still existing is evidenced by its action in this case. In the memorandum giving the reasons of the Department of State for determining to surrender the appellant, after stating the difference between the two governments as to the interpretation of this clause of the treaty, Mr. Secretary Knox said:

"The question is now for the first time presented as to whether or not the United States is under obligation under treaty to surrender to Italy for trial and punishment citizens of the United States fugitive from the justice of Italy, notwithstanding the interpretation placed upon the treaty by Italy with reference to Italian subjects. In this connection it should be observed that the United States, although, as stated above, consistently contending that the Italian interpretation was not the proper one, has not treated the Italian practice as a breach of the treaty obligation necessarily requiring abrogation, has not abrogated the treaty or taken any step looking thereto, and has, on the contrary, constantly regarded the treaty as in full force and effect and has answered the obligations imposed thereby and has invoked the rights therein granted. It should, moreover, be observed that even though the action of the Italian Government be regarded as a breach of the treaty, the treaty is binding until abrogated, and therefore the treaty not having been abrogated, its provisions are operative against us.

"The question would, therefore, appear to reduce itself to one of interpretation of the meaning of the treaty, the Government of the United States being now for the first time called upon to declare whether it regards the treaty as obliging it to surrender its citizens to Italy, notwithstanding Italy has not and insists it can not surrender its citizens to us. It should be observed, in the first place, that we have always insisted not only with reference to the Italian extradition treaty, but with reference to the other extradition treaties similarly phrased that the word 'persons' includes citizens. We are, therefore, committed to that interpretation. The fact that we have for reasons already given ceased generally to make requisition upon the Government of Italy for the surrender of Italian subjects under the treaty, would not require of necessity that we should, as a matter of logic or law, regard ourselves as free from the obligation of surrendering our citizens, we laboring under no such legal inhibition regarding surrender as operates against the government of Italy. Therefore, since extradition treaties need not be reciprocal, even in the matter of the surrendering of citizens, it would seem entirely sound to consider ourselves as bound to surrender our citizens to Italy even though Italy should not, by reason of the provisions of her municipal law be able to surrender its citizens to us."

The executive department having thus elected to waive any right to free itself from the obligation to deliver up its own citizens, it is the plain duty of this court to recognize the obligation to surrender the appellant as one imposed by the treaty as the supreme law of the land and as affording authority for the warrant of extradition.

Judgment affirmed.

---

On the right of a state to terminate a treaty because of a serious breach by the other party, see Chapter 6, Section 6.

## D. INTERNATIONAL AGREEMENTS IN UNITED STATES LAW: EXECUTIVE AGREEMENTS

### AUTHORITY TO MAKE INTERNATIONAL AGREEMENTS: LAW OF THE UNITED STATES

#### *RESTATEMENT (THIRD) § 303*

* * *

(2) The President, with the authorization or approval of Congress, may make an international agreement dealing with any matter that falls within the powers of Congress and of the President under the Constitution.

* * *

(4) The President, on his own authority, may make an international agreement dealing with any matter that falls within his independent powers under the Constitution.

### *1. Congressional–Executive Agreements*

### THE SOURCE AND LEGAL STATUS OF THE EXECUTIVE AGREEMENT

#### *HENKIN, FOREIGN AFFAIRS AND THE CONSTITUTION*

173–76 (1972) (footnotes omitted).*

Since our national beginnings Presidents have made some 1300 treaties with the consent of the Senate; they have made many thousands of other international agreements without seeking Senate consent. Some were authorized or approved by joint resolution of Congress; many were made by the President on his sole authority.

The Constitution does not expressly confer authority to make international agreements other than treaties,** but executive agreements, varying widely in formality and in importance, have been common from our early history. Where does the President find constitutional authority to make them? How does one distinguish an agreement which can be approved by the President with the approval of Congress, or on his own authority, from one requiring Senate consent? Are executive agreements subject to the same constitutional limitations as treaties, or to others? Do they have the same quality as law of the land, the same supremacy to state law, the same equality with acts of Congress?

* * *

Agreements made by joint authority of the President and Congress have come about in different ways. Congress has authorized the President to negotiate and conclude agreements on particular subjects—on postal relations, reciprocal trade, lend-lease, foreign assistance, nuclear reactors. Congress has authorized the President to conclude particular agreements already negotiated, as in the case of the Headquarters Agreement with the

* Reprinted with permission of Foundation Press.

** The Constitution does provide for "Agreements or Compacts" between States and foreign powers, with the consent of Congress. Art. I, sec. 10. * * *

United Nations and various multilateral agreements establishing international organizations, e.g., UNRRA, the International Bank and the International Monetary Fund, the International Refugee Organization. In some instances Congress has approved Presidential agreements by legislation or appropriation of funds to carry out their obligations.

Constitutional doctrine to support Congressional–Executive agreements is not clear or agreed. The Constitution expressly prescribes the treaty procedure and nowhere suggests that another method of making international agreements would do as well. * * *

Neither Congresses nor Presidents nor courts have been troubled by these conceptual difficulties and differences. Whatever their theoretical merits, it is now widely accepted that the Congressional–Executive agreement is a complete alternative to a treaty: the President can seek approval of any agreement by joint resolution of both houses of Congress instead of two-thirds of the Senate only. Like a treaty, such an agreement is the law of the land, superseding inconsistent state laws as well as inconsistent provisions in earlier treaties, in other international agreements or acts of Congress.

The Congressional–Executive agreement had strong appeal some years ago as an alternative to the treaty method. By permitting approval of an agreement by simple majority of both houses, it eliminates the veto by one-third-plus-one of the Senators present which in the past had effectively buried important treaties. It gives an equal role to the House of Representatives which has long resented the "undemocratic" anachronism that excludes it from the treaty-making process. Especially since so many treaties require legislative implementation if only by appropriation of funds, it assures approval of the agreement by both houses before ratification, virtually eliminating the danger that the House of Representatives might later refuse to join in giving effect to the agreement. It simplifies the parliamentary process: a treaty goes to the Senate for consent and, often, to the Senate again and to the House for implementation; a Congressional–Executive agreement can go to both houses in the first instance, and "consent" and implementation achieved in a single action. It eliminates issues about self-executing and non-self-executing agreements and about the consequences of inconsistency between international agreements and statutes: all such agreements are "executed" by Congress, every agreement has Congressional sanction, and the joint resolution approving it, clearly, can repeal any inconsistent statutes.

* * * [T]he Congressional–Executive agreement has not effectively replaced the treaty. * * * Perhaps enthusiasm for an alternative to the treaty method fell victim to the Bricker controversy in which "internationalists" who had earlier scorned the treaty process now found themselves resisting efforts to cripple it. But the constitutionality of the Congressional–Executive agreement is established, it is used regularly at least for trade and postal agreements, and remains available to Presidents for general use should the treaty process again prove difficult.

### *Notes*

1. The legislative branch has frequently recognized Congressional–Executive agreements as alternatives to treaties. After the First World War a House

Committee Report asserted the propriety of adherence to the World Court by Congressional Resolution instead of treaty, citing precedents. H.R.Rep. No. 1569, 68th Cong., 2nd Sess. 16 (1925). See also the joint resolution authorizing conclusion of the Headquarters Agreement with the United Nations, Ch. 482, 61 Stat. 756 (1947) (text of agreement included in resolution); U.N.R.R.A. Act of March 28, 1944, ch. 135, 58 Stat. 122; Bretton Woods Agreement Act (providing for participation in the International Monetary Fund and the International Bank for Reconstruction and Development), ch. 339, 59 Stat. 512 (1945); joint resolutions providing for membership and participation in the International Refugee Organization, ch. 185, 61 Stat. 214 (1947); F.A.O., ch. 342, 59 Stat. 529 (1945); U.N.E.S.C.O., ch. 700, 60 Stat. 712 (1946); W.H.O., ch. 469, 62 Stat. 441 (1948). Earlier, Congress had approved United States adherence to that part of the Versailles Treaty which established the International Labor Office, ch. 676, 48 Stat. 1182, 1183 (1934).

The UN Charter was approved as a treaty, but implementation was left largely to Congressional–Executive cooperation. See the United Nations Participation Act of 1945, ch. 583, 59 Stat. 619 (1945), as amended, 22 U.S.C.A. §§ 287–287*l* (1990); even "Article 43 agreements" to put forces at the disposal of the Security Council were to be approved by Congress, not consented to by the Senate only. See § 6, 59 Stat. 621, 22 U.S.C.A. 287d. See Chapter 11 infra on Article 43 agreements.

When the Executive Branch decided to seek approval of the UN Headquarters Agreement by joint resolution, it provided concerned foreign governments with an opinion of the Attorney General assuring them that the Congressional–Executive agreement would be the equivalent of a treaty and supreme law of the land. 40 Op.Att'y Gen. 469 (1946). While his opinion purported to speak only for the agreement in question, the arguments and authorities cited would seem to apply as well to any agreement.

The courts have approved Congressional–Executive agreements in a few cases involving matters within the delegated powers of Congress. In 1882 the Supreme Court held that postal conventions have equal status with treaties as part of the law of the land. Von Cotzhausen v. Nazro, 107 U.S. 215, 2 S.Ct. 503, 27 L.Ed. 540 (1882). See comments, S.Doc. No. 244, Sen.Misc.Doc., 78th Cong., 2d Sess. (1944); 19 Op.Att'y Gen. 513 (1882). See also B. Altman & Co. v. United States, 224 U.S. 583, 32 S.Ct. 593, 56 L.Ed. 894 (1912), where the Supreme Court considered a Congressional–Executive agreement to be a "treaty" within the meaning of a federal statute.

See generally, Lissitzyn, The Legal Status of Executive Agreements on Air Transportation, 17 J.Air L. & Comm. 436 (1950). For an early debate over the propriety and scope of executive agreements, see Borchard, Shall the Executive Agreement Replace the Treaty?, 53 Yale L.J. 644 (1944); McDougal & Lans, Treaties and Congressional–Executive or Presidential Agreements: Interchangeable Instruments of National Policy, 54 Yale L.J. 181, 534 (1945); Borchard, Treaties and Executive Agreements—A Reply, id. at 616. The debate has been resolved in their favor. See Restatement (Third) § 303, Comment *e*. For recent discussion, see Margolis, Executive Agreements and Presidential Power in Foreign Policy (1986).

In recent years Congressional–Executive agreements have been commonly used to establish U.S. military bases in other states, and to accelerate approval of international trade agreements. In 1974 Congress enacted the Trade Act, Pub.L. 93–618, 88 Stat. 1978, 1982, 2001, currently codified as amended at 19 U.S.C.A.

§§ 2101, 2111–2112, 2191 (1988), which provides for a "fast track" procedure for Congressional approval of trade agreements negotiated by the Executive. The "fast track" seeks to promote Executive–Congressional cooperation to ensure that trade agreements negotiated by the President will be implemented by Congress with appropriate legislation. This increased cooperation includes notice to Congress of an intention to conclude a trade agreement, and consultation between Executive and Congress on implementing legislation. See Koh, The Fast Track and United States Trade Policy, 18—Brooklyn J.Int'l L. 143 (1992); Homer & Bello, *U.S. Trade and Policy Series No. 20*—The Fast Track Debate: A Prescription for Pragmatism, 26 Int'l Lawyer 183 (1992). The "fast track" procedure has also been suggested as an appropriate mechanism for approving arms control agreements. See Note, Reinterpreting Advice and Consent: A Congressional Fast Track for Arms Control Treaties, 98 Yale L.J. 885 (1989); Note, Congress and Arms Sales: Tapping the Potential of the Fast–Track Guarantee Procedure, 97 Yale L.J. 1439 (1988).

2. It has been suggested that the Congressional–Executive Agreement might be more consistent with principles of democracy and representative government, but the U.S. Senate is not likely to agree to abandon the treaty process in which it has a special role under the Constitution. See Henkin, Constitutionalism, Democracy and Foreign Affairs (1990).

The control of Congress over Congressional–Executive agreements is at least as strong as that of the Senate over treaties. In 1962, Congress required the inclusion of members of prescribed Congressional committees on delegations for trade agreement negotiations. See Trade Expansion Act of 1962, Pub.L. 87–794, § 243, 76 Stat. 878, 19 U.S.C.A. § 1873 (1970). In approving agreements by joint resolution Congress has sometimes entered conditions or reservations; see, e.g., the resolution approving U.S. adherence to the International Refugee Organization, ch. 185, 61 Stat. 214 (1947); also the resolution authorizing the U.N. Headquarters Agreement, ch. 482, 61 Stat. 756, 758, 767–68 (1947), Note 1 above.

Who has the power to terminate a Congressional–Executive agreement is unresolved, but the President's authority seems no weaker than in regard to treaties. In some cases Congress purported to reserve for itself an equal right to annul authorized arrangements independently of the President. See, e.g., The Postal Service Act of 1960, Pub.L. No. 86–682, § 6103, 74 Stat. 688. The Postal Reorganization Act of 1970 does not contain such a provision. Pub.L. No. 91–375, ch. 50, § 5002, 84 Stat. 719, 766, 39 U.S.C.A. § 5002 (1970).

### 2. *Sole Executive Agreements*

#### *HENKIN, FOREIGN AFFAIRS AND THE CONSTITUTION*

179–82 (1972).*

There have indeed been suggestions, claiming support in *Belmont* [p. 236 below], that the President is constitutionally free to make any agreement on any matter involving our relations with another country, although for political reasons—especially if he will later require Congressional implementation—he will often seek Senate consent. As a matter of constitutional construction, however, that view is unacceptable, for it would wholly remove the "check" of Senate consent which the Framers struggled and compro-

* Footnotes omitted. Reprinted by permission of Foundation Press, Inc.

mised to write into the Constitution. One is compelled to conclude that there are agreements which the President can make on his sole authority and others which he can make only with the consent of the Senate, but neither Justice Sutherland nor any one else has told us which are which.

* * *

* * * In 1953, in the *Capps* case, Chief Judge Parker of the United States Court of Appeals for the Fourth Circuit refused to give effect to an executive agreement regulating the export of potatoes by Canada to the United States. (The Supreme Court, expressly declining to consider the questions that concern us, affirmed on other grounds.) Judge Parker might have limited himself to holding, as he did, that the executive agreement could not prevail in the face of an earlier inconsistent act of Congress, but he also said:

> "The answer is that while the President has certain inherent powers under the Constitution such as the power pertaining to his position as Commander in Chief of Army and Navy and the power necessary to see that the laws are faithfully executed, the power to regulate interstate and foreign commerce is not among the powers incident to the Presidential office, but is expressly vested by the Constitution in the Congress. * * * " [204 F.2d at 659]

Judge Parker's suggestion, it should be clear, would not only deny to many executive agreements effect as domestic law in the United States; it denies the President's power to make them at all. His argument is unpersuasive. It takes the narrowest view of the President's power, not even mentioning his foreign affairs powers. Judge Parker finds the President has no power because Congress does. If the President cannot make agreements on any matter on which Congress could legislate, there could be no executive agreements with domestic legal consequences, since, we have seen, the legislative power of Congress has few and far limits. If Judge Parker denied the President the power to make executive agreements only as to matters on which Congress has "express" powers to legislate, he was drawing a line between express and implied powers of Congress that makes little sense for any purpose. In either event it is difficult to see why the powers of Congress to legislate are any more relevant to determine the scope of Presidential power to commit the United States by executive agreement than by treaty.

Judge Parker's dictum does not accord with the practice either before or since he wrote: Presidents have made executive agreements on matters as to which Congress could legislate, notably international trade. Others have suggested other limitations: a sole executive agreement can be only "temporary" or of short duration; or, it can be effective only for the term of the President who makes it. None of these or similar suggestions has any apparent basis relevant to the scope of Presidential power generally, or to the Treaty Power, where any limitations on the power to make executive agreements should lie. One might suggest that the President must go to the Senate with "important" agreements, but even that "definition" would have at least one major qualification: executive agreements have been used for some very important agreements where either or both parties desired that the agreement remain confidential.

### *NATIONAL COMMITMENTS RESOLUTION*

U.S. Senate, 115 Cong.Rec. 17245 (1962).

Whereas accurate definition of the term "national commitment" in recent years has become obscured: Now, therefore, be it

*Resolved,* That (1) a national commitment for the purpose of this resolution means the use of the armed forces of the United States on foreign territory, or a promise to assist a foreign country, government, or people by the use of the armed forces or financial resources of the United States, either immediately or upon the happening of certain events, and (2) it is the sense of the Senate that a national commitment by the United States results only from affirmative action taken by the executive and legislative branches of the United States Government by means of a treaty, statute, or concurrent resolution of both Houses of Congress specifically providing for such commitment.

### *Notes*

1. "*Belmont* involved an agreement incidental to recognition of the Soviet Union, and Sutherland's opinion gave some emphasis to that fact. Recognition is indisputably the President's sole responsibility, and for many it is an 'enumerated' power implied in the President's express powers to appoint and receive Ambassadors. *Belmont,* then, might hold only that the President's specific and exclusive powers (principally those in respect of recognition, and his powers as Commander-in-Chief) support agreements on his sole authority. But, we have seen, the whole conduct of our foreign relations is exclusively the President's and that authority, too, has been said to be expressly 'enumerated,' in the clause vesting the 'executive Power.' Sutherland in fact seemed to find authority for the Litvinov Agreement not in the President's exclusive control of recognition policy but in his authority as 'sole organ,' his 'foreign affairs power' which supports not only recognition but much if not most other foreign policy." Henkin, Foreign Affairs and the Constitution 178 (1972). See also discussion on the scope of sole executive agreements, and particularly the *Capps Case,* p. 234 above.

2. Presidents have deployed U.S. forces to foreign countries in circumstances implying some executive agreement between the U.S. and receiving state. In 1990, for example, President Bush sent U.S. troops to Saudi Arabia to help defend it from attack after Iraq's invasion of Kuwait. See Chapter 11.

3. "Presidents have made numerous international agreements contemplated by a treaty, or which they considered appropriate for implementing treaty obligations, and no one seems to have questioned their authority to make them. Perhaps it is assumed that Senate consent to the original treaty implies consent to supplementary agreements; perhaps by such agreements the President takes care that the treaty is faithfully executed." Henkin, Foreign Affairs and the Constitution 176 (1972).

4. The President has concluded numerous agreements on his own authority to settle claims between the United States and another state. In Dames & Moore v. Regan, 453 U.S. 654, 101 S.Ct. 2972, 69 L.Ed.2d 918 (1981), the Supreme Court upheld the agreement with Iran arising out of the taking of United States

hostages, in which the United States agreed, *inter alia,* to terminate numerous cases in the courts of the United States and to have claims resolved by a joint arbitral tribunal. The Supreme Court upheld the validity of the agreement, noting that the power of the President to resolve international claims had been exercised for almost 200 years with Congressional acquiescence. The Court quoted Judge Learned Hand in Ozanic v. United States, 188 F.2d 228, 231 (2d Cir.1951):

> "The constitutional power of the President extends to the settlement of mutual claims between a foreign government and the United States, at least when it is an incident to the recognition of that government; and it would be unreasonable to circumscribe it to such controversies. The continued mutual amity between the nation and other powers again and again depends upon a satisfactory compromise of mutual claims; the necessary power to make such compromises has existed from the earliest times and been exercised by the foreign offices of all civilized nations."

453 U.S. at 683, 101 S.Ct. at 2988, 69 L.Ed.2d at 942. The Court postponed consideration of whether the agreement constituted a "taking" requiring compensation under the Fifth Amendment. For a note on the "taking" question, see Note 2, p. 188 above.

5. Congress has had before it numerous bills to limit or regulate sole executive agreements. In 1972, it adopted the Case Act, requiring the President to transmit to Congress all international agreements other than treaties within 60 days after their conclusion. If the President deems public disclosure of the agreement prejudicial to national security, he shall transmit it instead to the foreign affairs committees of both houses of Congress under injunction of secrecy to be removed only upon due notice from the President. See 1 U.S.C.A. § 112b. The Case Act was amended in 1977 and 1978 to make it applicable to agreements made by any department or agency of the United States government (1977) and to make it applicable to oral as well as written agreements (1978). 1 U.S.C.A. § 112b(a).

### *3. Executive Agreements as Law of the Land*

## UNITED STATES v. BELMONT

Supreme Court of the United States, 1937.
301 U.S. 324, 57 S.Ct. 758, 81 L.Ed. 1134.

MR. JUSTICE SUTHERLAND delivered the opinion of the Court.

This is an action at law brought by petitioner against respondents in a federal district court to recover a sum of money deposited by a Russian corporation (Petrograd Metal Works) with August Belmont, a private banker doing business in New York City under the name of August Belmont & Co. * * *

* * * In 1918, the Soviet Government duly enacted a decree by which it dissolved, terminated and liquidated the corporation (together with others), and nationalized and appropriated all of its property and assets of every kind and wherever situated, including the deposit account with Belmont. As a result, the deposit became the property of the Soviet Government, and so remained until November 16, 1933, at which time the Soviet Government released and assigned to petitioner all amounts due to that government from

American nationals, including the deposit account of the corporation with Belmont. Respondents failed and refused to pay the amount upon demand duly made by petitioner.

The assignment was effected by an exchange of diplomatic correspondence between the Soviet Government and the United States. The purpose was to bring about a final settlement of the claims and counterclaims between the Soviet Government and the United States; and it was agreed that the Soviet Government would take no steps to enforce claims against American nationals; but all such claims were released and assigned to the United States, with the understanding that the Soviet Government was to be duly notified of all amounts realized by the United States from such release and assignment. The assignment and requirement for notice are parts of the larger plan to bring about a settlement of the rival claims of the high contracting parties. The continuing and definite interest of the Soviet Government in the collection of assigned claims is evident; and the case, therefore, presents a question of public concern, the determination of which well might involve the good faith of the United States in the eyes of a foreign government. The court below held that the assignment thus effected embraced the claim here in question; and with that we agree.

That court, however, took the view that the situs of the bank deposit was within the State of New York; that in no sense could it be regarded as an intangible property right within Soviet territory; and that the nationalization decree, if enforced, would put into effect an act of confiscation. And it held that a judgment for the United States could not be had, because, in view of that result, it would be contrary to the controlling public policy of the State of New York. * * *

*First.* We do not pause to inquire whether in fact there was any policy of the State of New York to be infringed, since we are of opinion that no state policy can prevail against the international compact here involved.

* * *

We take judicial notice of the fact that coincident with the assignment set forth in the complaint, the President recognized the Soviet Government, and normal diplomatic relations were established between that government and the Government of the United States, followed by an exchange of ambassadors. The effect of this was to validate, so far as this country is concerned, all acts of the Soviet Government here involved from the commencement of its existence. The recognition, establishment of diplomatic relations, the assignment, and agreements with respect thereto, were all parts of one transaction, resulting in an international compact between the two governments. That the negotiations, acceptance of the assignment and agreements and understandings in respect thereof were within the competence of the President may not be doubted. Governmental power over internal affairs is distributed between the national government and the several states. Governmental power over external affairs is not distributed, but is vested exclusively in the national government. And in respect of what was done here, the Executive had authority to speak as the sole organ of that government. The assignment and the agreements in connection therewith did not, as in the case of treaties, as that term is used in the treaty making clause of the Constitution (Art. II, § 2), require the advice and consent of the Senate.

A treaty signifies "a compact made between two or more independent nations with a view to the public welfare." B. Altman & Co. v. United States, 224 U.S. 583, 600, 32 S.Ct. 593, 596, 56 L.Ed. 894, 910. But an international compact, as this was, is not always a treaty which requires the participation of the Senate. There are many such compacts, of which a protocol, a modus vivendi, a postal convention, and agreements like that now under consideration are illustrations. * * *

* * * And while this rule in respect of treaties is established by the express language of cl. 2, Art. VI, of the Constitution, the same rule would result in the case of all international compacts and agreements from the very fact that complete power over international affairs is in the national government and is not and cannot be subject to any curtailment or interference on the part of the several states. Compare United States v. Curtiss-Wright Export Corp., 299 U.S. 304, 316, 57 S.Ct. 216, 219, 81 L.Ed. 255, 260, 261 et seq. In respect of all international negotiations and compacts, and in respect of our foreign relations generally, state lines disappear. As to such purposes the State of New York does not exist. Within the field of its powers, whatever the United States rightfully undertakes, it necessarily has warrant to consummate. And when judicial authority is invoked in aid of such consummation, state constitutions, state laws, and state policies are irrelevant to the inquiry and decision. It is inconceivable that any of them can be interposed as an obstacle to the effective operation of a federal constitutional power. Cf. Missouri v. Holland, 252 U.S. 416, 40 S.Ct. 382, 64 L.Ed. 641; Asakura v. Seattle, 265 U.S. 332, 341, 44 S.Ct. 515, 516, 68 L.Ed. 1041, 1044. * * *

Judgment reversed.

### *Note*

In United States v. Pink, 315 U.S. 203, 62 S.Ct. 552, 86 L.Ed. 796 (1942), the United States, as assignee, sought to recover the assets in New York of a branch of a Russian corporation which had been nationalized by the Soviet Union. The New York courts held that since, under previously enunciated New York law, the nationalization could not be given extraterritorial effect, the United States as assignee stood no better than did the Russian government and was unable to collect. In reversing the state court, the Supreme Court said in part, 315 U.S. at 222, 224–25, 228–30, 62 S.Ct. at 561–65, 86 L.Ed. at 813–18:

> * * * [T]he Belmont case is determinative of the present controversy.
>
> * * *
>
> * * * [A]s we have seen, the Russian decree in question was intended to have an extraterritorial effect and to embrace funds of the kind which are here involved. Nor can there be any serious doubt that claims of the kind here in question were included in the Litvinov Assignment. It is broad and inclusive. It should be interpreted consonantly with the purpose of the compact to eliminate all possible sources of friction between these two great nations. * * * Strict construction would run counter to that national policy. For, as we shall see, the existence of unpaid claims against Russia and its nationals, which were held in this country, and which the Litvinov Assign-

ment was intended to secure, had long been one impediment to resumption of friendly relations between these two great powers.

* * *

If the priority had been accorded American claims [over foreign claims to the assets] by treaty with Russia, there would be no doubt as to its validity. Cf. Santovincenzo v. Egan, [284 U.S. 30, 52 S.Ct. 81, 76 L.Ed. 151 (1931) ]. The same result obtains here. The powers of the President in the conduct of foreign relations included the power, without consent of the Senate, to determine the public policy of the United States with respect to the Russian nationalization decrees. * * * That authority is not limited to a determination of the government to be recognized. It includes the power to determine the policy which is to govern the question of recognition. Objections to the underlying policy as well as objections to recognition are to be addressed to the political department and not to the courts. * * * Power to remove such obstacles to full recognition as settlement of claims of our nationals (Levitan, Executive Agreements, 35 Ill.L.Rev. 365, 382–385) certainly is a modest implied power of the President who is the "sole organ of the federal government in the field of international relations." United States v. Curtiss–Wright Corp., [299 U.S. at 320, 57 S.Ct. at 221, 81 L.Ed. at 262]. Effectiveness in handling the delicate problems of foreign relations requires no less. Unless such a power exists, the power of recognition might be thwarted or seriously diluted. No such obstacle can be placed in the way of rehabilitation of relations between this country and another nation, unless the historic conception of the powers and responsibilities of the President in the conduct of foreign affairs (see Moore, Treaties and Executive Agreements, 20 Pol.Sc.Q. 385, 403–417) is to be drastically revised. It was the judgment of the political department that full recognition of the Soviet Government required the settlement of all outstanding problems including the claims of our nationals. Recognition and the Litvinov Assignment were interdependent. We would usurp the executive function if we held that that decision was not final and conclusive in the courts.

"All constitutional acts of power, whether in the executive or in the judicial department, have as much legal validity and obligation as if they proceeded from the legislature, * * * " The Federalist, No. 64. A treaty is a "Law of the Land" under the supremacy clause (Art. VI, Cl. 2) of the Constitution. Such international compacts and agreements as the Litvinov Assignment have a similar dignity. United States v. Belmont, [301 U.S. at 331, 57 S.Ct. at 761, 81 L.Ed. 1139]. See Corwin, The President, Office & Powers (1940), pp. 228–240.

## "SELF-EXECUTING" EXECUTIVE AGREEMENTS

*HENKIN, FOREIGN AFFAIRS AND THE CONSTITUTION*

184–86 (1972) (footnotes omitted).*

One suggestion has had it that while the President can surely make some executive agreements, and perhaps even any agreement on any subject related to foreign affairs, such agreements are like treaties only in their international obligation. Congress, then, is presumably obligated to implement them, but, unlike treaties, they are never self-executing and cannot be effective as domestic law unless implemented by Congress.

* Reprinted with permission of Foundation Press.

If there was ever any basis for that view, the *Belmont* case [see p. 236 supra] surely rejects it as general doctrine. * * *

[I]t has been suggested that the doctrine of the *Belmont* case gives supremacy over state law only to executive agreements intimately related to the President's power of recognition, and that even such agreements will supersede only state public policy not formal state laws. Neither of these limitations was expressed—or implied—in *Belmont,* or in the *Pink* case decided five years later by a reconstituted Supreme Court. While *Pink* makes much of the relation of the Litvinov assignment to the recognition of the Soviet Government, the language and the reasoning of both cases would apply as well to any executive agreement and to any state law.

At least some executive agreements, then, can be self-executing and have some status as law of the land. As with treaties, of course, a self-executing executive agreement would surely lose its effect as domestic law in the face of a subsequent act of Congress. On the other hand, in the *Capps* case, we saw, an intermediate federal court held that an executive agreement—unlike a treaty—could not prevail against an earlier act of Congress; the Supreme Court expressly declined to consider that question. Yet many of the arguments why a treaty supersedes an earlier statute apply as well to executive agreements. The Supreme Court built its doctrine that treaties are equal to and can supersede acts of Congress on the Supremacy Clause of the Constitution, and, under *Belmont,* executive agreements, too, are supreme law of the land. If one sees the Treaty Power as basically a Presidential power (albeit subject to check by the Senate) there is no compelling reason for giving less effect to agreements which he has authority to make without the Senate. If one accepts Presidential primacy in foreign affairs in relation to Congress, one might allow his agreements to prevail even in the face of earlier Congressional legislation. If one grants the President some legislative authority in foreign affairs—as in regard to sovereign immunity—one might grant it to him in this respect too.

### *Note*

The Iran Hostage Agreement, upheld in Dames & Moore v. Regan, 453 U.S. 654, 101 S.Ct. 2972, 69 L.Ed.2d 918 (1981), also had legal effect in the United States, closing U.S. courts to certain claims. See, e.g., Harris Corp. v. National Iranian Radio & Television, 691 F.2d 1344 (11th Cir.1982). See generally Stein, Jurisprudence and Jurists' Prudence: The Iranian–Forum Clause Decisions of the Iran–U.S. Claims Tribunal, 78 A.J.I.L. 1 (1984); The U.S./Iranian Hostage Settlement, 75 A.S.I.L.Proc. 236 (1981); Norton & Collins, Reflections on the Iranian Hostage Settlement, 67 A.B.A.J. 428 (1981).

# Chapter 4

# STATES

## INTRODUCTORY NOTE

### SUBJECTS OF THE LAW AND INTERNATIONAL PERSONS

Subjects of international law include persons and entities capable of possessing international rights and duties under international law and endowed with the capacity to take certain types of action on the international plane. The term "international legal person" is commonly used in referring to such persons and entities. Questions of whether an entity is an international legal person arise in various contexts. Most commonly, they have related to the capacity to make treaties and agreements under international law, the capacity to make claims for breaches of international law, and the enjoyment of privileges and immunities from national jurisdiction. The question of international legal personality may also arise in regard to membership or participation in international bodies.

States are, of course, the principal examples of international persons. The attributes of statehood, as developed in customary law, provided the criteria for determining the "personality" of other entities. Indeed, at one time the generally held view was that only fully sovereign states could be persons in international law. The realities, however, were more complex and over time many different kinds of entities have been considered as capable of having international rights and duties and the capacity to act on the international plane. Such entities were often compared to states and distinctions were made by examining the degree of sovereignty they had retained or acquired. It had in fact long been evident that despite the dogma that only sovereign states could be subjects of international law, many other entities—some resembling states, others constituting organizations of states—were regarded as international legal persons for certain purposes and in some respects. Moreover, individuals and corporations or other juridical entities created by the laws of a state can also be persons under or subjects of international law when they are accorded rights, duties and other aspects of legal personality under customary international law or an international agreement. As in any legal system, not all subjects of international law are identical in their nature or their rights and one must constantly be aware of the relativity of the concept of international legal person.

The widening of the concept of international legal personality beyond the state is one of the more significant features of contemporary international law. This broadening is particularly evident in the case of public international organizations, supranational entities such as the European Community, and insurgent communities and movements of national liberation. But these developments should not obscure the primary and predominant role of the state as the subject of international law. To quote Wolfgang Friedmann:

> The states are the repositories of legitimated authority over peoples and territories. It is only in terms of state powers, prerogatives, jurisdictional limits and law-making capabilities that territorial limits and jurisdiction, responsibility for official actions, and a host of other questions of coexistence between nations can be determined. It is by virtue of their law-making power and monopoly that states enter into bilateral and multilateral compacts, that wars can be started or terminated, that individuals can be punished or extradited.
>
> This basic primacy of the state as a subject of international relations and law would be substantially affected, and eventually superseded, only if national entities were absorbed in a world state * * *.
>
> At present instead of witnessing the gradual absorption of national sovereignties and legal systems, we are faced with an opposite development: the proliferation of sovereignties * * *.

Friedmann, The Changing Structure of International Law 213–214 (1964).*

## SECTION 1. THE DETERMINATION OF STATEHOOD

### A. WHAT IS A STATE?

*RESTATEMENT (THIRD)*

**§ 201. State Defined**

Under international law, a state is an entity that has a defined territory and a permanent population, under the control of its own government, and that engages in, or has the capacity to engage in, formal relations with other such entities.

***Note***

Restatement (Third) § 206 states that the capacities, rights and duties of states include the following:

* Reprinted by permission of Columbia University Press and Stevens and Sons, Ltd.

(a) sovereignty over its territory and general authority over its nationals;

(b) status as a legal person, with capacity to own, acquire, and transfer property, to make contracts and enter into international agreements, to become a member of international organizations, and to pursue, and be subject to, legal remedies;

(c) capacity to join with other states to make international law, as customary law or by international agreement.

## B. WHEN DOES THE QUESTION OF STATEHOOD ARISE?

Controversies as to whether an entity should be considered as a state arise as a result of certain extraordinary political changes particularly in the following situations:

1. Break-up of an existing state into a number of states.
2. Secession or attempted secession by part of a territory of an existing state.
3. Cases in which foreign control is exercised over the affairs of a state, whether by treaty, unilateral imposition or delegation of authority.
4. Cases in which states have merged or formed a union.
5. Claims by constituent units of a union or federation to the attributes of statehood.
6. Territorial or non-territorial communities which have a special international status by virtue of treaty or customary law and which claim statehood for certain purposes.

In the recent past issues associated with the existence of new states have been generated by the break-up of the former U.S.S.R., Yugoslavia, and Czechoslovakia and the reunification of Germany.

Controversies that arise with respect to the existence of a new state occur on both the international and national levels. On the international level, the issue is likely to arise when the entity whose status is in controversy seeks admission or the right of participation in an international body open to states alone. Issues of statehood have therefore frequently arisen in connection with applications for membership in the United Nations or its affiliated organizations or in international conferences convened under its auspices. These issues are normally decided by decision of the international body concerned. Questions of statehood have also arisen in regard to the rights of entities to become parties to multilateral treaties or agreements open only to states. In some but not all of the cases involving treaties, the issue may be resolved by a collective decision.

National governments may also have to determine whether an entity is a state for purposes of bilateral relations. Normally this determination is made by the executive branch by recognition of the entity as a state. Such recognition may be explicit and formal or it may be implied in the initiation of diplomatic relations or from conclusion of a bilateral treaty. Questions of statehood also arise in national courts particularly in respect of entities which have not been recognized as states by the executive branch. Courts may have to decide whether an unrecognized entity should be regarded as a state for purposes of determining claims to property, issues of nationality, the right to sue, the validity of official acts, immunity from suit, and various other questions linked to statehood.

It should be noted that the question of whether an entity is or is not a state is distinct from the issue of whether a particular regime or authority is the government of that state. While the existence of an independent government is a requirement of statehood, governments change and conflicting claims of governmental authority may arise. In these cases, foreign governments and international organizations may have to decide which government should be considered the government of the state in question. The issues are not the same as those involved in determining statehood and are therefore treated separately in the material below.

## C. THE EFFECT OF RECOGNITION ON STATEHOOD: CONSTITUTIVE AND DECLARATORY VIEWS

The question of whether an entity is a state and should be so treated has given rise to two opposing theories. One theory is that the act of recognition by other states confers international personality on an entity purporting to be a state. In effect, the other states by their recognition "constitute" or create the new state. On this "constitutive" theory an observer or a court need only look at the acts of recognition (or lack thereof) to decide whether an entity is a state.

The opposing position is that the existence of a state depends on the facts and on whether those facts meet the criteria of statehood laid down in international law. Accordingly, a state may exist without being recognized. Recognition is merely declaratory. The primary function of recognition is to acknowledge the fact of the state's political existence and to declare the recognizing state's willingness to treat the entity as an international person, with the rights and obligations of a state.

Although distinguished jurists and some judicial authorities have supported the constitutive theory, the weight of authority and state practice support the declaratory position. As stated by the authoritative *Institut de Droit International* in 1936: "The existence of a new State with all the legal consequences attaching to this existence is not affected by the refusal of recognition by one or more states." [1936] 2 Annuaire de l'Institut de Droit Int'l 300. This view is adopted by the Inter-American Convention on Rights and Duties of States, 1933, 49 Stat. 3097, T.S. No. 8811, 165 L.N.T.S. 19 (Art. 3), and the Charter of the Organization of American States, 1948, 2 U.S.T. 2416, T.I.A.S. No. 2361, 119 U.N.T.S. 3 (Art. 9) (as amended by the Protocol of Amendment in 1967, 21 U.S.T. 607, T.I.A.S. No. 6487 (Art. 12)). See also Brownlie, Principles of Public International Law 88–91 (4th ed. 1990).

Some authorities, including Lauterpacht, Recognition in International Law (1947), adopt the "constitutive" theory, but contend that states have an obligation to recognize an entity that meets the qualifications of statehood.

Section 202(1) of the Restatement (Third) states that although a state is not required to accord formal recognition to any other state, it is required to treat as a state an entity that meets the requirements of statehood. A state is obligated not to recognize or treat as a state an entity that has attained the qualifications of statehood as a result of a threat or use of force in violation of the United Nations Charter. Restatement (Third) § 202(2).

Thus, unless an entity's existence is the result of an unlawful threat or use of force, in order to determine whether an entity is a state, it must be ascertained whether it meets the standards of international law. But such application may call for the determination of difficult questions of fact and law. Is there a government with the capacity to enter into relations with other states? Is it, in that sense, independent? In ascertaining these "facts," especially when they are in dispute, states and international bodies will generally give weight to recognition *vel non* by other states. Consequently, acts of recognition or refusals to recognize may have a significant and at times decisive role in determining controversial situations. For this reason, the theoretical gap between the declaratory and constitutive views is rather less in practice than in theory. The Reporters note that the position reflected in the Restatement (Third) § 202 is closer to the declaratory than the constitutive view, but that the practical differences between the two have diminished. "Even for the declaratory theory, whether an entity satisfies the requirements for statehood is, as a practical matter, determined by other states. * * * On the other hand, the constitutive theory lost much of its significance when it was accepted that states had the obligation * * * to treat as a state any entity that had the characteristics set forth in § 201. * * * See Meeker, Recognition and the Restatement, 41 N.Y.U.L.Rev. 83 (1966). Delays in recognizing or accepting statehood have generally reflected uncertainty as to the viability of the new state * * * or the view that it was created in violation of international law. * * * " Restatement (Third) § 202, Reporters' Note 1. The *ad hoc* Arbitration Commission (consisting of the Presidents of the Constitutional Courts of Belgium, France, Germany, Italy and Spain) established by the E.C.-sponsored Conference on Yugoslavia (see p. 253 infra) opined that "the existence or disappearance of the State is a question of fact; that the effects of recognition by other States are purely declaratory." Arbitration Commission Opinion No. 1, 31 I.L.M. 1494 (1992).

It is clear that an entity that meets the conditions of statehood cannot, because of the lack of recognition, be denied its rights or escape its obligations. "Its territory cannot be considered to be no-man's-land; there is no right to overfly without permission; ships flying its flag cannot be considered stateless, and so on." Mugerwa, Subjects of International Law, in Manual of Public International Law, 269 (Sorensen ed. 1968).* Nor can such a non-recognized entity evade the duties of states under international law. (In fact, non-recognized states are often charged with violations of international law and are the object of international claims by the very states refusing recognition.) These legal propositions are well supported by state practice and doctrine. They confirm the essential validity of the declaratory view and therefore the relevance of the legal conditions for determining whether an entity is a state.

* Reprinted with the permission of the Carnegie Endowment for International Peace.

## D. THE CONDITIONS OF STATEHOOD

### *1. Requirement of a Permanent Population and Defined Territory*

Philip C. Jessup, then United States representative to the Security Council, advocating the admission of Israel to the United Nations, said:

> The consideration of the application requires an examination of * * * the question of whether Israel is a State duly qualified for membership. Article 4 of the Charter of the United Nations specifies the following:
>
> > Membership in the United Nations is open to * * * peace-loving States which accept the obligations contained in the present Charter and, in the judgment of the Organization, are able and willing to carry out these obligations.
>
> * * * My Government considers that the State of Israel meets these Charter requirements.
>
> The first question which may be raised in analyzing Article 4 of the Charter and its applicability to the membership of the State of Israel, is the question of whether Israel is a State, as that term is used in Article 4 of the Charter. It is common knowledge that, while there are traditional definitions of a State in international law, the term has been used in many different ways. We are all aware that, under the traditional definition of a State in international law, all the great writers have pointed to four qualifications: first, there must be a people; second, there must be a territory; third, there must be a government; and, fourth, there must be capacity to enter into relations with other States of the world.
>
> In so far as the question of capacity to enter into relations with other States of the world is concerned, * * * I believe that there would be unanimity that Israel exercises complete independence of judgment and of will in forming and in executing its foreign policy. * * *
>
> When we look at the other classic attributes of a State, we find insistence that it must also have a Government. No one doubts that Israel has a Government. * * *
>
> According to the same classic definition, we are told that a State must have a people and a territory. Nobody questions the fact that the State of Israel has a people. * * *
>
> The argument seems chiefly to arise in connection with territory. One does not find in the general classic treatment of this subject any insistence that the territory of a State must be exactly fixed by definite frontiers. We all know that, historically, many States have begun their existence with their frontiers unsettled. Let me take as one example, my own country, the United States of America. Like the State of Israel in its origin, it had certain territory along the seacoast. It had various indeterminate claims to an extended territory westward. But, in the case of the United States, that land had not even been explored, and no one knew just where the American claims ended and where French and British and Spanish claims began. To the North, the exact delimitation of the frontier with the territories of Great Britain was not settled until

many years later. And yet, I maintain that, in the light of history and in the light of the practice and acceptance by other States, the existence of the United States of America was not in question before its final boundaries were determined.

The formulae in the classic treatises somewhat vary, one from the other, but both reason and history demonstrate that the concept of territory does not necessarily include precise delimitation of the boundaries of that territory. The reason for the rule that one of the necessary attributes of a State is that it shall possess territory is that one cannot contemplate a State as a kind of disembodied spirit. Historically, the concept is one of insistence that there must be some portion of the earth's surface which its people inhabit and over which its Government exercises authority. No one can deny that the State of Israel responds to this requirement. * * *

3 U.N. SCOR, 383 Mtg., Dec. 2, 1948, No. 128, pp. 9–12.

### *Notes*

1. A state does not cease to be a state because it is occupied by a foreign power. Restatement (Third) § 201, Comment *b*. Thus, Kuwait remained a state notwithstanding its occupation and putative annexation by Iraq in 1990. The United States never recognized the incorporation of Estonia, Latvia and Lithuania into the U.S.S.R. Treaties between the United States and those countries remained in force and their diplomatic representatives were regarded as duly accredited. When these countries regained their independence in 1991, the United States simply resumed full diplomatic relations. Vol. 2, No. 2 Foreign Pol'y Bull. 33 (Sept./Oct. 1991).

2. A state does not cease to exist when a previously functioning government becomes ineffective or defunct. A case in point is Somalia, the government of which no longer functioned effectively in 1992 when, under the authorization of the United Nations Security Council, United States forces assisted in establishing enough stability to permit distribution of food and other humanitarian resources needed to ameliorate widespread starvation. Cambodia has remained a state although it lacks a functioning government in the traditional sense, while being administered by the Supreme National Council under the U.N.-managed political settlement process established by the Paris Agreement on October 23, 1992. The SNC is an interim leadership group designed to serve as the embodiment of Cambodian national sovereignty in the transitional period leading to elections, to represent Cambodians abroad and to promote national reconciliation between the four Cambodian factions. Statement by Richard Solomon, Assistant Secretary of State for East Asian and Pacific Affairs, Vol. 2, No. 3 Foreign Pol'y Bull. 30 (Nov./Dec. 1991).

3. The requirement for a permanent population would prevent qualification of Antarctica as a state. Restatement (Third), § 201, Comment *c*. How many people does a "permanent population" imply? The Vatican, which is generally accepted as a state, see p. 299 infra, has a population of about 400 citizens and 800 residents. The proliferation of very small independent "sovereign" states, the "mini states", appears to confirm that no minimum number has been set. Nauru with 8,000 people has been considered a state as has Liechtenstein with 28,000 people. U.N. member states include several with fewer than 100,000 people. For consideration of problems created by "mini states", see J. Rapoport, Small States and Territories (a UNITAR study, 1971); Gunter, What

Happened to the United Nations Ministate Problem?, 71 A.J.I.L. 110 (1977). A significant number of "permanent" inhabitants will suffice even if large numbers of nomads move in and out of the territory. Restatement (Third), § 201, Comment *c*.

4. A new state does not have to extend nationality to its population as a condition of statehood. It is, however, true that when a new state is established in a territory, the inhabitants generally become nationals of that state. See Case Concerning Acquisition of Polish Nationality, 1923 P.C.I.J., Ser. B, No. 7, at 15.

5. With regard to territory, no rule prescribes a minimum. Monaco, for example, is only 1.5 square kilometers in size. One might speculate on whether an artificial installation on the sea-bed beyond national jurisdiction would have a territorial basis for a claim of statehood. See p. 320 infra. What about a "permanent colony" in outer space? See material on sovereignty over territory in outer space, p. 1368 infra.

### 2. *Requirement of a Government*

#### *LEAGUE OF NATIONS, COMMISSION OF JURISTS ON AALAND ISLANDS DISPUTE*

League of Nations O.J., Spec.Supp. 4, at 8–9 (1920).

[A Commission of Jurists appointed by the League in 1920 to consider certain aspects of a dispute concerning the *Aaland Islands* considered when Finland attained statehood after the civil war of 1917–18 in that country. The Jurists concluded that Finland did not attain statehood until an effective government was established. In their opinion they stated that:]

> * * * for a considerable time, the conditions required for the formation of a sovereign State did not exist. In the midst of revolution and anarchy, certain elements essential to the existence of a State, even some elements of fact, were lacking for a fairly considerable period. Political and social life was disorganized; the authorities were not strong enough to assert themselves; civil war was rife; further, the Diet, the legality of which had been disputed by a large section of the people, had been dispersed by the revolutionary party, and the Government had been chased from the capital and forcibly prevented from carrying out its duties; the armed camps and the police were divided into two opposing forces, and Russian troops, and after a time Germans also, took part in the civil war * * *. It is therefore difficult to say at what exact date the Finnish Republic, in the legal sense of the term, actually became a definitely constituted sovereign State. This certainly did not take place until a stable political organization had been created, and until the public authorities had become strong enough to assert themselves throughout the territories of the State without the assistance of foreign troops. It would appear that it was in May 1918, that the civil war was ended and that the foreign troops began to leave the country, so that from that time onward it was possible to reestablish order and normal political and social life, little by little.

#### *Notes*

1. Should the standard of effective government be less stringent when a territory is granted independence by a former sovereign? No one questioned

that the former Belgian Congo (now Zaire) was a state when it became independent though, like Finland in 1917, it was in a state of civil war and virtual anarchy. The same could be said of Burundi and Ruanda, both granted independence when they were without an effective government. See Higgins, Development of International Law Through the Political Organs of the United Nations 21–23 (1963). In contrast, Finland was engaged in a war of secession. Consider the following comment. "A new state formed by secession from a metropolitan state will have to demonstrate substantial independence, both formal and real, before it will be regarded as definitively created. On the other hand, the independence of an existing state is protected by international law rules against illegal invasion and annexation so that the state may, even for a considerable time, continue to exist as a legal entity despite lack of effectiveness. But where a new state is formed by grant of power from the former sovereign * * *, considerations of pre-existing rights are no longer relevant and independence is treated as a predominantly formal criterion." Crawford, The Criteria for Statehood in International Law, 48 Brit.Y.B.I.L. 120 (1976–77).

2. The *ad hoc* Arbitration Commission (consisting of the Presidents of the Constitutional Courts of Belgium, France, Germany, Italy and Spain) established by the E.C.-sponsored Conference on Yugoslavia (see p. 253 infra) was asked by the Chairman of the Conference, Lord Carrington of the United Kingdom, to give its opinion on whether the Socialist Federal Republic of Yugoslavia continued to exist as a state. In concluding that SFRY was in the process of dissolution, the Commission commented that "in the case of a federal-type State, which embraces communities that possess a degree of autonomy and, moreover, participate in the exercise of political power within the framework of institutions common to the Federation, the existence of the State implies that the federal organs represent the components of the Federation and wield effective power * * *." It then expressed its opinion that the "composition and workings of the essential organs of the Federation, be they the Federal Presidency, the Federal Council, the Council of the Republics and the Provinces, the Federal Executive Council, the Constitutional Court or the Federal Army, no longer meet the criteria of participation and representativeness inherent in a federal State * * *." Arbitration Commission Opinion No. 1, 31 I.L.M. 1494 (1992).

### *3. Requirement of Capacity to Engage in Relations With Other States*

Comment *e* to Restatement (Third) § 201 states as follows:

> *e. Capacity to conduct international relations.* An entity is not a state unless it has competence, within its own constitutional system, to conduct international relations with other states, as well as the political, technical and financial capabilities to do so. An entity which has the capacity to conduct foreign relations does not cease to be a state because it voluntarily turns over to another state some or all control of its foreign relations * * *.

### *Notes*

1. There have been examples in the past of states transferring control over foreign relations to another state. An example that persists is Liechtenstein, which transferred the control of its foreign relations to Switzerland, but was admitted as a party to the Statute of the International Court of Justice, for which only states qualify, and participated in *The Nottebohm Case* (Liechtenstein

v. Guatemala), 1955 I.C.J. 4, p. 397 infra. See Restatement (Third), § 201, Reporters' Note 4.

2. The establishment of the European Community did not terminate the statehood of the member states or vest the Community with statehood although the Community assumed international responsibility for certain matters, such as establishing uniform external tariffs, previously controlled by the member states. See Division of Powers between the European Communities and their Member States in the Field of External Relations (Timmermans & Voelker eds., 1981).

3. "Protectorates" or "Protected States" predominantly of the colonial era involved agreements by local rulers conferring authority over foreign affairs or other matters on an external state, usually an "imperial power". Although "protectorates" have virtually disappeared as a distinct legal category, small or weak states may still be subject to varying degrees of foreign control of a military, economic or political character. At one time—especially during the 1950's—foreign control was cited as a ground for excluding applicants for membership in the United Nations. This was clearly bound up with political and ideological factors. In the last three decades a large number of newly "independent" states have been admitted without question although they have often been heavily dependent in actuality on other powers for security and economic viability. The notable exceptions have been those "states" which have been regarded as "illegal" in the sense that their establishment was contrary to principles of international law, as for example Transkei and Rhodesia.

### *4. Emergence of Additional Criteria for Recognition of Statehood; Collective Recognition by the European Community*

Secretary of State Baker appeared to herald a new United States policy on the recognition of states in a speech before the September 1991 meeting of the Conference on Security and Cooperation in Europe. In addition to the traditional criteria for statehood, he indicated as relevant five principles closely related to those later enunciated by the E.C. Recognition was to be accorded in the light of the new states' adherence to the following:

> — Determining the future of the country peacefully and democratically, consistent with CSCE principles;
>
> — Respect for all existing borders, both internal and external, and change to those borders only through peaceful and consensual means;
>
> — Support for democracy and the rule of law, emphasizing the key role of elections in the democratic process;
>
> — Safeguarding of human rights, based on full respect for the individual and including equal treatment of minorities; and
>
> — Respect for international law and obligations, especially adherence to the Helsinki Final Act and the Charter of Paris.

Testimony of Ralph Johnson, Deputy Assistant Secretary of State for European and Canadian Affairs, October 17, 1991, Vol. 2, No. 3 Foreign Pol'y Bull. 39, 42 (Nov./Dec. 1991).

In connection with the emergence of new states in Eastern Europe an extraordinary European Political Cooperation (EPC) meeting of the Foreign Ministers of the European Community Member States issued on December

16, 1991, a Declaration on "Guidelines on the Recognition of New States in Eastern Europe and in the Soviet Union". The E.C. affirmed in the Declaration that the Community and its Member States would recognize, "subject to the normal standards of international practice and the political realities in each case," those new states that had constituted themselves on a democratic basis, had accepted the appropriate international obligations, and had committed themselves in good faith to negotiations and the peaceful settlement of outstanding issues. More specifically, the E.C. Guidelines required fulfillment of the following conditions as the foundation for recognition:

> — respect for the provisions of the Charter of the United Nations and the commitments subscribed to in the Final Act of Helsinki and in the Charter of Paris, especially with regard to the rule of law, democracy and human rights;
>
> — guarantees for the rights of ethnic and national groups and minorities in accordance with the commitments subscribed to in the framework of the CSCE [Conference on Security and Cooperation in Europe];
>
> — respect for the inviolability of all frontiers which can only be changed by peaceful means and by common agreement;
>
> — acceptance of all relevant commitments with regard to disarmament and nuclear non-proliferation as well as to security and regional stability;
>
> — commitment to settle by agreement, including where appropriate by recourse to arbitration, all questions concerning state succession and regional disputes.

The Declaration stated that the "commitment to these principles opens the way to recognition by the Community and its Member States and to the establishment of diplomatic relations." EPC Press Release 128/91 (Dec. 16, 1991), 31 I.L.M. 1486 (1992).

In a separate Declaration on Yugoslavia, 31 I.L.M. 1485 (1992), the ministers invited all Yugoslav republics to make requests for recognition by the E.C. by December 23, 1991. Each republic seeking E.C. recognition was required to state whether:

> — It wanted to be recognized as an independent state;
>
> — It accepted the commitments included in the general E.C. guidelines on recognition;
>
> — It accepted provisions of a draft Convention on Yugoslavia, especially those on human rights and rights of ethnic groups, developed by, and pending before, the E.C.-led Conference on Yugoslavia chaired by Lord Carrington;
>
> — It continued to support United Nations and E.C. efforts to reach a peaceful settlement of the disputes in Yugoslavia;
>
> — It agreed to adopt constitutional and political guarantees "ensuring that it has no territorial claims" against a neighboring E.C. country and that it would not use a name (e.g., Macedonia) that implied such

claims and would conduct "no hostile propaganda activities" against a neighboring E.C. country.

Those republics that responded positively to these conditions qualified to have their applications considered by an *ad hoc* Arbitration Commission, established by the Conference on Yugoslavia and consisting of the Presidents of the Constitutional Courts of Belgium, France, Germany, Italy and Spain. The President of the French Constitutional Court (Conseil Constitutionnel), Judge Robert Badinter, was chosen to act as Chairman.

The E.C. Guidelines appear to go well beyond the traditional qualifications for statehood under customary international law and appear to imply that recognition of statehood must be "earned" by meeting the standards articulated. One commentator has observed as follows:

> This extensive catalog of criteria, far in excess of traditional standards for recognition of statehood, confirms that the Community was not applying general international law in the determination of its position. Although some of the requirements reflected objective criteria that must be fulfilled if there is to be a well-founded claim to statehood, the more specific conditions were hand tailored to fit EC interests. * * *

Weller, The International Response to the Dissolution of the Socialist Federal Republic of Yugoslavia, 86 A.J.I.L. 569, 588 (1992) (footnotes omitted).

After receiving the opinion of the E.C. Arbitration Commission, the European Community and Austria and Switzerland recognized the former Yugoslav republics of Slovenia and Croatia on January 15, 1992. Recognition of Croatia by the E.C. was reportedly jeopardized at the last minute by release of Opinion No. 5 of the Arbitration Commission on January 11, 1992, 31 I.L.M. 1503 (1992), which indicated that Croatia had not yet provided all of the constitutional guarantees of the rights of minority groups called for in the E.C. Guidelines on recognition but had otherwise met the conditions of the Guidelines. N.Y. Times, Jan. 16, 1992, p. A6, col. 1. Thus, it is unclear that the E.C. followed its own guidelines in according recognition in this instance.

On December 25, 1991, a week after the formation of Commonwealth of Independent States to replace the former Soviet Union, President Bush made the following announcement:

> And so today, based on commitments and assurances given to us by some of these states, concerning nuclear safety, democracy, and free markets, I am announcing some important steps designed to begin this process.
>
> First, the United States recognizes and welcomes the emergence of a free, independent, and democratic Russia, led by its courageous President, Boris Yeltsin. Our Embassy in Moscow will remain there as our Embassy to Russia. We will support Russia's assumption of the U.S.S.R.'s seat as a Permanent Member of the United Nations Security Council. * * *
>
> Second, the United States also recognizes the independence of Ukraine, Armenia, Kazakhstan, Belarus, and Kirgizstan—all states that have made specific commitments to us. We will move quickly to establish diplomatic relations with these states and build new ties to

them. We will sponsor membership in the United Nations for those not already members.

Third, the United States also recognizes today as independent states the remaining six former Soviet Republics—Moldova, Turkmenistan, Azerbaijan, Tajikistan, Georgia, and Uzbekistan. We will establish diplomatic relations with them when we are satisfied that they have made commitments to responsible security policies and democratic principles, as have the other states we recognize today.

Vol. 2, Nos. 4 & 5 Foreign Pol'y Bull. 12 (Jan.–April 1992).

In connection with the emergence of new states associated with the break-up of the former Socialist Federal Republic of Yugoslavia, the United States initially declined to follow the E.C. lead on the ground that the parties to the Yugoslav conflict had first to reach a peaceful settlement through negotiation and with firm protections for minorities. N.Y. Times, Jan. 16, 1992, p. A6, col. 3. The United States did not recognize Slovenia, Croatia and Bosnia–Herzegovina until April 7, 1992, at which time the United States also announced that it was proceeding to establish diplomatic relations with each of them. What was previously the Socialist Federal Republic of Yugoslavia has thus become five separate entities: the states of Croatia, Slovenia, and Bosnia–Herzegovina, the remains of the former Republic of Yugoslavia (consisting of the Republics of Serbia and Montenegro) and the secessionist republic of Macedonia. Although the state of Macedonia appeared to have met the traditional criteria of statehood for some time, and it was found by the E.C. Arbitration Commission to meet the E.C. guidelines in January 1992, it has been recognized by only a handful of countries. Others, including the E.C., its member states and the United States, held off because of objections by Greece, a region of which is called Macedonia. The Greek government demanded that the Republic of Macedonia change its name, claiming that the right to use that name should belong exclusively to Greece. There appears to be no basis in international law or practice for Greece's position.

On April 7, 1993, the U.N. Security Council approved U.N. membership for Macedonia under the provisional name of the "Former Yugoslav Republic of Macedonia." As of May 27, 1993, the United States had still not recognized its statehood.

### *Notes*

1. The Arbitration Commission was established by the Peace Conference on Yugoslavia on August 27, 1991, as a body to which issues arising in connection with the break-up of the Socialist Federal Republic of Yugoslavia could be submitted for the rendering of opinions that would be transmitted to the Peace Conference. Through December 1992 the Commission had issued ten opinions and an interlocutory decision of July 4, 1992, upholding its authority to judge its own competence in the face of a challenge thereto by Serbia and Montenegro. Opinions 1 to 3 and 8 to 10 were in response to specific questions formulated by the Chairman of the Peace Conference. Opinions 4 to 7 considered the applications for international recognition submitted by four of the republics of the former Socialist Federal Republic of Yugoslavia. The interaction between the opinions of the Commission and the political decisions of the E.C. and its member states has been complex. For example, the E.C. and its members did not fully

accept the advice of the Commission when they recognized Croatia and failed to recognize Macedonia, while the E.C. and its members expressly cited the Commission's Opinion 10 of July 4, 1992, in refusing to accept the new Federal Republic of Yugoslavia (Serbia and Montenegro) as the sole successor to the former Socialist Federal Republic of Yugoslavia.

The Commission's Opinion 10 stated in part as follows:

> 1. * * * In Opinion No. 8, the Arbitration Commission concluded that the dissolution of the Socialist Federal Republic of Yugoslavia (SFRY) was complete and that none of the resulting entities could claim to be the sole successor to the SFRY.
>
> 2. On 27 April this year Montenegro and Serbia decided to establish a new entity bearing the name "Federal Republic of Yugoslavia" and adopted its constitution.
>
> The Arbitration Commission feels that, within the frontiers constituted by the administrative boundaries of Montenegro and Serbia in the SFRY, the new entity meets the criteria of international public law for a state, which were listed in Opinion No. 1 of 29 November 1991. However, as Resolution 757 (1992) of the UN Security Council points out, "the claim by the Federal Republic of Yugoslavia (Serbia and Montenegro) to continue automatically (the membership) of the former Socialist Federal Republic of Yugoslavia (in the United Nations) has not been generally accepted". As the Arbitration Commission points out in its ninth Opinion, the FRY is actually a new state and could not be the sole successor to the SFRY.
>
> 3. This means that the FRY (Serbia and Montenegro) does not *ipso facto* enjoy the recognition enjoyed by the SFRY under completely different circumstances. It is therefore for other states, where appropriate, to recognize the new state.
>
> 4. As, however, the Arbitration Commission pointed out in Opinion No. 1, while recognition is not a prerequisite for the foundation of a state and is purely declaratory in its impact, it is nonetheless a discretionary act that other states may perform when they choose and in a manner of their own choosing, subject only to compliance with the imperatives of general international law, and particularly those prohibiting the use of force in dealings with other states or guaranteeing the rights of ethnic, religious or linguistic minorities.
>
> Furthermore, the Community and its Member States, in their joint statement of 16 December 1991 on Yugoslavia and the Guidelines, adopted the same day, on the recognition of new states in Eastern Europe and in the Soviet Union, has set out the conditions for the recognition of the Yugoslav republics.
>
> 5. Consequently, the opinion of the Arbitration Commission is that:
>
> — the FRY (Serbia and Montenegro) is a new state which cannot be considered the sole successor to the SFRY;
>
> — its recognition by the Member States of the European Community would be subject to its compliance with the conditions laid down by general international law for such an act and the joint statement and Guidelines of 16 December 1991.

31 I.L.M. 1525 (1992).

2. One issue of central importance in the break-up of the Socialist Republic of Yugoslavia was the status of the pre-break-up frontiers of the constituent entities. The E.C. Arbitration Commission was asked to render its opinion on whether the internal frontiers between (i) Croatia and Serbia and (ii) Serbia and Bosnia–Herzegovina could be considered international boundaries under international law. Noting that Yugoslavia was in the process of dissolution, the Commission's opinion was that the new republics were entitled to the protection of their external boundaries under international law on the basis of the U.N. Charter, the Declaration on the Principles of International Law concerning Friendly Relations and Co-operation among States, the Helsinki Final Act and Article 11 of the Vienna Convention on Succession of States in respect of Treaties. The Commission added that, in the absence of agreement to the contrary between the states concerned, the preexisting frontiers enjoyed the protection of international law on the basis of the principle of *uti possidetis juris.* This principle, originally recognized in the disposition of border issues arising out of decolonization in Spanish America, has been recognized and applied by the I.C.J. in the *Case Concerning the Frontier Dispute (Burkina Faso v. Republic of Mali),* 1986 I.C.J. 554, 565, as a "general principle, which is logically connected with the phenomenon of the obtaining of independence, wherever it occurs." See also, Case Concerning Land, Island and Maritime Frontier Dispute (El Salvador v. Honduras; Nicaragua Intervening), 1992 I.C.J. 351, p. 331 infra. Finally, the Commission affirmed that no modification of preexisting frontiers by force would be recognized. Opinion No. 3, para. 2.

## E. IS THERE A DUTY OF RECOGNITION?

### *BROWNLIE, PRINCIPLES OF PUBLIC INTERNATIONAL LAW*

92 (4th ed. 1990).*

Lauterpacht and Guggenheim adopt the view that recognition is constitutive, but that there is a legal duty to recognize. This standpoint has been vigorously criticized[3] as bearing no relation to state practice and for its inconsistency, since in an oblique way it comes close to the declaratory view. In principle the legal duty can only be valid if it is in respect of an entity already bearing the marks of statehood and (although Lauterpacht does not express it thus) it is owed to the entity concerned. The argument postulates personality on an objective basis. However, discussion of Lauterpacht's views often reveals a certain confusion among the critics. Recognition, *as a public act of state,* is an optional and political act and there is no legal duty in this regard. However, in a deeper sense, if an entity bears the marks of statehood, other states put themselves at risk legally if they ignore the basic obligations of state relations. Few would take the view that the Arab neighbours of Israel can afford to treat her as a non-entity: the responsible United Nations organs and individual states have taken the view that Israel is protected, and bound, by the principles of the United Nations Charter governing the use of force. In this context of state *conduct* there is a duty to accept and apply certain fundamental rules of international law: there is a



3. See Kunz, 44 A.F. (1950), 713–19; Cohn, 64 L.Q.R. (1948), 404–8; Briggs, 43 A.F. (1949), 113–21. See also Jessup, 65 A.F. (1971), p. 214 and p. 217.

legal duty to "recognize" for certain purposes at least, but no duty to make an express, public, and political determination of the question or to declare readiness to enter into diplomatic relations by means of recognition. This latter type of recognition remains political and discretionary. Even recognition is not determinant of diplomatic relations, and absence of diplomatic relations is not in itself non-recognition of the state.

### *Notes*

1. How important is the issue of a duty of recognition? Consider the following comment of Waldock:

> Truth to tell, the establishment of such a duty, desirable though it is, would not really solve the central problem. For the duty could only be a duty to recognize when the conditions requisite for statehood are fulfilled. When there is no controversy as to the facts, there is not likely to be any political problem. Non-recognition will always be supported by allegations that the Government has been imposed on the people, or is a puppet Government, etc., and these allegations may or may not be true. We are then thrown back on the problem of who is to decide whether the new State or Government fulfils the required conditions, and the only ultimate solution is a collective recognition binding upon every State both inside and outside international organizations. Today, through the recognition practice of international organizations, we seem to have taken a step towards the principle of collective recognition.

Waldock, General Course on Public International Law, 106 Rec. des Cours 155 (1962–II).*

2. What is the significance of the "recognition practice" of international organizations? Does the admission of a new state to an international organization such as the United Nations imply collective recognition? Does it impose a duty on members to recognize the new state in both senses of recognition as used by Brownlie in the above excerpt? Is admission of a new state at the time of its independence "constitutive"? Consider the following comment:

> The prevailing opinion denies that acquisition of membership in the United Nations is equivalent to recognition by all Members of the Organisation. Admission to the Organisation certainly means that all Members must treat the new fellow member as an equal partner in law in all matters relating to the application of the Charter, particularly as far as the "Principles" embodied in Article 2 are concerned. To this extent common membership means that the newcomer is partially recognised. But apart from that, all States are free to decide whether to proceed to full recognition or limit their relations to the minimum.

Mosler, The International Society As A Legal Community, 140 Rec. des Cours 1, 60 (1974–IV).

## F. WHEN IS THERE A DUTY NOT TO RECOGNIZE?

### 1. *Recognition as Unlawful Intervention*

*HYDE, INTERNATIONAL LAW*
152–153 (2d rev. ed. 1945).*

§ 40. PRIOR TO RECOGNITION BY PARENT STATE

When recognition by foreign States precedes that accorded by the parent State, complaint on the part of the latter is to be anticipated. Nevertheless, the opinion has long prevailed in the United States that the propriety of recognition is not necessarily dependent upon the approval of such State. In harmony with the theory early advocated by Jefferson respecting the recognition of new governments, it has long been the accepted American doctrine that the right to accord recognition depends solely on the circumstance whether a new State has in fact come into being, and that the test of the existence of that fact is whether the conflict with the parent State has been substantially won. Statements of principle have not always drawn a sharp line of distinction between the time when the cause of the parent State was desperate or hopeless, and that when the contest was at an end. The point to be observed is, however, that the propriety of recognition, according to American theory, depends upon a fact, namely, the success of the revolutionary force, and that regardless of the illegitimacy thereof in the eyes of the parent State. Thus recognition based upon careful regard for such a fact is deemed to be consistent with the maintenance of friendly relations between the recognizing State and the parent State * * *.

The according of recognition to a country still in the throes of warfare against the parent State partakes of a different character. Such action constitutes participation in the conflict. It makes the cause of independence a common one between the aspirant for it and the outside State. Participation must be regarded as intervention, and therefore essentially antagonistic to that State.

#### *Notes*

1. United States concern about illegal recognition of the Confederacy during the Civil War was strongly expressed. See Hyde, at 153 n. 5. But the United States itself engaged in questionable recognition when it recognized Panama as a state two days after the latter declared its independence in 1903. Hyde, id., n. 6.

2. Recognition by five African governments of the secessionist territory of Biafra as a State during the Nigerian Civil War of 1967–1970 was criticized as unlawful by Nigeria. See Ijalaye, Was Biafra At Any Time a State in International Law?, 71 A.J.I.L. 551–559 (1971).

### 2. *Illegal States*

*RESOLUTION CONCERNING SOUTHERN RHODESIA*
Security Council of the United Nations, November 20, 1965.
1265th Meeting S.C.Res. 217, 20 SCOR, Resolutions and Decisions at 8.

The Security Council,

Deeply concerned about the situation in Southern Rhodesia,

* Footnotes omitted. Reprinted by permission of Little, Brown and Company.

Considering that the illegal authorities in Southern Rhodesia have proclaimed independence and that the Government of the United Kingdom of Great Britain and Northern Ireland, as the administering Power, looks upon this as an act of rebellion,

* * *

1. Determines that the situation resulting from the proclamation of independence by the illegal authorities in Southern Rhodesia is extremely grave, that the Government of the United Kingdom of Great Britain and Northern Ireland should put an end to it and that its continuance in time constitutes a threat to international peace and security;

* * *

3. Condemns the usurpation of power by a racist settler minority in Southern Rhodesia and regards the declaration of independence by it as having no legal validity;

4. Calls upon the Government of the United Kingdom to quell this rebellion of the racist minority;

5. Further calls upon the Government of the United Kingdom to take all other appropriate measures which would prove effective in eliminating the authority of the usurpers and in bringing the minority regime in Southern Rhodesia to an immediate end;

6. Calls upon all States not to recognize this illegal authority and not to entertain any diplomatic or other relations with it;

7. Calls upon the Government of the United Kingdom, as the working of the Constitution of 1961 has broken down, to take immediate measures in order to allow the people of Southern Rhodesia to determine their own future consistent with the objectives of General Assembly resolution 1514(XV);

8. Calls upon all States to refrain from any action which would assist and encourage the illegal regime and, in particular, to desist from providing it with arms, equipment and military materiel, and to do their utmost in order to break all economic relations with Southern Rhodesia, including an embargo on oil and petroleum products;

9. Calls upon the Government of the United Kingdom to enforce urgently and with vigour all the measures it has announced, as well as those mentioned in paragraph 8 above;

10. Calls upon the Organization of African Unity to do all in its power to assist in the implementation of the present resolution, in conformity with Chapter VIII of the Charter of the United Nations;

11. Decides to keep the question under review in order to examine what other measures it may deem it necessary to take.

Adopted at the 1265th meeting by 10 votes to none, with 1 abstention (France).

### *Notes*

1. At the time the above resolution was adopted, Rhodesia would have met the traditional criteria of statehood. Its government was clearly the effective

authority and had capacity to enter into foreign relations. Nonetheless, the Security Council resolution and previous General Assembly resolutions were accepted as definitive: Rhodesia was not recognized as a state by any government or treated as a state by any international organization. Does the decision in regard to Rhodesia confirm that a new requirement of statehood has been introduced—that a new state will not be recognized if it is a "minority regime" which violates the principle of self-determination? One commentator concluded that a new State must meet the requirement that "it shall not be based upon a systematic denial in its territory of certain civil and political rights, including in particular the right of every citizen to participate in the government of his country, directly or through representatives elected by regular, equal and secret suffrage." Fawcett, Security Council Resolutions on Rhodesia, 41 Brit.Y.B.I.L. 112 (1965–66).* How can one justify a requirement for new states that does not apply to existing states? The Rhodesian problem was eventually resolved in 1979–80 with the establishment of the state of Zimbabwe, which was generally recognized or accepted.

2. The U.N. General Assembly resolution on Transkei asserted both that Transkei's "independence" was sham and that the creation of Transkei was to consolidate apartheid and perpetuate white minority domination. G.A.Res. 31/6 G.A.O.R., 31st Sess., Supp. 39, p. 10 (1976). The latter point suggests that even if an independent state were created, it would be denied recognition in accordance with United Nations resolution if its establishment was considered a means to violate basic human rights.

Compare the decisions of the General Assembly and the Security Council calling on states to recognize the illegality of South Africa's presence in Namibia (South West Africa) and to refrain from any acts and any dealings with South Africa implying recognition of the legality of the presence and administration of South Africa. See International Court of Justice Advisory Opinion on Namibia [1971] I.C.J. 16, p. 485 infra.

3. Does non-recognition of a state imply that the entity is not expected to comply with duties of states under international law? Non-recognizing states have not hesitated to charge entities which they do not recognize as states with violations of international law. For example, the United States charged North Korea (which it did not recognize as a state) with illegal action when North Korea seized a United States naval vessel, the Pueblo, in 1968. 58 Dep't St.Bull. 196–97 (1968). See Mugerwa, Subjects of International Law, in Manual of Public International Law 269 (Sorensen ed. 1968).

4. Under international law states may not recognize "a territorial acquisition resulting from the threat or use of force." Declaration on Principles of International Law Concerning Friendly Relations and Cooperation among States in Accordance with the Charter of the United Nations, G.A.Res. 2625 (XXV) G.A.O.R., 25th Sess., Supp. 28, p. 121 (1970); 65 A.J.I.L. 243. Such recognition would be an improper interference in the internal affairs of the state of which the unlawfully acquired territory was a part. Restatement (Third) § 202(2). Thus, when following its invasion of Kuwait in August, 1990, Iraq announced a "comprehensive and eternal merger" with Kuwait, the U.N. Security Council unanimously adopted Resolution 662, calling upon "all States, international organizations and specialized agencies not to recognize that annexation, and to

refrain from any action or dealing that might be interpreted as indirect recognition of the annexation." S/RES/662 (1990). Most states did not recognize the secession of Biafra from Nigeria in 1967–70. The Confederate States of America were generally not recognized in 1861–65. It is uncertain whether acquisition of territory by lawful force, e.g., force used in self-defense against aggression, constitutes an exception. Consider the significance of such an exception in light of the unavailability as a general matter of an authoritative international determination of the factual issues frequently present when a use of force is claimed to be lawful. Consider the following comment:

> The number of examples of entities acquiring the characteristics of statehood allegedly through violation of law has not been large. Some states, particularly after a lapse of time, have been willing to accept a *fait accompli.* On a few occasions, the United Nations Security Council, or perhaps the General Assembly, might resolve the question. Compare the resolutions declaring North Korea and China aggressors against the Republic of Korea. S.C.Res. 82–85, 5 U.N. SCOR Resolutions and Decisions (S/INF/5/Rev. 1) at 4–7 (1950); G.A.Res. 498(V), 5 U.N.G.A.O.R., Supp. No. 20A at 1 (1951). In most instances, the issue is not subject to authoritative determination. For example, while many governments judged India's intervention in Bangladesh to be a violation of the Charter, but contrary arguments were made, justifying India's use of force as in support of self-determination or as humanitarian intervention. States generally recognized or treated Bangladesh as a state, and Bangladesh was admitted to the United Nations. See Franck & Rodley, After Bangladesh: The Law of Humanitarian Intervention by Military Force, 67 A.J.I.L. 275 (1973); Crawford, The Creation of States in International Law 115–18 (1979).

Restatement (Third) § 202, Reporters' Note 5.

5. Does non-recognition based on illegality risk being ineffective in the absence of other sanctions? Can it be justified in itself as a vindication of law? Lauterpacht has suggested that non-recognition "is the minimum of resistance which an insufficiently organized but law-abiding community offers to illegality; it is a continuous challenge to a legal wrong." Lauterpacht, Recognition in International Law 431 (1947).

## SECTION 2. RECOGNITION OF GOVERNMENTS

### A. CRITERIA OF RECOGNITION

Recognition of a state is not the same as recognition of its government although they often go together in the case of new states. Within existing states, governments come and go and normally the changes raise no question of recognition. When changes in government occur foreign governments are concerned primarily with the question of whether the new regime is in fact in control of the government. When the French monarchy was replaced by a popular government, Secretary of State Thomas Jefferson instructed the U.S. envoy in Paris that "[i]t accords with our principles to acknowledge any government to be rightful which is formed by the will of the nation substantially declared. * * * With such a government every kind of business may be done." Christopher, "Normalization of Diplomatic Relations," speech at Occidental College June 11, 1977. Daniel Webster, when

Secretary of State in 1852, expressed the United States' position which prevailed during the 19th century:

> From President Washington's time down to the present day it has been a principle, always acknowledged by the United States, that every nation possesses a right to govern itself according to its own will, to change its institutions at discretion, and to transact its business through whatever agents it may think proper to employ. This cardinal point in our policy has been strongly illustrated by recognizing the many forms of political power which have been successively adopted by France in the series of revolutions with which that country has been visited.

Quoted in Hyde at 159.

Although Webster was correct in expressing the position of the United States in the nineteenth century, the United States has in subsequent years applied on occasion standards for recognition other than that of effective control by the government. The varying United States practice as to recognizing governments has been summarized as follows in Restatement (Third) § 203, Reporters' Note 1:

> United States practice long reflected the view that recognition of governments was not a matter of international obligation but could be granted or withheld at will, to further national policy. United States policy has varied as to whether recognition should be withheld from a regime that has obtained power other than through constitutional processes. The case for withholding recognition was classically stated by President Wilson on March 11, 1913, after General Huerta overthrew the government of President Madero in Mexico. Based on the premise that a "just government rests always upon the consent of the governed," Wilson's view was that a regime taking control by force should not be dealt with on equal terms by other governments. 1 Hackworth, Digest of International Law 181 (1940). It was sometimes assumed that disapproval by foreign governments would undermine such a new regime and lead to its replacement, but that assumption has not been generally realized.
>
> At other times, however, United States policy has been to recognize the government in power despite distaste for the way it acceded to power, or for its ideology, policies, or personnel. The constitutionality of a regime's coming to power was often legally and factually difficult to determine and, in any event, the inquiry might seem improper and insulting to the country involved. It could also become awkward to continue to refuse to deal with a regime that was thriving in spite of non-recognition. In particular, withholding recognition of Latin American regimes was deemed by some states to be unlawful intervention in domestic affairs and intensified resentment against the United States in that region.
>
> Since 1970 the United States has moved away from its older recognition practice. "In recent years, U.S. practice has been to deemphasize and avoid the use of recognition in cases of changes of governments and to concern ourselves with the question of whether we wish to have diplomatic relations with the new governments." [1977] Digest of U.S. Practice in Int'l L. 19–21. Repeatedly, the State Department has responded to inquiries with the statement: "The question of recognition

> does not arise: we are conducting our relations with the new government." [1974] *Id.* at 13: [1975] *Id.* at 34. In some situations, however, the question cannot be avoided, for example, where two regimes are contending for power, and particularly where legal consequences within the United States depend on which regime is recognized or accepted.

In 1979, the United States recognized the People's Republic of China as the sole government of China and derecognized the regime in Taiwan. See p. 285 infra.

### *Notes*

1. Does Jefferson's "straightforward" statement on recognition mean that "effective power" alone is the prerequisite to recognition or is there a different standard in his reference to a government "formed by the will of the nation substantially declared"? Consider the following statement of a State Department legal adviser to the Senate Foreign Relations Committee:

> I think our present policy is more concerned with the acquiescence rather than the declaration of the will of the people. We have not generally concerned ourselves with asking, would the people, if given a free plebiscite, endorse that change of government.

United States Recognition of Foreign Governments: Hearings on S.Res. 205 Before the Comm. on For.Rel., 91st Cong., 1st Sess. 10 (1969) (Testimony of George Aldrich).

2. The criterion of constitutional legitimacy favored by Woodrow Wilson was similar to the Tobar or Betancourt Doctrine espoused in Latin America in 1907, which called for refusal to recognize any government that comes to power through extraconstitutional means until free elections are held and a government so elected assumes power. The doctrine was embodied in some treaties but in general was not followed in Latin America. However, a resolution of the Organization of American States did recommend that its member states exchange views when a government has been overthrown and take into account:

> Whether the de facto government proposes to take the necessary measures for the holding of elections within a reasonable period, giving its people the opportunity freely to participate in the consequent electoral processes. Res. XXVI.

OAS Second Special Inter-American Conference 1965, 5 I.L.M. 155 (1966). Although references are made to this, it has not precluded recognition of non-elected regimes.

3. During the periods in which the United States refused to recognize the U.S.S.R. (1920–1933) and the People's Government of China (1948–1979), it asserted as a condition of recognition that governments in effective control must be able and willing to live up to their international commitments. Both governments mentioned were charged with failures to observe international obligations. In retrospect, most observers would regard the United States' objections as based on ideological and political grounds. Is the requirement, as stated, legally meaningful? Does "ability" to live up to international commitments simply mean effective power to do so? Is "willingness" more than *pro forma* since no government would deny such willingness? On the other hand, does it leave room for states to deny recognition to internationally "lawless" regimes and therefore to apply sanctions against such behavior?

4. When conflicting governments contend for power and neither has complete effective power, should other criteria be applied? Should no action be taken until the conflict is resolved? What criteria should be followed by international bodies which must decide which regime should represent the state?

5. In February 1988, President Devalle of Panama tried to compel General Noriega to resign as commander of the Panamanian armed forces. Noriega refused and obtained a vote of the legislature to oust Devalle and install a new president approved by Noriega. In March, 1988, however, the United States Administration certified that Devalle was still the legitimate President of Panama with the result that United States banks could not release to the Noriega-backed regime deposits held in the name of the government of Panama. When Devalle's term ended in 1989, the United States Government ended the access of his representatives to the deposits.

6. There is a significant distinction between recognition of a government and maintaining diplomatic relations with it. Restatement (Third) § 203, Comment *d* states as follows:

> Recognition of a government is often effected by sending and receiving diplomatic representatives, but one government may recognize another yet refrain from assuming diplomatic relations with it. Similarly, breaking off relations does not constitute derecognition of the government. Some governments refrain from maintaining relations or terminate relations with each other in order to express disapproval, or from practical considerations, such as the absence of sufficient interests to warrant such relations, a lack of necessary personnel, or a desire to save the cost. Sometimes it is judged desirable to withdraw diplomatic personnel because of concern for their safety. When relations are not maintained directly they may be carried on through diplomatic channels provided by another government. Thus, the United States terminated relations with Cuba in 1961, but is represented in Cuba by the Swiss embassy in Havana, and Cuba is represented by the Czechoslovak embassy in Washington.

Deputy Secretary of State Warren Christopher stated as follows in a speech at Occidental College on June 11, 1977:

> * * * The premise of our present policy is that diplomatic relations do not constitute a seal of approval. Winston Churchill explained it best: "The reason for having diplomatic relations is not to confer a compliment, but to secure a convenience."
>
> * * *
>
> We maintain diplomatic relations with many governments of which we do not necessarily approve. The reality is that, in this day and age, coups and other unscheduled changes of government are not exceptional developments. Withholding diplomatic relations from these regimes, after they have obtained effective control, penalizes us. It means that we forsake much of the chance to influence the attitudes and conduct of a new regime. Without relations, we forfeit opportunities to transmit our values and communicate our policies. Isolation may well bring out the worst in the new government.

7. United States policy on diplomatic relations appears to have taken a new turn in connection with the emergence of the new states resulting from the dissolution of the former Soviet Union. On December 25, 1991, the United States recognized all twelve of the new states. President Bush also announced

the establishment of diplomatic relations with six that had made specific commitments apparently with respect to at least certain of the principles that now seem to be required by the United States as conditions to the recognition of statehood. See p. 250 supra. He also announced that diplomatic relations would be established with the other six (Moldova, Turkmenistan, Azerbaijan, Tajikistan, Georgia and Uzbekistan) when "we are satisfied that they have made commitments to responsible security policies and democratic principles as have the other states we recognize today." N.Y. Times, Dec. 26, 1991, at A16.

## THE TWO GOVERNMENTS OF CHINA

The Secretary General of the United Nations commented as follows in 1950 on the problem presented by the existence of two governments of China:

> The Chinese case is unique in the history of the United Nations, not because it involves a revolutionary change of government, but because it is the first in which two rival governments exist. It is quite possible that such a situation will occur again in the future and it is highly desirable to see what principle can be followed in choosing between the rivals. It has been demonstrated that the principle of numerical preponderance of recognition is inappropriate and legally incorrect. Is any other principle possible?
>
> It is submitted that the proper principle can be derived by analogy from Article 4 of the Charter. This Article requires that an applicant for membership must be able and willing to carry out the obligations of membership. The obligations of membership can be carried out only by governments which in fact possess the power to do so. Where a revolutionary government presents itself as representing a State, in rivalry to an existing government, the question at issue should be which of these two governments in fact is in a position to employ the resources and direct the people of the State in fulfilment of the obligations of membership. In essence, this means an inquiry as to whether the new government exercises effective authority within the territory of the State and is habitually obeyed by the bulk of the population.
>
> If so, it would seem to be appropriate for the United Nations organs, through their collective action, to accord it the right to represent the State in the Organization, even though individual Members of the Organization refuse, and may continue to refuse, to accord it recognition as the lawful government for reasons which are valid under their national policies.

Memorandum on Legal Aspects of Problems of Representation in the United Nations. U.N.Doc. S/1466 (1950).

### *Notes*

1. When the General Assembly considered the question of criteria for choosing between rival governments, the majority of governments rejected the "objective" test proposed by the United Kingdom based on "effective control over all or nearly all of the territory" and the "obedience of the bulk of population." Instead it recommended that, "whenever more than one authority claims to be

the government entitled to represent a Member State in the United Nations, and this question becomes a subject of controversy in the United Nations, the question should be considered in the light of the Purposes and Principles of the Charter and the circumstances of each case", G.A.Res. 396 (V) G.A.O.R., 5th Sess., Supp. 20, p. 24 (1950). This resolution was influenced obviously by the attitude toward Communist China, then engaged in armed hostilities against the United Nations Forces in Korea. However, the reluctance to adopt a purely factual test reflects a conception of "recognition" as involving value judgments. Such value judgments may be based on national interest in the specific sense of national policies and alliances. They may also be based on more general principles such as observance of human rights. The very broad formula adopted by the General Assembly left room for these conceptions. See Schachter, Problems of Law and Justice in Annual Review, United Nations Affairs 1951, 200–204 (Eagleton & Swift eds. 1952).

2. On September 22, 1992, the U.N. General Assembly by a vote of 127–6 with 26 abstentions adopted a resolution denying to the Federal Republic of Yugoslavia (consisting of Serbia and Montenegro) the right to succeed the Socialist Federal Republic of Yugoslavia as a member state of the United Nations. This action was influenced by the Federal Republic's involvement in hostilities in Bosnia-Herzegovina. The resolution determined that the Federal Republic of Yugoslavia "should apply for membership in the United Nations and that it shall not participate in the work of the General Assembly." G.A.Res. 47/1 Sept. 22, 1992, Vol. 3, No. 3 Foreign Pol'y Bull. 54 (Nov./Dec. 1992). South Africa had been suspended from the General Assembly in 1974 but remained a U.N. member.

## B. IS RECOGNITION NECESSARY?

### *STATEMENT OF MEXICAN FOREIGN MINISTER ESTRADA (1930)*

Whiteman, Digest of Int'l Law vol. 2, 85–86 (1963).

It is a well-known fact that some years ago Mexico suffered, as few nations have, from the consequences of that doctrine, which allows foreign governments to pass upon the legitimacy or illegitimacy of the régime existing in another country, with the result that situations arise in which the legal qualifications or national status of governments or authorities are apparently made subject to the opinion of foreigners.

Ever since the Great War, the doctrine of so-called "recognitions" has been applied in particular to the nations of this continent, although in well-known cases of change of régime occurring in European countries the governments of the nations have not made express declarations of recognition; consequently, the system has been changing into a special practice applicable to the Latin American Republics.

After a very careful study of the subject, the Government of Mexico has transmitted instructions to its Ministers or Chargés d'Affaires in the countries affected by the recent political crises, informing them that the Mexican Government is issuing no declarations in the sense of grants of recognition, since that nation considers that such a course is an insulting practice and one which, in addition to the fact that it offends the sovereignty of other nations, implies that judgment of some sort may be passed upon the internal affairs of those nations by other governments, inasmuch as the latter assume, in effect, an attitude of criticism, when they decide, favorably or unfavorably, as to the legal qualifications of foreign régimes.

### *Notes*

1. The Estrada Doctrine is generally understood to mean that recognition of governments is unnecessary once the state has been recognized. Should it not be construed more accurately as proposing (a) the sole criterion of effective control for deciding when to deal with a new government and (b) the avoidance of explicit and formal acts of recognition? What international policies would be served by this approach?

2. Baxter suggested that recognition is an "institution of law that causes more problems than it solves" and therefore should be rejected. "The partial withdrawal of law from this area of international relations will facilitate the maintenance of relations with states in which extraconstitutional changes of government are taking place, and that is a good thing." Baxter, Foreword to Galloway, Recognizing Foreign Governments p. xi (1978). If recognition in a formal sense has become unnecessary or a "non-problem," why did the People's Republic of China insist in 1979 on recognition by the United States as a condition of "normalization of relations"? Does that suggest that recognition cannot simply be replaced by the maintenance of diplomatic relations or a liaison office?

3. According to a State Department survey of 1969, "31 states indicated that they had abandoned traditional recognition policies and substituted the Estrada Doctrine or some equivalent by which they accepted whatever government was in effective control without raising the issue of recognition". Galloway at 10 and Appendix A. Mexico was among those countries, yet Mexico, the source of the Estrada Doctrine refused to recognize the Franco government of Spain for over three decades. Are many states prepared to abandon the institution of recognition as a political tool?

One study that favors the Estrada Doctrine recognizes that most states that express allegiance to the doctrine actually consider political factors in granting or withholding recognition. Galloway at 137–138.

4. Can the Estrada Doctrine be applied when there are rival claimants to power? Should foreign governments simply deal with both sets of officials regarding problems in areas where they respectively have de facto control until the conflict is resolved? See Jessup, A Modern Law of Nations 62–63 (1948), who observed that the Estrada Doctrine will not always save foreign governments from the necessity of choosing between rival claimants.

5. In April 1980, a change in the British policy concerning recognition of governments was announced by Lord Carrington to the House of Lords as follows:

> * * * [W]e have decided that we shall no longer accord recognition to Governments. The British Government recognise States in accordance with common international doctrine.
>
> Where an unconstitutional change of régime takes place in a recognised State, Governments of other States must necessarily consider what dealings, if any, they should have with the new régime, and whether and to what extent it qualifies to be treated as the Government of the State concerned * * *.

> We have * * * concluded that there are practical advantages in following the policy of many other countries in not according recognition to Governments. Like them, we shall continue to decide the nature of our dealings with regimes which come to power unconstitutionally in the light of our assessment of whether they are able themselves to exercise effective control of the territory of the State concerned and seem likely to do so.

Hansard, House of Lords, vol. 408, cols. 1121–1122. As a result, the question of whether a regime qualifies in the eyes of the United Kingdom as a government "will be left to be inferred from the nature of the dealings, if any, which [the UK Government] may have with it, and in particular on whether [the UK Government] are dealing with it on a normal Government to Government basis." 985 PARL. DEB. H.C. (5th ser.) 385 (1980). See Dixon, Recent Developments in United Kingdom Practice Concerning the Recognition of States and Governments, 22 Int'l Law. 555 (1988).

## *PETERSON, RECOGNITION OF GOVERNMENTS SHOULD NOT BE ABOLISHED*

77 A.J.I.L. 32, 46–50 (1983).*

In certain respects abolition [of recognition of governments] would create more confusion that it would cure. The idea that recognition applies only to states rests in part on a notion that recognition should apply only to subjects of international law, and not to their agents. However, the term "recognition" has a much broader meaning in international law. As in domestic law, "recognition" means taking formal cognizance of and giving legal effect to the existence of any number of situations, whether the emergence of a new entity (a state, a rebel group deserving belligerent status), a particular circumstance (war, foreign military occupation of a given territory), or a potentially controversial fact (claim to sovereignty over territory, existence of a foreign court ruling relevant to some case). If viewed in this broader perspective, there is nothing objectionable about applying recognition to the emergence of new governments.

Questions about the status of, communication with, and approval of new regimes are logically separate, but have tended to become intertwined. Advocates of abolition argue that current doctrines allowing governments great discretion about whether to recognize permit, if not encourage, identification of acknowledging status with approval, while communication is treated separately in all the informal ways previously discussed. They propose breaking the status-approval link by forming a link between status and communication. Under their alternative, status would be assumed once a government entered into formal communication (established diplomatic relations) with the new regime. Questions of approval would be left aside. This whole proposal rests on beliefs that governments must remain in as constant formal contact as possible and that the need for communication will overcome any disapproval of the new regime. Certainly, the expansion of

* Footnotes omitted. Reprinted by permission of the American Society of International Law.

"informal," "nonpolitical," and indirect forms of intergovernmental communication in the course of the 20th century supports their ideas.

Yet, on reflection, the situation seems far less simple. Creating a link between formal communications and the granting of status does not banish the possibility that questions of status will get mixed up with approval or disapproval of the new regime. Governments have long used severance of diplomatic relations to express strong disapproval of the current policies or postaccession political evolution of other governments. As noted earlier, this practice has become more common in recent years. It seems unlikely that such connections between communications and approval will be given up. Yet separating them will be necessary if linking status to formal communications is to break all links between approval and acceptance of status.

Then, too, the link between formal communications and acceptance of status rests on an inaccurate assumption and creates unnecessary complications. Such a link assumes that governments communicate mainly through diplomatic missions and cannot get along without them for long. This was largely true in the 19th century, but is not true today. Multilateral organizations, transgovernmental channels between agencies charged with similar tasks, contacts with state-owned enterprises or trade bodies, and various sorts of informal envoys all provide alternatives to diplomatic missions, as do the services of third parties. Many of these methods are cumbersome and ill-adapted to the discussion of important political issues, but they mean that governments are not faced with a choice between formal diplomatic relations and no contact at all. Moreover, the formal communications-status link does not work when diplomatic relations are absent. Finally and most seriously, a link between communications and status means that any failure to communicate during the early days of a regime's existence will be viewed as a sign of doubt about its status—regardless of the reason for the failure.

For all these reasons it is clear that separation of status and approval occurs only if all three questions are separated from one another. Total separation can best be realized by reforming the rules on recognition to require that decisions about status be guided by the effectivist rule. Nations could then base their decisions about communication on their relations with the other country or their ability to support a diplomatic mission without having to worry whether the lack of diplomatic relations suggests doubts about the new regime's status. Approval or disapproval can be indicated in many ways that have no relation to status or formal diplomatic relations, such as increasing or decreasing aid, encouraging or discouraging contacts between nationals, or commenting publicly on events in the other country.

Even if governments continue to insist upon links, the effectivist rule will still provide the best solution. A link between approval and communications creates some inconvenience, but it raises far fewer complications than a link between approval and status. An effectivist recognition rule would guide governments towards using the less inconvenient form of linkage.

* * *

Those who believe that the international community should refuse to accept regimes that come to power by means violating international law (for example, as a result of foreign imposition) have an additional reason to retain recognition of governments. Though refusal to continue diplomatic relations with the new regime might serve to indicate severe disapproval, its symbolic effectiveness is greatly reduced since there are many reasons for not having diplomatic relations that have no connection to the international legality or illegality of the new regime's origins. Particularly in a world where recognition normally followed an effectivist rule, nonrecognition would be an indication of severe disapproval. The danger that individual states might use such decisions as a new form of political response could be decreased by requiring that they be made collectively, as through the United Nations.

Thus, for both practical and doctrinal reasons, abolishing recognition of governments would be a mistake. This is not to argue that the existing institution is perfect. Far from it. Advocates of abolition are correct in their basic criticisms of recognition as it has been practiced, and in their insistence that any government in effective control of its state should have its status acknowledged and respected. If recognition of governments is to perform its proper functions, and confusion among acknowledgment of status, communication, and approval is to be avoided, recognition decisions must be based solely on whether the new government has control of its state. This effectivist rule would secure the advantages sought by advocates of abolition without causing the disadvantages attendant upon abolition.

### *Notes*

1. In view of the decisions taken by the United Nations in regard to Rhodesia and Namibia which involved non-recognition, is it not realistic to expect that non-recognition will be used (or recommended) by the U.N. against regimes considered to violate standards of self-determination, human rights or nonaggression? The Governments of some member states (e.g., Hungary and South Africa) had their credentials rejected on the ground that they did not represent the people of the country.

For a general defense of the use of recognition to further international aims, see Reisman & Suzuki, Recognition and Social Change in International Law in Toward World Order and Human Dignity 403–470 (Reisman & Weston, eds., 1976).

2. The Restatement (Third) takes the position that while a state is not required to accord formal recognition to the government of another state, a state is required to treat as the government of another state a regime that is in effective control of that state unless its control has been effected in violation of international law, in which event a state is required not to recognize or accept the regime as the government. Restatement (Third) § 203.

## C. UNRECOGNIZED GOVERNMENTS

### *1. Capacity of Unrecognized Governments to Bind the State*

## THE TINOCO CLAIMS ARBITRATION (GREAT BRITAIN v. COSTA RICA)

### *OPINION AND AWARD OF WILLIAM HOWARD TAFT, SOLE ARBITRATOR, 1923*

1 U.N.Rep. Int'l Arbitral Awards 369, 375 (1923).

[The case involved claims by Great Britain against Costa Rica for acts of a predecessor regime (the Tinoco regime) which had come to power by a coup and maintained itself in control for two years. The Tinoco regime was recognized by some governments but not by many leading powers (including Great Britain and the United States). When the Tinoco regime fell, the restored government nullified all of the Tinoco contracts, including an oil concession to a British company. Great Britain argued that the Tinoco Government was the only government in Costa Rica when the liabilities were created and that its acts could not be repudiated. Costa Rica argued that the Tinoco regime was not a government and that Great Britain was estopped by its non-recognition of Tinoco from claiming that Tinoco could confer rights on British subjects. In discussing the issue of recognition, the Arbitrator, United States Chief Justice Taft, stated:]

The non-recognition by other nations of a government claiming to be a national personality, is usually appropriate evidence that it has not attained the independence and control entitling it by international law to be classed as such. But when recognition *vel non* of a government is by such nations determined by inquiry, not into its *de facto* sovereignty and complete governmental control, but into its illegitimacy or irregularity of origin, their non-recognition loses something of evidential weight on the issue with which those applying the rules of international law are alone concerned. What is true of the non-recognition of the United States in its bearing upon the existence of a *de facto* government under Tinoco for thirty months is probably in a measure true of the non-recognition by her Allies in the European War. Such non-recognition for any reason, however, cannot outweigh the evidence disclosed by this record before me as to the *de facto* character of Tinoco's government, according to the standard set by international law.

Second. It is ably and earnestly argued on behalf of Costa Rica that the Tinoco government cannot be considered a *de facto* government, because it was not established and maintained in accord with the constitution of Costa Rica of 1871. To hold that a government which establishes itself and maintains a peaceful administration, with the acquiescence of the people for a substantial period of time, does not become a *de facto* government unless it conforms to a previous constitution would be to hold that within the rules of international law a revolution contrary to the fundamental law of the existing government cannot establish a new government. This cannot be, and is not, true.

[The Arbitrator rejected the claim of estoppel because Great Britain by non-recognition did not dispute the *de facto* existence of the Tinoco regime and because the successor Government had not been led by British non-recognition to change its position.]

### *Note*

In the *Tinoco* case, the *de facto* regime exercised authority throughout the country. Would the legal situation be different in respect of a *de facto* regime which controlled only a part of the country? The United States–Italian Claims Commission held that Yugoslavia was not liable for acts of the war-time state of Croatia, because Croatia was a puppet regime under German–Italian control and also because it was only a local authority with limited territorial control. Socony Vacuum Oil Co. Case, [1954] Int'l L.Rep. 55; [1956] id. 591.

### 2. *The International Personality of Insurgent Authority in Control of Specific Territory*

The category of *de facto* governments may also include organized insurgent groups which exercise governmental authority for a time over part of the territory of a state. Such groups may be regarded as "para-statal entities possessing a definite if limited form of international personality." G.G. Fitzmaurice, [1958] 2 Yb.I.L.C. at 32. Two specific attributes of such "personality" are indicated by state practice. First, the insurgent communities may be recognized as possessing belligerent rights against the *de jure* government and therefore as imposing neutrality on other states. See Lauterpacht, Recognition in International Law 187 (1947). Second, insurgent authorities in control of specific territory have also entered into agreements with governments and have therefore been considered to have treaty-making capacity. See [1958] 2 Yb.I.L.C. at 24. For example the Geneva Agreement of 1954 on the cessation of hostilities in Laos and Cambodia was signed by representatives of insurgent forces in control of some parts of the countries concerned although they were not recognized as de jure governments. However it has been argued that insurgent authorities cannot be "subjects of international law" or parties to treaties unless they represent the state "in the process of formation" and that "[a]ny detachment of insurgents cannot be entitled to such recognition. The treaties concluded with foreign authorities would have the level of a treaty only in a case where these authorities represent the State power, emerging in the course of the people's insurrection, and which is now in the process of formation." Lukashuk, Parties to Treaties—The Right of Participation, 135 Rec. des Cours 280–281 (1972–I).* It is evident that this position involves an element of "legitimacy" (as well as prediction) in addition to de facto control. It therefore provides more opportunity for political considerations.

The distinction between *de facto* and *de jure* recognition of insurgents is more than a matter of form; it has significant political and legal consequences. In Lauterpacht's words: "So long as the lawful government offers resistance which is not ostensibly hopeless or purely nominal, the *de jure* recognition of the revolutionary party as a government constitutes premature recognition which the lawful government is entitled to regard as an act of intervention contrary to international law. * * * [It] constitutes a drastic interference with the independence of the State concerned". Lauterpacht, Recognition in International Law 94–95 (1947).** This would not be the case for *de facto* recognition. However, *de facto* recognition of an insurgent authority has been considered as sufficient to support (as a matter of international law) sovereign immunity of the *de facto* government in the courts of the state granting such *de facto* (but not *de jure* ) recognition. The Arantzazu Mendi [1939] A.C. 256 (see p. 283 infra).

* Reprinted by permission of A.W. Sijthoff & Noordhoff International.

** Reprinted by Permission of the Cambridge University Press.

### Note

An insurgent authority with limited territorial control may nonetheless perform ordinary governmental functions in the area under its authority. It was held by a United States–Mexican Claims Commission in 1926 that the state of Mexico was liable for the acts of a local insurrectionary regime when such acts were of "purely governmental routine"—in the particular case, the sale of money orders. The Commission indicated that other types of acts by an insurrectionary regime would not subject the state to liability unless the *de facto* authority extended over a major portion of the territory of the state and over a majority of its people. Hopkins v. United Mexican States, 4 U.N.Rep. Int'l Arb. Awards 41 (1926). Is there sufficient reason to attribute to the state the responsibility for acts of a local revolutionary group which are of a routine administrative character? Is it justifiable to exclude from such attribution other "governmental acts" by the insurgents such as a contract for munitions or a large concession agreement?

## D. UNRECOGNIZED GOVERNMENTS IN MUNICIPAL LAW

### *1. The Validity of Acts of an Unrecognized Government*

## SALIMOFF & CO. v. STANDARD OIL OF N.Y.

N.Y. Court of Appeals, 1933.
262 N.Y. 220, 186 N.E. 679.

POUND, CH. J. The Soviet government, by a nationalization decree, confiscated all oil lands in Russia and sold oil extracted therefrom to defendants. The former owners of the property, Russian nationals, join in an equitable action for an accounting on the ground that the confiscatory decrees of the unrecognized Soviet government and the seizure of oil lands thereunder have no other effect in law on the rights of the parties than seizure by bandits. (Luther v. Sagor & Co., [1921] 1 K.B. 456; s.c., 3 K.B. 532; cited in Sokoloff v. National City Bank, 239 N.Y. 158, 164, 145 N.E. 917.) The complaints have been dismissed.

The question is as to the effect on the title of a purchaser from the unrecognized confiscating Soviet Russian government. Does title pass or is the Soviet government no better than a thief, stealing the property of its nationals and giving only a robber's title to stolen property? Plaintiffs contend that the Soviet decrees of confiscation did not divest them of title.

* * *

* * * The oil property confiscated was taken in Russia from Russian nationals. A recovery in conversion is dependent upon the laws of Russia. (Riley v. Pierce Oil Corp., 245 N.Y. 152, 154, 156 N.E. 647.) When no right of action is created at the place of wrong, no recovery in tort can be had in any other State on account of the wrong. The United States government recognizes that the Soviet government has functioned as a de facto or quasi government since 1917, ruling within its borders. It has recognized its existence as a fact although it has refused diplomatic recognition as one might refuse to recognize an objectionable relative although his actual existence could not be denied. It tells us that it has no disposition to ignore

the fact that such government is exercising control and power in territory of the former Russian empire. As was said by this court in Sokoloff v. National City Bank (supra, p. 165): "Juridically, a government that is unrecognized may be viewed as no government at all, if the power withholding recognition chooses thus to view it. In practice, however, since juridical conceptions are seldom, if ever, carried to the limit of their logic, the equivalence is not absolute, but is subject to self-imposed limitations of common sense and fairness, as we learned in litigations following our Civil War."

As a juristic conception, what is Soviet Russia? A band of robbers or a government? We all know that it is a government. The State Department knows it, the courts, the nations and the man on the street. If it is a government in fact, its decrees have force within its borders and over its nationals. "Recognition does not create the state." (Wulfsohn v. Russian S.F.S. Republic, 234 N.Y. 372, 375, 138 N.E. 24, 25.) It simply gives to a de facto state international status. Must the courts say that Soviet Russia is an outlaw and that the Provisional government of Russia as the successor of the Russian Imperial government is still the lawful government of Russia although it is long since dead? * * * The courts may not recognize the Soviet government as the de jure government until the State Department gives the word. They may, however, say that it is a government, maintaining internal peace and order, providing for national defense and the general welfare, carrying on relations with our own government and others. To refuse to recognize that Soviet Russia is a government regulating the internal affairs of the country, is to give to fictions an air of reality which they do not deserve.

### *Note*

1. Should decrees of a *de facto* government be accepted as valid for transferring assets located in the state of the forum but belonging to an entity subject to the law of the *de facto* government? The New York courts denied extraterritorial effect to Soviet decrees of nationalization prior to recognition of the U.S.S.R. in 1933. Bank deposits in New York of nationalized Soviet banks remained under the control of directors of the banks chartered by the Czarist Government. See Petrogradsky Mejdunarodny Kommerchesky Bank v. National City Bank, 253 N.Y. 23, 170 N.E. 479 (1930). Similarly, the nationalization decrees of the People's Republic of China were denied effect with respect to assets of the Bank of China in the United States as long as that Government was not accorded *de jure* recognition. See Bank of China v. Wells Fargo Bank, 104 F.Supp. 59 (N.D.Cal.1952), rev'd on other grounds, 209 F.2d 467 (9th Cir.1953).

### 2. *Municipal Law of Unrecognized Regime.*

## UPRIGHT v. MERCURY BUSINESS MACHINES CO.

Supreme Court of New York, Appellate Division, First Department, 1961.
13 A.D.2d 36, 213 N.Y.S.2d 417.

BREITEL, JUSTICE PRESIDING. Plaintiff, an individual, sues as the assignee of a trade acceptance drawn on and accepted by defendant in payment for business typewriters sold and delivered to it by a foreign corporation. The trade acceptance is in the amount of $27,307.45 and was assigned to plaintiff after dishonor by defendant.

Involved on this appeal is only the legal sufficiency of the first affirmative defense. It alleges that the foreign corporation is the creature of the East German Government, a government not recognized by the United States. It alleges, moreover, that such corporation is an enterprise controlled by and that it is an arm and instrument of such government.

On motion addressed to its sufficiency Special Term sustained the defense. For the reasons that follow the defense should have been stricken as legally insufficient * * *.

A foreign government, although not recognized by the political arm of the United States Government, may nevertheless have *de facto* existence which is juridically cognizable. The acts of such a *de facto* government may affect private rights and obligations arising either as a result of activity in, or with persons or corporations within, the territory controlled by such *de facto* government. This is traditional law (Russian Reinsurance Co. v. Stoddard, 240 N.Y. 149, 147 N.E. 703; M. Salimoff & Co. v. Standard Oil Co., 262 N.Y. 220, 186 N.E. 679, 89 A.L.R. 345 * * *.

* * *

So, too, only limited effect is given to the fact that the political arm has not recognized a foreign government. Realistically, the courts apprehend that political nonrecognition may serve only narrow purposes. While the judicial arm obligates itself to follow the suggestions of the political arm in effecting such narrow purposes, nevertheless, it will not exaggerate or compound the consequences required by such narrow purposes in construing rights and obligations affected by the acts of unrecognized governments (Sokoloff v. National City Bank, 239 N.Y. 158, 145 N.E. 917, 37 A.L.R. 712; M. Salimoff & Co. v. Standard Oil Co., supra). * * *

Applying these principles, it is insufficient for defendant merely to allege the nonrecognition of the East German Government and that plaintiff's assignor was organized by and is an arm and instrumentality of such unrecognized East German Government. The lack of jural status for such government or its creature corporation is not determinative of whether transactions with it will be denied enforcement in American courts, so long as the government is not the suitor.[1] * * *

The extent to which courts will recognize the legal effect of transactions within the territory of an unrecognized government, even where the transaction is materially affected by the action of such government, has been dramatically demonstrated. In M. Salimoff & Co. v. Standard Oil Co., 262 N.Y. 220, 186 N.E. 679, supra, it was held that one who took property by purchase from the unrecognized Russian government which had confiscated such property from its rightful owners nevertheless had good title as against the one-time lawful owners.

* * *

1. For, if the unrecognized government were allowed to sue, this would be deemed recognition of jural status (Russian Socialist Federated Soviet Republic v. Cibrario, 235 N.Y. 255, 139 N.E. 259). Note that the corporation perhaps could sue (see United States v. Insurance Companies, 22 Wall. 99, 89 U.S. 99, 22 L.Ed. 816, infra).

* * * [The internal acts of the East German Government, insofar as they concern the parties here, should be given effect generally. At least, this is so in the absence of allegation that defendant's property was expropriated by wrongful governmental force, or that for other reasons the transaction in suit or that directly underlying it violates public or national policy.

This case does not involve the issues, tendered by defendant in its argument, of jural status of the East German corporation, or of its incapacity to transfer title, or even of its capacity to sue in our courts. These have been long recognized as issues to be resolved by reference to the actual facts—the realities of life—occurring in the territory controlled by a *de facto* government, unless, of course, the contemplated juridical consequences of such "facts" can be properly related as inimical to the aims and purposes of our public or national policy [citations omitted]. Even the power of a rebel government in one of the Confederate States to create a corporation with capacity to sue the United States Government was admitted where such creation was not directly in furtherance of the rebellion (United States v. Insurance Companies, 22 Wall. 99, 89 U.S. 99, 22 L.Ed. 816).

* * * There are many things which may occur within the purview of an unrecognized government which are not evil and which will be given customary legal significance in the courts of nations which do not recognize the prevailing *de facto* government. In a time in which governments with established control over territories may be denied recognition for many reasons, it does not mean that the denizens of such territories or the corporate creatures of such powers do not have the juridical capacity to trade, transfer title, or collect the price for the merchandise they sell to outsiders, even in the courts of nonrecognizing nations * * *.

Of course, nonrecognition is a material fact but only a preliminary one. The proper conclusion will depend upon factors in addition to that of nonrecognition. Such is still the case even though an entity involved in the transaction be an arm or instrumentality of the unrecognized government. Thus, in order to exculpate defendant from payment for the merchandise it has received, it would have to allege and prove that the sale upon which the trade acceptance was based, or that the negotiation of the trade acceptance itself, was in violation of public or national policy. Such a defense would constitute one in the nature of illegality and if established would, or at least might, render all that ensued from the infected transaction void and unenforceable. Defendant buyer cannot escape liability merely by alleging and proving that it dealt with a corporation created by and functioning as the arm of and instrumentality of an unrecognized government.

* * *

Accordingly, the order of Special Term should be reversed, on the law, and the motion to strike the first affirmative defense granted * * * with leave, however, to defendant if it is so advised, to serve an amended answer within 20 days containing an affirmative defense asserting a violation of public policy with respect either to the underlying sale or the transfer of the trade acceptance in accordance with the views expressed in this opinion, or depending on any other theory not now passed upon. * * *

All concur except Steuer, J., who concurs in the result in a concurring opinion.

### *Notes*

1. English courts have generally refused to give effect to legislative acts of unrecognized governments and to legal acts pursuant to such laws. They have, for example, declined to recognize Rhodesian divorce decrees emanating from courts under the non-recognized regime of Ian Smith. See Adams v. Adams [1970] 3 A.E.R. 572. However in *Luther v. Sagor,* the English Court of Appeal gave effect to a Soviet confiscation decree of 1918 after receiving a letter from the Foreign Office stating that the British Government recognized the Soviet Government as the "*de facto* Government of Russia." The Court did not regard the distinction between *de facto* and *de jure* recognition as crucial, saying that since the British Government recognized the Soviet Government "as the Government really in possession of the powers of sovereignty, the acts of that Government must be treated with all the respect due to the acts of a duly recognized foreign sovereign State" Bankes, L.J. [1921] 3 K.B. at 543.

3. *Carl Zeiss Stiftung v. Rayner & Keeler* involved the validity of legislative and administrative acts of the East German Government (German Democratic Republic) which changed the structure of the plaintiff, the Carl Zeiss Stiftung. The Foreign Office certificate said that at the time in question the British Government recognized the Soviet Union as "*de jure* entitled to exercise governmental authority in respect of that zone * * * and have not recognized either *de jure* or *de facto* any other authority * * * in or in respect of that zone." On the basis of that certification, the Court of Appeal held that no effect could be given to the East German acts. The House of Lords reversed, holding that, since the acts of the East German Government were acts of a subordinate body exercising authority under the control of the Soviet Union as the occupying power, those acts were entitled to be regarded as the valid *lex domicilii* of the foundation (*Stiftung*) in question. [1967] 1 A.C. 853. See also Gur Corporation v. Trust Bank of South Africa Ltd., [1987] 1 Q.B. 599. Compare Carl Zeiss Stiftung v. V.E.B. Carl Zeiss, 293 F.Supp. 892 (S.D.N.Y.1968), modified, 433 F.2d 686 (2d Cir.1970), cert. denied, 403 U.S. 905, 91 S.Ct. 2205, 29 L.Ed.2d 680 (1971), in which the courts refused to give effect to the unrecognized East German Government's legislation concerning the Zeiss Foundation, distinguishing between acts of unrecognized governments "dealing solely with private, local and domestic matters," to which effect is given and acts "with respect to matters extending beyond the borders," to which it is not. 293 F.Supp. at 900. This case is cited by the Restatement (Third) in support of § 205(3), which states that "courts in the United States ordinarily give effect to acts * * * of a regime not recognized as the government of a state, if those acts apply to territory under the control of that regime and relate to domestic matters only."

### *3. Access to Courts*

## NATIONAL PETROCHEMICAL COMPANY OF IRAN v. M/T STOLT SHEAF

United States Court of Appeals, Second Circuit, 1988.
860 F.2d 551.

Before Cardamone, Pratt and Mahoney, Circuit Judges.

Cardamone, Circuit Judge:

The sole question presented on this appeal is whether National Petrochemical Company of Iran (NPC), a foreign corporation wholly owned by the government of Iran, is entitled to bring suit as a plaintiff in a diversity action in federal court. To answer such a question in this shoalstrewn area of the law, it is wise for courts to have in mind, like doctors taking the Hippocratic oath, that they must "first, do no harm." For the reasons that follow, we hold that NPC may maintain its action in the courts of the United States.

I

A brief background is necessary. In November of 1979 militants loyal to the Ayatollah Khomeini seized the United States Embassy in Tehran and took 52 American diplomatic personnel hostage. With the embassy and its personnel still in the militants' hands, on April 7, 1980 President Carter severed diplomatic relations with Iran and issued Executive Order No. 12,205, 45 Fed.Reg. 24,099 (1980), barring the sale to it of American products. As a result, NPC—which is a subsidiary of the National Iranian Oil Company that in turn is wholly owned by the government of Iran—found itself unable to procure essential chemicals such as ethylhexanol, orthoxylene, and ethylene dichloride from its usual sources in the United States. NPC's attempts to circumvent President Carter's trade embargo resulted in the transactions that brought about the instant litigation.

In the spring of 1980, NPC agreed to buy the needed chemicals from Monnris Enterprises (Monnris) of Dubai, United Arab Emirates. Monnris arranged to purchase them from Rotexchemie Brunst & Co. of Hamburg (Rotex), which contracted with United States sellers through its Geneva affiliate, Formula, S.A. (Formula). Rotex and Formula apparently fabricated shipping documents that concealed both the origin of the chemical cargo and its destination, and by such illegal methods were able to draw on the letters of credit issued by NPC before the cargoes were even shipped.

In August, 1980 Rotex chartered the defendant M/T Stolt Sheaf from the Liberian defendant Parcel Tankers, Inc. to carry the chemicals from Houston, Texas to Iran, via Barcelona, Spain. The remaining defendants are United States and Norwegian companies affiliated with Parcel Tankers and the M/T Stolt Sheaf. Rotex planned to deliver the embargoed goods to NPC in Iran, but when war broke out between Iran and Iraq in September, 1980 the chemicals were diverted to Taiwan, where Rotex resold them.

NPC * * * filed a complaint on September 30, 1986 in the United States District Court for the Southern District of New York (Owen, J.) alleging that the above named defendants had participated with the middlemen in fraud, conversion, falsifying bills of lading, all in breach of their duties and obligations under the bills of lading and the law. In a published decision, 671 F.Supp. 1009 (S.D.N.Y.1987), Judge Owen concluded—based upon a United States State Department letter written in connection with an unrelated case, Iran Handicraft & Carpet Export Center v. Marjan Int'l Corp., 655 F.Supp. 1275 (S.D.N.Y.1987)—that the United States has not recognized the Khomeini government of Iran. The district court therefore held that because NPC is a wholly-owned entity of an unrecognized foreign government, it is not entitled to bring suit in the courts of the United States. It dismissed NPC's complaint with prejudice. 671 F.Supp. at 1010.

On NPC's appeal from dismissal of its complaint, the United States has, for the first time, entered the litigation, submitting a brief as Amicus Curiae signed by attorneys from the Justice and State Departments, urging that NPC be granted access to the courts of the United States in this case.

II

We turn to an analysis of the law. Article III of the United States Constitution extends the federal judicial power to "all Cases ... between a State, or the Citizens thereof, and foreign States, Citizens or Subjects." U.S. Const., art. III, s 2, cl. 1. To effectuate this power, the United States Judicial Code provides diversity jurisdiction over any civil action arising between "a foreign state * * * as plaintiff and citizens of a State or of different States." 28 U.S.C. s 1332(a)(4) (1982).

To determine whether NPC as a wholly-owned entity of the Khomeini government of Iran should be granted access to federal court under s 1332(a)(4), it is helpful to review several well-established rules in this area of the law. In order to take advantage of diversity jurisdiction, a foreign state and the government representing it must be "recognized" by the United States. See Pfizer Inc. v. India, 434 U.S. 308, 319–20, 98 S.Ct. 584, 591–92, 54 L.Ed.2d 563 (1978); Calderone v. Naviera Vacuba S/A, 325 F.2d 76, 77 (2d Cir.1963); Land Oberoesterreich v. Gude, 109 F.2d 635, 637 (2d Cir.), cert. denied, 311 U.S. 670, 61 S.Ct. 30, 85 L.Ed. 431 (1940). As an incident to the President's express constitutional powers to appoint, U.S. Const., art. II, s 2, and to receive ambassadors, id. s 3, and to his implied power to maintain international relations, United States v. Curtiss–Wright Export Corp., 299 U.S. 304, 318–20, 57 S.Ct. 216, 220–21, 81 L.Ed. 255 (1936), the Supreme Court has acknowledged the President's exclusive authority to recognize or refuse to recognize a foreign state or government and to establish or refuse to establish diplomatic relations with it. See Banco Nacional de Cuba v. Sabbatino, 376 U.S. 398, 410, 84 S.Ct. 923, 930, 11 L.Ed.2d 804 (1964); Guaranty Trust Co. v. United States, 304 U.S. 126, 137, 58 S.Ct. 785, 791, 82 L.Ed. 1224 (1938); see also Restatement (Third) of the Foreign Relations Law of the United States s 204 (1987) (Restatement 3d).

For our purposes in this case, we also note that, under international law, a "state" is generally defined as "an entity that has a defined territory and a permanent population, under the control of its own government, and that engages in, or has the capacity to engage in, formal relations with other such entities." Restatement 3d s 201; see Texas v. White, 74 U.S. (7 Wall.) 700, 720, 19 L.Ed. 227 (1868). Although international law purports to require recognition of "states" that satisfy the elements of this definition, recognition of the particular government in control of another state is not mandatory. Further, a state derecognizes a governmental regime when it recognizes another regime as the legitimate government of that state. For example, when the United States recognized the People's Republic of China it derecognized the regime of the Taiwanese "Republic of China" which the United States had previously treated as the Chinese government. See Restatement 3d s 203, Comment f.

A break in diplomatic relations with another government does not automatically signify denial of access to federal courts. See Sabbatino, 376 U.S. 408–12, 84 S.Ct. 929–31. As the Supreme Court has observed, courts are hardly competent to assess how friendly or unfriendly our relationship with a foreign government is at any given moment, and absent some "definite touchstone for determination, we are constrained to consider any relationship, short of war, with a recognized sovereign power as embracing the privilege of resorting to United States courts." Id. at 410, 84 S.Ct. at 931; see Pfizer Inc., 434 U.S. at 319–20, 98 S.Ct. at 591–92. With these general rules in mind, we consider the circumstance of the instant case.

III

A. Recognition For Purposes of Federal Diversity Jurisdiction

The United States, as noted, severed diplomatic relations with Iran in 1980. In addition, NPC and Amicus concede that the President has never formally recognized the Khomeini government of Iran. The district court relied on a letter from the Assistant Legal Advisor for Management of the Department of State clarifying Iran's diplomatic status in connection with Iran Handicraft & Carpet Export Center v. Marjan Int'l Corp., 655 F.Supp. 1275 (S.D.N.Y.1987). The letter, dated December 26, 1985, stated in part: In response to your letter of December 13, 1985, the questions you posed and the answers of the State Department are as follows: "1. Has the United States recognized the Khomeini government of the Islamic Republic of Iran?" Answer: No. Id. at 1280 n. 4. Amicus contends that this response referred merely to the absence of formal recognition and was not intended to foreclose courts from entertaining suits by the Khomeini regime. NPC and Amicus argue that the Executive Branch has not prohibited the Khomeini regime's access to federal courts, and that the Executive Branch may recognize a government for the purposes of bringing suit despite the absence of formal recognition.

Appellees assert, to the contrary, that unlike diplomatic relations, the President's formal statement of recognition of a foreign government is a necessary condition to permitting it to sue in federal court. Certain language in the Supreme Court's decisions arguably supports such a requirement. See, e.g., Sabbatino, 376 U.S. at 410, 84 S.Ct. at 931 ("[T]he refusal to recognize has a unique legal aspect. It signifies this country's unwillingness to acknowledge that the government in question speaks * * * for the territory it purports to control.") (citations omitted); Guaranty Trust, 304 U.S. at 137, 58 S.Ct. at 791 ("[I]n conformity to generally accepted principles, the Soviet Government could not maintain a suit in our courts before its recognition by the political department of the Government."). Thus, appellees urge that NPC must be denied access to federal court based on the President's failure to extend formal recognition to the Khomeini government. We disagree and hold that the absence of formal recognition does not necessarily result in a foreign government being barred from access to United States courts.

Two reasons support this holding. First, as this century draws to a close, the practice of extending formal recognition to new governments has altered: The United States Department of State has sometimes refrained from announcing recognition of a new government because grants of recognition have been misinterpreted as pronouncements of approval. See 77 State Dep't Bull. 462–63 (Oct. 10, 1977) ("In recent years, U.S. practice has been to deemphasize and avoid the use of recognition in cases of changes of governments * * *"); Restatement 3d s 203, reporter's note 1 (commenting on recent deemphasis of formal recognition). As a result, the absence of formal recognition cannot serve as the touchstone for determining whether the Executive Branch has "recognized" a foreign nation for the purpose of granting that government access to United States courts.

Second, the power to deal with foreign nations outside the bounds of formal recognition is essential to a president's implied power to maintain international relations. Cf. United States v. Curtiss–Wright Export Corp., 299 U.S. 304, 318–20, 57 S.Ct. 216, 220–21, 81 L.Ed. 255 (1936). As part of this power, the Executive Branch must have the latitude to permit a foreign nation access to U.S. courts, even if that nation is not formally recognized by the U.S. government. This is because the president alone—as the constitutional guardian of foreign policy—knows what action is necessary to effectuate American relations with foreign governments. Cf. Sabbatino, 376 U.S. at 411 n. 12, 84 S.Ct. at 931 n. 12 (citing criticisms of any policy which would mandate formal recognition before a foreign nation could sue in U.S. courts).

This case serves as an excellent example. Relations between the United States and Iran over the past eight years have been less than friendly. Yet, the status of that relationship has not been unchanging. There have been periods of improvement, for example, release of the embassy hostages, and periods of worsening relations, most recently occasioned by the unfortunate downing of an Iranian civilian airliner by the U.S.S. Vincennes. It is evident that in today's topsy-turvy world governments can topple and relationships can change in a moment. The Executive Branch must therefore have broad, unfettered discretion in matters involving such sensitive, fast-changing, and complex foreign relationships. See Guaranty Trust, 304 U.S. at 137, 58 S.Ct. at 791 ("What government is to be regarded here as representative of a foreign sovereign state is a political rather than a judicial question, and is to be determined by the political department of the government."); Sabbatino, 376 U.S. at 410, 84 S.Ct. at 931 ("This Court would hardly be competent to undertake assessments of varying degrees of friendliness or its absence * * *"); Curtiss–Wright, 299 U.S. at 319, 57 S.Ct. at 220 ("In this vast external realm, with its important, complicated, delicate and manifold problems, the President alone has the power to speak or listen as a representative of the nation.").

### B. Deference to the Executive Branch

Determining that formal recognition is not necessary for Iran to gain access to U.S. courts does not end our inquiry. We must also consider whether the Executive Branch—despite its withholding of formal recognition—has evinced a willingness to permit Iran to litigate its claims in the U.S. forum. Several facts persuasively indicate such a willingness. For example, Iran and the United States entered into the Algerian Accords to resolve the embassy personnel hostage crisis; an ongoing Iran–United States Claims Tribunal at the Hague continues to adjudicate disputes between the two countries; and the 1955 Treaty of Amity, Economic Relations and Consular Rights between the United States and Iran remains in full force and effect. Standing alone, none of these indicia of Executive Branch willingness to allow Iran to proceed as a plaintiff in the United States courts would necessarily persuade us to reverse the district court and grant access.

Considering these factors in the aggregate, and not in isolation, as integral components of the United States overall relationship to Iran, the above recited connections strongly suggest that the Executive Branch has evinced an implicit willingness to permit the government of Iran to avail itself of a federal forum.

It is unnecessary to go further in examining other treaties, documents, or ties in order to ascertain the Executive Branch's intentions regarding Iran's access to the federal courts. The United States has submitted a Statement of Interest pursuant to 28 U.S.C. s 517 (1982) stating that "it is the position of the Executive Branch that the Iranian government and its instrumentality should be afforded access to our courts for purposes of resolution of the instant dispute." Because this Statement was not filed with Judge Owen, he was not apprised of the Executive Branch's position prior to ruling.

Appellees protest that for us to defer to what they term an "ad hoc, pro hac vice" directive to allow NPC's suit will encourage arbitrary and unpredictable pronouncements on the status of foreign governments, but we need not reach that question here because there is no indication that this is an arbitrary or ad hoc directive. This is not a case where the Executive Branch is attempting to prohibit a formally recognized government from bringing a single suit in the United States courts, nor is it a case where the Executive is arbitrarily allowing some suits by an unrecognized nation while disallowing others. Rather, here the Executive Branch—after entering into treaties with Iran, after establishing a claims tribunal to adjudicate disputes between the two countries, and after complying with U.S.–Iran agreements—expressly entered this case as Amicus requesting that Iran be given access to our courts. Under such circumstances, and as the sole branch authorized to conduct relations with foreign countries, the Executive clearly did not act arbitrarily. Accordingly, we hold that, for all the reasons stated, NPC must be permitted to proceed with its diversity suit in the Southern District of New York.

IV

The judgment of the district court dismissing NPC's complaint is reversed, the complaint is reinstated and the matter is remanded to the district court for further proceedings.

### *Notes*

1. The traditional rule generally applied by United States courts has been that an entity not recognized as a state or a regime not recognized as a government of a state cannot institute proceedings in the courts of a foreign state. Restatement (Third) § 205.

The United States Supreme Court in 1938 explained the principle of denial of access to a non-recognized government by stating that what government is to be regarded as the recognized representative of a foreign sovereign state is a political rather than a judicial question and is to be determined by the political department whose action in recognizing a foreign government is conclusive on all domestic courts. Guaranty Trust Co. of New York v. United States, 304 U.S. 126, 58 S.Ct. 785, 82 L.Ed. 1224 (1938).

2. In the *Sabbatino* case (p. 181 infra) the Supreme Court observed that the doctrine that non-recognition precluded suit by a foreign government had been much criticized and pointed out that since the precise question was not presented in the case (since Cuba was recognized, though diplomatic relations had been broken), the Court would intimate "no view on the possibility of access by an unrecognized government to United States courts." The severance of diplomatic relations did not imply the withdrawal of recognition and therefore did not preclude access: "It is the refusal to recognize which has a unique legal aspect, signifying this country's unwillingness to acknowledge that the government in question speaks as the sovereign authority for the territory it controls." The Court referred to the "possible incongruity" that would occur if a foreign power not recognized by the executive branch were accorded judicial recognition. 376 U.S. 398, 84 S.Ct. 923, 11 L.Ed.2d 804 (1964).

3. Withdrawal of recognition may prevent a government from maintaining an action already commenced. See Government of France v. Isbrandtsen–Moller, 48 F.Supp. 631 (S.D.N.Y.1943).

In 1970, the Republic of Viet Nam filed a suit against several American drug companies, alleging anti-trust violations. In 1975, the President of the Republic surrendered to North Viet Nam and in 1976 the territory of the Republic was joined to that of North Viet Nam to form a new state, the Socialist Republic of Viet Nam. At the time (1976), the United States recognized no government as the sovereign authority in the territory formerly known as South Viet Nam. The District Court dismissed the action on ground that the plaintiff no longer exists and "has not been succeeded by any government, entity or person that has capacity to sue in this court." On appeal, plaintiff argued the District Court erred in dismissing the action rather than suspending it in anticipation of recognition by the U.S. of a new government of Viet Nam. The Court of Appeals affirmed, noting that the trial court has discretion in deciding whether to suspend or dismiss a suit by a plaintiff whose recognition has been lost. In the circumstances of the case, the dismissal did not constitute an abuse of discretion. Republic of Vietnam v. Pfizer, Inc., 556 F.2d 892 (8th Cir.1977).

4. An unrecognized government cannot bring suit in an English court. Civil law countries generally deny *locus standi* to unrecognized governments. Brownlie, Principles of Public International Law 91 (4th ed.1990). However, in a few cases appearances by the unrecognized government have been allowed on the theory that the case involved private rather than public law. See cases cited in O'Connell, International Law 181 (2d ed. 1970).

5. Whether non-recognized governments may be defendants depends on their right to assert sovereign immunity. United States courts have taken the position that *de facto* governments in control of a state are entitled to claim sovereign immunity on behalf of the state.

In Wulfsohn v. Russian Socialist Federated Soviet Republic, 234 N.Y. 372, 138 N.E. 24 (1923), suit was brought against the Russian government to recover for the seizure of plaintiff's furs. The American court in refusing to grant relief invoked the doctrine of sovereign immunity, even though the Russian government had not been recognized by the United States. The court said in part: "[Our courts] may not bring a foreign sovereign before our bar, not because of comity, but because he has not submitted himself to our laws. Without his consent he is not subject to them." 234 N.Y. at 376, 138 N.E. at 26. The court also emphasized that the litigation did not involve property within the jurisdiction of the court: "The government itself is sued for an exercise of sovereignty within its own territories on the theory that such an act, if committed by an individual here, would be a tort under our system of municipal law." 235 N.Y. at 375, 138 N.E. at 25. The traditional rule that a foreign state may not be sued in the courts of another state without its consent must be considered in the light of those cases refusing to apply that rule where commercial activities conducted by the state, its instrumentalities or agents are involved. See p. 1133 infra.

6. The House of Lords decision in *Arantzazu Mendi,* [1939] A.C. 256, held that, since the insurgent authorities of Spain were recognized by the Executive Branch as a *de facto* government with administrative control over the larger part of Spain, that was sufficient to entitle that government to immunity from suit in an English court.

The opinion of the House of Lords has been criticized as dubious in equating an insurgent government in partial control of a state's territory with the state itself. See Brownlie, Principles of Public International Law 102 (4th ed. 1990).

## E. GOVERNMENTS–IN–EXILE

In contrast to *de facto* governments, governments-in-exile have been accorded *de jure* recognition but lack effective control over the territory of the state. In the past, most governments-in-exile based their claim to authority on continuity with a government which had formerly been in effective control of the state. States that continue to recognize such governments generally did so on the premise that the territory had been illegally occupied and that the legitimate government would be restored to power in the foreseeable future. Several countries occupied by German forces in World War II had exile governments recognized by the United States and the United Kingdom. See Brown, Sovereignty in Exile, 35 A.J.I.L. 666 (1941).

The legal consequences of such *de jure* recognition of governments-in-exile included recognition in municipal law of the control by the exile government of assets in the recognizing state. The recognizing governments also acknowledged the authority of the government-in-exile over its nationals abroad. It was also acknowledged that certain decrees of the government-in-exile applicable to events in the occupied territory would be given effect in the municipal courts of the recognizing states. In a case concerning a war-time decree of the Netherlands government-in-exile to protective possession over securities confiscated by the Nazis in Netherlands, the United States Circuit Court of Appeals upheld the validity of the decree in its application to occupied territory. Judge Charles Clark in his opinion said:

> Obviously absentee legislation intended to interfere with the occupant's *legitimate* rule should not be given effect. * * * The legitimate sovereign should be entitled to legislate over occupied territory insofar as such enactments do not interfere with the legitimate rule of the occupying power * * * [The decree in question] was aimed directly at preventing illegal seizure * * *

State of the Netherlands v. Federal Reserve Bank of New York, 201 F.2d 455 (2d Cir.1953).

The decrees of the governments-in-exile were not deprived of legal effect by subsequent *de jure* recognition of another government. In this connection see Boguslawski v. Gdynia–Ameryka Linie, [1950] 1 K.B. 157 (1949), affirmed [1951] 1 K.B. 162 (C.A.), affirmed sub nom. Gdynia Ameryka Linie Zeglugowe Spolka Akcyjna v. Boguslawski, [1953] A.C. 11 (1952), in which the plaintiff seamen sought to recover severance pay promised to them on July 3, 1945 by a minister of the Polish government-in-exile in London. The Foreign Secretary certified to the court that the British government had recognized the Polish government-in-exile in London as the government of Poland until midnight, July 5/6, 1945, and thereafter had recognized the new Provisional Government of National Unity (Lublin Government), which had been established June 28, 1945, as the government of Poland. The court held that the recognition of the Lublin Government by England did not operate retroactively to deprive of legal effect acts done in England by the exile government while it was still recognized by England. The court relied in part on the fact that the Polish merchant fleet, including defendant's vessels, was under the effective control of the exile government at the time the promise was made.

The wartime governments-in-exile took part in many international conferences and signed international agreements on behalf of their states. See Marek, Identity and Continuity of States in Public International Law 93–94, 439–40 (1968).

In recent years, governments-in-exile have been formed by movements seeking independence. They have often designated themselves as "provisional governments" and have been accorded recognition as such by sympathetic governments and by international bodies. An early example was the revolutionary "provisional government" of Algeria established in 1958, some years before it achieved control of Algeria. See Fraleigh, The Algerian Revolution as a Case Study in International Law, in The International Law of Civil War 179, (Falk ed., 1971). When governments-in-exile do not exercise stable control over territory in the country, they are not entitled under customary international law to belligerent status. Nevertheless, the Algerian Provisional Government and others have claimed such status and have received support for their claim. See Bedjaoui, Law and the Algerian Revolution 180 (1961). In 1970, Prince Sihanouk, who had been ousted as head of state in Cambodia, formed a government-in-exile in Peking which was recognized by China and by North Vietnam immediately. For an argument in favor of such recognition, see Barnes, U.S. Recognition Policy and Cambodia, in The Vietnam War and International Law, vol. 3, 149, 156 (Falk ed., 1972).

### *Notes*

1. "National liberation movements" have generally refrained from establishing themselves as governments-in-exile. Many such "liberation movements" have been accredited to international bodies within the United Nations and regional organizations such as the Organization of African Unity. What reasons may have led them to refrain from establishing a government-in-exile in a sympathetic state?

2. Can governments-in-exile be a means to promote basic political, civil and other human rights? Two commentators have suggested that the institution of governments-in-exile "provides dissident groups with an opportunity to organize, to seek international scrutiny of the conditions within a state, and to provide

alternative symbols for individuals within the state to identify with. * * * [I]t provides repositories of responsibility for the acts of regular or irregular forces of the exile government. * * * We suggest that claims for recognition * * * be granted in all those cases in which aspirant status within the state in question is denied or in which real political activity is severely sanctioned." Reisman & Suzuki, Recognition and Social Change in International Law, in Toward World Order and Human Dignity at 430 (Reisman & Weston eds., 1976).* Does past experience show that such exile governments can serve the aims listed? What problems would such recognition by foreign states create?

Consider the "phantom" governments-in-exile of Lithuania, Estonia, and Latvia which continued to be recognized by the United States and the United Kingdom notwithstanding the incorporation of those states in the Soviet Union. See Phantom Diplomats Carry on in Britain, Wall St.J., Dec. 9, 1970, at 1, col. 4.

## F. TERMINATION OF RECOGNITION

### *STATEMENT OF THE UNITED STATES ON WITHDRAWAL OF RECOGNITION FROM GOVERNMENT OF THE REPUBLIC OF CHINA (TAIWAN)*

80 Dep't State Bull. 26 (1979).

As of January 1, 1979, the United States of America recognizes the People's Republic of China as the sole legal government of China. On the same date, the People's Republic of China accords similar recognition to the United States of America. The United States thereby establishes diplomatic relations with the People's Republic of China.

On that same date, January 1, 1979, the United States of America will notify Taiwan that it is terminating diplomatic relations and that the Mutual Defense Treaty between the United States and the Republic of China is being terminated in accordance with the provisions of the Treaty. The United States also states that it will be withdrawing its remaining military personnel from Taiwan within four months.

In the future, the American people and the people of Taiwan will maintain commercial, cultural, and other relations without official government representation and without diplomatic relations.

The Administration will seek adjustments to our laws and regulations to permit the maintenance of commercial, cultural, and other nongovernmental relationships in the new circumstances that will exist after normalization.

### *Notes*

1. "A state derecognizes a regime when it recognizes another regime as the government. * * * Derecognition of one regime as the government without recognition of another regime has been rare. * * * [A] state may derecognize a regime without formally recognizing another, but any regime in effective control must be treated as the government." Restatement (Third) § 203, Comment *f.* So long as a state, as distinguished from its government, continues to meet the qualifications of statehood, its status as a state cannot be "derecognized."

2. If an entity ceases to possess the qualifications of statehood, it ceases to be a state and derecognition is unnecessary. Restatement (Third) § 202, Comment *g*. For example, derecognition of the German Democratic Republic was unnecessary when it was absorbed into the Federal Republic of Germany by accession to the Basic Law of the Federal Republic on October 3, 1990.

3. The Republic of China (Taiwan), which appears to meet the qualifications for statehood, is not a state because it claims to be part of China, not a separate state. The Taiwan Relations Act, 22 U.S.C.A. § 3301 et seq., exempts the Taiwan regime from some of the consequences of being unrecognized. Taiwan is accorded the right to sue and be sued in United States courts; its laws are given their normal application; and it has the right to own property in the United States. See p. 300 infra.

# SECTION 3. STATE SUCCESSION

## A. INTRODUCTION

The rights, capacities and obligations of a state appertain to the state as such and are not affected by changes in its government. If, however, a state acquires sovereignty over territory from another state, issues arise relating to the extent to which the former succeeds to the rights, capacities and obligations of the latter. Issues of state succession may arise when a state absorbs all of a predecessor state, a state takes over part of the territory of another state, a state becomes independent of another state of which it had formed a part, or a state arises because a predecessor state has separated into a number of states. Most successions in this century have resulted from peace treaties or from decolonization. More recently, major successions have included the unification of Germany (which involved an absorption by the Federal Republic of Germany of all of the territory of the German Democratic Republic without creating a new state), the merger of the Yemen Arab Republic (North Yemen) and the People's Democratic Republic of Yemen (South Yemen) to form the unified Republic of Yemen and the dissolution of the former U.S.S.R., the Socialist Federal Republic of Yugoslavia and the Czech and Slovak Republic.

The Reporters of the Restatement (Third) note that "[t]he international law and the practice of states as to succession have been uncertain and confused. In recent decades several views have emerged. Some suggest that the new state succeeds to no rights or obligations of its predecessor but begins with a *tabula rasa*. At the other pole is the view that a successor state is responsible for all obligations and enjoys all rights of its predecessor. Intermediate views have distinguished different circumstances of succession and different rights and obligations." Restatement (Third) § 208, Reporters' Note 1. The view adopted in the Restatement (Third) is that "succession has varying effects on state rights and duties." Id.

*CONFERENCE FOR PEACE IN YUGOSLAVIA*
*ARBITRATION COMMISSION OPINION NO. 9*

31 I.L.M. 1523 (1992).

[On May 18, 1992, the Chairman of the Arbitration Commission, the creation and function of which are discussed at p. 253 supra, received a letter from Lord Carrington, Chairman of the Conference for Peace in Yugoslavia, asking for the Commission's opinion on the following question:

Assuming that the dissolution of the former Socialist Federal Republic of Yugoslavia (SFRY) is now complete, "on what basis and by what means should the problems of the succession of states arising between the different states emerging from the SFRY be settled?

The Commission responded in part as follows:]

1. * * * In Opinion No. 8, the Arbitration Commission concluded that the dissolution of the Socialist Republic of Yugoslavia (SFRY) had been completed and that the state no longer existed.

New states have been created on the territory of the former SFRY and replaced it. All are successor states to the former SFRY.

2. As the Arbitration Commission pointed out in its first Opinion, the succession of states is governed by the principles of international law embodied in the Vienna Conventions of 23 August 1978 and 8 April 1983, which all Republics have agreed should be the foundation for discussions between them on the succession of states at the Conference for Peace in Yugoslavia.

The chief concern is that the solution adopted should lead to an equitable outcome, with the states concerned agreeing on procedures subject to compliance with the imperatives of general international law and, more particularly, the fundamental rights of the individual and of peoples and minorities.

3. In the declaration on former Yugoslavia adopted in Lisbon on 27 June 1992, the European Council stated that:

> "the Community will not recognize the new federal entity comprising Serbia and Montenegro as the successor State of the former Yugoslavia until the moment that decision has been taken by the qualified international institutions. They have decided to demand the suspension of the delegation of Yugoslavia at the CSCE and other international fora and organizations."

The Council thereby demonstrated its conviction that the Federal Republic of Yugoslavia (Serbia and Montenegro) has no right to consider itself the SFRY's sole successor.

4. The Arbitration Commission is therefore of the opinion that:

— the successor states to the SFRY must together settle all aspects of the succession by agreement;

— in the resulting negotiations, the successor states must try to achieve an equitable solution by drawing on the principles embodied in the 1978 and 1983 Vienna Conventions and, where appropriate, general international law;

— furthermore full account must be taken of the principle of equality of rights and duties between states in respect of international law;

— the SFRY's membership of international organizations must be terminated according to their statutes and that none of the successor states may thereupon claim for itself alone the membership rights previously enjoyed by the former SFRY;

— property of the SFRY located in third countries must be divided equitably between the successor states;

— the SFRY's assets and debts must likewise be shared equitably between the successor states;

— the states concerned must peacefully settle all disputes relating to succession to the SFRY which could not be resolved by agreement in line with the principle laid down in the United Nations Charter;

— they must moreover seek a solution by means of inquiry, mediation, conciliation, arbitration or judicial settlement;

— since, however, no specific question has been put to it, the Commission cannot at this stage venture an opinion on the difficulties that could arise from the very real problems associated with the succession to the former Yugoslavia.

### *Notes*

1. The majority of issues involving state succession to rights and obligations arise in the context of international agreements, which are discussed in Chapter 6. In 1978 a Convention on Succession of States in Respect of Treaties was adopted in Vienna, U.N.Doc. A/CONF. 80/31, 72 A.J.I.L. 971 (1978), and, in 1983, a Convention on the Succession of States in respect of State Property, Archives and Debts was adopted in Vienna, A/CONF. 117/14, 22 I.L.M. 306 [hereinafter cited as 1983 Succession Convention]. The United States has ratified neither, and it voted against adoption of the latter.

2. On state succession generally, see O'Connell, State Succession in Municipal Law and International Law (1967) [hereinafter cited as O'Connell, State Succession]. This Section will consider the effect of state succession on the internal legal system of the successor state, state succession to public debt and other contracts, the effect of state succession on property rights and state succession to obligations arising from violations of international law.

## B. STATE SUCCESSION AND THE INTERNAL LEGAL SYSTEM

With respect generally to the question of succession to the internal legal system of a territory, a distinction has traditionally been drawn between public law and private law. Public law, broadly, is that body of laws promulgated by the government for the effective administration of the country; it is political in character, concerns the relation of the population to the state, and pertains to the prerogatives of sovereignty. Private law, on the other hand, governs the relations between individual citizens and need not be directly affected by the administration of the country. See 1 O'Connell, State Succession 101–141.

The traditional view held that although private law survives a state succession and the rights of private parties are not affected by the change in sovereignty, public law does not survive. Id. at 104. This view, however, does not accord with state practice. An alternative approach, which seems closer to actual practice, is that if the public law of the new state and the public law of the predecessor state are consistent, succession takes place, but that if the laws are inconsistent, no succession occurs. In this view, succession is, in effect, a presumption, which can be rebutted by positive legislation of the new state. Id. at 107. State practice indicates that new states generally make legislative provision for continuity of the internal legal order, with the qualification that continuity must be consistent with the change in sovereignty. Id. at 118 et seq. Sometimes, both the predecessor state and the new state make legislative provision for succession with respect to the legal system. For instance, in the case of India, Britain provided for continuity of the legal system in the India Independence Act, 10 & 11 Geo. 6, c. 30, § 18 (1947). India provided for continuity in the Indian Constitution, Art. 372(2).

## C. SUCCESSION TO THE PUBLIC DEBT AND OTHER CONTRACTS

Public debts may be owed to another state, to an international organization, to a publicly or privately owned financial institution, or to a private person. In principle, a succession of states does not as such affect the rights and obligations of creditors with respect to public debts. 1983 Succession Convention, Art. 36, 22 I.L.M. 323. However, the issue of succession to obligations in the form of public debts is often resolved by agreement between the predecessor and successor states. See, e.g., Art. 23 of Federal Republic of Germany–German Democratic Republic: Treaty on the Establishment of German Unity, 30 I.L.M. 457, 478 (1991) and Financial and Economic Agreement between Indonesia and The Netherlands, art. 25, signed Dec. 27, 1949, 69 U.N.T.S. 252–257.

One important feature of the law in the area is the distinction drawn between the national public debt, which is owed by the state as a whole, and local public debt, which includes debts owed by the state in respect of a specific territory or specific assets and revenues and debts contracted by a political subdivision (e.g., a city or province). See generally 1 O'Connell, State Succession 369–453; Feilchenfeld, Public Debts and State Succession (1931).

In the case of national public debt, the 1983 Succession Convention provides that, in the absence of an agreement governing succession, if there is a transfer of part of the territory of a state, a separation of part of the territory of a state or a dissolution of a state, the public debt of the predecessor shall pass to the successor state "in an equitable proportion, taking into account, in particular, the property, rights and interests which pass to the successor state in relation to that * * * debt." Articles 37, 40 and 41, 22 I.L.M. 323–324. See Ottoman Public Debt Case, 1 R. Int'l Arb. Awards 529 (1925). If two or more states unite, the public debt of the predecessors passes to the successor. 1983 Succession Convention, Article 39. 22 I.L.M. 322. The result is the same if a state is absorbed by another state. Restatement (Third) § 209(2)(b). If the successor state were not responsible for the public debt of the predecessor(s), the creditors would have no source of payment and the successor state might be unjustly enriched by acquiring territory and assets without having to assume the debtor entity's obligations. Restatement (Third) § 209, Comment c. However, if the debtor entity retains fiscal independence, the debtor-creditor relationship is unaffected, and the entity remains responsible for repayment of the debt. See 1 O'Connell, State Succession 373, 375.

When Austria was made part of the German Reich in 1938, the United States delivered notes to the German Government indicating its belief that it was a general doctrine of international law that the substituted sovereign assumed the debts and obligations of the absorbed state. 1 Hackworth 545. The German Government replied that the law of state succession did not apply in the particular case because Austria had liquidated herself, that the debts were "political" in character, and that in the past the United States had failed to assume responsibility for the payment of debts. Gerner, Questions of State Succession Raised by the German Annexation of Austria, 32 A.J.I.L. 421 (1938). The United States rejected these contentions. Hyde 419. A separating state has generally not succeeded to the national (i.e., non-local) public debt of the predecessor state. See Zemanek, State Succession after Decolonization, 116 Rec. des Cours 180, 258 (1965–III).

Article 33 of the 1983 Succession Convention takes the position that the rules relating to public debt do not apply to public debt of a state held by creditors other than states and international institutions such as the World Bank. 22 I.L.M. 322. The Restatement (Third) § 209, Comment b, rejects this view and adopts the position that the rules also apply to public debt held by private creditors, citing the prevailing position in the International Law Commission.

Local public debts frequently take the form of obligations incurred for funds expended or used in connection with a particular project in the territory directly affected by separation or absorption. An example would be loans contracted with the International Bank for Reconstruction and Development. The Bank required that if such loans were extended to dependent territories, a separate Guarantee Agreement between the Bank and the colonial power be concluded. In most other cases, debts contracted by, or on behalf of, the separating territory are assigned to the successor state by agreement between the predecessor state and the new state. If no agreement is concluded, the new state nevertheless usually assumes the debts related to its territory which had been incurred before the separation or absorption. See Zemanek at 261–66; Feilchenfeld at 417–22.

Local debts may be obligations incurred by a fiscally autonomous governmental subdivision in the territory of the successor state before the creation of the new state. The general rule with regard to such local debts is that the change in sovereignty does not affect the local debts if the subdivision incurring those debts is unaffected by the change. If, moreover, the successor state impairs the repayment of the obligation, or causes the demise of the autonomy of the local authority which contracted the debt, the new state must assume repayment of the debt. See 1 O'Connell, State Succession at 452–54.

When the predecessor state is a party to contracts, these contracts are often governed by municipal law, and if the predecessor state remains in being (as was the case where a colony became independent), the contract between the predecessor state and a private party would remain valid, unless it was so connected with the territory of the new state that it would be impossible for the predecessor state to continue to perform the contract, in which case the successor state might be considered bound. If the private party has performed only part of the contract, but is prevented from completing performance because of the change in sovereignty, municipal law doctrines of frustration, *quantum meruit,* unjust enrichment, or restitution may become applicable. See 1 O'Connell 442–43.

If a contract between a private party and the state requires the construction and operation of public works or the extraction of minerals, it is clear that the contract is closely linked with the territory affected by change of sovereignty. However, it is also true that the successor state is not a party to the contract. Although the traditional law on this subject was unclear, compare West Rand Gold Mining Co., Ltd. v. The King, [1905] K.B. 391, with the Sopron–Koszeg Railway Case, [1929–30] Ann.Dig. 57, 59 (No. 54), economic development and concession agreements involving substantial investments by a foreign investor should be binding on the successor state. Restatement (Third) § 209, Comment *f.* Succession agreements may provide for the assumption of obligations under such agreements by the successor state.

### *Notes*

1. Section 209(2) of the Restatement (Third) states:

> (2) Subject to agreement between predecessor and successor states, responsibility for public debt of the predecessor, and rights and obligations under its contracts, remain with the predecessor state, except as follows:
>
> (a) where part of the territory of a state becomes territory of another state, local public debt, and the rights and obligations of the predecessor state under contracts relating to that territory, are transferred to the successor state;
>
> (b) where a state is absorbed by another state, the public debt, and rights and obligations under contracts of the absorbed state, pass to the absorbing state;
>
> (c) where part of a state becomes a separate state, local public debt, and rights and obligations of the predecessor state under contracts relating to the territory of the new state, pass to the new state.

Comment *d* to § 209 indicates that local debt includes both indebtedness incurred by a subdivision of the state (e.g., a city or province) and debts incurred by a state to finance a project located in a given locality. "[S]ince the successor state acquires control over the assets located in that territory, it assumes corresponding obligations." Restatement (Third) § 209, Comment *d.*

2. Among the significant differences between public debts and certain other contracts is the fact that termination of an obligation to pay a debt would unjustifiably enrich the state relieved of the repayment obligation, while termination of an executory contract would not necessarily do so. With respect to succession to public debts see Report of the International Law Commission on its 31st Session, G.A.O.R. 34 Sess., Supp. No. 10 (A/34/10) (1979) p. 95.

3. There was discussion in the International Law Commission of whether a convention on state succession to debts should include articles dealing with state succession with respect to "odious" debts. For a discussion of the issues and authorities relating to odious debt issues see the Ninth Report of the Special Rapporteur in 1977 I.L.C. Yrbk. Vol. II (Part One) p. 45. U.N. Doc. A/CN.4/301 and Add. I. The I.L.C. Report on the Work of its Thirty–third Session commented as follows on this report (footnotes omitted):

> (41) In his ninth report, the Special Rapporteur included a chapter entitled "Non-transferability of 'odious' debts". That chapter dealt, first, with the definition of "odious debts". The Special Rapporteur recalled *inter alia,* the writings of jurists who referred to "war debts" or "subjugation debts" and those who referred to "regime debts". For the definition of odious debts, he proposed an article C, which read as follows:
>
> *Article C. Definition of odious debts*
>
> For the purpose of the present articles, "odious debts" means:
>
> (a) all debts contracted by the predecessor State with a view to attaining objectives contrary to the major interests of the successor State or of the transferred territory;
>
> (b) all debts contracted by the predecessor State with an aim and for a purpose not in conformity with international law and, in particular, the principles of international law embodied in the Charter of the United Nations.
>
> (42) Second, the chapter dealt with the determination of the fate of odious debts. The Special Rapporteur reviewed State practice concerning "war debts", including a number of cases of the non-passing of such debts to a successor State, as well as cases of the passing of such debts. He further cited cases of State practice concerning the passing or non-passing to a successor State of "subjugation debts". He proposed the following article D, concerning the non-transferability of odious debts:
>
> *Article D. Non-transferability of odious debts*
>
> [Except in the case of the uniting of States,] odious debts contracted by the predecessor State are not transferable to the successor State.
>
> (43) The Commission, having discussed articles C and D, recognized the importance of the issues raised in connection with the question of "odious" debts, but was of the opinion initially that the rules formulated for each type of succession of States might well settle the issues raised by the question and might dispose of the need to draft general provisions on it. In completing the second reading of the draft, the Commission confirmed that initial view.

1981 I.L.C. Yrbk. Vol. II (Part Two) p. 78. The 1983 Succession Convention did not, in fact, deal with the issue of the non-transferability of odious debts.

## D. SUCCESSION TO STATE PROPERTY

When part of the territory of a state becomes territory of another state or a new state, the property of the predecessor state located in the territory concerned becomes the property of the successor state. Restatement (Third) § 209(1). Article 17 of the 1983 Succession Convention states that movable property of the predecessor state passes to the successor only if it is "connected with activity of the predecessor state in respect of territory to which the succession of states relates" 22 I.L.M. 314. "Except where the predecessor state wholly ceases to exist, property located outside the territory subject to the transfer of sovereignty (including intangibles, such as bank accounts) generally remains with the predecessor state." Restatement (Third) § 209, Reporters' Note 1.

If the successor state has violated the U.N. Charter in annexing a predecessor state with force, the unlawful successor should not be permitted to succeed to rights in property or to rights under contract, but should be responsible for the public debts of the predecessor. Restatement (Third) § 209, Comment *h*.

## E. SUCCESSION TO OBLIGATIONS ARISING FROM VIOLATIONS OF INTERNATIONAL LAW

It has been held that the successor state has no responsibility in international law for the international delicts of its predecessor. See Robert E. Brown Claim (United States v. Great Britain), American & British Claims Arbitration 187, 6 U.N.Rep.Int'l Arb. Awards 120 (1923) (Claimant sought compensation for refusal of local officials of the Boer Republics to issue licenses to exploit a goldfield. The United Kingdom contended that this was a delictual claim, and that it did not succeed to responsibility; the United States asserted that claimant's acquired rights were infringed and that Britain did succeed to the obligation to compensate Brown. The tribunal held that Brown had acquired a property right and that he had been injured by a denial of justice, but that this was a delict responsibility for which did not devolve on Britain.) See also Redward Claim (Hawaiian Claims) (Great Britain v. United States), American & British Claims, Arbitration 85, 160–61, 6 U.N.Rep.Int'l Arb. Awards 157 (1925) (Claimants had been wrongfully imprisoned by the Government of the Hawaiian Republic, which was subsequently annexed by the United States. The tribunal held that "legal liability for the wrong has been extinguished" with the disappearance of the Hawaiian Republic.) Thus if the claim has not been reduced to a money judgment, which may be considered a debt, or an interest on the part of the claimant in assets of fixed value, there is no acquired right in the claimant, and no obligation to which the successor state has succeeded. See 1 O'Connell, State Succession 482, 485–86.

### *Note*

Why should the successor state not be responsible for an international wrong if it has been enriched by the wrongful action of its predecessor? With respect to the Brown and Redward awards, it has been observed: "These cases date from the age of colonialism when colonial powers resisted any rule that would make them responsible for the delicts of states which they regarded as uncivilized. The authority of those cases a century later is doubtful. At least in some cases, it would be unfair to deny the claim of an injured party because the state that committed the wrong was absorbed by another state." Restatement (Third) § 209; Reporters' Note 7. See, generally, Czaplinski, State Succession and State Responsibility, 28 Can.Y.B.I.L. 339 (1990).

# SECTION 4. TERRITORIAL ENTITIES OTHER THAN STATES THAT HAVE INTERNATIONAL STATUS

## A. DEPENDENT ENTITIES AS PARTIES TO TREATIES

### *LISSITZYN, TERRITORIAL ENTITIES OTHER THAN STATES IN THE LAW OF TREATIES*

125 Rec. des Cours 5, 9–15 (1968–III).*

We must, therefore, be on guard against attaching too much significance to the characterisation of a particular entity as a "State." Indeed, depending on one's preference, certain entities which are not regarded as independent but which seem to participate in treaty relations can be described either as "dependent States" or as entities which, though not "States", possess a degree of international personality for this purpose.

* * *

* * * Such entities, in turn, fall into several broad subcategories:

(a) Members of composite States (i.e., federal unions, real unions and the like).

(b) "Dependent States" (protected States, protectorates, vassal States, "associated States", and the like).

(c) Colonial dependencies (self-governing colonies, non-self-governing colonies, condominia) and metropolitan political subdivisions.

(d) Territories administered under mandates or trusteeship agreements.

(e) Entities subject to special forms of international control or supervision other than mandates or trusteeships.

* * *

* * * An entity's rights and duties in international law need not be the same as those of States. It may have "a large measure" of international personality—that is, its capacities may be more limited than those of independent States. And practice, including the conclusion of international agreements, may provide the evidence that an entity has international personality.

Indeed, * * * the term "personality" is merely a short-hand symbol which denotes that an entity is endowed by international law with *some* legal capacities, but does not tell us what particular capacities it has. Different kinds of "international persons" have different capacities. It is the possession of some specific capacities that signifies that an entity has international personality, not the other way around. If an entity has treaty-making capacity, it is an "international person", but if we are told that an entity has "international personality," we cannot conclude that it has treaty-

* Footnotes omitted. Reprinted by permission of A.W. Sijthoff & Noordhoff International.

making capacity, since it may only possess some *other* capacity. Individuals, for example, may be regarded as "subjects of international law" for certain purposes, but we cannot conclude from this fact alone that they have treaty-making capacity. In this connection, it must also be pointed out that an entity may have the capacity to be a party to a treaty without being able to conclude treaties in its own name, if it has delegated the power to conclude treaties to another entity.

In considering the extent to which various kinds of dependent entities participate in treaty relations and the legal implications of such participation, we must bear in mind that the fact that a particular dependent entity appears to be named as a party to a certain treaty may have two radically different juridical explanations: First, it may be regarded as an international person possessing its own treaty-making capacity, whether or not it is a "State"; second, it may be regarded as having no distinct international personality or capacity of its own, but merely the authority to act as an agent or organ of the dominant State, which alone has the requisite capacity.

### *INTERNATIONAL LAW COMMISSION, REPORT ON THE LAW OF TREATIES, H. WALDOCK, SPECIAL RAPPORTEUR*

[1962] II Yb. I.L.C. 27, 36.

2. (a) In the case of a federation or other union of States, international capacity to be a party to treaties is in principle possessed exclusively by the federal State or by the Union. Accordingly, if the constitution of a federation or Union confers upon its constituent States power to enter into agreements directly with foreign States, the constituent State normally exercises this power in the capacity only of an organ of the federal State or Union, as the case may be.

(b) International capacity to be a party to treaties may, however, be possessed by a constituent State of a federation or union, upon which the power to enter into agreements directly with foreign States has been conferred by the Constitution:

(i) If it is a member of the United Nations, or

(ii) If it is recognized by the federal State or Union and by the other contracting State or States to possess an international personality of its own.

3. (a) In the case of a dependent State the conduct of whose international relations has been entrusted to another State, international capacity to enter into treaties affecting the dependent State is vested in the State responsible for conducting its international relations, except in the cases mentioned in sub-paragraph (b).

(b) A dependent State may, however, possess international capacity to enter into treaties if and in so far as:

(i) The agreements or arrangements between it and the State responsible for the conduct of its foreign relations may reserve to it the power to enter into treaties in its own name; and

(ii) The other contracting parties accept its participation in the treaty in its own name separately from the State which is responsible for the conduct of its international relations.

### *Notes*

1. Although colonies were not generally considered to have international personality or treaty-making capacity, they were allowed to become parties to many multilateral treaties. The Covenant of the League even allowed a "fully self-governing dominion or colony" to become a member of the League. India did so at a time when its foreign affairs were in law and in fact under British control. Prior to its independence in 1947, India became a party to other treaties which, in terms, were open only to states, such as the Chicago Convention on Civil Aviation. It was an original member of the United Nations and of the specialized agencies before independence. The Philippine Commonwealth was in much the same position.

2. In other cases, colonies became members of international organizations and parties to treaties with the authorization of the metropolitan power. It was generally considered that in these cases the metropolitan power remained ultimately responsible for the fulfillment of the commitments of the colony or possession. However, there is no legal reason why a treaty could not provide that a colony or other possession would be solely responsible for the performance of obligations within its competence without responsibility on the part of the metropolitan state. See Lissitzyn at 81–82.

3. For discussion of the treaty-making capacity of members of federal states or unions, see p. 433 infra.

## B. MANDATED AND TRUST TERRITORIES AND OTHER INTERNATIONALIZED TERRITORIES

The Mandate system was established at the end of World War I by the Allied and Associated Powers under Article 22 of the Covenant of the League of Nations. There were in all 15 mandated territories. Those in the Middle East became independent states, and the others in the Pacific and Africa (except for South West Africa) were transferred to the U.N. trusteeship system.

The U.N. trusteeship system had the same general aims as the Mandate system—namely, to promote "well-being and development" of the peoples and their eventual self-government or independence. The U.N. trust territories included some former mandated territories and only one additional territory, Italian Somaliland. As of 1992, all of the trust territories had achieved independence or "self-government" within another state, with the exception of a portion (i.e. Palau) of the Strategic Trust Territory of the Pacific Islands, of which the United States is the administering power.

Trust and mandated territories were administered by an administering authority or mandatory under agreements which provided for supervision by the United Nations Trusteeship Council or, in the case of the mandates, a League of Nations "Permanent Mandates Commission." These territories did not become part of the territory of the administering power. See Callas v. United States, 253 F.2d 838 (2d Cir.1958), cert. denied, 357 U.S. 936, 78 S.Ct. 1384, 2 L.Ed.2d 1550 (1958). Nor did the inhabitants acquire the nationality of the administering state. Sovereignty was considered to be vested in the people of the territory, but exercised, within strict limits of the agreements, by the administering power. Although the mandate and trust systems have virtually disappeared, the principles of international accountability and surveillance used in the mandate and trusteeship arrangements may have application in the future.

## C. ASSOCIATED STATES

Although the process of decolonization has in the great majority of cases resulted in the creation of fully independent states, some territories have passed through the status of associated states on the way to full independence, and a handful of them retain the status of associated states. The usual associated state is a territory that elects to combine complete internal independence with continued dependence upon another state in some measure in matters of international affairs and defense. Examples of states that have passed through the status of associated states are Antigua, St. Kitts–Nevis–Anguilla, Dominica, St. Lucia, St. Vincent and Grenada in association with the United Kingdom. All have since become independent states. The Cook Islands remain associated states with New Zealand, which is responsible for their defense and international affairs. It has been observed that "the intention behind association is to endow the States with competence less than that of full independence but greater than that of subordinacy. International law will have to accommodate them within its structure, though conundrums arise respecting the responsibility of the mother country for violations of international law or breaches of treaty obligations by the States and respecting the characterisation of a matter as one of internal affairs or one of external affairs." O'Connell, International Law 344 (2d ed. 1970).

Puerto Rico is a Commonwealth which is completely autonomous in internal affairs, but the United States is responsible for Puerto Rico's foreign affairs and defense. Puerto Rico has its own Constitution, under which the Governor and members of the legislature are elected and judges and officials of the executive branch are appointed. It also has its own tax system, civil and criminal laws, and determines its own budget. It has a Resident Commissioner in the United States House of Representatives, who is authorized to speak but not vote and to vote as well as speak in meetings of congressional committees to which appointed. Puerto Ricans are United States citizens but cannot vote in Presidential elections. See Leibowitz, The Commonwealth of Puerto Rico: Trying to Gain Dignity and Maintain Culture, 11 Ga.J.Int'l. & Comp.L. 211 (1981).

There has been considerable debate in Puerto Rico about whether Puerto Rico should, as an alternative to commonwealth status, become a state of, or become independent from, the United States. The position of the United States is that Puerto Rico is self-governing and that the decision to change its status is to be made by the Puerto Rican people.

### *Notes*

1. The special associated status of Puerto Rico was the subject of debate in the United Nations, particularly as to whether the island was a non-self-governing territory on which reports were required under Article 73(e) of the U.N. Charter. Since 1952, the United States has not submitted reports on the

ground that Puerto Rico is self-governing. See Cabranes, The Status of Puerto Rico, 16 I.C.L.Q. 531–9 (1967); Reisman, Puerto Rico and the International Process (1975).

2. The islands of Micronesia formerly comprised the Trust Territory of the Pacific Islands (Micronesia) established by the U.N. after World War II. Negotiations between the United States and their indigenous peoples have resulted in the creation of commonwealth status for the Northern Marianas and in free association with the United States for the Marshall Islands, the Federated States of Micronesia (the Caroline and Marshall Islands archipelagoes) and for Palau, although, with respect to Palau, arrangements have not been finalized.

The Covenant to Establish a Commonwealth of the Northern Marianas in Political Union with the United States of America became effective in 1976. As in the case of the Commonwealth of Puerto Rico, the people of the Northern Marianas are United States citizens, but unlike Puerto Rico, they have no representative in Congress. Foreign affairs and defense are under the control of the United States and designated provisions of the Constitution and federal law are applicable.

The Marshall Islands and the Federated States of Micronesia entered into Compacts of Free Association with the United States in 1986. Negotiations with Palau have produced a Free Association Compact, but it has not yet been approved by a plebiscite as required by the Palau constitution. A 1987 plebiscite producing a 67 percent vote in favor of the Compact was held to have been unconstitutional by the Palau Supreme Court. Pending establishment of a new status, the United States continues to fulfill its responsibilities in Palau as the administering power under U.N. Trusteeship.

Under the Compacts of Association between the United States and the Marshall Islands and the Federated States of Micronesia, the associated states are self-governing and have the capacity to conduct foreign affairs, including the capacity to enter into international agreements. Under Section 211 of the Compacts, the United States agrees to provide economic assistance and, under Section 311, for at least 15 years and thereafter as agreed, it has full authority and responsibility for security and defense matters, which include:

> "(1) the obligation to defend the Marshall Islands and the Federated States of Micronesia and their peoples from attack or threats thereof as the United States and its citizens are defended;
>
> (2) the option to foreclose access to or use of the Marshall Islands and the Federated States of Micronesia by military personnel or for the military purposes of any third country; and
>
> (3) the option to establish and use military areas and facilities in the Marshall Islands and the Federated States of Micronesia, subject to the terms of * * * separate agreements. * * *"

Moreover, under Section 313, each of the Associated States agrees to "refrain from actions which the Government of the United States determines, after appropriate consultation with those Governments, to be incompatible with its authority and responsibility for security and defense matters in or relating to the Marshall Islands and the Federated States of Micronesia." Both Associated States became members of the U.N. in 1991.

## D. OTHER INTERNATIONALIZED TERRITORIES

A historical example of an internationalized territory is that of the Free City of Danzig (once in Germany and now in Poland, known as Gdansk). The Free City of Danzig had a special autonomous status created by the Versailles Treaty and was under the protection of the League of Nations. Poland was entrusted with the conduct of foreign affairs, but, as a general rule, was required to obtain the consent of Danzig to treaties applicable to it. In 1932, the Permanent Court of International Justice concluded that Danzig was a state and a subject of international law. P.C.I.J.Adv.Opin. Treatment of Polish Nationals and Other Persons of Polish Origin in Danzig Territory 1932. P.C.I.J.Ser. A/B No. 44 pp. 23–25.

The Saar Territory also had a special international status from 1920 to 1935 and from 1947 to 1956. During the first period, it was governed by an international commission which entered into more than 30 treaties on its behalf. In the second period, it became a party to a number of multilateral treaties and was a member of the Council of Europe. Lissitzyn, Territorial Entities other than Independent States in the Law of Treaties, 125 Rec. des Cours 61–63 (1968–III).

A "Free Territory of Trieste" was envisaged by the 1947 Peace Treaty with Italy and a Permanent Statute for the Territory approved by the U.N. Security Council. However, the Statute was not implemented; an agreement between Italy and Yugoslavia superseded the arrangement.

An international regime for the city of Jerusalem was included in the U.N. General Assembly's Partition Plan for Palestine adopted in 1947. The U.N. Trusteeship Council adopted a draft statute in 1950, but the plan for territorial internationalization of Jerusalem was not carried out. See Lauterpacht, Jerusalem and The Holy Places (1968); Bovis, The Jerusalem Question 1917–1918 (1971).

For discussion of other internationalized territories, see Ydit, Internationalized Territories From the "Free City of Cracow" to the "Free City of Berlin" (1961). The territories discussed in this book include, in addition to those already mentioned, the Independent Republic of Cracow (1815–1846), the International Settlement of Shanghai (1863–1943), the International Zone of Tangier (1923–1953), and the territory of Memel (1920–1924).

## E. ENTITIES SUI GENERIS

Some territorial entities have an international legal status though they do not easily fit into any of the established categories mentioned in the previous sections.

### *1. The State of the Vatican City and the Holy See*

International treaties have been entered into by both the State of the Vatican City and the Holy See (i.e., the central administration of the Roman Catholic Church). The first designation was used for treaties which had a specific territorial application to the Vatican City (e.g., telecommunications). The Holy See has been more commonly used for purposes of international relations. It has been admitted as a full member of such specialized agencies of the United Nations as UNESCO, the World Health Organization, and the International Labor Organization, which under their constituent treaties are open only to states. Moreover, the Holy See has become a party to many of the major multinational conventions which are open to states alone. Diplomats (from many states) are accredited to the Holy See rather than to the State of Vatican City. See Graham, Vatican Diplomacy 28–30, 344–346 (1959) and Crawford, The Creation of States in International Law 152–60 (1979).

It has been the position of the Holy See that its international personality is based on its religious and spiritual authority and not its territorial enclave in Rome. The United Nations and other international organizations have taken no decision on that issue, though they use the name Holy See and no longer the State of the Vatican City. To acknowledge that international personality rested on the Holy See's religious authority might give rise to similar claims by the other religions, an issue that governments are not inclined to welcome. The problem has been avoided because of the ambiguity created by the fact that there is a territory, however small, and with a population of less than 1,200, which has been recognized by Italy as constituting the State of the Vatican City under the sovereignty of the Holy See. While no distinction is drawn by international organizations between the State of the Vatican City and the Holy See for purposes of membership or adherence to treaties, legal doctrine tends to regard them as two distinct legal persons. Consider the following comment by Hans Kelsen:

> The Head of the Church [i.e. the Holy See] is at the same time the Head of the State of the Vatican City. * * * But the State of the Vatican City, limited to a certain territory, must not be identified with the Church, which is tied to no limited territory. That means the territorial sphere of validity of the State of the Vatican City is limited, as every state territory is, whereas the territorial sphere of validity of the Roman Catholic Church is not limited.

Kelsen, Principles of International Law 252 (2d Rev. ed. Tucker 1966).* See also Ehler, The Recent Concordates, 104 Rec. des Cours 7–63 (1961–III).

### 2. *Taiwan (Formosa)*

The island of Taiwan has had an independent regime, the Republic of China, which has exercised full control over the island since the establishment of the People's Republic of China on the mainland in 1949 and has claimed to be the Government of China. On one view, the legal status of Taiwan remained undetermined even after the renunciation of Japanese claims in the Peace Treaty with Japan. On another view, Taiwan was legally part of China. Irrespective of these views, it was acknowledged that Taiwan was under the de facto authority of a government that engaged in foreign relations and entered into international agreements with other governments.

After the United States recognized the Government of the People's Republic of China and terminated its recognition of the regime in Taiwan in 1979, it continued to maintain economic and cultural agreements with the regime in control of Taiwan under a special arrangement. That arrangement involved the conduct of relations through a "nongovernmental" organization, the American Institute in Taiwan. The relevant legislation includes the following provisions:

## *TAIWAN RELATIONS ACT*

Pub.L. No. 94–83, April 10, 1979, 22 U.S.C. 3300 et seq.
18 I.L.M. 873 (1979).

* * *

Sec. 4. (a) The absence of diplomatic relations or recognition shall not affect the application of the laws of the United States with respect to Taiwan, and the laws of the United States shall apply with respect to Taiwan in the manner that the laws of the United States applied with respect to Taiwan prior to January 1, 1979.

(b) The application of subsection (a) of this section shall include, but shall not be limited to the following:

(1) Whenever the laws of the United States refer or relate to foreign countries, nations, states, governments, or similar entities, such terms shall include and such laws shall apply with respect to Taiwan. * * *

(c) For all purposes, including actions in any court in the United States, the Congress approves the continuation in force of all treaties and other international agreements, including multilateral conventions, entered into by the United States and the governing authorities on Taiwan recognized by the United States as the Republic of China prior to January 1, 1979, and in force between them on December 31, 1978, unless and until terminated in accordance with law.

(d) Nothing in this Act may be construed as a basis for supporting the exclusion or expulsion of Taiwan from continued membership in any international financial institution or any other international organization.

* * *

Sec. 6. (a) Programs, transactions, and other relations conducted or carried out by the President or any agency of the United States Government with respect to Taiwan shall, in the manner and to the extent directed by the President, be conducted and carried out by or through—

(1) The American Institute in Taiwan, a nonprofit corporation incorporated under the laws of the District of Columbia * * *.

### *Note*

For a discussion of the status of the Republic of China, see Chiu, The International Legal Status of The Republic of China, 8 Chinese Y.B. Int'l L. & A. 1 (1990).

# SECTION 5. THE INTERNATIONAL STATUS OF "PEOPLES" AND THEIR RIGHT OF SELF-DETERMINATION

## A. THE PRINCIPLE OF EQUAL RIGHTS AND SELF-DETERMINATION

### *UNITED NATIONS DECLARATION OF PRINCIPLES OF INTERNATIONAL LAW CONCERNING FRIENDLY RELATIONS AMONG STATES IN ACCORDANCE WITH THE CHARTER OF THE UNITED NATIONS*

General Assembly of the United Nations, A/Res. 2625 (XXV) (1970) G.A.O.R., 25th Sess., Supp. 28, at 121.

THE PRINCIPLE OF EQUAL RIGHTS AND SELF-DETERMINATION OF PEOPLES

By virtue of the principle of equal rights and self-determination of peoples enshrined in the Charter of the United Nations, all peoples have the right freely to determine, without external interference, their political status and to pursue their economic, social and cultural development, and every state has the duty to respect this right in accordance with the provisions of the Charter.

Every state has the duty to promote, through joint and separate action, realization of the principle of equal rights and self-determination of peoples, in accordance with the provisions of the Charter, and to render assistance to the United Nations in carrying out the responsibilities entrusted to it by the Charter regarding the implementation of the principle, in order:

(a) To promote friendly relations and co-operation among states; and

(b) To bring a speedy end to colonialism, having due regard to the freely expressed will of the peoples concerned;

and bearing in mind that subjection of peoples to alien subjugation, domination and exploitation constitutes a violation of the principle, as well as a denial of fundamental human rights, and is contrary to the Charter.

Every state has the duty to promote through joint and separate action universal respect for and observance of human rights and fundamental freedoms in accordance with the Charter.

The establishment of a sovereign and independent state, the free association or integration with an independent state or the emergence into any other political status freely determined by a people constitute modes of implementing the right of self-determination by that people.

Every state has the duty to refrain from any forcible action which deprives peoples referred to above in the elaboration of the present principle of their right to self-determination and freedom and independence. In their actions against, and resistance to, such forcible action in pursuit of the exercise of their right to self-determination, such peoples are entitled to seek and receive support in accordance with the purposes and principles of the Charter.

The territory of a colony or other non-self-governing territory has, under the Charter, a status separate and distinct from the territory of the state administering it; and such separate and distinct status under the Charter shall exist until the people of the colony or non-self-governing territory have exercised their right of self-determination in accordance with the Charter, and particularly its purposes and principles.

Nothing in the foregoing paragraphs shall be construed as authorizing or encouraging any action which would dismember or impair, totally or in part, the territorial integrity or political unity of sovereign and independent states conducting themselves in compliance with the principle of equal rights and self-determination of peoples as described above and thus possessed of a government representing the whole people belonging to the territory without distinction as to race, creed or colour.

Every state shall refrain from any action aimed at the partial or total disruption of the national unity and territorial integrity of any other state or country.

### *Notes*

1. Provisions on the right of all people to self-determination similar to the above text have been included as Article 1 of each of the International Covenants on Human Rights. The Covenants were concluded in 1966 and came into force in 1976. See Chapter 8.

2. The International Court of Justice, in advisory opinions in 1971 and 1975, stated that the principle of self-determination "as enshrined in the Charter of the United Nations" has through subsequent development of international law been accepted as a "right" of peoples in non-self-governing territories. I.C.J. Advisory Opinion on Namibia, [1971] I.C.J. at 31, quoted in Advisory Opinion on Western Sahara [1975] I.C.J. at 31–35, see excerpts at p. 133 supra. Judge Dillard, in a separate opinion in the *Western Sahara Case,* concluded that "the pronouncements of the Court thus indicate that a norm of international law has emerged applicable to the decolonization of those non-self-governing territories which are under the aegis of the United Nations." Id. at 121–2. It is to be noted, in this connection, that non-self-governing territories "under the aegis of the United Nations" refers to territories regarded as within Chapter XI of the Charter. Information on such territories must be furnished to the United Nations General Assembly. A list of criteria for determining non-self-governing territories may be found in the Annex to G.A.Res. 742 (VIII) G.A.O.R., 8th Sess., Supp. 17, at 22 (1953).

Though the Western Sahara opinion supports the legal right of self-determination, the events which followed the Opinion did not. See Franck, The Stealing of the Sahara, 70 A.J.I.L. 694 (1976).

## B. THE LEGAL RIGHT OF SELF-DETERMINATION IN THE POST-COLONIAL PERIOD

### *1. Defining "Peoples" Entitled to Self-Determination*

As indicated above, the concept of self-determination, expressed as a principle in the Charter, had become accepted as a "right" of peoples in non-self governing territories (i.e. colonies). However, the UN Resolutions and the two Covenants on Human Rights declared that "all peoples" have that right. Sir Gerald Fitzmaurice, writing in 1973 after his retirement as a judge of the International Court wrote that "juridically, the notion of a legal right of self-determination is nonsense, for how can an as yet judicially non-existent entity be the possessor of a legal right"? Fitzmaurice, The Future of Public International Law, in Livre du Centenaire, Ann. Inst. de Droit Int'l

1973 at 233, n. 85. Professor Thomas Franck noted the "incoherence" of the proclaimed right since the UN declarations accord the right "to all peoples" but at the same time assert that the right shall not authorize or encourage action which would impair "totally or in part, the territorial integrity or political unity of sovereign states. Franck concludes that for the right of self-determination to win acceptance as legitimate, the rule must make a persuasive distinction between "peoples" entitled and not entitled to self-determination. T. Franck, The Power of Legitimacy Among Nations 166 (1990). This would answer Fitzmaurice's criticism since the "self" would then be determined by authoritative international criteria.

Scholars and commentators have proposed such criteria for determining the "peoples" entitled to self-determination but there is little indication that most states are prepared to adopt generally applicable criteria. Many states probably would not accept the general principle that the right of self-determination applies to people within a sovereign state. India, for example, in becoming a party to the two Covenants on Human Rights made a reservation to the effect that the right of self-determination applied only to peoples under foreign domination and "not to sovereign independent states or to a section of a people or nation". See M. Halperin and D. Scheffer, Self–Determination in the New World Order 22–23 (1992).

### 2. *Separatist Movements*

Despite the opposition of many states to recognizing generally that the right of self-determination applies to peoples within existing states, claims of self-determination are being made by numerous organized movements that seek secession or autonomy. The dissolution of the U.S.S.R., Yugoslavia and Czechoslovakia has been regarded as evidence of effective self-determination. Many other European countries include active separatist or autonomy movements (e.g., Basques in Spain, Corsicans in France, Scots in Britain.) In Asia and Africa, the assertions of self-determination have recently increased in intensity and scope. For a list of self-determination movements as of 1992 see Halperin and Scheffer, op. cit. Appendix pp. 123–160. The UN Secretary–General declared in 1992 that "the cohesion of states is threatened by brutal ethnic, religious social, cultural and linguistic strife." Boutros–Ghali, Agenda for Peace, UN Doc. S/24111, para. 11 (1992), also in 31 I.L.M. 953, 948 (1992). The Secretary–General noting that the U.N. "has not closed its door" warned:

> "Yet if every ethnic, religious or linguistic group claimed statehood, there would be no limit to fragmentation and peace, security and economic well-being for all would become even more difficult to achieve."

Id. para. 17.

### 3. *Rights of Minorities*

Proposals have been made for criteria defining the "peoples" entitled to self-determination apart from colonial non-self-governing territories. However, no such criteria have received UN approval, apart from the decolonization context. International bodies have placed emphasis on recognizing and strengthening the rights of national minorities, while upholding the national unity and territorial integrity of existing states. See, for example, the Charter of Paris for a New Europe, signed in 1990 by the heads of state and governments of members of the Conference on Security and Cooperation in Europe (CSCE), 30 I.L.M. 195 (1991). The UN General Assembly also adopted on December 18, 1992, a "Declaration on The Rights of Persons Belonging to National or Ethnic, Religious and Linguistic Minorities" UN G.A.Res. 47/135, U.N.Doc. A/RES/47/135.

Will minority rights satisfy claims of self-determination? Some commentators point out that governments generally remain reluctant to grant minority groups rights that they fear will strengthen secessionist pressures. See Halperin and Scheffer, op. cit. at 60 (1992). The denial of minority rights and the absence of democratic rights for minority groups are regarded in many unofficial proposals as conditions for recognizing "people" entitled to self-determination. Other conditions suggested are that the claimant community possess a self-defined identity distinct from the rest of the country and that they inhabit a defined territory that largely supports secession. Some proposals would also require that a separation should not threaten armed conflict between the new and old states. For more extensive discussion of criteria, see Halperin and Scheffer id. pp. 71–93, A. Buchanan, Secession (1991); L. Buchheit, Secession, The Legitimacy of Self–Determination (1978); A. Heraclides, Secession, Self–Determination and Third Party Intervention, 43 J.Int.Aff. 399 (1992). R. Lapidoth, Sovereignty in Transition id. pp. 325–346.

### *Notes*

1. Should the right of self-determination (and secession) be denied to a self-defined people that share a common culture and language on the ground that they have democratic rights on a basis of equality with all other citizens? Consider, for example, self-determination claims by groups in Quebec and Scotland.

2. Is a probable danger of future transnational conflict a sufficient reason to deny secession by a minority group occupying a particular region of a country? In other words, would a likely threat to peace and security trump the right to self-determination?

## C. THE OBLIGATIONS IMPLIED BY THE RIGHT TO SELF–DETERMINATION

When a people has been internationally recognized as legally entitled to self-determination, what correlative obligations and rights arise for states and for international organizations?

### *1. Obligation to Ascertain the Will of the People*

The state in which—or against which—the claim of self-determination has been made by an appreciable minority would presumably be under an international obligation to ascertain (or permit the ascertainment of) the will of the relevant community. Under international practice, plebiscites have been a favored means for determining the free choice of the peoples. The United Nations has conducted plebiscites in several cases involving ex-colonial territories, though not in regard to claims of groups in sovereign states.

A critical issue is the determination of the area in which the plebiscite is to be held. Whether existing internal boundaries should apply; whether small enclaves of minority groups should be given separate rights; whether historic territorial claims should be recognized—these are issues that are likely to arise and for which there is no pre-determined answer. The difficulties are shown by the conflicts that arose in the wake of the dissolution of the U.S.S.R. and Yugoslavia. Plebiscites also are difficult where several choices are available and the required majority cannot be easily determined. See H.S. Johnson, Self-Determination Within the Community of Nations 71–98 (1967). Instead of voting, other means of ascertaining the will of the people may also be appropriate in cases where social structures enable such choices to be credibly determined. See E. Gordon, Resolution of the Bahrain Dispute 65 A.J.I.L. 560–568 (1971).

### 2. *International Responsibility for Violation of Obligation*

In principle, the failure of a responsible state to meet its obligation to support self-determination would be an international wrong giving rise to responsibility on the international level. The delict in question may also be of an erga omnes character, that is a violation of a legal duty owed to the international community (See Chapter 7). It would follow that all other states would be entitled to adopt counter-measures that would be proportional to the violation. Such measures could include material support to the groups claiming self-determination, suspension of the treaty rights of the violator, rupture of diplomatic relations, suspension of communications, severance of trade, denial of aid and loans.

If the situation arising from the delict threatens international peace, the UN Security Council might adopt sanctions of a mandatory character under Chapter VII. This would be in line with the precedent set in the case of Southern Rhodesia. See Chapter 11.

#### *Notes*

1. In the unlikely event that a large majority of the inhabitants of Hawaii would vote to secede from the United States to join a confederation of Japan and other Pacific rim countries, would the United States be obliged to recognize and accept the act of self-determination? Would it be legally precluded from employing force to prevent the secession?

2. In a case where the United Nations General Assembly or Security Council has recognized that a particular group is entitled to exercise the right of self-determination in a given area, can that right be conditioned on assurance that the new state would not threaten the peace and security of the state which has sovereignty or de facto control of the area in question? Would this condition be applicable to the claim of self-determination in regard to the West Bank and Gaza?

3. Would the International Court of Justice be an appropriate authority to pass on claims to self-determination through an advisory opinion requested by the UN General Assembly or Security Council? Would it be desirable for the UN to utilize a commission of legal experts to pass upon the claims of self-determination (as the League of Nations did in the *Aaland Islands Case*)?

## D. INTERNATIONAL "RECOGNITION" OF MOVEMENTS OF NATIONAL LIBERATION

An especially controversial aspect of international involvement in the exercise of self-determination has been granting national liberation movements access to international forums, particularly the United Nations and international conferences of states. The General Assembly adopted as a general criterion in respect of such invitations to national liberation movements in Africa that full participation as observers should be accorded to representatives of movements recognized by the Organization of African Unity, G.A.Res. 3280 (XXIX) G.A.O.R., 29th Sess., Supp. 31, at 5 (1974) and G.A.Res. 31/30, (XXXI) G.A.O.R., 31st Sess., Supp. 39, at 118 (1976). On this basis, African liberation movements have participated in U.N. bodies, in the specialized agencies and in international conferences on multilateral treaties convened by the United Nations. They also participated in the Diplomatic Conference on Humanitarian Law in Armed Conflicts. Specific resolutions by the General Assembly and international conferences have also accorded observer status to the Palestine Liberation Organization. See G.A.Res. 3237 (XXIX) G.A.O.R., 29th Sess., Supp. 31, at 4 (1974). The United Kingdom representative in opposing the resolution said:

> The United Nations had always been regarded as an organization of sovereign, independent States. Observer status had heretofore been confined to non-Member States and to regional organizations. The PLO was not the government of a State, was not recognized as such by anyone and does not purport to be one. Yet, under the draft resolution, it was being treated like a Member State except for the right to vote. That situation seemed to bring into question the nature of the United Nations.

11 U.N. Monthly Chronicle 39 (1974).

The Palestine Liberation Organization (PLO) reports that it has been recognized by more than 100 states of which a majority accord the PLO full diplomatic status. Although demands have been made for a Palestinian "homeland," no claim has been made that a state of Palestine exists. There is widespread acceptance of the PLO as the representative of the Palestinian people. This was the status accorded the PLO in 1974 in General Assembly Resolution 3236 (XXIX) G.A.O.R., 29th Sess., Supp. 31, at 4, calling for the invitation of the PLO to participate in all efforts, deliberations and conferences on the Middle East which are held under the auspices of the U.N. Although representatives of the United States have met officially with representatives of the PLO, the United States has not recognized or accepted any formal status for the PLO. In Klinghoffer v. S.N.C. Achille Lauro, 739 F.Supp. 854 (S.D.N.Y.1990), the District Court denied immunity to the PLO on the ground that it did not qualify as a state under international law. Representatives of Palestinians inhabiting the Occupied Territories (e.g., West Bank of the Jordan River and the Gaza Strip) rather than of the PLO participated in Mideast Peace talks in 1992.

## E. SELF-DETERMINATION EXTENDED

### 1. *Economic Self-Determination*

The concept of self-determination has also been extended to the right of people "to freely pursue their economic, social and cultural development" and "to freely dispose of their natural wealth and resources" (Article 1, Covenant on Civil and Political Rights and Covenant on Economic, Social and Cultural Rights.) In related actions, United Nations resolutions and declarations have proclaimed the "permanent sovereignty of peoples over their natural wealth and resources". See the Charter of Economic Rights and Duties of States. UN GA. Res. 3281 (XXIX) G.A.O.R., 29th Sess., Supp. 31, at 52 (1974) discussed in Chap. 17.

### 2. *Internal Self-Determination*

A more radical interpretation of the principle of self-determination holds that it embraces a right to internal democracy for all peoples irrespective of the status of the territory. Under this conception, self-determination goes beyond the rights of distinctive territorial communities to choose their own government and independence; it is a right of self-government for all peoples. Some support for this wide interpretation has been seen in the reference to "government representing the whole people belonging to the territory without distinction as to race, creed or colour" included in the penultimate paragraph of the 1970 Declaration on the Principles of Equal Rights and Self–Determination, p. 302 supra.

On recent developments, see T. Franck, "The Emerging Right to Democratic Governance" 86 A.J.I.L. 46–91 (1991); UNGA Resolutions 45/150 (1991) and 46/137 (1991), both stressing the importance of "periodic and genuine elections".

### *Notes*

1. One scholar concluded after the Southern Rhodesia Case that "where a territory is a self-determination unit no government will be recognized which comes into existence and seeks to control the territory as a state in violation of self-determination." J. Crawford, The Creation of States in International Law 105 (1979). Does this mean that a new government claiming statehood would have to show that it has been established by the decision of the people concerned expressed through a plebiscite or other acts of free choice? Were the recognitions of the successor states of the U.S.S.R. and Yugoslavia a confirmation of this principle? See p. 250 supra.

2. If the right to self-determination extends to "internal self-determination" (i.e. democracy), would there be a legal basis for collective measures against a government that does not have free elections and related democratic rights? See T. Franck loc. cit.

In June 1985, the Transitional Government of National Unity was installed in Namibia in response to a petition to the Republic of South Africa for a form of self-government. This transitional government governed Namibia until its resignation in February 1988 to permit the implementation of U.N. Security Council Resolution 435. S/RES/435 (1988). The May 1988 negotiations between Angola, Cuba and the Republic of South Africa led to the signing of the Geneva Protocol requiring the withdrawal of Cuban troops from Angola and South African troops from Namibia by April 21, 1990. The U.N. Transition Group (UNTAG) was set up in Namibia to supervise elections for the constituent assembly in November 1989. Independence was achieved on March 21, 1990.

## SECTION 6. ACQUISITION OF TERRITORIAL SOVEREIGNTY

### A. INTRODUCTION

As discussed in Section 1, in order to qualify as a state, an entity must have a defined territory and permanent population under the control of its own government which has the capacity to engage in relations with other states. Sovereignty over a specific territorial area is therefore an essential element of statehood.

There is obviously no question as to which states have acquired sovereignty over the great bulk of the earth's habitable territory, and some of the issues presented in connection with acquisition of sovereignty over territory are of more historical than contemporary significance. Nonetheless scores of controversies as to sovereignty over territory remain, including issues as to what state should be regarded as exercising sovereignty over certain islands, land areas subject to boundary disputes, and polar regions. For example, there is a dispute between Iran and the United Arab Emirates over the islands of Abu Musa and Greater and Lesser Tunb near the Strait of Hormuz at the entrance to the Persian Gulf through which 20 percent of the world's oil is transported. Sovereignty over the northern Kurile Islands seized by the Soviet Union at the end of World War II remain in dispute between Russia and Japan. The demarcation of the land frontier between Iraq and Kuwait under a 1963 agreement is being considered by a special commission pursuant to one of the conditions of the U.N. Security Council-supervised cease-fire ending the Persian Gulf War. This section will examine the international legal principles governing the acquisition of sovereignty over territory.

## B. BASIC PRINCIPLES

### ISLAND OF PALMAS CASE (UNITED STATES v. THE NETHERLANDS)

Permanent Court of Arbitration, 1928.
2 U.N.Rep.Int'l Arb. Awards 829.

[Palmas (also known as Miangas) is an isolated island of less than two square miles in area, lying about half way between Mindanao in the Philippine Islands and the most northerly of the Nanusa group in the former Dutch East Indies. It lies within the boundaries of the Philippines as ceded by Spain to the United States in 1898 by the Treaty of Paris. United States authorities learned in 1906 that the island was considered by the Netherlands to form a part of the Dutch possessions in that part of the world. After diplomatic correspondence, the United States and the Netherlands agreed in 1925 to submit to a member of the Permanent Court of Arbitration the question "whether the Island of Palmas (or Miangas) in its entirety forms a part of territory belonging to the United States of America or of Netherlands territory." The parties designated as sole arbitrator the Swiss jurist, Max Huber, who delivered his award on April 4, 1928.]

HUBER, Arbitrator: * * * The *United States,* as successor to the rights of Spain over the Philippines, bases its title in the first place on discovery. * * *

* * *

*The Netherlands* Government's main argument endeavours to show that the Netherlands, represented for this purpose in the first period of colonization by the East India Company, have possessed and exercised rights of sovereignty from 1677, or probably from a date prior even to 1648, to the present day. * * *

* * *

* * * [A]n element which is essential for the constitution of sovereignty should not be lacking in its continuation. So true is this, that practice, as well as doctrine, recognizes—though under different legal formulae and with certain differences as to the conditions required—that the continuous and peaceful display of territorial sovereignty (peaceful in relation to other States) is as good as a title. The growing insistence with which international law, ever since the middle of the 18th century, has demanded that the occupation shall be effective would be inconceivable, if effectiveness were required only for the act of acquisition and not equally for the maintenance of the right. If the effectiveness has above all been insisted on in regard to occupation, this is because the question rarely arises in connection with territories in which there is already an established order of things.

Territorial sovereignty, as has already been said, involves the exclusive right to display the activities of a State. This right has as corollary a duty: the obligation to protect within the territory the rights of other States, in particular their right to integrity and inviolability in peace and in war, together with the rights which each State may claim for its nationals in foreign territory. Without manifesting its territorial sovereignty in a manner corresponding to circumstances, the State cannot fulfill this duty. Territorial sovereignty cannot limit itself to its negative side, i.e. to excluding the activities of other States; for it serves to divide between nations the space upon which human activities are employed, in order to assure them at all points the minimum of protection of which international law is the guardian. * * *

Manifestations of territorial sovereignty assume, it is true, different forms, according to conditions of time and place. Although continuous in principle, sovereignty cannot be exercised in fact at every moment on every point of a territory. The intermittence and discontinuity compatible with the maintenance of the right necessarily differ according as inhabited or uninhabited regions are involved, or regions enclosed within territories in which sovereignty is incontestably displayed or again regions accessible from, for instance, the high seas. * * *

* * *

It is admitted by both sides that international law underwent profound modifications between the end of the Middle–Ages and the end of the 19th century, as regards the rights of discovery and acquisition of uninhabited regions or regions inhabited by savages or semi-civilised peoples. Both Parties are also agreed that a juridical fact must be appreciated in the light of the law contemporary with it, and not of the law in force at the time when a dispute in regard to it arises or fails to be settled. The effect of discovery by Spain is therefore to be determined by the rules of international law in force in the first half of the 16th century * * *.

If the view most favourable to the American arguments is adopted—with every reservation as to the soundness of such view—that is to say, if we consider as positive law at the period in question the rule that discovery as such, i.e. the mere fact of seeing land, without any act, even symbolical, of taking possession, involved *ipso jure* territorial sovereignty and not merely an "inchoate title", a *jus ad rem,* to be completed eventually by an actual and durable taking of possession within a reasonable time, the question arises whether sovereignty yet existed at the critical date, i.e. the moment of conclusion and coming into force of the Treaty of Paris.

As regards the question which of different legal systems prevailing at successive periods is to be applied in a particular case (the so-called intertemporal law), a distinction must be made between the creation of rights and the existence of rights. The same principle which subjects the act creative of a right to the law in force at the time the right arises, demands that the existence of the right, in other words its continued manifestation, shall follow the conditions required by the evolution of law. International law in the 19th century, having regard to the fact that most parts of the globe were under the sovereignty of States members of the community of nations, and that territories without a master had become relatively few, took account of a tendency already existing and especially developed since the middle of the 18th century, and laid down the principle that occupation, to constitute a claim to territorial sovereignty, must be effective, that is, offer certain guarantees to other States and their nationals. It seems therefore incompatible with this rule of positive law that there should be regions which are neither under the effective sovereignty of a State, nor without a master, but which are reserved for the exclusive influence of one State, in virtue solely of a title of acquisition which is no longer recognized by existing law, even if such a title ever conferred territorial sovereignty. For these reasons, discovery alone, without any subsequent act, cannot at the present time suffice to prove sovereignty over the Island of Palmas (or Miangas); and in so far as there is no sovereignty, the question of an abandonment properly speaking of sovereignty by one State in order that the sovereignty of another may take its place does not arise.

If on the other hand the view is adopted that discovery does not create a definitive title of sovereignty, but only an "inchoate" title, such a title exists, it is true, without external manifestation. However, according to the view that has prevailed at any rate since the 19th century, an inchoate title of discovery must be completed within a reasonable period by the effective occupation of the region claimed to be discovered. This principle must be applied in the present case, for the reasons given above in regard to the rules determining which of successive legal systems is to be applied (the so-called intertemporal law). Now, no act of occupation nor, except as to a recent period, any exercise of sovereignty at Palmas by Spain has been alleged. But even admitting that the Spanish title still existed as inchoate in 1898 and must be considered as included in the cession under Article III of the Treaty of Paris, an inchoate title could not prevail over the continuous and peaceful display of authority by another State; for such display may prevail even over a prior, definitive title put forward by another State. * * *

* * *

In the last place there remains to be considered *title arising out of contiguity.* Although States have in certain circumstances maintained that islands relatively close to their shores belonged to them in virtue of their geographical situation, it is impossible to show the existence of a rule of positive international law to the effect that islands situated outside territorial waters should belong to a State from the mere fact that its territory forms the *terra firma* (nearest continent or island of considerable size). * * *

*The Netherlands' arguments* contend that the East India Company established Dutch sovereignty over the Island of Palmas (or Miangas) as early as the 17th century, by means of conventions with the princes of Tabukan (Taboekan) and Taruna (Taroena), two native chieftains of the Island of Sangi (Groot Sangihe), the principal island of the Talautse Isles (Sangi Islands), and that sovereignty has been displayed during the past two centuries.

* * *

* * * The questions to be solved in the present case are the following:

*Was the island of Palmas (or Miangas) in 1898 a part of territory under Netherlands' sovereignty?*

*Did this sovereignty actually exist in 1898 in regard to Palmas (or Miangas)* and are the facts proved which were alleged on this subject? * * *

* * * Since the contract of 1885 with Taruna and that of 1899 with Kandahar–Taruna comprise Palmas (or Miangas) within the territories of a native State under the suzerainty of the Netherlands and since it has been established that in 1906 on the said island a state of things existed showing at least certain traces of display of Netherlands sovereignty, it is now necessary to examine what is the nature of the facts invoked as proving such sovereignty, and to what periods such facts relate. This examination will show whether or not the Netherlands have displayed sovereignty over the Island of Palmas (or Miangas) in an effective continuous and peaceful manner at a period at which such exercise may have excluded the acquisition of sovereignty, or a title to such acquisition, by the United States of America. * * *

[After a detailed examination of the acts of the Dutch East India Company and the Netherlands State tending to establish a display of sovereignty over the Island of Palmas, the arbitrator continued:]

The claim of the United States to sovereignty over the Island of Palmas (or Miangas) is derived from Spain by way of cession under the Treaty of Paris. The latter Treaty, though it comprises the island in dispute within the limits of cession, and in spite of the absence of any reserves or protest by the Netherlands as to these limits, has not created in favour of the United States any title of sovereignty such as was not already vested in Spain. The essential point is therefore to decide whether Spain had sovereignty over Palmas (or Miangas) at the time of the coming into force of the Treaty of Paris. * * *

* * *

The acts of indirect or direct display of Netherlands sovereignty at Palmas (or Miangas), especially in the 18th and early 19th centuries are not numerous, and there are considerable gaps in the evidence of continuous display. But apart from the consideration that the manifestations of sovereignty over a small and distant island, inhabited only by natives, cannot be expected to be frequent, it is not necessary that the display of sovereignty should go back to a very far distant period. It may suffice that such display existed in 1898, and had already existed as continuous and peaceful before that date long enough to enable any Power who might have considered herself as possessing sovereignty over the island, or having a claim to sovereignty, to have, according to local conditions, a reasonable possibility for ascertaining the existence of a state of things contrary to her real or alleged rights.

It is not necessary that the display of sovereignty should be established as having begun at a precise epoch; it suffices that it had existed at the critical period preceding the year 1898. It is quite natural that the establishment of sovereignty may be the outcome of a slow evolution, of a progressive intensification of State control. This is particularly the case, if sovereignty is acquired by the establishment of the suzerainty of a colonial Power over a native State, and in regard to outlying possessions of such a vassal State.

Now the evidence relating to the period after the middle of the 19th century makes it clear that the Netherlands Indian Government considered the island distinctly as a part of its possessions and that, in the years immediately preceding 1898, an intensification of display of sovereignty took place.

Since the moment when the Spaniards, in withdrawing from the Moluccas in 1666, made express reservations as to the maintenance of their sovereign rights, up to the contestation made by the United States in 1906, no contestation or other action whatever or protest against the exercise of territorial rights by the Netherlands over the Talautse (Sangi) Isles and their dependencies (Miangas included) has been recorded. The peaceful character of the display of Netherlands sovereignty for the entire period to which the evidence concerning acts of display relates (1700–1906) must be admitted.

* * *

The conditions of acquisition of sovereignty by the Netherlands are therefore to be considered as fulfilled. It remains now to be seen whether the United States as successors of Spain are in a position to bring forward an equivalent or stronger title. This is to be answered in the negative.

The title of discovery, if it had not been already disposed of by the Treaties of Münster and Utrecht would, under the most favourable and most extensive interpretation, exist only as an inchoate title, as a claim to establish sovereignty by effective occupation. An inchoate title however cannot prevail over a definite title founded on continuous and peaceful display of sovereignty.

The title of contiguity, understood as a basis of territorial sovereignty, has no foundation in international law. * * *

The Netherlands title of sovereignty, acquired by continuous and peaceful display of State authority during a long period of time going probably back beyond the year 1700, therefore holds good. * * *

## *Notes*

1. Pursuant to General Assembly resolution 3292 (XXIX), the I.C.J. rendered an advisory opinion in the *Western Sahara Case,* 1975 I.C.J. 12, on two questions affecting the legal status of the Western Sahara. Question I was whether the Western Sahara (Rio de Oro and Sakiet El Hamra) was *terra nullius* at the time of its colonization by Spain. In concluding it was not, the Court stated, 1975 I.C.J. at 38–39:

> 77. In the view of the Court, for the purposes of the present Opinion, "the time of colonization by Spain" may be considered as the period beginning in 1884, when Spain proclaimed a protectorate over the Rio de Oro [on the basis of agreements entered into with the chiefs of local tribes]. * * *
>
> * * *
>
> 79. Turning to Question I, the Court observes that the request specifically locates the question in the context of "the time of colonization by Spain", and it therefore seems clear that the words "Was Western Sahara * * * a territory belonging to no one (*terra nullius* )?" have to be interpreted by reference to the law in force at that period. The expression "*terra nullius* " was a legal term of art employed in connection with "occupation" as one of the accepted legal methods of acquiring sovereignty over territory. "Occupation" being legally an original means of peaceably acquiring sovereignty over territory otherwise than by cession or succession, it was a cardinal condition of a valid "occupation" that the territory should be *terra nullius*—a territory belonging to no-one—at the time of the act alleged to constitute the "occupation" (cf. Legal Status of Eastern Greenland, P.C.I.J., Series A/B, No. 53, pp. 44 f. and 63 f.). In the view of the Court, therefore, a determination that Western Sahara was a "*terra nullius* " at the time of colonization by Spain would be possible only if it were established that at that time the territory belonged to no-one in the sense that it was then open to acquisition through the legal process of "occupation".

> 80. Whatever differences of opinion there may have been among jurists, the State practice of the relevant period indicates that territories inhabited by tribes or peoples having a social and political organization were not regarded as *terra nullius.* It shows that in the case of such territories the acquisition of sovereignty was not generally considered as effected unilaterally through "occupation" of *terra nullius* by original title but through agreements concluded with local rulers. On occasion, it is true, the word "occupation" was used in a non-technical sense denoting simply acquisition of sovereignty; but that did not signify that the acquisition of sovereignty through such agreements with authorities of the country was regarded as an "occupation" of a "*terra nullius* " in the proper sense of these terms. On the contrary, such agreements with local rulers, whether or not considered as an actual "cession" of the territory, were regarded as derivative roots of title, and not original titles obtained by occupation of *terra nullius.*
>
> 81. In the present instance, the information furnished to the Court shows that at the time of colonization Western Sahara was inhabited by peoples which, if nomadic, were socially and politically organized in tribes and under chiefs competent to represent them. * * *

Question II was what were the legal ties between this territory and the Kingdom of Morocco and the Mauritanian entity at the time of its colonization by Spain.

Can the Court's view that the Western Sahara was not *terra nullius* because it was inhabited by socially and politically organized tribes be squared with the conclusion of the Permanent Court of Arbitration in the *Island of Palmas Case* that the Netherlands could acquire sovereignty over Palmas by "occupation," when Palmas was inhabited by natives who presumably were also to some extent socially and politically organized?

For a critique of the advisory opinion on the *terra nullius* issue see Smith, Sovereignty over Unoccupied Territories—The Western Sahara Decision, 9 Case W.Res.J.Int'l L. 135–143 (1977). Consider the following comment of the author (footnotes omitted):

> If a territory is not *terra nullius,* the result is that some politically organized group must be exercising traditional acts of sovereignty in relation to it. If those traditional acts include, as the court in the *Island of Palmas* case indicates, the right to exclude the activities of other States, as well as the ability to protect the rights of other nationals in the territory, then the Western Sahara Court would be hard-pressed to name the party displaying these acts of sovereignty in Western Sahara. * * * [T]he Court in the *Island of Palmas* case defines sovereignty in such a way as to disqualify all of the parties with an interest in Western Sahara. * * *
>
> Indeed, Morocco and Mauritania are disqualified because of the Court's determination later in the opinion that they lacked sufficient ties of territorial sovereignty [*sic* ] to Western Sahara. The burden similarly cannot be placed on the tribes of Western Sahara simply because they were incapable of exercising the acts of sovereignty required by the *Palmas* decision over the vast majority of the territory. Thus, the Court's conclusion that Western Sahara was not *terra nullius* in 1884 is not consistent with the fact that there was no country or group of individuals in a position to occupy the territory at that time.

Id. at pp. 140–141. The author also suggests that the strongest argument in support of the position that the Western Sahara was not *terra nullius* is that Spain did not proceed on the basis that it was establishing sovereignty over *terra nullius,* but claimed a protectorate over Rio de Oro on the basis of agreements entered into with chiefs of the local tribes. Id. at 141–143. Note, however, the initiation of the claim of The Netherlands to sovereignty over the Island of Palmas was also based on agreements with native chieftains. What does the Court in *Western Sahara* mean when it says that such agreements with local leaders were regarded as "derivative roots of title, and not original titles obtained by occupation of *terra nullius* "?

2. How "effective" does the Dutch occupation of Palmas seem to have been? Could it be said that "effectiveness was established negatively from the absence of any competing manifestations of sovereignty, and that it was only because the Netherlands had taken more interest in the Island than Spain that it was adjudged entitled?" 1 O'Connell 472. On the problem of "effectiveness" of occupation, compare the *Eastern Greenland Case,* p. 317 infra and the *Clipperton Island* arbitration, 2 U.N.Rep.Int'l Arb.Awards 1105, 26 A.J.I.L. 390 (1931), in which France was held entitled to sovereignty over a small unpopulated guano island situated in the Pacific Ocean about 670 miles southwest of Mexico. The French claim was based on the fact that a French naval officer had in 1858 cruised to the island, proclaimed French sovereignty, made detailed geographic

notes, and landed some members of his crew. The party left no sign of sovereignty on the island, but notified French and Hawaiian officials in Honolulu, and had a declaration of sovereignty published in a Honolulu journal. No further action was taken by France or any other state until 1897, when France protested to the United States the presence on the island of three persons who had raised an American flag at the approach of a French vessel. The United States disclaimed in 1898 any interest in the island, but meanwhile Mexico had sent a gunboat to the island and had had the Mexican flag raised. Mexico claimed that it had always enjoyed sovereignty over Clipperton by virtue of Spanish discovery, or in the alternative, that the French "occupation" from 1858 to 1897 had been ineffective and that the island was in 1897 *terra nullius.* The Arbitrator held that Spanish discovery had not been proved, nor had Spanish exercise of sovereign rights; the island was therefore capable of appropriation in 1858. Turning to the question whether France had effectively occupied the island, the Arbitrator held that although the exercise of effective, exclusive authority ordinarily required the establishment of an administration capable of securing respect for the sovereign's rights, this was not necessary in the case of uninhabited territory which is at the occupying state's absolute and undisputed disposition from the latter's first appearance. Should the *Clipperton Island Case* be limited to situations closely paralleling its facts; i.e., small unpopulated islands? Compare the materials on the polar regions, p. 1361 infra.

3. On April 2, 1924, Secretary of State Hughes wrote to the Norwegian Minister, H.H. Bryn, in regard to the legal effect of Amundsen's explorations in the Antarctic:

> In the penultimate paragraph of your letter you state that, in order to avoid any misunderstanding, you would add that possession of all the land which Mr. Amundsen may discover will, of course, be taken in the name of His Majesty, the King of Norway. In my opinion rights similar to those which in earlier centuries were based upon the acts of a discoverer, followed by occupation or settlement consummated at long and uncertain periods thereafter, are not capable of being acquired at the present time. Today, if an explorer is able to ascertain the existence of lands still unknown to civilization, his act of so-called discovery, coupled with a formal taking of possession, would have no significance, save as he might herald the advent of the settler; and where for climatic or other reasons actual settlement would be an impossibility, as in the case of the Polar regions, such conduct on his part would afford frail support for a reasonable claim of sovereignty. * * *

The Norwegian Minister replied on November 12, 1924, that the Norwegian Government did not intend "to invoke a possible discovery of new land as a basis for a claim to sovereignty. It only meant that the Norwegian Government claimed the right to priority in acquiring subsequently the sovereignty by settlement or by other procedure sanctioned by International Law." Both notes are quoted in 1 Hackworth 399–400. For further discussion of the issues related to acquisition of sovereignty over the Antarctic, see p. 1361 infra.

4. What is the significance of the rule of "intertemporal law" as articulated by the Arbitrator in the principal case? Is it a just criticism of this formulation that it would require every state constantly to examine its title to each portion of its territory "in order to determine whether a change in the law had necessitated, as it were, a reacquisition?" Jessup, The Palmas Island Arbitration, 22 A.J.I.L. 735, 740 (1928). See also de Visscher, Theory and Reality in Public International Law 211–12 (rev. ed. Corbett trans. 1968).

# LEGAL STATUS OF EASTERN GREENLAND CASE (DENMARK v. NORWAY)

Permanent Court of International Justice, 1933.
P.C.I.J., Ser. A/B, No. 53, 3 Hudson, World Ct.Rep. 148.

[A Norwegian proclamation of 1931 purported to place portions of Eastern Greenland under Norwegian sovereignty, on the theory that the territory was *terra nullius,* rather than Danish territory. Denmark thereupon instituted proceedings against Norway in the Permanent Court of International Justice, both states being bound by the "optional clause" of the Court's Statute, asking that the Court declare the Norwegian decree invalid.

[The Court first discussed the history of Greenland, as well as the history of the Danish and Norwegian monarchies, noting that the crowns of the two countries had been united from 1380 to 1814 A.D. By the Treaty of Kiel of 1814, the King of Denmark ceded to Sweden the Kingdom of Norway, excluding, however, his rights in Greenland and other territories.]

The first Danish argument is that the Norwegian occupation of part of the East coast of Greenland is invalid because Denmark has claimed and exercised sovereign rights over Greenland as a whole for a long time and has obtained thereby a valid title to sovereignty. The date at which such Danish sovereignty must have existed in order to render the Norwegian occupation invalid is the date at which the occupation took place, viz., July 10th, 1931.

The Danish claim is not founded upon any particular act of occupation but alleges—to use the phrase employed in the Palmas Island decision of the Permanent Court of Arbitration, April 4th, 1928—a title "founded on the peaceful and continuous display of State authority over the island". It is based upon the view that Denmark now enjoys all the rights which the King of Denmark and Norway enjoyed over Greenland up till 1814. Both the existence and the extent of these rights must therefore be considered, as well as the Danish claim to sovereignty since that date.

It must be borne in mind, however, that as the critical date is July 10th, 1931, it is not necessary that sovereignty over Greenland should have existed throughout the period during which the Danish Government maintains that it was in being. Even if the material submitted to the Court might be thought insufficient to establish the existence of that sovereignty during the earlier periods, this would not exclude a finding that it is sufficient to establish a valid title in the period immediately preceding the occupation.

Before proceeding to consider in detail the evidence submitted to the Court, it may be well to state that a claim to sovereignty based not upon some particular act or title such as a treaty of cession but merely upon continued display of authority, involves two elements each of which must be shown to exist: the intention and will to act as sovereign, and some actual exercise or display of such authority.

Another circumstance which must be taken into account by any tribunal which has to adjudicate upon a claim to sovereignty over a particular territory, is the extent to which the sovereignty is also claimed by some other Power. In most of the cases involving claims to territorial sovereignty which have come before an international tribunal, there have been two competing claims to the sovereignty, and the tribunal has had to decide which of the two is the stronger. One of the peculiar features of the present case is that up to 1931 there was no claim by any Power other than Denmark to the sovereignty over Greenland. Indeed, up till 1921, no Power disputed the Danish claim to sovereignty.

It is impossible to read the records of the decisions in cases as to territorial sovereignty without observing that in many cases the tribunal has been satisfied with very little in the way of the actual exercise of sovereign rights, provided that the other State could not make out a superior claim. This is particularly true in the case of claims to sovereignty over areas in thinly populated or unsettled countries.

[The Court described the establishment of Nordic colonies in Greenland as early as the 10th century, and acknowledgments by these colonies of the sovereignty of the King of Norway. It then held that, although the original colonies disappeared at an early date, there was no abandonment by the King of his rights in Greenland. The Court then noted that a re-awakening of interest in Greenland during the 18th century led to the re-establishment of colonies in 1721, and that thereafter there was "a manifestation and exercise of sovereign rights." The Court rejected Norway's contention that in the legislative and administrative acts of the 18th century the term "Greenland" was not used in the geographic sense but only in reference to the colonized areas of western Greenland. As evidence supporting this conclusion, the Court relied on Danish treaties in which the other contracting party had agreed to the exclusion of Greenland from the scope of the treaty: this showed, said the Court, "a willingness on the part of the States with which Denmark has contracted to admit her right to exclude Greenland. * * * To the extent that these treaties constitute evidence of recognition of her sovereignty over Greenland in general, Denmark is entitled to rely upon them." After discussing Danish activity in Greenland from 1814 to 1915, the Court summarized:]

In view of the above facts, when taken in conjunction with the legislation she had enacted applicable to Greenland generally, the numerous treaties in which Denmark, with the concurrence of the other contracting Party, provided for the non-application of the treaty to Greenland in general, and the absence of all claim to sovereignty over Greenland by any other Power, Denmark must be regarded as having displayed during this period of 1814 to 1915 her authority over the uncolonized part of the country to a degree sufficient to confer a valid title to the sovereignty.

[The Court then discussed the effect of various communications which Denmark had addressed to other states between 1915 and 1921, asking recognition of Denmark's rights in Greenland, and rejected the Norwegian contentions that Denmark thereby admitted that it possessed no sovereignty over uncolonized parts of Greenland and that it was "estopped" from claiming a long-established sovereignty over the whole island.]

The period subsequent to the date when the Danish Government issued the Decree of May 10th, 1921, referred to above, witnessed a considerable increase in the activity of the Danish Government on the eastern coast of Greenland. * * *

Even if the period from 1921 to July 10th, 1931, is taken by itself and without reference to the preceding periods, the conclusion reached by the Court is that during this time Denmark regarded herself as possessing sovereignty over all Greenland and displayed and exercised her sovereign rights to an extent sufficient to constitute a valid title to sovereignty. When considered in conjunction with the facts of the preceding periods, the case in favour of Denmark is confirmed and strengthened.

It follows from the above that the Court is satisfied that Denmark has succeeded in establishing her contention that at the critical date, namely, July 10th, 1931, she possessed a valid title to the sovereignty over all Greenland.

This finding constitutes by itself sufficient reason for holding that the occupation of July 10th, 1931, and any steps taken in this connection by the Norwegian Government, were illegal and invalid.

[The Court also held, as separate and independent grounds for its conclusion, that: (1) Norway had "debarred herself from contesting Danish sovereignty over the whole of Greenland" by becoming a party to various bilateral and multilateral agreements in which Greenland had been described as Danish or in which Denmark had excluded Greenland from the operation of the agreement, and (2) Norway had given express undertakings to the Danish government by which it promised not to contest Danish sovereignty over the whole of Greenland. * * *]

## *Notes*

1. As understood by the Court, were the numerous recognitions by *third states* of Denmark's sovereignty in Greenland mere evidence of Danish sovereignty or an actual element in the root of title? Would recognition by these third states without prior Danish occupation of parts of Greenland have aided Denmark in its claim? In the *Island of Palmas* arbitration, supra, did Spanish acquiescence in Dutch pretensions of sovereignty over the island amount, in the Arbitrator's view, to mere evidence of Dutch sovereignty or to an actual element in establishing the existence of sovereignty? Did the basis on which the Arbitrator found the island to be Dutch differ from that on which Danish sovereignty was found over Greenland? See generally Jennings, The Acquisition of Territory in International Law 36–41 (1963). If Spain could have been shown to have recognized Dutch sovereignty over Palmas, as Norway was held to have recognized Danish sovereignty in the *Eastern Greenland Case,* would Spain (and therefore the United States) have been "estopped" from contesting the rights of the Netherlands in the island? See Jennings at 41–43; McNair, The Law of Treaties 487 (1962).

2. For comment on the *Eastern Greenland Case,* see Preuss, The Dispute Between Denmark and Norway over the Sovereignty of East Greenland, 26 A.J.I.L. 469 (1932); Hyde, The Case Concerning the Legal Status of Greenland, 27 A.J.I.L. 732 (1933). For discussion of the formation of rules of international law relating to the acquisition of sovereignty over territory, see Schwarzenberger, Title to Territory: Response to a Challenge, 51 A.J.I.L. 308 (1957). Questions of treaty interpretation often affect sovereignty over territory. See the Case Concerning the Temple of Preah Vihear (Cambodia v. Thailand), 1962 I.C.J. 6; Johnson, The Case Concerning the Temple of Preah Vihear, 11 I.C.L.Q. 1183 (1962).

3. Disputes have arisen over the sovereignty to various small islands dotting the oceans. Although sovereignty over many has not been claimed, strategic location and possible oil and mineral reserves enhance their current attractiveness. The Spratly and Parcel Islands in the South China Sea have been claimed by Vietnam, China and the Philippines. For an analysis of each of these countries' claims, see Park, The South China Sea Disputes: Who Owns the Islands and the Natural Resources?, 5 Ocean Dev. and Int'l L.J. 27 (1978), Chiu and Park, Legal Status of the Parcel and Spratly Islands, 3 Ocean Dev. and Int'l L.J. 1 (1975–76) and Cheng, Dispute over the South China Sea Islands, 10 Tex.Int'l L.J. 265 (1975). Similarly, Japan and China dispute the sovereignty over the Senkaku Islands in the East China Sea. See Cheng, The Sino–Japanese Dispute Over the Tiao-yu-tai (Senkaku) Islands and the Law of Territorial Acquisition, 14 Va.J.Int'l L. 221 (1971).

4. The Beagle Channel Islands, which lie between the Atlantic and Pacific oceans, were the subject of dispute between Argentina and Chile from 1905 to 1984. Although both countries agreed in 1971 that the British Government should arbitrate their dispute (10 I.L.M. 1182 (1971)), the award of the islands to Chile (Declaration of Her Majesty Queen Elizabeth II, April 18, 1977, 17 I.L.M. 632 (1978)) was not honored by Argentina. On Jan. 8, 1979, Chile and Argentina agreed to submit their dispute for resolution by the Pope, 18 I.L.M. (1979). The dispute was resolved in a Treaty of Peace and Friendship signed at the Vatican on January 23, 1984.

5. The Falkland Islands or Islas Malvinas have been the subject of a dispute eventuating in armed conflict in 1982 between Argentina and the United Kingdom. The islands were occupied by Argentine forces, which were defeated by British forces. See Franck, Dulce et Decorum Est: The Strategic Role of Legal Principles in the Falklands War, 77 A.J.I.L. 109 (1983) and Beck, The Falklands Islands as an International Problem (1988).

6. On when and how sovereignty can be claimed over newly emerged islands, see Note, Eruptions in International Law: Emerging Volcanic Islands and the Law of Territorial Acquisition, 11 Cornell Int'l L.J. 121 (1978); Note, Legal Claims to Newly Emerged Islands, 15 San Diego L.Rev. 525 (1978).

7. Is occupation a means by which private persons can acquire sovereignty over parts of the universe? On efforts to create one's own island by reliance on occupation, see Comment, To Be or Not to Be: The Republic of Minerva—Nation Founding by Individuals, 12 Colum.J.Trans.L. 520 (1973); United States v. Ray, 423 F.2d 16 (5th Cir.1970) (United States granted an injunction against the building up of a reef outside of the territorial waters of the Florida coast into an island to be known as the Grand Capri Republic or Atlantis, Isle of Gold).

## C. CONTIGUITY

### *LAUTERPACHT, SOVEREIGNTY OVER SUBMARINE AREAS*

[1950] Brit.Y.B.Int'l L. 376, 428–29.*

The award of Dr. Huber in the case of the *Island of Palmas* has occasionally been cited as proving the assertion that international law does

* Footnotes omitted. Reprinted by permission of the Oxford University Press from The British Yearbook of International Law, vol. 27, published by Oxford University Press for the Royal Institute of International Affairs.

not recognize the title of contiguity. Even if that were the correct interpretation of the award it is doubtful whether, notwithstanding the high authority of the arbitrator, it could dispose of a doctrine which has figured prominently in the practice of states. However, it is doubtful whether this is the intended effect of the award. The arbitrator, it is true, held that "it is impossible to show the existence of a rule of positive international law to the effect that islands situated outside territorial waters should belong to a state from the fact that its territory forms the *terra firma.*" However, it must be borne in mind that the award related only to islands; that, in a sense, it was *obiter* inasmuch as the claim of the United States was not based mainly on contiguity; that the arbitrator admitted that a group of islands may form "in law a unit, and that the fate of the principal part may involve the rest"; and that he held in effect, with regard to occupation of territories which form a geographical unit, that the appropriation must be presumed, in the initial stages, to extend to the whole unit (a rule which is one of the main aspects of the doctrine of contiguity) and that the only consideration to which contiguity must cede is that of actual adverse display of sovereignty by the competing state.

* * * [I]t is difficult to understand fully the judgment of the Permanent Court of International Justice in the case of the *Legal Status of Eastern Greenland* unless due weight is given to that part of the pronouncement of the Court which extended the legal consequences of display of sovereignty to uninhabited and uncolonized parts of Greenland forming an integral part of the territories which the Court considered to have been occupied by means of the display of some state activity. * * *

In fact, the apparent antinomy of effectiveness and contiguity begins to wear thin as soon as we realize—and the award in the case of *Island of Palmas* and other cases clearly urge that consideration—that effectiveness need not be as complete as appears at first sight and that contiguity is not as theoretical and arbitrary as may appear at first sight. This explains why those who are skeptical of contiguity as a title occasionally suggest that a mere proclamation may satisfy the requirement of effectiveness—provided that it has the support of contiguity. The fact is that as a rule the conceptions of effectiveness and contiguity often provide no more than an argumentative starting-point. There is a sound core in both, though in case of conflicting claims mere contiguity when confronted with effective occupation, which is not *per se* illegal, must yield to the latter as representing a superior title. But effectiveness is not a magic formula which can be applied with mathematical precision. It is effectiveness relative to the situation and to the circumstances. It may range from the requirement of intensive administration in every "nook and corner" in a densely populated and developed area to mere "state activity" manifesting itself in the conclusion of treaties and conferment of concessions by an authority situated in a narrowly circumscribed part of the territory or even outside it; and it may even assume the form of a mere proclamation. When that point is reached there is little to choose between contiguity and "effectiveness" of occupation. Contiguity in such cases may be an essential condition which gives the only element of substance to such otherwise abstract occupation. In that sense contiguity is a factor more potent than effectiveness reduced to the very shadow of its natural self. Conversely, the claim of contiguity is *pro tanto* much stronger when there is only a remote prospect of occupation by rival states to oppose it—as is the case in the matter of submarine areas. While effectiveness in the shape of "notional" occupation exhibits a somewhat formal and nebulous complexion, contiguity assumes, in comparison, a distinct degree of reality. * * *

### *Note*

On contiguity as a basis for the continental shelf doctrine, see p. 1277 infra.

## D. "PRESCRIPTION" OR "TITLE FOUNDED ON LONG AND PEACEFUL POSSESSION"

### *BRIERLY, THE LAW OF NATIONS*

167–71 (6th ed. Waldock 1963).*

*Prescription* as a title to territory is ill defined and some writers deny its recognition altogether. International law does appear, however, to admit that, by a process analogous to the prescription of municipal law, long possession may operate either to confirm the existence of a title the precise origin of which cannot be shown or to extinguish the prior title of another sovereign. * * *

In the absence of definite evidence that the possession began as a wrongful assumption of a sovereignty already belonging to another state, peaceful and continuous possession raises a presumption that the original assumption of sovereignty was in conformity with international law and has the effect of consolidating the claimant's title. Possession of territory consists in the exercise or display of state authority in or in regard to the territory in question. In the *Island of Palmas Arbitration* M. Huber spoke of the acquisition of sovereignty by way of continuous and peaceful display of state authority as "so-called prescription" and also said that "the continuous and peaceful display of territorial sovereignty (peaceful in relation to other states) is as good as a title. * * *" Again, even in the *Eastern Greenland* case, which is commonly referred to as the leading case on "occupation", the Court emphasized that Denmark did not found her claim upon any "particular act of occupation" but alleged a title "founded on the peaceful and continuous display of state authority"; and it awarded the sovereignty to Denmark on the basis of the latter's display of state authority with regard to the whole of Greenland during successive periods of history.

In fact, it is neither very easy nor very necessary to draw a precise line between an ancient title derived from an original "occupation" and one founded simply on long and peaceful possession. For in the *Island of Palmas* case M. Huber emphasized that proof of an original taking of possession is not enough and that possession must be maintained by display of State authority; and, on the other hand, both he in that case and the Court in the *Eastern Greenland* case pointed out that proof of peaceful possession in the most recent period before the rival claimant attempts to assume the sovereignty is sufficient by itself to establish a title to the territory—without proof of a long historic possession. The truth seems to be

* Footnotes omitted. Reprinted by permission of the Clarendon Press, Oxford.

that peaceful display of state authority is by itself a valid title to sovereignty and that proof either of an original act of occupation or of the long duration of a display of state authority is important primarily as confirming the peaceful and nonadverse character of the possession. Peaceful display of state authority over a long period excludes the existence of any valid prior title in another state and makes it unnecessary to rely upon the principle of extinctive prescription by long adverse possession.

The principle of extinctive prescription under which the passage of time operates ultimately to bar the right of a prior owner to pursue his claim against one who, having wrongfully displaced him, has continued for a long time in adverse possession is recognized in almost all systems of municipal law and it appears equally to be admitted by international law. * * * It is a nice question as to exactly how far diplomatic and other paper forms of protest by the dispossessed state suffice to "disturb" the possession of the interloper so as to prevent the latter from acquiring a title by prescription. Paper protests may undoubtedly be effective for a certain length of time to preserve the claim of the dispossessed state. If, however, the latter makes no effort at all to carry its protests farther by referring the case to the United Nations or by using other remedies that may be open to it, paper protests will ultimately be of no avail to stop the operation of prescription. Thus it was largely for the purpose of avoiding any risk of the extinguishment of its claims by prescription that in 1955 the United Kingdom filed a unilateral application with the International Court challenging alleged encroachments by Argentina and Chile on the Falkland Islands Dependencies.

## E. THE PROCESS OF CONSOLIDATION

Does the "ambiguity in actual cases based essentially on effective possession" suggest the question "whether the various factors contributing to building a title cannot usefully and instructively be subsumed under the one heading of a process of 'consolidation', and regarded as being for essential purposes all part of one legal process, or 'mode' of acquisition of territorial sovereignty"? Jennings, The Acquisition of Territory in International Law 23–24 (1963). See the materials collected in 2 Whiteman 1224–29. This approach has been advocated by Charles de Visscher, who regards "proven long use," which is admitted to be the "foundation" of a process of consolidation, as representing merely "a complex of interests and relations which in themselves have the effect of attaching a territory or an expanse of sea to a given State. It is these interests and relations, varying from one case to another, and not the passage of a fixed term, unknown in any event to international law, that are taken into direct account by the judge in order to decide *in concreto* on the existence or nonexistence of a consolidation by historic titles." de Visscher, Theory and Reality in Public International Law 209 (rev. ed. Corbett trans. 1968). Compare Lissitzyn, International Law Today and Tomorrow 17 (1965) ("Not infrequently, the real problem is which of two contestants has the stronger claim [based on a process of consolidation and other factors]."). Does the de Visscher formulation permit undue weight to be given to political, as opposed to legal, claims to territory? Although Jennings at 25–26, has expressed misgivings on this point, he views the de Visscher analysis as "a penetrating and illuminating observation of the way Courts actually tackle questions of title to territorial sovereignty." The doctrine results, he maintains, in the subtle shift of factors such as recognition, acquiescence, and estoppel from *evidence* of a state's sovereign possession (i.e., of a "situation ripe for prescription") to "*themselves* decisive ingredients in the process of creating title." Id. at 25–26. See generally Blum, Historic Titles in International Law (1965).

## F. PRINCIPLE OF *UTI POSSIDETIS JURIS*

### CASE CONCERNING THE FRONTIER DISPUTE (BURKINA FASO v. REPUBLIC OF MALI)

International Court of Justice, 1986.
1986 I.C.J. 554.

[Burkina Faso (previously Republic of Upper Volta) and the Republic of Mali submitted to a Chamber of the I.C.J. pursuant to a special agreement the question "[w]hat is the line of the frontier" of the Upper Volta and the Republic of Mali in "a band of territory extending from the sector Koro (Mali) Djibo (Upper Volta) up to and including the region of Béli." Prior to analyzing the evidence and drawing the line of the frontier, the Chamber (Judges Lachs, Ruda, Bedjaoui, Luchaire, Abi–Saab) commented as follows on the principle of *uti possidetis*: ]

19. The characteristic feature of the legal context of the frontier determination to be undertaken by the Chamber is that both States involved derive their existence from the process of decolonization which has been unfolding in Africa during the past 30 years. Their territories, and that of Niger, were formerly part of the French colonies which were grouped together under the name of French West Africa (AOF). Considering only the situation which prevailed immediately before the accession to independence of the two States, and disregarding previous administrative changes, it can be said that Burkina Faso corresponds to the colony of Upper Volta, and the Republic of Mali to the colony of Sudan (formerly French Sudan). It is to be supposed that the Parties drew inspiration from the principle expressly stated in the well-known resolution (AGH/Res. 16 (I)), adopted at the first session of the Conference of African Heads of State and Government, meeting in Cairo in 1964, whereby the Conference solemnly declared that all member States of the Organization of African Unity "solemnly ... pledge themselves to respect the frontiers existing on their achievement of national independence", inasmuch as, in the preamble to their Special Agreement, they stated that the settlement of the dispute by the Chamber must be "based in particular on respect for the principle of the intangibility of frontiers inherited from colonization". It is clear from this text, and from the pleadings and oral arguments of the Parties, that they are in agreement as regards both the applicable law and the starting-point for the legal reasoning which is to lead to the determination of the frontier between their territories in the disputed area.

20. Since the two Parties have, as noted above, expressly requested the Chamber to resolve their dispute on the basis, in particular, of the "principle of the intangibility of frontiers inherited from colonization", the Chamber

cannot disregard the principle of *uti possidetis juris,* the application of which gives rise to this respect for intangibility of frontiers. Although there is no need, for the purposes of the present case, to show that this is a firmly established principle of international law where decolonization is concerned, the Chamber nonetheless wishes to emphasize its general scope, in view of its exceptional importance for the African continent and for the two Parties. In this connection it should be noted that the principle of *uti possidetis* seems to have been first invoked and applied in Spanish America, inasmuch as this was the continent which first witnessed the phenomenon of decolonization involving the formation of a number of sovereign States on territory formerly belonging to a single metropolitan State. Nevertheless the principle is not a special rule which pertains solely to one specific system of international law. It is a general principle, which is logically connected with the phenomenon of the obtaining of independence, wherever it occurs. Its obvious purpose is to prevent the independence and stability of new States being endangered by fratricidal struggles provoked by the challenging of frontiers following the withdrawal of the administering power.

21. It was for this reason that, as soon as the phenomenon of decolonization characteristic of the situation in Spanish America in the 19th century subsequently appeared in Africa in the 20th century, the principle of *uti possidetis,* in the sense described above, fell to be applied. The fact that the new African States have respected the administrative boundaries and frontiers established by the colonial powers must be seen not as a mere practice contributing to the gradual emergence of a principle of customary international law, limited in its impact to the African continent as it had previously been to Spanish America, but as the application in Africa of a rule of general scope.

22. The elements of *uti possidetis* were latent in the many declarations made by African leaders in the dawn of independence. These declarations confirmed the maintenance of the territorial status quo at the time of independence, and stated the principle of respect both for the frontiers deriving from international agreements, and for those resulting from mere internal administrative divisions. The Charter of the Organization of African Unity did not ignore the principle of *uti possidetis,* but made only indirect reference to it in Article 3, according to which member States solemnly affirm the principle of respect for the sovereignty and territorial integrity of every State. However, at their first summit conference after the creation of the Organization of African Unity, the African Heads of State, in their Resolution mentioned above (AGH/Res. 16(I)), adopted in Cairo in July 1964, deliberately defined and stressed the principle of *uti possidetis juris* contained only in an implicit sense in the Charter of their organization.

23. There are several different aspects to this principle, in its well-known application in Spanish America. The first aspect, emphasized by the Latin genitive *juris,* is found in the pre-eminence accorded to legal title over effective possession as a basis of sovereignty. Its purpose, at the time of the achievement of independence by the former Spanish colonies of America, was to scotch any designs which non-American colonizing powers might have

on regions which had been assigned by the former metropolitan State to one division or another, but which were still uninhabited or unexplored. However, there is more to the principle of *uti possidetis* than this particular aspect. The essence of the principle lies in its primary aim of securing respect for the territorial boundaries at the moment when independence is achieved. Such territorial boundaries might be no more than delimitations between different administrative divisions or colonies all subject to the same sovereign. In that case, the application of the principle of *uti possidetis* resulted in administrative boundaries being transformed into international frontiers in the full sense of the term. This is true both of the States which took shape in the regions of South America which were dependent on the Spanish Crown, and of the States Parties to the present case, which took shape within the vast territories of French West Africa. *Uti possidetis,* as a principle which upgraded former administrative delimitations, established during the colonial period, to international frontiers, is therefore a principle of a general kind which is logically connected with this form of decolonization wherever it occurs.

24. The territorial boundaries which have to be respected may also derive from international frontiers which previously divided a colony of one State from a colony of another, or indeed a colonial territory from the territory of an independent State, or one which was under protectorate, but had retained its international personality. There is no doubt that the obligation to respect pre-existing international frontiers in the event of a State succession derives from a general rule of international law, whether or not the rule is expressed in the formula *uti possidetis.* Hence the numerous solemn affirmations of the intangibility of the frontiers existing at the time of the independence of African States, whether made by senior African statesmen or by organs of the Organization of African Unity itself, are evidently declaratory rather than constitutive: they recognize and confirm an existing principle, and do not seek to consecrate a new principle or the extension to Africa of a rule previously applied only in another continent.

25. However, it may be wondered how the time-hallowed principle has been able to withstand the new approaches to international law as expressed in Africa, where the successive attainment of independence and the emergence of new States have been accompanied by a certain questioning of traditional international law. At first sight this principle conflicts outright with another one, the right of peoples to self-determination. In fact, however, the maintenance of the territorial status quo in Africa is often seen as the wisest course, to preserve what has been achieved by peoples who have struggled for their independence, and to avoid a disruption which would deprive the continent of the gains achieved by much sacrifice. The essential requirement of stability in order to survive, to develop and gradually to consolidate their independence in all fields, has induced African States judiciously to consent to the respecting of colonial frontiers, and to take account of it in the interpretation of the principle of self-determination of peoples.

26. Thus the principle of *uti possidetis* has kept its place among the most important legal principles, despite the apparent contradiction which

explained its coexistence alongside the new norms. Indeed it was by deliberate choice that African States selected, among all the classic principles, that of *uti possidetis*. This remains an undeniable fact. In the light of the foregoing remarks, it is clear that the applicability of *uti possidetis* in the present case cannot be challenged merely because in 1960, the year when Mali and Burkina Faso achieved independence, the Organization of African Unity which was to proclaim this principle did not yet exist, and the abovementioned resolution calling for respect for the pre-existing frontiers dates only from 1964.

### *Note*

The *ad hoc* Arbitration Commission established by the European Community in 1991 to render advice on various issues relating to the dissolution of the former Socialist Republic of Yugoslavia rendered an opinion on January 11, 1992, that, in the absence of agreement of the relevant states to the contrary, the preexisting frontiers between Croatia and Serbia and Serbia and Bosnia–Herzegovina were entitled to protection under principles of international law, citing the U.N. Charter, the Declaration on the Principles of International Law concerning Friendly Relations and Co-operation among States, other international instruments, and the principle of *uti possidetis* applied in the principal case. For another application of the principle of *uti possidetis* see *Case Concerning Land, Island and Maritime Frontier Dispute (El Salvador v. Honduras, Nicaragua intervening)* at p. 331 infra.

## G. OTHER "MODES" OF ACQUIRING TERRITORIAL SOVEREIGNTY

### *1. Accretion*

Accretion is the expansion of a state's territory by operation of nature, for example, by the gradual shifting of the course of a river, the recession of the sea, or the building up of river deltas. The concept is of minor importance, but for detailed discussions see 1 Oppenheim 696–98; 1 O'Connell 492–95; 2 Whiteman 1084–85.

### *2. Cession*

#### *HACKWORTH, DIGEST OF INTERNATIONAL LAW*

Vol. 1, pp. 421–22 (1940).

Cession of territory involves the transfer of sovereignty by means of an agreement between the ceding and the acquiring states. It is a *derivative* mode of acquisition. The cession may comprise a portion only of the territory of the ceding state or it may comprise the totality of its territory. In the latter situation, as for example in the treaty of August 22, 1910 between Japan and Korea, the ceding state disappears and becomes merged into the acquiring state.

The consent of the population of ceded territory is not essential to the validity of the cession, although Grotius (bk. II, ch. vi, sec. 4) apparently held the opposite view. It is worthy of note, however, that in recent years cessions of territory have frequently been conditioned upon the will of the people as expressed in a plebiscite.

### *3. Conquest*

*DECLARATION ON PRINCIPLES OF INTERNATIONAL LAW CONCERNING FRIENDLY RELATIONS AND CO-OPERATION AMONG STATES IN ACCORDANCE WITH THE CHARTER OF THE UNITED NATIONS*

G.A.Res. 2625 (XXXV 1970).

The General Assembly,

* * *

*Having considered* the principles of international law relating to friendly relations and co-operation among States,

1. *Solemnly proclaims* the following principles:

* * *

Every State has the duty to refrain in its international relations from the threat or use of force against the territorial integrity or political independence of any State, or in any other manner inconsistent with the purposes of the United Nations. Such a threat or use of force constitutes a violation of international law and the Charter of the United Nations and shall never be employed as a means of settling international issues.

* * *

The territory of a State shall not be the object of military occupation resulting from the use of force in contravention of the provisions of the Charter. The territory of a State shall not be the object of acquisition by another State resulting from the threat or use of force. No territorial acquisition by another State resulting from the threat or use of force shall be recognized as legal. Nothing in the foregoing shall be construed as affecting:

(a) Provisions of the Charter or any international agreement prior to the Charter regime and valid under international law; or

(b) The powers of the Security Council under the Charter.

#### *Notes*

1. On August 1, 1990, the armed forces of Iraq invaded and occupied Kuwait. On August 2, the U.N. Security Council unanimously condemned the invasion and demanded that Iraq withdraw all forces immediately and unconditionally. S/RES/660 (1990). On August 9, 1990, the Council unanimously adopted Resolution 662 which stated, in part:

> *Gravely alarmed* by the declaration by Iraq of a "comprehensive and eternal merger" with Kuwait,
>
> *Demanding,* once again, that Iraq withdraw immediately and unconditionally all its forces to the positions in which they were located on 1 August 1990,
>
> *Determined* to bring the occupation of Kuwait by Iraq to an end and to restore the sovereignty, independence and territorial integrity to Kuwait,

*Determined also* to restore the authority of the legitimate Government of Kuwait,

*1. Decides* that annexation of Kuwait by Iraq under any form and whatever pretext has no legal validity, and is considered null and void;

*2. Calls upon* all States, international organizations and specialized agencies not to recognize that annexation, and to refrain from any action or dealing that might be interpreted as an indirect recognition of the annexation;

*3. Further demands* that Iraq rescind its actions purporting to annex Kuwait * * *.

2. Following the Arab–Israeli war in June, 1967, Israel took certain measures to accomplish the "administrative unification" of Jerusalem. The General Assembly, by a vote of 99 to 0, with 20 abstentions, adopted the following resolution:

*The General Assembly,*

*Deeply concerned* at the situation prevailing in Jerusalem as a result of the measures taken by Israel to change the status of the City,

1. *Considers* that these measures are invalid;

2. *Calls upon* Israel to rescind all measures already taken and to desist forthwith from taking any action which would alter the status of Jerusalem;

3. *Requests* the Secretary–General to report to the General Assembly and the Security Council on the situation and the implementation of the present resolution not later than one week from its adoption.

G.A.Res. 2253 (S–V) G.A.O.R., 5th Emerg.Spec.Sess., Supp. 1, at 4 (1967).

The action by the General Assembly was followed by a series of Security Council resolutions to the same effect, see S.C.Res. 252 (XXIII 1968) p. 9; S.C.Res. 267 (XXIV 1969) p. 3; S.C.Res. 271, id. p. 5; and S.C.Res. 298 (XXVI 1971) p. 6. The General Assembly reaffirmed its earlier resolution in G.A.Res. 31/106 (XXXI 1976) p. 50. Israel has failed to comply with these resolutions.

3. May a state that is not a member of the United Nations extend its sovereignty by armed conquest of another state? In Military and Paramilitary Activities In and Against Nicaragua (Nicaragua v. United States of America), 1986 I.C.J. 14, para. 190, the I.C.J. held that the principles of the U.N. Charter relating to the threat or use of force were part of customary international law with the character of *jus cogens.* See p. 893 infra. See also Jennings, The Acquisition of Territory in International Law 53–55 (1963); U.N. Charter, Art. 2(6). If such conquest does take place, does a member-state of the United Nations violate its obligations under the Charter by recognition of a change of sovereignty?

4. If international law no longer permits a state to gain "title" to territory by resorting to war, what is the present status of territory conquered and annexed at a time when international law did recognize such a "title" as valid? Does the doctrine of the "intertemporal law" apply? What is the present status of territory recently conquered and annexed by armed force, e.g., Goa, which was conquered and annexed by India in 1961? Will the answer depend on whether or not India's "title" is recognized by other states? See Oppenheim at 704–705 Jennings at 61–65. What is the effect, if any, of Portugal's establishment in 1962 of a Goan government-in-exile (2 Whiteman 1144)?

5. Is the conquering state's position in any way improved through its forcing the conquered state to agree to a treaty of cession? Article 52 of the Vienna Convention on the Law of Treaties states that a treaty (including presumably a treaty of cession) is void "if its conclusion has been procured by the threat or use of force in violation of the principles of international law embodied in the Charter of the United Nations." See p. 492 infra. See also Jennings at 56–61.

6. Is there any basis for concluding that an occupation of territory by a lawful use of armed force in the exercise of the right of self-defense under Article 51 of the Charter can give rise to a valid title to territory? See Schwebel, What Weight to Conquest, 64 A.J.I.L. 344–47 (1970).

7. In the Arab–Israeli war in June 1967, Israeli armed forces occupied Gaza, the West Bank, Sinai, and the Golan Heights. In 1968, Israel began establishing civilian settlements in these territories. Was this permitted under international law? See Letter of Herbert J. Hansell, Legal Adviser to the U.S. Department of State, of April 21, 1978, 17 I.L.M. 777 (1978) (reaching the conclusion that, as a belligerent occupant, Israel had no right to establish such settlements); G.A.Res. 3215 (XXXII) (1977) at 13 (to the same effect by vote of 131 to 1, with the abstentions of Costa Rica, Fiji, Guatemala, Malawi, Nicaragua, Papua, New Guinea, and United States). On whether Israel had the right to develop new oil fields in Sinai and the Gulf of Suez, see Memorandum of Law of the U.S. Department of State of Oct. 1, 1976, 16 I.L.M. 733 (1977) (reaching a negative answer), and the Response of the Ministry of Foreign Affairs of Israel of August 1, 1977, 17 I.L.M. 432 (1978) (giving an affirmative answer). On a possible justification for these measures, see p. 1031 infra. Note that armed occupation is different from conquest.

## H. BOUNDARY DISPUTES

### *1. Extent of Land Territory*

### *RESTATEMENT (SECOND) 1965*

#### § 12. Land, River, and Lake Boundaries

(1) The boundary separating the land areas of two states is determined by acts of the states expressing their consent to its location.

(2) Unless consent to a different rule has been expressed,

(a) when the boundary between two states is a navigable river, its location is the middle of the channel of navigation;

(b) when the boundary between two states is a non-navigable river or a lake, its location is the middle of the river or lake.

**Comment:**

*a. Land boundaries.* * * * Many boundary disputes have been settled by peaceful means including, in particular, boundary conventions and arbitration, as in the case of the continental land boundaries of the United States. Because, in a majority of cases, the location of land boundaries between states is defined by agreement (frequently as interpreted by arbitration) almost no specific principles of international law have developed in this field.

*b. Thalweg doctrine.* The rule locating the boundary in the middle of the channel of navigation rather than the middle of the stream is called the "thalweg" doctrine. See Louisiana v. Mississippi, 202 U.S. 1, 26 S.Ct. 408, 50 L.Ed. 913 (1906); New Jersey v. Delaware, 291 U.S. 361, 54 S.Ct. 407, 78 L.Ed. 847 (1934).

*c. Effect of natural shift.* In disputes between the states of the United States, the Supreme Court has applied the distinction between accretion and avulsion, under which the boundary between two states shifts with the gradual shifting of the channel caused by erosion and deposit of alluvium (accretion) but does not shift when the river is suddenly diverted from the previous channel (avulsion). See Nebraska v. Iowa, 143 U.S. 359, 12 S.Ct. 396, 36 L.Ed. 186; Arkansas v. Tennessee, 246 U.S. 158, 38 S.Ct. 301, 62 L.Ed. 638 (1918); 12 A.J.I.L. 648 (1918). * * *

## CASE CONCERNING LAND, ISLAND AND MARITIME FRONTIER DISPUTE (EL SALVADOR v. HONDURAS; NICARAGUA INTERVENING)

International Court of Justice, 1992.
1992 I.C.J. 351.

[A dispute over land, island and maritime boundaries between Honduras and El Salvador festered for many years and erupted in the "Soccer War". Soccer teams from the two countries took part in a World Cup qualifying final in San Salvador in 1969. Honduran fans were beaten and the Honduran flag insulted. Mobs in Honduras beat Salvadorans. Thereafter, Salvadoran planes and warships attacked Honduran air bases and islands in the Gulf of Fonseca. Honduras responded with land and air attacks. In four days 2,000 people died, mostly Honduran civilians. Honduras forced the return of 130,000 Salvadoran migrant workers.

In 1972, after extensive negotiations, El Salvador and Honduras reached agreement on most of their land boundary which had not previously been delimited, leaving thirteen sectors unsettled. Mediation begun in 1978 led to the conclusion of a General Treaty of Peace in 1980 which defined the boundary in seven sectors of the land frontier. A Joint Frontier Commission was established to delimit the boundary in the remaining six sectors. When the Commission failed to reach agreement, the parties concluded a Special Agreement in 1986 to submit unresolved issues to a five-judge Chamber of the I.C.J. The Special Agreement also vested a Special Demarcation Commission with responsibility for demarcation of the actual frontier line in accordance with the judgment of the Chamber. El Salvador and Honduras agreed that the Chamber's basic task was "to delimit" the boundary, i.e. "to indicate what are the geographical points of a line susceptible of defining the frontier." It would then be the responsibility of the Special Commission "to demarcate it by a technical operation." Opinion, para. 39.

In an exceedingly complex decision, rendered on September 11, 1992, the Chamber (Judge Sette–Camara, President; Judges Oda and Jennings;

Judges ad hoc Valtiros and Torres Bernardez) delimited the boundary in the six disputed sectors. It also ruled on the legal status of the islands of El Tigre, Meanguera and Meanguerita in the Gulf of Fonseca and on the legal situation of the maritime areas within and without the closing line of the Gulf of Fonseca. Nicaragua was permitted to intervene with respect to the maritime areas aspect of the case.

Article 5 of the Special Agreement provided that the Chamber was to take into account the rules of international law applicable between the Parties, including where pertinent the rules of the General Treaty of Peace. These included Article 26 of the General Treaty, which stated as follows:

> For the delimitation of the frontier line in areas subject to controversy, the Joint Frontier Commission shall take as a basis the documents which were issued by the Spanish Crown or by any other Spanish authority, whether secular or ecclesiastical, during the colonial period, and which indicate the jurisdictions or limits of territories or settlements. It shall also take account of other evidence and arguments of a legal, historical, human or any other kind, brought before it by the Parties and admitted under international law.

The Chamber regarded Article 26 as a rule relating to evidence that could properly be adduced by the parties in the proceeding *sub judice.* Opinion, para. 48.

After the independence of Central America was proclaimed in 1821, Honduras and El Salvador were originally part of the Federal Republic of Central America, which included also Costa Rica, Guatemala and Nicaragua. When the Republic broke up in 1839, Honduras and El Salvador became independent states. It was accepted by the Chamber and the parties that the new boundaries following independence should, in accordance with the principle of *uti possidetis juris* generally applied in Spanish America, follow the administrative boundaries utilized during the colonial period.

The Chamber observed that the 1821 *uti possidetis* boundary when ascertained was not frozen for all time but was susceptible to change by subsequent adjudication, agreement, acquiescence or recognition involving the affected parties. Opinion, para. 67. For example, it concluded that one portion of the boundary was different from that of the 1821 boundary as a result of acquiescence by Honduras evidenced by its conduct from 1881 until 1972. Opinion, para. 80.

The complexities of the decision were largely attributable to the difficulties of delineating the *uti possidetis* boundary when, as in the case presented, documentary evidence is fragmentary and often ambiguous and conflicting. With respect to application of the principle of *uti possidetis juris* under such circumstances the Chamber commented as follows:]

42. * * * [I]n the Arbitral Award of the Swiss Federal Council of 24 March 1922 concerning certain boundary questions between Colombia and Venezuela, it had been observed that:

> "This general principle [of *uti possidetis juris* ] offered the advantage of establishing an absolute rule that there was not in law in the old Spanish America any *terra nullius;* while there might exist many regions which had never been occupied by the Spaniards and many

> unexplored or inhabited by non-civilized natives, these regions were reputed to belong in law to whichever of the Republics succeeded to the Spanish province to which these territories were attached by virtue of the old Royal ordinances of the Spanish mother country. These territories, although not occupied in fact were by common consent deemed to by occupied in law from the first hour by the new Republic * * *" (*UNRIAA,* Vol. I, p. 228.)

Thus the principle of *uti possidetis juris* is concerned as much with title to territory as with the location of boundaries; certainly a key aspect of the principle is the denial of the possibility of *terra nullius.*

43. To apply this principle is not so easy when, as in Spanish Central America, there were administrative boundaries of different kinds or degrees; for example, besides "provinces" (a term of which the meaning was different at different periods), there were *Alcaldías Mayores* and *Corregimientos* and later on, in the 18th century, *Intendencias,* as well as the territorial jurisdictions of a higher court (*Audiencias* ), Captaincies–General and Vice–Royalties; and indeed the territories which became El Salvador and Honduras were, before 1821, all part of the same larger administrative area, the Captaincy–General or Kingdom of Guatemala. Furthermore, the jurisdictions of general administrative bodies such as those referred to did not necessarily coincide in territorial scope with those of bodies possessing particular or special jurisdictions, e.g., military commands. Besides, in addition to the various civil territorial jurisdictions, general or special, there were the ecclesiastical jurisdictions, which were supposed to be followed in principle, pursuant to general legislation, by the territorial jurisdiction of the main civil administrative units in Spanish America; such adjustment often needed, however, a certain span of time within which to materialize. Fortunately, in the present case, insofar as the sectors of the land boundary are concerned, the Parties have indicated to which colonial administrative divisions they claim to have succeeded; the problem is to identify the areas, and their boundaries, which corresponded to these divisions, to be referred to herein, for the sake of simplicity, as "provinces" which in 1821 became respectively El Salvador and Honduras, initially as constituent States of the Federal Republic of Central America. Moreover it has to be remembered that no question of international boundaries could ever have occurred to the minds of those servants of the Spanish Crown who established administrative boundaries; *uti possidetis juris* is essentially a retrospective principle, investing as international boundaries administrative limits intended originally for quite other purposes.

44. Neither Party has however produced any legislative or similar material indicating specifically, with the authority of the Spanish Crown, the extent of the territories and the location of the boundaries of the relevant provinces in each area of the land boundary. Both Parties have instead laid before the Chamber numerous documents, of different kinds, some of which, referred to collectively as "titles" (*títulos* ), concern grants of land in the areas concerned by the Spanish Crown, from which, it is claimed, the provincial boundaries can be deduced. Some of these actually record that a particular landmark or natural feature marked the boundary of the provinces at the time of the grant; but for the most part this is not so, and the Chamber is asked, in effect, to conclude, in the absence of other evidence

of the position of a provincial boundary, that where a boundary can be identified between the lands granted by the authorities of one province and those granted by the authorities of the neighbouring province, this boundary may be taken to have been the provincial boundary and thus the line of the *uti possidetis juris.* Thus it was the territorial aspect of that principle rather than its boundary aspect that was the one mainly employed by both Parties in their arguments before the Chamber. The location of boundaries seemed often, in the arguments of the Parties, to be incidental to some "claim", or "title", or "grant", respecting a parcel of territory, within circumambient boundaries only portions of which are now claimed to form an international boundary. It is rather as if the disputed boundaries must be constructed like a jig-saw puzzle from certain already cut pieces so that the extent and location of the resulting boundary depend upon the size and shape of the fitting piece.

45. The term "title" has in fact been used at times in these proceedings in such a way as to leave unclear which of several possible meanings is to be attached to it; some basic distinctions may therefore perhaps be usefully stated. As the Chamber in the *Frontier Dispute* case observed, the word "title" is generally not limited to documentary evidence alone, but comprehends "both any evidence which may establish the existence of a right, and the actual source of that right" (*I.C.J. Reports 1986,* p. 564, para. 18). In one sense, the "title" of El Salvador or of Honduras to the areas in dispute, in the sense of the source of their rights at the international level, is, as both Parties recognize, that of succession of the two States to the Spanish Crown in relation to its colonial territories; the extent of territory to which each State succeeded being determined by the *uti possidetis juris* of 1821. Secondly, insofar as each of the two States inherited the territory of particular administrative units of the colonial structure, a "title" might be furnished by, for example, a Spanish Royal Decree attributing certain areas to one of those. As already noted, neither Party has been able to base its claim to a specific boundary line on any "titles" of this kind applicable to the land frontier. * * * [T]he *títulos* submitted to the Chamber recording the grant of particular lands to individuals or to Indian communities cannot be considered as "titles" in this sense; they could rather be compared to "colonial *effectivités* " as defined by the Chamber formed to deal with the *Frontier Dispute:* "the conduct of the administrative authorities as proof of the effective exercise of territorial jurisdiction in the region during the colonial period" (*I.C.J. Reports 1986,* p. 586, para. 63). These, or some of them, are however "titles" in a third, municipal-law, sense, in that they evidence the right of the grantees to ownership of the land defined in them. In some cases, the grant of the "title" in this third sense was not perfected; but the record, particularly of any survey carried out, nevertheless remains a "colonial effectivity" which may be of value as evidence of the position of the provincial boundary. * * *

[When the Chamber found no persuasive documentary evidence of the location of the boundary at the time the states gained their independence, resort was had to other evidence. On some occasions the Chamber attached weight to a topographical feature such as a watershed that provided a readily identifiable and convenient boundary. Opinion, paras. 46, 101, 114. On another it invoked equity *infra legem* to adopt a boundary proposed in negotiations between Honduras and El Salvador in 1869 which remained unratified by the parties but was apparently not the subject of disagreement. Opinion, paras. 262–63.

The sixth disputed sector involved the location of a boundary formed by the Goascorán River that flows into the Gulf of Fonseca. As stated by the Chamber:]

306. * * * Honduras contends that in 1821 the river Goascorán constituted the boundary between the colonial units to which the two States have succeeded, that there has been no material change in the course of the river since 1821, and that the boundary therefore follows the present stream, flowing into the Gulf north-west of the Islas Ramaditas in the Bay of La Union. El Salvador however claims that it is a previous course followed by the river which defines the boundary, and that this course, since abandoned by the stream, can be traced, and it reaches the Gulf at Estero La Cutú.

* * *

308. The contention of El Salvador that a former bed of the river Goascorán forms the *uti possidetis juris* boundary depends, as a question of fact, on the assertion that the Goascorán formerly was running in that bed, and that at some date it abruptly changed its course to its present position. On this basis El Salvador's argument of law is that where a boundary is formed by the course of a river, and the stream suddenly leaves its old bed and forms a new one, this process of "avulsion" does not bring about a change in the boundary, which continues to follow the old channel. No record of an abrupt change of course having occurred has been brought to the Chamber's attention, but were the Chamber satisfied that the river's course was earlier so radically different from its present one, then an avulsion might reasonably be inferred. While the area is low and swampy, so that different channels might well receive different proportions of the total run-off at different times, there does not seem to be a possibility of the change having occurred slowly by erosion and accretion, to which, as El Salvador concedes, different legal rules may apply.

309. There is no scientific evidence that the previous course of the Goascorán was such that it debouched in the Estero La Cutú * * *, rather than in any of the other neighbouring inlets in the coastline * * *.

310. It is apparently El Salvador's case that whether the change in the river's course occurred before or after 1821 does not affect the matter. Its contentions may be understood as covering two different hypotheses. If the river still followed the alleged "old" course (to the Estero La Cutú) in 1821, the river was the boundary which by the operation of the *uti possidetis juris* became transformed into the international frontier. That frontier would then, according to El Salvador, have been maintained as it was, notwithstanding a subsequent avulsion of the river, by virtue of a rule of international law to that effect. If however the change of the river's course occurred before 1821 (but after it had become identified as a provincial boundary), and no further change of course took place after 1821, then El Salvador's claim to the "old" course as the modern boundary would have to rest on an alleged persistence, during the colonial period, of the "old" course

as boundary, on the basis of a rule concerning avulsion which would be a rule, not of international law, but of Spanish colonial law. * * *

* * *

312. In the Chamber's view, however, any claim by El Salvador that the boundary follows an old course of the river abandoned at some time *before* 1821 must be rejected. It is a new claim and inconsistent with the previous history of the dispute. * * *

[The Chamber concluded on the basis of the evidence submitted, which included 18th century cartographic material and the conduct of the parties in 19th century negotiations, that the 1981 course of the Goascorán was the same as the present course and it delimits the relevant portion of the boundary. The Chamber then turned to the question of which state had jurisdiction over each of the islands of El Tigre, Meanguera and Meanguerita in the Gulf of Fonseca.]

332. It is the contention of Honduras that the law applicable to the island dispute by virtue of these provisions is solely the *uti possidetis juris* of 1821. El Salvador on the other hand initially (in its Memorial) relied heavily on the exercise or display of sovereignty over the islands, contending that the island dispute was, in its view, a dispute as to attribution of territory rather than a dispute over the delimitation of a frontier. Subsequently, however, it maintained that the dispute over the islands can be viewed in two possible ways: while it is able to rely on effective possession of the islands as the basis of its sovereignty thereof on the ground that this is a case where sovereignty has to be attributed, it is equally able to rely on historical formal title-deeds as unquestionable proof of its sovereignty of the islands in accordance with the principle of the *uti possidetis juris* of 1821. In the view of El Salvador, its rights over the islands are not merely confirmed but fortified by the combined effect of the application of the two criteria. While questioning whether Article 26 of the General Treaty of Peace is applicable to the islands at all, El Salvador also points to the final sentence of Article 26, which in its view was directed, even in the context of land boundaries, to balancing the application of Spanish colonial titles with "more modern concepts"; it concludes that the Chamber is bound to apply the modern law of the acquisition of territory, and to look at the effective exercise and display of State sovereignty over the islands as well as historical titles.

333. The Chamber has no doubt that the starting-point for the determination of sovereignty over the islands must be the *uti possidetis juris* of 1821. The islands of the Gulf of Fonseca were discovered in 1522 by Spain, and remained under the sovereignty of the Spanish Crown for three centuries. When the Central American States became independent in 1821, none of the islands were *terra nullius;* sovereignty over the islands could not therefore be acquired by occupation of territory. The matter was one of the succession of the newly-independent States to all former Spanish islands in the Gulf. The Chamber will therefore consider whether it is possible to establish the appurtenance in 1821 of each disputed island to one or the other of the various administrative units of the Spanish colonial structure in Central America. For this purpose, it may have regard not only to legislative and administrative texts of the colonial period, but also to "colonial *effectivités*"

* * *. In the case of the islands, there are no land titles of the kind which Chamber has taken into account in order to reconstruct the limits of the *uti possidetis juris* on the mainland; and the legislative and administrative texts are confused and conflicting. The attribution of individual islands to the territorial administrative divisions of the Spanish colonial system, for the purposes of their allocation to the one or the other newly independent State, may well have been a matter of some doubt and difficulty, judging by the evidence and information submitted. It should be recalled that when the principle of the *uti possidetis juris* is involved, the *jus* referred to is not international law but the constitutional or administrative law of the pre-independence sovereign, in this case Spanish colonial law; and it is perfectly possible that that law itself gave no clear and definite answer to the appurtenance of marginal areas, or sparsely populated areas of minimal economic significance. For this reason, it is particularly appropriate to examine the conduct of the new States in relation to the islands during the period immediately after independence. Claims then made, and the reaction—or lack of reaction—to them may throw light on the contemporary appreciation of what the situation in 1821 had been, or should be taken to have been. * * *

[The Chamber reviewed the facts, including evidences of title and colonial *effectivités,* on which El Salvador and Honduras based their claims to the islands in the Gulf and observed that many of the historical events relied on can be, and have been, interpreted in different ways and thus used to support the arguments of either Party.]

341. The Chamber considers it unnecessary to analyse in any further detail the arguments of each Party directed to showing that that Party acquired sovereignty over some or all of the islands of the Gulf by the application of the *uti possidetis juris* principle. It has reached the conclusion * * * that the material available to the Chamber * * * is too fragmentary and ambiguous to be sufficient for any firm conclusion to be based upon it. The Chamber must therefore proceed * * * to consider the conduct of the Parties in the period following independence, as indicative of the then view of what must have been the 1821 position. This may further be supplemented by considerations independent of the *uti possidetis juris* principle, in particular the possible significance of the same conduct, or the conduct of the Parties in more recent years, as possibly constituting acquiescence. * * *

343. The difficulty with application to the present case of principles of law [relating to the acquisition of territory, invoked by El Salvador] is however that they were developed primarily to deal with the acquisition of sovereignty over territories available for occupation, i.e., *terra nullius.* Both Parties however assert a title of succession from the Spanish Crown, so that the question arises whether the exercise or display of sovereignty by the one Party, particularly when coupled with lack of protest by the other, could indicate the presence of an *uti possidetis juris* title in the Party so exercising sovereignty, where the evidence on the basis of documentary titles or colonial *effectivités* was ambiguous. * * *

345. In the present case both Parties have argued their respective claims with regard to the operation of the *uti possidetis juris* on the basis, in

effect, that this is a principle the application of which is automatic: on independence, the boundaries of the relevant colonial administrative divisions are transformed into international frontiers. In the first place, it should not be overlooked that Spanish colonial divisions in Spanish America did not individually have any "original" or "historic" titles, as those concepts are understood in international law. The original title belonged exclusively to the Spanish Crown, not the internal administrative subdivisions established by it; and it was equally the Spanish Crown which had sovereignty of the colonial territories. Secondly, as the Chamber's examination of the sectors of the land boundary has shown, in practice the operation of the principle is more complex. Where the relevant administrative boundary was ill-defined or its position disputed, in the view of the Chamber the behavior of the two newly independent States in the years following independence may well serve as a guide to where the boundary was, either in their shared view, or in the view acted on by one and acquiesced in by the other * * *. This aspect of the matter is of particular importance in relation to the status of the islands, by reason of their history.

346. Shortly after independence in 1821, the newly independent Central American States were united by the Constitution of 1824 in the Federal Republic of Central America, successor of Spain in the sovereignty over, *inter alia,* the islands. Uninhabited or sparsely inhabited, the islands were left dormant for some years, since the economic value of their exploitation was little. The problem of their appurtenance to one or the other of the riparian States thus did not raise any interest or inspire any dispute until the break-up of the Federal Republic and the years nearing the mid-19th century. The well-protected waters of the Gulf of Fonseca, with its mouth extending over some 19 nautical miles, the good navigation channels, and the possibility of construction of safe and comfortable ports, had long commended the Gulf to pirates and buccaneers in search of a haven; from the 1840's onward the attention of the big powers, interested in having a foothold in Central America, began to be attracted to the islands of the Gulf.

347. Thus it was not until a number of years after the independence of the two States that the question of the appurtenance of the islands of the Gulf to the one or the other became of significant import. What then occurred appears to the Chamber to be highly material. The islands were not *terra nullius,* and in legal theory each island already appertained to one of the three States surrounding the Gulf as heir to the appropriate part of the Spanish colonial possessions, so that *acquisition* of territory by occupation was not possible; but the effective possession by one of the Gulf States of any island of the Gulf could constitute an *effectivité,* though a post-colonial one, throwing light on the contemporary appreciation of the legal situation. Possession backed by the exercise of sovereignty may be taken as evidence confirming the *uti possidetis juris* title. The Chamber does not find it necessary to decide whether such possession could be recognized even in contradiction of such a title, but in the case of the islands, where the historical material of colonial times is confused and contradictory, and the accession to independence was not immediately followed by unambiguous acts of sovereignty, this is practically the only way in which the *uti possidetis juris* could find formal expression so as to be judicially recognized and determined.

[The Chamber dealt first with El Tigre, reviewing the historical events concerning it from 1833 onward. Noting that Honduras has remained in effective possession and control of the island since 1849, the Chamber concluded that the conduct of the Parties in the years following the dissolution of the Federal Republic of Central America was consistent with the contemporary assumption that El Tigre appertained to Honduras and that this assumption also implied belief that Honduras was entitled to the island by succession from Spain, or, at least, that such succession by Honduras was not contradicted by any known colonial title. Opinion, paras. 348–355.

Regarding Meanguera and Meanguerita, the Chamber observed that throughout the argument the two islands were treated by both Parties as constituting a single insular unity. The smallness of Meanguerita, its contiguity to the larger island, and the fact that it is uninhabited made it appropriate to treat it as a "dependency" of Meanguera.

The Chamber noted that the initial formal manifestation of the dispute occurred in 1854, when a circular letter made widely known El Salvador's claim to Meanguera. Furthermore, in 1856 and 1879 El Salvador's official journal carried reports concerning administrative acts relating to it without reactions or protest by Honduras. The Chamber observed that from the late 19th century documentary evidence of extensive *effectivités* of El Salvador established that the presence of El Salvador on Meanguera intensified, still without objection or protest from Honduras.

It was only in January 1991 that the Government of Honduras first made any protest to the Government of El Salvador concerning Meanguera, which was rejected by the latter Government. This protest was regarded by the Chamber as having been made too late to affect the presumption of acquiescence on the part of Honduras. Opinion, para. 364. The conduct of Honduras vis-a-vis earlier *effectivités* revealed some form of tacit consent to the situation. Id. The Chamber stated its conclusions with respect to the disputed islands as follows:]

368. * * * It is the Chamber's duty, under Article 5 of the Special Agreement, to take into account the "rules of International Law applicable between the Parties, including, where pertinent, the provisions of the General Treaty of Peace". In relation to the islands in dispute, the "documents which were issued by the Spanish Crown or by any other Spanish authority, whether secular or ecclesiastical", do not appear sufficient to "indicate the jurisdictions or limits of territories or settlements" in terms of Article 26 of that Treaty, so that no firm conclusion can be based upon such material, taken in isolation, for deciding between the two claims to an *uti possidetis juris* title. Under the final sentence of Article 26, the Chamber is however entitled to consider both the effective interpretation of the *uti possidetis juris* by the Parties, in the years following independence, as throwing light on the application of the principle and the evidence of effective possession and control of an island by one Party without protest by the other, as pointing to acquiescence. The evidence as to possession and control, and the display and exercise of sovereignty, by Honduras over El Tigre and by El Salvador over Meanguera (to which Meanguerita is an appendage), coupled in each case with the attitude of the other Party, clearly shows however, in the view of the Chamber, that Honduras was treated as having succeeded to

Spanish sovereignty over El Tigre, and El Salvador to Spanish sovereignty over Meanguera and Meanguerita.

[The Court went on to consider the legal regime of the waters of the Gulf of Fonseca, the portion of the dispute in which Nicaragua was permitted to intervene. The Chamber held that the Gulf constitutes an historic bay, Opinion paras. 384–393, 404–405, and that, as in the case of the land and island disputes, the principle of *uti possidetis juris* controlled. The Chamber noted that the bay had been a single State bay during the greater part of its known history and had not been divided or apportioned between the different administrative units which became the three coastal States. There had been no attempt to divide and delimit the waters according to the principle of *uti possidetis juris.* The delimitation effected between Nicaragua and Honduras in 1900, which was substantially an application of the method of equidistance, was not in any way inspired by the application of the *uti possidetis juris.* The Chamber therefore concluded that a joint succession of the three States to the maritime area had occurred, and their joint sovereignty over the area was held to be the logical outcome of the principle of *uti possidetis juris* itself. Opinion, para. 405. The Chamber found that the waters of the Gulf are subject to a condominium regime and that all three states have equivalent legal rights in the Gulf waters up to the bay closing line. (Excluded from this regime are a belt extending three miles from the littoral of the three states, which is subject to the exclusive sovereignty of the coastal state, and those areas subject to special treaty or customary delimitations.) Opinion, para. 414. The waters of the Gulf are subject to existing rights of innocent passage through both the three-mile belt and the waters held under joint sovereignty. The Chamber also found that there is a territorial sea proper seaward of the closing line of the Gulf and, since there is a condominium of the waters of the Gulf, there is a tripartite presence at the closing line and the three coastal States are entitled to the territorial sea, the continental shelf and the exclusive economic zone outside the bay. Opinion, para. 418. Finally the Chamber laid down general principles applicable to delimiting entitlements of the three states to these maritime areas seaward of the closing line of the Gulf. Opinion, paras. 419–420.]

* * *

### *Notes*

1. On international boundaries, see generally 1 Oppenheim 661–670; 1 Hackworth 713–83; 3 Whiteman 1–871; Hyde 439–50, 489–510; Boggs, International Boundaries (1940); Jones, Boundary Making (1945). With particular reference to the thalweg doctrine, see 1 Hyde 443–49. Disputes often arise concerning the proper interpretation of agreements establishing boundaries. See, *e.g.,* the case concerning the Temple of Preah Vihear (Cambodia v. Thailand), 1962 I.C.J. 6 and the demarcation of the boundary between the Republic of Iraq and Kuwait established in a 1963 Agreement required by the U.N. Security Counsel as a condition of the 1991 cease-fire. S/RES 687 (1992). The latter demarcation was effected by the U.N. Iraq–Kuwait Boundary Demarcation Commission. The Security Council adopted Resolution 773 on August 26, 1992, which stated in part:

> *Recalling* in this connection that through the demarcation process the Commission is not reallocating territory between Kuwait and Iraq, but it is

simply carrying out the technical task necessary to demarcate for the first time the precise coordinates of the boundary set out in the Agreed Minutes between the State of Kuwait and the Republic of Iraq regarding the restoration of Friendly Relations, Recognition and Related Matters signed by them on 4 October 1963, and that this task is being carried out in the special circumstances following Iraq's invasion of Kuwait and pursuant to resolution 687 (1991) * * *.

* * *

4. *Underlines* its guarantee of the inviolability of the above-mentioned international boundary and its decision to take as appropriate all necessary measures to that end in accordance with the Charter, as provided for in paragraph 4 of resolution 687 (1991) * * *

Vol. 3, No. 3 Foreign Pol'y Bull. 57–58 (Nov./Dec. 1992).

2. The Egypt–Israel Arbitration Tribunal: Award in Boundary Dispute Concerning the Taba Area (September 29, 1988), 27 I.L.M. 1421 (1988), involved resolution of a controversy between Egypt and Israel concerning the location of nearly 100 "pillars" of demarcation originally erected in 1906 and 1907. The 1979 Israel–Egypt Treaty of Peace established that the permanent international boundary between Egypt and Israel is "the recognized international boundary between Egypt and the former mandated territory of Palestine." A joint Israeli–Egyptian Commission was established for the purpose, inter alia, of "organiz[ing] the demarcation of the international boundary." When this commission failed to agree on the location of the pillars demarcating the boundary line, the issues were submitted to arbitration. In the course of its award, the tribunal stated:

* * * If a boundary line is once demarcated jointly by the parties concerned, the demarcation is considered as an authentic interpretation of the boundary agreement even if deviations may have occurred or if there are some inconsistencies with maps. This has been confirmed in practice and legal doctrine, especially for the case that a long time has elapsed since demarcation. Ress concludes an examination of cases with the following statement:

"If the parties have considered over a long time the demarcated frontier as valid, this is an authentic interpretation of the relevant international title." (Ress, *The Delimitation and Demarcation of Frontiers in International Treaties and Maps,* Institute of International Public Law and International Relations in Thessaloniki 1985, pp. 435–37, especially 437; see also Münch, "Karten im Völkerrecht", *Gedächtnisschrift für Friedrich Klein,* Munich 1977, p. 344). It may also be referred to the Judgment of the International Court of Justice in the *Temple* case where the Court states:

"In general, when two countries establish a frontier between them, one of the primary objects is to achieve stability and finality. This is impossible if the line so established can, at any moment, and on the basis of a continuously available process, be called in question, and its rectification claimed, whenever any inaccuracy by reference to a clause in the parent treaty is discovered. Such a process could continue indefinitely, and finality should never be reached so long as possible errors still remained to be discovered. Such a frontier, so far from being stable, would be completely precarious." (1962 *ICJ Reports* 34)

27 I.L.M. 105–106. See Kaikobad, Some Observations on the Doctrine of Continuity and Finality of Boundaries, 1983 Brit.Y.B.I.L. 119 (1983), where the author suggests that the principle of finality and stability in various manifestations constitutes one of the more fundamental and important precepts in the law of international boundaries.

3. A state may have less than absolute authority over resources below the surface of its territory. For example, prevailing authority supports the rule that a state may not draw more from liquid resources below the surface that straddle national boundaries than its proportional share of the common pool. See generally Lagoni, Oil and Gas Deposits Across National Frontiers, 73 A.J.I.L. 215 (1979).

### 2. *Airspace*

#### *CONVENTION ON INTERNATIONAL CIVIL AVIATION*

Signed at Chicago, December 7, 1944.
61 Stat. 1180, T.I.A.S. 1591, 15 U.N.T.S. 295.

Art. 1. The contracting States recognize that every State has complete and exclusive sovereignty over the airspace above its territory.

#### *Notes*

1. 49 U.S.C.A. § 1508(a) provides: "The United States of America is declared to possess and exercise complete and exclusive national sovereignty in the airspace of the United States, including the airspace above all inland waters and airspace above those portions of the adjacent marginal high seas, bays, and lakes, over which by international law or treaty or convention the United States exercises national jurisdiction."

2. On the rights of states over the airspace above the seas adjacent to their land territory, see p. 1240 infra.

3. Since 1950, the United States has promulgated regulations establishing Air Defense Identification Zones (ADIZs) which extend at some points several hundred miles beyond the territorial sea. See 14 CFR 99 et seq. (1979); 49 U.S.C.A. §§ 1521–23 (amending 49 U.S.C.A. §§ 701–705). Foreign aircraft entering ADIZs are required to file flight plans and to make periodic position reports. Canada established ADIZs in 1951.

In 1956, during the Algerian conflict, France established a "zone of special responsibility," extending some eighty miles from the coast of Algeria, within which aircraft were required to file detailed information regarding their flight, to stay within assigned corridors, and to maintain contact with ground identification stations. See McDougal, Lasswell & Vlasic, Law and Public Order in Space 307–11 (1963). Some ten states other than the U.S. and Canada have maintained ADIZs.

4. On what basis, if any, can these extensions of jurisdiction be justified? See Note, Air Defense Identification Zones, Creeping Jurisdiction in the Airspace, 18 Va.J.Int'l L. 485, 497–505 (1978), concluding (1) that extant international conventions tend to reject claims of jurisdiction over airflights beyond the territorial sea, (2) that self-defense cannot be a justification because of the absence of an imminent threat and of proportionality, and (3) that the practice of establishing ADIZs has not become customary international law.

5. Originally, a state's authority over airspace above its territory was thought to extend *usque ad coelum.* More recently, efforts have been made to define more precise limits and, specifically, to determine where airspace ends and outer space begins. For a discussion of the various criteria of delimitation that have been proposed, see U.N.Doc. A/AC. 105/C. 2/7 (1970).

6. In the 1982 Law of the Sea Convention, the maximum breadth of the territorial sea is twelve miles. See p. 1245 infra. The boundary affects aircraft routes through straits and archipelagic waters that are between six and twenty-four miles wide, imposing a substantial limitation on the absolute sovereignty of the coastal states. Aircraft are guaranteed a "right of transit" through these areas so long as they conform to certain procedures, such as continuous monitoring of specified radio channels. See Articles 37–39, 42, 44, 53–54, discussed in greater detail at p. 1262 infra. See also Grandison and Meyer International Straits, Global Communications and the Evolving Law of the Sea, 8 Vand.J.Transnat'l L. 393 (1974–75); McNees, Freedom of Transit Through International Straits, 6 J.Mar.L. 175 (1974–75).

# Chapter 5

# ORGANIZATIONS, COMPANIES AND INDIVIDUALS IN INTERNATIONAL LAW

This chapter concerns entities other than states. The material deals with the legal status and capacity in international law of public international organizations, intergovernmental and nongovernmental associations, transnational (or multinational) companies and consortia. It also includes material on the position of the individual in international law.

## SECTION 1. INTERNATIONAL ORGANIZATIONS

The proliferation of international organizations has been a notable feature of international relations during the last fifty years. Such organizations are either nongovernmental or intergovernmental, a basic distinction for legal purposes. Within each of these categories, the organizations exhibit remarkable diversity in function, structure, and effect.

### PUBLIC INTERNATIONAL ORGANIZATIONS

In international law, the term "international organization" is generally used to refer to organizations composed entirely or mainly of states and usually established by treaty. The treaty is, as a rule, the constitutive instrument. These organizations are often referred to as public or intergovernmental international organizations. Hundreds of such organizations are now in existence. They vary widely in scope, structure and function. The United Nations includes nearly all the states of the world as members and a wide range of functions. Linked to the United Nations are autonomous "specialized agencies" for example FAO (the Food and Agriculture Organization), WHO (World Health Organization), and ICAO (International Civil Aviation Organization). The World Bank and the International Monetary

Fund are also specialized agencies of the United Nations operating under their own statutes. Many international organizations are regional bodies, either broad in scope or specialized. Still others are concerned with a particular commodity or with an activity in a particular area. See generally, Chapters 17, 18, and 19.

The Restatement (Third) Part II, Chapter 2, Introductory Note, states:

> International organizations are created by international agreements and are governed by the law pertaining to such agreements. The law of international organizations has become a separate subdivision of international law, much as in national legal systems the law of corporations developed independently of the law of contracts even while retaining links to it. Particularly when organs of an international organization are authorized by its constitutive agreement to make decisions, allocate funds, admit and expel members and interpret or even amend the constitutive agreement, the organization can be said to have a law of its own, a kind of "international constitutional law."

Typically, an international organization has a plenary organ in which all member states are represented, a smaller body entrusted with certain important decisions (e.g., an executive committee or council), and a secretariat or staff to carry out administrative, representative, advisory, and technical functions. The larger international organizations also have subsidiary bodies such as commissions and agencies which are under the authority of the principal organs but which often have considerable authority delegated to them. The United Nations has well over a hundred such subsidiary bodies performing executive, advisory, rule-making, and even judicial functions. Such prominent international organizations as the U.N. Children's Fund (UNICEF), the U.N. Development Program and the High Commissioner for Refugees are in this category.

## NONGOVERNMENTAL INTERNATIONAL ORGANIZATIONS

While international law is concerned mainly with intergovernmental organizations, nongovernmental organizations (commonly known as NGOs) play an active role on the international scene and in some cases have a recognized legal status under treaties and other international arrangements. The Charter of the United Nations provides for consultative arrangements between the Economic and Social Council and nongovernmental organizations (Article 71) and some hundreds of such NGOs have consultative status under that provision. Similar arrangements exist in other intergovernmental organizations. The numerous international nongovernmental organizations range over the entire array of human activity. They include worldwide organizations involved in humanitarian, health, human rights and environmental matters; professional and scientific associations; the federations and international unions made up of national associations representing labor or employers; religious bodies; scientific academies; and so on. Many of these organizations have been accorded the right to express their views to official international bodies and in some circumstances they perform functions delegated to them by international instruments or governmental decisions. A notable example is the distinctive role of the International Committee of the Red Cross, a nongovernmental body, which has important functions under the Geneva Conventions on the Laws of the War and in delivering humanitarian supplies to areas ravaged by hostilities or famine. Some scientific bodies, though nongovernmental, have also been accorded official functions by international governmental organizations. Nonetheless, nongovernmental organizations in general have not been accorded the status of international legal persons. Their legal capacity and their rights are governed by applicable municipal law. But see Hondius, European Convention on the Recognition of the Legal Personality of International Nongovernmental Organizations, 7 The Philanthropist 6 (1988).

NGOs have played increasingly important roles in the human rights and environmental areas. For example, organizations such as Amnesty International and the Americas Watch Committee have assisted the U.N. Human Rights Commission in its efforts to monitor human rights violations around the world and organizations such as Greenpeace and Friends of the Earth have played watchdog roles in identifying violators of environmental restrictions. See, e.g., Steiner, Diverse Partners: Non-Governmental Organizations in the Human Rights Movement (1991); Cohen, The Role of Nongovernmental Organizations in the Drafting of the Convention on the Rights of the Child, 12 Hum.Rts.Q. 137 (1990); Neier, Lillich, Fruhling, Posner, & Shifter, Transitions in the Midst of Crisis: the Role of the Nongovernmental Organization in Transitions to Democracy and the Rule of Law, 5 Am.U.J.Int'l L. & Pol'y. 970 (1990); Weissbrodt, The Role of International Organizations in the Implementation of Human Rights and Humanitarian Law in Situations of Armed Conflict, 21 Vand.J.Transnat'l L. 313 (1988).

## MULTINATIONAL PUBLIC ENTERPRISES

States have also created entities of an international character to conduct activities of a financial or commercial character for state enterprises and private companies. Such entities are generally established by treaty but unlike the public international organizations they are for the most part institutions under municipal law. Many operate like private corporations and have sometimes been called "international public corporations." However, that expression has been used in such different senses that it tends to mislead. See Yokota, How Useful is the Notion of International Public Corporation Today? in Essays in Honour of Judge Manfred Lachs 551 (Makarczyk ed., 1984).

An example of a public multinational financial institution is the Bank of International Settlements, established by a 1930 Convention of six states. It operates under a Swiss Charter and is governed by Swiss law to the extent not inconsistent with the Convention. Another European organization known as EUROFIMA (which buys railroad equipment for national railway systems) is also a treaty organization which operates in a commercial manner under its conventions and statutes; matters not covered by these instruments are subject to the municipal law of the headquarters state. Several multinational public enterprises operate as consortia in the fields of aviation and shipping. Scandinavian Air Lines and Air Afrique are examples. See section 4.

An important multinational enterprise—INTELSAT, the International Telecommunications Satellite Organization, was established by a 1973 treaty among a large number of states. It is an operating organization composed of members that are public or private entities responsible for national aspects of global satellite communications. See 23 U.S.T. 3813, TIAS No. 7532. Unlike the other multinational enterprises referred to above, the INTELSAT Agreement does not accept the municipal law of its headquarters state as residual law. Instead, it provides that legal disputes are to be resolved by an arbitration tribunal on the basis of the INTELSAT Agreement itself and "generally accepted principles of law." See Chapter 18 at p. 1480.

## SECTION 2. INTERNATIONAL LEGAL PERSONALITY AND POWERS OF INTERNATIONAL ORGANIZATIONS

The material that follows deals primarily with the question of whether international governmental organizations are legal persons and the implications of that conclusion. The attribution of international legal personality involves the capacity to perform legal acts on the international plane rather than within a municipal law system. In practice, international organizations have exercised international legal capacity in a variety of ways. "International organizations have concluded treaties, made use of the high seas with ships flying their own flag, created international peace forces, convened international conferences with representatives of States and other international organizations, organized internally the functioning and procedure of their organs, sent diplomatic representatives to member and non-member States, have received permanent missions from member States, undertaken administration tasks in certain territories, presented protests to States and brought claims into the international plane, and have participated in the activities of other international organizations with envoys, observers, etc." Rama-Montalo, International Legal Personality and Implied Powers of International Organizations, 44 Brit.Y.B.I.L. 123 (1970).

In exercising international legal capacity and correlatively in assuming international responsibility for their acts, international organizations draw a distinction in terms of legal powers and obligations between the organization and its member states. That distinction also requires that the organization possess organs capable of exercising such legal capacity and responsibilities on the international plane. Standing conferences of states under multilateral conventions or loose associations such as the British Commonwealth lack such organs and consequently do not exercise the attributes of international personality. An international organization may also have been denied such international personality by its constitutive instrument or decisions of its members. An example is the Bank for International Settlements which, though international in purpose and composition, was granted legal capacity in the municipal law of each of its member states but not international legal capacity.

Although it is now recognized that most international governmental organizations have international legal personality, there are still doctrinal controversies (with practical implications) on certain legal issues, namely:

(1) Whether international personality is an inherent (or objective) attribute of international organization or whether it depends on the constitutive instrument and the powers expressly or impliedly granted to it.

(2) Whether there is a precise category of legal rights and duties derived from the fact of international personality or whether the rights and duties depend on the powers and functions of the international organization.

(3) Whether the denial of international personality by the member states means that the entity cannot be regarded as an international organization under international law.

## A. CAPACITY TO BRING CLAIMS AGAINST STATES

### REPARATION FOR INJURIES SUFFERED IN THE SERVICE OF THE UNITED NATIONS

International Court of Justice, Advisory Opinion, 1949.
1949 I.C.J. 174.

THE COURT. * * * The first question asked of the Court is as follows:

"In the event of an agent of the United Nations in the performance of his duties suffering injury in circumstances involving the responsibility of a State, has the United Nations, as an Organization, the capacity to bring an international claim against the responsible *de jure* or *de facto* government with a view to obtaining the reparation due in respect of the damage caused (a) to the United Nations, (b) to the victim or to persons entitled through him?"

It will be useful to make the following preliminary observations:

(a) The Organization of the United Nations will be referred to usually, but not invariably, as "the Organization".

(b) Questions I(a) and I(b) refer to "an international claim against the responsible *de jure* or *de facto* government." The Court understands that these questions are directed to claims against a State, and will, therefore, in this opinion, use the expression "State" or "defendant State."

(c) The Court understands the word "agent" in the most liberal sense, that is to say, any person who, whether a paid official or not, and whether permanently employed or not, has been charged by an organ of the Organization with carrying out, or helping to carry out, one of its functions—in short, any person through whom it acts.

(d) As this question assumes an injury suffered in such circumstances as to involve a State's responsibility, it must be supposed, for the purpose of this Opinion, that the damage results from a failure by the State to perform obligations of which the purpose is to protect the agents of the Organization in the performance of their duties.

(e) The position of a defendant State which is not a member of the Organization is dealt with later, and for the present the Court will assume that the defendant State is a Member of the Organization. * * *

Competence to bring an international claim is, for those possessing it, the capacity to resort to the customary methods recognized by international law for the establishment, the presentation and the settlement of claims. Among these methods may be mentioned protest, request for an enquiry, negotiation, and request for submission to an arbitral tribunal or to the Court in so far as this may be authorized by the Statute.

This capacity certainly belongs to the State; a State can bring an international claim against another State. Such a claim takes the form of a claim between two political entities, equal in law, similar in form, and both the direct subjects of international law. It is dealt with by means of negotiation, and cannot, in the present state of the law as to international jurisdiction, be submitted to a tribunal, except with the consent of the States concerned.

When the Organization brings a claim against one of its Members, this claim will be presented in the same manner, and regulated by the same procedure. It may, when necessary, be supported by the political means at the disposal of the Organization. In these ways the Organization would find a method for securing the observance of its rights by the Member against which it has a claim.

But, in the international sphere, has the Organization such a nature as involves the capacity to bring an international claim? In order to answer this question, the Court must first enquire whether the Charter has given the Organization such a position that it possesses, in regard to its Members, rights which it is entitled to ask them to respect. In other words, does the Organization possess international personality? This is no doubt a doctrinal expression, which has sometimes given rise to controversy. But it will be used here to mean that if the Organization is recognized as having that personality, it is an entity capable of availing itself of obligations incumbent upon its Members.

To answer this question, which is not settled by the actual terms of the Charter, we must consider what characteristics it was intended thereby to give to the Organization.

The subjects of law in any legal system are not necessarily identical in their nature or in the extent of their rights, and their nature depends upon the needs of the community. Throughout its history, the development of international law has been influenced by the requirements of international life, and the progressive increase in the collective activities of States has already given rise to instances of action upon the international plane by certain entities which are not States. This development culminated in the establishment in June 1945 of an international organization whose purposes and principles are specified in the Charter of the United Nations. But to achieve these ends the attribution of international personality is indispensable.

The Charter has not been content to make the Organization created by it merely a centre "for harmonizing the actions of nations in the attainment of these common ends" (Article 1, para. 4). It has equipped that centre with organs, and has given it special tasks. It has defined the position of the Members in relation to the Organization by requiring them to give it every assistance in any action undertaken by it (Article 2, para. 5), and to accept and carry out the decisions of the Security Council; by authorizing the General Assembly to make recommendations to the Members; by giving the Organization legal capacity and privileges and immunities in the territory of each of its Members; and by providing for the conclusion of agreements between the Organization and its Members. Practice—in particular the conclusion of conventions to which the Organization is a party—has confirmed this character of the Organization, which occupies a position in certain respects in detachment from its Members, and which is under a duty to remind them, if need be, of certain obligations. It must be added that the Organization is a political body, charged with political tasks of an important character, and covering a wide field, namely, the maintenance of international peace and security, the development of friendly relations among nations, and the achievement of international cooperation in the solution of problems of an economic, social, cultural or humanitarian character (Article 1); and in dealing with its Members it employs political means. The "Convention on the Privileges and Immunities of the United Nations" of 1946 creates rights and duties between each of the signatories and the Organization (see, in particular, Section 35). It is difficult to see how such a convention could operate except upon the international plane and as between parties possessing international personality.

In the opinion of the Court, the Organization was intended to exercise and enjoy, and is in fact exercising and enjoying, functions and rights which can only be explained on the basis of the possession of a large measure of international personality and the capacity to operate upon an international plane. It is at present the supreme type of international organization, and it could not carry out the intentions of its founders if it was devoid of international personality. It must be acknowledged that its Members, by entrusting certain functions to it, with the attendant duties and responsibilities, have clothed it with the competence required to enable those functions to be effectively discharged.

Accordingly, the Court has come to the conclusion that the Organization is an international person. That is not the same thing as saying that it is a State, which it certainly is not, or that its legal personality and rights and duties are the same as those of a State. Still less is it the same thing as saying that it is "a super-State," whatever that expression may mean. It does not even imply that all its rights and duties must be upon the international plane, any more than all the rights and duties of a State must be upon that plane. What it does mean is that it is a subject of international law and capable of possessing international rights and duties, and that it has capacity to maintain its rights by bringing international claims.

The next question is whether the sum of the international rights of the Organization comprises the right to bring the kind of international claim described in the Request for this Opinion. That is a claim against a State to obtain reparation in respect of the damage caused by the injury of an agent of the Organization in the course of the performance of his duties. Whereas a State possesses the totality of international rights and duties recognized by international law, the rights and duties of an entity such as the Organization must depend upon its purposes and functions as specified or implied in its constituent documents and developed in practice. The functions of the Organization are of such a character that they could not be effectively discharged if they involved the concurrent action, on the international plane, of fifty-eight or more Foreign Offices, and the Court concludes that the Members have endowed the Organization with capacity to bring international claims when necessitated by the discharge of its functions.

[With respect to Question I(a), the Court continued:]

* * * It cannot be doubted that the Organization has the capacity to bring an international claim against one of its Members which has caused injury to it by a breach of its international obligations towards it. The damage specified in Question I(a) means exclusively damage caused to the interests of the Organization itself, to its administrative machine, to its property and assets and to the interests of which it is the guardian. It is clear that the Organization has the capacity to bring a claim for this damage. As the claim is based on the breach of an international obligation on the part of the Member held responsible by the Organization, the Member cannot contend that this obligation is governed by municipal law, and the Organization is justified in giving its claim the character of an international claim.

When the Organization has sustained damage resulting from a breach by a Member of its international obligations, it is impossible to see how it can obtain reparation unless it possesses capacity to bring an international claim. It cannot be supposed that in such an event all the Members of the Organization, save the defendant State, must combine to bring a claim against the defendant for the damage suffered by the Organization.

The Court is not called upon to determine the precise extent of the reparation which the Organization would be entitled to recover. It may, however, be said that the measure of the reparation should depend upon the amount of the damage which the Organization has suffered as the result of the wrongful act or omission of the defendant State and should be calculated in accordance with the rules of international law. * * *

[With respect to Question I(b), the Court stated:]

* * *

The Court is here faced with a new situation. The questions to which it gives rise can only be solved by realizing that the situation is dominated by the provisions of the Charter considered in the light of the principles of international law.

The question * * * presupposes that the injury for which the reparation is demanded arises from a breach of an obligation designed to help an agent of the Organization in the performance of his duties. It is not a case in which the wrongful act or omission would merely constitute a breach of the general obligations of a State concerning the position of aliens; claims made under this head would be within the competence of the national State and not, as a general rule, within that of the Organization.

The Charter does not expressly confer upon the Organization the capacity to include, in its claim for reparation, damage caused to the victim or to persons entitled through him. The Court must therefore begin by enquiring whether the provisions of the Charter concerning the functions of the Organization, and the part played by its agents in the performance of those functions, imply for the Organization power to afford its agents the limited protection that would consist in the bringing of a claim on their behalf for reparation for damage suffered in such circumstances. Under international law, the Organization must be deemed to have those powers which, though not expressly provided in the Charter, are conferred upon it by necessary implication as being essential to the performance of its duties. This principle of law was applied by the Permanent Court of International Justice to the International Labour Organization in its Advisory Opinion No. 13 of July 23rd, 1926 (Series B., No. 13, p. 18), and must be applied to the United Nations.

Having regard to its purposes and functions already referred to, the Organization may find it necessary, and has in fact found it necessary, to entrust its agents with important missions to be performed in disturbed parts of the world. Many missions, from their very nature, involve the agents in unusual dangers to which ordinary persons are not exposed. For the same reason, the injuries suffered by its agents in these circumstances will sometimes have occurred in such a manner that their national State would not be justified in bringing a claim for reparation on the ground of diplomatic protection, or, at any rate, would not feel disposed to do so. Both to ensure the efficient and independent performance of these missions and to afford effective support to its agents, the Organization must provide them with adequate protection. * * *

* * * For that purpose, it is necessary that, when an infringement occurs, the Organization should be able to call upon the responsible State to remedy its default, and, in particular, to obtain from the State reparation for the damage that the default may have caused to its agent.

In order that the agent may perform his duties satisfactorily, he must feel that this protection is assured to him by the Organization, and that he may count on it. To ensure the independence of the agent, and, consequently, the independent action of the Organization itself, it is essential that in performing his duties he need not have to rely on any other protection than that of the Organization (save of course for the more direct and immediate protection due from the State in whose territory he may be). In particular, he should not have to rely on the protection of his own State. If he had to rely on that State, his independence might well be compromised, contrary to the principle applied by Article 100 of the Charter. And lastly, it is essential that—whether the agent belongs to a powerful or to a weak State; to one more affected or less affected by the complications of international life; to one in sympathy or not in sympathy with the mission of the agent—he should know that in the performance of his duties he is under the protection of the Organization. This assurance is even more necessary when the agent is stateless.

Upon examination of the character of the functions entrusted to the Organization and of the nature of the missions of its agents, it becomes clear that the capacity of the Organization to exercise a measure of functional protection of its agents arises by necessary intendment out of the Charter.

The obligations entered into by States to enable the agents of the Organization to perform their duties are undertaken not in the interest of the agents, but in that of the Organization. When it claims redress for a breach of these obligations, the Organization is invoking its own right, the right that the obligations due to it should be respected. On this ground, it asks for reparation of the injury suffered, for "it is a principle of international law that the breach of an engagement involves an obligation to make reparation in an adequate form"; as was stated by the Permanent Court in its Judgment No. 8 of July 26th, 1927 (Series A., No. 9, p. 21). In claiming reparation based on the injury suffered by its agent, the Organization does not represent the agent, but is asserting its own right, the right to secure respect for undertakings entered into towards the Organization.

Having regard to the foregoing considerations, and to the undeniable right of the Organization to demand that its Members shall fulfil the obligations entered into by them in the interest of the good working of the Organization, the Court is of the opinion that, in the case of a breach of these obligations, the Organization has the capacity to claim adequate reparation, and that in assessing this reparation it is authorized to include the damage suffered by the victim or by persons entitled through him.

The question remains whether the Organization has "the capacity to bring an international claim against the responsible *de jure* or *de facto* government with a view to obtaining the reparation due in respect of the damage caused (a) to the United Nations, (b) to the victim or to persons entitled through him" when the defendant State is not a member of the Organization.

In considering this aspect of Questions I(a) and (b), it is necessary to keep in mind the reasons which have led the Court to give an affirmative answer to it when the defendant State is a Member of the Organization. It has now been established that the Organization has capacity to bring claims on the international plane, and that it possesses a right of functional protection in respect of its agents. Here again the Court is authorized to assume that the damage suffered involves the responsibility of a State, and it is not called upon to express an opinion upon the various ways in which that responsibility might be engaged. Accordingly the question is whether the Organization has capacity to bring a claim against the defendant State to recover reparation in respect of that damage or whether, on the contrary, the defendant State, not being a member, is justified in raising the objection that the Organization lacks the capacity to bring an international claim. On this point, the Court's opinion is that fifty States, representing the vast majority of the members of the international community, had the power, in conformity with international law, to bring into being an entity possessing objective international personality, and not merely personality recognized by them alone, together with capacity to bring international claims.

Accordingly, the Court arrives at the conclusion that an affirmative answer should be given to Questions I(a) and (b) whether or not the defendant State is a Member of the United Nations.

Question II is as follows:

"In the event of an affirmative reply on point I(b), how is action by the United Nations to be reconciled with such rights as may be possessed by the State of which the victim is a national?"

* * * When the victim has a nationality, cases can clearly occur in which the injury suffered by him may engage the interest both of his national State and of the Organization. In such an event, competition between the State's right of diplomatic protection and the Organization's right of functional protection might arise, and this is the only case with which the Court is invited to deal.

In such a case, there is no rule of law which assigns priority to the one or to the other, or which compels either the State or the Organization to refrain from bringing an international claim. The Court sees no reason why the parties concerned should not find solutions inspired by goodwill and common sense, and as between the Organization and its Members it draws attention to their duty to render "every assistance" provided by Article 2, paragraph 5, of the Charter.

Although the bases of the two claims are different, that does not mean that the defendant State can be compelled to pay the reparation due in respect of the damage twice over. International tribunals are already familiar with the problem of a claim in which two or more national States are interested, and they know how to protect the defendant State in such a case.

The question of reconciling action by the Organization with the rights of a national State may arise in another way; that is to say, when the agent bears the nationality of the defendant State.

The ordinary practice whereby a State does not exercise protection on behalf of one of its nationals against a State which regards him as its own national, does not constitute a precedent which is relevant here. The action of the Organization is in fact based not upon the nationality of the victim, but upon his status as agent of the Organization. Therefore it does not matter whether or not the State to which the claim is addressed regards him as its own national, because the question of nationality is not pertinent to the admissibility of the claim. * * *

* * *

[The individual opinions of Judges Alvarez and Azevedo, and the dissenting opinion of Judges Krylov and Badawi Pasha and the dissenting opinion by Judge Hackworth are omitted.]

### *Notes*

1. Does the opinion of the Court rest upon the "implied powers doctrine" as many writers have assumed or does it base its conclusion on the finding of international personality in the objective characteristics of the organization? What difference does it make? Consider the following comment:

> If all these activities have their legal basis in the personality of the organization, it is sufficient that an organization should possess international personality for it to have the legal capacity to perform them. On the other hand, if they have their basis in implied powers the question will be posed in different terms for each organization. Likewise, member States

> will in each case possess the right to claim that certain activity of the organization does not conform to, or goes beyond, the purposes and functions expressed or implied in the constitutional provisions and therefore to refuse to collaborate financially or otherwise in its carrying out; they will be entitled to do so on the simple ground of legality, because it is their right as members to insist that the limitation of sovereignty which results from their agreement to be bound by a majority decision will only be applied in that frame of activities which they consented to grant the organization in subscribing to the constituent instrument.[1] If all these activities are based on the international personality of the organization, they cannot be assailed simply on the ground that they are not expressly foreseen in the constitutional provisions. But, if they have their basis in the implied powers doctrine, an international tribunal might hold them to be unlawful on the ground that they do not constitute a "necessary implication" or that they are not "essential to the performance of its duties" or that they are not "within the scope of the functions of the organization".

Rama–Montaldo, 44 Brit.Y.B.I.L. at 123–134.*

2. A close reading of the Court's opinion suggests that it followed both doctrinal approaches but used each for different conclusions. It referred to the "characteristics of the organization" and to activities which "can only be based on a large measure of international personality and the capacity to operate upon an international plane." It concluded, on that basis, that the organization had the capacity to maintain its rights by international claims that is, "to negotiate, to conclude a special agreement and to prosecute a claim before an international tribunal." But after the Court reached this conclusion, it turned to a different question, to wit: whether the general right to bring a claim "comprises the right to bring the kind of international claim described in the Request for this Opinion." In answering this question, the Court did not rely on inherent legal personality; it said the answer depended on the "purposes and functions as specified or implied in its constituent documents and developed in practice." This led the Court to consider the powers of the Organization to protect its agents as relevant to the particular claim.

3. May members act only through the organization and not independently on matters covered by the functions of the organization? This question arose in a case involving the European Community. The relevant issue was whether a treaty on European road transport (ERTA) could be negotiated by the Community. The Court of Justice of the European Community referred to the powers of the Community and said:

> This Community authority excludes the possibility of a concurrent authority on the part of member States, since any initiative taken outside the framework of the common institutions would be incompatible with the unity of the Common Market and the uniform application of Community law.

ERTA Case, 47 I.L.R. 278, 305 (1971).

Would this conclusion be appropriate for the United Nations or one of its specialized agencies?

1. Cf. I.C.J. Reports, 1962, p. 167: "Save as they have entrusted the organization with the attainment of these common ends the Member States retain their freedom of action."

4. Some scholars have argued that international organizations that meet certain criteria (e.g., are not under the jurisdiction of any state) have in law and practice "objective legal personality" and that they may therefore perform any international act which they are in a practical position to perform, subject only to the following legal limitations: (1) constitutional provisions forbidding acts for certain purposes or procedures; (2) the principle that the acts do not impose obligations on member states unless they have so agreed or on third parties without a special legal basis. See Seyersted, Objective International Personality of Intergovernmental Organizations (1963); also Balladore Pallieri, quoted in Rama–Montaldo, at 118–20. One difficulty in demonstrating that this position has been followed is that acts carried out by international organizations are virtually always said to be legally justified on the basis of constitutional powers and functions rather than on grounds of inherent powers. Consequently the acts, if challenged, are regarded as valid or invalid in terms of the delegated or implied purposes and competence of the organization. This has been evident in the cases brought before the International Court of Justice involving challenges to the legal authority of the United Nations. See, for example, Advisory Opinions on U.N. Administrative Tribunal, 1954 I.C.J. 47, on Certain Expenses of the United Nations, 1962 I.C.J. 151, discussed below and at p. 359 and on Namibia, 1971 I.C.J. 16, p. 511 infra. There is little reason to expect that any international organizations will assert a general inherent legal power to perform "sovereign" international acts on grounds of their objective legal personality irrespective of the constitutional definition of their functions and powers.

## B. WHO ACTS FOR AN INTERNATIONAL ORGANIZATION?

The constitutive instrument of each international organization prescribes the powers and functions of the organization and also identifies the organs entitled to exercise the powers granted to the organization. As indicated in the *Reparations Case* on p. 348 and in note 4 above, it is necessary to show that an organization has been given expressly or by implication the power to perform the acts in question. The question may also arise whether the acts in question were performed or authorized by the organs empowered to do so by the constituent instrument. If that were not the case, would the action, be an act of the organization? Would it be legally effective if not taken or authorized by the proper organ?

These questions were considered in an advisory opinion of the International Court of Justice concerning Certain Expenses of the United Nations, 1962 I.C.J. 151. The "expenses" referred to were incurred by the United Nations for the United Nations peacekeeping forces in the Suez area and the former Belgian Congo (now Zaire). The General Assembly had included them in the budget as expenses of the Organization. The legality of that decision was questioned by several member states—principally, the U.S.S.R. and France, who both refused to pay. They claimed that the expenses and the underlying actions were not authorized by the proper organ of the United Nations—namely, the Security Council.

The Court, by a majority opinion, ruled that the General Assembly had the authority to decide that the expenses were those of the Organization. In regard to the contention that the action had been taken by the "wrong" organ the Court's opinion declared:

> It is agreed that the action in question is within the scope of the functions of the Organization but it is alleged that it has been initiated or carried out in a manner not in conformity with the division of functions among the several organs which the Charter prescribes. If the action was taken by the wrong organ, it was irregular as a matter of the internal structure, but this would not necessarily mean that the expense incurred was not an expense of the Organization. Both national and international law contemplate cases in which the body corporate or politic may be bound, as to third parties, by an ultra vires act of an agent.

1962 I.C.J. 151, 168.

Although this excerpt refers to the action as binding in respect of third parties, the opinion also supports the conclusion that the Assembly's action is binding on its members. One judge, Sir Gerald Fitzmaurice, thought the latter point should "not be pressed too far." He considered that the Organization may be bound by *ultra vires* acts toward parties outside the Organization but he doubted that the same principle could apply as between the Organization and the member states *inter se.* In that respect he said:

> There can be no doubt that, in principle at least, expenditures incurred in excess of the powers of the expending body are invalid expenditures. * * * If an instrument such as the Charter of the United Nations attributes given functions in an exclusive manner to one of its organs constituted in a certain way—other and different functions being attributed to other and differently constituted organs—this can only be because, in respect of the performance of the functions concerned, importance was attached to the precise constitution of the organ concerned.

1962 I.C.J. 200.

## C. TREATY-MAKING CAPACITY

International organizations have long assumed a capacity to enter into agreements with states, irrespective of whether that power could be found expressed or implied in its constitutive instrument. Fitzmaurice, usually cautious, concluded as far back as 1953 that: "* * * the necessary attribute of international personality, is the power to enter, directly, or mediately, into relationship (by treaty or otherwise) with other international persons." Fitzmaurice, The Law and Procedure of the International Court of Justice, 30 Brit.Y.B.I.L. 2 (1953). However, attributing treaty-making capacity to international personality does not dispose of the question whether a particular treaty falls within the purposes and competence of the international organization. For that question, one must look to the constitution and the powers granted or implied by it; it is not determined by the existence of international personality.

The U.N. Convention on Treaties Concluded Between States and International Organizations or Between Two or More International Organizations provides: "The capacity of an international organization to conclude treaties is governed by the relevant rules of that organization" (Article 6).

The International Law Commission which prepared the draft convention commented on the above article, as follows:

> A question naturally arises as to the nature and characteristics of the "relevant rules" in the matter of an organization's capacity, and it might be tempting to answer this question in general terms, particularly with regard to the part played by *practice.* That would obviously be a mistake which the text of draft article 6 seeks to avert by specifying that "the capacity of an international organization to conclude treaties is governed by the relevant rules of *that* organization".
>
> It should be clearly understood that the question how far practice can play a creative part, particularly in the matter of international organizations' capacity to conclude treaties, cannot be answered uniformly for all international organizations. This question, too, depends on the "rules of the organization"; indeed, it depends on the highest category of those rules—those which form, in some degree, the constitutional law of the organization and which govern in particular the *sources* of the organization's rules. It is theoretically conceivable that, by adopting a rigid legal framework, an organization might exclude practice as a source of its rules. Even without going as far as that, it must be admitted that international organizations differ greatly from one another as regards the part played by practice and the form which it takes, *inter alia* in the matter of their capacity to conclude international agreements. There is nothing surprising in this; the part which practice has played in this matter in an organization like the United Nations, faced in every field with problems fundamental to the future of all mankind, cannot be likened to the part played by practice in a technical organization engaged in humble operational activities in a circumscribed sector.

I.L.C.Rep. 295–96 (1981).

### *Note*

For a discussion of the 1986 Vienna Convention on Treaties Between States and International Organizations, See Gaja, A "New" Vienna Convention on Treaties Between States and International Organizations or Between International Organizations: A Critical Commentary, 1987 Brit.Y.B.Int'l L. 253–269 (1987).

## D. *LOCUS STANDI* BEFORE INTERNATIONAL TRIBUNALS

Under national law, a legal person normally has the capacity to sue and be sued in national courts. International legal personality should logically involve an analogous capacity before international tribunals. This depends, however, on the law governing the tribunal or on the special agreement establishing an arbitral body. The principal international judicial organ, the International Court of Justice, hears only states in contentious proceedings as parties. Advisory opinions may, in contrast, be requested only by certain international organizations—namely, the U.N. General Assembly and the Security Council and, when so authorized by the General Assembly, other U.N. organs and the specialized agencies (Article 96 of the Charter).

One indirect method for overcoming the barrier to *locus standi* of international organizations before the Court is found in section 30 of the Convention on the Privileges and Immunities of the United Nations, which provides that if a difference arises between the United Nations on the one hand and a member state on the other hand in regard to the interpretation or application of the Convention, a request shall be made for an advisory opinion in accordance with the Charter. The opinion of the Court shall be accepted as decisive. Thus in effect, a dispute between the Organization and a state can be the subject of a binding decision by the Court on the basis of a proceeding which, in substance, would be akin to a contentious proceeding. For further discussion on the role of international organizations before the International Court of Justice, see Chapter 10 on Peaceful Settlement of Disputes.

International organizations may be parties to arbitration proceedings in disputes with states. The Headquarters Agreement of 1947 between the United Nations and the United States provided for arbitration in case of disputes under that agreement, and many similar arbitration clauses have been introduced in agreements between international organizations and states.

## E. RESPONSIBILITY OF INTERNATIONAL ORGANIZATIONS

Since international legal personality gives intergovernmental organizations the right to make claims and enter into treaties, it also involves legal responsibility for acts of a delictual or contractual character. If an international organization can be a "plaintiff" on the international plane, it must also be a "defendant" when the circumstances warrant it. In practice, international organizations have long accepted responsibility for tortious acts of its officials, agents, and others (such as troops) acting under their control. Most international organizations have also assumed financial responsibility for contractual obligations *vis-à-vis* states. The member states of the organizations do not, as a rule, incur individual responsibility for the acts or engagements of the organization except as they may bear the costs through the agreed procedures for meeting the financial expenses of the organization.

Questions of responsibility of international organizations have arisen most conspicuously in connection with the peace-keeping activities of the United Nations. These involved complex legal and political issues as to the financial costs incurred in the large-scale peace-keeping activities and the obligation of member states to bear these costs when they regarded the actions as ultra vires. Some of the issues were considered by the International Court in its advisory opinion on Certain Expenses of the United Nations, 1962 I.C.J. 151, 333. Responsibility for damage and personal injuries by military forces provided by member states but acting under the authority of the United Nations were also assumed by the United Nations. Agreements with the governments which contributed troops and with the host (i.e., territorial) governments provided the terms of financial responsibility and the procedures for settling particular cases. For detailed discussions of various aspects of responsibility in respect of United Nations peacekeeping, see Bowett et al., United Nations Forces (1964). The legal issues were especially difficult in regard to the peace-keeping activities in the Congo (now Zaire) in the period 1961–1964. Their complexity is brought out in the article by Salmon, Les Accords Spaak—U Thant du 20 Fevrier 1965, 11 Ann. Francais 468 (1965). See also U.N. Jur.Yb. 41 (1965).

It is well accepted that conduct of an organ or personnel of an international organization within the territory of a state cannot, by reason of that fact alone, be attributed to the territorial state. This is recognized in agreements concluded by the organizations with the host states. For examples of agreements and analysis of legal issues, see Report of 27th Session International Law Commission relating to State Responsibility (draft article 13), [1975] 2 Yb.I.L.C. 87–91. Responsibility of the United Nations for violations of the laws of war by peace-keeping forces under its authority has been considered by the *Institut de Droit International* at its sessions in 1971 (Zagreb) and 1975 (Wiesbaden) on the basis of reports by de Visscher and Hambro. See 54–I Ann. de l'Institut de Droit Int'l 1 (1971); 54–II id. 149 (1971); 56–I id. 81–117, 475–94 (1975).

The contractual responsibilities of international organizations *vis-à-vis* private persons have also generated a substantial body of law and practice especially with respect to applicable law, terms of contracts and settlement of disputes. See Valticos, Les contrats conclus par les organisations internationales avec des personnes privées, 57–I Ann. de l'Institut de Droit Int'l 1 (1977); Jenks, The Proper Law of International Organization (1962).

An issue that has attracted recent attention is the circumstances under which member states of an international organization may be secondarily or concurrently liable to third parties for debts of the organization. This issue was the focus of decisions by the English Court of Appeals in Maclaine Watson & Co. Ltd. v. Department of Trade & Indus., [1988] 3 All E.R. 257, and by the House of Lords in J.H. Rayner Ltd. v. Department of Trade & Indus., [1989] 3 W.L.R. 969, which arose out of the defaults by the International Tin Council (ITC) on contracts to purchase tin and on bank loans entered into as a part of its efforts to support the price of tin through maintenance of a buffer stock. The ITC was an international organization established with "international legal personality" by the Sixth International Tin Agreement to which more than 20 states and the European Community were parties. The Court of Appeals rejected secondary or concurrent liability of the member states, and the House of Lords affirmed.

On the basis of an examination of these English cases, the principal textual authorities, and state practice, Amerasinghe concludes that "the better view is that there is no presumption, when the constituent instrument does not indicate such an intention, that members of an international organization are concurrently or secondarily liable for its obligations. The presumption is thus the reverse. However, though there is no evidence of this in the sources, policy reasons also suggest the need to limit this rule on the basis of estoppel: the presumption of nonliability could be displaced by evidence that members (some or all of them) or the organization with the approval of members gave creditors reason to assume that members (some or all of them) would accept concurrent or secondary liability even without an express or implied intention to that effect in the constituent instrument." Amerasinghe, Liability to Third Parties of Member States of International

Organizations: Practice, Principle and Judicial Precedent, 85 A.J.I.L. 259, 280 (1991).

## F. IMMUNITIES OF INTERNATIONAL ORGANIZATIONS

The Restatement (Third) § 467 states as follows:

(1) Under international law, an international organization generally enjoys such privileges and immunities from the jurisdiction of a member state as are necessary for the fulfillment of the purposes of the organization, including immunity from legal process, and from financial controls, taxes, and duties.

(2) Under the law of the United States, international organizations are entitled to the privileges and immunities provided by international agreements to which the United States is party, and organizations designated by the President under the International Organizations Immunities Act are entitled to the privileges and immunities provided in that Act.

The major international organizations enjoy the immunities referred to in subsection (1) under their charters and supplementary agreements. See the discussion in Chapter 13 beginning at p. 1214. Comments *a* and *d* of the Restatement elaborate as follows on the scope of international organization immunities:

*a. Privileges and immunities by international agreement and under customary law.* * * *

The provisions in international agreements dealing with privileges and immunities of international organizations do not distinguish between immunity from jurisdiction to prescribe, to adjudicate, or to enforce by nonjudicial means. The immunities contemplated are principally immunities from judicial process and police interference, but immunity from any exercise of jurisdiction could be claimed if it is necessary for the fulfillment of the purposes of the organization. See also Comment *c*. Compare § 463.

* * *

*d. Applicability of restrictive theory of immunity.* It appears that the restrictive theory that limits the immunity of a state from legal process (see § 451) does not apply to the United Nations, to most of its Specialized Agencies, or to the Organization of American States. These organizations enjoy immunity from jurisdiction to adjudicate in all cases, both under their charters and other international agreements (see Comment *b*), and under the law of the United States. Whether other international organizations enjoy absolute or restricted immunity under international law is unclear, but at least until that question is authoritatively resolved they will probably be accorded only restricted immunity under the law of the United States. See Reporter's Note 4.

International organizations are absolutely immune from suits arising out of their internal operations, including their relations with their employees. See, e.g., Mendaro v. World Bank, 717 F.2d 610 (D.C.Cir.1983). The issue whether restrictive or absolute immunity is applicable in other situations is discussed in Oparil, Immunity of International Organizations in United States Courts: Absolute or Restrictive?, 24 Vand. J. Transnat'l L. 689 (1991).

Immunity may be waived by the organization's charter. Thus, Article VII, Section 3 of the World Bank's Articles of Agreement has been held to constitute a waiver of immunity from suits "arising out of its external commercial contracts and activities." Mendaro v. World Bank, supra at 618. Immunity may also be waived by an appropriate organ or officer of the organization. Waiver must be express. Such organ or officer may also waive the immunity of the organization in a particular case, and may agree to arbitration but, at least without specific authorization, immunity from any measure of execution may not be waived. See Restatement (Third) § 467, Comment *e.*

## G. ORGANIC JURISDICTION OF INTERNATIONAL ORGANIZATIONS

### *SEYERSTED, JURISDICTION OVER ORGANS AND OFFICIALS OF STATES, THE HOLY SEE AND INTERGOVERNMENTAL ORGANIZATIONS*

14 I.C.L.Q. 69–71, 77–78 (1965).*

It follows from the practice described in the preceding sections, which has attained the force of customary law, that intergovernmental organisations have general and exclusive legislative and administrative jurisdiction in internal matters and that they also have compulsory judicial power over their organs and officials as such. This jurisdiction is *inherent,* i.e., it may be exercised, with the exceptions indicated below, by all intergovernmental organisations without specific authorisation in their constitutions or otherwise.

It is to the same practice that one must look, in the first place, for a *delimitation* of this jurisdiction. In cases of doubt, one may perhaps also seek some guidance in the parallel delimitations within democratic States between those powers which these may exercise by executive action and those which require formal statute.

1. *Internal relations stricto sensu.* The inherent jurisdiction exercised by intergovernmental organisations comprises in the first place all relations between and within the organisation and its organs and officials as such. It comprises also relations with member States (and their representatives) in their capacity as members of the organs of the organisation.

Such internal relations *stricto sensu* include in the first place organisational matters, which usually are of an internal nature or have important internal aspects. But functional matters also often have internal aspects *stricto sensu.*

Thus, the rules of procedure enacted for the several deliberative organs of most organisations regulate in the first place relations within the organ

* Footnotes omitted. Reprinted by permission of the British Institute of International and Comparative Law.

concerned, notably the rights and duties of the individual members thereof *vis-à-vis* the organ as a whole. And the terms of reference for a subsidiary organ which are adopted by the superior organ establishing it regulate, *inter alia,* the relations between these two organs. Financial regulations govern relations within the secretariat as well as relations between the secretariat and other organs, such as the plenary organ, the executive council and the auditors. * * *

Similarly, administrative tribunals adjudicate disputes arising out of the relationship of employment between the organisation and its officials.

States, including the host State, refrain from exercising any jurisdiction in these relations. * * *

Such internal jurisdiction is directly and *ipso facto* binding only upon the organs and the officials and, to a very limited extent, upon the members. And it is binding upon them only in their capacity as officials or members of organs, not when they act in their capacity as private individuals or States, respectively. It is thus *organic jurisdiction.* Confined to organic relations, its validity cannot be contested by any outside party. It is indirectly, or prejudicially, binding also upon such parties just as the acts performed by a *State* in the exercise of *its* organic jurisdiction must be recognised as valid by other States and their nationals, even if the Act of State doctrine is not recognised in other respects.

2. *Bilateral external relations.* The organic jurisdiction extends also to the field of external relations (*actes de liaison* ), i.e., relations with other subjects of municipal or international law, such as the conclusion of contracts and treaties and the performance of unilateral acts. It even extends to those functions which the organisation performs with regard to relations between other subjects of international law *inter se.* But in both respects the organisation has inherent jurisdictional powers only over the organs of the organisation and not over the other party or parties.

* * *

5. *Constitutional limitations.* Although no constitutional authorisation is necessary in order to enable an intergovernmental organisation to exercise organic jurisdiction, such jurisdiction cannot, of course, be exercised in conflict with any provision of the constitution.

Any constitutional provision, which might exclude the exercise by the organisation of its organic jurisdiction in any particular respect, would clearly be binding upon the organisation. * * *

* * *

Constitutional provisions concerning the *manner* in which decisions shall be made must also be observed in the enactment of regulations and in the making of executive decisions. * * *

### *Notes*

1. The internal autonomy of international organization has been extensively considered in the literature and in decisions of international tribunals. See advisory opinions of the International Court of Justice on Effect of Awards of Compensation Made by the U.N. Administrative Tribunal, 1954 I.C.J. 27, on

Judgments of the Administrative Tribunal of I.L.O. on Complaints against UNESCO, 1956 I.C.J. 77, and on Application for Review of Judgment of U.N. Administrative Tribunal, 1973 I.C.J. 166. See also Meron, The United Nations Secretariat: The Rules and Practice (1977) which reveals the tension between the legal principles of internal autonomy of the organization and the actuality of political pressure by member governments.

2. Internal judicial organs have been established within international organizations to adjudicate disputes between the organization and its staff members. The U.N. Administrative Tribunal includes within its jurisdiction not only the United Nations, but also some of the specialized agencies. The Administrative Tribunal of the I.L.O. similarly has an extended jurisdiction beyond the I.L.O. itself, including by special agreement, several of the specialized agencies located in Europe (e.g., UNESCO, FAO, and WHO). The European Economic Community did not have to create a special tribunal, since its Court of Justice had jurisdiction with respect to complaints of staff members. A considerable body of case-law has been developed by the several tribunals concerned with the rights and obligations of international organizations vis-à-vis international officials. In particular, procedural rights analogous to due process have been defined in a great variety of situations of international employment. See Bastid, Have the U.N. Administrative Tribunals Contributed to the Development of International Law in Transnational Law in a Changing Society 299–312 (Friedmann, Henkin, Lissitzyn, eds. 1972); Meron, supra.

## SECTION 3. MEMBERSHIP AND REPRESENTATION IN INTERNATIONAL ORGANIZATIONS

1. Membership in international organizations is generally limited to states. In some cases other governmental entities have also been admitted to membership.

States become members by:

(a) becoming parties to the constitutive treaty establishing the organization;

(b) by admission through votes of one or more of the principal organs. (In the United Nations, for example, an applicant state must receive the approval of the Security Council, including the affirmative vote of the five permanent members and two-thirds of the General Assembly.);

(c) by succession in accordance with the rules of the organization. (Generally a successor state has been required to be elected as a new member; if a successor state is admitted by virtue of succession (rather than election) it succeeds to both the rights and obligations of its predecessor.)

2. Requirements of membership

Some organizations are open to all states that accept the obligations of the constitution. Regional organizations limit membership to states within a defined region. The constitution may impose other qualifications. For example, the U.N. Charter declares, that membership is open to "peace loving" states and requires that members be "able and willing to carry out the obligations of the Charter." Whether an applicant was truly independent and viable was debated in several cases. In recent years, many ministates, including some associated states that do not conduct their own foreign relations or defense, have been admitted to membership even though it appeared that they were dependent politically and economically on other states.

3. Representation of States

States are represented in international organization by representatives or delegations appointed by the government. Changes in régime or form of government do not affect the rights or obligations of a member. In a number of instances, competing authorities have claimed to be the government with the right to represent the state. The decision as to which claimant has the right to appoint representatives is made by the organization, generally by accepting or rejecting credentials submitted by the claimants. Many states have argued that the decision should be taken on "objective" criteria, in particular, which claimant is in effective control of the state and able to employ the resources and direct the people in fulfillment of the obligations of membership. Others have maintained that the willingness of a regime to fulfill the purposes of the Organization and to abide by its principles is also relevant. See discussion in Chapter 4 at p. 260 on the recognition of governments.

The credentials of a delegation were rejected in some instances because the government in question was considered to be "unrepresentative" or to have violated principles of the constituent instrument. South Africa was denied participation in the U.N. General Assembly on these grounds. Objection to that action as illegal was registered by the United States on the ground that it was an indirect suspension of the rights of membership without conforming to the Charter's condition for such suspension, in particular, an affirmative vote by the Security Council. See Kirgis, International Organizations in their Legal Setting, 123–44, 500–34 (1977 with 1982 supplement); Halberstam, Excluding Israel from the General Assembly By a Rejection of its Credentials, 78 A.J.I.L. 179–192 (1984); Jhabvala, The Credentials Approach to Representation in the U.N. General Assembly, 7 Cal.W.Int'l L.J. 615 (1977).

4. On September 22, 1992, the U.N. General Assembly took the unprecedented step of denying the Federal Republic of Yugoslavia (Serbia and Montenegro) the right to succeed the Socialist Federal Republic of Yugoslavia as a member of the United Nations. This action was related to the former's involvement in the hostilities in Bosnia–Herzegovina. See note 2 at p. 265 supra.

5. Non-state entities are members of some international organizations. The Universal Postal Union, for example, includes postal administrations of territories that are not in themselves states. While representatives and delegations are normally designated by governments, the International Labour Organization constitution provides for tri-partite representation of labor, employers and governments.

## SECTION 4. INTERGOVERNMENTAL COMPANIES, CONSORTIA, AND PRODUCERS ASSOCIATIONS

### A. INTERGOVERNMENTAL COMPANIES AND CONSORTIA

Since the Second World War a new type of international corporate institution, public in purpose, but private, or mixed public and private, in legal form, has developed. These corporations have been instituted on a bilateral or multilateral basis for the fulfillment of certain joint purposes by participating governments, by a combination of governments and private enterprises, or by private companies representing government-approved monopolies. Such multinational companies are a form of organization intermediate between the public international organization and private corporations operating on an international scale.

These corporations deal with matters which are beyond the scope of any one state or corporation created by one state. See generally, Fligler, Multinational Public Enterprises (1967). See also, Adam, Les Etablissements Publics Internationaux (1957). The establishment of the European Company for Financing Railway Equipment (EUROFIMA) was approved by a convention of October 20, 1955, 378 U.N.T.S. 225, between sixteen European countries for the purpose of unifying and improving the construction and performance of railway rolling stock. EUROFIMA was established as a Swiss company, and is governed in its organizational and operational aspects by Swiss law. It is nevertheless an international company, the capital of which is subscribed by national railway administrations. The company is governed primarily by the Statute of the company and secondarily by the law of the headquarters state (Switzerland). The Statute is to be given effect notwithstanding contrary provisions of the law of the headquarters state. In practice, Swiss law governs most of the contracts concluded by the company. See Adam, Société Européenne pour le Financement du Matériel Ferroviaire (EUROFIMA), 3 Eur.Yb. 70 (1957).

In the field of river navigation, the International Moselle Company was formed by France, Luxembourg and the Federal Republic of Germany in 1956. Convention Concerning the Canalization of the Moselle, October 27, 1956, Journal Officiel Français 460 (1957); J. du Droit Int'l (Clunet) 264 (1958). The company is organized as a limited liability company under German law (*Gesellschaft mit beschränkter Haftung* or GmbH) and is registered in the Trade Registry of Germany.

Scandinavian Airlines System (SAS) was formed in 1952 by a consortium agreement between the national airline companies of Denmark, Norway, and Sweden. The consortium agreement is published in Council of Europe, European Companies 41 (1952); see also Nelson, Scandinavian Airlines System: Cooperation in the Air, 20 J.Air L. & Comm. 178 (1953). More recently, Air Afrique was formed by eleven states which were former French African territories (Cameroun, Central African Republic, Chad, Congo (Brazzaville), Dahomey, Gabon, Ivory Coast, Mauritania, Niger, Senegal, and Upper Volta), in cooperation with a French company which had previously used the name "Air Afrique" and which owns stock in the new company. The company was formed as a private *société anonyme* which has the nationality of each of the contracting states, and has a *siège social* in the capitals of each of the member countries. The treaty was signed March 28, 1961; see 17 Rev. Française de Droit Aérien 329 (1963).

In Latin America, intergovernmental corporations have been seen as instruments for economic integration and common market arrangements. They have been promoted by the Inter-American Development Bank and by regional integration bodies. For a comprehensive group of studies, see Corporaciones Públicas Multinacionales para el desarrollo y la integración de la América Latina (Kaplan, compilador) 1972.

## B. INTERGOVERNMENTAL PRODUCERS ASSOCIATIONS

Still another form of intergovernmental organization has been the intergovernmental producers association, most prominently exemplified by OPEC, the Organization of Petroleum Exporting Countries. A number of similar organizations have been established by intergovernmental agreements of states engaged in the production of primary commodities. Examples have included producers of bauxite, copper, iron ore, and of agricultural commodities such as coffee, cocoa, bananas, and sisal. Their main objective is to secure fair (i.e., higher) prices for their product and to coordinate national action so as to increase the return to producers and to promote national control over the industry concerned. The associations engage in joint price fixing sometimes backed by export limits, production quotas, and market allocations. See p. 1412 infra. The developed market-economy countries have criticized such intergovernmental associations as cartel-like attempts to raise costs artificially and impose restraints on international trade. They maintain that artificial price fixing will lead to substitution and lower demand in the long run.

In contrast, the developing countries have strongly supported such associations as legitimate means of increasing their share of revenues and increasing their bargaining power vis-à-vis the industrialized states and multinational companies. They have succeeded in obtaining United Nations recognition of the right of states to form such producers associations in Article 5 of the Charter of Economic Rights and Duties (1974), which reads as follows:

> All States have the right to associate in organizations of primary commodity producers in order to develop their national economies to achieve stable financing for their development, and in pursuance of their aims, to assist in the promotion of sustained growth of the world economy, in particular accelerating the development of developing countries. Correspondingly all States have the duty to respect that right by refraining from applying economic and political measures that would limit it.

Although the producers associations have been described as cartels or cartel-like, their supporters have resisted that description, as seen in the following comment on OPEC:

> If one applies the definition of export cartels used by Western countries (for example, the Webb–Pomerene Act of the United States),

> the OPEC organization does not pass the test. An export cartel not only must include rigid agreements on prices, but also related agreements in such key areas as production control and market sharing. The export cartel must also be responsible for monitoring the activities of its constituent members with a view to policing violations and penalizing violators. The OPEC member governments do not perform any of these cartel functions. Their agreement on oil-export prices is strictly voluntary, and does not carry with it sanctions or rewards. Moreover, the agreements leave to the discretion of each member government the setting and changing of prices within a range considered reasonable by OPEC members. A close scrutiny of OPEC's statutes and resolutions shows that the Organization does not have supranational powers. Member countries do not delegate to any central body their policy- or decision-making powers. Indeed, they jealously guard their sovereignty, and consider their freedom of action to be paramount.
>
> This relatively low level of authority that member countries provide the OPEC organization has so far not proven a source of weakness. On the contrary, it has enabled the organization to weather dramatic changes in world oil conditions and in its members' policies.

Mikdashi, The OPEC Process, 104 Daedalus No. 4, 207–208 (Fall 1975).*

The foregoing comment suggests that OPEC, although an intergovernmental association, does not make a distinction in terms of legal powers and functions between the organization and its member states. Nor is it clear that the organization exercises powers on the international plane rather than solely within the national systems of its member states and other countries. For these reasons, it may not be clear that OPEC and similar producers associations should be regarded as international legal persons. It may well be that some of the associations will evolve in that direction as they are entrusted with organizational tasks and responsibilities and enter into agreements with states. See Pollard, Law and Policy of Producers' Associations (1984); Hveem, The Political Economy of Third World Producer Associations (1978); Rangarajan, Commodity Conflict (1978); Schachter, Sharing the World's Resources (1977).

## SECTION 5. TRANSNATIONAL CORPORATIONS UNDER INTERNATIONAL LAW

In the last few decades, considerable attention has been given to the international role of private corporations which are incorporated in (and often have their headquarters in) one state and carry out operations in a number of countries. Such transnational (or multinational) corporations have become the focus of considerable controversy because of their economic and, in some cases, political power, the mobility and complexity of their operations, and the difficulties they create for national states—both "home" and "host" states—which seek to exercise legal authority over them. Such

* Reprinted by permission of the American Academy of Arts and Sciences from Daedalus, Fall 1975.

corporations are "private," nongovernmental entities, they are subject to applicable national law, and they are not international legal persons in the technical sense. That is, they are not generally subject to obligations, and generally do not enjoy rights, under international law. However, in some cases they have entered into agreements with governments under which the parties have agreed that principles of public international law or general principles of law, rather than national law, will govern the transaction. See p. 739 infra.

In the European Community, private enterprises are accorded legal standing to participate in community procedures. Private enterprises are subject to direct regulation by the Community organs, and have a corresponding right to appeal against decisions of the executive organs of the Community. For a more detailed discussion of the law of the European Communities, see Chapter 19, Section 2 infra. For most purposes, however, private corporations are treated in international law as the nationals of a particular state, whether the state of incorporation or the state where the corporation maintains its headquarters (*siège social*). Corporations, like individuals, must in most instances rely on the protection of their governments, and do not have access to international legal proceedings to protect their rights. See Barcelona Traction Case, 1970 I.C.J. 3, p. 406 infra.

The principal emphasis in recent years has been on efforts to develop international measures to regulate the conduct of the transnational corporations across national lines and to define the rights and duties of home and host states in respect of the corporation's activities. Foremost among these measures have been a proposed Code of Conduct for Transnational Corporations which was under consideration and negotiation by the United Nations for years (see p. 1454 infra) and Guidelines on the Treatment of Foreign Direct Investment published by the World Bank Group in 1992 (see p. 1459 infra). Proposals have also been made for a multilateral treaty under which transnational corporations which meet certain conditions would be qualified to apply for a charter from an international body which would entitle it to protection under the treaty and oblige it to comply with a set of rules and international surveillance. See, e.g., Ball, Proposal for an International Charter in Global Companies 171–172 (Ball ed., 1975). An "international companies law" of this kind does not seem likely to be realized in the foreseeable future, but the effort to develop a "code" in the form of binding rules or guidelines is likely to continue. The following extracts provide some indication of the issues presented by attempts to develop international regulation of transnational corporations.

## *UNITED NATIONS: THE IMPACT OF MULTINATIONAL CORPORATIONS ON THE DEVELOPMENT PROCESS AND ON INTERNATIONAL RELATIONS*

Report of the "Group of Eminent Persons".

U.N.Doc. E/5500/Add 1 (1974).

Multinational corporations are important actors on the world stage.

The report entitled, Multinational Corporations in World Development,[1] aptly describes their current significance and recent trends. The total value of international production controlled by such corporations now exceeds that of international trade. * * *

Multinational corporations are enterprises which own or control production or service facilities outside the country in which they are based. Such enterprises are not always incorporated or private; they can also be co-operatives or state-owned entities.[2]

Most countries have recognized the potential of multinational corporations and have encouraged the expansion of their activities in one form or another within their national borders. The role of foreign private investment in development is indeed acknowledged in the International Development Strategy for the Second United Nations Development Decade.[3] At the same time, certain practices and effects of multinational corporations have given rise to widespread concern and anxiety in many quarters and a strong feeling has emerged that the present *modus vivendi* should be reviewed at the international level.

Opinions vary on the contribution of multinational corporations to world economic development and international relations, on the problems created by them and on the ways in which they should be treated. This was amply borne out in the discussions of the Group and in the views expressed during the hearings by representatives of Governments, labour and consumer organizations, by executives of multinational corporations and by members of the academic community. All, including the multinational corporations themselves, expressed concern of one kind or another.

Home countries are concerned about the undesirable effects that foreign investment by multinational corporations may have on domestic employment and the balance of payments, and about the capacity of such corporations to alter the normal play of competition. Host countries are concerned about the ownership and control of key economic sectors by foreign enterprises, the excessive cost to the domestic economy which their operations may entail, the extent to which they may encroach upon political sovereignty and their possible adverse influence on sociocultural values. Labour interests are concerned about the impact of multinational corporations on employment and workers' welfare and on the bargaining strength of trade unions. Consumer interests are concerned about the appropriateness, quality and price of the goods produced by multinational corporations. The multinational corporations themselves are concerned about the possible nationalization or expropriation of their assets without adequate compensation and about restrictive, unclear and frequently changing government policies.

1. United Nations publication, Sales No. 73.11.A.11.

2. There is general agreement in the Group that the word "enterprise" should be substituted for corporation, and a strong feeling that the word transnational would better convey the notion that these firms operate from their home bases across national borders. However, the term "multinational corporations" is used in this report in conformity with Economic and Social Council resolution 1721 (LIII). See also alternative definitions in Multinational Corporations in World Development.

3. International Development Strategy: Action Programme of the General Assembly for the Second United Nations Development Decade (United Nations publication, Sales No. E.71.11.A.2), para. 50.

From all these expressions of concern, one conclusion emerges: fundamental new problems have arisen as a direct result of the growing internationalization of production as carried out by multinational corporations. We believe that these problems must be tackled without delay, so that tensions are eased and the benefits which can be derived from multinational corporations are fully realized.

## *CHARNEY, TRANSNATIONAL CORPORATIONS AND DEVELOPING PUBLIC INTERNATIONAL LAW*

Duke L.J. 748, 762–69 (1983).*

### I. Introduction

Currently, one of the most significant developments in public international law is the apparent creation of law applicable to transnational corporations (TNC). Although public international law has addressed international economic issues for some time, recently, in light of expanded TNC activity and increased third world leverage in international affairs, greater attention has been focused on the establishment of rules to govern TNC behavior. These developments are partly explained as an effort by the third world to increase its international power vis-a-vis the power of both the TNCs and the western developed world, with whom the TNCs are generally aligned, but there are also additional factors encouraging them. First, because one country usually cannot unilaterally regulate TNC power and behavior, even the western, developed countries have an interest in these developments. Second, TNCs themselves recognize the benefits of a uniform regulatory scheme that would avoid many of the difficulties produced by varying national requirements. Although these new rules will be aimed at TNCs, international practice has largely precluded TNCs from directly participating in *this* rule-making process.

* * *

There is evidence that TNCs have had international legal personality and have participated in the international legal system for some time. Examples of such participation include application of public international law to contracts with state entities and participation in dispute settlement forums established either by treaty or intergovernmental organizations. Some principles of public international law have become so widely accepted that they have been viewed as binding on the TNCs' international activities. Finally, TNCs advise international organizations when their interests are at stake and it is clear that they play a direct role in influencing national behavior on relevant international matters.

Some commentators have suggested ignoring the fiction of "juridical actors." They argue that since the real actors are those natural persons who have both a stake in and the power to affect the decisions, it is immaterial what fictional entity has formal international personality. On the basis of this analysis, many TNCs, or at least their leaders, have always been and will continue to be participants in the international legal system.

While this view is helpful in some cases, it is often necessary to distinguish the personalities of organizations such as TNCs and state entities from those of their human representatives and constituents. Because TNCs are corporate personalities and have substantial power at their disposal, decisions about whether they should participate in the law-making process and be held accountable for violations of the law are significant. For example, the TNCs' influence upon and accountability to rules of international law appear to be a function of the extent to which it may *directly* participate in the international legal process. In an effort to limit that influence, states continue to regard the nation-state government as the main (if not sole) participant in the international legal system and to exclude, or at least to severely limit, the non-state entities' role. This resistance to TNC participation is motivated not merely by a nostalgic desire to return to the days when the state was "sovereign," but by the nation-states' belief that a power struggle is taking place between themselves and the TNCs. It is well-documented that there are a number of TNCs that are economically more powerful than all but the largest nation-states. Furthermore, the nonterritorial and globe-circling activities of these TNCs make them less subject to the will of individual nation-states and enable them to play states off against each other. TNC involvement, particularly with third world governments, has often resulted in substantial TNC influence on host governments, and that influence has not always served those governments' best interests.

Some maintain that TNC activities are actually just a new form of western colonialism while others view the TNC as a more benign force that is ultimately subject to state control even without major new international initiatives. Regardless of which view is correct, the international community is moving toward greater international regulation of international business without allowing direct business participation.

Currently, TNC directors appear to agree with many national governments that TNCs ought not to participate directly in the international legal system—a position evidenced by the fact that TNCs have not overtly sought broad international legal personality. In fact, when George Ball proposed that the major TNCs should be subject to international rather than national incorporation, the business community was unenthusiastic. * * *

TNCs benefit from their international nonstatus. Nonstatus immunizes them from direct accountability to international legal norms and permits them to use sympathetic national governments to parry outside efforts to mold their behavior. TNCs also enjoy some immunity from third world derision at the U.N. General Assembly and other multinational forums because national governments are willing to insulate them from these and other international pressures. Broad international legal personality would destroy these defenses. On the other hand, TNCs are eager to influence international decision making. They are willing participants to the extent that they can obtain *specific* international legal personality without loss of the benefits that the lack of *general* personality provides. In the future, it will become increasingly difficult for them to have it both ways.

* * *

There are strong arguments for expanding the role of TNCs in the international legal system. Nation-states aside, TNCs are the most powerful actors in the world today and to not recognize that power would be unrealistic. The international economy depends heavily on the services they provide and they have far greater influence and economic power than unorganized human beings or most other nongovernmental organizations. In fact, even the influence of intergovernmental organizations, which depends on the continued financial and political support of nation-state sponsors, cannot be compared to the power of many TNCs. This argument for increased TNC participation is further supported by the conclusion, reached earlier in this article, that the continued viability of the international legal system depends upon the close conformity of public international law to international realities.

### *Notes*

1. The author goes on to urge the development of methods of expanding the role of TNCs in the process of international norm development. For example, TNCs might be accredited as non-voting participants in international conferences or TNCs might be involved in expert groups which could participate in international conferences. Such groups could observe the negotiations, participate in information exchanges, issue reports and interact with state representatives to develop new norms. Id. pp. 780–783. Are such forms of informal participation likely to be fruitful? Do you agree with the author's conclusion:

> The international legal community has failed to give these [TNCs and other non-state entities possessing comparable economic power] a role because of the power struggles among nation-states and the perceived threats to the nation-state system that they represent. Continuing this conflict imposes unnecessary costs on the international legal system. The effectiveness of international law depends largely upon the legitimacy of its rules. Because the law development process is the vehicle by which these rules are legitimized, a process that excludes powerful international actors will become less legitimate in the eyes of the excluded actors and will breed disrespect for the international system as a whole.

Id. p. 787.

2. The literature on the transnational corporation has been voluminous. See Bergsten, Horst and Moran, American Multinationals and American Interests (1978); Vernon, Storm over the Multinationals (1977); Baranson, Technology and the Multinationals (1978); Conference on the Regulation of Transnational Corporations, 15 Colum.J.Transnat'l L. 367 (1976). For consideration of questions of applicable law, conflicts of jurisdiction, and international registration, see 57–I Ann. de l'Institut de Droit Int'l 266–386 (1977). The reports of the U.N. Commission on Transnational Corporations and the studies of the U.N. Centre on Transnational Corporations (CTC) are highly informative on the policies of governments and practices of multinational companies. After years of effort the U.N. Commission produced a draft Code of Conduct for Transnational Corporations which is set forth in the document supplement. See p. 1454 infra. "Guidelines for Multinational Enterprises" have been adopted by the Organization for Economic Cooperation and Development (OECD), composed of governments of the industrialized market-economy countries. 15 I.L.M. 969 (1976). In 1992 the World Bank Group published Guidelines on the Treatment of Foreign Direct Investment, 31 I.L.M. 1366. See p. 1459 infra.

# SECTION 6. INDIVIDUALS IN INTERNATIONAL LAW

## A. THE STATUS OF THE INDIVIDUAL IN INTERNATIONAL LAW

In discussing the status of individuals in international law, Jessup commented as follows in 1948:

> For the purposes of this context * * * international law or the law of nations must be defined as law applicable to states in their mutual relations and to individuals in their relations with states. International law may also, under this hypothesis, be applicable to certain interrelationships of individuals themselves, where such interrelationships involve matters of international concern. So long, however, as the international community is composed of states, it is only through an exercise of their will, as expressed through treaty or agreement or as laid down by an international authority deriving its power from states, that a rule of law becomes binding upon an individual. When there is created some kind of international constituent assembly or world parliament representative of the people of the world and having authority to legislate, it will then be possible to assert that international law derives authority from a source external to the states. This would be true even though states might well have been the original creators of such a representative legislature. The inescapable fact is that the world is today organized on the basis of the coexistence of states, and that fundamental changes will take place only through state action * * *.

Jessup, A Modern Law of Nations 17–18 (1948). (Footnotes omitted). *

## MAVROMMATIS PALESTINE CONCESSIONS (JURISDICTION)

## (GREECE v. GREAT BRITAIN)

Permanent Court of International Justice, 1924.
P.C.I.J., Ser. A, No. 2, p. 11–12.

[The Greek Government brought a suit against Great Britain arising out of the alleged refusal of the Palestine Government, and therefore, the British Government, to recognize rights acquired by M. Mavrommatis, a Greek national, under contracts and agreements concluded with him by the authorities of the Ottoman Empire, the predecessor sovereign in Palestine. The British Government filed a preliminary objection to the jurisdiction of the Court. In upholding its jurisdiction, the Court observed:]

* * *

In the case of the Mavrommatis concessions it is true that the dispute was at first between a private person and a State—i.e. between M. Mavrommatis and Great Britain. Subsequently, the Greek Government took up the case. The dispute then entered upon a new phase; it entered the domain of international law, and became a dispute between two States. Henceforward therefore it is a dispute which may or may not fall under the jurisdiction of Permanent Court of International Justice.

Article 26 of the Mandate, in giving jurisdiction to the Permanent Court of International Justice, does not, in fact, merely lay down that there must be a dispute which requires to be settled. It goes on to say that the dispute must be between the Mandatory and another Member of the League of Nations. This is undoubtedly the case in the present suit, since the claimant State Greece, like Great Britain, has from the outset belonged to the League of Nations. It is an elementary principle of international law that a State is entitled to protect its subjects, when injured by acts contrary to international law committed by another State, from whom they have been unable to obtain satisfaction through the ordinary channels. By taking up the case of one of its subjects and by resorting to diplomatic action or international judicial proceedings on his behalf, a State is in reality asserting its own rights—its right to ensure, in the person of its subjects, respect for the rules of international law.

The question, therefore, whether the present dispute originates in an injury to a private interest, which in point of fact is the case in many international disputes, is irrelevant from this standpoint. Once a State has taken up a case on behalf of one of its subjects before an international tribunal, in the eyes of the latter the State is sole claimant. The fact that Great Britain and Greece are the opposing Parties to the dispute arising out of the Mavrommatis concessions is sufficient to make it a dispute between two States within the meaning of Article 26 of the Palestine Mandate.

### *Note*

Customary international law and international agreements have created obligations of states in favor of natural and juridical persons. The customary law of state responsibility, under which a state may be responsible to another state for certain injuries to aliens, is an important example, discussed in Chapter 9.

Under the traditional law of state responsibility, as seen in the *Mavrommatis Case,* supra, certain injuries to foreign nationals were considered to be offenses against the state of which they were nationals. Once the injured alien exhausts available remedies under the legal system of the state causing the injury, the state of which the injured party is a national may seek reparation in a state-to-state claim. See p. 677 infra.

Subsequent to World War II, international human rights agreements have created obligations and responsibilities for states with respect to all natural persons subject to their jurisdiction and a customary international law of human rights has been developing. This is discussed in Chapter 8. The developing law of human rights deals with the obligations of states with respect to all human beings, not only aliens. It reflects general acceptance that every individual should have rights which all states should respect and protect. Thus, observance of human rights is not the state's business alone (and within its "domestic jurisdiction"), but is a matter of international concern and an appropriate subject for regulation by international law. See Chapter 8, Section 1.

On the international personality of individuals, see, generally, Korowicz, The Problem of the International Personality of Individuals, 50 A.J.I.L. 533 (1956); Waldock, General Course on Public International Law, 106 Rec. des Cours 5, 192 (1962–II). See also Chapter 8.

### *LAUTERPACHT, INTERNATIONAL LAW AND HUMAN RIGHTS*

27–29 (1973).*

The position of the individual as a subject of international law has often been obscured by the failure to observe the distinction between the recognition, in an international instrument, of rights enuring to the benefit of the individual and the enforceability of these rights at his instance. The fact that the beneficiary of rights is not authorised to take independent steps in his own name to enforce them does not signify that he is not a subject of the law or that the rights in question are vested exclusively in the agency which possesses the capacity to enforce them. Thus, in relation to the current view that the rights of the alien within foreign territory are the rights of his State and not his own, the correct way of stating the legal position is not that the State asserts its own exclusive right but that it enforces, in substance, the right of the individual who, as the law now stands is incapable of asserting it in the international sphere. Conversely, there seems to be no warrant for the disposition to allow the question of enforceability of rights to be influenced by the doctrine that individuals cannot be subjects of international law. The question whether individuals in any given case are subjects of international law and whether that quality extends to the capacity of enforcement must be answered pragmatically by reference to the given situation and to the relevant international instrument. That instrument may make them subjects of the law without conferring upon them procedural capacity; it may aim at, and achieve, both these objects.

The legal position in the matter is well illustrated by the question whether individuals can acquire rights directly by treaty independently of municipal legislation. Prior to the Advisory Opinion of the Permanent Court of International Justice in the case concerning the Jurisdiction of the Courts of Danzig in the matter of Danzig railway officials, that question was generally answered in the negative—though even then some caution would have been indicated having regard to the law of some countries, such as the United States in which duly ratified treaties are a self-executing part of municipal law. Similarly, there had already existed treaties—such as that establishing the Central American Court of Justice, the provisions relating to the Mixed Arbitral Tribunals in the Peace Treaties of 1919, and the Polish–German Upper Silesian Convention—which conferred upon individuals direct rights of international action. However, it was the Advisory Opinion, given in 1928, in the case concerning the Jurisdiction of the Courts of Danzig, which dealt a decisive blow to the dogma of the impenetrable barrier separating individuals from international law. In that case Poland

* Footnotes omitted. Reprinted by permission of Stevens and Sons, Ltd.

contended that the agreement between her and Danzig regulating the conditions of employment of Danzig officials whom she had taken over into her railway service was an international treaty which created rights and obligations as between Poland and Danzig only; that as that agreement had not been incorporated into Polish municipal law it did not create rights and obligations for individuals; that Poland's responsibility was limited to that owed to Danzig; and that therefore Danzig courts, before which the officials had brought an action in the matter, had no jurisdiction. The Court rejected this contention. It said:—

> It may be readily admitted that, according to a well established principle of international law, the *Beamtenabkommen,* being an international agreement, cannot, as such, create direct rights and obligations for private individuals. But it cannot be disputed that the very object of an international agreement, according to the intention of the contracting Parties, may be the adoption by the parties of some definite rules creating individual rights and obligations and enforceable by the national courts. That there is such an intention in the present case can be established by reference to the terms of the *Beamtenabkommen.*

This pronouncement is among the most important rendered by the Court. On the first occasion on which it was directly confronted with the traditional argument, it rejected it * * *. It laid down, in effect, that no considerations of theory can prevent the individual from becoming the subject of international rights if States so wish. That affirmation by the Permanent Court of International Justice of the right of individuals to acquire rights directly under treaties was not an isolated event. It was followed—and the coincidence is significant—by other judicial decisions pointing in the same direction.

## *O'CONNELL, INTERNATIONAL LAW*

Vol. 1, 108–109 (2d ed. 1970).*

* * * The individual as the end of community is a member of the community, and a member has status: he is not an object. It is not a sufficient answer to assert that the State is the medium between international law and its own nationals, for the law has often fractured this link when it failed in its purpose. For example, in the areas of black and white slavery, human rights and protection of minorities, international law has selected the individual as a member of the international community for rights and duties, even against the national State. * * *

Theory and practice establish that the individual has legally protected interests, can perform legally prescribed acts, can enjoy rights and be the subject of duties under municipal law deriving from international law; and if personality is no more than a sum of capacities, then he is a person in international law, though his capacities may be different from and less in number and substance than the capacities of States. An individual, for example, cannot acquire territory, he cannot make treaties and he cannot have belligerent rights. But he can commit war crimes, and piracy, and

* Some footnotes omitted. Reprinted by permission of Stevens and Sons, Ltd.

crimes against humanity and foreign sovereigns, and he can own property which international law protects, and he can have claims to compensation for acts arising *ex contractu* or *ex delicto.* He may not be able to pursue his claims and take action to protect his property without the intervention of his own State, but it is still his claim and still his interest which the machinery of enforcement is designed to facilitate.

The statements of doctrine of the International Court on this matter have tended to reflect the object theory which was current when they were made. The Court in the *Mavrommatis* case said that only when the national State takes up the complaint of its subject does the matter enter "the domain of international law." What, then, was the nature of the dispute before it became one between two States? It certainly was not a dispute in municipal law, because there was no municipal law on the subject. The Court would have to say that the dispute was not a legal one at all, and became such only when taken up by the Greek Government. This would be an unacceptable answer when Mavrommatis' whole position was based on the assertion that international law regulated his rights and property. In many similar instances the law officers would advise their governments that Mr. X should be compensated or his claim acknowledged, and their advice is surely in reference to law. The contention that X's claim is no claim in law at all until X's government takes it up is based upon the theory that States alone have capacity in international law and that the "object" of the law has no claim in law. The *Mavrommatis* approach on these lines demonstrates how artificial is the supposed distinction between the claim when it was a non-legal one and the claim when it became a legal one; it was still the same claim based upon the same legal propositions; the only difference was a change in the formal identity of the claimant.

Even if international law does directly create rights and duties in the individual it would not follow that the national State of the individual is no more than a technique for securing recognition of them. International law endows the national State with discretion to act in relation to these rights and duties, and if discretion to act is legal competence then it is true to say that the national State has capacity over and above the capacity of the individual.

## B. THE STATUS OF THE INDIVIDUAL UNDER THE LAW OF THE EUROPEAN COMMUNITIES

### *TOTH, THE INDIVIDUAL AND EUROPEAN LAW*

24 I.C.L.Q. 659, 660–62 (1975).*

* * *

In the substantive law of the European Communities the position of the individual is determined by the fact that so far as he is concerned the Treaties contain basically three different kinds of provisions. A first category of provisions do not go beyond the traditional concept of an international

* Footnotes omitted. Reprinted by permission of the British Institute of International and Comparative Law.

treaty obligation. They are addressed to, and create mutual rights and obligations between, the member States only. These must be executed (implemented) by the member States in order to become effective. They are not directly applicable to individuals; and if they affect individuals at all they can only do so indirectly, i.e., as a result of national implementation and as national, not Community, measures. A second category of provisions are addressed to Community institutions only, requiring them to adopt implementing measures in realisation of a Community objective specified in the Treaty. Individuals are affected not by the Treaty provisions themselves but by these implementing measures (the so-called secondary legislation). These may be of two different kinds, i.e., directly applicable (regulations and decisions addressed to individuals, exceptionally also directives and decisions addressed to member States) and non-directly applicable (directives and decisions addressed to member States). The latter may affect individuals only if and when further implemented by the member State to which the measure is addressed. A third class of provisions were originally addressed to and created obligations for the member States only, but were subsequently declared by the European Court to be of such a nature as to produce direct effects in the legal relations between the member States and individuals. Accordingly, these apply to individuals directly, i.e., without legislative intervention by the member States, creating for them rights enforceable in the municipal courts. Such directly applicable Community provisions have an overriding effect over conflicting national rules, whether earlier or later in time, and whether laid down in ordinary statutes or in the Constitution itself.

* * *

The status of the individual in substantive Community law determines his position with respect to remedies. The main consideration here is that beside other individuals, there are two main actors on the Community scene against which the individual may wish to seek protection: the Community institutions (more precisely, the Council and the Commission) and the member States. Legal protection against the former is necessary partly to counterbalance their considerable lawmaking and executive powers which are not at the present time subject to sufficient political control by an elected body such as the European Parliament, and partly to make up for the lack of a clear separation of legislative and executive powers between the two institutions—both being requirements inherent in the very concept of *Rechtsstaat.* Legal protection against member States is necessary because these, as sovereign bodies, are in the position of suppressing the individual's rights or justified legal or economic interests in the area of Community activities, which interests may, and often do, conflict with their own. According to these requirements, individuals have a dual system of remedies open to them: i.e., before the European Court of Justice and before national courts.

### *Note*

For discussion of the right of an individual to assert a claim based on violation of human rights under the European human rights regime see p. 658 infra.

## C. THE LEGAL RESPONSIBILITY OF INDIVIDUALS IN INTERNATIONAL LAW

Failure by a government to comply with international obligations is a violation of law by the state, and claims for such violation are properly addressed by the government of the offended state to that of the violating state. Ordinarily, the officials, or other persons, who committed the act constituting the violation are not held personally responsible for it under international law.

In some circumstances, and in some measure, however, international law has recognized individual responsibility. There are innumerable references, for example, to individuals committing "an offense against the law of nations." Compare the power of the United States Congress to define and punish offenses against the law of nations. U.S. Const. Art. 1, § 8. One view has it that piracy, for example, is an individual violation of international law, although the punishment of it is left to states, and any state may punish the offender. See, e.g., United States v. Smith, 18 U.S. (5 Wheat.) 153, 161–62, 5 L.Ed. 57 (1820), 2 Moore, International Law 951 et seq. (1906). Another view is that international law prescribes no crime of piracy for individuals, but merely permits states to apply their national laws to punish piracy even when the accused is not subject to the state's jurisdiction under accepted principles, i.e., if he is not a national of the state and the act of piracy was not committed in that state's territorial waters or against one of its vessels. "Under international law piracy is only a special ground of state jurisdiction * * * The law of nations on the matter is permissive only. It justifies state action within limits and fixes those limits." Harvard Research in International Law, Piracy, 26 A.J.I.L.Supp. 739, 754, 759–60 (1932). See the discussion of permissible bases for the exercise of legislative jurisdiction in Chapter 12. For the provision on piracy in the Geneva Convention on the High Seas, and in the United Nations Convention on the Law of the Sea, see p. 1301.

There is similar disagreement as to how to categorize criminal responsibility for violations of the rules of war, which may be punished by the enemy or by "international authorities." Ex parte Quirin, 317 U.S. 1, 63 S.Ct. 1, 87 L.Ed. 3 (1942). The Geneva Conventions on the treatment of prisoners of war authorized a belligerent state to try individual members of enemy forces who violate the provisions of the Convention; they also require the state whose military authorities have committed these violations to bring them to punishment. Similar provisions apply to offenses against civilian populations in violation of the Convention Relative to the Protection of Civilian Persons in Time of War, 6 U.S.T. 3516, T.I.A.S. No. 3365, 75 U.N.T.S. 287 (1949). For a famous instance during the Vietnam War, see United States v. Calley, 46 C.M.R. 1131 (A.C.M.R.1973), aff'd, 22 C.M.A. 534, 48 C.M.R. 19 (1973), petition for writ of habeas corpus granted sub nom., Calley v. Callaway, 382 F.Supp. 650 (M.D.Ga.1974), rev'd, 519 F.2d 184 (5th Cir.1975), cert. denied, 425 U.S. 911, 96 S.Ct. 1505, 47 L.Ed.2d 760 (1976). Compare also the provisions in the conventions on the suppression of aircraft hijacking and sabotage, which require any party to make the offense punishable by severe penalties and either to extradite, or to investigate and prosecute, if appropriate, an alleged offender. Hague Convention for the Suppression of Unlawful Seizure of Aircraft, December 16, 1970, 22 U.S.T. 1641, T.I.A.S. No.

7192; Montreal Convention for Suppression of Unlawful Acts Against the Safety of Civilian Aviation, September 23, 1971, 24 U.S.T. 565, T.I.A.S. No. 7570.

The Convention on the Prevention and Punishment of the Crime of Genocide, Dec. 9, 1948, 78 U.N.T.S. 277, provides that persons committing genocide and related enumerated offenses "shall be punished, whether they are constitutionally responsible rulers, public officials or private individuals," and the contracting parties undertake to enact the necessary legislation to provide effective penalties for guilty persons. (Articles IV and V). "Persons charged with genocide * * * shall be tried by a competent tribunal of the State in the territory of which the act was committed, or by such international penal tribunal as may have jurisdiction. * * *" (Article VI). No such international penal tribunal has been established. The United States has ratified the Convention and has enacted legislation rendering genocide a punishable crime. Genocide Convention Implementation Act of 1988, 18 U.S.C.A. § 1091.

### 1. *Trials of Individuals as War Criminals*

## INTERNATIONAL MILITARY TRIBUNAL (NUREMBERG) JUDGMENT AND SENTENCES

41 A.J.I.L. 172–75, 220–21 (1946).

JUDGMENT

On 8 August 1945, the Government of the United Kingdom of Great Britain and Northern Ireland, the Government of the United States of America, the Provisional Government of the French Republic, and the Government of the Union of Soviet Socialist Republics entered into an Agreement establishing this Tribunal for the Trial of War Criminals whose offenses have no particular geographical location. In accordance with Article 5, the following Governments of the United Nations have expressed their adherence to the Agreement:

Greece, Denmark, Yugoslavia, the Netherlands, Czechoslovakia, Poland, Belgium, Ethiopia, Australia, Honduras, Norway, Panama, Luxembourg, Haiti, New Zealand, India, Venezuela, Uruguay, and Paraguay.

By the Charter annexed to the Agreement, the constitution, jurisdiction, and functions of the Tribunal were defined.

The Tribunal was invested with power to try and punish persons who had committed Crimes against Peace, War Crimes, and Crimes against Humanity as defined in the Charter.

The Charter also provided that at the Trial of any individual member of any group or organization the Tribunal may declare (in connection with any act of which the individual may be convicted) that the group or organization of which the individual was a member was a criminal organization.

In Berlin, on 18 October 1945, in accordance with Article 14 of the Charter, an Indictment was lodged against the defendants named in the caption * * *, who had been designated by the Committee of the Chief Prosecutors of the signatory Powers as major war criminals.

A copy of the Indictment in the German language was served upon each defendant in custody, at least 30 days before the Trial opened.

This Indictment charges the defendants with Crimes against Peace by the planning, preparation, initiation, and waging of wars of aggression, which were also wars in violation of international treaties, agreements, and assurances; with War Crimes; and with Crimes against Humanity. The defendants are also charged with participating in the formulation or execution of a common plan or conspiracy to commit all these crimes. The Tribunal was further asked by the Prosecution to declare all the named groups or organizations to be criminal within the meaning of the Charter.

* * *

### THE CHARTER PROVISIONS

The individual defendants are indicted under Article 6 of the Charter, which is as follows:

> Article 6. The Tribunal established by the Agreement referred to in Article 1 hereof for the trial and punishment of the major war criminals of the European Axis countries shall have the power to try and punish persons who, acting in the interests of the European Axis countries, whether as individuals or as members of organizations, committed any of the following crimes:
>
> The following acts, or any of them, are crimes coming within the jurisdiction of the Tribunal for which there shall be individual responsibility:
>
> (a) Crimes Against Peace: namely, planning, preparation, initiation or waging of a war of aggression, or a war in violation of international treaties, agreements or assurances, or participation in a common plan or conspiracy for the accomplishment of any of the foregoing:
>
> (b) War Crimes: namely, violations of the laws or customs of war. Such violations shall include, but not be limited to, murder, ill-treatment or deportation to slave labor or for any other purpose of civilian population of or in occupied territory, murder or ill-treatment of prisoners of war or persons on the seas, killing of hostages, plunder of public or private property, wanton destruction of cities, towns or villages, or devastation not justified by military necessity:
>
> (c) Crimes Against Humanity: namely, murder, extermination, enslavement, deportation, and other inhumane acts committed against any civilian population, before or during the war, or persecutions on political, racial, or religious grounds in execution of or in connection with any crime within the jurisdiction of the Tribunal, whether or not in violation of the domestic law of the country where perpetrated.
>
> Leaders, organizers, instigators, and accomplices, participating in the formulation or execution of a common plan or conspiracy to commit any of the foregoing crimes are responsible for all acts performed by any persons in execution of such plan.

These provisions are binding upon the Tribunal as the law to be applied to the case.

* * *

It was submitted that international law is concerned with the actions of sovereign States, and provides no punishment for individuals; and further, that where the act in question is an act of State, those who carry it out are not personally responsible, but are protected by the doctrine of the sovereignty of the State. In the opinion of the Tribunal, both these submissions must be rejected. That international law imposes duties and liabilities upon individuals as well as upon States has long been recognized. In the recent case of Ex parte Quirin (1942, 317 U.S. 1), before the Supreme Court of the United States, persons were charged during the war with landing in the United States for purposes of spying and sabotage. The late Chief Justice Stone, speaking for the Court, said:

> From the very beginning of its history this Court has applied the law of war as including that part of the law of nations which prescribes for the conduct of war, the status, rights, and duties of enemy nations as well as enemy individuals.

He went on to give a list of cases tried by the Courts, where individual offenders were charged with offenses against the laws of nations, and particularly the laws of war. Many other authorities could be cited, but enough has been said to show that individuals can be punished for violations of international law. Crimes against international law are committed by men, not by abstract entities, and only by punishing individuals who commit such crimes can the provisions of international law be enforced.

The provisions of Article 228 of the Treaty of Versailles already referred to illustrate and enforce this view of individual responsibility.

The principle of international law, which under certain circumstances, protects the representatives of a state, cannot be applied to acts which are condemned as criminal by international law. The authors of these acts cannot shelter themselves behind their official position in order to be freed from punishment in appropriate proceedings. Article 7 of the Charter expressly declares:

> The official position of Defendants, whether as heads of State, or responsible officials in Government departments, shall not be considered as freeing them from responsibility, or mitigating punishment.

On the other hand the very essence of the Charter is that individuals have international duties which transcend the national obligations of obedience imposed by the individual state. He who violates the laws of war cannot obtain immunity while acting in pursuance of the authority of the state if the state in authorizing action moves outside its competence under international law.

It was also submitted on behalf of most of these defendants that in doing what they did they were acting under the orders of Hitler, and therefore cannot be held responsible for the acts committed by them in carrying out these orders. The Charter specifically provides in Article 8:

> The fact that the Defendant acted pursuant to order of his Government or of a superior shall not free him from responsibility, but may be considered in mitigation of punishment.

The provisions of this article are in conformity with the law of all nations. That a soldier was ordered to kill or torture in violation of the international law of war has never been recognized as a defense to such acts of brutality, though, as the Charter here provides, the order may be urged in mitigation of the punishment. The true test, which is found in varying degrees in the criminal law of most nations, is not the existence of the order, but whether moral choice was in fact possible.

## TRIALS OF WAR CRIMINALS BEFORE THE NUREMBERG MILITARY TRIBUNALS UNDER CONTROL COUNCIL LAW NO. 10, 1946–1949, VOL. III (1951)

"The Justice Case" (Case 3), Opinion and Judgment,
954, 955, 964, 970–972, 974–975, 979, 983–984.

The indictment contains four counts, as follows:

(1) Conspiracy to commit war crimes and crimes against humanity. The charge embraces the period between January 1933 and April 1945.

(2) War crimes, to wit: violations of the laws and customs of war, alleged to have been committed between September 1939 and April 1945.

(3) Crimes against humanity as defined by Control Council Law No. 10, alleged to have been committed between September 1939 and April 1945.

(4) Membership of certain defendants in organizations which have been declared to be criminal by the judgment of the International Military Tribunal in the case against Goering, et al.

* * *

In declaring that the expressed determination of the victors to punish German officials who slaughtered their own nationals is in harmony with international principles of justice, we usurp no power; we only take judicial notice of the declarations already made by the chief executives of the United States and her former Allies. The fact that C.C.Law 10 on its face is limited to the punishment of German criminals does not transform this Tribunal into a German court. The fact that the four powers are exercising supreme legislative authority in governing Germany and for the punishment of German criminals does not mean that the jurisdiction of this Tribunal rests in the slightest degree upon any German law, prerogative, or sovereignty. We sit as a Tribunal drawing its sole power and jurisdiction from the will and command of the Four occupying Powers. * * *

* * * As to the punishment of persons guilty of violating the laws and customs of war (war crimes in the narrow sense), it has always been recognized that tribunals may be established and punishment imposed by the state into whose hands the perpetrators fall. These rules of international law were recognized as paramount, and jurisdiction to enforce them by

the injured belligerent government, whether within the territorial boundaries of the state or in occupied territory, has been unquestioned. (Ex parte Quirin, [317 U.S. 1, 63 S.Ct. 1, 87 L.Ed. 3 (1942) ]; In re Yamashita, 327 U.S. 1, [66 S.Ct. 340, 90 L.Ed. 499 (1946) ].) However, enforcement of international law has been traditionally subject to practical limitations. Within the territorial boundaries of a state having a recognized, functioning government presently in the exercise of sovereign power throughout its territory, a violator of the rules of international law could be punished only by the authority of the officials of that state. The law is universal, but such a state reserves unto itself the exclusive power within its boundaries to apply or withhold sanctions. Thus, notwithstanding the paramount authority of the substantive rules of common international law, the doctrines of national sovereignty have been preserved through the control of enforcement machinery. It must be admitted that Germans were not the only ones who were guilty of committing war crimes; other violators of international law could, no doubt, be tried and punished by the state of which they were nationals, by the offended state if it can secure jurisdiction of the person, or by an international tribunal if of competent authorized jurisdiction.

Applying these principles, it appears that the power to punish violators of international law in Germany is not solely dependent on the enactment of rules of substantive penal law applicable only in Germany. Nor is the apparent immunity from prosecution of criminals in other states based on the absence there of the rules of international law which we enforce here. Only by giving consideration to the extraordinary and temporary situation in Germany can the procedure here be harmonized with established principles of national sovereignty. In Germany an international body (the Control Council) has assumed and exercised the power to establish judicial machinery for the punishment of those who have violated the rules of the common international law, a power which no international authority without consent could assume or exercise within a state having a national government presently in the exercise of its sovereign powers.

* * *

The defendants claim protection under the principle *nullum crimen sine lege,* though they withheld from others the benefit of that rule during the Hitler regime. Obviously the principle in question constitutes no limitation upon the power or right of the Tribunal to punish acts which can properly be held to have been violations of international law when committed. By way of illustration, we observe that C.C.Law 10, article II, paragraph 1(*b* ), "War Crimes," has by reference incorporated the rules by which war crimes are to be identified. In all such cases it remains only for the Tribunal, after the manner of the common law, to determine the content of those rules under the impact of changing conditions.

Whatever view may be held as to the nature and source of our authority under C.C.Law 10 and under common international law, the *ex post facto* rule, properly understood, constitutes no legal nor moral barrier to prosecution in this case.

Under written constitutions the *ex post facto* rule condemns statutes which define as criminal, acts committed before the law was passed, but the *ex post facto* rule cannot apply in the international field as it does under constitutional mandate in the domestic field. Even in the domestic field the prohibition of the rule does not apply to the decisions of common law courts, though the question at issue be novel. International law is not the product of statute for the simple reason that there is as yet no world authority empowered to enact statutes of universal application. International law is the product of multipartite treaties, conventions, judicial decisions and customs which have received international acceptance or acquiescence. It would be sheer absurdity to suggest that the *ex post facto* rule, as known to constitutional states, could be applied to a treaty, a custom, or a common law decision of an international tribunal, or to the international acquiescence which follows the event. To have attempted to apply the *ex post facto* principle to judicial decisions of common international law would have been to strangle that law at birth. As applied in the field of international law, the principle *nullum crimen sine lege* received its true interpretation in the opinion of the IMT in the case versus Goering, et al. The question arose with reference to crimes against the peace, but the opinion expressed is equally applicable to war crimes and crimes against humanity. The Tribunal said:

> In the first place, it is to be observed that the maxim *nullum crimen sine lege* is not a limitation of sovereignty, but is in general a principle of justice. To assert that it is unjust to punish those who in defiance of treaties and assurances have attacked neighboring states without warning is obviously untrue, for in such circumstances the attacker must know that he is doing wrong, and so far from it being unjust to punish him, it would be unjust if his wrong were allowed to go unpunished. * * *

C.C.Law 10 is not limited to the punishment of persons guilty of violating the laws and customs of war in the narrow sense; furthermore, it can no longer be said that violations of the laws and customs of war are the only offenses recognized by common international law. The force of circumstance, the grim fact of worldwide interdependence, and the moral pressure of public opinion have resulted in international recognition that certain crimes against humanity committed by Nazi authority against German nationals constituted violations not alone of statute but also of common international law. * * *

As the prime illustration of a crime against humanity under C.C.Law 10, which by reason of its magnitude and its international repercussions has been recognized as a violation of common international law, we cite "genocide" which will shortly receive our full consideration. A resolution recently adopted by the General Assembly of the United Nations is in part as follows:

* * *

> "The General Assembly therefore—
>
> Affirms that genocide is a crime under international law which the civilized world condemns, and for the commission of which principals and accomplices—whether private individuals, public officials, or statesmen, and whether the crime is committed on religious, racial, political or any other grounds—are punishable; * * *."

The General Assembly is not an international legislature, but it is the most authoritative organ in existence for the interpretation of world opinion. Its recognition of genocide as an international crime is persuasive evidence of the fact. We approve and adopt its conclusions. Whether the crime against humanity is the product of statute or of common international law, or, as we believe, of both, we find no injustice to persons tried for such crimes. They are chargeable with knowledge that such acts were wrong and were punishable when committed.

The defendants contend that they should not be found guilty because they acted within the authority and by the command of German laws and decrees. Concerning crimes against humanity, C.C.Law 10 provides for punishment whether or not the acts were in violation of the domestic laws of the country where perpetrated (C.C.Law 10, art. II, par. 1(*c*)) * * *.

The foregoing provisions constitute a sufficient, but not the entire, answer to the contention of the defendants. The argument that compliance with German law is a defense to the charge rests on a misconception of the basic theory which supports our entire proceedings. The Nuremberg Tribunals are not German courts. They are not enforcing German law. The charges are not based on violation by the defendants of German law. On the contrary, the jurisdiction of this Tribunal rests on international authority. It enforces the law as declared by the IMT Charter and C.C.Law 10, and within the limitations on the power conferred, it enforces international law as superior in authority to any German statute or decree. It is true, as defendants contend, that German courts under the Third Reich were required to follow German law (i.e., the expressed will of Hitler) even when it was contrary to international law. But no such limitation can be applied to this Tribunal. Here we have the paramount substantive law, plus a Tribunal authorized and required to apply it notwithstanding the inconsistent provisions of German local law. The very essence of the prosecution case is that the laws, the Hitlerian decrees and the Draconic, corrupt, and perverted Nazi judicial system themselves constituted the substance of war crimes and crimes against humanity and that participation in the enactment and enforcement of them amounts to complicity in crime. We have pointed out that governmental participation is a material element of the crime against humanity. Only when official organs of sovereignty participated in atrocities and persecutions did those crimes assume international proportions. It can scarcely be said that governmental participation, the proof of which is necessary for conviction, can also be a defense to the charge.

### *Notes*

1. The second of the foregoing passages is from one of the Nuremberg trials carried out under the authority of the Allied Control Council, pursuant to Law No. 10. In these trials the judicial machinery was part of the occupation administration for the American zone, the Office of Military Government (OMGUS). See generally Taylor, Nuremberg Trials, International Conciliation No. 450 (1959); Taylor, Nuremberg and Vietnam (1970).

2. The General Assembly, by unanimous vote, affirmed the principles of international law recognized in the Nuremberg Charter and Judgment. G.A.Res. 95(I) U.N.Doc. A/236 (1946). Is the reasoning of the tribunals quoted above persuasive as to the criminal responsibility of individuals obeying state

orders? See Lauterpacht, International Law and Human Rights 38–47 (1950); Schneeberger, The Responsibility of the Individual under International Law, 35 Geo.L.J. 481 (1947); Levy, Criminal Responsibility of Individuals and International Law, 12 U.Chi.L.Rev. 313 (1945); Manner, The Legal Nature and Punishment of Criminal Acts of Violence Contrary to the Laws of War, 37 A.J.I.L. 407 (1943).

3. In 1950, pursuant to a request from the General Assembly, the International Law Commission prepared a Draft Code of Offenses Against the Peace and Security of Mankind, offenses which would be crimes under international law for which individuals would be responsible. [1950] 2 Yb.I.L.C. 253; [1951] 2 Yb.I.L.C. 43. Because the Draft Code raised problems related to the effort to define aggression, the General Assembly postponed consideration of the Draft Code until it could consider both problems together. In 1974, the Assembly adopted a definition of aggression, G.A.Res. 3314(XXIX) G.A.O.R., 29th Sess., Supp. 31 (1974) p. 897 infra. Article 5(2) provided: "A war of aggression is a crime against international peace. Aggression gives rise to international responsibility." In 1978, the Draft Code of Offenses Against the Peace and Security of Mankind was reactivated, the General Assembly inviting comments on the 1954 draft. G.A.Res. 33/97(XXXIII) (1978). The United States opposed reconsideration of the Draft Code as a useless exercise. It argued that the likelihood of achieving consensus was small, a consolidated code would add nothing to existing conventions and declarations, and the 1974 definition of aggression was too imprecise to serve as the basis for a criminal indictment. Reply of the United States, UN Doc. A/35/210/Add. 1 at 11 (1980), and UN Doc. A/C.6/35/SR. 12 at 9 (Oct. 7, 1980).

In 1981 the Draft Code was nonetheless referred back by the General Assembly to the International Law Commission, where a new controversy over individual and state criminal responsibility arose. The 1954 Draft Code was addressed to individuals and not to states (Article 1), but the Commission questioned "whether new subjects of law, in the form of the State or certain other groups, have not emerged in the criminal area." [1983] I Yb.I.L.C. 22. Although the Commission divided sharply on this question, the prevailing opinion was that criminal responsibility of the State must be included in the Code. [1983] I Yb.I.L.C. 23. However, after soliciting the opinions of member states, the Commission reversed its position and stated it would limit criminal responsibility to individuals. [1983] I Yb.I.L.C. 29–30. See Gross, Some Observations on the Draft Code of Offences Against the Peace and Security of Mankind, 13 Isr.Yb.H.Rts. 9–51 (1983); Ferencz, Current Developments: The Draft Code of Offences Against the Peace and Security of Mankind, 75 A.J.I.L. 674 (1981).

The work of the International Law Commission on the Code of Crimes has since been focused on preparing articles for a draft code of crimes for which individuals are responsible. At its 43d session in 1991, the Commission adopted the Draft Code of Crimes Against the Peace and Security of Mankind consisting of 26 articles including articles on the crimes of aggression; threat of aggression; intervention; colonial domination; genocide; apartheid; systematic or mass violations of human rights; exceptionally serious war crimes; recruitment, use, financing and training of mercenaries; international terrorism; illicit drug trafficking; and wilful and severe damage to the environment. 30 I.L.M. 1584 (1991). Article 5 of the 1991 draft provides that prosecution of an individual does relieve a State of responsibility under international law for an act or omission attributable to it. Article 6 states that any "State in whose territory an individual alleged to have committed a crime against the peace and security of mankind is present shall either try or extradite him." 30 I.L.M. 1585 (1991). For commentary on the draft see I.L.C. Tenth Report on the Draft Code of

Crimes Against the Peace and Security of Mankind at pp. 31–59, A/CN.4/L.469 20 March 1992.

Questions of individual responsibility for violations of the laws of war received wide public attention during the Vietnam war. The killing of prisoners in custody and the massacre of Vietnamese civilians (most notoriously in the Son My–My Lai cases) resulted in some court-martials of American soldiers, see p. 380 supra, and stimulated demands for punishment of higher officials in both military and civilian positions. There was abundant evidence that higher-ranking military commanders knew or were in a position to know that the laws of war in respect of treatment of the civilian population and of prisoners of war were being violated in numerous situations. See Taylor, Nuremberg and Vietnam, chapters 5–7 (1970). Although no punitive action was taken against the senior military commanders, the issue of their individual responsibility was widely discussed and the precedent of Nuremberg invoked. Civilian officials, including the President and the Secretary of State, were also charged with complicity in atrocities and as bearing the principal responsibility for the widespread bombing of civilian populations in both Vietnam and Cambodia.

Proposals for setting up an international criminal court on a permanent basis have been made in the United Nations and advocated by nonofficial bodies. A UN Committee on International Criminal Jurisdiction submitted reports (including a draft statute for an international criminal court) in 1951 and in 1953. See 9 GAOR, Supp. 12 (A/2625) (1953). No action was taken to proceed with the report, and it seems improbable that an international criminal court will be established in the near future. See International Criminal Law 513–627 (Mueller & Wise eds., 1965). For a documented history and analysis of past efforts to establish an International Criminal Court see Ferencz, An International Criminal Court: A Step Toward World Peace (1980). As requested by the U.N. General Assembly, the International Law Commission has recently been considering the possibility of establishing an international criminal court and has considered draft provisions dealing with this project. See I.L.C. Tenth Report on the Draft Code of Crimes Against the Peace and Security of Mankind pp. 3–30, 59–69, A/CN.4/442 20 March 1992.

4. Iraq's aggression against Kuwait in August 1990 gave rise to charges that Saddam Hussein's government and military forces committed crimes against the peace and war crimes, and proposals were made that the perpetrators be brought to trial, possibly in absentia. One proposal called for trial by an ad hoc tribunal established under the authority of the U.N. Security Council. Compare O'Brien, The Nuremberg Precedent and the Gulf War, 31 Va.J.I.L. 391 (1991) and Moore, War Crimes and the Rule of Law in the Gulf Crisis, 31 Va.J.I.L. 403 (1991). The U.N. Human Rights Commission appointed a Special Rapporteur in 1991 to investigate and report on human rights violations in Iraq. This Special Rapporteur submitted a series of reports to the Commission and the U.N. General Assembly. See the Report to the Commission on Human Rights of 18 February 1992, U.N. Doc. E/CN.4/1992/31, and an interim report on human rights violations in the southern marsh area of Iraq forwarded to the U.N. General Assembly on 10 August 1992. U.N. Doc. A/47/367.

## BALKANS WAR-CRIMES COMMISSION RESOLUTION

S.C.Res. 780 (1992).

THE SECURITY COUNCIL,

* * *

RECALLING paragraph 10 of its resolution 764 * * * of 13 July 1992, in which it reaffirmed that all parties are bound to comply with the obligations under international humanitarian law and in particular the Geneva Conventions of 12 August 1949, and that persons who commit or order the commission of grave breaches of the Conventions are individually responsible in respect of such breaches,

RECALLING also its resolution 771 * * * of 13 August 1992, in which, inter alia, it demanded that all parties and others concerned in the former Yugoslavia, and all military forces in Bosnia and Herzegovina, immediately cease and desist from all breaches of international humanitarian law,

EXPRESSING once again its grave alarm at continuing reports of widespread violations of international humanitarian law occurring within the territory of the former Yugoslavia and especially in Bosnia and Herzegovina, including reports of mass killings and the continuance of the practice of "ethnic cleansing,"

1. REAFFIRMS its call, in paragraph 5 of resolution 771 (1992), upon States and, as appropriate, international humanitarian organizations to collate substantiated information in their possession or submitted to them relating to the violations of humanitarian law, including grave breaches of the Geneva Conventions being committed in the territory of the former Yugoslavia, and requests States, relevant United Nations bodies, and relevant organizations to make this information available within thirty days of the adoption of this resolution and as appropriate thereafter, and to provide other appropriate assistance to the Commission of Experts referred to in paragraph 2 below;

2. REQUESTS the Secretary-General to establish, as a matter of urgency, an impartial Commission of Experts to examine and analyze the information submitted pursuant to resolution 771 * * * and the present resolution, together with such further information as the Commission of Experts may obtain through its own investigations or efforts of other persons or bodies pursuant to resolution 771 (1992), with a view to providing the Secretary-General with its conclusions on the evidence of grave breaches of the Geneva Conventions and other violations of international humanitarian law committed in the territory of the former Yugoslavia;

3. ALSO REQUESTS the Secretary-General to report to the Council on the establishment of the Commission of Experts;

4. FURTHER REQUESTS the Secretary-General to report to the Council on the conclusions of the Commission of Experts and to take account of these conclusions in any recommendations for further appropriate steps called for by resolution 771 (1992);

5. DECIDES to remain actively seized of the matter.

### *Notes*

1. The Balkans War Crimes Commission is to be modelled on the Allied War Crimes Commission set up in 1943, which collected the evidence of Nazi atrocities that was used in Nuremberg and other trials of Nazis. The Security Council took no action to establish a tribunal to try those who might be indicted on the basis of evidence collected by the Commission of war crimes and crimes against humanity.

The United States urged creation of a war-crimes tribunal in August 1992, a proposal also endorsed by Cyrus R. Vance and Lord Owen, the heads of the joint United Nations–European Community mediation effort. On December 16, 1992, the United States published a list of Serbian and Croatian political and military figures as possible war criminals at the U.N.–E.C.–sponsored Yugoslavia Conference involving 29 states. The names and details of their alleged crimes were supplied to the U.N. War Crimes Commission, which has the responsibility of determining whether prosecution is warranted. The alleged crimes against humanity include murders of men, women and children, mass executions, torture and forced expulsion of civilians from their villages, many carried out under the banner of "ethnic cleansing".

On May 25, 1993, the U.N. Security Council adopted by a vote of 15–0 a resolution establishing an 11–judge court for the trial of individuals accused of serious violations of international humanitarian law committed in the former Yugoslavia since 1991. S.C.Res. 808 (1993). The judges will be elected by the U.N. General Assembly acting on Security Council recommendation. The Court is expected to have a trial and appeals chamber and a prosecutor. It would not try individuals *in absentia* and would therefore necessarily rely on governmental cooperation, including extradition.

2. On December 3, 1992, the Security Council unanimously adopted a resolution authorizing the use of force to establish a secure environment for humanitarian relief operations in Somalia. S.C.Res. 794 (1992). The resolution also stated that the Council strongly condemned "all violations of international humanitarian law occurring in Somalia, including in particular the deliberate impeding of the delivery of food and medical supplies essential for the survival of the civilian population, and affirms that those who commit or order the commission of such acts will be held individually responsible in respect of such acts."

## D. TERRORISTS IN INTERNATIONAL LAW

In the past thirty years the international community has witnessed a substantial increase in domestic and international terrorist activities. This development has been accompanied by a dramatic increase in state-provided training, financing and logistical support to terrorist organizations.

Efforts by the international community to combat acts of terrorism by individuals have led to the conclusion of several multilateral conventions. These conventions are directed at specific types of terrorist conduct—aircraft sabotage and hijacking,[1] attacks on diplomats,[2] and hostage-taking.[3] They

1. Convention for the Suppression of Unlawful Seizure of Aircraft, 22 U.S.T. 1641, T.I.A.S. No. 7192; Convention for the Suppression of Unlawful Acts against the Safety of Civil Aviation, 24 U.S.T. 565, T.I.A.S. No. 7570.

2. Convention on the Prevention and Punishment of Crimes Against Internationally

3. See note 3 on page 392.

oblige states to prosecute an alleged offender found within their territory or to extradite him or her.

### 1. *Terrorism as an International Crime*

Directed specifically against terrorism is the Convention to Prevent and Punish the Acts of Terrorism Taking the Form of Crimes Against Persons and Related Extortion That Are of International Significance, to which the United States is a party and (as of 1992) ten Latin American countries are parties. 27 U.S.T. 3949, T.I.A.S. No. 8413.

After a series of terrorist acts in 1985, the United Nations General Assembly unanimously passed a resolution which:

> 1. *Unequivocally condemns,* as criminal, all acts, methods and practices of terrorism wherever and by whomever committed, including those which jeopardize friendly relations among States and their security; * * *
>
> 4. *Appeals* to all States that have not yet done so to consider becoming party to the existing international conventions relating to various aspects of international terrorism * * *
>
> 6. *Calls upon* all States to fulfill their obligations under international law to refrain from organizing, instigating, assisting or participating in terrorist acts in other States, or acquiescing in activities within their territory directed toward the commission of such acts. * * *

U.N.G.A.Res. 40/61 G.A.O.R., 40th Sess., Supp. 53 (1985). The Security Council also adopted a resolution in December 1985 condemning all acts of hostage taking and abduction and declaring that all states are obliged to prevent such acts. S.C.Res. 579 U.N.Doc. S/RES/579 (1985).

### 2. *The Obligation to Extradite and the Political Offense Exception*

Persons accused of terrorism have claimed that they are engaged in political activities and come within the "political offense" exception to extradition. This claim has often been successful because of the strong tradition in many states of providing asylum and protection for political offenders. Two regional conventions, however, attempt to limit the application of the "political offense" doctrine to terrorist acts. See The European Convention on the Suppression of Terrorism, 15 I.L.M. 1272 (1976), and the Agreement on the Application of the European Convention for the Suppression of Terrorism (the Dublin Agreement), 19 I.L.M. 325 (1980). See also the Supplementary Extradition Treaty between the United States and the United Kingdom, Treaty Doc. 99–8 99th Cong., 1st Sess.1985, which came into force in 1986. For a discussion of the political offense exception and extradition in general, see Hannay, International Terrorism and the Political Offense Exception, 18 Col.J.Transnat'l L. 381 (1980), and p. 1113 infra.

Protected Persons, including Diplomatic Agents, 28 U.S.T. 1975, T.I.A.S. No. 8532.

3. International Convention against the Taking of Hostages, adopted by the General Assembly on December 17, 1979. U.N. Doc. A/Res/34/146.

### 3. *State Responsibility in Cases of Terrorism*

Unless a state is party to a convention obliging it to extradite or prosecute, it is debatable whether the State violates international law if it offers a safe haven to a terrorist. However, states allowing terrorists to use their territory as a base for their operations incur international responsibility. The well-established rule of international law forbidding states to permit their territory to be used as a base for armed bands of whatever nature to operate against in the territory of another state has been suggested as a basis for international claims against states providing support for terrorists. See Lillich & Paxman, State Responsibility for Injuries to Aliens Occasioned by Terrorist Activities, 26 Am.U.L.Rev. 217 (1977), and p. 718 infra.

### 4. *International Sanctions Against Terrorism*

None of the multilateral antiterrorist conventions provides for economic or other sanctions against states that assist terrorists or offer them a safe haven. A framework for cooperation in the application of a specific sanction has been established, however, in the Bonn Declaration on Hijacking. 17 I.L.M. 1285 (1975). Under this Declaration, the United States, Japan, and four Western European states have agreed to halt air traffic service with any country that refuses to extradite or prosecute airplane hijackers or refuses to return the aircraft, passengers and crew. The Declaration has attracted widespread support and may serve as a model for future economic sanctions against states actively supporting terrorism. See Murphy, Recent International Legal Developments in Controlling Terrorism, 4 Chin.Yb.I.L. and Affs. 97, 107–08, 118–19 (1984); Comment, Skyjacking and the Bonn Declaration of 1978, 10 Cal.W.Int'l L.J. 123 (1980); and Murphy, Punishing International Terrorists: The Legal Framework for Policy Initiatives (1985).

The United States adopted several countermeasures against Libya on the basis of evidence that the Libyan government supported terrorist action directed against United States nationals and United States installations and vehicles. The measures adopted in 1986 included partial severance of trade and financial relations. See Statement of President on January 7, 1986, in 86:2108 State Dept.Bull. 36–39 (1986). See also Executive Orders 12543 and 12544 of January 7, 1986. Id. On counter-measures and sanctions generally, see Chapter 7, Section 7.

On April 14, 1986, the United States launched bombing raids on Libyan targets as a response to Libya's alleged involvement in a terrorist bombing of a Berlin nightclub frequented by United States servicemen, and it justified the military action as an act of self-defense consistent with Article 51 of the U.N. Charter. See p. 922 infra. On the legality of the extraterritorial use of force against individual terrorists and against states harboring such terrorists, see Chapter 11.

In the aftermath of the terrorist bombing of Pan Am Flight 103 over Lockerbie, Scotland, in December, 1987, and following a long investigation, the United States and the United Kingdom indicted two Libyan nationals in 1992 and demanded that they be turned over for prosecution to the United States or the United Kingdom. The Libyan Government took the position that, in the absence of an extradition treaty with either the United States or the United Kingdom, its only obligation under the 1971 Montreal Aircraft

Sabotage Convention (Convention for the Suppression of Unlawful Acts against the Safety of Civil Aviation, 24 U.S.T. 565, T.I.A.S. No. 7570), to which all three states are parties, was to investigate and prosecute, if appropriate, or to extradite. Libya conducted an investigation and decided it had an inadequate basis on which to prosecute. It declined to extradite on the ground that Libyan law precluded extradition of Libyan nationals to another country. The request by the French Government for extradition of alleged Libyan terrorists involved in the destruction of U.T.A. Flight 773 was also rebuffed by the Libyan Government. The U.N. Security Council then unanimously adopted a resolution urging the Libyan Government "immediately to provide a full and effective response to [the requests to cooperate fully in establishing responsibility for the terrorist acts] so as to contribute to the elimination of international terrorism." S.C.Res. 731, 47th Sess., 3033d Mtg., U.N.Doc. S/RES/731 (1992). Subsequently, the Security Council, by vote of 10–0 with 5 abstentions (China, Cape Verde, India, Monaco, and Zimbabwe), determined that "the failure by the Libyan Government to demonstrate, by concrete actions, its renunciation of terrorism, and, in particular, its continued failure to respond fully and effectively to the requests in Resolution 731 constitute a threat to international peace and security." Acting under Chapter VII of the Charter, the Council imposed sanctions on Libya, including termination of air traffic, a prohibition on sale of aircraft and arms and related components and services, and a reduction in the size of Libyan diplomatic and consular missions.

## SECTION 7. NATIONALITY UNDER INTERNATIONAL LAW

### A. NATIONALITY OF INDIVIDUALS

#### 1. *Significance of Nationality*

An individual's nationality is significant under international law at a number of points. A state has jurisdiction to prescribe with respect to its nationals located outside its territory when it could not do so with respect to aliens. See p. 1057 infra. A state may accord diplomatic protection to its national in any case in which the national has been injured by another state's violation of international law. See p. 677 infra. It may intercede diplomatically on behalf of an alien only under special circumstances, for example, when human rights violations under a human rights treaty or customary international law are involved. See p. 632 infra. Extradition treaties may provide that a state need not extradite its own nationals. See p. 1114 infra.

In 1923, the Permanent Court of International Justice in the *Tunis and Morocco Nationality Decrees Case,* (1923) P.C.I.J., Ser.B., No. 4, p. 4, held that whether a state treated an individual as its national was a matter within its exclusive domestic jurisdiction. In the intervening years some international law constraints, which are discussed in the materials that follow, have developed on the untrammelled power of a state to confer its nationality on an individual or to withdraw it.

A focus of considerable attention has been whether the individual has a right to a nationality or, in other words, to be protected from statelessness. The right also encompasses the right to change one's nationality and the right not to be arbitrarily deprived of one's nationality. See Chan, The Right to a Nationality As a Human Right, 12 Hum.Rts.L.J. 1–14 (1991).

Although there is significant support for the proposition that a right to nationality should be recognized as a human right protected under international law, there has been substantial resistance to this recognition on the part of states. As recently as 1989, an attempt to guarantee the right to nationality in a Protocol to the European Convention on Human Rights failed. Id. at p. 7.

### *Notes*

1. A stateless individual has no right to invoke the diplomatic protection of any state. If expelled by the country of residence, no state is required to accept him or her. A number of international agreements reduce the circumstances under which statelessness can occur. The Protocol to the Convention Relating to the Status of Refugees, 19 U.S.T. 6223, T.I.A.S. No. 6577, 606 U.N.T.S. 267, 1968, to which the United States is a party, accords protection under certain circumstances to stateless refugees. The United States is not a party to the United Nations Convention relating to the Status of Stateless Persons, 360 U.N.T.S. 117 (1954), or to the United Nations Convention on the Reduction of Statelessness. U.N.Doc. A/Conf. 9/15. The latter would prohibit denationalization except for serious acts of disloyalty if it would render the individual stateless, and it would prohibit denationalization based on marriage to a foreign national if the result would be statelessness.

2. Restatement (Third) § 211, Comment *c* states as follows with respect to termination of nationality:

> Traditional international law did not question the authority of a state to terminate the nationality of any of its nationals. Increasingly, the law has accepted some limitations on involuntary termination of nationality, both to prevent statelessness (Comment *g*) and in recognition that denationalization can be an instrument of racial, religious, ethnic, or gender discrimination, or of political repression. There has also been a growing recognition of a human right to nationality. See § 701, Reporters' Note 6. International law does not forbid denationalization for treason, espionage, or other serious offenses against the state, or the cancellation of naturalization for fraud in obtaining it.

Article 15(1) of the Universal Declaration of Human Rights, G.A.RES 217 (III 1948), provides that everyone "has a right to a nationality" and Article 15(2) states that no one "shall be arbitrarily deprived of his nationality nor denied the right to change his nationality." See Lauterpacht, International Law and Human Rights (1968) at 346–350.

Article 20 of the American Convention on Human Rights provides as follows:

Right to Nationality

1. Every person has the right to a nationality.

2. Every person has the right to the nationality of the State in whose territory he was born if he does not have the right to any other nationality.

3. No one shall be arbitrarily deprived of his nationality or of the right to change it.

In an advisory opinion on whether proposed amendments to the Costa Rica Constitution violated Article 20, the Inter-American Court of Human Rights opined that nationality is an inherent right of all human beings and that a state's regulation of nationality is subject to a state's obligations to protect the human rights of individuals. Re Amendments to the Naturalization Provisions of the Constitution of Costa Rica, Advisory Opinion of 19 January 1984, OC-4/84, reported in 5 Hum.Rts.L.J. 161 (1984).

3. While nationality is a concept of international law, citizenship is a concept of the municipal law of many but not all states. Citizenship is a status that usually entails full political rights, including the right to vote and hold public office. A citizen under municipal law is usually a national under international law, but not all nationals are citizens under municipal law. Restatement (Third) § 211, Comment *h*.

### 2. *Limits on the Conferring of Nationality*

#### *CONVENTION ON CERTAIN QUESTIONS RELATING TO THE CONFLICT OF NATIONALITY LAWS*

Signed at The Hague, April 12, 1930.
179 L.N.T.S. 89, 5 Hudson, Int'l Legislation 359.

Art. 1. It is for each State to determine under its own law who are its nationals. This law shall be recognised by other States in so far as it is consistent with international conventions, international custom, and the principles of law generally recognised with regard to nationality.

Art. 2. Any question as to whether a person possesses the nationality of a particular State shall be determined in accordance with the law of that State.

Art. 3. Subject to the provisions of the present Convention, a person having two or more nationalities may be regarded as its national by each of the States whose nationality he possesses.

#### *Notes*

1. What limits does international law, particularly "international custom" and "the principles of law generally recognised with regard to nationality," impose on the power of states to legislate on matters of nationality? The Harvard Research laid down the rule in 1929 that the power of a state to confer its nationality was "not unlimited," observing that although it might be difficult to specify the limitations imposed by international law on the power of a state to confer its nationality, "it is obvious that some limitations do exist." The Law of Nationality, Art. 2, 23 A.J.I.L.Spec.Supp. 11, 24–27 (1929). The Hague Codification Conference of 1930 was unable to agree upon a more precise formulation than that adopted in Article 1 of the Convention on Certain Questions Relating to the Conflict of Nationality Laws, quoted above, but a number of participating governments asserted that states were not obligated under international law to

recognize nationality conferred upon a person in the absence of some generally recognized relationship or connection between the person and the state claiming him as its national. The German government, for example, stated:

> * * * [A] State has no power, by means of a law or administrative act, to confer its nationality on all the inhabitants of another State or on all foreigners entering [its] territory. Further, if the State confers its nationality on the subjects of other States without their request, when the persons in question are not attached to it by any particular bond, as, for instance, origin, domicile or birth, the States concerned will not be bound to recognise such naturalisation.

League of Nations Docs.1929. V. 1, at 13.

The United States was of the opinion that there were "certain grounds generally recognised by civilised States upon which a State may properly clothe individuals with its nationality at or after birth, but * * * no State is free to extend the application of its laws of nationality in such a way as to reach out and claim the allegiance of whomsoever it pleases. The scope of municipal laws governing nationality must be regarded as limited by consideration of the rights and obligations of individuals and of other States." Id. at 145–46. Although certain governments participating in the Conference questioned the existence of rules of international law, other than those laid down in treaties, that limited a state's freedom in matters of nationality, the text of Article 1 of the Convention on Certain Questions Relating to the Conflict of Nationality Laws was adopted by an overwhelming majority. As of 1991, twenty-five states, including the United States have become party to the Convention.

Compare Hyde 1066: "In a broad sense international law limits the right of a State to impress its national character upon an individual, or to prevent that character from being lost or transferred. The freedom of action of each member of the family of nations is, however, wide. That circumstance, as well as the modern practice of States to declare by statute what persons are deemed to be nationals by birth, and how nationality may be acquired or lost, serves to obscure from view the final test of the reasonableness of the local law." What circumstances make it "reasonable" for a state to confer its nationality upon an individual? While states confer nationality at birth exclusively on the basis of descent from nationals (*jure sanguinis*) and on the basis of birth within the territory of the state (*jure soli*), the majority have enacted legislation that combines elements of both systems, with one or the other serving as a principal standard. U.N. Secretariat, Laws Concerning Nationality, U.N.Doc. ST/LEG/SER.B/4 (1954), supplemented by ST/LEG/SER.B/9 (1959).

## NOTTEBOHM CASE (LIECHTENSTEIN v. GUATEMALA)

International Court of Justice, 1955.
1955 I.C.J. 4.

[Nottebohm had been a German national from his birth in Germany in 1881 until his naturalization in Liechtenstein in 1939, shortly after the outbreak of war in Europe. In 1905, he had taken up residence in Guatemala and engaged in substantial business dealings in that country. Thereafter, he sometimes went to Germany on business, to other countries on holidays, and to Liechtenstein in order to visit a brother who lived there after 1931. In early 1939, Nottebohm went to Europe and eventually applied for naturalization in Liechtenstein on October 9, 1939. Nottebohm sought and received dispensation from residence requirements, paid his fees and gave security for the payment of taxes, and completed the naturalization process by taking an oath of allegiance on October 20, 1939. He obtained a Liechtenstein passport, had it visaed by the Guatemalan consul in Zurich, and returned to Guatemala to resume his business activities. At his request, Guatemalan authorities made appropriate changes regarding Nottebohm's nationality in the Register of Aliens and in his identity document.

[On July 17, 1941, the United States blacklisted Nottebohm and froze his assets in the United States. War broke out between the United States and Germany, and between Guatemala and Germany, on December 11, 1941. Nottebohm was arrested by Guatemalan authorities in 1943 and deported to the United States, where he was interned until 1946 as an enemy alien. He applied upon his release for readmission to Guatemala, but his application was refused. Nottebohm then took up residence in Liechtenstein, but Guatemala had in the meantime taken measures against his properties in that country, culminating in confiscatory legislation of 1949.

[Liechtenstein instituted proceedings against Guatemala in the International Court of Justice, asking the Court to declare that Guatemala had violated international law "in arresting, detaining, expelling and refusing to readmit Mr. Nottebohm and in seizing and retaining his property" and consequently was bound to pay compensation. Guatemala's principal argument in reply was that the Liechtenstein claim was inadmissible on grounds of the claimant's nationality.

[The Court rejected Liechtenstein's argument that Guatemala was precluded from contesting Nottebohm's nationality, because it had on several occasions acknowledged Nottebohm's claim of Liechtenstein nationality. It then continued:]

Since no proof has been adduced that Guatemala has recognized the title to the exercise of protection relied upon by Liechtenstein as being derived from the naturalization which it granted to Nottebohm, the Court must consider whether such an act of granting nationality by Liechtenstein directly entails an obligation on the part of Guatemala to recognize its effect, namely, Liechtenstein's right to exercise its protection. In other words, it must be determined whether that unilateral act by Liechtenstein is one which can be relied upon against Guatemala in regard to the exercise of protection. The Court will deal with this question without considering that of the validity of Nottebohm's naturalization according to the law of Liechtenstein.

* * *

* * * [T]he issue which the Court must decide is not one which pertains to the legal system of Liechtenstein. It does not depend on the law or on the decision of Liechtenstein whether that State is entitled to exercise its protection, in the case under consideration. To exercise protection, to apply to the Court, is to place oneself on the plane of international law. It is

international law which determines whether a State is entitled to exercise protection and to seise the Court.

* * *

The practice of certain States which refrain from exercising protection in favour of a naturalized person when the latter has in fact, by his prolonged absence, severed his links with what is no longer for him anything but his nominal country, manifests the view of these States that, in order to be capable of being invoked against another State, nationality must correspond with the factual situation. * * *

The character thus recognized on the international level as pertaining to nationality is in no way inconsistent with the fact that international law leaves it to each State to lay down the rules governing the grant of its own nationality. The reason for this is that the diversity of demographic conditions has thus far made it impossible for any general agreement to be reached on the rules relating to nationality, although the latter by its very nature affects international relations. It has been considered that the best way of making such rules accord with the varying demographic conditions in different countries is to leave the fixing of such rules to the competence of each State. On the other hand, a State cannot claim that the rules it has thus laid down are entitled to recognition by another State unless it has acted in conformity with this general aim of making the legal bond of nationality accord with the individual's genuine connection with the State which assumes the defence of its citizens by means of protection as against other States.

* * *

According to the practice of States, to arbitral and judicial decisions and to the opinions of writers, nationality is a legal bond having as its basis a social fact of attachment, a genuine connection of existence, interests and sentiments, together with the existence of reciprocal rights and duties. It may be said to constitute the juridical expression of the fact that the individual upon whom it is conferred, either directly by the law or as the result of an act of the authorities is in fact more closely connected with the population of the State conferring nationality than with that of any other State. Conferred by a State, it only entitles that State to exercise protection vis-á-vis another State, if it constitutes a translation into juridical terms of the individual's connection with the State which has made him its national.

* * *

Since this is the character which nationality must present when it is invoked to furnish the State which has granted it with a title to the exercise of protection and to the institution of international judicial proceedings, the Court must ascertain whether the nationality granted to Nottebohm by means of naturalization is of this character or, in other words, whether the factual connection between Nottebohm and Liechtenstein in the period preceding, contemporaneous with and following his naturalization appears to be sufficiently close, so preponderant in relation to any connection which may have existed between him and any other State, that it is possible to regard the nationality conferred upon him as real and effective, as the exact juridical expression of a social fact of a connection which existed previously or came into existence thereafter.

Naturalization is not a matter to be taken lightly. * * * In order to appraise its international effect, it is impossible to disregard the circumstances in which it was conferred, the serious character which attaches to it, the real and effective, and not merely the verbal preference of the individual seeking it for the country which grants it to him.

At the time of his naturalization does Nottebohm appear to have been more closely attached by his tradition, his establishment, his interests, his activities, his family ties, his intentions for the near future to Liechtenstein than to any other State? * * *

At the date when he applied for naturalization Nottebohm had been a German national from the time of his birth. He had always retained his connections with members of his family who had remained in Germany and he had always had business connections with that country. His country had been at war for more than a month, and there is nothing to indicate that the application for naturalization then made by Nottebohm was motivated by any desire to dissociate himself from the Government of his country.

He had been settled in Guatemala for 34 years. He had carried on his activities there. It was the main seat of his interests. He returned there shortly after his naturalization, and it remained the centre of his interests and of his business activities. He stayed there until his removal as a result of war measures in 1943. He subsequently attempted to return there, and he now complains of Guatemala's refusal to admit him. There, too, were several members of his family who sought to safeguard his interests.

In contrast, his actual connections with Liechtenstein were extremely tenuous. No settled abode, no prolonged residence in that country at the time of his application for naturalization: the application indicates that he was paying a visit there and confirms the transient character of this visit by its request that the naturalization proceedings should be initiated and concluded without delay. No intention of settling there was shown at that time or realized in the ensuing weeks, months or years—on the contrary, he returned to Guatemala very shortly after his naturalization and showed every intention of remaining there. If Nottebohm went to Liechtenstein in 1946, this was because of the refusal of Guatemala to admit him. No indication is given of the grounds warranting the waiver of the condition of residence, required by the 1934 Nationality Law, which waiver was implicitly granted to him. There is no allegation of any economic interests or of any activities exercised or to be exercised in Liechtenstein, and no manifestation of any intention whatsoever to transfer all or some of his interests and his business activities to Liechtenstein. It is unnecessary in this connection to attribute much importance to the promise to pay the taxes levied at the time of his naturalization. The only links to be discovered between the Principality and Nottebohm are the short sojourns already referred to and the presence in Vaduz of one of his brothers: but his brother's presence is referred to in his application for naturalization only as a reference to his good conduct. Furthermore other members of his family have asserted Nottebohm's desire to spend his old age in Guatemala.

These facts clearly establish, on the one hand, the absence of any bond of attachment between Nottebohm and Liechtenstein and, on the other hand, the existence of a long-standing and close connection between him and Guatemala, a link which his naturalization in no way weakened. That naturalization was not based on any real prior connection with Liechtenstein, nor did it in any way alter the manner of life of the person upon whom it was conferred in exceptional circumstances of speed and accommodation. In both respects, it was lacking in the genuineness requisite to an act of such importance, if it is to be entitled to be respected by a State in the position of Guatemala. It was granted without regard to the concept of nationality adopted in international relations.

Naturalization was asked for not so much for the purpose of obtaining a legal recognition of Nottebohm's membership in fact in the population of Liechtenstein, as it was to enable him to substitute for his status as a national of a belligerent State that of a national of a neutral State, with the sole aim of thus coming within the protection of Liechtenstein but not of becoming wedded to its traditions, its interests, its way of life or of assuming the obligations—other than fiscal obligations—and exercising the rights pertaining to the status thus acquired.

Guatemala is under no obligation to recognize a nationality granted in such circumstances. Liechtenstein consequently is not entitled to extend its protection to Nottebohm vis-á-vis Guatemala and its claim must, for this reason, be held to be inadmissible. * * *

For these reasons, the court, by eleven votes to three, holds that the claim submitted by the Government of the Principality of Liechtenstein is inadmissible.

[Dissenting opinions of Judges Klaestad and Read, and of Judge *ad hoc* Guggenheim, are omitted.]

### *Notes*

1. Is nationality an absolute or a relative concept? Does the freedom of a state under international law to make a person its national depend on the consequences to be attached to the nationality bestowed? Would Guatemala have been under the obligation to recognize Nottebohm as a Liechtenstein national in regard to claims accrued during his actual presence in Liechtenstein?

2. The Restatement takes the position, based on the *Nottebohm* case, that other states need not accept nationality conferred on an individual by another state when it is not based on a "genuine link" between the conferring state and the individual. Restatement (Third) § 211. Comment *c* notes as follows:

> The precise contours of this concept, however, are not clear. Laws that confer nationality on ground of birth in a state's territory (*ius soli*) or birth to parents who are nationals (*ius sanguinis*) are universally accepted as based on genuine links. Voluntary naturalization is generally recognized by other states but may be questioned when there are no other ties to the state, *e.g.,* a period of residence in the state. The comparative "genuineness" and strength of links between a state and an individual are relevant also for resolving competing claims between two states asserting nationality, or between such states and a third state.

See Brownlie, Principles of International Law 407–420 (4th ed. 1990).

### 3. *Involuntary Nationality*

The imposition by a state of its nationality on an individual against his or her will, or if that nationality has been renounced, may violate international law. A state is not required to recognize a nationality imposed by another state or an individual against his or her will on the basis of a link such as marriage to a national, a specified period of residence, acquisition of real property in the state's territory, bearing of a child there or having a particular ethnic or national origin. Another state is not required to recognize a nationality that the individual has renounced. Restatement (Third) § 211, Comment *d.* "However legislation that operates only prospectively and gives the alien a reasonable opportunity to avoid the imposition of nationality would probably not violate international law. Laws that provide that a woman automatically acquires her husband's nationality upon marriage are questionable if the woman objects, under the principle of gender equality now internationally recognized, *e.g.,* in the Convention on the Nationality of Women, 49 Stat. 2957, T.S. No. 875 (1934), and in the Universal Declaration of Human Rights and the principal human rights covenants." Restatement (Third) § 211, Reporters' Note 2.

### 4. *Dual Nationality*

## UNITED STATES EX REL. MERGÉ v. ITALIAN REPUBLIC

Italian–United States Conciliation Commission, 1955.
3 Collection of Decisions No. 55.
14 U.N.R.I.A.A. 236.

[The claimant had acquired United States nationality upon her birth in New York in 1909. At the age of 24, she married an Italian national in Rome and thereby acquired, according to Italian law, Italian nationality as well. She lived in Italy with her husband until 1937, at which time she accompanied her husband to Japan, where the latter had been sent as a translator and interpreter for the Italian Embassy in Tokyo. The United States Consulate General there registered the claimant, at her request, as a United States national. The claimant remained with her husband in Japan until 1946, at which time she returned to the United States for a period of nine months on a passport issued to her by the United States consulate in Yokohama. She then returned to Italy to rejoin her husband. Immediately upon her arrival, she registered as a United States national at the American Embassy in Rome. In 1948, the United States submitted to Italy a claim based on Article 78 of the Italian Peace Treaty (February 10, 1947, T.I.A.S. 1648) for compensation for the loss, as a result of the war, of a grand piano and other personal property located in Italy and owned by the claimant. Italy rejected the claim on the ground that the claimant was an Italian national, and the dispute relating to the claimant's double nationality was submitted to the Conciliation Commission.

[The first sub-paragraph of Article 78, § 9(a), of the peace treaty provided that the term "United Nations nationals" was to mean "individuals who are nationals of any of the United Nations." The Commission first considered whether this definition had been intended to avoid the double nationality problem, by allowing claims by all United Nations nationals whether or not they were also Italian nationals. After concluding that the treaty did not resolve the issue, the Commission considered the applicable general principles of international law:]

In this connection two solutions are possible: a) the principle according to which a State may not afford diplomatic protection to one of its nationals against the State whose nationality such person also possesses; b) the principle of effective or dominant nationality.

The two principles just mentioned are defined in [The Hague Convention on Certain Questions Relating to the Conflict of Nationality Laws of 1930]: the first (Art. 4) within the system of public international law; the second (Art. 5) within the system of private international law.

Art. 4 * * * is as follows:

> "A State may not afford diplomatic protection to one of its nationals against a State whose nationality such person also possesses."

The same Convention, in Art. 5, indicates effective nationality as the criterion to be applied by a third State in order to resolve the conflicts of laws raised by dual nationality cases. Such State

> "shall, of the nationalities which any such person possesses, recognize exclusively in its territory either the nationality of the country in which he is habitually and principally resident, or the nationality of the country with which in the circumstances he appears to be most closely connected."

This rule, although referring to the domestic jurisdiction of a State, nevertheless constitutes a guiding principle also in the international system. * * *

The Hague Convention, although not ratified by all the Nations, expresses a *communis opinio juris,* by reason of the near-unanimity with which the principles referring to dual nationality were accepted. * * *

It is not a question of adopting one nationality to the exclusion of the other. Even less when it is recognized by both Parties that the claimant possesses the two nationalities. The problem to be explained is, simply, that of determining whether diplomatic protection can be exercised in such cases.

A prior question requires a solution: are the two principles which have just been set forth incompatible with each other, so that the acceptance of one of them necessarily implies the exclusion of the other? If the reply is in the affirmative, the problem presented is that of a choice; if it is in the negative, one must determine the sphere of application of each one of the two principles.

The Commission is of the opinion that no irreconcilable opposition between the two principles exists; in fact, to the contrary, it believes that they complement each other reciprocally. The principle according to which a State cannot protect one of its nationals against a State which also considers him its national and the principle of effective, in the sense of dominant, nationality, have both been accepted by the Hague Convention (Articles 4 and 5) and by the International Court of Justice (Advisory Opinion of April 11, 1949 and the Nottebohm Decision of April 6, 1955). If these two principles were irreconcilable, the acceptance of both by the Hague

Convention and by the International Court of Justice would be incomprehensible. * * *

The principle, based on the sovereign equality of States, which excludes diplomatic protection in the case of dual nationality, must yield before the principle of effective nationality whenever such nationality is that of the claiming State. But it must not yield when such predominance is not proved, because the first of these two principles is generally recognized and may constitute a criterion of practical application for the elimination of any possible uncertainty.

* * * In view of the principles accepted, it is considered that the Government of the United States of America shall be entitled to protect its nationals before this Commission in cases of dual nationality, United States and Italian, whenever the United States nationality is the effective nationality.

In order to establish the prevalence of the United States nationality in individual cases, habitual residence can be one of the criteria of evaluation, but not the only one. The conduct of the individual in his economic, social, political, civic and family life, as well as the closer and more effective bond with one of the two States must also be considered.

It is considered that in this connection the following principles may serve as guides:

(a) The United States nationality shall be prevalent in cases of children born in the United States of an Italian father and who have habitually lived there.

(b) The United States nationality shall also be prevalent in cases involving Italians who, after having acquired United States nationality by naturalization and having thus lost Italian nationality, have reacquired their nationality of origin as a matter of law as a result of having sojourned in Italy for more than two years, without the intention of retransferring their residence permanently to Italy.

(c) With respect to cases of dual nationality involving American women married to Italian nationals, the United States nationality shall be prevalent in cases in which the family has had habitual residence in the United States and the interests and the permanent professional life of the head of the family were established in the United States.

(d) In case of dissolution of marriage, if the family was established in Italy and the widow transfers her residence to the United States of America, whether or not the new residence is of an habitual nature must be evaluated, case by case, bearing in mind also the widow's conduct, especially with regard to the raising of her children, for the purpose of deciding which is the prevalent nationality.

United States nationals who did not possess Italian nationality but the nationality of a third State can be considered "United Nations nationals" under the Treaty, even if their prevalent nationality was the nationality of the third State.

In all other cases of dual nationality, Italian and United States, when, that is, the United States nationality is not prevalent in accordance with the above, the principle of international law, according to which a claim is not admissible against a State, Italy in our case, when this State also considers the claimant as its national and such bestowal of nationality is, as in the case of Italian law, in harmony * * * with international custom and generally recognized principles of law in the matter of nationality, will reacquire its force.

Examining the facts of the case in bar, * * * the Commission holds that Mrs. Mergé can in no way be considered to be dominantly a United States national within the meaning of Article 78 of the Treaty of Peace, because the family did not have its habitual residence in the United States and the interests and the permanent professional life of the head of the family were not established there. In fact, Mrs. Mergé has not lived in the United States since her marriage, she used an Italian passport in traveling to Japan from Italy in 1937, she stayed in Japan from 1937 until 1946 with her husband, an official of the Italian Embassy in Tokyo, and it does not appear that she was ever interned as a national of a country enemy to Japan.

Inasmuch as Mrs. Mergé, for the foregoing reasons, cannot be considered to be dominantly a United States national within the meaning of Article 78 of the Treaty of Peace, the Commission is of the opinion that the Government of the United States of America is not entitled to present a claim against the Italian Government in her behalf. * * *

[Petition of the United States rejected.]

### *Notes*

1. In Iran v. United States, Case No. A/18, 5 Iran–U.S. Claims Tribunal Reports 251 (1984), the Tribunal held that it could exercise jurisdiction over a claim by a dual national of the United States and Iran against Iran when the claimant's United States nationality was dominant and effective based on all relevant factors, such as habitual residence, center of interests, family ties, participation in public life and other evidence of attachment. See Crook and James, Remarks at Panel on Decisions of the Iran–U.S. Claims Tribunal, A.S.I.L.Proc. 222–27 (1984). On the Tribunal generally, see Chapter 9.

The U.N. Compensation Commission established by the Security Council to supervise the compensation of victims of international law violations by Iraq in connection with its invasion of Kuwait, however, has ruled that Iraqi nationals may file claims if they "have bona fide nationality of any other state," evidently without having to demonstrate that the other nationality is the dominant and effective one. Brower, International Law: On the Edge of Credibility in the Wake of Iraq's Invasion and Occupation of Kuwait, A.S.I.L.Proc. 478, 480 (1992).

2. See also the *Alexander Tellech Claim* (United States v. Austria and Hungary), Tripartite Claims Commission, 1928 Decisions and Opinions 71, 6 U.N.R.I.A.A. 248. Claimant was born in the United States of Austrian parents in 1895, thereby acquiring both Austrian and United States nationality. He lived in the United States until the age of five, when he accompanied his parents to Austria. In 1914, the claimant was interned "as an agitator engaged in propaganda in favor of Russia"; after sixteen months in an internment camp, he was impressed into military service. The Commission rejected a United States claim, put forward on Tellech's behalf, for compensation for time lost and for alleged suffering and privation, on the ground that Tellech was a citizen of Austria as well as of the United States and that he had voluntarily taken "the

risk incident to residing in Austrian territory and subjecting himself to the duties and obligations of an Austrian citizen arising under the municipal laws of Austria."

3. The *Canevaro Case* (Italy v. Peru), Hague Court Reports (Scott) 284 (Perm.Ct.Arb.1912), involved a claim asserted against Peru by three individuals on whose behalf Italy had intervened. Two of the claimants were Italian nationals, but Peru contended that the third individual, Canevaro, had no right to be considered an Italian claimant. The tribunal noted that Canevaro was considered a Peruvian citizen under Peruvian law because he was born on Peruvian territory and was considered an Italian citizen under Italian law because he was born of an Italian father. It also found that Canevaro had on several occasions acted as a Peruvian citizen, both by running as a candidate for the Senate (of which only Peruvian citizens can be members) and by successfully defending his election, and, particularly, by accepting the office of Consul General for the Netherlands, after having secured the authorization of both the Peruvian Government and the Peruvian Congress. It therefore held that whatever Canevaro's status as a national might be in Italy, the Government of Peru had a right to consider him a Peruvian citizen and to deny his status as an Italian claimant.

4. In addition to the issue of whether a state of which an individual is a national may assert an international claim against another state of which the individual is also a national or against a third state, dual nationality issues may arise in the context of military service and taxation. An individual who is a national of two states is exposed to obligatory military service in each, and may be subject to taxation on worldwide income in each. The latter exposure is present only rarely, because nearly all states tax the worldwide income of only those individuals who are residents. The United States is one of a very small number of states that taxes the worldwide income of its citizens even if they reside in another state. See Gustafson & Pugh, Taxation of International Transactions 34–35 (CCH 1991). For a discussion of the United States rules relating to dual nationality, see Kelly, Dual Nationality, the Myth of Election, and a Kinder, Gentler State Department, 23 Inter–Am.L.Rev. 421 (1991–1992).

## B. NATIONALITY OF CORPORATIONS

### CASE CONCERNING THE BARCELONA TRACTION, LIGHT AND POWER COMPANY, LIMITED (BELGIUM v. SPAIN), SECOND PHASE

International Court of Justice, 1970.
1970 I.C.J. 3.

[Rejecting the claim of Belgium, the court said in part:]

28. * * * The claim is presented on behalf of natural and juristic persons, alleged to be Belgian nationals and shareholders in the Barcelona Traction, Light and Power Company, Limited. The submissions of the Belgian Government make it clear that the object of its Application is reparation for damage allegedly caused to these persons by the conduct, said to be contrary to international law, of various organs of the Spanish State towards that company and various other companies in the same group.

* * *

30. The States which the present case principally concerns are Belgium, the national State of the alleged shareholders, Spain, the State whose organs are alleged to have committed the unlawful acts complained of, and Canada, the State under whose laws Barcelona Traction was incorporated and in whose territory it has its registered office ("head office" in the terms of the by-laws of Barcelona Traction).

31. Thus the Court has to deal with a series of problems arising out of a triangular relationship involving the State whose nationals are shareholders in a company incorporated under the laws of another State, in whose territory it has its registered office; the State whose organs are alleged to have committed against the company unlawful acts prejudicial to both it and its shareholders; and the State under whose laws the company is incorporated, and in whose territory it has its registered office.

32. In these circumstances it is logical that the Court should first address itself to what was originally presented as the subject-matter of the third preliminary objection: namely the question of the right of Belgium to exercise diplomatic protection of Belgian shareholders in a company which is a juristic entity incorporated in Canada, the measures complained of having been taken in relation not to any Belgian national but to the company itself.

33. When a State admits into its territory foreign investments or foreign nationals, whether natural or juristic persons, it is bound to extend to them the protection of the law and assumes obligations concerning the treatment to be afforded them. * * *

35. * * * In the present case it is therefore essential to establish whether the losses allegedly suffered by Belgian shareholders in Barcelona Traction were the consequence of the violation of obligations of which they were the beneficiaries. In other words: has a right of Belgium been violated on account of its nationals' having suffered infringement of their rights as shareholders in a company not of Belgian nationality?

36. Thus it is the existence or absence of a right, belonging to Belgium and recognized as such by international law, which is decisive for the problem of Belgium's capacity.

> "This right is necessarily limited to intervention [by a State] on behalf of its own nationals because, in the absence of a special agreement, it is the bond of nationality between the State and the individual which alone confers upon the State the right of diplomatic protection, and it is as a part of the function of diplomatic protection that the right to take up a claim and to ensure respect for the rules of international law must be envisaged." (Panevezys–Saldutiskis Railway, Judgment, 1939, P.C.I.J., Series A/B, No. 76, p. 16.)

It follows that the same question is determinant in respect of Spain's responsibility towards Belgium. Responsibility is the necessary corollary of a right. In the absence of any treaty on the subject between the Parties, this essential issue has to be decided in the light of the general rules of diplomatic protection.

37. In seeking to determine the law applicable to this case, the Court has to bear in mind the continuous evolution of international law. Diplomatic protection deals with a very sensitive area of international relations,

since the interest of a foreign State in the protection of its nationals confronts the rights of the territorial sovereign, a fact of which the general law on the subject has had to take cognizance in order to prevent abuses and friction. From its origins closely linked with international commerce, diplomatic protection has sustained a particular impact from the growth of international economic relations, and at the same time from the profound transformations which have taken place in the economic life of nations. These latter changes have given birth to municipal institutions, which have transcended frontiers and have begun to exercise considerable influence on international relations. One of these phenomena which has a particular bearing on the present case is the corporate entity.

38. In this field international law is called upon to recognize institutions of municipal law that have an important and extensive role in the international field. This does not necessarily imply drawing any analogy between its own institutions and those of municipal law, nor does it amount to making rules of international law dependent upon categories of municipal law. All it means is that international law has had to recognize the corporate entity as an institution created by States in a domain essentially within their domestic jurisdiction. This in turn requires that, whenever legal issues arise concerning the rights of States with regard to the treatment of companies and shareholders, as to which rights international law has not established its own rules, it has to refer to the relevant rules of municipal law. Consequently, in view of the relevance to the present case of the rights of the corporate entity and its shareholders under municipal law, the Court must devote attention to the nature and interrelation of those rights.

* * *

40. There is, however, no need to investigate the many different forms of legal entity provided for by the municipal laws of States, because the Court is concerned only with that exemplified by the company involved in the present case: Barcelona Traction—a limited liability company whose capital is represented by shares. * * *

41. Municipal law determines the legal situation not only of such limited liability companies but also of those persons who hold shares in them. Separated from the company by numerous barriers, the shareholder cannot be identified with it. The concept and structure of the company are founded on and determined by a firm distinction between the separate entity of the company and that of the shareholder, each with a distinct set of rights. The separation of property rights as between company and shareholder is an important manifestation of this distinction. So long as the company is in existence the shareholder has no right to the corporate assets.

* * *

44. Notwithstanding the separate corporate personality, a wrong done to the company frequently causes prejudice to its shareholders. But the mere fact that damage is sustained by both company and shareholder does not imply that both are entitled to claim compensation. Thus no legal conclusion can be drawn from the fact that the same event caused damage simultaneously affecting several natural or juristic persons. Creditors do

not have any right to claim compensation from a person who, by wronging their debtor, causes them loss. In such cases, no doubt, the interests of the aggrieved are affected, but not their rights. Thus whenever a shareholder's interests are harmed by an act done to the company, it is to the latter that he must look to institute appropriate action; for although two separate entities may have suffered from the same wrong, it is only one entity whose rights have been infringed.

* * *

48. The Belgian Government claims that shareholders of Belgian nationality suffered damage in consequence of unlawful acts of the Spanish authorities and, in particular, that the Barcelona Traction shares, though they did not cease to exist, were emptied of all real economic content. It accordingly contends that the shareholders had an independent right to redress, notwithstanding the fact that the acts complained of were directed against the company as such. Thus the legal issue is reducible to the question of whether it is legitimate to identify an attack on company rights, resulting in damage to shareholders, with the violation of their direct rights.

* * *

50. In turning now to the international legal aspects of the case, the Court must, as already indicated, start from the fact that the present case essentially involves factors derived from municipal law—the distinction and the community between the company and the shareholder—which the Parties, however widely their interpretations may differ, each take as the point of departure of their reasoning. If the Court were to decide the case in disregard of the relevant institutions of municipal law it would, without justification, invite serious legal difficulties. It would lose touch with reality, for there are no corresponding institutions of international law to which the Court could resort. Thus, the Court has, as indicated, not only to take cognizance of municipal law but also to refer to it. It is to rules generally accepted by municipal legal systems which recognize the limited company whose capital is represented by shares, and not to the municipal law of a particular State, that international law refers. * * *

51. On the international plane, the Belgian Government has advanced the proposition that it is inadmissible to deny the shareholders' national State a right of diplomatic protection merely on the ground that another State possesses a corresponding right in respect of the company itself. In strict logic and law this formulation of the Belgian claim to *jus standi* assumes the existence of the very right that requires demonstration. In fact the Belgian Government has repeatedly stressed that there exists no rule of international law which would deny the national State of the shareholders the right of diplomatic protection for the purpose of seeking redress pursuant to unlawful acts committed by another State against the company in which they hold shares. This, by emphasizing the absence of any express denial of the right, conversely implies the admission that there is no rule of international law which expressly confers such a right on the shareholders' national State.

52. International law may not, in some fields, provide specific rules in particular cases. In the concrete situation, the company against which

allegedly unlawful acts were directed is expressly vested with a right, whereas no such right is specifically provided for the shareholder in respect of those acts. Thus the position of the company rests on a positive rule of both municipal and international law. As to the shareholder, while he has certain rights expressly provided for him by municipal law * * *, appeal can, in the circumstances of the present case, only be made to the silence of international law. Such silence scarcely admits of interpretation in favour of the shareholder.

* * *

70. In allocating corporate entities to States for purposes of diplomatic protection, international law is based, but only to a limited extent, on an analogy with the rules governing the nationality of individuals. The traditional rule attributes the right of diplomatic protection of a corporate entity to the State under the laws of which it is incorporated and in whose territory it has its registered office. These two criteria have been confirmed by long practice and by numerous international instruments. This notwithstanding, further or different links are at times said to be required in order that a right of diplomatic protection should exist. Indeed, it has been the practice of some States to give a company incorporated under their law diplomatic protection solely when it has its seat (*siège social*) or management or centre of control in their territory, or when a majority or a substantial proportion of the shares has been owned by nationals of the State concerned. Only then, it has been held, does there exist between the corporation and the State in question a genuine connection of the kind familiar from other branches of international law. However, in the particular field of the diplomatic protection of corporate entities, no absolute test of the "genuine connection" has found general acceptance. Such tests as have been applied are of a relative nature, and sometimes links with one State have had to be weighed against those with another. In this connection reference has been made to the *Nottebohm* case. In fact the Parties made frequent reference to it in the course of the proceedings. However, given both the legal and factual aspects of protection in the present case the Court is of the opinion that there can be no analogy with the issues raised or the decision given in that case.

71. In the present case it is not disputed that the company was incorporated in Canada and has its registered office in that country. The incorporation of the company under the law of Canada was an act of free choice. Not only did the founders of the company seek its incorporation under Canadian law but it has remained under that law for a period of over fifty years. It has maintained in Canada its registered office, its accounts and its share registers. Board meetings were held there for many years; it has been listed in the records of the Canadian tax authorities. Thus a close and permanent connection has been established, fortified by the passage of over half a century. This connection is in no way weakened by the fact that the company engaged from the very outset in commercial activities outside Canada, for that was its declared object. Barcelona Traction's links with Canada are thus manifold.

* * *

76. * * * [T]he record shows that from 1948 onwards the Canadian Government made to the Spanish Government numerous representations which cannot be viewed otherwise than as the exercise of diplomatic protection in respect of the Barcelona Traction company. Therefore this was not a case where diplomatic protection was refused or remained in the sphere of fiction. It is also clear that over the whole period of its diplomatic activity the Canadian Government proceeded in full knowledge of the Belgian attitude and activity.

77. It is true that at a certain point the Canadian Government ceased to act on behalf of Barcelona Traction, for reasons which have not been fully revealed, though a statement made in a letter of 19 July 1955 by the Canadian Secretary of State for External Affairs suggests that it felt the matter should be settled by means of private negotiations. The Canadian Government has nonetheless retained its capacity to exercise diplomatic protection; no legal impediment has prevented it from doing so; no fact has arisen to render this protection impossible. It has discontinued its action of its own free will.

* * *

79. The State must be viewed as the sole judge to decide whether its protection will be granted, to what extent it is granted, and when it will cease. It retains in this respect a discretionary power the exercise of which may be determined by considerations of a political or other nature, unrelated to the particular case. Since the claim of the State is not identical with that of the individual or corporate person whose cause is espoused, the State enjoys complete freedom of action. Whatever the reasons for any change of attitude, the fact cannot in itself constitute a justification for the exercise of diplomatic protection by another government, unless there is some independent and otherwise valid ground for that.

* * *

81. The cessation by the Canadian Government of the diplomatic protection of Barcelona Traction cannot, then, be interpreted to mean that there is no remedy against the Spanish Government for the damage done by the allegedly unlawful acts of the Spanish authorities. It is not a hypothetical right which was vested in Canada, for there is no legal impediment preventing the Canadian Government from protecting Barcelona Traction. Therefore there is no substance in the argument that for the Belgian Government to bring a claim before the Court represented the only possibility of obtaining redress for the damage suffered by Barcelona Traction and, through it, by its shareholders.

* * *

83. The Canadian Government's right of protection in respect of the Barcelona Traction company remains unaffected by the present proceedings. * * *

* * *

88. It follows from what has already been stated above that, where it is a question of an unlawful act committed against a company representing

foreign capital, the general rule of international law authorizes the national State of the company alone to make a claim.

* * *

92. Since the general rule on the subject does not entitle the Belgian Government to put forward a claim in this case, the question remains to be considered whether nonetheless, as the Belgian Government has contended during the proceedings, considerations of equity do not require that it be held to possess a right of protection. It is quite true that it has been maintained, that, for reasons of equity, a State should be able, in certain cases, to take up the protection of its nationals, shareholders in a company which has been the victim of a violation of international law. Thus a theory has been developed to the effect that the State of the shareholders has a right of diplomatic protection when the State whose responsibility is invoked is the national State of the company. Whatever the validity of this theory may be, it is certainly not applicable to the present case, since Spain is not the national State of Barcelona Traction.

93. On the other hand, the Court considers that, in the field of diplomatic protection as in all other fields of international law, it is necessary that the law be applied reasonably. It has been suggested that if in a given case it is not possible to apply the general rule that the right of diplomatic protection of a company belongs to its national State, considerations of equity might call for the possibility of protection of the shareholders in question by their own national State. This hypothesis does not correspond to the circumstances of the present case.

94. In view, however, of the discretionary nature of diplomatic protection, considerations of equity cannot require more than the possibility for some protector State to intervene, whether it be the national State of the company, by virtue of the general rule mentioned above, or, in a secondary capacity, the national State of the shareholders who claim protection. In this connection, account should also be taken of the practical effects of deducing from considerations of equity any broader right of protection for the national State of the shareholders. It must first of all be observed that it would be difficult on an equitable basis to make distinctions according to any quantitative test: it would seem that the owner of 1 per cent. and the owner of 90 per cent. of the share-capital should have the same possibility of enjoying the benefit of diplomatic protection. The protector State may, of course, be disinclined to take up the case of the single small shareholder, but it could scarcely be denied the right to do so in the name of equitable considerations. In that field, protection by the national State of the shareholders can hardly be graduated according to the absolute or relative size of the shareholding involved.

95. The Belgian Government, it is true, has also contended that as high a proportion as 88 per cent. of the shares in Barcelona Traction belonged to natural or juristic persons of Belgian nationality, and it has used this as an argument for the purpose not only of determining the amount of the damages which it claims, but also of establishing its right of action on behalf of the Belgian shareholders. Nevertheless, this does not alter the Belgian Government's position, as expounded in the course of the proceedings, which implies, in the last analysis, that it might be sufficient for one single share to

belong to a national of a given State for the latter to be entitled to exercise its diplomatic protection.

96. The Court considers that the adoption of the theory of diplomatic protection of shareholders as such, by opening the door to competing diplomatic claims, could create an atmosphere of confusion and insecurity in international economic relations. The danger would be all the greater inasmuch as the shares of companies whose activity is international are widely scattered and frequently change hands. It might perhaps be claimed that, if the right of protection belonging to the national States of the shareholders were considered as only secondary to that of the national State of the company, there would be less danger of difficulties of the kind contemplated. However, the Court must state that the essence of a secondary right is that it only comes into existence at the time when the original right ceases to exist. As the right of protection vested in the national State of the company cannot be regarded as extinguished because it is not exercised, it is not possible to accept the proposition that in case of its non-exercise the national States of the shareholders have a right of protection secondary to that of the national State of the company. Furthermore, study of factual situations in which this theory might possibly be applied gives rise to the following observations.

97. The situations in which foreign shareholders in a company wish to have recourse to diplomatic protection by their own national State may vary. It may happen that the national State of the company simply refuses to grant it its diplomatic protection, or that it begins to exercise it (as in the present case) but does not pursue its action to the end. It may also happen that the national State of the company and the State which has committed a violation of international law with regard to the company arrive at a settlement of the matter, by agreeing on compensation for the company, but that the foreign shareholders find the compensation insufficient. Now, as a matter of principle, it would be difficult to draw a distinction between these three cases so far as the protection of foreign shareholders by their national State is concerned, since in each case they may have suffered real damage. Furthermore, the national State of the company is perfectly free to decide how far it is appropriate for it to protect the company, and is not bound to make public the reasons for its decision. To reconcile this discretionary power of the company's national State with a right of protection falling to the shareholders' national State would be particularly difficult when the former State has concluded, with the State which has contravened international law with regard to the company, an agreement granting the company compensation which the foreign shareholders find inadequate. If, after such a settlement, the national State of the foreign shareholders could in its turn put forward a claim based on the same facts, this would be likely to introduce into the negotiation of this kind of agreement a lack of security which would be contrary to the stability which it is the object of international law to establish in international relations.

* * *

99. It should also be observed that the promoters of a company whose operations will be international must take into account the fact that States have, with regard to their nationals, a discretionary power to grant diplo-

matic protection or to refuse it. When establishing a company in a foreign country, its promoters are normally impelled by particular considerations; it is often a question of tax or other advantages offered by the host State. It does not seem to be in any way inequitable that the advantages thus obtained should be balanced by the risks arising from the fact that the protection of the company and hence of its shareholders is thus entrusted to a State other than the national State of the shareholders.

100. In the present case, it is clear from what has been said above that Barcelona Traction was never reduced to a position of impotence such that it could not have approached its national State, Canada, to ask for its diplomatic protection, and that, as far as appeared to the Court, there was nothing to prevent Canada from continuing to grant its diplomatic protection to Barcelona Traction if it had considered that it should do so.

101. For the above reasons, the Court is not of the opinion that, in the particular circumstances of the present case, *jus standi* is conferred on the Belgian Government by considerations of equity.

* * *

103. Accordingly,

THE COURT rejects the Belgian Government's claim by fifteen votes to one, twelve votes of the majority being based on the reasons set out in the present Judgment.

### *Notes*

1. For comment, see Higgins, Aspects of the Case Concerning the Barcelona Traction, Light and Power Company, Ltd., 11 Va.J.Int'l L. 327 (1971); Lillich, The Rigidity of Barcelona, 65 A.J.I.L. 522 (1971); Comment, 3 N.Y.U.J.Int'l L. & P. 391 (1970); discussion in [1971] A.S.I.L.Proc. 333, 340–358, 360–365. See Jiménez de Aréchaga, International Responsibility of States for Acts of the Judiciary, in Transnational Law in a Changing Society 171–187 (Friedmann, Henkin & Lissitzyn eds. 1972), for a discussion of the merits of the case which were not reached by the Court.

2. Restatement (Second) (1965) § 172 provides: "When a domestic corporation, in which an alien is directly or indirectly a shareholder, is injured by action attributable to a state that would be wrongful under international law if the corporation were an alien corporation, the state is not responsible under international law for the injury to the corporation. The state is, however, responsible for the consequent injury to the alien to the extent of his interest in the corporation, if

(a) a significant portion of the stock of the corporation is owned by the alien or other aliens of whatever nationality,

(b) the state knows or has reason to know of such ownership at the time of the conduct causing the injury to the corporation,

(c) the corporation fails to obtain reparation for the injury,

(d) such failure is due to causes over which the alien or other alien shareholders cannot exercise control, and

(e) a claim for the injury to the corporation has not been voluntarily waived or settled by the corporation."

The bulk of foreign investment is carried on by subsidiary corporations which are organized under the laws of the state where the business will be conducted and are controlled by a multinational corporation organized under the laws of another state. Capital-exporting states, including the United States, as the states of which the parent company is a national, have protested and made international claims when the properties of the foreign subsidiary have been expropriated by the state in which it is incorporated. See Restatement (Third) § 213, Reporter's Note 3, § 713, Comment *e* and the Barcelona Traction Case (Belgium v. Spain) at p. 412 supra. The United States is a party to a number of treaties of friendship, commerce and navigation that provide for rights in favor of alien shareholders in domestic corporations of either party. See, e.g., Article VI of the United States Treaty with Pakistan on Friendship and Commerce, 12 U.S.T. 110, T.I.A.S. No. 4683, 404 U.N.T.S. 259.

# Chapter 6

# THE LAW OF TREATIES

## SECTION 1. DEFINITION AND GOVERNING LAW

Treaties, as we noted in chapter 2 (section 3) are a principal source of obligation in international law. The term "treaty" is used generally to cover the binding agreements between subjects of international law that are governed by international law. In addition to the term "treaty," a number of other appellations are used to apply to international agreements. Some of the more common are convention, pact, protocol, charter, covenant, declaration as well as the words treaty or international agreement. Other terms are act, statute, *modus vivendi,* exchange of notes, and on occasion, communiqué or agreed statement. The particular appellation given to an agreement has in itself no legal effect. Some of the terms used follow habitual uses, others are used to denote solemnity (e.g., covenant or charter) or the supplementary character of the agreement (e.g., protocol). The United Nations Charter in Article 102 requires the registration of "every treaty and every international agreement entered into by a Member of the United Nations." This applies whatever the form or descriptive name used for the agreement. The phrase "international agreement" is used here.

In concluding what purports or appears to be an "agreement," the states concerned may sometimes intend to create only political or moral, as opposed to legal, commitments.

Such "nonbinding agreements" are referred to in some cases as "gentlemen's agreements" and in other contexts as political or moral undertakings. Whether they are intended to be nonbinding in a legal sense is not always clear. Nor is it always clear what legal consequences flow from such agreements. These questions will be considered below.

### A. THE VIENNA CONVENTION ON THE LAW OF TREATIES

The Vienna Convention on the Law of Treaties, concluded in 1969, is the principal authoritative source of the law of treaties, and it will therefore be the focus of this chapter. The Convention is regarded as in large part (but not entirely) declaratory of existing law, and on that basis it has been invoked and applied by tribunals and by states even prior to its entry into force and in regard to nonparties as well as parties. Some of its provisions have gone beyond existing law or have altered previously established rules. These provisions are generally characterized as "progressive development" in keeping with the terms used in Article 13 of the U.N. Charter and the Statute of the International Law Commission. As we shall see, the distinction between the declaratory and the "new" law of the Convention is not readily apparent from the text and sometimes subject to conflicting assessments. It is perhaps more significant that states tend to refer to all of the provisions of the Convention as an authoritative source of law, thus gradually transforming its innovative features into customary law through such application. It is natural that a Convention which was concluded with virtually unanimous approval of the international community, after some two decades of study and deliberation, should be applied by legal advisors and courts as the primary source of law. It still remains possible for a nonparty state to challenge a particular provision on the ground that it goes beyond existing law and has not become part of general international law since its inclusion. However, the tendency of states and tribunals to turn to the Convention for authority makes it highly likely that it will be regarded in its entirety as having become part of general international law.

The Convention entered into force on January 27, 1980 upon ratification by the 35th state and, as of 1991, there were 66 parties. The Convention had not been ratified by the United States as of 1991. However, the Department of State, in submitting the Convention to the Senate, stated that the Convention "is already recognized as the authoritative guide to current treaty law and practice." S.Exec.Doc.L., 92d Cong. 1st Sess. (1971) p. 1.

Work on the Vienna Convention was first undertaken by the International Law Commission in 1949. From its outset, it was assumed that the task was primarily that of codification and draft articles would eventually form an international treaty. At one point, there was support for an "expository code" in lieu of a treaty. It was thought that this would allow for declaratory and expository material in the code that would not be permissible in a Convention. However, the Commission decided in 1961 (and reaffirmed in 1965) that a multilateral convention would be more effective. The Convention was concluded in 1969 in two sessions of a plenipotentiary conference of states held under United Nations auspices in Vienna. During the twenty-year period of preparation, numerous drafts and commentaries were prepared by special rapporteurs of the International Law Commission and considered in detail by the Commission and by the Legal Committee of the U.N. General Assembly. The four special rapporteurs were the leading British international lawyers of the period: James Brierly, Sir Hersch Lauterpacht, Sir Gerald Fitzmaurice and Sir Humphrey Waldock (the latter three were elected successively as judges on the International Court). The detailed reports by these rapporteurs and the summary records of the International Law Commission are a voluminous and valuable collection of the *travaux préparatoires* essential for understanding and interpretation. They have been published in the annual Yearbooks of the International Law Commission. The records of the Vienna conferences at which the treaty was finally concluded are also essential for interpretation. They have been published as U.N. documents of the United Nations Conference on the Law of Treaties, Official Records, First (and Second) Session. A useful guide to these records is contained in Rosenne, The Law of Treaties: Guide to the Legislative History of the Vienna Convention (1970). Substantive studies dealing with the legislative history of the treaty include: Sinclair, The Vienna Convention on the Law of Treaties (2d ed. 1984); Elias, The Modern Law of Treaties (1974); Haraszti, Some Fundamental Problems of the Law of Treaties (1973); Kearney & Dalton, The Treaty on Treaties, 64 A.J.I.L. 495 (1970).

## THE SCOPE OF THE VIENNA CONVENTION

The Convention is limited to treaties concluded between states (Article 1). It deliberately excluded treaties between states and international organizations or between international organizations themselves. These treaties are the subject of another convention which was concluded in 1986; it is not much different in any major respects. See section 2 infra.

The Vienna Convention applies only to agreements in written form. It expressly recognizes, however, that this limitation is without prejudice to the legal force of non-written agreements or to the application to them of any of the rules set forth in the Convention to which they would be subject under international law independently of the Convention (Article 3).

The Convention declares that it is non-retroactive (Article 4). However, in this connection also it is said that the principle is "without prejudice to the application of any rules set forth in the present Convention to which treaties would be subject under international law independently of the Convention."

These latter two provisions both acknowledge the continued application of customary law and, where relevant, of general principles of law to treaties, whether covered or not by the Convention. A clause in the preamble to the Convention affirms that rules of customary international law will continue to govern questions not regulated by the Convention.

The distinction between those rules of the Convention which are customary law (or general international law) and those provisions which are extensions or changes of existing law can be made only on the basis of a particular examination of the provision in question and its relationship to existing law. In most cases where this question has arisen the answer cannot easily be given. Ian Sinclair, a leading participant and commentator, has said that: "It is only in rare cases, and then by implication rather than by express pronouncement, that one can determine where the Commission has put forward a proposal by way of progressive development rather than by way of codification" (Sinclair at p. 14).

## THE VIENNA CONVENTION AS CUSTOMARY INTERNATIONAL LAW

## FISHERIES JURISDICTION CASE (UNITED KINGDOM v. ICELAND)

International Court of Justice, 1974.
1974 I.C.J. 3, 18.

International law admits that a fundamental change in the circumstances which determined the parties to accept a treaty, if it has resulted in a radical transformation of the extent of the obligations imposed by it, may, under certain conditions, afford the party affected a ground for invoking the termination or suspension of the treaty. This principle, and the conditions and exceptions to which it is subject, have been embodied in Article 62 of the Vienna Convention on the Law of Treaties, which may in many respects be considered as a codification of existing customary law on the subject of the termination of a treaty relationship on account of change of circumstances.

## ADVISORY OPINION ON NAMIBIA

International Court of Justice, Advisory Opinion, 1971.
1971 I.C.J. 16, 47.*

The rules laid down by the Vienna Convention on the Law of Treaties concerning termination of a treaty relationship on account of breach [Article 603] (adopted without a dissenting vote) may in many respects be considered as a codification of existing customary law on the subject.

## GOLDER CASE (GOLDER v. UNITED KINGDOM)

European Court of Human Rights, 1975.
(1975) ECHR, Ser.A, No. 18.

The submissions made to the Court were in the first place directed to the manner in which the Convention, and particularly Article 6 § 1, should be interpreted. The Court is prepared to consider, as do the Government and the Commission, that it should be guided by Articles 31 to 33 of the Vienna Convention of 23 May 1969 on the Law of Treaties. That Convention has not yet entered into force and it specifies, at Article 4, that it will not be retroactive, but its Articles 31 to 33 enunciate in essence generally accepted principles of international law to which the Court has already referred on occasion. In this respect, for the interpretation of the European Convention account is to be taken of those Articles subject, where appropriate, to "any relevant rules of the organization"—the Council of Europe—within which it has been adopted (Article 5 of the Vienna Convention).

* See p. 511, * for the complete title of this opinion.

## B. THE DEFINITION OF A TREATY

### *JIMÉNEZ DE ARÉCHAGA, INTERNATIONAL LAW IN THE PAST THIRD OF A CENTURY*

159 Rec. des Cours 35–37 (1978–I).*

Although the definition of an international treaty seems at first sight to be a purely academic question, judicial experience shows that the determination of whether a certain instrument constitutes a treaty has important practical consequences.

For instance, in two cases before the International Court of Justice the question whether an instrument was a treaty had decisive significance for the establishment of the Court's jurisdiction with respect to the dispute.

In the *Anglo–Iranian Oil Co.* case the jurisdiction of the court was invoked on the basis of Iran's acceptance of the optional clause, dating from 1932, which referred to disputes "relating to the application of treaties or conventions accepted by Persia and subsequent to the ratification of this declaration."

The United Kingdom invoked as a treaty subsequent to 1932 a concession contract of 1933, signed between the Government of Iran and the Anglo–Persian Oil Company, contending that this agreement had:

> "a double character, the character of being at once a concessionary contract between the Iranian Government and the Company and a treaty between the two Governments."

The Court could not, however,

> "accept the view that the contract signed between the Iranian Government and the Anglo–Persian Oil Company has a double character. It is nothing more than a concessionary contract between a government and a foreign corporation. The United Kingdom Government is not a party to the contract; there is no privity of contract between the Government of Iran and the Government of the United Kingdom."

From this pronouncement of the Court it results that an agreement between a State and a private company, even a multinational one, even if it is (as Anglo–Iranian was then) half-owned by a government, cannot be considered as a treaty in international law, but only as a contract. The Court's dictum implies that a treaty requires that two or more States become bound *vis-à-vis* each other.

It would be wrong however to assume that the Court thus endorsed a restrictive definition of a treaty as an agreement concluded between *two or more States.*

In a subsequent decision, in 1962, the Court accepted that the notion of "treaty" also covered an agreement between a State and an international organization which constituted a subject of international law enjoying the *ius tractatum.* In the jurisdictional phase of the *South West Africa* cases, the Court decided, for the purpose of establishing its jurisdiction, that the Mandate with respect to South West Africa was a "treaty or convention" as required by Article 37 of the Statute.

* Footnotes omitted. Reprinted by permission of A.W. Sijthoff & Noordhoff International.

The court declared that although the Mandate:

"took the form of a resolution of the Council of the League * * *. It cannot be correctly regarded as embodying only an executive action in pursuance of the Covenant. The Mandate, in fact and in law, is an international agreement having the character of a treaty or convention."

The Court further recognized that the Mandate was a treaty "to which the League of Nations itself was one of the Parties."

In the light of this judicial pronouncement it may be concluded that in contemporary international law the traditional definition of a treaty as an agreement between two or more States must be enlarged to include other types of agreement which today constitute a large percentage of the treaties concluded: agreements between States and international organizations and between international organizations *inter se.* There may also be trilateral agreements involving two States and an international organization. The traditional concept must be replaced by the notion that a treaty is an agreement between two or more subjects of international law.

The definition of a treaty as an agreement between subjects of international law is not in itself sufficient. There may be agreements between States which do not constitute international treaties. McNair gives the example of a purchase by the United Kingdom Government of one thousand tons of chilled beef from the Government of the Argentine Republic upon the basis of a standard form of contract used in the meat trade.

Another example of an interstate contract and not a treaty could be the purchase of a building or a piece of land for a legation, when this transaction is subject to the municipal law of one of the parties or to that of a third State. A third instance, involving an international organization, would be a loan or a guarantee agreement between the World Bank and a State, which, as has occurred in the past, is made subject to the laws of the State of New York. This is the reason why the codification in the Vienna Convention adds a requirement to the definition of a treaty: the agreement must be "governed by international law."

When is an agreement governed by international law? Is this a matter of choice or of intention of the parties? In principle, the intention of the parties, express or implied, would appear to be controlling. However, there are cases in which the nature and object of the agreement make it impossible to subject it to any system of municipal law; such an agreement must be governed by international law, whatever the intention of parties. A case in point is the cession of a small piece of land by France to Switzerland to permit the enlargement of Geneva Airport. Despite the comparatively trivial importance of this agreement, it had to be embodied in a treaty since it involved the transfer of sovereignty over State territory.

The deliberations at the Vienna Conference reveal that the phrase "governed by international law" is designed to cover other meanings and implications as well.

It was suggested at the Conference that it was necessary to add to the definition the requirement that to be a treaty the agreement "must produce legal effects" or must "create rights and obligations."

These suggestions were designed to exclude from the concept of "treaties" the declarations of principle, communiqués, political instruments or "gentlemen's agreements" which represent a concurrence of wills but without producing legal effects.

However, it may be unwise to exclude political declarations or joint communiqués *en bloc* and in principle from the concept of treaties. In a given case, the terms of one of those instruments may be sufficiently precise to produce legal effects under international law. It is a question to be determined in each case in the light of the circumstances.

Consequently these above-mentioned amendments were not accepted but were deemed superfluous: the production of legal effects or the creation or declaration of rights and obligations are already implicit in the phrase "governed by international law."

## UNILATERAL STATEMENTS AS THE FOUNDATION FOR A TREATY

## LEGAL STATUS OF EASTERN GREENLAND (NORWAY v. DENMARK)

Permanent Court of International Justice, 1933.
[1933] P.C.I.J. Ser. A/B, No. 53, 71.

What Denmark desired to obtain from Norway was that the latter should do nothing to obstruct the Danish plans in regard to Greenland. The declaration which the Minister for Foreign Affairs gave on July 22nd, 1919, on behalf of the Norwegian Government, was definitely affirmative: "I told the Danish Minister to-day that the Norwegian Government would not make any difficulty in the settlement of this question".

The Court considers it beyond all dispute that a reply of this nature given by the Minister for Foreign Affairs on behalf of his Government in response to a request by the diplomatic representative of a foreign Power, in regard to a question falling within his province, is binding upon the country to which the Minister belongs.

## NUCLEAR TESTS CASE (AUSTRALIA & NEW ZEALAND v. FRANCE)

International Court of Justice, 1974.
1974 I.C.J. 253.

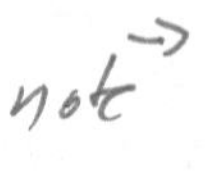

43. It is well recognized that declarations made by way of unilateral acts, concerning legal or factual situations, may have the effect of creating legal obligations. Declarations of this kind may be, and often are, very specific. When it is the intention of the State making the declaration that it should become bound according to its terms, that intention confers on the declaration the character of a legal undertaking, the State being thenceforth legally required to follow a course of conduct consistent with the declaration. An undertaking of this kind, if given publicly, and with an intent to be bound, even though not made within the context of international negotia-

tions, is binding. In these circumstances, nothing in the nature of a *quid pro quo* nor any subsequent acceptance of the declaration, nor even any reply or reaction from other States, is required for the declaration to take effect, since such a requirement would be inconsistent with the strictly unilateral nature of the juridical act by which the pronouncement by the State was made.

44. Of course, not all unilateral acts imply obligation; but a State may choose to take up a certain position in relation to a particular matter with the intention of being bound—the intention is to be ascertained by interpretation of the act. When States make statements by which their freedom of action is to be limited, a restrictive interpretation is called for.

45. With regard to the question of form, it should be observed that this is not a domain in which international law imposes any special or strict requirements. Whether a statement is made orally or in writing makes no essential difference, for such statements made in particular circumstances may create commitments in international law, which does not require that they should be couched in written form. Thus the question of form is not decisive. As the Court said in its Judgment on the preliminary objections in the case concerning the *Temple of Preah Vihear:*

> Where * * * as is generally the case in international law, which places the principal emphasis on the intentions of the parties, the law prescribes no particular form, parties are free to choose what form they please provided their intention clearly results from it. (*ICJ Reports 1961,* p. 31.)

The Court further stated in the same case: "* * * the sole relevant question is whether the language employed in any given declaration does reveal a clear intention * * *" (*ibid.,* p. 32).

46. One of the basic principles governing the creation and performance of legal obligations, whatever their source, is the principle of good faith. Trust and confidence are inherent in international co-operation, in particular in an age when this co-operation in many fields is becoming increasingly essential. Just as the very rule of *pacta sunt servanda* in the law of treaties is based on good faith, so also is the binding character of an international obligation assumed by unilateral declaration. Thus interested States may take cognizance of unilateral declarations and place confidence in them, and are entitled to require that the obligation thus created be respected.

* * * The Court must however form its own view of the meaning and scope intended by the author of a unilateral declaration which may create a legal obligation, and cannot in this respect be bound by the view expressed by another State which is in no way a party to the text.

49. Of the statements by the French Government now before the Court, the most essential are clearly those made by the President of the Republic. There can be no doubt, in view of his functions, that his public communications or statements, oral or written, as Head of State, are in international relations acts of the French State. His statements, and those of members of the French Government acting under his authority, up to the last statement made by the Minister of Defence (of 11 October 1974), constitute a whole. Thus, in whatever form these statements were expressed, they must be held

to constitute an engagement of the State, having regard to their intention and to the circumstances in which they were made.

50. The unilateral statements of the French authorities were made outside the Court, publicly and *erga omnes,* even though the first of them was communicated to the Government of Australia. As was observed above, to have legal effect, there was no need for these statements to be addressed to a particular State, nor was acceptance by any other State required. The general nature and characteristics of these statements are decisive for the evaluation of the legal implications, and it is to the interpretation of the statements that the Court must now proceed. The Court is entitled to presume, at the outset, that these statements were not made *in vacuo,* but in relation to the tests which constitute the very object of the present proceedings, although France has not appeared in the case.

## FRONTIER DISPUTE CASE (BURKINA FASO v. MALI)

International Court of Justice, 1986.
1986 I.C.J. 554.

39. The statement of Mali's Head of State on 11 April 1975 was not made during negotiations or talks between the two Parties; at most, it took the form of a unilateral act by the Government of Mali. Such declarations "concerning legal or factual situations" may indeed "have the effect of creating legal obligations" for the State on whose behalf they are made, as the Court observed in the *Nuclear Tests Cases* (*ICJ Reports 1974,* pp. 267, 472). But the Court also made clear in those cases that it is only "when it is the intention of the State making the declaration that it should become bound according to its terms" that "that intention confers on the declaration the character of a legal undertaking" (*ibid.*). Thus it all depends on the intention of the State in question, and the Court emphasized that it is for the Court to "form its own view of the meaning and scope intended by the author of a unilateral declaration which may create a legal obligation" (*ibid.,* pp. 269, 474). In the case concerning *Military and Paramilitary Activities in and against Nicaragua (Nicaragua v. United States of America, Merits 1986),* the Court examined a communication transmitted by the Junta of National Reconstruction of Nicaragua to the Organization of American States, in which the Junta listed its objectives; but the Court was unable to find anything in that communication "from which it can be inferred that any legal undertaking was intended to exist" (*ICJ Reports 1986,* p. 132, para. 261). The Chamber considers that it has a duty to show even greater caution when it is a question of a unilateral declaration not directed to any particular recipient.

40. In order to assess the intentions of the author of a unilateral act, account must be taken of all the factual circumstances in which the act occurred. For example, in the *Nuclear Tests Cases,* the Court took the view that since the applicant States were not the only ones concerned at the possible continuance of atmospheric testing by the French Government, that Government's unilateral declarations had "conveyed to the world at large, including the Applicant, its intention effectively to terminate these tests" (*ICJ Reports 1974,* p. 269, para. 51; p. 474, para. 53). In the particular

circumstances of those cases, the French Government could not express an intention to be bound otherwise than by unilateral declarations. It is difficult to see how it could have accepted the terms of a negotiated solution with each of the applicants without thereby jeopardizing its contention that its conduct was lawful. The circumstances of the present case are radically different. Here, there was nothing to hinder the Parties from manifesting an intention to accept the binding character of the conclusions of the Organization of African Unity Mediation Commission by the normal method: a formal agreement on the basis of reciprocity. Since no agreement of this kind was concluded between the Parties, the Chamber finds that there are no grounds to interpret the declaration made by Mali's Head of State on 11 April 1975 as a unilateral act with legal implications in regard to the present case.

### *Notes*

1. The Commission's Special Rapporteur, Sir Humphrey Waldock, commented upon the phrase "governed by international law," as follows:

> * * * [T]he element of subjection to international law is so essential a part of an international agreement that it should be expressly mentioned in the definition. There may be agreements between States, such as agreements for the acquisition of premises for a diplomatic mission or for some purely commercial transaction, the incidents of which are regulated by the local law of one of the parties or by a private law system determined by reference to conflict of laws principles. Whether in such cases the two States are *internationally* accountable to each other at all may be a nice question; but even if that were held to be so, it would not follow that the basis of their international accountability was a *treaty* obligation. At any rate, the Commission was clear that it ought to confine the notion of an "international agreement" for the purposes of the law of treaties to one the whole formation and execution of which (as well as the *obligation* to execute) is governed by international law.

[1962] II Yb.I.L.C. 32.

The Commission concluded that the element of intention is embraced in the phrase "governed by international law" and therefore it was not necessary to refer to intention in the definition.

2. How is one to know when international law applies and when it does not? A clear case for the application of international law would possibly be a "political" agreement, e.g., a treaty of alliance or cession of territory. In other cases, it has been suggested that "it is in reality the intention of the parties that determines the application of private law or of public international law. In the absence of express stipulation, that intention is to be deduced by methods similar to those employed by the private international lawyer who ascertains the 'proper law' of a contract: it depends on all the material circumstances of the case. Very clear evidence will have to be required before it can be assumed that sovereign states have contracted on the basis of private law * * *. On the other hand, it would probably not be justified to speak of a presumption that public international law applies." Mann, The Law Governing State Contracts, 21 Brit. Y.B.I.L. 11, 28 (1944).* Is it possible to draw up a list of "material" circumstances that will suggest that an agreement is governed by international law? Is

* Reprinted by permission from the British Yearbook of International Law. Published by the Oxford University Press for the Royal Institute of International Affairs.

it material that the agreement is concluded by "two organs of government not empowered to conduct foreign relations"?

3. Are the only systems of law open to contracting states either public international law or the municipal law of one or both of the contracting states (or of a third state)? See Mann at p. 19; McNair, The Law of Treaties 4–5 (1961), suggesting that states may also enter into agreements governed by the terms of the contract, supplemented as necessary by general principles of law.

## C. NONBINDING AGREEMENTS

### *SCHACHTER, THE TWILIGHT EXISTENCE OF NONBINDING INTERNATIONAL AGREEMENTS*

71 A.J.I.L. 296 (1977).*

International lawyers generally agree that an international agreement is not legally binding unless the parties intend it to be. Put more formally, a treaty or international agreement is said to require an intention by the parties to create legal rights and obligations or to establish relations governed by international law. If that intention does not exist, an agreement is considered to be without legal effect ("sans porteé juridique"). States are, of course, free to enter into such nonbinding agreements, whatever the subject matter of the agreement. However, questions have often arisen as to the intention of the parties in this regard. The main reason for this is that governments tend to be reluctant (as in the case of the Helsinki Final Act) to state explicitly in an agreement that it is nonbinding or lacks legal force. Consequently inferences as to such intent have to be drawn from the language of the instrument and the attendant circumstances of its conclusion and adoption. Emphasis is often placed on the lack of precision and generality of the terms of the agreement. Statements of general aims and broad declarations of principles are considered too indefinite to create enforceable obligations and therefore agreements which do not go beyond that should be presumed to be nonbinding.[9] It is also said, not implausibly, that mere statements of intention or of common purposes are grounds for concluding that a legally binding agreement was not intended. Experience has shown that these criteria are not easy to apply especially in situations where the parties wish to convey that their declarations and undertakings are to be taken seriously, even if stated in somewhat general or "programmatic" language. Thus, conflicting inferences were drawn as to the intent of the parties in regard to some of the well-known political agreements during

* Some footnotes omitted. Reprinted by permission of the American Society of International Law.

9. O'Connell, [International Law, (2d ed. 1970)] at 199–200. But other jurists have noted that vague and ill-defined provisions appear in agreements which do not lose their binding character because of such indefiniteness. See P. Reuter, Introduction au Droit des Traités 44 (1972); G.G. Fitzmaurice, Report on the Law of Treaties to the International Law Commission. [1956] 2 Y.B.Int.Law Comm. 117, UN Doc. A/CN.4/101 (1956). The latter commented that "it seems difficult to refuse the designation of treaty to an instrument—such as, for instance, a treaty of peace and amity, or of alliance—even if it only establishes a bare relationship and leaves the consequences to rest on the basis of an implication as to the rights and obligations involved, without these being expressed in any definite articles." Id.

the Second World War, notably the Cairo, Yalta, and Potsdam agreements.[10] No doubt there was a calculated ambiguity about the obligatory force of these instruments at least in regard to some of their provisions and this was reflected in the way the governments dealt with them.[11] After all, imprecision and generalities are not unknown in treaties of unquestioned legal force. If one were to apply strict requirements of definiteness and specificity to all treaties, many of them would have all or most of their provisions considered as without legal effect. Examples of such treaties may be found particularly among agreements for cultural cooperation and often in agreements of friendship and trade which express common aims and intentions in broad language. Yet there is no doubt that they are regarded as binding treaties by the parties and that they furnish authoritative guidance to the administrative officials charged with implementation. Other examples of highly general formulas can be found in the UN Charter and similar "constitutional" instruments the abstract principles of which have been given determinate meaning by the international organs (as, for example, has been done in regard to Articles 55 and 56 of the Charter).[12] These cases indicate that caution is required in drawing inferences of nonbinding intention from general and imprecise undertakings in agreements which are otherwise treated as binding. However, if the text or circumstances leave the intention uncertain, it is reasonable to consider vague language and mere declarations of purpose as indicative of an intention to avoid legal effect.[13] Other indications may be found in the way the instrument is dealt with after its conclusion—for example, whether it is listed or published in national treaty collections, whether it is registered under Article 102 of the Charter, whether it is described as a treaty or international agreement of a legal character in submissions to national parliaments or courts.[14] None of

**10.** Statements by officials of the British and U.S. Governments indicated that they did not consider the Yalta and Potsdam agreements as binding. For the U.K. views, see references in Münch, supra note 8, at 5 n. 22. For the U.S. position, see infra note 11. A contrary point of view was expressed in 1969 by a representative of the USSR at the Vienna Conference on the Law of Treaties. He declared that the Yalta and Potsdam agreements as well as the Atlantic Charter provided for "rights and obligations" and laid down "very important rules of international law." UN Doc. A/Conf. 39/11 Add. 1, at 226 (para. 22). Sir Hersch Lauterpacht considered that the Yalta and Potsdam agreements "incorporated definite rules of conduct which may be regarded as legally binding on the States in question." 1 Oppenheim, International Law 788 (7th ed. H. Lauterpacht, ed. 1948). On the other hand, Professor Briggs suggested that the Yalta agreement on the Far Eastern territories may be considered only as "the personal agreement of the three leaders." Briggs, The Leaders' Agreement of Yalta, 40 AJIL 376, at 382 (1946).

**11.** The Yalta Agreement was published by the State Department in the Executive Agreements Series (No. 498) and was also published in U.S. Treaties in Force (1963). However, in 1956 the State Department stated to the Japanese Government in an aide-mémoire that "the United States regards the so-called Yalta Agreement as simply a statement of common purposes by the heads of the participating governments and * * * not as of any legal effect in transferring territories." 35 Dept. State Bull. 484 (1956). But see Briggs, supra note 10, for statements by the U.S. Secretary of State that an agreement was concluded by the leaders.

**12.** See memorandum of State Department quoted infra note 24. See also L. Sohn and T. Buergenthal, International Protection of Human Rights 505–14, 946–47 (1973).

**13.** See Münch, supra note 8, at 8; O'Connell, supra note 6, at 199. But cf. Reuter and Fitzmaurice, supra note 9.

**14.** The appellation of an instrument has but little evidentiary value as to its legal effect in view of the wide variety of terms used to designate binding treaties and the accepted rule that form and designation are immaterial in determining their binding effect. Thirty-nine different appellations for treaties are listed in Myers, The Names and Scope of Treaties, 51 AJIL 574 (1957).

these acts can be considered as decisive evidence but together with the language of the instruments they are relevant. The level and authority of the governmental representatives who have signed or otherwise approved the agreement may also be relevant but here too, some caution is necessary in weighing the evidentiary value. Chiefs of state and foreign ministers do enter into nonbinding arrangements and lower officials may, if authorized, act for a state in incurring legally binding obligations. If a lower official, without authority, purports to conclude an agreement, the supposed agreement may be entirely void and without any effect. It would, in consequence, have to be distinguished from the kind of nonbinding agreement which is treated by the parties as an authorized and legitimate mutual engagement.

We should bear in mind that not all nonbinding agreements are general and indefinite. Governments may enter into precise and definite engagements as to future conduct with a clear understanding shared by the parties that the agreements are not legally binding. The so-called "gentlemen's agreements" fall into this category. They may be made by heads of state or governments or by ministers of foreign affairs and, if authorized, by other officials. In these cases the parties assume a commitment to perform certain acts or refrain from them. The nature of the commitment is regarded as "nonlegal" and not binding. There is nonetheless an expectation of, and reliance on, compliance by the parties. An example is the agreement made in 1908 by the United States and Japan, through their foreign ministers, relating to immigration which was observed for nearly two decades, although probably not considered binding. On the multilateral level, some gentlemen's agreements have been made by governments with regard to their activities in international organizations, particularly on voting for members of representative bodies which have to reflect an appropriate distribution of seats among various groups of states (as for instance, the London agreement of 1946 on the distribution of seats in the Security Council). It has been suggested that a gentlemen's agreement is not binding on the states because it is deemed to have been concluded by the representatives in their personal names and not in the name of their governments. This reasoning is rather strained in the case of agreements which are intended to apply to government action irrespective of the individual who originally represented the government. It seems more satisfactory to take the position, in keeping with well-established practice, simply that it is legitimate for governments to enter into gentlemen's agreements recognizing that they are without legal effect.

This still leaves us with questions as to the nature of the commitment accepted by the parties in a nonbinding agreement and what precisely is meant by stating that the agreement is without legal effect. We shall begin with the latter point.

It would probably be generally agreed that a nonbinding agreement, however seriously taken by the parties, does not engage their legal responsibility. What this means simply is that noncompliance by a party would not be a ground for a claim for reparation or for judicial remedies. This point, it should be noted, is quite different from stating that the agreement need not be observed or that the parties are free to act as if there were no such agreement. As we shall indicate below, it is possible and reasonable to conclude that states may regard a nonbinding undertaking as controlling even though they reject legal responsibility and sanctions. * * *

A second proposition that would command general (though not unanimous) agreement is that nonbinding agreements are not "governed by international law." Exclusion from the Vienna Convention on the Law of Treaties follows from the conclusion that such agreements are not governed by international law, a requirement laid down in the definition in Article 2(a). * * * The *travaux préparatoires* of the Vienna Convention on the Law of Treaties confirm the conclusion that nonbinding agreements were intended to be excluded from the Convention on the ground that they are not governed by international law.[19]

The conclusion that nonbinding agreements are not governed by international law does not however remove them entirely from having legal implications. Consider the following situations. Let us suppose governments in conformity with a nonbinding agreement follow a course of conduct which results in a new situation. Would a government party to the agreement be precluded from challenging the legality of the course of conduct or the validity of the situation created by it? A concrete case could arise if a government which was a party to a gentlemen's agreement on the distribution of seats in an international body sought to challenge the validity of the election. In a case of this kind, the competent organ might reasonably conclude that the challenging government was subject to estoppel in view of the gentlemen's agreement and the reliance of the parties on that agreement.

* * *

Still another kind of legal question may arise in regard to nonbinding agreements. What principles or rules are applicable to issues of interpretation and application of such agreements? As we have already seen, customary law and the Vienna Convention do not "govern" the agreements. But if the parties (or even a third party such as an international organ) seek authoritative guidance on such issues, it would be convenient and reasonable to have recourse to rules and standards generally applicable to treaties and international agreements insofar as their applicability is not at variance with the nonbinding nature of these agreements. For example, questions as to territorial scope, nonretroactivity, application of successive agreements, or criteria for interpretation could be appropriately dealt with by reference to

**19.** At the Vienna conference a Swiss amendment was proposed to exclude nonbinding agreements such as "political declarations and gentlemen's agreements." In the opinion of the Swiss legal adviser (Bindschedler), such nonbinding agreements were governed by international law and had legal consequences and therefore would not be excluded by the definition in Article 2. The amendment was not adopted presumably because most representatives thought that such nonbinding agreements were not governed by international law. Taking a different position, the USSR representative opposed the Swiss amendment because he considered that some of the agreements referred to by the Swiss delegate should be covered by the Vienna Convention (mentioning the Atlantic Charter, Yalta, and Potsdam agreements). See supra note 10. As indicated by its preparatory work, the International Law Commission intended to exclude the nonbinding agreements from the scope of the Vienna Convention and thought this would be done by the definition of international agreements as those governed by international law. See Report of the International Law Commission to the General Assembly [1959] 2 Y.B.Int.Law Comm. 96–97, UN Doc. A/4169 (1959). For earlier references, see Brierly, Report [1950] id. 228, UN Doc. A/CN.4/23 (1950); Lauterpacht, Report [1953] id. 96–99, UN Doc. A/CN.4/63 (1953).

the Vienna Convention even though that Convention does not in terms govern the agreements. * * * It may be useful, however, to indicate what may reasonably be meant by an understanding that an agreement entails a political or moral obligation and what expectations are created by that understanding.

Two aspects may be noted. One is internal in the sense that the commitment of the state is "internalized" as an instruction to its officials to act accordingly. Thus, when a government has entered into a gentlemen's agreement on voting in the United Nations, it is expected that its officials will cast their ballots in conformity with the agreement though no legal sanction is applicable. Or when governments have agreed, as in the Helsinki Act, on economic cooperation or human rights, the understanding and expectation is that national practices will be modified, if necessary, to conform to those understandings. The political commitment implies, and should give rise to, an internal legislative or administrative response. These are often specific and determinate acts.

The second aspect is "external" in the sense that it refers to the reaction of a party to the conduct of another party. The fact that the states have entered into mutual engagements confers an entitlement on each party to make representations to the others on the execution of those engagements. It becomes immaterial whether the conduct in question was previously regarded as entirely discretionary or within the reserved domain of domestic jurisdiction. By entering into an international pact with other states, a party may be presumed to have agreed that the matters covered are no longer exclusively within its concern. When other parties make representations or offer criticism about conduct at variance with the undertakings in the agreement, the idea of a commitment is reinforced, even if it is labelled as political or moral.

* * *

The fact that nonbinding agreements may be terminated more easily than binding treaties should not obscure the role of the agreements which remain operative. De Gaulle is reported to have remarked at the signing of an important agreement between France and Germany that international agreements "are like roses and young girls; they last while they last." As long as they do last, even nonbinding agreements can be authoritative and controlling for the parties. There is no *a priori* reason to assume that the undertakings are illusory because they are not legal. To minimize their value would exemplify the old adage that "the best is the enemy of the good." It would seem wiser to recognize that nonbinding agreements may be attainable when binding treaties are not and to seek to reinforce their moral and political commitments when they serve ends we value.

# SECTION 2. CONCLUSION AND ENTRY INTO FORCE

## A. CAPACITY

*OPPENHEIM'S INTERNATIONAL LAW*

1217–20 (9th ed., Jennings & Watts, eds. 1992).

§ 595 **Treaty-making capacity of states.** Every state possesses treaty-making capacity. However, a state possesses this capacity only so far as it is sovereign. States which are not fully sovereign can become parties only to such treaties as they are competent to conclude. No hard and fast rule defines the competence of less than fully sovereign states: everything depends upon the special case. The constitutions of federal states may contain provisions on the competence, if any, of the member states to conclude international treaties with foreign states, and on the extent to which they do so in their own right or on behalf of the federal state. Similarly, protected states may conclude treaties if so authorised by the protecting state or the treaty establishing the protectorate. In some cases territories or territorial unions which are not fully sovereign states have been admitted to some international organisations, thus recognising in them a measure of treaty-making power. On occasion a dependent territory, such as a colony, may conclude a bilateral treaty with a foreign state; but this will normally only be with the express consent of the parent state, given either ad hoc or generally for particular categories of treaties, covering matters of particular interest to the territory. In such cases the territory is probably to be regarded as not exercising a treaty-making power in its own right but as exercising as a delegate the treaty-making power of the parent state which remains ultimately responsible in international law. Difficult questions often arise over whether an agreement concluded with non-recognised communities constitute treaties, particularly those negotiated as part of the process by which they achieve independence. Particular mention may be made of the problems which, if there are deep differences over the recognition of entities as states, can arise over the implementation of signature or accession clauses of multilateral treaties which are cast in terms applying to 'all States'. These problems are now usually in practice avoided by a formula opening signature or accession to states which are members of the United Nations or a specialised agency, or by having for the treaty more than one depositary.

An instrument is void as a treaty if concluded in disregard of the international limitations upon the capacity of the parties to conclude treaties. It may sometimes not be easy to determine whether a treaty actually restricts a state's capacity to conclude subsequent treaties, or whether it merely imposes obligations with which its subsequent treaties must not conflict; in the former case a treaty purportedly concluded in excess of capacity will be void, while in the latter the matter is more likely to be seen as one of international responsibility. The Court of Justice of the European Communities has held that in certain circumstances the member states have ceased to have any right to conclude treaties with third countries, the European Economic Community alone having the right to do so in those circumstances.

§ 596 **Treaty-making capacity of international organisations.** The capacity of international organisations to conclude international agreements is now beyond doubt, where such capacity is expressly provided in their constitutive instruments or where it is indispensable for the fulfilment of the purposes and functions for which they were set up. Many international organisations have concluded international agreements with member states, with states which are not members, and with other international organisations.

Although international agreements concluded between states and international organisations or between international organisations are not dealt with by the Vienna Convention on the Law of Treaties 1969, this does not affect the legal force of such agreements or the application to them of any of the rules set forth in the Convention, to which they would be subject under international law independently of the Convention. By and large it was believed that the law governing treaties between states applied, *mutatis mutandis,* to agreements concluded by and between international organisations, although certain special characteristics of such agreements would have to be taken into account. A Resolution adopted by the Vienna Conference recommended that the General Assembly should refer to the International Law Commission the study of the question of such agreements. This the Assembly did in 1969, and in 1982 the Commission completed its work on the matter and submitted final draft Articles for a Convention to the Assembly. These draft Articles formed the basis for the Convention on the Law of Treaties between States and International Organizations or between International Organizations which was adopted in 1986 at the conclusion of a conference held in Vienna. In effect, the 1986 Convention applies to the treaties with which it deals the same rules as those laid down by the 1969 Convention for treaties between states, with such adaptations as are necessary because of the characteristics of international organisations.

## *RESTATEMENT (THIRD)*

### § 311 Capacity and Authority to Conclude International Agreements

(1) Every state has capacity to conclude international agreements.

(2) A person is authorized to represent a state for purposes of concluding an international agreement if (a) he produces full powers or (b) such authority clearly appears from the circumstances.

(3) A state may not invoke a violation of its internal law to vitiate its consent to be bound unless the violation was manifest and concerned a rule of fundamental importance.

**Source Note:**

Subsection (1) follows Article 6 of the Vienna Convention, and Subsections (2) and (3) are adapted from Articles 7(1) and 46 respectively.

**Comment:**

*a. Agreements by subdivisions of states.* The term "state" in this section, as throughout this Restatement, means a nation-state as defined in

§ 201. A State of the United States or a subdivision of another state is not a state having capacity to conclude an international agreement. As to the status of agreements concluded by such subdivisions, see § 301, Comment *g* and § 302, Comment *f.*

**§ 301 Comment:**

*g. Agreements by subdivisions of states.* The constitutions of some states permit the making of certain agreements by their subdivisions, such as States of the United States, German Laender, Canadian provinces, or Swiss cantons. See § 201, Reporters' Note 9. Some of those agreements are international agreements within the scope of this section. For example, if both states and subdivisions of states are parties to an agreement, the rules of this Part can apply. They can apply also to some agreements among subdivisions only. See § 486, Reporters' Note 6. For the status of agreements entered into by States of the United States, see § 302, Comment *f.*

**§ 302 Comment:**

*f. Agreements by States of the United States.* The United States Constitution provides: "No State shall enter into any Treaty, Alliance or Confederation." Article I, Section 10, clause 1. A State may, however, enter into an "Agreement or Compact ... with a foreign power" with the consent of Congress. Id., clause 3. What distinguishes a treaty, which a State cannot make at all, from an agreement or compact, which it can make with Congressional consent, has not been determined. That would probably be deemed a political decision. Hence, if Congress consented to a State agreement with a foreign power, courts would not be likely to find that it was a "treaty" for which Congressional consent was unavailing.

By analogy with inter-State compacts, a State compact with a foreign power requires Congressional consent only if the compact tends "to the increase of political power in the States which may encroach upon or interfere with the just supremacy of the United States." Virginia v. Tennessee, 148 U.S. 503, 519, 13 S.Ct. 728, 734, 37 L.Ed. 537 (1893). In general, agreements involving local transborder issues, such as agreements to curb a source of pollution, to coordinate police or sewage services, or to share an energy source, have been considered not to require Congressional consent. Such agreements are not international agreements under the criteria stated in § 301(1), but other State compacts might be. See § 301, Comment *g;* compare Comment *d* to that section.

## *Notes*

1. *Component States of Federal Unions.* Many of the most important members of the modern community of nations are federal states; i.e., single international persons made up of entities having some degree of autonomy or sovereignty in domestic affairs. Among these are Australia, Brazil, Canada, Germany, India, Mexico, Switzerland, and the United States. The question may arise whether a constituent state of such a union, e.g., New York, has the capacity to enter into an agreement with another state. It may safely be assumed, first of all, that the capacity of one constituent state to enter into an agreement with another constituent state belonging to the same federal union is a question solely of the constitutional law of that union. The constituent states of Germany and Switzerland, for example, retain the right to conclude treaties

among themselves without the consent of the central government (1 Oppenheim 176–77), while the states of the United States must receive the approval of Congress before entering into "any Agreement or Compact" (U.S. Const., Art. I, sec. 10). On the other hand, it is not clear whether the capacity of constituent states to enter into agreements with foreign states is regulated only by the union's constitutional law. Where the constituent state is authorized by the union's constitution to enter into agreements with foreign states, does the constituent state on that basis alone have capacity under international law to enter into an agreement, or does the constituent state under such circumstances act only as an agent or organ of the federal union? Under what circumstances might the answer to this question be of practical importance? Of what significance would it be that the constitutional law of the federal union required (as in Germany and the United States) that the federal legislature or executive approve agreements proposed to be concluded between constituent and foreign states, and that this procedure was followed? Note that in an American court a foreign state may not sue a state of the Union without its consent. Principality of Monaco v. Mississippi, 292 U.S. 313, 54 S.Ct. 745, 78 L.Ed. 1282 (1934).

The United States Congress is sometimes called upon to approve proposed agreements between states of the United States and foreign countries or subdivisions thereof. These typically relate to the construction or maintenance of international highways and bridges. See, e.g., P.L. 85–145 (Joint Resolution consenting to agreement between New York State and Canada providing for continued existence of the Buffalo and Fort Erie Public Bridge Authority), 71 Stat. 367 (1957); P.L. 85–877 (Act authorizing Minnesota to negotiate and enter into highway agreement with Canadian province of Manitoba), 72 Stat. 1701 (1958); Zimmerman & Wendell, The Interstate Compact since 1925, at 79–84 (1951). The State Department occasionally opposes approval of proposed agreements on the ground that they would infringe the federal treaty-making and other powers. See, e.g., 5 Hackworth 24–25; the 1956 hearings before a subcommittee of the Senate Foreign Relations Committee on the proposed Great Lakes Basin compact between two Canadian provinces and several states of the United States, 84th Cong., 2d Sess. 6–8, 13–21 (1956).

What would be the status of an agreement concluded between a state of the United States and a foreign country without the approval of Congress, where the state has represented to the foreign country that it has the capacity under United States law to enter into such an agreement, and the foreign state, not unreasonably, relies on the state's representation? Is this the same situation as one in which the head of a state falsely represents to the head of another state that he possesses the constitutional authority to bind his state in an international agreement without the consent of the legislature? See section 5B infra.

It sometimes occurs that not only does the constitutional law of the federal union expressly permit constituent states to enter into agreements with foreign states, but that foreign states also recognize some degree of international legal personality in those states. See Triska & Slusser, The Theory, Law, and Policy of Soviet Treaties 63–64, 158–59, 427 (1962); 1 Whiteman 406–13. But see Dolan, The Member–Republics of the U.S.S.R. as Subjects of the Law of Nations, 4 I.C.L.Q. 629 (1955).

2. The International Law Commission had proposed that the article on capacity include a second paragraph providing that members of a federal union have treaty-making capacity if and to the extent provided in the federal constitution. France regarded the provision as in accord with existing practice. Strong

opposition came from Canada on several grounds, in particular stating that it could lead to interpretation by international bodies of the constitutions of federal states. In the final stages, the paragraph was deleted. See Kearney & Dalton at 506–508.

## CAPACITY OF SELF–GOVERNING TERRITORIES

What is the treaty-making capacity of political entities that have never been states and whose international relations are exercised by a dominant state, but which are more or less self-governing in respect of internal affairs? India, for example, beginning with the Treaty of Versailles in 1919, became a separate party to numerous international agreements, as did many other members of the British Commonwealth. The Philippine Commonwealth, before attaining independence, became a party to international agreements, as did Southern Rhodesia. See Lissitzyn, Territorial Entities Other Than Independent States in the Law of Treaties, 125 Rec. des Cours 5 (1968–III).

Sir Humphrey Waldock concluded that the parties to agreements with the territories do not and cannot "legally look upon the self-governing territory as a distinct juridical person and a responsible party to the treaty entirely separate from the parent State." First Report on the Law of Treaties, [1962] 2 Yb.I.L.C. 27, 37. Compare the following conclusions:

> * * * It may, indeed, be doubted that international law contains any objective criteria of international personality or treaty-making capacity. The very act or practice of entering into international agreements is sometimes the only test that can be applied to determine whether an entity has such personality or capacity, or, indeed, "statehood." * * * Perhaps the only limitation on the possession and exercise of treaty-making capacity by a political subdivision is lack of consent to the exercise of such capacity by the dominant (or "sovereign") entity to which the subdivision is subordinate. Once such consent has been given, the capacity comes into being or is exercised whenever another entity is willing and able to enter into an agreement with the subdivision that is intended to be governed by international law. The very exercise of treaty-making capacity by a subordinate entity endows it with legal personality under international law. It makes little sense, therefore, to make possession of such personality a prerequisite to the conclusion of treaties. * * *

Lissitzyn, Efforts to Codify or Restate the Law of Treaties, 62 Colum.L.Rev. 1166, 1183–84 (1962).* What are the essential elements of the process of consent described above?

### *Note & Question*

Article 305 of the 1982 Convention on the Law of the Sea provides that the Convention is open for signature to various entities (other than states) and international organizations, provided that they have competence over matters governed by the Convention and to enter treaties in respect of these matters.

Articles 306 and 307 provide that the entities referred to in Article 305 may ratify or accede to the convention in the same way as states.

Do the foregoing provisions alter Waldock's conclusion that the parties to the treaty cannot "legally look upon the self-governing territory as a distinct juridical person and a responsible party to the treaty entirely separate from the parent state"?

## B. FULL POWERS, ADOPTION, AND AUTHENTICATION

### 1. *Full Powers*

*SINCLAIR, THE VIENNA CONVENTION ON THE LAW OF TREATIES*

29–33 (2d ed. 1984).*

The first stage in the treaty-making process is to establish the authority of the representatives of the negotiating State or States concerned to perform the necessary formal acts involved in the drawing up of the text of a treaty or in the conclusion of a treaty. This authority is in principle determined by the issuance of a formal document entitled a "full power" which designates a named individual or individuals to represent the State for the purpose of negotiating and concluding a treaty. * * *

Article 7 of the Vienna Convention * * * sets out the general rule that a person is considered as representing a State for the purpose of adopting or authenticating the text of a treaty or for the purpose of expressing the consent of the State to be bound by a treaty if:

(*a*) he produces full powers; or

(*b*) it appears from the practice of the States concerned or from other circumstances that their intention was to consider that person as representing the State for such purposes and to dispense with full powers.

Thus the general rule is expressed in suitably flexible terms. Subparagraph (*b*) is intended to preserve the modern practice of States to dispense with full powers in the case of agreements in simplified form.

* * * Implicitly the Commission recognized that the non-production of full powers might involve a certain risk for one or other of the States concerned, in the sense that it might be subsequently claimed that an act relating to the conclusion of a treaty had been performed without authority.

Partly to guard against this risk and also to respect accepted international practice, paragraph 2 of Article 7 of the Convention establishes that, "in virtue of their functions and without having to produce full powers", Heads of State, Heads of Government and Ministers for Foreign Affairs are considered as representing their State for the purpose of all acts relating to the conclusion of a treaty. Heads of diplomatic missions are likewise considered as representing their State *ex officio* and without the need to produce full powers, but only for the purpose of adopting the text of a treaty between the accrediting State and the State to which they are accredited. Finally, representatives accredited by States to an international conference

* Footnotes omitted. Reprinted by permission of Manchester University Press.

or to an international organisation or one of its organs enjoy similar powers, but only for the purpose of adopting the text of a treaty in that conference, organisation or organ. * * *

An interesting point which was raised at the conference is the relationship between this rule about inherent capacity to perform certain acts relating to the conclusion of treaties and the rule set out in Article 46 of the Convention concerning the violation of provisions of internal law regarding competence to conclude treaties. It will be recalled that Article 46 establishes the principle that a State may not invoke the fact that its consent to be bound by a treaty has been expressed in violation of a provision of its internal law regarding competence to conclude treaties unless that violation was manifest and concerned a rule of its internal law of fundamental importance. The question is: does paragraph 2 of Article 7 raise an incontestable presumption as a matter of international law that the designated office-holders are *ex officio* entitled to perform the specified acts without the need to produce full powers notwithstanding that, as a matter of internal law, they are not empowered to do so? It would seem that the presumption is incontestable. * * *

Article 8 of the Convention forms the corollary to Article 7. It provides that an act relating to the conclusion of a treaty performed by a person who cannot be considered under Article 7 as authorised to represent a State for that purpose is without legal effect unless afterwards confirmed by that State. Cases of this kind are, of course, very rare, but the Commission's commentary cites two or three relevant examples from diplomatic history where State representatives had signed treaties in the absence of authority to do so. The *rationale* of the rule embodied in Article 8 would appear to be, as the Commission suggested, that "where there is no authority to enter into a treaty * * * the State must be entitled to disavow the act of its representative". An important point, which the text of Article 8 does not entirely resolve, is whether the subsequent confirmation must be expressed or can be implied from the conduct of the State concerned. The drafting history demonstrates fairly conclusively that confirmation can be so implied. * * *

### *Note*

Is a state bound by apparent authority to conclude agreements? Two decisions of the Permanent Court of International Justice indicate that a state is bound when it is not evident to the other party that the official acting for the state has exceeded his authority. See Case on Legal Status of Eastern Greenland, 1933 P.C.I.J., Ser. A/B, No. 53, at 71, p. 317 supra; Free Zones Case, 1932 P.C.I.J., Ser. A/B, No. 46. See also discussion in section 5 below relating to invalidity under Article 46 of the Vienna Convention.

## *2. Adoption and Authentication of the Test of a Treaty*

### *SINCLAIR, THE VIENNA CONVENTION ON THE LAW OF TREATIES*

33–36 (2nd ed. 1984).

The next stage in the conclusion of a treaty is the adoption of the text. In the Convention itself there is no definition of the term 'adoption', but it would appear to mean the formal act whereby the form and content of the proposed treaty are settled. Historically, the adoption of the text of a treaty took place by the agreement of all the States participating in the negotiations. Unanimity could therefore be said to constitute the classical rule—a rule which was considered so obvious as hardly to require stating in terms.

Unanimity must, by the nature of things, remain the unqualified rule for the adoption of the text of a bilateral treaty. If the parties to a proposed bilateral treaty have not reached agreement on the terms of the treaty, there is self-evidently no *consensus ad idem* and no text to be 'adopted'. The negotiations will obviously continue until the outstanding points in dispute have been settled and the necessary wording for the treaty agreed upon.

Unanimity likewise remains the rule for the category of treaties known, for purposes of convenience, as 'restricted multilateral treaties'. A 'restricted multilateral treaty' may be defined as a treaty whose object and purpose are such that the application of the treaty in its entirety between all the parties is an essential condition of the consent of each one to be bound by the treaty. Examples of restricted multilateral treaties are treaties establishing very close co-operation between a limited number of States, such as treaties of economic integration, treaties between riparian States relating to the development of a river basin or treaties relating to the building of a hydro-electric dam, scientific installations or the like. Treaties of this nature, particularly treaties providing for economic integration, are of growing significance in current practice. The most notable illustration is the series of treaties providing for the establishment of the European Communities. The essential characteristic of such treaties is that they incorporate a nexus of clearly interdependent rights and obligations, the fulfilment of which in their entirety by all the States involved is a precondition for the staged progress towards the objectives set out in the treaty. Thus unanimity remains the rule for the adoption of the text of such a treaty, and unanimity remains the rule for its entry into force. In principle, unanimity is also required for the admission of a new member to a grouping of this nature, in the sense that the consent of all the original member States, as well as of the applicant State, to be bound by an agreement embodying conditions of admission is required as a condition precedent to admission.

Article 9 of the Convention accordingly sets out, in paragraph 1, the general rule that the adoption of the text of a treaty takes place by the consent of the States participating in its drawing up. But it is obvious that this rule is not appropriate to the process whereby the texts of treaties are adopted at international conferences. Accordingly, Article 9(2) of the Convention establishes the general rule that 'the adoption of the text of a treaty at an international conference takes place by the vote of two-thirds of the States present and voting unless by the same majority they shall decide to apply a different rule'.

* * *

We have already noted that this particular provision constitutes progressive development rather than codification. At the conference some doubts were expressed about the substance of this rule, particularly in view of the differing types of international conference to which it might be thought to be applicable. * * * There was general agreement that the rule set out in Article 9(2) did not automatically apply to treaties adopted within international organisations if the relevant rules of the organisation provided otherwise; * * *

* * *

It would accordingly seem that the rule set out in Article 9(2) applies essentially to major international conferences—that is to say, large conferences attended by a great number of States. If such conferences are convened within the framework of international organisations, then any special rules of the organisation for the adoption of treaties will apply, notwithstanding Article 9(2); * * *

## C. EXPRESSION OF CONSENT TO BE BOUND

Articles 11 to 17 of the Convention deal with the ways in which states express their consent to be bound by a treaty. Article 11 lists the various means of expressing consent as signature, exchange of instruments constituting a treaty, ratification, acceptance, approval or accession. It adds to this list "any other means if so agreed." This last phrase would include for example the exchange of unsigned *notes verbales* as a means of consent to a treaty.

### *1. Signature*

The report of the International Law Commission on the draft of the present Article 12 observes that the article deals with signature only as a means by which the definitive consent of a state to be bound by the treaty is expressed. It does not deal with signature subject to "ratification" or subject to "acceptance" or "approval."

The following comments of the Commission explain the provisions of Article 12:

> (3) *Paragraph 1* of the article admits the signature of a treaty by a representative as an expression of his State's consent to be bound by the treaty in three cases. The first is when the treaty itself provides that such is to be the effect of signature as is common in the case of many types of bilateral treaties. The second is when it is otherwise established that the negotiating States were agreed that signature should have that effect. In this case it is simply a question of demonstrating the intention from the evidence. The third case, which the Commission included in the light of the comments of Governments, is when the intention of an individual State to give its signature that effect appears from the full powers issued to its representative or was expressed during the negotiation. It is not uncommon in practice that even when ratification is regarded as essential by some States from the point of view of their own requirements, another State is ready to express its consent to be bound definitively by its signature. In such a case, when the intention to be bound by signature alone is made clear, it is superfluous to insist upon ratification; and under paragraph 1(c) signature will have that effect for the particular State in question.
>
> (4) *Paragraph 2* covers two small but not unimportant subsidiary points. Paragraph 2(a) concerns the question whether initialling of a text may constitute a signature expressing the State's consent to be

bound by the treaty. In the 1962 draft [51] the rule regarding initialling of the text was very strict, initialling being treated as carrying only an authenticating effect and as needing in all cases to be followed by a further act of signature. In short it was put on a basis similar to that of signature *ad referendum.* Certain Governments pointed out, however, that in practice initialling, especially by a Head of State, Prime Minister or Foreign Minister, is not infrequently intended as the equivalent of full signature. The Commission recognized that this was so, but at the same time felt that it was important that the use of initials as a full signature should be understood and accepted by the other States. It also felt that it would make the rule unduly complicated to draw a distinction between initialling by a high minister of State and by other representatives, and considered that the question whether initialling amounts to an expression of consent to be bound by the treaty should be regarded simply as a question of the intentions of the negotiating States. Paragraph 2(a) therefore provides that initialling is the equivalent of a signature expressing such consent when it is established that the negotiating States so agreed.

(5) *Paragraph 2*(b) concerns signature ad referendum which, as its name implies, is given provisionally and subject to confirmation. When confirmed, it constitutes a full signature and will operate as one for the purpose of the rules in the present article concerning the expression of the State's consent to be bound by a treaty. * * *

[1966] II Yb.I.L.C. 196.

### 2. *Ratification, Acceptance, and Accession*

Article 14 sets out the rules determining cases where ratification is necessary in addition to signature to establish the state's consent to be bound.

The word "ratification" as used here and throughout the Convention refers only to ratification on the international plane. It is distinct and separate from the procedural act of "ratification" under municipal law such as parliamentary ratification or approval. The International Law Commission commented on the changing use of "ratification" in its report, as follows:

(2) The modern institution of ratification in international law developed in the course of the nineteenth century. Earlier, ratification had been an essentially formal and limited act by which, after a treaty had been drawn up, a sovereign confirmed, or finally verified, the full powers previously issued to his representative to negotiate the treaty. It was then not an approval of the treaty itself but a confirmation that the representative had been invested with authority to negotiate it and, that being so, there was an obligation upon the sovereign to ratify his representative's full powers, if these had been in order. Ratification came, however, to be used in the majority of cases as the means of submitting the treaty-making power of the executive to parliamentary control, and ultimately the doctrine of ratification underwent a funda-

51. Article 10, para. 3 of that draft.

mental change. It was established that the treaty itself was subject to subsequent ratification by the State before it became binding. Furthermore, this development took place at a time when the great majority of international agreements were formal treaties. Not unnaturally, therefore, it came to be the opinion that the general rule is that ratification is necessary to render a treaty binding.

(3) Meanwhile, however, the expansion of intercourse between States, especially in economic and technical fields, led to an ever-increasing use of less formal types of international agreements, amongst which were exchanges of notes, and these agreements are usually intended by the parties to become binding by signature alone. On the other hand, an exchange of notes or other informal agreement, though employed for its ease and convenience, has sometimes expressly been made subject to ratification because of constitutional requirements in one or the other of the contracting States.

Id. at 197.

It will be noted that the Convention does not take a stand on whether ratification is required when a treaty is silent on the matter. Some authorities had previously maintained that ratification is necessary when the treaty or the surrounding circumstances do not evidence an intent to dispense with ratification. The Commission had originally included a residuary rule requiring ratification if the treaty is silent on the matter. That rule was dropped after governments opposed it. At the Conference, the issue was revived with one group favoring ratification as a residuary rule, with a second group favoring signature as the residuary means. Both were defeated. The Convention, accordingly, does not adopt any presumption in favor of signature or ratification as a means of expressing definitive consent to be bound when the treaty is silent on the question. Actually, the issue is largely theoretical since as the Commission noted "total silence on the subject is exceptional."

The references in paragraph two of Article 14 to "acceptance" and "approval" were included because of an increased use of these terms for an expression of consent to be bound either without signature or after a non-binding prior signature. The Commission report commented as follows:

(10) Acceptance has become established in treaty practice during the past twenty years as a new procedure for becoming a party to treaties. But it would probably be more correct to say that "acceptance" has become established as a name given to two new procedures, one analogous to ratification and the other to accession. For, on the international plane, "acceptance" is an innovation which is more one of terminology than of method. If a treaty provides that it shall be open to signature "subject to acceptance", the process on the international plane is like "signature subject to ratification". Similarly, if a treaty is made open to "acceptance" without prior signature, the process is like accession. In either case the question whether the instrument is framed in the terms of "acceptance", on the one hand, or of ratification or acceptance, on the other, simply depends on the phraseology used in the treaty. Accordingly the same name is found in connexion with two different procedures; but there can be no doubt that to-day "acceptance"

takes two forms, the one an act establishing the State's consent to be bound after a prior signature and the other without any prior signature.

(11) "Signature subject to acceptance" was introduced into treaty practice principally in order to provide a simplified form of "ratification" which would allow the government a further opportunity to examine the treaty when it is not necessarily obliged to submit it to the State's constitutional procedure for obtaining ratification. Accordingly, the procedure of "signature subject to acceptance" is employed more particularly in the case of treaties whose form or subject matter is not such as would normally bring them under the constitutional requirements of parliamentary "ratification" in force in many States. In some cases, in order to make it as easy as possible for States with their varying constitutional requirements to enter into the treaty, its terms provide for either ratification or acceptance. Nevertheless, it remains broadly true that "acceptance" is generally used as a simplified procedure of "ratification".

(12) The observations in the preceding paragraph apply *mutatis mutandis* to "approval", whose introduction into the terminology of treaty-making is even more recent than that of "acceptance". "Approval", perhaps, appears more often in the form of "signature subject to approval" than in the form of a treaty which is simply made open to "approval" without signature. But it appears in both forms. Its introduction into treaty-making practice seems, in fact, to have been inspired by the constitutional procedures or practices of approving treaties which exist in some countries.

Id. at 198–99.

Article 15 deals with accession which is the traditional means by which a state becomes a party to a treaty of which it is not a signatory. On the question of whether accession may take place prior to entry into force of the treaty, the Commission report commented:

(2) Divergent opinions have been expressed in the past as to whether it is legally possible to accede to a treaty which is not yet in force and there is some support for the view that it is not possible.[57] However, an examination of the most recent treaty practice shows that in practically all modern treaties which contain accession clauses the right to accede is made independent of the entry into force of the treaty, either expressly by allowing accession to take place before the date fixed for the entry into force of the treaty, or impliedly by making the entry into force of the treaty conditional on the deposit, *inter alia,* of instruments of accession. The modern practice has gone so far in this direction that the Commission does not consider it appropriate to give any currency, even in the form of a residuary rule, to the doctrine that treaties are not open to accession until they are in force. In this connexion it recalls the following observation of a previous Special Rapporteur: [58]

**57.** See Sir G. Fitzmaurice's first report on the law of treaties, Yearbook of the International Law Commission, 1956, vol. II, pp. 125–26; and Mr. Brierly's second report, Yearbook of the International Law Commission, 1951, vol. II, p. 73.

**58.** See Sir H. Lauterpacht, Yearbook of the International Law Commission, 1953, vol. II, p. 120.

> "Important considerations connected with the effectiveness of the procedure of conclusion of treaties seem to call for a contrary rule. Many treaties might never enter into force but for accession. Where the entire tendency in the field of conclusion of treaties is in the direction of elasticity and elimination of restrictive rules it seems undesirable to burden the subject of accession with a presumption which practice has shown to be in the nature of an exception rather than the rule."

Accordingly, in the present article accession is not made dependent upon the treaty having entered into force.

Id. at 199.

### *Note*

A common type of provision is: "This treaty shall come into force upon the expiration of ninety days from the date of exchange of ratifications." May a state, having ratified, withdraw its ratification before ninety days have passed? Another common provision is: "This treaty shall come into force upon the receipt by the depositary of instruments of ratification of ______ states." If twelve ratifications are required, may a state which was among the first to ratify withdraw its ratification before the twelfth ratification has been received? The Universal Copyright Convention provides in Article IX(1) that the convention shall come into force "three months after the deposit of twelve instruments of ratification, acceptance or accession." 216 U.N.T.S. 132, 144. The Convention entered into force among the ratifying states on September 16, 1955. On August 19, 1955, the Philippine Republic deposited an instrument of accession with the Director–General of UNESCO (the depositary of the Convention). According to Article IX(2), such an instrument of accession became effective when three months had passed. On November 15, 1955 (less than a week before the date on which the Philippine accession would have become effective), the Philippine Government purported to withdraw its accession. How should the depositary act? See U.S. Dep't of State, Treaties in Force 271 n. 14 (1969). For comparable situations, see Summary of the Practice of the Secretary–General as Depositary of Multilateral Agreements, U.N.Doc. ST/LEG/7, at 28 (1959). What arguments might be made in support of, as well as in opposition to, the proposition that the Philippine Republic became and still is a party to the Universal Copyright Convention?

## D. OBLIGATION NOT TO DEFEAT OBJECT OF A TREATY

What are the obligations of a state which has signed a treaty subject to ratification? The Permanent Court of International Justice appears to have taken the position that, if ratification takes place, a signatory state's misuse of its rights prior to ratification may amount to a violation of its treaty obligations. Case of Certain German Settlers in Polish Upper Silesia, 1926 P.C.I.J., Ser. A, No. 7, at 30. The International Law Commission considered that this obligation begins when a state agrees to enter into negotiations for the conclusion of a treaty. *A fortiori,* it would attach also to a state which has actually ratified, acceded, or accepted a treaty if there is an interval before the treaty enters into force.

At the Conference, the Commission proposal was criticized for imposing a duty on states which had undertaken to negotiate. It was acknowledged that this was not an existing rule. Moreover, it was suggested that the object of a treaty could not easily be determined when it was still in negotiation. States might be discouraged from entering negotiations if they were then under a vague obligation. The proposal relating to negotiations was then defeated.

Whether Article 18 as it now stands is declaratory of prior customary law is uncertain. There is some authority for that conclusion (see McNair, The Law of Treaties 199, 204 (1961)), but the matter is not free from doubt. It may be expected, nonetheless, that Article 18 will be invoked from time to time against states which have signed but not ratified and against states which have consented to be bound in the interval prior to entry into force. It should be noted that the two paragraphs have limitations. Where the state has not yet consented to be bound, the obligation continues "until it has made its intention clear not to become a party to the treaty." In the case of a state which has consented to be bound but the treaty has not yet entered into force, the obligation is made conditional on the absence of undue delay in entry into force.

### *Notes*

1. What actions by a signatory state would defeat the object and purpose of a treaty that has not entered into force for the parties? The United States and the former U.S.S.R. signed the Strategic Arms Limitation Treaty II in 1979 but did not ratify it. Each accused the other from time to time of violating terms of the unratified treaty which imposed limits on the number of missiles.

In April 1986, the President ordered the elimination of two nuclear submarines in order to keep within the terms of the unratified treaty. Is the principle of Article 18 applicable to such actions or are they motivated by a mutual intent to comply with the treaty even if it has not entered into force legally? Would a failure to dismantle a missile scheduled to be eliminated defeat the object of the treaty if it could later be dismantled?

2. Consider Restatement (Third) § 312, Comment *i:*

> *Obligations prior to entry into force.* Under Subsection (3), a state that has signed an agreement is obligated to refrain from acts that would defeat the object and purpose of the agreement. It is often unclear what actions would have such effect. The application of that principle has raised issues with regard to the Second Strategic Arms Limitation Treaty signed in 1979 but not ratified. Testing a weapon in contravention of a clause prohibiting such a test might violate the purpose of the agreement, since the consequences of the test might be irreversible. Failing to dismantle a weapon scheduled to be dismantled under the treaty might not defeat its object, since the dismantling could be effected later. The obligation under Subsection (3) continues until the state has made clear its intention not to become a party or if it appears that entry into force will be unduly delayed.

## E. RESERVATIONS

### *1. What is a Reservation?*

A reservation is "a unilateral statement, however phrased or named, made by a State, when signing, ratifying, acceding to, accepting or approving a treaty, whereby it purports to exclude or to vary the legal effect of certain provisions of the treaty in their application to that State." In the context of bilateral agreements, a reservation is closely analogous to a counter-offer by the reserving state, and the legal situation is clear, whether the reservation is accepted or rejected by the other state. The most difficult problems concerning reservations, however, have arisen when one or more of the parties to a multilateral treaty objects to another state's attempt to become a party subject to one or more reservations.

### *Notes*

1. The United States and Canada concluded a treaty concerning the Niagara River which provided for the allocation as between the two countries of the hydro-electric power produced. The U.S. Senate in its resolution of advice and consent included a "reservation" that the United States reserves the right to provide by legislation for the use of the U.S. share of electric power and that no project for the use of that share should be undertaken until specifically authorized by Congress. Canada did not express any objection to the reservation, saying it was none of its concern. The N.Y. Power Authority requested a license for a project to use the U.S. share of the power, but it was refused by the Federal Power Commission on the ground that Congress had not legislated and therefore the project was contrary to the reservation incorporated into the treaty. What legal objection could be made to this opinion? See Power Authority of N.Y. v. Federal Power Commission, 247 F.2d 538 (D.C.Cir.1957) which held that the "reservation" had not the effect of law, vacated as moot, 355 U.S. 64, 78 S.Ct. 141, 2 L.Ed.2d 107 (1957). What is the basis for that decision? For critical comment, see Henkin, The Treaty Makers and the Law Makers: The Niagara Power Reservation, 56 Colum.L.Rev. 1151 (1956).

2. The International Law Commission, in its commentary on Article 2(d), noted that "States not infrequently make declarations as to their understanding of some matter or as to their interpretation of a particular provision. Such a declaration may be a mere clarification of the State's position or it may amount to a reservation, according as it does or does not vary or exclude the application of the terms of the treaty as adopted. ([1966] II Yb.I.L.C. 189–90). The U.N. Convention on the Law of the Sea of 1982 excludes reservations other than those specifically authorized. However, it allows declarations of understanding provided they do not purport to exclude or modify the legal effect of provisions of the Convention. Article 309. See text below.

3. Suppose a state attaches an "interpretative statement" to its ratification which by its terms indicates that the state will become a party only if that interpretation is accepted. If the interpretation appears inconsistent with the treaty provisions, do other parties have to consider it to be a reservation and to reject it if they disagree? It has been suggested that "the better course" would be to accept the characterization of interpretation but refuse to accept the interpretation and force the issue to some form of adjudication. Bowett, Reservations to Non–Restricted Multilateral Treaties, 48 Brit.Y.B.I.L. 69 (1976–77). If an interpretative statement is not accepted by other parties, does it exclude the affected provision or prevent the treaty from entering into force between the "objecting" and "declaring" states?

4. Suppose a reservation does not purport to modify the terms of a treaty but only the legal effect of those terms? For example, a state may designate a particular area as falling within a legal category in the treaty. A Court of Arbitration ruled in 1977 that Article 2(d) of the Vienna Convention also covered

"statements purporting to exclude or modify the *legal effect* of certain provisions in their application to the reserving State." Arbitration between the United Kingdom and France on the Delimitation of the Continental Shelf, Decision of 30 June 1977. 18 I.L.M. 397, 418, para. 55 (1979).

5. Is a state obliged to include declarations of understanding or intent in its instrument of ratification? Strictly speaking there is no such requirement since the other party or parties need not accept understandings that are not reservations. However, states often communicate such declarations of understanding and interpretive comments to make their position clear. For bilateral treaties, the United States does this as a rule in a protocol of exchange of instruments of ratification. See Restatement (Third) § 314, Reporters' Note 1.

### 2. *Permissibility and Acceptance of Reservations*

## RESERVATIONS TO THE CONVENTION ON GENOCIDE

International Court of Justice, Advisory Opinion, 1951.
1951 I.C.J. 15.

[After a dispute had arisen concerning the legal effect of reservations made by several states to the Genocide Convention of 1948 (78 U.N.T.S. 277), the General Assembly adopted a resolution on November 16, 1950, G.A.Res. 478 (V) (1950), asking the International Court of Justice for an advisory opinion on the questions, *inter alia:*]

In so far as concerns the Convention on the Prevention and Punishment of the Crime of Genocide in the event of a State ratifying or acceding to the Convention subject to a reservation made either on ratification or on accession, or on signature followed by ratification:

I. Can the reserving State be regarded as being a party to the Convention while still maintaining its reservation, if the reservation is objected to by one or more of the parties to the Convention but not by others?

II. If the answer to Question I is in the affirmative, what is the effect of the reservation as between the reserving State and:

(a) The parties which object to the reservation?

(b) Those which accept it?

[In answering these questions, the Court stated:]

All three questions are expressly limited by the terms of the Resolution of the General Assembly to the Convention on the Prevention and Punishment of the Crime of Genocide * * *. [T]he replies which the Court is called upon to give to them are necessarily and strictly limited to that Convention. The Court will seek these replies in the rules of law relating to the effect to be given to the intention of the parties to multilateral conventions.

* * *

It is well established that in its treaty relations a State cannot be bound without its consent, and that consequently no reservation can be effective against any State without its agreement thereto. It is also a generally recognized principle that a multilateral convention is the result of an agreement freely concluded upon its clauses and that consequently none of the contracting parties is entitled to frustrate or impair, by means of unilateral decisions or particular agreements, the purpose and *raison d'être* of the convention. To this principle was linked the notion of the integrity of the convention as adopted, a notion which in its traditional concept involved the proposition that no reservation was valid unless it was accepted by all the contracting parties without exception, as would have been the case if it had been stated during the negotiations.

This concept, which is directly inspired by the notion of contract, is of undisputed value as a principle. However, as regards the Genocide Convention, it is proper to refer to a variety of circumstances which would lead to a more flexible application of this principle. Among these circumstances may be noted the clearly universal character of the United Nations under whose auspices the Convention was concluded, and the very wide degree of participation envisaged by Article XI of the Convention. Extensive participation in conventions of this type has already given rise to greater flexibility in the international practice concerning multilateral conventions. More general resort to reservations, very great allowance made for tacit assent to reservations, the existence of practices which go so far as to admit that the author of reservations which have been rejected by certain contracting parties is nevertheless to be regarded as a party to the convention in relation to those contracting parties that have accepted the reservations—all these factors are manifestations of a new need for flexibility in the operation of multilateral conventions.

It must also be pointed out that although the Genocide Convention was finally approved unanimously, it is nevertheless the result of a series of majority votes. The majority principle, while facilitating the conclusion of multilateral conventions, may also make it necessary for certain States to make reservations. This observation is confirmed by the great number of reservations which have been made of recent years to multilateral conventions.

* * *

The Court * * * must now determine what kind of reservations may be made and what kind of objections may be taken to them.

The solution of these problems must be found in the special characteristics of the Genocide Convention. * * * The Genocide Convention was * * * intended by the General Assembly and by the contracting parties to be definitely universal in scope. It was in fact approved on December 9th, 1948, by a resolution which was unanimously adopted by fifty-six States.

The objects of such a convention must also be considered. The Convention was manifestly adopted for a purely humanitarian and civilizing purpose. It is indeed difficult to imagine a convention that might have this dual character to a greater degree, since its object on the one hand is to safeguard the very existence of certain human groups and on the other to confirm and endorse the most elementary principles of morality. In such a convention the contracting States do not have any interests of their own; they merely have, one and all, a common interest, namely, the accomplishment of those high purposes which are the *raison d'être* of the convention. Consequently, in a convention of this type one cannot speak of individual advantages or disadvantages to States, or of the maintenance of a perfect contractual balance between rights and duties. The high ideals which inspired the Convention provide, by virtue of the common will of the parties, the foundation and measure of all its provisions.

* * *

The object and purpose of the Genocide Convention imply that it was the intention of the General Assembly and of the States which adopted it that as many States as possible should participate. The complete exclusion from the Convention of one or more States would not only restrict the scope of its application, but would detract from the authority of the moral and humanitarian principles which are its basis. It is inconceivable that the contracting parties readily contemplated that an objection to a minor reservation should produce such a result. But even less could the contracting parties have intended to sacrifice the very object of the Convention in favour of a vain desire to secure as many participants as possible. The object and purpose of the Convention thus limit both the freedom of making reservations and that of objecting to them. It follows that it is the compatibility of a reservation with the object and purpose of the Convention that must furnish the criterion for the attitude of a State in making the reservation on accession as well as for the appraisal by a State in objecting to the reservation.

Any other view would lead either to the acceptance of reservations which frustrate the purposes which the General Assembly and the contracting parties had in mind, or to recognition that the parties to the Convention have the power of excluding from it the author of a reservation, even a minor one, which may be quite compatible with those purposes.

It has nevertheless been argued that any State entitled to become a party to the Genocide Convention may do so while making any reservation it chooses by virtue of its sovereignty. The Court cannot share this view. It is obvious that so extreme an application of the idea of State sovereignty could lead to a complete disregard of the object and purpose of the Convention.

On the other hand, it has been argued that there exists a rule of international law subjecting the effect of a reservation to the express or tacit assent of all the contracting parties. This theory rests essentially on a contractual conception of the absolute integrity of the convention as adopted. This view, however, cannot prevail if, having regard to the character of the convention, its purpose and its mode of adoption, it can be established that the parties intended to derogate from that rule by admitting the faculty to make reservations thereto.

It does not appear, moreover, that the conception of the absolute integrity of a convention has been transformed into a rule of international law. The considerable part which tacit assent has always played in estimating the effect which is to be given to reservations scarcely permits one to state that such a rule exists, determining with sufficient precision the effect of objections made to reservations. In fact, the examples of objections made to reservations appear to be too rare in international practice to have given rise to such a rule. It cannot be recognized that the report which was adopted on the subject by the Council of the League of Nations on June 17th, 1927, has had this effect. At best, the recommendation made on that date by the Council constitutes the point of departure of an administrative practice which, after being observed by the Secretariat of the League of Nations, imposed itself, so to speak, in the ordinary course of things on the Secretary–General of the United Nations in his capacity of depositary of conventions concluded under the auspices of the League. But it cannot be concluded that the legal problem of the effect of objections to reservations has in this way been solved. * * *

* * *

It results from the foregoing considerations that Question I, on account of its abstract character, cannot be given an absolute answer. The appraisal of a reservation and the effect of objections that might be made to it depend upon the particular circumstances of each individual case.

Having replied to Question I, the Court will now examine Question II * * *.

[E]ach State which is a party to the Convention is entitled to appraise the validity of the reservation, and it exercises this right individually and from its own standpoint. As no State can be bound by a reservation to which it has not consented, it necessarily follows that each State objecting to it will or will not, on the basis of its individual appraisal within the limits of the criterion of the object and purpose stated above, consider the reserving State to be a party to the Convention. * * *

The disadvantages which result from this possible divergence of views—which an article concerning the making of reservations could have obviated—are real; they are mitigated by the common duty of the contracting States to be guided in their judgment by the compatibility or incompatibility of the reservation with the object and purpose of the Convention. It must clearly be assumed that the contracting States are desirous of preserving intact at least what is essential to the object of the Convention; should this desire be absent, it is quite clear that the Convention itself would be impaired both in its principle and in its application.

It may be that the divergence of views between parties as to the admissibility of a reservation will not in fact have any consequences. On the other hand, it may be that certain parties who consider that the assent given by other parties to a reservation is incompatible with the purpose of the Convention, will decide to adopt a position on the jurisdictional plane in respect of this divergence and to settle the dispute which thus arises either by special agreement or by the procedure laid down in Article IX of the Convention.

Finally, it may be that a State, whilst not claiming that a reservation is incompatible with the object and purpose of the Convention, will nevertheless object to it, but that an understanding between that State and the reserving State will have the effect that the Convention will enter into force between them, except for the clauses affected by the reservation.

Such being the situation, the task of the Secretary–General would be simplified and would be confirmed to receiving reservations and objections and notifying them.

* * *

For these reasons,

The Court is of Opinion,

In so far as concerns the Convention on the Prevention and Punishment of the Crime of Genocide, in the event of a State ratifying or acceding to the Convention subject to a reservation made either on ratification or on accession, or on signature followed by ratification,

*On Question I:*

by seven votes to five,

that a State which has made and maintained a reservation which has been objected to by one or more of the parties to the Convention but not by others, can be regarded as being a party to the Convention, if the reservation is compatible with the object and purpose of the Convention; otherwise, that State cannot be regarded as being a party to the Convention.

*On Question II:*

by seven votes to five,

(a) that if a party to the Convention objects to a reservation which it considers to be incompatible with the object and purpose of the Convention, it can in fact consider that the reserving State is not a party to the Convention;

(b) that if, on the other hand, a party accepts the reservation as being compatible with the object and purpose of the Convention, it can in fact consider that the reserving State is a party to the Convention * * *.

### *Notes*

1. Vice President Guerrero, and McNair, Read, and Hsu Mo, JJ., joined in a dissenting opinion which argued that Question I should have been answered in the negative; i.e., that if a party to the Convention objected to a reservation made by another state, the reserving state could not be considered a party to the Convention. Question II was therefore irrelevant. The dissenting Judges attempted to show that "the practice of governments [had] resulted in a rule of law requiring the unanimous consent of all parties to a treaty before a reservation can take effect and the State proposing it can become a party," (1951 I.C.J. 32) and pointed out that the practice of the League of Nations and of the United Nations Secretariat (in their roles as depositaries of certain conventions) had conformed to this principle. It was then noted that the states negotiating a treaty were free to modify the above rule, and frequently did so, by expressly providing in the treaty for the effect of reservations, but that the states participating in the adoption of the Genocide Convention had not included such a provision and therefore should be taken as having intended to contract on the basis of the "unanimity" rule. The dissenters also criticized the Court's distinction between "compatible" and "incompatible" reservations on the grounds that it represented an innovation in the law of treaties and that the subjective nature of the distinction made it unworkable. The joint dissenting opinion concluded that "the integrity of the terms of the Convention [was] of greater importance than mere universality in its acceptance," and expressed skepticism that the effect of the majority opinion could be limited to the Genocide Convention, as opposed to "humanitarian" conventions generally. Id. at 46, 47.

2. In 1986, the United States Senate gave its consent to ratification of the Convention on Genocide subject to two reservations. One reservation related to the dispute settlement clause in Article IX. It provided that the specific consent of the United States shall be required before a dispute to which the United States is a party may be submitted to the Court. Is this reservation substantially the same as the reservations of the U.S.S.R. and other Soviet bloc states considered in the Advisory Opinion? A second reservation of the United States is discussed below.

The Soviet Union argued at the time of the controversy concerning the reservations to the Genocide Convention that any state could become a party to a general multilateral convention subject to any reservation it wished to advance, regardless of the objections of other parties. Later, however, writers of the Soviet Union expressed their approval of the rules laid down in the Court's advisory opinion and in the Vienna Convention. See Triska & Slusser, The Theory, Law and Policy of Soviet Treaties 84, 87–88 (1962).

3. The *Advisory Opinion on Reservations to the Genocide Convention* was widely endorsed by governments. It gave impetus to the adoption of the flexible system for reservations to multilateral conventions adopted in the Vienna Convention, in particular Article 20(4). The Court's opinion also emphasized the legislative character of many new multilateral conventions and especially those intended to benefit individuals. In these cases, it was deemed desirable to encourage the widest participation and therefore to allow states to participate even though they were not prepared to accept every provision. See Restatement (Third) § 313, Reporters' Note 1.

4. At the same time, both the Advisory Opinion and the Vienna Convention set limits to the permissibility of reservations. In particular, a reservation could not be accepted if it was incompatible with the object and purpose of the Convention. See Article 19 of the Vienna Convention. But query whether this test of permissibility can be maintained in the absence of an authoritative means of determining whether the reservation is compatible with object and purpose? If each state is free to make that determination, and there is no agreed means of compulsory judicial settlement or collective decision procedure, does not the test of impermissibility lose its practical significance? Judge Ruda believes it does. See Ruda, Reservations to Multilateral Conventions, 146 Rec. des Cours 95, 190 (1975–III). Bowett in contrast lays stress on the requirement of permissibility as a matter of treaty interpretation that is not dependent on the reactions of the states parties. See his comments below. Whether this is meaningful in practice would seem to depend on the readiness of states parties to the Convention to have recourse to the Court or to other third party determinations to settle differences of views as to compatibility. Thus far (as of 1993), no such cases involving interstate disputes as to compatibility have been brought to international tribunals. However, the Inter-American Court of Human Rights has given an advisory opinion on a question of incompatibility raised by a request for interpretation. A summary of the opinion is given below.

5. The I.C.J. Advisory Opinion highlights the character and object of the Genocide Convention. By implication it suggests that some multilateral conventions should have a different regime for reservations. What other regimes are possible? Consider the following:

(1) the "classical rule" requiring consent of every contracting state;

(2) the exclusion of all reservations;

(3) the acceptance of reservations by a decision of a collective body or by the approval of a qualified majority of parties;

(4) the rejection of reservations if a qualified majority (e.g., two thirds) of the parties object to it;

Does the Vienna Convention allow for all of these alternative regimes? Does it require any of them in particular treaties?

6. Can one identify certain multilateral conventions which by their character and purpose require that the treaty be applied in its entirety by all parties? See Article 20(2) of the Vienna Convention. Should this hold true only for treaties with a small number of parties? Would it apply to an arms control treaty? Is it especially applicable to economic integration treaties such as the treaties establishing common markets? See Ruda at 186.

7. Reservations have been made on several occasions by states adhering to treaties that were constituent instruments (i.e., constitutions) of international organizations. In all these cases the practice has been to refer the reservation to the body of the organization in question. The Vienna Convention now expresses this as a rule unless the treaty provides otherwise. For prior debate on this issue, see Schachter, The Question of Treaty Reservation at the 1959 General Assembly, 54 A.J.I.L. 372 (1960).

8. Reservations are most commonly made to multilateral treaties on human rights. Is a permissive flexible system desirable in these cases? See the advisory opinion of the Inter-American Court of Human Rights below. Is it desirable to exclude incompatible reservations to human rights treaties by providing for the rejection of reservations if two thirds of the contracting states object to the reservation? A clause to this effect is included in the U.N. Convention on the Elimination of All Forms of Racial Discrimination 1966. 660 U.N.T.S. 195, Article 20(2). The United States had preferred no reservation clause at all. See Lerner, The U.N. Convention on the Elimination of All Forms of Racial Discrimination 96 (2d ed. 1980).

## EXCLUSION OF RESERVATIONS

Are there reasons why some general multilateral conventions of a "legislative" character should not allow any reservations at all, irrespective of compatibility? Consider the reservations clause and the accompanying clause on declarations included in the U.N. Convention on the Law of the Sea, 1982.

### Article 309

No reservations or exceptions may be made to this Convention unless expressly permitted by other articles of this Convention.

### Article 310

Article 309 does not preclude a State, when signing, ratifying or acceding to this Convention, from making declarations or statements, however phrased or named, with a view, *inter alia,* to the harmonization of its laws and regulations with the provisions of this Convention, provided that such declarations or statements do not purport to exclude or to modify the legal effect of the provisions of this Convention in their application to that State.

### *Note*

Why have reservations to the Law of the Sea Convention generally been prohibited? Is the element of complete reciprocity more important in this case than in other multilateral legislative treaties? Will it result in the nonparticipation of states that object only to one or two provisions? A Report of the U.S. delegation in 1980 said:

> Since the Convention is an overall "package deal" reflecting different priorities of different states, to permit reservations would inevitably permit one State to eliminate the "quid" of another State's "quo". Thus there was general agreement in the Conference that in principle reservations could not be permitted.

Reports of the United States Delegation to the Third United Nations Conference on the Law of the Sea 83 (Nordquist & Park eds., 1983).

## *BOWETT, RESERVATIONS TO NON-RESTRICTED MULTILATERAL TREATIES*

48 Brit.Y.B.I.L. 67, 88–90 (1976–77).*

An examination of recent State practice on reservations suggests that there is considerable uncertainty over the operation of the rules now embodied in the Vienna Convention.

The primary source of uncertainty is the failure to perceive the difference between the issue of the "permissibility" of a reservation and the issue of the "opposability" of a reservation to a particular Party.

The issue of "permissibility" is the preliminary issue. It must be resolved by reference to the treaty and is essentially an issue of treaty interpretation; it has nothing to do with the question of whether, as a matter of policy, other Parties find the reservation acceptable or not. The consequence of finding a reservation "impermissible" may be either that the reservation alone is a nullity (which means that the reservation cannot be accepted by a Party holding it to be impermissible) or that the impermissible reservation nullifies the State's acceptance of the treaty as a whole.

The issue of "opposability" is the secondary issue and pre-supposes that the reservation is permissible. Whether a Party chooses to accept the reservation, or object to the reservation, or object to both the reservation and the entry into force of the treaty as between the reserving and the objecting State, is a matter for a policy decision and, as such, not subject to the criteria governing permissibility and not subject to judicial review.

It therefore follows that State practice would be clearer, and more logical, if objections to reservations stated whether the objection was based on the view that the reservation was impermissible or not. This would enable the reserving State to argue the matter of permissibility, if this were the ground of objection, whereas it cannot argue with a policy objection. It should also be incumbent upon a State objecting on the ground of impermissibility to state whether, in its view, the effect is to nullify the reservation or to nullify the acceptance of the treaty by the reserving State. Without such a statement of the legal consequences which a Party attaches to its objection on the ground of impermissibility, it is impossible to determine whether there is a treaty relationship or not.

Where the objection is not on the ground of impermissibility the matter is simpler, since Articles 20 and 21 of the Vienna Convention effectively indicate what legal consequences flow from acceptance, objection, or objection to both the reservation and any treaty relationship.

If this analysis is correct, it seems possible to formulate the following propositions which might provide useful guidance to States:

1. The test of a true reservation is whether it seeks to exclude or modify the legal effect of the provisions of the treaty to which the reservation is attached, and by this test a reservation must be distinguished from declarations or other interpretative statements however named. The latter, whilst not reservations, need not be accepted and raise an issue of treaty interpretation.

2. The permissibility of reservations under contemporary law is governed by the rules set out in Article 19 of the Vienna Convention; in essence, these rules assume the general permissibility of reservations to the non-restricted multilateral treaty except where reservations are expressly or impliedly prohibited or are incompatible with the object and purpose of the treaty. The criterion of "compatibility" does not apply to reservations which are prohibited, expressly or impliedly, or to a reservation which is expressly permitted.

3. A reservation which is expressly permitted and which requires no subsequent acceptance is one the legal effect of which is capable of being deduced from the treaty itself. Thus, a reservations clause permitting reservations to an article in general terms does not mean that all reservations to that article are *ipso facto* permissible and require no subsequent acceptance, although a reservation excluding the article *in toto* might be of this nature.

4. Therefore, in relation to reservations to an article to which reservations are allowed, the permissibility of any particular reservation will depend upon its fulfilling certain criteria, namely:

(i) that it is a true reservation;

(ii) that it is a reservation to that article and does not seek to modify the effect of some other article to which reservations are not allowed;

(iii) that it does not seek to modify rules of law which derive from some other treaty or from customary international law;

(iv) that it is not incompatible with the object and purpose of the treaty.

5. When a reservation is "impermissible" according to the rules set out in conclusions 2, 3 and 4 above, the inconsistency in the reserving State's expression of a will to be bound by the treaty and the formulation of an impermissible reservation must be resolved as a matter of construction of what the State really intended. It is suggested that the following is the proper test:

(i) a reservation not incompatible with the object and purpose of the treaty may be severed and should be disregarded as a nullity;

(ii) a reservation incompatible with the object and purpose of the treaty and not severable invalidates the State's acceptance of the treaty.

6. The question of "permissibility" is always a question to be resolved as a matter of construction of the treaty and does *not* depend on the reactions of the Parties. Therefore, though each Party may have to determine whether it regards a reservation as permissible, in the absence of any "collegiate" system it must do so on the basis of whether the treaty permits such a reservation. The issue of "permissibility" is thus entirely separate from the issue of "opposability", that is to say whether a Party accepts or does not accept a reservation which is permissible.

7. Parties may not accept an impermissible reservation.

8. As to permissible reservations, with non-restricted multilateral treaties, a reservation which is expressly authorized in the sense of conclusion 3 above requires no acceptance and takes effect with the reserving State's acceptance of the treaty. That apart, permissible reservations may meet with the following three reactions from other Parties:

(i) acceptance of the reservation: the effect is that the treaty is in force and the reservation takes full effect between the reserving and accepting States, on a reciprocal basis;

(ii) objection to the reservation: the effect is that the treaty is in force, but *minus* the provision affected by the reservation *to the extent of the reservation.* The reservation is not "opposable" to the objecting State;

(iii) objection to the reservation and an express objection to the treaty's entering into force: the effect is that the reserving and objecting States are not in any treaty relationship. Neither the treaty nor the reservation is "opposable" to the objecting State.

9. The objecting State, exercising either of the last two options set out in conclusion 8 above, is free to object on any ground: that is to say, its objection is not confined to the ground of "incompatibility" with the object and purpose of the treaty.

10. Both reservations and objections may be withdrawn in writing, taking effect on communication to the objecting or reserving State, as the case may be. The effect of withdrawal is to restore the original treaty text in the case of the withdrawal of a reservation. In the case of the withdrawal of an objection, this is equivalent to an acceptance of the reservation.

### *Notes*

1. Bowett's point 8(ii) above restates Article 21(3) of the Vienna Convention. Does this rule mean that the legal effect is precisely the same for a state that accepts the reservation and for a state that objects to the reservation but does not object to the treaty coming into force between it and the reserving state? If a reservation excludes a particular treaty provision, both the accepting state and the objecting state are not bound by the provision. If a reservation modifies a treaty provision, the modified provision applies to the accepting state. An objecting state may exclude the provision only "to the extent of the reservation". Is the result in legal effect the same? Two leading commentators think

so. See Ruda, Reservations to Multilateral Conventions at 200, and Sinclair, The Vienna Convention on the Law of Treaties at 77.

2. In the light of the foregoing, consider the Understanding attached by the United States to its ratification of the International Covenant on Civil and Political Rights modifying the provision that "the Covenant shall extend to all parts of federal States without any limitations or exceptions" (Article 50). The understanding obliges the United States to implement all provisions of the Covenant over whose subject matter the Federal Government exercises legislative and judicial jurisdiction but with respect to provisions over whose subject matter state or local governments exercise jurisdiction, the United States is committed only "to take appropriate measures to the end" that the state or local governments "take appropriate measures for the fulfillment of this Covenant." See Chapter 8, p. 628 infra. The same "State Rights" reservation was proposed to the Convention on the Elimination of All Forms of Racial Discrimination. See President's Message to the Senate concerning four human rights treaties, 95th Cong. 2d Sess.1978. For a contracting state that objects to this reservation but does not object to the treaty entering into force for the United States, Article 50 would not apply "to the extent of the reservation." Hence the objecting state would not be entitled to complain that Article 50 has been violated by a failure to give effect to the Covenant in its entirety. The objecting state would then be in the same position as an accepting state in this respect, a somewhat surprising result.

3. If some states object to a reservation on grounds of impermissibility (e.g., incompatibility) and others accept it, is the reserving state's ratification to be counted by the depositary in determining the number of states needed to bring the treaty into force? What criteria should apply? See U.N. Secretary General, Report on Depositary Practice in Relation to Reservations, U.N.Doc. A/5687, p. 96–97 (1964).

## IMPORTANCE OF RESERVATIONS

How important are reservations in the overall treaty relations among states? Have the new flexible rules increased participation in multilateral treaties? Neither question is easy to answer since international lawyers have rarely done research on such empirical questions. One statistical survey examined multilateral conventions that entered into force between 1919–1971. It found, surprisingly, that 85% of the 1164 conventions had no reservations at all. Even fewer reservations were found in the conventions (839) that were limited to certain states because of subject or geography; 92% had no reservations. Gamble, Reservations to Multilateral Treaties: A Macroscopic View of State Practice, 74 A.J.I.L. 372, 379 (1980).

Most reservations did not deal with the substantive provisions of the treaties. They related to dispute settlement, nonrecognition of other parties, compatibility with specific domestic laws, and colonial territories. Of the substantive reservations, the greater number were adjudged to be minor. Id. at 384–85. For similar findings, see Schachter, Nawaz & Fried, Toward Wider Acceptance of U.N. Treaties 154–56 (1971), indicating that most reservations to U.N. treaties were not substantive.

Although reservations are relatively infrequent to treaties generally (on average, a state has made only one reservation to a multilateral treaty every ten years), reservations may be significant in enabling states to join certain kinds of multilateral treaties. Most evident in that category are the human rights treaties. For example, the Convention on Discrimination against Women has drawn reservations from 44 countries, including a number of substantive significance. Treaties dealing with private law and judicial procedure also attract reservations, nearly always on narrow points. See Gamble at 386. Whether reservations have significantly increased since 1971 has not been determined.

Whatever the overall statistics show, it also is evident that in particular cases, reservations may allow states to participate when they otherwise would not. However, reservations give rise to disputes when they are considered by some states to weaken substantially the effect of the convention and to be incompatible with the object and purpose of the treaty.

### *Note*

Adopted in 1979 by the U.N. General Assembly, the Convention on the Elimination of All Forms of Discrimination against Women is the most comprehensive international treaty protecting the human rights of women. Article 1 expresses the basic core of the Convention: "Discrimination against women, denying or limiting as it does their equality of rights with men, is fundamentally unjust and constitutes an offence against human dignity." The Convention now has more than a hundred signatories, but numerous countries conditioned their ratification on substantive reservations. Therefore, while the Convention purports to prohibit "all forms" of discrimination against women, many state parties have refused to accept the full import of this goal. "The Women's Convention may face the paradox of maximizing its universal application at the cost of compromising its integrity." Rebecca J. Cook, Reservations to the Convention on the Elimination of All Forms of Discrimination Against Women, 30 Va.J.Int'l L. 643 (1990).

Professor Cook explains that in formulating the treaty, the drafters sought to promote widespread adherence by permitting compatible reservations to the responsibilities of membership. After considerable debate, the drafters agreed to the following article on reservations:

Article 28

> 1. The Secretary–General of the United Nations shall receive and circulate to all States the text of reservations made by States at the time of ratification or accession.
>
> 2. A reservation incompatible with the object and purpose of the present Convention shall not be permitted.
>
> 3. Reservations may be withdrawn at any time by notification to this effect addressed to the Secretary–General of the United Nations who shall then inform all States thereof. Such notification shall take effect on the date on which it is received.

Cook argues that only reservations that contemplate the provision of means to move progressively toward equality between men and women are compatible with the "object and purpose of the treaty" as provided by Article 28(2) of the Women's Convention and Article 19(c) of the Vienna Convention. She writes:

> If, within the reserving state, the impact of the reservation is minor, so as to approach if not actually fall under the principle *de minimis non curat*

*lex,* the reservation can be tolerated in the name of promoting universal membership in the Convention. If, however, the impact on women is significant in denying equality or equality of opportunity with men, the reservation must be rejected and the cause of integrity of the Convention must prevail. The significance of a reservation is determined prospectively by an interaction of qualitative and quantitative factors. A minor quantitative exclusion may be permissible, such as in the case of reservations by Belgium, Luxembourg, Spain and the United Kingdom stating that succession to the monarchy shall favor males over females without regard to order of birth. This clearly postpones the succession of the Monarch's oldest daughter to the youngest son, and the symbolism of the discrimination reflects the values and perceptions of more than the few individuals directly concerned. Such a symbolic though quantitatively limited reservation may be compared to a reservation of qualitatively trivial impact on women that affects them in sizeable numbers. A reservation that, for instance, precludes women eligible for regular training and promotion in the military from hand to hand military combat roles may be permissible, provided that, as in the case of a quantitative exclusion, the party to the Convention otherwise maintains progressive development towards elimination of cultural and related environments that have historically conditioned the prevailing discrimination.

To propose that compatibility of reservations is specific to the circumstances of individual countries, and that countries with such features as a large differential literacy rate between men and women or with many households headed by women are different from other countries, suggests that legal determination of compatibility arises not from the object and purpose of the Convention *per se,* but from specific applications of treaty provisions to individual countries. In other words, compatibility may seem determinable not as a function of interpretation of the treaty as a whole, but from socio-political measurements of effects of reservations on women. It is proposed, however, that the universal aspiration of the Convention compels recognition that state parties are located at different points on the road to achievement of the Convention's obligation of result and that they may progress at different rates.

The Women's Convention mandates relative assessments of reservations for the purpose of legal determination of compatibility. This is implicit in the approach to eliminating discrimination taken in the Convention, which is designed not simply to bring women to a level of rights enjoyed by men, but to permit women to maximize the potential for their development and self-realization without regard to comparisons between their optimal achievements and those of men. Similarly relevant are obligations of state parties. In those societies where women have an advanced capacity for development and self-realization, relatively few additional obligations under the Convention are assumed. In those societies, however, where women suffer multiple discriminations, a state assumes a larger obligation. Accordingly, performance of states parties under the Convention, and the compatibility of their reservations, will be specific to their circumstances. There are, however, certain reservations which, despite the particular circumstances of a given state party, will clearly be unacceptable.

30 Va.J.Int'l L. at 679–81.

Several Islamic states have acceded to the treaty with a general reservation that they will not comply with any requirements that conflict with Sharia law. Cook is dubious of the validity of this type of cultural reservation:

> Reservations to Article 2 that exclude the establishment of means to amend national laws and culture to eliminate discrimination against women are highly questionable since one of the primary objectives of the Convention is an obligation of means. In other words, exclusion of the means to move towards its ultimate goals obstructs and compromises compliance with the object and purpose of the Convention.

Id. at 689.

Cook also expresses skepticism about the validity of many other treaty reservations, such as ones relating to the admission of women into the military, the eligibility of women for night work, the civil and contractual capacity of women, and the status of women in marriage and family relations. She concludes:

> The repetition of a state's assertion of its legal authority to apply its domestic law in preference to the principles advanced in the Convention soon becomes explicable as a refusal rather than a willingness to be bound by the Convention. That is, when a state's obligations under the Convention are trivial or minor in contrast to the treaty obligations it declines to accept, it is unconvincing for the state to claim party status and for other states parties to claim that they are in a legal relationship under the Convention with the reserving state. The state's participation in the Convention may be an act of legal form but a fiction of legal, political and social substance.

Id. at 707.

### 3. *Reservations to Human Rights Treaties*

## ADVISORY OPINION ON RESERVATIONS

Inter–American Court on Human Rights,
Ser. A, No. 2 (1982).

[Two states ratified the American Convention on Human Rights with reservations. The depository, the Organization of American States, on the basis of an opinion of its legal adviser, ruled that the ratifications could not be effective until at least one contracting state accepted them. In the absence of an express acceptance, acceptance by a contracting state could only be implied at the end of a one-year period of non-objection. Article 20(5). This would mean that the ratifying states might not be bound by the Human Rights Convention for the year following their ratification. Their inhabitants would consequently be denied the protection of the Convention for that time even though the states had expressed their consent to be bound.

In its Advisory Opinion, the Inter–American Court held that the reserving states should be considered parties as of the date of their ratification even though the reservations had not been accepted by any other contracting state. The court emphasized that the requirements of acceptance and reciprocity were not appropriate for a human rights treaty which must be seen "for what in reality it is: a multilateral legal instrument or framework enabling states to make binding unilateral commitments not to violate the human rights of individuals within their jurisdiction." Advisory Opinion, para. 33. On this theory, reciprocity loses its relevance and reservations may be considered as authorized by the treaty provided they are not incompatible with the object and purpose of the treaty. Consequently the two states which ratified with reservations should be considered as legally bound from the date of their ratification.] For comments see Buergenthal, The Advisory Practice of the Inter-American Human Rights Court, 79 A.J.I.L. 1, 20–33 (1985).

## ADVISORY OPINION ON RESTRICTION TO THE DEATH PENALTY

Inter-American Court on Human Rights,
Adv.Op. No. OC–3 (1983) Ser. A, No. 3, 23 I.L.M. 320 (1984).

[One of the questions put to the Court by the Inter-American Commission on Human Rights concerned a reservation made by Guatemala relating to the imposition of the death penalty. Article 4(2) of the Convention prohibits, *inter alia,* the death penalty for crimes to which it had not applied previously under the domestic law of the state. Article 4(4) prohibits the application of the death penalty for "political offences or related common crimes." The reservation of Guatemala was made to the latter provision "inasmuch as the Constitution of the Republic of Guatemala only excludes from the application of the death penalty political crimes but not common crimes related to political crimes."

The question presented to the Court was whether this reservation can be invoked to justify the application of the death penalty to common crimes connected with political crimes to which that penalty did not previously apply. The Court concluded that "Article 4(2) contains an absolute prohibition on the extension of the death penalty." It concluded therefore that the reservation restricted by its own wording to Article 4(4) does not allow the reserving state to extend by subsequent legislation the death penalty for crimes to which that penalty was not previously applied.

In reaching these conclusions, the Court emphasized the fact that derogations from Article 4 were not permitted by the Convention. It linked incompatibility with nonderogability in the following passage.]

Consequently, the first question which arises when interpreting a reservation is whether it is compatible with the object and purpose of the treaty, Article 27 of the Convention allows the States Parties to suspend, in time of war, public danger, or other emergency that threatens their independence or security, the obligations they assumed by ratifying the Convention, provided that in doing so they do not suspend or derogate from certain basic or essential rights, among them the right to life guaranteed by Article 4. It would follow therefrom that a reservation which was designed to enable a State to suspend any of the non-derogable fundamental rights must be deemed to be incompatible with the object and purpose of the Convention and, consequently, not permitted by it. The situation would be different if the reservation sought merely to restrict certain aspects of a non-derogable right without depriving the right as a whole of its basic purpose. Since the reservation referred to by the Commission in its submission does not appear to be of a type that is designed to deny the right to life as such, the Court concludes that to that extent it can be considered, in principle, as not being incompatible with the object and purpose of the Convention.

[23 I.L.M. 320, 341, para. 61.

The Court then stated it must interpret the reservation in a manner most consistent with the object and purpose of the Convention. In particular a reservation should not be construed to limit the exercise of rights to a greater extent than is provided in the reservation. Accordingly, the Court considered it necessary to interpret the Guatemalan reservation to be limited to allow the continuance of its death penalty for common crimes related to political offenses but not to permit applying the death penalty to new offenses. The Court's reasoning is indicated in the following passage:]

Since the reservation modifies or excludes the legal effects of the provision to which it is made, the best way to demonstrate the effect of the modification is to read the provision as it has been modified. The substantive part of the reservation "only excludes political crimes from the application of the death penalty, but not common crimes related to political crimes." It is clear and neither ambiguous nor obscure, and it does not lead to a result that is absurd or unreasonable applying the ordinary meaning to the terms, to read the article as modified by the reservation as follows: "4(4) In no case shall the capital punishment be inflicted for political offenses," thus excluding the related common crimes from the political offenses that were reserved. No other modification of the Convention can be derived from this reservation, nor can a State claim that the reservation permits it to extend the death penalty to new crimes or that it is a reservation also to Article 4(2).

[Id. at 345, para. 73.]

### *Notes*

1. Was the Court justified in concluding that the Guatemalan reservation was not incompatible with the object and purpose of the Convention—in particular of Article 4(4) which states that "in no case should capital punishment be inflicted for political offenses or related common crimes"? Did the reservation not allow Guatemala to impose the death penalty for "related common crimes"? Why would this exception be consistent with the purpose of the Convention?

2. A member of the Inter-American Court has stressed the significance of the advisory opinion in linking nonderogability of rights and incompatibility. See Buergenthal at 25. Query, whether this should not also have applied to the non-derogable right in Article 4(4)? If so, the Court should have ruled the reservation impermissible. Was it better on balance to allow the reservation so that Guatemala could be a party without derogating from the other "more basic" provisions of Article 4?

## *UNITED STATES RESERVATION TO THE GENOCIDE CONVENTION*

Reprinted in 28 I.L.M. 754 (1989).

[The United States Senate has given its consent to ratification of the Genocide Convention in 1986, subject to a number of conditions, including:]

That nothing in the Convention requires or authorizes legislation or other action by the United States of America prohibited by the Constitution of the United States as interpreted by the United States.

### *Notes*

1. Is a reservation such as that of the United States which would permit non-compliance with the international convention (because of inconsistent internal law of the State) compatible with the object and purpose of the Convention? Is it plausible in the light of U.S. constitutional law to consider that the above U.S. reservation to the Genocide Convention would actually result in the United States claiming a right of non-compliance with any obligation of that Convention? If a contracting state objects to the reservation on grounds of incompatibility but does not object to the entry into force of the Convention between it and the U.S., what is the legal situation?

2. After the President of the United States signed the two International Covenants, plus the American Convention on Human Rights and the International Convention on Elimination of Racial Discrimination, he submitted them to the Senate for its advice and consent together with several reservations. The accompanying message said "Whenever a provision is in conflict with United States law, a reservation, understanding or declaration has been recommended." Message from the President transmitting four treaties on human rights, 95th Congress 2nd Session, Sen.Exec. C, D, E and F, iii–iv (1978). An accompanying communication from the Secretary of State said that the treaties contain provisions that appear to be in conflict with, or go beyond, the requirements of United States law and that the reservations and understandings were "designed to harmonize the treaties with existing provisions of domestic law" Id. at vi. Are these reservations compatible with Article 2 of the Covenant on Civil and Political Rights which expressly requires all parties to adopt measures necessary to give effect to the Covenant? Is a reservation or group of reservations designed to reduce the obligations of a state to the level of existing domestic law compatible with the object of a Convention that its obligations be observed by all parties? See Schachter, The Obligation of the Parties to Give Effect to the Covenant on Civil and Political Rights, 73 A.J.I.L. 462, 464–65 (1979).

## F. ENTRY INTO FORCE AND PROVISIONAL APPLICATION

The obvious rule, laid down in Article 24 of the Vienna Convention, is that a treaty enters into force in such manner and upon such date as it may provide or as the negotiating states may agree. Failing such provision, the treaty enters into force as soon as all negotiating states have consented to be bound.

How can a treaty, which has not entered into force, govern such matters as authentication, signature and ratifications, depositary functions, reservations, or entry into force which have to be dealt with prior to the treaty's coming into force? Article 24(4) makes explicit what was always tacitly assumed, namely that such provisions must apply from the time of adoption of the text. They are considered to have been accepted as governing provisions when the text is adopted.

The desire to apply a treaty even before it has come into force has led to an increasing use of "provisional application." Some treaties so provide; in other cases the negotiating states have so agreed in some other manner. Article 25 of the Vienna Convention recognizes this practice. It also makes explicit the right of termination of such provisional application, requiring that the terminating state notify the other states between which the treaty is being applied of its intention not to become a party to the treaty.

Although Article 25 applies to a treaty "pending its entry into force," that phrase may be construed to cover the situation of states which have not definitively consented to be bound (i.e., treaty not in force for them), even if the treaty is in force for others. Statements at the Vienna Conference support this interpretation. See Sinclair, The Vienna Convention on the Law of Treaties at 46. Provisional application may also relate to a part of a treaty.

Provisional application has assumed increasing importance in recent years because of the felt need to act quickly in regulating new problems and because of the delays in obtaining ratification or accession by the considerable number of states now required for entry into force of general multilateral treaties (for example, the Vienna Convention requires 35 adherences). A great many governments which have negotiated and voted for multilateral treaties often take years to consent to be bound. Such delays frequently have little to do with the substance of the treaties and are caused by extraneous factors (e.g., administrative or translation difficulties, parliamentary objections to marginal clauses, or lack of qualified personnel to handle the large volume of treaties). For an analysis of the slow rate of treaty adherence and its causes, see Schachter, Nawaz, and Fried, Toward the Wider Acceptance of UN Treaties (1971).

### *Notes*

1. The United States has on occasion accepted the obligations of treaties on a provisional basis before the ratification process was completed. In some cases this was done in regard to treaties which "were beyond the authority of the President to enter into on a permanent basis." Restatement (Third) § 312, Reporters' Note 7. How far the implied authority of the President might extend in regard to such treaties is uncertain. Id.

2. The Department of State publishes an annual list of *Treaties in Force* for the United States. After entry into force most treaties to which the United States is a party are published singly in a series entitled Treaties and Other International Agreements (T.I.A.S.). Subsequently bound volumes entitled United States Treaties and Other International Agreements (U.S.T.) are published. Agreements registered or recorded with the United Nations are published in the United Nations Treaty Series (U.N.T.S.).

## SECTION 3. OBSERVANCE, APPLICATION, AND INTERPRETATION

### A. OBSERVANCE

#### *1. Pacta Sunt Servanda and Good Faith (Article 26)*

Lord McNair, The Law of Treaties 493 (1961), prefaces his discussion of the binding effect of treaties with the following remarks:

> In every uncodified legal system there are certain elementary and universally agreed principles for which it is almost impossible to find

specific authority. In the Common Law of England and the United States of America, where can you find specific authority for the principle that a man must perform his contracts? Yet almost every decision on a contract presupposes the existence of that principle. The same is true of international law. No Government would decline to accept the principle *pacta sunt servanda,* and the very fact that Governments find it necessary to spend so much effort in explaining in a particular case that the *pactum* has ceased to exist, or that the act complained of is not a breach of it, either by reason of an implied term or for some other reason, is the best acknowledgment of that principle.

* * *

In the *Chorzów Factory Case (Jurisdiction),* the Permanent Court of International Justice stated that it was "a principle of international law that the breach of an [international] engagement involves an obligation to make reparation in an adequate form. Reparation * * * is the indispensable complement of a failure to apply a convention and there is no necessity for this to be stated in the convention itself." 1927 P.C.I.J., Ser.A, No. 9, at 21. Occasionally, agreements will specifically refer to the obligation of the parties to observe the provisions therein. The United Nations Charter (the preamble of which states that one of the aims of the organization is "to establish conditions under which * * * respect for the obligations arising from treaties * * * can be maintained") provides in Article 2(2) that all Members shall "fulfill in good faith the obligations assumed by them in accordance with the present Charter."

The International Law Commission said in its commentary of 1966:

> (2) There is much authority in the jurisprudence of international tribunals for the proposition that in the present context the principle of good faith is a legal principle which forms an integral part of the rule *pacta sunt servanda.* * * * [T]he Permanent Court of International Justice, in applying treaty clauses prohibiting discrimination against minorities, insisted in a number of cases, that the clauses must be so applied as to ensure the absence of discrimination in fact as well as in law; in other words, the obligation must not be evaded by a merely literal application of the clauses. Numerous precedents could also be found in the jurisprudence of arbitral tribunals.

[1966] II Yb.I.L.C. 211.

### 2. *Internal Law and Treaty Observance (Article 27)*

The Vienna Convention restates in Article 27 the long-accepted rule of customary law that a state may not invoke its internal law as a justification for its failure to perform a treaty. See Advisory Opinion on Treatment of Polish Nationals and Other Persons of Polish Origin in Danzig Territory, 1932 P.C.I.J., Ser. A/B, No. 44, at 22. Where a state has a domestic rule of law that a later statute supersedes an earlier treaty (as is the case in the United States) a domestic court will apply the statute rather than the treaty. However, the state remains internationally bound by the treaty and responsible if it violates its provisions. Of importance in this connection is the principle widely accepted in national legal systems that domestic law should be construed insofar as possible to avoid violating a state's international obligation. See Lauritzen v. Larsen, 345 U.S. 571, 578, 73 S.Ct. 921, 926, 97 L.Ed. 1254 (1953); M. Sorensen, Report Concerning Obligations of a State Party to a Treaty as Regards its Municipal Law in Human Rights in National and International Law 13 (A.H. Robertson ed., 1968).

A constitutional provision has no higher status in international law than any other provision of internal law except in one respect. A state may invoke the fact that its consent to be bound by a treaty was expressed in violation of its internal law as invalidating such consent if (and only if) the violation was "manifest and concerned a rule of its internal law of fundamental importance." Article 46 of the Vienna Convention. This aspect of the problem is dealt with in Section 5B, infra.

## B. APPLICATION

### *1. Non-Retroactivity and the Intertemporal Problem (Article 28)*

A treaty may by its terms or by implication apply to a fact or situation prior to the entry into force of the treaty. In the absence of such provision, its provisions do not bind a party in respect of an act or fact which occurred, or a situation which ceased to exist, before the entry into force of a treaty. Article 28 makes this explicit.

But consider its application in the case of a legal or other concept which has changed its meaning over time. Should the concept be interpreted as understood at the time it was adopted or at the time of its application? Would the latter interpretation violate the rule against retroactive application?

The International Court of Justice faced this issue in its *Advisory Opinion on Namibia* (p. 511 infra) when it had to interpret terms of the Mandate for Southwest Africa. These terms included "sacred trust," and "well-being and development" of the indigenous inhabitants. The opinion of the Court included the following conclusions relating to this problem:

> Mindful as it is of the primary necessity of interpreting an instrument in accordance with the intentions of the parties at the time of its conclusion, the Court is bound to take into account the fact that the concepts embodied in Article 22 of the Covenant * * * were not static, but were by definition evolutionary, as also, therefore, was the concept of the sacred trust. The parties to the Covenant must consequently be deemed to have accepted them as such.

The Court consequently reached the following conclusion:

> * * * That is why, viewing the institutions of 1919, the Court must take into consideration the changes which have occurred in the supervening half-century, and its interpretation cannot remain unaffected by the subsequent development of law, through the Charter of the United Nations and by way of customary law.

The Court further added:

> * * * Moreover, an international instrument has to be interpreted and applied within the framework of the entire legal system prevailing at the time of interpretation.

1971 I.C.J. 31.

The interpretation of the International Court and Article 28 are aspects of the broader subject of intertemporal law. The following resolution on that subject was adopted by the *Institut de Droit International* in 1975 after several years of study and debate.

### *THE INTERTEMPORAL PROBLEM IN PUBLIC INTERNATIONAL LAW*

Resolution adopted by the Institut de Droit International at its Wiesbaden Session. 56 Ann. de l'Institut de Droit Int'l 537 (preamble omitted) (1975).

1. Unless otherwise indicated, the temporal sphere of application of any norm of public international law shall be determined in accordance with the general principle of law by which any fact, action or situation must be assessed in the light of the rules of law that are contemporaneous with it.

2. In application of this principle:

(a) any rule which relates to a single fact shall apply to facts that occur while the rule is in force;

(b) any rule which relates to the repetition or succession of identical facts shall apply even though only one or some of such facts should occur after the entry into force of the rule;

(c) any rule which relates to an actual situation shall apply to situations existing while the rule is in force, even if these situations have been created previously;

(d) any rule which relates to a certain period of time, or to the existence of a situation during a defined period, shall apply only to periods the initial and terminal dates of which lie within the time when the rule is in force;

(e) any rule which relates to the end of a period shall apply to any case where the period has come to an end at a time when the rule is in force;

(f) any rule which relates to the licit or illicit nature of a legal act, or to the conditions of its validity, shall apply to acts performed while the rule is in force;

(g) any rule which relates to the continuous effects of a legal act shall apply to effects produced while the rule is in force, even if the act has been performed prior to the entry into force of the rule;

(h) any rule which relates to the substance of a legal status shall apply even if the status has been created or acquired prior to the entry into force of the rule.

3. States and other subjects of international law shall, however, have the power to determine by common consent the temporal sphere of application of norms, notwithstanding the rules laid down in Paragraphs 1 and 2 and subject to any imperative norm of international law which might restrict that power.

This provision shall be without prejudice to obligations which may ensue for contracting parties from previous treaties to which they are parties and from the provisions of which they cannot depart even by common consent.

4. Wherever a provision of a treaty refers to a legal or other concept without defining it, it is appropriate to have recourse to the usual methods of interpretation in order to determine whether the concept concerned is to be interpreted as understood at the time when the provision was drawn up or as understood at the time of its application. Any interpretation of a treaty must take into account all relevant rules of international law which apply between the parties at the time of application.

5. The solution of such intertemporal problems as might arise within international Organizations is reserved.

6. In order to eliminate any cause of uncertainty or dispute, it is desirable that every international instrument should include express provisions indicating the solution which ought to be given to such intertemporal problems as might arise in the course of its application.

## 2. *Territorial Application*

### *SINCLAIR, THE VIENNA CONVENTION ON THE LAW OF TREATIES*

89–92 (2d ed. 1984).*

The proposed rule was justified on the basis that "State practice, the jurisprudence of international tribunals and the writings of jurists appear to support the view that a treaty is to be presumed to apply to all the territory of each party unless it otherwise appears from the treaty". * * *

The phrase "the entire territory of each party" was intended to be a comprehensive term designed to embrace all the land and appurtenant territorial waters and air space which constitute the territory of the State.

There was little discussion of this provision at the Vienna conference. * * * The Australian delegation, having surveyed the problems confronting States parts of whose territories were regarded as distinct for the purposes of various phases of the treaty-making process, concluded that "[Article 29] was only a residual rule of interpretation and could not in any way be construed as a norm requiring a State to express its consent to be bound by treaties without first establishing whether the treaty was acceptable and applicable to all the component parts of the State". The United Kingdom delegation stated, in a brief intervention, their understanding that "the expression 'its entire territory' applied solely to the territory over which a party to the treaty in question exercised its sovereignty".

It is clear that the opening words of Article 29 of the Convention impart a considerable degree of flexibility into the operation of the basic rule. But in what circumstances will a different intention appear from the treaty or be otherwise established? In other words, what exceptions are there to the residual rule?

* Footnotes omitted. Reprinted by permission of Manchester University Press.

It would appear that exceptions to the residual rule can be either express or implied. The obvious express exception is a territorial application clause in the treaty itself. But there can be other kinds of express exception. The device whereby, on signature or ratification, a State makes a declaration as to the territorial effect or extent of the act of signature or ratification has long been known and accepted in State practice. Thus, in ratifying the Convention on the High Seas in 1963, the United Kingdom government declared that "ratification of this Convention on behalf of the United Kingdom does not extend to the States in the Persian Gulf enjoying British protection". * * *

A word of caution is, however, necessary here. A reservation on the territorial application of certain types of treaty may be excluded because such a reservation would be incompatible with the object and purpose of the treaty. There are certain treaties, principally in the field of disarmament or humanitarian law, which are clearly intended to be world-wide in their application. It is arguable that the nature of such treaties would preclude the making of a reservation designed to limit their territorial application.

I have so far concentrated on express provisions operating as exceptions to the residual rule. What about implied exceptions? The principal implied exception is a treaty adopted by, or within the framework of, a regional organisation or intended to apply only within a particular region. Where such a treaty is "silent" as to its territorial application, its regional character may be such as to create a presumption that territorial units outside the region which are dependent upon a State within the region are excluded. * * *

The context of a particular treaty can also constitute an implied exception to the residual rule. An example would be a treaty which specified a particular zone of application (thereby impliedly excluding any dependent territories not included within the zone).

Thus it would appear that the operation of the residual rule on territorial application is subject to a number of exceptions. In cases where a particular treaty is silent upon its territorial application, declarations made by a State on signature or ratification, the specific terms of an instrument of ratification or accession or a valid reservation can operate to exclude the rule. Furthermore, the regional character, or the particular context, of a treaty may impliedly operate to exclude the rule, in so far as the regional character or context is indicative of the intention of the parties that the treaty should have a limited territorial application.

### *3. Application of Successive Treaties Relating to the Same Subject Matter (Article 30)*

The tremendous increase in the number of treaties and the diversity of international organizations engaged in treaty-making (regional, functional, and global) have resulted in numerous treaties which overlap and sometimes create conflicting obligations. One question raised is whether inconsistent treaties *vis-à-vis* different parties are valid. It has been suggested that a treaty should be invalid if it involves a breach of obligations previously undertaken by one or more of its parties. The Vienna Convention bypasses this problem of invalidity and that of responsibility for breach arising from inconsistent treaties. Article 30 approaches the problem as one of priorities. It provides in substance:

(a) If a treaty says that it is subject to, or is not to be considered as incompatible with, another treaty, that other treaty will prevail.

(b) As between parties to a treaty who become parties to a later, inconsistent, treaty, the earlier treaty will apply only where its provisions are not incompatible with the later treaty.

(c) As between a party to both treaties and a party to only one of them, the treaty to which both are parties will govern the mutual rights and obligations of the States concerned.

These provisions do not meet the problem raised by a series of treaties which required application of a later treaty even *vis-à-vis* states parties only to the earlier treaty. The problem was raised in the following statement made at the Vienna Conference by the representative of the International Bureaus for the Protection of Intellectual and Industrial Property:

> However, a special situation existed in international Unions such as those administered by B.I.R.P.I., which included the Unions instituted by the 1883 Paris Convention for the Protection of Industrial Property and the 1886 Berne Convention for the Protection of Literary and Artistic Works. Those Conventions had been revised on several occasions but each revision was merely a different version of the original Convention, which continued to exist. There was only one Union constituted by each original Convention.
>
> Technically, each original Convention and its revising Acts were separate and successive treaties, each calling for ratification. A State, however, sometimes acceded to the most recent Act of a Union, without declaring that its accession was valid for the previous Acts. In its relations with States parties to the most recent Act, no problem arose. In its relations with States members of the Union but not parties to the most recent Act, on the other hand, the acceding State was understood to have tacitly accepted all the previous texts, so that its relations with the States parties only to the earlier texts were governed by those earlier texts. The legal position was arguable, but the system was the only practicable one. The Union was more important than the Convention which had set it up. Without that tacit acceptance system, the State acceding to the latest text would have no relations with half the membership of the Union.

Vienna Conference on the Law of Treaties, First Sess. 31st mtg. statement by Woodley.

Is the problem raised by the above statement met by Article 5 of the Vienna Convention? The following comments by Sinclair at pp. 97–98 * are pertinent:

> First, and perhaps most important, it is clear that the rules laid down in Article 30 are intended to be residuary rules—that is to say, rules which will operate in the absence of express treaty provisions regulating priority. Paragraph 2 of the commentary to the proposal

* Reprinted by permission of Manchester University Press.

submitted by the Commission had already drawn attention to the fact that "treaties not infrequently contain a clause intended to regulate the relation between the provisions of the treaty and those of another treaty or of any other treaty related to the matters with which the treaty deals" and that "whatever the nature of the provision, the clause has necessarily to be taken into account in appreciating the priority of successive treaties relating to the same subject matter". But the Commission's proposal was not (and indeed the text of Article 30 is not) drafted in such a way as to make it clear that the proposed rules were residuary in nature. However, in response to a comment made at the conference, Sir Humphrey Waldock confirmed 'that the rules in paragraphs 3, 4 and 5 were thus designed essentially as residuary rules'.

Second, the chairman of the Drafting Committee, in introducing the revised text of what later became Article 30 at the 91st meeting of the Committee of the Whole, clarified the meaning to be attached to the concept of compatability as used in paragraph 3 of the Article.

* * *

This is clearly relevant to the type of problem which arises when there coexist two international Conventions on the same subject-matter, one adopted within a regional framework and one within a universal framework. A good example is afforded by the European Convention on Human Rights and the United Nations Covenants on Human Rights. Quite apart from any conflict of substantive provisions, there would inevitably, unless special provision had been made, have been a conflict between the implementation provisions of the two Conventions. For this reason, Article 44 of the United Nations Covenant on Civil and Political Rights states that the provisions for the implementation of the present Covenant shall apply without prejudice to the procedures prescribed in the field of human rights by or under the constituent instruments and the conventions of the United Nations and of the specialised agencies and shall not prevent the States Parties to the present Covenant from having recourse to other procedures for settling a dispute in accordance with general or special international agreements in force between them.

Third, it seems clear that, in determining which treaty is the 'earlier' and which the 'later', the relevant date is that of the adoption of the text and not that of its entry into force. Adoption of the second treaty manifests the new legislative intent. But, of course, the rules laid down in Article 30 have effect for each individual party to a treaty only as from the date of entry into force of the treaty for that party.

Finally, it would seem that the expression 'relating to the same subject-matter' must be construed strictly. It will not cover cases where a general treaty impinges indirectly on the content of a particular provision of an earlier treaty. Accordingly, a general treaty on the reciprocal enforcement of judgments will not affect the continued applicability of particular provisions concerning the enforcement of judgments contained in an earlier treaty dealing with third-party liability in the field of nuclear energy. This is not a question of the application of successive treaties relating to the same subject-matter, but is rather a question of treaty interpretation involving consideration of the maxim *generalia specialibus non derogant.*

## C. INTERPRETATION OF TREATIES

### 1. *Organs of Interpretation and Interpretation by the Parties*

## JESSE LEWIS (THE DAVID J. ADAMS) CLAIM (UNITED STATES v. GREAT BRITAIN)

Claims Arbitration under the Special Agreement
of August 18, 1910, 1921, Nielsen Rep. 526.
6 U.N.R.I.A.A. 85.

[By the Treaty of London of 1818, 8 Stat. 248, the United States renounced for its nationals the right to fish in Canadian waters, with the proviso that American fishermen should be permitted to enter Canadian bays and harbors "for the purpose of shelter and of repairing damages therein, of purchasing wood, and of obtaining water, and for no other purpose whatever." In 1886, the American fishing schooner *David J. Adams,* having entered Canadian waters for the purpose of purchasing fresh bait, was seized by Canadian authorities for alleged violations of the Treaty of 1818 and of the applicable Canadian legislation. A Canadian court condemned the vessel, finding that it had violated the Treaty and legislation. On behalf of the vessel's owner, the United States subsequently claimed damages from the British Government on the ground, *inter alia,* that the seizure and condemnation were wrongful because based on an erroneous interpretation of the Treaty. The British agent argued, *inter alia,* that the Arbitral Tribunal was not competent to re-examine the Canadian court's interpretation.]

THE TRIBUNAL * * * Great Britain and Canada, acting in the full exercise of their sovereignty and by such proper legislative authority as was established by their municipal public law, had enacted and were entitled to enact such legislative provisions as they considered necessary or expedient to secure observance of the said Treaty; and, so far as they are not inconsistent with the said Treaty, those provisions are binding as municipal public law of the country on any person within the limits of British jurisdiction. At the time of the seizure of the *David J. Adams* such legislation was embodied in the British Act of 1819 (59 George III, C. 38), and the Canadian Acts of 1868 (31 Vict. 61), 1871 (34 Vict., C. 23).

Great Britain and Canada, acting by such proper judicial authority as was established by their municipal law, were fully entitled to interpret and apply such legislation and to pronounce and impose such penalty as was provided by the same, but such judicial action had the same limits as the aforesaid legislative action, that is to say so far as it was not inconsistent with the said Treaty.

In this case the question is not and cannot be to ascertain whether or not British law has been justly applied by said judicial authorities, nor to consider, revise, reverse, or affirm a decision given in that respect by British Courts. On the contrary, any such decision must be taken as the authorized expression of the position assumed by Great Britain in the subject matter, and, so far as such decision implies an interpretation of said treaty, it must be taken as the authorized expression of the British interpretation.

The fundamental principle of the juridical equality of States is opposed to placing one State under the jurisdiction of another State. It is opposed to the subjection of one State to an interpretation of a Treaty asserted by another State. There is no reason why one more than the other should impose such an unilateral interpretation of a contract which is essentially bilateral. The fact that this interpretation is given by the legislative or judicial or any other authority of one of the Parties does not make that interpretation binding upon the other Party. Far from contesting that principle, the British Government did not fail to recognize it. * * *

For that reason the mere fact that a British Court, whatever be the respect and high authority it carries, interpreted the treaty in such a way as to declare the David J. Adams had contravened it, cannot be accepted by this Tribunal as a conclusive interpretation binding upon the United States Government. Such a decision is conclusive from the national British point of view; it is not from the national United States point of view. * * * [T]he duty of this international Tribunal is to determine, from the international point of view, how the provisions of the treaty are to be interpreted and applied to the facts, and consequently whether the loss resulting from the forfeiture of the vessel gives rise to an indemnity. * * *

[The Tribunal then held that the Canadian court's interpretation and application of the Treaty had not been erroneous.]

### *Notes*

1. A unilateral interpretation of an international agreement, whether made by the executive, legislative, or judicial organs of one of the contracting states, is not binding upon other contracting states. See McNair, The Law of Treaties 345–50 (1961); Hyde 1460–61; Degan, L'Interprétation des accords en droit international 17–18 (1963); 1 Juris–Classeur de Droit International, Fasc. 12–C, para. 7. Would it nevertheless be prudent for contracting states to protest what they believe to be an erroneous interpretation or application of a treaty by the government or courts of another contracting state? In the *Case Concerning the Temple of Preah Vihear* (Cambodia v. Thailand), 1962 I.C.J. 6, the contending states each claimed sovereignty over a small area of frontier territory in which the ruins of the ancient Temple of Preah Vihear were located. Cambodia relied on a 1907 map which showed the Temple area to be a part of French Indochina, now Cambodia. Thailand (formerly Siam) argued that the map was erroneous because it had not been drawn in accordance with a 1904 Siamese–French treaty. The Court emphasized, in holding for Cambodia, that the map had been produced by the French at Siamese request, and that the Siamese had never protested the alleged error; this was enough, the Court concluded, to amount to Siamese acquiescence in the map as drawn. Did the *Temple Case* involve interpretation or modification of the 1904 treaty? See the materials on modification of international agreements, pp. 484–86 infra.

In connection with the interpretation of the Hay–Pauncefote treaty of 1901 between the United States and Great Britain, the Counselor of the Department of State (Lansing) referred in a memorandum of 1913 to a treaty concluded between the United States and Panama in 1903. The Panama Treaty was "a matter of common knowledge and a subject of public discussion," he wrote, pointing out that Great Britain had made no protest or criticism of provisions exempting Panamanian ships from canal tolls until 1912. "It may fairly be urged," concluded the Counselor, "that the Panama Treaty was a contemporaneous interpretation of the Hay–Pauncefote Treaty, and that Great Britain gave assent to the interpretation by permitting the Governments of the United States and of Panama to act under its provisions without interposing any objections." 5 Hackworth 253–54. See generally de Visscher, Problèmes d'Interprétation Judiciaire en Droit International Public 168–81 (1963); MacGibbon, The Scope of Acquiescence in International Law, 31 Brit.Y.B.I.L. 143, 146–47 (1954).

In 1988, the Senate included in its resolution ratifying the INF Treaty between the United States and the Soviet Union a condition making all executive branch statements to the Senate the main source for interpreting the agreement after the text itself. In a letter to the Senate, President Reagan registered strong disapproval of this condition. Reagan argued that the Senate had no power to alter the traditional principles of treaty interpretation by subordinating sources such as the intent of the parties, the negotiating record, and subsequent practices to the unilateral declarations of the United States. "[T]he principles of treaty interpretation recognized and repeatedly invoked by the courts may not be limited or changed by the Senate alone, and those principles will govern any future disputes over the interpretation of this treaty," concluded the President. 27 I.L.M. 1413 (1988).

2. What is the legal effect of an interpretation made by the parties to an international agreement? See Ste. Ruegger et Boutet v. Ste. Weber et Howard, [1933–34] Ann.Dig. 404 (No. 179) (Trib. civ. de la Seine, France), in which the court held itself bound by an interpretation recorded by exchange of notes between the French Minister of Foreign Affairs and the British Ambassador, of a treaty between the two countries. The Court said that although a "unilateral" interpretation had only an "advisory effect," an interpretation agreed upon by both governments had the effect of adding an additional clause to the treaty. Should *interpretation* by the parties to a bilateral treaty always be regarded as an *amendment* of the treaty? What practical results might depend upon the distinction?

3. An interpretation agreed upon by all the parties to a treaty is commonly called an "authentic," as distinct from a "unilateral," interpretation. See Degan at 18–19; de Visscher, Problèmes d'Interprétation Judiciare en Droit International Public 20–21 (1963). Many modern treaties contain clauses providing that disputes concerning the interpretation or application of the treaty shall be settled by an independent and impartial authority such as an *ad hoc* arbitral tribunal or by a permanent body such as the International Court of Justice.

4. If a multilateral treaty is under consideration, it is ordinarily impractical to obtain the assent of every party to a given interpretation. What is the legal effect of an interpretation made by fewer than all the parties? Should non-participating states be bound by the interpretation made by the other contracting states if the former do not protest within a reasonable time? Should an interpretation reached by fewer than all the contracting states be given greater weight than a "unilateral" interpretation? In Philippson v. Imperial Airways, Ltd., [1939] A.C. 332, the House of Lords held that the term "High Contracting Party" as used in the Warsaw Convention on International Air Transportation, 1929, 49 Stat. 3000, 137 L.N.T.S. 11, included a state that had signed the treaty but had not yet ratified it. The British Embassy in the United States informed

the Secretary of State of the decision, and stated that the British Government's interpretation of "High Contracting Party" was that the term included only states that were finally bound by the treaty's provisions. On October 6, 1939, the Secretary of State expressed his agreement with the British Government's position. 4 Hackworth 373; 5 Hackworth 199, 250–51. Could either the United States or the United Kingdom thereafter assert against the other a different interpretation of "High Contracting Party," as used in the Warsaw Convention? Would other parties to the Warsaw Convention be bound by the United States–United Kingdom interpretation if they did not protest within a reasonable time? What would be reasonable time? What would be the position of states acceding to the Convention in years subsequent to 1939? Would these be bound by the United States–United Kingdom interpretation if, upon accession, they did not reserve their position on that question?

5. May a court in a third state interpret a treaty at the request of private litigants? Would such judicial determinations contravene sovereign rights of the states that are parties to the Treaty? Should the court in the third state apply the act of state doctrine? See Occidental of Umm v. A Certain Cargo of Petroleum, 577 F.2d 1196 (5th Cir.1978), cert. denied, 442 U.S. 928, 99 S.Ct. 2857, 61 L.Ed.2d 296 (1979); Buttes Gas and Oil Co. v. Hammer (House of Lords) 1982 A.C. 888, reprinted in 21 I.L.M. 92 (1982). On Act of State, see Chapter 3.

6. Which organ or organs are responsible for the interpretation of international agreements, such as the Charter of the United Nations, that serve as constitutions for international organizations? The San Francisco Conference failed to include in the Charter any specific provisions relating to the Charter's interpretation, instead leaving to the organs and member-states of the United Nations the freedom to determine for themselves the meaning of Charter provisions. The Committee on Legal Problems offered the following suggestions, which were subsequently approved by the Conference:

> In the course of the operations from day to day of the various organs of the Organization, it is inevitable that each organ will interpret such parts of the Charter as are applicable to its particular functions. This process is inherent in the functioning of any body which operates under an instrument defining its functions and powers. It will be manifested in the functioning of such a body as the General Assembly, the Security Council, or the International Court of Justice. Accordingly, it is not necessary to include in the Charter a provision either authorizing or approving the normal operation of this principle.
>
> Difficulties may conceivably arise in the event that there should be a difference of opinion among the organs of the Organization concerning the correct interpretation of a provision of the Charter. Thus, two organs may conceivably hold and may express or even act upon different views. Under unitary forms of national government the final determination of such a question may be vested in the highest court or in some other national authority. However, the nature of the Organization and of its operation would not seem to be such as to invite the inclusion in the Charter of any provision of this nature. If two Member States are at variance concerning the correct interpretation of the Charter, they are of course free to submit the dispute to the International Court of Justice as in the case of any other treaty. Similarly, it would always be open to the General Assembly or to the Security Council, in appropriate circumstances, to ask the International Court of Justice for an advisory opinion concerning the meaning of a

provision of the Charter. Should the General Assembly or the Security Council prefer another course, an *ad hoc* committee of jurists might be set up to examine the question and report its views, or recourse might be had to a joint conference. In brief, the members or the organs of the Organization might have recourse to various expedients in order to obtain an appropriate interpretation. It would appear neither necessary nor desirable to list or to describe in the Charter the various possible expedients.

It is to be understood, of course, that if an interpretation made by any organ of the Organization or by a committee of jurists is not generally acceptable it will be without binding force. In such circumstances, or in cases where it is desired to establish an authoritative interpretation as a precedent for the future, it may be necessary to embody the interpretation in an amendment to the Charter. This may always be accomplished by recourse to the procedure provided for amendments.

13 U.N.C.I.O. Docs. 709. What difficulties might be expected to arise under the above "process" of interpretation? Does the availability of an Advisory Opinion by the International Court of Justice mitigate the danger of deadlock?

Under the Treaty of Rome, establishing the European Economic Community, 298 U.N.T.S. 11, a Court of Justice was set up and empowered to "ensure observance of law and justice in the interpretation and application of [the] Treaty." Article 164; see also Articles 173, 174, and 177. The Court's decisions are enforceable under Articles 187 and 192.

### *2. Problems and Methods of Treaty Interpretation (Articles 31–32)*

#### *JIMÉNEZ DE ARÉCHAGA, INTERNATIONAL LAW IN THE PAST THIRD OF A CENTURY*

159 Rec. des Cours 42–48 (1978–I).*

Legal rules concerning the interpretation of treaties constitute one of the Sections of the Vienna Convention which were adopted without a dissenting vote at the Conference and consequently may be considered as declaratory of existing law.

The four Articles devoted to the interpretation of treaties are based on the jurisprudence established by the World Court and distil the essence of such fundamental principles as could properly be treated as rules of international law on the subject, "and not merely guidelines for States" applicable to all treaties, whatever their nature or content. No suggestion was made, as is proposed by certain writers, that different rules or methods of interpretation should apply to what are described as *traités-lois* and to other types of instruments, such as *traité-contrats.* This distinction is not adopted by the Convention.

A divergence of views arose however at the Conference concerning the basic approach on the interpretation of treaties.

There is a fundamental opposition between two schools of thought: the first one asserts that the primary task in the interpretation of treaties is to

* Footnotes omitted. Reprinted by permission of A.W. Sijthoff & Noordhoff International.

ascertain the common or real intention of the parties; the second school defines as the objective of treaty interpretation the determination of the meaning of a text. According to the first approach, "the prime, indeed, the only legitimate object, is to ascertain and give effect to the intentions or presumed intentions of the parties"; according to the second, the fundamental objective is "to establish what the text means according to the ordinary or apparent signification of its terms; its approach is therefore through the study and analysis of the text." The test which distinguishes at the practical level one approach from the other is the position assigned to the *travaux préparatoires* of the treaty. The first school places on the same level the text of the treaty and its *travaux préparatoires,* since both serve to determine the real intention of the parties; the second school considers the text above all as the basic material for interpretation and the *travaux préparatoires* are only taken into account as a secondary or supplementary means of interpretation.

The proposals submitted to the Vienna Conference by the International Law Commission were inspired by the textual approach; primacy was accorded to the text of the treaty as the basis for its interpretation. The Commission said in its commentary that its proposal "is based on the view that the text must be presumed to be the authentic expression of the intentions of the parties; and that, in consequence, the starting point of interpretation is the elucidation of the meaning of the text, not an investigation *ab initio* into the intentions of the parties."

PROVISIONS OF THE VIENNA CONVENTION REGARDING INTERPRETATION

Article 31, paragraph 1, of the Convention establishes what may be described as the "golden rule" of interpretation:

> "A treaty shall be interpreted in good faith in accordance with the ordinary meaning to be given to the terms of the treaty in their context and in the light of its object and purpose."

According to this and the subsequent paragraphs of Article 31, the interpretation of a treaty is to be carried out on the basis of what may be described as intrinsic materials, that is to say, texts and related instruments which have been agreed to by the parties. The process of interpretation must begin with an analysis of the specific provisions of the treaty concerning the question in dispute; it goes on to consider the context, that is to say, other provisions of the treaty, including its preamble, annexes and related instruments made in connection with the conclusion of the treaty, taking particularly into account the object and purpose of the treaty, as it appears from these intrinsic materials. It is important to remark that "the object and purpose of the treaty" is mentioned not as an independent element as in the Harvard Draft Convention but at the end of paragraph 1. This was done deliberately, in order to make clear that "object and purpose" are part of the context, the most important one, but not an autonomous element in interpretation, independent of and on the same level as the text, as is advocated by the partisans of the teleological method of interpretation. The latter method emphasizes the general purpose of the treaty, which is assigned an existence of its own, independent of the original intentions of the parties. In this way, gaps can be filled, corrections made, texts expanded or supplemented, so long as it is in furtherance of the general purpose attributed to the treaty by the interpreter.

Paragraph 3 of Article 31 then proceeds to indicate further intrinsic materials to be taken into account together with the context, and these have also been the object of the express or implied consent or consensus of the parties: subsequent agreements, subsequent practice and relevant rules of international law. This is a process of interpretation which has been aptly described by Max Huber as one of *encerclement progressif* of an agreed text: the text is departed from only gradually, in concentric circles, proceeding from the central to the peripheral. The only concession made to the "intention of the parties" school is that, according to paragraph 4, "a special meaning shall be given to a term if it is established that the parties so intended." However, as the Court has recently stressed, the party which invokes a special meaning must "demonstrate convincingly the use of the term with that special meaning."

On the other hand, and this is an essential feature of the approach proposed by the International Law Commission and adopted by the Conference, the extrinsic materials, that is to say, those which have not been the object of the specific agreement of the parties, such as the preparatory work of the treaty and the circumstances of its conclusion, are described as "supplementary means of interpretation" and are governed by a separate article. This Article 32 provides that:

> "Recourse may be had to supplementary means of interpretation, including the preparatory work of the treaty and the circumstances of its conclusion, in order to confirm the meaning resulting from the application of Article 31, or to determine the meaning when the interpretation according to Article 31,
>
> (a) leaves the meaning ambiguous or obscure; or
>
> (b) leads to a result which is manifestly absurd or unreasonable."

The separation between Articles 31 and 32 is not to be viewed as establishing two distinct and successive phases in the process of interpretation, or as providing that *travaux préparatoires* are to be only examined when, after exhausting the intrinsic materials of Article 31, an ambiguity or obscurity remains or the result is manifestly absurd or unreasonable. In the task of analysis, there need be no such succession in time and the process is largely a simultaneous one. As Sir Humphrey Waldock said in his commentary on the Article, "all the various elements, as they were present in any given case, would be thrown into the crucible and their interaction would give the legally relevant interpretation." * * *

Consequently, preparatory work is frequently examined and often taken into account. It may be difficult in practice to establish the borderline between confirming a view previously reached and actually forming it, since this belongs to the mental processes of the interpreter. In any case, the importance of *travaux préparatoires* is not to be underestimated and their relevance is difficult to deny, since the question whether a text can be said to be clear is in some degree subjective. On the other hand, the separation between Articles 31 and 32 and the restrictions contained in the latter provision constitute a necessary safeguard which strengthens the textual approach and discourages any attempt to resort to preparatory work in order to dispute an interpretation resulting from the intrinsic materials set out in Article 31.

## *Notes*

1. In one of its first opinions, the International Court of Justice declined to "deviate from the consistent practice of the Permanent Court of International Justice, according to which there is no occasion to resort to preparatory work if the text of a convention is sufficiently clear in itself." Conditions of Admission of a State to Membership in the United Nations, Advisory Opinion, 1947–48 I.C.J. 57, 63. In a number of other cases as well, the Court displayed a readiness to assume that a treaty was clear, and consequently to dispense with preparatory work. See Lauterpacht at 121–24; Fitzmaurice, The Law and Procedure of the International Court of Justice: Treaty Interpretation and Certain Other Treaty Points, 28 Brit.Y.B.I.L. 1, 6 (1951). It is not entirely clear whether the Court has modified its attitude in more recent years so as to display a greater readiness to resort to preparatory work. Compare Lauterpacht, pp. 124–27, 138–41, with Fitzmaurice, The Law and Procedure of the International Court of Justice 1951–4: Treaty Interpretation and Other Treaty Points, 33 Brit.Y.B.I.L. 203, 215–20 (1957). See also Hogg, The International Court: Rules of Treaty Interpretation, 43 Minn.L.Rev. 369, 445 (1959).

2. Is preparatory work really of any significant value in ascertaining the true intentions of the contracting parties? While the texts of many treaties often contain accidental and even deliberate ambiguities and omissions, the records of international conferences are also sometimes less than successful in depicting the true course of negotiations. See the comments by Sir Eric Beckett upon Lauterpacht's report to the Institute of International Law on the interpretation of treaties, [1950] 1 Ann. de l'Institut de Droit Int'l 435, 442–44, and Lauterpacht's reply in [1952] 1 id. 197, 214–16. Haraszti, a Hungarian jurist, emphasizes that the preparatory work has interpretative value only where it throws light on the "joint intention of the parties" and relates to the text actually agreed upon. Haraszti, Some Fundamental Problems of the Law of Treaties 122–125 (1973).

3. Should the consideration of *travaux préparatoires* be barred by the fact that not all the parties to a dispute participated in the conference or negotiations that led to the conclusion of the treaty? In the *Case Concerning the Jurisdiction of the International Commission of the River Oder,* 1929 P.C.I.J., Ser. A, No. 23, the Permanent Court of International Justice ruled that preparatory work relevant to the interpretation of disputed articles of the Treaty of Versailles was inadmissible because three of the states involved in the proceeding had not taken part in the Conference which prepared the treaty. Should the admissibility of preparatory work against a non-participating state be influenced by the fact that the materials had been published or were otherwise available for study? The rule in the *River Oder Case* is probably no longer followed by the International Court of Justice, and it has been rejected by the International Law Commission. See Rosenne, Travaux Préparatoires, 12 I.C.L.Q. 1378, 1380–81 (1963); International Law Commission, Draft Articles on the Law of Treaties, art. 70 (commentary), [1964] II Yb.I.L.C. 205.

4. If there is no specific language on the point in controversy and no evidence of a common intention of the parties, may a tribunal seized of the dispute interpret the treaty? The International Court replied affirmatively with

respect to a treaty that gave an arbitral tribunal competence to pass on claims of private persons based on the treaty. Ambatielos Case, 1953 I.C.J. 110.

5. Would the practice of single states in the application of a multilateral agreement have increased relevance if it tended to demonstrate recognition by those states of obligations later sought to be avoided by them through a narrow interpretation of the agreement? Compare the situation in which a single state, without protest from other parties, has consistently applied an agreement in such a way as to avoid obligations later sought to be imposed upon it. What are the respective roles of estoppel and acquiescence as interpretative aids in such situations? See Bowett, Estoppel Before International Tribunals and Its Relation to Acquiescence, 33 Brit.Y.B.I.L. 176 (1957).

6. May the subsequent conduct of the parties to the Treaty determine the meaning of provisions that were ambiguous? See Article 31(3) of the Vienna Convention. United States courts have often relied on subsequent conduct as evidence of the intent of the parties. See Sumitomo Shoji America v. Avagliano, 457 U.S. 176, 102 S.Ct. 2374, 72 L.Ed.2d 765 (1982). Subsequent conduct was relied on by a federal court to find that the term "accident" as used in the Warsaw Convention on liability for aviation accidents included "hijackings." Husserl v. Swiss Air Transport Co., Ltd., 351 F.Supp. 702 (S.D.N.Y.1972). See also Day v. Trans World Airlines, Inc., 528 F.2d 31 (2d Cir.1975); Restatement (Revised) § 325, Reporters' Note 5.

7. To what extent, if at all, ought special rules to be applied in the interpretation of such international agreements as the Charter of the United Nations and other constitutive instruments of international organizations, or of multilateral conventions concerned with the regulation of matters of social or humanitarian significance? Consider the following statement of Judge Azevedo, dissenting from the Advisory Opinion Concerning the Competence of the General Assembly for the Admission of a State to the United Nations, 1950 I.C.J. 4, 23:

> * * * [T]he interpretation of the San Francisco instruments will always have to present a teleological character if they are to meet the requirements of world peace, co-operation between men, individual freedom and social progress. The Charter is a means and not an end. To comply with its aims one must seek the methods of interpretation most likely to serve the natural evolution of the needs of mankind.
>
> Even more than in the applications of municipal law, the meaning and the scope of international texts must continually be perfected, even if the terms remain unchanged.

Are the original intentions of the parties, assuming that these can be discovered, any longer relevant to an interpretation based on the "teleological" approach, or would it be more important to discover the "emergent purpose" of the treaty, i.e., the objects or purposes revealed by the operation and practical application of the treaty? Consider the statement of the European Court of Human Rights that the European Convention on Human Rights should be construed "in the light of modern-day conditions obtaining in the democratic societies of the Contracting States and not solely according to what might be presumed to have been in the minds of the drafters of the Convention." Deumeland Case, 86 I.L.R. 376, 408 (1986). See generally Fitzmaurice, The Law and Procedure of the International Court of Justice 1951–4: Treaty Interpretation and Other Treaty Points, 33 Brit.Y.B.I.L. 203, 207–09 (1957); Gordon, The World Court and the Interpretation of Constitutive Treaties, 59 A.J.I.L. 794 (1965). McDougal, Lasswell & Miller, The Interpretation of Agreements and World Public Order (1967);

Schachter, Interpretation of the Charter in the Political Organs of the United Nations, in Law, State and International Legal Order (Engel & Metall eds. 1964).

It has been suggested that the International Court of Justice has recognized and applied, in its interpretation of treaties, the "principle of maximum effectiveness." Under this rule, other things being equal, "texts are presumed to have been intended to have a definite force and effect, and should be interpreted so as to have such force and effect rather than so as not to have it, and so as to have the *fullest* value and effect consistent with their wording (so long as the meaning be not strained) and with the other parts of the text." Fitzmaurice at 28 Brit.Y.B.I.L. 8 (1951) (emphasis in original). What is the difference between the "principle of maximum effectiveness" and the "teleological" approach? See id.; Lauterpacht, Restrictive Interpretation and the Principle of Effectiveness in the Interpretation of Treaties, 26 Brit.Y.B.I.L. 48, 72–75 (1949).

### *3. Treaties in Pluri-Lingual Texts (Article 33)*

Many international agreements are drawn up in more than one language. Where each version is formally authenticated (e.g., through signature), and the parties have not provided that one version should prevail in the event of disagreement, are all versions equally authoritative? The parties often expressly provide that all versions are equally authoritative (see, e.g., multilateral conventions drawn up under the auspices of the United Nations). When the parties have not otherwise provided, there is considerable authority for the proposition that the two or more texts should be interpreted with reference to one another so as to give corresponding provisions a common meaning. See generally Hardy, The Interpretation of Plurilingual Treaties by International Courts and Tribunals, 37 Brit.Y.B.I.L. 72 (1961); International Law Commission, Draft Articles on the Law of Treaties, [1966] II Yb.I.L.C. 224–26.

The Permanent Court of International Justice expressed itself on the question of reconciling versions in the different languages in the *Mavrommatis Palestine Concession Case,* P.C.I.J., Ser. A, No. 2 (1924). It stated that "where two versions possessing equal authority exist, one of which appears to have a wider bearing than the other, it [the Court] is bound to adopt the more limited interpretation which can be made to harmonize with both versions and which, as far as it goes, is doubtless in accordance with the common intention of the Parties." P.C.I.J., Ser. A, No. 2, p. 10.

In *Nicaragua v. U.S.* (Jurisdiction) (1984), the International Court of Justice relied in part on the French text of Article 36(5) of the Statute of the International Court to resolve an issue of interpretation which the judges considered as equivocal, and which was left open in the English text. 1984 I.C.J. 406–407 (paras. 30, 31).

Should a different approach be taken where it can be shown that the parties used one language in negotiating and establishing the text, even though the treaty itself declared the texts in all the languages as authentic? In the *Mavrommatis Case,* the Permanent Court supported its choice of the more restrictive text (which was the English version) by noting also that the original text was English. Even jurists who strongly favor equality of all language texts recognize that, if no common meaning can be found, a text used in the negotiations would reflect the intention of the parties more than the versions in translation. The problem of ascertaining which text was used is complicated when a negotiating conference, such as those under UN auspices, have versions in 6 languages distributed to the delegates, all of which are declared equally authentic. See Haraszti, Some Fundamental Problems of the Law of Treaties 183 (1973). Germer, Interpretation of Plurilingual Treaties, 11 Harv.Int'l L.J. 400, 413 (1970).

## D. TREATIES AND THIRD STATES

A third state, in international law usage and as defined in the Vienna Convention, is any state not a party to the treaty in question (Article 2(1)(h)). In principle a treaty creates neither obligations nor rights for third states without their consent. The maxim *pacta tertiis nec nocent nec prosunt* is often quoted. The principle is firmly established as a general rule but questions have arisen as to possible exceptions with respect both to rights and to obligations. The International Law Commission and the Vienna conference considered that the basic principle should be maintained without any exception. They sought to meet the cases of possible exceptions through doctrinal explanation and flexible articles. The following excerpts from the report of the Commission express the rationale for Articles 34 to 38.

### *1. Obligations for Third States (Article 35)*

(1) The primary rule, formulated in the previous article, is that the parties to a treaty cannot impose an obligation on a third State without its consent. That rule is one of the bulwarks of the independence and equality of States. The present article also underlines that the consent of a State is always necessary if it is to be bound by a provision contained in a treaty to which it is not a party. Under it two conditions have to be fulfilled before a non-party can become bound: first, the parties to the treaty must have intended the provision in question to be the means of establishing an obligation for the State not a party to the treaty; and secondly, the third State must have expressly agreed to be bound by the obligation. The Commission appreciated that when these conditions are fulfilled there is, in effect, a second collateral agreement between the parties to the treaty, on the one hand, and the third State on the other; and that the juridical basis of the latter's obligation is not the treaty itself but the collateral agreement. However, even if the matter is viewed in this way, the case remains one where a provision of a treaty concluded between certain States becomes directly binding upon another State which is not and does not become a party to the treaty.

[1966] II Yb.I.L.C. 227.

### *Notes*

1. Is there an implied exception to the rule enunciated above in Article 2 paragraph 6 of the U.N. Charter? The International Court of Justice in its advisory opinion in the *Namibia Case,* p. 511 infra, declared that the non-member states of the U.N. must "act in accordance with" the decisions of the United Nations which terminated the mandate for South–West Africa (Namibia) and declared the presence of South Africa in Namibia illegal. See Advisory Opinion, 1971 I.C.J. 16. See Article 2(6) of U.N. Charter.

2. May obligations be imposed by a treaty on an aggressor state which is not a party? See Article 75 of the Vienna Convention.

3. Would a treaty for demilitarization of a territory be binding on third states? See Antarctic Treaty. The concept of an "objective régime" is considered at p. 483 below.

### 2. *Rights of Third States Under Treaties (Article 36)*

* * *

(7) *Paragraph 1* lays down that a right may arise for a State from a provision of a treaty to which it is not a party under two conditions. First, the parties must intend the provision to accord the right either to the particular State in question, or to a group of States to which it belongs, or to States generally. The intention to accord the right is of cardinal importance, since it is only when the parties have such an intention that a legal right, as distinct from a mere benefit, may arise from the provision. Examples of stipulations in favour of individual States, groups of States or States generally have already been mentioned in paragraph (2). The second condition is the assent of the beneficiary State. The formulation of this condition in the present tense "and the State assents thereto" leaves open the question whether juridically the right is created by the treaty or by the beneficiary State's act of acceptance. In one view, as already explained, the assent of the intended beneficiary, even though it may merely be implied from the exercise of the right, constitutes an "acceptance" of an offer made by the parties; in the other view the assent is only significant as an indication that the right is not disclaimed by the beneficiary. The second sentence of the paragraph then provides that the assent of the State is to be presumed so long as the contrary is not indicated. This provision the Commission considered desirable in order to give the necessary flexibility to the operation of the rule in cases where the right is expressed to be in favour of States generally or of a large group of States. * * *

(8) *Paragraph 2* specifies that in exercising the right a beneficiary State must comply with the conditions for its exercise provided for in the treaty or established in conformity with the treaty. The words "or established in conformity with the treaty" take account of the fact that not infrequently conditions for the exercise of the right may be laid down in a supplementary instrument or in some cases unilaterally by one of the parties. For example, in the case of a provision allowing freedom of navigation in an international river or maritime waterway, the territorial State has the right in virtue of its sovereignty to lay down relevant conditions for the exercise of the right provided, of course, that they are in conformity with its obligations under the treaty. * * *

[1966] II Yb.I.L.C. 229.

### *Notes*

1. Will states be discouraged from creating rights in favor of third states (*e.g.*, freedom of transit through Panama Canal) by fear they would be limiting their action in the future? If the parties may freely revoke such rights of third states, the "rights" may be more nominal than legal. Is the compromise, as set forth in Article 37(2), satisfactory from the standpoint of third states?

2. In a case relating to the Kiel Canal, the Permanent Court of International Justice held that the Versailles treaty which provided that the Canal was to

be open to all vessels of nations at peace with Germany had provided a "treaty guarantee * * * for the benefit of all nations of the world." The "S.S. Wimbledon," 1923 P.C.I.J., Ser. A, No. 1, at 22. Would Germany have the right to close the Canal to any non-party under Article 37(2)?

3. Are rights in third states to most-favored nation treatment revocable by the parties?

### 3. *Objective Régimes Created by Treaty*

(4) The Commission considered whether treaties creating so-called "objective régimes", that is, obligations and rights valid *erga omnes,* should be dealt with separately as a special case. Some members of the Commission favoured this course, expressing the view that the concept of treaties creating objective régimes existed in international law and merited special treatment in the draft articles. In their view, treaties which fall within this concept are treaties for the neutralization or demilitarization of particular territories or areas, and treaties providing for freedom of navigation of international rivers or maritime waterways; and they cited the Antarctic Treaty as a recent example of such a treaty. Other members, however, while recognizing that in certain cases treaty rights and obligations may come to be valid *erga omnes,* did not regard these cases as resulting from any special concept or institution of the law of treaties. They considered that these cases resulted either from the application of the principle in [Article 36] or from the grafting of an international custom upon a treaty under the process which is the subject of the reservation in the present article. Since to lay down a rule recognizing the possibility of the creation of objective régimes directly by treaty might be unlikely to meet with general acceptance, the Commission decided to leave this question aside in drafting the present articles on the law of treaties. It considered that the provision in Article [36], regarding treaties intended to create rights in favour of States generally, together with the process mentioned in the present article, furnish a legal basis for the establishment of treaty obligations and rights valid *erga omnes,* which goes as far as is at present possible. Accordingly, it decided not to propose any special provision on treaties creating so-called objective régimes.

[1966] II Yb.I.L.C. 231.

### *Notes*

1. Can it be said that the Antarctic Treaty, p. 1366, imposes obligations *erga omnes* by virtue of "custom" when only a small number of states have become parties to the treaty? What is the legal basis for states which have made a territorial arrangement outside of their national jurisdiction to consider that arrangement to be binding on non parties? If a substantial number of non-party states express approval of the treaty provisions (such as those on demilitarization and environmental protection) but deny that the treaty expresses customary law, can it be maintained that the treaty is binding on those states? For positions of governments on this issue, see U.N. Secretary General, Report on Antarctica, U.N. Doc. A/39/583 Part II (1984).

2. If two states enter into a treaty for cession of territory, are third states free to refuse to recognize the effects of the treaty as, for example, on the nationality of the inhabitants? Are such treaties "dispositive," as suggested by

McNair, The Law of Treaties 256–59 (1961)? Would the Antarctic Treaty regime be opposable to third states on the ground that the states party to the treaty include all those which have claims to territorial sovereignty? For discussion of sovereignty claims, see Chapter 15. See also Antarctic Resources Policy: Scientific, Legal and Political Issues (Vicuña, ed., 1983); Cahier, Le Probléme des Effets des Traités a L'Égard des États Tiers, 143 Rec. des Cours 595, 660–79 (1974–III).

3. What is the effect of Article 2(6) of the United Nations Charter on states that are not members of the Organization?

## SECTION 4. AMENDMENT AND MODIFICATION OF TREATIES

### *KEARNEY & DALTON, THE TREATY ON TREATIES*

64 A.J.I.L. 495, 523–525 (1970).*

Article 40 on the amendment of multilateral treaties provides needed clarification in an area of treaty law in which there had been a good deal of custom but relatively little formulation of customary international law. The Harvard Draft, for example, has no provisions regarding amendment, and the subject is not even mentioned in the Eighth Edition of Oppenheim's International Law (1955). As the Commission's commentary points out, "the development of international organization and the tremendous increase in multilateral treaty-making have made a considerable impact on the process of amending treaties." A mere glance at the maze of supplementary protocols, declarations of rectification and implementing agreements spawned by the General Agreement on Tariffs and Trade is convincing proof.

Article 40 provides residuary rules that safeguard the rights of parties to a treaty to participate in the amending process by requiring notification to all parties of any proposed amendment and by specifying their right to participate in the decision to be taken on the proposal and in the negotiation and conclusion of any amendatory agreement. The right to become party to the new agreement is also extended to every state entitled to become a party to the treaty.

Paragraphs 4 and 5 contain a much needed clarification of the relationships between the various parties to an original treaty and a series of amending agreements, particularly with regard to a state that becomes a party to an amended treaty. In that case, the state, unless it expresses a different intention, becomes both a party to the treaty as amended and a party to the unamended treaty vis-à-vis any party to the treaty not bound by the amendment.

The distinction between Article 40 on amendments and Article 41 on modification is based upon whether the proposal to change the treaty is directed to all the parties or only a part of them. The Commission's rationale for Article 41 was that it dealt not with the amendment of a treaty

* Footnotes omitted. Reprinted by permission of the American Society of International Law.

but with an *inter se* agreement "in which two or a small group of parties set out to modify the treaty between themselves alone without giving the other parties the option of participating in it. * * *" The commentary indicates considerable dubiety in the Commission regarding such agreements: "An *inter se* agreement is more likely [than an amendment] to have an aim and effect incompatible with the object and purpose of the treaty. History furnishes a number of instances of *inter se* agreements which substantially changed the regime of the treaty and which overrode the objections of interested States. * * *" Reflecting this view, Article 41 provides:

> 1. Two or more of the parties to a multilateral treaty may conclude an agreement to modify the treaty as between themselves alone if:
>
> (a) the possibility of such a modification is provided for by the treaty; or
>
> (b) the modification in question is not prohibited by the treaty and:
>
> (i) does not affect the enjoyment by the other parties of their rights under the treaty or the performance of their obligations;
>
> (ii) does not relate to a provision, derogation from which is incompatible with the effective execution of the object and purpose of the treaty as a whole.

Moreover, paragraph 2 lays down the procedural requirement that the parties contemplating such a modification agreement must notify the other parties to the treaty of their "intention" to conclude the agreement and what the "modification" is, unless the treaty itself dispenses with the requirement. This cautionary approach is a reasonable one, even though the vast majority of *inter se* agreements are unexceptionable. As Jiménez de Aréchaga, the distinguished Uruguayan jurist, pointed out in the committee of the whole, regional arrangements are an important example of *inter se* agreements:

> "In technical conventions, such as those on air navigation or postal relations, the *inter se* procedure had become a necessity of everyday international life and to prohibit such agreements, or render them unnecessarily difficult, would give to a single party a right of veto in matters when there was a genuine need to keep abreast of developments."

The strict limitations on action listed in Article 41 do not apply if the action to amend is instituted under Article 40. Some concern was expressed in the committee of the whole that selection of the one or the other approach might be based upon an intent to avoid a particular procedural requirement. The likelihood appears small, however, and while there may be some overlapping of amendments and modifications, the basic distinction is fair and workable.

The only instance in which the conference completely deleted one of the Commission's draft articles was in connection with the articles on amendment and modification. The International Law Commission had proposed an article on modification of treaties by subsequent practice. The text read as follows:

> "A treaty may be modified by subsequent practice in the application of the treaty establishing the agreement of the parties to modify its provisions." * * *

Substantial concern over the unpredictable effects of the article was expressed in the committee of the whole. The U.S. Delegation urged deletion of the article. It voiced concern that relatively low-ranking officials might interpret a treaty erroneously and follow a course of conduct which, unknown to governments, could lead to modification of the treaty. Some of the African states also expressed concern. On a roll-call vote, 54 states voted for deletion of the article; only 15 voted for its retention.

## *Notes*

1. Should the deletion of the proposed article on modification by subsequent practice mean that no such modification will be permissible? Would not a consistent practice by the parties furnish persuasive evidence of their common agreement to a change? In 1963, an international arbitration tribunal in a dispute between France and the United States concerning the bilateral Air Transport Services Agreement of 1946 concluded that the subsequent practice of the two parties was relevant not only to the interpretation of the treaty but also to its modification by tacit consent. The Tribunal found that the conduct of the parties (in particular, the acts of officials concerned with aviation services) established a right "not by virtue of the Agreement of 1946 but rather by virtue of an agreement that implicitly came into force at a later date." Decision of Arbitration Tribunal concerning International Air Transport Services Agreement between France and the United States, digested in 58 A.J.I.L. 1016–1030 (1964), see especially 1023–1027. The full text of the decision is in 3 I.L.M. 668 (1964).

2. Whether all parties to a treaty had the right to participate in negotiation of a revision was a disputed question prior to the Vienna Convention. Some writers said that there was no such right. See Hoyt, The Unanimity Rule in the Revision of Treaties (1959). The International Law Commission declined to accept that view. It considered that "the very nature of the legal relations established by a treaty requires that every party should be consulted in regard to any amendment or revision of the treaty." The fact that this has not always happened, the Commission stated, was not a sufficient reason to set aside the principle. [1966] II Yb.I.L.C. 233. The Commission was also concerned to assure all parties to a treaty that they would be notified when some parties intend to include an agreement to modify the treaty as between themselves alone. See Article 41(2).

3. Multilateral agreements, especially those which are the constituent instruments of international organizations, nearly always contain specific rules for amendment. Generally, these rules permit amendment by approval of a qualified majority (often, two-thirds of the parties). In most of the constituent instruments of international organizations states which do not accept the amended treaty are required by the terms of the treaty to cease to be parties. In the absence of a provision to this effect, the non-assenting parties are in principle unaffected by the amendment in their relations with the amending parties. The U.N. Charter states that amendments shall come into force for all members when they have been adopted and ratified by two-thirds of the members, including all the permanent members of the Security Council (Article 108).

# SECTION 5. INVALIDITY OF TREATIES

## A. GENERAL PROVISIONS RELATING TO INVALIDITY

The International Law Commission considered it important to provide that the validity of a treaty may be impeached only through the application of the Vienna Convention (Article 42). It was also considered desirable to state explicitly that a state which is no longer bound by a treaty because of invalidity or termination does not escape an obligation to which it is subject under international law independently of the treaty (Article 43).

Prior to the Vienna Convention, there was some doubt whether an invalid provision of a treaty may be struck out without declaring the entire treaty invalid. Some judges in separate opinions in the I.C.J. *Norwegian Loans*, 1957 I.C.J. 9, and *Interhandel*, 1959 I.C.J. 6, cases had favored separability in the case of the alleged nullity of a unilateral declaration under Article 36(2) of the Statute of the Court by reason of an allegedly invalid reservation. The Commission favored separability provided that it did not materially upset the balance of interests on the basis of which the parties consented to be bound. This is made clear in Article 44(3). In cases of fraud and corruption only the victim state may invoke invalidity, and then it has the option of invalidating the whole treaty or only the clauses to which the fraud or corruption relate (Article 44(4)). In cases where the treaty is absolutely void (as in cases of coercion or conflict with *jus cogens*) there is no separability; the treaty is entirely null and void (Article 44(5)).

The Commission was aware that provisions on invalidity involved possible abuse. A party may become aware of a ground for invalidity but "continue with the treaty and only raise the matter at a much later date when it desires for quite other reasons to put an end to its obligations under the treaty." [1966] II Yb.I.L.C. 239. Article 45 seeks to meet that situation. A state is prohibited from claiming invalidity if after becoming aware of the facts it has agreed that the treaty remains in force or by reason of its conduct must be considered to have acquiesced in the validity of the treaty or its continuation in force. This rule does not apply where the treaty is absolutely void as in cases of coercion or *jus cogens.*

The principle of acquiescence played a role in two cases before the International Court of Justice: the case of the Arbitral Award of the King of Spain, 1960 I.C.J. 192, 213–214 and the case of The Temple of Preah Vihear, 1962 I.C.J. 6, 23–32.

## B. ULTRA VIRES TREATIES

As we saw earlier, a state may not invoke its internal law as justification for failure to perform a treaty. This general principle is qualified, however, by the rule stated in Article 46 of the Vienna Convention. That provision permits a state to assert as a ground of invalidity of a treaty the fact that its consent to be bound was expressed in violation of a provision of its internal law concerning the competence to conclude treaties. A state may invoke that fact only if "the violation was manifest and concerned a rule of internal law of fundamental importance." Article 46. Accordingly, in the special circumstances stated, the question of constitutional competence to conclude a treaty—a matter of internal law—becomes internationally relevant. The rule, it should be noted, may be relied upon only by the state whose consent was expressed in contravention of its own constitutional provision or other rule of fundamental importance.

The requirement that the violation must be "manifest" is of particular interest. Article 46(2) says that "a violation is manifest if it would be objectively evident to any State dealing with the matter in accordance with normal practice and good faith." Article 46(2). It is conceivable that a head of state might enter into a treaty in contravention of an unequivocal and well-known fundamental principle of his national law. But such cases are rare. See [1966] II Yb.I.L.C. 241–42. Normally when a head of state or government ratifies or accedes to a treaty, a strong presumption exists that he or she has acted within constitutional authority. Even if doubts were expressed in that respect, it is unlikely that another state would find a violation "manifest" or objectively evident.

Studies of treaty practice have confirmed the perception that constitutional incompetence has not actually resulted in invalidating treaties. Hans Blix, in a study prior to the Vienna Convention, concluded that in fact "no treaty has been found that has been admitted to be invalid or held by an international tribunal to be invalid, because concluded by a constitutionally incompetent authority or in an unconstitutional manner * * *. Furthermore, there is no lack of treaties made in violation of constitutions, or by constitutionally incompetent authorities, and yet admitted to be valid in international law." Blix, Treaty–Making Power 373–374 (1960). A similar conclusion was reached by a later study. See Wildhaber, Treaty–Making Power and Constitutions 146–82 (1971). The latter also observes on the basis of an comparative analysis that the constitutional competence to enter into treaties "are almost never really clear." Id. at 181.

The provision in the United States Constitution that the President may not enter into a "treaty" without the advice and consent of the Senate is of particular interest. McNair commented that that requirement possesses "an international notoriety so that other states cannot hold a State bound by a treaty when in fact there has been no compliance with constitutional requirements of this type." McNair, The Law of Treaties 63 (1961). A different conclusion is drawn by Henkin in the following comment:

> But the power of the President to make many agreements without the Senate casts some doubt on "the fundamental importance" of Senate consent; in any event, failure to obtain such consent cannot be a "manifest" violation of the Constitution since no one can say with certainty when it is required.

Henkin, Foreign Affairs and the Constitution 427, n. 21 (1972).

The Restatement (Third) contains the following comment on this point:

> Some agreements such as the U.N. Charter on the agreement creating NATO are of sufficient dignity, formality and importance that, in the unlikely event that the President attempted to make such an agreement on his own authority, his lack of authority might be regarded as "manifest".

Restatement (Third) § 311, Comment *c.*

### *Notes*

1. As of 1993, Article 46 has not been invoked by any state as a basis for a claim of invalidity. However, the article was invoked in the U.S. Senate in connection with two bilateral agreements to which the United States adhered. One was an agreement between the United States and Israel in 1975 connected with the withdrawal of Israel from the Sinai peninsula, which involved a number of commitments by the United States with respect to meeting Israeli's supply needs and defense requirements. The Legislative Counsel to the Senate took the position that since the agreement was concluded without the advice and consent of the Senate, it was without force under domestic law. Moreover, since it violated in that respect a rule of fundamental importance and since Israel should reasonably have known of this constitutional defect, the agreement was without force in international law. The State Department rejected that position and no action was taken by the Senate. The Department of State memorandum is reproduced in 15 I.L.M. 198 (1976). For an analysis of the issues, see Meron, Article 46 of the Vienna Convention on the Law of Treaties (ultra vires treaties), 49 Brit.Y.B.I.L. 175–199 (1978).

2. The question of constitutional competence was also raised in the Senate in regard to the agreement between the United States and Panama concluded in 1977 with respect to the Panama Canal. In this case, the issue related to an alleged violation by Panama of its constitutional requirements for entering into an agreement of the character of the Canal treaty. A group of U.S. Senators contended that the Panama constitution clearly required a plebiscite to approve a treaty. They asserted that the plebiscite conducted prior to ratification did not meet that requirement because subsequently the United States, on the advice of the Senate, included a number of reservations, conditions and understandings in the instruments of ratification. While these were accepted by the President of Panama, they were not submitted to a second plebiscite. Several Senators argued that the violation was "manifest" and concerned a rule of fundamental importance. They maintained that unless this was corrected by renegotiation, Panama would be able in the future to claim invalidity because of the constitutional defect. Sen.Exec. Report 95–12 of the Comm. on Foreign Relations, 95 Cong., 2d Sess. (1978). Also 71 A.J.I.L. 635–43 (1978). The Government of Panama responded that under Panamanian law, a second plebiscite was not required. Panama had accepted the Senate's conditions, reservations and understandings but regarded them as interpretations of the treaties, not as alterations or amendments. The Executive Branch of the U.S. Government considered the legal position of Panama as "reasonable." They did not see any violation of Panama law and certainly no manifest violations within the meaning of Article 46. Meron, at 190.

Would there be a basis for a future Panamanian Government to seek to invalidate the agreements on the ground of Article 46? Would Article 45 apply in that event?

3. The reluctance of tribunals to look behind the ostensible authority of a foreign minister to commit his state was evidenced in the *Eastern Greenland Case* decided by the Permanent Court of International Justice in 1933. P.C.I.J., Ser. A/B, No. 53. The case involved a dispute between Norway and Denmark regarding Norwegian occupation of parts of Greenland. The Norwegian Foreign Minister had informed Denmark orally that the "Norwegian Government would not make any difficulty in the settlement of this question." Before the court,

Norway contended that under its constitution the foreign minister could not enter into a binding international agreement on "matters of importance" without approval of the "King in Council." The Court rejected the Norwegian claim that this constitutional limitation invalidated the commitment of the foreign minister. It was sufficient, the Court found, that the foreign minister acted "within his province" in replying to an inquiry of the Danish Government. Presumably, the Court meant "within his province" under international customary law (see Full Powers). In view of that oral statement, Norway was held bound to refrain from contesting Danish sovereignty and from occupying any part of Greenland.

## C. ERROR, FRAUD, AND CORRUPTION

### *1. Error (Article 48)*

In regard to error as a ground of invalidity, the International Law Commission had the following comments:

> (1) In municipal law error occupies a comparatively large place as a factor which vitiates consent to a contract. Some types of error found in municipal law are, however, unlikely to arise in international law. Moreover, treaty-making processes are such as to reduce to a minimum the risk of errors on material points of substance. In consequence, the instances in which errors of substance have been invoked as affecting the essential validity of a treaty have not been frequent. Almost all the recorded instances concern geographical errors, and most of them concern errors in maps. In some instances, the difficulty was disposed of by a further treaty; in others the error was treated more as affecting the application of the treaty than its validity and the point was settled by arbitration. * * *
>
> * * *
>
> (7) Under paragraph 1 error affects consent only if it was an essential error in the sense of an error as to a matter which formed an essential basis of the consent given to the treaty. Furthermore, such an error does not make the treaty automatically void, but gives a right to the party whose consent to the treaty was caused by the error to invoke the error as invalidating its consent. On the other hand, if the invalidity of the treaty is established in accordance with the present articles, the effect will be to make the treaty void *ab initio*.
>
> (8) *Paragraph 2* excepts from the rule cases where the mistaken party in some degree brought the error upon itself. The terms in which the exception is formulated are drawn from those used by the Court in the sentence from its judgment in the *Temple* case * * *. The Commission felt, however, that there is substance in the view that the Court's formulation of the exception "if the party contributed by its own conduct to the error, or could have avoided it, or if the circumstances were such as to put that party on notice of a possible error" is so wide as to leave little room for the operation of the rule. This applies particularly to the words "or could have avoided it." Accordingly, without questioning the Court's formulation of the exception in the context of the particular case, the Commission concluded that, in codifying the general rule

regarding the effect of error in the law of treaties, those words should be omitted.

(9) *Paragraph 3,* in order to prevent any misunderstanding, distinguishes errors in the *wording* of the text from errors in the treaty. The paragraph merely underlines that such an error does not affect the validity of the consent and falls under the provisions of article 74 relating to the correction of errors in the texts of treaties.

[1966] II Yb.I.L.C. 243–244.

For more detailed discussion of error, see Elias, The Modern Law of Treaties 154–61 (1974).

### 2. *Fraud (Article 49)*

Fraud as a ground for invalidity was separated from error because in the Commission's words:

> Fraud, when it occurs, strikes at the root of an agreement in a somewhat different way from innocent misrepresentation and error. It does not merely affect the consent of the other party to the terms of the agreement; it destroys the whole basis of mutual confidence between the parties.

[1966] II Yb.I.L.C. 244.

The Commission noted a "paucity of precedents" in international law with regard to fraud. However, it decided against defining fraud and stated that it proposes only a broad concept comprised in the term "fraud" ("dol" in French and "dolo" in Spanish) rather than the detailed connotations the term has in domestic law. It added that the expression "fraudulent conduct" ("conduite frauduleuse") is designed "to include any false statements, misrepresentations or other deceitful proceedings by which a State is induced to give a consent to a treaty which it would not otherwise have given." Id. at 245.

### 3. *Corruption (Article 50)*

Although some members of the International Law Commission considered that corruption fell within the category of fraud, the majority considered that corruption was sufficiently distinct and required a special article. The Commission commented:

> (4) The strong term "corruption" is used in the article expressly in order to indicate that only acts calculated to exercise a substantial influence on the disposition of the representative to conclude the treaty may be invoked as invalidating the expression of consent which he has purported to give on behalf of his State. The Commission did not mean to imply that under the present article a small courtesy or favour shown to a representative in connexion with the conclusion of a treaty may be invoked as a pretext for invalidating the treaty.
>
> (5) Similarly, the phrase "directly or indirectly by another negotiating State" is used in the article in order to make it plain that the mere fact of the representative's having been corrupted is not enough. The Commission appreciated that corruption by another negotiating State, if it occurs, is unlikely to be overt. But it considered that, in order to be a

> ground for invalidating the treaty, the corrupt acts must be shown to be directly or indirectly imputable to the other negotiating State.

Id.

## D. COERCION

### 1. *Coercion of a Representative*

The Commission considered coercion of a representative of such gravity that the consent of a state so obtained shall be without any legal effect. It referred to a case of "third-degree methods of pressure" against the President and Foreign Minister of Czechoslovakia in 1939 to extract their signatures to a treaty creating a German protectorate over Bohemia and Moravia. It also referred generally to instances in which members of legislatures were coerced to procure ratification of a treaty. Id. at 246. Coercion was also used to include a threat to ruin the career of a representative by exposing a private indiscretion as well as a threat to injure a member of his family.

### 2. *Coercion of a State*

The Commission considered this principle as established law. It said:

> (1) The traditional doctrine prior to the Covenant of the League of Nations was that the validity of a treaty was not affected by the fact that it had been brought about by the threat or use of force. However, his doctrine was simply a reflection of the general attitude of international law during that era towards the legality of the use of force for the settlement of international disputes. With the Covenant and the Pact of Paris there began to develop a strong body of opinion which held that such treaties should no longer be recognized as legally valid. The endorsement of the criminality of aggressive war in the Charters of the Allied Military Tribunals for the trial of the Axis war criminals, the clear-cut prohibition of the threat or use of force in Article 2(4) of the Charter of the United Nations, together with the practice of the United Nations itself, have reinforced and consolidated this development in the law. The Commission considers that these developments justify the conclusion that the invalidity of a treaty procured by the illegal threat or use of force is a principle which is *lex lata* in the international law of to-day.
>
> (2) Some jurists, it is true, while not disputing the moral value of the principle, have hesitated to accept it as a legal rule. They fear that to recognize the principle as a legal rule may open the door to the evasion of treaties by encouraging unfounded assertions of coercion, and that the rule will be ineffective because the same threat or compulsion that procured the conclusion of the treaty will also procure its execution, whether the law regards it as valid or invalid. These objections do not appear to the Commission to be of such a kind as to call for the omission from the present articles of a ground of invalidity springing from the most fundamental provisions of the Charter, the relevance of which in the law of treaties as in other branches of international law cannot to-day be regarded as open to question.

Id. at 246.

The proposed article led to a major confrontation at the Vienna Conference when a number of states proposed an amendment to define "force" to include "economic or political pressure" (referred to as the nineteen-state amendment). An account by the U.S. representative to the Vienna Conference and his colleague follows:

> The proponents of the amendment made it quite clear in the committee of the whole that their amendment was directed toward "economic needs." The representative of Tanzania described "the withdrawal of economic aid or of promises of aid [and] the recall of economic experts" as the type of conduct which should be prohibited. The Algerian representative advanced the thesis:
>
>> * * * the era of the colonial treaty was past or disappearing, but there was no overlooking the fact that some countries had resorted to new and more insidious methods, suited to the present state of international relations, in an attempt to maintain and perpetuate bonds of subjection. Economic pressure, which was a characteristic of neo-colonialism, was becoming increasingly common in relations between certain countries and the newly independent States.
>>
>> Political independence could not be an end in itself; it was even illusory if it was not backed by genuine economic independence. That was why some countries had chosen the political, economic and social system they regarded as best calculated to overcome under-development as quickly as possible. That choice provoked intense opposition from certain interests which saw their privileges threatened and then sought through economic pressure to abolish or at least restrict the right of peoples to self-determination. Such neo-colonialist practices, which affected more than two-thirds of the world's population and were retarding or nullifying all efforts to overcome under-development, should therefore be denounced with the utmost rigour.
>
> Statements of this character reinforced the already deep misgivings as to the effect of the amendment held by the states concerned with the stability of treaties.
>
> The scope of the phrase "threat or use of force" in Article 2, paragraph 4, of the United Nations Charter, as is well known, has been for many years the source of acrimonious dispute. The legislative history of the San Francisco Conference is clear as to its original intent. The Chilean delegate made that point:
>
>> * * * The Brazilian delegation to the 1945 San Francisco Conference had proposed the inclusion of an express reference to the prohibition of economic pressure, and its proposal had been rejected. Consequently, any reference to the principles of the Charter in that respect must be a reference to the kind of force which all the Member States had agreed to prohibit, namely, physical or armed force.
>
> The discussions were complicated by the fact that the United Nations Special Committee on Principles of International Law concerning Friendly Relations and Cooperation Among States had been studying

the "threat or use of force" issue since 1964, and action by the Conference could only cut across the deliberations of that body. The question was also raised whether the conference was attempting to amend the United Nations Charter. The basic problem was well summed up by the Dutch representative:

> In itself, the rule stated in article [52] was perfectly clear and precise. He supported the principle underlying the article, namely, the principle that an aggressor State should not, in law, benefit from a treaty it had forced its victim to accept. Nevertheless, it must be borne in mind that there was a fundamental difference of opinion as to the meaning of the words 'threat or use of force' in Article 2, paragraph 4, of the United Nations Charter. If those words could be interpreted as including all forms of pressure exerted by one State on another, and not just the threat or use of armed force, the scope of article [52] would be so wide as to make it a serious danger to the stability of treaty relations.

The course of the debate had made it clear that if the amendment were put to the vote it would carry by quite a substantial majority. On the other hand, in private discussions it had been made quite clear to the proponents that adoption could wreck the conference because states concerned with the stability of treaties found the proposal intolerable.

To reduce tension, discussion of the article was adjourned and private negotiations resorted to. A compromise solution was reached after some days of cooling off. The amendment was withdrawn. In its place, a draft declaration condemning threat or use of pressure in any form by a state to coerce any other state to conclude a treaty was unanimously adopted by the committee. Although at one point during the plenary it appeared that the compromise might be unraveling, it was adhered to by both sides. The declaration finally approved by the conference in 1969 is annexed to the Final Act.

Kearney & Dalton, 64 A.J.I.L. at 533–535.*

The International Law Commission also considered that a treaty imposed by illegal force should be void, as opposed to voidable. It said in this connection:

> Even if it were conceivable that after being liberated from the influence of a threat or of a use of force a State might wish to allow a treaty procured from it by such means, the Commission considered it essential that the treaty should be regarded in law as void *ab initio.* This would enable the State concerned to take its decision in regard to the maintenance of the treaty in a position of full legal equality with the other State. If, therefore, the treaty were maintained in force, it would in effect be by the conclusion of a new treaty and not by the recognition of the validity of a treaty procured by means contrary to the most fundamental principles of the Charter of the United Nations.

[1966] II Yb.I.L.C. 247.

* Footnotes omitted. Reprinted by permission of the American Society of International Law.

The question of the time element in the application of the article was dealt with by the Commission in the following comments:

> The Commission considered that there is no question of the article having retroactive effects on the validity of treaties concluded prior to the establishment of the modern law. "A juridical fact must be appreciated in the light of the law contemporary with it." The present article concerns the conditions for the valid conclusion of a treaty—the conditions, that is, for the *creation* of a legal relation by treaty. An evolution of the law governing the conditions for the carrying out of a legal act does not operate to deprive of validity a legal act already accomplished in conformity with the law previously in force. The rule codified in the present article cannot therefore be properly understood as depriving of validity *ab initio* a peace treaty or other treaty procured by coercion prior to the establishment of the modern law regarding the threat or use of force.
>
> (8) As to the date from which the modern law should be considered as in force for the purposes of the present article, the Commission considered that it would be illogical and unacceptable to formulate the rule as one applicable only from the date of the conclusion of a convention on the law of treaties. As pointed out in paragraph (1) above, the invalidity of a treaty procured by the illegal threat or use of force is a principle which is *lex lata.* Moreover, whatever differences of opinion there may be about the state of the law prior to the establishment of the United Nations, the great majority of international lawyers to-day unhesitatingly hold that article 2, paragraph 4, together with other provisions of the Charter, authoritatively declares the modern customary law regarding the threat or use of force. The present article, by its formulation, recognizes by implication that the rule which it lays down is applicable at any rate to all treaties concluded since the entry into force of the Charter. On the other hand, the Commission did not think that it was part of its function, in codifying the modern law of treaties, to specify on what precise date in the past an existing general rule in another branch of international law came to be established as such. Accordingly, it did not feel that it should go beyond the temporal indication given by the reference in the article to "the principles of the Charter of the United Nations."

Id.

### *Notes*

1. Would the seizure of hostages for the purpose of coercing their government to grant certain concessions and benefits to the state that seized the hostages constitute a use of force or threat of force against the political independence of the state whose nationals were seized? Would an agreement granting the benefits demanded be void under Article 52?

2. When the United States and Iran reached agreements (known as the Algerian Accords) in 1980 that called for the release of U.S. diplomats and other U.S. nationals, were those agreements void under Article 52 because they were procured by the use of force against the United States? Could either side have refused to perform on the ground that the treaty was void *ab initio?* The main provisions of the agreement provided for the release of the hostages plus a

declaration of nonintervention by the U.S. and the unblocking of Iranian assets frozen in the U.S. in response to the seizure. The United States gave nothing to Iran beyond releasing Iranian assets. In fact Iran received back less than its assets, since a part was placed in escrow to pay creditors and other claimants of United States nationality. See Chapter 7, Section 9. Can one say that an arrangement of this kind was "procured by" the use of threat of force, even if force was initially used against the United States? See Schachter, International Law in the Hostages Crisis in American Hostages in Iran 325, 369–373 (Christopher, *et al.*, 1985).

## E. CONFLICT WITH A PEREMPTORY NORM (JUS COGENS)

### *INTERNATIONAL LAW COMMISSION REPORT*

[1966] II Yb.I.L.C. 169, 247–49.

(1) The view that in the last analysis there is no rule of international law from which States cannot at their own free will contract out has become increasingly difficult to sustain, although some jurists deny the existence of any rules of *jus cogens* in international law, since in their view even the most general rules still fall short of being universal. The Commission pointed out that the law of the Charter concerning the prohibition of the use of force in itself constitutes a conspicuous example of a rule in international law having the character of *jus cogens.* Moreover, if some Governments in their comments have expressed doubts as to the advisability of this article unless it is accompanied by provision for independent adjudication, only one questioned the existence of rules of *jus cogens* in the international law of to-day. Accordingly, the Commission concluded that in codifying the law of treaties it must start from the basis that to-day there are certain rules from which States are not competent to derogate at all by a treaty arrangement, and which may be changed only by another rule of the same character.

(2) The formulation of the article is not free from difficulty, since there is no simple criterion by which to identify a general rule of international law as having the character of *jus cogens.* Moreover, the majority of the general rules of international law do not have that character, and States may contract out of them by treaty. It would therefore be going much too far to state that a treaty is void if its provisions conflict with a rule of general international law. Nor would it be correct to say that a provision in a treaty possesses the character of *jus cogens* merely because the parties have stipulated that no derogation from that provision is to be permitted, so that another treaty which conflicted with that provision would be void. Such a stipulation may be inserted in any treaty with respect to any subject-matter for any reasons which may seem good to the parties. The conclusion by a party of a later treaty derogating from such a stipulation may, of course, engage its responsibility for a breach of the earlier treaty. But the breach of the stipulation does not, simply as such, render the treaty void (see article 26). It is not the form of a general rule of international law but the particular nature of the subject-matter with which it deals that may, in the opinion of the Commission, give it the character of *jus cogens.*

(3) The emergence of rules having the character of *jus cogens* is comparatively recent, while international law is in process of rapid development.

The Commission considered the right course to be to provide in general terms that a treaty is void if it conflicts with a rule of *jus cogens* and to leave the full content of this rule to be worked out in State practice and in the jurisprudence of international tribunals. Some members of the Commission felt that there might be advantage in specifying, by way of illustration, some of the most obvious and best settled rules of *jus cogens* in order to indicate by these examples the general nature and scope of the rule contained in the article. Examples suggested included (a) a treaty contemplating an unlawful use of force contrary to the principles of the Charter, (b) a treaty contemplating the performance of any other act criminal under international law, and (c) a treaty contemplating or conniving at the commission of acts, such as trade in slaves, piracy or genocide, in the suppression of which every State is called upon to co-operate. Other members expressed the view that, if examples were given, it would be undesirable to appear to limit the scope of the article to cases involving acts which constitute crimes under international law; treaties violating human rights, the equality of States or the principle of self-determination were mentioned as other possible examples. The Commission decided against including any examples of rules of *jus cogens* in the article for two reasons. First, the mention of some cases of treaties void for conflict with a rule of *jus cogens* might, even with the most careful drafting, lead to misunderstanding as to the position concerning other cases not mentioned in the article. Secondly, if the Commission were to attempt to draw up, even on a selective basis, a list of the rules of international law which are to be regarded as having the character of *jus cogens,* it might find itself engaged in a prolonged study of matters which fall outside the scope of the present articles.

* * *

(6) The second matter is the non-retroactive character of the rule in the present article. The article has to be read in conjunction with article [64] (Emergence of a new rule of *jus cogens* ), and in the view of the Commission, there is no question of the present article having retroactive effects. It concerns cases where a treaty is void *at the time of its conclusion* by reason of the fact that its provisions are in conflict with an already existing rule of *jus cogens.* The treaty is wholly void because its actual conclusion conflicts with a peremptory norm of general international law from which no States may derogate even by mutual consent. Article [64], on the other hand, concerns cases where a treaty, valid when concluded, becomes void and terminates by reason of the subsequent establishment of a new rule of *jus cogens* with which its provisions are in conflict. The words "*becomes* void and *terminates*" make it quite clear, the Commission considered, that the emergence of a new rule of *jus cogens* is not to have retroactive effects on the validity of a treaty. The invalidity is to attach only as from the time of the establishment of the new rule of *jus cogens.* The non-retroactive character of the rules in articles [53] and [64] is further underlined in article [71], paragraph 2 of which provides in the most express manner that the *termination* of a treaty as a result of the emergence of a new rule of *jus cogens* is not to have retroactive effects.

### *Notes*

1. Although the draft article on peremptory norms generated much controversy at the Vienna conference, a revised draft was adopted by a vote of 72 in

favor, 3 against, and 18 abstentions. Three changes were made to meet objections:

— The words "at the time of its conclusion" were added to make clear the non-retroactive character of the rule.

— It was made explicit that the peremptory norms were the norms recognized by the international community as a whole as those from which no derogation was permitted.

— It was agreed that a party to a dispute involving *jus cogens* may submit it to the International Court for a decision in all cases in which the procedures for settlement (indicated in Article 65) have failed to produce a solution within twelve months.

The adoption of this compulsory jurisdiction compromissory clause made it possible for states apprehensive over the possible destabilizing effect of the *jus cogens* article to support the adoption of the Vienna Convention. For detailed accounts, see Sinclair, The Vienna Convention on the Law of Treaties 203–226 (2d ed. 1984); Elias, The Modern Law of Treaties 177–187, 192–194 (1974); Sztucki, Jus Cogens and the Vienna Convention (1974).

2. What are the rules of *jus cogens* today? A former President of the International Court of Justice has suggested the following answer:

> The substantive contents of *jus cogens* are likely to be constantly changing in accordance with the progress and development of international law and international morality. *Jus cogens* is not an immutable natural law but an evolving concept: the last phrase in the definition envisages the modification of *jus cogens* by the same process which led to its establishment.
>
> Such subsequent rules may originate in a treaty whose norms become generally accepted. A treaty of this nature, containing a new rule of *jus cogens,* would not be void, even if some of its provisions conflicted with an established rule of *jus cogens:* the new rules of *jus cogens* would simply modify or replace the old ones. Otherwise, international society would be deprived of the necessary means of development of its notions of public policy through processes of international legislation. For instance, the traditional definition of piracy may be extended to cover hijacking of aeroplanes or the opium and drug conventions expanded to include synthetic drugs.

Jiménez de Aréchaga, 159 Rec. des Cours 9, 64–67 (1978–I). * See Chapter 2 supra.

* Footnotes omitted. Reprinted by permission of A.W. Sijthoff & Noordhoff International.

*SINCLAIR, THE VIENNA CONVENTION ON THE LAW OF TREATIES*

222–224 (2d ed. 1984).*

Whatever their doctrinal point of departure, the majority of jurists would no doubt willingly concede to the sceptics that there is little or no evidence in positive international law for the concept that nullity attaches to a treaty concluded in violation of *jus cogens.* But they would be constrained to admit that the validity of a treaty between two States to wage a war of aggression against a third State or to engage in acts of physical or armed force against a third State could not be upheld; and, having made this admission, they may be taken to have accepted the principle that there may exist norms of international law so fundamental to the maintenance of an international legal order that a treaty concluded in violation of them is a nullity.

Some (among whom may be counted your author) would be prepared to go this far, but would immediately wish to qualify this acceptance of the principle involved by sketching out the limits within which it may be operative in present-day international law. In the first place, they would insist that, in the present state of international society, the concept of an "international legal order" of hierarchically superior norms binding all States is only just beginning to emerge. Ideological differences and disparities of wealth between the individual nation States which make up the international community, combined with the contrasts between the objectives sought by them, hinder the development of an over-arching community consensus upon the content of *jus cogens.* Indeed, it is the existence of these very differences and disparities which constitute the principal danger implicit in an unqualified recognition of *jus cogens;* for it would be only too easy to postulate as a norm of *jus cogens* a principle which happened neatly to serve a particular ideological or economic goal. In the second place, they would test any assertion that a particular rule constitutes a norm of *jus cogens* by reference to the evidence for its acceptance as such by the international community as a whole, and they would require that the burden of proof should be discharged by those who allege the *jus cogens* character of the rule. Applying this test, and leaving aside the highly theoretical case of a treaty purporting to deny the application of the principle *pacta sunt servanda,* it would seem that sufficient evidence for ascribing the character of *jus cogens* to a rule of international law exists in relation to the rule which requires States to refrain in their international relations from the threat of force against the territorial integrity or political independence of any other State. There is ample evidence for the proposition that, subject to the necessary exceptions about the use of force in self-defence or under the authority of a competent organ of the United Nations or a regional agency acting in accordance with the Charter, the use of armed or physical force against the territorial integrity or political independence of any State is now prohibited. This proposition is so central to the existence of any international legal order of individual nation States (however nascent that international legal order may be) that it must be taken to have the character of *jus cogens.* Just as national legal systems begin to discard, at an early stage of their

* Footnotes omitted. Reprinted by permission of Manchester University Press.

development, such concepts as "trial by battle," so also must the international legal order be assumed now to deny any cover of legality to violations of the fundamental rule embodied in Article 2(4) of the Charter.

Beyond this, uncertainty begins, and one must tread with considerable caution. The dictates of logic, and overriding considerations of morality, would appear to require that one should characterise as *jus cogens* those rules which prohibit the slave trade and genocide; but the evidence is ambivalent, since the treaties which embody these prohibitions contain normal denunciation clauses. Of course, it may be argued that the presence or absence of normal denunciation clauses should not be taken as being decisive; denunciation clauses are regularly embodied in treaties for traditional, rather than practical, reasons. In any event, it is likely that the prohibitions may now be taken to form part of general international law binding all States regardless of whether they are parties to the treaties embodying them. The unenforceability of any treaty contemplating genocide or the slave trade is further assured by the fact that such a treaty would contravene the Charter of the United Nations, which prevails in the event of conflict.

To sum up, there is a place for the concept of *jus cogens* in international law. Its growth and development will parallel the growth and development of an international legal order expressive of the consensus of the international community as a whole. Such an international legal order is, at present, inchoate, unformed and only just discernible. *Jus cogens* is neither Dr. Jekyll nor Mr. Hyde; but it has the potentialities of both. If it is invoked indiscriminately and to serve short-term political purposes, it could rapidly be destructive of confidence in the security of treaties; if it is developed with wisdom and restraint in the overall interest of the international community it could constitute a useful check upon the unbridled will of individual States.

## *Notes*

1. See Chapter 2 supra at pp. 92–93 for a discussion of what is meant by the "international community of states."

2. Although Article 66 of the Vienna Convention provides for compulsory adjudication of disputes concerning the application of Articles 53 and 64, up to now (1993) no cases have been brought to the International Court under this provision. However, jurists and governments have not been hesitant to propose their own ideas of peremptory norms. For examples see Sinclair at 217. The International Law Commission has suggested such norms in its proposed list of international crimes. See Chapter 7, Section 5. At the U.N. Conference on the Law of the Sea, a number of governments maintained that the principle of the common heritage of mankind with respect to areas beyond national jurisdiction had acquired the character of a peremptory norm. However, a proposal to that effect was not included in the Convention on the Law of the Sea. See Chapter 14. The General Assembly adopted a resolution in 1979 declaring that the agreements between Egypt and Israel (known as the Camp David Agreements) "have no validity." G.A.Res. 34/65 B (XXXIV 1979). The legal premise appeared to be that the agreements were considered to violate *jus cogens* norms. See Gaja, Jus Cogens Beyond the Vienna Convention, 172 Rec. des Cours 279, 282 (1981–III).

4. Would the compulsory adjudication clause of Article 66 of the Vienna Convention significantly reduce the risk that Articles 53 and 64 would "destroy the security of treaties"? Would it restrain governments from attacking treaties regarded by them as unjust? Could they not use Article 66 to impugn treaties which are alleged to be contrary to such Charter principles as sovereign equality, or such "fundamental principles" as the non-acquisition of territory by the threat or use of force? (See Chapter 4, Section 6). Would the International Court now have wide latitude to declare treaties to be void on the basis of such principles?

5. It has been suggested that the concept of *jus cogens* has inspired the distinction between international delicts and international crimes proposed in the International Law Commission's Draft Articles on State Responsibility. An international crime was defined as a violation of an "international obligation so essential for the protection of fundamental interests of the international community that its breach is recognized as a crime by that community as a whole." Article 19 of the Draft Articles. [1976] II Yb.I.L.C. The Commission observed, however, that the "category of international obligations admitting of no derogation is much broader than the category of obligations whose breach is necessarily an international crime." Id. at 120. See generally, Chapter 7 infra.

6. Article 64 deals with the emergence of a new rule of *jus cogens.* The treaty becomes void but, as stated in Article 71, the termination does not affect any right, obligation, or legal situation created through the execution of the treaty "provided that those rights, obligations or situations may thereafter be maintained only to the extent that their maintenance is not in itself in conflict with the new peremptory norm of general international law." Does this proviso throw doubt on executed settlements?

7. The International Law Commission suggested that any alteration of a rule of *jus cogens* would probably be effected by conclusion of a general multilateral treaty. But would not such a treaty when concluded contravene unlawfully the rule of *jus cogens* it purports to alter? Does this make the idea of *jus cogens* almost meaningless in that context?

8. The Restatement (Third) accepts the provisions of Articles 53 and 64 as customary law. However, it adds that inasmuch as the United States is not a party to the Convention and therefore the judicial safeguards do not apply to it, "the United States is likely to take a particularly restrictive view of these doctrines, and they can be applied as international law accepted by the United States only with caution." § 331, Reporters' Note 4. The Restatement also declares in § 331, Comment *e,* that in view of the uncertainty as to the scope of *jus cogens,* there is a particularly strong need "for an impartial determination of its applicability. A domestic court should not on its own authority refuse to give effect to an agreement on the ground that it violates a peremptory norm."

## SECTION 6. TERMINATION OR SUSPENSION OF TREATIES

### A. TERMINATION OR WITHDRAWAL UNDER THE TERMS OF A TREATY OR BY CONSENT OF THE PARTIES

Most treaties today contain clauses (a) fixing their duration or (b) the date of termination or (c) an event or condition to bring about termination or

(d) a right to denounce or withdraw from the treaty. The clauses themselves are varied. Whether they apply in a particular case is a matter of interpretation. Article 54 of the Vienna Convention contains the self-evident rule that a treaty may be terminated in accordance with its own provisions. It also provides that a treaty may be terminated at any time by consent of all its parties.

### *Notes*

1. Who has the right to act for a state in terminating a treaty? In principle, this is left to municipal law just as is the competence to express consent to be bound. But suppose the termination of the treaty is declared by an organ of the state lacking constitutional authority to take such action definitively. The Vienna Convention does not deal with this question. In Article 67, it mentions only the state officials who do not have to produce full powers for acts of termination; it follows in this respect the general principle of Article 7. Article 46 deals with the violation of domestic law regarding competence to conclude a treaty. It has been suggested that a similar rule should be applied in case of termination and that if there are no relevant constitutional provisions directly relating to termination, those relating to the competence to conclude treaties should apply. See Haraszti, Some Fundamental Problems of the Law of Treaties 251–253 (1973). Haraszti (a Hungarian) cites as an instance of such unlawful termination the denunciation of the Warsaw Pact by Hungary "at the time of the counter-revolution of 1956." He also observes that in the United States the President has terminated treaties without obtaining or seeking the advice and consent of the Senate. In 1979, however, when the President terminated the Mutual Defense Treaty with the Republic of China (Taiwan) in accordance with its terms, his right to do so without obtaining the advice and consent of the Senate was challenged in the Senate and in a judicial proceeding brought by U.S. citizens on constitutional grounds. See p. 227 supra.

2. Does a clause providing for unilateral termination of a treaty give a party a right to terminate one or more clauses of the treaty without abrogating the rest of the treaty? When the other party or parties refused to accept such partial termination, termination of the entire agreement was necessitated. See 5 Hackworth 309–14; McNair, The Law of Treaties 476–478 (1961).

3. May a denunciation or withdrawal be revoked before the end of the period when it would take effect? Article 68 of the Vienna Convention answers in the affirmative. In proposing this rule, the International Law Commission commented that the right to revoke the notice is implicit in the rule that it is not to become effective until a certain date and other parties should take that into account. Accordingly, there would be no grounds for requiring consent of the other parties.

4. What happens if the denunciations or withdrawals reduce the parties to a multilateral treaty to a number below that required for its entry into force? The Vienna Convention (Article 55) states that that fact alone shall not result in termination. If the negotiating states consider that a minimum number should be necessary for maintaining the treaty in force, it should be so stated.

5. Is the term "denunciation" applicable to action in accordance with Article 54? Although the Convention does not use that term in Article 54 denunciation is often used in referring to acts of unilateral termination whether in accordance with the treaty or on other grounds. It has no independent legal significance.

6. Many agreements have special provisions for withdrawal or release under particular circumstances. These are often preferred to general unilateral withdrawal provisions because they indicate an awareness of contingencies under which release from obligations would be acceptable. In some cases they provide for special procedures under which a party can seek to be released from all or some of its obligations. See General Agreement on Tariffs and Trade (GATT) Article XXV(5), Article XXVIII. When agreements identify the circumstances that would trigger release, the determination whether those circumstances have occurred may be left to the party itself or referred to an international organ authorized to grant a waiver to the party. The latter type is found in the International Monetary Fund Agreement and various commodity agreements. For a general review of withdrawal and release provisions in international agreements, see Bilder, Managing the Risks of International Agreement 52–55, 98–104 (1981).

## B. DENUNCIATION OR WITHDRAWAL FROM A TREATY WHICH CONTAINS NO PROVISION REGARDING TERMINATION

### *INTERNATIONAL LAW COMMISSION REPORT*

[1966] II Yb.I.L.C. 169, 250–251.

* * *

(2) In principle, the answer to the question must depend on the intention of the parties in each case, and the very character of some treaties excludes the possibility that the contracting States intended them to be open to unilateral denunciation or withdrawal at the will of an individual party. Treaties of peace and treaties fixing a territorial boundary are examples of such treaties. Many treaties, however, are not of a kind with regard to which it can be said that to allow a unilateral right of denunciation or withdrawal would be inconsistent with the character of the treaty. * * *

(4) Some members of the Commission considered that in certain types of treaties, such as treaties of alliance, a right of denunciation or withdrawal after reasonable notice should be implied in the treaty unless there are indications of a contrary intention. Other members took the view that, while the omission of any provision for it in the treaty does not exclude the possibility of implying a right of denunciation or withdrawal, the existence of such a right is not to be implied from the character of the treaty alone. According to these members, the intention of the parties is essentially a question of fact to be determined not merely by reference to the character of the treaty but by reference to all the circumstances of the case. This view prevailed in the Commission.

### *Notes*

1. At the Vienna Conference, the Commission's position relating to the "nature" of the treaty was not accepted. The majority considered that a right of denunciation may be implied by the nature of the treaty irrespective of evidence of intention. Treaties of alliance and of commerce were cited as examples of such treaties. Accordingly, Article 56 contains an express provision permitting denunciation or withdrawal on the basis of the nature of the treaty. See Sinclair, The Vienna Convention on the Law of Treaties at 102.

2. Treaties, such as those for a territorial arrangement or boundary, are said to preclude an implied right of denunciation since by their nature they have been executed. Cuba stated that a lease agreement can never be perpetual and that an implied right of denunciation exists. U.N. Conference on Law of Treaties, vol. I p. 336–37. This was clearly directed to the Guantanamo Bay lease to the United States.

## *UNITED NATIONS CONFERENCE ON INTERNATIONAL ORGANIZATION*

Commission I: Commentary on Withdrawal.
San Francisco, 1945. 1 U.N.C.I.O. Docs. 616–17.

The Committee adopts the view that the Charter should not make express provision either to permit or to prohibit withdrawal from the Organization. The Committee deems that the highest duty of the nations which will become Members is to continue their cooperation within the Organization, for the preservation of international peace and security. If, however, a Member because of exceptional circumstances feels constrained to withdraw, and leave the burden of maintaining international peace and security on the other Members, it is not the purpose of the Organization to compel that member to continue its cooperation in the Organization.

It is obvious, however, that withdrawal or some other forms of dissolution of the Organization would become inevitable if, deceiving the hope of humanity, the Organization was revealed to be unable to maintain peace or could do so only at the expense of law and justice.

Nor would it be the purpose of the Organization to compel a Member to remain in the Organization if its rights and obligations as such were changed by Charter amendment in which it has not concurred and which it finds itself unable to accept, or if an amendment duly accepted by the necessary majority in the Assembly or in a general conference fails to secure the ratification necessary to bring such amendment into effect.

It is for these considerations that the Committee has decided to abstain from recommending insertion in the Charter of a formal clause specifically forbidding or permitting withdrawal.

### *Notes*

1. Commission I's Rapporteur stated on June 23, 1945 that "the absence of * * * [a withdrawal] clause is not intended to impair the right of withdrawal, which each state possesses on the basis of the principle of the sovereign equality of the members. The Commission would deplore any reckless or wanton exercise of the right of withdrawal but recognizes that, under certain exceptional circumstances, a state may feel itself compelled to exercise this right." 6 U.N.C.I.O. Doc. 5, 149. The Plenary Session of the Conference approved the Report. The sole objection was raised by the Soviet delegate, who interpreted the Commentary as "condemn[ing] beforehand the grounds on which any state may find it necessary to exercise its right of withdrawal from the Organization. Such right is an expression of state sovereignty and should not be reviled, in advance, by the International Organization." 1 U.N.C.I.O. 619–20. What weight should be assigned to the above statements, as well as to the Commentary on Withdrawal, in the interpretation of the Charter? See Kelsen, The Law of the United

Nations 127 (1950). For a discussion of contemporaneous United States views on the problem of withdrawal, see id. at 129 n. 1. See, in general, Feinberg, Unilateral Withdrawal from an International Organization, 39 Brit.Y.B.I.L. 189 (1963).

On the withdrawal of Indonesia from the United Nations in 1965 and its return in 1966, see 4 I.L.M. 364 (1965); Livingstone, Withdrawal from the United Nations—Indonesia, 14 I.C.L.Q. 637 (1965); Schwelb, Withdrawal from the United Nations: The Indonesian Intermezzo, 61 A.J.I.L. 661 (1967).

2. In recommending acceptance by the United States of the Constitution of the World Health Organization, Congress included in its Joint Resolution a reservation to the effect that, "in the absence of any provision * * * for withdrawal from the Organization, the United States reserves its right to withdraw from the Organization on a one-year notice * * *." 62 Stat. 441–42. See 19 Dep't St.Bull. 310 (1948). The World Health Assembly unanimously accepted the United States reservation by a Resolution of July 2, 1948. See Feinberg at 202–203. In 1949 and 1950, a number of states of the Soviet bloc announced their withdrawal from WHO, but their notifications to the Director-General were rejected on the ground that the WHO Constitution made no provision for withdrawal. The Organization continued to regard the absent states as members, and when the Soviet Union and the other "inactive members" began to resume full participation in 1957, it was agreed that the Organization would accept a token payment of five percent in settlement of the absentee states' financial obligations for the intervening years. See generally id. at 202–208, and sources cited. After a number of states had withdrawn from and then returned to UNESCO, the Organization's Constitution was amended in 1954 to provide specifically for withdrawal. Id. at 209–11. In all the remaining Specialized Agencies of the United Nations, withdrawal is specifically authorized under the conditions stated.

## C. TERMINATION OF A TREATY IMPLIED BY THE CONCLUSION OF A SUBSEQUENT TREATY

### *INTERNATIONAL LAW COMMISSION REPORT*

[1966] II Yb.I.L.C. 169, 252–253.

(1) The present article deals with cases where the parties, without expressly terminating or modifying the first treaty, enter into another treaty which is so far incompatible with the earlier one that they must be considered to have intended to abrogate it. Where the parties to the two treaties are identical, there can be no doubt that, in concluding the second treaty, they are competent to abrogate the earlier one; for that is the very core of the rule contained in article [54]. Even where the parties to the two treaties are not identical, the position is clearly the same if the parties to the later treaty include all the parties to the earlier one; for what the parties to the earlier treaty are competent to do together, they are competent to do in conjunction with other States. The sole question therefore is whether and under what conditions the conclusion of the further incompatible treaty must be held by implication to have terminated the earlier one. This question is essentially one of the construction of the two treaties in order to determine the intentions of the parties with respect to the maintenance in force of the earlier one.

(2) *Paragraph 1* therefore seeks to formulate the conditions under which the parties to a treaty are to be understood as having intended to terminate it by concluding a later treaty conflicting with it. The wording of the two clauses in paragraph 1 is based upon the language used by Judge Anzilotti in his separate opinion in the *Electricity Company of Sofia and Bulgaria* case, where he said:

> There was no express abrogation. But it is generally agreed that, beside express abrogation, there is also tacit abrogation resulting from the fact that the new provisions are incompatible with the previous provisions, or that the whole matter which formed the subject of these latter is henceforward governed by the new provisions.

That case, it is true, concerned a possible conflict between unilateral declarations under the Optional Clause and a treaty, and the Court itself did not accept Judge Anzilotti's view that there was any incompatibility between the two instruments. Nevertheless, the two tests put forward by Judge Anzilotti for determining whether a tacit abrogation had taken place appeared to the majority of the Commission to contain the essence of the matter.

(3) *Paragraph 2* provides that the earlier treaty shall not be considered to have been terminated where it appears from the circumstances that a later treaty was intended only to suspend the operation of the earlier one. Judge Anzilotti, it is true, in the above-mentioned opinion considered that the declarations under the Optional Clause, although in his view incompatible with the earlier treaty, had not abrogated it because of the fact that the treaty was of indefinite duration whereas the declarations were for limited terms. But it could not be said to be a general principle that a later treaty for a fixed term does not abrogate an earlier treaty expressed to have a longer or indefinite duration. It would depend entirely upon the intention of the States in concluding the second treaty, and in most cases it is probable that their intention would have been to cancel rather than suspend the earlier treaty.

### *Notes*

1. A question of termination may arise when a later treaty is incompatible with an earlier treaty in respect of its major or essential, though not all of its, provisions. Should the compatible provisions remain in effect? This question arose in 1939 in regard to a treaty between the U.S. and the Ottoman Empire of 1830 which had been in effect with Egypt as a successor to the Turkish Empire. Provisions of that treaty relating to capitulations were superseded by the Montreux Convention of 1937. The United States took the position that the entire treaty of 1830 was "wiped out" by the Montreux Convention, even though some of the provisions of the earlier treaty were technically compatible with the Montreux Convention. 5 Hackworth 306.

2. It will be recalled that Article 30 of the Vienna Convention also deals with successive treaties relating to the same subject (pp. 468–71 supra). But that article concerns the priority of inconsistent obligations of treaties which are in force. It does not become applicable unless it has been determined under Article 59 that the parties did *not* intend to terminate or suspend the earlier treaty by the later treaty.

## D. TERMINATION AS A CONSEQUENCE OF A BREACH BY A PARTY

### *INTERNATIONAL LAW COMMISSION REPORT*

[1966] II Yb.I.L.C. 169, 253–255.

(1) The great majority of jurists recognize that a violation of a treaty by one party may give rise to a right in the other party to abrogate the treaty or to suspend the performance of its own obligations under the treaty. A violation of a treaty obligation, as of any other obligation, may give rise to a right in the other party to take nonforcible reprisals, and these reprisals may properly relate to the defaulting party's rights under the treaty. Opinion differs, however, as to the extent of the right to abrogate the treaty and the conditions under which it may be exercised. Some jurists, in the absence of effective international machinery for securing the observance of treaties, are more impressed with the innocent party's need to have this right as a sanction for the violation of the treaty. They tend to formulate the right in unqualified terms, giving the innocent party a general right to abrogate the treaty in the event of a breach. Other jurists are more impressed with the risk that a State may allege a trivial or even fictitious breach simply to furnish a pretext for denouncing a treaty which it now finds embarrassing. These jurists tend to restrict the right of denunciation to "material" or "fundamental" breaches and also to subject the exercise of the right to procedural conditions.

(5) The Commission was agreed that a breach of a treaty, however serious, does not *ipso facto* put an end to the treaty, and also that it is not open to a State simply to allege a violation of the treaty and pronounce the treaty at an end. On the other hand, it considered that within certain limits and subject to certain safeguards the right of a party to invoke the breach of a treaty as a ground for terminating it or suspending its operation must be recognized. Some members considered that it would be dangerous for the Commission to endorse such a right, unless its exercise were to be made subject to control by compulsory reference to the International Court of Justice. The Commission, while recognizing the importance of providing proper safeguards against arbitrary denunciation of a treaty on the ground of an alleged breach, concluded that the question of providing safeguards against arbitrary action was a general one which affected several articles. It, therefore, decided to formulate in the present article the substantive conditions under which a treaty may be terminated or its operation suspended in consequence of a breach, and to deal with the question of the procedural safeguards in article 62.

(6) *Paragraph 1* provides that a "material" breach of a bilateral treaty by one party entitles the other to *invoke* the breach as a ground for terminating the treaty or suspending its operation in whole or in part. The formula "invoke as a ground" is intended to underline that the right arising under the article is not a right arbitrarily to pronounce the treaty terminated. If the other party contests the breach or its character as a "material" breach, there will be a "difference" between the parties with regard to which the normal obligations incumbent upon the parties under the Charter and under general international law to seek a solution of the question through

pacific means will apply. The Commission considered that the action open to the other party in the case of a material breach is to invoke either the termination or the suspension of the operation of the treaty, in whole or in part. The right to take this action arises under the law of treaties independently of any right of reprisal, the principle being that a party cannot be called upon to fulfill its obligations under a treaty when the other party fails to fulfil those which it undertook under the same treaty. This right would, of course, be without prejudice to the injured party's right to present an international claim for reparation on the basis of the other party's responsibility with respect to the breach.

(7) *Paragraph 2* deals with a material breach of a multilateral treaty, and here the Commission considered it necessary to distinguish between the right of the other parties to react jointly to the breach and the right of an individual party specially affected by the breach to react alone. Subparagraph (*a*) provides that the other parties may, by a unanimous agreement, suspend the operation of the treaty or terminate it and may do so either only in their relations with the defaulting State or altogether as between all the parties. When an individual party reacts alone the Commission considered that its position is similar to that in the case of a bilateral treaty, but that its right should be limited to suspending the operation of the treaty in whole or in part as between itself and the defaulting State. In the case of a multilateral treaty the interests of the other parties have to be taken into account and a right of suspension normally provides adequate protection to the State specially affected by the breach. Moreover, the limitation of the right of the individual party to a right of suspension seemed to the Commission to be particularly necessary in the case of general multilateral treaties of a law-making character. Indeed, a question was raised as to whether even suspension would be admissible in the case of law-making treaties. The Commission felt, however, that it would be inequitable to allow a defaulting State to continue to enforce the treaty against the injured party, whilst itself violating its obligations towards that State under the treaty. Moreover, even such treaties as the Genocide Convention and the Geneva Conventions on the treatment of prisoners of war, sick and wounded allowed an express right of denunciation independently of any breach of the convention. The Commission concluded that general law-making treaties should not, simply as such, be dealt with differently from other multilateral treaties in the present connexion. Accordingly, subparagraph (*b*) lays down that on a material breach of a multilateral treaty any party specially affected by the breach may *invoke* it as a *ground* for suspending the operation of the treaty in whole or in part *in the relations between itself and the defaulting State.*

(8) *Paragraph 2(c)* is designed to deal with the problem raised in the comments of Governments of special types of treaty, e.g. disarmament treaties, where a breach by one party tends to undermine the whole régime of the treaty as between all the parties. In the case of a material breach of such a treaty the interests of an individual party may not be adequately protected by the rules contained in paragraphs 2(*a*) and (*b*). It could not suspend the performance of its own obligations under the treaty vis-à-vis the defaulting State without at the same time violating its obligations to the other parties. Yet, unless it does so, it may be unable to protect itself

against the threat resulting from the arming of the defaulting State. In these cases, where a material breach of the treaty by one party radically changes the position of every party with respect to the further performance of its obligations, the Commission considered that any party must be permitted without first obtaining the agreement of the other parties to suspend the operation of the treaty with respect to itself generally in its relations with all the other parties. Paragraph 2(*c*) accordingly so provides.

(9) *Paragraph 3* defines the kind of breach which may give rise to a right to terminate or suspend the treaty. Some authorities have in the past seemed to assume that any breach of any provision would suffice to justify the denunciation of the treaty. The Commission, however, was unanimous that the right to terminate or suspend must be limited to cases where the breach is of a serious character. It preferred the term "material" to "fundamental" to express the kind of breach which is required. The word "fundamental" might be understood as meaning that only the violation of a provision directly touching the *central* purposes of the treaty can ever justify the other party in terminating the treaty. But other provisions considered by a party to be essential to the effective execution of the treaty may have been very material in inducing it to enter into the treaty at all, even though these provisions may be of an ancillary character. Clearly, an unjustified repudiation of the treaty—a repudiation not sanctioned by any of the provisions of the present articles—would automatically constitute a material breach of the treaty; and this is provided for in sub-paragraph (*a*) of the definition. The other and more general form of material breach is that in sub-paragraph (*b*), and is there defined as a violation of a provision essential to the accomplishment of any object or purpose of the treaty.

### *Notes*

1. At the Vienna conference, paragraph 5 was added to the draft of the Commission. Its objective was to ensure that the rules providing for termination as a consequence of breach would not cause the termination or suspension of the many conventions of a humanitarian character which protect the "human person." Reference was made to the Geneva Conventions for the Protection of Victims of War and to conventions relating to refugees and human rights. It was considered desirable to make it clear that a material breach in these cases should not lead to abrogation or suspension of the treaty. The general view is that such treaties are essentially for the benefit of individuals and they involve obligations which should not be dependent on reciprocal performance by the states parties. Compare the reasoning of the International Court in its *Advisory Opinion on Reservations to the Convention on Genocide,* p. 446 supra.

2. A state may choose to ignore a violation by another state of a treaty to which both are parties. See Charlton v. Kelly, 229 U.S. 447, 33 S.Ct. 945, 57 L.Ed. 1274 (1913), where the Supreme Court held that inasmuch as the executive branch of government had waived its "right to free itself from the obligation to deliver up its own citizens" pursuant to an extradition treaty with Italy that had been interpreted by Italian authorities as excluding the extradition from Italy of Italian citizens, the courts were compelled to recognize the treaty as binding and in full force.

3. Does a violation by one party of a single article or group of articles of an agreement justify another party in regarding itself as freed of all obligations under the agreement? In his report to the Security Council on problems

concerning the Armistice Agreements concluded between Israel and various Arab states in 1949, the Secretary–General stated:

> 16. As a matter of course, each party considers its compliance with the stipulations of an armistice agreement as conditioned by compliance of the other party to the agreement. Should such a stand be given the interpretation that any one infringement of the provisions of the agreement by one party justifies reactions by the other party which, in their turn, are breaches of the armistice agreement, without any limitation as to the field within which reciprocity is considered to prevail, it would in fact mean that the armistice régime could be nullified by a single infringement by one of the parties. Although such an interpretation has never been given from responsible quarters, it appears to me that a lack of clarity has prevailed. From no side has it been said that a breach of an armistice agreement, to whatever clause it may refer, gives the other party a free hand concerning the agreement as a whole, but a tendency to regard the agreements, including the cease-fire clauses, as entities may explain a feeling that in fact, due to infringements of this or that clause, the obligations are no longer in a strict sense fully binding, and specifically that a breach of one of the clauses, other than the cease-fire clause, may justify action in contravention of that clause.
> * * *
>
> 18. The very logic of the armistice agreements shows that infringements of other articles cannot serve as a justification for an infringement of the cease-fire article. If that were not recognized, it would mean that any one of such infringements might not only nullify the armistice régime, but in fact put in jeopardy the cease-fire itself. For that reason alone, it is clear that compliance with the said article can be conditioned only by similar compliance of the other party.

11 SCOR, Supp. Apr.–June 1956, at 34–35, U.N.Doc. S/3596, at 6–7 (1956). See the International Law Commission's comment on the separability of treaty provisions, [1966] II Yb.I.L.C. 237–39 (Art. 41).

4. Article 60 provides for a right to terminate or suspend the operation of a treaty in part. Is the right to partial abrogation subject to the limitations laid down by Article 44 relating to separability or is the injured party free to abrogate particular clauses as it chooses? See Haraszti at 325 n. 40.

5. Whether termination for breach is permissible will often depend on determination of whether a violation has occurred. Specific and unambiguous provisions make such determination easier but there are often good reasons to avoid excessive specificity and instead to allow for leeway in interpretation. Provisions for verifying compliance are included in many treaties and are of critical importance to treaties concerning armaments, truce arrangements and environmental protection. A good summary of treaty provisions and problems relating to protection against nonperformance will be found in Bilder, Managing the Risks of International Agreement 106–194 (1981). See generally, Rosenne, Breach of Treaty (1985).

6. In *Rainbow Warrior* (New Zealand v. France), 82 I.L.R. 499 (1990), a French–New Zealand Arbitration Tribunal addressed the question of whether a state can justify breach of treaty obligations by referring to exceptions within the law of state responsibility, such as *force majeure,* distress, and necessity. (Circumstances precluding wrongfulness in law of state responsibility is treated in Chapter 7, on international responsibility and remedies.) The Tribunal answered this question in the affirmative, holding that both the customary law

of treaties and the customary law of state responsibility were relevant and applicable in ascertaining the consequences, if any, of a breach of treaty:

> The reason is that the general principles of International Law concerning State responsibility are equally applicable in the case of breach of treaty obligation, since in the international law field there is no distinction between contractual and tortious responsibility, so that any violation by a State of any obligation, of whatever origin, gives rise to State responsibility and consequently, to the duty of reparation.

Id. at 551.

## ADVISORY OPINION ON NAMIBIA

International Court of Justice, Advisory Opinion, 1971.
1971 I.C.J. 16.*

[In 1966, the General Assembly adopted a resolution in which, *inter alia,* it decided that South Africa's Mandate to what became known as Namibia (South West Africa) was terminated. G.A.Res. 2145 (XXI) (1966). This resolution did not induce South Africa to terminate or relax its control of the territory, and the situation was put on the agenda of the Security Council, which on January 30, 1970, reaffirmed the General Assembly resolution and declared, *inter alia*, "that the continued presence of the South African authorities in Namibia is illegal and that consequently all acts taken by the Government of South Africa on behalf of or concerning Namibia after the termination of the Mandate are illegal and invalid." S.C.Res. 276, U.N.Doc. S/INF/25, at 1. South Africa remained adamant and refused to cooperate with the U.N. Council for Namibia which had been set up by the General Assembly in 1967 and which had begun to issue Travel Documents and Identity Certificates for inhabitants of Namibia. On July 29, 1970, the Security Council adopted a resolution submitting to the International Court of Justice for an advisory opinion the following question: "What are the legal consequences for States of the continued presence of South Africa in Namibia, notwithstanding Security Council resolution 276 (1970)?" S.C.Res. 284.

On June 21, 1971, the Court answered this question as follows:]

by 13 votes to 2,

(1) that, the continued presence of South Africa in Namibia being illegal, South Africa is under obligation to withdraw its administration from Namibia immediately and thus put an end to its occupation of the Territory;

by 11 votes to 4,

(2) that States Members of the United Nations are under obligation to recognize the illegality of South Africa's presence in Namibia and the invalidity of its acts on behalf of or concerning Namibia, and to refrain from any acts and in particular any dealings with the Government of

* The complete title of this opinion is: Legal Consequences for States of the Continued Presence of South Africa in Namibia (South West Africa), notwithstanding Security Council Resolution 276 (1970).

South Africa implying recognition of the legality of, or lending support or assistance to, such presence and administration;

(3) that it is incumbent upon States which are not Members of the United Nations to give assistance, within the scope of subparagraph (2) above, in the action which has been taken by the United Nations with regard to Namibia.

[1971 I.C.J. 16, at 58.

In the course of its reasoning, the Court rejected South Africa's suggestion that Class C Mandates were "in their practical effect not far removed from annexation," as well as the contention that such Mandates were not terminable without the Mandatory's consent.]

93. In paragraph 3 of the operative part of the resolution the General Assembly "*Declares* that South Africa has failed to fulfil its obligations in respect of the administration of the Mandated Territory and to ensure the moral and material well-being and security of the indigenous inhabitants of South West Africa and has, in fact, disavowed the Mandate". In paragraph 4 the decision is reached, as a consequence of the previous declaration "that the Mandate conferred upon His Britannic Majesty to be exercised on his behalf by the Government of the Union of South Africa is *therefore* terminated * * *". (Emphasis added.) It is this part of the resolution which is relevant in the present proceedings.

94. In examining this action of the General Assembly it is appropriate to have regard to the general principles of international law regulating termination of a treaty relationship on account of breach. For even if the mandate is viewed as having the character of an institution, as is maintained, it depends on those international agreements which created the system and regulated its application. As the Court indicated in 1962 "this Mandate, like practically all other similar Mandates" was "a special type of instrument composite in nature and instituting a novel international régime. It incorporates a definite agreement * * *" (I.C.J. Reports 1962, p. 331). The Court stated conclusively in that Judgment that the Mandate " * * * in fact and in law, is an international agreement having the character of a treaty or convention" (I.C.J. Reports 1962, p. 330). The rules laid down by the Vienna Convention on the Law of Treaties concerning termination of a treaty relationship on account of breach (adopted without a dissenting vote) may in many respects be considered as a codification of existing customary law on the subject. In the light of these rules, only a material breach of a treaty justifies termination, such breach being defined as:

(a) a repudiation of the treaty not sanctioned by the present Convention; or

(b) the violation of a provision essential to the accomplishment of the object or purpose of the treaty (Art. 60, para. 3).

95. General Assembly resolution 2145 (XXI) determines that both forms of material breach had occurred in this case. By stressing that South Africa "has, in fact, disavowed the Mandate", the General Assembly declared in fact that it had repudiated it. The resolution in question is therefore to be viewed as the exercise of the right to terminate a relationship

in case of a deliberate and persistent violation of obligations which destroys the very object and purpose of that relationship.

* * *

96. It has been contended that the Covenant of the League of Nations did not confer on the Council of the League power to terminate a mandate for misconduct of the Mandatory and that no such power could therefore be exercised by the United Nations, since it could not derive from the League greater powers than the latter itself had. For this objection to prevail it would be necessary to show that the mandates system, as established under the League, excluded the application of the general principle of law that a right of termination on account of breach must be presumed to exist in respect of all treaties, except as regards provisions relating to the protection of the human person contained in treaties of a humanitarian character (as indicated in Art. 60, para. 5, of the Vienna Convention). The silence of a treaty as to the existence of such a right cannot be interpreted as implying the exclusion of a right which has its source outside of the treaty, in general international law, and is dependent on the occurrence of circumstances which are not normally envisaged when a treaty is concluded.

* * *

101. It has been suggested that, even if the Council of the League had possessed the power of revocation of the Mandate in an extreme case, it could not have been exercised unilaterally but only in cooperation with the mandatory Power. However, revocation could only result from a situation in which the Mandatory had committed a serious breach of the obligations it had undertaken. To contend, on the basis of the principle of unanimity which applied in the League of Nations, that in this case revocation could only take place with the concurrence of the Mandatory, would not only run contrary to the general principle of law governing termination on account of breach, but also postulate an impossibility. For obvious reasons, the consent of the wrongdoer to such a form of termination cannot be required.

### *Note*

Was the Court correct in saying that there is a general principle of law that a right of termination on account of breach must be presumed to exist in respect of all treaties? Briggs has noted that the Court produces no evidence in support. Moreover, he finds that Article 60 does not recognize that proposition. In the case of multilateral treaties, a material breach may be invoked only *as a ground for termination or suspension* under paragraph 2(a). Paragraphs 2(b) and 2(c) permit invocation of a material breach only as a ground for suspension, not termination. Briggs points out that the International Law Commission stated that "the breach of a treaty, however serious, does not *ipso facto* put an end to the treaty and * * * it is not open to a state simply to allege a violation of the treaty and pronounce the treaty at an end * * *." (See [1966] II Yb.I.L.C. at 253–255 quoted supra, p. 507.) The statement of the Court, according to Briggs, is *obiter dicta* since the *Namibia Case* did not involve a claim by a state of a unilateral right to terminate a treaty for breach. The analogy should have been with the collective right of termination set forth in paragraph 2a of Article 60. See Briggs, Unilateral Denunciation of Treaties, 68 A.J.I.L. 51, 56–57 (1974).

## APPEAL RELATING TO THE JURISDICTION OF THE ICAO COUNCIL

## (INDIA v. PAKISTAN)

International Court of Justice, 1972.
1972 I.C.J. 46.

[Pakistan had brought a complaint against India before the Council of the International Civil Aviation Organization (ICAO) on the ground that India had violated provisions of the 1944 Chicago Convention on International Civil Aviation and the International Air Services Transport Agreement. The basis for the complaint was that India had unilaterally suspended flights of Pakistan aircraft over Indian territory. The ICAO Council assumed jurisdiction on the basis of the jurisdictional clauses in the treaties. India appealed to the International Court of Justice charging that the treaties had been suspended by India on ground of a breach by Pakistan (in particular, the hijacking of an Indian plane, allegedly with compliance of Pakistan). Therefore, it claimed the ICAO Council had no jurisdiction.

Pakistan objected to the Court's taking jurisdiction on the ground that India's contention that the treaties were not in force or in operation meant that India did not have standing to bring a case on the basis of the treaty jurisdictional clauses. The Court rejected the Pakistan challenge and in so doing declared:]

Nor in any case could a merely unilateral suspension per se render jurisdictional clauses inoperative, since one of their purposes might be, precisely, to enable the validity of the suspension to be tested. If a mere allegation, as yet unestablished, that a treaty was no longer operative could be used to defeat its jurisdictional clauses, all such clauses would become potentially a dead letter, even in cases like the present, where one of the very questions at issue on the merits, and as yet undecided, is whether or not the treaty is operative—i.e., whether it has been validly terminated or suspended. The result would be that means of defeating jurisdictional clauses would never be wanting.

[With respect to the jurisdiction of the ICAO Council, India claimed that its right to unilateral termination or suspension for material breach had been properly exercised and accordingly the treaties no longer were in force. It followed that the ICAO Council could not have jurisdiction. India's conduct in suspending Pakistan flights was therefore outside of, not under, the treaties. In regard to this, the Court stated:]

* * * it involves a point of principle of great general importance for the jurisdictional aspects of this—or of any—case. This contention is to the effect that since India, in suspending overflights in February 1971, was not invoking any right that might be afforded by the Treaties, but was acting outside them on the basis of a general principle of international law, "therefore" the Council, whose jurisdiction was derived from the Treaties, and which was entitled to deal only with matters arising under them, must be incompetent. Exactly the same attitude has been evinced in regard to the contention that the Treaties were suspended in 1965 and never revived,

or were replaced by a special régime. The Court considers however, that for precisely the same order of reason as has already been noticed in the case of its own jurisdiction in the present case, a mere unilateral affirmation of these contentions—contested by the other party—cannot be utilized so as to negative the Council's jurisdiction. The point is not that these contentions are necessarily wrong but that their validity has not yet been determined. Since therefore the Parties are in disagreement as to whether the Treaties ever were (validly) suspended or replaced by something else; as to whether they are in force between the Parties or not; and as to whether India's action in relation to Pakistan overflights was such as not to involve the Treaties, but to be justifiable *aliter et aliunde;*—these very questions are in issue before the Council, and no conclusions as to jurisdiction can be drawn from them, at least at this stage, so as to exclude *ipso facto* and *a priori* the competence of the Council.

32. To put the matter in another way, these contentions are essentially in the nature of replies to the charge that India is in breach of the Treaties: the Treaties were at the material times suspended or not operative, or replaced,—hence they cannot have been infringed. India has not of course claimed that, in consequence, such a matter can never be tested by any form of judicial recourse. This contention, if it were put forward, would be equivalent to saying that questions that prima facie may involve a given treaty, and if so would be within the scope of its jurisdictional clause, could be removed therefrom at a stroke by a unilateral declaration that the treaty was no longer operative. The acceptance of such a proposition would be tantamount to opening the way to a wholesale nullification of the practical value of jurisdictional clauses by allowing a party first to purport to terminate, or suspend the operation of a treaty, and then to declare that the treaty being now terminated or suspended, its jurisdictional clauses were in consequence void, and could not be invoked for the purpose of contesting the validity of the termination or suspension,—whereas of course it may be precisely one of the objects of such a clause to enable that matter to be adjudicated upon. Such a result, destructive of the whole object of adjudicability, would be unacceptable.

### *Notes*

1. As in the *Advisory Opinion on Namibia,* the Court in the above case relied on the Vienna Convention on the Law of Treaties as authoritative even prior to the entry into force of that Convention.

2. Did the Court in this case clear up the ambiguity of the *obiter dicta* in the *Namibia* opinion about the unilateral right of a state to terminate a treaty for breach?

3. Briggs commented on the decision as follows:

> The court properly confined itself to upholding its own jurisdiction and that of the ICAO Council; but it may be noted that much of the rationale advanced by the Court to restrict claims of a unilateral right under general international law to terminate or suspend jurisdictional treaties for breach would appear to have cogency in relation to all treaties, whether or not they contain jurisdictional clauses.

Briggs, Unilateral Denunciation of Treaties: The Vienna Convention and the International Court of Justice, 68 A.J.I.L. 60–61 (1974).*

4. Is a party affected by a breach obliged to continue performance of a treaty which the other party is violating during the period when the required process of dispute settlement is in progress? Is the aggrieved party restricted in taking counter-measures (including non-compliance) when the treaty itself provides for negotiation, arbitration or other means of settlement? These questions were considered by an arbitral tribunal in a dispute between France and the United States concerning an Air Services Agreement. The tribunal held that the aggrieved state (the United States) was entitled to take counter-measures including suspension of its performance under the treaty when such measures were not disproportionate to the breach, notwithstanding the agreement for arbitration. Case Concerning the Air Services Agreement between France and the United States, Award of December 9, 1978. 18 U.N.R.I.A.A. 417. The decision is dealt with in more detail below in Chapter 7, Section 7 on counter-measures. See also Damrosch, Retaliation or Arbitration or Both, 74 A.J.I.L. 785 (1980).

## E. FUNDAMENTAL CHANGE OF CIRCUMSTANCES

### *INTERNATIONAL LAW COMMISSION REPORT*

[1966] II Yb.I.L.C. 169, 256–258.

(1) Almost all modern jurists, however reluctantly, admit the existence in international law of the principle with which this article is concerned and which is commonly spoken of as the doctrine of *rebus sic stantibus.* Just as many systems of municipal law recognize that, quite apart from any actual *impossibility* of performance, contracts may become inapplicable through a fundamental change of circumstances, so also treaties may become inapplicable for the same reason. Most jurists, however, at the same time enter a strong *caveat* as to the need to confine the scope of the doctrine within narrow limits and to regulate strictly the conditions under which it may be invoked; for the risks to the security of treaties which this doctrine presents in the absence of any general system of compulsory jurisdiction are obvious. The circumstances of international life are always changing and it is easy to allege that the changes render the treaty inapplicable.

* * *

(6) The Commission concluded that the principle, if its application were carefully delimited and regulated, should find a place in the modern law of treaties. A treaty may remain in force for a long time and its stipulations come to place an undue burden on one of the parties as a result of a fundamental change of circumstances. Then, if the other party were obdurate in opposing any change, the fact that international law recognized no legal means of terminating or modifying the treaty otherwise than through a further agreement between the same parties might impose a serious strain on the relations between the States concerned; and the dissatisfied State might ultimately be driven to take action outside the law. The number of cases calling for the application of the rule is likely to be comparatively

small. As pointed out in the commentary to article 51, the majority of modern treaties are expressed to be of short duration, or are entered into for recurrent terms of years with a right to denounce the treaty at the end of each term, or are expressly or implicitly terminable upon notice. In all these cases either the treaty expires automatically or each party, having the power to terminate the treaty, has the power also to apply pressure upon the other party to revise its provisions. Nevertheless, there may remain a residue of cases in which, failing any agreement, one party may be left powerless under the treaty to obtain any legal relief from outmoded and burdensome provisions. It is in these cases that the *rebus sic stantibus* doctrine could serve a purpose as a lever to induce a spirit of compromise in the other party. Moreover, despite the strong reservations often expressed with regard to it, the evidence of the acceptance of the doctrine in international law is so considerable that it seems to indicate a recognition of a need for this safety-valve in the law of treaties.

(7) In the past the principle has almost always been presented in the guise of a tacit condition implied in every "perpetual" treaty that would dissolve it in the event of a fundamental change of circumstances. The Commission noted, however, that the tendency to-day was to regard the implied term as only a fiction by which it was attempted to reconcile the principle of the dissolution of treaties in consequence of a fundamental change of circumstances with the rule *pacta sunt servanda.* In most cases the parties gave no thought to the possibility of a change of circumstances and, if they had done so, would probably have provided for it in a different manner. Furthermore, the Commission considered the fiction to be an undesirable one since it increased the risk of subjective interpretations and abuse. For this reason, the Commission was agreed that the theory of an implied term must be rejected and the doctrine formulated as an objective rule of law by which, on grounds of equity and justice, a fundamental change of circumstances may, under certain conditions, be invoked by a party as a ground for terminating the treaty. It further decided that, in order to emphasize the objective character of the rule, it would be better not to use the term "*rebus sic stantibus* " either in the text of the article or even in the title, and so avoid the doctrinal implication of that term.

### *Notes*

1. Consider the five conditions that have to be met under Article 62 before a "fundamental change of circumstances" can be invoked as a ground of termination:

— The change must have been of a fundamental character.

— The change must have been unforeseen (if the treaty contains provisions for certain contingencies, e.g., economic hardships, the condition is not unforeseen).

— The circumstances which have changed must have been "an essential basis of the consent to be bound by the treaty."

— The effect of the change must be to transform radically the extent of the obligations of the party invoking the change as a ground of termination.

— The obligations in question are "still to be performed under the treaty" (hence, the article does not apply to treaties whose provisions have been fully executed).

2. Would the principle of Article 62 apply to settlements of a territorial nature? Note the explicit exclusion of a treaty if it "establishes a boundary." The International Law Commission rejected suggestions that the exception for boundary treaties might be inconsistent with the principle of self-determination. It considered that if a boundary treaty were not excepted, the rule "might become a source of dangerous friction." But the Commission also said: "By excepting treaties establishing a boundary from its scope, the present article would not exclude the operation of the principle of self-determination in any case where the conditions for its legitimate operation existed." [1966] II Yb.I.L.C. 259. A territorial settlement need not establish a boundary, e.g., it may transfer an island or a zone such as the Canal Zone. Since these actions would not establish a boundary, the issue would be whether the treaty was fully executed or whether in some respects it is executory. In the *Free Zones Case* (P.C.I.J., Ser. A/B, No. 46), Switzerland claimed that *rebus sic stantibus* did not apply to the territorial clauses which had been executed. France, however, noted that certain personal rights were created and that France, for example, had a continuing obligation to abstain from levying customs duties on individuals. The Court did not find it necessary to pass on this point but it exemplifies the case of a continuing obligation as part of a territorial settlement.

3. May a state invoke a fundamental change which has resulted from its own acts? An example mentioned in the International Law Commission was whether a state which had transformed itself from an agricultural to an industrial country could claim that change as a ground for terminating a treaty which was based on the previous agricultural character of the country. Since it could not be said that industrialization was a breach of the treaty, the exception in paragraph 2(b) of Article 62 would not apply. However, when a change is the result of a breach by a party, that party cannot invoke the change as a ground for termination.

4. Does Article 62 apply to treaties which have a fixed duration? Under customary international law, *rebus sic stantibus* was considered inapplicable to treaties containing a fixed term, however long the duration. See Jiménez de Aréchaga, 159 Rec. des Cours at 48. But the Commission considered that a fundamental change of circumstances may occur when a treaty has a fixed term and that it was desirable to apply the rule to such treaties wherever the necessary conditions were met. Is Article 62 in that respect *de lege ferenda?*

5. Does Article 62 permit an automatic extinction of a treaty? Does it provide for an unchallengeable unilateral right to terminate? By its terms, Article 62 confers a right to call for termination. Procedural requirements are laid down for this, as for other grounds of termination, in Articles 65 and 66. These provisions come into play if the claim to termination is disputed. They require that negotiation or other procedures of settlement be used as agreed by the parties. If no solution is reached, a compulsory conciliation procedure may be instituted by any party to the dispute; however, the Conciliation Commission's conclusions are not binding on the parties (Annex V of Vienna Convention). Accordingly, it remains open to a party to maintain its right to terminate on grounds of Article 62, provided that it has complied with the notification and procedural requirements. How effective this will prove in limiting claims based on fundamental change remains to be seen. The Vienna Convention does,

however, exclude the right to an absolutely unlimited right to unilateral termination, such as was apparently asserted by the United States in 1941 when the President suspended the operation of the International Load Line Convention of 1930 on grounds of changed shipping conditions brought about by the war in Europe. See 5 Hackworth 355–56; Briggs, The Attorney–General Invokes Rebus Sic Stantibus, 36 A.J.I.L. 89 (1942).

6. International tribunals, while recognizing the principle of *rebus sic stantibus,* have "generally avoided giving it effect, usually on the ground that it was not applicable to the facts at hand." Restatement Second, Comment to Article 153. This is borne out by the two cases most often cited in this connection. The first is the *Case of the Free Zones* between France and Switzerland decided by the P.C.I.J. in 1932 (see p. 437 supra), in which the Court found that the circumstances which had changed were not those on the basis of which the parties entered into the treaty. The second case is the *Fisheries Jurisdiction Case* between the United Kingdom and Iceland decided by the International Court of Justice in 1973. In that case, the Court considered the applicability of the principle of fundamental change of circumstances in the light of the Vienna Convention. The relevant excerpts from the decision of the Court are given below.

For a detailed treatment of doctrine and state practice prior to the Vienna Convention, see Haraszti, Treaties and the Fundamental Change of Circumstances, 146 Rec. des Cours 1 (1975–III).

7. May a private party invoke the doctrine of changed circumstances to defeat the application of a treaty? A claimant in a suit against an airline for loss of cargo argued that the limits on liability of the Warsaw Convention of 1929 did not apply because fundamental changes of circumstances had occurred since its conclusion. The U.S. Supreme Court recognized that a party to a treaty might invoke changed circumstances as an excuse for terminating its treaty obligations. However, when the states parties continue to assert the vitality of the treaty, a private person who finds the continued existence of the treaty inconvenient may not invoke the doctrine of changed circumstances. Trans World Airlines, Inc. v. Franklin Mint, 466 U.S. 243, 104 S.Ct. 1776, 80 L.Ed.2d 273 (1984).

## THE FISHERIES JURISDICTION CASE (UNITED KINGDOM v. ICELAND)

International Court of Justice, 1973.

1973 I.C.J. 3.

[On April 14, 1972, the United Kingdom filed an Application before the International Court of Justice instituting proceedings against Iceland challenging the proposed extension of Iceland's exclusive fisheries jurisdiction from 12 to 50 miles around its shores. The United Kingdom founded the Court's jurisdiction on Article 36, paragraph 1, of the Court's Statute and a March 11, 1961, Exchange of Notes between the two countries under which the United Kingdom recognized Iceland's claim to a 12–mile fisheries limit in return for Iceland's agreement that any dispute as to the extension of Icelandic fisheries jurisdiction beyond the 12–mile limit "shall, at the request of either party, be referred to the International Court of Justice."

The Government of Iceland notified the Court by letter dated May 29, 1972 that Iceland was not willing "to confer" jurisdiction on the Court and would not appoint an Agent. Thereupon, the Government of the United Kingdom requested the Court to grant interim measures of protection under Article 41 of the Court's Statute, which the Court proceeded to do, while ordering hearings on the question of its jurisdiction to deal with the merits.

In its decision of February 2, 1973, the Court, finding by 14 to 1 that it had jurisdiction, regretted the absence of Iceland in the proceedings, noted its obligations under the Statute to establish its own jurisdiction, and observed that in so doing it would "consider those objections which might, in its view, be raised against its jurisdiction."

With respect to questions relating to fundamental change of circumstances, the decision of the Court contained the following paragraphs:]

31. It should be observed at the outset that the compromissory clause has a bilateral character, each of the parties being entitled to invoke the Court's jurisdiction; it is clear that in certain circumstances it could be to Iceland's advantage to apply to the Court. The argument of Iceland appears, however, to be that, because of the general trend of development of international law on the subject of fishery limits during the last ten years, the right of exclusive fisheries jurisdiction to a distance of 12 miles from the baselines of the territorial sea has been increasingly recognized and claimed by States, including the applicant State itself. It would then appear to be contended that the compromissory clause was the price paid by Iceland for the recognition at that time of the 12-mile fishery limit by the other party. It is consequently asserted that if today the 12-mile fishery limit is generally recognized, there would be a failure of consideration relieving Iceland of its commitment because of the changed legal circumstances. It is on this basis that it is possible to interpret the Prime Minister's statement to the Althing on 9 November 1971, to the effect that it was unlikely that the agreement would have been made if the Government of Iceland had known how these matters would evolve.

32. While changes in the law may under certain conditions constitute valid grounds for invoking a change of circumstances affecting the duration of a treaty, the Icelandic contention is not relevant to the present case. The motive which induced Iceland to enter into the 1961 Exchange of Notes may well have been the interest of obtaining an immediate recognition of an exclusive fisheries jurisdiction to a distance of 12 miles in the waters around its territory. It may also be that this interest has in the meantime disappeared, since a 12-mile fishery zone is now asserted by the other contracting party in respect of its own fisheries jurisdiction. But in the present case, the object and purpose of the 1961 Exchange of Notes, and therefore the circumstances which constituted an essential basis of the consent of both parties to be bound by the agreement embodied therein, had a much wider scope. That object and purpose was not merely to decide upon the Icelandic claim to fisheries jurisdiction up to 12 miles, but also to provide a means whereby the parties might resolve the question of the validity of any further claims. This follows not only from the text of the agreement but also from the history of the negotiations, that is to say, from the whole set of circumstances which must be taken into account in determining what induced both parties to agree to the 1961 Exchange of Notes.

34. It is possible that today Iceland may find that some of the motives which induced it to enter into the 1961 Exchange of Notes have become less compelling or have disappeared altogether. But this is not a ground justifying the repudiation of those parts of the agreement the object and purpose of which have remained unchanged. Iceland has derived benefits from the executed provisions of the agreement, such as the recognition by the United Kingdom since 1961 of a 12–mile exclusive fisheries jurisdiction, the acceptance by the United Kingdom of the baselines established by Iceland and the relinquishment in a period of three years of the pre-existing traditional fishing by vessels registered in the United Kingdom. Clearly it then becomes incumbent on Iceland to comply with its side of the bargain, which is to accept the testing before the Court of the validity of its further claims to extended jurisdiction. Moreover, in the case of a treaty which is in part executed and in part executory, in which one of the parties has already benefited from the executed provisions of the treaty, it would be particularly inadmissible to allow that party to put an end to obligations which were accepted under the treaty by way of *quid pro quo* for the provisions which the other party has already executed.

* * *

35. In his letter of 29 May 1972 to the Registrar, the Minister for Foreign Affairs of Iceland refers to "the changed circumstances resulting from the ever-increasing exploitation of the fishery resources in the seas surrounding Iceland." Judicial notice should also be taken of other statements made on the subject in documents which Iceland has brought to the Court's attention. Thus, the resolution adopted by the Althing on 15 February 1972 contains the statement that "owing to changed circumstances the Notes concerning fishery limits exchanged in 1961 are no longer applicable."

36. In these statements the Government of Iceland is basing itself on the principle of termination of a treaty by reason of change of circumstances. International law admits that a fundamental change in the circumstances which determined the parties to accept a treaty, if it has resulted in a radical transformation of the extent of the obligations imposed by it, may, under certain conditions, afford the party affected a ground for invoking the termination or suspension of the treaty. This principle, and the conditions and exceptions to which it is subject, have been embodied in Article 62 of the Vienna Convention on the Law of Treaties, which may in many respects be considered as a codification of existing customary law on the subject of the termination of a treaty relationship on account of change of circumstances.

37. One of the basic requirements embodied in that Article is that the change of circumstances must have been a fundamental one. In this respect the Government of Iceland has, with regard to developments in fishing techniques, referred in an official publication on *Fisheries Jurisdiction in Iceland,* enclosed with the Foreign Minister's letter of 29 May 1972 to the Registrar, to the increased exploitation of the fishery resources in the seas surrounding Iceland and to the danger of still further exploitation because of an increase in the catching capacity of fishing fleets. The Icelandic statements recall the exceptional dependence of that country on its fishing for its

existence and economic development. In his letter of 29 May 1972 the Minister stated:

> "The Government of Iceland, considering that the vital interests of the people of Iceland are involved, respectfully informs the Court that it is not willing to confer jurisdiction on the Court in any case involving the extent of the fishery limits of Iceland * * *"

In this same connection, the resolution adopted by the Althing on 15 February 1972 had contained a paragraph in these terms:

> "That the Governments of the United Kingdom and the Federal Republic of Germany be again informed that because of the vital interests of the nation and owing to changed circumstances the Notes concerning fishery limits exchanged in 1961 are no longer applicable and that their provisions do not constitute an obligation for Iceland."

38. The invocation by Iceland of its "vital interests," which were not made the subject of an express reservation to the acceptance of the jurisdictional obligation under the 1961 Exchange of Notes, must be interpreted, in the context of the assertion of changed circumstances, as an indication by Iceland of the reason why it regards as fundamental the changes which in its view have taken place in previously existing fishing techniques. This interpretation would correspond to the traditional view that the changes of circumstances which must be regarded as fundamental or vital are those which imperil the existence or vital development of one of the parties.

39. The Applicant, for its part, contends that the alterations and progress in fishing techniques have not produced in the waters around Iceland the consequences apprehended by Iceland and therefore that the changes are not of a fundamental or vital character. In its Memorial, it points out that, as regards the capacity of fishing fleets, increases in the efficiency of individual trawlers have been counter-balanced by the reduction in total numbers of vessels in national fleets fishing in the waters around Iceland, and that the statistics show that the total annual catch of demersal species has varied to no great extent since 1960.

40. The Court, at the present stage of the proceedings, does not need to pronounce on this question of fact, as to which there appears to be a serious divergence of views between the two Governments. If, as contended by Iceland, there have been any fundamental changes in fishing techniques in the waters around Iceland, those changes might be relevant for the decision on the merits of the dispute, and the Court might need to examine the contention at that stage, together with any other arguments that Iceland might advance in support of the validity of the extension of its fisheries jurisdiction beyond what was agreed to in the 1961 Exchange of Notes. But the alleged changes could not affect in the least the obligation to submit to the Court's jurisdiction, which is the only issue at the present stage of the proceedings. It follows that the apprehended dangers for the vital interests of Iceland, resulting from changes in fishing techniques, cannot constitute a fundamental change with respect to the lapse or subsistence of the compromissory clause establishing the Court's jurisdiction.

43. Moreover, in order that a change of circumstances may give rise to a ground for invoking the termination of a treaty it is also necessary that it should have resulted in a radical transformation of the extent of the obligations still to be performed. The change must have increased the burden of the obligations to be executed to the extent of rendering the performance something essentially different from that originally undertaken. In respect of the obligation with which the Court is here concerned, this condition is wholly unsatisfied; the change of circumstances alleged by Iceland cannot be said to have transformed radically the extent of the jurisdictional obligation which is imposed in the 1961 Exchange of Notes. The compromissory clause enabled either of the parties to submit to the Court any dispute between them relating to an extension of Icelandic fisheries jurisdiction in the waters above its continental shelf beyond the 12-mile limit. The present dispute is exactly of the character anticipated in the compromissory clause of the Exchange of Notes. Not only has the jurisdictional obligation not been radically transformed in its extent; it has remained precisely what it was in 1961.

* * *

44. In the United Kingdom Memorial it is asserted that there is a flaw in the Icelandic contention of change of circumstances: that the doctrine never operates so as to extinguish a treaty automatically or to allow an unchallengeable unilateral denunciation by one party; it only operates to confer a right to call for termination and, if that call is disputed, to submit the dispute to some organ or body with power to determine whether the conditions for the operation of the doctrine are present. In this connection the Applicant alludes to Articles 65 and 66 of the Vienna Convention on the Law of Treaties. Those Articles provide that where the parties to a treaty have failed within 12 months to achieve a settlement of a dispute by the means indicated in Article 33 of the United Nations Charter (which means include reference to judicial settlement) any one of the parties may submit the dispute to the procedure for conciliation provided in the Annex to the Convention.

45. In the present case, the procedural complement to the doctrine of changed circumstances is already provided for in the 1961 Exchange of Notes, which specifically calls upon the parties to have recourse to the Court in the event of a dispute relating to Iceland's extension of fisheries jurisdiction. Furthermore, any question as to the jurisdiction of the Court, deriving from an alleged lapse through changed circumstances, is resolvable through the accepted judicial principle enshrined in Article 36, paragraph 6, of the Court's Statute, which provides that "in the event of a dispute as to whether the Court has jurisdiction, the matter shall be settled by the decision of the Court." In this case such a dispute obviously exists, as can be seen from Iceland's communications to the Court, and to the other Party, even if Iceland has chosen not to appoint an Agent, file a Counter-Memorial or submit preliminary objections to the Court's jurisdiction; and Article 53 of the Statute both entitles the Court and, in the present proceedings, requires it to pronounce upon the question of its jurisdiction. This it has now done with binding force.

## F. WAR BETWEEN CONTRACTING PARTIES

### TECHT v. HUGHES

Court of Appeals of New York, 1920.

229 N.Y. 222, 128 N.E. 185, cert. denied, 254 U.S. 643, 41 S.Ct. 14, 65 L.Ed. 454.

[An American citizen died intestate in New York, where he owned real property, on December 27, 1917, twenty days after the outbreak of war between the United States and Austria–Hungary. One of the decedent's two daughters, Mrs. Techt, had previously married a citizen of Austria–Hungary and had, under Federal legislation then in force, thereby lost her United States citizenship and acquired that of her husband. The New York statute allowed citizens and "alien friends" to take and hold real property. Mrs. Techt's sister claimed the whole property on the ground that Mrs. Techt was an "alien enemy," but the Appellate Division pointed out that neither Mrs. Techt nor her husband had been interned or subjected to other restrictions as enemy nationals and held that Mrs. Techt was an "alien friend." 188 App.Div. 743, 177 N.Y.S. 420 (First Dep't 1919). On the sister's appeal, Mrs. Techt also relied on the Treaty of 1848 between the United States and Austria, 9 Stat. 944, which provided that nationals of either state could take real property by descent, sell it within two years, and remove the proceeds thereof. The Court of Appeals decided that Mrs. Techt, despite the absence of restrictions, was not an alien friend and not entitled to the statute's protection. Her claim therefore depended entirely upon the continuing effectiveness, despite the state of war, of the Treaty of 1848.]

CARDOZO, J. * * * The support of the statute failing, there remains the question of the treaty. The treaty, if in force, is the supreme law of the land (Const. U.S. art. 6) and supersedes all local laws inconsistent with its terms * * *. The plaintiff has an estate of inheritance, if the treaty is in force.

* * *

The effect of war upon the existing treaties of belligerents is one of the unsettled problems of the law. The older writers sometimes said that treaties ended ipso facto when war came. 3 Phillimore, Int.L. 794. The writers of our own time reject these sweeping statements. 2 Oppenheim, Int.L. § 99; Hall, Int.L. 398, 401; Fiore, Int.L. (Borchard's Transl.) § 845. International law to-day does not preserve treaties or annul them, regardless of the effects produced. It deals with such problems pragmatically, preserving or annulling as the necessities of war exact. It establishes standards, but it does not fetter itself with rules. When it attempts to do more, it finds that there is neither unanimity of opinion nor uniformity of practice. "The whole question remains as yet unsettled." Oppenheim, supra. This does not mean, of course, that there are not some classes of treaties about which there is general agreement. Treaties of alliance fall. Treaties of boundary or cession, "dispositive" or "transitory" conventions, survive. Hall, Int.L. pp. 398, 401; 2 Westlake, Int.L. 34; Oppenheim, supra. So, of course, do treaties which regulate the conduct of hostilities. Hall, supra; 5 Moore, Dig.Int.L. 372; Society for Propagation of the Gospel v. Town of New Haven, 8 Wheat. 464, 494, 5 L.Ed. 662.

Intention in such circumstances is clear. These instances do not represent distinct and final principles. They are illustrations of the same principle. They are applications of a standard. When I ask what that principle or standard is, and endeavor to extract it from the long chapters in the books, I get this, and nothing more: That provisions compatible with a state of hostilities, unless expressly terminated, will be enforced, and those incompatible rejected.

> Treaties lose their efficacy in war only if their execution is incompatible with war. Les traités ne perdent leur efficacité en temps de guerre que si leur exécution est incompatible avec la guerre elle-même.

Bluntschli, Droit International Codifié, sec. 538.

That in substance was Kent's view, here as often in advance of the thought of his day:

> All those duties, of which the exercise is not necessarily suspended by the war, subsist in their full force. The obligation of keeping faith is so far from ceasing in time of war that its efficacy becomes increased, from the increased necessity of it.

1 Kent, Comm. p. 176.

That, also, more recently, is the conclusion embodied by the Institute of the International Law in the rules voted at Christiania in 1912, which defined the effects of war on international conventions. In these rules, some classes of treaties are dealt with specially and apart. Treaties of alliance, those which establish a protectorate or a sphere of influence, and generally treaties of a political nature, are, it is said, dissolved. Dissolved, too, are treaties which have relation to the cause of war. But the general principle is declared that treaties which it is reasonably practicable to execute after the outbreak of hostilities must be observed then, as in the past. The belligerents are at liberty to disregard them only to the extent and for the time required by the necessities of war. * * *

This, I think, is the principle which must guide the judicial department of the government when called upon to determine during the progress of a war whether a treaty shall be observed, in the absence of some declaration by the political departments of the government that it has been suspended or annulled. A treaty has a two-fold aspect. In its primary operation, it is a compact between independent states. In its secondary operation, it is a source of private rights for individuals within states. Head Money Cases, 112 U.S. 580, 598, 5 Sup.Ct. 247, 28 L.Ed. 798. Granting that the termination of the compact involves the termination of the rights, it does not follow, because there is a privilege to rescind, that the privilege has been exercised. The question is not what states may do after war has supervened, and this without breach of their duty as members of the society of nations. The question is what courts are to presume that they have done. * * *

President and Senate may denounce the treaty, and thus terminate its life. Congress may enact an inconsistent rule, which will control the action of the courts. * * * The treaty of peace itself may set up new relations, and terminate earlier compacts, either tacitly or expressly. The proposed treaties with Germany and Austria give the victorious powers the privilege of choosing the treaties which are to be kept in force or abrogated. But until some one of these things is done, until some one of these events occurs, while war is still flagrant, and the will of the political departments of the government unrevealed, the courts, as I view their function, play a humbler and more cautious part. It is not for them to denounce treaties generally en bloc. Their part it is, as one provision or another is involved in some actual controversy before them, to determine whether, alone or by force of connection with an inseparable scheme, the provision is inconsistent with the policy or safety of the nation in the emergency of war, and hence presumably intended to be limited to times of peace. The mere fact that other portions of the treaty are suspended, or even abrogated, is not conclusive. The treaty does not fall in its entirety unless it has the character of an indivisible act. * * *

To determine whether it has this character, it is not enough to consider its name or label. No general formula suffices. We must consult in each case the nature and purpose of the specific articles involved. * * *

I find nothing incompatible with the policy of the government, with the safety of the nation, or with the maintenance of the war in the enforcement of this treaty, so as to sustain the plaintiff's title. We do not confiscate the lands or goods of the stranger within our gates. If we permit him to remain, he is free during good behavior to buy property and sell it. Trading with Enemy Act Oct. 6, 1917, 40 Stat. 411, c. 106. * * * A public policy not outraged by purchase will not be outraged by inheritance.

The plaintiff is a resident; but even if she were a nonresident, and were within the hostile territory, the policy of the nation would not divest her of the title whether acquired before the war or later. Custody would then be assumed by the Alien Property Custodian. The proceeds of the property, in the event of sale, would be kept within the jurisdiction. * * *

I do not overlook the statements which may be found here and there in the works of authors of distinction (Hall, supra; Halleck, Int.L. [4th Ed.] 314; Wheaton, Int.L. [5th Ed.] 377) that treaties of commerce and navigation are to be ranked in the class of treaties which war abrogates or at least suspends. Commerce is friendly intercourse. Friendly intercourse between nations is impossible in war. Therefore treaties regulating such intercourse are not operative in war. But stipulations do not touch commerce because they happen to be embodied in a treaty which is styled one to regulate or encourage commerce. We must be on our guard against being misled by labels. Bluntschli's warning, already quoted, reminds us that the nature and not the name of covenants determines whether they shall be disregarded or observed. * * *

Restrictions upon ownership of land by aliens have a history all their own, unrelated altogether to restrictions upon trade. * * * When removed, they cease to exist for enemies as well as friends, unless the statute removing them enforces a distinction. * * * More than that, the removal, when effected by treaty, gives reciprocal privileges to the subjects of each state, and is thus of value to one side as much as to the other. For this reason, the inference is a strong one, as was pointed out by the Master of the Rolls in Sutton v. Sutton, 1 Russ. & M. 664, 675, that the privileges, unless expressly revoked are intended to endure. Cf. 2 Westlake, p. 33; also Halleck, Int.L., supra. There, as in Society of Propagation of the Gospel v.

Town of New Haven, 8 Wheat. 464, 494, 5 L.Ed. 662, the treaty of 1794 between the United States and England, protecting the citizens of each in the enjoyment of their landed property, was held not to have been abrogated by the war of 1812. Undoubtedly there is a distinction between those cases and this, in that there the rights had become vested before the outbreak of the war. None the less, alike in reasoning and in conclusion, they have their value and significance. If stipulations governing the tenure of land survive the stress of war, though contained in a treaty which is described as one of amity, it is not perceived why they may not also survive, though contained in a treaty which is described as one of commerce. In preserving the right of inheritance for citizens of Austria when the land inherited is here we preserve the same right for our citizens when the land inherited is there. * * * Congress has not yet commanded us, and the exigencies of war, as I view them, do not constrain us, to throw these benefits away.

No one can study the vague and wavering statements of treaties and decision in this field of international law with any feeling of assurance at the end that he has chosen the right path. One looks in vain either for uniformity of doctrine or for scientific accuracy of exposition. There are wise cautions for the statesmen. There are few precepts for the judge. All the more, in this uncertainty, I am impelled to the belief that, until the political departments have acted, the courts, in refusing to give effect to treaties, should limit their refusal to the needs of the occasion; that they are not bound by any rigid formula to nullify the whole or nothing; and that, in determining whether this treaty survived the coming of war, they are free to make choice of the conclusion which shall seem the most in keeping with the traditions of the law, the policy of the statutes, the dictates of fair dealing, and the honor of the nation.

Judgment affirmed.

### *Notes*

1. What did the court mean by its reference to the "compatibility" of the treaty with "the policy or safety of the nation in the emergency of war"? How is this "compatibility" related to the intentions of the parties? What standards of "compatibility" did the court have in mind, and to what sources of policy did it look? Would the following statement of Secretary of State Lansing, if it had been brought to the court's attention, have required a different result? "[I]n view of the present state of war between the United States and Austria–Hungary and Germany, the Department does not regard these provisions [relating to inheritance of real property] as now in operation." Letter to the Alien Property Custodian, September 10, 1918, 5 Hackworth 379. The Supreme Court stated in Clark v. Allen, 331 U.S. 503, 513, 67 S.Ct. 1431, 1437, 91 L.Ed. 1633 (1947), that "[w]here the relevant historical sources and the instrument itself give no plain indication that it is to become inoperative in whole or in part on the outbreak of war, we are left to determine as *Techt v. Hughes,* supra, indicates, whether the provision under which rights are asserted is incompatible with national policy in time of war." The court held that a treaty provision similar to that involved in *Techt v. Hughes* was not incompatible with national policy. Compare Karnuth v. United States ex rel. Albro, 279 U.S. 231, 49 S.Ct. 274, 73 L.Ed. 677 (1929), in which Article III of the Jay Treaty of 1794, 8 Stat. 116, which provided for the free passage and repassage of British and United States citizens across the Canadian border, was held to have been abrogated by the war of 1812. The

Court pointed out that the treaty provision was "wholly promissory and prospective and necessarily ceases to operate in a state of war, since the passing and repassing of citizens or subjects of one sovereignty into the territory of another is inconsistent with the condition of hostility." The Court held that the "provision belongs to the class of treaties which does not survive war" between the parties. 279 U.S. at 240, 49 S.Ct. at 277, 73 L.Ed. at 682.

2. The Vienna Convention does not contain any provision concerning the effect of the outbreak of hostilities upon treaties. The International Law Commission explained that it:

> * * * considered that the study of this topic would inevitably involve a consideration of the effect of the provisions of the Charter concerning the threat or use of force upon the legality of the recourse to the particular hostilities in question; and it did not feel that this question could conveniently be dealt with in the context of its present work upon the law of treaties.

[1966] II Yb.I.L.C. 176 (para. 29).

## *THE EFFECTS OF ARMED CONFLICTS ON TREATIES RESOLUTION OF THE INSTITUT DE DROIT INTERNATIONAL*

Adopted 1985 (Helsinki Session).

### Article 1

For the purposes of this Resolution, the term "armed conflict" means a state of war or an international conflict which involve armed operations which by their nature or extent are likely to affect the operation of treaties between States parties to the armed conflict or between States parties to the armed conflict and third States, regardless of a formal declaration of war or other declaration by any or all of the parties to the armed conflict.

### Article 2

The outbreak of an armed conflict does not *ipso facto* terminate or suspend the operation of treaties in force between the parties to the armed conflict.

### Article 3

The outbreak of an armed conflict renders operative, in accordance with their own provisions, between the parties treaties which expressly provide that they are to be operative during an armed conflict or which by reason of their nature or purpose are to be regarded as operative during an armed conflict.

### Article 4

The existence of an armed conflict does not entitle a party unilaterally to terminate or to suspend the operation of treaty provisions relating to the protection of the human person, unless the treaty otherwise provides.

### Article 5

The outbreak of an armed conflict does not *ipso facto* terminate or suspend the operation of bilateral treaties in force between a party to that conflict and third States.

The outbreak of an armed conflict between some of the parties to a multilateral treaty does not *ipso facto* terminate or suspend the operation of that treaty between other contracting States or between them and the States parties to the armed conflict.

ARTICLE 6

A treaty establishing an international organization is not affected by the existence of an armed conflict between any of its parties.

ARTICLE 7

A State exercising its right of individual or collective self-defence in accordance with the Charter of the United Nations is entitled to suspend in whole or in part the operation of a treaty incompatible with the exercise of that right, subject to any consequences resulting from a later determination by the Security Council of that State as an aggressor.

ARTICLE 8

A State complying with a resolution by the Security Council of the United Nations concerning action with respect to threats to the peace, breaches of the peace or acts of aggression shall either terminate or suspend the operation of a treaty which would be incompatible with such resolution.

ARTICLE 9

A State committing aggression within the meaning of the Charter of the United Nations and Resolution 3314 (XXIX) of the General Assembly of the United Nations shall not terminate or suspend the operation of a treaty if the effect would be to benefit that State.

ARTICLE 10

This Resolution does not prejudge rights and duties arising from neutrality.

ARTICLE 11

At the end of an armed conflict and unless otherwise agreed, the operation of a treaty which has been suspended should be resumed as soon as possible.

### *Notes*

1. What are the implications of the distinction drawn in the above resolution between rights of states acting in self-defense and rights of aggressor states? If contradictory claims as to legality are made by the parties to armed conflicts and no authoritative determination is made by the U.N. Security Council, would states in conflict be entitled to determine unilaterally whether they may suspend treaties considered incompatible with their exercise of the right of self-defense? Would the practical effects be different if the above resolution were followed instead of the rationale in *Techt v. Hughes*?

2. The resolution adopted by the Institut in 1985 followed several years of study and discussion. For reports and comments see Annuaire of the Institut, volumes 59–I, p. 201–284 (1981), 59–II, p. 175–244 (1981), 61–I, p. 1–25 (1985), 61–II (1986).

3. The hostilities between the United States and Iran following the Iranian Revolution in 1979 raised some question of whether their bilateral treaties still remained in force. Concurring in Sedco, Inc. v. National Iranian Oil Company

and the Islamic Republic of Iran, 84 I.L.R. 521 (Iran–U.S.Cl.Trib. Mar. 27, 1986), Judge Brower rejected Iran's claim that the Treaty of Amity, Economic Relations, and Consular Rights between the United States and Iran was no longer applicable because of the souring of relations. Judge Brower pointed to statements by Iran subsequent to the Iranian Revolution referring to the continued validity of the treaty and Iran's failure to give notice of termination pursuant to the terms of the treaty.

# SECTION 7. STATE SUCCESSION IN RESPECT OF TREATIES

## A. GENERAL COMMENTS ON SUCCESSION TO TREATY OBLIGATIONS AND RIGHTS

### 1. *Introduction*

"Succession of states" refers to the fact of replacement of one state by another in the responsibility for the international relations of territory. That factual event is to be distinguished from its legal consequences, such as the transfer of rights or obligations on the occurrence of that event. This section deals with the rights and obligations in respect of treaties which derive from the factual change in the state responsible for international relations of a territory.

The replacement of one state by another is different, of course, from the changes in government which take place without affecting the legal identity of the state (see Chapter 4). Even a "social revolution" is considered only to change the régime and not the continuity of the state.

Succession of states has been a persistent feature of international history. The consolidation of national states, the creation of empires and their break-up, the secession of states, annexation, merger and consolidation, and, after the Second World War, decolonization are the historical events which have given rise to the legal questions of inheritance or devolution of rights and obligations in regard to treaties. From 1950 to 1980, the problems of state succession were most prominently associated with decolonization and the legal answers were largely addressed to those problems.

In the 1990's, new problems of succession arose, particularly in Europe. The unification of the two German states in 1990 raised questions of succession with respect to hundreds of treaties of practical importance. Even more complicated were the treaty succession issues presented by the dissolution of the Soviet Union in 1991 into 15 states, with perhaps more to come. The break-up of Yugoslavia into 5 states in 1992 and the splitting of Czechoslovakia into two also raised problems of treaty succession that included novel aspects. In 1993 it would be rash to predict (as the Restatement (Third) did in 1987) that a wave of emerging states is unlikely (section 208, Reporters note 4). Secessionist movements are on the increase in many countries and it is almost certain that new states will emerge. It is also safe to anticipate that some existing states will merge or be absorbed into other states and that some boundaries will be changed. Treaty succession questions will require solutions for these cases as for those that result from the splitting of states.

The legal consequences of state succession arise in respect of matters other than treaties. For example, questions arise in regard to the "inheritance" of state property, fiscal claims, the public debt of the replaced state, state contracts and concessions, nationality and transmissibility of state responsibility. These matters are dealt with separately from the questions which arise in regard to treaties. (See Chapter 7, on responsibility of states.)

### 2. *Devolution Agreements*

In a number of cases, predecessor and successor states have made agreements concerning the "devolution" of rights and obligations under treaties. Such agreements were generally used by the United Kingdom when transferring sovereignty to former colonial territories. Some other colonial powers also had such agreements. Under their terms, they deal only with the transfer of treaty rights and obligations from predecessor to successor. They do not in themselves bind other states parties to the predecessor's treaties. The International Law Commission has commented on such agreements, as follows:

> (18) The practice of States does not admit, therefore, the conclusion that a devolution agreement should be considered as by itself creating a legal nexus between the successor State and third States parties, in relation to treaties applicable to the successor State's territory prior to its independence. Some successor States and some third States parties to one of those treaties have undoubtedly tended to regard a devolution agreement as creating a certain presumption of the continuance in force of certain types of treaties. But neither successor States nor third States nor depositaries have as a general rule attributed automatic effects to devolution agreements. Accordingly, State practice as well as the relevant principles of the law of treaties would seem to indicate that devolution agreements, however important as general manifestations of the attitude of successor States to the treaties of their predecessors, should be considered as *res inter alios acta* for the purposes of their relations with third States.

[1974] II (I) Yb.I.L.C. 186.

In the case of the "reunification" of Germany, the problems of treaty succession of the two states were dealt with principally by three treaties entered into by the two German states. One of the treaties, the Treaty of Final Settlement of 1990 was also signed by the four main allies of World War Two, terminated the rights and responsibilities of the four powers and the quadripartite treaties relating to Germany. 29 I.L.M. 1186 (1990). This treaty also known as the Two Plus Four treaty also provided that the current external borders of the two states shall be final. The right of united Germany to belong to alliances was also recognized.

Another treaty, the treaty on Unification of September 18, 1990 recognized that the treaties in force in the Federal Republic (i.e., West Germany) before unification now extend to the territory of the former East German state (G.D.R.). With respect to treaties of the former G.D.R. the Unification Treaty calls for consultation with the other parties to settle the questions of continuity, adjustment or termination. A third treaty (the "State Treaty") established the union between the two parts of Germany and laid down fundamental constitutional principles. As indicated, these treaties on unification still leave open for consultation which treaties of the former GDR will continue in force for that territory. It is recognized that "GDR treaties with ideological-political contents inconsistent with the attitude of the unified state are no longer valid." H. Steinberger, Germany Reunified: International and Constitutional Problems. 1992 Brigham Young U.L.Rev. 23.

### *3. Unilateral Declarations by Successor States*

A number of newly independent states have made unilateral declarations of a general character regarding the continuation of treaties of their predecessor states. Such declarations have varied in form but have generally provided for the provisional application of such treaties during a period in which the new state would examine the treaties and determine which would be adopted and which terminated. Such declarations were designed to avoid sudden discontinuity and also to avoid an assumption of universal succession. They came to be known as "pick and choose" declarations. For examples of such declarations, see [1974] II (I) Yb.I.L.C. 188–192. The International Law Commission described the legal effect of such agreements, as follows:

> Accordingly, the legal effect of the declarations seems to be that they furnish bases for a *collateral* agreement in simplified form between the newly independent State and the individual parties to its predecessor's treaties for the provisional application of the treaties after independence. The agreement may be express but may equally arise from the conduct of any individual State party to any treaty covered by the declaration, in particular from acts showing that it regards the treaty as still having application with respect to the territory.

[1974] II (I) Yb.I.L.C. 192.

### *4. The Vienna Convention on the Succession of States in Respect of Treaties*

The comprehensive Vienna Convention on the Succession of States in Respect of Treaties was concluded in 1978 by a conference convened by the United Nations. One hundred states participated in the conference.

The Vienna Convention on Succession of States was the culmination of work commenced by the International Law Commission in 1962 and carried out by the Commission and Governments on the basis of draft articles and commentaries prepared by special rapporteurs during the decade 1964 to 1974. The conference which adopted the Convention took place in Vienna in two sessions in 1977 and 1978. The Convention was opened for signature on August 23, 1978 "in a single copy in the Arabic, Chinese, English, French, Russian and Spanish languages, each text being equally authentic." It is to enter into force when 15 states have ratified or acceded to it. As of 31 December 1991, only nine states had adhered to the Convention.

The Convention by its terms applies only in respect of a succession of states which has occurred after the entry into force of the Convention except as otherwise agreed. Agreements to apply the Convention to earlier treaties may be made by declarations of successor states in relation to any other state accepting such declaration (Article 7).

The Convention includes the "saving clause" that the non-retroactivity provision is without prejudice to the application of any rules to which states would be subject under international law independently of the Convention. As this Convention like the Vienna Convention on the Law of Treaties is in large part intended to codify customary law, many of its articles may be considered as declaratory of existing law. However, it cannot be presumed that all articles are declaratory. The U.S. State Department Legal Advisor stated that the rules of the Vienna Convention were "generally regarded as declarative of existing customary international law by the United States" Robert Owen quoted in M. Leich, Digest of US Practice (1980) 1041 n. 43.

The material which follows will deal with the major features of the new Convention. Explanatory material is taken largely from the authoritative commentary of the International Law Commission in its report of 1974. That report and earlier special reports of the rapporteurs also contain extensive material on cases and treaty practice. References to articles in the material that follows are to the articles of the Convention.

### 5. *The Restatement (Third)*

§ 210 of the Restatement (Third) provides:

**§ 210. State Succession: International Agreements**

(1) When part of the territory of a state becomes territory of another state, the international agreements of the predecessor state cease to have effect in respect of that territory and the international agreements of the successor state come into force there.

(2) When a state is absorbed by another state, the international agreements of the absorbed state are terminated and the international agreements of the absorbing state become applicable to the territory of the absorbed state.

(3) When part of a state becomes a new state, the new state does not succeed to the international agreements to which the predecessor state was party, unless, expressly or by implication, it accepts such agreements and the other party or parties thereto agree or acquiesce.

(4) Pre-existing boundary and other territorial agreements continue to be binding notwithstanding Subsections (1)–(3).

The above text is generally consistent with the Vienna Convention but varies from it in certain respects. For example, it rejects the distinction made in the Vienna Convention between newly independent states emerging from colonialism and states ensuing from separation of parts of a State. See Section D below.

## B. TREATIES NOT AFFECTED BY SUCCESSION OF STATES (TERRITORIAL TREATIES)

*INTERNATIONAL LAW COMMISSION REPORT*

[1974] II (I) Yb.I.L.C. 157, 196, 201 and 206.

(1) Both in the writings of jurists and in State practice frequent reference is made to certain categories of treaties, variously described as of a

"territorial," "dispositive," "real" or "localized" character, as binding upon the territory affected notwithstanding any succession of States. The question of what will for convenience be called in this commentary "territorial treaties" is at once important, complex and controversial. In order to underline its importance the Commission need only mention that it touches such major matters as international boundaries, rights of transit on international waterways or over another State, the use of international rivers, demilitarization or neutralization of particular localities, etc.

* * *

(17) The weight of the evidence of State practice and of legal opinion in favour of the view that in principle a boundary settlement is unaffected by the occurrence of a succession of States is strong and powerfully reinforced by the decision of the United Nations Conference on the Law of Treaties to except from the fundamental change of circumstances rule a treaty which establishes a boundary. Consequently, the Commission considered that the present draft must state that boundary settlements are not affected by the occurrence of a succession of States as such. Such a provision would relate exclusively to the effect of the succession of States on the boundary settlement. It would leave untouched any other ground of claiming the revision or setting aside of the boundary settlement, whether self-determination or the invalidity or termination of the treaty. Equally, of course, it would leave untouched any legal ground of defence to such a claim that might exist. In short, the mere occurrence of a succession of States would neither consecrate the existing boundary if it was open to challenge nor deprive it of its character as legally established boundary, if such it was at the date of the succession of States.

* * *

Running through the precedents and the opinions of writers are strong indications of a belief that certain treaties attach a régime to territory which continues to bind it in the hands of any successor State. Not infrequently other elements enter into the picture, such as an allegation of fundamental change of circumstances or the allegedly limited competence of the predecessor State, and the successor State in fact claims to be free of the obligation to respect the régime. Nevertheless, the indications of the general acceptance of such a principle remain. * * * The evidence does not, however, suggest that this category of treaties should embrace a very wide range of so-called territorial treaties. On the contrary, this category seems to be limited to cases where a State by a treaty grants a right to use territory, or to restrict its own use of territory, which is intended to attach to territory of a foreign State or, alternatively, to be for the benefit of a group of States or of all States generally. There must in short be something in the nature of a territorial régime.

### *Notes*

1. Was it consistent for newly independent states to demand freedom to continue or terminate treaties of predecessor states but insist that boundary treaties remain in force? Even when boundary disputes have arisen between a newly independent state and another state, the new states have not claimed they were free from the obligation to respect boundaries made in treaties of their

predecessor colonial rulers. See Charter of the Organization of African Unity Art. III(3).

2. Does Article 11 bar a successor state from challenging an existing boundary based on a treaty? What grounds might be advanced for such challenge?

3. Article 12 relates to "other territorial régimes" not affected by succession. Why did not this Article (and Article 11) simply provide for succession, i.e., continuity of rights and obligations, instead of declaring that the territorial régime is not affected by succession? In either case, there would be a rule of continuity. Is it not artificial to separate succession in respect of the territorial régime from succession in respect of the treaty establishing that régime? On the other hand, does it favor stability if the territorial régime (or boundary régime) is regarded as established by an executed treaty and that this legal situation rather than the treaty passed to the successor state? For discussion see [1974] II (I) Yb.I.L.C. 201 (paragraphs 18–20) and 206 (para. 36.)

4. Note the distinction drawn in Article 12 between territorial régimes for the benefit of a particular territory and those for the benefit of a group of states or of all states. Is this distinction useful in clarifying the territorial régimes covered by Article 12? Consider examples in the two categories.

5. Note that paragraph 3 of Article 12 excludes from that article treaties for the establishment of foreign military bases. Would such treaties otherwise have been binding on successor states? The United Kingdom had in 1941 granted to the United States military bases in British colonies in the West Indies. When these colonies were approaching independence, the United States declared that the future of the bases must be a matter of agreement with the newly independent states. Would the U.S. have had legal grounds to insist on the retention of the bases irrespective of the successor's consent? See Esgain, Military Servitudes and the New Nations, in The New Nations in International Law and Diplomacy 42–97 (O'Brien ed. 1963).

## C. THE "MOVING TREATY-FRONTIERS" RULE

### *INTERNATIONAL LAW COMMISSION REPORT*

[1974] II (I) Yb.I.L.C. 157, 208.

(1) [Article 15] concerns the application of a rule, which is often referred to by writers as the "moving treaty-frontiers" rule, in cases where territory not itself a State undergoes a change of sovereignty and the successor State is an already existing State. The article thus concerns cases which do not involve a union of States or merger of one State with another, and equally do not involve the emergence of a newly independent State. The moving treaty-frontiers principle also operates in varying degrees in certain other contexts. But in these other contexts it functions in conjunction with other rules, while in the cases covered by the present article—the mere addition of a piece of territory to an existing State—the moving treaty-frontiers rule appears in pure form. Although in a sense the rule underlies much of the law regarding succession of States in respect of treaties, the present case constitutes a particular category of succession of States, which the Commission considered should be in a separate part. Having regard to its relevance in other contexts, the Commission decided to place it in part II of the draft, immediately after the general provisions in part I.

(2) Shortly stated, the moving treaty-frontiers rule means that, on a territory's undergoing a change of sovereignty, it passes automatically out of the treaty régime of the predecessor sovereign into the treaty régime of the successor sovereign. It thus has two aspects, one positive and the other negative. The positive aspect is that the treaties of the successor State begin automatically to apply in respect of the territory in question as from the date of the succession. The negative aspect is that the treaties of the predecessor State, in turn, cease automatically to apply in respect of such territory as from that date.

### *Notes*

1. Paragraph (a) of Article 15 provides that treaties of the predecessor state cease to be in force in respect of the territory to which the succession relates. It does not affect the continued application of the treaties of the predecessor apart from their territorial scope. However, would the predecessor state still be bound by a treaty if the separated territory was a large or important area for the application of the treaty? What rule would provide a ground for termination?

2. Assuming the factual conditions for the application of the "moving treaty-frontier" rule in accordance with Article 15, would the successor be bound to consider the treaties of the predecessor state as in force for the territory transferred?

3. How should the German unification have been treated under the principles of the Vienna succession treaty? Since the unification did not create a new state but only an enlarged Federal Republic of Germany, the "moving frontier" rule would seem to apply. However, this would have meant that all the GDR treaties would cease to be in force (Article 14), a result that was not desired (as noted above). If the uniting of the two states was treated as creating a new state, the treaties of both states would remain in force unless otherwise agreed or unless it appears that the application of the treaty would be incompatible with its object or "would radically change the conditions for the operation of the treaty" (Article 30). This formula was not satisfactory in the German case because many of the GDR treaties had ideological or political elements incompatible with the unified state. Accordingly, the question of succession of the GDR treaties was left open, pending consultation with the other states parties to them. See H. Steinberger, Germany Reunified, 1992 Brigham Young U.L.Rev. 23.

## D. THE NEWLY INDEPENDENT STATE

### *INTERNATIONAL LAW COMMISSION REPORT*

[1974] II (I) Yb.I.L.C. 157, 211–217, 237, 239.

(2) The question of a newly independent State's inheritance of the treaties of its predecessor has two aspects: (a) whether that State is under an *obligation* to continue to apply those treaties to its territory after the succession of States, and (b) whether it is *entitled* to consider itself as a party to the treaties in its own name after the succession of States. These two aspects of succession in the matter of treaties cannot in the view of the Commission be treated as if they were the same problem. If a newly independent State were to be considered as automatically bound by the

treaty obligations of its predecessor, reciprocity would, it is true, require that it should also be entitled to invoke the rights contained in the treaties. And, similarly, if a newly independent State were to possess and to assert a right to be considered as a party to its predecessor's treaties, reciprocity would require that it should at the same time be subject to the obligations contained in them. But reciprocity does not demand that, if a State should be *entitled* to consider itself a party to a treaty it must equally be *bound* to do so. Thus, a State which signs a treaty subject to ratification has a right to become a party but is under no obligation to do so. In short, the question whether a newly independent State is under an *obligation* to consider itself a party to its predecessor's treaties is legally quite distinct from the question whether it may have a *right* to consider or to make itself a party to those treaties.

Clearly, if a newly independent State is under a legal *obligation* to assume its predecessor's treaties, the question whether it has a right to claim the status of a party to them becomes irrelevant. The first point, therefore, is to determine whether such a legal obligation does exist in general international law, and it is this point to which the present article is directed.

(3) The majority of writers take the view, supported by State practice, that a newly independent State begins its life with a clean slate, except in regard to "local" or "real" obligations. The clean slate is generally recognized to be the "traditional" view on the matter. It has been applied to earlier cases of newly independent States emerging either from former colonies (i.e., the United States of America; the Spanish American Republics) or from a process of secession or dismemberment (i.e., Belgium, Panama, Ireland, Poland, Czechoslovakia, Finland). * * *

* * *

(6) The metaphor of the clean slate is a convenient way of expressing the basic concept that a newly independent State begins its international life free from any *obligation* to continue in force treaties previously applicable with respect to its territory simply by reason of that fact. But even when that basic concept is accepted, the metaphor appears in the light of existing State practice to be at once too broad and too categoric. It is too broad in that it suggests that, so far as concerns the newly independent States, the prior treaties are wholly expunged and are without any relevance to its territory. The very fact that prior treaties are often continued or renewed indicates that the clean slate metaphor does not express the whole truth. The metaphor is too categoric in that it does not make clear whether it means only that a newly independent State is not *bound* to recognize any of its predecessor's treaties as applicable in its relations with other States, or whether it means also that a newly independent State is not *entitled* to claim any right to be or become a party to any of its predecessor's treaties. As already pointed out, a newly independent State may have a clean slate in regard to any *obligation* to continue to be bound by its predecessor's treaties without it necessarily following that the new independent State is without any *right* to establish itself as a party to them.

(2) * * * Moreover, although modern depositary and State practice does not support the thesis that a newly independent State is under any general obligation to consider itself a successor to treaties previously applicable in

respect of its territory, it does appear to support the conclusion that a newly independent State has a general *right of option* to be a party to certain categories of multilateral treaties in virtue of its character as a successor State. A distinction must, however, be drawn in this connexion between multilateral treaties in general and multilateral treaties of a restricted character, for it is only in regard to the former that a newly independent State appears to have an actual right of option to establish itself as a party *independently of the consent of the other States parties and quite apart from the final clauses of the treaty.*

(9) * * * If the conclusions drawn by the Commission from the modern practice are correct what the principle confers upon a newly independent State is simply a *right of option* to establish itself as a separate party to the treaty in virtue of the legal nexus established by its predecessor between the territory to which the succession of States relates and the treaty. It is not a right to "succeed" to its predecessor's participation in the treaty in the sense of a right to step exactly, and only to step exactly, into the shoes of its predecessor. The newly independent State's right is rather to *notify its own consent to be considered as a separate party to the treaty.* In short, a newly independent State whose territory was subject to the régime of a multilateral treaty at the date of the State's succession is entitled, simply in virtue of that fact, to establish itself as a separate party to the treaty.

(2) * * * If in the case of many multilateral treaties that legal nexus appears to generate an actual right for the newly independent State to establish itself as a party or a contracting State, this does not appear to be so in the case of bilateral treaties.

* * *

(12) From the evidence adduced in the preceding paragraphs, the Commission concludes that succession in respect of bilateral treaties has an essentially voluntary character: voluntary, that is, on the part not only of the newly independent State but also of the other interested State. On this basis the fundamental rule to be laid down for bilateral treaties appears to be that their continuance in force after independence is a matter of agreement, express or tacit, between the newly independent State and the other State party to the predecessor State's treaty.

### *Notes*

1. A newly independent state is defined in Article 2, paragraph 1(f). To meet the definition, the new state must have been a "dependent territory for the international relations of which the predecessor state was responsible." Is this definition adequate to distinguish between separation of a part of a state (Article 34) and the creation of a newly independent state? What criteria apply in case of secession?

2. Are newly independent states entitled to automatic admission to international organizations of which their predecessor states were members? Article 4 of Convention provides that the rules of the international organization concerning acquisition of membership shall apply. See commentary of International Law Commission on Article 4 in [1974] II (I) Yb.I.L.C. 177–180. In practice, the United Nations and the specialized agencies have recognized that a new state resulting from secession would have to apply for membership irrespective of its

inclusion in a member state. When British India, a UN member split into India and Pakistan, the UN General Assembly decided that India (the larger part) continued as the UN member whereas Pakistan was required to apply for membership. On the basis of an opinion by the UN Legal Department, the Legal Committee of the General Assembly declared that as a general principle a member state did not cease to be a member because its boundary or constitution had been changed. It would be necessary to show that it ceased to exist as a legal personality before it would lose its membership. The new state formed from the territory would have to submit a new application for membership. See Schachter, 25 Brit.Y.B.I.L. (1948) at 101–109.

3. When the USSR dissolved in 1990, Russia, the largest and most important Republic, was accepted as a continuing member. It was also accepted by the General Assembly and the Security Council as the successor to the USSR under Article 23, thus confirming permanent membership and the veto right on Russia. The actual text of the article was not amended; it still includes the Union of Soviet Socialist Republics. Ukraine and Belarus (formerly Byelorussia) that had been original members of the UN continued as members. All of the other Republics were admitted by separate votes to membership. They were also admitted to most of the specialized agencies of the United Nations through the normal admission procedure.

4. Are the successor states to the Soviet Union to be treated as "newly independent states" and therefore not bound to maintain in force its predecessors treaties in their respective territories? In view of the actual conditions of the USSR is it plausible to conclude that since none of the component states had been truly self-governing, they were now "newly independent" and therefore the "clean slate" rule applied? An alternative view would be that although state power in the USSR was concentrated in the Communist Party and Russia was dominant, the other republics were not excluded as such from having its citizens take part in the central government. They could appropriately be distinguished from colonies ruled by a metropolitan power. On this premise, they would be "separating" states and the rule of continuity would apply—that is, any treaty in force in respect of the entire territory of the USSR would continue in force for each successor state (See infra). The Restatement (Third) written prior to the USSR dissolution would apply the clean slate rule to any new state that separated from the predecessor state. See § 210(3). It considers that the distinction between former dependent territories and other separated areas does not reflect consistent practice and would be difficult to apply. Section 210, Reporters' Note 4.

Would the effect of the Restatement rule in regard to the former USSR mean that the new Republics (other than Russia, Ukraine, Belarus) be free to reject all the multilateral treaties to which the USSR had been a party? Would it not be plausible to consider that the Soviet régime constitutionally provided for participation on a formally equal basis to all its Republics? See discussion infra, Chapter 11, p. 1042 on succession to arms control treaties of the USSR.

4. Note that under Article 17(3) the participation of a newly independent state in a treaty must have the concurrence of all the parties, if "by reason of the limited number of the negotiating states and the object and purpose of the treaty" the treaty should be so construed. Is there an analogy between this paragraph and Article 20(2) of the Vienna Convention on the Law of Treaties?

5. When a newly independent state chooses to become a party, does it inherit the reservations, acceptances, and objections of the predecessor exactly as

they were at the date of the succession? Is it free to withdraw in regard to itself any such reservation or objection of the predecessor? See Article 20 of the Convention. For state practice, see commentary of the Commission in [1974] II (I) Yb.I.L.C. 222–227.

6. Although the "clean slate" metaphor applies to bilateral treaties (since the successor state as stated in Article 24 has neither an obligation nor a right to become a party), in actual practice there has been a considerable measure of continuity in respect of bilateral treaties in certain categories. Such "*de facto* continuity" is frequent in regard to agreements on air transport, trade, technical assistance, tax, visa requirements and powers of consuls. The International Law Commission took note of such continuity but concluded that the continuity derived from mutual consent and not from a sense of a legal rule. They noted that the unilateral declarations (supra) and the devolution agreements assumed that, in general, bilateral treaties required the consent of the other contracting party for their continuance in force. See commentary in Commission report of 1974, id. at 236–241.

7. Article 24 provides that consent to continuity of a bilateral treaty may be inferred from conduct of the two states concerned. Would this mean that the two states need only continue to apply the treaty without any formalities as to its continuance? Would a mere listing of a treaty as in force constitute evidence of consent? Consider the relation of this clause to the principle of good faith and acquiescence as expressed in Article 45 of the Vienna Convention on the Law of Treaties.

8. The Restatement (Third) does not adopt the distinction between former colonies and new states arising from succession. Section 210, Reporters' Note 4 says that the distinction:

> does not reflect consistent practice and would be difficult to apply. Moreover, some "dependent territories", such as the British dominions, had a greater voice in making international agreements applicable to their territory than some "separated states" such as Bangladesh.

9. Has the international trend in the period after decolonization supported a presumption of continuity in cases of dissolution or secession rather than the rupture sanctioned by the clean slate theory? Should a presumption of continuity make allowance for negotiation in particular cases for exceptions? See comments of Crawford and Williamson in 86 Proc.Am.Soc.Int.L. 10–23 (1992).

## E. UNITING AND SEPARATION OF STATES

### 1. *Uniting of States*

#### *INTERNATIONAL LAW COMMISSION REPORT*

[1974] II (I) Yb.I.L.C. 157, 253–258.

(1) These articles deal with a succession of States arising from the uniting in one State of two or more *States,* which had separate international personalities at the date of the succession. They cover the case where one State merges with another State even if the international personality of the latter continues after they have united. The case of the emergence of a newly independent State from the combining of two or more territories, not already States at the date of the succession, has been dealt with separately

in part III, article 29. The transfer of a mere *territory* to an existing State also falls under an earlier provision of the draft articles, namely the moving treaty-frontier rule set out in article 14.

(2) The succession of States envisaged in the present articles does not take into account the particular form of the internal constitutional organization adopted by the successor State. The uniting may lead to a wholly unitary State, to a federation or to any other form of constitutional arrangement. In other words, the degree of separate identity retained by the original States after their uniting, within the constitution of the successor State, is irrelevant for the operation of the provisions set forth in these articles.

(3) Being concerned only with the uniting of two or more States in one *State*, associations of States having the character of intergovernmental organizations such as, for example, the United Nations, the specialized agencies, OAS, the Council of Europe, CMEA, etc., fall completely outside the scope of the articles; as do some hybrid unions which may appear to have some analogy with a uniting of States but which do not result in a new *State* and do not therefore constitute a succession of *States*.

* * *

(27) In the light of the above practice and the opinion of the majority of writers, the Commission concluded that a uniting of States should be regarded as in principle involving the continuance in force of the treaties of the States in question *ipso jure*. This solution is also indicated by the need of preserving the stability of treaty relations. As sovereign States, the predecessor States had a complex of treaty relations with other States and ought not to be able at will to terminate those treaties by uniting in a single State. The point has particular weight today in view of the tendency of States to group themselves in new forms of association.

(28) Consequently, the Commission formulated the rule embodied in article 30 as the corresponding article of the 1972 draft, on the basis of the *ipso jure* continuity principle duly qualified by other elements which need also to be taken into account; i.e. the agreement of the States concerned, the compatibility of the treaties in force prior to the uniting of the States with the situation resulting from it, the effects of the change on the operation of the treaty and the territorial scope which those treaties had under their provisions.

## *Notes*

1. How does one distinguish a uniting of states from the "moving frontier" case? When Texas, then an independent state, was admitted to the United States in 1845, the United States considered that Texas's pre-union treaties lapsed. However, Great Britain and France objected, arguing that Texas could not, by joining the U.S., exonerate itself from its existing treaties. Later, the U.S. view seems to have been accepted by Great Britain. [1974] II (I) Yb.I.L.C. 254.

2. Recent examples of union of sovereign states are those of Egypt and Syria in 1958 into the United Arab Republic (later dissolved) and of Tanganyika and Zanzibar into the United Republic of Tanzania (1964). In both cases, the

treaties of the individual constituent states were continued in force within their regional limits.

3. May the evolution of the European Economic Community lead to its being treated as a union of states for purposes of Article 31? Although the Community has treaty-making authority in some areas, it is not at present regarded as a state and *a fortiori* it is not a successor state in respect of treaties of its member states. The pre-Community treaties of member states are dealt with by the Treaty of Rome (the constituent instrument of the EEC) in terms of the compatibility of obligations of successive treaties relating to the same subject matter. See Article 234 of the Treaty of Rome. When new members have joined the EEC they have been required to become bound by certain prior treaties made by the EEC. This is therefore a matter of express agreement rather than by operation of law consequent on succession.

4. The Restatement (Third), distinguishes between absorption of one state by another and the merger of two or more states into a new state that is a federal union. Section 210, Comment *c* states:

*Federal union.* It is sometimes difficult to distinguish between an absorption of one state by another and the merger of two or more states into a federal union. See Reporters' Note 2. In a federal union, the effect on preexisting obligations may depend on the constitutional character of the union and the nature of the preexisting rights and obligations. If the constituent entities have no power under the union to maintain pre-existing agreements, their obligations terminate when the union comes into effect. If the agreement remains within the power of a constituent entity, the agreement continues in force in the territory of that entity.

In general, when the constituent states merging to form a federal union had each been a party to a multilateral agreement, the federal union becomes a party to the agreement and the constituent entities cease to be parties. However, membership in an international organization is generally not treated as automatic for a new federal union but must be conferred, even if the constituent entities had all been members of the organization.

### 2. *Separation of States*

#### *INTERNATIONAL LAW COMMISSION REPORT*

[1974] II (I) Yb.I.L.C. 157, 260, and 265.

(1) These articles deal with questions of succession in respect of treaties in cases where a part or parts of the territory of a State separate to form one or more independent States. The situations covered by the articles presuppose a predecessor State and one or more successor States, namely, the new State or States established in part or parts of the former territory of the predecessor State. The articles regulate the effect of such a succession of States on treaties in force at the date of the succession of States in respect of the whole or part of the territory of the predecessor State from the standpoint of:

(a) The successor or successor States, whether or not the predecessor State continues to exist (article 34) and

(b) of the predecessor State, when it continues to exist (article 35). * * *

* * *

(23) From a purely theoretical point of view, there may be a distinction between dissolution and separation of part of a State. In the former case, the predecessor State disappears; in the latter case, the predecessor State continues to exist after the separation. This theoretical distinction might have implications in the field of succession in respect of treaties, but it does not necessarily follow that the effects of the succession of States in the two categories of cases must be different for the parts which become new States. In other words, it is possible to treat the new States resulting from the dissolution of an old State as parts separating from that State.

* * *

(25) * * * The Commission concluded that although some discrepancies might be found in State practice, still that practice was sufficiently consistent to support the formulation of a rule which, with the necessary qualifications, would provide that treaties in force at the date of the dissolution should remain in force *ipso jure* with respect to each State emerging from the dissolution. The fact that the situation may be regarded as one of "separation of part or parts of a State" rather than one of "dissolution" does not alter this basic conclusion.

(27) The available evidence of practice during the United Nations period appears to indicate that, at least in some circumstances, the separated territory which becomes a sovereign State may be regarded as a newly independent State to which in principle the rules of the present draft articles concerning newly independent States should apply. * * *

### *Notes*

1. Who determines whether a separated part of a state shall be considered as a newly independent state or as governed by Article 34? When Singapore separated from Malaysia in 1965, it chose to act as a newly independent state not bound by the treaty obligations of its predecessor except insofar as it consented. Assuming the Convention was in force, could Singapore's action have been challenged on the ground that it had not been a "dependent territory" of the Federation of Malaysia and therefore could not release itself from treaty obligations in accordance with Article 34?

2. Consider contemporary examples of territorial units in which separatist movements are strong. If successful, would the new states have grounds to characterize themselves as "newly independent" for purposes of the Convention on Succession of States in Respect of Treaties? Would they have reasons to favor application of Article 34 instead?

# Chapter 7

# INTERNATIONAL RESPONSIBILITY AND REMEDIES

## SECTION 1. GENERAL PRINCIPLES OF INTERNATIONAL RESPONSIBILITY

If a state by its act or omission breaches an international obligation, it incurs international responsibility. If the consequence is an injury to another state, the delinquent state is responsible to make reparation or give satisfaction for the breach to the injured state. Thus when an international wrongful act occurs, it creates new legal relations between the states concerned independent of their consent. A state injured by a violation may seek redress by claims made through diplomatic channels or through a procedure of dispute settlement to which the states concerned have agreed. Under some circumstances, the injured state may take measures of self-help or counter-measures not involving use of force.

In the *Corfu Channel Case,* the International Court of Justice held Albania liable for certain omissions, in particular the absence of a warning of the danger of mines laid in her territorial waters. The International Court stated:

> These grave omissions involve the international responsibility of Albania. The Court therefore reaches the conclusion that Albania is responsible under international law for the explosions which occurred * * * and for the damage and loss of human life which resulted from them and that there is a duty upon Albania to pay compensation to the United Kingdom.

1949 I.C.J. 23.

In the much quoted words of the Permanent Court of International Justice:

> It is a principle of international law that the breach of an agreement involves an obligation to make reparation in an adequate form. Reparation therefore is the indispensable complement of a failure to

apply a convention and there is no necessity for this to be stated in the convention itself.

Chorzów Factory Case (Jurisdiction) 1927 P.C.I.J., Ser.A, No. 9, p. 21.

As these statements indicate, responsibility arises whenever there is a breach of an international obligation, whatever its origin. There is no distinction in this respect between breach of an agreement or a violation of a rule of international law. Moreover, since any violation of an obligation resulting in injury to another state gives rise to international responsibility, the substantive grounds for such responsibility are as numerous and varied as the norms of international law.

International responsibility in the general sense is therefore distinct from the rules that determine the legality or illegality of conduct. The latter are sometimes described as "primary" rules, the breach of which is the source of responsibility. The general rules of responsibility are referred to as "secondary," inasmuch as they determine the legal consequences of failure to fulfill obligations established by the primary rules. See Report of the I.L.C., [1973] II Yb.I.L.C. 169–70. This does not mean, of course, that all breaches are treated in the same way. The gravity of a wrongful act and its consequences affect responsibility. Other distinctions are also relevant. But, in the language of the International Law Commission:

> [I]t is one thing to define a rule and the obligation it imposes, and another to determine whether there has been a breach of that obligation and what should be the consequences. Only the second aspect comes within the sphere of responsibility proper.

Id. at 170.

Accordingly, the material in this chapter deals with the general conditions under which a state may be held to have committed an international delict which gives rise to international responsibility. It also deals with the consequences that an internationally wrongful act may have such as the obligation of reparation and the procedures that may be used for redress. Specifically, the following questions are addressed:

— What is the "act of a state" under international law: when is an act or omission by human beings (individually or collectively) attributable to the state? (Section 2.)

— Is it a necessary element of a wrongful act that it include fault on the part of those responsible for the act? (Section 3.)

— Is there a general duty on the part of a state to take steps to prevent harm to other states? (Section 3.)

— Does breach of an international obligation by a state towards another state infringe the right of that state irrespective of actual injury or damage to it? (Section 4.)

— If a state violates a rule of customary law or a multilateral treaty, is it internationally responsible to all other states bound by the custom or treaty? (Section 4.)

— Should a distinction be made in legal consequences among wrongful acts based on the importance to the international community of the obligation violated? Should some violations of fundamental rules be treated as international crimes rather than as international delicts? (Section 5.)

— What circumstances generally preclude wrongfulness and responsibility for acts that are not in conformity with international obligations? Such circumstances may include prior consent of the injured state, distress, necessity, *force majeure,* self-defense. (Section 6.)

— Under what conditions may a state injured by a wrongful act take counter-measures that would otherwise be unlawful. (Section 7.)

— What requirements are imposed on a state responsible for a wrongful act? What are the forms of reparation? (Section 8.)

— What procedures are available for the injured state to obtain reparation? (Section 9.)

## SECTION 2. THE ACT OF STATE UNDER INTERNATIONAL LAW RULES OF ATTRIBUTION

*REPORT OF INTERNATIONAL LAW COMMISSION*

[1973] II Yb.I.L.C. 161, 189.

* * *

(3) Since the State can act physically only through actions or omissions by human beings or human collectivities, the problems posed by this fundamental notion of the "act of the State" which have to be resolved in the present chapter have a common denominator. The basic task is to establish when, according to international law, it is the State which must be regarded as acting: what actions or omissions can in principle be considered as conduct of the State, and in what circumstances, such conduct must have been engaged in, if it is to be actually attributable to the State as a subject of international law. In that connexion, it must first of all be pointed out that, in theory, there is nothing to prevent international law from attaching to the State the conduct of human beings or collectivities whose link with the State might even have no relation to its organization; for example, any actions or omissions taking place in its territory could be considered acts of the State. In practice, however, we find that what is, as a general rule, attributed to the State at the international level are the acts of members of its "organization," in other words, the acts of its "organs" or "agents." This is the basic principle. The purpose of the present chapter of the draft will, in fact, be to define and complete this principle, to determine its scope and limitations and the derogations to which it is subject.

(4) From this point of view, once the basic rule has been laid down which attributes to the State the acts of its organs, the question arises whether the activities of certain categories of organs should be excluded from the "acts of the State." Another point to be considered is whether or not, in addition to the conduct of organs which form part of the State machinery, it is appropriate to attribute to the State, at the international level, the conduct of organs of public institutions other than the State itself,

or of persons who, though not "organs" in the proper sense of the term, engage in what are in fact public activities, or of organs of another subject of international law placed at the disposal of the State in question. Attention will then be given to the question whether or not it is appropriate to regard as "acts of the State" the conduct of organs or, more generally, of persons whose activities are in principle attributed to the State, when such conduct is adopted in circumstances which cast doubt on the legitimacy of that attribution. This question arises, for example, where an organ exceeds its competence or acts contrary to the requirements of internal law concerning its activities. We next have to consider the treatment to be accorded to the conduct of private individuals acting solely in that capacity, and the basis on which the conduct of the State organs in connexion with acts by private individuals may be regarded as a source of responsibility. Lastly, consideration will be given to the case of the conduct of organs of other subjects of international law acting in the territory of the State and to problems relating to the retroactive attribution to a State of acts of a victorious insurrectionary movement.

The following Draft Articles on State Responsibility were adopted by the I.L.C. between 1973 and 1975.

## *DRAFT ARTICLES ON STATE RESPONSIBILITY*

[1975] II Yb. I.L.C. 59–60.

### Article 5

#### Attribution to the State of the Conduct of its Organs

For the purposes of the present articles, conduct of any State organ having that status under the internal law of that State shall be considered as an act of the State concerned under international law, provided that organ was acting in that capacity in the case in question.

### Article 6

#### Irrelevance of the Position of the Organ in the Organization of the State

The conduct of an organ of the State shall be considered as an act of that State under international law, whether that organ belongs to the constituent, legislative, executive, judicial or other power, whether its functions are of an international or an internal character and whether it holds a superior or a subordinate position in the organization of the State.

### Article 7

#### Attribution to the State of the Conduct of Other Entities Empowered to Exercise Elements of the Governmental Authority

1. The conduct of an organ of a territorial governmental entity within a State shall also be considered as an act of that State under international law, provided that organ was acting in that capacity in the case in question.

2. The conduct of an organ of an entity which is not part of the formal structure of the State or of a territorial governmental entity, but which is empowered by the internal law of that State to exercise elements of the governmental authority, shall also be considered as an act of the State under

international law, provided that organ was acting in that capacity in the case in question.

### Article 8

### Attribution to the State of the Conduct of Persons Acting in Fact on Behalf of the State

The conduct of a person or group of persons shall also be considered as an act of the State under international law if

(a) it is established that such person or group of persons was in fact acting on behalf of that State; or

(b) such person or group of persons was in fact exercising elements of the governmental authority in the absence of the official authorities and in circumstances which justified the exercise of those elements of authority.

### Article 9

### Attribution to the State of the Conduct of Organs Placed at its Disposal by Another State or by an International Organization

The conduct of an organ which has been placed at the disposal of a State by another State or by an international organization shall be considered as an act of the former State under international law, if that organ was acting in the exercise of elements of the governmental authority of the State at whose disposal it has been placed.

### Article 10

### Attribution to the State of Conduct of Organs Acting Outside Their Competence or Contrary to Instructions Concerning Their Activity

The conduct of an organ of a State, of a territorial governmental entity or of an entity empowered to exercise elements of the governmental authority, such organ having acted in that capacity, shall be considered as an act of the State under international law even if, in the particular case, the organ exceeded its competence according to internal law or contravened instructions concerning its activity.

### Article 11

### Conduct of Persons Not Acting on Behalf of the State

1. The conduct of a person or a group of persons not acting on behalf of the State shall not be considered as an act of the State under international law.

2. Paragraph 1 is without prejudice to the attribution to the State of any other conduct which is related to that of the persons or groups of persons referred to in that paragraph and which is to be considered as an act of the State by virtue of articles 5 to 10.

### Article 12

### Conduct of Organs of Another State

1. The conduct of an organ of a State acting in that capacity, which takes place in the territory of another State or in any other territory under

its jurisdiction, shall not be considered as an act of the latter State under international law.

2. Paragraph 1 is without prejudice to the attribution to a State of any other conduct which is related to that referred to in that paragraph and which is to be considered as an act of that State by virtue of articles 5 to 10.

### Article 13

#### Conduct of Organs of an International Organization

The conduct of an organ of an international organization acting in that capacity shall not be considered as an act of a State under international law by reason only of the fact that such conduct has taken place in the territory of that State or in any other territory under its jurisdiction.

### Article 14

#### Conduct of Organs of an Insurrectional Movement

1. The conduct of an organ of an insurrectional movement, which is established in the territory of a State or in any other territory under its administration, shall not be considered as an act of that State under international law.

2. Paragraph 1 is without prejudice to the attribution to a State of any other conduct which is related to that of the organ of the insurrectional movement and which is to be considered as an act of that State by virtue of articles 5 to 10.

3. Similarly, paragraph 1 is without prejudice to the attribution of the conduct of the organ of the insurrectional movement to that movement in any case in which such attribution may be made under international law.

### Article 15

#### Attribution to the State of the Act of an Insurrectional Movement Which Becomes the New Government of a State or Which Results in the Formation of a New State

1. The act of an insurrectional movement which becomes the new government of a State shall be considered as an act of that State. However, such attribution shall be without prejudice to the attribution to that State of conduct which would have been previously considered as an act of the State by virtue of articles 5 to 10.

2. The act of an insurrectional movement whose action results in the formation of a new State in part of the territory of a pre-existing State or in a territory under its administration shall be considered as an act of the new State.

## *Notes*

1. Problems of attribution require that clear distinctions be made between matters governed by international law and matters governed by national law. The following examples are illustrative. Whether an entity (or a person) is an organ of the state is determined by national law. The fact that the organ's conduct is attributed to the state does not confer international status or personality on the organ. The criteria for determining attribution in international law are independent of those in national law. Hence, conduct may be internationally attributable to the state even when, in national law, there would be no such

attribution. This may be the case, for example, for certain acts of private persons exercising functions of a governmental character without any authorization to do so. See Draft Articles 8 and 11(2), [1975] II Yb.I.L.C. 60.

2. Does separation of powers within a national government affect attribution? As the above rules indicate, it makes no difference in regard to attribution whether the organ was part of the executive, legislative, or judicial branch. Nor does it make any difference whether the organ had or had not any responsibility for foreign affairs. A state may be internationally accountable for officials performing entirely domestic duties, irrespective of whether their conduct had been endorsed or known to the officials charged with international matters.

3. Would attributing judicial conduct to the state run counter to the principle of independence of the judiciary or to the doctrine of res judicata? These tenets have been invoked in the past to negate attribution of judicial acts, but in recent years the responsibility of the state for acts of its judicial organs has been generally recognized. Thus, a state is responsible if a judgment denies immunity to an ambassador or is incompatible with an extradition treaty. If the judgment is not subject to appeal and is contrary to international law, an international delict is imputable to the state. On the other hand, if a judgment that is not appealable is contrary to national law, the state would not be responsible save in exceptional cases (for example, bad faith and discriminatory intent) where the "primary" international law rule was violated. See de Aréchaga, International Responsibility, in Manual of Public International Law 550–53 (Sorensen, ed. 1968).

4. The doctrine of legislative (or parliamentary) supremacy has no bearing on whether the acts of a legislative organ are attributable to the state. The Permanent Court has stated that from the standpoint of international law "municipal laws are merely facts which express the will and constitute the activities of states in the same manner as do legal decisions or administrative measures". Polish Upper Silesia Case, 1926 P.C.I.J.Ser. A, No. 7, p. 19.

Thus, if a state has incurred a treaty obligation which requires legislation, the failure of the legislature to enact such legislation results in responsibility of the state unless it took other means to fulfill the obligation. Moreover, the fact that, under national law, a legislative enactment prevails over a prior treaty obligation would not absolve the state from responsibility resulting from the non-performance of treaty obligations.

5. As Article 6 above makes clear even a "subordinate organ" may engage in conduct attributable to a state. Would this be the case if recourse may be had to a superior organ to correct the wrongful or injurious conduct?

Should the probable availability of local remedies in cases of wrongful conduct affect the principle of attribution? For a discussion of local remedies rule, see p. 588 infra.

6. Federal states have sometimes sought to deny responsibility for conduct of their constituent states and provinces. See Hyde, International Law 948 (2d rev. ed.). However, many arbitral awards have upheld attribution in cases involving injuries suffered by aliens. See de Aréchaga, in Manual of Public International Law at 557. A federal state is also responsible for the fulfillment of treaty obligations in its entire territory irrespective of internal division of powers. Exceptions to this may be made in the treaty itself or in related circumstances. See Article 29 of Vienna Convention on the Law of Treaties.

7. Questions as to responsibility of a state for *ultra vires* acts of its officials, for conduct of private persons, and for acts of insurrectional movements have arisen mainly in regard to injuries to aliens. These questions are dealt with in Chapter 9. A more general discussion of these problems of attribution will be found in the detailed commentary of the International Law Commission to Articles 10, 11, 14, 15. See I.L.C.Rep., [1975] II Yb.I.L.C. 61–106. See also The International Law Commission's Draft Articles on State Responsibility: Part I, Articles 1–35 (Rosenne, ed. 1991).

## SECTION 3. OBJECTIVE RESPONSIBILITY AND THE REQUIREMENT OF LEGAL INTEREST

### *BROWNLIE, PRINCIPLES OF PUBLIC INTERNATIONAL LAW*

423–28 (2nd ed. 1973).*

Technically, objective responsibility rests on the doctrine of the voluntary act: provided that agency and causal connexion are established, there is a breach of duty by result alone. Defences, such as act of third party, are available, but the defendant has to exculpate himself. In the conditions of international life, which involve relations between highly complex communities, acting through a variety of institutions and agencies, the public law analogy of the *ultra vires* act is more realistic than a seeking for subjective *culpa* in specific natural persons who may, or may not, "represent" the legal person (the state) in terms of wrongdoing. Where, for example, an officer in charge of a cruiser on the high seas orders the boarding of a fishing vessel flying another flag, there being no legal justification for the operation, and the act being in excess of his authority, a tribunal will not regard pleas that the acts were done in good faith, or under a mistake of law, with any favour. Moreover, in municipal systems of law, the precise mode of applying a *culpa* doctrine, especially in the matter of assigning the burden of proof, may result in a regime of objective responsibility.

It is believed that the practice of states and the jurisprudence of arbitral tribunals and the International Court have followed the theory of objective responsibility as a general principle (which may be modified or excluded in certain cases). Objective tests of responsibility were employed by the General Claims Commission set up by a Convention between Mexico and the United States in 1923 in the well-known *Neer* and *Roberts* claims, and in the *Caire* claim, Verzijl, President of the Franco–Mexican Claims Commission, applied the doctrine of the objective responsibility of the State, that is to say, a responsibility for those acts committed by its officials or its organs, and which they are bound to perform, despite the absence of *faute* on their part * * * The State also bears an international responsibility for all acts committed by its officials or its organs which are delictual according to international law, regardless of whether the official organ has acted within the limits of his competency or has exceeded those limits * * * However, in order to justify the admission of this objective responsibility of the State for acts committed by its officials or organs outside their competence, it is necessary that they should have acted, at least apparently, as authorised

* Footnotes omitted. Reprinted by permission of Clarendon Press, Oxford.

officials or organs, or that, in acting, they should have used powers or measures appropriate to their official character. * * *

A considerable number of writers support this point of view, either explicitly, or implicitly, by considering the questions of imputability, causation, and legal excuses without adverting to the questions of *culpa* and *dolus.* At the same time certain eminent opinions have supported the Grotian view that *culpa* or *dolus malus* provide the proper basis of state responsibility in all cases. A small number of arbitral awards give some support to the *culpa* doctrine: for example, in the *Home Missionary Society* case, the tribunal referred to a "well-established principle of international law that no government can be held responsible for the act of rebellious bodies of men committed in violation of its authority, where it is itself guilty of no breach of good faith, or of no negligence in suppressing insurrection". However, many of the awards cited in this connexion are concerned with the standard of conduct required by the law *in a particular context,* for example claims for losses caused by acts of rebellion, of private individuals, of the judiciary, and so on.

The fact that an *ultra vires* act of an official is accompanied by malice on his part, i.e. an intention to cause harm, without regard to whether or not the law permits the act, does not affect the responsibility of his state. Indeed, the principle of objective responsibility dictates the irrelevance of intention to harm, *dolus,* as a condition of liability; and yet general propositions of this sort should not lead to the conclusion that *dolus* cannot play a significant role in the law. Proof of *dolus* on the part of leading organs of the state will solve the problem of "imputability" in the given case, and, in any case, the existence of a deliberate intent to injure may have an effect on remoteness of damage as well as helping to establish the breach of duty. Malice may justify the award of "penal" damages.

Motive and intention are frequently a specific element in the definition of permitted conduct. Thus the rule is stated that expropriation of foreign property is unlawful if the object is that of political reprisal or retaliation. Again, action ostensibly in collective defence against an aggressor will cease to be lawful if the state concerned in the action is proved to be intent on using the operation for purposes of annexation. Similarly, where conduct on its face unlawful is sought to be justified on the grounds of necessity or self-defence, the intention of the actor is important, since it may remove all basis for the defences. Difficulty may arise in many cases where states have legal powers not conditioned by the existence of particular motives for their exercise: if such powers are used in such a way as to cause damage to another state, or to disregard human rights, is the conduct involved rendered illegal?

### *Notes*

1. The element of "fault" is sometimes raised in connection with the assertion that states have a general duty to prevent the use of its territory to cause significant harm to other states. For example, Oppenheim's International Law at 291 (8th ed., Lauterpacht, 1955) says "a State is bound to prevent such use of its territory, as having regard to the circumstances, is unduly injurious to the inhabitants of the neighboring state." Since many lawful activities within states may adversely affect neighboring states or common areas such as the high

seas, the issue is presented whether the international responsibility to prevent harm should be conditioned on some element of fault such as negligence, lack of good faith or intentional failure to comply with international standards. These issues have arisen mainly in connection with trans-boundary pollution of the atmosphere, rivers or other common waters. They also arise in respect of damage to the high seas and outer space. These matters of international environmental law are treated later in Chapter 16.

2. State responsibility in these cases has sometimes been considered under the principles of abuse of right or liability without fault. However, the trend has been to move away from these abstract and vague notions to defining conduct required of states to prevent harm to other states. Thus, the obligation to avoid harmful environmental damage has been stated as an obligation to take such measures as may be necessary to ensure that activities within the jurisdiction or control of a state conform to international rules and standards for the protection of the environment of other states or areas beyond national jurisdiction. See Restatement (Third) § 601. Many such obligations are specified in treaties relating to common waters and marine areas as well as to Antarctic and Outer Space. These "primary rules" of conduct determine the elements that are pertinent in deciding whether the obligation has been wrongfully violated.

3. A strong criticism of the International Law Commission work on responsibility has been made by Philip Allott. He objects to the basic idea that "every intentionally wrongful act of a State entails the international responsibility of that State."

He argues:

> Two especially vicious consequences result from using responsibility as a general and independent category in international law. First, it consecrates the idea that wrong-doing is the behavior of a general category known as "states" and is not the behavior of morally responsible human beings. It therefore obscures the fact that breaches of international law are attributable formally to the legal persons known as states but morally to the human beings who determine the behavior of states.
>
> Second, if responsibility exists as a legal category, it must be given legal substance. In particular, general conditions of responsibility have to be created which are then applicable to all rights and duties. The net result is that the deterrent effect of the imposition of responsibility is seriously compromised, not only by rationalizing it (the first vicious consequence) but also by leaving room for argument in every conceivable case of potential responsibility (the second vicious consequence). When lawyers leave room for argument there is much room for injustice.

State Responsibility and the Unmaking of International Law, 29 Harv.Int'l L.J. 1 (1988). Do you consider Allott's criticism well founded? Are the dangers he envisages likely consequences of the basic idea?

## SECTION 4. THE REQUIREMENT OF INJURY

It is sometimes said that a breach of an obligation gives rise to responsibility irrespective of injury caused to another state unless the obligation itself (i.e., the primary rule of conduct) requires such injury as a condition of a breach. For example, the obligation of a state to protect the embassy of a foreign government is breached only if damage occurs to that embassy; negligence in protection is not itself a breach. However, if the primary rule does not make injury an essential element of a violation, an obligation may be breached even though no specific injury is caused to another state. Does this mean that as a general rule the breach of the obligation is itself the wrongful act giving rise to responsibility and that no injury need be shown? The International Law Commission suggested that in 1973. It said:

> For examples we need only turn to the conventions on human rights or the majority of the international labour conventions. If one of these international obligations is violated, the breach thus committed does not normally cause any economic injury to the other States parties to the convention, or even any slight to their honour or dignity. Yet it manifestly constitutes an internationally wrongful act, so that if we maintain at all costs that 'damage' is an element in any internationally wrongful act, we are forced to the conclusion that any breach of an international obligation towards another State involves some kind of 'injury' to that other State. But this is tantamount to saying that the 'damage' which is inherent in any internationally wrongful act is the damage which is at the same time inherent in any breach of an international obligation. Reference to the breach of an international obligation thus seemed to the Commission fully sufficient to cover that aspect as well, without the addition of anything further.

I.L.C.Rep., [1973] II Yb.I.L.C. 183.

Does it follow from the examples given in the above passage, that the breach of an obligation by one state *always* infringes the rights of all other states to whom that obligation is owed? Are there not some obligations based on customary law or rules in multilateral treaties that may be violated with respect to one state (or a few states) without infringing the rights of all others bound? For example, the basic rule of territorial sovereignty binding on all states would be breached by one state entering illicitly the territory of another; but that breach does not infringe the rights of all other states or give rise to responsibility to them by the offending state. How do we distinguish these obligations from those referred to in the I.L.C. statement quoted above?

Objecting to the view advanced by the I.L.C. in its report on state responsibility, de Aréchaga and Tanzi have written:

> The requirement of damage is really an expression of the fundamental legal principle that no one can maintain an action unless he has an interest of a legal nature. It is always the element of damage suffered by one State that entitles that particular State to claim against the State which caused the damage, and demand redress.

Jimenez de Aréchaga & Attila Tanzi, International State Responsibility, in International Law: Achievements and Prospects 347, 349 (M. Bedjaoui ed., 1991) (footnote omitted).

The International Court of Justice commented on this question in its judgment in the *Barcelona Traction Case* brought by Belgium against Spain. The following excerpts from the Court's Judgment rendered in 1970 are pertinent.

## CASE CONCERNING THE BARCELONA TRACTION, LIGHT AND POWER COMPANY, LIMITED (BELGIUM v. SPAIN), SECOND PHASE

International Court of Justice, 1970.
1970 I.C.J. 3.

[Rejecting the claim of Belgium, the Court said in part:]

28. * * * The claim is presented on behalf of natural and juristic persons, alleged to be Belgian nationals and shareholders in the Barcelona Traction, Light and Power Company, Limited. The submissions of the Belgian Government make it clear that the object of its Application is reparation for damage allegedly caused to these persons by the conduct, said to be contrary to international law, of various organs of the Spanish State towards that company and various other companies in the same group.

* * *

30. The States which the present case principally concerns are Belgium, the national State of the alleged shareholders, Spain, the State whose organs are alleged to have committed the unlawful acts complained of, and Canada, the State under whose laws Barcelona Traction was incorporated and in whose territory it has its registered office ("head office" in the terms of the by-laws of Barcelona Traction).

31. Thus the Court has to deal with a series of problems arising out of a triangular relationship involving the State whose nationals are shareholders in a company incorporated under the laws of another State, in whose territory it has its registered office; the State whose organs are alleged to have committed against the company unlawful acts prejudicial to both it and its shareholders; and the State under whose laws the company is incorporated, and in whose territory it has its registered office.

32. In these circumstances it is logical that the Court should first address itself to what was originally presented as the subject-matter of the third preliminary objection: namely the question of the right of Belgium to exercise diplomatic protection of Belgian shareholders in a company which is a juristic entity incorporated in Canada, the measures complained of having been taken in relation not to any Belgian national but to the company itself.

33. When a State admits into its territory foreign investments or foreign nationals, whether natural or juristic persons, it is bound to extend to them the protection of the law and assumes obligations concerning the treatment to be afforded them. These obligations, however, are neither absolute nor unqualified. In particular, an essential distinction should be drawn between the obligations of a State towards the international community as a whole, and those arising vis-à-vis another State in the field of diplomatic protection. By their very nature the former are the concern of all States. In view of the importance of the rights involved, all States can be held to have a legal interest in their protection; they are obligations *erga omnes*.

34. Such obligations derive, for example, in contemporary international law, from the outlawing of acts of aggression, and of genocide, as also from

the principles and rules concerning the basic rights of the human person, including protection from slavery and racial discrimination. Some of the corresponding rights of protection have entered into the body of general international law (Reservations to the Convention on the Prevention and Punishment of the Crime of Genocide, Advisory Opinion, I.C.J. Reports 1951, p. 23); others are conferred by international instruments of a universal or quasi-universal character.

35. Obligations the performance of which is the subject of diplomatic protection are not of the same category. It cannot be held, when one such obligation in particular is in question, in a specific case, that all States have a legal interest in its observance. In order to bring a claim in respect of the breach of such an obligation, a State must first establish its right to do so, for the rules on the subject rest on two suppositions:

> "The first is that the defendant State has broken an obligation towards the national State in respect of its nationals. The second is that only the party to whom an international obligation is due can bring a claim in respect of its breach." (Reparation for Injuries Suffered in the Service of the United Nations, Advisory Opinion, I.C.J. Reports 1949, pp. 181–82.)

In the present case it is therefore essential to establish whether the losses allegedly suffered by Belgian shareholders in Barcelona Traction were the consequence of the violation of obligations of which they were the beneficiaries. In other words: has a right of Belgium been violated on account of its nationals having suffered infringement of their rights as shareholders in a company not of Belgian nationality?

### *Notes*

1. The concept of *erga omnes* obligations expressed by the Court was endorsed by the International Law Commission and applied to the obligations, the breach of which constituted "international crimes." I.L.C.Rep., [1976] II (Pt.2) Yb.I.L.C. 95–122. (For list of international crimes proposed by the I.L.C., see Section 5 below.) The Restatement (Third) also accepted the category of *erga omnes* obligations. It included in that category customary law obligations in respect of human rights and protection of the environment. See Restatement (Third) § 902.

2. Notwithstanding the apparent acceptance of the *erga omnes* concept, no state has invoked it in judicial proceedings since its enunciation in the *Barcelona Case.* Some years before *Barcelona* a similar idea had been asserted in a case brought in the International Court by Ethiopia and Liberia against South Africa for violation of the League of Nations mandate under which South Africa administered the territory of South West Africa. Ethiopia and Liberia asserted that as former members of the League they had a legal interest to vindicate the rights of that community of states in the mandate allegedly violated by South Africa. The Court in denying their legal standing referred to their claim as analogous to the *actio popularis* in Roman law under which a citizen could request the courts to protect a public interest. The Court observed that the *actio popularis* was "not known to international law at present * * *." South West Africa Cases, 1966 I.C.J. 45.

3. When the Court subsequently endorsed the *erga omnes* conception in the *Barcelona Traction Case,* did it imply support of the right of any state to bring an

action to protect a "public" or "collective" interest of the community? Such right, if recognized, would be similar to the *actio popularis.* However, on the international level the exercise of the right would require a jurisdictional basis. It could not be exercised unless the respondent state specifically agreed to jurisdiction or had consented in a treaty or by acceptance of compulsory jurisdiction under Article 35(2) of the Statute of the Court. See Chapter 10. Query whether it would contribute to wider law observance if every state could bring judicial action against a law violator (subject to jurisdictional requirements) for that state's infringement of collective interests. By increasing the class of potential plaintiffs, legal actions for breaches of law might become more common and thus enhance observance of norms that are in the interest of all states. On the other hand, would that very consequence make states more reluctant to submit in advance to jurisdiction of the Court? See discussion in Schachter, International Law in Theory and Practice, 178 Rec. des Cours 192–201 (1982–V); Schwelb, The Actio Popularis and International Law, 2 Isr.Yb. H.Rts. 47 (1972).

4. Recognition of *erga omnes* obligations has consequences beyond judicial proceedings. States considered to have a legal interest in vindicating important community or collective interests may assert that interest in relevant non-judicial arenas such as international organs. Or, more important, they may take counter-measures unilaterally or jointly against offending states. (See Section 7 below.) Would such counter-measures strengthen compliance with basic rules of conduct? Is there a danger that in the absence of judicial control every state could "appoint itself as the avenger of the international community * * * in the name of higher values as determined by itself" and thus add to international chaos. See P. Weil, Towards Relative Normativity in International Law, 77 A.J.I.L. 413, 433 (1983).

5. Under what circumstances would a state be regarded as having its rights infringed when another state breaches an obligation that applies generally to all states or to a large group of states under customary or treaty law? The International Law Commission has sought to answer this by giving a broad meaning to "injured states" in respect of breaches of customary law and multilateral treaties. I.L.C.Rep. 54–59 (1985). They have suggested that states are injured states for purposes of responsibility:

> (a) when the right infringed by the breach was established in favor of such state or group of states (for example, the state of nationality of an injured foreigner);
>
> (b) when the infringement of the right affects the enjoyment of the right or the performance of obligations by other states, those other states are injured;
>
> (c) where the obligation was established to protect human rights and fundamental freedoms, all states are deemed to be injured by the breach (the Commission observed that in this situation, the legal interests are not allocable to any particular state);
>
> (d) where a multilateral treaty has established a "collective interest" all parties are injured if the breach by one affects that interest;
>
> (e) lastly, all states are considered as "injured states" when the breach of the obligation is an international crime.

Note that the last three categories are in keeping with the principle of *erga omnes* obligations. What is the likely consequence of allowing all the states in these categories to invoke the responsibility of the offending state? Would it deter violations? Would the injured states be more likely to take counter-measures or bring charges in international bodies? Is there danger of abuse of these rights in the absence of controls by international judicial or political organs? See J. Charney, Third State Remedies in International Law, Mich. J.Int'l L. 57 (1989).

## SECTION 5. INTERNATIONAL CRIMES AND INTERNATIONAL DELICTS

### *INTERNATIONAL LAW COMMISSION DRAFT ARTICLES ON STATE RESPONSIBILITY*

[1976] II (Pt.2) Yb.I.L.C. 75.

#### ARTICLE 19

*International Crimes and International Delicts*

1. An act of a State which constitutes a breach of an international obligation is an internationally wrongful act, regardless of the subject-matter of the obligation breached.

2. An internationally wrongful act which results from the breach by a State of an international obligation so essential for the protection of fundamental interests of the international community that its breach is recognized as a crime by that community as a whole, constitutes an international crime.

3. Subject to paragraph 2, and on the basis of the rules of international law in force, an international crime may result, *inter alia,* from:

(a) a serious breach of an international obligation of essential importance for maintenance of international peace and security, such as that prohibiting aggression;

(b) a serious breach of an international obligation of essential importance for safeguarding the right of self-determination of peoples, such as that prohibiting the establishment or maintenance by force of colonial domination;

(c) a serious breach on a widespread scale of an international obligation of essential importance for safeguarding the human being, such as those prohibiting slavery, genocide, apartheid;

(d) a serious breach of an international obligation of essential importance for the safeguarding and preservation of the human environment, such as those prohibiting massive pollution of the atmosphere or of the seas.

4. Any internationally wrongful act which is not an international crime in accordance with paragraph 2, constitutes an international delict.

#### *Notes*

1. An exposition of the authorities and reasons in support of the distinction between international crimes and delicts is included in the Report of the International Law Commission for 1976. I.L.C.Rep., [1976] II (Pt.2) Yb.I.L.C. 95–

122. Draft Article 19 was approved unanimously by the International Law Commission in 1976. The discussion in the Commission and in its commentary emphasized that a wrongful act would be an international crime only if so recognized by the "international community as a whole." This did not mean unanimity according to the Commission members, but it did require agreement of "all the essential components of the international community." [1976] II (Pt.2) Yb.I.L.C. at 119. At that time, the "essential components" were considered to include the "Western Countries" the "socialist Countries" and the "Third World." Query whether in 1993, these three categories are appropriate to describe the "essential components" of the international community. Is it possible today to define the international community in a way to express its pluralist character without requiring unanimity?

2. After its adoption by the I.L.C., Article 19 received a mixed reception by governments in the Sixth (Legal) Committee of the U.N. General Assembly. The United States, in particular, opposed the draft mainly on the ground that the concept of a crime of state implied penal responsibility. In its view, the imposition of "criminal penalties" against a state required international judicial authority with compulsory powers to determine guilt and penalties. Several other "Western" and Latin–American states shared this view and expressed objections to the draft article. Many of the supporters of Article 19, however, pointed out that the article did not provide for "penal responsibility" and that the question of the legal consequences of a crime of state was to be considered later in Part II of the Articles on Responsibility. Most governments including the United States agreed that there were wrongful acts more serious than others because they affect fundamental common interests and such violations may call for special legal consequences.

3. Some countries, especially in Western Europe, questioned Article 19 because it implied the right of states not injured by the violation to take action against the violator. They observed this would open the way for unilateral action by powerful states ("self-appointed policemen") without any judicial determination of the crime. On the other hand, proponents of Article 19 emphasized the importance of recognizing that all states were affected by violations of rules of a fundamental character and every state should therefore be able to take counter-measures that were appropriate and proportionate to the violation. An intermediate position suggested by several states would recognize that non-injured states had a legal interest in crimes *erga omnes* but would require that the right be implemented within the framework of international institutions rather than unilaterally.

4. Note that Article 19 does not deal with the legal consequences of an international crime. That critical aspect was left to Part Two of the I.L.C. Draft Articles on State Responsibility. Accordingly, a Draft on the legal consequences of an international crime was subsequently submitted by the special rapporteur for Part II (the regime of responsibility). The draft (Article 14 of Part Two) read as follows:

Article 14

1. An international crime entails all the legal consequences of an internationally wrongful act and, in addition, such rights and obligations as are determined by the applicable rules accepted by the international community as a whole.

2. An international crime committed by a State entails an obligation for every other state:

(a) not to recognize as legal the situation created by such crime, and,

(b) not to render aid or assistance to the state which has committed such crime in maintaining the situation created by such crime; and

(c) to join other states in affording mutual assistance in carrying out the obligations under subparagraphs (a) and (b).

The above proposal by the Special Rapporteur of Part II (Professor Riphagen) did not impose criminal penalties. It provided rather for "solidarity" by imposing obligations on non-injured states not to render assistance to the violator or recognize as legal the situation created by the violation. In this way, the community interest would be recognized by "multilateralizing" injury. However the proposed article did not go as far as to require judicial determination of the violation or collective sanctions (such as economic boycott) against the violator. Do you think it would be desirable to move toward those requirements?

5. Professor Weiler suggested in 1987 that the proponents of Article 19 had a "prophetic vision" by which they hoped to breathe new life into the U.N. Charter system which seemed at the time to have failed to deter the grave violations referred to in Article 19. Weiler wrote:

> The very acceptance of the concept of a Crime of State, "let loose" in the evolving international legal order and its law-making processes will, according to this prophetic vision, generate and prod the international community to evolve, flesh out and perfect whatever rudimentary regime of consequences is initially worked out.

J. Weiler, in International Crimes of State: A Critical Analysis of the ILC's Draft Article 19 on State Responsibility 332 (Weiler, Cassesse, Spinedi eds. 1989).

In what ways could the concept of "international crimes" and a special regime of responsibility be fleshed out so as to strengthen international order?

6. In the light of U.N. actions in 1991–93 can we expect that grave violations of essential rules such as those against aggression, genocide, and environmental devastation will be addressed by the U.N. Security Council and other international bodies that have competence to act under the Charter and other multilateral instruments? Would such "enforcement" measures by international organs be more likely if international law doctrine included the category of international crimes while leaving it to the institutionalized international community to take protective measures? Oppenheim's International Law 536 n. 14 (Jennings & Watts, eds., 9th ed. 1992) concludes that "unless the criminal responsibility of states is to be reduced to the vanishing point of law, its enforcement must be placed in the hands of impartial international agencies operating within the ambit of a politically organized international society." Does this suggest the need for a body more "impartial" than the U.N. Security Council?

7. The legislative history of Article 19 and the doctrinal and policy issues raised are well presented in a collective work edited by J. Weiler, A. Cassesse, and M. Spinedi entitled International Crimes of State: A Critical Analysis of the ILC's Draft Article 19 on State Responsibility (1989). It includes contributions by 27 authoritative jurists. The bibliographical appendix lists 147 items on the subject up to 1987.

# SECTION 6. CIRCUMSTANCES PRECLUDING WRONGFULNESS

Normally an act of state that is not in conformity with an international obligation is an internationally wrongful act entailing responsibility on the part of the state. However, under some special circumstances an inference of wrongfulness is precluded. The circumstances that are generally considered to have this effect are: consent, *force majeure* and fortuitous events, distress and necessity. Two other categories of state conduct may also be considered to exclude wrongfulness: self-defense and counter-measures. Counter-measures will be dealt with in the following section. Self-defense is treated in Chapter 11 on the use of force. The present section will deal with the other circumstances.

When any of these special circumstances is present, the obligation in question is not breached. "The act of the State in question cannot be characterized as wrongful for the good reason that, because of the presence of a certain circumstance, the State committing the act was not under an international obligation *in that case* to act otherwise." I.L.C.Rep., [1979] II (Pt.2) Yb.I.L.C. 108 (emphasis in original).

## A. CONSENT

The International Law Commission has adopted the following article on consent as part of its articles on responsibility of states:

> Article 29. Consent
>
> 1. The consent validly given by a State to the commission by another State of a specified act not in conformity with an obligation of the latter State towards the former State precludes the wrongfulness of the act in relation to that State to the extent that the act remains within the limits of that consent.
>
> 2. Paragraph 1 does not apply if the obligation arises out of a peremptory norm of general international law. For the purposes of the present draft articles, a peremptory norm of general international law is a norm accepted and recognized by the international community of States as a whole as a norm from which no derogation is permitted and which can be modified only by a subsequent norm of general international law having the same character.

I.L.C.Rep., [1979] II (Pt.2) Yb.I.L.C. 109.

### *Notes*

1. The entry of foreign troops into territory of another state which would normally be unlawful becomes lawful (as a rule) if it took place with the consent of that state. Many cases involving such entry of troops have occurred and a number were considered by the U.N. General Assembly and Security Council. The basic principle of consent as a legitimating factor was not challenged. Differences of opinion arose, however, on whether consent had been validly expressed on behalf of the state, whether rights of other states were violated or whether a peremptory norm was infringed. Among such cases were those involving the entry of Soviet troops into Hungary (1956), Czechoslovakia (1968)

and Afghanistan (1981); the entry of U.S. troops in Grenada (1984) and into Lebanon (1958). See Chapter 11 on these cases. See also Schachter, The Right of States to Use Armed Force, 82 Mich.L.Rev. 1620 (1984); L. Doswald–Beck, The Legal Validity of Military Intervention By Invitation of the Government, 56 Brit.Y.B.I.L. 190 (1985). Many cases not involving military action also recognize that when a state entitled to observance of an obligation agrees to its non-observance, the other state does not commit a lawful act by such nonobservance. See Russian Indemnity Case, 3 U.N.R.I.A.A. 446.

2. May consent be implied or presumed? The I.L.C. considered that consent to be valid must be "*really expressed*," but such expression may be by conduct as well as words. It cannot, however, be presumed. [1979] II (Pt.2) Yb.I.L.C. 112 (emphasis in original). Is it truly consent if there are elements of coercion? Would implicit threats of invasion invalidate consent? Would threats of economic retaliation?

3. Does consent to be valid require the support of the people? Is internal law decisive or are standards of international law relevant to determine the "will" of the state? These questions arise in several cases involving military intervention, including those referred to in note 1 supra. See Chapter 11.

4. Consent precludes the wrongfulness of an act only in relation to the state giving consent. However, an act consented to by one state may be a breach toward another state. Sending troops into one country may involve a breach to another (as for example where a treaty of neutralization is violated). Injury to nationals of a consenting state in violation of an international convention may also involve a breach toward other parties to the convention. The conventions on human rights are pertinent.

5. Note that the I.L.C. text considers that even freely given consent would not absolve a state from responsibility where the obligation was *jus cogens*. Does this involve an extension of the *jus cogens* principle beyond that laid down in the Vienna Convention on the Law of Treaties? See Articles 53 and 64 of the Convention on the Law of Treaties, 1155 U.N.T.S. 331; 8 I.L.M. 679 (1969). The Commission bases its view on "logical principles" rather than on practice. I.L.C.Rep., [1979] II (Pt.2) Yb.I.L.C. 114. Would a government be free to consent to give up sovereignty and become a "protectorate" or province of another state? Can self-determination be asserted as *jus cogens* and a plebiscite demanded as a condition of state consent to giving up sovereign rights to another?

## B. FORCE MAJEURE AND FORTUITOUS EVENT

Article 31 of the I.L.C. Draft Articles on State Responsibility reads:

> 1. The wrongfulness of an act of a State not in conformity with an international obligation of that State is precluded if the act was due to an irresistible force or to an unforeseen external event beyond its control which made it materially impossible for the State to act in conformity with that obligation or to know that its conduct was not in conformity with that obligation.
>
> 2. Paragraph 1 shall not apply if the State in question has contributed to the occurrence of the situation of material impossibility.

I.L.C.Rep., [1979] II (Pt.2) Yb.I.L.C. 122.

### *Notes*

1. *Force majeure* and fortuitous events are frequently invoked as reasons for excluding wrongfulness. Although the use of the two terms is not uniform in practice, the situations covered by them have one common feature: "the State organs are involuntarily placed in a situation which makes it *materially impossible* for them either to adopt conduct in conformity with the requirements of an international obligation incumbent on their State or to realize that the conduct they are engaging in is not of the character required." I.L.C.Rep., [1979] II (Pt.2) Yb.I.L.C. 124.

2. Examples of such situations have often arisen when vessels or aircraft have entered the territory of another state without prior consent. Such entry may be due to bad weather or defects in function of equipment that made entry unavoidable or made it impossible for the pilot to know he had made an error. While such situations are not treated as international wrongs, disputes about them arise because facts and motives may not be verifiable. For example, the shooting down in 1983 by a Soviet military plane of a Korean passenger plane in flight over the U.S.S.R. in eastern Asia was followed by charges and countercharges as to whether the plane had erroneously diverted from its course or had done so intentionally. If fortuitous events such as failure of equipment had been responsible for the pilot to go off course and not to know that, then the flight was not intentionally wrongful. See Report of the International Civil Aviation Organization on the case, 13 December 1983, 23 I.L.M. 937 (1984). The controversy about the facts continued after the foregoing report.

3. *Force majeure* has also been invoked as a ground for a state to avoid payment of its debt. Two cases that reached the Permanent Court of International Justice involved pleas by debtor states that they were unable to pay in gold as required by the loan agreement. In both cases, the defense was unsuccessful on the ground that it was not in fact impossible for the states to pay in gold or equivalent value. See Case Concerning Serbian Loans, 1929 P.C.I.J., Ser. C., No. 16–III, pp. 211–29 and Case Concerning Brazilian Loans, 1929 P.C.I.J., Ser. A., No. 20/21, pp. 33–40.

Would *force majeure* in the sense of "material impossibility" apply when the debtor state could not pay without imposing severe hardships on its inhabitants? Would such condition be an "irresistible force"? If inability to pay had been caused by an unexpected collapse in prices of a commodity that was a major source of export earnings of the debtor state would the precipatory cause be regarded as a "fortuitous event"? See below for discussion of "distress" and "necessity" as possible grounds for non-payment.

4. In some cases the state claiming *force majeure* may have contributed to the occurrence of the event. It may, for example, have failed to provide adequate guidance to an aircraft that intruded into foreign territory. It would seem doubtful in that case that the state should be able to disclaim responsibility because of *force majeure.* See I.L.C.Rep., [1979] II (Pt.2) Yb.I.L.C. 125–26.

## C. DISTRESS

Article 32 of the I.L.C. Draft Articles on State Responsibility reads:

> 1. The wrongfulness of an act of a State not in conformity with an international obligation of that State is precluded if the author of the conduct which constitutes the act of that State had no other means, in a

situation of extreme distress, of saving his life or that of persons entrusted to his care.

2. Paragraph 1 shall not apply if the State in question has contributed to the occurrence of the situation of extreme distress or if the conduct in question was likely to create a comparable or greater peril.

I.L.C.Rep., [1979] II (Pt.2) Yb.I.L.C. 133.

### *Notes*

1. "Distress" differs from *force majeure* and fortuitous event in that in case of distress, conformity with the obligation is possible but would result in loss of life. Distress has been invoked as an excuse when a frontier was violated by a vessel or aircraft to save lives in peril. See Lissitzyn, Treatment of Aerial Intruders, 47 A.J.I.L. 588 (1953). Multilateral conventions on the law of the sea and marine pollution contain exculpatory provisions for both *force majeure* and distress. See U.N. Convention on the Law of the Sea 1982, Article 18(2) and 39(1)(e); Convention on Prevention of Pollution by Oil 1954, 327 U.N.T.S. 8, Article V.

2. Would "distress" be a legitimate ground for a state to refuse to pay a debt if such payment would require so substantial a reduction in living standards as to cause starvation or higher rates of infant mortality? Leaders of some debtor countries have raised this issue.

## D. NECESSITY

Article 33 of the I.L.C. Draft Articles on State Responsibility reads:

Article 33. State of necessity

1. A state of necessity may not be invoked by a State as a ground for precluding the wrongfulness of an act of that State not in conformity with an international obligation of the State unless:

(*a*) the act was the only means of safeguarding an essential interest of the State against a grave and imminent peril; and

(*b*) the act did not seriously impair an essential interest of the State toward which the obligation existed.

2. In any case, a state of necessity may not be invoked by a State as a ground for precluding wrongfulness:

(*a*) if the international obligation with which the act of the State is not in conformity arises out of a peremptory norm of general international law; or

(*b*) if the international obligation with which the act of the State is not in conformity is laid down by a treaty which, explicitly or implicitly, excludes the possibility of invoking the state of necessity with respect to that obligation; or

(*c*) if the State in question has contributed to the occurrence of the state of necessity.

I.L.C.Rep., [1980] II (Pt.2) Yb.I.L.C. 34.

## *Notes*

1. Necessity as a ground for precluding wrongfulness differs from *force majeure* in that the latter involves material impossibility to conform with the obligation or to realize the conduct is contrary to the obligation. In that sense, *force majeure* involves an unintentional breach. A state of necessity, however, involves a deliberate act not to conform with the obligation. It is intentional conduct considered necessary to safeguard "an essential interest of the State against a grave and imminent peril" (Article 33). The state organs which have to decide on the conduct to take are free to make a deliberate and fully conscious choice.

2. What are the "essential interests of the State" that justify breaking international obligations when such interests are endangered? The existence of the state is mentioned as one. Others suggested by the I.L.C. are: the maintenance of conditions in which essential services can function, the keeping of domestic peace, the survival of part of its population, the ecological preservation of all or some of its territory. I.L.C.Rep., [1980] II (Pt.2) Yb.I.L.C. 39–52.

3. Necessity is similar to self-defense in that both involve a right to act to safeguard essential state interests. Self-defense involves a danger caused by the state acted against, in particular by that state's use or threat of armed force. In contrast, a state of necessity is independent of any conduct of the state injured by the violation of the obligation. For example, a state may invoke necessity to avoid payment of a financial debt on the ground the payment would clearly entail such disruption of its public services as to jeopardize public order and economic life of the country. The Greek government offered this defense for its failure to pay awards of an arbitral tribunal to Belgium. Société Commercial de Belgique (Socobel) Case, P.C.I.J., Ser. C, No. 87, pp. 101, 141. The Belgian government questioned the fact of inability to pay and also declared that such inability, if verified, would only justify a suspension of payment, not a final discharge of the debt. The Court implicitly accepted the basic principle that, if verified, the inability of Greece to pay would justify nonpayment. P.C.I.J., Ser. A/B, No. 78, p. 19.

4. Would a "state of necessity" justify an incursion into foreign territory to rescue or protect endangered persons detained by hostile forces not under the control of the territorial state? Belgium advanced that ground to justify the entry of its parachutists into the Congo (now Zaire) in 1960 to protect endangered Belgian nationals. See McNemar, The Postindependence War in the Congo, in The International Law of Civil War, 244 (Falk ed., 1971). Other rescue actions such as those by Israel in Entebbe, Uganda (1976) and by the United States in Iran (1980) to free imprisoned hostages were justified as self-defense rather than as necessity. See Schachter, International Law in the Hostage Crisis, in American Hostages in Iran 325 (Christopher et al., 1985). See Chapter 11. On military necessity in time of war, see Downey, The Law of War and Military Necessity, 47 A.J.I.L. 251 (1958).

5. Does "necessity know no law"? Since "necessity" has been and can be used for inadmissible and often unstated purposes, should it not be excluded as a justification for violations of international obligations? Many leading jurists have so argued. Consider the views of de Aréchaga & Tanzi:

> It may be concluded, therefore, that there is no general principle allowing the defence of necessity. There are particular rules of international law making allowance for varying degrees of necessity, but these cases have a meaning and a scope entirely outside the traditional doctrine. Thus, for

instance, vessels in distress are allowed to seek refuge in a foreign port, even if it is closed; in the case of famine in a country, a foreign ship proceeding to another port may be detained and its cargo expropriated; neutral states may exercise the traditional right of angary with respect to foreign ships lying in their ports. In these cases—in which adequate compensation must be paid to the injured parties—it is not the doctrine of necessity which provides the foundation of the particular rules, but humanitarian considerations, which do not apply to the state as a body politic.

Jimenez de Aréchaga & Attila Tanzi, International State Responsibility in International Law: Achievements and Prospects 347, 355 (M. Bedjaoui ed., 1991). See also Brierly, The Law of Nations 403 (6th ed., Waldock, 1963).

Those who favor necessity argue that it has been recognized in international life and for doctrine to deny its applicability would not check abuses in fact. See Oppenheim, International Law 297 (8th ed., Lauterpacht, 1955), Garcia Amador, Third Report on State Responsibility, [1958] II Yb.I.L.C. 47. These writers favor laying down restrictive conditions for the application of necessity to prevent it from becoming a readily available pretext for violating obligations. Are the restrictive conditions in the International Law Commission's Article 33 adequate and realistic? See Commission analysis in its report of 1980, pp. 104–111.

6. Are there obligations in respect of which the plea of necessity should be excluded *a priori?* Article 33 excludes obligations based on *jus cogens* norms, particularly in cases of noncompliance with the prohibition of aggression. Some treaties also explicitly or implicitly exclude necessity as an excuse for nonperformance. The non-derogable provisions of human rights treaties cannot be infringed on grounds of necessity.

7. Should a state that justifiably invokes necessity be required nonetheless to pay compensation for material damage due to its violation of the obligation? Such payment of compensation would not be reparation for "a wrongful act" but is there any reason why it could not be a separate "primary" obligation of the state that caused injury by its own deliberate act?

## E. SELF-DEFENSE

A lawful measure of self-defense may also involve conduct contrary to an international obligation. If self-defense is in accord with the U.N. Charter, it would preclude a finding of wrongfulness. See Chapter 11 on the use of force.

## RAINBOW WARRIOR (NEW ZEALAND v. FRANCE)

82 I.L.R. 499 (France–New Zealand Arbitration Tribunal 1990).

[Using two high explosive devices, a team of French agents destroyed the *Rainbow Warrior,* a civilian vessel owned by Greenpeace International, at its moorings in Auckland Harbor, New Zealand on July 10, 1985. A serious dispute ensued between France, which requested the extradition of two captured agents (Major Alain Mafart and Captain Dominique Prieur), and New Zealand, which sought reparations for the incident. Unable to reach a settlement, France and New Zealand submitted their disagreements to the Secretary General of the United Nations for binding arbitration.

The Secretary General's ruling, issued on July 6, 1986, required France to pay reparations of US $7 million and to cease interfering in certain of New Zealand's trade affairs with the European Economic Community. As to extradition, the Secretary General ordered that Mafart and Prieur be transferred to a French military facility on the isolated island of Hao in French Polynesia for a three-year period. The ruling stipulated that the two agents were "prohibited from leaving the island for any reason, except with the mutual consent of the two Governments." France and New Zealand formalized their understanding of the Secretary General's ruling in an exchange of letters described as the "1986 Agreement" or the "First Agreement."

About five months after the transfer of the two agents to Hao, France asked New Zealand for permission to transport Major Mafart to a hospital in Paris to undergo urgent medical treatment for an abdominal pain of unknown cause. In the midst of negotiations to acquire New Zealand's consent, France transferred Mafart to Paris. After voicing strong objection to France's unilateral action, New Zealand sent a physician, Dr. R.S. Croxson, to Paris in order to examine Mafart. Although he expressed doubt as to the necessity of an emergency evacuation, Croxson confirmed that Mafart's medical condition required sophisticated tests that were unavailable in Hao. Croxson continued to observe Mafart on a regular basis; on February 12, 1988, he informed New Zealand that Mafart's medical condition no longer warranted his continued stay in Paris. Instead of returning Mafart to Hao, France declared him "repatriated for health reasons" on March 11, 1988.

A similar episode occurred with Captain Prieur. On May 3, 1988, France requested New Zealand's permission to transfer Prieur to Paris because she was pregnant. New Zealand asked to examine Prieur on Hao before consenting to the transfer. France agreed. However, when French authorities learned that Prieur's father was dying of cancer, they decided "for obvious humanitarian reasons" to fly her to Paris before arrangements to obtain New Zealand's consent were completed.

Soon thereafter, New Zealand and France submitted their dispute to an arbitral tribunal. New Zealand demanded (1) a declaration that France had breached its obligations by failing to obtain New Zealand's consent prior to the removal of Mafart and Prieur from Hao and (2) an order that France must return the two agents to the island for the balance of their three-year sentences. France denied international responsibility on the theories of force majeure and distress. The Tribunal commented as follows:]

### Circumstances Precluding Wrongfulness

76. Under the title "Circumstances Precluding Wrongfulness" the International Law Commission proposed in Articles 29 to 35 a set of rules which include three provisions, on *force majeure* and fortuitous event (Article 31), distress (Article 32), and state of necessity (Article 33), which may be relevant to the decision on this case. * * *

77. [T]here are several reasons for excluding the applicability of the excuse of force majeure in this case. As pointed out in the report of the International Law Commission, Article 31 refers to "a situation facing the subject taking the action, which leads it, as it were, despite itself, to act in a

manner not in conformity with the requirements of an international obligation incumbent on it." Force majeure is "generally invoked to justify involuntary, or at least unintentional conduct"; it refers "to an irresistible force or an unforeseen external event against which it has no remedy and which makes it 'materially impossible' for it to act in conformity with the obligation," since "no person is required to do the impossible." * * *

New Zealand is right in asserting that the excuse of force majeure is not of relevance in this case because the test of its applicability is of absolute and material impossibility, and because a circumstance rendering performance more difficult or burdensome does not constitute a case of force majeure. Consequently, this excuse is of no relevance in the present case.

78. Article 32 of the Articles drafted by the International Law Commission deals with another circumstance which may preclude wrongfulness in international law, namely, that of the "distress" of the author of the conduct which constitutes the act of the State whose wrongfulness is in question. * * * The commentary of the International Law Commission explains that " 'distress' means a situation of extreme peril in which the organ of the State which adopts that conduct has, at that particular moment, no means of saving himself or persons entrusted to his care other than to act in a manner not in conformity with the requirements of the obligation in question." * * * The question therefore is to determine whether the circumstances of distress in a case of extreme urgency involving elementary humanitarian considerations affecting the acting organs of the State may exclude wrongfulness in this case.

79. In accordance with the previous legal considerations, three conditions would be required to justify the conduct followed by France in respect to Major Mafart and Captain Prieur:

(1) the existence of very exceptional circumstances of extreme urgency involving medical or other considerations of an elementary nature, provided always that a prompt recognition of the existence of those exceptional circumstances is subsequently obtained from the other interested party or is clearly demonstrated.

(2) The reestablishment of the original situation of compliance with the assignment in Hao as soon as the reasons of emergency invoked to justify the repatriation had disappeared.

(3) The existence of a good faith effort to try to obtain the consent of New Zealand in terms of the 1986 Agreement.

### The Case of Major Mafart

80. The New Zealand reaction to the French initiative for the removal of Major Mafart appears to have been conducted in conformity with the above considerations. * * *

81. The sending of Dr. Croxson to examine Major Mafart the same day of the arrival of the latter in Paris [implied] that if the alleged conditions of urgency justifying the evacuation were verified, consent would very likely have been given to what was until then a unilateral removal. * * * Dr. Croxson's first report, of 14 December 1987, accepts that Major Mafart needed "detailed investigations which were not available in Hao[.]" * * *

83. [Dr. Croxson's] sixth report, dated 12 February 1988, on the other hand, evidences that there was by that time a clear obligation of the French authorities to return Major Mafart to Hao, by reason of the disappearance of the urgent medical emergency which had determined his evacuation. This report, together with the absence of other medical reports showing the recurrence of the symptoms which determined the evacuation, demonstrates that Major Mafart should have been returned to Hao at least on 12 February 1988, and that failure to do so constituted a breach by the French Government of its obligations under the First Agreement. * * *

88. Both parties recognized that the return of Major Mafart to Hao depended mainly on his state of health. Thus, the French Ministry of Foreign Affairs in its note of 30 December 1987 to the New Zealand Embassy referring to France's respect for the 1986 Agreement had said that Major Mafart will return to Hao when his state of health allowed.

Consequently, there was no valid ground for Major Mafart continuing to remain in metropolitan France and the conclusion is unavoidable that this omission constitutes a material breach by the French Government of the First Agreement. * * *

### The Case of Captain Prieur

89. As to the situation of Captain Prieur, the French authorities advised the New Zealand Government, on 3 May 1988, that she was pregnant, adding that a medical report indicated that "this pregnancy should be treated with special care * * *" The advice added that "the medical facilities on Hao are not equipped to carry out the necessary medical examinations and to give Mrs. Prieur the care required by her condition." * * *

93. The facts * * *, which are not disputed, show that New Zealand would not oppose Captain Prieur's departure, if that became necessary because of special care which might be required by her pregnancy. * * *

94. On the other hand, it appears that during the day of 5 May the French Government suddenly decided to present the New Zealand Government with the fait accompli of Captain Prieur's hasty return for a new reason, the health of Mrs. Prieur's father, who was seriously ill, hospitalized for cancer. * * *

96. [D]uring the day of 5 May 1988, France did not seek New Zealand's approval in good faith for Captain Prieur's sudden departure; and accordingly, the return of Captain Prieur, who left Hao on Thursday, 5 May at 11:30 p.m. (French time) and arrived in Paris on Friday, 6 May, thus constituted a violation of the obligations under the 1986 Agreement. * * *

97. Moreover, France continued to fall short of its obligations by keeping Captain Prieur in Paris after the unfortunate death of her father on 16 May 1988. * * *

99. In summary, the circumstances of distress, of extreme urgency and the humanitarian considerations invoked by France may have been circumstances excluding responsibility for the unilateral removal of Major Mafart without obtaining New Zealand's consent, but clearly these circumstances entirely fail to justify France's responsibility for the removal of Captain

Prieur and from the breach of its obligations resulting from the failure to return the two officers to Hao (in the case of Major Mafart once the reasons for their removal had disappeared). There was here a clear breach of its obligations and a breach of material character.

## SECTION 7. COUNTER-MEASURES AND SELF-HELP

A state injured by another state's violation of an international obligation is entitled to take measures against the offending state. Article 11. I.L.C.Rep. 55–61 (1992). Such unilateral measures are sometimes described as self-help or in recent usage as counter-measures. More specific legal terms are used to describe three different kinds of counter-measures; as follows:

(i) Reprisal refers to a counter-measure that would be unlawful if not for the prior illegal act of the state against which they were taken. Reprisals under traditional international law generally involved use of force but they also include nonforcible measures.

(ii) Reciprocal measures or measures "by way of reciprocity" refer to nonperformance by the injured state of its obligations toward the offending state when such obligations correspond to or are directly connected with the obligations breached.

(iii) Retorsion refers to counter-measures of the injured state against the offending state that are generally permissible in international law irrespective of the prior breach (for example, suspending diplomatic relations or bilateral aid).

### A. CONDITIONS FOR RESORTING TO COUNTERMEASURES (SELF-HELP)

The Restatement (Third) includes the following section on self-help:

#### § 905. Unilateral Remedies

(1) Subject to Subsection (2), a state victim of a violation of an international obligation by another state may resort to countermeasures that might otherwise be unlawful, if such measures

(a) are necessary to terminate the violation or prevent further violation, or to remedy the violation; and

(b) are not out of proportion to the violation and the injury suffered.

(2) The threat or use of force in response to a violation of international law is subject to prohibitions on the threat or use of force in the United Nations Charter as well as to Subsection (1).

The International Law Commission's Draft Articles on State Responsibility (Part Two) contain a similar provision in Article 13:

> Any measure taken by an injured State * * * shall not be out of proportion to the gravity of the internationally wrongful act and of the effects thereof.

However, Article 14 of the Draft Articles significantly qualifies Article 13 by prohibiting an injured State from engaging in certain counter-measures, regardless of their proportionality. Article 14 reads as follows:

> 1. An injured State shall not resort, by way of countermeasure, to:
>
> (a) the threat or use of force [in contravention of Article 2, paragraph 4, of the United Nations Charter];
>
> (b) any conduct which:
>
> (i) is not in conformity with the rules of international law on the protection of fundamental human rights;
>
> (ii) is of serious prejudice to the normal operation of bilateral or multilateral diplomacy;
>
> (iii) is contrary to a peremptory norm of general international law;
>
> (iv) consists of a breach of an obligation towards any State other than the State which has committed the internationally wrongful act.
>
> 2. The prohibitions set forth in paragraph 1(a) include not only armed force but also any extreme measures of political or economic coercion jeopardizing the territorial integrity or political independence of the State against which they are taken.

Draft Article 12 states several further conditions on the resort to counter-measures:

> 1. Subject to the provisions set forth in paragraphs 2 and 3, no measure of the kind indicated in the preceding article [Article 11, countermeasures by an injured State] shall be taken by an injured State prior to:
>
> (a) the exhaustion of all the amicable settlement procedures available under general international law, the United Nations Charter or any other dispute settlement instrument to which it is a party; and
>
> (b) appropriate and timely communication of its intention.
>
> 2. The condition set forth in subparagraph (a) of the preceding paragraph does not apply:
>
> (a) where the State which has committed the internationally wrongful act does not cooperate in good faith in the choice and the implementation of available settlement procedures;
>
> (b) to interim measures of protection taken by the injured State, until the admissibility of such measures have been decided upon by an international body within the framework of a third party settlement procedure;
>
> (c) to any measures taken by the injured State if the State which has committed the internationally wrongful act fails to comply with an interim measure of protection indicated by the said body.

3. The exceptions set forth in the preceding paragraph do not apply wherever the measure envisaged is not in conformity with the obligation to settle disputes in such a manner that international peace and security, and justice, are not endangered.

### *Notes and Questions*

1. Should every human rights violation imply an absolute prohibition on equivalent counter-measures, or should a distinction be made between categories of human rights? Most agree that a state cannot engage in counter-measures affecting the life and physical integrity of nationals of the wrongdoing state. However, should, for example, it be lawful for a state, if the freedom of movement of its nationals has been restricted by another state, to impose similar constraints on the movement of the nationals of the other state?

2. Does paragraph 1(b)(ii) of Article 14 prohibit the suspension of diplomatic relations as a counter-measure at the bilateral or multilateral level? To what extent should a regime of counter-measures be designed to resolve rather than to aggravate international disputes, and how does your answer to this question affect your interpretation of the purposes behind paragraph 1(b)(ii)?

3. Is paragraph 1(b)(iii) of Article 14 necessary? Isn't it true that no departure is ever allowed from rules of *jus cogens*?

4. Does Article 14 adequately protect third-party states from the effects of an injured state's counter-measures? Given the increasing political and economic interdependence of nations, do you expect that counter-measures normally could be taken against a wrongdoing state without having any spillover effects on third parties? Should the regime of counter-measures be nullified simply because of the possibility of incidental or unintended effects on third parties?

5. Does paragraph 2 of Article 14, proscribing the use of extreme political or economic coercion as a counter-measure on the theory that such actions are potentially as injurious as use of armed force, effectively eliminate virtually all counter-measures? How broadly is this prohibition to be construed? Couldn't the appropriateness of extreme measures of political and economic coercion simply be determined by using the test of proportionality?

## CASE CONCERNING AIR SERVICES AGREEMENT BETWEEN FRANCE AND THE UNITED STATES, ARBITRAL AWARD OF DEC. 9, 1978

18 U.N.R.I.A.A. 417, 443–46.

[The United States claimed that France had violated the bilateral Air Services Agreement of 1946 by refusing to allow a smaller Pan Am plane to be substituted for a 747 aircraft in Pan Am flights to Paris from London. The French contended that the proposed change (a "change of gauge") was not authorized by the Agreement without French consent. The U.S. disagreed. After fruitless discussions, France compelled Pan Am to cease its flights to Paris. The U.S. protested and proposed arbitration. It also set in motion action under U.S. law to suspend the French flights to Los Angeles that were authorized by the 1946 Agreement and had been long established. The case was then submitted to arbitration under a compromise that put two questions to the tribunal: (1) did the U.S. carrier have the right to change gauge? (2) did the U.S. have the right to suspend French traffic to Los Angeles in retaliation for the suspension of Pan Am flights to Paris? The Tribunal answered both questions affirmatively.

[With respect to the second issue, France had questioned the U.S. right to retaliate on two grounds. First, it contended that retaliation was illegal because the Treaty provided for arbitration and the retaliatory measures were undertaken when the arbitral compromise was being negotiated. Second, it argued that the U.S. retaliation (the suspension of long-established Paris–Los Angeles flights of Air France) was grossly disproportionate to the French suspension of a new service from London to Paris. On these issues the Tribunal commented as follows:]

If a situation arises which, in one State's view, results in the violation of an international obligation by another State, the first State is entitled, within the limits set by the general rules of international law pertaining to the use of armed force, to affirm its rights through "counter-measures." (para. 81)

It is generally agreed that all counter-measures must, in the first instance, have some degree of equivalence with the alleged breach; this is a well-known rule. In the course of the present proceedings, both Parties have recognized that the rule applies to this case, and they both have invoked it. It has been observed, generally, that judging the "proportionality" of counter-measures is not an easy task and can at best be accomplished by approximation. In the Tribunal's view, it is essential, in a dispute between States, to take into account not only the injuries suffered by the companies concerned but also the importance of the questions of principle arising from the alleged breach. The Tribunal thinks that it will not suffice, in the present case, to compare the losses suffered by Pan Am on account of the suspension of projected services with the losses which the French companies would have suffered as a result of the counter-measures; it will also be necessary to take into account the importance of the positions of principle which were taken when the French authorities prohibited changes of gauge in third countries. (para. 83)

Can it be said that the resort to such counter-measures, which are contrary to international law but justified by a violation of international law allegedly committed by the State against which they are directed, is restricted if it is found that the Parties previously accepted a duty to negotiate or an obligation to have their dispute settled through a procedure of arbitration or of judicial settlement? (para. 84)

It is tempting to assert that when Parties enter into negotiations, they are under a general duty not to aggravate the dispute, this general duty being a kind of emanation of the principle of good faith. (para. 85)

Though it is far from rejecting such an assertion, the Tribunal is of the view that, when attempting to define more precisely such a principle, several essential considerations must be examined. (para. 86)

The Tribunal recalls the terms of Article VIII of the 1946 Agreement.

This Article provides for an obligation of continuing consultation between the Parties. In the context of this general duty, the Agreement establishes a clear mandate to the Parties to make good faith efforts to negotiate on issues of potential controversy, several other provisions of the Agreement and the Annex state requirements to consult in specific circumstances, when the possibility of a dispute might be particularly acute. Finally, Article X imposes on the Parties a special consultation requirement when, in spite of previous efforts, a dispute has arisen. (para. 88)

But the present problem is whether, on the basis of the above-mentioned texts, counter-measures are prohibited. The Tribunal does not consider that either general international law or the provisions of the Agreement allow it to go that far. (para. 89)

Indeed, it is necessary carefully to assess the meaning of counter-measures in the framework of proportionality. Their aim is to restore equality between the Parties and to encourage them to continue negotiations with mutual desire to reach an acceptable solution. In the present case, the United States of America holds that a change of gauge is permissible in third countries; that conviction defined its position before the French refusal came into play; the United States counter-measures restore in a negative way the symmetry of the initial positions. (para. 90)

It goes without saying that recourse to counter-measures involves the great risk of giving rise, in turn, to a further reaction, thereby causing an escalation which will lead to a worsening of the conflict. Counter-measures therefore should be a wager on the wisdom, not on the weakness of the other Party. They should be used with a spirit of great moderation and be accompanied by a genuine effort at resolving the dispute. But the Arbitral Tribunal does not believe that it is possible, in the present state of international relations, to lay down a rule prohibiting the use of counter-measures during negotiations, especially where such counter-measures are accompanied by an offer for a procedure affording the possibility of accelerating the solution of the dispute. (para. 91)

* * *

However, the lawfulness of such counter-measures has to be considered still from another viewpoint. It may indeed be asked whether they are valid in general, in the case of a dispute concerning a point of law, where there is arbitral or judicial machinery which can settle the dispute. Many jurists have felt that while arbitral or judicial proceedings were in progress, recourse to counter-measures, even if limited by the proportionality rule, was prohibited. Such an assertion deserves sympathy but requires further elaboration. If the proceedings form part of an institutional framework ensuring some degree of enforcement of obligations, the justification of counter-measures will undoubtedly disappear, but owing to the existence of that framework rather than solely on account of the existence of arbitral or judicial proceedings as such. (para. 94)

Besides, the situation during the period in which a case is not yet before a tribunal is not the same as the situation during the period in which that case is *sub judice*. So long as a dispute has not been brought before the tribunal, in particular because an agreement between the Parties is needed to set the procedure in motion, the period of negotiation is not over and the rules mentioned above remain applicable. This may be a regrettable solution, as the Parties in principle did agree to resort to arbitration or judicial settlement, but it must be conceded that under present-day international law States have not renounced their right to take counter-measures in such situations. In fact, however, this solution may be preferable as it facilitates States' acceptance of arbitration or judicial settlement procedures. (para. 95)

The situation changes once the tribunal is in a position to act. To the extent that the tribunal has the necessary means to achieve the objectives justifying the counter-measures, it must be admitted that the right of the Parties to initiate such measures disappears. In other words, the power of a tribunal to decide on interim measures of protection, regardless of whether this power is expressly mentioned or implied in its statute (at least as the power to formulate recommendations to this effect), leads to the disappearance of the power to initiate counter-measures and may lead to an elimination of existing counter-measures to the extent that the tribunal so provides as an interim measure of protection. As the object and scope of the power of the tribunal to decide on interim measures of protection may be defined quite narrowly, however, the power of the Parties to initiate or maintain counter-measures, too, may not disappear completely. (para. 96)

As far as the action undertaken by the United States Government in the present case is concerned, the situation is quite simple. Even if arbitration under Article X of the Agreement is set in motion unilaterally, implementation may take time, and during this period counter-measures are not excluded: a State resorting to such measures, however, must do everything in its power to expedite the arbitration. This is exactly what the Government of the United States has done. (para. 98)

The Tribunal's Reply to Question (B) consists of the above observations as a whole. These observations lead to the conclusion that, under the circumstances in question, the Government of the United States had the right to undertake the action that it undertook under Part 213 of the Economic Regulations of the C.A.B. (para. 99)

## *Notes*

1. Should a distinction be made between a counter-measure in the nature of reprisal and nonperformance of an obligation in response to a breach of the same or equivalent obligation by the other party? The latter has been referred to in international law jurisprudence as the principle of *inadimplenti non est inadimplendum* (no performance is due to a nonperformer), described by Judge Anzilotti as "so just, so equitable, so universally recognized". Dissenting opinion in River Meuse Case, 1937 P.C.I.J., Ser. A/B, No. 70, p. 50 (1937). In the above *Air Services Case,* could the U.S. action to suspend flights to Los Angeles have been regarded as permissible nonperformance of an obligation similar to that allegedly breached by France? If so, would "necessity and proportionality" have been required? What criteria are relevant for differentiating nonperformance as a measure of reciprocity from nonperformance as a measure of self-help subject to limitations imposed by international law? For general discussion of reciprocity and unilateral remedies, see Zoller, Peacetime Unilateral Remedies 14–27 (1984).

2. Is a reprisal generally impermissible where an agreement between the parties provides for arbitration or judicial settlement? An affirmative answer was given by the *Institut de Droit International* in 1934, 38 Ann. de l'Inst. 709

(1934). The International Law Commission also took that view in 1979, I.L.C.Rep. 319 (1979), as did Bowett, Economic Coercion and Reprisal of States, 13 Va.J.Int.L. 1 (1972) and Dumbauld, Interim Measures of Protection in International Controversies 182–84 (1932). Why did the tribunal in the *Air Services Case* take a different position? See Damrosch, Retaliation or Arbitration or Both, 74 A.J.I.L. 785, 802, 807 (1980). Damrosch maintains that a victim state should not be required to "embark on lengthy and expensive litigation" before it may suspend its performance in the event of breach. Id. at 806. The "interplay and even escalation of responses before a dispute reaches a tribunal can serve important purposes." Id. at 807.

3. Article 12 of the International Law Commission's Draft Articles on State Responsibility (Part Two) requires an injured state, prior to engaging in counter-measures, (1) to exhaust "all the amicable settlement procedures available under general international law, the United Nations Charter or any other dispute settlement instrument to which it is a party," and (2) to communicate its intentions to the state in breach. However, the injured state may take interim measures of protection until a competent tribunal decides on the admissibility of such interim measures. I.L.C.Rep. 61–69 (1992). By requiring the injured state to exhaust *all* amicable procedures, would Article 12 give undue advantage to the wrongdoing state? Given the time-consuming nature of international dispute settlement mechanisms, is it fair to expect the injured state to defer the taking of counter-measures potentially for many years? Does Article 12 give the wrongdoing state an incentive to employ delaying tactics in negotiation? Would a fairer approach be to make the exhaustion of amicable settlement procedures a parallel obligation, rather than a precondition, for resort to counter-measures—that is, the injured state could take counter-measures until such time as the wrongdoing state agreed to a dispute settlement procedure? Or would the immediate imposition of counter-measures put the injured state in an unfair position of strength in any ensuing negotiations agreed to by the wrongdoing state?

4. When U.S. diplomats and other U.S. nationals were held as hostages in Tehran in 1979–1980, the U.S. took counter-measures by freezing (i.e., blocking) Iranian assets, to prevent Iran from withdrawing its funds in U.S. banks. The "freeze" continued after the U.S. instituted proceedings against Iran in the International Court of Justice. Other counter-measures such as a trade embargo also were taken. The Court in its decision condemned Iran for allowing and condoning the seizure of the Embassy and detention of U.S. nationals. 1980 I.C.J. 3. It mentioned the U.S. counter-measures of an economic character but did not hold them to be wrongful. Id. at 17–18, 28–29. However, two judges (Soviet and Syrian nationals) declared that the U.S. blocking of Iranian assets was a coercive act aimed to influence the outcome of the dispute and therefore incompatible with the U.S. submission to the Court. United States Diplomatic and Consular Staff in Tehran Case, 1980 I.C.J. 3, 53–54, 63–65. Should self-help measures be precluded during judicial proceedings "since they are designed to bring about the termination of the conflict without regard to the impartial determination the parties agreed to seek when they assented to the Tribunal's jurisdiction." Stein, Contempt, Crisis and the Court, 76 A.J.I.L. 512 (1982). What if the tribunal is unable to protect the aggrieved State from injury during the pendency of the case? In the Tehran hostages case, the Court's order for provisional measures of protection was ineffective. Is that why the Court refrained from criticizing the economic counter-measures taken by the United

States in the hostages case? See Schachter, International Law in the Hostage Crisis, in American Hostages in Iran, 325, 339–45 (Christopher et al., 1984).

5. The tribunal in the *Air Services Case* (supra) said that counter-measures must have "some degree of equivalence with the breach" (para. 83). This suggests a "tit for tat" response to a breach. But is that always permissible? Would the United States have had the right to hold Iranian diplomats as hostages because the Iranians held U.S. diplomats? Are not some counter-measures, although "equivalent," impermissible because contrary to peremptory norms or recognized humanitarian principles? How difficult, in practice, are the concepts of "proportionality" and "equivalence" to apply? Is it always possible to weigh the equivalence of counter-measures against the wrongful act?

6. May counter-measures against a state's wrongful conduct take the form of sanctions against individuals because they are nationals of the offending state? May the assets of individuals be frozen or seized on the ground that the state of which they are nationals has acted wrongfully? A U.S. Court held such action permissible with respect to Cuban nationals in the U.S. Sardino v. Federal Reserve Bank, 361 F.2d 106 (2d Cir.1966). The Court observed that "the Constitution protects the alien from arbitrary action by our government but not from reasonable response to such action by his own". Id. at 111. Does international law also impose a limit? For example if the state whose nationals were affected maintains that the "freeze" of assets was disproportionate or arbitrary, an international law issue would be raised. See Restatement (Third) § 905. Would retaliatory action against individuals for the wrongs of their states raise human rights issues based on invidious discrimination or disproportionate penalties? See Narenji v. Civiletti, 617 F.2d 745 (D.C.Cir.1979), upholding U.S. regulations that required Iranian students in the U.S. during the hostage crisis to report to the Immigration Service for a check on their compliance with their visas. United States legislation on counter-measures generally includes procedural provisions to protect individuals affected from arbitrary action. See Zoller, Enforcing International Law Through U.S. Legislation, 42–57 (1985).

7. There is considerable disagreement over whether states belonging to a so-called "self-contained regime"—defined generally as an international body creating both substantive obligations *and* special procedures in the event of a breach—may resort to countermeasures based on general international law in addition to the remedies specified by the regime's constitutive instrument. The European Economic Community (EEC) is perhaps the most prominent example of a "self-contained regime"; another common example is a human rights "system," such as the European Convention or the Covenant on Civil and Political Rights. The EEC Court has expressed the view that member states forfeited their freedom to engage in unilateral measures under the general international law of countermeasures as a consequence of joining the community. However, Gaetano Arangio–Ruiz, special rapporteur on state responsibility to the International Law Commission, has generally concluded otherwise:

> [A] State joining a so-called 'self-contained' regime does not thereby restrict—by a kind of autolimitation—the rights or *facultes* of unilateral reaction it possesses under general international law to such an extent as to render the accepted 'regime' unsusceptible of derogation or integration. Of course, any State accepting the 'regime' shall be bound, when confronted with a breach of a 'regime's' obligation on the part of another participating State, to react—if it wishes to react—first of all in conformity with the provisions of the relevant 'regime'.

Henkin also has stated, with respect to the principal human rights treaties, that the stipulated procedures were intended to supplement rather than to supplant remedies available under the general international law. Which view do you believe is most sound? Do states have an obligation, at a minimum, to utilize the express mechanisms of the "self-contained regime" simultaneously with any unilateral countermeasures? To what extent, if any, does the view expressed by Arangio–Ruiz and Henkin jeopardize the efficacy of international bodies such as the EEC?

8. Must a state show injury in order to resort to countermeasures, or is a mere breach of international law sufficient for a state to act? Is there an inherent risk in a regime of countermeasures that a powerful nation could assume for itself a role as the "world's police" to enforce its own conception of the law? Riphagen, the special rapporteur on state responsibility, has observed that the International Law Commission should "take the greatest care, in devising the conditions of lawful resort to such actions, to ensure that the factual inequalities among States do not unduly operate to the advantage of the strong and rich over the weak and needy." I.L.C.Rep. 327 (1991).

9. Riphagen also has noted that respect for humanitarian principles is another substantive restriction on resort to countermeasures. Other substantive limitations on countermeasures include the inviolability of specially protected persons (such as diplomatic envoys) and the obligations embodied in *jus cogens* and *erga omnes*. See I.L.C.Rep. 331–32 (1991).

## B. COUNTERMEASURES TO VIOLATION OF MULTILATERAL TREATY OR GENERAL CUSTOMARY LAW

As a rule a state injured by a breach of a multilateral treaty may suspend its performance of obligations toward the state that acted wrongfully. Article 60(2) of the Vienna Convention on the Law of Treaties provides that a party "specially affected by the breach may invoke it as a ground for suspending the operations of the agreement in whole or in part between itself and the defaulting state." A similar right of suspension by an injured state toward the violating state would seem appropriate in case of a breach of customary law. However, a number of exceptions to this broad right appear to be required. Consider the following:

1. Suspending performance of the obligation toward a defaulting state may adversely affect the rights of all other parties to the multilateral treaty. In that case the counter-measure would injure third states as well as the offending state. An example is a breach of a multilateral treaty concerning pollution. If a party suspends its restraints on pollution with respect to a state guilty of violation it almost surely will also injure other states parties to the treaty. In some cases, nonperformance may adversely affect a collective interest such as protection of the high seas, Antarctic or outer space. When a unilateral remedy against a violator by way of nonperformance would entail damage to a collective interest, there is good reason to bar unilateral nonperformance.

2. Where obligations are intended to protect individuals irrespective of nationality, to allow nonperformance as a retaliation for a breach would injure individuals who are the objects of protection. The Vienna Convention of Treaties does not allow for suspension of provisions for "the protection of

the human person contained in treaties of a humanitarian character". Art. 60(5).

3. Multilateral treaties may provide expressly for responses to violations by collective decisions or other procedures. Such express stipulations are generally construed to exclude other responses by injured parties. See Restatement (Third) § 905, Comment *a*.

4. A violation of a peremptory rule of international law (e.g., on genocide, aggression, slave trade) obviously should not be a ground for an injured state or any state to suspend its compliance with that obligation. Other fundamental principles of international intercourse as, for example, immunities of diplomats, may have a similar status in this respect. A violation of diplomatic immunity by one state does not entitle the injured state to engage in similar violations.

The International Law Commission's Draft Articles on State Responsibility (Part Two) include provisions covering the above situations. See Articles 5, 14. I.L.C.Rep. 73–86, 93–99 (1992).

## C. RETORSION

### *1. Examples of Retorsion*

Retorsion as indicated above refers to retaliatory measures that an aggrieved state is legally free to take whether or not the offending state committed an illegal act. In practice, most retaliatory acts fall into this category. Typical examples of such retaliatory actions are rupture of diplomatic relations, cessation of trade in general or in specific items (e.g., strategic materials), curtailment of migration from the offending government, and denial of benefits available to the offending government. See Wild, Sanctions and Treaty Enforcement (1934); Lowenfeld, Trade Controls for Political Ends (2d ed. 1983); Zoller, Peacetime Unilateral Measures (1984).

Retorsion is often an "equivalent" act of retaliation in response to an unfriendly act. For example, the expulsion of a diplomat is commonly followed by that diplomat's state declaring as *persona non grata* a diplomat of equivalent rank from the first state. The rupture of diplomatic relations falls within the scope of a state's discretion. It may follow an unfriendly act of another state that is not itself illegal (as, for example, an expulsion of nationals) or it may be a response to conduct considered unlawful. Trade boycotts or denial of trade benefits may similarly be directed against "unfriendly" acts or illegal conduct.

Whether or not they are effective in advancing their objectives depends on the particular circumstances. In many cases, economic boycotts or denial of specific benefits have not resulted in changing the policies of the offending states. This has been most evident when the target state's conduct is a manifestation of a basic political position. For example, the economic sanctions adopted by the United States against "unfriendly" regimes in China, Cuba, Iran, Libya and the U.S.S.R. are often considered to have failed to change the behavior of those states. See Doxey, Economic Sanctions in International Law (1980); Hufbauer, Schott & Elliott, Economic Sanctions Reconsidered (1990). However, some studies show that economic sanctions have probably influenced the offending state's behavior in a number of cases though it is difficult to say whether such sanctions were decisive in that respect. See Hufbauer et al. id. for analyses of more than a hundred cases of economic sanctions and their apparent effects.

U.S. legislation provides for retorsion in response to illegal acts in various situations:

— The first "Hickenlooper Amendment" directs the President to suspend foreign aid to any state that nationalized properties of U.S. nationals without providing for compensation as required by international law. Foreign Assistance Act of 1961, as amended 22 U.S.C.A. § 2370(e).

— The U.S. Foreign Assistance Act also denies assistance "to the government of any country which engages in a consistent pattern of gross violations of internationally recognized human rights," including torture, prolonged detention without charges "or other flagrant denial of the right to life, liberty and security of person". 22 U.S.C.A. § 2151h(a).

— Legislation provides for countervailing duties and other countermeasures in response to violations of rules on trade (e.g., dumping).

— Legislation on air carriers, fishermen, and taxation also prescribes measures against foreign states that violate treaty rights of the United States. See generally Zoller, Enforcing International Law Through U.S. Legislation (1985).

### 2. *Legal Limits on Retorsion*

Since states are generally free to refuse to trade with others or to deny benefits and to take other action that falls under the heading of retorsion, the question of their legality does not normally arise. However, their legality may be questioned when the counter-measures are directed to an unlawful end. Consider the example of a state discontinuing trade with an offending country and imposing as a condition for the resumption of trade a change in the internal or foreign policy of the offending state. Apropos of that example, Schachter has written:

> In that case, an otherwise discretionary act, the retorsion, is used as a means of coercing the object of that retorsion to give up its sovereign right, quite apart from the alleged violation of law that gave rise to the retorsion. There is good reason to consider such use of retorsion as illegal because of its improper objective. One may characterize it as an abuse of rights, but it is more precise to refer to a primary rule that precludes such coercion. The rule is expressed in the unanimously agreed Declaration of Principles of International Law Concerning Friendly Relations (adopted by the United Nations General Assembly in 1970) in the following language:
>
> > "No State may use or encourage the use of economic, political or any other type of measures to coerce another State in order to obtain from it the subordination of the exercise of its sovereign rights and to secure from it advantages of any kind."
>
> The fact that retorsion is used when the target of its use has violated an international law obligation would not legally entitle the government using it to demand that the offending State give up its sovereign rights.

> It is most unlikely that this broad principle will be challenged. However, its application in actual cases is not always readily apparent except in rather extreme situations (such as a demand that the offending State change its government or cease relations with another State). Nonetheless, even acknowledging the impropriety of these "extreme" cases (which are by no means hypothetical) can be a significant step toward recognizing that in some cases otherwise legal acts may be rendered illicit because of the wrongful end sought.

Schachter, International Law in Theory and Practice, 178 Rec. des Cours 185–86 (1982–V).

Should acts of retorsion be subject to requirements of proportionality? In practice, retaliatory measures tend to have "a degree of equivalence" to the offense. Diplomatic or trade relations are rarely, if ever, suspended for minor or isolated offenses. While states are not legally required to maintain diplomatic or trade relations—or, in general, to be friendly—an "unfriendly act" that is disproportionate to an offense and causes substantial damage to another state may be viewed as "an abuse of rights" and therefore illegitimate. Oppenheim, International Law 345 (8th ed., Lauterpacht, 1955) concludes that states are legally precluded from taking measures that would otherwise be permitted if such measures "would inflict upon another State an injury which cannot be justified by a legitimate consideration of its own advantage". Is this general formulation of an "abuse of rights" principle verifiable as a rule of customary international law? If not, should it be favored as a rule *de lege ferenda?*

## D. COLLECTIVE SANCTIONS

1. Counter-measures against an offending state for violation of an international obligation may be taken by aggrieved states through joint or parallel action. Such action, commonly called collective sanctions, have generally involved severance of diplomatic relations, trade boycotts and, in some cases, cessation of air or sea traffic. These measures, if not contrary to treaty obligations, fall within the discretionary authority of states (retorsion). Where they are contrary to treaty obligations or customary law obligations, they may be legally justified as reprisals by states injured by the offending state's violation. In several cases states not directly injured have joined in collective counter-measures on the ground that the violation affected a collective interest or a common concern of the international community. While such instances might have been characterized as responses to violations of *erga omnes* obligations, the states taking the action have rarely, if ever, explicitly referred to that doctrine. Nonetheless, their emphasis on the common concern of states in combatting such acts as aggression, terrorism or gross violations of human rights is in keeping with the concept of *erga omnes* obligations.

2. Collective sanctions of a non-military character may be adopted by the U.N. Security Council as mandatory enforcement measures under Chapter VII of the U.N. Charter, particularly Article 41. Decisions of the Council under that article must be based on a determination of the existence of a threat to, or breach of, peace or an act of aggression. Article 39 of the Charter. The Council may then require U.N. members to sever economic

and diplomatic relations and to interrupt, wholly or partially, all means of communication, including air traffic, postal and radio. Article 41. It may also order military action under Article 42. See Chapter 11. Collective sanctions under Article 41 were ordered by the Council in 1968 against the "illegal racist minority regime" in Southern Rhodesia (now Zimbabwe). S.C.Res. 253 (XXIII), (1968). See Chapter 11, p. 990. In 1977 the Security Council also adopted a mandatory resolution under Chapter VII requiring all states to cease providing South Africa with arms and related material of all types. S.C.Res. 418 (XXXII), (1977). That resolution included a determination that the acts and policies of South Africa constituted a threat to international peace and security. See Chapter 11, pp. 986–87.

Almost immediately after the Iraqi invasion of Kuwait in August 1990, the Security Council imposed a sweeping trade and financial embargo on Iraq. S.C.Res. 661 (1990). See generally Oscar Schachter, United Nations Law in the Gulf Conflict, 85 Am.J.Int'l L. 452, 454–57 (1991). Most recently, in May 1992, the Security Council declared trade sanctions and an oil embargo on Yugoslavia, comprising Serbia and Montenegro, in response to the Serbian-led rebellion against Bosnia. S.C.Res. 757 (1992).

3. Obligatory collective sanctions have been held to be required, in at least one case, on the basis of a declaratory resolution of the U.N. Security Council. In 1970, the Security Council affirmed a General Assembly resolution that declared South Africa's mandate over South West Africa (Namibia) terminated. The Council then declared that the presence of South African authorities in Namibia was illegal and that their acts concerning Namibia were illegal and invalid. An advisory opinion of the International Court of Justice in 1971 held that all states are legally obliged to draw the consequences of the illegal presence of South Africa by not recognizing its administration or acts performed by it in the territory (with some exceptions required in the interest of the inhabitants). Advisory Opinion Concerning Namibia, 1971 I.C.J. 16. See p. 511.

Does this opinion of the Court indicate that all states may have a duty to take appropriate measures (particularly, non-recognition of illegal acts) when an offending state has committed a serious breach of law of concern to the international community? Does it depend on a binding decision by the Security Council?

4. In a case where the Security Council has called on parties to a dispute to negotiate a peaceful settlement and has not recommended "sanction", may states not parties to the dispute impose a trade embargo against one of the disputing states? The issue arose in 1983 during the war between Argentina and Great Britain over the Argentine action in the Falkland (Malvinas) Islands. Members of the European Economic Community and the United States imposed financial and trade restrictions on Argentina on the ground that Argentina had violated article 2(4) of the Charter. See Acevedo, The U.S. Measures Against Argentina Resulting from the Malvinas Conflict, 78 A.J.I.L. 323 (1984).

5. Trade restrictions and other retaliatory measures were taken by some states against Iran because of the seizure and detention of U.S. diplomats and other persons in Tehran in 1979–80. Although the Security Council had censured Iran for its breach of fundamental rules of diplomatic

law, it had not called on states to take economic or diplomatic sanctions against Iran. The retaliatory actions were not challenged on legal grounds. On the seizure of the diplomats and Security Council action in that case, see the I.C.J. decision in Chapter 10, Section 4.

6. A threat of collective sanctions was included in the Bonn Declaration on Hijacking, adopted in 1975 by the United States, Japan, France, Italy, West Germany and Great Britain. See Chapter 5, Section 6C on Terrorism.

## SECTION 8. REPARATION FOR THE BREACH OF AN INTERNATIONAL OBLIGATION

### *JIMÉNEZ DE ARÉCHAGA, INTERNATIONAL LAW IN THE PAST THIRD OF A CENTURY*

159 Rec. des Cours 285–87 (1978–I).*

Leaving aside the possibility of sanctions which may be applied by an international organization in the event of international crimes, a State discharges the responsibility incumbent upon it for breach of an international obligation by making reparation for the injury caused.

Reparation is the generic term which describes the various methods available to a State for discharging or releasing itself from such responsibility. The forms of reparation may consist in restitution, indemnity or satisfaction.

The basic principles governing reparation were established by the Permanent Court of International Justice as follows:

> "* * * reparation must, as far as possible, wipe out all the consequences of the illegal act and re-establish the situation which would, in all probability, have existed if that act had not been committed. Restitution in kind, or, if this is not possible, payment of a sum corresponding to the value which a restitution in kind would bear; the award, if need be, of damages for loss sustained which would not be covered by restitution in kind or payment in place of it—such are the principles which should serve to determine the amount of compensation due for an act contrary to international law." P.C.I.J. Series A No. 17, pp. 47–48.

(1) RESTITUTION

Restitution in kind is designed to re-establish the situation which would have existed if the wrongful act or omission had not taken place, by performance of the obligation which the State failed to discharge: revocation of the unlawful act, return of a property wrongfully removed or abstention from further wrongful conduct. The Permanent Court of International Justice implied, in the above passage, that restitution is the normal form of reparation and indemnity could only take its place if restitution in kind "is not possible".

* Footnotes omitted. Reprinted by permission of A.W. Sijthoff & Noordhoff International.

Often, an arbitration agreement or *compromis* confers discretion on the arbitrator to select the most adequate form of reparation in a given case. In such cases, the tribunal will take into consideration the practical difficulties or inconveniences which may be involved in restitution in kind and select pecuniary compensation instead. The same discretion is vested in the International Court of Justice under Article 36(2) of its Statute. For these reasons, although restitution in kind remains the basic form of reparation, in practice, and in the great majority of cases, monetary compensation takes its place.

(2) INDEMNITY

This is "the most usual form of reparation" since "money is the common measure of valuable things." Since monetary compensation must, as far as possible, "wipe out all the consequences of the illegal act" and correspond "to the value which a restitution in kind would bear", loss of profits are included and the value of a confiscated property must be determined at the time of payment and not at that of confiscation. The indemnity should compensate for all damage which follows as a consequence of the unlawful act, including "a profit which would have been possible in the ordinary course of events" but not prospective gains which are highly problematical, "too remote or speculative" or "possible but contingent and undeterminate damage." The basic test is the certainty of the damage. It is not essential that the damage should have already taken place for compensation to be recoverable. For instance, the future damaging consequences which will certainly result from nuclear fall-out warrant compensation even before the actual damage has occurred. Punitive or exemplary damages, inspired by disapproval of the unlawful act and as a measure of deterrence or reform of the offender, are incompatible with the basic idea underlying the duty of reparation. Imposition of such damages goes beyond the jurisdiction conferred on the International Court of Justice by its Statute and that normally attributed to arbitral tribunals, which are not invested "with a repressive power".

(3) SATISFACTION

This third form of reparation is appropriate for non-material damage or moral injury to the dignity or personality of the State.

The forms of satisfaction must be considered, in contemporary law and practice, as limited to the presentation of official regrets and apologies, the punishment of the guilty minor officials and particularly the formal acknowledgment or judicial declaration of the unlawful character of the act.

The International Court of Justice, following the precedent of arbitral awards, has asserted that a judicial declaration of the unlawful character of an act constitutes "in itself appropriate satisfaction."

## *Notes*

1. The issue of whether restitution-in-kind or indemnity should take precedence in the international law of reparations was faced squarely in Texaco Overseas Petroleum Co. and California Asiatic Oil Co. v. The Government of the Libyan Arab Republic, 17 I.L.M. 1 (1978); see p. 136 supra. In reaching that issue, the sole arbitrator (Professor Dupuy) held, *inter alia,* that arbitration clauses, contractual references to "general principles of law" as the governing law, and/or characterizations of an agreement as one for "economic develop-

ment" were sufficient to create an "internationalized" contractual relationship which could not be lawfully affected by national legal action (in this case, nationalization measures against claimants' concessions). The Arbitrator then held that under international law, restitution-in-kind was the "normal sanction for non-performance of contractual obligations." Id. at 36. The only proviso to his order requiring the Libyan government to "perform and give full effect" to the concession agreements it had breached, was an indication that the order might be reversed upon a showing that compliance was not dependent solely upon the will of the parties. Id. at 36–37.

The award against the Government of Libya was rendered in defendant's absence; Libya did not participate in any stage of the proceedings. In fact, Libya had already stated that it would compensate the claimants. Rigaux, Des dieux et des héros, [1978] Revue Critique de Droit Int'l Privé 439–440. Several months after the Arbitrator announced his decision the parties settled their dispute for 152 million dollars in crude oil; Von Mehren, Introductory Note, 17 I.L.M. 2 (1978).

2. A conclusion contrary to that in the *Texaco Case* was reached by Judge Lagergren in an earlier award rendered in BP v. Libya (Arbitral Award of Aug. 1, 1974 and Oct. 10, 1983). After extensive review of the authorities, Judge Lagergren decided that restitution would not be a proper remedy in case of confiscation of a concession in breach of the concession agreement. 53 I.L.R. 297, 346–48 (1979).

3. Even if restitution-in-kind should be the preferred remedy for disputes based on treaties between states, query whether that principle holds when a state contracts with individuals? Should an individual be able to invoke an "international contract law" to force a sovereign authority to act in a specified way with regard to activities within the authority's own territory?

The International Law Commission's articles on state responsibility (Part Two) include the following:

Article 7

> If the internationally wrongful act is a breach of an international obligation concerning the treatment to be accorded by a State, within its jurisdiction, to aliens, whether natural or juridical persons, and the State which has committed the internationally wrongful act does not re-establish the situation as it existed before the breach, the injured State may require that State to pay to it a sum of money corresponding to the value which a re-establishment of the situation, as it existed before the breach, would bear.

I.L.C.Rep. 238 (1984).

4. Compensation may include both direct and indirect damage. In case of an oil spill or destruction of a ship lost revenue may be included. But on the whole, rules as to calculation of damages, interest, loss of profits etc. are not clear. See Whiteman, Damages in International Law, 3 vols. (1943). Should punitive or "exemplary" damages be awarded if the offense is serious and intentional or repetitive? There is some authority holding that punitive awards against states are not permissible. See Judge Parker's opinion in *Lusitania Cases* (U.S. v. Germany 1923). 7 U.N.Rep. Int'l Arb. Awards 201 (1923). Should exception be made for an international crime? See Section 5 above.

5. Since the primary obligation of the violating state is to undo the wrong and discontinue the acts that caused the violation, tribunals have occasionally

issued orders directing the respondent state to take such steps. In the Iranian hostage case, the International Court of Justice ordered Iran to release the hostages and turn over the premises and archives of the U.S. Embassy to the protecting Power. 1980 I.C.J. 3, 45–46. Specific performance may be especially important in cases involving continuing environmental damage, an increasingly important topic of international claims. See Chapter 16.

## SECTION 9. INTERNATIONAL PROCEDURES TO IMPLEMENT OBLIGATIONS OF REPARATION

An injured state that is legally entitled to reparation from a state responsible for a wrongful act may bring a claim through diplomatic channels or through any procedure for dispute settlement to which the states have agreed. Diplomatic channels normally involve exchanges and negotiations between the parties. Dispute settlement procedures may be bilateral as, for example, through a commission composed of representatives of the two states. Other procedures of dispute settlement may involve third parties; either states or individuals. Dispute settlement procedures embrace a variety of arrangements provided for in existing treaties or ad hoc agreements. They include bilateral commissions, conciliation and mediation procedures, arbitration and judicial settlement. See United Nations, A Survey of Treaty Provisions for the Pacific Settlement of International Disputes 1949–1962 (UN Pub. 66 V.5 1966).

Claims commissions and arbitral tribunals have been established by many countries to deal with cases in which the violation and international obligations concerns the treatment of nationals or certain other persons of the injured state. Examples are the several claims commissions between Mexico and the United States and, more recently, the Iran–U.S. Arbitral Tribunal established by treaty to adjudicate claims of U.S. nationals for injuries by Iran. See Section C below and Chapter 9 on these and other claims tribunals.

### A. PROCEDURAL REQUIREMENTS

Interstate claims and settlement procedures, although diverse in character, present a few common problems of a procedural character. They include the following:

#### *1. Standing to Make Claims*

States may present claims through diplomatic channels or to tribunals only if they have the requisite legal interest. As discussed above in Section 3, this depends on determining to whom the obligation is owed and on the meaning of "injury." Although the concept of certain *erga omnes* obligations has been recognized in principle, as of 1986 no judicial or arbitral proceeding has taken place where the claimant's standing was based on the *erga omnes* concept.

The issue of standing to bring a claim has been considered by the International Court of Justice in the following cases: Nottebohm Case (Liechtenstein v. Guatemala), 1955 I.C.J. 4; South West Africa Cases, 1966

I.C.J. 6; Barcelona Traction (Belgium v. Spain), 1970 I.C.J. 3. Cases concerning intervention by third parties have also considered the meaning of "legal interest". See Chapter 10.

Several international conventions allow *any* party to the convention to bring a case against another party for breach of an obligation before a court or commission provided both parties have accepted an optional protocol or clause to that effect. See e.g., Convention on the Elimination of All Forms of Racial Discrimination 660, U.N.T.S. 195 (1965).

### 2. *Laches*

Whether international law includes a rule of laches has come up in several cases. An opinion of the U.S.–Mexican General Claims Commission stated that "no rule of international law put[s] a limit on * * * the presentation of an international claim to an international tribunal." George W. Cook Claim, 4 U.N.R.I.A.A. 3, 214. Some tribunals have denied remedies when the action was brought after a long lapse of time on the ground that the respondent government was placed in an unfair position in making its defense. See Ralston, The Law of Procedure of International Tribunals, 375–83 (1926) and Supplement 185–87 (1936). The *Institut de Droit International* concluded in 1925 that "it is left to the unfettered discretion of the international tribunal" to determine whether there has been undue delay. 32 Ann. de l'Inst. de Droit Int'l 558–60 (1925). An arbitral tribunal endorsed this principle in the *Ambatielos Case* when it denied a British contention that the claim of Greece should be rejected because of undue delay in its presentation. Ambatielos Case, Award of 1956, 12 U.N.R.I.A.A. 83, 103–04 (1963).

### 3. *Negotiation as a Pre-requisite to Settlement Procedures*

Most agreements on dispute settlement provide that negotiation, consultation or "diplomacy" be resorted to before a claim can be submitted to a tribunal or other procedure for settlement. Even when that has not been specified in an agreement, tribunals have treated negotiation as an implied condition. As one court stated, a requirement that negotiation take place may be implied to show that a dispute actually exists and that "a difference of views is in question which has not been capable of being otherwise overcome" Chorzów Case (Interpretation of Judgments 7 and 8) 1927 P.C.I.J., Ser. A, No. 13, p. 10–11. Several cases have dealt with the meaning of the obligation to negotiate. In the *Mavrommatis Case* the Permanent Court of International Justice commented:

> "Negotiations do not of necessity always presuppose a more or less lengthy series of notes and despatches; it may suffice that a discussion has been commenced and * * * a deadlock is reached, or if finally a point is reached at which one of the parties definitely declares himself unable or refuses to give way."

1924 P.C.I.J., Ser. A, No. 2, p. 13.

The International Court of Justice in the *North Sea Continental Shelf Case* observed that

> the parties are under an obligation to enter into negotiation with a view to reaching an agreement * * *; they are under an obligation so to

> conduct themselves that the negotiations are meaningful, which will not be the case when either of them insists upon its own position without contemplating any modification of it.

1969 I.C.J. 3, 47–48.

What criteria may a court employ to determine whether a party that purports to be ready to negotiate and engages in discussion takes positions that they know have no chance of acceptance? Can it satisfy itself that negotiation in that case is a sham or futile?

### 4. *Exhaustion of Local Remedies*

A well-established rule of customary international law is that a state seeking remedies for denial of rights to its nationals must exhaust remedies in national courts and administrative agencies before instituting international proceedings. Although originally confined to the context of diplomatic protection of aliens, today international tribunals apply the "rule of local remedies" to the field of human rights as well. The rule confers on the host or respondent state an important initial role in the international dispute settlement process. C.F. Amerasinghe, explains the justification for the rule as follows:

> The rule sprang up primarily as an instrument designed to ensure respect for the sovereignty of host States in a particular area of international dispute settlement. Basically this is the principal reason for its survival today and also for its projection into international systems of human rights protection. Whether in the modern law of diplomatic protection or in the conventional law of human rights protection, the raison d'être of the rule is the recognition given by members of the international community to the interest of the host State, flowing from its sovereignty, in settling international disputes of a certain kind by its own means before international mechanisms are invoked.

Local Remedies in International Law 359 (1990).

The "rule of local remedies" ensures that "the State where the violation has occurred should have an opportunity to redress it by its own means, within the framework of its own domestic legal system." Interhandel Case (Switzerland v. U.S.), 1959 I.C.J. 6. This requirement means that a remedy must be sought until the highest court rules on the issue.

Will this not be futile where it is clear that the law is established by statute or precedent and that no court is competent to overrule it? What if it is clear that the courts are totally subservient to the executive who has taken the decision being challenged? See Panevezys Railway Case, 1939 P.C.I.J., Ser. A/B, No. 76, p. 18.

Are exceptions to the exhaustion of remedies rule warranted where the individual injured has only a transitory connection or none at all with the offending state? An example is that of a passenger in a plane shot down while in flight when that passenger had no link with the state. Should he be required to go to the courts of the offending state? The issue arose in a case brought by Israel against Bulgaria but the Court did not consider the Bulgarian contention that the injured Israeli had failed to seek remedies in Bulgarian courts. 1959 I.C.J. 127. Another example would involve an injury to a person in his own country caused by a space object or missile of a foreign state. Should that person be required to go to the courts of the responsible state before he or his state can claim damages? There is no such requirement in the Convention on Liability for Damage caused by Space Objects 1972. See Article IX. See also Chapter 9 on exhaustion of local remedies rule.

For the International Court of Justice's most recent discussion of the rule of local remedies, see Case Concerning Elettronica Sicula S.p.A. (ELST) (United States v. Italy), 1989 I.C.J. 15, 28 I.L.M. 1111, relevant portions of which are reprinted infra at p. 696.

### 5. *Manifestation of Consent to Third Party Settlement*

International claims "cannot in the present state of the law as to international jurisdiction be submitted to a tribunal except with the consent of the states concerned". Advisory Opinion of International Court of Justice on Reparation of Injuries, 1949 I.C.J. 177–78. Such consent may be manifested by agreements to general categories of cases such as agreements for claims commissions or arbitration. See Chapter 10 on jurisdictional clauses for arbitration and submission to jurisdiction of the International Court of Justice.

While the requirement of consent is unqualified, it has long been clear that consent need not be express but may be inferred from conduct conclusively establishing it. "The submission of arguments on the merits without making reservations in regard to the question of jurisdiction" has been held to confer the necessary consent. See Case Concerning Minorities in Upper Silesia, 1928 P.C.I.J., Ser. A, No. 16, p. 24. See also the Asylum Case (Colombia–Peru), 1950 I.C.J. 266, 267–68. The term *forum prorogatum* has been applied to jurisdiction based on conduct implying consent. See Chapter 10, Section 4. See also Rosenne, The Law and Practice of the International Court of Justice, 357–59 (1965).

## B. ENFORCEMENT AND EXECUTION OF INTERNATIONAL AWARDS

Awards and orders of international tribunals holding states responsible for wrongful acts have generally been complied with. See Schachter, The Enforcement of International Judicial and Arbitral Awards, 54 A.J.I.L. 1 (1960). Cases of noncompliance have been relatively infrequent and nearly always based on objections by the defaulting state to the jurisdiction of the tribunal or on other grounds of nullity.

In cases of noncompliance the successful state may have recourse to national and international measures against the defaulting state.

### 1. *Execution Against Assets of Non-complying State*

In the Tehran hostages case, the International Court of Justice ruled that Iran was obliged to make reparation to the United States for the injury caused by the seizure and detention of U.S. nationals in Tehran. It left for future decision the determination of the form and amount, failing agreement of the parties. 1980 I.C.J. 45. Subsequently the parties reached agreement on settlement and no award of damages was requested by the United States.

If an award of monetary damages had been made by the Court and Iran did not comply, would the United States have been entitled to execute the award from the assets of the Iranian state and its agencies in the United States? Would such action have required a decision of the Security Council to give effect to the judgment in accordance with Article 94 of the U.N. Charter?

Or would execution by the United States have been a permissible act of self-help? Are the conclusions the same for binding arbitral awards as for judgments of the International Court of Justice?

Suppose the defaulting state had assets in a third state not a party to the dispute, would the successful state have been legally entitled to those assets to satisfy the judgment? Would the third state have been under a duty to transfer those assets? If no duty exists, would the third state be entitled to transfer the assets by recognizing the international award as binding and governed by principles of comity applicable to foreign judgments?

An affirmative answer to the latter question was suggested by the governments of France, the United Kingdom and the United States when they were faced with a demand that gold in their custody as fiduciaries and claimed by Albania should be used to pay the damages awarded by the International Court against Albania in the *Corfu Channel Case,* 1949 I.C.J. 4. The three governments were of the opinion that the required amount of gold could be paid to the United Kingdom to satisfy the Court's award provided that it was decided by arbitration that Albania was entitled to a share of the gold held by the three governments. Although the arbitrator did so decide, Italy contested the decision and then objected to the International Court determining the issue in the absence of Albania. 1949 I.C.J. 9, 10. In consequence the gold was not transferred to any of the claimants.

Whether or not the fiduciaries had the right to use the gold to meet the British claim to execution depends on their rights under the agreement delegating fiduciary powers to them. See Oliver, The Monetary Gold Decision in Perspective, 49 A.J.I.L. 216 (1955). The reasoning underlying the position of the fiduciary governments would support the right of a third state holding funds to meet a demand of a state entitled to execution under a binding decision of an international judicial or arbitral tribunal. See Schachter, The Enforcement of International Judicial and Arbitral Awards, 54 A.J.I.L. 1, 9–12 (1960).

### 2. *Execution Through Domestic Courts of State in Which Funds of Judgment Debtor Are Located*

In the case of *Socobel v. Greece,* a private Belgian company was awarded damages against Greece by an international arbitral tribunal. See 47 A.J.I.L. 508 (1953). When Greece did not pay, the Belgian company sought to attach funds of the Greek government in Belgium. The Belgian Court allowed an attachment as a conservatory action pending an *exequator* from the Belgian government certifying the validity and binding character of the arbitral award. The Belgian Court also held that the funds of Greece were not entitled to immunity against execution because they were related to business done by Greece in Belgium.

Can it be maintained that courts of a third state are under an obligation to recognize and enforce judgments of international tribunals that are binding on the parties in accordance with international law? Should it be regarded as a matter of comity? Would the municipal court have to ensure that competing claims are met? See M.E. O'Connell, 85 Proc.Am.S.Int'l L. 439 (1991).

A separate question may be raised whether an award of a "non-national" tribunal is entitled to be treated as a foreign arbitral award made in a contracting state for purposes of recognition and enforcement under the U.N. Convention on Recognition and Enforcement of Arbitral Awards (the so-called New York Convention of 1958). See Paulsson, Arbitration Unbound: Award Detached from the Law of its Country of Origin, 30 I.C.L.Q. 358 (1981).

### 3. *Enforcement Provisions in Multilateral Treaties*

As indicated, the U.N. Charter provides that the Security Council may take measures to give effect to a judgment of the International Court when requested to do so. Article 94. No such action has been taken by the Council to date (June 1986).

The Convention on International Civil Aviation of 1944 also refers to possible noncompliance by a contracting state with a decision of the International Court or of an arbitral tribunal in a matter covered by the convention. The contracting states are obliged to exclude the airline of a contracting state from operating in their territory if the Council of the International Civil Aviation Organization has determined that the airline is not in compliance with the final decision of the International Court or arbitral tribunal. Article 87 of the Convention on International Civil Aviation. 61 Stat. 1180, 15 U.N.T.S. 295. See also Constitution of International Labor Organization, Article 33.

### 4. *Establishment of a Fund for Payment of Awards*

An unusual arrangement to ensure execution of awards was included in the Algiers Accord between the United States and Iran for arbitration of claims of nationals of each country against the other state arising out of debts, contracts, expropriations and other measures affecting property rights. Official claims of the United States arising out of contracts for goods and services were also covered. See Chapter 10, Section 3D.

As part of the settlement agreement, a portion of the Iranian assets frozen in the United States was set aside to provide a fund out of which claims of U.S. nationals against Iran could be satisfied. Three separate dollar accounts were established. Two were in the Bank of England to cover bank loans; they amounted to about $5 billion. The third dollar account, amounting to $1 billion (plus interest) was in the Central Bank of the Netherlands and was to be used to pay nonbank claimants. This third account has been used to pay U.S. claimants for awards made by the Arbitral Tribunal. See Panel on Iran–United States Litigation, A.S.I.L.Proc. 3–30 (1983).

An earlier arrangement for funds to pay claims was the provision in the Peace Treaties of 1947 which gave the victorious states a right to retain the property of the enemy states situated in their territory and to liquidate such property for the purpose of paying claims which the government and their nationals had against the enemy country. See Mann, Enemy Property and the Paris Peace Treaties, 64 L.Q.Rev. 402 (1948).

### C. CLAIMS SETTLEMENT BY THE UNITED STATES

In 1794 the United States and Great Britain concluded the Jay Treaty under which several hundred claims based on maritime seizures were referred to a mixed commission for arbitration. See Hyde, International Law 1587–88 (1945). A number of arbitration cases involving the United States took place in the 19th century, one of the more notable being the U.S. claims against Great Britain for damage covered by the Confederate warship Alabama. See Hyde, id. at 1592–93.

Several claims commissions were established, beginning in 1868, to deal with U.S.—Mexican claims, mostly against Mexico but some against the U.S. The two U.S.—Mexico Claims Commissions set up in 1923 dealt with more than 6000 claims and in doing so created a significant body of case law on state responsibility. See Feller, The Mexican Claims Commissions 1923–1934 (1935).

As indicated above the United States and Iran in the agreement known as the Algiers Declarations established an arbitral Tribunal to which some 3000 claims were submitted. The agreement is in 20 I.L.M. 223 (1981). See Chapter 10, Section 3D.

After the Second World War, several lump-sum settlement agreements were made by the United States with countries in Europe and later with China. "Foreign Claims Settlement Commissions" were created in the United States to distribute funds received from foreign governments to the U.S. nationals entitled to receive them. The Commissions have considered each claim separately and determined its validity and amount on the basis of "principles of international law, justice and equity" 22 U.S.C.A. §§ 1621–1645. See Lillich & Weston, International Claims: Their Settlement by Lump Sum Agreements (1975).

## SECTION 10. REMEDIES OF PRIVATE PERSONS IN DOMESTIC COURTS FOR VIOLATIONS OF INTERNATIONAL LAW

The Restatement (Third), § 906, states:

> A private person, whether natural or juridical, injured by a violation of an international obligation by a state, may bring a claim against that state or assert that violation as a defense
>
> * * *
>
> b) in a court or other tribunal of that state pursuant to its law; or
>
> c) in a court or other tribunal of the injured person's state of nationality or of a third state, pursuant to the law of such state, subject to limitations under international law.

## A. OBLIGATION TO PROVIDE A REMEDY TO INJURED PERSONS

1. Is a state required by international law to provide a remedy to injured persons in its domestic courts for a violation of international law by that state? Schachter observes:

> There is no general requirement in international law that states provide such remedies. By and large, international law leaves it to them to meet their obligations in such ways as the state determines * * * However, in some cases there are obligations of means—that is, specific requirements as to the procedures and agencies that are to be used for the fulfillment of obligations of result. Such obligations of means are specified in treaties of various kinds, particularly those which are intended to benefit private persons.
>
> "* * * Some treaties require that individuals have a right to a remedy by a competent authority, leaving it to the state to decide whether that authority would be executive, administrative or judicial. In other cases, treaties do not expressly confer a right to judicial remedies but an implication to that effect can be drawn."

Schachter, International Law in Theory and Practice, 178 Rec. des Cours 232–33 (1982–V).

The Restatement (Third) declares in § 907, Comment *a*:

> International agreements, even those directly benefiting private persons, generally do not create private rights or provide for a private cause of action in domestic courts, but there are exceptions with respect to both rights and remedies * * *

2. Whether a treaty that says nothing about individual rights or remedies may be interpreted as conferring such rights or remedies may be easy to determine in some cases but difficult in others. For example, treaties concerned with rights of property by descent or inheritance have long been treated in the United States as conferring rights upon individuals. See Head Money Cases, 112 U.S. 580, 598, 5 S.Ct. 247, 28 L.Ed. 798 (1884). Similarly, treaties according nationals of the contracting states equal treatment have been construed to give individuals judicial remedies. See Asakura v. Seattle, 265 U.S. 332, 44 S.Ct. 515, 68 L.Ed. 1041 (1924). However, treaties concerned with the use of force such as the UN Charter, and other political treaties, have been interpreted as not conferring enforceable rights on individuals injured by violations. The courts in the United States have tended to deny relief either because the treaty was deemed not to confer individual rights or remedies, or on the ground that the issues raised were "political questions" which should be left to the political branches of government. See United States v. Berrigan, 283 F.Supp. 336, 342 (D.Md.1968); Sanchez–Espinoza v. Reagan, 568 F.Supp. 596 (D.D.C.1983), affirmed, 770 F.2d 202 (D.C.Cir.1985); Tel–Oren v. Libyan Arab Republic, 726 F.2d 774 (D.C.Cir.1984), certiorari denied, 470 U.S. 1003, 105 S.Ct. 1354, 84 L.Ed.2d 377 (1985). On the latter case, see Chapter 8, pp. 654–55. For individual remedies for human rights violations see Chapter 8, Section 1. See also Chapter 3 on self-executing treaties, pp. 212–21.

3. For an example of a treaty provision expressly addressing individual remedies, see Article 2(3) of the International Covenant on Civil and Political Rights which obliges each state party to ensure "an effective remedy" to any person whose rights have been violated. It also requires that the right to such remedy be determined by "a competent authority provided for by the legal system of the state" and that the remedies granted be enforced by the state. See Schachter, The Obligation to Implement the Covenant in Domestic Law, in The International Bill of Rights 311 (Henkin ed. 1981).

4. Does international customary law require a state to provide a judicial remedy for an alien injured by a breach of international law? See Mann, The Consequences of an International Wrong in International and National Law, 48 Brit.Y.B.I.L. 1 (1975–76); cf. Banco Nacional de Cuba v. Chase Manhattan Bank, 658 F.2d 875 (2d Cir.1981). See generally Chapter 9.

## B. LIMITATIONS ON INDIVIDUAL REMEDIES IN DOMESTIC COURTS

1. Suits brought against foreign states may be barred by sovereign immunity unless such immunity has been waived. Whether a treaty conferring remedies to injured individuals constitutes a waiver is a matter of treaty interpretation. In the United States and other countries that have adopted the restrictive theory of immunity, suits against states may be brought in cases to which the immunity does not apply. See generally Chapter 13, Section 1. Even where sovereign immunity applies, suit may ordinarily be brought against a responsible official. See Restatement (Third) § 131, Reporters' Note 4.

2. Relief by a domestic court may also be barred in the United States by the act of state doctrine and related doctrines. See Chapter 3, p. 180.

3. Remedies in domestic courts are also limited by jurisdictional requirements. The forum state must have jurisdiction to adjudicate and the substantive law must be within its legislative jurisdiction. See further Chapter 12. Suits brought by foreign nationals may be limited by rules of the forum including the principle of *forum non conveniens.*

4. Suits against the United States require the consent of the United States. Such consent, by statute, to cover tort and contract claims, may include cases involving violations of international obligations. See Restatement (Third) § 907, Reporters' Note 2. Jurisdiction of federal courts over suits by aliens for torts in violation of treaties to which the United States is a party or in violation of the law of nations is provided by the Alien Tort Law. See Filartiga v. Pena–Irala, 630 F.2d 876 (2d Cir.1980), discussed in Chapter 2, p. 126 and Chapter 8, pp. 653–54. See Randall, Federal Jurisdiction Over International Law Claims, 18 N.Y.U.J.Int.L. and Pol. 1 (1985); Burley, The Alien Tort Statute and the Judiciary Act of 1789, 83 AJIL 461 (1989).

# Chapter 8

# HUMAN RIGHTS

That international law was traditionally seen as governing only relations between states did not preclude the development of customary norms or conventional international obligations dealing with the condition and treatment of individuals in whom states had an interest—notably their diplomats or other nationals. In principle, such duties and obligations were seen as owing by one state to another state, although, of course, they redounded to the benefit of individuals. See Chapter 7. State responsibility for injury to aliens (Chapter 9), for example, is not seen as creating rights for the alien under international law; he or she benefits because the law sees an offense to the individual as an offense against the state whose nationality the individual bears; remedies for violation of these norms are accorded only to the state, although the individual has to exhaust local remedies under domestic law before his government may pursue its remedies under international law. Diplomatic privileges and immunities (Chapter 13), provisions about the rights of nationals commonly found in treaties of friendship, commerce and navigation, limitations and safeguards in extradition treaties, restrictions on prescriptive jurisdiction, the laws of war, all in fact afford protection to individuals, although in principle the obligation and the remedies for violation run from state to state. The fact that these norms and agreements reflected very largely a state's interests in protecting its own nationals against other states confirmed the identification of an individual with his own state, and discouraged any tendency to grant independent status to the individual. That, in turn, rendered it unthinkable that international law should concern itself with protecting the interests of the individual against his own government, even less that it might give the individual international remedies against his own government.

## THE ORIGINS OF CONTEMPORARY INTERNATIONAL HUMAN RIGHTS LAW

### *HENKIN, THE INTERNATIONALIZATION OF HUMAN RIGHTS*

Proceedings of the General Education Seminar, Vol. 6, No. 1 (Fall 1977) p. 7–9.*

Historically, how a state treated persons within its territory was its own affair, implicit in its sovereignty over its own territory and in the freedom to act there as it would unless specifically forbidden by international law. International law developed one early exception when it recognized that how a country treats an alien is the proper concern of the government whose nationality he/she bore. The exception might be seen as essentially political, not humanitarian. Long ago, we know, a government which offended a citizen of Rome offended Rome, and if an American is abused elsewhere today, the United States is offended. (It was widely accepted, therefore, that injustice to a stateless person was not a violation of international law since no state was offended; surely, there was no state that could invoke a remedy for such injustice.) But even if that exception is seen as a political expression of our nation-state system, rather than humanitarian, it is significant that governments were offended by violations of the "human rights" of their nationals. In our day this law has been controversial insofar as it has been invoked to protect alien property, but it is not commonly challenged as regards treatment of the alien person, and at least some security for at least some property is also widely recognized as a human right.

In order to determine whether an alien was mistreated, there had to be some standard of treatment, and traditional international law, at least as seen in the West, developed the idea of an international standard of justice. I know of no accepted philosophical foundation for this international standard and no agreed legal definition of its contents, nor are there enough cases from which one might derive a clear sense of what it imports. Americans would probably recognize in it something very like "fairness." In any case, this international notion of justice obviously long antedated the universalization of human rights. The standard for the treatment of aliens invoked by their national governments and acquiesced in by host governments was often higher than that applied by these countries to their own citizens at home. The international standard, then, was not a universal human rights standard, and governments that invoked it did not suggest that it applied also to how governments treated their own citizens. That treatment was not the concern of international law or the business of other governments, and in fact governments rarely concerned themselves with domestic injustice elsewhere. The few major-power intercessions, for example, that of the United States in the nineteenth century in response to Russian programs, did not invoke international law. In that instance as in other examples of "quiet diplomacy," intercession invoked a general morality and occurred only when violations were egregious and dramatic, and when there was a demand for it by a domestic constituency with affinity for the victims in the other country (as in the United States, for example, the Irish, the Jews, and others).

The treatment of aliens was not the only exception to the principle that how a government acts at home is a matter of local concern only. In the seventeenth century, Catholic princes negotiated agreements about the

* Reprinted by permission of Proceedings of the General Education Seminar.

treatment of Catholics by Protestant princes, and vice versa, and later, governments began to negotiate protections for ethnic minorities with which they identified, even those who as a matter of law held the nationality of the country in which they lived. In the late nineteenth and early-twentieth century, minority treaties were virtually imposed by the major powers on smaller ones in Central and Eastern Europe because it was believed that violation of minority rights led to intervention and war. The mandate system of the League of Nations, following World War I, required a commitment by the mandatory power to promote the welfare of the local population. It has been argued that such clauses did not reflect *bona fide* concern for human rights but were only a "sop" to justify keeping "the natives" in continued tutelage; whatever the reason, "primitive" human rights provisions appeared in international legal documents. (Such a clause in the mandate for South West Africa became the basis for a suit in the International Court of Justice and contributed to the termination of the mandate and the emergence of Namibia.) A clear example of early internationalization of human rights is slavery; in the nineteenth century, when major countries abolished slavery in their own countries, an international standard developed that slavery was unacceptable and the slave trade was outlawed.

The contribution of the International Labor Organization also should not be overlooked. The ILO was organized after World War I to promote common basic standards for labor and social welfare. Sixty years later we have more than a hundred international conventions promulgated by the ILO, widely adhered to and fairly well observed. Again, one might find political-economic rather than humanitarian motivations for what the ILO achieved: perhaps, indeed, the ILO was the West's fearful answer to socialism which had gained its first bridgehead in the USSR; perhaps the convention reflected a desire by developed states to reduce "unfair competition" from countries with sub-standard labor conditions. Whatever the reason(s), international human rights were planted and grew.

Real, full-blown internationalization of human rights came in the wake of Hitler and World War II. ["Crimes against humanity" were among the charges in the Nuremberg Charter. See p. 879 below.] The United Nations Charter includes legal obligations in respect to human rights and virtually all states today are parties to the Charter. The Universal Declaration has achieved universal recognition, and the two principal international covenants, one on Civil and Political Rights, the other on Economic, Social and Cultural Rights, have now come into effect. There are other conventions dealing with particular rights, and the Genocide Convention and the Convention on the Elimination of all Forms of Racial Discrimination have many adherents. Corresponding programs have internationalized human rights on a regional basis in Europe and Latin America.

### *Notes*

1. Since the above paragraph was written, the Organization of African Unity adopted the Charter on Human and Peoples' Rights (The Banjul Charter) and established a commission to promote the aims of the Charter. See p. 673 below.

2. "Human rights" is a term in common usage but not authoritatively defined. Such rights are said to include those "moral-political claims which, by

contemporary consensus, every human being has or is deemed to have upon his society or government," claims which are recognized "as of right," not by love, or grace, or charity. Henkin, Rights: American and Human, 79 Colum.L.Rev. 405 (1979); Henkin, The Rights of Man Today 1–3 (1978).

The Universal Declaration has been recognized as the authoritative articulation and enumeration of the essential human rights of individuals. Rights of peoples to self-determination and to "economic self-determination" were added by the International Covenants. There have been suggestions also of additional "generations" of rights, e.g., rights to peace, a healthful environment, economic and political development. See, e.g., Crawford, The Rights of Peoples 159–166 (1988); Alston, A Third Generation of Solidarity Rights: Progressive Development or Obfuscation of International Human Rights Law?, 29 Neth.Int'l L.Rev. 307 (1982); Marks, Emerging Human Rights: A New Generation for the 1980s?, 33 Rutgers L.Rev. 435 (1981). See also pp. 610–11 infra.

It is common practice to distinguish, and to treat as a separate subject, the humanitarian law applicable during hostilities. See chapter 11 infra. In fact, the two bodies of law overlap and individuals in war and hostilities enjoy rights under the law of human rights. See generally Meron, Human Rights and Humanitarian Norms as Customary Law (1989). See also the symposium on Human Rights and Humanitarian Law, in 91/1 Bull.Human Rts. 1–61 (1992).

International Human Rights generally, the Universal Declaration, and, notably, the International Covenant on Civil and Political Rights, address the rights of natural persons only. The Covenant on Economic, Social, and Cultural Rights, however, recognizes some rights for trade unions. Article 8(1). Compare the European Convention on Human Rights, some of whose provisions also would apply to juridical persons. Article 25 of that Convention expressly accords a right of petition to "any person, nongovernmental organization or group of individuals claiming to be a victim of a violation." The First Protocol to the Convention provides: "[e]very natural or legal person is entitled to the peaceful enjoyment of his possessions." Article 1. See also Respect for the Right of Everyone to Own Property Alone as Well as in Association with Others and Its Contribution to the Economic and Social Development of Member States, G.A.Res. 45/98 (22 January 1991). See Buergenthal, To Respect and to Ensure: State Obligations and Permissible Derogations, in The International Bill of Rights 72, 73 (Henkin ed. 1981). See Restatement (Third) § 701, Reporters' Note 6.

International human rights law cuts across all states and many different cultures. This has given rise to an examination of the nature of human rights from different cultural perspectives. See, e.g., Human Rights in Cross–Cultural Perspectives: A Quest for Consensus (An–Na'im, ed. 1992).

3. The literature of international human rights continues to grow. See generally Forsythe, The Internationalization of Human Rights (1991); Cassese, Human Rights in a Changing World (1990); Donnelly, Universal Human Rights in Theory and Practice (1989); Henkin, The Age of Rights (1989); MacFarlane, The Theory and Practice of Human Rights (1985); Vincent, Human Rights and International Relations (1986); Sieghart, The Lawful Rights of Mankind: An Introduction to the International Legal Code of Human Rights (1985); Human Rights and International Law (Meron, ed. 1984); Roberts, Human Rights in the World: An Introduction to the Study of the International Protection of Human Rights (2nd ed. 1982); The International Dimensions of Human Rights (Vasak, ed. 1982); McDougal, Lasswell & Chen, Human Rights and World Public Order

(1980). For earlier writings see Henkin, The Rights of Man Today, Chapter 3 (1978); Sohn & Buergenthal, The International Protection of Human Rights (1973); Lauterpacht, International Law and Human Rights (1950, 1973). Books designed for teaching international human rights include Lillich, International Human Rights: Problems of Law, Policy and Practice (1991); Newman & Weissbrodt, International Human Rights Law: Law, Policy and Process (1990); Meron, Human Rights in International Law: Legal and Policy Issues (1984). There is also a specialized literature, for example, on the European Convention, the American Convention and the African Charter. See pp. 656–76 infra. For compilations of human rights documents see Brownlie, Basic Documents on Human Rights (3rd ed. 1991); Lillich, International Human Rights Instruments: A Compilation of Treaties, Agreements, and Declarations of Especial Interest to the United States (looseleaf, 1983–1990); Center for the Study of Human Rights, Columbia University, Twenty-Four Human Rights Documents (1992); United Nations, Human Rights: Status of International Instruments (1987); Blaustein, Clark & Sigler, Human Rights Source Book (1987); Council of Europe, Human Rights in International Law: Basic Texts (1985).

# SECTION 1. INTERNATIONAL HUMAN RIGHTS LAW

## A. THE SUBSTANTIVE LAW OF HUMAN RIGHTS

The international law of human rights includes numerous (and increasing) international agreements and other instruments, as well as recognized corpus of principles of customary law. Three principal instruments—the Universal Declaration of Human Rights, the International Covenant on Civil and Political Rights (and its Optional Protocol) and the International Covenant on Economic, Social and Cultural Rights have, together, acquired the universal designation of "the International Bill of Rights."

The law of human rights begins with the United Nations Charter.

### *1. Charter of the United Nations*

Article 55

With a view to the creation of conditions of stability and well-being which are necessary for peaceful and friendly relations among nations based on respect for the principle of equal rights and self-determination of peoples, the United Nations shall promote:

a. higher standards of living, full employment, and conditions of economic and social progress and development;

b. solutions of international economic, social, health, and related problems; and international cultural and educational co-operation; and

c. universal respect for, and observance of, human rights and fundamental freedoms for all without distinction as to race, sex, language, or religion.

Article 56

All Members pledge themselves to take joint and separate action in co-operation with the Organization for the achievement of the purposes set forth in Article 55.

### *Notes*

1. See also the references to human rights in the Preamble to the U.N. Charter, Articles 1(3), 62(2), 68, 76(c). And see Article 13(1)(b), providing that the General Assembly "shall initiate studies and make recommendations for the purpose," *inter alia,* of "assisting in the realization of human rights and fundamental freedoms * * *."

2. There has been continuing controversy as to whether the human rights provisions of the U.N. Charter create binding legal obligations on member states to respect the human rights of their inhabitants and, if so, which are the rights that are the subject of this obligation. Compare Re Drummond Wren, [1945] O.R. 778, [1945] 4 D.L.R. 674 (Ontario High Court), in which the court declared a restrictive racial covenant void, *inter alia,* as against public policy, citing the Charter provisions on human rights as indicative of public policy, with Sei Fujii v. California, 217 P.2d 481, rehearing denied, 218 P.2d 595 (Cal.App.1950). In the latter case the California District Court of Appeal held the Alien Land Law invalid on the ground that it conflicted with the human rights provisions of the United Nations Charter. On appeal, however, the California Supreme Court held the statute invalid under the Fourteenth Amendment, but expressly rejected the lower court's view that the Charter provisions on human rights had become the "supreme law of the land." 38 Cal.2d 718, 722–25, 242 P.2d 617, 621–22 (1952). The California Supreme Court observed that the Charter provisions lacked the mandatory quality and definiteness that would indicate an intent to create enforceable rights. *Sei Fujii,* also discussed p. 217 supra. Compare also Oyama v. California, 332 U.S. 633, 649–50, 673, 68 S.Ct. 269, 276–77, 288, 92 L.Ed. 249, 259 (1948), in which the Court held a section of the Alien Land Law unconstitutional as violative of the Fourteenth Amendment. In concurring opinions, Justices Black, Douglas, Rutledge and Murphy referred to the section's inconsistency with the United Nations Charter. Efforts to invoke the human rights provisions of the U.N. Charter in United States courts have not been successful, the Charter being held not to be self-executing. See p. 217 above. It has been urged that the issue be reexamined. See, e.g., Newman, Keynote Address, Conference on Human Rights Law in State and Federal Courts, 17 U.S.F.L.Rev. 2 (1982); Strossen, Recent U.S. and International Judicial Protection of Individual Rights: A Comparative Legal Process Analysis and Proposed Synthesis, 41 Hastings L.J. 805 (1990).

The issue has also been recast as whether the provisions of the Charter, taken together with later developments, notably the Universal Declaration of Human Rights, various covenants and conventions, resolutions of the U.N. General Assembly and of other international bodies, and the practices and declarations of states, have created binding legal obligations. Those who find such legal obligation argue either that the documents and developments have filled out and concretized the obligations left inchoate or undefined by the Charter; or that the Charter, together with what came after, have created a customary law of human rights. See Schwelb, The International Court of Justice and the Human Rights Clause of the Charter, 66 A.J.I.L. 337 (1972); Sohn, Protection of Human Rights through International Legislation, in 1 Rene Cassin, Amicorum Discipulorumque Liber 325 (1969); also Lauterpacht, International Law and Human Rights 145–60 (1950, 1973). On this view, all members of the U.N. are legally bound, and the binding obligations would require at least respect for those rights that are not disputed, for example, those which international law had always included in the concept of "justice" not to be denied to an alien, as well as freedom from slavery, systematic racial discrimination and genocide, perhaps also from systematic patterns of torture and arbitrary detention. See, for example, the numerous resolutions of the General Assembly and those of the Security Council declaring apartheid to be contrary to the principles of the Charter (p. 986 infra); also the Draft Articles on State Responsibility, in the Report of the International Law Commission, 33 GAOR Supp. 10 (A/33/10) at 193 (1978). Article 19(3)(c) would provide that an international crime may result from "a serious breach on a widespread scale of an international obligation of essential importance for safeguarding the human being, such as those prohibiting slavery, genocide and apartheid." For a contrary view see Watson, Legal Theory, Efficacy and Validity of Human Rights Norms, U.Ill.L.F. 609 (1979). See generally Schachter, International Law in Theory and Practice 335–42 (1991).

The customary law of human rights is discussed in the Restatement (Third), Part VII, Introductory Note, and §§ 702, 703. See p. 615 below.

3. It has been suggested that the U.N. Charter should be seen together with the Nuremberg Charter, the latter judging the past, the U.N. Charter prescribing for the future. The Nuremberg Charter applied a customary international law of human rights in charging the Nazi war criminals, *inter alia,* with "crimes against humanity." See Charter of the International Military Tribunal, August 8, 1945, 59 Stat. 546–47. See p. 879 below. The U.N. Charter codifies that customary law and renders applicable to all states at least such human rights law as was invoked at Nuremberg.

### 2. *The International Bill of Rights: The Declaration and the Covenants*

#### *UNIVERSAL DECLARATION OF HUMAN RIGHTS*

Adopted and Proclaimed by G.A.Res. 217A (III) (10 Dec. 1948).

PREAMBLE

*Whereas* recognition of the inherent dignity and of the equal and inalienable rights of all members of the human family is the foundation of freedom, justice and peace in the world,

*Whereas* disregard and contempt for human rights have resulted in barbarous acts which have outraged the conscience of mankind, and the advent of a world in which human beings shall enjoy freedom of speech and belief and freedom from fear and want has been proclaimed as the highest aspiration of the common people,

*Whereas* it is essential, if man is not to be compelled to have recourse, as a last resort, to rebellion against tyranny and oppression, that human rights should be protected by the rule of law,

*Whereas* it is essential to promote the development of friendly relations between nations,

*Whereas* the peoples of the United Nations have in the Charter reaffirmed their faith in fundamental human rights, in the dignity and worth of the human person and in the equal rights of men and women and have determined to promote social progress and better standards of life in larger freedom,

*Whereas* Member States have pledged themselves to achieve, in cooperation with the United Nations, the promotion of universal respect for and observance of human rights and fundamental freedoms,

*Whereas* a common understanding of these rights and freedoms is of the greatest importance for the full realization of this pledge,

*Now, therefore,*

The General Assembly

*Proclaims* this Universal Declaration of Human Rights as a common standard of achievement for all peoples and all nations, to the end that every individual and every organ of society, keeping this Declaration constantly in mind, shall strive by teaching and education to promote respect for these rights and freedoms and by progressive measures, national and international, to secure their universal and effective recognition and observance, both among the peoples of Member States themselves and among the peoples of territories under their jurisdiction.

*Article 1*

All human beings are born free and equal in dignity and rights. They are endowed with reason and conscience and should act towards one another in a spirit of brotherhood.

*Article 2*

Everyone is entitled to all the rights and freedoms set forth in this Declaration, without distinction of any kind, such as race, colour, sex, language, religion, political or other opinion, national or social origin, property, birth or other status.

Furthermore, no distinction shall be made on the basis of the political, jurisdictional or international status of the country or territory to which a person belongs, whether it be independent, trust, non-self-governing or under any other limitation of sovereignty.

*Article 3*

Everyone has the right to life, liberty and security of person.

*Article 4*

No one shall be held in slavery or servitude; slavery and the slave trade shall be prohibited in all their forms.

*Article 5*

No one shall be subjected to torture or to cruel, inhuman or degrading treatment or punishment.

*Article 6*

Everyone has the right to recognition everywhere as a person before the law.

*Article 7*

All are equal before the law and are entitled without any discrimination to equal protection of the law. All are entitled to equal protection against any discrimination in violation of this Declaration and against any incitement to such discrimination.

*Article 8*

Everyone has the right to an effective remedy by the competent national tribunals for acts violating the fundamental rights granted him by the constitution or by law.

*Article 9*

No one shall be subjected to arbitrary arrest, detention or exile.

*Article 10*

Everyone is entitled in full equality to a fair and public hearing by an independent and impartial tribunal, in the determination of his rights and obligations and of any criminal charge against him.

*Article 11*

1. Everyone charged with a penal offence has the right to be presumed innocent until proved guilty according to law in a public trial at which he has had all the guarantees necessary for his defence.

2. No one shall be held guilty of any penal offence on account of any act or omission which did not constitute a penal offence, under national or international law, at the time when it was committed. Nor shall a heavier penalty be imposed than the one that was applicable at the time the penal offence was committed.

*Article 12*

No one shall be subjected to arbitrary interference with his privacy, family, home or correspondence, nor to attacks upon his honour and reputation. Everyone has the right to the protection of the law against such interference or attacks.

*Article 13*

1. Everyone has the right to freedom of movement and residence within the borders of each State.

2. Everyone has the right to leave any country, including his own, and to return to his country.

*Article 14*

1. Everyone has the right to seek and to enjoy in other countries asylum from persecution.

2. This right may not be invoked in the case of prosecutions genuinely arising from non-political crimes or from acts contrary to the purposes and principles of the United Nations.

*Article 15*

1. Everyone has the right to a nationality.

2. No one shall be arbitrarily deprived of his nationality nor denied the right to change his nationality.

*Article 16*

1. Men and women of full age, without any limitation due to race, nationality or religion, have the right to marry and to found a family. They are entitled to equal rights as to marriage, during marriage and at its dissolution.

2. Marriage shall be entered into only with the free and full consent of the intending spouses.

3. The family is the natural and fundamental group unit of society and is entitled to protection by society and the State.

*Article 17*

1. Everyone has the right to own property alone as well as in association with others.

2. No one shall be arbitrarily deprived of his property.

*Article 18*

Everyone has the right to freedom of thought, conscience and religion; this right includes freedom to change his religion or belief, and freedom, either alone or in community with others and in public or private, to manifest his religion or belief in teaching, practice, worship and observance.

*Article 19*

Everyone has the right to freedom of opinion and expression; this right includes freedom to hold opinions without interference and to seek, receive and impart information and ideas through any media and regardless of frontiers.

*Article 20*

1. Everyone has the right to freedom of peaceful assembly and association.

2. No one may be compelled to belong to an association.

*Article 21*

1. Everyone has the right to take part in the government of his country, directly or through freely chosen representatives.

2. Everyone has the right to equal access to public service in his country.

3. The will of the people shall be the basis of the authority of government; this will shall be expressed in periodic and genuine elections which shall be by universal and equal suffrage and shall be held by secret vote or by equivalent free voting procedures.

*Article 22*

Everyone, as a member of society, has the right to social security and is entitled to realization, through national effort and international co-operation and in accordance with the organization and resources of each State, of the economic, social and cultural rights indispensable for his dignity and the free development of his personality.

*Article 23*

1. Everyone has the right to work, to free choice of employment, to just and favourable conditions of work and to protection against unemployment.

2. Everyone, without any discrimination, has the right to equal pay for equal work.

3. Everyone who works has the right to just and favourable remuneration ensuring for himself and his family an existence worthy of human dignity, and supplemented, if necessary, by other means of social protection.

4. Everyone has the right to form and to join trade unions for the protection of his interests.

*Article 24*

Everyone has the right to rest and leisure, including reasonable limitation of working hours and periodic holidays with pay.

*Article 25*

1. Everyone has the right to a standard of living adequate for the health and well-being of himself and of his family, including food, clothing, housing and medical care and necessary social services, and the right to security in the event of unemployment, sickness, disability, widowhood, old age or other lack of livelihood in circumstances beyond his control.

2. Motherhood and childhood are entitled to special care and assistance. All children, whether born in or out of wedlock, shall enjoy the same social protection.

*Article 26*

1. Everyone has the right to education. Education shall be free, at least in the elementary and fundamental stages. Elementary education shall be compulsory. Technical and professional education shall be made generally available and higher education shall be equally accessible to all on the basis of merit.

2. Education shall be directed to the full development of the human personality and to the strengthening of respect for human rights and fundamental freedoms. It shall promote understanding, tolerance and friendship among all nations, racial or religious groups, and shall further the activities of the United Nations for the maintenance of peace.

3. Parents have a prior right to choose the kind of education that shall be given to their children.

*Article 27*

1. Everyone has the right freely to participate in the cultural life of the community, to enjoy the arts and to share in scientific advancement and its benefits.

2. Everyone has the right to the protection of the moral and material interests resulting from any scientific, literary or artistic production of which he is the author.

*Article 28*

Everyone is entitled to a social and international order in which the rights and freedoms set forth in this Declaration can be fully realized.

*Article 29*

1. Everyone has duties to the community in which alone the free and full development of his personality is possible.

2. In the exercise of his rights and freedoms, everyone shall be subject only to such limitations as are determined by law solely for the purpose of securing due recognition and respect for the rights and freedoms of others and of meeting the just requirements of morality, public order and the general welfare in a democratic society.

3. These rights and freedoms may in no case be exercised contrary to the purposes and principles of the United Nations.

*Article 30*

Nothing in this Declaration may be interpreted as implying for any State, group or person any right to engage in any activity or to perform any act aimed at the destruction of any of the rights and freedoms set forth herein.

### *Notes*

1. The Universal Declaration was adopted on November 10, 1948, by a vote of 48 to 0 with eight abstentions: Byelorussian S.S.R., Czechoslovakia, Poland, Saudi Arabia, Ukrainian S.S.R., U.S.S.R., Union of South Africa, and Yugoslavia. The Communist states of Europe later accepted the Universal Declaration, expressly in the Final Act of the Conference on Security and Cooperation in Europe (Helsinki 1975). No new state or government has questioned or expressed any reservations about the principles of the Universal Declaration, and it continues to be cited with unanimous approval or acquiescence in resolutions of international bodies.

2. There has been debate about the legal status of the Declaration. At the time of its adoption, the U.S. representative in the General Assembly said: "It is not a treaty; it is not an international agreement. It is not and does not purport to be a statement of law or of legal obligation." 19 Dep't State Bull. 751 (1948). See also Lauterpacht, International Law and Human Rights 408–417 (1950, 1973). But compare the following, from Sohn & Buergenthal, International Protection of Human Rights 518–19, 522 (1973):

> The duty to "observe faithfully and strictly" not only the provisions of the Charter but also of the Universal Declaration was proclaimed by the General Assembly in the 1960 Declaration on the Granting of Independence to Colonial Countries and Peoples. Similarly, the 1963 Declaration on the Elimination of All Forms of Racial Discrimination recognized that every State shall "fully and faithfully observe the provisions of * * * the Universal Declaration of Human Rights." Both declarations were adopted unanimously.
>
> Taking the above mentioned developments into account, the unofficial Assembly for Human Rights, which met in Montreal in March 1968, stated that the "Universal Declaration of Human Rights constitutes an authoritative interpretation of the Charter of the highest order, and has over the

years become a part of customary international law." Montreal Statement of the Assembly for Human Rights 2 (New York, 1968); reprinted in 9 Journal of the International Commission of Jurists, No. 1, p. 94, at 95 (June 1968). In the Declaration of Teheran, the official International Conference on Human Rights, which met at Teheran in April–May 1968, reached a similar conclusion and proclaimed that the "Universal Declaration of Human Rights states a common understanding of the peoples of the world concerning the inalienable and inviolable rights of all members of the human family and constitutes an obligation for the members of the international community." Final Act of the International Conference on Human Rights 3, at 4, para. 2 (UN Doc. A/CONF. 32/41; UN Publ. E.68.XIV.2). The General Assembly of the United Nations in December 1968 endorsed the Proclamation of Tehran "as an important and timely reaffirmation of the principles embodied in the Universal Declaration of Human Rights." General Assembly, Resolution 2442 (XXIII), 19 Dec. 1968; 23 GAOR, Suppl. No. 18 (A/7218), at 49. See also the statement by the Secretary–General emphasizing the proclamation by the Teheran Conference that the Universal Declaration constitutes "an obligation for the members of the international community." Introduction to the Annual Report of the Secretary–General on the Work of the Organization, Sept. 1968, 23 GAOR, Suppl. No. 1A (A/7201/Add.1), at 13.

* * *

The Secretary–General, in his 1971 Survey of International Law (A/CN.4/245, at 196), noted that the "Universal Declaration is not in terms a treaty instrument;" he pointed out, however, that:

> "During the years since its adoption the Declaration has come, through its influence in a variety of contexts, to have a marked impact on the pattern and content of international law and to acquire a status extending beyond that originally intended for it. In general, two elements may be distinguished in this process: first, the use of the Declaration as a yardstick by which to measure the content and standard of observance of human rights; and, second, the reaffirmation of the Declaration and its provisions in a series of other instruments. These two elements, often to be found combined, have caused the Declaration to gain a cumulative and pervasive effect."

See Schwelb, The Influence of the Universal Declaration of Human Rights on International and National Law, 53 A.S.I.L.Proc. 217 (1959). See also the separate opinion of Vice President Ammoun in Advisory Opinion on the Continued Presence of South Africa in Namibia (South West Africa), [1971] I.C.J. 16, 76; Lillich, Civil Rights, in Human Rights in International Law (Meron ed. 1984); Nickel, Making Sense of Human Rights: Philosophical Reflections on the Universal Declaration of Human Rights (1987); Ramcharan, The Concept and Present Status of International Protection of Human Rights: Forty Years after the Universal Declaration (1989); Humphrey, No Distant Millennium: The International Law of Human Rights (1989).

3. The Restatement concludes: "Few states would agree that any action by a state contrary to any provision of the Declaration is, for that reason alone, a violation of the Charter or of customary international law. On the other hand, almost all states would agree that some infringements of human rights enumerated in the Declaration are violations of the Charter or of customary internation-

al law. See § 702." Restatement (Third), Introductory Note to Part VII. See p. 627 below.

4. It has been suggested that the Universal Declaration, after the U.N. Charter, is the most influential instrument of the second half of the twentieth century. It underlies the entire international law of human rights, but, as the Declaration itself contemplated, its principal influence may have been to secure the recognition of human rights by states and instil the idea and the principles of human rights into the national constitutions and laws of virtually all states. The Universal Declaration has been copied or incorporated by reference in numerous constitutions of new states.

## THE PRINCIPAL COVENANTS

### *HENKIN, THE INTERNATIONAL BILL OF RIGHTS: THE UNIVERSAL DECLARATION AND THE COVENANTS*

in International Enforcement of Human Rights 6–9 (Bernhardt & Jolowicz, eds. 1987).

After the Universal Declaration was adopted, there were various views as to how best to secure its "universal and effective recognition and observance." Although some continued to insist that a binding international law of human rights was neither desirable nor feasible, the view that prevailed was that the Declaration should be converted into an international human rights covenant that would clearly be of binding character in international law.

* * *

* * * [T]he Universal Declaration was bifurcated into two distinct and different covenants, a Covenant on Civil and Political Rights, and another Covenant on Economic, Social, and Cultural Rights. Over the objection of the more developed states, which questioned the relevance and propriety of such provisions in covenants on human rights, both Covenants begin with the right of peoples to self-determination and to sovereignty over their natural resources. Then the two covenants go different ways.

In the Covenant on Civil and Political Rights states undertake to respect and ensure the rights recognized by the Covenant for all persons subject to their jurisdiction and to enact any laws and adopt any other measures necessary to that end. The rights recognized in the Covenant, following the first twenty-one articles of the Universal Declaration, generally spell out the same rights in greater detail and sometimes with qualifications. Unlike the Declaration, however, the Covenant includes a right not to be imprisoned for debt, and makes special mention of the rights of children and of minorities; it also requires states to prohibit propaganda for war or incitement to racial hatred. On the other hand, the right to enjoy private property and not to be arbitrarily deprived of one's property, found in Article 17 of the Universal Declaration, is missing from the Covenant. That omission doubtless was not a rejection of the essential right but was the result of sharp disagreement on the scope and definition of the right, and perhaps a spill-over of the controversy over the protection of properties of foreign nationals.

The Covenant also spells out permissible limitations on particular rights when necessary for national security, public order (*ordre public*), public health and morals or the rights and freedoms of others. Article 4 permits derogation from most (not all) rights in time of proclaimed public emergency which threatens the life of the nation, to the extent strictly required by the exigencies of the situation.

Unlike the Declaration, the Covenant, since it created legal obligations, addressed the need to provide measures for their enforcement * * *. While in legal principle every state party is a promisee and entitled to request compliance by any other state party, ordinarily no other state has any interest in doing so and is especially reluctant to demand compliance or threaten sanctions for violation at the expense of its friendly relations and diplomatic capital.

It has been necessary, therefore, to develop special "enforcement machinery," that would monitor compliance and bring to bear international influence and world opinion so as to help deter or terminate violations. The International Covenant on Civil and Political Rights established a Human Rights Committee of experts as its principal monitoring body. Within one year of adherence to the Covenant, and thereafter upon request, states parties are required to report to the Committee on measures taken to give effect to the rights recognized in the Covenant. [See p. 634 below.] In addition, member states may, if they wish, declare that they agree to be subject to complaints to the Committee by other state parties. (Article 41). [See p. 634 below.] Under a separate, optional protocol to the Covenant, member states may agree to submit to communications—i.e., complaints—to the Committee lodged against them by or on behalf of private persons claiming to be victims of violation. [See p. 640 below.]

### *Notes*

1. The drafters of the Covenants initially intended to write only one instrument. The original drafts included only political and civil rights, but economic and social rights were added early. Western states then fought for, and obtained, a division into two covenants. They insisted that economic and social rights were essentially aspirations or plans, not rights, since their realization depended on economic resources and on controversial economic theory and ideology. These, they said, were not appropriate subjects for binding obligations and should not be allowed to dilute the legal character of provisions honoring political-civil rights; states prepared to assume obligations to respect political-civil rights should not be discouraged from doing so by requiring of them impossible social-economic commitments * * *. There was wide agreement and clear recognition that the means required to enforce or induce compliance with social-economic undertakings were different from the means required for civil-political rights. See Henkin, Introduction, The International Bill of Rights 9–10 (1981).

The Covenant on Civil and Political Rights is drafted in terms of the individual's rights, whereas the Covenant on Economic, Social and Cultural Rights speaks to the states. Is that significant? Under the Covenant on Civil and Political Rights, states parties are obligated to respect and ensure the rights recognized in the Covenant without delay or exception. A state party to the Covenant on Economic, Social and Cultural Rights undertakes "to take steps * * * to the maximum of its available resources, with a view to achieving progressively the full realization of the rights recognized * * *." (Article 2).

The Covenant on Civil and Political Rights came into effect on March 23, 1976. The Covenant on Economic, Social and Cultural Rights came into effect on January 3, 1976. As of January 1, 1993, 100 states have adhered to the Covenant on Civil and Political Rights, and 60 states have adhered to the Protocol. (The Second Optional Protocol to the Covenant on Civil and Political Rights aiming at the abolition of the death penalty entered into force on July 11, 1991; as of January 1, 1993, ten states have adhered to it). As of January 1993, 104 states have adhered to the Covenant on Economic, Social and Cultural Rights.

2. By Article 2 of the International Covenant on Civil and Political Rights, states parties undertake to respect and ensure the rights indicated "to all individuals within its territory and subject to its jurisdiction." Is the Covenant violated if a state party does not respect the rights of persons on the high seas? In the territory of another state? See Buergenthal, To Respect and Ensure: State Obligations and Permissible Derogations, in The International Bill of Rights 73–77 (Henkin ed. 1981).

The obligation of states "to respect and ensure" the rights recognized by the Covenant on Civil and Political Rights apparently includes an obligation to protect individuals against violations of their human rights by private persons. Contrast the principle in United States Constitutional jurisprudence that the Constitution protects only against "state action." See Tribe, American Constitutional Law, 350–53, 1688–1720 (2d ed. 1988). Compare the provision in the Restatement (Third) § 702, that a state violates customary law if, as a matter of state policy, it "encourages or condones" certain infringements of human rights. See p. 615 below. Does a state party violate the Covenant if it kidnaps a person in the territory of another state and brings him back for trial? See United States v. Alvarez-Machain, ___ U.S. ___, 112 S.Ct. 2188, 119 L.Ed.2d 441 (1992); Lutz, State Sponsored Abductions: The Human Rights Ramifications of Alvarez–Machain, 9 World Pol'y J. 687 (1992). See also the discussion of the case in Chapter 3, p. 177.

3. The Covenant on Economic, Social and Cultural Rights obligates states to recognize and progressively achieve the following rights: the right to work (Art. 6); to just and favorable working conditions (Art. 7); to trade unions (Art. 8); to social security (Art. 9); to protection of and assistance to the family, mothers and children (Art. 10); to adequate food, clothing and housing (Art. 11); to the highest attainable standard of physical and mental health (Art. 12); to education (Art. 13); and the right to take part in cultural life, to enjoy the benefits of scientific progress and its applications, and to benefit from the protection of the moral and material interests resulting from any scientific, literary or artistic production of which a person is the author (Art. 15). What obligations do parties to the Covenants assume? To whom? See Schachter, International Law in Theory and Practice 345–51 (1991).

By Article 2(1) of the International Covenant on Economic, Social and Cultural Rights, states undertake to realize the rights indicated "individually and through international assistance and cooperation, especially economic and technical." Does this provision create obligations for a state party to assist other states parties to realize the economic and social and cultural rights of their inhabitants? Compare the arguments of advocates of a "right to development," some of whom suggest that persons in need have claims upon wealthy nations for assistance. Rich, The Right to Development as an Emerging Human Right, 23 Va.J.I.L. 287 (1983); Espiell, The Right of Development as a Human Right, 16

Tex.I.L.J. (1981). See generally the U.N. Declaration on the Right of Development, G.A.Res. 41/128 (1986), G.A.O.R. 41st Sess., Supp. 53, at 86, which recognized "[t]he right of development" as "an inalienable human right." (Article 1). The Declaration was adopted by a vote of 146 to 1 (the U.S.), with eight abstentions (including Japan and the Britain); and there has been uncertainty whether the Declaration is intended to state the customary law. For a discussion of the right to development, and of the possible tension between individual and collective rights, see Schachter, International Law in Theory and Practice 331–32 (1991); Henkin, The Age of Rights 191–93 (1989). See also Crawford, The Rights of Peoples 65–66 (1988); International Law and Development (De Waart, Peters & Denters, eds. (1988); International Law of Development (Snyder & Slinn, eds. 1987).

4. For a comprehensive guide to interpretation of the Covenant on Civil and Political Rights, see The International Bill of Rights: The Covenant on Civil and Political Rights (Henkin, ed., 1981). As of 1993, a guide to the Covenant on Economic, Social and Cultural Rights by Louis Sohn was approaching publication.

5. Other international human rights agreements were concluded before and after the Covenants. The Slavery Convention of 1926 and the Genocide Convention of 1948 are early examples. Human rights conventions since the Covenants generally develop and expand the protections provided in the Covenant on particular subjects. The following is the status of some of the principal agreements as of January 1, 1993:

| Title of Agreement | Date of Entry into Force | Citation | U.S. Party | No. of Parties |
|---|---|---|---|---|
| International Convention on the Elimination of All Forms of Racial Discrimination | 1–4–69 | 660 U.N.T.S. 195 | No | 130 |
| Convention against Discrimination in Education | 5–22–62 | 429 U.N.T.S. 95 | No | 76 |
| International Convention on the Suppression and Punishment of the Crime of Apartheid | 7–18–76 | Annex to G.A.Res. 3068 (XVIII) | No | 91 |
| Convention on the Prevention and Punishment of the Crime of Genocide | 1–12–51 | 7 U.N.T.S. 277 | Yes | 102 |
| Convention on the Non–Applicability of Statutory Limitations to War Crimes and Crimes against Humanity | 11–11–70 | 754 U.N.T.S. 73 | No | 31 |
| Slavery Convention of 1926 | 3–9–27 | 60 U.N.T.S. 253 [a] | Yes | 95 |

a. 46 Stat. 2183, T.S. 778 (1929). The United States is also party to the 1953 Protocol amending the Convention, 7 U.S.T. 479, T.I.A.S. No. 3532, 182 U.N.T.S. 51 (adhered to by 44 states), but not to other amendments that went into force in 1955, 212 U.N.T.S. 176 (47 parties).

| Title of Agreement | Date of Entry into Force | Citation | U.S. Party | No. of Parties |
|---|---|---|---|---|
| Supplementary Convention on the Abolition of Slavery, the Slave Trade, and Institutions and Practices Similar to Slavery | 4–30–57 | 266 U.N.T.S. 3[b] | Yes | 105 |
| Abolition of Forced Labor Convention | 1–17–59 | 320 U.N.T.S. 291 | Yes | 108 |
| Convention for the Suppression of the Traffic in Persons and of the Exploitation of the Prostitution of Others | 7–25–51 | 96 U.N.T.S. 271 | No | 60 |
| Convention on the Nationality of Married Women | 8–11–58 | 309 U.N.T.S. 65 | No | 57 |
| Convention on the Reduction of Statelessness | 12–13–75 | A/CONF.9/15,1961 | No | 15 |
| Convention Relating to the Status of Stateless Persons | 6–6–60 | 360 U.N.T.S. 117 | No | 36 |
| Convention Relating to the Status of Refugees | 4–22–54 | 189 U.N.T.S. 137 | No | 106 |
| Protocol Relating to the Status of Refugees | 10–4–67 | 606 U.N.T.S. 267 [c] | Yes | 108 |
| Convention on the International Right of Correction | 8–24–62 | 435 U.N.T.S. 91 | No | 12 |
| Convention on the Political Rights of Women | 7–7–54 | 193 U.N.T.S. 135 [d] | Yes | 96 |
| Convention on the Elimination of all Forms of Discrimination Against Women | 9–3–81 | A/Res./34/180 | No | 111 |
| Convention Against Torture and Other Cruel, Inhuman or Degrading Treatment or Punishment | 6–26–87 | Ga.Res. 39/46 [e] | No | 64 |
| Convention on the Rights of the Child | 9–2–90 | G.A.Res. 44/25 | No | 107 |
| Second Optional Protocol to the International Covenant on Civil and Political Rights Aiming at the Abolition of the Death Penalty | 7–11–91 | G.A.Res. 44/128 | No | 11 |

**b.** 18 U.S.T. 3201, T.I.A.S. No. 6418.

**c.** 19 U.S.T. 6223, T.I.A.S. No. 6577.

**d.** 27 U.S.T. 1909, T.I.A.S. No. 8285.

**e.** The Senate has given consent to ratification of the Torture Convention, with reservations, see [Senate] Treaty Doc. 100–20, but the Senate declared that the President should not ratify the Convention until Congress had enacted implementing legislation. As of early 1993, Congress had not taken legislative action and the U.S. had not deposited its instrument of ratification. See p. 626 infra for a discussion of international human rights law and the United States.

In 1990, the United Nations General Assembly passed a resolution adopting the Convention on the Rights of Migrant Workers. As of early 1993, the Convention had not entered into force and only two states (Mexico and Morocco) had signed the Convention. See G.A.Res. 45/158, reprinted in, 30 I.L.M. 517 (1991).

The United Nations and some of its Specialized Agencies have also promoted other human rights conventions, declarations and guidelines, e.g.,

— Discrimination (Employment and Occupation) Convention;

— Convention Against Discrimination in Education;

— Equal Remuneration Convention;

— Convention on the Reduction of Statelessness;

— Universal Declaration on the Eradication of Hunger and Malnutrition;

— Standard Minimum Rules for the Treatment of Prisoners;

— Declaration on the Protection of all Persons from Being Subjected to Torture and Other Cruel, Inhuman or Degrading Treatment or Punishment;

— Declaration on the Granting of Independence to Colonial Countries and Peoples;

— Declaration on the Elimination of Discrimination Against Women;

— Declaration on Territorial Asylum;

— Declaration of the Rights of the Child;

— Declaration on the Promotion among Youth of the Ideals of Peace, Mutual Respect and Understanding between Peoples;

— Declaration on Social Progress and Development;

— Declaration on the Rights of Mentally Retarded Persons;

— Declaration of the Principles of International Cultural Co-operation;

— Declaration on the Elimination of all Forms of Intolerance and of Discrimination Based on Religion or Belief;

— Declaration on Race and Racial Prejudice;

— Convention Concerning Minimum Standards of Social Security;

— International Convention on the Protection of the Rights of Migrant Workers and Members of Their Families;

— Convention Concerning Employment Policy;

— Convention on Consent to Marriage and Minimum Age for Marriage and Registration of Marriages;

— International Convention Against Apartheid in Sports.

The texts of many of these instruments are collected in Human Rights, A Compilation of International Instruments (United Nations Publication, Doc. No. ST/HR/1/Rev. 2, 1983). See also United Nations Action in the Field of Human Rights (U.N.Doc. No. ST/HR/2/Rev. 2, 1988).

6. Since it came into existence after the First World War, the International Labor Organization has promoted more than 100 conventions dealing with conditions of labor and other social conditions; a number of them have been

widely ratified. International Labor Office, International Labor Conventions and Recommendations, chart of ratifications, Jan. 1, 1993. See generally Valticos, International Labor Law (1979); Galenson, The International Labour Organisation: An American View (1981). For a summary and review of the structure of the ILO, see International Labour Office, International Labour Standards 197–204 (1982). UNESCO has also promoted agreements on human rights matters within its particular jurisdiction, e.g., the UNESCO Convention Against Discrimination in Education, 429 U.N.T.S. 93 (1960).

7. The Covenants were to transform the provisions of the Universal Declaration into binding treaties, but there are significant differences between the Declaration and the Covenants. Some of the rights set forth in the Declaration, notably Article 14 (asylum) and Article 17 (property), have no counterpart in the Covenants. Failure to include a right to property reflected principally international differences, particularly intense at the time, as to the obligation to compensate aliens for nationalized properties. See Chapter 9. On the other hand, the Covenant on Civil and Political Rights includes the right of peoples to self-determination and to freely dispose of their natural resources (Article 1); procedural protections for aliens against expulsion (Article 13); the right not to be compelled to testify against oneself (Article 14(3)(g)); compensation for miscarriage of justice (Article 14(6)); freedom from double jeopardy (Article 14(7)); the prohibition of propaganda for war or of advocacy of national, racial or ethnic hatred (Article 20); the right of a child to a name and a nationality (Article 24); protection for cultural, religious and linguistic rights of minorities (Article 27). The Covenant also spells out limitations on rights referred to in the Declaration (Art. 29(2)). See p. 619 below. See Restatement (Third) § 701, Reporters' Note 6. The socio-economic provisions in the Declaration are much expanded in the Covenant on Economic, Social and Cultural Rights.

Some of the differences between the Declaration and the Covenants reflect the difference between a declaration and international agreements, and what states sought to achieve by each. The differences reflect also the changing composition of international society; there were 58 members in the U.N. in 1948, 122 in 1966 when the Covenants were adopted. Most of the additional members were new states that had recently been colonies, and their admission into the international system changed the balance between traditional and new states, between developed and developing, between "libertarian," "socialist," and various "mixed" societies.

The right to self-determination was included in Article 1 of the Covenant on Economic, Social and Cultural Rights and in Article 1 of the Covenant on Civil and Political Rights, over objections that these are political principles, not legal rights; that, in any event, they are not rights of individuals but of "peoples," and not a continuing responsibility of a state towards its own inhabitants. Note the reservation of the United Kingdom to Article 1 of the Covenant on Civil and Political Rights. But see Jenks, Human Rights, Social Justice and Peace: The Broader Significance of the ILO Experience, in International Protection of Human Rights, Proceedings of the Seventh Nobel Symposium 227 (Eide & Schou eds. 1967). On the meaning of the right of self-determination in the Covenant, see Cassesse, The Self-Determination of Peoples, in The International Bill of Rights (Henkin ed. 1981). On self-determination generally, see Chapter 4, p. 302. Do the procedures for "enforcement" provided in those covenants, p. 634 infra, apply as well to this right?

See generally An–Na'im, Human Rights in Cross–Cultural Perspective: A Quest for Consensus (1991); The Rights of Peoples (Crawford, ed. 1988); Meron, Human Rights Law–Making in the United Nations (1986); Meron, Norm–Making and Supervision in International Human Rights, 76 A.J.I.L. 754 (1982); Meron, On A Hierarchy of International Human Rights, 80 A.J.I.L. 1 (1986); Capotorti, Human Rights: The Hard Road Towards Universality, in The Structure and Process of International Law (MacDonald & Johnston eds. 1983).

On particular rights, see The International Law and Policy of Human Welfare (MacDonald & Johnston eds. 1978); McKean, Equality and Discrimination Under International Law (1983); Hertzberg & Zannuto, The Protection of Human Rights in the Criminal Process Under International Instruments and National Constitutions (1981); Burgers, The United Nations Convention Against Torture: A Handbook on the Convention Against Torture and other Cruel, Inhuman or Degrading Treatment or Punishment (1988); Goodwin–Gill, International Law and the Movement of Persons Between States (1978), and The Refugee in International Law (1983); Hevener, International Law and the Status of Women (1983); Khushalani, Dignity and Honour of Women as Basic and Fundamental Human Rights (1982). See generally Human Rights: A Topical Bibliography, Center for the Study of Human Rights, Columbia University (1983); Human Rights, An International and Comparative Law Bibliography (Friedman & Sherman eds. 1985).

### *3. Customary International Law of Human Rights*

### *Restatement (Third) § 702*

A state violates international law if, as a matter of state policy, it practices, encourages or condones

(a) genocide,

(b) slavery or slave trade,

(c) the murder or causing the disappearance of individuals,

(d) torture or other cruel, inhuman or degrading treatment or punishment,

(e) prolonged arbitrary detention,

(f) systematic racial discrimination, or

(g) consistent patterns of gross violations of internationally recognized human rights.

### *Notes*

1. The Restatement (Third) Comments on this section include:

*a. Scope of customary law of human rights.* This section includes as customary law only those human rights whose status as customary law is generally accepted (as of 1987) and whose scope and content are generally agreed. See § 701, Reporters' Note 6. The list is not necessarily complete, and is not closed: human rights not listed in this section may have achieved the status of customary law, and some rights might achieve that status in the future. See Comments *j, k,* and *l.*

* * *

*j. Systematic religious discrimination.* The United Nations Charter (Articles 1, 13, 55) links religious discrimination with racial discrimination and treats them alike; to the extent that racial discrimination violates the Charter religious discrimination does also. Religious discrimination is also treated identically with racial discrimination in the principal covenants and in the constitutions and laws of many states. There is as yet no convention on the elimination of religious discrimination, and there has been no concerted attack on such discrimination comparable to that on *apartheid,* but there is a strong case that systematic discrimination on grounds of religion as a matter of state policy is also a violation of customary law. See Reporters' Note 8.

*k. Right to property.* The Universal Declaration of Human Rights includes the right to own and not to be arbitrarily deprived of property. See § 701, Reporters' Note 6, and § 711, Comment *d.* There is, however, wide disagreement among states as to the scope and content of that right, which weighs against the conclusion that a human right to property generally has become a principle of customary law. All states have accepted a limited core of rights to private property, and violation of such rights, as state policy, may already be a violation of customary law. Invasions of rights in private property that have not achieved the status of customary law may nonetheless violate a particular international agreement or, where the victim is a foreign national, the principles of customary law governing state responsibility to foreign nationals. See §§ 711–713.

*l. Gender discrimination.* The United Nations Charter (Article 1(3)) and the Universal Declaration of Human Rights (Article 2) prohibit discrimination in respect of human rights on various grounds, including sex. Discrimination on the basis of sex in respect of recognized rights is prohibited by a number of international agreements, including the Covenant on Civil and Political Rights, the Covenant on Economic, Social and Cultural Rights, and more generally by the Convention on the Elimination of All Forms of Discrimination Against Women, which, as of 1987, had been ratified by 91 states and signed by a number of others. The United States had signed the Convention but had not yet ratified it. See Introductory Note to this Part. The domestic laws of a number of states, including those of the United States, mandate equality for, or prohibit discrimination against, women generally or in various respects. Gender-based discrimination is still practiced in many states in varying degrees, but freedom from gender discrimination as state policy, in many matters, may already be a principle of customary international law. Discrimination by a state that does not constitute a violation of customary law may violate a particular international agreement if practiced by a state party.

*m. Consistent pattern of gross violations of human rights.* The acts enumerated in clauses (a) to (f) are violations of customary law even if the practice is not consistent, or not part of a "pattern," and those acts are inherently "gross" violations of human rights. Clause (g) includes other infringements of recognized human rights that are not violations of customary law when committed singly or sporadically (although they may be forbidden to states parties to the International Covenants or other particular agreements); they become violations of customary law if the state is guilty of a "consistent pattern of gross violations" as state policy. A violation is gross if it is particularly shocking because of the importance of the right or the gravity of the violation. All the rights proclaimed in the Universal

Declaration and protected by the principal International Covenants (see § 701, Reporters' Note 6) are internationally recognized human rights, but some rights are fundamental and intrinsic to human dignity. Consistent patterns of violation of such rights as state policy may be deemed "gross" *ipso facto.* These include, for example, systematic harassment, invasions of the privacy of the home, arbitrary arrest and detention (even if not prolonged); denial of fair trial in criminal cases; grossly disproportionate punishment; denial of freedom to leave a country; denial of the right to return to one's country; mass uprooting of a country's population; denial of freedom of conscience and religion; denial of personality before the law; denial of basic privacy such as the right to marry and raise a family; and invidious racial or religious discrimination. A state party to the Covenant on Civil and Political Rights is responsible even for a single, isolated violation of any of these rights; any state is liable under customary law for a consistent pattern of violations of any such right as state policy.

Reporters' Note 10 adds:

"*Consistent pattern of gross violations.*" This phrase derives from Res. 1503 of the United Nations Economic and Social Council, which authorized the Subcommission on Prevention of Discrimination and Protection of Minorities of the Commission on Human Rights to appoint a "working group" to consider communications "which appear to reveal a consistent pattern of gross and reliably attested violations of human rights and fundamental freedoms," even by states not parties to any relevant international agreement. Res. 1503, 48 U.N. ESCOR Supp. No. 1A at 8–9. The Subcommission has been implementing that resolution annually since that time. See the annual reports of the United Nations Commission on Human Rights to the Economic and Social Council. See also, for example, the action taken in respect of Chile, Report of the United Nations Commission on Human Rights on its 32d session, 60 U.N. ESCOR Supp. No. 3 (1976); the report dealing with Malawi, Report of the United Nations Commission on Human Rights on its 36th session, U.N. ESCOR Supp. No. 3 (1980). United Nations bodies have recommended measures against particular "consistent patterns of gross violation," notably *apartheid.* See § 703, Reporters' Note 10.

2. Does the practice of states support § 702 of the Restatement? The Reporters' Notes to § 701 state:

1. *Human rights law and sources of international law.* Ordinarily, international law does not assume restrictions on state autonomy. But the universal acceptance of human rights in principle, and active international concern with human rights, has led to some readiness to conclude that states have assumed human rights obligations. There is a disposition to find legal obligation in indeterminate language about human rights in international agreements, *e.g.,* the United Nations Charter (see Introductory Note to this Part). There is some willingness to find that the practice of states, perhaps under constitutional, political, or moral impetus, is practice with a sense of international legal obligation creating a customary international law of human rights, even though many states sometimes violate these rights, see § 102(2). Absorption into international law of principles common to national legal systems generally is only a secondary source of international law (§ 102(4)), but there is a willingness to conclude that prohibitions common to the constitutions or laws of many states are general principles that have been absorbed into international law.

2. *Practice creating customary human rights law.* International human rights law governs relations between a state and its own inhabitants. Other states are only occasionally involved in monitoring such law through ordinary diplomatic practice. Therefore, the practice of states that is accepted as building customary international law of human rights includes some forms of conduct different from those that build customary international law generally. See § 102, Comment *b.* Practice accepted as building customary human rights law includes: virtually universal adherence to the United Nations Charter and its human rights provisions, and virtually universal and frequently reiterated acceptance of the Universal Declaration of Human Rights even if only in principle; virtually universal participation of states in the preparation and adoption of international agreements recognizing human rights principles generally, or particular rights; the adoption of human rights principles by states in regional organizations in Europe, Latin America, and Africa (see Introductory Note to this Part); general support by states for United Nations resolutions declaring, recognizing, invoking, and applying international human rights principles as international law; action by states to conform their national law or practice to standards or principles declared by international bodies, and the incorporation of human rights provisions, directly or by reference, in national constitutions and laws; invocation of human rights principles in national policy, in diplomatic practice, in international organization activities and actions; and other diplomatic communications or action by states reflecting the view that certain practices violate international human rights law, including condemnation and other adverse state reactions to violations by other states. The International Court of Justice and the International Law Commission have recognized the existence of customary human rights law. See Case Concerning the Barcelona Traction, Light & Power Co., Ltd. (Belgium v. Spain), [1970] I.C.J. Rep. 32, quoted in § 703, Reporters' Note 3; § 702, Reporters' Notes 3, 4. See, generally McDougal, Lasswell and Chen, Human Rights and World Public Order 266 *et seq.,* 313 *et seq.* (1980). Some of these practices may also support the conclusion that particular human rights have been absorbed into international law as general principles common to the major state legal systems. See § 702, Reporters' Note 1.

Compare Chapter 2 supra.

3. Section 702 of the Restatement has been invoked in U.S. courts by undocumented aliens whom the United States was unable to deport and who were in detention. They claimed, *inter alia,* that they were being arbitrarily detained in violation of international law. The Court so held in Rodriguez–Fernandez v. Wilkinson, 505 F.Supp. 787 (D.Kan.1980), aff'd, 654 F.2d 1382 (10th Cir.1981). See also Fernandez–Roque v. Smith, 600 F.Supp. 1500 (D.Ga.1985), rev'd sub nom., Garcia–Mir v. Smith, 766 F.2d 1478 (11th Cir.1985), cert. denied, 475 U.S. 1022, 106 S.Ct. 1213, 89 L.Ed.2d 325 (1986). For a discussion of U.S. Constitutional protections afforded aliens, see pp. 176–77 above. The Circuit Court of Appeals apparently accepted that the detention violated international law, but held that the courts could not give relief against such a violation. See p. 176 supra.

4. An early invocation of a customary law of human rights is found in the Nuremberg Charter, which charged Nazi leaders with "crimes against humanity." See pp. 879–83 below.

For an application of customary law of human rights in a suit against a foreign official, see *Filartiga*, p. 653 below.

5. Are human rights norms *jus cogens?* See Restatement (Third) § 702, Comment *n* and Reporters' Note 11, Schachter, International Law in Theory and Practice 342–45 (1991). On *jus cogens* generally, see Chapter 6, p. 496.

6. What limitations upon the scope of rights do international instruments permit? Professor Henkin writes:

> As in even the most enlightened and libertarian national rights systems, most of the rights in the Covenant [on Civil and Political Rights] are not absolute. The freedom of expression, in the classic reference, does not permit one falsely to cry "fire" in a crowded theater; the most libertarian societies do not permit slander; all countries impose some limits on freedom of movement in some circumstances to protect national security or public order. In the rights jurisprudence of the United States these permissible limitations are not expressed in the Constitution, although sometimes read into general phrases: search and seizure is forbidden only if "unreasonable," punishment only if "cruel and unusual," infringements on liberty only if they deny "due process of law."
>
> The Framers of the Covenant sought to define the permissible scope of limitations as strictly as possible, although inevitably in general phrases. For example, the freedom of movement within a country or the right to leave it "shall not be subject to any restrictions except those which are provided by law, are necessary to protect national security, public order (*ordre public*), public health or morals, or the rights and freedoms of others, and are consistent with the other rights recognized" in the Covenant (Article 12(3)). Or, "the Press and the public may be excluded from all or part of a trial for reasons of morals, public order (*ordre public*) or national security in a democratic society, or when the interest of the private lives of the parties so requires, or to the extent strictly necessary in the opinion of the court in special circumstances where publicity would prejudice the interests of justice" (Article 14(1)). One can debate the merits of these and other limitations or their particular formulations, but few would question that in principle some such limitations are inevitable and probably desirable. The limitations themselves, however, are governed by law, not by the whim of the state. Whether a particular limitation on a right is permissible under the Covenant is a question of international law, and the state's action can be scrutinized and challenged as a violation of the Covenant * * *.

Introduction, The International Bill of Rights: The Covenant on Civil and Political Rights 21–22 (Henkin ed. 1981). See also Kiss, Permissible Limitations on Rights, in id, at 290.

Limitations are to be distinguished from permissible derogations from rights in emergencies.

## DEROGATIONS FROM RIGHTS IN EMERGENCIES

### *COVENANT ON CIVIL AND POLITICAL RIGHTS*

999 U.N.T.S. 171, 6 I.L.M. 368 (1967).

#### Article 4

1. In time of public emergency which threatens the life of the nation and the existence of which is officially proclaimed, the States Parties to the

present Covenant may take measures derogating from their obligations under the present Covenant to the extent strictly required by the exigencies of the situation, provided that such measures are not inconsistent with their other obligations under international law and do not involve discrimination solely on the ground of race, colour, sex, language, religion or social origin.

2. No derogation from articles 6, 7, 8 (paragraphs 1 and 2), 11, 15, 16 and 18 may be made under this provision.

3. Any State Party to the present Covenant availing itself of the right of derogation shall immediately inform the other States Parties to the present Covenant, through the intermediary of the Secretary–General of the United Nations, of the provisions from which it has derogated and of the reasons by which it was actuated. A further communication shall be made, through the same intermediary, on the date on which it terminates such derogation.

### *Notes*

1. Paragraph 2 of Article 4 prohibits derogations from, among others, guarantees to the right to life (Article 6), against torture (Article 7), and against slavery and servitude (Article 8).

2. Does the availability of derogations from human rights obligations render the agreements that embody them ineffectual? Henkin comments:

> A different question is whether the derogations and limitations permitted by the agreements are so large as to render the undertakings illusory, especially since they are, in the first instance at least, interpreted and applied by every acting state for itself, and—to date—no other state (or international body) scrutinizes that interpretation and application in fact. Those are subjects for fuller exposition another day, but, in a preliminary word, I do not think these and other "loopholes" render the undertakings illusory, or derogate from the quality of any rights created. In my view the derogation clauses are not destructive of the obligations (or the rights) so long as they are in fact interpreted and applied as written and intended, and the other states and the international bodies scrutinize their interpretation and application. Similarly, I do not consider undertakings to realize economic, social, and cultural rights "progressively" as essentially illusory. The economic-social undertakings were made legal obligations in order to establish the idea of economic-social benefits as rights and to increase the likelihood of their enjoyment; it was not clear what else was expected to flow [from] making them legal obligations. Even those purposes may be sufficient to support law and rights; the future may show whether there are in fact other purposes and consequences for seeing, and continuing to see, international covenants as law and as creating rights.

Henkin, International Human Rights as "Rights," 1 Cardozo L.Rev. 446–47 (1979).

3. Is derogation permissible of a principle of human rights that has the character of *jus cogens?* See Restatement (Third) § 702, Comment *n.* See generally Chapter 6, p. 653.

## LAWLESS CASE

[1961] European Court of Human Rights, Ser. A. no. 1.

*As to whether, despite Articles 5 and 6 of the [European Convention for the Protection of Human Rights and Fundamental Freedoms], the detention of G.R. Lawless was justified by the right of derogation allowed to the High Contracting Parties in certain exceptional circumstances under Article 15 of the Convention.*

20. *Whereas* the Court is called upon to decide whether the detention of G.R. Lawless from 13th July to 11th December 1957 under the Offences against the State (Amendment) Act, 1940, was justified, despite Articles 5 and 6 of the Convention, by the right of derogation allowed to the High Contracting Parties in certain exceptional circumstances under Article 15 of the Convention;

21. *Whereas* Article 15 reads as follows:

"(1) In time of war or other public emergency threatening the life of the nation any High Contracting Party may take measures derogating from its obligations under this Convention to the extent strictly required by the exigencies of the situation, provided that such measures are not inconsistent with its other obligations under international law.

(2) No derogation from Article 2, except in respect of deaths resulting from lawful acts of war, or from Articles 3, 4 (paragraph 1) and 7 shall be made under this provision.

(3) Any High Contracting Party availing itself of this right of derogation shall keep the Secretary–General of the Council of Europe fully informed of the measures which it has taken and the reasons therefor. It shall also inform the Secretary–General of the Council of Europe when such measures have ceased to operate and the provisions of the Convention are again being fully executed."

22. *Whereas* it follows from these provisions that, without being released from all its undertakings assumed in the Convention, the Government of any High Contracting Party has the right, in case of war or public emergency threatening the life of the nation, to take measures derogating from its obligations under the Convention other than those named in Article 15, paragraph 2, provided that such measures are strictly limited to what is required by the exigencies of the situation and also that they do not conflict with other obligations under international law; whereas it is for the Court to determine whether the conditions laid down in Article 15 for the exercise of the exceptional right of derogation have been fulfilled in the present case;

(a) *As to the existence of a public emergency threatening the life of the nation.*

23. *Whereas* the Irish Government, by a Proclamation dated 5th July 1957 and published in the Official Gazette on 8th July 1957, brought into force the extraordinary powers conferred upon it by Part II of the Offences against the State (Amendment) Act, 1940, "to secure the preservation of public peace and order;"

24. *Whereas,* by letter dated 20th July 1957 addressed to the Secretary–General of the Council of Europe, the Irish Government expressly stated

that "the detention of persons under the Act is considered necessary, to prevent the commission of offences against public peace and order and to prevent the maintaining of military or armed forces other than those authorised by the Constitution;"

* * *

27. *Whereas* the Commission, following the investigation carried out by it in accordance with Article 28 of the Convention, expressed a majority opinion in its Report that in "July 1957 there existed in Ireland a public emergency threatening the life of the nation within the meaning of Article 15, paragraph 1, of the Convention;"

28. *Whereas,* in the general context of Article 15 of the Convention, the natural and customary meaning of the words "other public emergency threatening the life of the nation" is sufficiently clear; whereas they refer to an exceptional situation of crisis or emergency which affects the whole population and constitutes a threat to the organised life of the community of which the State is composed; whereas, having thus established the natural and customary meaning of this conception, the Court must determine whether the facts and circumstances which led the Irish Government to make their Proclamation of 5th July 1957 come within this conception; whereas the Court, after an examination, find this to be the case; whereas the existence at the time of a "public emergency threatening the life of the nation," was reasonably deduced by the Irish Government from a combination of several factors, namely: in the first place, the existence in the territory of the Republic of Ireland of a secret army engaged in unconstitutional activities and using violence to attain its purposes; secondly, the fact that this army was also operating outside the territory of the State, thus seriously jeopardising the relations of the Republic of Ireland with its neighbour; thirdly the steady and alarming increase in terrorist activities from the autumn of 1956 and throughout the first half of 1957;

29. *Whereas,* despite the gravity of the situation, the Government had succeeded, by using means available under ordinary legislation, in keeping public institutions functioning more or less normally, but whereas the homicidal ambush on the night of 3rd to 4th July 1957 in the territory of Northern Ireland near the border had brought to light, just before 12th July—a date, which, for historical reasons is particularly critical for the preservation of public peace and order—the imminent danger to the nation caused by the continuance of unlawful activities in Northern Ireland by the IRA and various associated groups, operating from the territory of the Republic of Ireland;

30. *Whereas,* in conclusion, the Irish Government were justified in declaring that there was a public emergency in the Republic of Ireland threatening the life of the nation and were hence entitled, applying the provisions of Article 15, paragraph 1, of the Convention for the purposes for which those provisions were made, to take measures derogating from their obligations under the Convention;

(b) *As to whether the measures taken in derogation from obligations under the Convention were "strictly required by the exigencies of the situation".*

31. *Whereas* Article 15, paragraph 1, provides that a High Contracting Party may derogate from its obligations under the Convention only "to the extent strictly required by the exigencies of the situation;" whereas it is therefore necessary, in the present case, to examine whether the bringing into force of Part II of the 1940 Act was a measure strictly required by the emergency existing in 1957;

* * *

35. *Whereas* it was submitted that in view of the means available to the Irish Government in 1957 for controlling the activities of the IRA and its splinter groups the Irish Government could have taken measures which would have rendered superfluous so grave a measure as detention without trial; whereas, in this connection, mention was made of the application of the ordinary criminal law, the institution of special criminal courts of the type provided for by the Offences against the State Act, 1939, or of military courts; whereas it would have been possible to consider other measures such as the sealing of the border between the Republic of Ireland and Northern Ireland;

36. *Whereas,* however, considering, in the judgment of the Court, that in 1957 the application of the ordinary law had proved unable to check the growing danger which threatened the Republic of Ireland; whereas the ordinary criminal courts, or even the special criminal courts or military courts, could not suffice to restore peace and order; whereas, in particular, the amassing of the necessary evidence to convict persons involved in activities of the IRA and its splinter groups was meeting with great difficulties caused by the military, secret and terrorist character of those groups and the fear they created among the population; whereas the fact that these groups operated mainly in Northern Ireland, their activities in the Republic of Ireland being virtually limited to the preparation of armed raids across the border was an additional impediment to the gathering of sufficient evidence; whereas the sealing of the border would have had extremely serious repercussions on the population as a whole, beyond the extent required by the exigencies of the emergency;

Whereas it follows from the foregoing that none of the above-mentioned means would have made it possible to deal with the situation existing in Ireland in 1957; whereas, therefore, the Administrative detention—as instituted under the Act (Amendment) of 1940—of individuals suspected of intending to take part in terrorist activities, appeared, despite its gravity, to be a measure required by the circumstances;

37. *Whereas,* moreover, the Offences against the State (Amendment) Act of 1940, was subject to a number of safeguards designed to prevent abuses in the operation of the system of administrative detention; whereas the application of the Act was thus subject to constant supervision by Parliament, which not only received precise details of its enforcement at regular intervals but could also at any time, by a Resolution, annul the Government's Proclamation which had brought the Act into force; whereas the Offences against the State (Amendment) Act 1940, provided for the establishment of a "Detention Commission" made up of three members, which the Government did in fact set up, the members being an officer of the Defense Forces and two judges; whereas any person detained under this Act

could refer his case to that Commission whose opinion, if favourable to the release of the person concerned, was binding upon the Government; whereas, moreover, the ordinary courts could themselves compel the Detention Commission to carry out its functions;

Whereas, in conclusion, immediately after the Proclamation which brought the power of detention into force, the Government publicly announced that it would release any person detained who gave an undertaking to respect the Constitution and the Law and not to engage in any illegal activity, and that the wording of this undertaking was later altered to one which merely required that the person detained would undertake to observe the law and refrain from activities contrary to the 1940 Act; whereas the persons arrested were informed immediately after their arrest that they would be released following the undertaking in question; whereas in a democratic country such as Ireland the existence of this guarantee of release given publicly by the Government constituted a legal obligation on the Government to release all persons who gave the undertaking;

Whereas, therefore, it follows from the foregoing that the detention without trial provided for by the 1940 Act, subject to the above-mentioned safeguards, appears to be a measure strictly required by the exigencies of the situation within the meaning of Article 15 of the Convention;

38. *Whereas,* in the particular case of G.R. Lawless, there is nothing to show that the powers of detention conferred upon the Irish Government by the Offences against the State (Amendment) Act 1940, were employed against him, either within the meaning of Article 18 of the Convention, for a purpose other than that for which they were granted, or within the meaning of Article 15 of the Convention, by virtue of a measure going beyond what was strictly required by the situation at that time; * * *

## *Notes*

1. The substantive provisions in the European Convention are comparable to those in the International Covenant on Civil and Political Rights. See p. 619 above. Article 15 of the Convention provides for derogation from rights in emergency but forbids derogations from the right to life (Article 2), and the guarantees against torture (Article 3), slavery (Article 4), and *ex post facto* criminal law (Article 7).

2. For a comprehensive study of derogations, see Despouy, The Administration of Justice and the Human Rights of Detainees: Question of Human Rights and States of Emergency, U.N.Doc. E/CN.4/Sub. 2/1992/23/Rev. 1 (2 November 1992); International Commission of Jurists, States of Emergency: Their Impact on Human Rights (1983). See also Chowdhury, The Rule of Law in a State of Emergency: The Paris Minimum Standards of Human Rights Norms in a State of Emergency (1989); Grossman, States of Emergency: Latin America and the United States, in Constitutionalism and Rights 176–96 (Henkin & Rosenthal eds., 1990); Buergenthal, To Respect and to Ensure: State Obligations and Permissible Derogations, in The International Bill of Rights 72, 78–86 (Henkin ed., 1981); Higgins, Derogation Under Human Rights Treaties, 48 Brit.Y.B. Int'l L. 281 (1975–76).

In Silva v. Uruguay, the Human Rights Committee expressed its views on the derogations clause of Article 4(1) of the Covenant on Civil and Political Rights stating:

> According to Article 4(1) of the Covenant, the States Parties may take measures derogating from their obligations under that instrument in a situation of public emergency which threatens the life of the nation and the existence of which has been formally proclaimed. * * *
>
> Although the sovereign right of a State Party to declare a state of emergency is not questioned * * * the Human Rights Committee is of the opinion that a State, by merely invoking the existence of exceptional circumstances, cannot evade the obligations which it has undertaken by ratifying the Covenant. Although the substantive right to take derogatory measures may not depend on a formal notification being made pursuant to Article 4(3) of the Covenant, the State Party concerned is duty-bound to give a sufficiently detailed account of the relevant facts when it invokes Article 4(1) of the Covenant in proceedings under the Optional Protocol. * * * If the respondent Government does not furnish the required justification itself, as it is required to do under Article 4(2) of the Optional Protocol and Article 4(3) of the Covenant, the Human Rights Committee cannot conclude that valid reasons exist to legitimise a departure from the normal legal régime prescribed by the Covenant.

Silva v. Uruguay, 1 Selected Decision H.R.C. 65 (1981). See also I/A Court H.R., Advisory Opinion OC–8/87, Habeas Corpus in Emergency Situations (Arts. 27(2), 25(1) and 7(6) of the American Convention on Human Rights) (30 January 1987).

In 1984 at Siracusa, Italy, a colloquium sponsored by the American Association of the International Commission of Jurists (a nongovernmental body) produced the Siracusa Principles on the Limitation and Derogation Provisions in the International Covenant on Civil and Political Rights.

3. Should derogations from human rights treaties be permitted? Would states ratify the treaties if derogations were not permitted? What is the effect of continuous or repeated derogations? Professor Henkin writes:

> The relation of rights to remedies to enjoyment raises other questions for the international law of human rights. In principle, whether the human rights agreements are being honored, whether the individuals are in fact enjoying the human rights promised, is not immediately legally (or philosophically) relevant. For the short term, at least, failure of one or more states to carry out their international human rights undertakings does not vitiate the character of the undertakings as legal obligations, or the rights and duties they create. But if international human rights obligations fail to make any difference in fact over an extended time; if the states that undertook these obligations act continuously and consistently as though they had not, or as if they were not legal obligations; if the promisee-states do not seek to have the undertakings enforced, and otherwise acquiesce in violations and act as though no obligations exist—then one would have to consider whether there are legal obligations and consequent rights and duties. One might then ask whether, despite the legal forms followed and the legal words used, legal obligations were intended and were consummated; or, perhaps, whether despite original intentions to make law, the obligations were ended by implied mutual agreement or acquiescence, or lapsed from "desuetude." (In regard to economic-social rights, in particular, the future may provide evidence belying the assumption that legal obligations were intended.)

Henkin, International Human Rights as "Rights," 1 Cardozo L.Rev. 446 (1979).

## INTERNATIONAL HUMAN RIGHTS LAW FOR THE UNITED STATES

*HENKIN, THE AGE OF RIGHTS*

74–77 (1990) (footnotes omitted).

From the beginning, the international human rights movement was conceived by the United States as designed to improve the condition of human rights in countries other than the United States (and a very few like-minded liberal states). United States participation in the movement was also to serve the cause of human rights in other countries. To that end, the United States promoted and actively engaged in establishing international standards and machinery. It did not strongly favor but it also did not resist the move to develop international agreements and international law, but, again, it saw them as designed for other states. * * *

The reasons why the United States has maintained its distance from the international human rights agreements are not obvious. At one time, some lawyers in the United States questioned the constitutional authority of the treaty makers to adhere to such agreements: it was said that the agreements dealt with matters that under the United States Constitution were reserved to the States; or were delegated exclusively to Congress; or were not a proper subject for a treaty because they were only of "domestic concern." Each of these legal objections was long ago refuted. Thirty-five years ago some feared that United States adherence to international human rights agreements would threaten then-existing institutions and practices, such as racial segregation; now, Americans are happy to say, those practices are outlawed, independently of international agreements. Thirty-five years ago Senator Bricker's proposed constitutional amendment sought to prevent the use of treaties to "nationalize" human rights matters and to give Congress authority to deal with them. Today, as a result of new constitutional interpretations, individual rights are already national, Congress already has power to legislate about them.

And yet, resistance to United States adherence remains strong. In some measure, resistance to United States participation builds on differences between constitutional rights and international human rights. In particular, American constitutional rights are individualistic and deeply democratic in their eighteenth-century conception. Self-government is the basic right on which all others depend: *Representative government is freedom,* Thomas Paine said. In contemporary international human rights, on the other hand, popular sovereignty does not imply any particular system of government; individual participation in government is only one right among others, and the form of participation is not defined. * * *

But the resistance in the United States is deeper. There is resistance to imposing national standards on some matters that have long been deemed "local"; even more, there is resistance to accepting international standards, and international scrutiny, on matters that have been for the United States to decide. A deep isolationism continues to motivate many Americans, even some who are eager to judge others as by interceding on behalf of human rights in other countries.

### *Notes*

1. The Introductory Note to Part VII, Protection of Persons (Natural and Juridical), of the Restatement (Third) provides:

> *Human rights in United States foreign relations law.* The United Nations Charter and the Charter of the Organization of American States, both of which include human rights provisions, are treaties of the United States. The human rights conventions to which the United States is a party (see § 701, Comment *e,* and chart above) are also treaties of the United States. Obligations assumed by the United States in these agreements are law of the land, either directly if the provisions are self-executing or upon implementation by Congress. See § 111. The customary international law of human rights, § 702, is also law of the United States. § 111(1). Federal statutes refer to "internationally recognized human rights" and have legislated national policy toward governments guilty of "consistent patterns of gross violations" of such rights. See § 702, Reporters' Note 10. The United States has frequently reiterated its acceptance of the Universal Declaration, and whatever legal character it has applies to the United States.
>
> * * * In 1978, President Carter transmitted to the Senate the International Covenant on Civil and Political Rights, the International Covenant on Economic, Social and Cultural Rights, the Convention on the Elimination of All Forms of Racial Discrimination, and the American Convention on Human Rights. In 1980, President Carter submitted to the Senate the Covenant on the Elimination of All Forms of Discrimination against Women. If the Senate consents and the President proceeds with ratification of these treaties, they will become law of the United States. Even in the absence of ratification by the United States, some provisions of these covenants and conventions reflect principles of customary international law and thus are part of the law of the United States. * * *.

Restatement (Third), Introductory Note to Part VII 149–50 (footnotes omitted). See also Buergenthal, The U.S. and International Human Rights, 9 Hum.Rts.L.J. 141 (1988).

2. The Genocide Convention was signed by President Truman in 1948 and was before the Senate until 1986. The principal human rights Covenants were open for signature in 1966, but the United States did not sign them until 1977. The Covenant on Civil and Political Rights lay before the Senate until 1992, and the Covenant on Economic, Social and Cultural Rights is still before the Senate as of early 1993. The Bush Administration did not ask for Senate action on that Covenant or on two other conventions signed and transmitted to the Senate by President Carter in 1977.

3. As of 1993, the U.S. Senate has consented to the ratification of three major human rights agreements.

*a. Genocide.* The Convention on the Prevention and Punishment of the Crime of Genocide was before the United States Senate from 1949 to 1986. In February 1986, the Senate gave its consent, subject to several reservations and other conditions. One of these required the President to delay ratification until Congress enacted legislation, required by the Convention, to make genocide a crime. Congress passed the Genocide Convention Implementation Act in 1988 and the U.S. ratified the Convention in 1989. The Genocide Convention has been invoked by U.S. courts. See Matter of Extradition of Demjanjuk, 612 F.Supp. 544 (N.D.Ohio 1985), and related cases found at 612 F.Supp. 571 (N.D.Ohio 1985) (denying writ of habeas corpus), 776 F.2d 571 (6th Cir.1985), cert. denied, 475 U.S. 1016, 106 S.Ct. 1198, 89 L.Ed.2d 312 (1986).

*b. Torture.* In 1988 the United States signed the U.N. Convention Against Torture. The Senate gave consent in 1990, with reservations and required the President to delay ratification until Congress had adopted implementing legislation. See 136 Cong.Rec. S17486, 101st Cong., 2d Sess. (Oct. 27, 1990). As of early 1993, Congress had not acted and the U.S. had not deposited its instrument of ratification. In 1992 Congress enacted the Torture Victim Protection Act, Pub.L. 102–256, March 12, 1992, 106 Stat. 73, 28 U.S.C.A. § 1350), but it was not intended to, and does not in fact, implement the Torture Convention. See p. 612, note e.

*c. Civil and Political Rights.* In 1992, President Bush requested Senate consent to ratification of the Covenant on Civil and Political Rights with a number of Reservations, Understandings and Declarations. The Senate gave its consent and the United States ratified the Covenant subject to the following.

### *U.S. RESERVATIONS, UNDERSTANDINGS AND DECLARATIONS TO THE INTERNATIONAL COVENANT ON CIVIL AND POLITICAL RIGHTS*

138 Cong.Rec. S4781, S4783 (April 2, 1992).

*Resolved, (two-thirds of the Senators present concurring therein),* That the Senate advise and consent to the ratification of the International Covenant on Civil and Political Rights, adopted by the United Nations General Assembly on December 16, 1966, and signed on behalf of the United States on October 5, 1977, (Executive E, 95–2), subject to the following reservations, understandings, declarations and proviso:

I. The Senate's advice and consent is subject to the following reservations:

(1) That Article 20 does not authorize or require legislation or other action by the United States that would restrict the right of free speech and association protected by the Constitution and laws of the United States.

(2) That the United States reserves the right, subject to its Constitutional constraints, to impose capital punishment on any person (other than a pregnant woman) duly convicted under existing or future laws permitting the imposition of capital punishment, including such punishment for crimes committed by persons below 18 years of age.

(3) That the United States considers itself bound by Article 7 to the extent that "cruel, inhuman or degrading treatment or punishment" means the cruel and unusual treatment or punishment prohibited by the Fifth, Eighth and/or Fourteenth Amendments to the Constitution of the United States.

(4) That because U.S. law generally applies to an offender the penalty in force at the time the offense was committed, the United States does not adhere to the third clause of paragraph 1 of Article 15.

(5) That the policy and practice of the United States are generally in compliance with and supportive of the Covenant's provisions regard-

ing treatment of juveniles in the criminal justice system. Nevertheless, the United States reserves the right, in exceptional circumstances, to treat juveniles as adults, notwithstanding paragraphs 2(b) and 3 of Article 10 and paragraph 4 of Article 14. The United States further reserves to these provisions with respect to individuals who volunteer for military service prior to age 18.

II. The Senate's advice and consent is subject to the following understandings, which shall apply to the obligations of the United States under this Covenant:

(1) That the Constitution and laws of the United States guarantee all persons equal protection of the law and provide extensive protections against discrimination. The United States understands distinctions based upon race, colour, sex, language, religion, political or other opinion, national or social origin, property, birth or any other status—as those terms are used in Article 2, paragraph 1 and Article 26—to be permitted when such distinctions are, at minimum, rationally related to a legitimate governmental objective. The United States further understands the prohibition in paragraph 1 of Article 4 upon discrimination, in time of public emergency, based "solely" on the status of race, colour, sex, language, religion or social origin not to bar distinctions that may have a disproportionate effect upon persons of a particular status.

(2) That the United States understands the right to compensation referred to in Articles 9(5) and 14(6) to require the provision of effective and enforceable mechanisms by which a victim of an unlawful arrest or detention or a miscarriage of justice may seek and, where justified, obtain compensation from either the responsible individual or the appropriate governmental entity. Entitlement to compensation may be subject to the reasonable requirements of domestic law.

(3) That the United States understand[s] the reference to "exceptional circumstances" in paragraph 2(a) of Article 10 to permit the imprisonment of an accused person with convicted persons where appropriate in light of an individual's overall dangerousness, and to permit accused persons to waive their right to segregation from convicted persons. The United States further understands that paragraph 3 of Article 10 does not diminish the goals of punishment, deterrence, and incapacitation as additional legitimate purposes for a penitentiary system.

(4) That the United States understands that subparagraphs 3(b) and (d) of Article 14 do not require the provision of a criminal defendant's counsel of choice when the defendant is provided with court-appointed counsel on grounds of indigence, when the defendant is financially able to retain alternative counsel, or when imprisonment is not imposed. The United States further understands that paragraph 3(e) does not prohibit a requirement that the defendant make a showing that any witness whose attendance he seeks to compel is necessary for his defense. The United States understands the prohibition upon double jeopardy in paragraph 7 to apply only when the judgment of acquittal has been rendered by a court of the same governmental unit, whether

the Federal Government or a constituent unit, as is seeking a new trial for the same cause.

(5) That the United States understands that this Convention shall be implemented by the Federal Government to the extent that it exercises legislative and judicial jurisdiction over the matters covered therein, and otherwise by the state and local governments; to the extent that state and local governments exercise jurisdiction over such matters, the Federal Government shall take measures appropriate to the Federal system to the end that the competent authorities of the state or local governments may take appropriate measures for the fulfillment of the Convention.

III. The Senate's advice and consent is subject to the following declarations:

(1) That the United States declares that the provisions of Articles 1 through 27 of the Covenant are not self-executing.

(2) That it is the view of the United States that States Party to the Covenant should wherever possible refrain from imposing any restrictions or limitations on the exercise of the rights recognized and protected by the Covenant, even when such restrictions and limitations are permissible under the terms of the Covenant. For the United States, Article 5, paragraph 2, which provides that fundamental human rights existing in any State Party may not be diminished on the pretext that the Covenant recognizes them to a lesser extent, has particular relevance to Article 19, paragraph 3, which would permit certain restrictions on the freedom of expression. The United States declares that it will continue to adhere to the requirements and constraints of its Constitution in respect to all such restrictions and limitations.

(3) That the United States declares that it accepts the competence of the Human Rights Committee to receive and consider communications under Article 41 in which a State Party claims that another State Party is not fulfilling its obligations under the Covenant.

(4) That the United States declares that the right referred to in Article 47 may be exercised only in accordance with international law.

IV. The Senate's advice and consent is subject to the following proviso, which shall not be included in the instrument of ratification to be deposited by the President:

Nothing in this Covenant requires or authorizes legislation, or other action, by the United States of America prohibited by the Constitution of the United States as interpreted by the United States.

### *Notes*

1. President Carter had recommended generally similar reservations to the Covenant on Civil and Political Rights in 1978. See Message from the President of the United States Transmitting Four Treaties Pertaining to Human Rights, 95th Cong., 2d Sess. iii-xxiii (Feb. 23, 1978). See also Int'l Human Rights Law Group, U.S. Ratification of the Human Rights Treaties 85–103 (Lillich, ed. 1981). In seeking Senate consent to ratification of the Covenant, the Bush Administration indicated that it would not seek implementing legislation on the ground

that none was necessary, even though the United States declared the Covenant non-self-executing. The United Nations Secretary–General accepted the U.S. ratification, noting the "package" of declarations, understandings and reservations. Was the position of the Bush Administration legally defensible? Was implementing legislation unnecessary? See generally Clark, The Vienna Convention Reservations Regime and the Convention on Discrimination Against Women, 85 A.J.I.L. 281 (1991). For the effect of a Senate declaration that a treaty is not to be self-executing, see Chapter 3. Some have suggested that the Bush Administration package is inconsistent with the object and purpose of the treaty and therefore makes ratification nugatory. Do you agree? See Chapter 3 supra.

For the texts of reservations and declarations to the Covenant by other states, see Note by the Secretary–General, Reservations, Declarations, Notifications and Objections Relating to the International Covenant on Civil and Political Rights and the Optional Protocol Thereto, U.N.Doc. CCPR/C/2/Rev.3 (12 May 1992). See also Higgins, The United Nations: Still a Force for Peace, 52 Mod.L.Rev. 1, 11–17 (1982).

2. One international human rights agreement that has been increasingly invoked in the United States is the Protocol Relating to the Status of Refugees (see p. 653 below). The definition of refugee contained in the Protocol was before the Supreme Court in I.N.S. v. Stevic, 467 U.S. 407, 104 S.Ct. 2489, 81 L.Ed.2d 321 (1984). Whether the Protocol is self-executing (see p. 653 below), and whether some of its provisions were violated, was argued in the challenge to the Haitian Interdiction Program, Haitian Refugee Center, Inc. v. Gracey, 600 F.Supp. 1396 (D.D.C.1985), affirmed, 809 F.2d 794 (D.C.Cir.1987), and in several proceedings brought by Cuban nationals claiming asylum, e.g., Fernandez–Roque v. Smith, 567 F.Supp. 1115 (N.D.Ga.1983), and subsequent proceedings. See also Bertrand v. Sava, 684 F.2d 204 (2d Cir.1982); Pierre v. United States, 525 F.2d 933, 935 (5th Cir.1976), vacated and remanded to dismiss as moot, 434 U.S. 962, 98 S.Ct. 498, 54 L.Ed.2d 447 (1977).

Litigation concerning the interdiction of Haitian boats continued into the 1990s. One of the grounds of appeal relied upon by lawyers for the Haitian asylum-seekers concerned interpretation of U.S. legislation intended to reflect the provision in the Protocol to the Refugee Convention concerning the obligation not to return refugees to a place where they fear persecution ("non-refoulement"). Circuit Courts of Appeal have divided as to whether the interdiction program was consistent with the legislation. Compare Haitian Refugee Center, Inc. v. Baker, 953 F.2d 1498 (11th Cir.1992), cert. denied, ___ U.S. ___, 112 S.Ct. 1245, 117 L.Ed.2d 477 (1992) (interdiction program was consistent with the legislation), with Haitian Centers Council, Inc. v. McNary, 969 F.2d 1350 (2d Cir.1992). The Supreme Court granted certiorari in the *McNary* case and reversed the judgment sub nom. Sale v. Haitian Centers Council, Inc. (No. 92–344, June 21, 1993). The Court held, inter alia, that Article 33 of the Convention Relating to the Status of Refugees, which provides that no state shall expel or return ("refouler") a refugee to a state where his or her life or freedom is threatened because of race, religion, nationality or political beliefs, was not intended to have extraterritorial effect. The U.S. interdiction program was not in violation of Article 33 because it took place outside U.S. territorial waters. The Court stated the interdiction program may "violate the spirit of Article 33," but because "* * * the text of Article 33 cannot reasonably be read to say anything at all about a nation's actions toward aliens outside its own territory, it does not prohibit such actions."

3. Restatement (Third) § 701, Reporters' Note 7, states:

Courts in the United States have increasingly looked to international human rights standards as law in the United States or as a guide to United States law. See cases cited in § 702, Reporters' Notes 5 and 6; compare Reporters' Note 5 to this section. There are numerous references to the Universal Declaration, *e.g.,* Zemel v. Rusk, 381 U.S. 1, 14, n. 13, 85 S.Ct. 1271, 1279, n. 13, 14 L.Ed.2d 179 (1963); Kennedy v. Mendoza–Martinez, 372 U.S. 144, 161, n. 16, 83 S.Ct. 554, 564, n. 16, 9 L.Ed.2d 644 (1965). Several cases have cited the United Nations Standard Minimum Rules for the Treatment of Prisoners (10 GAOR, U.N.Doc. A/Conf. 6/C.1/L.1, 1955), to help determine rights under the due process and the cruel and unusual punishment clauses of the United States Constitution. See Estelle v. Gamble, 429 U.S. 97, 103–104 and n. 8, 97 S.Ct. 285, 290–291 and n. 8, 50 L.Ed.2d 251 (1976); Detainees of Brooklyn House of Detention for Men v. Malcolm, 520 F.2d 392, 396 (2d Cir.1975); Morgan v. Lavallee, 526 F.2d 221 (2d Cir.1975); Lareau v. Manson, 507 F.Supp. 1177, 1187 and n. 9 (D.Conn.1980), affirmed in part, 651 F.2d 96 (2d Cir.1981); see also United States *ex rel.* Wolfish v. Levi, 439 F.Supp. 114, n. 20 (S.D.N.Y.1977), affirmed in part and reversed in part, 573 F.2d 118 (2d Cir.1978), reversed, Bell v. Wolfish, 441 U.S. 520, 99 S.Ct. 1861, 60 L.Ed.2d 447 (1979). In Sterling v. Cupp, 290 Or. 611, 625 P.2d 123 (1981), the Supreme Court of Oregon enjoined prison officials from assigning female guards to certain duties in relation to male prisoners, citing the United Nations standards and other international human rights instruments to support its conclusion that "needlessly harsh, degrading, or dehumanizing treatment of prisoners" violated the Oregon Constitution. 625 P.2d at 131, n. 21.

## B. IMPLEMENTATION AND ENFORCEMENT OF HUMAN RIGHTS

### *RESTATEMENT (THIRD) INTRODUCTION TO PART VII*

International human rights law and agreements have the same status and the same binding character as other international law and agreements. However, international law generally is largely observed because violations directly affect the interests of states, which are alert to deter, prevent, or respond to violations. See Introductory Note to Part I, Chapter 1. Violations of the international law of human rights, on the other hand, generally injure the inhabitants of the violating state; ordinarily, other states are not directly affected by such violations and their concern for human rights in other states has been uneven. Moreover, states are generally reluctant to submit their actions in respect to human rights to scrutiny by other states. Special international "machinery" has been created to monitor compliance with international human rights law, but the effectiveness of those bodies and procedures in helping induce compliance has been variable. (The European Convention regime has had conspicuous success.) The condition of human rights varies widely even among states that have adhered to international human rights agreements.

### 1. *Enforcement of International Agreements*

*CONVENTION ON THE PREVENTION AND PUNISHMENT OF THE CRIME OF GENOCIDE*

General Assembly of the United Nations, December 9, 1948.
78 U.N.T.S. 277.

* * *

ARTICLE VIII

Any Contracting Party may call upon the competent organs of the United Nations to take such action under the Charter of the United Nations as they consider appropriate for the prevention and suppression of acts of genocide or any of the other acts enumerated in article III.

ARTICLE IX

Disputes between the Contracting Parties relating to the interpretation, application or fulfillment of the present Convention, including those relating to the responsibility of a State for genocide or for any of the other acts enumerated in article III, shall be submitted to the International Court of Justice at the request of any of the parties to the dispute.

* * *

#### *Notes*

1. No dispute under the Genocide Convention has reached the International Court of Justice. There have been efforts to persuade one or more states to bring a proceeding against the Pol Pot and the Khmer Rouge in Cambodia, later against Iraq and against Serbia (over "ethnic cleansing"). As of 1993 no such proceedings have been brought. What deters states from instituting proceedings charging genocide?

On May 25, 1993, the Security Council established a War Crimes Tribunal to prosecute serious violations of international humanitarian law, committed in the territory of the former Yugoslavia since 1991, including "mass killing, organised and systematic detention and rape of women, and the continuance of the practice of 'ethnic cleansing' * * *." S.C.Res. 827 (May 25, 1993). See p. 1031 infra.

2. In ratifying the Genocide Convention, the United States reserved the right not to go to the Court unless the U.S. agrees to do so in a particular case. See Chapter 10.

3. A human rights issue reached the Court in the South West Africa Case, in which Ethiopia and Liberia instituted proceedings against the Republic of South Africa charging violation of the undertaking in Article 27 of the Mandate "to promote to the utmost the material and moral well-being and the social progress of the inhabitants" of South West Africa. In its first judgment, 31 Dec. 1962, [1962] I.C.J. 319, a majority of the Court found that the Mandate was an international agreement and that any Member of the League could object to violations and bring the dispute to court as one between them and the Mandatory power. But in its final judgment the majority held that the petitioner states had not established any legal rights or interest appertaining to them in the subject matter of the present claims. [1966] I.C.J. 6.

## *INTERNATIONAL COVENANT ON CIVIL AND POLITICAL RIGHTS*

General Assembly of the United Nations, December 16, 1966.
999 U.N.T.S. 171, 6 I.L.M. 368 (1967).

* * *

### Article 40

1. The States Parties to the present Covenant undertake to submit reports on the measures they have adopted which give effect to the rights recognized herein and on the progress made in the enjoyment of those rights: (a) within one year of the entry into force of the present Covenant for the States Parties concerned and (b) thereafter whenever the Committee so requests.

2. All reports shall be submitted to the Secretary–General of the United Nations who shall transmit them to the Committee for consideration. Reports shall indicate the factors and difficulties, if any, affecting the implementation of the present Covenant.

3. The Secretary–General of the United Nations may after consultation with the Committee transmit to the specialized agencies concerned copies of such parts of the reports as may fall within their field of competence.

4. The Committee shall study the reports submitted by the States Parties to the present Covenant. It shall transmit its reports and such general comments as it may consider appropriate to the States Parties. The Committee may also transmit to the Economic and Social Council these comments along with the copies of the reports it has received from States Parties to the present Covenant.

5. The States Parties to the present Covenant may submit to the Committee observations on any comments that may be made in accordance with paragraph 4 of this article.

### Article 41

1. A State Party to the present Covenant may at any time declare under this article that it recognizes the competence of the Committee to receive and consider communications to the effect that a State Party claims that another State Party is not fulfilling its obligations under the present Covenant. Communications under this article may be received and considered only if submitted by a State Party which has made a declaration recognizing in regard to itself the competence of the Committee. No communication shall be received by the Committee if it concerns a State Party which has not made such a declaration. * * *

### Article 42

1. (a) If a matter referred to the Committee in accordance with article 41 is not resolved to the satisfaction of the States Parties concerned, the Committee may, with the prior consent of the States Parties concerned, appoint an *ad hoc* Conciliation Commission (hereinafter referred to as "the Commission"). * * *

### Article 44

The provisions for the implementation of the present Covenant shall apply without prejudice to the procedures prescribed in the field of human rights by or under the constituent instruments and the conventions of the United Nations and of the specialized agencies and shall not prevent the States Parties to the present Covenant from having recourse to other procedures for settling a dispute in accordance with general or special international agreements in force between them.

### Article 45

The Committee shall submit to the General Assembly, through the Economic and Social Council, an annual report on its activities.

* * *

## IMPLEMENTATION MACHINERY OF THE INTERNATIONAL COVENANT ON CIVIL AND POLITICAL RIGHTS

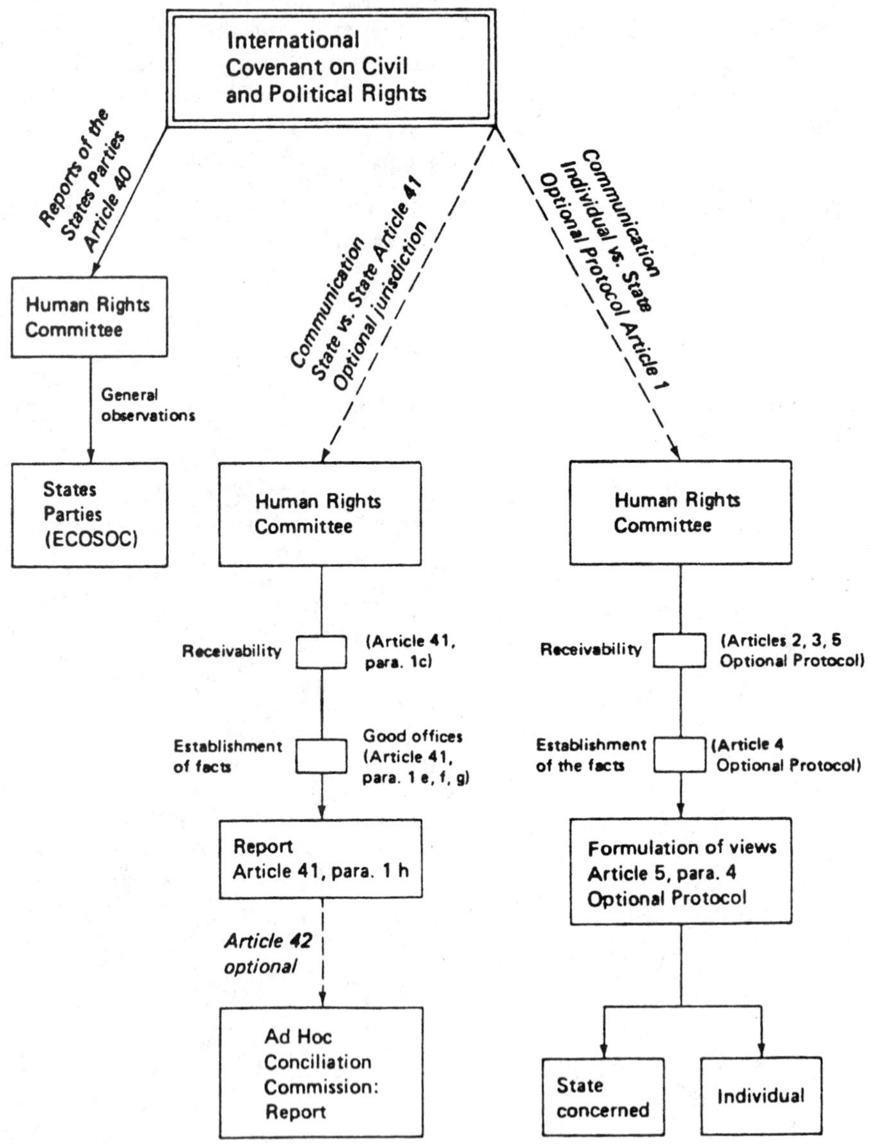


Vasak, International Dimensions of Human Rights 685 (1982)

### *Notes*

1. Article 28 of the Covenant on Civil and Political Rights provides for the establishment of the Human Rights Committee, the Covenant's principal organ of implementation. The Committee consists of eighteen members, nationals of states parties, who serve in their personal capacities. The Committee considers the reports submitted by states parties under Article 40.

The Committee has established guidelines for the form and content of reports. See U.N.Doc. A/40/600 (1985). The first part of the report should describe the general legal framework within which civil and political rights in the state are protected. The second part is to deal with the legislative, administrative and other measures in force to protect each of the rights under the Covenant, and include information about limitations or restrictions on their exercise. See United Nations Centre for Human Rights/United Nations Institute for Training and Research, Manual on Human Rights Reporting, U.N.Doc. HR/PUB/91/1 (1991). The Manual not only covers reporting under the Civil and Political Covenant, but also canvasses reporting under the Covenant on Economic, Social and Cultural Rights; the Convention on the Elimination of All Forms of Discrimination; the Convention on the Suppression and Punishment of the Crime of Apartheid; the Convention on the Elimination of All Forms of Discrimination Against Women; and the Convention Against Torture and Other Cruel, Inhuman or Degrading Treatment or Punishment.

The Committee has invited states to send representatives to discuss their reports and to answer questions. The Committee also considers information from other sources. During the Cold War there had been controversy within the Committee as to what sources of information may be used.

The Committee is authorized only to make general comments on reports. The states concerned are not required to take any action on the Committee's comments, nor are the Committee's conclusions submitted to an authoritative political organ empowered to make formal and specific recommendations to the government concerned. Pursuant to Article 45 the Committee submits to the General Assembly an annual report on its activities. In these reports, the Committee has not restricted itself to reporting compliance of states, but has included general comments on the substance of particular articles of the Covenant. See, e.g., Report of the Human Rights Committee, G.A.O.R. 47th Sess. No. 40 (A/47/40) (1992). For a compilation of comments by the Committee, see Compilation of General Comments and General Recommendations Adopted by Human Rights Treaty Bodies 1–35, U.N.Doc. HRI/GEN/1 (4 Sept. 1992).

2. For parties that have agreed, pursuant to Article 41, the Committee may receive and consider communications by one state party claiming that another state party is in violation of the Covenant. This procedure assumes that bilateral negotiations have failed and domestic remedies exhausted. The Committee is to make available its "good offices" to help settle the dispute. If a settlement is not achieved, the Committee is required to submit a report which is to be confined to a brief statement of the facts and the Committee's view on the possibilities of an amicable solution. The parties then have three months to decide whether to accept the Committee's report.

The Committee also receives and considers communications from individuals claiming a violation by a state, if the state is a party to the Optional Protocol. See p. 640 infra.

3. The United Nations meets the expenses of and provides services to the Human Rights Committee, but strictly, the Committee is not a U.N. agency; it is a body established by the states parties to the Covenant. (It is not to be confused with the Human Rights Commission, a United Nations agency and sub-organ of the Economic and Social Council). Analogous committees have been established by other human rights conventions, notably the Committee on the Elimination of Racial Discrimination (CERD), established by the Convention on the Elimination of All Forms of Racial Discrimination; the Committee on the Elimination of Discrimination Against Women (CEDAW), established by the Convention on the Elimination of All Forms of Discrimination Against Women; and the Committee Against Torture (CAT), established by the Convention Against Torture and Other Cruel, Inhuman or Degrading Treatment or Punishment. About these Treaty Committees Henkin has written:

### *HENKIN, INTERNATIONAL LAW: POLITICS, VALUES AND FUNCTIONS*

216 Rec. des Cours 255–61 (1989–IV) (footnotes omitted).

The impressive array of international standards adopted in the various covenants and conventions indicates the readiness of the international State system in principle to sacrifice State values of autonomy and impermeability in order to promote the human values of human rights. The character of the enforcement machinery established by the agreements indicates how strong still is the commitment to State values, and how resistant States still are to derogations from their autonomy and to the penetration of their society, even for purposes of promoting the human values they have willingly embraced. International agreements, developed by State representatives committed to State values, have eschewed "intrusive" means of enforcement. The Genocide Convention (1948), still following a pattern established for treaties generally, provided for resort to the International Court of Justice by any party to a dispute relating to the "interpretation, application or fulfilment of the present Convention". (No State has brought any such dispute to the Court.) The principal international covenants and conventions do not contain such an "ICJ clause" or any comparable provision for compulsory dispute resolution. They do not provide for institutions with authority to take initiative to monitor compliance and investigate possible violations. They do not provide generally for a body that might receive complaints of violation, examine them, and issue a judgment and a directive to a State found guilty of a violation to "cease and desist".

* * *

With small differences, treaty committees follow a pattern established for the Human Rights Committee in the Covenant on Civil and Political Rights and the Committee on Racial Discrimination in the Convention on the Elimination of Racial Discrimination. Committee members are elected by the States parties. They are to be nationals of States parties but may include no more than one national of the same State, with

> "consideration being given to equitable geographical distribution [of membership] and to the representation of the different forms of civilizations as well as of the principal legal systems".

Committee members are to be persons of "high moral character and recognized competence in the field of human rights" and serve in their personal capacities, not as government representatives.

* * *

State reporting is the least "intrusive" enforcement machinery, reflecting the international system's strong commitment to values of State autonomy and impermeability. (It reflects too some abiding feeling that a "sovereign State" is not to be accused or adjudged, surely not without its consent.) State values are respected also in the limitations on committee consideration of the reports. The Human Rights Committee "shall study the reports". It may make only "general comments" and its comments (and the "observations" of the State party) are reported to the Economic and Social Council, a political body. State values and inter-State political forces have been reflected also in various aspects of the committee's operations: in the rules of procedure adopted by the committee; in the kind and degree of attention given to reports by committee members. The committee members serve in their personal capacity and solemnly declare their impartiality, yet the kind and amount of "cross-examination" of State representatives about the reports often differ with the degree of independence which the member enjoys from his (her) own Government in fact, and with relations between that Government and the reporting State. The process is inevitably influenced by the disposition of political forces in the system generally—"Cold War" or "détente", considerations of "Third World solidarity" and "non-alignment".

Political forces have moved enforcement small steps beyond reporting, in different measure for different conventions. Differences reflect the degree of the international system's commitment to the particular rights involved in a particular convention, and corresponding political pressures to accept more intrusive monitoring. The time at which a convention was adopted may be significant, as later draftsmen learned from experience under earlier bodies, and States were reassured (or habituated) by that experience. Thus, the Covenant on Civil and Political Rights, applying to all rights, had to settle for the reporting system as the lowest common denominator of agreement. * * *

The slow development of enforcement machinery reflects the tensions in the international system between its new commitment to human values and its traditional commitment to values of State autonomy and impermeability. Slowly the treaty committees—notably the Human Rights Committee and the Committee on Racial Discrimination—have gained experience, confidence and acceptance, becoming less "politicized" and more effective. Slowly more States have accepted the jurisdiction of these committees to consider private complaints. States have not become much more willing to scrutinize or be scrutinized by other States; they have become less unwilling to respond to intercession by a respected multilateral body in limited circumstances.

Experience has afforded important lessons in the politics of enforcement of the special law of human rights. It had been anticipated that States would be reluctant to submit to complaints that they were violating their obligations under the Covenant and other conventions, but that they would be less reluctant to submit to State complaints than to private complaints.

Therefore, the Convention on the Elimination of Racial Discrimination provided for inter-State complaints but made submission to private complaint optional. The Covenant made both procedures optional, but relegated State submissions to private complaint to a separate protocol so as not to discourage adherence to the Covenant.

* * *

Many States, we must conclude, remain reluctant to submit to individual complaints—because they resist penetration of the State veil, are unwilling to have their citizens act independently in the international arena, and fear they might be embarrassed by accusations. But slowly an increasing number of States are becoming less unwilling to submit to the possibility of such complaints before a respected international body in a discreet process. On the other hand, States remain unwilling to expend political capital and to jeopardize their friendly relations by complaining of human rights violations by another State; States are unwilling to invite such complaints against themselves. States have made significant steps towards accepting third party resolution of disputes involving traditional State interests; they have not yet recognized that human rights everywhere are every State's proper interest.

## *OPTIONAL PROTOCOL TO THE INTERNATIONAL COVENANT ON CIVIL AND POLITICAL RIGHTS*

General Assembly of the United Nations, December 16, 1966.
999 U.N.T.S. 171, 6 I.L.M. 383 (1967).

### ARTICLE 1

A State Party to the Covenant that becomes a Party to the present Protocol recognizes the competence of the Committee to receive and consider communications from individuals, subject to its jurisdiction, claiming to be victims of a violation by that State Party of any of the rights set forth in the Covenant. No communication shall be received by the Committee if it concerns a State Party to the Covenant which is not a Party to the present Protocol.

### *Notes*

1. Compare Part II of the International Convention on the Elimination of All Forms of Racial Discrimination, 660 U.N.T.S. 195, 1966, which provides for a Committee on the Elimination of Racial Discrimination, requires parties to report to the Committee on compliance, and provides for state complaints against other states. In addition, Article 14 provides that a state may by declaration recognize the competence of the Committee to consider communications from individual victims or groups of victims.

2. Although the Protocol to the International Covenant on Civil and Political Rights speaks of "communications from individuals * * * claiming to be victims of a violation," the Human Rights Committee early concluded that it may receive communications on behalf of such individuals from other persons or organizations. See Report of the Human Rights Committee, 32 GAOR Supp. 44

(A/32/44) at 1 (1977). That is now reflected in Rule 90(1)(b) of the Committee's Rules.

3. Since the Committee began its work under the Optional Protocol at its second session in 1977, 468 communications have been placed before it (as of 1991). See 46 U.N.GAOR Supp. (No. 40) at 160, U.N.Doc. A/46/40 (1991). Of the 468 communications, 119 were concluded by Committee views expressed under Article 5(4) of the Optional Protocol; 124 were declared inadmissible; 70 were discontinued or withdrawn; 46 were declared admissible but have not yet been concluded; and 109 were pending at the pre-admissibility stage. See Compilation of General Comments and General Recommendations Adopted by Human Rights Treaty Bodies 1–35, 81–82, U.N.Doc. HRI/GEN/1 (4 Sept. 1992). See generally McGoldrick, The Human Rights Committee: Its Role in the Development of the International Covenant on Civil and Political Rights (1991); Higgins, The United Nations: Still a Force for Peace, 52 Mod.L.Rev. 1 (1989).

The Committee defines and clarifies the Optional Protocol as it presents its views on the cases it finds admissible. For example, the Committee has required authors of communications to justify their authority to act on behalf of an alleged victim. It has declared that only individuals, not organizations, may submit communications. The Committee has also explained its understanding of many of the substantive provisions of the Covenant on Civil and Political Rights, including the right to life (Art. 6), the right not to be subjected to torture (Art. 7), the right to liberty and security of person (Art. 9), the rights to family life and protection of the family (Articles 17 and 23), and others. See 39 U.N.GAOR Supp. (No. 40) at 118, U.N.Doc. A/39/40 (1984); 40 U.N.GAOR Supp. (No. 40) at 142, U.N.Doc. A/40/40 (1985).

## *INTERNATIONAL COVENANT ON ECONOMIC, SOCIAL AND CULTURAL RIGHTS*

General Assembly of the United Nations, December 16, 1966.
993 U.N.T.S. 3, 6 I.L.M. 360 (1967).

* * *

### Article 16

1. The States Parties to the present Covenant undertake to submit in conformity with this part of the Covenant reports on the measures which they have adopted and the progress made in achieving the observance of the rights recognized herein.

2. (a) All reports shall be submitted to the Secretary–General of the United Nations who shall transmit copies to the Economic and Social Council for consideration in accordance with the provisions of the present Covenant.

(b) The Secretary–General of the United Nations shall also transmit to the specialized agencies copies of the reports, or any relevant parts therefrom, from States Parties to the present Covenant which are also members of these specialized agencies in so far as these reports, or parts therefrom, relate to any matters which fall within the responsibilities of the said agencies in accordance with their constitutional instruments.

* * *

### Article 19

The Economic and Social Council may transmit to the Commission on Human Rights for study and general recommendation or as appropriate for information the reports concerning human rights submitted by States in accordance with articles 16 and 17, and those concerning human rights submitted by the specialized agencies in accordance with article 18.

* * *

IMPLEMENTATION OF THE INTERNATIONAL COVENANT ON ECONOMIC, SOCIAL AND CULTURAL RIGHTS

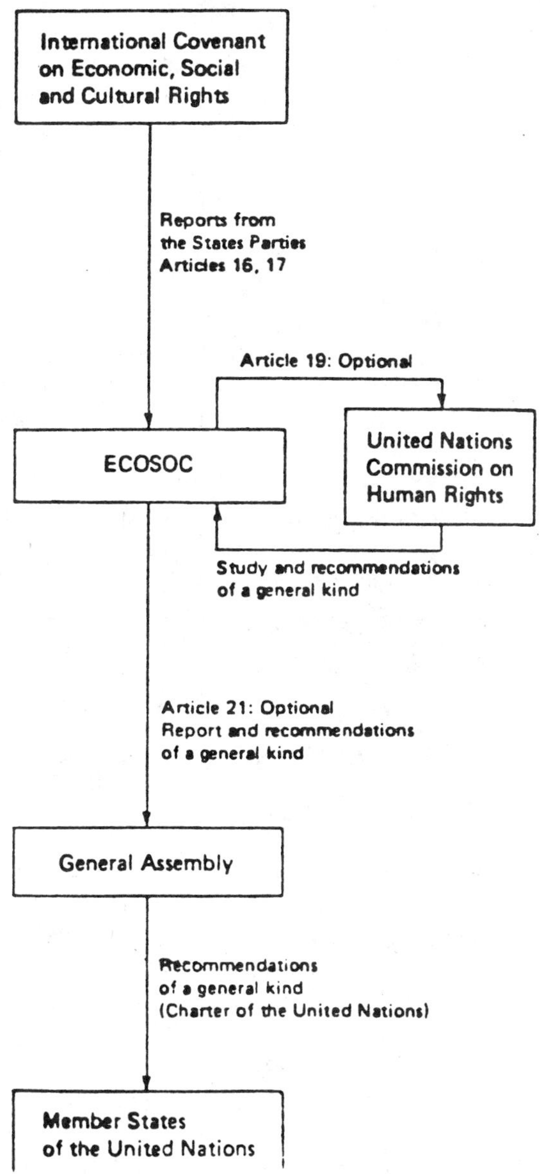


Vasak, International Dimensions of Human Rights 686 (1982)

## *Notes*

1. The Economic and Social Council established a Committee on Economic, Social and Cultural Rights to consider the reports submitted by the states parties. G.A.Res. 1985/17 (28 May 1985). The character and function of this

Committee parallel those of the Human Rights Committee established by Article 28 of the Covenant on Civil and Political Rights, see p. 637 supra.

2. Does the Economic and Social Committee "monitor" compliance? Could the Committee determine whether a state is "achieving progressively the full realization of the rights" set out in the Covenant? Could the Committee determine the optimal use of a state's "available resources" and the "appropriate means" to bring about the realization of the rights recognized in the Covenant?

## INTERSTATE ENFORCEMENT

All international human rights agreements make some provision for the settlement of disputes between parties about the interpretation or application of the agreement. The Covenant on Civil and Political Rights includes an optional clause (Article 41) by which a state may declare that it recognizes, on a reciprocal basis, the competence of the Human Rights Committee to receive and consider "communications" that it is not fulfilling its obligations under the Covenant. As of early 1993, over 27 states have made declarations under Article 41. The Convention on the Elimination of all Forms of Racial Discrimination (CERD), and the Convention Against Torture includes similar provisions, but the CERD provision (Article 11) is not optional and requires no special declaration.

Do these provisions supplement or replace the ordinary interstate remedies for violations of international law?

### *HENKIN, HUMAN RIGHTS AND "DOMESTIC JURISDICTION"*

Human Rights, International Law and The Helsinki Accord
21, 29–31, 33 (Buergenthal ed. 1977).*

Breach of a human rights obligation, like violation of any international legal obligation, is an international wrongful act for which the international legal system provides remedies. It has been suggested, however, that the only remedies for the violation of a human rights agreement are those specified in the agreement. In particular, unless expressly so provided, one party does not have a remedy against another for failure to live up to the agreement. That view is ill-founded.

The duty to carry out international obligations is the heart of the international legal system; and that prime duty implies an ancillary duty to cease and desist from a violation and to give other satisfaction to the state or states to which the obligation was due. The injured state may seek reparation and ask that the violator take measures to prevent repetition, offer an apology, punish the persons who committed the violation, pay a symbolic sum of money, or afford other relief.

Except for the few universal obligations, enforceable perhaps by any state (in a kind of *actio popularis* ), a breach of an international obligation is a wrong to the particular state or states to which that obligation is due, and

* Footnotes omitted. Reprinted by permission of Allanheld, Osmun & Co., Publishers, Inc. and the American Society of International Law.

only such state or states may enforce that obligation and seek a remedy for its violation. An international agreement creates obligations between parties and gives each party a legal interest in having it carried out; it may be enforced by one party against another even if it is an agreement for the benefit of a third entity not party to the agreement. * * *

The argument that human rights agreements are not directly enforceable between the parties * * * seems to be based * * * on the view that, as a matter of interpretation, human rights agreements in general, and particular human rights agreements, contemplate no remedies between parties, but only whatever remedies are expressly provided. It is assumed that states are willing to enter into agreements about human rights but are unwilling to have them enforced among the parties; the quest for special enforcement machinery, it is said, also reflects the intention that ordinary interstate remedies be excluded.

These arguments are not persuasive. International human rights agreements are like other international agreements, creating legal obligations between the parties and international responsibility for their violation. They are essentially mutual undertakings among states for the benefit of third parties (the inhabitants of the countries party to the agreement) and in principle are enforceable by the promisees, that is, the other parties to the agreement. *Prima facie,* surely, and in the absence of any expressed or clearly implied intention to supersede them, the usual remedies for breach of an international obligation are available here. * * *

* * *

No human rights agreements, even those that establish elaborate enforcement machinery, expressly or by clear implication exclude the ordinary interstate remedies. In fact, the principal human rights agreements clearly imply the contrary: that every party to the agreement has a legal interest in having it observed by other parties and can invoke ordinary legal remedies to enforce it.

* * *

There is no suggestion * * * that the human rights of all individuals everywhere can be protected by all states. Human rights agreements generally do not create universal legal interests for all states: they create legal interests for the parties to the agreement by virtue of the legal obligations assumed by them *inter sese.* The remedies to be invoked are not by way of some extraordinary *actio popularis;* they are the ordinary remedies available to parties to an agreement against violation by another party. The distinction is fundamental and clear. In the *South West Africa* Cases, for example, the majority denied the standing of Ethiopia and Liberia to enforce the human rights provisions of the mandate because they "were not parties to them * * *. Not being parties to the instruments of mandate, they could draw from them only such rights as are unequivocally conferred." The implication is that, even for the majority of the court, had the petitioners been parties to the mandate agreement they would have had a legal interest to enforce it and could have availed themselves of the usual remedies for vindicating that interest.

### Notes

1. For a contrary view, see Frowein, The Interrelationship between the Helsinki Final Act, the International Covenants on Human Rights, and the European Convention on Human Rights, in Human Rights, International Law and the Helsinki Accord 71, 78–80 (Buergenthal ed. 1977). See Restatement (Third) § 703, Reporters' Note 2.

2. In the *Soering* case, the European Court of Human Rights ruled that under Article 3 of the European Convention on Human Rights (which prohibits torture, inhuman or degrading treatment) the United Kingdom could not extradite a person to the U.S. to be tried for a capital offense because of the possibility that upon conviction the person would be confined on "death row" which is inhuman and degrading and would violate Article 3. The Soering Case, [1989] Eur.Ct.H.R., Ser.A. No. 161. See p. 661 infra. But see Pratt and Morgan v. Jamaica, Communications Nos. 210/1986 and 225/1987, in Report of the Human Rights Committee, U.N.G.A.O.R., 44th Sess., Supp. No. 40 (A/44/40) at 215, 231, where the Committee held that the Covenant on Civil and Political Rights was not violated by a lengthy stay on death row.

For state enforcement of human rights upon violation by other states, see p. 644.

## INDIVIDUAL RIGHTS AND REMEDIES UNDER INTERNATIONAL AGREEMENTS

### *HENKIN, INTERNATIONAL HUMAN RIGHTS AS "RIGHTS"*

1 Cardozo L.Rev. 438 (1979).*

Because the international law of human rights is made by states assuming obligations (the state as legislator), the international instruments focus at first on the state's obligations: it is the state's undertaking that creates the law. But under that law after it is in effect, the focus shifts sharply. The instruments are designated as dealing with the "rights" of individuals and there is reference to individual "rights" in every article. But the state's obligation and the individual's right are not necessarily correlative, or even in the same legal order. There are different possible perspectives on the relation between them:

1. The simple, undaring view sees international human rights agreements essentially, if not exclusively, in interstate terms. The agreements constitute undertakings by each state-party to every other state-party, creating rights and obligations between them. * * *

In this prospective the only rights and duties created by international human rights agreements are the duty of every state-party to act as it had promised, and the right of every other state-party to have that promise to it kept. The individual has no international legal rights; he is only the "incidental beneficiary" of rights and duties between the state-parties. The individual has no international remedies; he is only the "incidental" beneficiary of the remedies available between states-parties. * * *

2. A second perspective would see the international agreements, while creating rights and duties for the states-parties, as also giving the individual

* Footnotes omitted. Reprinted by permission of The Cardozo Law Review.

rights against his society under international law (in addition to any rights he has under his national constitutional-legal system). The language of the agreements clearly declares these individual rights in every clause: "Every human being has the inherent right to life"; "No one shall be held in slavery;" "Everyone has the right to liberty and security of the person;" "Everyone shall be free to leave any country, including his own." The individual has these international legal rights even though they are enforceable only by interstate remedies, by governments or international bodies acting in his behalf. Under the Optional Protocol to the Covenant on Civil and Political Rights providing for consideration by the Human Rights Committee of individual complaints, or under the provision in the European Convention that the European Commission "may receive petitions" from any person claiming to be the victim of a violation, the individual enforces his own right by his own remedy.

* * *

3. A third perspective, which is independent of but might be combined with either of the two set forth, would suggest that the states-parties, as legislators, have legislated "human rights" into international law giving them status as affirmative independent values. That status is supported and furthered by the rights and duties which were established, whether the rights be those of states or of individuals. While directly creating status or values, independent of rights and duties, is an unusual conception in international law, since law is made wholly by way of states assuming obligations, one can say, perhaps, that every state-party assumes two different kinds of obligations corresponding to the two roles I have described. Acting with other states (the state as legislator), each state agrees to recognize and give legal status in the international system to "human rights" as claims that every individual has—or should have—upon his own society. In addition, each state (the state as obligor) undertakes to respect and ensure these values for its own citizens, thereby also creating rights in other states, and perhaps in individuals.

### *Note*

Compare the opinion of Judge Bork in Tel–Oren v. Libyan Arab Republic, 726 F.2d 774 (D.C.Cir.1984), pp. 654–55 infra.

## 2. *Enforcement of Customary Law of Human Rights*

### *RESTATEMENT (THIRD) § 703*

Comment *b* and Reporters' Notes 3 and 4

*b. Remedies for violation of customary law of human rights.* Since the obligations of the customary law of human rights are *erga omnes* (obligations to all states), § 702, Comment *o*, any state may pursue remedies for their violation, even if the individual victims were not nationals of the complaining state and the violation did not affect any other particular interest of that state. For the remedies available to individual victims against the state or state officials, see Comment *c*.

* * *

3. *Remedies for violation of customary law of human rights.* Ordinarily, violations of customary law entail remedies for the state that is the victim of the violation. The customary law of human rights, however, protects individuals subject to each state's jurisdiction, and the international obligation runs equally to all other states, with no state a victim of the violation more than any other. Any state, therefore, may make a claim against the violating state. Where the complaining and the accused states have agreed to means for settling disputes between them generally—for example, by accepting the jurisdiction of the International Court of Justice or submitting to arbitration—such means are available for alleged violations of this section.

In the *Barcelona Traction* case, Reporters' Note 2, at 32, the International Court of Justice said:

> In particular, an essential distinction should be drawn between the obligations of a State towards the international community as a whole, and those arising vis-à-vis another State in the field of diplomatic protection. By their very nature the former are the concern of all States. In view of the importance of the rights involved, all States can be held to have a legal interest in their protection; they are obligations *erga omnes.*
>
> Such obligations derive, for example, in contemporary international law, from the outlawing of acts of aggression, and of genocide, as also from the principles and rules concerning the basic rights of the human person, including protection from slavery and racial discrimination. Some of the corresponding rights of protection have entered into the body of general international law * * *; others are conferred by international instruments of a universal or quasi-universal character.
>
> Obligations the performance of which is the subject of diplomatic protection are not of the same category. It cannot be held, when one such obligation in particular is in question, in a specific case, that all States have a legal interest in its observance.

The Court seemed to distinguish diplomatic protection in general, including protection for ordinary violations of human rights, which is available only for nationals of the complaining state (see Reporters' Note 2), from protection against violations of the "basic rights of the human person" set forth in this section, as to which "all States can be held to have a legal interest in their protection."

4. *Remedies regardless of nationality of individual victim.* Remedies available to states parties under international human rights agreements (Subsection (1)), and remedies available to all states for violation by any state of the customary law of human rights (Subsection (2)), do not depend on the nationality of the individual victim. But see Reporters' Note 2, distinguishing between interstate claims and diplomatic protection under international human rights agreements. In practice, states are more likely to intercede on behalf of individuals who are their own nationals or with whom they have other links. But see the South West Africa cases, Reporters' Note 1.

### *Notes*

1. There have been suggestions that a state may intervene in another state that commits gross human rights violations. Is this consistent with Article 2(4) of the U.N. Charter? Is it permissible if carried out pursuant to authorization by the Security Council? See Chapter 11 infra. See generally the Declaration of Minimum Standards, adopted by an expert meeting convened by the Institute for Human Rights (2 December 1990).

2. The Restatement (Third) § 703, Comment *f* adds the following:

> *State sanctions for human rights violations by another state.* A state may criticize another state for failure to abide by recognized international human rights standards, and may shape its trade, aid or other national policies so as to dissociate itself from the violating state or to influence that state to discontinue the violations.

3. On obligations and remedies *erga omnes* generally, see Schachter, International Law in Theory and Practice 208–13 (1991). See Chapter 7, Section 4. See also Meron, Human Rights and Humanitarian Norms as Customary Law (1989).

## ENFORCEMENT BY POLITICAL BODIES

### *HENKIN, INTERNATIONAL LAW: POLITICS, VALUES AND FUNCTIONS*

216 Rec. des Cours 9, 265–67 (1989–IV) (footnotes omitted).

International human rights law benefits significantly from enforcement also by political bodies. In general, international political bodies have attended only to the enforcement of norms of extraordinary political significance such as the law of the Charter on the use of force, but political bodies have devoted extraordinary efforts to promoting law on human rights and for that and other reasons they have not avoided the demands of enforcement of—inducing compliance with—that law.

If law is politics, enforcement of law in the inter-State system is also heavily political. Political influence brought to bear in the organs and suborgans of the United Nations determined the enforcement machinery that found its way into covenants and conventions. (Political forces, I have suggested, have influenced also how that machinery has worked.) But United Nations bodies themselves have also been an arena for charges of human rights violations, sometimes evoking resolutions of condemnation.

The Members of the United Nations have been divided as to their readiness to address charges of specific human rights violations. Some States have resisted the airing of such charges on the ground that these were not the proper business of the Organization, which is forbidden "to intervene in matters which are essentially within the domestic jurisdiction of any State" (Art. 2(7)). In fact, United Nations practice long ago rejected that objection, in effect reflecting the conclusion that human rights violations were not a matter of domestic jurisdiction, or that United Nations discussion of them is not intervention, or both. United Nations practice in this regard has been determined not according to legal principle but by negotiation and majority vote.

Sensitivity to State values, reluctance to scrutinize and be scrutinized, have generally discouraged United Nations consideration of charges of specific violations. For a while, dominant forces in the Organization succeeded in preventing consideration of the thousands of complaints of human rights violations that poured into the United Nations Secretariat. In time, the Economic and Social Council was moved to authorize a subcommission of the Human Rights Commission to appoint a "working group" to meet for a short period each year, in confidence, to consider communications "which appear to reveal a consistent pattern of gross violations of human rights and fundamental freedoms". In time, the proceedings became less limited and less confidential and increasingly the United Nations Human Rights Commission has been appointing "rapporteurs", adopting resolutions, and issuing reports. At all times, moreover, some charges of violation have made their way to the agenda of the larger United Nations bodies, the Economic and Social Council and the General Assembly, and infrequently also the Security Council.

One cannot appraise these activities with precision or with confidence, but clearly they have served as some inducement to terminate or mitigate violations, perhaps even as some deterrent. Political bodies, however, are subject to their own political laws. The larger bodies—notably the United Nations General Assembly—are more visible, more newsworthy, therefore more "politicized", therefore less likely to apply human rights norms judicially, impartially. In such bodies, human rights are more susceptible to being subordinated to non-human rights considerations. There, voting, including "bloc-voting", has led to "selective targeting" of some States, sometimes exaggerating their violations, and overlooking those of other States, including some that are guilty of gross violations. Smaller political bodies, such as the Human Rights Commission, are also inhabited by government representatives concerned for State values and friendly relations, but increasingly they are able to be somewhat less "political", more evenhanded, as well as more activist in the cause of human rights.

### *QUESTION OF THE VIOLATION OF HUMAN RIGHTS AND FUNDAMENTAL FREEDOMS, INCLUDING POLICIES OF RACIAL DISCRIMINATION AND SEGREGATION AND OF APARTHEID, IN ALL COUNTRIES, WITH PARTICULAR REFERENCE TO COLONIAL AND OTHER DEPENDENT COUNTRIES AND TERRITORIES*

The Economic and Social Council, 1967.
E.S.C.Res. 1235, 42 ESCOR Supp. 1 (E/4393) at 17.

* * *

2. *Authorizes* the Commission on Human Rights and the Sub-Commission on Prevention of Discrimination and Protection of Minorities, in conformity with the provisions of paragraph 1 of the Commission's resolution 8 (XXIII), to examine information relevant to gross violations of human rights and fundamental freedoms, as exemplified by the policy of apartheid as practised in the Republic of South Africa and in the Territory of South West Africa under the direct responsibility of the United Nations and now illegally occupied by the Government of the Republic of South Africa, and to

racial discrimination as practised notably in Southern Rhodesia, contained in the communications listed by the Secretary–General pursuant to Economic and Social Council resolution 728 F (XXVIII) of 30 July 1959; * * *

### *PROCEDURE FOR DEALING WITH COMMUNICATIONS RELATING TO VIOLATIONS OF HUMAN RIGHTS AND FUNDAMENTAL FREEDOMS*

The Economic and Social Council, 1970.
E.S.C.Res. 1503, 48 ESCOR Supp. 1A (E/4832/Add. 1) at 8 (footnotes omitted).

*Noting* resolutions 7 (XXVI) and 17 (XXV) of the Commission on Human Rights and resolution 2 (XXI) of the Sub–Commission on Prevention of Discrimination and Protection of Minorities,

1. *Authorizes* the Sub–Commission on Prevention of Discrimination and Protection of Minorities to appoint a working group consisting of not more than five of its members, with due regard to geographical distribution, to meet once a year in private meetings for a period not exceeding ten days immediately before the sessions of the Sub–Commission to consider all communications, including replies of Governments thereon, received by the Secretary–General under Council resolution 728 F (XXVIII) of 30 July 1959 with a view to bringing to the attention of the Sub–Commission those communications, together with replies of Governments, if any, which appear to reveal a consistent pattern of gross and reliably attested violations of human rights and fundamental freedoms within the terms of reference of the Sub–Commission; * * *

### *Notes*

1. Under what authority did the Economic and Social Council adopt this procedure? Is the assumption that "gross violations of human rights" constitute violations of the U.N. Charter or of other international agreements? Of customary law? Is the authority of the working group limited to charges against states members of the U.N., or states that have adhered to the international covenants on human rights or other relevant conventions? See Buergenthal, Human Rights, International Law, and the Helsinki Accord (1977). Sohn, Human Rights: Their Implementation by the United Nations, in Human Rights in International Law (Meron ed. 1984).

2. Human rights questions considered by the U.N. Human Rights Commission on the Economic and Social Council frequently come also to the U.N. General Assembly. The Assembly also has other human rights questions on its agenda every year, notably, on apartheid in South Africa.

For a discussion of U.N. bodies concerned with human rights, see The United Nations and Human Rights (U.N. Office of Public Information, 1968); United Nations Action in the Field of Human Rights (1988); Meron, Human Rights Law–Making in the United Nations (1986). The General Assembly has considered human rights issues in the context of other subjects within its jurisdiction; because they endangered relations between states and international peace and security (e.g., the issue of Indians in South Africa, G.A.Res. 44 (1946); apartheid, G.A.Res. 721 (1953)); because they raised questions under principles of international law (e.g., the case of the Russian wives, G.A.Res. 285 (1949)); because they raised questions under peace treaties and basic principles of the

Charter (violations by Bulgaria and Hungary, G.A.Res. 272 (1949) and G.A.Res. 385 (1950)).

See also the Security Council Resolution imposing a mandatory arms embargo against the Republic of South Africa in response to racial repression, p. 986 infra.

### *3. National Enforcement of International Human Rights Obligations*

#### *HENKIN, INTRODUCTION*

The International Bill of Rights: The Covenant on Civil and Political Rights 7 (Henkin, ed. 1981)(footnote omitted).

The international law of human rights parallels and supplements national law, superseding and supplying the deficiencies of national constitutions and laws; but it does not replace, and indeed depends on, national institutions. The constituency in every society that supports human rights law is different from the constituency that supports, say, international trade agreements, or military alliances, or peaceful settlements, or even international organization and cooperation. The pressures on a government to adhere to international human rights law are also different from those to adhere to other law, and indeed, a state's adherence to human rights conventions is far less important if in fact it behaves at home, toward its own, consistently with their terms.

In other respects, too, international law and politics see human rights in the context of the international political system. Although human rights are universal, they are the claims of an individual upon his society, not on other societies. Although the society in which one lives may be crucial to life and dignity, although a right to change one's society might well be deemed fundamental, the individual does not have an absolute right to join another society and seek his rights there. Even those who are oppressed at home do not yet have an international human right to asylum elsewhere; those who are starving at home do not have an internationally recognized human right to be taken in by the more affluent societies or to be fed by them.

#### *COVENANT ON CIVIL AND POLITICAL RIGHTS*

999 U.N.T.S. 171, 6 I.L.M. 368 (1967).

* * *

ARTICLE 2

1. Each State Party to the present Covenant undertakes to respect and to ensure to all individuals within its territory and subject to its jurisdiction the rights recognized in the present Covenant, without distinction of any kind, such as race, colour, sex, language, religion, political or other opinion, national or social origin, property, birth or other status.

2. Where not already provided for by existing legislative or other measures, each State Party to the present Covenant undertakes to take the

necessary steps, in accordance with its constitutional processes and with the provisions of the present Covenant, to adopt such legislative or other measures as may be necessary to give effect to the rights recognized in the present Covenant.

3. Each State Party to the present Covenant undertakes:

(*a*) To ensure that any person whose rights or freedoms as herein recognized are violated shall have an effective remedy, notwithstanding that the violation has been committed by persons acting in an official capacity;

(*b*) To ensure that any person claiming such a remedy shall have his right thereto determined by competent judicial, administrative or legislative authorities, or by any other competent authority provided for by the legal system of the state, and to develop the possibilities of judicial remedy;

(*c*) To ensure that the competent authorities shall enforce such remedies when granted.

* * *

### *Notes*

1. The United States deposited its instrument of ratification of the Covenant on Civil and Political Rights on June 8, 1992. The Covenant entered into force for the United States on September 8, 1992. See Treaty Action (Multilateral), 3 Dept. State Dispatch (No. 48, 1992). (As to the Genocide Convention, see p. 627 supra). The U.S. is also a party to the Protocol Relating to the Status of Refugees, 1966, and this Protocol has been invoked in United States courts. See I.N.S. v. Stevic, 467 U.S. 407, 104 S.Ct. 2489, 81 L.Ed.2d 321 (1984). See Note 2, p. 631 above. For cases holding that the human rights provisions of the U.N. Charter are not self-executing, see Frolova v. Union of Soviet Socialist Republics, 761 F.2d 370 (7th Cir.1985), and cases cited there at 374 n. 5. And see Chapter 3, p. 216 above.

Human rights norms recognized as customary international law (p. 615 above) are law in the U.S. and can be enforced against the U.S. in appropriate proceedings. For the suggestion that cases arising under customary international law arise under U.S. law under § 1331, see Restatement (Third) § 703, Reporters' Note 7. For a discussion of the extent to which international human rights law is a part of U.S. law generally, see p. 626 above. For the view that the courts will not compel the President to respect customary international law, see pp. 175–76, Chapter 3.

2. In some situations, aliens may obtain a remedy in United States courts for human rights violations by foreign officials. See Filartiga v. Pena–Irala, 630 F.2d 876 (2d Cir.1980). Dr. Joel Filartiga and his daughter, Dolly, Paraguayan nationals residing in the United States, brought suit in the Eastern District of New York against Americo Pena–Irala (Pena), a former police official in Paraguay who was in New York on an expired visa. Filartiga claimed that Pena had kidnapped and tortured his son to death in retaliation for the father's political opposition to the Paraguayan government. Alleging that such torture was a violation of international law, they invoked the jurisdiction of the district court under the Alien Tort Statute, 28 U.S.C. § 1350, which gives the district court jurisdiction over a civil action by an alien for a tort only, committed in violation of the law of nations or a treaty of the United States. The district court

dismissed the claim for lack of jurisdiction. On appeal, the Court of Appeals for the Second Circuit reversed. It said in part:

> In light of the universal condemnation of torture in numerous international agreements, and the renunciation of torture as an instrument of official policy by virtually all of the nations of the world (in principle if not in practice), we find that an act of torture committed by a state official against one held in detention violates established norms of the international law of human rights, and hence the law of nations. * * *
>
> * * *
>
> * * * Accordingly, we must conclude that the dictum in Dreyfus v. von Finck, supra, 534 F.2d at 31, to the effect that "violations of international law do not occur when the aggrieved parties are nationals of the acting state," is clearly out of tune with the current usage and practice of international law. The treaties and accords cited above, as well as the express foreign policy of our own government, all make it clear that international law confers fundamental rights upon all people vis-a-vis their own governments. While the ultimate scope of those rights will be a subject for continuing refinement and elaboration, we hold that the right to be free from torture is now among them. * * * [W]e believe it is sufficient here to construe the Alien Tort Statute, not as granting new rights to aliens, but simply as opening the federal courts for adjudication of the rights already recognized by international law. * * *
>
> Although the Alien Tort Statute has rarely been the basis for jurisdiction during its long history, there can be little doubt that this action is properly brought in federal court. This is undeniably an action by an alien, for a tort only, committed in violation of the law of nations. * * *
>
> * * *
>
> * * * In the modern age, humanitarian and practical considerations have combined to lead the nations of the world to recognize that respect for fundamental human rights is in their individual and collective interest. Among the rights universally proclaimed by all nations, as we have noted, is the right to be free of physical torture. Indeed, for purposes of civil liability, the torturer has become—like the pirate and slave trader before him—*hosti humani generis,* an enemy of all mankind. Our holding today, giving effect to a jurisdictional provision enacted by our First Congress, is a small but important step in the fulfillment of the ageless dream to free all people from brutal violence.

Id. at 880–890 (footnotes omitted).

Compare Tel–Oren v. Libyan Arab Republic, 517 F.Supp. 542 (D.D.C.1981). In that case representatives of twenty-nine persons who died in a terrorist attack on a bus in Israel filed suit in a United States district court against Libya, the P.L.O., the Palestine Information Office, the National Association of Arab Americans and the Palestine Congress of North America. The complaints charged the defendants with torts in violation of both international law and criminal statutes of the United States. The plaintiffs asserted that the district court had jurisdiction under the Alien Tort Claims Act, 28 U.S.C.A. § 1350. Addressing the jurisdictional issue, the district court said:

For jurisdiction to vest under § 1350, three elements must be present: 1) the claim must be made by an *alien,* 2) it must be for a *tort,* and 3) the tort must be *in violation of the law of nations or the treaties of the United States.*

* * *

* * * [§ 1350] serves merely as an entrance into the federal courts and in no way provides a cause of action to any plaintiff. Somewhere in the law of nations or in the treaties of the United States, the plaintiffs must discern and plead a cause of action that, if proved, would permit the Court to grant relief. The plaintiffs cite no cause of action given to them by the law of nations or by treaties of the United States. Just as discussed under § 1331, an action predicated on a treaty or on more general norms of international law must have at its basis a specific right to a private claim. Plaintiffs have demonstrated no such entitlement. "[T]o interpret international human rights law to create a federal private right of action overstates the level of agreement among nations on remedies for human rights violation." Note, Torture as a Tort in Violation of International Law: Filartiga v. Pena-Irala, 33 Stan.L.Rev. 353, 357 (1981) * * *. In short, unless treaties to which the United States is a party or even the law of nations generally provide a private right of action, no jurisdictional grant, be it § 1331 or § 1350, can aid a plaintiff seeking relief in federal district court.

* * *

* * * [I]t behooves the court to discern promptly in cases such as the instant whether international law has expressly or impliedly entrusted individuals with the authority to enforce its precepts. Because that determination may ultimately cloak a court with potent authority over a foreign land, the query is jurisdictional, not merely a demurrer to the plaintiff's complaint. Absent the clear indication, not present here, that nations intend to subject themselves to such worldwide jurisprudential assaults, jurisdiction under § 1350 will not vest.

517 F.Supp. at 548–50.

The judgment of the district court was affirmed, 726 F.2d 774 (D.C.Cir., 1984), cert. denied, 470 U.S. 1003, 105 S.Ct. 1354, 84 L.Ed.2d 377 (1985). There was no opinion of the court. While Judge Edwards' analysis of § 1350 generally followed that of the court in Filartiga, Judge Bork argued that Congress gave the federal courts jurisdiction only when international law created a private tort. *Filartiga* was followed in other cases, see e.g., Forti v. Suarez-Mason, 672 F.Supp. 1531 (N.D.Cal.1987), and has been accepted as the better reasoned opinion. See p. 166, Chapter 3. Congress may have implicitly confirmed the *Filartiga* interpretation when it enacted the Torture Victim Protection Act, see note 3 below. On the Alien Tort Statute, see Randall, Federal Jurisdiction Over International Law Claims: Inquiries into the Alien Tort Statute, 18 N.Y.U.J.Int'l L. & Pol. 1 (1985); Casto, The Federal Court's Protective Jurisdiction Over Torts Committed in Violation of the Law of Nations, 18 Conn.L.Rev. 467 (1986); Burley, The Alien Tort Statute and the Judiciary Act of 1789: A Badge of Honor, 83 A.J.I.L. 461 (1989).

See the discussion of the individual's rights under international law, p. 646 above.

3. § 1350 provides jurisdiction for suits by aliens only. Could a citizen bring a suit under 28 U.S.C.A. § 1331, on the ground that a suit in tort for

torture in violation of international law is a case arising under the laws of the United States? See Restatement (Third) § 131, Comment *e* and Reporters' Note 4. The argument was rejected in Handel v. Artukovic, 601 F.Supp. 1421 (D.C.Cal.1985). In 1992, however, Congress enacted the Torture Victim Protection Act, Pub.L. 102–256, 106 Stat. 73 (Mar. 12, 1992), codified at, 28 U.S.C.A. § 1350, providing a remedy in damages for victims of torture. The Act applies whether the victim is an alien or a U.S. national. The Act does not expressly indicate the constitutional basis for the jurisdiction of the federal courts but presumably it confers jurisdiction pursuant to Article III, Section 2 of the Constitution, on the basis that the cases would be arising under the laws of the United States. Does this suggest that Congress considers torture (and by implication other violations of customary international law) to be violations of U.S. law and therefore within 28 U.S.C.A. § 1331?

4. Congress has provided "sanctions" for violations of human rights in other countries by denying economic aid and military sales to "any country which engages in a consistent pattern of gross violations of internationally recognized human rights, including torture or cruel, inhuman, or degrading treatment or punishment, prolonged detention without charges, or other flagrant denial of the right to life, liberty and the security of the person." 22 U.S.C.A. § 2151n(a). See also 22 U.S.C.A. § 2304. Compare the "Jackson–Vanik" Amendment conditioning trade benefits for communist countries on their permitting emigration. See Trade Act of 1974, § 402, 19 U.S.C.A. § 2432 (1976). See Restatement (Third) § 702, Reporters' Note 9. See generally U.S. Legislation Relating Human Rights to U.S. Foreign Policy, prepared by International Human Rights Law Group (3d ed. Sept. 1982). The U.S. imposed trade sanctions against South Africa for its policy of apartheid. See the Comprehensive Anti–Apartheid Act of 1986, 22 U.S.C.A. §§ 5001–5016. See Clarizio, Clements & Geetter, United States Policy Toward South Africa, 11 Hum.Rts.Q. 249 (1989). See also p. 174, for a discussion of the sanctions imposed by states of the U.S. See generally Henkin, The Age of Rights, chap. 5 (1990).

In 1992 Congress enacted the Cuban Democracy Act of 1992, 22 U.S.C.A. §§ 6001–6010, which announces the policy of the U.S. "to seek a peaceful transition to democracy" in Cuba "through the careful application of sanctions directed at the Castro government" and "to make clear to other countries that * * * the United States will take into account their willingness to cooperate in such a policy * * *." 22 U.S.C.A. § 6002. The Act declares that countries that "provide assistance to Cuba" shall not be eligible for assistance under the Foreign Assistance Act of 1961 or for assistance or sales under the Arms Export Control Act. 22 U.S.C.A. § 6003(b). The Act also restricts trade with Cuba by U.S. firms and closes or limits access to U.S. ports to vessels engaged in trade with Cuba. 22 U.S.C.A. § 6005.

5. On the interplay between human rights and domestic enforcement generally see Randall, Federal Courts and the International Human Rights Paradigm (1990); Bayefsky, International Human Rights Law: Use in the Canadian Charter of Rights and Freedoms Litigation (1992).

## SECTION 2. REGIONAL HUMAN RIGHTS LAW

Both the Council of Europe and the Organization of American States have established major, comprehensive human rights programs for those regions, parallel to, and in important respects more effective than, that of the United Nations. In 1981, African states moved toward a regional human rights system when the Organization of African Unity adopted the African Charter of Human and People's Rights. The League of Arab States established a Commission on Human Rights in 1968, but it appears to have been inactive. For a comparative appraisal of regional human rights regimes, see Weston, Lukes & Hnatt, Regional Human Rights Regimes: A Comparison and Appraisal, 20 Vand.J.Transnat'l L. 585 (1987).

## A. THE EUROPEAN HUMAN RIGHTS SYSTEM

The European Convention for the Protection of Human Rights and Fundamental Freedoms (213 U.N.T.S. 221, 1950) entered into force on September 3, 1953. It was drafted under sponsorship of the Council of Europe, and open to accession by all members of the Council. By early 1993 it had been ratified by all twenty-one Council members, but not all members have ratified the various protocols to the Convention. See Chart Showing Signatures and Ratifications of Council of Europe Conventions and Agreements (Council of Europe Legal Affairs, May 1993).

Although France was one of the original signatories to the Convention, it did not ratify the Convention until May 3, 1974. The instrument of ratification was accompanied by two reservations relating to Articles 5, 6 and 75(1), and a declaration of interpretation relating to Articles 10 and 63. After the Cold War, some former members of the Soviet bloc reportedly moved to join the Council of Europe and become parties to the European Convention.

### 1. *The Rights and Freedoms Protected*

While there are sometimes significant differences in their formulation, the substantive provisions of the European Convention are comparable to those in the International Covenant on Civil and Political Rights. They include: the right to life; freedom from torture and inhuman or degrading treatment; freedom from slavery, servitude or forced labor; liberty and security of person, and detention only in accordance with procedures prescribed by law; the right to a fair and public hearing in determining civil rights and obligations, or criminal charges; respect for privacy and family life; freedom of thought, conscience and religion; freedom of expression, peaceful assembly and association; the right to marry and found a family; freedom from invidious discrimination. Everyone whose rights are violated shall have a remedy. Subsequent protocols added protection for property; the right to an education; a provision for free elections; no deprivation of liberty for inability to fulfil a contractual obligation; freedom of movement and residence and the right to leave the country; the right to enter the territory of the state of which one is a national; freedom from expulsion from the country of one's nationality, and no collective expulsion of aliens. Unlike the International Covenant, the European Convention contains no reference to a right of peoples to self-determination and to "economic self-determination" (International Covenant, Article 1); to the rights of persons belonging to ethnic, religious or linguistic minorities (Article 27); the right to recognition everywhere as a person before the law (Article 16), and the right to equality before the law and the equal protection of the law, Article 26 (but cf. European Convention Article 14, forbidding discrimination on grounds of sex, race, color etc. in the enjoyment of rights). There is also no European counterpart to the International Covenant's prohibition on war propaganda or advocacy of national, racial or religious hatred that constitutes incitement to discrimination (Article 20). And there is no mention of rights of the child (International Covenant, Article 24). Unlike the International Covenant, the European Convention protects property. The Convention also provides that no one shall be deprived of the right to enter his own country, while the Covenant provides that no one shall be *arbitrarily* deprived of that right (Article 12(4)). The Convention provides explicitly that no one may be expelled from the territory of the state of which he is a national (Protocol 4, Article 3).

In 1985, the adherence of a seventh member brought into force Protocol 6 prohibiting capital punishment in time of peace. Protocol 7 gives additional substantive protections—restrictions on expulsion of aliens, the right to review of a conviction by a higher tribunal, the right of a victim of a miscarriage of justice to be compensated, freedom from double jeopardy, and the equality of spouses in respect of marriage. Protocol 7 entered into force in 1988 and had 12 adherents as of January 1, 1993. Protocol 8, designed to accelerate the procedures of the European Commission and the Court came into force in 1990 and had 23 ratifications by 1993.

### 2. *The System of Implementation and Enforcement*

The authors of the European Convention constructed an elaborate institutional framework to supervise the observance of the rights listed in the Convention. This machinery consists of an organ of inquiry and conciliation (the Commission), a political decision-making organ (the Committee of Ministers of the Council of Europe), and a judicial organ (the European Court of Human Rights).

The Committee of Ministers consists of one representative for each member state of the Council of Europe. In addition to appointing the Human Rights Commission, the Committee takes a case when the Commission fails to secure a friendly settlement to a dispute and the parties and the Commission do not refer the case to the European Court. See generally Council of Europe, Collection of Recommendations, Resolutions and Declarations of the Committee of Ministers Concerning Human Rights, 1949–1987 (1989).

The Commission is comprised of 21 members, no two of whom are nationals of the same state. They are elected by the Committee of Ministers of the Council of Europe, and serve in their individual capacities for 6 year terms. Every state that is a member of the Council of Europe has—whether or not it has ratified the Convention—one judge on the European Court. Judges are elected for 9 year terms by the European Parliamentary Assembly, and serve in their individual capacities.

Any claim submitted by a state party under Article 24, or by an individual under Article 25 of the European Convention, must be submitted to the Commission. The Commission determines the admissibility of applications, establishes the facts of each admitted case, attempts to achieve a friendly settlement and, in the event of failure, draws up a report on the facts and states its opinion as to whether a state has breached an obligation under the Convention. The Commission transmits its report to the Council of Ministers, which may prepare proposals for resolving unsettled cases. The Commission may also submit a case to the European Court. This unusual procedure, with a quasi-judicial organ submitting a case to a judicial organ, permits individual claims to get before the Court. For a detailed sketch of the operation of the Convention, see the chart below.

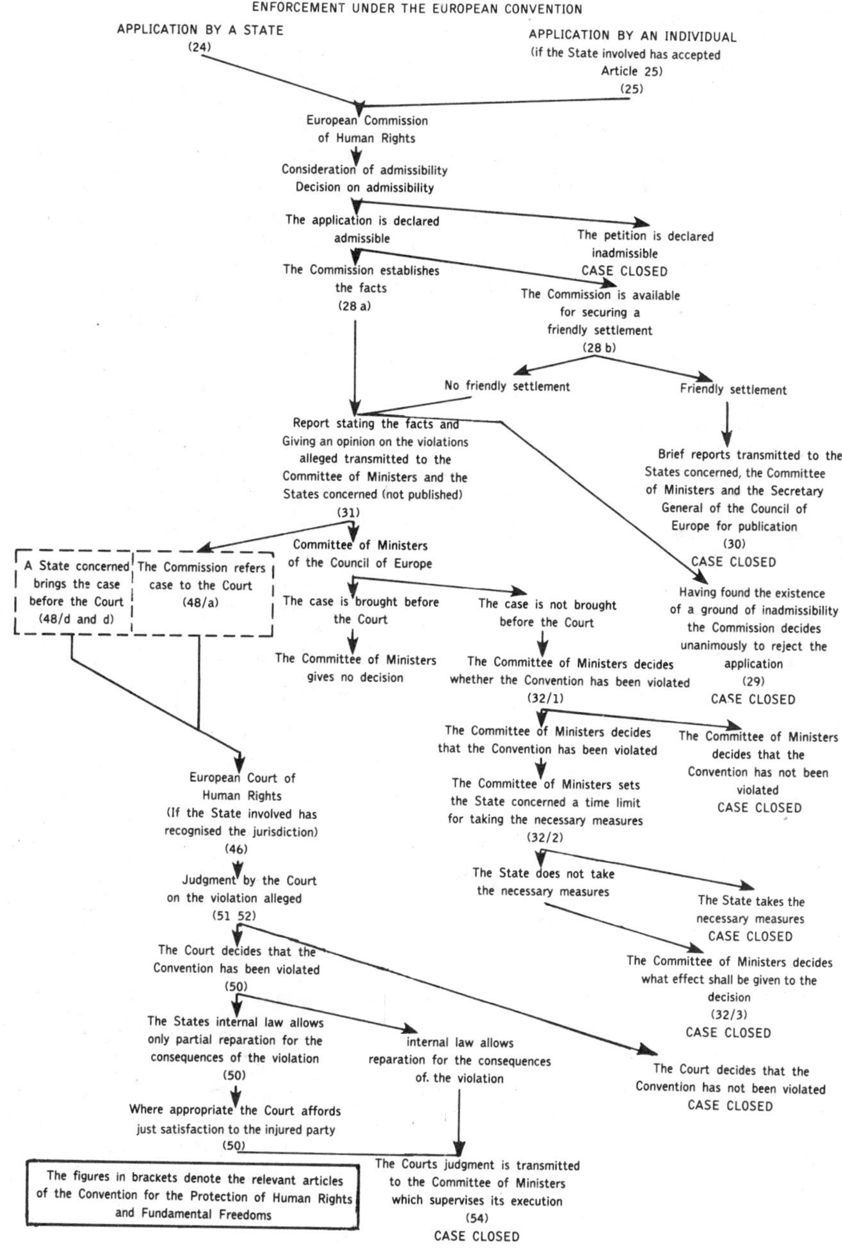


Council of Europe, What is the Council of Europe Doing to Protect Human Rights 29 (1977)

[D10152]

The European Court of Human Rights is established by Articles 38–66 of the Convention. No case can be brought directly before the Court. It must first come before the Commission in the form of an application, be declared admissible and be investigated by the Commission. The Court receives a case only after the Commission has acknowledged its failure to reach a friendly settlement (Article 47). The Court has jurisdiction with respect to any state party to the Convention that has accepted compulsory jurisdiction or has given its consent for a particular case (Article 48).

As of 1993 the Court had decided nearly 400 cases. Its first action, in 1961, involved a complaint charging the Republic of Ireland with violations of Articles 5 and 6. In the Lawless Case, [1961], Eur.Ct.H.R.Ser.A. no. 1, the Court described the kind of public emergency that would permit derogations from the Convention (Article 15) and found that detaining Lawless without a trial did not constitute a violation of the Convention. See p. 621 above.

Article 6 guarantees of a fair public trial, presumption of innocence, and right to legal counsel, have generated numerous cases. The Court has ruled on the reasonableness of time spent by prisoners in detention before trial and on the appropriate length of judicial proceedings. Neumeister Case, [1968] Eur.Ct.H.R.Ser.A. no. 5; Stogmuller Case, [1969] Eur.Ct.H.R.Ser.A. no. 7; Matznetter Case, [1969] Eur.Ct.H.R.Ser.A. no. 8. The Court found implied in Article 6(1) a right of access to the courts, which included a right to obtain counsel by a prisoner. Golder Case, [1975] Eur.Ct.H.R.Ser.A. no. 18.

In several cases during the 1980s and 1990s the Court has looked with ill favor on lengthy trial proceedings and concluded that any unreasonable delay not the fault of the defendant violates Article 6(1). See the Eckle Case, [1982] Eur.Ct.H.R.Ser.A. no. 51; the Case of Foti and Others, [1982] Eur.Ct.H.R.Ser.A. no. 56; the Case of Albert and Le Compte, [1982] Eur.Ct. H.R.Ser.A. no. 81; the Maj Case, [1991] Eur.Ct.H.R.Ser.A. no. 196–D.

Claims brought under Articles 5 and 6 have provided the Court with opportunities to examine a number of issues concerning criminal practice and procedure in various states. See the Airey Case, [1980] Eur.Ct. H.R.Ser.A. no. 32 and the Artico Case, [1980] Eur.Ct.H.R.Ser.A. no. 37 (guarantee of legal counsel); the Adolf Case, [1982] Eur.Ct.H.R.Ser.A. no. 49 and the Minelli Case, [1983] Eur.Ct.H.R.Ser.A. no. 62 (innocent until proven guilty); the Barbera, Messegue and Jabardo Case, [1988] Eur.Ct.H.R.Ser.A. no. 146 (right to a fair trial).

The Court has also scrutinized state acts alleged to have unreasonably deprived persons of liberty. See Guzzardi Case, [1980] Eur.Ct.H.R.Ser.A. no. 39 (Mafioso defendant confined on island); Winterwerp Case, [1980] Eur.Ct. H.R.Ser.A. no. 33 and Case of X v. The United Kingdom, [1981] Eur.Ct. H.R.Ser.A. no. 46 (procedures for confinement in mental institutions); Vagrancy Cases, [1971] Eur.Ct.H.R.Ser.A. no. 10 (jailing persons under vagrancy statutes); the Thynne, Wilson and Gunnell Case [1990] Eur.Ct.H.R.Ser.A. no. 190 (indeterminate prison sentence).

The Court has examined alleged violations of Articles 11 and 14 relating to state actions discriminating against unions (see Belgium Police Case, [1975] Eur.Ct.H.R.Ser.A. no. 19, and Swedish Engine Driver's Union Case, [1976] Eur.Ct.H.R.Ser.A. no. 20), violations of Article 2's education guarantees (see Belgian Linguistic Cases, [1968] Eur.Ct.H.R.Ser.A. no. 4, and the Case of Campbell and Cosans, [1982] Eur.Ct.H.R.Ser.A. no. 48), violations of Article 10's guarantee of freedom of expression (see the Sunday Times case, [1979] Eur.Ct.H.R.Ser.A. no. 28), violations of Article 8's guarantee of privacy (see the case of Silver and Others, [1983] Eur.Ct.H.R.Ser.A. no. 61, Malone Case [1984] Eur.Ct.H.R.Ser.A. no. 82, the Dudgeon Case, [1981] Eur.Ct. H.R.Ser.A. no. 45, the Kruslin case [1990] Eur.Ct.H.R.Ser.A. no. 176–A and the Huvig case [1990] Eur.Ct.H.R.Ser.A. no. 176–B) and the award of reparations as just satisfaction to an injured party under Article 50 (see Neumeister Reparation Case, [1974] Eur.Ct.H.R.Ser.A. no. 17).

In the *Soering* case the Court prohibited the extradition to the United States of a suspect charged with a capital offense because if convicted he might be sent to "death row" which would violate the guarantee of "physical integrity" contained in Article 3. See p. 646 supra. Soering was ultimately extradited for a lesser offense, when the U.S. agreed that it would try him for the noncapital offense only. See Britain Extradites Soering, 6 Int'l Enforcement Reporter 26 (Issue 1, 1990).

In another case, the Netherlands Supreme National Court enjoined the Dutch military authorities from handing a member of the United States Armed Forces over to U.S. authorities pursuant to the Status of Forces Agreement between the Netherlands and the U.S. because if convicted he might be subject to the death penalty contrary to the Sixth Protocol to the European Convention on Human Rights to which the Netherlands was a party. The Court ruled that the Sixth Protocol took precedence over its obligations under the Status of Forces Agreement. Hoge Raad der Nederlanden [HR], 16 Rechtspraak van de Week [Rvd W] Nr. 76, 343 (1990) (Short v. Netherlands). See also the Opinion of the Netherlands Advocaat-General, reprinted in 29 I.L.M. 1375 (1990).

The number and variety of cases coming before the Court has increased and includes cases concerning the prohibition of forced labor, the right to respect and private family life, home and correspondence, the right to marry, the freedom of expression, the right to peaceful assembly, the right to trade union freedom, the right to effective remedy, the right to education, and the right to free elections. For a comprehensive listing of cases, see European Court of Human Rights, Aperçus: Survey of Activities 1959–1990 (1991). See also the European Rights Case Digest published periodically by the British Institute of Human Rights. For reports of cases before the European Court, see the Human Rights Law Journal.

### *Notes*

1. See generally Cassese, Human Rights and the European Community: Methods of Protection (1991); Cassese, Human Rights and the European Community: Substantive Law (1991); Clapham, Human Rights and the European Community: A Critical Overview (1991); Janis, European Human Rights Law (1990); Fawcett, Application of the European Convention on Human Rights (1987). For earlier writing see Robertson, Human Rights in Europe (2d ed. 1977); Castberg, The European Convention on Human Rights (1974); Jacobs, The European Convention on Human Rights (1975); Fawcett, The Application of the European Convention on Human Rights (1969). See also, van Dijk & van Hoof, Theory and Practice of the European Convention on Human Rights (1984);

Mastny, Human Rights and Security: Europe on the Eve of a New Era (1991); Merrills, The Development of International Law by the European Court of Human Rights (1988); Morrisson, The Dynamics of Development in the European Human Rights Convention System (1981); Beddard, Human Rights and Europe: a Study of the Machinery of Human Rights (1980); Drzemczewski, European Human Rights Convention in Domestic Law (1983); Vasak, The Council of Europe, in The International Dimensions of Human Rights 457 (Vasak ed. 1982).

2. The European Court of Justice, the judicial organ of the European Economic Communities (EEC), has found and given effect to some implied "fundamental," "basic" human rights in the law of the Communities. The Court has also developed a doctrine by which provisions of EEC law that are "directly effective" grant individual rights that must be upheld in national courts of member states.

> A number of cases * * * refer to certain Community law rights or protections as "fundamental" or "basic." The notion seems to be that these rights * * * exist whether or not the Treaty of secondary legislation specifically mentions them, and that the institutions must in any event respect them. These general principles of law provide important basic protections.
>
> The term "basic rights" has also come to designate another set of rights, ones that are typically more political or social than economic in character, and include what we know as human rights. The *Stauder* case shows early recognition of that fact. However, * * * certain Member State courts also exerted a good deal of pressure on the Court of Justice to guarantee basic rights protection. These national courts, notably German and Italian, served notice that the supremacy of Community law over national law in their legal orders might depend on the Community's respect for human rights and other fundamental freedoms embodied in national constitutions and international conventions, and on the Court of Justice's readiness to ensure such respect.

Bermann, Goebel, Davey & Fox, Cases and Materials on European Community Law 142 (1993). See also Stauder v. City of Ulm, Sozialamt, Case 29/69 [1969] ECR 419 ("Interpreted in this way the provision at issue contains nothing capable of prejudicing the fundamental human rights enshrined in the general principles of community law and protected by the Court."); Nold v. Commission, Case 4/73, [1974] ECR 49.

## THE EUROPEAN SOCIAL CHARTER

In 1961, the countries of Western Europe adopted the European Social Charter, 529 U.N.T.S. 89; it came into force on 26 February 1965. The following states have become parties: Austria, Belgium, Cyprus, Denmark, Finland, France, Germany, Greece, Iceland, Ireland, Italy, Luxembourg, Malta, The Netherlands, Norway, Portugal, Sweden, Spain, Turkey, and the United Kingdom. The Charter expresses the resolution of the parties "to make every effort in common to improve the standard of living and to promote the social well-being of both their urban and rural populations by means of appropriate institutions and action." In Part I, the parties "accept as the aim of their policy, to be pursued by all appropriate means, both national and international in character, the attainment of conditions in which the following rights and principles may be effectively realized." Part II lists undertakings in various categories, e.g., the right to work, the right to a fair remuneration, the right to bargain collectively, the rights of children, the right of employed women to protection, the right to Social Security, the right to social and medical assistance. Article 20 provides:

1. Each of the Contracting Parties undertakes:

(a) to consider Part I of this Charter as a declaration of the aims which it will pursue by all appropriate means, as stated in the introductory paragraph of that Part;

(b) to consider itself bound by at least five of the following Articles of Part II of this Charter: Articles 1, 5, 6, 12, 13, 16 and 19;

(c) in addition to the Articles selected by it in accordance with the preceding sub-paragraph, to consider itself bound by such a number of Articles or numbered paragraphs of Part II of the Charter as it may select, provided that the total number of Articles or numbered paragraphs by which it is bound is not less than 10 Articles or 45 numbered paragraphs.

2. The Articles or paragraphs selected in accordance with subparagraphs (b) and (c) of paragraph 1 of this Article shall be notified to the Secretary–General of the Council of Europe at the time when the instrument of ratification or approval of the Contracting Party concerned is deposited.

3. Any Contracting Party may, at a later date, declare by notification to the Secretary–General that it considers itself bound by any Articles or any numbered paragraphs of Part II of the Chapter which it has not already accepted under the terms of paragraphs 1 of this Article. Such undertakings subsequently given shall be deemed to be an integral part of the ratification or approval, and shall have the same effect as from the thirtieth day after the date of the notification.

4. The Secretary–General shall communicate to all the signatory Governments and to the Director–General of the International Labour Office any notification which he shall have received pursuant to this Part of the Charter.

5. Each Contracting Party shall maintain a system of labour inspection appropriate to national conditions.

The chart below describes the Charter's implementation procedures. See also Harris, The European Social Charter (1984).

IMPLEMENTATION OF EUROPEAN SOCIAL CHARTER

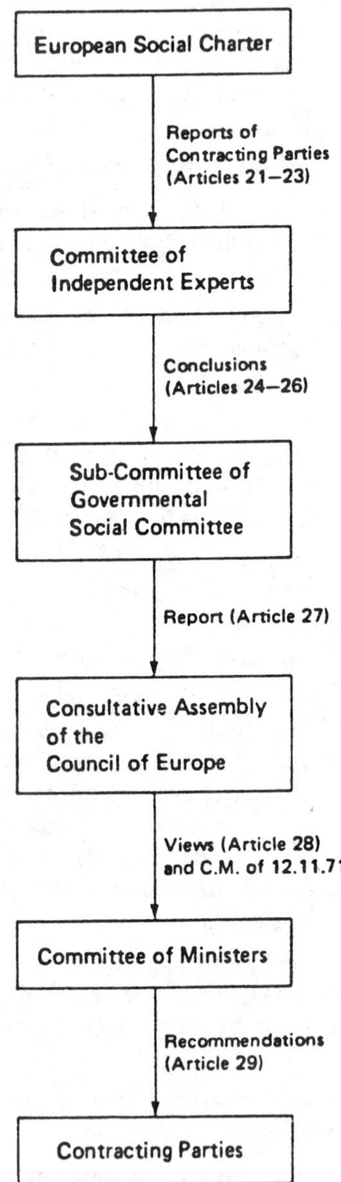


Vasak, International Dimensions of Human Rights 686 (1982).

## *Note*

In 1989, the European Economic Communities adopted a Community Charter of Fundamental Social Rights of Workers, now known as the Social Charter of 1989. It was endorsed at the Strasbourg European Council meeting by all the member states (except the United Kingdom). See Watson, The Community Social Charter, 28 Common Mkt.L.Rev. 37 (1991); Dominick, Toward a Community Bill of Rights: The EC Charter of Fundamental Social Rights, 14 Fordham Int'l L.J. 639 (1990–91); Bercusson, The EC's Charter of Fundamental Rights of

Workers, 53 Mod.L.Rev. 624 (1990); Hepple, The Implementation of the Community Charter of Fundamental Social Rights, 53 Mod.L.Rev. 643 (1990).

## THE CONFERENCE ON SECURITY AND COOPERATION IN EUROPE (CSCE)

(THE HELSINKI FINAL ACT, 1975)

The human rights norms established in the Helsinki Final Act are not strictly regional human rights law, since both European and North Atlantic states are parties to the CSCE. The Final Act (also known as the Helsinki Accords) was signed on August 1, 1975, by the leaders of 35 Eastern and Western European states, as well as the U.S. and Canada. It was the result of an interlude of Cold War détente and represented an important political bargain in which Western states accepted the political status quo in Europe and the Communist states made human rights commitments. See Human Rights, International Law, and the Helsinki Accord (Buergenthal, ed. 1977).

### *HENKIN, THE AGE OF RIGHTS*

57–58 (1990) (footnote omitted).

At the Conference on Security and Cooperation in Europe the participating states agreed to discuss human rights together with other matters relating to security and cooperation. In the Final Act, the participants declared it to be among the principles guiding relations between them that they would respect human rights and fundamental freedoms and promote and encourage their effective exercise. In addition:

> In the field of human rights and fundamental freedoms, the participating States will act in conformity with the purposes and principles of the Charter of the United Nations and with the Universal Declaration of Human Rights. They will also fulfill their obligations as set forth in the international declarations and agreements in this field, including inter alia the International Covenants on Human Rights, by which they may be bound. (1(a)VII)

They also agreed to fulfill in good faith obligations under international law generally (1(a)X). Later in the act (Basket III) the participating states "make it their aim," "declare their readiness," and "express their intention" to implement cooperation in humanitarian and other fields, including human contacts, information, and cooperation and exchange in culture and in education. These human rights provisions were the condition and the price of other provisions of great political importance desired by other participants. Western participants saw them as the condition of and an integral aspect of détente at which the whole Final Act aimed.

While Helsinki was not intended to be a legally binding agreement, and does not add legally binding human rights obligations, it clearly precludes any suggestion that matters it deals with are within domestic jurisdiction and beyond the reach of appropriate inquiry and recourse.

### *Note*

The participants in the Helsinki Accords declared their resolve, in the period following the 1975 conference, to implement the provisions of the Final Act and began this process through an exchange of views at a series of multilateral conferences in Belgrade (1977), Madrid (1979) and in Vienna (1986), which largely became arenas for charges that members of the Soviet bloc were violating human rights. After the Cold War the CSCE changed in character and focus. Successive meetings in 1989–91 at Paris, Vienna, Bonn, Copenhagen and Moscow reflected common agreement and commitment, and produced important documents on the Human Dimension of the CSCE. These documents, particularly the documents produced at the Copenhagen and Moscow meetings, elaborated the commitment to human rights in important detail and gave prominent emphasis to democracy as a major human right and as a foundation for other human rights. See generally the following three articles by Buergenthal, Democratization and Europe's New Public Order, in CSCE and the New Blueprint for Europe 53 (Wyatt, ed. 1991); The Copenhagen CSCE Meeting: A New Public Order for Europe, 11 Hum.Rts.L.J. 217 (1990); CSCE Human Dimension: The Birth of a System, 1 Collected Course of the Academy of European Law 163 (No. 2, 1990). See also Lucas, The Conference on Security and Cooperation in Europe and the Post–Cold War Era (1990).

## B. THE INTER–AMERICAN HUMAN RIGHTS SYSTEM

Organizations of the states in the Western Hemisphere have been concerned with human rights since the Second World War. The Charter of the Organization of American States includes the provision: "Each State has the right to develop its cultural, political and economic life freely and naturally. In this free development the State shall respect the rights of the individual and the principles of universal morality" (originally Chapter III, Art. 13; now Chapter IV, Art. 16). These have been deemed to be words of legal obligation. Thomas & Thomas, The Organization of American States 223 (1963).

The American Declaration on the Rights and Duties of Man was adopted in 1948, seven months before the Universal Declaration was approved. It is generally accepted that the American Declaration was not intended to have legally binding character and has not acquired such character since. See LeBlanc, The OAS and the Promotion and Protection of Human Rights 13 (1977). But see pp. 669–70 infra.

In 1959, the Fifth Meeting of Consultation of Ministers of Foreign Affairs resolved that the Inter–American Council of Jurists should prepare a Convention on Human Rights, and also one to create an Inter–American Court for the Protection of Human Rights. The Meeting decided also to organize an Inter–American Commission on Human Rights. The American Convention on Human Rights was signed in San Jose, Costa Rica on 22 November 1969, and came into force in June 1978. As of 1986, 19 states have ratified the Convention. Elections to the Inter–American Court of Human Rights created by the Convention first took place in May 1979. Terms are for six years and are staggered. Article 52 of the Convention permits nationals of all member states of the O.A.S. to serve on the Court, whether or not the member state is a party to the Convention. Thomas

Buergenthal of the United States—which is not a party to the Convention—has served on the Court.

### 1. *The Rights and Freedoms Protected*

Substantively, the American Declaration and the American Convention parallel the Universal Declaration and the International Covenant on Civil and Political Rights. The American Declaration, however, includes a chapter containing 10 articles setting forth the individual's duties (compare Article 29(1) of the Universal Declaration). The American Convention protects the accepted political-civil rights, although some in terms significantly different from those in the International Covenant on Civil and Political Rights. In the American Convention, for example, the right to life "shall be protected by law and, in general, from the moment of conception" (Art. 4(1)). The protected rights include: the right to life, freedom from torture and inhuman treatment, freedom from slavery and servitude, the right to liberty and security, the right to a fair trial, freedom from retroactivity of the criminal law, the right to respect for private and family life, freedom of conscience and religion, freedom of thought and expression, freedom of assembly, freedom of association, freedom to marry and found a family, the right to property, freedom of movement, freedom from exile, prohibition of the collective expulsion of aliens, the right to participate in free elections, the right to an effective remedy if one's rights are violated, the right to recognition as a person before the law, the right to compensation for miscarriage of justice, the right of reply, the right to a name, the rights of the child, the right to a nationality, the right to equality before the law, the right of asylum. Like the European Convention but unlike the International Covenant, it will be noted, the American Convention includes protection for property, and freedom from exile and collective expulsion for aliens. Unlike both the International Covenant and the European Convention, the American Convention recognizes a right of reply (to anyone injured by inaccurate or offensive statements or ideas) and the right of asylum. But the American Convention does not include the right to an education or other economic-social rights. It commits the states parties, in Article 26, to work to achieve progressively "by legislation or other appropriate means, the full realization of the rights implicit in the economic, social, educational, scientific, and cultural standards set forth in the Charter of the Organization of American States. * * * "

### 2. *Implementation of Human Rights in the Inter-American System*

The Inter-American Commission of Human Rights was created in 1960 and was elevated to the status of an organ of the OAS in 1970. As such, its competence has been to "further respect" for human rights; the quoted words were interpreted to grant authority "to promote" but not "to protect" human rights. Almost immediately and for some years, however, an "activist" commission read its mandate very broadly. In 1965, it was granted authority "to examine" private communications alleging violation of rights. It has exercised its authority with "mixed" success, high in the Dominican Republic in 1965–66, least notable as regards Cuba or Haiti (which refused to cooperate with the Commission). See generally Buergenthal, Protecting

Human Rights in the Americas: Selected Problems (1990); Organization of American States, Basic Documents Pertaining to Human Right in the Inter-American System (1988); Quiroga, The Battle of Human Rights: Gross, Systematic Violations and the Inter-American System (1988). See also Mower, Regional Human Rights: A Comparative Study of the West European and Inter-American Systems, (1991).

With the coming into force of the American Convention, the Inter-American Commission has become one of two organs having "competence with respect to matters relating to the fulfillment of the commitments" made by states parties to the Convention (Article 33). The Commission, however, unlike its counterpart in the European system, received its "judicial" character only at the 1969 Convention. The Commission had been a controversial investigative body and advocate for human rights since its formation in 1960 and it still reflects the tension between its "activist" and "judicial" roles—a tension which may affect the respect given its judgments. The European Commission, on the other hand, was formed as an enforcement arm of the European Convention and given only quasi-judicial functions—and its role in the European human rights system is widely appreciated.

The Inter-American Court of Human Rights is the second organ responsible for supervising adherence of states parties to the Convention. The enforcement duties of the Commission and Court are stated in Articles 46–61 (in Documents Supplement), and described in the chart below.

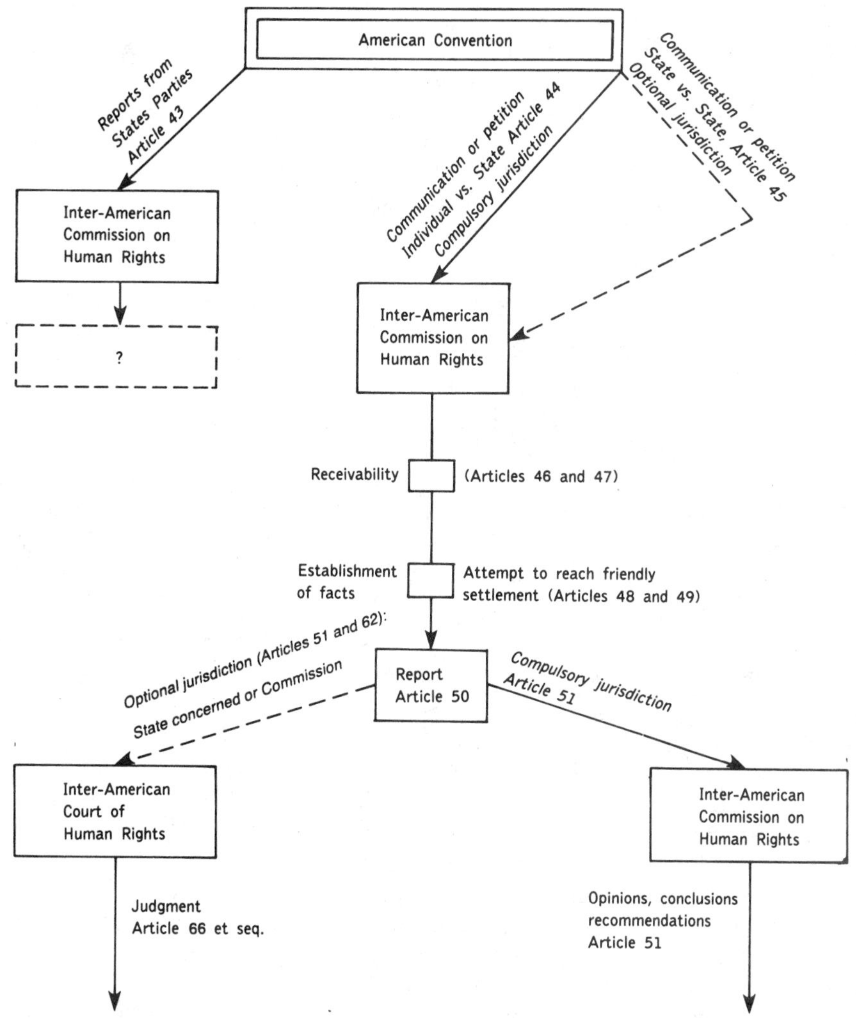


Vasak, International Dimensions of Human Rights 684 (1982)

[D10151]

## Notes

1. The Court was established in 1978. Fourteen O.A.S. states (Costa Rica, Peru, Venezuela, Honduras, Ecuador, Argentina, Uruguay, Colombia, Guatemala, Suriname, Panama, Chile, Nicaragua and Trinidad and Tobago) have recognized the jurisdiction of the Court as binding. According to Article 62 of the Convention, any state party may accept the jurisdiction of the Court in a specific case. The Inter-American Court of Human Rights, as of early 1993, has issued 12 advisory opinions and addressed 8 contentious cases.

2. In 1989, the Inter-American Court of Human Rights issued an advisory opinion on the legal effect to be given to the American Declaration on the Rights and Duties of Man. Colombia requested the Court to determine whether the

Court had the authority under the Inter–American Convention on Human Rights to render advisory opinions interpreting the Declaration. The Court decided that it had such authority provided that the interpretation of the Declaration was necessary to resolve a question related to either the American Convention or one of the "other treaties" over which the Court has advisory jurisdiction. The Court noted that the American Declaration is an authoritative interpretation of the OAS Charter. Interpretation of the American Declaration of the Rights and Duties of Man in the Context of Article 64 of the American Convention on Human Rights, Advisory Opinion OC–10/89, July 14, 1989, Series A No. 10.

What implications are raised by the Court's advisory opinion on the American Declaration on the Rights and Duties of Man, p. 666 above? Newman & Weissbrodt have translated the Spanish version of Court's opinion on the Declaration as concluding: "The fact that the Declaration is not a treaty does not * * * import the conclusion that it lacks legal effect, nor is the Court prevented from interpreting it * * *." Newman & Weissbrodt, International Human Rights 303 (1990). Has the Court in effect expanded its advisory jurisdiction to include the customary international law of human rights? Does the advisory opinion on "other treaties" in the case discussed in Note 3.*a* below, together with the Court's opinion on the American Declaration support the conclusion that the Court can also issue advisory opinions concerning other "non-binding resolutions," such as the Universal Declaration of Human Rights?

3. The Court's advisory opinions include:

*a.* In response to a series of questions posed by the government of Peru relating to the Court's jurisdiction to issue advisory opinions, the Court found that it had advisory jurisdiction "with regard to any provision dealing with the protection of human rights set forth in any international treaty applicable in the American states, regardless of whether it be bilateral or multilateral, whatever be the principal purpose of such a treaty, and whether or not non-Member States of the inter-American system are or have a right to become parties thereto." I/A Court H.R., "Other Treaties" Subject to the Advisory Jurisdiction of the Court (Art. 64 American Convention on Human Rights), Advisory Opinion OC–1/82 of September 24, 1982. Series A No. 1. Does this mean the Court can issue advisory opinions relating, for example, to an American state's duties under the Universal Declaration and the Covenants?

*b.* In response to developments in Guatemala, the Inter–American Commission on Human Rights requested the Court's opinion on whether the imposition of the death penalty by a state, for crimes for which such punishment was not provided in domestic law at the time of the adoption of the American Convention, constituted a violation of the Convention, even if the state had filed a reservation to the relevant provision in the Convention. The Court found that the Convention "imposes an absolute prohibition on the extension of the death penalty," and that a state party cannot apply the death penalty to additional crimes, even if a reservation to the relevant provision in the Convention had been entered at the time of ratification. I/A Court H.R., Restrictions to the Death Penalty (Arts. 4(2) and 4(4) American Convention on Human Rights), Advisory Opinion OC–3/83 of September 8, 1983. Series A No. 3. See Chapter 6, Section 2E.

*c.* Responding to a request by Costa Rica, the Court advised that the compulsory licensing of journalists through mandatory membership in an association for the practice of journalism is incompatible with Article 13 of the

American Convention on Human Rights if it denies a person access to the full use of the news media as a means of expressing opinions or imparting information. The Court also found that Costa Rica's proposed law requiring compulsory licensing of journalists would infringe Article 13 of the Convention because the law would prevent certain people from joining the association. See I/A Court H.R., Compulsory Membership in an Association Prescribed by Law for the Practice of Journalism (Arts. 13 and 29 American Convention on Human Rights), Advisory Opinion OC–5/85 of November 13, 1985 Series A No. 5.

*d.* Advising on an issue submitted by the Inter–American Commission, the Court has determined that exhaustion of local remedies is not required where an individual's indigence or a general fear in the legal community to represent the individual, prevents the complainant from invoking local remedies. The Court also determined that where the State subject of the complaint demonstrates that there are local remedies, the complainant must show that the exceptions to exhaustion of local remedies within the Convention (Article 46(2)) apply and that the individual was prevented from obtaining the legal counsel necessary for the protection of rights guaranteed by the Convention. I/A Court H.R., Exceptions to the Exhaustion of Local Remedies (Art. 46(1), 46(2)(a) and 46(2)(b) American Convention on Human Rights) Advisory Opinion OC–11/90 of August 10, 1990, 12 Human Rts.L.J. 20 (1990).

*e.* In 1991, the Court declined to answer questions put to it by Costa Rica as to whether its draft legislation for the establishment of a Court of Criminal Appeals fulfilled the requirements of Article 8(2)(h) of the American Convention on Human Rights (the right of appeal). The Inter–American Commission gave evidence that it had before it a number of cases involving alleged violations by Costa Rica of Article 8(2)(h). In 1986, the Commission had given Costa Rica six months to rectify the situation in the hope that many of the cases could be resolved without further intervention by the Commission. By 1991, after a decision by the Supreme Court of Costa Rica that Article 8(2)(h) was self-executing, the legislation for the Court of Criminal Appeals had not yet been passed. The Court held that a reply to the questions presented by Costa Rica could, in the guise of an advisory opinion, result in a determination of contentious cases not yet brought before the Court, without giving the victims of the alleged human rights abuses the opportunity to participate in the proceedings before the Court. I/A Court H.R., Advisory Opinion OC–12/91 of December 6, 1991, Compatibility of Draft Legislation with Article 8(2)(h) of the American Convention on Human Rights, 10 Annual Report of the Inter–American Court of Human Rights 114 (1991).

4. *Contentious cases.* Beginning in 1987, the Court considered a series of cases submitted by the Inter–American Commission concerning disappearances in Honduras. The Court awarded compensation to the next of kin in two of the cases. I/A Court H.R., Velasquez Rodriguez Case, Compensatory Damages, Judgment of July 21, 1989 (Art. 63(1) American Convention on Human Rights) Series C No. 7; I/A Court H.R., Godinez Cruz Case, Compensatory Damages, Judgment July 21, 1989 (Art. 63(1) American Convention on Human Rights) Series C No. 8. In another case, the Court held that the responsibility of the Government of Honduras for the deaths of two Costa Rican citizens who had allegedly entered Honduras and disappeared had not been proved. I/A Court H.R., Fairen Garbi and Solis Corrales Case, Judgment of March 15, 1989, Series C. No. 6. In all three cases, the Court dealt with harassment and assassination of witnesses, finally indicating provisional measures ordering the Honduran government to do everything within its power to stop the harassment. The

Court also considered a number of preliminary objections by Honduras, including failure to exhaust local remedies and ruled that where a pattern of disappearances was proven, local remedies such as habeas corpus were non-existent or ineffective because of the failure of government officials to reveal the whereabouts of the victims and because of persistent harassment of persons trying to invoke local remedies. See, e.g., I/A Court H.R., Godinez Cruz Case, Judgment of January 20, 1989. Series C No. 5., at 116. The Court also made strong statements on the burden and standard of proof to be applied in cases of wide-scale disappearances where the State subject of the complaint has most control over the evidence. See Godinez Cruz Case (above) and Valasquez Rodriguez Case, Judgment of July 29, 1988, 8 Annual Report of the Inter-American Court of Human Rights 35 (1988).

In another case, at the request of the Inter-American Commission, the Court ordered provisional measures to protect fourteen members of human rights organizations in Chunima, Guatemala. See Provisional Measures Requested by the Inter-American Commission on Human Rights with Regard to Guatemala (Chunima Case), Order of August 1, 1991, 10 Annual Report of the Inter-American Court of Human Rights 52 (1991). In 1990, the Court made a similar order in relation to a situation in Peru which was later corrected to the Court's satisfaction. See Provisional Measures Requested by the Inter-American Commission on Human Rights in the Matter of Peru (Bustios-Rojas Case), Order of January 17, 1991, 10 Annual Report of the Inter-American Court of Human Rights 15 (1991).

The Commission also brought to the Court a contentious case against Suriname concerning the killing of seven civilians by soldiers. Suriname claimed it was not responsible for the killings, but later, during the Court hearing, accepted responsibility. The Court retained jurisdiction in the case to decide on appropriate compensation to the next of kin. See Aloeboetoe et al. Case, Judgment of December 4, 1991, 10 Annual Report of the Inter-American Court of Human Rights 57 (1991). The Court also considered, and rejected, preliminary objections in two cases submitted to it by the Commission. See Gangaram Panday Case, Preliminary Objections, Judgment of December 4, 1991, 10 Annual Report of the Inter-American Court of Human Rights 64 (1991); and Neira Alegria et al. Case, Preliminary Objections, Judgment of December 11, 1991, 10 Annual Report of the Inter-American Court of Human Rights 75 (1991).

5. Since 1980, the Inter-American Commission has heard several complaints against the United States alleging violations of the American Declaration of the Rights and Duties of Man, the American Convention on Human Rights, and of the customary law of human rights. See, e.g., the "*Baby Boy*" Case, Case No. 2141, Inter-Am.C.H.R. 25, OEA.Ser.L/V/II.54, doc. 9 rev. 1 (1981) (*Roe v. Wade* does not violate the right to life granted by American Declaration and the American Convention); The *Roach* Case, Case No. 9647, Inter-Am.C.H.R. 147, OEA/Ser.L/V/II.71, doc. 9 rev. 1 (1987) (U.S. death sentence for crime committed by juvenile under 18 is not a violation of a customary norm, although such a norm may be emerging); The *Celestine* case, Case No. 10,031, Inter-Am.C.H.R. res. 23/89, OEA/Ser.L./V/II.76, doc. 44 (1989) (facts did not establish that U.S. applied death penalty in racially discriminatory manner). There have also been charges before the Commission that the United States violated the Declaration and customary law when it invaded Panama in 1989, and when it interdicted vessels carrying Haitian asylum seekers on the high seas.

6. On the promotion and protection of human rights in the Americas, see Davidson, The Inter–American Court of Human Rights (1992); Buergenthal, Norris & Shelton, Protecting Human Rights in the Americas (3rd ed. 1990); Frost, The Evolution of the Inter–American Court of Human Rights: Reflections of Present and Former Judges, 14 Hum.Rts.Q. 171 (1992); Grossman, Proposals to Strengthen the Inter–American System of Protection of Human Rights, 32 Germ.Y.B.Int'l L. 264 (1990); Shelton, Improving Human Rights Protections: Recommendations for Enhancing the Effectiveness of the Inter–American Commission and the Inter–American Court of Human Rights, 3 Am.U.J.Int'l L. & Pol'y 323 (1988); Norris, The Individual Petition Procedure of the Inter–American System for the Protection of Human Rights, in Guide to International Human Rights Practice (Hannum, ed. 1984); Buergenthal, The Inter–American Court of Human Rights, 76 A.J.I.L. 231 (1982).

7. The American Convention deals with economic and social rights in Article 26. In 1988, the General Assembly of the Organization of American States adopted the Additional Protocol to the American Conventions on Economic, Social and Cultural Rights (Protocol of San Salvador). As of 1993, the Protocol had 15 signatures, but only one accession. See Annual Report of the Inter–American Commission on Human Rights, 1991, at 287–339, OEA/Serv.L./V/II/.81, doc. 6 (14 February 1992).

## C. THE AFRICAN HUMAN RIGHTS SYSTEM

The Organization of African Unity has, for most of its existence, been concerned with colonialism and its vestiges, with apartheid in South Africa, Namibia, and Rhodesia (now Zimbabwe), and the economic development of post-colonial African states. In 1979 the OAU decided to draft an "African Charter on Human and Peoples' Rights."

The African Charter was drafted over a two-year period in Banjul, the Gambia. The Assembly of Heads of State and Government of the OAU adopted the Charter in 1981 and officially named it the "Banjul Charter." OAU Doc. CAB/LEG/67/3 rev. 5, reprinted in 21 I.L.M. 58 (1982). The Charter entered into force on October 21, 1986, after it was ratified by a majority of OAU member states. As of early 1993, 42 states are party to the Charter. See generally Mbaye, Les Droits de L'Homme en Afrique (1992); Human Rights in Africa: Cross–Cultural Perspectives (An–Na'im & Deng, eds. 1990); Shivji, The Concept of Human Rights in Africa (1989); Howard, Human Rights in Commonwealth Africa (1986); Rembe, Africa and Regional Protection of Human Rights (1985); Eze, Human Rights in Africa (1984); See also Peter, Human Rights in Africa: A Comparative Study of the African Human and Peoples' Rights Charter and the New Tanzanian Bill of Rights (1990). For a compilation of relevant documents, see Naldi, Documents of the Organization of African Unity (1992); The International Law of Human Rights in Africa: Basic Documents and Annotated Bibliography (Hamalengwa, Flinterman & Dankwa, eds. 1988).

### *1. The Rights and Freedoms Protected*

The Banjul Charter speaks to both rights owed by a state to its people and duties owed by citizens to the state. The Charter also speaks to the rights of "peoples" within states.

For individuals, the Charter protects the right to equal protection of the law; the right to life; freedom from slavery, torture and cruel, inhuman or degrading punishment and treatment; the right to liberty and freedom from arbitrary arrest or detention; the presumption of innocence in a criminal trial, and the right to counsel; freedom of conscience, profession, religion, expression, association, assembly and movement; the right to leave and return to one's own country; the right to seek and obtain asylum when persecuted; the right to participate freely in government; the right to property; the right to work under equitable and satisfactory conditions; the right to enjoy the best attainable state of physical and mental health; the right to an education; freedom from discrimination; prohibition of mass expulsion of aliens.

The Charter guarantees the right of "peoples" to existence and to self-determination. It specifically reserves to "colonized" or "oppressed" peoples the right to free themselves by resorting to any means recognized by the international community, and states that all such peoples shall have the right to receive assistance from Charter states. Also included is the right of peoples to economic, social and cultural development; the right to freely dispose of their wealth and natural resources. State parties are required to eliminate all forms of foreign economic exploitation. Peoples have the right to a general satisfactory environment favorable to their development.

The Charter lists duties owed by a citizen to his state. They include the duty not to discriminate against others; to protect the family and respect and maintain parents; to serve the state and contribute to its defense; and to pay taxes in the interest of society.

### 2. *The System of Implementation and Enforcement*

The Charter establishes an African Commission on Human and Peoples' Rights to promote and ensure protection of human rights in Africa. The Commission's mandate is generally three-fold: to promote respect for human rights through studies, seminars, conferences, the dissemination of information and cooperation with local agencies; to "ensure" the protection of human rights under conditions laid down by the Charter; and to interpret the provisions of the Charter. The Commission is therefore quasi-judicial in character, but only renders reports to the states concerned with a particular case and to the Assembly of Heads of State and Government. It is up to the states concerned or the Assembly to take any action in response to violations described in the reports. In these respects, the Commission is not unlike the human rights commissions of the European and American Conventions. However, the Charter does not create a court to which states and the Commission can refer cases when settlement is otherwise unattainable. See Welch, The African Commission on Human and Peoples' Rights: A Five Year Report and Assessment, 14 Hum.Rt.Q. 43 (1992).

### *Note*

The Arab League, founded in 1945, decided in 1968 to establish a Permanent Arab Commission on Human Rights (Res. 2443, 3 Sept. 1968). Its essential aim is to promote respect for human rights, rather than to take measures to protect them. The Commission has focused on alleged human rights abuses by Israel in the occupied territories rather than on human rights problems within the Arab states. See Boutros–Gali, The League of Arab States, in Vasak, at 575; Rembe, Human Rights in Africa: Some Selected Problems (1984).

In 1990, a Draft Arab Convention on the Prevention of Torture and Inhuman or Degrading Treatment was prepared by a Committee of Experts and presented to all Arab states and the League of Arab states for its consideration. As of 1993, it had not come into effect.

---

### *HENKIN, INTERNATIONAL LAW: POLITICS, VALUES AND FUNCTIONS*

216 Rec. des Cours 9, 272–73, 336–37 (1989–IV).

This, briefly, is the story to date of the international system's move towards commitment to human values through an international law of human rights. The idea of human rights has been universally accepted. Excellent international standards have been developed and incorporated into national constitutions and international instruments. The Universal Declaration is repeatedly invoked, the various covenants and conventions are adhered to by States from every region and of every ideological hue. More than half of the States have adhered to the International Covenant on Civil and Political Rights and the International Covenant on Economic, Social and Cultural Rights; even larger numbers of States are parties to the Genocide Convention, the Convention on the Elimination of All Forms of Racial Discrimination, the Convention on the Elimination of All Forms of Discrimination against Women. The Convention on Torture is still new but it too is likely to achieve wide support. Customary law of human rights continues to grow, and some of it is *jus cogens.*

But the condition of human rights leaves something to be desired in every country, and much to be desired in many countries. The development of a national human rights culture depends primarily on internal forces, but an international human rights culture can strongly influence domestic progress. International law generally has managed with reasonable success, thanks to a culture of compliance and to horizontal enforcement; international human rights law is still developing its culture of compliance. The move from State values to human values represented by the new international law of human rights has not yet gone so far as to induce States to accept "intrusive" monitoring and impartial judgment of State compliance. In a system of States subject to the politics of States, State resistance to enforcement has limited the effectiveness of treaty machinery as well as the political influence of international bodies. Regional groupings in Europe and America have had far better success, but the African human rights movement is still developing, and human rights law and enforcement are hardly noticeable in other regions. Bilateral enforcement by individual States has had marginal impact. Non-governmental monitors are effective, but insufficient.

International standards have contributed to a universal human rights culture which has been slowly taking root around the world. Those who have insisted on converting a universal declaration of human rights into an international law of human rights have placed faith in the power of norms to add strength to that culture and to shape the behaviour of States in respect of rights more quickly. But the added influence of law depends largely on the ability of the system to induce compliance with that law and persistent resistance to effective inducements may put into question the normative quality of the norms.

There is a need to take the international law of human rights seriously by taking inducements to comply more seriously. An international culture of compliance with human rights may require the system to promote, and States to accept, more intrusive enforcement of human rights, to move farther from State values to human values. Much may depend on the changing international political climate. Might the USSR yet agree to, and the Third World join in, new enforcement machinery? Might the United States improve its international co-operation and participation in the International Human Rights Movement? Will such new developments transform political inducements to comply with international human rights law, so as to make the international system more responsive to human values in fact as it is in principle?

* * *

One can state with substantial confidence that systemic attention to human values will continue to increase. Egregious violations of human rights will continue to command world attention and machinery for inducing compliance will continue to evolve. Additional conventions will come into effect—such as the Convention on the Rights of the Child, and some day perhaps one on the elimination of religious intolerance. The customary law of human rights will grow slowly. Despite past frustrations, the idea of a United Nations High Commissioner for Human Rights is not dead. I hope (but cannot be confident) that the United States, whose human rights record at home is commendable but whose resistance to important international human rights activity has been deplorable, will adhere to covenants and conventions and improve its participation in the Human Rights Movement generally. Regional machinery will grow even stronger in Europe (perhaps attracting even some Eastern neighbours) and in Latin America. It will evolve in Africa, and will burgeon in parts of Asia and in the Arab world. The politicization of human rights in the universal organizations, notably in the United Nations, can be reduced, and might result in greater activism in support of human rights, especially as regards egregious, "consistent patterns of gross violations".

# Chapter 9

# RESPONSIBILITY FOR INJURY TO ALIENS

Under ordinary circumstances and in the absence of an international agreement to the contrary a state is not obligated under international law to admit nationals of another state into its territory, and it incurs no international responsibility if it deports them. If aliens are admitted, they may be subjected to restrictions on the duration of their stay, where they may travel, and the activities they may engage in. Moreover, a national of one state who comes within the territorial jurisdiction of another, whether as a transient or as a permanent resident, becomes thereby subject generally to the legal regime applicable to nationals of that state, except to the extent that a special regime is applicable to aliens. For example, aliens may be excluded from engaging in various commercial or other gainful activity, from owning real property, from such civil and political rights as the right to vote or to hold public office, and from such duties as fulfilling a military service obligation. Generally, however, aliens' substantive and procedural rights are neither better nor worse than those of local nationals, and they do not carry with them the rights and protections they may enjoy under the law of the state of their nationality.

Under customary international law, however, an alien may properly seek from the state of which he or she is a national, and it may properly accord, diplomatic protection against an act or omission by a foreign state causing injury to the alien that may give rise to international responsibility. A state is entitled to communicate with its national who is arrested or charged with a crime by another state, to give assistance and to have a representative present at the trial. The protecting state may intercede to protect its national's human rights, personal safety, property or other interests. See Restatement (Third) § 713, Comment *c.* Under circumstances to be examined in this Chapter, if the alien has suffered an injury as a result of a violation of a substantive rule of international law attributable to a foreign state, the state of which he or she is a national may assert, on the state-to-state level, a claim against the offending state that is based on the injury to the alien. The injured alien may be a natural or a judicial person (e.g., a corporation). Normally, the injured alien must exhaust remedies under the laws and through the institutions of the state to which the wrongful conduct is attributable. In the event that such alien is unable to obtain redress for the injury under the laws and through the institutions of that state, what originated as the claim of the private party can be elevated to the international plane, provided that the state of which the private party is a national elects to assert a claim against the allegedly responsible state.

Most international claims are of this variety; that is, they are derivative in the sense that they involve not a wrong inflicted directly on one state by another, but rather injury caused by one state to a national of another state. State responsibility arises only if the act or omission of the state causing the injury is wrongful under international law. The injury may be caused directly by action of the foreign state—for example, physical injury to the person or confiscation of the property of an alien by an agent or organ of the state—or it may be caused by a failure by the state to provide redress for an injury inflicted on the alien by some private person—for example, a failure of the state to provide judicial remedies to an alien on whom physical or economic injury has been inflicted by a resident of that state.

The customary law of responsibility for injury to aliens, both individual and juridical, and the law of human rights, examined in Chapter 8, which deals with the obligations of states to all human beings, not just to aliens, have developed separately. The latter reflects "general acceptance * * * that how a state treats individual human beings, including its own citizens, in respect of their human rights, is not the state's own business alone and therefore exclusively within its 'domestic jurisdiction,' but is a matter of international concern and a proper subject for regulation by international law." Restatement (Third) Part VII, Introductory Note.

Notwithstanding differences in the development and origins of the customary law of responsibility for injury to aliens and the law of human rights there is a substantial overlap and a growing interrelationship between them.

> The difference in history and in jurisprudential origins between the older law of responsibility for injury to aliens and the newer law of human rights should not conceal their essential affinity and their increasing convergence. The law of responsibility to aliens posited and invoked an international standard of justice for individuals, even if dogmas of the international system limited the application of that standard to foreign nationals. That standard of justice, like contemporary human rights law, derived from historic conceptions of natural law, as reflected in the conscience of contemporary mankind and the major cultures and legal systems of the world. As the law of human rights developed, the law of responsibility for injury to aliens, as applied to natural persons, began to refer to violation of their "fundamental human rights," and states began to invoke contemporary human rights norms as the basis for claims for injury to their nationals.

Id.

The law of state responsibility retains vitality in providing protection against injuries to individual aliens that do not rise to the level of violations of human rights and against injuries to judicial persons that have no "human" rights.

When the wrongful conduct attributable to a state results in injury to a national of another state, the latter state may resort to any of the remedial measures available to a state that has been the object of a breach of international law, which are discussed in Chapter 7. Although the underlying injury is to an alien individual or private legal entity, the liability runs from the responsible state to the state of which the injured alien or entity is a national. Thus, assertion of a claim based on state responsibility arising out of an injury to a private party requires the interposition of the state of which he is a national. The derivative nature of the state's claim based on injury to its national becomes important in connection with such matters as the measure of reparation and circumstances under which action by the national may effect a settlement or a waiver of any claim of his state based on state responsibility. See p. 701 infra. The principles of nationality, discussed at p. 394 supra, play an important role in connection with state responsibility.

During the last 35 years or so there have been a number of studies of the law of state responsibility for injury to aliens. One, with draft articles, was prepared for the International Law Commission by its Special Rapporteur, F.V. Garcia-Amador, and was considered by the Commission between 1956 and 1960. Beginning in 1962, a new Special Rapporteur, Roberto Ago, prepared a report for the Commission dealing with state responsibility in specific contexts. See Report of International Law Commission on the Work of its 32d Session, G.A.O.R., 35th Sess.Supp. No. 10 (A/35/10) (1980). Dr. Garcia-Amador's study and a draft convention with commentary prepared by Sohn and Baxter are contained in Garcia-Amador, Sohn & Baxter, Recent Codification of the Law of State Responsibility for Injuries to Aliens (1974). The most recent survey is found in Chapter 2, Part VII of the Restatement (Third).

## SECTION 1. CONFLICTING VIEWS ON BASIC PRINCIPLES

### A. THE INTERNATIONAL MINIMUM STANDARD OF JUSTICE AND THE PRINCIPLE OF EQUALITY

The traditional view of the customary law of state responsibility as espoused by the United States and many other states, including, in particular, most of the industrialized states of the West, was summarized in 5 Hackworth at 471–72 as follows:

> The state has the right to expect that the alien shall observe its laws and that his conduct shall not be incompatible with the good order of the state and of the community in which he resides or sojourns. It has the obligation to give him that degree of protection for his person and property which he and his state have the right to expect under local law, under international law, and under treaties and conventions between his state and the state of residence. Failure of the alien or of the

state to observe these requirements may give rise to responsibility in varying degrees, the alien being amenable to the local law or subject to expulsion from the state, or both, and the state being responsible to the alien or to the state of which he is a national.

We are here concerned primarily with responsibility of the state. * * * It does not arise merely because an alien has been injured or has suffered loss within the state's territory. If the alien has suffered an injury at the hands of a private person his remedy usually is against that person, and state responsibility does not arise in the absence of a dereliction of duty on the part of the state itself in connection with the injury, as for example by failure to afford a remedy, or to apply an existing remedy. When local remedies are available the alien is ordinarily not entitled to the interposition of his government until he has exhausted those remedies. * * * This presupposes the existence in the state of orderly judicial and administrative processes. In theory an unredressed injury to an alien constitutes an injury to his state, giving rise to international responsibility.

If the alien receives the benefits of the same laws, protection, and means of redress for injuries which the state accords to its own nationals, there is no justifiable ground for complaint unless it can be shown that the system of law or its administration falls below the standard generally recognized as essential by the community of nations. The mere fact that the law and procedure of the state in which the alien resides differ from those of the country of which he is a national does not of itself afford justification for complaint. * * *

Elihu Root said:

> There is a standard of justice, very simple, very fundamental, and of such general acceptance by all civilized countries as to form a part of the international law of the world. The condition upon which any country is entitled to measure the justice due from it to an alien by the justice which it accords to its own citizens is that its system of law and administration shall conform to this general standard. If any country's system of law and administration does not conform to that standard, although the people of the country may be content or compelled to live under it, no other country can be compelled to accept it as furnishing a satisfactory measure of treatment to its citizens. * * *

Proceedings of the American Society of International Law 20–21, 22 (1910).

The relationship between the international minimum standard of justice and the principle of equality of aliens and nationals was highlighted in the diplomatic correspondence between the United States and Mexico on the obligation of Mexico under international law to compensate United States owners of agrarian properties expropriated by the Mexican government. Some excerpts that capture the substance and the flavor of the debate follow:

*Secretary Hull to the Mexican Ambassador, July 21, 1938:* During recent years the Government of the United States has upon repeated occasions made representations to the Government of Mexico with regard to the continuing expropriation by Your Excellency's Government of agrarian properties owned by American citizens, without adequate, effective and prompt compensation being made therefor.

* * *

If it were permissible for a government to take the private property of the citizens of other countries and pay for it as and when, in the judgment of the government, its economic circumstances and its local legislation may perhaps permit, the safeguards which the constitutions of most countries and established international law have sought to provide would be illusory. Governments would be free to take property far beyond their ability or willingness to pay, and the owners thereof would be without recourse. We cannot question the right of a foreign government to treat its own nationals in this fashion if it so desires. This is a matter of domestic concern. But we cannot admit that a foreign government may take the property of American nationals in disregard of the rule of compensation under international law. * * *

* * *

*The Mexican Minister for Foreign Affairs (Hay) to the American Ambassador, August 3, 1938:* * * * My Government maintains, on the contrary, that there is in international law no rule universally accepted in theory nor carried out in practice which makes obligatory the payment of immediate compensation nor even of deferred compensation, for expropriations of a general and impersonal character like those which Mexico has carried out for the purpose of redistribution of the land. * * *

* * *

* * * Nevertheless Mexico admits, in obedience to her own laws, that she is indeed under obligation to indemnify in an adequate manner; but the doctrine which she maintains on the subject, which is based on the most authoritative opinions of writers of treatises on international law, is that the time and manner of such payment must be determined by her own laws. * * *

The republics of our continent have let their voice be heard since the first Pan American Conference, vigorously maintaining the principle of equality between nationals and foreigners, considering that the foreigner who voluntarily moves to a country which is not his own, in search of a personal benefit, accepts in advance, together with the advantages which he is going to enjoy, the risks to which he may find himself exposed. It would be unjust that he should aspire to a privileged position * * *.

* * *

*Secretary Hull to the Mexican Ambassador, August 22, 1938:* * * *

The Government of the United States merely adverts to a self-evident fact when it notes that the applicable and recognized authorities on international law support its declaration that, under every rule of law and equity, no government is entitled to expropriate private property, for whatever purpose, without provision for prompt, adequate, and effective payment therefor. In addition, clauses appearing in the constitutions of almost all nations today, and in particular in the constitutions of the American republics, embody the principle of just compensation. These, in themselves, are declaratory of the like principle in the law of nations.

* * *

The Mexican Government refers to the fact that, when it undertook suspension of the payment of its agrarian debt, the measure affected equally Mexicans and foreigners. It suggests that if Mexico had paid only the latter to the exclusion of its nationals, she would have violated a rule of equity.

* * *

The doctrine of equality of treatment, like that of just compensation, is of ancient origin. It appears in many constitutions, bills of rights and documents of international validity. The word has invariably referred to equality in lawful rights of the person and to protection in exercising such lawful rights. There is now announced by your Government the astonishing theory that this treasured and cherished principle of equality, designed to protect both human and property rights, is to be invoked, not in the protection of personal rights and liberties, but as a chief ground of depriving and stripping individuals of their conceded rights. It is contended, in a word, that it is wholly justifiable to deprive an individual of his rights if all other persons are equally deprived, and if no victim is allowed to escape. * * *

19 Dep't of State, Press Releases 50–52, 136–37, 140, 143–44 (1938).

### *Notes*

1. On March 18, 1938, the Mexican Government expropriated the properties in Mexico of certain foreign-owned oil companies operating there, including a number of United States-owned companies.

Mexico agreed in 1938 to the establishment of a joint commission to settle agrarian claims accumulated since 1927, and made a good faith down payment of $1 million. By the Mexican–United States Agreement of 1941, which resolved all prior agrarian and other claims exclusive of those arising out of the petroleum seizures, Mexico agreed to pay $40 million in annual installments, as against claims totalling more than $350 million. After voluminous diplomatic exchange, a Mexican–United States settlement of claims arising out of the expropriation of oil properties was finally achieved in 1942. The United States, on behalf of the United States oil companies that estimated the total value of their holdings at $260 million, settled for a sum approximating $24 million payable in installments over several years, plus interest at three per cent.

2. In 1961, The Asian–African Legal Consultative Committee, on which ten Afro–Asian states (Burma, Ceylon, India, Indonesia, Iraq, Japan, Morocco, Pakistan, Sudan, and the then U.A.R.) were represented, adopted a set of Principles Concerning Admission and Treatment of Aliens. Article 12 provided that a state has the right to acquire, expropriate or nationalize an alien's property in return for compensation determined in accordance with "local laws, regulations and

orders." The Committee thus rejected the concept of an international minimum standard of justice under which aliens might have to be accorded more favorable treatment than nationals. For this reason, the delegation of Japan refused to accept the Article 12 formulation. Report of Fourth Session of Asian–African Legal Consultative Committee, Tokyo 49 (1961). This position, initially championed by the Latin American countries, was espoused during the last four decades by a majority of the developing countries and was reflected in resolutions of various United Nations Organs. See p. 687 infra.

## B. STATE RESPONSIBILITY AS CUSTOMARY INTERNATIONAL LAW

During much of the post-World War II period, criticisms were levelled at the traditional law of state responsibility by representatives of a variety of developing states that objected to being bound by rules formulated without their participation, in many cases, before they emerged as independent states. A direct attack on the continued viability of the principles of state responsibility was made by Guha Roy in Is the Law of Responsibility of States for Injuries to Aliens a Part of Universal International Law?, 55 A.J.I.L. 863, 888–90 (1961): *

> The law of responsibility * * * is not founded on any universal principles of law or morality. Its sole foundation is custom, which is binding only among states where it either grew up or came to be adopted. It is thus hardly possible to maintain that it is still part of universal international law. Whatever the basis of obligation in international law in the past, when the international community was restricted to only a few states, including those, fewer still, admitted into it from time to time, the birth of a new world community has brought about a radical change which makes the traditional basis of obligation outmoded.
>
> Once it is found that the right of diplomatic protection of their nationals abroad, claimed by states as a customary right, is not universally binding, the structure of this law as part of universal international law crumbles, for this right is assumed to be the sole basis of a state's claim to stretch out its protecting hand to its nationals in the territory of another state independently of its consent. Its elimination from universal international law necessarily means that, even outside the limited zone of the applicability of this law, the responsibility of a state for injuries to aliens remains in every case in which it may be held to be responsible exactly in the same way as in the case of its own nationals, but it remains its responsibility not to the home state of the injured alien but to the injured alien himself. In other words, it ceases to be an international responsibility and becomes a responsibility only under the municipal law of the state concerned. * * *
>
> * * * From the point of view of a state which is not party to any understanding with other states about the treatment of their nationals in one another's territory, what is ordinarily presented as the international standard of justice seems to be open to five objections.

First, a national of one state, going out to another in search of wealth or for any other purpose entirely at his own risk, may well be left to the consequences of his own ventures, even in countries known to be dangerous. For international law to concern itself with his protection in a state without that state's consent amounts to an infringement of that state's sovereignty. Secondly, a standard open only to aliens but denied to a state's own citizens inevitably widens the gulf between citizens and aliens and thus hampers, rather than helps, free intercourse among peoples of different states. Thirdly, the standard is rather vague and indefinite. Fourthly, the very introduction of an external yardstick for the internal machinery of justice is apt to be looked upon as an affront to the national system, whether or not it is below the international standard. Fifthly, a different standard of justice for aliens results in a twofold differentiation in a state where the internal standard is below the international standard. Its citizens as aliens in other states are entitled to a higher standard than their fellow citizens at home. Again, the citizens of other states as aliens in it are also entitled to a better standard than its own citizens.

For a considerable number of years, the International Law Commission tried unsuccessfully to reach agreement on a codification of the law of state responsibility for injury to aliens. Fundamentally differing views on the basic principles of state responsibility were the principal stumbling block. See Lillich, "The Current Status of the Law of State Responsibility" in International Law of State Responsibility for Injuries to Aliens 16–21 (Lillich ed. 1983).

Efforts of the U.N. Centre and Commission on Transnational Corporations since 1975 to develop a multilateral Code of Conduct on Transnational Corporations, discussed at p. 1454 infra, also remain incomplete in substantial part because of these fundamental differences. The 1985 Report of the Centre on Transnational Corporations on Work on the Formulation of the United Nations Code of Conduct on Transnational Corporations, E/C. 10/1985/s/2, summarized as follows, at p. 15–18, the views in opposition to the traditional view of state responsibility for injury to aliens supported by the United States and many other industrialized states, which embraces the international minimum standard of treatment that states must accord to aliens (footnotes omitted):

(ii) *Latin American views*

38. The theoretical foundations, as well as the practical implications of the traditional law of State responsibility, have been questioned by a number of Latin American officials and jurists. * * *

39. The basis of the objection, which was elaborated by Calvo, had two main elements. First, Calvo maintained that a sovereign independent State was entitled, by reason of the principle of equality, to complete freedom from interference in any form, whether by diplomacy or by force, from other States. Second, aliens were entitled to no greater rights and privileges than those available to nationals. Accordingly, the national courts of the host State had exclusive jurisdiction over disputes involving aliens, and aliens could seek redress only in such national courts. Thus, the Latin American response to the internation-

al minimum standard was the doctrine of national treatment. According to that doctrine, customary international law merely requires a host State to accord to aliens essentially the same rights as those enjoyed by nationals.

40. Latin American States sought to reinforce this doctrine by appropriate provisions in their national constitutions and laws and by "Calvo" clauses in concessions and other State contracts which enjoined aliens to seek redress exclusively in national courts. The doctrine was further reaffirmed in a resolution adopted by the Seventh International Conference of American States, held in Montevideo in 1933, which provided as follows:

> "[The Conference] reaffirms once more, as a principle of international law, the civil equality of the foreigner with the national as the maximum limit of protection to which he may aspire in the positive legislation of the State".

The Conference adopted the Convention on Rights and Duties of States, article 9 of which asserted that "foreigners may not claim rights other or more extensive than those of * * * nationals." [The United States attached a reservation to this article.] * * *.

* * *

42. In sum, the impact of the Calvo doctrine on the legal traditions of Latin American States is reflected in the following propositions: (a) international law requires the host State to accord national treatment to aliens; (b) national law governs the rights and privileges of aliens; (c) national courts have exclusive jurisdiction over disputes involving aliens, who may therefore not seek redress by recourse to diplomatic protection; (d) international adjudication is inadmissible for the settlement of disputes with aliens. Latin American nations have demonstrated their attachment to those principles by rejecting, with a few exceptions, the International Convention for Settlement of Investment Disputes, and by the opposition of most of them to the conclusion of bilateral investment treaties.

(iii) *Views of socialist countries*

43. The emergence of the socialist countries of Eastern Europe involved extensive nationalizations of private property, which challenged the philosophical assumptions underpinning the traditional doctrine of State responsibility. Although socialist countries subsequently undertook to pay compensation for nationalized foreign economic interests under lump-sum compensation settlements, they have rejected the traditional idea of an international minimum standard. Socialist countries maintain that the regulation of alien property falls exclusively within the province of national law.

44. * * * Accordingly, the treatment of a foreign company falls outside the purview of international law. This position is reinforced by the principle that international law is exclusively concerned with the regulation of relations between States. Such a regime does not apply to relations between a State and an entity, such as a transnational corpora-

tion, which lacks international legal personality and is not a subject of international law. Furthermore, equality of treatment between foreign and domestic enterprises is incompatible with the structure of the political and economic system of a socialist State. Socialist countries thus reject the traditional doctrine of State responsibility which, in their view, was developed to protect foreign economic interests. Such a doctrine is seen as having no validity in contemporary international law, and contravenes the basic principles of international law, namely, "principles of respect for state sovereignty, non-interference in internal affairs, equality of States * * * good neighbourly fulfilment of international obligations."

* * *

(iv) *The emergence of new States*

46. The emergence of new nations from colonialism after the Second World War and their efforts to assert their economic independence and to restructure their internal economic systems has also had an impact on traditional principles of State responsibility. The new nations, especially in Africa and Asia, generally challenged the universal validity of those principles on the ground that they had been developed without their participation or consent. Furthermore, the principles of State responsibility were assailed as unjust, inequitable and essentially colonial in character. In fact, the application of those principles to the newly independent States was seen as perpetuating an exploitative system beneficial to the developed market economies.

47. This period has witnessed, therefore, a great number of nationalizations in developing countries, particularly in the natural resource sector. In taking those measures, these countries have maintained that nationalization was a legitimate exercise of national sovereignty which did not admit of qualifications or limitations, and that the sovereign right to restructure the economic order to guarantee their economic independence would be frustrated if it were encumbered by the traditional doctrine of State responsibility. In addition, they have generally departed from the traditional standards on compensation.

## *Notes*

1. In reviewing the materials that follow it will be useful to keep in mind that, in recent years, the sharp edge of the debate over the basic principles of state responsibility for injury to aliens has been blunted as a result of pressures from a number of quarters. These have included the collapse of communism in the former U.S.S.R. and Eastern Europe and the effort in those states to move toward privatization and market economies. This has been accompanied in the developing world by a growing recognition that moves toward freer markets and privatization of business are more likely to encourage economic development than continued reliance on government-owned enterprises and managed economies. Many developing countries have increasingly acknowledged that foreign private investment has an essential role to play in fostering economic development and that to encourage an inflow of foreign private investment and its concomitant technical and managerial knowhow, it is necessary to enhance the legal security of foreign investment. The needs for capital in the developing

world, the republics of the former U.S.S.R. and the states of Eastern Europe emerging from communism and, for that matter, in the rest of the world far outstrip the available supply. The developing world and the states of Eastern Europe must compete for scarce capital and the competition has become all the keener as a result of the Third World debt crises and recession in most of the industrialized states. These developments, which create a compelling need in many of the developing states and emerging states of Europe to attract foreign private capital, have been accompanied by a widespread willingness to move beyond acerbic debates over doctrinal differences with respect to the basic principles of state responsibility and to consider more specific substantive and procedural arrangements to enhance the investment climate and legal security for foreign private investment, in which both capital-importing and capital-exporting states have come to share a common interest. See note at p. 690 infra.

2. Another issue to consider in connection with the materials that follow is what extent the development of the international law of human rights as a source of state responsibility has the potential for facilitating a reconciliation of the varying views as to the basic principles of state responsibility. Certain instances of action or inaction by agents of a state that fail to meet the international minimum standard of justice or "ordinary standards of civilization" of the traditional law of state responsibility have been accepted as violations of human rights in the Universal Declaration on Human Rights or the Covenant on Civil and Political Rights. See p. 678 supra and p. 708 infra.

## C. CONFLICTING PRINCIPLES AS APPLIED TO TREATMENT OF ALIEN PROPERTY

The issue framed during the 1930's in the United States–Mexican correspondence on the Mexican expropriations of agrarian properties, p. 680 supra, namely the obligation of a state under international law to compensate aliens whose property has been expropriated, became a particular focus of debates in the United Nations on the principles of state responsibility under customary law during the 1960's and 1970's. United Nations General Assembly Resolution on Permanent Sovereignty over Natural Resources, G.A.Res. 1803, (XVII 1962), provided that, in case of nationalization, the alien owner shall be paid "appropriate compensation, in accordance with the rules in force in the State taking such measures in the exercise of its sovereignty and in accordance with international law." For the background of this resolution, see the Protection of Private Property Invested Abroad, a Report by the Committee on International Trade and Investment, Section on International and Comparative Law, American Bar Association 18 (1963). The United States unilaterally interpreted "appropriate" to mean "prompt, adequate and effective." See Schwebel, The Story of the U.N. Declaration on Permanent Sovereignty over Natural Resources, 49 A.B.A.J. 463 (1963).

The Trade and Development Board of UNCTAD adopted Resolution 88 (XII), 12 U.N. TDOR, Supp. 1 at 1, U.N. Doc TD/B/423 (1972) stating, in part, that it

> 2. *Reiterates* that * * * such measures of nationalization as States may adopt in order to recover their natural resources are the expression of a sovereign power in virtue of which it is for each State to fix the amount of compensation and the procedure for these measures, and any dispute which may arise in that connexion falls within the sole jurisdic-

tion of its courts, without prejudice to what is set forth in General Assembly resolution 1803 (XVII);

* * *

On December 17, 1973, the U.N. General Assembly adopted Resolution 3171, on Permanent Sovereignty over Natural Resources, (XXVIII 1973), which, after recalling, among others, its Resolution 1803 (XVII), stated, in part:

The General Assembly

* * *

1. *Strongly reaffirms* the inalienable rights of States to permanent sovereignty over all their natural resources, on land within their international boundaries as well as those in the sea-bed and the subsoil thereof within their national jurisdiction and in the superjacent waters;

2. *Supports resolutely* the efforts of the developing countries and of the peoples of the territories under colonial and racial domination and foreign occupation in their struggle to regain effective control over their natural resources;

3. *Affirms* that the application of the principle of nationalization carried out by States, as an expression of their sovereignty in order to safeguard their natural resources, implies that each State is entitled to determine the amount of possible compensation and the mode of payment, and that any disputes which might arise should be settled in accordance with the national legislation of each State carrying out such measures * * *.

The vote was 109 in favor, one against (United Kingdom) and 17 abstaining (including the United States and most developed countries).

On May 1, 1974, the General Assembly adopted a Declaration on the Establishment of a New International Economic Order, G.A.Res. 3201 (S–VI 1974), which stated, in part:

1. * * * The benefits of technological progress are not shared equitably by all members of the international community. The developing countries, which constitute 70 per cent of the world's population, account for only 30 per cent of the world's income. It has proved impossible to achieve an even and balanced development of the international community under the existing international economic order. The gap between the developed and the developing countries continues to widen in a system which was established at a time when most of the developing countries did not even exist as independent States and which perpetuates inequality. * * *

* * *

4. The new international economic order should be founded on full respect for the following principles:

* * *

(e) Full permanent sovereignty of every State over its natural resources and all economic activities. In order to safeguard these resources, each State is entitled to exercise effective control over them and their exploitation with means suitable to its own situation, including the right to nationalization or transfer of ownership to its nationals, this right being an expression of the full permanent sovereignty of the State. No State may be subjected to economic, political or any other type of coercion to prevent the free and full exercise of this inalienable right.

Then, on December 12, 1974, the General Assembly adopted Resolution 3281, the Charter of Economic Rights and Duties of States, (XXIX 1974). Paragraph 2 of Article 2 of Chapter II dealt with nationalization as follows:

Each State has the right:

* * *

(c) To nationalize, expropriate or transfer ownership of foreign property, in which case appropriate compensation should be paid by the State adopting such measures, taking into account its relevant laws and regulations and all circumstances that the State considers pertinent. In any case where the question of compensation gives rise to a controversy, it shall be settled under the domestic law of the nationalizing State and by its tribunals, unless it is freely and mutually agreed by all States concerned that other peaceful means be sought on the basis of the sovereign equality of States and in accordance with the principle of free choice of means.

The vote on Article 2, Paragraph 2(c), was 104 in favor, 16 against (including the United States and many developed states) with 6 abstentions.

Lillich has commented on the foregoing developments in the institutions of the United Nations in The Valuation of Nationalized Property in International Law, Vol. 3, 191–95 (1976),* as follows:

The frontal assault on the substantive norms of Resolution 1803 (XVII) has coincided with a renewed attack on its procedural counterpart, the diplomatic protection of nationals abroad. Despite unsuccessful attempts during the past century, especially by the Latin American States, to restrict diplomatic protection, the Permanent Court of International Justice described this doctrine as "an elementary principle of international law," a view that has been reaffirmed by the International Court of Justice upon more than one occasion. Yet both the UNCTAD resolution [Resolution 88(XII), 12 U.N. TDOR, Supp. 1 at 1, U.N.Doc. TD/B/423 (1972)] and Resolution 3171 (XXVIII) purport to demolish, at least insofar as the nationalization of foreign-owned property is concerned, what one experienced observer has called "one of the most fundamental pillars of international law." [39] Abolishing the right of diplomatic protection, moreover, would emasculate whatever substantive norms governing compensation do exist, since, as Mr. Justice Holmes

* Some footnotes omitted. Reprinted by permission of University Press of Virginia.

39. Freeman, Recent Aspects of the Calvo Doctrine and the Challenge to International Law, 40 A.J.I.L. 121, 122 (1946) * * *.

once remarked, "[l]egal obligations that exist but cannot be enforced are ghosts that are seen in the law but that are elusive to the grasp." [40]

That the sponsors and supporters of the UNCTAD resolution intended to immunize themselves from potential international responsibility is apparent from the language of their resolution, which states that "any dispute" concerning a State's nationalization of foreign-owned property "falls within the sole jurisdiction of its courts * * *." Similarly, Resolution 3171 (XXVIII) provides that "any disputes which might arise should be settled in accordance with the national legislation of each State carrying out such measures," surely an open invitation to nationalizing States to enact measures making their domestic courts the final decisionmakers on the amount, if any, of "possible" compensation. Taken together, the two resolutions can be read as a thinly disguised attempt to endow the Calvo Doctrine, which maintains "that aliens are not entitled to rights and privileges not accorded to nationals, and that therefore they may seek redress for grievances only before the local authorities," with limited international status. * * *

* * *

* * * [D]espite the fact that the Calvo Doctrine, both in general and as incorporated in the UNCTAD resolution and Resolution 3171 (XXVIII), is couched in procedural terms, the real issue involved is the international responsibility of the State. Its opponents simply do not want any question raised as to compliance with their international obligations; they do not wish to run the risks of an adverse award that might result from submission to arbitration. They wish to encourage foreign capital to invest and they would like foreign talent to assist in developing the country but they also wish to be completely free to take any measures they desire without being subject to a demand for compensation arising out of violations of rights. In brief, they would have the benefits of their bargain but not its obligations.

* * *

### *Note*

It has been suggested "that the opposing positions, when stated in the abstract, are in head-on contradiction, but the conflict may not be as sharp when the issues are placed in a more specific context. When a controversy arises over expropriation, it is almost certain that issues of fair treatment and 'appropriate' compensation will be raised within the negotiating or settlement framework established by the expropriating government. The argument then is not on the issue of national competence, but about the specific circumstances and the criteria to be applied." Schachter, The Evolving International Law of Development, 15 Colum.J.Transnat'l L. 1, 8 (1976). If this is so, the nationalizing government, even if committed ideologically to exclusive national competence, is likely to be influenced by principles followed in other countries and by their own perceived interest in maintaining the confidence of foreign investors. Thus, in most cases in recent years settlements have been negotiated or submitted to arbitration, not imposed by the courts of the expropriating states. Id. More-

**40.** The Western Maid, 257 U.S. 419, 433 (1922).

over, as suggested above, in recent years without necessarily abandoning their doctrinal positions on the law of state responsibility, many developing countries have moved toward encouraging foreign investment perceived to be needed for their economic development by improving the legal protection it enjoys and have adopted specific substantive and procedural measures toward this end that are inconsistent with the doctrinal positions they espoused in the debates of the 1960s and 1970s. These measures have included entry into hundreds of bilateral treaties for the protection of foreign investment, discussed at page 764 infra, adherence to the Convention for the Settlement of Investment Disputes Between States and Nationals of Other States, discussed at p. 1459 infra, and participation in the Multilateral Investment Guaranty Agency, discussed at p. 1460 infra. For other commentary, see Weston, The Charter of Economic Rights and Duties of States and the Deprivation of Foreign–Owned Wealth, 75 A.J.I.L. 437 (1981); Brower & Tepe, The Charter of Economic Rights and Duties of States: A Reflection or Rejection of International Law?, 9 Int'l. Lawyer 295 (1975); W.D. Rogers, Of Missionaries, Fanatics, and Lawyers: Some Thoughts on Investment Disputes in The Americas, 72 A.J.I.L. 1 (1978).

## SECTION 2. CONDITIONS AND PROCEDURAL ASPECTS OF ASSERTION OF CLAIM

### A. GENERAL CONSIDERATIONS

International law imposes no duty on a state to press on the international level a claim based on injury caused by a foreign state to one of the former's nationals. Under the law of the United States, as well as most other states, the injured national has no legally enforceable right to compel his government to espouse his claim. See Borchard, The Diplomatic Protection of Citizens Abroad 355–98 (1915); Distribution of the Alsop Award, Opinion of J. Reuben Clark, Solicitor, Department of State, 7 A.J.I.L. 382, 384 (1913). Moreover, if the claim is espoused by the United States, it becomes an international claim and as such is appropriate for international negotiations between the United States and the state that has allegedly caused the injury. From the time the claim is espoused, the United States enjoys exclusive control over the handling and disposition of the claim. Sometimes, the states concerned will agree to a lump-sum settlement of all outstanding claims. See Lillich and Weston, International Claims: Their Settlement by Lump–Sum Agreements (1975). If not settled through negotiation, the states concerned might elect to submit the claim or claims to the International Court of Justice, to an ad hoc arbitral tribunal or to a special regime of arbitral tribunals established by the two states to hear all outstanding claims by nationals of one against the other. An example of the third approach is the Iran–United States Claims Tribunal established by the Algiers Accords in 1980. See Steward and Sherman, "Developments at the Iran–United States Claims Tribunal: 1981–1983," 24 Va.J.Int'l.L. 1 (1984).

In Administrative Decision V (United States v. Germany), Mixed Claims Commission, 1924, [1923–25] Administrative Decisions and Opinions 145, 190, 7 U.N.Rep.Int'l Arb.Awards 119, 152, Umpire Parker stated: "In exercising such control [the nation] is governed not only by the interest of the particular claimant but by the larger interests of the whole people of the nation and must exercise an untrammelled discretion in determining when and how the claim will be presented and pressed, or withdrawn or compromised, and the private owner will be bound by the action taken. Even if payment is made to the espousing nation in pursuance of an award, it has complete control over the fund so paid to and held by it and may, to prevent fraud, correct a mistake, or protect the national honor, at its election return the fund to the nation paying it or otherwise dispose of it." Thus, it is clear that the Executive may waive or settle a claim by the United States against a foreign state based on its responsibility for an injury to a United States national despite the latter's objection.

The claim asserted on the international plane by the state of which the injured alien is a national remains derivative in a number of respects. See Restatement (Third) § 713, Comment *a.* Thus, the injured party enjoys broad rights to settle its claim against the foreign state before it is espoused by the state of which he is a national and, by such settlement, defeat any claim by that state. Moreover, the injured person is generally required to exhaust his remedies under the local law of the foreign state before the state of which he is a national may assert a claim. See p. 693 infra. In addition, the measure of compensation that may be recovered by the state is based on the injury to its national; compensation normally does not encompass any element of recompense for injury to the state. See p. 755 infra.

Remedies available to a state whose national has suffered injury in violation of international law, including international claims procedures and other diplomatic steps or international responses, are discussed in Chapter 7. See also Restatement (Third) § 713. This state may also invoke any measures embodied in a treaty between the two states, including arbitration or adjudication. For example, treaties of friendship, commerce and navigation and other bilateral investment treaties frequently provide for resort to the International Court of Justice or to arbitration. With respect to economic rights guaranteed to nationals of member states of the European Communities, special remedies under the Rome Treaty are available. See p. 658 supra.

The customary law of state responsibility developed primarily out of claims practice, negotiation and agreement concerning liability and compensation and by decisions of arbitral tribunals and claims commissions established pursuant to international agreements, such as the General Claims Convention of 1923 between the United States and Mexico, 43 Stat. 1730. See p. 706 infra. See, e.g., Sohn & Buergenthal, International Protection of Human Rights, Chapters 1 and 2 (1973). Claims made by or against the United States are summarized in 8 Whiteman, Digest of International Law 697–906 (1967) and in the annual Report of U.S. Practice in International Law.

More recently a customary law of human rights has developed principally on the basis of the human rights provisions of the U.N. Charter and the Universal Declaration of Human Rights and various international agreements, such as the International Covenant on Civil and Political Rights. While their origins are different, there is a substantial overlap between state responsibility for violations of human rights of aliens and state responsibility for failing to accord a minimum standard of justice to aliens under traditional customary law principles, and to the extent of the overlap the operative rules may be regarded as having merged. See Restatement (Third) Part VII and Chapter 8 supra.

## B. EXHAUSTION OF LOCAL REMEDIES

Generally a state may not espouse a claim based on injury inflicted on its national by another state unless its national has first exhausted all administrative and judicial remedies available in the defendant state. The rationale for this prerequisite is to give the allegedly responsible state an opportunity to remedy the wrong under its own domestic institutions before the claim can be elevated to the international plane. See generally Amerasinghe, Local Remedies in International Law (1990) and Trindade, The Application of the Rule of Exhaustion of Local Remedies in International Law (1983).

## CLAIM OF FINNISH SHIPOWNERS (FINLAND v. GREAT BRITAIN)

Dr. Algot Bagge, Sole Arbitrator, 1934.
3 U.N.Rep.Int'l Arbitral Awards, 1479.

[Thirteen ships belonging to Finnish nationals were used by the British government in wartime service during 1916 and 1917. The Finnish government made a claim on Great Britain in 1920 for compensation on behalf of the shipowners, who had failed to obtain payment for the use of the vessels and for the loss of three of them. The claim was rejected by the British government, and the shipowners brought proceedings against the Crown before the Admiralty Transport Arbitration Board, set up under the Indemnity Act of 1920 to deal with claims for payment or compensation for the use or loss of requisitioned vessels. The Board denied compensation in a 1926 judgment, by which it found that the ships had been requisitioned by or on behalf of the former Russian government and that Great Britain had used them pursuant to an agreement with Russia. The shipowners did not appeal, although the Indemnity Act provided for recourse to the Court of Appeal. Finland again took up the claims of the shipowners and, after diplomatic approaches to Great Britain had again failed, brought the matter in 1931 to the attention of the Council of the League of Nations. The British government there contended, *inter alia,* that there was no foundation for a diplomatic claim because the shipowners had failed to exhaust their municipal remedies. Finland argued in reply, *inter alia,* that the Board's decision had turned on a question of fact—i.e., whether Russia or Great Britain had requisitioned the ships—and that there therefore could have been no successful appeal. On the recommendation of the Council, the two states agreed to submit to arbitration the question whether the Finnish shipowners had exhausted "the means of recourse placed at their disposal by British law."

[A. BAGGE, Sole Arbitrator: ]

The Finnish Government * * * contend that even if there existed a technical right of appeal from the judgment of the Arbitration Board, such right was illusory and ineffective in that any appeal, having regard to the findings of fact of the Board, was bound to fail. The failure to appeal therefore cannot be treated as a failure to exhaust local remedies within the meaning of the international rule. It is no objection to an international claim that there exists some theoretical or technical possibility of resort to municipal jurisdictions. The local remedy must be really available and it must be effective and adequate.

The contention of the Finnish Government that the local remedy must be effective, also expressed by Borchard (Diplomatic Protection of Citizens Abroad § 383) to the effect that "the rule that local remedies must be exhausted before diplomatic interposition is proper is in its application subject to the important condition that the local remedy is effective in securing redress" is, it appears, approved of by the British Government (British Countermemorial No. 21).

* * *

The Finnish Government have expressly declared that they do not suggest that in the present case there has been any failure of British law or British courts to fulfil the requirements of international law. But they allege that the remedies open to the shipowners were, anyhow, not effective: Generally, in regard to the remedies under the Indemnity Act, because damages corresponding to the loss sustained cannot under Section 2 of the Indemnity Act be recovered. Secondly, because in consequence of the provisions of the Indemnity Act that appeal is allowed only on points of law, the only remedy open to the shipowners was barred, as the decision of the Arbitration Board that there was a Russian and not an English requisition, was a finding of fact from which there was no appeal. And, in this respect, the Finnish Government * * * argue that there [was no necessity to appeal because there were reasonable grounds for believing that the appeal would not be successful]. * * *

* * *

The international claim of the Finnish Government * * * is not based on the fact of the rejection of the claim of the Finnish shipowners being a breach of international law. * * * [H]ere the alleged fact, creating liability under international law, is an initial breach of international law, consisting in the alleged taking and using of the Finnish ships without paying for it.

* * * [I]t appears that the *raison d'être* of the local remedies rule, in a case of an alleged initial breach of international law, can be solely that all the contentions of fact and propositions of law which are brought forward by the claimant Government in the international procedure as relevant to their contention that the respondent Government have committed a breach of international law by the act complained of, must have been investigated and adjudicated upon by the municipal Courts up to the last competent instance, thereby also giving the respondent Government a possibility of doing justice in their own, ordinary way. * * *

[The Arbitrator then held that an appeal from the decision of the Board would have been ineffective to change the result; nor were other remedies (such as recourse to the War Compensation Court or to the Crown by petition of right) available to the shipowners. He therefore held that the shipowners had "exhausted the means of recourse placed at their disposal by British law."]

### *Notes*

1. In the Interhandel Case (Switzerland v. United States) (Preliminary Objections), 1959 I.C.J. 6, Interhandel, a Swiss corporation, brought an action in the U.S. District Court to recover shares of a United States corporation that the United States had vested in 1942 as German assets. The District Court dismissed the complaint and the Court of Appeals affirmed. While Interhandel's petition for certiorari was pending before the Supreme Court, the Swiss Government commenced proceedings against the United States in the International Court on behalf of Interhandel. The Supreme Court subsequently reversed the Court of Appeals and remanded the case to the District Court. The International Court found that local remedies in the United States had not been exhausted.

2. As held in the *Finnish Shipowners Case,* there is no need to exhaust local remedies if it is established that such resort would be futile or such remedies are nonexistent. Velasquez–Rodriguez Case (Prel. Objections), I–A Court H.R., Series C: Decision and Judgments, No. 1 (1987). If it were shown that the Finnish shipowners had lost before the Arbitration Board because they had failed to call an available witness, would the Arbitrator have held that local remedies had been exhausted? Compare the Ambatielos Claim (Greece v. United Kingdom), 12 U.N.Rep.Int'l Arb. Awards 83, decided in 1956 by a special arbitral commission which held that failure to call an essential witness in a British proceeding necessitated the rejection of a Greek national's claim. See Bagge, Intervention on the Ground of Damage Caused to Nationals, with Particular Reference to Exhaustion of Local Remedies and the Rights of Shareholders, [1958] Brit.Y.B.I.L. 162, 167–68. If an alien claimant loses on a point of law before a court of first instance, is he obliged to appeal even if the appellate courts regard the applicable point of law as well settled? See the Panevezys–Saldutiskis Ry. Case (Estonia v. Lithuania), P.C.I.J., Ser. A/B, No. 76 (1939), in which the Court stated that if it could be substantiated that the highest Lithuanian court had already given a decision in a previous case adverse to the Estonian company's claim, there would be no need to appeal in order to satisfy the local remedies rule. Id. at 18. The Court held, however, that the highest Lithuanian court had not yet pronounced upon the applicable point of law, and the Estonian claim was rejected. Id. at 20–21. See Restatement (Third) § 713, Comment *f*; § 902, Comment *k*.

3. An exception to the local remedies rule may be applicable if "the state of the alien's nationality, which has espoused his claim, is asserting on its own behalf a separate and preponderant claim for direct injury to it arising out of the same wrongful conduct." Restatement (Second) § 208(c). See the Interhandel Case (Switzerland v. United States) (Preliminary Objections), 1959 I.C.J. 6, and the dissenting opinions. The argument has also been advanced that the local remedies rule should be inapplicable where a state has injured aliens who have established no voluntary "contacts" with the respondent state. See Meron, The Incidence of the Rule of Exhaustion of Local Remedies, [1959] Brit.Y.B.I.L. 83. Israel resorted to the latter argument in the Case of the Aerial Incident of 27th July 1955 (Israel v. Bulgaria), [1959] I.C.J. 127, in order to counter Bulgaria's contention that Israeli nationals who had been aboard an aircraft shot down by Bulgarian anti-aircraft fire over Bulgarian territory should be required to exhaust remedies available in Bulgarian courts. The Court, in dismissing Israel's claim on other grounds, did not find it necessary to reach the local remedies issue.

## CASE CONCERNING ELETTRONICA SICULA S.p.A. (ELSI)

## (UNITED STATES OF AMERICA v. ITALY)

International Court of Justice, 1989.
1989 I.C.J. 15, 28 I.L.M. 1111.

[The United States instituted proceedings against Italy in respect of a dispute arising out of the requisition by the Government of Italy of the plant and related assets of Raytheon–Elsi S.p.A., previously known as Elettronica Sicula S.p.A. (ELSI), an Italian company 100 percent owned by the Raytheon Company ("Raytheon") (and to the extent of less than one percent of the ELSI shares) by Machlett Laboratories Incorporated ("Machlett"), a United States subsidiary of Raytheon. The United States alleged that the requisition deprived Raytheon of the right and capacity to conduct an orderly liquidation of ELSI's assets and resulted in losses to Raytheon of $12,679,000. The United States alleged that the requisition violated the Treaty of Friendship, Commerce and Navigation of 1948 and a Supplementary Agreement of 1951 between Italy and the United States. Following the requisition, ELSI's directors voted to file a voluntary petition in bankruptcy. In the bankruptcy proceedings conducted by an Italian court what little remained after disposition of ELSI's assets and payment of bankruptcy administration expenses was distributed to creditors; Raytheon received nothing on its equity investment in ELSI and had to repay bank loans to ELSI that Raytheon had guaranteed. Prior to concluding on the merits that the actions of the Italian Government did not constitute breaches of the treaty or supplementary agreement, the Court discussed the contention by Italy that Raytheon had failed to exhaust its local remedies in Italy as follows (28 I.L.M. 1124–1128)]

48. It is common ground between the Parties that the Court has jurisdiction in the present case, under Article 36, paragraph 1, of its Statute, and Article XXVI of the Treaty of Friendship, Commerce and Navigation, of 2 June 1948 ("the FCN Treaty"), between Italy and the United States; which Article reads:

> "Any dispute between the High Contracting Parties as to the interpretation or the application of this Treaty, which the High Contracting Parties shall not satisfactorily adjust by diplomacy, shall be submitted to the International Court of Justice, unless the High Contracting Parties shall agree to settlement by some other pacific means."

The jurisdiction is thus confined to questions of "the interpretation or the application" of the FCN Treaty and Protocols and of the Agreement Supplementing the Treaty between the United States of America and the Italian Republic, of 26 September 1951 (which Agreement is hereinafter called "the Supplementary Agreement"), Article IX of which provides that it is to "constitute an integral part" of the FCN Treaty. This same jurisdiction may accordingly be exercised by this Chamber, created by the Court to deal with this case by virtue of Article 26, paragraph 2, of its Statute, and Articles 17 and 18 of its Rules, at the request of and after consultation with the Parties.

49. While the jurisdiction of the Chamber is not in doubt, an objection to the admissibility of the present case was entered by Italy in its Counter-Memorial, on the ground of an alleged failure of the two United States corpora-

tions, Raytheon and Machlett, on whose behalf the United States claim is brought, to exhaust the local remedies available to them in Italy. This objection, which the Parties agreed should be heard and determined in the framework of the merits, must, therefore, be considered at the outset.

50. The United States questioned whether the rule of the exhaustion of local remedies could apply at all to a case brought under Article XXVI of the FCN Treaty. That Article, it was pointed out, is categorical in its terms, and unqualified by any reference to the local remedies rule; and it seemed right, therefore, to conclude that the parties to the FCN Treaty, had they intended the jurisdiction conferred upon the Court to be qualified by the local remedies rule in cases of diplomatic protection, would have used express words to that effect; as was done in an Economic Co-operation Agreement between Italy and the United States of America also concluded in 1948. The Chamber has no doubt that the parties to a treaty can therein either agree that the local remedies rule shall not apply to claims based on alleged breaches of that treaty; or confirm that it shall apply. Yet the Chamber finds itself unable to accept that an important principle of customary international law should be held to have been tacitly dispensed with, in the absence of any words making clear an intention to do so. This part of the United States response to the Italian objection must therefore be rejected.

51. The United States further argued that the local remedies rule would not apply in any event to the part of the United States claim which requested a declaratory judgment finding that the FCN Treaty had been violated. The argument of the United States is that such a judgment would declare that the United States own rights under the FCN Treaty had been infringed; and that to such a direct injury the local remedies rule, which is a rule of customary international law developed in the context of the espousal by a State of the claim of one of its nationals, would not apply. The Chamber, however, has not found it possible in the present case to find a dispute over alleged violation of the FCN Treaty resulting in direct injury to the United States, that is both distinct from, and independent of, the dispute over the alleged violation in respect of Raytheon and Machlett. The case arises from a dispute which the Parties did not "satisfactorily adjust by diplomacy"; and that dispute was described in the 1974 United States claim made at the diplomatic level as a "claim of the Government of the United States of America on behalf of Raytheon Company and Machlett Laboratories, Incorporated". The Agent of the United States told the Chamber in the oral proceedings that "the United States seeks reparation for injuries suffered by Raytheon and Machlett". And indeed, as will appear later, the question whether there has been a breach of the FCN Treaty is itself much involved with the financial position of the Italian company, ELSI, which was controlled by Raytheon and Machlett.

52. Moreover, when the Court was, in the *Interhandel* case, faced with a not dissimilar argument by Switzerland that in that case its "principal submission" was in respect of a "direct breach of international law" and therefore not subject to the local remedies rule, the Court, having analysed that "principal submission", found that it was bound up with the diplomatic protection claim, and that the Applicant's arguments "do not deprive the dispute * * * of the character of a dispute in which the Swiss Government appears as having adopted the cause of its national * * *" (*Interhandel, Judgment, I.C.J. Reports 1959*, p. 28). In the present case, likewise, the Chamber has no doubt that the matter which colours and pervades the United States claim as a whole, is the alleged damage to Raytheon and

Machlett, said to have resulted from the actions of the Respondent. Accordingly, the Chamber rejects the argument that in the present case there is a part of the Applicant's claim which can be severed so as to render the local remedies rule inapplicable to that part.

* * *

56. The damage claimed in this case to have been caused to Raytheon and Machlett is said to have resulted from the "losses incurred by ELSI's owners as a result of the involuntary change in the manner of disposing of ELSI's assets": and it is the requisition order that is said to have caused this change, and which is therefore at the core of the United States complaint. It was, therefore, right that any local remedy against the Italian authorities, calling in question the validity of the requisition of ELSI's plant and related assets, and raising the matter of the losses said to result from it, should be pursued by ELSI itself. In any event, both in order to attempt to recover control of ELSI's plant and assets, and to mitigate any damage flowing from the alleged frustration of the liquidation plan, the first step was for ELSI—and only ELSI could do this—to appeal to the Prefect against the requisition order. After the bankruptcy, however, the pursuit of local remedies was no longer a matter for ELSI's management but for the trustee in bankruptcy * * *.

57. After the trustee in bankruptcy was appointed, he, acting for ELSI, by no means left the Italian authorities and courts unoccupied with ELSI's affairs. It was he who, under an Italian law of 1934, formally requested the Prefect to make his decision within 60 days of that request; which decision was itself the subject of an unsuccessful appeal by the Mayor to the President of Italy. On 16 June 1970, the trustee, acting for the bankrupt ELSI, brought a suit against the Acting Minister of the Interior and the Acting Mayor of Palermo, asking the court to adjudge that the defendants should

> "pay to the bankrupt estate of Raytheon–Elsi * * * damages for the illegal requisition of the plant machinery and equipment * * * for the period from April 1 to September 30, 1968, in the aggregate amount of Lire 2,395,561,600 plus interests * * *"

On 2 February 1973, the Court of Palermo, as indicated above (paragraph 43), rejected the claim. The trustee in bankruptcy then appealed to the Court of Appeal of Palermo; which Court gave a judgment on 24 January 1974 which "partly revising the judgment of the Court of Palermo" ordered payment by the Ministry of the Interior of damages of 114,014,711 lire with interest. Appeal was taken finally to the Court of Cassation which upheld the decision of the Court of Appeal, by a decision of 26 April 1975.

58. It is pertinent to note that this claim for damages (paragraph 42 above), as it came before the Court of Palermo in the action brought by the trustee, was described by that Court as being based *(inter alia)* upon the argument of the trustee in bankruptcy.

> "that the requisition order caused an economic situation of such gravity that it immediately and directly triggered the bankruptcy of the company"

* * *

Similarly the Court of Appeal of Palermo had to consider whether there was a "causal link between the requisition order and the company's bankruptcy". It is thus apparent that the substance of the claim brought to the adjudication of the Italian courts is essentially the claim which the United States now brings before this Chamber. The arguments were different, because the municipal court was applying Italian law, whereas this Chamber applies international law; and, of course, the parties were different. Yet it would seem that the municipal courts had been fully seized of the matter which is the substance of the Applicant's claim before the Chamber. For both claims turn on the allegation that the requisition, by frustrating the orderly liquidation, triggered the bankruptcy, and so caused the alleged losses.

59. With such a deal of litigation in the municipal courts about what is in substance the claim now before the Chamber, it was for Italy to demonstrate that there was nevertheless some local remedy that had not been tried; or at least, not exhausted. This burden Italy never sought to deny. It contended that it was possible for the matter to have been brought before the municipal courts, citing the provisions of the treaties themselves, and alleging their violation. This was never done. In the actions brought before the Court of Palermo, and subsequently the Court of Appeal of Palermo, and the Court of Cassation, the FCN Treaty and its Supplementary Agreement were never mentioned. This is not surprising, for, as Italy recognizes, the way in which the matter was pleaded before the courts of Palermo was not for Raytheon and Machlett to decide but for the trustee. Furthermore, the local remedies rule does not, indeed cannot, require that a claim be presented to the municipal courts in a form, and with arguments, suited to an international tribunal, applying different law to different parties: for an international claim to be admissible, it is sufficient if the essence of the claim has been brought before the competent tribunals and pursued as far as permitted by local law and procedures, and without success.

60. The question, therefore, reduces itself to this: ought Raytheon and Machlett, suing in their own right, as United States corporations allegedly injured by the requisition of property of an Italian company whose shares they held, have brought an action in the Italian courts, within the general limitation-period (five years), alleging violation of certain provisions of the FCN Treaty between Italy and the United States; this mindful of the fact that the very question of the consequences of the requisition was already in issue in the action brought by its trustee in bankruptcy, and that any damages that might there be awarded would pass into the pool of realized assets, for an appropriate part of which Raytheon and Machlett had the right to claim as creditors?

* * *

62. * * * In the present case * * * it was for Italy to show, as a matter of fact, the existence of a remedy which was open to the United States stockholders and which they failed to employ. * * *

63. It is never easy to decide, in a case where there has in fact been much resort to the municipal courts, whether local remedies have truly been "exhausted". But in this case Italy has not been able to satisfy the Chamber that there clearly remained some remedy which Raytheon and Machlett,

independently of ELSI, and of ELSI's trustee in bankruptcy, ought to have pursued and exhausted.

### *Notes*

1. A state may waive the requirement of exhaustion of local remedies, allowing claims against it to be brought by another state directly to an international tribunal. See Article V of the Convention establishing the Mexican–United States General Claims Commission, Sept. 8, 1923, 43 Stat. 1730 T.S. 678, 4 Malloy 4441, providing that no claim should be "disallowed or rejected by the Commission by the application of the general principle of international law that the legal remedies must be exhausted as a condition precedent to the validity or allowance of any claim." See Freeman, The International Responsibility of States for Denial of Justice 435–36 (1938). Where two states have agreed to arbitrate existing disputes, will they be held impliedly to have waived the local remedies rule? Authority on this point is not uniform. Amerasinghe concludes that "it would seem the better view is that whether such treaties are signed before or after the disputes arise, no waiver of the local remedies may be generally implied," citing, *inter alia,* the *ELSI* case. Amerasinghe, Local Remedies in International Law 258 (1990). Compare Garcia–Amador's view that "there can be no hard and fast rule applicable to every case, for it will always have to be ascertained whether the true purpose of the treaty was to exclude the application of the [local remedies] principle in the claim under consideration." Garcia–Amador, Sohn & Baxter, Recent Codification of the Law of State Responsibility for Injuries to Aliens (1974). An example involving an implied waiver is the Claims Settlement Declaration establishing the Iran–United States Claims Tribunal. The Declaration called for submission of claims by nationals of either party to arbitration "whether or not filed with any court" and stated that claims referred to the arbitration tribunal shall "be considered excluded from the jurisdiction of the courts of Iran; or of the United States, or of any other court." Award No. 93–2–3 [1983], 4 Iran–U.S. Claims Tribunal Reports 102 (1983).

2. The implied waiver issue may also be presented if a state agrees in a contract with an alien to arbitrate any dispute that may arise under the contract. There is substantial support for the position that there is generally an implied waiver in these circumstances although under certain circumstances the waiver may be subject to limitations. See Amerasinghe, supra note 1 at 260–268. Article 26 of the ICSID Convention, see p. 1459 infra, states as follows:

> Consent of the parties to arbitration under this Convention shall, unless otherwise stated, be deemed consent to such arbitration to the exclusion of any other remedy. A Contracting State may require the exhaustion of local administrative or judicial remedies as a condition of its consent to arbitration under this Convention.

The Report of the Executive Directors on the Convention comments that

> It may be presumed that when a State and an investor agree to have recourse to arbitration, and do not reserve the right to have recourse to other remedies or require prior exhaustion of other remedies, the intention of the parties is to have recourse to arbitration to the exclusion of any other remedy.

Doc. ICSID/2 at 10–11.

## C. WAIVER BY ALIEN (CALVO CLAUSE)

It is generally agreed that if an alien injured by a state in a manner wrongful under international law waives or settles the claim prior to diplomatic intervention by the state of which he is a national, then the waiver or settlement is effective as a defense on behalf of the respondent state, provided the waiver or settlement is not made under duress. Should the result be different if the waiver or settlement is made after the injury, but also after the alien's state has espoused the claim? See Restatement (Third) § 713, Reporters' Note 6.

More troublesome problems have been raised by the efforts of Latin American states to avoid foreign diplomatic intervention through various devices, including waivers required of aliens in advance, which limit their rights to those available under domestic law and secured by domestic legal remedies. As noted above at p. 684, such efforts have been reflected in widespread adoption of statutory and constitutional provisions embodying the Calvo Doctrine.

A number of states have not stopped with the enactment of provisions of law embodying the Calvo Doctrine, but have gone on to require of aliens doing business within their territory adherence to a so-called "Calvo Clause", requiring that in every state contract with an alien, the alien must agree to submit all disputes to the courts of the host state and renounce all claims to diplomatic intercession by the state of which the alien is a national. Shea, The Calvo Clause 24 (1955). Id. The relevant articles in the constitutions of a number of Latin American states have provided an exception for cases of denial of justice, but in some it has been expressly provided that an adverse judicial decision is not to be equated with a denial of justice. Id. at 25.

Article 18 of an agreement between the North American Dredging Company and the Government of Mexico involved in the North American Dredging Co. Case (United States v. Mexico), General Claims Commission, 1926 [1927] Opinions of Commissioners 21, 22, 4 U.N.Rep.Int'l Arb. Awards 26, 26–27 (1951), provided:

> The contractor and all persons who, as employees or in any other capacity, may be engaged in the execution of the work under this contract either directly or indirectly, shall be considered as Mexicans in all matters, within the Republic of Mexico, concerning the execution of such work and the fulfilment of this contract. They shall not claim, nor shall they have, with regard to the interests and the business connected with this contract, any other rights or means to enforce the same than those granted by the laws of the Republic to Mexicans, nor shall they enjoy any other rights than those established in favor of Mexicans. They are consequently deprived of any rights as aliens, and under no conditions shall the intervention of foreign diplomatic agents be permitted, in any matter related to this contract.

It should be noted that insofar as the clause emphasizes the duty of an alien to submit to the law of any foreign state in whose territory he happens to be, or the necessity of exhausting local remedies before a claim may arise under international law or diplomatic intervention properly be made (see p. 693 supra), the clause merely restates the otherwise existing obligations of the alien. See Lipstein, The Place of the Calvo Clause in International Law,

[1945] Brit.Y.B.I.L. 130. The controversy regarding the proper interpretation of the Calvo Clause, the extent to which it may be given effect by an international tribunal, and the ability of a private individual to prevent his state from entering a claim on his behalf, is thoroughly discussed in Shea, supra, *passim,* and sources there cited.

In its opinion in the *North American Dredging Co. Case,* supra at 27–30, 4 U.N.Rep.Arb. Awards at 30–32, the Commission stated:

> 14. Reading this article [article 18 quoted supra] as a whole, it is evident that its purpose was to bind the claimant to be governed by the laws of Mexico and to use the remedies existing under such laws. * * * But this provision did not, and could not, deprive the claimant of his American citizenship and all that that implies. It did not take from him his undoubted right to apply to his own Government for protection if his resort to the Mexican tribunals or other authorities available to him resulted in a denial or delay of justice as that term is used in international law. In such a case the claimant's complaint would be not that his contract was violated but that he had been denied justice. The basis of his appeal would be not a construction of his contract, save perchance in an incidental way, but rather an internationally illegal act.
>
> 15. What, therefore, are the rights which claimant waived and those which he did not waive in subscribing to article 18 of the contract? (a) He waived his right to conduct himself as if no competent authorities existed in Mexico; as if he were engaged in fulfilling a contract in an inferior country subject to a system of capitulations; and as if the only real remedies available to him in the fulfillment, construction, and enforcement of this contract were international remedies. All these he waived and had a right to waive. (b) He did not waive any right which he possessed as an American citizen as to any matter not connected with the fulfillment, execution, or enforcement of this contract as such. (c) He did not waive his undoubted right as an American citizen to apply to his Government for protection against the violation of international law (internationally illegal acts) whether growing out of this contract or out of other situations. (d) He did not and could not affect the right of his Government to extend to him its protection in general or to extend to him its protection against breaches of international law. But he did frankly and unreservedly agree that in consideration of the Government of Mexico awarding him this contract, he did not need and would not invoke or accept the assistance of his Government with respect to the fulfillment and interpretation of his contract and the execution of his work thereunder. * * *

The Commission, however, rejected the claim, stating:

> 18. If it were necessary to demonstrate how legitimate are the fears of certain nations with respect to abuses of the right of protection and how seriously the sovereignty of those nations within their own boundaries would be impaired if some extreme conceptions of this right were recognized and enforced, the present case would furnish an illuminating example. The claimant, after having solemnly promised in writing that it would not ignore the local laws, remedies, and authorities, behaved from the very beginning as if article 18 of its contract had

no existence in fact. It used the article to procure the contract, but this was the extent of its use. It has never sought any redress by application to the local authorities and remedies which article 18 liberally granted it and which, according to Mexican law, are available to it, even against the Government, without restrictions, both in matter of civil and of public law. * * *

20. Under article 18 of the contract declared upon the present claimant is precluded from presenting to its Government any claim relative to the interpretation or fulfillment of this contract. If it had a claim for denial of justice, for delay of justice or gross injustice, or for any other violation of international law committed by Mexico to its damage, it might have presented such a claim to its Government, which in turn could have espoused and presented it here. Although the claim as presented falls within the first clause of Article I of the Treaty, describing claims coming within this Commission's jurisdiction, it is not a claim that may be rightfully presented by the claimant to its Government for espousal and hence is not cognizable here * * *.

See also the Mexican Union Railway, Ltd. Case (Great Britain v. Mexico), Mexico–Great Britain Claims Commission, 1930, 5 U.N.Rep.Int'l Arb. Awards 115, in which the majority of the Commission stated its conviction that no person could "deprive the Government of his country of its undoubted right to apply international remedies to violations of international law committed to his hurt. * * * For the Government the contract is *res inter alios acta,* by which its liberty of action can not be prejudiced." Id. at 120.

### *Notes*

1. There have been no significant judicial or arbitral decisions with respect to the effect of a Calvo Clause since the arbitrations referred to above, which left considerable doubt as to its effectiveness. Note, The Calvo Clause, 6 Texas Int'l L. Forum 289 (1971). The United States and certain other states deny the validity of the Calvo Doctrine and the Clause on the ground that the right of protection is not the national's to waive. See [1976] Digest of U.S. Practice in Int'l Law 435. Is this position sound? Because the state's claim is essentially derivative, an individual can waive or settle any claim based on the injury attributable to the foreign state after the injury and before any intercession by the state of which he is a national, and this waiver or settlement will defeat the state claim. See p. 701 supra. To this extent, therefore, an agreement between a national and a foreign state can preempt the state's opportunity to assert a diplomatic claim for injury to its national. This being so, why can he not also effectively defeat his state's right to intervene before the fact through execution of an agreement containing a Calvo Clause?

2. The parties to the International Convention on the Settlement of Investment Disputes between States and Nationals of Other States, 1965, T.I.A.S. No. 6090, 17 U.S.T. 1270, 575 U.N.T.S. 159, have agreed not to espouse diplomatically claims of their nationals in respect of disputes submitted to arbitration under the Convention. See p. 1459 infra.

## D. NATIONALITY OF CLAIMANT

A state may generally assert a claim against another state arising out of an injury for which the latter is responsible to an individual or a juridical entity, such as a corporation, only if the injured party has the nationality of the claimant state. The principles governing the circumstances under which an individual or a corporation may be treated as a national of the claimant state for various purposes, including the law of state responsibility, have been examined in Chapter 5 at p. 394.

A state allegedly responsible for an injury to an alien with multiple nationality may refuse a claim or intercession by another state if the injured person (i) is also a national of the respondent state or (ii) is also a national of both a third state and the respondent state and the respondent state treats the person as its national for purposes of the conduct causing the injury. A claim or intercession may not be refused, however, if the nationality of the claimant state is "dominant" as a result of the injured alien's stronger ties to that state based on all relevant factors, such as extended residence, family relationships and the like. See p. 402 supra. Generally, no state may assert a claim or intercede diplomatically on behalf of a stateless person, but human rights of a stateless person are protected under international human rights law, discussed at p. 395 supra, which applies to all persons subject to a state's jurisdiction regardless of their nationality. Restatement (Third) § 713, Comments *d* and *e*.

If the claimant changes his nationality after the injury on which the claim is based has occurred, or assigns his claim to a person of another nationality, or dies and leaves heirs of a different nationality, is it likely that the claim will be espoused by any government? The frequently reiterated position of the U.S. Department of State was formulated as follows by an Assistant Legal Adviser in 1960:

> * * * Under generally accepted principles of international law and practice, a claim may properly be espoused by one government against another government only on behalf of a national of the government espousing the claim, who had that status at the time the claim arose and continuously thereafter to the date of presentation of the claim. It has been the long-standing practice of the Department to decline to espouse claims which have not been continuously owned by United States nationals.

8 Whiteman 1243. A similar position has been taken by the U.S. Foreign Claims Settlement Commission. Id. at 1245–47. See, further, 5 Hackworth 804–09. The rule, of course, may be modified by agreement between the governments of the claimant and the respondent states.

## E. ATTRIBUTION OF CONDUCT TO A STATE

This section deals with attribution of acts or omissions to states in the context of injuries to the person or property of aliens. The general rules relating to the attribution of conduct to the state have been considered in Chapter 7. In addition to being responsible for violations of its obligations under international law resulting from action or inaction of the executive, legislative or judicial branch of its government or the government of any political subdivision, a state may be responsible if the violation results from action or inaction by any "organ, agency, official, employee, or other agent of a government or of any political subdivision, acting within the scope of authority or under color of such authority." Restatement (Third) § 207.

## WILLIAM T. WAY CLAIM
## (UNITED STATES v. MEXICO)

United States and Mexico General Claims Commission, 1928.
[1928–29] Opinions of Commissioners 94.
4 U.N.Rep.Int'l Arbitral Awards 391.

[The United States claimed twenty-five thousand dollars on behalf of the brother and half-brother of Clarence Way, a United States citizen who had been shot and killed by Mexican arresting officers. It appeared that the local Alcalde, motivated by personal grievances, had issued a warrant for Way's arrest that was void on its face, under Mexican law, for failure to state the charge on which arrest was to be made. The arresting officers had been supplied with arms, and the warrant directed them "to use such means as may be suitable" in order to bring in the prisoner.

[The United States originally based its claim solely upon the alleged failure of Mexican authorities to punish the guilty parties with sufficient severity. At the oral argument, however, the United States agent put forward the alternative theory of Mexico's direct responsibility for Way's murder because occasioned by the illegal act of an official of the Mexican state of Sinaloa. The Commission rejected the first ground, and then turned to the second:]

The Commission has in other cases extensively considered cognate questions relating to responsibility of a Government for its officials, including such as are sometimes called "minor officials."

* * *

It is believed to be a sound principle that, when misconduct on the part of persons concerned with the discharge of governmental functions, whatever their precise status may be under domestic law, results in a failure of a nation to live up to its obligations under international law, the delinquency on the part of such persons is a misfortune for which the nation must bear the responsibility.

It appears from the record that the Alcalde of Aguacaliente de Baca exercised certain judicial functions. He is classified under the Code of Criminal Procedure of Sinaloa as a part of the "judicial police." Under international law a nation has responsibility for the conduct of judicial officers. However, there are certain other broad principles with respect to personal rights which appear applicable to the instant case. These principles are recognized by the laws of Mexico, the laws of the United States and under the laws of civilized countries generally, and also under international law. There must be some ground for depriving a person of his liberty. He is entitled to be informed of the charge against him if he is arrested on a warrant. Gross mistreatment in connection with arrest and imprisonment is not tolerated, and it has been condemned by international tribunals. It seems scarcely to be necessary to say that guarantees of this nature were violated when the Alcalde who, as it appears from the decision of the Sinaloa court, had authority to issue proper warrants, issued a void warrant as the court held, a warrant stating no charge, and directed the execution of that so-called warrant by armed men who killed a cultured and inoffensive man, who evidently had sought to avoid trouble with the Alcalde. For this tragic violation of personal rights secured by Mexican law and by international law, it is proper to award an indemnity in favor of the claimants. The sum of $8,000.00 may be awarded in the light of precedents which it is proper to consider in connection with the instant case.

### *Notes*

1. The General Claims Commission was set up under the United States–Mexican Convention signed September 8, 1923, 43 Stat. 1730, 4 Malloy 4441. Article I of the treaty referred to a Commission of three members all claims of citizens of Mexico and the United States "whether corporations, companies, associations, partnerships or individuals" including "all claims for losses or damages originating from acts of officials or others acting for either Government and resulting in injustice."

2. There is ample support in diplomatic practice and arbitral awards for attribution to the state of conduct of minor officials whether of the national government or political subdivisions. See [1983] II Yb.I.L.C. 161. It is well established that failure to accord reasonable police protection to an alien or to punish a violation of an alien's rights will give rise to state responsibility. See p. 716 infra.

3. Article 10 of the Draft Articles on State Responsibility prepared under the auspices of the International Law Commission attributes to a state conduct of "an organ of the State * * * such organ having acted in that capacity even if, in the particular case, the organ exceeded its competence according to internal law or contravened instructions concerning its activity." See Report of the International Law Commission on the Work of its 31st Session, G.A.O.R. 34th Sess., Supp. No. 10 (A/34/10) (1979) p. 241–42. For references to international practice, see [1972] II Yb. I.L.C. 72–153.

4. The consistent practice of the United States has been to accept responsibility under international law for acts or omissions of agents of its constituent states and to require such acceptance by the national government of foreign states. The United States paid an indemnity to Italy because authorities of the City of New Orleans failed to prevent the lynching of Italian nationals being held for trial. Moore, Digest of International Law 837 (1906).

5. A state would be responsible for acts of an entity that is not part of the governmental structure but has been empowered to exercise functions akin to those normally exercised by the state. For example, a railway or mining company to which police powers have been granted may engage the responsibility of the state for injury to an alien. The International Court of Justice held in the Case Concerning United States Diplomatic and Consular Staff in Tehran, 1980 I.C.J.Rep. 3, 29, that the conduct of the militants who had seized the embassy and staff "might be considered as itself directly imputable to the Iranian State only if it were established that, in fact, * * * the militants acted on behalf of the State * * *."

6. Private persons employed by a state to abduct a person from foreign territory may have their conduct attributed to the state on whose behalf the abduction was conducted. See *The Eichmann Case,* p. 1083 supra. Private persons may also assume public functions in times of emergency. In these cases, there may be no formal link with the machinery of the state. As indicated in Article 8 of the International Law Commission Draft Articles on State Responsi-

bility, quoted at p. 548, the International Law Commission considered that the state should bear responsibility if the persons were in fact exercising governmental authority and the circumstances justified such exercise.

## F. CIRCUMSTANCES UNDER WHICH OTHERWISE UNLAWFUL CONDUCT CAUSING INJURY TO AN ALIEN IS NOT WRONGFUL

As discussed in Chapter 7 at p. 561, conduct attributable to a state causing damage to an alien that would otherwise violate international law may be found not to be wrongful because of special circumstances, such as *force majeure,* distress and necessity. In the context of state responsibility for injury to aliens, circumstances involving an exercise of the police power or power to regulate the state's currency may preclude an inference that such conduct is wrongful. For example, conduct that is reasonably necessary for the maintenance of public order, safety or health or the enforcement of laws of the state (including revenue laws) that do not depart from the international minimum standard of justice would normally not be violative of international law. To be lawful, the conduct of the state must be reasonably necessary to achieve the indicated objective and that objective should be consistent with international legal standards. Restatement (Second) § 197 (1965).

Conduct of a state reasonably necessary to control the value of its currency or to protect its foreign exchange resources is normally lawful even though it results in injury to an alien's economic interests, subject to the rules set down in the Articles of the International Monetary Fund if it is a party thereto. See p. 735 infra. For example, devaluation of currency that causes damage to an alien does not generally violate international law and the same is usually true with respect to application to an alien of a requirement that foreign funds held within the territory of the state be surrendered against payment in local currency at the official rate of exchange. Restatement (Second) § 198 (1965).

Moreover, conduct attributable to a state and causing damage to an alien will generally not be deemed wrongful if it is reasonably necessary to protect life or property in case of disaster or other serious emergency. See the discussion of distress and necessity at p. 563 supra.

Conduct attributable to a state that would otherwise be lawful under the foregoing principles may not be so if it involves unreasonable discrimination against nationals of a state. See Restatement (Third) § 712, Comments *g* and *i* and discussion at p. 728 infra.

Application of the rules relating to circumstances under which a reasonable exercise of police powers or currency control preclude a finding of wrongfulness may be closely related to or may overlap determination of whether a taking of property of an alien, which under customary international law principles would call for compensation to the injured alien, has occurred. The line between a taking of property and permissible regulation of an alien is discussed at p. 734 infra.

# SECTION 3. SUBSTANTIVE BASES OF RESPONSIBILITY

## A. GENERAL

### RESTATEMENT (THIRD)

### § 711. State Responsibility for Injury to Nationals of Other States

A state is responsible under international law for injury to a national of another state caused by an official act or omission that violates

(a) a human right that, under § 701, a state is obligated to respect for all persons subject to its authority;

(b) a personal right that, under international law, a state is obligated to respect for individuals of foreign nationality; or

(c) a right to property or another economic interest that, under international law, a state is obligated to respect for persons, natural or juridical, of foreign nationality, as provided in § 712.

**Comment:**

*a. Human rights, "denial of justice," and injury.* This chapter deals with a state's responsibility for injury to nationals of other states. * * * Any injury to an alien for which a state is responsible under this chapter has sometimes been characterized as a "denial of justice." More commonly the phrase "denial of justice" is used narrowly, to refer only to injury consisting of, or resulting from, denial of access to courts, or denial of procedural fairness and due process in relation to judicial proceedings, whether criminal or civil. As regards natural persons, most injuries that in the past would have been characterized as "denials of justice" are now subsumed as human rights violations under clause (a). Clauses (b) and (c) include injuries that are not commonly recognized as violations of human rights but for which a state is nonetheless responsible under international law when the victim is a foreign national. See Comment *e* and § 712.

* * *

*b. International human rights as minimum standard.* Under international law, a state is responsible for injury to foreign nationals resulting from violation of their internationally recognized human rights, as well as for injury resulting from violation of other interests for which international law provides special protections to foreign nationals. Under clause (a), the state is responsible for injury due to violation of those rights which the state is obligated to respect for all persons subject to its authority, whether pursuant to international human rights agreements to which it is party, or under the customary law of human rights (§ 702); aliens enjoy these rights equally with the state's own nationals. Clause (b) declares that, in respect of foreign nationals, a state is responsible also for injury due to violation of those internationally recognized * * * [personal] rights that may not fall under § 702 and would not be protected by international law as regards the state's own nationals in the absence of international agreement. Under clause (c), a state is responsible for injury to property and other economic interests of foreign nationals that may not be recognized as human rights, and that are protected for foreign juridical persons as well as for foreign individuals. See § 712. A foreign national may also enjoy other rights under special treaties, such as those of the European Economic Community; under the Convention or the Protocol relating to the Status of Refugees (see Reporters' Note 7); under a treaty of friendship, commerce, and navigation between the state of his nationality and the state in which he resides or is present; or under the domestic law of the state of his residence or of another state.

c. *Obligation to respect human rights of foreign nationals as customary law.* A state's responsibility to individuals of foreign nationality under customary law includes the obligation to respect the civil and political rights articulated in the principal international human rights instruments—the Universal Declaration and the International Covenant on Civil and Political Rights—as rights of human beings generally (see Introductory Note to this Part), but not political rights that are recognized as human rights only in relation to a person's country of citizenship, such as the right to vote and hold office, or the right to return to one's country (Universal Declaration, Articles 13(2), 21; Covenant on Civil and Political Rights, Articles 12(4), 25). See § 701, Reporters' Note 6. Thus, a state party to the Covenant on Civil and Political Rights is responsible for any violation of any of its provisions in relation to any human being subject to its jurisdiction, regardless of the individual's nationality; but every state, whether or not a party to the Covenant, is responsible for denying to nationals of another state any right specified in the Covenant that is guaranteed by rules of customary law relating to the protection of foreign nationals. Customary law also holds a state responsible for "consistent patterns of gross violations" of human rights of any persons subject to its jurisdiction. § 702(g). As regards foreign nationals, however, a state is responsible even for a single violation of many of the civil and political rights proclaimed in the Universal Declaration (other than those applicable only to citizens), even if it is not "gross." See § 702, Comment *m*.

The Universal Declaration proclaims also certain economic, social, and cultural rights, later developed in the Covenant on Economic, Social and Cultural Rights. See Introductory Note to this Part, and § 701, Reporters' Note 6. The traditional responsibility of states under customary law does not include the obligation to extend such rights to foreign nationals. See Reporters' Note 2. Customary law, however, requires that foreign nationals be accorded the equal protection of the laws and forbids unreasonable distinctions between aliens and nationals. Distinctions between aliens and nationals in regard to some economic, social or cultural rights may not be unreasonable. See Comments *f* and *g* and Reporters' Note 3.

### *Notes*

1. The Reporters state that "[i]t is generally accepted that states may invoke recognized international human rights standards on behalf of their nationals; attempts to invoke protections going beyond international human rights standards, as in clauses (b) and (c) of this section, might be resisted by some states." Reporters Note 1. The differences of view with respect to the content and theoretical basis of the customary law of state responsibility and the

limited success of the many efforts at codification of the law of state responsibility discussed at p. 684 supra provide the backdrop for the Reporters' caveat with respect to acceptance of the protections reflected in clauses (b) and (c). To the extent that conduct causing injury to an alien constitutes a violation of a human right recognized and accepted by the great majority of developed and less developed states representing the entire spectrum of political organization and philosophy, these differences of view appear to have been sapped of much of their significance.

2. Following the invasion by Iraq of Kuwait, the U.N. Security Council confirmed the responsibility under international law of Iraq for the widespread violations by Iraq of the human and property rights of nationals of Kuwait and many third countries caused by the invasion and occupation. S/RES/674 (1990), 29 I.L.M. 1561 (1990). Subsequently, the Security Council adopted Resolution 687 (1991), S/RES/687, 30 I.L.M. 847 (1991), which reaffirmed in paragraph 16 that responsibility and established a fund and institutions and procedures for processing, evaluating and payment of claims. In paragraph 17 of the resolution, the Council decided "that all Iraqi statements made since 2 August 1990 repudiating its foreign debt are null and void", and demanded that "Iraq adhere scrupulously to all of its obligations concerning servicing and repayment of its foreign debt". The Council also decided, in paragraph 18 of the resolution, "to create a fund to pay compensation for claims that fall within the scope of paragraph 16 * * * and to establish a Commission that will administer the fund".

In paragraph 19 of the resolution, the Security Council directed the Secretary–General "to develop and present to the Security Council for decision * * * recommendations for the fund to meet the requirement for the payment of claims established in accordance with paragraph 18 * * *, and for a programme to implement the decisions in paragraphs 16, 17 and 18 * * *, including: administration of the fund; mechanisms for determining the appropriate level of Iraq's contribution to the fund based on a percentage of the value of the exports of petroleum and petroleum products from Iraq not to exceed a figure to be suggested to the Council by the Secretary–General, taking into account the requirements of the people of Iraq, Iraq's payment capacity as assessed in conjunction with the international financial institutions taking into consideration external debt service, and the needs of the Iraqi economy; arrangements for ensuring that payments are made to the fund; the process by which funds will be allocated and claims paid; * * * and the composition of the Commission designated [in paragraph 18]".

The United Nations Compensation Fund is administered by the United Nations Compensation Commission which was established by Security Council Resolution 692 (1991) of May 2, 1991, and which functions under the authority of the Security Council. The Commission is charged with responsibility for dealing with a variety of complex administrative, financial, legal and policy issues, including the mechanism for determining the level of contribution by Iraq to the Fund; the allocation of funds and payments of claims; the procedures for evaluating losses, listing claims and verifying their validity; and resolving disputed claims. See Report of the Secretary General Pursuant to Paragraph 19 of Security Council Resolution 687 (1991) S/22559 2 May 1991, 30 I.L.M. 1706 (1991). The Security Council decided in Resolution 705 S/RES/705 (1991), on May 30, 1991, that the compensation to be paid by Iraq into the United Nations Compensation Fund shall not exceed 30 percent of the annual value of the exports of petroleum and petroleum products from Iraq. 30 I.L.M. 1715. See

Report by the Secretary–General Pursuant to Paragraph 5 of Security Council Resolution 706 (1991), S/23006 4 September 1991, 30 I.L.M. 1722. The Security Council then authorized Iraq to make a first sale of $1.6 billion of oil. As of the end of 1992, however, Iraq had refused to resume international sales of oil on the ground that the U.N. compensation arrangements constituted an interference in Iraq's internal affairs. Even if Iraq exported 2.5 million barrels of oil a day, as it did in 1989, the amount contributed to the Compensation Fund would be about $6.3 billion a year. It would take many years at that rate to fund compensation for the estimated $100 to $200 billion in losses caused by Iraq's violations of international law. See Lillich, Brower, Bettauer, Magraw, Glod and others, Panel Discussion on Claims Against Iraq: The UN Compensation Commission and Other Remedies, 86 A.S.I.L.Proc. 477–500 (1992).

## B. DENIAL OF PROCEDURAL JUSTICE

## B.E. CHATTIN CLAIM
## (UNITED STATES v. MEXICO)

United States and Mexico General Claims Commission, 1927.
[1927] Opinions of Commissioners 422.
4 U.N.Rep.Int'l Arbitral Awards 282.

VAN VOLLENHOVEN, PRESIDING COMMISSIONER. 1. This claim is made by the United States of America against the United Mexican States on behalf of B.E. Chattin, an American national. Chattin, who since 1908 was an employee (at first freight conductor, thereafter passenger conductor) of the Ferrocarril Sud–Pacífico de México (Southern Pacific Railroad Company of Mexico) and who in the Summer of 1910 performed his duties in the State of Sinaloa, was on July 9, 1910, arrested at Mazatlán, Sinaloa, on a charge of embezzlement; was tried there in January, 1911, convicted on February 6, 1911, and sentenced to two years' imprisonment; but was released from the jail at Mazatlán in May or June, 1911, as a consequence of disturbances caused by the Madero revolution. He then returned to the United States. It is alleged that the arrest, the trial and the sentence were illegal, that the treatment in jail was inhumane, and that Chattin was damaged to the extent of $50,000.00, which amount Mexico should pay. * * *

* * *

3. The circumstances of Chattin's arrest, trial and sentence were as follows. In the year 1910 there had arisen a serious apprehension on the part of several railroad companies operating in Mexico as to whether the full proceeds of passenger fares were accounted for to these companies. The Southern Pacific Railroad Company of Mexico applied on June 15, 1910, to the Governor of the State of Sinaloa, in his capacity as chief of police of the State, co-operating with the federal police, in order to have investigations made of the existence and extent of said defrauding of their lines within the territory of his State. On or about July 8, 1910, one Cenobio Ramírez, a Mexican employee (brakeman) of the said railroad, was arrested at Mazatlán on a charge of fraudulent sale of railroad tickets of the said company, and in his appearance before the District Court in that town he accused the conductor Chattin—who since May 9, 1910, had charge of trains operating

between Mazatlán and Acaponeta, Nayarit—as the principal in the crime with which he, Ramírez, was charged; whereupon Chattin also was arrested by the Mazatlán police, on July 9, (not 10), 1910. On August 3 (not 13), 1910, his case was consolidated not only with that of Ramírez, but also with that of three more American railway conductors (Haley, Englehart and Parrish) and of four more Mexicans. After many months of preparation and a trial at Mazatlán, during both of which Chattin, it is alleged, lacked proper information, legal assistance, assistance of an interpreter and confrontation with the witnesses, he was convicted on February 6, 1911, by the said District Court of Mazatlán as stated above. The case was carried on appeal to the Third Circuit Court at Mexico City, which court on July 3, 1911, affirmed the sentence. In the meantime (May or June, 1911) Chattin had been released by the population of Mazatlán which threw open the doors of the jail in the time elapsing between the departure of the representatives of the Diaz regime and the arrival of the Madero forces. * * *

* * *

12. The next allegation on the American side is that Chattin's trial was held in an illegal manner. The contentions are: * * * (c) that the proceedings were unduly delayed; (d) that an exorbitant amount of bail was required; (e) that the accused was not duly informed of the accusations; * * * (h) that there were no oaths required of the witnesses; * * * and (j) that the hearings in open court which led to sentences of from two years' to two years and eight months' imprisonment lasted only some five minutes. * * *

* * *

15. For undue delay of the proceeding (allegation c), there is convincing evidence in more than one respect. The formal proceedings began on July 9, 1910. Chattin was not heard in court until more than one hundred days thereafter. The stubs and perhaps other pieces of evidence against Chattin were presented to the Court on August 3, 1910; Chattin, however, was not allowed to testify regarding them until October 28, 1910. Between the end of July, and October 8, 1910, the Judge merely waited. * * * If the necessity of new evidence was not seriously felt before October, 1910, this means that the Judge either has not in time considered the sufficiency of Ramírez's confession as proof against Chattin, or has allowed himself an unreasonable length of time to gather new evidence. * * * Another remarkable proof of the measure of speed which the Judge deemed due to a man deprived of his liberty, is in that, whereas Chattin appealed from the decree of his formal imprisonment on July 11, 1910—an appeal which would seem to be of rather an urgent character—"the corresponding copy for the appeal" was not remitted to the Appellate Court until September 12, 1910; this Court did not render judgment until October 27, 1910; and though its decision was forwarded to Mazatlán on October 31, 1910, its receipt was not established until November 12, 1910.

16. The allegation (d) that on July 25, 1910, an exorbitant amount of bail, to-wit a cash bond in the sum of 15,000.00 pesos, was required for the accused is true; but it is difficult to see how in the present case this can be held an illegal act on the part of the Judge.

17. The allegation (e) that the accused has not been duly informed regarding the charge brought against him is proven by the record, and to a painful extent. The real complainant in this case was the railroad company, acting through its general manager; this manager, an American, not only was allowed to make full statements to the Court on August 2, 3, and 26, 1910, without ever being confronted with the accused and his colleagues, but he was even allowed to submit to the Court a series of anonymous written accusations, the anonymity of which reports could not be removed (for reasons which he explained); these documents created the real atmosphere of the trial. Were they made known to the conductors? Were the accused given an opportunity to controvert them? There is no trace of it in the record, nor was it ever alleged by Mexico. * * * It is not shown that the confrontation between Chattin and his accusers amounted to anything like an effort on the Judge's part to find out the truth. Only after November 22, 1910, and only at the request of the Prosecuting Attorney, was Chattin confronted with some of the persons who, between July 13 and 21, inclusive, had testified of his being well acquainted with Ramírez. It is regrettable, on the other hand, that the accused misrepresents the wrong done him in this respect. He had not been left altogether in the dark. According to a letter signed by himself and two other conductors dated August 31, 1910, he was perfectly aware even of the details of the investigations made against him; so was the American vice-consul on July 26, 1910, and so was one H.M. Boyd, a dismissed employee of the same railroad company and friend of the conductors, as appears from his letter of October 4, 1910. Owing to the strict seclusion to which the conductors contend to have been submitted, it is impossible they could be so well-informed if the charges and the investigations were kept hidden from them.

* * *

19. The allegation (h) that the witnesses were not sworn is irrelevant, as Mexican law does not require an "oath" (it is satisfied with a solemn promise, *protesta,* to tell the truth), nor do international standards of civilization.

* * *

21. The allegation (j) that the hearings in open court lasted only some five minutes is proven by the record. This trial in open court was held on January 27, 1911. It was a pure formality, in which only confirmations were made of written documents, and in which not even the lawyer of the accused conductors took the trouble to say more than a word or two.

22. The whole of the proceedings discloses a most astonishing lack of seriousness on the part of the Court. * * * Neither during the investigations nor during the hearings in open court was any such thing as an oral examination or cross-examination of any importance attempted. It seems highly improbable that the accused have been given a real opportunity during the hearings in open court, freely to speak for themselves. It is not for the Commission to endeavor to reach from the record any conviction as to the innocence or guilt of Chattin and his colleagues; but even in case they were guilty, the Commission would render a bad service to the Government

of Mexico if it failed to place the stamp of its disapproval and even indignation on a criminal procedure so far below international standards of civilization as the present one * * *.

29. Bringing the proceedings of Mexican authorities against Chattin to the test of international standards (paragraph 11), there can be no doubt of their being highly insufficient. Inquiring whether there is convincing evidence of these unjust proceedings (paragraph 11), the answer must be in the affirmative. Since this is a case of alleged responsibility of Mexico for injustice committed by its judiciary, it is necessary to inquire whether the treatment of Chattin amounts even to an outrage, to bad faith, to wilful neglect of duty, or to an insufficiency of governmental action recognizable by every unbiased man (paragraph 11); and the answer here again can only be in the affirmative.

30. * * * Irregularity of court proceedings is proven with reference to absence of proper investigations, insufficiency of confrontations, withholding from the accused the opportunity to know all of the charges brought against him, undue delay of the proceedings, making the hearings in open court a mere formality, and a continued absence of seriousness on the part of the Court. Insufficiency of the evidence against Chattin is not convincingly proven; intentional severity of the punishment is proven, without its being shown that the explanation is to be found in unfairmindedness of the Judge. * * * Taking into consideration, on the one hand, that this is a case of direct governmental responsibility, and, on the other hand, that Chattin, because of his escape, has stayed in jail for eleven months instead of for two years, it would seem proper to allow in behalf of this claimant damages in the sum of $5,000.00, without interest.

[Opinion of Nielsen and dissent of MacGregor, Commissioners, are omitted.]

### *Notes*

1. The Restatement (Third) treats denials of basic due process in criminal proceedings, exemplified by the facts in the *B.E. Chattin Claim,* as violations of the human rights of aliens. As examples of injuries that would be treated under customary international law as unlawful failures to afford a minimum standard of justice to an alien and that under contemporary law are accepted as violations of human rights under the Universal Declaration of Human Rights or the Covenant on Civil and Political Rights, the Restatement Reporters cite (1) denials of due process in criminal proceedings (e.g., arbitrary arrest; unlawful or prolonged detention; unreasonably delayed or unfair trial; being tried twice for the same offense; denial of right to defend oneself and confront witnesses or to communicate with representatives of one's government; and (2) arbitrary and unreasonable use of force by governmental representatives (e.g., excessive use of force by state officials; inhuman treatment and torture to elicit "confession"). Restatement (Third) § 711, Reporters' Note 2. The Reporters further comment on the relevant state practice and decisions as follows:

> Claims were also made on behalf of aliens for other actions violating rights later recognized in the Universal Declaration, such as freedom of speech, freedom of religion, freedom to travel within a country, and the right

to marry or obtain a divorce. See, e.g., 8 Whiteman, Digest 402; L. of N. Doc. C. 26.M.21. 1929, II, 32; Freeman 511. There is some authority in international law to support such claims, but these freedoms might be restricted to resident aliens, and might be denied in time of national emergency.

There were also claims for injury due to denial to foreign nationals of benefits enjoyed by nationals, such as social security or aid to indigents or incompetents, or due to other discrimination between aliens and nationals or against aliens of particular nationality. See 3 Hackworth 650–52; 8 Whiteman, Digest 387. International law forbids some such discriminations, but others are permitted. See § 712, Comments *f* and *i*. Compare the corresponding jurisprudence under the "equal protection" clause of the Fourteenth Amendment of the United States Constitution, § 722.

There appears to be no record, however, of a state objecting to imprisonment of its nationals for debt, although that is prohibited by Article 11 of the Covenant on Civil and Political Rights. * * *

Restatement (Third) § 711, Reporters' Note 2.

2. There are denials of procedural justice that would be unlawful under customary international law that would not rise to the level of human rights violations. An example would be denial of access to domestic courts in civil proceedings for the determination of an alien's rights. Von Bokkelen Claim, 2 Moore, Int'l Arb. 842. International agreements commonly guarantee reasonable access to a court or other tribunal on the same basis as nationals. See, e.g., Friendship, Commerce and Navigation Treaty between the United States and the Netherlands, March 27, 1956, Art. V(1), 8 U.S.T. 2043, T.I.A.S. No. 3942, 285 U.N.T.S. 231. See also Ruden and Co. (United States v. Peru), 2 Moore, Int'l Arb. 1653 (1870); Johnson Claim (United States v. Peru), 2 Moore, Int'l Arb. 1656; Council of Europe, Convention for the Protection of Human Rights and Fundamental Freedoms, art. 6(1), Eur.T.S. No. 5 (1950), Cmd. No. 8969 (T.S. No. 71) (1953), 213 U.N.T.S. 221; U.N. Universal Declaration of Human Rights, Art. 10 (1948), [1948] U.N.Yb.Hum.Rights 458; American Declaration of The Rights and Duties of Man, art. XVIII (1948), 43 A.J.I.L.Supp. 133, 136 (1949), United Nations Covenant on Civil and Political Rights arts. 9(3), 14, at p. 608. Consider the relationship between state immunity, discussed at p. 1046 supra, and denial of procedural justice. Can the dismissal of an action by an alien against the state on the ground of immunity give rise to a proper claim of denial of justice? See Restatement (Second) § 180(2) (1965).

3. It is well settled that mere error in a decision or relatively minor procedural irregularities do not constitute unlawful denials of procedural justice. The injustice must be egregious. The decision must be "so obviously wrong that it cannot have been made in good faith and with reasonable care," or "a serious miscarriage of justice" must otherwise be "clear." See e.g., Herrera v. Canevaro & Co., [1927–28] Ann.Dig. 219 (Sup.Ct.Peru). Examples of procedural insufficiencies or mistakes for which states have not been held responsible under international law include failure of a witness to take an oath, incorrect but good faith misapplication or misinterpretation of the law, and improper dismissal of a case for lack of jurisdiction (when another forum was available). Restatement (Third) § 711, Reporter's Note 2(B).

## C. FAILURE TO PROTECT ALIENS OR TO APPREHEND AND PROSECUTE THOSE WHO WRONGFULLY INFLICT INJURY ON ALIENS

### LAURA M.B. JANES CLAIM (UNITED STATES v. MEXICO)

United States and Mexico General Claims Commission, 1926.
[1927] Opinions of Commissioners 108.
4 U.N.Rep.Int'l Arb.Awards 82.

[By the Commission:] * * * 3. Byron Everett Janes, for some time prior to and until the time of his death on July 10, 1918, was Superintendent of Mines for the El Tigre Mining Company at El Tigre. On or about July 10, 1918, he was deliberately shot and killed at this place by Pedro Carbajal, a former employee of the Mining Company who had been discharged. The killing took place in the view of many persons resident in the vicinity of the company's office. The local police *Comisario* was informed of Janes' death within five minutes of the commission of the crime and arrived soon thereafter at the place where the shooting occurred. He delayed for half an hour in assembling his policemen and insisted that they should be mounted. The El Tigre Mining Company furnished the necessary animals and the posse, after the lapse of more than an hour from the time of the shooting, started in pursuit of Carbajal who had departed on foot. The posse failed to apprehend the fugitive. Carbajal remained at a ranch six miles south of El Tigre for a week following the shooting, and it was rumored at El Tigre that he came to that place on two occasions during his stay at the ranch. Subsequently information was received that Carbajal was at a mescal plant near Carrizal, about seventy-five miles south of El Tigre. This information was communicated to Mexican civil and military authorities, who failed to take any steps to apprehend Carbajal, until the El Tigre Mining Company offered a reward, whereupon a local military commander was induced to send a small detachment to Carrizal, which, upon its return reported that Carbajal had been in this locality but had left before the arrival of the detachment, and that it was therefore impossible to apprehend him.

4. It is alleged in the Memorial that the Mexican authorities took no proper steps to apprehend and punish Carbajal; that such efforts as were made were lax and inadequate; that if prompt and immediate action had been taken on one occasion there is reason to believe that the authorities would have been successful; that it was only after a money reward for the capture of Carbajal had been offered that some dilatory steps were taken to apprehend him in a nearby town where he was staying. * * *

* * *

10. * * * With respect to these preliminary steps, we feel justified in reaching the conclusion that they were inefficient and dilatory. From an examination of the evidence on this point accompanying the Memorial, and more particularly from an examination of the records produced by the Mexican Government, we are constrained to reach the conclusion that there was clearly such a failure on the part of the Mexican authorities to take

prompt and efficient action to apprehend the slayer as to warrant an award of indemnity. * * *

* * *

17. Carbajal, the person who killed Janes, was well known in the community where the killing took place. Numerous persons witnessed the deed. The slayer, after killing his victim, left on foot. There is evidence that a Mexican police magistrate was informed of the shooting within five minutes after it took place. The official records with regard to the action taken to apprehend and punish the slayer speak for themselves. Eight years have elapsed since the murder, and it does not appear from the records that Carbajal has been apprehended at this time. Our conclusions to the effect that the Mexican authorities did not take proper steps to apprehend and punish the slayer of Janes is based on the record before us consisting of evidence produced by both Governments.

18. The respondent Government has not denied that, under the Convention of September 8, 1923, acts of authorities of Sonora may give rise to claims against the Government of Mexico. The Commission is of the opinion that claims may be predicated on such acts.

* * *

[Separate opinion of NEILSEN, COMMISSIONER, omitted.]

### *Notes*

1. In the *William E. Chapman Claim* (United States v. Mexico), the United States and Mexico General Claims Commission held Mexico liable for failure of Mexican authorities (i) to take appropriate steps to protect a U.S. Consul who was shot and seriously wounded at Puerto Mexico after threats to United States diplomatic and consular representatives had been communicated to Mexican authorities and (ii) to take proper steps to apprehend and punish the person who did the shooting. 4 U.N.Rep.Int'l Arb.Awards 632.

2. Restatement (Second) § 183 provides: "A state is responsible under international law for injury to the person or property of an alien caused by conduct that is not itself attributable to that state, if

> (a) the conduct is either (i) criminal under the law of the state, (ii) generally recognized as criminal under the laws of states that have reasonably developed legal systems, or (iii) an offense against public order, and
>
> (b) either (i) the injury results from the failure of the state to take reasonable measures to prevent the conduct causing the injury, or (ii) the state fails to take reasonable steps to detect, prosecute, and impose an appropriate penalty on the person or persons responsible for the conduct if it falls within Clause (a)(i)."

The Restatement (Third) treats injuries to aliens of these types as violations of international law that fall short of violations of human rights and that are therefore covered by § 711(b). Restatement (Third) § 711, Reporters' Note 2(B).

Compare Art. 13(2) of the Sohn & Baxter Draft Convention on the International Responsibility of States for Injuries to Aliens, 55 A.J.I.L. 545, 575 (1961): "Failure to exercise due diligence to apprehend, or to hold after apprehension as required by the laws of the State, a person who has committed against an alien any [criminal] act * * * is wrongful, to the extent that such conduct deprives that alien or any other alien of the opportunity to recover damages from the person who has committed the act." The *Janes Case* is expressly disapproved in the Explanatory Note; the authors state that "the opportunity to see the criminal punished" is "not recognized by any mature legal system as a legally protected right." Draft No. 12 with Explanatory Notes, at 138–39 (1961). See also Article 7(3) of a draft convention presented to the International Law Commission in 1961, [1961] II Yb.I.L.C. 47, U.N.Doc.A/CN.4/34 & Addendum.

### *LILLICH & PAXMAN, STATE RESPONSIBILITY FOR INJURIES TO ALIENS OCCASIONED BY TERRORIST ACTIVITIES*

26 Am.U.L.Rev. 217–221, 245–249, 276, 305–307 (1977).*

Scarcely a day passes without press reports of another act of transnational terrorism, whether it be an aerial hijacking like the June 1976 takeover of the Air France airliner flown to Uganda, a political kidnapping such as the spectacular seizure in December 1975 of the oil ministers from the Organization of Petroleum Exporting Countries (OPEC) in Vienna, or an indiscriminate act of violence designed to achieve publicity for its perpetrators or their cause. Such acts obviously present a serious challenge to the existing international legal order. At the outset, it has become apparent that, in Brian Jenkins' words, "[i]nternational law and the rules of warfare as they now exist are inadequate to cope with this new mode of conflict." Yet attempts to remedy the substantive gaps and structural defects of international law, both within and without the United Nations, have met with relatively little success. The United Nations Security Council debate following the Entebbe rescue operation revealed once again the wide divergence in the world community over how—and, indeed, perhaps even whether—to approach the transnational terrorism phenomenon.

Just because there has been little progress in formulating new norms and creating new procedures does not mean, of course, that international law has nothing to contribute to the effort to combat such terrorism. As Jenkins states, "[i]f international law is to have greater weight in this area of conflict, new laws must be created;" yet he adds this significant qualification: "or old ones modified to deal with the unique problems of international terrorism." One important body of traditional international law which provides a significant, if in some cases relatively marginal, sanction against transnational terrorism is the law of state responsibility for injuries to aliens. Derived from state practice, arbitral decisions and codification attempts over many years, this body of international law offers a rich vein of relevant precedent that can be worked for profit.

Although rarely speaking directly to transnational terrorism, the norms governing state responsibility provide by analogy ample insights into how they might be applied in the terrorism context. In the first place, "such activities when emanating directly from the Government itself or indirectly from organizations receiving from it financial or other assistance or closely associated with it by virtue of the constitution of the State concerned,

* Some footnotes omitted. Reprinted by permission of the American University Law Review.

amount to a breach of International Law." Secondly, while the duty of a state to prevent the commission of acts injurious to foreign states, including acts injurious to their nationals as well, does not imply an obligation to suppress all inimical conduct by private persons or groups, "States are under a duty to prevent and suppress such subversive activity against foreign Governments as assumes the form of armed hostile expeditions or attempts to commit common crimes against life or property." Finally, even when a state does not incur responsibility for breach of the first two duties, it may render itself liable internationally as an "accessory-after-the-fact" if it "fails to take reasonable steps to apprehend and punish the wrongdoer, or if the punishment is so trivial as to be contemptuous of the wrong done to the alien." This duty to take reasonable steps to apprehend and punish arguably includes a duty to extradite if a state apprehends the wrongdoer but does not submit him to prosecution.

[The authors discuss in detail the authorities bearing on a state's responsibility for failure to prevent injuries to aliens and their property and conclude:]

That a state has a general duty under international law to prevent whenever possible injuries to aliens caused by ordinary individuals is apparent. The present survey of arbitral decisions, state practice, and codification attempts solidly substantiates the point. Moreover, that duty extends to injuries caused by terrorists. Yet the duty is not absolute, for states are not held accountable for all injuries to all aliens inflicted by such individuals. What is required is that they exercise "due diligence" with regard to the prevention of these injuries. That means essentially that states are to take all reasonable measures under the circumstances to prevent terrorist acts.

"Due diligence," in turn, depends upon certain basic assumptions about the ability of the state to fulfill its duty. First, it assumes that the state has the means to provide protection. If the state lacks such means, or if the possibility of providing protection is very remote, then frequently no responsibility for the injury will be imposed. * * *

Second, "due diligence" assumes that the state had the opportunity to prevent the act but failed to do so. In the terrorism context, opportunity would be linked most often to the question of some sort of prior notice. Where states have been put on actual notice or "alerted in good time" of an imminent threat of terrorism, another element to establish liability under the principles of state responsibility would be present. Indeed, Sohn and Baxter have suggested that being put on constructive notice, as, for example, when a number of terrorist acts have occurred in the past in the same area, may be sufficient to satisfy the notice test. * * *

Having been put on notice, the final question becomes: what did the state do to avert the danger, or indeed could the danger have been averted? Here again the actions of the state are judged by their reasonableness under the circumstances. Where the state neglects or fails to take reasonable measures, responsibility will attach. In addition, where the state itself or its officials are involved in the promotion of terrorism, responsibility obviously runs directly to the state.

* * *

What of the situation where it is general knowledge that terrorists have been active in kidnapping either alien corporate officials or persons with special international status? The local authorities can be assumed to have knowledge of the likelihood of it happening again, yet they may lack the means to provide protection for every foreigner. Thus the local authorities notify the aliens of the inability to afford them protection, and advise them to employ their own body guards. The local authorities concentrate their limited resources on prevention, but a major effort is directed to after-the-fact pursuit and prosecution. After the next kidnapping will state responsibility arise? Since the local authorities were unable to prevent it—an assumption reasonable in these circumstances—liability probably will not be imposed. * * *

What of the actions of the authorities after a kidnapping when negotiations are being undertaken by the parties? What would be the significance of the fact that the authorities so bungled the situation as to cause the death of the hostage? A statement made by Huber in the *British Property in Spanish Morocco* Case suggests that there continued to be a duty: the authorities must take steps "as far as possible to avert the consequences of such acts." The deaths of the Israeli Olympic athletes held hostage in Munich in 1972 arguably may be regarded as a breach of this duty. Liability certainly would exist in this case if the German authorities actually acted in the wholly reckless manner that has been suggested.[112]

The most difficult aspect of applying traditional state responsibility norms to terrorist situations is that the latter rarely conform to the neat prior-notice pattern. Surprise attacks are endemic to terrorism; neither the authorities nor the victim know in advance what is to happen. How then, can responsibility be assigned if there really is no opportunity to prevent the act other than comprehensive surveillance efforts? Huber, it will be recalled, held in the *Ziat, Ben Kiran* Case that the suddenness of the act vitiated responsibility based upon the duty to protect rationale.

**112.** In the early morning hours of 5 September 1972, eight members of the Black September movement infiltrated the Israeli pavilion, assassinated two Israeli athletes and took nine other ones hostage. In exchange for the hostages, the Arab terrorists demanded that Israel release 234 Arab prisoners. When the Israeli Government refused to cooperate, arrangements were made with the West German Government to have the terrorists and their hostages flown to Cairo, but at the airport police marksmen opened fire on the terrorists, in the process killing all nine Israeli hostages. The German authorities were able to arrest the three terrorists who survived the shooting.

Officials of other governments, journalists, and legal scholars have criticized the police action at the airport as a hasty and ill-conceived use of force. On 20 September 1972, the West German Government issued a "white paper" about the incident which took the position that all reasonable security measures had been taken by the Munich police. Although the Israelis had requested special protection and the police had received information regarding possible political incidents, they had received no specific threats against the Israeli athletes. Had such information been received, however, even massive security measures, given the terrorists' method of operation, would not necessarily have prevented the initial attack. West Germany advanced no explanation for the disastrous outcome of the police action at the airport. Arguably, state responsibility may arise for injuries resulting from such an action. Liability also might be based on the ground that the security measures were inadequate, especially in light of the fact that the victims of the incident had made special protection demands. Although the West German Government has not admitted responsibility on either ground, it has paid 3,200,000 Deutsche Mark to the families of the Israeli victims. Rousseau, Chronique Des Faits Internationaux, 77 R.G.D.I.P., supra note 31, at 1145–49 (1973).

[On the basis of a thorough review of the authorities dealing with state responsibility for failure to apprehend or punish terrorists, the authors summarize their conclusions as follows:]

While the acts of terrorists are usually front page material, word of their prosecution, punishment, or release—especially the latter—rarely is thought to be newsworthy. Unfortunately, it is increasingly common for states to adopt, either voluntarily or under threats of additional terrorist acts, a lenient policy toward the punishment of terrorists. While undeniably justified, the widespread indignation over the recent release by France of Abu Daoud, the Palestinian terrorist leader allegedly responsible for the deaths of the Israeli Olympic athletes in Munich, was nevertheless somewhat selective. * * * Failure to extradite transnational terrorists, while offering an attractive basis for claiming that a state responsibility norm has been violated, has not yet been recognized as a basis for such an international claim absent the existence of a treaty. Arguably, it should be, but at present states simply may have to "rely upon the goodwill of the requested state" in extraditing terrorists. Similarly, failure to apprehend and punish transnational terrorists, while also an attractive basis for imposing state responsibility obligations, has not been recognized as generating international liability in the absence of a treaty commitment condemning the particular terrorist act and creating a specific duty of prosecution or extradition.

* * *

The review of international law sources contained in this part * * * suggests that states are under certain duties with respect to the apprehension, prosecution, and punishment of terrorists. Failure to comply with these duties may give rise to claims based upon traditional state responsibility principles.

The ease with which the duty may be imposed depends upon whether local or nonlocal terrorism is involved. The duty applies most clearly to cases arising within the borders of a single country; that is, where both the terrorist act and the arrest, trial, and punishment take place in one state. On the other hand, where the act occurs in one country and the terrorist flees to another country, the existence of the duty, if any, is clouded by the customary international law practice concerning asylum and extradition. * * *

* * *

### *Note*

Lillich and Paxman conclude (at pp. 307–309) that a state may be held responsible for injury to aliens arising from, inter alia, its (a) subsidization and support of terrorists; (b) complicity with terrorists; (c) encouraging, counseling, and creating opportunity for terrorists; (d) failing to use due diligence to prevent terrorist acts; and (e) failure to apprehend or punish terrorists.

## D. INJURY TO ECONOMIC INTERESTS OF ALIENS

### *1. Non-Commercial Risks of International Business*

A principal focus of the law of state responsibility in recent decades has been the extent to which it is a source of legal protection for the economic interests of alien investors against non-commercial risks. These non-commercial risks have been described as follows in Pugh, Legal Protection of International Transactions Against Non–Commercial Risks, in Lawyer's Guide to International Business Transactions 301–311 (Surrey & Shaw eds., 1963): *

> International business transactions in many [developing] areas of the world involve an important measure of non-commercial risks. * * * To a large extent non-commercial risks are the inevitable results of the turbulent currents of political, economic and social change which are surging in these areas, and their existence is a fact of international business that sets operations in the developing countries off sharply from operations in the industrialized world. * * *
>
> What are these non-commercial risks? In their starkest forms they are familiar enough. Examples that jump to mind are expropriation by the foreign government without adequate compensation, violation by the foreign government of a concession or other agreement, imposition of foreign exchange restrictions that prevent remittance of profits abroad and import restrictions that prevent importation of necessary equipment or raw materials. While such events may be catastrophic in their impact on a foreign enterprise they are, in a sense, simpler to isolate and to achieve a measure of protection against then less obvious factors that may be encountered.
>
> "Creeping expropriation" is a short-hand term that has gained wide currency to describe the great variety of more subtle measures that can be employed by a foreign government to interfere with business operations and impair the rights of the foreign investor. Residence and labor permits for key United States personnel or import permits for essential materials and equipment may be unreasonably delayed or refused. Taxes that discriminate in substance, if not in form, against foreign-owned business may be imposed. Profits may be restricted by governmental price controls or reduced as a result of governmentally-subsidized competition. In these cases, the problem of securing legal protection is often aggravated by the difficulties of defining the violation of the foreigner's rights and of evaluating the amount of the loss that can be said to have resulted.
>
> Beyond this, there is an area of risk of substantial loss to the foreign business resulting from local governmental interference against which no effective legal protection is possible. Governments in the developing countries commonly play a far more pervasive role in business operations than is usual in the industrialized countries of the West. Achieving industrial progress in a backward economy requires extensive economic planning and, in many cases, requires the local government to become involved to a marked degree in certain commercial and industrial undertakings. As a result of the extent of the local government's role in business operations in developing countries and the severe shortage of trained civil servants in many of these countries, the rights of the

foreign businessman may be more seriously impaired through governmental inefficiency than through governmental design.

The non-commercial risks in international business transactions are particularly accentuated in the case in which the United States firm makes a direct investment abroad. Here substantial assets of the investor are exposed to expropriation or nationalization, or to requisition or damage in the event of war or insurrection. In addition, the investor faces the risk that currency restrictions will preclude remittance of profits home in U.S. dollars and the risk that if it should be decided to contract or abandon the venture, it may be impossible to repatriate in dollars some or all of the dollar capital originally invested. Devaluation of the local currency may seriously diminish the real return on the investment. Then, too, because of the extent of the involvement of a direct investment in the local economy, the exposure to government harassment or interference at any number of points is maximized.

Non-commercial risks must also be reckoned with when the United States firm makes no direct contribution of capital but merely makes an investment in the form of rights to patents, trademarks, secret processes and formulae and similar industrial property or in the form of technical or managerial services to a firm owned by local interests. * * * [S]uch contributions normally will be supplied under some sort of contractual arrangement, such as a license agreement, a technical assistance agreement or a management contract, calling for periodic payments in U.S. dollars. In such cases, valuable intangible property including patents, secret processes and other know-how, rights to which have been transferred to the foreign enterprise, may be exposed to seizure along with the assets of the foreign enterprise to which they have been made available. * * * In addition, currency inconvertibility may prevent remittance of the consideration in dollars to the United States supplier of know-how or the imposition of local taxes may deprive the supplier of a fair return on the know-how supplied. * * *

Non-commercial risks are also faced by a United States firm that does no more than sell goods into the foreign market. Whenever goods are exported to a less developed country on terms other than under irrevocable letter of credit, there is likely to be a significant element of non-commercial risk. The longer the period of the credit extended, of course, the greater the risk. Where heavy capital goods are sold on credit extending over a number of years, the magnitude of the risk may be substantial. The risks here take a number of forms. For example, there is risk that U.S. dollars will not be available to meet the prescribed payments of principal and interest. If payment is called for in local currency, the risk of currency depreciation or devaluation is present. There is the danger that after fabrication of the goods and the shipment from the point of fabrication, the export may be prevented by the imposition of * * * restrictions by the foreign government.

* * *

Recognizing that non-commercial risks pose an important obstacle to foreign investment, most of the developing countries of the non-communist world have taken steps to grant special assurances to foreign investors against many of the more serious of these risks in an effort to encourage the desperately needed inflow of foreign private capital.

Such assurances may be negotiated on an ad hoc basis and embodied in a concession agreement or a guarantee agreement. In recent years, however, it has become increasingly common to find such assurances made available to the foreign investor pursuant to broad investment incentive programs. * * *

In terms of content, the benefits granted under the typical investment encouragement program go well beyond assurances against non-commercial risks. Typically, they include positive incentives such as tax reductions or holidays, assurances against tax increases, low interest loans supplied or guaranteed by the government, and establishment of tariff barriers to protect the investment from foreign competition. Of particular interest here is the extent to which such programs attempt to protect the foreign investor against non-commercial risks.

Since the primary focus of most investment incentive programs is on encouraging direct investments of foreign capital, their major concern is with the risks associated with such investment. Thus, the investment incentive program may include specific guarantees against expropriation without compensation. In some cases, a specific guarantee against expropriation under any circumstances for a prescribed period may be granted. * * *

* * *

A basic feature of every investment incentive program is guarantees with respect to the remittance of profits and the repatriation of capital. In some cases, the remittance of profits from an approved investment is guaranteed without limitation. In others, the guarantee may cover annual remittance of a certain percentage of profits or profits representing a certain percentage return on invested capital. In the case of guarantees with respect to repatriation of capital, it is common to find a fixed percentage of capital (for example, twenty percent) as the maximum which may be repatriated in any year with the additional limitation that there be no repatriation for an initial period of years. * * *

Where loans by the United States firm accompany an approved investment, assurances can commonly be obtained with respect to the availability and transferability of foreign exchange required for the interest and principal payments called for under an approved loan agreement.

Another common feature of investment incentive programs is assurances concerning exemptions from import restrictions and import levies with respect to equipment and raw materials that may be needed in connection with the enterprise. Often assurances are also afforded concerning the right of the investor to hire key foreign technical and managerial personnel notwithstanding the limitations on hiring such personnel that might otherwise obtain under local law.

Some capital-importing countries have accepted, either in ad hoc concession or guarantee agreements or under investment incentive programs, arbitration of disputes with foreign investors.

### *Note*

The protection under customary international law against the non-commercial risks faced by private parties making investments and supplying know how, goods and services to developing countries is discussed in this chapter. Also discussed are bilateral investment treaties and treaties of friendship, commerce and navigation which afford varying degrees of legal protection against such risks and the role of United States courts and United States laws in providing legal security for international trade and investment. Other sources of existing and potential legal security against non-commercial risks are discussed in connection with international investment in Chapter 17 at p. 1444 infra. National programs offering insurance against non-commercial risks and various multilateral efforts to improve the legal climate for private investment in developing countries, including the World Bank Convention on the Settlement of Investment Disputes and the Convention for a Multilateral Investment Guarantee Agency, are discussed in Chapter 17 at p. 1459 and p. 1460, infra, respectively.

## 2. *Expropriation and Nationalization of Alien-Owned Property*

### a. *Introduction*

In 1964 Mr. Justice Harlan observed in Banco Nacional de Cuba v. Sabbatino, 376 U.S. 398, 428–29, 84 S.Ct. 923, 940–41, 11 L.Ed.2d 804 (1964):

> There are few if any issues in international law today on which opinion seems to be so divided as the limitations on a State's power to expropriate the property of aliens. There is, of course, authority, in international judicial and arbitral decisions, in the expressions of national governments, and among commentators for the view that a taking is improper under international law if it is not for a public purpose, is discriminatory, or is without provision for prompt, adequate, and effective compensation. However, Communist countries, although they have in fact provided a degree of compensation after diplomatic efforts, commonly recognize no obligation on the part of the taking country. Certain representatives of the newly independent and underdeveloped countries have questioned whether rules of state responsibility toward aliens can bind nations that have not consented to them and it is argued that the traditionally articulated standards governing expropriation of property reflect "imperialist" interests and are inappropriate to the circumstances of emergent states.
>
> The disagreement as to relevant international law standards reflects an even more basic divergence between the national interests of capital importing and capital exporting nations and between the social ideologies of those countries that favor state control of a considerable portion of the means of production and those that adhere to a free enterprise system.

While the differences to which Mr. Justice Harlan referred have not been eliminated, their practical importance has been much diminished. Influenced by the dramatic decline of communism and the worldwide shortage of capital, many developing countries have moved toward privatization and freer economies in an effort to accelerate economic development. Thus, states are now placing increasing emphasis on attracting private investment from abroad, and in order to achieve success in this endeavor, it is essential to improve the legal security enjoyed by foreign investors. It is obviously incompatible with enhancing the legal security of private foreign investment and the confidence of potential investors to attack the traditional customary international law rules of state responsibility that remain a significant source of legal security for the foreign investor. Because the doctrinal positions of the Latin American, the socialist states and the developing states in Africa and Asia are deeply rooted, it has been impossible to fashion compromises on the basic rules of state responsibility that will command widespread support. Hence, there has been a shift of focus from the general substantive customary rules of state responsibility to specific mechanisms, both substantive and procedural, that will increase the legal protection of foreign investors in the developing world. For example, a large and growing number of developing states have embraced such arrangements as bilateral investment treaties according specific legal protections to foreign investors, discussed at p. 764 infra, the concept of compulsory arbitration of investment disputes between foreign investors and foreign states in which investments are made, discussed at p. 1459 infra, and insurance of foreign investments against non-commercial risks by bilateral and multilateral agencies, discussed at pp. 1448 and 1460 infra. By focussing more narrowly on specific measures such as these, substantial progress in improving the legal security of foreign investments and the investment climate has been made.

Before examining the areas in which there has been substantial recent progress, the current state of the substantive customary rules of state responsibility that protect the property rights of foreign investors can be usefully examined.

Since the end of colonialism following World War II, the differing views on the basic principles of state responsibility, examined at p. 679 supra, have been reflected in, and to a considerable extent have been focussed on, divergent views on the international law principles applicable to taking of alien-owned property. Along with certain other capital-exporting states, the United States has maintained that a taking of property for public purposes is contrary to international law unless it is accompanied by "prompt, adequate and effective compensation." In contrast, as highlighted in the exchange of notes between the United States and Mexico in connection with the Mexican expropriations of agrarian properties, p. 680 supra, the traditional Latin American view, subsequently espoused by many developing countries in Africa and Asia as well, is that the international legal obligation of the state to pay compensation to an alien whose property has been taken involves no more than a duty to compensate the alien to the extent that its own nationals are compensated under local law. Others would deny any international legal responsibility on the part of a state to pay compensation to an alien whose property has been taken. See p. 684 supra.

It should be noted that under certain circumstances the taking of property will be wrongful under international law (with the result that a duty to make reparation will arise) quite independently of whether compensation has been paid. One case about which there is no room for dispute is when the taking is in violation of a treaty. In the Case Concerning the

Factory at Chorzów (Claim for Indemnity), P.C.I.J., Ser. A, No. 17 (1928), the Permanent Court held the taking to be in violation of the German–Polish Convention concerning Upper Silesia and that, accordingly, compensation equivalent to restitution of the property in kind was called for. See the discussion at p. 756 infra. There is support for the view that a taking not for a public purpose would violate international law, see Restatement (Third) § 712(1)(a), and that a taking that involves discrimination against aliens is wrongful under international law. See Restatement (Third) § 712(1)(b).

The heart of the problem, however, is to what extent does international law impose a duty to pay compensation in the event of a taking of alien property by a state which is for a public purpose, non-discriminatory and not violative of a treaty. Or to rephrase the question, to what extent must compensation be paid, if such a taking is to be lawful under international law?

## *RESTATEMENT (THIRD)*

### § 712. Economic Injury to Nationals of Other States

A state is responsible under international law for injury resulting from:

(1) a taking by the state of the property of a national of another state that

(a) is not for a public purpose, or

(b) is discriminatory, or

(c) is not accompanied by provision for just compensation;

For compensation to be just under this Subsection, it must, in the absence of exceptional circumstances, be in an amount equivalent to the value of the property taken and be paid at the time of taking, or within a reasonable time thereafter with interest from the date of taking, and in a form economically usable by the foreign national. * * *

* * *

(3) other arbitrary or discriminatory acts or omissions by the state that impair property or other economic interests of a national of another state.

### *Notes*

1. The public purpose requirement is included in the United States treaties of friendship, commerce and navigation, see p. 761 infra, and bilateral investment treaties, see p. 766 infra. Presumably because "public purpose" is a broad and expanding concept, challenges to expropriations on the ground that they are not for a public purpose have been rare. The few decisions applying the rule have also involved a denial of compensation by the taking state. Walter Fletcher Smith, 2 U.N.Rep.Int'l Arb. 913 (1929); Finlay Claim, 39 Br. & For. State Papers 410 (1849); Banco Nacional De Cuba v. Sabbatino, 193 F.Supp. 375, 384 (S.D.N.Y.1961), aff'd, 307 F.2d 845 (2d Cir.1962), rev'd on other grounds, 376 U.S. 398, 84 S.Ct. 923, 11 L.Ed.2d 804 (1964). Article 10, paragraph (1)(a) of the Draft Convention on the Responsibility of States for Injuries to Aliens, prepared by Sohn and Baxter, provides that a taking is wrongful "if it is not for a public purpose clearly recognized as such by a law of general application in effect at the

time of the taking," 55 A.J.I.L. 545, 553 (1961). The accompanying comment observes:

> * * * It is not without significance that what constitutes a "public purpose" has rarely been discussed by international tribunals and that in no case has property been ordered restored to its former owner because the taking was considered to be for other than a public purpose. This unwillingness to impose an international standard of public purpose must be taken as reflecting great hesitancy upon the part of tribunals and of States adjusting claims through diplomatic settlement to embark upon a survey of what the public needs of a nation are and how these may best be satisfied * * *. Id. at 555–56.

Consider a taking by a state of an alien's property for the personal use of an official of the state. See Restatement (Third) § 712, Comment *e*.

2. With respect to discrimination as a basis for finding a taking of an alien's property by a state to violate international law, it has been noted that "[d]iscrimination implies unreasonable distinction. Takings that invidiously single out property of persons of a particular nationality would be unreasonable; classifications, even if based on nationality, that are rationally related to the state's security or economic policies might not be unreasonable." Restatement (Third) § 712, comment *f*.

*b. Requirement of Compensation*

The focus of most of the controversies relating to the law of expropriation is on the issue of compensation and whether that issue is to be determined under international law.

The proposition that compensation in the event of expropriation of the property of an alien must be determined under international law was adopted in U.N. General Assembly Resolution 1803 (XVII) on Permanent Sovereignty over Natural Resources, (adopted in 1962 by the General Assembly by 87 votes to two, with twelve abstentions), which refers to "appropriate compensation, in accordance with the rules in force in the State taking such measures in the exercise of its sovereignty and in accordance with international law."

However, an effort to undermine this position is reflected in subsequent resolutions adopted by various United Nations organs set forth at page 687 supra, which reflected support among the socialist states, the Latin American countries and many developing countries for the proposition that the issue of compensation is to be determined not under international law but under the national law of the expropriating state.

In Resolution 3171 (XXVIII) on Permanent Sovereignty over Natural Resources, p. 688 supra, adopted in 1974, the General Assembly refers to "possible compensation" and affirms that "any disputes which might arise should be settled in accordance with the national legislation of each State carrying out such measures".

The Charter of Economic Rights and Duties of States, p. 689 supra, adopted by the U.N. General Assembly on December 12, 1974, (G.A.Res. 3281 (XXIX)), states that "appropriate compensation should be paid by the [expropriating] State, * * * taking into account its relevant laws and regulations and all circumstances that the State considers pertinent." However, settlement is to be under the domestic law of and in domestic tribunals of the nationalizing state unless it agreed to submit the matter to some other peaceful means of settlement.

The Restatement (Third) adopts the view maintained by the United States and many other states that the adequacy of compensation is a matter to be determined under international law. § 712, p. 727 supra. This was also the position adopted by the arbitrator in Texaco Overseas Petroleum Company, et al. v. Libyan Arab Republic, 17 I.L.M. 1 (1978), who concluded that unlike Resolution 3171 and the Charter of Economic Rights and Duties of States, Resolution 1803(XVII) was authoritative evidence of customary international law because it was supported by states representing all geographical areas and all economic systems. See p. 140 supra. The question whether this view will ultimately prevail over the view that compensation should be determined solely by reference to the law of the expropriating state may remain open in the eyes of many developing states, but there has been a decided shift in recent years toward acceptance by a growing number of these states that expropriation disputes may properly be governed by international standards embodied in bilateral treaties. A significant manifestation of this shift is the large number of bilateral investment treaties entered into by over 80 developing states that specifically provide that full compensation must be paid to a foreign investor whose property has been expropriated. "* * * [I]t is not unreasonable to assume that as long as states want and need capital and technology from abroad, they will, on the whole, be prepared to give assurance in agreements and practice that they will abide by the requirements of international law in respect of compensation. Our experience to date tends to confirm this despite some UN speeches. States are more likely, of course, to accept this obligation when the foreign investor is perceived as beneficial and the interests of both sides are mutually reciprocal." Schachter, Compensation for Expropriation, 78 A.J.I.L. 121, 129–30 (1984).

It is also significant that in all of the arbitral decisions since 1971, the sole arbitrator or arbitral body has concluded that the issue of compensation was to be determined under customary international law or under the terms of a friendship, commerce and navigation treaty where applicable. See Norton, A Law of the Future or a Law of the Past? Modern Tribunals and the International Law of Expropriation, 85 A.J.I.L. 474, 479–88 (1991).

### c. *The Measure of Compensation*

Assuming that there is a duty under international law to pay compensation to an alien whose property is expropriated, the inquiry shifts to what is the proper measure of compensation due under international law.

Comment *d* to Restatement (Third) § 712 states:

> *d. Just compensation.* The elements constituting just compensation are not fixed or precise, but, in the absence of exceptional circumstances, compensation to be just must be equivalent to the value of the property taken and must be paid at the time of taking or with interest from that date and in an economically useful form.
>
> There must be payment for the full value of the property, usually "fair market value" where that can be determined. Such value should

take into account "going concern value", if any, and other generally recognized principles of valuation.

Provision for compensation must be based on value at the time of taking; as in United States domestic law, if compensation is not paid at or before the time of taking but is delayed pending administrative, legislative, or judicial processes for fixing compensation, interest must be paid from the time of taking.

Compensation should be in convertible currency without restriction on repatriation, but payment in bonds may satisfy the requirement of just compensation if they bear interest at an economically reasonable rate and if there is a market for them through which their equivalent in convertible currency can be realized.

Various forms of payment have been provided in negotiated settlements which would not be held to satisfy the requirement of just compensation, e.g., payment in nonconvertible currency that can be used for investment in productive assets in the taking state, or even payment in kind, as in the case of expropriation of investment in natural resources.

In exceptional circumstances, some deviation from the standard of compensation set forth in Subsection (1) might satisfy the requirement of just compensation. Whether circumstances are so exceptional as to warrant such deviation, and whether in the circumstances the particular deviation satisfies the requirement of just compensation, are questions of international law. An instance of exceptional circumstances that has been specifically suggested and extensively debated, but never authoritatively passed upon by an international tribunal, involves national programs of agricultural land reform. See Reporters' Note 3. A departure from the general rule on the ground of exceptional circumstances is unwarranted if (i) the property taken had been used in a business enterprise that was specifically authorized or encouraged by the state; (ii) the property was an enterprise taken for operation as a going concern by the state; (iii) the taking program did not apply equally to nationals of the taking state; or (iv) the taking itself was otherwise wrongful under Subsection (1)(a) or (b). * * *

Reporters' Note 3 adds:

The land reform exception has been supported on the ground that takings of agricultural land, unlike takings of mineral resources or of a going business concern, typically do not generate funds from which the government could make compensation. If a requirement of compensation fully in accord with the standard set forth in Subsection (1) would prevent the program, the obligation to compensate might be satisfied by a lower standard. Latin American states that have framed this exception have not denied that aliens had to be treated no less favorably than nationals as to compensation. * * *

### *Notes*

1. The formulation that under international law compensation for expropriated property must be "adequate, prompt and effective" is sometimes referred to as the "Hull formula," in recognition of its assertion by Secretary of State

Hull in his exchanges with the Mexican Minister of Foreign Relations in 1938, see p. 681 supra. The Hull formula has been consistently asserted by the United States in diplomatic exchanges and international tribunals to be the standard of compensation required under international law. Restatement (Third) § 712, Comment *c*. Thus, at the time of the adoption of U.N. General Assembly Resolution 1803(XVII) in 1962, p. 687 supra, the United States, after unsuccessfully proposing the Hull formula as the standard of compensation under international law, voted for the "appropriate compensation" formulation, but asserted the view that "appropriate" was the equivalent of the Hull formula. See p. 687 supra. The Restatement (Second) §§ 185, 187 (1965) defined "just" compensation in the black letter text as equivalent to "adequate, prompt and effective" compensation. This omission of the Hull formula from the black letter text in the Restatement (Third) has been criticized by a Legal Adviser to the Department of State. Robinson, Expropriation in the Restatement Revised, 78 A.J.I.L. 176 (1984). In fact, while the Hull formula has been incorporated in a large number of bilateral treaties negotiated by the United States and other capital-exporting states between themselves and with a growing number of developing states, it has been rejected by many developing states as reflecting customary international law and has not been adopted in multilateral agreements or declarations. Restatement (Third) § 712, Comment *c*. It is doubtful whether the Hull formula as such represents customary international law. Schachter, Compensation for Expropriation, 78 A.J.I.L. 121, 122–23 (1984). However, in 1985 Gann concluded that if one looks beyond the formulation articulated by arbitral tribunals to study the actual awards, there has been "little (if any) retreat in the level of protection to foreign investment afforded by tribunals since the 1965 Restatement." Gann, Compensation Standard for Expropriation, 23 Col.J.Trans.L. 615, 616 (1985). In a 1991 review of arbitral decisions, including seven decisions rendered by Chambers of the Iran–U.S. Claims Tribunal and two disputes arbitrated under the auspices of the International Centre for Settlement of Investment Disputes (ICSID), Norton concluded that, with one exception, every arbitral tribunal that had considered the issue during the period from 1971 to 1991 had "affirmed that customary international law requires a state expropriating the property of a foreign national to pay the full value of that property measured, where possible, by the market price. * * * Although no tribunal has expressly invoked the Hull formula, the result has been the same." Norton, A Law of the Future or a Law of the Past? Modern Tribunals and the International Law of Expropriation, 85 A.J.I.L. 474, 488 (1991).

2. To what extent is there a difference in substance between the formulation of "appropriate" compensation adopted in U.N. Resolution 1803(XVII) and "just" compensation adopted by the Restatement? Consider the following comment by Schachter (footnotes omitted):

> * * * [A] case can be made for considering that just compensation should now be replaced by "appropriate compensation." Judge Jiménez de Aréchaga, a former President of the International Court, has favored "appropriate" because in his view, "it conveys better [than 'just' or 'adequate'] the complex circumstances which may be present in each case." He also suggests that the concept brings in the principle of "unjust enrichment." There might also be a practical advantage to "appropriate compensation" because it has received the support of a great many capital-importing countries and these countries might then be more willing to accept the international obligation and international procedures for dispute settlement.

On the other hand, the draft *Restatement,* taking a more traditional position, can justify its choice of "just" over "appropriate" by the fact that "just compensation" has been used widely in national constitutions (e.g., the Fifth Amendment), in legislation and in many treaties. It may also be said that "appropriate" would create uncertainty precisely because it would replace "just." It might then be argued—as does Jiménez de Aréchaga—that "appropriate" allows for consideration of factors that would not be within the ambit of "just." For example, it might be considered "appropriate" to give weight to the needs and capabilities of the expropriating state. Some would consider this desirable, others unjust. * * *

Schachter, Compensation for Expropriation, 78 A.J.I.L. 121, 127–29 (1984).

3. Whether the formulation is "appropriate" or "just" compensation, there is obviously much room for disagreement and a large measure of flexibility for the tribunal or the negotiators called upon to resolve the issue of what level of compensation is called for in a particular case. Even under the Hull formula, there is ample room for disagreement concerning the precise meaning of the adjectives "adequate," "prompt" and "effective." It is equally clear that they are interrelated. For example, undue delay in payment or payment that cannot be converted into a usable economic benefit to the dispossessed alien can affect the "adequacy" of the compensation arrangements.

4. What criteria are or should be relevant or controlling in valuing the expropriated facilities? Book value, replacement value or fair market value of the expropriated assets or fair market value of the "going concern"? To what extent should the value reflect lost future profits of the enterprise and other intangibles such as "good will" or managerial and technical know how? To what extent, if at all, should adequacy of compensation be affected by other factors not bearing directly on current value of the expropriated business, such as the circumstances under which the investment was originally made, a history of large profits to the alien owners without commensurate benefits to the local economy, past environmental damage caused by the project and the ability of the expropriating state to pay?

To what extent does an approach based on the "full value" or the fair market value of the expropriated properties or enterprise preclude taking into account, in determining what constitutes adequate compensation, factors not bearing on the amount of the loss to the alien whose property has been taken? For example, does it rule out considering the unavailability of foreign exchange resources to the taking state that would be needed to pay immediately the full value the property would have in an economy with a balance of payments surplus? Does it rule out weighing the relationship between past profits drawn off and the amount of investment or the various past benefits conferred on the economy by the investment?

Is the suggestion persuasive that in exceptional cases, such as an agricultural land reform program, some deviation from the standard of just compensation may be permitted? If so, what other circumstances might be treated as exceptional?

5. To what extent does permitting payment in bonds meet the problem of the developing state that lacks the foreign exchange resources to pay adequate compensation in convertible currency? In Restatement (Second) § 189, Comment *b,* it was observed:

> Payment in state bonds that are not in fact marketable does not satisfy the requirement of promptness unless the maturity date of the bonds is within a reasonable time under the circumstances. Payment in marketable bonds promptly delivered satisfies the requirement, but if they can be sold only at a discount, payment in this manner will not satisfy the requirement of full value specified in § 188. Furthermore, if the proceeds of the bonds, either at maturity or on sale, are in local currency, the requirements of convertibility specified in § 190 must be satisfied.

Compare Restatement (Third), § 712, Comment *d*, p. 729 supra. Are there policy considerations that support under limited circumstances treating bonds as adequate compensation if their face amount, as opposed to their fair market value, equals the value of the property taken? What bearing does the currency in which the obligations to pay principal and interest are expressed have on this problem?

6. In the 1977 TOPCO arbitration, p. 136 supra and p. 741 infra, the sole arbitrator concluded that the proper standard under customary international law was "appropriate compensation" as reflected in the 1962 General Assembly Resolution 1803 (XVII). He went on to hold that *restitutio in integrum* was the proper remedy and to order Libya to resume performance under the concession agreements. Norton infers that this result was the equivalent of damages equal to the full value of the expropriated properties and concludes as follows:

> * * * Recent international tribunals have consistently affirmed a requirement under international law that full compensation be paid for expropriations of foreign property. A theoretical debate persists over the scope of possible exceptions to that standard, but the recent decisions suggest that only truly extraordinary circumstances would be likely to support such exceptions. This affirmation of a full compensation standard is explained, in part, by the increasingly widespread recognition that such a standard fosters foreign investment vital to economic development. But it also appears to arise from the preference of arbitrators for judicial and arbitral precedents as sources of international law because these precedents have greater legitimacy, integrity and determinacy than other available sources.

Norton, supra note 2 at 503.

7. The focus of debates between the developing and developed countries in the United Nations and elsewhere shifted in the 1970's to the concept of what has been called a New International Economic Order, and the discussions have reflected the demands of the developing countries for greater participation in, and benefit from, the international economic system. See, e.g., the U.N. Declaration on the Establishment of a New Economic Order, G.A.Res. 3201(S–VI), p. 688 supra. During the 1960's and 1970's, the stance of many developing countries involved a heavy emphasis on the right of expropriation without compensation and a condemnation of the exploitative activities of the multinational companies, positions vigorously rejected by developed countries of the non-communist world. In recent years, there has been a significant shift in the attitude of many developing countries toward foreign investment. Foreign investments involving exploitation of natural resources for the most part had been taken over by the developing states, and their governments began to acquire the knowledge and experience needed to enable them to regulate foreign investment. In addition, increased aspirations for enhanced economic development and diminished progress toward that objective, coupled with widespread moves toward privatization and freer economies, have encouraged an acknowl-

edgement that foreign private investment has an important role to play in economic development through the transfer of resources, technological knowhow, and managerial expertise. Although basic differences remain on such issues as the duty to compensate the alien whose property has been expropriated, there has been a palpable tendency to downplay issues like this one, on which compromise on the doctrinal level may not be possible, and to move on to adopting practical substantive and procedural measures that will contribute to the legal security of foreign investment in developing countries. The most significant of these from the point of view of substantive norms is the striking proliferation of bilateral investment treaties between developing and developed countries in which full compensation is required, often by specific reference to the Hull formula of prompt, adequate and effective compensation. See p. 766 infra.

8. On September 25, 1992, the World Bank Group published a Report to the Development Committee and Guidelines on the Treatment of Foreign Direct Investment set forth in the Document Supplement and 31 I.L.M. 1366 (1992). The Development Committee is a Joint Ministerial Committee of the Boards of Governors of the IMF and the World Bank. Its approval and publication of the Report and Guidelines are particularly significant because of the almost universal membership of the sponsoring institutions and because of their central role in international development. In a forward to the publication, the President of the World Bank Group indicated that the Development Committee agreed "without reservation" to call the guidelines to the attention of the member states. He further stated that the guidelines may "assist in the progressive development of international law in this important area." Ibid. With respect to expropriation, Part IV of the guidelines provides in part that "[a] State may not expropriate or otherwise take in whole or in part a foreign private investment in its territory, or take measures which have similar effects, except where this is done in accordance with applicable legal procedures, in pursuance in good faith of a public purpose, without discrimination on the basis of nationality and against the payment of appropriate compensation." The guideline goes on to state that compensation will be deemed "appropriate" if it is "adequate, effective and prompt." Adequacy is generally to be based on the fair market value of the asset taken. Fair market value may be determined by a method agreed to by the expropriating state and the foreign investor or by a tribunal designated by them. In the event that such agreement is not achieved, the guideline sets forth in detail the circumstances under which compensation will be deemed to be adequate, effective and prompt.

### d. *What Constitutes a "Taking" of Property?*

Under certain circumstances an interference with an alien's property rights that falls short of an outright expropriation may constitute an effective or constructive taking of property giving rise to an obligation on the part of the responsible state to compensate the alien whose property rights have been impaired. "A 'taking of property' includes not only an outright taking of property but also any such unreasonable interference with the use, enjoyment, or disposal of property as to justify an inference that the owner thereof will not be able to use, enjoy, or dispose of the property within a reasonable period of time after the inception of such interference." Article 10, Draft Convention On the International Responsibility of States for Injuries to Aliens, 55 A.J.I.L. 545, 553–54 (1961).

On the other hand, although conduct attributable to the state interferes with or impairs the alien's property rights, it may be deemed not to constitute such a taking of his property because the conduct represents a reasonable exercise of the state's power to regulate matters related to public order, safety or health, its currency, foreign exchange resources, balance of payments or emergency situations. See p. 707 supra.

French v. Banco Nacional de Cuba, 23 N.Y.2d 46, 295 N.Y.S.2d 433 (1968), involved these facts: Plaintiff's assignor had invested in a Cuban farm in 1957 when the Cuban Government permitted foreign investors to turn the proceeds from their enterprises into U.S. dollars and exempted such proceeds from export tax. Under this regime, plaintiff's assignor acquired certificates executed by defendant bank and the Cuban Government's Currency Stabilization Fund stating he would receive for Cuban pesos from defendant bank U.S. $150,000 which would be exempt from the export tax. On July 15, 1959, the Currency Stabilization Fund suspended processing of the certificates. Plaintiff, to whom the certificates were assigned, brought an action for $150,000, plus interest. In holding that the dishonoring of the certificates was an act of state, under the doctrine enunciated by the Supreme Court in *Banco Nacional de Cuba v. Sabbatino,* p. 181, according to which the Courts of the United States will not (subject to the qualifications introduced by the Second Hickenlooper Amendment, see p. 193 infra) inquire into the validity of acts of a foreign state within its territory, the New York Court of Appeals observed, 295 N.Y.S.2d at 442–43:

> Indeed, if the act of state doctrine was decisive in the situation presented in the *Sabbatino* case, then, it must surely be so here—again, unless the Hickenlooper Amendment requires a different result. In the present case, although there are circumstances which undoubtedly imposed serious losses upon the plaintiff's assignor, manifestly, they do not reach the level of an outright "taking" or "expropriation" with which the court was confronted in *Sabbatino.*
>
> The Government of Cuba, by its Decision No. 346, has actually done nothing more than enact an exchange control regulation similar to regulations enacted or promulgated by many other countries, including our own. * * * A currency regulation which alters either the value or character of the money to be paid in satisfaction of contracts is not a "confiscation" or "taking." (Cf. Norman v. Baltimore & O.R.R. Co., 294 U.S. 240, 55 S.Ct. 407, 79 L.Ed. 885; Nortz v. United States, 294 U.S. 317, 55 S.Ct. 428, 79 L.Ed. 907, and Perry v. United States, 294 U.S. 330, 55 S.Ct. 432, 79 L.Ed. 912 [Gold Clause Cases].) As one authoritative writer in the field has stated (Mann, Money in Public International Law, 96 Recueil Des Cours [1959] 1, 90), "A legislator who reduces rates of interest or renders agreements invalid or incapable of being performed or prohibits exports, or renders performance more expensive by the imposition of taxes or tariffs does not take property. Nor does he take property if he depreciates currency or prohibits payment in foreign currency or abrogates gold clauses. Expectations relating to the continuing intrinsic value of all currency or contractual terms such as the gold clause are, like favorable business conditions and good will, 'transient circumstances, subject to changes,' and suffer from 'congenital infirmity' that they may be changed by the competent legislator. They are not property, their change is not deprivation." * * *

[After concluding the Second Hickenlooper Amendment could not apply because there was no taking of property and that therefore the act of state doctrine must be applied, the Court went on to discuss whether, assuming that the action of the Government of Cuba *had* constituted a taking (as the dissenting judges had concluded), the taking would have violated international law, 295 N.Y.S. at 449–50:]

> * * * This being so, it is not necessary to reach the further question whether the action of the Cuban Government offended principles of international law. Since, however, our dissenting brethren have concluded that such action did constitute a taking of property to which a claim of title or other right is asserted and have gone on to urge that it violated international law, we treat that question—of international law—briefly.
>
> This is not an era, surely, in which there is anything novel or internationally reprehensible about even the most stringent regulation of national currencies and the flow of foreign exchange. Such practices have been followed, as the exigencies of international economics have required—and despite resulting losses to individuals—by capitalist countries and communist countries alike, by the United States and its allies as well as by those with whom our country has had profound differences. They are practices which are not even of recent origin but which have been recognized as a normal measure of government for hundreds of years, if not, indeed, as long as currency has been used as the medium of international exchange. (See Winkler, Foreign Bonds, an Autopsy—A Study of Defaults and Repudiations of Government Obligations [1933], p. 21; Mann, The Legal Aspects of Money [2d ed., 1953], p. 337.)
>
> In short, the control of national currency and of foreign exchange is an essential governmental function; the state which coins money has "power to prevent its outflow" (Ling Su Fan v. United States, 218 U.S. 302, 311, 31 S.Ct. 21, 54 L.Ed. 1049, see, also, Nortz v. United States, 294 U.S. 317, 330, 55 S.Ct. 428, supra); and as the court observed in Perry v. United States, 294 U.S. 330, 356, 55 S.Ct. 432, 437, supra, "[t]he same reasoning is applicable to the imposition of restraints upon transactions in foreign exchange." (See, also, Restatement, 2d, Foreign Relations Law of the United States, § 198, Comment *b.*) The Restatement finds no violation of international law in such a currency measure "if it is reasonably necessary in order to control the value of the currency or to protect the foreign exchange resources of the state" (§ 198). The Restatement goes on to recite that "the application to an alien of a requirement that foreign funds held within the territory of the state be surrendered against payment in local currency at the official rate of exchange is not wrongful under international law, even though the local currency is less valuable on the free market than the foreign funds surrendered." Thus, if the Cuban Government could, under the example cited, have properly required an alien within its borders to surrender American dollars "against payment" in pesos, as a measure "reasonably necessary * * * to protect the foreign exchange resources of the state" (Restatement, 2d Foreign Relations Law of the United States, § 198), the present refusal of the Cuban Government to surrender American dollars

in order to protect its dollar reserves, though harsh in its effect, would also seem to be within the limits of international legality.

In the case before us—whatever other economic measures the Cuban Government may have taken (and they are not reflected by evidence in the record)—there is no question that the actions complained of were aimed at protecting Cuba's scarce "foreign exchange resources." The testimony of the defendant's president that these actions were essential to prevent the wiping out of Cuba's foreign currency reserves is uncontradicted. Accordingly, that country's refusal to exchange * * * pesos for dollars, though it may be deplored, may not be characterized as so unreasonable or unjust as to outrage current international standards of governmental conduct. * * *

### *Notes*

1. The following Comment accompanies Restatement (Third) § 712(1):

> *g. Expropriation or regulation.* Subsection (1) applies not only to avowed expropriations in which the government formally takes title to property, but also to other actions of the government that have the effect of "taking" the property, in whole or in large part, outright or in stages ("creeping expropriation"). A state is responsible as for an expropriation of property under Subsection (1) when it subjects alien property to taxation, regulation, or other action that is confiscatory, or that prevents, unreasonably interferes with, or unduly delays, effective enjoyment of an alien's property or its removal from the state's territory. Depriving an alien of control of his property, as by an order freezing his assets, might become a taking if it is long extended. A state is not responsible for loss of property or for other economic disadvantage resulting from bona fide general taxation, regulation, forfeiture for crime, or other action of the kind that is commonly accepted as within the police power of states, if it is not discriminatory, comment *f,* and is not designed to cause the alien to abandon the property to the state or sell it at a distress price. As under United States constitutional law, the line between "taking" and regulation is sometimes uncertain. See Reporters' Note 6.

Compare the foregoing with the provisions concerning what constitutes a taking under the First Hickenlooper Amendment, 22 U.S.C.A. § 2370(e)(1), p. 171 infra, and under the OPIC investment insurance program, p. 1448 infra. Under the latter, a taking includes, *inter alia,* any action which is taken, authorized, ratified or condoned by the Government of the Project Country which for a period of one year results in preventing the investor from "exercising effective control over the use or disposition of a substantial portion of its property or from constructing the Project or operating the same." Under this test would appointment of a "receiver" to manage the enterprise constitute a "taking"? On June 6, 1992, the Government of Zaire announced that it was requisitioning the assets of all foreign-owned companies, including subsidiaries of Chevron Corporation, Mobil Corporation, Royal Dutch Shell Group of the United Kingdom and the Netherlands and Petrofina of Italy. The measure was described by the Zaire Government as temporary and its announced purpose was to ease chronic fuel shortages. The companies affected were to be compensated but there was concern that Zaire lacked sufficient convertible currency resources to permit reimbursement of the companies. In January 1990, the zaire traded at 300 to the dollar; in June 1992 the official exchange rate was over 200,000, and the black market rate 250,000, to the dollar.

For a recent decision of the I.C.J. rejecting the argument of the United States that the requisition of an Italian subsidiary of two related United States corporations constituted a taking of property without compensation which violated the terms of the United States–Italy FCN Treaty of 1948 and a Supplementary Agreement of 1951, see Case Concerning Elettronica Sicula S.p.A. (ELSI) (United States v. Italy), 1989 I.C.J. 15, 28 I.L.M. 1111, at paras. 116–18.

For international cases distinguishing a taking of property from lawful regulation see Harga Engineering Co. v. Islamic Rep. of Iran, 2 Iran–U.S. C.T.R. 499 (1982) (claim that the Iranian state bank had taken claimant's bank accounts by dishonoring claimant's check and frustrating its attempts to authenticate its officer's signature dismissed) and Kugele v. Polish State, [1931–32] Ann.Dig. 69 (claim that a series of license fees imposed by Poland constituted a taking because they compelled claimant to close his brewery dismissed). Also compare the majority and concurring opinions in Starrett Housing Corp. v. Islamic Rep. of Iran, 23 I.L.M. 1090 (1984).

For a commentary on the "conceptional labyrinth that separates the so-called police power from the so-called power of eminent domain," see Weston, "Constructive Takings" under International Law: A Modest Foray into the Problem of "Creeping Expropriation", 16 Va.J.Int'l L. 101, 153–54 (1975). See also Christie, What Constitutes a Taking of Property Under International Law, [1962] Brit.Y.B.I.L. 307.

2. Article 21 of the Harvard Research Draft Convention on the Rights and Duties of Neutral States in Naval and Aerial War, 33 A.J.I.L.Supp. 167, 359 (1939), states: "A belligerent may, within its territory or within territory held in military occupation, in case of urgent necessity, requisition a neutral vessel privately owned and operated, or cargo owned by nationals of a neutral State, if the vessel or the cargo was brought into such territory voluntarily and not as the result of compulsion or pressure exercised by the belligerent or by an allied belligerent; provided that this privilege may be exercised by a belligerent only if it pays the fair market value, under prevailing conditions, of the vessel or cargo requisitioned." Article 22 provides that: "A belligerent has no duty to pay compensation for damage to a neutral vessel or other neutral property or persons, when such damage is incidental to a belligerent's act of war against the armed forces of its enemy and not in violation of the provisions of this Convention or of the law of war."

### *3. Breach by a State of Its Undertaking to an Alien*

Contractual arrangements between states and aliens are a common phenomenon in international society. These arrangements may cover a great variety of matters. The agreements involved may be similar to agreements between private parties in a purely commercial context. A private supplier may sell goods or services to a foreign government or grant to it rights to patents or know-how under a licensing arrangement. Alternatively, they may involve special features related to the fact that the agreement is between an alien investor and a foreign government. A private company may enter into a concession agreement with a foreign government calling for the exploitation, development and marketing by the private company of mineral resources owned by the foreign government. A private investor may enter into a contractual arrangement with a foreign government pursuant to an investment incentive program under which an investment in productive facilities is made by the private investor in consideration for various guarantees and incentives afforded by the foreign government. The undertakings made by the state under such varied arrangements differ widely and these differences may be relevant to the question of whether state responsibility under international law attaches as a result of its breach of a particular undertaking.

When does a breach of an undertaking by a state to an alien constitute a violation of international law? At one extreme, consider in connection with the materials that follow the validity of the position that since only states have rights and obligations under international law, a state can limit its exercise of sovereignty only by international agreement with another state or international organization and consequently a state cannot limit its exercise of sovereignty by agreement with an alien.

At the other extreme, it has been argued that the doctrine of *pacta sunt servanda* (agreements must be observed) as a rule of international law applies in the case of any agreement between a state and an alien relating to an investment or mineral concession. See, e.g., Schwebel, International Protection of Contractual Arrangements, 53 Proc.A.S.I.L. 266 (1959); Kissam & Leach, Sovereign Expropriation of Property and Abrogation of Concession Contracts, 28 Fordham L.Rev. 177, 194–214 (1959); Brandon, Legal Aspects of Private Foreign Investments, 18 Fed.Bar J. 298, 337–40 (1958); Ray, Law Governing Contracts Between States and Foreign Nationals, 2 Institute on Private Investments Abroad, 5 (1960). Does it follow from this view that contractual obligations assumed by a state are no less binding than treaty obligations?

### *a. Choice and Effect of Governing Law*

A necessary step in determining whether a breach or repudiation giving rise to state responsibility has occurred will be to ascertain, in accordance with the principles of the conflict of laws or private international law what body of law (or bodies of law) governs questions of the validity, interpretation, and performance of the contract. As pointed out in the Saudi Arabia v. Arabian American Oil Company (Aramco) Arbitration Award, 27 Int'l L.Rep. 117, 165 (1958):

> It is obvious that no contract can exist *in vacuo,* i.e., without being based on a legal system. The conclusion of a contract is not left to the unfettered discretion of the Parties. It is necessarily related to some positive law which gives legal effects to the reciprocal and concordant manifestations of intent made by the parties. The contract cannot even be conceived without a system of law under which it is created. Human will can only create a contractual relationship if the applicable system of law has first recognized its power to do so.

Compare Sohn & Baxter, Responsibility of States for Injuries to the Economic Interests of Aliens, 55 Am.J.Int'l L. 545, 569 (1961): "[Every contract] draws its binding force, its meaning, and its effectiveness from a legal system, which must be so developed and refined as to be capable of dealing with the great range of problems to which the performance and violation of promises gives rise. *Pacta sunt servanda* is undoubtedly the basic norm of any system of law dealing with agreements, but the principle speaks on such a high level of abstraction that it affords little or no guidance in the resolution of concrete legal disputes relating to agreements. What is *pactum* and when and how and if it is to be *servandum* are questions which must be answered by a system of law capable of reacting in a sophisticated manner to these problems. What that system of law is can be determined by the private international law of the forum, whether national or international."

The choice of governing law problem can be quite complex in relation to an agreement between a state and an alien. When a contract is entered into between a state and a private party national of another state, the parties are free under conflict of laws principles to designate the body or bodies of law that shall govern the validity, interpretation and performance of the agreement and, if they so choose, to withdraw the agreement from the exclusive application of the law of the contracting state or any other domestic legal system. The generally unfettered freedom of the contracting state and the foreign private party to choose the governing law was reflected in a resolution adopted by the *Institut de Droit International* in 1979 stating that "[t]he parties may in particular choose as the proper law of the contract either one or several domestic legal systems or the principles common to such systems or the general principles of law or the principles applied in international economic relations, or international law, or a combination of these sources of law." Ann.Inst. de Droit Int'l Vol. 58 Part II at p. 195. National and international tribunals will generally accept the choice by the contracting parties of governing law as binding, and it will only be in the rare case that the parties by design or inadvertence will fail to choose what law will govern a significant contract. In connection with the materials that follow, consider what factors are likely to influence the negotiations as to this issue.

Should the parties fail to designate a governing law, the agreement would, under the principles of the conflict of laws, usually be governed by the law of the state with which it has the closest links.

In the absence of an explicit choice of governing law, the determination of governing law may be complicated by questions such as whether there should be a presumption in favor of the municipal law of the contracting state or whether reference of disputes under the agreement to an international arbitral tribunal implies a choice as to governing law, or at least, as found by Arbitrator Cavin in the Sapphire–N.I.O.C. Arbitration, 13 Int'l and Comp.L.Q. 987, 1011–15 (1964), a rejection of municipal law of the contracting state as controlling. See Lalive, Contracts Between a State or a State Agency and a Foreign Company, 13 I.C.L.Q. 987 (1964). Determining the governing law or "the proper law of the contract" may swing the door open to problems concerning the content of that law. For example, if municipal law of the contracting state is selected, does it encompass the municipal law relating to public or administrative contracts under which in certain circumstances the contracting state may not be bound if the public interest otherwise requires? Is it municipal law as it existed on the date of the agreement or as it may be amended from time to time? The parties may include a so-called "stabilization clause" stating that the agreement will be governed by municipal law in force at the time the agreement is concluded. See p. 754 infra. The purpose is to protect the foreign investor from risk of changes in municipal law detrimental to its interests.

The 1933 concession granted by Persia to the Anglo–Persian Oil Company provided that differences between the parties were to be settled by arbitration and that an award of the arbitrators was to be based on "the judicial principles contained in Article 38 of the Statutes of the Permanent Court of International Justice." Does such a choice of law provision render international law directly applicable to the agreement? Does it follow that the agreement could not be altered or terminated by the application of municipal law? See Anglo–Iranian Oil Case, Pleadings, Oral Arguments and Documents 267, 268 (I.C.J.1952). Would such an agreement be subject to adjustment in accordance with fundamentally changed circumstances to the same extent that a treaty would? See p. 516 supra.

Compare Article 46 of the 1954 agreement between Iran and the consortium of oil companies which provided: "In view of the diverse nationalities of the parties to this Agreement, it shall be governed by and interpreted and applied in accordance with principles of law common to Iran and the several nations in which the other parties to this Agreement are incorporated, and in the absence of such common principles, then by and in accordance with principles of law recognized by civilized nations in general, including such of those principles as may have been applied by international tribunals." 2 Hurewitz, Diplomacy in the Near and Middle East 377 (1956).

## TEXACO OVERSEAS PETROLEUM COMPANY ET AL. v. LIBYAN ARAB REPUBLIC

International Arbitral Award Jan. 19, 1977.

*TRANSLATION OF AWARD ON THE MERITS IN FRENCH, JOURNAL DU DROIT INTERNATIONAL*

Vol. 104, No. 2 (1977) at p. 350, published in 17 I.L.M. 1 (1978).

[On September 1, 1973 and February 11, 1974, Libya promulgated decrees purporting to nationalize all of the rights, interests and property of Texaco Overseas Petroleum Company ("TOPCO") and California Asiatic Oil Company ("CAOC") in Libya granted to them jointly by the Government of Libya under 14 Deeds of Concession.

TOPCO and CAOC requested arbitration and appointed an arbitrator. The Libyan Government refused to accept arbitration and did not appoint an arbitrator. Pursuant to the arbitration provision in their Deeds of Concession, TOPCO and CAOC requested the President of the International Court of Justice to appoint a sole arbitrator to hear and determine the disputes. The Libyan Government opposed such request and filed a memorandum with the President contending, *inter alia,* that the disputes were not subject to arbitration because the nationalizations were sovereign acts.

After considering the Libyan Government's objections, the President of the International Court of Justice, on December 18, 1974, appointed Rene–Jean Dupuy, Secretary General of The Hague Academy of International Law and Professor of Law at the University of Nice, as the Sole Arbitrator. The Libyan Government did not participate in the subsequent proceedings.

On January 19, 1977, the Sole Arbitrator delivered an Award on the Merits in favor of TOPCO and CAOC. The Sole Arbitrator held that (a) the

Deeds of Concession are binding on the parties, (b) by adopting the measures of nationalization the Libyan Government breached its obligations under the Deeds of Concession and (c) the Libyan Government was legally bound to perform the Deeds of Concession in accordance with their terms.

Following the rendering of the Award on the Merits, Libya, TOPCO and CAOC reached a settlement of their disputes. Libya agreed to provide TOPCO and CAOC over the next 15 months with $152 million of Libyan crude oil, and TOPCO and CAOC agreed to terminate the arbitration proceedings. The Sole Arbitrator's award on the merits stated, in part, as follows (footnotes omitted):]

1. The present arbitration arises out of 14 Deeds of Concession concluded between the competent Libyan Authorities (Petroleum Commission or Petroleum Ministry, depending on the date of the contracts) and the above-mentioned companies * * *.

* * *

2. The wording of these fourteen contracts is a copy of the text of a model contract annexed to the text of the Libyan Law on Petroleum of 1955. This relationship is indicated by a statement appearing at the top of the deeds of concession to the effect that the deed of concession is concluded on its date "under the authority of the Petroleum Law of 1955".

* * *

22. * * * [T]he juridical value and, consequently, the binding nature of the Deeds of Concession in dispute can only be judged on the basis of the law which is applicable to them because it is obvious that, if—assuming arguendo—these contracts were governed by Libyan law, the result would have been that their binding nature could be affected *a priori* by legislative or regulatory measures taken within the Libyan national legal order (quite apart from the questions of responsibility which the adoption of such legal measures might, should the case arise, entail in conformity with Libyan municipal law).

But the Deeds of Concession in dispute are not controlled by Libyan law or, more exactly, are not controlled by Libyan law alone. It is incontestable that these contracts were international contracts, both in the economic sense because they involved the interests of international trade and in the strict legal sense because they included factors connecting them to different states * * *.

23. What was the law applicable to these contracts? It is this particular question that the parties intended to resolve in adopting Clause 28 of the Deeds of Concession in a form which must be recalled here:

> "This concession shall be governed by and interpreted in accordance with the principles of the law of Libya common to the principles of international law and in the absence of such common principles then by and in accordance with the general principles of law, including such of those principles as may have been applied by international tribunals."

Thus, a complex system to determine the law applicable or the "choice of law" has been provided by the contracting parties involving a two-tier system:

— the principles of Libyan law were applicable to the extent that such principles were common to principles of international law;

— alternatively, in the absence of such conformity, reference was made to general principles of law.

24. Two questions must therefore be decided by the Tribunal in order to rule on the binding nature of the Deeds of Concession which are in dispute:

— first question: Did the parties have the right to select the law which was to govern their contract?

— second question: Under what circumstances was the choice of law applicable and what consequence should be derived from the international character of the contracts?

* * *

25. The answer to this first question is beyond any doubt: all legal systems, whatever they are, apply the principle of the autonomy of the will of the parties to international contracts. * * *

* * *

36. Under what circumstances was the choice of applicable law made and what consequences should be derived therefrom as to the internationalization of the Deeds of Concession in dispute?

* * *

* * * [T]he internationalization of contracts entered into between States and foreign private persons can result in various ways which it is now time to examine.

41. a.a) At the outset, it is accepted that the reference made by the contract, in the clause concerning the governing law, to the general principles of law leads to this result. These general principles, being those which are mentioned in Article 38 of the Statute of the International Court of Justice, are one of the sources of international law: they may appear alone in the clause or jointly with a national law, particularly with the law of the contracting State.

* * *

There are many international contracts comparable to the contracts in dispute which refer to the general principles of law. It will suffice to cite here: the contract between Iran and Agip Mineraria of 24 August 1954 (Art. 40), the contract between Iran and the Consortium of 19 September 1954 (Art. 46), the contract between Kuwait and Kuwait Shell Petroleum Company of 15 January 1961 (Art. 35), and the contract between the United Arab Republic and Pan America U.A.R. Oil Company, of 23 October 1963 (Art. 42).

42. International arbitration case law confirms that the reference to the general principles of law is always regarded to be a sufficient criterion for the internationalization of a contract. * * *

It should be noted that the invocation of the general principles of law does not occur only when the municipal law of the contracting State is not suited to petroleum problems. Thus, for example, the Iranian law is without doubt particularly well suited for oil concessions but this does not prevent the contracts executed by Iran from referring very often to these general principles. The recourse to general principles is to be explained not only by the lack of adequate legislation in the State considered (which might have been the case, at one time, in certain oil Emirates). It is also justified by the need for the private contracting party to be protected against unilateral and abrupt modifications of the legislation in the contracting State: it plays, therefore, an important role in the contractual equilibrium intended by the parties.

* * *

44. b.b) Another process for the internationalization of a contract consists in inserting a clause providing that possible differences which may arise in respect of the interpretation and the performance of the contract shall be submitted to arbitration.

Such a clause has a twofold consequence:

— on the one hand, * * * the institution of arbitration shall be that established by international law.

— on the other hand, as regards the law applicable to the merits of the dispute itself, the inclusion of an arbitration clause leads to a reference to the rules of international law.

Even if one considers that the choice of international arbitration proceedings cannot by itself lead to the exclusive application of international law, it is one of the elements which makes it possible to detect a certain internationalization of the contract. The *Sapphire International Petroleum Ltd.* award is quite explicit: "If no positive implication can be made from the arbitral clause, it is possible to find there a negative intention, namely to reject the exclusive application of Iranian law" (35 Int'l L.R. 136 (1963), at 172); this is what led the arbitrator in that case, in the absence of any explicit reference to the law applicable, not to apply automatically Iranian law, thus dismissing any presumption in its favor. It is therefore unquestionable that the reference to international arbitration is sufficient to internationalize a contract, in other words, to situate it within a specific legal order—the order of the international law of contracts.

45. (c) A third element of the internationalization of the contracts in dispute results from the fact that it takes on a dimension of a new category of agreements between States and private persons: economic development agreements * * *.

Several elements characterize these agreements: in the first place, their subject matter is particularly broad: they are not concerned only with an isolated purchase or performance, but tend to bring to developing countries investments and technical assistance, particularly in the field of research and exploitation of mineral resources, or in the construction of factories on a turnkey basis. Thus, they assume a real importance in the development of the country where they are performed: it will suffice to mention here the importance of the obligations assumed in the case under consideration by the concession holders in the field of road and port infrastructures and the training on the spot of qualified personnel. The party contracting with the State was thus associated with the realization of the economic and social progress of the host country.

In the second place, the long duration of these contracts implies close cooperation between the State and the contracting party and requires permanent installations as well as the acceptance of extensive responsibilities by the investor.

Finally, because of the purpose of the cooperation in which the contracting party must participate with the State and the magnitude of the investments to which it agreed, the contractual nature of this type of agreement is reinforced: the emphasis on the contractual nature of the legal relation between the host State and the investor is intended to bring about an equilibrium between the goal of the general interest sought by such relation and the profitability which is necessary for the pursuit of the task entrusted to the private enterprise. The effect is also to ensure to the private contracting party a certain stability which is justified by the considerable investments which it makes in the country concerned. The investor must in particular be protected against legislative uncertainties, that is to say the risks of the municipal law of the host country being modified, or against any government measures which would lead to an abrogation or rescission of the contract. Hence, the insertion, as in the present case, of so-called stabilization clauses: these clauses tend to remove all or part of the agreement from the internal law and to provide for its correlative submission to *sui generis* rules as stated in the *Aramco* award, or to a system which is properly an international law system. From this latter point of view, the following considerations should be noted, which were mentioned in the *Sapphire* award, and which stress the interest of the internationalization of the contract:

> "Such a solution seems particularly suitable for giving the guarantees of protection which are indispensable for foreign companies, since these companies undergo very considerable risks in bringing financial and technical aid to countries in the process of development. It is in the interest of both parties to such agreements that any disputes between them should be settled according to the general principles universally recognized and should not be subject to the particular rules of national laws. * * *" (35 Int'l L.R. 136 (1963), at 175–176.)

* * *

46. The Tribunal must specify the meaning and the exact scope of internationalization of a contractual relationship so as to avoid any misunderstanding: indeed to say that international law governs contractual relations between a State and a foreign private party neither means that the latter is assimilated to a State nor that the contract entered into with it is assimilated to a treaty.

* * *

47. This Tribunal * * * shall * * * consider as established today the concept that legal international capacity is not solely attributable to a State and that international law encompasses subjects of a diversified nature. If States, the original subjects of the international legal order, enjoy all the capacities offered by the latter, other subjects enjoy only limited capacities which are assigned to specific purposes. * * * In other words, stating that a contract between a State and a private person falls within the international legal order means that for the purposes of interpretation and performance of the contract, it should be recognized that a private contracting party has

specific international capacities. But, unlike a State, the private person has only a limited capacity and his quality as a subject of international law does enable him only to invoke, in the field of international law, the rights which he derives from the contract.

* * *

* * * [A]s stated by Professor Garcia Amador ("International Responsibility", 2 Y.B.Int'l L.Comm'n 1, U.N.Doc. A/CN.4/119 (1959), at 32):

> "* * * In the matter of contracts, the international personality and capacity of the individual [that is to say the private person, natural or fictitious] depend on the recognition granted to them by the State in its legal relations with him. Agreements which provide in one form or another for the application of a legal system or of principles alien to municipal law, or for the settlement of disputes by international means and procedures, differ from those governed exclusively by municipal law in that the contractual relation between a State and a private person is raised to an international plane, thus necessarily conferring upon that person the necessary degree of international personality and capacity."

Thus, the internationalization of certain contracts entered into between a State and a private person does not tend to confer upon a private person competences comparable to those of a State but only certain capacities which enable him to act internationally in order to invoke the rights which result to him from an internationalized contract.

49. The above quotation from Mr. Garcia Amador is all the more appropriate as it refers to the conclusion of agreements which are "governed exclusively by municipal law," implying thereby that some agreements may be governed both by municipal law and by international law. It is precisely this latter kind of hypothesis which is to be found in the case under consideration since the clause of the contracts under dispute relating to the applicable law refers to the "principles of Libyan law which are common to the principles of international law." It is significant in this respect that, in a formula in which it must be assumed that each term has been weighed, the parties concerned referred not to Libyan law itself, but to "the principles of Libyan law." Indeed, the parties thereby wanted to demonstrate that they intended the Arbitral Tribunal to base itself on the spirit of the Libyan law as expressed in the fundamental principles of that law, rather than by its rules which may be contingent and variable since these rules depended, in the last instance, on the unilateral will—even arbitrariness—of one of the contracting parties: hence, the reference which is also made to the principles of international law.

It follows that the reference made by the contracts under dispute to the principles of Libyan law does not nullify the effect of internationalization of the contracts which has already resulted from their nature as economic development agreements and recourse to international arbitration for the settlement of disputes. The application of the principles of Libyan law does not have the effect of ruling out the application of the principles of international law, but quite the contrary: it simply requires us to combine the two in verifying the conformity of the first with the second.

* * *

51. Applying the principles stated above, the Arbitral Tribunal will refer:

(1) On the one hand, as regards the principles of Libyan law: regardless of the source of Libyan law taken into consideration, whether we refer to the Sharia, the Sacred Law of Islam (a special reference should be made to Surah 5 of the Koran which begins with the verse: "O ye believers, perform your contracts!") or to the Libyan Civil Code which includes on this point two basic articles illustrating the value which Libyan law attaches to the principle of the respect of the word given:

— Article 147, under which "The contract makes the law of the parties. It can be revoked or altered only by mutual consent of the parties or for reasons provided by the law;"

— Article 148, under which "A contract must be performed in accordance with its contents and in compliance with the requirements of good faith,"

one is led to the same conclusion, that is: that Libyan law recognizes and sanctions the principle of the binding force of contracts.

(2) On the other hand, as regards the principles of international law: from this second point of view, it is unquestionable, as written by Professor Jessup * * * that the maxim " 'pacta sunt servanda' is a general principle of law; it is an essential foundation of international law."

No international jurisdiction whatsoever has ever had the least doubt as to the existence, in international law, of the rule *pacta sunt servanda:* it has been affirmed vigorously both in the *Aramco* award in 1958 and in the *Sapphire* award in 1963. One can read, indeed, in the *Sapphire* award, that "it is a fundamental principle of law, which is constantly being proclaimed by international Courts, that contractual undertakings must be respected. The rule 'pacta sunt servanda' is the basis of every contractual relationship" (35 Int'l L.R. 136 (1963), at 181). This Tribunal cannot but reaffirm this in its turn by stating that the maxim *pacta sunt servanda* should be viewed as a fundamental principle of international law.

52. The conformity, on this essential point, of the principles of Libyan law with the principles of international law relieves the Tribunal from discussing the matter further. * * *

* * *

[The arbitrator then considered whether the deeds of concession could be regarded as administrative contracts under civil law which the State would be entitled, under certain circumstances, to amend unilaterally or even abrogate in the public interest. The arbitrator concluded this position was untenable for two reasons. First, the deeds of concession did not meet the definition of administrative contracts under Libyan law. One element of this definition was that the contract confer upon the government rights and powers not usually found in a civil contract, such as the power to amend or abrogate the contract unilaterally if the public interest requires, or—in the terminology of French law—rights and powers going beyond the ambit of ordinary law (*clauses exorbitantes du droit common*). With respect to this element he stated:]

In the case under consideration * * * it is obvious that the Government of Libya had intended to deal with its partners on a footing of equality with respect to the Deeds of Concession in dispute and that these contracts do not include any clause going beyond the ambit of ordinary law; quite the contrary, it is indeed stipulated that laws or regulations, the effect of which might be to amend the contractual rights of the concession holders, cannot be applied to the concession holders unless accepted by them. * * *

* * *

* * * But when the State or the administrative authority has formally undertaken to waive its right, in regard to the contracting party, to use its prerogatives as a public power, failing the contracting party's agreement, it is difficult to imagine that such State or such administrative authority could have demonstrated more clearly that it intended to deal on an equal footing with its partner. This Tribunal cannot therefore but conclude * * * that the so-called stabilization clause "is a negation of one of the principal characteristics of an administrative contract," i.e., its basically and essentially inegalitarian nature. Lastly, resorting to international arbitration would confirm, if need be, the idea that the parties had intended to deal on a footing of equality.

[The second reason cited by the arbitrator was that the distinction between administrative contracts and civil contracts was a creature of the French legal system (and others based upon it) and it could not be regarded as a "principle of international law" or as a "general principle of law."]

* * *

It is clear from an international point of view that it is not possible to criticize a nationalization measure concerning nationals of the State concerned, or any measure affecting aliens in respect of whom the State concerned has made no particular commitment to guarantee and maintain their position. On the assumption that the nationalizing State has concluded with a foreign company a contract which stems from the municipal law of that State and is completely governed by that law the resolution of the new situation created by nationalization will be subject to the legal and administrative provisions then in force.

62. But the case is totally different where the State has concluded with a foreign contracting party an internationalized agreement, either because the contract has been subjected to the municipal law of the host country, viewed as a mere law of reference, applicable as of the effective date of the contract, and "stabilized" on that same date by specific clauses, or because it has been placed directly under the aegis of international law. Under these two assumptions, the State has placed itself within the international legal order in order to guarantee vis-à-vis its foreign contracting party a certain legal and economic status over a certain period of time. In consideration for this commitment, the partner is under an obligation to make a certain amount of investments in the country concerned and to explore and exploit at its own risks the petroleum resources which have been conceded to it.

Thus, the decision of a State to take nationalizing measures constitutes the exercise of an internal legal jurisdiction but carries international consequences when such measures affect international legal relationships in which the nationalizing State is involved.

* * *

67. * * * [T]he State, by entering into an international agreement with any partner whatsoever, exercises its sovereignty whenever the State is not subject to duress and where the State has freely committed itself through an untainted consent.

As recognized in the award delivered in the case between the Government of Saudi Arabia and Aramco, it is not incompatible for a State to grant a concession while desiring not to alienate its sovereignty:

> "* * * By reason of its very sovereignty within its territorial domain, the State possesses the legal power to grant rights which it forbids itself to withdraw before the end of the Concession with the reservation of the Clauses of the Concession Agreement relating to its revocation. Nothing can prevent a State, in the exercise of its sovereignty, from binding itself irrevocably by the provisions of a concession and from granting to the concessionnaire irretractable rights. Such rights have the character of acquired rights. * * * " (52 Rev.Crit.D.I.P. 272 (1963), at 315; 27 Int'l L.R. 117 (1963), at 168.)

* * *

* * *

70. * * * Clause 16 of the Deeds of Concession contains a stabilization clause with respect to the rights of the concession holder. As consideration for the economic risks to which the foreign contracting parties were subjected, the Libyan State granted them a concession of a minimum duration of 50 years and, more specifically, containing a non-aggravation clause, Clause 16, which provided:

> "The Government of Libya will take all steps necessary to ensure that the company enjoys all the rights conferred by this concession. The contractual rights expressly created by this concession shall not be altered except by mutual consent of the parties."

Another paragraph was added to this provision under the Royal Decree of December 1961 and became an integral part of the contract on the basis of the Agreement of 1963. It provides:

> "This Concession shall throughout the period of its validity be construed in accordance with the Petroleum Law and the Regulations in force on the date of execution of the agreement of amendment by which this paragraph (2) was incorporated into the concession agreement. Any amendment to or repeal of such Regulations shall not affect the contractual rights of the Company without its consent."

71. Such a provision, the effect of which is to stabilize the position of the contracting party, does not, in principle, impair the sovereignty of the Libyan State. Not only has the Libyan State freely undertaken commitments but also the fact that this clause stabilizes the petroleum legislation and regulations as of the date of the execution of the agreement does not

affect in principle the legislative and regulatory sovereignty of Libya. Libya reserves all its prerogatives to issue laws and regulations in the field of petroleum activities in respect of national or foreign persons with which it has not undertaken such a commitment. Clause 16 only makes such acts invalid as far as contracting parties are concerned—with respect to whom this commitment has been undertaken—during the period of applicability of the Deeds of Concession. Any changes which may result from the adoption of new laws and regulations must, to affect the contracting parties, be agreed to by them. This is so not because the sovereignty of Libya would be reduced, but simply by reason of the fact that Libya has, through an exercise of its sovereignty, undertaken commitments under an international agreement, which, for its duration, is the law common to the parties.

Thus, the recognition by international law of the right to nationalize is not sufficient ground to empower a State to disregard its commitments, because the same law also recognizes the power of a State to commit itself internationally, especially by accepting the inclusion of stabilization clauses in a contract entered into with a foreign private party.

* * *

73. Thus, in respect of the international law of contracts, a nationalization cannot prevail over an internationalized contract, containing stabilization clauses, entered into between a State and a foreign private company. The situation could be different only if one were to conclude that the exercise by a State of its right to nationalize places that State on a level outside of and superior to the contract and also to the international legal order itself, and constitutes an "act of government" ("acte de gouvernement") which is beyond the scope of any judicial redress or any criticism.

* * *

91. Therefore, one should note that the principle of good faith, which had already been mentioned in Resolution 1803 (XVII), has an important place even in Resolution 3281 (XXIX) called "The Charter of Economic Rights and Duties of States". One should conclude that a sovereign State which nationalizes cannot disregard the commitment undertaken by the contracting State: to decide otherwise would in fact recognize that all contractual commitments undertaken by a State have been undertaken under a purely permissive condition on its part and are therefore lacking of any legal force and any binding effect. From the point of view of its advisability, such a solution would gravely harm the credibility of States since it would mean that contracts signed by them did not bind them; it would introduce in such contracts a fundamental imbalance because in these contracts only one party—the party contracting with the State—would be bound. In law, such an outcome would go directly against the most elementary principle of good faith and for this reason it cannot be accepted.

* * *

[The arbitrator then analyzed at length Libyan law and international law relating to remedies for breach of contractual obligations and held that the injured complainants were entitled to *restitutio in integrum* and that Libya was required to perform specifically its contractual obligations with respect to the complainants, stating that] "* * * this Tribunal must hold that *restitutio in integrum* is, both under the principles of Libyan law and under the principles of international law, the normal sanction for non-performance of contractual obligations and that it is inapplicable only to the extent that restoration of the *status quo ante* is impossible * * *"

* * *

### *Notes*

1. Consider the bases for what Professor Dupuy refers to as "internationalization" of the contract. What, if anything, does "internationalization" connote beyond the specific features on which the characterization is based? Does it imply that international remedies would be available to the private party for breach by the state that would not be available for violation by the state of other contracts? What, if anything, does the concept of internationalization contribute to the analysis of what law governs the contract? Dupuy makes clear that "internationalization" does not imply that the private party is assimilated to a state or the contract to a treaty. Is it more than a label for a contract between an alien and a state that is explicitly to be governed by international law (or general principles of law) rather than by the municipal law of the contracting state? Dupuy states that the private party under an internationalized contract is given "a limited capacity to invoke, in the field of international law, the rights that he derives from the contract." What is meant by invoking contractual rights "in the field of international law?"

2. Dupuy suggests that in the case of international development contracts, the contract may be "internationalized" whether or not there is an international arbitration clause or a clause selecting as the governing law a body of law other than that of the contracting state. Is there any basis for concluding that an international development contract involves obligations on the international level different from other contracts? See Fatouros, International Law and the Internationalized Contract, 74 A.J.I.L. 134–141 (1980). Consider the following (footnotes omitted):

> * * * [P]olitical and economic factors also bear in a more subtle way on the "internationalizing" of large-scale economic development agreements. The "host" state and the private company are not the only parties in interest; the home state of the company may be heavily involved and indeed often is. Its political, financial and other economic interests may be implicated in the concession or development agreement. The government may have urged the grant of the concession by the host government and encouraged the private firm to proceed. In many cases, it will have helped to provide financing directly or indirectly and it may have insured the company against political risks. In some cases, a bilateral treaty between the two states will apply to the investment and impose obligations in that respect on the contracting state. Prosper Weil has observed that these relations are indicative of the international "enracinement" of many development agreements. He has suggested that this reality must be reflected in the relevant international law principles that apply on the inter-state level. This could mean that the Calvo doctrine espoused by many states would not apply so as to exclude the home state of the company from asserting its rights and interest, in disputes concerning the contract and its performance. State practice confirms the role of the home states in extending diplomatic protection to private companies in cases of development agreements of a

certain magnitude and salience. Host states tend to accept such "protection" as legitimate. In this sense, it may be said that the development agreements are "internationalized." But this is not the same as saying that they have become directly subject to international law or that their alleged breach by the state in itself involves a violation of international law.

In sum, we need to be cautious in employing the phrase "internationalized" contracts. We may use the term in a descriptive sense for contracts which have the transnational features we have discussed—namely, non-national governing law, non-national arbitration, or international economic and political significance. However, we cannot infer from these features that the contracts have been transposed to another "legal order" or that they have become subject to international law in the same way as a treaty between two States.

To be sure, the international law of State responsibility applies to these so-called international contracts just as it does to all other contracts and transactions between states and foreign nationals. The application of the rules of state responsibility will have to take cognizance of the special contractual provisions for non-national law and arbitration and also, when appropriate, the interest of the state to which the private party belongs. But these special features do not alter the basic principles of State responsibility applicable to injury to non-nationals resulting from contractual violations. * * *

Schachter, International Law in Theory and Practice 310–311 (1991).

*b. Breach of Undertaking as a Violation of International Law*

It is apparent from the foregoing that, under the applicable principles of conflict of laws, the law governing the interpretation, validity and performance of the contract may be determined to be the municipal law of the contracting state, principles of law applied in common by two or more municipal law systems, principles of public international law, general principles of law, some other body of law, custom or some combination of these. Indeed, various aspects of the contractual relationship may be governed by different bodies of law. Having determined the governing law, the problem shifts to seeking the content of that law as applied to the particular contractual undertaking involved. To what extent under the governing principles are contracting parties held to their undertakings under an inflexible application of *pacta sunt servanda?* To what extent, if at all, is either party afforded leeway in meeting its obligations? To what extent can the rights and duties of the parties be adjusted to meet changing conditions?

Then, assuming that a breach of contractual obligation by the contracting state is established under the law governing the agreement, when, in the absence of a treaty violation or a denial of procedural justice, will such a breach constitute a violation of international law thereby providing the substantive basis for a claim of state responsibility?

## *RESTATEMENT (THIRD)*

### § 712. Economic Injury to Nationals of Other States

A state is responsible under international law for injury resulting from:

* * *

(2) a repudiation or breach by the state of a contract with a national of another state

(a) where the repudiation or breach is (i) discriminatory; or (ii) motivated by non-commercial considerations, and compensatory damages are not paid; or

(b) where the foreign national is not given an adequate forum to determine his claim of repudiation or breach, or is not compensated for any repudiation or breach determined to have occurred. * * *

## *Notes*

In the Explanatory Note to Article 12 of the Draft Convention on the International Responsibility of States for Injuries to Aliens, 55 A.J.I.L. at 570, Sohn and Baxter comment:

"Doctrine and jurisprudence have attempted to maintain a middle course by limiting State responsibility for a violation of a concession or contract to those cases in which there has been a 'denial of justice' in litigation in the courts of the respondent State respecting an alleged breach of the contract and to cases in which the breach of the contract or concession has been characterized as 'arbitrary' or 'tortious.' These highly flexible and indefinite standards suggest that there is a certain amount of discretion in the respondent State to interpret or modify the terms of the agreement in a reasonable and non-discriminatory way but call for a response in damages on the international plane when there has been a violation of certain requirements laid down by international law. What constitutes a departure from these requirements cannot be set down with definiteness or precision. * * *"

2. The Restatement Reporters comment on § 712(2) as follows:

*h. Repudiation or breach of contract by state.* A state party to a contract with a foreign national is liable for a repudiation or breach of that contract under applicable national law, but not every repudiation or breach by a state of a contract with a foreign national constitutes a violation of international law. Under Subsection (2), a state is responsible for such a repudiation or breach only if it is discriminatory, Comment *f,* or if it is akin to an expropriation in that the contract is repudiated or breached for governmental rather than commercial reasons and the state is not prepared to pay damages. A state's repudiation or failure to perform is not a violation of international law under this section if it is based on a bona fide dispute about the obligation or its performance, if it is due to the state's inability to perform, or if nonperformance is motivated by commercial considerations and the state is prepared to pay damages or to submit to adjudication or arbitration and to abide by the judgment or award.

With respect to any repudiation or breach of a contract with a foreign national, a state may be responsible for a denial of justice under international law if it denies to the alien an effective domestic forum to resolve the dispute and has not agreed to any other forum; or if, having committed itself to a special forum for dispute settlement, such as arbitration, it fails to honor such commitment; or if it fails to carry out a judgment or award rendered by such domestic or special forum. See Comment *j.*

> A breach of contract by a state may sometimes constitute "creeping expropriation," Comment *g*, for example, if the breach makes impossible the continued operation of the project that is the subject of the contract.

For discussion of the treatment under international law of breaches by a state of different types of contracts, see Restatement (Third) § 712, Reporters' Notes 9 and 10.

3. The Guidelines on the Treatment of Foreign Direct Investment published by the Development Committee of the World Bank Group and the IMF on September 25, 1992, 31 I.L.M. 1366 (1992), discussed at p. 734 supra, take the position that only under limited conditions may a state unilaterally terminate, amend or otherwise disclaim liability under a contract with a foreign private investor for other than commercial reasons. These conditions are that the action be taken (i) in accordance with applicable legal procedures, (ii) in pursuance in good faith of a public purpose, (iii) without discrimination on the basis of nationality, and (iv) against the payment of appropriate compensation. The appropriateness of compensation will be determined under the standards applicable to instances of expropriation. Guideline IV, Section 11, 31 I.L.M. 1383 (1992). See p. 734 supra.

4. Agreements between states and foreign investors sometimes contain "stabilization clauses" stating that the law in force at the time of execution of the agreement will govern. An early example was Article 21 of the 1933 Concession granted by Persia to the Anglo Persian Oil Company which provided:

> This Concession shall not be annulled by the Government and the terms therein contained shall not be altered either by general or special legislation in the future, or by administrative measures or any other acts whatever of the executive authorities.

Another was considered in the TOPCO Arbitration, supra p. 749. In addition to freezing tax laws and customs laws and other regulatory regimes that might adversely affect profitability of the project, these clauses are often intended to prevent repudiation of the contract or expropriation of the project. It has been argued that a state cannot be bound by such a clause because it would be inconsistent with its sovereignty. Saudia Arabia v. Aramco Award, 27 Int'l L.Rep. 117 (1958); Kuwait v. Aminol Award, 21 I.L.M. 976 (1982). The better view, however, seems that expressed by Dupuy, namely that entering into such an undertaking is itself an exercise of sovereignty that is binding on the state. In the *Kuwait v. Aminol Award,* the tribunal concluded that the contract before it had such a long duration (i.e., 60 years) that the tribunal would not presume that the stabilization clause was intended to preclude nationalization unless that were expressly so stipulated, id. paras. 94–95, but decided that the stabilization clause had a legal effect in respect of nationalization by reinforcing requirements for proper indemnification as a condition of the taking. Id. para. 96. Under the formulation of § 712(2) of the Restatement (Third) if a state breaches a stabilization clause in an economic development agreement with a foreign private investor, for example, by imposing on the project exchange controls or tax increases that otherwise apply to nationals and aliens alike, would such a breach without more be a violation of international law? See Restatement (Third) § 712, Reporters' Note 10, where the view is expressed that "[i]f coupled with an arbitration clause, such a stabilization clause will be given effect by the arbitrator."

Liberian Eastern Timber Corporation (LETCO) v. Government of Liberia, 26 I.L.M. 647 (1987), an ICSID arbitration, involved a timber concession agreement governed by Liberian law with a stabilization clause. The tribunal expressed the view that the stabilization clause must be respected. "Otherwise, the contracting state may easily avoid its contractual obligations by legislation. Such legislation action could only be justified by nationalization which [is for a bona fide public purpose, is nondiscriminatory and is accompanied by payment of appropriate compensation]" 26 I.L.M. 667 (1987). Why should it be lawful to breach a stabilization clause by enactment of a law nationalizing the alien concessionaire?

5. Often under the investment incentive program of developing countries, instruments of approval are issued. Under a typical procedure, "the prospective investor must apply to the competent state agency, designated and quite often created by the basic investment law, in order to have its investment approved or 'registered.' * * * The final instrument of approval is very often the product of extensive negotiations. By that instrument, the state grants to the investor some or all of the assurances and privileges provided for in the investment incentive law, while the investor undertakes certain obligations with respect to the form, amount, and other elements of the investment. The precise form of the instrument varies in the different countries. It is usually an act of the executive branch of government: an administrative decree, a decision of the cabinet or of certain ministers, or some other administrative act." Fatouros, Government Guarantees to Foreign Investors, 122–23 (1962). Do such unilateral undertakings by a state fall outside the area of "contract"? Fatouros concludes that such instruments "are of a mixed character, both contractual and noncontractual." Id. at 196; see the discussion id. at 192–209. If an undertaking constitutes no more than a unilateral act by the state, can a breach thereof constitute a breach of international law? To what extent are the principles in the contractual area applicable? Should general principles of estoppel come into play? See, e.g., MacGibbon, Estoppel in International Law, 7 I.C.L.Q. 468 (1958); Friedmann, Some Impacts of Social Organization on International Law, 50 A.J.I.L. 475, 506 (1956).

## SECTION 4. REPARATION

When an act or omission attributed to a state causes injury to an alien in violation of international law, the state of which the injured alien is a national has, as against the responsible state, the remedies generally available between states for violation of customary international law, discussed in Chapter 7 at p. 570 supra, and any special remedies available under an applicable treaty. Restatement (Third) § 713.

The violation of international law creates an obligation on the part of the delinquent to make reparation for the wrong to the state injured by the violation. Reparation may consist in an indemnity or money damages, restitution or satisfaction. See the discussion at p. 583 supra. When a state asserts a claim based on responsibility of another state for an injury to one of its nationals, the state's claim is essentially derivative in nature, some of the implications of which have been discussed at p. 692 above. Another implication is that, when a state's claim arises from an injury to one of its nationals, reparation often takes the form of a monetary payment measured by the damages suffered by its national; the injury to the dignity or sovereignty of the state is frequently treated as having only theoretical or symbolic significance.

As the Permanent Court of International Justice observed in the Case Concerning the Factory at Chorzów (Merits), P.C.I.J.Ser.A, No. 17, at 28 (1928):

> "* * * Rights or interests of an individual the violation of which rights causes damage are always in a different plane to rights belonging to a State, which rights may also be infringed by the same act. The damage suffered by an individual is never therefore identical in kind with that which will be suffered by a State; it can only afford a convenient scale for the calculation of the reparation due to the State."

In appropriate circumstances, reparation might also include additional monetary damages for the injury to the claimant state. For discussion of the relationship between the injury to an individual and to a state of which he is a national in fixing the measure of reparation, see the opinions in Laura M.B. Janes Claim (United States v. Mexico), [1927] Opinions of Commissioner 108, 4 U.N.Int'l Arb.Awards 82.

The entire reparation is paid to the claimant state and disbursed to its national claimants at its discretion. On the legal status of reparation received by the United States, see William v. Heard, 140 U.S. 529 (1891); Opinion of J. Reuben Clark, Solicitor for the Department of State, 7 A.J.I.L. 382 (1913). See generally 3 Whiteman, Damages in International Law 2035–59 (1943) [Hereinafter cited as Whiteman, Damages]; 5 Hackworth 763–801.

In the *Chorzów Factory Case,* the Permanent Court of International Justice also indicated that:

> The essential principle contained in the actual notion of an illegal act—a principle which seems to be established by international practice and in particular by the decisions of arbitral tribunals—is that reparation must, as far as possible, wipe out all the consequences of the illegal act and reestablish the situation which would, in all probability, have existed if that act had not been committed. Restitution in kind, or, if this is not possible, payment of a sum corresponding to the value which a restitution in kind would bear; the award, if need be, of damages for loss sustained which would not be covered by restitution in kind or payment in place of it—such are the principles which should serve to determine the amount of compensation due for an act contrary to international law.

P.C.I.J.Ser.A, No. 17, at 41. In the majority of cases restitution is impossible because of changed circumstances, and the reparation must consist of monetary compensation.

In 1974, two arbitral tribunals reached different conclusions on whether restitution is an appropriate remedy in a case of confiscation of an oil concession in breach of the concession agreement. Compare Texaco Overseas Petroleum Company v. Libya, supra at p. 750 (Dupuy: restitution is an appropriate remedy), with BP v. Libya, (unpublished, Aug. 1, 1974) (Judge Lagergren: restitution cannot be ordered). See also p. 584 supra.

The Permanent Court also distinguished between the case in which the payment of "fair compensation" can render lawful under international law an expropriation or other taking of property (see p. 726 supra), and the case in which the taking is wrongful under international law even if such compensation is paid. Id. at 46. In the former case, the Court indicated that the measure of compensation was the value of the property at the time of the taking plus interest to the date of payment. The *Chorzów Factory Case* itself involved the latter since the taking there was in violation of a specific treaty prohibition against expropriation (even if compensation were paid). The Court stated that in this situation the measure of damages was the value that the undertaking would have had at the time of indemnification had the expropriation not taken place, plus any losses sustained as a result of the expropriation. Id. at 48. Thus, the Court allowed damages for loss of profits realized between the seizure and the indemnification.

Reparation has been held to include compensation for lost profits when the violation of international law consists in tortious conduct resulting in loss or destruction of property if the profits were reasonably certain and not speculative. See Irene Roberts Case (United States v. Venezuela), Ralston, Venezuelan Arbitrations of 1903, 142, 144, 9 U.N.Rep.Int'l Arb.Awards 204, 207–08; 3 Whiteman, Damages at 1840–58. If the profits were speculative in view of the circumstances, they have generally not been included in the measure of reparation. In cases involving contract claims, lost profits may be allowed where they are reasonable and within the contemplation of the parties. See The Shufeldt Claim (United States v. Guatemala), Dep't of State Arb.Ser. No. 3, 851, 877–78, 2 U.N.Rep.Int'l Arb.Awards 1079, 1099 (1930); 3 Whiteman, Damages at 1858–66. When a tribunal is not permitted by the *compromis* to grant reparation for anticipated profits, or when it feels that the profits are too speculative to measure, it can normally grant interest in lieu of profits.

In claims for personal injuries the measure of reparation for the injury to the individual is the loss to the individual claimant. Damages have included medical expenses, loss of earnings, George Henry Clapham Claim (Great Britain v. Mexico), 5 U.N.Rep.Int'l Arb.Awards 201, 203–04 (1931), pain and suffering, 1 Whiteman, Damages at 588–89, and mental anguish, Opinion in the Lusitania Cases (United States v. Germany), Mixed Claims Commission, [1923–25] Administrative Decisions and Opinions 17, 21–22, 7 U.N.Rep.Int'l Arb.Awards 32, 36–37 (1923). Damages may be reduced where the claimant has contributed to the injury. Lillie S. Kling Claim (United States v. Mexico), General Claims Commission, [1930–31] Opinions of Commissioners 36, 49–50, 4 U.N.Rep.Int'l Arb.Awards 575, 585 (1930).

Problems sometimes arise in attributing responsibility to the delinquent state for the damages suffered by an individual claimant. A state is ordinarily responsible only for the damages caused by its delinquency. Where the delinquency is a failure to apprehend and punish a private person who has injured an alien or his property, the offending state has not damaged the claimant except in so far as the state's delinquency prevents the claimant from bringing a damage action against the responsible person. If, as is often the case, an action against the private wrongdoer would be fruitless, the delinquent state has not caused any damage to the claimant. International tribunals have generally avoided such a result by finding that the delinquent state's lack of diligence in apprehending or punishing the private wrongdoer amounted to condoning the injury and imposed derivative liability on the state, or by finding that the claimant suffered "grief," "mistrust and lack of safety" resulting from the state's failure to apprehend or punish the wrongdoer. See Poggioli Case (Italy v. Venezuela) Ralston, Venezuelan Arbitrations of 1903, 847, 869, 10 U.N.Rep.Int'l Arb.Awards 669, 689; Laura M.B. Janes Claim (United States v. Mexico), General Claims Commission, [1927] Opinions of Commissioners 108, 120, 4 U.N.Rep.Int'l Arb.Awards 82. Under either theory damages have usually been measured by the loss suffered by the individual claimant rather than by the gravity of the state's delinquency. See 1 Whiteman, Damages at 39; Brierly, The Theory of Implied State Complicity in International Claims, [1928] Brit. Y.B.I.L. 42; Freeman, The International Responsibility of States for Denial of Justice 367–69 (1938). But cf. The William T. Way Claim (United States v. Mexico), see p. 1079 supra; The "I'm Alone" Case (Canada v. United States), 3 U.N.Rep.Int'l Arb.Awards 1609 (1935); Claims of Richeson et al. (United States v. Panama), 6 U.N.Rep.Int'l Arb.Awards 325 (1933); 1 Whiteman, Damages at 721–744, 788.

Another source of difficulty may arise in determining whether the delinquent state is liable for particular items of damage suffered by individual claimants. This problem arises particularly when the *compromis* conferring jurisdiction on a tribunal limits its jurisdiction to claims "resulting from" some specified event. Tribunals generally speak of "proximate cause" and tend to disallow damages which are "remote," "speculative," or not proximately caused by the delinquency. See Administrative Decision No. II, (United States v. Germany), Mixed Claims Commission, 1923, [1923–25] Administrative Decisions and Opinions 5, 12–13, 7 U.N.Rep.Int'l Arb.Awards 23, 29–30. Whatever particular damages will be allowed depends on the particular circumstances of each case. See 3 Whiteman, Damages at 1765–1874.

International tribunals generally award interest either from the date of the obligation to make reparation or from the date of the award. The rate varies depending on the nature of the claim and on the rate of interest generally prevailing at the time and place of the injury. See 2 O'Connell at 1211–13; 1 Oppenheim at 353 n. 1; 3 Whiteman, Damages at 1913–2006. Tribunals frequently allow individual claimants the cost of preparing their claims. However, in the absence of an agreement to the contrary, the governments bear their own costs in preparing or defending their claims and share the cost of the tribunal equally. 3 Whiteman, Damages at 2024–28.

## SECTION 5. SUCCESSION TO INTERNATIONAL RESPONSIBILITY

Although the problem of state succession arises in other contexts, especially in connection with determining whether a successor state succeeds to rights and duties embodied in international agreements, see p. 530 supra, it also arises in the context of state responsibility with the focus on the extent to which the successor state is responsible for violations of international law by the predecessor. See the discussion in Chapter 4 at p. 293.

# SECTION 6. BILATERAL TREATIES

## A. INTRODUCTION

A large number of bilateral treaties have been entered into between industrialized capital exporting countries and developing countries that have as one of their objectives or as their sole objective increasing the legal protection to private parties of one of the contracting states that invest or engage in other business transactions in the other contracting state against non-commercial risks of the kinds discussed at p. 721. These treaties may be divided into two categories. The first encompasses treaties of friendship, commerce and navigation ("FCN treaties") which, as the title implies, cover a wide range of trade relations in addition to providing legal protection against non-commercial risks. The second category encompasses bilateral investment treaties that have been concluded by capital-exporting countries with developing countries that focus specifically on protection of the foreign investor against specified non-commercial risks, such as the taking of the investor's property without compensation and, in some cases, violation by a contracting state of contracts with nationals of the other contracting state. Many of these investment treaties have their roots in the Draft Convention on the Protection of Foreign Property prepared under the auspices of the Organization for Economic Co-operation and Development (OECD) and adopted in 1967 by the OECD Council, stating the belief that the Draft Convention would be useful in the preparation of bilateral agreements for the protection of foreign property. See p. 1453 infra. Bilateral FCN and investment treaties are discussed generally in Bilateral Treaties for International Investment, International Chamber of Commerce (Paris 1977).

## B. FRIENDSHIP, COMMERCE AND NAVIGATION TREATIES

During the 1950's and 1960's the United States negotiated a network of bilateral treaties of friendship, commerce and navigation, designed primarily for the protection and encouragement of United States private trade and investment abroad. See Walker, Modern Treaties of Friendship, Commerce, and Navigation, 42 Minn.L.Rev. 805 (1958); Rubin, Private Foreign Investment 76 (1956); Wilson, U.S. Commercial Treaties and International Law (1960); American Bar Association, Commercial Treaty Index (1976).

The basic thrust of these agreements is to obligate each contracting state to grant at least national and most-favored-nation treatment to citizens and companies of the other contracting state. With respect to some activities, however, such as those related to national security, transport, utilities and exploitation of national resources, most-favored-nation treatment may be all that is guaranteed.

The United States Treaty with Pakistan on Friendship and Commerce, which was signed November 12, 1959, and entered into force on February 12, 1961, 12 U.S.T. 110, T.I.A.S. No. 4683, 404 U.N.T.S. 259, reflects the basic pattern of the post-World War II FCN treaties. The role of the treaties in providing legal security for international trade and investment can be examined with reference to its provisions. For a detailed comparative analysis of the United States FCN treaties see The Protection of Private

Property Invested Abroad, Report by the Committee on International Trade and Investment, Section of International and Comparative Law, American Bar Association 39–58 (1963).

The treaties specifically prohibit discriminatory treatment of nationals of the other contracting state. Thus, Article 6(3) of the Pakistan treaty states:

> (3) Neither Party shall take unreasonable or discriminatory measures that would impair the legally acquired rights or interests within its territories of nationals and companies of the other Party in the enterprises which they have established, in their capital, or in the skills, arts or technology which they have supplied.

With respect to exchange restrictions, Article 12 of the Pakistan treaty provides:

> (1) Nationals and companies of either Party shall be accorded by the other Party national treatment and most-favored-nation treatment with respect to payments, remittances and transfers of funds or financial instruments between the territories of the two Parties as well as between the territories of such other Party and of any third country.
>
> (2) Neither Party shall impose exchange restrictions as defined in paragraph 5 of the present Article except to the extent necessary to prevent its monetary reserves from falling to a low level, to effect an increase in the reserves in order to bring them up to an adequate level, or both. It is understood that the provisions of the present Article do not alter the obligations either Party may have to the International Monetary Fund or preclude imposition of particular restrictions whenever the Fund specifically authorizes or requests a Party to impose such particular restrictions.
>
> (3) If either Party imposes exchange restrictions in accordance with paragraph 2 of the present Article, it shall, after making whatever provision may be necessary to assure the availability of foreign exchange for goods and services essential to the health and welfare of its people, make reasonable provision for the withdrawal, in foreign exchange in the currency of the other Party, of: (a) the compensation referred to in Article 6, paragraph 4, (b) earnings, whether in the form of salaries, interest, dividends, commissions, royalties, payments for technical services, or otherwise, and (c) amounts for amortization of loans, depreciation of direct investments, and capital transfers, giving consideration to special needs for other transactions. If more than one rate of exchange is in force, the rate applicable to such withdrawals shall be a rate which is specifically approved by the International Monetary Fund for such transactions or, in the absence of a rate so approved, an effective rate which, inclusive of any taxes or surcharges on exchange transfers, is just and reasonable.
>
> (4) Exchange restrictions shall not be imposed by either Party in a manner unnecessarily detrimental or arbitrarily discriminatory to the claims, investments, transport, trade, and other interests of the nationals and companies of the other Party, nor to the competitive position thereof.

> (5) The term "exchange restrictions" as used in the present Article includes all restrictions, regulations, charges, taxes, or other requirements imposed by either Party which burden or interfere with payments, remittances or transfers of funds or of financial instruments between the territories of the two Parties.

To what extent do these guarantees represent a significant measure of legal protection to a United States enterprise beyond that accorded under customary international law? Do they constitute meaningful limitations on a State's otherwise virtually untrammelled freedom to regulate its monetary policy? Do they lend any protection against currency depreciation or devaluation? Do they shift to the State imposing the controls a burden of justification that is to some extent susceptible of objective proof? See Fatouros, Government Guarantees to Foreign Investors 218 (1962).

On expropriation, Article 6 of the treaty provides as follows:

> (4) Property of nationals and companies of either Party shall not be taken within the territories of the other Party except for a public purpose, nor shall it be taken without the prompt payment of just compensation. Such compensation shall be in an effectively realizable form and shall represent the full equivalent of the property taken; and adequate provision shall have been made at or prior to the time of taking for the determination and payment thereof.
>
> (5) Nationals and companies of either Party shall in no case be accorded, within the territories of the other Party, less than national treatment and most-favored-nation treatment with respect to the matters set forth in paragraphs 2 and 4 of the present Article. Moreover, enterprises in which nationals and companies of either Party have a substantial interest shall be accorded, within the territories of the other Party, not less than national treatment and most-favored-nation treatment in all matters relating to the taking of privately owned enterprises into public ownership and to the placing of such enterprises under public control.

What do these provisions add to the protection afforded under customary international law? To what extent are these provisions undermined by the exchange provision escape clauses of Article 12(3) under which a contracting State is required to make "reasonable provision" for the withdrawal in foreign exchange of compensation only after providing for goods and services essential for the health and welfare of its people?

Other provisions of interest contained in the Pakistan treaty include the following:

> Art. 7. (1) Enterprises which nationals and companies of either Party are permitted to establish or acquire, within the territories of the other Party, shall be permitted freely to conduct their activities therein, upon terms no less favorable than other enterprises of whatever nationality engaged in similar activities. Such nationals and companies shall enjoy the rights to continued control and management of such enterprises, and to do all other things necessary or incidental to the effective conduct of their affairs.

(2) Each Party reserves the right to limit the extent to which aliens may establish or acquire interests in enterprises engaged within its territories in activities for gain (business activities) provided that in any event not less than most-favored-nation treatment shall be accorded. However, new limitations imposed by either Party upon the extent to which alien nationals or companies are permitted to carry on such activities within its territories shall not be applied as against enterprises which are engaged in such activities therein at the time such limitations are adopted and which are owned or controlled by nationals and companies of the other Party.

* * *

Art. 9. * * * (3) Nationals and companies of either Party shall be accorded within the territories of the other Party national treatment and most-favored-nation treatment with respect to acquiring, by purchase, lease or otherwise, and with respect to owning and possessing, personal property of all kinds, both tangible and intangible. * * *

(4) Nationals and companies of either Party shall be accorded within the territories of the other Party national treatment and most-favored-nation treatment with respect to disposing of property of all kinds.

Art. 10. (1) Nationals and companies of either Party shall be accorded, within the territories of the other Party, national treatment and most-favored-nation treatment with respect to obtaining and maintaining patents of invention, and with respect to rights in trademarks, trade names, trade labels and industrial property of every kind. * * *

Art. 11. (1) Nationals of either Party residing within the territories of the other Party, and companies of either Party engaged in trade or other gainful pursuit or in scientific, educational, religious or philanthropic activities within the territories of the other Party, shall not be subject to the payment of taxes, fees or charges imposed upon or applied to income, capital, transactions, activities or any other object, or to requirements with respect to the levy and collection thereof, within the territories of such other Party, more burdensome than those borne by nationals and companies of such other Party.

* * *

(3) Nationals and companies of either Party shall in no case be subject, within the territories of the other Party, to the payment of taxes, fees or charges imposed upon or applied to income, capital, transactions, activities or any other object, or to requirements with respect to the levy and collection thereof, more burdensome than those borne by nationals, residents and companies of any third country.

To what extent do the quoted treaty provisions in their entirety lend protection against various types of creeping expropriation, such as wage and labor controls, price controls, import and export restrictions, confiscatory taxation, or unfair competition from an enterprise owned by the local government or private interests? Note that the treaties provide no protection, beyond the prohibition of discriminatory treatment and the other general provisions set forth, supra, against violation by a Contracting State of specific contractual or other assurances made to an alien investor.

Some of the treaty provisions afford a measure of protection to the United States firm supplying know-how to an enterprise in Pakistan under a license agreement, technical or managerial services agreement or some other contractual arrangement. Because the know-how supplier's return is typically cast in the form of a current royalty or fee payment, the extent of the treaty protection against exchange restrictions that would inhibit or preclude the remittance of such payments in foreign exchange is of particular significance. Also, industrial property rights (such as patents or trademarks) recognized under the laws of the Contracting State and owned by a United States enterprise would enjoy the same protection against expropriation and discriminatory treatment as other property. National and most-favored-nation treatment is accorded with respect to the obtaining and maintaining of patents, trademarks and other industrial property.

The treaties also contain provisions specifically aimed at providing protection for the United States firm exporting goods to the other Contracting State. To a considerable extent these provisions overlap similar arrangements applicable under the General Agreement on Tariffs and Trade. See p. 1399 supra. Article 14(1) of the Pakistan treaty guarantees the exporter's products most-favored-nation treatment as to customs duties and other charges that may be imposed, as to the methods by which such duties and charges are imposed and as to all related rules and formalities. Within the other Contracting State, the exporter's goods are guaranteed national treatment as to sale, distribution, internal taxation, storage and use. Pakistan treaty, Art. 16(1).

If a Contracting State finds it necessary to impose quantitative restrictions on imports, there is a requirement for notice to exporters affected as well as a guarantee that, if allotments are made benefitting any third country, exporters protected by the treaty shall be afforded a proportionate share of such allotments. Pakistan treaty, Art. 14(3).

Article 17 of the Pakistan treaty states:

> 1. Each Party undertakes: (a) that enterprises owned or controlled by its Government, and that monopolies or agencies granted exclusive or special privileges within its territories, shall make their purchases and sales involving either imports or exports affecting the commerce of the other Party solely in accordance with commercial considerations, including price, quality, availability, marketability, transportation and other conditions of purchase or sale; and (b) that the nationals, companies and commerce of such other Party shall be afforded adequate opportunity, in accordance with customary business practice, to compete for participation in such purchases and sales.
>
> 2. Each Party shall accord to the nationals, companies and commerce of the other Party fair and equitable treatment, as compared with that accorded to the nationals, companies and commerce of any third country, with respect to: (a) the governmental purchase of supplies, (b) the awarding of concessions and other government contracts, and (c) the sale of any service sold by the Government or by any monopoly or agency granted exclusive or special privileges.

In addition to the limitations on the protection accorded the exporter by the provisions already mentioned, many of the exporter's rights depend on reciprocity, and they are subject to advantages that either Contracting State may accord to its own fisheries or to adjacent countries "to facilitate frontier traffic" or by virtue of a customs union or free trade area. Pakistan treaty, Art. 14. Also each Contracting State retains the right to impose controls on imports (or exports) "that have effect equivalent to, or which are necessary to make effective, exchange restrictions." Pakistan treaty, Art. 14(7).

With respect to enforcement of treaty rights, Article 5(1) provides:

> 1. Nationals and companies of either Party shall be accorded national treatment and most-favored-nation treatment with respect to access to the courts of justice and to administrative tribunals and agencies within the territories of the other Party, in all degrees of jurisdiction, both in pursuit and in defense of their rights. It is understood that companies of either Party not engaged in activities within the territories of the other Party shall enjoy such access therein without any requirement of registration or domestication.

The treaty does not provide for international judicial or arbitral enforcement of rights vested in private parties by its terms, but it does call for resolution of disputes between the Contracting States arising out of the treaty ultimately by recourse to the International Court of Justice if other means of settlement fail. Art. 23(2).

In evaluating the significance of the FCN treaties, one must consider not only their substantive coverage or lack of coverage but also the fact that the very existence of the treaty may reflect a favorable climate for United States trade and investment in the other contracting state. One must also keep in mind that relatively few FCN treaties have been concluded with the developing countries of Africa, Asia and Latin America where the need for the protection they afford is often important. All such treaties, moreover, are terminable by either party on notice.

In recent years the United States has ceased negotiation of FCN treaties with developing countries and has shifted its efforts to negotiating reciprocal bilateral investment treaties which focus principally on providing the nationals of each contracting state with liberalized access to the market of the other contracting state and on providing enhanced legal protection against noncommercial risks.

### *Note*

For an extensive discussion of the scope of various provisions of the United States FCN Treaty with Italy of 1948 and a Supplementary Agreement of 1951, see Case Concerning Elettronica Sicula S.p.A. (ELSI) (United States v. Italy), 1989 I.C.J. 15, 28 I.L.M. 1111, the facts of which are summarized at p. 696 supra. See also Murphy, The ELSI Case: An Investment Dispute at the International Court of Justice, 16 Yale J.Int'l L. 391 (1991).

## C. BILATERAL INVESTMENT TREATIES (BITs)

Hundreds of bilateral investment treaties (BITs) have entered into force since the first such treaty was entered into by the Federal Republic of Germany and Pakistan in 1959. Salacuse, BIT by BIT: The Growth of

Bilateral Investment Treaties and Their Impact on Foreign Investment in Developing Countries, 24 Int'l Law. 655, 657 (1990). All the major capital-exporting states and more than 80 developing countries have become parties to these arrangements. Germany has led the way, having entered into more than 70. Id. at 657. In recent years, the United States has placed increasing reliance on investment treaties, denominated Treaties Concerning the Reciprocal Encouragement and Protection of Investments, and has signed treaties with 18 countries. Treaties with Bangladesh, Cameroon, Egypt, Grenada, Morocco, Panama, Senegal, Turkey and Zaire are in effect. Treaties with Argentina, the Czech and Slovak Republic, Congo, Haiti, Kazakhstan, Romania, Russia, Sri Lanka and Tunisia await ratification. Others are being negotiated. The United States treaties differ from many entered into by European countries in that their purpose is not merely protection of investments but also ensuring free access (with limited exceptions) of investors of each contracting state to the market of the other contracting state.

Treaties for the protection of foreign private investors in the Czech and Slovak Republic, Kazakhstan, Romania and Russia represent radical departures from the past and reflect the dramatic change in the legal climate for foreign investment in those economies. Perhaps most striking, however, is the signing by the United States on November 14, 1991, of a treaty with Argentina, 31 I.L.M. 124 (1991), because Argentina, which has also recently signed treaties with Germany, Switzerland, Belgium/Luxembourg and the United Kingdom, agreed in the treaty with the United States to abandon the Calvo Doctrine and accept dispute settlement between the investor and the host government by binding arbitration under the rules of ICSID or UNCITRAL or other institution agreed by the parties with no requirement for prior exhaustion of remedies in the host country. Article VII, 31 I.L.M. 132. Moreover, the treaty embodies the rule that expropriation must be accompanied by "prompt, adequate and effective compensation"—the Hull formula, which has been an anathema to most Latin American countries since the 1930s. Article IV(1), 31 I.L.M. at 131.

BITs typically grant rights to, and impose obligations on, both contracting states on a reciprocal basis. The treaties normally encompass such matters as general standards of treatment of foreign investment, protection against expropriation, compensation for losses from armed conflict or internal disorder, currency transfers and convertibility, and settlement of disputes.

The United States BITs are exemplified by the Treaty with Turkey, which entered into force on May 18, 1990 and which is included in the Document Supplement.

### 1. *Standards of Treatment*

Most United States investment treaties call for according "fair and equitable treatment" to covered investments and, with a variety of exceptions and qualifications, provide for national treatment or most-favored-nation treatment, whichever is more favorable to the investor. Exceptions typically exclude sectors of the economy, such as public utilities, transport, and defense, that are not open to foreign investment.

### 2. *Expropriation*

A central feature of all of the investment treaties is the provisions relating to expropriation. All call for payment of full compensation, either invoking the Hull formula or some equivalent formulation. Many of these treaties go beyond the usual provisions of the FCN treaties in covering indirect takings of property of nationals of the other contracting state, and some cover violation of contractual undertakings given by a contracting state to a national of the other contracting state.

Article III of the United States–Turkey Treaty, 25 I.L.M. at 92 (1985), provides in part, as follows:

> 1. Investments shall not be expropriated or nationalized either directly or indirectly through measures tantamount to expropriation or nationalization ("expropriation") except for a public purpose; in a non-discriminatory manner; upon payment of prompt, adequate and effective compensation; and in accordance with due process of law and the general principles of treatment provided for in Article II(2) [National treatment or most-favored-nation treatment, whichever is more favorable to the investor].
>
> 2. Compensation shall be equivalent to the fair market value of the expropriated investment at the time the expropriatory action was taken or became known. Compensation shall be paid without delay; be fully realizable; and be freely transferable. In the event that payment of compensation is delayed, such compensation shall be paid in an amount which would put the investor in a position no less favorable than the position in which he would have been, had the compensation been paid immediately on the date of expropriation.
>
> 3. A national or company of either Party that asserts that all or part of its investment has been expropriated shall have a right to prompt review by the appropriate judicial or administrative authorities of the other Party to determine whether such expropriation and any compensation therefor conforms to the principles of this Article.

### 3. *Losses from Armed Conflict or Internal Disorder*

Most treaties provide that foreign investors will be accorded national or most-favored-nation treatment with respect to losses resulting from armed conflict, civil disturbance and the like. For example, Article III(4) of the United States–Turkey Treaty, 25 I.L.M. at 92, provides that "[n]ationals or companies of either Party whose investments suffer losses in the territory of the other Party owing to war, insurrection, civil disturbance or other similar events shall be accorded treatment by such other Party not less favorable than that accorded to its own nationals or companies of any third country, whichever is the most favorable treatment, as regards any measures it adopts in relation to such losses." For an ICSID arbitral award interpreting provisions of the Sri Lanka–United Kingdom Bilateral Investment Treaty concerning protection against losses owing to war or other armed conflict, revolution, a state of national emergency, revolt, insurrection or riot, see Asian Agricultural Products Ltd. v. Sri Lanka, 30 I.L.M. 580 (1990).

### 4. *Transfers and Convertibility of Payments*

Investment treaties typically include general provisions guaranteeing free transferability in convertible currency of "returns" on investment, broadly defined to include both remittance of current payments, such as interest, dividends, rents, royalties and service fees, and repatriation of capital, including gain from the sale of the investment. However, frequently there are qualifications which give the contracting party some flexibility to impose controls required to protect the value of its currency and its balance of payments. For example, Article 7 of The Netherlands–Philippines Treaty for the Promotion and Protection of Investment, Tractatenblad (Neth.) No. 86, 1985, provides:

> 1. Each Contracting Party shall in respect of investments permit nationals of the other Contracting Party the unrestricted transfer in free convertible currency of their investments and of the earnings from it to the country designated by those nationals, subject to the right of the former Contracting Party to impose equitably and in good faith such measures as may be necessary to safeguard the integrity and independence of its currency, its external financial position and balance of payments, consistent with its rights and obligations as a member of the International Monetary Fund.

Article IV of the United States–Turkey Treaty, 25 I.L.M. at 93, does not accord comparable leeway:

> 1. Each Party shall permit all transfers related to an investment to be made freely and without delay into and out of its territory. Such transfers include: (a) returns; (b) compensation pursuant to Article III; (c) payments arising out of an investment dispute; (d) principal and interest payments arising under loan agreements; and (e) proceeds from the sale or liquidation of all or any part of an investment.
>
> 2. Transfers shall be made in a freely convertible currency at the prevailing market rate of exchange on the date of transfer with respect to spot transactions in the currency or currencies to be transferred.

### 5. *Settlement of Disputes*

Most recent United States BITs provide for two dispute settlement mechanisms: one to deal with disputes between a contracting state and a foreign investor and the other to deal with disputes between the two contracting states.

With respect to disputes in the first category, many recent treaties provide for eventual resolution of disputes under the rules and procedures of the International Centre for Settlement of Investment Disputes (ICSID). For example, Article VI of the United States–Turkey Treaty, 25 I.L.M. at 94, provides, in part, as follows:

> 1. For purposes of this Article, an investment dispute is defined as a dispute involving (a) the interpretation or application of an investment agreement between a Party and a national or company of the other Party; (b) the interpretation or application of any investment authorization granted by a Party's foreign investment authority to such national

or company; or (c) an alleged breach of any right conferred or created by this Treaty with respect to an investment.

2. In the event of an investment dispute between a Party and a national or company of the other Party, the parties to the dispute shall initially seek to resolve the dispute by consultations and negotiations in good faith. If such consultations or negotiations are unsuccessful, the dispute may be settled through the use of non-binding, third-party procedures upon which such national or company and the Party mutually agree. If the dispute cannot be resolved through the foregoing procedures, the dispute shall be submitted for settlement in accordance with any previously agreed, applicable dispute settlement procedures.

3. (a) The national or company concerned may choose to consent in writing to the submission of the dispute to the International Centre for Settlement of Investment Disputes ("Centre") for settlement by arbitration, at any time after one year from the date upon which the dispute arose, provided:

(i) the dispute has not, for any reason, been submitted by the national or company for resolution in accordance with any applicable dispute settlement procedures previously agreed to by the parties to the dispute; and

(ii) the national or company concerned has not brought the dispute before the courts of justice or administrative tribunals or agencies of competent jurisdiction of the Party that is a party to the dispute.

(b) Each Party hereby consents to the submission of an investment dispute to the Centre for settlement by arbitration.

Frequently, disputes between the contracting states may be settled upon the demand of either party by an ad hoc arbitral proceeding. See, e.g., Article VII of the United States–Turkey Treaty, 25 I.L.M. at 96.

### 6. *Significance of the Bilateral Investment Treaty Network*

Salacuse sums up his evaluation of the bilateral investment treaties as follows:

> Despite the lack of proof of [the treaties'] effectiveness, the BIT movement as a whole may be seen as part of an ongoing process to create a new international law of foreign investment to respond to the demands of the new global economy that has so rapidly emerged within the last few years. While the world has developed a relatively elaborate legal structure for trade in the form of the General Agreement on Tariffs and Trade, it has yet to create similar structure for international investment. Such a multilateral arrangement, a General Agreement on Direct International Investment, is many years away and will only be achieved through a gradual step-by-step approach. The negotiations on trade-related investment measures in the current Uruguay Round of GATT represent an important initiative for that organization, and the results may contribute to a new international law on foreign investment. The BIT movement of the past thirty years has also been an important step in this direction. Although BITs themselves only bind

the two countries concerned and are probably not sufficiently widespread to constitute customary international law, the process of study, consultation, discussion, and negotiation that has been part of the BIT movement has certainly laid a foundation for the creation of an international investment framework that may eventually attract the consensus of the nations of the world.

24 Int'l Law. 675 (footnotes omitted).

Salacuse cites, as an example of a multilateral investment treaty that has clearly been influenced by the bilateral treaties, the Agreement Among Brunei, Indonesia, Malaysia, The Philippines, Singapore, and Thailand for the Promotion and Protection of Investments, December 12, 1987, 27 I.L.M. 612 (1988). 24 Int'l Law. 675.

### *Note*

For a discussion of bilateral investment treaties, see Alvarez, Vandevelde, Propp, Gunawardana and others, Panel Discussion on The Development and Expansion of Bilateral Investment Treaties, A.S.I.L. Proc. 532–557 (1992).

## SECTION 7. PROTECTION UNDER UNITED STATES LAW FOR INTERNATIONAL TRADE AND INVESTMENT

### A. SOVEREIGN IMMUNITY, THE ACT OF STATE DOCTRINE AND THE SECOND HICKENLOOPER AMENDMENT

A United States national seeking to obtain legal redress in United States courts for injury to property attributable to conduct of a foreign state or its instrumentality may be faced with a claim of sovereign immunity, discussed at p. 1126 supra, as well as an invocation of the act of state doctrine, discussed at p. 180 supra. To what extent does the Second Hickenlooper Amendment, which is set forth at p. 193 supra, meaningfully improve the legal position of the United States national?

In connection with the materials on state immunity, the act of state doctrine and the Second Hickenlooper Amendment, consider under what circumstances a United States national can invoke the aid of United States courts if his property has been taken without compensation by a foreign state. What are the possibilities if the property seized is brought into the United States? How would the rights and remedies of the United States national be affected by whether the property is in the possession of the foreign state or some private party deriving its title through the foreign state? If the property does not find its way into the United States, under what circumstances, if any, could relief be obtained in United States courts?

### *Notes*

1. The decision of the Supreme Court in *Banco Nacional de Cuba v. Sabbatino,* p. 181 supra, involved a taking of property by the government of a recognized state within its own territory that was alleged to have been in violation of a rule of customary international law as to which there was

substantial controversy. The Supreme Court has not had occasion to decide a case involving a taking of property by a foreign state since *Sabbatino* in which one of these factors was not present.

In Alfred Dunhill of London, Inc. v. Republic of Cuba, 425 U.S. 682, 96 S.Ct. 1854, 48 L.Ed.2d 301 (1976), the Supreme Court held that repudiation by a state agency of an obligation to repay amounts paid by a United States importer of cigars did not constitute an act of state on the ground that an act of state implies a formal act of sovereignty. Four justices of the majority expressed the view that commercial transactions engaged in by a foreign state should be excepted from the act of state doctrine. This was based on the analogy of the commercial activity exception to the sovereign immunity doctrine and the fact that with respect to commercial transactions, unlike expropriation, there is broad international agreement as to the applicable rules, 425 U.S. at 695–706, 96 S.Ct. at 1861–1866. This exception has not been embraced by the lower courts. See, e.g., Braka v. Bancomer S.A., 762 F.2d 222 (2d Cir.1985).

While the act of state doctrine does not encompass takings of property located outside the territorial jurisdiction of the taking state at the time of the taking, e.g., Republic of Iraq v. First National City Bank, 241 F.Supp. 567 (S.D.N.Y.1965), aff'd, 353 F.2d 47 (2d Cir.1965), cert. denied, 382 U.S. 1027, 86 S.Ct. 648, 15 L.Ed.2d 540 (1966), a court may give effect to an act of state even as to assets in the United States when it serves the policy objectives of the United States to do so. Banco Nacional de Cuba v. Chemical Bank New York Trust Co., 658 F.2d 903 (2d Cir.1981).

2. After the reversal and remand by the Supreme Court in *Sabbatino* and enactment of the Second Hickenlooper Amendment, when the *Sabbatino* case again came before the Court of Appeals, Banco Nacional de Cuba v. Farr, 383 F.2d 166 (2d Cir.1967), cert. denied, 390 U.S. 956, 88 S.Ct. 1038, 19 L.Ed.2d 1151 (1968), the Court reaffirmed its prior decision rejecting the act of state doctrine and noted, in a dictum, that if the compensation standards of the statute were different from, they tended to be more exacting upon expropriating states than, the customary international law standards applied in the first *Sabbatino Case* and reapplied in the second. 383 F.2d at 183–85.

3. No President has made a determination that the foreign policy interests of the United States required application of the act of state doctrine in a case to which the Second Hickenlooper Amendment applied. However, in connection with the Algiers Accords containing the agreement between the United States and Iran of January 1981, President Carter gave assurances that the courts would be advised that adjudication of claims brought by the government of Iran to recover property allegedly removed from Iran by the Shah or his family should not be considered legally barred by the act of state doctrine.

4. The Second Hickenlooper Amendment act of state exception is limited to actions asserting title to specific property within the United States; it does not apply to claims for compensation for a taking of property or to assets of a nationalizing state not related to the taking on which the action is based that may come within the jurisdiction. See Banco Nacional de Cuba v. First National Bank of New York, 270 F.Supp. 1004 (S.D.N.Y.1967), rev'd, 431 F.2d 394 (2d Cir.1970), rev'd, 406 U.S. 759, 92 S.Ct. 1808, 32 L.Ed.2d 466 (1972); French v. Banco Nacional de Cuba, 23 N.Y.2d 46, 295 N.Y.S.2d 433, 242 N.E.2d 704 (1968); compare Ramirez de Arellano v. Weinberger, 745 F.2d 1500 (D.C.Cir.1984), vac'd, 471 U.S. 1113, 105 S.Ct. 2353, 86 L.Ed.2d 255 (1985). If the property taken is located in the United States the plaintiff need not attach or reduce the property

to possession, and, as long as it was in the United States when the action is commenced, it need not remain in the United States during the pendency of the action. Restatement (Third) § 444, Comment *e*.

5. Under § 1605(a)(3) of the Foreign Sovereign Immunities Act, a state is not immune from jurisdiction to adjudicate with respect to property taken in violation of international law which is present in the United States in connection with a commercial activity carried on by the taking state therein. It is unclear if the act of state doctrine is raised in such a case, whether the court should apply the standards of customary international law or treaty or the more specific standards of the First Hickenlooper Amendment. See Restatement (Third) § 444, Comment *d*.

## B. FIRST HICKENLOOPER AMENDMENT

### *FOREIGN ASSISTANCE ACT OF 1961 SECTION 301(d)*

77 Stat. 386 (1963), 78 Stat. 1013 (1964), as amended, 22 U.S.C.A. § 2370(e).

(e)(1) The President shall suspend assistance to the government of any country to which assistance is provided under this chapter or any other Act when the government of such country or any other government agency or subdivision within such country on or after January 1, 1962—

(A) has nationalized or expropriated or seized ownership or control of property owned by any United States citizen or by any corporation, partnership, or association not less than 50 per centum beneficially owned by United States citizens, or

(B) has taken steps to repudiate or nullify existing contracts or agreements with any United States citizen or any corporation or partnership, or association not less than 50 per centum beneficially owned by United States citizens, or

(C) has imposed or enforced discriminatory taxes or other exactions, or restrictive maintenance or operational conditions, or has taken other actions, which have the effect of nationalizing, expropriating, or otherwise seizing ownership or control of property so owned,

and such country, government agency, or government subdivision fails within a reasonable time (not more than six months after such action, or, in the event of a referral to the Foreign Claims Settlement Commission of the United States within such period as provided herein, not more than twenty days after the report of the Commission is received) to take appropriate steps, which may include arbitration, to discharge its obligations under international law toward such citizen or entity, including speedy compensation for such property in convertible foreign exchange, equivalent to the full value thereof, as required by international law, or fails to take steps designed to provide relief from such taxes, exactions, or conditions, as the case may be; and such suspension shall continue until the President is satisfied that appropriate steps are being taken, and the provisions of this subsection shall not be waived with respect to any country unless the President determines and certifies that such a waiver is important to the national interests of the United States. Such certification shall be reported immediately to Congress.

Upon request of the President (within seventy days after such action referred to in subparagraphs (A), (B), or (C) of this paragraph), the Foreign Claims Settlement Commission of the United States * * * is hereby authorized to evaluate expropriated property, determining the full value of any property nationalized, expropriated, or seized, or subjected to discriminatory or other actions as aforesaid, for purposes of this subsection and to render an advisory report to the President within ninety days after such request. Unless authorized by the President, the Commission shall not publish its advisory report except to the citizen or entity owning such property. * * *

(2) [Second Hickenlooper Amendment, set forth at p. 193 supra.]

### *Note*

Until amended by the Foreign Assistance Act of 1973, P.L. No. 93–183, 87 Stat. 722 (1973), to provide for waiver when certified by the President to be in the national interest, the First Hickenlooper Amendment, 22 U.S.C.A. § 2370(e)(1), dealing with suspension of foreign aid, contained a no-waiver clause. Prior to the 1973 change, the clause had been invoked only once, against Ceylon in 1963. In the case of the dispute between International Petroleum Company, Ltd. (IPC), a wholly-owned subsidiary of Standard Oil of New Jersey, and Peru in 1969, the Nixon Administration strained to avoid applying it by finding that resort to Peruvian administrative remedies and ongoing negotiations constituted "appropriate steps" adequate to make invocation unnecessary. Even after those remedies had been exhausted and negotiations had broken down, the First Hickenlooper Amendment was not applied, and since then it has never been invoked. See Lillich, Requiem for Hickenlooper, 69 A.J.I.L. 97–100.

# Chapter 10

# PEACEFUL SETTLEMENT OF DISPUTES

## SECTION 1. THE OBLIGATION TO SETTLE DISPUTES BY PEACEFUL MEANS

### A. THE CHARTER OBLIGATIONS

Article 2, paragraph 3 of the U.N. Charter provides:

> 3. All Members shall settle their international disputes by peaceful means in such a manner that international peace and security, and justice, are not endangered.

Article 33 of the Charter states:

> 1. The parties to any dispute, the continuance of which is likely to endanger the maintenance of international peace and security, shall, first of all, seek a solution by negotiation, enquiry, mediation, conciliation, arbitration, judicial settlement, resort to regional agencies or arrangements, or other peaceful means of their own choice.
>
> 2. The Security Council shall, when it deems necessary, call upon the parties to settle their dispute by such means.

Articles 34–38 of the Charter authorize the Security Council to recommend procedures and terms of settlement. Article 36(3) provides:

> 3. In making recommendations under this Article the Security Council should also take into consideration that legal disputes should as a general rule be referred by the parties to the International Court of Justice in accordance with the provisions of the Statute of the Court.

*Notes*

1. Does the obligation to settle disputes by peaceful means signify more than the obligation of Article 2(4) to avoid use of force or threat of force? Are states obliged to settle all their disputes or only those "the continuance of which

is likely to endanger the maintenance of international peace and security" (Article 33)?

2. May the United Nations Security Council require a state to settle a dispute that the Council deems likely to endanger international peace? Compare the Council's authority under Chapter VI and Chapter VII of the Charter.

3. Does the obligation of Article 2(3) preclude a state from using force to vindicate its legal rights? See Chapter 11.

## B. TREATY OBLIGATIONS OF PEACEFUL SETTLEMENT

Many treaties—multilateral and bilateral—have included obligations to settle disputes by peaceful means. Some cover broad categories of disputes; others refer to disputes of specified character.

### *1. The General Act of 1928*

The most notable attempt to establish obligations of peaceful settlement of all disputes was the General Act for the Pacific Settlement of International Disputes adopted in Geneva by the League of Nations in 1928. It is sometimes referred to as the Geneva Act. Chapter I of the Act provides for the conciliation of legal disputes if the parties so agree; if they do not agree, or if conciliation fails, Chapter II requires the submission of the dispute to arbitration or to the Permanent Court of International Justice. Non-legal disputes are to be submitted to conciliation under Chapter I; if conciliation fails, the dispute is to be referred to an arbitral tribunal for settlement under Chapter III. A novel and striking aspect of Chapter III is its provision that, failing agreement to the contrary by the parties, the tribunal should decide the dispute *ex aequo et bono* if no rule of positive international law could dispose of the controversy. The significance of this provision is not clear, and its practical importance has not been great. In 1949, the General Assembly of the United Nations revised the Act in some minor respects, but previous adherences are still effective. Revised General Act, G.A.Res. 268 (IV) (1949).

Whether the General Act of 1928 was still in force was questioned by parties in three cases before the International Court of Justice: The Nuclear Tests Cases, 1974 I.C.J. 253; the Trial of Pakistani Prisoners of War Case, 1973 I.C.J. 328; and the Aegean Sea Continental Shelf Case, 1978 I.C.J. 3. The Court did not find it necessary to determine the present status of the 1928 Act.

The General Act was acceded to by 22 states but some states later denounced it. The 1949 Revised General Act has had only seven accessions. The United States did not become a party to either of the General Acts.

### *2. Other Dispute Settlement Treaties*

Between the two World Wars, many bilateral treaties were concluded providing for conciliation or arbitration of disputes between states. Generally, they exclude some categories of disputes such as those involving "vital interests" or domestic matters. The United States entered into about 20 bilateral treaties for conciliation and arbitration. Over 200 such treaties are reproduced in the U.N. Systematic Survey of Treaties for the Pacific Settlement of International Disputes 1928–1948 (1949).

After the United Nations Charter came into force, new treaties that dealt solely with peaceful settlement decreased sharply. Only 8 such treaties were concluded from 1949–1962. This is understandable, since the Charter itself includes obligations of pacific settlement. However, regional treaties were still thought to be useful to spell out obligations of dispute settlement and their implementation. In 1957, a European Convention on the Peaceful Settlement of Disputes was concluded, and in 1964 the African states concluded a Protocol on Conciliation and Arbitration to implement the general dispute settlement obligation in the Charter of African Unity. For texts, see U.N. Survey of Treaty Provisions for the Pacific Settlement of International Disputes 1949–1962 (1966).

### *3. Dispute Clauses in Treaties on Other Matters*

In addition to these specialized dispute settlement treaties, many treaties dealing with other matters contain broadly stated obligations to settle disputes through negotiation, conciliation, arbitration or judicial settlement. Some only repeat the U.N. Charter provisions. See for example, the NATO treaty of 1949, Articles 1 and 7 (34 U.N.T.S. 342) and the Warsaw Pact of 1955 (219 U.N.T.S. 3). Multilateral agreements for regional cooperation, and numerous bilateral and multilateral treaties on economic matters, or transport and communications and social questions have dispute settlement clauses applicable to differences arising under those treaties. For texts, see U.N. Survey, supra. Writing in 1976, Sohn noted that out of 17,000 treaties registered with the League of Nations or the United Nations, some 4,000 include compromissory clauses providing for the pacific settlement of disputes relating to the interpretation and application of the treaty itself. He writes:

> They present a rich and wonderous mosaic. The methods of settlement employed range from bilateral negotiations through conciliation and various forms of arbitration to reference to the International Court of Justice or other permanent tribunals.
>
> Some clauses take the form of a single sentence; others embody extensive codes of structural and procedural provisions, sometimes even offering alternative methods of settlement for different kinds of disputes.

Sohn, Settlement of Disputes Relating to the Interpretation and Application of Treaties, 136 Rec. des Cours 205, 259 (1976–II).

The United States is a party to more than 70 bilateral and multilateral treaties that include compromissory clauses providing for non-judicial and judicial settlement. Morrison, Treaties as a Source of Jurisdiction Especially in U.S. Practice, in The International Court of Justice at a Crossroads 58, 61 (Damrosch ed., 1987).

Many of these clauses bind all disputants to submit to the procedure at the unilateral request of one of them. For example, the Multilateral Protocol for Regulating Poppy Cultivation and Opium Production of 1953 requires submission to the International Court of Justice "at the request of any of the parties to the dispute." Other clauses state simply that the dispute shall be submitted to arbitration or other means of settlement. While such clauses are mandatory, they require that all the parties to the dispute agree on the submission. The Antarctic Treaty, for example, says that "any dispute shall, with the consent of all parties to the dispute, be referred to the International Court of Justice for settlement."

The International Court of Justice and its predecessor, the Permanent Court of International Justice (PCIJ), have considered the non-judicial remedies in compromissory clauses in a number of cases. An enlightening analysis of those cases is found in Scheffer, Non Judicial Remedies and the Jurisdiction of the International Court of Justice, 27 Stan.J.Int'l L. 83 (1991).

The most common clauses in bilateral agreements provide for settlement through bilateral negotiations, consultation or other contacts of the parties. They do not involve third parties and therefore do not provide for binding decisions. Mixed commissions are often utilized. A recent example is the treaty between the United States and the Soviet Union on anti-ballistic missiles (ABM Treaty), 23 U.S.T. 3435, TIAS No. 7503, which provides for a Standing Consultative Commission to deal with questions of compliance under the treaty. See Caldwell, The Standing Consultative Commission, in Verification and Arms Control (Potter ed. 1985).

Other clauses in bilateral treaties provide for reference to permanent organs or to arbitration and judicial settlement. See Sections 3 and 4.

Elaborate treaty provisions for dispute settlement are contained in the U.N. Convention on the Law of Sea of 1982. They include a variety of procedures for binding and non-binding decisions on disputes arising under the Convention and allow for considerable flexibility in the choice of procedures. However, every contracting party must signify, at the time it expresses its consent to be bound, its choice of the basic procedure or forum it is willing to accept. Part XV and Annexes V, VI, and VII of the Convention on the Law of the Sea, 1982. See Chapter 14.

## C. THE MEANING OF "DISPUTE"

The obligation of peaceful settlement applies to "disputes," not to all disagreements between states. A difference in views, or a sense of injury, does not necessarily mean that a dispute exists. International case-law and commentary have considered the term "dispute" as a technical term. The failure of an applicant to show the existence of a dispute has been a ground for rejecting cases brought to the International Court and its predecessor, the Permanent Court. See Electricity Company of Sofia, 1939 P.C.I.J. Ser. A/B, No. 77, 64, 83; Northern Cameroons Case, 1963 I.C.J. 33–34; Nuclear Tests Cases, 1974 I.C.J. 260, 270–271.

A dispute requires a degree of specificity and contestation. In the *Mavrommatis Case,* the International Court defined dispute "as a disagreement on a point of law or fact, a conflict of legal views or interests between two persons." 1924 P.C.I.J. Ser. A, No. 2, at 11–12.

There is authority that a disagreement is not a dispute if its resolution would not have any practical effect on the relations of the parties. In the *Northern Cameroons Case,* the International Court was faced with a disagreement on the interpretation of a United Nations trusteeship agreement that was no longer in force. Moreover, the applicant made no claim for reparation. In declining to adjudicate the claim, the Court said:

> The Court's judgment must have some practical consequences in the sense that it can affect existing legal rights or obligations thus removing uncertainty from their legal relations. No judgment on the merits in this case would satisfy these essentials of the judicial function.

1963 I.C.J. at 33–34.

In the *Nuclear Tests Cases* brought by Australia and New Zealand against France, the majority of the Court considered that French government statements that the tests have ceased meant that a dispute between the parties no longer existed. 1974 I.C.J. at 270–71. However, four dissenting judges noted that the claims and legal grounds advanced by the applicants were rejected by the French government on legal grounds. They said: "these circumstances in themselves suffice to qualify the present dispute as a 'dispute in regard to which the parties are in conflict as to their legal rights' and as a 'legal dispute' * * *." Joint Dissenting Opinion of Judges de Aréchaga, Dillard, Onyeama and Waldock, id. at 366. Compare the doctrine of "mootness" in domestic courts. See Rosenberg, Smit and Korn, Elements of Civil Procedure 200–06 (4th ed. 1985).

Is prior negotiation necessary to determine that a dispute exists? The PCIJ declared in one of the *Chorzów Cases:* "The manifestation of a dispute in a specific manner, as for instance by diplomatic negotiations, is not required." But the Court added that it is "desirable" that a State should not summon another State to appear before the Court without having endeavored to make it clear that the difference between them "has not been capable of being otherwise overcome." 1927 P.C.I.J. Ser. A, No. 13, at 10–11.

The obligation to settle disputes by peaceful means is not limited to legal disputes. Neither the Charter provisions nor the other general treaty provisions requiring dispute settlement restrict the term disputes to legal disputes. The question of whether a dispute is "legal" arises when a treaty provides that a specific means of settlement shall be employed for legal disputes. Some treaties, for example, provide for settlement of non-legal disputes by conciliation or arbitration and for submission of legal disputes to the International Court. Although the International Court and other judicial tribunals are in a broad sense limited to deciding disputes on the basis of law, the parties to a dispute may refer a case to the International Court for a decision *ex aequo et bono* (see Article 38, para. 2, of the Statute). Apart from this exception, it seems clear from Article 38 that the Court must decide in accordance with international law. However, this does not preclude the Court from deciding an issue of fact "which if established would constitute a breach of an international obligation." Article 36(2) of the Statute.

Disputes regarding the interpretation or application of a treaty are recognized as essentially legal, even though they arise in political contexts and the legal question "forms only one element in a wider and long standing political dispute." Case Concerning the U.S. Diplomats in Tehran, 1980 I.C.J. 19–20. In that case the Court found unacceptable the view that "because a legal dispute submitted to the Court is only an aspect of a political dispute, the Court should decline to resolve for the parties the legal question at issue between them." Id. See also Nicaragua v. United States, 1984 I.C.J. 439–40 (Jurisdiction and Admissibility). These cases are discussed below in Section 4 on the International Court. See also Restatement (Third) § 903, Comment *d.*

## SECTION 2. NON-ADJUDICATORY PROCEDURES

### A. NEGOTIATION

*LACHS, THE LAW AND THE SETTLEMENT OF INTERNATIONAL DISPUTES, IN DISPUTE SETTLEMENT THROUGH THE UNITED NATIONS*

287–9 (Raman ed. 1977).*

* * * The first stage of settlement is reserved to negotiations. From time immemorial States have resorted to that means. No reminder is needed that the obligation is not limited to entering into such negotiations but includes the obligation "also to pursue them as far as possible with a view to concluding agreements."

We may all agree that in fact ours is an age of negotiation. It dominates almost all fields of international relations, not only those which can cover the shaping of new law but also the settlement of disputes.

* * *

Contemporary States resort to negotiations very frequently, probably owing to the fact that they are rather anxious to retain control to the very end over the decisions arising out of differences which divide them. There are of course many international disputes and problems which cannot be solved otherwise; some concern the international community at large, but also on a bilateral level. There is a wide field of lawmaking in which, again, movement is only possible by way of negotiation through special channels devised for the purpose.

In such settings the distinction between the legal and extralegal, between rights and interests, which appears so sharply before a tribunal, is overshadowed in the common strivings towards peaceful reconciliation, and in the outcome, too, much new law may gradually take shape. Again out of disputes, patterns of future co-operation are laid down.

Diplomacy, however, has its limits. And many factors, serve to divert, distort, or protract the course of negotiations, notably the complexity of the interests involved, the incidence of pressures, political factors, all sorts of considerations extraneous to the central issues in a dispute or disagreement. They may go on endlessly, leaving issues requiring urgent solutions in suspense and thus increasing tension. Very frequently they break down, producing the same effect or worse. The complications and intricacies of contemporary life demand ever new devices to deal with such failures. In any case, the obligation to negotiate, to which I referred earlier, does not imply an obligation actually to reach agreement. The obligation is only to try one's best.

* Footnotes omitted. Reprinted with the permission of Oceana Publications, Inc.

*REPORT OF THE SPECIAL COMMITTEE ON PRINCIPLES OF INTERNATIONAL LAW CONCERNING FRIENDLY RELATIONS AND CO-OPERATION AMONG STATES*

U.N. Doc. A/5746, [1964] U.N.Jur.Yb. 65.

[The debate focused upon the issue of whether direct negotiations should be accorded special legal emphasis as against the other means of peaceful settlement recognized by international law and set forth in the Charter. The report said in part:]

* * *

156. A number of representatives urged that direct negotiation was the fundamental means of resolving international disputes and had been established as such by international law and State practice. * * * [B]y its very nature it most adequately met the need for the prompt and flexible settlement of international disputes, * * * it better preserved the equality of the parties, * * * it could be used for the settlement of both political and legal disputes, and * * * it offered the most effective means for the peaceful settlement of disputes. Moreover, direct negotiations best promoted compromise, and prevented disputes from acquiring proportions which made them a threat to international peace and security, since they made it possible for conflicts to be dealt with as soon as they arose. Furthermore, direct negotiation was a means which did not oblige third States to take up a specific position on disputes which did not affect their interests or threaten international peace and security. * * * In addition, the means of direct negotiation, while it brought about the settlement of disputes, could at the same time bring into being rules regulating future relations between the States concerned, thus promoting the development of international law through the conclusion of multilateral and bilateral agreements. * * *

158. Other representatives, however, while recognizing the great importance of direct negotiation, which was the very essence of diplomacy, felt that it should not be given priority over the other means of settlement of disputes, since that would be to distort the principles which were the foundation of the entire existing system of peaceful settlement of disputes. In their view, the constant trend in the development of international law in this regard since the nineteenth century had been to transcend the stage of negotiation and to establish and improve more institutional means of settlement based on recourse to third parties or organs. * * * Direct negotiation had disadvantages, demonstrated by history, which, according to the representatives in question, ruled it out as the ideal, principal or exclusive means of peaceful settlement of international disputes. Thus, direct negotiation did not allow the facts to be established objectively and impartially, nor enable third parties to exercise a moderating influence on the dispute, nor prevent the putting forward of exaggerated claims which might aggravate the dispute, nor ensure equal terms, since usually one of the parties was in a weaker position than the other; nor could it be used for the solution of certain types of disputes, nor guarantee the solution of a dispute since either party could choose to be intransigent at any moment. * * *

### *Notes*

1. Judge Lachs refers to negotiators who "go on endlessly, leaving issues requiring urgent solutions in suspense and thus increasing tension." Are these *bona fide* negotiations? May the aggrieved party withdraw? In the *North Sea Continental Shelf Case,* the International Court said:

> The parties are under an obligation to enter into negotiations with a view to arriving at an agreement * * *. [T]hey are under an obligation so to conduct themselves that the negotiations are meaningful, which will not be the case when either of the parties insists upon its own position without contemplating any modification of it.

1969 I.C.J. 3, 47–48.

2. Multilateral negotiations in large international bodies and conferences obviously differ from negotiations between two states or among small groups. Where large numbers of participants are involved, blocs of like-minded states and coalitions of divergent groups generally play a significant role. Committees and working groups are often the principal arenas of negotiation. Leadership of some states or of individuals can be critical in reaching consensus. The chairmen of committees and secretariat personnel frequently seek compromise proposals. When the object is to achieve broad agreement, consensus procedures rather than voting are generally favored. Voting may however be resorted to for political ends. Several recent studies have thrown light on the complexities of multilateral negotiation. See Kaufmann, Conference Diplomacy (1968); Buzan, Negotiating by Consensus: Developments in Technique at the United Nations Conference on the Law of the Sea, 75 A.J.I.L. 324 (1981); Benedick, Ozone Diplomacy: New Directions in Safeguarding the Planet (1991).

## B. GOOD OFFICES, MEDIATION, CONCILIATION, AND INQUIRY

### *BRIERLY, THE LAW OF NATIONS*

373–76 (6th ed. Waldock, 1963).*

#### § 4. Good Offices, Mediation, Conciliation

In these modes of composing a quarrel, the intervention of a third party aims, not at *deciding* the quarrel *for* the disputing parties, but at inducing them to decide it for themselves. The difference between the two first terms is not important; strictly a state is said to offer 'good offices' when it tries to induce the parties to negotiate between themselves, and to 'mediate' when it takes a part in the negotiations itself, but clearly the one process merges into the other. Both, moreover, are political processes, which hardly fall within international law. The Hague Conventions for the Pacific Settlement of International Disputes declare it to be desirable that powers strangers to a dispute should offer their good offices and mediation, and such an offer is not to be regarded as an unfriendly act.

The same Conventions also introduced a new device for the promotion of peaceful settlements, in Commissions of Inquiry, whose function was simply to investigate the facts of a dispute and to make a report stating them; this report was not to have the character of an award, and the parties were free to decide what effect, if any, they would give it. The Commission was to be constituted for each occasion by agreement between the parties. This machinery was used with good effect in the Dogger Bank dispute between Great Britain and Russia in 1904.

The idea underlying these Commissions, that if resort to war can only be postponed and the facts clarified and published, war will probably be averted altogether, inspired the so-called 'Bryan treaties,' the first of which was concluded between Great Britain and the United States in 1914. Under these the parties agreed to refer 'all disputes of every nature whatsoever' which cannot be otherwise settled to a standing 'Peace Commission' for investigation and report, and not to go to war until the report was received, which had to be within a year. The Commission consisted of one national and one non-national chosen by each party, and a fifth, not a national of either party, chosen by agreement. No disputes whatsoever were excluded from the operation of these treaties.

The method of the 'Bryan treaties' was extensively adopted in later developments of international organization, and as it is essentially different from the method of arbitration on the one hand, and not precisely the same as that of mediation on the other, it is convenient to refer to it as 'conciliation.' It has been defined as 'the process of settling a dispute by referring it to a commission of persons whose task it is to elucidate the facts and * * * to make a report containing proposals for a settlement, but not having the binding character of an award or judgment'. Conciliation, therefore, differs from arbitration, because in it terms of settlement are merely proposed, and not dictated to the disputing states; it is therefore unlike arbitration, a method appropriate to any dispute whatsoever. In the period between the two Great Wars machinery of conciliation was set up by many treaties between particular states, notably by those of Locarno in 1925. These so-called 'arbitration conventions' set up a 'Permanent Conciliation Commission' usually of five persons, consisting of one national of each of the signatory states and three non-nationals; disputes 'as to the respective rights' of the parties might by agreement be referred to the Commission, but if not settled there, they were to be referred to arbitration or to the Permanent Court; other disputes were to be referred to the Commission. Its task was to 'elucidate questions in dispute, to collect with that object all necessary information by means of inquiry or otherwise, and to endeavour to bring the parties to an agreement * * * at the close of its labours the Commission shall draw up a report'.

Treaties of conciliation have scarcely fulfilled the hopes placed in them; for, although nearly 200 commissions have been established, they have been little used, the number of cases dealt with by them being not much more than ten. There have, however, been a few encouraging examples of the use of conciliation in more recent years which have led to a revival of interest in this procedure for settling international disputes, and the development of its use in engaging the attention of international lawyers.

### *Notes*

1. The United States eventually concluded forty-eight "Bryan peace treaties" similar to that described above by Professor Brierly; many of these are still in force, but seem never to have been invoked. See 6 Hackworth at 5; Hyde at

1570–72; Report of the Secretary–General on Methods of Factfinding, U.N.Doc. A/5694, at 29–33 (May 1, 1964). On the General Act for the Pacific Settlement of International Disputes of 1928, the Locarno treaties of 1925, and the numerous other bilateral and multilateral conciliation conventions concluded between the wars, see generally 2 Oppenheim at 16–20, 88–96; Hyde at 1572–78. See also Habicht, Post–War Treaties for the Pacific Settlement of International Disputes (1931); U.N. Secretariat, Systematic Survey of Treaties for the Pacific Settlement of International Disputes, 1928–1948 (1949); U.N. Secretariat, A Survey of Treaty Provisions for the Pacific Settlement of International Disputes, 1949–1962 (1966). For a recent general survey, see J. Merrills, International Dispute Settlement (2d ed. 1991).

2. Conciliation for dispute settlement is provided in the Vienna Convention on the Law of Treaties and the Vienna Convention on Succession of States in respect of Treaties. In both conventions, conciliation may be requested by any party to the dispute relating to the convention. The dispute is then referred to a conciliation commission which would seek to bring about an amicable settlement. The commission may make proposals to the parties, but such proposals are not binding on the parties. See Kearney & Dalton, The Treaty on Treaties, 64 A.J.I.L. 495, 553–55 (1970); Lavalle, The Dispute Settlement Provisions of the Vienna Convention on Succession of States in Respect of Treaties, 73 A.J.I.L. 407 (1979). Conciliation procedures are also in other multilateral treaties, including the Covenant on Civil and Political Rights (Article 42). The U.N. Convention on the Law of the Sea of 1982 provides for compulsory (but non-binding) conciliation at the request of any party to a dispute relating to certain fisheries, scientific research and boundary questions. Article 297(3).

3. Should the purely recommendatory character of a conciliation commission's proposals be reinforced by declaring in the rules that the parties are in no way bound or estopped by the findings of the commission? A proposal to this effect made by Fitzmaurice to the *Institut de Droit International* was not carried. See 2 Ann. de l'Institut de Droit Int'l 214 (1961). If a conciliation commission (e.g., under the Vienna Convention on the Law of Treaties) should find in favor of a state claiming invalidity of a treaty, would that finding furnish a good legal basis for that state to take steps to release it from the treaty commitment? Conversely, would a finding that there was no right to terminate estop a state from taking such action? It has been suggested that in determining the obligations of a party to the conciliation, the finding of the conciliator on the law and facts should be given weight but not treated as conclusive. Schachter, International Law in Theory and Practice, 178 Rec. des Cours 206 (1982–V).

4. Are conciliation commissions more effective if their procedure resembles that of negotiation (e.g., a round-table conference without rules of procedure)? Or is it generally desirable to have rules of procedure of a quasi-judicial nature? Both approaches have been followed in the bilateral conciliation commissions established after 1945. For consideration of the approaches, see 48–I Ann. de l'Institut de Droit Int'l 5 (1959), 49–II id., 214 (1961). When a commission faces a disagreement on a question of fact and seeks to interrogate witnesses or experts, should the proceedings be of a judicial nature? See Fox, Conciliation in International Disputes: The Legal Aspects, in Report of David Davies Memorial Institute 93 (1972). For general treatment of conciliation, see also Cot, International Conciliation (Eng. trans. 1972).

5. The Hague Convention of 1907 on Pacific Settlement provided for international commissions of inquiry charged with the duty of establishing the

facts in international disputes. Fact-finding commissions were utilized in several disputes and a number of bilateral treaties provided for commissions of inquiry (*commissions d'enquête*). See Bar–Yaacov, The Handling of International Disputes By Means of Inquiry (1974); Report of the U.N. Secretary–General on Methods of Fact–Finding, UN Doc A/5694 (1965) and A/6228 (1966).

6. Mediation is distinguished from conciliation and fact-finding in that the mediator is expected to have a more active role by furthering negotiation and making proposals to the parties. Techniques of mediation have been extensively studied by political scientists, historians, and social psychologists and a large body of research findings and analysis (along with historical and anecdotal narrative) is available. Flexibility and adaptation to the particular circumstances characterize the more successful efforts. Most observers agree that little is gained by giving these techniques precise procedural rules or legal structures.

7. Mediators and conciliators may be individuals, committees, or institutional bodies. Heads of governments and experienced diplomats have often performed that role. In some cases, they can exercise leverage because of their ability to benefit or withhold benefits from the parties. They may have a representative role acting on behalf of the United Nations or an international regional agency. They may facilitate negotiation by providing information and ideas, by subdividing ("fractionating") issues, by offering services (such as monitoring compliance or providing resources), or even offering guarantees. Each dispute reveals its distinctive features and requires its own combination of methods.

Studies of interest include J. Merrills, International Dispute Settlement (2d ed. 1991); D. Pruitt and J. Rubin, Social Conflict: Escalation, Stalemate and Settlement (1986); I.W. Zartman, Ripe for Resolution (1985); V. Pechota, Complementary Structures of Third Party Settlement in International Disputes (UNITAR Study), reprinted in Dispute Settlement Through the United Nations 149–220 (V. Raman ed., 1977); O. Young, The Intermediaries, Third Parties in International Crises (1967).

8. Third-party dispute settlement has sometimes been carried out by non-governmental organizations and private individuals. In 1993, for example, a Roman Catholic lay society in Rome played a key role in bringing an end to a bloody civil war in Mozambique that had gone on for almost a decade. See C.R. Hume, The Mozambique Peace Process, in the Diplomatic Record 1993. A protracted dispute between Argentina and Chile concerning the Beagle Channel was settled through the mediation of Cardinal Samore, designated by the Pope after Argentina had rejected the decision of an arbitral tribunal. See Wetter, 1 The International Arbitral Process 276 (1979). The International Committee of the Red Cross and the Society of Friends (Quakers) have both carried out mediation efforts through "quiet diplomacy." See J. Pictet, The Red Cross as a Factor in World Peace, in Int. Review of the Red Cross 571 (No. 80, Nov. 1967); R. Warren, The Conflict Intersystem and the Change Agent, 8 J. Conflict Resolution 231–41 (1964).

## C. DISPUTE SETTLEMENT THROUGH THE UNITED NATIONS AND OTHER INTERNATIONAL ORGANIZATIONS

### *AGENDA FOR PEACE*

Report of the UN Secretary–General UN Doc. A/47/277, S/24111 (June 17, 1992), reprinted in 31 I.L.M. 953 (1992).

PREVENTIVE DIPLOMACY

The most desirable and efficient employment of diplomacy is to ease tensions before they result in conflict—or, if conflict breaks out, to act swiftly to contain it and resolve its underlying causes. Preventive diplomacy may be performed by the Secretary–General personally or through senior staff or specialized agencies and programmes, by the Security Council or the General Assembly, and by regional organizations in cooperation with the United Nations. Preventive diplomacy requires measures to create confidence; it needs early warning based on information gathering and informal or formal fact-finding; it may also involve preventive deployment and, in some situations, demilitarized zones.

*Measures to Build Confidence*

Mutual confidence and good faith are essential to reducing the likelihood of conflict between States. Many such measures are available to Governments that have the will to employ them. Systematic exchange of military missions, formation of regional or subregional risk reduction centres, arrangements for the free flow of information, including the monitoring of regional arms agreements, are examples. I ask all regional organizations to consider what further confidence-building measures might be applied in their areas and to inform the United Nations of the results. I will undertake periodic consultations on confidence-building measures with parties to potential, current or past disputes and with regional organizations, offering such advisory assistance as the Secretariat can provide.

*Fact-Finding*

Preventive steps must be based upon timely and accurate knowledge of the facts. Beyond this, an understanding of developments and global trends, based on sound analysis, is required. And the willingness to take appropriate preventive action is essential. Given the economic and social roots of many potential conflicts, the information needed by the United Nations now must encompass economic and social trends as well as political developments that may lead to dangerous tensions.

(*a*) An increased resort to fact-finding is needed, in accordance with the Charter, initiated either by the Secretary–General, to enable him to meet his responsibilities under the Charter, including Article 99, or by the Security Council or the General Assembly. Various forms may be employed selectively as the situation requires. A request by a State for the sending of a United Nations fact-finding mission to its territory should be considered without undue delay.

(*b*) Contacts with the Governments of Member States can provide the Secretary–General with detailed information on issues of concern. I ask that all Member States be ready to provide the information needed for effective preventive diplomacy. I will supplement my own contacts by regularly sending senior officials on missions for consultations in capitals or other locations. Such contacts are essential to gain insight into a situation and to assess its potential ramifications.

(*c*) Formal fact-finding can be mandated by the Security Council or by the General Assembly, either of which may elect to send a mission under its immediate authority or may invite the Secretary–General to take the necessary steps, including the designation of a special envoy. In addition to collecting information on which a decision for further action can be taken, such a mission can in some instances help to defuse a dispute by its presence, indicating to the parties that the Organization, and in particular the Security Council, is actively seized of the matter as a present or potential threat to international security.

(*d*) In exceptional circumstances the Council may meet away from Headquarters as the Charter provides, in order not only to inform itself directly, but also to bring the authority of the Organization to bear on a given situation.

PEACEMAKING

Mediation and negotiation can be undertaken by an individual designated by the Security Council, by the General Assembly or by the Secretary–General. There is a long history of the utilization by the United Nations of distinguished statesmen to facilitate the processes of peace. They can bring a personal prestige that, in addition to their experience, can encourage the parties to enter serious negotiations. There is a wide willingness to serve in this capacity, from which I shall continue to benefit as the need arises. Frequently it is the Secretary–General himself who undertakes the task. While the mediator's effectiveness is enhanced by strong and evident support from the Council, the General Assembly and the relevant Member States acting in their national capacity, the good offices of the Secretary–General may at times be employed most effectively when conducted independently of the deliberative bodies. Close and continuous consultation between the Secretary–General and the Security Council is, however, essential to ensure full awareness of how the Council's influence can best be applied and to develop a common strategy for the peaceful settlement of specific disputes.

## *Notes and Questions*

1. Preventive diplomacy and peacemaking by the United Nations are based on several Charter provisions, beginning with the principle of Article 2(3) that

> "All Members shall settle their international disputes by peaceful means in such a manner that international peace and security, and justice, are not endangered."

Note that this applies to all international disputes. Its unqualified language appears to oblige states to settle all their disputes with other states, whether or not their continuance endangers peace. In fact, there are numerous inter-state disputes that states feel no need to settle and that do not endanger peace. Note also that Article 2(3) requires that the settlement of a dispute shall not endanger "justice," a requirement that does not appear in Chapter VI on Pacific Settlement of Disputes.

2. Article 33 of Chapter VI also imposes an obligation of peaceful settlement, but here it refers to a dispute or situation "the continuance of which is

likely to endanger the maintenance of international peace and security." This may suggest that a bilateral dispute would not be covered unless it threatened wider repercussions, but this limitation has not been recognized in practice.

3. Questions have arisen as to the responsibility of the Security Council under Article 34 to investigate any dispute or "situation" in order to determine whether the continuance of the dispute or situation is likely to endanger the maintenance of international peace and security. Is the Council empowered to investigate situations involving internal conflict or mistreatment of inhabitants of a country when it is evident that peace and security may eventually be endangered? Would a finding to that effect mean that the situation in question is no longer a matter "essentially within the domestic jurisdiction" of the state concerned and therefore that the limitation of Article 2(7) of the Charter does not apply? Note that in the report of the Secretary-General quoted above, reference is made to the "economic and social roots of many potential conflicts" and the need to "encompass economic and social trends as well as political developments that may lead to dangerous tensions." United Nations organs have long recognized that internal conflicts, particularly when characterized by racism, and or massive deprivation of basic human rights, are of international concern and endanger international peace. See O. Schachter, The United Nations and Internal Conflict, in Law and Civil War in the Modern World 231–46 (J.N. Moore ed., 1974); also reprinted in Dispute Settlement Through the United Nations (Raman ed., 1977).

4. In some cases the U.N. Security Council authorized the Secretary-General to seek to facilitate settlement of internal disputes between competing factions in a country. It did so in respect to the former Belgian Congo (now Zaire) in 1961–1963. G. Abi-Saab, The United Nations Operation in the Congo, 1960–1964, 124–38 (1978). More recently, it did so in regard to Somalia in 1992–1993. U.N. Security Council Resolutions 767 and 775 (1992) (characterizing the internal situation of Somalia as a threat to peace and security). Such peace-making efforts have been associated with "peacekeeping" forces. See Chapter 11. It is now recognized that humanitarian assistance may facilitate dispute settlement in a situation where disorder and material shortages aggravate a conflict. The Secretary-General in his Agenda for Peace Report (supra) noted, for example, that assistance to displaced persons can be essential to solving a conflict. Para. 40, Agenda for Peace Report. The High Commissioner for Refugees, the Children's Fund (UNICEF), the World Food Program, the World Health Organization, and other humanitarian bodies have become an important part of many efforts to achieve settlement of conflict.

## REGIONAL ORGANIZATIONS

1. Regional organizations such as the Organization of American States (OAS), the Organization of African Unity (OAU), the Arab League, the Conference on Security and Cooperation in Europe (CSCE), the Association of South-East Asian States (ASEAN), and others have also had active roles in non-adjudicatory dispute settlement. The on-going conflicts in ex-Yugoslavia in 1992–1993 were dealt with through joint efforts of mediators appointed by the U.N. Secretary-General and the European Community. Similarly, efforts toward settlement of the civil war in El Salvador were carried out by representatives of the OAS and the U.N. Secretary-General in

1991–1993. In regard to the conflict in Somalia, the U.N. conciliation efforts were joined by the OAU, the League of Arab States, and Organization of the Islamic Conference.

2. In some cases regional bodies have been perceived by one of the parties to the conflict as partial to the other and therefore as unsuitable for a mediatory role. From that standpoint the United Nations was preferred since its larger membership provided more assurance of even-handed treatment. Regional organizations also lack the resources and experience of the United Nations, particularly in regard to peacekeeping forces and large-scale fact-finding. The experience in 1992 and 1993 in regard to the conflicts in ex-Yugoslavia, Somalia, and Haiti underlined the relative weakness of the respective regional bodies and the need for United Nations involvement. In regard to Yugoslavia, see Weller, The International Response to the Dissolution of the Socialist Federal Republic of Yugoslavia, 86 Am.J.Int'l L. 569 (1992). On the OAU, see B. Andemicael, The OAU and the UN (UNITAR Pub. 1976).

## PUBLIC DEBATE AND PARLIAMENTARY DIPLOMACY IN DISPUTE SETTLEMENT

As a rule, negotiating mechanisms that are flexible and relatively informal are preferable for seeking resolution of difficult disputes. This is especially true when bargaining (i.e., the trading of concessions) is the dominant mode of negotiation. However, when there are marked disparities in bargaining strength, weaker parties will tend toward formal, rule-oriented structures or to larger forums in which they can obtain political support.

It is almost axiomatic that negotiation and mediation can be more effectively carried out in private rather than in public meetings. When institutional mechanisms provide generally for public meetings, it is often essential to use informal private negotiating mechanisms (as, for example, the Security Council consultations that are now standard procedures).

Notwithstanding the advantages of private negotiations, "parliamentary diplomacy" and public statements may help sometimes to further settlement by placing pressure on the parties. On the other hand, a public debate may complicate settlement procedures by increasing tensions, stimulating domestic rigidity, and adding ideological elements to the dispute.

The role of international institutions in facilitating negotiation may be substantially reduced when the governing bodies adopt positions or express views in favor of one side. When an organization is perceived by the party as hostile, it loses its opportunity to act itself as a third-party intermediary or to have its officials perform that role. Does this imply that international bodies should renounce their role of expressing international policy or applying principles of law to particular situations? May their positions, when based on a general consensus, generate pressure for negotiation even though the organization does not act in a mediational role? These questions have been raised in major disputes brought to the United Nations when one side has been supported by large majorities in the General Assembly or Security Council.

Difficulties in determining who should be the parties to multilateral negotiation may require a variety of procedural stratagems, e.g., separate meetings, proxy representation, composite delegations, unofficial observers, etc. As questions of participation are often linked to substantive issues, the preliminary negotiations on the question of invitations and composition of delegations will often be partly determinative of the issues to be considered.

It has often been suggested that regional (or sub-regional) machinery be used before recourse is had to the United Nations. There is little evidence that the regional bodies have been more effective in dealing with high-intensity conflicts. Even conceding that regional bodies may be better for dispute-settlement involving countries of the region, it is questionable whether the idea of regional primacy should deter or delay action in other bodies when it appears that regional measures will not be taken or are inadequate. As indicated above, joint efforts have been used in recent conflicts in ex-Yugoslavia, Somalia, and El Salvador.

Individual governments or *ad hoc* groups of governments often have a role in facilitating negotiations between disputing states. Such "facilitators" may report to appropriate international organs such as the Security Council, but this may not be helpful in cases in which such reports are likely to provoke the taking of one-sided positions that could impede the negotiation.

Post-settlement arrangements may influence the choice of settlement mechanisms. Mediators (whether governments or international organs) may contribute to the solution of the difficulties by accepting a role in security or economic arrangements to be carried out after an agreed settlement. For example, the U.N. may provide observers to supervise demilitarization. The World Bank played a key role in settling the Indus River dispute by providing development funds.

## SECTION 3. ARBITRATION

### A. ROLE OF ARBITRATION IN SETTLEMENT OF DISPUTES

Arbitration, in contrast to conciliation, leads to a binding settlement of a dispute on the basis of law. The arbitral body is composed of judges who are normally appointed by the parties but who are not subject to their instructions. The arbitral body may be established *ad hoc* by the parties or it may be a continuing body set up to handle certain categories of disputes. Arbitration differs from judicial settlement in that the parties have competence as a rule to appoint arbitrators, to determine the procedure and, to a certain extent, to indicate the applicable law.

The history of international arbitration can be traced as far back as ancient Greece, and its use as a means of peaceful settlement was frequent even during the Middle Ages. See generally Ralston, International Arbitration from Athens to Locarno 153–89 (1929). The process fell into disuse, however, until its revival in the nineteenth century by a series of arbitrations between the United States and the United Kingdom arising out of the Jay Treaty (1794) and the Treaty of Ghent (1814). See Simpson & Fox, International Arbitration 1–4 (1959); Hyde at 1587–88. A number of other international arbitrations occurred later in the nineteenth century, one of the most important of which concerned the claims of the United States against the United Kingdom for damages arising out of the activities of the Confederate warship Alabama. See Simpson & Fox at 8–9; Hyde 1592–93. A system of rules and procedures was by this time gradually receiving general acceptance and in 1875 the *Institut de Droit International* completed an influential draft code of arbitral procedure. See Projet de réglement pour la procédure arbitrale internationale, 1 Ann. de l'Institut de Droit Int'l 126 (1877).

At the Hague Peace Conference of 1899 arbitration was one of the most important topics under discussion. The resulting Convention for the Pacific Settlement of International Disputes, 32 Stat. 1799, 2 Malloy 2016, contained, in addition to provisions on good offices, mediation, and inquiry, a number of articles on international arbitration, the object of which was stated in Article XV to be "the settlement of differences between States by judges of their own choice, and on the basis of respect for law." Article XVI set out the parties' recognition that, "[i]n questions of a legal nature, and especially in the interpretation or application of International Conventions," international arbitration was the "most effective, and at the same time the most equitable, means of settling disputes which diplomacy has failed to settle." Article XVIII specified that an agreement to arbitrate implied the legal obligation to submit to the terms of the award. The Convention did not impose any specific obligation to arbitrate; it merely attempted to set up institutions and procedures that could be utilized when and if two or more states desired to submit a dispute to arbitration. Detailed rules on procedure were therefore set out in the Convention, and the so-called Permanent Court of Arbitration was established. The latter was in no sense a "permanent court"—it was, however, possible to convene a Court from among a permanent panel of arbitrators. Under the method of selection laid down by Article XLIV of the revised Convention of 1907, 36 Stat. 2199, 2 Malloy 2220, each party to the Convention was eligible to nominate a maximum of four persons "of known competency in questions of international law, of the highest moral reputation, and disposed to accept the duties of Arbitrator." When two states decided to refer a dispute to the Court, they could select two arbitrators from among those nominated by the states party to the Convention. Only one of those selected could be a national or a nominee of the selecting state. The four arbitrators would then choose an umpire. Detailed provision was made for the selection of an umpire if the arbitrators were unable to agree upon a single individual. On the Permanent Court of Arbitration, see generally Francois, La Cour Permanente d'Arbitrage, son Origine, sa Jurisprudence, son Avenir, 85 Rec. des Cours 460 (1955–I).

Since World War II, states have looked with less favor on the adoption of general multilateral conventions for compulsory arbitration. However, support for arbitration as a preferred means of adjudication still finds wide support among states. This was demonstrated in the U.N. Conference on the Law of the Sea by the preference for arbitration as the means to be used in default of any other choice of settlement machinery (see Chapter 14). Moreover, states continue to have recourse to arbitration on an *ad hoc* basis. In some cases, arbitration has been used even when hostilities between the parties had broken out. A successful example is the *Rann of Kutch Case* between India and Pakistan, decided in 1968, which involved a territorial dispute. For detailed account, see Wetter, The International Arbitral Process, vol. I, 250–275 (1979). Repudiation of arbitral awards has been relatively rare. See Schachter, The Enforcement of International Judicial and Arbitral Decisions, 54 A.J.I.L. 1 (1960). On nullity, see 799 infra.

The texts of many international arbitral awards have been reprinted in volumes published by the United Nations, entitled Reports of International Arbitral Awards (U.N.R.I.A.A.). Nineteen volumes have appeared, the last in 1990. A full listing of public international law arbitrations from 1794 to 1989 can be found in Stuyt, Survey of International Arbitrations 1794–1989 (1990). International arbitral decisions also are published in International Legal Materials and in International Law Reports. See also Lauterpacht, Aspects of the Administration of International Justice 10–11 (1991) (listing numerous *ad hoc* arbitral decisions reported in the International Law Reports since 1945).

The Restatement (Third) deals with interstate arbitration in § 904.

## B. THE UNDERTAKING TO ARBITRATE AND THE "COMPROMIS d'ARBITRAGE"

Generally, parties to a dispute undertake to submit the controversy to arbitration and, in the same instrument, specify the method by which the arbitral tribunal is to be constituted, the questions it is to answer, and the procedures by which it shall arrive at a decision. The undertaking to arbitrate may also appear as an independent agreement or as a part thereof. Standing by itself, the undertaking to arbitrate usually does not dispose of all the detailed questions that must be settled before arbitration actually takes place. It may, as a minimum, specify the manner in which the arbitrators are to be selected. Other questions remain to be answered by the parties in a subsequent agreement, sometimes called the *compromis d'arbitrage.* The contents of the *compromis* were described by the International Law Commission in Article 2 of its Model Rules on Arbitral Procedure:

> 1. Unless there are earlier agreements which suffice for the purpose, for example in the undertaking to arbitrate itself, the parties having recourse to arbitration shall conclude a *compromis* which shall specify, as a minimum:
>
> (a) The undertaking to arbitrate according to which the dispute is to be submitted to the arbitrators;
>
> (b) The subject-matter of the dispute and, if possible, the points on which the parties are or are not agreed;
>
> (c) The method of constituting the tribunal and the number of arbitrators.
>
> 2. In addition, the *compromis* shall include any other provisions deemed desirable by the parties, in particular:
>
> (i) The rules of law and the principles to be applied by the tribunal, and the right, if any, conferred on it to decide *ex aequo et bono* as though it had legislative functions in the matter;

(ii) The power, if any, of the tribunal to make recommendations to the parties;

(iii) Such power as may be conferred on the tribunal to make its own rules of procedure;

(iv) The procedure to be followed by the tribunal; provided that, once constituted, the tribunal shall be free to override any provisions of the *compromis* which may prevent it from rendering its award;

(v) The number of members required for the constitution of a *quorum* for the conduct of the hearings;

(vi) The majority required for the award;

(vii) The time limit within which the award shall be rendered;

(viii) The right of the members of the tribunal to attach dissenting or individual opinions to the award, or any prohibition of such opinions;

(ix) The languages to be employed in the course of the proceedings;

(x) The manner in which the costs and disbursements shall be apportioned;

(xi) The services which the International Court of Justice may be asked to render.

This enumeration is not intended to be exhaustive. [1958] II Yb.I.L.C. 83. The parties to the *compromis* may confer jurisdiction on the arbitrators only to answer particular questions of law or fact, or they may give the tribunal power to decide on the merits a single controversy or a series of related disputes. One of the parties may admit liability, and the tribunal may therefore be asked only to determine damages. Any provision in the *compromis* relating to the law to be applied by the tribunal is essential to interpreting the award and to determining its value as a precedent. It is also important to note whether the award is to be accepted by the parties as final and binding or as merely advisory.

Questions of procedure not answered in the *compromis* must be settled by the tribunal. The *compromis* will normally give the tribunal the express power to perform this task, although it is often maintained that such a provision is unnecessary inasmuch as any arbitral tribunal has the inherent power to determine its procedures in a way not inconsistent with the *compromis.* Precedents established by past tribunals are often of great value, as are codes of procedure such as that prepared by the International Law Commission in 1958. For general information on the procedural aspects of arbitration, see Carlston, The Process of International Arbitration (1946); Simpson & Fox, International Arbitration 147 (1959).

### *Notes*

1. "International law does not lay down hard and fast rules concerning the character or weight of evidence in international arbitrations or rules which closely approximate the technical rules followed in proceedings before domestic courts; admissibility of evidence and the weight to be attached to it is largely

left to the arbitral tribunal. For the most part the rules followed by such tribunals are more elastic and more liberal than those generally followed by domestic courts." 6 Hackworth at 98. See generally Simpson & Fox at 192; Sandifer, Evidence before International Tribunals (rev. ed. 1975). See also White, The Use of Experts by International Tribunals (1965).

2. Bilateral treaties concluded between Western states often provide for the arbitration or judicial settlement of disputes arising out of the treaty. Article 27(2) of the Treaty of Friendship, Commerce and Navigation between the United States and Germany 1954, 7 U.S.T. 1839, provides, for example, as follows:

> Any dispute between the Parties as to the interpretation or the application of the present Treaty which the Parties do not satisfactorily adjust by diplomacy or some other agreed means shall be submitted to arbitration or, upon agreement of the Parties, to the International Court of Justice.

Such clauses have been inserted in many post-war commercial treaties concluded by the United States. See Wilson, United States Commercial Treaties and International Law 23 (1960). For a case in which the International Court of Justice held that a state was under a duty to submit to arbitration under the provisions of a bilateral treaty, see the Ambatielos Case (Greece v. United Kingdom), Merits: Obligation to Arbitrate, 1953 I.C.J. 10. For the ensuing arbitration and its result, see The Ambatielos Claim, 12 U.N.R.I.A.A. 83 (1956).

3. The five Paris Peace Treaties of 1947 provided, at the Soviet Union's insistence, for reference of disputes arising under the treaties to arbitral tribunals rather than to the International Court of Justice. Bulgaria, Hungary and Rumania were subsequently able to frustrate arbitration of disputes arising under the human rights provisions of the treaties by the simple expedient of refusing to appoint an arbitrator on their behalf. The International Court of Justice then ruled in an Advisory Opinion that the Secretary–General of the United Nations could not appoint a third arbitrator under the authority granted to him by the Peace Treaties until both parties to the dispute had appointed their arbitrators. 1950 I.C.J. 221. Article XLV of the Pact of Bogotá, signed on April 30, 1948, contains an elaborate scheme designed to prevent the frustration of the arbitral procedure through a refusal by one party to appoint an arbitrator. 30 U.N.T.S. 55, 100.

4. Does arbitration always lead to a binding award? Consider Article 12 of the Air Transport Agreement between the United States and Italy, Feb. 6, 1948, 62 Stat. 3729, T.I.A.S. No. 1902, 73 U.N.T.S. 113:

> Except as otherwise provided in the present Agreement or its Annex, any dispute between the contracting parties relative to the interpretation or application of the present Agreement or its Annex, which cannot be settled through consultation, shall be submitted for an advisory report to a tribunal of three arbitrators, one to be named by each contracting party, and the third to be agreed upon by the two arbitrators so chosen, provided that such third arbitrator shall not be a national of either contracting party.
>
> * * * The executive authorities of the contracting parties will use their best efforts under the powers available to them to put into effect the opinion expressed in any such advisory report. * * *

On June 30, 1964, the two governments signed a *compromis* to establish an arbitral tribunal in accordance with Article 12 of their Air Transport Agreement. On July 17, 1965, the tribunal rendered a decision upholding the contentions of the United States, with the arbitrator designated by Italy filing a dissenting opinion. In June 1966, Italy denounced the bilateral agreement pursuant to Article 9 thereof. See 4 I.L.M. 974 (1965).

5. Normally, an arbitration agreement is limited to disputes between the parties to it. However, in some cases agreements have allowed third states to bring claims. See, for example, Protocol between Germany and Venezuela 1903, Article VI, 9 U.N.R.I.A.A. 105–106.

## C. PROBLEMS RELATING TO THE EFFECTIVENESS OF INTERNATIONAL ARBITRATION AGREEMENTS

Three persistent problems are related to international arbitration agreements: (1) the severability of an arbitration clause from the remainder of a contract or treaty, (2) the claim of denial of justice by refusal to arbitrate, and (3) the authority of a truncated international arbitral tribunal. These problems arise in public international arbitration between states or between a state and a private entity and in international commercial arbitration between private parties. See Schwebel, International Arbitration: Three Salient Problems (1987).

### THE SEVERABILITY OF THE ARBITRATION AGREEMENT

The issue of severability arises when a contract or treaty containing an arbitration clause is claimed to be invalid or to have been terminated or suspended. In these circumstances it has been often argued that the nullification of the contract also vitiates the arbitral obligations of the parties. If the contract is invalid or no longer in force, it is claimed that the obligation to arbitrate fails with the agreement of which it is part. The argument against severability has been generally rejected on three principal grounds. First, an arbitration clause will ordinarily be comprehensive in terms and encompass "any dispute" arising out of or relating to the contract, including disputes over the validity of the agreement. See Delaume, Transnational Contracts: Applicable Law and Settlement of Disputes 59–61 (1985). Second, if one party could deny the other a right to arbitration by the mere allegation that the agreement lacked initial or continuing validity, then the simple expedient of declaring the agreement void would always be open to a party to avoid its arbitral obligation. Losinger & Co. Case, P.C.I.J., Ser. C, No. 78, 113–16 (1936). See Schwebel, International Arbitration 4 (1987). Third, it has been legally presumed that the parties to an agreement containing an arbitral clause conclude not one but two agreements: the principal substantive agreement and a second separable agreement providing for arbitration. Id., at 5. But see Wetter, Salient Features of Swedish Arbitrations Clauses, [1983] Y.B. of the Arbitration Institute of the Stockholm Chamber of Commerce 33, 35 ("such a conception is almost always very far from [the parties] minds as well as from those of their legal advisors.").

Despite these arguments in favor of severability, it has been claimed that two situations may be inappropriate for its application. Where the issue is not whether the principal agreement is valid, but whether it was actually concluded at all, there may be room to challenge the existence of the arbitration clause. See Jennings, Nullity and Effectiveness in International Law, in Cambridge Essays in International Law 66–67 (1965). Second, where the issue is whether the agreement to arbitrate is valid, the decision of the arbitral tribunal on the matter may generally be reviewed in a national court. See, e.g., French Code of Civil Procedure, as amended by Decree No. 81–500 of 12 May 1981, reprinted in 20 I.L.M. 917–22 (1981).

The major international arbitration agreements recognize the severability of the principal contract and an arbitration clause. The 1976 Arbitration Rules (Article 21(2)) adopted by the United Nations Commission on International Trade Law provides "an arbitration clause which forms part of a contract and which provides for arbitration under these Rules shall be treated as an agreement independent of the other terms of the contract." See also the 1985 Model Law on International Commercial Arbitration (Article 16(1)) ("A decision by the arbitral tribunal that the contract is null and void shall not entail *ipso jure* the invalidity of the arbitration clause"); the Rules of the Court of Arbitration of the International Chamber of Commerce (Article 8(4)) ("the arbitrator shall not cease to have jurisdiction by reason of any claim that the contract is null and void * * * provided he upholds the validity of the agreement to arbitrate."); Resolution on Arbitration between states, State Enterprises or state entities, and foreign enterprises, 63 Annuaire de L'institut de Droit International 324 (1990–II) (Article 3(a)) ("Unless the arbitration agreement provides otherwise * * * [t]he arbitration agreement is separable from the legal relationship to which it refers * * *"). See further Schwebel, International Arbitration 13–23 (1987).

In the Appeal Relating to the Jurisdiction of the ICAO Council (Judgement), 1972 I.C.J. 46, the International Court of Justice addressed the issue of severability. In the case, India took the position that the Council of the International Civil Aviation Organization (ICAO) lacked jurisdiction to hear Pakistan's complaint under the 1944 Chicago Civil Aviation Convention and a Transit Agreement against India for prohibiting the flight of civil aircraft over Indian territory. India maintained that as the Convention and Transit Agreement had been terminated or suspended between India and Pakistan, those international agreements could not furnish the ICAO Council with a basis for jurisdiction. The Court rejected India's argument and held that a party to a treaty cannot defeat the provision for adjudication or arbitration that the treaty contains by contending that it has terminated the treaty. The Court stated:

> The acceptance of such a proposition would be tantamount to opening the way to a wholesale nullification of the practical value of jurisdictional clauses by allowing a party first to purport to terminate, or suspend the operation of a treaty, and then to declare that the treaty being now terminated or suspended, its jurisdictional clauses were in consequence void, and could not be invoked for the purpose of contesting the validity of the termination or suspension * * * Such a result, destructive of the whole object of adjudicability, would be unacceptable.

Id. at 64–65. See also Schwebel, International Arbitration (1987); Mann, The Consequences of an International Wrong in International and National Law, 48 Brit.Y.B.Int'l L. 60, n. 3 (1976–77).

In TOPCO v. Libya, Preliminary Award of 27 November 1975, 55 I.L.R. 389, Libya maintained before sole arbitrator René–Jean Dupuy that the arbitration clauses contained in Deeds of Concession were rendered void by the nationalization of the property subject to the Deeds. The arbitrator extensively canvassed international and municipal case law, as well as the opinion of publicists, in affirming the principle "of the autonomy or the independence of the arbitrations clause. This principle * * * has the consequence of permitting the arbitration clause to escape the fate of the contract which it contains * * *." Id. at 407.

## DENIAL OF JUSTICE BY REFUSAL TO ARBITRATE

Consider a situation where a contract between a state and an alien contains an arbitration clause that provides arbitration shall be the exclusive remedy for the settlement of disputes and the state refuses to arbitrate. The question has been raised whether such a refusal constitutes a denial of justice under international law. See Mann, State Contracts and International Arbitration, 42 Brit.Y.B.Int'l L. 1 (1967). Mann concludes that:

> denial of justice in the strict and narrow sense of the term implied the failure to afford access to the tribunals of the respondent State itself. But there is no reason of logic or justice why the doctrine of denial of justice should not be so interpreted as to comprise the relatively modern case of the repudiation of an arbitration clause. The respondent State which, wilfully and as a result of its own initiative, has failed to implement an arbitration clause, can hardly allege that it has afforded justice in general or the agreed justice in particular, or complain that it is aggrieved by being held responsible for its own deliberate acts.

Id., at 27–28.

The Restatement (Third) § 712, Comment *h* declares "a state may be responsible for a denial of justice under international law * * * if, having committed itself to a special forum for dispute settlement, such as arbitration, it fails to honor such commitment. * * *"

Mann suggests a controversial exception for general legislation, not directed specifically at a contracting alien, adopted after the conclusion of the contract containing an arbitration clause. Mann maintains that a State which acts in accordance with the law cannot be said to frustrate the arbitration clause or commit a denial of justice. Schwebel, however, maintains that it is not state law but international law that protects the contractual relationship between a state and an alien. Schwebel claims "[i]f the alien's right to arbitration is negated by the contracting State, a wrong under international law ensues, whatever the law governing the contract, the arbitration agreement or the arbitral process, no less than a wrong under international law ensues if a State takes the property of an alien without just compensation whether or not the right to that property derives from its municipal law * * * The essential point is that international law sets up certain restraint upon the action which a State may legitimately take in its treatment of aliens." Schwebel, International Arbitration 66–67 (1987).

Sompong Sucharitkul, a member of the International Law Commission, has been critical of rules, including denial of justice, that would preclude a state from altering its obligations to arbitrate. He states that there is:

> nothing sacrosanct, nothing final about arbitration, least of all the peremptory character, the impossibility of derogation from an obligation to arbitrate. This would be more effective than international law, more powerful than supra-national law. It would be almost divine if once the State permits itself to submit to arbitration, it cannot allegedly derogate from this submission. However, it should be pointed out that the character of arbitration is itself voluntary, it is in itself extra-legal and conciliatory.

Sucharitkul, in Colloquium on International Trade Agreements 359 (1969), quoted in Schwebel, International Arbitration 107 (1987). See also Amerasinghe, State Responsibility for Injuries to Aliens 118 (1967).

The claim of denial of justice by refusal to arbitrate has been raised by states at various times. In the arbitrations involving Texaco Overseas Petroleum Company (TOPCO) and California Asiatic Oil Company v. the Government of the Libyan Arab Republic, 53 I.L.R. 389; and Libyan American Oil Company (LIAMCO) v. Government of the Libyan Arab Republic, 62 I.L.R. 141, the United States delivered the following note of protest to Libya over its decrees affecting the interests of TOPCO and LIAMCO:

> The concession agreements governing the operations of the oil companies specifically provide * * * for arbitration of disputes not otherwise settled. * * * The United States Government understands that the companies in question have requested arbitration; it expects that the Government of the Libyan Arab Republic will respond positively to their request since failure to do so would constitute a denial of justice and an additional breach of international law.

[1975] Digest of United States Practice in International Law 490 (1976).

In Elf Aquitaine Iran v. National Iranian Oil Company, 11 Y.B. Commercial Arbitration 98 (1986), the sole arbitrator stated that "[i]t is a recognized principle of international law that a state is bound by an arbitration clause contained in an agreement * * * and cannot thereafter unilaterally set aside the access of the other party to the system envisaged by the parties in their agreement for the settlement of disputes." Id., at 104. The arbitrator concluded that "[t]he existing precedents demonstrate * * * that a government bound by an arbitration clause cannot validly free itself of this obligation by an act of its own will such as, for example, by changing its internal law, or by a unilateral cancellation of the contract or of the concession." This unpublished portion of the Preliminary Award of 1982 is reproduced in Schwebel, International Arbitration 101 (1987).

## THE AUTHORITY OF TRUNCATED TRIBUNALS

The problem that arises in the case of a truncated arbitral tribunal is whether the tribunal has the power to issue a binding award when an arbitrator refuses to participate in the final award on his own initiative or on the instruction of a party, or when an arbitrator withdraws and a party fails to designate a replacement. This is a problem that has arisen in interstate arbitration and in arbitrations between states and aliens. Schwebel concludes that the weight of the law supports the authority of a truncated arbitral tribunal to render a binding award, but notes that the cases and the legal opinion of scholars are divided. Schwebel, International Arbitration 153 (1987). See also the extensive comments by members of the International Law Commission and other commentators on the authority of truncated tribunals, id., at 154–180.

The Iran–United States Claim Tribunal was confronted with the purposeful absence of arbitrators appointed by Iran. For example, in Case Number 17, 1 Iran–U.S. Claim Tribunal Rept. 415 (1982), Chamber Three of the Tribunal issued an award that was signed by only two of the three judges; the third judge from Iran, Judge Sani, informed the Tribunal that he would not sign the award because he had not been notified of the deliberative session of the Chamber during which the award was decided. One of the other judges responded that the case had been heard on September 1 and 2, 1982 and that during the following four months there had been numerous deliberations. Citing the *travaux prépatatoires* of the UNCITRAL Rules, which the Iranian–U.S. Claims Tribunal had incorporated into its own rules, the arbitrator signing the award contended the "under international law, Judge Sani cannot frustrate the work of the Chamber or the Tribunal by wilfully absenting himself and refusing to sign an award." Id., at 425. Similar absences of Iranian Judges occurred in nine other cases, but the Tribunal or the Chambers within it proceeded to give awards. Iran initially mounted a challenge to the awards in the Courts of the Netherlands, but ultimately discontinued its claims. Schwebel maintains that in view of such discontinuance, "it may be concluded that Iran has acquiesced in the validity of those awards." Schwebel, International Arbitration: Three Salient Problems 253 (1987). See also Resolution on Arbitration between states, State Enterprises, or state entities, and foreign enterprises, 63 Annuaire de L'institut de Droit International 324 (1990–II) (Article 3(c)) ("A Party's refusal to participate in the arbitration, whether by failing to appoint an arbitrator pursuant to the arbitration agreement, or through the withdrawal of an arbitrator, or by resorting to other obstructionist measures, neither suspends the proceedings nor prevents the rendition of a valid award.").

## D. SOME SUBSTANTIVE PROBLEMS OF ARBITRATION

### *MODEL RULES ON ARBITRAL PROCEDURE*

[1958] 2 Yb. I.L.C. 83.

* * *

#### Article 35

The validity of an award may be challenged by either party on one or more of the following grounds:

(a) That the tribunal has exceeded its powers;

(b) That there was corruption on the part of a member of the tribunal;

(c) That there has been a failure to state the reasons for the award or a serious departure from a fundamental rule of procedure;

(d) That the undertaking to arbitrate or the *compromis* is a nullity.

* * *

## IN THE MATTER OF THE INTERNATIONAL TITLE TO THE CHAMIZAL TRACT

Award of the International Boundary Commission, 1911.
[1911] For.Rel.U.S. 573, 586, 597–98.

[The United States and Mexico attempted in the Treaty of Guadalupe Hidalgo of 1848 and in the Gadsden Treaty of 1853 to fix the boundary line between their respective territories. Because the Colorado and Rio Grande Rivers constantly shifted their channels, the two countries agreed in 1884 that the dividing line should continue to "follow the center of the normal channel" of each river, "notwithstanding any alterations in the banks or in the course of those rivers, provided that such alterations be effected by natural causes through the slow and gradual erosion and deposit of alluvium * * *." Other changes brought about by the force of the current, such as the sudden abandonment of an existing river bed and the opening of a new one ("avulsion"), were to produce no change in the dividing line, which should continue to follow the middle of the original channel bed, even though this should become wholly dry or obstructed by deposits. 24 Stat. 1011, 1 Malloy 1159. In 1889, an International Boundary Commission was created by agreement between the United States and Mexico and charged with the task of deciding whether changes in the course of the Colorado River and the Rio Grande had occurred "through avulsion or erosion" for the purposes of the 1884 treaty. 26 Stat. 1512, 1 Malloy 1167.

In 1895 a dispute arose over a tract of land in El Paso, Texas known as "El Chamizal." Each country claimed the entire tract. The Boundary Commission was unable to agree on the boundary line, and a convention was signed by the two governments on June 24, 1910, establishing a commission to "decide solely and exclusively as to whether the international title to the Chamizal tract is in the United States of America or Mexico." 36 Stat. 2481, 2483. In rendering the award, the Presiding Commissioner of the arbitral tribunal, with the Mexican Commissioner concurring in part, said:]

* * * [T]he Presiding Commissioner and the Mexican Commissioner are of opinion that the accretions which occurred in the Chamizal tract up to the time of the great flood in 1864 should be awarded to the United States of America, and that inasmuch as the changes which occurred in that year did not constitute slow and gradual erosion within the meaning of the Convention of 1884, the balance of the tract should be awarded to Mexico.

[The American Commissioner dissented. At the session of the Commission in which the award was read, the agent for the United States protested against the decision and award, *inter alia,* on the following grounds:]

1. Because it departs from the terms of submission in the following particulars:

a. Because in dividing the Chamizal tract it assumes to decide a question not submitted to the commission by the convention of 1910 and a question the commission was not asked to decide by either party at any stage of the proceedings;

b. Because it fails to apply the standard prescribed by the Treaty of 1884;

c. Because it applied to the determination of the issue of erosion or avulsion a ruling or principle not authorized by the terms of the submission or by the principles of international law or embraced in any of the treaties or conventions existing between the United States and Mexico;

d. Because it departs from the jurisdictional provision of the Treaty of 1889 creating the International Boundary Commission.

[Shortly after the Commission had adjourned, the United States notified Mexico that "[f]or the reasons set forth by the American commissioner in his dissenting opinion, and by the American agent in his suggestion of protest, [it did] not accept this award as valid or binding." [1911] For.Rel.U.S. 598. The United States suggested the negotiation of a new boundary convention to settle the matter, but Mexico declined on the ground that the matter had been finally adjudicated and that there remained only the admittedly difficult task of relocating the line of 1864.]

---

No further action was taken until the conclusion in 1963 of a treaty by which the disputed territory was divided between the two countries. 15 U.S.T. 21, T.I.A.S. No. 5515, 505 U.N.T.S. 185. The agreement entered into force on January 14, 1964. See generally 3 Whiteman at 680–99. For a discussion of the controversy from a Mexican point of view, see Gomez Robledo, México y el Arbitraje Internacional 161 (1965). See also Carlston, The Process of International Arbitration 151–55 (1946).

### *Note*

Agreements to arbitrate have often formulated the issue as an "exclusive disjunction" (i.e., "either—or") permitting only one of two decisions. When arbitrators decide on a third solution, the result may be declared a nullity because of the deviation from the *compromis* (as in the *Chamizal Case*). In the much praised award in the *Island of Palmas Case* (p. 309 supra), the arbitrator, Huber, dealt with the issue squarely, asserting that the parties could not have intended him to return a *non liquet* (i.e., no decision). Is there not a danger that, if arbitrators depart from the compromissory restrictions, the decision will not be carried out? Would such decisions make states more reluctant to submit disputes to arbitration? One commentator, in discussing the dilemma of an arbitrator faced with an unsatisfactory either-or choice, suggested that "[o]nly if the alternative decisions available will be repudiated by the losing party * * * should a nondecision be delivered." Reisman, Nullity and Revision 550 (1971).* Does this proposal involve, in effect, a modification of the *compromis* by implicit agreement of the parties?

## FRAUD

### *HYDE, 2 INTERNATIONAL LAW CHIEFLY AS INTERPRETED AND APPLIED BY THE UNITED STATES*

1640–42 (2d ed. 1945).*

In the cases of Weil and of La Abra Silver Mining Company before the American–Mexican Commission of July 4, 1868, when the United States discovered that, through fraud on the part of American claimants, it had been made the instrument of wrong towards a friendly State, by means of impositions upon the arbitral tribunal as well as upon itself, it repudiated the acts and made reparation.

The Department of State is rightly indisposed to seek enforcement of an award favorable to an American citizen, which is deemed unjust, by reason, for example, of the founding of the claim on the tortious conduct of the claimant, or of irregularities in the arbitral proceedings, or of the existence of documents adverse to the claimant and not submitted to the tribunal.

To quote Judge Ralston:

> "The United States, upon a number of occasions, has seen fit to consent to the reopening of awards believed unjust. This was the case with the Venezuelan Claims Commission of 1866, whose awards were reopened and reviewed by the Commission of 1885, upon which sat two Americans and one Venezuelan. Awards under the Mexican treaty of 1848 were set aside by the courts in the case of the Gardiner claim, and were reviewed through act of Congress referring the Atocha claim to the Court of Claims. In the interest of rejected claims, Congress reopened two of the awards of the commission under the Chinese Claims Treaty of 1858, permitting the Attorney–General to decide one case finally and the Court of Claims the other. In the case of the *Caroline* the Secretary of State, against the protest of the claimant, returned to Brazil money which had been paid after a diplomatic settlement, and Congress appropriated a large sum to reimburse Brazil for moneys paid the United States representative, but which never reached the Treasury."

It will be observed that the foregoing discussions have reference to the attitude of the governments concerned rather than of arbitral tribunals upon which fraud may have been perpetrated by a litigating State.

In his decision of December 15, 1933, Mr. Justice Roberts, as Umpire in the cases of the Sabotage Claims against Germany, made the following statement:

> "The petition, in short, avers the Commission has been misled by fraud and collusion on the part of witnesses and suppression of evidence on the part of some of them. The Commission is not *functus officio.* It still sits as a court. To it in that capacity are brought charges that it has been defrauded and misled by perjury, collusion, and suppression. No tribunal worthy its name or of any respect may allow its decision to stand if such allegations are well-founded. Every tribunal has inherent power to reopen and to revise a decision induced by fraud. If it may correct its own errors and mistakes *a fortiori* it may, while it still has

* Footnotes omitted. Reprinted by permission of Little, Brown & Co.

jurisdiction of a cause, correct errors into which it has been led by fraud and collusion."

The Commission exercising the jurisdiction which it undoubtedly possessed, on June 15, 1939, set aside, revoked and annulled an earlier decision of October 16, 1930, reached at Hamburg; and it went further, and, passing upon the merits of the claims, found that the liability of Germany had been established. * * *

### *CARLSTON, THE PROCESS OF INTERNATIONAL ARBITRATION*

185–92 (1946).*

From the foregoing review of authorities one can only conclude * * * that the concept of "essential error" is vague. Yet it is believed that a certain legal analysis of the problem can be made with a view to clarifying and restricting the issues involved. No one would gainsay that merely a mistake or a questionable application of the law would not give rise to nullity. Accordingly, the exception has been advanced that the error must relate to the principal object of the *compromis,* not merely an accessory error which can be readily corrected by the parties requesting a modification of the award on that point. Balasko classifies essential error as a "gross error of fact or of law." Hall remarks, in this connection, that there is "ample room for the commission, under the influence of sentiment, of personal or national prejudices, or erroneous theories of law, and views unconsciously biased by national interests, of grave injustice, for which the injured state has no remedy." Occasion has already been taken to distinguish essential error from cases involving fraud of the parties. The problem, therefore, narrows to the status of those arbitral opinions which are based upon an erroneous appreciation by the arbitrators of the facts or of the law. If the error of fact were owing to the fact that both the tribunal and the parties were ignorant of evidence later discovered, the procedure of revision would be open to them. With regard to the error of law, there is much force in the view of Ulloa that:

> "The *error of law* should be discarded, because its appreciation cannot be left to the appreciation of the prejudiced State, which will always discover allegations on which to base it. The error of law is only a manifestation of the incapacity of the arbitrator, imputable to the parties who have selected him and must suffer the consequences."

But if the error in law should consist in a failure to apply an applicable rule of law stipulated in the *compromis,* nullity may result. The reasoning of the tribunal in the *Trail Smelter* case is pertinent in this connection:

> The formula "essential error" originated in a text voted by the International Law Institute in 1876. From its inception, its very authors were divided as to its meaning * * *
>
> The Tribunal is of the opinion that the proper criterion lies in a distinction not between "essential" errors in law and other such errors, but between "manifest" errors, such as that in the Schreck case or such

* Footnotes omitted. Reprinted by permission of Columbia University Press.

as would be committed by a tribunal that would overlook a relevant treaty or base its decision on an agreement admittedly terminated, and other errors in law.

* * * When the arbitral award is lacking in one or more of the conditions required for its validity, as established by the practice of States, the tribunal may be said to have committed an essential error. For essential error, if it is to serve any useful purpose, should be deemed to refer to the absence of one or more of the various objective, definite, established legal conditions necessary for the validity of the award. If essential error is to be considered in any other light, that is, as referring to error or mistake generally, the ascertainment of its existence would require not only an examination of the tribunal's action and its award in the light of the *compromise,* as does excess of jurisdiction, but an examination of the intrinsic merit of the reasons which dictated the award, an examination of the facts and documents submitted, in short, a new examination of the case on the merits.

### *Notes*

1. Is Carlston's definition of essential error completely circular? Would it not be simpler to recognize the propriety of reopening and correcting a decision involving a clear mistake of law, as suggested in the *Trail Smelter Case?* In the *Lehigh Valley Railroad Case* between U.S. and Germany (1940), the arbitral commission stated:

> Where the decision involves a material error the Commission not only has the power but is under a duty, upon a proper showing, to reopen and correct a decision to accord with the facts and applicable rules.

6 Hackworth at 132.

2. "The term 'essential error' has also been used to indicate error caused by the production of false evidence. To those possessing the background of the English common law, however, the term seems to suggest more aptly judicial error in the appreciation of the facts or law of a case than fraud. It is believed that clearer thinking would be aided if the term were no longer used to indicate cases involving fraud in the production of evidence; such cases involve more properly a violation of a fundamental rule of procedure. Little purpose is served in continuing to consider such cases as involving 'essential error,' when in the minds of many that term is suggestive of an unconscionable decision." Carlston, The Process of International Arbitration 186 (1946). The term "essential error" has also been commonly used to indicate an unjust decision. See id. at 187–89.

3. The distinction between "a mere error in law" that does not justify revision and those "manifest" errors that do justify revision is a difficult one. Hyde criticized the formulation of the *Trail Smelter* tribunal, quoted by Carlston in the principal text above, as "vague" and suggested the following: "It is submitted that when the decision to which objection is made was based upon a supposition which it is inconceivable that the States at variance would, for any reason, have agreed for purposes of adjudication, to accept as a test of the propriety of the conduct of either, a sufficient ground for revision exists, the judicial error in such case being the misconception on the part of the court of the basis on which its conclusion was sought." Hyde at 1636.

4. A succinct analysis of case-law on scope of review of arbitral awards is contained in Reisman, Nullity and Revision 423–41 (1971).

## E. THE IRAN–UNITED STATES CLAIMS TRIBUNAL

The most active arbitral tribunal today is the Iran–United States Claims Tribunal established under the Declaration of Algeria. 20 I.L.M. 223 (1981).

The Tribunal, which has its seat at The Hague, has jurisdiction over private claims of nationals of the U.S. against Iran and nationals of Iran against the United States. However, it may not decide claims arising under a contract which contained a forum-selection clause specifying the Iranian courts. In one of the earliest cases, the Tribunal ruled that it also has no jurisdiction over "direct" claims by one government against the nationals of the other. Case No. A/2, decision of 19 December 1981, reprinted in 21 I.L.M. 78 (1982).

The Tribunal consists of nine members, of which three are chosen by Iran, three by the U.S., and three by the six thus appointed. The arbitration rules of the United Nations Commission on International Trade Law (UNCITRAL) govern the appointment of arbitrators and the procedure of the Tribunal. See Baker & Davis, The UNCITRAL Arbitration Rules in Practice: The Experience of the Iran–United States Claims Tribunal (1992). If the parties fail to agree on any of the three arbitrators chosen jointly, according to these rules, the Secretary–General of the Permanent Court of Arbitration at The Hague shall designate an appointing authority who may exercise his discretion in appointing an arbitrator to the disputed position. Art. 7(b), UNCITRAL Arbitration Rules, 15 I.L.M. 701, 705 (1976). Pursuant to this provision, the Secretary–General designated the President of the Supreme Court of the Netherlands as the appointing authority. Appointments were made by him in two cases, including the appointment of the President of the Tribunal in 1985.

The appointing authority also has the power to rule on challenges to the continued presence of a judge who refuses to withdraw and has done so in several cases. Articles 10–12, UNCITRAL Arbitration Rules. In the 1984 decision of the Tribunal on dual nationality (see Chapter 5, Section 7) the dissenting Iranian members declared that "[t]he composition of the so-called neutral arbitrators, itself the result of the imposed mechanism of the UNCITRAL Rules, is so unbalanced as to have made the Tribunal lose all credibility to adjudicate any dispute between the Islamic Republic of Iran * * * and the United States." Case No. A/18, decision of 6 April 1984, 5 Iran–U.S. Claims Tribunal Reports 251, 266.

All decisions and awards of the Tribunal are final and binding. They are enforceable against either government in the courts of any nation in accordance with its laws. A fund was also established in the Central Bank of the Netherlands for payment of the awards to U.S. claimants. See Chapter 7, Section 9B.

The Tribunal is required to decide cases on the basis of respect for law, applying choice of law rules and principles of commercial and international law which it determines to be applicable. See supra, p. 405 n. 1. For a statement on the implications of this provision, see L. Damrosch, et al., Panel on Decisions of Iran–United States Claims Tribunal, 78 A.S.I.L.Proc. 221, 227–33 (1984). See also Khan, The Iran–United States Claims Tribunal: Controversies, Cases and Contribution (1990); D. Caron, The Nature of the

Iran-United States Claims Tribunal and the Evolving Structure of International Dispute Resolution, 84 Am.J. Int'l L. 104 (1990).

Tribunal decisions are published in a series entitled *Iran–United States Claims Tribunal Reports* (Grotius Press) and in two bi-weekly looseleaf services: *Iranian Assets Litigation Reporter* (Andrews Publications) and *Mealy's Litigation Reports: Iran Claims.* The more important decisions are reprinted in International Legal Materials and summarized in the Judicial Decisions section of the American Journal of International Law.

## F. THE RECENT GROWTH OF INTERNATIONAL ARBITRATION

The tremendous growth of international commerce after the Second World War has led to a concomitant growth in the settlement of disputes arising from such commerce through arbitration. The leading institution in this field has been the International Court of Arbitration of the International Chamber of Commerce in Paris, France. Under its auspices and rules, a steadily growing number of disputes are settled. The United Nations Commission on International Trade Law has made international arbitration one of its preoccupations. It has developed the UNCITRAL Arbitration Rules that may be used both in *ad hoc* and institutionally supervised arbitration. Many arbitration institutions, including the American Arbitration Association (AAA), will administer arbitrations, under either their own rules or the UNCITRAL Rules. The Iran–United States Claims Tribunal also conducts its proceedings under the UNCITRAL Rules. The Center for Public Resources (CPR) has evolved another set of rules that parties may adopt for the arbitration of their disputes. The number of institutions that administer international arbitrations is growing apace. On these developments, see H. Smit, The Future of International Commercial Arbitration, 25 Colum. J. Transnat'l L. 9 (1986). On the AAA International Arbitration Rules, which are an adaptation of the UNCITRAL Rules, see H. Smit, The New International Arbitration Rules of the American Arbitration Association, 2 Am.Rev.Int.Arb. 1 (1992). On the CPR Rules, see H. Smit, The Center for Public Resources' Rules for non-Administered Arbitration of International Disputes: A Critical and Comparative Commentary, 2 Am.Rev. Int.Arb. 3 (1992). UNCITRAL has also developed a Model Law on International Commercial Arbitration, which has been adopted by a number of states in the United States and abroad. See, J.S. McClendon, State International Arbitration Laws: Are They Needed or Desirable, 1 Am.Rev.Int.Arb. 245 (1990); B.E. Shifman, Developments in Adoption of the 1985 UNCITRAL Model Law on International Commercial Arbitration, 1 Am.Rev.Int.Arb. 281 (1990).

A most important advantage of international arbitration is that its awards are recognized and enforced in a large number of countries. As of August 1992, the New York Convention on the Recognition and Enforcement of Foreign Arbitral Awards of June 10, 1958, had been ratified by 89 states, including nearly all major commercial nations. 330 U.N.T.S. 38. On this Convention, see A.J. van den Berg, The New York Arbitration Convention of 1958 (1981); World Arbitration Reporter (Parker School of Foreign and Comparative Law ed., 1988). This feature of international arbitration offers particular advantages in relations with foreign states. An arbitration clause in a contract with a foreign state ensures not only that there will be a forum to adjudicate any dispute that may arise under the contract, but also that any award rendered in such a dispute will be enforceable virtually anywhere in the world. In this respect, awards entitled to recognition and enforcement under the New York Convention enjoy more effective enforcement than other awards or judgments, including those of the International Court of Justice. On international arbitration generally, see A. Lowenfeld, International Litigation and Arbitration Ch. 4 (1993).

# SECTION 4. THE INTERNATIONAL COURT OF JUSTICE

*CHARTER OF THE UNITED NATIONS*

[See Articles 92–96]

---

*STATUTE OF THE INTERNATIONAL COURT OF JUSTICE*

[See Articles 34–38]

### *Notes*

1. The parties to the Statute include all members of the United Nations and one non-member (Switzerland) by resolutions of the General Assembly pursuant to Article 93(2) of the United Nations Charter. The conditions upon which the Court is open to states which are not parties to the Statute are laid down in Security Council Resolution 9 of October 15, 1946, adopted pursuant to Article 35(2) of the Statute. See 1 SCOR, 2d Ser. No. 19, at 467–68.

2. Under Article 96(1), the General Assembly and the Security Council may request an advisory opinion on any legal question. Pursuant to Article 96(2) of the United Nations Charter, the General Assembly has authorized four organs of the United Nations and fifteen specialized agencies to request advisory opinions of the Court on legal questions within the scope of their activities.

3. There are fifteen judges on the Court elected by the Security Council and the General Assembly, each body voting separately. Nominations are made by national groups rather than by governments. See Articles 2–12 of the Statute. The judges may include no more than one national of any state. A "gentlemen's agreement" among members of the United Nations generally governs the distribution of seats among the various regions of the world. In 1993, the Court had 4 judges from western Europe, 2 from eastern Europe, 3 from Africa, 3 from Asia, 2 from Latin–America, and one from the United States. Judges serve for nine years, with 5 judges rotating off each three years. Judges may be re-elected and often are. If a party in a case does not have a judge of its nationality, it may designate an *ad hoc* judge (Article 31).

4. The Court generally has decided cases by a full bench. It may, however, form chambers, composed of three or more judges to deal with a particular case or a category of cases (Articles 25–26). Ad hoc chambers were used in four recent cases: Gulf of Maine Area Case (Canada v. U.S.), 1984 I.C.J. 246; Frontier Dispute (Burkina Faso v. Mali), 1986 I.C.J. 554; ELSI Case (U.S. v. Italy), 1989 I.C.J. 15; and Land, Island and Maritime Frontier Dispute (El Salvador v. Honduras), 1987 I.C.J. 10. One of the most criticized aspects of the use of

chambers is the extent to which the parties may influence or control the selection of the judges. Judge Oda has noted that, although the jurisprudence of the Court is intended to reflect the diversity of the world's legal systems:

> In the case of all four of the ad hoc Chambers that have been constituted during recent years, consideration of "the main forms of civilization and the principal legal systems of the world" apparently was not in the minds of the parties in proposing the judges to sit on the Chamber or of the Court as a whole in electing the Chamber. Excluding national and ad hoc judges, the Chamber for the Gulf of Maine case had three Western European judges (from France, the Federal Republic of Germany and Italy); the Chamber for the Frontier Dispute (Burkina Faso v. Mali) case, one African (Algeria), one Eastern European (Poland) and on Latin American (Argentina); the Chamber for the Elettronica Sicula S.p.A. (ELSI) case (U.S./Italy), two Asians (India and Japan) and one Western European (United Kingdom) (one of the Asians was the then President of the Court); and the Chamber for the El Salvador/Honduras case, one Latin American (Brazil), one Asian (Japan) and one Western European (United Kingdom). This record suggests that no consistent geographical consideration has guided the choice of the judges of the Chambers. It may also be asked, when there are five main regions according to United Nations practice, by what criteria is the Court to choose three judges from among these five regions?

Shigeru Oda, Note and Comment, Further Thoughts on the Chambers Procedure of the International Court of Justice, 82 Am.J. Int'l L. 556, 557 (1988). Do you agree that the objectivity, neutrality, and reputation of the Court is threatened by a system that allows the parties to have their dispute heard by an ad hoc chamber because they fear that the composition of the full court may not suit their goals? Consider an opposing view in favor of the use of Chambers by Judge Schwebel:

> The workings of this process to date show that it affords the Court the opportunity to settle international disputes in a fashion that meets the needs of the parties and the international community, and does not detract from the integrity of the Court. It has not "fractionalized" or "regionalized" international law in any degree. It has not thrown into question the universal character of international law. It may be that sometimes the parties may desire, or settle upon, a Chamber of regional complexion; other times they will not. That happens in ad hoc arbitration as well.

Stephen Schwebel, Ad Hoc Chambers of the International Court of Justice, 81 Am.J. Int'l L. 831, 850 (1987).

The Court also has a standing chamber of five judges to determine cases by summary procedure where speedy action is required (Article 29). All questions are decided by a majority vote of the judges present. In case of a tie the President has a casting vote (Article 55).

## RECOURSE TO THE COURT

During the period 1946–July 31, 1991, the Court had 86 cases presented to it. It rendered 52 judgments and 21 advisory opinions. It also issued 249 orders, mostly of a procedural character but including some indicating provisional measures.

Many of the judgments and advisory opinions have been of major significance for the clarification and development of international law.

Nonetheless, international lawyers and students of international relations have noted and often deplored the fact that states have not chosen to submit most of their legal disputes to the Court. Even though resolutions have been adopted by unanimous votes in the General Assembly calling for greater use of the International Court, relatively few disputes are submitted to the Court.

The following comments sum up the reasons generally given for the reluctance of states to submit their disputes to the Court.

It is no great mystery why they are reluctant to have their disputes adjudicated. Litigation is uncertain, time consuming, troublesome. Political officials do not want to lose control of a case that they might resolve by negotiation or political pressures. Diplomats naturally prefer diplomacy; political leaders value persuasion, manoeuvre and flexibility. They often prefer to "play it by ear," making their rules fit the circumstances rather than submit to pre-existing rules. Political forums, such as the United Nations, are often more attractive, especially to those likely to get wide support for political reasons. We need only compare the large number of disputes brought to the United Nations with the few submitted to adjudication. One could go on with other reasons. States do not want to risk losing a case when the stakes are high or be troubled with litigation in minor matters. An international tribunal may not inspire confidence, especially when some judges are seen as "political" or as hostile. There is apprehension that the law is too malleable or fragmentary to sustain "true" judicial decisions. In some situations, the legal issues are viewed as but one element in a complex political situation and consequently it is considered unwise or futile to deal with them separately. Finally we note the underlying perception of many governments that law essentially supports the *status quo* and that courts are not responsive to demands for justice or change. Schachter, International Law in Theory and Practice, 178 Rec. des Cours 208 (1982–V).

See also de Visscher, chapters II and IV, in Theory and Reality in International Law (rev.ed., Corbett trans., 1968); Jessup, The Price of Justice (1971); The Future of the International Court of Justice (Gross ed. 1976) (especially contributions by Fitzmaurice, Gross, Jessup and Kearney); Jiménez de Aréchaga, International Law in the Past Third of a Century, 159 Rec. des Cours 167–169 (1978–I); Falk, Reviving the World Court (1986). A general work on the Court is Rosenne, The Law and Practice of the International Court (2d ed. 1985).

## A. JURISDICTION

The Court has two kinds of jurisdiction: to decide contentious cases between states and to render advisory opinions. Only states may be parties to a contentious case, not international organizations or private persons. The jurisdiction of the Court in contentious cases is based on the consent of the parties, express or implied (Article 36 of the Statute). Consent may be given *ad hoc* or by prior agreement in a treaty (Article 36(1)) or by accepting compulsory jurisdiction under Article 36(2). In the latter case, the case must be a "legal dispute." No such limitation is imposed in Article 36(1). However, Article 38 states that the function of the Court is to "decide in accordance with international law such disputes as are submitted to it."

See Restatement (Revised) § 903, Comment *d*.

### *ROSENNE, THE LAW AND PRACTICE OF THE INTERNATIONAL COURT*

Vol. 1, p. 332–35, 344, 357–59 (1965).*

The statutory basis for the conventional jurisdiction of the Court is Article 36(1). * * * By this, the Court has jurisdiction over all "cases" which the parties refer to it, and over all matters specially provided for in treaties and conventions in force.

In practice, two generic types of agreement for referring a matter to the Court can be discerned. The classic method by which the parties refer a case to the Court is by a special agreement (*compromis*). This is an agreement whereby two or more States agree to refer a particular and defined matter to the Court for decision. The distinguishing feature of the special agreement as a title of jurisdiction is that jurisdiction is conferred and the Court is seised of the defined issues of the concrete case by the mere notification to the Court of the agreement. Only if an agreement has that double effect can it be regarded as a true special agreement, as that expression is used in the Statute and Rules of Court, so as to lead to the application of the special procedure, reminiscent of the procedure of classical international arbitration, which those texts specify. * * *

The more usual method of conferring jurisdiction under this head is by a compromissory clause in a multilateral or bilateral treaty. The treaty may be one providing for the reference of a given dispute to the Court, a general treaty of peaceful settlement of disputes, or a treaty regulating some other topic and containing a compromissory clause. The effect of such a provision is to establish the jurisdiction of the Court, as between the parties, to the extent specified in the compromissory clause. * * * That * * * a treaty is in force creates as between its parties the necessary elements of mutuality and reciprocity in the general sense, but whether specific jurisdiction to entertain the concrete case exists has to be determined in the usual way. The compromissory clause may also regulate the seising of the Court, for instance by specifying what preliminary conditions have to be met and how the proceedings may be instituted: and if the unilateral institution of proceedings by application is envisaged, the result will be to establish a form of compulsory jurisdiction. However, that compulsory jurisdiction will be based on Article 36(1) of the Statute and not on Article 36(2), which means that it will not have the variable scope characteristic of the compulsory jurisdiction properly so-called * * *. If the treaty is a multilateral one and the proceedings raise a question of the construction of that treaty * * *, its other parties have a right to intervene, under Article 63 of the Statute. * * *

[T]he principle of *forum prorogatum* which emerges from the decisions of the two Courts is that jurisdiction may be conferred by the tacit consent of

* Footnotes omitted. Reprinted by permission of A.W. Sijthoff & Noordhoff International.

the parties, deduced from their conduct in pleading to the merits of a claim (including a counter-claim) without raising the question of jurisdiction. Tacit consent is thus clearly distinguishable from informal consent, a fact which may be of importance * * * in connexion with the question: What organ of the State is competent to perform the act expressing the consent of the State? * * *

The doctrine is neatly summarized in the *Haya de la Torre* case: "The Parties have in the present case consented to the jurisdiction of the Court. All the questions submitted to it have been argued on the merits, and no objection has been made to a decision on the merits. This conduct of the Parties is sufficient to confer jurisdiction on the Court." * * *

In considering whether jurisdiction has been conferred by the tacit consent of the respondent, the Court will have regard to the whole of its conduct, and not merely to isolated phenomena, and it will not exercise jurisdiction if the whole of that State's conduct in the case is consistent with an intention that it should not exercise jurisdiction. * * *

### *Notes*

1. Most cases brought before the Court have been brought under compromissory clauses in treaties. Several have been based on the General Act for Peaceful Settlement (Section 1 supra). Others have been based on pre–1945 treaties that apply because the present International Court succeeded to the jurisdiction of the Permanent Court of International Justice under Article 37 of the Statute.

2. Nearly 250 treaties currently in force provide for resolution of disputes by the International Court. 39 I.C.J.Yb. 1985. The United States is a party to more than 70 of them.

3. A case brought under a treaty clause does not require a special agreement; it is begun by a unilateral application. Under a special agreement (*compromis*) the Court is limited to the questions put by the parties; under a treaty clause, the Court determines the relevant issues of law raised by the application. States that bind themselves by a treaty may be reluctant subsequently to adjudicate a particular case under that treaty. Some have refused to appear in such cases but nonappearance does not defeat jurisdiction. See Case Concerning U.S. Diplomatic Personnel in Tehran, 1980 I.C.J. 3, discussed below.

4. Some general multilateral conventions provide for compulsory jurisdiction through optional protocols such as those to the Vienna Conventions on Diplomatic Relations and on Consular Relations. Other conventions have jurisdictional clauses that allow any party to bring the dispute to the Court. Some of these conventions expressly allow reservations; others are silent on reservations but have had reservations made to them. See I.C.J. Advisory Opinion on Reservation to the Genocide Convention, Chapter 6. Some conventions exclude such reservations.

5. A few treaties give the Court "appellate jurisdiction." For example, the Convention on International Civil Aviation (1944) provides for appeals to the Court from decisions of the Council of the International Civil Aviation Organization (ICAO). See Case Between India and Pakistan Relating to Jurisdiction of ICAO Council, 1972 I.C.J. 46 (see Chapter 6, p. 514 supra). The Court has also used its advisory jurisdiction to review judgments of international administrative

tribunals. These cases have been brought by the organizations concerned under special procedures for advisory opinions and do not come within the contentious jurisdiction of the Court.

6. Relatively informal agreements between states for referring disputes to the Court may be sufficient for jurisdiction under Article 36(1). See the Fisheries Jurisdiction Cases, 1973 I.C.J. 3, 49 (discussed above at p. 519). Would an unsigned press communiqué expressing an intention to refer cases to the Court be adequate? The Court gave a negative reply in the Aegean Sea Continental Shelf Case, 1978 I.C.J. 3.

7. Many bilateral treaties include provisions for compulsory jurisdiction of disputes relating to the interpretation and application of the Treaty. Treaties of Friendship, Commerce and Navigation entered into by the United States with some 30 countries have such clauses. One was invoked by the United States in its case against Iran concerning the hostages in Tehran (discussed below) and another was invoked by Nicaragua in its proceeding against the United States for military and paramilitary activity against Nicaragua (infra).

8. Article 36(1) also states that "the jurisdiction of the Court * * * comprises all matters specially provided for in the Charter of the United Nations." Are there any such matters? The only possible provision is Article 36(3) of the Charter which authorizes the Security Council to "recommend" that parties refer their disputes to the Court. However, as 7 judges declared in the Corfu Channel Case, 1949 I.C.J. 31, a recommendation is an inadequate basis for compulsory jurisdiction. Is there room for the view that the Security Council may "decide" under chapter 7 that a state must submit a dispute to the Court?

## COMPULSORY JURISDICTION UNDER THE OPTIONAL CLAUSE

Article 36(2) of the Statute provides:

> 2. The states parties to the present Statute may at any time declare that they recognize as compulsory *ipso facto* and without special agreement, in relation to any other state accepting the same obligation, the jurisdiction of the Court in all legal disputes concerning:
>
> a. the interpretation of a treaty;
>
> b. any question of international law;
>
> c. the existence of any fact which, if established, would constitute a breach of an international obligation;
>
> d. the nature or extent of the reparation to be made for the breach of an international obligation.

Article 36(3) of the Statutes states:

> 3. The declarations referred to above may be made unconditionally or on condition of reciprocity on the part of several or certain states, or for a certain time.

The position as of 1986 in respect of declarations accepting compulsory jurisdiction under Article 36(2) is summarized in the following note of the Restatement (Third) § 903, Reporters' Note 2:

As of 1986, 57 states had made declarations under Article 36(2) of the Statute of the Court accepting compulsory jurisdiction of the Court; 11 of these declarations have expired or have been terminated. Forty-six declarations are in force; 44 by members of the United Nations, and two by non-members (Liechtenstein and Switzerland). Declarations in effect are by states of Western Europe, the Americas, Africa, Asia, and the Pacific; there are no declarations by states of Eastern Europe. Several of the declarations antedate the International Court of Justice and originally conferred jurisdiction on the Permanent Court of International Justice, but under Article 36(5) of the Statute of the International Court of Justice such declarations are deemed to be acceptances of the jurisdiction of the successor Court.

Some of the declarations are without limit of time; others are for a specific period (usually five or ten years), in many instances with an automatic renewal clause. Many declarations reserve the right to terminate by a notice of withdrawal effective upon receipt by the Secretary-General of the United Nations. Some declarations specify that they apply only to disputes arising after the declaration was made or concerning situations or facts subsequent to a specified date. Seventeen declarations are without any reservation; the remaining declarations are accompanied by a variety of reservations. Many states have modified their reservations, some of them several times.

The most common reservation excludes disputes committed by the parties to other tribunals or which the parties have agreed to settle by other means of settlement. Another common reservation excludes disputes relating to matters that are "exclusively" or "essentially" within the domestic jurisdiction of the declarant state; some of these reservations provide in addition that the question whether a dispute is essentially within the domestic jurisdiction is to be determined by the declaring state (a so-called "self-judging" clause). Several declarations exclude disputes arising under a multilateral treaty "unless all parties to the treaty affected by the decision are also parties to the case before the Court" or, more broadly, "unless all parties to the treaty are also parties to the case before the Court." Some reservations exclude disputes as to a particular subject, such as territorial or maritime boundaries or other law of the sea issues.

A few declarations, using various formulas, exclude disputes arising out of hostilities to which the declarant state is a party; the most comprehensive of these reservations is that of India which excludes "disputes relating to or connected with facts or situations of hostilities, armed conflicts, individual or collective actions taken in self-defense, resistance to aggression, fulfillment of obligations imposed by international bodies, and other similar or related acts, measures or situations in which India is, has been or may in future be involved." A reservation of the United Kingdom made in 1957 excluded disputes "relating to any question which, in the opinion of the Government of the United Kingdom, affects the national security of the United Kingdom or of any of its dependent territories"; this clause was restricted in the United Kingdom's 1958 declaration to certain past disputes and was omitted in its 1963 declaration.

An increasing number of states have added to their declarations clauses designed to avoid surprise suits by states that accept the Court's jurisdiction and immediately bring a case against another state. For instance, some states have excluded any dispute that was brought before the Court by a party to a dispute less than 12 months after the party had accepted the jurisdiction of the Court with respect to that category of disputes. Many states have reserved the right to modify or terminate a declaration peremptorily by means of a notification to the Secretary-General of the United Nations, with effect from the moment of that notification.

In 27 contentious cases (as of 1986), objections were raised as to the Court's jurisdiction or the admissibility of an application; the Court dismissed almost half of these cases. A few cases were terminated by the Court when it was informed that the defendant had not previously accepted the Court's jurisdiction and was not willing to accept it *ad hoc* for the particular case. Several cases were discontinued by agreement between the parties. See [1985–86] I.C.J. Y.B. 48, 50, 123, 124.

## SOME DECLARATIONS RECOGNIZING AS COMPULSORY THE JURISDICTION OF THE COURT

### Guinea-Bissau

*[Translation from the French]* 7 VIII 89.

In accordance with Article 36, paragraph 2, of the Statute of the International Court of Justice, the Republic of Guinea–Bissau accepts as compulsory *ipso facto* and without special agreement, in relation to any other State accepting the same obligation, the jurisdiction of the Court in all legal disputes referred to in Article 36, paragraph 2, of the Statute thereof.

This declaration will remain in force until six months following the date on which the Government of Guinea–Bissau makes known its intention of terminating it.

New York, 7 August 1989.

(*Signed*) Raul A. de Melo Cabral,
Chargé d'affaires a.i.

### United Kingdom of Great Britain and Northern Ireland [1]

1 I 69.

1. I have the honour, by direction of Her Majesty's Principal Secretary of State for Foreign and Commonwealth Affairs, to declare on behalf of the Government of the United Kingdom of Great Britain and Northern Ireland that they accept as compulsory *ipso facto* and without special convention, on condition of reciprocity, the jurisdiction of the International Court of Justice, in conformity with paragraph 2 of Article 36 of the Statute of the Court, until such time as notice may be given to terminate the acceptance, over all

1. This declaration replaced that of 27 November 1963 (U.N.T.S., I, No. 6995, Vol. 482), notice of the withdrawal and termination of which was given by letter of 1 January 1969, received by the Secretary–General of the United Nations on that date.

disputes arising after 24 October 1945, with regard to situations or facts subsequent to the same date, other than:

(i) any dispute which the United Kingdom

(*a*) has agreed with the other Party or Parties thereto to settle by some other method of peaceful settlement; or

(*b*) has already submitted to arbitration by agreement with any State which had not at the time of submission accepted the compulsory jurisdiction of the International Court of Justice.

(ii) disputes with the government of any other country which is a Member of the Commonwealth with regard to situations or facts existing before 1 January 1969;

(iii) disputes in respect of which any other Party to the dispute has accepted the compulsory jurisdiction of the International Court of Justice only in relation to or for the purpose of the dispute; or where the acceptance of the Court's compulsory jurisdiction on behalf of any other Party to the dispute was deposited or ratified less than twelve months prior to the filing of the application bringing the dispute before the Court.

2. The Government of the United Kingdom also reserves the right at any time, by means of a notification addressed to the Secretary-General of the United Nations, and with effect as from the moment of such notification, either to add to, amend or withdraw any of the foregoing reservations, or any that may hereafter be added.

New York, 1 January 1969.

(*Signed*) L.C. Glass

United States of America

26 VIII 46.

I, Harry S. Truman, President of the United States of America, declare on behalf of the United States of America, under Article 36, paragraph 2, of the Statute of the International Court of Justice, and in accordance with the Resolution of 2 August 1946 of the Senate of the United States of America (two-thirds of the Senators present concurring therein), that the United States of America recognizes as compulsory *ipso facto* and without special agreement, in relation to any other State accepting the same obligation, the jurisdiction of the International Court of Justice in all legal disputes hereafter arising concerning—

(a) the interpretation of a treaty;

(b) any question of international law;

(c) the existence of any fact which, if established, would constitute a breach of an international obligation;

(d) the nature or extent of the reparation to be made for the breach of an international obligation;

*Provided,* that this declaration shall not apply to—

(a) disputes the solution of which the parties shall entrust to other tribunals by virtue of agreements already in existence or which may be concluded in the future; or

(b) disputes with regard to matters which are essentially within the domestic jurisdiction of the United States of America as determined by the United States of America; or

(c) disputes arising under a multilateral treaty, unless (1) all parties to the treaty affected by the decision are also parties to the case before the Court, or (2) the United States of America specially agrees to jurisdiction; and

*Provided further,* that this declaration shall remain in force for a period of five years and thereafter until the expiration of six months after notice may be given to terminate this declaration.

(*Signed*) Harry S. TRUMAN

Done at Washington this fourteenth day of August 1946.

### *Notes*

1. The United States acceptance of compulsory jurisdiction was terminated by President Reagan on October 7, 1985, with effect six months from that date. The termination was linked to the decision of the International Court in November 1984 in the case brought by Nicaragua against the United States for military and para-military activities in and against Nicaragua, 1984 I.C.J. 392. A summary of the case is on p. 837.

2. In explaining the motives for the decision to terminate acceptance of the compulsory jurisdiction clause, the Legal Adviser of the State Department observed that the United States had never successfully brought another state before the Court under the compulsory jurisdiction clause although it tried to do so several times. Sofaer, Statement to Senate Foreign Relations Committee, December 4, 1985, 86:2106 State Dept. Bull. 67 (1986). See p. 849 below. One reason he noted was that under the principle of reciprocity the respondent state could invoke the U.S. reservation involving matters essentially within domestic jurisdiction as determined by the United States, as was done by Bulgaria in 1960 in a case brought by the United States against Bulgaria for an aerial incident injuring United States nationals. See Gross, Bulgaria Invokes the Connally Amendment, 56 A.J.I.L. 357 (1962).

3. France brought a case against Norway based on the acceptance of compulsory jurisdiction by both States. The French Declaration of acceptance contained a clause similar to that in the U.S. acceptance. Norway argued it had the right to rely on the restrictions in the French declaration and claimed that the matter fell within the national jurisdiction of Norway. The Court held that, in accordance with the condition of reciprocity, "Norway, equally with France, is entitled to except from the compulsory jurisdiction of the Court disputes understood by Norway to be essentially within its national jurisdiction". The French application was therefore rejected. The Court declared that it was not called upon to examine the validity of the reservation since the question of its validity was not presented by the issues in the proceedings inasmuch as both parties relied on the reservation. Case of Certain Norwegian Loans, 1957 I.C.J. 9. Judge Lauterpacht in a separate opinion maintained that a self-judging reserva-

tion was invalid and, if not separable, invalidated the acceptance of compulsory jurisdiction. 1957 I.C.J. 34. Similar views were expressed by Lauterpacht and 3 other judges in the Interhandel Case, 1959 I.C.J. 95, 54, 75, 85.

4. In the *Norwegian Loans Case* the Court relied on the fact that both the Norwegian and French declarations were made on condition of reciprocity as provided for in paragraph 3 of Article 36. Suppose such condition had not been included in the declarations, should the Court have decided that Norway could invoke the French reservation on the basis of the clause in Article 36(2) that jurisdiction is accepted "in relation to any other state accepting the same obligation." Do these words mean that every acceptance impliedly includes a condition of reciprocity? Professor Brown Weiss points out in an illuminating study of reciprocity that

> The current theory of reciprocity under the Optional Clause has three primary postulates:
>
> 1. Jurisdiction exists under the Optional Clause only to the extent that both parties have accepted a common commitment
> 2. Determination of reciprocity takes place only at the moment the Court is seised of a case
> 3. Reciprocity applies only to the scope and substance of the commitments, not to the formal conditions of their creation, duration or extinction.

E. Brown Weiss, Reciprocity and the Optional Clause, in the International Court of A Crossroads 84 (L. Damrosch ed., 1987).

5. The U.S. argued in the Nicaragua Case of 1984 that it should benefit from an implied condition in Nicaragua's declaration permitting Nicaragua to terminate its declaration at will with immediate effect. The Court refused to apply reciprocity to such temporal conditions of termination or modification, though the Court has recognized that the temporal conditions which exclude disputes prior to a given date are covered by reciprocity.

6. May a state that accepted compulsory jurisdiction withdraw such acceptance when it learns that a case is about to be brought against it? May a state accept compulsory jurisdiction to bring a specific case and immediately thereafter withdraw its acceptance to avoid being sued in another matter? Would such "hit-and-run" tactics be contrary to the principle of reciprocity or good faith?

7. When the United States terminated its acceptance, its spokesmen observed that a majority of judges in 1985 came from states that had not accepted compulsory jurisdiction and that only 47 countries in all had such acceptances. In what respect do these facts bear on the desirability or not of U.S. continued acceptance? Brown Weiss concluded that "acceptance of the compulsory jurisdiction of the Court by less than one-third of the countries that are parties to the Statute of the Court has not in practice resulted in significant inequities for those states that have accepted the Optional Clause" (loc. cit at 105).

## OBJECTIONS TO JURISDICTION OR ADMISSIBILITY

*JIMÉNEZ DE ARÉCHAGA, INTERNATIONAL LAW IN THE PAST THIRD OF A CENTURY*

159 Rec. des Cours, 155–158 (1978–I).*

### PRELIMINARY OBJECTIONS

While before municipal tribunals an objection of incompetence must be examined *in limine litis* for reasons of economy of procedure, in the international field there are more substantial grounds which make it necessary to deal with questions of jurisdiction as independent and preliminary issues.

As the Court explained in 1972:

> "For the party raising a jurisdictional objection, its significance will also lie in the possibility it may offer of avoiding, not only a decision, but even a hearing, on the merits—a factor which is of prime importance in many cases. An essential point of legal principle is involved here, namely that a party should not have to give an account of itself on issues of merits before a tribunal which lacks jurisdiction in the matter, or whose jurisdiction has not yet been established." [280]

In harmony with these views, the Rules of Court provide in Article 79(3) for the suspension of the proceedings on the merits as soon as a preliminary objection is filed. An amendment introduced in the Rules in 1972 states in Article 79(6) that this is done "in order to enable the Court to determine its jurisdiction at the preliminary stage of the proceedings".

The difficulty which exists in this respect in the international field is that sometimes the issues involved in a preliminary objection, even one of jurisdiction, may touch upon the merits or "at least involve some consideration of them". For instance, in the *Right of Passage over Indian Territory* case, the Court had to determine when the dispute arose, since the acceptance of jurisdiction only applied to disputes which had arisen after a certain date. In that case the Court joined the objection to the merits on the ground that "it is not at present in possession of sufficient evidence to enable it to pronounce on these questions [281]".

The 1972 amendments to the Rules of Procedure of the Court provide a different solution to the difficulties encountered in the *Right of Passage over Indian Territory* case. The new Rules have eliminated the express authorization to join a preliminary objection to the merits. Paragraph 6 of Article 79 empowers the Court to request the parties to argue at the preliminary stage all questions, even touching on the merits, which bear on the jurisdictional issue, and to present those specific aspects of the merits which it is indispensable to know in order to decide a preliminary objection of jurisdiction. Thus, in the case referred to above, the Court, if acting under the present Rules, would have had to determine, at the preliminary stage, the date at which the dispute originated, as it did without difficulty, and without prejudging the merits, in its final decision [282].

* Some footnotes omitted. Reprinted by permission of A.W. Sijthoff & Noordhoff International.

**280.** ICAO Council case, ICJ Reports 1972, p. 56.

**281.** ICJ Reports 1957, p. 152.

**282.** Right of Passage over Indian Territory case, ICJ Reports 1960, pp. 33–36.

Besides objections against jurisdiction, other issues may be raised as preliminary objections, such as for instance, those concerning the admissibility of an application. A common aspect of all preliminary objections is that their effect is, if they are upheld, to prevent further proceedings on the merits in the case.

There are objections of admissibility which may be decided with logical independence and complete separation from the merits, such as the link of nationality of the protected person, a ground which was raised both in the *Nottebohm* and *Barcelona Traction* cases. The nonexhaustion of local remedies also operated as a dilatory preliminary objection to admissibility in the *Interhandel* case; in other cases and depending on the circumstances, this particular objection may be so closely intertwined with the merits that it would cease to have an exclusively preliminary character. A decision of the Court to the effect that an objection raised as preliminary "does not possess in the circumstances of the case an exclusively preliminary character" does not dispose completely of the objection, which remains available to be raised by the interested party as a possible defence on the merits; the Court only rejects the submission that such an objection has, in the circumstances of the case, a preliminary character.

This system is based on the realization that it is possible to present as a preliminary objection [of] inadmissibility what in effect constitutes an issue going to the very heart of the merits and thus devoid of a genuine preliminary character.

For instance, in the *Nuclear Tests* cases Judges Gros and Petrén took the position that the question whether there were rules of customary law forbidding atmospheric nuclear tests should have been taken up by the Court as a preliminary question concerning the admissibility of the application. If the Court, in preliminary proceedings, reached the conclusion that the invoked rules of customary law did not exist, then, according to those Judges, the Court should have declared the application inadmissible and without object [283].

This does not in my view constitute a proper application of the preliminary objection procedure. To decide as a preliminary point and *in limine litis* whether there is a rule of customary law supporting the rights invoked by the applicant, would concentrate into the preliminary phase the core of the case, the central issue concerning the merits, namely whether there is a rule of customary law forbidding atmospheric nuclear tests. Such a decision, if taken as preliminary, would have been reached without affording the parties the full opportunities granted by the Statute to plead their cases and furnish evidence in support.

As stated in the joint dissenting opinion in that case, the question whether an objection is to be decided in preliminary proceedings or at the stage of the merits "necessarily depends on whether the objection is genuinely of a preliminary character or whether it is too closely linked to the merits to be susceptible of a just decision without first having pleadings on the merits." [284]

**283.** ICJ Reports 1973, p. 288 and p. 304; and ICJ Reports 1974, pp. 304–305.

**284.** Joint dissenting opinion, ICJ Reports 1974, p. 363.

## NUCLEAR TESTS CASE
## (AUSTRALIA v. FRANCE)

International Court of Justice, 1974.
1974 I.C.J. 253.

* * *

15. It is to be regretted that the French Government has failed to appear in order to put forward its arguments on the issues arising in the present phase of the proceedings, and the Court has thus not had the assistance it might have derived from such arguments or from any evidence adduced in support of them. The Court nevertheless has to proceed and reach a conclusion, and in doing so must have regard not only to the evidence brought before it and the arguments addressed to it by the Applicant, but also to any documentary or other evidence which may be relevant. It must on this basis satisfy itself, first that there exists no bar to the exercise of its judicial function, and secondly, if no such bar exists, that the Application is well founded in fact and in law.

* * *

16. The present case relates to a dispute between the Government of Australia and the French Government concerning the holding of atmospheric tests of nuclear weapons by the latter Government in the South Pacific Ocean. Since in the present phase of the proceedings the Court has to deal only with preliminary matters, it is appropriate to recall that its approach to a phase of this kind must be, as it was expressed in the *Fisheries Jurisdiction* cases, as follows:

> "The issue being thus limited, the Court will avoid not only all expressions of opinion on matters of substance, but also any pronouncement which might prejudge or appear to prejudge any eventual decision on the merits." (I.C.J. Reports 1973, pp. 7 and 54.)

It will however be necessary to give a summary of the principal facts underlying the case.

* * *

18. As the United Nations Scientific Committee on the Effects of Atomic Radiation has recorded in its successive reports to the General Assembly, the testing of nuclear devices in the atmosphere has entailed the release into the atmosphere, and the consequent dissipation in varying degrees throughout the world, of measurable quantities of radio-active matter. It is asserted by Australia that the French atmospheric tests have caused some fall-out of this kind to be deposited on Australian territory; France has maintained in particular that the radio-active matter produced by its tests has been so infinitesimal that it may be regarded as negligible, and that such fall-out on Australian territory does not constitute a danger to the health of the Australian population. These disputed points are clearly matters going to the merits of the case, and the Court must therefore refrain, for the reasons given above, from expressing any view on them.

* * *

51. In announcing that the 1974 series of atmospheric tests would be the last, the French Government conveyed to the world at large, including the Applicant, its intention effectively to terminate these tests. It was bound to assume that other States might take note of these statements and rely on their being effective. The validity of these statements and their legal consequences must be considered within the general framework of the security of international intercourse, and the confidence and trust which are so essential in the relations among States. It is from the actual substance of these statements, and from the circumstances attending their making, that the legal implications of the unilateral act must be deduced. The objects of these statements are clear and they were addressed to the international community as a whole, and the Court holds that they constitute an undertaking possessing legal effect. The Court considers that the President of the Republic, in deciding upon the effective cessation of atmospheric tests, gave an undertaking to the international community to which his words were addressed. It is true that the French Government has consistently maintained, for example in a Note dated 7 February 1973 from the French Ambassador in Canberra to the Prime Minister and Minister for Foreign Affairs of Australia, that it "has the conviction that its nuclear experiments have not violated any rule of international law," nor did France recognize that it was bound by any rule of international law to terminate its tests, but this does not affect the legal consequences of the statements examined above. The Court finds that the unilateral undertaking resulting from these statements cannot be interpreted as having been made in implicit reliance on an arbitrary power or reconsideration. The Court finds further that the French Government has undertaken an obligation the precise nature and limits of which must be understood in accordance with the actual terms in which they have been publicly expressed.

52. Thus the Court faces a situation in which the objective of the Applicant has in effect been accomplished, inasmuch as the Court finds that France has undertaken the obligation to hold no further nuclear tests in the atmosphere in the South Pacific.

53. The Court finds that no question of damages arises in the present case, since no such claim has been raised by the Applicant either prior to or during the proceedings, and the original and ultimate objective of Applicant has been to seek protection "against any further atmospheric test" * * *.

* * *

56. It may be argued that although France may have undertaken such an obligation, by a unilateral declaration, not to carry out atmospheric nuclear tests in the South Pacific Ocean, a judgment of the Court on this subject might still be of value because, if the judgment upheld the Applicant's contentions, it would reinforce the position of the Applicant by affirming the obligation of the Respondent. However, the Court having found that the Respondent has assumed an obligation as to conduct, concerning the effective cessation of nuclear tests, no further judicial action is required. The Applicant has repeatedly sought from the Respondent an assurance that the tests would cease, and the Respondent has, on its own initiative, made a series of statements to the effect that they will cease. Thus the Court concludes that, the dispute having disappeared, the claim

advanced by Australia no longer has any object. It follows that any further finding would have no *raison d'être.*

* * *

62. For these reasons,

THE COURT,

by nine votes to six,

finds that the claim of Australia no longer has any object and that the Court is therefore not called upon to give a decision thereon.

### *Notes*

1. Does it make a difference whether the objective of Australia was to have the tests terminated from the date of its application or the date of the judgment? If the former, would the dispute have an object, e.g., a declaration of illegality as "satisfaction," or a basis for a future claim of damages? Can an issue be regarded as moot when it concerns the continued applicability of a rule of customary international law?

2. The Court considered it unnecessary to decide that it was properly seised of the dispute and had jurisdiction to entertain it since it found that the dispute had disappeared. Its action, in its view, rested on "inherent jurisdiction" to provide for orderly settlement of all matters in dispute. Consider the following comment in a joint dissenting opinion of 5 judges: "If the so-called inherent jurisdiction" is considered by the Court to authorize it to decide that France is now under an obligation to terminate atmospheric nuclear tests in the South Pacific Ocean, why does the "inherent jurisdiction" not also authorize it, on the basis of that same international obligation, to decide that "the French Republic shall not carry out any further such tests". 1974 I.C.J. 325–26.

3. If the Australian objective was to bring about a cessation of tests after the judgment, did the dispute cease when the French statements were made even if those statements did not amount to a legal undertaking? For a closely reasoned analysis of the meaning of "dispute" in this context, see Macdonald and Hough, The Nuclear Tests Case Revisited, 20 Germ.Y.B.I.L. 337 (1977). Other commentaries on the case include: Franck, Word Made Law, 69 A.J.I.L. 612–21 (1975); Lellouche, The Nuclear Tests Cases, 16 Harv.Int'l L.J. 614 (1975); McWhinney, International Law–Making and the Judicial Process: The World Court and the French Nuclear Tests Case, 3 Syracuse J.Int'l L. & Comm. 9 (1975).

## AEGEAN SEA CONTINENTAL SHELF CASE (GREECE v. TURKEY)

International Court of Justice, 1976.

(Request for the Indication of Interim Measures of Protection)

1976 I.C.J. 3.

[In 1974, the Turkish Government began to explore for petroleum in submarine areas of the Aegean Sea claimed by Greece as part of the continental shelf appertaining to certain Greek islands. Following Greek protests and unsuccessful negotiations, Greece referred the matter simultaneously to the International Court and to the Security Council. In its application to the Court, Greece specified as a basis of jurisdiction the General Act of 1928 and a joint communiqué issued in 1975. Greece also requested that the Court indicate interim measures of protection under Article 41 of the Statute pending judgment on the merits. In particular, it requested that both countries be enjoined from conducting further exploration or research in the contested areas. The Court declined to indicate the interim measures of protection requested by Greece. The following excerpts are from its order of September 11, 1976:]

* * *

30. Whereas, according to the information before the Court, the seismic exploration undertaken by Turkey, of which Greece complains, is carried out by a vessel traversing the surface of the high seas and causing small explosions to occur at intervals under water; whereas the purpose of these explosions is to send sound waves through the seabed so as to obtain information regarding the geophysical structure of the earth beneath it; whereas no complaint has been made that this form of seismic exploration involves any risk of physical damage to the seabed or subsoil or to their natural resources; whereas the continued seismic exploration activities undertaken by Turkey are all of the transitory character just described, and do not involve the establishment of installations on or above the seabed of the continental shelf; and whereas no suggestion has been made that Turkey has embarked upon any operations involving the actual appropriation or other use of the natural resources of the areas of the continental shelf which are in dispute;

31. Whereas seismic exploration of the natural resources of the continental shelf without the consent of the coastal State might, no doubt, raise a question of infringement of the latter's exclusive right of exploration; whereas, accordingly, in the event that the Court should uphold Greece's claims on the merits, Turkey's activity in seismic exploration might then be considered as such an infringement and invoked as a possible cause of prejudice to the exclusive rights of Greece in areas then found to appertain to Greece;

* * *

33. Whereas, in the present instance, the alleged breach by Turkey of the exclusivity of the right claimed by Greece to acquire information concerning the natural resources of areas of continental shelf, if it were established, is one that might be capable of reparation by appropriate means; and whereas it follows that the Court is unable to find in that alleged breach of Greece's rights such a risk of irreparable prejudice to rights in issue before the Court as might require the exercise of its power under Article 41 of the Statute to indicate interim measures for their preservation;

* * *

36. Whereas, independently of its request regarding the preservation of its rights, Greece requested the Court during the public sitting to indicate interim measures of protection in order to prevent the aggravation or extension of the dispute; whereas, before this request could be entertained, the Court would have to determine whether, under Article 41 of the Statute, the Court has such an independent power to indicate interim measures

having that object; whereas, however, for the reasons now to be explained, the Court does not find it necessary to examine this point;

* * *

41. Whereas both Greece and Turkey, as Members of the United Nations, have expressly recognized the responsibility of the Security Council for the maintenance of international peace and security; whereas, in the above-mentioned resolution, the Security Council has recalled to them their obligations under the United Nations Charter with respect to the peaceful settlement of disputes, in the terms set out in paragraph 39 above; whereas, furthermore, as the Court has already stated, these obligations are clearly imperative in regard to their present dispute concerning the continental shelf in the Aegean; and whereas it is not to be presumed that either State will fail to heed its obligations under the Charter of the United Nations or fail to heed the recommendations of the Security Council addressed to them with respect to their present dispute;

42. Whereas, accordingly, it is not necessary for the Court to decide the question whether Article 41 of the Statute confers upon it the power to indicate interim measures of protection for the sole purpose of preventing the aggravation or extension of a dispute * * *.

### *Notes*

1. What is the test of irreparable prejudice implicit in the Court's decision? Is it that any injury could be compensated by monetary payment to Greece? Would the acquisition of seismic information enable one party to have advantages in negotiating delimitation or joint venture agreements which would prejudice the other side? In view of this possibility, should Turkey have had the burden of showing that there would be no irreparable injury?

2. The Court did not find it necessary to pronounce on its jurisdiction as to the merits, even on a prima facie basis. However, several judges, in separate opinions, considered that the Court should have first decided the basic question of its own jurisdiction. For example, Judge Mosler stated that Article 41 was not "an independent source of jurisdiction on the same footing and quality as article 36. * * * In view of the provisional character of the requested order, it is sufficient that the Court when it actually indicates interim measures should have reached the provisional conviction based on a summary examination of the material before it * * * that it had jurisdiction on the merits of the case." Id. at 25. Judges Lachs, Morozov, Ruda, and Tarazi also regarded a finding of jurisdiction as essential; Tarazi and Morozov suggested a full finding on jurisdiction. In support of majority, see Jiménez De Aréchaga 159 Rec. des Corrs at 160–63; Elias, The International Court of Justice and the Indication of Provisional Measures of Protection (Amado Memorial Lecture 1978, published by United Nations). For a flexible approach to Article 41, see Mendelson, Measures of Protection in Cases of Contested Jurisdiction, 46 Brit.Y.B.I.L. 259 (1972–73).

3. Interim measures of protection under Article 41 have been "indicated" by the International Court of Justice in four cases: the Anglo–Iranian Oil Case, 1951 I.C.J. 89; the Fisheries Jurisdiction Case (Request for the Indication of Interim Measures of Protection), 1972 I.C.J. 12; Nuclear Tests Cases, 1973 I.C.J. 99, 135; Case Concerning United States Diplomatic and Consular Staff in Tehran, 1979 I.C.J. 23; and Case Concerning Military and Para-military Activities In and Against Nicaragua, 1984 I.C.J. 4. They were refused in the Interhan-

del Case, 1957 I.C.J. 105; the Case of the Trial of Pakistani Prisoners of War, 1973 I.C.J. 328; and the Aegean Sea Continental Shelf Case, p. 820 supra.

4. Can it be maintained that interim measures under Article 41 should be entirely independent of the requirements of consent under Article 36? It has been suggested that when the Court has jurisdiction *ratione personae* under Article 35, it may order interim measures against any state party to the Statute. However, no judge has accepted this view, which runs counter to the premise of consent to the Court's jurisdiction under Article 36.

## CASE CONCERNING UNITED STATES DIPLOMATIC AND CONSULAR STAFF IN TEHRAN

## (UNITED STATES OF AMERICA v. IRAN)

Order of Provisional Measures, 15 December 1979.
1979 I.C.J. 7.

### Request for the Indication of Provisional Measures

Having regard to the Application by the United States of America filed in the Registry of the Court on 29 November 1979, instituting proceedings against the Islamic Republic of Iran in respect of a dispute concerning the situation in the United States Embassy in Tehran and the seizure and holding as hostages of members of the United States diplomatic and consular staff in Iran;

* * *

1. Whereas in the above-mentioned Application the United States Government invokes jurisdictional provisions in certain treaties as bases for the Court's jurisdiction in the present case; whereas it further recounts a sequence of events, beginning on 4 November 1979 in and around the United States Embassy in Tehran and involving the invasion of the Embassy premises, the seizure of United States diplomatic and consular staff and their continued detention; and whereas, on the basis of the facts there alleged, it requests the Court to adjudge and declare:

> (a) That the Government of Iran, in tolerating, encouraging, and failing to prevent and punish the conduct described in the preceding Statement of Facts [*in the Application* ], violated its international legal obligations to the United States as provided by
>
> — Articles 22, 24, 25, 27, 29, 31, 37 and 47 of the Vienna Convention on Diplomatic Relations,
>
> — Articles 28, 31, 33, 34, 36 and 40 of the Vienna Convention on Consular Relations,
>
> — Articles 4 and 7 of the Convention on the Prevention and Punishment of Crimes against Internationally Protected Persons, including Diplomatic Agents, and
>
> — Articles II(4), XIII, XVIII and XIX of the Treaty of Amity, Economic Relations, and Consular Rights between the United States and Iran, and
>
> — Articles 2(3), 2(4) and 33 of the Charter of the United Nations;

(b) That pursuant to the foregoing international legal obligations, the Government of Iran is under a particular obligation immediately to secure the release of all United States nationals currently being detained within the premises of the United States Embassy in Tehran and to assure that all such persons and all other United States nationals in Tehran are allowed to leave Iran safely;

(c) That the Government of Iran shall pay to the United States, in its own right and in the exercise of its right of diplomatic protection of its nationals, reparation for the foregoing violations of Iran's international legal obligations to the United States, in a sum to be determined by the Court; and

(d) That the Government of Iran submit to its competent authorities for the purpose of prosecution those persons responsible for the crimes committed against the premises and staff of the United States Embassy and against the premises of its Consulates;

2. Having regard to the request dated 29 November 1979 and filed in the Registry the same day, whereby the Government of the United States of America, relying on Article 41 of the Statute and Articles 73, 74 and 75 of the Rules of Court, asks the Court urgently to indicate, pending the final decision in the case brought before it by the above-mentioned Application of the same date, the following provisional measures:

(a) That the Government of Iran immediately release all hostages of United States nationality and facilitate the prompt and safe departure from Iran of these persons and all other United States officials in dignified and humane circumstances.

(b) That the Government of Iran immediately clear the premises of the United States Embassy, Chancery and Consulate of all persons whose presence is not authorized by the United States Chargé d'Affaires in Iran, and restore the premises to United States control.

(c) That the Government of Iran ensure that all persons attached to the United States Embassy and Consulate should be accorded, and protected in, full freedom within the Embassy and Chancery premises, and the freedom of movement within Iran necessary to carry out their diplomatic and consular functions.

(d) That the Government of Iran not place on trial any person attached to the Embassy and Consulate of the United States and refrain from any action to implement any such trial.

(e) That the Government of Iran ensure that no action is taken which might prejudice the rights of the United States in respect of the carrying out of any decision which the Court may render on the merits, and in particular neither take nor permit action that would threaten the lives, safety, or well-being of the hostages;

* * *

8. Whereas on 9 December 1979 a letter, dated the same day and transmitted by telegram, was received from the Minister for Foreign Affairs of Iran, which reads as follows:

* * *

I have the honour to acknowledge receipt of the telegrams concerning the meeting of the International Court of Justice on 10 December 1979, at the request of the Government of the United States of America, and to submit to you below the position of the Government of the Islamic Republic of Iran in this respect.

1. First of all, the Government of the Islamic Republic of Iran wishes to express its respect for the International Court of Justice, and for its distinguished members, for what they have achieved in the quest for just and equitable solutions to legal conflicts between States. However, the Government of the Islamic Republic of Iran considers that the Court cannot and should not take cognizance of the case which the Government of the United States of America has submitted to it, and in a most significant fashion, a case confined to what is called the question of the "hostages of the American Embassy in Tehran".

2. For this question only represents a marginal and secondary aspect of an overall problem, one such that it cannot be studied separately, and which involves, *inter alia,* more than 25 years of continual interference by the United States in the internal affairs of Iran, the shameless exploitation of our country, and numerous crimes perpetrated against the Iranian people, contrary to and in conflict with all international and humanitarian norms.

3. The problem involved in the conflict between Iran and the United States is thus not one of the interpretation and the application of the treaties upon which the American Application is based, but results from an overall situation containing much more fundamental and more complex elements. Consequently, the Court cannot examine the American Application divorced from its proper context, namely the whole political dossier of the relations between Iran and the United States over the last 25 years. This dossier includes, *inter alia,* all the crimes perpetrated in Iran by the American Government, in particular the *coup d'état* of 1953 stirred up and carried out by the CIA, the overthrow of the lawful national government of Dr. Mossadegh, the restoration of the Shah and of his régime which was under the control of American interests, and all the social, economic, cultural, and political consequences of the direct interventions in our internal affairs, as well as grave, flagrant and continuous violations of all international norms, committed by the United States in Iran.

4. With regard to the request for provisional measures, as formulated by the United States, it in fact implies that the Court should have passed judgment on the actual substance of the case submitted to it, which the Court cannot do without breach of the norms governing its jurisdiction. Furthermore, since provisional measures are by definition intended to protect the interests of the parties, they cannot be unilateral, as they are in the request submitted by the American Government.

In conclusion, the Government of the Islamic Republic of Iran respectfully draws the attention of the Court to the deep-rootedness and the essential character of the Islamic revolution of Iran, a revolution of a whole oppressed nation against its oppressors and their masters; any examination of the numerous repercussions thereof is a matter essentially and directly within the national sovereignty of Iran.

* * *

13. Noting that the Government of Iran was not represented at the hearing; and whereas the non-appearance of one of the States concerned cannot by itself constitute an obstacle to the indication of provisional measures;

14. Whereas the treaty provisions on which, in its Application and oral observations, the United States Government claims to found the jurisdiction of the Court to entertain the present case are the following:

(i) the Vienna Convention on Diplomatic Relations of 1961, and Article 1 of its accompanying Optional Protocol concerning the Compulsory Settlement of Disputes;

(ii) the Vienna Convention on Consular Relations of 1963, and Article 1 of its accompanying Optional Protocol concerning the Compulsory Settlement of Disputes;

(iii) Article XXI, paragraph 2, of the Treaty of Amity, Economic Relations, and Consular Rights of 1955 between the United States of America and Iran; and

(iv) Article 13, paragraph 1, of the Convention of 1973 on the Prevention and Punishment of Crimes against Internationally Protected Persons, including Diplomatic Agents;

* * *

18. Whereas, accordingly, it is manifest from the information before the Court and from the terms of Article I of each of the two Protocols that the provisions of these Articles furnish a basis on which the jurisdiction of the Court might be founded with regard to the claims of the United States under the Vienna Conventions of 1961 and 1963;

19. Whereas, so far as concerns the rights claimed by the United States with regard to two of its nationals who, according to the declaration by Mr. David D. Newsom referred to in paragraph 7 above, are not personnel either of its diplomatic or of its consular mission, it appears from the statements of the United States Government that these two private individuals were seized and are detained as hostages within the premises of the United States Embassy or Consulate in Tehran; whereas it follows that the seizure and detention of these individuals also fall within the scope of the applicable provisions of the Vienna Conventions of 1961 and 1963 relating to the inviolability of the premises of Embassies and Consulates; whereas, furthermore, the seizure and detention of these individuals in the circumstances alleged by the United States clearly fall also within the scope of the provisions of Article 5 of the Vienna Convention of 1963 expressly providing that consular functions include the functions of protecting, assisting and safeguarding the interests of nationals; and whereas the purpose of these functions is precisely to enable the sending State, through its consulates, to ensure that its nationals are accorded the treatment due to them under the general rules of international law as aliens within the territory of the foreign State;

20. Whereas, accordingly, it is likewise manifest that Article I of the Protocols concerning the compulsory settlement of disputes which accompany the Vienna Conventions of 1961 and 1963 furnishes a basis on which the jurisdiction of the Court might be founded with regard to the claims of the United States in respect of the two private individuals in question;

21. Whereas, therefore, the Court does not find it necessary for present purposes to enter into the question whether a basis for the exercise of its powers under Article 41 of the Statute might also be found under Article XXI, paragraph 2, of the Treaty of Amity, Economic Relations, and Consular Rights of 1955, and Article 13, paragraph 1, of the Convention on the Prevention and Punishment of Crimes against Internationally Protected Persons, including Diplomatic Agents, of 1973;

22. Whereas, on the other hand, in the above-mentioned letter of 9 December 1979 the Government of Iran maintains that the Court cannot and should not take cognizance of the present case, for the reason that the question of the hostages forms only "a marginal and secondary aspect of an overall problem" involving the activities of the United States in Iran over a period of more than 25 years; and whereas it further maintains that any examination of the numerous repercussions of the Islamic revolution of Iran is essentially and directly a matter within the national sovereignty of Iran;

23. Whereas, however important, and however connected with the present case, the iniquities attributed to the United States Government by the Government of Iran in that letter may appear to be to the latter Government, the seizure of the United States Embassy and Consulates and the detention of internationally protected persons as hostages cannot, in the view of the Court, be regarded as something "secondary" or "marginal," having regard to the importance of the legal principles involved; whereas the Court notes in this regard that the Secretary–General of the United Nations has indeed referred to these occurrences as "a grave situation" posing "a serious threat to international peace and security" and that the Security Council in resolution 457 (1979) expressed itself as deeply concerned at the dangerous level of tension between the two States, which could have grave consequences for international peace and security;

24. Whereas, moreover, if the Iranian Government considers the alleged activities of the United States in Iran legally to have a close connection with the subject-matter of the United States Application, it remains open to that Government under the Court's Statute and Rules to present its own arguments to the Court regarding those activities either by way of defence in a Counter–Memorial or by way of a counter-claim filed under Article 80 of the Rules of Court; whereas, therefore, by not appearing in the present proceedings, the Government of Iran, by its own choice, deprives itself of the opportunity of developing its own arguments before the Court and of itself filing a request for the indication of provisional measures; and whereas no provision of the Statute or Rules contemplates that the Court should decline to take cognizance of one aspect of a dispute merely because that dispute has other aspects, however important;

25. Whereas it is no doubt true that the Islamic revolution of Iran is a matter "essentially and directly within the national sovereignty of Iran;" whereas however a dispute which concerns diplomatic and consular premises

and the detention of internationally protected persons, and involves the interpretation or application of multilateral conventions codifying the international law governing diplomatic and consular relations, is one which by its very nature falls within international jurisdiction.

26. Whereas accordingly the two considerations advanced by the Government of Iran in its letter of 9 December 1979 cannot, in the view of the Court, be accepted as constituting any obstacle to the Court's taking cognizance of the case brought before it by the United States Application of 29 November 1979.

27. Whereas in that same letter of 9 December 1979 the Government of Iran also puts forward two considerations on the basis of which it contends that the Court ought not, in any event, to accede to the United States request for provisional measures in the present case;

28. Whereas, in the first place, it maintains that the request for provisional measures, as formulated by the United States, "in fact implies that the Court should have passed judgment on the actual substance of the case submitted to it"; whereas it is true that in the *Factory at Chorzów* case the Permanent Court of International Justice declined to indicate interim measures of protection on the ground that the request in that case was "designed to obtain an interim judgment in favour of a part of the claim" (*Order of 21 November 1927, P.C.I.J., Series A, No. 12,* at p. 10); whereas, however, the circumstances of that case were entirely different from those of the present one, and the request there sought to obtain from the Court a final judgment on part of a claim for a sum of money; whereas, moreover, a request for provisional measures must by its very nature relate to the substance of the case since, as Article 41 expressly states, their object is to preserve the respective rights of either party; and whereas in the present case the purpose of the United States request appears to be not to obtain a judgment, interim or final, on the merits of its claims but to preserve the substance of the rights which it claims *pendente lite;*

* * *

33. Whereas by the terms of Article 41 of the Statute the Court may indicate such measures only when it considers that circumstances so require in order to preserve the rights of either party;

34. Whereas the circumstances alleged by the United States Government which, in the submission of that Government, require the indication of provisional measures in the present case may be summarized as follows:

(i) On 4 November 1979, in the course of a demonstration outside the United States Embassy compound in Tehran, demonstrators attacked the Embassy premises; no Iranian security forces intervened or were sent to relieve the situation, despite repeated calls for help from the Embassy to the Iranian authorities. Ultimately the whole of the Embassy premises was invaded. The Embassy personnel, including consular and non-American staff, and visitors who were present in the Embassy at the time were seized. Shortly afterwards, according to the United States Government, its consulates in Tabriz and Shiraz, which had been attacked earlier in 1979, were also seized, without any action being taken to prevent it;

(ii) Since that time, the premises of the United States Embassy in Tehran, and of the consulates in Tabriz and Shiraz, have remained in the hands of the persons who seized them. These persons have ransacked the archives and documents both of the diplomatic mission and of its consular section. The Embassy personnel and other persons seized at the time of the attack have been held hostage with the exception of 13 persons released on 18 and 20 November 1979. Those holding the hostages have refused to release them, save on condition of the fulfilment by the United States of various demands regarded by it as unacceptable. The hostages are stated to have frequently been bound, blindfolded, and subjected to severe discomfort, complete isolation and threats that they would be put on trial or even put to death. The United States Government affirms that it has reason to believe that some of them may have been transferred to other places of confinement;

(iii) The Government of the United States considers that not merely has the Iranian Government failed to prevent the events described above, but also that there is clear evidence of its complicity in, and approval of, those events;

(iv) The persons held hostage in the premises of the United States Embassy in Tehran include, according to the information furnished to the Court by the Agent of the United States, at least 28 persons having the status, duly recognized by the Government of Iran, of "member of the diplomatic staff" within the meaning of the Vienna Convention on Diplomatic Relations of 1961; at least 20 persons having the status, similarly recognized, of "members of the administrative and technical staff" within the meaning of that Convention; and two other persons of United States nationality not possessing either diplomatic or consular status. Of the persons with the status of member of the diplomatic staff, four are members of the Consular Section of the Embassy;

(v) In addition to the persons held hostage in the premises of the Tehran Embassy, the United States Chargé d'Affaires in Iran and two other United States diplomatic agents are detained in the premises of the Iranian Ministry for Foreign Affairs, in circumstances which the Government of the United States has not been able to make entirely clear, but which apparently involve restriction of their freedom of movement, and a threat to their inviolability as diplomats;

* * *

38. Whereas there is no more fundamental prerequisite for the conduct of relations between States than the inviolability of diplomatic envoys and embassies, so that throughout history nations of all creeds and cultures have observed reciprocal obligations for that purpose; and whereas the obligations thus assumed, notably those for assuring the personal safety of diplomats and their freedom from prosecution, are essential, unqualified, and inherent in their representative character and their diplomatic function;

39. Whereas the institution of diplomacy, with its concomitant privileges and immunities, has withstood the test of centuries and proved to be an instrument essential for effective co-operation in the international community, and for enabling States, irrespective of their differing constitutional and

social systems, to achieve mutual understanding and to resolve their differences by peaceful means;

40. Whereas the unimpeded conduct of consular relations, which have also been established between peoples since ancient times, is no less important in the context of present-day international law, in promoting the development of friendly relations among nations, and ensuring protection and assistance for aliens resident in the territories of other States; and whereas therefore the privileges and immunities of consular officers and consular employees, and the inviolability of consular premises and archives, are similarly principles deep-rooted in international law;

41. Whereas, while no State is under any obligation to maintain diplomatic or consular relations with another, yet it cannot fail to recognize the imperative obligations inherent therein, now codified in the Vienna Conventions of 1961 and 1963, to which both Iran and the United States are parties;

42. Whereas continuance of the situation the subject of the present request exposes the human beings concerned to privation, hardship, anguish and even danger to life and health and thus to a serious possibility of irreparable harm;

43. Whereas in connection with the present request the Court cannot fail to take note of the provisions of the Convention on the Prevention and Punishment of Crimes against Internationally Protected Persons, including Diplomatic Agents, of 1973, to which both Iran and the United States are parties;

* * *

47. Accordingly,

THE COURT,

unanimously,

1. *Indicates,* pending its final decision in the proceedings instituted on 29 November 1979 by the United States of America against the Islamic Republic of Iran, the following provisional measures:

A. (i) The Government of the Islamic Republic of Iran should immediately ensure that the premises of the United States Embassy, Chancery and Consulates be restored to the possession of the United States authorities under their exclusive control, and should ensure their inviolability and effective protection as provided for by the treaties in force between the two States, and by general international law;

(ii) The Government of the Islamic Republic of Iran should ensure the immediate release, without any exception, of all persons of United States nationality who are or have been held in the Embassy of the United States of America or in the Ministry of Foreign Affairs in Tehran, or have been held as hostages elsewhere, and afford full protection to all such persons, in accordance with the treaties in force between the two States, and with general international law;

(iii) The Government of the Islamic Republic of Iran should, as from that moment, afford to all the diplomatic and consular personnel of the United States the protection, privileges and immunities to which they are entitled under the treaties in force between the two States, and under general international law, including immunity from any form of criminal jurisdiction and freedom and facilities to leave the territory of Iran;

B. The Government of the United States of America and the Government of the Islamic Republic of Iran should not take any action and should ensure that no action is taken which may aggravate the tension between the two countries or render the existing dispute more difficult of solution;

2. *Decides* that, until the Court delivers its final judgment in the present case, it will keep the matters covered by this Order continuously under review.

## CASE CONCERNING UNITED STATES DIPLOMATIC AND CONSULAR STAFF IN TEHRAN (UNITED STATES OF AMERICA v. IRAN)

Judgment of May 24, 1980.
1980 I.C.J. 3.

[The following summary is taken from the Yearbook of the International Court of Justice 1980 (at 119–25) with some excerpts from the Judgment:]

* * *

Iran took no part in the proceedings. It neither filed pleadings nor was represented at the hearing, and no submissions were therefore presented on its behalf. Its position was however defined in two letters addressed to the Court by its Minister for Foreign Affairs on 9 December 1979 and 16 March 1980 respectively. In these the Minister maintained *inter alia* that the Court could not and should not take cognizance of the case.

### The Facts (paras. 11–32)

The Court expresses regret that Iran did not appear before it to put forward its arguments. The absence of Iran from the proceedings brought into operation Article 53 of the Statute, under which the Court is required, before finding in the Applicant's favour, to satisfy itself that the allegations of fact on which the claim is based are well founded.

In that respect the Court observes that it has had available to it, in the documents presented by the United States, a massive body of information from various sources, including numerous official statements of both Iranian and United States authorities. This information, the Court notes, is wholly concordant as to the main facts and has all been communicated to Iran without evoking any denial. The Court is accordingly satisfied that the allegations of fact on which the United States based its claim were well founded.

ADMISSIBILITY (PARAS. 33–44)

Under the settled jurisprudence of the Court, it is bound, in applying Article 53 of its Statute, to investigate, on its own initiative, any preliminary question of admissibility or jurisdiction that may arise.

On the subject of admissibility, the Court, after examining the considerations put forward in the two letters from Iran, finds that they do not disclose any ground for concluding that it could not or should not deal with the case. Neither does it find any incompatibility with the continuance of judicial proceedings before the Court in the establishment by the Secretary–General of the United Nations, with the agreement of both States, of a Commission given a mandate to undertake a fact-finding mission to Iran, hear Iran's grievances and facilitate the solution of the crisis between the two countries.

[The Court referred to the contention of Iran that the issues raised by the United States cannot be examined separately from the "overall problem" involving "more than 25 years of continual interference by the United States in the internal affairs of Iran". In response the Court commented that:]

* * * legal disputes between sovereign States by their very nature are likely to occur in political contexts, and often form only one element in a wider and long-standing political dispute between the States concerned. Yet never has the view been put forward before that, because a legal dispute submitted to the Court is only one aspect of a political dispute, the Court should decline to resolve for the parties the legal questions at issue between them. Nor can any basis for such a view of the Court's functions or jurisdiction be found in the Charter or the Statute of the Court: if the Court were, contrary to its settled jurisprudence, to adopt such a view, it would impose a far-reaching and unwarranted restriction upon the role of the Court in the peaceful solution of international disputes.

JURISDICTION (PARAS. 45–55)

Four instruments having been cited by the United States as bases for the Court's jurisdiction to deal with its claims, the Court finds that three, namely the Optional Protocols to the two Vienna Conventions of 1961 and 1963 on, respectively, Diplomatic and Consular Relations, and the 1955 Treaty of Amity, Economic Relations, and Consular Rights between the United States and Iran, do in fact provide such foundations.

[The Court noted that the Protocols provided for arbitration or conciliation before resort to the Court. However, it found that neither party had proposed arbitration or conciliation; consequently, they had no application. In any case "they are not to be understood as laying down a precondition of the applicability of the precise and categorical provision contained in Article 1 establishing the compulsory jurisdiction of the Court * * * " (para. 48). With regard to the 1955 Treaty of Amity, the Court referred to the dispute settlement clause which provides that any dispute "not satisfactorily adjusted by diplomacy shall be submitted to the International Court * * * " (Article XXI, para. 2). The Court observed that "the refusal of the Iranian government to enter into any discussion of the matter" meant "beyond any doubt" that there existed a "dispute not satisfactorily adjusted by diplomacy" (para. 51). The Court also observed in regard to the article in the 1955 treaty:]

While that Article does not provide in express terms that either party may bring a case to the Court by unilateral application, it is evident, as the United States contended in its Memorial, that this is what the parties intended. Provisions drawn in similar terms are very common in bilateral treaties of amity or of establishment, and the intention of the parties in accepting such clauses is clearly to provide for such a right of unilateral recourse to the Court, in the absence of agreement to employ some other pacific means of settlement.

The Court, however, does not find it necessary in the present Judgment to enter into the question whether Article 13 of the fourth instrument so cited, namely the 1973 Convention on the Prevention and Punishment of Crimes against Internationally Protected Persons including Diplomatic Agents, provides a basis for the exercise of its jurisdiction with respect to the United States' claims thereunder.

MERITS, ATTRIBUTABILITY TO THE IRANIAN STATE OF THE ACTS COMPLAINED OF, AND VIOLATION BY IRAN OF CERTAIN OBLIGATIONS (PARAS. 56–94)

The Court has also, under Article 53 of its Statute, to satisfy itself that the claims of the Applicant are well founded in law. To this end, it considers the acts complained of in order to determine how far, legally, they may be attributed to the Iranian State (as distinct from the occupiers of the Embassy) and whether they are compatible or incompatible with Iran's obligations under treaties in force or other applicable rules of international law, while the Ayatollah declared that the detention of the hostages would continue until the new Iranian parliament had taken a decision as to their fate.

The Iranian authorities' decision to continue the subjection of the Embassy to occupation, and of its staff to detention as hostages, gave rise to repeated and multiple breaches of Iran's treaty obligations, additional to those already committed at the time of the seizure of the Embassy (1961 Convention: Arts. 22, 24, 25, 26, 27 and 29; 1963 Convention: *inter alia,* Art. 33; 1955 Treaty, Art. II(4)).

With regard to the Chargé d'Affaires and the two other members of the United States mission who have been in the Iranian Ministry of Foreign Affairs since 4 November 1979, the Court finds that the Iranian authorities have withheld from them the protection and facilities necessary to allow them to leave the Ministry in safety. Accordingly, it appears to the Court that in their respect there have been breaches of Articles 26 and 29 of the 1961 Vienna Convention.

Taking note, furthermore, that various Iranian authorities have threatened to have some of the hostages submitted to trial before a court, or to compel them to bear witness, the Court considers that, if put into effect, that intention would constitute a breach of Article 31 of the same Convention.

(c) *Possible existence of special circumstances* (paras. 80–89)

The Court considers that it should examine the question whether the conduct of the Iranian Government might be justified by the existence of special circumstances, for the Iranian Minister for Foreign Affairs had alleged in his two letters to the Court that the United States had carried out criminal activities in Iran. The Court considers that, even if these alleged activities could be considered as proven, they would not constitute a defence to the United States' claims, since diplomatic law provides the possibility of breaking off diplomatic relations, or of declaring *persona non grata* members of diplomatic or consular missions who may be carrying on illicit activities. The Court concludes that the Government of Iran had recourse to coercion against the United States Embassy and its staff instead of making use of the normal means at its disposal.

(d) *International responsibility* (paras. 90–92)

The Court finds that Iran, by committing successive and continuing breaches of the obligations laid upon it by the Vienna Conventions of 1961 and 1963, the 1955 Treaty, and the applicable rules of general international law, has incurred responsibility towards the United States. As a consequence, there is an obligation on the part of the Iranian State to make reparation for the injury caused to the United States. Since, however, the breaches are still continuing, the form and amount of such reparation cannot yet be determined.

At the same time the Court considers it essential to reiterate the observations it made in its Order of 15 December 1979 on the importance of the principles of international law governing diplomatic and consular relations. After stressing the particular gravity of the case, arising out of the fact that it is not any private individuals or groups that have set at naught the inviolability of an embassy, but the very government of the State to which the mission is accredited, the Court draws the attention of the entire international community to the irreparable harm that may be caused by events of the kind before the Court. Such events cannot fail to undermine a carefully constructed edifice of law, the maintenance of which is vital for the security and well-being of the international community.

(e) *United States operation in Iran on 24–25 April 1980* (paras. 93 and 94)

With regard to the operation undertaken in Iran by United States military units on 24–25 April 1980, the Court says that it cannot fail to express its concern. It feels bound to observe that an operation undertaken in those circumstances, from whatever motive, is of a kind calculated to undermine respect for the judicial process in international relations. Nevertheless, the question of the legality of that operation can have no bearing on the evaluation of Iran's conduct on 4 November 1979. The findings reached by the Court are therefore not affected by that operation.

* * *

For these reasons, the Court gave the following decision:

"THE COURT,

1. By thirteen votes to two,

*Decides* that the Islamic Republic of Iran, by the conduct which the Court has set out in this Judgment, has violated in several respects, and is still violating, obligations owed by it to the United States of America under international conventions in force between the two countries, as well as under long-established rules of general international law;

2. By thirteen votes to two,

*Decides* that the violations of these obligations engage the responsibility of the Islamic Republic of Iran towards the United States of America under international law;

3. Unanimously,

*Decides* that the Government of the Islamic Republic of Iran must immediately take all steps to redress the situation resulting from the events of 4 November 1979 and what followed from these events, and to that end:

*(a)* must immediately terminate the unlawful detention of the United States Chargé d'affaires and other diplomatic and consular staff and other United States nationals now held hostage in Iran, and must immediately release each and every one and entrust them to the protecting Power (Article 45 of the 1961 Vienna Convention on Diplomatic Relations);

*(b)* must ensure that all the said persons have the necessary means of leaving Iranian territory, including means of transport;

*(c)* must immediately place in the hands of the protecting Power the premises, property, archives and documents of the United States Embassy in Tehran and of its Consulates in Iran;

4. Unanimously,

*Decides* that no member of the United States diplomatic or consular staff may be kept in Iran to be subjected to any form of judicial proceedings or to participate in them as a witness;

5. By twelve votes to three,

*Decides* that the Government of the Islamic Republic of Iran is under an obligation to make reparation to the Government of the United States of America for the injury caused to the latter by the events of 4 November 1979 and what followed from these events;

6. By fourteen votes to one,

*Decides* that the form and amount of such reparation, failing agreement between the Parties, shall be settled by the Court, and reserves for this purpose the subsequent procedure in the case.

Judge Lachs appended a separate opinion, and Judges Morozov and Tarazi dissenting opinions to the Judgment.

## *Notes*

1. Was the Court justified in criticizing the attempt of the United States to rescue the hostages during the pendency of the case? Are measures of self-help, if otherwise legal, precluded when judicial proceedings are under way? One commentator suggests they are not permissible "for they are designed to bring about the termination of the conflict without regard to the impartial determinations the parties agreed to seek when they assented to the tribunal's jurisdiction." Stein, Contempt, Crisis and the Court, 76 A.J.I.L. 499, 512 (1982).

The Court pointed out that the United States had requested the Court to expedite the case. Did that imply an undertaking to let the proceedings run their course?

2. The Court's reprimand to the United States also referred to the Order of Provisional Measures, stating that no action was to be taken "which might aggravate the tension between the two countries." 1980 I.C.J. 43. Should Iran's failure to comply with the Court's order of provisional measures have relieved the United States of its duty to do so? Apparently the Court did not regard reciprocity as a condition of compliance. Assuming a state disobeys an order of provisional measures, may the Court impose penalties on that state? Should the Court have applied the equitable notion of "clean hands" to deny relief to a moving party (as the United States was)? Was it pertinent that Iran's non-compliance and continued violation of basic international law was relatively much more serious? See Schachter, International Law in the Hostages Crisis, in American Hostages in Iran 325, 344–45 (Christopher et al. eds., 1985).

3. Note that the Court did not pass upon the legality of the rescue mission under international law. The majority avoided taking issue with the U.S. position that the rescue was a justifiable self-help action because the individuals were in imminent danger of execution as evidenced by Iranian threats. Two dissenting judges, Tarazi (Syria) and Morozov (U.S.S.R.) considered that the United States was not entitled to reparations because of the rescue mission and the economic counter-measures taken against Iran. In their view these measures violated international law and the Court's provisional measures order. 1980 I.C.J. 65.

4. Iran released the hostages in January 1981, seven months after the Court's judgment. Under the Declarations of Algeria by which Iran and the United States expressed their commitments for release of the hostages, withdrawal of sanctions and settlement of claims, the United States agreed to withdraw all claims pending against Iran before the International Court of Justice. Para. 11 of Declaration of Algeria, 20 I.L.M. 223 (1981).

5. Iran's refusal to appear before the Court followed four earlier instances of non-appearance by respondent states: Iceland in 1972 (*Fisheries Cases*), India in 1973 (*Case Concerning Prisoners of War*), France in 1974 (*Nuclear Tests Cases*), Turkey in 1976 (*Aegean Sea Continental Shelf Case*). All five cases involved objections to jurisdiction at preliminary stages in connection with requests for provisional measures. The non-appearing states brought their objections to the notice of the Court (as did Iran in the hostages case) by letters and other communications that did not constitute official memorials or other documents called for by the Court's rules. The Statute of the Court does not provide for default. Article 53 of the Statute requires the Court to satisfy itself that it has jurisdiction and, if so, that the claim of the applicant is well founded in fact and law. What advantages does a state get by non-appearance? What action may the Court take against a state that boycotts the proceedings? See Fitzmaurice, The Problem of the Non–Appearing Defendant Government, 51 Brit.Y.B.I.L. 94–96 (1980); Thirlway, Non-appearance Before the International Court of Justice (1985).

6. The United States appeared in the case brought against it by Nicaragua in order to contest jurisdiction and admissibility, but withdrew after the Court found it had jurisdiction. This was the first case of non-appearance after a finding of jurisdiction by the Court. The reasons for United States withdrawal

are summarized in a State Department statement of January 18, 1985, 24 I.L.M. 246 (1985).

## CASE CONCERNING MILITARY AND PARAMILITARY ACTIVITIES IN AND AGAINST NICARAGUA

## (NICARAGUA v. UNITED STATES)

International Court of Justice, 1984.
1984 I.C.J. 169 (Provisional Measures).
1984 I.C.J. 392 (Jurisdiction).

[The following summary of the Court's decisions is taken from the Yearbook of the International Court of Justice 1984–85, pp. 135–47:]

On 9 April 1984 the Government of Nicaragua filed an Application instituting proceedings against the United States of America, accompanied by a request for the indication of provisional measures, in respect of a dispute concerning responsibility for military and paramilitary activities in and against Nicaragua. As basis for the jurisdiction of the Court it invoked [the] declaration[s] accepting the Court's jurisdiction deposited by the two States under Article 36 of the Statute of the Court.

On 13 April 1984, by a letter from its Ambassador to the Netherlands, the Government of the United States of America informed the Court that it had appointed an Agent for the purposes of the case while indicating its conviction that the Court was without jurisdiction to deal with the Application and was *a fortiori* without jurisdiction to indicate the provisional measures requested by Nicaragua.

Having heard the oral observations of both Parties on the request for provisional measures at public sittings on 25 and 27 April 1984, the Court held on 10 May 1984 a public sitting at which it delivered an Order (I.C.J. Reports 1984, p. 169) indicating such measures. The operative provisions of this Order are as follows:

"THE COURT,

A. Unanimously,

*Rejects* the request made by the United States of America that the proceedings on the Application filed by the Republic of Nicaragua on 9 April 1984, and on the request filed the same day by the Republic of Nicaragua for the indication of provisional measures, be terminated by the removal of the case from the list;

B. *Indicates,* pending its final decision in the proceedings instituted on 9 April 1984 by the Republic of Nicaragua against the United States of America, the following provisional measures:

1. Unanimously,

The United States of America should immediately cease and refrain from any action restricting, blocking or endangering access to or from Nicaraguan ports, and, in particular, the laying of mines;

2. By fourteen votes to one,

The right to sovereignty and to political independence possessed by the Republic of Nicaragua, like any other State of the region or of the world, should be fully respected and should not in any way be jeopardized by any military and paramilitary activities which are prohibited by the principles of international law, in particular the principle that States should refrain in their international relations from the threat or use of force against the territorial integrity or the political independence of any State, and the principle concerning the duty not to intervene in matters within the domestic jurisdiction of a State, principles embodied in the United Nations Charter and the Charter of the Organization of American States.

IN FAVOUR: *President* Elias; *Vice–President* Sette–Camara; *Judges* Lachs, Morozov, Nagendra Singh, Ruda, Mosler, Oda, Ago, El–Khani, Sir Robert Jennings, de Lacharrière, Mbaye, Bedjaoui.

AGAINST: *Judge* Schwebel.

3. Unanimously,

The Governments of the United States of America and the Republic of Nicaragua should each of them ensure that no action of any kind is taken which might aggravate or extend the dispute submitted to the Court;

4. Unanimously,

The Governments of the United States of America and the Republic of Nicaragua should each of them ensure that no action is taken which might prejudice the rights of the other Party in respect of the carrying out of whatever decision the Court may render in the case;

C. Unanimously,

*Decides* further that, until the Court delivers its final judgment in the present case, it will keep the matters covered by this Order continuously under review;

D. Unanimously,

*Decides* that the written proceedings shall first be addressed to the questions of the jurisdiction of the Court to entertain the dispute and of the admissibility of the Application;

And reserves the fixing of the time-limits for the said written proceedings, and the subsequent procedure, for further decision."

*

Judges Mosler and Sir Robert Jennings appended a joint separate opinion to the Order of the Court (I.C.J. Reports 1984, p. 189) and Judge Schwebel appended a dissenting opinion (ibid., pp. 190–207).

*

In accordance with Article 41, paragraph 2, of the Statute of the Court, the Registrar immediately notified the Parties and the Security Council of the indication of these measures.

*

By an Order of 14 May 1984 the President of the Court fixed the following time-limits for the filing of pleadings addressed to the questions of jurisdiction and admissibility: 30 June 1984 for the Memorial of Nicaragua, and 17 August 1984 for the Counter–Memorial of the United States (I.C.J. Reports 1984, p. 209). These pleadings were filed within the prescribed time-limits.

On 15 August 1984, before the expiration of the time-limits allowed for the filing of pleadings relating to jurisdiction and admissibility, the Republic of El Salvador filed a Declaration of Intervention in the case under the terms of Article 63 of the Statute. In its Declaration, the Government of El Salvador stated that the purpose of its intervention was to enable it to maintain that the Court had no jurisdiction to entertain Nicaragua's application. In this connection, it referred to certain multilateral treaties on which Nicaragua relies in its dispute with the United States.

Having regard to the written observations on that Declaration submitted by the Parties in accordance with Article 83 of the Rules of Court, on 4 October 1984 the Court made an Order of which the operative provisions are as follows:

"THE COURT,

(i) By nine votes to six,

*Decides* not to hold a hearing on the Declaration of Intervention of the Republic of El Salvador.

IN FAVOUR: *President* Elias; *Vice–President* Sette–Camara; *Judges* Lachs, Morozov, Nagendra Singh, Oda, El–Khani, Mbaye, Bedjaoui.

AGAINST: *Judges* Ruda, Mosler, Ago, Schwebel, Sir Robert Jennings, de Lacharrière.

(ii) By fourteen votes to one,

*Decides* that the Declaration of intervention of the Republic of El Salvador is inadmissible inasmuch as it relates to the current phase of the proceedings brought by Nicaragua against the United States of America.

IN FAVOUR: *President* Elias; *Vice–President* Sette–Camara; *Judges* Lachs, Morozov, Nagendra Singh, Ruda, Mosler, Oda, Ago, El–Khani, Sir Robert Jennings, de Lacharrière, Mbaye, Bedjaoui.

AGAINST: *Judge* Schwebel."

From 8 to 18 October 1984, the Court held nine public sittings during which speeches were made on behalf of Nicaragua and the United States on the questions of jurisdiction and admissibility. The Judge *ad hoc* appointed by Nicaragua under Article 31 of the Statute of the Court, Mr. C.-A. Colliard, participated in the work of the Court from this stage of the proceedings. (See p. 44.)

At a public sitting held on 26 November 1984, the Court delivered its Judgment (I.C.J. Reports 1984, p. 392). An analysis of the Judgment is given below.

*Proceedings and Submissions of the Parties (paras. 1–11)*

After recapitulating the various stages in the proceedings and setting out the submissions of the Parties (paras. 1–10), the Court recalls that the case concerns a dispute between the Government of the Republic of Nicaragua and the Government of the United States of America arising out of military and paramilitary activities in Nicaragua and in the waters off its coasts, responsibility for which is attributed by Nicaragua to the United States. In the present phase, the case concerns the Court's jurisdiction to entertain and pronounce upon this dispute, as well as the admissibility of Nicaragua's Application referring it to the Court (para. 11).

*I. The Question of the Jurisdiction of the Court to Entertain the Dispute (paras. 12–83)*

*A. The Declaration of Nicaragua and Article 36, Paragraph 5, of the Statute of the Court (paras. 12–51)*

To found the jurisdiction of the Court, Nicaragua relied on Article 36 of the Statute of the Court and the declarations accepting the compulsory jurisdiction of the Court made by the United States and itself.

*The Relevant Texts and the Historical Background to Nicaragua's Declaration (paras. 12–16)*

On 6 April 1984 the Government of the United States deposited with the Secretary-General of the United Nations a notification signed by the Secretary of State, Mr. George Shultz (hereinafter referred to as "the 1984 notification"), referring to the declaration of 1946, and stating that:

> "the aforesaid declaration shall not apply to disputes with any Central American State or arising out of or related to events in Central America, any of which disputes shall be settled in such manner as the parties to them may agree.
>
> "Notwithstanding the terms of the aforesaid declaration, this proviso shall take effect immediately and shall remain in force for two years, so as to foster the continuing regional dispute settlement process which seeks a negotiated solution to the interrelated political, economic and security problems of Central America."

In order to be able to rely upon the United States declaration of 1946 to found jurisdiction in the present case, Nicaragua has to show that it is a "State accepting the same obligation" as the United States within the meaning of Article 36, paragraph 2, of the Statute.

For this purpose, it relies on a declaration made by it on 24 September 1929 pursuant to Article 36, paragraph 2, of the Statute of the Permanent Court of International Justice, the predecessor of the present Court, which provided that:

> "The Members of the League of Nations and the States mentioned in the Annex to the Covenant may, either when signing or ratifying the Protocol to which the present Statute is adjoined, or at a later moment, declare that they recognize as compulsory *ipso facto* and without special agreement, in relation to any other Member or State accepting the same obligation, the jurisdiction of the Court * * *"

in any of the same categories of dispute as listed in Article 36, paragraph 2, of the Statute of the present Court.

Nicaragua relies further on Article 36, paragraph 5, of the Statute of the present Court, which provides that:

> "Declarations made under Article 36 of the Statute of the Permanent Court of International Justice and which are still in force shall be deemed, as between the parties to the present Statute, to be acceptances of the compulsory jurisdiction of the International Court of Justice for the period which they still have to run and in accordance with their terms."

The Judgment recalls the circumstances in which Nicaragua made its declaration: on 14 September 1929, as a Member of the League of Nations, it signed the Protocol of Signature of the Statute of the Permanent Court of International Justice [1]: this Protocol provided that it was subject to ratification and that instruments of ratification were to be sent to the Secretary-General of the League of Nations. On 24 September 1929 Nicaragua deposited with the Secretary-General of the League a declaration under Article 36, paragraph 2, of the Statute of the Permanent Court which reads:

[*Translation from the French*]

> "On behalf of the Republic of Nicaragua I recognize as compulsory unconditionally the jurisdiction of the Permanent Court of International Justice.
>
> Geneva, 24 September 1929.
>
> (*Signed*) T.F. MEDINA."

The national authorities in Nicaragua authorized its ratification, and, on 29 November 1939, the Ministry of Foreign Affairs of Nicaragua sent a telegram to the Secretary-General of the League of Nations advising him of the despatch of the instrument of ratification. The files of the League, however, contain no record of an instrument of ratification ever having been received and no evidence has been adduced to show that such an instrument of ratification was ever despatched to Geneva. After the Second World War,

1. While a State admitted to membership of the United Nations automatically becomes a party to the Statute of the International Court of Justice, a State member of the League of Nations only became a party to that of the Permanent Court of International Justice if it so desired, and, in that case, it was required to accede to the Protocol of Signature of the Statute of the Court.

Nicaragua became an original Member of the United Nations, having ratified the Charter on 6 September 1945; on 24 October 1945 the Statute of the International Court of Justice, which is an integral part of the Charter, came into force.

*The Arguments of the Parties (paras. 17–23) and the Reasoning of the Court (paras. 24–42)*

This being the case, the United States contends that Nicaragua never became a party to the Statute of the Permanent Court and that its 1929 declaration was therefore not "still in force" within the meaning of the English text of Article 36, paragraph 5, of the Statute of the present Court.

In the light of the arguments of the United States and the opposing arguments of Nicaragua, the Court sought to determine whether Article 36, paragraph 5, could have applied to Nicaragua's declaration of 1929.

The Court notes that the Nicaraguan declaration was valid at the time when the question of the applicability of the new Statute, that of the International Court of Justice, arose, since under the system of the Permanent Court of International Justice a declaration was valid only on condition that it had been made by a State which had signed the Protocol of Signature of the Statute. It had not become binding under that Statute, since Nicaragua had not deposited its instrument of ratification of the Protocol of Signature and it was therefore not a party to the Statute. However, it is not disputed that the 1929 declaration could have acquired binding force. All that Nicaragua need have done was to deposit its instrument of ratification, and it could have done that at any time until the day on which the new Court came into existence. It follows that the declaration had a certain potential effect which could be maintained for many years. Having been made "unconditionally" and being valid for an unlimited period, it had retained its potential effect at the moment when Nicaragua became a party to the Statute of the new Court.

In order to reach a conclusion on the question whether the effect of a declaration which did not have binding force at the time of the Permanent Court could be transposed to the International Court of Justice through the operation of Article 36, paragraph 5, of the Statute of that body, the Court took several considerations into account.

As regards the French phrase *"pour une durée qui n'est pas encore expirée"* applying to declarations made under the former system, the Court does not consider it to imply that *"la durée non expirée"* (the unexpired period) is that of a commitment of a binding character. The deliberate choice of the expression seems to denote an intention to widen the scope of Article 36, paragraph 5, so as to cover declarations which have not acquired binding force. The English phrase "still in force" does not expressly exclude a valid declaration of unexpired duration, made by a State not party to the Protocol of Signature of the Statute of the Permanent Court, and therefore not of binding character.

With regard to the considerations governing the transfer of the powers of the former Court to the new one, the Court takes the view that the primary concern of those who drafted its Statute was to maintain the greatest possible continuity between it and the Permanent Court and that their aim was to ensure that the replacement of one Court by another should not result in a step backwards in relation to the progress accomplished towards adopting a system of compulsory jurisdiction. The logic of a general system of devolution from the old Court to the new resulted in the ratification of the new Statute having exactly the same effects as those of the ratification of the Protocol of Signature of the old Statute, i.e., in the case of Nicaragua, a transformation of a potential commitment into an effective one. Nicaragua may therefore be deemed to have given its consent to the transfer of its declaration to the International Court of Justice when it signed and ratified the Charter, thus accepting the Statute and its Article 36, paragraph 5.

Concerning the publications of the Court referred to by the Parties for opposite reasons, the Court notes that they have regularly placed Nicaragua on the list of those States that have recognized the compulsory jurisdiction of the Court by virtue of Article 36, paragraph 5, of the Statute. The attestations furnished by these publications have been entirely official and public, extremely numerous and have extended over a period of nearly 40 years. The Court draws from this testimony the conclusion that the conduct of States parties to the Statute has confirmed the interpretation of Article 36, paragraph 5, of the Statute, whereby the provisions of this Article cover the case of Nicaragua.

*The Conduct of the Parties (paras. 43–51)*

Nicaragua also contends that the validity of Nicaragua's recognition of the compulsory jurisdiction of the Court finds an independent basis in the conduct of the Parties. It argues that its conduct over 38 years unequivocally constitutes consent to be bound by the compulsory jurisdiction of the Court and that the conduct of the United States over the same period unequivocally constitutes its recognition of the validity of the declaration of Nicaragua of 1929 as an acceptance of the compulsory jurisdiction of the Court. The United States, however, objects that the contention of Nicaragua is inconsistent with the Statute and, in particular that compulsory jurisdiction must be based on the clearest manifestation of the State's intent to accept it. After considering Nicaragua's particular circumstances and noting that Nicaragua's situation has been wholly unique, the Court considers that, having regard to the source and generality of statements to the effect that Nicaragua was bound by its 1929 declaration, it is right to conclude that the constant acquiescence of that State in those affirmations constitutes a valid mode of manifestation of its intent to recognize the compulsory jurisdiction of the Court under Article 36, paragraph 2, of the Statute. It further considers that the estoppel on which the United States has relied and which would have barred Nicaragua from instituting proceedings against it in the Court, cannot be said to apply to it.

*Finding:* the Court therefore finds that the Nicaraguan declaration of 1929 is valid and that Nicaragua accordingly was, for the purposes of Article 36, paragraph 2, of the Statute of the Court, a "State accepting the same obligation" as the United States at the date of filing of the Application and could therefore rely on the United States declaration of 1946.

*B. The Declaration of the United States (paras. 52–76)*
*The Notification of 1984 (paras. 52–66)*

The acceptance of the jurisdiction of the Court by the United States on which Nicaragua relies is the result of the United States declaration of 14 August 1946. However, the United States argues that effect should be given to the letter sent to the Secretary–General of the United Nations on 6 April 1984 (see p. [636] above). It is clear that if this notification were valid as against Nicaragua at the date of filing of the Application, the Court would not have jurisdiction under Article 36 of the Statute. After outlining the arguments of the Parties in this connection, the Court points out that the most important question relating to the effect of the 1984 notification is whether the United States was free to disregard the six months' notice clause which, freely and by its own choice, it has appended to its declaration, in spite of the obligation it has entered into vis-à-vis other States which have made such a declaration. The Court notes that the United States has argued that the Nicaraguan declaration, being of undefined duration, is liable to immediate termination, and that Nicaragua has not accepted "the same obligation" as itself and may not rely on the time-limit proviso against it. The Court does not consider that this argument entitles the United States validly to derogate from the time-limit proviso included in its 1946 declaration. In the Court's opinion, the notion of reciprocity is concerned with the scope and substance of the commitments entered into, including reservations, and not with the formal conditions of their creation, duration or extinction. Reciprocity cannot be invoked in order to excuse departure from the terms of a State's own declaration. The United States cannot rely on reciprocity since the Nicaraguan declaration contains no express restriction at all. On the contrary, Nicaragua can invoke the six months' notice against it, not on the basis of reciprocity, but because it is an undertaking which is an integral part of the instrument that contains it. The 1984 notification cannot therefore override the obligation of the United States to submit to the jurisdiction of the Court vis-à-vis Nicaragua.

*The United States Multilateral Treaty Reservation (paras. 67–76)*

The question remains to be resolved whether the United States declaration of 1946 constitutes the necessary consent of the United States to the jurisdiction of the Court in the present case, taking into account the reservations which were attached to the declaration. Specifically, the United States had invoked proviso (*c*) to that declaration, which provides that the United States acceptance of the Court's compulsory jurisdiction shall not extend to

> "disputes arising under a multilateral treaty, unless (1) all parties to the treaty affected by the decision are also parties to the case before the Court, or (2) the United States of America specially agrees to jurisdiction".

This reservation will be referred to as the "multilateral treaty reservation."

The United States argues that Nicaragua relies in its Application on four multilateral treaties, and that the Court, in view of the above reservation, may exercise jurisdiction only if all treaty parties affected by a prospective decision of the Court are also parties to the case.

The Court notes that the States which, according to the United States, might be affected by the future decision of the Court, have made declarations of acceptance of the compulsory jurisdiction of the Court, and are free, any time, to come before the Court with an application instituting proceedings, or to resort to the incidental procedure of intervention. These States are therefore not defenceless against any consequences that may arise out of adjudication by the Court and they do not need the protection of the multilateral treaty reservation (in so far as they are not already protected by Article 59 of the Statute). The Court considers that obviously the question of what States may be affected is not a jurisdictional problem and that it has no choice but to declare that the objection based on the multilateral treaty reservation does not possess, in the circumstances of the case, an exclusively preliminary character.

*Finding:* the Court finds that, despite the United States notification of 1984, Nicaragua's Application is not excluded from the scope of the acceptance by the United States of the compulsory jurisdiction of the Court. The two declarations afford a basis for its jurisdiction.

*C. The Treaty of Friendship, Commerce and Navigation of 21 January 1956 as a Basis of Jurisdiction (paras. 77–83)*

In its Memorial, Nicaragua also relies, as a "subsidiary basis" for the Court's jurisdiction in this case, on the Treaty of Friendship, Commerce and Navigation which it concluded at Managua with the United States on 21 January 1956 and which entered into force on 24 May 1958. Article XXIV, paragraph 2, reads as follows:

> "Any dispute between the Parties as to the interpretation or application of the present Treaty, not satisfactorily adjusted by diplomacy, shall be submitted to the International Court of Justice, unless the Parties agree to settlement by some other pacific means."

Nicaragua submits that this treaty has been and is being violated by the military and paramilitary activities of the United States as described in the Application. The United States contends that, since the Application presents no claims of any violation of the treaty, there are no claims properly before the Court for adjudication, and that, since no attempt to adjust the dispute by diplomacy has been made, the compromissory clause cannot operate. The Court finds it necessary to satisfy itself as to jurisdiction under the treaty inasmuch as it has found that the objection based upon the multilateral treaty reservation in the United States declaration does not debar it from entertaining the Application. In the view of the Court, the fact that a State has not expressly referred, in negotiations with another State, to a particular treaty as having been violated by the conduct of that other State, does not debar that State from invoking a compromissory clause in that treaty. Accordingly, the Court finds that it has jurisdiction under the 1956 Treaty to entertain the claims made by Nicaragua in its Application.

### *II. The Question of the Admissibility of Nicaragua's Application (paras. 84–108)*

The Court now turns to the question of the admissibility of Nicaragua's Application. The United States contended that it is inadmissible on five separate grounds, each of which, it is said, is sufficient to establish such inadmissibility, whether considered as a legal bar to adjudication or as "a matter requiring the exercise of prudential discretion in the interest of the integrity of the judicial function".

The *first ground of inadmissibility* (paras. 85–88) put forward by the United States is that Nicaragua has failed to bring before the Court parties whose presence and participation is necessary for the rights of those parties to be protected and for the adjudication of the issues raised in the Application. In this connection, the Court recalls that it delivers judgments with binding force as between the Parties in accordance with Article 59 of the Statute, and that States which consider they may be affected by the decision are free to institute separate proceedings or to employ the procedure of intervention. There is no trace, either in the Statute or in the practice of international tribunals, of an "indispensable parties" rule which would only be conceivable in parallel to a power, which the Court does not possess, to direct that a third State be made a party to proceedings. None of the States referred to can be regarded as being in a position such that its presence would be truly indispensable to the pursuance of the proceedings.

The *second ground of inadmissibility* (paras. 89–90) relied on by the United States is that Nicaragua is, in effect, requesting that the Court in this case determines the existence of a threat to peace, a matter falling essentially within the competence of the Security Council because it is connected with Nicaragua's complaint involving the use of force. The Court examines this ground of inadmissibility at the same time as the *third ground* (paras. 91–98) based on the position of the Court within the United Nations system, including the impact of proceedings before the Court on the exercise of the inherent right of individual or collective self-defence under Article 51 of the Charter. The Court is of the opinion that the fact that a matter is before the Security Council should not prevent it from being dealt with by the Court and that both proceedings could be pursued *pari passu*. The Council has functions of a political nature assigned to it, whereas the Court exercises purely judicial functions. Both organs can therefore perform their separate but complementary functions with respect to the same events. In the present case, the complaint of Nicaragua is not about an ongoing war [or] armed conflict between it and the United States, but about a situation demanding the peaceful settlement of disputes, a matter which is covered by Chapter VI of the Charter. Hence, it is properly brought before the principal judicial organ of the United Nations for peaceful settlement. This is not a case which can only be dealt with by the Security Council in accordance with the provisions of Chapter VII of the Charter.

With reference to Article 51 of the Charter, the Court notes that the fact that the inherent right of self-defence is referred to in the Charter as a "right" is indicative of a legal dimension, and finds that if, in the present proceedings, it became necessary for the Court to judge in this respect between the Parties, it cannot be debarred from doing so by the existence of a procedure requiring that the matter be reported to the Security Council.

A *fourth ground of inadmissibility* (paras. 99–101) put forward by the United States is the inability of the judicial function to deal with situations involving ongoing armed conflict, since the resort to force during an ongoing armed conflict lacks the attributes necessary for the application of the judicial process, namely a pattern of legally relevant facts discernible by the means available to the adjudicating tribunal. The Court observes that any judgment on the merits is limited to upholding such submissions of the Parties as has been supported by sufficient proof of relevant facts and that ultimately it is the litigant who bears the burden of proof.

The *fifth ground of inadmissibility* (paras. 102–108) put forward by the United States is based on the non-exhaustion of the established processes for the resolution of the conflicts occurring in Central America. It contends that the Nicaraguan Application is incompatible with the Contadora process to which Nicaragua is a party.

The Court recalls its earlier decisions that there is nothing to compel it to decline to take cognizance of one aspect of a dispute merely because that dispute has other aspects (*United States Diplomatic and Consular Staff in Tehran* case, *I.C.J., Reports 1980,* p. 19, para. 36), and the fact that negotiations are being actively pursued during the proceedings is not, legally, any obstacle to the exercise by the Court of its judicial function (*Aegean Sea Continental Shelf* case, *I.C.J. Reports 1978,* p. 12, para. 29). The Court is unable to accept either that there is any requirement of prior exhaustion of regional negotiating processes as a precondition to seising the Court or that the existence of the Contadora process constitutes in this case an obstacle to the examination by the Court of Nicaragua's Application.

The Court is therefore unable to declare the Application inadmissible on any of the grounds the United States has advanced.

*Findings (paras. 109–111)*

* * *

*Status of the Provisional Measures (para. 112)*

The Court states that its Order of 10 May 1984 and the provisional measures indicated therein remain operative until the delivery of the final judgment in the case.

*Operative Clause (para. 113)*

"For these reasons,

THE COURT,

(1)(a) *finds,* by eleven votes to five, that it has jurisdiction to entertain the Application filed by the Republic of Nicaragua on 9 April 1984, on the basis of Article 36, paragraphs 2 and 5, of the Statute of the Court;

IN FAVOUR: *President* Elias; *Vice-President* Sette-Camara; *Judges* Lachs, Morozov, Nagendra Singh, Ruda, El-Khani, de Lacharrière, Mbaye, Bedjaoui; *Judge* ad hoc Colliard;

AGAINST: *Judges* Mosler, Oda, Ago, Schwebel and Sir Robert Jennings;

(b) *finds,* by fourteen votes to two, that it has jurisdiction to entertain the Application filed by the Republic of Nicaragua on 9 April 1984, in so far as that Application relates to a dispute concerning the interpretation or application of the Treaty of Friendship, Commerce and Navigation between the United States of America and the Republic of Nicaragua signed at Managua on 21 January 1956, on the basis of Article XXIV of that Treaty;

IN FAVOUR: *President* Elias; *Vice-President* Sette–Camara; *Judges* Lachs, Morozov, Nagendra Singh, Mosler, Oda, Ago, El–Khani, Sir Robert Jennings, de Lacharrière, Mbaye, Bedjaoui; *Judge* ad hoc Colliard;

AGAINST: *Judges* Ruda and Schwebel;

(c) *finds,* by fifteen votes to one, that it has jurisdiction to entertain the case;

IN FAVOUR: *President* Elias; *Vice-President* Sette–Camara; *Judges* Lachs, Morozov, Nagendra Singh, Ruda, Mosler, Oda, Ago, El–Khani, Sir Robert Jennings, de Lacharrière, Mbaye, Bedjaoui; *Judge* ad hoc Colliard;

AGAINST: *Judge* Schwebel;

(2) *finds,* unanimously, that the said Application is admissible."

## *Notes*

1. Five judges dissented from that part of the Court's judgment relating to Nicaragua's 1929 declaration accepting compulsory jurisdiction. The dissenting judges considered that the declaration was not an "acceptance" within the meaning of Article 36(5) of the Court's statute inasmuch as it was not "in force" because it was never ratified. 1984 I.C.J. 461, 471, 514, 533, 558. Was the Court's use of the French text of Article 36(5) helpful to resolve the question of interpretation as to what is meant by "in force"? Was Nicaragua's "subsequent conduct" indicating its belief that it was bound by the 1929 declaration a valid reason to consider it bound? Was the U.S. objection a technical one that should not have overridden Nicaragua's assertion that it was bound?

2. Was the Court justified in denying the right of the U.S. to modify its acceptance on the ground that the six-month notice clause applied? Should that clause have been given effect even though Nicaragua had no similar clause in its acceptance and could have terminated it at any time? What does reciprocity mean in this connection? See opinions of dissenting Judges Ago and Jennings, 1984 I.C.J. 514, 533. See notes pp. 814–15 on reciprocity.

3. Two judges dissented from the finding of the Court that it had jurisdiction on the basis of a dispute settlement clause in the Treaty of Friendship, Commerce and Navigation of 1956. One of the dissenting judges, Judge Ruda of Argentina considered that negotiation had not taken place and that such negotiation was a pre-condition of submission to the Court. Id. at 454. Judge Schwebel in a dissenting opinion declared that the bilateral treaty "is a purely commercial agreement whose terms do not relate to the use or misuse of force in international relations." He observed that the treaty expressly precluded its application to "traffic in arms" and to measures "necessary to protect the essential security interests" of a party. Schwebel, Dissenting Opinion, para. 117–29. Other judges, however, noted that Nicaragua had alleged violations of specific provisions of the bilateral treaty (for example, that mining of ports and territorial waters and attacks on airports endangered traffic and trade in violation of the treaty), and that it would be up to Nicaragua to prove such treaty violations in the proceedings on the merits. In their view, the allegations were sufficient to support a finding of jurisdiction. See, e.g., Ago, Separate Opinion, para. 2.

4. Was the Court justified in rejecting the U.S. argument, based on its reservation excluding disputes under a multilateral treaty unless all parties to the Treaty affected by the decision were also parties to the case? The pleadings showed that El Salvador, Costa Rica and Honduras were involved in the charges and counter-charges. It was not clear that Nicaragua's complaint rested on multi-lateral treaties alone; Nicaragua had also argued violations of customary law on use of force. If so, would the U.S. reservation apply? Was the Court warranted in holding that this issue, as well as the question of whether Nicaragua's neighbors would be affected by the decision, could not be answered until the Court dealt with the merits? Judge Schwebel contended that the Court was nullifying the jurisdictional bar inserted by the United States in its acceptance. Schwebel, Dissenting Opinion, para. 71–72. See L. Damrosch, Multilateral Disputes, in The International Court of Justice at a Crossroads 376 (Damrosch ed., 1987).

5. Note the distinction in the Court's decision between jurisdiction and admissibility. A similar distinction was drawn in the *Tehran Hostages Case* (p. 823). Although the United States contended in the *Nicaragua Case* that the case was "inadmissible" on five separate grounds, the Court unanimously decided the application admissible. Is admissibility the same as "justiciability," that is, whether the dispute is a legal dispute capable of judicial determination? If the claim presents a legal question, is the Court entitled to abstain from acting on it because political issues are also involved, or because military hostilities are under way, or because the matter has been or is before the U.N. Security Council? Should a claim of self-defense be treated as justiciable? For a lively debate on these questions among international lawyers and public officials, see Proceedings of the American Society of International Law for 1985 and 1986.

6. About one year after the decision on jurisdiction and admissibility in the *Nicaragua Case,* the United States terminated its acceptance of compulsory jurisdiction, for reasons linked to the decision of the Court in the *Nicaragua Case.* 24 I.L.M. 1742–45. See also statement of Legal Adviser of State Department to Senate Committee on Foreign Relations, extracts from which follow.

## STATEMENT OF LEGAL ADVISER OF STATE DEPARTMENT

### *ABRAHAM D. SOFAER, TO SENATE FOREIGN RELATIONS COMMITTEE*

December 4, 1985.

86 Dept.State Bull. 67, 70–71 (No. 2106, Jan.1986).

THE NICARAGUA CASE

* * *

Even more disturbing, for the first time in its history, the Court has sought to assert jurisdiction over a controversy concerning claims related to an ongoing use of armed force. This action concerns every state. It is inconsistent with the structure of the UN system. The only prior case involving use-of-force issues—the *Corfu Channel* case—went to the Court after the disputed actions had ceased and the Security Council had determined that the matter was suitable for judicial consideration. In the Nicaragua case, the Court rejected without a soundly reasoned explanation our arguments that claims of the sort made by Nicaragua were intended by the UN Charter exclusively for resolution by political mechanisms—in particular, the Security Council and the Contadora process—and that claims to the exercise of the inherent right of individual and collective self-defense were excluded by Article 51 of the Charter from review by the Court.

I cannot predict whether the Court's approach to these fundamental Charter issues in the jurisdictional phase of the Nicaragua case will be followed in the Court's judgment on the merits. Nevertheless, the record gives us little reason for confidence. It shows a Court majority apparently prepared to act in ways profoundly inconsistent with the structure of the Charter and the Court's place in that structure. The Charter gives to the Security Council—not the Court—the responsibility for evaluating and resolving claims concerning the use of armed force and claims of self-defense under article 51. With regard to the situation in Central America, the Security Council exercised its responsibility by endorsing the Contadora process as the appropriate mechanism for resolving the interlocking political, security, economic, and other concerns of the region.

### Implications for U.S. National Security

The fact that the ICJ indicated it would hear and decide claims about the ongoing use of force made acceptance of the Court's compulsory jurisdiction an issue of strategic significance. Despite our deep reluctance to do so and the many domestic constraints that apply, we must be able to use force in our self-defense and in the defense of our friends and allies. We are a law-abiding nation, and when we submit ourselves to adjudication of a subject, we regard ourselves as obliged to abide by the result. For the United States to recognize that the ICJ has authority to define and adjudicate with respect to our right of self-defense, therefore, is effectively to surrender to that body the power to pass on our efforts to guarantee the safety and security of this nation and of its allies.

* * *

We recognize that this nation has a special obligation to support the ICJ and all other institutions that advance the rule of law in a world full of terror and disorder. Our belief in this obligation is what led us to set an example by accepting the Court's compulsory jurisdiction in 1946 and by continuing that acceptance long after it became clear that the world would not follow suit and that our acceptance failed to advance our interests in any tangible manner.

Yet, the President also is responsible to the American people and to Congress to avoid potential threats to our national security. The ICJ's decisions in the Nicaragua case created real and important additional considerations that made the continued acceptance of compulsory jurisdiction unacceptable, despite its symbolic significance. We hope that, in the long run, this action, coupled with our submission of disputes under article 36(1), will strengthen the Court in the performance of its proper role in the international system established by the UN Charter and the Court's own Statute.

### *Notes*

1. Consider the contention in the above statement that the competence of the Security Council under Article 51 excludes adjudication by the Court of the legality of self-defense where the court has jurisdiction by virtue of a treaty provision or an acceptance under Article 36(2) rather than an agreed submission. The Council is authorized to take measures necessary to maintain peace and security. When it takes such measures, is a decision by the Council on the legality of the use of force implied? Is the Council an appropriate body to make legal determinations? Would a decision by the International Court on legality impose an obstacle (legal or political) to Council action? Suppose the Council is seized of the dispute but takes no action or does no more than request the parties to settle their dispute by peaceful means (as the Council did in the Nicaraguan case); should that decision deprive a state from seeking a judgment on the legality of the use of force by another state when that other state accepted jurisdiction in accordance with Article 36 of the statute of the Court? What if the respondent state is protected by the veto (its own or an ally's) from an adverse decision by the Council?

2. If the right of self-defense is non-justiciable (as implied by the Legal Adviser's comment on the right of the United States to decide the issue for itself), does that mean in effect that there is no legal restraint on use of force? Is it consistent with the notion of a legal right to exclude determination by a competent judicial body? If states have accepted compulsory jurisdiction of the Court by treaty or a declaration under Article 36(2) without excluding issues of self-defense or cases involving use of force, should the Court abstain from adjudicating the issue of self-defense? See Schachter, 80 A.S.I.L.Proc. 210 (1986).

3. Is there good reason to consider that the Court cannot generally decide factual issues concerning the use of force? See Judgment (Merits) in Nicaragua v. United States, 1986 I.C.J. 97–98 (Chapter 11, p. 911 infra). Even if the Court has a limited capacity to find the truth in cases of past or ongoing hostilities, does it follow that it should hold the case to be inadmissible or to deny jurisdiction? Would it be appropriate in such cases for the Court to consider the merits as argued by the parties and then—if the Court is not satisfied the applicant's claim is well founded in fact or law—to deny the relief requested? See Article 53 of the Statute.

4. Consider the observation of the Legal Adviser (above) that "no state" can rely on the International Court to decide questions of illegal intervention "properly and fairly." Does that assume that the judges (or most of them) are incapable of deciding such issues "fairly and properly" because of political bias? Or does it suggest that the judicial process is unable to produce answers to the issues because the issues are not answerable by "judicial standards"?

On the objectivity of the Court, and related issues, see Schachter, International Law in Theory and Practice, 178 Rec. des Cours 69–73 (1982–V); Falk, Reviving the World Court (1986); Rosenne, The Composition of the Court, in The Future of the International Court of Justice 377–95 (Gross ed. 1976); Suh, Voting Behavior of National Judges in International Courts, 63 A.J.I.L. 224 (1969).

On the question whether the Court may and should deal with cases involving use of force, see O. Schachter, Disputes Involving the Use of Force, in The International Court of Justice at a Crossroads 223–41 (L. Damrosch ed., 1987); R. Bilder, Judicial Procedures Relating to the Use of Force, 31 Va.J.Int'l L. 249 (1991); T. Gill, Litigation Strategy at the International Court (1989).

## NON-APPEARANCE

The non-appearance of the United States in the merits phase of the *Nicaragua* Case was not unprecedented. Five prior cases—beginning with Iceland in 1972 (*Fisheries* cases), then followed by India in 1973, by France (*Nuclear Tests* cases), Turkey (*Aegean Sea Continental Shelf* case), and Iran (*Tehran Hostages* case)—had occurred and had raised issues regarding the consequences of such failure to appear. The Statute of the Court does not provide for, or permit, default judgments under Article 53.

In the event of non-appearance by the respondent state, the Court has taken the position that it must examine the matter on its own and take "special care" to act with circumspection. Schachter argues that in effect this means that the non-appearing accused state acquires an advantage. It does not have to face questions by the Court, and the Court takes special care to make sure its views are considered. The applicant state is also handicapped since it cannot properly consider and answer arguments of the non-participating "respondent" state.

The Institut de Droit International after some years of study and debate reached the following conclusions in a resolution adopted in 1991:

Article 1

Each State entitled under the Statute to appear before the Court and with respect to which the Court is seized of a case is *ipso facto,* by virtue of the Statute, a party to the proceedings, regardless of whether it appears or not.

Article 2

In considering whether to appear or to continue to appear in any phase of proceedings before the Court, a State should have regard to its duty to co-operate in the fulfillment of the Court's judicial functions.

Article 3

In the event that a State fails to appear in a case instituted against it, the Court should, if circumstances so warrant:

(a) invite argument from the appearing party on specific issues which the Court considers have not been canvassed or have been inadequately canvassed in the written or oral pleadings;

(b) take whatever other steps it may consider necessary, within the scope of its powers under the Statute and the Rules of Court, to maintain equality between the parties.

Article 4

Notwithstanding the non-appearance of a State before the Court in proceedings to which it is a party, that State is, by virtue of the Statute, bound by any decision of the Court in that case, whether on jurisdiction, admissibility, or the merits.

Article 5

A State's non-appearance before the Court is in itself no obstacle to the exercise by the Court of its functions under Article 41 of the Statute.

### *Note*

For further discussion on non-appearance, see Elkind, Non–Appearance Before the International Court of Justice: Functional and Comparative Analysis (1984); Thirlway, Non–Appearance Before the International Court of Justice (1985); Charney, Disputes Implicating the Institutional Credibility of the Court: Problems of Non–Appearance, Non–Participation, and Non–Performance, in The International Court of Justice at a Crossroads 288 (L. Damrosch ed., 1987).

## INTERVENTION

A state may intervene in a case between other states in two kinds of situations. Under Article 62 of the Statute, a state which considers that "it has an interest of a legal nature in the case" may be permitted to intervene by the Court. The other situation applies when the state requesting intervention is a party to the convention which is before the Court. In that case the state has the right to intervene and if it uses that right, the treaty interpretation given by the Court will be binding on it. Article 63 of the Statute. The case-law on intervention is summarized in the Restatement (Third) § 903, Reporters' Note 7:

> In the Permanent Court of International Justice, there was only one case of intervention, by the Government of Poland in the Wimbledon Case, which involved the interpretation of the Peace Treaty of Versailles of 1919. P.C.I.J., ser. A, No. 1 at 11–13 (1923). In 1951, the International Court of Justice allowed Cuba to intervene in the Haya de la Torre Case between Colombia and Peru, which involved the interpretation of the 1928 Havana Convention on Asylum, to which Cuba was a party. [1951] I.C.J.Rep. 71, 76–77. In later cases involving permissive interventions under Article 62, the Court took a more restrictive attitude and refused to grant permission to intervene. See Nuclear Tests Cases, Reporters' Note 3, [1974] I.C.J.Rep. 530, 535 (Fiji's application to intervene lapsed when the proceedings were terminated because the main case "no longer has any object"); Case Concerning the Continental Shelf (Tunisia/Libyan Arab Jamahiriya) (Application of Malta for Permission to Intervene), [1981] I.C.J.Rep. 3, 19 (Malta's interests were no greater than those of other Mediterranean states, and her application was so restricted by various reservations that the decision in the case could not affect any of her legal interests); Case Concerning the Continental Shelf (Libyan Arab Jamahiriya/Malta) (Application of Italy for Permission to Intervene), [1984] I.C.J.Rep. 3, 18–28 (to permit Italy to intervene would introduce a fresh dispute; Article 62 was not intended as an alternative means of bringing an additional dispute as a case before the Court); Case Concerning Military and Paramilitary Activities in and Against Nicaragua (Nicaragua v. United States) (Declaration of Intervention of the Republic of El Salvador), [1984] I.C.J.Rep. 215, 216 (although El Salvador's declaration invoked Article 63, this declaration addressed the

substance of the dispute and was inadmissible at the stage of proceedings relating only to the Court's jurisdiction). Later, in a decision concluding that it had jurisdiction of the case, the Court noted that if Costa Rica, El Salvador, and Honduras should find that "they might be affected by the future decision of the Court" in the case, they would be free to institute proceedings against Nicaragua or resort to the incidental procedures for intervention under Articles 62 and 63 of the Statute. [1984] I.C.J.Rep. 392, 425. No further action was taken by Costa Rica or Honduras, but proceedings against them were instituted by Nicaragua in 1986. 25 Int'l Leg.Mat. 1290, 1293 (1986) (applications by Nicaragua); [1986] I.C.J.Rep. 548, 551 (procedural orders); [1987] *id.* 182 (order recording the discontinuance by Nicaragua of the proceedings against Costa Rica).

See also Sztucki, Intervention under Article 63 of the I.C.J. Statute in the Phase of Preliminary Proceedings: The Salvadoran Incident, 79 A.J.I.L. 1005 (1985).

A less restrictive position was taken by a Chamber of the Court in allowing Nicaragua to intervene in a case between El Salvador and Honduras concerning their maritime frontier. The Chamber recognized that Nicaragua had a legal interest in the case by virtue of its co-ownership of the waters of the Gulf of Fonseca which was one area in dispute between the parties. The Chamber made it clear that its permission to Nicaragua to intervene did not make Nicaragua a party to the dispute. Maritime Frontier Case, I.C.J. Reports 1990, pp. 92, 133–34. Accordingly, Nicaragua would not be bound by the decision (or protected by it) under the terms of Article 59 of the Statute. It may be asked whether in view of Nicaragua's co-ownership of the waters in litigation, it should not have been treated as a party bound by the decision and protected by it. For a critical view of the Chamber's decision on this point, see D.W. Greig, Third Party Rights and Intervention Before the International Court, 32 Va.J.Int'l L. 285, 321–30 (1992).

The issue of intervention came up before the International Court in a different way when it was argued that the two states parties to a treaty at issue were "necessary parties" and therefore their failure to intervene should preclude the Court from adjudicating the case. The case concerned the claim of Nauru that the three states that were trustees from Nauru under a U.N. trusteeship agreement breached their obligations by marketing Nauru's phosphate resources and failing to restore the property after the phosphate was removed. The Court ruled that the failure of the two trustees, New Zealand and the United Kingdom to intervene did not bar Nauru from proceeding with its claim against Australia, the third trustee. Case Concerning Certain Phosphate Lands in Nauru, Preliminary Objection, I.C.J. Reports 1992, p. 240. See generally Weeramantry, Nauru: Environmental Damage Under International Trusteeship (1992).

For an illuminating analysis of issues before the Court concerning intervention, see D.W. Greig, op. cit. supra.

## PROVISIONAL MEASURES OF PROTECTION

The Court has the "power to indicate, if it considers the circumstances so require, any provisional measures which ought to be taken to preserve the respective rights of the parties." Art. 41 of the Statute. This right is analogous to the common law interlocutory injunction under which parties may be enjoined from acting in a way to prejudice the outcome during the proceedings. The two criteria most often invoked for such provisional relief are urgency and irreparable injury.

May the Court impose provisional measures without dealing first on jurisdiction? As Judge Jiménez de Aréchaga said: "In cases where there is no reasonable probability, prima facie ascertained by the Court, of jurisdiction on the merits it would be devoid of sense to indicate provisional measures to ensure the execution of a judgment the Court will never render." Aegean Sea Case, I.C.J. Reports 1976, p. 15. In the Fisheries Jurisdiction Case, the Court declared:

> On a request for provisional measure, the Court need not, before indicating them, finally satisfy itself that it has jurisdiction on the merits of the case, yet it ought not to act under Article 41 of the Statute of the Court if the absence of jurisdiction on the merits is manifest.

I.C.J. Reports 1972, pp. 15–16. The Court has imposed provisional measures in six cases, including the Nicaragua Case, before determining definitively the issue of jurisdiction. Judge Schwebel, in a separate opinion in the Nicaragua Case (Jurisdiction), urged that the Court give parties time to argue issues of jurisdiction in depth and to take the necessary time itself to deliberate issues of jurisdiction in depth. I.C.J. Reports 1984, p. 207 (Sep.Op. Schwebel).

In 1992, Libya requested that the Court impose provisional measures enjoining the United Kingdom and the United States from taking measures against Libya pursuant to a Security Council decision intended to coerce Libya to surrender Libyans accused of terrorist activities to the two respondent countries. In particular, the individuals were accused of planting a bomb on Pan–Am Flight No. 103 that caused the plane to crash over Lockerbie, Scotland. Libya based its jurisdictional claim on the Compromissory Clause in the Montreal Convention of 1971 on Suppression of Unlawful Acts Against Safety of Civil Aviation. Libya contended that the Convention recognized its right to prosecute the individuals accused of crimes covered by the Convention and its right not to surrender them to another country. The Court denied the Libyan request by eleven votes to five. The majority considered that the Security Council Resolution 745 (1992) requiring Libya to surrender the accused individuals imposed a legal duty on Libya and any indication of provisional measures would run "a serious risk of conflicting with the work of the Security Council." The Court noted that while it was not called on to determine definitively the legal effect of the Security Council resolution, the rights claimed by Libya were not "now" appropriate for protection by provisional measures. I.C.J. Reports 1992, pp. 3, 15.

For analysis of provisional measures in the I.C.J., see B. Oxman, Jurisdiction and the Power to Indicate Provisional Measures, in The International Court of Justice at a Crossroads 323 (Damrosch ed., 1987). For a wider discussion of interim measures of protection, particularly in regard to human rights, see R. Macdonald, Interim Measures in International Law, with Special Reference to the European System for the Protection of Human Rights in 52 Zaö. R.V. (Heidelberg, J. Int'l L.) 703–40 (1992).

## B. ADVISORY OPINIONS

The Court may give an advisory opinion on "any legal question" requested by a body authorized by or in accordance with the U.N. Charter Article 65 of the Statute of the Court. The Charter in Article 96 states that the General Assembly or the Security Council may request advisory opinions. In addition other organs of the United Nations may be so authorized by the General Assembly.

Four organs of the United Nations and 15 specialized agencies have been authorized to request advisory opinions. A state may not request an advisory opinion. It may, however, request an authorized international organization to make such request.

As of February 1993, the Court has rendered 22 advisory opinions. Twelve were in response to requests by the U.N. General Assembly, one (the *Namibia Case*) was requested by the Security Council and one by the Economic and Social Council. Three of the specialized agencies (UNESCO, WHO and IMCO) requested one opinion each. Five advisory opinions were given at the request of the U.N. Committee on Applications for Review of Administrative Tribunal Judgments. This U.N. Committee was established in 1955 specifically for the purpose of requesting advisory opinions of the Court to review decisions of the U.N. Administrative Tribunal. U.N.G.A.Res. 957(X), (1955).

Although an advisory opinion has no binding effect in itself, some international agreements provide that disputes relating to the interpretation and application of the agreement shall be submitted to the Court for an opinion that will be accepted as binding by the parties to the dispute. One example is the following provision in the General Convention on Privileges and Immunities of the United Nations.

### *CONVENTION ON THE PRIVILEGES AND IMMUNITIES OF THE UNITED NATIONS*

Adopted by the General Assembly, February 13, 1946.
1 U.N.T.S. 15.

Sec. 30. All differences arising out of the interpretation or application of the present convention shall be referred to the International Court of Justice, unless in any case it is agreed by the parties to have recourse to another mode of settlement. If a difference arises between the United Nations on the one hand and a Member on the other hand, a request shall be made for an advisory opinion on any legal question involved in accordance with Article 96 of the Charter and Article 65 of the Statute of the Court. The opinion given by the Court shall be accepted as decisive by the parties.

### *RESERVATION BY THE UNION OF SOVIET SOCIALIST REPUBLICS TO THE CONVENTION ON THE PRIVILEGES AND IMMUNITIES OF THE UNITED NATIONS*

Deposited on September 22, 1953.
173 U.N.T.S. 369.

The Soviet Union does not consider itself bound by the provision of section 30 of the Convention which envisages the compulsory jurisdiction of the International Court and, in regard to the competence of the International Court in differences arising out of the interpretation and application of the Convention, the Soviet Union will, as hitherto, adhere to the position that, for the submission of a particular dispute for settlement by the International Court, the consent of all the parties to the dispute is required in every individual case. This reservation is equally applicable to the provision contained in the same section, whereby the advisory opinion of the International Court shall be accepted as decisive.

### *Notes*

1. Substantially identical reservations to the Convention were filed by other Communist countries that were members of the United Nations. The same states made similar reservations to the Convention on the Privileges and Immunities of the Specialized Agencies, adopted by the General Assembly on November 21, 1947, 33 U.N.T.S. 261. See, e.g., Accession of Czechoslovakia, Dec. 29, 1966, 586 U.N.T.S. 246.

May the advisory jurisdiction of the Court be used in cases of disputes where one or more of the parties to the dispute does not consent to the Court's advisory jurisdiction? See the opinion of the Court in the *Western Sahara Case* below.

2. In Applicability of Article VI, Section 22, of the Convention on the Privileges and Immunities of the United Nations, [1989] I.C.J. 177, the United Nations Economic and Social Council requested an advisory opinion on behalf of the Sub–Commission on Prevention of Discrimination and Protection of Minorities. Article VI, Section 22 of the Convention on the Privileges and Immunities of the United Nations confers immunity on experts performing missions for the United Nations.

In 1985, the Sub–Commission had appointed Mr. Mazilu, a Romanian national, as a special rapporteur and requested that he compile a report concerning human rights and youth. Mazilu had been expected to present his report in Geneva at the 1987 session of the Sub–Commission, but he failed to attend and the Sub–Commission was informed by the Permanent Representative of Romania in Geneva, and by a telegram bearing Mazilu's name, that his health had prevented his attendance. The U.N. made several unsuccessful attempts to contact Mazilu by mail and subsequent letters by Mazilu to the U.N. stated that he had not received any communication from the U.N. and that his Government had refused him permission to travel. There was no reference to illness in these letters.

On 31 December 1987, Mazilu's term as a member of the Sub–Commission expired. Several requests by the U.N. in January 1988 to Romanian authorities for Mazilu to be allowed to travel to Geneva received no response and a missive from Mazilu was received stating that communications between him and the

U.N. were being obstructed. He wrote that pressure by the Romanian authorities had been exercised against him to compel his retirement from the Romanian Ministry of Foreign Affairs and to persuade him to inform the Sub–Commission that he was unable to compile the report. Romanian officials responded that Mazilu had requested retirement from the Foreign Ministry and suggested that the individual appointed to take Mazilu's place produce the report.

Mazilu failed to attend the 1988 session of the Sub–Commission and the United Nations was unable to locate him. In August 1988, Romania notified the U.N. that Mazilu was unable to finish his report because of his ill health. The Sub–Commission then requested the U.N. Secretary–General to attempt to establish contacts with the Romanian government over the matter. Romania responded that any attempt by the U.N. to intervene would be regarded as interference in the internal affairs of Romania and that the affair was an internal affair between a citizen and his government. In September 1988, the Sub–Commission requested that the Secretary–General invoke the Convention on Privileges and Immunities and request the assistance of the Romanian authorities in enabling Mazilu to complete his report. The Secretary–General complied with the request, but no response was received from the Romanian government. In January 1989, Romania sent an *Aide Mémoire* to the U.N. repeating that Mazilu could not complete the report because of ill health. It further maintained that Section 22 of the Convention did not apply to a special rapporteur and that, in any event, it did not apply to an expert in his country of residence or nationality, but only in countries to which he had been sent on a mission for the acts connected with that mission.

At this point the U.N. Economic and Social Council requested the advisory opinion from the Court on the applicability of Section 22. Romania argued that the Court lacked jurisdiction to give an advisory opinion because of Romania's reservation to Section 30 of the Convention. The reservation was substantially identical to that of the Soviet Union reproduced above. Romania argued that its consent was required for the Court to have jurisdiction to render an advisory opinion on the matter. The Court held unanimously that it had jurisdiction under Article 96 of the U.N. Charter and that Romania's reservation to Section 30 did not apply to advisory opinions. The Court reasoned that advisory opinions are not binding on states and, therefore, the consent of states are not required for jurisdiction. The Court noted, however, that in certain circumstances where consent was not required for jurisdiction, the Court might consider lack of consent as a compelling reason not to entertain the request for an advisory opinion. The Court nevertheless ruled that this exception was not available to Romania on the facts of the case. Having cleared the jurisdictional hurdle, the Court went on to hold that Section 22 applied to a special rapporteur in Mazilu's position and that persons eligible for immunity under the Convention could claim it in the states of which they were nationals or in which they were ordinarily resident, except where the state concerned had made specific reservations precluding its applicability and Romania had not made such a reservation. The Court also held that a special rapporteur retains immunity status until the tasks assigned have been completed.

## WESTERN SAHARA CASE

International Court of Justice, Advisory Opinion, 1975.
1975 I.C.J. 12.

[For the facts of case, see Chapter 4, p. 314 supra]

The Court:

* * *

25. Spain has made a number of observations relating to the lack of its consent to the proceedings, which, it considers, should lead the Court to decline to give an opinion. These observations may be summarized as follows:

(a) In the present case the advisory jurisdiction is being used to circumvent the principle that jurisdiction to settle a dispute requires the consent of the parties.

(b) The questions, as formulated, raise issues concerning the attribution of territorial sovereignty over Western Sahara.

(c) The Court does not possess the necessary information concerning the relevant facts to enable it to pronounce judicially on the questions submitted to it.

26. The first of the above observations is based on the fact that on 23 September 1974 the Minister for Foreign Affairs of Morocco addressed a communication to the Minister for Foreign Affairs of Spain recalling the terms of a statement by which His Majesty King Hassan II had on 17 September 1974 proposed the joint submission to the International Court of Justice of an issue expressed in the following terms:

> "You, the Spanish Government, claim that the Sahara was *res nullius*. You claim that it was a territory or property left uninherited, you claim that no power and no administration had been established over the Sahara: Morocco claims the contrary. Let us request the arbitration of the International Court of Justice at The Hague * * * It will state the law on the basis of the titles submitted * * *"

Spain has stated before the Court that it did not consent and does not consent now to the submission of this issue to the jurisdiction of the Court.

27. Spain considers that the subject of the dispute which Morocco invited it to submit jointly to the Court for decision in contentious proceedings, and the subject of the questions on which the advisory opinion is requested, are substantially identical; thus the advisory procedure is said to have been used as an alternative after the failure of an attempt to make use of the contentious jurisdiction with regard to the same question. Consequently, to give a reply would, according to Spain, be to allow the advisory procedure to be used as a means of bypassing the consent of a State, which constitutes the basis of the Court's jurisdiction. If the Court were to countenance such a use of its advisory jurisdiction, the outcome would be to obliterate the distinction between the two spheres of the Court's jurisdiction, and the fundamental principle of the independence of States would be affected, for States would find their disputes with other States being submitted to the Court, by this indirect means, without their consent; this might

result in compulsory jurisdiction being achieved by majority vote in a political organ. Such circumvention of the well-established principle of consent for the exercise of international jurisdiction would constitute, according to this view, a compelling reason for declining to answer the request.

28. In support of these propositions Spain has invoked the fundamental rule, repeatedly reaffirmed in the Court's jurisprudence, that a State cannot, without its consent, be compelled to submit its disputes with other States to the Court's adjudication. It has relied, in particular, on the application of this rule to the advisory jurisdiction by the Permanent Court of International Justice in the *Status of Eastern Carelia* case (P.C.I.J., Series B, No. 5), maintaining that the essential principle enunciated in that case is not modified by the decisions of the present Court in the cases concerning the Interpretation of Peace Treaties with Bulgaria, Hungary and Romania, First Phase (I.C.J. Reports 1950, p. 65) and the Legal Consequences for States of the Continued Presence of South Africa in Namibia (South West Africa) notwithstanding Security Council Resolution 276 (1970) (I.C.J. Reports 1971, p. 16). Morocco and Mauritania, on the other hand, have maintained that the present case falls within the principles applied in those two decisions and that the *ratio decidendi* of the *Status of Eastern Carelia* case is not applicable to it.

* * *

31. In the proceedings concerning the Interpretation of Peace Treaties with Bulgaria, Hungary and Romania, First Phase, this Court had to consider how far the views expressed by the Permanent Court in the *Status of Eastern Carelia* case were still pertinent in relation to the applicable provisions of the Charter of the United Nations and the Statute of the Court. It stated, *inter alia:*

> "This objection reveals a confusion between the principles governing contentious procedure and those which are applicable to Advisory Opinions.
>
> "The consent of States, parties to a dispute, is the basis of the Court's jurisdiction in contentious cases. The situation is different in regard to advisory proceedings even where the Request for an Opinion relates to a legal question actually pending between States. The Court's reply is only of an advisory character: as such, it has no binding force. It follows that no State, whether a Member of the United Nations or not, can prevent the giving of an Advisory Opinion which the United Nations considers to be desirable in order to obtain enlightenment as to the course of action it should take. The Court's Opinion is given not to the States, but to the organ which is entitled to request it; the reply of the Court, itself an 'organ of the United Nations', represents its participation in the activities of the organization, and, in principle, should not be refused." (I.C.J. Reports 1950, p. 71.)

32. The Court, it is true, affirmed in this pronouncement that its competence to give an opinion did not depend on the consent of the interested States, even when the case concerned a legal question actually pending between them. However, the Court proceeded not merely to stress its judicial character and the permissive nature of Article 65, paragraph 1, of

the Statute but to examine, specifically in relation to the opposition of some of the interested States, the question of the judicial propriety of giving the opinion. Moreover, the Court emphasized the circumstances differentiating the case then under consideration from the *Status of Eastern Carelia* case and explained the particular grounds which led it to conclude that there was no reason requiring the Court to refuse to reply to the request. Thus the Court recognized that lack of consent might constitute a ground for declining to give the opinion requested if, in the circumstances of a given case, considerations of judicial propriety should oblige the Court to refuse an opinion. In short, the consent of an interested State continues to be relevant, not for the Court's competence, but for the appreciation of the propriety of giving an opinion.

33. In certain circumstances, therefore, the lack of consent of an interested State may render the giving of an advisory opinion incompatible with the Court's judicial character. An instance of this would be when the circumstances disclose that to give a reply would have the effect of circumventing the principle that a State is not obliged to allow its disputes to be submitted to judicial settlement without its consent. If such a situation should arise, the powers of the Court under the discretion given to it by Article 65, paragraph 1, of the Statute, would afford sufficient legal means to ensure respect for the fundamental principle of consent to jurisdiction.

* * *

39. The above considerations are pertinent for a determination of the object of the present request. The object of the General Assembly has not been to bring before the Court, by way of a request for advisory opinion, a dispute or legal controversy, in order that it may later, on the basis of the Court's opinion, exercise its powers and functions for the peaceful settlement of that dispute or controversy. The object of the request is an entirely different one: to obtain from the Court an opinion which the General Assembly deems of assistance to it for the proper exercise of its functions concerning the decolonization of the territory.

40. The General Assembly, as appears from paragraph 3 of resolution 3292 (XXIX), has asked the Court for an opinion so as to be in a position to decide "on the policy to be followed in order to accelerate the decolonization process in the territory * * * in the best possible conditions, in the light of the advisory opinion * * * ". The true object of the request is also stressed in the preamble of resolution 3292 (XXIX), where it is stated "that it is highly desirable that the General Assembly, in order to continue the discussion of this question at its thirtieth session, should receive an advisory opinion on some important legal aspects of the problem."

* * *

42. Furthermore, the origin and scope of the dispute, as above described, are important in appreciating, from the point of view of the exercise of the Court's discretion, the real significance in this case of the lack of Spain's consent. The issue between Morocco and Spain regarding Western Sahara is not one as to the legal status of the territory today, but one as to the rights of Morocco over it at the time of colonization. The settlement of this issue will not affect the rights of Spain today as the administering

Power, but will assist the General Assembly in deciding on the policy to be followed in order to accelerate the decolonization process in the territory. It follows that the legal position of the State which has refused its consent to the present proceedings is not "in any way compromised by the answers that the Court may give to the questions put to it" (Interpretation of Peace Treaties with Bulgaria, Hungary and Romania, First Phase, I.C.J. Reports 1950, p. 72).

43. A second way in which Spain has put the objection of lack of its consent is to maintain that the dispute is a territorial one and that the consent of a State to adjudication of a dispute concerning the attribution of territorial sovereignty is always necessary. The questions in the request do not however relate to a territorial dispute, in the proper sense of the term, between the interested States. They do not put Spain's present position as the administering Power of the territory in issue before the Court: resolution 3292 (XXIX) itself recognizes the current legal status of Spain as administering Power. Nor is in issue before the Court the validity of the titles which led to Spain's becoming the administering Power of the territory, and this was recognized in the oral proceedings. The Court finds that the request for an opinion does not call for adjudication upon existing territorial rights or sovereignty over territory. Nor does the Court's Order of 22 May 1975 convey any implication that the present case relates to a claim of a territorial nature.

44. A third way in which Spain, in its written statement, has presented its opposition to the Court's pronouncing upon the questions posed in the request is to maintain that in this case the Court cannot fulfil the requirements of good administration of justice as regards the determination of the facts. The attribution of territorial sovereignty, it argues, usually centres on material acts involving the exercise of that sovereignty, and the consideration of such acts and of the respective titles inevitably involves an exhaustive determination of facts. In advisory proceedings there are properly speaking no parties obliged to furnish the necessary evidence, and the ordinary rules concerning the burden of proof can hardly be applied. That being so, according to Spain, the Court should refrain from replying in the absence of facts which are undisputed, since it would not be in possession of sufficient information such as would be available in adversary proceedings.

45. Considerations of this kind played a role in the case concerning the *Status of Eastern Carelia.* In that instance, the non-participation of a State concerned in the case was a secondary reason for the refusal to answer. The Permanent Court of International Justice noted the difficulty of making an enquiry into facts concerning the main point of a controversy when one of the parties thereto refused to take part in the proceedings.

46. Although in that case the refusal of one State to take part in the proceedings was the cause of the inadequacy of the evidence, it was the actual lack of "materials sufficient to enable it to arrive at any judicial conclusion upon the question of fact" (P.C.I.J., Series B, No. 5, p. 28) which was considered by the Permanent Court, for reasons of judicial propriety, to prevent it from giving an opinion. Consequently, the issue is whether the Court has before it sufficient information and evidence to enable it to arrive at a judicial conclusion upon any disputed questions of fact the determina-

tion of which is necessary for it to give an opinion in conditions compatible with its judicial character.

47. The situation in the present case is entirely different from that with which the Permanent Court was confronted in the *Status of Eastern Carelia* case. Mauritania, Morocco and Spain have furnished very extensive documentary evidence of the facts which they considered relevant to the Court's examination of the questions posed in the request, and each of these countries, as well as Algeria and Zaire, have presented their views on these facts and on the observations of the others. The Secretary–General has also furnished a dossier of documents concerning the discussion of the question of Western Sahara in the competent United Nations organs. The Court therefore considers that the information and evidence before it are sufficient to enable it to arrive at a judicial conclusion concerning the facts which are relevant to its opinion and necessary for replying to the two questions posed in the request.

## *Notes*

1. The *Eastern Carelia Case* to which the Court refers arose out of a dispute between Finland and the U.S.S.R. when the latter was not a member of the League of Nations and refused to take any part in its proceedings or in the Court. For the Court's refusal to render an advisory opinion, see 1923 P.C.I.J., Ser. B, No. 5, p. 7.

2. The International Court also had occasion to consider its competence to render opinions in the absence of consent by states concerned in the Advisory Opinion on Interpretation of the Peace Treaties, referred to in the Western Sahara Opinion. Although the Court gave an advisory opinion that the three absent, non-consenting states (Bulgaria, Hungary, and Romania) were obliged to comply with the dispute-settlement clauses of the peace treaties, these states did not appoint members of the treaty commissions. In a subsequent opinion, the Court declared that their failure to make such appointments meant that the commissions could not function. 1950 I.C.J. 221.

3. In the instant case, the Court observed that "consent of an interested State continues to be relevant, not for the Court's competence, but for the appreciation of the propriety of giving an opinion." What circumstances would be relevant to "propriety" of giving an opinion requested by the General Assembly or Security Council? Would there have to be evidence of a genuine United Nations need for an opinion as distinct from the resolution of a dispute?

4. Would it be desirable for the General Assembly to authorize a special committee to request advisory opinions on legal disputes between states, provided that all states parties to the dispute should have consented to the procedure? It has been suggested that states would be willing to agree to nonbinding advisory jurisdiction in regard to disputes in which they would not accept the contentious jurisdiction of the Court. See Szasz, Enhancing the Advisory Jurisdiction of the World Court, in The Future of the International Court of Justice 499 (Gross ed., 1976).

5. Should use of the Court be encouraged, by having the General Assembly (through a committee) act as a conduit whereby regional and functional multinational bodies could submit requests for advisory opinions? A proposal has also been made that national courts be authorized to submit questions of international law which have come up before them to the I.C.J. for advisory opinions.

Assuming that this proposal were adopted, would it have been desirable for the U.S. Supreme Court in the *Sabbatino* case to have requested an opinion from the International Court on issues concerning the international law applicable to the right of nationalization and requirements of compensation? See Jessup, The Price of International Justice 76–82 (1971). For a valuable review of advisory opinions, see Pomerance, The Advisory Function of the International Court in the League and U.N. Eras (1973).

6. Compare the competence of the Inter–American Court on Human Rights to give advisory opinions. See Buergenthal, The Advisory Practice of the Inter–American Human Rights Court, 79 A.J.I.L. 1 (1985).

## SECTION 5. SPECIALIZED INTERNATIONAL TRIBUNALS

While the U.N. Charter describes the International Court of Justice as "the principal judicial organ" of the United Nations and the U.N. is the most comprehensive international organization in terms of purposes and members, states have not limited themselves to the I.C.J. as the sole institution for the resolution of disputes. See International Courts for the Twenty–First Century, Part III, specialized International Tribunals and Procedures 161–252 (Janis, ed. 1992); Merrills, International Dispute Settlement (2d ed. 1991). There are increasingly important areas of contention, the resolution of which states have allocated to other tribunals. As discussed above, many disputes that apparently fall within the jurisdiction of the International Court of Justice are regularly submitted to arbitration by states as a deliberate choice. See Lauterpacht, Aspects of the Administration of International Justice 10–11 (1991).

Moreover, modern treaty practice has witnessed the development of treaty provisions for the compulsory settlement of disputes by reference to special tribunals instead of through the International Court of Justice. See generally Oellers–Frahm and Wühler, Dispute Settlement in Public International Law, Texts and Materials (1984). Following World War II special "Claims Commissions" and "Conciliation Commissions" were established to resolve claims—ordinarily involving property claims of Allied nationals—arising out of the war. Similarly, particular treaty regimes have provided for the settlement of specialized classes of disputes falling within the scope of the treaty. Notable examples are found in the General Agreement on Tariffs and Trade, the International Coffee Agreements, the Convention on the Prevention of Marine Pollution by Dumping of Wastes and Other Matter, and the International Energy Agency Dispute Settlement Center. See Lauterpacht, Aspects of the Administration of International Justice 12 (1991).

Perhaps the most important group of specialized tribunals have been set up by the various human rights agreements. Starting with the European Commission and the European Court of Human Rights set up by the 1950 European Commission on Human Rights, the system for the protection of human rights has expanded to include the Inter–American Commission on Human Rights (1960), the Inter–American Court of Human Rights (1979), the African Commission on Human and Peoples' Rights (1986), and since it began its work in 1977, the United Nations Human Rights Committee, acting pursuant to the International Covenant on Civil and Political Rights and the Optional Protocol to the Covenant. See Chapter 8 infra.

As discussed above, there are also Administrative Tribunals of various international organizations. These are not inter-state tribunals in the true sense, but they are "international" in the sense that they operate outside the legal control of any state and apply and develop an organic body of law that is independent of the law of any particular state. See Amerasinghe, The Law of International Civil Service (1988). The principal tribunals within this category are those established within the United Nations, the International Labor Organization, and the World Bank. Their principal function is to hear complaints by staff members relating to alleged breaches of terms of employment.

### *E. LAUTERPACHT, ASPECTS OF THE ADMINISTRATION OF INTERNATIONAL JUSTICE*

14–22 (1991) (footnotes omitted).

* * * [T]he case for a specialist tribunal is strong where it is foreseen that there will be many cases with similar issues, to be decided over a relatively short time span, and in which the knowledge gained in deciding one will be of direct relevance in deciding others. For this reason, the weight of case numbers aside, it makes sense to assign to a claims commission a series of claims arising out of a given occurrence, such as the claims against Germany arising out of the First World War or the claims against Iran arising out of the events of 1979–1980. Similarly, in relation to the question of how the international judicial system can contribute to the evolution and application of international standards for the protection of the environment, it seems likely that the use of an expert tribunal will be helpful.

In principle, there can be no objection to the multiplication of international tribunals provided that there is sufficient work for them. It is only if an existing tribunal is capable of coping with the additional flow of work, and yet is not adopted for that purpose, that one needs to question the value of establishing the additional forum. A good illustration of what probably is an unnecessary duplication of arrangements is to be found in the prospective establishment of the Law of the Sea Tribunal under the 1982 Convention on the Law of the Sea. Part XV of this Convention contains an elaborate structure for the settlement of disputes which offers the parties a choice of recourse to a new Law of the Sea Tribunal, or to the ICJ, or to one kind of specially constituted arbitral tribunal for some purposes and to another arbitral tribunal for more limited purposes. Given the apparent reluctance of some States to commit themselves to the jurisdiction of the ICJ because its membership is geographically divorced from the region in which the case arises, one can understand the provision of arbitration as an alternative. But why should it be necessary to provide for a complete additional tribunal?

The political origin of the LOS Tribunal appears to lie in the initiative taken by the United States at a relatively early stage in the negotiations. This initiative reflected the firm belief of that country that the comprehensive regulation of so important an area of the law as that relating to the sea must be accompanied by effective judicial machinery for the settlement of disputes. Coupled with this was the concern felt at that time, because of the criticism of the ICJ, especially by developing countries in the UN General Assembly, following its judgment in the *South West Africa Cases,* that that Court would not be acceptable as the exclusive forum for settling disputes arising under any new Convention. Once the idea of an additional tribunal had taken root, there appeared to be no inclination to question it. But that does not mean that an institution conceived nearly a quarter of a century ago, but not yet born, must necessarily be allowed to reach term; and the justification for it may properly be reviewed in the light of evolving circumstances.

Basically, the LOS Tribunal will not be very different from the ICJ—except that it will consist of 21 members (not 15 as in the ICJ) who are not expected to be full-time judges. Its jurisdiction, which comprises all disputes submitted to it in accordance with the Convention, is therefore essentially concerned with traditional maritime matters of a kind which the ICJ is perfectly competent to handle and has repeatedly dealt with in the past. This is in a sense recognized by the fact that recourse to the ICJ is itself a permitted option under the Convention's dispute settlement system.

There is, however, one category of disputes that might arise under the Convention with which the ICJ is not able to deal under its Statute as framed at present, namely, that which involves the exercise of procedural rights directly by non-State entities, whether natural or legal persons. However, this prospect is quite narrow. It is limited to disputes that may arise under Articles 187 and 292 of the Convention. The first of these Articles foresees the reference to the Sea–Bed Disputes Chamber of the LOS Tribunal of a range of disputes arising in connection with the exploitation of the seabed beyond the limits of national jurisdiction and involving as parties not only States Parties to the Convention but also the Authority (an international organization), the Enterprise (likewise an international organization), State enterprises (which are, of course, not States) and national or juridical persons (which are likewise not States). In view of the provision in Article 34 of the Statute of the ICJ that "only States may be parties to disputes before the Court", it is clear that the ICJ would not be authorized to deal with these cases. Nor would the ICJ be permitted to deal with a case arising under Article 292 of the Convention, on the prompt release of vessels, if the parties (of which one would in this situation be a non-State entity) were to agree to submit the case to an international tribunal.

Do these two extensions of the competence of the LOS Tribunal to cases involving non-State parties warrant the construction of a whole additional judicial system to deal with LOS Convention problems—especially when the new Tribunal is not given an exclusive jurisdiction over such questions? That question appears to have occasioned little, if any, specific discussion in the LOS Conference. Now that one can, admittedly with the benefit of hindsight, review the situation with more detachment and see how transient was the impact of the *South West Africa* judgment, one may well wonder whether some of the effort that went into constructing a tribunal that so closely parallels the ICJ could not have been better employed in determining how the Statute of the ICJ itself might have been revised to enable that body to deal with these additional categories of cases. It is sometimes difficult to reject the thought that a number of States—once the proposal for a new tribunal had been launched by the United States—accorded an undeclared priority to creating twenty-one more judicial posts in the world. If this is the reason for the establishment of the new LOS Tribunal, it is not a sufficient one.

The international community would do well to consider whether, even at this late stage, and within the framework of the Decade of International Law that is to run from now to 2000, there would not be advantage in amending the Statute of the ICJ so as also to permit access to the Court in the limited class of cases that seems to be the only advance that the LOS Tribunal has to offer over the ICJ. If such amendments to the Statute of the ICJ were to be made, the Law of the Sea Treaty could at the same time—perhaps even as part of the same process—be amended to delete the provisions for the establishment and operation of the LOS Tribunal. The justification for such a development would not lie simply in the considerable financial savings that would be achieved (though they should not be lightly dismissed), nor in the elimination of a risk of diversity of approach and substantive decision between two major international tribunals. The real justification would lie in the simple good sense of not doing something unnecessary.

## *Note*

The establishment of an international criminal court to try individuals accused of international crimes has been under consideration by the United Nations for several decades. See Bridge, The Case for an International Court of Criminal Justice and the Formulation of International Criminal Law, in International Courts for the Twenty-First Century 213–231 (Janis, ed., 1992). The principal reason for the establishment of an international criminal court is that "since 1945 notorious cases of crimes against humanity * * * have gone unpublished * * * and in many cases, serious crimes against peace or humanity have been committed by persons who were at the time members of the Government of a State." Report of the International Law Commission 1992, G.A.O.R. 47th Sess., Supp. No. 10, at 155–56. The Working Group to the Commission has recommended that an international criminal court "should not have compulsory jurisdiction, in the sense of a general jurisdiction which a State party to the Statute is obliged to accept *ipso facto* and without further agreement. Nor would it have exclusive jurisdiction, in the sense of a jurisdiction which excludes the concurrent jurisdiction of States in criminal cases. It should not be a full-time body, but rather an established structure which could be called into operation when required." Id. at 161–62.

In 1992, the U.N. Security Council adopted Resolution 780, which calls on states to collect information on grave breaches of humanitarian law occurring in the hostilities in the former Yugoslavia for possible use in special courts set up to try individuals accused of war crimes. See Chapter 11, p. 1031 infra, for an account of the War Crimes Tribunal established by the Security Council to hear allegations of serious violations of international humanitarian law in connection with the continuing fighting in the former Yugoslavia.

# Chapter 11

# THE USE OF FORCE

## SECTION 1. THE USE OF FORCE BETWEEN STATES

### A. THE TRADITIONAL LAW

The international system consists principally of states, defined politically and territorially (see Chapter 4, Section 1, p. 246 supra), and in principle implies the autonomy of every state, both its freedom from coercion and the integrity of its territory. All invasions of either a state's independence or of its territory have sometimes been subsumed in the term "intervention." The extreme form of intervention, of course, is resort to armed force to conquer another state's territory, sometimes even to swallow it and terminate its existence as a state.

The traditional law governing uses of force and resort to war was radically transformed by the U.N. Charter. In particular respects, however, it is not agreed whether the traditional law survived or was modified by the Charter. The traditional law as it relates to the permissible uses of force in peacetime is presented in Section 1A; the changes effected by the Charter are discussed in Section 1C. For the Law of War, as it was before the Charter and as it is today, see Section 4A.

#### INTERVENTION

*HENKIN, HOW NATIONS BEHAVE*

153–54 (2d ed. 1979).*

Every nation resists interference in its affairs, and no nation admits that it has in fact interfered in another's affairs. Indeed, many of the acts specifically prohibited by international law are forms of foreign intervention or other improper interference, e.g., aggression, lesser territorial intrusions,

* Reprinted by permission of Columbia University Press.

forms of espionage; in addition, customary international law prohibits "intervention" generally. By treaty and in various declarations and resolutions of international bodies, nations have unanimously and repeatedly accepted absolute prohibitions on "intervention" in the affairs of other states.

Prohibitions of intervention and interference, it should be clear, are part of the quest for an ideal of equally sovereign and independent nations. Complete independence is, of course, an illusory goal; if, indeed, it was ever otherwise, today the interdependence of all nations is a commonplace. Some act of any nation may reverberate everywhere. Big powers, in particular, affect domestic affairs in other nations by their mere existence. American political and economic policies, whether of action or inaction, may "intervene" in the national life of other states as effectively as would sending the Marines. In a sense, to "intervene" to influence the policy of another government is the very purpose of all diplomacy and of all international agreements. International society could not deal with all these interventions by general "rule" even if it wished to. The broadest of the prohibitions on intervention has never been held to reach every action that clearly affected the interests or "independence" of other nations. There has been little success, however, in defining or enumerating the forms of intervention that are forbidden; many nations have been particularly reluctant to agree to any suggestion or implication that intervention—by any means, for any purpose—was permissible.

### *Note*

"Intervention" is a concept of uncertain legal significance. "Unfortunately there is no satisfactory agreement among jurists as to the meaning and content of intervention in international law. Not only the authorities, but also the practices of states are in confusion." Thomas and Thomas, Non–Intervention 67 (1956). Many writers employ the term in the sense of "dictatorial interference" by a state in the internal or external affairs of another state, which usually involves a threat or use of force. Cf., e.g., id. at 68; 1 Oppenheim 305; Brierly, The Law of Nations 402 (6th ed. Waldock, 1963); Hyde 245–47. See generally Intervention in World Politics (Bull, ed. 1984). The term has too often been used also for other attempts by one state to influence another state, for any purpose, by any means. Although among jurists there has long been a wide consensus that intervention in the strict sense is a violation of a state's sovereignty and generally contrary to international law, there have been many instances of such intervention in the practice of states.

Even before the U.N. Charter, there was little agreement as to the exceptional circumstances that may justify intervention. Among such circumstances suggested have been threats to the safety of nationals of the intervening state, previous unlawful intervention or threat of intervention by another state, chronic disregard by a state of its international obligations, the needs of self-defense or self-preservation of the intervening state, and collective decision to put an end to inhumane treatment by a government of all or some of its own nationals (humanitarian intervention). The legal sufficiency of most of these circumstances as justification for intervention has been challenged. The legality of extending armed assistance to a government at its request against its domestic opponents also remains highly controversial and may not be regarded as "intervention" under some definitions.

On unilateral intervention for humanitarian purposes, see p. 930 infra; on collective intervention under the authority of the United Nations, notably of the Security Council, see p. 962 infra.

### *1. Permissible Coercive Measures and Uses of Force Short of War*

States have traditionally utilized coercive measures short of war in attempting to prevail in disputes with other states. The severance of diplomatic relations is one such measure. The maintenance of such relations is not required by international law, and the severance of such relations is therefore not contrary to international law. See Restatement (Third) § 203(3), § 905, Comment *a*; Stone, Legal Controls of International Conflict 288 (rev. ed. 1959). See also Chapter 7, Section 7, pp. 570–83, on countermeasures and self-help.

## RETORSION

A variety of coercive measures may be encompassed within the term "retorsion," which refers to measures that are "unfriendly" but are not prohibited by international law, taken by one state against another in response to a perceived offense (whether or not the offense is a violation of an international norm). The First Hickenlooper Amendment to the U.S. Foreign Assistance Act is commonly cited as an instance of retorsion. 77 Stat. 386 (1963), 78 Stat. 1013 (1964), as amended, 22 U.S.C.A. § 2370(e). Other forms of retorsion include: the shutting of ports to vessels of an unfriendly state, imposition of travel restrictions or denial of entry visas for its nationals, revocation of tariff concessions not guaranteed by treaty (or other trade restrictions), the display of naval forces near the waters of an unfriendly state. For a detailed account of several recent acts of retorsion, see von Glahn, Law Among Nations[:] An Introduction to Public International Law 637–40 (6th ed. 1992).

## REPRISAL

### *HACKWORTH, DIGEST OF INTERNATIONAL LAW*

Vol. 6, 154–55 (1943).

On October 19, 1914 a German official and two German officers from German Southwest Africa were killed at the Portuguese post of Naulilaa in Angola under the following circumstances: A party of Germans had crossed into Angola to discuss with the Portuguese authorities the importation of food supplies into German Southwest Africa. Due to difficulties in interpreting, misunderstandings arose between the parties. In the course of a discussion a Portuguese officer seized the bridle of a German official's horse and the official struck him. At that time a German officer drew his pistol. The Portuguese officer ordered his men to fire and the official and two officers were killed. Portuguese authorities subsequently interned the German interpreter and a German soldier. The authorities of German Southwest Africa did not communicate with the Portuguese authorities, but in alleged reprisal for the incident German troops attacked and destroyed certain forts and posts in Angola. These events took place prior to the entry of Portugal into the World War. After the war, the Portuguese Government claimed damages on account of the incident. Alois de Meuron, a Swiss lawyer, was designated on August 15, 1920 as arbitrator to determine in conformance with paragraph 4 of the annex to articles 297–298 of the Treaty of Versailles the amount of the Portuguese claims. On February 9, 1928 two other arbitrators, both Swiss nationals, Robert Guex and Robert Fazy, were added to the tribunal. In an award rendered July 31, 1928 the arbitrators stated that the death of the German official and of the two German officers was not the consequence of an act contrary to the law of nations on the part of the Portuguese authorities. They declared that the *sine qua non* of the right to exercise reprisals is a motive furnished by a preliminary act contrary to the law of nations and that, even had such an act on the part of the Portuguese authorities been established, the German argument that the reprisals were justified would have been rejected because reprisals are only permissible when they have been preceded by an unsatisfied demand. The use of force, they stated, is only justified by necessity. They also stated that, even if it were admitted that the law of nations does not demand that reprisals be in approximate proportion to the offense, it would, nevertheless, certainly be necessary to consider as excessive and illegal reprisals out of all proportion to the act motivating them. They found that there was obvious disproportion between the incident at Naulilaa and the reprisals which followed, and defined reprisals as follows:

> "Reprisals are an act of self-help (Selbsthilfehandlung) on the part of the injured state, an act corresponding *after an unsatisfied demand* to an act contrary to the law of nations on the part of the offending state. They have the effect of momentarily suspending, in the relations between the two states, the observance of such or such a rule of the law of nations. They are limited by the experiences of humanity and the rules of good faith applicable in relations between state and state. They would be illegal if a preliminary act contrary to the law of nations had not furnished a reason for them. * * *" [Translation.]

For the tribunal's full opinion, see 2 U.N.Rep.Int'l Arb.Awards 1011 (1949).

## *Note*

Compare the Joint Resolution of April 22, 1914, relating to the occupation of Veracruz, which stated that "the President is justified in the employment of the armed forces of the United States to enforce his demands for unequivocal amends for certain affronts and indignities committed against the United States" by Mexico. The Resolution further stated that "the United States disclaims any hostility to the Mexican people or any purpose to make war upon Mexico." 38 Stat. 770. See 1 Hackworth at 151; 6 Hackworth at 152.

## SELF-DEFENSE

## THE CAROLINE

2 Moore, Digest of International Law 412 (1906).

[During an insurrection in Canada in 1837, the insurgents secured recruits and supplies from the American side of the border. There was an encampment of one thousand armed men organized at Buffalo, and located at Navy Island in Upper Canada; there was another encampment of insurgents at Black Rock, on the American side. The Caroline was a small steamer employed by these encampments. On December 29, 1837, while moored at Schlosser, on the American side of the Niagara River, and while occupied by some thirty-three American citizens, the steamer was boarded by an armed body of men from the Canadian side, who attacked the occupants. The latter merely endeavored to escape. Several were wounded; one was killed on the dock; only twenty-one were afterwards accounted for. The attacking party fired the steamer and set her adrift over Niagara Falls. In 1841, upon the arrest and detention of one Alexander McLeod, in New York, on account of his alleged participation in the destruction of the vessel, Lord Palmerston avowed responsibility for the destruction of the Caroline as a public act of force in self-defense, by persons in the British service. He therefore demanded McLeod's release. McLeod was, however, tried in New York, and acquitted. In 1842 the two Governments agreed on principle that the requirements of self-defense might necessitate the use of force. Mr. Webster, Secretary of State, denied, however, that the necessity existed in this particular case, while Lord Ashburton, the British Minister, apologized for the invasion of American territory. Said Mr. Webster in the course of a communication to the British Minister, August 6, 1842 *:]

The President sees with pleasure that your Lordship fully admits those great principles of public law, applicable to cases of this kind, which this government has expressed; and that on your part, as on ours, respect for the inviolable character of the territory of independent states is the most essential foundation of civilization. And while it is admitted on both sides that there are exceptions to this rule, he is gratified to find that your Lordship admits that such exceptions must come within the limitations stated and the terms used in a former communication from this department to the British plenipotentiary here. Undoubtedly it is just, that, while it is admitted that exceptions growing out of the great law of self-defense do exist, those exceptions should be confined to cases in which the "necessity of that self-defence is instant, overwhelming, and leaving no choice of means, and no moment for deliberation."

### *Notes*

1. *Proportionality.* In an earlier letter to the British authorities, Mr. Webster included a requirement of proportionality: "It will be for [Her Majesty's Government] to show, also, that the local authorities of Canada, even supposing the necessity of the moment authorized them to enter the territories of The United States at all, did nothing unreasonable or excessive; since the act, justified by the necessity of self-defence, must be limited by that necessity, and kept clearly within it." Mr. Webster to Mr. Fox (April 24, 1841), 29 British and Foreign State Papers 1129, 1138 (1857).

* The statement of facts is taken from Hyde, International Law 239 (1945). [Ed.]

2. *Self-defense under the U.N. Charter.* For the law as to self-defense since the U.N. Charter, see p. 911 infra. See generally Greenwood, Self-Defence and the Conduct of International Armed Conflict, in International Law at a Time of Perplexity: Essays in Honour of Shabtai Rosenne 273 (Dinstein, ed. 1989).

## 2. *War in Traditional International Law*

## WAR AS A LAWFUL INSTRUMENT OF NATIONAL POLICY

### *OPPENHEIM, INTERNATIONAL LAW*

Vol. 2, 177–78 (7th ed. Lauterpacht, 1952).*

Prior to the General Treaty for the Renunciation of War the institution of war fulfilled in International Law two contradictory functions. In the absence of an international organ for enforcing the law, war was a means of self-help for giving effect to claims based or alleged to be based on International Law. Such was the legal and moral authority of this notion of war as an arm of the law that in most cases in which war was in fact resorted to in order to increase the power and the possessions of a State at the expense of others, it was described by the States in question as undertaken for the defence of a legal right. This conception of war was intimately connected with the distinction, which was established in the formative period of International Law and which never became entirely extinct, between just and unjust wars. At the same time, however, that distinction was clearly rejected in the conception of war as a legally recognised instrument for challenging and changing rights based on existing International Law. In the absence of an international legislature it fulfilled the function of adapting the law to changed conditions. Moreover, quite apart from thus supplying a crude substitute for a deficiency in international organisation, war was recognised as a legally admissible instrument for attacking and altering existing rights of States independently of the objective merits of the attempted change. As Hyde, writing in 1922, said: "It always lies within the power of a State * * * to gain political or other advantages over another, not merely by the employment of force, but also by direct recourse to war." International Law did not consider as illegal a war admittedly waged for such purposes. It rejected, to that extent, the distinction between just and unjust wars. War was in law a natural function of the State and a prerogative of its uncontrolled sovereignty.

### *Note*

"It was not a cynic who once suggested that international law establishes order in unimportant matters but not in important ones. Doubtless, the comment referred in particular to the anomaly of international law before our times, which set up rules about international conduct in time of peace but did not forbid nations to commit the ultimate 'aggression' against international order, the resort to war. That incongruity had its explanations, principally in the failure of early attempts to distinguish just wars (to be permitted, even encouraged) from unjust wars (to be outlawed). Third nations also wished to avoid becoming involved in the wars of others and wished to go their way in relation to both belligerent sides without having to decide which was in 'the right.' And, in

* Footnotes omitted. Reprinted by permission of Langsmans, Green & Co., Publisher.

fact, one cannot say that the anomaly nullified international law. Indeed, nations were more likely to observe the international law of peace, knowing that if their interests were too gravely jeopardized they could go to war to vindicate them and establish a new basis for new relations in a revised international order with different international obligations." Henkin, How Nations Behave 135–36 (2d ed. 1979).*

If states were not prepared to go to war in its legal sense, whether for reasons given by Henkin or for other reasons, they remained bound by the legal restraints on resort to force expressed in rules such as those on non-intervention, reprisal, and self-defense. See Waldock, The Regulation of the Use of Force by Individual States, 81 Rec. des Cours 457 (1952); Brownlie, International Law and the Use of Force by States 21 (1963).

## THE STATE OF WAR IN INTERNATIONAL LAW

The concern of states to regulate the conduct and the impact of war was an early impetus to the development of international law. The first systematic international law treatise, that of Grotius, was entitled *De Jure Belli Ac Pacis (Of the Law of War and Peace).* International law writers postulated a dichotomy between war and peace and distinguished laws for nations at peace from laws for nations at war. "Belligerent" states, those at war, had the duty to observe the rules of war, and to respect the neutrality of non-belligerent states. These rules were designed to limit the spread of armed conflict and to promote a modicum of humanity in battle. Neutral states were expected to follow the relevant rules if they were to avoid the conflict. See p. 875 below.

In order to determine whether the rules of war or of neutrality applied it was necessary to determine whether a state of war existed between states. Such a determination was not always easy to make. State practice during the nineteenth century suggests that a state of war resulted when one party declared war or intended a state of war to exist. This practice provided states obvious advantages. If a state of war did not exist unless war was declared or intended, a state could refrain from declaring war so as to avoid the necessity of complying with the laws of war. Also, other nations could not then invoke the laws of neutrality. Some writers argued for an objective test, notably evidence of large-scale fighting. This view seemed more realistic as states began to initiate and engage in hostilities without formal declarations of war. For a critical discussion of the concept of war, see Grob, The Relativity of War and Peace (1949). On the difficulty of determining when armed hostilities constituted war, see Brownlie, International Law and the Use of Force by States 38–40 (1963). In cases of civil war, the concept of belligerency traditionally determined the application of the laws of war and neutrality: only when revolutionary factions attained the status of "belligerents" did the traditional laws come into play. In recent times, however, the practice of formally recognizing a state of belligerency fell into disuse. See p. 940 below.

Early in the Twentieth Century, new interest in defining war was stimulated by agreements to outlaw war as a method of settling disputes—the League of Nations Covenant and the Pact of Paris. See Treaty Providing for the Renunciation of War as an Instrument of National Policy (Kellogg–Briand Treaty), Aug. 27, 1928, p. 879 below. Without a workable definition of "war," the limitations imposed by these treaties upon the parties could not be determined. See Eagleton, The Attempt to Define War, [1933] Int'l Conciliation No. 291.

## NEUTRALITY

### *OPPENHEIM, INTERNATIONAL LAW*

Vol. 2, 653–54 (7th ed. Lauterpacht, 1952).*

* * * Such States as do not take part in a war between other States are neutrals. The term "neutrality" is derived from the Latin *neuter*. Neutrality may be defined as the attitude of impartiality adopted by third States towards belligerents and recognised by belligerents, such attitude creating rights and duties between the impartial States and the belligerents. Whether or not a third State will adopt an attitude of impartiality at the outbreak of war is not a matter for International Law but for international politics. Therefore, unless a previous treaty stipulates it expressly, no duty exists for a State, according to International Law, to remain neutral when war breaks out. Every sovereign State, as an independent member of the Family of Nations, is master of its own resolutions, and the question of remaining neutral or not at the outbreak of war is, in the absence of a treaty stipulating otherwise, one of policy and not of law. However, all States which do not expressly declare the contrary by word or action are supposed to be neutral, and the rights and duties arising from neutrality come into existence, and remain in existence, through the mere fact of a State taking up an attitude of impartiality, and not being drawn into the war by the belligerents. A special assertion of intention to remain neutral is not, therefore, legally necessary on the part of neutral States, although they often expressly and formally proclaim their neutrality.

### *Notes*

1. Neutrality was a legal status accorded to certain non-belligerents. In order to qualify for treatment as a neutral, a state had to assume an attitude of impartiality toward the belligerents. Policies adopted by the neutral state had to be applied equally to all parties at war. See Harvard Research in International Law, Draft Convention on Rights and Duties of Neutral States in Naval and Aerial War, 33 A.J.I.L. Spec.Supp. 175, 232–34 (1939); Eagleton, The Duty of Impartiality on the Part of a Neutral, 34 A.J.I.L. 99 (1940). In return for assuming the duty of impartiality toward belligerents, the neutral was guaranteed the inviolability of his territory and freedom from belligerent acts. On the early development of the law of neutrality, see Jessup & Deak, Neutrality, Volume I: The Origins (1935); 2 Oppenheim at 623–42; Örvik, The Decline of Neutrality 1914–1941 11–37 (1953); Hall, The Rights and Duties of Neutrals

* Footnotes omitted. Reprinted by permission of Langsmans, Green & Co., Publisher.

(1874). On the Declaration of Paris, see 2 Oppenheim at 460–63; Stone at 457; Smith, The Declaration of Paris in Modern War, 55 L.Q.Rev. 237 (1939).

2. The Hague Peace Conferences of 1899 and 1907 led to two conventions defining the rights of neutrals. See Convention Respecting the Rights and Duties of Neutral Powers and Persons in Case of War on Land, Oct. 18, 1907, 36 Stat. 2310, T.S. No. 540; Convention Concerning the Rights and Duties of Neutral Powers in Naval War, Oct. 18, 1907, 36 Stat. 2415, T.S. No. 545. As of January 1, 1993, 34 states were party to the former Convention, 30 to the latter.

3. What were thought to be firm principles of the law of neutrality were repeatedly violated during the First and Second World Wars, particularly in regard to shipping, blockades and confiscation of properties. On long-range blockades generally, see Tucker, The Law of War and Neutrality at Sea 278–82, 316–17 (International Law Studies of the Naval War College, 1957); McDougal & Feliciano, Law and Minimum World Public Order 484–88 (1961); Alford, Modern Economic Warfare (International Law Studies of the Naval War College, 1963); Medlicott, The Economic Blockade (Vol. 1, 1952; Vol. 2, 1959). See also Smith, The Law and Custom of the Sea 131–37 (3d ed. 1959).

4. *Neutrality and the U.N. Charter.* For a discussion of neutrality under the U.N. Charter see p. 940 infra.

## B. PRE-UNITED NATIONS EFFORTS TO DISCOURAGE OR OUTLAW WAR

### HAGUE CONVENTION II

*CONVENTION RESPECTING THE LIMITATION OF THE EMPLOYMENT OF FORCE FOR THE RECOVERY OF CONTRACT DEBTS, SIGNED AT THE HAGUE, OCTOBER 18, 1907*

36 Stat. 2241, T.S. 537.

* * *

ARTICLE 1

The contracting Powers agree not to have recourse to armed force for the recovery of contract debts claimed from the Government of one country by the Government of another country as being due to its nationals.

This undertaking is, however, not applicable when the debtor State refuses or neglects to reply to an offer of arbitration, or, after accepting the offer, prevents any *compromis* from being agreed on, or, after the arbitration, fails to submit to the award. * * *

### THE LEAGUE OF NATIONS

*BOWETT, THE LAW OF INTERNATIONAL INSTITUTIONS*

17–18 (4th ed. 1982).*

The creation of a league of States, dedicated to the maintenance of peace, had long been advocated in philosophical and juristic writings and in

 Footnotes omitted.

the aims of private organisations. The immediate source of the League of Nations was, however, a proposal introduced at the Peace Conference of Paris in 1919. In the drafting of the Covenant of the League the major powers played the decisive role; it emerged as a fusion of President Wilson's third draft and the British proposals emanating from the Phillimore Committee.

The League's objective was "to promote international co-operation and to achieve international peace and security." The system of collective security envisaged in the Covenant rested, essentially, on the notions of disarmament (Art. 8), pacific settlement of disputes and the outlawry of war (Arts. 11–15), a collective guarantee of the independence of each member (Art. 10), and sanctions (Arts. 16 and 17). The League's disarmament programme failed dismally. As envisaged in the Covenant, the pacific settlement of disputes likely to lead to a rupture of the peace was obligatory; parties to the dispute could choose to go to arbitration, judicial settlement or to the Council of the League. It was obligatory to accept the award or a unanimous report of the Council and an obligation on all members not to go to war with any State so accepting. The members agreed to respect and preserve the "territorial integrity and existing political independence" of all members against external aggression. War, as such, was not made illegal but only where begun without complying with the requirements of the Covenant with regard to prior resort to pacific settlement of the dispute. A State resorting to war in violation of its undertaking with regard to pacific settlement was deemed to have committed an act of war against all other members. Yet it was left to each member to decide whether a breach had occurred or an act of war had been committed, so that even the obligation to apply economic sanctions under Article 16(1) was dependent on the member's own view of the situation. Military sanctions could be recommended by the Council, but the decision on whether to apply them rested with each member.

Such was the system; in itself a not unworkable one. After an initial success in dealing with the Graeco–Bulgarian crisis of 1925, and a less spectacular achievement in the Chaco dispute of 1928, the League witnessed the invasion of Manchuria in 1931, the Italo–Abyssinian War of 1934–35, the German march into the Rhineland in 1936, into Austria in 1938, into Czechoslovakia in 1939, the Soviet Union's invasion of Finland in 1939 and, finally, the German invasion of Poland in 1939. Apart from half-hearted economic sanctions against Italy in 1935, no sanctions were ever really applied by the League. To this extent the failure of the League was due, not to the inadequacies of the Covenant, but to the apathy and reluctance of the member States to discharge their obligations.

## *COVENANT OF THE LEAGUE OF NATIONS, JUNE 28, 1919*

1 Hudson International Legislation 1 (1931).

* * *

### ARTICLE XVI

Should any Member of the League resort to war in disregard of its covenants under Articles 12, 13 or 15, it shall *ipso facto* be deemed to have committed an act of war against all other Members of the League, which hereby undertake immediately to subject it to the severance of all trade or financial relations, the prohibition of all intercourse between their nationals and the nationals of the covenant-breaking State, and the prevention of all financial, commercial or personal intercourse between the nationals of the covenant-breaking State and the nationals of any other State, whether a Member of the League or not.

It shall be the duty of the Council in such case to recommend to the several Governments concerned what effective military, naval or air force the Members of the League shall severally contribute to the armed forces to be used to protect the covenants of the League.

The Members of the League agree, further, that they will mutually support one another in the financial and economic measures which are taken under this Article, in order to minimise the loss and inconvenience resulting from the above measures, and that they will mutually support one another in resisting any special measures aimed at one of their number by the covenant-breaking State, and that they will take the necessary steps to afford passage through their territory to the forces of any of the Members of the League which are co-operating to protect the covenants of the League.

* * *

### *Note*

*Failure of the Covenant.* The provisions of Article 16 of the Covenant were given their decisive test in the War between Italy and Abyssinia (Ethiopia). Italy invaded Abyssinia on October 3, 1935. Despite the absence of any procedural provisions in the Covenant, machinery for the implementation of Article 16 was swiftly devised. The League Council, after hearing the plea of Abyssinia, appointed a Committee of Six to draw up a report. On October 11, the Council adopted the report of the Committee which had found that the Italian Government had resorted to war in violation of the Covenant. Within sixteen days of the outbreak of war the League drew up a series of proposals suggesting to its members the implementation of embargoes extending to arms, financial credit, exports and imports and calling for mutual economic help to those innocent countries adversely affected by the embargo. The sanctions, however, fell short in many ways of those prescribed in Article 16 of the Covenant. Due to weakness and vacillation on the part of Britain and France, the export embargo did not extend to coal, steel and oil, the commodities most vital to Italy. The subsequent refusal of the League to take further measures when the initial sanctions proved inadequate exposed its impotence. In the face of British, French and Russian fears of war with Italy, the controversial oil embargo was never adopted.

The failure of the League to prevent the obvious aggression of Italy and to deal effectively with the aggressor undermined the credibility of a regime of international law under which war was to be abolished as an instrument of national policy. The standard used in assessing aggression is discussed in Wright, The Test of Aggression in the Italo–Ethiopian War, 30 A.J.I.L. 45 (1936). For a description of the League actions, see Spencer, The Italian–Ethiopian Dispute and the League of Nations, 31 A.J.I.L. 614 (1937). The relevant documents are set forth in League of Nations—Dispute Between Ethiopia and Italy, 30 A.J.I.L. Supp. 1 (1936).

On the League of Nations generally, see Walters, A History of the League of Nations (1960); Scott, The Rise and Fall of the League of Nations (1973); Joyce, Broken Star: The Story of the League of Nations, 1919–1939 (1978); Ostrower, Collective Insecurity: The United States and the League of Nations During the Early Thirties (1979); The League of Nations in Retrospect: Proceedings of the Symposium (1983); Northedge, The League of Nations: Its Life and Times, 1920–1946 (1986).

### *GENERAL TREATY FOR THE RENUNCIATION OF WAR (KELLOGG–BRIAND PACT)*

August 27, 1928, 46 Stat. 2343, 94 L.N.T.S. 57.

Art. I. The High Contracting Parties solemnly declare in the names of their respective peoples that they condemn recourse to war for the solution of international controversies, and renounce it as an instrument of national policy in their relations with one another.

Art. II. The High Contracting Parties agree that the settlement or solution of all disputes or conflicts of whatever nature or of whatever origin they may be, which may arise among them, shall never be sought except by pacific means.

#### *Notes*

1. The treaty became effective on July 24, 1929, is still in force and some new states, e.g., Barbados and Fiji, have adhered to it. As of January 1, 1993, 66 states were parties.

2. The "Saavedra Lamas Treaty," signed by certain American states at Rio de Janeiro on October 10, 1933, and by the U.S. in 1934, condemns wars of aggression and provides in Article 1 that "the settlement of disputes or controversies of any kind * * * shall be effected only by the pacific means which shall have the sanction of international law." 6 Hackworth at 9.

## THE NUREMBERG CHARTER AND TRIALS

An International Military Tribunal was established at the end of World War II by the London Agreement among the United States of America, the French Republic, the United Kingdom of Great Britain and Northern Ireland, and the Union of Soviet Socialist Republics "for the trial of war criminals whose offenses have no particular geographical location whether they be accused individually or in their capacity as members of organizations or groups or in both capacities." The original indictment presented to the Tribunal on October 6, 1945, charged the German defendants under Article VI of the Charter of the International Military Tribunal with committing Crimes against the Peace, War Crimes and Crimes against Humanity. An additional charge which merged with the others alleged that the defendants had planned and conspired to commit these same acts.

Crimes against the Peace were defined by Article VI as:

> planning, preparation, initiation, or waging of a war of aggression, or a war in violation of international treaties, agreements, assurances, or

participation in a common plan or conspiracy for the accomplishment of any of the foregoing.

The Charter and the subsequent judgment never adopted a definition of aggressive war. Although the United States representative tried to have such a definition included in the Charter, his efforts were rebuffed. In the end, the Tribunal apparently accepted the argument that the acts perpetrated by Germany speak for themselves; that under any seriously propounded definition of aggression the German leaders were guilty.

Since one of the central concerns of the Nuremberg Tribunal was the imputation of individual criminal responsibility, its use of the concept of aggressive war was influenced by the notion of a criminal conspiracy. Both the proof by the prosecution and the judgment of the Tribunal detail how the Nazi leaders in deliberate fashion planned the Second World War. The judgment describes the seizure of power by the Nazi Party, the intentions of its leaders, and finally the specific aggressive acts of the government. Aggressive war in these terms was the pursuit of an expansionist policy through deliberate criminal acts.

## JUDGMENT OF THE INTERNATIONAL MILITARY TRIBUNAL

Nuremberg, Sept. 30, 1946, reprinted in, 41 A.J.I.L. 186–218 (1946).

The charges in the Indictment that the defendants planned and waged aggressive wars are charges of the utmost gravity. War is essentially an evil thing. Its consequences are not confined to the belligerent states alone, but affect the whole world.

To initiate a war of aggression, therefore, is not only an international crime; it is the supreme international crime differing only from other war crimes in that it contains within itself the accumulated evil of the whole.

The first acts of aggression referred to in the Indictment are the seizure of Austria and Czechoslovakia; and the first war of aggression charged in the Indictment is the war against Poland begun on the 1st September 1939.

Before examining that charge it is necessary to look more closely at some of the events which preceded these acts of aggression. The war against Poland did not come suddenly out of an otherwise clear sky; the evidence has made it plain that this war of aggression, as well as the seizure of Austria and Czechoslovakia, was premeditated and carefully prepared, and was not undertaken until the moment was thought opportune for it to be carried through as a definite part of the preordained scheme and plan.

For the aggressive designs of the Nazi Government were not accidents arising out of the immediate political situation in Europe and the world; they were a deliberate and essential part of Nazi foreign policy.

From the beginning, the National Socialist movement claimed that its object was to unite the German people in the consciousness of their mission and destiny, based on inherent qualities of race, and under the guidance of the Fuehrer.

For its achievement, two things were deemed to be essential: The disruption of the European order as it has existed since the Treaty of Versailles, and the creation of a Greater Germany beyond the frontiers of 1914. This necessarily involved the seizure of foreign territories.

War was seen to be inevitable, or at the very least, highly probable, if these purposes were to be accomplished. The German people, therefore, with all their resources, were to be organized as a great political-military army, schooled to obey without question any policy decreed by the State. * * *

The Charter defines as a crime the planning or waging of war that is a war of aggression or a war in violation of international treaties. The Tribunal has decided that certain of the defendants planned and waged aggressive wars against 12 nations, and were therefore guilty of this series of crimes. This makes it unnecessary to discuss the subject in further detail, or even to consider at any length the extent to which these aggressive wars were also "wars in violation of international treaties, agreements, or assurances."

These treaties are set out in Appendix C of the Indictment. * * *

The jurisdiction of the Tribunal is defined in the Agreement and Charter, and the crimes coming within the jurisdiction of the Tribunal, for which there shall be individual responsibility, are set out in Article 6. The law of the Charter is decisive, and binding upon the Tribunal. * * *

The Charter makes the planning or waging of a war of aggression or a war in violation of international treaties a crime; and it is therefore not strictly necessary to consider whether and to what extent aggressive war was a crime before the execution of the London Agreement. * * *

The question is, what was the legal effect of this [the Kellogg–Briand] Pact? The nations who signed the pact or adhered to it unconditionally condemned recourse to war for the future as an instrument of policy, and expressly renounced it. After the signing of the Pact, any nation resorting to war as an instrument of national policy breaks the Pact. In the opinion of the Tribunal, the solemn renunciation of war as an instrument of national policy necessarily involves the proposition that such a war is illegal in international law; and that those who plan and wage such a war, with its inevitable and terrible consequences, are committing a crime in so doing. War for the solution of international controversies undertaken as an instrument of national policy certainly includes a war of aggression, and such a war is therefore outlawed by the Pact. * * *

### *Notes*

1. *Aggressive wars.* The Tribunal, following its Charter, distinguishes a war of aggression from one in breach of international agreements, but deals only briefly with the latter. Appendix C to the indictment sets out the various agreements which Germany is charged with having breached.

The defense argued on behalf of the German defendants that although a nation could not wage aggressive war without transgressing international law, it could use war as an instrument of self-defense, and that the nation itself must be the sole judge of whether its actions were in self-defense. If action in self-defense is permissible, who is to judge when a nation is an aggressor? Is it realistic to outlaw aggressive war without providing for a tribunal to arbitrate whether a particular course of conduct is aggressive? In rejecting the plea of self-defense, the Tribunal adopted the test stated in the *Caroline* case, p. 872 supra.

The International Military Tribunal was criticized as necessarily biased since the victors could not impartially judge their adversaries. For example, it was pointed out that although the German "invasion" of Poland was found to be aggressive, this action by the Germans was executed in concert with the Union of Soviet Socialist Republics which was never accused of aggressive conduct before the International Military Tribunal. For a survey of the "aggressive" acts of the various governments, see Hankey, Politics, Trials and Errors 10–16 (1950).

It has also been argued that the question of aggression is so predominantly a political question that it should be settled through the political arm of government, not by a court. Instead of the Nuremberg procedure should there have been a determination by the Allies that Germany was the aggressor and appropriate political measures taken against its leaders?

Could a defeated nation ever hope to punish the leaders of a victorious aggressor nation? Would a victorious aggressor, or nations involved in wars where there is no clear victor, ever submit to the jurisdiction of an international tribunal with the possibility that their leaders might be declared perpetrators of crimes against the peace?

2. *The trial generally.* See, in general, Agreement for the Prosecution and Punishment of the Major War Criminals of the European Axis (the London Agreement), 59 Stat. 1544, 82 U.N.T.S. 279; Taylor, Nuremberg Trials, [1949] Int'l Conciliation No. 450, at 243; Memorandum submitted by the Secretary-General, The Charter and Judgment of the Nürnberg Tribunal, U.N.Doc. A/ACN. 4/5 (1949); Hankey, Politics, Trials and Errors (1950); Taylor, The Nuremberg Trials, 55 Colum.L.Rev. 488 (1955); Jackson, The Nürnberg Case (1947); Wright, The Law of the Nuremberg Trial, 41 A.J.I.L. 38 (1947); Finch, The Nuremberg Trial and International Law, 41 A.J.I.L. 20 (1947); Jessup, Crime of Aggression, 62 Pol.Sci.Q. 1 (1947); Schick, Crimes Against the Peace, 38 J.Crim.L. & Crim. 445 (1948). The Charter of the Tribunal—the underlying jurisdictional document—was annexed to the London Agreement, supra. For the Indictment, see U.S. Dep't of State, Trial of War Criminals 23 (Dep't of State pub. no. 2420, European Ser. No. 10, 1945). A similar Tribunal was established in the Far East. For a discussion of the Tokyo war crimes trials, in which several major Japanese leaders were found guilty and sentenced to death, see Keenan & Brown, Crimes against International Law (1950). The International Military Tribunals should not be confused with the tribunals convened by the various occupying powers under their own authority. The judgment of one of the latter tribunals is reproduced, in part at p. 880 supra.

3. *Nuremberg principles and Vietnam.* In United States v. Mitchell, 246 F.Supp. 874 (D.Conn.1965), the defendant, charged with having failed to report for induction as ordered, defended on the ground, *inter alia,* that the war in Vietnam was a war of aggression within the meaning of the Treaty of London, and that under the treaty he would be responsible for participating even though ordered to do so. The trial court charged the jury that the Treaty did not interfere "in any manner in respect to this defendant fulfilling his duty under this order." (Quoted at 386 U.S. 972, 87 S.Ct. 1162, 18 L.Ed.2d 132 (1967)). He was convicted and his conviction was affirmed, 369 F.2d 323 (2d Cir.1966); the

Supreme Court denied certiorari, Douglas J. dissenting from the denial of certiorari with a brief opinion, 386 U.S. 972, 87 S.Ct. 1162, 18 L.Ed.2d 132 (1967). See also the dissenting opinion of Justices Stewart and Douglas from the denial of certiorari in Mora v. McNamara, 389 U.S. 934, 88 S.Ct. 282, 19 L.Ed.2d 287 (1967).

Most of the cases arising out of the Vietnam war raised issues under the U.S. Constitution, but some also addressed arguments that the United States was violating international law. Some courts rejected the substantive arguments, some declared them to be "political questions" and non-justiciable. See Sugarman, Judicial Decisions Concerning the Constitutionality of United States Military Activity in Indo–China, 13 Colum.J.Transnat'l L. 470 (1974). See also Henkin, Viet Nam in the Courts of the United States: "Political Questions," 63 A.J.I.L. 284 (1969). See p. 178 supra on political questions.

4. *Nuremberg principles today.* There have been suggestions that an international tribunal be established and the President of Iraq and others be brought to trial for committing "crimes against the peace" by invading Kuwait in 1990. See Count I of the Draft Indictment of Saddam Hussein. Ad Hoc United Nations Criminal Tribunal v. Saddam Hussein and the Military, Political and Economic Advisors of Iraq, reprinted in, 20 Den.J.Int'l L. & Policy 91, 91–92 (1991); Beres Toward Prosecution of Iraqi Crimes Under International Law: Jurisprudential Foundations and Jurisdictional Choices, 22 Cal.W.Int'l L.J. 127 (1991–92): O'Brien, The Nuremberg Precedent and the Gulf War, 31 Vir.J.I.L. 391 (1991); Masterton, The Persian Gulf War Crimes Trials, [1991] Army Lawyer 7 (1991); Moore, War Crimes and the Rule of Law in the Gulf Crisis, 31 Va.J.I.L. 403 (1991).

What are the prospects for future application of the concept of "crimes against the peace?" See p. 1031 below for an account of the War Crimes Tribunal established in 1993 to try serious breaches of humanitarian law in the former Yugoslavia.

See generally, Taylor, The Anatomy of the Nuremberg Trials: A Personal Memoir (1992); Harris, A Call For An International War Crimes Court: Learning From Nuremberg, 23 U.Toledo L.Rev. 229 (1992); Lippman, Nuremberg: 45 years later, 7 Conn.J.Int'l L. 1, 30–32 (1991). For earlier analysis see Schick, The Nuremberg Trial and the International Law of the Future, 41 A.J.I.L. 770 (1947); Janeczek, Nuremberg Judgement in the Light of International Law 126–31 (1949). See also Taylor, Nuremberg and Vietnam: An American Tragedy (1970).

5. *State responsibility.* The Nuremberg Charter sought to establish the individual responsibility of the Nazi leaders. For the view that a serious violation of an international obligation of critical importance for the maintenance of international peace and security may constitute an international crime for which a state may be criminally liable, see Article 19(3) of Part I of the Draft Articles on State Responsibility, provisionally adopted by the International Law Commission on its first reading, printed in [1980] II (Pt. 2) Y.B.Int'l Law Comm. 30. See generally, International Crimes of State: A Critical Analysis of the ILC's Draft Article 19 on State Responsibility (Weiler, Cassese & Spinedi, eds. 1989). On crimes against humanity generally, see Bassiouni, Crimes Against Humanity in International Criminal Law (1992).

## THE NUREMBERG AND THE U.N. CHARTERS

*TAYLOR, NUREMBERG & VIETNAM: AN AMERICAN TRAGEDY*

78–79 (1970).*

The United Nations and the Nuremberg trials were virtually twin offspring of the Allied negotiations and agreements with respect to the peace that would follow victory. It was at the Moscow Conference in October, 1943, that Eden, Hull and Molotov issued joint declarations pledging their countries to the establishment of an international organization to maintain peace and security, and to the post-war trial and punishment of German war criminals. It was at the San Francisco Conference in the spring of 1945 that the United Nations was organized, and that the first discussions looking to the establishment of an international war crimes tribunal were conducted among the four principal Allies—Britain, France, the Soviet Union and the United States. The Charter of the United Nations was signed at San Francisco on June 26, 1945, and the Agreement embodying the Charter of the International Military Tribunal was signed on August 8, 1945, at London.

Different as the twins were, they shared the same two basic purposes: promoting peaceful rather than warlike settlement of international disputes, and humanitarian governmental policies. Thus the Charter of the United Nations declared the organization's purposes to be "the prevention and removal of threats to the peace * * * and the suppression of acts of aggression or other breaches of the peace," while the London Charter specified as "crimes against peace" the "planning, preparation, initiation, or waging of a war of aggression, or a war in violation of international treaties, agreements or assurances." The United Nations was dedicated to "encouraging respect for human rights and for fundamental freedoms for all without distinction as to race, sex, language, or religion," and the London Charter condemned not only "war crimes" but also "crimes against humanity," including "persecutions on political, racial, or religious grounds." Essentially, the Nuremberg trials were intended to bring the weight of law and criminal sanctions to bear in support of the peaceful and humanitarian principles that the United Nations was to promote by consultation and collective action. * * *

## C. THE UNITED NATIONS CHARTER

### *1. Overview*

## THE LAW OF THE CHARTER

The United Nations Charter laid the foundation of a "new world order" after the Allied victory in the Second World War. Originally an international agreement open only to states that had declared war against the Axis powers, it has become a universal agreement open to all states. Membership in the United Nations and adherence to the Charter have been the aim of every entity that aspired to and achieved statehood. Since the United Nations is open only to states, acceptance for membership constitutes com-

* Reprinted by permission of Random House.

pelling proof of statehood. Some older states that had not sought membership (e.g., the Principality of Liechtenstein) and other states that had been denied membership during the ideological conflict of the Cold War (e.g., North Korea) are likely to become members, rendering U.N. membership virtually universal; but a referendum in Switzerland in 1992 failed to support an application for U.N. membership.

The U.N. Charter declares the aims of the Charter and the purposes of the United Nations Organization. See the Preamble and Article 1. The Charter prescribes international norms outlawing the threat or use of force, the principal norms on which the new order stands, and now universally recognized as *jus cogens.* The Charter establishes the United Nations Organization to maintain international peace and security, as well as to promote friendly relations and international cooperation among nations in solving international problems of economic, social, cultural or humanitarian character and in promoting respect for human rights.

The principal legal norms of the Charter are contained in Articles 2(3) and 2(4). Article 2(3) commits members to settle their disputes by peaceful means. By Article 2(4) member states undertake to refrain from the threat or use of force against the territorial integrity or political independence of other states or in any other manner inconsistent with the purposes of the United Nations. See p. 890 infra.

The Charter does not attempt to outlaw only "war" or "aggression;" it prohibits the "threat or use of force," however it be characterized. Chapter VII of the Charter gives the U.N. Security Council authority to determine the existence of any threat to the peace, breach of peace or act of aggression and to make recommendations or decide what measures shall be taken to maintain or restore international peace or security. By Article 51, "[n]othing in the present Charter shall impair the inherent right of individual or collective self-defence if an armed attack occurs * * *." See p. 911 infra.

## THE UNITED NATIONS ORGANIZATION

The principal purpose of the United Nations Organization is "[t]o maintain international peace and security, and to that end: to take effective collective measures for the prevention and removal of threats to the peace, and for the suppression of acts of aggression or other breaches of the peace, and to bring about by peaceful means, and in conformity with the principles of justice and international law, adjustment or settlement of international disputes or situations which might lead to the breach of the peace * * *." U.N. Charter, Article 1(1). The members of the U.N. conferred primary responsibility for the maintenance of international peace and security on the U.N. Security Council. Id., Article 24 and Chapter VII. The United Nations has other purposes as well, and organs of the U.N. other than the Security Council have responsibility to further those purposes (as well as some role in maintaining international peace and security). Article 1 of the Charter specifically mentions as additional purposes the development of friendly relations among nations (Article 1(2)), and international cooperation in solving, economic, social, cultural, and humanitarian problems (Article 1(3)).

These areas of cooperation are elaborated in Chapters IX and X of the Charter.

A general limitation on the purposes and powers of the United Nations is laid down in Article 2(7) of the Charter: "Nothing contained in the present Charter shall authorize the United Nations to intervene in matters which are essentially within the domestic jurisdiction of any state." This provision, however, "shall not prejudice the application of enforcement measures under Chapter VII." Id.

The principal organs of the United Nations include the General Assembly, the Security Council, the Secretariat, and the International Court of Justice. Article 7(1) of the Charter lists also as principal organs the Economic and Social Council, which is concerned with cooperation on economic, social and cultural matters, including human rights (Article 62), and the Trusteeship Council. Pursuant to Article 7(2), subsidiary organs may be created when necessary; these have been created in substantial numbers and for a variety of purposes.

*The General Assembly*

All members of the United Nations are members of the General Assembly (Articles 9(1) and 18(1)). The General Assembly may discuss, and make recommendations on, any matters within the scope of the Charter. (Article 10). However, it may make recommendations on disputes or situations with regard to which the Security Council is exercising its powers only upon the Security Council's request (Article 12(1)).

The General Assembly may make only recommendations, but its resolutions, both in form and content, frequently purport to be more than recommendations. On the contribution to law-making of General Assembly resolutions, see Chapter 2 supra. On the role of the General Assembly in peacekeeping, see p. 997 infra.

Each member of the General Assembly has one vote. Decisions on important questions are made by a two-thirds majority of the members present and voting. Important questions include those enumerated in Article 18(2) and any additional categories of questions decided by a majority of the members present and voting (Article 18(3)).

*The Security Council*

The Security Council consists of five permanent and now—as a result of amendment—ten non-permanent members. The permanent members are the People's Republic of China, France, the United Kingdom, the United States, and, since early 1992, Russia, which succeeded to the seat of the U.S.S.R. The non-permanent members are elected by the General Assembly for two-year terms with due regard to the contribution of members to the purposes of the U.N. and to equitable geographical distribution. (Article 23(1)).

The Security Council's principal task is to ensure international peace and security. In the discharge of this task, it may exercise the powers granted by Chapters VI–VIII of the Charter. The Security Council was given authority also to exercise the functions of the U.N. relating to "strategic areas," including the approval of trusteeship agreements (Article 83).

Article 52 of the Charter authorizes regional arrangements and agencies for dealing with matters relating to the maintenance of international peace and security. The Security Council may utilize regional arrangements for enforcement action under its authority (Article 53).

*The Secretariat*

The Secretariat is headed by the Secretary–General, who is appointed for a five-year term by the General Assembly upon the recommendation of the Security Council (Article 97). The Secretary–General is the organization's chief administrative officer. He may bring to the attention of the Security Council any matter that in his opinion may threaten international peace and security (Article 99). He shall also perform such other functions as may be entrusted to him by the other organs (Article 98).

*The International Court of Justice*

Article 92 of the Charter declares the International Court of Justice "the principal judicial organ of the United Nations." The Court functions in accordance with its Statute, which is annexed to the Charter. See Chapter 10 supra.

### *Note*

The authority of the Security Council is set forth in Chapters V through VII of the Charter: its composition in Article 23, its functions and powers in Articles 24–26, its voting procedure in Articles 27–32. Member States delegate to the Security Council "primary responsibility for the maintenance of international peace and security" (Article 24) and "agree to accept and carry out the decisions of the Security Council" (Article 25). Chapter VI, Articles 33–38, define the authority of the Council in the pacific settlement of disputes.

## THE LAW OF THE CHARTER DURING THE COLD WAR

For some 40 years the United Nations Organization and its activities were hampered, and often thwarted, by the Cold War. The Security Council was largely incapacitated in its principal role of maintaining international peace and security by lack of agreement (and by veto) of the permanent members. The Council did contribute to peacekeeping when the Big Powers agreed, but agreement was often elusive. As a consequence, the General Assembly sought to assume part of the Security Council's responsibility (see, e.g., the Uniting for Peace Resolution, G.A.Res. 337(V) (1950), G.A.O.R., 5th Sess., Supp. 20, at 10), but it too was hampered by the Cold War and by the enlarged membership dominated by new, developing states.

The Cold War and its effects on the U.N. doubtless influenced the interpretation of the normative principles of the Charter and weakened compliance with those norms, but there was never a serious suggestion that the United Nations, and notably the Security Council's inability to act in times of crisis, invalidated or weakened the Charter norms proscribing the threat or use of force. The end of the Cold War has revived the Security Council, enabling it to play its intended role (e.g., in the Gulf War) and has encouraged the Council to extend its authority and activities (e.g., in actions in Somalia and in the former Yugoslavia).

### *HENKIN, HOW NATIONS BEHAVE*

137–38 (2nd ed. 1979).*

Unlike the limited restraints in the Covenant of the League and the provisions of the Kellogg–Briand Pact, the Charter's prohibition on unilateral force was to apply universally: members were bound by it; they were to see to it that nonmembers also complied. For the first time, nations tried to bring within the realm of law those ultimate political tensions and interests that had long been deemed beyond control by law. They determined that even sincere concern for national "security" or "vital interests" should no longer warrant any nation to initiate war. They agreed, in effect, to forgo the use of external force to change the political status quo. Nations would be assured their fundamental independence, the enjoyment of their territory, their freedom—a kind of right to be let alone. With it, of course, came the corresponding obligation to let others alone, not to use force to resolve disputes, or even to vindicate one's "rights." Change—other than internal change through internal forces—would have to be achieved peacefully, by agreement. Henceforth there would be order, and international society could concentrate on meeting better the needs of justice and welfare.

This most political of norms has been the target of "realists" from the beginning. They have questioned whether it is viable, even whether it is clearly desirable. Some who approved the norm in 1945 began to ask later whether it was acceptable. A "realist" would suggest that the law could have worked only if the United States and the Soviet Union had been prepared to cooperate to enforce peace. A lawyer might ask whether the law remains law, according to the principle of *rebus sic stantibus,* when the assumptions on which it was based have failed, when the circumstances in which it was made and those for which it was contemplated have radically changed.

For me, the changing facts and faces of international law have not detracted from the validity of the law of the Charter and have only reinforced its desirability. Consider, first, the argument based on the failure of the original conception of the United Nations: it has not established an effective international police system; it has not developed and maintained machinery for peaceful settlement of disputes (making self-help unnecessary and undesirable). But the draftsmen of the Charter were not seeking merely to replace "balance of power" by "collective security"; they were determined, according to the Preamble, to abolish "the scourge of war." All the evidence is persuasive that they sought to outlaw war, whether or not the U.N. organization succeeded in enforcing the law or in establishing peace and justice. And none of the original members, nor any one of the many new members, has ever claimed that the law against the use of force is undesirable now that the United Nations is not what had been intended.

* Footnotes omitted. Reprinted by permission of Columbia University Press.

### *Notes*

1. Henkin argues also that the other "changed circumstances"—the failure of Allied cooperation that gave way to the ideological confrontation of the Cold War, the development and proliferation of terrible weapons of mass destruction, and the transformation of the political system by the emergence of new nations and the "Third World"—did not render Article 2(4) less valid or less desirable. Henkin, How Nations Behave 138–39 (2d ed. 1979). The revival of the Security Council has put an end to arguments that the Charter norms against the use of force (Articles 2(3) and 2(4)) may have been voided under the doctrine of *rebus sic stantibus* (p. 888 supra), but its long dormant state encouraged arguments for inferring exceptions, for example to permit the use of force for humanitarian intervention or to defend or promote democracy. See p. 929 infra.

On the continuing validity and viability of Article 2(4) during the Cold War, compare Franck, Who Killed Article 2(4)? Or Changing Norms Governing the Use of Force by States, 64 A.J.I.L. 809 (1970), with Henkin, The Reports of the Death of Article 2(4) Are Greatly Exaggerated, 65 A.J.I.L. 544 (1971). See also Henkin, How Nations Behave 146–53 (2d ed. 1979); Schachter, In Defense of International Rules on the Use of Force, 53 U.Chi.L.Rev. 113 (1986). For the impact of the Cold War on the interpretation of the law of the Charter, see pp. 962–64 infra. See also Henkin, The Use of Force: Law and U.S. Policy, in Right v. Might: International Law and the Use of Force 37, 38–41 (2d ed. 1991); Macdonald, The Use of Force by States in International Law, in International Law: Achievements and Prospects 715, 719–31 (Bedjaoui, ed. 1991).

2. U.S. actions, e.g., in Grenada, Nicaragua, and Panama gave rise to charges that for the United States the law of the Charter was inapplicable when important national interests were at stake. Official U.S. representatives, however, continued to insist on the validity of the law of the Charter, and sought to justify U.S. actions under that law and to judge the actions of other states by that standard. But the United States withdrew from the proceedings brought against it by Nicaragua before the International Court of Justice. See p. 837 supra.

3. Henkin concludes that even during the Cold War there were fewer violations of the Charter than was commonly assumed. The principal "wars" were civil wars with external involvement, as to which the law of the Charter did not speak clearly. See p. 949 infra. The Cold War may have encouraged violations by smaller developing powers who expected that ideological conflict between the super powers would incapacitate the Security Council and provide them immunity from other adverse consequences (e.g., the Iran–Iraq War 1981–1988 and wars between Ethiopia and its neighbors). See Henkin, How Nations Behave 112–118 (2nd ed. 1979).

The end of the Cold War contributed to the disintegration of states (e.g., the U.S.S.R., Yugoslavia, and Czechoslovakia), and to conflict between newly independent states, as between Serbia and Croatia, and Serbia and Bosnia. See p. 988 infra.

## 2. *The Prohibition of the Use of Force*

### *CHARTER OF THE UNITED NATIONS*

San Francisco, June 26, 1945

* * *

ARTICLE 2

* * *

4. All Members shall refrain in their international relations from the threat or use of force against the territorial integrity or political independence of any state, or in any other manner inconsistent with the Purposes of the United Nations.

* * *

### *SCHACHTER, INTERNATIONAL LAW IN THEORY AND PRACTICE*

110–113 (1991) (footnotes omitted).

The basic provision restricting the use of force (or its threat) in international relations is Article 2, paragraph 4, of the Charter. * * *

The paragraph is complex in its structure and nearly all of its key terms raise questions of interpretation. We know that the principle was intended to outlaw war in its classic sense, that is, the use of military force to acquire territory or other benefits from another State. Actually the term "war" is not used in Article 2(4). It had been used in the League of Nations Covenant and the Kellogg–Briand Pact of 1928, but it had become evident in the 1930s that States engaged in hostilities without declaring war or calling it war. The term "force" was chosen as a more factual and wider word to embrace military action.

"Force" has its own ambiguities. It is sometimes used in a wide sense to embrace all types of coercion: economic, political and psychological as well as physical. Governments in the United Nations have from time to time sought to give the prohibition in Article 2(4) the wider meaning particularly to include economic measures that were said to be coercive. Although support was expressed by a great many states in the Third World for this wider notion, it was strongly resisted by the Western States. * * *

Even limited to armed force, the term raises questions of interpretation. Some center on the notion of "indirect" force. Does a State indirectly employ force when it allows its territory to be used by troops fighting in another country? Does a State use force when it provides arms to insurgents or to one side in a war? Does troop training as expert advice amount to indirect force? These questions have tended to be treated under the rubric of "intervention", a concept which has often been dealt with independently of Article 2(4) and defined as dictatorial interference by a State in the affairs of another State. However, Article 2(4) remains the most explicit Charter rule against intervention through armed force, indirect and direct, and it is pertinent to consider such actions as falling within the scope of the prohibition. * * *

* * *

A * * * basic question of interpretation is presented by the peculiar structure of the article. It is generally presumed that the prohibition was intended to preclude all use of force except that allowed as self-defence or authorized by the Security Council under Chapter VII. Yet the article is not drafted that way. The last 23 words contain qualifications. The article requires States to refrain from force or threat of force when that is "against the territorial integrity or political independence of any State" or "inconsistent with the purposes of the United Nations". If these words are not redundant, they must qualify that all-inclusive prohibition against force. Just how far they do qualify the prohibition is difficult to determine from a textual analysis alone.

The problem of interpretation has arisen in regard to two types of justification for the use of force. One such justification concerns the use of force solely to vindicate or secure a legal right. Thus it has been claimed that a State is allowed to use force to secure its lawful passage through waters of an international strait or to compel compliance with an arbitral or judicial award. One may extend this to other cases where a State considers that its rights have been violated. The textual argument based on the qualifying clause of Article 2(4) is that such force is not directed against the territorial integrity or political independence of the target state nor is it inconsistent with United Nations purposes. In its simplest form, it is the argument that force for a benign end does not fall within the qualifying language of Article 2(4). The argument, if accepted, would go a long way to cut down on the scope of Article 2(4). * * *

One answer to this argument is that the Charter itself requires that disputes be settled by peaceful means (Article 2, para. 3) and that the first declared purpose of the Charter is to remove threats to the peace and to suppress breaches of the peace. Consequently any use of force in international relation would be inconsistent with a Charter purpose. The only exceptions would be self-defense under Article 51 and military enforcement measures under Chapter VII.

A second answer is that any coercive incursion of armed troops into a foreign State without its consent impairs that State's territorial integrity, and any use of force to coerce a State to adopt a particular policy or action must be considered as an impairment of that State's political independence. On these premises it does not matter that the coercive action may have only a short-term effect nor does it matter that the end sought by the use of force is consistent with a stated purpose of the Charter. As long as the act of force involves a non-consensual use of a State's territory or compels a State to take a decision it would not otherwise take, Article 2(4) has been violated.

This position has been taken by the great majority of States and by most international lawyers. It finds support in the two decisions of the International Court of Justice concerned with the legality of the use of force[: *The Corfu Channel case* and *The Nicaragua case* ].

### *Notes*

1. Article 2(3) provides: "All Members shall settle their international disputes by peaceful means in such a manner that international peace and security, and justice, are not endangered." This is also a legal undertaking, but

in practice it has been subordinated to Article 2(4). As long as a state does not resort to force, there has been no disposition to find a violation of law in failure to settle disputes peacefully, as by leaving them unsettled.

2. Unlike earlier efforts to outlaw "war" or "aggression," Article 2(4) does not mention either term. The framers avoided them because these terms lend themselves to circumvention. There could be hostilities without a declared war, and uses of force that did not acquire the character of war. Aggression had long resisted definition, and who was the aggressor could be falsified and might not always be easy to determine. The framers also sought to outlaw even war as a "duel" by mutual consent, when neither side could properly be seen as aggressor.

The Charter was intended to outlaw war as well as all lesser uses of force, but the language used was not without ambiguity. Is only military force forbidden or does the prohibition include the use of "economic" force and other coercive measures? Is the threat of force forbidden only if a threat is expressed or clearly implied, or is it forbidden also to create threatening situations, as when one state builds up armed forces and armaments that could threaten another? Does the prohibition of the threat or use of force against the territorial integrity of another state forbid only force designed permanently to deprive another state of any part of its territory or does it also forbid any forcible invasion of another's territory however temporary? Does the prohibition of force against the "political independence" of another state forbid only force designed to end the latter's independence and render it a "puppet," or does it also bar force designed to coerce a state to act against its will, even once, in any circumstances? Is force forbidden even if its purpose is humanitarian, to save human lives, or to help a people achieve "self-determination?" Is the use of force permissible to install a legitimate, democratic government? Does Article 2(4) forbid a state to give military support to insurgents? to the incumbent government battling insurgents? to either side in a civil war? The relation of the prohibition in Article 2(4) to the right of self-defense (Article 51) is considered at p. 911 infra.

During the drafting of Article 2(4), Brazil proposed including a prohibition against the use of "economic measures" against a state. See 6 Docs. of the U.N. Conf. on Int'l Org. 335. The proposal was rejected, but it is not clear whether the rejection reflected a belief that economic aggression was not included within the term "force" or whether "force" was a broad enough term to cover it without specific mention. Goodrich, Hambro and Simons state:

> It seems reasonable to conclude that while various forms of economic and political coercion may be treated as threats to the peace, as contrary to certain of the declared purposes and principles of the Organisation, or as violating agreements entered into or recognised principles of international law, they are not to be regarded as coming necessarily under the prohibition of Article 2(4), which is to be understood as directed against the use of armed force.

Goodrich, Hambro & Simons, Charter of the United Nations 49 (3rd ed. 1969). See p. 896 on the definition of aggression.

For a discussion of the meaning of Article 2(4), including many of the issues addressed in the following pages, see Schachter, The Right of States to Use Armed Force, 82 Mich.L.Rev. 1620 (1984). Schachter concludes (at 1633):

> Admittedly, the article does not provide clear and precise answers to all the questions raised. Concepts such as "force," "threat of force" or "politi-

cal independence" embrace a wide range of possible meanings. Their application to diverse circumstances involves choices as to these meanings and assessments of the behavior and intentions of various actors. Differences of opinion are often likely even among "disinterested" observers; they are even more likely among those involved or interested. But such divergences are not significantly different from those that arise with respect to almost all general legal principles.

The foregoing analysis shows that article 2(4) has a reasonably clear core meaning. That core meaning has been spelled out in interpretive documents such as the Declaration of Principles of International Law, adopted unanimously by the General Assembly in 1970. The International Court and the writings of scholars reflect the wide area of agreement on its meaning. It is therefore unwarranted to suggest that article 2(4) lacks the determinate content necessary to enable it to function as a legal rule of restraint.

On the modern prohibition of the use of force, see Law and Force in the New International Order (Damrosch & Scheffer, eds. 1991); Henkin, The Use of Force: Law and U.S. Policy, in Right v. Might: International Law and the Use of Force 37–69 (2nd ed. 1991); Schachter, In Defense of International Rules on the Use of Force, 53 U.Chi.L.Rev. 113 (1986); O'Brien, The Conduct of Just and Limited War (1981); Walzer, Just and Unjust Wars (1977); Hoffmann, International Law and the Control of Force, in The Relevance of International Law 34–66 (Deutsch & Hoffmann, eds., 1971); Falk, Legal Order in a Violent World (1968); Brownlie, International Law and the Use of Force by States (1963); McDougal & Feliciano, Law and Minimum World Public Order (1961); Stone, Legal Controls of International Conflict (1959).

3. In Military and Paramilitary Activities in and against Nicaragua (Nicaragua v. United States), 1984 I.C.J. 169, the Court indicated provisional measures, including: "The United States of America should immediately cease and refrain from any action restricting, blocking or endangering access to or from Nicaraguan ports, and, in particular, the laying of mines." Does that "order" imply that in the Court's view such actions violate Article 2(4)? Other principles of international law?

4. The Charter proscribes the use of force "against another state." Does it forbid also force against a non-sovereign entity? For a discussion of the issue in connection with British intervention in the Imamate of Oman, see the Verbatim Record of the Security Council, 12 SCOR (783d mtg) at 7, S/PV 783 (20 August 1957).

5. The Charter does not purport to make Article 2(4) binding on nonmember states, but Article 2(6) provides: "The Organization shall ensure that states which are not Members of the United Nations act in accordance with these Principles so far as may be necessary for the maintenance of peace and security." It is commonly accepted that in substance Article 2(4) has become a principle of customary law binding on all states, and has acquired the character of *jus cogens.* See Restatement (Third) § 102, Comment *k* and Reporters' Note 6. In the *Nicaragua* case, p. 911 infra, the International Court of Justice, after ruling that limitations on the Court's exercise of jurisdiction in the case precluded it from considering Nicaragua's claim under the U.N. Charter, went on to consider the claim under customary law which the Court held to be virtually identical to the law of the Charter as regards the use of force and the right of self-defense.

6. A violation of Article 2(4) is clearly a breach of international obligations to the victim of the threat or use of force. The International Court of Justice has said, moreover, that the principles of international law outlawing acts of aggression are obligations *erga omnes,* to the international community as a whole. See Barcelona Traction, Light and Power Company, Ltd., 1970 I.C.J. 3. See also Military and Paramilitary Activities in and against Nicaragua (Nicaragua v. United States) (Schwebel, J., dissenting), 1984 I.C.J. 169, 190.

The Draft Articles on State Responsibility provide that an international crime may result from "a serious breach of an international obligation of essential importance to maintenance of international peace and security, such as prohibiting aggression." Article 19(3)(a), printed in [1980] II (Pt. 2) Y.B.Int'l L.Comm. 30. See generally, International Crimes of State: A Critical Analysis of the ILC's Draft Article 19 on State Responsibility (Weiler, Cassese & Spinedi, eds. 1989).

For the argument that issues concerning Article 2(4) or the corresponding customary law are not justiciable before the International Court of Justice see p. 82 supra.

7. The term aggression does not appear in Article 2(4) of the Charter, but it appears in the following Charter provisions:

Article 1

The purposes of the United Nations are:

1. To maintain international peace and security, and to that end: to take effective collective measures for the prevention and removal of threats to the peace, and for the suppression of acts of aggression or other breaches of the peace. * * *

* * *

Article 39

The Security Council shall determine the existence of any threat to the peace, breach of the peace, or act of aggression and shall make recommendations, or decide what measures shall be taken in accordance with Articles 41 and 42, to maintain or restore international peace and security.

* * *

What is the relation of Article 39 to Article 2(4)? Is the Security Council's authority under Article 39 limited to situations caused by violations of Article 2(4)? See Goodrich, Hambro & Simons, Charter of the United Nations 306 (3rd ed. 1969).

## THE THREAT OF FORCE

### *SECRETARY-GENERAL OF THE UNITED NATIONS, REPORT ON THE QUESTION OF DEFINING AGGRESSION*

U.N.Doc. A/2211 at 52 (October 3, 1952) (footnotes omitted).

#### 1. What Constitutes a Threat to Use Force?

367. This occurs where a State, in order to force its will on another State, threatens to use force against it. The most typical form of this threat

is the ultimatum in which the State to which it is addressed is given a time-limit in which to accept the demands made upon it, and told that if it rejects these demands war will be declared on it or certain coercive measures such as a naval blockade, bombardment, or occupation of a given territory, will be taken. However, the threat to use force is not always made in so crude and open a form. There are sometimes veiled threats which may be very effective, but are difficult to detect.

368. Again, the threat of force differs from the employment of force in the same way as the threat to kill differs from murder. The person who utters the threat may not intend to carry it out, and the threat is then only a form of intimidation and "blackmail". He may also change his mind and not resort to action.

369. De Brouckère, in his report of 1 December 1926 to the Committee of the Council of the League of Nations, stated:

> "We find in history many instances of violence and aggression which have not led to war, either because the victim was too weak or too faint-hearted to offer any resistance, or because the matter was settled, by negotiation or through the mediation of a third party, before the state of war was established. The fact is that a state of war does not really exist until the country attacked takes up the challenge and thus admits the existence of a state of war." [See League of Nations document A.14.1927.V, p. 68.]

370. Similarly, a country's weakness may lead it to yield to a threat of aggression before the potential aggressor needs to take action to achieve the desired result.

### 2. The International Law Commission Considers the Question From The Penal Standpoint

371. At its third session (1951), the International Law Commission, in preparing a draft Code of Offences against the Peace and Security of Mankind, considered the question whether the threat to resort to an act of aggression ought to be considered as actual aggression.

372. After deciding, by ten votes to one, that the threat of employment of force was an offence, it decided, by six votes to four, that such a threat did not constitute aggression. [A/CN.4/SR.109, paragraph 106.]

373. In the list of offences against peace drawn up by the International Law Commission, the threat to resort to an act of aggression occupies the second place [this offence is defined thus: "(2) Any threat by the authorities of a State to resort to an act of aggression against another State." A/1858, paragraph 59], the first in the list being aggression itself. In the comments accompanying the text of the draft code, the Commission points out that Article 2, paragraph 4, of the United Nations Charter prescribes that all Members shall "refrain in their international relations from the threat or use of force".

374. It must be borne in mind that in drafting its draft Code of Offences against the Peace and Security of Mankind, the International Law Commission was thinking in terms of the punishment of individuals called to personal account for their crimes. The problem confronting organs of an international institution and governments at the moment when the act is

committed is somewhat different, namely, what action to take in respect of a State which resorts to aggression or the threat of aggression.

### *Note*

Professor Schachter writes:

> What is meant by a "threat of force" has received rather less consideration [than what is meant by "the use of force"]. Clearly a threat to use military action to coerce a State to make concessions is forbidden. But in many situations the deployment of military forces or missiles has unstated aims and its effect is equivocal. However, the preponderance of military strength in some States and their political relations with potential target States may justifiably lead to an inference of a threat of force against the political independence of the target State. An examination of the particular circumstances is necessary to reach that conclusion, but the applicability of Article 2(4) in principle can hardly be denied. Curiously, it has not been invoked much as an explicit prohibition of such implied threats. The explanation may lie in the subtleties of power relations and the difficulty of demonstrating coercive intent. Or perhaps more realistically, it may be a manifestation of the general recognition and tolerance of disparities of power and their effect in maintaining dominant and subordinate relationships between unequal States. However, such toleration, wide as it may be, is not without limits. A blatant and direct threat of force to compel another State to yield territory or make substantial political concessions (not required by law) would have to be seen as illegal under Article 2(4), if the words "threat of force" are to have any meaning.

Schachter, International Law in Theory and Practice 111 (1991) (footnotes omitted). See also Sadurska, Threats of Force, 82 A.J.I.L. 239 (1988).

## DEFINING AGGRESSION

### *FRIEDMANN, THE CHANGING STRUCTURE OF INTERNATIONAL LAW*

254–55 (1964).*

* * * There is no reason to believe that the nations of the world could not theoretically agree on the concepts of "invasion," "armed attacks" or "blockade." Differences are primarily ones of objectives; they are essentially of a political and ideological, not of a logical, character. Hence, the controversy as to whether an attempt at definition should be abandoned altogether and the decision whether an unlawful aggression has occurred in a particular case be left to the competent authority, or whether an agreed definition of various types of aggression should be regarded as an indispensable though not automatic guide for the decision-maker, does not perhaps touch the fundamental problem.

Basic disagreements can be reflected either in definitions so vague and ambiguous as to give effective liberty of action, or in a reluctance to entrust the decision to an impartial authority. The unwillingness of the nations, up to date, to entrust full authority over war and peace to the United Nations or to any international body, may be attributed to three major factors: (a)

* Some footnotes omitted. Reprinted by permission of Columbia University Press.

the continuing struggle between the conflicting demands of national sovereignty and international order, expressed in the claims and limitations of the national right of self-defence; (b) the development of means of destruction so swift and devastating that the traditional time lag between the development of an armed attack and the organisation of defence has become largely obsolete; (c) the enormously increased importance of political and ideological warfare, which has created new forms of "indirect" aggression, not amenable to the established criteria and definitions of aggression.

### *Note*

At the San Francisco Conference, and for many years thereafter, the United States opposed the elaboration of a definition of aggression. President Truman summarized the United States position in his annual report to Congress, 1950:

> At the San Francisco Conference on International Organization (1945) there was a movement to insert a definition of aggression in the United Nations Charter. The United States opposed this proposal. It took the position that a definition of aggression cannot be so comprehensive as to include all cases of aggression and cannot take into account the various circumstances which might enter into the determination of aggression in a particular case. Any definition of aggression is a trap for the innocent and an invitation to the guilty. The United States position prevailed at San Francisco, and the Charter adopted a system whereby the appropriate U.N. organ, in the first instance the Security Council, would determine on the basis of the facts of a particular case whether aggression has taken place.

5 Whiteman, Digest of International Law 740 (1965).

On October 3, 1952, the Secretary–General, acting in compliance with G.A.Res. 599, submitted a comprehensive report on the question of defining aggression. U.N. Doc. A/2211, excerpts from which are reproduced at p. 894 supra, and at p. 901 infra. In 1967, the General Assembly decided to expedite the efforts to define aggression, and established a Special Committee on the Question of Defining Aggression. See G.A.Res. 2330. The Committee finally adopted a definition by consensus in 1974 and recommended it for adoption by the General Assembly.

### *RESOLUTION ON THE DEFINITION OF AGGRESSION*

G.A.Res. 3314(XXIX) (1974), G.A.O.R. 29th Sess., Supp. 31, at 42 (footnotes omitted).

*The General Assembly,*

* * *

*Deeply convinced* that the adoption of the Definition of Aggression would contribute to the strengthening of international peace and security,

1. *Approves* the Definition of Aggression, the text of which is annexed to the present resolution;

* * *

3. *Calls upon* all States to refrain from all acts of aggression and other uses of force contrary to the Charter of the United Nations and the Declaration on Principles of International Law concerning Friendly Rela-

tions and Co-operation among States in accordance with the Charter of the United Nations; [G.A.Res. 2625, 25 GAOR Supp. 28 (A/8028) at 121 (1970).]

4. *Calls the attention* of the Security Council to the Definition of Aggression, as set out below, and recommends that it should, as appropriate, take account of that Definition as guidance in determining, in accordance with the Charter, the existence of an act of aggression.

## ANNEX

## DEFINITION OF AGGRESSION

*The General Assembly,*

* * *

*Recalling* that the Security Council, in accordance with Article 39 of the Charter of the United Nations, shall determine the existence of any threat to the peace, breach of the peace or act of aggression and shall make recommendations, or decide what measures shall be taken in accordance with Articles 41 and 42, to maintain or restore international peace and security,

* * *

*Bearing in mind* that nothing in this Definition shall be interpreted as in any way affecting the scope of the provisions of the Charter with respect to the functions and powers of the organs of the United Nations,

* * *

*Believing* that, although the question whether an act of aggression has been committed must be considered in the light of all the circumstances of each particular case, it is nevertheless desirable to formulate basic principles as guidance for such determination,

*Adopts* the following Definition of Aggression:

### *Article 1*

Aggression is the use of armed force by a State against the sovereignty, territorial integrity or political independence of another State, or in any other manner inconsistent with the Charter of the United Nations, as set out in this Definition.

*Explanatory note:* In this Definition the term "State:"

(a) Is used without prejudice to questions of recognition or to whether a State is a Member of the United Nations;

(b) Includes the concept of a "group of States" where appropriate.

### *Article 2*

The first use of armed force by a State in contravention of the Charter shall constitute *prima facie* evidence of an act of aggression although the Security Council may, in conformity with the Charter, conclude that a determination that an act of aggression has been committed would not be justified in the light of other relevant circumstances, including the fact that the acts concerned or their consequences are not of sufficient gravity.

*Article 3*

Any of the following acts, regardless of a declaration of war, shall, subject to and in accordance with the provisions of article 2, qualify as an act of aggression:

(a) The invasion or attack by the armed forces of a State of the territory of another State, or any military occupation, however temporary, resulting from such invasion or attack, or any annexation by the use of force of the territory of another State or part thereof;

(b) Bombardment by the armed forces of a State against the territory of another State or the use of any weapons by a State against the territory of another State;

(c) The blockade of the ports or coasts of a State by the armed forces of another State;

(d) An attack by the armed forces of a State on the land, sea or air forces, marine and air fleets of another State;

(e) The use of armed forces of one State which are within the territory of another State with the agreement of the receiving State, in contravention of the conditions provided for in the agreement or any extension of their presence in such territory beyond the termination of the agreement;

(f) The action of a State in allowing its territory, which it has placed at the disposal of another State, to be used by that other State for perpetrating an act of aggression against a third State;

(g) The sending by or on behalf of a State of armed bands, groups, irregulars or mercenaries, which carry out acts of armed force against another State of such gravity as to amount to the acts listed above, or its substantial involvement therein.

*Article 4*

The acts enumerated above are not exhaustive and the Security Council may determine that other acts constitute aggression under the provisions of the Charter.

*Article 5*

1. No consideration of whatever nature, whether political, economic, military or otherwise, may serve as a justification for aggression.

2. A war of aggression is a crime against international peace. Aggression gives rise to international responsibility.

3. No territorial acquisition or special advantage resulting from aggression is or shall be recognized as lawful.

*Article 6*

Nothing in this Definition shall be construed as in any way enlarging or diminishing the scope of the Charter, including its provisions concerning cases in which the use of force is lawful.

*Article 7*

Nothing in this Definition, and in particular article 3, could in any way prejudice the right of self-determination, freedom and independence, as derived from the Charter, of peoples forcibly deprived of that right and referred to in the Declaration on Principles of International Law concerning Friendly Relations and Co-operation among States in accordance with the Charter of the United Nations, particularly peoples under colonial and racist régimes or other forms of alien domination; nor the right of these peoples to struggle to that end and to seek and receive support, in accordance with the principles of the Charter and in conformity with the above-mentioned Declaration.

*Article 8*

In their interpretation and application the above provisions are interrelated and each provision should be construed in the context of the other provisions.

### *Notes*

1. An explanatory note to Article 1 was included in the text of the Resolution. Explanatory notes to Articles 3 and 5 were included in the Report of the Special Committee on the Question of Defining Aggression, 29 GAOR, Supp. 19 (A/9619 and Corr. 1) at 5 (1974).

2. The United States acquiesced in the adoption of this definition. For its comments on the definition and on each of its articles, see the statement of Robert Rosenstock, the U.S. Representative to the Special Committee, 70 Dep't State Bull. 498 (1974). Have the fears the United States expressed in opposition to defining aggression been realized? Has the U.N. definition served any useful purpose?

3. There were two approaches to the definition of aggression during the years of debate in the United Nations. Some favored an "enumerative" definition that would include a list of the acts that constitute aggression; others favored a general definition similar to that of Article 2(4) of the Charter. The 1974 Resolution contains elements of both. Article 1 follows the general definition of the Charter, and limits the definition of aggression to armed force, despite the suggestion by a number of states that aggression includes other forms of hostile acts. Article 3, however, sets out a number of acts that constitute aggression and Article 4 indicates that the list is not exhaustive. The threat of force was not included in Article 1, and "[t]he economic, ideological and other modes of aggression were carefully considered * * * but the result was an interpretation that they did not fall within the term 'aggression' as it had been used in the Charter." Broms, The Definition of Aggression, 154 Rec. des Cours 299, 386 (1977–I). The 1974 Resolution has had mixed reviews on the ground that it glosses over or avoids many disputed issues. See generally, Nyiri, The United Nations Search for a Definition of Aggression (1989); Stone, Conflict Through Consensus: UN Approaches to Aggression (1977); Ferencz, Defining Aggression, 2 vols. (1975); also Bennett, A Linguistic Critique of the Definition of Aggression, 31 Germ.Y.B.Int'l L. 481 (1988); Brown–John, The 1974 Definition of Aggression: A Query, 15 Can.Y.B.Int'l L. 301 (1977); Garvey, The U.N. Definition of "Aggression": Law and Illusion in the Context of Collective Security, 17 Va.J.Int'l L. 177 (1977); Stone, Hopes and Loopholes in the 1974 Definition of Aggression, 71 A.J.I.L. 224 (1977).

A list of acts of aggression similar to that in Article 3 of the Resolution is contained in Article 12 of the International Law Commission's Draft Code of Crimes Against the Peace and Security of Mankind. See McCaffrey, The Fortieth Session of the International Law Commission, 83 A.J.I.L. 153 (1989).

4. The 1952 Report on the Question of Defining Aggression contained a suggestion that "unilateral action to deprive a State of the economic resources derived from the fair practice of international trade, or to endanger its economy" may be an act of aggression. U.N.Doc. A/2211 at 58. The concept of economic aggression was criticized by others as "liable to extend the concept of aggression almost indefinitely." Id. Economic coercion was not included in the 1974 definition of aggression but several resolutions have denounced such coercion as subverting sovereign rights. See, e.g., Article 32 of the Charter of Economic Rights and Duties of States, G.A.Res. 3281(XXIX), reprinted in, 14 I.L.M. 251 (1975); Declaration of the Principles of International Law Concerning Friendly Co-operation among States, G.A.Res. 2265(XXV); Declaration on the Inadmissibility of Intervention in Domestic Affairs of States and the Protection of their Independence and Sovereignty, G.A.Res. 2131 (XX), p. 905 infra. Compare Article 16 of the Charter of the Organization of American States: "No State may use or encourage the use of coercive measures of an economic or political character in order to force the sovereign will of another State and obtain from it advantages of any kind." 119 U.N.T.S. 3, T.I.A.S. No. 2361, 2 U.S.T. 2394 (1948). For a defense of economic measures used for political purposes in the context of the Arab–Israeli dispute, see Shihata, Destination Embargo of Arab Oil: Its Legality under International Law, 68 A.J.I.L. 591 (1974). See generally, The Arab Oil Weapon (Paust & Blaustein, eds. 1977); Economic Coercion and the New International Economic Order (Lillich, ed. 1976); Almond, An Assessment of Economic Warfare: Developments from the Persian Gulf, 31 Va.J.Int'l L. 645 (1991); Edwards, The Iraqi Oil "Weapon" in the 1991 Gulf War: A Law of Armed Conflict Analysis, 40 Naval L.Rev. 105 (1992). On the use of economic force under Article 2(4) of the Charter. See p. 892 supra.

6. On agreements procured by the use or threat of force, see Article 52 of the 1969 Vienna Convention on the Law of Treaties, 1155 U.N.T.S. 331, reprinted in, 8 I.L.M. 679 (1969). See p. 492 supra.

## INDIRECT AGGRESSION

Charges of "indirect aggression" were not uncommon during the ideological conflict of the Cold War, and to some extent during the years of resistance to colonialism and of external support for "peoples liberation movements." In the changed world order after the Cold War, instances of indirect aggression may be less frequent, but are not excluded.

### *FRIEDMANN, THE CHANGING STRUCTURE OF INTERNATIONAL LAW*

262 (1964).*

It is the increasingly numerous and important forms of attack upon the integrity of a state by other than the traditional means of military attack, usually styled "indirect" or "ideological" aggression, that give rise to prob-

* Footnotes omitted. Reprinted by permission of Columbia University Press.

lems of altogether different dimensions and that affect some of the foundations of traditional international law. These attacks range from many types of ideological and political propaganda and psychological warfare, by radio, by aerial leaflets, etc., to the organisation of subversive, political movements inside another country, the systematic infiltration of political agents, and the systematic economic strangulation of a regime by comprehensive trade boycott.

The legal problems arising from these important but often highly elusive forms of interference with the integrity of a state are further complicated by the fact that they are often intertwined with civil strife and the ensuing question whether assistance to one or both sides in a civil conflict, ranging from military assistance to the supply of arms, political and economic help, is permitted or prohibited by international law. In modern civil wars, military assistance to one or the other side may often be a means of deliberately supporting one political or social order as against another. * * *

### *Notes*

1. Brownlie writes:

> Charges of "aggression" are frequently based on allegations of military aid to, and control over, rebels in a civil war. If rebels are effectively supported *and controlled* by another state that state is responsible for a "use of force" as a consequence of the agency. Thus aid to rebels by foreign states has been held by the General Assembly to be inconsistent with the principles of the United Nations Charter, with implicit reference to Article 2, paragraphs 3 and 4. However, in cases in which aid is given but there is no agency established, and there is no exercise of control over the rebels by the foreign government, it is very doubtful if it is correct to describe the responsibility of that government in terms of a use of force or armed attack. Unfortunately the resolutions referred to above and the other relevant materials do not draw this distinction. The illegality of aid to rebel groups has been established in a variety of ways. It has been described as "intervention in the internal affairs of a state" and as "indirect aggression." In resolution 380(V) of 17 November 1950, the General Assembly included "fomenting civil strife" in its strong condemnation of aggression.

Brownlie, International Law and the Use of Force 370 (1963).*

The 1952 report of the Secretary General on the Question of Defining Aggression (U.N.Doc. A/2211, Oct. 3, 1952), p. 894 supra, product of the earlier days of the United Nations, included extended discussion of "indirect aggression." See Section VII at 55. "The characteristic of indirect aggression appears to be that the aggressor state, without itself committing hostile acts as a State, operates through third parties who are either foreigners or nationals seemingly acting on their own initiative. * * * The concept of indirect aggression has been construed to include certain hostile acts or certain forms of complicity in hostilities in progress." Id. at 56. The report also considered "cases of indirect aggression which do not constitute acts of participation in hostilities in progress, but which are designed to prepare such acts, to undermine a country's power of resistance, or to bring about a change in its political or social system." Id. at 55. Among examples proposed by spokesmen of various countries were: intervention in another state's internal or foreign affairs; violation of the political

* Footnotes omitted. Reprinted by permission of the Clarendon Press, Oxford.

integrity of a country by subversive action; incitement to civil war; maintenance of a fifth column; ideological aggression and propaganda. Id. at 55–56.

The term "indirect aggression" is not included in the definition of aggression adopted by the General Assembly, but some elements in the definition may be deemed indirect, e.g., Art. 3(g), p. 900 supra. Note that Article 4 states that the acts enumerated in Article 3 are not exhaustive.

See Nicaragua v. United States, p. 911 below.

2. "A hostile propaganda attack carried on by one state against another of such a magnitude as to endanger the security of the state against which it is directed can be classified as aggression—as ideological aggression. It is nothing short of an attack against the international personality of a state. Inasmuch as it does not involve the use of armed force it can qualify as indirect aggression, although it would seem to make for greater clarity to label it simply as aggression. To fall within the category of aggression it must in general be directed by a state against another state. It is states (and in some instances other entities) which are precluded from spreading hostile propaganda against or within other states * * *." Thomas & Thomas, The Concept of Aggression in International Law 88–89 (1972).*

## THREAT OR USE OF LIMITED FORCE

## THE CUBAN MISSILE CRISIS, 1962

*WHITEMAN, DIGEST OF INTERNATIONAL LAW*

Vol. 4, 523–24 (1965).

On the evening of October 22, 1962, President John F. Kennedy announced to his fellow U.S. citizens that "This Government, as promised, has maintained the closest surveillance of the Soviet military buildup on the island of Cuba. Within the past week unmistakeable evidence has established the fact that a series of offensive missile sites is now in preparation on that imprisoned island." He added that "This urgent transformation of Cuba into an important strategic base—by the presence of these large, long-range, and clearly offensive weapons of sudden mass destruction—constitutes an explicit threat to the peace and security of all the Americas, in flagrant and deliberate defiance of the Rio Pact of 1947, the traditions of this nation and hemisphere, the Joint Resolution of the 87th Congress, the Charter of the United Nations, and my own public warnings to the Soviets on September 4 and 13 [1962]." On the following day, October 23, the Council of the Organization of American States, meeting as the Provisional Organ of Consultation, called for "the immediate dismantling and withdrawal from Cuba of all missiles and other weapons with any offensive capability" and recommended that "the member states, in accordance with Articles 6 and 8 of the Inter-American Treaty of Reciprocal Assistance [1947], take all measures, individually and collectively, including the use of armed force, which they may deem necessary to ensure that the Government of Cuba cannot continue to receive supplies which may threaten the peace and

* Footnotes omitted. Reprinted by permission of Southern Methodist University Press.

security of the Continent and to prevent the missiles in Cuba with offensive capability from ever becoming an active threat to the peace and security of the Continent."

On that same day—October 23, 1962—President Kennedy by Proclamation ordered the interdiction by U.S. forces of the delivery of offensive weapons to Cuba. The substantive portions of the Proclamation provided that in accordance with the resolution of the Organ of Consultation of the American Republics of October 23, 1962, "and to defend the security of the United States," the forces under the President's command were ordered, beginning at 2 p.m. Greenwich time October 24, 1962, to interdict the delivery of offensive weapons and associated matériel to Cuba. To enforce this order, the Secretary of Defense was ordered to take appropriate measures to prevent the delivery of the prohibited matériel to Cuba, "employing the land, sea and air forces of the United States in cooperation with any forces that may be made available by other American States." The Secretary of Defense was authorized to make designations "within a reasonable distance of Cuba, of prohibited or restricted zones and of prescribed routes." Further, the Proclamation specified:

> Any vessel or craft, which may be proceeding toward Cuba may be intercepted and may be directed to identify itself, its cargo, equipment and stores and its ports of call, to stop, to lie to, to submit to visit and search, or to proceed as directed. Any vessel or craft which fails or refuses to respond to or comply with directions shall be subject to being taken into custody. Any vessel or craft which it is believed is en route to Cuba and may be carrying prohibited matériel or may itself constitute such matériel shall, wherever possible, be directed to proceed to another destination of its own choice and shall be taken into custody if it fails or refuses to obey such directions. All vessels or craft taken into custody shall be sent into a port of the United States for appropriate disposition.
>
> In carrying out this order, force shall not be used except in case of failure or refusal to comply with directions, or with regulations or directives of the Secretary of Defense, issued hereunder, after reasonable efforts have been made to communicate them to the vessel or craft, or in case of self-defense. In any case, force shall be used only to the extent necessary.

Proclamation No. 3504, 47 Dep't State Bull. 717 (1962), 27 Fed.Reg. 10401 (1962).

### *Note*

Was the U.S. action in Cuba a threat or use of force? Against the territorial integrity or political independence of Cuba? Of the Soviet Union? Of States whose ships were prevented from going to Cuba? Was it "in any other manner inconsistent with the purposes of the United Nations?" See MacChesney, Some Comments on the "Quarantine" of Cuba, 57 A.J.I.L. 592, 596 (1963); also Henkin, The UN and Its Supporters, 78 Pol.Sci.Q. 504, 527, 528 (1963). But see Wright, The Cuban Quarantine, 57 A.J.I.L. 546 (1963). Wright rejected also the argument that the U.S. action was a "pacific blockade" under traditional international law; that it was permissible in self-defense under Article 51, quoted below; that it was justified under the authority of the Organization of

American States, as officially argued by the Deputy Legal Adviser of the State Department.

For the suggestion that international law was not "relevant" in the Cuban Missile Crisis, see p. 40 supra.

## NON–INTERVENTION

The U.N. Charter does not speak to intervention by states (as distinguished from intervention by the U.N. "in matters which are essentially within the domestic jurisdiction of any state," which is precluded by Article 2(7)). Insofar as intervention is used strictly to refer to "dictatorial interference" by use or threat of force, p. 890 supra, it is to be considered in the light of the prohibition of Article 2(4). Other international instruments have inveighed against intervention, but usually without defining it.

### *DECLARATION ON THE INADMISSIBILITY OF INTERVENTION INTO THE DOMESTIC AFFAIRS OF STATES*

G.A.Res. 2131(XX) (1965).

*The General Assembly,*

*Deeply concerned* at the gravity of the international situation and the increasing threat to universal peace due to armed intervention and other direct or indirect forms of interference threatening the sovereign personality and the political independence of States,

*Considering* that the United Nations, in accordance with their aim to eliminate war, threats to the peace and acts of aggression, created an Organization, based on the sovereign equality of States, whose friendly relations would be based on respect for the principle of equal rights and self-determination of peoples and on the obligation of its Members to refrain from the threat or use of force against the territorial integrity or political independence of any State,

*Recognizing* that, in fulfilment of the principle of self-determination, the General Assembly, by the Declaration on the Granting of Independence to Colonial Countries and Peoples contained in resolution 1514 (XV) of 14 December 1960, stated its conviction that all peoples have an inalienable right to complete freedom, the exercise of their sovereignty and the integrity of their national territory, and that, by virtue of that right, they freely determine their political status and freely pursue their economic, social and cultural development,

*Recalling* that in the Universal Declaration of Human Rights the Assembly proclaimed that recognition of the inherent dignity and of the equal and inalienable rights of all members of the human family is the foundation of freedom, justice and peace in the world, without distinction of any kind,

*Reaffirming* the principle of non-intervention, proclaimed in the charters of the Organization of American States, the League of Arab States and of the Organization of African Unity and affirmed at the Conferences of

Montevideo, Buenos Aires, Chapultepec and Bogotá, as well as in the decisions of the Afro–Asian Conference at Bandung, the First Conference of Heads of State or Government of Non–Alligned Countries at Belgrade, in the Programme for Peace and International Co-operation adopted at the end of the Second Conference of Heads of State or Government of Non–Aligned Countries at Cairo, and in the declaration on subversion adopted in Accra by the Heads of State and Government of the African States,

*Recognizing* that full observance of the principle of the non-intervention of States in the internal and external affairs of other States is essential to the fulfillment of the purposes and principles of the United Nations,

*Considering* that armed intervention is synonymous with aggression and, as such, is contrary to the basic principles on which peaceful international co-operation between States should be built,

*Considering further* that direct intervention, subversion and all forms of indirect intervention are contrary to these principles and, consequently, constitute a violation of the Charter of the United Nations,

*Mindful* that violation of the principle of non-intervention poses a threat to the independence, freedom and normal political, economic, social and cultural development of countries, particularly those which have freed themselves from colonialism, and can pose a serious threat to the maintenance of peace,

*Fully aware* of the imperative need to create appropriate conditions which would enable all States, and in particular the developing countries, to choose without duress or coercion their own political, economic and social institutions,

*In the light of the foregoing considerations, solemnly declares:*

1. No State has the right to intervene, directly or indirectly, for any reason whatever, in the internal or external affairs of any other State. Consequently, armed intervention and all other forms of interference or attempted threats against the personality of the State or against its political, economic and cultural elements, are condemned;

2. No State may use or encourage the use of economic, political or any other type of measures to coerce another State in order to obtain from it the subordination of the exercise of its sovereign rights or to secure from it advantages of any kind. Also, no State shall organize, assist, foment, finance, incite or tolerate subversive, terrorist or armed activities directed towards the violent overthrow of the régime of another State, or interfere in civil strife in another State;

3. The use of force to deprive peoples of their national identity constitutes a violation of their inalienable rights and of the principle of non-intervention;

4. The strict observance of these obligations is an essential condition to ensure that nations live together in peace with one another, since the practice of any form of intervention not only violates the spirit and letter of the Charter but also leads to the creation of situations which threaten international peace and security;

5. Every State has an inalienable right to choose its political, economic, social and cultural systems, without interference in any form by another State;

6. All States shall respect the right of self-determination and independence of peoples and nations, to be freely exercised without any foreign pressure, and with absolute respect for human rights and fundamental freedoms. Consequently, all States shall contribute to the complete elimination of racial discrimination and colonialism in all its forms and manifestations;

7. For the purpose of this Declaration, the term "State" covers both individual States and groups of States;

8. Nothing in this Declaration shall be construed as affecting in any manner the relevant provisions of the Charter of the United Nations relating to the maintenance of international peace and security, in particular those contained in Chapters VI, VII and VIII.

### *Note*

On September 24, 1965, the Soviet Union, stating that international tension was increasing because of acts of aggression and intervention into domestic affairs of states, called for consideration of a declaration of principles of non-intervention. Draft declarations were submitted to the First Committee of the General Assembly by the Soviet Union, by a group of Latin American States, and by a group of Afro–Asian states. Debate failed to resolve the differences in the drafts and, after consultation among the sponsors, a new draft was introduced and sponsored by a 57–member group of Afro–Asian and Latin American states. The First Committee approved this draft, without amendments, by a vote of 100 to none with five abstentions. 20 GAOR, First Comm. 434, U.N.Doc. A/C.1/SR 1422 (Dec. 20, 1965). The following day the General Assembly adopted the draft by a vote of 109 to none with one abstention. 20 GAOR, U.N.Doc. A/PV. 1407 (Dec. 21, 1965). The United Kingdom abstained from both votes. It objected to the failure to define accurately and precisely the terms used in the draft and the failure to take sufficient time to allow all nations to study the declaration and to present their views. 20 GAOR, First Comm. 430–31, U.N.Doc. A/C.1/SR 1422 (Dec. 20, 1965).

## THE CONTINUING VALIDITY OF THE RULE OF NON–INTERVENTION

### *BULL, CONCLUSION*

Intervention in World Politics 184–87 (Bull, ed. 1984).*

On the one hand, great inequalities of power provide the conditions in which intervention is possible. On the other hand, the motives which give rise to it are widespread and insistent: economic motives such as the desire to acquire or to preserve access to resources; ideological motives such as the desire to promote social revolution or national liberation, or to oppose it; security motives such as concern to affect the global distribution of power; perhaps even humanitarian motives, such as concern to uphold human

* Reprinted by permission of Clarendon Press, Oxford.

rights against tyrannical regimes. In a world political system as marked as is our own by interconnectedness and mutual sensitivity and vulnerability, such motives are scarcely to be avoided: our access to resources, the survival of our values and ways of living, our military security, and the human rights of others very often do depend on events within the jurisdiction of other states, which we can determine by intervening in them. Nor are such motives necessarily unworthy or discreditable. * * *

Does this mean that it would be better to abandon the rule of non-intervention rather than maintain a pretence that states are bound by it? Normative structures may be conceived readily enough, in which this rule would have no place. In a world in which power and the authority to use it were concentrated in a central international authority, perhaps developing out of a strengthened United Nations, the rights of the authority to interfere coercively within the spheres of jurisdiction of the component political units might be unlimited. In a world in which power and authority were in the hands of regional international organizations, bodies such as the European Community, the Socialist Commonwealth of the Soviet Union and its allies, the Organization of African States, or the Association of South–East Asian Nations might similarly have unlimited powers of interference within particular regions, and the rule of non-intervention would have no place, except in relations among the various regional bodies. We may also imagine a world in which, in place of a rule of non-intervention, there was a rule confining rights of intervention to a limited number of great powers, each of which would be licensed to play the role of policeman in a particular part of the world: such a conception of international order, based on an understanding among a small number of regionally dominant great powers (the United States, the Soviet Union, Britain, China, India) briefly attracted the attention of planners of the post-war world during the Second World War, as an alternative to the United Nations system more in tune with the realities which then prevailed; in this kind of system the rule of non-intervention would play a role only in relations among the great powers.

In fact, however, the rule of non-intervention is essentially bound up with the rule that states are entitled to rights of independence or sovereignty. A state within whose sphere of jurisdiction there may be legitimate coercive interference by a world authority, a regional body, or a great power licensed to act as a policeman, is not independent or sovereign. Proposals to abandon the rule of non-intervention, along one or another of the lines sketched out above, are in effect proposals to abandon the principle that states have rights to independence, and to construct world order upon a quite different basis.

Whatever the merits of these and other visions of an alternative world order, it has to be recognized that none commands any significant degree of support among the political forces which prevail in the world today. There is an overwhelming consensus behind the principle that all states are entitled to rights of independence or sovereignty.

The consensus behind the rule that states have rights of sovereignty extends to its corollary, that they have the duty of non-intervention. The evidence that states today are willing to attach reservations and qualifications in principle to their adherence, as well as to violate it from time to time in practice, does not detract from this consensus, nor does it detract from the vital role which the rule plays in helping to define the basis of the present world order. Nor is it clear that the degree of disregard of the rule of non-intervention manifest in world politics at the present time is basically novel or unusual. The impression we have that the post–1945 period is one which is specially marked by interventionism is the result less, I suspect, of a greater incidence or severity of acts of coercive interference than in earlier periods, than it is of changes in our consciousness or perceptions: in a world in which intervention has come to be defined more broadly, condemned more loudly, resented more bitterly, reported more faithfully, we are more willing to recognize acts of intervention for what they are than we were in earlier phases in the history of international politics.

If there is a way forward now, it lies not in seeking to replace the rule of non-intervention with some other rule, but rather in considering how it should be modified and adapted to meet the particular circumstances and needs of the present time.

### *Notes*

1. The volume edited by Hedley Bull includes, in addition to Bull's Introduction, and Conclusion and his essay on Intervention in the Third World, other articles of interest: Hoffmann, The Problem of Intervention; Higgins, Intervention and International Law; Windsor, Superpower Intervention; Moisi, Intervention in French Foreign Policy; Luttwak, Intervention and Access to Natural Resources; Akehurst, Humanitarian Intervention; Falk, Intervention and National Liberation; Luard, Collective Intervention.

2. For the application of the principle of non-intervention under customary law to outlaw support for rebels against an established government, see Case Concerning Military and Paramilitary Activities in and against Nicaragua (Nicaragua v. United States) (Merits), 1986 I.C.J. 14, 106–110.

## INTERVENTION BY INVITATION

### *SCHACHTER, THE RIGHT OF STATES TO USE ARMED FORCE*

82 Mich.L.Rev. 1620, 1644–45 (1984).*

A separate comment is called for by the kind of case presented by the request of the Governor–General of Grenada for military intervention by the United States and neighboring states. That request was premised on the "vacuum of authority" resulting from an attempted coup d'état and a danger of foreign intervention. A factual question was raised as to whether the Governor–General made his request prior to the intervention or whether it was "concocted" after the invasion had been agreed upon and set in motion. Another question was raised as to whether the Governor–General had the constitutional authority to make such a request. On both these points, there was reason to doubt that the Governor–General's "request" constituted an adequate legal justification for the armed intervention. However, apart from these questions specifically related to Grenada, there is the broader issue of principle concerning intervention on invitation of the government.

We have already observed that authoritative legal opinion (manifested in the above-mentioned resolution of the Insitut de Droit International) considers that intervention on either side in a civil war interferes with the right of the people to decide the issue for themselves. However, in the absence of a civil war, recognized governments have a right to receive external military assistance and outside states are free to furnish such aid. But a problem arises if such outside military force is used to impose restrictions on the "political independence" of the country, as, for example, by limiting the choice of the population in regard to the composition of the government or the policies it should follow. In such cases, we would conclude that the foreign armies, though invited by the government, are using military force to curtail the political independence of the state, and therefore it is an action that contravenes article 2(4). A different conclusion may be reached when a foreign force is invited by the government to help put down an attempted coup or to assist in restoring law and order. This would not violate article 2(4). Recent examples include French and British military support of African governments facing internal disorder. The line between the two situations may not always be easy to draw. An initial intervention of a limited character may evolve into a more protracted use of foreign forces to repress internal democracy and political expression. There is good reason therefore to place a heavy burden on any foreign government which intervenes with armed forces even at the invitation of the constitutional authority to demonstrate convincingly that its use of force has not infringed the right of the people to determine their political system and the composition of their government. It cannot be assumed that governments will, as a rule, invite foreign interventions that leave the people entirely free to make their own political determinations, though on occasion this may be the case.

## *Notes*

1. Among the justifications claimed by the United States for the invasion of Panama in 1989, President Bush included the following:

> In the early morning of December 20, 1989, the democratically elected Panamanian leadership announced the formation of a government, assumed power in a formal swearing-in ceremony, and welcomed the assistance of the U.S. Armed Forces in removing the illegitimate Noriega regime.

Communication from the President of the United States Transmitting a Report on the Development Concerning the Deployment of United States Forces to Panama on December 20, 1989, House Doc. 101–127, 101st Cong., 2d Sess., at 1 (1990). In summing up the justifications for the invasion the President repeated that the deployment of U.S. forces "was welcomed by the democratically elected government of Panama." Id. at 2. See the President's letter to Congress, p. 924 infra.

It appears that several hours before the invasion began, a U.S. representative in Panama informed Giullermo Endaro, who had apparently been the majority's choice in a recent election, that the invasion was about to take place. Endaro was then taken to a U.S. military base in the Panama Canal Zone where the Oath of Office was administered to him. The United States did not claim that Endaro invited the invasion or was asked to consent to it, or that if he had not done so the invasion would not have taken place. Did Endaro's "welcome" of the invasion constitute an invitation by the government, justifying it under international law? Was it justified as a use of force to give effect to the wishes of the Panamanian people? See the discussion of the invasion of Panama, p. 924 infra. See also Hargrove, Intervention by Invitation and the Politics of the New World Order; Mullerson, Intervention by Invitation; Wedgewood, Commentary on Intervention by Invitation; and Ferencz, Commentary on What International Law Demands and How States Respond, all in Law and Force in the New International Order 111–185 (Damrosch & Scheffer, eds. 1991).

2. In the Nicaragua Case (Merits), the International Court of Justice said:

> As the Court has stated, the principle of non-intervention derives from customary international law. It would certainly lose its effectiveness as a principle of law if intervention were to be justified by a mere request for assistance made by an opposition group in another State—supposing such a request to have actually been made by an opposition to the régime in Nicaragua in this instance. Indeed, it is difficult to see what would remain of the principle of non-intervention in international law if intervention, which is already allowable at the request of the government of a State, were also to be allowed at the request of the opposition. This would permit any State to intervene at any moment in the internal affairs of another State, whether at the request of the government or at the request of its opposition. Such a situation does not in the Court's view correspond to the present state of international law.

Military and Paramilitary Activities in and against Nicaragua (Nicaragua v. United States), 1986 I.C.J. 14, 126.

### 3. *The Self-Defense Exception: Article 51*

*CHARTER OF THE UNITED NATIONS*

San Francisco, June 26, 1945.

* * *

ARTICLE 51

Nothing in the present Charter shall impair the inherent right of individual or collective self-defence if an armed attack occurs against a Member of the United Nations, until the Security Council has taken measures necessary to maintain international peace and security. Measures taken by Members in the exercise of this right of self-defence shall be immediately reported to the Security Council and shall not in any way affect the authority and responsibility of the Security Council under the present Charter to take at any time such action as it deems necessary in order to maintain or restore international peace and security.

* * *

## MILITARY AND PARAMILITARY ACTIVITIES IN AND AGAINST NICARAGUA (NICARAGUA v. UNITED STATES OF AMERICA)

1986 I.C.J. 14, 103–123.

[In 1984 the Republic of Nicaragua brought a proceeding against the United States charging the U.S. with military and paramilitary activities against Nicaragua. The U.S. denied the jurisdiction of the Court, and when the Court concluded that it had jurisdiction, the U.S. discontinued its participation in the case. See Chapter 10.

Nicaragua accused the United States of attacks on oil pipelines, storage and port facilities in Nicaragua, Nicaraguan naval patrol boats, and the mining of Nicaraguan ports; violation of Nicaraguan air space; as well as training, arming, equipping, financing and supplying the Contra forces and otherwise aiding military and paramilitary activities against Nicaragua. Nicaragua claimed that these acts constituted violations of Article 2(4) of the U.N. Charter as well as corresponding principles of customary law. The United States charged that Nicaragua had supplied arms and given others support from its territory to armed opposition to the Government of El Salvador, and that U.S. actions were designed to interdict that support. The United States justified its activities against Nicaragua as acts in collective self-defense with El Salvador.

Because of reservations in the U.S. declaration accepting the compulsory jurisdiction of the Court, the Court concluded that it could not consider the Nicaraguan claims under the U.N. Charter, but that the principles as to the use of force incorporated in the Charter "correspond, in essentials, to those found in customary international law" and proceeded to adjudicate Nicaragua's claims accordingly, in effect construing Articles 2(4) and 51 of the Charter. The Court (by twelve votes to three) decided that by the actions indicated the U.S. had breached its obligations under customary law not to use force against another state and not to intervene in the affairs of another state or to violate its sovereignty and not to interrupt peaceful maritime commerce, as well as in breach of its obligation under the Treaty of Friendship, Commerce and Navigation between the two states. The Court rejected claims that the Acts were justified as being in collective self-defense with the Government of El Salvador.

In its judgment the Court said:]

195. In the case of individual self-defence, the exercise of this right is subject to the State concerned having been the victim of an armed attack. Reliance on collective self-defence of course does not remove the need for this. There appears now to be general agreement on the nature of the acts which can be treated as constituting armed attacks. In particular, it may be considered to be agreed that an armed attack must be understood as including not merely action by regular armed forces across an international border, but also "the sending by or on behalf of a State of armed bands, groups, irregulars or mercenaries, which carry out acts of armed force against another State of such gravity as to amount to" (*inter alia* ) an actual armed attack conducted by regular forces, "or its substantial involvement therein". This description, contained in Article 3, paragraph (*g*), of the Definition of Aggression annexed to General Assembly resolution 3314 (XXIX), may be taken to reflect customary international law. The Court sees no reason to deny that, in customary law, the prohibition of armed attacks may apply to the sending by a State of armed bands to the territory of another State, if such an operation, because of its scale and effects, would have been classified as an armed attack rather than as a mere frontier incident had it been carried out by regular armed forces. But the Court does

not believe that the concept of "armed attack" includes not only acts by armed bands where such acts occur on a significant scale but also assistance to rebels in the form of the provision of weapons or logistical or other support. Such assistance may be regarded as a threat or use of force, or amount to intervention in the internal or external affairs of other States. It is also clear that it is the State which is the victim of an armed attack which must form and declare the view that it has been so attacked. There is no rule in customary international law permitting another State to exercise the right of collective self-defence on the basis of its own assessment of the situation. Where collective self-defence is invoked, it is to be expected that the State for whose benefit this right is used will have declared itself to be the victim of an armed attack.

196. The question remains whether the lawfulness of the use of collective self-defence by the third State for the benefit of the attacked State also depends on a request addressed by that State to the third State. A provision of the Charter of the Organization of American States is here in point: and while the Court has no jurisdiction to consider that instrument as applicable to the dispute, it may examine it to ascertain what light it throws on the content of customary international law. The Court notes that the OAS Charter includes, in Article 3(*f*), the principle that: "an act of aggression against one American State is an act of aggression against all the other American States" and a provision in Article 27 that:

> "Every act of aggression by a State against the territorial integrity or the inviolability of the territory or against the sovereignty or political independence of an American State shall be considered an act of aggression against the other American States."

* * *

199. At all events, the Court finds that in customary international law, whether of a general kind or that particular to the inter-American legal system, there is no rule permitting the exercise of collective self-defence in the absence of a request by the State which regards itself as the victim of an armed attack. The Court concludes that the requirement of a request by the State which is the victim of the alleged attack is additional to the requirement that such a State should have declared itself to have been attacked.

* * *

201. To justify certain activities involving the use of force, the United States has relied solely on the exercise of its right of collective self-defence. However the Court, having regard particularly to the non-participation of the United States in the merits phase, considers that it should enquire whether customary international law, applicable to the present dispute, may contain other rules which may exclude the unlawfulness of such activities. It does not, however, see any need to reopen the question of the conditions governing the exercise of the right of individual self-defence, which have already been examined in connection with collective self-defence. On the other hand, the Court must enquire whether there is any justification for the activities in question, to be found not in the right of collective self-defence against an armed attack, but in the right to take counter-measures in response to conduct of Nicaragua which is not alleged to constitute an armed

attack. It will examine this point in connection with an analysis of the principle of non-intervention in customary international law.

* * *

211. The Court has recalled above (paragraphs 193 to 195) that for one State to use force against another, on the ground that that State has committed a wrongful act of force against a third State, is regarded as lawful, by way of exception, only when the wrongful act provoking the response was an armed attack. Thus the lawfulness of the use of force by a State in response to a wrongful act of which it has not itself been the victim is not admitted when this wrongful act is not an armed attack. In the view of the Court, under international law in force today—whether customary international law or that of the United Nations system—States do not have a right of "collective" armed response to acts which do not constitute an "armed attack". Furthermore, the Court has to recall that the United States itself is relying on the "inherent right of self-defence" (paragraph 126 above), but apparently does not claim that any such right exists as would, in respect of intervention, operate in the same way as the right of collective self-defence in respect of an armed attack. In the discharge of its duty under Article 53 of the Statute, the Court has nevertheless had to consider whether such a right might exist; but in doing so it may take note of the absence of any such claim by the United States as an indication of *opinio juris.*

* * *

229. The Court must thus consider whether, as the Respondent claims, the acts in question of the United States are justified by the exercise of its right of collective self-defence against an armed attack. The Court must therefore establish whether the circumstances required for the exercise of this right of self-defence are present and, if so, whether the steps taken by the United States actually correspond to the requirements of international law. For the Court to conclude that the United States was lawfully exercising its right of collective self-defence, it must first find that Nicaragua engaged in an armed attack against El Salvador, Honduras or Costa Rica.

230. As regards El Salvador, the Court has found (paragraph 160 above) that it is satisfied that between July 1979 and the early months of 1981, an intermittent flow of arms was routed via the territory of Nicaragua to the armed opposition in that country. The Court was not however satisfied that assistance has reached the Salvadorian armed opposition, on a scale of any significance, since the early months of 1981, or that the Government of Nicaragua was responsible for any flow of arms at either period. Even assuming that the supply of arms to the opposition in El Salvador could be treated as imputable to the Government of Nicaragua, to justify invocation of the right of collective self-defence in customary international law, it would have to be equated with an armed attack by Nicaragua on El Salvador. As stated above, the Court is unable to consider that, in customary international law, the provision of arms to the opposition in another State constitutes an armed attack on that State. Even at a time when the arms flow was at its peak, and again assuming the participation of the Nicaraguan Government, that would not constitute such armed attack.

231. Turning to Honduras and Costa Rica, the Court has also stated (paragraph 164 above) that it should find established that certain trans-border incursions into the territory of those two States, in 1982, 1983 and 1984, were imputable to the Government of Nicaragua. Very little information is however available to the Court as to the circumstances of these incursions or their possible motivations, which renders it difficult to decide whether they may be treated for legal purposes as amounting, singly or collectively, to an "armed attack" by Nicaragua on either or both States. The Court notes that during the Security Council debate in March/April 1984, the representative of Costa Rica made no accusation of an armed attack, emphasizing merely his country's neutrality and support for the Contadora process (S/PV.2529, pp. 13–23); the representative of Honduras however stated that "my country is the object of aggression made manifest through a number of incidents by Nicaragua against our territorial integrity and civilian population" (ibid., p. 37). There are however other considerations which justify the Court in finding that neither these incursions, nor the alleged supply of arms to the opposition in El Salvador, may be relied on as justifying the exercise of the right of collective self-defence.

232. The exercise of the right of collective self-defence presupposes that an armed attack has occurred; and it is evident that it is the victim State, being the most directly aware of that fact, which is likely to draw general attention to its plight. It is also evident that if the victim State wishes another State to come to its help in the exercise of the right of collective self-defence, it will normally make an express request to that effect. Thus in the present instance, the Court is entitled to take account, in judging the asserted justification of the exercise of collective self-defence by the United States, of the actual conduct of El Salvador, Honduras and Costa Rica at the relevant time, as indicative of a belief by the State in question that it was the victim of an armed attack by Nicaragua, and of the making of a request by the victim State to the United States for help in the exercise of collective self-defence.

233. The Court has seen no evidence that the conduct of those States was consistent with such a situation, either at the time when the United States first embarked on the activities which were allegedly justified by self-defence, or indeed for a long period subsequently. So far as El Salvador is concerned, it appears to the Court that while El Salvador did in fact officially declare itself the victim of an armed attack, and did ask for the United States to exercise its right of collective self-defence, this occurred only on a date much later than the commencement of the United States activities which were allegedly justified by this request. The Court notes that on 3 April 1984, the representative of El Salvador before the United Nations Security Council, while complaining of the "open foreign intervention practised by Nicaragua in our internal affairs" (S/PV.2528, p. 58), refrained from stating that El Salvador had been subjected to armed attack, and made no mention of the right of collective self-defence which it had supposedly asked the United States to exercise. Nor was this mentioned when El Salvador addressed a letter to the Court in April 1984, in connection with Nicaragua's complaint against the United States. It was only in its Declaration of Intervention filed on 15 August 1984, that El Salvador referred to requests addressed at various dates to the United States for the

latter to exercise its right of collective self-defence (para. XII), asserting on this occasion that it had been the victim of aggression from Nicaragua "since at least 1980". In that Declaration, El Salvador affirmed that initially it had "not wanted to present any accusation or allegation [against Nicaragua] to any of the jurisdictions to which we have a right to apply", since it sought "a solution of understanding and mutual respect" (para. III).

234. As to Honduras and Costa Rica, they also were prompted by the institution of proceedings in this case to address communications to the Court; in neither of these is there mention of armed attack or collective self-defence. As has already been noted (paragraph 231 above), Honduras in the Security Council in 1984 asserted that Nicaragua had engaged in aggression against it, but did not mention that a request had consequently been made to the United States for assistance by way of collective self-defence. On the contrary, the representative of Honduras emphasized that the matter before the Security Council "is a Central American problem, without exception, and it must be solved regionally" (S/PV.2529, p. 38), i.e., through the Contadora process. The representative of Costa Rica also made no reference to collective self-defence. Nor, it may be noted, did the representative of the United States assert during that debate that it had acted in response to requests for assistance in that context.

235. There is also an aspect of the conduct of the United States which the Court is entitled to take into account as indicative of the view of that State on the question of the existence of an armed attack. At no time, up to the present, has the United States Government addressed to the Security Council, in connection with the matters the subject of the present case, the report which is required by Article 51 of the United Nations Charter in respect of measures which a State believes itself bound to take when it exercises the right of individual or collective self-defence. The Court, whose decision has to be made on the basis of customary international law, has already observed that in context of that law, the reporting obligation enshrined in Article 51 of the Charter of the United Nations does not exist. It does not therefore treat the absence of a report on the part of the United States as the breach of an undertaking forming part of the customary international law applicable to the present dispute. But the Court is justified in observing that this conduct of the United States hardly conforms with the latter's avowed conviction that it was acting in the context of collective self-defence as consecrated by Article 51 of the Charter. This fact is all the more noteworthy because, in the Security Council, the United States has itself taken the view that failure to observe the requirement to make a report contradicted a State's claim to be acting on the basis of collective self-defence (S/PV.2187).

236. Similarly, while no strict legal conclusion may be drawn from the date of El Salvador's announcement that it was the victim of an armed attack, and the date of its official request addressed to the United States concerning the exercise of collective self-defence, those dates have a significance as evidence of El Salvador's view of the situation. The declaration and the request of El Salvador, made publicly for the first time in August 1984, do not support the contention that in 1981 there was an armed attack capable of serving as a legal foundation for United States activities which began in the second half of that year. The States concerned did not behave

as though there were an armed attack at the time when the activities attributed by the United States to Nicaragua, without actually constituting such an attack, were nevertheless the most accentuated; they did so behave only at a time when these facts fell furthest short of what would be required for the Court to take the view that an armed attack existed on the part of Nicaragua against El Salvador.

237. Since the Court has found that the condition *sine qua non* required for the exercise of the right of collective self-defence by the United States is not fulfilled in this case, the appraisal of the United States activities in relation to the criteria of necessity and proportionality takes on a different significance. As a result of this conclusion of the Court, even if the United States activities in question had been carried on in strict compliance with the canons of necessity and proportionality, they would not thereby become lawful. If however they were not, this may constitute an additional ground of wrongfulness. On the question of necessity, the Court observes that the United States measures taken in December 1981 (or, at the earliest, March of that year—paragraph 93 above) cannot be said to correspond to a "necessity" justifying the United States action against Nicaragua on the basis of assistance given by Nicaragua to the armed opposition in El Salvador. First, these measures were only taken, and began to produce their effects, several months after the major offensive of the armed opposition against the Government of El Salvador had been completely repulsed (January 1981), and the actions of the opposition considerably reduced in consequence. Thus it was possible to eliminate the main danger to the Salvadorian Government without the United States embarking on activities in and against Nicaragua. Accordingly, it cannot be held that these activities were undertaken in the light of necessity. Whether or not the assistance to the *contras* might meet the criterion of proportionality, the Court cannot regard the United States activities summarised in paragraphs 80, 81 and 86, i.e., those relating to the mining of the Nicaraguan ports and the attacks on ports, oil installations, etc., as satisfying that criterion. Whatever uncertainty may exist as to the exact scale of the aid received by the Salvadorian armed opposition from Nicaragua, it is clear that these latter United States activities in question could not have been proportionate to that aid. Finally on this point, the Court must also observe that the reaction of the United States in the context of what it regarded as self-defence was continued long after the period in which any presumed armed attack by Nicaragua could reasonably be contemplated.

238. Accordingly, the Court concludes that the plea of collective self-defence against an alleged armed attack on El Salvador, Honduras or Costa Rica, advanced by the United States to justify its conduct toward Nicaragua, cannot be upheld; and accordingly that the United States has violated the principle prohibiting recourse to the threat or use of force by the acts listed in paragraph 227 above, and by its assistance to the *contras* to the extent that this assistance "involve[s] a threat or use of force" (paragraph 228 above).

* * *

### *Note*

Judge Schwebel's dissent was based largely on his conclusion that Nicaragua's support of the insurgency in El Salvador was so extensive and persistent as to amount to an armed attack justifying collective self-defense by the United States, and that this warranted military activities not only in El Salvador but against Nicaraguan territory as well. Moreover, in his view, judgment for Nicaragua was unwarranted because it had pressed false testimony on the Court in a deliberate effort to conceal its wrongs. Schwebel voted with the majority holding that the United States violated customary law by failing to make known the existence and location of the mines it had laid.

Judge Oda objected to the Court's consideration of the Nicaraguan claim as arising under customary law. In his view, the multilateral treaty reservation denied the Court jurisdiction of any proceeding based on such a treaty, and even if the treaty and customary law could be disentangled, the Court could not entertain the case and decide it on principles of customary law. Moreover, the claim presented a political dispute, not a legal dispute under 36(2).

Judge Jennings agreed with Oda that the U.S. multilateral treaty reservation must be respected and the Court could not exercise jurisdiction and apply customary law in lieu of the multilateral treaties. Therefore, he voted against the Court's decisions on the use of force, on intervention and on self-defense. However Jennings and Oda both joined the majority in holding that the laying of mines by the United States breached United States obligations under a bilateral treaty.

Seven of the judges who voted with the majority appended separate opinions dealing with various aspects of the judgment.

### *SCHACHTER, INTERNATIONAL LAW IN THEORY AND PRACTICE*

141–46 (1991) (footnotes omitted).

A critical question affecting both law and policy on self-defense concerns the degree of uncertainty or indeterminacy that inheres in the proclaimed legal limits. Some indeterminancy results from the key standards of necessity and proportionality, concepts that leave ample room for diverse opinions in particular cases. Other sources of uncertainty can be traced to differing interpretations of the events that would permit forcible defensive action. Varying views have been advanced by governments and scholars relating to the kinds of illegal force that would trigger the right of an armed defensive response. While strong positions have been taken by nearly all States against "preventive" or "preemptive" war, some uncertainty remains as to threats of force that credibly appear as likely to result in imminent attack. Other issues, highlighted by the *Nicaragua* case, concern the illegal use of force through subversion, supply of arms, and logistic support of armed forces as sufficient ground for defensive response. It is not entirely clear to what extent self-defense responding to an armed attack embraces the use of force as a deterrent to future attacks. Nor is there agreement on the circumstances that would permit a State to intervene (or "counterintervene") in an internal conflict under the principle of collective self-defense. Even more unsettling is the uncertainty about the first use of nuclear weapons, the targeting of civilian centers and the proportionality of retaliatory action.

These controversial issues indicate that the rules of self-defense fall far short of a code of conduct that would provide precise "hard law" for many cases likely to arise. * * *

* * *

Notwithstanding its relative indeterminacy, self-defense as a legal norm can have an ascertainable relationship to the policies and actions of governments. The "defensist" principle—namely, that self-defense is the only legitimate reason to use force against another State—has been expressed as the strategic policy of most States. Evidence for this is not only found in governmental statements to international bodies, where they may be expected. Recent studies by political scientists and students of military strategy confirm the practical implication of defensist doctrine. When States proclaim the principle of self-defense as governing the use of force, they have a stake in its credibility to other States and to their own citizens. For such States to be credible, their weapons, training and contingent planning must reflect a defensist strategy. Their good faith can be tested by their willingness to consider ways to reduce threats and resolve conflicts without using force. Hence, a defensist posture is not merely one of restraint but a source of policy that goes beyond the essentially negative rules of the law. It has obvious implications for such protective activities as monitoring and inspection. It calls for limitations on weaponry and balance among adversaries. The danger that systems which purport to be defensive may be perceived as offensive and therefore "destabilizing" becomes a matter of central concern. The most obvious consequence of defensist doctrine is that States no longer consider that they may invade other States for objectives that were considered in prior periods as legitimate and appropriate. Thus, the naked use of force for economic gain, or to avenge past injustices, or civilize "inferior" people, or vindicate honor, or achieve "manifest destiny", is no longer asserted as national policy. Seen in the perspective of history, this is a profound change in the relations of States.

* * *

The more controversial questions of self-defense have been raised by actions and claims that would expand a State's right to use force beyond the archetypical case of an armed attack on the territory or instrumentality of that State. Such expanded conceptions of self-defense are exemplified by the following uses of force by States claiming self-defense:

(1) the use of force to rescue political hostages believed to face imminent danger of death or injury;

(2) the use of force against officials or installations in a foreign State believed to support terrorists acts directed against nationals of the State claiming the right of defense;

(3) the use of force against troops, planes, vessels or installations believed to threaten imminent attack by a State with declared hostile intent;

(4) the use of retaliatory force against a government or military force so as to deter renewed attacks on the State taking such action;

(5) the use of force against a government that has provided arms or technical support to insurgents in a third State;

(6) the use of force against a government that has allowed its territory to be used by military forces of a third State considered to be a threat to the State claiming self-defense;

(7) the use of force in the name of collective defense (or counterintervention) against a government imposed by foreign forces and faced with large-scale military resistance by many of its people.

* * * Nearly all the cases have been discussed in U.N. bodies and, although opinions have been divided, it is clear that most governments have been reluctant to legitimize expanded self-defense actions that go beyond the paradigmatic case. Thus, no U.N. resolution has approved the use of force in any of the cases that I have listed. In the few cases where resolutions were adopted that passed judgment on the legality of the action, they denied the validity of the self-defense claim. In many cases, resolutions were not adopted, but the majority of States that addressed the issue of lawfulness criticized the actions as contrary to the Charter. Few ventured to defend the legality of the self-defense claims. * * *

* * * the general reluctance to approve uses of force under expanded conceptions of self-defense is itself significant. Such reluctance is evidence of a widespread perception that widening the scope of self-defense will erode the basic rule against unilateral recourse to force. The absence of binding judicial or other third-party determinations relating to the use of force adds to the apprehension that a more permissive rule of self-defense will open the way to further disregard of the limits on force. The refusal of the United States to take part in the proceedings of the International Court on the merits in the *Nicaragua* case and by its non-compliance with the judgment against it has given new emphasis to this point.

It is true that some international lawyers believe that legitimate self-defense should be construed more liberally. They argue that the absence of effective collective remedies against illegal force makes it necessary, indeed inevitable, that States take defensive action on the basis of their own perceptions of national interest and capabilities. In addition to the imperatives of national security, they cite the responsibility of powerful States to maintain international order. They call for a liberal construction of self-defense, stressing that the words of the Charter should be interpreted "in context" so as to yield "reasonable" meanings required by the "purpose and object" of the text. Unilateral acts that stretch the meaning of self-defense are treated as "State practice", although there is no general *opinio juris* to support their "acceptance as law". Conduct that violates text and earlier interpretations may be viewed as new or emerging law based on the efficacy of accomplished facts in shaping the law. Some of these arguments, if accepted, would extend the concept of self-defense so broadly as to allow almost any unilateral use of force taken in the name of law and order. There is no evidence that governments by and large would favor this result. On the contrary, the records of the United Nations, as already mentioned, show strong resistance to widening self-defense to permit force except where there has been an armed attack or threat of imminent attack. It does not seem likely that this resistance will disappear in the foreseeable future.

This does not mean, of course, that the law of self-defense will remain static. The kaleidoscopic events of our era will continue to create new pressures for resort to force. The role of international law cannot be limited to repeating the old maxims. What its role should be calls for further consideration.

### *Notes*

1. The end of the Cold War and the revival of the Security Council raised additional questions about the relation of the right of self-defense to the authority of the Security Council and about the implications of the "until" clause of Article 51. How does the availability of the Security Council affect the right of self-defense? Is the victim of an armed attack required to bring the matter to the attention of the Security Council before taking any military measures in self-defense? Can states continue to use armed force in self-defense after the Security Council is "seized" of the matter? After the Security Council has considered the matter, made determinations, recommendations, decisions? See p. 967 infra.

During the years when the Security Council was largely neutralized (p. 977 below), victims of an armed attack had to defend themselves indefinitely, alone or with the assistance of allies, not only "until the Security Council has taken measures necessary to maintain international peace and security." In such circumstances, does the right of self-defense under article 51 justify only such action as necessary to beat back the attack? Does it justify retaliation, limited perhaps by the principle of proportionality? Does it remove all the prohibitions of Article 2(4), so that the victim of an armed attack is in effect warranted in engaging in a "just war" against the aggressor, limited only by the traditional rules of war? May the victim carry the war to the territory of the aggressor? To the territories of allies of the aggressor? Are other states forbidden to help the aggressor? Obligated to help the victim?

If the victim of an armed attack, acting in lawful self-defense under Article 51, succeeds in conquering territory of the aggressor, is annexation of such territory lawful? See Chapter 4, p. 328.

2. Brownlie addressed the question of lawful defensive measures in the face of indirect aggression:

> In so far as there is a use of force by forces controlled by a foreign state, this may be met by lawful measures of self-defence including forcible measures proportionate to the danger. Yet it is very difficult in this context to say what are proportionate measures. In the case of sporadic incursions by armed bands by land or sea effective measures may be taken to prevent incursion without any operations against the parent state. Interception may occur on the frontier or at the limit of territorial waters. However, preventive action has been taken against armed bands on a number of occasions and the legality of such action will depend on the status of anticipatory action in the modern law. More delicate problems arise in the case of the state which gives military aid to an aggressor, or which gives aid to, or exercises control over, rebel groups or other irregular forces. It is suggested that so far as possible defensive measures should be confined to the territory of the defending state and the hostile forces themselves unless there is clear evidence of a major invasion across a frontier which calls for

extensive military operations which may not be confined merely to protecting the frontier line. The precise difficulty in the case of indirect aggression is to avoid major breaches of the peace of wide territorial extent arising from defensive measures based on vague evidence of foreign complicity.

In the present connexion it might be argued that "armed attack" in Article 51 of the Charter refers to a trespass, a direct invasion, and not to activities described by some jurists as "indirect aggression". But providing there is a control by the principal, the aggressor state, and an actual use of force by its agents, there is an "armed attack".

Brownlie, International Law and the Use of Force, 372–73 (1963).*

3. On April 14, 1986, the United States bombed targets in Libyan territory, killing both military and civilian persons and inflicting substantial damage. President Reagan announced that the United States had "launched a series of strikes against the headquarters, terrorist facilities, and military assets that support Muammar Qadhafi's subversive activities." The President's statement justified the action as being in response, in particular, to a bombing of a Berlin nightclub frequented by U.S. servicemen in which one was killed and many wounded. Reagan described the attack as "a mission fully consistent with Article 51 of the UN Charter. We believe that this preemptive action against terrorist installations will not only diminish Colonel Qadhafi's capacity to export terror, it will provide him with incentives and reasons to alter his criminal behavior." Presidential Statement of April 14, 1986, U.S. Dept. of State, Selected Documents No. 24.

Was the action of the United States justified as a use of force in self-defense under Article 51? Was it in response to an "armed attack against a member of the United Nations" within the meaning of that article? Note the reference to the bombing as a "preemptive action."

In October 1985 Israel launched an air attack on the Headquarters of the Palestine Liberation Organization (PLO) in Tunisia, in response to terrorist activities attributed to the PLO. The Security Council condemned the action as an "act of armed aggression against Tunisian territory in flagrant violation of the Charter." S.C.Res. 573 (1985). The United States abstained. See 80 A.J.I.L. 165 (1980).

Compare the use or threat of force to apprehend alleged terrorists who are in another state's jurisdiction or control. In 1985, four United States military planes intercepted an Egyptian aircraft over the Mediterranean Sea compelling it to land in Italy so that alleged terrorists aboard the aircraft could be prosecuted for seizing a vessel, taking hostages, and murder. Was the action lawful under the Charter? See Schachter, In Defense of International Rules on the Use of Force, 53 U.Chi.L.Rev. 113, 139–40 (1986).

On April 14, 1993, it was reported that Kuwaiti authorities had thwarted a terrorist plot to assassinate former President George Bush while on a visit to Kuwait. An investigation by U.S. intelligence agencies concluded that the highest levels of the Iraqi government had directed its agents to carry out the

* Footnotes omitted. Reprinted by permission of the Clarendon Press, Oxford.

assassination. On June 26, 1993, United States forces fired 23 Tomahawk missiles at Iraqi intelligence headquarters, from war ships stationed in the Persian Gulf and the Red Sea. At a special session of the Security Council, the U.S. representative said "[T]his was a direct attack on the United States, an attack that required a direct United States response. Consequently, President Clinton yesterday instructed the United States armed forces to carry out a military operation against the headquarters of the Iraqi Intelligence Service in Baghdad. We responded directly, as we were entitled to do, under Article 51 of the United Nations Charter, which provides for the exercise of self defense in such cases."

Assuming the facts as reported, was the U.S. action justified under Article 51 as a response to an armed attack? Was it necessary? proportional? Was the U.S. action justifiable under Security Council resolutions relating to Iraq, supra pp. 970–972:

4. In 1974, in response to a suggestion by Rostow that the United States endorse the right of reprisal under Article 51 of the United Nations Charter, Acting Secretary of State Kenneth Rush wrote:

> [I]t is the established policy of the United States that a State is responsible for the international use of armed force originating from its territory, whether that force be direct and overt or indirect and covert. This equally is the announced policy of the United Nations, expressly reflected, * * *, in the General Assembly's resolution 2625 on Principles of International Law concerning Friendly Relations and Cooperation among States. The definition of aggression recently forwarded by a UN Special Committee to the General Assembly also maintains this accepted principle of international law.
>
> You would add a complementary principle, namely, that where a State cannot or will not fulfill its international legal obligations to prevent the use of its territory for the unlawful exercise of force, the wronged State is entitled to use force, by way of reprisal, to redress, by self-help, the violation of international law which it has suffered.
>
> As you know, resolution 2625 also contains the following categorical statement: "States have a duty to refrain from acts of reprisal involving the use of force." That injunction codifies resolutions of the Security Council which have so affirmed.
>
> The United States has supported and supports the foregoing principle. Of course we recognize that the practice of States is not always consistent with this principle and that it may sometimes be difficult to distinguish the exercise of proportionate self-defense from an act of reprisal. Yet, essentially for reasons of the abuse to which the doctrine of reprisals particularly lends itself, we think it desirable to endeavor to maintain the distinction between acts of lawful self-defense and unlawful reprisals.

68 A.J.I.L. 736 (1974).*

* Footnotes omitted. Reprinted by permission of American Society of International Law.

## THE INVASION OF PANAMA AND ITS JUSTIFICATION

*COMMUNICATION FROM THE PRESIDENT OF THE UNITED STATES TRANSMITTING A REPORT ON THE DEVELOPMENT CONCERNING THE DEPLOYMENT OF UNITED STATES FORCES TO PANAMA ON DECEMBER 20, 1989*

House Doc. 101–127, 101st Cong., 2d Sess. (1990).

THE WHITE HOUSE,
*Washington, DC, December 21, 1989.*

HON. THOMAS S. FOLEY,
*Speaker of the House of Representatives,*
*Washington, DC.*

DEAR MR. SPEAKER: On December 15, 1989, at the instigation of Manuel Noriega, the illegitimate Panamanian National Assembly declared that a state of war existed between the Republic of Panama and the United States. At the same time, Noriega gave a highly inflammatory anti-American speech. A series of vicious and brutal acts directed at U.S. personnel and dependents followed these events.

On December 16, 1989, a U.S. Marine officer was killed without justification by Panama Defense Forces (PDF) personnel. Other elements of the PDF beat a U.S. Naval officer and unlawfully detained, physically abused, and threatened the officer's wife. These acts of violence are directly attributable to Noriega's dictatorship, which created a climate of aggression that places American lives and interests in peril.

These and other events over the past two years have made it clear that the lives and welfare of American citizens in Panama were increasingly at risk, and that the continued safe operation of the Panama Canal and the integrity of the Canal Treaties would be in serious jeopardy if such lawlessness were allowed to continue.

Under these circumstances, I ordered the deployment of approximately 11,000 additional U.S. forces to Panama. In conjunction with the 13,000 U.S. Forces already present, military operations were initiated on December 20, 1989, to protect American lives, to defend democracy in Panama, to apprehend Noriega and bring him to trial on the drug-related charges for which he was indicted in 1988, and to ensure the integrity of the Panama Canal Treaties.

In the early morning of December 20, 1989, the democratically elected Panamanian leadership announced formation of a government, assumed power in a formal swearing-in ceremony, and welcomed the assistance of U.S. Armed Forces in removing the illegitimate Noriega regime.

The deployment of U.S. Forces is an exercise of the right of self-defense recognized in Article 51 of the United Nations charter and was necessary to protect American lives in imminent danger and to fulfill our responsibilities under the Panama Canal Treaties. It was welcomed by the democratically elected government of Panama. The military operations were ordered pursuant to my constitutional authority with respect to the conduct of foreign relations and as Commander in Chief.

In accordance with my desire that Congress be fully informed on this matter, and consistent with the War Powers Resolution, I am providing this report on the deployment of U.S. Armed Forces to Panama.

Although most organized opposition has ceased, it is not possible at this time to predict the precise scope and duration of the military operations or how long the temporary increase of U.S. Forces in Panama will be required. Nevertheless, our objectives are clear and largely have been accomplished. Our additional Forces will remain in Panama only so long as their presence is required.

Sincerely,

George Bush.

### *Notes*

1. Critics of the Panama invasion have concluded that the alleged justifications were not the real reasons for U.S. intervention and that its purpose was to abduct General Noriega and to bring him to trial in the U.S. for conspiracy to smuggle drugs into the United States. However, assuming the facts and characterizations as alleged, was the Panama invasion justified under international law? Compare the article by the then Legal Adviser to the U.S. Department of State, Sofaer, The Legality of the United States Actions in Panama, 29 Colum.J.Trans.L. 281 (1991) and the letter to the President of the U.N. Security Council from the U.S. Permanent Representative to the United Nations. U.N.Doc. S/21035, with Henkin, The Invasion of Panama Under International Law: A Gross Violation, 29 Colum.J.Trans.L. 293 (1991). See also Agora: U.S. Forces in Panama: Defenders, Aggressors or Human Rights Activists, 84 A.J.I.L. 494 (1990).

2. One of the principal justifications invoked by President Bush appears to be the right of self-defense under Article 51. See Sofaer, note 1 supra. Do you agree? Was the invasion necessary? Proportional? Are the U.S. justifications consistent with the opinion of the International Court of Justice in the *Nicaragua* Case (Merits), p. 911 supra? Note that the Legal Advisor did not mention the Nicaragua case. Compare Henkin, note 1 supra.

## ANTICIPATORY SELF-DEFENSE

During the nuclear confrontation of the Cold War the legal and political literature were addressed to the possibility of a nuclear "first strike" to preempt an impending nuclear attack and strategies to defend against such an horrific eventuality. With the end of the Cold War those debates lost their immediacy, but it remains important to consider whether a state may act in anticipation of an impending attack with nuclear, chemical, biological or even conventional weapons.

### *SCHACHTER, THE RIGHT OF STATES TO USE ARMED FORCE*

82 Mich.L.Rev. 1620, 1633–35 (1982) (footnotes omitted).

The very fact that states have turned to self-defense to justify the use of force indicates that the text of article 2(4) is not so loose or uncertain as to allow credible self-serving interpretation in all cases. The question then arises whether self-defense provides a wide-open legal loophole in the prohibition against force and whether its apparent availability as a legal justification in recent cases has deprived article 2(4) of much of its significance.

The readiness of states to justify their use of force on the basis of self-defense indicates the importance of defining that "inherent" right in order to limit the latitude of states to interpret it freely in their interest. In the comments that follow, we will consider the principal legal issues that have arisen in regard to legitimate self-defense.

#### The Requirement of an Armed Attack and Anticipatory Defense

Our first question—whether self-defense requires an armed attack or whether it is permissible in anticipation of an attack—has given rise to much controversy among international lawyers. The text of article 51 does not answer the question directly. It declares that "[n]othing in the present Charter shall impair the inherent right of individual or collective self-defense if an armed attack occurs." On one reading this means that self-defense is limited to cases of armed attack. An alternative reading holds that since the article is silent as to the right of self-defense under customary law (which goes beyond cases of armed attack), it should not be construed by implication to eliminate that right. The drafting history shows that article 51 was intended to safeguard the Chapultepec Treaty which provided for collective defense in case of armed attack. The relevant commission report of the San Francisco Conference declared "the use of arms in legitimate self-defense remains admitted and unimpaired." It is therefore not implausible to interpret article 51 as leaving unimpaired the right of self-defense as it existed prior to the Charter. The main interpretive difficulty with this is that the words "if an armed attack occurs" then become redundant, a conclusion which should not be reached without convincing evidence that such redundant use was in keeping with the drafters intention. The link with the Chapultepec Treaty provides a reason for the inclusion of the words "if an armed attack occurs" and explains why it was not said that self-defense is limited to cases of armed attack.

Much of the debate in recent years has focused on the consequences of adopting one or the other interpretation, especially in the light of the apprehension over nuclear missiles. Even as far back as 1946, the U.S. Government stated that the term "armed attack" should be defined to include not merely the dropping of a bomb but "certain steps in themselves preliminary to such action." In recent years, the fear that nuclear missiles, could, on the first strike, destroy the capability for defense and allow virtually no time for defense has appeared to many to render a requirement of armed attack unreasonable. States faced with a perceived danger of immediate attack, it is argued, cannot be expected to await the attack like sitting ducks. In response to this line of reasoning, others argue that the existence of nuclear missiles has made it even more important to maintain a legal barrier against preemptive strikes and anticipatory defense. It is conceded by them that states facing an imminent threat of attack will take defensive measures irrespective of the law, but it is preferable to have states make that choice governed by necessity than to adopt a principle that would make it easier for a state to launch an attack on the pretext of anticipatory defense.

Both of the foregoing positions express apprehensions that are reasonable. It is important that the right of self-defense should not freely allow the use of force in anticipation of an attack or in response to a threat. At the same time, we must recognize that there may well be situations in which the imminence of an attack is so clear and the danger so great that defensive action is essential for self-preservation. It does not seem to me that the law should leave such defense to a decision *contra legem.* Nor does it appear necessary to read article 51 in that way—that is, to exclude completely legitimate self-defense in advance of an actual attack. In my view it is not clear that article 51 was intended to eliminate the customary law right of self-defense and it should not be given that effect. But we should avoid interpreting the customary law as if it broadly authorized preemptive strikes and anticipatory defense in response to threats.

The conditions of the right of anticipatory defense under customary law were expressed generally in an eloquent formulation by the U.S. Secretary of State Daniel Webster in a diplomatic note to the British in 1842 * * * [in which he asserted] that self-defense must be confined to cases in which "the necessity of that self-defense is instant, overwhelming, and leaving no choice of means, and no moment for deliberation."

The Webster formulation of self-defense is often cited as authoritative customary law. It cannot be said that the formulation reflects state practice (which was understandably murky on this point when war was legal), but it is safe to say it reflects a widespread desire to restrict the right of self-defense when no attack has actually occurred. A recent case in point concerns the Israeli bombing of a nuclear reactor in Iraq in 1981, which the Israeli government sought to justify on the ground of self-defense. Israel cited the Iraqi position that it was at war with Israel and claimed that the reactor was intended for a nuclear strike. Many governments and the UN Security Council rejected the Israeli position. In the debates in the Security Council on this question, several delegates referred to the Caroline Case formulation of the right of anticipatory defense as an accepted statement of customary law. We may infer from these official statements recognition of the continued validity of an "inherent" right to use armed force in self-defense prior to an actual attack but only where such an attack is imminent "leaving no moment for deliberation."

### *Notes*

1. Compare the following views:

> a. Under the Charter, alarming military preparations by a neighboring state would justify a resort to the Security Council, but would not justify resort to anticipatory force by the state which believed itself threatened.
>
> The documentary record of the discussions at San Francisco does not afford conclusive evidence that the suggested interpretation of the words "armed attack" in Article 51 is correct, but the general tenor of the discussions, as well as the careful choice of words throughout Chapters VI and VII of the Charter relative to various stages of aggravation of dangers to the peace, support the view stated.

Jessup, A Modern Law of Nations 166–67 (1948) (footnotes omitted).

> b. It was to avoid and eliminate the political and military dangers of letting the nations judge by themselves the vital issues of attack and defence that the relevant provisions of the United Nations Charter were formulated. But the inability of the UN, as at present organised, to act swiftly has handed the power of decision back to the national states. * * * But while this immensely increases the necessity for a reliable international detection organisation and mechanism, in the absence of effective international machinery the right of self-defense must probably now be extended to the defence against a clearly imminent aggression, despite the apparently contrary language of Article 51 of the Charter. The dangers of such an interpretation should not be underestimated. It means that the United States or the Soviet Union may, on the basis of plausible but inaccurate information, send a bomber or missile force to the other country to destroy the force believed to be poised for aggression.

Friedmann, The Changing Structure of International Law 259–60 (1964) (footnotes omitted).

> c. If there were clear evidence of an attack so imminent that there was no time for political action to prevent it, the only meaningful defense for the potential victim might indeed be the pre-emptive attack and—it may be argued—the scheme of Article 2(4) together with Article 51 was not intended to bar such attack. But this argument would claim a small and special exception for the special case of the surprise nuclear attack; today, and one hopes for a time longer, it is meaningful and relevant principally only as between the Soviet Union and the United States * * * But such a reading of the Charter, it should be clear, would not permit (and encourage) anticipatory self-defense in other, more likely situations between nations generally.
>
> * * *
>
> Surely, any extension of Article 51 is especially to be resisted, for whatever is allowed to come within its "armed attack" exception to Article 2(4) might permit full-scale war against the "attacker" and bring in allies on both sides.

Henkin, How Nations Behave 143–45 (2nd ed. 1979) (footnotes omitted).

d. The United States was right in the Cuban Missile crisis not to say that the deployment of missiles in Cuba by the Soviet Union constituted an "armed attack" that would give rise to the right of self-defense. I agree that it would be too dangerous for the world community to allow unilateral uses of force simply because there were some deployments of weapons or modernization of weapons. On the other hand, to say that a nation has to be a sitting duck (to use Professor Myres McDougal's phrase) and wait until the bombs are actually dropping on its soil—that cannot be right either. When attack is initiated and is underway, even though the attacker has not actually arrived in the victim state, measures can be taken. There should be agreement on that principle.

But there are hard cases. Egyptian President Gamal Abdel Nasser announced the blockade of the Gulf of Aqaba in 1967; Israel attacked. I think most people felt that was justified self-defense. But when Israel attacked the nuclear reactor in Iraq in 1981, most people—maybe with the exception of McDougal and one or two others—argued that that went too far. And yet, if anticipatory self-defense cannot cover the Iraqi reactor case (and I have no doubt that nuclear reactor was not for peaceful purposes only), how are we going to deal with a Saddam Hussein who may be preparing to use weapons of mass destruction against his neighbors?

Gardner, Commentary on the Law of Self–Defense, in Law and Force in the New International Order 51–52 (Damrosch & Scheffer, eds. 1991).

2. The official justification of United States action in the 1963 Cuban missile crisis (p. 903 supra) did not invoke anticipatory self-defense, but some writers sought to justify the quarantine on that basis. See, e.g., MacChesney, Some Comments on the "Quarantine" of Cuba, 57 A.J.I.L. 592 (1963). For an opposing view, see Henkin, How Nations Behave 295–96 (2d ed. 1979). Some who argued against limiting the right to self-defense to cases where an armed attack occurs may have had in mind particularly a right to anticipate a nuclear attack. See, e.g., McDougal, The Soviet Cuban Quarantine and Self–Defense, 57 A.J.I.L. 597, 599–601 (1963).

3. In 1981, Israel bombed a nuclear reactor under construction in Iraq and sought to justify its action by claiming a right of "anticipatory" self-defense. Was the threat to Israel such as to bring it within a "liberal" reading of Article 51? Was the alleged Iraqi threat "immediate" within the formula or the spirit of *The Caroline?* Was it relevant that Iraq had continued to maintain that she was in a state of war with Israel? See D'Amato, Israel's Air Strike Upon the Iraqi Nuclear Reactor, 77 A.J.I.L. 584 (1983); G. Fischer, Le bombardment par Israël d'un réacteur nucléaire irakien, 1981 Annuaire Français de Droit International 147. For a discussion of this action in the Security Council, see U.N.Docs. S/PV.2285–88, along with S.C.Res. (487), reprinted in, 20 I.L.M. 993 (1981).

Compare the claim that the United States bombing attack on Libya in 1986 in response to terrorist activities was a "preemptive action" and "fully consistent with article 51." See p. 922 supra.

### 4. *Claims of Permissible Use of Force for Benign Purposes*

Article 2(4) of the Charter prohibits the use of force against the territorial integrity or political independence of another state in absolute terms. Article 51 declares that nothing in the Charter shall impair the inherent right of self-defense if an armed attack occurs. See p. 911. During the years of the Cold War there were suggestions that the Charter should be interpreted to permit also intervention by force for certain benign purposes, including: intervention to end or prevent gross violations of human rights; to protect one's nationals; to extricate hostages; to promote or maintain democracy, socialism or self-determination. Governments and publicists generally have found no basis for such exceptions to Article 2(4), with the possible exception of the "Entebbe principle" permitting the rescue of hostages, p. 936 infra. In the 1990's, with growing disorder in some regions, notably in the former Yugoslavia, there were renewed claims for a right of unilateral intervention.

## HUMANITARIAN INTERVENTION

### *SCHACHTER, INTERNATIONAL LAW IN THEORY AND PRACTICE*

178 Rec. des Cours 9, 143–44 (1985–V) (footnotes omitted).

[A] broad exception to the prohibition in Article 2(4) has been proposed by some international lawyers for humanitarian intervention. The argument has been made that in cases of large-scale atrocities or acute deprivation, armed intervention by outside States would be a justifiable exception to the Article 2(4) prohibition. The argument rests not on the interpretation of "territorial integrity" and other qualifying phrases, but on an overriding need to act in the interest of basic humanitarian values. It is accepted that such necessity arises only when effective peaceful measures are unavailable. The argument has powerful emotional appeal, especially when large-scale genocide occurs or innocent persons are tortured or killed as hostages. The brutalities of the last decade have often seemed to cry out for effective humanitarian intervention through the use of force.

Nonetheless, governments by and large (and most jurists) would not assert a right to forcible intervention to protect the nationals of another country from atrocities in their own country. An exception was the intervention of Indian troops to protect Bengalis in East Pakistan during the 1971 civil war in Pakistan. India's ethnic links and the refugee influx in its own territory as well as hostility to Pakistan were factors influencing its military intervention. It is interesting that despite considerable sympathy for the oppressed Bengalis, a large majority of the United Nations General Assembly called on India to withdraw its forces.

The reluctance of governments to legitimize foreign invasion in the interest of humanitarianism is understandable in light of past abuses by powerful States. States strong enough to intervene and sufficiently interested in doing so tend to have political motives. They have a strong temptation to impose a political solution in their own national interest. Most governments are acutely sensitive to this danger and they show no disposition to open up Article 2(4) to a broad exception for humanitarian intervention by means of armed force.

But a somewhat different position has been taken when a State uses force to rescue or protect its own nationals in imminent peril of injury in a foreign country. Such action has sometimes been called a type of humanitarian intervention, although it is much more circumscribed than the broad principle discussed above. Examples of such rescue of nationals in danger include: the Belgian action in Stanleyville in 1961, the United States forces in the Dominican Republic in 1965, the Israeli rescue action in Entebbe, the United States unsuccessful attempt in 1980 to liberate the hostages in Iran and the more successful "rescue" of Americans in Grenada in 1983. * * *

### Notes

1. *The humanitarian intervention debate.* Prior to the U.N. Charter, though war was not unlawful, it was rare for a state to employ military force in the territory of another state for the purpose of protecting the indigenous population against abuses by their own government. The use of force to protect nationals, sometimes called humanitarian intervention, was justified on grounds of self-defense. See note 2 below.

There has been considerable debate as to the legality of humanitarian intervention since the U.N. Charter came into force. Compare the following views:

a. "There is general agreement that, by virtue of its personal and territorial authority, a state can treat its own nationals according to discretion. But a substantial body of opinion and of practice has supported the view that there are limits to that discretion and that when a state commits cruelties against and persecution of its nationals in such a way as to deny their fundamental human rights and to shock the conscience of mankind, the matter ceases to be of sole concern to that state and even intervention in the interest of humanity might be legally permissible. However, the fact that, when resorted to by individual states, it may be—and has been—abused for selfish purposes tended to weaken its standing as a lawful practice."

1 Oppenheim's International Law 442–43 (9th ed., Jennings & Watts, eds. 1992) (footnotes omitted).

b. In a book titled Law and Civil War in the Modern World, Brownlie and Lillich had the following exchange:

> "It is clear to the present writer that a jurist asserting a right of forcible humanitarian intervention has a very heavy burden of proof. Few writers familiar with the modern materials of state practice and legal opinion on the use of force would support such a view. In the first place, it is significant that the very small number of writers cited in support of this view by Lillich include two, McDougal and Reisman, who lean heavily on a flexible and teleological interpretation of treaty texts. Leading modern authorities who either make no mention of humanitarian intervention and whose general position militates against its legality, or expressly deny its existence include Brierly, Castrén, Jessup, Jiménez de Aréchaga, Briggs, Schwarzenberger, Goodrich, Hambro, and Simons, Skubiszewski, Friedmann, Waldock, Bishop, Sørenson, and Kelsen. In the lengthy discussions over the years in the United Nations bodies of the definition of aggression and the principles of international law concerning international relations and cooperation among states, the variety of opinions canvassed has not revealed even a substantial minority in favor of the legality of humanitarian intervention. The *Repertory of Practice of United Nations Organs* provides no support; nor does the International Law Commission's Draft Declaration of the Rights and Duties of States. The voluminous materials in Whiteman's *Digest* lack even a passing reference to humanitarian intervention. Counting heads is not, of

course, a sound way of resolving issues of principle. However, quite apart from the weight of the opinion of experts cited above, it is the writer's view that these authorities are reporting and reflecting the universal consensus of government opinion and practice since 1945. Their views thus combine both policy in the sense of the reasonable expectations of states and the normative quality of rules based on *consensus.* With due respect to Lillich, it must be said that, if a new view is to be put forward, either it should be based on a much more substantial exposition of the practice, doctrine, and general development of the law relating to the use of force by states or the view should be offered *tout court* as a proposal to change existing law."

Brownlie, Humanitarian Intervention, in Law and Civil War in the Modern World 218–19 (Moore, ed., 1974) (footnotes omitted). Lillich replied:

"If, as Falk has remarked, 'the renunciation of intervention does not substitute a policy of nonintervention; it involves the development of some form of collective intervention,' then concomitantly the failure to develop effective international machinery to facilitate humanitarian interventions arguably permits a state to intervene unilaterally in appropriate situations. Writing a decade ago, Ronning wisely observed that 'it is as useless to outlaw intervention without providing a satisfactory substitute as it was to outlaw war when no satisfactory substitute was available.' He also posed the difficult question, which becomes more relevant every year,

> whether refusal to compromise on the principle of absolute non-intervention will not threaten the very principle itself. It can of course continue to be honored in countless declarations and protests, but if it does not square with the hard facts of international politics, that will be the extent of its honor.

Although Brownlie does not consider this question, events during the past decade reveal a widening 'credibility gap' between the absolute non-intervention approach to the Charter which he espouses and the actual practice of states."

Lillich, Humanitarian Intervention: A Reply to Dr. Brownlie and a Plea for Constructive Alternatives, in Law and Civil War in the Modern World 229, 247–48 (Moore, ed. 1974) (footnotes omitted). Does the revival of the U.N. Security Council since the end of the Cold War undercut Lillich's complaint about the lack of "effective international machinery?" See p. 981 infra for a discussion on humanitarian intervention pursuant to U.N. authorization.

c. "The majority of scholars who have analyzed the Article 2(4) prohibition on the use of force would agree with the absolutist interpretation posited by Sir Humphrey Waldock when he wrote:

> [A]rticle 2(4) prohibits entirely any threat or use of force between independent states except in individual or collective self-defense under article 51 or in execution of collective measures under the Charter for maintaining or restoring peace.

"Not only is there widespread agreement among scholars on the absolutist interpretations of article 2(4), but the prevailing view of the member states of the United Nations, as exemplified in General Assembly resolutions, also strongly supports the view that the Charter prohibits all unilateral uses of force except in self-defense.

"There is, nevertheless, a growing minority of writers which argues that because 'humanitarian intervention seeks neither a territorial change nor a challenge to the political independence of the state involved,' it is inaccurate to conclude that it is precluded by article 2(4). This analysis contradicts both the plain meaning of article 2(4)'s language and the intent of its drafters to prohibit absolutely the use of force except in self-defense.

"In order to interpret article 2(4) as allowing an exception to the use of force for humanitarian intervention, it is necessary to argue that where *the purpose* of the intervention is neither to impair territorial integrity nor to challenge political independence, then there is no violation of the article. The language of article 2(4), however, prohibits all uses of force 'against the territorial integrity or political independence of a state,' and makes no exception for use of force when there is no evil purpose to violate territorial integrity or political independence. What matters is not the purpose of the violation, but the act of violating itself. An armed intervention, even if undertaken for the purpose of protecting human rights, violates the very essence of territorial integrity and, since it would necessarily require a change in authority structures to assure respect for human rights, would also be against the political independence of the target state.

"Not only does an interpretation of the Charter that allows for humanitarian intervention contradict the clear language of article 2(4), but it also fails to take account of the fact that it was the unabashed *intent of the framers* to assure that there would be no exception to the prohibition on the use of force other than for self-defense. Indeed, none of those advocating a *restrictive interpretation* of article 2(4) have even attempted to answer the persuasive evidence put forth that the territorial integrity and political independence language of the article was intended to strengthen, rather than weaken, the prohibition on the use of force. Ultimately, it is difficult to escape the conclusion of Brownlie and others that is 'extremely doubtful' whether humanitarian intervention survived the "general prohibition of resort to force to be found in the U.N. Charter."

Wolf, Humanitarian Intervention, IX Mich.Y.B.Int'l Leg.Stud. 333, 339–40 (1988) (footnotes omitted).* Despite these strict views as to the meaning of the Charter, Wolf concludes:

> The argument against a right of humanitarian intervention is based primarily on an absolute interpretation of the article 2(4) prohibition on the use of force and the fear of abusive invocation of the doctrine. The reality of current state practice, however, has rendered the absolute prohibition of the Charter meaningless. Thus, there exists a compelling need for a contemporary and realistic interpretation of article 2(4) based on state practice that recognizes an exception to the Charter prohibition when force is required to prevent mass slaughter.

Id., at 368.

d. As state practice supporting humanitarian intervention as an exception to Article 2(4), Lillich and Wolf cite three of the instances of the protection of nationals referred to by Schachter above, as well as India's action in Bangladesh in 1971, the Vietnamese invasion of Cambodia in 1978, and the 1979 Tanzanian invasion of Uganda. Should these episodes be characterized instead as violations of the Charter? The British Foreign Office has stated:

> II.21. The state practice to which advocates of the right of humanitarian intervention have appealed provides an uncertain basis on which to rest

* Reprinted with permission. Mr. Wolf's views are expressed in his personal capacity.

such a right. Not the least this is because history has shown that humanitarian ends are almost always mixed with other less laudable motives for intervening, and because often the 'humanitarian' benefits of an intervention are either not claimed by the intervening state or are only put forward as an *ex post facto* justification of the intervention. * * * The two most discussed instances of alleged humanitarian intervention since 1945 are the Indian invasion of Bangladesh in 1971 and Tanzania's invasion of Uganda in 1979. But, although both did result in unquestionable benefits for * * * the people of East Bengal and Uganda, India and Tanzania were reluctant to use humanitarian ends to justify their invasion of a neighbor's territory. Both preferred to quote the right to self-defence under Article 51. And in each case the self-interest of the invading state was clearly involved.

II.22. * * * [T]he overwhelming majority of contemporary legal opinion comes down against the existence of a right of humanitarian intervention, for three main reasons: first, the UN Charter and the corpus of modern international law do not seem specifically to incorporate such a right; secondly, state practice in the past two centuries, and especially since 1945, at best provides only a handful of genuine cases of humanitarian intervention, and, on most assessments, none at all; and finally, on prudential grounds, that the scope for abusing such a right argues strongly against its creation. * * * In essence, therefore, the case against making humanitarian intervention an exception to the principle of non-intervention is that its doubtful benefits would be heavily outweighed by its costs in terms of respect for international law.

United Kingdom Foreign Office Policy Document No. 148, reprinted in, 57 Brit.Y.B.Int'l L. 614 (1986). For the attitudes of other states towards humanitarian intervention, see Schachter, The Right of States to Use Armed Force, 82 Mich.L.Rev. 1620, 1628–33 (1984).

e. The writers who accept humanitarian intervention usually demand "that there be no (overriding) selfish interests involved on the side of the intervenor; a demand formulated long ago by Rougier as that of *'desintéressment'* ..." Verwey, Humanitarian Intervention Under International Law, 32 Neth.Int'l L.Rev. 357, 371 (1985).

f. For other recent argument on humanitarian intervention, see inter alia the essays by Farer, Kartashkin, Meron and Damrosch, in Law and Force in the New International Order 185–223 (Damrosch & Scheffer, eds. 1991). See also Téson, Humanitarian Intervention: An Inquiry into Law and Morality (1988); Ronzitti, Rescuing Nationals Abroad Through Military Coercion and Intervention on Grounds of Humanity (1985); Humanitarian Intervention and the United Nations (Lillich, ed. 1973); Akehurst, Humanitarian Intervention, in Intervention in World Politics (Bull, ed. 1984); Bayzler, Re-examining the Doctrine of Humanitarian Intervention in Light of the Atrocities in Kampuchea and Ethiopia, 23 Stan.J.Int'l L. 547 (1987); Fairley, State Actors, Humanitarian Intervention and International Law: Reopening Pandora's Box, 10 Ga.J.Int'l Comp.L. 29 (1980); Franck & Rodley, After Bangladesh: The Law of Humanitarian Intervention by Military Force, 67 A.J.I.L. 275 (1973); Henkin, Use of Force: Law and U.S. Policy, in Right v. Might Use of Force 37 (2nd ed. 1991); Jhavala, Unilateral Humanitarian Intervention and International Law, 21 Indian J.Int'l L. 208 (1981); Nafziger, Self–Determination and Humanitarian Intervention in a Community of Power, 20 Den.J.Int'l L. & Pol'y 9 (1991); Rodley, Human Rights and Humanitarian Intervention: The Case Law of the World Court, 38 Int'l &

Comp.L.Q. 321 (1989); Scheffer, Toward a Modern Doctrine of Humanitarian Intervention, 4 Fla.Int'l L.J. 435 (1989). See Restatement (Third) § 703, Comment *e.*

2. *Protection of nationals.* The intervention by a state to protect its nationals and ensure their humane treatment in another state was traditionally justified on the grounds of self-defense. Bowett, writing in 1958, took the position that such intervention to protect nationals had been lawful before the U.N. Charter as self-defense and remained lawful thereafter under Article 51. Bowett, Self–Defence in International Law 87–90 (1958). See also his later essay, The Use of Force for the Protection of Nationals Abroad, in The Current Legal Regulation of the Use of Force 39 (Cassese, ed. 1986). Friedmann wrote that:

> The conditions under which a state may be entitled, as an aspect of self-defense, to intervene in another state to protect its nationals from injury, were formulated by Professor Waldock in 1952 as follows: "There must be (1) an imminent threat of injury to nationals, (2) a failure or inability on the part of the territorial sovereign to protect them and (3) measures of protection strictly confined to the object of protecting them against injury" * * * This was invoked, among other reasons, by the British Government in support of its armed intervention in Egypt during the Suez Canal crisis of 1956. Since, unlike in the Dominican Republic in April, 1965, there was no breakdown of organized government in Egypt nor any physical threat to foreign nationals, the United States had much greater legal justification for its original, limited intervention in protection of its nationals in the Dominican crisis than did Great Britain in the Suez crisis.

Friedmann, United States Policy and the Crisis of International Law, 59 A.J.I.L. 857, 867 n. 10 (1965). See generally, 1 Oppenheim's International Law 440–42 (9th ed. Jennings & Watts, eds. 1992). For the law prior to the Charter, see the opinion of Judge Huber in *The Spanish Zones of Morocco Claims,* 2 U.N.R.I.A.A. 615 (1925).

The right to intervene to protect nationals was one of the grounds invoked by the United States for its invasion of Grenada in 1983. See p. 1008 infra. See also Joyner, The United States Action in Grenada, 78 A.J.I.L. 131 (1984). It was also used as a justification by the U.S. for the invasion of Panama in 1989. See p. 924 above; also Use of Force, Protection of Nationals—Deployment of U.S. Forces to Panama (U.S. *Digest,* Ch. 14, § 1), reprinted in 84 A.J.I.L. 545 (1990). Schachter suggests:

> Reliance on self-defence as a legal ground for protecting nationals in emergency situations of peril probably reflects a reluctance to rely solely on the argument of humanitarian intervention as an exception to Article 2(4) or on the related point that such intervention is not "against the territorial integrity or political independence" of the territorial State and that it is not inconsistent with the Charter. Many governments attach importance to the principle that any forcible incursion into the territory of another State is a derogation of that State's territorial sovereignty and political independence, irrespective of the motive for such intervention or its long term consequences. Accordingly, they tend to hold to the sweeping prohibition of Article 2(4) against the use or threat of force except where self-defence or Security Council enforcement action is involved.

Schachter, International Law in Theory and Practice: General Course in Public International Law, 178 Rec. des Cours 8, 148 (1982–V) (footnotes omitted).

By no means have all writers agreed that the right to intervene to protect nationals survived the U.N. Charter. Professor Brownlie, for example, argues:

> * * * [I]t is very doubtful if * * * intervention [to protect nationals] has any basis in the modern law. The instances in which states have purported to exercise it, and the terms in which it is delimited, show that it provides infinite opportunities for abuse. Forcible intervention is now unlawful. It is true that the protection of nationals presents particular difficulties and that a government faced with a deliberate massacre of a considerable number of nationals in a foreign state would have cogent reasons of humanity for acting, and would also be under very great political pressure. The possible risks of denying the legality of action in a case of such urgency, an exceptional circumstance, must be weighed against the more calculable dangers of providing legal pretexts for the commission of breaches of the peace in the pursuit of national rather than humanitarian interest.

Brownlie, International Law and the Use of Force by States 301 (1963). See also Ronzitti, Rescuing Nationals Abroad through Military Coercion and Intervention on Grounds of Humanity 64 (1985). As regards the U.S. invasion of Panama in 1989, Henkin argues, *inter alia,* that the alleged protection of U.S. nationals could not be justified under Article 51 as a use of force in self-defense since no "armed attack" had occurred. Henkin, The Invasion of Panama Under International Law: A Gross Violation, 29 Colum.J.Transnat'l L. 293, 305–06 (1991). On Panama, see p. 924.

3. *Extricating hostages.* Consider the intervention by Israel in Uganda to release Israeli hostages from a hijacked plane at Entebbe, and the U.S. attempt to rescue U.S. hostages in Iran after the U.S. embassy was seized. Henkin maintains that in hostage situations there may be a limited right to intervene "to liberate hostages if the territorial state cannot or will not do so." Henkin, Use of Force: Law and U.S. Policy, in Right v. Might: International Law and the Use of Force 37, 41–42 (2nd ed. 1991). Henkin would not limit this protection to hostages that are nationals of the intervening state. Provided the "use of force is strictly limited to what is necessary to save lives," an intervening state could act to rescue its own nationals, the territorial state's nationals, or the nationals of a third state. Id. But see the Security Council debate on the Entebbe Incident, where the Israeli (and U.S.) representatives defended Israel's action as self-defense because the hostages were its nationals. U.N.Doc. S/PV.1939, at 51–59 (July 1976), reprinted in 15 I.L.M. 1224 (1976).

## INTERVENTION FOR DEMOCRACY

### *REISMAN, COERCION AND SELF-DETERMINATION: CONSTRUING CHARTER ARTICLE 2(4)*

78 A.J.I.L. 642, 643–45 (1984) (footnotes omitted).*

If some unilateral coercions are effectively treated as legitimate, the challenge to contemporary lawyers is not to engage in automatic indiscriminate denunciations of unilateral resorts to coercion by states as violations of Article 2(4). They must begin to develop a set of criteria for appraising the lawfulness of unilateral resorts to coercion.

A sine qua non for any action—coercive or otherwise—I submit, is the maintenance of minimum order in a precarious international system. Will a particular use of force enhance or undermine world order? When this requirement is met, attention may be directed to the fundamental principle of political legitimacy in contemporary international politics: the enhancement of the ongoing right of peoples to determine their own political destinies. That obvious point bears renewed emphasis for it is the main purpose of contemporary international law: Article 2(4) is the means. The basic policy of contemporary international law has been to maintain the political independence of territorial communities so that they can continue to express their desire for political community in a form appropriate to them.

Article 2(4), like so much in the Charter and in contemporary international politics, rests on and must be interpreted in terms of this key postulate of political legitimacy in the 20th century. Each application of Article 2(4) must enhance opportunities for ongoing self-determination. Though all interventions are lamentable, the fact is that some may serve, in terms of aggregate consequences, to increase the probability of the free choice of peoples about their government and political structure. Others have the manifest objective and consequence of doing exactly the opposite. There is neither need nor justification for treating in a mechanically equal fashion Tanzania's intervention in Uganda to overthrow Amin's despotism, on the one hand, and Soviet intervention in Hungary in 1956 or Czechoslovakia in 196[8] to overthrow popular governments and to impose an undesired regime on a coerced population, on the other. Here, as in all other areas of law, it is important to remember that norms are instruments devised by human beings to precipitate desired social consequences. One should not seek point-for-point conformity to a rule without constant regard for the policy or principle that animated its prescription, and with appropriate regard for the factual constellation in the minds of the drafters.

Coercion should not be glorified, but it is naive and indeed subversive of public order to insist that it never be used, for coercion is a ubiquitous feature of all social life and a characteristic and indispensable component of law. The critical question in a decentralized system is not whether coercion has been applied, but whether it has been applied in support of or against community order and basic policies, and whether it was applied in ways whose net consequences include increased congruence with community goals and minimum order.

## *SCHACHTER, THE LEGALITY OF PRO-DEMOCRATIC INVASION*

78 A.J.I.L. 645, 649–50 (1984).*

The difficulty with Reisman's argument is not merely that it lacks support in the text of the Charter or in the interpretation that states have given Article 2(4) in the past decades. It would introduce a new normative basis for recourse to war that would give powerful states an almost unlimited right to overthrow governments alleged to be unresponsive to the popular will or to the goal of self-determination. The implications of this for interstate violence in a period of superpower confrontation and obscurantist rhetoric are ominous. That invasions may at times serve democratic values must be weighed against the dangerous consequences of legitimizing armed attacks against peaceful governments. It will be recalled that the International Court of Justice in the *Corfu Channel* case rejected the defense of the United Kingdom that it had used armed force in the cause of international justice. The Court's pronouncement on this bears repetition:

> The Court cannot accept such a line of defence. The Court can only regard the alleged right of intervention as the manifestation of a policy of force, such as cannot, whatever be the present defects in international organization, find a place in international law. Intervention is perhaps still less admissible in the particular form it would take here; for, from the nature of things, it would be reserved for the most powerful States, and might easily lead to perverting the administration of international justice itself.

The Court's measured phrases remind us of the historic realities of abuse by powerful states for supposedly good causes. It is no answer to say that invasions should be allowed where there is no abuse and only for the higher good of self-determination. In the absence of an effective international mechanism to restrain force, individual governments would have the latitude to decide on the "reality" of democracy and self-determination in various countries. The test one side would favor would not be acceptable to others. Ideological confrontations would sooner or later become clashes of power.

These considerations are so evident that we can be quite sure that governments will not adopt the suggested reinterpretation of Article 2(4) as law. Not even its espousal by a powerful state would make it law. In short, it is not, will not, and should not be law. Yet there is a reason for concern that the thesis has been put forward by an international lawyer of standing. In this period of tension and unilateral action, arguments such as those presented may influence policy in favor of armed intervention. The fragility of international organization enhances the danger. This is surely not the time for international lawyers to weaken the principal normative restraint against the use of force. The world will not be made safe for democracy through new wars or invasions of the weak by the strong.

### *Notes*

1. *The "Reagan Doctrine."* A Reagan doctrine has been traced back to a speech by President Reagan on March 1, 1985. He said, "freedom movements arise and assert themselves. They're doing so on almost every continent populated by man—in the hills of Afghanistan, in Angola, in Kampuchea, in Central America * * * They're our brothers, these freedom fighters, and we owe them our help." See Reisman, Allocating Competences to Use Coercion in the Post–Cold War World: Practices, Conditions, and Prospects, in Law and Force in the New International Order 26, 34 n. 13 (Damrosch & Scheffer, eds. 1991). This and subsequent statements were interpreted as asserting the right of the United States (or any other state) to intervene by force to defend, maintain, restore or impose democratic government. See Kirkpatrick & Gerson, The Reagan Doctrine, Human Rights, and International Law, in Right v. Might: International Law and the Use of Force 19 (2nd ed. 1991). A similar view was implied by President Bush among his justifications for the 1989 invasion of Panama. See p.

924 supra. Compare the Reagan doctrine with the statement by President Johnson that the "American nations cannot, must not, and will not permit the establishment of another Communist government in the Western Hemisphere."

2. *The "Brezhnev Doctrine."* During the Cold War, the Reagan doctrine's counterpart was the Soviet Union's Brezhnev doctrine. The Brezhnev doctrine had its genesis in the Soviet invasion of Czechoslovakia on September 25, 1968; it asserted the right of socialist states to intervene in another socialist state when socialism there was threatened. See the reported statement of Leonid Brezhnev on the occasion of the invasion of Czechoslovakia, reprinted in 7 I.L.M. 1323 (1968). The U.S.S.R. did not reassert the Brezhnev doctrine after Czechoslovakia, and some believe that the Soviet Union disavowed it in the Final Act of the Conference on Security and Cooperation in Europe (Helsinki 1975). In 1991, the doctrine was unequivocally rejected by Mikhail Gorbachev. See generally Moore & Turner, International Law and the Brezhnev Doctrine (1987); Jones, The Soviet Concept of 'Limited Sovereignty' from Lenin to Gorbachev: The Brezhnev Doctrine (1990).

3. See generally the essays on intervention against illegitimate régimes by Lukashuk, Franck, Burley and Nanda, in Law and Force in the New International Order 143–184 (Damrosch & Scheffer, eds. 1991); Schachter, Is There a Right to Overthrow an Illegitimate Regime, in Le Droit international au service de la justice et du development: mélanges Michel Virally 423 (1991); Reisman, Old Wine in New Bottles: The Reagan and Brezhnev Doctrines in Contemporary International Law and Practice, 13 Yale J.Int'l L. 171 (1988); Henkin, The Use of Force: Law and U.S. Policy, in Right v. Might: International Law and the Use of Force 37, 44 (2nd ed. 1991). Henkin argues that:

> Self-determination as a justification for the use of force to end colonialism has lost its raison d'être, but some have invoked a people's right to "internal self-determination" to support the use of force by one state to preserve or impose democracy in another * * * Some see this view as the foundation of the so-called Reagan Doctrine, construed as including a claim of the right to intervene by force in another state to preserve or impose democracy.
>
> The claim has received no support by any other government. Like the use of force to impose or maintain socialism or any other ideology, the use of force for democracy clearly would be contrary to the language of Article 2(4), to the intent of the framers, and to the construction long given to that article by the United States.
>
> At bottom, all suggestions for exceptions to article 2(4) imply that, contrary to the assumptions of the Charter's framers, there are universally recognized values higher than peace and the autonomy of states. In general, the claims of peace and state autonomy have prevailed.

Id.

4. What are the implications of the Reagan and Brezhnev doctrines for the principle of "sovereign equality of states" enshrined in the U.N. Charter? The International Court of Justice appears to have rejected both doctrines in the *Nicaragua* case (Merits):

> The finding of the United States Congress also expressed the view that the Nicaraguan Government had taken "significant steps towards establishing a totalitarian Communist dictatorship". However the régime in Nicaragua be defined, adherence by a State to any particular doctrine does not

> constitute a violation of customary international law; to hold otherwise would make nonsense of the fundamental principle of State sovereignty, on which the whole of international law rests, and the freedom of choice of the political, social, economic and cultural system of a State. Consequently, Nicaragua's domestic policy options, even assuming that they correspond to the description given of them by the Congress finding, cannot justify on the legal plane the various actions of the [U.S.] complained of. The Court cannot contemplate the creation of a new rule opening up a right of intervention by one State against another on the ground that the latter has opted for some particular ideology or political system.

Case Concerning Military and Paramilitary Activities in and against Nicaragua (Nicaragua v. United States), 1986, I.C.J. 14, 133.

5. During the years of decolonization there was support for the view that states may intervene to promote the process of self-determination. See Friedmann, Intervention and International Law, 25 Int'l Spectator 40, 59–61 (1971). Professor Friedmann wrote:

> [S]elf-determination * * * suffers from grave ambiguities and contradictions as a criterion to justify unilateral intervention by outside states. The difficulties became evident enough when the post-war successor states to the Austro–Hungarian Empire were formed in 1919, in implementation of President Wilson's principle of self-determination. They are no less evident today. Self-determination was a reasonably clear goal as long as colonies strove for independence from their colonial masters or "protectors." But once the new states were established, usually within the former colonial boundaries, they became as adamant against attempts of ethnic minorities to secede, or to form political associations with their ethnic brethren in other states, as any colonial empire. And it is always possible to qualify the legitimacy of a quest for self-determination by adding such words as "genuine."

Id. But see Article 7 of the Resolution on the Definition of Aggression which provides that nothing in the definition is intended to prejudice the "right to self-determination" and the right of "peoples forcibly deprived of that right * * * to struggle to that end and to seek and receive support, in accordance with the principles of the Charter and in conformity with the [Declaration on Friendly Relations]. G.A.Res. 3314 (XXIX) (1974). See also The Principle of Equal Rights and Self–Determination of Peoples in the Declaration on Principles of International Law Concerning Friendly Relations and Co-operation Among States in Accordance with the Charter of the United Nations, G.A.Res. 2625 (XXXV) (1970).

### 5. *Belligerency and Neutrality Under the Charter*

The United Nations Charter prohibits any threat or use of force, but presumably was designed also to abolish the state of war. If so, the concepts of belligerency and neutrality were also to be eliminated by the Charter. If the U.N. takes action against an aggressor, member states may be obliged to assist and cannot remain neutral. See Henkin, How Nations Behave 140 (2d ed. 1979). Unfortunately, the U.N. Charter did not put an end to large scale hostilities, however denominated, and issues about the rights and duties of both the participants in hostilities and of nonparticipants have continued to arise. See pp. 1025–34 infra. Surely it is important to assure that parties to hostilities observe the rules designed to make hostilities less inhumane.

Even in U.N. actions against aggression, there is a need to attend to the laws of war and to humanitarian law.

## *NORTON, BETWEEN THE IDEOLOGY AND THE REALITY: THE SHADOW OF THE LAW OF NEUTRALITY*

17 Harv.Int'l L.J. 249–52, 276–77, 307, 309–11 (1976).*

Since the signing of the United Nations Charter, the customary law of neutrality has been caught between an international legal order which purports to outlaw war and hence make neutrality obsolete, and an international political environment characterized by frequent armed conflicts in which there is a need to regulate the relations of belligerent and non-belligerent states. The results have been confused, if not chaotic. With the juridical status of armed conflicts uncertain, third states have most often refrained from taking a formal stance of neutrality. But where the need for *some* legal rule has been acute and where the particular rule of the customary law has suited their interests, states have invoked that customary law and defended its continued vitality. Neutrality has for some three decades, therefore, led a sort of "juridical half-life," suspended between an ideology which denies its premises and a reality which finds it useful, if not necessary.

* * *

Neutral status was seriously challenged during and between the two world wars by the series of efforts to outlaw aggressive war which successfully culminated in article 2(4) of the United Nations Charter. Under the international legal order established by the Charter, resort to armed force by a state was henceforth usually to be regarded as aggression. The objects of such aggression would be entitled to defend themselves, but self-defense was to be primarily an interim measure until the collective security mechanism of the United Nations could be organized to meet the armed aggression. There were envisioned, then, three essential categories of the use of armed force: aggression; self-defense; and collective self-defense. Future international armed conflicts would be between an aggressor and either an individual state exercising its right of self-defense or the United Nations acting collectively. In either event, an attitude of impartiality toward the belligerents, the very essence of traditional neutrality, would be impermissible.[7]

Most commentators recognized from the outset that this system was not seamless, and accordingly that there still might be a place in the interstices for the traditional law of neutrality. The principal problem was the authori-

* Some footnotes omitted. Reprinted by permission of Harvard International Law Journal Association.

7. In principle no Member of the United Nations is entitled, at its discretion, to remain neutral in a war in which the Security Council has found a particular State guilty of a breach of the peace or of an act of aggression and in which it has called upon the Member of the United Nations concerned either to declare war upon that State or to take military action indistinguishable from war. This is the cumulative effect of Article 2(5) of the Charter (in which Members undertake to give the United Nations every assistance in any action it takes in accordance with the Charter); of Article 25 (in which Members undertake to accept and to comply with the decisions of the Security Council); and of the provisions of Chapter VII of the Charter in the matter of "enforcement action." * * *

tative designation of the aggressor. In every instance of armed conflict each party might be expected to characterize its opponent as the aggressor. The Security Council was empowered to make authoritative determinations on this issue and then to authorize collective security actions or make other recommendations binding on member states. But in the absence of a Security Council decision, individual states might not wish or be able to ascertain for themselves which of the belligerents was the aggressor. In such a situation, it was recognized that assuming the status of a traditional neutral was probably permissible. This was, however, expected to be an unusual situation.

The unusual situation soon became the rule. Because of the Cold War split among the permanent members of the Security Council, that body never assumed the collective security role initially envisioned for it. For the same reason, and because in most instances of armed conflict designation of an aggressor was impossible or likely to have adverse political consequences, the Security Council never designated aggressors. The originally anticipated interstitial situation in which assumption of a neutral status might be permissible under the Charter has arisen, therefore, in every international armed conflict of the last three decades.

But, despite this development, it has not proven possible simply to revert to the earlier system in which non-belligerent states were always entitled, if not obligated, to become neutrals. War is still outlawed. This ideological premise creates difficult issues for non-belligerent states in several respects. First, every instance of international armed conflict is still subject to United Nations debate and theoretically to authoritative resolution by the Security Council. To declare neutrality may to some extent legitimize the legal status of the conflict and impede its potential resolution by the appropriate international bodies. Secondly, belligerents no longer uniformly characterize armed hostilities as "war." It is, therefore, no longer certain under exactly what circumstances a non-belligerent is entitled to declare itself a neutral for legal purposes. In the absence of a formal acknowledgement of a state of war by the belligerents, it is unclear whether a non-belligerent, by the very fact of its non-belligerence, is automatically entitled to any of the rights or subject to any of the duties of the traditional law of neutrality. But if a non-belligerent does issue a declaration of neutrality under these circumstances, it creates the possible anomaly of applying the law of neutrality between belligerents and neutrals despite the fact that the belligerents do not themselves recognize a legal state of war. Finally, the outlawry of aggressive war raises the classical issues of the *bellum justum* for third states: may they unilaterally designate the aggressor and discriminate in favor of its victim; or, alternatively, are they *obligated* under certain circumstances to so designate and discriminate?

* * *

The reasons for the general reluctance of states to rely upon the customary law of neutrality are perspicuous: one is ideological, the other practical. The ideological problem stems from the outlawry of war, which creates several theoretical issues for would-be neutrals: the permissibility of their assuming a legal status which implicitly acknowledges the legitimacy of an armed conflict, often while the subject is being deliberated by the

United Nations; ambiguous juridical relationships caused by belligerents' unwillingness to characterize hostilities as "war;" and the difficult burdens of designating aggressors and victims. State practice confirms and clarifies these dilemmas. Because aggressive war is outlawed, belligerent states have justified their conduct of armed hostilities by other principles of international law thought to have an even more compelling normative import; that is to say, each has made its cause a *bellum justum.* At the very least, this has entailed structuring the facts of a conflict to permit the argument that one's own state was the victim of an aggressive attack and hence entitled to the right of self-defense under article 51 of the Charter. But in recent conflicts this almost ritualized claim has nearly always been joined with a more substantive claim of right. Thus, in Algeria the FLN's claim was based on the right of self-determination; in Korea, the partially successful reliance on United Nations sanctions supported a theory of the exercise of collective security; in both Korea and Vietnam, each side alleged the other's Great Power imperialist interference in local or regional matters to justify its own intervention; and in all the conflicts involving to a greater or lesser extent civil wars, the issue of intervention in the internal affairs of a state was raised. Such normative claims, often phrased in absolutist terms, do not readily admit strict impartiality for third parties. It is not, therefore, surprising that third states should have avoided taking the legal status of neutrality.

Practical considerations have also dissuaded non-belligerents from becoming neutrals in the legal sense:

> It is advantageous for third States not to be forced to apply rules of neutrality, which only serve to restrict commercial relations between these States and their citizens on the one hand and conflicting States and other neutral States on the other, without, however, conferring any real additional benefits. In peacetime conditions, they are able to protect themselves and their citizens quite as well and even better.
>
> * * *

It would, however, seem indisputable that under some circumstances—notably the absence of binding Security Council decisions—the customary law of neutrality retains its legal validity and should be applicable. Moreover, practice suggests that states will sometimes find it mutually advantageous to apply the customary law, and that on other occasions non-belligerents should at least have the option of relying upon that law to protect their interests. * * * .

These conclusions are applicable to armed conflicts of a primarily international nature. With respect to conflicts wholly between parties within pre-existing international boundaries (concededly not always a clear-cut distinction), recent practice suggests that the institution of neutrality is defunct, or at least moribund. The cases of Algeria and Nigeria provide somewhat contradictory reasons for its demise. In Algeria and many other former colonies, the cause of self-determination has been thought by an increasingly large segment of the international community to be so compellingly a just one that impartiality should not be permissible. * * * In Nigeria it was the very inviolability of international borders, the principle of *uti posseditis,* conjoined with the principle precluding international intervention into subjects of domestic jurisdiction that seemed to preclude other states' invocation of the law of neutrality. This phenomenon will presumably recur at least in other secessionist conflicts. Where there may be some remaining theoretical potential for a resurrection of the law of neutrality in civil conflicts may be in "wars of national liberation" in already independent states or in possible armed conflicts in states currently ruled by racial minorities, e.g., Rhodesia and South Africa. Both of these situations would involve heavily normative considerations, however, and most likely preclude reliance on the customary law of neutrality. Civil wars of many sorts will undoubtedly continue to pose a major international problem, but the institution of neutrality is thus unlikely to play a significant role in the resolution of that problem.

* * *

It is neither realistic nor desirable to expect the international community to renounce the ideal of outlawing war because it has not, as yet, succeeded. But until a system can be devised which will realize this ideal, the problems associated with the use of force will persist and will, ironically, be exacerbated by the existence of the ideal itself. Caught between this reality and the failed ideal, the law of neutrality will continue its shadowy existence.

### *Notes*

1. Compare also Henkin, Force, Intervention and Neutrality in Contemporary International Law, 57 A.S.I.L.Proc. 147, 159–61 (1963), with Deak, Neutrality Revisited, in Transnational Law in a Changing Society 137 (Friedmann, Henkin & Lissitzyn eds., 1972).

2. Beginning with their attack on Israel in 1948, some Arab states claimed a state of war and belligerency as justification, e.g., for barring passage through the Suez Canal or international straits of Israeli vessels, and vessels of other states plying to and from Israel. For a rejection of this claim, see Security Council Resolution 2322, at 3 (1951). The 1979 Peace Treaty between Egypt and Israel expressly terminated such state of war. See Egypt–Israel Peace Treaty, March 26, 1979, 18 I.L.M. 362 (1979).

Iraq has continued to claim it is in a state of war with Israel, having formally declared war against it. Israel characterized Iraq as a belligerent in its justification for bombing an Iraqi nuclear reactor. See p. 929, Note 3 above.

The Iran–Iraq war in the 1980s saw frequent invocation of the neutral-belligerent distinction, particularly as it relates to states that shipped oil from Iran. See Comment, Air Attacks on Neutral Shipping in the Persian Gulf: The Legality of the Iraqi Exclusion Zone and Iranian Reprisals, 8 Bost.Coll.Int'l & Comp.L.Rev. 517 (1985).

3. The "neutral state" continues to be mentioned in documents such as the Geneva Convention Relative to the Protection of Civilian Persons in Time of War (Art. 11), and the Geneva Convention Relative to the Treatment of Prisoners of War (Art. 11).

# SECTION 2. INTERVENTION IN CIVIL WAR

## A. THE TRADITIONAL LAW

Intervention by foreign powers in civil war and other domestic strife was regarded traditionally as a special form of foreign intervention, subject to the limitations imposed by traditional law on intervention generally. See pp. 868, 905 supra. Since the Second World War, objections to external intervention have invoked also the principle of "self-determination" and the prohibition on the use of force in Article 2(4). Such intervention has also sometimes become the concern of U.N. organs because it threatened international peace. During the Cold War, revolution and internal wars became entangled in international ideological conflict, and some claimed to be wars of self-determination and "peoples' liberation," inviting external supporters. See p. 940 supra.

Even before the U.N. Charter, intervention in civil war was, for international law, a particularly troublesome form of intervention. Henkin writes:

> Not surprisingly, revolutionary movements sought external assistance for themselves, but condemned as intervention any assistance to the governments against which they were rebelling. Not surprisingly, governments (including those which themselves came to power by revolution) saw objectionable "intervention" when other nations supported rebellion, whether by financial, political, or military means. Not surprisingly, governments saw no objectionable "intervention" in financial, military, or political support for themselves, even to shore them up against possible rebellion.
>
> The result was that international society struggled to achieve consensus and law on such questions as: What kinds of assistance may be given to legitimate governments? At what point does such assistance cease to be permissible because the government's right and power to rule are being challenged? At what stage may nations begin to accord rebels limited rights as "insurgents"? When may they decide to accord them belligerent rights equal to those of the government previously in power? When may they recognize them as the legitimate government? What are the rights and duties of states in regard to one side or the other in fullblown civil war? The absence of international standards or procedures for recognition has left nations with wide discretion as to when and whom to recognize, which they are able to exploit for their own 'interventionist' political interests. Some of these issues became acute during the Civil War in Spain, when the actions of several countries battered whatever norms there might have been about intervention or neutrality or about that assertion of neutrality which becomes a kind of intervention because it accords belligerent status to rebel forces.

How Nations Behave at 155 (2d ed. 1979).*

The Spanish Civil War was a watershed for international law on intervention in civil war. In February of 1936, the Spanish Popular Front came to power in Spain through an electoral victory.[1] Influential members of several rightist parties first attempted to seize power peaceably, but when this effort failed, started a revolt in Morocco headed by General Franco. From the start of hostilities, Germany and Italy intervened by transporting the rebel troops of General Franco to the mainland. Aid to the Franco government continued despite the Non–Intervention Agreements which both Germany and Italy signed. On November 18, 1936, they recognized the rebels as the legitimate government of Spain.[2]

The incumbent Republican government appealed for assistance. After initial vacillation, the French Cabinet decided not to intervene, but it did permit the private sale of arms to the Republican Government.[3] If France had been willing to provide the guns and ammunition Spain sought, the rebellion might have been crushed. The flow of French arms was completely ended pursuant to the Non–Intervention Agreements. Great Britain and the United States adopted arms embargoes as part of their non-intervention policy.

At the initiative of Great Britain and France, an attempt was made to end intervention in the Spanish Civil War through the exchange of unilateral pledges by twenty-seven European governments. The agreements to prevent shipments of arms, ammunition and implements of war were to be supervised by the International Committee for the Application of the Agreement Regarding Non–Intervention in Spain. From its first meeting on September 9, 1936, until the middle of November, 1936, the Committee heard charges of intervention by the various powers. It is generally recognized that Germany and Italy violated the agreements on a major scale from the beginning. Although the Soviet Union maintained strict neutrality in the first stages of the war, it began to intervene in October, 1936, by sending significant quantities of Soviet equipment to the Republican Government.

The United States was not a party to the Non–Intervention Agreements, but it maintained a policy of strict neutrality, including an absolute embargo against the shipment of arms to Spain. The refusal of the United States to sell arms, combined with the non-intervention policy of the British and French, deprived the Spanish Republic of adequate armaments while the rebels received supplies from Germany and Italy. American policy was criticized as a departure from traditional American practice of selling arms freely, especially to established governments. It was defended as a further development in its neutralist position.

With the fall of Catalonia in February of 1939, the world concluded that the Spanish Civil War was over. France and Britain accorded official recognition to the government of General Franco on February 27; the United States extended recognition on April 1.

1. The classic analysis of the international law implications of the Spanish Civil War is Padelford, International Law and Diplomacy in the Spanish Civil Strife (1939).

2. Recognition of the rebels as the legitimate government of Spain came when the fall of Madrid was anticipated by many observers, but it has been criticized as premature recognition, forbidden by international law.

3. The policy of non-intervention adopted by the French Government appears to have been influenced by a fear of provoking Germany into more open intervention, leading to a world war.

The Non-Intervention Pact departed from the traditional doctrine that, in a civil war, the Government but not the rebels may receive assistance from outside, at least until the rebels have been granted the status of belligerency. This status was never accorded to the Franco forces, who moved directly from rebels to full recognition as the government of Spain. Germany and Italy, while nominally parties to this Pact, not only violated it by providing massive supplies and armed contingents—of which the German bombing squadron that obliterated Guernica is the most notorious example—but they also circumvented the problem of inequality of status between Government and rebels by recognizing the Franco rebels as the Government of Spain in November, 1936, simultaneously with the conclusion of the Non-Intervention Pact. This shows how, in the absence of international machinery, the discretion enjoyed by individual governments in granting or withholding recognition to other governments, could by-pass the distinctions made by the traditional doctrine between the status of governments and of rebels in a civil war.

### *Notes*

1. Does the history of the Spanish Civil War, and in particular the Non-Intervention Pact, illustrate the obsolescence of the traditional rule under which neutral governments are enjoined from assisting either side in a war by military supplies, but private manufacturers and traders are permitted to do so? At a time when many governments directly control the manufacture of arms, would such a rule create a state of imbalance that would not be acceptable to the states prejudiced by the application of this rule? Can a government disclaim responsibility for the movement of arms from its territory to any other power, or disclaim the power to regulate or interdict such supplies?

On the question of government responsibility for private arms supplies, see Friedmann, The Growth of State Control over the Individual and its Effect upon the Rules of International State Responsibility, 19 Brit.Y.B.I.L. 118 (1938).

2. Supplying arms to a belligerent is one example of an act that may violate the neutral duty of impartiality. See p. 875 supra. The recruitment and training of troops in one state to launch an attack against another state is another example. Title 18 U.S.C.A. § 960 provides:

> Whoever, within the United States, knowingly begins or sets on foot or provides or prepares a means for or furnishes the money for, or takes part in, any military or naval expedition or enterprise to be carried on from thence against the territory or dominion of any foreign prince or state, or of any colony, district, or people with whom the United States is at peace, shall be fined not more than $3,000 or imprisoned not more than three years, or both.

In 1959, the Department of Justice asked the Department of State for its opinion whether an organization formed in California and called the "Tibetan Brigade," which reportedly intended to go into Tibet in order to "aid the Tibetans in their revolt against the Chinese Communist tyranny," might be acting in violation of 18 U.S.C.A. § 960. The Department of State replied that Communist China should not be considered a state within the meaning of the statute, since at the time the Communist régime was not recognized by the United States as the legitimate government. Furthermore the United States could not be considered at peace with Communist China. See 5 Whiteman 254–55.

Following the abortive action against the Castro régime by Cuban refugees and their sympathizers on April 15, 1961, the Attorney General of the United States stated that none of their activities had violated the neutrality laws of the United States. While conceding that the laws prohibit the departure from the United States of a group organized as a military expedition against a nation with whom the United States is at peace, he contended that the departure of several persons at the same time with the intent of joining an insurgent group was not criminal. 5 Whiteman 275–76.

Are U.S. neutrality laws affected by the U.N. Charter or by the United Nations Participation Act of 1945, 22 U.S.C.A. §§ 287–287e?

3. In 1989, the United Nations General Assembly adopted an International Convention against the Recruitment Use, Financing and Training of Mercenaries. As of January 1, 1993, the Convention had 17 of the 22 signatures required to bring it into force. See U.N.Doc. A/Res/44/34, reprinted in 29 I.L.M. 89 (1990).

## SUPPORTING GOVERNMENTS OR RECOGNIZING INSURGENTS

### *FRIEDMANN, THE CHANGING STRUCTURE OF INTERNATIONAL LAW*

265–66 (1964).*

* * * A distinction has often been made between support for the incumbent government and support for insurgents, on the ground "that a foreign state commits an international delinquency by assisting insurgents in spite of being at peace with the legitimate government." [4] But since there is a very wide measure of discretion in the speed and manner in which any individual state may recognize insurgents in another state either as belligerents or as the legitimate government, the value of this distinction is highly doubtful. At most it may be said that, in extreme cases of foreign assistance to rebels in the guise of their immediate recognition as the legitimate government, at a time when they had no substantial control of the country, as was notably the case in the almost immediate recognition of the Franco government by Germany and Italy after the rebellion, is a thinly disguised interference in the affairs of another state, utterly at variance with established principles of recognition. Apart from such extreme cases, the parties in a civil strife seriously contesting the control of the country, must probably be taken as equals. Any, reasonably precise, definition of the rights and duties of other states with regards to the parties in a civil war is made extremely difficult by the fact that civil war usually arises from clashes of political philosophy and bitter social tensions, and that therefore the sympathies of governments and political groups outside the state torn by civil war are usually deeply engaged on one side or the other. This tends to mould legal interpretations of rights of intervention and duties of abstention even more in the direction of political sympathies, than in other situations. Thus, in the Spanish Civil War from 1936–38, which deeply stirred official and

* Some footnotes omitted. Reprinted by permission of Columbia University Press.

4. Oppenheim, International Law, Vol. 2 (7th ed., Lauterpacht, 1952), p. 660. See also Jessup, The International Problem of Governing Mankind (1947), p. 33 et seq.

non-official political opinion abroad, those favoring the cause of the incumbent Republican Government of Spain affirmed the widely supported doctrine that in the case of civil war, the legal government but not the insurgents are entitled to assistance, at least up to the point when the insurgents have become sufficiently established to attain the status of belligerency. This attitude was strengthened by the blatant intervention of Nazi Germany and Fascist Italy on the side of Franco, from the very outbreak of revolution. For reasons of policy rather than law, the Western governments came to treat both sides as equals, by concluding a non-intervention pact to which the Fascist Powers, as well as the Soviet Union, were also parties. This pact, based on the principle of abstention from assistance to either side proved a complete failure, not because of the underlying principle but because the Fascist Powers, and to a lesser extent the Soviet Union, ignored the obligations undertaken in the pact so that the disparity between the assistance granted to the Franco faction by states in league with him and the failure of the Republican Government to obtain aid from the Western Powers, became even greater. Legally, however, a case can be made for the theory underlying the nonintervention pact, provided, of course, that it is genuinely observed by all sides. Quincy Wright has contended, with powerful support in the legal literature, that "in a situation of civil strife, the state is temporarily inhibited from acting. A government beset by civil strife is not in a position to invite assistance in the name of the state." * * *

## B. CIVIL STRIFE AND THE UNITED NATIONS CHARTER

### *HENKIN, HOW NATIONS BEHAVE*

155–57 (2d ed. 1979).*

When, in the U.N. Charter, the nations decided to outlaw wars and the use of force, they said nothing explicit about internal wars; clearly, they did not intend to prohibit revolution or civil war. The Charter, too, though it enshrines principles of "independence," "sovereign equality," and "self-determination," says nothing explicit about outside intervention in internal struggles. It is not commonly insisted that the Charter itself forbids intervention in internal wars by political and economic means. The question that has divided lawyers is whether the Charter provision that members shall not use or threaten force against the political independence or territorial integrity of another member forbids also intervention by force in a civil war.

For this purpose one might perhaps distinguish different kinds of intervention. One can readily argue the unlawfulness of "subversive" intervention: it is just as much a violation for an outside power to use force subtly or covertly to subvert an existing government and impose a puppet government as it is to send its armies to conquer the victim and impose a puppet government. On this view, the Charter bars external participation in internal struggle by force, at least if this intervention threatens the political independence or territorial integrity of the victim. The United

* Some footnotes omitted. Reprinted by permission of Columbia University Press.

Nations has in effect taken this position when its resolutions condemned "indirect aggression"; the definition of aggression which it adopted, the Declaration of Principles on Friendly Relations, the Charter of Economic Rights and Duties of States, all condemn "indirect aggression."

Some lawyers have argued that, when nations come to the support of one side or the other in cases of independent insurrection or *bona fide* civil war, it is not a violation of the norms of the U.N. Charter * but only of some customary rule against such intervention which, if it was ever sound, may not have recovered from the wounds it suffered in the Spanish Civil War. Many believed that there is no agreed norm forbidding active military support for the recognized government of a country, at least before rebellion has made great headway. The United States has invoked the right to give such aid to Greece, Lebanon, Nationalist China, and South Vietnam. The Soviet Union claimed a similar justification in Hungary. Some may even assert the right to recognize and support rebel causes, as in Angola (against Portugal), and even in the Congo in 1964–65. International law was not much invoked when different powers supported different factions competing for authority, as in Angola in 1975–76, or even when India recognized Bangladesh, or Tanzania recognized Biafra while civil war was still in progress.

In our time, some forces for intervention have been particularly strong and unlikely to heed an uncertain law. The difficulties of defining and preventing "unlawful intervention" have been multiplied where domestic and international interests are entangled and internal conflicts have special international significance. There were interventions to help end colonialism, as when Tunisia actively supported the Algerian rebels, and when other nations supported rebels against Portuguese rule in Angola. The major interventions involved, of course, Communist expansionism and Western efforts to contain it. Even interventions not unlike those of past days, and not obviously related to colonialism or communism, have looked different in our times—for example, Egyptian troops in Yemen in the 1960s, and open, full-blown and continuing intervention in Lebanon in 1976–77.**

* It is argued that even if intervention is not considered a use of force against the territorial integrity or political independence of the victim state [Article 2(4)], it may yet constitute a threat to international peace, especially when nations intervene on both sides. No doubt, in a given case, U.N. organs may conclude that such competing interventions threaten the peace, and may invoke their authority accordingly. It has been suggested that even civil war itself (without intervention) may constitute a threat to the peace which the United Nations is authorized to suppress.

** Our times also raised special problems of intervention where there is no internal war. We were not too far from traditional accusations of foreign intervention when West Germany protested recognition of East Germany as a separate state, but this division—and those in Vietnam, Korea, China—was hardly a traditional instance of rebellion or secession. The People's Republic of China continued to protest recognition of the Nationalist regime in Taiwan, whether as the Government of China or even as having authority over Taiwan.

## INTERVENTION BY FORCE IN CIVIL WARS

### *SCHACHTER, THE RIGHT OF STATES TO USE ARMED FORCE*

82 Mich.L.Rev. 1620, 1641–45 (1984).*

Foreign military interventions in civil wars have been so common in our day that the proclaimed rule of nonintervention may seem to have been stood on its head. Talleyrand's cynical quip comes to mind: "non-intervention is a word that has the same meaning as intervention." Indeed, virtually all the interventions that occur today are carried out in the name of nonintervention; they are justified as responses to prior interventions by the other side. No state today would deny the basic principle that the people of a nation have the right, under international law, to decide for themselves what kind of government they want, and that this includes the right to revolt and to carry on armed conflict between competing groups. For a foreign state to support, with "force," one side or the other in an internal conflict, is to deprive the people in some measure of their right to decide the issue by themselves. It is, in terms of article 2(4), a use of force against the political independence of the state engaged in civil war.

The states that intervene do not challenge this legal principle; they generally proclaim it as the basis for their "counter-intervention." They are often able to do so with some plausibility, because in almost every civil war the parties have sought and received some outside military support. A preeminent difficulty in applying the rule of nonintervention in these circumstances arises from the equivocal position of the established government. Other states are free as a general rule (in the absence of contrary treaties) to furnish arms, military training and even combat forces to that government at its request. On the other hand, they may not do the same for an opposing force; that would clearly violate the sovereignty and independence of the state.

Consequently, governments commonly receive foreign military aid and they may request more such aid when faced with an armed insurrection. At that point two questions arise: (1) is there an obligation to cease aid to the established regime because that now involves taking sides in an internal conflict? And (2) if such aid to the government constitutes foreign intervention, does it permit counter-intervention to support the other side? Concretely, if the Nicaraguan Sandinista regime receives Cuban and Soviet military supplies and advisors, is the United States free to support the armed opposition by training, arms and technical advice? An answer to the first question involves an assessment of the particular circumstances and of the presumption that the government is entitled to continued aid. The relevant general principle, in keeping with the concept of political independence and non-intervention, would be that when an organized insurgency occurs on a large scale involving a substantial number of people or control over significant areas of the country, neither side, government or insurgency, should receive outside military aid. Such outside support would be contrary to the right of the people to decide the issue by their own means. It would be immaterial whether the insurgency was directed at overthrow of the government or at secession (or autonomy) of a territorial unit.

* Footnotes omitted. Reprinted by permission of the Michigan Law Review.

The second and more difficult question is whether an illegal intervention on one side permits outside states to give military aid to the other party (whether government or insurrectionists). Such counter-intervention may be justified as a defense of the independence of the state against foreign intervention; it may then be viewed as "collective self-defense" in response to armed attack. True, it may also further "internationalize" a local conflict and increase the threat to international peace. The Vietnam War is the outstanding example. Despite the danger, the law does not proscribe such counter-intervention. It is not that two wrongs make a right but that the grave violation of one right allows a defensive response. The political solution is to avoid its necessity by a strict application of a nonintervention rule applied to both sides. To achieve this it is probably essential in most cases to have international mechanisms (peacekeeping forces or observer teams) to monitor compliance with a *cordon sanitaire* and a ban on assistance.

A related problem of practical importance is the clarification of what kinds of military aid qualify as illicit intervention. The UN resolutions on nonintervention leave this to ad hoc judgments, but a strong case can be made for the specifications of impermissible acts. Such specification would give more determinate content to the principle of nonintervention and, in that respect, strengthen it. In line with this view, the Institut de Droit International, in its resolution on nonintervention, has designated the following acts as impermissible when done to support either party in a civil war:

> (a) sending armed forces or military volunteers, instructors or technicians to any party to a civil war, or allowing them to be sent or to set out;
>
> (b) drawing up or training regular or irregular forces with a view to supporting any party to a civil war, or allowing them to be drawn up or trained;
>
> (c) supplying weapons or other war material to any party to a civil war, or allowing them to be supplied;
>
> * * *
>
> (e) making their territories available to any party to a civil war, or allowing them to be used by any such party, as bases of operations or of supplies, as places of refuge, for the passage of regular or irregular forces, or for the transit of war material. The last mentioned prohibition includes transmitting military information to any of the parties.

The Institut also declared that outside states should use "all means to prevent inhabitants of their territories, whether natives or aliens, from raising contingents and collecting equipment, from crossing the border or from embarking from their territories with a view to fomenting or causing a civil war." They also have a duty to disarm and intern any force of either party to a civil war which enters their territory. However, the Institut's resolution does not prohibit humanitarian aid for the benefit of victims of a civil war nor does it exclude economic or technical aid that is not likely to have a substantial impact on the outcome of a civil war. While it cannot be said that these declarations of the Institut are clearly existing law in every detail, they are a persuasive interpretation of the general rule against nonintervention and should influence state practice.

Two additional principles have been proposed for placing limits on counter-intervention. One is that the counter-intervention should be limited to the territory of the state where the civil war takes place. The fact that the prior intervention was illegal (i.e., in violation of the rule of non-intervention) would not justify legally the use of force by a third state in the violator's territory. This territorial limitation on counter-intervention has been observed in nearly all recent civil wars. However, it apparently has been abandoned by the United States insofar as its "counter-intervention" on the side of the El Salvador regime has extended to support of anti-Sandinista forces fighting on Nicaraguan soil. The United States had justified this action under the collective self-defense provision of article 51, presumably on the ground that Nicaragua has engaged in an armed attack on El Salvador. The United States also "counter-intervened" against Nicaragua by mining approaches to Nicaraguan ports. The legality of the U.S. actions has been challenged by Nicaragua in a case brought by it in April 1984 against the United States in the International Court of Justice. If the Court takes up the merits of the Nicaraguan complaint (overriding U.S. objections to the jurisdiction of the Court), it will have an opportunity to clarify the limits of collective self-defense and of counter-intervention under the UN charter.

The second limitation arises from the principle of proportionality. It calls for limits on the technological level of weapons used in a counter-intervention. This is essentially a no-first-use rule. High-technology weapons of mass destruction should not be introduced into the internal conflict by any outside intervening state, whatever its right to intervene. On the whole, this rule of restraint has been followed in recent civil wars, though the Vietnam War involved exceptions. There is good reason to consider it as a legal restriction and not merely a prudential principle. It is, however, less clear that state practice conforms to a rule of proportionality in regard to the quantum of military aid on one side or the other. Proportionality would require some rough equivalence between the counter-intervention and the illicit aid given the other side. However, when an established regime faces a strong indigenous insurgency which has some outside aid, the counter-intervening government favoring the regime is likely to be under great pressure to give massive support to that regime, even if relatively minor aid from the outside is given to the insurgents. U.S. military aid to El Salvador is a current example. It demonstrates the difficulty of applying a principle of proportionality in the absence of agreed limits by both sides on the quantum and character of outside aid.

## *Notes*

1. See generally Resolution on Principles of Non–Intervention of the Institute of International Law, 56 Annuaire de l'Institut de Droit International 119–56, 411–74 (1975, Wiesbaden Session) (resolution and accompanying reports and discussion); Vincent, Non-intervention and International Order (1974); J.N. Moore, Law and Civil War in the Modern World (1974); Bowett, Self–Defense in International Law (1958); Falk, Legal Order in a Violent World, Part II (19), in

Intervention in International Politics (Bull ed. 1984); Farer, Harnessing Rogue Elephants: a Short Discourse on Foreign Intervention in Civil Strife, 82 Harv. L.Rev. 511 (1969).

2. As to whether intervention in a state by one outside power justifies counter-intervention by another, see Cutler, the Right to Intervene, 64 Foreign Affairs 96 (1985). Compare Schachter, The Right of States to Use Armed Force, 82 Mich.L.Rev. at 1641–45; Schachter, In Defense of International Rules on the Use of Force, 53 U.Chi.L.Rev. 113, 120–21, 137–38 (1986); Henkin, The Use of Force: Law and U.S. Policy, in Might v. Right: International Law and the Use of Force 37, 50–65 (2d ed. 1991).

## *FALK, INTERNATIONAL LAW AND THE UNITED STATES ROLE IN THE VIETNAM WAR*

75 Yale L.J. 1122–27 (1966).*

The central issue is whether an externally abetted internal war belongs in either traditional legal category of war—"civil" or "international." Four sub-inquiries are relevant. What are the legal restraints, if any, upon national discretion to treat a particular internal war as an international war? What rules and procedures are available to determine whether foreign participation in an internal war constitutes "military assistance," "intervention," "aggression" or "an armed attack"? What responses are permissible by the victim of "aggression" or "an armed attack"? Finally, what should be the roles of national, regional, and global actors in interpreting and applying the relevant rules?

If the internal war is regarded as a "civil" war, then the legally permitted response to intervention is restricted to counter-intervention; an intervening nation whose own territory is not the scene of conflict may not attack the territory of a state intervening on the other side.[5] If foreign intervention were held to convert an "internal" war into an "international" war, the intervention could be regarded as an armed attack that would justify action in self-defense proportionate to the aggression. The victim of aggression is entitled, if necessary, to attack the territory of the aggressor expanding the arena of violence to more than a single political entity.[6] Given the commitment of international law to limiting the scope, duration, and intensity of warfare, it would appear desirable severely to restrict or perhaps to deny altogether, the discretion of nations to convert an internal war into an international war by characterizing external participation as

* Some footnotes omitted. Reprinted by permission of the Yale Law Journal Company and Fred B. Rothman & Company for the Yale Law Journal, V. 75.

5. The assertion in the text must be qualified to the extent that the United States decision to bomb North Viet Nam is treated as a law-creating precedent (rather than as a violation).

6. If the conceptions of "aggression" and "armed attack" are so vague that nations can themselves determine their content, a self-serving legal description of the desired course of state action can be given and is not subject to criticism in a strict sense. A critic would be required to stress that an expansive definition of "armed attack," although not forbidden by prior rules of law, was an unwise legal claim because of its status as a precedent available to others and because of its tendency to expand the scope and magnify the scale of a particular conflict.

"aggression" rather than as "intervention."[7]

* * *

The appraisal of a claim by a national government that an act of intervention is "aggression" is a complex task even if performed with utter impartiality. It depends on assessing very confused facts as to the extent and phasing of external participation, as well as upon interpreting the intentions of the participating nations. For instance, one must distinguish in the behavior of an international rival between a program of unlimited expansion through violence and intervention to assure the fair play of political forces in a particular domestic society. In the context of contemporary international politics, a crucial assessment is whether Communism or specific Communist states propose unlimited expansion by using unlawful force or whether they rely upon persuasion and permissible levels of coercion. It is difficult to obtain adequate evidence on the limits of permissible political and paramilitary coercion. Arguably, even a program of maximum expansion should be countered by self-limiting responses aimed at neutralizing Communist influence on internal wars and at building a world order that minimizes the role of military force. We must also not overlook the welfare of the society torn by internal war. The great powers tend to wage their struggles for global dominance largely at the expense of the ex-colonial peoples. These considerations support a conservative approach to internal wars, an approach treating them as civil wars, and permitting a neutralizing response as a maximum counteraction. * * *

* * *

Civil strife can be analyzed in terms of three different types of violent conflict.[16] A Type I conflict involves the direct and massive use of military force by one political entity across a frontier of another—Korea or Suez. To neutralize the invasion it may be necessary to act promptly and unilaterally, and it is appropriate either to use force in self-defense or to organize collective action under the auspices of a regional or global institution. A Type II conflict involves substantial military participation by one or more foreign nations in an internal struggle for control, e.g., the Spanish Civil War. To neutralize this use of military power it may be necessary, and it is appropriate, to take offsetting military action confined to the internal arena, although only after seeking unsuccessful recourse to available procedures for peaceful settlement and machinery for collective security. A third type of conflict, Type III, is an internal struggle for control of a national society, the outcome of which is virtually independent of external participation. * * *

These three models are analytical tools designed to clarify the nature and consequences of policy choices. Reasonable men may disagree on the proper classification of a particular war, especially if they cannot agree on the facts. * * *

* * *

7. It is important to distinguish between the factual processes of coercion and the legal labels used to justify or protest various positions taken by the participants. Aggression is a legal conclusion about the nature of a particular pattern of coercion.

16. These "types" are analytical rather than empirical in character. In actual experience a particular occasion of violence is a mixture of types, although the nature of the mixture is what makes one classification more appropriate than another.

Two general issues bear on an interpretation of the rights and duties of states in regard to internal wars of either Type II or III. First, to what extent does the constituted elite—the incumbent regime—enjoy a privileged position to request outside help in suppressing internal challenges directed at its control? Traditional international law permits military assistance to the incumbent regime during early stages of an internal challenge. However, once the challenging faction demonstrates its capacity to gain control and administer a substantial portion of the society, most authorities hold that a duty of neutrality or nondiscrimination governs the relations of both factions to outside states. A state may act in favor of the incumbent to neutralize a Type III conflict only until the challenge is validated as substantial. A crucial question is whether outside states can themselves determine the point at which the challenge is validated, or whether validation is controlled, or at least influenced, by international procedures and by objective criteria of validation. * * *

### *Note*

Since the Second World War there have been many instances of external participation in situations of internal disorder, strife or civil war: U.S. support for Greek and Turkish governments fighting Communist guerrilla bands (1947); the Soviet Union's interventions in Hungary (1956), Czechoslovakia (1968), and Afghanistan (1979); by India in Bangladesh (1971); civil war in Lebanon (1958 and 1982); the sending of U.S. marines to the Dominican Republic (1965); internal and interstate war in the Horn of Africa (since 1974); interventions in civil war in Angola and Southern Africa (since 1975); Vietnam's invasion of Kampuchea to depose the Pol Pot regime (1979); external roles in civil war in El Salvador and Nicaragua (since 1978); by several countries, notably Cuba and South Africa, in Angola (beginning in 1978); French and Libyan involvement in civil war in Chad (since 1983); and the U.S. invasion of Grenada (1983). The most extensive involvement by the United States in foreign civil strife since the last world war was in Vietnam.

## VIETNAM

### *HENKIN, HOW NATIONS BEHAVE*

304–308 (2d ed. 1979).*

Even the barest, briefest narrative of American involvement in Indochina must go back at least to 1954. At a political conference in Geneva following years of fighting, France signed a cease-fire and agreed to transfer sovereignty to a "State of Vietnam." The Final Declaration of the Conference affirmed the unity of Vietnam and envisioned holding elections in July 1956. But while the rival governments in North and South Vietnam committed themselves to unifying the country, the South Vietnamese government did not accept the Geneva Conference and the United States did not sign the Final Declaration, although it announced that it would abide by the Declaration's terms.

It soon appeared that the South Vietnam government would not agree to general elections, claiming that the elections could not be free in the

* Footnotes omitted. Reprinted by permission of Columbia University Press.

Communist-controlled North. The United States supported that view. Instead, it led in the establishment of the South–East Asia Collective Defense Treaty (SEATO), and a protocol to that treaty made its provisions applicable to Cambodia, Laos, and "the free territory under the jurisdiction of the state of Vietnam."

General elections were not held in 1956, and in the years that followed Communist-led dissident groups (known as the Vietcong, or later, the National Liberation Front) engaged in terroristic activities, rebellion and war against the South Vietnamese government. Supported by Southern Communists trained in North Vietnam, the Vietcong made important headway and by the end of 1960 controlled substantial areas of South Vietnam.

United States support for the South began early and increased slowly. In the early years it helped build up the South Vietnamese army; in 1961 it began to send combat advisers to accompany combat-support units, and by 1963 there were some 16,000 U.S. military personnel in South Vietnam. Following a coup d'état apparently with U.S. knowledge if not support, President Johnson concluded that stronger U.S. support was necessary. In August 1964 a North Vietnamese attack on two U.S. destroyers in the Gulf of Tonkin led to a resolution by Congress authorizing the President "to take all necessary measures to repel any armed attack against the forces of the United States and to prevent further aggression," and to assist any member or protocol State of SEATO "requesting assistance in defense of its freedom." In October 1964 American aircraft began to attack supply trails in Laos; in March 1965 they began to bomb in North Vietnam; in April 1965 President Johnson sent combat troops. Beginning in the latter months of 1965, North Vietnamese troops entered the South to support the Vietcong. In 1967 the United States began to bomb in Laos, and in 1970 in Cambodia, claiming that the Communists were using those territories to support their aggression, and the local governments were unwilling or unable to prevent them. Despite intermittent efforts by both sides and by third parties to end the war, it continued for years more, terminating finally with the Paris agreements of 1973.

* * *

There are at least three possible models to characterize the Vietnam War and the U.S. role in it, and the judgment of international law will largely depend on which characterization it accepts.

Model A saw the war as civil war within an independent South Vietnam, with North Vietnam an outside state helping one side, the United States another outside state helping the other. Military intervention in civil war was not acceptable under traditional international law, but that law may never have recovered from the wounds it suffered at many hands during the Spanish Civil War. On its face at least, such external intervention is not obviously a violation of Article 2(4) of the U.N. Charter as a use of force against the political independence or territorial integrity of another state, if the support was bona fide and the intervenor was not seeking to dominate the side it supported and establish a puppet regime.

On this view of the Vietnam War, neither the United States nor North Vietnam violated a vital contemporary norm of international law, as long as both confined themselves to supporting activity. But U.S. bombing of North Vietnam added an unacceptable dimension, converting an essentially civil war into an international war. (In the Spanish Civil War, intervenors did not, nor claimed the right to, attack each other's territory.) Indeed, world reaction to U.S. participation appeared to harden appreciably after the United States began to bomb in the North, in part perhaps because the world saw the war as an internal affair in South Vietnam and held the United States responsible for expanding it.

A second view (Model B) also saw the war as civil war, not between the Vietcong and the Saigon Government in a separate independent South Vietnam, but within the single state of Vietnam, between North Vietnam and the Vietcong on one hand and Saigon forces on the other. In such a war, U.S. intervention, even bombing North Vietnam, was—again—perhaps a violation of traditional international norms against intervention in civil war, but not clearly of the U.N. Charter. Bombing Laos or Cambodia would be more difficult to justify, even if one viewed those countries as tacit supporters of North Vietnam; toleration of mutual interventions in civil war does not contemplate attacks by one intervenor against another.

Officially, the United States saw the war in Vietnam in yet a third perspective (Model C). North Vietnam launched an armed attack against the territorial integrity and political independence of an independent country, the Republic of South Vietnam, using the Vietcong as its agent. This was a use of force in clear violation of Article 2(4) of the Charter. In the face of this armed attack, the Republic of South Vietnam had its inherent right of self-defense under Article 51 of the Charter, and the United States could come to its aid in collective self-defense—as indeed, it had obligated itself to do in the South East Asian Collective Defense Treaty. The United States and the Republic of South Vietnam had every right to carry the war to the territory of the aggressor in order to defeat the aggression; they could carry the war to the territory of any other countries that involved themselves in the aggression, or permitted the aggressor to use their territory for its aggressive purposes, i.e., Laos and Cambodia.

### *Notes*

1. On August 10, 1964, Congress passed the "Gulf of Tonkin Resolution", H.J.Res. 1145, 78 Stat. 384:

> *Resolved by the Senate and House of Representatives of the United States of America in Congress assembled,* That the Congress approves and supports the determination of the President, as Commander in Chief, to take all necessary measures to repel any armed attack against the forces of the United States and to prevent further aggression.
>
> SEC. 2. The United States regards as vital to its national interest and to world peace the maintenance of international peace and security in southeast Asia. Consonant with the Constitution of the United States and the Charter of the United Nations and in accordance with its obligations under the Southeast Asia Collective Defense Treaty, the United States is, therefore, prepared, as the President determines, to take all necessary steps, including the use of armed force, to assist any member or protocol state of the Southeast Asia Collective Defense Treaty requesting assistance in defense of its freedom.

SEC. 3. This resolution shall expire when the President shall determine that the peace and security of the area is reasonably assured by international conditions created by action of the United Nations or otherwise, except that it may be terminated earlier by concurrent resolution of the Congress.

2. The Tonkin Gulf Resolution was repealed in 1971 by Pub.L. No. 91–672 § 12, 84 Stat. 2055. Henkin wrote: "[i]n the political context of Vietnam–Cambodia repeal of the Tonkin Resolution did not in fact constitute a Congressional decision to end the war." "Its repeal * * * could properly be interpreted only as withdrawing authority for new military actions in the area in the future. That Congress repealed the resolution while appropriating funds for continuance of the war and rejecting resolutions for its termination could leave no doubt that repeal was not intended as the equivalent of a resolution to terminate the war * * *." Foreign Affairs and the Constitution at 108, 351 n. 47.

The war was ended by the Agreement on Ending the War and Restoring Peace in Vietnam, signed at Paris, January 27, 1973. See 12 I.L.M. 48 (1973).

For the history of U.S. involvement in Vietnam, see Kahin & Lewis, The United States in Vietnam (1967); Buttinger, Vietnam: The Unforgettable Tragedy (1977). A convenient compendium of the principal documents and articles is contained in The Vietnam War and International Law (Falk ed. 1968–74). See also Falk, International Law and the United States Role in the Vietnam War, 75 Yale L.J. 1122 (1966); Moore, The Lawfulness of Military Assistance to the Republic of Vietnam, 61 A.J.I.L. 1 (1967); Falk's response at 76 Yale L.J. 1095 (1967); Falk, The Six Legal Dimensions of the Vietnam War (1968). Compare also their contributions to Symposium on the United States Military Action in Cambodia, 1970, in the Light of International and Constitutional Law, 65 A.J.I.L. 1 (1971). See generally J.N. Moore, Law and the Indo–China War (1972).

3. In the 1990's, The United Nations became involved in civil wars, rebellion, and other disorder in Yugoslavia, Somalia and Cambodia; was its involvement legally justified? See Section 3 infra. Does it portend a larger role for the United Nations than originally contemplated?

## THE CHARTER'S CONTINUING RESTRAINTS ON THE USE OF FORCE

### *SCHACHTER, THE RIGHT OF STATES TO USE ARMED FORCE*

82 Mich.L.Rev. 1620–21, 1623–24, 1645–46 (1984).*

When the United Nations (UN) Charter was adopted, it was generally considered to have outlawed war. States accepted the obligation to settle all disputes by peaceful means and to refrain from the use or threat of use of force in their international relations. Only two exceptions were expressly allowed: force used in self-defense when an armed attack occurs, and armed action authorized by the UN Security Council as an enforcement measure. These provisions were seen by most observers as the heart of the Charter and the most important principles of contemporary international law. They have been reaffirmed over and over again in unanimous declarations of the United Nations, in treaties and in statements of political leaders.

Yet as we are all acutely aware, there is widespread cynicism about their effect. Reality seems to mock them. Wars take place, countries are invaded, armed force is used to topple governments, to seize territory, to avenge past injustice, to impose settlements. Threats of force, open or implicit, pervade the relations of states. The menace of a nuclear holocaust hangs over all nations, great or small. Collective security, as envisaged in the Charter, has had little practical effect. Our personal lives are deeply affected by the expectation of violence, by the vast resources devoted to armaments, and perhaps most insidiously, by the belief that little can be done to replace force as the ultimate arbiter in conflicts between nations.

It is no wonder that the obligations of the Charter are widely seen as mere rhetoric, at best idealistic aspirations, or worse as providing a pretext or "cover" for aggression. This evaluation, devastating as it may appear for international law, cannot be dismissed or minimized. But there is the other aspect of reality. Never before in history has there been such widespread and well-founded recognition of the costs and horrors of war. That awareness and its objective basis are powerful factors in strengthening the conscious self-interest in avoiding armed conflict.

It does not follow, of course, that rules of law must be seen as an effective remedy. At the present time, peace is often perceived as "secured" by the balance of power between West and East and the deterrent effect of nuclear arms. It is widely maintained that these factors, not the legal rules of the UN Charter, are what count. But even if countervailing power and the fear of nuclear devastation are restraints on use of force, it is abundantly clear that they have not prevented many armed conflicts, nor have they led to acceptance of a complete prohibition on the use of force. We do not, for our present purposes, have to consider in detail why this is so. It is sufficient to recognize that in numerous situations governments are not deterred from the use or threat of force by considerations of power, fear of destruction or, for that matter, by law. We generally attribute such decisions to judgments of self-interest and rational assessments of probable gains and costs. We may also recognize that nonrational factors—emotions, drives for power, ignorance—have an important role. There is rather more uncertainty about the influence of law and morality on such decisions. The reasons for this uncertainty do not arise from an absence of reference to legal and moral rules. On the contrary, every time a government uses force or responds to such use by others, it invokes the law along with considerations of morality and humanity. This very fact generates cynicism since it seems possible for every action to find support in law and there appears to be no effective higher authority to settle the matter. These facts understandably lead many to conclude that the legal rules on the use of force may be used to rationalize and justify almost any use of force and, therefore, that they can have little if any influence on the actual decision to use force.

One question raised by these observations is whether the existing rules on the use of force are so vague and uncertain as to allow a state to offer a plausible legal justification for virtually any use of force it chooses to exercise.

If we take the realistic view that governments deciding on the use of force take into account the diverse considerations referred to earlier—the probable costs and benefits, the responses of other states and the public, the effect on future claims by other states, the value of law-compliance to international order—we may conclude that the issue of permissibility under the law is a factor that would normally be considered. That this is often the case is shown, at least in some degree, by the fact that in virtually every case the use of force is sought to be justified by reference to the accepted Charter rules. While such justification may be no more than a rationalization of an action chosen solely on grounds of interest and power, the felt need to issue a legal justification is not without importance. It demonstrates that states require a basis of legitimacy to justify their actions to their own citizens and, even more, to other states whose cooperation or acquiescence is desired. The fact that claims of legitimacy are also self-serving does not mean that they do not influence conduct by the actors or by those to whom they are addressed. Even if we label those claims as hypocritical ("the tribute that vice pays to virtue"), they require credibility and for that reason must be confirmed by action. We need not treat this as a categorical imperative that holds good in every case in order to recognize that in a great many situations there is a link between conduct and the perceived restraints of law. Power and interest are not superseded by law, but law cannot be excluded from the significant factors influencing the uses of power and the perception of interests.

* * *

It would be a mistake to conclude that the international law of force is so vague and fragmentary as to allow governments almost unlimited latitude to use force. International texts and the legal positions taken by governments reveal a coherent body of principles that apply to a wide range of conduct involving armed force. These principles are grounded in two major interests, both widely accepted as basic to our international system. The first is the paramount interest in the sovereignty and independence of nation-states. The second is the common interest in restraints on the unbridled exercise of power. Such restraints are no longer seen as "mere" ideals. The fear of nuclear war and mass destruction has made them a prime necessity for survival.

It is true that the efficacy of law is limited because the system lacks effective central authority and is characterized by vast discrepancies in the power of states. Fear of nuclear devastation has not eliminated the Hobbesian element in that system. Powerful states may violate international obligations; they may do so with relative impunity or they may pay a price. But they also have a stake in stability and an acute sense of countervailing power. A decentralized legal system can operate because of these factors of self-interest and reciprocal reactions.

Moreover, the system is not wholly decentralized. As we have indicated, collective judgments are continuously being made both within and outside of formal institutions. Decisions of international bodies add both to the specificity and density of agreed law and affect the costs that result from illegitimate conduct. However inadequate this may seem in comparison to a mature national legal system, it should not be scorned as an element in maintaining peace. To consider its inadequacy a reason for ignoring the restraints can only add to the present insecurity. A world in which power and self-interest alone are expected to restrain force would not be a safer world. We may move dangerously in that direction by weakening existing law on the ground that it lacks impartial organs of application and enforcement. The best would then become the enemy of the good.

## SECTION 3. COLLECTIVE USE OF FORCE

The League of Nations, the first "universal" organization established for the purpose of maintaining international peace, failed and effectively died in the Second World War. The reason for its failure was the unwillingness or inability of the principal world powers to resist Nazi–Fascist aggression. That reason includes subsidiary reasons commonly cited: the dominance of narrow nationalism among the Big Powers over their willingness to cooperate, the failure of the United States to participate, the unwillingness of France and Great Britain to act decisively to make the League work, suspicious hostility between them and the U.S.S.R. preventing cooperation against aggressive fascism.

The League of Nations did not purport to outlaw war, only to impose a "cooling-off period" to permit collective conciliation, arbitration or adjudication. Collective action against violation of the League system was limited to diplomatic and economic sanctions, although the League Council had the duty to recommend what military assistance League members should contribute to "the armed forces to be used to protect the covenants of the League." Art. 16(2). For the relevant provisions of the League Covenant, see 877 supra.

### A. THE UNITED NATIONS

The principal purpose of the United Nations is:

> To maintain international peace and security, and to that end: to take effective collective measures for the prevention and removal of threats to the peace, and for the suppression of acts of aggression or other breaches of the peace, and to bring about by peaceful means, and in conformity with the principles of justice and international law, adjustment or settlement of international disputes or situations which might lead to a breach of the peace;

Charter of the United Nations, Article 1(1).

The primary responsibility for achieving that purpose was lodged in the Security Council. (Article 24). The Security Council was given the authority to pursue that purpose by peaceful means (Chapter VI) and also by collective military action if necessary (Chapter VII). Additionally, the General Assembly as well as the Secretary–General were given authority which might be used for keeping the peace. See Articles 10–15 and 99.

#### *1. The Collective Use of Force Under the Charter*

The 51 states that signed the Charter of the United Nations in San Francisco on June 26, 1945, believed that the new Organization's principal function would be to maintain peace and security through an authoritative institution and process, including, if necessary, the use of collective force against an aggressor. To that end, the Charter entrusted executive authority and "primary responsibility" to the Security Council, and within the Council, to the five Permanent Members, whose unanimity is required for non-procedural decisions. By design, enforcement action under Chapter VII of the Charter cannot be taken against any Permanent Member, or against any state without the consent (or acquiescence) of all Permanent Members. Four of the five Permanent Members were the major Allied powers of World War II. Their collaboration was expected to lay the foundation for German and European reconstruction and for world-wide security from aggression. The fifth Permanent Member was China, the "awakening giant," expected to play a major role in the post-war world. Two of the World's great powers, Germany and Japan, were excluded as the recently defeated enemies.

By 1947, the Cold War had split the former Allies into opposing ideological blocs. This led to the partition of Germany. West Germany became a major ally of the United States, East Germany a satellite of the Soviet Union, and the mutual exercise of the veto in the Security Council long prevented either Germany from becoming a member of the United Nations. After the Communist takeover in China, the United States opposed the seating of the Communist government in any organ of the United Nations, so that the more than 700 million inhabitants of mainland China remained for many years without effective representation in the United Nations. The incapacitation of one of the major pillars of the new organization—a security system built on the unified action of the world's five leading powers—shattered a second pillar; the Permanent Military Force envisaged in Articles 43–47 of the Charter could not be established because the major powers could not agree on the essentials of composition, command structure, territorial facilities, and conditions of action.

The void left by the absence of an international security system was temporarily, but only partly, filled by what may be called a "second phase" of collective security within the United Nations. After the collapse of the Charter's plan for a Security Council guided by the major powers acting in concert and supported by a permanent force, a strong Secretary-General and a more active General Assembly gave the United Nations a general "watchdog" function in international conflicts and the power to intervene actively in a "peacekeeping" role on an *ad hoc* basis (at least in some conflicts). The composition and function of these peacekeeping forces, however, were different from those of military forces envisaged under Chapter VII of the Charter. The peacekeeping forces were made up in the main of units from smaller states and they operated with the consent of the member states concerned. Their function was—and still is—to discourage hostilities, not to restore or maintain peace.

The "second phase" of United Nations collective security changed radically during the 1960s and 1970s. The principal reason was the explosive rate at which colonial and dependent territories attained statehood and almost automatic membership in the United Nations. This accentuated the discrepancy between power and responsibility. Under the original scheme of the Charter, the proliferation of new states would not have affected the predominance of the Security Council and the privileged position within the Council of the Permanent Members. But as the Security Council remained paralyzed, and as the functions and power of the General Assembly—in which each member has one vote—increased, a change in attitude of the major powers occurred as control slipped from their hands. This change was reflected in the crisis provoked by French and Soviet resistance to the advisory opinion of the International Court of Justice in *Certain Expenses of the United Nations,* see p. 997 infra, a reaction against the increasing domination of the General Assembly by smaller and poorer states.

The policy of the United States also tended in that direction. When, in 1950, the United States sponsored the "Uniting for Peace" resolution, which purports to confer on (or recognize in) the General Assembly powers to "recommend" collective measures when the Security Council is unable to act, the U.S. was still certain of a comfortable two-thirds majority in the General Assembly for action that it strongly sponsored. But that situation changed. In the aftermath of the Arab–Israeli war of June 1967, it was the Soviet Union—which had bitterly opposed the Uniting for Peace Resolution as usurping the functions of the Security Council—that invoked the Resolution when it failed to obtain a Security Council resolution condemning Israel as the aggressor, and it was the United States that opposed the convocation of the Assembly. In the General Assembly, neither the United States nor the U.S.S.R. thought it advisable to pursue its own draft resolution, and threw their support to conflicting resolutions introduced by smaller powers. The voting showed an almost even division among the members and it was not possible to obtain the required two-thirds majority.

Further political change brought further change to the United Nations. The continued proliferation of new states and the emergence of the "Third World" with substantial political solidarity; the acceptance of the People's Republic of China as the government of China to be represented in the U.N. and its aspirations to be the Big Power representative of the developing nations; conflict between the Soviet Union and China and improved relations between China and the United States—all further modified the U.N. peacekeeping system. It became possible for a combination of smaller members, sometimes with the support of one or both of the Communist powers, to authorize a United Nations operation to which the United States (and the United Kingdom) were opposed. In time, despite the stand earlier taken by the United States as to peacekeeping expenses, the U.S. and the U.K. began to see their interest in a voluntary rather than a compulsory assessment for the cost of all but basic administrative expenses for U.N. operations. That would help contain the power of the majority of non-Western and economically underdeveloped states in the General Assembly. At the same time, the U.N. majority was unwilling or unable to use the U.N. effectively. The U.N. played no role in the Vietnam War. It had little role in restoring or maintaining peace between African states such as Ethiopia and Somalia. It remained virtually irrelevant to the resolution of civil wars and other internal conflicts, even where they spilled out of national borders, and the result was largely determined by outsiders (e.g. Bangladesh in 1971; Angola in 1974; Western Sahara in 1975; Afghanistan in 1980; Chad in 1984).

The end of the Cold War, and increased cooperation by the Permanent Members of the Security Council in the late 1980s and early 1990s, have led commentators to suggest that a "third phase" of collective security in the United Nations may have begun. This phase might be characterized by a new willingness and ability by the Security Council to fulfill its primary responsibility under the Charter for the maintenance of international peace and security, as seen in the Gulf War of 1990–91, in modest but potentially stronger measures in connection with the conflict in the former Yugoslavia, and in the 1992–93 relief effort in Somalia.

The future of collective security and enforcement actions under Chapter VII of the Charter remains to be seen. Will cooperation continue? Will the Council's decision-making process avoid bias and the appearance of bias? Will the Security Council's structure, composition, and procedures, be reformed to reflect the world of the end-of-century, with more (or different) Permanent Members? Will the authority and the mandate of the Security Council continue to expand? Will the U.N. mobilize the financial and political resources to enable it to meet the challenges that clamor for collective action, perhaps even by force—against massive violations of human rights, ethnic strife, rampant hunger and floods of refugees?

In addition to possible future Security Council actions to maintain and restore peace, the U.N. remains available to mobilize and serve as an umbrella for peacekeeping personnel where the countries involved and the dominant political forces do not resist. The 1992–93 U.N. attempt at a Cambodian solution, and the U.N. authorization of military intervention in Somalia for humanitarian purposes, are attempts to extend U.N. collective security activities to what has been called "saving failed states."

The revival of the Security Council, and a growing role for the Secretary-General, may spill over to the other U.N. organs and other U.N. activities. The U.N. has social, economic and other humanitarian purposes. The decline of the General Assembly's role in matters of peace and security may encourage members to seek to expand its role in other domains.

## THE SECURITY COUNCIL AND CHAPTER VII OF THE CHARTER

### *CHARTER OF THE UNITED NATIONS*

San Francisco, June 26, 1945.

#### ACTION WITH RESPECT TO THREATS TO THE PEACE, BREACHES OF THE PEACE, AND ACTS OF AGGRESSION

*Article 39*

The Security Council shall determine the existence of any threat to the peace, breach of the peace, or act of aggression and shall make recommendations, or decide what measures shall be taken in accordance with Article 41 and 42, to maintain or restore international peace and security.

*Article 40*

In order to prevent an aggravation of the situation, the Security Council may, before making the recommendations or deciding upon the measures provided for in Article 39, call upon the parties concerned to comply with such provisional measures as it deems necessary or desirable. Such provisional measures shall be without prejudice to the rights, claims, or position of the parties concerned. The Security Council shall duly take account of failure to comply with such provisional measures.

*Article 41*

The Security Council may decide what measures not involving the use of armed force are to be employed to give effect to its decisions, and it may call upon the Members of the United Nations to apply such measures. These may include complete or partial interruption of economic relations and of rail, sea, air, postal, telegraphic, radio, and other means of communication, and the severance of diplomatic relations.

*Article 42*

Should the Security Council consider that measures provided for in Article 41 would be inadequate or have proved to be inadequate, it may take such action by air, sea or land forces as may be necessary to maintain or restore international peace or security. Such action may include demonstrations, blockade, and other operations by air, sea, or land forces of Members of the United Nations.

*Article 43*

1. All Members of the United Nations, in order to contribute to the maintenance of international peace and security, undertake to make available to the Security Council, on its call and in accordance with a special agreement or agreements, armed forces, assistance, and facilities, including rights of passage, necessary for the purpose of maintaining international peace and security.

2. Such agreement or agreements shall govern the numbers and types of forces, their degree of readiness and general location, and the nature of the facilities and assistance to be provided.

3. The agreement or agreements shall be negotiated as soon as possible on the initiative of the Security Council. They shall be concluded between the Security Council and Members or between the Security Council and groups of Members and shall be subject to ratification by the signatory states in accordance with their respective constitutional processes.

***Note***

See also Articles 2(6), 2(7), 9–12, 18, 23–25, 27, 34, 44–50, 103, 107 of the United Nations Charter.

## *SKYBISZEWSKI, USE OF FORCE BY INTERNATIONAL INSTITUTIONS AND LEGAL ASPECTS OF COLLECTIVE SECURITY*

Manual of Public International Law 785–88 (Sorensen, ed. 1968) (cross references omitted).*

The organ of the United Nations which is charged with the "primary responsibility for the maintenance of international peace and security" is the SC [Security Council]. In carrying out its duties under this responsibility, the Council acts on behalf of all the members of the Organization. While

* Reprinted with permission from St. Martin's Press.

in the pacific settlement of disputes, under Chapter VI of the Charter, the Council may only adopt recommendations and thus cannot bind the addressees of its resolutions, in matters involving "any threat to the peace, breach of the peace, or act of aggression", including the threat or use of force and handled under Chapter VII of the Charter, the Council has powers of decision.

When the nature or characteristics of a dispute or situation, which has been brought to the attention of the Council either by a state (Art. 35), or the Secretary–General (Art. 99), point to the inadequacy of peaceful methods and dictate the necessity of some executive action on the part of the United Nations, the first act of the Council is to make a determination under Article 39. By virtue of this provision the Council ascertains "the existence of any threat to the peace, breach of the peace, or act of aggression". None of these terms has been defined by the Charter, and the Council is free to arrive at its conclusions on the basis of whatever factual and other considerations it regards proper to take into account. * * *

Once the SC has resolved that there exists a threat to the peace, breach of the peace or act of aggression, it has the competence (i) to call upon the parties to comply with certain provisional measures, or (ii) to make recommendations, or (iii) to employ measures not involving the use of armed force or (iv) to use force. The Council may combine any of these possibilities with another as circumstances require.

(i) The Council's competence to order "such provisional measures as it deems necessary or desirable" is dealt with in Article 40. The Council calls upon the parties concerned to comply with the provisional measures, that is, the parties are bound to conform to them. The purpose of the provisional measures is "to prevent an aggravation of the situation". The provisional measures are "without prejudice to the rights, claims, or position of the parties concerned". The Council takes "account of failure to comply with such provisional measures". * * *

(ii) The Council may desist from adopting mandatory decisions and instead make recommendations (Art. 39). Sometimes, the recommendations of the Council authorize full-fledged military action by individual members, or they initiate a United Nations peace-keeping operation, including the setting up of appropriate mechanisms for that purpose * * *

(iii) The Council may, further, call upon the members to apply "measures not involving the use of armed force" against the delinquent state. According to Article 41, such measures "may include complete or partial interruption of economic relations and of rail, sea, air, postal, telegraphic, radio, and other means of communication, and the severance of diplomatic relations". They are the non-military preventive or enforcement measures of the United Nations. * * *

(iv) Finally, as a measure of last resort, the Council has the competence to order the use of force. The Council does so when it comes to the conclusion that the non-military steps referred to under (iii) "would be inadequate or have proved to be inadequate". * * *

### *Note*

The Security Council has found threats to the peace, breaches of the peace or acts of aggression on only six occasions: in 1950 when South Korea was invaded by North Korea; in 1980 when Argentina sought to recover the Falkland Islands; in 1987 when Iraq launched war against Iran; in 1990, in the Iraqi invasion of Kuwait; in 1991, in the ethnic warring in the former Yugoslavia; and in 1992, when clan warfare prevented relief aid from reaching victims in Somalia. As of 1993, the Security Council authorized the use of collective force in only two cases, in Korea and the Gulf War.

## 2. *Collective Actions to Maintain or Restore Peace and Security*

### KOREA

On June 25, 1950 the United States and a Commission established to aid reunification of North and South Korea, informed the United Nations that North Korean forces had invaded South Korea. A resolution adopted at an emergency meeting of the Security Council determined that the North Korean action constituted a breach of the peace and called for the immediate cessation of hostilities and the withdrawal of the North Korean units. S.C.Res. 82 (1950). There were no negative votes on the Council. (The Soviet delegate had been absent since January of 1959 because of a dispute over the representation of China).

The Security Council met on June 27 and, having noted that "urgent military measures are required to restore international peace and security," recommended "that the Members of the United Nations furnish such assistance to the Republic of Korea as may be necessary to repel the armed attack and to restore international peace and security in the area." S.C.Res. 83 (1950). This resolution was the first collective security effort authorized under the Charter. Again, the Soviet delegate was absent and thus unable to exercise his veto.

A Security Council resolution of July 7, 1950, requested the United States to appoint the commander of a unified command to which all Members were urged to provide assistance, including forces. The unified command was authorized to use the United Nations flag. S.C.Res. 84 (1950). The Soviet delegate returned to the Security Council on August 1, 1950, and blocked any further action by the Council. On October 7, 1950 the General Assembly, noting that the objectives of the Security Council had not yet been attained, established the United Nations Commission for the Unification and Rehabilitation of Korea. G.A.Res. 376(V) (1950).

The Korean conflict continued until the conclusion of an armistice agreement (T.I.A.S. No. 2782) at Panmunjom on July 27, 1953, between the Commander-in-Chief, United Nations Command, and the respective commanders of the North Korean and Communist Chinese forces. Although some of the principal provisions in the Armistice agreement were not carried out and there were several incidents, hostilities have not been resumed. See Henkin, How Nations Behave at 77–79.

A conference convened in Geneva in 1954 failed to reach a political solution to the conflict. On June 15, however, the fifteen members of the United Nations forces and the Republic of Korea signed a declaration containing the two fundamental principles upon which Korean reunification should be based. These were a justification of United Nations intervention and the proposition that genuinely free elections under United Nations supervision were necessary for a "unified, independent and democratic Korea." The declaration stated further that the Communists had rejected all efforts to obtain agreement on these fundamental points, and that it was better to face disagreement than to raise false hopes. 30 Dep't State Bull. 973 (1954); 31 id. 948 (1954). See generally U.S. Dep't of State, Korea's Independence (U.S. Dep't of State Pub. 2933, 1947); Korea, 1945–48 (U.S. Dep't of State Pub. 3305, 1948); Hoyt, The United States Reaction to the Korean Attack, 55 A.J.I.L. 45 (1961); Goodrich, Korea (1950); 5 Whiteman 102–09, 789–95, 1113–18 (1965).

### *Notes*

1. *Abstention by a Permanent Member.* The U.S.S.R. long maintained that the Council's resolution recommending that states assist South Korea was illegal because it did not have the affirmative vote of all the permanent members of the Security Council. The practice of the Security Council since that time has rejected the Soviet position and established that abstention (or absence) does not constitute a veto. For example, in 1990 China, a Permanent Member, abstained from voting on Resolution 678, authorizing the use of force to expel Iraq from Kuwait, but the legality of the resolution or of the subsequent use of force has not been questioned. (China abstained also 1992, when the Security Council imposed sanctions on the Khmer Rouge in Cambodia and when it called for a naval blockade of Serbia and Montenegro). For the practice of the Council in this respect, see Bailey, The Procedure of the U.N. Security Council 224–25 (2d ed. 1988).

2. *Collective action or collective self-defense.* The Resolutions passed by the Council in June and July of 1950 make no mention of Chapter VII of the Charter or of any specific Charter articles. Does that matter? Does the Security Council have power to make any recommendation whatsoever for the maintenance of international peace and security, or is it restricted to the specific measures set out in Chapter VII? See Dinstein, War, Aggression and Self-Defence 255–65 (1988); Bowett, U.N. Forces 32–59 (1964); Goodrich, Korea 102–21 (1956). See also the advisory opinion of the International Court of Justice in *Certain Expenses of the United Nations,* p. 997 infra. Some commentators have argued that the action taken in Korea is more appropriately characterized as an action taken in collective self-defence rather than an enforcement action under the Charter. See Stone, Legal Controls of International Conflict 234–37 (2nd ed. 1959). Was Article 51 of the Charter applicable even though neither North Korea nor South Korea was a member of the United Nations?

3. *Presidential authority.* President Truman sent U.S. armed forces to Korea, assumed the Unified Command and appointed General McArthur to command the U.N. forces, all without seeking authorization from Congress. Did he act within his Constitutional authority? Did the U.N. Charter, a treaty to which the United States is a party, supply the necessary authority since treaties are the law of the land and the President "shall take care that laws the be faithfully executed?" (U.S. Const., Art. 2, sec. 2) Was it relevant that the Council resolution was only a recommendation, not a mandatory decision legally binding on the United States? Some members of Congress questioned the President's authority but their objections were not pressed. 96 Cong. rec. 9320 (daily ed. June 28, 1950). Congress in effect ratified the President's action

through the appropriation of funds and by legislation. See Henkin, Congress, the President and the United Nations, 3 Pace Y.B.Int'l L. 1 (1991).

## THE PERSIAN GULF WAR 1990–91

The end of the Cold War and the thaw in relations between the United States and the Soviet Union resulted in a revitalized Security Council that faced its first major test when Iraq invaded Kuwait on August 2, 1990. The Security Council unanimously condemned the invasion and demanded that Iraq "withdraw immediately and unconditionally all its armed forces." S.C.Res. 660 (1990). The U.S. imposed comprehensive economic sanctions against Iraq, and the Soviet Union, the European Community, Japan, Germany and other countries followed. On August 6, 1992, the Security Council formalized these sanctions.

*Security Council Resolution 661*
August 6, 1990

*The Security Council* * * *

* * *

*Acting* under Chapter VII of the Charter of the United Nations, * * *

3. *Decides* that all States shall prevent:

(a) The import into their territories of all commodities and products originating in Iraq or Kuwait or exported therefrom after the date of the present resolution;

(b) Any activities by their nationals or in their territories which would promote * * * the export * * * of any commodities or products from Iraq or Kuwait; * * *

(c) The sale or supply by their nationals or from their territories * * * of any commodities or products, including weapons or any other military equipment * * * but not including supplies intended strictly for medical purposes, and, in humanitarian circumstances, foodstuffs, to any person or body in Iraq or Kuwait * * *

4. *Decides* that all States shall not make available to the Government of Iraq or to any commercial, industrial or public utility undertaking in Iraq or Kuwait any funds or any other financial or economic resources * * * except payments exclusively for strictly medical or humanitarian purposes * * *

5. *Calls upon* all States, including States non-members of the United Nations, to act strictly in accordance with the provisions of the present resolution notwithstanding any contract entered into or licence granted before the date of the present resolution;

6. *Decides* to establish * * * a Committee of the Security Council consisting of all the members of the Council, to undertake the following tasks * * *

(a) To examine the reports on the progress of the implementation of the present resolution which will be submitted by the Secretary–General;

(b) To seek from all States further information regarding the action taken by them concerning the effective implementation of * * * the present resolution * * *

### *Note*

This Security Council resolution provided a legal basis under U.S. law, for the sanctions the Council had imposed. See the U.N. Participation Act, 22 U.S.C.A. § 287c.

---

Despite the economic and military embargo established by Resolution 661, some Iraqi ships were reported to be sailing in and out of Iraqi ports apparently carrying embargoed goods, and there was concern that some countries were violating the embargo. The United States took the position that Resolution 661 authorized the use of military force to stop Iraqi ships suspected of carrying prohibited cargo, but other states, including the Soviet Union, disputed that view. The United States took no action to enforce the sanctions until, after intensive negotiations, the Security Council adopted Resolution 665 authorizing the use of "measures commensurate to the specific circumstances as may be necessary * * * to halt all inward and outward maritime shipping in order to inspect and verify their cargoes and destinations and to ensure strict implementation of * * * resolution 661 * * *." S.C.Res. 665 (1991).

Later, the Security Council adopted Resolution 666 to ensure that permissible food shipments went to those most in need and not to the Iraqi military. The Council also adopted Resolution 670, directing states to take steps to ensure that their aircraft, and aircraft flying over their territory, were in compliance with Resolution 661. The Council also considered action it might take against states not complying with Resolution 661.

During the time the Security Council was engaged in implementing Resolution 661, there was a dramatic military buildup in the Persian Gulf. U.S. forces were rushed early to the Gulf area, and many troops entered Saudi Arabia pursuant to agreement between the two countries to deter and help defend Saudi Arabia against possible attack by Iraq. By the end of November 1990, it was reported, the U.S. had more than 250,000 military personnel in the region, part of a planned deployment of 400,000 troops by mid-January. Other states, including Egypt, Saudi Arabia, Britain, France, Argentina and Canada, had reportedly deployed between 200,000 and 250,000 troops. When Iraq remained adamant in refusing to withdraw from Kuwait, the Security Council, on November 29, adopted Resolution 678 to authorize the use of military force to eject Iraq from Kuwait.

*Security Council Resolution 678*
November 29, 1990

*The Security Council* * * *

*Noting that,* despite all efforts by the United Nations, Iraq refuses to comply with its obligation to implement resolution 660 (1990) * * * in flagrant contempt of the Security Council,

*Mindful* of its duties and responsibilities under the Charter of the United Nations for the maintenance and preservation of international peace and security,

*Determined* to secure full compliance with its decisions,

*Acting* under Chapter VII of the Charter,

1. *Demands* that Iraq comply fully with resolution 660 (1990) and all subsequent relevant resolutions, and decides, while maintaining all its decisions, to allow Iraq one final opportunity, as a pause of goodwill, to do so;

2. *Authorizes* Member States co-operating with the Government of Kuwait, unless Iraq on or before 15 January 1991 fully implements, as set forth in paragraph 1 above, the foregoing resolutions, to use all necessary means to uphold and implement resolution 660 (1990) and all subsequent relevant resolutions and to restore international peace and security in the area;

3. *Requests* all States to provide appropriate support for the actions undertaken in pursuance of paragraph 2 of the present resolution;

4. *Requests* the States concerned to keep the Security Council regularly informed on the progress of actions undertaken pursuant to paragraphs 2 and 3 of the present resolution; * * *

### *SCHACHTER, UNITED NATIONS LAW IN THE GULF CONFLICT*

85 A.J.I.L. 452–63 (1991) (Footnotes omitted).*

Probably the most controversial issue faced by the Council during the gulf conflict was whether the sanctions under Article 41 would prove to be adequate to achieve the Council's objective. After the first two months, it was evident that the embargo was largely effective, particularly in stopping Iraq's oil exports and in cutting off the supply of significant imports of a technical and military nature. There appeared to be little doubt that the Iraqi economy was substantially damaged. However, it was much less clear whether such damage, even if continued, would bring about the demanded change in policy on the part of the Iraqi leadership and, if so, when. The United States Government concluded by November 1990 that military action would probably be required to compel Iraq to withdraw from Kuwait. It persuaded most of the other Council members to support a resolution authorizing the states cooperating with Kuwait to take the necessary means to uphold and implement the prior resolutions and to restore peace and security in the area. This authorization was to be effective on January 16, 1991, if Iraq did not comply by that date. The two members of the Council opposed to the resolution (Cuba and Yemen) questioned its validity on the ground that the Council had authorized the use of force without determining that the Article 41 sanctions would be inadequate. In their view, that determination was required when force was authorized under the terms of Article 42.

There are two possible answers to this point. One is that Article 42 was not being applied; this issue is examined below. The other answer is that even if Article 42 was applied, the Council discussion showed that members considered that the economic sanctions would not be adequate to achieve the withdrawal of Iraq. Whether this supposition was well-founded can only be a matter of speculation inasmuch as armed force was used on January 16, 1991.

* * *

The legal concept of collective self-defense was invoked in the gulf conflict almost immediately after the invasion by Iraq. Kuwait requested the aid of other countries and steps were taken by the United States, the United Kingdom and Saudi Arabia to lend assistance. The Security Council in its Resolution 661, which, as we saw, adopted sanctions under Article 41, also included in its preamble a paragraph that affirmed "the inherent right of individual or collective self-defence, in response to the armed attack by Iraq against Kuwait."

* * *

In affirming the applicability of collective self-defense in the gulf situation, the Council recognized (again by implication) that third states had the right to use force to aid Kuwait, even though those states themselves had not been attacked and had no treaty or other special links with Kuwait. * * *

* * *

The right of collective self-defense, however, came into question a few weeks after the United Nations imposed the sanctions under Article 41. The perception that such sanctions were not likely to bring about an Iraqi withdrawal had led to proposals for military action. The United States, the United Kingdom, and some other governments considered that such action would be permissible collective self-defense, based on the necessity to compel the aggressor to withdraw unconditionally. As against this position, it was argued by other governments and some international lawyers that the right of self-defense no longer applied when the Security Council had adopted measures it considered necessary to repel the armed attack. This argument rested on the language of Article 51, which safeguarded the right of self-defense "until the Council has taken measures necessary to maintain international peace and security." If these words are taken literally, the right of self-defense would be overridden whenever the Security Council adopted measures considered necessary in case of an armed attack on a state. This would be an implausible—indeed, absurd—interpretation. A Council decision that calls on an invader to withdraw and to cease hostilities is certainly a necessary measure, but it could not be intended to deprive the victim state of its right to defend itself when the invader has not complied with the Council's order. A reasonable construction of the provision in Article 51 would recognize that the Council has the authority to adopt a measure that would require armed action to cease even if that action was undertaken in self-defense. However, this would not mean that *any* measure would preempt self-defense. The intent of the Council as expressed in its decision would determine whether the right to use force in self-defense had been suspended by the Council.

In the Iraq–Kuwait case, the principal argument that collective self-defense was superseded by Council action relied on the fact that the Council had adopted mandatory economic sanctions under Article 41. It was obvious that such economic sanctions were adopted in the hope that they would be effective in bringing about the withdrawal of Iraqi forces. While this was the hope, the resolutions contained no indication that self-defense rights were meant to be terminated by the adoption of sanctions. Indeed, the very resolution, No. 661, that first adopted the economic sanctions included the preambular paragraph, referred to above, affirming rights of individual and collective self-defense. * * *

* * *

The controversy over preemption ended when the Security Council adopted Resolution 678 on November 29, 1990, authorizing the states cooperating with Kuwait to use "all necessary means to uphold and implement" the Council's resolutions if Iraq did not unconditionally withdraw on or before January 15, 1991. It was amply clear that necessary means included the use of armed force to bring about Iraq's withdrawal and compliance with other provisions of the twelve resolutions adopted between August 2 and November 29. As of January 16, Resolution 678 was treated as the legal basis of the large-scale military action by the coalition of states that brought about the defeat of Iraq at the end of February 1991 and its withdrawal from Kuwait.

The precise Charter basis of Resolution 678 was somewhat uncertain. The resolution itself declared that the Council was acting under chapter VII, but it did not specify which article of chapter VII. It thus left several possibilities open to conjecture. One was that chapter VII in general provided an adequate legal basis. Another view was that a resolution authorizing armed force necessarily came within Article 42 and had to meet the requirements of that article. Still a third position was that the authorization came properly within the scope of collective self-defense and that the Council was exercising its authority under Article 51 (which is also in chapter VII).

A good case can be made for this latter position. * * * One reason for treating Resolution 678 as falling within Article 51 is that it authorized the group of states identified as cooperating with Kuwait in resisting the invasion to take the necessary means to achieve the objectives previously declared by the Council and, in addition, to restore peace and security in the area. It is significant in this respect that the Council did not decide that the armed forces of the cooperating states were to be placed at the disposal or under the control of the Security Council. No United Nations command was set up; no reference was made to a United Nations force or to use of the UN flag. These were features of the UN-authorized force in Korea; their omission here is further evidence that the Security Council intended to leave the choice of means, timing, command and control to the participating states.

It may be asked why a new resolution was required when the Council had already affirmed the right of collective self-defense soon after the invasion. Moreover, collective self-defense action did not require Council approval or authorization; member states were free anyway to use force against the aggressor within the limits of self-defense. However, the resolution served the political purpose of underlining the general support of the United Nations for the military measures if Iraq did not withdraw before January 16, 1991. In addition, the resolution, supported by all of the cooperating states committed to collective action, clarified the objectives of the collective defense action. * * * To characterize the military action as collective self-defense rather than as a United Nations action does not imply that the use of force was wholly a matter of discretion for the cooperating states; nor does it mean that the Council lacked authority to place limits on the military action. Article 51 expressly recognizes that, in cases of self-defense, the Council retains the authority and responsibility to take such action as it deems necessary to restore international peace and security. This language makes it clear that the Council may decide on the limits and objectives of the military action authorized as collective self-defense.

Resort to collective self-defense (*jus ad bellum* ) is also subject to requirements of necessity and proportionality, even though these conditions are not expressly stated in Article 51. * * *

It is worth noting that the debate in the Council and elsewhere on whether the use of force was "necessary" self-defense took a direction rather different from the way the issue had previously been discussed by international lawyers. The argument advanced by opponents of the use of force contended, as noted above, that the economic embargo would prove to be effective in due course; hence, in their view, force was not required as a matter of self-defense. * * *

The criterion of necessity thus debated is quite different from the view previously accepted that an illegal armed attack on a large scale is in itself sufficient to meet the requirement of necessity for self-defense. * * *

* * *

It has generally been assumed that the Council's authority to apply armed force under chapter VII can only be found in Article 42. This assumption was also evidenced in statements made by some of the Security Council members. This is not surprising. For one thing, Article 42 is the only provision in the Charter that expressly empowers a UN organ "to take action by air, sea, or land forces" as may be necessary to maintain or restore international peace and security. Moreover, Article 39, the "basic" provision of chapter VII, authorizes the Council to "decide what measures shall be taken in accordance with Articles 41 and 42, to maintain or restore international peace and security." A reasonable inference is that if the Council decides on measures, they should be under either Article 41 (i.e., not involving force) or Article 42 (if military action is taken). Hence, if Resolution 678 is a "measure decided on" by the Council involving armed force, Article 42 would necessarily apply.

The argument is not entirely compelling. Although Article 42 is the only Charter article that expressly empowers a UN organ to take action by armed force, it does not follow that other provisions may not also apply. This point was made by the International Court of Justice in its advisory opinion in the *Expenses* case. The Court then rejected the argument that the armed force authorized by the United Nations in the Middle East and the Congo had to be based on Article 42. It declared, "The Court cannot accept so limited a view of the powers of the Security Council * * *." The Court's Delphic comment does not point to any alternative article, but it suggests that the Council could act on a liberal construction of its authority derived from its general powers to maintain and restore international peace and security. * * *

There are, of course, advantages to constitutional interpretation of such flexibility in cases where decisions are generally acceptable. On the other hand, invoking UN authority for coercive armed force touches an especially sensitive area, often with far-reaching effects. Confusion or uncertainty about the precise legal basis may well create friction. By avoiding reference in Resolution 678 to any particular article of chapter VII, the Council left the matter in doubt, giving rise to questions of authority that may require specific legal grounds. One hypothesis, suggested earlier, is that Resolution 678 is more compatible with an authorization of collective self-defense than with a conception of the Council as itself taking action by air, sea or land forces. There is no reason to doubt that the Council has authority under Article 51 to express approval of collective defense actions in a particular case. This may not be incompatible with Article 42 since its terms are flexible, allowing for a variety of actions.

To put it in another way, Resolution 678 may be read as consistent with both Article 51 and Article 42. In regard to the latter, the Council's resolution is an example of "action" taken by the Council involving the use of military forces. The word "action" does not have to mean that those armed forces are under the control or command of the Council. That such command and control was contemplated under other articles of chapter VII should not be read into Article 42. Recognizing Article 42 as a relevant source of authority together with Article 51 would not in itself enhance the Council's authority over the armed forces. It should not be forgotten that Article 51 gives the Council full authority and responsibility in cases of self-defense to take measures to maintain and restore international peace and security.

To be sure, the use of the term "action" in Article 42 may mean "enforcement" in a mandatory sense rather than an authorization. But even if Article 42 allows for mandatory "action," this should embrace the lesser power to recommend or authorize action. It does not make sense to require a mandatory decision where a recommendation or authorization would suffice to achieve the desired action.

If we assume that the Council's Resolution 678 is also a form of "action" within the meaning of Article 42, the question arises (as it did in the Council) whether the conditions of that article have been met. One such condition is that the Council shall have made the determination required in Article 39. The Council did so when in Resolution 660 it found that a breach of the peace had occurred. It also took provisional measures under Article 40 when it ordered withdrawal and negotiation.

Article 42 requires that the Council, before acting under that article, "consider that measures provided for in Article 41 would be inadequate or have proved to be inadequate." At least two members of the Council argued that the Council never did decide that the sanctions under Article 41 would be inadequate; consequently, they questioned the legal validity of Resolution 678. While it is true that the Council did not formally declare the inadequacy of the economic sanctions under Article 41, the debates indicate that several members believed that the sanctions would prove to be inadequate to bring about a withdrawal by Iraq. Moreover, it is not unreasonable to infer that the Council decision authorizing the cooperating states to use force ("all necessary means") impliedly recognized that sanctions would not prove adequate to compel Iraqi withdrawal. The defiant position taken by the Iraqi regime even after six months of sanctions added support to the belief that military action was needed to bring about its compliance. Whether a longer period would have been effective remains conjectural, but there is no doubt that the Council had the legal right to decide on the need for military action.

### *Notes*

1. After Resolution 678 the Security Council adopted no further resolutions on the Gulf until after the cease-fire. As of 1992–93, the Council continued to monitor the cease-fire and to adopt other resolutions to assure Iraqi compliance. The Council has sought also to protect Kurds and Shiites, inhabitants of Iraq, against gross violations of their human rights. See p. 981 infra. What is the basis for the Security Council's authority? How long does it continue? What is its scope?

2. Schachter states that the action taken in the Gulf can be characterized either as one of collective self-defense authorized by the Security Council or as an action taken under Article 42. Does the characterization have legal or practical consequences? See generally Moore, The Gulf Crisis: Enforcing the Rule of Law (1992); Agora: The Gulf Crisis in International and Foreign Relations Law, 85 A.J.I.L. 63–109, 506–535 (1991); The Gulf War: The Law of International Sanctions, 85 A.S.I.L. Proc. 169 (1991); Chayes, The Use of Force in the Persian Gulf, in Law and Force in the New International Order (Damrosch & Scheffer, eds. 1991); Murphy, De Jure War in the Gulf: Lex Specialis of Chapter VII Actions Prior to, During, and in the Aftermath of the United Nations War Against Iraq, 5 N.Y. Int'l L. Rev. 71 (1991); see also The Gulf War: Collective Security, War Powers and Laws of War, 85 A.S.I.L. Proc. 1 (1991); Quigley, The United States and The United Nations in the Persian Gulf War: New Order or Disorder?, 25 Cornell Int'l L.J. 1 (1992).

For compilations of documents and references to texts and periodical literature, see The Kuwait Crisis: Basic Documents (Lauterpacht, Greenwood, Weller & Bethlehem, eds. 1991); Gulf War Legal and Diplomatic Documents, 13 Houston J. Int'l L. 281 (1991); Bibliography, The International Legal Implications of Iraq's Invasion of Kuwait: A Research Guide, 23 N.Y.U.J. Int'l L. & Pol. 231 (1991).

3. The Gulf War raised long dormant issues under Article 51 of the Charter. Article 51 provides that states may exercise the "inherent" right of individual or collective self-defense "until the Security Council has taken measures necessary to maintain international peace and security." Can the Council order the cessation of action taken in self-defense, despite the fact that it is an "inherent" right? Does the right to act in self-defense cease as soon as the Council is seized of the matter or only when the Council has taken measures?

Will any action by the Council suspend the right to self-defense or does it come to an end only when the measures taken by the Security Council are successful and peace and security are restored? Who determines whether the measures taken have been effective? Once the Council has taken necessary measures, does the right of self-defense cease, or is it merely suspended, possibly to be revived at a later date? Professor Chayes has commented:

> One of the most serious, relevant, and fateful questions concerning the use of force under international law is what actions were open—and under what circumstances—to the forces of the United States and other countries arrayed against Iraq in the Persian Gulf region in 1990. The unspoken assumption of high government officials and certain commentators in the early months of the Iraq–Kuwait crisis was that the United States and its coalition partners, even in the absence of a further attack by Iraq or authorization of the Security Council, remained legally free to take military action upon their own decision. That was the position taken in early August 1990 by the United States on the question of the use of naval force in the Persian Gulf to enforce the U.N. sanctions. The U.S. Secretary of State and others said that such action was permissible as an exercise of the right of collective self-defense of Kuwait under Article 51 of the U.N. Charter, and thus required no further Security Council action.
>
> * * *
>
> Among the most important of the controverted questions—not because it was necessarily the most probable but because it throws the issues into sharpest relief—was the suggestion noted earlier that the United States was free, even in the absence of further provocation by Iraq or authorization by the Security Council, to use force against Iraq by virtue of some continuing right of collective self-defense emanating from the original attack on Kuwait. In other words, so the argument runs, the original deployments in Saudi Arabia and the Persian Gulf region were made in response to the armed attack on Kuwait and thus could be seen as an exercise of the inherent right of collective self-defense. The Security Council could be said to have acknowledged this position in its reference in Resolution 665 to "Member States co-operating with the government of Kuwait which are deploying maritime forces to the area." It rests with each of those states, perhaps in consultation with Kuwait and others whose forces were also at risk, to decide whether the measures taken in response to the Iraqi aggression were sufficient, and if not, what further action would be needed.
>
> The textual argument against this position, it seems to me, is very strong. Article 51 is not an affirmative grant of a right of self-defense but a statement of the situations in which the exercise of an "inherent right" is not precluded by the Charter. But those situations are subject to a limit of time. They endure only "until the Security Council has taken the measures necessary to maintain international peace and security."
>
> Who is to judge whether measures authorized by the Security Council are sufficient to maintain international peace and security? Again, the text of the Charter argues strongly that the function belongs to the Security Council. Article 39 says the Council shall "decide what measures shall be taken in accordance with Articles 41 and 42 to maintain or restore international peace and security." The same phrase, "measures necessary to maintain international peace and security," is the key to the temporal limitation on the inherent right of self-defense in Article 51. Even more

telling is Article 42, the article that empowers the Security Council to adopt measures involving the use of force, which begins: "Should the Security Council consider that measures provided for in Article 41 [i.e., diplomatic and economic sanctions] would be inadequate or have proved to be inadequate * * *." It seems clear that all of these provisions of Chapter VII—which is entitled "Action with Respect to Threats to the Peace, Breaches of the Peace, and Acts of Aggression"—are interlocking and that the critical phrase, "measures necessary to maintain international peace and security," carries the same meaning in all of them.

In the larger scheme of the Charter, it is the Security Council that has "primary responsibility for the maintenance of international peace and security," which is recognized as primarily a political rather than a legal task. To carry out that responsibility, the Council, once seized of a matter under Chapter VII, must have the authority to make the political judgments as to the requirements of the situation and the measures necessary to deal with it. Security Council preemption, moreover, reinforces the fundamental objective of Article 2(4) and Article 51 to confine the permissible occasions for the unilateral use of force to the narrowest possible range, where it is immediately and universally apparent that armed response is required.

During the Cold War, when the Security Council was immobilized by reciprocal vetoes, the argument was perhaps available that a state acting in individual or collective self-defense could not be expected to forgo continuing action simply because the Council was debating the situation, with no likelihood of a serious substantive outcome. This also would be the case if the Council's action is plainly incommensurate with the seriousness of the situation. In those instances it would be a plausible argument that the Council was simply not exercising its functions, so that the preemption contemplated by Article 51 when the Council was truly addressing the situation does not come into operation.

From the beginning of the Iraq–Kuwait crisis, as has been widely acknowledged, the Security Council worked "as it was supposed to work" according to the design of its framers. It cannot be argued that the Council failed to address the situation with appropriate gravity or to adopt measures with real impact or to strengthen those measures as the need became apparent. If the United Nations works as intended, judgments as to the ultimate objectives of U.N. action, the sufficiency of the measures to be taken, how long to wait for the sanctions to take effect, and the like are consigned to the Council, which acts by a majority of nine out of fifteen members, including the concurring or abstaining votes of the permanent members. In the process of reaching those decisions the United States necessarily has a very important voice. Indeed, there is both scope and need for American leadership. The United States can ensure by use of the veto that the Council will not act against its interests. But if the United States cannot induce the necessary number of other Security Council members to agree that additional measures involving the use of force are necessary, the Charter would clearly seem to preclude unilateral action.

Chayes, The Use of Force in the Persian Gulf, in Law and Force in the New International Order 3–7 (Damrosch & Scheffer, eds. 1991) (footnotes omitted). See also Greig, Self–Defence and the Security Council: What Does Article 51 Require?, 40 Int'l Comp.L.Q. 366 (1991); Gardner, Commentary on the Law of Self–Defense, in Law and Force in the New International Order (Damrosch &

Scheffer, eds. 1991); Penna, The Right to Self–Defense in the Post–Cold War Era: The Role of the United Nations, 20 Den.J.Int'l L. & Pol'y. 41 (1991); Mullerson, Self–Defense in the Contemporary World, in Law and Force in the New International Order (Damrosch & Scheffer, eds. 1991).

4. Do the usual requirements for action taken in self-defense—necessity and proportionality—apply to an action authorized by the Council? Does the Council have the authority to suspend these requirements? See Implementing Limitations on the Use of Force: The Doctrine of Proportionality and Necessity, 86 A.S.I.L.Proc. 39 (1992).

5. In Korea, the Security Council "recommended" that "member states" come to the defense of South Korea. In the Gulf War, the Council "authorized" military action by states cooperating with Kuwait. Are these differences of legal significance? In Korea the Security Council recommended a Unified Command controlled by the United States and authorized the use of the U.N. flag. The Security Council did not seek to exercise any control over the actions either in Korea or in the Gulf. Schachter states "the problems of authority and control are almost certain to complicate any future large scale enforcement action." Schachter, International Law in Theory and Practice 398 (1991). Is it possible for the Security Council, perhaps with the assistance of the Military Staff Committee, directly to command a multinational force? Is it desirable? In 1992, in Somalia, the Security Council "authorized the Secretary–General and the Member States concerned to make the necessary arrangements for the unified command and control of the forces involved" and "to establish appropriate mechanisms for coordination between the United Nations and their military forces." It also invited the Secretary–General to send "a small * * * liaison staff to the Field Headquarters of the unified command." See S.C.Res. 794 (1992), p. 983 infra.

6. *The laws of war.* Do the laws of war apply to actions authorized by the Security Council? Who is responsible if the laws of war are contravened or if abuses of human rights are committed by member states authorized by the Council to take action? See Conditions of Application of Humanitarian Rules of Armed Conflict to Hostilities in which United Nations Forces may be engaged, 54 (II) Ann. de l'Institut de Droit Int. 449–54 (1971); Conditions of Application of Rules, other than Humanitarian Rules, of Armed Conflict to Hostilities in which United Nations Forces may be Engaged, 56 (II) Ann. de l'Institut de Droit Int. 541–45 (1975). On the laws of war see Section 4 infra.

7. *Presidential authority.* As in the Korean War, the United States was the major power behind the coalition forces in the Gulf War. President Bush claimed constitutional authority to deploy forces in war against Iraq, pursuant to the Security Council Resolution 678, without Congressional approval. Members of Congress and many publicists denied that the President had the authority to act without Congressional authorization, especially in view of the War Powers Resolution. Would it make any difference if Security Council Resolution 678 had purported to be mandatory rather than only "authorizing" military action? Congress gave the President the authority he requested in 2 H.J.Res. 77, 102d Cong., 1st Sess., 137 Cong.Rec. 443 (1991). On the dispute between the President and the Congress, see U.S. Policy to Reverse Iraq's Occupation of Kuwait, 137 Cong.Rec. S323–04, 102d Cong., 1st Sess. (1991); The Situation in the Middle East[:] Expressing Sense of Congress that Congress Must Approve an Offensive Action against Iraq, 137 Cong.Rec. H390–01, 102d Cong., 1st Sess. (1991); See also the arguments of counsel for the President in Dellums v. Bush, 752 F.Supp.

1141 (1991); Henkin, Congress, the President and the United Nations, 3 Pace Y.B. Int'l L. 1 (1991); also, Scheffer, Use of Force After the Cold War: Panama, Iraq, and the New World Order, in Right v. Might: International Law and the Use of Force 109, 148–152 (2nd ed. 1991); Glennon, The Constitution and Chapter VII of the United Nations Charter, 85 A.J.I.L. 74 (1991).

### *3. United Nations Collective Action for Humanitarian Purposes*

The end of the Cold War and the revival of the Security Council made possible its action in the Gulf War, the kind of action for which the Council was designed. It also encouraged resort to the Security Council for collective military action in situations involving widespread atrocities against civilian populations or massive human suffering resulting from the breakdown of domestic order and from internal hostilities.

#### IRAQ

Some have cited United Nations action in the aftermath of the Gulf War as a precedent for collective humanitarian intervention generally. After the cease-fire in February 1991, there were reports of wide-spread human rights violations committed by Iraqi forces against Iraq's Kurdish and Shiite populations, causing nearly two million refugees to flee towards the Turkish and Iranian borders. On April 5, 1991, the Security Council adopted Resolution 688, which, while recalling Article 2(7) of the Charter and reaffirming its commitment to the sovereignty, territorial integrity and political independence of Iraq, condemned "the repression of the Iraqi civilian population in many parts of Iraq * * * the consequences of which threaten peace and security in the region," and demanded that Iraq cease the repression and allow "immediate access by international humanitarian organizations to all those in need of assistance in all parts of Iraq." Resolution 688 authorized the Secretary–General to pursue humanitarian efforts through U.N. agencies and to send a mission to the region, but did not authorize any use of force to protect the refugees. See S.C.Res. 688 (1991), reprinted in, 30 I.L.M. 858 (1991).

In April, 1992, Britain, France and the United States sent forces into Northern Iraq to create "safe havens" to which the Iraqi Kurdish refugee population could return. The United States stressed the humanitarian nature of the operation and invoked Resolution 688 "to establish several encampments in northern Iraq, where relief supplies * * * w[ould] be made available in large quantities and distributed in an orderly way." See Adelman, Humanitarian Intervention: The Case of the Kurds, 4 Int'l J. Refugee L. 4, 4–5 n. 1 (1992). The United States also declared that "[a]dequate security w[ould] be provided at those sites by U.S., British and French ground forces, consistent with United Nations Resolution 688." Id. Given that a cease fire had been put in place, does Resolution 688 support the unilateral establishment of "safe havens" inside Iraq by the United States, France and Britain? Does Resolution 678 provide support for such havens?, see p. 971 supra.

## *SECRETARY-GENERAL OF THE UNITED NATIONS, REPORT ON THE WORK OF THE ORGANIZATION*

U.N. Doc. A/46/1 at 10–11 (Sept. 1991).

I believe that the protection of human rights has now become one of the keystones in the arch of peace. I am also convinced that it now involves more a concerted exertion of international influence and pressure through timely appeal, admonition, remonstrance or condemnation and, in the last resort, an appropriate United Nations presence, than what was regarded as permissible under traditional international law.

It is now increasingly felt that the principle of non-interference with the essential domestic jurisdiction of States cannot be regarded as a protective barrier behind which human rights could be massively or systematically violated with impunity. The fact that, in diverse situations, the United Nations has not been able to prevent atrocities cannot be cited as an argument, legal or moral, against the necessary corrective action, especially where peace is also threatened. Omissions or failures due to a variety of contingent circumstances do not constitute a precedent. The case for not impinging on the sovereignty, territorial integrity and political independence of States is by itself indubitably strong. But it would only be weakened if it were to carry the implication that sovereignty, even in this day and age, includes the right of mass slaughter or of launching systematic campaigns of decimation or forced exodus of civilian populations in the name of controlling civil strife or insurrection. With the heightened international interest in universalizing a regime of human rights, there is a marked and most welcome shift in public attitudes. To try to resist it would be politically as unwise as it is morally indefensible. It should be perceived as not so much a new departure as a more focused awareness of one of the requirements of peace. * * *

* * *

* * * We need not impale ourselves on the horns of a dilemma between respect for sovereignty and the protection of human rights. The last thing the United Nations needs is a new ideological controversy. What is involved is not the right of intervention but the collective obligation of States to bring relief and redress in human rights emergencies.

It seems to be beyond question that violations of human rights imperil peace, while disregard of the sovereignty of States would spell chaos. The maximum caution needs to be exercised lest the defence of human rights becomes a platform for encroaching on the essential domestic jurisdiction of States and eroding their sovereignty. Nothing would be a surer prescription for anarchy than an abuse of this principle.

Some caveats are, therefore, most necessary at this point. First, like all other basic principles, the principle of protection of human rights cannot be invoked in a particular situation and disregarded in a similar one. To apply it selectively is to debase it. Governments can, and do, expose themselves to charges of deliberate bias; the United Nations cannot. Second, any international action for protecting human rights must be based on a decision taken in accordance with the Charter of the United Nations. It must not be a unilateral act. Third, and relatedly, the consideration of proportionality is of the utmost importance in this respect. Should the scale or manner of international action be out of proportion to the wrong that is reported to have been committed, it is bound to evoke a vehement reaction, which, in the long run, would jeopardize the very rights that were sought to be defended.

### *Note*

As of 1993, the United Nations had not authorized coercive force against the expressed will of the government of a state in order to terminate or prevent atrocities against a civilian population. Does the Secretary-General's report advocate such actions? Is this what the Security Council authorized in Iraq after the Gulf War?

## SOMALIA 1992–93

In 1992, the Security Council authorized United Nations Operations in Somalia (UNOSOM) to alleviate hunger and starvation there. S.C.Res. 733 (1992). On November 24 and November 30, 1992, the Secretary-General transmitted letters to the President of the Security Council reporting on the continuing deterioration of humanitarian conditions in Somalia, and on the civil strife between various factions and clans preventing UNOSOM from implementing the earlier Security Council mandate to provide relief assistance. See U.N.Docs. S/24859 and S/24868; S.C.Res. 733, 746, 751, 767 and 775 (1992). The Secretary-General urged military action pursuant to Article 39 of the Charter, to ensure that UNOSOM succeeded in its relief mission; in his opinion "no government exist[ed] in Somalia that could request and allow such use of force." U.N.Doc. S/24868, at 3. He emphasized that the purpose of the force would be to bring the violence against the international relief effort to an end and that in order to achieve this goal it would be necessary to disarm the various warring factions, irregular forces and gangs. On December 3, 1992 the Security Council adopted a resolution authorizing the use of "military force" to establish "a secure environment for humanitarian relief operations in Somalia."

*Security Council Resolution 794*
December 3, 1992

*The Security Council* * * *

*Recognizing* the unique character of the present situation in Somalia and *mindful* of its deteriorating, complex and extraordinary nature, requiring an immediate and exceptional response;

*Determining* that the magnitude of the human tragedy caused by the conflict in Somalia, further exacerbated by the obstacles being created to the distribution of humanitarian assistance, constitutes a threat to international peace and security * * *

* * *

*Expressing grave alarm* at the continuing reports of widespread violations of international humanitarian law occurring in Somalia * * *

* * *

*Determined* * * * to restore peace, stability and law and order with a view to facilitating the process of a political settlement under the auspices of the United Nations, aimed at national reconciliation in Somalia * * *

* * *

2. *Demands* that all parties, movements and factions in Somalia take all measures necessary to facilitate the efforts of the United Nations * * * and humanitarian organizations to provide humanitarian assistance to the affected population in Somalia;

* * *

5. *Strongly condemns* all violations of international humanitarian law occurring in Somalia * * * and *affirms* that those who commit or order the commission of such acts will be held individually responsible in respect of such acts;

* * *

7. *Endorses* the recommendation by the Secretary–General * * * that action under Chapter VII of the Charter * * * should be taken in order to establish a secure environment for humanitarian relief operations in Somalia as soon as possible;

8. *Welcomes* the offer by a Member State * * * concerning the establishment of an operation to create such a secure environment;

9. *Welcomes also* offers by other Member States to participate in that operation;

10. *Acting* under Chapter VII of the Charter of the United Nations, *authorizes* the Secretary–General and Member States cooperating to implement the offer referred to in paragraph 8 above to use all necessary means to establish as soon as possible a secure environment for humanitarian relief operations in Somalia;

11. *Calls* on all Member States which are in a position to do so to provide military forces and to make additional contributions, in cash or in kind, in accordance with paragraph 10 . . .;

12. *Authorizes* the Secretary–General and the Member States concerned to make the necessary arrangements for the unified command and control of the forces involved, which will reflect the offer referred to in paragraph 8 above;

13. *Requests* the Secretary–General and the Member States acting under paragraph 10 above to establish appropriate mechanisms for coordination between the United Nations and their military forces;

### *Notes*

1. The "Member State" to which the cryptic paragraph 8 of Resolution 794 refers is the United States.

2. There was little initial Somali resistance to the military intervention authorized by the Security Council for the protection of humanitarian aid. Would the authorization of force be within the authority of the Security Council under Chapter VII if taken in the face of active objection by a government in control of its territory? Would it be consistent with Article 2(7)? Did it matter

that Somalia was perceived to be in a state of anarchy without an effective government? Was there a threat to the peace or a breach of the peace in Somalia within the meaning of Article 39 of the Charter? Is a determination of threat to international peace and security a necessary prerequisite to Security Council action on humanitarian grounds? Is there any other legal basis for such action?

Does the United Nation action in Iraq and Somalia reflect a greater willingness on the part of the Security Council to involve itself in internal conflicts? Do these actions evince a changing conception of state sovereignty and "domestic jurisdiction?"

3. Following the Security Council resolution to authorize military intervention for humanitarian purposes in Somalia, there have been suggestions for interventions in Sudan, Togo and Liberia to put an end to civil strife and disorder. Does the Security Council have the power to declare any situation a threat to international peace and security and to recommend or decide on measures to be taken? Does the Security Council have the power to authorize the use of force in the absence of a threat to international peace and security? Can it intervene where it appears that a state's civil and governmental structures have failed and the state is incapable of sustaining itself? Might the Trusteeship provisions of the Charter provide any basis for actions? See p. 296 infra. Could the Security Council establish a U.N. "protectorate" or a "suzerainty," See Brierly, The Law of Nations 133–37, 181–89 (6th ed. 1963). See generally, Helman & Ratner, Saving Failed States, 89 For. Pol'y 3 (Winter 1992–93).

4. The military relief action taken in Somalia was sanctioned by the Security Council, but some have suggested that the conditions prompting U.N. intervention would justify unilateral intervention as well—a so-called "Bush Doctrine." Does this suggestion have any merit as a matter of law? See the discussion of unilateral humanitarian intervention, p. 930 supra.

5. The authority of the Security Council to authorize military action for humanitarian purposes remains the subject of debate. See, e.g., Scheffer, Toward a Modern Doctrine of Humanitarian Intervention, 23 U. Toledo L.Rev. 253 (1992); Nanda, Tragedies in Northern Iraq, Liberia, Yugoslavia, and Haiti—Revising the Validity of Humanitarian Intervention Under International Law—Pt. 1, 20 Den.J.Int'l L. & Pol'y 305 (1992); Delbruck, A Fresh Look at Humanitarian Intervention Under the Authority of the United Nations, 67 Ind.L.J. 887 (1992); Chopra & Weiss, Sovereignty Is No Longer Sacrosanct: Codifying Humanitarian Intervention, 6 Ethics & Int'l Aff. 95 (1992); Myers, A New Remedy for Northern Ireland: The Case for United Nations Peacekeeping Intervention in an Internal Conflict, 11 N.Y.Sch.J.Int'l & Comp.L. 1 (1990); Gehrke, The Mozambique Crisis: A Case for United Nations Military Intervention, 24 Cornell Int'l L.J. 135 (1991). See also Weissbrodt, The Role of International Organizations in the Implementation of Human Rights and Humanitarian Law in Situations of Armed Conflict, 21 Vand.J.Transnat'l L. 313 (1988).

### *4. U.N. Sanctions Not Involving Military Force*

Article 41 of the Charter authorizes the Security Council to impose embargoes and other sanctions "not involving the use of armed force." Presumably the Council may impose such sanctions "to give effect to its decisions" for the purpose of maintaining or restoring international peace and security.

The Security Council has used economic sanctions and embargoes as a prelude to military action, as in Iraq before the Gulf War. The sanctions were reported to have a profound effect on Iraq's economy but did not produce an Iraqi withdrawal from Kuwait and the Security Council therefor authorized the use of military force. See pp. 970–81 supra. The sanctions remained in place throughout the war and continued under the terms of the cease-fire contained in Resolution 687 (1991). Pursuant to Article 50 of the Charter the Council established a committee to oversee the implementation of the sanctions and to examine requests for assistance from member states adversely affected by them. For legal issues raised by the sanctions see Schachter, United Nations Law in the Gulf Conflict, 85 A.J.I.L. 452 (1991). See also The Kuwait Crisis: Sanctions and Their Economic Consequences (Bethlehem, ed. 1991).

Late in 1991, the Security Council imposed sanctions against Serbia and Montenegro for their refusal to cease hostilities as ordered by the Security Council. Earlier, the Security Council imposed sanctions against Rhodesia (see p. 990 below) and South Africa for circumstances which it determined were threats to international peace and security.

## SOUTH AFRICA

In 1963, "having considered the question of race conflict in South Africa resulting from the policies of apartheid," and "[b]eing convinced that the situation in South Africa is seriously disturbing international peace and security," the Security Council resolved that it "strongly deprecates the policies of South Africa in its perpetuation of racial discrimination as being inconsistent with the principles contained in the Charter of the United Nations and contrary to its obligations as a Member of the United Nations," and "solemnly calls upon all States to cease forthwith the shipment of arms, ammunition of all types, and military vehicles to South Africa." S.C.Res. 181 (1963).

In 1970, reiterating its "condemnation of the evil and abhorrent policies of apartheid and the measures being taken by the Government of South Africa to enforce and extend those policies beyond its borders"; convinced "that the situation resulting from the continued application of the policies of apartheid and the constant build-up of the South African military and police forces * * * constitutes a potential threat to international peace and security; and recognizing that the extensive arms build-up of the military force of South Africa poses a real threat to the security and sovereignty of independent African States opposed to the racial policies of the Government of South Africa," the Security Council called upon all the States to strengthen the arms embargo of 1963 in several respects. S.C.Res. 282 (1970).

The use of the words "seriously disturbing international peace and security" in 1963, and "constitutes a potential threat to international peace and security" in 1970, was designed to meet objections of the U.S. which was not "prepared to agree that the situation in South Africa is one which now calls for the kind of action appropriate in cases of threats to the peace or breaches of the peace under Chapter VII of the United Nations Charter."

U.N. Sec. Council Off. Rec. Plenary Meeting 1056, August 7, 1963. The U.S. voted for the 1963 resolution and abstained in 1970.

In 1977, in response to repeated calls from African states, the Council unanimously adopted Resolution 418 which transformed the recommendation of voluntary sanctions into a mandatory decision. The Council determined that "the acquisition by South Africa of arms and related *matériel* constitutes a threat to the maintenance of international peace and security." It decided that "all states shall cease forthwith any provision to South Africa of arms and related *matériel* of all types."

The General Assembly repeatedly called on the Security Council to declare any military or nuclear collaboration with South Africa a threat to the peace and to impose mandatory economic sanctions, See, e.g., the fifteen resolutions adopted on January 23, 1979. G.A.Res. 33/183 A through O. The Council did not impose mandatory economic sanctions, but in 1985 it urged all member states to suspend all new investments in South Africa. See S.C.Res. 596 (1985).

South African legislation establishing apartheid was repealed in the late 1980s and brought an end to many of the sanctions states had imposed on South Africa. As of early 1993, the mandatory arms embargo remains in place.

## LIBYA

On December 21, 1988, Pan Am flight 103, carrying a large number of U.S. and British citizens, exploded while in flight over Lockerbie, Scotland. On November 14, 1991, after an extended investigation, a U.S. grand jury indicted two Libyans, charging they had caused a bomb to be placed on board the plane. On November 27, 1991, the U.S. and British governments, in a joint statement, demanded that Libya "must surrender for trial all those charged with the crime." See U.N. Doc. S/23308, annex (1991). All three states are parties to the Convention for the Suppression of Unlawful Acts against the Safety of Civil Aviation (the Montreal Convention), Article 7 of which provides:

> The Contracting State in the territory of which the alleged offender is found shall, if it does not extradite him, be obliged, without exception whatsoever and whether or not the offence was committed in its territory, to submit the case to its competent authorities for the purpose of prosecution. * * *

The Montreal Convention, reprinted in 10 I.L.M. 1154 (1971). On January 31, 1992, the Security Council adopted a resolution expressing concern over investigations that had implicated officials of the Libyan government in the bombing, deploring that Libya had failed to cooperate fully in establishing responsibility for the bombing, and urging Libya to comply with the U.S. and British demand to surrender the suspects. S.C.Res. 731 (1992).

On March 3, 1992, Libya instituted proceedings in the International Court of Justice (ICJ) seeking provisional measures to enjoin the U.S. and Britain from taking action calculated to coerce Libya to surrender the accused individuals to any jurisdiction outside Libya. In accordance with

Article 7 of the Montreal Convention, Libya indicated that it would undertake to prosecute the individuals accused of the bombing. Before the ICJ ruled on Libya's request for provisional measures, the Security Council, acting under Article VII of the Charter, resolved that Libya must comply with the requests by the U.S. and Britain to deliver those charged with the bombing for trial and imposed sanctions on Libya in an attempt to compel compliance. S.C.Res. 748 (1992). All member states of the United Nations were required to cut air access with Libya and prohibit exports of aircraft, weapons and technical data related to weapons until the Security Council has decided that Libya has complied with the Resolution.

On April 14, 1992, the ICJ issued Orders denying Libya's request for provisional measures. Case Concerning Questions of Interpretation and Application of 1971 Montreal Conventions Arising from Aerial Incident at Lockerbie, 1992 I.C.J. 3, 114.

Professor Tomuschat has written:

> The two Orders of the Court * * * are based on extremely narrow grounds. The reader has more to guess than to actually glean from the text of the decisions, inasmuch as the juridical rationale is condensed in three short paragraphs * * * which essentially underline the importance of Resolution 784 (1992) for the outcome of the controversy between Libya and the defendant states. Considering that this resolution was adopted under Chapter VII of the Charter, the Court additionally refers to Article 103 of the Charter, according to which Charter commitments take precedence over any other treaty commitments of a member state of the United Nations. In these circumstances, concludes the Court, it would not be appropriate to indicate provisional measures since such a step might impair the legal effects of Resolution 748.

Tomuschat, The Lockerbie Case Before the International Court of Justice, Int'l Comm. of Jurists Review 38, 41 (No. 48, June 1992). See also Franck, The "Powers of Appreciation": Who is the Ultimate Guardian of UN Legality?, 86 A.J.I.L. 519 (1992).

## SERBIA AND MONTENEGRO (THE FORMER YUGOSLAVIA)

The former Socialist Federal Republic of Yugoslavia had been composed of six republics (Slovenia, Croatia, Serbia, Bosnia–Hercegovina, Montenegro and Macedonia) with ethnic populations of Serbs, Croats, Slovenes, Albanians, Macedonians. Negotiations among the republics to achieve a loose federation of fully or semi-sovereign states was carried on in the spring of 1990 following demands by Croatia and Slovenia for a looser federation to dilute existing Serbian political domination. The negotiations failed apparently because of Serbia's demand for a tighter federation to preserve its dominant political status and further attempts to negotiate the political future and territorial integrity of the former Yugoslavia were unsuccessful. On June 25, 1991 Slovenia and Croatia declared their independence. On June 27, 1991, armed forces controlled by Serbia attacked the provisional Slovenian militia, which appealed for international assistance from the European Community (EC), the Conference on Security and Cooperation in

Europe (CSCE), and the United Nations. By July 1991, Serbia had initiated hostilities against Croatia, claiming that minority Serbians in Croatia had the right to secede. Subsequently, a number of states recognized the former Yugoslavian Republics of Slovenia, Croatia and Bosnia–Hercegovina as independent states.

On September 25, 1991, the Security Council finally convened and unanimously adopted Resolution 713 expressing support for the collective efforts of the EC and CSCE to bring about peace. The Council then decided under Chapter VII of the Charter "that all States shall, for the purposes of establishing peace and stability in Yugoslavia, immediately implement a general and complete embargo on all deliveries of weapons and military equipment to Yugoslavia until the Security Council decides otherwise * * *." S.C.Res. 713 (1991). The Security Council did not invoke article 2(4) and there was no suggestion that an international act of aggression had taken place.

As ethnic fighting worsened during 1992–93, spilling over into Bosnia–Hercegovina, U.N. action remained modest and largely ineffective. The fighting continued to worsen in Croatia and Bosnia–Hercegovina, with reports of Serbian atrocities and "ethnic cleansing." On May 30, 1992 the Security Council tightened its embargo with respect to Serbia and Montenegro, by prohibiting the import and export of commodities to or from these states. The Council also ordered that all air links with Serbia and Montenegro be severed. S.C.Res. 757 (1992). The Council later approved the U.N. Protection Force to keep separate Serbs and Croats that had been warring in Croatia. On October 6, 1992, the Security Council banned military flights over Bosnia and Hercegovina. S.C.Res. 781 (1992). On November 16, 1992, in order to combat wide-spread violations of the Security Council's economic sanctions, the Council decided to impose a naval blockade of the Adriatic Sea and Danube River. S.C.Res. 787 (1992). As of early 1993, the Council was still considering enforcement measures for violations of the "no-fly" zone over Bosnia–Hercegovina. See generally, Weller, The International Response to the Dissolution of the Socialist Federal Republic of Yugoslavia, 86 A.J.I.L. 569 (1992).

Do the strictures of Article 2(7) limit the options available to the Security Council for action it may take in the former Yugoslavia? Or were the obstacles to more effective U.N. action largely political?

### *Notes*

1. *Cambodia.* In October 1991, the four warring Cambodian factions signed the Agreements Elaborating the Framework for a Comprehensive Political Settlement of the Cambodian Conflict, reprinted in 31 I.L.M. 174 (1992), and consented to host a U.N. Peacekeeping force to help return the country to normalcy. The peace process, however, showed signs of faltering with the Khmer Rouge's refusal to disarm and to allow voter registration in areas it controlled; and with its threats not to participate in the elections called for by the Accords (The Khmer Rouge also engaged in hostilities against U.N. personnel). In order to combat the Khmer Rouge's growing intransigence, the Security Council on November 30, 1992, called on states to prevent petroleum products from reaching the Khmer Rouge and requested states to respect a moratorium on the export of logs. S.C.Res 792 (1992). The Security Council indicated it

would hold elections with or without the Khmer Rouge and expressed its intent to impose stronger sanctions if necessary. See generally Ratner, The Cambodian Settlement Agreements, 87 A.J.I.L. 1 (1993). The Security Council did not determine that the situation in Cambodia is a threat to international peace and security. Is there authority for the Security Council to impose sanctions without such a determination? Can the existence of a threat to international peace and security go without saying? See p. 994 below on the U.N. Cambodian peacekeeping mission.

2. *Rhodesia.* Another early case of Security Council sanction (in addition to South Africa) involved Rhodesia, predecessor of Zimbabwe.

On November 11, 1965, the government of Ian Smith purported to declare the independence of Rhodesia (called by most states Southern Rhodesia) from the United Kingdom. The British Governor–General was relieved of his authority, and a new constitution perpetuating domination of the country by its European minority was promulgated. The General Assembly on the same day requested the Security Council to consider the Rhodesian situation "as a matter of urgency." G.A.Res. 2024 (1965). Thirty-five states also signed a letter calling for an emergency meeting of the Council. U.N.Doc. S/6902. On November 12 and 20, the Council called upon states not to recognize the Smith regime and to refrain from supplying the latter with war materials or petroleum products. S.C.Res. 216 and 217 (1965).

In December, 1966, the Security Council adopted a resolution declaring the situation a threat to international peace and security. The resolution called upon member states to prohibit the import into their territories of certain specified commodities originating in Southern Rhodesia, and to prohibit the sale or supply of arms, military supplies, aircraft, motor vehicles, and oil and oil products to Rhodesia. S.C.Res. 232 (1966). For a report on the implementation of the resolution by member states, see U.N.Doc. S/7781 and Adds. 1 to 5. The resolution was implemented in the United States by Exec. Order No. 11322, 3 CFR 243 (Comp.1967).

On May 29, 1968, the Security Council adopted a resolution calling for total economic, political and cultural isolation of Southern Rhodesia. S.C.Res. 253 (1968); 7 I.L.M. 897 (1968). The resolution was adopted unanimously.

With the resolution of the dispute leading to the establishment of the State of Zimbabwe, the embargo was terminated by the Security Council. S.C.Res. 460 (1979).

3. In light of the experience of the use of United Nations sanctions not involving military force, consider their effectiveness as an instrument of international order. In what circumstances are they likely to succeed? What can be done to make them more effective? On the effectiveness of sanctions generally see Hufbauer, Schott & Elliot, Economic Sanctions Reconsidered: History and Current Policy (2d ed. 1990); Lapidoth, Some Reflections on the Law and Practice on the Imposition of Sanctions by the Security Council, 30 Archiv des Völkerrechts 114 (1992).

### 5. *U.N. Peacekeeping Activities to Maintain International Peace*

During the Cold War and the frustration of the Security Council, the principal U.N. contribution to international peace and security consisted of various forms of "peacekeeping"—efforts to prevent hostilities from erupting or resuming. The Security Council established some peacekeeping arrangements pursuant to its authority under Chapter VI. The General Assembly exercised authority to recommend peacekeeping arrangements under Article 14. All the organs of the United Nations, including the Secretary–General, have contributed to peacekeeping by various forms of "preventive diplomacy."

In tracing the major peacekeeping activities that the United Nations has undertaken, it is important to direct attention to the changing roles of the United Nations organs involved in the peacekeeping process. In the early instances, the United Nations sought to establish an international military force that could cope with an act of aggression, a threat to the peace, or a breach of the peace. In later cases—in the Sinai and on the Golan Heights following the 1973 Israel–Arab War, in Lebanon in 1978—the UN forces are a deterrent "presence" in effect asked for by the States involved.

## THE ARAB–ISRAELI CONFLICT

After the cessation of fighting between Israel and the Arab states that followed the Israeli declaration of independence on May 14, 1948, friction with Egypt continued. The Egyptians had obstructed Israeli commerce through the Gulf of Aquaba and through the Suez Canal, and Israeli complaints to the Security Council on four occasions between 1950 and 1955 failed to achieve results. President Nasser then announced, on July 26, 1956, the nationalization of the Suez Canal Company. The principal shareholders of the latter were the United Kingdom and various private interests in the United Kingdom and in France. Efforts by the French, British and United States governments in the United Nations failed to persuade Egypt to return the Canal to international status.

On October 29, 1956, Israeli forces invaded Egypt. On October 31, the Security Council approved by a vote of 7–2–2 a resolution introduced by Yugoslavia that placed the question before the General Assembly. As a procedural matter, the resolution was not defeated by the negative votes of France and the United Kingdom. See Article 27(2) of the Charter. The resolution (S.C.Res. 119) noted the grave situation created by the action against Egypt and called for the convocation of an emergency special session of the General Assembly pursuant to the "Uniting for Peace" Resolution.

On November 5, 1956, the General Assembly passed a resolution establishing "a United Nations Command for an emergency international Force to secure and supervise the cessation of hostilities." G.A.Res. 1000. By November 7, the fighting had stopped.

On November 8, Major–General E.L.M. Burns of Canada was appointed Chief of the United Nations Command of the United Nations Emergency Force (UNEF). See U.N.Doc. A/3317. With Egyptian approval the UNEF was established on Egyptian territory. Israel indicated that "on no account" would she "agree to the stationing of a foreign force, no matter how called, in her territory or in any of the areas occupied by her." See U.N.Docs. A/3313 and A/3314; N.Y. Times, November 8, 1956, at 1, col. 2. See generally Friedmann & Collins, The Suez Canal Crisis of 1956, in Scheinman

& Wilkinson, International Law and Political Crisis: An Analytic Casebook 91 (1968).

After some delay and further resolutions of the U.N. General Assembly, on March 8, 1957, the Secretary General confirmed full Israeli withdrawal behind the armistice lines.

Ten years later, on May 18, 1967, the United Arab Republic decided to terminate the presence of the U.N. Emergency Force from the territory of the United Arab Republic and the Gaza Strip. The U.N. Secretary General U Thant accepted the authority of the UAR to take this action and instructed UNEF to withdraw. See Special Report of the Secretary General, May 18, 1967, U.N.Doc. A/6669 (1967). The United States announced that it viewed with dismay the withdrawal of UNEF without action by either the General Assembly or the Security Council. See the letter of Ernest A. Gross challenging the legal right of the UAR to withdraw UNEF unilaterally and the propriety of the Secretary General's compliance. N.Y. Times, May 26, 1967 at 44.

As the UNEF troops withdrew, large UAR units took their place. Tension in the Middle East increased rapidly. Israeli Premier Eshkol warned that any interference with the freedom of Israeli shipping would be taken as an act of aggression.

The efforts of the major powers to avert the outbreak of war were unavailing. On June 5, 1967, Israel, claiming attacks by its Arab neighbors, launched a major invasion of Arab territory. See U.N.Docs. S/PV 1347 at 3, 17–20; 1348 at 73–75 (1967). Within a week the Israeli troops were completely victorious and a large portion of Arab territory had been occupied. The Security Council's demand for an immediate cease-fire was eventually honored by the parties. Resolution 242, among other things, called for the withdrawal of Israeli forces "from territories" occupied by them. For the text of resolution 242 and other resolutions, see 6 I.L.M. 604–08 (1967). The efforts of the Soviet Union to have a resolution adopted requiring the withdrawal of Israeli troops were unsuccessful. See generally Bowie, The Suez Crisis 1956 (1974).

Despite Resolution 242, there was no progress towards a peaceful settlement, and Israel remained in control of the territories seized in the 1967 war. On October 6, 1973, Egyptian, Syrian and Iraqi forces launched a surprise attack on Israel, but after some initial successes they were repelled. Under pressure from the United States and the U.S.S.R., Israel agreed to withdraw its forces from Egyptian soil and disengagement agreements were signed between Israel–Egypt and Israel–Syria. The Security Council established the U.N. Emergency Force (UNEF) to monitor disengagement between Egypt and Israel (S.C.Res. 340 (1973)), and the U.N. Disengagement Observer Force (UNDOF) (S.C.Res. 350 (1974)) for the buffer zone between Israel and Syria.

In the intervening years, the General Assembly adopted resolutions calling on Israel to withdraw from the occupied territories, and recognizing the right of the "Palestinian people" to self-determination; it gave observer status to the Palestine Liberation Organization. See G.A.Res. 3237 (1974).

In 1978–79, with U.S. support and intermediation, Israel and Egypt negotiated a peace treaty under which Israel agreed to withdraw from the Sinai, and Egypt agreed to end the state of war and to establish normal relations with Israel. The treaty was signed on March 26, 1979. See 28 I.L.M. 362 (1979). Other Arab states rejected it and a plan to have the agreement monitored by U.N. forces was abandoned because of Soviet opposition.

Upon U.S. initiative, preliminary negotiations between Israel, Arab states and Palestinian representatives began in 1992 in search for a comprehensive peace. As of 1993, two United Nations peacekeeping forces remain in the Middle East, UNDOF and the United Nations Interim Force in Lebanon (UNIFIL). UNDOF continues to monitor the Golan Heights buffer zone between Israel and Syria. Israel had also occupied southern Lebanon in retaliation for PLO raids launched from bases in that area. In 1978, UNIFIL was established to oversee the withdrawal of Israeli forces and assist the government of Lebanon in ensuring the return of its effective authority in the area. See S.C.Res. 425 and 426. UNIFIL has been unable to fulfill its mandate completely but has managed to reduce the level of violence and the risk of wider conflict between Israeli and Arab forces.

## CYPRUS

After negotiations with Greece, Turkey, and representatives of the Greek and Turkish Cypriot communities, the United Kingdom granted independence to the Republic of Cyprus. Treaty concerning the Establishment of the Republic of Cyprus, August 16, 1960, 382 U.N.T.S. 8.

Differences between the Greek and Turkish Cypriot communities soon manifested themselves during the drafting of constitutional provisions that were to guarantee the rights of the respective groups, and communal fighting broke out in late 1963. Although the conflict was domestic in character, the fact that each side was supported by a guarantor state (as established in the Treaty of Guarantee, 382 U.N.T.S. 8) gave the struggle international overtones. The Security Council considered the Cyprus situation from February 18 to March 4, 1964, and unanimously approved on the latter date a resolution establishing a United Nations Peace–Keeping Force in Cyprus (UNFICYP). S.C.Res. 186. UNFICYP was mobilized and in operation by March 27, 1964.

In August, 1964, fighting broke out and Turkey made several air attacks against Greek Cypriots. Turkey claimed that UNFICYP was unable to stop either the continued arming of the Greek community or its military offensive against the Turkish community. Widespread fighting ceased, but tensions remained high. In September, the Secretary–General reported that UNFICYP was able to maintain the peace, but that both sides were continuing to build their military strength.

In the following years, little progress was made toward the solution of the island's problems. Both sides remained armed and occasional, isolated fighting broke out. See generally Ehrlich, Cyprus 1958–1967 (1974).

In 1974, the delicate balance was shattered when a coup by Greek officers overthrew President Makarios, apparently in a move toward uniting Cyprus with Greece. Turkish troops, however, invaded Cyprus and overthrew the rebel regime. The U.N. ordered a cease-fire, but by the time real cease-fire took hold Turkish troops controlled forty per cent of the island. President Makarios resumed control of the Government until he died, but the island remained effectively divided and efforts to resolve the dispute and reestablish an agreed unified government did not succeed. The presence of UNFICYP on Cyprus has continued.

In 1992, Canada announced that it was withdrawing its military units from the peacekeeping forces in Cyprus and in early 1993, negotiations on a final settlement sponsored by the Secretary–General had not succeeded. Has the extended presence of the U.N. peacekeeping forces hampered the settlement process? Would the absence of peacekeepers force a solution? See generally Rossides, Cyprus and the Rule of Law, 17 Syracuse J.Int'l L. & Com. 23 (1991).

## CAMBODIA

For many years, Cambodia has suffered from civil war, interventions, genocide and other gross violations of human rights, and massive dislocations of its population. In March 1970, Cambodia's hereditary king, Norodom Sihanouk, was overthrown by General Lon Nol, who instituted authoritarian rule under the name of the Khmer Republic. In 1975, the Khmer Rouge gained control of Cambodia, renaming it Democratic Kampuchea, and attempted a total restructuring of Cambodian society, committing mass state-sponsored killing and other violations of human rights. In 1979, Vietnam invaded Cambodia and installed a régime known as the People's Republic of Kampuchea, which controlled most of Cambodia during the 1980's. After the Vietnamese invasion, four factions conducted a guerilla war in an attempt to gain control of Cambodia.

In 1991, the four Cambodian warring factions endorsed a United Nations plan designed to help rebuild Cambodia and signed a number of agreements aimed at a comprehensive settlement. See Paris Conference on Cambodian Agreements Elaborating the Framework for a Comprehensive Political Settlement of the Cambodian Conflict, U.N.Doc. A/46/608 and S/233177, reprinted in 31 I.L.M. 174 (1992). Under the 1991 Paris Agreements the four warring factions agreed to create a Supreme National Council (SNC), composed of representatives of the factions, to act as the "unique * * * source of authority" and embody Cambodian sovereignty. The SNC delegated to the United Nations all authority necessary to ensure the implementation of the comprehensive settlement. In 1992, the United Nations set up the U.N. Transitional Authority (UNTAC) to monitor the disarmament of the four Cambodian warring factions and supervise free elections. UNTAC is comprised of over 15,000 personnel and has been given authority within Cambodia, including aspects of civil administration. In order to create a neutral environment for elections, the warring factions "delegated" to UNTAC control of five Ministries and supervision of others, access to all governmental documents, and power to issue binding directives and replace personnel. See Ratner, The Cambodian Settlement Agreements, 87 A.J.I.L. 1 (1993). When the Khemer Rouge appeared to be threatening the implementation of the Paris peace accords, the Security Council imposed sanctions. See p. 989 above.

Is the U.N. peacekeeping mission in Cambodia, including the extensive authority of UNTAC, within the authority of the Security Council? Is the Cambodian situation similar to that of Somalia in that there has been a break-down of effective government? See p. 983 supra. Do United Nations actions in Cambodia and Somalia require reexamination of the broad view of state sovereignty discussed in Chapter 1?

### *Notes*

1. As of early 1993, the United Nations was continuing the following peacekeeping operations:

**United Nations Peacekeepers On Current Missions**

| | | PERSONNEL |
|---|---|---|
| **Angola** | Angola Verification Mission | 479 |
| **Arab–Israeli conflict** | Truce Supervision Organization | 272 |
| **Balkans** | Protection Force | 22,500 |
| **Cambodia** | Transitional Authority in Cambodia | 17,531 |
| **Cyprus** | Peacekeeping Force in Cyprus | 2,197 |
| **El Salvador** | Observer Mission in El Salvador | 595 |
| **Golan Heights** | Disengagement Observer Force | 1,350 |
| **India and Pakistan** | Military Observer Group | 38 |
| **Iraq and Kuwait** | Iraq–Kuwait Observation Mission | 409 |
| **Lebanon** | Interim Force in Lebanon | 5,805 |
| **Somalia** | Operation in Somalia | 550 |
| **Western Sahara** | Mission for the Referendum in the Western Sahara | 365 |

*Source: United Nations Secretary General*

2. On December 11, 1992, the Security Council voted unanimously to send some 700 U.N. personnel to the former Yugoslavian republic of Macedonia. The mission's mandate is to seek to prevent the hostilities in other parts of the former Yugoslavia from spreading into Macedonia. This is apparently the first time the United Nations peacekeepers have been deployed in support of "preventive diplomacy" as called for by the Secretary–General in his Agenda for Peace. See p. 1001 supra.

3. The peacekeeping activities of the United Nations have depended on the consent of states and parties involved. Do any of the organs of the U.N. have authority to establish peacekeeping missions in the absence of such consent? Should the United Nations seek to extend its peacekeeping role to conflicts where it is not invited to participate?

4. U.N. peacekeeping efforts sometimes replace or give way to efforts by individual or groups of states. In 1982 the Lebanese governments asked France, Britain and the United States to send troops to bolster U.N. forces attempting to police a fragile ceasefire in Lebanon's civil war. Frequent attacks by the various militias culminated in a bomb attack on the U.S. troop barracks, killing 250 marines. Gradually all Western troops were withdrawn and only the U.N. force

remains. A similar attempt at non-U.N. peacekeeping in Chad's Civil War ended in failure for different reasons. The Organization of African Unity asked several African states to send troops to police a cease-fire. However, the states sending troops could not afford the cost of sustaining the operation and eventually withdrew their contingents.

On the other hand, United States troops continue to monitor the peace between Egypt and Israel in Sinai. These troops are there at the request of the two governments.

5. *The Congo.* During the years 1960–64, the United Nations was involved in peacekeeping operations in the Congo. In early 1960, the Congo obtained its independence. Within a week of independence, there had been mutinies in the Congolese army and attacks on Belgians and other Europeans. On July 8, Belgium dispatched troops to the Congo for the announced purpose of protecting its nationals. On July 11, the mineral-rich province of Katanga announced its secession.

On July 12, President Kasavubu and Prime Minister Lumumba of the Republic of the Congo requested United Nations assistance in a telegram to the Secretary–General. See U.N.Doc. S/4382.

On July 14, the Security Council approved a resolution authorizing the Secretary–General "to provide the Government of the Republic of the Congo with such military assistance as may be necessary until, through the efforts of the Congolese Government with the technical assistance of the United Nations, the national security forces may be able, in the opinion of the Government, to fully meet their tasks." S.C.Res. 143.

The Security Council became embroiled in a debate on the right of the United Nations forces to enter Katanga. See the Secretary–General's memorandum of August 12, U.N.Doc. S/4417/Add.6. During September, the Soviet Union vetoed several resolutions that would have reaffirmed the power of the United Nations forces to maintain law and order. An impasse developed and continued until the adoption on September 17 of a United States-sponsored resolution (S.C.Res. 157) that called for an emergency meeting of the General Assembly as provided for in the "Uniting for Peace" Resolution. On September 20, the General Assembly passed a resolution confirming the functions of the United Nations forces and requesting the Secretary–General to continue his support of the Central Government of the Congo. G.A.Res. 1474.

Despite the presence of United Nations forces, civil strife in the Congo continued. On February 21, 1961, the Security Council reaffirmed its previous resolutions and urged that the United Nations act to prevent the occurrence of a civil war in the Congo. It called for the withdrawal of all foreign military personnel and called upon all states to take measures to prevent persons from joining the civil strife. The Council also urged the restoration of order through the convening of the Parliament and the reorganization of Congolese armed units. See S.C.Res. 161.

Further resolutions of the Security Council were necessary before foreign mercenaries were removed, the secession of Katanga ended, and law and order restored.

On the role of law in the crisis in the Congo, see Abi–Saab, The United Nations Operation in the Congo 1960–64 (1978). See Secretary–General of the United Nations report on the withdrawal of the United Nations Force in the

Congo and on other aspects of the United Nations operation, June 29, 1964, U.N.Doc. S/5784.

Under what Articles of the Charter could the Activities of the ONUC force have been justified? See Miller (pseudonym for Schachter), Legal Aspects of the United Nations Action in the Congo, 55 A.J.I.L. 1 (1961). Compare the withdrawal of the United Nations forces from the Congo with the withdrawal of forces from Egypt in 1967. Was the withdrawal of the forces in either case required by international law?

6. Other early U.N. peacekeeping missions include: The Security Force in West Irian (UNSF) which operated during 1962–63; and the Transition Assistance Group (UNTAG) which was deployed in Namibia in 1989–90. There have also been numerous United Nations Observer Missions, generally set up to oversee the implementation of cease-fire agreements. More recently, there have been missions for other purposes: overseeing elections in Namibia (UNTAG, 1989–90); supervising the implementation of the Comprehensive Political Settlement Agreements in Cambodia (UNAMIC, 1992–); supervising the referendum in Western Sahara (MINURSO, 1991–); monitoring compliance with human rights agreements in El Salvador (ONUSAL, 1991–).

7. On peacekeeping generally, see Durch & Blechman, Keeping the Peace: The United Nations in the Emerging World Order (1992); Fermann, Bibliography on International Peacekeeping (1992); White, The United Nations and the Maintenance of International Peace and Security (1990); The Blue Helmets: A Review of United Nations Peace-keeping (2d ed. 1990); Rikhye, United Nations and Peacekeeping: Results, Limits and Prospects (1988); James, The Politics of Peacekeeping (1984); Higgins, United Nations Peacekeeping 1946–79: Documents and Commentary, 4 vols. (1981); United Nations Peace–Keeping (Cassese, ed. 1978); Rikhye, Harbottle & Egge, The Thin Blue Line: International Peacekeeping and Its Future (1974); Bowett, United Nations Forces (1964); Heathcote, Peacekeeping by United Nations Forces (1963); Goodrich & Simons, The United Nations and the Maintenance of International Peace and Security (1955).

### 6. *Enforcement Action by the General Assembly*

## CERTAIN EXPENSES OF THE UNITED NATIONS

International Court of Justice, Advisory Opinion, 1962.
1962 I.C.J. 151.

* * *

Article 24 of the Charter provides:

> "In order to ensure prompt and effective action by the United Nations, its Members confer on the Security Council primary responsibility for the maintenance of international peace and security * * * "

The responsibility conferred is "primary", not exclusive. This primary responsibility is conferred upon the Security Council, as stated in Article 24, "in order to ensure prompt and effective action." To this end, it is the Security Council which is given a power to impose an explicit obligation of compliance if for example it issues an order or command to an aggressor under Chapter VII. It is only the Security Council which can require enforcement by coercive action against an aggressor.

The Charter makes it abundantly clear, however, that the General Assembly is also to be concerned with international peace and security.

Article 14 authorizes the General Assembly to "recommend measures for the peaceful adjustment of any situation, regardless of origin, which it deems likely to impair the general welfare or friendly relations among nations, including situations resulting from a violation of the provisions of the present Charter setting forth the purposes and principles of the United Nations." The word "measures" implies some kind of action, and the only limitation which Article 14 imposes on the General Assembly is the restriction found in Article 12, namely, that the Assembly should not recommend measures while the Security Council is dealing with the same matter unless the Council requests it to do so. Thus while it is the Security Council which, exclusively, may order coercive action, the functions and powers conferred by the Charter on the General Assembly are not confined to discussion, consideration, the initiation of studies and the making of recommendations; they are not merely hortatory. Article 18 deals with *"decisions"* of the General Assembly "on important questions". These "decisions" do indeed include certain recommendations, but others have dispositive force and effect. Among these latter decisions, Article 18 includes suspension of rights and privileges of membership, expulsion of Members, "and budgetary questions". In connection with the suspension of rights and privileges of membership and expulsion from membership under Articles 5 and 6, it is the Security Council which has only the power to recommend and it is the General Assembly which decides and whose decision determines status; but there is a close collaboration between the two organs. Moreover, these powers of decision of the General Assembly under Articles 5 and 6 are specifically related to preventive or enforcement measures.

By Article 17, paragraph 1, the General Assembly is given the power not only to "consider" the budget of the Organization, but also to "approve" it. The decision to "approve" the budget has a close connection with paragraph 2 of Article 17, since thereunder the General Assembly is also given the power to apportion the expenses among the Members and the exercise of the power of apportionment creates the obligation, specifically stated in Article 17, paragraph 2, of each Member to bear that part of the expenses which is apportioned to it by the General Assembly. When those expenses include expenditures for the maintenance of peace and security, which are not otherwise provided for, it is the General Assembly which has the authority to apportion the latter amounts among the Members. The provisions of the Charter which distribute functions and powers to the Security Council and to the General Assembly give no support to the view that such distribution excludes from the powers of the General Assembly the power to provide for the financing of measures designed to maintain peace and security.

The argument supporting a limitation on the budgetary authority of the General Assembly with respect to the maintenance of international peace and security relies especially on the reference to "action" in the last sentence of Article 11, paragraph 2. This paragraph reads as follows:

> "The General Assembly may discuss any questions relating to the maintenance of international peace and security brought before it by any Member of the United Nations, or by the Security Council, or by a State which is not a Member of the United Nations in accordance with Article 35, paragraph 2, and, except as provided in Article 12, may make recommendations with regard to any such question to the State or

States concerned or to the Security Council, or to both. Any such question on which action is necessary shall be referred to the Security Council by the General Assembly either before or after discussion."

The Court considers that the kind of action referred to in Article 11, paragraph 2, is coercive or enforcement action. This paragraph which applies not merely to general questions relating to peace and security, but also to specific cases brought before the General Assembly by a State under Article 35, in its first sentence empowers the General Assembly, by means of recommendations to States or to the Security Council, or to both, to organize peace-keeping operations at the request, or with the consent, of the States concerned. This power of the General Assembly is a special power which in no way derogates from its general powers under Article 10 or Article 14, except as limited by the last sentence of Article 11, paragraph 2. This last sentence says that when "action" is necessary the General Assembly shall refer the question to the Security Council. The word "action" must mean such action as is solely within the province of the Security Council. It cannot refer to recommendations which the Security Council might make, as for instance under Article 38, because the General Assembly under Article 11 has a comparable power. The "action" which is solely within the province of the Security Council is that which is indicated by the title of Chapter VII of the Charter, namely "Action with respect to threats to the peace, breaches of the peace, and acts of aggression". If the word "action" in Article 11, paragraph 2, were interpreted to mean that the General Assembly could make recommendations only of a general character affecting peace and security in the abstract, and not in relation to specific cases, the paragraph would not have provided that the General Assembly may make recommendations on questions brought before it by States or by the Security Council. Accordingly, the last sentence of Article 11, paragraph 2, has no application where the necessary action is not enforcement action.

The practice of the Organization throughout its history bears out the foregoing elucidation of the term "action" in the last sentence of Article 11, paragraph 2. Whether the General Assembly proceeds under Article 11 or under Article 14, the implementation of its recommendations for setting up commissions or other bodies involves organizational activity—action—in connection with the maintenance of international peace and security. Such implementation is a normal feature of the functioning of the United Nations. Such committees, commissions or other bodies or individuals, constitute, in some cases, subsidiary organs established under the authority of Article 22 of the Charter. The functions of the General Assembly for which it may establish such subsidiary organs include, for example, investigation, observation and supervision, but the way in which such subsidiary organs are utilized depends on the consent of the State or States concerned.

## 7. *The Role of the Secretary-General*

### *SECRETARY-GENERAL OF THE UNITED NATIONS, REPORT ON THE WORK OF THE ORGANIZATION*

U.N.Doc. A/37/1 at 3 (Sept. 1982).

In order to avoid the Security Council becoming involved too late in critical situations, it may well be that the Secretary-General should play a more forthright role in bringing potentially dangerous situations to the attention of the Council within the general framework of Article 99 of the Charter. My predecessors have done this on a number of occasions, but I wonder if the time has not come for a more systematic approach. Most potential conflict areas are well known. The Secretary-General has traditionally, if informally, tried to keep watch for problems likely to result in conflict and to do what he can to pre-empt them by quiet diplomacy. The Secretary-General's diplomatic means are, however, in themselves quite limited. In order to carry out effectively the preventive role foreseen for the Secretary-General under Article 99, I intend to develop a wider and more systematic capacity for fact-finding in potential conflict areas. Such efforts would naturally be undertaken in close co-ordination with the Council. Moreover, the Council itself could devise more swift and responsive procedures for sending good offices missions, military or civilian observers or a United Nations presence to areas of potential conflict. Such measures could inhibit the deterioration of conflict situations and might also be of real assistance to the parties in resolving incipient disputes by peaceful means.

### *Notes*

1. Both the U.S.S.R. and the United States reacted negatively to Secretary-General Pérez de Cuéllar's 1982 desire to develop a "wider and more sympathetic capacity" for fact finding in areas of potential conflict. Nevertheless, Pérez de Cuéllar initiated steps to achieve that goal. He created the Office of Research and Collection of Information (ORCI) and sought reform in the political offices of the Seretariat to make it more effective in conflict prevention. 1992 saw the sixth Secretary-General, Boutros-Ghali, attempting to continue these reforms.

2. The Office of the Secretary-General has the potential to be a strong force in helping to settle or prevent international conflict, but different Secretaries-General have realized that potential differently. The first Secretary-General, Trygve Lie, established the role of the Office under Article 99 of the Charter. He interpreted his powers broadly, for example, undertaking to investigate the Greek frontier dispute in 1946 and to monitor tensions in Korea in 1950. The second Secretary-General, Dag Hammarskjöld, appointed in 1953, was widely regarded as an innovator in the Office. Hammarskjöld played an important role in helping to prevent conflict between the U.S. and the People's Republic of China in the aftermath of the Korean War. He launched the practice of maintaining a "U.N. presence" in regions of potential conflict, and developed the Secretary-General's role in "preventive diplomacy," without instruction from either the Security Council or the General Assembly. Hammarskjöld brought the Congo question before the Security Council in 1960 and was instrumental in resolving the conflict. But some states criticized his broad conception of the Secretary-General's "executive powers." U Thant's humanitarian activities in India and Pakistan in 1971 added another dimension to preventive diplomacy, but he and his successor, Kurt Waldheim, apparently took a narrower view of their role in the maintenance of international peace and security than their predecessors. Javier Pérez de Cuéllar played an important,

though unsuccessful role in attempts to resolve the Falkland/Malvinas war, and he was instrumental in ending the Iran–Iraq war, as well as in negotiating the Afghanistan settlement. He was also prominent in the Central American peace process, brokering the peace in El Salvador on the eve of his retirement. Since assuming office in 1992, Boutros Boutros–Ghali has been "activist" and pursuing new directions. See, e.g., the Agenda for Peace below.

On the Office of the Secretary–General see, Franck, Nation Against Nation, Chapters 7 and 8 (1985); Bourloyannis, Fact-finding by the Secretary General of the United Nations, 22 N.Y.U.J.Int'l L. & Pol. 641 (1990); Ramcharan, The Office of the Secretary General of the United Nations, 13 Dalhousie L.J. 742 (1990); Boudreau, Sheathing the Sword: The U.N. Secretary General and the Prevention of International Conflict (1991); Ramcharan, The International Law and Practice of Early Warning and Preventive Diplomacy: The Emerging Global Watch (1991); Gordenker, The U.N. Secretary General and the Maintenance of Peace (1967). See also Ramcharan, The Good Offices of the United Nations Secretary General in the Field of Human Rights, 76 A.J.I.L. 130 (1982).

### 8. *The Future Role of the United Nations*

With the end of the Cold War there has been increased hope that the United Nations will finally realize the aspirations of its founders and meet world needs at the start of the 21st Century. United Nations actions in Somalia, in Cambodia, in the former Yugoslavia, and possible action elsewhere may point to new tasks and a broader conception of collective security within the United Nations.

## THE AGENDA FOR PEACE

In June 1992, the Secretary–General issued a report entitled "An Agenda for Peace," which recommended ways of strengthening the United Nations powers "for preventive diplomacy, for peacemaking and for peace-keeping." The Secretary–General wrote:

> 14. Since the creation of the United Nations in 1945, over 100 major conflicts around the world have left some 20 million dead. The United Nations was rendered powerless to deal with many of these crises because of the vetoes—279 of them—cast in the Security Council, which were a vivid expression of the divisions of that period.
>
> 15. With the end of the cold war there have been no such vetoes since 31 May 1990, and demands on the United Nations have surged. Its security arm, once disabled by circumstances it was not created or equipped to control, has emerged as a central instrument for the prevention and resolution of conflicts and for the preservation of peace. Our aims must be:
>
> - To seek to identify at the earliest possible stage situations that could produce conflict, and to try through diplomacy to remove the sources of danger before violence results;
> - Where conflict erupts, to engage in peacemaking aimed at resolving the issues that have led to conflict;
> - Through peace-keeping, to work to preserve peace, however fragile, where fighting has been halted and to assist in implementing agreements achieved by the peacemakers;

- To stand ready to assist in peace-building in its differing contexts: rebuilding the institutions and infrastructures of nations torn by civil war and strife; and building bonds of peaceful mutual benefit among nations formerly at war;
- And in the largest sense, to address the deepest causes of conflict: economic despair, social injustice and political oppression. It is possible to discern an increasingly common moral perception that spans the world's nations and peoples, and which is finding expression in international laws, many owing their genesis to the work of this Organization.

U.N.Doc. A/47/227 and S/2411 (17 June 1992), reprinted in, 31 I.L.M. 953 (1992). See also Report of the Special Committee on the Charter of the United Nations and on the Strengthening of the Role of the Organization, G.A.O.R., 46th Sess., Supp. 33 (1991); Chapter 10, p. 784.

### *Notes*

1. In the Agenda for Peace, the Secretary–General outlines a program of "preventive diplomacy," "peacemaking," and peacekeeping. Techniques for "preventive diplomacy" would include measures to build confidence, fact-finding, the development of early warning systems, preventive deployment of U.N. forces, and the establishment of demilitarized zones. "Peacemaking" would draw on the Security Council's powers under the Charter, but may also entail pressure exerted by the General Assembly, mediation, negotiation, resort to the International Court of Justice, the development of "peace-enforcement units," as envisioned by Article 40 of the Charter, under the command of the Secretary–General, and post-conflict peace building. "Peacekeeping" would continue in the established pattern. See Weiss, New Challenges for U.N. Military Operations: Implementing the Agenda for Peace, 16 Wash.Q. 51 (1993).

2. Numerous proposals have been made for strengthening the role of the Security Council. Presently, the Council meets only at the request of a member of the United Nations; it has been proposed that it meet at regular intervals as well. Another suggestion would have the Council establish committees to oversee the implementation of Council resolutions and to monitor trouble spots. See Nicol, The United Nations Security Council: Towards Greater Effectiveness 125–29 (1982). Others have suggested establishing an independent investigation process and requiring the Council to discuss every conflict or potential conflict. See White, The United Nations and the Maintenance of International Peace and Security 87–89 (1990). Writing before the end of the Cold War, Sohn suggested "establishing regional monitoring groups within the framework of the Security Council * * *. Each regional monitoring group would watch events in a particular region and, in cooperation with the Secretary–General, collect information on any situation likely to endanger peace." Sohn, The Security Council's Role in the Settlement of International Disputes, 78 A.J.I.L. 402, 404 (1984).

3. The Agenda for Peace recommends Security Council negotiations, supported by the Council's Military Staff Committee, to implement the special agreements provided for in Article 43 of the Charter, under which Member States make available to the Security Council forces, assistance and facilities for purposes determined by the Security Council. Henkin has commented:

> 9. Article 43 provides that all Members, "in order to contribute to the maintenance of international peace and security, *undertake* to make avail-

able to the Security Council, on its call and in accordance with a special agreement or agreements, armed forces, assistance, and facilities, including rights of passage, necessary for the purpose of maintaining international peace and security."

Article 43 is mandatory. It creates a legal obligation for Member states to make available to the Security Council forces, assistance and facilities, and to do so in accordance with a special agreement or agreements. It creates a legal obligation for states to negotiate such agreements on the initiative of the Security Council "as soon as possible."

10. Because of the Cold War, the Security Council was unable to take the initiative, and Article 43 agreements between the Security Council and Member states have not been negotiated. But, in my view, the failure to do so during the past 47 years has not vitiated the obligation to do so. The Council may take that initiative at any time; in my view, the Security Council is required to take that initiative. If the Security Council takes the initiative, if it calls on Member states to negotiate such agreements with the Council, Member states are legally obligated to negotiate such agreements in good faith, to bring such agreements into effect, to proceed to carry them out.

After such agreements are concluded, the forces designated by such agreements are available for the Security Council, "on its call." In particular, Members *shall* (are legally obligated to) hold national air-force contingents "immediately available," "for combined international enforcement action." (Article 45).

11. The Charter sets forth the authority and the responsibility of the Security Council and the obligations of U.N. Members pursuant to Council decisions. But the Council consists of its Members and can act only through its Members. It would seem to be the duty (if not the legal obligation) of Council members, not least the permanent Members, to see to it that the Council fulfills its role and its responsibilities. It is the responsibility of the Council members to see to it that the Council makes the determinations, and the recommendations or decisions, contemplated by Articles 39 to 42. It is the responsibility of Council members to see to it that the Council takes the initiative to negotiate and conclude Article 43 agreements.

Thus, as I read these provisions, the United States, as a member of the Security Council, has a responsibility to join with other members of the Council to have the Council take the initiative to negotiate Article 43 agreements with Member states. Then, after the Security Council has taken such initiative, the United States as a Member of the U.N., is legally obligated to negotiate such an agreement with the Security Council.

12. I have referred to the obligations of the United States as a Member of the U.N. in respect of decisions of the Security Council. It is probably unnecessary to recall here that in fact the Security Council can do nothing under Chapter VII of the Charter over the objection (the veto) of the United States or of another of the permanent members (United Kingdom, France, Russia, China). (Article 27(3)). The United States therefore can prevent any Security Council action that might entail legal obligations it does not wish to assume. But if it (or another permanent member) does not exercise the veto and a mandatory resolution is adopted, the United States is obligated to comply with it.

Arming the United Nations Security Council—The Collective Security Participation Resolution, S.J.Res. 325, Hearing before the Senate Comm. on Foreign Relations, S.Hrg. 102–873, 102d Cong., 2d Sess. (24 September 1992). Compare Krylov, International Peacekeeping and enforcement actions After the Cold War, in Law and Force in the New International Order 94, 98–99 (Damrosch & Scheffer, eds. 1991).

4. In response to the Agenda for Peace, the U.S. Senate introduced a defense authorization bill that requires the President to prepare a report by 1994 responding to the Secretary–General's recommendations and their implications for U.S. policy. See 138 Cong.Rec. S17711, S17725, S17735, 102d Cong., 2d Sess. (Oct. 8, 1992).

## B. REGIONAL ORGANIZATIONS AND COLLECTIVE SECURITY

### *CHARTER OF THE UNITED NATIONS*

San Francisco, June 26, 1945.

REGIONAL ARRANGEMENTS

*Article 52*

1. Nothing in the present Charter precludes the existence of regional arrangements or agencies for dealing with such matters relating to the maintenance of international peace and security as are appropriate for regional action, provided that such arrangements or agencies and their activities are consistent with the Purposes and Principles of the United Nations.

2. The Members of the United Nations entering into such arrangements or constituting such agencies shall make every effort to achieve pacific settlement of local disputes through such regional arrangements or by such regional agencies before referring them to the Security Council.

3. The Security Council shall encourage the development of pacific settlement of local disputes through such regional arrangements or by such regional agencies either on the initiative of the state concerned or by reference from the Security Council.

* * *

### *SCHACHTER, AUTHORIZED USES OF FORCE BY THE UNITED NATIONS AND REGIONAL ORGANIZATIONS*

The New International Order and the Use of Force, 65, 86–88 (Damrosch & Scheffer, eds. 1991) (footnotes omitted).*

The U.N. Charter recognizes in its Chapter VIII that regional arrangements and agencies are appropriate means for maintaining peace and security, provided that their activities are consistent with the purposes and principles of the Charter. Indeed, Article 52 of the Charter requires states to make every effort to achieve peaceful settlement of "local disputes" through regional arrangements or agencies before referring such disputes to the U.N. Security Council. The idea that disputes and threats to the peace involving states within a region should preferably be dealt with primarily by regional bodies has been an early and persistent influence. At San Francisco the Security Council was perceived as a forum of last resort when states were unable to resolve conflicts between them through the peaceful means listed in Chapter VI or through regional instrumentalities.

* * *

The Charter in Article 53 expressly directs the Security Council to utilize the regional arrangements or agencies covered by Chapter VIII for enforcement action where appropriate. The regional bodies are indirectly authorized to undertake enforcement action inasmuch as Article 53 states that they may not do so without the authorization of the Security Council. Thus the failure of the Council to grant permission for enforcement action would bar such action. A permanent member could therefore prevent enforcement action by a regional organization. Cases have come before the Security Council involving decisions of the Organization of American States (O.A.S.) to apply diplomatic and economic measures that were in the nature of sanctions as envisaged in Article 41 of the U.N. Charter. In these cases, the Council did not decide that those measures were covered by Article 53. The majority of members maintained that such non-forcible coercive measures were within the competence of individual states. Since states were free to sever trade or diplomatic relations, they could do so by concerted action under the aegis of a regional organization. The reasoning is not wholly compelling since concerted action by a regional body to impose sanctions of the kind contemplated in Chapter VII (Article 41) would appear to be within the meaning of enforcement action in Article 53.

* * *

Apart from collective self-defense, regional organizations may institute peacekeeping operations that do not involve coercive measures against a state. This has been done in a number of cases. However, it has not always been agreed that the regional peacekeeping operation has actually received the consent of the territorial sovereign. Questions of this kind have come up where it was uncertain who, if anyone, may legitimately grant such consent in the absence of effective and recognized governmental authority. This emerged as a problem when U.S. forces together with troops from several Caribbean countries intervened in Grenada, claiming *inter alia* that they had been authorized to do so by a regional body (the Organization of Eastern Caribbean States) to bring peace and order to a country in a condition of anarchy. The General Assembly condemned the intervention as a violation of the Charter. However, there was no international criticism of a regional peacekeeping force of West African states that sought to bring an end to a bloody internal conflict in Liberia in 1990. This was clearly not an enforcement action or collective defense, nor was there an invitation from a government enjoying international recognition. A case of this kind would suggest an interpretation of peacekeeping by regional bodies that allows for a collective military intervention to help end an internal conflict when a government has been deposed or no longer has effective authority.

It is probable that peacekeeping actions and perhaps limited enforcement will be employed by regional organizations more frequently in the future. They are likely to be used to assist in monitoring and border patrol and perhaps to help to provide order to a country in internal conflict or near-anarchy.

### *1. The Inter–American System*

The Inter–American system of collective security includes two principal international agreements; the 1947 Inter–American Treaty of Reciprocal Assistance (The Rio Treaty), 21 U.N.T.S. 77, T.I.A.S. No. 2361, and the Charter of the Organization of American States (OAS Charter), 119 U.N.T.S. 3, T.I.A.S. No. 2361. See in particular Articles 1, 3, 6, 8 & 9 or the Rio Treaty, and Articles 14–19, 24 & 25 of the OAS Charter. Also relevant are the 1928 Convention on the Rights and Duties of States (The Montevideo Convention) and the 1926 Convention for the Maintenance, Preservation, and Reestablishment of Peace. See 1 García–Amador, The Inter–American System: Treaties, Conventions & Other Documents 261–326 (Pt. 2, 1983).

The Rio Treaty was an outgrowth of the Act of Chapultepec (Resolution on "Reciprocal Assistance and American Solidarity"), T.I.A.S. No. 1543 (1945). The Act contained a provision recognizing that aggression or the threat of aggression would warrant consultation among the American Republics with a view to collective measures of defense. The Charter of the Organization of American States entered into force for the United States on December 13, 1951. As of January 1993, there were 33 Member States in the Organization.

### *Notes*

1. *Relationship with the United Nations.* A former legal adviser of the State Department described the relation as follows:

> The appropriate relationship between the United Nations and regional organizations such as this one, the OAS, can be summarized in terms I think of six principles.
>
> One, the members of the United Nations pursuant to articles 33 and 52 of the charter should seek to deal with threats to the peace within a geographical region through regional arrangements before coming to the United Nations. This is precisely what the members of the OAS have done in the Dominican case.
>
> Second, regional organizations should not of course take enforcement action without the authorization of the Security Council. But in the Dominican Republic the Organization of American States did not take the kind of action that would require Security Council approval.
>
> Third, action taken by regional organizations must be consistent with the purposes and principles of the United Nations. This is obviously the case with the actions of the OAS in the Dominican Republic case.
>
> Fourth, the Security Council should at all times be kept fully informed of actions undertaken by regional organizations. The OAS is keeping the Security Council fully informed; witness the report you have just had from Dr. Mora through Mr. Mayobre this afternoon. And the Council has also

arranged to keep itself informed through a representative of the Secretary–General.

Fifth, the Security Council has the competence to deal with any situation which might threaten international peace and security. This competence is not at issue here.

But sixth, the Security Council should not seek to duplicate or interfere with action through regional arrangements so long as those actions remain effective and are consistent with our charter. The purposes of the United Nations Charter will hardly be served if two international organizations are seeking to do things in the same place with the same people at the same time.

As a matter of sound practice and the wise use of discretion, the Security Council under present conditions should keep itself fully informed but not undertake any activity, either diplomatic or on the ground, which would hinder the efforts and the responsibilities of the competent organization. It will serve the purposes of the United Nations Charter best if the OAS achieves what it has set out to accomplish, and that is to restore peace and achieve reconciliation so that the Dominican people can develop their own democratic institutions.

Stevenson, Principles of U.N.–OAS Relationship in the Dominican Republic, 52 Dep't State Bull. 975, 976–77 (1965).

David Scheffer adds:

Chapter VIII of the Charter (Articles 52–54) refers to enforcement action that may be taken by "regional arrangements or agencies." Although such regional arrangements typically would be established by treaty among its members (for example, the North Atlantic Treaty Organization and the Organization of American States), Chapter VIII is open to a more flexible interpretation encompassing arrangements which could fall short of formal treaty-based defense organizations. If it had exhibited more explicit organizational trappings, the multinational force that was created in 1990 to confront Iraqi aggression might have qualified for a Chapter VIII "arrangement" and therefore have been authorized by the Security Council to use military force pursuant to that chapter rather than Chapter VII. The fact that the principal participants (the United States, the United Kingdom, and France) of the multinational force arrayed against Iraq were from outside the Middle East might have appeared awkward in any such arrangement, but Chapter VIII does not necessarily limit the composition of regional arrangements to member states of the geographical region in question.

Scheffer, Commentary on Collective Security, in Law and Force in the New International Order 101, 107–08 (Damrosch & Scheffer, eds. 1991).

2. Meeker suggests that the Cuban quarantine of 1962 was justified under the Charter as an action taken by a "regional organization":

It is clear that collective action for peace and security which the Security Council may take under Chapter VII does not contravene Article 2, paragraph 4. It is also clear that individual or collective self-defense against armed attack, in accordance with Article 51, does not violate the Charter. Here it may be noted that the United States, in adopting the defensive quarantine of Cuba, did not seek to justify it as a measure required to meet an "armed attack" within the meaning of Article 51. Nor did the United States seek to sustain its action on the ground that Article 51 is not an all-

> inclusive statement of the right of self-defense and that the quarantine was a measure of self-defense open to any country to take individually for its own defense in a case other than "armed attack." Indeed, as shown by President Kennedy's television address of October 22 and by other statements of the Government, reliance was not placed on either contention, and the United States took no position on either of these issues.
>
> The quarantine was based on a collective judgment and recommendation of the American Republics made under the Rio Treaty. It was considered not to contravene Article 2, paragraph 4, because it was a measure adopted by a regional organization in conformity with the provisions of Chapter VIII of the Charter. The purposes of the Organization and its activities were considered to be consistent with the purposes and principles of the United Nations as provided in Article 52. This being the case, the quarantine would no more violate Article 2, paragraph 4, than measures voted by the Council under Chapter VII, by the General Assembly under Articles 10 and 11, or taken by United Nations Members in conformity with Article 51.
>
> Finally, in relation to the Charter limitation on threat or use of force, it should be noted that the quarantine itself was a carefully limited measure proportionate to the threat and designed solely to prevent any further build-up of strategic missile bases in Cuba.

Meeker, Defensive Quarantine and the Law, 57 A.J.I.L. 523, 524 (1963).*

For other expressions of this argument in support of the United States action, see Chayes, The Legal Case for U.S. Action in Cuba, 47 Dept. State Bull. 763 (1962); Chayes, The Cuban Missile Crisis (1974). Henkin expressed doubts about this justification. See p. 929 supra. See Comment, in Chayes, The Cuban Missile Crisis 150–53 (1974). Also How Nations Behave 291–92 (2d ed. 1979). On the OAS generally, see p. 666 supra.

The OAS is considered a Regional Organization within Art. 52 of the U.N. Charter.

3. The 1983 U.S. intervention in Grenada was said to be in response to a request for help from a group of Caribbean states called the Organization of Eastern Caribbean States. Is this group a regional organization within Article 52? Was the invasion of Grenada in 1983 by the United States and several Caribbean states a lawful "regional action" under the U.N. Charter? Moore argues:

> The Grenada mission by the OECS countries and Barbados, Jamaica and the United States is a paradigm of a lawful regional peacekeeping action under Article 52. It was undertaken in a context of civil strife and breakdown of government following the brutal murder of Maurice Bishop and members of his cabinet in an attempted coup. It was in response to a request for assistance in restoring human rights and self-determination from the only constitutional authority on the island, Governor–General Sir Paul Scoon. * * *
>
> Jointly requested or participated in by almost one-third of the membership of the Organization of American States, the Grenada mission is also consistent with the OAS Charter. * * * Articles 22 and 28 of the OAS Charter make clear that regional peacekeeping or defensive actions in

> accordance with special regional treaties do not violate the noninterventionist provisions. * * *
>
> Thus, on several grounds—request by lawful authority and action under "treaties in force" and "special treaties"—the peacekeeping and humanitarian protective action of the OECS in the Grenada mission is consistent with the Charter of the OAS. Moreover, since the Grenada mission is rooted in rights recognized by the UN Charter, under Article 137 of the revised Charter of the OAS, they could not be impaired by the OAS Charter in any event. Article 137 provides: "None of the provisions of this Charter shall be construed as impairing the rights and obligations of the Member States under the Charter of the United Nations."

J.N. Moore, Grenada and the International Double Standard, 78 A.J.I.L. 145, 154–59 (1984) (footnotes omitted).*

Christopher Joyner disagrees:

> An especially intriguing facet of the entire diplomatic episode—and a second espoused legal justification as well—is that the United States was invited by at least five members of the Organization of Eastern Caribbean States (OECS) to intervene militarily into Grenada. Created in 1981, the OECS contains within its charter a quasi-collective security provision. * * *
>
> While "collective defence" as such is called for in the Treaty, nowhere is there stipulated the option to invite outside assistance against a member state. Further, it is difficult to fathom how a treaty among seven small states could legally promote an invasion by the United States against one of its own members at the behest of the others. To be sure, considerable doubt also exists about whether the invasion of Grenada is consistent with the original intent of the signers, or for that matter, those specified treaty provisions relating to "external defence" and "arrangements for collective security against external aggression."
>
> Several reasons rebut the use of this Treaty to legitimize U.S. intervention in Grenada. First, the United States is not a party to the Treaty and therefore legally lies outside the ambit of its concerns. (Interestingly enough, neither are Barbados and Jamaica, which also participated in the invasion.) Second, Article 8 specifically deals with "collective defence and the preservation of peace and security against external aggression." No external aggressor existed: Grenada, the state in question, was a Treaty member. In addition, the OECS Treaty makes no mention of any collective security or defensive measures to be taken against a member of the organization, should such an occasion arise. There is, in short, no provision for military action in instances other than those involving "external aggression, including mercenary aggression," and such a case was absent in the October 1983 Grenada episode.

Joyner, Reflections on the Lawfulness of Invasion, 78 A.J.I.L. 131, 135–37, 142 (1984) (footnotes omitted).*

See also the editorial comment, Vagts, International Law Under Time Pressure, 78 A.J.I.L. 169 (1984), and the communication by 9 Professors of Law, Boyle et al., International Lawlessness—Grenada, 78 A.J.I.L. 172 (1984).

4. The OAS has monitored and taken political action in regard to uses of force in the region. On December 22, 1989, after the U.S. invasion of Panama,

the OAS, by a vote of twenty to one, with five abstentions, adopted a resolution "to deeply regret the intervention" and "[t]o call for the withdrawal of the foreign troops used for the military intervention. * * *" OAS Doc. CP/Res. 534 (800/89), in Acts of the Special Session of the Permanent Council of the OEA/Ser.G., CP/ACLA 800/89. On October 3, 1991, in response to the overthrow of the President of Haiti by military coup, the OAS unanimously recommended that its member states take "action to bring about the diplomatic isolation of those who hold power illegally in Haiti" and "suspend their economic, financial, and commercial ties * * *." OAS Doc. OEA/Ser.F/V.1/MRE/RES.1/91, corr. 1, paras. 5, 6 (1991). The trade embargo was strengthened on May 17, 1992. OAS Doc. OEA/Ser.F/V.1/MRE/RES.3/92 (1992), reprinted in 86 A.J.I.L. 667 (1992).

5. On June 19, 1954, the government of Guatemala alleged that armed attacks were being made against its territory by forces based in Honduras and Nicaragua and aided by the United States.

The OAS took up the question, basing its action on a Declaration approved by the Tenth Inter–American Conference in March 1954 that had stated, in part:

> That the domination or control of the political institutions of any American state by the international communist movement, extending to this Hemisphere the political system of an extra-continental power, would constitute a threat to the sovereignty and political independence of the American States, endangering the peace of America, and would call for a Meeting of Consultation to consider the adoption of appropriate action in accordance with existing treaties.

For the full text of the Declaration, see 48 A.J.I.L.Supp. 123 (1954).

On June 26, 1954, the government of Guatemala invited the Inter–American Peace Committee to send a fact-finding mission to Guatemala. Before the mission could arrive, however, the government of Guatemala was replaced by the anti-Communist regime of Carlos Castillo Armas. On July 2, the new government informed the Security Council that the problem had ceased to exist and that there was no reason to keep the question on the Council's agenda. See Thomas & Thomas, The Organization of American States 302–13 (1963).

Compare the provisions of the Rio Treaty with those of Chapter VIII of the United Nations Charter. Should Guatemala have gone to the OAS before appealing to the Security Council? Was the choice primarily one of legal analysis? See Claude, The OAS and the United Nations, Int'l Conciliation No. 547, at 30–34 (1964). Compare the Guatemalan situation with the 1956 Suez crisis. What are the similarities? See Fawcett, Intervention in International Law, 2 Rec. des Cours 344, 372 (1961).

On May 6, 1965, the Third Plenary Session of the parties adopted the following resolution:

> 1. To request governments of member states that are willing and capable of doing so to make contingents of their land, naval, air or police forces available to the Organization of American States, within their capabilities, and to the extent they can do so, to form an inter-American force that will operate under the authority of this Tenth Meeting of Consultation.
>
> 2. That this Force will have as its sole purpose, in a spirit of democratic impartiality, that of cooperating in the restoration of normal conditions in the Dominican Republic, in maintaining the security of its inhabitants and the inviolability of human rights, and in the establishment of an atmosphere

of peace and conciliation that will permit the functioning of democratic institutions.

4 I.L.M. 594 (1965), 59 A.J.I.L. 986 (1965), 52 Dep't State Bull. 862 (1965). Argentina, Bolivia, Brazil, Colombia, Costa Rica, Dominican Republic, El Salvador, Guatemala, Haiti, Honduras, Nicaragua, Panama, Paraguay, and the United States voted for the resolution. Chile, Ecuador, Mexico, Peru, and Uruguay voted against it, and Venezuela abstained.

6. On the OAS generally, see Levin, The Organization of American States and the United Nations: Relations in the Peace and Security Field (1974); Lima, Intervention in International Law with Reference to the Organization of American States (1971); The Inter–American System: Treaties, Conventions and Other Documents: A Compilation (1983); The Organization of American States and International Law, 80 A.S.I.L.Proc. 1 (1986); cf., Acevedo, The Right of Members of the Organization of American States to Refer Their "Local Disputes Directly to the United Nations Security Council," 4 Am.U.J.Int'l L. & Pol'y 25 (1989); Caminos & Lavalle, New Departures in the Exercise of Inherent Powers by the UN and OAS Secretaries–General: The Central American Situation, 83 A.J.I.L. 395 (1989).

### 2. *Organization of African Unity (OAU)*

The heads of state of thirty-two African countries signed the Charter of the Organization of African Unity on May 25, 1963. 479 U.N.T.S. 39, 58 A.J.I.L. 873 (1964). The agreement entered into force on September 13, 1963. Article 2 of the Charter provides that the promotion of the unity and solidarity of the African states and the defense of the sovereignty, territorial integrity, and independence of these states shall be among the purposes of the Organization. The states agree to coordinate and harmonize their policies in several fields, among which is that of "defense and security." In Article 3, the agreement sets forth the following principles, to which the parties declare their adherence:

> 1. the sovereign equality of all Member States;
>
> 2. non-interference in the internal affairs of States;
>
> 3. respect for the sovereignty and territorial integrity of each State and for its inalienable right to independent existence;
>
> 4. peaceful settlement of disputes by negotiation, mediation, conciliation or arbitration;
>
> 5. unreserved condemnation, in all its forms, of political assassination as well as of subversive activities on the part of neighbouring States or any other State; * * *

Article 20 authorizes the establishment of a Defense Commission.

The OAU's first opportunity to play a role in peacekeeping arose with the 1963 border dispute between Algeria and Morocco. A long-standing dispute over mineral-rich land flared up following Algerian independence in July 1962, and by October 1963 small skirmishes had yielded to military occupation of border towns and a general mobilization in Algeria. First attempts to arrange a cease-fire were not successful. The parties to the dispute were induced, however, to seek an all-African rather than a United Nations settlement as the result of a meeting arranged in Mali by Emperor

Haile Selassie and President Modibo Keita. An extraordinary session of the OAU was convened, at which the Council of Ministers appointed an *ad hoc* commission and charged it with the tasks of ascertaining responsibility for the hostilities and of recommending a settlement. The commission met in Mali and in the Ivory Coast, receiving documents from both sides. On February 20, 1964, the two governments announced that an agreement had been reached. Withdrawal of forces was to take place, and a demilitarized zone was to be established. In April, prisoners were exchanged. The two states had reestablished diplomatic relations by May 1965, and the respective heads of state had met at the border.

The OAU has been less successful in dealing with subsequent problems within the sphere of its concern. It did not play an effective role in the dispute over the Western Sahara (see Chapter 4, p. 314 supra), in efforts to curtail the atrocities of the Idi Amin regime in Uganda, or in resolving the long Rhodesian crisis before the creation of the State of Zimbabwe. Nor did the OAU play a role in the Civil war in Chad. Peacekeeping troops were sent by individual African states.

### *Notes*

1. In 1992, the OAU welcomed the United Nations military presence in Somalia to establish a secure environment for the distribution of relief aid but the Organization has not contributed to the military forces. See p. 983 supra. In 1990, the OAU endorsed the peacekeeping efforts of the Economic Community of West African States (ECOWAS) in Liberia. ECOWAS brokered a cease-fire between warring factions, but it was shattered on October 15, 1992 when the National Patriotic Front launched surprise attacks on the ECOWAS peacekeeping force. See generally, Final Communique, ECOWAS Doc. ECW/HSG/XV/7/Rev. 1 (1992); U.S. Policy Toward Liberia, U.S. Dept. of State Dispatch (November 30, 1992).

2. For a discussion of the 1963 border conflict between Algeria and Morocco, see Boutro–Ghali, The Addis Ababa Charter, Int'l Conciliation No. 546 (1964); Wild, The Organization of African Unity and the Algerian–Moroccan Border Conflict: A Study of New Machinery for Peacekeeping and for the Peaceful Settlements of Disputes among African States, 20 Int'l Org. 18 (1966).

3. On the OAU generally see, Documents of the Organization of African Unity (Naldi, ed. 1992); The Organization of African Unity, 1963–1988 (Akindele, ed. 1988); Andemicael, The OAU and the UN: Relations Between the Organization of African Unity and the United Nations (1976); El Ayouty, The OAU After 10 Years: Comparative Perspectives (1975); Naldi, Peacekeeping Attempts by the Organization of African Unity, 34 Int'l & Comp.L.Q. 593 (1985); Ramphul, The Role of International and Regional Organizations in the Peaceful Settlement of Internal Disputes (With Special Emphasis on the Organization of African Unity), 13 Georgia J.Int'l & Comp.L. 371 (1983); M'Baye & Ndiaye, The Organization of African Unity, in The International Dimensions of Human Rights (Vasak, ed. 1982).

4. *Other regional bodies.*

*a. The Arab League.*

The Arab League is a regional, political organisation of comprehensive aims. * * *

* * *

Under Article V [of the League Pact] the League Members renounce recourse to force to resolve disputes between them and, whilst they do not accept the jurisdiction of the Council of the League to mediate or arbitrate as compulsory over such disputes, if they do have recourse to the Council its decision is binding. In practice the League Council has used the more informal processes of conciliation on many occasions in dealing with inter-regional disputes, without any formal acceptance of the Council's jurisdiction under Article V. Indeed, in the Kuwait crisis in 1961, the Council established an Inter–Arab Force as a "peace-keeping" operation in view of the dispute between Kuwait and Iraq. The Council did the same in June 1976 in Lebanon.

Under Article VI each Member has a right to summon the Council immediately in the event of aggression, whether by another League Member or an outside State. The Council may then, by unanimous vote (excepting the aggressor State), decide upon measures to check the aggression. This collective security function is further specified in a separate collective security pact, based upon Article 51 of the UN Charter and on the notion that aggression against any League Member is aggression against all; the pact entered into force on August 23, 1952, and established a Permanent Joint Defence Council and Permanent Military Commission. On the occasion of the Anglo–French aggression against Egypt in 1956, involving the landing of troops in Suez, the collective security machinery failed to bring assistance to Egypt. Prior to the Arab/Israeli war of June 1967, Egypt, Jordan and the PLA (Palestine Liberation Army) instituted a joint military command, although it is clear that no integration of armed forces comparable to that which has occurred in NATO and the Warsaw Pact has yet happened.

Bowett, The Law of International Institutions 229–231 (4th ed. 1982) (footnote omitted).

During the early days of the 1990 Persian Gulf crisis, the Arab League, in a bitterly divided vote, urged its members to participate in the military deployment approved by the Security Council to protect Saudi Arabia and other Arab states against Iraqi aggression. On the Arab League generally, see Pogany, The Arab League and Peacemaking in Lebanon (1987); Pogany, The League of Arab States: An Overview, 21 Bracton L.J. 41 (1989). For earlier works see Hassouna, League of Arab States and Regional Disputes (1975); MacDonald, League of Arab States (1965); Khalil, The Arab States and the Arab League (2 vol. 1962).

*b. Association of South–East Asian Nations (ASEAN).*

ASEAN is an organization comprised of six rapidly developing nations in Southeast Asia: Indonesia, Malaysia, the Philippines, Singapore, Thailand, and Brunei. In 1991, these states together had a population estimated at 320 million and a gross national product of over $260 billion. The 1967 Bangkok Declaration that brought the organization into existence declared that ASEAN was designed to improve the economic well-being of its members, but ASEAN has also a regional security component. The 1969 declaration provided that one of the purposes of the Association is to "promote regional peace and stability." It has been noted that all the members face threats from internal insurgency movements supported by external assistance and fear the power of Mainland China and Japan. See Krause, U.S. Economic Policy Toward ASEAN 5–6 (1982). See also Unger, ASEAN, in Negotiating World Order: The Artisanship and Architecture of Global Diplomacy, chap. 11 (1986).

In January 1992, the states met to consider, among other things, a new approach to security cooperation in light of the declining regional military presence of the United States. In July 1992, another conference was held to discuss regional security after China had threatened to use force in the South China Sea in furtherance of its claim in the territorial dispute over the Paracel and Spratly Islands. See pp. 1253–54 infra. A representative of China attended the meeting and gave assurances to the group that it did not intend to threaten or use force in the settlement of the dispute.

Does either the Arab Leage or ASEAN qualify as regional organizations within the meaning of Article 52? Compare generally Bowett, The Law of International Institutions 229 (4th ed. 1982), with Goodrich, Hambro & Simons, Charter of the United Nations 351 (3d ed. 1969).

## C. COLLECTIVE SELF–DEFENSE ARRANGEMENTS

During the decades of ideological conflict, bipolarism and the Cold War, groups of states established organizations principally for "collective self-defense," but some had additional cooperative purposes. The most important politically was the North Atlantic Treaty Organization (NATO); the Communist bloc responded by establishing the Warsaw Pact. In other parts of the world groups of states established the Southeast Asia Treaty Organization (SEATO), the Central Treaty Organization (CENTO), and the ANZUS Council.

Some of these organizations withered early. The end of the Cold War has cast doubt whether any of these organizations will survive.

### *FRIEDMANN, THE CHANGING STRUCTURE OF INTERNATIONAL LAW*

258 (1964).*

The development of non-universal regional defence organisations, whether based on Article 51 or Article 52 of the Charter, is not a phase in the progress towards universal security. It is, as Josef Kunz rightly observed some years ago, writing of the newly formed Inter–American Treaty Organisation, "a substitute, an *Ersatz* for the nonexisting general collective security and sanctions." Collective defence organizations such as NATO, the Warsaw Pact group, or the Organisation of American States represent groupings of powers made necessary by the corresponding power of the enemy and the inability of most existing national states to defend themselves singly. Such coalitions and even mergers of defence organisations create bigger units but they do not point the way toward world security. If, eventually, the defence organisations of the many sovereign states were merged into only two or three collective defence mechanisms, corresponding to the super-states of Orwell's *1984*, national sovereignties would be correspondingly reduced in number, but the change would be from the power

* Footnote omitted. 

balances of numerous big and small national states to the more massive and potentially more destructive balance of power between two or three blocks of super-Powers. The organisation of peace differs from that of any other human interest in that it can only be universal. It permits, or even demands, decentralisation, but the amalgamation of states in larger non-universal groups which can be entirely positive in the fields of human rights, social welfare or economic integration, only reduces the number of potential belligerents.

## *Notes*

1. *North Atlantic Treaty Organization (NATO).* The North Atlantic Treaty was signed in Washington on April 4, 1949, T.I.A.S. No. 1964. The original parties were Belgium, Canada, Denmark, France, Iceland, Italy, Luxembourg, the Netherlands, Norway, Portugal, the United Kingdom, and the United States. It entered into force on August 24, 1949. Greece and Turkey acceded in 1951, T.I.A.S. No. 2390, 126 U.N.T.S. 350, and the Federal Republic of Germany in 1955, T.I.A.S. No. 3428, 243 U.N.T.S. 308. France withdrew its military contingents from the NATO commands in 1966, but has continued to be a member of NATO.

The Treaty states as its objectives collective self-defense (Articles 3–6) and also peaceful settlement of disputes involving a member (Article 1) and development of mutual relations, conditions of stability and well-being, and economic collaboration (Article 2).

A Council attends to implementation of the Treaty with such subsidiary bodies as may be necessary, including a European defense committee (Article 9). The defense committee was established, but in 1959 it was absorbed into the Council. The Council has established a number of other committees as well as the position of Secretary General, who is the Chairman of the Council and the administrative head of the organization.

The Treaty does not obligate a member to come to the aid of any other member when an armed attack occurs. A member need take only "such action as it deems necessary" to restore and maintain the security of the North Atlantic area (Article 5). The treaty also recognizes that each state's response must be in accord with its own constitutional processes (Article 11). Unified commands (Supreme Allied Commander in Europe and Supreme Commander for the North Atlantic) were formed with regional planning groups. Within the system of co-operation developed, there has been a substantial measure of integration. While there is no legal obstacle to a member state's withdrawing its forces from NATO commitments, in practice such withdrawal is difficult. Nevertheless, the absence of a legal obligation to come to a member state's defense kept alive concern about United States response in case of an armed attack in Europe.

The end of the Cold War has called into question the continued importance of the NATO alliance. In 1990, NATO explicitly decided to "enhance the political component" of the alliance. The Communique for the December 1990 ministerial meeting of the North Atlantic Council stated: "the risks that Allies now face in Europe arise less from a likelihood of deliberate aggression against Allied territory by former adversaries, than from the unforeseeable strategic consequences of instabilities that might emerge in a period of rapid and wide-spread political and economic transformation." See NAC Ministerial Communique, December 1990, paras. 2 and 4 respectively, reprinted in 38 NATO Rev. 22 (No. 6, Dec. 1990). The London Declaration on a Transformed North Atlantic

Alliance proposed a joint declaration on a commitment to nonaggression to be made by NATO, Warsaw Pact countries, and other states in the Conference on Security and Cooperation in Europe (CSCE). NATO also invited members of the Warsaw Pact to establish diplomatic liaisons. See The London Declaration on a Transformed North Atlantic Alliance, U.S. Dept. of State, Selected Doc. No. 38 (July 1990). NATO has also approved the membership of a unified Germany. Some commentators are uncertain as to NATO's future and suggest that it may be superseded, or absorbed into the CSCE, with links to the European Communities. See, e.g., Dean, The Post–Cold War Security System in Europe—An Evaluation, 24 Cornell Int'l L.J. 457 (1991).

On NATO generally, see NATO at 40: Confronting a Changing World (1990); NATO After Forty Years (1990); Schmitz, Defending the NATO Alliance: Global Implications (1987); Shea, NATO 2000: A Political Agenda for a Political Alliance (1990); Stromseth, The North Atlantic Treaty and European Security after the Cold War, 24 Cornell Int'l L.J. 479 (1991); Symposium, NATO and the European Community: Forging the Alliance, [1991] Detroit Coll.L.Rev. 279 (1991). For earlier analysis, see Stein & Hay, Law and Institutions in the Atlantic Area, 1031–1108 (1967); Moore, NATO and the Future of Europe (1958); Ball, NATO and the European Union Movement (1959). On the Conference on Security and Cooperation in Europe, see generally The Helsinki Process and the Future of Europe (Wells, ed. 1990); Flynn & Scheffer, Limited Collective Security, 80 For.Pol'y 77 (1990).

The Soviet Union attacked the legality of NATO in the General Assembly in 1949, claiming that the treaty violated international law and the Charter and that it was of an aggressive character. See 3 U.N.GAOR, pt. 2 at 63–65 (April 14, 1949). Ambassador Austin of the United States answered the Soviet charges in part as follows, 20 Dep't State Bull. 552, 553–54 (1949):

> The paramount authority of the Security Council of the United Nations in enforcement action is clearly recognized. At the same time, the treaty is based on the inherent right, recognized in article 51 of the Charter, of collective self-defense against armed attack pending the time when the Security Council has taken the measures necessary to maintain international peace and security. Measures to be taken in the exercise of this right must be reported immediately to the Security Council and cannot in any way affect the authority and responsibility of that organ for the maintenance of peace. * * *
>
> The prominent characteristic of article 51 is the expression in it of a cause for action which is recognized the world over, and which commanded agreement at San Francisco, namely: "The inherent right of individual or collective self-defense." Great progress had already been made immediately before the meeting in San Francisco in implementation of that inherent right. The states of the Western Hemisphere had, by treaties, developed a system of their own in the hemisphere for the operation of measures of self-defense. The Chapultepec conference had finished its work only two months before the meeting at San Francisco. There it had crystallized the basic principles of this system of hemispheric self-defense in the Act of Chapultepec. At San Francisco, therefore, where the adoption of this act by the American republics was brought to the attention of the negotiators of the Charter of the United Nations, the question arose how the legitimate operation of such a regional system was to be fitted into a general global system.

Although the Soviet Union continued to attack the NATO Treaty it sponsored the Warsaw Pact of 1955, which has a similar structure and legal foundation.

Should NATO be considered a collective defense organization under Article 51 of the Charter, or a regional organization under Chapter VIII? Compare the provisions of the NATO Treaty with those of the Warsaw Pact, following.

For the treaty documents, see 63 Stat. 2241, T.I.A.S. No. 1964, 34 U.N.T.S. 243.

2. *Warsaw Pact.* Writing at the height of the Cold War, Bowett described the nature of the Pact:

> This Organization began with the signature of a Treaty of Friendship, Co-operation and Mutual Assistance at Warsaw on May 14, 1955, a treaty of twenty years' duration, to which there are now eight parties, Albania, Bulgaria, Czechoslovakia, German Democratic Republic, Hungary, Poland, Roumania and the U.S.S.R.; China sends observers to the Political Consultative Committee.
>
> The Organization is a direct counterpart of NATO, and, as the preamble recites, was prompted by the re-armament of Western Germany and its inclusion in NATO consequent upon the formation of WEU. The treaty reaffirms the obligations of Article 2(4) of the UN Charter, and contains an undertaking to work for general disarmament and to consult on all international questions relating to the common interests of the Members; membership is open to all other States "irrespective of their social and state systems" ready to assist in preserving peace. It is, therefore, in practice only and not by its terms confined to Eastern Europe; this is consistent with the repeated invitation by the U.S.S.R. to the Western Powers to join in a general European security treaty.
>
> The crux of the security system lies in Article 4 whereby, on the basis of Article 51 of the UN Charter, an armed attack in Europe on any Member gives rise to the individual and collective obligation to render "immediate assistance * * * by all the means it may consider necessary, including the use of armed force".

Bowett, The Law of International Institutions 201–202 (1963). Footnotes omitted.*

The end of the Cold War, the demise of the U.S.S.R. and political changes in Eastern Europe, have prompted several commentators to conclude that the Warsaw Pact has ceased to exist. See, e.g., Risse–Kappen, Political Changes and the Prospects of Peace in a New Europe, 24 Cornell Int'l L.J. 407 (1991). East Germany formally withdrew from the Pact in 1990, prior to the unification of Germany, and other Pact members pronounced the end of the doctrine that considered the West as an "ideological enemy." Pact members also resolved to study ways to transform the organization into a democratic alliance to help stabilize Europe. In November 1990, Poland's Foreign Minister prophesied that the Warsaw Pact "will disappear because it no longer corresponds to the international situation existing in that part of Europe."

For general commentary on the Warsaw Pact, see Dean, Meeting Gorbachev's Challenge: How to Build Down the NATO–Warsaw Pact Confrontation (1989); Lewis, The Warsaw Pact: Arms Doctrine and Strategy (1982); Jones,

* Reprinted by permission of Fredrick A. Praeger, Inc.

Soviet Influence in Eastern Europe: Political Autonomy and the Warsaw Pact (1981); Soviet Allies: The Warsaw Pact and the Issue of Reliability (Nelson, ed. 1984). See also Karbonski, The Warsaw Pact, Int'l Conciliation, No. 573 (1969).

3. *Southeast Asia Treaty Organization (SEATO).* This organization was created by the Manila Treaty of September 8, 1954, with the United States, the United Kingdom, France, Pakistan, the Philippines, Thailand, Australia, and New Zealand as members. Pakistan is no longer a member. A separate Protocol put Cambodia, Laos, and Vietnam within the protected area, so that these states, although not members, could benefit from the organization's protection. As an organization for collective self-defense, it is based on the notion that an armed attack upon any member constitutes a danger to the peace and security of the others. However, each member state agrees only to "act to meet the common danger in accordance with its constitutional processes" (Article IV(1)). SEATO provided an organizational framework for providing military assistance to South–Vietnam in its struggle with North–Vietnam.

On June 30, 1977, the organizational aspects of SEATO were dissolved, but the collective defense treaty remains in force. For the treaty documents, see 6 U.S.T. 81, T.I.A.S. No. 3170, 209 U.N.T.S. 28; The CENTO Council (Central Treaty Organization, 1960). On these organizations, see generally Collective Defence in South East Asia: The Manila Treaty and Its Implications (1956); Geneva Agreements on Vietnam, South East Asia Treaty Organization, Charter of the United Nations (1968). See also Bowett, The Law of International Institutions 195–96, 199 (4th ed. 1982).

4. *Other Arrangements.* There are a number of additional organizations inspired by the notion of collective self-defense. These include the Central Treaty Organization (CENTO), which originated with the Bagdad Pact of 1955, U.N.T.S. 3032 (1955), and the ANZUS Council, created by the tripartite security pact between Australia, New Zealand, and the United States of April 29, 1952, T.I.A.S. No. 2493. In 1986, New Zealand withdrew from the treaty and implemented a nuclear free zone. See McLachlan, ANZUS: The Treaty Reappraised, [1985] New Zealand L.J. 271; Hewison, Withdrawal from ANZUS, [1986] New Zealand L.J. 87; Chinkin, Suspension of Treaty Relationship: The ANZUS Alliance, 7 UCLA Pac.Basin L.J. 114 (1990).

For a list of other possible collective self-defense treaties, see Goodrich, Hambro & Simons, Charter of the UN 349–50 (3d ed. 1969). For some purposes, the League of Arab States may be considered a collective self-defense organization. It has not been suggested that the OAU be considered a collective self-defense organization.

On regional collective security arrangements generally, see Scheffer, Commentary on Collective Security, in Law and Force in the New International Order 101, 107–08 (Damrosch & Scheffer, eds. 1991). See also Farer, The Role of Regional Collective Security Arrangements, in Collective Security in a Changing World, ch. 7 (Weiss, ed. 1993); Monro, Pacts for Peace: UN, NATO, SEATO, CENTO, and OAS (1967).

# SECTION 4. THE LAW OF WAR AND THE CONTROL OF WEAPONS

## A. THE LAW OF WAR

The traditional rules of war addressed three subjects: the definition of war; the conduct of war—the regulation of weapons, treatment of prisoners and injured participants, treatment of enemy nationals, their property, treatment of the populations of occupied territories, and protection for non-military ships; and the relations between neutral states and belligerent states. Deviations from the laws of war were violations of international law although war and acts of war, *per se,* were not unlawful. See p. 873 above.

The adoption of the U.N. Charter and its provisions outlawing the use of force (p. 889 above) cast doubt on whether the state of war has remained part of international law. It raised questions about the continued validity of conceptions of belligerency and neutrality. See p. 875 above. However, there has been universal agreement that "humanitarian law"—the rules governing the conduct of war—remain part of international law and are applicable in hostilities, lawful or unlawful under the Charter. See, generally, the essays in Les Dimensions Internationales du Droit Humanitaire, UNESCO (1986). See p. 940 supra.

In describing the content of those laws one must consider that the rationale of each rule since, the weapons and conditions they addressed in the Nineteenth and early Twentieth Centuries may no longer exist. Those who developed rules governing the use of weapons could not have foreseen nuclear missiles and sophisticated lethal and non-lethal poisonous gases. However, old norms, interpreted in light of the values they were designed to promote, may be applicable to modern weapons. Guerrilla wars and undeclared wars, although not "total" wars in the sense of World Wars I and II, raise the same issues. Indeed, the rules of warfare which were not scrupulously observed in the total wars of this century may find application in today's more limited conflicts.

Increasingly sophisticated weaponry as seen in the United Nations action against Iraq in 1991 suggests the need for a reexamination of the Law of War. In addition to limiting the use of chemical and biological weapons, can limitations be devised for so-called "smart bombs?" Are the distinctions between military and civilian targets still meaningful? Can they be redrawn with greater precision? Will they be observed? For that matter, in "total" war with "smart bombs" and other super-weapons, is the distinction between military personnel and civilian population still viable? Can it be strengthened?

### *1. Regulation of Weapons*

### REGULATION OF CONVENTIONAL, BIOLOGICAL AND CHEMICAL WEAPONS

Classic conceptions of the use of weapons in war began with the proposition that the amount of force required to overpower the enemy may be used, but kinds and degrees of force that were not necessary for that military purpose were barred by the concept of humanity. Furthermore, for a long time the notions of chivalry and sportsmanship required that a certain amount of fairness and mutual respect should prevail even during armed hostilities.

The conventions that have sought to limit the use of weapons developed norms focusing upon four types of armaments: (1) bullets; (2) poisons and poisoned weapons; (3) gases; and (4) aerial bombardment. These norms sought to limit the introduction of new techniques that appear to be particularly destructive or inhumane. The rationale behind decisions to limit certain types of weapons and not others was not always clear; generally, international agreements attempted to eliminate weapons that cause unnecessary suffering. See Declaration of St. Petersburg (1868) infra. Mustard gas, for example, incapacitated soldiers but also burned flesh and internal organs; the dum-dum bullet expanded on impact, tearing great wounds in its victims. For the earliest treaty regulating bullets, see Declaration Renouncing the Use, in Time of War, of Explosive Projectiles under 400 Grammes Weight, Dec. 11, 1868, Hertslet, Treaties and Conventions between Great Britain and Foreign Powers 79 (1877). See also Declaration Respecting Expanding Bullets, July 29, 1899 [1907] Gr.Brit.T.S. No. 32; Scott (ed.). The Hague Conventions and Declarations of 1899 and 1907, at 227 (3d ed. 1918).

Concentrated aerial bombardment introduced by Germany during the First World War and condemned by the Allies as inhumane, became accepted practice during World War II. For an early but unsuccessful attempt to regulate aerial bombardment, see Declaration Prohibiting the Discharge of Projectiles and Explosives from Balloons, Oct. 18, 1907, 36 Stat. 2439, T.S.No. 546. The use of incendiary and explosive shells and bombs was another hazard that developed along with air power. Though they were widely condemned when used, attempts to eliminate them (and later, flamethrowers, fire and napalm) have failed. So, too, have attempts to eliminate concentration bombing as practiced in World War II. See Spaight, Air Power and War Rights 259–95 (3d ed. 1947); Stone, Legal Controls of Armed Conflict 629–31 (rev. 3d. 1959). More successful have been bans on poisonous weapons, which were generally observed during the Second World War. See Protocol for the Prohibition of the Use in War of Asphyxiating, Poisonous or Other Gases, June 17, 1925, 94 L.N.T.S. 65; and of Bacteriological Methods of Warfare, June 17, 1925, 94 L.N.T.S. 65; 2 Dep't of the Army, International Law 44 (Pub. No. 27–161–2, 1962). But see reports of experts appointed by the U.N. Secretary–General, of the use of chemical weapons in the Iran–Iraq war, S/164333, S/17127, S/17130, U.N.Chronicle, at 3 (March 1984); id., at 24 (March 1985). See also McCormack, International Law and the Use of Chemical Weapons in the Gulf War, 21 Cal.W.Int'l L.J. 1 (1990–91). McCormack writes:

> Despite overwhelming evidence that Iraq used both nerve and mustard gas on an increasing scale [during the Iran–Iraq war] killing and injuring thousands of soldiers and civilians in flagrant breach of its obligations under the Geneva Protocol of 1925, the international community has not universally condemned Iraq. Because of their silence, governments from all countries have encouraged future violations of the Geneva Protocol.

Id., at 29. There were also reports of the Iraqi use of chemical weapons against its own Kurdish population during that time. See comment, The Iraqi Use of Chemical Weapons Against the Kurds: A Case Study in the

Regulation of Chemical Weapons in International Law, 9 Dick.J.Int'l L. 121 (1991).

On June 1, 1990, the United States and the Soviet Union entered into a bilateral Agreement on the Destruction and Non-proliferation of Chemical Weapons and on Measures to Facilitate the Multilateral Convention Banning Chemical Weapons. See 29 I.L.M. 932 (1990); Recent Developments, 32 Harv.Int'l L.J. 497 (1991). See p. 1042 infra on the status of arms control agreements to which the former Soviet Union had been bound. This followed the condemnation of the use of chemical weapons, see the Final Declaration of the Paris Conference on the Prohibition of Chemical Weapons, Jan. 11, 1989, reprinted in Arms Control Rep. 704.B.388.2 (1989).

On September 3, 1992, after 24 years of negotiation, the Geneva Conference on Disarmament approved a draft treaty that would forbid states parties from using, producing or stockpiling poison gas or lethal chemical weapons. Under the terms of the treaty, states are obliged to negotiate as soon as possible procedures for the disposal of existing chemical weapons by the year 2010 at the latest, and to submit to rigorous verification arrangements. On January 13–15, 1993, 120 states signed the draft treaty, including the United States, India, China, Israel and Iran. On earlier attempts to obtain superpower adherence to a chemical weapons treaty, see the work of the U.N. Ad Hoc Working Group on Chemical Weapons to the Committee on Disarmament, U.N.Doc. CD/358.

The outlawing of war by the U.N. Charter, (see p. 889 infra) has not been deemed to have had any effect on law regulating weapons. It is accepted that issues about the legality of war should not release participants from humanitarian restraints. Presumably, it is hoped that even an aggressor violating the law of the Charter may comply with limitations on the weapons used, if only in order to induce similar restraint by the victims fighting in self-defense. The various conventions limiting the uses of weapons have been maintained and updated.

### *Note*

On weapons regulation generally, see Symposium, International Law and the Rules of War: The Crisis Over Kuwait, [1991] Duke J.Comp. & Int'l L. 1–135; Roach, Certain Conventional Weapons: Arms Control or Humanitarian Law?, 105 Mil.L.Rev. 3 (1984); Paust, Controlling Prohibited Weapons and the Illegal Use of Permitted Weapons, 28 McGill L.J. 608–27 (1983); Levie, Humanitarian Restrictions on Chemical and Biological Weapons, 13 U.Toledo L.Rev. 1192 (1982); Fenrick, New Developments in the Law Concerning the Use of Conventional Weapons in Armed Conflict, 19 Can.Y.B.Int'l L. 229 (1981). For earlier analysis, see 2 Oppenheim, International Law 341–45 (7th ed. Lauterpacht, ed. 1952); McDougal & Feliciano, Law and Minimum World Public Order 614–71 (1961).

## THE LEGALITY OF POSSESSION AND USE OF NUCLEAR WEAPONS

The outlawing of war has coincided with the coming of the nuclear age and nuclear deterrence raising issues about the legality of nuclear weapons.

Arguments that the use of nuclear weapons is contrary to customary international law usually emphasize four sources: (1) Article 23(a) of the Hague Regulations prohibiting poisons and poisoned weapons; (2) the Protocol of 1925 which prohibits the use not only of poisonous and other gases but also of "analogous liquids, materials or devices;" (3) Article 23(c) of the Hague Regulations which prohibits weapons calculated to cause unnecessary suffering; and (4) the 1868 Declaration of St. Petersburg which lists as contrary to humanity those weapons which "needlessly aggravate the sufferings of disabled men or render their death inevitable." Two facts are relevant. In 1945, near the end of the Second World War, the United States used atomic bombs against the Japanese cities of Hiroshima and Nagasaki. In 1961, the General Assembly passed a resolution declaring that the use of nuclear weapons is a violation of the United Nations Charter and of international law. See below. See generally International Law Association, Report of the Fiftieth Conference 192 (1962). The United States voted against the resolution and challenged its view of the law. It should be noted that during the Cold War the major antagonists, while avowing their own restraint, have each recognized the possibility of the use of nuclear weapons. Since these weapons are deemed to be essential to the military capacity of major powers, it is likely that their use would be determined by the demands of military strategy and not by possible proscriptions of international law.

Big powers insisted that they had to develop and retain nuclear weapons as a deterrent to the use of such weapons by other states, and to aggression with conventional weapons. Even some who insisted that the use of nuclear weapons was illegal or immoral conceded that it is not unlawful or immoral to keep them as a deterrent. Compare National Conference of Catholic Bishops, Pastoral Letter on War and Peace—Challenge of Peace: God's Promise and Our Response, reprinted in Castelli, The Bishops and the Bomb 274 (1983).

The end of the Cold War and the fragmentation of the U.S.S.R. have reduced the fear of nuclear war between superpowers, but have not mooted questions as to the legality of using nuclear weapons. These developments, moreover, have generated new fears of nuclear proliferation and continuing attempts by additional states to develop nuclear capabilities. See Levin, Where Have All the Weapons Gone? The Commonwealth of Independent States' Struggle to Stop the Proliferation of Nuclear Weapons and the New Role of the International Atomic Energy Agency, 24 N.Y.U.J.Int'l L. & Pol. 957 (1992); Spector, Repentant Nuclear Proliferants, 88 For.Pol'y 21 (Fall 1992). See also p. 1039 on arms control.

Difficulty in determining the limitations imposed by contemporary international law has led to the suggestion that a new convention be adopted to outlaw the use of nuclear weapons. See G.A.Res. 33/71B (1978). The problem of enforcing such a ban has directed attention to the development of inspection systems. There have also been suggestions for agreement on "no-first-use" of nuclear weapons. See the discussion of disarmament and arms-control, pp. 1039–45 infra. Theorists see limitations on the use of nuclear weapons in mutual deterrence or in political forces in international relations. Explicit norms, incorporated in a convention, are, according to this analysis, of secondary importance. See, e.g., Dahlitz, Nuclear Arms Control (1983).

### *DECLARATION ON THE PROHIBITION OF THE USE OF NUCLEAR AND THERMONUCLEAR WEAPONS*

G.A.Res. 1653 (XVI) (1961).

The General Assembly * * * declares that:

1. (a) The use of nuclear and thermo-nuclear weapons is contrary to the spirit, letter and aims of the United Nations, and, as such, a direct violation of the Charter of the United Nations;

(b) The use of nuclear and thermo-nuclear weapons would exceed even the scope of war and cause indiscriminate suffering and destruction to mankind and civilization and, as such, is contrary to the rules of international law and the laws of humanity;

(c) The use of nuclear and thermo-nuclear weapons as a war directed not against an enemy or enemies alone but also against mankind in general, since the peoples of the world not involved in such a war will be subjected to all the evils generated by the use of such weapons;

(d) Any State using nuclear and thermo-nuclear weapons is to be considered as violating the Charter of the United Nations, as acting contrary to the laws of humanity and as committing a crime against mankind and civilization.

The resolution was adopted by a vote of 55 to 20, with 26 abstentions. (The United States, United Kingdom, France, Australia, Canada, China, and Italy voted no.) G.A.Res. 1653 (1961). The United States has strongly and repeatedly reiterated its view that the resolution does not reflect the state of international law.

### *Notes*

1. In an action against the Japanese government, Japanese citizens argued that the Japanese government had unlawfully waived their claims for damages resulting from the atomic bombs dropped at Hiroshima and Nagasaki by the United States in 1945. The court stated:

> [T]here is not an established theory among international jurists in connection with the difference of poison, poison gas, bacterium, etc. from atomic bombs. However, judging from the fact that the St. Petersburg Declaration declares that "* * * considering that the use of a weapon which increases uselessly the pain of people who are already placed out of battle and causes their death necessarily is beyond the scope of this purpose, and considering that the use of such a weapon is thus contrary to humanity * * *" and that article 23(e) of the Hague Regulations respecting War on Land prohibits "the employment of such arms, projectiles, and material as cause unnecessary injury," we can safely see that besides poison, poison-gas and bacterium the use of the means of injuring the enemy which causes at least the same or more injury is prohibited by international law. The destructive power of the atomic bomb is tremendous, but it is doubtful whether atomic bombing really had an appropriate military effect at that time and whether it was necessary. It is a deeply sorrowful reality that the atomic bombing on both

cities of Hiroshima and Nagasaki took the lives of many civilians, and that among the survivors there are people whose lives are still imperilled owing to the radial rays, even today 18 years later. In this sense, it is not too much to say that the pain brought by the atomic bombs is severer than that from poison and poison-gas, and we can say that the act of dropping such a cruel bomb is contrary to the fundamental principle of the laws of war that unnecessary pain must not be given.

The Shimoda Case, Judgment of the Tokyo District Court, 7 Dec. 1963, reprinted in 8 Japanese Ann.Int'l L. 212, 241–42 (1964).

2. Builder and Graubard analyze the legality of nuclear weapons as follows:

In the absence of express international agreement relating to the matter, the question of the legality of the use of the atomic weapon must be judged by reference: (a) to existing international instruments relating to the limits of the use of violence in war; (b) to the distinction, which many believe to be fundamental, between combatants and noncombatants; and (c) to the principles of humanity, which, to some degree, must be regarded as forming part of the law of war.

It may be advisable to sum up the necessarily tentative conclusions reached on the legality of the use of nuclear weapons:

(1) Considerations of humanity, requirements of civilisation or other formative factors are no substitute for prohibitive rules of international law and, by themselves, do not constitute evidence of rules prohibiting the use of nuclear weapons.

(2) The principle of the exemption of the civilian population from being an intentional object of warfare as an abstraction from relevant rules of international law has been so whittled down during the Second World War and in post–1945 treaties of a humanitarian character as to cease to offer any reliable guidance. At the most, it still excludes the use of the most powerful nuclear weapons against the civilian population, provided that this sector of the population complies with two requirements—

(a) the civilians concerned must not be connected with the war effort, and

(b) be remote from important target areas.

(3) It is possible to argue that the radiation and, in the case of "unclean" nuclear weapons, their fall-out effects

(a) make applicable to nuclear weapons the rules of international customary law by which the use of poison and poisoned weapons is prohibited, as well as Article 23(a) of the Hague Regulation of 1899 and 1907 on Land Warfare, and

(b) the Geneva Protocol on Poisonous Gases and Analogous Materials of 1925, the provisions of which were treated in the post–1919 period as declaratory of existing international law.

(4) On the assumption of the illegality in principle of the use of all nuclear weapons, the legality of their use by way of reprisals must be accepted within the limits within which reprisals are admitted in international law, but cannot be justified or excused on any other ground.

(5) If nuclear weapons of a calibre which does not allow for exemption from warfare of the civilian population as defined under (2)(a) and (b) above

are used, or this sector of the enemy population is made the intentional object of nuclear attack, it is a tenable proposition that such acts amount also to crimes against humanity. * * *

Builder & Graubard, The International Law of Armed Conflict: Implications for the Concept of Assured Destruction 32 (1982) (footnotes omitted).

3. The illegality of nuclear weapons under international law was raised in U.S. courts, without success, as a defense to criminal charges stemming from civil protests against such weapons. See, e.g., United States v. Kabat, 797 F.2d 580 (8th Cir.1986), cert. denied, 481 U.S. 1030, 107 S.Ct. 1958, 95 L.Ed.2d 530 (1987); United States v. Montgomery, 772 F.2d 733 (11th Cir.1985); United States v. Brodhead, 714 F.Supp. 593 (D.Mass.1989). See also Boyle, Defending Civil Resistance Under International Law (1987); Lippman, Civil Resistance: Revitalizing International Law in the Nuclear Age, 13 Whittier L.Rev. 17 (1992); Citizen Initiatives under International Law, 82 A.S.I.L. Proc. 555 (1988). The illegality of such weapons was also asserted as a ground for challenging the production and deployment of nuclear weapons. See, e.g., United States v. Thompson, 90–10118, disposition (unpublished) tabled at, 931 F.2d 898 (9th Cir.1991); United States v. Allen, 760 F.2d 447 (2d Cir.1985). See also Pauling v. McElroy, 164 F.Supp. 390 (D.D.C.1958), aff'd, 278 F.2d 252 (D.C.Cir.1960), cert. denied, 364 U.S. 835, 81 S.Ct. 61, 5 L.Ed.2d 60 (1960); Greenham Women Against Cruise Missiles v. Reagan, 591 F.Supp. 1332 (S.D.N.Y.1984), aff'd, 755 F.2d 34 (2d Cir.1985).

4. On the legality of nuclear weapons generally, see Singh & McWhinney, Nuclear Weapons and Contemporary International Law (1988); Falk, Meyerowitz & Sanderson, Nuclear Weapons and International Law (1981); Van Boven, Fundamental Rights and Nuclear Arms, 19 Den.J.Int'l L. & Pol'y 55 (1990–91); Weeramantry, The Law, Nuclear Weapons and the Real World, 19 Den.J.Int'l L. & Pol'y 55 (1990–91); Bleimaier, Nuclear Weapons and Crimes Against Humanity Under International Law, 33 Catholic Lawyer 161 (1990); Green, Nuclear Weapons and the Law of Armed Conflict, 17 Den.J.Int'l L. & Pol'y 1 (1988); Meyerowitz, The Opinions of Legal Scholars on the Legal Status of Nuclear Weapons, 24 Stan.J. Int'l L. 111 (1987). For earlier work, see Spaight, The Atomic Problem (1948); Schwarzenberger, The Legality of Nuclear Weapons (1958); Singh, Nuclear Weapons and International Law (1959); Rosas, International Law and the Use of Nuclear Weapons, in Essays in Honor of Erik Casteren 73–95 (1979).

## 2. *International Humanitarian Law*

### *McCOUBREY, INTERNATIONAL HUMANITARIAN LAW: THE REGULATION OF ARMED CONFLICTS*

1–4 (1990) (footnotes omitted).

International humanitarian law is that branch of the laws of armed conflict which is concerned with the protection of the victims of armed conflict, meaning those rendered *hors de combat* by injury, sickness or capture, and also civilians. It is founded upon the ideas that the legitimate scope of military action is not unlimited and that those who are or have been rendered non-combatant are entitled to impartial humanitarian concern and that both they and those charged with their care and welfare in the rendering of humanitarian aid are not legitimate targets in hostilities.

These principles are deceptively easy to state but much less so to express as legal norms which are reasonably capable of practical application in the extreme circumstances of armed conflict and herein lies one of the most urgent problems in the development of this area of law. International humanitarian law, or 'Geneva' law, as such is now found primarily in the four 1949 Geneva Conventions, the two 1977 Additional Protocols and associated materials. It is a sub-part of one of two major divisions of the modern law of armed conflict, which are the *jus ad bellum* and the *jus in bello.* The first of these is concerned with the legitimacy of resort to armed force, which is now permissible only in pursuit of the 'inherent right of self-defence', as variously defined, preserved by article 51 of the United Nations Charter as an exception to the general ban upon resort to armed force contained in article 2(4). The second makes provision for the legal regime applicable during an armed conflict in progress and, it must be stressed, these provisions are generally applicable irrespective of the lawfulness or otherwise of the original resort to armed force by any of the parties to the conflict.

* * *

Beyond the questions of appropriate categorization of the laws of armed conflict there is a seeming paradox which must be considered in there being laws, and certainly 'humanitarian' laws, of armed conflict at all. If public international law represents the outer edge of 'legal' orders, then the laws of armed conflict must represent the most tenuous upper reaches of the 'legal' atmosphere. Armed conflict is the ultimate breakdown of the international 'social' and legal order, much as is interpersonal violence in a municipal context, and one which public international law is largely concerned to avert. It is therefore prima facie curious to find a structure of legal norms which is designed to regulate the conduct of a state of international relations which is in essence a descent into extra-legal violence. Certainly, there is no modern municipal legal equivalent in rules and principles designed to regulate the 'proper' conduct of interpersonal violence. * * *

### *Note*

McCoubrey defines international humanitarian law as that which protects human beings during armed conflict; other writers have used the term more broadly to refer to the entire legal regime for the regulation of war.

On international humanitarian law generally, see Beigbeder, The Role and Status of International Humanitarian Volunteers and Organizations: The Right and Duty to Humanitarian Assistance (1991); Humanitarian Law of Armed Conflict (Delissen & Tanja, eds. 1991); Implementation of International Humanitarian Law (Kalshoven & Sandoz, eds. 1989); the Collection of Papers on the Protection of the Human Being in Armed Conflicts, 9 Australian YB. Int'l L. (1985); International Dimensions of Humanitarian Law (UNESCO 1988); Bourloyannis, The Security Council of the United Nations and the Implementation of International Humanitarian Law, 20 Den.J.Int'l L. & Pol'y 335 (1992); Austin, The Law of International Armed Conflicts, in International Law: Achievements and Prospects 765, 770–87 (Bedjaoui, ed. 1991); Weissbrodt, The Role of International Organizations in the Implementation of Human Rights and Humanitarian Law in Situations of Armed Conflict, 21 Vand.J. Transnat'l L. 313 (1988).

## TREATMENT OF PRISONERS OF WAR AND THE SICK AND WOUNDED

Humanitarian treatment of prisoners of war was not emphasized until the second half of the nineteenth century. See 2 Oppenheim at 367–96; Stone at 651–79. The Hague Regulations did not prevent many of the hardships that prisoners suffered during World War I, but they did provide an enlightened basis for regulation. Besides the failure to anticipate the problems that arose in World War I, the chief defects of the regulations were a lack of specificity and the absence of any enforcement procedures. After the First World War, a conference at Geneva adopted new, more elaborate rules. See Convention Relating to the Treatment of Prisoners of War, July 27, 1929, 47 Stat. 2021, T.S. No. 846, 118 L.N.T.S. 343. Like the prior rules, the new rules did not anticipate the new modes of warfare adopted in the world war that followed their acceptance.

The outlawing of war by the U.N. Charter has not been deemed to affect the humanitarian laws of war. In the interstate wars between Israel and the Arab states, for example, both sides assumed that they were bound by the relevant conventions—and claimed to be abiding by them. See p. 991 supra.

The Geneva Convention Relative to the Treatment of Prisoners of War, Aug. 12, 1949, 3 U.S.T. 3316, T.I.A.S. No. 3364, 75 U.N.T.S. 135, is now the authoritative statement. An outstanding innovation of the Convention, in addition to its application to all cases of declared war, is its partial application to all other armed conflicts, including internal wars. If one of the participants in a conflict is not a party to the Convention, the powers who are parties are nevertheless bound in their mutual relations. The Convention defines prisoners in a way calculated to include every person likely to be captured in the course of hostilities. Full and primary responsibility for the treatment of prisoners of war falls upon the Detaining Power, not upon individuals. The Detaining Power is under a general obligation to treat prisoners humanely. They must receive maintenance and medical attention. Medical and scientific experiments are prohibited, as are reprisals for breaches of the laws of war other than breaches of the Convention itself. See Stone, Legal Controls of International Conflicts 656 n. 21 (rev. ed. 1959); 2 Oppenheim at 562 n. 3. Prisoners are to be treated alike, regardless of race, nationality, religious beliefs, or political opinions.

At the time of detention, the prisoner is required to give a minimum of information. He is not to be subjected to torture and may retain his personal effects. Conditions at the detention camps must meet standards provided in the Convention. The work that the prisoner is required to perform must not be inherently dangerous, humiliating, or directly connected with the operations of the war. The prisoner must be permitted contact with his family and correspondence privileges. Procedures must be established for registering complaints against the administration of the detention camp. Penal and disciplinary sanctions, including procedures for determining guilt, are prescribed by the Convention. Additional articles regulate repatriation, and information to the outside regarding prisoners.

The Convention elaborates the idea introduced in the 1929 Convention, of a Protecting Power appointed by mutual agreement, which determines whether the provisions of the conventions are being followed. When the belligerents are unable to agree upon such an appointment, the Detaining Power is required to request a neutral state, an impartial organization, or a humanitarian organization to substitute for the Protecting Power. Each contracting party undertakes to provide penal sanctions against persons who violate the established norms. Parties to the conventions are obligated to search out those persons alleged to have committed such breaches.

Many of the general provisions of the Geneva Convention Relative to the Treatment of Prisoners of War are incorporated directly into the Geneva Convention for the Amelioration of the Condition of the Wounded and Sick in Armed Forces in the Field, Aug. 12, 1949, 6 U.S.T. 3114, T.I.A.S. No. 3362, 75 U.N.T.S. 31. The Geneva Convention for the Amelioration of the Condition of the Wounded, Sick, Shipwrecked Members of the Armed Forces at Sea, Aug. 12, 1949, 6 U.S.T. 3217, T.I.A.S. No. 3363, 75 U.N.T.S. 85, is similar. As of 1993, there were 159 parties to the four Geneva Conventions.

Issues have arisen about the applicability of the Geneva Conventions to civil wars, or to hostilities between recognized governments and "liberation movements," or terrorist groups. See Bond, The Rules of Riot (1974); Kalshoven, Applicability of Customary International Law in Non-international Armed Conflicts, in Current Problems of International Law 267 (Cassese ed. 1975); Taubenfeld, The Applicability of the Laws of War in Civil War, in Law and Civil War in the Modern World 499 (Moore ed. 1974).

In 1977 two additional protocols were adopted to fill gaps in the Conventions, since the Conventions do not address some problems of modern warfare, notably guerrilla war. Unfortunately, the 1977 Protocols proved to be as controversial as the types of armed conflict they governed. As of 1993, the newer instruments had more than sixty parties. See generally Best, Humanity in Warfare (1980); Venthley, Guerilla Warfare (1983); Draper, The Implementation and Enforcement of the Geneva Conventions of 1949 and of the Two Additional Protocols, 164 Rec. des Cours 1 (1979); Schindler, The Different Types of Armed Conflicts According to the Geneva Conventions and Protocols, No. 3 id. at 117; Cassese, The Status of Rebels Under the 1977 Geneva Protocol on Non-International Armed Conflict, 30 Int'l and Comp.L.J. 416–39 (1981); Protocols Additional to the Geneva Conventions on the Law of War, A.S.I.L.Proc. (1980); Aldrich, New Life for the Laws of War, 75 A.J.I.L. 764 (1981); Levie, Protection of War Victims (1979–80). On the earlier Conventions, see Draper, The Red Cross Conventions (1958); Pictet, The Geneva Conventions of 12 August, 1949: Commentary (1952–60). See also The Law of Non–International Armed Conflict: Protocol II to the 1949 Geneva Conventions (Levie, ed. 1987); Ramcharan, The Role of International Bodies in the Implementation and Enforcement of Humanitarian Law and Human Rights Law in Non–International Armed Conflicts, 33 Am.U.L.Rev. 99 (1983).

The treatment of prisoners of war in the 1991 Gulf conflict does not seem to have produced any significant new issues. See generally Meron, Prisoners of War, Civilians and Diplomats in the Gulf Crisis, 85 A.J.I.L. 104 (1991).

## ENEMY NATIONALS AND THEIR PROPERTY WITHIN BELLIGERENT TERRITORY

At one time, belligerents were permitted to confiscate private as well as public enemy property, moveable and immovable, including debts. This practice was reversed in respect of private property through treaties that provided that enemy subjects and private property could be withdrawn at the outbreak of war. The last case of outright confiscation of private property occurred in 1793, but it is not clear whether such confiscation today would violate customary international law. See 2 Oppenheim at 326. Compare the treatment of private fishing vessels, The Paquete Habana, p. 58 supra. Customary law permits the seizure of public enemy property and the prohibition of the withdrawal of private enemy property.

In the early stages of the First World War, states scrupulously avoided confiscatory acts against enemy states, but most states eventually adopted exceptional war measures which, though not amounting to confiscation, inflicted great loss and injury. At the end of both the First and Second World Wars, the peace treaties included provisions giving nationals of the victorious states recourse against the vanquished states for loss of property. Nationals of the vanquished country, however, could apply only to their own states for compensation. The United States never recognized any obligation to compensate for the seizure of enemy property.

Regulation of enemy property has been recognized in the United States as within the war power of the federal government. See Hays, Enemy Property in America (1923); Gathings, International Law and American Treatment of Alien Enemy Property (1940); Council on Foreign Relations, The Postwar Settlement of Property Rights 16–22 (1945). Eight months after the United States entered the First World War, Congress passed the "Trading with the Enemy Act," 40 Stat. 411 (1917). See 50 U.S.C.A. §§ 21–24 for the current presidential authority to supervise enemy aliens. The "Trading with the Enemy Act" prohibited all trade with persons or firms resident within enemy territory or resident outside the United States and doing business within such territory or with nationals of an ally of an enemy state unless authorized by license. All business enterprises whose stock was held by enemies or allies of enemies, and all persons holding property of or indebted to enemies, were required to register with the Alien Property Custodian. At first empowered only to administer such property, the Alien Property Custodian was later authorized to manage and dispose of property. In the Second World War, government control of foreign-owned property was instituted more than a year before the entry of the United States. Following the initial executive order relating to Norwegian and Danish property within the United States, the property of all the governments and nations of continental Europe (except Turkey), of Japan and of China was frozen. After the United States entered the war, the authority of the Secretary of the Treasury was widened to include liquidation or supervision of Axis-controlled business enterprises located in the United States. Nearly two years after the first freezing order, President Roosevelt established the Office of the Alien Property Custodian.

In accordance with principles enunciated in the Potsdam and Paris agreements, the United States passed the "War Claims Act of 1948," 62 Stat. 1240, which provided that owners of alien property seized during the Second World War would not be compensated.

Treaties after a war often provide that the victorious powers may retain seized enemy property; its former owners are to be compensated by their own governments. See, e.g., Article 79 of the 1947 Peace Treaty with Italy, 61 Stat. 1245, T.I.A.S. No. 1648, 49 U.N.T.S. 1; Chapter 6, [Bonn] Convention on the Settlement of Matters Arising Out of the War and Occupation, 1952, 6 U.S.T. 4411, T.I.A.S. No. 3425, 332 U.N.T.S. 219; Tag v. Rogers, 267 F.2d 664 (D.C.Cir.1959), cert. denied, 362 U.S. 904 (1960); DeVries, The International Responsibility of the United States for Vested German Assets, 51 A.J.I.L. 18 (1957).

On the treatment of enemy property, see generally Stone at 434–36; 2 Oppenheim at 326–32. An extensive study of the practice during World War II throughout the world, is Domke, Trading with the Enemy in World War II (1943), and Domke, The Control of Alien Property (1947). The treatment of enemy property under the peace treaties at the conclusion of the Second World War is considered in Mann, Enemy Property and the Paris Peace Treaties, 64 L.Q.Rev. 492 (1948). See also Martin, The Treatment of Enemy Property under the Peace Treaties of 1947, 34 Grotius Soc.Trans. 77 (1948).

Alien enemy control during the First and Second World Wars included internment of dangerous foreign nationals. Benefiting from the experience at the outbreak of the First World War, the government was able to increase the efficiency and incidence of internment at the beginning of the Second World War. On December 7, 1941, a presidential proclamation provided for the internment of Japanese nationals. Subsequent decrees applied to German, Italian, Hungarian, Bulgarian and Rumanian nationals. By October 5, 1943, 14,807 aliens had been taken into custody. See Hoover, Alien Enemy Control, 29 Iowa L.Rev. 398 (1944). Presidential authority for the supervision of enemy aliens is contained in 50 U.S.C.A. § 21. *Habeas corpus* was available to these persons, although the only justiciable question was whether they belonged to the category of persons designated by legislation as liable to seizure. In general, the right of enemy aliens, whether seized or not, to use the court was limited to defensive actions. See Brandon, Legal Control Over Resident Enemy Aliens in Time of War in the United States and in the United Kingdom, 44 A.J.I.L. 382 (1950).

Additional protection is provided by the "Geneva Convention Relative to the Protection of Civilian Persons in Time of War," Aug. 12, 1949, 6 U.S.T. 3516, T.I.A.S. No. 3365, 75 U.N.T.S. 287. It prohibits violence to life and person and allows no distinction based on race, religion, or political opinion. It defines situations in which an alien may leave the territory of the belligerent and provides that the regulation of those aliens remaining may depart from the provisions regulating such aliens in peace time only to the extent required by war time control and security. Aliens must be allowed to receive relief, necessary medical care and religious comfort. They must be allowed to move from exposed areas. They may not be compelled to work on any task related to military operations and when working they must be accorded working conditions equal to those of the belligerent's nationals.

There is also an elaborate set of rules regulating treatment of internees. See Stone, Legal Controls of International Conflicts 684–92. As of 1993, 165 states were parties to the Convention.

In 1992, the Security Council adopted Resolution 771, which called on states and international humanitarian organizations to collect information relating to violations of humanitarian law, including grave breaches of the Geneva Conventions, committed during the hostilities in the territory of the former Yugoslavia. On September 22, 1992, the United States submitted a report to the Security Council, in accordance with resolution 771, charging numerous instances of willful killing, torture of prisoners, abuse of civilians, deliberate attacks on noncombatants, mass forcible expulsions and deportation of civilians, and wanton devastation and destruction of property. See 3 For.Pol'y Bull. 49 (No. 3, 1992). The report stated that the United States was working with other states on a resolution to create a U.N. commission to establish the facts in connection with these charges, and to "prepare for possible prosecution of individuals found guilty of those crimes." Id.

On May 25, 1993, the Security Council established a War Crimes Tribunal to prosecute serious breaches of international humanitarian law in the former Yugoslavia. S.C.Res. 827 (1993). The mandate of the Tribunal includes trying those accused of "mass killing, organised and systematic detention and rape of women, and the continuance of the practice of 'ethnic cleansing * * *.'" Id. See Chapter 8, p. 633.

The rape of women by belligerent or occupying forces has been a perennial atrocity addressed by international law in only general terms and not effectively deterred or punished. See Khushalani, Dignity and Honour of Women as Basic and Fundamental Human Rights 63–64 (1982). In 1993, during the hostilities in the former Yugoslavia, it was reported that there had been as many as 20,000 cases of rape of Muslim women committed by Serbian troops as a matter of state policy and strategy of war. There were demands for international enforcement of the Geneva Convention against such atrocities, including war crime trials, as well as enforcement through complaints under the Convention Against Torture. An analogous atrocity had been the forced enrollment of women into brothels as was done to Korean women by Japan in the Second World War. See Hicks, They Won't Allow Japan to Push the Comfort Women Aside, Int'l Herald Trib., Feb. 10, 1993.

## TREATMENT OF THE POPULATION OF OCCUPIED TERRITORY

When belligerent occupation has been established in accordance with the requirements of international law, the occupying power assumes broad legal powers that it would not have merely as a belligerent. These powers and reciprocal duties reflect the divergent and common interests of the occupying power and the local inhabitants. Both have a common interest in the maintenance of law and order. The occupying power desires to minimize the diversion of its resources from other war operations, while the local inhabitants want to conduct their lives without violence and undue coercion.

Humane treatment of the inhabitants not only serves the values of decency, but is a precondition of administering the territory with a minimal expenditure of force. See McDougal & Feliciano, Law and Minimum World Public Order 790–808 (1961).

Belligerent occupation creates a complicated scheme of legal relations involving not only the occupant and the inhabitants, but also the temporarily ousted sovereign. Customary rules articulating these relationships have been strongly influenced by the Hague Regulations and the Geneva Convention Relative to the Protection of Civilian Persons in Time of War. For the purposes of the latter instrument, the character of the war is irrelevant. Specifically, the fact that one of the parties to the conflict had violated a norm of international law in initiating hostilities would not affect the applicability of the Convention. The occupant is empowered to maintain order and utilize the resources of the country for its own military needs. The occupying power may confer rights only against itself and it may not force the people to swear allegiance to it. The precise extent of its power is uncertain, particularly with respect to effecting changes in fundamental institutions. See Stone, Legal Controls of International Conflict, 688–89, 723–32 (rev. ed. 1959).

Ordinarily, the occupying power is expected to rely on the organs of the subservient government, such as the courts, for maintaining law and order. When these institutions prove inadequate, the belligerent may replace them with institutions of a military nature. In punishing war crimes or activity directed against the occupying power, the courts are forbidden to apply any retroactive law or to depart from the principle of proportionality in punishment. Death penalties are permissible in certain types of cases only. Collective penalties, intimidation, terrorism, taking of hostages and acts of reprisal against the civilian population are prohibited. Since, in reaction to a recalcitrant civilian population, an occupying power might well adopt penal measures without regard to these niceties, the practicality of such rules has been questioned. See McDougal & Feliciano, Law and Minimum World Public Order 797 (1961). Discrimination on the grounds of race, religion or political opinion is also forbidden. In general, all forcible mass transfers of population are prohibited, except where required by security or military necessity. The occupying power is also required to provide certain welfare services.

On the treatment of the population of occupied territory see generally Stone, Legal Controls of International Conflict, 697–706, 723–26, 727–32 (rev. ed. 1959); 2 Oppenheim at 438–56; 2 Dep't of the Army at 163–73; McDougal & Feliciano at 732; von Glahn, The Occupation of Enemy Territory (1957); Gutteridge, The Protection of Civilians in Occupied Territory, 5 Y.B. World Aff. 290 (1951).

The extended occupation by Israel since the war of 1967 of territories previously in Arab hands has raised some novel problems. It has been argued that international law does not contemplate long, indefinite occupation. The United States has declared Israel's program of establishing settlements in West Bank territories a violation of international law. Israel has claimed that the Geneva Convention applied only to territories occupied in war that belonged to another sovereign state, and that since the termination of the British Mandate and the failure of the UN Partition Plan of 1947 when the Arab states rejected and defeated it by going to war, the territories in question do not belong to Jordan or any one else. See Letter of the State Department Legal Adviser Concerning the Legality of Israeli Settlements in the Occupied Territories, 17 I.L.M. 777 (1978). A discussion of the Israeli position is found in Blum, The Missing Reversioner: Reflections on the Status of Judea and Samaria, 3 Israel L.Rev. 279, 281–95 (1968).

The U.N. in effect rejected these arguments when it called on Israel to cancel an order expelling a number of Palestinians from the West Bank in 1988 and from Gaza in 1992. See S.C.Res. 607 (1988) and Res. 799 (1992). In addition to denying the applicability to those territories of the rules governing occupation, Israel has also argued that the prohibition on expulsion in the Geneva Convention applied only to mass displacement of population but did not forbid the expulsion of individuals as a form of punishment or as a security measure. See generally, the debate between Falk and Weston, The Relevance of International Law to Palestinian Rights in the West Bank and Gaza: In Legal Defense of the Intifada, 32 Harv.Int'l L.J. 129 (1991). Peace talks between Israel and its neighbors began in 1992 and if successful might terminate the occupation character of the Israeli presence in the West Bank.

Extended occupation has raised issues also about Israel's right to exploit the natural resources of Sinai or of the sea-bed off the shores of occupied lands. See Gerson, Off–Shore Oil Exploration by a Belligerent Occupant: The Gulf of Suez Dispute, 71 A.J.I.L. 725 (1977).

## ENEMY SHIPS

The law of war included also limitations in favor of enemy merchantmen. Unlike armed ships and other public vessels, an enemy merchant ship was not to be attacked unless it refused to submit to visit and capture. See generally 2 Oppenheim at 465–97; Stone at 571–607. These rules were widely disregarded in both World Wars, notably by submarines, which found it difficult to visit and capture. Prohibitions on submarine warfare against merchant ships were made explicit between the wars. See Treaty for the Limitation and Reduction of Naval Armaments (London Naval Treaty of 1930), April 22, 1930, pt. IV, Art. 22, 46 Stat. 2858, 2881, T.S. No. 830, 112 L.N.T.S. 65, 88; 2 Hackworth at 690–95; 6 Hackworth at 466.

After visit, a merchant vessel could be taken to port and adjudicated a prize, and thereafter its disposition was governed by municipal law. For a description of American prize practice, see Gilmore & Black, The Law of Admirality 40 (2d ed. 1975); 2 Whiteman at 1–138. Immunities were granted to hospital ships, to vessels with religious, scientific, or philanthropic missions and also to coastal fishing boats.

The rules as to treatment of enemy ships have not been reviewed since the U.N. Charter, and their present status is uncertain.

### *Note*

In the *Nicaragua* case (Merits), the Court observed that the laying of mines in the waters of another state without any warning or notification is not only an unlawful act but also a breach of the principles of humanitarian law. The Court stated:

> [I]f a State lays mines in any waters whatever in which the vessels of another State have right of access or passage, and fails to give any warning or notification whatsoever, in disregard of the security of peaceful shipping, it commits a breach of the principles of humanitarian law underlying the specific provisions [Articles 3 and 4] of [Hague] Convention No. VIII of 1907. Those principles were expressed in the *Corfu Channel* case as follows:
>
> "certain general and well recognized principles namely: elementary considerations of humanity, even more exacting in peace than in war" (I.C.J. Reports 1949, p. 22).

1986 I.C.J. 14, 112.

### *3. The Law of War and Environmental Protection*

#### *1977 PROTOCOL I ADDITIONAL TO THE GENEVA CONVENTIONS 1949*

Official Record of the Diplomatic Conference on the Reaffirmation and Development of International Humanitarian Law applicable in Armed Conflicts
6 U.S.T. 3516, T.I.A.S. No. 3364.

ARTICLE 35—BASIC RULES

* * *

3. It is prohibited to employ methods or means of warfare which are intended, or may be expected, to cause widespread, long-term and severe damage to the natural environment.

* * *

ARTICLE 55—PROTECTION OF THE NATURAL ENVIRONMENT

1. Care shall be taken in warfare to protect the natural environment against widespread, long-term and severe damage. This protection includes a prohibition of the use of methods or means of warfare which are intended or may be expected to cause such damage to the natural environment and thereby to prejudice the health and survival of the population.

#### *1977 CONVENTION ON THE PROHIBITION OF MILITARY OR ANY OTHER HOSTILE USE OF ENVIRONMENTAL MODIFICATION TECHNIQUES (ENMOD CONVENTION)*

31 U.S.T. 333, T.I.A.S. No. 9614.

ARTICLE I

1. Each State Party to this Convention undertakes not to engage in military or any other hostile use of environmental modification techniques having widespread, long-lasting or severe effects as the means of destruction, damage or injury to any other State Party.

2. Each State Party to this Convention undertakes not to assist, encourage or induce any State, group of States or international organization to engage in activities contrary to the provisions of paragraph 1 of this article.

Article II

As used in article I, the term 'environmental modification techniques' refers to any technique for changing—through the deliberate manipulation of natural processes—the dynamics, composition or structure of the Earth, including its biota, lithosphere, hydrosphere and atmosphere, or of outer space.

### *Notes*

1. The United States has taken the position that Article 35(3) of the 1977 Protocol I, additional to the Geneva Conventions "is too broad and ambiguous and is not a part of customary law." See Matheson, The United States Position on the Relation of Customary Law to the 1977 Protocols Additional to the 1949 Geneva Conventions, 2 Am.U.J.Int'l L. & Pol'y 419, 420–21 (1987). As of early 1993, the 1977 Protocol I, Additional to the 1949 Geneva Conventions had been ratified or acceded to by more than 102 states, not including the United States.

2. The Conference of the Committee on Disarmament, which was the drafting body of the ENMOD Convention, appended four nonbinding "Understandings" in explanation of portions of the Convention. The understandings with regard to Articles I and II provide:

*Understanding relating to Article I*

It is the understanding of the Committee that, for the purposes of this Convention, the terms "widespread", "long-lasting" and "severe" shall be interpreted as follows:

(*a*) "widespread": encompassing an area on the scale of several hundred square kilometres;

(*b*) "long-lasting": lasting for a period of months, or approximately a season;

(*c*) "severe": involving serious or significant disruption or harm to human life, natural and economic resources or other assets.

It is further understood that the interpretation set forth above is intended exclusively for this Convention and is not intended to prejudice the interpretation of the same or similar terms if used in connexion with any other international agreement.

*Understanding relating to Article II*

It is the understanding of the Committee that the following examples are illustrative of phenomena that could be caused by the use of environmental modification techniques as defined in Article II of the Convention: earthquakes; tsunamis; an upset in the ecological balance of a region; changes in weather patterns (clouds, precipitation, cyclones of various types and tornadic storms); changes in climate patterns; changes in ocean currents; changes in the state of the ozone layer; and changes in the state of the ionosphere.

It is further understood that all the phenomena listed above, when produced by military or any other hostile use of environmental modification techniques, would result, or could reasonably be expected to result, in widespread, long-lasting or severe destruction, damage or injury. Thus, military or any other hostile use of environmental modification techniques as defined in Article II, so as to cause those phenomena as a means of destruction, damage or injury to another State Party, would be prohibited.

It is recognized, moreover, that the list of examples set out above is not exhaustive. Other phenomena which could result from the use of environmental modification techniques as defined in Article II could also be appropriately included. The absence of such phenomena from the list does not in any way imply that the undertaking contained in Article I would not be applicable to those phenomena, provided the criteria set out in that Article were met.

As of 1993, the ENMOD Convention had been ratified by more than 50 states, including the United States, Great Britain and the former U.S.S.R. On September 15, 1992, the state parties to the ENMOD Convention convened a Review Conference as provided for in Article 8 of the treaty. The United States urged the Conference to preserve the Convention without change, but developing countries sought to widen the Convention's prohibitions to include deliberate environmental changes through the use of herbicides. See International Environment Daily (BNA) (Sept. 17, 1992).

3. Professor Falk has proposed a Convention on the Crime of Ecocide, which would prohibit and criminalize deliberate acts to "destroy, in whole or in part, a human ecosystem," including the use of nuclear, biological, chemical or other weapons of mass destruction, chemical herbicides to defoliate and destroy natural forests for military purposes, and the extreme use of bombs and artillery. See Falk, Revitalizing International Law, chap. 9, Appendix 2, at 187 (1984).

4. During the 1991 Gulf War Iraqi forces reportedly opened valves at the Mina al-Ahamadi and Mina al-Gakr oil terminals and pumped large quantities of crude oil into the Persian Gulf. Toward the end of the conflict Iraq set massive fires in Kuwaiti oil fields. After the cease-fire, the Security Council adopted a resolution that declared Iraq was "liable under international law for any direct loss, damage, including environmental damage and the depletion of natural resources, or injury * * * as a result of Iraq's unlawful invasion and occupation of Kuwait." S.C.Res. 687, at ¶ 16 reprinted in, 30 I.L.M. 846 (1991). Would Protocol I, the ENMOD Convention or Professor Falk's Ecocide Convention apply to Iraq's actions in the Gulf war? Professor Oxman writes:

> One of the questions arising out of Iraq's military occupation of Kuwait and the ensuing armed conflict is whether existing treaties and customary international law regulating armed conflict adequately address and serve as a deterrent to acts of environmental degradation, sometimes styled environmental terrorism. Particular attention has focused on Iraq's decision to release large quantities of oil into the Persian Gulf from Kuwait and to ignite large numbers of Kuwaiti oil wells.
>
> * * *
>
> The hard questions in considering environmental limitations on the conduct of armed conflict did not arise in Iraq's case. The fact that Iraq was an occupying power in Kuwait placed it under special obligations with respect to property located there. To most observers, both the oil spill and fires would represent precisely the kind of vindictive and wanton destruction that has long been excluded by the laws of war. This basic principle is manifested in many specific rules, such as the prohibition on pillage. Even if one could imagine some military advantages from the smoke and the oil

slicks in impeding the adversary, the magnitude of the destruction done by the oil spill and the fires is wholly out of proportion to such military objectives. It violates one of the most fundamental principles of the law of armed conflict, namely the prohibition on damage that is excessive in relation to the military objectives involved.

As the Iraqi case demonstrates, many of the rules governing armed conflict that are designed to protect civilian lives, health, and property also have the collateral effect of protecting the environment. Moreover, increased knowledge of the environmental consequences of particular types of events affects the application of those rules, often broadening their restraining effect. To put it differently, military planners need to consider the effects of their actions on the environment if only because failure to do so may result in unlawful injury to civilians or non-military objects.

* * *

Therefore, perhaps the most important environmental question is whether the protection of civilians and civilian objects, not merely from destruction or injury directed at them, but from so-called collateral destruction or injury, is adequate. I trust the philosophical answer to this question will be "no" as long as wars persist.

The practical question must recognize that rules of protection, to be effective, must be widely accepted by governments and respected by their armed forces precisely when they are engaged in armed conflict, presumably in defense or pursuit of what they consider vital interests. One might put the question as follows: Have we done the best we can for the moment?

* * *

Both environmentalists and members of the armed forces would be justified in asking if myriad questions regarding the legality of virtually all modern methods or means of warfare should be resolved on the basis of the words *may be expected* and the words *widespread, long-term and severe.* Given the following "legislative history" in the official report on this ambiguous text, one wonders what the fuss is about anyway: "It appeared to be a widely shared assumption that battlefield damage incidental to conventional warfare would not normally be proscribed by this provision." *Long-term* was regarded as being "measured in decades," perhaps "twenty or thirty years * * * being a minimum."

Precisely because armed conflict is always bad for the environment, it would seem that any text attempting to deal with the problem of environmental restraints in a simple and sweeping fashion either would admonish us to think about and try to balance the competing values at stake, at best, or would descend into meaningless or hyperbole (undone by deft interpretations), at worst.

It makes more sense to assume the applicability of the general restraints of the laws of war, such as the principle of proportionality, and ask whether there are specific situations, not covered by rules restraining injuries to civilians and property, that require more detailed regulation. The Environmental Modification Convention, to which the United States is party, is an example of such an approach. That convention is regularly reviewed. If appropriate, such a review could become the occasion for discussion of these issues.

> Specific rules regarding not only dams, dikes, and nuclear electric generating stations, but regarding the remnants of war, are set forth in Protocol I. Perhaps there is a need for other specific rules. Protocol I itself indicates that there may be other types of installations containing dangerous forces where attack should be closely regulated. Indeed, some installations may be dangerous precisely because they contain biological or chemical weapons, creating a direct collision between environmental and health concerns on the one hand and the traditional distinction between military and civilian targets on the other. Resolution of this conflict requires a risk/benefit analysis implied in the principle of proportionality. Whatever the command structure, one trusts that both operational and supervisory military and civilian officials participate in decisions involving potentially catastrophic targeting.
>
> It is not easy to decide whether new rules are needed or desirable, not to mention negotiable in a helpful form. In this field, perhaps more so than in other fields of law, one must consider perverse effects. The practical impact of a particular protective legal rule may be to increase the likelihood of damage to an installation or site that would not otherwise have been a profitable object of attack.

Oxman, Environmental Warfare, 22 Ocean Dev. & Int'l L. 433, 433–436 (1991) (footnotes omitted).

In setting conditions for the cease-fire in the 1991 Gulf War, the Security Council adopted a resolution that included apparently the first determination under international law of state liability for harm to the environment and for the depletion of natural resources. Iraq was declared "liable under international law for any direct loss, damage, including environmental damage and the depletion of natural resources * * * as a result of Iraq's unlawful invasion and occupation of Kuwait." S.C.Res. 687 (1991). See Tinker, "Environmental Security" in the United Nations: Not a Matter for the Security Council, 59 Tenn. L.Rev. 787 (1992).

5. On the environmental implications of the Gulf War, see Arkin, Durrant & Cherni, On Impact: Modern Warfare and the Environment—A Case Study of the Gulf War (1991); The Gulf War: Environment as a Weapon, 85 A.S.I.L.Proc. 214 (1991); Okorodudu–Fabara, Oil in the Persian Gulf War: Legal Appraisal of an Environmental Warfare, 23 St. Mary's L.J. 123 (1991); Robinson, International Law and the Destruction of Nature in the Gulf War, 21 Env'l Pol'y & L. 216 (1991); Szsasz, Environmental Destruction as a Method of Warfare: International Law Applicable to the Gulf War, 15 Disarmament 128 (1992); Toukan, The Gulf War and the Environment: The Need for a Treaty Prohibiting Ecological Destruction as a Weapon of War, 15 Fletcher Forum of World Aff. 95 (1991).

6. On the implications between the Laws of War for the environment generally, see Environmental Protection and the Law of War: A Fifth Geneva Convention on the Protection of Environment in Time of Armed Conflict (Plant, ed.1992); Westing, Environmental Hazards of War: Releasing Dangerous Forces in an Industrialized World (1990); Environmental Warfare: A Technical, Legal and Policy Appraisal (Westing, ed.1984); Almond, The Use of the Environment as an Instrument of War, 2 Y.B.Int'l Env'l L. 455 (1991); Blix, Arms Control Treaties Aimed at Reducing the Military Impact on the Environment, in Essays in International Law in Honour of Judge Manfred Lachs 704 (1984); Bothe, The Protection of the Environment in Times of Armed Conflict, 34 Germ.Y.B.Int'l L. 54 (1991); Drucker, The Military Commander's Responsibility for the Environ-

ment, 11 Env'l Ethics 135 (1989); Falk, Environmental Warfare and Ecocide: Fact, Appraisal and Proposal, 9 Revue Belge de Droit International 1 (1973); Goldblat, Legal Protection of the Environment Against the Effects of Military Activities, 22 Bull. Peace Proposals 399 (1991); Johnstone, Ecocide and the Geneva Convention, 49 For.Aff. 711 (1971); Schafer, The Relationship between International Law of Armed Conflict and Environmental Protection: The Need to Regulate What Types of Conduct are Permissible During Hostilities, 19 Cal.W.Int'l L.J. 285 (1989); Singh, The Environmental Law of War and the Future of Mankind, in The Future of the International Law of the Environment 419 (Dupuy, ed.1985); Westing, Environmental Warfare, 15 Env'l L. 645 (1985).

## B. ARMS CONTROL AND DISARMAMENT

### *COT & BONIFACE, DISARMAMENT AND ARMS CONTROL*

International Law: Achievements and Prospects 811–12 (Bedjaoui, ed.1991) (footnotes omitted).

1. Although the concepts of disarmament and arms control are frequently used interchangeably, they none the less apply to separate situations and are distinct from one another. Disarmament may be defined as the process arising from any measure taken on the basis of a legal obligation entailing a reduction in the existing level of armaments. It can range from a reduction in a specific type of armaments to the complete destruction of national arsenals, or any stage in between. Disarmament may be general or total, but it may also be partial and/or regional.

2. Arms control is a more recent concept, originating in the United States in the early 1960s.

The purpose of arms control is not only to limit the volume and growth of arsenals, but also to control the uses to which existing weapons are put.

"Unlike disarmament as such, arms control is compatible with the pursuit of the arms race. All it presupposes is that there will be an international dialogue to steer this race towards an equilibrium between the powers."

3. There are in fact two possible interpretations of arms control. It may be considered as a stop-gap, or the lesser of two evils: according to this view, genuine disarmament having proved to be unattainable in the immediate future, one might as well impose the strictest limits possible on the arms race. However, arms control may also be chosen for its own merits. It is then based on the view that in the nuclear age, the antithesis of armament and disarmament is outmoded. "Arms control aims to diminish the risk of conflict by means of limited measures applicable to different aspects of armaments, without for all that calling into question the contribution of weapons to the security of the State".

4. The advocates of the theory of nuclear deterrence hold that nuclear weapons can play a part in maintaining security. They claim that the damage that could be caused by a nuclear war is so great that it prevents conflicts from arising between countries possessing nuclear arms including conflicts limited to the use of conventional weapons. Whatever gains they might expect to make, the belligerents would be sure to suffer even greater

losses. The goal of arms control is thus to safeguard peace, and peace is not automatically endangered by the existence of arsenals. Consequently, it is merely necessary to avoid the arms race having any destabilizing effects whence the idea of managing it and making it predictable, or, in short, controlling it. It is no coincidence that the concepts of nuclear deterrence and arms control came into being simultaneously.

5. Arms control, like disarmament, must be distinguished from the laws of war. Their purpose is simply to regulate the use of weapons during a conflict and not to limit or reduce their numbers in time of peace. Accordingly, the 1925 Geneva protocol prohibiting the use of chemical weapons has to do with the laws of war, while an agreement on the limitation or elimination of chemical weapons concerns arms control or disarmament. Similarly, an undertaking not to be the first to use nuclear weapons comes under the laws of war rather than arms control or disarmament.

6. Confidence-building measures are also distinct from arms control, even though they were confused initially. Confidence-building measures may be defined as any exchange of information, or any means allowing or providing for an exchange of information, concerning military postures, without, however, regulating the existing level of armaments.

Although these measures improve the international climate, they do not deal with the existence, size or growth of the arsenals. Accordingly, the Soviet–American agreement concerning the establishment of a direct communications link, signed in Geneva on 20 June 1963, can be classified as a confidence-building measure, and does not come under the process of arms control.

---

After the First World War, disarmament was high on the international agenda as a promising way of maintaining international peace and security. The victorious nations imposed limitations on German rearmament and sought also to regulate their own armaments. The emphasis was on the weapons of the previous war; e.g., disarmament conferences at London and Washington concluded agreements establishing ratios on battleships for the major powers. See Treaty for the Limitation and Reduction of Naval Armaments (London Naval Treaty of 1930), April 22, 1930, 46 Stat. 2858, T.S. No. 830, 112 L.N.T.S. 65; Washington Treaty: Limitation of Naval Armament (1922), 43 Stat. 1655, T.S. No. 671, 25 L.N.T.S. 201. The fear of poison gas also led to prohibitions on the use of particular weapons. See 1019 above.

Planning for peace following the Second World War emphasized not disarmament but collective security. Under the U.N. Charter, the Permanent Members of the Security Council would make armed forces available to the Council in order to deter, prevent, or suppress aggression. See U.N. Charter, Article 43. The Big Powers would, of course, remain armed for this purpose, but it was hoped that they would not require major arsenals; the rest of the world, surely, could disarm and remain unarmed. The failure of that original conception required instead reliance on self-defense and collective self-defense under Article 51, or on regional peace-keeping, all of which depended on the maintenance of arms. The emergence of nuclear weapons made the quest for means of eliminating or controlling them seem urgent, but the international system never succeeded in overcoming the fears and other drives that have led to ever-more and ever-more-terrible weapons of mass destruction. The dream, and the formal commitment to disarmament, however, has never faded, although it soon ceased to have high priority.

In fact, arms control negotiations have never been long in abeyance, and a number of agreements were concluded and are in force:

— Antarctic Treaty

(Signed: 1 December 1959; entered into force: 23 June 1961.)

— Treaty banning nuclear weapon tests in the atmosphere, in outer space and under water (Partial Test Ban Treaty)

(Signed: 5 August 1963; entered into force: 10 October 1963.)

— Treaty on principles governing the activities of states in the exploration and use of outer space, including the moon and other celestial bodies (Outer Space Treaty)

(Signed: 27 January 1967; entered into force: 10 October 1967.)

— Treaty for the prohibition of nuclear weapons in Latin America (Treaty of Tlatelolco)

(Signed: 14 February 1967; entered into force: 22 April 1968.)

— Treaty on the non-proliferation of nuclear weapons (Non–Proliferation Treaty)

(Signed: 1 July 1968; entered into force: 5 March 1970.)

— Treaty on the prohibition of the emplacement of nuclear weapons and other weapons of mass destruction on the sea-bed and the ocean floor and in the subsoil thereof (Sea–Bed Treaty)

(Signed: 11 February 1971; entered into force: 18 May 1972.)

— Agreement on measures to reduce the risk of outbreak of nuclear war between the U.S. and the USSR (U.S.–Soviet Nuclear Accidents Agreements)

(Signed: 30 September 1971; entered into force: 30 September 1971.)

— Convention on the prohibition of the development, production and stockpiling of bacteriological (biological) and toxin weapons and on their destruction

(Signed: 10 April 1972; entered into force: 26 March 1975.)

— U.S.–Soviet treaty on the limitation of anti-ballistic missile systems (SALT ABM Treaty)

(Signed: 26 May 1972; entered into force: 3 October 1972.)

— US–Soviet interim agreement on certain measures with respect to the limitation of strategic offensive arms (SALT Interim Agreement)

(Signed: 26 May 1972; entered into force: 3 October 1972.)

— U.S.–Soviet agreement on the prevention of nuclear war

(Signed: 22 June 1973; entered into force: 22 June 1973.)

— Protocol to the U.S.–Soviet treaty on the limitation of anti-ballistic missile systems

(Signed: 3 July 1974; entered into force: 25 May 1976.)

— Document on confidence-building measures and certain aspects of security and disarmament, included in the Final Act of the Conference on Security and Co-operation in Europe

(Signed: August 1975.)

— French–Soviet agreement on the prevention of the accidental or unauthorized use of nuclear weapons (French–Soviet Nuclear Accidents Agreement)

(Concluded through an exchange of letters on 16 July 1976 between the foreign ministers of France and the USSR; entered into force: 16 July 1976.)

— Convention on the prohibition of military or any other hostile use of environmental modification techniques (ENMOD Convention)

(Signed: 18 May 1977; entered into force: 5 October 1978.)

— British–Soviet agreement on the prevention of an accidental outbreak of nuclear war (British–Soviet Nuclear Accidents Agreement)

(Signed: 10 October 1977; entered into force: 10 October 1977.)

— U.S.–Soviet arms limitation agreements (Strategic Arms Limitation Talks (Salt II)) (signed: June 1979; never entered into force)

— Conventional Forces in Europe Treaty (originally negotiated between members of NATO the Warsaw Pact) (signed 19 November 1990; not in force).

The U.S. and the Soviet Union signed the U.S.–Soviet treaty on the Limitation of Underground Nuclear Weapons Tests (Threshold Test Ban Treaty) (signed 3 July 1974) and the U.S.–Soviet Treaty on Underground Nuclear Explosions for Peaceful Purposes (Peaceful Nuclear Explosions Treaty) (Signed 28 May 1976) (both entered into force 11 December 1990). In 1987 the U.S.S.R. and the United States signed the Treaty on the Elimination of Intermediate–Range Nuclear Forces (INF) (not in force). On July 31, 1991 the U.S. and the Soviet Union signed Treaty on the Reduction and Limitation of Strategic Offensive Arms (the START treaty) and less than two years later, on December 29, 1992, Russia and the United States entered into the START II treaty to reduce ground-based multiple warhead missiles. Neither treaty, however, is in force. On the effect of succession to former Soviet Union arms control treaties see notes below.

The two treaties with the greatest number of adherents are the Treaty Banning Nuclear Weapons (118 states parties as of January 1992) and the Treaty on the Non–Proliferation of Nuclear Weapons (149 states parties as of January 1992).

### *Notes*

1. The fragmentation of the Soviet Union into 15 independent republics, each of which has declared its independence and been recognized by the United States has raised issues regarding succession to arms control treaties binding on the former Soviet Union. Bunn and Rhinelander write:

> Two seemingly inconsistent rules of international law have been advanced to deal with the problem of inheritance of treaties when a state breaks apart to form two or more new states: "continuity" and "clean slate." [See Chapter 6 supra]. Under the continuity rule, any treaty that was in force for the entire territory of the predecessor state is presumed to

continue in force for each separating state. Under the clean slate rule, generally applied to newly independent former colonies, the new states may wipe their individual slates clean and choose whether or not to join treaties that were brought into force for their territories when under colonial rule by the predecessor states. Because the problem has come up most frequently since World War II when colonies achieved independence, there are more recent cases where the clean slate rule has been applied than the continuity rule. For cases such as Russian succession to the obligations of the Soviet Union, however, the continuity rule remains strong.

* * *

Russia was certainly not a colony, a dependent trust or mandated territory, of the Soviet Union. Were Belarus, Kazakhstan and Ukraine? They are not the same as the Belgian, British, French, Dutch, Italian, etc. dependent colonies in other regions of the world from the metropolitan governments that entered into treaties for them. Belarus and Ukraine, though part of the Soviet Union, had sufficient status in 1945 to be charter members of the United Nations and to join arms control treaties in their own name between 1945 and their independence. * * *

* * *

* * * Application of the continuity rule would not make each former republic a nuclear-weapon state party to the NPT [nonproliferation treaty] just because the Soviet Union was such a party and the treaty applied throughout Soviet territory. Such a result would mean each could control nuclear weapons, which would be wholly inconsistent with the purpose of the treaty. The NPT was intended to hold the line at the number of nuclear-weapon states that had "manufactured and exploded a nuclear weapon or other nuclear explosive device prior to January 1, 1967." That was five: Britain, China and France as well as the Soviet Union and the United States.

The 1978 Vienna Convention contains an exception to the continuity rule if "it appears from the treaty or is otherwise established that the application of the treaty in respect of the successor State would be incompatible with the object and purpose of the treaty * * *." Clearly, this exception is applicable to succession to the NPT by republics other than Russia. That means they are non-nuclear-weapon states under the NPT, and must join it in that capacity if they wish to become members.

What has happened in the former republics so far is consistent with this view. Tactical nuclear weapons from all the republics that had them other than Russia have been moved to Russia, except for some remaining in Belarus and Ukraine, and removal of these is promised before July 1, 1992. Strategic nuclear weapons exist only in Belarus, Kazakhstan and Ukraine besides Russia, and removal of the last of these from Kazakhstan is promised by 1999. Both Belarus and Ukraine have promised to join the NPT as non-nuclear-weapon states and to become nuclear-free zones. While Kazakhstan's position is more ambiguous, U.S. representatives are negotiating with it as well as with Belarus, Russia and Ukraine about further removal of nuclear weapons.

Bunn & Rhinelander, Who Inherited the Former Soviet Union's Obligations Under Arms Control Treaties with the United States? Memorandum to the Committee on Foreign Relations (10 March 1992). See also State Succession and Relations with Federal States, 86 A.S.I.L.Proc. 1, 6–10 (1992); Saxer, The

Transformation of the Soviet Union: From a Socialist Federation to a Commonwealth of Independent States, 14 Loyola L.A.Int'l & Comp.L.J. 581, 691–92 (1992); Chapter 6, Section 7 supra.

2. In 1992, the United States attempted to curb the proliferation of nuclear weapons and technological knowledge from economically insecure states of the former Soviet Union (e.g., Russia, Byelarus and Ukrainia) by providing financial aid to enable those states to destroy nuclear weapons and retain scientists. See the report in Arms Control 8 (18 May 1992).

3. For a complete bibliography on disarmament, see Burns, Arms Control and Disarmament: A Bibliography (1977).

For a treatment of the legal problems of disarmament, see Henkin, Arms Control and Inspection in American Law (1958); Berman & Maggs, Disarmament Inspection Under Soviet Law (1967); Aronowitz, Legal Aspects of Arms Control Verification in the United States (1965); Barnet & Falk, Security in Disarmament (1965). See also Henkin, Disarmament, The Lawyer's Interest, in Proc. 4th Hammarskjöld Forum, 1, (1964).

4. Failure to disarm and the maintenance of armed forces and even sophisticated weapons, without more, have not been deemed a threat of force in violation of Article 2(4) of the U.N. Charter.

5. Henkin writes:

> A "sophisticated" explanation for the lack of any comprehensive agreement on disarmament is that nations do not throw on the bargaining table, and put out of their own control, the "basics" of national survival. The skepticism about disarmament which has come to many with years of frustration existed from the beginning with some traditional diplomatists and masters of "real politik," who found no serious disarmament in their own experience or in diplomatic history and had no room for it in their theories of how nations behave. Perhaps, for a while, the terrible War and the awesome new atomic bomb, which moved nations to create the United Nations, might possibly have moved them to the even more radical adjustments of comprehensive disarmament under supra-national controls, like that called for by the original Acheson–Lilienthal Plan of 1946 for international control of the atom. But that it did not happen then suggests that nothing has happened to make nations change their ways. To date, these skeptics can, of course, say they told us so.
>
> Those who do not accept that nations are inherently beyond this "salvation," may yet recognize that only unusual fears and crises move nations to radical readjustments, and comprehensive, supervised disarmament with its political consequences would be radical indeed. One might have thought, perhaps, that the big weapons would shake the inertia of nations, but it has not happened. Perhaps one adequate explanation is that both sides have come to believe that big weapons cannot in fact be disarmed. How to make a bomb is knowledge that cannot be eradicated, and some groups, somewhere, some day, can start to make one. Nuclear stockpiles, also, can be hidden beyond the reach of any practicable detection, and even delivery vehicles can be "hardened" and made difficult to destroy or detect. Against these dangers, no nation will wish to give up its nuclear deterrent, unless perhaps it were replaced by some yet-to-be devised, effective, and reliable international force beyond the ken of present political planning.

Henkin, Disarmament, the Lawyer's Interest, in Proceedings of the Fourth Hammarskjöld Forum, 1, 16–17 (1964).

6. Although arms-control progress has been small, writing on the subject continues to proliferate. See Achieving Effective Arms Control, Committee on International Arms and Security Affairs, Association of the Bar of the City of New York (1985); Clarke & Mowlan (eds.), Debate on Disarmament (1982); World Military Expenditures and Arms Transfers, U.S. Arms Control and Disarmament Agency (1985); Fischer, Preventing War in the Nuclear Age (1984); Miller & Feininder (eds.), Nuclear Weapons and Law (1984).

# Chapter 12

# BASES OF JURISDICTION

## SECTION 1. JURISDICTION UNDER INTERNATIONAL LAW

### A. JURISDICTION DEFINED: THE DIFFERENT FORMS OF JURISDICTION

The term jurisdiction is commonly used to describe authority to affect legal interests. Traditionally, three kinds of jurisdiction are distinguished: legislative, judicial, and executive or enforcement jurisdiction. See generally Restatement, Second, Conflict of Laws § 9 (1971). It is generally recognized that rules of general import may be formulated not only by legislatures, but also by other institutions of government, such as administrative agencies, and even courts. For that reason, the Restatement (Third) prefers to use the term prescription. Similarly, recognizing that adjudicatory functions may be exercised by governmental institutions other than courts, the Restatement (Third) prefers the term jurisdiction to adjudicate over the term judicial jurisdiction. Restatement (Third), Part IV, Introductory Note.

The Restatement, Second, Foreign Relations Law of the United States § 6, Comment *a,* distinguished only between prescriptive and enforcement jurisdiction and defined the latter term as "the capacity * * * to enforce a rule of law, whether this capacity be exercised by the judicial or the executive branch." The Restatement (Third) does distinguish between jurisdiction to adjudicate and jurisdiction to enforce. It defines jurisdiction to adjudicate as "the authority of a state to subject particular persons or things to its judicial process" and jurisdiction to enforce as the authority of a state "to use the resources of government to induce or compel compliance with its law." Restatement (Third), Part IV, Introductory Note.

In the materials that follow, the terms legislative, judicial, and executive jurisdiction will be used interchangeably with the terms jurisdiction to prescribe, to adjudicate, and to enforce.

Jurisdiction may be defined on several levels. The legislative, judicial or executive powers of particular institutions must, in the first instance, be defined under municipal law. Municipal law may again operate on more than one level. For example, in the United States, the legislative, judicial, and executive powers of the federal branches of government are defined first in the Constitution. The federal Constitution sets limits beyond which the legislative, judicial, and executive branches of federal and state governments, in exercising their powers, may not go. Similarly, conflict of laws rules also define the limits of legislative, judicial, and executive jurisdiction. These limits may, but need not, be the same as those prescribed by constitutional law. Thus, a court in the United States may deny recognition to a foreign judgment or refuse to apply a foreign law because, under its conflicts rules, the foreign court or legislature sought to extend its jurisdiction too far; and it may do so, even if recognition of what the foreign institution did would not run afoul of constitutional limitations. See, e.g., Grubel v. Nassauer, 210 N.Y. 149, 103 N.E. 1113 (1913).

While, therefore, legislative, judicial, and executive jurisdiction already have to be defined on several levels under municipal law, international law provides still a different level. It defines the limits states and other international legal persons may not exceed in exercising jurisdiction. The extent to which the pertinent rules of international law are operative in municipal law systems depends, of course, on the status of international law within those systems. On this aspect, see Chapter 3. But, within the international system, rules of international law operate directly on the subjects of international law whose powers they delimit.

## B. INTERNATIONAL LAW RULES OF JURISDICTION GENERALLY

International law has not yet developed a comprehensive set of rules defining with reasonable precision all forms of jurisdiction that may be exercised by states and other international legal persons. Rather, international law has given principal attention to the reach of a state's jurisdiction—legislative, judicial, or executive—in criminal matters.

The Restatement (Third) states in Comment *f* to § 403 that the criteria for jurisdiction to prescribe "apply to criminal as well as to civil regulation." But Reporters' Note 8 states that in "applying the principle of reasonableness, the exercise of criminal (as distinguished from civil) jurisdiction in relation to acts committed in another state may be perceived as particularly intrusive." However, Comment *b* to § 421, which deals with Jurisdiction to Adjudicate, states that it applies to the exercise of "criminal as well as of civil jurisdiction."

The Restatement (Third) does not refer to judicial decisions or to other authority that broadly extend to jurisdiction in civil matters the limitations imposed by international law on the exercise of criminal jurisdiction. Furthermore, there appears to be no recorded instance of a state's having objected to another state's exercising judicial jurisdiction in a civil matter on a so-called exorbitant basis of jurisdiction (such as the plaintiff's nationality under Article 14 of the French Civil Code) on the ground that international law precludes reliance on such a basis. On jurisdiction to adjudicate, see Section 7 of this Chapter.

In more recent times, foreign sovereigns have increasingly objected to the exercise of extraterritorial legislative jurisdiction in the economic sphere through statutes that threaten both criminal and administrative and civil sanctions. See Section 6 of this Chapter. Administrative and some forms of civil sanctions, such as injunctions and punitive damages, may, indeed, affect the person on whom they are imposed as seriously as do criminal sanctions and may therefore be regarded as coming within the realm of criminal jurisdiction for the purposes here discussed. It may well be argued, however, that international law limitations on the exercise of administrative and civil jurisdiction are still in a stage of development and that broad generalizations should be treated with circumspection.

The exercise of executive jurisdiction in any form on the territory of another state is generally regarded as limited by international law, regardless of whether the enforcement measure is of a criminal or civil nature. See Section 8 of this Chapter.

The permissible nature and scope of jurisdiction under international law vary with the international legal person whose jurisdiction is at issue. As the International Court of Justice has taught in Reparation for Injuries Suffered in the Service of the United Nations, [1949] I.C.J. 174, p. 348 supra, the powers of an international legal person are a function of the role it plays in the world community.

The classical view is that a state does not have to establish a valid basis for its exercise of jurisdiction and that the burden of establishing that its exercise of jurisdiction violates international law rests upon the person asserting the violation. See the *Lotus Case,* p. 63 supra. More recently, the view has been espoused that, especially when it acts extraterritorially, a state must demonstrate affirmatively the existence of an appropriate basis of jurisdiction. An alternative view is that the exercise of all forms of jurisdiction is subject to an overall limitation of reasonableness. This is the position taken in the Restatement (Third) § 403. See also Schachter, International Law in Theory and Practice, 178 Rec. des Cours 240–42 (1982–V).

Thus far, international law, in defining the limits of jurisdiction, has concerned itself principally with defining the jurisdiction of states. However, as international entities with varying measures of international legal personality continue to develop, international law will increasingly have to concern itself with their jurisdiction. Indeed, the assertion by the European Economic Community of extra-territorial legislative jurisdiction in antitrust matters and of its own powers in certain maritime areas of the Community (see p. 1538 infra) make clear that international law will also play a significant role in defining the jurisdiction of international legal persons other than states.

## C. INTERNATIONAL LAW CRITERIA FOR DETERMINING JURISDICTION

### 1. *Basic Principles*

Under international law, the jurisdiction of a state depends on the interest that state, in view of its nature and purposes, may reasonably have in exercising the particular jurisdiction asserted and on the need to reconcile that interest with the interests of other states in exercising jurisdiction. The nature and significance of the interests of a state in exercising jurisdiction depend on the relation of the transaction, occurrence, or event, and of the person to be affected, to the state's proper concerns.

Whatever happens on the territory of a state is of that state's primary concern (the territorial principle). A state also has a significant interest in exercising jurisdiction over persons or things that possess its nationality (the nationality principle) and in protecting its nationals (the passive nationality principle). In addition, a state has an evident interest in protecting itself against acts, even if performed outside of its territory and by persons that owe it no allegiance, that threaten its existence or its proper functioning as a state (the protective principle). And, finally, certain activities are so universally condemned that any state has an interest in exercising jurisdiction to combat them (the universal principle).

## *RESTATEMENT (THIRD)*

### § 402. Bases of Jurisdiction to Prescribe

Subject to § 403, a state has jurisdiction to prescribe law with respect to

(1)(a) conduct that, wholly or in substantial part, takes place within its territory;

(b) the status of persons, or interests in things, present within its territory;

(c) conduct outside its territory that has or is intended to have substantial effect within its territory;

(2) the activities, interests, status, or relations of its nationals outside as well as within its territory; and

(3) certain conduct outside its territory by persons not its nationals that is directed against the security of the state or against a limited class of other state interests.

### § 404. Universal Jurisdiction to Define and Punish Certain Offenses

A state has jurisdiction to define and prescribe punishment for certain offenses recognized by the community of nations as of universal concern, such as piracy, slave trade, attacks on or hijacking of aircraft, genocide, war crimes, and perhaps certain acts of terrorism, even where none of the bases of jurisdiction indicated in § 402 is present.

### *Notes*

1. The Restatement (Third) provides in § 403 for an overall limitation on the exercise of jurisdiction. This limitation, it is stated in Comment *a,* "has emerged as a principle of international law." To what extent is this statement borne out by the materials that follow? Is the imposition of this requirement likely to alleviate the problems that arise in cases of conflicts of jurisdiction? See Section 6 of this Chapter. Or would it be more appropriate to provide that national institutions should read this limitation into national law whenever possible?

2. Section 403 of the Restatement (Third) does not impose the limitation of reasonableness upon the exercise of jurisdiction on the basis of the universal principle. Is there no room for such a limitation when jurisdiction is exercised on that basis?

3. According to § 402(c), a state has jurisdiction to prescribe law with respect to "conduct outside its territory that * * * is intended to have substantial effect within its territory." Is, as this section states, mere intent sufficient? See Section 2(A)(2) of this Chapter. See also Restatement (Third) §§ 415–16, which, in antitrust and securities laws cases, require actual effect within the state's territory.

## *RESTATEMENT (THIRD)*

### § 403. Limitations on Jurisdiction to Prescribe

(1) Even when one of the bases for jurisdiction under § 402 is present, a state may not exercise jurisdiction to prescribe law with respect to a person or activity having connections with another state when the exercise of such jurisdiction is unreasonable.

(2) Whether exercise of jurisdiction over a person or activity is unreasonable is determined by evaluating all relevant factors, including, where appropriate:

(a) the link of the activity to the territory of the regulating state, *i.e.*, the extent to which the activity takes place within the territory, or has substantial, direct, and foreseeable effect upon or in the territory;

(b) the connections, such as nationality, residence, or economic activity, between the regulating state and the person principally responsible for the activity to be regulated, or between that state and those whom the regulation is designed to protect;

(c) the character of the activity to be regulated, the importance of regulation to the regulating state, the extent to which other states regulate such activities, and the degree to which the desirability of such regulation is generally accepted;

(d) the existence of justified expectations that might be protected or hurt by the regulation;

(e) the importance of the regulation to the international political, legal, or economic system;

(f) the extent to which the regulation is consistent with the traditions of the international system;

(g) the extent to which another state may have an interest in regulating the activity; and

(h) the likelihood of conflict with regulation by another state.

(3) When it would not be unreasonable for each of two states to exercise jurisdiction over a person or activity, but the prescriptions by the two states are in conflict, each state has an obligation to evaluate its own as well as the other state's interest in exercising jurisdiction, in light of all the relevant

factors; including those set out in Subsection (2); a state should defer to the other state if that state's interest is clearly greater.

Since each state is part of the world community, rules defining its jurisdiction must take due account of the needs of that community and, specifically, of the need not to encroach unnecessarily on the interests of other members. This has been a significant consideration in delimiting in different fashion the extraterritorial reach of the various kinds of jurisdiction.

The extent to which recognized bases of jurisdiction provide the premises for the exercise of the various forms of jurisdiction will be considered in the sections that follow.

# SECTION 2. JURISDICTION TO PRESCRIBE BASED ON THE TERRITORIAL PRINCIPLE

## A. SCOPE

A state's territorial authority extends both horizontally and vertically. Traditionally, a state has exercised authority over its land territory for virtually all purposes. However, the measure of a state's authority over its maritime areas is more limited and decreases as the maritime areas become more distant from the state's shores. Similarly, although a state exercises its jurisdiction above as well as below the surface of its territory and maritime areas, the measure of its control decreases as the distance from the surface becomes greater. On the extent of land territory and authority below and above the surface, see Chapter 4. On the extent of maritime areas and related airspace, see Chapter 14.

Subject to the limitation that a state may exercise jurisdiction only in pursuit of purposes that are its proper concern, the territorial principle provides the premise for the exercise of jurisdiction not only with respect to transactions, persons, or things within the territory, but also with respect to certain consequences produced within the territory by persons acting outside it.

### *1. With Respect to Persons and Things Within the Territory*

It is well settled that a state may exercise jurisdiction with respect to all persons or things within its territory. See, e.g., Marshall, C.J., in The Schooner Exchange v. McFaddon, 11 U.S. (7 Cranch) 116, 136, 3 L.Ed. 287 (1812), p. 1129 infra:

> The jurisdiction of the nation within its own territory is necessarily exclusive and absolute. It is susceptible of no limitation not imposed by itself. Any restriction upon it, deriving validity from an external source, would imply a diminution of its sovereignty to the extent of the restriction, and an investment of that sovereignty to the same extent in that power which could impose such restriction. All exceptions, therefore, to the full and complete power of a nation within its own territories, must be traced up to the consent of the nation itself.

### 2. *With Respect to Persons and Things Without the Territory—Objective Territorial Principle*

## UNITED STATES v. ALUMINUM CO. OF AMERICA

Court of Appeals of the United States, Second Circuit, 1945.
148 F.2d 416.

Before L. HAND, SWAN and A. HAND, CIRCUIT JUDGES.

[The complaint alleged that defendants Alcoa and Aluminum, Limited (a Canadian corporation formed to take over the properties of Alcoa outside the United States) had illegally conspired in restraint of domestic and foreign commerce with respect to the manufacture and sale of aluminum ingot. The Government's appeal from dismissal of its complaint, 44 F.Supp. 97 (S.D.N.Y. 1941), was referred to the Court of Appeals, because a quorum of six qualified Justices of the Supreme Court was wanting. One of the central issues in the case was whether the participation of Aluminum, Limited, in an "alliance" with a number of foreign producers constituted a violation of § 1 of the Sherman Act (15 U.S.C.A. § 1), which provides in relevant part that "every contract, combination * * * or conspiracy, in restraint of trade or commerce among the several States, or with foreign nations, is declared to be illegal." In the course of holding that "Limited" violated the Act, the court (per L. Hand, C.J.) stated:]

Whether "Limited" itself violated that section depends upon the character of the "Alliance." It was a Swiss corporation, created in pursuance of an agreement entered into on July 3, 1931, the signatories to which were a French corporation, two German, one Swiss, a British, and "Limited." The original agreement, or "cartel," provided for the formation of a corporation in Switzerland which should issue shares, to be taken up by the signatories. This corporation was from time to time to fix a quota of production for each share, and each shareholder was to be limited to the quantity measured by the number of shares it held, but was free to sell at any price it chose. The corporation fixed a price every year at which it would take off any shareholder's hands any part of its quota which it did not sell. No shareholder was to "buy, borrow, fabricate or sell" aluminum produced by anyone not a shareholder except with the consent of the board of governors, but that must not be "unreasonably withheld." * * * However, * * * until 1936, when the new arrangement was made, imports into the United States were not included in the quotas. * * *

The agreement of 1936 abandoned the system of unconditional quotas, and substituted a system of royalties. Each shareholder was to have a fixed free quota for every share it held, but as its production exceeded the sum of its quotas, it was to pay a royalty, graduated progressively in proportion to the excess; and these royalties the "Alliance" divided among the shareholders in proportion to their shares. * * * Although this agreement, like its predecessor, was silent as to imports into the United States, when that question arose during its preparation, as it did, all the shareholders agreed that such imports should be included in the quotas. * * *

Did either the agreement of 1931 or that of 1936 violate § 1 of the Act? The answer does not depend upon whether we shall recognize as a source of liability a liability imposed by another state. On the contrary we are concerned only with whether Congress chose to attach liability to the conduct outside the United States of persons not in allegiance to it. That being so, the only question open is whether Congress intended to impose the liability, and whether our own Constitution permitted it to do so: as a court of the United States, we cannot look beyond our own law. Nevertheless, it is quite true that we are not to read general words, such as those in this Act, without regard to the limitations customarily observed by nations upon the exercise of their powers * * *. We should not impute to Congress an intent to punish all whom its courts can catch, for conduct which has no consequences within the United States. * * * On the other hand, it is settled law—as "Limited" itself agrees—that any state may impose liabilities, even upon persons not within its allegiance, for conduct outside its borders that has consequences within its borders which the state reprehends; and these liabilities other states will ordinarily recognize. * * * Restatement of Conflict of Laws § 65. It may be argued that this Act extends further. Two situations are possible. There may be agreements made beyond our borders not intended to affect imports, which do affect them, or which affect exports. Almost any limitation of the supply of goods in Europe, for example, or in South America, may have repercussions in the United States if there is trade between the two. Yet when one considers the international complications likely to arise from an effort in this country to treat such agreements as unlawful, it is safe to assume that Congress certainly did not intend the Act to cover them. Such agreements may on the other hand intend to include imports into the United States, and yet it may appear that they have had no effect upon them. That situation might be thought to fall within the doctrine that intent may be a substitute for performance in the case of a contract made within the United States; or it might be thought to fall within the doctrine that a statute should not be interpreted to cover acts abroad which have no consequence here. We shall not choose between these alternatives; but for argument we shall assume that the Act does not cover agreements, even though intended to affect imports or exports, unless its performance is shown actually to have had some effect upon them. Where both conditions are satisfied, the situation certainly falls within such decisions as United States v. Pacific & Arctic R. & Navigation Co., 228 U.S. 87, 33 S.Ct. 443, 57 L.Ed. 742; Thomsen v. Cayser, 243 U.S. 66, 37 S.Ct. 353, 61 L.Ed. 597, Ann.Cas.1917D, 322 and United States v. Sisal Sales Corporation, 274 U.S. 268, 47 S.Ct. 592, 71 L.Ed. 1042. * * * It is true that in those cases the persons held liable had sent agents into the United States to perform part of the agreement; but an agent is merely an animate means of executing his principal's purposes, and, for the purposes of this case, he does not differ from an inanimate means; besides, only human agents can import and sell ingot.

Both agreements would clearly have been unlawful, had they been made within the United States; and it follows from what we have just said that both were unlawful, though made abroad, if they were intended to affect imports and did affect them.

[The Court went on to find that the 1936 agreement intended to set up a quota system for imports and that, absent a showing by "Limited" that imports were not in fact affected, the agreement violated § 1 of the Act.]

### Notes

1. The territorial principle has not only been universally accepted by States, but it has had a significant development in modern times. This development has been a necessary consequence of the increasing complexity of the "act or omission" which constitutes crime under modern penal legislation. The "act or omission" need not consist of an isolated action or failure to act. Not infrequently it appears as an event consisting of a series of separate acts or omissions. These separate acts or omissions need not be simultaneous with respect to time or restricted to a single State with respect to place. Indeed, with the increasing facility of communication and transportation, the opportunities for committing crimes whose constituent elements take place in more than one State have grown apace. To meet these conditions, the jurisdiction of crime founded upon the territorial principle has been expanded in several ways.

> In the first place, national legislation and jurisprudence have developed the so-called subjective territorial principle which establishes the jurisdiction of the State to prosecute and punish for crime commenced within the State but completed or consummated abroad. * * *
>
> In the second place, national legislation and jurisprudence have developed the so-called objective territorial principle which establishes the jurisdiction of the State to prosecute and punish for crime commenced without the State but consummated within its territory. * * *

Harvard Research in International Law, Jurisdiction with Respect to Crime, 29 A.J.I.L.Supp. 435, 484, 487–88 (1935).

2. * * * [The objective territorial principle] is often said to apply where the offence "takes effect" or "produces its effects" in the territory. In relation to elementary cases of direct physical injury, such as homicide, this is unexceptionable, for here the "effect" which is meant is an essential ingredient of the crime. Once we move out of the sphere of direct physical consequences, however, to employ the formula of "effects" is to enter upon a very slippery slope; for here the effects within the territory may be no more than an element of alleged consequential damage which may be more or less remote. * * * [T]o extend the notion of effects, without qualification, from the simple cases of direct physical injury to cases such as defamation, sedition, and the like, is to introduce a dangerous ambiguity into the basis of the doctrine. If indeed it were permissible to found objective territorial jurisdiction upon the territoriality of more or less remote repercussions of an act wholly performed in another territory, then there were virtually no limit to a State's territorial jurisdiction.

Jennings, Extraterritorial Jurisdiction and the United States Antitrust Laws 33 Brit.Y.B.I.L. 146, 159 (1957).*

3. The approach of the *Alcoa* case has been extended quite far. In Continental Ore Co. v. Union Carbide & Carbon Corp., 370 U.S. 690, 82 S.Ct. 1404, 8 L.Ed.2d 777 (1962), the plaintiff contended that a Canadian company, that had been appointed by the Canadian government as the exclusive wartime agent to purchase and allocate vanadium for Canadian industries, had violated the American anti-trust laws by not purchasing vanadium from the plaintiff in Canada. The Supreme Court upheld the lower court's ruling that the Sherman Act extended its extraterritorial reach to this conduct and that the act of state doctrine was inapplicable since the incriminated conduct had not been required

by the Canadian authorities. To the same effect, see United States v. The Watchmakers of Switzerland Information Center, Inc., 133 F.Supp. 40 (S.D.N.Y. 1955).

4. "Nearly all European writers have been critical of the United States' notion of extra-territorial application of a State's laws to aliens. The European Advisory Committee on the Restatement * * * criticized the Restatement rule of extra-territorial jurisdiction, stating:

> In our view, the exercise of jurisdiction based on territory is not justified in cases where all that has occurred within the territory is the effects of certain conduct and not at least part of the conduct itself."

Riedweg, The Extra–Territorial Application of Restrictive Trade Legislation—Jurisdiction and International Law, International Law Association, Report of the Fifty-first Conference 357, 372–73 (1964).

5. The Court of Justice of the European Communities has thus far attempted to avoid deciding whether the antitrust provisions of the EEC Treaty have extraterritorial effect. It has done this by attributing the conduct of a subsidiary within the EEC to its parent outside and by thus finding conduct of the parent within the Community. The actual effect of this construction has, however, been to apply the EEC provisions extraterritorially in order to reach, among others, American enterprises outside of the EEC. See generally 2 Smit & Herzog, The Law of the European Economic Community § 85.19.

6. Does the United States have jurisdiction to legislate in regard to Noriega's participation in Panama in international drug trafficking that resulted in 2,141 pounds of cocaine being illegally brought into the United States? For an affirmative answer, see United States v. Noriega, 746 F.Supp. 1506 (S.D.Fla. 1990). Did the United States properly seize Noriega in Panama? See United States v. Alvarez–Machain, p. 1116 infra.

7. For the argument that the extraterritorial reach given by U.S. courts to U.S. laws varies with the subject regulated, see Turley, "When in Rome": Multinational Misconduct and the Presumption Against Extraterritoriality, 84 NW.U.L.Rev. 598 (1990). See also Degnan & Kane, The Exercise of Jurisdiction Over and Enforcement of Judgements Against Alien Defendants, 39 Hastings L.J. 799 (1988).

8. Two growing areas of transnational litigation which bring up complex questions of jurisdiction are securities fraud and Civil RICO. For an argument in favor of expanding extraterritorial jurisdiction in RICO cases, see Goldsmith and Rinne, Civil RICO, Foreign Defendants, and "ET", 73 Minn.L.Rev. 1023 (1989). On transnational securities fraud, see Note, Subject Matter Jurisdiction over Transnational Securities Fraud: A Suggested Roadmap to the New Standard of Reasonableness, 71 Cornell L.Rev. 919 (1986).

## *RESTATEMENT (THIRD)*

### § 415. Jurisdiction to Regulate Anti–Competitive Activities

(1) Any agreement in restraint of United States trade made in the United States, and any conduct or agreement in restraint of such trade that is carried out in significant measure in the United States, are subject to the jurisdiction to prescribe of the United States, regardless of the nationality or

place of business of the parties to the agreement or of the participants in the conduct.

(2) Any agreement in restraint of United States trade that is made outside of the United States, and any conduct or agreement in restraint of such trade that is carried out predominantly outside of the United States, are subject to the jurisdiction to prescribe of the United States, if a principal purpose of the conduct or agreement is to interfere with the commerce of the United States, and the agreement or conduct has some effect on that commerce.

(3) Other agreements or conduct in restraint of United States trade are subject to the jurisdiction to prescribe of the United States if such agreements or conduct have substantial effect on the commerce of the United States and the exercise of jurisdiction is not unreasonable.

### *Notes*

1. This section is part of a subchapter entitled "Principles of Jurisdiction Applied". Other sections in this subchapter deal with jurisdiction in tax, antitrust, and securities matters. See §§ 411–16.

2. Does the quoted provision reflect current law? Note that § 415 requires effect on United States commerce.

3. For applications of a "jurisdictional rule of reason," see Timberlane Lumber Co. v. Bank of America National Trust & Saving Ass'n, 549 F.2d 597 (9th Cir.1976). In (this and other) cases, the courts, applying the jurisdictional rule of reason, found it reasonable for the U.S. antitrust laws to reach conduct abroad. Do these cases support imposition of a requirement of reasonableness as a matter of international law? The difficulty of interest balancing by national courts has been duly noted. See Laker Airways v. Sabena et al., 731 F.2d 909, 951–52 (D.C.Cir.1984):

> When one State exercises its jurisdiction and another in protection of its interests attempts to quash the first exercise of jurisdiction, it is simply impossible to judicially balance these totally contradictory and mutually negating actions.

See also British Airways Board v. Laker Airways (House of Lords, 1984), 23 I.L.M. 727 (1984); Schachter, International Law in Theory and Practice, 178 Rec. des Cours 253 (1982–V). On conflicts of jurisdiction, see Section 6 of this Chapter.

## *MODEL PENAL CODE*

10 U.L.A. 433 (1974).

### § 1.03. Territorial Applicability

(1) Except as otherwise provided in this Section, a person may be convicted under the law of this State of an offense committed by his own conduct or the conduct of another for which he is legally accountable if:

(a) either the conduct which is an element of the offense or the result which is such an element occurs within this State; or

(b) conduct occurring outside the State is sufficient under the law of this State to constitute an attempt to commit an offense within the State; or

(c) conduct occurring outside the State is sufficient under the law of this State to constitute a conspiracy to commit an offense within the State and an overt act in furtherance of such conspiracy occurs within the State; or

(d) conduct occurring within the State establishes complicity in the commission of, or an attempt, solicitation or conspiracy to commit, an offense in another jurisdiction which also is an offense under the law of this State; or

(e) the offense consists of the omission to perform a legal duty imposed by the law of this State with respect to domicile, residence or a relationship to a person, thing or transaction in the State; or

(f) the offense is based on a statute of this State which expressly prohibits conduct outside the State, when the conduct bears a reasonable relation to a legitimate interest of this State and the actor knows or should know that his conduct is likely to affect that interest.

(2) Subsection (1)(a) does not apply when either causing a specified result or a purpose to cause or danger of causing such a result is an element of an offense and the result occurs or is designed or likely to occur only in another jurisdiction where the conduct charged would not constitute an offense, unless a legislative purpose plainly appears to declare the conduct criminal regardless of the place of the result.

(3) Subsection (1)(a) does not apply when causing a particular result is an element of an offense and the result is caused by conduct occurring outside the State which would not constitute an offense if the result had occurred there, unless the actor purposely or knowingly caused the result within the State.

(4) When the offense is homicide, either the death of the victim or the bodily impact causing death constitutes a "result," within the meaning of Subsection (1)(a) and if the body of a homicide victim is found within the State, it is presumed that such result occurred within the State.

(5) This State includes the land and water and the air space above such land and water with respect to which the State has legislative jurisdiction.

### *Note*

Are these provisions compatible with international law?

# SECTION 3. JURISDICTION BASED ON NATIONALITY

## A. JURISDICTION BASED ON NATIONALITY OVER NATURAL PERSONS

### BLACKMER v. UNITED STATES

Supreme Court of the United States, 1932.
284 U.S. 421, 52 S.Ct. 252, 76 L.Ed. 375.

HUGHES, C.J.: * The petitioner, Harry M. Blackmer, a citizen of the United States resident in Paris, France, was adjudged guilty of contempt of the Supreme Court of the District of Columbia for failure to respond to subpoenas served upon him in France and requiring him to appear as a witness on behalf of the United States at a criminal trial in that court. Two subpoenas were issued, for appearances at different times, and there was a separate proceeding with respect to each. The two cases were heard together, and a fine of $30,000 with costs was imposed in each case, to be satisfied out of the property of the petitioner which had been seized by order of the court. The decrees were affirmed by the Court of Appeals of the District [49 F.2d 523], and this Court granted writs of certiorari * * *.

The subpoenas were issued and served, and the proceedings to punish for contempt were taken, under the provisions of the Act of July 3, 1926, c. 762, 44 Stat. 835, U.S.C., tit. 28, §§ 711–718 (28 U.S.C.A. §§ 711–718). The statute provides that whenever the attendance at the trial of a criminal action of a witness abroad, who is "a citizen of the United States or domiciled therein," is desired by the Attorney General, or any assistant or district attorney acting under him, the judge of the court in which the action is pending may order a subpoena to issue, to be addressed to a consul of the United States and to be served by him personally upon the witness with a tender of traveling expenses. Sections 2, 3 of the act (28 U.S.C.A. §§ 712, 713). Upon proof of such service and of the failure of the witness to appear, the court may make an order requiring the witness to show cause why he should not be punished for contempt, and, upon the issue of such an order, the court may direct that property belonging to the witness and within the United States may be seized and held to satisfy any judgment which may be rendered against him in the proceeding. Sections 4, 5 (28 U.S.C.A. §§ 714, 715). Provision is made for personal service of the order upon the witness and also for its publication in a newspaper of general circulation in the district where the court is sitting. Section 6 (28 U.S.C.A. § 716). If, upon the hearing, the charge is sustained, the court may adjudge the witness guilty of contempt and impose upon him a fine not exceeding $100,000, to be satisfied by a sale of the property seized. Section 7 (28 U.S.C.A. § 717). This statute and the proceedings against the petitioner are assailed as being repugnant to the Constitution of the United States.

First. The principal objections to the statute are that it violates the due process clause of the Fifth Amendment. These contentions are: (1) That the "Congress has no power to authorize United States consuls to serve process except as permitted by treaty;" (2) that the act does not provide "a valid method of acquiring judicial jurisdiction to render personal judgment against defendant and judgment against his property;" (3) that the act "does not

* Some footnotes omitted.

require actual or any other notice to defendant of the offense or of the Government's claim against his property;" (4) that the provisions "for hearing and judgment in the entire absence of the accused and without his consent" are invalid; and (5) that the act is "arbitrary, capricious and unreasonable."

While it appears that the petitioner removed his residence to France in the year 1924, it is undisputed that he was, and continued to be, a citizen of the United States. He continued to owe allegiance to the United States. By virtue of the obligations of citizenship, the United States retained its authority over him, and he was bound by its laws made applicable to him in a foreign country. Thus, although resident abroad, the petitioner remained subject to the taxing power of the United States. Cook v. Tait, 265 U.S. 47, 54, 56, 44 S.Ct. 444, 68 L.Ed. 895. For disobedience to its laws through conduct abroad, he was subject to punishment in the courts of the United States. United States v. Bowman, 260 U.S. 94, 102, 43 S.Ct. 39, 67 L.Ed. 149. With respect to such an exercise of authority, there is no question of international law,[6] but solely of the purport of the municipal law which establishes the duties of the citizen in relation to his own government. While the legislation of the Congress, unless the contrary intent appears, is construed to apply only within the territorial jurisdiction of the United States, the question of its application, so far as citizens of the United States in foreign countries are concerned, is one of construction, not of legislative power. American Banana Co. v. United Fruit Co., 213 U.S. 347, 357, 29 S.Ct. 511, 53 L.Ed. 826, 16 Ann.Cas. 1047; United States v. Bowman, supra; Robertson v. Labor Board, 268 U.S. 619, 622, 45 S.Ct. 621, 69 L.Ed. 1119. Nor can it be doubted that the United States possesses the power inherent in sovereignty to require the return to this country of a citizen, resident elsewhere, whenever the public interest requires it, and to penalize him in case of refusal. Compare Bartue and the Duchess of Suffolk's Case, 2 Dyer's Rep. 176b, 73 Eng.Rep. 388; Knowles v. Luce, Moore 109, 72 Eng.Rep. 473. What in England was the prerogative of the sovereign in this respect pertains under our constitutional system to the national authority which may be exercised by the Congress by virtue of the legislative power to prescribe the duties of the citizens of the United States. It is also beyond controversy that one of the duties which the citizen owes to his government is to support the administration of justice by attending its courts and giving his testimony whenever he is properly summoned. * * * And the Congress may provide for the performance of this duty and prescribe penalties for disobedience.

In the present instance, the question concerns only the method of enforcing the obligation. The jurisdiction of the United States over its absent citizen, so far as the binding effect of its legislation is concerned, is a jurisdiction in personam, as he is personally bound to take notice of the laws that are applicable to him and to obey them. United States v. Bowman, supra. But for the exercise of judicial jurisdiction in personam, there must be due process, which requires appropriate notice of the judicial action and an opportunity to be heard. For this notice and opportunity the statute provides. The authority to require the absent citizen to return and testify necessarily implies the authority to give him notice of the requirement. As

6. "The law of Nations does not prevent a State from exercising jurisdiction over its subjects travelling or residing abroad, since they remain under its personal supremacy." Oppenheim, International Law (4th Ed.) vol. 1, § 145, p. 281; * * * Hyde, International Law, vol. 1, § 240, p. 424; Borchard, Diplomatic Protection of Citizens Abroad, § 13, pp. 21, 22.

his attendance is needed in court, it is appropriate that the Congress should authorize the court to direct the notice to be given, and that it should be in the customary form of a subpoena. Obviously, the requirement would be nugatory, if provision could not be made for its communication to the witness in the foreign country. The efficacy of an attempt to provide constructive service in this country would rest upon the presumption that the notice would be given in a manner calculated to reach the witness abroad. * * * The question of the validity of the provision for actual service of the subpoena in a foreign country is one that arises solely between the government of the United States and the citizen. The mere giving of such a notice to the citizen in the foreign country of the requirement of his government that he shall return is in no sense an invasion of any right of the foreign government and the citizen has no standing to invoke any such supposed right. While consular privileges in foreign countries are the appropriate subjects of treaties, it does not follow that every act of a consul, as, e.g., in communicating with citizens of his own country, must be predicated upon a specific provision of a treaty. The intercourse of friendly nations, permitting travel and residence of the citizens of each in the territory of the other, presupposes and facilitates such communications. In selecting the consul for the service of the subpoena, the Congress merely prescribed a method deemed to assure the desired result but in no sense essential. The consul was not directed to perform any function involving consular privileges or depending upon any treaty relating to them, but simply to act as any designated person might act for the government in conveying to the citizen the actual notice of the requirement of his attendance. The point raised by the petitioner with respect to the provision for the service of the subpoena abroad is without merit.

As the Congress could define the obligation, it could prescribe a penalty to enforce it. And, as the default lay in disobedience to an authorized direction of the court, it constituted a contempt of court, and the Congress could provide for procedure appropriate in contempt cases. * * *

Decrees affirmed.

MR. JUSTICE ROBERTS took no part in the consideration and decision of this case.

### *Notes*

1. In Skiriotes v. Florida, 313 U.S. 69, 61 S.Ct. 924, 85 L.Ed. 1193 (1941), the Supreme Court affirmed defendant's conviction for violation of a state statute making it criminal to use diving equipment in the taking of sponges off the coast of Florida. Defendant had been arrested in Florida, but argued that the state had no power to try him because he had used the proscribed equipment while six miles from shore. The Court avoided the question of the extent of Florida's territorial waters, and, assuming from the record that Skiriotes was a citizen of the United States and of Florida, concluded that Florida might regulate the conduct of its "citizens" upon the high seas with respect to matters in which it had a legitimate interest and when there was no conflict with acts of Congress. Id. at 77.

2. A number of statutory provisions, in addition to that applied to Blackmer, apply specifically to the conduct or income of United States nationals abroad. See, e.g., 18 U.S.C.A. § 2381 (proscribing treason by anyone "owing

allegiance to the United States" "within the United States or elsewhere"); 18 U.S.C.A. § 953 (punishing unauthorized attempts by "any citizen of the United States, wherever he may be," to influence a foreign government in its relations with the United States); Internal Revenue Code § 1 (imposing an income tax on "all citizens of the United States, wherever resident"); 50 U.S.C.A.App. § 453 (requiring "every male citizen of the United States," *inter alia,* to register for military service). In the United Kingdom, statutes provide for the punishment of not only treason, but also homicide, bigamy, perjury, and other crimes, when committed abroad by a British subject. 10 Halsbury's Laws of England 322–24 (Simonds ed. 1955). See also 2 O'Connell at 898–99; 2 Hackworth at 203–06. India has provided that its criminal law applies to Indian nationals everywhere, no matter how minor the offense. Indian Penal Code § 4 (3d ed. Raju 1965). Non-common law states also claim comprehensive jurisdiction over crimes committed by nationals abroad. In France, for example, a citizen can be prosecuted in France for any *crime* (roughly equivalent to a felony) and many *délits* (misdemeanors) committed abroad. Code de Procédure Pénale, Art. 689 (Dalloz 1966); see Delaume, Jurisdiction over Crimes Committed Abroad: French and American Law, 21 Geo.Wash.L.Rev. 173 (1952); 1 Travers, Le Droit Pénal International 584–631 (1920). See also German Penal Code (Strafgesetzbuch) § 3 (German criminal law applicable to Germans whether act committed in Germany or abroad), § 4 (German criminal law applicable to persons acquiring German citizenship after criminal act has been committed).

3. Under what circumstances will a United States statute be held to apply to conduct by United States nationals taking place outside United States territory, when the statute does not expressly so provide? In United States v. Bowman, 260 U.S. 94, 43 S.Ct. 39, 67 L.Ed. 149 (1922), the Supreme Court held that a statute punishing conspiracy to defraud a United States-owned corporation was applicable to conduct taking place on the high seas. The court stated that to limit the statute's scope to "the strictly territorial jurisdiction" would be greatly to curtail its usefulness and to leave open "a large immunity for frauds as easily committed by citizens on the high seas and in foreign countries as at home." In such cases, the Court continued, Congress had not "thought it necessary to make specific provision in the law that the *locus* shall include the high seas and foreign countries, but allows it to be inferred from the nature of the offense." Id. at 98. The conviction of three United States nationals was accordingly affirmed on the ground that they were "certainly subject to such laws as [the United States] might pass to protect itself and its property." Id. at 102. Cf. Steele v. Bulova Watch Co., 344 U.S. 280, 73 S.Ct. 252, 97 L.Ed. 319 (1952); Ramirez & Feraud Chili Co. v. Las Palmas Food Co., 146 F.Supp. 594 (S.D.Cal. 1956), aff'd per curiam, 245 F.2d 874 (9th Cir.1957), cert. denied, 355 U.S. 927, 78 S.Ct. 384, 2 L.Ed.2d 357 (1958), construing the Lanham Act to reach infringement of trademarks by United States nationals in foreign countries but producing adverse economic effects in the United States. But cf. Vanity Fair Mills Inc. v. T. Eaton Co., 234 F.2d 633 (2d Cir.1956), cert. denied, 352 U.S. 871, 77 S.Ct. 96, 1 L.Ed.2d 76 (1956), reh. denied, 352 U.S. 913, 77 S.Ct. 144, 1 L.Ed.2d 120 (1956), holding that the Lanham Act did not provide a remedy for trademark infringement by a Canadian corporation in Canada, even though the infringement caused economic harm to plaintiff in the United States.

4. The statute involved in Blackmer v. United States, the principal case, is now codified as 28 U.S.C.A. § 1783, and is incorporated by reference into Fed.R.Civ.P. 45(e)(2) and Fed.R.Crim.P. 17(e)(2). It provides in relevant part that a United States court may order the issuance of a subpoena requiring the

appearance as a witness of a "national or resident of the United States who is in a foreign country" if such testimony is "necessary in the interest of justice." Would the Court in the principal case have reached the same result if Blackmer had been an alien, domiciled in the United States? Is it unreasonable for a state to assert legislative jurisdiction over its domiciliaries when they are abroad? Compare Milliken v. Meyer, 311 U.S. 457, 462, 61 S.Ct. 339, 342, 85 L.Ed. 278 (1940) ("Domicile in the state is alone sufficient to bring an absent defendant within the reach of the state's jurisdiction for purposes of a personal judgment by means of appropriate substituted service.") The word "resident" in 28 U.S.C.A. § 1783 was, in the 1948 revision of the Judicial Code, substituted for "or domiciled therein." Would an alien's residence or domicile in the United States provide a reasonable basis for the assertion of legislative jurisdiction with regard to an act committed outside the United States? See Smit, International Aspects of Federal Civil Procedure, 61 Colum.L.Rev. 1031, 1048–49 (1961).

5. Once it is established that a defendant is a national of a state, may that state exercise jurisdiction over him? Does your answer depend on whether an international or national concept of nationality is applied? Cf. Grubel v. Nassauer, 210 N.Y. 149, 103 N.E. 1113 (1913) (denying recognition to an Austrian judgment rendered against an Austrian who had emigrated to the United States before the Austrian proceedings had been commenced). Would domicile be a more appropriate basis for jurisdiction? Cf. Friedmann, The Changing Structure of International Law 235–36 (1984). Should a distinction be drawn depending on whether civil or criminal jurisdiction is exercised?

6. It has been held that a state has jurisdiction to try and punish one of its nationals for an offense committed abroad even though he is also a national of the state in which the offense was committed. Coumas v. Superior Court, 31 Cal.2d 682, 192 P.2d 449 (1948); Tomoya Kawakita v. United States, 343 U.S. 717, 72 S.Ct. 950, 96 L.Ed. 1249 (1952).

## B. JURISDICTION BASED ON NATIONALITY OVER LEGAL PERSONS

## *RESTATEMENT (THIRD)*

### § 414. Jurisdiction with Respect to Activities of Foreign Branches and Subsidiaries

(1) Subject to §§ 403 and 441, a state may exercise jurisdiction to prescribe for limited purposes with respect to activities of foreign branches of corporations organized under its laws.

(2) A state may not ordinarily regulate activities of corporations organized under the laws of a foreign state on the basis that they are owned or controlled by nationals of the regulating state. However, under §§ 403 and subject to § 441, it may not be unreasonable for a state to exercise jurisdiction for limited purposes with respect to activities of affiliated foreign entities.

(a) by direction to the parent corporation in respect of such matters as uniform accounting, disclosure to investors, or preparation of consolidated tax returns of multinational enterprises; or

(b) by direction to either the parent or the subsidiary in exceptional cases, depending on all relevant factors, including the extent to which

(i) the regulation is essential to implementation of a program to further a major national interest of the state exercising jurisdiction;

(ii) the national program of which the regulation is a part can be carried out effectively only if it is applied also to foreign subsidiaries;

(iii) the regulation conflicts or is likely to conflict with the law or policy of the state where the subsidiary is established.

(c) In the exceptional cases referred to in paragraph (b), the burden of establishing reasonableness is heavier when the direction is issued to the foreign subsidiary than when it is issued to the parent corporation.

### *Notes*

1. The traditional rule is that a state has jurisdiction over legal persons organized under its laws. Many states, in addition, assert jurisdiction over legal persons whose principal place of business or registered office (*siège social*) is located in their territories, without encountering objections assertedly based on international law. States have further sought to regulate activities by legal persons organized or having their principal places of business abroad when these persons are owned or controlled by nationals. All three of these criteria can be found in United States law. See Restatement (Third) § 414, Reporters' Note 4. It is particularly the jurisdiction exercised over foreign legal persons owned or controlled by nationals that has led to objections by foreign states. See, e.g., the Siberian pipeline dispute, involving export prohibitions imposed by the United States pursuant to the Export Administration Act of 1979, 50 U.S.C.A. app. 2404, upon "any person subject to the jurisdiction of the United States." The regulations issued to effectuate these prohibitions purported to extend their effect to foreign persons, not owned or controlled by United States persons, who had agreed, in licensing contracts concluded with United States persons, to abide by export prohibitions that might be promulgated by the United States. See, e.g., Export of Oil and Gas Equipment to the Soviet Union, Statement on Extension of U.S. Sanctions, 18 Weekly Comp.Pres.Doc. 820 (June 18, 1982). The European Economic Community and several of its member states protested and ordered persons in their territories to perform their contracts and deliver the pipeline materials to their Russian purchasers. See Legal Serv. E.C.Com., European Communities: Comments on the U.S. Regulations Concerning Trade with the U.S.S.R., reprinted in 21 I.L.M. 891 (1982); N.Y. Times, Aug. 24, 1982, at D1, col. 3; N.Y. Times, July 23, 1982, at A1, col. 6 (government of France compelling all French companies to honor pipeline-related contracts with the Soviet Union); United Kingdom: Statement and Order Concerning the American Export Embargo with Regard to the Soviet Gas Pipeline (Aug. 2, 1982), reprinted in 21 I.L.M. 851 (1982) (British government order to four British companies with the largest pipeline contracts not to comply with the U.S. embargo). Were the European objections based on solid international law grounds? What if the "person subject to the jurisdiction of the United States" owns, but does not control, the foreign person? For a statement of the U.S. position, see Dam, Extraterritoriality and Conflicts of Jurisdiction, 1983 A.S.I.L.Proc. 370 (1983).

2. Other areas in which the United States has endeavored to extend the extraterritorial reach of its legislation include shipping, tax, export control, anti-boycott legislation, foreign corrupt practices, and securities law.

In McCullouch v. Sociedad Nacional de Marineros de Honduras, 372 U.S. 10, 83 S.Ct. 671, 9 L.Ed.2d 547 (1963), the Supreme Court refused to apply the National Labor Relations Act to maritime operations of foreign flag vessels employing alien seamen, even though the foreign corporations owning the vessels were wholly owned by American corporations and the vessels were operating in a regular course of trade between foreign and United States ports. The Court referred specifically to complications in international relations that might ensue from the application of the Act to such operations.

Compare United States v. Mitchell, 553 F.2d 996 (5th Cir.1977) (Marine Mammal Protection Act of 1972 held to protect animals only within U.S. territory and therefore inapplicable to U.S. citizens committing violations abroad) with United States v. King, 552 F.2d 833 (9th Cir.1976) (conspiracy by U.S. citizens to distribute narcotics in Japan held a violation of 21 U.S.C.A. § 959 because defendants' intent was to import drugs into the U.S.).

On the extraterritorial reach of United States tax laws, see Restatement (Third) §§ 411–13. On the controversial "unitary tax" imposed by many States, see Container Corp. of America v. Franchise Tax Board, 463 U.S. 159, 103 S.Ct. 2933, 77 L.Ed.2d 545 (1983) (upholding the California unitary tax on a Delaware corporation, headquartered in Illinois); Restatement (Third) § 412, Reporters' Note 7.

On the other subjects mentioned, see Restatement (Third) § 414, Reporters' Notes 3–8. On the conflicts with foreign sovereigns that have arisen as a consequence, see Section 6 infra.

3. The federal act prohibiting discrimination in employment was held to lack extraterritorial scope in an action complaining of discrimination in employment by a United States corporation in Saudi Arabia. Boureslan v. Aramco, 857 F.2d 1014 (5th Cir.1988), reh'g granted 863 F.2d 8 (5th Cir.1988), aff'd 892 F.2d 1271, aff'd 499 U.S. ___, 111 S.Ct. 1227, 113 L.Ed.2d 274 (1991). To the same effect Pfeiffer v. Wm. Wrigley Jr. Co., 755 F.2d 554 (7th Cir.1985) (age discrimination in employment); Independent Union of Flight Attendants v. Pan American World Airways, Inc., 923 F.2d 678 (9th Cir.), opinion withdrawn on rehearing, 966 F.2d 457 (9th Cir.1992) (Railway Labor Act does not apply extraterritorially).

4. May a state assert on the international level the rights of a corporation that neither is organized under its law nor has a principal office within its territory on the ground that the corporation is owned or controlled by shareholders who are nationals of the state? On this question, see the Barcelona Traction Case, 1970 I.C.J. 3, discussed in Chapter 9.

## C. JURISDICTION BASED ON THE NATIONALITY OF THE VICTIM

### UNITED STATES v. FAWAZ YUNIS

United States Court of Appeals, District of Columbia Circuit, 1991.
288 U.S.App.D.C. 129, 924 F.2d 1086.

Opinion for the Court filed by CHIEF JUDGE MIKVA.

MIKVA, CHIEF JUDGE: Appellant Fawaz Yunis challenges his convictions on conspiracy, aircraft piracy, and hostage-taking charges stemming from the hijacking of a Jordanian passenger aircraft in Beirut, Lebanon. He appeals from orders of the district court denying his pretrial motions relating to jurisdiction, illegal arrest, alleged violations of the Posse Comitatus Act, and the government's withholding of classified documents during discovery. Yunis also challenges the district court's jury instructions as erroneous and prejudicial.

Although this appeal raises novel issues of domestic and international law, we reject Yunis' objections and affirm the convictions.

## I. Background

On June 11, 1985, appellant and four other men boarded Royal Jordanian Airlines Flight 402 ("Flight 402") shortly before its scheduled departure from Beirut, Lebanon. They wore civilian clothes and carried military assault rifles, ammunition bandoleers, and hand grenades. Appellant took control of the cockpit and forced the pilot to take off immediately. The remaining hijackers tied up Jordanian air marshals assigned to the flight and held the civilian passengers, including two American citizens, captive in their seats. The hijackers explained to the crew and passengers that they wanted the plane to fly to Tunis, where a conference of the Arab League was under way. The hijackers further explained that they wanted a meeting with delegates to the conference and that their ultimate goal was removal of all Palestinians from Lebanon.

After a refueling stop in Cyprus, the airplane headed for Tunis but turned away when authorities blocked the airport runway. Following a refueling stop at Palermo, Sicily, another attempt to land in Tunis, and a second stop in Cyprus, the plane returned to Beirut, where more hijackers came aboard. These reinforcements included an official of Lebanon's Amal Militia, the group at whose direction Yunis claims he acted. The plane then took off for Syria, but was turned away and went back to Beirut. There, the hijackers released the passengers, held a press conference reiterating their demand that Palestinians leave Lebanon, blew up the plane, and fled from the airport.

An American investigation identified Yunis as the probable leader of the hijackers and prompted U.S. civilian and military agencies, led by the Federal Bureau of Investigation (FBI), to plan Yunis' arrest. After obtaining an arrest warrant, the FBI put "Operation Goldenrod" into effect in September 1987. Undercover FBI agents lured Yunis onto a yacht in the eastern Mediterranean Sea with promises of a drug deal, and arrested him once the vessel entered international waters. The agents transferred Yunis to a United States Navy munitions ship and interrogated him for several days as the vessel steamed toward a second rendezvous, this time with a Navy aircraft carrier. Yunis was flown to Andrews Air Force Base from the aircraft carrier, and taken from there to Washington, D.C. In Washington, Yunis was arraigned on an original indictment charging him with conspiracy, hostage taking, and aircraft damage. A grand jury subsequently returned a superseding indictment adding additional aircraft damage counts and a charge of air piracy.

Yunis filed several pretrial motions, among them a motion to suppress statements he made while aboard the munitions ship. In *United States v. Yunis (Yunis I)*, 859 F.2d 953 (D.C.Cir.1988), this court reversed a district court order suppressing the statements, and authorized their introduction at trial. We revisited the case on a second interlocutory appeal relating to discovery of classified information, reversing the district court's disclosure order. *United States v. Yunis (Yunis II),* 867 F.2d 617 (D.C.Cir.1989).

Yunis admitted participation in the hijacking at trial but denied parts of the government's account and offered the affirmative defense of obedience to military orders, asserting that he acted on instructions given by his superiors in Lebanon's Amal Militia. The jury convicted Yunis of conspiracy, 18 U.S.C. § 371 (1988), hostage taking, 18 U.S.C. § 1203 (1988), and air piracy, 49 U.S.C.app. § 1472(n) (1988). However, it acquitted him of three other charged offenses that went to trial: violence against people on board an aircraft, 18 U.S.C. § 32(b)(1) (1988), aircraft damage, 18 U.S.C. § 32(b)(2) (1988), and placing a destructive device aboard an aircraft, 18 U.S.C. § 32(b)(3) (1988). The district court imposed concurrent sentences of five years for conspiracy, thirty years for hostage taking, and twenty years for air piracy. Yunis appeals his conviction and seeks dismissal of the indictment.

## II. Analysis

Yunis argues that the district court lacked subject matter and personal jurisdiction to try him on the charges of which he was convicted, that the indictment should have been dismissed because the government seized him in violation of the Posse Comitatus Act and withheld classified materials useful to his defense, and that the convictions should be reversed because of errors in the jury instructions. We consider these claims in turn.

### *A. Jurisdictional Claims*

[The Court's discussion of the Hostage Taking Act has been omitted.]

* * *

Nor is jurisdiction precluded by norms of customary international law. The district court concluded that two jurisdictional theories of international law, the "universal principle" and the "passive personal principle," supported assertion of U.S. jurisdiction to prosecute Yunis on hijacking and hostage-taking charges. *See Yunis,* 681 F.Supp. at 899–903. Under the universal principle, states may prescribe and prosecute "certain offenses recognized by the community of nations as of universal concern, such as piracy, slave trade, attacks on or hijacking of aircraft, genocide, war crimes, and perhaps certain acts of terrorism," even absent any special connection between the state and the offense. *See* Restatement (Third) of the Foreign Relations Law of the United States §§ 404, 423 (1987) [hereinafter Restatement]. Under the passive personal principle, a state may punish non-nationals for crimes committed against its nationals outside of its territory, at least where the state has a particularly strong interest in the crime. *See id.* at § 402 comment g; *United States v. Benitez,* 741 F.2d 1312, 1316 (11th Cir.1984) (passive personal principle invoked to approve prosecution of Colombian citizen convicted of shooting U.S. drug agents in Colombia), *cert. denied,* 471 U.S. 1137 (1985).

Relying primarily on the Restatement, Yunis argues that hostage taking has not been recognized as a universal crime and that the passive personal principle authorizes assertion of jurisdiction over alleged hostage takers only where the victims were seized because they were nationals of the prosecuting state. Whatever merit appellant's claims may have as a matter of international law, they cannot prevail before this court. Yunis seeks to portray international law as a self-executing code that trumps domestic law whenever the two conflict. That effort misconceives the role of judges as appliers of international law and as participants in the federal system. Our duty is to enforce the Constitution, laws, and treaties of the United States, not to conform the law of the land to norms of customary international law. *See* U.S. CONST. art. VI. As we said in *Committee of U.S. Citizens Living in Nicaragua v. Reagan,* 859 F.2d 929 (D.C.Cir.1988): "Statutes inconsistent with principles of customary international law may well lead to international law violations. But within the domestic legal realm, that inconsistent statute simply modifies or supersedes customary international law to the extent of the inconsistency." *Id.* at 938. *See also Federal Trade Comm'n v. Compagnie de Saint–Gobain–Pont–a–Mousson,* 636 F.2d 1300, 1323 (D.C.Cir. 1980) (U.S. courts "obligated to give effect to an unambiguous exercise by Congress of its jurisdiction to prescribe even if such an exercise would exceed the limitations imposed by international law").

To be sure, courts should hesitate to give penal statutes extraterritorial effect absent a clear congressional directive. *See Foley Bros. v. Filardo,* 336 U.S. 281, 285 (1949); *United States v. Bowman,* 260 U.S. 94, 98 (1922). Similarly, courts will not blind themselves to potential violations of international law where legislative intent is ambiguous. *See Murray v. The Schooner Charming Betsy,* 6 U.S. (2 Cranch) 64, 118 (1804) ("[A]n act of congress ought never to be construed to violate the law of nations, if any other possible construction remains * * *."). But the statute in question reflects an unmistakable congressional intent, consistent with treaty obligations of the United States, to authorize prosecution of those who take Americans hostage abroad no matter where the offense occurs or where the offender is found. Our inquiry can go no further.

* * *

### III. Conclusion

For the foregoing reasons, the convictions are

*Affirmed.*

2. A number of states have statutes asserting extraterritorial criminal legislative jurisdiction based on the victim's possessing their nationality. See the *Lotus Case,* p. 63 supra. It is disputed whether this is a permissible basis of jurisdiction, although no objections to its exercise have been made in recent years. See, e.g., Restatement (Third) § 402, Comment *g;* O'Connell, International Law 828–29 (2d ed. 1970) (tentatively accepting it); Brownlie, Principles of Public International Law 303 (4th ed. 1990) (calling it least justifiable of all bases); Mann, The Doctrine of Jurisdiction in International Law, 111 Rec. des Cours 39–41, 92–93 (1964–I) (noting that it has been severely criticized). However, on October 12, 1984, the United States amended 18 U.S.C.A. § 7 to provide, in paragraph 7, that the "special maritime and territorial jurisdiction of the United States, as used in this title, includes * * * [a]ny place outside the jurisdiction of any nation with respect to an offense by or against a national of the United States". See also Restatement (Third) § 402, Comment *g.*

## D. JURISDICTION BASED ON THE NATIONALITY OF VEHICLES AND OBJECTS

### *1. Maritime Vessels*

Vessels are usually considered to possess the nationality of the state whose flag they fly. But, as in the case of persons, international law requires that there be a "genuine link" between the state and the vessel. For a more detailed discussion, see Chapter 14.

### *2. Aircraft and Space Vehicles*

*CONVENTION ON INTERNATIONAL CIVIL AVIATION*

Signed at Chicago, December 7, 1944.
61 Stat. 1180, T.I.A.S. No. 1591, 15 U.N.T.S. 295.

Art. 17. Aircraft have the nationality of the State in which they are registered.

Art. 18. An aircraft cannot be validly registered in more than one State, but its registration may be changed from one State to another.

Art. 19. The registration or transfer of registration of aircraft in any contracting State shall be made in accordance with its laws and regulations.

*Notes*

1. As of January 1, 1992, this Convention was in force for 167 states, including the United States.

2. Whether Articles 17 and 19 of the Chicago Convention, and corresponding provisions of earlier agreements, merely codify rules that would be binding as customary international law in the absence of agreement is a question still under debate, particularly in the context of the "genuine link" requirement of the International Court of Justice in the *Nottebohm Case* (p. 397 supra), and of the Geneva Convention on the High Seas (Art. 5). Compare, e.g., McDougal *et al.* at 553–54, with Cheng, The Law of International Air Transport 130–31 (1962).

3. 49 U.S.C.A. § 140(f) provides that a certificate of aircraft registration with the United States shall be "conclusive evidence of nationality for international purposes."

4. The International Civil Aviation Organization (ICAO) Legal Committee has proposed amendments to the Chicago Convention that would transfer certain functions and duties from the state of registry to the state of the operator. These amendments were considered by the ICAO Assembly at its 1980 session. See ICAO L/C Working Draft No. 861, published with the 23d Session of the Legal Committee (1978) and ICAO Doc. 9238–LC/1802, 132–133. [As of January 1, 1992, these amendments to the Chicago Convention had not entered into force.] See also the related amendments to the Convention on Damage Caused by Foreign Aircraft to Third Parties on the Surface (signed in Rome on October 7, 1952, reproduced in 19 J. Air L. & Commerce 447 (1952) and embodied in a Protocol to the ICAO Conference in September 1978). This issue is discussed in Fitzgerald, The International Civil Aviation Organization and the Development of Conventions on International Air Law (1947–1978), 3 Annals Air & Space L. 51, 75 (1978).

6. Article 77 of the Chicago Convention provides that "[t]he [ICAO] Council shall determine in what manner the provisions of this Convention relating to nationality of aircraft shall apply to aircraft operated by international operating agencies." The ICAO Council made this determination in 1968. See ICAO Doc. 8722–C/976 (1968). Thus far, international organizations have chosen to operate their aircraft only on a national basis. Fitzgerald at 75.

## *TREATY ON PRINCIPLES GOVERNING THE ACTIVITIES OF STATES IN THE EXPLORATION AND USE OF OUTER SPACE, INCLUDING THE MOON AND OTHER CELESTIAL BODIES*

Done at London, Moscow, and Washington, January 27, 1967.
18 U.S.T. 2410, T.I.A.S. No. 6347, 610 U.N.T.S. 205.

Art. 8. A State Party to the Treaty on whose registry an object launched into outer space is carried shall retain jurisdiction and control over such object, and over any personnel thereof, while in outer space or on a celestial body. Ownership of objects launched into outer space, including objects landed or constructed on a celestial body, and of their component parts, is not affected by their presence in outer space or on a celestial body or by their return to the Earth. Such objects or component parts found beyond the limits of the State Party to the Treaty on whose registry they are carried shall be returned to that State Party, which shall, upon request, furnish identifying data prior to their return.

### *Notes*

1. As of January 1, 1992, this Convention was in force for 98 states, including the United States.

2. The Convention on Registration of Objects Launched into Outer Space, 1023 U.N.T.S. 15, 28 U.S.T. 695, T.I.A.S. No. 8480, provides for registration of such objects with the Secretary–General of the United Nations. The Convention entered into force for the United States on September 15, 1976. As of January 1, 1992, 44 states had become parties to the Convention.

3. For an interesting comment on choice of law in space, see Comment, "Oh I have slipped the surly bonds of earth: Multinational Space Stations and Choice of Law, 78 Calif.L.Rev. 1375 (1990).

## *CONVENTION ON INTERNATIONAL CIVIL AVIATION*

Signed at Chicago, December 7, 1944.
61 Stat. 1180, T.I.A.S. No. 1591, 15 U.N.T.S. 295.

Art. 1. The contracting States recognise that every State has complete and exclusive sovereignty over the airspace above its territory.

* * *

Art. 5. Each contracting State agrees that all aircraft of the other contracting States, being aircraft not engaged in scheduled international air services shall have the right, subject to the observance of the terms of this Convention, to make flights into or in transit nonstop across its territory and to make stops for non-traffic purposes without the necessity of obtaining prior permission, and subject to the right of the State flown over to require landing. Each contracting State nevertheless reserves the right, for reasons of safety of flight, to require aircraft desiring to proceed over regions which are inaccessible or without adequate air navigation facilities to follow prescribed routes, or to obtain special permission for such flights.

Such aircraft, if engaged in the carriage of passengers, cargo, or mail for remuneration or hire on other than scheduled international air services, shall also, subject to the provisions of Article 7, have the privilege of taking on or discharging passengers, cargo, or mail, subject to the right of any State where such embarkation or discharge takes place to impose such regulations, conditions or limitations as it may consider desirable.

Art. 6. No scheduled international air service may be operated over or into the territory of a contracting State, except with the special permission or other authorisation of that State, and in accordance with the terms of such permission or authorisation.

## *Notes*

1. The Convention goes on to provide a legal framework regulating flights of civil aircraft (excluding state aircraft, which include aircraft used in military, customs, and police services). Under Article 3 state aircraft are not permitted to fly over or land in the territory of a state without authorization by special agreement or otherwise.

2. Do aircraft enjoy a right of "innocent passage" through the air space of a foreign state in the absence of the latter's express agreement? (On the right of innocent passage of vessels through a foreign state's territorial waters, see p. 1254, infra.) The International Air Services Transit Agreement (59 Stat.1693, 84 U.N.T.S. 389, E.A.S. 487) grants limited transit and landing rights to scheduled aircraft. Would such aircraft have any rights in the air space of a state that was not a party to the IAST Agreement or to a special bilateral agreement? As a matter of practice, no state concedes or claims a right of innocent passage for aircraft in the air space of another state, absent international agreement. Statements made by delegates to the Geneva Conference on the Law of the Sea (1958) indicate a widespread conviction that aircraft enjoy no right of innocent passage, such comparable privileges as exist being solely the result of international agreement. See, e.g., 3 U.N.Conf. on the Law of the Sea, Off.Rec. 8, 104 (United Kingdom), 26 (United States), 90–91 (Canada) (1958); 1 id. at 336 (comments by International Civil Aviation Organization) (1958).

3. During the negotiations over the L.O.S.C., the right of denying innocent passage to aircraft was reasserted. See, e.g., 65 Dep't St.Bull. 261 (1971) (statement of Mr. Stevenson, the U.S. representative to the Conference on the Law of the Sea). The United States and many other nations maintained this position, while arguing at the same time for a "right of transit" through the airspace above the territorial sea of states bordering on straits or archipelagic waters. See McNees, Freedom of Transit Through International Straits, 6 J.Mar.L. 175 (1975).

4. Does a right of "entry in distress" exist for aircraft? Article 25 of the Convention on International Civil Aviation provides: "Each contracting State undertakes to provide such measures of assistance to aircraft in distress in its territory as it may find practicable * * *." Whether the foregoing provision

imposes any obligation with respect to state aircraft, or whether states not parties to the Chicago Convention are under any similar obligation with respect to aircraft of any type, are still open questions. The *ad hoc* committee of the General Assembly on the peaceful uses of outer space, however, "considered that certain substantive rules of international law already exist concerning rights and duties with respect to aircraft and airmen landing on foreign territory through accident, mistake or distress. The opinion was expressed that such rules might be applied in the event of similar landings of space vehicles." U.N.Doc. A/4141, p. 67 (1959). A problem related to that of landing rights is raised when an aircraft enters another state's air space either because of navigational error or because it is forced by bad weather to do so. In 1946, five United States airmen were killed when their unarmed transport was shot down over Yugoslavia. The United States claimed that the plane had been forced by bad weather to deviate from its course; Yugoslavia denied that there was bad weather in the vicinity of the incident and alleged that the aircraft had ignored landing signals. In paying an indemnity, "inspired by human feelings," to the United States on behalf of the families of the airmen, Yugoslavia reserved its position on the facts. See Lissitzyn, The Treatment of Aerial Intruders in Recent Practice and International Law, 47 A.J.I.L. 559, 569–73 (1953). Numerous subsequent disputes involving a number of Western and Soviet-bloc states were characterized by disagreement over factual issues such as the location of aircraft, the reason for their presence in foreign territory, and whether they had been warned to land. Id. at 573–85. The conclusion has been offered, however, that "there is a right of entry for all foreign aircraft, state or civil, when such entry is due to distress not deliberately caused by persons in control of the aircraft and there is no reasonably safe alternative. * * * Foreign aircraft and their occupants may not be subjected to penalties or to unnecessary detention by the territorial sovereign for entry under such circumstances or for entry caused by a mistake at least when the distress or mistake has not been due to negligence chargeable to the persons in control of the aircraft." Id. at 588–89. In July 1955, an Israeli passenger plane was shot down, with the loss of 58 lives, by Bulgarian aircraft after it had strayed from its course and penetrated Bulgarian territory. Attempts by Israel, the United Kingdom, and the United States to call Bulgaria to account in the International Court of Justice were defeated on jurisdictional grounds. See generally Gross, The Jurisprudence of the World Court: Thirty-Eighth Year (1959), 57 A.J.I.L. 751, 753–71 (1963). In May 1960, a United States U-2 reconnaissance plane was shot down while flying over the Soviet Union at an altitude of approximately 60,000 to 68,000 feet. The United States did not protest the Soviet action; nor did it protest the trial, conviction and imprisonment for espionage of the American pilot. When Soviet fire brought down a United States RB-47 two months later, however, the United States made vigorous protests on the ground that the aircraft had been over the high seas at the time of its interception. The Soviet Union claimed that the American plane had deliberately intruded into Soviet air space and had disobeyed an order to land. See Lissitzyn, Some Legal Implications of the U-2 and RB-47 Incidents, 56 A.J.I.L. 135 (1962).

5. On September 1, 1983, a Korean civil airplane, with 269 persons aboard, was shot down by the U.S.S.R. while flying without permission through Soviet airspace. Did the U.S.S.R. violate international law? Does the answer depend on (1) whether the plane was in Soviet airspace as the result of a navigational error or other inadvertence, (2) whether a proper directive to land had been given and disregarded, or (3) whether the plane was engaged in spying on Soviet

military installations? See Note, Legal Argumentation in International Crises: The Downing of Korean Airlines Flight 007, 97 Harv.L.Rev. 1198 (1984). See also Chapter 7, Section 6.

## *CONVENTION ON INTERNATIONAL CIVIL AVIATION*

Signed at Chicago, December 7, 1944.
61 Stat. 1190, T.I.A.S. No. 1591, 15 U.N.T.S. 295.

Art. 12. Each contracting State undertakes to adopt measures to insure that every aircraft flying over or maneuvering within its territory and that every aircraft carrying its nationality mark, wherever such aircraft may be, shall comply with the rules and the regulations relating to the flight and maneuver of aircraft there in force. Each contracting State undertakes to keep its own regulations in these respects uniform, to the greatest possible extent, with those established from time to time under this Convention. Over the high seas, the rules in force shall be those established under this Convention. Each contracting State undertakes to insure the prosecution of all persons violating the regulations applicable.

### *Notes*

1. An aircraft took off from Rabat (Morocco) on October 22, 1956, carrying five representatives of the insurgent Algerian "Front de Liberation Nationale," who had been invited by the Sultan of Morocco to attend a conference in Tunis. The aircraft was registered in France, but owned and operated by a state-controlled Moroccan corporation. The pilots were French nationals. After refuelling at Palma, the aircraft took off from Tunis, but was almost immediately ordered by the French government to direct its course toward Algiers. The pilot changed course accordingly, and the plane and its passengers were taken into custody upon arrival in Algeria. A strong protest from the Moroccan government accused France of an act of "pure piracy." France argued that the aircraft's registration in France justified the French action. See La Pradelle, L'enlèvement aérien des Chefs Fellagah, 19 Revue Generale de l'Air 235 (1956). The dispute was submitted to arbitration in 1958, but the tribunal adjourned after the Moroccan delegation walked out. Verplaetse, International Law in Vertical Space 73 (1960).

2. On whether a state may intercept a foreign aircraft over the high seas, see Note 12, p. 1077 infra.

## *CONVENTION ON OFFENCES AND CERTAIN OTHER ACTS COMMITTED ON BOARD AIRCRAFT*

Opened for signature at Tokyo, September 14, 1963.
704 U.N.T.S. 219, 20 U.S.T. 2941, T.I.A.S. No. 6768.

### ARTICLE 3

1. The State of registration of the aircraft is competent to exercise jurisdiction over offences and acts committed on board.

2. Each Contracting State shall take such measures as may be necessary to establish its jurisdiction as the State of registration over offences committed on board aircraft registered in such State.

3. This Convention does not exclude any criminal jurisdiction exercised in accordance with national law.

ARTICLE 4

A Contracting State which is not the State of registration may not interfere with an aircraft in flight in order to exercise its criminal jurisdiction over an offence committed on board except in the following cases:

(a) the offence has effect on the territory of such State;

(b) the offence has been committed by or against a national or permanent resident of such State;

(c) the offence is against the security of such State;

(d) the offence consists of a breach of any rules or regulations relating to the flight or manoeuvre of aircraft in force in such State;

(e) the exercise of jurisdiction is necessary to ensure the observance of any obligation of such State under a multilateral international agreement.

### *Notes*

1. The Convention entered into force for the United States and eleven other states on December 4, 1969. As of January 1, 1992, 143 states had become parties. Omitted articles describe the powers of the aircraft commander to restrain persons while the aircraft is in flight and to disembark such persons and to deliver them to the authorities of a contracting state in whose territory the aircraft may land. The Convention also establishes procedures for the investigation of offences and for the resolution of conflicts of jurisdiction. Article 11 obliges contracting states to "take all appropriate measures to restore control of [an] aircraft to its lawful commander or to preserve his control of the aircraft" in the event of an unlawful seizure by a person on board or an attempt at such seizure.

2. A Rumanian national, aboard a foreign aircraft en route to the United States, sexually accosted a nine-year old Norwegian girl. He was ruled subject to an American court's jurisdiction in United States v. Georgescu, 723 F.Supp. 912 (E.D.N.Y.1989). Is there a proper international law basis for this ruling?

## *CONVENTION FOR THE SUPPRESSION OF UNLAWFUL SEIZURE OF AIRCRAFT (HIJACKING)*

Signed at The Hague, December 16, 1970.
22 U.S.T. 1641, T.I.A.S. No. 7192.

[See Articles 1–14]

---

### *Notes*

1. As of January 1, 1992, this Convention had entered in force for 147 states, including the U.S.

2. On September 23, 1971, a Convention for the Suppression of Unlawful Acts Against the Safety of Civil Aviation (Sabotage), 24 U.S.T. 564, T.I.A.S. No.

7570, was signed in Montreal, Canada. As of January 1, 1992, the Convention had entered into force for 146 states, including the U.S. This Convention is in many respects similar to the 1970 Convention, but is primarily designed to control attacks and sabotage against civil aircraft in flight and on the ground rather than "unlawful seizure" (hijacking). Article 1 of the 1971 Convention reads as follows:

> 1. Any person commits an offence if he unlawfully and intentionally:
>
> (a) performs an act of violence against a person on board an aircraft in flight if that act is likely to endanger the safety of that aircraft; or
>
> (b) destroys an aircraft in service or causes damage to such an aircraft which renders it incapable of flight or which is likely to endanger its safety in flight; or
>
> (c) places or causes to be placed on an aircraft in service, by any means whatsoever, a device or substance which is likely to destroy that aircraft, or to cause damage to it which renders it incapable of flight, or to cause damage to it which is likely to endanger its safety in flight; or
>
> (d) destroys or damages air navigation facilities or interferes with their operation, if any such act is likely to endanger the safety of aircraft in flight; or
>
> (e) communicates information which he knows to be false, thereby endangering the safety of an aircraft in flight.
>
> 2. Any person also commits an offence if he:
>
> (a) attempts to commit any of the offences mentioned in paragraph 1 of this Article; or
>
> (b) is an accomplice of a person who commits or attempts to commit any such offence.

Article 2(b) of the Convention provides:

> an aircraft is considered to be in service from the beginning of the preflight preparation of the aircraft by ground personnel or by the crew for a specific flight until twenty-four hours after any landing; the period of service shall, in any event, extend for the entire period during which the aircraft is in flight as defined in paragraph (a) of this Article.

Article 2(a) is substantially identical with Article 3(1) of the 1970 Convention. Article 5 is similar to Article 4 of the 1970 Convention, but adds another clause: "(a) when the offence is committed in the territory of that State." There are some other differences between the two conventions. For the text of the 1971 Convention, see 26 ICAO Bulletin, No. 10 (October 1971), at 15; 10 I.L.M. 1151 (1971).

3. The Conventions of 1970 and 1971 were inspired by mounting international concern with the increasingly frequent hijacking of aircraft in flight and attacks upon aircraft on the ground as well as in flight. They greatly increased the permissible scope of state action in combatting hijackings.

4. The Tokyo and the Hague Conventions apply when an aircraft is unlawfully seized while "in flight." Article 1(3) of the Tokyo Convention defines an aircraft to be in flight from "* * * the moment when power is applied for purpose of takeoff until the landing run ends." Compare Article 3(1) of the Hague Convention.

5. On what bases of jurisdiction are the Hague and Tokyo Conventions premised? Does the grant of jurisdiction to any ratifying state within whose borders the alleged offender is found extend customary international law? Note that Article 4(2) obligates the state to exercise jurisdiction in these circumstances.

6. Under Article 4 of the Hague Convention, several states may have concurrent jurisdiction. May this lead to problems, since the Convention has no provision establishing the priority of their claims? See Abramovsky, Multilateral Conventions for the Suppression of Unlawful Seizures and Interference with Aircraft, Part I: The Hague Convention, 13 Colum.J.Transnat'l L. 381, 396 (1974) (concluding that the state in which the offender is apprehended would enjoy a primary *de facto* right to exercise jurisdiction).

7. Does Article 7 of the Hague Convention require a state to prosecute an alleged offender, if it does not extradite him? Since many hijackings are politically motivated, a state desiring to harbor fugitives may claim the traditional exemption from extradition for "political offenses." Article 8(1) of the Hague Convention defines the hijacking offence as an extraditable offence for those member states that are already linked by an extradition treaty, but does this categorization extend beyond the described situation? See the discussion of this issue in Abramovsky, id. at 401–405 and Abramovsky, id., Part II: The Montreal Convention, 14 Colum.J.Transnat'l L. 296, 298–99 (1975) (concluding that most states prefer to maintain the exemption even in the context of aircraft hijacking, despite the problems of defining a "political offence").

On June 25, 1985, the United States, the United Kingdom and Northern Ireland signed a Supplementary Extradition Treaty providing that the "political offense exception" shall not apply to specified crimes of violence (typically committed by terrorists), including offenses under the 1970 Hague Hijacking Convention, the 1971 Montreal Aircraft Sabotage Convention, the 1973 New York Convention on the Prevention and Punishment of Crimes Against Internationally Protected Persons, Including Diplomatic Agents, and the 1979 Hostage Convention. The United Kingdom is already a party to the European Convention on the Suppression of Terrorism, which permits Council of Europe members not to regard as political a range of offenses similar to those included in the U.S.—U.K. Convention. See generally Leich, Contemporary Practice of the United States Relating to International Law, 79 A.J.I.L. 1045 (1985).

8. At the 20th Extraordinary Session of the ICAO Assembly in 1973, several proposals were made with the aim of broadening the effectiveness of international control over interference with aircraft. See Abramovsky, id. Part III: The Legality and Political Feasibility of a Multilateral Air Security Enforcement Convention, 14 Colum.J.Transnat'l L. 451 (1975). A new multilateral convention was proposed, establishing an International Commission with the power to investigate alleged violations of the enforcement provisions of the Tokyo, Hague, and Montreal Conventions. It provided for sanctions against states that refused to comply with the Commission's recommendations. Among the contemplated sanctions was the collective suspension of flights to and from such a state. See LC/Working Draft No. 820, ICAO Doc. 9050–LC/169–2 at 265 (1973). On the compatibility of these sanctions with those provided for in Article 41 of the U.N. Charter, see Abramovsky, Part III at 470–474; see also, Fitzgerald, Recent Proposals for Concerted Action Against States in Respect of Unlawful Interference with International Civil Aviation, 40 A.J.I.L. 161 (1974).

France proposed that the provisions of the Hague Convention be incorporated into the Chicago Convention p. 1072 supra by amendment of the latter. Failure to ratify the amendment would constitute grounds for expulsion from the ICAO. See LC/Working Draft No. 821, ICAO Doc. 9050–LC/169–2, at 274 (1973). See Abramovsky, Part III at 457 (arguing that adoption of this proposal would politicize, if not destroy, the ICAO).

None of the proposals were passed by the ICAO assembly. Since 1973, international efforts to control hijacking have consisted mainly of calling upon states to join the 1970 and 1971 Conventions and to upgrade airport security measures. See, e.g., G.A.Res. 32/8 (XXXII 1977), as discussed in 78:2015 Dep't St.Bull. 53–55 (June 1978) and ICAO Council Resolution of 2 December 1977, as discussed in 33 ICAO Bulletin 19 (January 1978).

9. Faced with an apparent impasse in efforts to impose international sanctions on "haven" states, what may states do unilaterally? On August 10, 1973, a Lebanese airplane which had been chartered by Iraqi Airways was intercepted within Lebanese air space by Israeli military jets and forced to land inside Israel. The Israelis hoped to capture a leader of the Popular Front for the Liberation of Palestine whom Arab states had refused to extradite despite the fact that the leader's organization publicly claimed responsibility for killing passengers and crew members of unlawfully seized aircraft. The Israelis were condemned by the United Nations Security Council and the ICAO. See S.C.Res. 337, (XXVIII 1973), ICAO Doc. 9050–LC/169–1, at 196 (1973).

On the international law aspects of the Entebbe incident, see p. 718 supra.

In 1974, the United States Congress enacted the following provision:

> (a) Whenever the President determines that a foreign nation is acting in a manner inconsistent with the Convention for the Suppression of Unlawful Seizure of Aircraft, or if he determines that a foreign nation permits the use of territory under its jurisdiction as a base of operations or training or as a sanctuary for, or in any way arms, aids, or abets, any terrorist organization which knowingly uses the illegal seizure of aircraft or the threat thereof as an instrument of policy, he may, without notice or hearing and for as long as he determines necessary to assure the security of aircraft against unlawful seizure, suspend (1) the right of any air carrier or foreign air carrier to engage in foreign air transportation, and the right of any person to operate aircraft in foreign air commerce, to and from that foreign nation, and (2) the right of any foreign air carrier to engage in foreign air transportation, and the right of any foreign person to operate aircraft in foreign air commerce, between the United States and any foreign nation which maintains air service between itself and that foreign nation. * * *

49 U.S.C.A. § 1514. See also 49 U.S.C.A. § 1515, which grants the Secretary of Transportation the power to withhold, revoke, or impose conditions upon the operating authority of any nation that fails to maintain the security measures set by the Convention on International Civil Aviation.

10. An alternative to unilateral action is the conclusion of bilateral treaties. See, e.g., the agreement between the United States and Cuba providing for the return or prosecution of hijackers of aircraft and ships, Memorandum of Understanding on Hijacking of Aircraft and Vessels and Other Offenses, Dep't St. Press Rel. No. 35 (Feb. 15, 1973); 24 U.S.T. 737, T.I.A.S. No. 7579.

11. On December 18, 1985, the U.N. Security Council adopted Resolution 579, condemning all acts of hostage-taking and abduction. On January 14, 1986,

the U.N. General Assembly adopted a Resolution (G.A.Res. 40/61 (XL 1986)), condemning "as criminal, all acts, methods and practices of terrorism wherever and by whomever committed." Do these resolutions provide a basis for the view that the acts condemned are covered by the universality principle?

12. To what extent may a state use force against a state promoting or harboring terrorists? In October 1985, United States airplanes intercepted over the high seas, and then directed to and forced down on a United States airbase in Sicily, an Egyptian airplane that carried terrorists who had seized on the high seas the Achille Lauro, an oceangoing vessel of Italian registry, and who had killed one of its American passengers. Egypt protested this action. N.Y. Times, Oct. 11, 1985, at 1, col. 1. Was its protest well-founded? Note that the Law of the Sea Convention, in Articles 95 and 96, declares immune from interference by other states warships and other vessels used for non-commercial purposes of another state that are on the high seas. See also Section 8, p. 1110.

13. On June 15, 1985, a TWA plane was hijacked on a flight from Cairo to Rome and forced to fly to various cities, ending up finally in Beirut. After the passengers had been discharged, the plane was blown up on the airfield in Beirut. N.Y. Times, June 15, 1985, Sec. 1, p. 1, col. 6. To what extent are any of the conventions discussed in this Section applicable to the activities of the hijackers? See United States v. Fawaz Yunis, 924 F.2d 1086 (D.C.Cir.1991) (finding the Hostage Taking Act, 18 U.S.C.A. § 1203, and the Antihijacking Act of 1974, 49 U.S.C.A.App. §§ 1472(n), applicable to hijacking by an alien of a Jordanian plane with American passengers in Beirut). On this case, see also p. 1064 supra.

14. On December 27, 1985, gunmen sprayed gunfire and detonated grenades in an airport lounge in Vienna. On the same day, gunmen did the same at the El–Al check-in counter at the Rome airport. Many persons, including Americans, were killed; many others were wounded. N.Y. Times, Dec. 28, 1985, Sec. 1, p. 1, col. 4. Are the provisions of any of the conventions discussed in this Section applicable? Does the United States have jurisdiction to prosecute the perpetrators? Would it be entitled to their extradition? On these questions, see Section 9 of this Chapter. Could the United States seize the perpetrators in a foreign state or intercept a vessel on, or an airplane flying over, the high seas in order to seize them? See Section 8 of this Chapter.

## *ANTIHIJACKING ACT OF 1974*

Act of August 5, 1974, Pub.L. No. 93–366 amending
the U.S. Federal Aviation Act of 1958.
[49 U.S.C.A. §§ 1301, 1472.]

### *Notes*

1. In United States v. Cordova, 89 F.Supp. 298 (E.D.N.Y.1950), it was held that an aircraft was not a "vessel" within the meaning of 18 U.S.C.A. § 7(1) and that a United States Court therefore had no jurisdiction to try and punish a defendant accused of assaulting certain persons (including the pilot) on a United States aircraft flying over the high seas between Puerto Rico and New York. Congress thereupon amended 18 U.S.C.A. § 7 by an Act of July 12, 1952 (69 Stat. 589), adding a new subsection (5) so that the "special maritime and territorial jurisdiction of the United States" now extends to:

Any aircraft belonging in whole or in part to the United States, or any citizen thereof, or to any corporation created by or under the laws of the United States, or any State, Territory, district, or possession thereof, while such aircraft is in flight over the high seas, or over any other waters within the admiralty and maritime jurisdiction of the United States and out of the jurisdiction of any particular State.

2. An Act to Implement the Convention on Offenses and Certain Other Acts Committed on Board Aircraft, and For Other Purposes, enacted on October 14, 1970 (84 Stat. 921), amending the U.S. Federal Aviation Act of 1958, included a new section defining the "special aircraft jurisdiction of the United States." The Antihijacking Act of 1974 amended this section to conform its provisions to the Hague Convention. Note, however, that the Hague Convention, by its terms (Article 3(2)), is not applicable "to aircraft used in military, customs or police services." Does the Act go beyond the Convention in any other respects? See also 49 U.S.C.A. § 1514, which was also part of the Antihijacking Act. The Act is discussed in Note, The Antihijacking Act of 1974: A Step Beyond the Hague Convention, 16 South Texas L.J. 356 (1974–75).

3. Note that U.S.C.A. § 1401(b) permits the registration in the United States only of aircraft owned by citizens or lawful residents of the United States and not registered in any foreign country. United States citizens are not forbidden, however, to own or otherwise hold interests in aircraft that are registered in a foreign country. Under what circumstances, if any, might jurisdiction asserted by the United States on the basis of 18 U.S.C.A. § 7(5) supra be unlawful under international law? Does the same problem exist for jurisdiction asserted on the basis of 49 U.S.C.A. § 1301(38)? On what bases of jurisdiction are §§ 1301 and 1472 premised?

4. United States v. Pliskow, 354 F.Supp. 369 (E.D.Mich.1973), aff'd, 480 F.2d 927 (6th Cir.1973), held that the defendant, who boarded a plane with dynamite, a gun, and notes indicating his intent to hijack, had not violated the then applicable statute, because he was captured prior to the airplane's starting its engines. Could the same decision be reached under the 1974 statute? See the definition of "in flight" in § 1301 and the prohibition of attempts in § 1472(i)(3).

5. The sections of Title 18 referred to in Section 1472(k) provide punishment for assaults, maimings, theft, receipt of stolen property, murder, manslaughter, attempted murder or manslaughter, and rape.

## *TREATY ON PRINCIPLES GOVERNING THE ACTIVITIES OF STATES IN THE EXPLORATION AND USE OF OUTER SPACE, INCLUDING THE MOON AND OTHER CELESTIAL BODIES*

Done at London, Moscow, and Washington, January 27, 1967.
18 U.S.T. 2410, T.I.A.S. No. 6347, 610 U.N.T.S. 205.

[SEE ARTICLES 1–8]

---

### *Notes*

1. 10 U.S.C.A. § 805 extends to "all places" United States criminal jurisdiction over personnel subject to the Uniform Code of Military Justice. As of

January 1, 1976, Congress had considered, but not passed, legislation which would extend U.S. criminal jurisdiction generally to "aerospace." See S.1, 93d Cong., 1st Sess. (1973); S.1400, id., and S.1 94th Cong., 1st Sess. (1974). See also Menter, Jurisdiction Over Man–Made Orbital Satellites, 2 J.Space L. 19 (1974).

2. Under 18 U.S.C.A. § 7(5), the "special maritime and territorial jurisdiction of the United States" includes:

> Any aircraft belonging in whole or in part to the United States * * * while such aircraft is in flight over the high seas, or over any other waters within the admiralty and maritime jurisdiction of the United States * * *.

Does this provision extend United States jurisdiction to a United States space shuttle in outer space or on a celestial body?

3. On Dec. 21, 1981, Section 7 of Title 18 of the U.S.C.A. was amended to add paragraph 6, reading as follows:

> (6) Any vehicle used or designed for flight or navigation in space and on the registry of the United States pursuant to the Treaty on Principles Governing the Activities of States in the Exploration and Use of Outer Space, Including the Moon and Other Celestial Bodies and the Convention on Registration of Objects Launched into Outer Space, while that vehicle is in flight, which is from the moment when all external doors are closed on Earth following embarkation until the moment when one such door is opened on Earth for disembarkation or in the case of a forced landing, until the competent authorities take over the responsibility for the vehicle and for persons and property aboard.

4. The Agreement on the Rescue of Astronauts, the Return of Astronauts, and the Return of Objects Launched into Outer Space, 19 U.S.T. 7570, T.I.A.S. No. 6599, 672 U.N.T.S. 119, came into force on December 3, 1968. By January 1, 1992, 88 states had become parties. See generally Houben, A New Chapter of Space Law, 15 Neth.Int'l L.Rev. 121 (1968); Christol, The Modern International Law of Outer Space 152 (1982). The Agreement provides, in part, as follows:

> Art. 1. Each Contracting Party which receives information or discovers that the personnel of a spacecraft have suffered accident or are experiencing conditions of distress or have made an emergency or unintended landing in territory under its jurisdiction or on the high seas or in any other place not under the jurisdiction of any State shall immediately:
>
> (a) Notify the launching authority or, if it cannot identify and immediately communicate with the launching authority, immediately make a public announcement by all appropriate means of communication at its disposal;
>
> (b) Notify the Secretary–General of the United Nations, who should disseminate the information without delay by all appropriate means of communication at his disposal.
>
> Art. 2. If, owing to accident, distress, emergency or unintended landing, the personnel of a spacecraft land in territory under the jurisdiction of a Contracting Party, it shall immediately take all possible steps to rescue them and render them all necessary assistance. It shall inform the launching authority and also the Secretary–General of the United Nations of the steps it is taking and of their progress. If assistance by the launching authority would help to effect a prompt rescue or would contribute substantially to the effectiveness of search and rescue operations, the launching

authority shall co-operate with the Contracting Party with a view to the effective conduct of search and rescue operations. Such operations shall be subject to the direction and control of the Contracting Party, which shall act in close and continuing consultation with the launching authority.

Art. 3. If information is received or it is discovered that the personnel of a spacecraft have alighted on the high seas or in any other place not under the jurisdiction of any State, those Contracting Parties which are in a position to do so shall, if necessary, extend assistance in search and rescue operations for such personnel to assure their speedy rescue. They shall inform the launching authority and the Secretary–General of the United Nations of the steps they are taking and of their progress.

Art. 4. If, owing to accident, distress, emergency or unintended landing, the personnel of a spacecraft land in territory under the jurisdiction of a Contracting Party or have been found on the high seas or in any other place not under the jurisdiction of any State, they shall be safely and promptly returned to representatives of the launching authority.

Art. 5. (1) Each Contracting Party which receives information or discovers that a space object or its component parts has returned to Earth in territory under its jurisdiction or on the high seas or in any other place not under the jurisdiction of any State, shall notify the launching authority and the Secretary–General of the United Nations.

(2) Each Contracting Party having jurisdiction over the territory on which a space object or its component parts has been discovered shall, upon the request of the launching authority and with assistance from that authority if requested, take such steps as it finds practicable to recover the object or component parts.

(3) Upon request of the launching authority, objects launched into outer space or their component parts found beyond the territorial limits of the launching authority shall be returned to or held at the disposal of representatives of the launching authority, which shall, upon request, furnish identifying data prior to their return.

(4) Notwithstanding paragraphs 2 and 3 of this article, a Contracting Party which has reason to believe that a space object or its component parts discovered in territory under its jurisdiction, or recovered by it elsewhere, is of a hazardous or deleterious nature may so notify the launching authority, which shall immediately take effective steps, under the direction and control of the said Contracting Party, to eliminate possible danger of harm.

(5) Expenses incurred in fulfilling obligations to recover and return a space object or its component parts under paragraphs 2 and 3 of this article shall be borne by the launching authority.

Art. 6. For the purposes of this Agreement, the term "launching authority" shall refer to the State responsible for launching, or, where an international intergovernmental organization is responsible for launching, that organization, provided that that organization declares its acceptance of the rights and obligations provided for in this Agreement and a majority of the States members of that organization are Contracting Parties to this Agreement and to the Treaty on Principles Governing the Activities of States in the Exploration and Use of Outer Space, including the Moon and Other Celestial Bodies.

5. The Convention on International Liability for Damage Caused by Space Objects, 24 U.S.T. 2389, T.I.A.S. No. 7762, which as of January 1, 1992, had been ratified by 82 parties, provides for absolute liability of the launching state for damage caused by a space object on the surface of the earth or to aircraft in flight.

This Convention was invoked for the first time in January, 1978, when Canada billed the U.S.S.R. for six million dollars spent in locating and cleaning up radioactive debris from the disintegration of the Soviet's Cosmos 954. The Canadian claim is reproduced at 18 I.L.M. 899 (1979). Since then, the U.S.S.R. has paid. For a discussion of the legal issues involved, See Dembling, Cosmos 954 & The Space Treaties, 6 J. Space L. 129 (1978); Gorove, Cosmos 954; Issues of Law and Policy, id. at 137. See also Wilkins, Substantive Bases for Recovery for Injuries Sustained by Private Individuals as a Result of Fallen Space Objects, id. at 161; Christol, The Modern Law of Outer Space 59 (1982).

### *3. Other Things*

The notion that inanimate things, like vessels and aircraft, may stand in a sufficiently close relationship to a particular state to provide a basis for the exercise of jurisdiction by that state over the thing and the persons using it naturally leads to the question whether this notion can be extended to other material, and perhaps even immaterial, things. For example, states may seek to exercise jurisdiction over artistic creations and cultural artifacts on the ground that they are part of the national patrimony. See, e.g., Convention on the Illicit Movement of Art Treasures, entered into force in April 24, 1972, for the United States on December 2, 1983, 823 U.N.T.S. 231, reprinted in 10 I.L.M. 289 (1971). American efforts to control beyond its borders the flow of technology created in the United States have also raised the question whether technology can be regarded as national so as to justify the exercise of jurisdiction on the basis of nationality by the state where it was created. For arguments against this basis for asserting jurisdiction, see Legal Serv. of the Comm'n of the European Communities, European Communities: Comments on the U.S. Regulations Concerning Trade with the U.S.S.R., reprinted in 21 I.L.M. 891 (1982).

# SECTION 4. JURISDICTION BASED ON PROTECTION OF CERTAIN STATE, UNIVERSAL, AND OTHER INTERESTS

## A. PROTECTIVE PRINCIPLE

### *RESTATEMENT (THIRD)*

#### § 402. Bases of Jurisdiction to Prescribe

Subject to § 403, a state has jurisdiction to prescribe law with respect to

(1) * * *

(2) * * *

(3) certain conduct outside its territory by persons not its nationals that is directed against the security of the state or against a limited class of other state interests.

### *Notes*

1. In United States v. Archer, 51 F.Supp. 708 (S.D.Cal.1943), the court regarded the federal statute making it a crime for either an alien or a United States citizen to commit perjury before a diplomatic or consular office, 11 Stat. 61, 22 U.S.C.A. § 1203, as resting on the protective principle and convicted thereunder an alien who committed perjury before a vice consul in Mexico in connection with an application for a non-immigrant visa. See also United States v. Rodriguez, 182 F.Supp. 479 (S.D.Cal.1960), reversed on other grounds sub nom. Rocha v. United States, 288 F.2d 545 (9th Cir.1961), cert. denied, 366 U.S. 948, 81 S.Ct. 1902, 6 L.Ed.2d 1241 (1961).

2. Compare Restatement, (Third) § 402(3) with the following articles from the Harvard Research in International Law, Jurisdiction with Respect to Crime, 29 A.J.I.L.Supp. 435, 440 (1935):

> Art. 7. A state has jurisdiction with respect to any crime committed outside its territory by an alien against the security, territorial integrity or political independence of that state, provided that the act or omission which constitutes the crime was not committed in exercise of a liberty guaranteed the alien by the law of the place where it was committed.
>
> Art. 8. A state has jurisdiction with respect to any crime committed outside its territory by an alien which consists of a falsification or counterfeiting, or an uttering or falsified copies or counterfeits, of the seals, currency, instruments of credit, stamps, passports, or public documents, issued by that state or under its authority.

3. In 1972, Israel amended its Penal Law to include the following provision:

> The courts in Israel are competent to try under Israeli law a person who has committed abroad an act which would be an offense if it had been committed in Israel and which harmed or was intended to harm the State of Israel, its security, property or economy or its transport or communications links with other countries.

Passed by the Knesset on the 6th Nisan, 5732 (March 21, 1972), 5732 (1972) Sefer Ha–Chukkim 52. Can this provision be supported by the protective principle? See Note, Extraterritorial Jurisdiction and Jurisdiction Following Forcible Abduction: A New Israeli Precedent in International Law, 72 Mich.L.Rev. 1087 (1974).

## B. UNIVERSALITY PRINCIPLE

### *RESTATEMENT (THIRD) § 404, p. 1049 supra.*

### *UNITED NATIONS CONVENTION ON THE LAW OF THE SEA*

#### ART. 100

#### *Note*

"It has long been recognized and well settled that persons and vessels engaged in piratical operations on the high seas are entitled to the protection of no nation and may be punished by any nation that may apprehend or capture them. This stern rule of international law refers to piracy in its international-law sense and not to a variety of lesser maritime offenses so designated by municipal law." 2 Hackworth at 681. On piracy, see p. 380 supra.

### *LETTER OF 15 JUNE 1960 FROM THE REPRESENTATIVE OF ARGENTINA TO THE PRESIDENT OF THE SECURITY COUNCIL*

U.N. Doc. S/4336.

I have the honour, on the instructions of my Government, to request you to call an urgent meeting of the Security Council to consider the violation of the sovereign rights of the Argentine Republic resulting from the illicit and clandestine transfer of Adolf Eichmann from Argentine territory to the territory of the State of Israel, contrary to the rules of international law and the Purposes and Principles of the Charter of the United Nations and creating an atmosphere of insecurity and mistrust incompatible with the preservation of international peace.

An explanatory memorandum is attached. * * *

(Signed) Mario Amadeo
Ambassador

EXPLANATORY MEMORANDUM

In view of the failure of the diplomatic representations made by it to the Government of Israel the Argentine Government is now compelled, in defence of fundamental rights, to request that the case be dealt with by the Security Council, the case being in its view explicitly covered by the provisions of Article 34 and Article 35, paragraph 1, of the United Nations Charter.

The facts which have led to this situation are as follows:

1. Having learned from reports which had become known to world public opinion that Adolf Eichmann had been captured in Argentine territory by "volunteer groups" which transferred him to the territory of Israel and there delivered him to the authorities of that country, the Argentine Government approached the Government of Israel with a request for information in that connexion.

2. The Government of Israel, through its Embassy at Buenos Aires, replied to this request in a note of 3 June 1960 in which it stated that Eichmann had in fact been transferred to Israel from Argentine territory. After stating that Eichmann had consented to the transfer, the Government of Israel's note concluded with the statement that "if the volunteer group violated Argentine law or interfered with matters within the sovereignty of Argentina, the Government of Israel wishes to express its regret."

3. In view of the recognition of the authenticity of the facts reported in connexion with Eichmann's capture, the Argentine Government * * * made the most formal protest against the illegal act committed to the detriment of a fundamental right of the Argentine State, and requested appropriate reparation for the act, namely the return of Eichmann, for which it set a

time-limit of one week, and the punishment of those guilty of violating Argentine territory. The Argentine Government stated that, failing compliance with this request, it would refer the matter to the United Nations. * * *

It is unnecessary to adduce further considerations in order to underline the gravity of the resulting situation. The illicit and clandestine transfer of Eichmann from Argentine territory constitutes a flagrant violation of the Argentine State's right of sovereignty, and the Argentine Government is legally justified in requesting reparation. That right cannot be qualified by any other considerations, even those invoked by the Government of Israel with regard to the importance attaching to the trial of a man accused of exterminations in concentration camps, although the Argentine Government and people understand those reasons to the full. Any contrary interpretation would be tantamount to approving the taking of the law into one's own hands and the subjecting of international order to unilateral acts which, if repeated, would involve undeniable dangers for the preservation of peace.

Before appealing to the Security Council, the Argentine Government endeavoured, in accordance with the Charter of the United Nations, to reach a satisfactory solution through the normal diplomatic channels of negotiation. In these endeavours the close friendship between Argentina and the State of Israel played a part. Those endeavours have, however, been without success. In these circumstances, the only remaining recourse is to the Security Council. A political question is involved which, apart from gravely prejudicing Argentine sovereignty, constitutes a precedent dangerous for international peace and security, for the maintenance of which the Security Council bears primary responsibility.

The Argentine Government hopes that the Security Council will attach to this question all the importance which it merits, and will take decisions involving just reparation for the rights violated.

### *Notes*

1. On which bases of jurisdiction could Israel rely in its capture and execution of Eichmann? Is the fact that Israel did not exist as a state when Eichmann committed the acts for which he was prosecuted significant in this context?

2. Israel disputed the Council's competence to deal with the incident in a letter of June 21, 1960 (U.N.Doc. S/4341), stating that Argentina's unilateral allegations did not suffice to bring the dispute within the terms of Article 34 of the Charter and expressing the conviction that the difficulties between the two countries could best be settled by direct negotiations. At its 865th meeting on June 22, 1960, however, the Council included the matter in its agenda without objection. The Israeli representative was invited to take a seat at the Council table. For the debate, see U.N. Docs. S/P.V. 865–68; see also the summary contained in the Security Council's report to the General Assembly for the year ending July 15, 1960, 15 GAOR Supp. 2 (A/4494), p. 19–24. On June 23, 1960, the Security Council adopted a resolution by eight votes to none, with two abstentions (Poland and the Soviet Union) and one member (Argentina) not participating in the vote. The operative parts of the resolution (S/4349) were as follows:

*The Security Council,* * * *

> 1. *Declares* that acts such as that under consideration, which affect the sovereignty of a Member State and therefore cause international friction, may, if repeated, endanger international peace and security;
>
> 2. *Requests* the Government of Israel to make appropriate reparation in accordance with the Charter of the United Nations and the rules of international law * * *.

3. On August 3, 1960, the following joint communiqué was published in Jerusalem and Buenos Aires:

> The Governments of Israel and the Republic of Argentina, animated by the wish to comply with the resolution of the Security Council of June 23, 1960, in which the hope was expressed that the traditionally friendly relations between the two countries will be advanced, have decided to regard as closed the incident that arose out of the action taken by Israeli nationals which infringed fundamental rights of the State of Argentina.

See Lord Russell of Liverpool, The Trial of Adolf Eichmann xvi–xvii (1962); Pearlman, the Capture and Trial of Adolf Eichmann 79 (1963); Papdatos, The Eichmann Trial 60 n. 54 (1964). Eichmann was charged under the Nazis and Nazi Collaborators (Punishment) Law (5710–1950, No. 64, 4 Laws of the State of Israel 154) with commission of the following crimes in Germany or countries occupied by Germany during World War II—crimes against the Jewish people [§ 1(a)(1) ], crimes against humanity [§ 1(a)(2) ], war crimes [§ 1(a)(3) ], and membership in a hostile organization [§ 3]—in the indictment of February 21, 1961. On December 11, 1961, the District Court of Jerusalem found Eichmann guilty on all counts of the indictment (Criminal Case No. 40/61). An appeal was dismissed on May 29, 1962 (Criminal Appeal No. 336/61). In the course of its Judgment, the court overruled the defense contention that there was no jurisdiction because the defendant had been captured in a foreign country in violation of international law. For a complete English translation of the judgments, see 36 Int'l L.Reports 5 (1968). A bibliography on the Eichmann trial is included in Mueller & Wise, eds., International Criminal Law 370–71 (1965).

4. See also Matter of Demjanjuk, 612 F.Supp. 544 (N.D.Ohio 1985), approving a request for extradition to Israel of a person charged with crimes committed in Nazi concentration camps in Eastern Europe, even though the usual condition for extradition that the crimes had been committed in the territory of the requesting state was not met. Cf. also Matter of Barbie, [1983] Gaz.Pal.Jur. 710 (Cass.Crim. Oct. 6, 1983).

The district court's decision in the *Demjanjuk* case was affirmed on appeal. 776 F.2d 571 (6th Cir.1985), cert. denied, 475 U.S. 1016, 106 S.Ct. 1198, 89 L.Ed.2d 312 (1986). After Demjanjuk had been convicted in Israel, questions arose as to whether Demjanjuk was in fact the person who was accused of the crimes involved. This prompted an unusual order by the Court of Appeals issued *sua sponte* directing the United States to respond to reports that the prosecution had failed to disclose information to that effect.

5. Could and should the United States enact criminal legislation covering terrorist attacks anywhere in the world? Or should such legislation be limited to terrorist attacks upon United States instrumentalities, ships, bases, diplomatic or consular buildings, nationals or residents? Survivors and representatives of persons murdered in an attack on a civilian bus in Israel brought suit against several defendants alleging violations of the law of nations, treaties of the United States, as well as the law of the United States. The Court of Appeals

upheld dismissal for lack of subject matter jurisdiction, ruling that terrorist attacks did not violate the law of nations or other federal law. Tel–Oren v. Libyan Arab Republic, 726 F.2d 774, (D.C.Cir.1984), cert. denied, 470 U.S. 1003, 105 S.Ct. 1354, 84 L.Ed.2d 377 (1985).

6. On illegal capture and abduction, see also p. 1110 infra.

7. Note that the Restatement (Third) § 404 does not impose the limitation of reasonableness on the exercise of universal jurisdiction. Should it do so in cases in which there is another state that is better situated effectively to exercise its jurisdiction? On this question, see Schachter, International Law in Theory and Practice 179 Rec. des Cours 263–64 (1982—V).

8. Does the possible absence of any link between the state exercising universal jurisdiction and the person over whom it is exercised require more extensive safeguards for the protection of that person? See id. at 264–65.

9. A number of recent multilateral conventions provide for punishment or extradition of persons guilty of specified crimes, such as hijacking, hostage taking, and terrorism, regardless of the absence of any of the traditional bases of jurisdiction other than the universality principle. On these conventions, see Section 3(D)(2) of this Chapter. Have the parties to these conventions in effect extended the universality principle to these crimes? Could they do so? See id. at 262–63.

10. For an argument in favor of expanding the universality principle of jurisdiction to terrorism and other offenses the community of nations widely condemns, see Randall, Universal Jurisdiction Under International Law, 66 Tex.L.Rev. 785. See also Note, Extraterritorial Jurisdiction Over Acts of Terrorism Committed Abroad: Omnibus Diplomatic Security and Antiterrorism Act of 1988, 72 Cornell L.Rev. 599; Comment, The Omnibus Diplomatic Security and Antiterrorism Act of 1986: Prescribing and Enforcing United States Law against Terrorist Violence Overseas, 37 UCLA L.Rev. 985 (1990).

11. Iraq has been accused of systematically murdering and displacing Kurds in Northern Iraq and Shiites in Southern Iraq. After Iraq had been driven from Kuwait, the United Nations was urged to set up a tribunal for the prosecution of Saddam Hussein and others under his command for war crimes. These proposals continue to be pressed. See, e.g., N.Y.Times, Magazine Section, Jan. 3, 1993.

Similar proposals have been made in regard to the "cleansing" of Muslims and Croatians by Serbs in the civil strife in former Yugoslavia. To-date, no tribunal has been set up for this purpose.

Should the United Nations create a standing tribunal to adjudicate claims based on the universality principle? Who should be able to bring an action in such a tribunal? The idea of creating such a tribunal continues to engage the interest of many. For a recent work addressing this subject, see Taylor, The Anatomy of the Nuremberg Trials: A Personal Memoir (1992).

# SECTION 5. JURISDICTION BASED ON AGREEMENT WITH STATE HAVING JURISDICTION

## *RESTATEMENT, SECOND, FOREIGN RELATIONS LAW OF THE UNITED STATES (1965)*

### § 25. Jurisdiction Conferred by International Agreement With Territorial State

A state has jurisdiction to prescribe and enforce a rule of law in the territory of another state to the extent provided by international agreement with the other state.

### *Notes*

1. By article II of the Hay–Bunau–Varilla Convention of 1903 (33 Stat. 234, T.S. No. 431) the United States was granted, "in perpetuity the use, occupation and control" of the Panama Canal Zone. Article III of this Convention provided that the United States was to exercise its rights as "if it were the sovereign of the territory within which said lands and waters are located to the entire exclusion of the exercise by the Republic of Panama of any such sovereign rights, power or authority." On this Convention, see Smit, The Panama Canal: A National or International Waterway?, 76 Colum.L.Rev. 965 (1976).

By Treaties of Sept. 7, 1977, 16 I.L.M. 1022 (1977), the rights of the United States over the Canal Zone were substantially modified. The new Canal Treaty acknowledges "the Republic of Panama's sovereignty over its territory," stresses that Panama is the "territorial sovereign," declares the entire territory of Panama to be "under the flag of the Republic of Panama," and provides that Panama "shall reassume plenary jurisdiction over the former Canal Zone upon entry into force of this treaty." Canal Treaty, Preamble, para. (3), and arts. I(2), III(1), VII(1), and XI(1). What is the international legal effect of the quoted provisions? See Smit, The Proposed Panama Canal Treaties: A Triple Failure, 17 Colum.J.Transnat'l L. 1 (1978).

2. By an agreement of February 23, 1903, Cuba leased to the United States certain territory in Guantanamo for use by the latter as a naval station. Article III of the agreement recited the United States' recognition of Cuba's continuing "ultimate sovereignty" over the leased territory and Cuba's consent that the United States should exercise "complete jurisdiction and control over and within" the leased areas. 1 Malloy 358. A later agreement of the same year fixed the conditions of the lease and also provided for the mutual extradition of persons committing offenses against the laws of Cuba or the United States in areas under their respective control. 1 Malloy 360. Limited jurisdictional rights were granted to the United States when it leased naval and air bases in certain British territories during World War II. Article I of the agreement of March 27, 1941, 55 Stat. 1560, limited United States jurisdiction in the leased areas to "all the rights, power and authority * * * necessary for the establishment, use, operation and defence * * * or appropriate for their control." On leases of territory, see, in general, 1 O'Connell 361–63.

3. During the nineteenth and the early part of the twentieth centuries, a number of European states entered into agreements with weaker states, usually Asian or African, by which the latter relinquished their jurisdiction over individuals within their territory having the nationality of the other contracting parties, this jurisdiction being exercised instead by each state over its own

nationals through special courts set up for the purpose. See 1 Oppenheim § 381 (8th ed. Lauterpacht 1955). On United States consular jurisdiction in Morocco, see Case Concerning Rights of Nationals of the United States of America in Morocco (France v. United States), 1952 I.C.J. 176; Nadelmann, American Consular Jurisdiction in Morocco and the Tangier International Jurisdiction, 49 A.J.I.L. 506 (1955). By a note of October 6, 1956 the United States relinquished its extraterritorial rights in Morocco, 35 Dep't St.Bull. 844 (1956). See Young, The End of American Consular Jurisdiction in Morocco, 51 A.J.I.L. 402 (1957).

4. Another example of jurisdiction based on agreement arises out of the trusteeship arrangements under Chapter XII of the United Nations Charter and the mandate system under the Covenant of the League of Nations. The trustee state, while not sovereign of the trust territory, has the power to prescribe and enforce rules of law. Under the Trusteeship Agreement for the former Japanese Mandated Islands, the United States was given full powers of administration, legislation and jurisdiction. 61 Stat. 3302, T.I.A.S. No. 1665, 8 U.N.T.S. 189. The powers of the trustee state are exercised under the supervision of the Trusteeship Council of the United Nations.

5. The territory of South West Africa, of which the Republic of South Africa is the mandatory, is the only League of Nations mandate in which the mandatory still exercises jurisdiction. The International Court of Justice decided in 1950 that the supervisory functions provided for in the mandate were to be exercised by the United Nations. Advisory Opinion on the International Status of South West Africa, 1950 I.C.J. 128. The Court subsequently held that the mandate was still in existence and that charges of violations of the mandate and Charter were justiciable before the court. South West Africa Cases, Preliminary Objections, 1962 I.C.J. 319. However, the Court, in effect, reversed its 1962 decision by holding in 1966 that Liberia and Ethiopia lacked a legal right or interest in South Africa's administration of South West Africa, and dismissed their action against South Africa. South West Africa Cases, (2d Phase) 1966 I.C.J. 6. Thereafter, the General Assembly passed a resolution declaring that South Africa's mandate over South West Africa was terminated, and that "South West Africa comes under the direct responsibility of the United Nations." G.A.Res. 2145, (XXI 1966) at 2. The Republic of South Africa, however, continued to exercise jurisdiction over South West Africa.

On June 12, 1968, the General Assembly renamed the territory Namibia, G.A.Res. 2372 (XX 1968) at 1, but this was disregarded by South Africa. Its continued presence was declared in violation of Res. 2145 by a series of Security Council resolutions, S.C.Res. 264 (XXIV 1969); S.C.Res. 269, id. (1969); S.C.Res. 276, 25 id. (1970); S.C.Res. 283, id. (1970); S.C.Res. 301 (XXVI 1971); and by the International Court of Justice, 1971 I.C.J. 16. On Sept. 27, 1974, the U.N. Council for Namibia asked all nations to refrain from exploiting the mineral resources of Namibia as long as the government of South Africa continued to exercise its authority there, Namibia Decree No. 1, 29 GAOR Supp. 24A (A/9624/Add. 1) at 27 (1974). For a discussion of the legal effectiveness of this decree, see Schermers, The Namibia Decree in National Courts, 26 I.C.L.Q. 81 (1977). In 1985, the Steering Committee of the United Nations Council for Namibia decided to institute legal proceedings in The Netherlands against individuals who violate Decree No. 1. U.N. Doc. A/AC. 131/194 (1985), 80 A.J.I.L. 442 (1986). See generally Herman, The Legal Status of Namibia and of the United Nations Council for Namibia, 13 Can.Y.B.I.L. 306 (1975). The United Nations General Assembly has adopted a declaration in support of self-determination, G.A.Res. S–9/2 (S–IX 1978), and the Western states have proposed a formula for settlement to the Security Council, 17 I.L.M. 762 (1978).

6. After World War II, the United States continued to control islands captured from Japan, including Okinawa and the other Ryukyu Islands. Article 3 of the 1951 Treaty of Peace with Japan gave to the United States, pending the creation, at the option of the United States, of a United Nations trusteeship administered by the United States, "the right to exercise all and any powers of administration, legislation and jurisdiction over the territory and inhabitants of these islands, including the territorial waters." 3 U.S.T. 3169, T.I.A.S. No. 2490, 136 U.N.T.S. 45. At the time the United States denied any intent of acquiring permanent possession of the islands and stated that Japan retained "residual sovereignty." 25:637 Dep't St.Bull. 455, 463 (1951). It asserted that the interests of peace and security justified its continued control of the islands. See 30:758 Dep't.St.Bull. 17 (1954); 3 Whiteman 595–600. A number of cases held that the United States did not acquire Okinawa and the Ryukyus. See United States v. Ushi Shiroma, 123 F.Supp. 145 (D.Hawaii 1954) (native of Okinawa held not to be a national of the United States; United States possesses *de facto,* not *de jure,* sovereignty); Burna v. United States, 240 F.2d 720 (4th Cir.1957) (Okinawa is a "foreign country" within meaning of Federal Tort Claims Act). By Agreement of June 17, 1971, 3 U.S.T. 3172, T.I.A.S. No. 2490, the United States relinquished in favor of Japan all rights it had under the 1951 Treaty of Peace over the islands.

7. States may also agree to exercise jurisdiction jointly over a territory. The resulting arrangement, the so-called condominium, may call for a joint or some form of divided administration of the conjoint sovereignty of the parties. Under one such agreement the United Kingdom and France governed the New Hebrides. Protocol respecting the New Hebrides, Aug. 6, 1914, [1922] Gr.Brit. T.S. 7, Cmd. at 1681, 10 L.N.T.S. 333. See generally 1 Oppenheim at 565–67; 1 O'Connell 360–31; El–Erian, Condominium and Related Situations in International Law (1952). In 1981, the New Hebrides declared their independence.

8. By the Treaty of Uquair of 1922, Saudi Arabia and Kuwait agreed that a defined territory between the two states would be joint and common and that in this territory they would share equal rights (*mashaa'* or *mushtaraqa*). A similar treaty was concluded at the same time between Saudi Arabia and Iraq. In 1965, Saudi Arabia and Kuwait divided the joint territory into two parts, one of which was annexed to Kuwait and the other to Saudi Arabia. The 1965 Treaty preserved the interests each State had in the mineral resources in these parts, which it described as a one-half undivided interest. On these arrangements, see Lagoni, Oil and Gas Deposits Across National Frontiers, 73 A.J.I.L. 215 (1979); Onorato, Apportionment of an International Common Petroleum Deposit, 17 I.C.L.Q. 85 (1968). What rights does each of these states have to the mineral resources in these parts? In Getty Oil Co. v. Kuwait Petroleum Co. et al., Case No. 83 Civ. 0566 (S.D.N.Y.1983), Judge Pollack held that the parties were entitled to take equal parts of the oil in the ground and that, if one party took more, it had to account for the excess.

9. The United States Coast Guard stopped a Panamanian ship on the high seas, searched it, and found 20 tons of marijuana. Two crew members were prosecuted and convicted in a U.S. district court. Their conviction was upheld on the ground that Panama had agreed to the U.S. prosecution. United States v. Robinson 843 F.2d 1 (1st Cir.1988), cert. denied, 488 U.S. 834, 109 S.Ct. 93, 102 L.Ed.2d 69 (1988).

## *AGREEMENT BETWEEN THE PARTIES TO THE NORTH ATLANTIC TREATY REGARDING THE STATUS OF THEIR FORCES*

Signed at London, June 19, 1951.
4 U.S.T. 1792, T.I.A.S. No. 2846, 199 U.N.T.S. 67.

### ARTICLE VII

1. Subject to the provisions of this Article,

(a) the military authorities of the sending State shall have the right to exercise within the receiving State all criminal and disciplinary jurisdiction conferred on them by the law of the sending State over all persons subject to the military law of that State;

(b) the authorities of the receiving State shall have jurisdiction over the members of a force or civilian component and their dependents with respect to offenses committed within the territory of the receiving State and punishable by the law of that State.

2. (a) The military authorities of the sending State shall have the right to exercise exclusive jurisdiction over persons subject to the military law of that State with respect to offences, including offences relating to its security, punishable by the law of the sending State, but not by the law of the receiving State.

(b) The authorities of the receiving State shall have the right to exercise exclusive jurisdiction over members of a force or civilian component and their dependents with respect to offences, including offences relating to the security of that State, punishable by its law but not by the law of the sending State.

(c) For the purposes of this paragraph and of paragraph 3 of this Article a security offence against a State shall include (i) treason against the State; (ii) sabotage, espionage or violation of any law relating to official secrets of that State, or secrets relating to the national defence of that State.

3. In cases where the right to exercise jurisdiction is concurrent the following rules shall apply:

(a) The military authorities of the sending State shall have the primary right to exercise jurisdiction over a member of a force or of a civilian component in relation to (i) offences solely against the property or security of that State, or offences solely against the person or property of another member of the force or civilian component of that state or of a dependent; (ii) offences arising out of any act or omission done in the performance of official duty.

(b) In the case of any other offence the authorities of the receiving State shall have the primary right to exercise jurisdiction.

(c) If the State having the primary right decides not to exercise jurisdiction, it shall notify the authorities of the other State as soon as practicable. The authorities of the State having the primary right shall give sympathetic consideration to a request from the authorities of the other State for a waiver of its right in cases where that other State considers such waiver to be of particular importance.

4. The foregoing provisions of this Article shall not imply any right for the military authorities of the sending State to exercise jurisdiction over persons who are nationals of or ordinarily resident in the receiving State, unless they are members of the force of the sending State.

5. (a) The authorities of the receiving and sending States shall assist each other in the arrest of members of a force or civilian component or their dependents in the territory of the receiving State and in handing them over to the authority which is to exercise jurisdiction in accordance with the above provisions.

(b) The authorities of the receiving State shall notify promptly the military authorities of the sending State of the arrest of any member of a force or civilian component or a dependent.

(c) The custody of an accused member of a force or civilian component over whom the receiving State is to exercise jurisdiction shall, if he is in the hands of the sending State, remain with that State until he is charged by the receiving State.

6. (a) The authorities of the receiving and sending States shall assist each other in the carrying out of all necessary investigations into offences, and in the collection and production of evidence, including the seizure and, in proper cases, the handing over of objects connected with an offence. The handing over of such objects may, however, be made subject to their return within the time specified by the authority delivering them.

(b) The authorities of the Contracting Parties shall notify one another of the disposition of all cases in which there are concurrent rights to exercise jurisdiction.

7. (a) A death sentence shall not be carried out in the receiving State by the authorities of the sending State if the legislation of the receiving State does not provide for such punishment in a similar case.

* * *

8. Where an accused has been tried in accordance with the provisions of this Article by the authorities of one Contracting Party and has been acquitted, or has been convicted and is serving, or has served, his sentence or has been pardoned, he may not be tried again for the same offence within the same territory by the authorities of another Contracting Party. However, nothing in this paragraph shall prevent the military authorities of the sending State from trying a member of its force for any violation of rules of discipline arising from an act or omission which constituted an offence for which he was tried by the authorities of another Contracting Party.

9. Whenever a member of a force or civilian component or a dependent is prosecuted under the jurisdiction of a receiving State he shall be entitled—

(a) to a prompt and speedy trial;

(b) to be informed, in advance of trial, of the specific charge or charges made against him;

(c) to be confronted with the witnesses against him;

(d) to have compulsory process for obtaining witnesses in his favour, if they are within the jurisdiction of the receiving State;

(e) to have legal representation of his own choice for his defence or to have free or assisted legal representation under the conditions prevailing for the time being in the receiving State;

(f) if he considers it necessary, to have the services of a competent interpreter; and

(g) to communicate with a representative of the Government of the sending State and, when the rules of the court permit, to have such a representative present at his trial.

* * *

### *Notes*

1. The N.A.T.O. Status of Forces Agreement is supplemented by bilateral agreements between the United States and Canada (T.I.A.S. No. 3074), Denmark (T.I.A.S. No. 4002), Norway (T.I.A.S. No. 2950), Greece (T.I.A.S. No. 3649), the Netherlands (T.I.A.S. No. 3174) and Turkey (T.I.A.S. No. 3020). Iceland, although a member of N.A.T.O., is not a party to the Status of Forces Agreement; the status of United States forces in that country is regulated solely by bilateral agreement (T.I.A.S. No. 2295). Large numbers of United States military personnel are stationed in non-N.A.T.O. countries; their status is usually regulated by bilateral agreement. See, e.g., the agreements with Korea (T.I.A.S. No. 6226), Japan (T.I.A.S. No. 4510), and Australia (T.I.A.S. No. 5349). Excerpts from other status of forces agreements are included in the appendices to Stanger, Criminal Jurisdiction over Visiting Armed Forces (Naval War College International Law Studies 1957–58) (1965). No agreement relating to the status of United States forces at the time they were present in South Vietnam has been made public. For detailed discussion of the operation of status of forces agreements to which the United States is a party, see Stanger at 141–266 and the annual Hearings before a Subcommittee of the Senate Committee on Armed Services to Review the Operation of Article VII of the NATO Status of Forces Treaty, Together with * * * Other Criminal Jurisdictional Arrangements (1954). See also Health, Status of Forces Agreements as a Basis for United States Custody of an Accused, 49 Mil.L.Rev. 45 (1970); Norton, United States Obligations Under Status of Forces Agreements: A New Method of Extradition?, 5 Ga.J.Int'l & Comp.L. 1 (1975); Schwenk, Jurisdiction of Receiving State Over Forces of Sending Under NATO Status of Forces Agreement, 6 Int'l Lawyer 525 (1972); Note, NATO Status of Forces Agreement not an Exclusive Remedy for Member of United States Forces or Civilian Component, 7 Vand.J.Transnat'l L. 5211 (1974).

For bilateral status of forces agreements concluded between the Soviet Union and the German Democratic Republic, Hungary, and Poland, see 52 A.J.I.L. 210–27 (1958). For a treaty signed October 16, 1968, on the status of Soviet troops temporarily stationed in Czechoslovakia, see I.L.M. 1331–39 (1968).

On status of military forces generally, see Lazareff, Status of Military Forces Under Current International Law (1971).

2. The United States Supreme Court has, in a series of decisions, sharply limited the power of United States military authorities to try by court martial civilian employees or civilian dependents of members of United States forces. See Reid v. Covert; Kinsella v. Krueger, 354 U.S. 1, 77 S.Ct. 1222, 1 L.Ed.2d 1148

(1957); Kinsella v. United States ex rel. Singleton, 361 U.S. 234, 80 S.Ct. 297, 4 L.Ed.2d 268 (1960); Grisham v. Hagan, 361 U.S. 278, 80 S.Ct. 310, 4 L.Ed.2d 279 (1960); McElroy v. United States ex rel. Guagliardo, Wilson v. Bohlender, 361 U.S. 281, 80 S.Ct. 305, 4 L.Ed.2d 282 (1960). On these rulings, see Stanger at 176–83; Ehrenhaft, Policing Civilians Accompanying the United States Armed Forces Overseas: Can United States Commissioners Fill the Jurisdictional Gap?, 36 Geo.Wash.L.Rev. 273 (1967).

## WILSON v. GIRARD

Supreme Court of the United States, 1957.
354 U.S. 524, 77 S.Ct. 1409, 1 L.Ed. 1544.

PER CURIAM. Japan and the United States became involved in a controversy whether the respondent Girard should be tried by a Japanese court for causing the death of a Japanese woman. The basis for the dispute between the two Governments fully appears in the affidavit of Robert Dechert, General Counsel of the Department of Defense, an exhibit to a government motion in the court below, and the joint statement of Secretary of State John Foster Dulles and Secretary of Defense Charles E. Wilson, printed as appendices to this opinion.

Girard, a Specialist Third Class in the United States Army, was engaged on January 30, 1957, with members of his cavalry regiment in a small unit exercise at Camp Weir range area, Japan. Japanese civilians were present in the area, retrieving expended cartridge cases. Girard and another Specialist Third Class were ordered to guard a machine gun and some items of clothing that had been left nearby. Girard had a grenade launcher on his rifle. He placed an expended 30–caliber cartridge case in the grenade launcher and projected it by firing a blank. The expended cartridge case penetrated the back of a Japanese woman gathering expended cartridge cases and caused her death.

The United States ultimately notified Japan that Girard would be delivered to the Japanese authorities for trial. Thereafter, Japan indicted him for causing death by wounding. Girard sought a writ of habeas corpus in the United States District Court for the District of Columbia. The writ was denied, but Girard was granted declaratory relief and an injunction against his delivery to the Japanese authorities. 152 F.Supp. 21. The petitioners appealed to the Court of Appeals for the District of Columbia, and, without awaiting action by that court on the appeal, invoked the jurisdiction of this Court under 28 U.S.C. § 1254(1), 28 U.S.C.A. § 1254(1). Girard filed a cross-petition for certiorari to review the denial of the writ of habeas corpus. We granted both petitions. * * *

A Security Treaty between Japan and the United States, signed September 8, 1951, was ratified by the Senate on March 20, 1952, and proclaimed by the President effective April 28, 1952 [3 U.S.T. 3329, T.I.A.S. 2491]. Article III of the Treaty authorized the making of Administrative Agreements between the two Governments concerning "[t]he conditions which shall govern the disposition of armed forces of the United States of America in and about Japan * * *." Expressly acting under this provision, the two Nations, on February 28, 1952, signed an Administrative Agreement covering, among other matters, the jurisdiction of the United States over offenses committed in Japan by members of the United States armed forces, and providing that jurisdiction in any case might be waived by the United States. This Agreement [3 U.S.T. 3341, T.I.A.S. 2492] became effective on the same date as the Security Treaty (April 28, 1952) and was considered by the Senate before consent was given to the Treaty.

Article XVII, paragraph 1, of the Administrative Agreement provided that upon the coming into effect of the "Agreement between the Parties to the North Atlantic Treaty regarding the Status of their Forces," [4 U.S.T. 1792, T.I.A.S. 2846] signed June 19, 1951, the United States would conclude with Japan an agreement on criminal jurisdiction similar to the corresponding provisions of the NATO Agreement. The NATO Agreement became effective August 23, 1953, and the United States and Japan signed on September 29, 1953, effective October 29, 1953, a Protocol Agreement [4 U.S.T. 1846, T.I.A.S. 2848] pursuant to the covenant in paragraph 1 of Article XVII.

Paragraph 3 of Article XVII, as amended by the Protocol, dealt with criminal offenses in violation of the laws of both Nations and provided:

> 3. In cases where the right to exercise jurisdiction is concurrent the following rules shall apply:
>
> (a) The military authorities of the United States shall have the primary right to exercise jurisdiction over members of the United States armed forces or the civilian component in relation to
>
> > (i) offenses solely against the property or security of the United States, or offenses solely against the person or property of another member of the United States armed forces or the civilian component or of a dependent;
> >
> > (ii) offenses arising out of any act or omission done in the performance of official duty.
>
> (b) In the case of any other offense the authorities of Japan shall have the primary right to exercise jurisdiction.
>
> (c) If the State having the primary right decides not to exercise jurisdiction, it shall notify the authorities of the other State as soon as practicable. The authorities of the State having the primary right shall give sympathetic consideration to a request from the authorities of the other State for a waiver of its right in cases where that other State considers such waiver to be of particular importance.

Article XXVI of the Administrative Agreement established a Joint Committee of representatives of the United States and Japan to consult on all matters requiring mutual consultation regarding the implementation of the Agreement; and provided that if the Committee "* * * is unable to resolve any matter, it shall refer that matter to the respective governments for further consideration through appropriate channels."

In the light of the Senate's ratification of the Security Treaty after consideration of the Administrative Agreement, which had already been signed, and its subsequent ratification of the NATO Agreement, with knowledge of the commitment to Japan under the Administrative Agreement, we are satisfied that the approval of Article III of the Security Treaty authorized the making of the Administrative Agreement and the subsequent Protocol embodying the NATO Agreement provisions governing jurisdiction to try criminal offenses.

The United States claimed the right to try Girard upon the ground that his act, as certified by his commanding officer, was "done in the performance of official duty" and therefore the United States had primary jurisdiction. Japan insisted that it had proof that Girard's action was without the scope of his official duty and therefore that Japan had the primary right to try him.

The Joint Committee, after prolonged deliberations, was unable to agree. The issue was referred to higher authority, which authorized the United States representatives on the Joint Committee to notify the appropriate Japanese authorities, in accordance with paragraph 3(c) of the Protocol, that the United States had decided not to exercise, but to waive, whatever jurisdiction it might have in the case. The Secretary of State and the Secretary of Defense decided that this determination should be carried out. The President confirmed their joint conclusion.

A sovereign nation has exclusive jurisdiction to punish offenses against its laws committed within its borders, unless it expressly or impliedly consents to surrender its jurisdiction. The Schooner Exchange v. M'Faddon, 7 Cranch 116, 136, 3 L.Ed. 287. Japan's cession to the United States of jurisdiction to try American military personnel for conduct constituting an offense against the laws of both countries was conditioned by the covenant of Article XVII, section 3, paragraph (c) of the Protocol that

> "* * * The authorities of the State having the primary right shall give sympathetic consideration to a request from the authorities of the other State for a waiver of its right in cases where that other State considers such waiver to be of particular importance."

The issue for our decision is therefore narrowed to the question whether, upon the record before us, the Constitution or legislation subsequent to the Security Treaty prohibited the carrying out of this provision authorized by the Treaty for waiver of the qualified jurisdiction granted by Japan. We find no constitutional or statutory barrier to the provision as applied here. In the absence of such encroachments, the wisdom of the arrangement is exclusively for the determination of the Executive and Legislative Branches.

The judgment of the District Court in No. 1103 is reversed, and its judgment in No. 1108 is affirmed.

MR. JUSTICE DOUGLAS took no part in the consideration or decision of this case.

[Appendices omitted.]

## *AGREEMENT BETWEEN THE UNITED NATIONS AND CYPRUS CONCERNING THE STATUS OF THE UNITED NATIONS PEACE-KEEPING FORCE IN CYPRUS*

492 U.N.T.S. 57 (1964).

* * *

11. Members of the Force shall be subject to the exclusive jurisdiction of their respective national States in respect of any criminal offenses which may be committed by them in Cyprus.

12. (a) Members of the Force shall not be subject to the civil jurisdiction of the courts of Cyprus or to other legal process in any matter relating to their official duties. In a case arising from a matter relating to the official duties of a member of the Force and which involves a member of the Force and a Cypriot citizen, and in other disputes as agreed, the procedure provided in paragraph 38(b) shall apply to the settlement.

(b) In those cases where civil jurisdiction is exercised by the courts of Cyprus with respect to members of the Force, the courts or other Cypriot authorities shall grant members of the Force sufficient opportunity to safeguard their rights. If the Commander certifies that a member of the Force is unable because of official duties or authorized absence to protect his interests in a civil proceeding in which he is a participant the aforesaid court or authority shall at his request suspend the proceeding until the elimination of the disability, but for not more than ninety days. Property of a member of the Force which is certified by the Commander to be needed by him for the fulfillment of his official duties shall be free from seizure for the satisfaction of a judgment, decision or order, together with other property not subject thereto under the law of Cyprus. The personal liberty of a member of the Force shall not be restricted by a court or other Cypriot authority in a civil proceeding, whether to enforce a judgment, decision or order, to compel an oath of disclosure, or for any other reason. * * *

* * *

15. Military police of the Force may take into custody any Cypriot citizen committing an offence or causing a disturbance on the premises referred to in paragraph 19, without subjecting him to the ordinary routine of arrest, in order immediately to deliver him to the nearest appropriate Cypriot authorities for the purpose of dealing with such offence or disturbance.

16. The Cypriot authorities may take into custody a member of the Force, without subjecting him to the ordinary routine of arrest in order immediately to deliver him, together with any weapons or items seized, to the nearest appropriate authorities of the Force: (a) when so requested by the Commander, or (b) in cases in which the military police of the Force are unable to act with the necessary promptness when a member of the Force is apprehended in the commission or attempted commission of a criminal offence that results or might result in serious injury to persons or property, or serious impairment of other legally protected rights.

* * *

18. The Commander and the Cypriot authorities shall assist each other in the carrying out of all necessary investigations into offences in respect of which either or both have an interest, in the production of witnesses, and in the collection and production of evidence, including the seizure and, in proper cases, the handing over, of things connected with an offence. The handing over of any such things may be made subject to their return within the time specified by the authority delivering them. Each shall notify the other of the disposition of any case in the outcome of which the other may have an interest or in which there has been a transfer of custody under the provisions of paragraphs 15 and 16 of these arrangements. The government will ensure the prosecution of persons subject to its criminal jurisdiction who are accused of acts in relation to the Force or its members which, if committed in relation to the Cypriot army or its members, would have rendered them liable to prosecution. The Secretary–General will seek assurances from Governments of Participating States that they will be prepared to exercise jurisdiction with respect to crimes or offences which may be committed against Cypriot citizens by members of their national contingents serving with the Force. * * *

### *Notes*

1. Agreements were also concluded by the United Nations with Egypt, 260 U.N.T.S. 61, on the status of the United Nations Emergency Force (UNEF) in Egyptian territory, and with the Republic of the Congo, 414 U.N.T.S. 229, on the status of the United Nations Force in the Congo (ONUC). For comprehensive analysis and discussion, see Bowett, United Nations Forces (1964); Seyersted, United Nations Forces in the Law of Peace and War (1966).

2. Recently, United Nations military forces have been in Saudi Arabia, Cambodia, the former Yugoslavian republics (Slovenia, Serbia, Croatia, Bosnia–Herzegovina, Montenegro, and Macedonia) and Somalia. To what extent were these troops subject to the jurisdiction of Saudi Arabia?

In the case of Cambodia, although there was no stable government at the time, by Resolution 745 (1992), the Security Council decided to establish the Transitional Authority in Cambodia in order to contribute to the restoration and maintenance of peace and the holding of free elections, in line with agreements signed by the principal parties in Paris on October 23, 1991. To what extent are these troops subject to the jurisdiction of Cambodia?

As an interim arrangement to create conditions for peace and security required for the negotiation of an overall settlement of the Yugoslav crisis, the Security Council passed Resolution 743 (1992), which established a United Nations Protection Force for an initial period of 12 months. Later, Resolution 758 (1992) extended its mandate to allow for the deployment of additional personnel in Bosnia–Herzegovinia. Additional contributions have been authorized by Resolutions 761, 762, and 764 (1992). To what extent are these troops subject to the jurisdiction of the republic in which they are situated?

In the case of Somalia, where the civilian population of the country was starving as a civil war raged between gangs led by war-lords, the Secretary–General of the United Nations urged military action to ensure that United Nations relief efforts could achieve their goal of feeding the starving population. In his opinion "no government exist[ed] in Somalia that could request and allow such use of force." U.N. Doc. S/24868, at 3. On December 3, 1992, the Security Council adopted a resolution authorizing the use of military force to establish "a secure environment for humanitarian relief operations in Somalia." To what extent are the troops and the relief agents under the jurisdiction of Somalia?

## SECTION 6. CONFLICTS OF JURISDICTION

Bases of jurisdiction frequently overlap. For example, a state may, on the basis of the nationality principle, reach its nationals abroad, but the conduct of the nationals of that state may, on the basis of the territorial principle, also be within the jurisdiction of the foreign state in which these nationals act. Similarly, one state may have jurisdiction under the subjective territorial principle and another under the objective territorial or the protective principle.

These overlaps lead to particularly vexing problems when one of the states having jurisdiction prohibits conduct that the other state having jurisdiction commands. These problems are exemplified by United States v. The Bank of Nova Scotia, p. 1098.

However, there may also be conflicts of jurisdiction when one state prohibits conduct that the other state does not command, but permits or encourages. In those cases, the permitting state, if it is sufficiently concerned, may turn the permission into a command. The inclination to do so becomes particularly strong if, as United States courts initially ruled, a United States court would not apply a coercive United States law extraterritorially if the foreign state where the conduct was required forbade it. Many of the so-called blocking statutes, p. 1105 infra, were enacted in an effort to accommodate nationals or residents subject to foreign extraterritorial prohibitions and provide them with a proper defense in American courts. As might have been expected, the response of American courts to the emergence of these statutes has been to limit, if not eliminate, the availability of this defense.

The imposition of the limitation of reasonableness by Restatement (Third) § 403 would reduce the area of overlap and, as a consequence, the possibility of conflicts of jurisdiction. But it would not eliminate the possibility of conflicts altogether. Indeed, it might aggravate the conflict by giving a state the opportunity to argue that reasonableness, and therefore international law, is on its side.

In an attempt to deal with these conflicts of jurisdiction, the Restatement (Third) provides in Section 441, reproduced infra, its suggested solution. Whether its attempt is successful should be considered in the light of the materials that follow.

### UNITED STATES v. THE BANK OF NOVA SCOTIA

United States Court of Appeals, Eleventh Circuit, 1982.

691 F.2d 1384, cert. denied, 462 U.S. 1119, 103 S.Ct. 3086, 77 L.Ed. 1348 (1983).

LEWIS R. MORGAN, SENIOR CIRCUIT JUDGE: *

The Bank of Nova Scotia appeals from an order of the United States District Court for the Southern District of Florida holding the Bank of Nova

* Some footnotes omitted; others renumbered.

Scotia in civil contempt for failing to comply with an order of the court enforcing a grand jury subpoena duces tecum. The Bank of Nova Scotia (the Bank) presents three arguments against enforcing the subpoena. The Bank first contends that there were insufficient grounds to enforce the subpoena. The Bank also contends that enforcing the subpoena would violate due process. Finally, the Bank argues that the subpoena should not be enforced as a matter of comity between nations. We find that Bank's contentions to be without merit, and therefore we affirm the district court.

## I. Facts

The Bank of Nova Scotia is a Canadian chartered bank with branches and agencies in forty-five countries, including the United States and the Bahamas. A federal grand jury conducting a tax and narcotics investigation issued a subpoena duces tecum to the Bank calling for the production of certain records maintained at the Bank's main branch or any of its branch offices in Nassau, Bahamas and Antigua, Lesser Antilles, relating to the bank accounts of a customer of the Bank.[1] The subpoena was served on the Bank's Miami, Florida agency on September 23, 1981. The Bank declined to produce the documents asserting that compliance with the subpoena without the customer's consent or an order of the Bahamian courts would violate Bahamian bank secrecy laws.[2]

1. The Bank investigated and found no documents which were requested located at its Antigua branch. Accordingly, that part of the subpoena is not in issue.

2. Banks and Trust Companies Regulations Act of 1965, 1965 Bah.Acts No. 64, as amended by the Banks and Trust Companies Regulation (Amendment) Act, 1980, 1980 Bah. Acts No. 3, and Section 19 of the Banks Act, III Bah.Rev.Laws, c. 96 (1965), as amended by the Banks Amendment Act 1980, 1980 Bah. Acts No. ______. Both Section 10 and Section 19 are identical. Section 10 of the Bank and Trust Companies Regulation Act as amended provides:

Preservation of secrecy

10.—(1) No person who has acquired information in his capacity as—

(a) director, officer, employee or agent of any licensee or former licensee;

(b) counsel and attorney, consultant or auditor of the Central Bank of The Bahamas, established under section 3 of the Central Bank of The Bahamas Act 1974, or as an employee or agent of such counsel and attorney, consultant or auditor;

(c) counsel and attorney, consultant, auditor, accountant, receiver or liquidator of any licensee or former licensee or as an employee or agent of such counsel and attorney, consultant, auditor, accountant, receiver or liquidator;

(d) auditor of any customer of any licensee or former licensee or as an employee or agent of such auditor;

(e) the Inspector under the provisions of this Act,

shall, without the express or implied consent of the customer concerned, disclose to any person any such information relating to the identity, assets, liabilities, transactions, accounts of a customer of a licensee or relating to any application by any person under the provisions of this Act, as the case may be, except—

(i) for the purpose of the performance of his duties or the exercise of his functions under this Act, if any; or

(ii) for the purpose of the performance of his duties within the scope of his employment; or

(iii) when a licensee is lawfully required to make disclosure by any court of competent jurisdiction within The Bahamas, or under the provisions of any law of The Bahamas.

—(2) Nothing contained in this section shall—

(a) prejudice or derogate from the rights and duties subsisting at common law between a licensee and its customer; or

(b) prevent a licensee from providing upon a legitimate business request in the normal course of business a general credit rating with respect to a customer.

—(3) Every person who contravenes the provisions of subsection (1) of this section shall be guilty of an offense against this Act and shall be liable on summary conviction to a fine not exceeding fifteen thousand

A hearing was held on the government's motion to compel the Bank to comply with the subpoena on January 13, 1982. * * * The Bank also presented an affidavit showing that compliance with the subpoena could expose the Bank to prosecution under the Bahamian bank secrecy law. The affidavit also showed that the government could obtain an order of judicial assistance from the Supreme Court of the Bahamas allowing disclosure if the subject of the grand jury investigation is a crime under Bahamian law and not solely criminal under United States tax laws. The government did not make a showing that the documents sought are relevant and necessary to the grand jury's investigation.

After the district court entered an order compelling the Bank to comply with the subpoena, the Bank's Miami agent appeared before the grand jury and formally declined to produce the documents called for by the subpoena. The district court held the Bank in civil contempt and the Bank brings this appeal.

II. Relevance of the Documents

The Bank urges this court to follow the Third Circuit's holdings in In re Grand Jury Proceedings, 486 F.2d 85 (Schofield I), (3rd Cir.1973), and In re Grand Jury Proceedings, 507 F.2d 963 (Schofield II), (3rd Cir.1975), cert. denied, 421 U.S. 1015, 95 S.Ct. 2424, 44 L.Ed.2d 685 (1975), and require the government to show that the documents sought are relevant to an investigation properly within the grand jury's jurisdiction and not sought primarily for another purpose. * * *

The guidelines established by the Third Circuit in *Schofield* are not mandated by the Constitution; the Third Circuit imposed the requirements under that court's inherent supervisory power. *Schofield,* 486 F.2d at 89; *McLean,* 565 F.2d at 320. We decline to impose any undue restrictions upon the grand jury investigative process pursuant to this court's supervisory power. * * *

While it is true courts should not impinge upon the political prerogatives of the government in the sensitive area of foreign relations, Chicago and Southern Air Lines v. Waterman Steamship Corp., 333 U.S. 103, 111, 68 S.Ct. 431, 436, 92 L.Ed. 568 (1948), accepting the Bank's position would be a greater interference with foreign relations than the procedures employed here. In essence, the Bank would require the government to chose between impeding the grand jury's investigation and petitioning the Supreme Court of the Bahamas for an order of disclosure.

This court is cognizant that international friction has been provoked by enforcement of subpoenas such as the one in question. See, Restatement

dollars or to a term of imprisonment not exceeding two years or to both such fine and imprisonment.

The government argues the Bank would not be successfully prosecuted by Bahamian authorities if it complied with the subpoena. In this regard it argues that because Section 10(2)(a) expressly preserves the common law relationship between bank and customers, the Bank is authorized to disclose the requested information. See Tournier v. National Provincial and Union Bank of England, [1924] 1 K.B. 461 (Banker may disclose banking information concerning a customer where the banker is compelled by law to disclose information); Barclay's Bank International, Ltd. v. McKinney, No. 474 (Bah.S.Ct. Feb. 16, 1979). Although the determination of foreign law is reviewable on appeal, F.R.Civ.P. 44.1, we shall assume for purposes of this appeal that the Bank will be subject to criminal sanctions in the Bahamas.

(Revised) of Foreign Relations Law of the United States § 420, Reporter's Note 1. See generally, Rio Tinto Zinc Corp. v. Westinghouse Electric Corp., [1978] A.C. 547, 616, 629–31, 639–40, 650 (H.L.) (criticizing the United States for claims of "jurisdiction over foreigners in respect to acts done outside the jurisdiction of that country"). But as recognized in United States v. First National City Bank, 379 U.S. 378, 384–85, 85 S.Ct. 528, 531–32, 13 L.Ed.2d 365 (1965), the various federal courts remain open to the legislative and executive branches of our government if matters such as this prove to have international repercussions. See, e.g., Convention on Double Taxation of Income, September 27, 1951. United States–Switzerland, 2 U.S.T. 1751, T.I.A.S. No. 2316 (Swiss–US Tax Treaty providing for exchange of information for, inter alia, the prevention of fraud.)

III. Due Process

The Bank contends that compliance with the subpoena would require it to violate the Bahamian bank secrecy law and therefore enforcing the subpoena and imposing contempt sanctions for noncompliance violates due process under Société Internationale pour Participations Industrielles v. Rogers, 357 U.S. 197, 78 S.Ct. 1087, 2 L.Ed.2d 1255 (1958). The Bank argues that once it has shown Bahamian law bars production of the documents and that it is a disinterested custodian of the documents due process prohibits enforcement of the subpoena. We disagree.

The Bank attempts to fashion a due process defense to the contempt proceedings because of its lack of purposeful involvement or responsibility in the subject matter before the court. In essence, the Bank asserts it is fundamentally unfair to require a "mere stakeholder" to incur criminal liability in the Bahamas. The Bank's position does not withstand analysis.

In *Societe Internationale* a Swiss holding company brought an action to recover assets seized under the Trading with the Enemy Act. The district court had ordered production of certain banking records of a Swiss bank pursuant to the government's discovery request. The holding company failed to comply with the court's order, after good faith efforts were made to comply, on the grounds that compliance would violate Swiss penal laws. The district court then dismissed the suit with prejudice due to noncompliance with the production order. In reversing the district court, the Supreme Court did not erect an absolute bar to sanctions being imposed for noncompliance with summons or subpoenas whenever compliance is prohibited by foreign law. *Societe Internationale,* 357 U.S. at 105–06, 78 S.Ct. 1092–93; United States v. Vetco, Inc., 644 F.2d 1324, 1329 (9th Cir.1981), cert. denied, 454 U.S. 1098, 102 S.Ct. 671 (1981). *Societe Internationale* held only that the sanction of outright dismissal of that plaintiff's complaint could not be imposed where that plaintiff had acted in good faith, was unable to comply because of foreign law, and was entitled to a hearing on the merits in order for the Trading with the Enemy Act to withstand constitutional challenge. *Societe Internationale,* 352 U.S. at 211–12, 78 S.Ct. at 1095–96. Compare, National Hockey League v. Metropolitan Hockey Club, Inc., 427 U.S. 639, 96 S.Ct. 2778, 49 L.Ed.2d 747 (1976), and Roadway Express, Inc. v. Piper, 447 U.S. 752, 767 n. 14, 100 S.Ct. 2455, 2464 n. 14, 65 L.Ed.2d 488 n. 14 (1980). (emphasizing bad faith vs. inability to comply dichotomy). See United States v. Vetco, 644 F.2d at 1329–30. The Court left the district court free to impose other sanctions. *Societe Internationale,* 357 U.S. at 213, 78 S.Ct. at 1096. *Societe Internationale* does not stand for the proposition that a lawfully issued grand jury subpoena may be resisted on constitutional grounds where compliance would violate foreign criminal law. See, e.g., United States v. Vetco, Inc., 644 F.2d at 1329; Ohio v. Arthur Andersen & Co., 570 F.2d 1370 (10th Cir.1978), cert. denied, 439 U.S. 833, 99 S.Ct. 114, 58 L.Ed.2d 129 (1979); SEC v. Banca Della Suizzera Italiance, 92 F.R.D. 111 (S.D.N.Y.1981).

The Bank has failed to bring itself within the holding of *Societe Internationale.* The district court found the Bank had not made a good faith effort to comply with the subpoena in its order of June 11, 1982. Record at 140. The Bahamian government has not acted to prevent the Bank from complying with the subpoena. Finally, the Bank is not being denied a constitutionally required forum to recover confiscated assets.[3]

## IV. Comity

The Bank's final contention is that comity between nations precludes enforcement of the subpoena. The Bank argues that the district court improperly analyzed this case under the balancing test of the Restatement (Second) of Foreign Relations Law of the United States § 40 (1965) adopted in In re Grand Jury Proceedings, United States v. Field, 532 F.2d 404 (5th Cir.1976), cert. denied, 429 U.S. 940, 97 S.Ct. 354, 50 L.Ed.2d 309 (1976).[4] The district court concluded that because compliance with the subpoena may cause the Bank to violate Bahamian penal laws, it was appropriate to follow the balancing test adopted in *Field.* Because we conclude this case is controlled by *Field,* we affirm the court below.

In *Field* contempt penalties were upheld against a nonresident alien who, having been subpoenaed to testify before a grand jury while present in the United States, refused to answer questions before the grand jury, despite the witness' assertion that the very act of testifying would subject him to criminal penalties in his country of residence. Id. at 405. The grand jury was investigating the use of foreign banks in evading tax enforcement. Field was an officer of a bank located in the Grand Cayman Islands, British West Indies, and was subpoenaed to testify about matters concerning his bank and its clients. Id. at 405–06. After balancing the competing interests

**3.** It is difficult to fashion due process protections recognizing the differential argued by the Bank, i.e., stakeholder vs. participant. If fairness is the key, as is asserted here, then it seems hardly offensive to "traditional notions of fair play and substantial justice," Milliken v. Meyer, 311 U.S. 457, 463, 61 S.Ct. 339, 343, 85 L.Ed. 278 (1940), to subject entities who do business in the United States and thereby voluntarily bring themselves within the jurisdiction of our courts and legislatures to the burdens of United States law.

**4.** Section 40 reads:

Limitations on Exercise of Enforcement Jurisdiction

Where two states have jurisdiction to prescribe and enforce rules of law and the rules they may prescribe require inconsistent conduct upon the part of a person, each state is required by international law to consider, in good faith, moderating the exercise of its enforcement jurisdiction, in the light of such factors as

(a) vital national interests of each of the states,

(b) the extent and the nature of the hardship that inconsistent enforcement actions would impose upon the person,

(c) the extent to which the required conduct is to take place in the territory of the other state.

(d) the nationality of the person, and

(e) the extent to which enforcement by action of either state can reasonably be expected to achieve compliance with the rule prescribed by that state.

of the United States and the Cayman Islands under the Restatement approach, the court affirmed the district court's imposition of contempt sanctions against Field. Id. at 407–09.

The situation before us is similar to that in *Field* in all material respects. The Bank has been subpoenaed while subject to the jurisdiction of our courts and has been required to disclose information before a grand jury even though the very fact of disclosure may subject the Bank to criminal sanctions by a foreign sovereign.

The Bank attempts to distinguish *Field* from the case before us on four grounds. The Bank first asserts that the Bank itself is not under investigation by the grand jury, unlike the situation in *Field.* See United States v. Payner, 447 U.S. 727, 100 S.Ct. 2439, 65 L.Ed.2d 468 (1980) (Castle Bank and Trust Company of Nassau, Bahamas under investigation in 1972 as part of narcotics investigation known as "Operation Trade Winds"). A careful reading of *Field* reveals that the fact that Castle Bank and Trust Company was under investigation did not affect the court's analysis. That court was concerned with the proliferation of foreign secret bank accounts utilized by Americans to evade income taxes and conceal crimes. In re Grand Jury Proceedings, United States v. Field, 523 F.2d at 407–08. The instant subpoena calls for the production of certain records relating to bank accounts of a United States citizen pursuant to a tax and narcotics investigation.

Second, the Bank argues this case is distinguishable from *Field* because documentary evidence is requested here rather than testimonial evidence as in *Field.* The distinction, while real, is immaterial. The case before us concerns the relations among nations; whether the subpoena will be enforced is a matter of international comity. Id. at 407. Comity is "a nation's expression of understanding which demonstrates due regard both to international duty and convenience and to the rights of persons protected by its own laws." Somportex Limited v. Philadelphia Chewing Gum Corp., 453 F.2d 435 (3rd Cir.1971), cert. denied, 405 U.S. 1017, 92 S.Ct. 1294, 31 L.Ed.2d 479 (1972). Whether the requested information is testimonial or documentary, the effect on the competing state interests will be the same. The deference accorded the Bahamian interest is not to be diminished by the form of the requested information.

Third, the bank argues this case is distinguishable from *Field* because the instant subpoena calls for information located in the Bahamas instead of the United States. This argument is without merit for two reasons. First, the disclosure to the grand jury will occur in this country. See United States v. Vetco, Inc., 644 F.2d at 1332. Second, the affront to the Bahamas occurs no matter where the information is originally located; the interest of the Bahamas in preserving the secrecy of these records is impinged by the fact of disclosure itself.

Finally, the Bank contends the government "could avoid rather than provoke disrespect for the sovereignty of a friendly nation" by pursuing the alternative of applying for an order of judicial assistance permitting disclosure from the Supreme Court of the Bahamas. Brief of Appellant at 18. See United States v. Vetco, Inc., 644 F.2d at 1332; United States v. First National City Bank, 396 F.2d 897 (2d Cir.1968); Restatement (Revised) of

Foreign Relations Law of the United States § 420 (Tent.Draft No. 3, 1982). Applying for judicial assistance, however, is not a substantially equivalent means for obtaining production because of the cost in time and money and the uncertain likelihood of success in obtaining the order. According to the affidavit from a member of the Honorable Society of Lincoln's Inn, England, and of the Bahamas Bar, the Supreme Court of the Bahamas does not have power to order disclosure if the subject of the investigation is criminal only under the tax laws of the United States. Therefore, it is not clear to any degree of certainty that the Bahamian court would order disclosure of all the requested documents.[5]

The judicial assistance procedure does not afford due deference to the United States' interests. In essence, the Bank asks the court to require our government to ask the courts of the Bahamas to be allowed to do something lawful under United States law. We conclude such a procedure to be contrary to the interests of our nation and outweigh the interests of the Bahamas.

In *Field* the vital role of a grand jury's investigative function to our system of jurisprudence and the crucial importance of the collection of revenue to the "financial integrity of the republic" outweighed the Cayman Islands' interest in protecting the right of privacy incorporated into its bank secrecy laws. In re Grand Jury Proceedings. United States v. Field, 532 F.2d at 407–08. The United States' interest in the case before us has not been diminished since *Field* was decided. The Bank asserts the Bahamas' interest in the right of privacy; this interest is similarly outweighed. A Bahamian court would be able to order production of these documents. Banks and Trust Companies Regulation Act, 1965 Bah.Acts No. 64, § 10(I)(iii), as amended 1980 Bah.Acts No. 3. In addition, numerous officials, employees, attorneys, and agents of the Bank of Nova Scotia or the Central Bank of the Bahamas may disclose information regarding the account in the performance of their various functions under the Bank Act. Id. § 10(1)(a–e). It is incongruous to suggest that a United States court afford greater protection to the customer's right of privacy than would a Bahamian court simply because this is a foreign tribunal. In re Grand Jury Proceedings. United States v. Field, 535 F.2d at 408. A statute that is "hardly a blanket guarantee of privacy" does not present a Bahamian interest sufficient to outweigh the United States' interest in collecting revenues and insuring an unimpeded and efficacious grand jury process. See United States v. Payner, 447 U.S. 727, 731, 100 S.Ct. 2439, 2444, 65 L.Ed.2d 468 n. 4 (1980) (predecessor statute identical in relevant parts held not to create a reasonable expectation of privacy).

## V. Conclusion

Absent direction from the Legislative and Executive branches of our federal government, we are not willing to emasculate the grand jury process whenever a foreign nation attempts to block our criminal justice process. It is unfortunate the Bank of Nova Scotia suffers from differing legal commands of separate sovereigns, but as we stated in *Field:*

5. The Bank conceded at oral argument that if the grand jury is conducting a tax investigation the documents could not be obtained through the judicial assistance procedure.

> In a world where commercial transactions are international in scope, conflicts are inevitable. Courts and legislatures should take every reasonable precaution to avoid placing individuals in the situation [the Bank] finds [it]self. Yet, this court simply cannot acquiesce in the proposition that United States criminal investigations must be thwarted whenever there is conflict with the interest of other states.

In re Grand Jury Proceedings. United States v. Field, 535 F.2d at 410.

For the reasons stated above, the judgment entered by the district court is

Affirmed.

### *Notes*

1. For a subsequent decision to the same effect, see In re Societe Nationale Industrielle Aerospatiale et al., 782 F.2d 120 (8th Cir.1986), vac'd and rem'd, 482 U.S. 522, 107 S.Ct. 2542, 96 L.Ed.2d 461 (1987).

2. Initially, United States courts ruled that they would not require acts that would run afoul of the law of the foreign country in which they were to be performed. See, e.g., United States v. General Electric Co., 115 F.Supp. 835 (D.N.J.1953). See also Restatement (Third) § 441, Reporters' Notes 1 and 3. In United States v. First National City Bank, 396 F.2d 897 (2d Cir.1968), the Second Circuit stated, in dictum, that it would follow this rule even if the foreign prohibition was of a civil nature only. In this case, Citibank had argued that it should not be compelled to produce documents located in its German branch, because its disclosure would expose it to a civil damage suit in Germany. The Court ultimately ruled that Citibank had failed to show that this was a realistic danger.

3. Around the time these early decisions were rendered, foreign countries started to enact statutes forbidding, in specified circumstances, compliance with a foreign court order or law. Much cited examples are the Ontario Business Records Protection act, 1947 Ont.Rev.Stat. c. 54, and the Dutch Economic Competition Act of 1956, Staatsblad 1956, No. 401, § 39. For further examples, see Restatement (Third) § 442, Reporters' Note 4.

4. The response by American courts has been twofold. First, they have construed the pertinent foreign laws not to prohibit the conduct required by American law. See, e.g., First National City Bank of New York v. Internal Revenue Service, 271 F.2d 616 (2d Cir.1959), cert. denied, 361 U.S. 948, 80 S.Ct. 402, 4 L.Ed.2d 381 (1960); United States v. First National City Bank, 396 F.2d 897 (2d Cir.1968). It should be noted in this connection that the impact of blocking statutes, which prohibit the production of information in aid of foreign litigation, may be avoided by producing the information not in the foreign state but in the United States. These statutes generally do not prohibit that the person who possesses the information carry it to the state that requires its production. Once it has been carried to that state, its production can there be effectuated without running afoul of the prohibition. Cf. In re Anschuetz & Co., GmbH, 754 F.2d 602 (5th Cir.1985). Of course, a blocking statute might be construed to prohibit production in the state requiring production, but that would give it the very extraterritorial effect that is alleged to be objectionable to the state that enacted it.

5. The second type of response of American courts has taken the form of their being exacting in determining whether the person subject to the American

command had made a good faith effort to avoid the foreign prohibition. The requirement that the person seeking to invoke a foreign prohibition as an excuse for non-compliance with an American command must make a good faith effort to avoid, or seek dispensation from, the foreign prohibition, finds a solid basis in the Supreme Court's decision in Société Internationale pour des Participations Industrielles et Commerciales, S.A. v. Rogers, 357 U.S. 197, 78 S.Ct. 1087, 2 L.Ed.2d 1255 (1958). See Note, Extraterritorial Discovery: An Analysis Based on Good Faith, 83 Colum.L.Rev. 1320 (1983).

6. In an effort to avoid being caught in the vise of conflicting demands, a number of litigants have sought the assistance of foreign courts in resisting the commands of American courts. This type of judicial confrontationism has not led to success for those who practiced it. A number of courts have issued injunctions enjoining litigants from complying with foreign court orders. See Marc Rich & Co. A.G. v. United States, 736 F.2d 864 (2d Cir.1984); see also Restatement (Third) § 403, Reporters' Note 7. But these injunctions have not proved effective. American courts, faced with foreign injunctions, have generally insisted upon compliance with their orders. See, e.g., Laker Airways, Ltd. v. Sabena, Belgian World Airlines, 731 F.2d 909 (D.C.Cir.1984). Their insistence has been facilitated by the circumstance that, in this game of judicial daring, the actual confrontation does not occur until the court that issued the injunction imposes sanctions for its disobedience. Thus far, no court has taken this ultimate step. Indeed, it is generally recognized that this type of judicial confrontation is to be avoided as incompatible with proper relations between members of the world community. See Restatement (Third) § 403, Reporters' Note 7. Cf. also British Airways Board v. Laker Airways, [1985] A.C. 58 (reversing an injunction enjoining Laker from pursuing an antitrust action in an American court).

7. The principal case reflects the most recent American response to foreign efforts to prohibit recourse to American procedures seeking information abroad. See also in re Grand Jury Proceedings, 691 F.2d 1384 (11th Cir.1982), cert. denied, 462 U.S. 1119, 103 S.Ct. 3086, 77 L.Ed.2d 1348 (1983); Remington Products, Inc. v. North American Philips Corp., 107 F.R.D. 642 (D.C.Conn.1985) (precluding reliance on Dutch blocking statute); Graco, Inc. v. Kremlin, Inc., 101 F.R.D. 503 (N.D.Ill.1984) (rejecting reliance on the French blocking statute). But see Reinsurance Co. v. Administratia Asigurarilor de stat, 902 F.2d 1275 (7th Cir.1990). Cf. also In re Anschuetz & Co., GmbH, 754 F.2d 602 (5th Cir.1985). For a discussion of the steadily increasing number of foreign blocking statutes, see Restatement (Third) § 442, Reporters' Note 4. See also Lowe, Blocking Extraterritorial Jurisdiction: The British Protection of Trading Interests Act, 75 A.J.I.L. 257 (1981).

8. The Restatement (Third) § 442 deals in a separate section with conflicts of jurisdiction in obtaining disclosure abroad. As foreign enterprises increasingly become involved in American commerce, they increasingly are sued in American courts. When, in such actions, documents must be served, or disclosure obtained abroad, foreign states involved have, with growing measure, objected to the performance of the necessary procedural acts on their territory. These objections have often been defended as based on international law. The performance of such acts is, it has been argued, an infringement upon the foreign state's sovereignty. When the procedural act is performed by a private person, such as service by a person not a party over 18 years of age or a deposition before a private person agreed upon by the parties, the argument may be based on a misconception of American procedural rules. See Smit, Interna-

tional Cooperation in Civil Litigation: Some Observations on the Rules of International Law and Reciprocity, 9 Neth.Int.L.Rev. 137 (1963). Even if the procedural act is performed by a government official, in the absence of a clearly expressed objection, international law would not appear to be breached. The Supreme Court so ruled in Blackmer v. United States, 284 U.S. 421, 52 S.Ct. 252, 76 L.Ed. 375 (1932), p. 832 supra. In this case, involving service by an American consul of a subpoena on a United States citizen in Paris, Chief Justice Hughes stated that France could hardly be assumed to object to such service. On these problems generally, see Smit, International Aspects of Federal Civil Procedure, 61 Colum.L.Rev. 1031 (1961); Smit, International Litigation Under the United States Code, 65 Colum.L.Rev. 1015 (1965). For a recent decision dealing with the international law aspects of the making of service in proceedings before the Federal Trade Commission, see Federal Trade Commission v. Compagnie de Saint–Gobain–Pont–a–Mousson, 636 F.2d 1300 (D.C.Cir.1980). See also Restatement (Third) § 437, Reporters' Note 3; Oliver, International Law and Foreign Investigatory Subpoenas Sought to Be Enforced Without the Consent or Cooperation of the Territorial Sovereign: Impasse of Accommodation? 19 San Diego L.Rev. 409 (1982).

9. When the foreign objection takes the form of a statutory prohibition, conflicts of jurisdiction become aggravated. The Hague Conference on Private International Law has produced a Convention on Service of Judicial and Extrajudicial Documents Abroad and a Convention on the Taking of Evidence Abroad in Civil or Commercial Matters (23 U.S.T. 2555, T.I.A.S. No. 7444, 847 U.N.T.S. 231). While the purpose of these Conventions was to eliminate problems, they appear to have added to them. Foreign contracting states have argued that the Conventions preclude resort to otherwise available municipal law procedures. This argument has been extensively discussed and litigated. See, e.g., Oxman, The Choice Between Direct Discovery and Other Means of Obtaining Evidence Abroad: The Impact of the Hague Evidence Convention, 37 U.Miami L.Rev. 733 (1983).

In Societe Nationale Industrielle Aerospatiale v. U.S. District Court of Southern District Iowa, 482 U.S. 522, 107 S.Ct. 2542, 96 L.Ed.2d 461 (1987), the Supreme Court ruled the Hague Evidence Convention not to be exclusive. However, in Volkswagenwerk Aktiengesellschaft v. Schlunk, 486 U.S. 694, 108 S.Ct. 2104, 100 L.Ed.2d 722 (1988), the Court ruled The Hague Service Convention exclusive. The language of the Service Convention, the Court ruled, dictated this result. However, it significantly alleviated the impact of this ruling by finding that domestic rules could be used if the service on the foreign defendant were made in the United States. Why are foreign states so insistent upon a litigant's traveling the Convention route? Would the procedure not be more flexible if a litigant were left the choice between domestic and Convention rules?

10. The Restatement (Third) contains provisions dealing with conflicts of jurisdiction generally (§ 441) and in regard to disclosure (§ 442).

## *RESTATEMENT (THIRD)*

### § 441. Foreign State Compulsion

(1) In general, a state may not require a person

(a) to do an act in another state that is prohibited by the law of that state or by the law of the state of which he is a national; or

(b) to refrain from doing an act in another state that is required by the law of that state or by the law of the state of which he is a national.

(2) In general, a state may require a person of foreign nationality

(a) to do an act in that state even if it is prohibited by the law of the state of which he is a national; or

(b) to refrain from doing an act in that state even if it is required by the law of the state of which he is a national.

### *Notes*

1. To what extent do the materials in this Section provide support for these provisions as a matter of international or United States foreign relations law? What difference does it make whether they are the one or the other?

2. For discussion of the resolution of conflicts of jurisdiction arising from acts committed on foreign vessels in territorial waters, see ch. 14, sec. 2, A1–2 infra.

3. For additional decisions rejecting the foreign compulsion doctrine, see United States v. Davis, 767 F.2d 1025 (2d Cir.1981); Laker Airways v. Sabena, 731 F.2d 909 (D.C.Cir.1984). But see United States v. First Nat'l Bank of Chicago, 699 F.2d 341 (7th Cir.1983) (refusing to compel disclosure forbidden by Greek law).

## SECTION 7. JURISDICTION TO ADJUDICATE

A state may not exercise its judicial functions within the territory of another state without the latter's consent. See Section 5 of this Chapter. Conversely, a state may normally exercise its judicial functions in regard to persons or things within its territory. Questions, analogous to those that have arisen in the area of legislative jurisdiction, may arise when a state exercises within its territory judicial authority over persons or things outside of its territory. And these questions become particularly acute when the judicial authority is sought to be exercised over persons or things that have no reasonable relation to the state that seeks to exercise judicial jurisdiction.

However, many states have habitually exercised adjudicatory authority over persons outside of their borders in the absence of some contact that would be considered sufficient under due process limitations developed in the United States. The overwhelming majority of states permit criminal prosecutions *in absentia* of the accused. And leading civil law countries exercise adjudicatory authority in civil cases on bases such as the nationality or residence of the plaintiff or the mere presence of unrelated property. For a more detailed discussion, see Rosenberg, Smit & Dreyfuss, Elements of Civil Procedure 226 (5th ed. 1990) and authorities cited. While these bases have been characterized as exorbitant or extraordinary, they have, thus far, not been asserted, on authoritative grounds, to be violative of international law.

The Restatement (Third) states that "increasingly, they [i.e., states] object to the improper exercise of jurisdiction [i.e. jurisdiction on an extravagant basis] as itself a violation of international principles." Section 421, Introductory Note. Although the Restatement (Third) refers to no source supporting this statement, it would appear that good grounds exist for international law limitations on the exercise of a state's extraterritorial judicial jurisdiction, at least in criminal and administrative matters. For example, in *Alvarez–Machain* case, see p. 1116 infra, it might be argued that prosecuting in the United States a person abducted in violation of international law constituted itself a violation of international law. See note 2, p. 1124 infra. Whether the same is true in civil matters is considerably more doubtful.

The Restatement (Third) has attempted to formulate the proper criteria in the provisions set forth below.

## *RESTATEMENT (THIRD)*

### § 421. Jurisdiction to Adjudicate

(1) A state may exercise jurisdiction through its courts to adjudicate with respect to a person or thing if the relationship of the state to the person or thing is such as to make the exercise of jurisdiction reasonable.

(2) In general, a state's exercise of jurisdiction to adjudicate with respect to a person or thing is reasonable if, at the time jurisdiction is asserted:

(a) the person or thing is present in the territory of the state, other than transitorily;

(b) the person, if a natural person, is domiciled in the state;

(c) the person, if a natural person, is resident in the state;

(d) the person, if a natural person, is a national of the state;

(e) the person, if a corporation or comparable juridical person, is organized pursuant to the law of the state;

(f) a ship, aircraft or other vehicle to which the adjudication relates is registered under the laws of the state;

(g) the person, whether natural or juridical, has consented to the exercise of jurisdiction;

(h) the person, whether natural or juridical, regularly carries on business in the state;

(i) the person, whether natural or juridical, had carried on activity in the state, but only in respect of such activity;

(j) the person, whether natural or juridical, had carried on outside the state an activity having a substantial, direct, and foreseeable effect within the state, but only in respect of such activity; or

(k) the thing that is the subject of adjudication is owned, possessed, or used in the state, but only in respect of a claim reasonably connected with that thing.

(3) A defense of lack of jurisdiction is generally waived by any appearance by or on behalf of a person or thing (whether as plaintiff, defendant, or third party), if the appearance is for a purpose that does not include a challenge to the exercise of jurisdiction.

* * *

### § 423. Jurisdiction to Adjudicate in Enforcement of Universal and Other Non-Territorial Crimes

A state may exercise jurisdiction through its courts to enforce its criminal laws that punish universal crimes or other non-territorial offenses within the state's jurisdiction to prescribe.

## SECTION 8. JURISDICTION TO ENFORCE

### § 431. Jurisdiction to Enforce

(1) A state may employ judicial or nonjudicial measures to induce or compel compliance or punish noncompliance with its laws or regulations, provided it has jurisdiction to prescribe in accordance with §§ 402 and 403.

(2) Enforcement measures must be reasonably related to the laws or regulations to which they are directed; punishment for noncompliance must be preceded by an appropriate determination of violation and must be proportional to the gravity of the violation.

(3) A state may employ enforcement measures against a person located outside its territory

(a) if the person is given notice of the claims or charges against him that is reasonable in the circumstances;

(b) if the person is given an opportunity to be heard, ordinarily in advance of enforcement, whether in person or by counsel or other representative; and

(c) when enforcement is through the courts, if the state has jurisdiction to adjudicate.

***Notes***

1. Does this section purport to state a rule of American foreign relations law or of international law? The Introductory Note to this Section states that enforcement measures "are subject, under international law, to the requirement of reasonableness". Is this statement correct?

2. What is the effect of a state's having improperly exercised its executive jurisdiction on its subsequent exercise of judicial jurisdiction? If, for example, a state improperly seizes a person accused of a crime outside of its borders, may it nevertheless properly exercise judicial jurisdiction over this person in the United States? The traditional rule of international law is that of "*male captus, bene detentus,*" i.e., that a person who has been improperly seized may nevertheless properly be tried. This rule has been argued to follow from the principle that, under international law, only the state in the territory of which the person was captured may complain of the improper exercise of executive jurisdiction. However, states have exercised judicial jurisdiction over persons improperly seized, even if the state in the territory of which they were seized objected. See p. 1083 supra. Furthermore, courts have generally sustained the exercise of judicial jurisdiction over persons improperly seized in a foreign country. Leading cases to this effect are Ker v. Illinois, 119 U.S. 436, 7 S.Ct. 225, 30 L.Ed. 421 (1886) and Frisbie v. Collins, 342 U.S. 519, 72 S.Ct. 509, 96 L.Ed. 541 (1952). The Second Circuit has grafted an exception upon the *Ker–Frisbie* doctrine in the case of a

seizure abroad that was attended by brutality. United States v. Toscanino, 500 F.2d 267 (2d Cir.1974). This decision appears to apply a rule of American rather than international law. In any event, the *Toscanino* rule has not been applied in cases that did not involve egregiously brutal conduct. See Restatement (Third) § 433, Reporters' Note 3; Note, Jurisdiction After International Kidnapping: A Comparative Study, 8 B.C.Int'l & Comp.L.Rev. 237 (1985). The *Ker–Frisbie* doctrine was reaffirmed in United States v. Alvarez–Machain, 504 U.S. ___, 112 S.Ct. 2188, 119 L.Ed.2d 441 (1992), reproduced at p. 1116 infra. The notes following this case explore the implications of this decision. See 1124 infra.

3. Is a state's judicial and executive jurisdiction more extensive in cases of the exercise of universal legislative jurisdiction than in other cases? May, in such cases, a state exercise executive jurisdiction on the territory of another state? Does the propriety of a state's exercising executive jurisdiction in such cases on the territory of another state depend on whether the person against whom the jurisdiction is exercised (a) is a national of the state exercising it, (b) performed the acts for which he is called to account within the territory of the state exercising it, (c) did the incriminated acts against a national of the state exercising it, or (d) is not called to account for his conduct by the state on the territory of which the jurisdiction is exercised? In October 1985, United States warplanes intercepted, and forced down on a United States airbase in Sicily, an Egyptian airplane flying over the high seas that carried terrorists who had seized on the high seas the Achille Lauro, an oceangoing vessel of Italian registry, and who had killed one of its American passengers. Egypt protested. N.Y. Times, October 11, 1985, at 1, col. 1. Was its protest well-founded in international law? See Restatement (Third) § 423, supra, p. 1110. See also Lowenfeld & Glynn, Analyzing the Applicable Laws in the Achille Lauro Aftermath, 194:87 N.Y.L.J.V., p. 1, col. 3, Nov. 1, 1985. But cf. Art. 82 of the 1982 Law of the Sea Convention on Immunity of Warships and Other Government Ships Operated for Non–Commercial Purposes.

## SECTION 9. EXTRADITION

Extradition is the surrender of an individual accused or convicted of a crime by the state within whose territory he is found to the state under whose laws he is alleged to have committed or to have been convicted of the crime. Until the nineteenth century the extradition of fugitives was rare and was a matter of sovereign discretion rather than of obligation. With the dramatic improvements in transportation in the nineteenth century, the number of criminals fleeing to foreign states increased and states began to conclude bilateral treaties providing for their extradition. In Factor v. Laubenheimer, 290 U.S. 276, 287, 54 S.Ct. 191, 193, 78 L.Ed. 315 (1933), the court noted that "[t]he principles of international law recognize no right to extradition apart from treaty. While a government may, if agreeable to its own constitution and laws, voluntarily exercise the power to surrender a fugitive from justice to the country from which he has fled * * * the legal right to demand his extradition and the correlative duty to surrender him to the demanding country exist only when created by treaty." In fact, the municipal law of many states prevents arrest and extradition of a fugitive except pursuant to a treaty operating as internal law or a statute providing for extradition. See 2 O'Connell 793–94; Valentine v. United States ex rel.

Neidecker, 299 U.S. 5, 9, 57 S.Ct. 100, 102, 81 L.Ed. 5 (1936). In the United States, international extradition is governed by federal law. See 18 U.S.C.A. §§ 3184–3195. The States have no power to extradite fugitives to foreign countries. On extradition generally, see Restatement (Third) §§ 476–79; Bassiouni, International Extradition (1983); Mich.Yb.Int.Leg.Stud., Transnational Aspects of Criminal Procedure (1983).

Since most instances of extradition arise under bilateral or multilateral treaties, many of the problems raised by extradition are questions of treaty interpretation. Most bilateral treaties contain a list of acts for which a fugitive may be extradited. Multilateral and some bilateral treaties stipulate merely that the act for which extradition is sought be a crime in both the asylum and requisitioning states punishable by a certain minimum penalty, usually imprisonment for at least one year.

Difficult problems arise under the treaties that list extraditable crimes when the act committed by the fugitive is punishable in the requisitioning state and listed in the treaty, but not punishable in the asylum state because the law of the latter defines the crime differently. See The Eisler Extradition Case, 43 A.J.I.L. 487 (England 1949). In such a situation, if the asylum state applies its own law to define the crime, it may violate its obligations under the treaty. See 4 Hackworth 117–18. If the asylum state applies the law of the requisitioning state, it would be extraditing the fugitive for an act that was not an offense under its own law. The solution to the problem may be found in the requirement of "double criminality,"—i.e., that extradition is available only when the act is punishable under the law of both states. The name of the offense and the elements that make it criminal need not be precisely the same providing that the fugitive could be punished for the act in both states. See Harvard Research in International Law, Draft Convention on Extradition, 29 A.J.I.L.Spec.Supp. 81–86 (1935); 1 Oppenheim 958; Re Clark, [1929] 3 D.L.R. 737.

Under the requirement of "double criminality" the act must be characterized as a crime by the law of the asylum state. However, in Factor v. Laubenheimer, 290 U.S. 276, 54 S.Ct. 191, 78 L.Ed. 315 (1933), the Court approved extradition to Great Britain for the crime of receiving money knowing it to have been fraudulently obtained although the law of Illinois, where the fugitive was found, did not make such an act criminal. The Court felt that the extradition treaty between the United States and Great Britain did not require "double criminality" for the particular offense, and stressed the fact that the offense was criminal under the laws of several of the States. For criticism, see Hudson, The Factor Case and Double Criminality in Extradition, 28 A.J.I.L. 274 (1934); cf. Borchard, The Factor Extradition Case, 28 A.J.I.L. 742 (1934). See also Restatement (Third) § 477, Comment *d.*

The principle of "double criminality" would also require that the act be criminal in both states when it was committed. In Peters v. Egnor, 888 F.2d 713 (10th Cir.1989), the British Theft Act and the American federal securities fraud statute were found "substantially analogous" and therefore to meet the requirement of dual criminality. But see United States ex rel. Oppenheim v. Hecht, 16 F.2d 955 (2d Cir.1927), granting extradition for an act which was made criminal in the United States after it had been committed. Treaties frequently provide that extradition shall not take place if the prosecution of the fugitive is barred by a statute of limitations in either the asylum state or requisitioning state. See e.g., Extradition Treaty between the United States and Great Britain, Dec. 22, 1931, art. 5, 47 Stat. 2122, T.S. 849, 163 L.N.T.S. 59.

Special problems may arise when the crime for which extradition is sought was not committed on the territory of the state requesting extradition. In 1977, Abu Daoud, alleged to have participated in the massacre of Israeli athletes at the Munich Olympic Games, was arrested in France. Both West–Germany and Israel sought his extradition. The *Chambre d'Accusation* of the Paris Court of Appeals, four days after Daoud's arrest, after a proceeding lasting only 20 minutes, released Daoud, and France expelled him to Algeria where he was accorded a hero's welcome. The ground given for rejection of the West–German request was that the request had not been "confirmed at the same time by diplomatic channel." The reasons for denial of the Israeli request were more complex. The Paris Court held that, at the time Daoud allegedly committed the crime, he could not have been prosecuted for it in France even if his victims had been French nationals, and that, therefore, he could not be extradited to Israel, even though Israeli law did permit his prosecution on the ground that the victims were Israeli citizens. The Paris Court also held that, although the French Penal Code was amended in 1975 to give France jurisdiction on the passive personality basis, this amendment could not be given retroactive effect. No reason was given why Daoud was not prosecuted in France for having entered on a false passport. On this case, see Liskofsky, The Abu Daoud Case: Law or Politics, 7 Is.Yb.H.Rtg. 66 (1977).

In the eighteenth century, extradition was most frequently sought and granted for what are now termed political offenses. By the nineteenth century public opinion in Western Europe turned against the extradition of fugitives accused of only political offenses. Belgium, which enacted the first extradition law in 1833, incorporated the principle of non-extradition for political offenses into the law. Today, most treaties exempt fugitives accused of political offenses from extradition. Though the principle has been almost universally accepted, "political offenses" have never been precisely defined. The first attempt to delineate the principle was the "attentat" clause in many treaties, which provides that the murder of the head of a foreign government or a member of his family is not to be considered a political offense. See, e.g., Treaty of Extradition between the United States and Venezuela, Art. 3, 43 Stat. 1698, T.S. 675, 49 L.N.T.S. 435. Some treaties extend the exclusion to any murder or attempt on life in general. See, e.g., Extradition Treaty between Italy and Finland, 1928, Art. 3(3), 111 L.N.T.S. 295. However, in 1934 in the absence of such a clause in the applicable treaty, the Turin Court of Appeal refused to extradite the assassins of King Alexander of Yugoslavia to France on the ground that the crime was political. In re Pavelic, [1933–34] Ann.Dig. No. 158 (Italy).

In 1892, Switzerland adopted a law which provided that a crime was not to be considered political if it was primarily a common offense even though it had a political motivation or purpose. The decision on extradition was left to the highest Swiss Court. See 2 O'Connell 802; 1 Oppenheim 967. Some treaties provide that "[c]riminal acts which constitute clear manifestations of anarchism or envisage the overthrow of the bases of all political organizations" shall not be considered political offenses. Treaty of Extradition between the United States and Brazil, Art. V(6), 15 U.S.T. 2093, T.I.A.S. No. 5691, 532 U.N.T.S. 177. British and American courts have held that for an offense to be political it must be committed in furtherance of a political movement or in the course of a struggle to control the government of a state. In re Castioni, [1891] 1 Q.B. 149, 156, 166; In re Ezeta, 62 Fed. 972, 999 (D.C.Cal.1894). However, this strict rule has been relaxed recently to provide refuge for private individuals fleeing totalitarian states. See Regina v. Governor of Brixton Prison, Ex parte Kolczynski, [1955] 1 Q.B. 540 (1954). For a discussion of political offenses, see Regina v. Governor of Brixton Prison, Ex parte Schtraks, [1964] A.C. 556, 581–84, 587–92 (H.L.); Garcia Mora, Crimes Against Humanity and the Principle of Nonextradition of Political Offenders, 62 Mich.L.Rev. 927 (1964); Harvard Research at 107–19; Spanish–German Extradition Treaty case, [1925–26] Ann.Dig. No. 234 (Germany 1926). Treaties also frequently prohibit extradition for purely military offenses. See Convention on Extradition between the United States and Sweden, Art. V(4), 14 U.S.T. 1845, T.I.A.S. No. 5496, 494 U.N.T.S. 141.

The United States and the United Kingdom signed on June 25, 1985, a Supplementary Extradition Treaty that excludes from the category of "political offenses" specified crimes of violence that are typically committed by terrorists. See also p. 1075 supra. The category of excluded crimes would include crimes committed by the so-called Irish Republic Army. At least some courts have refused extradition for such crimes on the ground that they are "political". See, e.g., Matter of Doherty, 599 F.Supp. 270 (S.D.N.Y. 1984); see also Restatement (Third) § 478, Reporters' Note 6. The European Convention on the Suppression of Terrorism permits Council of Europe members not to regard as political similar offenses typically committed by terrorists. See Leich, Contemporary Practice of the United States Related to International Law, 79 A.J.I.L. 1045 (1985).

According to the principle of specialty, the requisitioning state may not, without the permission of the asylum state, try or punish the fugitive for any crimes committed before the extradition except the crimes for which he was extradited. The permission of the asylum state is also required for the requisitioning state to re-extradite the fugitive to a third state. United States ex rel. Donnelly v. Mulligan, 74 F.2d 220 (2d Cir.1934). See also United States v. Rauscher, 119 U.S. 407, 7 S.Ct. 234, 30 L.Ed. 425 (1886); Harvard Research, at 213–19; Restatement (Third) § 478.

The majority of extradition treaties contain provisions exempting nationals of the asylum state from extradition. The usual provision is that neither party shall be obligated to surrender its nationals, thus leaving the matter in the discretion of the asylum state. The policy, which is most commonly reflected in civil law jurisdictions, apparently stems from a feeling that individuals should not be withdrawn from the jurisdiction of their own courts. See Harvard Research, at 125. However, the courts in many civil law countries have broad jurisdiction to try and punish their nationals for crimes committed in other countries. See id. at 445. The United States surrenders nationals (unless exempted by treaty) as a matter of obligation, even in the absence of reciprocity. Charlton v. Kelly, 229 U.S. 447, 33 S.Ct. 945, 57 L.Ed. 1274 (1913). Great Britain generally surrenders nationals. See Extradition Act, 1870, 33 & 34 Vict. c. 52, § 26; 1 Oppenheim 956. Multilateral extradition conventions which recognize the principle of non-extradition of nationals generally provide that if the asylum state refuses to extradite a national it shall itself prosecute the person claimed. See, e.g., Convention on Extradition, signed at Montevideo, Art. 2, 49 Stat. 3111, T.S. 882, 165 L.N.T.S. 45.

Depending on municipal law, extradition may be exclusively an executive function or may require a judicial hearing. The United States requires a judicial hearing of the evidence against the fugitive, 18 U.S.C.A. § 3184. Article 9 of the 1931 Extradition Treaty between the United States and Great Britain provides: "The extradition shall take place only if the evidence be found sufficient, according to the laws of the High Contracting Party applied to * * * to justify the committal of the prisoner for trial, in case the crime or offense had been committed in the territory of such High Contracting Party * * *." 47 Stat. 2125. "If, on such hearing, [the judge] deems the evidence sufficient to sustain the charge under the provisions of the proper treaty or convention, he shall certify the same, together with a copy of all the testimony taken before him, to the Secretary of State * * *." 18 U.S.C.A. § 3184. The Secretary of State then may grant or refuse extradition. See 4 Hackworth 49–50, 186ff. The function of the judicial hearing is to permit the fugitive to insure that the proceedings comply with the applicable statutes and treaties. He may produce evidence that he did not commit the offense or object that the offense was political. The decision of the committing magistrate on the sufficiency of the evidence is not subject to correction by appeal. Collins v. Miller, 252 U.S. 364, 369, 40 S.Ct. 347, 349, 64 L.Ed. 616 (1920). However, the fugitive may petition for a writ of habeas corpus to challenge the legality of his detention and may urge upon the Secretary of State that his extradition not be granted. See 4 Hackworth 174–75.

Where extradition is not possible because of the lack of a treaty or for some other reason, or where extradition is not feasible because of the time and expense involved, states may resort to other methods of surrendering or recovering fugitives. If the fugitive is not a national of the asylum state, it may deport him as an undesirable alien or exclude him (i.e., deny him permission to enter the country). In either case, the fugitive may be turned over directly to the state that desires to prosecute him, or may be sent to a third state from which his extradition is possible. The United States and Mexico and the United States and Canada have frequently resorted to exclusion or deportation in order to deliver fugitives to each other without going through the process of extradition. See Evans, Acquisition of Custody over the International Fugitive Offender—Alternatives to Extradition: A Survey of United States Practice, 40 Brit.Y.B.I.L. 77 (1964).

On kidnapping of fugitives, see generally Note, Extraterritorial Jurisdiction and Jurisdiction Following Forcible Abduction: A New Israeli Precedent in International Law, 72 Mich.L.Rev. 1087 (1974); Shearer, Extradition in International Law 72–76 (1971); Sponsler, International Kidnapping, 5 Int.Law. 27 (1971); O'Higgins, Unlawful Seizure and Irregular Extradition, 36 Brit.Y.B.I.L. 279 (1960); Garcia-Mora, Criminal Jurisdiction of a State over Fugitives Brought From a Foreign Country by Force or Fraud: A

Comparative Study, 32 Ind.L.J. 427 (1957). See also Section 8 of this Chapter.

## UNITED STATES v. HUMBERTO ALVAREZ-MACHAIN

Supreme Court of the United States, 1992.
504 U.S. ___, 112 S.Ct. 2188, 119 L.Ed.2d 441.

THE CHIEF JUSTICE delivered the opinion of the Court.*

The issue in this case is whether a criminal defendant, abducted to the United States from a nation with which it has an extradition treaty, thereby acquires a defense to the jurisdiction of this country's courts. We hold that he does not, and that he may be tried in federal district court for violations of the criminal law of the United States.

Respondent, Humberto Alvarez-Machain, is a citizen and resident of Mexico. He was indicted for participating in the kidnap and murder of United States Drug Enforcement Administration (DEA) special agent Enrique Camarena-Salazar and a Mexican pilot working with Camarena, Alfredo Zavala-Avelar.[1] The DEA believes that respondent, a medical doctor, participated in the murder by prolonging agent Camarena's life so that others could further torture and interrogate him. On April 2, 1990, respondent was forcibly kidnapped from his medical office in Guadalajara, Mexico, to be flown by private plane to El Paso, Texas, where he was arrested by DEA officials. The District Court concluded that DEA agents were responsible for respondent's abduction, although they were not personally involved in it. United States v. Caro-Quintero, 745 F.Supp. 599, 602-604, 609 (CD Cal 1990).[2]

Respondent moved to dismiss the indictment, claiming that his abduction constituted outrageous governmental conduct, and that the District Court lacked jurisdiction to try him because he was abducted in violation of the extradition treaty between the United States and Mexico. Extradition Treaty, May 4, 1978, [1979] United States-United Mexican States, 31 U.S.T. 5059, T.I.A.S. No. 9656 (Extradition Treaty or Treaty). The District Court rejected the outrageous governmental conduct claim, but held that it lacked jurisdiction to try respondent because his abduction violated the Extradition Treaty. The district court discharged respondent and ordered that he be repatriated to Mexico. Caro-Quintero, supra, at 614.

* Some footnotes omitted; others renumbered.

1. Respondent is charged in a sixth superseding indictment with: conspiracy to commit violent acts in furtherance of racketeering activity (in violation of 18 U.S.C. §§ 371, 1959 [18 U.S.C.A. §§ 371, 1959]); committing violent acts in furtherance of racketeering activity (in violation of 18 U.S.C. § 1959(a)(2) [18 U.S.C.A. § 1959(a)(2)]); conspiracy to kidnap a federal agent (in violation of 18 U.S.C. §§ 1201(a)(5), 1201(c) [18 U.S.C.A. §§ 1201(a)(5), 1201(c)]); kidnap of a federal agent (in violation of 18 U.S.C. § 1201(a)(5) [18 U.S.C.A. § 1201(a)(5)]); and felony murder of a federal agent (in violation of 18 U.S.C. §§ 1111(a), 1114 [18 U.S.C.A. §§ 1111(a), 1114]). App 12-32.

2. Apparently, DEA officials had attempted to gain respondent's presence in the United States through informal negotiations with Mexican officials, but were unsuccessful. DEA officials then, through a contact in Mexico, offered to pay a reward and expenses in return for the delivery of respondent to the United States. United States v. Caro-Quintero, 745 F.Supp. 599, 602-604 (CD Cal. 1990).

The Court of Appeals affirmed the dismissal of the indictment and the repatriation of respondent, relying on its decision in United States v. Verdugo–Urquidez, 939 F.2d 1341 (CA9 1991), cert. pending, No. 91–670. 946 F.2d 1466 (1991). In Verdugo, the Court of Appeals held that the forcible abduction of a Mexican national with the authorization or participation of the United States violated the Extradition Treaty between the United States and Mexico.[3] Although the Treaty does not expressly prohibit such abductions, the Court of Appeals held that the "purpose" of the Treaty was violated by a forcible abduction, * * * which, along with a formal protest by the offended nation, would give a defendant the right to invoke the Treaty violation to defeat jurisdiction of the district court to try him. The Court of Appeals further held that the proper remedy for such a violation would be dismissal of the indictment and repatriation of the defendant to Mexico.

In the instant case, the Court of Appeals affirmed the district court's finding that the United States had authorized the abduction of respondent, and that letters from the Mexican government to the United States government served as an official protest of the Treaty violation. Therefore, the Court of Appeals ordered that the indictment against respondent be dismissed and that respondent be repatriated to Mexico. 946 F.2d at 1467. We granted certiorari, * * * and now reverse.

Although we have never before addressed the precise issue raised in the present case, we have previously considered proceedings in claimed violation of an extradition treaty, and proceedings against a defendant brought before a court by means of a forcible abduction. We addressed the former issue in United States v. Rauscher, 119 U.S. 407, 7 S.Ct. 234, 30 L.Ed. 425 (1886); more precisely, the issue of whether the Webster–Ashburton Treaty of 1842, 8 Stat. 576, which governed extraditions between England and the United States, prohibited the prosecution of defendant Rauscher for a crime other than the crime for which he had been extradited. Whether this prohibition, known as the doctrine of specialty, was an intended part of the treaty had been disputed between the two nations for some time. Rauscher, 119 U.S. at 411, 7 S.Ct., at 236. Justice Miller delivered the opinion of the Court, which carefully examined the terms and history of the treaty; the practice of nations in regards to extradition treaties; the case law from the states; and the writings of commentators, and reached the following conclusion:

> "[A] person who has been brought within the jurisdiction of the court *by virtue of proceedings under an extradition treaty,* can only be tried for one of the offences described in that treaty, and for the offence with which he is charged in the proceedings for his extradition, until a reasonable time and opportunity have been given him, after his release or trial upon such charge, to return to the country from whose asylum he had been forcibly taken under those proceedings." Id., at 430, 7 S.Ct., at 246 (emphasis added).

3. Rene Martin Verdugo–Urquidez was also indicted for the murder of agent Camarena. In an earlier decision, we held that the Fourth Amendment did not apply to a search by United States agents of Verdugo–Urquidez' home in Mexico. United States v. Verdugo–Uriquidez, 494 U.S. 259, 110 S.Ct. 1056, 108 L.Ed.2d 222 (1990).

In addition, Justice Miller's opinion noted that any doubt as to this interpretation was put to rest by two federal statutes which imposed the doctrine of specialty upon extradition treaties to which the United States was a party. * * * Unlike the case before us today, the defendant in Rauscher had been brought to the United States by way of an extradition treaty; there was no issue of a forcible abduction.

In Ker v. Illinois, 119 U.S. 436, 7 S.Ct. 225, 30 L.Ed. 421 (1886), also written by Justice Miller and decided the same day as Rauscher, we addressed the issue of a defendant brought before the court by way of a forcible abduction. Frederick Ker had been tried and convicted in an Illinois court for larceny; his presence before the court was procured by means of forcible abduction from Peru. A messenger was sent to Lima with the proper warrant to demand Ker by virtue of the extradition treaty between Peru and the United States. The messenger, however, disdained reliance on the treaty processes, and instead forcibly kidnapped Ker and brought him to the United States.[4] We distinguished Ker's case from Rauscher, on the basis that Ker was not brought into the United States by virtue of the extradition treaty between the United States and Peru, and rejected Ker's argument that he had a right under the extradition treaty to be returned to this country only in accordance with its terms. We rejected Ker's due process argument more broadly, holding in line with "the highest authorities" that "such forcible abduction is no sufficient reason why the party should not answer when brought within the jurisdiction of the court which has the right to try him for such an offence, and presents no valid objection to his trial in such court." * * *

In Frisbie v. Collins, 342 U.S. 519, 72 S.Ct. 509, 96 L.Ed. 541, rehearing denied, 343 U.S. 937, 72 S.Ct. 768, 96 L.Ed. 1344 (1952), we applied the rule in Ker to a case in which the defendant had been kidnapped in Chicago by Michigan officers and brought to trial in Michigan. We upheld the conviction over objections based on the due process clause and the Federal Kidnapping Act. * * *

The only differences between Ker and the present case are that Ker was decided on the premise that there was no governmental involvement in the abduction, 119 U.S. at 443, 7 S.Ct., 229; and Peru, from which Ker was abducted, did not object to his prosecution.[5] Respondent finds these differences to be dispositive, as did the Court of Appeals in Verdugo, 939 F.2d, at 1346, contending that they show that respondent's prosecution, like the prosecution of Rauscher, violates the implied terms of a valid extradition treaty. The Government, on the other hand, argues that Rauscher stands as an "exception" to the rule in Ker only when an extradition treaty is invoked, and the terms of the treaty provide that its breach will limit the jurisdiction of a court. * * * Therefore, our first inquiry must be whether the abduction of respondent from Mexico violated the extradition treaty between the

4. Although the opinion does not explain why the messenger failed to present the warrant to the proper authorities, commentators have suggested that the seizure of Ker in the aftermath of a revolution in Peru provided the messenger with no "proper authorities" to whom the warrant could be presented. See Kester, Some Myths of United States Extradition Law, 76 Geo.L.J. 1441, 1451 (1988).

5. Ker also was not a national of Peru, whereas respondent is a national of the country from which he was abducted. Respondent finds this difference to be immaterial. Tr. of Oral Arg. 26.

United States and Mexico. If we conclude that the Treaty does not prohibit respondent's abduction, the rule in Ker applies, and the court need not inquire as to how respondent came before it.

In construing a treaty, as in construing a statute, we first look to its terms to determine its meaning. Air France v. Saks, 470 U.S. 392, 397, 105 S.Ct. 1338, 1341, 84 L.Ed.2d 289 (1985); Valentine v. United States ex rel. Neidecker, 299 U.S. 5, 11, 57 S.Ct. 100, 103, 81 L.Ed. 5 (1936). The Treaty says nothing about the obligations of the United States and Mexico to refrain from forcible abductions of people from the territory of the other nation, or the consequences under the Treaty if such an abduction occurs. Respondent submits that Article 22(1) of the Treaty which states that it "shall apply to offenses specified in Article 2 [including murder] committed before and after this Treaty enters into force," 31 U.S.T., at 5073–5074, evidences an intent to make application of the Treaty mandatory for those offenses. However, the more natural conclusion is that Article 22 was included to ensure that the Treaty was applied to extraditions requested after the Treaty went into force, regardless of when the crime of extradition occurred.

More critical to respondent's argument is Article 9 of the Treaty which provides:

> "1. Neither Contracting Party shall be bound to deliver up its own nationals, but the executive authority of the requested Party shall, if not prevented by the laws of that Party, have the power to deliver them up if, in its discretion, it be deemed proper to do so.
>
> "2. If extradition is not granted pursuant to paragraph 1 of this Article, the requested Party shall submit the case to its competent authorities for the purpose of prosecution, provided that Party has jurisdiction over the offense." Id., at 5065.

According to respondent, Article 9 embodies the terms of the bargain which the United States struck: if the United States wishes to prosecute a Mexican national, it may request that individual's extradition. Upon a request from the United States, Mexico may either extradite the individual, or submit the case to the proper authorities for prosecution in Mexico. In this way, respondent reasons, each nation preserved its right to choose whether its nationals would be tried in its own courts or by the courts of the other nation. This preservation of rights would be frustrated if either nation were free to abduct nationals of the other nation for the purposes of prosecution. More broadly, respondent reasons, as did the Court of Appeals, that all the processes and restrictions on the obligation to extradite established by the Treaty would make no sense if either nation were free to resort to forcible kidnapping to gain the presence of an individual for prosecution in a manner not contemplated by the Treaty. Verdugo, supra, at 1350.

We do not read the Treaty in such a fashion. Article 9 does not purport to specify the only way in which one country may gain custody of a national of the other country for the purposes of prosecution. In the absence of an extradition treaty, nations are under no obligation to surrender those in their country to foreign authorities for prosecution. Rauscher, 119 U.S., at 411–412, 7 S.Ct. at 236; Factor v. Laubenheimer, 290 U.S. 276, 287, 54 S.Ct. 191, 193, 78 L.Ed. 315 (1933); cf. Valentine v. United States ex rel. Neidecker, supra, 299 U.S., at 8–9, 57 S.Ct., at 102 (United States may not extradite a citizen in the absence of a statute or treaty obligation). Extradition treaties exist so as to impose mutual obligations to surrender individuals in certain defined sets of circumstances, following established procedures. See 1 J. Moore, A Treatise on Extradition and Interstate Rendition, § 72 (1891). The Treaty thus provides a mechanism which would not otherwise exist, requiring, under certain circumstances, the United States and Mexico to extradite individuals to the other country, and establishing the procedures to be followed when the Treaty is invoked.

The history of negotiation and practice under the Treaty also fails to show that abductions outside of the Treaty constitute a violation of the Treaty. As the Solicitor General notes, the Mexican government was made aware, as early as 1906, of the Ker doctrine, and the United States' position that it applied to forcible abductions made outside of the terms of the United States–Mexico extradition treaty. Nonetheless, the current version of the Treaty, signed in 1978, does not attempt to establish a rule that would in any way curtail the effect of Ker. Moreover, although language which would grant individuals exactly the right sought by respondent had been considered and drafted as early as 1935 by a prominent group of legal scholars sponsored by the faculty of Harvard Law School, no such clause appears in the current treaty.[6]

Thus, the language of the Treaty, in the context of its history, does not support the proposition that the Treaty prohibits abductions outside of its terms. The remaining question, therefore, is whether the Treaty should be interpreted so as to include an implied term prohibiting prosecution where the defendant's presence is obtained by means other than those established by the Treaty. See Valentine, 299 U.S., at 17, 57 S.Ct., at 106 ("Strictly the question is not whether there had been a uniform practical construction denying the power, but whether the power had been so clearly recognized that the grant should be implied").

Respondent contends that the Treaty must be interpreted against the backdrop of customary international law, and that international abductions are "so clearly prohibited in international law" that there was no reason to include such a clause in the Treaty itself. Brief for Respondent 11. The international censure of international abductions is further evidenced, according to respondent, by the United Nations Charter and the Charter of the Organization of American States. Id., at 17, 57 S.Ct., at 106. Respondent does not argue that these sources of international law provide an independent basis for the right respondent asserts not to be tried in the United States, but rather that they should inform the interpretation of the Treaty terms.

6. In Article 16 of the Draft Convention on Jurisdiction with Respect to Crime, the Advisory Committee of the Research in International Law proposed:

"In exercising jurisdiction under this Convention, no State shall prosecute or punish any person who has been brought within its territory or a place subject to its authority by recourse to measures in violation of international law or international convention without first obtaining the consent of the State or States whose rights have been violated by such measures." Harvard Research in International Law, 29 Am J Int'l L 442 (Supp 1935).

The Court of Appeals deemed it essential, in order for the individual defendant to assert a right under the Treaty, that the affected foreign government had registered a protest. Verdugo, 939 F.2d, at 1357 ("in the kidnapping case there must be a formal protest from the offended government after the kidnapping"). Respondent agrees that the right exercised by the individual is derivative of the nation's right under the Treaty, since nations are authorized, notwithstanding the terms of an extradition treaty, to voluntarily render an individual to the other country on terms completely outside of those provided in the Treaty. The formal protest, therefore, ensures that the "offended" nation actually objects to the abduction and has not in some way voluntarily rendered the individual for prosecution. Thus the Extradition Treaty only prohibits gaining the defendant's presence by means other than those set forth in the Treaty when the nation from which the defendant was abducted objects.

This argument seems to us inconsistent with the remainder of respondent's argument. The Extradition Treaty has the force of law, and if, as respondent asserts, it is self-executing, it would appear that a court must enforce it on behalf of an individual regardless of the offensiveness of the practice of one nation to the other nation. In Rauscher, the Court noted that Great Britain had taken the position in other cases that the Webster–Ashburton Treaty included the doctrine of specialty, but no importance was attached to whether or not Great Britain had protested the prosecution of Rauscher for the crime of cruel and unusual punishment as opposed to murder.

More fundamentally, the difficulty with the support respondent garners from international law is that none of it relates to the practice of nations in relation to extradition treaties. In Rauscher, we implied a term in the Webster–Ashburton Treaty because of the practice of nations with regard to extradition treaties. In the instant case, respondent would imply terms in the extradition treaty from the practice of nations with regards to international law more generally. Respondent would have us find that the Treaty acts as a prohibition against a violation of the general principle of international law that one government may not "exercise its police power in the territory of another state." Brief for Respondent 16. There are many actions which could be taken by a nation that would violate this principle, including waging war, but it cannot seriously be contended an invasion of the United States by Mexico would violate the terms of the extradition treaty between the two nations.

In sum, to infer from this Treaty and its terms that it prohibits all means of gaining the presence of an individual outside of its terms goes beyond established precedent and practice. * * * The general principles cited by respondent simply fail to persuade us that we should imply in the United States–Mexico Extradition Treaty a term prohibiting international abductions.

Respondent and his amici may be correct that respondent's abduction was "shocking," Tr. of Oral Arg. 40, and that it may be in violation of general international law principles. Mexico has protested the abduction of respondent through diplomatic notes, App. 33–38, and the decision of whether respondent should be returned to Mexico, as a matter outside of the

Treaty, is a matter for the Executive Branch.[7] We conclude, however, that respondent's abduction was not in violation of the Extradition Treaty between the United States and Mexico, and therefore the rule of Ker v. Illinois is fully applicable to this case. The fact of respondent's forcible abduction does not therefore prohibit his trial in a court in the United States for violations of the criminal laws of the United States.

The judgment of the Court of Appeals is therefore reversed, and the case is remanded for further proceedings consistent with this opinion.

So ordered.

JUSTICE STEVENS, with whom JUSTICE BLACKMUN and JUSTICE O'CONNOR join, dissenting.

The Court correctly observes that this case raises a question of first impression. The case is unique for several reasons. It does not involve an ordinary abduction by a private kidnaper, or bounty hunter, as in Ker v. Illinois, 119 U.S. 436, 7 S.Ct. 225, 30 L.Ed. 421 (1886); nor does it involve the apprehension of an American fugitive who committed a crime in one State and sought asylum in another, as in Frisbie v. Collins, 342 U.S. 519, 72 S.Ct. 509, 96 L.Ed. 54 (1952). Rather, it involves this country's abduction of another country's citizen; it also involves a violation of the territorial integrity of that other country, with which this country has signed an extradition treaty.

A Mexican citizen was kidnaped in Mexico and charged with a crime committed in Mexico; his offense allegedly violated both Mexican and American law. Mexico has formally demanded on at least two separate occasions that he be returned to Mexico and has represented that he will be prosecuted and punished for his alleged offense. It is clear that Mexico's demand must be honored if this official abduction violated the 1978 Extradition Treaty between the United States and Mexico. In my opinion, a fair reading of the treaty in light of our decision in United States v. Rauscher, 119 U.S. 407, 7 S.Ct. 234, 30 L.Ed. 425 (1886), and applicable principles of international law, leads inexorably to the conclusion that the District Court, United States v. Caro–Quintero, 745 F.Supp. 599 (CDCal.1990), and the Court

7. The Mexican government has also requested from the United States the extradition of two individuals it suspects of having abducted respondent in Mexico, on charges of kidnapping. App. 39–66.

The advantage of the diplomatic approach to the resolution of difficulties between two sovereign nations, as opposed to unilateral action by the courts of one nation, is illustrated by the history of the negotiations leading to the treaty discussed in Cook v United States, supra. The United States was interested in being able to search British vessels which hovered beyond the 3–mile limit and served as supply ships for motor launches which took intoxicating liquor from them into ports for further distribution in violation of prohibition laws. The United States initially proposed that both nations agree to searches of the other's vessels beyond the 3–mile limit; Great Britain rejected such an approach, since it had no prohibition laws and therefore no problem with United States vessels hovering just beyond its territorial waters. The parties appeared to be at loggerheads; then this Court decided Cunard Steamship Co. v. Mellon, 262 U.S. 100, 43 S.Ct. 504, 67 L.Ed. 894 (1923), holding that our prohibition laws applied to foreign merchant vessels as well as domestic within the territorial waters of the United States, and that therefore the carrying of intoxicating liquors by foreign passenger ships violated those laws. A treaty was then successfully negotiated giving the United States the right to seizure beyond the 3–mile limit (which it desired), and giving British passenger ships the right to bring liquor into United States waters so long as the liquor supply was sealed while in those waters (which Great Britain desired). Cook v. United States, supra.

of Appeals for the Ninth Circuit, 946 F.2d 1466 (1991) (per curiam), correctly construed that instrument.

* * *

III

A critical flaw pervades the Court's entire opinion. It fails to differentiate between the conduct of private citizens, which does not violate any treaty obligation, and conduct expressly authorized by the Executive Branch of the Government, which unquestionably constitutes a flagrant violation of international law, and in my opinion, also constitutes a breach of our treaty obligations. Thus, at the outset of its opinion, the Court states the issue as "whether a criminal defendant, abducted to the United States from a nation with which it has an extradition treaty, thereby acquires a defense to the jurisdiction of this country's courts." Ante, at 2190. That, of course, is the question decided in Ker v. Illinois, 119 U.S. 436, 7 S.Ct. 225, 30 L.Ed. 421 (1886); it is not, however, the question presented for decision today.

The importance of the distinction between a court's exercise of jurisdiction over either a person or property that has been wrongfully seized by a private citizen, or even by a state law enforcement agent, on the one hand, and the attempted exercise of jurisdiction predicated on a seizure by federal officers acting beyond the authority conferred by treaty, on the other hand, is explained by Justice Brandeis in his opinion for the Court in Cook v. United States, 288 U.S. 102, 53 S.Ct. 305, 77 L.Ed. 641 (1933). That case involved a construction of a prohibition era treaty with Great Britain that authorized American agents to board certain British vessels to ascertain whether they were engaged in importing alcoholic beverages. A British vessel was boarded 11½ miles off the coast of Massachusetts, found to be carrying unmanifested alcoholic beverages, and taken into port. The Collector of Customs assessed a penalty which he attempted to collect by means of libels against both the cargo and the seized vessel.

The Court held that the seizure was not authorized by the treaty because it occurred more than 10 miles off shore. The Government argued that the illegality of the seizure was immaterial because, as in Ker, the Court's jurisdiction was supported by possession even if the seizure was wrongful. Justice Brandeis acknowledged that the argument would succeed if the seizure had been made by a private party without authority to act for the Government, but that a different rule prevails when the Government itself lacks the power to seize. * * *

* * *

The Court's failure to differentiate between private abductions and official invasions of another sovereign's territory also accounts for its misplaced reliance on the 1935 proposal made by the Advisory Committee on Research in International Law. See ante, at 2194–2195, and n. 13. As the text of that proposal plainly states, it would have rejected the rule of the Ker case. The failure to adopt that recommendation does not speak to the issue the Court decides today. The Court's admittedly "shocking" disdain for customary and conventional international law principles, see ante, at 2195, is thus entirely unsupported by case law and commentary.

IV

As the Court observes at the outset of its opinion, there is reason to believe that respondent participated in an especially brutal murder of an American law enforcement agent. That fact, if true, may explain the Executive's intense interest in punishing respondent in our courts. Such an explanation, however, provides no justification for disregarding the Rule of Law that this Court has a duty to uphold. * * *

* * *

I suspect most courts throughout the civilized world—will be deeply disturbed by the "monstrous" decision the Court announces today. For every Nation that has an interest in preserving the Rule of Law is affected, directly or indirectly, by a decision of this character. As Thomas Paine warned, an "avidity to punish is always dangerous to liberty" because it leads a Nation "to stretch, to misinterpret, and to misapply even the best of laws." To counter that tendency, he reminds us:

> "He that would make his own liberty secure must guard even his enemy from oppression; for if he violates this duty he establishes a precedent that will reach to himself."

I respectfully dissent.

### *Notes*

1. It is a well-settled rule of international law that international agreements must be construed in accordance with good faith. Good faith is objective good faith; it imposes a standard of objective reasonableness. See Chapter 6. When a treaty is construed to accord with objective good faith, its provisions are supplemented by reference to the law, not to the subjective intentions of the parties. The pertinent question, in determining what the law requires, is not what the parties actually intended, but, instead, what they would have intended if they had thought of the possibility of including the lacking provision in the treaty. See Smit, Frustration of Contract: A Comparative Attempt at Consolidation, 58 Colum.L.Rev. 287 (1958). Is there any reasonable doubt that, if, at the time of the negotiation and conclusion of the Treaty, the parties had considered the possibility that either party would engage in abduction in violation of international law, they would have included in the Treaty a provision prohibiting this? Does the Court give any consideration to the possible implication of this prohibition on the basis of objective good faith rather than the parties' actual intentions?

2. The Court did not dispute that the forcible abduction of the accused from Mexico violated international law. Should it also have considered whether the exercise of personal jurisdiction made possible by this forcible abduction constituted a violation of international law? Might the answer to that question depend on whether the abduction was effectuated by private persons or upon the direction of U.S. government officials? Is the notion of *male captus bene detentus* applicable in the latter case, which can more appropriately be described as *male captus male detentus*? See M.J. Glennon, State-Sponsored Abduction: A Comment on United States v. Alvarez–Machain, 86 A.J.I.L. 746 (1992).

3. Another question is whether the U.S. prosecutor and the Executive had the constitutional power to keep in custody and prosecute a person whose presence they had procured in violation of international law and elementary

principles of proper governmental conduct? If they did not, would dismissal of the charges be the appropriate sanction? Cf. on this problem, M. Halberstam, In Defense of the Supreme Court Decision in Alvarez–Machain, 86 A.J.I.L. 736, 738–43 (1992).

4. Upon remand, the District Court dismissed the charges on the ground that the prosecution had failed to produce adequate proof of its charges. See Seth Mydons, Judge Clears Mexican in Agent's Killing, N.Y. Times, December 15, 1992, at A20.

5. For an instance in which FBI agents lured a person accused of hijacking a Jordanian airplane in Beirut with American passengers aboard onto a yacht in the Mediterranean with the promise of a drug deal and arrested him when the vessel entered international waters, see United States v. Fawaz Yunis, 924 F.2d 1086 (D.C.Cir.1991) (upholding the court's jurisdiction). If, in the principal case, the American anti-drug enforcement officers had lured the Mexican doctor to the United States, would international law have been violated? Would such a stratagem have been implicitly prohibited by the extradition treaty?

# Chapter 13

# IMMUNITY FROM JURISDICTION

## SECTION 1. JURISDICTIONAL IMMUNITIES OF FOREIGN STATES

Under international law, states and other international legal persons enjoy certain immunities from the exercise of jurisdiction. In addition, such immunities may be granted by municipal law. Of course, when an immunity exists under international law, its denial by municipal law may create a claim for violation of international law. But nothing prevents a state from granting more extensive immunities than those granted by international law. In states that do not recognize the supremacy of international law over national law, such as the United States, national law may grant a lesser measure of immunity than that prescribed by international law.

Consequently, in determining the jurisdictional immunities to which an international legal person is entitled, both international and municipal law must be studied. This is a circumstance worth noting, because both the United States and the United Kingdom have enacted statutes on this subject and other states are following their example.

Since jurisdiction may be exercised on the legislative, the judicial, and the enforcement level, immunities from jurisdiction may also operate on these three levels. However, traditionally, primary consideration has been given to immunity from judicial and enforcement jurisdiction.

Originally, jurisdictional immunities were regarded as being absolute. A state could invoke them, irrespective of the nature of its sovereign activities. This absolute form of immunity is based on the conception that all states are equal and that no one state may exercise authority over any other. It is aptly described by Chief Justice Marshall in The Schooner Exchange v. M'Faddon, p. 1129 infra.

As states have become involved increasingly in commercial activities, the pressures towards limiting immunity have grown apace. As a consequence, the absolute approach to jurisdictional immunities has been forced into broad retreat. However, a number of states still embrace it, although their espousal of the absolute doctrine is frequently formal rather than substantive. While proclaiming that the absolute doctrine is part of prevailing international law, most of these countries have agreed that their instrumentalities engaged in commercial activities may be sued in foreign courts.

At present, a pragmatic functional approach has largely taken the place of the conceptual absolute one. Under this functional approach, the problems attendant upon exercising jurisdiction over a foreign state are balanced against the propriety of denying persons the benefits of exercising jurisdiction that they would enjoy if their claims were asserted against a private person rather than a foreign state. This functional approach has led to the emergence of a restrictive or relative doctrine. This restrictive doctrine denies immunity claimed by a foreign state in regard to an activity or property that is commercial rather than public or, as it is often expressed, that belongs to the sphere of *ius gestionis* rather than that of *ius imperii.* This development has greatly enhanced the significance of distinguishing between the three types of jurisdiction against which a plea of immunity is advanced. For since the factual premises for the exercise of these types of jurisdiction may differ, the propriety of a claim of immunity may depend on the particular form of jurisdiction from the exercise of which immunity is sought.

Problems of jurisdictional immunities arise when an action is brought in the tribunals of one state against another state or its instrumentalities or property. When such an action is brought, the first question that arises is whether the local tribunal has judicial jurisdiction over the foreign state. This question is one of immunity from judicial jurisdiction. The second question that arises is whether the forum has the authority to evaluate the foreign state's conduct under the rules of law applicable to such conduct. This raises a question of immunity from legislative jurisdiction. This question has received scant attention. The third question that arises is when a foreign state or its property is immune from non-judicial enforcement measures. This is a question of immunity from jurisdiction to enforce.

The efforts to restrict immunity from judicial jurisdiction are increasingly taking legislative form. The United States enacted the Foreign Sovereign Immunities Act in 1976, 90 Stat. 2891, 28 U.S.C.A. §§ 1330, 1332, 1391, 1441, 1602–1611, as amended by Pub.L. 100–640, 102 Stat. 3333 (1988). The 1988 amendments deal with sovereign immunity in admiralty cases and arbitration. The United Kingdom enacted its State Immunity Act in 1978, 26 & 27 Eliz. 2, Ch. 33, 17 I.L.M. 1123. Canada enacted its Act to Provide for State Immunity in Canadian courts in 1982, 29, 30 & 31 Eliz. 2, Ch. 93, 21 I.L.M. 798 (1982). Australia, Pakistan, Singapore, and South Africa have enacted similar statutes. See U.N.Leg.Ser.U.N.Doc. ST/LEG/SER.B/20 (1982). And other states may follow suit. On sovereign immunity policy in New Zealand, see Hastings, Sovereign Immunity in New Zealand, 1990 N.Z.L.J. 214 (1990).

All of the statutes enacted thus far embrace a restrictive view of immunity. The provisions of the Foreign Sovereign Immunities Act of 1976 are treated in some detail below. On the State Immunity Act 1978, see Mann, The State Immunity Act 1978, 50 B.Y.I.L. 43 (1981); Bud, The State Immunity Act of 1978: An English Update, 13 Int.Law. 619 (1979); Delaume, The State Immunity Act of the United Kingdom, 73 A.J.I.L. 185 (1979); Shaw, The State Immunity Act of 1978, 128 N.L.J. 1136 (1978); Higgins, Recent Developments in the Law of Sovereign Immunity of the United Kingdom, 71 A.J.I.L. 423 (1977); Fox, Enforcement Jurisdiction, Foreign State Property and Diplomatic Immunity, 34 Int'l & Comp.L.Q. 115 (1985); Davidson, State Immunity in the English Courts: A Lingering Death, 33 N.Ir.Legal Q. 171 (1982); Fox, State Immunity: The House of Lords Decision in I Congresso del Portido, 88 Law A.Rev. 94 (1982); Marasinghe, The Modern Law of Sovereign Immunity, 54 Mod.L.Rev. 664 (1991); Note, Reciprocal Influence of British and United States Law: Foreign Sovereign Immunity Law from the Schooner Exchange to the State Immunity Act of 1978, 13 Vand.J.Transn.L. 761 (1980); Note, A Comparative Analysis of the British State Immunity Act of 1978, 3 B.C.Int. & Comp.L.Rev. 175 (1979). On the Canadian Act, see Molot & Jewett, The State Immunity Act of Canada, 20 Can.Y.Int.L. 79 (1982); Jewett & Molot, State Immunity Act—Basic Principles, 61 Can.B.Rev. 843 (1983); Note, The Canadian State Immunity Act, 14 Law & Pol'y Int'l Bus. 1197 (1983).

The Council of Europe has developed a European Convention on State Immunity And Additional Protocol, Basle, May 16, 1972, 11 I.L.M. 470 (1972). This Convention enumerates the specific instances in which a contracting state is not immune from jurisdiction in the courts of another contracting state. These include the case in which a state "has on the territory of the State of the forum an office, agency or other establishment through which it engages, in the same manner as a private person, in an industrial, commercial or financial activity, and the proceedings relate to that activity" (Art. 7). On this Convention, see Sinclair, The European Convention on State Immunity, 22 Int. & Comp.L. 254 (1973). See also Dellapenna, Foreign State Immunity in Europe, 5 N.Y.Int'l L.R. 51 (1992).

The International Law Association has also produced a Draft Convention on Foreign Sovereign Immunity. See Note, International Law Association Draft Convention on Foreign Sovereign Immunity: A Comparative Approach, 23 Va.J.Int.L. 635 (1983).

In 1978, the International Law Commission began preparing draft articles on the jurisdictional immunities of states and their property. The Commission completed the first reading of the draft articles during its 1986 session. See Report of the International Law Commission to the General Assembly, 41 U.N. GAOR Supp. (No. 10) at 9–24, U.N. Doc. A/41/10 (1986), reprinted in [1986] 2. Y.B.Int'l L.Comm'n, U.N. Doc. A/CN.4/1986/Add.1 (Part 2). The ILC adopted the first reading in 1986, and substantial progress has since been made on the second reading. A diplomatic conference is likely to follow approval upon the second reading. See Morris, The International Law Commission's Draft Convention on Jurisdictional Immunities of States and Their Property, 17 Denv.J.Int'l L. & Pol'y 395 (1989); Greig, Specific Exceptions to Immunity Under the International Law Commission's Draft Articles, 38 Int'l & Comp.L.Q. 560 (1989); Greig, Forum State Jurisdiction and Sovereign Immunity Under the International Law Commission's Draft Articles, 38 Int'l & Comp.L.Q. 243 (1989); Balas & Pauknerova, The Czechoslovak Approach to the Draft Convention on Jurisdictional Immunities of States and Their Property, 12 Mich.J.Int'l L. 874 (1991); Note, The International Law Commission's Draft Articles on the Jurisdictional Immunities of States and Their Property: The Commercial Contract Exception, 27 Colum.J.Transnat'l L. 657 (1989). On state immunity, see further Gamal Moursi Badr, Preparing Students For Practice in International Law: On Teaching the Law of International Transactions: State Immunity: An Analytical and Prognostic View (Martinus Niihoff Publishers) (1984); Christoph H. Shrever, State Immunity: Some Recent Developments (Grotius Publications Limited) (1988).

## A. THE ABSOLUTE FORM OF SOVEREIGN IMMUNITY

### THE SCHOONER EXCHANGE v. McFADDON

Supreme Court of the United States, 1812.
11 U.S. (7 Cranch) 116, 3 L.Ed. 287.

[A libel was brought against the schooner Exchange by two American citizens who claimed that they owned and were entitled to possession of the ship. They alleged that the vessel had been seized on the high seas in 1810 by forces acting on behalf of the Emperor of France and that no prize court of competent jurisdiction had pronounced judgment against the vessel. No one appeared for the vessel, but the United States Attorney for Pennsylvania appeared on behalf of the United States Government to state that the United States and France were at peace, that a public ship (known as the Balaou) of the Emperor of France had been compelled by bad weather to enter the port of Philadelphia, and was prevented from leaving by the process of the court. The United States Attorney stated that, even if the vessel had in fact been wrongfully seized from the libellants, property therein had passed to the Emperor of France. It was therefore requested that the libel be dismissed with costs and the vessel released. The District Court dismissed the libel, the Circuit Court reversed (4 Hall's L.J. 232), and the United States Attorney appealed to the Supreme Court.]

MARSHALL, C.J.: * * * The jurisdiction of the nation within its own territory is necessarily exclusive and absolute. It is susceptible of no limitation not imposed by itself. * * *

This full and absolute territorial jurisdiction being alike the attribute of every sovereign * * * would not seem to contemplate foreign sovereigns nor their sovereign rights as its objects. One sovereign being in no respect amenable to another; and being bound by obligations of the highest character not to degrade the dignity of his nation, by placing himself or its sovereign rights within the jurisdiction of another, can be supposed to enter a foreign territory only under an express license, or in the confidence that the immunities belonging to his independent sovereign station, though not expressly stipulated, are reserved by implication, and will be extended to him.

This perfect equality and absolute independence of sovereigns, and this common interest impelling them to mutual intercourse, and an interchange of good offices with each other, have given rise to a class of cases in which every sovereign is understood to waive the exercise of a part of that complete exclusive territorial jurisdiction, which has been stated to be the attribute of every nation.

1st. One of these is admitted to be the exemption of the person of the sovereign from arrest or detention within a foreign territory. * * *

2d. A second case, standing on the same principles with the first, is the immunity which all civilized nations allow to foreign ministers. * * *

3d. A third case in which a sovereign is understood to cede a portion of his territorial jurisdiction is, where he allows the troops of a foreign prince to pass through his dominions. * * *

[The Court concluded that the territorial sovereign's license to foreign armies must be express, and not merely implied, but that a different rule applied in the case of foreign ships.] * * * If there be no prohibition, the ports of a friendly nation are considered as open to the public ships of all powers with whom it is at peace, and they are supposed to enter such ports and to remain in them while allowed to remain, under the protection of the government of the place. * * *

When private individuals of one nation spread themselves through another as business or caprice may direct, mingling indiscriminately with the inhabitants of that other, or when merchant vessels enter for the purposes of trade, it would be obviously inconvenient and dangerous to society, and would subject the laws to continual infraction, and the government to degradation, if such individuals or merchants did not owe temporary and local allegiance, and were not amenable to the jurisdiction of the country. * * *

But in all respects different is the situation of a public armed ship. She constitutes a part of the military force of her nation; acts under the immediate and direct command of the sovereign; is employed by him in national objects. He has many and powerful motives for preventing those objects from being defeated by the interference of a foreign state. Such interference cannot take place without affecting his power and his dignity. The implied license therefore under which such vessel enters a friendly port, may reasonably be construed, and it seems to the Court, ought to be construed, as containing an exemption from the jurisdiction of the sovereign, within whose territory she claims the rights of hospitality.

Upon these principles, by the unanimous consent of nations, a foreigner is amenable to the laws of the place; but certainly in practice, nations have not yet asserted their jurisdiction over the public armed ships of a foreign sovereign entering a port open for their reception.

Bynkershoek, a jurist of great reputation, has indeed maintained that the property of a foreign sovereign is not distinguishable by any legal exemption from the property of an ordinary individual, and has quoted several cases in which courts have exercised jurisdiction over causes in which a foreign sovereign was made a party defendant.

Without indicating any opinion on this question, it may safely be affirmed, that there is a manifest distinction between the private property of the person who happens to be a prince, and that military force which supports the sovereign power, and maintains the dignity and the independence of a nation. A prince, by acquiring private property in a foreign country, may possibly be considered as subjecting that property to the territorial jurisdiction; he may be considered as so far laying down the prince, and assuming the character of a private individual; but this he cannot be presumed to do with respect to any portion of that armed force, which upholds his crown, and the nation he is entrusted to govern. * * *

It seems then to the Court, to be a principle of public law, that national ships of war, entering the port of a friendly power open for their reception, are to be considered as exempted by the consent of that power from its jurisdiction.

* * *

The arguments in favor of this opinion which have been drawn from the general inability of the judicial power to enforce its decisions in cases of this description, from the consideration, that the sovereign power of the nation is alone competent to avenge wrongs committed by a sovereign, that the questions to which such wrongs give birth are rather questions of policy than of law, that they are for diplomatic, rather than legal discussion, are of great weight, and merit serious attention. But the argument has already been drawn to a length, which forbids a particular examination of these points.
* * *

If the preceding reasoning be correct, the Exchange, being a public armed ship, in the service of a foreign sovereign, with whom the government of the United States is at peace, and having entered an American port open for her reception, on the terms on which ships of war are generally permitted to enter the ports of a friendly power, must be considered as having come into the American territory, under an implied promise, that while necessarily within it, and demeaning herself in a friendly manner, she should be exempt from the jurisdiction of the country. * * *

[Judgment of the Circuit Court reversed, and judgment of the District Court, dismissing the libel, affirmed.]

### *Notes*

1. Early attempts to limit the scope of sovereign immunity to judicial jurisdiction came in cases involving claims arising from the operation of commercial vessels by foreign governments. However, in Berizzi Bros. Co. v. S.S. Pesaro, 271 U.S. 562, 46 S.Ct. 611, 70 L.Ed. 1088 (1926), the Supreme Court rejected the argument, accepted in a prior stage of the case by the District Court, that Italy was not entitled to immunity in an *in rem* proceeding brought to enforce a claim for cargo damage against a merchant vessel owned and operated by Italy.

2. In 1938, Lord Maugham, in Compania Naviera Vascongado v. S.S. Cristina, [1938] A.C. 485, 521–22, commented:

> Half a century ago foreign Governments very seldom embarked in trade with ordinary ships, though they not infrequently owned vessels destined for public uses, and in particular hospital vessels, supply ships, and surveying or exploring vessels. There were doubtless very strong reasons for extending the privilege long possessed by ships of war to public ships of the nature mentioned; but there has been a very large development of State-owned commercial ships since the Great War, and the question whether the immunity should continue to be given to ordinary trading ships has become acute. Is it consistent with sovereign dignity to acquire a tramp steamer and to compete with ordinary shippers and ship-owners in the markets of the world? Doing so, is it consistent to set up the immunity of a sovereign

if, owing to the want of skill of captain and crew, serious damage is caused to the ship of another country? Is it also consistent to refuse to permit proceedings to enforce a right of salvage in respect of services rendered, perhaps at great risk, by the vessel of another country? Is there justice or equity, or for that matter is international comity being followed, in permitting a foreign Government, while insisting on its own right of indemnity [*sic* ], to bring actions in rem or in personam against our own nationals?

My Lords, I am far from relying merely on my own opinion as to the absurdity of the position which our Courts are in if they must continue to disclaim jurisdiction in relation to commercial ships owned by foreign Governments. The matter has been considered over and over again of late years by foreign jurists, by English lawyers, and by business men, and with practical unanimity they are of opinion that, if Governments or corporations formed by them choose to navigate and trade as shipowners, they ought to submit to the same legal remedies and actions as any other shipowner. This was the effect of the various resolutions of the Conference of London of 1922, of the conference of Gothenburg of 1923 and of the Genoa Conference of 1925. Three Conferences not being deemed sufficient, there was yet another in Brussels in the year 1926. It was attended by Great Britain, France, Germany, Italy, Spain, Holland, Belgium, Poland, Japan and a number of other countries. The United States explained their absence by the statement that they had already given effect to the wish for uniformity in the laws relating to State-owned ships by the Public Vessels Act, 1925 (1925 c. 428). The Brussels Conference was unanimously in favour of the view that in times of peace there should be no immunity as regards State-owned ships engaged in commerce; and the resolution was ratified by Germany, Italy, Holland, Belgium, Estonia, Poland, Brazil and other countries, but not so far by Great Britain. (Oppenheim, International Law, 5th ed., vol. i., p. 670.)

3. The Brussels Convention on the Unification of Certain Rules Relating to Immunity of State-owned Vessels, signed April 10, 1926, 176 L.N.T.S. 199, provides in Article 1 that "Seagoing vessels owned or operated by States, cargoes owned by them, and cargoes and passengers carried on Government vessels, and the States owning or operating such vessels, or owning such cargoes, are subject in respect of claims relating to the operation of such vessels or the carriage of such cargoes to the same rules of liability and to the same obligations as those applicable to private vessels, cargoes and equipments." The same procedures are to be available to enforce such liabilities and obligations as would be available in the case of privately owned merchant vessels and cargoes and their owners. These provisions do not apply, however, to warships and other vessels "used at the time a cause of action arises exclusively on Governmental and non-commercial service," nor shall such vessels be subject to seizure, attachment or other *in rem* proceedings. When such vessels are involved in controversies relating to collision, salvage, general average, repairs, supplies, or other contracts relating to the vessel, the claimant is entitled to institute proceedings in the courts of the state owning or operating the vessel, without that state being permitted to avail itself of its immunity. A supplementary protocol, signed May 24, 1934, prohibits attachment or seizure of vessels chartered by Governments for non-commercial service, without reference to the status of the vessel at the time the cause of action arose. The convention applies only as between parties to it; these were, as of January 1, 1988: Argentina, Belgium, Brazil, Chile, Denmark, Egypt, Estonia, France, Germany, Greece, Hungary, Italy, Libya, Malagasy Republic, Netherlands, Norway, Portugal, Somalia, Surinam, Sweden,

Switzerland, Syrian Arab Republic, Turkey, United Kingdom, Uruguay, Zaire. In accordance with Article 7, the treaty ceased to have effect between belligerent states during World War II; it came into renewed force between Germany and most of the Allied Powers on November 1, 1953. Poland, which had ratified in 1936, denounced the Convention on March 17, 1952, and rejoined on July 16, 1976. Romania, which had joined on August 4, 1937, denounced on September 21, 1959. [As of January 1, 1992, the United States had still not become a party to the Convention.] See Knauth's Benedict on Admiralty, Vol. 6A, Doc. 8–4, Sec. 8–38, 39 (7th ed. 1958 and 1988 Supp.), and [1976] Int'l Mar. Committee Documentation 235, 352, and succeeding years.

4. The Soviet Union and other communist states embraced a doctrine of absolute immunity premised on the notion that a state's immunity is the natural consequence of its sovereignty. To accommodate the needs of practice, the Soviet Union concluded a large number of bilateral treaties under which its trade delegations in foreign countries were subject to local jurisdiction with respect to their commercial activities.

In the United States, the problem was addressed by the Soviet Union's organizing a corporation formed under local law to conduct its commercial activities. See, generally, Triska and Slusser, The Theory, Law and Policy of Soviet Treaties, 324–33 (1962) and Sucharitkul, State Immunities and Trading Activities in International Law 152–61 (1959). Now that the formerly communist states have opted for a more market-oriented approach, they are likely to accept a more restrictive approach to sovereign immunity.

Between 1948 and 1958, the United States concluded fourteen treaties requiring that each party waive sovereign immunity for state-controlled enterprises engaged in commercial activities. The practice to include a provision to this effect was discontinued in 1958. See Setser, the Immunity Waiver for State–Controlled Business Enterprises in United States Commercial Treaties, 55 A.S.I.L. Proc. 89 (1961).

## B. THE RESTRICTIVE FORM OF SOVEREIGN IMMUNITY

### *1. The "Commercial" Exception*

## DRALLE v. REPUBLIC OF CZECHOSLOVAKIA

Supreme Court of Austria, 1950.
[1950] Int'l L.Rep. 155.*

[The German cosmetics firm of Georg Dralle had had a branch office since 1910 at Bodenbach, in Bohemia, which subsequently became part of Czechoslovakia. The branch office was the registered owner in Austria of trademarks used by the German firm in connection with the sale of its goods in Austria. When the branch was nationalized by Czechoslovakia in 1945, the nationalized firm claimed the Austrian trademarks and requested the Austrian customers of the German firm not to offer the latter's goods for sale under the trademarks in question. The German firm applied for an injunction to restrain the Czechoslovakian firm from using the trademarks in Austria. The defendant claimed to be immune from the jurisdiction of the Austrian courts, and claimed in any event to be entitled to use the

* Reprinted by permission of Butterworth & Co. (Publishers) Ltd., H. Lauterpacht, Editor.

trademarks in question. The plaintiff was awarded an injunction; this decree was affirmed by the appellate court, and the defendant appealed to the Supreme Court.]

[The Court]: * * * In view of the fact that we are here concerned with a question of international law we have to examine the practice of the courts of civilised countries and to find out whether from that practice we can deduce a uniform view; this is the only method of ascertaining whether there still exists a principle of international law to the effect that foreign States, even in so far as concerns claims belonging to the realm of private law, cannot be sued in the courts of a foreign State.

The first court to enunciate the principle that in matters belonging purely to the realm of private law foreign States cannot claim immunity was the Court of Cassation of Naples in a judgment of March 27, 1886 (*Giurisprudenza Italiana,* 1886, I, 1, 228). A few months later the Court of Cassation of Florence (in a judgment of July 16, 1886: *Giurisprudenza Italiana,* 1886, I, 1, 486) followed this decision. The Court of Cassation of Rome did likewise on July 1 and October 12, 1893 (*Giurisprudenza Italiana,* 1893, I, 1, 1213). The case was concerned with the following facts:

On May 17, 1866, the Austrian Government made an agreement with a certain firm by the name of Fisola by which the latter undertook to build fortifications along the Venetian border. When Venetia had ceased to be part of Austria, the Austrian State refused to pay for the work. The Court of Cassation of Rome decided in favour of municipal jurisdiction, mainly on the ground that a distinction must be made between a case in which a Government acts in its capacity of *ente politico* and a case in which it acts in its capacity of *ente civile.* In the former case its acts cannot be subject to adjudication by foreign tribunals, while in the latter case the Government acts in the capacity of a legal personality of private law and is, therefore, subject to the rules of private law. * * *

[The Court then referred to more recent cases in which this view was affirmed by Italian courts: Corte di cassazione 1925 No. 1456; Corte 1926 No. 1661; and the judgment of August 3, 1935, reported in *Giurisprudenza Italiana,* 1935, I, 1, 109.]

In 1903, in the case of Société Anonyme de Chemins de Fer Liégeois–Luxemburgeois v. The Netherlands (June 11, 1903, *Clunet,* 1904, 417), the Belgian Court of Cassation followed this practice. The plaintiff company had agreed with the Netherlands Railway Administration to enlarge a station building which was being used by both parties, and it claimed from the Netherlands a sum of money payable by the latter and which the plaintiff company had advanced. The Court of Cassation rejected the plea to the jurisdiction on the ground that "the immunity of foreign States from the jurisdiction of foreign courts can be invoked only where their sovereignty is affected thereby; this was the case only in so far as concerned acts relating to the political life of a State. Where, on the other hand, the State, in taking account of the needs of the community, does not confine itself to its political role, but on the contrary acquires and possesses property, concludes agreements, constitutes itself creditor and debtor and even engages in commerce, it does not set in motion executive power, but merely does what private individuals can do; in such a case it acts like a private individual.

* * *" The Court of Cassation added that in all these cases the competence of the municipal courts derives not from the consent of the defendant State, but from the nature of the act and the capacity in which the State has intervened. * * *

[The court then discusses decisions of Swiss and Egyptian courts adopting this view.]

Among States which in principle recognise immunity from jurisdiction even where *acta gestionis* of private law are concerned are Germany (*RGZ.* 62, 165; 103, 274), England (in particular a judgment given in 1880) [probably *The Parlement Belge,* 5 P.D. 197], the United States (in particular a judgment given in 1812 [The Schooner Exchange v. McFaddon, 11 U.S. (7 Cranch) 110]—see the digest of the jurisprudence of the United States of America in *Revue génèrale de Droit international public,* 1936, pp. 603 seq.), Czechoslovakia, Poland (judgment of the Supreme Court of Warsaw of March 2, 1936, *Annuario di diritto comparato,* II/III p. 768) and Portugal (judgment delivered in 1923 and referred to in *Revue génèrale de Droit international public,* 1934, p. 545), also France (in particular a judgment of January 24, 1849, DP. 49, 1, 9). The French courts, however, have deviated from this jurisprudence in so far as concerns a foreign State regularly engaged in commerce in France. * * *

[The Court then reviewed certain decisions of Greek, Roumanian and Brazilian tribunals which adopted the restrictive view of state immunity.]

This survey shows that today it can no longer be said that jurisprudence generally recognises the principle of exemption of foreign States in so far as concerns claims of a private character, because the majority of courts of different civilised countries deny the immunity of a foreign State, and more particularly because exceptions are made even in those countries which today still adhere to the traditional principle that no State is entitled to exercise jurisdiction over another State * * *.

The Resolution passed by the Imperial Economic Conference of the British Empire in 1923 is proof that this movement has also made headway in the Anglo-Saxon countries; the Resolution stated expressly that a Dominion engaged in trade in another Dominion is not, for that reason, entitled to claim freedom from taxation (Harvard Research, 608: "shall not in its character as such be treated as entitled to any sovereign immunity from taxation either directly or through the claims of superiority to the jurisdiction of municipal courts").

A similar recommendation is contained in the Report of the World Economic Conference held at Geneva in 1927 (Harvard Research, 607).

International treaties too have on several occasions recognised the principle that *acta jure gestionis* are not exempt from jurisdiction. Thus, Article 233 of the Treaty of St. Germain (and similarly the other Treaties concluded near Paris) provide that the Austrian Government if it engages in international trade shall not, in relation to such trade, be or be regarded as being, entitled to claim rights, privileges and immunities of sovereignty. * * *

Other treaties too contain similar provisions which are not limited in their application to particular States, as e.g., Article 30 of the Paris Air

Navigation Convention of October 13, 1919, and Article 2 of the Warsaw Convention for the Unification of Certain Rules regarding Air Transport, of October 12, 1929. Similarly, the various draft agreements of international associations contain proposals, pointing in the same direction * * *.

[A] detailed draft with reasoned arguments was prepared by the Harvard Law School in 1932; its Article II contains the following provision:

> A State may be made a respondent in a proceeding in a court of another State, when in the territory of such other State it engages in an industrial, commercial, financial or other business enterprise in which private persons may there engage, or does an act there in connection with such an enterprise wherever conducted, and the proceeding is based upon the conduct of such enterprise or upon such act.
>
> The foregoing provision shall not be construed to allow a State to be made a respondent in a proceeding relating to its public debt.

The authors of the draft refer in particular to the jurisprudence of Italy, Belgium and the Egyptian Mixed Tribunals and state that even if the distinction between *acta jure gestionis* and *acta jure imperii* has not been generally recognised, it is time to lay down such a distinction in an international codification (Harvard Research, 606). It is worth mentioning that the introduction (p. 473) refers to a remark made by Chief Justice Marshall, the author of the judgment given in 1812 which is still a leading decision, who said in that judgment that a Head of State who descends into the market place must be treated like any private trader. The various proposals of international associations show that the classic doctrine of unlimited immunity no longer corresponds to the view expressed in legal practice.

Neither does the literature on the subject present a uniform picture. The Supreme Court must now consider legal doctrine briefly because the *communis opinio doctorum* is also regarded as a source of international law.

[After examining the views of a number of writers of different nationalities, the Court continued]:

Accordingly, there clearly is no *communis opinio doctorum.* The Supreme Court therefore reaches the conclusion that it can no longer be said that by international law so-called *acta gestionis* are exempt from municipal jurisdiction. This subjection of the *acta gestionis* to the jurisdiction of States has its basis in the development of the commercial activity of States. The classic doctrine of immunity arose at a time when all the commercial activities of States in foreign countries were connected with their political activities, either by the purchase of commodities for their diplomatic representatives abroad, or by the purchase of war material for war purposes, etc. Therefore there was no justification for any distinction between private transactions and acts of sovereignty. Today the position is entirely different; States engage in commercial activities and, as the present case shows, enter into competition with their own nationals and with foreigners. Accordingly, the classic doctrine of immunity has lost its meaning and, *ratione cessante,* can no longer be recognised as a rule of international law. * * * For these reasons the Supreme Court reaches the conclusion that in the present case the question of jurisdiction must be answered in the affirmative. * * *

*LETTER OF ACTING LEGAL ADVISER, JACK B. TATE, TO DEPARTMENT OF JUSTICE, MAY 19, 1952*

26 Dep't State Bull. 984 (1952).

The Department of State has for some time had under consideration the question whether the practice of the Government in granting immunity from suit to foreign governments made parties defendant in the courts of the United States without their consent should not be changed. The Department has now reached the conclusion that such immunity should no longer be granted in certain types of cases. In view of the obvious interest of your Department in this matter I should like to point out briefly some of the facts which influenced the Department's decision.

A study of the law of sovereign immunity reveals the existence of two conflicting concepts of sovereign immunity, each widely held and firmly established. According to the classical or absolute theory of sovereign immunity, a sovereign cannot, without his consent, be made a respondent in the courts of another sovereign. According to the newer or restrictive theory of sovereign immunity, the immunity of the sovereign is recognized with regard to sovereign or public acts (*jure imperii*) of a state, but not with respect to private acts (*jure gestionis*). There is agreement by proponents of both theories, supported by practice, that sovereign immunity should not be claimed or granted in actions with respect to real property (diplomatic and perhaps consular property excepted) or with respect to the disposition of the property of a deceased person even though a foreign sovereign is the beneficiary.

The classical or virtually absolute theory of sovereign immunity has generally been followed by the courts of the United States, the British Commonwealth, Czechoslovakia, Estonia, and probably Poland.

The decisions of the courts of Brazil, Chile, China, Hungary, Japan, Luxembourg, Norway, and Portugal may be deemed to support the classical theory of immunity if one or at most two old decisions anterior to the development of the restrictive theory may be considered sufficient on which to base a conclusion.

The position of the Netherlands, Sweden, and Argentina is less clear since although immunity has been granted in recent cases coming before the courts of those countries, the facts were such that immunity would have been granted under either the absolute or restrictive theory. However, constant references by the courts of these three countries to the distinction between public and private acts of the state, even though the distinction was not involved in the result of the case, may indicate an intention to leave the way open for a possible application of the restrictive theory of immunity if and when the occasion presents itself.

A trend to the restrictive theory is already evident in the Netherlands where the lower courts have started to apply that theory following a

Supreme Court decision to the effect that immunity would have been applicable in the case under consideration under either theory.

The German courts, after a period of hesitation at the end of the nineteenth century have held to the classical theory, but it should be noted that the refusal of the Supreme Court in 1921 to yield to pressure by the lower courts for the newer theory was based on the view that that theory had not yet developed sufficiently to justify a change. In view of the growth of the restrictive theory since that time the German courts might take a different view today.

The newer or restrictive theory of sovereign immunity has always been supported by the courts of Belgium and Italy. It was adopted in turn by the courts of Egypt and of Switzerland. In addition, the courts of France, Austria, and Greece, which were traditionally supporters of the classical theory, reversed their position in the 20's to embrace the restrictive theory. Rumania, Peru, and possibly Denmark also appear to follow this theory.

Furthermore, it should be observed that in most of the countries still following the classical theory there is a school of influential writers favoring the restrictive theory and the views of writers, at least in civil law countries, are a major factor in the development of the law. Moreover, the leanings of the lower courts in civil law countries are more significant in shaping the law than they are in common law countries where the rule of precedent prevails and the trend in these lower courts is to the restrictive theory.

Of related interest to this question is the fact that ten of the thirteen countries which have been classified above as supporters of the classical theory have ratified the Brussels Convention of 1926 under which immunity for government owned merchant vessels is waived. In addition, the United States which is not a party to the Convention, some years ago announced and has since followed, a policy of not claiming immunity for its public owned or operated merchant vessels. Keeping in mind the importance played by cases involving public vessels in the field of sovereign immunity, it is thus noteworthy that these ten countries (Brazil, Chile, Estonia, Germany, Hungary, Netherlands, Norway, Poland, Portugal, Sweden) and the United States have already relinquished by treaty or in practice an important part of the immunity which they claim under the classical theory.

It is thus evident that with the possible exception of the United Kingdom little support has been found except on the part of the Soviet Union and its satellites for continued full acceptance of the absolute theory of sovereign immunity. There are evidences that British authorities are aware of its deficiencies and ready for a change. The reasons which obviously motivate state trading countries in adhering the theory with perhaps increasing rigidity are most persuasive that the United States should change its policy. Furthermore, the granting of sovereign immunity to foreign governments in the courts of the United States is most inconsistent with the action of the Government of the United States in subjecting itself to suit in these same courts in both contract and tort and with its long established policy of not claiming immunity in foreign jurisdictions for its merchant vessels. Finally, the Department feels that the widespread and increasing practice on the part of governments of engaging in commercial activities makes necessary a practice which will enable persons doing business with them to have their rights determined in the courts. For these reasons it will hereafter be the Department's policy to follow the restrictive theory of sovereign immunity in the consideration of requests of foreign governments for a grant of sovereign immunity.

It is realized that a shift in policy by the executive cannot control the courts but it is felt that the courts are less likely to allow a plea of sovereign immunity where the executive has declined to do so. There have been indications that at least some Justices of the Supreme Court feel that in this matter courts should follow the branch of the Government charged with responsibility for the conduct of foreign relations.

In order that your Department, which is charged with representing the interests of the Government before the courts, may be adequately informed it will be the Department's practice to advise you of all requests by foreign governments for the grant of immunity from suit and of the Department's action thereon.

### *Notes*

1. A private firm in Cologne sued the Empire of Iran in order to obtain payment of a bill for 292 DM ($73) rendered to the latter for repairs made on the heating system in the Iranian Embassy at the request of the Ambassador. The question of sovereign immunity was raised before the local court, which decided that the defendant, as a sovereign state, was immune under international law from German jurisdiction. The plaintiff appealed from this decision, and the case was referred to the Supreme Constitutional Court of the Federal Republic of Germany, which, after a comprehensive review of the authorities, reversed, stating:

> A summary evaluation of jurisprudence, of rules contained in treaties, of attempts at codification, and of the teachings of publicists, shows that unlimited state immunity can no longer be regarded as a rule of customary international law. One must agree with the Austrian Supreme Court, as it concluded in its decision of May 10, 1950 [the *Dralle* case] * * * "that it can no longer be said that, according to established international law, so-called acta gestionis are excluded from municipal jurisdiction." * * * Decision of April 30, 1963, 16 BVerfG 27, 16 N.J.W. 1732, 19 L.Z. 171.

2. In 1960, the Asian–African Legal Consultative Committee received the final report of the Committee on Immunity of States in Respect of Commercial and Other Transactions of a Private Character, in which India, Burma, Ceylon, Indonesia, Japan, Iraq, and the United Arab Republic had been represented. A delegation from Pakistan attended the 1960 session, as did an observer from Iran. The following are excerpts from the final report:

> 4. All the delegations except that of Indonesia were of the view that a distinction should be made between different types of state activity and immunity to foreign states should not be granted in respect of their activities which may be called commercial or of private nature. The Indonesian delegate, however, adhered to the view that immunity should continue to be granted to all the activities of the foreign state irrespective of their nature provided they were carried on by the government itself. * * *
>
> 9. The Committee having taken the view of all the delegations into consideration decided to recommend as follows: * * * (ii) A State which enters into transactions of a commercial or private character, ought not to

raise the plea of sovereign immunity if sued in the courts of a foreign state in respect of such transactions. If the plea of immunity is raised it should not be admissible to deprive the jurisdiction of the Domestic Courts.

12. * * * The Delegation of Indonesia dissented on the recommendation contained in clause (ii) which was agreed upon by all other Delegations.

The Indonesian Government summarized its views as follows:

States should be immune from legal proceedings before Foreign Courts for all their acts, regardless of whether such acts are of a public or private character. * * *

Asian–African Legal Consultative Committee, Third Session, Colombo, 1960 (Secretariat of the Committee, New Delhi, India, n.d.), 66–69, 81.

3. Of the twenty-nine states that returned a completed questionnaire distributed by the International Law Commission, fourteen reported that they granted full immunity. See Materials on Jurisdictional Immunities of States and Their Property, U.N.Doc. No. E/F.81V.10.

4. On the restrictions upon sovereign immunity recognized by the 1991 Draft Articles of the International Law Commission, see 30 I.L.M. 1554 (1991).

## *FOREIGN SOVEREIGN IMMUNITIES ACT OF 1976*

[28 U.S.C.A. § 1602].

The Congress finds that the determination by United States courts of the claims of foreign states to immunity from the jurisdiction of such courts would serve the interests of justice and would protect the rights of both foreign states and litigants in United States courts. Under international law, states are not immune from the jurisdiction of foreign courts insofar as their commercial activities are concerned, and their commercial property may be levied upon for the satisfaction of judgments rendered against them in connection with their commercial activities. Claims of foreign states to immunity should henceforth be decided by courts of the United States and of the States in conformity with the principles set forth in this chapter.

### *Notes*

1. What criteria determine whether the foreign state's activity or property is commercial rather than public? Are they criteria of international law, the law of the forum state, or the law of the foreign state? See also the Decision of April 30, 1963 of the German Constitutional Court, 16 BVerfG 63, 19 L.Z 175, p. 1139 supra (national law may be used to draw the distinction, but may not deviate from the views of the preponderance of states as to what belongs to the region of state authority in its narrow and proper sense).

2. In the United States, whether a foreign state's act is commercial is determined by reference to the Foreign Sovereign Immunities Act of 1976 (F.S.I.A.). Prior to the enactment of the F.S.I.A., some argued that the purpose of the foreign state's act was determinative, while others looked at the nature of the act. For a discussion, see Victory Transport, Inc. v. Comisaria General de Abastecimiento y Transportes, 336 F.2d 354 (2d Cir.1964), cert. denied, 381 U.S. 934, 85 S.Ct. 1763, 14 L.Ed.2d 698 (1965). The Foreign Sovereign Immunities Act of 1976, 28 U.S.C.A. § 1603(d), provides the following definition:

> A "commercial activity" means either a regular course of commercial conduct or a particular commercial transaction or act. The commercial character of an activity shall be determined by reference to the nature of the course of conduct or particular transaction or act, rather than by reference to its purpose.

The Harvard Research in International Law, Competence of Courts in Regard to Foreign States, Art. 11, 25 A.J.I.L.Supp. 451, 597, provides that a state engages in a commercial activity when it "engages in an * * * enterprise in which private persons may engage." The Restatement (Third) § 451 adopts the latter criterion ("claims arising out of activities of the kind that may be carried on by private persons"). Which of these formulations is the most appropriate?

3. A number of authorities have approached the problem by seeking to determine what is political and considering all other activity commercial. See *Victory Transport,* Note 2, supra. The German Supreme Constitutional Court in its decision of April 30, 1963, p. 907 supra, in which a private firm sued the Empire of Iran for non-payment of a bill allegedly incurred in the repair of the Iranian Embassy's heating system, said: "It is obvious that the conclusion of such a contract does not fall within the core of the state's political authority." 16 BVerfG at 64, 19 L.Z. at 175. Compare the principle suggested by Lalive, L'Immunité de Jurisdiction des Etats et des Organisations Internationales, 84 Rec. des Cours 205, 285 (1953–III): "The foreign state enjoys jurisdictional immunity only for certain acts of public authority."

4. In 1960, the United States claimed immunity through diplomatic channels in a suit brought in Italy by an Italian company that had built sewers for the U.S. Logistic Command in Italy on the ground that the case arose from activity of the U.S. Government in its capacity as a sovereign. The Italian Court of Cassation upheld the decision below denying immunity on the ground that the transaction was of a private law nature even though done for a military purpose. Governo degli Stati Uniti di America c. Soc. I.R.S.A., [1963] Foro Ital. 1405, 47 Revista de Diritto Internazionale 484 (May 13, 1963).

The State Department, however, took the following position in 1962 with respect to a claim of immunity on behalf of the Industrial Bank of the Argentine Republic:

> [T]he activities for the defendant Bank in extending credits to private persons for the purpose of inducing them to invest in the economy of Argentina by bringing and operating their industrial plants there, importing raw materials for use therein, and constructing a plant to furnish hydroelectric power for such plants, even though the power plant was to be owned by the Government of Argentina, are all acts of a private nature (*jure gestionis*) for which the Bank is not entitled to claim sovereign immunity regardless of its relationship to the Government of Argentina. It may be assumed that all acts of a government whether of a public (*jure imperii*) or private nature (*jure gestionis*) are done for some public purpose. It is obvious, however, that this cannot be the criterion else the restrictive theory of sovereign immunity would be meaningless. It is the nature of the activity engaged in by the Government which is controlling and not whether it serves some public policy.

Letter to Argentine Embassy, dated April 19, 1962, concerning Mirabella v. Banco Industrial De La Republica Argentina, 38 Misc.2d 128, 237 N.Y.S.2d 499 (1963).

## REPUBLIC OF ARGENTINA v. WELTOVER, INC.

Supreme Court of the United States, 1992.
___ U.S. ___, 112 S.Ct. 2160, 119 L.Ed.2d 394.

JUSTICE SCALIA delivered the opinion of the Court.*

This case requires us to decide whether the Republic of Argentina's default on certain bonds issued as part of a plan to stabilize its currency was an act taken "in connection with a commercial activity" that had a "direct effect in the United States" so as to subject Argentina to suit in an American court under the Foreign Sovereign Immunities Act of 1976, 28 U.S.C. § 1602 *et seq.*

I

Since Argentina's currency is not one of the mediums of exchange accepted on the international market, Argentine businesses engaging in foreign transactions must pay in U.S. dollars or some other internationally accepted currency. In the recent past, it was difficult for Argentine borrowers to obtain such funds, principally because of the instability of the Argentine currency. To address these problems, petitioners, the Republic of Argentina and its central bank, Banco Central (collectively Argentina), in 1981 instituted a foreign exchange insurance contract program (FEIC), under which Argentina effectively agreed to assume the risk of currency depreciation in cross-border transactions involving Argentine borrowers. This was accomplished by Argentina's agreeing to sell to domestic borrowers, in exchange for a contractually predetermined amount of local currency, the necessary U.S. dollars to repay their foreign debts when they matured, irrespective of intervening devaluations.

Unfortunately, Argentina did not possess sufficient reserves of U.S. dollars to cover the FEIC contracts as they became due in 1982. The Argentine government thereupon adopted certain emergency measures, including refinancing of the FEIC-backed debts by issuing to the creditors government bonds. These bonds, called "Bonods," provide for payment of interest and principal in U.S. dollars; payment may be made through transfer on the London, Frankfurt, Zurich, or New York market, at the election of the creditor. Under this refinancing program, the foreign creditor had the option of either accepting the Bonods in satisfaction of the initial debt, thereby substituting the Argentine government for the private debtor, or maintaining the debtor/creditor relationship with the private borrower and accepting the Argentine government as guarantor.

When the Bonods began to mature in May 1986, Argentina concluded that it lacked sufficient foreign exchange to retire them. Pursuant to a Presidential Decree, Argentina unilaterally extended the time for payment, and offered bondholders substitute instruments as a means of rescheduling the debts. Respondents, two Panamanian corporations and a Swiss bank who hold, collectively, $1.3 million of Bonods, refused to accept the rescheduling, and insisted on full payment, specifying New York as the place where payment should be made. Argentina did not pay, and respondents then

* Footnotes omitted.

brought this breach-of-contract action in the United States District Court for the Southern District of New York, relying on the Foreign Sovereign Immunities Act of 1976 as the basis for jurisdiction. Petitioners moved to dismiss for lack of subject-matter jurisdiction, lack of personal jurisdiction, and *forum non conveniens.* The District Court denied these motions, 753 F.Supp. 1201 (S.D.N.Y.1991), and the Court of Appeals affirmed, 941 F.2d 145 (CA2 1991). We granted Argentina's petition for certiorari, which challenged the Court of Appeals' determination that, under the Act, Argentina was not immune from the jurisdiction of the federal courts in this case.

II

The Foreign Sovereign Immunities Act of 1976, 28 U.S.C. § 1602 *et seq.* (FSIA), establishes a comprehensive framework for determining whether a court in this country, state or federal, may exercise jurisdiction over a foreign state. Under the Act, a "foreign state *shall* be immune from the jurisdiction of the courts of the United States and of the States" unless one of several statutorily defined exceptions applies. § 1604 (emphasis added). The FSIA thus provides the "sole basis" for obtaining jurisdiction over a foreign sovereign in the United States. See *Argentine Republic v. Amerada Hess Shipping Corp.*, 488 U.S. 428, 434–439, 109 S.Ct. 683, 688–690, 102 L.Ed.2d 818 (1989). The most significant of the FSIA's exceptions—and the one at issue in this case—is the "commercial" exception of § 1605(a)(2), which provides that a foreign state is not immune from suit in any case

> "in which the action is based upon a commercial activity carried on in the United States by the foreign state; or upon an act performed in the United States in connection with a commercial activity of the foreign state elsewhere; or upon an act outside the territory of the United States in connection with a commercial activity of the foreign state elsewhere and that act causes a direct effect in the United States." § 1605(a)(2).

In the proceedings below, respondents relied only on the third clause of § 1605(a)(2) to establish jurisdiction, 941 F.2d, at 149, and our analysis is therefore limited to considering whether this lawsuit is (1) "based * * * upon an act outside the territory of the United States"; (2) that was taken "in connection with a commercial activity" of Argentina outside this country; and (3) that "cause[d] a direct effect in the United States." The complaint in this case alleges only one cause of action on behalf of each of the respondents, viz., a breach-of-contract claim based on Argentina's attempt to refinance the Bonods rather than to pay them according to their terms. The fact that the cause of action is in compliance with the first of the three requirements—that it is "based upon an act outside the territory of the United States" (presumably Argentina's unilateral extension)—is uncontested. The dispute pertains to whether the unilateral refinancing of the Bonods was taken "in connection with a commercial activity" of Argentina, and whether it had a "direct effect in the United States." We address these issues in turn.

A

Respondents and their *amicus,* the United States, contend that Argentina's issuance of, and continued liability under, the Bonods constitute a "commercial activity" and that the extension of the payment schedules was taken "in connection with" that activity. The latter point is obvious enough, and Argentina does not contest it; the key question is whether the activity is "commercial" under the FSIA.

The FSIA defines "commercial activity" to mean:

> "[E]ither a regular course of commercial conduct or a particular commercial transaction or act. The commercial character of an activity shall be determined by reference to the nature of the course of conduct or particular transaction or act, rather than by reference to its purpose." 28 U.S.C. § 1603(d).

This definition, however, leaves the critical term "commercial" largely undefined: The first sentence simply establishes that the commercial nature of an activity does *not* depend upon whether it is a single act or a regular course of conduct, and the second sentence merely specifies what element of the conduct determines commerciality (*i.e.,* nature rather than purpose), but still without saying what "commercial" means. Fortunately, however, the FSIA was not written on a clean slate. As we have noted, see *Verlinden B.V. v. Central Bank of Nigeria,* 461 U.S. 480, 486–489, 103 S.Ct. 1962, 1967–1969, 76 L.Ed.2d 81 (1983), the Act (and the commercial exception in particular) largely codifies the so-called "restrictive" theory of foreign sovereign immunity first endorsed by the State Department in 1952. The meaning of "commercial" is the meaning generally attached to that term under the restrictive theory at the time the statute was enacted. See *McDermott Int'l, Inc. v. Wilander,* 498 U.S. ___, ___, 111 S.Ct. 807, ___, 112 L.Ed.2d 866 (1991) ("[W]e assume that when a statute uses [a term of art], Congress intended it to have its established meaning"); *NLRB v. Amax Coal Co.,* 453 U.S. 322, 329, 101 S.Ct. 2789, 2794, 69 L.Ed.2d 672 (1981); *Morissette v. United States,* 342 U.S. 246, 263, 72 S.Ct. 240, 249–250, 96 L.Ed. 288 (1952).

This Court did not have occasion to discuss the scope or validity of the restrictive theory of sovereign immunity until our 1976 decision in *Alfred Dunhill of London, Inc. v. Republic of Cuba,* 425 U.S. 682, 96 S.Ct. 1854, 48 L.Ed.2d 301. Although the Court there was evenly divided on the question whether the "commercial" exception that applied in the foreign-sovereign-immunity context also limited the availability of an act-of-state defense, compare *id.,* at 695–706, 96 S.Ct., at 1861–1867 (plurality) with *id.,* at 725–730, 96 S.Ct., at 1875–1878 (Marshall, J., dissenting), there was little disagreement over the general scope of the exception. The plurality noted that, after the State Department endorsed the restrictive theory of foreign sovereign immunity in 1952, the lower courts consistently held that foreign sovereigns were not immune from the jurisdiction of American courts in cases "arising out of purely commercial transactions," *id.,* at 703, 96 S.Ct., at 1865–66; citing, *inter alia, Victory Transport, Inc. v. Comisaria General,* 336 F.2d 354 (CA2 1964), cert. denied, 381 U.S. 934, 85 S.Ct. 1763, 14 L.Ed.2d 698 (1965), and *Petrol Shipping Corp. v. Kingdom of Greece,* 360 F.2d 103 (CA2), cert. denied, 385 U.S. 931, 87 S.Ct. 291, 17 L.Ed.2d 213 (1966). The plurality further recognized that the distinction between state sovereign acts, on the one hand, and state commercial and private acts, on the other, was not entirely novel to American law. * * * The plurality stated that the restrictive theory of foreign sovereign immunity would not bar a suit based upon a foreign state's participation in the marketplace in the manner of a private citizen or corporation. 425 U.S., at 698–705, 96 S.Ct., at 1863–1866. A foreign state engaging in "commercial" activities "do[es] not exercise powers peculiar to sovereigns"; rather, it "exercise[s] only those powers that can also be exercised by private citizens." *Id.,* at 704, 96 S.Ct., at 1866. The dissenters did not disagree with this general description, see *id.,* at 725, 96 S.Ct., at 1875–1876. Given that the FSIA was enacted less than six months after our decision in *Alfred Dunhill* was announced, we think the plurality's contemporaneous description of the then-prevailing restrictive theory of sovereign immunity is of significant assistance in construing the scope of the Act.

In accord with that description, we conclude that when a foreign government acts, not as regulator of a market, but in the manner of a private player within it, the foreign sovereign's actions are "commercial" within the meaning of the FSIA. Moreover, because the Act provides that the commercial character of an act is to be determined by reference to its "nature" rather than its "purpose," 28 U.S.C. § 1603(d), the question is not whether the foreign government is acting with a profit motive or instead with the aim of fulfilling uniquely sovereign objectives. Rather, the issue is whether the particular actions that the foreign state performs (whatever the motive behind them) are the *type* of actions by which a private party engages in "trade and traffic or commerce," Black's Law Dictionary 270 (6th ed. 1990). See, *e.g., Rush–Presbyterian–St. Luke's Medical Center v. Hellenic Republic,* 877 F.2d 574, 578 (CA7), cert. denied, 493 U.S. 937, 110 S.Ct. 333, 107 L.Ed.2d 322 (1989). Thus, a foreign government's issuance of regulations limiting foreign currency exchange is a sovereign activity, because such authoritative control of commerce cannot be exercised by a private party; whereas a contract to buy army boots or even bullets is a "commercial" activity, because private companies can similarly use sales contracts to acquire goods, see, *e.g., Stato di Rumania v. Trutta* [1926] Foro It. I 584, 585–586, 589 (Corte di Cass. del Regno, Italy), translated and reprinted in part in 26 Am.J.Int'l L. 626–629 (Supp.1932).

The commercial character of the Bonods is confirmed by the fact that they are in almost all respects garden-variety debt instruments: they may be held by private parties; they are negotiable and may be traded on the international market (except in Argentina); and they promise a future stream of cash income. We recognize that, prior to the enactment of the FSIA, there was authority suggesting that the issuance of public debt instruments did not constitute a commercial activity. *Victory Transport,* 336 F.2d, at 360 (dicta). There is, however, nothing distinctive about the state's assumption of debt (other than perhaps its purpose) that would cause it always to be classified as *jure imperii,* and in this regard it is significant that *Victory Transport* expressed confusion as to whether the "nature" or the "purpose" of a transaction was controlling in determining commerciality, *id.,* at 359–360. Because the FSIA has now clearly established that the "nature" governs, we perceive no basis for concluding that the issuance of debt should be treated as categorically different from other activities of foreign states.

Argentina contends that, although the FSIA bars consideration of "purpose," a court must nonetheless fully consider the *context* of a transaction in order to determine whether it is "commercial." Accordingly, Argentina claims that the Court of Appeals erred by defining the relevant conduct in what Argentina considers an overly generalized, acontextual manner and by essentially adopting a *per se* rule that all "issuance of debt instruments" is "commercial." See 941 F.2d, at 151 (" '[I]t is self-evident that issuing public debt is a commercial activity within the meaning of [the FSIA]' "), quoting *Shapiro v. Republic of Bolivia,* 930 F.2d 1013, 1018 (CA2 1991). We have no occasion to consider such a *per se* rule, because it seems to us that even in full context, there is nothing about the issuance of these Bonods (except perhaps its purpose) that is not analogous to a private commercial transaction.

Argentina points to the fact that the transactions in which the Bonods were issued did not have the ordinary commercial consequence of raising capital or financing acquisitions. Assuming for the sake of argument that this is not an example of judging the commerciality of a transaction by its purpose, the ready answer is that private parties regularly issue bonds, not just to raise capital or to finance purchases, but also to refinance debt. That is what Argentina did here: by virtue of the earlier FEIC contracts, Argentina was *already* obligated to supply the U.S. dollars needed to retire the FEIC-insured debts; the Bonods simply allowed Argentina to restructure its existing obligations. Argentina further asserts (without proof or even elaboration) that it "received consideration [for the Bonods] in no way commensurate with [their] value," Brief for Petitioners 22. Assuming that to be true, it makes no difference. Engaging in a commercial act does not require the receipt of fair value, or even compliance with the common-law requirements of consideration.

Argentina argues that the Bonods differ from ordinary debt instruments in that they "were created by the Argentine Government to fulfill its obligations under a foreign exchange program designed to address a domestic credit crisis, and as a component of a program designed to control that nation's critical shortage of foreign exchange." *Id.,* at 23–24. In this regard, Argentina relies heavily on *De Sanchez v. Banco Central de Nicaragua,* 770 F.2d 1385 (CA5 1985), in which the Fifth Circuit took the view that "[o]ften, the essence of an act is defined by its purpose"; that unless "we can inquire into the purposes of such acts, we cannot determine their nature"; and that, in light of its purpose to control its reserves of foreign currency, Nicaragua's refusal to honor a check it had issued to cover a private bank debt was a sovereign act entitled to immunity. *Id.,* at 1393. Indeed, Argentina asserts that the line between "nature" and "purpose" rests upon a "formalistic distinction [that] simply is neither useful nor warranted." Reply Brief for Petitioners 8. We think this line of argument is squarely foreclosed by the language of the FSIA. However difficult it may be in some cases to separate "purpose" (*i.e.,* the *reason* why the foreign state engages in the activity) from "nature" (*i.e.,* the outward form of the conduct that the foreign state performs or agrees to perform), see *De Sanchez, supra,* at 1393, the statute unmistakably commands that to be done. 28 U.S.C. § 1603(d). We agree with the Court of Appeals, see 941 F.2d, at 151, that it is irrelevant *why* Argentina participated in the bond market in the manner of a private actor; it matters only that it did so. We conclude that Argentina's issuance of the Bonods was a "commercial activity" under the FSIA.

B

The remaining question is whether Argentina's unilateral rescheduling of the Bonods had a "direct effect" in the United States, 28 U.S.C. § 1605(a)(2). In addressing this issue, the Court of Appeals rejected the suggestion in the legislative history of the FSIA that an effect is not "direct" unless it is both "substantial" and "foreseeable." * * *

That suggestion is found in the House Report, which states that conduct covered by the third clause of § 1605(a)(2) would be subject to the jurisdiction of American courts "consistent with principles set forth in section 18, Restatement of the Law, Second, Foreign Relations Law of the United States (1965)." H.R.Rep. No. 94–1487, pp. 1, 19, U.S.Code Cong. & Admin.News 1976, pp. 6604, 6618 (1976). Section 18 states that American laws are not given extraterritorial application except with respect to conduct that has, as a "direct and foreseeable result," a "substantial" effect within the United States. Since this obviously deals with jurisdiction to *legislate* rather than jurisdiction to *adjudicate,* this passage of the House Report has been charitably described as "a bit of a *non sequitur,*" *Texas Trading & Milling Corp. v. Federal Republic of Nigeria,* 647 F.2d 300, 311 (CA2 1981), cert. denied, 454 U.S. 1148, 102 S.Ct. 1012, 71 L.Ed.2d 301 (1982). Of course the generally applicable principle *de minimis non curat lex* ensures that jurisdiction may not be predicated on purely trivial effects in the United States. But we reject the suggestion that § 1605(a)(2) contains any unexpressed requirement of "substantiality" or "foreseeability." As the Court of Appeals recognized, an effect is "direct" if it follows "as an immediate consequence of the defendant's * * * activity," 941 F.2d, at 152.

The Court of Appeals concluded that the rescheduling of the maturity dates obviously had a "direct effect" on respondents. It further concluded that that effect was sufficiently "in the United States" for purposes of the FSIA, in part because "Congress would have wanted an American court to entertain this action" in order to preserve New York City's status as "a preeminent commercial center." *Id.,* at 153. The question, however, is not what Congress "would have wanted" but what Congress enacted in the FSIA. Although we are happy to endorse the Second Circuit's recognition of "New York's status as a world financial leader," the effect of Argentina's rescheduling in diminishing that status (assuming it is not too speculative to be considered an effect at all) is too remote and attenuated to satisfy the "direct effect" requirement of the FSIA. *Ibid.*

We nonetheless have little difficulty concluding that Argentina's unilateral rescheduling of the maturity dates on the Bonods had a "direct effect" in the United States. Respondents had designated their accounts in New York as the place of payment, and Argentina made some interest payments into those accounts before announcing that it was rescheduling the payments. Because New York was thus the place of performance for Argentina's ultimate contractual obligations, the rescheduling of those obligations necessarily had a "direct effect" in the United States: Money that was supposed to have been delivered to a New York bank for deposit was not forthcoming. We reject Argentina's suggestion that the "direct effect" requirement cannot be satisfied where the plaintiffs are all foreign corporations with no other connections to the United States. We expressly stated in

*Verlinden* that the FSIA permits "a foreign plaintiff to sue a foreign sovereign in the courts of the United States, provided the substantive requirements of the Act are satisfied," 461 U.S., at 489, 103 S.Ct., at 1969.

Finally, Argentina argues that a finding of jurisdiction in this case would violate the Due Process Clause of the Fifth Amendment, and that, in order to avoid this difficulty, we must construe the "direct effect" requirement as embodying the "minimum contacts" test of *International Shoe Co. v. Washington,* 326 U.S. 310, 316, 66 S.Ct. 154, 158, 90 L.Ed. 95 (1945). Assuming, without deciding, that a foreign state is a "person" for purposes of the Due Process Clause, cf. *South Carolina v. Katzenbach,* 383 U.S. 301, 323–324, 86 S.Ct. 803, 815–816, 15 L.Ed.2d 769 (1966) (States of the Union are not "persons" for purposes of the Due Process Clause), we find that Argentina possessed "minimum contacts" that would satisfy the constitutional test. By issuing negotiable debt instruments denominated in U.S. dollars and payable in New York and by appointing a financial agent in that city, Argentina " 'purposefully avail[ed] itself of the privilege of conducting activities within the [United States],' " *Burger King Corp. v. Rudzewicz,* 471 U.S. 462, 475, 105 S.Ct. 2174, 2183, 85 L.Ed.2d 528 (1985), quoting *Hanson v. Denckla,* 357 U.S. 235, 253, 78 S.Ct. 1228, 1240, 2 L.Ed.2d 1283 (1958).

* * *

We conclude that Argentina's issuance of the Bonods was a "commercial activity" under the FSIA; that its rescheduling of the maturity dates on those instruments was taken in connection with that commercial activity and had a "direct effect" in the United States; and that the District Court therefore properly asserted jurisdiction, under the FSIA, over the breach-of-contract claim based on that rescheduling. Accordingly, the judgment of the Court of Appeals is

*Affirmed.*

### *Notes*

1. In what circumstances can a foreign state be sued in the United States on bonds it has issued? In the principal case, the Court stressed that the bonds were denominated in U.S. dollars and payable in New York. Would a clause in the bond declaring New York law applicable suffice? Would it be sufficient if the bonds were denominated in U.S. dollars and the holders were U.S. citizens or residents, but no place of payment were specified? How can a foreign state avoid being subjected to suit in the United States on bonds it has issued? Would a clause selecting a foreign forum be sufficient?

2. Would the New York court have had in personam competence under New York law if the FSIA had not supplied its own bases? Is it appropriate for the United States to subject a foreign state to suit in New York if the foreign state would not have been subject to suit if it had been a private entity? See Smit, Note 1 at p. 1149, infra.

3. In Foremost–McKesson, Inc. v. The Islamic Republic of Iran, 905 F.2d 438 (D.C.Cir.1990), the American plaintiff brought an action against Iran asserting that Iran had used its majority position in an Iranian corporate joint venture wrongfully to deprive plaintiffs of benefits to which it was entitled. Iran pleaded sovereign immunity. The Court ruled that Iran's alleged wrongful conduct was commercial and also found the requisite direct effect under the third clause of

Section 1605(a)(2). The Court distinguished the case at bar from that adjudicated in Zedan v. Kingdom of Saudi Arabia, 849 F.2d 1511 (D.C.Cir.1988), in which it found the circumstance that the plaintiff had not received the contractually stipulated payment for work done in Saudi Arabia after his return to the United States not to produce the statutorily required effect in the United States. In the *Foremost* case, the complaint alleged a constant flow of capital, management personnel, engineering data, machinery and equipment between the United States and Iran. See also Texas Trading & Milling Corp. v. Federal Republic of Nigeria, 647 F.2d 300 (2d Cir.1981), cert. denied, 454 U.S. 1148, 102 S.Ct. 1012, 71 L.Ed.2d 301 (1982).

## *FOREIGN SOVEREIGN IMMUNITIES ACT OF 1976*

[See 28 U.S.C.A. §§ 1602–06].

### *Notes*

1. On the Foreign Sovereign Immunities Act of 1976 generally, see Smit, The Foreign Sovereign Immunities Act of 1976: A Plea For Drastic Surgery, 1980 Proc.A.S.I.L. 49; Kahale & Vega, Immunity and Jurisdiction: Toward a Uniform Body of Law in Actions Against Foreign States, 18 Colum.J.Transnat'l L. 211 (1979); Brower, Bistline & Loomis, The Foreign Sovereign Immunities Act of 1976 in Practice, 73 A.J.I.L. 200 (1979); Carl, Suing Foreign Governments in American Courts: The United States Foreign Sovereign Immunities Act in Practice, 33 Southw.L.J. 1007 (1979); Delaume, Three Perspectives on Sovereign Immunity, 71 A.J.I.L. 379 (1977); Peay, The Foreign Sovereign Immunities Act of 1975: Reflections on Old Problems in a New Bill, 5 Black L.J. 270 (1976); Simmons, The Foreign Sovereign Immunities Act of 1976: Giving the Plaintiff his Day in Court, 46 Fordham L.Rev. 543 (1977); Von Mehren, The Foreign Sovereign Immunities Act of 1976, 17 Colum.L.Transnat'l L. 33 (1978); Note, Sovereign Immunity, 18 Harv.Int'l L.J. 429 (1977); Hill, A Policy Analysis of the American Law of Foreign State Immunity, 50 Fordh.L.Rev. 155 (1981); Feldman, The United States FSIA of 1976 In Perspective: A Founder's View; 35 Int'l & Comp.L.Q. 302 (1986); Lacroix, The Theory and Practice of the Foreign Sovereign Immunities Act: Untying the Gordian Knot, 5 Int'l Tax & Bus.Law. 144 (1987); Foreign Governments in United States Court: [A Panel], 1991 Proc. A.S.I.L. 251.

2. Following the decision in Trendtex Trading Corp. v. Central Bank of Nigeria, [1977] 2 W.L.R. 356, in which the Court of Appeals held the restrictive doctrine to apply not only to *in rem,* but also to *in personam* cases, the United Kingdom enacted the State Immunity Act of 1978, 17 I.L.M. 1123 (1978). See p. 1127 supra.

3. The Report of the Senate Judiciary Committee states that the Foreign Sovereign Immunities Act codifies "the so-called 'restrictive' principle of sovereign immunity, as formerly recognized in international law" Sen.Rep. No. 94–1310, 94th Cong.2d Sess., p. 9 (1976). Is this an accurate statement?

4. Does Section 1604 properly reflect the developments in this area? In *Victory Transport,* p. 1140, note 2 *supra,* the Second Circuit stated: "Sovereign immunity is a derogation from the normal exercise of jurisdiction by the courts and should be accorded only in clear cases. * * * We are disposed to deny a claim of sovereign immunity * * * unless it is plain that the activity in question

falls within one of the categories of strictly political or public acts * * *." Even before the Act was enacted, it had been stated that "a subtle shift has occurred—from a doctrine granting immunity unless the activity is 'commercial' to a doctrine denying immunity unless the activity is 'political'." Note, Sovereign Immunity of States Engaged in Commercial Activities, 65 Colum.L.Rev. 1086, 1100 (1965). See also Lord Denning in Rahimtoola v. Nizam of Hyderabad, [1958] A.C. 379, 422–23. See further, Note 3 supra. The Senate Judiciary Report on the Act states that, "since sovereign immunity is an affirmative defense which must be specially pleaded, the burden will remain on the foreign state to produce evidence in support of its claims of immunity." Sen.Rep. No. 94–1310, 94th Cong.2d Sess., p. 17 (1976). Is this statement supported by the text of the Act?

5. Why does Section 1605(a)(2) provide for non-immunity only if the action is based on a commercial activity carried on in, or having a substantial contact with, the United States or on an act performed or having a direct effect there? Should a foreign state, subject to suit in the United States under generally prevailing rules of adjudicatory authority, be allowed a plea of sovereign immunity because the commercial activity or act on which the claim for relief is based occurred abroad and caused no direct effect in, and had no substantial contact with, the United States? Does this provision improperly commingle rules of sovereign immunity and rules of judicial competence? See Section 1330(a) and (b) of the Act providing that, subject to certain qualifications, personal jurisdiction exists as to any claim for relief with regard to which the foreign state is not entitled to immunity under Sections 1605–1607.

6. In Yessenin–Volpin v. Novosti Press Agency, 443 F.Supp. 849 (S.D.N.Y. 1978), the court upheld a claim of immunity in an action alleging a libel in a publication distributed in the United States on the ground that the libel was not "an act outside of the territory of the United States in connection with a commercial activity of the foreign state elsewhere." Acknowledging that the act had produced a direct effect in the United States, the court held that it had not been performed "in connection with a commercial activity." Although Novosti did engage in commercial activities, the court ruled that the publications in which the alleged libels appeared were official commentary of the Soviet government and therefore could not be regarded as published in the course of a commercial activity.

7. Do the activities of O.P.E.C., and specifically the fixing of crude oil prices, constitute a commercial activity? On this question, see International Ass'n of Machinists and Aerospace Workers v. OPEC, 477 F.Supp. 553 (C.D.Cal. 1979), aff'd on act of state grounds, 649 F.2d 1354 (9th Cir.1981).

8. For commentary on the effectiveness of the commercial activity exception in the FSIA, see Donoghue, Taking the "sovereign" out of the Foreign Sovereign Immunities Act: A Functional Approach To The Commercial Activity Exception, 17 Yale J.Int'l L. 489 (1992); Vazquez, The Relationship Between The FSIA's Commercial Activity Exception And The Due–Process Clause, 1991 Proc. A.S.I.L. 257; Note, Nationalized and Denationalized Commercial Enterprises Under The Foreign Sovereign Immunities Act, 90 Colum.L.Rev. 2278 (1990); Note, The Foreign Sovereign Immunities Act: Inconsistencies In Application Of The Commercial Activity Direct Effect Exception, 5 Emory Int'l L.Rev. 211 (1991); Note, De Sanchez v. Banco Central De Nicaragua, 770 F.2d 1385 (5th Cir.1985): Too Many Exceptions To The Commercial Activities Exception Of The Foreign Sovereign Immunities Act of 1976?, 14 Brook.J.Int'l L. 715 (1988); Note,

Foreign Sovereign Immunities Act—Commercial Activity Exception—United States May Exercise Jurisdiction Over A Foreign Sovereign Who Has Issued Promissory Notes To A U.S. Corporation—Shapiro v. Republic of Bolivia, 930 F.2d 1013, 21 Ga.J.Int'l & Comp.L. 539 (1991).

## *2. Other Restrictions Upon Absolute Immunity*

# CLAIMS TO IMMOVABLES OR PROPERTY ACQUIRED BY GIFT OR SUCCESSION, OR ARISING FROM NON-COMMERCIAL TORTS

*FOREIGN SOVEREIGN IMMUNITIES ACT OF 1976*

[28 U.S.C.A. § 1605].

GENERAL EXCEPTIONS TO THE JURISDICTIONAL IMMUNITY OF A FOREIGN STATE

(a) A foreign state shall not be immune from the jurisdiction of courts of the United States or of the States in any case—

* * *

(4) in which rights in property in the United States acquired by succession or gift or rights in immovable property situated in the United States are in issue;

(5) not otherwise encompassed in paragraph (2) above, in which money damages are sought against a foreign state for personal injury or death, or damage to or loss of property, occurring in the United States and caused by the tortious act or omission of that foreign state or any official or employee of that foreign state while acting within the scope of his office or employment; except this paragraph shall not apply to—

(A) any claim based upon the exercise or performance or the failure to exercise or perform a discretionary function regardless of whether the discretion be abused, or

(B) any claim arising out of malicious prosecution, abuse of process, libel, slander, misrepresentation, deceit, or interference with contract rights;

### *1. Property Within the Forum State*

Section 1605(a)(4) of the FSIA provides for denial of immunity in regard to claims to immovable property situated in the United States, irrespective of whether the property is of a commercial nature. This denial extends even to property used for diplomatic or consular purposes. See Sen.Rep. No. 94–1310, 94th Cong.2d Sess., p. 20 (1976).

Most courts and commentators have concluded that a foreign state's immunity from jurisdiction does not extend to proceedings for the determination of possession of, or an interest in, immovable or real property located in the territory of a state exercising jurisdiction. Restatement (Third) § 455(1) and (2). The reason usually given for this exception to state immunity is that real property, unless it is used for diplomatic or consular purposes, is "so indissolubly connected with the territory of a State that the State of the situs cannot permit the exercise of any other jurisdiction in respect thereof * * *." Harvard Research in International Law, Competence of Courts in Regard to Foreign States, Art. 9, 26 A.J.I.L.Supp. 451, 578 (1932). It has also been asserted that a state, by acquiring real property located in the territory of another state, voluntarily submits itself to the jurisdiction of the situs state (i.e., "waives" its immunity) in matters regarding its interests in the property. Storelli v. Government of the French Republic, [1923–24] Ann.Dig. 129 (Court of Rome, Italy, 1924); see also Restatement (Third) § 455, Comment b.

May a state rely on its immunity in order to resist eminent domain or other proceedings directed against its property by the state in which the property is located? Cf. Georgia v. City of Chattanooga, 264 U.S. 472, 44 S.Ct. 369, 68 L.Ed. 796 (1924). On the expropriation or requisition of a foreign state's chattels, see the position taken by the United States in 1941 in connection with the seizure of eighteen aircraft purchased in the United States by Peru. A memorandum prepared by the Legal Adviser's Office stated that "[e]very state undoubtedly possesses the right in case of emergency and subject to compensation to seize any foreign property on its territory." [1941] 7 For.Rel. 518. In proceedings before the Court of Claims, Switzerland did not argue that the United States had violated international law in requisitioning certain property belonging to the Swiss government. Swiss Confederation v. United States, 108 Ct.Cl. 388, 70 F.Supp. 235 (1947); Swiss Federal Railways v. United States, 125 Ct.Cl. 444, 112 F.Supp. 357 (1953).

According to the Senate Judiciary Committee Report, "[t]here is general agreement that a foreign state may not claim immunity when the suit against it relates to rights in property, real or personal, obtained by gift or inherited by the foreign state and situated or administered in the country where suit is brought." Sen.Rep. No. 94–1310, 94th Cong.2d Sess., p. 20 (1976). What is the basis for this denial of immunity?

### 2. *Torts Within the Forum State*

Section 1605(a)(5) denies immunity for most non-commercial torts causing "personal injury or death, or damage to or loss of property." As to the basis in international law for this denial of immunity, see Sen.Rep. No. 94–1310, 94th Cong.2d Sess., pp. 20–21 (1976). On the scope of this provision, see Restatement (Third) § 454.

### 3. *Torts Outside the Forum State*

In the beginning, section 1605(a)(5) was generally ruled inapplicable when the tort or injury occurred outside of the United States. See Persinger v. Islamic Republic of Iran, 729 F.2d 835 (D.C.Cir.1984), cert. denied, 469 U.S. 881, 105 S.Ct. 247, 83 L.Ed.2d 185 (1984) (detention of hostages in U.S. embassy in Iran held not to have occurred in the United States); Asociacion de Reclamantes v. United Mexican States, 735 F.2d 1517 (D.C.Cir.1984), cert. denied, 470 U.S. 1051, 105 S.Ct. 1751, 84 L.Ed.2d 815 (1985); Australian Government Aircraft Factories v. Lynne, 743 F.2d 672 (9th Cir.1984), cert. denied, 469 U.S. 1214, 105 S.Ct. 1189, 84 L.Ed.2d 335 (1985); McKeel v. Islamic Republic of Iran, 722 F.2d 582 (9th Cir.1983), cert. denied, 469 U.S. 880, 105 S.Ct. 243, 83 L.Ed.2d 182 (1984); Harris v. VAO Intourist, 481 F.Supp. 1056 (E.D.N.Y.1979). But see De Sanchez v. Banco Central De

Nicaragua, 515 F.Supp. 900 (E.D.La.1981) (conversion of a check drawn on a U.S. bank by foreign central bank is within this Section).

Notwithstanding these earlier rulings, attempts to sue foreign states for wrongful conduct outside of the United States have continued. Initially, the courts resisted these attempts. See, e.g., Frolova v. U.S.S.R., 761 F.2d 370 (7th Cir.1985) (alleged violation of human rights did not occur in the United States). See also Siderman v. The Republic of Argentina et al., 965 F.2d 699 (9th Cir.1992) (torture outside of the United States does not confer jurisdiction under the FSIA).

An effort was therefore made to create a basis for jurisdiction outside of the FSIA, and, specifically, to base it on the Alien Torts Claims Act. The Second Circuit approved these efforts in Filartiga v. Pena–Irala, 630 F.2d 876 (2d Cir.1980) and the Letelier v. Republic of Chile, 748 F.2d 790 (2d Cir.1984), cert. denied, 471 U.S. 1125, 105 S.Ct. 2656, 86 L.Ed.2d 273 (1985). However, the Supreme Court has ruled differently.

## ARGENTINE REPUBLIC v. AMERADA HESS SHIPPING CORP.

Supreme Court of the United States, 1989.
488 U.S. 428, 109 S.Ct. 683, 102 L.Ed.2d 818.

CHIEF JUSTICE REHNQUIST delivered the opinion of the Court.*

Two Liberian corporations sued the Argentine Republic in a United States District Court to recover damages for a tort allegedly committed by its armed forces on the high seas in violation of international law. We hold that the District Court correctly dismissed the action, because the Foreign Sovereign Immunities Act of 1976 (FSIA), 28 U.S.C. § 1330 *et seq.,* does not authorize jurisdiction over a foreign state in this situation.

Respondents alleged the following facts in their complaints. Respondent United Carriers, Inc., a Liberian corporation, chartered one of its oil tankers, the Hercules, to respondent Amerada Hess Shipping Corporation, also a Liberian corporation. The contract was executed in New York City. Amerada Hess used the Hercules to transport crude oil from the southern terminus of the Trans–Alaska Pipeline in Valdez, Alaska, around Cape Horn in South America, to the Hess refinery in the United States Virgin Islands. On May 25, 1982, the Hercules began a return voyage, without cargo but fully fueled, from the Virgin Islands to Alaska. At that time, Great Britain and petitioner Argentine Republic were at war over an archipelago of some 200 islands—the Falkland Islands to the British, and the Islas Malvinas to the Argentineans—in the South Atlantic off the Argentine coast. On June 3, United States officials informed the two belligerents of the location of United States vessels and Liberian tankers owned by United States interests then traversing the South Atlantic, including the Hercules, to avoid any attacks on neutral shipping.

By June 8, 1982, after a stop in Brazil, the Hercules was in international waters about 600 nautical miles from Argentina and 500 miles from the Falklands; she was outside the "war zones" designated by Britain and

* Some footnotes omitted; others renumbered.

Argentina. At 12:15 Greenwich mean time, the ship's master made a routine report by radio to Argentine officials, providing the ship's name, international call sign, registry, position, course, speed, and voyage description. About 45 minutes later, an Argentine military aircraft began to circle the Hercules. The ship's master repeated his earlier message by radio to Argentine officials, who acknowledged receiving it. Six minutes later, without provocation, another Argentine military plane began to bomb the Hercules; the master immediately hoisted a white flag. A second bombing soon followed, and a third attack came about two hours later, when an Argentine jet struck the ship with an air-to-surface rocket. Disabled but not destroyed, the Hercules reversed course and sailed to Rio de Janeiro, the nearest safe port. At Rio de Janeiro, respondent United Carriers determined that the ship had suffered extensive deck and hull damage, and that an undetonated bomb remained lodged in her No. 2 tank. After an investigation by the Brazilian Navy, United Carriers decided that it would be too hazardous to remove the undetonated bomb, and on July 20, 1982, the Hercules was scuttled 250 miles off the Brazilian coast.

Following unsuccessful attempts to obtain relief in Argentina, respondents commenced this action in the United States District Court for the Southern District of New York for the damage that they sustained from the attack. United Carriers sought $10 million in damages for the loss of the ship; Amerada Hess sought $1.9 million in damages for the fuel that went down with the ship. Respondents alleged that petitioner's attack on the neutral Hercules violated international law. They invoked the District Court's jurisdiction under the Alien Tort Statute, 28 U.S.C. § 1350, which provides that "[t]he district courts shall have original jurisdiction of any civil action by an alien for a tort only, committed in violation of the law of nations or a treaty of the United States." Amerada Hess also brought suit under the general admiralty and maritime jurisdiction, 28 U.S.C. § 1333, and "the principle of universal jurisdiction, recognized in customary international law." Complaint of Amerada Hess ¶ 5, App. 20. The District Court dismissed both complaints for lack of subject-matter jurisdiction, 638 F.Supp. 73 (1986), ruling that respondents' suits were barred by the FSIA.

A divided panel of the United States Court of Appeals for the Second Circuit reversed. 830 F.2d 421 (1987). The Court of Appeals held that the District Court had jurisdiction under the Alien Tort Statute, because respondents' consolidated action was brought by Liberian corporations, it sounded in tort ("the bombing of a ship without justification"), and it asserted a violation of international law ("attacking a neutral ship in international waters, without proper cause for suspicion or investigation"). *Id.*, at 424–425. Viewing the Alien Tort Statute as "no more than a jurisdictional grant based on international law," the Court of Appeals said that "who is within" the scope of that grant is governed by "evolving standards of international law." *Id.*, at 425, citing *Filartiga v. Pena–Irala,* 630 F.2d 876, 880 (CA2 1980). The Court of Appeals reasoned that Congress' enactment of the FSIA was not meant to eliminate "existing remedies in United States courts for violations of international law" by foreign states under the Alien Tort Statute. 830 F.2d, at 426. The dissenting judge took the view that the FSIA precluded respondents' action. *Id.*, at 431. We granted certiorari, 485 U.S. 1005, 108 S.Ct. 1466, 99 L.Ed.2d 697 (1988), and now reverse.

We start from the settled proposition that the subject-matter jurisdiction of the lower federal courts is determined by Congress "in the exact degrees and character which to Congress may seem proper for the public good." *Cary v. Curtis,* 44 U.S. (3 How.) 236, 245, 11 L.Ed. 576 (1845); see *Insurance Corp. of Ireland v. Compagnie des Bauxites de Guinee,* 456 U.S. 694, 701, 102 S.Ct. 2099, 2103, 72 L.Ed.2d 492 (1982) (jurisdiction of lower federal courts is "limited to those subjects encompassed within the statutory grant of jurisdiction"). In the FSIA, Congress added a new chapter 97 to Title 28 of the United States Code, 28 U.S.C. §§ 1602–1611, which is entitled "Jurisdictional Immunities of Foreign States." Section 1604 provides that "[s]ubject to existing international agreements to which the United States [was] a party at the time of the enactment of this Act[,] a foreign state shall be immune from the jurisdiction of the courts of the United States and of the States except as provided in sections 1605 to 1607 of this chapter." The FSIA also added § 1330(a) to Title 28; it provides that "[t]he district courts shall have original jurisdiction without regard to amount in controversy of any nonjury civil action against a foreign state * * * as to any claim for relief in personam with respect to which the foreign state is not entitled to immunity under sections 1605–1607 of this title or under any applicable international agreement." § 1330(a).

We think that the text and structure of the FSIA demonstrate Congress' intention that the FSIA be the sole basis for obtaining jurisdiction over a foreign state in our courts. Sections 1604 and 1330(a) work in tandem: § 1604 bars federal and state courts from exercising jurisdiction when a foreign state is entitled to immunity, and § 1330(a) confers jurisdiction on district courts to hear suits brought by United States citizens and by aliens when a foreign state is not entitled to immunity. As we said in Verlinden, the FSIA "must be applied by the district courts in every action against a foreign sovereign, since subject-matter jurisdiction in any such action depends on the existence of one of the specified exceptions to foreign sovereign immunity." Verlinden B.V. v. Central Bank of Nigeria, 461 U.S. 480, 493, 103 S.Ct. 1962, 1971, 76 L.Ed.2d 81 (1983).

The Court of Appeals acknowledged that the FSIA's language and legislative history support the "general rule" that the Act governs the immunity of foreign states in federal court. 830 F.2d, at 426. The Court of Appeals, however, thought that the FSIA's "focus on commercial concerns" and Congress' failure to "repeal" the Alien Tort Statute indicated Congress' intention that federal courts continue to exercise jurisdiction over foreign states in suits alleging violations of international law outside the confines of the FSIA. Id., at 427. The Court of Appeals also believed that to construe the FSIA to bar the instant suit would "fly in the face" of Congress' intention that the FSIA be interpreted pursuant to " 'standards recognized under international law.' " Ibid., quoting H.R.Rep., at 14.

Taking the last of these points first, Congress had violations of international law by foreign states in mind when it enacted the FSIA. For example, the FSIA specifically denies foreign states immunity in suits "in which rights in property taken in violation of international law are in issue." 28 U.S.C. § 1605(a)(3). Congress also rested the FSIA in part on its power under Art. I, § 8, cl. 10, of the Constitution "[t]o define and punish Piracies and Felonies committed on the high Seas, and Offenses against the Law of

Nations." See H.R.Rep., at 12; S.Rep., at 12. From Congress' decision to deny immunity to foreign states in the class of cases just mentioned, we draw the plain implication that immunity is granted in those cases involving alleged violations of international law that do not come within one of the FSIA's exceptions.

As to the other point made by the Court of Appeals, Congress' failure to enact a *pro tanto* repealer of the Alien Tort Statute when it passed the FSIA in 1976 may be explained at least in part by the lack of certainty as to whether the Alien Tort Statute conferred jurisdiction in suits against foreign states. Enacted by the First Congress in 1789, the Alien Tort Statute provides that "[t]he district courts shall have original jurisdiction of any civil action by an alien for a tort only, committed in violation of the law of nations or a treaty of the United States." 28 U.S.C. § 1350. The Court of Appeals did not cite any decision in which a United States court exercised jurisdiction over a foreign state under the Alien Tort Statute, and only one such case has come to our attention—one which was decided after the enactment of the FSIA.[1]

In this Court, respondents argue that cases were brought under the Alien Tort Statute against foreign states for the unlawful taking of a prize during wartime. Brief for Respondents 18–25. The Alien Tort Statute makes no mention of prize jurisdiction, and § 1333(2) now grants federal district courts exclusive jurisdiction over "all proceedings for the condemnation of property taken as a prize." In *The Santissima Trinidad,* 20 U.S. (7 Wheat.) 283, 353–354, 5 L.Ed. 454 (1822), we held that foreign states were not immune from the jurisdiction of United States courts in prize proceedings. That case, however, was not brought under the Alien Tort Statute but rather as a libel in admiralty. Thus there is a distinctly hypothetical cast to the Court of Appeals' reliance on Congress' failure to repeal the Alien Tort Statute, and respondents' arguments in this Court based on the principle of statutory construction that repeals by implication are disfavored.

We think that Congress' failure in the FSIA to enact an express *pro tanto* repealer of the Alien Tort Statute speaks only faintly, if at all, to the issue involved in this case. In light of the comprehensiveness of the statutory scheme in the FSIA, we doubt that even the most meticulous draftsman would have concluded that Congress also needed to amend *pro tanto* the Alien Tort Statute and presumably such other grants of subject-matter jurisdiction in Title 28 as § 1331 (federal question), § 1333 (admiralty), § 1335 (interpleader), § 1337 (commerce and antitrust), and § 1338 (patents, copyrights, and trademarks). Congress provided in the FSIA that "[c]laims of foreign states to immunity should *henceforth* be decided by courts of the United States in conformity with the principles set forth in this chapter," and very likely it thought that should be sufficient. § 1602 (emphasis added); see also H.R.Rep., at 12; S.Rep., at 11 (FSIA "intended to preempt any other State and Federal law (excluding applicable international agreements) for according immunity to foreign sovereigns").

1. See *Von Dardel v. Union of Soviet Socialist Republics,* 623 F.Supp. 246 (DC 1985) (alternative holding). The Court of Appeals did cite its earlier decision in *Filartiga v. Pena-Irala,* 630 F.2d 876 (1980), which involved a suit under the Alien Tort Statute by a Paraguayan national against a Paraguayan police official for torture; the Paraguayan Government was not joined as a defendant.

For similar reasons we are not persuaded by respondents' arguments based upon the rule of statutory construction under which repeals by implication are disfavored. This case does not involve two statutes that readily could be seen as supplementing one another, see *Wood v. United States,* 41 U.S. (16 Pet.) 342, 363, 10 L.Ed. 987 (1842), nor is it a case where a more general statute is claimed to have repealed by implication an earlier statute dealing with a narrower subject. See *Morton v. Mancari,* 417 U.S. 535, 549–551, 94 S.Ct. 2474, 2482–2483, 41 L.Ed.2d 290 (1974). We think that Congress' decision to deal comprehensively with the subject of foreign sovereign immunity in the FSIA, and the express provision in § 1604 that "a foreign state shall be immune from the jurisdiction of the courts of the United States and of the States except as provided in sections 1605–1607," preclude a construction of the Alien Tort Statute that permits the instant suit. See *Red Rock v. Henry,* 106 U.S. 596, 601–602, 1 S.Ct. 434, 438–439, 27 L.Ed. 251 (1883); *United States v. Tynen,* 78 U.S. (11 Wall.) 88, 92, 20 L.Ed. 153 (1871). The Alien Tort Statute by its terms does not distinguish among classes of defendants, and it of course has the same effect after the passage of the FSIA as before with respect to defendants other than foreign states.

Respondents also argue that the general admiralty and maritime jurisdiction, § 1333(1), provides a basis for obtaining jurisdiction over petitioner for violations of international law, notwithstanding the FSIA. Brief for Respondents 42–49. But Congress dealt with the admiralty jurisdiction of the federal courts when it enacted the FSIA. Section 1605(b) expressly permits an *in personam* suit in admiralty to enforce a maritime lien against a vessel or cargo of a foreign state. Unless the present case is within § 1605(b) or another exception to the FSIA, the statute conferring general admiralty and maritime jurisdiction on the federal courts does not authorize the bringing of this action against petitioner.

Having determined that the FSIA provides the sole basis for obtaining jurisdiction over a foreign state in federal court, we turn to whether any of the exceptions enumerated in the Act apply here. These exceptions include cases involving the waiver of immunity, § 1605(a)(1), commercial activities occurring in the United States or causing a direct effect in this country, § 1605(a)(2), property expropriated in violation of international law, § 1605(a)(3), inherited, gift, or immovable property located in the United States, § 1605(a)(4), noncommercial torts occurring in the United States, § 1605(a)(5), and maritime liens, § 1605(b). We agree with the District Court that none of the FSIA's exceptions applies on these facts. * * *

Respondents assert that the FSIA exception for noncommercial torts, § 1605(a)(5), is most in point. * * * Section 1605(a)(5) is limited by its terms, however, to those cases in which the damage to or loss of property occurs *in the United States.* Congress' primary purpose in enacting § 1605(a)(5) was to eliminate a foreign state's immunity for traffic accidents and other torts committed in the United States, for which liability is imposed under domestic tort law. See H.R.Rep., at 14, 20–21; S.Rep., at 14, 20–21.

In this case, the injury to respondents' ship occurred on the high seas some 5,000 miles off the nearest shores of the United States. Despite these telling facts, respondents nonetheless claim that the tortious attack on the

Hercules occurred "in the United States." They point out that the FSIA defines "United States" as including all "territory and waters, continental and insular, subject to the jurisdiction of the United States," § 1603(c), and that their injury occurred on the high seas, which is within the admiralty jurisdiction of the United States, see *The Plymouth,* 70 U.S. (3 Wall.) 20, 36, 18 L.Ed. 125 (1866). They reason, therefore, that "by statutory definition" petitioner's attack occurred in the United States. * * *

We find this logic unpersuasive. We construe the modifying phrase "continental and insular" to restrict the definition of United States to the continental United States and those islands that are part of the United States or its possessions; any other reading would render this phrase nugatory. Likewise, the term "waters" in § 1603(c) cannot reasonably be read to cover all waters over which United States courts might exercise jurisdiction. When it desires to do so, Congress knows how to place the high seas within the jurisdictional reach of a statute. We thus apply "[t]he canon of construction which teaches that legislation of Congress, unless contrary intent appears, is meant to apply only within the territorial jurisdiction of the United States." *Foley Brothers v. Filardo,* 336 U.S. 281, 285, 69 S.Ct. 575, 577, 93 L.Ed. 680 (1949); see also *Weinberger v. Rossi,* 456 U.S. 25, 32, 102 S.Ct. 1510, 1516, 71 L.Ed.2d 715 (1982). Because respondents' injury unquestionably occurred well outside the 3–mile limit then in effect for the territorial waters of the United States, the exception for noncommercial torts cannot apply.

The result in this case is not altered by the fact that petitioner's alleged tort may have had effects in the United States. Respondents state, for example, that the Hercules was transporting oil intended for use in this country and that the loss of the ship disrupted contractual payments due in New York. * * * Under the commercial activity exception to the FSIA, § 1605(a)(2), a foreign state may be liable for its commercial activities "outside the territory of the United States" having a "direct effect" inside the United States. But the noncommercial tort exception, § 1605(a)(5), upon which respondents rely, makes no mention of "territory outside the United States" or of "direct effects" in the United States. Congress' decision to use explicit language in § 1605(a)(2), and not to do so in § 1605(a)(5), indicates that the exception in § 1605(a)(5) covers only torts occurring within the territorial jurisdiction of the United States. Respondents do not claim that § 1605(a)(2) covers these facts.

We also disagree with respondents' claim that certain international agreements entered into by petitioner and by the United States create an exception to the FSIA here. * * * Respondents point to the Geneva Convention on the High Seas, Apr. 29, 1958, [1962] 13 U.S.T. 2312, T.I.A.S. No. 5200, and the Pan American Maritime Neutrality Convention, Feb. 20, 1928, 47 Stat. 1989, 1990–1991, T.S. No. 845. * * * These conventions, however, only set forth substantive rules of conduct and state that compensation shall be paid for certain wrongs. They do not create private rights of action for foreign corporations to recover compensation from foreign states in United States courts. Cf. *Head Money Cases,* 112 U.S. 580, 598–599, 5 S.Ct. 247, 253–254, 28 L.Ed. 798 (1884); *Foster v. Neilson,* 27 U.S. (2 Pet.) 253, 314, 7 L.Ed. 415 (1829). Nor do we see how a foreign state can waive its immunity under § 1605(a)(1) by signing an international agreement that contains no mention of a waiver of immunity to suit in United States courts or even the availability of a cause of action in the United States. We find similarly unpersuasive the argument of respondents and *Amicus Curiae* Republic of Liberia that the Treaty of Friendship, Commerce and Navigation, Aug. 8, 1938, United States–Liberia, 54 Stat. 1739, T.S. No. 956, carves out an exception to the FSIA. Brief for Respondents 52–53; Brief for the Republic of Liberia as *Amicus Curiae* 11. Article I of this Treaty provides, in pertinent part, that the nationals of the United States and Liberia "shall enjoy freedom of access to the courts of justice of the other on conforming to the local laws." The FSIA is clearly one of the "local laws" to which respondents must "conform" before bringing suit in United States courts.

We hold that the FSIA provides the sole basis for obtaining jurisdiction over a foreign state in the courts of this country, and that none of the enumerated exceptions to the Act apply to the facts of this case. The judgment of the Court of Appeals is therefore

*Reversed.*

JUSTICE BLACKMUN, with whom JUSTICE MARSHALL joins, concurring in part.

I join the Court's opinion insofar as it holds that the FSIA provides the sole basis for obtaining jurisdiction over a foreign state in federal court.

I, however, do not join the latter part of the Court's opinion to the effect that none of the FSIA's exceptions to foreign sovereign immunity apply in this case. * * * I believe it inappropriate to decide here, in the first instance, whether any exceptions to the FSIA apply in this case. * * *

### Notes

1. For a discussion of this decision, see Note, Obtaining Jurisdiction Over Foreign Sovereigns: The Alien Tort Statute Meets The Foreign Sovereign Immunities Act—Argentine Republic v. Amerada Hess Shipping Corp., 31 Harv. Int'l L.J. 368 (1990).

2. The decision in the principal case left complainants of a foreign state's wrongful conduct abroad only reliance on Section 1605(a)(2) of the FSIA. In Nelson v. Saudi Arabia, 923 F.2d 1528 (11th Cir.1991), the American plaintiff sued Saudi Arabia to recover for his detention and torture in Saudi Arabia. He alleged that he had been recruited in the United States as a monitoring systems engineer in a Saudi Arabian hospital, but was detained and tortured in retaliation for reporting safety violations. The court found that the action was "based upon" a commercial activity, i.e., the plaintiff's recruitment, carried on in the United States. The Supreme Court has granted certiorari, and the United States is urging reversal. For discussion of the case, see Romano, Extension of the Commercial Activity Exception of the Foreign Sovereign Immunities Act to a Human Rights Violation: Nelson v. Saudi Arabia, 5 N.Y.Int'l L.Rev. 24 (1992); Note, Nelson v. Saudi Arabia: An Unrestricted Reading of Foreign Sovereign Immunity, 23 U.Miami Inter–Am.L.Rev. 541 (1991–92).

3. If the FSIA had used the "arising from" terminology customarily used by long-arm statutes, would the result in the *Nelson* case have been the same? See Smit, The Foreign Sovereign Immunity Act of 1976: A Plea for Drastic Surgery, 1980 Proc.A.S.I.L. 49, 59. Is the ruling in the principal case constitutional? Cf. Helicopteros Nacionales de Colombia, S.A. v. Hall, 466 U.S. 408, 104 S.Ct. 1868, 80 L.Ed.2d 404 (1984) (limited commercial activities in the United

States do not provide constitutional basis for the exercise of jurisdiction in regard to wrongful death occasioned abroad).

4. In the *Nelson* case, could Saudi Arabia properly rely on the act-of-state doctrine? See pp. 1165–1170 infra.

5. Can a foreign state be sued in a United States court for a murder in the United States ordered by one of its officials? See Liu v. The Republic of China, 892 F.2d 1419 (9th Cir.1989) (federal choice of law rule points to California law on the issue of the liability of China for the acts of its officials.)

6. It has been said since the ruling in the principal case that the FSIA is the sole means by which to gain jurisdiction over a foreign state, and therefore if a plaintiff's claim does not fit within any of the exceptions to Congress' broad recognition of immunity to other nations contained in the FSIA, then plaintiff's complaint must be dismissed. Is this statement true? For a negative answer see Princz v. Federal Republic of Germany, 1992 WL 437971 (D.D.C.1992).

## C. WAIVER OF IMMUNITY

### *FOREIGN SOVEREIGN IMMUNITIES ACT OF 1976*

[See 28 U.S.C.A. §§ 1605(a)(1) and 1610].

The Act distinguishes between three kinds of waiver: (1) waiver of immunity from jurisdiction (Section 1605(a)(1)); (2) waiver of immunity from attachment in aid of execution or from execution (Section 1610(a)–(c)); and (3) waiver of immunity from attachment prior to the entry of judgment (Section 1610(d)). In addition, counterclaims, regulated in Section 1607, may be regarded as a particular form of waiver. See p. 917 infra. The first two forms of waiver may be effectuated "either explicitly or by implication," while immunity from pre-judgment attachment may be waived only "explicitly." All three forms of waiver are effective "notwithstanding any withdrawal of the waiver which the foreign state may purport to effect except in accordance with the terms of the waiver."

In Siderman de Blake v. The Republic of Argentina et al., 965 F.2d 699 (9th Cir.1992), the plaintiff sought to recover for torture and wrongful seizure of property by Argentine authorities. In response to Argentina's plea of sovereign immunity, the court ruled, *inter alia,* that Argentina had waived this defense by requesting the assistance of California state courts in proceedings conducted against the plaintiff in Argentina in pursuit of the very conduct that formed the basis for plaintiff's action:

> "Here, we confront a situation where Argentina apparently not only envisioned United States court participation in its persecution of the Sidermans, but by its actions deliberately implicated our courts in that persecution. The Sidermans have presented evidence that a year after Jose, Lea and Carlos Siderman fled Argentina in fear for their lives, the Argentine military authorities altered the Tucuman provincial land records to show that they had held title only to 127, as opposed to 127,000 acres of land in the Province, and that in their last-minute efforts to raise cash they had thus sold property which did not belong to them. The Tucuman Public Prosecutor then initiated criminal proceedings against Jose Siderman for this 'fraudulent' sale, and had the

Tucuman Supreme Court enlist the aid of our courts, via a letter rogatory, in serving him with process. 'The letter rogatory, dated May 11, 1980, informed the Presiding Judge of the Los Angeles Superior Court that criminal proceedings were pending against Jose Siderman in the Supreme Court of Tucuman. It requested the court's assistance in serving papers on Siderman, who was living in Los Angeles at the time. While the court complied with the request, the record is not clear as to the subsequent course of lawsuit. In their papers in support of jurisdiction, the Sidermans suggest that the Argentine military authorities sought to obtain Jose's return to Argentina in order to further torture and perhaps even to kill him.'

Shortly after the Los Angeles Superior Court received Argentina's letter rogatory, indeed, Argentina requested that the Italian authorities arrest Siderman, who had travelled to Italy for a wedding, and extradite him to Argentina for having allegedly forged certain travel documents. Siderman was detained in Italy for seven months, twenty-seven days of which time was spent in prison, before an Italian court dismissed the charges against him as pretextual and denied Argentina's extradition request.

We conclude that the Sidermans have presented evidence sufficient to support a finding that Argentina has implicitly waived its sovereign immunity with respect to their claims for torture. The evidence indicates that Argentina deliberately involved United States courts in its efforts to persecute Jose Siderman. If Argentina has engaged our courts in the very course of activity for which the Sidermans seek redress, it has waived its immunity as to that redress."

### *Notes*

1. A waiver may be contained in a treaty with a foreign state. On whether a waiver by treaty waives immunity from pre-judgment attachment, see p. 1175, Note 7 infra.

2. An explicit waiver may also be contained in a contract with a private party. See Sen.Rep. No. 94–1310, 94th Cong.2d Sess., p. 17 (1976). Can an explicit waiver also be effectuated by a unilateral act? What law determines the effectiveness of such a waiver? Can an effective waiver be included in a contract that is invalid under the applicable law?

3. Implicit waiver may be deduced from conduct signifying an intent to waive. A prominent example is the filing of a general appearance. See Flota Maritima Browning De Cuba, S.A. v. Motor Vessel Cuidad De La Habana, 335 F.2d 619 (4th Cir.1964) (holding ineffective an attempt to raise the plea of immunity at a later stage in the action). See also Flota Maritima Browning de Cuba, S.A. v. Snobl, 363 F.2d 733 (4th Cir.1966), cert. denied, 385 U.S. 837, 87 S.Ct. 82, 17 L.Ed.2d 71 (1966). Other examples are the signing of an arbitration clause, a forum selection clause, and a choice-of-law clause, and assertion of a counterclaim.

4. Can failure to appear be construed as a waiver? In Von Dardel On Behalf of Raoul Wallenberg et al. v. U.S.S.R., 623 F.Supp. 246 (D.D.C.1985), the

Court gave an affirmative answer. But see Frolova v. U.S.S.R., 761 F.2d 370 (7th Cir.1985), in which the Court raised the defense of sovereign immunity on its own motion. See also Subsection F, on Procedure for Claiming Immunity, p. 1177 infra.

5. The provision that a waiver may not be withdrawn except in accordance with its terms is designed to overrule legislatively decisions such as Rich v. Naviera Vacuba, S.A., 197 F.Supp. 710 (E.D.Va.1961), aff'd, 295 F.2d 24 (4th Cir.1961). See Sen.Rep. No. 94–1310, 94th Cong.2d Sen., p. 18 (1976).

6. In Foremost–McKesson, Inc. v. The Islamic Republic of Iran, 905 F.2d 438 (D.C.Cir.1990), Iran had answered that the action was barred by the Algiers Accord (Executive Order No. 12, 294, 46 Fed.Reg. 14, 111 (1981)). Foremost then pursued its claims before the Iran–United States Claims Tribunal. When this Tribunal had concluded its adjudication, Foremost revived its action. Iran then moved for leave to amend its answer to assert sovereign immunity. The Court rejected Foremost's argument that Iran had waived the immunity defense by failing to include it in its original answer. It ruled that, although a waiver could be implicit, Iran's original answer did not reflect an intention to forego the defense.

7. Can an ambassador extraordinary and plenipotentiary to the United Nations waive his state's immunity in an action brought on a promissory note executed by the ambassador on behalf of his state under a loan made by the plaintiff to finance the renovation of that state's permanent mission to the United Nations? In First Fidelity Bank, N.A. v. The Government of Antigua & Barbuda Permanent Mission, 877 F.2d 189 (2d Cir.1989), the Second Circuit ruled that the ambassador's authority presented a question of fact to be determined upon a proper hearing. Neither the majority nor the dissent considered the relevance of the attorney for the foreign state's having signed the waiver, nor that it had been signed by the ambassador after the foreign state had negotiated a settlement with the plaintiff through the ambassador. Judge Newman dissented.

## THE EFFECT OF AN ARBITRATION AGREEMENT

On the circumstances in which an arbitration agreement may be regarded as a waiver of immunity, see Restatement (Third) § 456, Reporters' Note 3. Should an arbitration clause in an agreement between two states be treated in the same manner for this purpose as an arbitration clause in an agreement between a state and an individual? See the commentary on Art. 20 of the I.L.C. Draft, which states that submission to arbitration by a state entails an implied acceptance of the supervisory jurisdiction of a court of another state otherwise competent to determine questions connected with the arbitration agreement. An agreement to submit to settlement pursuant to the Convention on the Settlement of Investment Disputes Between States and Nationals of Other States, 17 U.S.T. 1270, T.I.A.S. No. 6090, raises no question of waiver, since the decision of the tribunal has the force of a judgment in the States adhering to the Convention (Art. 54(1)).

In 1988, the FSIA was amended to deal with problems that had arisen in regard to arbitration agreements to which a foreign state was a party. Subsection 6 was added to Section 1605(a) to permit an action to enforce such an arbitration agreement if (A) the arbitration takes place or is intended to take place in the United States, (B) the agreement or award is or may be governed by a treaty or other international agreement in force for the United States calling for the recognition and enforcement of arbitral awards, (C) the underlying claim, save for the agreement to arbitrate, could have been brought in a United States court under this section or section 1607, or (D) paragraph (1) of this subsection is otherwise applicable." On this amendment, see Atkison & Ramsey, Proposed Amendment of the Foreign Sovereign Immunity Act, 79 A.J.I.L. 770, 771–74 (1985).

The 1988 Amendment also added subsection 6 to Section 1610(a) providing for execution of a judgment based on an arbitral award rendered against the foreign state, provided such execution not be inconsistent with the arbitration agreement.

For further reading on the FSIA and arbitration agreements, see Kahale, New Legislation in the United States Facilitates Enforcement of Arbitral Agreements and Awards Against Foreign States, 6 J. Int'l Arb. 57 (1989).

Are these limitations desirable? Restatement (Third) § 456(2)(b) provides that an agreement to arbitrate is a waiver of immunity from jurisdiction in an action to compel arbitration or to enforce the award. Is this the preferable rule?

## COUNTERCLAIMS

*FOREIGN SOVEREIGN IMMUNITIES ACT OF 1976*

[28 U.S.C.A. § 1607].

COUNTERCLAIMS

In any action brought by a foreign state, or in which a foreign state intervenes, in a court of the United States or of a State, the foreign state shall not be accorded immunity with respect to any counterclaim—

(a) for which a foreign state would not be entitled to immunity under section 1605 of this chapter had such claim been brought in a separate action against the foreign state; or

(b) arising out of the transaction or occurrence that is the subject matter of the claim of the foreign state; or

(c) to the extent that the counterclaim does not seek relief exceeding an amount or differing in kind from that sought by the foreign state.

### *Notes*

1. Subsection (a) is based upon article 1 of the European Convention on State Immunity, 11 I.L.M. 470 (1972).

2. Subsection (b) is inspired by the compulsory counterclaim rule of the Federal Rules of Civil Procedure, Fed.R.Civ.P. 13(a). See also Restatement (Third) § 456(2)(a)(i). Cf. also Alfred Dunhill of London, Inc. v. Republic of Cuba, 425 U.S. 682, 96 S.Ct. 1854, 48 L.Ed.2d 301 (1976).

3. Subsection (c) codifies the holding in National City Bank of New York v. Republic of China, 348 U.S. 356, 75 S.Ct. 423, 99 L.Ed. 389 (1955).

## D. THE NATURE OF THE RESTRICTIONS ON IMMUNITY

### *1. The Relation Between Immunity From Legislative Jurisdiction And The Act–of–State Doctrine*

Section 1605 of the Foreign Sovereign Immunities Act of 1976 speaks of immunity "from the jurisdiction of the courts." This type of immunity is distinguished from "immunity from attachment and execution" treated in Sections 1609–1611. The terminology used leaves uncertain whether the Act also deals with immunity from the exercise of legislative jurisdiction.

The Restatement (Third) § 461, Comment h, states that the F.S.I.A. "assumes that foreign states are not immune from United States jurisdiction to prescribe" in suits against foreign states that the Act permits. While the accuracy of this statement is subject to dispute (see p. 1167 infra), it leaves open whether foreign states are immune from jurisdiction to prescribe in all other cases.

The Act's failure to distinguish in specific terms between immunity from judicial jurisdiction and immunity from legislative jurisdiction may be explained by the circumstance that, once immunity from judicial jurisdiction is found, the court cannot reach the question of whether there is also immunity from legislative jurisdiction. Under the absolute doctrine of sovereign immunity, the question of immunity from legislative jurisdiction could therefore not arise.

But when the restrictive doctrine gained ground, the distinction became significant. This probably went largely unnoticed, because in most cases adjudicated by the courts the claim arose from, or was related to, the same commercial activity or property that, through seizure or attachment, provided the basis for the exercise of judicial jurisdiction. As a consequence, in such cases denial of immunity from judicial jurisdiction necessarily implied denial of immunity from legislative jurisdiction. However, this was not true in cases in which the commercial activity or property that provided the basis for the exercise of judicial jurisdiction was different from the activity or property from which the claim for relief arose.

This situation was presented in New York and Cuba Mail S.S. Co. v. Republic of Korea, 132 F.Supp. 684 (S.D.N.Y.1955), in which the attachment of funds of the Korean government on deposit in a New York bank provided the basis for the exercise of judicial jurisdiction, but the claim arose from a collision with defendant's vessel in Pusan, Korea. The State Department took the position that the funds were immune from attachment, but declined to suggest that the foreign state was entitled to claim immunity "inasmuch as the particular acts out of which the cause of action arose are not shown to be of purely governmental character." The State Department subsequently relinquished its position that a foreign state could claim immunity from judicial jurisdiction even if the property attached was commercial (see its statement in Stephen v. Zivnostenska Banka, Nat. Corp., 15 A.D.2d 111, 116, 222 N.Y.S.2d 128, 133–34 (1st Dep't 1961)), but the distinction it in effect made between immunity from judicial jurisdiction and immunity from legislative jurisdiction remained very much alive. Specifically, this distinction had to be made not only when an *in rem* type of action was brought and the property proceeded against had nothing to do with the claim for relief asserted (for another instance, see Chemical Natural Resources, Inc. v. Republic of Venezuela, 420 Pa. 134, 215 A.2d 864 (1966)), but also when a foreign state did substantial commercial business within the United States, but the claim for relief asserted did not arise from that business. Indeed, as American courts increasingly came to require a lesser and lesser measure of business done to support judicial competence in regard to unrelated claims (see, e.g., Bryant v. Finnish Nat. Airline, 15 N.Y.2d 426, 260 N.Y.S.2d 625, 208 N.E.2d 439 (1965)), the possibility that judicial competence over foreign states would be premised on commercial activities unrelated to those from which the claim for relief arose became correspondingly larger.

It might therefore have been expected that the Foreign Sovereign Immunities Act of 1976 would pay particular attention to immunity from legislative jurisdiction. This, however, does not appear to be the case. The Act's failure to address immunity from legislative jurisdiction with particularity may be explained in part by the circumstance that the Act provides principally for *in personam* judicial competence in regard to claims that are related to the activity or to the act upon which judicial competence is based. See Title 28, Section 1330(b), in conjunction with Section 1605. However, while this type of specific competence is most likely to be the most frequent basis of judicial competence, the Act does provide for judicial competence in cases in which the claim asserted did not arise from the activity or act that provides the basis of competence. See Sections 1605(a)(3) and (b). See also Nelson v. Saudi Arabia, 923 F.2d 1528 (11th Cir.1991), cert. granted, ___ U.S. ___, 112 S.Ct. 2937, 119 L.Ed.2d 562 (1992), discussed at p. 1159 supra, in which the Eleventh Circuit allowed an action seeking recovery for wrongful detention and torture in Saudi Arabia on the ground that the plaintiff had been recruited for employment in a Saudi Arabian hospital in the United States. In addition, there may be circumstances in which a foreign state has waived immunity from judicial, but not immunity from legislative, jurisdiction. Cf. Restatement (Third) § 456, which distinguishes between waiver of immunity from judicial jurisdiction and waiver of immunity from attachment and, in Subchapters A, B, and C of Chapter 5, deals separately with immunity from jurisdiction to prescribe, to adjudicate, and to enforce. In those cases, the question of whether the Act also deals with immunity from legislative jurisdiction therefore remains most pertinent. Endeavors to provide an answer to this question may take the following provision as a starting point.

## *FOREIGN SOVEREIGN IMMUNITIES ACT OF 1976*

[28 U.S.C.A. § 1606].

### Extent of Liability

As to any claim for relief with respect to which a foreign state is not entitled to immunity under section 1605 or 1607 of this chapter, the foreign state shall be liable in the same manner and to the same extent as a private individual under like circumstances; but a foreign state except for an agency or instrumentality thereof shall not be liable for punitive damages; if, however, in any case wherein death was caused, the law of the place where the action or omission occurred provides, or has been construed to provide, for damages only punitive in nature, the foreign state shall be liable for actual or compensatory damages measured by the pecuniary injuries resulting from such death which were incurred by the persons for whose benefit the action was brought.

---

Is this provision to be read as providing that, once there is no immunity from judicial jurisdiction, the liability of the foreign state is to be determined on the assumption that the acts for which the foreign state is called to account were those of a private individual? If so, it would require rejection of claims of immunity from legislative jurisdiction in all cases in which there is no immunity from judicial jurisdiction.

Support for the view that denial of immunity from judicial jurisdiction implies denial of immunity from legislative jurisdiction may also be derived from Section 1605(a)(3). After all, the taking of property in violation of international law is rather typical of acts that are normally regarded as public rather than commercial. See *Victory Transport,* p. 1140 supra. It would, therefore, make little sense to deny immunity from judicial jurisdiction in an action "in which rights in property taken in violation of international law are in issue," unless the court were authorized to adjudicate such rights. Clearly, the court could do so only if it would not be barred from making such an adjudication by the act of state doctrine or a claim of immunity from legislative jurisdiction. For if it would be so barred, Section 1605(a)(3) would encourage an action that would become an exercise in futility once the merits were reached.

The Senate Judiciary Committee Report on the Act states that since "* * * this section deals solely with issues of immunity, it in no way affects existing law on the extent to which, if at all, the 'act of state' doctrine may be applicable." Sen.Rep. No. 94–1310, 94th Cong.2d Sess., p. 19 (1976). The act of state doctrine applies typically in an action in which the validity or legality of an act of a foreign state performed within that state's territory is drawn into question. When applicable, it precludes American courts from judging the validity or legality of such an act. See, e.g., Oetjen v. Central Leather Co., 246 U.S. 297, 38 S.Ct. 309, 62 L.Ed. 726 (1917). The doctrine has also been extended to cases in which a foreign state, rather than a private party, invoked it to preclude examination of the validity or legality of its own sovereign act. Cf., e.g., Alfred Dunhill of London, Inc. v. Republic of Cuba, 425 U.S. 682, 96 S.Ct. 1854, 48 L.Ed.2d 301 (1976) at p. 190 supra. For a more detailed treatment of the act-of-state doctrine, see p. 188 supra. It would appear, however, that in such cases the reviewability of the act of a foreign sovereign should be determined by reference to rules of immunity from legislative jurisdiction rather than act of state. Not only are the reasons for abstaining from review of the act of a foreign state less weighty in cases between private parties, rules of immunity from legislative jurisdiction may be grounded in international law, while the act of state doctrine admittedly is a product of municipal lawmaking. See Banco Nacional de Cuba v. Sabbatino, 376 U.S. 398, 84 S.Ct. 923, 11 L.Ed.2d 804 (1964). See also Letelier v. Republic of Chile, 488 F.Supp. 665 (D.D.C.1980), in which the court rejected the argument that the officials who ordered the assassination of Letelier acted within Chile and were therefore covered by the act-of-state doctrine on the ground that "[t]o hold otherwise would totally emasculate the purpose and effectiveness of the Foreign Sovereign Immunities Act." (at 674).

On the relationship between the FSIA and the act-of-state doctrine, see Achebe, The Act of State Doctrine and Foreign Sovereign Immunities Act of 1976: Can They Coexist?, 13 Md.J.Int'l L. & Trade 247 (1989); Leacock, The Commercial Activity Exception To The Act Of State Doctrine Revisited: Evolution Of A Concept, 13 N.C.J.Int'l L. & Com.Reg. 1 (1988); Note, Act Of State And Sovereign Immunity: The Marcos Cases—Republic of the Philippines v. Marcos, 818 F.2d 1473; In re Grand Jury Proceedings, John Doe # 700, 817 F.2d 1108 (9th Cir.1987); Republic of the Philippines v. Marcos, 806 F.2d 344 (2nd Cir.1986); 29 Harv.Int'l L.J. 127 (1988).

On the act-of-state doctrine and state sponsored terrorism under the FSIA, see Paust, Federal Jurisdiction Over Extraterritorial Acts of Terrorism and NonImmunity For Foreign Violators Of International Law Under The FSIA And The Act Of State Doctrine, 23 Va.J.Int'l L. 191 (1983); Note, A Proposal To Deny Foreign Sovereign Immunity To Nations Sponsoring Terrorism, 6 Am.U.J.Int'l L. & Pol'y 77 (1990). On the act-of-state doctrine and international business transactions under the FSIA, see Ebenroth & Teitz, Winning (Or Losing) By Default: The Act of State Doctrine, Sovereign Immunity And Comity In International Business Transactions, 19 Int'l Law. 225 (1985).

Whatever the proper analysis, the question of whether there is immunity from legislative jurisdiction will arise when the act-of-state doctrine does not apply. Not only does that doctrine not apply to acts done without the foreign sovereign's territory (see p. 189 supra); since the *Dunhill* decision, it also does not apply to commercial acts of the foreign state, even if performed inside its territory. Furthermore, the act-of-state doctrine does not apply in all cases in which the Hickenlooper amendment (see p. 193 supra) is applicable. In all of these situations, the question of whether, regardless of the act-of-state doctrine, the foreign sovereign may claim immunity from legislative jurisdiction must therefore be addressed.

The Foreign Sovereign Immunities Act does not address that question in explicit terms. However, it may be argued that recognizing immunity from legislative jurisdiction in the situation covered by Section 1605(a)(3) would deprive this provision of its practical significance. On the other hand, the Act's legislative history, by acknowledging that the Act does not purport to affect act-of-state principles, gives potent support to the view that non-immunity from the jurisdiction of American courts does not necessarily imply non-immunity from the exercise of legislative jurisdiction. Under that view, immunity from legislative jurisdiction may be available to a foreign state in all cases in which the claim for relief arises from a foreign sovereign's public act other than the act that provides the basis for judicial competence.

The Restatement (Third) § 461 states that "A state is not immune from the jurisdiction to prescribe of another state except to the extent provided in respect of diplomatic and consular activities, §§ 464–66." Does this provision state prevailing international law? When, in an action brought against a foreign state which is not immune from judicial jurisdiction, a question arises as to the propriety of a governmental act of that foreign state either within or without that state's territory, is that state entitled to immunity from legislative jurisdiction?

### *Notes*

1. The Senate Judiciary Report on the Act states: "The bill is not intended to affect the substantive law of liability." Sen.Rep. No. 94–1310, 94th Cong.2d Sess., p. 11 (1976). Is this statement borne out by the provisions of Section 1606? What about other provisions of the Act? See Section 1605(a)(5).

2. By reference to what law is an American court to determine whether the plaintiff suffered "actual or compensatory damages measured by the primary injuries * * * incurred by the persons for whose benefit the actions was brought," whether the persons referred to were the proper persons to bring the actions, and whether the damages "resulted" from the death? See Engle, Choosing Law For Attributing Liability Under The Foreign Sovereign Immunities Act: A Proposal For Uniformity, 15 Fordham Int'l L.J. 1060 (1991/92). Does it make any difference whether the action is pending in a state or federal court?

### *2. The Applicable Federal Common Law*

To what extent do the federal courts, when proceeding under the FSIA, have to apply federal common law? As made clear by Section 1606, the courts will have to put the appropriate constructions on its provisions. But this is not all. In almost every action under the FSIA, unless federal common law is deemed controlling, the court will have to determine the rights and obligations of the parties by reference to the law indicated by the proper conflict of law rules. Are these conflict of laws rules those of the state in which the federal court is sitting or judge-made federal conflict of laws rules? The usual rule is that a federal court should apply the conflict of laws rules of the state in which it sits. Klaxon Co. v. Stentor Electric Mfg. Co., 313 U.S. 487, 61 S.Ct. 1020, 85 L.Ed. 1477 (1941). However, there is, of course, a strong federal interest in the proper adjudication of cases involving foreign states. It is that interest that prompted enactment of the FSIA in the first place. And it is that interest that moved the court in Liu v. The Republic of China, 892 F.2d 1419 (9th Cir.1989) and Harris v. Polskie Linie Lotnicze, 820 F.2d 1000 (9th Cir.1987), to rule that in FSIA cases federal common law provides the applicable choice of law rule. The advantage of this approach is that it ensures that all federal courts will apply the same law to disputes involving foreign states. This will, in turn, safeguard the federal interest in maintaining consistency in United States relations with foreign states. Indeed, a strong argument could be made for the federation's formulating its own rules for the resolution of disputes involving foreign states. The foreign relations power provides adequate constitutional support for such an approach. See Chapter 3 supra. And it would ensure that, in matters involving foreign nations, the United States would speak with a unitary voice.

## E. THE ROLE OF THE EXECUTIVE BRANCH

### *FOREIGN SOVEREIGN IMMUNITIES ACT OF 1976*

[28 U.S.C.A. § 1602].

FINDINGS AND DECLARATION OF PURPOSE

* * * Claims of foreign states to immunity should henceforth be decided by courts of the United States and of the States in conformity with the principles set forth in this chapter.

---

In Ex parte Republic of Peru, 318 U.S. 578, 63 S.Ct. 793, 87 L.Ed. 1014 (1943), Chief Justice Stone, in ruling upon Peru's claim of sovereign immunity, stated:

> Here the State Department has not left the Republic of Peru to intervene in the litigation through its ambassador as in the case of *The Navemar* [303 U.S. 68, 58 S.Ct. 432, 82 L.Ed. 667 (1938)]. The department has allowed the claim of immunity and caused its actions to be certified to the district court through the appropriate channels. The certification and the request that the vessel be declared immune must be accepted by the courts as a conclusive determination by the political arm of the Government that the continued retention of the vessel interferes with the proper conduct of our foreign relations. Upon the submission of this certification to the district court, it became the court's duty, in conformity to established principles, to release the vessel and to proceed no further in the cause. * * *

In Republic of Mexico v. Hoffman (The Baja California), 324 U.S. 30, 65 S.Ct. 530, 89 L.Ed. 729 (1945), Chief Justice Stone, in affirming denial of a plea of sovereign immunity, stated:

> * * * More important, and we think controlling in the present circumstances, is the fact that, despite numerous opportunities like the present to recognize immunity from suit of a vessel owned and not possessed by a foreign government, this government has failed to do so. We can only conclude that it is the national policy not to extend the immunity in the manner now suggested, and that it is the duty of the courts, in a matter so intimately associated with our foreign policy and which may profoundly affect it, not to enlarge an immunity to an extent which the government, although often asked, has not seen fit to recognize.

Section 1602 is intended to free the courts from the obligation of absolute obedience to the executive. As stated in the Senate Judiciary Committee Report, "[a] principal purpose of this bill is to transfer the determination of sovereign immunity from the executive branch to the judicial branch. * * * The Department of State would be freed from pressures from foreign governments to recognize their immunity from suit and from any adverse consequences resulting from an unwillingness of the Department to support that immunity." Sen.Rep. 94–1370, 94th Cong.2d Sess. p. 9 (1976).

### *Notes*

1. Does the Act intend to overrule the *Republic of Peru* and *Republic of Mexico* cases? If it does, how well does it express this intent? Can the Act constitutionally overrule these cases? Compare the action of the President in regard to claims upon Iran in Dames & Moore v. Regan, 453 U.S. 654, 101 S.Ct. 2972, 69 L.Ed.2d 918 (1981), discussed in Chapter 3, Section 2(D).

2. Does the Act preclude any role of the Executive in adjudication of claims of sovereign immunity? See Letter from the Legal Adviser of the State Department to the Attorney General (Nov. 10, 1976), 75 Dep't St. Bull. 649–50 (1976):

> * * * the Executive Branch will, of course, play the same role in sovereign immunity cases that it does in other types of litigation—e.g., appearing as *amicus curiae* in cases of significant interest to the Government. Judicial construction of the new statute will be of general interest to the Department of State, since the statute, like the Tate letter, endeavors to incorporate international law on sovereign immunity into domestic United States law and practice. If a court should misconstrue the new statute, the United States may well have an interest in making its views on the legal issues known to an appellate court.

In addition, the Executive may wish to express its views to the courts in cases not covered by the Act.

3. Under the Act, may the Executive suggest upon the record that the foreign state claims sovereign immunity without taking a position on the claim? The State Department has done so in Jackson v. People's Republic of China, 550 F.Supp. 869 (N.D.Ala.1982). See also Libyan American Oil Co. v. Libya, 684 F.2d 1032 (D.C.Cir.1981). The statements of the United States in these cases can be found in 22 I.L.M. 1077 (1983) and 20 I.L.M. 161 (1981). For a discussion of practical difficulties encountered by a foreign state that did not wish to employ private counsel for this purpose, see Carl, Suing Foreign Governments in American Courts: The United States Foreign Sovereign Immunities Act in Practice, 33 Southw.L.J. 1007, 1056–57 (1979).

4. May the Act's intent to deprive the Executive of a conclusive say in this area be carried over into the act-of-state doctrine? On the role of the Executive in the latter area, see p. 193 supra.

## F. PROCEDURAL PROBLEMS

### *1. Judicial Competence in Sovereign Immunity Cases*

### SUBJECT MATTER COMPETENCE

1. Actions against foreign states

#### *FOREIGN SOVEREIGN IMMUNITIES ACT OF 1976*

[28 U.S.C.A. § 1330(a)].

ACTIONS AGAINST FOREIGN STATES

(a) The district courts shall have original jurisdiction without regard to amount in controversy of any nonjury civil action against a foreign state as defined in section 1603(a) of this title as to any claim for relief in personam with respect to which the foreign state is not entitled to immunity either under sections 1605–1607 of this title or under any applicable international agreement.

* * *

[28 U.S.C.A. § 1332(a)(2), (3), and (4)]

DIVERSITY OF CITIZENSHIP * * *

(a) The district courts shall have original jurisdiction of all civil actions where the matter in controversy exceeds the sum or value of $50,000, exclusive of interest and costs, and is between—

* * *

(2) citizens of a State and citizens or subjects of a foreign state;

(3) citizens of different States and in which citizens or subjects of a foreign state are additional parties; and

(4) a foreign state, defined in section 1603(a) of this title, as plaintiff and citizens of a State or of different States.

* * *

[28 U.S.C.A. § 1441(d)]

ACTIONS REMOVABLE GENERALLY

* * *

(d) Any civil action brought in a State court against a foreign state as defined in section 1603(a) of this title may be removed by the foreign state to the district court of the United States for the district and division embracing the place where such action is pending. Upon removal the action shall be tried by the court without jury. Where removal is based upon this subsection, the time limitations of section 1446(b) of this chapter may be enlarged at any time for cause shown.

## *Notes*

1. Is Section 1330(a) constitutional? In Verlinden B.V. v. Central Bank of Nigeria, 461 U.S. 480, 103 S.Ct. 1962, 76 L.Ed.2d 81 (1983), the Supreme Court reversed a decision by the Second Circuit Court of Appeals that there was no constitutional subject matter jurisdiction in the action brought by the Dutch plaintiff. The Supreme Court ruled that there was federal question jurisdiction because the action arose under the FSIA. Is this reasoning persuasive? Or did *Verlinden* present a case of "protective" jurisdiction? See Smit, in International Contracts, Foreign Sovereign Immunity—American Style 255 (1981).

2. In which actions against a foreign state do the district courts have subject matter competence? Are the Act's provisions exclusive? What *in rem* actions can be brought in state courts? The Supreme Court has ruled that the FSIA provides the only bases for proceeding against a foreign state. See Section 1610(d). Can they be removed to a federal court?

3. Is there ever a right to trial by jury in an action against a foreign state? The Act proceeds on the assumption that, since there is no right to trial by jury in an action against the U.S. Government, there is none in a suit against a foreign state. See Section 1441(d) (last sentence); cf. Sen.Rep. No. 94–1310, 94th Cong.2d Sess., p. 12 (1976). Does this conclusion necessarily follow? See Icenogle v. Olympic Airways, S.A., 82 F.R.D. 36 (D.D.C.1979) (holding plaintiff entitled to trial by jury in action against foreign corporation qualifying as "foreign state" under the Act).

Compare Ruggiero v. Compania Peruana De Vapores, 639 F.2d 872 (2d Cir.1981) (holding that denial of right to trial by jury does not violate Seventh Amendment), with Rex v. Compania Peruana de Vapores, S.A., 660 F.2d 61 (3d Cir.1981), cert. denied, 456 U.S. 926, 102 S.Ct. 1971, 72 L.Ed.2d 441 (1982) (holding foreign state instrumentality entitled to jury trial). Cf. also Williams v. Shipping Corp. of India, 653 F.2d 875 (4th Cir.1981), cert. denied, 455 U.S. 982, 102 S.Ct. 1490, 71 L.Ed.2d 691 (1982) (ruling absence of right to jury trial not to prevent removal from state court); Greeley v. KLM Royal Dutch Airlines, 85 F.R.D. 697 (S.D.N.Y.1979) (no jury trial in action removed under FSIA). See further Restatement (Third) § 458(4). On this question, see also Smit, The Foreign Sovereign Immunities Act of 1976: A Plea for Drastic Surgery, 1980 Proc.A.S.I.L. 49.

2. Actions by foreign states

A foreign state may bring an action in a federal court when the requirements of 28 U.S.C.A. § 1332(a)(4) are met. If the foreign state elects to bring the action in a state court, may it be removed to a federal court? Under 28 U.S.C.A. § 1441(b), unless that action asserts a claim arising under federal law, it may be removed by the defendant only if none of the defendants are citizens of the state in which the action is brought. It may therefore be crucial whether an action brought by a foreign state in a state court arises under federal law. If it does, any action involving a foreign state may be brought in, or removed to, a federal court, regardless of whether the foreign state is the plaintiff or the defendant. It would appear beyond question that this is the preferable rule. If the FSIA had been more skillfully drafted, it would straightforwardly have so provided. See Smit, The Foreign Sovereign Immunities Act of 1976: A Plea for Drastic Surgery, 1980 A.S.I.L.Proc. 49, 57. It does not so provide and, unfortunately, 28 U.S.C.A. § 1332(a)(4), which was added at the time of enactment of the FSIA, provides an argument against the preferable rule stated. For if any action involving a foreign state raises a question of federal law, this subsection would be superfluous.

As the law presently stands, however, it is possible to permit most actions involving a foreign state to be brought in, or removed to, a federal court while perhaps preserving some room for application of 28 U.S.C.A. § 1332(a)(4). The prevailing, and preferable, view is that, in cases involving foreign states, the applicable conflict of laws rules are federal. The Ninth Circuit has consistently so ruled. Liu v. The Republic of China, 892 F.2d 1419 (9th Cir.1989); Harris v. Polskie Linie Lotnicze, 820 F.2d 1000 (9th Cir.1987). Consequently, in all cases involving a foreign state in which it is necessary to apply conflict of laws rules, federal law must be applied. And such cases may therefore be removed to the federal court as arising under federal law, regardless of whether the foreign state is the plaintiff or the defendant.

It is only when an action brought by a foreign state raises no question of federal conflict of laws, that 28 U.S.C.A. § 1332(a)(4) retains its relevance. It may be difficult to conceive of such cases, since the very presence of a foreign state in the action would appear to necessitate reference to conflict of laws rules. However, this may well have escaped the notice of the legislature. After all, the applicability of conflict of laws rules often escapes notice. And it is certainly plausible that it escaped the notice of the draftsmen of the FSIA, which in many other respects appears deficient. Of course, if the view that the federal courts must apply federal law to all cases involving foreign states, regardless of conflict of laws rules, were adopted, all cases brought by foreign states could be brought in, or removed to, federal courts.

## 2. *In Personam Competence*

### *FOREIGN SOVEREIGN IMMUNITIES ACT OF 1976*

[28 U.S.C.A. § 1330(b) and (c)].

ACTIONS AGAINST FOREIGN STATES

* * *

(b) Personal jurisdiction over a foreign state shall exist as to every claim for relief over which the district courts have jurisdiction under subsection (a) where service has been made under section 1608 of this title.

(c) For purposes of subsection (b), an appearance by a foreign state does not confer personal jurisdiction with respect to any claim for relief not arising out of any transaction or occurrence enumerated in sections 1605–1607 of this title.

### *Notes*

1. Note that Section 1605(b) attempts to convert traditional *in rem* actions in admiralty into *in personam* actions. Is this merely window-dressing? See the proviso at the end of Section 1605(b). The 1988 Amendments which added subsections (c) and (d) seek to eliminate the problems this attempted conversion occasioned.

2. For an application of Section 1605(b), see O'Connell Machinery Co. v. M.V. "Americana", 734 F.2d 115 (2d Cir.1984). The limitation on liens against state-owned vessels is criticized by Yiannopoulos, Foreign Sovereign Immunity and the Arrest of State–Owned Ships: The Need For An Admiralty Foreign Sovereign Immunity Act, 57 Tul.L.Rev. 1274 (1983).

3. The 1988 amendments, in addition to dealing with problems that had arisen in arbitration, eliminate some of the problems that had arisen under the FSIA's provisions relating to the converted in rem actions. On these amendments, see Atkeson & Ramsey, 79 A.J.I.L. 770, 778 (1985). For a judicial circumvention of the forfeiture rule of Section 1605(b), see Velidor v. L/P/G Benghazi, 653 F.2d 812 (3d Cir.1981) (ruling that personal claim survives).

4. Was it desirable for the new Act to create its own bases of *in personam* competence or would it have been preferable to rely on generally prevailing bases? See Smit, Note 1, p. 1149 supra. For decisions finding lack of *in personam* competence under the Act, see Carey v. National Oil Corp., 592 F.2d 673 (2d Cir.1979); Harris v. VAO Intourist, Moscow, 481 F.Supp. 1056 (E.D.N.Y. 1979); Vencedora Oceanica Navigacion, S.A. v. Compagnie Nationale Algerienne De Navigation (C.N.A.N.), 730 F.2d 195 (5th Cir.1984); Upton v. Empire of Iran, 459 F.Supp. 264 (D.D.C.1978), aff'd mem., 607 F.2d 494 (D.C.Cir.1979); Berkovitz v. Islamic Republic of Iran, 735 F.2d 329 (9th Cir.1984) (all holding that in a personal injury case the direct effect within the meaning of Section 1605(a)(2) occurs at the place of injury). However, in other cases, the courts have been inclined to be more liberal. In Texas Trading & Milling Corp. v. Federal Republic of Nigeria, 647 F.2d 300 (2d Cir.1981), cert. denied, 454 U.S. 1148, 102 S.Ct. 1012, 71 L.Ed.2d 301 (1982), the issuance of letters of credit payable in New York on a sale transacted abroad was held sufficient to create competence under the Act. In addition, when a foreign state instrumentality engages in commercial activities within the United States, the courts have been more inclined to

find the requisite direct effect in the United States in financial loss to a plaintiff in the United States resulting from a wrongful act abroad. See, e.g., Sugarman v. Aeromexico, Inc., 626 F.2d 270 (3d Cir.1980); Ministry of Supply, Cairo v. Universe Tankships, Inc., 708 F.2d 80 (2d Cir.1983); De Sanchez v. Banco Central De Nicaragua, 515 F.Supp. 900 (E.D.La.1981). See further Restatement (Third) §§ 453–54. And in the *Nelson* case supra, the court found commercial activities in the United States sufficient to create jurisdiction in relation to a claim of unlawful detention and torture in the foreign country.

5. In an action against a foreign state, may *in personam* competence also be premised on a basis available under federal or state law not embodied in the Act? Cf. Fed.R.Civ.P. 4(e); Miller, Service of Process on State, Local, and Foreign Governments under Rule 4, 46 F.R.D. 101 (1969). For a negative answer, see Harris v. VAO Intourist Moscow, Note 4 supra. Cf. also the *Amerada Hess Shipping Co.* case supra, in which the Supreme Court ruled the bases of subject matter competence provided by the FSIA to be the only ones available.

6. Was it desirable to let the existence of *in personam* competence under Section 1330(b) depend on whether service has been properly made under Section 1608? For a negative answer, see Smit, Note 1, p. 1149 supra.

7. The service provisions in Section 1605(b)(1) and (2) were changed by the 1988 Amendments. Subsections (c) and (d) were also added by these Amendments.

### 3. *In Rem Competence*

*FOREIGN SOVEREIGN IMMUNITIES ACT OF 1976*

[28 U.S.C.A. § 1610(d) ].

EXCEPTIONS TO THE IMMUNITY FROM ATTACHMENT OR EXECUTION

* * *

(d) The property of a foreign state, as defined in section 1603(a) of this chapter, used for a commercial activity in the United States, shall not be immune from attachment prior to the entry of judgment in any action brought in a court of the United States or of a State, or prior to the elapse of the period of time provided in subsection (c) of this section, if—

(1) the foreign state has explicitly waived its immunity from attachment prior to judgment, notwithstanding any withdrawal of the waiver the foreign state may purport to effect except in accordance with the terms of the waiver, and

(2) the purpose of the attachment is to secure satisfaction of a judgment that has been or may ultimately be entered against the foreign state, and not to obtain jurisdiction.

#### *Notes*

1. Is a contractual waiver of "any sovereign immunity" an "explicit" waiver of immunity from attachment within the meaning of this provision? Or must the waiver provision state in so many words that the immunity waived includes immunity from pre-judgment attachment? How likely would it be for

foreign lawyers to know of such a requirement and to include so explicit a provision?

2. If immunity from pre-judgment attachment has been waived explicitly, may an *in rem* action be brought against a foreign state or its property in a federal or state court? See Section 1610(d)(2) and (e).

3. Was it desirable to eliminate pre-judgment attachment? How likely are foreign states sued *in personam* to make their assets scarce when the time for execution arrives? See Smit, Note 1, p. 1149 supra. On whether attachments laid before the Act became effective continue their effect after the effective date of the Act, see, e.g., Amoco Overseas Oil Co. v. Compagnie Nationale Algerienne De Navigation, 459 F.Supp. 1242 (S.D.N.Y.1978); National American Corp. v. Federal Republic of Nigeria, 448 F.Supp. 622 (S.D.N.Y.1978).

4. Would a waiver of immunity contained in a contract concluded before the Act entered into force and at that time effectively waiving immunity from attachment become ineffective for failure of explicitness when the Act entered into force? Would an affirmative answer be compatible with the constitutional ban on the impairment of contracts?

5. The limitations imposed by the Act upon pre-judgment attachment raised significant problems at the time of the Iranian Hostage Crisis, when Iran announced the withdrawal of its funds from the United States. Most claimants laid attachments first and worried about the consequences later. The courts were understandably eager to find a proper legal basis for these attachments. See, e.g., Note 7 infra. Some litigants sought injunctions against debtors of Iran rather than attachments. The President, in order to protect their rights, then issued an order freezing all such assets. The order was upheld in Dames & Moore v. Regan, 453 U.S. 654, 101 S.Ct. 2972, 69 L.Ed.2d 918 (1981), discussed in Chapter 3, Section 2(D). By the Algerian Accords, provision was made for U.S. claimants to present their claims to a United States—Iran Tribunal sitting in The Hague. Part of the frozen funds were released to Iran; another part was remitted to the custody of the Dutch Government with provision for payment out of these funds of awards rendered by the Tribunal. On this Tribunal, see Chapter 10.

6. An amendment was proposed permitting, under specified conditions, pre-judgment attachment against instrumentalities of a foreign state. See Atkeson & Ramsey, Proposed Amendments of the Foreign Sovereign Immunity Act, 79 A.J.I.L. 770, 776–77, 787 (1985). The conditions statutorily specified include the moving party's posting a bond of at least 50 percent of the value of the property attached. See proposed Section 1610(d)(i)(E), id. at 789. Is this an appropriate requirement? This proposed amendment was not adopted.

7. Does a waiver of immunity in a Treaty of Friendship, Commerce, and Navigation waive immunity from pre-judgment attachment? For an affirmative answer, see Behring International, Inc. v. Imperial Iranian Air Force, 475 F.Supp. 383 (D.N.J.1979), aff'd, 699 F.2d 657 (3d Cir.1983). Note that Section 1604 of the Act provides that a foreign state shall be immune from the jurisdiction of the courts "[S]ubject to existing international agreements."

### 4. *Service of Process*

*FOREIGN SOVEREIGN IMMUNITIES ACT OF 1976*

90 Stat. 2891, 28 U.S.C.A.

[See Section 1608(a), (b), and (c) ]

#### *Notes*

1. Was it necessary to create special service provisions for actions against foreign states? Cf. Smit, Note 1, p. 1171 supra. See Petrol Shipping Corp. v. Kingdom of Greece, 360 F.2d 103 (2d Cir.1966) (holding that Federal Civil Rule 4 does not provide for service on a foreign state, but upholding service by mail under local district court rule); Hellenic Lines, Ltd. v. Moore, 345 F.2d 978 (D.C.Cir.1965) (holding improper service on the foreign state's ambassador in Washington); Caravel Office Building Co. v. The Peruvian Air Attache, 347 A.2d 280 (D.C.App.1976) (upholding service by registered mail on air attache as proper service on Peru); Alberti v. Empresa Nicaraguense de la Carne, 705 F.2d 250 (7th Cir.1983) (service by mail on foreign ambassador improper). In New England Merchants National Bank v. Iran Power Generation and Transmission Co., 495 F.Supp. 73 (S.D.N.Y.1980), the court permitted substituted service under Fed.R.Civ.P. 4(i). See also Note, Amenability of Foreign Sovereign to Federal In Personam Jurisdiction, 14 Va.J. Int'l L. 487, 489–91 (1974); Miller, Service of Process on State, Local, and Foreign Governments under Rule 4, Federal Rules of Civil Procedure, 46 F.R.D. 101, 121–22 (1969).

2. Was it desirable to let the availability of the form of service prescribed in Section 1608(a)(3) depend on the impossibility of making service under Section 1608(a)(1) and (2)? See Carl, Note 1, p. 1149 supra, at 1022–28.

3. On August 24, 1967, the United States ratified the Convention on the Service Abroad of Judicial and Extrajudicial Documents in Civil or Commercial Matters. As of January 1, 1992 the following countries had also ratified this Convention: Antigua & Barbuda, Barbados, Belgium, Botswana, Canada, China, Cyprus, Czechoslovakia, Denmark, Egypt, Finland, France, Germany, Greece, Israel, Italy, Japan, Luxembourg, Malawi, the Netherlands, Norway, Pakistan, Portugal, Seychelles, Spain, Sweden, Turkey, and the United Kingdom. For a report on how this Convention is working, see 28 I.L.M. 1556 (1989) and Weis, The Federal Rules and the Hague Conventions: Concerns of Conformity and Comity, 50 U.Pitt.L.Rev. 903 (1989). What is the relationship between the Convention's and the Act's provisions on service?

4. In 40 D 6262 Realty Corp. v. United Arab Emirates Government, 447 F.Supp. 710 (S.D.N.Y.1978), petitioners had affixed a notice of petition to the premises occupied by the defendant and had mailed a copy to the defendant's Permanent Mission. The Court held the service improper as not authorized by either Section 1608(a)(1), (a)(2), or (a)(3). Could the service have been held proper under the *Petrol Shipping* approach? See Note 1 supra. See also Gray v. Permanent Mission of the People's Republic of the Congo to the United Nations, 443 F.Supp. 816 (S.D.N.Y.1978) (holding insufficient under the Act service made upon the defendant's "secretary").

5. For the regulations of the Secretary of State prescribing the form of the notice of suit required by Section 1608(a)(3) and (4), see Title 22, CFR 93.1–93.2, 16 I.L.M. 159 (1977).

6. Section 1608(b) is inspired by Fed.R.Civ.P. 4(i). Would closer adherence to the Rule's provisions have been desirable? See Smit, Note 1, p. 1171 supra.

### 5. *Procedures for Claiming Immunity*

A foreign state may be required to follow certain procedures in asserting its immunity, provided that these procedures do not unreasonably restrict its opportunity effectively to assert its immunity.

#### *Notes*

1. The Foreign Sovereign Immunities Act does not address the problem of how sovereign immunity is to be claimed.

2. For a ruling that a ship's master is not the proper person "to vindicate the owner's sovereignty," see The Gul Djemal, 264 U.S. 90, 44 S.Ct. 244, 68 L.Ed. 574 (1924).

3. On whether the Executive may suggest immunity on the record under the Act, see Note 2, p. 1169 supra.

4. May the court raise the sovereign immunity defense on its own motion? The court did so in Frolova v. U.S.S.R., 761 F.2d 370 (7th Cir.1985) (on the ground that absence of sovereign immunity is a prerequisite to subject matter competence and may therefore be raised upon the court's own motion). But in Von Dardel On Behalf of Raoul Wallenberg et al. v. U.S.S.R., 623 F.Supp. 246 (D.D.C.1985), the Court construed the failure of the U.S.S.R. to appear and raise the defense as a waiver.

5. The appellate courts have ruled that a rejection by a district court of a claim to immunity is immediately appealable under the collateral order doctrine. See Foremost–McKesson v. Islamic Republic of Iran, 905 F.2d 438, 443 (D.C.Cir. 1990), and cases cited.

## G. IMMUNITY FROM EXECUTION

*FOREIGN SOVEREIGN IMMUNITIES ACT OF 1976*

[See 28 U.S.C.A. §§ 1609–1611].

Before the Foreign Sovereign Immunities Act of 1976 entered into force, the U.S. State Department took the position that the property of a foreign state was absolutely immune from execution. This position had also been adopted by American courts, the leading case being Dexter & Carpenter v. Kunglig Jarnvagtsstyvelsen, 43 F.2d 705 (2d Cir.1930), cert. den., 282 U.S. 896, 51 S.Ct. 181, 75 L.Ed. 789 (1931).

However, the United States position in this regard appeared not to be required by international law. Eminent authority supported the view that, under international law, the restrictive doctrine of immunity could properly be extended to deny immunity from execution to commercial as distinguished from public, property of a foreign state. See, e.g., Lauterpacht, The Problem of Jurisdictional Immunities of Foreign States, 1951 Brit.Y.B.I.L. 220, 241–43; Lalive, L'Immunité de Jurisdiction des Etats et des Organisations Internationales, 84 Rec. des Cours 205, 274–75 (1953–III); Restatement, Second, The Foreign Relations Law of the United States, § 69, Reporter's Note 2 (1965).

The Foreign Sovereign Immunities Act of 1976 changed prior United States practice and rulings by permitting execution on a foreign state's commercial property in the circumstances statutorily specified. It is to be noted that the commercial property upon which execution may be levied need not in all circumstances be used for the commercial activity from which the claims for relief arose. But cf. Section 1610(a)(2).

A proposed amendment to the Act that would substantially broaden execution permitted under the Act (see Atkeson & Ramsey, Proposed Amendments to the Foreign Sovereign Immunities Act, 79 A.J.I.L. 770, 777–78 (1985)), was not adopted. It would have permitted execution on any property belonging to an agency or instrumentality of a foreign state engaged in commercial activity in the United States when the judgment relates to a claim for which there is no immunity. Should the Act be amended to permit even broader execution? Does the decision that follows provide the proper approach?

## FIRST NATIONAL CITY BANK v. BANCO PARA EL COMERCIO EXTERIOR DE CUBA

Supreme Court of the United States, 1983.
462 U.S. 611, 103 S.Ct. 2591, 77 L.Ed.2d 46.

JUSTICE O'CONNOR delivered the opinion of the Court.*

In 1960 the Government of the Republic of Cuba established respondent Banco Para el Comercio Exterior de Cuba (Bancec) to serve as "[a]n official autonomous credit institution for foreign trade * * * with full juridical capacity * * * of its own. * * *" Law No. 793, Art. 1 (1960), App. to Pet. for Cert.2d. In September 1960 Bancec sought to collect on a letter of credit issued by petitioner First National City Bank (now Citibank) in its favor in support of a contract for delivery of Cuban sugar to a buyer in the United States. Within days after Citibank received the request for collection, all of its assets in Cuba were seized and nationalized by the Cuban Government. When Bancec brought suit on the letter of credit in United States District Court, Citibank counterclaimed, asserting a right to set off the value of its seized Cuban assets. The question before us is whether Citibank may obtain such a setoff, notwithstanding the fact that Bancec was established as a separate juridical entity. Applying principles of equity common to international law and federal common law, we conclude that Citibank may apply a setoff.

### I

* * *

On February 1, 1961, Bancec brought this diversity action to recover on the letter of credit in the United States District Court for the Southern District of New York.

* * *

On March 8, 1961, after Bancec had been dissolved, Citibank filed its answer, which sought a setoff for the value of its seized branches, not an

* Some footnotes omitted; others renumbered.

affirmative recovery of damages.[1] On July 7, 1961, Bancec filed a stipulation signed by the parties stating that Bancec had been dissolved and that its claim had been transferred to the Ministry of Foreign Trade, and agreeing that the Republic of Cuba may be substituted as plaintiff. The District Court approved the stipulation, but no amended complaint was filed.

* * *

A bench trial was held in 1977, after which the District Court granted judgment in favor of Citibank. 505 F.Supp. 412 (1980). The court rejected Bancec's contention that its separate juridical status shielded it from liability for the acts of the Cuban Government.

* * *

The United States Court of Appeals for the Second Circuit reversed. 658 F.2d 913 (2nd Cir.1981). * * *

* * *

* * * We reverse, and remand the case for further proceedings.

II

A

As an initial matter, Bancec contends that the Foreign Sovereign Immunities Act of 1976, 28 U.S.C. §§ 1602–1611 (FSIA), immunizes an instrumentality owned by a foreign government from suit on a counterclaim based on actions taken by that government. * * *

We disagree. The language and history of the FSIA clearly establish that the Act was not intended to affect the substantive law determining the liability of a foreign state or instrumentality, or the attribution of liability among instrumentalities of a foreign state. Section 1606 of the FSIA provides in relevant part that "[a]s to any claim for relief with respect to which a foreign state is not entitled to immunity * * *, the foreign state shall be liable in the same manner and to the same extent as a private individual under like circumstances * * *." The House Report on the FSIA states:

> "The bill is not intended to affect the substantive law of liability. Nor is it intended to affect * * * the attribution of responsibility between or among entities of a foreign state; for example, whether the proper entity of a foreign state has been sued, or whether an entity sued is liable in whole or in part for the claimed wrong." H.R.Rep. No. 94–1487, p. 12 (1976), U.S.Code Cong. & Admin.News 1976, pp. 6604, 6610.

Thus, we conclude that the FSIA does not control the determination of whether Citibank may set off the value of its seized Cuban assets against Bancec's claim.

1. Citibank's answer alleged that the suit was "brought by and for the benefit of the Republic of Cuba by and through its agent and wholly-owned instrumentality, * * * which is in fact and law and in form and function an integral part of and indistinguishable from the Republic of Cuba." App. 113.

B

We must next decide which body of law determines the effect to be given to Bancec's separate juridical status. Bancec contends that internationally recognized conflict-of-law principles require the application of the law of the state that establishes a government instrumentality—here Cuba—to determine whether the instrumentality may be held liable for actions taken by the sovereign.

We cannot agree. As a general matter, the law of the state of incorporation normally determines issues relating to the *internal* affairs of a corporation. Application of that body of law achieves the need for certainty and predictability of result while generally protecting the justified expectations of parties with interests in the corporation. See Restatement (Second) of Conflict of Laws § 302, Comments *a* & *e,* (1971). Cf. Cort v. Ash, 422 U.S. 66, 84, 95 S.Ct. 2080, 2090, 45 L.Ed.2d 26 (1975). Different conflicts principles apply, however, where the rights of third parties *external* to the corporation are at issue. See Restatement (Second) of Conflict of Laws, supra, § 301. To give conclusive effect to the law of the chartering state in determining whether the separate juridical status of its instrumentality should be respected would permit the state to violate with impunity the rights of third parties under international law while effectively insulating itself from liability in foreign courts. We decline to permit such a result.[2]

Bancec contends in the alternative that international law must determine the resolution of the question presented. Citibank, on the other hand, suggests that federal common law governs. The expropriation claim against which Bancec seeks to interpose its separate juridical status arises under international law, which, as we have frequently reiterated, "is part of our law * * *." The Paquete Habana, 175 U.S. 677, 700, 20 S.Ct. 290, 299, 44 L.Ed. 320 (1900). As we set forth below, * * * the principles governing this case are common to both international law and federal common law, which in these circumstances is necessarily informed both by international law principles and by articulated congressional policies.

2. Pointing out that 28 U.S.C. § 1606, see supra, at 2597, contains language identical to the Federal Tort Claims Act (FTCA), 28 U.S.C. § 2674, Bancec also contends alternatively that the FSIA, like the FTCA, requires application of the law of the forum State—here New York—including its conflicts principles. We disagree. Section 1606 provides that "[a]s to any claim for relief with respect to which a foreign state is not entitled to immunity * * *, the foreign state shall be liable in the same manner and to the same extent as a private individual under like circumstances." Thus, where state law provides a rule of liability governing private individuals, the FSIA requires the application of that rule to foreign states in like circumstances. The statute is silent, however, concerning the rule governing the attribution of liability *among* entities of a foreign state. In Banco Nacional de Cuba v. Sabbatino, 376 U.S. 398, 425, 84 S.Ct. 923, 938, 11 L.Ed.2d 804 (1964), this Court declined to apply the State of New York's act of state doctrine in a diversity action between a United States national and an instrumentality of a foreign state, concluding that matters bearing on the Nation's foreign relations "should not be left to divergent and perhaps parochial state interpretations." When it enacted the FSIA, Congress expressly acknowledged "the importance of developing a uniform body of law" concerning the amenability of a foreign sovereign to suit in United States courts. H.R.Rep. No. 94–1487, p. 32 (1976). See Verlinden B.V. v. Central Bank of Nigeria, 461 U.S. 480, 489, 103 S.Ct. 1962, 1969, 76 L.Ed.2d 81 (1983). In our view, these same considerations preclude the application of New York law here.

III

A

Before examining the controlling principles, a preliminary observation is appropriate. The parties and *amici* have repeatedly referred to the phrases that have tended to dominate discussion about the independent status of separately constituted juridical entities, debating whether "to pierce the corporate veil," and whether Bancec is an "alter ego" or a "mere instrumentality" of the Cuban Government. In Berkey v. Third Avenue Ry. Co., 244 N.Y. 84, 155 N.E. 58 (1926), Justice (then Judge) Cardozo warned in circumstances similar to those presented here against permitting worn epithets to substitute for rigorous analysis.

> "The whole problem of the relation between parent and subsidiary corporations is one that is still enveloped in the mists of metaphor. Metaphors in law are to be narrowly watched, for starting as devices to liberate thought, they end often by enslaving it." Id., at 94, 155 N.E., at 61.

With this in mind, we examine briefly the nature of government instrumentalities.

Increasingly during this century, governments throughout the world have established separately constituted legal entities to perform a variety of tasks. The organization and control of these entities vary considerably, but many possess a number of common features. A typical government instrumentality, if one can be said to exist, is created by an enabling statute that prescribes the powers and duties of the instrumentality, and specifies that it is to be managed by a board selected by the government in a manner consistent with the enabling law. The instrumentality is typically established as a separate juridical entity, with the powers to hold and sell property and to sue and be sued. Except for appropriations to provide capital or to cover losses, the instrumentality is primarily responsible for its own finances. The instrumentality is run as a distinct economic enterprise; often it is not subject to the same budgetary and personnel requirements with which government agencies must comply.

These distinctive features permit government instrumentalities to manage their operations on an enterprise basis while granting them a greater degree of flexibility and independence from close political control than is generally enjoyed by government agencies. These same features frequently prompt governments in developing countries to establish separate juridical entities as the vehicles through which to obtain the financial resources needed to make large-scale national investments.

> "[P]ublic enterprise, largely in the form of development corporations, has become an essential instrument of economic development in the economically backward countries which have insufficient private venture capital to develop the utilities and industries which are given priority in the national development plan. Not infrequently, these public development corporations * * * directly or through subsidiaries, enter into partnerships with national or foreign private enterprises, or they offer shares to the public." Friedmann, Government Enterprise: A Comparative Analysis, in Government Enterprise: A Comparative Study 303, 333–334 (W. Friedmann & J. Garner eds. 1970).

Separate legal personality has been described as "an almost indispensable aspect of the public corporation." Id., at 314. Provisions in the corporate charter stating that the instrumentality may sue and be sued have been construed to waive the sovereign immunity accorded to many governmental activities, thereby enabling third parties to deal with the instrumentality knowing that they may seek relief in the courts. Similarly, the instrumentality's assets and liabilities must be treated as distinct from those of its sovereign in order to facilitate credit transactions with third parties. Id., at 315. Thus what the Court stated with respect to private corporations in Anderson v. Abbott, 321 U.S. 349, 64 S.Ct. 531, 88 L.Ed. 793 (1944), is true also for governmental corporations:

> "Limited liability is the rule, not the exception; and on that assumption large undertakings are rested, vast enterprises are launched, and huge sums of capital attracted." Id., at 362, 64 S.Ct., at 537.

Freely ignoring the separate status of government instrumentalities would result in substantial uncertainty over whether an instrumentality's assets would be diverted to satisfy a claim against the sovereign, and might thereby cause third parties to hesitate before extending credit to a government instrumentality without the government's guarantee. As a result, the efforts of sovereign nations to structure their governmental activities in a manner deemed necessary to promote economic development and efficient administration would surely be frustrated. Due respect for the actions taken by foreign sovereigns and for principles of comity between nations, see Hilton v. Guyot, 159 U.S. 113, 163–164, 16 S.Ct. 139, 143, 40 L.Ed. 95 (1895), leads us to conclude—as the courts of Great Britain have concluded in other circumstances [3]—that government instrumentalities established as juridical

3. The British courts, applying principles we have not embraced as universally acceptable, have shown marked reluctance to attribute the acts of a foreign government to an instrumentality owned by that government. In *I Congreso del Partido,* [1983] A.C. 244, a decision discussing the so-called "restrictive" doctrine of sovereign immunity and its application to three Cuban state-owned enterprises, including Cubazucar, Lord Wilberforce described the legal status of government instrumentalities:

> "State-controlled enterprises, with legal personality, ability to trade and to enter into contracts of private law, though wholly subject to the control of their state, are a well-known feature of the modern commercial scene. The distinction between them, and their governing state, may appear artificial: but it is an accepted distinction in the law of England and other states. Quite different considerations apply to a state-controlled enterprise acting on government directions on the one hand, and a state, exercising sovereign functions, on the other." Id., at 258 (citation omitted).

Later in his opinion, Lord Wilberforce rejected the contention that commercial transactions entered into by state-owned organizations could be attributed to the Cuban Government. "The status of these organizations is familiar in our courts, and it has never been held that the relevant state is in law answerable for their actions." Id., at 271. See also Trendtex Trading Corp. v. Central Bank of Nigeria, [1977] Q.B. 529, in which the Court of Appeal ruled that the Central Bank of Nigeria was not an "alter ego or organ" of the Nigerian Government for the purpose of determining whether it could assert sovereign immunity. Id., at 559.

In C. Czarnikow Ltd. v. Rolimpex, [1979] A.C. 351, the House of Lords affirmed a decision holding that Rolimpex, a Polish state trading enterprise that sold Polish sugar overseas, could successfully assert a defense of *force majeure* in an action for breach of a contract to sell sugar. Rolimpex had defended on the ground that the Polish Government had instituted a ban on the foreign sale of Polish sugar. Lord Wilberforce agreed with the conclusion of the court below that, in the absence of "clear evidence and definite findings" that the foreign government took the action "purely in order to extricate a state enterprise from contractual liability," the enterprise cannot be regarded as an organ of the state. Rolimpex, he concluded, "is not so closely connected with the government of Poland that it is precluded from relying on the entities distinct and independent from their sovereign should normally be treated as such.

We find support for this conclusion in the legislative history of the FSIA. * * *

Thus, the presumption that a foreign government's determination that its instrumentality is to be accorded separate legal status is buttressed by this congressional determination. We next examine whether this presumption may be overcome in certain circumstances.

B

In discussing the legal status of *private* corporations, courts in the United States [4] and abroad,[5] have recognized that an incorporated entity—described by Chief Justice Marshall as "an artificial being, invisible, intangible, and existing only in contemplation of law"—is not to be regarded as legally separate from its owners in all circumstances. Thus, where a corporate entity is so extensively controlled by its owner that a relationship of principal and agent is created, we have held that one may be held liable for the actions of the other. See NLRB v. Deena Artware, Inc., 361 U.S. 398, 402–404, 80 S.Ct. 441, 443, 44 L.Ed.2d 400 (1960). In addition, our cases have long recognized "the broader equitable principle that the doctrine of corporate entity, recognized generally and for most purposes, will not be regarded when to do so would work fraud or injustice." Taylor v. Standard Gas Co., 306 U.S. 307, 322, 59 S.Ct. 543, 550, 83 L.Ed. 669 (1939). See Pepper v.

ban [on foreign sales] as government intervention. * * * " Id., at 364.

4. See 1 W. Fletcher, Cyclopedia of the Law of Private Corporations § 41 (rev.perm. ed. 1983):

> "[A] corporation will be looked upon as a legal entity as a general rule, and until sufficient reason to the contrary appears; but, when the notion of legal entity is used to defeat public convenience, justify wrong, protect fraud, or defend crime, the law will regard the corporation as an association of persons." Id., at 389 (footnote omitted).

See generally H. Henn, Handbook of the Law of Corporations § 146 (2d ed. 1970); I. Wormser, Disregard of the Corporate Fiction and Allied Corporation Problems 42–85 (1927).

5. In Case Concerning The Barcelona Traction, Light & Power Co., 1970 I.C.J. 3, the International Court of Justice acknowledged that, as a matter of international law, the separate status of an incorporated entity may be disregarded in certain exceptional circumstances:

> "Forms of incorporation and their legal personality have sometimes not been employed for the sole purposes they were originally intended to serve; sometimes the corporate entity has been unable to protect the rights of those who entrusted their financial resources to it; thus inevitably there have arisen dangers of abuse, as in the case of many other institutions of law. Here, then, as elsewhere, the law, confronted with economic realities, has had to provide protective measures and remedies in the interests of those within the corporate entity as well as of those outside who have dealings with it: the law has recognized that the independent existence of the legal entity cannot be treated as an absolute. It is in this context that the process of 'lifting the corporate veil' or 'disregarding the legal entity' has been found justified and equitable in certain circumstances or for certain purposes. The wealth of practice already accumulated on the subject in municipal law indicates that the veil is lifted, for instance, to prevent the misuse of the privileges of legal personality, as in certain cases of fraud or malfeasance, to protect third persons such as a creditor or purchaser, or to prevent the evasion of legal requirements or of obligations.
>
> * * *
>
> "In accordance with the principle expounded above, the process of lifting the veil, being an exceptional one admitted by municipal law in respect of an institution of its own making, is equally admissible to play a similar role in international law * * *." Id., at 38–39.

On the application of these principles by European courts, see Cohn & Simitis, "Lifting the Veil" in the Company Laws of the European Continent, 12 Int'l & Comp.L.Q. 189 (1963); Hadari, The Structure of the Private Multinational Enterprise, 71 Mich.L.Rev. 729, 771, n. 260 (1973).

Litton, 308 U.S. 295, 310, 60 S.Ct. 238, 246, 84 L.Ed. 281 (1939). In particular, the Court has consistently refused to give effect to the corporate form where it is interposed to defeat legislative policies. E.g., Anderson v. Abbot, 321 U.S., at 362–363, 64 S.Ct., at 537–538. * * *

C

We conclude today that similar equitable principles must be applied here. In National City Bank v. Republic of China, 348 U.S. 356, 75 S.Ct. 423, 99 L.Ed. 389 (1955), the Court ruled that when a foreign sovereign asserts a claim in a United States court, "the consideration of fair dealing" bars the state from asserting a defense of sovereign immunity to defeat a setoff or counterclaim. Id., at 365, 75 S.Ct., at 429. See 28 U.S.C. § 1607(c). As a general matter, therefore, the Cuban Government could not bring suit in a United States court without also subjecting itself to its adversary's counterclaim. Here there is apparently no dispute that, as the District Court found, and the Court of Appeals apparently agreed, see 658 F.2d, at 916, n. 4, "the devolution of [Bancec's] claim, however viewed, brings it into the hands of the Ministry [of Foreign Trade], or Banco Nacional," each a party that may be held liable for the expropriation of Citibank's assets. 505 F.Supp., at 425. See Banco Nacional de Cuba v. First National City Bank, 478 F.2d, at 194. Bancec was dissolved even before Citibank filed its answer in this case, apparently in order to effect "the consolidation and operation of the economic and social conquests of the Revolution," particularly the nationalization of the banks ordered by Law No. 891.[6] Thus, the Cuban Government and Banco Nacional, not any third parties that may have relied on Bancec's separate juridical identity, would be the only beneficiaries of any recovery.[7]

In our view, this situation is similar to that in the *Republic of China* case.

> "We have a foreign government invoking our law but resisting a claim against it which fairly would curtail its recovery. It wants our law, like any other litigant, but it wants our law free from the claims of justice." 348 U.S., at 361–362, 75 S.Ct., at 427 (footnote omitted).[8]

6. Law No. 930, the law dissolving Bancec, contains the following recitations:

"WHEREAS, the measures adopted by the Revolutionary Government in pursuance of the Program of the Revolution have resulted, within a short time, in profound social changes and considerable institutional transformations of the national economy.

"WHEREAS, among these institutional transformations there is one which is specially significant due to its transcendence in the economic and financial fields, which is the nationalization of the banks ordered by Law No. 891, of October 13, 1960, by virtue of which the banking functions will hereafter be the exclusive province of the Cuban Government.

"WHEREAS, the consolidation and the operation of the economic and social conquests of the Revolution require the restructuration into a sole and centralized banking system, operated by the State, constituted by the [Banco Nacional], which will foster the development and stimulation of all productive activities of the Nation through the accumulation of the financial resources thereof, and their most economic and reasonable utilization." App. to Pet. for Cert. 14d–15d.

7. The parties agree that, under the Cuban Assets Control Regulations, 31 CFR pt. 515 (1982), any judgment entered in favor of an instrumentality of the Cuban Government would be frozen pending settlement of claims between the United States and Cuba.

8. See also First National City Bank v. Banco Nacional de Cuba, 406 U.S., at 770–773, 92 S.Ct., at 1814–1816 (Douglas, J., concurring in result); Federal Republic of Germany v. Elicofon, 358 F.Supp. 747 (EDNY 1972), aff'd, 478 F.2d 231 (CA2 1973), cert. denied, 415 U.S. 931, 94 S.Ct. 1443, 39 L.Ed.2d 489 (1974). In

Giving effect to Bancec's separate juridical status in these circumstances, even though it has long been dissolved, would permit the real beneficiary of such an action, the Government of the Republic of Cuba, to obtain relief in our courts that it could not obtain in its own right without waiving its sovereign immunity and answering for the seizure of Citibank's assets—a seizure previously held by the Court of Appeals to have violated international law. We decline to adhere blindly to the corporate form where doing so would cause such an injustice. See Bangor Punta Operations, Inc. v. Bangor & Aroostook R. Co., supra, 417 U.S., at 713, 94 S.Ct., at 2584.

Respondent contends, however, that the transfer of Bancec's assets from the Ministry of Foreign Trade or Banco Nacional to Empresa and Cuba Zucar effectively insulates it from Citibank's counterclaim. We disagree. Having dissolved Bancec and transferred its assets to entities that may be held liable on Citibank's counterclaim, Cuba cannot escape liability for acts in violation of international law simply by retransferring the assets to separate juridical entities. To hold otherwise would permit governments to avoid the requirements of international law simply by creating juridical entities whenever the need arises. * * * We therefore hold that Citibank may set off the value of its assets seized by the Cuban Government against the amount sought by Bancec.

IV

Our decision today announces no mechanical formula for determining the circumstances under which the normally separate juridical status of a government instrumentality is to be disregarded.[9] Instead, it is the product of the application of internationally recognized equitable principles to avoid the injustice that would result from permitting a foreign state to reap the benefits of our courts while avoiding the obligations of international law.

The District Court determined that the value of Citibank's Cuban assets exceeded Bancec's claim. Bancec challenged this determination on appeal, but the Court of Appeals did not reach the question. It therefore remains open on remand. The judgment of the Court of Appeals is reversed, and the case is remanded for further proceedings consistent with this opinion.

It is so ordered.

*Elicofon*, the District Court held that a separate juridical entity of a foreign state not recognized by the United States may not appear in a United States court. A contrary holding, the court reasoned, "would permit non-recognized governments to use our courts at will by creating 'juridical entities' whenever the need arises." 358 F.Supp., at 757.

**9.** The District Court adopted, and both Citibank and the Solicitor General urge upon the Court, a standard in which the determination whether or not to give effect to the separate juridical status of a government instrumentality turns in part on whether the instrumentality in question performed a "governmental function." We decline to adopt such a standard in this case, as our decision is based on other grounds. We do observe that the concept of a "usual" or a "proper" governmental function changes over time and varies from nation to nation. Cf. New York v. United States, 326 U.S. 572, 580, 66 S.Ct. 310, 313, 90 L.Ed. 326 (1946) (opinion of Frankfurter, J.) ("To rest the federal taxing power on what is 'normally' conducted by private enterprise in contradiction to the 'usual' governmental functions is too shifting a basis for determining constitutional power and too entangled in expediency to serve as a dependable legal criterion"); id., at 586, 66 S.Ct., at 316 (Stone, C.J., concurring); id., at 591, 66 S.Ct., at 318 (Douglas, J., dissenting). See also Friedmann, The Legal Status and Organization of the Public Corporation, 16 Law & Contemp.Prob. 576, 589–591 (1951).

JUSTICE STEVENS, with whom JUSTICE BRENNAN and JUSTICE BLACKMUN join, concurring in part and dissenting in part.

Today the Court correctly rejects the contention that American courts should readily "pierce the corporate veils" of separate juridical entities established by foreign governments to perform governmental functions. Accordingly, I join Parts I, II, III–A, and III–B of the Court's opinion. But I respectfully dissent from Part III–C, in which the Court endeavors to apply the general principles it has enunciated. Instead I would vacate the judgment and remand the case to the Court of Appeals for further proceedings.

* * *

Of course, the Court may have reached a correct assessment of the transactions at issue. But I continue to believe that the Court should not decide factual issues that can be resolved more accurately and effectively by other federal judges, particularly when the record presented to this Court is so sparse and uninformative.[1]

### *Note*

In Letelier v. Republic of Chile, 748 F.2d 790 (2d Cir.1984), it was held that a judgment rendered against Chile for damages resulting from the murder of the former Chilean Ambassador in Washington, D.C. could not be executed by levying on the assets of Linea Aerea Nacional—Chile, a corporation the stock of which is wholly owned by Chile.

## H. POLITICAL SUBDIVISIONS AND INSTRUMENTALITIES OF A FOREIGN STATE ENJOYING IMMUNITY

### *FOREIGN SOVEREIGN IMMUNITIES ACT OF 1976*

[28 U.S.C.A. § 1603(a) and (b)].

#### DEFINITIONS

For purposes of this chapter—

(a) A "foreign state," except as used in section 1608 of this title, includes a political subdivision of a foreign state or an agency or instrumentality of a foreign state as defined in subsection (b).

(b) An "agency or instrumentality of a foreign state" means any entity—

(1) which is a separate legal person, corporate or otherwise, and

1. Nor do I agree that a contrary result "would cause such an injustice." Ante, at 2603. Petitioner is only one of many American citizens whose property was nationalized by the Cuban Government. It seeks to minimize its losses by retaining $193,280.30 that a purchaser of Cuban sugar had deposited with it for the purpose of paying for the merchandise, which was delivered in due course. Having won this lawsuit, petitioner will simply retain that money. If petitioner's contentions in this case had been rejected, the money would be placed in a fund comprised of frozen Cuban assets, to be distributed equitably among all the American victims of Cuban nationalizations. Ante, at 2602–2603, n. 24. Even though petitioner has suffered a serious injustice at the hands of the Cuban Government, no special equities militate in favor of giving this petitioner a preference over all other victims simply because of its participation in a discrete, completed, commercial transaction involving the sale of a load of Cuban sugar.

(2) which is an organ of a foreign state or political subdivision thereof, or a majority of whose shares or other ownership interest is owned by a foreign state or political subdivision thereof, and

(3) which is neither a citizen of a State of the United States as defined in section 1332(c) and (d) of this title, nor created under the laws of any third country.

* * *

*Notes*

1. The enumeration of entities comprehended within the term "foreign state" is intended to be exhaustive. Consequently, "[a]n entity which does not fall within the definitions of sections 1603(a) or (b) would not be entitled to sovereign immunity in any case before a Federal or State court." Sen.Rep. No. 94–1310, 94th Cong.2d Sess., p. 15 (1976).

2. Whether entities comprehended within the definition of foreign state are entitled to immunity depends on the other provisions of the Act. The scope of entitlement to immunity may depend on whether a foreign state or a political division or an instrumentality or agency thereof is involved. See Section 1610(b).

3. In Edlow Int'l Co. v. Nuklearna Elextrarna Krsko, 441 F.Supp. 827 (D.D.C.1977), an action against a Yugoslavian "workers organization" for brokerage fees in connection with a sale of uranium oxide was dismissed for want of subject matter competence under Section 1330(a) on the ground that the workers organization was not an "agency or instrumentality of a foreign state." Does this decision point up the undesirability of defining subject matter competence by reference to whether immunity is unavailable? See p. 1171 supra. For an analysis of this decision, see 5 B'klyn J.Int'l L. 191 (1979).

4. The question of whether Novosti, a Soviet information agency, came within the definition of "foreign state" was raised in Yessenin–Volpin v. Novosti Press Agency, 443 F.Supp. 849 (D.C.N.Y.1978). The court, stressing the difficulty of applying the Act's definitions under "concepts which exist in socialist states such as the Soviet Union," held that "Novosti is either an organ of the U.S.S.R. or 'owned' by the U.S.S.R."

## SECTION 2. IMMUNITIES OF STATE REPRESENTATIVES

### A. GENERAL PRINCIPLES

The FSIA provides for the immunity of foreign states and political subdivisions and agencies and instrumentalities of a foreign state. According to the legislative history cited in Note 1 above, an entity that is not comprehended within the definitions of these entities given in Sections 1603(a) and (b) is not entitled to sovereign immunity. However, the FSIA does not deal with the sovereign immunity that may be claimed by the foreign officials that are not entities within the FSIA's definitions. To the extent foreign officials are in the diplomatic or consular service of a foreign state, their immunities are prescribed by international agreements, general international law, and local law. If they are state representatives to international organizations, their immunities are regulated by applicable international agreements and local law. But if they are representatives of a foreign state that do not come within any of these categories, the extent of their immunity depends on general international or local law. As the materials that follow will demonstrate, the immunity representatives of foreign states enjoy is a function of the nature of their office and the applicable international agreement or local law.

## CHUIDIAN v. PHILIPPINE NATIONAL BANK

United States Court of Appeals, Ninth Circuit, 1990.
912 F.2d 1095.

Before WALLACE, THOMPSON and O'SCANNLAIN, CIRCUIT JUDGES.

WALLACE, CIRCUIT JUDGE:

Chuidian, a Philippine citizen, sued Daza, a Philippine citizen and an official of the Philippine government, after Daza instructed the Philippine National Bank (Bank) to dishonor a letter of credit issued by the Republic of the Philippines to Chuidian. The district court dismissed for lack of subject matter jurisdiction, and Chuidian timely appeals. We have jurisdiction pursuant to 28 U.S.C. § 1291, and we affirm.

I

Chuidian owns interests in various businesses in California. In 1985, the Philippine Export and Foreign Loan Guarantee Corporation (Guarantee Corporation), an instrumentality of the Republic of the Philippines government under then-President Ferdinand Marcos, sued several of Chuidian's companies in Santa Clara County Superior Court. Chuidian counterclaimed. The parties settled the Santa Clara County litigation in late 1985. As part of the settlement, the Bank, a state-owned bank, issued an irrevocable letter of credit to Chuidian on behalf of the Guarantee Corporation, payable at the Bank's Los Angeles branch.

Shortly thereafter, on February 26, 1986, the government of President Marcos was overthrown, and replaced by the current government of President Corazon Aquino. The new regime formed the Presidential Commission on Good Government (Commission), an executive agency charged with recovering "ill-gotten wealth" accumulated by Marcos and his associates. Philippine Executive Order No. 1, § 2(a) (Feb. 28, 1986). The Commission was given the authority "[t]o enjoin or restrain any actual or threatened commission of acts by any person or entity that may render moot and academic, or frustrate, or otherwise make ineffectual the efforts of the Commission. * * *" *Id.*, § 3(d).

Daza was a duly appointed member of the Commission. In March 1986, acting pursuant to section 3(d) of the executive order, Daza instructed the Bank not to make payment on the letter of credit issued to Chuidian. According to Daza, the Commission suspected that Marcos and Chuidian had entered into a fraudulent settlement of the Santa Clara County litigation to pay off Chuidian for not revealing certain facts about Marcos's involvement in Chuidian's business enterprises. As a result, the Commission wished to examine the propriety of the settlement, and, in order to secure payment in the event of a decision against Chuidian, needed to prevent payment under the letter of credit.

When the Bank, pursuant to Daza's order, refused to make payment under the letter of credit, Chuidian sued the Bank in Los Angeles County Superior Court. The Bank removed the action to federal district court pursuant to 28 U.S.C. § 1441(d). Chuidian later added as defendants Daza and several other individuals, asserting intentional interference in his contractual relations with the Bank.

In an unrelated action, the Guarantee Corporation sought to reopen the Santa Clara County litigation and set aside the settlement giving rise to the letter of credit. Like Daza, the Guarantee Corporation asserted that the settlement was the product of a collusive arrangement between Chuidian and Marcos. The Guarantee Corporation also intervened in Chuidian's suit against Daza, arguing that Chuidian should not recover because the settlement giving rise to the letter of credit was invalid.

After protracted procedural maneuvering, Daza moved to dismiss on grounds of defective service of process and sovereign immunity. Daza also moved for sanctions pursuant to rule 11, Fed.R.Civ.P. The district court granted the motion to dismiss, holding that Daza had sovereign immunity for acts committed in his official capacity as a member of the Commission, and that Chuidian's allegations that Daza had acted beyond his authority lacked merit. The court denied Daza's request for rule 11 sanctions. Chuidian appeals from the dismissal, and Daza cross-appeals from the denial of sanctions.

II

The parties agree that absent a finding of sovereign immunity, the district court had subject matter jurisdiction to consider Chuidian's claims. Nevertheless, because the question is one of first impression in this circuit and is sufficiently in doubt, we determined that it should be considered by us sua sponte.

Chuidian and Daza are both citizens of the Philippines. Therefore, no diversity jurisdiction exists. *See* 28 U.S.C. § 1332. Likewise, Chuidian's underlying claims do not present a federal question. *See* 28 U.S.C. § 1331.

Federal courts have jurisdiction over suits against foreign sovereigns under the Foreign Sovereign Immunity Act, 28 U.S.C. §§ 1602–1611 (Act), even where the parties are not diverse and the underlying claims do not present a federal question. *Verlinden B.V. v. Central Bank of Nigeria,* 461 U.S. 480, 489–94, 103 S.Ct. 1962, 1969–74, 76 L.Ed.2d 81 (1983) (*Verlinden*); 28 U.S.C. § 1330(a). Nevertheless, we do not base our jurisdiction on the Act. To do so would be insufficient for this case because some of the claims presented do not raise an issue of sovereign immunity. For those which do involve sovereign acts, the district court did not rely upon the Act, and the parties dispute whether it applies. We need not resolve this question since a more secure basis for jurisdiction exists which places the entire controversy properly before us without regard to the applicability of 28 U.S.C. § 1330(a).

The claim against Daza's co-defendant, the Bank, is properly in federal court pursuant to 28 U.S.C. § 1441(d). At all relevant times, the Philippine government owned a majority interest in the Bank. Thus, the Bank qualifies as an "agency or instrumentality of a foreign state" under 28 U.S.C. § 1603(b). *See* 28 U.S.C. § 1608(b)(2). Section 1441(d) provides that in any state court action against a foreign state (including an agency or instrumentality of a foreign state), the foreign state may remove the proceeding to federal court. We have not previously considered whether removal pursuant to section 1441(d) transfers the entire action or only the claim against the removing entity. We now decide that jurisdictional issue.

The Fifth Circuit faced an identical question in *Arango v. Guzman Travel Advisors Corp.*, 621 F.2d 1371, 1375 (5th Cir.1980) (*Arango* ). Arango stated a claim against Dominicana, an instrumentality of the government of the Dominican Republic and several private parties. Dominicana removed pursuant to section 1441(d). The Fifth Circuit held that where a sovereign defendant in a multi-party suit removes under section 1441(d), "the entire action against all defendants accompanies it to federal court." *Id.* at 1375. The court relied upon two passages from the legislative history of section 1441(b). First, Congress spoke of removal of "the action" rather than of "the claim," suggesting that removal would not effect a separation of the claims. Second, Congress acknowledged that co-defendants might be involuntarily removed under section 1441(d). "New subsection (d) of section 1441 permits the removal of any such *action* at the discretion of the foreign state, even if there are multiple defendants *and some of these defendants desire not to remove the action.*" H.R.Rep. No. 94–1487, 94th Cong.2d Sess., *reprinted in* 1976 U.S.Code Cong. & Admin.News 6604, 6631 (emphasis added) (House Report). The Fifth Circuit reasoned that such involuntary removal could occur only if section 1441(d) envisioned removal of the entire action. *Arango,* 621 F.2d at 1375.

We agree with the reasoning of the Fifth Circuit and hold that section 1441(d) requires, in the case of a removal by a foreign sovereign, that the federal court initially exercise jurisdiction over claims against co-defendants even if such claims could not otherwise be heard in federal court. Thus, the proper removal by Daza's co-defendant Bank also transferred the claims against Daza to federal court, without regard to whether the Act provides an independent basis for hearing those claims. Therefore, given that the claims were properly in federal court, we next consider whether the Act or some other form of sovereign immunity barred adjudication on the merits.

### III

The central issue in this appeal is whether Daza is entitled to sovereign immunity for acts committed in his official capacity as a member of the Commission. Daza argues that he qualifies as an "agency or instrumentality of a foreign state," 28 U.S.C. § 1603(b), and hence is entitled to immunity pursuant to the Act, 28 U.S.C. § 1604. Chuidian contends either that Daza is not covered by the Act, or, in the alternative, that this case falls within the exceptions to immunity expressly provided by the Act. *See* 28 U.S.C. §§ 1605–07. The government, in a "Statement of Interest of the United States," takes a third position. Under the government's view, Daza is not covered by the Act because he is an individual rather than a corporation or an association, but he is nevertheless entitled to immunity under the general principles of sovereign immunity expressed in the Restatement (Second) of Foreign Relations Law § 66(b).

A.

We initially consider whether the Act applies to an individual such as Daza acting in his official capacity as an employee of a foreign sovereign. Resolution of this issue necessitates a brief recitation of the evolution of the law of sovereign immunity.

* * * According to the Restatement, immunity extended to:

(a) the state itself;

(b) its head of state * * *;

(c) its government or any governmental agency;

(d) its head of government * * *;

(e) its foreign minister * * *;

(f) any other public minister, official, or agent of the state with respect to acts performed in his official capacity if the effect of exercising jurisdiction would be to enforce a rule of law against the state[.]

Restatement (Second), § 66.

In practice, however, the determination of whether a suit was barred under the principles of the Restatement was made not by the courts but by the State Department. * * *

During the 1970s, Congress became concerned that the law of sovereign immunity under the practice of the Tate letter was leaving immunity decisions subject to diplomatic pressures rather than to the rule of law.

* * *

As a result, in 1976 Congress enacted the Act, largely codifying the existing common law of sovereign immunity. The principal change envisioned by the statute was to remove the role of the State Department in determining immunity. Sovereign immunity could be obtained only by the provisions of the Act, and only by the courts interpreting its provisions; "suggestions" from the State Department would no longer constitute binding determinations of immunity. * * *

The Act is "the sole basis for obtaining [subject matter] jurisdiction over a foreign state in our courts." *Argentine Republic v. Amerada Hess Shipping Corp.*, 488 U.S. 428, 109 S.Ct. 683, 688, 102 L.Ed.2d 818 (1989) (*Amerada Hess*); *Liu v. Republic of China*, 892 F.2d 1419, 1424 (9th Cir.1989). Therefore, if Daza is considered a "foreign state" for purposes of the Act, our decision on immunity must be based upon the provisions of that statute.

The Act, 28 U.S.C. § 1603, provides:

For purposes of this chapter—

(a) A "foreign state" * * * includes a political subdivision of a foreign state or an agency or instrumentality of a foreign state as defined in subsection (b).

(b) An "agency or instrumentality of a foreign state" means any entity—

(1) which is a separate legal person, corporate or otherwise, and

(2) which is an organ of a foreign state or political subdivision thereof, or a majority of whose shares or other ownership interest is owned by a foreign state or political subdivision thereof, and

(3) which is neither a citizen of a State of the United States * * * nor created under the laws of any third country.

The government and Chuidian argue that the definition of "agency or instrumentality of a foreign state" in section 1603(b) includes only agencies, ministries, corporations, and other associations, and is not meant to encompass individuals. Such a reading draws some significant support from the legislative history of section 1603(b), which reads in part:

> The first criterion [section 1603(b)(1)] * * * is intended to include a corporation, association, foundation or any other entity which, under the law of the foreign state where it was created, can sue or be sued in its own name * * *.
>
> The second criterion [section 1603(b)(2)] requires that the entity be either an organ of a foreign state * * * or that a majority of the entity's shares or other ownership interest be owned by a foreign state. * * *
>
> As a general matter, entities which meet the definition of an "agency or instrumentality of a foreign state" could assume a variety of forms, including a state trading corporation, a mining enterprise, a transport organization such as a shipping line or airline, a steel company, a central bank, an export association, a governmental procurement agency or a department or ministry * * *.

House Report at 6614.

This language from the House Report indicates that Congress was primarily concerned with *organizations* acting for the foreign state, and may not have expressly contemplated the case of *individuals* acting as sovereign instrumentalities. At least one court has so concluded. *Republic of the Philippines v. Marcos,* 665 F.Supp. 793, 797 (N.D.Cal.1987) (*Marcos*) ("The terminology of [section 1603(b)]—'agency', 'instrumentality', 'entity', 'organ'—makes it clear that the statute is not intended to apply to natural persons.").

Chuidian and the United States thus argue that Daza's immunity cannot be evaluated under the provisions of the Act. Chuidian argues that Daza therefore cannot be granted immunity: the Act provides the sole source of sovereign immunity, and Daza does not qualify under its definition of a foreign state. The government, on the other hand, urges us to apply the pre-Act common law of immunity. In its view, the Act replaces common law only in the context of "foreign states" as defined by section 1603(b); elsewhere—i.e., for entities covered by the common law but not covered by the Act—common law principles remain valid. The government further argues that Daza is immune under the common law principles of the Second Restatement; Chuidian contends that even if the old common law applies, an exception to immunity is applicable.

We are persuaded by neither of these arguments. While section 1603(b) may not explicitly include individuals within its definition of foreign instrumentalities, neither does it expressly exclude them. The terms "agency," "instrumentality," "organ," "entity," and "legal person," while perhaps more readily connoting an organization or collective, do not in their typical legal usage necessarily exclude individuals. Nowhere in the text or legislative history does Congress state that individuals are *not* encompassed within the section 1603(b) definition; indeed, aside from some language which is more commonly associated with the collective, the legislative history does not even hint of an intent to exclude individual officials from the scope of the Act. Such an omission is particularly significant in light of numerous statements that Congress intended the Act to codify the existing common law principles of sovereign immunity. As pointed out above, pre–1976 common law expressly extended immunity to individual officials acting in their official capacity. If in fact the Act does not include such officials, the Act contains a substantial unannounced departure from prior common law.

The most that can be concluded from the preceding discussion is that the Act is ambiguous as to its extension to individual foreign officials. Under such circumstances, we decline to limit its application as urged by Chuidian and the government. We conclude that the consequences of such a limitation, whether they be the loss of immunity urged by Chuidian or the reversion to pre-Act common law as urged by the government, would be entirely inconsistent with the purposes of the Act.

It is generally recognized that a suit against an individual acting in his official capacity is the practical equivalent of a suit against the sovereign directly. *Monell v. Department of Social Services,* 436 U.S. 658, 690 n. 55, 98 S.Ct. 2018, 2035 n. 55, 56 L.Ed.2d 611 (1978) ("[O]fficial-capacity suits generally represent only another way of pleading an action against an entity of which an officer is an agent."); *Morongo Band of Mission Indians v. California State Board of Equalization,* 858 F.2d 1376, 1382 n. 5 (9th Cir.1988) ("A claim alleged against a state officer acting in his official capacity is treated as a claim against the state itself."), *cert. denied,* 488 U.S. 1006, 109 S.Ct. 787, 102 L.Ed.2d 779 (1989). Thus, to take Chuidian's argument first, we cannot infer that Congress, in passing the Act, intended to allow unrestricted suits against individual foreign officials acting in their official capacities. Such a result would amount to a blanket abrogation of foreign sovereign immunity by allowing litigants to accomplish indirectly what the Act barred them from doing directly. It would be illogical to conclude that Congress would have enacted such a sweeping alteration of existing law implicitly and without comment. Moreover, such an interpretation would defeat the purposes of the Act: the statute was intended as a comprehensive codification of immunity and its exceptions. The rule that foreign states can be sued only pursuant to the specific provisions of sections 1605–07 would be vitiated if litigants could avoid immunity simply by recasting the form of their pleadings.

Similarly, we disagree with the government that the Act can reasonably be interpreted to leave intact the pre–1976 common law with respect to foreign officials. Admittedly, such a result would not effect the sweeping changes which would accompany the rule suggested by Chuidian: the government merely proposes that immunity of foreign states be evaluated under the Act and immunity of individuals be evaluated under the (substantially similar) provisions of the Second Restatement. Nevertheless, such a rule would also work to undermine the Act.

The principal distinction between pre–1976 common law practice and post–1976 statutory practice is the role of the State Department. If individual immunity is to be determined in accordance with the Second Restatement, presumably we would once again be required to give conclusive weight to the State Department's determination of whether an individual's activities fall within the traditional exceptions to sovereign immunity. *See Ex Parte Peru,* 318 U.S. at 589, 63 S.Ct. at 800; Restatement (Second) § 69 note 1. As observed previously, there is little practical difference between a suit against a state and a suit against an individual acting in his official capacity. Adopting the rule urged by the government would promote a peculiar variant of forum shopping, especially when the immunity question is unclear. Litigants who doubted the influence and diplomatic ability of their sovereign adversary would choose to proceed against the official, hoping to secure State Department support, while litigants less favorably positioned would be inclined to proceed against the foreign state directly, confronting the Act as interpreted by the courts without the influence of the State Department.

Absent an explicit direction from the statute, we conclude that such a bifurcated approach to sovereign immunity was not intended by the Act. First, every indication shows that Congress intended the Act to be comprehensive, and courts have consistently so interpreted its provisions. *Amerada Hess,* 109 S.Ct. at 688 ("[T]he text and structure of the [Act] demonstrate Congress' intention that the [Act] be the *sole* basis for obtaining jurisdiction over a foreign state in our courts.") (emphasis added). Yet the rule urged by the government would in effect make the statute optional: by artful pleading, litigants would be able to take advantage of the Act's provisions or, alternatively, choose to proceed under the old common law.

Second, a bifurcated interpretation of the Act would be counter to Congress's stated intent of removing the discretionary role of the State Department. *See* House Report at 6605–06. Under the government's interpretation, the pre–1966 common law would apply, in which the State Department had a discretionary role at the option of the litigant. But the Act is clearly intended as a mandatory rather than an optional procedure. To convert it to the latter by allowing suits against individual officials to proceed under the old common law would substantially undermine the force of the statute. There is no showing that Congress intended such a limited effect in passing a supposedly comprehensive codification of foreign sovereign immunity.

Furthermore, no authority supports the continued validity of the pre–1976 common law in light of the Act. Indeed, the American Law Institute recently issued the Restatement (Third) of Foreign Relations Law, superseding the Second Restatement relied upon by the government in this action. The new restatement deletes in its entirety the discussion of the United States common law of sovereign immunity, and substitutes a section analyzing such issues exclusively under the Act. Restatement (Third) of Foreign Relations Law, §§ 451 *et seq.* (1986).

For these reasons, we conclude that Chuidian's suit against Daza for acts committed in his official capacity as a member of the Commission must be analyzed under the framework of the Act. We thus join the majority of courts which have similarly concluded that section 1603(b) can fairly be read to include individuals sued in their official capacity. *Kline v. Kaneko,* 685 F.Supp. 386, 389 (S.D.N.Y.1988) ("The [Act] does apply to individual defendants when they are sued in their official capacity."); *American Bonded Warehouse Co. v. Compagnie Nationale Air France,* 653 F.Supp. 861, 863 (N.D.Ill.1987) ("Defendants Francois Bachelet and Joe Miller, sued in their respective capacities as employees of Air France [an instrumentality of the government of France], are also protected by the [Act]."); *Mueller v. Diggelman,* No. 82 CIV 5513 (S.D.N.Y.1983) (LEXIS, gen-fed library, dist. file) (judges and clerks of foreign court, sued in their official capacities, entitled to immunity under the Act); *Rios v. Marshall,* 530 F.Supp. 351, 371, 374 (S.D.N.Y.1981) (official of British West Indies Central Labour Organization, an instrumentality of the British West Indies, protected under the Act); *but see Marcos,* 665 F.Supp. at 797 (Act not applicable to Philippine solicitor general).

* * *

Affirmed

### *Notes*

1. Is the court in the principal case correct in concluding that a foreign official who cannot be categorized as an agency or instrumentality cannot claim immunity? Note that Section 1603(b), in defining the concepts of agency and instrumentality, speaks of "entity."

2. Does it necessarily follow, as assumed by the court in the principal case, that recognition of immunity outside the scope of the FSIA restores the Department of State to its former role?

3. Should the Restatement (Third) have dealt with the immunity of foreign official generally? Is a member of a foreign royal house entitled to immunity?

4. In 1988, the U.S. Department of State published its Guidance for Law Enforcement Officers with Regard to Personal Rights and Immunities of Foreign Diplomatic and Consular Personnel, 27 I.L.M. 1617 (1988).

5. For a ruling that the successor government could waive the former Philippines president's immunity, see In re Doe, 860 F.2d 40 (2d Cir.1988).

6. President Noriega was ruled to lack immunity notwithstanding his holding a diplomatic passport in United States v. Noriega, 746 F.Supp. 1506 (S.D.Fla.1990).

## ARCAYA v. PÁEZ

United States District Court, Southern District of New York, 1956.
145 F.Supp. 464, aff'd per curiam, 244 F.2d 958 (2d Cir.1957).

DIMOCK, DISTRICT JUDGE. This is a libel action. Plaintiff is a Venezuelan citizen residing in New York. Defendant now moves for summary judgment dismissing the complaint, on the ground of immunity of defendant by virtue of his status as Consul General of Venezuela in New York and his status as permanent representative of Venezuela to the United Nations with the rank of Envoy Extraordinary and Minister Plenipotentiary, and on the further ground that the court lacks jurisdiction of the subject matter because of defendant's status as such permanent representative. * * *

An accredited resident representative to the United Nations, with the rank of Envoy Extraordinary and Minister Plenipotentiary is entitled in the territory of the United States to all privileges and immunities accorded to diplomatic envoys accredited to the United States. * * *

Defendant raises questions of two kinds: the question of jurisdiction of the court over suits against diplomatic representatives and the question of the immunity of diplomatic representatives even though the court may have jurisdiction.

On the question of jurisdiction, the power of the District Court to entertain an action against a consul seems to be conceded, as indeed it must be perforce section 1351 of title 28 of the United States Code. The power to entertain actions against "ambassadors or other public ministers of foreign states * * * not inconsistent with the law of nations" is, however, vested exclusively in the Supreme Court by section 1251.

On the question of immunity, a consul is not immune from suit except when the action is based upon acts which he has committed within the scope of his duties. * * *

An ambassador or minister is, however, absolutely immune from suit even though it be based upon personal transactions. * * *

The court must, of course, determine its own jurisdiction without reference to the views of the Department of State. The questions of the diplomatic status enjoyed by a given defendant and the immunity to be accorded him are, however, questions where a determination of the Department of State is binding upon the court. United States of Mexico v. Schmuck, 293 N.Y. 264, 56 N.E.2d 577.

Having stated these principles, I return to the record in the particular case. The complaint alleges that, while plaintiff was exiled from Venezuela for political reasons, defendant publicized certain Venezuelan newspaper articles therein quoted which reflect unfavorably on the political, professional, social and moral standing of plaintiff. This is alleged to have been accomplished by posting in the consulate, by circularization to its mailing list and by personal distribution to visitors to the consulate and others.

When the action was commenced on March 16, 1956, defendant's only office under the Government of Venezuela was consul general. Nevertheless he communicated with the Venezuelan Ambassador in Washington and, as a result, the Venezuelan Ambassador wrote the Secretary of State a letter, dated April 10, 1956, requesting that the Department of State suggest to this court that the suit should be dismissed upon a plea of immunity on behalf of the Government of Venezuela. By a letter dated three days later, the Minister of Foreign Relations of Venezuela advised defendant, that, by order of the President and by order of that Ministry, defendant had been appointed Alternate Representative of the Delegation of the Republic of Venezuela before the United Nations with a rank of Envoy Extraordinary and Minister Plenipotentiary. * * *

I understand from [a letter of September 17, 1956, from the Legal Adviser to the State Department to the Court] that the questions that the Department undertook to answer were (1) whether subsequent acquisition by defendant of diplomatic status would defeat the court's previously acquired jurisdiction of the subject matter and (2) whether defendant is entitled to all of the privileges and immunities of a representative to the United Nations. The first is answered in the negative and the second in the affirmative.

I do not feel that I ought to accept without examination a determination by the Department of State that the court did not lose any jurisdiction it had theretofore possessed when defendant was appointed representative to the United Nations. The determination that defendant is entitled to the privileges and immunities of the office of representative to the United Nations does, however, conclude me under the doctrine of Matter of United States of Mexico v. Schmuck, 293 N.Y. 264, 56 N.E.2d 577, supra. The question whether the appointment was colorable is therefore no longer open before me.

That leaves for my decision the question (1) whether the court obtained jurisdiction of the subject matter before defendant's appointment as representative and, if so, the question (2) whether jurisdiction was ousted by that appointment and, if not, the question (3) whether defendant has immunity from this suit as consul and, if not, the question (4) whether one of the immunities of a representative to the United Nations is immunity from further prosecution of a suit begun before the acquisition of status as such representative.

The answer to question one, whether the court obtained jurisdiction of the subject matter, must, as I said above, be in the affirmative. Section 1351 of title 28 of the United States Code expressly gives jurisdiction of suits against consuls to the district courts.

The second question, whether that jurisdiction was ousted by defendant's appointment as representative, was correctly answered in the negative by the Legal Adviser to the Department of State. It is true that the jurisdiction of the Supreme Court over suits against ministers is exclusive under section 1251 of title 28 of the United States Code. It is also true that it has been held (although I have some doubt as to the correctness of the ruling) that the bestowal of the *privileges and immunities* of diplomatic envoys upon representatives to the United Nations, by section 15 of the Joint Resolution of August 4, 1947, above quoted, deprives all courts except the Supreme Court of jurisdiction of suits against them. Friedberg v. Santa Cruz, 274 App.Div. 1072, 86 N.Y.S.2d 369. Granting, however, the correctness of that ruling that the Supreme Court alone would have jurisdiction of a suit originally instituted against a representative to the United Nations, the acquisition of that status by a defendant after the district court had obtained jurisdiction of the subject matter of the suit would not oust the district court of jurisdiction. * * *

A question similar to the one now before me was decided by the District Court of Appeals of California, in Earle v. De Besa, 109 Cal.App. 619, 293 P. 885. There, an action had been validly commenced against an alien in the state courts of California. Some time before the trial was concluded, the defendant was appointed Consul General of the Republic of Peru. The defendant thereupon moved to dismiss the complaint on the ground that the state court had no jurisdiction over actions against a consul, citing the forerunner of 28 U.S.C.A. § 1351 which gives exclusive jurisdiction over actions against consuls to the federal courts. The California courts denied the motion, holding that, since valid jurisdiction had been obtained at the commencement of the action, it was not destroyed by a subsequent change of status of the defendant.

I therefore do not believe that defendant's appointment as representative to the United Nations affected the jurisdiction of this court.

The third question, whether defendant was immune when this suit was brought, involves the determination of an issue of fact. The State Department, though requested to suggest this immunity to this court by the Venezuelan Ambassador, merely submitted a copy of his letter without comment. The determination of the question is therefore left to the courts.

As I stated at the beginning of this opinion, a consul is immune from only such suits as are grounded upon transactions within the scope of his official authority. * * *

[A] consul's duties are commercial but * * * they may be enlarged by special authority. To be effective such an enlargement must, however, "be recognized by the government within whose dominions he assumes to exercise it." The Venezuelan Ambassador here asserted such an enlargement in his letter of April 10, 1956, to the Secretary of State. He said:

> "I communicated to Mr. Páez my belief that once the newspapers and the American reading public had been informed of the truth concerning the subject matter of Dr. Arcaya's misrepresentations and concerning Dr. Arcaya's own political history, his baseless complaints and accusations would thenceforth, seen in proper perspective, lose all credibility and news value.
>
> "It was therefore in pursuance of his duties as a responsible agent of the Republic of Venezuela that Mr. Páez wrote a letter to 'The New York Times' published in the issue of March 12, 1956 and it was also pursuant to those duties that he informed appropriate persons concerning information appearing in the Venezuelan newspapers which served to clarify the matters involved in Doctor Arcaya's charges. The Government of Venezuela feels not only that it was within the duties of Mr. Páez to do so but that he would have been remiss in carrying out his official instructions had he failed to do so."

If the alleged enlargement of defendant's duties had been "recognized by the government within whose dominions" it was assumed to be exercised, the Department of State would surely have so advised the court instead of submitting the letter without comment.

I must therefore decide the question whether, on the record before me, the acts with which defendant is charged were within his commercial duties. * * * I can find nothing to indicate that defendant's alleged acts were within the scope of his authority. I must therefore deny defendant's motion for summary judgment dismissing the case insofar as the motion is based upon diplomatic immunity of defendant as consul general.

That leaves the fourth and final question, whether defendant's immunity as a "diplomatic envoy," conferred by virtue of his status as representative to the United Nations under the terms of section 15 of the Joint

Resolution of August 4, 1947, prevents the prosecution of this action against him.

This involves a question which, so far as revealed by the researches of any of those concerned, is novel: where a court has acquired jurisdiction over a defendant, what is its duty when that defendant obtains diplomatic immunity? * * *

In [Magdalena Steam Navigation v. Martin, 2 El. & El. 94, 114] Lord Campbell had occasion to discuss the rationale of diplomatic immunity under the law of nations. There the Envoy Extraordinary and Minister of Plenipotentiary of the Republics of Guatemala and New Granada was sued upon a cause of action which accrued after he had acquired that status. In granting judgment for the defendant, Lord Campbell said, p. 111, "The great principle is to be found in Grotius de Jure Belli et Pacis, 2, c. 18, s. 9, 'Omnis coactio abesse a legato debet' " * * *.

Lord Campbell was * * * of the opinion that the immunity of ambassadors was not limited to freedom from service of process. He regarded the ambassador's protection from the necessity of retaining an attorney in an action for libel, of subpoenaing witnesses for his defense and of personally attending the trial where he might be needed to instruct his legal advisors, as part of the protection to which he was entitled under the law of nations. No one has suggested that any court has ever held otherwise or suggested any good reason why a court should do so.

I am clear therefore that this action should not at present be permitted to proceed against this defendant. I do not believe, however, that the action should be dismissed. If the summons had been served on defendant after he had attained the rank of a diplomatic envoy he would have been the victim of an unlawful act upon which plaintiff could base no rights. Here, however, plaintiff has lawfully served a summons on him. By that act plaintiff obtained at least two valuable rights: the right to prosecute the action without further service of process and the right to prosecute the action despite the subsequent expiration of the period limited for the institution of an action for libel. Must plaintiff lose these rights because of defendant's promotion? I see no reason for such a deprivation. It will not interfere with defendant's efficiency as alternate representative to the United Nations to have the action pend dormant while he fulfills the duties of his new office. If and when defendant loses his status and the immunity that goes with it, plaintiff ought to be allowed to proceed with his action. * * *

The motion is therefore granted to the extent of staying the action for such time and only for such time as defendant retains his status as Alternate Resident Representative of the Republic of Venezuela to the United Nations with the rank of Envoy Extraordinary and Minister Plenipotentiary. * * *

### *Notes*

1. The FSIA does not deal with immunity from jurisdiction of a head of state. This immunity continues to be governed by non-statutory rules. The Restatement (Second), Foreign Relations Law § 66 (1965), extended the sovereign immunity enjoyed by a foreign state to its head and members of its official party. However, the Restatement (Third) does not contain a similar provision. But cf. Restatement (Third) § 464, Comment i and Reporters' Note 13. The State

Department, relying on "international authority" and "international custom," has continued issuing suggestions of immunity for heads of state after enactment of the FSIA. Are the courts free to disregard these suggestions? They have not done so. See, e.g., Psinakis v. Marcos (N.D.Cal.1975), 1975 Dig.U.S.Prac.Int'l 342, 344; Chong Boon Kim v. Kim Young (Haw.Cir.Ct.1963), 58 A.J.I.L. 186. Should the immunity of a head of state be co-extensive with that enjoyed by a state or with that enjoyed by a diplomatic or consular agent? On these problems, see Note, Resolving the Confusion Over Head of State Immunity: The Defined Rights of Kings, 86 Colum.L.Rev. 169 (1986); Note, The Dictator, Drugs and Diplomacy by Indictment: Head–Of–State Immunity in United States v. Noriega, [683 F.Supp. 1373], 4 Conn.J.Int'l L. 729 (1989).

2. In 1986, both Duvalier, then the President of Haiti, and Marcos, then the President of the Philippines, left their countries and took up residence abroad, Duvalier in France and Marcos in the United States. After their departure, actions were brought against them in the United States to recover large amounts assertedly wrongfully taken while they were President. Attachments were laid on assets allegedly owned by them in the United States. Switzerland, in a highly unusual move, instructed Swiss banks temporarily to freeze funds on deposit in the name of Duvalier. The following actions related to Duvalier's assets. The Republic of Haiti v. Crown Charters, Inc. et al., 667 F.Supp. 839 (S.D.Fla.1987); In re Letter of Request for Judicial Assistance from the Tribunal Civil de Port-au-Prince, Republic of Haiti, 669 F.Supp. 403 (S.D.Fla.1987). The United States made available to the new Philippine government a list of assets Marcos had brought with him to Hawaii. Were these actions likely to lead to success? To what extent are the doctrines of immunity from jurisdiction and act-of-state applicable in the premises? Marcos never resigned or was deposed as president. Was he entitled to the immunity of a head of state? Should the opinion of the State Department be regarded as decisive? Cf. Republic of Philippines v. Westinghouse Elec. Corp., 821 F.Supp. 292 (D.N.J.1993).

## B. DIPLOMATIC REPRESENTATIVES

### *HACKWORTH, DIGEST OF INTERNATIONAL LAW*

Vol. 4, pp. 513–14 (1942).

In a letter of March 16, 1906 to the Secretary of Commerce and Labor, Secretary Root said:

> There are many and various reasons why diplomatic agents, whether accredited or not to the United States, should be exempt from the operation of the municipal law at [sic] this country. The first and fundamental reason is the fact that diplomatic agents are universally exempt by well recognized usage incorporated into the Common law of nations, and this nation, bound as it is to observe International Law in its municipal as well as its foreign policy, cannot, if it would, vary a law common to all. * * *
>
> The reason of the immunity of diplomatic agents is clear, namely: that Governments may not be hampered in their foreign relations by the arrest or forcible prevention of the exercise of a duty in the person of a governmental agent or representative. If such agent be offensive and

his conduct is unacceptable to the accredited nation it is proper to request his recall; if the request be not honored he may be in extreme cases escorted to the boundary and thus removed from the country. And rightly, because self-preservation is a matter peculiarly within the province of the injured state, without which its existence is insecure. Of this fact it must be the sole judge: it cannot delegate this discretion or right to any nation however friendly or competent. It likewise follows from the necessity of the case, that the diplomatic agent must have full access to the accrediting state, else he cannot enter upon the performance of his specific duty, and it is equally clear that he must be permitted to return to the home country in the fulfillment of official duty. As to the means best fitted to fulfil these duties the agent must necessarily judge: and of the time required in entering and departing, as well as in the delay necessary to wind up the duties of office after recall, he must likewise judge.

For these universally accepted principles no authority need be cited.

### *Notes*

1. "It is enough that an ambassador has requested immunity, that the State Department has recognized that the person for whom it was requested is entitled to it, and that the Department's recognition has been communicated to the court." Carrera v. Carrera, 84 U.S.App.D.C. 333, 174 F.2d 496, 497 (1949).

The Diplomatic List maintained by the Department of State (the "Blue List") reflects only a ministerial act and not a determination by the executive of a right to immunity. See Trost v. Tompkins, 44 A.2d 226 (Munic.Ct.App.D.C.1945). Cf. also United States v. Dizdar, 581 F.2d 1031 (2d Cir. 1978). Restatement (Third) § 464, Reporters' Note 1. See 22 U.S.C.A. § 254a–e, p. 951 infra, and Haley v. State, 200 Md. 72, 88 A.2d 312 (1952) (immunity denied because official notice of defendant's status had not been communicated to Department of State). The State Department also maintains a "White List" of employees of diplomatic missions. See Carrera v. Carrera, supra; Restatement (Third) § 464, Reporters' Note 1.

Which members of a diplomat's family are entitled to immunity? See O'Keefe, Privileges and Immunities of the Diplomatic Family, 25 Int'l & Comp. L.Q. 329 (1976).

2. In its 1958 articles on diplomatic privileges and immunities, which served as the basis for the Vienna Convention on Diplomatic Relations, the International Law Commission noted that diplomatic privileges and immunities had in the past been justified on the basis of the "extraterritoriality" theory or on the basis of the "representative character" theory. According to the former, the premises of the mission represented a sort of extension of the territory of the sending state; according to the latter, privileges and immunities were based on the idea that the diplomatic mission personified the sending state. The Commission then observed that a "third theory" appeared to be gaining ground in modern times; i.e., the "functional necessity" theory, "which justifies privileges and immunities as being necessary to enable the mission to perform its functions." The Commission stated that it had been guided by this third theory "in solving problems on which practice gave no clear pointers, while also bearing in mind the representative character of the head of the mission and of the mission itself." 2 Ybk.I.L.C. 95 (1958). What is the significance of the "functional necessity" theory to the scope and extent of diplomatic immunities? Does it

imply an obligation on the part of the sending state to waive the immunity of one of its diplomatic agents in situations where it can be established that such waiver would not interfere with the functions of the mission? See Kerley, Some Aspects of the Vienna Conference on Diplomatic Intercourse and Immunities, 56 A.J.I.L. 88, 91–93 (1962). Compare Section 20 of the Convention on the Privileges and Immunities of the United Nations, infra. See Garretson, The Immunities of Representatives of Foreign States, 41 N.Y.U.L.Rev. 67, 71 (1966). For other support for the "functional necessity" theory of diplomatic immunities, see Restatement (Revised) § 464, Comment a; Harvard Research in International Law, Diplomatic Privileges and Immunities, 26 A.J.I.L.Supp. 15, 26 (Introductory Comment) (1932). This theory has become increasingly important as nations increase the size of their delegations, and as the number of nations and organizations appointing diplomats has grown. See Ling, A Comparative Study of the Privileges and Immunities of United Nations Member Representatives and Officials with the Traditional Privileges and Immunities of Diplomatic Agents, 33 Wash. & Lee L.Rev. 91 (1976).

3. Until 1978, diplomatic immunity was provided for by an Act of Congress enacted on April 30, 1790. This legislation extended civil and criminal immunity to all diplomats, diplomatic administrators, their family members and staff. By 1978, this amounted to over 30,000 individuals. The Department of State urged that this law be repealed in favor of legislation which would conform to the narrower provisions of the Vienna Convention on Diplomatic Relations, p. 1202 infra. On Sept. 30, 1978, the 95th Congress acquiesced by enacting Pub.L. 95–393, 92 Stat. 808 which is codified at 22 U.S.C.A. § 254a–e and 28 U.S.C.A. § 1364. See the Diplomatic Relations Act, p. 1204 infra.

4. Diplomatic agents are generally free to travel in the receiving state, subject to restrictions for national security reasons. Vienna Convention on Diplomatic Relations Art. 26. Travel restrictions had been imposed by the U.S.S.R. The United States retaliated, invoking Art. 47(2) of the Convention, which permits retaliation against a state that has interpreted the Convention restrictively. See Restatement (Third) § 464, Reporters' Note 5.

5. On diplomatic immunity generally, see Restatement (Third) §§ 464–66; Satow, Guide to Diplomatic Practice (5th ed. 1979); B. Sen, A Diplomat's Handbook on International Law and Practice (2d ed. 1979); Denza, Diplomatic Law: Commentary on the Vienna Convention on Diplomatic Relations (1976); Brown, Diplomatic Immunity: State Practice Under the Vienna Convention, 37 Int'l & Comp.L.Q. 53 (1988).

## *VIENNA CONVENTION ON DIPLOMATIC RELATIONS*

Signed April 18, 1961.
500 U.N.T.S. 95.

[See Articles 22–41.]

### *Notes*

1. The Convention entered into force on April 24, 1964, after 22 states had deposited instruments of ratification. As of January 1, 1992, 156 states were parties to the convention. For a full account and analysis of the proceedings in the conference that led to the adoption of the convention, see Kerley, Some Aspects of the Vienna Conference on Diplomatic Intercourse and Immunities, 56 A.J.I.L. 88 (1962).

2. Although Article 32(2) of the Vienna Convention provides that waiver "must always be express," it also provides in Article 32(3) that, when a diplomatic agent brings suit, waiver is implied as to a counterclaim directly related to the principal claim. Can the diplomat waive or only his state? See Note, Foreign Relations—Sovereign Immunity—Ambassador Status Is One Factor In Determining Agent's Authority To Waive Immunity. First Fidelity Bank v. Government of Antigua & Barbuda, 877 F.2d 189, 14 Suffolk Transnat'l L.J. 286 (1990). On waiver generally, see Restatement (Third) § 464, Reporters' Note 15.

3. For a study on abuse of diplomatic and consular privileges prompted by the killing of a U.K. policewoman by a member of the Libyan consular staff, see Higgins, U.K. Foreign Affairs Committee Report on the Abuse of Diplomatic Immunities and Privileges: Government Response and Report, 80 A.J.I.L. 135 (1986).

4. On the diplomatic courier and pouch, see 1985 I.L.C.Rep. 83–120, Draft Articles on the Status of the Diplomatic Courier and the Diplomatic Bag Not Accompanied by Diplomatic Courier.

5. In Latin America, there have been a number of instances of granting asylum or refuge in diplomatic missions to political figures who have incurred the disfavor of the state in which the mission is established. The practice of granting diplomatic asylum is the subject of a number of Latin American Conventions on Asylum (Havana, 1928), (Montevideo, 1933), (Caracas, 1954), which provide for asylum only for political refugees and in cases of humanitarian concern. Even in those cases, the asylum may generally be granted only for limited time. The right to grant diplomatic asylum is not recognized by the United States (2 Hackworth 622) or the United Kingdom (2 McNair, International Law Opinions 74–76 (1956)). In the Asylum Case, 1950 I.C.J. 266, the International Court of Justice observed:

> A decision to grant diplomatic asylum involves a derogation from the sovereignty of that State. It withdraws the offender from the jurisdiction of the territorial State and constitutes an intervention in matters which are exclusively within the competence of that State. Such a derogation from territorial sovereignty cannot be recognized unless its legal basis is established in each particular case.

Id. at 274–75. For other portions of the Asylum Case, see p. 72 supra. In 1956, the Department of State authorized the United States Legation in Budapest to grant refuge to Cardinal Mindszenty, threatened by the arrival of Soviet troops. He stayed there for many years. For other instances in which a U.S. Embassy has granted sanctuary to threatened persons, see 1978 Dig. of U.S.Prac. in Int'l L. 568–71; 75 A.J.I.L. 142–47 (1981). For a statement of U.S. policy, see Dep't State Bull., Oct. 1980 p. 50. If a refugee is granted diplomatic asylum, can he be forcibly removed by agents of the territorial state?

For a discussion of the relationship between Art. 41 of the Vienna Convention and the right of the embassy to grant asylum, see Note, Toward Codification of Diplomatic Asylum, 8 N.Y.U.J.Int'l L. & Pol. 435 (1976). See generally Restatement (Third) § 466, Comment b and Reporters' Note 3.

6. In what other ways may host nations protect diplomatic agents? Title 18 U.S.C.A. § 112 provides, in part, that "[w]hoever assaults, strikes, wounds, imprisons, or offers violence to a foreign official, official guest or internationally protected person or makes any other violent attack upon the person or liberty of such person," shall be subject to fine or imprisonment, or both. In addition, the

statute prohibits demonstrations within one hundred feet of foreign government buildings, and makes the destruction or attempted injury to the property of a foreign government or of its officials a felony. The Act extends the jurisdiction of the United States to any offender found within its territory, irrespective of the nationality of the victim or the defendant, or the place where the crime was committed.

7. The U.N. has also been active in this area. On Dec. 14, 1973, the General Assembly adopted The Convention on the Prevention and Punishment of Crimes against Internationally Protected Persons, see 28 GAOR, Supp. 30, U.N.Doc. A/9030 (1973), 28 U.S.T. 1975, T.I.A.S. No. 8532. The Convention has been ratified by a large number of nations, including the U.S., the U.K., and the U.S.S.R.

8. In the Iranian Hostage Case, p. 823 infra, the International Court of Justice granted both specific relief and damages for violation of the relevant provisions of the Vienna Conventions on Diplomatic Relations and on Consular Relations.

9. When the United States invaded Panama, President Noriega sought refuge in the mission of the Vatican in Panama. The United States negotiated with the Vatican emissary the terms of President Noriega's surrender.

## *DIPLOMATIC RELATIONS ACT*

[See 22 U.S.C.A. § 254a–e]

### *Notes*

1. This legislation was enacted on Sept. 30, 1978, and became effective 90 days later. For a discussion of the Act, see Note, 10 Case W.Res.J.I.L. 827 (1978).

2. Local communities sometimes object to the immunities, including the immunity from property taxes, diplomats enjoy. See, e.g., United States v. Glen Cove, 322 F.Supp. 149 (E.D.N.Y.1971), aff'd, 450 F.2d 884 (2d Cir.1971); Note, Immunity of Foreign Consulate Property from Real Property Taxation, 38 Albany L.Rev. 976 (1974).

3. What measures can properly be taken against illegal parking by diplomats? In New York City, the police tow illegally parked cars with diplomatic plates to the City pound, but release them without payment of a fine or a towing charge. Is this permissible under international law and applicable conventions?

4. Persons injured by diplomatic personnel traditionally have been denied relief under United States law. Section 254e directs the Director of the Office of Foreign Missions to require liability insurance of all mission members. This provision must be read in conjunction with 28 U.S.C.A. § 1364, which grants to the district courts competence, without regard to the amount in controversy, over all civil actions brought directly against the diplomats' insurer. Can the insurer require the diplomat to invoke his immunity? See also the Department of State's Regulations on Compulsory Liability Insurance for Diplomatic Missions and Personnel, 22 CFR 151 et seq. (1980), 18 I.L.M. 871 (1979).

5. Section 254c allows the President to extend more or less favorable treatment on the basis of reciprocity. For an example, see Union of Soviet

Socialist Republics—United States: Agreement on Privileges and Immunity of Embassy Staff, 17 I.L.M. 56 (1979).

6. In 1982, Congress adopted the Foreign Missions Act, 22 U.S.C.A. § 4301, authorizing the Secretary of State to determine the treatment to be extended to the mission of a foreign state. See Restatement (Third) § 464, Reporters' Note 5.

*VIENNA CONVENTION ON DIPLOMATIC RELATIONS*

Signed April 18, 1961.
500 U.N.T.S. 95.

* * *

Art. 40. (1) If a diplomatic agent passes through or is in the territory of a third State, which has granted him a passport visa if such visa was necessary, while proceeding to take up or to return to his post, or when returning to his own country, the third State shall accord him inviolability and such other immunities as may be required to ensure his transit or return. The same shall apply in the case of any members of his family enjoying privileges or immunities who are accompanying the diplomatic agent, or travelling separately to join him or to return to their country.

(2) In circumstances similar to those specified in paragraph 1 of this Article, third States shall not hinder the passage of members of the administrative and technical or service staff of a mission, and of members of their families, through their territories.

(3) Third States shall accord to official correspondence and other official communications in transit, including messages in code or cipher, the same freedom and protection as is accorded by the receiving State. They shall accord to diplomatic couriers, who have been granted a passport visa if such visa was necessary, and diplomatic bags in transit the same inviolability and protection as the receiving State is bound to accord.

(4) The obligations of third States under paragraphs 1, 2 and 3 of this Article shall also apply to the persons mentioned respectively in those paragraphs, and to official communications and diplomatic bags, whose presence in the territory of the third State is due to *force majeure.*

* * *

### Note

The immunities of a diplomat while in transit through the territory of a third state have long been the subject of considerable controversy. For a concise summary, see Harvard Research in International Law, Diplomatic Privileges and Immunities, 26 A.J.I.L.Supp. 15, 85–88 (Art. 15) (1932). See also Bergman v. De Sieyes, 170 F.2d 360 (2d Cir.1948) (immunity upheld) (opinion by L. Hand, C.J.). The article recommended by the Harvard Research provided that a third state should permit the transit of a diplomatic agent across its territory for the purpose of traveling to, or from, his post in the receiving state (whether or not the other end of his journey was the territory of the sending state), granting only such privileges and immunities as were necessary to facilitate the transit. These privileges and immunities were subject to the conditions that the third state has recognized the government of the sending state and that it be informed of the agent's official character. Id. Under Article 40 of the Vienna Convention, would the ambassador from the People's Republic of North Korea to Cuba be entitled to passage through the United States in order to take up his post? As a preliminary problem, would North Korea be entitled to claim the benefits of Article 40? See Article 48 which restricts the states eligible to become parties to the Convention to "all states Members of the United Nations or of any of the specialized agencies or parties to the Statute of the International Court of Justice, and * * * [to] any other state invited by the General Assembly of the United Nations to become a party to the Convention." See Hearings Before the Subcommittee of the Committee on Foreign Relations, United States Senate, on Executive H, 88th Cong., 1st Sess. (Vienna Convention on Diplomatic Relations), 89th Cong., 1st Sess. at 30, 64 (1965). If the Swiss ambassador to Cuba were ordered by his government to travel to the Swiss embassy in Ottawa in order to participate in a conference there, would he be entitled to the benefits of Article 40 while in transit through the United States? If the trip to Canada were for personal reasons (e.g., a vacation), would he be entitled to immunity? See United States v. Rosal, 191 F.Supp. 663 (S.D.N.Y.1960).

## C. CONSULS

### *O'CONNELL, INTERNATIONAL LAW*

Vol. II, p. 914 (2d ed. 1970).*

The institution of the consul derives from the practice in medieval Italy of electing a representative from among the foreign merchants resident in a city, and until very recently consular functions were principally commercial and not diplomatic, though judicial jurisdiction over nationals of the consul's State was sometimes vested in consuls, especially in undeveloped countries. Today, however, the distinction between commercial and diplomatic activity is difficult to maintain. Much formal diplomatic negotiation is in fact trade promotion, and much trade promotion leads to diplomatic overtures. This fusion of functions has led inevitably to a fusion of the diplomatic and consular services, so that a career officer may be posted on one tour to an embassy secretariat, on the next to a trade mission, and on the next to a consulate proper. Some embassies make no pretense even of keeping the consular service distinct, and house it in the same building, and to some extent with the same personnel.

Traditionally, consuls were concerned only with commercial and like matters, but in recent times they have come to represent all manner of governmental activity, such as supervising treaty implementation and performing duties with respect to government-owned merchant ships. These functions are not very distinguishable from those of diplomats. * * *

* Footnotes omitted. Reprinted by permission of Sweet & Maxwell, Ltd.

## *VIENNA CONVENTION ON CONSULAR RELATIONS*

Signed at Vienna, April 24, 1963.
596 U.N.T.S. 261, 21 U.S.T. 77, T.I.A.S. No. 6820.

[See Articles 41–55]

### *Note*

The United Nations Conference on Consular Relations adopted, on April 24, 1963, the Vienna Convention on Consular Relations and two optional protocols, one of which provides for settlement of disputes by the International Court of Justice. The Convention entered into force on March 19, 1967. As of January 1, 1992, 138 states, including the United States, had ratified the Convention.

Article 5 of the Convention contains a list of consular functions. These cover a wide spectrum and include, among others, protecting in the receiving state the interests of the sending state and of its nationals; furthering the development of commercial, economic, cultural and scientific relations; ascertaining conditions and developments in the commercial, economic, cultural and scientific life of the receiving state; issuing passports, visas, and travel documents; helping and assisting nationals of the sending state; serving as a notary or civil registrar; assisting nationals in connection with decedents' estates, guardianships for persons lacking legal capacity and representation and preservation of rights before local tribunals; transmitting documents or executing letters rogatory or commissions to take evidence for courts of the sending state; exercising rights of supervision and inspection of vessels and aircraft of the sending state; and extending assistance to such vessels and aircraft and their crews, including conducting investigations and settling disputes.

Article 17 provides that a consular officer may be authorized to perform diplomatic acts without effect upon his consular status. Articles 3 and 70 deal with the performance of consular functions by diplomatic personnel. Other omitted articles deal, *inter alia,* with the appointment and admission of consular officers, the *exequatur* (authorization from the receiving state admitting the head of a consular post to the exercise of his functions, no longer used by the United States), miscellaneous facilities and privileges to be granted by the receiving state, protocol matters, and the termination of consular functions. Article 31, on the inviolability of consular premises, provides that authorities of the receiving state shall not enter "that part of the consular premises which is used exclusively for the purpose of the work of the consular post" except by permission, which may be "assumed" in the case of "fire or other disaster requiring prompt protective action." In 1948, New York police authorities entered the Soviet Consulate General in order to provide medical assistance for, and to investigate the fall from a third-story window of a Soviet national who had refused to return to the Soviet Union. As a consequence of this and other incidents, consular relations between the United States and the Soviet Union were broken off. See Preuss, Consular Immunities: The Kasenkina Case, 43 A.J.I.L. 37 (1949), and compare Article 17 of the Consular Convention between the United States and the Soviet Union, p. 1209 infra. Article 31 of the Vienna Convention further provides that the consular premises and furnishings, as well as other post property, "shall be immune from any form of requisition for purposes of national defense or public utility," but then states that "if expropriation is necessary for such purposes," all possible steps shall be taken not to impede consular functions and that "prompt, adequate and effective compensation" shall be paid to the sending state. The latter clause was not included in the International Law Commission draft articles, and the reason for its addition by the Conference is not clear. It has been stated that "[t]he trend before 1948 was to grant absolute consular immunity from military requisition and expropriation, irrespective of considerations of military defense or public utility," but that since World War II there are indications that expropriation or requisition of consular property may be permissible under conditions similar to those stated in Article 31 of the Vienna Convention. Lee, Consular Law and Practice 283–84 (1961). The United States broke off consular relations with Communist China in 1950 when the latter requisitioned certain property serving as United States consular premises. 22 Dep't State Bull. 119 (1950). The United States resumed diplomatic relations with Communist China in 1979.

## ARCAYA v. PÁEZ

[See p. 1195 supra]

### *Notes*

1. Shortly after the decision in the *Arcaya Case,* the Secretary of State informed the chiefs of foreign missions in the United States that:

> It has appeared to the Government of the United States that the functions and status of consular officers and employees, as determined by international law and practice and applicable treaties, are essentially incompatible with the functions and status of principal representatives to the United Nations and members of their staffs entitled to diplomatic privileges and immunities under the Headquarters Agreement between the United States and the United Nations, signed June 26, 1947.
>
> The Chiefs of Mission are accordingly advised that hereafter the Government of the United States must decline to recognize, in a consular capacity, or in any other non-diplomatic capacity, any person who is entitled to diplomatic immunity pursuant to Section 15 of the above-mentioned Headquarters Agreement. In the case of the several Governments who presently have one or more of their representatives in the United States recognized in a consular capacity and also accredited to the United Nations pursuant to Section 15 of the above-mentioned Headquarters Agreement, the Secretary of State would appreciate being advised, as soon as possible, whether the Government concerned prefers that the individual's exequatur or other consular recognition be revoked, or prefers to terminate, by appropriate notification to the Secretary General, his accreditation to the United Nations. * * *
>
> The Government of the United States will continue to recognize, in a dual capacity, members of diplomatic missions in Washington who also perform consular functions. The Government of the United States will also accept as consular officers and employees persons who from time to time may perform functions and duties in connection with their government's representation to the United Nations, provided that such officers and employees do not thereby become entitled to claim diplomatic immunity.

Dep't of State Circular of January 16, 1958, quoted in Lee at 190–91.

2. For a comparison of diplomatic and consular immunities, see Restatement (Third) § 466, Comment *a* and Reporters' Note 1. The principal difference is that consular personnel enjoy immunity only in regard to their official acts, while diplomatic personnel enjoy personal immunity. The State Department normally leaves to the court whether an act was done in the performance of official consular functions. The United States has bilateral consular conventions with a large number of countries. For a partial listing, and a brief discussion of their terms, see Restatement (Third) § 465, Reporters' Note 3.

3. As pointed out by the court in Arcaya v. Páez, p. 1195 supra, all civil actions and proceedings brought in the United States against consuls or vice consuls of foreign states must be brought in the federal district courts. 28 U.S.C.A. § 1351. The Supreme Court has held, however, that divorce proceedings may be brought against consuls in the state courts. Ohio ex rel. Popovici v. Agler, 280 U.S. 379, 50 S.Ct. 154, 74 L.Ed. 489 (1930). Until 1978, 28 U.S.C.A. § 1351, as it then read, was construed to render only the federal courts competent to hear cases against consular personnel. As a consequence, since the federal courts do not hear cases under state criminal law, consular personnel were in fact immune from prosecution under state law. This situation was changed when Congress, by the Diplomatic Relations Act of 1978, amended 28 U.S.C.A. § 1351 to make clear that it provided for exclusive federal competence only in civil cases. This statutory provision does not apply to members of the family of consular personnel. They remain subject to normal federal and state rules of judicial competence.

## *CONSULAR CONVENTION BETWEEN THE UNITED STATES AND THE UNION OF SOVIET SOCIALIST REPUBLICS*

Signed at Moscow, June 1, 1964.
19 U.S.T. 5018, T.I.A.S. No. 6570.

* * *

Art. 17. The consular archives shall be inviolable at all times and wherever they may be. Unofficial papers shall not be kept in the consular archives.

The buildings or parts of buildings and the land ancillary thereto, used for the purposes of the consular establishment and the residence of the head of the consular establishment, shall be inviolable.

The police and other authorities of the receiving state may not enter the building or that part of the building which is used for the purposes of the consular establishment or the residence of the head of the consular establishment without the consent of the head thereof, persons appointed by him, or the head of the diplomatic mission of the sending state.

Art. 18. (1) The consular establishment shall have the right to communicate with its Government, with the diplomatic mission and the consular establishments of the sending state in the receiving state, or with other diplomatic missions and consular establishments of the sending state, making use of all ordinary means of communication. In such communications, the consular establishment shall have the right to use code, diplomatic couriers, and the diplomatic pouch. The same fees shall apply to consular establishments in the use of ordinary means of communication as apply to the diplomatic mission of the sending state.

(2) The official correspondence of a consular establishment, regardless of what means of communication are used, and the sealed diplomatic pouch bearing visible external marks of its official character, shall be inviolable and not subject to examination or detention by the authorities of the receiving state.

Art. 19. (1) Consular officers shall not be subject to the jurisdiction of the receiving state in matters relating to their official activity. The same applies to employees of the consular establishment, if they are nationals of the sending state.

(2) Consular officers and employees of the consular establishment who are nationals of the sending state shall enjoy immunity from the criminal jurisdiction of the receiving state.

(3) This immunity from the criminal jurisdiction of the receiving state of consular officers and employees of the consular establishment of the sending state may be waived by the sending state. Waiver must always be express.

* * *

### *Notes*

1. In what important respects do the immunity provisions of the United States–Soviet Union Consular Convention differ from corresponding articles of the Vienna Convention, supra? See the Report of the Senate Committee on Foreign Relations on the Consular Convention with the Soviet Union, S.Exec. Doc. No. 4, 89th Cong., 1st Sess. (1965), and compare the Minority Report, id. at 2. After a long struggle between proponents and opponents of the Convention, the Senate gave its advice and consent, on March 16, 1967, to ratification by the United States. 56 Dep't State Bull. 545 (1967). See the Secretary of State's news conference of May 27, 1966, 54 id. 918 (1966), and his statement before the Senate Committee on Foreign Relations on January 23, 1967, 56 id. 247 (1967). The Convention entered into force on July 13, 1968, 59 id. 32 (1968). For an analysis of the convention, see Lay, The United States–Soviet Consular Convention, 59 A.J.I.L. 876 (1965); Note, Soviet Consular Convention: Post–Vienna, 10 Harv. Int'l L.J. 360 (1969).

2. Consular conventions have also been concluded between the United States and Hungary, July 6, 1973, 24 U.S.T. 1141, T.I.A.S. No. 7641 and between the United States and Poland, July 6, 1973, 24 U.S.T. 1231, T.I.A.S. No. 2642. The Soviet Union and other Communist states were especially active during the last two decades in concluding consular treaties, both among themselves and with other states. For a description and analysis of trends in consular law and practice, including bilateral treaty developments, see Lee, Consular Law and Practice 303–23 (1961).

## D. SPECIAL MISSIONS

In adopting a set of draft articles on diplomatic intercourse and immunities, the International Law Commission observed, in 1958, that these dealt only with permanent diplomatic missions and that it was desirable as well to clarify the status of "itinerant envoys, diplomatic conferences and special missions sent to a State for limited purposes." In 1960, the Commission adopted a preliminary set of draft articles on special missions and recommended that these be referred to the forthcoming Vienna Conference on Diplomatic Intercourse and Immunities. The Conference, however, decided that the draft articles were unsuitable for inclusion in the Vienna Convention and referred the articles back to the General Assembly, which in turn requested the International Law Commission to undertake further study of the problem. The Commission considered a revised draft and reexamined it in the light of comments from member states. See Report of the International Law Commission, 22 GAOR, Supp. No. 9 (A/6709/Rev. 1), at 2–4. On Dec. 8, 1969, the General Assembly approved a Convention on Special Missions, see G.A.Res 2530 (XXIV 1970) at 99. The Convention entered into force on June 21, 1985. As of December 31, 1991, the United States had not become a party but there were 13 signatories and 25 parties to the Convention.

The Restatement (Third), in contrast to its predecessor, does not contain a provision recognizing that an official representative of a foreign state on special mission enjoys immunity to the extent required by the performance of his official duties. This immunity is now covered by the general provision on diplomatic immunity. See Restatement (Third) § 464, Comment i and Reporters' Note 13.

## E. REPRESENTATIVES TO INTERNATIONAL ORGANIZATIONS

### *CONVENTION ON THE PRIVILEGES AND IMMUNITIES OF THE UNITED NATIONS*

Adopted by the General Assembly, February 13, 1946.
1 U.N.T.S. 15, 21 U.S.T. 1418, T.I.A.S. No. 6900.

* * *

Art. IV. § 11. Representatives of Members to the principal and subsidiary organs of the United Nations and to conferences convened by the United Nations, shall, while exercising their functions and during the journey to and from the place of meeting, enjoy the following privileges and immunities:

(a) Immunity from personal arrest or detention and from seizure of their personal baggage, and, in respect of words spoken or written and all acts done by them in their capacity as representatives, immunity from legal process of every kind;

(b) Inviolability for all papers and documents;

(c) The right to use codes and to receive papers or correspondence by courier or in sealed bags;

(d) Exemption in respect of themselves and their spouses from immigration restrictions, aliens registration or national service obligations in the state they are visiting or through which they are passing in the exercise of their functions;

(e) The same facilities in respect of currency or exchange restrictions as are accorded to representatives of foreign governments on temporary official missions;

(f) The same immunities and facilities in respect of their personal baggage as are accorded to diplomatic envoys, and also;

(g) Such other privileges, immunities and facilities not inconsistent with the foregoing as diplomatic envoys enjoy, except that they shall have no right to claim exemption from customs duties on goods imported (otherwise than as part of their personal baggage) or from excise duties or sales taxes.

§ 12. In order to secure, for the representatives of Members to the principal and subsidiary organs of the United Nations and to conferences convened by the United Nations, complete freedom of speech and independence in the discharge of their duties, the immunity from legal process in respect of words spoken or written and all acts done by them in discharging their duties shall continue to be accorded, notwithstanding that the persons concerned are no longer the representatives of Members.

* * *

§ 14. Privileges and immunities are accorded to the representatives of Members not for the personal benefit of the individuals themselves, but in order to safeguard the independent exercise of their functions in connection with the United Nations. Consequently a Member not only has the right but is under a duty to waive the immunity of its representative in any case where in the opinion of the Member the immunity would impede the course of justice, and it can be waived without prejudice to the purpose for which the immunity is accorded.

§ 15. The provisions of Sections 11, 12 * * * are not applicable as between a representative and the authorities of the state of which he is a national or of which he is or has been the representative.

§ 16. In this article the expression "representatives" shall be deemed to include all delegates, deputy delegates, advisers, technical experts and secretaries of delegations.

* * *

## *Notes*

1. As of January 1, 1992, one hundred and twenty-seven states were parties to the Convention on the Privileges and Immunities of the United Nations. For the states that are parties, see the Multilateral Treaties List of Signatures, Ratifications, Accessions, Etc., ST./LEG/SER. D/12, p. 35. The United States ratified the Convention in 1970.

2. Section 15 of Article V of the Agreement between the United Nations and the United States Regarding the Headquarters of the United Nations, 61 Stat. 3416, T.I.A.S. No. 1676, 11 U.N.T.S. 11, provides as follows:

(1) Every person designated by a Member as the principal resident representative to the United Nations of such Member or as a resident representative with the rank of ambassador or minister plenipotentiary,

(2) such resident members of their staffs as may be agreed upon between the Secretary–General, the Government of the United States and the Government of the Member concerned,

(3) every person designated by a Member of a specialized agency, as defined in Article 57, paragraph 2, of the Charter, as its principal resident representative, with the rank of ambassador or minister plenipotentiary, at the headquarters of such agency in the United States, and

(4) such other principal resident representatives of Members to a specialized agency and such resident members of the staffs of representatives of a specialized agency as may be agreed upon between the principal executive officer of the specialized agency, the Government of the United States and the Government of the Member concerned,

shall, whether residing inside or outside the headquarters district, be entitled in the territory of the United States to the same privileges and immunities, subject to corresponding conditions and obligations, as it accords to diplomatic envoys accredited to it. In the case of Members whose governments are not recognized by the United States, such privileges and immunities need be extended to such representatives, or persons on the staffs of such representatives, only within the headquarters district, at their residences and offices outside the district, in transit between the district and such residences and offices, and in transit on official business to or from foreign countries.

The United States insists that it may control the entry of aliens into the United States to safeguard its security. See Note 4, p. 1218 infra. The United States has in fact limited some representatives to a 25 mile radius over the objections by their states. See Restatement (Third) § 470, Reporters' Note 2.

3. In 1986, the United States informed the U.S.S.R. that it would have to reduce the number of members of its mission, and those of Ukraine and Byelorussia, to the United Nations. The U.N. Secretary General referred the dispute to the appropriate U.N. Committee. It would appear to be covered by Article 15(2) of the Headquarters Agreement, Note 2 supra. If the dispute had arisen between the United States and the United Nations, it would have been subject to compulsory arbitration under Article 21 of the Headquarters Agreement.

4. Section 7(b) of the International Organizations Immunities Act, 22 U.S.C.A. § 288d(b), infra, accords representatives to international organizations, as well as officers and employees of such organizations, immunity "from suit and legal process relating to acts performed by them in their official capacity and falling within their functions as such representatives, officers, or employees."

On the immunities of representatives to international organizations, see generally Restatement (Third) § 470; Gross, Immunities and Privileges of Delegations to the United Nations, 16 Int'l Org. 483 (1962); Ling, Comparative Study of The Privileges and Immunities of UN Member Representatives and Officials with the Traditional Privileges and Immunities of Diplomatic Agents, 33 Wash. & Lee L.Rev. 91 (1976); Amerasinghe, Liability To Third Parties Of Member States Of International Organizations: Practice, Principle, and Judicial Precedent, 85 A.J.I.L. 259 (1991).

5. The privileges and immunities of member representatives to international organizations are treated in the Vienna Convention on the Representation of States in Their Relations with International Organizations of a Universal Character, U.N.Doc. No. A/CONF. 67/16, March 14, 1975, which has not yet entered into force. The United States abstained on the vote on the final text on the

ground that the Convention would unduly expand privileges and immunities. See 1975 Dig.U.S.Prac. 38–40.

6. Is a representative to the United Nations entitled to the privileges and immunities of a diplomat *in transitu* while he travels to and from the Headquarters District? Does a comparison of the Vienna Convention with the Headquarters Agreement and the International Organizations Immunities Act, p. 1217 infra, reveal any significant advantages enjoyed by diplomatic agents in transit through the United States over representatives to the United Nations? See Hearings Before the Subcommittee of the Senate Committee on Foreign Relations, on Executive H, 88th Cong., 1st Session (Vienna Convention on Diplomatic Relations), 89th Cong., 1st Sess. at 15–16 (1965).

7. 28 U.S.C.A. § 1351, as amended by the Diplomatic Relations Act of 1978, gives the district courts exclusive original competence over all civil actions against diplomatic personnel. It is apparently intended also to cover members to missions to international organizations, such as the United Nations and the Organization of American States. See Restatement (Third) § 470, Reporters' Note 4.

8. A number of decisions by American courts have given effect to the immunity from legal process of representatives to international organizations. See, e.g., Anonymous v. Anonymous, 44 Misc.2d 14, 252 N.Y.S.2d 913 (N.Y.Family Ct.1964) and cases cited in Restatement (Third) § 470, Reporters' Note 2.

## SECTION 3. IMMUNITIES OF INTERNATIONAL ORGANIZATIONS, THEIR AGENTS, OFFICIALS, AND INVITEES

The modern law relating to the immunities of international organizations has developed principally from the experience of the League of Nations and the International Labor Organization, although some aspects of its origin can be traced back into the nineteenth century. This body of law began as little more than "a general principle resting on the questionable analogy of diplomatic immunities; it has become a complex body of rules set forth in detail in conventions, agreements, statutes and regulations." Jenks, International Immunities XXXV (1961). As the scope and importance of the activities of international organizations have increased in the postwar world, so have the extent and significance of their immunities and those of their officials. The bases for their immunities differ in important respects from those for the granting of jurisdictional immunities to foreign states. Like states, international organizations require jurisdictional immunities in order to carry on their functions without interference from municipal courts and administrators; unlike states, however, international organizations do not enjoy a long history of respect for their authority or the means of taking reciprocal reprisals against infringements of that authority. Two main questions are raised in the following materials: In what essential respects do the immunities of international organizations differ from those of states? To what extent is the trend towards limiting the immunities of states likely to apply to international organizations? As a corollary to the latter question, what procedures and practices can organizations adopt that will forestall abuse and consequent criticism and curtailment of their immunities?

## *CONVENTION ON THE PRIVILEGES AND IMMUNITIES OF THE UNITED NATIONS*

Adopted by the General Assembly, February 13, 1946.
1 U.N.T.S. 15, 21 U.S.T. 1418, T.I.A.S. No. 6900.

[See Articles II and V]

### *Notes*

1. In an *Aide-Mémoire* to the Permanent Representative of a Member State of October 27, 1963, the Secretary General of the United Nations gave the following legal opinion concerning the proposed accession by that State to the Convention subject to a reservation denying to any United Nations official (or an expert on mission for the United Nations) of that state's nationality any privilege or immunity under the Convention, 1963 U.N. Jur'l Yb. 188:

> 1. * * *.
>
> 2. In the opinion of the Secretary-General, a closer examination of the true legal operation of this reservation, as so interpreted, will leave no doubt that it is incompatible with the United Nations Charter. * * *
>
> 3. Numerous privileges and immunities specified in article V are not ordinarily understood to have practical application as between an official of the United Nations and his Government of nationality. Such an official will have no occasion, unless in rare circumstances, to require immunity from immigration restrictions in his own country, or privileges in respect of exchange facilities, or repatriation facilities in time of international crisis; he cannot by definition require immunity from alien registration, and it would be exceptional for him to have reason to claim duty-free entry for his personal effects on taking up his post in the country.
>
> 4. The situation is quite otherwise in the matter of his official acts, and it is here that the reservation cannot be reconciled with the Charter. Section 18(*a*) in article V requires that officials of the United Nations be "immune from legal process in respect of words spoken or written and all acts performed by them in *their official capacity*" (emphasis supplied). It follows that your country, in proposing the reservation quoted above, has (no doubt unintentionally) reserved the right to prosecute United Nations officials of its nationality for words spoken or written or for any acts performed by them in their official capacity, indeed for actions which are in effect the acts of the Organization itself. It would equally be the consequence of the reservation that your country would be reserving jurisdiction to its national courts to entertain private lawsuits against its citizens for acts performed by them as officials of the United Nations.
>
> 5. Article 105 of the Charter provides in its second paragraph that officials of the Organization shall "enjoy such privileges and immunities as are necessary for the independent exercise of their functions in connection with the Organization." Likewise, by the second paragraph of Article 100 each Member of the United Nations "undertakes to respect the exclusively international character of the responsibilities of the Secretary-General and the staff." It needs no argument to demonstrate that the reservation by a Member of the right, even in the abstract, to exercise jurisdiction over the official acts of the United Nations staff, either through its courts or through

other organs or authorities of the State, would be incompatible with the independent exercise and exclusively international character of the responsibilities of such officials of the Organization. This derogation from the clear terms of the Charter would in no way be affected by the common nationality of the international official and the prosecuting authority. The Secretary-General cannot believe that the legal effect of the reservation in question, although indisputable when examined in this light, was consciously intended.

2. Absent special agreement or legislation in each Member State, would the United Nations be entitled to the privileges and immunities of Article 105 of the Charter?

Before the United States acceded to the Convention in 1970, were the substantive obligations of the Convention nonetheless binding on the United States? The Legal Counsel, speaking as the representative of the Secretary-General of the United Nations, stated in 1968:

> With regard to the legal framework of the regime of privileges and immunities of the United Nations, * * * in the first place, Article 105 of the Charter accorded such privileges and immunities as were "necessary." By paragraphs 1 and 2, it imposed an obligation on all Members of the United Nations to accord such privileges and immunities as were necessary for the fulfillment of the purposes of the Organization or for the independent exercise of the functions of representatives and officials, irrespective of whether or not they had acceded to the Convention. In accordance with paragraph 3, the purpose of the Convention was merely to determine the details of the application of the first two paragraphs of the same Article. In the second place, the Convention, in determining the details of certain privileges and immunities, in effect provided the minimum privileges and immunities which the Organization required in all Member States. Additional privileges and immunities necessary for special situations, such as at the Headquarters in New York or for peace-keeping or development missions in various areas of the world, were provided for by special agreements. In the third place, ninety-six Member States had acceded to the Convention while, in most of the remaining Member States as well as in some non-member States, the provisions of the Convention had been made applicable by special agreements. It could thus be said that in the nearly twenty-two years since the adoption of the Convention by the General Assembly, the standards and principles of the Convention had been so widely accepted that they had now become a part of the general international law governing the relations of States and the United Nations.

Annual Report of the Secretary-General, 23 GAOR, Supp. 1 (A/7201), at 208–09 (1968) (summary record).

As of December 31, 1991, 96 States, but not the United States, had acceded to the companion Convention on the Privileges and Immunities of the Specialized Agencies, adopted by the General Assembly on November 21, 1947, 33 U.N.T.S. 261, which provides in detail for the immunities of organizations related to the United Nations under Articles 57 and 63 of the Charter. The constitutions of many of these organizations, however, provide themselves for some degree of immunity, as do the constituent instruments of many non-related organizations. See, e.g., Article 16 of the Constitution of the Food and Agriculture Organization, T.I.A.S. No. 4803, and the other provisions cited in Jenks, International Immunities 3–5 (1961). What might account for the United States' failure to accede to this convention on privileges and immunities? See the provisions of the International Organizations Immunities Act, p. 1217 infra, and the Headquarters Agreement, p. 1212 supra.

3. Unlike the Charter, the Covenant of the League of Nations provided only for the immunity of League officials (in addition to representatives of members of the League), who were to be entitled to "diplomatic privileges and immunities" when they were "engaged on the business of the League." The only protection intended for the League itself was a provision that League property was to be "inviolable." Covenant, Art. 7(4), (5). On the relevance of the experience of the League and the International Labour Organisation to the development of the immunities of the United Nations and other postwar organizations, see Jenks at 12–16. A *modus vivendi* was entered into by the League and the Swiss Federal Government on September 18, 1926, by which Switzerland recognized that the League possessed international personality and legal capacity and that it could not "in principle, according to the rules of international law, be sued before the Swiss Courts without its express consent." The archives and premises of the League were recognized as inviolable, and certain customs and fiscal exemptions were granted. In addition, the League's staff was granted certain immunities from Swiss civil and criminal jurisdiction. See Hill, Immunities and Privileges of Officials of the League of Nations 14–23, 138–98 (1947).

4. The Permanent Court of International Justice began to sit at The Hague in 1922. The government of the Netherlands gave effect to the immunities and privileges of the judges envisaged by Article 19 of the Court's Statute and to the immunities and privileges of Court officials envisaged by Article 7(4) of the Covenant in a series of regulations; these were replaced in 1928 by an agreement between the Dutch Foreign Minister and the President of the Court, in which judges and officials continued to be assimilated to corresponding diplomatic representatives and officials. Hill at 21–23; see generally id. at 50–57, and the 1928 Agreement and supplementary rules, id. at 199–202 (Annex III), 1 Hudson, International Legislation 597 (1931). On the status of the International Court of Justice, see Articles 19, 32(8), and 42(3) of the Statute, the site agreement between the Netherlands and the President of the Court, 8 U.N.T.S. 61, and the recommendations contained in the General Assembly Resolution 90, U.N.Doc.A/64/Add. 1 at 176–79 (1946). The Court as an institution continues to be assimilated to the diplomatic corps. For discussion, see 5 Repertory of Practice of United Nations Organs 362–66 (1955); Jenks at 93–95. The privileges and immunities of other international tribunals, including the European Court of Human Rights and the Court of Justice of the European Communities, are discussed id. at 95–101.

5. The immunities of international organizations and their officials and premises, archives, documents and communications are treated in Restatement (Third) § 467–470. On these immunities generally, see Jenks, International Immunities (1961) and Bowett, The Law of International Institutions (3d ed. 1975).

## *INTERNATIONAL ORGANIZATIONS IMMUNITIES ACT*

[See 22 U.S.C.A. § 288a–e]

### *Notes*

1. For the international organizations designated as entitled to the benefits of the International Organizations Immunities Act, see the table following 22

U.S.C.A. § 288, supplemented by executive orders appearing in current issues of the Federal Register and in supplementary volumes of Title 3 of the Code of Federal Regulations.

2. 22 U.S.C.A. §§ 288(f)(1)–288(f)(2) authorize the President to extend to the European Space Research Organization and the Organization of Eastern Caribbean States as well as to the Organization of African Unity respectively the privileges of the International Organizations Immunities Act. 22 U.S.C.A. §§ 288(g)–288(i) permit the extension of the privileges and immunities enjoyed by accredited diplomatic missions to the Organization of American States, the Commission of European Communities, and the Liaison Office of the People's Republic of China.

3. Legislation concerning the legal status, privileges and immunities of the United Nations and the specialized agencies, as well as of other international organizations, has been enacted in many states. See the statutes, regulations and other instruments collected in Legislative Texts and Treaty Provisions concerning the Legal Status, Privileges and Immunities of International Organizations, ST./LEG/SER.B/10, 11 (1959, 1961), as supplemented by extracts reproduced in successive issues, beginning in 1962, of the United Nations Juridical Yearbook. Legislation has been enacted in the United Kingdom that is comparable in scope to that of the United States. See the International Organizations (Immunities and Privileges) Act, 1950 (14 Geo. 6, c. 14), and 7 Halsbury's Laws of England § 586 for the organizations designated by Order in Council as entitled to the benefits of the Act. For a case applying the Act, see Zoernsch v. Waldock, [1964] 2 All E.R. 256 (C.A.) (suit against a member and the secretary of the European Commission of Human Rights for alleged "negligence and corruption in running the business * * * of the Commission * * *").

4. Problems concerning the immunities and privileges of international organizations are particularly likely to arise in those states in which the organizations have their headquarters, or in which they carry on extensive activities. The "Headquarters Agreement" between the United States and the United Nations was authorized by Congress on August 4, 1947, 61 Stat. 756, and entered into force on November 21, 1947, T.I.A.S. No. 1676, 61 Stat. 3416. In addition to provisions concerning the privileges and immunities of representatives of members of the United Nations, discussed at supra, the Headquarters Agreement contains the following Article guaranteeing the communication and transit privileges of the Organization, its officials, and representatives of members:

> Art. IV. § 11. The federal, state or local authorities of the United States shall not impose any impediments to transit to or from the headquarters district of (1) representatives of Members or officials of the United Nations, or of specialized agencies as defined in Article 57, paragraph 2, of the Charter, or the families of such representatives or officials, (2) experts performing missions for the United Nations or for such specialized agencies, (3) representatives of the press, or of radio, film or other information agencies, who have been accredited by the United Nations (or by such a specialized agency) in its discretion after consultation with the United States, (4) representatives of non-governmental organizations recognized by the United Nations for the purpose of consultation under Article 71 of the Charter, or (5) other persons invited to the headquarters district by the United Nations or by such specialized agency on official business. The appropriate American authorities shall afford any necessary protection to

such persons while in transit to or from the headquarters district. This section * * * does not impair the effectiveness of generally applicable laws and regulations as to the operation of means of transportation.

§ 12. The provisions of Section 11 shall be applicable irrespective of the relations existing between the Governments of the persons referred to in that section and the Government of the United States.

In the joint resolution, which authorized the President to conclude the Headquarters Agreement, it was provided in Section 6 (61 Stat. at 767) that nothing in the agreement should be construed as "in any way diminishing, abridging, or weakening the right of the United States to safeguard its own security and completely to control the entrance of aliens into any territory of the United States other than the headquarters district and its immediate vicinity, * * * and such areas as it is reasonably necessary to traverse in transit between the same and foreign countries." For the 1953 dispute involving the application of this provision by the United States, see infra.

Article III of the Agreement (§§ 7–10) deals with "Law and Authority in the Headquarters District." The Headquarters District is itself inviolable, and United States officials may not enter the district in order to perform official duties, nor may legal process be served there, without the consent of the Secretary–General, but the United Nations is obligated to prevent the Headquarters District from becoming a refuge (§ 9). Federal, state and local law apply within the district (§ 7), except insofar as inconsistent with United Nations regulations made "for the purpose of establishing therein conditions in all respects necessary for the full exercise of its [the Organization's] functions" (§ 8). The United Nations is given no enforcement jurisdiction other than that inherent in its power to deny entry to or expel persons from the District (§ 10). For a discussion and summary of regulations promulgated by the U.N., pursuant to the Headquarters Agreement, see 5 Rep'y of Practice of United Nations Organs 340–42 (1955). See People v. Coumatos, 224 N.Y.S.2d 504 (Gen.Sess.N.Y.Co.1961), 507 (1962) (prosecution for grand larceny committed by United Nations employee in Headquarters District; held, defendant not entitled to immunity, and New York law applicable within District in absence of inconsistent United Nations regulations). The United States has also concluded a headquarters agreement with the Organization of American States (181 U.N.T.S. 147), and Switzerland has such agreements with a large number of organizations. See Jenks, International Immunities 7 (1961). The United Nations has concluded a number of special headquarters agreements on behalf of its economic commissions, political missions (such as those in Korea, Egypt, Lebanon, Jordan, and the Congo), and technical assistance missions in various countries. See id. at 8–10. Numerous agreements have also been concluded in connection with the stationing of United Nations forces. See supra.

5. How do the privileges and immunities of the United Nations in the United States, as contained in the International Organizations Immunities Act and in the Headquarters Agreement, compare to those specified in the Convention on the Privileges and Immunities of the United Nations, supra? To what extent does the immunity enjoyed by the United Nations and its officials differ from that enjoyed by a foreign state and its officials? To what extent do the limitations imposed by the International Organizations Immunities Act on the immunities and privileges of United Nations officials who are United States citizens go beyond the limitations of the Convention?

## LUTCHER S.A. CELULOSE E PAPEL v. INTER-AMERICAN DEVELOPMENT BANK

United States Court of Appeals, District of Columbia Circuit, 1967.
127 U.S.App.D.C. 238, 382 F.2d 454.

BURGER, CIRCUIT JUDGE. Appellants brought suit in the District Court for damages and injunctive relief claiming that the Bank had violated loan agreements with Lutcher S.A. Celulose e Papel by participating in loans made to competitors of Lutcher. This appeal followed the District Court's denial of preliminary injunctive relief and the grant of the Bank's motion to dismiss on the ground that the Bank is immune from suit and that the complaint failed to state a claim for which relief could be granted.

Appellant Lutcher S.A. is a Brazilian corporation organized in 1959 to engage in lumbering operations and the processing of paper pulp; F. Lutcher Brown is president and majority shareholder of Lutcher S.A.

Appellee is an international lending institution established in 1959 by joint action and subscription of the United States of America and all Latin American nations, Cuba excepted. Its stated purpose is "to contribute to the acceleration of the process of economic development of the member countries, giving priority to those loans and guarantees that will contribute most effectively to their economic growth."

The complaint alleges that from 1961 to 1964 the Bank made loans to Lutcher aggregating $8,700,000. In the same period it also made loans aggregating $5,000,000 to another Brazilian corporation engaged in lumbering and pulp processing, Papel e Celulose Catarinense Ltda., referred to as the Klabin group. Klabin operated the largest pulp and paper facility in Brazil and had a "monopoly in the newsprint industry." The Bank also made loans of $15,500,000 to another borrower to expand the largest pulp and paper and newsprint facility in Chile. These loans were made over Brown's protests that the Bank had inaccurate information about the state of the pulp market in Brazil and in Latin America and that these loans could jeopardize Lutcher's financial and competitive position.

In 1965 the Klabin group came to the Bank to obtain clearances to enable it to borrow additional funds from other sources, and Lutcher again urged the Bank to study the market situation. The Bank stated it would have an independent study made. In reliance on this, Appellants' complaint continues, Lutcher made payments owed the Bank. But in February, 1966, it is claimed, the Bank decided not to have a market study made. It appearing that the Bank was about to approve the Klabin request, Appellants brought this action to enjoin the Bank from doing so and to recover damages.

Appellants allege that the Bank "knowingly carried out wrongful acts with reckless disregard" for Appellants by lending to competitors and breached "an implied obligation" not to hinder Lutcher in fulfilling its contract with the Bank. The complaint alleges the Bank "impliedly warranted" to act "prudently" in considering loan applications from applicants in competition with Lutcher. Appellants view the duty of the Bank in these terms: "As a Development bank, the Inter-American Bank should have assisted Lutcher S.A. and by all means avoided any direct action detrimental to Lutcher S.A." They also claim that the Bank breached the 1965 agreements to make a market study, in reliance upon which Lutcher had incurred new debts and taken actions which it might otherwise not have taken.

Appellee contends, apart from argument on the merits, that it is immune from suit by virtue of specific legislation. The International Organizations Immunities Act provides that international organizations may be designated by the President so that they "shall enjoy the same immunity from suit and every form of judicial process as is enjoyed by foreign governments, except to the extent that such organizations may expressly waive their immunity for the purpose of any proceedings or by the terms of any contract." In 1960 President Eisenhower designated the Bank an international organization entitled to immunity, hence the question of the Bank's immunity turns on whether it has waived immunity from suit.

The answer in this case must be found in the Agreement establishing the Bank. The relevant provision is paragraph 1, Section 3 of Article XI; it provides:

> "Actions may be brought against the Bank only in a court of competent jurisdiction in the territories of a member in which the Bank has an office, has appointed an agent for the purpose of accepting service or notice of process, or has issued or guaranteed securities."

This provision is hardly a model of clarity; Appellants argue it constitutes a waiver of immunity. The Bank urges that such an interpretation "would wipe out Section 2(b) of the Immunities Act," a result which it says can be avoided by interpreting the provision as only a partial waiver, allowing suit by bondholders, creditors, and beneficiaries of its guarantees, on the theory that in such cases vulnerability to suit contributes to the effectiveness of the Bank's operation.

Unless this provision is read as merely describing the available forum for such suits and actions as to which waiver had been otherwise made, it must itself be a waiver of immunity. We do not read it as a venue provision for actions resulting from individual waivers; rather it is a provision waiving immunity and laying venue for the suits permitted. The terms are clear that "actions may be brought against the Bank"; had the drafters intended this clause to be only a venue provision, the language would more likely have provided, in essence, that actions brought against the Bank pursuant to any waiver of immunity could be brought in certain named courts. We conclude the absence of such limitation was purposeful. The subscribing nations were certainly alert to the problem and it was entirely appropriate to resolve the immunity question in the organic law of the Bank rather than leave it to case-by-case decision. That this was a deliberate choice is indicated by the title of Article XI, "Status, Immunities and Privileges," and the fact that the second paragraph of Section 3 expressly prohibits suits by members. The drafters thus manifested full awareness of the immunity problem and we conclude they must have been aware that they were waiving immunity in broad terms rather than treating narrowly a venue problem. * * *

In 1960 President Eisenhower issued, as we noted, his Executive Order qualifying the Bank for immunities available under the terms of the International Organizations Immunities Act. In 1962 President Kennedy amended President Eisenhower's Order by another Order, which is entitled as intended "to provide for an exception to the Inter–American Development Bank's immunity from suit specified in the International Organizations Immunities Act." This Order added the following clause to the Eisenhower Order:

> "*Provided,* That such designation shall not be construed to affect in any way the applicability of the provisions of Section 3, Article XI, of the Articles of Agreement of the Bank. * * *"

As amended, the Order tracks the Orders qualifying the International Finance Corporation and the World Bank. Its effect could only have been to reinforce the waiver of immunity. * * *

The Bank contends that, while Section 3 does waive immunity, it does so only with respect to suits brought by "bondholders, and other like creditors and the beneficiaries of its guarantees." The Bank seems to rest its argument on a broad assurance that it knows "the purpose and effect of the complex of statutory, international agreement and executive order provisions is this." The distinction made by the Bank is surely not necessary, as the Bank suggests it is, to preserve Section 2(b) of the Immunities Act, since that section expressly contemplates waiver.

There is an indication in Section 3 that bondholders have a special status under the agreement. The status conferred however is not that of the Bank's waiver of immunity, but rather the Bank's willingness to defend suits where it "has issued or guaranteed securities" even though venue might not otherwise lie in that jurisdiction. The status is conferred in the phrase which is disjunctively connected with other phrases laying venue—"in the territories of a member in which the Bank has an office, has appointed an agent for purpose of accepting service or notice of process, or has issued or guaranteed securities."

In fact, there are two features of Section 3 that militate against the Bank's argument. First, the drafters of the Agreement indicated that when they wanted to make an exception to waiver of immunity they knew how to do so. Prudently concerned with possible interference in bank operations by member countries, the drafters explicitly and expressly provided in paragraph 2 of Section 3 that *members* could not sue the Bank. This insured that members would not, in the Bank's words, intrude into "essential policy decisions * * * entrusted to its officers and Board." Second, the drafters stated that the Bank could be sued "in the territories of a member in which the Bank has an office, has appointed an agent for the purpose of accepting service or notice of process, or has issued or guaranteed securities." They must have contemplated that the Bank would establish offices in the areas intended to be served. Provision for suit in *any* member country where the Bank has an office must have been designed to facilitate suit for some class other than creditors and bondholders, i.e., borrowers; creditors suing to enforce bond obligations would more likely sue in United States Courts.

It is true, as the Bank argues, that the Agreement of the Asian Development Bank limits suit to "cases arising out of or in connection with the exercise of its powers to borrow money, to guarantee obligations, to buy and sell or underwrite the sale of securities" and that the Treasury Department stated that the Asian Bank's "immunities, exemptions and privileges * * * are similar to those embodied in the charters of the World Bank and the Inter-American Development Bank." The Department was indeed correct; the agreements of the Inter-American Bank and the Asian Bank are similar with respect to "immunities, exemptions and privileges." But similar does not mean identical, and the difference in language with respect to immunity from suit—only one of many privileges and immunities treated in the two agreements—is quite significant. Article 50 of the Asian Bank Agreement provides:

> 1. The Bank *shall enjoy immunity* from every form of legal process, *except in cases arising out of or in connection with the exercise of its powers to borrow money,* to guarantee obligations, or to buy and sell or underwrite the sale of securities, in which cases actions may be brought against the Bank in a court of competent jurisdiction in the territory of a country in which the Bank has its principal or a branch office, or has appointed an agent for the purpose of accepting service or notice of process, or has issued or guaranteed securities. (Emphasis added.)

Section 3 of Article XI of the Inter-American Bank Agreement states:

> "*Actions may be brought* against the Bank only in a court of competent jurisdiction in the territories of a member in which the Bank has an office, has appointed an agent for the purpose of accepting service or notice of process, or has issued or guaranteed securities." (Emphasis added.)

The Asian Bank Agreement explicitly reserves immunity except for certain situations, which are specifically spelled out. The Inter-American Bank Agreement has no reservation of immunity and mentions no category of cases in paragraph one in which the Bank cannot be sued. After this difference, the language of the two provisions becomes very similar, but the difference is a clear and telling one. It is quite impossible to argue in the face of it that the Inter-American Bank's Agreement implicitly provides an immunity which the Asian Bank's Agreement explicitly sets forth. * * *

There is no support in the common law doctrine of sovereign immunity for the Bank's argument. The doctrine has developed around the nature and function of the defendant, not the type of action a particular suit represents. No case is cited to us in which the immunity of the sovereign, be it domestic or foreign, depended on the identity of the suitor.

Even if we accepted the rationale of the distinction urged by the Bank as relevant to waiver, it would not necessarily yield the result desired by the Bank. There is no reason to believe that suits by creditors are less harassing to Bank management, or less expensive than are other kinds of suits. Just as it is necessary for the Bank to be subject to suits by bondholders in order to raise its lending capital, it may be that responsible borrowers committing large sums and plans on the strength of the Bank's agreement to lend would be reluctant to enter into borrowing contracts if thereafter they were at the mercy of the Bank's good will, devoid of means of enforcement. Suits by non-member creditors can affect the management of the Bank just as much as suits by borrowers—perhaps more; the Bank may have market power with respect to borrowers that would enable it to insist on loan contracts insulating its management functions, which it may not have with respect to creditors. * * *

The District Judge concluded that "where delicate, complex issues of international economic policy are involved, jurisdiction should be denied." But the complaint does not raise large or delicate international policy issues but rather purports to allege what at best is a simple breach of agreement and possible tort.

Turning to this alternative ground, we agree with the District Judge that the complaint does not state a cause of action for which relief is available. * * *

Affirmed.

### *Notes*

1. To what extent should an international organization having competence to influence "delicate, complex issues of international economic policy" be entitled to the deference accorded by courts in the United States and other countries to foreign states when the latter act within their territory or otherwise within their competence in international law so as to give effect to important public interests? Compare Banco Nacional de Cuba v. Sabbatino, p. 181 supra. Would a foreign state have been entitled to immunity under circumstances comparable to those present in the principal case?

2. In Curran v. City of New York et al., 191 Misc. 229, 77 N.Y.S.2d 206 (Sup.Ct.1947), a taxpayer brought suit against the City of New York, Trygve Lie, Secretary–General of the United Nations, and others in order to set aside city action making possible the location of U.N. headquarters in New York. The Secretary–General appeared specially and moved for the dismissal of the complaint against him on the ground that the court had no jurisdiction because he was being sued in respect of acts performed by him in his official capacity, citing sections 2(b) [22 U.S.C.A. § 288a(b)] and 7(b) [22 U.S.C.A. § 288d(b)] of the International Organizations Immunities Act, p. 965 supra. The United States Attorney brought to the court's attention the State Department's certification of "the immunity of the United Nations and of Lie as its Secretary General," and requested that the service of process on him be vacated and the complaint dismissed for lack of jurisdiction. The court so ruled. Compare Westchester County on Complaint of Donnelly v. Ranollo, 187 Misc. 777, 67 N.Y.S.2d 31 (City Ct. New Rochelle 1946), in which the personal chauffeur of the Secretary–General was charged with speeding while driving the latter on official business. Immunity was claimed on the basis of section 7(b) of the International Organizations Immunities Act, on the ground that the defendant had been performing an act in his official capacity and within his functions, but the court held that the Act and the Charter conferred immunity only upon "those personnel whose activities are such as to be necessary to the actual execution of the purposes and deliberations of the United Nations as distinguished from those household servants and personnel who merely serve the personal comfort, convenience or luxury of the delegates and Secretariat who actually perform the true functions of the Organization." 187 Misc. at 781, 67 N.Y.S.2d at 35. In the absence of State Department certification that immunity was in the public interest, the court refused to grant immunity except upon a trial of the issue of fact, i.e., whether defendant had been acting in his official capacity and within his functions. For criticism of the *Ranollo* case, see Preuss, Immunity of Officers and Employees of the United Nations for Official Acts: The Ranallo [*sic* ] Case,

41 A.J.I.L. 555 (1947); Jenks, International Immunities 119 (1961). Although the State Department subsequently indicated that it thought immunity should be granted, the United Nations decided not to press the claim of immunity and to pay the fine. Preuss at 557. Following this case, the United Nations no longer claimed immunity in respect of traffic violations for its drivers or other officials driving in the course of duty. Jenks at 119.

3. The Diplomatic Relations Act, 22 U.S.C.A. § 254e, extends the requirement of compliance with the Director of the Office of Foreign Missions' regulations on liability insurance to the individuals described in Section 19 of the Convention on Privileges and Immunities of the United Nations. Article V, section 15, of the Headquarters Agreement, p. 959 supra, makes representatives to the United Nations subject to the same obligation. The State Department regulations on this subject may be found at 22 CFR 151 et seq. (1980); 18 I.L.M. 871 (1979).

Prior to the adoption of these provisions, immunity had usually been waived in those accident cases involving United Nations vehicles for which a settlement could not be reached; furthermore, a 1946 resolution of the General Assembly had instructed the Secretary–General to ensure that the drivers of official United Nations vehicles, as well as staff members who owned or operated cars, carry liability insurance. G.A.Res. 22E (1946). See also Jenks at 119–20.

May the insurer of an insured representative to the United Nations insist that the insured invoke his or her immunity?

4. In United States v. Coplon, 84 F.Supp. 472 (S.D.N.Y.1949), espionage activities by a Soviet employee of the Secretariat were held not to fall within the categories set up by the International Organizations Immunities Act or the United Nations Charter. Defendant himself, not the Secretariat, had claimed immunity.

How can the United States proceed against one of the officials entitled, under the Convention, to complete immunity? See Articles 18 and 19 of the Convention, supra, and compare 22 U.S.C.A. § 288d(b). See Jenks at 30.

If the United Nations, or an official entitled to immunity, were to initiate legal proceedings in a United States court, would the defendant have the right to assert a counterclaim? See Restatement (Third) § 469, Reporters' Note 4.

5. In addition to the possibility that an international organization will waive its immunity or that of one of its officials from suit in a municipal court, there may be available to a private claimant certain procedures within the organization by which judicial redress may be obtained. The Administrative Tribunals of the United Nations and of the International Labour Organisation are competent "to determine disputes between international organisations and their officials and persons claiming through such officials concerning the terms of appointment and tenure of officials and the rights of officials and pensioners under the applicable staff and pension regulations." Jenks at 161. The ILO Tribunal was originally the League of Nations Tribunal and has been granted by agreement jurisdiction in respect of the World Health Organisation, the Food and Agriculture Organisation, UNESCO, the International Telecommunication Union, the World Meteorological Organisation, the European Organisation for Nuclear Research, the International Atomic Energy Agency, and GATT. By agreement the U.N. Administrative Tribunal has jurisdiction over the International Civil Aviation Organization and the Inter-governmental Maritime Consultative Organization. See further Jessup, Transnational Law 82–94 (1956), partic-

ularly on the law applied by the Tribunals. In 1954, the International Court of Justice ruled in an advisory opinion that the General Assembly did not have the right to refuse to give effect to a compensation award made by the United Nations Administrative Tribunal. Effect of Awards of Compensation Made by the United Nations Administrative Tribunal (Advisory Opinion), 1954 I.C.J. 47. The United Nations has adopted the practice of including arbitration clauses in its commercial contracts. Jessup at 100.

6. Does the restrictive doctrine also apply to international organizations? Cf. Broadbent v. OAS, 628 F.2d 27 (D.C.Cir.1980) (the U.S. argued to this effect, but the court did not reach the issue); Tuck v. Pan American Health Organization, 668 F.2d 547 (D.C.Cir.1981) (issue not reached, since there would be immunity in any event); Mendaro v. The World Bank, 717 F.2d 610 (D.C.Cir. 1983) (finding immunity in suit of former employee). See generally Restatement (Third) § 467, Reporters' Note 4; Glenn et al., Immunities Of International Organizations, 22 Va.J.Int'l L. 247 (1982); Oparil, Immunity Of International Organizations In United States Courts: Absolute Or Restrictive? 24 And.J.Transnat'l L. 689 (1991).

## *ADMISSION OF REPRESENTATIVES OF NON–GOVERNMENTAL ORGANIZATIONS ENJOYING CONSULTATIVE STATUS*

Legal Opinion of the Secretariat of the United Nations.
April 10, 1953, U.N.Doc. E/2397.

* * *

2. [T]he Women's International Democratic Federation, a non-governmental organization in consultative relationship with the Council in Category B, designated Mrs. Margarette Rae Luckock as its representative to attend the seventh session of the Commission on the Status of Women, which adjourned on 3 April 1953, and thereafter to attend the current session of the Economic and Social Council. The World Federation of Trade Unions, a non-governmental organization in consultative relationship with the Council in Category A, designated Mr. Jan Dessau as its representative to attend the current session of the Council. Both representatives made application for a visa at appropriate United States Consulates and the Secretariat of the Economic and Social Council made notification to the United States Mission to the United Nations of these applications, in accordance with established procedures.

3. The representative of the United States reported to the Economic and Social Council at its 679th plenary meeting on 9 April 1953 that his Government had found it impossible to grant these applications. He explained the position of his Government as follows:

> In denying these applications, my Government has found it necessary to invoke the right to safeguard its security which it reserved to itself in Section 6 of the Joint Resolution (Public Law 357) of the 80th Congress, which authorized the United States to enter into the Headquarters Agreement, and in the note of its Representative, dated November 21, 1947, bringing the Headquarters Agreement into effect.

4. Section 11(4) of the Headquarters Agreement provides: [p. 1218 supra].

5. Section 13(a) of the Headquarters Agreement reads as follows:

(a) Laws and regulations in force in the United States regarding the entry of aliens shall not be applied in such manner as to interfere with the privileges referred to in Section 11. When visas are required for persons referred to in that Section, they shall be granted without charge and as promptly as possible.

6. These are the only provisions in the Headquarters Agreement bearing upon the right of transit to the Headquarters District on the part of properly designated representatives of non-governmental organizations. Nothing in the text of the Headquarters Agreement reserves to the United States the authority to deny a visa to any of the classes of persons specified in Section 11. Indeed, Section 13(d) specifies that, *except* as provided above, "* * * the United States retains full control and authority over the entry of persons or property into the territory of the United States * * *."

7. By Joint Resolution (Public Law 357—80th Congress) the Senate and House of Representatives of the United States Congress authorized the President of the United States to bring the Headquarters Agreement into effect on the part of the United States.

8. Section 6 of the Joint Resolution stated that nothing in the Agreement should be construed as in any way diminishing, abridging or weakening the right of the United States to safeguard its own security and completely to control the entry of aliens into any territory of the United States other than the Headquarters District and its immediate vicinity, and such areas as it was reasonably necessary to traverse in transit between the same and foreign countries.

9. The Secretary–General of the United Nations was authorized to bring the Headquarters Agreement into force by the General Assembly, which approved the text of the Agreement in its resolution 169(II). But in the event that the provision in section 6 of the Joint Resolution had been intended by the United States to constitute a reservation, it was never made known to the General Assembly as such, and it was never considered by the General Assembly nor accepted by it.

* * *

12. Finally, even if the United States had intended to formulate a reservation, it would not appear from a reading of section 6 of the Joint Resolution that it could have application to the present cases. It refers to control by the United States of the entrance of aliens into any territory of the United States *other than* the Headquarters District, its immediate vicinity, and the necessary area of transit.

13. It appears from the foregoing that persons falling within the classes referred to in section 11 of the Headquarters Agreement are entitled to transit to and from the Headquarters District, and that this right of transit has not been made the subject of any reservation.

### *Notes*

1. As a result of negotiations between the Secretary–General and the United States government, it was agreed that the Headquarters Agreement was not to be used as a cover for activities directed against United States security. It

was recognized that the United States (1) had a right to grant visas "valid only for transit to and from the Headquarters District and sojourn in its immediate vicinity;" (2) had the authority "to make any reasonable definition, consistent with the purposes of the Agreement, of the 'immediate vicinity' of the Headquarters District, of the necessary routes of transit, and of the time and manner of expiration of the visas following the completion of official functions;" and (3) had a right to deport persons abusing the privileges of residence in activities outside their official capacity. On the other hand, with respect to "aliens in transit to the Headquarters District exclusively on official business of, or before, the United Nations," it was recognized that "the rights of the United States are limited by the Headquarters Agreement to those mentioned." As for borderline cases, i.e., where there might be evidence that a person was coming to the United States for purposes detrimental to United States security, the United States gave assurances that "timely" decisions would be made at "the highest levels," and that the Secretary–General would be kept informed. Report by the Secretary–General to the Economic and Social Council, July 27, 1953, U.N.Doc.E/2492 at 2–3. The possibility of submitting future disputes to arbitration, as provided in the Headquarters Agreement, was discussed in the Council as the only alternative to a failure of negotiations. See Liang, The Question of Access to the United Nations Headquarters of Representatives of Non–Governmental Organizations in Consultative Status, 48 A.J.I.L. 434, 445–50 (1954).

2. Henrique Galvão, a former colonial officer under the Salazar regime in Portugal, had been convicted by a Portuguese court of involuntary manslaughter in connection with the seizure of a vessel on which he made his way to Brazil, where he was received as a political refugee. In a letter dated November 4, 1963, he requested a hearing before the Fourth Committee for the purpose of proposing a solution to problems of Portuguese administration in Angola. U.N.Doc.A/C.4/600/Add.5. The Fourth Committee requested an opinion as to the legal implications of the possible appearance before it of Mr. Galvão. The Legal Opinion of the Secretariat of the United Nations of November 15, 1963, U.N.Doc.A/C.4/621; 1963 U.N.Jur'l Ybk. 164, stated as follows:

* * *

4. Apart from police protection * * * the obligations imposed on the host Government by the Headquarters Agreement are limited to assuring the right of access to the Headquarters and an eventual right of departure. The Headquarters Agreement does not confer any diplomatic status upon an individual invitee because of his status as such. He therefore cannot be said to be immune from suit or legal process during his sojourn in the United States and outside of the Headquarters district.

5. Two other provisions of the Headquarters Agreement serve to reinforce the right of access to the Headquarters. Section 13(a) specifies that the laws and regulations in force in the United States regarding the *entry* of aliens shall not be applied in such manner as to interfere with the privilege of transit to the Headquarters district. This provision, however, clearly assures admission to the United States without conferring any other privilege or immunity during the sojourn. Similarly, section 13(b) interposes certain limitations on the right of the host Government to require the departure of persons invited to the Headquarters district while they continue in their official capacity; but this plainly relates to restrictions on the power of deportation and not, conversely, on a duty to bring about departure. Moreover, section 13(d) makes clear that, apart from the two foregoing

restrictions, "the United States retains full control and authority over the entry of persons or property into the territory of the United States and the conditions under which persons may remain or reside there."

6. It is thus clear that the United Nations would be in no position to offer general assurances to Mr. Galvão concerning immunity from legal process during his sojourn in the United States. It might be that individual citizens of the United States might have civil causes of action against him and could subject him to service of process. While the Federal Government might have no intention, and might lack jurisdiction, to initiate any criminal proceedings against him, it is a known fact that there are legal limitations on the powers of the executive branch of the United States Government to ensure against any type of proceeding by another branch of the Government, including the judicial branch.

7. Moreover, * * * the attention of the Committee has already been invited to the possibility that extradition proceedings might be instituted against Mr. Galvão during his presence in this country. By an Extradition Convention of 7 May 1908 between Portugal and the United States persons may be delivered up who are charged, among other crimes, with piracy or with mutiny or conspiracy by two or more members of the crew or other persons on board of a vessel on the high seas, for the purpose of rebelling against the authority of the captain of the vessel, or by fraud or violence taking possession of the vessel, or with assault on board ships upon the high seas with intent to do bodily harm, or with abduction or detention of persons for any unlawful end. The extradition is also to take place for the participation in any of such crimes as an accessory before or after the fact. The Convention contains the usual exception for any crime or offence of a political character, or for acts connected with such crimes or offences (Articles II and III).

* * *

9. There is no precedent in the history of the Headquarters Agreement which would indicate whether an application of Federal Regulations restricting departure of an alien, by reason of proceedings against him not related to his presence at the United Nations, would constitute an impediment to transit "from the Headquarters district" within the meaning of section 11 of the Agreement. There is likewise no precedent which would indicate whether compliance by the Federal Government with the terms of an extradition treaty would conflict with the right of transit of an invitee from the Headquarters district. In this connexion it is important to note that what the United States Government has undertaken not to do, by the terms of section 11, is to "impose" any impediment to transit from the Headquarters. To the extent that the presence of Mr. Galvão in the United States might in one manner or another give rise to proceedings against him by operation of existing law in relation to preexisting facts (such as previous activities on his part), it could be argued that this did not constitute an action taken by the Government to impose an impediment on his departure. * * *

* * *

11. In these circumstances, it must be recognized that a situation could arise by which the Fourth Committee was deprived of the advantage of receiving oral testimony from Mr. Galvão. Should he not be prepared to

> attend because of the inability of the host Government to confer upon him a general immunity, it is clear that his abstention from appearing would be his own, and not the affirmative imposition of an impediment to his transit. For it might only be at the moment of his attempted departure from the United States that an arbitrable dispute could arise as to whether he was entitled to depart notwithstanding proceedings which might in the meantime have been instituted against him. * * *

On November 14, 1963 the Fourth Committee approved Galvão's request for a hearing and decided to request the Secretary–General to consult with the United States government "with a view to ensuring that petitioners coming to the United States for the purpose of testifying before a committee should enjoy the necessary protection during their transit to and from the Headquarters district." 18 U.N.GAOR, 4th Comm. 324–25 (1963). Galvão appeared before the Committee on December 9, 1963, id. at 525–529, and apparently left the United States without incident on the following day. See 3 I.L.M. 169 (1964).

Is the Secretariat's interpretation of the Headquarters Agreement open to criticism? See the debate in the Fourth Committee on November 13, 1963, 18 U.N.GAOR, 4th Comm. 305–09 (1963), quoted in part at 1963 U.N.Jur'l Yb. 166–67 n. 7. Note that Section 27 of the Headquarters Agreement provides that the agreement "shall be construed in the light of its primary purposes to enable the United Nations at its headquarters in the United States, fully and efficiently to discharge its responsibilities and fulfill its purposes." 61 Stat. at 3434. Compare the Secretariat's note to the Under–Secretary for Economic and Social Affairs, November 26, 1963, 1963 U.N.Jur'l Yb. 167, in which it is stated that "[t]he essential element in the right of access [to meetings of U.N. organs and to offices of the U.N.] is that representatives of governments, officials of the Organization and other persons invited on official business shall not be impeded in their transit to or from the United Nations offices in connexion with meetings or other activities in which they are entitled to participate." It was further noted that the Secretary–General had taken the position that derogation from "the foregoing principles of access * * * would be disruptive to the functioning of United Nations organs and contrary to the clear obligations of Member States under the Charter." Id. at 168.

3. For the status of Permanent Observers at the United Nations of non-member states, see the Legal Counsel's memorandum to the Acting Secretary–General, August 22, 1962, 1962 U.N.Jur'l Ybk. 237. Cf. Pappas v. Francisci, 119 N.Y.S.2d 69 (Sup.Ct.1953) (Italian observer held not entitled to immunity).

# Chapter 14

# THE LAW OF THE SEA

"A law of the sea is as old as nations, and the modern law of the sea is virtually as old as modern international law. For three hundred years it was probably the most stable and least controversial branch of international law. It was essentially reaffirmed and codified as recently * * * as 1958. By 1970 it was in disarray." Henkin, How Nations Behave 212 (2d ed. 1979). In the 1990's there has been again general agreement on the legal regime that should govern the seas, but one aspect—mining the sea-bed beyond national jurisdiction—has been controversial and unresolved.

The history of the law of the sea reflects a constant struggle between states that asserted special rights to vast areas of the sea and other states that insisted on the freedom to navigate and fish in all the ocean spaces. Exceptions to the freedom of the seas (*mare liberum*) developed slowly, as coastal states pressed for control over marine traffic and resources near their shores. Important inroads on the freedom of the seas, principally in favor of coastal states, and the definition of the "high seas" as the area "beyond national jurisdiction" in the 1982 United Nations Convention on the Law of the Sea (see p. 1297), suggests examination of coastal state rights before dealing with the seas "beyond national jurisdiction." Therefore, after stating the basic principles (Section 1), Section 2 of this Chapter traces the development of the rights of coastal states as exceptions to the freedom of the seas, culminating in codification in the Law of the Sea Convention which permits coastal states to exercise authority over a "territorial sea," "the continental shelf," and an "exclusive economic zone." Section 3 sets forth the law of the extensive areas of the sea that remain "beyond national jurisdiction," are subject to "the regime of the high seas," and open to all for reasonable use, with due consideration for the rights of other states to use them similarly. Three smaller but important subjects (the marine environment, scientific research, and the settlement of sea disputes) are considered in sections 4 through 6. Section 7 closes this Chapter with a discussion of the law that applies in all parts of the sea to the instrument that first opened the seas to human voyagers—the ship.

## SOURCES OF THE LAW OF THE SEA

The law of the sea was largely customary law, until it was codified and developed by the International Law Commission in a major undertaking culminating in the first United Nations Conference on the Law of the Sea in 1958. That Conference adopted four conventions: on the Territorial Sea and the Contiguous Zone (15 U.S.T. 1606, T.I.A.S. No. 5639, 516 U.N.T.S. 205); on the High Seas (13 U.S.T. 2312, T.I.A.S. No. 5200, 450 U.N.T.S. 82); on the Continental Shelf (15 U.S.T. 471, T.I.A.S. No. 5578, 499 U.N.T.S. 311); and on Fishing and Conservation of the Living Resources of the High Seas (17 U.S.T. 138, T.I.A.S. No. 5969, 559 U.N.T.S. 285). As of January 1993 the Convention on the High Seas had 57 parties; the Territorial Sea Convention had 45 parties; the Continental Shelf Convention, 53; the Fishing and Conservation Convention, 36. Insofar as the Conventions merely codify customary law, they reflect law binding also on states that have not adhered to them. The Conventions have also contributed to the development of customary law. Compare the *North Sea Continental Shelf Cases*, p. 1280 infra. (A Second Law of the Sea Conference in 1960 to determine the width of the territorial sea, an issue left unresolved in the 1958 Convention, did not succeed.)

In the following decades, the proliferation of new states and other forces pressed for a new recodification as well as for important substantive changes. Initiatives in the U.N. General Assembly, beginning in 1967, to deal with the resources of the sea-bed "beyond national jurisdiction" led to the Third U.N. Law of the Sea Conference, at which virtually the whole of the law of the sea was reexamined. The Conference began in 1973, and after eight years of negotiation, it produced the Draft Convention on the Law of the Sea (Informal Text), A/CONF.62/WP.10/Rev.3 (1980). The Draft Convention was considered virtually complete. However, the Reagan administration which took office in the United States in 1981 proposed a number of changes to it, particularly with regard to the sea-bed mining provisions (Part IX). These proposals were, for the most part, rejected and the final draft was approved on April 30, 1982, by a vote of 130 states in favor, 4 against and 17 abstentions. The four states voting against were the United States, Israel, Turkey and Venezuela. The new Convention contains 320 articles and nine annexes (containing 125 additional articles). A/CONF.62/122 (1982), reprinted in 21 I.L.M. 1245 (1982). It was signed in Jamaica, December 10, 1982, by 119 states and will come into force one year after 60 states ratify it. As of January 1993, 52 states have ratified the treaty.

In 1983 President Reagan proclaimed the establishment of a 200-mile Exclusive Economic Zone for the United States, an act he said was in accord with the existing maritime law and practice as confirmed by the 1982 Convention. The President's Statement reads in part:

> The United States has long been a leader in developing customary and conventional law of the sea. Our objectives have consistently been to provide a legal order that will, among other things, facilitate peaceful, international uses of the oceans and provide for equitable and effective

management and conservation of marine resources. The United States also recognizes that all nations have an interest in these issues.

Last July I announced that the United States will not sign the UN Law of the Sea Convention that was opened for signature on December 10. * * *

However, the convention * * * contains provisions with respect to traditional uses of the oceans which generally confirm existing maritime law and practice and fairly balance the interests of all states.

Today I am announcing three decisions to promote and protect the oceans interests of the United States in a manner consistent with those fair and balanced results in the convention and international law.

First, the United States is prepared to accept and act in accordance with the balance of interests relating to traditional uses of the oceans—such as navigation and overflight. In this respect, the United States will recognize the rights of other states in the waters off their coasts, as reflected in the convention, so long as the rights and freedoms of the United States and others under international law are recognized by such coastal states.

Second, the United States will exercise and assert its navigation and overflight rights and freedoms on a worldwide basis in a manner that is consistent with the balance of interests reflected in the convention. The United States will not, however, acquiesce in unilateral acts of other states designed to restrict the rights and freedoms of the international community in navigation and overflight and other related high seas uses.

Third, I am proclaiming today an exclusive economic zone in which the United States will exercise sovereign rights in living and nonliving resources within 200 nautical miles of its coast.

83 Dep't State Bull. No. 2075 at 70–71 (1983).

The failure of the United States to support the final text of the treaty resulted in uncertainty as to the state of the law of the sea and the status of the Convention before it goes into force or in relation to states that do not become parties to it. The U.S. appeared ready to accept as customary law virtually all the provisions except those relating to mining in the deep sea-bed. Many states, in particular developing states, argued that the Convention was a "package deal" reflecting not only compromises as to the terms of particular articles, but "trade-offs" between articles and subjects. In particular, they insisted that they had agreed to provisions favorable to the interests of developed states (notably the United States) in some sections of the treaty in order to achieve agreement on the provisions they wanted, notably the regime for deep sea-bed mining. Consequently, they argued that such sections cannot be treated as reflecting agreed customary law unless the entire treaty—including the deep sea-bed regime—is recognized as customary law. However, all agree that many of its provisions duplicate provisions in the 1958 Conventions, and many others are clearly established customary law of the sea.

The Restatement (Third), Part V, Introductory Note concludes:

For purposes of this Restatement, therefore, the Convention as such is not law of the United States. However, many of the provisions of the Convention follow closely provisions in the 1958 conventions to which the United States is a party and which largely restated customary law as of that time. Other provisions in the LOS Convention set forth rules that, if not law in 1958, became customary law since that time, as they were accepted at the Conference by consensus and have influenced, and came to reflect, the practice of states. See § 102, Reporters' Note 2. In particular, in March 1983 President Reagan proclaimed a 200–nautical-mile exclusive economic zone for the United States and issued a policy statement in which the United States in effect agreed to accept the substantive provisions of the Convention, other than those dealing with deep sea-bed mining, in relation to all states that do so with respect to the United States. Thus, by express or tacit agreement accompanied by consistent practice, the United States, and states generally, have accepted the substantive provisions of the Convention, other than those addressing deep sea-bed mining, as statements of customary law binding upon them apart from the Convention. See Case Concerning Delimitation of the Maritime Boundary of the Gulf of Maine (Canada/United States), [1984] I.C.J.Rep. 246, 294 (the provisions of the LOS Convention concerning the continental shelf and the exclusive economic zone "were adopted without any objections" and may "be regarded as consonant at present with general international law on the question"). In a few instances, however, there is disagreement whether a provision of the Convention reflects customary law. See, *e.g.,* § 514, Reporters' Note 4, and § 515, Comment *b.* Some provisions of the Convention, notably those accepting particular arrangements for settling disputes, clearly are not customary law and have not been accepted by express or tacit agreement.

Id. (footnotes omitted).

In the *Gulf of Maine Case,* a Chamber of the International Court of Justice stated:

> Turning lastly to the proceedings of the Third United Nations Conference on the Law of the Sea and the final result of that Conference, the Chamber notes in the first place that the Convention adopted at the end of the Conference has not yet come into force and that a number of States do not appear inclined to ratify it. This, however, in no way detracts from the consensus reached on large portions of the instrument and, above all, cannot invalidate the observation that certain provisions of the Convention, concerning the continental shelf and the exclusive economic zone were adopted, without any objections.

1984 I.C.J. 53. See also *Case Concerning Continental Shelf* (Libya v. Malta), 1985 I.C.J. 13, 30 (it is the clear duty of the Court to consider if relevant, provisions of the 1982 Law of the Sea Convention that are binding as rules of customary law); *Case Concerning the Arbitral Award of 31 July 1989* (Guinea–Bissau v. Senegal), 1990 I.C.J. 64, 72 (guidance may be found in the 1982 Convention, although it has not yet entered into force) (Evensen, J., separate opinion); *Case Concerning Passage Through the Great Belt* (Finland v. Denmark) (application for provisional measures), 1991 I.C.J. 12, 13 (account has to be taken of the provisions of the 1982 Law of the Sea Convention that reflect customary law).

In referring to the Convention, therefore, it may be desirable to note the continuity between the 1982 Convention and its antecedents.

For discussions of the Third LOS Conference, see Law of the Sea: United States Policy Dilemma (Oxman, Caron & Burdi, eds. 1983); Allott, Power Sharing in the Law of the Sea, 77 A.J.I.L. 1 (1983). For a collection of documents on the Third Law of the Sea Conference, see Platzöder, Third United Nations Conference on the Law of the Sea: Documents, 18 vols. (1982–1988). For the perspectives of different states on the Third Law of the Sea Conference and on the law of the sea generally, see The International Law of the Sea (Blishchenko & Gureyev, eds. 1988); The Law of the Sea: Problems from the East Asian Perspective (Park & Park, eds. 1987); Szekely, Latin America and the Development of the Law of the Sea, 2 vols. (1986); Singh, The United Nations Convention on the Law of the Sea (1985); Rembe, Africa and the International Law of the Sea (1980); El–Hakim, The Middle Eastern States and the Law of the Sea (1979). On the law of the sea generally, see New Directions in the Law of the Sea, 11 vols. (Nordquist, et al., eds.); O'Connell, The Law of the Sea (Shearer, ed. 1982); The Law of the Sea in the 1990s: A Framework for Further Cooperation (Kuribayashi & Miles, eds. 1992); A Handbook on the New Law of the Sea, 2 vols. (Dupuy, ed. 1991). For an indication of provisions of the 1982 Convention that do not apply to the United States, or whose applicability is in doubt, see Restatement (Third), Part V, Introductory Note, n. 4.

The 1982 Convention has remained in abeyance, but the Preparatory Commission established by resolution pursuant to Part XI of the Draft Convention has met periodically and pursued its work at a leisurely pace. The number of states that have adhered to the covenant have grown slowly and as of December 1992, fifty-two states had ratified the Convention (60 are required to bring the Convention into effect). It is commonly recognized that a number of states are poised to ratify the Convention and bring it into effect but see no reason to do so as long as the United States (and other industrialized states) will not join, especially since the implementation of key sections of the Convention depends on their financial and technological commitment of those states.

The years since 1982 have wrought radical changes in the political context of the Convention and in the economic assumptions that underlay it. It has become clear that deep sea-bed mining will not in fact be economical for a long time, perhaps for decades, and that no country has any economic reason (and few have political reasons) for proceeding with sea-bed mining. In the 1990s, doubt as to the economic viability of deep sea-bed mining muted the debate about its legality, but the issue has not been resolved. The changed world order following the end of the Cold War has also largely overtaken the ideological differences that underlay some of the compromises of the "package deal"; the general commitment to "privatization" and free market principles, and democracy, may also have outdated some of the provisions of Part XI and its annexes to which the United States objected. In the early 1990s the Secretary General has been pursuing informed negotiations with a view to removing the obstacles, notably in Part XI of the Convention and its annexes, to widespread ratification of the Convention. The Clinton Administration will doubtless be pressed to re-examine the U.S. position.

In November 1992, an independent panel of U.S. experts said:

> Fundamental United States interests would be served by removing the obstacles to widespread ratification of the 1982 United Nations Convention on the Law of the Sea. U.S. interests in the Convention include those related to the use and protection of the oceans, international trade and economic growth, as well as national interests in order, stability, and orderly change in international relations.

The panel went on to enumerate fundamental U.S. interests in security, in free movement of trade and communications, and in the environment as supporting ratification of the 1982 Convention. Panel on the Law of Ocean Uses, Letter dated November 25, 1992. See also Panel on the Law of Ocean Uses, U.S. Interests and the United Nations Convention on the Law of the Sea (June 1990).

Failure to bring the 1982 Convention into force (see p. 1232 supra) has doubtless encouraged some disposition particularly to coastal states to encroach further on the commonage. A statement by Chilean officials has been interpreted as launching a new doctrine of the "presential sea" in which the coastal state has a "presence" which underlies rights in a zone of sea far beyond the 200 mile Exclusive Economic Zone. See the articles by Vicuña, Clingan, Jr., Joyner & DeCola in 24 Ocean Dev. & Int'l L. 81–121 (1993).

See generally El–Baghdadi, The Seabed's Mineral Resources and the Conditions Affecting the Regime to Regulate Their Exploitation, 26 J. World Trade L. 85 (1992); Schmidt, Common Heritage or Common Burden? The United States Position on the Development of a Regime for Deep Seabed Mining in the Law of the Sea Conventions (1989).

### *Note*

The Law of the Sea is commonly used to describe that part of international law that deals with the relations, activities and interests of states involving the sea. It is distinct from other branches of sea-related law. Admiralty or maritime law, for example, deals primarily with relations, activities and interests of private persons involved in the transport of passengers or goods. Those relations are generally governed by domestic law, but various aspects are now regulated by international agreement. The International Maritime Organization (IMO) has included among its concerns maritime safety and marine pollution, and the draft Law of the Sea Convention contains some rules of maritime law as well, for example, those relating to penal jurisdiction in the event of collision.

## SECTION 1. THE BASIC PRINCIPLES: FREEDOM AND "COMMONAGE"

For hundreds of years after Hugo Grotius prevailed in his famous controversy with John Selden (see historical introduction), international law saw the seas as belonging to everyone or to no one, and *mare liberum* as the fundamental principle of the law of the seas (although subject in war to the laws of war, p. 1033 supra). That status and that principle applied throughout the seas. Exceptions, principally in favor of coastal states, developed slowly, and historically, at least, were seen—and resisted—as carved out of the commonage, as derogations from freedom. Zones of "national jurisdiction" for the coastal states—the territorial sea, the continental shelf, the exclusive economic zone—are later developments, some very recent, creating distinctions between them and the rest of the seas and giving the latter the distinguishing label, the "high seas."

### *HENKIN, CHANGING LAW FOR THE CHANGING SEAS*

Uses of the Seas 69, 70–71 (Gullion ed. 1968).*

For hundreds of years the basic principle of the law of the seas has been freedom. With it—or beneath it—has been the principle that the sea belonged to everyone, or to no one. In particular, unlike land, the sea could not be acquired by nations and made subject to national sovereignty.

Freedom of the seas has meant freedom to use the seas, and no uses have been barred. The principal use has been navigation—for fishing, trade, travel, war. In time, the seas began to lend themselves to tunneling, laying of cables, submarine travel, scientific research. Today, the seas are a principal area of military deployment and manoeuvre and harbor "permanently" sophisticated military weapons and equipment. The seas have recreational and scientific importance. They have long been a repository for waste, recently also for atomic waste. Unless modified, the principle of freedom would presumably apply also to future uses—to transportation, sojourn, or other human activity in the waters below or on the sea bed.

Freedom has extended also to the air above the seas and it, too, has been open to all for aviation and its various purposes. There has been no agreement, however, as to "who owns the seabed," as to whether the "commonage" of the seas applies as well to the seabed and its subsoil. Some have urged that the seas are not subject to national acquisition only because that would interfere with freedom, particularly for navigation, but there is no similar reason for denying national acquisition and sovereignty in the seabed and its subsoil.

Freedom of the seas, and the principle that they belong to all, or none, has meant also freedom for all nations to exploit sea resources, principally to fish and to keep one's catch. Those who insisted that the seas were common property might have had difficulty explaining why individual nations could appropriate the fish that belonged to all. But the theoretical questions bothered only theoreticians. Fishing was older than international law; no nation had any interest in insisting that fishing was generally prohibited; besides, the fish reproduced themselves and seemed plentiful and inexhaustible. Even when it proved that fish were not in fact always and everywhere plentiful and inexhaustible, the freedom to fish in the seas at large survived unimpaired. It seemed unlikely that a different rule would apply as man began to extract other resources, organic or inorganic, from the waters, or to the waters themselves, although questions might arise if new processes for extraction required major, "permanent" installations that unduly interfered with navigation or other established rights.

Again, there has been disagreement as to whether the resources on or beneath the seabed are similarly subject to appropriation by anyone. * * *

If, however, it is now (or will soon be) possible for any nation to extract a wealth of oil and manganese in parts of the sea far from any coast, may it lawfully do so, and, if so, on what terms, subject to what limitations? Or are these minerals the property of all, not to be extracted at all without the consent of "the community," and only on its terms?

## SECTION 2. DEROGATIONS FROM "COMMONAGE" IN FAVOR OF COASTAL STATES

The territorial sea resulted from early recognition that the coastal state had special interests in waters adjacent to its shores for some purposes; in time, the various interests combined into "sovereignty" over a "territorial sea." See Jessup, The Law of Territorial Waters and Maritime Jurisdiction (1927). Coastal states also claimed the need to protect their territorial interests (or their territorial sea) against acts outside the territorial sea. A "contiguous zone" in which the coastal state could act against smugglers developed early; later, some claimed rights to act against polluters or "pirate broadcasters." There developed also a right for the coastal state of "hot pursuit," even on the high seas, of violators of its special zones and interests.

Preference or exclusive rights for the coastal state to natural resources in or beneath waters adjacent to the coast (but beyond the territorial sea) developed more recently; the Truman Proclamation justified the doctrine of the continental shelf in the interest of conservation and as "reasonable and just." See p. 1277 infra. Other coastal states thought it reasonable and just that the coastal state have preferred or exclusive fishing rights in coastal areas even beyond the territorial sea, leading to an exclusive economic zone, with exclusive rights for the coastal state in all natural resources of their "patrimonial sea." See pp. 1291–92.

The 1982 Convention completed a process of development in the customary law of the seas that confirmed authority for coastal states, but different authority in different coastal zones.

### *RESTATEMENT (THIRD) § 511*

Subject to §§ 512–15, a coastal state may exercise jurisdiction over the following coastal zones:

(a) The territorial sea: a belt of sea that may not exceed 12 nautical miles, measured from a baseline which is either the low-water line along the coast, or the seaward limit of the internal waters of the coastal state or in the case of an archipelagic state the seaward limit of the archipelagic waters;

(b) The contiguous zone: a belt of sea contiguous to the territorial sea that may not extend beyond 24 nautical miles from the baselines from which the breadth of the territorial sea is measured;

(c) The continental shelf: the sea-bed and subsoil of the submarine areas that extend beyond the coastal state's territorial sea

(i) throughout the natural prolongation of the state's land territory to the outer edge of the continental margin, subject to certain limitations based on geological and geographical factors; or

(ii) to a distance of 200 nautical miles from the baselines from which the breadth of the territorial sea is measured, where there is no continental margin off the coast or where the continental margin does not extend to that distance;

(d) The exclusive economic zone: a belt of sea beyond the territorial sea that may not exceed 200 nautical miles from the baselines from which the breadth of the territorial sea is measured.

**Comment:**

*a. Different coastal state authority in different zones.* The authority of the coastal state is different in the different zones defined in this section. The coastal state exercises sovereignty in the territorial sea; limited policing rights in the contiguous zone; sovereign rights over the natural resources of the continental shelf and over economic exploitation of the exclusive economic zone; and limited jurisdiction within the exclusive economic zone with regard to marine scientific research, the protection and preservation of the marine environment, and artificial islands and certain installations and structures. *Compare* § 512 and § 513 *with* § 514 and § 515. With respect to matters falling within its authority in the particular zone, the coastal state generally has jurisdiction to prescribe, to adjudicate, and to enforce by nonjudicial measures, but such jurisdiction is not necessarily exclusive. See Introductory Note to Part IV.

* * *

*d. Exercise of coastal state jurisdiction optional.* Under international law, every coastal state is entitled to exercise authority in areas of the sea adjacent to its coast, as indicated in this chapter. There is, however, no duty for a state to assert or exercise such authority or to do so to the fullest extent permissible. The United States, for instance, has refused to extend its territorial sea beyond three miles, to claim certain areas as historic waters, or to draw straight baselines in certain areas where its coast is deeply indented or where there is a fringe of islands along the coast, thus diminishing the sea areas to which its jurisdiction could have been extended. See United States v. California, 381 U.S. 139, 167–68, 175, 85 S.Ct. 1401, 1416–17, 1421, 14 L.Ed.2d 296 (1965); United States v. Louisiana, 394 U.S. 11, 72–73, 89 S.Ct. 773, 806–807, 22 L.Ed.2d 44 (1969). See also Reporters' Notes 3, 4, and 5.

In respect of coastal zones other than the continental shelf, the jurisdiction of the coastal state and the limits and content of that jurisdiction depend on a proclamation or other express act by the state, but the rights of the coastal state in the continental shelf are automatic and do not depend on exercise or assertion of authority. *Compare* Article 77(3) of the LOS Convention *with* Articles 3, 33, 47, and 57.

*e. Internal waters and ports.* Internal waters are waters wholly or largely surrounded by a state's land territory, as well as sea waters on the landward side of the baseline of the territorial sea or of the archipelagic waters. 1958 Convention on the Territorial Sea and the Contiguous Zone,

Article 5(1); LOS Convention, Articles 8(1) and 50. Under international law, a coastal state's sovereignty over its land territory extends to its internal waters, including bays. See Comment *f.* A state also has complete sovereignty over its seaports, but there are special rules for roadsteads and offshore terminals. 1958 Convention on the Territorial Sea, Article 9; LOS Convention, Articles 12, 60, 218, and 220.

## A. THE TERRITORIAL SEA

*U.N. CONVENTION ON THE LAW OF THE SEA (1982)*

U.N.Doc. A/CONF. 62/122; 21 I.L.M. 1261 (1982).

ARTICLE 2

*Legal Status of the Territorial Sea, of the Air Space Over the Territorial Sea and of its Bed and Subsoil*

1. The sovereignty of a coastal State extends, beyond its land territory and internal waters and, in the case of an archipelagic State, its archipelagic waters, to an adjacent belt of sea, described as the territorial sea.

2. This sovereignty extends to the air space over the territorial sea as well as to its bed and subsoil.

3. The sovereignty over the territorial sea is exercised subject to this Convention and to other rules of international law.

### *Note*

The analogous articles in the 1958 Convention on the Territorial Sea and the Contiguous Zone (Articles 1 and 2) do not include the reference to archipelagic states. The 1982 Convention contains a new Part IV, Articles 46–54, prescribing specially for such states. See p. 1249 below.

### *1. Definition and Delimitation: Historic Development*

After state claims to vast expanses of ocean had ceased, during the seventeenth century, to obtain international respect in law or in practice, there remained the idea that a littoral state might properly claim special interests in at least certain areas of adjacent waters, the inviolability of which was necessary to its safety and protection. The doctrine of the territorial sea is traditionally regarded as having been based on the maxim laid down by the Dutch jurist Bynkershoek in the early eighteenth century that a state's dominion extended only so far out to sea as its cannon would reach; this, in turn, is regarded as having given rise to the doctrine of a three-mile belt of territorial waters, three miles supposedly being the approximate range of eighteenth-century, shore-based cannons. Bynkershoek seems only to have been the first writer to record a "cannon shot" rule that had already been applied in the practice of Mediterranean states to exempt from wartime capture all merchant vessels lying within actual gun range of neutral ports or fortresses. See Walker, Territorial Waters: The Cannon Shot Rule, 22 Brit.Y.B.I.L. 210, 213–22 (1945). This rule did not involve a continuous belt of waters, but merely constructed zones or "pockets" of adjacent sea within which prizes could not be taken without violating a duty owed to the neutral state. In the North, however, the German jurist

Pufendorf envisaged as early as 1672 a maritime belt for defensive purposes (id. at 224), and Denmark (which had at various times claimed the whole ocean between Iceland and Norway, as well as the Baltic Sea) claimed for certain purposes a belt of waters, adjacent to her territories and measured in leagues. Under pressure from other states, Denmark was forced in 1745 to reduce her jurisdiction for neutrality purposes to one league, but this was the Scandinavian league of four nautical miles and not the three-mile league used in the rest of Europe. Kent, The Historical Origins of the Three-Mile Limit, 48 A.J.I.L. 537, 538–45 (1954). When French privateers captured two British ships in 1761, within the limits of the neutral waters proclaimed by Denmark, the French government replied to the Danish protest by proposing that the belt of neutral waters surrounding Danish territories be limited to three miles, i.e., the possible range of cannon. This was the first meeting of the two separate principles previously applied to fix the outward limit of neutral waters. Id. at 548–50. Denmark did not accept the French proposal, and in 1779 Sweden also adopted the Scandinavian league as the limit of her jurisdiction. Id. at 550–51.

The doctrine of a continuous belt of territorial sea, one league or three marine miles wide, received its first explicit statement in 1782, on the basis of the Italian writer Galiani's conclusion that it would be unreasonable for the neutrality of particular waters to depend on whether or not forts were built on the adjacent shores, and on the range of the guns which might be mounted therein. Walker at 228–29. Galiani's proposal of a standard three-mile limit probably had no relation to the actual or supposed range of contemporary cannons, but simply represented a convenient standard measure, just as had the league in the North. The cannon shot tradition, however, was to linger for many years in diplomatic practice and in writings on international law.

The first acceptance in state practice of the three-mile belt of territorial sea occurred in 1793, when the United States, forced to define its neutral waters in the war between France and Great Britain, proposed that the belligerents should respect United States neutrality up to "*the utmost range of a cannon ball,* usually stated at one sea league," this being the smallest breadth claimed by any state. 1 Moore, Digest of International Law 702–703 (1906). France and Great Britain agreed, and the three-mile limit was subsequently applied in British and United States prize courts. See Walker at 230 n. 1.

Thereafter, the three-mile limit was applied for a number of purposes, and states came to rely on the comprehensive notion of the territorial sea as a basis for the exercise of, *inter alia,* fishing, police, and revenue jurisdiction. After inclusion in a number of European treaties regulating fishing rights, and after adoption by a number of Asian and South American states, the three-mile limit was world-wide by the end of the nineteenth century, with comparatively few exceptions (notably the Scandinavian countries—four miles, Russia—three to twelve miles at different times, and Spain and Portugal—each claiming six miles). Brierly, The Law of Nations 203–204 (6th ed., Waldock, 1963). Difficulties were caused, however, by the practice of some states asserting jurisdiction for customs and fishing purposes in zones contiguous to, but outside, the three-mile territorial sea. The North Sea Fishery Convention of 1882 adopted a three-mile limit, while excepting certain prized areas from this rule, but even the renunciation by Great Britain in 1876 of customs jurisdiction in a contiguous zone did not persuade other states to do likewise. Id. at 204–05.

By this time, the traditional association of the three-mile limit with the cannon shot doctrine had been rendered obsolete. When, for example, in 1862 Spain protested the failure of United States ships to respect its six-mile belt of territorial waters off the coast of Cuba, arguing that six miles was not unreasonable in view of the increased range of cannon, Secretary of State Seward replied that if the sovereignty of a coastal state were continually to be subject to change with "improvements of the science of ordnance," the consequent uncertainty would provoke endless conflicts. The "more practical limit" of three miles had been generally recognized by nations, concluded Seward, and no state could extend unilaterally a jurisdiction derived in the first place only from the law of nations. 1 Moore, Digest of International Law 707, 716 (1906).

State practice remained apparently fairly constant up to and during the first three decades of the twentieth century, but considerable deep-rooted dissatisfaction with the three-mile territorial sea was revealed in the surveys conducted by the Preparatory Committee for the League of Nations' Hague Codification Conference of 1930, at which the subject of territorial waters was to be one of the three topics chosen for codification. The Committee reported that its survey of governments showed agreement that "a state has sovereignty over a belt of sea round its coast," but that there was a lack of unanimity on the question of the breadth of this belt. "According to the majority," stated the Committee, "the breadth is three nautical miles. No reply disputes that territorial waters include such a three-mile belt, but there are several which contemplate a greater breadth. Some present the claim of individual States to a greater breadth as one established in international law, a contention which is expressly rejected by other replies; others mention such a greater breadth without stating whether they regard it as already recognized by international law; others recommend an extension of territorial waters as a matter to be agreed to but involving an innovation. The breadth proposed in some replies is four miles, in others six or eighteen. * * * Most States agree, to a greater or lesser extent, that exercise of particular specified rights by the coastal State outside its territorial waters, i.e., on the high seas, can be accepted as legitimate—at any rate, as a compromise and as the result of a convention on the subject." 2 Conference for the Codification of International Law: Bases of Discussion 17, 33, 34 (1929). The number of states opposing the three-mile limit was sufficient to prevent the Conference from reaching agreement on this point (id. at 210–211), and some states interpreted this failure as leaving every state free to fix its own limit.

Thereafter and especially after the 1945 Truman proclamations with regard to the continental shelf and the conservation of fisheries, many states extended their claims to six or twelve miles, or even more. See 28 Dep't St.Bull. 486–87 (1953).

In 1951, pursuant to a recommendation of the General Assembly, the International Law Commission began work on the régime of the territorial sea. Although substantial progress was made in most areas, this body also failed to reach agreement on the breadth of the territorial sea, and in its final report, adopted at the eighth session (1956), the Commission recommended the following Article ([1956] II Yb.I.L.C. 265):

ARTICLE 3

(1) The Commission recognizes that international practice is not uniform as regards the delimitation of the territorial sea.

(2) The Commission considers that international law does not permit an extension of the territorial sea beyond twelve miles.

(3) The Commission, without taking any decision as to the breadth of the territorial sea up to that limit, notes, on the one hand, that many states have fixed a breadth greater than three miles and, on the other hand, that many states do not recognize such a breadth when that of their own territorial sea is less.

(4) The Commission considers that the breadth of the territorial sea should be fixed by an international conference.

The Geneva Conference on the Law of the Sea failed to achieve the two-thirds majority that was necessary for decision on a definite limit of territorial waters. Just prior to the opening of the Conference, some twenty-one states still claimed three miles as the breadth of their territorial seas (the Scandinavian states still claimed four miles), thirteen states claimed six miles (two of these claimed this distance only for fishing purposes), and twelve states asserted dominion over a belt of sea nine to twelve miles wide. In addition, nine states claimed apparently all the waters above the continental shelves adjacent to their territories, and there were a variety of miscellaneous claims. Sorenson, The Law of the Sea, [1958] Int'l Conciliation No. 520, at 244. But there was agreement (Article 24) that the contiguous zone, "a zone of high seas contiguous to its territorial sea," may not extend beyond twelve miles from shore, which implied that the territorial sea was to be at most something less than twelve miles wide.

In the work of the First Committee (on the territorial sea and contiguous zone), two major approaches to the problem could be discerned. First, a group led by the United States and the United Kingdom struggled to retain the traditional three-mile limit, admitting, however, some willingness to compromise on the question of exclusive fishing rights. Second, the Soviet bloc (supported by the Arab states and by a number of the newly independent nations of Africa and Asia) favored the right of coastal states to choose their own limit for the territorial sea, up to twelve miles from the baseline. The latter group received occasional, and ultimately decisive, support from states such as Canada, Iceland, Mexico and other Latin American nations concerned primarily with the conservation and exploitation of fishery resources in their offshore waters. Heinzen, The Three–Mile Limit: Preserving the Freedom of the Seas, 11 Stan.L.Rev. 597, 652–53 (1959). Midway in the Conference, the United Kingdom proposed as a compromise a six-mile territorial sea. 3 U.N. Conf. on the Law of the Sea, Off.Rec. 103–04 (1958). The United States (after first deploring the British retreat) then attempted to make the United Kingdom proposal even more attractive to fishing states by suggesting in addition that the coastal state would have the right to regulate fishing in the contiguous zone, subject to the preservation of the fishing rights of other states which had exploited these waters during the previous five years. Id. at 153. The United States proposal was still not satisfactory to the fishing states, especially Canada, but came closest to acceptance by the full Conference. 2 id. at 39.

The failure of the 1958 Conference to reach agreement on the two most important problems before it—the breadth of the territorial sea and the extent of fishing rights in the contiguous zone—motivated the decision to convene a second Conference on the Law of the Sea in 1960. Between 1958 and 1960, a number of additional states had extended their territorial sea beyond three miles. See 4 Whiteman at 19–33. The United States in the interim determined that the "area of compromise which could produce a proposal capable of acceptance at the Conference of 1960 was not broad and was, in general, the area between the previous United States proposal and the previous Canadian proposal at the 1958 Conference, thus incorporating a 6–mile territorial sea with some kind of 6–mile contiguous fishing zone." Id. at 120. Accordingly, the United States and Canada ultimately placed before the 1960 Conference a joint proposal based on the 1958 United States compromise suggestion: a territorial sea of six miles, plus a contiguous zone of six additional miles in which the coastal state would enjoy exclusive fishing rights; the "vested interests" of other states in the resources of the contiguous zone would, however, be preserved, but only for a period of ten years, after which they would expire. Second U.N. Conf. on the Law of the Sea, Off.Rec.Annexes 173 (1960). The proposal was intended to recognize the special interest of some states (notably Iceland, Norway, and Canada) in the exploitation of their coastal fisheries, while allowing a period during which the adverse effects of exclusion on foreign fishermen could be mitigated. It was expected that the proposal would receive the necessary two-thirds approval, but opposition led by the Soviet and Arab blocs succeeded by one vote in blocking adoption of the proposal. Second U.N. Conf. on the Law of the Sea, Off.Rec. Summary Rec. 30 (1960). The United States and the United Kingdom emphasized that the non-acceptance of the compromise proposal left the legal situation where it had been previous to the Conference, and stated their intention to continue to adhere to the three-mile limit and not to recognize any larger claim as valid against them without their agreement. See generally Dean, The Second Geneva Conference on the Law of the Sea, 54 A.J.I.L. 751 (1960).

After 1960, with the continuing proliferation of states and the emergence of the "Third World," the drive for a twelve-mile territorial sea became stronger and the opposition to it eroded. The United States indicated its readiness to accept the twelve-mile zone, provided passage through international straits were assured. See p. 1261 infra. But developing coastal states no longer saw widening the territorial sea beyond twelve miles as the way to extending their exclusive jurisdiction over resources and joined to develop instead the concept of a far-wider "patrimonial sea" or "exclusive economic zone." See pp. 1291–92 infra.

## BREADTH OF THE TERRITORIAL SEA

*U.N. CONVENTION ON THE LAW OF THE SEA (1982)*

U.N.Doc. A/CONF. 62/122; 21 I.L.M. 1261 (1982).

ARTICLE 3

Every State has the right to establish the breadth of its territorial sea up to a limit not exceeding 12 nautical miles, measured from baselines determined in accordance with this Convention.

* * *

ARTICLE 5

Except where otherwise provided in this Convention, the normal baseline for measuring the breadth of the territorial sea is the low-water line along the coast as marked on large-scale charts officially recognized by the coastal State.

### *Notes*

1. The 1982 Convention laid to rest a long controversy as to the breadth of the territorial sea. It could not be resolved in the negotiations on the 1958 Conventions, which accordingly contained no provision on the matter. The Second United Nations Conference on the Law of the Sea in 1960, convened specially for the purpose of resolving the issue, reached no agreement.

Coastal states that had pressed for a wide territorial sea, some up to 200 (or more) miles, did so particularly to obtain exclusive fishing rights. During the years of negotiations leading up to the 1982 Convention, coastal states began to claim large exclusive fishing zones. Increasing acceptance of such zones and the move to a 200 mile Exclusive Economic Zone (see p. 1291 infra) eliminated the pressure for a large territorial sea and led to acceptance of the 12 mile limit on the territorial sea.

2. Under the 1982 Convention a state "has the right" to establish a territorial sea "to a limit not exceeding" 12 miles. The United States had resisted extending its own territorial sea beyond three miles, perhaps in the hope of inducing others to exercise similar restraint. In 1988, however, President Reagan issued a Proclamation declaring that "[t]he territorial sea of the United States henceforth extends to 12 nautical miles from the baselines of the United States determined in accordance with international law." Presidential Proclamation on the Territorial Sea of the United States, December 27, 1988, reprinted in 28 I.L.M. 284 (1989).

As of the early 1990s, state practice had taken a marked swing from three miles to twelve miles as the width most commonly claimed. Most coastal states have claimed from three to twelve miles: ten claimed three miles; six claimed from four to six miles; 110 claimed twelve miles. Seventeen, apparently, continued to claim twenty miles or greater, with twelve states claiming 200 miles. Law of the Sea Bulletin 39 (No. 15, May 1990). The 1982 Convention probably states the present customary law, and claims beyond 12 miles will doubtless be challenged.

3. Important consequences for the maritime right of innocent passage (and for aircraft, which have no right of innocent passage over the territorial sea) flow from the extension of the territorial sea to 12 miles. The United States representative at the 1958 Geneva Conference pointed out:

> One of the merits of the three mile limit was that it was safest for shipping. Many landmarks still used for visual plotting by small craft were not visible at a range of 12 miles; only 20 per cent. of the world's lighthouses had a range that exceeded that distance; radar navigation was of only marginal utility beyond 12 miles; and many vessels (which frequently did not want to enter the territorial sea) did not carry sufficient cable or appropriate equipment to anchor at the depths normally found outside the 12 mile-limit. * * * One further objection to extending the territorial sea was that, in time of war, a neutral state would have greater difficulty in safeguarding the broader belt of territorial waters against the incursions of ships of belligerents.

III 1958 Sea Conference Records 26. See also *Fisheries Jurisdiction Case* (Jurisdiction), 1973 I.C.J. 3, 28 n. 8 (Fitzmaurice, J. dissenting) (broader territorial sea presents difficulty for states in the discharge of their territorial sea responsibilities of policing; marking channels, reefs and other obstacles; giving notice of dangers to navigation; and providing rescue services).

4. The method of measuring the territorial sea involves highly technical geographical considerations and was long controversial. See, for example, Fisheries Case (United Kingdom v. Norway), 1951 I.C.J. 116. In response to intensified exploitation of Norwegian coastal waters by British fishing vessels, the Norwegian government had issued a decree in 1935 which delimited Norway's northern territorial waters on the basis of straight baselines drawn along the most seaward points on the islands ("skjaergaard") which line the coast. Contending that international law required the baseline to be the actual low-water mark (except in the case of bays), the United Kingdom instituted proceedings in the International Court of Justice after its negotiations with Norway had failed. There was no objection to Norway's use of four miles as the breadth of its territorial sea, in view of Norway's historic claim to a four-mile territorial sea. The Court prefaced its decision with a discussion of the geographic and economic characteristics of the coastal regions of the Norwegian mainland, as well as of the "skjaergaard" of some 120,000 islands, rocks, and reefs, in the course of which it stressed the pronounced indentations and convolution of the coast and the dependence of the local population on fishing as a means of survival. The Court found, by a vote of ten to two, that the method of delimitation used by Norway was not contrary to international law, and, by a vote of eight to four, that the baselines drawn by the 1935 Decree did not violate international law.

On various aspects of the Anglo–Norwegian Fisheries Case, see 4 Whiteman at 137–94; Waldock, The Anglo–Norwegian Fisheries Case, 28 Brit.Y.B.I.L. 114 (1951); Fitzmaurice, The Law and Procedure of the International Court of Justice, 1951–54, 31 Brit.Y.B.I.L. 371 (1954); Johnson, The Anglo–Norwegian Fisheries Case, 1 I.C.L.Q. 145 (1952); Evensen, Anglo–Norwegian Fisheries Case and Its Legal Consequences, 46 A.J.I.L. 609 (1952). See also Blum, Historic Titles in International Law (1965).

The *Fisheries Case* has been often cited as denying the claims of coastal states to determine their own jurisdiction. The Court said (at 132): "The delimitation of the sea areas has always an international aspect; it cannot be dependent merely upon the will of the coastal State as expressed in its municipal law." The *Fisheries Case* is also cited to support the principle that a state is not bound by a rule of customary international law if it expressed dissent while the law was developing. See 1951 I.C.J. at 131. See Chapter 2, p. 87 above.

5. The 1982 Convention generally follows the 1958 Convention as to the method of measuring the territorial sea. See in particular Article 5 (normal baseline) and Article 7 (straight baselines). A new Article 6 provides that for islands situated on atolls or having fringed reefs, the baseline is the seaward low-water line of the reef. Where the coastline is highly unstable, Article 7(2) permits the coastal state to select the appropriate points along such baselines which remain effective until changed by the coastal state. Article 11 adds that "[o]ffshore installations and artificial islands shall not be considered as permanent harbour works" to be regarded as part of the coast for the purpose of delimiting the territorial sea. Article 14 adds that "[t]he coastal state may determine baselines in turn by any of the methods provided for in the foregoing articles to suit different conditions."

6. In 1965, the United States Supreme Court resolved a dispute between the Federal Government and the State of California over the definition of "inland waters" on the California coast. United States v. California, 381 U.S. 139, 85 S.Ct. 1401, 14 L.Ed.2d 296 (1965). The United States had ceded various submerged lands to coastal states under the Submerged Lands Act of 1953. See p. 1285 below. Under the Act, the United States owned the lands "lying seaward of the ordinary low-water mark, and outside of the inland waters, extending seaward three nautical miles * * *." The Court applied the recently "settled" international rule defining inland waters, contained in the Convention on the Territorial Sea and the Contiguous Zone (T.I.A.S. No. 639), which had been ratified by the United States. The provision of the 1958 Convention used by the Court is carried over into the 1982 Law of the Sea Convention unchanged (Art. 10).

In United States v. Alaska, ___ U.S. ___, 112 S.Ct. 1606, 118 L.Ed.2d 222 (1992), the Supreme Court pointed out that in *U.S. v. California* it held that "international law recognized the seaward expansion of sovereignty through artificial additions to the coastline." As between state and federal government, however, the Court in the *Alaska* case upheld the power of the Secretary of the Army to condition a permit to build an artificial addition on the Alaskan coastline, on Alaska's stipulation that the construction would not alter the location of the existing federal-state boundary.

On jurisdiction over internal waters and ports, and the law governing islands, see p. 1332 below.

## BAYS

If an area of sea meets the legal requirements to be considered a bay, it becomes internal waters so that there is no right of innocent passage. See p. 1254 infra.

Attempts to establish, for international legal purposes, a geographic definition for bays occurred with some frequency during the nineteenth century, especially in the Anglo–French Fisheries Convention of 1839 and in the North Sea Fisheries Convention of 1882 (both of which provided that the mouth of a "bay" might be no more than ten miles wide in order for the coastal state to claim exclusive fishing rights therein). At the same time, however, a number of states claimed, on historic or other grounds, bays the openings of which were of greater width.

The International Law Commission, in its final report adopted in 1956, recommended a closing line of fifteen miles as a compromise between the ten-mile rule and the twenty-four mile rule supported by those states claiming a twelve-mile territorial sea. The Commission's definition also included, however, a proviso that the total area of the enclosed body of water must be at least as great as that of the semicircle whose diameter is the line drawn across the mouth thereof. See [1956] I Yb.I.L.C. 190–93, 195–97; [1956] II Yb.I.L.C. 268–69. The twenty-four mile closing line was restored by the First Committee at the Geneva Conference in 1958, 3 U.N.Conf. on the Law of the Sea, Off.Rec. 144–46 (1958), and this limit was approved by the full Conference by a vote of 49 to 19, with nine abstentions. 2 id. at 63.

The 1982 Convention, Art. 10, retains the 24–mile closing line adopted in the 1958 Convention and is identical with Article 7 of that Convention in other respects, too.

The Restatement (Third) § 511, Comment *f*, states:

> A coastal state may designate a bay as its internal waters if it has prescribed characteristics. It must be a well-marked indentation in the coast, not a mere curvature. Its area must be as large as, or larger than, that of the semicircle whose diameter is a line drawn across the mouth of the indentation. The closing line of a bay is drawn between its natural entrance points; the line may not exceed 24 nautical miles, but a 24–mile line may be drawn within the bay in such manner as to enclose the maximum area of water that is possible with a line of that length. 1958 Convention on the Territorial Sea and the Contiguous Zone, Article 7; LOS Convention, Article 10.
>
> In addition, international law recognizes "historic" bays that have been considered internal waters even though they do not satisfy criteria for a bay. 1958 Convention on the Territorial Sea and the Contiguous Zone, Article 7(6); LOS Convention, Article 10(6).

Article 7(6) of the 1958 Convention on the Territorial Sea and Contiguous Zone provides that states were free to claim "so-called 'historic' bays" even if these did not meet the geographic criteria of the rest of Article 7. For background, see [1962] II Yb.I.L.C. 1. Article 10(6) of the 1982 Convention says only that its provisions do not apply to historic bays.

In the *Continental Shelf Case* (Libya v. Tunisia), 1982 I.C.J. 18, the Court noted that historic bays had been purposefully left for later consideration when Article 7 of the 1958 Convention was drafted and that the 1982 Convention had failed to address the issue. The Court concluded:

> It seems clear that the matter continues to be governed by general international law which does not provide for a '*single régime*' for 'historic waters' or 'historic bays,' but only for a particular régime for each of the concrete, recognised cases of 'historic waters' or 'historic bays.'

1982 I.C.J. at 73.

The United States has long characterized "bays" according to two principles: a geographic test, based on a maximum closing line of ten miles and a minimum area of enclosed waters, or an "historic" test. If either principle applied, the U.S. would consider the waters a bay and internal waters of the United States. Delaware and Chesapeake Bays have long been considered as forming part of the internal waters of the United States. 1 Moore, Digest of International Law 735–39, 741–42 (1906). Other important "historic" bays are the Bay of Chaleurs, Conception Bay, and Miramichi Bay (all Canadian). Canada claims as well all of Hudson's Bay, but this claim has been disputed by the United States. See, in general, 4 Whiteman at 233–58. It should be noted that some "historic" bays may now be able to qualify as geographic bays under the liberalized criteria adopted in Article 7 of the 1958 Convention and Article 10 of the 1982 Convention.

Another controversial claim to an historic bay is Libya's claim to the Gulf of Sidra. That claim and its rejection by the United States played a role in a 1981 incident in the Gulf where United States jets shot down two Libyan fighters which were challenging the presence of United States ships in Gulf waters and United States jets in the airspace above. In 1986, the United States again engaged Libyan forces in the Gulf when a naval fleet crossed the Libyan-set boundary to assert the right to innocent passage in waters beyond 12 miles from the Libyan shore. See 87 Dept. State Bull. 69 (1987); Blum, The Gulf of Sidra Incident, 80 A.J.I.L. 668 (1986).

On bays generally, see Westerman, The Juridical Bay (1987); Bouchez, The Regime of Bays in International Law (1964); Scovazzi, Bays and Straight Baselines in the Mediterranean, 19 Ocean Dev. & Int'l L. 401 (1988); Goldie, Historic Bays in International Law: An Impressionistic Overview, 11 Syracuse J.Int'l L. & Com. 211 (1984).

The 1982 Convention includes a special regime requiring cooperation by states bordering "enclosed or semi-enclosed seas," defined as "a gulf, basin, or sea surrounded by two or more States and connected to the open seas by a narrow outlet or consisting entirely or primarily of the territorial seas and exclusive economic zones of two or more coastal States." (Part IX, Arts. 122–23). See Symmons, The Maritime Zones of Islands (1979).

## ARCHIPELAGOES AND ARCHIPELAGIC STATES

In a note of December 12, 1955 to the United Nations, the Philippine government referred to its position that "all waters around, between and connecting the different islands belonging to the Philippine Archipelago irrespective of their widths or dimensions, are necessary appurtenances of its land territory, forming an integral part of the national or inland waters, subject to the exclusive sovereignty of the Philippines," and that other water areas (specified in the Spanish cession of 1898 to the United States, and in other United States agreements) were considered as territorial waters. 4 Whiteman at 282–83. On December 14, 1957, the Indonesian government stated that the "Indonesian archipelago" had historically been considered as an "entity," and that all waters "around, between and connecting" the islands of the archipelago were consequently to be considered as "inland or national waters subject to the absolute sovereignty of Indonesia." The peaceful passage of foreign vessels was guaranteed to the extent they did not infringe Indonesian sovereignty or security. Id. at 284. The United States refused to recognize the validity of the Philippine and Indonesian claims and

Australia and Japan refused to recognize the validity of the Indonesian claim. Id. at 283–85. In Civil Aeronautics Board v. Island Airlines, Inc., 235 F.Supp. 990 (D.Hawaii 1964), aff'd, 352 F.2d 735 (9th Cir.1965), it was held that each island of the Hawaiian archipelago had its own territorial sea and that the intervening waters were high seas. For the State Department position in *Island Airlines,* see 4 Whiteman at 281. See also Dellapenna, The Philippines Territorial Water Claim in International Law, 5 J.L. & Econ.Dev. 45 (1970).

Writing about archipelagic states in connection with the delimitation of the maritime boundary between the Republic of China (Taiwan) and the Philippines, Professor Chiu states:

> Until recently few international law scholars and few countries have paid much attention to the special legal problems concerning mid-ocean archipelagos. The question of whether a group of islands can be considered as a unit in delimiting a territorial sea has, according to most authorities, been adequately solved by general rules concerning the delimitation of the territorial sea of the mainland or island. The 1929 Harvard Draft on the Law of the Territorial Sea contains no provision relating to groups of islands or archipelagos. Article 7 of the Draft provides that the territorial sea of islands should be measured in a similar way to that of the mainland. It is a contention of this article that no different rule should be established for groups of islands or archipelagos, except that, if the outer fringe of islands is sufficiently close to form one complete belt of marginal sea, then the waters within such belt should be considered as territorial waters.
>
> At the Hague Codification Conference, convened by the League of Nations in 1930, the question of archipelagos was raised by Portugal, which submitted the following proposal as a basis of discussion:
>
> > In the case of an archipelago, the islands forming the archipelago shall be deemed to be a unit and the breadth of the territorial sea shall be measured from the islands most distant from the centre of the archipelago.
>
> The United States proposed the total deletion of the archipelago concept. After discussion, the Conference did not attempt to draft an article on this subject. Only a few writers discussed this problem after the Conference, and, with the exception of Munch, none of them made any concrete proposal.
>
> When the United Nations International Law Commission (ILC) began to draft its text on the law of the sea, only cursory attention was paid to the question of archipelagos.
>
> In J.P.A. François's Third Report on the Regime of the Territorial Sea to the United Nations International Law Commission, he included a draft article on the "groups of islands" as follows:
>
> > 1. The term "groups of islands," in the juridical sense, shall be determined to mean three or more islands enclosing a portion of the sea when joined by straight lines not exceeding five miles in length except that one such line may extend to a maximum of ten miles.

> 2. The straight lines specified in the preceding paragraph shall be the baseline for measuring the territorial sea. Waters lying within the area bounded by such lines and the islands themselves shall be considered as inland waters.

> Because of the divergent views expressed by several members of the Commission and the press of time, in 1956 François suggested leaving the matter to the diplomatic conference to be convened. His suggestion was adopted by the Commission and the matter was shelved. The Draft Articles on the Law of the Sea submitted to the 1958 UNCLOS I at Geneva contain no provision on archipelagos at all. At the Conference, only two countries—the Philippines and Yugoslavia—raised the question of archipelagos, and the Convention on the Territorial Sea and Contiguous Zone, which was adopted by the 1958 Conference, is silent on the problem.

> At the UNCLOS II in 1960 the Philippines again raised the archipelago question, but the Conference did not take any action on it. It was not until the early 1960s that scholars of international law began to pay attention to the special problems of the archipelagos. In the meantime a number of former archipelago colonies had become independent. They are likely to make archipelago claims to protect or expand their maritime interests.

> At UNCLOS III, Part VII of the Informal Single Negotiating Text, issued in 1975 and entitled "Archipelagos," contains two sections, the first of which relates to archipelagic states, i.e., states constituted wholly by one or more archipelagos which may include other islands, and the second to oceanic archipelagos belonging to continental states. Section one contains 14 articles (117–130), while section two contains only one article (131), which provides that "the provisions of section 1 are without prejudice to the status of oceanic archipelagos forming an integral part of the territory of a continental state." In other words, continental states' archipelagos can also apply the so-called archipelagic principle to their archipelagos in delimiting maritime boundaries. The benefit of this method of delimitation is obvious. A state can draw straight baselines joining the outermost points of the outermost islands and drying reefs of the archipelago. After discussion at the Fourth Session of the Conference, held between March 15 and May 7, 1976, the informal text was revised and distributed on May 6, 1976. In the revised text, Part VII became Chapter VII and was renamed "Archipelagic States." The revised text contains no article on oceanic archipelagos of a continental state. In other words, a continental state cannot apply the archipelagic principle in delimiting its oceanic archipelagos. This approach was later formally adopted in the 1982 Convention. The UNCLOS official records and press releases do not disclose why continental states with archipelagos agreed to such an arrangement.

Chiu, Some Problems Concerning the Delimitation of the Maritime Boundary Between the Republic of China and the Philippines, 3 Chinese Y.B.I.L. 1, 10–12 (1983) (footnotes omitted).

The problems of security, communications and fishing faced by the Philippines and Indonesia were countered by the interests of other states in the use of the intervening waters and their airspace for international transport (and, to a lesser extent, for fishing of their own). See, generally, McDougal & Burke, The Public Order of the Oceans 411–15 (1962). If no special consideration were given to the facts that a group of islands was relatively close-knit and under the sovereignty of a single state, it might be expected that each constituent island would be entitled to its own territorial sea and that the archipelago as a whole would be entitled to no extraordinary jurisdiction over intervening waters. See, e.g., Harvard Research in International Law, The Law of Territorial Waters, art. 7, 23 A.J.I.L.Spec. Supp. 241, 275–76 (1929). The International Court of Justice, in the *Anglo–Norwegian Fisheries Case,* 1951 I.C.J. 116, observed that attempts to subject groups of islands to "conditions analogous to the limitations concerning bays" had not gone "beyond the stage of proposals" Id. at 131, and the International Law Commission decided in 1955 that a proposed article setting narrow limits on an archipelagic state's discretion to enclose intervening waters should be deleted. [1955] I Yb.I.L.C. 217–18. Lack of technical information was cited as one of the obstacles to agreement. [1956] II Yb.I.L.C. 270.

The claims of archipelagic states were largely accepted in the 1982 Convention which provides in pertinent part:

Article 46

Use of Terms

For the purposes of this Convention:

(a) "archipelagic State" means a State constituted wholly by one or more archipelagos and may include other islands;

(b) "archipelago" means a group of islands, including parts of islands, interconnecting waters and other natural features which are so closely interrelated that such islands, waters and other natural features form an intrinsic geographical, economic and political entity, or which historically have been regarded as such.

Article 47

Archipelagic Baselines

1. An archipelagic State may draw straight archipelagic baselines joining the outermost points of the outermost islands and drying reefs of the archipelago provided that within such baselines are included the main islands and an area in which the ratio of the area of the water to the area of the land, including atolls, is between 1 to 1 and 9 to 1.

2. The length of such baselines shall not exceed 100 nautical miles, except that up to 3 per cent of the total number of baselines enclosing any archipelago may exceed that length, up to a maximum length of 125 nautical miles. * * *

---

The territorial sea, contiguous zone, exclusive economic zone, and the continental shelf of an archipelagic state are measured from these baselines

(Art. 48). The archipelagic state has sovereignty over all the waters enclosed by these baselines as well as over the airspace, seabed and subsoil (Art. 49). But archipelagic states agree to respect (1) existing agreements with other states and traditional fishery rights and other activities of immediately adjacent neighboring states and submarine cables laid by other states (Art. 51). There is a right to innocent passage within archipelagic waters (Art. 52). The archipelagic state may designate sea lanes and air routes suitable for continuous and expeditious passage, analogous to those established by states bordering international straits. See p. 1265 infra. All ships and aircraft have the right of "archipelagic sea lane passage" (Art. 53).

As of 1988, eleven states claimed archipelagic status and nine had published geographical coordinates of territorial sea using straight baselines. See Smith, Global Maritime Claims, 20 Ocean Dev. & Int'l L. 92 (1989).

On Archipelagoes generally, see United Nations, Analytical Studies on the Law of the Sea Convention—Archipelagic States (1990); Rajan, The Legal Regime of Archipelagos, 29 Germ.Y.B.Int'l L. 441 (1987); Herman, The Modern Concept of Off-Lying Archipelago in International Law, 23 Can. Y.B.Int'l L. 172 (1985); Tolentino, Archipelagoes under the Convention on the Law of the Sea, 28 Far Eastern L.Rev. 1 (1984); Coquia, Development of the Archipelagic Doctrine as a Recognized Principle of International Law, 58 Philippine L.J. 13 (1983).

## ISLANDS

### *U.N. CONVENTION ON THE LAW OF THE SEA (1982)*

U.N.Doc. A/CONF. 62/122; 21 I.L.M. 1261 (1982).

#### Article 121

#### Régime of islands

1. An island is a naturally formed area of land, surrounded by water, which is above water at high tide.

2. Except as provided for in paragraph 3, the territorial sea, the contiguous zone, the exclusive economic zone and the continental shelf of an island are determined in accordance with the provisions of this Convention applicable to other land territory.

3. Rocks which cannot sustain human habitation or economic life of their own shall have no exclusive economic zone or continental shelf.

According to the Conciliation Commission in *Jan Mayern Case,* reprinted in 20 I.L.M. 797 (1981), the 1982 Convention "reflect[s] the present status of international law," with respect to islands. The 1982 Convention's definition repeats that of the 1958 Convention, but restricts the conditions under which an island may have an exclusive economic zone and continental shelf. See Jaywardene, The Regime of Islands in International Law (1990).

Small islands have become increasingly important because of the possibility of exploiting gas and oil resources in the seabed of their adjacent waters. In the South China Sea, for example, the People's Republic of

China, Taiwan, Vietnam, the Philippines and Malaysia have been in dispute over the Paracel Islands and Spratly Islands for many years for this reason. China and Vietnam have engaged in hostilities over their competing claims to the Spratly Islands and in 1992 China reportedly stationed military forces on the Islands over the protests of the other claimants. See generally Johnston & Valencia, Pacific Ocean Boundary Problems: Status and Solutions (1991); Bennett, The People's Republic of China and the use of International Law in the Spratly Islands dispute, 28 Stan.J.Int'l L. 425 (1992); Chang, China's Claim of Sovereignty over Spratly and Paracel Islands: A Historical and Legal Perspective, 23 Case W.Res.J.Int'l L. 399 (1991).

In *Case Concerning the Land, Island and Maritime Frontier Dispute* (El Salvador v. Honduras: Nicaragua intervening), 1992 I.C.J. 351, the Court put an end to a century-old territorial dispute between El Salvador and Honduras; the Court held, among other things, that El Salvador is entitled to possession of the islands in the Gulf of Fonseca. In *Case Concerning Maritime Delimitation and Territorial Questions Between Qatar and Bahrain* (Qatar v. Bahrain), Qatar instituted proceedings against Bahrain in "respect of certain disputes between the two States relating to sovereignty over the Hawar Islands, sovereign rights over the shoals of Dibal and Qit'at Jaradah, and the delimitation of the maritime areas of the two States." Order, 1992 I.C.J. 237. See also the arbitral decision in the Case Concerning Delimitation of Maritime Areas Between Canada and the French Republic, involving the delimitation of the continental shelf off Canada and the French islands of St. Pierre and Miquelon, reprinted in 31 I.L.M. 1149 (1992).

### 2. *Passage Through the Territorial Sea*

#### a. *Innocent Passage*

*U.N. CONVENTION ON THE LAW OF THE SEA (1982)*

U.N.Doc. A/CONF. 62/122; 21 I.L.M. 1261 (1982).

ARTICLE 17

*Right of Innocent Passage*

Subject to this Convention, ships of all States, whether coastal or land-locked, enjoy the right of innocent passage through the territorial sea.

ARTICLE 18

*Meaning of Passage*

1. Passage means navigation through the territorial sea for the purpose of:

(a) traversing that sea without entering internal waters or calling at a roadstead or port facility outside internal waters; or

(b) proceeding to or from internal waters or a call at such roadstead or port facility.

2. Passage shall be continuous and expeditious. However, passage includes stopping and anchoring, but only in so far as the same are incidental to ordinary navigation or are rendered necessary by *force majeure*

or distress or for the purpose of rendering assistance to persons, ships or aircraft in danger or distress.

ARTICLE 19

*Meaning of Innocent Passage*

1. Passage is innocent so long as it is not prejudicial to the peace, good order or security of the coastal State. Such passage shall take place in conformity with this Convention and with other rules of international law.

2. Passage of a foreign ship shall be considered to be prejudicial to the peace, good order or security of the coastal State if in the territorial sea it engages in any of the following activities:

(a) any threat or use of force against the sovereignty, territorial integrity or political independence of the coastal State, or in any other manner in violation of the principles of international law embodied in the Charter of the United Nations;

(b) any exercise or practice with weapons of any kind;

(c) any act aimed at collecting information to the prejudice of the defence or security of the coastal State;

(d) any act of propaganda aimed at affecting the defence or security of the coastal State;

(e) the launching, landing or taking on board of any aircraft;

(f) the launching, landing or taking on board of any military device;

(g) the loading or unloading of any commodity, currency or person contrary to the customs, fiscal, immigration or sanitary laws and regulations of the coastal State;

(h) any act of wilful and serious pollution contrary to this Convention;

(i) any fishing activities;

(j) the carrying out of research or survey activities;

(k) any act aimed at interfering with any systems of communication or any other facilities or installations of the coastal State;

(*l*) any other activity not having a direct bearing on passage.

ARTICLE 20

*Submarines and Other Underwater Vehicles*

In the territorial sea, submarines and other underwater vehicles are required to navigate on the surface and to show their flag.

## Notes

1. "The right of innocent passage seems to be the result of an attempt to reconcile the freedom of ocean navigation with the theory of territorial waters. While recognizing the necessity of granting to littoral states a zone of waters along the coast, the family of nations was unwilling to prejudice the newly gained freedom of the seas. As a general principle, the right of innocent passage requires no supporting argument or citation of authority; it is firmly established in international law." Jessup, The Law of Territorial Waters and Maritime Jurisdiction 120 (1927).

2. The 1982 Convention spells out in detail the kinds of laws and regulations relating to innocent passage that the coastal state may adopt. "Such laws and regulations shall not apply to the design, construction, manning or equipment of foreign ships unless they are giving effect to generally accepted international rules or standards" (Art. 21(2)). Compare the general language of Article 17 of the 1958 Convention. Article 22 authorizes the coastal state to establish sea lanes and traffic separation schemes, especially for ships carrying nuclear or other dangerous or toxic substances. The duties of the coastal state are also given greater specificity. It may not discriminate against the ships of any state or against ships carrying cargoes to, from or on behalf of any State (Art. 24(1)(b)). As under the 1958 Convention, "the coastal state shall give appropriate publicity to any dangers to navigation, of which it has knowledge * * * " (Art. 24(2)). Is that requirement less stringent than that suggested in the *Corfu Channel Case*, p. 1257 infra? By Article 26 the coastal state may not levy charges for passage, only for any specific service rendered the ship, and without discrimination.

3. For a suggestion that the right to "innocent passage" was not violated by a United States military search and seizure of a United States vessel in foreign territorial waters, see United States v. Conroy, 589 F.2d 1258 (5th Cir.1979), cert. denied, 444 U.S. 831, 100 S.Ct. 60, 62 L.Ed.2d 40 (1979), discussed at Note 5, p. 1351 below.

4. A warship's right of innocent passage under customary law was unclear. Jessup concluded in 1927 that "the sound rule seems to be that they [warships] should not enjoy an absolute legal right to pass through a state's territorial waters any more than an army may cross the land territory." The Law of Territorial Waters and Maritime Jurisdiction 120 (1927). The Hague Codification Conference confined itself to observing that states ordinarily "will not forbid the passage of foreign warships" and "will not require a previous authorisation or notification." 24 A.J.I.L.Supp. 246 (1930). For a collection of views, see 4 Whiteman at 404–17.

The 1958 Convention on the Territorial Sea and the Contiguous Zone provides:

> Article 23. If any warship does not comply with the regulations of the coastal State concerning passage through the territorial sea and disregards any request for compliance which is made to it, the coastal State may require the warship to leave the territorial sea.

The 1982 Convention, Article 30, repeats the 1958 Convention but adds the word "immediately."

Did the inclusion of Article 23 in the 1958 Convention imply that warships have a right of innocent passage through a foreign state's territorial sea? The International Law Commission had adopted an additional article, which was to have preceded the present Article 23, providing that a coastal state might make the passage of warships through its territorial sea "subject to previous authorization or notification." [1956] II Yb.I.L.C. 276. After lengthy discussion and the rejection of several amendments, the Commission's text was approved by the First Committee (3 U.N.Conf. on the Law of the Sea, Off.Rec. 127–31), but, after a majority of the Plenary Meeting had voted to delete the words "authorization or," vigorous opposition from the Afro–Asian–Soviet bloc prevented the article as a whole from obtaining the necessary two-thirds approval. 2 id. at 66–68. Many of these states have, on ratifying the Convention, made reservations asserting the coastal state's right to require warships to seek previous authorization before passing through the territorial sea. See Slonim, The Right of Innocent Passage and the 1958 Geneva Conference on the Law of the Sea, 5 Colum.J.Transnat'l L. 96 (1966).

Is it persuasive, with respect to the innocent passage of warships, that Article 14(6) of the 1958 Convention, and Article 20 of the 1982 Convention provide that "submarines are required to navigate on the surface and to show their flag"? See [1956] II Yb.I.L.C. 273; 3 U.N.Conf. on the Law of the Sea, Off.Rec. 111–12 (1958). The 1958 Convention, while putting warships in a separate subsection, included it in the section entitled "Right of Innocent Passage" and the article providing that ships of all states shall enjoy the right of innocent passage was in a subsection entitled "Rules applicable to all ships." On the other hand, a subsection applicable to Government ships other than warships expressly provided that the rules applicable to all ships shall apply, while no such provision appears in the subsection applicable to warships. The 1982 Convention places warships and other government ships operated for non-commercial purposes in the same subsection of a section entitled "Innocent Passage in the Territorial Sea." The right of innocent passage is set forth in a subsection applicable to all ships. And see Delupis, Foreign Warships and Immunity for Espionage, 78 A.J.I.L. 53 (1984). See also, Jin, The Question of Innocent Passage of Warships after the UNCLOS III, 13 Marine Pol'y 56 (1989); Oxman, The Régime of Warships under the United Nations Convention on the Law of the Sea, 24 Va.J.Int'l L. 809 (1984); Sadurska, Foreign Submarines in Swedish Waters: The Erosion of an International Norm, 10 Yale J.Int'l L. 34 (1984).

5. The Restatement (Third) § 512 states:

> Subject to § 513, the coastal state has the same sovereignty over its territorial sea, and over the air space, sea-bed and subsoil thereof, as it has in respect of its land territory.

*b. International Straits*

## CORFU CHANNEL CASE
## (UNITED KINGDOM v. ALBANIA)

International Court of Justice, 1949.
1949 I.C.J. 4.

[The United Kingdom sought to hold Albania responsible for damage caused to British Warships by mines moored in the Corfu Channel in Albanian territorial waters. Albania, in turn, charged that, on another occasion, British warships had passed through the channel without the permission of Albanian authorities, and sought satisfaction.]

* * *

To begin with, the foundation for Albania's responsibility, as alleged by the United Kingdom, must be considered. On this subject, the main position of the United Kingdom is to be found in its submission No. 2: that the minefield which caused the explosions was laid between May 15th, 1946, and October 22nd, 1946, by or with the connivance or knowledge of the Albanian Government.

* * *

The obligations incumbent upon the Albanian authorities consisted in notifying, for the benefit of shipping in general, the existence of a minefield in Albanian territorial waters and in warning the approaching British warships of the imminent danger to which the minefield exposed them. Such obligations are based, not on the Hague Convention of 1907, No. VIII, which is applicable in time of war, but on certain general and well-recognized principles, namely: elementary considerations of humanity, even more exacting in peace than in war; the principle of the freedom of maritime communication; and every State's obligation not to allow knowingly its territory to be used for acts contrary to the rights of other States.

In fact, Albania neither notified the existence of the minefield, nor warned the British warships of the danger they were approaching.

* * *

In fact, nothing was attempted by the Albanian authorities to prevent the disaster. These grave omissions involve the international responsibility of Albania.

The Court therefore reaches the conclusion that Albania is responsible under international law for the explosions which occurred on October 22nd, 1946, in Albanian waters, and for the damage and loss of human life which resulted from them, and that there is a duty upon Albania to pay compensation to the United Kingdom.

* * *

In the second part of the Special Agreement, the following question is submitted to the Court:

> (2) Has the United Kingdom under international law violated the sovereignty of the Albanian People's Republic by reason of the acts of the Royal Navy in Albanian waters on the 22nd October and on the 12th and 13th November 1946 and is there any duty to give satisfaction?

The Court will first consider whether the sovereignty of Albania was violated by reason of the acts of the British Navy in Albanian waters on October 22nd, 1946.

On May 15th, 1946, the British cruisers Orion and Superb, while passing southward through the North Corfu Channel, were fired at by an Albanian battery in the vicinity of Saranda. It appears from the report of the commanding naval officer dated May 29th, 1946, that the firing started when the ships had already passed the battery and were moving away from it; that from 12 to 20 rounds were fired; that the firing lasted 12 minutes and ceased only when the ships were out of range; but that the ships were not hit although there were a number of "shorts" and of "overs". An Albanian note of May 21st states that the Coastal Commander ordered a few shots to be fired in the direction of the ships "in accordance with a General Order founded on international law."

The United Kingdom Government at once protested to the Albanian Government, stating that innocent passage through straits is a right recognized by international law. There ensued a diplomatic correspondence in which the Albanian Government asserted that foreign warships and merchant vessels had no right to pass through Albanian territorial waters without prior notification to, and the permission of, the Albanian authorities. This view was put into effect by a communication of the Albanian Chief of Staff, dated May 17th, 1946, which purported to subject the passage of foreign warships and merchant vessels in Albanian territorial waters to previous notification to and authorization by the Albanian Government. The diplomatic correspondence continued, and culminated in a United Kingdom note of August 2nd, 1946, in which the United Kingdom Government maintained its view with regard to the right of innocent passage through straits forming routes for international maritime traffic between two parts of the high seas. The note ended with the warning that if Albanian coastal batteries in the future opened fire on any British warship passing through the Corfu Channel, the fire would be returned.

* * *

It is, in the opinion of the Court, generally recognized and in accordance with international custom that States in time of peace have a right to send their warships through straits used for international navigation between two parts of the high seas without the previous authorization of a coastal State, provided that the passage is innocent. Unless otherwise prescribed in an international convention, there is no right for a coastal State to prohibit such passage through straits in time of peace.

The Albanian Government does not dispute that the North Corfu Channel is a strait in the geographical sense; but it denies that this Channel belongs to the class of international highways through which a right of passage exists, on the grounds that it is only of secondary importance and not even a necessary route between two parts of the high seas, and that it is used almost exclusively for local traffic to and from the ports of Corfu and Saranda.

It may be asked whether the test is to be found in volume of traffic passing through the Strait or in its greater or lesser importance for international navigation. But in the opinion of the Court the decisive criterion is rather its geographical situation as connecting two parts of the high seas and the fact of its being used for international navigation. Nor can it be decisive that this Strait is not a necessary route between two parts of the high seas, but only an alternative passage between the Aegean and the Adriatic Seas. It has nevertheless been a useful route for international maritime traffic.
* * *

* * *

Having regard to these various considerations, the Court has arrived at the conclusion that the North Corfu Channel should be considered as belonging to the class of international highways through which passage cannot be prohibited by a coastal State in time of peace.

On the other hand, it is a fact that the two coastal States did not maintain normal relations, that Greece had made territorial claims precisely with regard to a part of Albanian territory bordering on the Channel, that Greece had declared that she considered herself technically in a state of war with Albania, and that Albania, invoking the danger of Greek incursions, had considered it necessary to take certain measures of vigilance in this region. The Court is of opinion that Albania, in view of these exceptional circumstances, would have been justified in issuing regulations in respect of the passage of warships through the Strait, but not in prohibiting such passage or in subjecting it to the requirement of special authorization.

* * *

## *Notes*

1. The *Corfu Channel* decision has been criticized for giving insufficient weight to functional considerations, i.e., failing to balance "the interest which the coastal state has in its own territorial sea against that which the international maritime community has in traversing that passage." 1 O'Connell at 563.

2. Article 16(4) of the 1958 Convention provides:

> There shall be no suspension of the innocent passage of foreign ships through straits which are used for international navigation between one part of the high seas and another part of the high seas or the territorial sea of a foreign state.

The International Law Commission, in its final version of the predecessor of Article 16(4), limited the right of passage through straits to those which are "normally used for international navigation between two parts of the high seas." [1956] II Yb.I.L.C. 273. In the First Committee, however, the word "normally" was deleted and the article was further amended to its present form by a vote of 31–30–10, over vigorous objection by the Arab states. (Prior to the occupation of the Sinai Peninsula by Israeli forces in 1967, Egypt and Saudi Arabia controlled the Straits of Tiran which provided the sole access to the Gulf of Aqaba, on which Israel has several miles of frontage.) 3 U.N.Conf. on the Law of the Sea, Off.Rec. 93–96, 100 (1958). In the Plenary Meeting, a motion by the United Arab Republic for a separate vote on paragraph 4 of Article 16 was defeated by a vote of 34–32–6; the article was then approved in full. Several Arab states, however, entered reservations to this provision.

3. By the terms of the Treaty of Lausanne (Convention relating to the Régime of the Straits, signed at Lausanne, July 24, 1923, 28 L.N.T.S. 115), the Dardanelles and the Bosphorus came under the supervision of an international commission, the only one of its type ever to function. Vessels of commerce were to be allowed free passage in time of war and in peace, but limits were placed on the number of naval vessels permitted to transit the Straits into the Black Sea; Turkey was permitted to take defensive measures against enemy ships in time of war (Annex to Art. 2 of the Treaty of Lausanne), but the Straits were demilitarized (Art. 4). The Straits Commission functioned as a supervisor of transit, assuring that warships could pass through the Straits without undue hindrance, upon occasion making representations to Turkey on this subject. The Commission was terminated upon conclusion of the Montreux Convention of 1936 (Convention concerning the Régime of the Straits, signed at Montreux, July 20, 1936, entered into force Nov. 9, 1936, 173 L.N.T.S. 213, 7 Hudson, International Legislation 386 (1941)). The Montreux Convention transferred the functions of the Straits Commission to Turkey (Art. 24), the littoral state, which thus reasserted its sovereignty. Restrictions on the number of warships transiting the Straits into the Black Sea were maintained. Turkey assumed responsibility for assuring free passage. Free and unlimited navigation for merchant vessels was retained (Art. 2), but Turkey was granted the right to remilitarize the Straits. The Montreux Convention was to remain in force for twenty years from the date of its entry into force, and was subject to denunciation upon two years'

notice after 1956; the right of free transit for merchant vessels is to continue without time limitation. Apparently, none of the parties had sought to denounce the Convention. See 4 Whiteman at 417–47; see also Baxter, The Law of International Waterways 159–68 (1964). For materials on the problem of the Gulf of Aqaba, see 4 Whiteman at 465–80.

## THE 1982 CONVENTION AND INTERNATIONAL STRAITS

In response to pressures to widen the territorial sea (p. 1244 supra), the United States and several other powers indicated a willingness to accept a twelve-mile territorial sea provided they were assured passage through international straits. They were not content with mere rights of "innocent passage" through such straits since there had been disagreement as to whether warships were entitled to innocent passage, and submarines were explicitly required to surface; also, the meaning of innocent passage had been disputed and in any event left passing vessels substantially at the mercy of the coastal state. The result was a new regime for international straits with a right of "transit passage."

## TRANSIT PASSAGE

### *U.N. CONVENTION ON THE LAW OF THE SEA (1982)*

U.N.Doc. A/CONF. 62/122; 21 I.L.M. 1261 (1982).

Article 37

*Scope of This Section*

This section applies to straits which are used for international navigation between one part of the high seas or an exclusive economic zone and another part of the high seas or an exclusive economic zone.

Article 38

*Right of Transit Passage*

1. In straits referred to in article 37, all ships and aircraft enjoy the right of transit passage, which shall not be impeded; except that, if the strait is formed by an island of a State bordering the strait and its mainland, transit passage shall not apply if there exists seaward of the island a route through the high seas or through an exclusive economic zone of similar convenience with respect to navigational and hydrographical characteristics.

2. Transit passage means the exercise in accordance with this Part of the freedom of navigation and overflight solely for the purpose of continuous and expeditious transit of the strait between one part of the high seas or an exclusive economic zone and another part of the high seas or an exclusive economic zone. However, the requirement of continuous and expeditious transit does not preclude passage through the strait for the purpose of entering, leaving or returning from a State bordering the strait, subject to the conditions of entry to that State.

3. Any activity which is not an exercise of the right of transit passage through a strait remains subject to the other applicable provisions of this Convention.

ARTICLE 39

*Duties of Ships and Aircraft During Transit Passage*

1. Ships and aircraft, while exercising the right of transit passage, shall:

(a) proceed without delay through or over the strait;

(b) refrain from any threat or use of force against the sovereignty, territorial integrity or political independence of States bordering the strait, or in any other manner in violation of the principles of international law embodied in the Charter of the United Nations;

(c) refrain from any activities other than those incident to their normal modes of continuous and expeditious transit unless rendered necessary by *force majeure* or by distress;

(d) comply with other relevant provisions of this Part.

2. Ships in transit passage shall:

(a) comply with generally accepted international regulations, procedures and practices for safety at sea, including the International Regulations for Preventing Collisions at Sea;

(b) comply with generally accepted international regulations, procedures and practices for the prevention, reduction and control of pollution from ships.

3. Aircraft in transit passage shall:

(a) observe the Rules of the Air established by the International Civil Aviation Organization as they apply to civil aircraft, state aircraft will normally comply with such safety measures and will at all times operate with due regard for the safety of navigation;

(b) at all times monitor the radio frequency assigned by the competent internationally designated air traffic control authority or the appropriate international distress radio frequency.

ARTICLE 40

*Research and Survey Activities*

During transit passage, foreign ships, including marine scientific research and hydrographic survey ships, may not carry out any research or survey activities without the prior authorization of the States bordering straits.

### *Notes*

1. The 1982 Convention provides that bordering states may designate sea lanes and prescribe traffic separation schemes where necessary to promote safe passage (Art. 41), and may make laws and regulations for safety, regulation of traffic, prevention of pollution and fishing, enforcing customs, immigration, fiscal and sanitary laws (Art. 42). User states and border states shall by agreement cooperate in navigation and safety aids and prevention of pollution from ships (Art. 43). International straits not covered by this regime (see Art.

36) shall be governed by "innocent passage" which shall not be suspended (Art. 45).

2. Does the "transit passage" regime modify the rules governing the exercise of civil and criminal jurisdiction of the coastal state in its territorial sea, p. 1336 infra?

## INTERNATIONAL CANALS

"The right of free passage through international straits is a product of state practice hardening into customary international law and thence into treaty. The right of free passage through interoceanic canals is a consequence of the opening of each waterway to usage by the international community. It is the origin of the right in a series of individual grants which distinguishes the law relating to canals from the law of straits. The privilege of free passage through the three major interoceanic canals, Suez, Panama, and Kiel, has been created in each case by a treaty to which the territorial sovereign, acting freely or under the pressure of other powers, has been a party." Baxter, The Law of International Waterways 168–69 (1964).*

The right of free passage through the Suez Canal is usually said to be founded on the Convention of Constantinople of 1888 (79 Brit. & For. State Papers 18, reprinted in 3 A.J.I.L.Supp. 123 (1909)), although some writers maintain that the international character of the canal had already been established by concessions of 1854 and 1866. The Convention was signed by Great Britain, Germany, France, Austria–Hungary, Italy, the Netherlands, Russia, Spain, and the Ottoman Empire (then holding sovereignty over Egypt); after the Canal's nationalization in 1956, Egypt reaffirmed its obligations under the Convention (265 U.N.T.S. 299; 272 U.N.T.S. 225). The Convention provides in Article I that the Canal "shall always be free and open, in time of war as in time of peace, to every vessel of commerce or of war, without distinction of flag," and in Article IV that "no right of war, no act of hostility, nor any act having for its object the obstruction of the free navigation of the Canal, shall be committed in the Canal and its ports of access, as well as within a radius of three marine miles from those ports, even though the Ottoman Empire should be one of the belligerent Powers." The Convention also includes restrictions on warships and fortifications. In practice, rights under Article I have usually been regarded as granted to all states whether or not they adhere to the Convention. See 1 O'Connell at 643–48; Baxter at 89–91, 169–70, 183 n. 162. During the two World Wars, the United Kingdom justified measures inconsistent with the Convention as necessary to prevent the Canal's destruction; after 1948, Egypt justified anti-Israeli restrictions on the basis of its "inherent" right of self-defense. See 1 O'Connell at 647–48; Gross, Passage Through the Suez Canal of Israel-bound Cargo and Israel Ships, 51 A.J.I.L. 530 (1957). The Suez Canal was opened to Israel-bound cargoes pursuant to the Egypt–Israel Peace Treaty Art. 5 (28 I.L.M. 362 (1979)). On November 18, 1965, Egypt justified the shutting of the canal to Rhodesian vessels on the ground that the two countries were in a state of war. N.Y. Times, November 19, 1965, p. 2.

The regime of the Panama Canal was governed by the Hay–Pauncefote Treaty of 1901 between the United States and Great Britain (32 Stat.1903), the rules of which were expressly stated to be "substantially as embodied in the Convention of Constantinople." The agreement provided in Article III that "the canal shall be free and open to the vessels of commerce and of war of all nations observing these Rules, on terms of entire equality, so that there shall be no discrimination against any such nation, or its citizens or subjects, in respect of the conditions or charges of traffic, or otherwise." The foregoing language was substantially reproduced in the 1903 treaty by which the United States acquired the Canal Zone from Panama. See Baxter at 170–71. The Panama Canal Treaties were replaced by new ones in 1979. See 16 I.L.M. 1022 and 1040 (1977).

The Kiel Canal had not, prior to the Treaty of Versailles of 1919, been held out by Germany as an international waterway open without restriction to all states. Article 380 of the Treaty of Versailles, however, provided that "the Kiel Canal and its approaches shall be maintained free and open to the vessels of commerce and of war of all nations at peace with Germany on terms of entire equality." 112 Brit. & For. State Papers 1, 189. The Permanent Court of International Justice, in the Case of the S.S. Wimbledom, P.C.I.J., Ser. A, No. 1 (1923), referred to the Canal as "an international waterway * * * for the benefit of all nations of the world" (id. at 22), even though only twenty-eight states were parties to Article 380. In 1936, Germany denounced Article 380 without effective protest from other states.

The legal position of states that are not parties to treaties guaranteeing passage through international canals has been rationalized by the doctrine of "international servitudes," by the "third-party beneficiary" concepts drawn from municipal law, by the theory that certain treaties are "dispositive" in nature in the sense that they create "real rights" that attach to a territory and are therefore not dependent on the treaty which created them, and by analogy to treaties, such as the United Nations Charter, that have an objective, legislative character, in that they create international status that must be recognized by all states, whether contracting parties or not. Baxter states that "the preferable theory concerning the rights of nonsignatories is that a state may, in whole or in part, dedicate a waterway to international use, which dedication, if relied upon, creates legally enforceable rights in favor of the shipping of the international community. A treaty, a unilateral declaration—perhaps even a concession—may be the instrument whereby the dedication is effected. Its form is not important; what is important is that it speaks to the entire world or to a group of states who are to be the beneficiaries of the right of free passage." Baxter at 182–83. See generally 2 Hackworth at 769; 3 Whiteman at 10761; Baxter, The Law of International Waterways, *passim* (1964); 1 O'Connell at 640–51.

### c. *Archipelagic Sea–Lane Passage*

## *RESTATEMENT (THIRD) § 513(4)*

(4) In archipelagic waters, (a) all ships have the right of innocent passage; and (b) all ships and aircraft enjoy the right of archipelagic sea lanes passage.

* * *

**Comment:**

* * *

*k. Archipelagic sea lanes passage.* Under Subsection (4), foreign ships (and aircraft) enjoy the right of passage through designated archipelagic sea lanes (and air routes), which must include all normal passage routes used for international navigation or overflight. Where there are two routes of similar convenience between the same entry and exit points, only one needs to be designated. The sea lanes and air routes are to be designated by agreement between the archipelagic state and the competent international organization (principally IMO). LOS Convention, Article 53. Such passage is generally subject to the same standards as transit passage through straits, Article 54, but the Convention explicitly provides that archipelagic sea lanes passage is allowed in "the normal mode"; for instance, submarines may travel under water. *Compare* Articles 38(2) and 39(1)(c) *with* 53(3). If the archipelagic state has not designated archipelagic sea lanes or routes, "the right of archipelagic sea lanes passage may be exercised through the routes normally used for international navigation." *Id.* Article 53(12). In archipelagic waters other than the designated sea lanes, ships of all states enjoy the right of innocent passage similar to the one they possess in the territorial sea, except in inland waters delimited by straight lines drawn across mouths of rivers, bays, and entrances to ports. See *id.* Articles 50 and 52(1).

### *Note*

Restatement (Third) § 513, Reporters' Note 4 states:

> Acceptance by the major maritime states of the concept of archipelagic state was conditional on acceptance of the right of archipelagic sea lanes passage. Such sea lanes are defined in detail in Article 53 of the LOS Convention. The main rules relating to international straits apply, with such modifications as may be necessary, to archipelagic sea lanes passage. See LOS Convention, Arts. 46–54.

In 1992, the Japanese government came under intense pressure not to use the Strait of Malacca, one of the world's most heavily traveled sea lanes, to transport a large quantity of plutonium to Japan. As a result, vessels transporting the plutonium followed a high seas route instead. Was Japan entitled to use the Strait of Malacca? See Restatement (Third) § 513(3), Comment *j,* and Reporters' Note 3. See also de Yturriaga, Straits Used for International Navigation (1991); Langdon, The Extent of Transit Passage: Some Practical Anomalies, 14 Marine Pol'y 130 (1990); Mahmoudi, Customary International Law and Transit Passage, 20 Ocean Dev. & Int'l L. 157 (1989); Caminos, The Legal Regime of Straits in the 1982 United Nations Convention on the Law of the Sea, 205 Rec. des Cours 9 (1987); Valencia & Marsh, Access to Straits and Sealanes in Southeast Asian Seas: Legal, Economic and Strategic Considerations, 16 J. Maritime L. & Com. 513 (1985).

### 3. *The Contiguous Zone*

## CHURCH v. HUBBART

Supreme Court of the United States, 1804.
6 U.S. (2 Cranch) 187, 2 L.Ed. 249.

[The brigantine Aurora, an American vessel, was seized "four or five leagues" off the coast of Brazil by Portuguese authorities, for alleged illicit trade with the shore. To recover the loss, the vessel's owner sued on two insurance policies issued by the defendant. Each policy, however, had excluded losses arising out of illicit trade with the Portuguese. The insurer relied on the exclusions, but plaintiff argued, *inter alia,* that a seizure so far from shore was unlawful because it was outside the Portuguese territorial jurisdiction. The Circuit Court directed a verdict for the insurer, and the owner appealed. In the course of his opinion, Chief Justice Marshall stated:]

That the law of nations prohibits the exercise of any act of authority over a vessel in the situation of the Aurora, and that this seizure is, on that account, a mere marine trespass, not within the exception, cannot be admitted. To reason from the extent of protection a nation will afford to foreigners, to the extent of the means it may use for its own security, does not seem to be perfectly correct. It is opposed by principles which are universally acknowledged. The authority of a nation, within its own territory, is absolute and exclusive. The seizure of a vessel, within the range of its cannon, by a foreign force, is an invasion of that territory, and is a hostile act which it is its duty to repel. But its power to secure itself from injury may certainly be exercised beyond the limits of its territory. Upon this principle, the right of a belligerent to search a neutral vessel on the high seas, for contraband of war, is universally admitted, because the belligerent has a right to prevent the injury done to himself, by the assistance intended for his enemy: so too, a nation has a right to prohibit any commerce with its colonies. Any attempt to violate the laws made to protect this right, is an injury to itself, which it may prevent, and it has a right to use the means necessary for its prevention. These means do not appear to be limited within any certain marked boundaries, which remain the same, at all times and in all situations. If they are such as unnecessarily to vex and harass foreign lawful commerce, foreign nations will resist their exercise. If they are such as are reasonable and necessary to secure their laws from violation, they will be submitted to. * * *

If this right be extended too far, the exercise of it will be resisted. It has occasioned long and frequent contests, which have sometimes ended in open war. The English, it will be well recollected, complained of the right claimed by Spain to search their vessels on the high seas, which was carried so far, that the *guarda costas* of that nation seized vessels not in the neighborhood of their coasts. This practice was the subject of long and fruitless negotiations, and at length, of open war. The right of the Spaniards was supposed to be exercised unreasonably and vexatiously, but it never was contended, that it could only be exercised within the range of the cannon from their batteries. Indeed, the right given to our own revenue cutters, to visit vessels four leagues from our coast, is a declaration that, in the opinion of the American government, no such principle as that contended for has a real existence. Nothing, then, is to be drawn from the laws or usages of nations, which gives to this part of the contract before the court, the very limited construction which the plaintiff insists on, or which proves that the seizure of the Aurora, by the Portuguese governor, was an act of lawless violence.

The argument that such act would be within the policy, and not within the exception, is admitted to be well founded. That the exclusion from the insurance of "the risk of illicit trade with the Portuguese," is an exclusion only of that risk, to which such trade is by law exposed, will be readily conceded. It is unquestionably limited and restrained by the terms "illicit trade." No seizure, not justifiable under the laws and regulations established by the crown of Portugal, for the restriction of foreign commerce with its dependencies, can come within this part of the contract, and every seizure which is justifiable by those laws and regulations, must be deemed within it.

[The judgment below was reversed, and a new trial ordered, because the trial court had admitted improperly authenticated documents.]

## *Notes*

1. Marshall, writing in 1804, suggested that a state's power to secure itself from injury may be exercised beyond the limits of its territory, and that the means "do not appear to be limited within any certain marked boundaries." In time, however, the coastal state's rights to act were confined to a limited contiguous zone. Might the coastal state have authority to act beyond the contiguous zone for some purposes? See pp. 1274–76 infra. Compare the right of a coastal state to act against "pirate broadcasting" from the high seas. See p. 1302 infra.

2. "The exercise of jurisdiction in contiguous zones of the high seas becomes necessary in view of the inadequacy under modern conditions of any reasonable breadth of territorial waters; whatever we may regard as the breadth of marginal sea now accepted under international law, there are occasions and purposes for which jurisdiction must be exercised farther out from shore. This differs from an attempt to declare such areas territorial waters subject to the full sovereignty of the coastal state." Bishop, The Exercise of Jurisdiction for Special Purposes in High Seas Beyond the Outer Limit of Territorial Waters (paper prepared for the sixth conference of the Inter–American Bar Ass'n, 1949), reprinted in 99 Cong.Rec. 2493 (1953).

3. What is the scope of the proposition that a state may exercise such jurisdiction on the high seas as is "reasonable and necessary" to prevent the violation of its laws? Does a privilege to prevent violations encompass the privilege to punish attempted violations or past violations?

## *U.N. CONVENTION ON THE LAW OF THE SEA (1982)*

U.N.Doc. A/CONF. 62/122; 21 I.L.M. 1261 (1982).

### ARTICLE 33

### *Contiguous Zone*

1. In a zone contiguous to its territorial sea, described as the contiguous zone, the coastal State may exercise the control necessary to:

(a) prevent infringement of its customs, fiscal, immigration or sanitary laws and regulations within its territory or territorial sea;

(b) punish infringement of the above laws and regulations committed within its territory or territorial sea.

2. The contiguous zone may not extend beyond 24 nautical miles from the baselines from which the breadth of the territorial sea is measured.

## *Notes*

1. Article 24 of the 1958 Convention was essentially the same except that the outer-limit of the zone was set at twelve miles. See also Restatement (Third) § 513, Comment *f.*

Article 24 of the 1958 Convention was based on a text adopted by the International Law Commission at its eighth session in 1956. The Commission's commentary on the article provided:

> (1) International law accords States the right to exercise preventive or protective control for certain purposes over a belt of the high seas contiguous to their territorial sea. It is, of course, understood that this power of control does not change the legal status of the waters over which it is exercised. These waters are and remain a part of the high seas and are not subject to the sovereignty of the coastal State, which can exercise over them only such rights as are conferred on it by the present draft or are derived from international treaties.
>
> (2) Many States have adopted the principle that in the contiguous zone the coastal State may exercise customs control in order to prevent attempted infringements of its customs and fiscal regulations within its territory or territorial sea, and to punish infringements of those regulations committed within its territory or territorial sea. The Commission considered that it would be impossible to deny to States the exercise of such rights.
>
> (3) Although the number of States which claim rights over the contiguous zone for the purpose of applying sanitary regulations is fairly small, the Commission considers that, in view of the connexion between customs and sanitary regulations, such rights should also be recognized for sanitary regulations.
>
> (4) The Commission did not recognize special security rights in the contiguous zone. It considered that the extreme vagueness of the term "security" would open the way for abuses and that the granting of such rights was not necessary. The enforcement of customs and sanitary regulations will be sufficient in most cases to safeguard the security of the State. In so far as measures of self-defence against an imminent and direct threat to the security of the State are concerned, the Commission refers to the general principles of international law and the Charter of the United Nations.
>
> (5) Nor was the Commission willing to recognize any exclusive right of the coastal State to engage in fishing in the contiguous zone. The Preparatory Committee of The Hague Codification Conference found, in 1930, that the replies from Governments offered no prospect of an agreement to extend the exclusive fishing rights of the coastal State beyond the territorial sea [2 Conference for the Codification of International Law, Bases of Discussion 34 (1930)]. The Commission considered that in that respect the position has not changed. * * *
>
> (9) The Commission considers that the breadth of the contiguous zone cannot exceed twelve miles from the coast, the figure adopted by the

> Preparatory Committee of The Hague Codification Conference (1930) [2 Conference for the Codification of International Law, Bases of Discussion 34 (1930) ]. Until such time as there is unanimity in regard to the breadth of the territorial sea, the zone should be measured from the coast and not from the outer limit of the territorial sea. States which have claimed extensive territorial waters have in fact less need for a contiguous zone than those which have been more modest in their delimitation.

[1956] II Yb.I.L.C. 294–95. The Commission's decision not to include "immigration" as one of the matters over which a coastal state could exercise jurisdiction outside its territorial waters was overruled at the Geneva Conference, at which the present third paragraph of Article 24 was also adopted. 3 U.N.Conf. on the Law of the Sea, Off.Rec. 181–82, 198–99 (1958). See generally Mason, Alien Stowaways, the Immigration and Naturalization Service and Shipowners, 12 Tulane Mar.L.J. 361 (1988).

In United States v. F/V Taiyo Maru, 395 F.Supp. 413 (D.Maine 1975), a Japanese ship was found fishing illegally and was seized in the United States exclusive fishing zone, nine miles offshore and beyond the then three mile territorial sea limit. The defendants argued that the seizure was not permitted by Article 24 of the 1958 Convention, but the court held that the list in Article 24 of purposes for which a contiguous zone may be established is not exhaustive. Id., at 419. See also United States v. Postal, 589 F.2d 862, 876 n. 20 (5th Cir.1979), cert. denied, 444 U.S. 832, 100 S.Ct. 61, 62 L.Ed.2d 40 (1979); Ridell, Hot Pursuit from a Fisheries Zone, 70 A.J.I.L. 95 (1976).

2. Compare Article 24 of the 1958 Convention (and Article 33 of the 1982 Convention) with Harvard Research in International Law, The Law of Territorial Waters, Art. 20, 23 A.J.I.L. Spec.Supp. 241, 333–34 (1929): " * * * On the high sea adjacent to the marginal sea * * * a state may take such measures as may be necessary for the enforcement within its territory or territorial waters of its customs, navigation, sanitary or police laws or regulations, or for its immediate protection." See also Case of the Virginius, 2 Moore, Digest of International Law 895, 980 (1906).

3. What is the scope of the jurisdiction permitted in the contiguous zone? May a coastal state prescribe rules with which foreign vessels in the contiguous zone must comply? Would such rules have to relate to infringement of customs, fiscal, immigration or sanitary interests within the coastal state's territory or territorial sea? See McDougal & Burke, The Public Order of the Oceans 608–21 (1962). May a coastal state enforce such rules against foreign ships while the latter are in the contiguous zone? What is the scope of jurisdiction to "prevent" violations within the coastal state's territory or territorial sea? Might legitimate "preventive" measures include the arrest of a smuggling vessel or the confiscation of contraband? Would the Portuguese action upheld in Church v. Hubbart, supra, be allowable under the 1982 Convention. See McDougal & Burke, supra at 621–30; Lowe, The Development of the Contiguous Zone, 52 Brit.Y.B.I.L. 109 (1981); Varghese, Territorial Sea and Contiguous Zone: Concept and Development, 9 Cochin U.L.Rev. 436 (1985); Symonides, Origin and Legal Essence of the Contiguous Zone, 20 Ocean Dev. & Int'l L. 203 (1989).

It is the position of the United States that there exists off its coast "a 9-mile contiguous zone of high seas seaward of the territorial sea for the purposes of the customs, fiscal, immigration, and sanitary controls described in Article 24 of the Convention on the Territorial Sea and Contiguous Zone, and for the purposes of exclusive fisheries rights under Public Law 89–658 of October 14, 1966." 37

Fed.Reg. 11906 (15 June 1972). In 1988, the United States extended its territorial sea to 12 miles, see p. 1245 supra, but it has apparently not yet formally announced a larger contiguous zone. Under Article 33 of the 1982 Convention the U.S. may exercise control in a contiguous zone up to 24 miles from its baseline of territorial sea.

4. Could a coastal state take any action against an offending foreign vessel that hovered just outside the contiguous zone? In comparison to the flexible standard laid down in Church v. Hubbart, supra, and in light of the considerations that necessitate the exercise of jurisdiction beyond territorial waters, how satisfactory is the Convention Article? "It should be observed," said Hyde, "that the privilege * * * is not measured by exact limits and might be rendered illusory if it were. The geographical features of the coasts of maritime States vary so greatly that needed privileges of self-protection on the high sea are not alike and do not lend themselves to arrangements that lay down uniform geographical or linear tests." 1 Hyde 462. See also McDougal & Burke, supra at 606–07; Jessup, The United Nations Conference on the Law of the Sea, 59 Colum.L.Rev. 234, 244 (1959). Is the enumeration of categories in the Article intended to be exclusive? Is the International Law Commission commentary, supra, or the specific rejection by the Geneva Conference of certain categories, conclusive on this question?

5. Since the 1982 Convention now provides for a 200 mile exclusive economic zone (p. 1291 infra) and defines the continental shelf as extending even beyond that zone in some cases (p. 1279 infra), has the significance of the contiguous zone changed?

## CUSTOMS ZONES, HOVERING, AND HOT PURSUIT

From the early part of the eighteenth century, the United Kingdom enforced laws sometimes referred to as "hovering acts" which authorized the search and seizure, on the high seas at varying distances (up to eight or even 100 leagues) from the coast, of British and foreign ships suspected of having an intention to smuggle goods ashore. See Masterson, Jurisdiction in Marginal Seas With Special Reference to Smuggling 1–162 (1929); Jessup, The Law of Territorial Waters and Maritime Jurisdiction 77–79 (1927). No state protested these acts, and Sir William Scott defended them in the case of *Le Louis,* 2 Dodson Adm.Rep. 210, 245 (1817), as founded on the "common courtesy" and "common convenience" of nations. The United States and a number of Latin American countries, on becoming independent, adopted similar customs zones, usually of twelve miles, and some European states also authorized seizures outside territorial waters. Jessup at 80–91, see also Masterson at 175–206. In 1876, however, the United Kingdom reversed its policy and, in repealing the "hovering acts," took the position that a state could not, under international law, exercise jurisdiction on the high seas against vessels of other states. Jessup at 79. The new British doctrine gained the adherence of some other states, notably Germany and Japan, but the United States and a number of other countries continued to regard contiguous zone jurisdiction in customs matters as a right sanctioned by state practice. Brierly; The Law of Nations 205 (6th ed. Waldock 1963).

Prior to the advent of Prohibition, the United States did not attempt to board foreign vessels beyond the three-mile territorial sea except when the vessel was bound for the United States, or when it had been caught violating United States laws in the territorial sea and was then "hotly pursued." See Cook v. United States, 288 U.S. 102, 112–13, 53 S.Ct. 305, 308–09, 77 L.Ed. 641 (1933). The widespread smuggling of liquor, after 1920, from British and other ships led Congress to provide, in the Tariff Act of 1922, that even foreign vessels not bound for the United States might be boarded, searched, and seized beyond the three-mile limit. Hyde, 780–82. It nevertheless continued to be the consistent United States policy to release vessels seized beyond this limit which had not been bound for the United States, except in cases where it appeared that the vessel had already been in contact with the shore. See Cook v. United States, supra. The "shore contact" rule was applied in The Grace and Ruby, 283 Fed. 475 (D.Mass.1922), to justify forfeiture of a British schooner seized outside the three-mile limit but which had used its boat and members of its crew to assist in ferrying liquor ashore. A British protest was answered by the State Department with a reference to the incident of the Araunah, in which the United Kingdom had acquiesced in a Russian seizure on the high seas of a British vessel engaged in illegal seal hunting by means of its canoes operating close to the shore. [1922] 1 For.Rel.U.S. 592–93. In the Henry L. Marshall, 286 Fed. 260 (S.D.N.Y.1922), aff'd, 292 Fed. 486 (2d Cir.1923), cert. denied, 263 U.S. 712, 44 S.Ct. 38, 68 L.Ed. 519 (1923), the "shore contact" rule was applied even though contact was made through shore-based boats, rather than the ship's own. Although the ship was ostensibly of British registry, the United Kingdom did not press a protest because the registration had been fraudulently obtained; the State Department nevertheless vigorously asserted the validity of the principle involved. [1923] 1 For.Rel.U.S. 163–64; Jessup at 251–53.

The United States and the United Kingdom finally entered into a treaty in 1924, 43 Stat. 1761, under which the United Kingdom agreed not to protest restrictions imposed on British vessels by the United States within an hour's sailing distance from the latter's coast, and the United States agreed that it would not enforce the Prohibition laws against liquor carried by British vessels in United States waters as sealed cargo destined for foreign ports or as sea stores. Similar treaties were concluded between the United States and other countries. See 1 Hackworth at 678–79. In 1925, the northern European coastal states (from Norway and Denmark to the U.S.S.R.) concluded the Treaty of Helsingfors, 42 L.N.T.S. 75, 4 Whiteman 489, which authorized, as among the parties, a twelve-mile contiguous zone off their respective coasts for the purpose of suppressing contraband traffic in liquor.

In the Anti–Smuggling Act of 1935, 49 Stat. 517, Congress provided that the President, upon finding that vessels hovering beyond the twelve-mile limit of "customs waters" were assisting or threatening to assist "the unlawful introduction or removal into or from the United States of any merchandise or person," might declare a "customs-enforcement area" extending not more than one hundred miles from the vicinity of the offending vessels and not more than fifty miles from the outward limit of United States customs waters (i.e., not more than sixty-two miles from the United States coastline). Within such a customs-enforcement area, United States customs officers were to have the same enforcement powers (including the power of seizure and arrest) as they would have at any place in the United

States. The Act expressly disclaimed the intention to authorize jurisdiction in violation of any international agreement, and the provisions relating to customs-enforcement areas were not regarded in the United States as in themselves authorizing the violation of customary rules of international law. See generally Jessup, The Anti–Smuggling Act of 1935, 31 A.J.I.L. 101 (1937). Only five such zones were established, Briggs, The Law of Nations 375 (2d ed. 1952), and the only seizure made under the 1935 Act that provoked a protest from a foreign government did not involve a customs-enforcement area but a conspiracy. In The Reidun, 14 F.Supp. 771 (E.D.N.Y. 1936), libels were dismissed against a Norwegian vessel seized in New York for having transshipped liquor while 500 to 600 miles from the nearest point of the United States customs waters or enforcement areas on the ground that the place of transshipment was not "adjacent to the customs waters of the United States" within the meaning of the Anti–Smuggling Act. However, an amended libel which charged that the vessel had been fitted out in Belgium for the purpose of smuggling, in violation of Section 3(a) of the Act was subsequently sustained. 15 F.Supp. 112 (E.D.N.Y.1936). The court stated: "Congress may very well have intended to mete out punishment to those who conspire outside of the territorial jurisdiction to violate laws of the nation by subjecting them to apprehension or punishment when found within the jurisdiction. If the *Reidun* was fitted out as alleged and did cause merchandise to be smuggled into the United States in defiance of its revenue laws, it ran the hazard of punishment by coming within the customs enforcement areas." Id. at 113. Does the foregoing rationale express a theory of territorial and maritime jurisdiction, or does it depend upon some other principle? Compare United States v. Aluminum Company of America, supra p. 1052. The Norwegian Government protested the seizure of the *Reidun,* and the vessel was released upon that government's assurances that it would take steps to prevent Norwegian vessels from violating United States revenue laws.

How does the contiguous zone provision in the 1982 Convention affect a coastal state's enforcement of its customs laws? Could the United States proclaim a "customs-enforcement area" pursuant to the Anti–Smuggling Act if this area extended beyond the contiguous zone? Could a coastal state board and search a foreign vessel hovering beyond its territorial sea but within the contiguous zone? If contraband or false manifests were found, could the coastal state order the forfeiture of the vessel or of its cargo? Would such an order be "punitive" or "preventive" action, within the meaning of the contiguous zone provision? Does that provision exclude the application of the "shore contact" doctrine to ships beyond the contiguous zone? Within the contiguous zone, does the "shore contact" rule add anything to the coastal state's ability to enforce its customs laws?

For the United States program to interdict vessels suspected of bringing undocumented aliens to the United States, see p. 1305 below.

## RIGHT OF HOT PURSUIT

### *U.N. CONVENTION ON THE LAW OF THE SEA (1982)*

U.N.Doc. A/CONF. 62/122; 21 I.L.M. 1261 (1982).

ARTICLE 111

1. The hot pursuit of a foreign ship may be undertaken when the competent authorities of the coastal State have good reason to believe that the ship has violated the laws and regulations of that State. Such pursuit must be commenced when the foreign ship or one of its boats is within the internal waters, the territorial sea or the contiguous zone of the pursuing State, and may only be continued outside the territorial sea or the contiguous zone if the pursuit has not been interrupted. It is not necessary that, at the time when the foreign ship within the territorial sea or the contiguous zone receives the order to stop, the ship giving the order should likewise be within the territorial sea or the contiguous zone. If the foreign ship is within a contiguous zone, as defined in article 33, the pursuit may only be undertaken if there has been a violation of the rights for the protection of which the zone was established.

2. The right of hot pursuit shall apply *mutatis mutandis* to violations in the exclusive economic zone or on the continental shelf, including safety zones around continental shelf installations, of the laws and regulations of the coastal State applicable in accordance with this Convention to the exclusive economic zone or the continental shelf, including such safety zones.

3. The right of hot pursuit ceases as soon as the ship pursued enters the territorial sea of its own country or of a third State.

4. Hot pursuit is not deemed to have begun unless the pursuing ship has satisfied itself by such practicable means as may be available that the ship pursued or one of its boats or other craft working as a team and using the ship pursued as a mother ship are within the limits of the territorial sea, or, as the case may be, within the contiguous zone or the exclusive economic zone or above the continental shelf. The pursuit may only be commenced after a visual or auditory signal to stop has been given at a distance which enables it to be seen or heard by the foreign ship.

5. The right of hot pursuit may be exercised only by warships or military aircraft, or other ships or aircraft clearly marked and identifiable as being on government service and specially authorized to that effect.

6. Where hot pursuit is effected by an aircraft:

(a) The provisions of paragraphs 1 to 4 shall apply *mutatis mutandis:*

(b) The aircraft giving the order to stop must itself actively pursue the ship until a ship or aircraft of the coastal State, summoned by the aircraft, arrives to take over the pursuit, unless the aircraft is itself able to arrest the ship. It does not suffice to justify an arrest outside the territorial sea that the ship was merely sighted by the aircraft as an offender or suspected offender, if it was not both ordered to stop and pursued by the aircraft itself or other aircraft or ships which continue the pursuit without interruption.

7. The release of a ship arrested within the jurisdiction of a State and escorted to a port of that State for the purposes of an inquiry before the

competent authorities may not be claimed solely on the ground that the ship, in the course of its voyage, was escorted across a portion of the exclusive economic zone or the high seas, if the circumstances rendered this necessary.
* * *

### *Notes*

1. This provision essentially repeats that in Article 23 of the 1958 Convention on the High Seas except for the addition of paragraph 2 extending the doctrine of hot pursuit, *mutatis mutandis,* to violations in the exclusive economic zone or on the continental shelf. See p. 1296 infra. See Restatement (Third) § 513, Comment *g.*

2. How does the right of "hot pursuit" relate to a coastal state's rights in the contiguous zone? Is a situation conceivable in which a coastal state may be unable legally to seize a vessel hovering in the contiguous zone, but may nevertheless pursue the vessel to the high seas and seize it there? See generally Allen, Doctrine of Hot Pursuit: A Functional Interpretation Adaptable to Emerging Maritime Law Enforcement Technology and Practices, 20 Ocean Dev. & Int'l L. 30 (1989); Poulantzas, The Right of Hot Pursuit in International Law (1969).

## COASTAL STATE AUTHORITY IN OTHER "ZONES"

*a. Security Zones*

The Preparatory Committee for the Hague Codification Conference of 1930 recommended, as a basis of discussion, that a coastal state might exercise jurisdiction on the high seas adjacent to territorial waters to prevent "interference with its security by foreign ships." 2 Conference for the Codification of International Law, Bases of Discussion 34 (1930). However, the Conference itself reached no agreement on the subject. In 1956 the International Law Commission rejected the granting of special security rights in the contiguous zone. [1956] 2 Yb.I.L.C. 295. It explained that "the extreme vagueness of the term 'security' would open the way for abuses and that the granting of such rights was not necessary * * *. In so far as measures of self-defence against an imminent and direct threat to the security of the State are concerned, the Commission refers to the general principles of international law and the Charter of the United Nations." Id. The First Committee at the Geneva Conference of 1958 recommended that the coastal state be permitted to take measures in the contiguous zone "necessary to prevent and punish * * * violations of its security," 2 U.N.Conf. on the Law of the Sea, Off.Rec. 117 (1958), but security jurisdiction was dropped in the plenary meeting. Id. at 40. See p. 1268 supra.

State practice and the views of writers prior to 1958 in the matter of security zones were inconclusive. In reliance on the principle of reasonableness advanced in Church v. Hubbart, p. 1266 supra, it might be urged that "a neutral State may reasonably demand that belligerent operations at sea be conducted at such a distance from its territory as may be necessary in order to safeguard it from injury or interference." Hyde at 2348. During World War I, a number of South American states had proposed a declaration by the American Republics that belligerents must refrain from hostile acts within a "reasonable" distance from the shores. Id. After the outbreak of World

War II in 1939, the Foreign Ministers of the American Republics issued the "Declaration of Panama," 1 Dep't State Bull. 331 (1939), which enunciated the "inherent right" of the American states "to have those waters adjacent to the American continent * * * free from the commission of any hostile act by any non-American belligerent * * *." Such waters were defined by a system of straight lines which extended in many places several hundred miles out from the shore. See generally Fenwick, The Declaration of Panama, 34 A.J.I.L. 116 (1940). In response to an inquiry regarding the propriety of the Declaration under international law, the Department of State called the Declaration "a practical measure designed to maintain certain vital interests," and a "statement of principle, based on the inherent right of self-protection rather than a formal proposal for the modification of international law." 7 Hackworth at 703–704. The zone was also defended on the ground of its "inherent reasonableness." The battle in 1939 involving the Graf Spee, and certain other engagements, occasioned a joint protest by the American Republics to the belligerent powers. The replies were alike in rejecting the right of the American states to impose a modification of international law upon other states without their consent. 7 Hackworth at 704–708. The Naval War College affirmed the right of the belligerent states not to recognize the binding nature of the Panama Declaration, calling the latter "without precedent" in the extent of neutral waters for which it called. U.S. Naval War College, International Law Situations 80 (1939).

What is the effect of war, or armed conflict not labeled "war," on the jurisdiction which a state may exercise in adjacent waters? The International Law Commission, in its 1956 articles which served as bases for discussion by the Geneva Conference, stated that the draft regulated the law of the sea "in time of peace only." [1956] 2 Yb.I.L.C. 256. Saudi Arabia proposed in the Conference's First Committee a similar qualification to be included in the title to the articles on the Territorial Sea and the Contiguous Zone. 3 U.N.Conf. on the Law of the Sea, Off.Rec. 156 (1958). A Yugoslav amendment would have ensured the applicability of the Convention in case of "armed conflict" as well, (id. at 195), but no action was taken by the Committee or by the Conference. During the Algerian war, French forces intercepted on the high seas a number of vessels suspected of carrying arms destined for Algerian revolutionaries. Germany protested the interception of its vessels as a violation of international law. 4 Whiteman at 513–14. To what extent is the literal application of the Conventions subject to temporary suspension in time of crisis not amounting to war or even armed conflict, but affecting a nation's security? Did the United States have the right in meeting the threat posed by the installing of Soviet missiles in Cuba (see p. 903) in October, 1962 to intercept on the high seas vessels bound for Cuba? To what extent and under what conditions may a state use areas of the high seas for activities that require the exclusion of unauthorized vessels? May a state forbid foreign vessels to enter an area in which it is conducting tests of nuclear weapons or guided missiles? See generally 4 Whiteman 553–631; McDougal & Schlei, The Hydrogen Bomb Tests in Perspective: Lawful Measures for Security, 64 Yale L.J. 648 (1955). Compare Margolis, The Hydrogen Bomb Experiments and International Law, 64 Yale L.J. 629 (1955). Compare Nuclear Tests (Australia v. France, New Zealand v. France), 1974 I.C.J. 253, 535.

The Restatement (Third) § 511, Comment *k*, states that "[i]nternational law has not recognized coastal state assertions of special zones to protect security * * *."

*b. Air Defense Zones*

Some states have asserted the right to create air identification zones extending far beyond the contiguous zone. Restatement (Third) § 521, Reporters' Note 2 states:

> *Overflight and air defense.* The United States has established air defense areas, air defense identification zones (ADIZ), and, for Alaska, a distant early warning identification zone (DEWIZ). Some of these zones extend several hundred miles into the sea. Pilots entering these zones are obliged to report promptly and to provide specified data to United States authorities; a foreign aircraft not complying with this requirement is not permitted to enter the air space of the United States. See 14 C.F.R. § 99.23. Similar zones have been established by other states. These zones have been generally accepted. It is uncertain, however, whether a coastal state can apply such regulations to aircraft passing through its declared air defense zone but not planning to enter its airspace. See Note, "Air Defense Identification Zones: Creeping Jurisdiction in the Airspace," 18 Va.J.Int'l L. 485 (1978); 4 Whiteman, Digest of International Law 496–97 (1965). See also § 511, Comment *k*.

*c. Anti–Pollution Zones*

In 1970, Canada declared an "anti-pollution" zone up to 100 nautical miles from her Arctic coast, forbade pollution in that zone, imposed penalties and civil liability for violations (including unintentional violations), and authorized comprehensive regulation and inspection of vessels to prevent pollution. 18–19 Elizabeth II, c. 47 (1969–70), reprinted in 9 I.L.M. 543 (1970). See Henkin, Arctic Anti–Pollution: Does Canada Make—or Break—International Law?, 65 A.J.I.L. 131 (1971).

Pollution control is now the subject of a number of conventions, and is dealt with in the 1982 Convention Part XII "Protection and Preservation of the Marine Environment." See p. 1321 infra. The Restatement concludes that international law has not yet recognized coastal state authority in a special zone to protect the environment. Restatement (Third) § 511, Comment *k*.

## B. ECONOMIC RESOURCES BEYOND THE TERRITORIAL SEA

### *SCHACHTER, INTERNATIONAL LAW IN THEORY AND PRACTICE*

275–77 (1991).*

Viewed from a lawyer's perspective, the first notable action in derogation of the *res communis* was the claim by the United States in 1945 to full sovereignty over the continental shelf. That claim expressed in the Truman Proclamation has been generally seen as the start of the process of territorial expansion in ocean space. The shelf was claimed by the United States as an extension of the land-mass of the adjacent State and thus naturally appurtenant to it. Over a decade or so, the United States position was adopted by others and then embodied in the 1958 Geneva Convention on the Continental Shelf. It did not give rise to controversy since the extension of national authority over the shelf did not impinge very much on the traditional uses of the seas—fishing and navigation. * * * What was important as technology developed were the hydrocarbon resources, oil and gas, that were found and exploited on the shelf. These resources are still the most valuable of the resources of the sea * * *.

Although the appropriation of the shelf by coastal States did not appear to challenge the freedom of the seas, it had an influence on the claims made in the 1940s and 1950s by some coastal States to exclusive rights to fish or to engage in whaling in a 200–mile zone off their coasts [see p. 1288 below] * * *. In due course, the demands for preferential and exclusive fishing zones spread to other coastal countries and were more vigorously expressed. * * *

### *Note*

Demands for special rights of protection for coastal States were followed by claims of preferential rights to resources. Such rights were embodied in treaties and given judicial imprimatur in the fisheries cases involving Iceland decided by the International Court in 1974 [see p. 1289 below]. In a short period of time preferential rights evolved into exclusive rights over a fishing zone generally of 200 miles. In the course of the ten-year period of negotiation of the United Nations Convention on the Law of the Sea, these zones became the 200–mile exclusive economic zones in which coastal States exercised "sovereign rights" over all resources. The principle of the exclusive economic zone was gradually given legal force by unilateral acts of coastal States and received acceptance as a major principle of the new Convention.

## *1. The Continental Shelf*

### *POLICY OF THE UNITED STATES WITH RESPECT TO THE NATURAL RESOURCES OF THE SUBSOIL AND SEA BED OF THE CONTINENTAL SHELF*

Presidential Proclamation 2667, September 28, 1945.
10 Fed.Reg. 12303 (1945).

WHEREAS the Government of the United States of America, aware of the long range world-wide need for new sources of petroleum and other minerals, holds the view that efforts to discover and make available new supplies of these resources should be encouraged; and

WHEREAS its competent experts are of the opinion that such resources underlie many parts of the continental shelf off the coasts of the United States of America, and that with modern technological progress their utilization is already practicable or will become so at an early date; and

WHEREAS recognized jurisdiction over these resources is required in the interest of their conservation and prudent utilization when and as development is undertaken; and

WHEREAS it is the view of the Government of the United States that the exercise of jurisdiction over the natural resources of the subsoil and sea bed of the continental shelf by the contiguous nation is reasonable and just, since the effectiveness of measures to utilize or conserve these resources would be contingent upon cooperation and protection from the shore, since the continental shelf may be regarded as an extension of the land-mass of the coastal nation and thus naturally appurtenant to it, since these resources frequently form a seaward extension of a pool or deposit lying within the territory, and since self-protection compels the coastal nation to keep close watch over activities off its shores which are of the nature necessary for utilization of these resources;

NOW, THEREFORE, I, HARRY S. TRUMAN, President of the United States of America, do hereby proclaim the following policy of the United States of America with respect to the natural resources of the subsoil and sea bed of the continental shelf.

Having concern for the urgency of conserving and prudently utilizing its natural resources, the Government of the United States regards the natural resources of the subsoil and sea bed of the continental shelf beneath the high seas but contiguous to the coasts of the United States as appertaining to the United States, subject to its jurisdiction and control. In cases where the continental shelf extends to the shores of another State, or is shared with an adjacent State, the boundary shall be determined by the United States and the State concerned in accordance with equitable principles. The character as high seas of the waters above the continental shelf and the right to their free and unimpeded navigation are in no way thus affected.

### *Notes*

1. A White House press release issued on the same day as the Truman Proclamation noted that "[g]enerally, submerged land which is contiguous to the continent and which is covered by no more than 100 fathoms (600 feet) of water is considered as the continental shelf." 4 Whiteman 758. See, in general, 4 Whiteman at 752–64. On President Truman's proclamation, also issued on September 28, 1945, relating to the conservation and protection of fishing resources in areas of the high seas contiguous to United States waters, see 4 Whiteman at 945–62. See p. 1289 infra.

2. In 1951, in the *Abu Dhabi* case, Lord Asquith of Bishopstone concluded that the doctrine of the continental shelf was unknown to international law in 1939 and had not yet become part of the corpus of international law in 1951. See 1 Int'l & Comp.L.Q. 247 (1952).

The International Law Commission adopted draft articles on the continental shelf and related subjects at its third session in 1951. In its commentary to Article 2 (providing that the continental shelf was "subject to the exercise by the coastal State of control and jurisdiction for the purpose of exploring it and exploiting its natural resources"), the Commission noted that "though numerous proclamations have been issued over the past decade, it can hardly be said that such unilateral action has already established a new customary law." [1951] 2 Yb.I.L.C. 141–42. See also Kunz, Continental Shelf and International Law: Confusion and Abuse, 50 A.J.I.L. 828, 829, 832 (1956).

Compare the suggestion made in the North Sea Continental Shelf cases that emerging customary law "became crystallized in the adoption of the Continental Shelf Convention," p. 1280 infra.

## DEFINITION OF THE CONTINENTAL SHELF

### *U.N. CONVENTION ON THE LAW OF THE SEA (1982)*

U.N.Doc. A/CONF. 62/122; 21 I.L.M. 1261 (1982).

ARTICLE 76

1. The continental shelf of a coastal State comprises the sea-bed and subsoil of the submarine areas that extend beyond its territorial sea throughout the natural prolongation of its land territory to the outer edge of the continental margin, or to a distance of 200 nautical miles from the baselines from which the breadth of the territorial sea is measured, where the outer edge of the continental margin does not extend up to that distance.

* * *

3. The continental margin comprises the submerged prolongation of the land mass of the coastal State, and consists of the sea-bed and subsoil of the shelf, the slope and the rise. It does not include the deep ocean floor with its oceanic ridges or the subsoil thereof.

### *Notes*

1. The 1958 Convention contained the following definition of the Continental Shelf:

> Art. 1. For the purpose of these articles, the term "continental shelf" is used as referring (a) to the seabed and subsoil of the submarine areas adjacent to the coast but outside the area of the territorial sea, to a depth of 200 metres or, beyond that limit, to where the depth of the superjacent waters admits of the exploitation of the natural resources of the said areas; (b) to the seabed and subsoil of similar submarine areas adjacent to the coasts of islands.

The wide expansion of the definition of the continental shelf in the 1982 Convention as compared with the 1958 Convention is related to the acceptance of the exclusive economic zone of 200 miles, p. 1291 infra.

2. Sections 4–7 of Article 76 of the 1982 Convention provide for defining the outer edge of the continental margin wherever it extends beyond 200 nautical miles. It shall not exceed 350 miles from the baseline or 100 nautical miles from the 2500 meter isobath. (Only the 350 mile limit applies on submarine ridges, Article 76(6)). A Commission on the Limits of the Continental Shelf is to be established which shall make recommendations to coastal states, but the limits established by the coastal state "taking into account these recommendations" shall be final and binding. Article 76(8).

Do states not party to the 1982 Convention need to take into account recommendations of the Commission? If they do not, can they claim the expanded provision of Article 76 on the basis of customary law? Compare Note 3 below.

3. States generally were prepared to accept a very wide "continental shelf," but the geographically disadvantaged states sought to share in as much of the continental shelf as exceeded the 200 mile zone which would accrue to coastal states under the new Exclusive Economic Zone. The 1982 Convention, Article 82, provides:

> 1. The coastal State shall make payments or contributions in kind in respect of the exploitation of the non-living resources of the continental shelf beyond 200 nautical miles from the baselines from which the breadth of the territorial sea is measured.
>
> 2. The payments and contributions shall be made annually with respect to all production at a site after the first five years of production at that site. For the sixth year, the rate of payment or contribution shall be 1 per cent of the value or volume of production at the site. The rate shall increase by 1 per cent for each subsequent year until the twelfth year and shall remain at 7 per cent thereafter. Production does not include resources used in connection with exploitation.
>
> 3. A developing State which is a net importer of a mineral resource produced from its continental shelf is exempt from making such payments or contributions in respect of that mineral resource.
>
> 4. The payments or contributions shall be made through the Authority, which shall distribute them to States Parties to this Convention, on the basis of equitable sharing criteria, taking into account the interests and needs of developing States, particularly the least developed and the land-locked among them.

Can a state not party to the Convention claim that the extended definition of the continental shelf is customary law if it does not accept also the obligations of Art. 82? See Restatement (Third) Introductory Note to Part V. See generally, Jewett, The Evolution of the Legal Regime of the Continental Shelf, 22 Can. Y.B.Int'l L. 153 (1984), and 23 Can.Y.B.Int'l L. 201 (1985).

## DELIMITATION OF THE CONTINENTAL SHELF BETWEEN STATES

## THE NORTH SEA CONTINENTAL SHELF CASES

International Court of Justice, 1969.
1969 I.C.J. 3.

[In 1966, a dispute arose between the Federal Republic of Germany on one side and The Netherlands and Denmark on the other concerning the delimitation of the boundaries of their respective continental shelves in the North Sea. The United Kingdom had concluded agreements with Norway, Denmark and The Netherlands on the boundaries of their respective continental shelf claims. Denmark, The Netherlands and Germany, however, had not agreed with each other on boundaries in the eastern part of the North Sea. On March 31, 1966, Denmark and The Netherlands reached agreement on the boundary line between their respective claims. This line, based on the principle of the "equidistant line" begins at a point on the boundary line separating the United Kingdom's shelf from the eastern half of the North Sea, and extends to a point off the coast of West Germany, thus preventing Germany from extending its continental shelf to the United Kingdom boundary line in the middle of the North Sea. The Federal Republic of Germany is not a party to the Convention on the Continental Shelf.

[Special agreements were concluded between the Federal Republic of Germany and The Netherlands and between the Federal Republic of Germany and Denmark providing for the submission to the International Court of Justice of the disagreement between Germany and its neighbor states over the proper delimitation of the continental shelf in the North Sea. The Court handed down its decision on February 29, 1969. North Sea Continental Shelf Cases (Federal Republic of Germany v. Denmark; Federal Republic of Germany v. Netherlands), 1969 I.C.J. 3.

[The Court first rejected the argument of Denmark and the Netherlands that the rule of equidistance has a *priori* character of inherent necessity because it gave expression to, and translated into linear terms, a principle of proximity inherent in the basic concept of the continental shelf, causing every part of the shelf to appertain to the nearest coastal state and to no other. It then considered the contention of Denmark and the Netherlands that although prior to the 1958 Geneva Conference, continental shelf law was only in the formative stage, and State practice lacked uniformity, yet "the process of the definition and consolidation of the emerging customary law took place through the work of the International Law Commission, the reaction of governments to that work and the proceedings of the Geneva Conference"; and that this emerging customary law became "crystallized in the adoption of the Continental Shelf Convention by the Conference." The Court rejected this contention as applied to this issue, stating:]

Whatever validity this contention may have in respect of at least certain parts of the Convention, the Court cannot accept it as regards the delimitation provision (Article 6), the relevant parts of which were adopted almost unchanged from the draft of the International Law Commission that formed the basis of discussion at the Conference. The status of the rule in the Convention therefore depends mainly on the processes that led the Commission to propose it. These processes have already been reviewed. * * * [T]he Court considers this review sufficient for present purposes also, in order to show that the principle of equidistance, as it now figures in Article 6 of the Convention, was proposed by the Commission with considerable hesitation, somewhat on an experimental basis, at most *de lege ferenda,* and not at all *de lege iata* or as an emerging rule of customary international law. This is clearly not the sort of foundation on which Article 6 of the Convention could be said to have reflected or crystallized such a rule.

1969 I.C.J. at 38. [The Court buttressed this conclusion by pointing out that Article 6 was one of the provisions in respect of which Article 12 permitted any state to attach a reservation on signing, ratifying or acceding. The Court further concluded that neither the effect of the Geneva Convention nor state practice since its signing justified the inference that delimitation according to the principle of equidistance rises to the level of a mandatory rule of customary law. See the excerpt of the Court's opinion at p. 80 supra. Having decided that neither the equidistance method nor any other method of delimitation was obligatory, the Court stressed as the basic applicable legal principles (1) that delimitation must be the object of agreement between the states concerned and (2) that such agreement must be arrived at in accordance with equitable principles. In its judgment (eleven votes to six) the Court stated:]

[T]he principles and rules of international law applicable to the delimitation as between the Parties * * * are as follows:

(1) delimitation is to be effected by agreement in accordance with equitable principles, and taking account of all the relevant circumstances, in such a way as to leave as much as possible to each Party all those parts of the continental shelf that constitute a natural prolongation of its land territory into and under the sea, without encroachment on the natural prolongation of the land territory of the other;

(2) if, in the application of the preceding sub-paragraph, the delimitation leaves to the Parties areas that overlap, these are to be divided between them in agreed proportions or, failing agreement, equally, unless they decide on a régime of joint jurisdiction, user, or exploitation for the zones of overlap or any part of them;

[I]n the course of the negotiations, the factors to be taken into account are to include:

(1) the general configuration of the coasts of the Parties, as well as the presence of any special or unusual features;

(2) so far as known or readily ascertainable, the physical and geological structure, and natural resources, of the continental shelf areas involved;

(3) the element of a reasonable degree of proportionality, which a delimitation carried out in accordance with equitable principles ought to bring about between the extent of the continental shelf areas appertaining to the coastal State and the length of its coast measured in the general direction of the coastline, account being taken for this purpose of the effects, actual or prospective, of any other continental shelf delimitations between adjacent States in the same region.

1969 I.C.J. at 53.

### *Note*

The Court's disposition of the cases is criticized in Friedmann, The North Sea Continental Shelf Cases, 64 A.J.I.L. 229 (1970). For other aspects of the Court's opinion see Chapter 2, p. 78 supra.

## *U.N. CONVENTION ON THE LAW OF THE SEA (1982)*

U.N.Doc. A/CONF. 62/122; 21 I.L.M. 1261 (1982).

### Article 83

### *Delimitation of the Continental Shelf Between States With Opposite or Adjacent Coasts*

1. The delimitation of the continental shelf between States with opposite or adjacent coasts shall be effected by agreement on the basis of international law, as referred to in Article 38 of the Statute of the International Court of Justice, in order to achieve an equitable solution.

2. If no agreement can be reached within a reasonable period of time, the States concerned shall resort to the procedures provided for in Part XV.

3. Pending agreement as provided for in paragraph 1, the States concerned, in a spirit of understanding and co-operation, shall make every effort to enter into provisional arrangements of a practical nature and, during this transitional period, not to jeopardize or hamper the reaching of the final agreement. Such arrangements shall be without prejudice to the final delimitation.

4. Where there is an agreement in force between the States concerned, questions relating to the delimitation of the continental shelf shall be determined in accordance with the provisions of that agreement.

### *Notes*

1. Article 83 (and the identical Article 74 dealing with delimitation of exclusive economic zones) reflect the inability of states to achieve a formula for maritime boundary delimitation between continental shelves or exclusive economic zones of different states. The inability to agree has resulted in numerous arbitrations and adjudications to delimit maritime boundaries. Between 1969 and 1984 the International Court of Justice heard three maritime boundary cases, two as a full court, one as chamber. By 1993, three additional cases on delimitation had been brought before the Court: *Case Concerning the Land, Island and Maritime Frontier Dispute* (El Salvador v. Honduras: Nicaragua intervening) (Merits), 1992 I.C.J. 351; *Case Concerning Maritime Delimitation and Territorial Question Between Qatar and Bahrain* (Qatar v. Bahrain), see Order 1992 I.C.J. 237; and *Case Concerning the Arbitral Award of 31 July 1989* (Guinea–Bissau v. Senegal), 1989 I.C.J. 126. See also *Case Concerning Passage Through the Great Belt* (Finland v. Denmark) (Provisional Measures), 1992 I.C.J. 348.

The *North Sea Continental Shelf Cases,* p. 1280 above, and the *Continental Shelf Case* between Libya and Tunisia, relied on "equitable principles" to divide a shelf where there was no interruption in the natural prolongation of the coasts, but gave no clear guidelines as to the applicable principles. The Court did not try to elucidate equitable principles, beyond a few statements such as that parties should not refashion nature and that special effects or circumstances could be taken into account.

In the *Gulf of Maine Case* (1984 I.C.J. 246), the Chamber seemed to abandon any quest for principles to apply to delimitation cases generally. The Chamber said:

> 111. A body of detailed rules is not to be looked for in customary international law. * * * and not [to be tested] by deduction from preconceived ideas. It is therefore unrewarding, especially in a new and still unconsolidated field like that involving the quite recent extension of the claims of States to areas which were until yesterday zones of the high seas, to look to general international law to provide a ready-made set of rules that can be used for solving any delimitation problems that arise. A more useful course is to seek a better formulation of the fundamental norm, on which the Parties were fortunate enough to be agreed, and whose existence in the legal convictions not only of the Parties to the present dispute, but of all States, is apparent from an examination of the realities of international legal relations.

112. The Chamber therefore wishes to conclude this review * * * by attempting a more complete and, in its opinion, more precise reformulation of the "fundamental norm" already mentioned. For this purpose it will, *inter alia,* draw also upon the definition of the "actual rules of law * * * which govern the delimitation of adjacent continental shelves—that is to say, rules binding upon States for all delimitations" which was given by the Court in its 1969 Judgment in the *North Sea Continental Shelf* cases (*I.C.J. Reports 1969,* pp. 46–47, para. 85). What general international law prescribes in every maritime delimitation between neighbouring States could therefore be defined as follows:

(1) No maritime delimitation between States with opposite or adjacent coasts may be effected unilaterally by one of those States. Such delimitation must be sought and effected by means of an agreement, following negotiations conducted in good faith and with the genuine intention of achieving a positive result. Where, however, such agreement cannot be achieved, delimitation should be effected by recourse to a third party possessing the necessary competence.

(2) In either case, delimitation is to be effected by the application of equitable criteria and by the use of practical methods capable of ensuring, with regard to the geographic configuration of the area and other relevant circumstances, an equitable result. Id. at 299.

The Chamber concluded that, in the absence of agreement, states will have to seek third party determination of maritime boundaries. No principle applies in the absence of agreement. (The equidistance line, for example, cannot be applied in the absence of agreement.)

As for the principles that should guide the third party, the Chamber said:

There has been no systematic definition of the equitable criteria that may be taken into consideration for an international maritime delimitation, and this would in any event be difficult *a priori,* because of their highly variable adaptability to different concrete situations * * * Here again the essential consideration is that none of the potential methods has intrinsic merits which would make it preferable to another in the abstract * * *. Above all there must be willingness to adopt a combination of different methods whenever that * * * may be relevant in the different phases of the operation and with reference to different segments of the line.

Id. at pp. 312, 315.

All these I.C.J. cases indicate that in applying equitable principles geography is the primary concern; economic conditions and environmental concerns are excluded. Nevertheless, geography was "modified" to some extent to achieve a more equitable result. The concavity of the Federal Republic of Germany's coast was taken into account in the *North Sea Cases.* A line dictated by the general direction of the coasts was modified by the presence of islands in the *Libya–Tunisia Case.* The proportionality of the coasts was considered in the *Gulf of Maine Case.*

The International Court of Justice Chamber also looked for the first time at a unitary boundary for both the shelf and the water column. While it reiterated the dual character of its task throughout the opinion, the Chamber did not indicate how the line it drew would be different if it were delimiting the shelf only. It seemed to imply that in the absence of a clear, natural division in the continental shelf between adjacent states, it will be possible to divide both water column and shelf using the same principles. Again, the exact nature of those principles remains unclear. Compare Restatement (Third) § 511. See Feldman, Tunisia–Libya Continental Shelf Case: geographic justice or judicial compromise?, 77 A.J.I.L. 219 (1983); Schneider, The Gulf of Maine Case, 79 A.J.I.L. 539 (1985); Legault and Hankey, From Sea to Seabed, 79 A.J.I.L. 961 (1985). See generally, International Maritime Boundaries (Charney & Alexander, eds., 1993); Evans, Relevant Circumstances and Maritime Delimitation (1989); Weil, The Law of Maritime Delimitations—Reflections (1989); Jagota, Maritime Boundary (1984). See also Charney, Ocean Boundaries Between Nations: A Theory for Progress, 78 A.J.I.L. 582 (1984).

2. In the United States, controversy over the continental shelf has centered chiefly upon the rights of the federal government as opposed to those of the coastal states. In 1947, the Supreme Court held that the United States was "possessed of paramount rights in, and full dominion and power over, the lands, minerals and other things" underlying the Pacific Ocean seaward of the low-water mark on the coast of California and outside of inland waters, to the extent of three nautical miles, and that California had "no title thereto or property interest therein." United States v. California, 332 U.S. 19, 67 S.Ct. 1658, 91 L.Ed. 1889 (1947), reh'g denied, 332 U.S. 804, 805, 68 S.Ct. 20, 21, 92 L.Ed. 382 (Decree) (1947). In United States v. Louisiana, 339 U.S. 699, 70 S.Ct. 914, 94 L.Ed. 1216 (1950), the Court followed the *California* decision and held that the United States possessed identical rights over areas underlying the Gulf of Mexico, to the extent (27 miles from the coast) claimed by Louisiana. Noting that the one difference between Louisiana's claim and the earlier claim of California was that the former state claimed rights "twenty-four miles seaward of the three-mile belt," the Court (per Douglas, J.) stated: "If, as we held in California's case, the three-mile belt is in the domain of the Nation rather than that of the separate States, it follows *a fortiori* that the ocean beyond that limit also is. The ocean seaward of the marginal belt is perhaps even more directly related to the national defense, the conduct of foreign affairs, and world commerce than is the marginal sea." 339 U.S. at 705. On the same day as the Louisiana decision, the Court held that Texas had no interest in the undersea areas contiguous to its coast, even though Texas argued that it had acquired both proprietary and sovereign rights in a 9–mile marginal belt prior to annexation by the United States. United States v. Texas, 339 U.S. 707, 70 S.Ct. 918, 94 L.Ed. 1221 (1950), reh'g denied, 340 U.S. 907, 71 S.Ct. 277, 95 L.Ed. 656 (1950). The United States was held to be possessed of paramount rights in, and full dominion and power over, the undersea areas extending to the edge of the continental shelf in the Gulf of Mexico first claimed by Texas in 1947. 339 U.S. at 715–20; 340 U.S. 900–901 (Decree) (1950).

On May 22, 1953, Congress passed the Submerged Lands Act, 67 Stat. 29, 43 U.S.C.A. §§ 1301–15, by which the United States relinquished to the coastal states all of its rights in submerged lands within certain geographical limits, and confirmed the rights of the United States beyond those limits. The Act defined the areas relinquished to the states in terms of state boundaries as they existed at the time a state became a member of the Union, but not extending beyond three geographic miles in the Atlantic and Pacific Oceans or beyond three marine leagues (9 miles) in the Gulf of Mexico. On August 7, 1953, Congress approved the Outer Continental Shelf Lands Act, 67 Stat. 462, 43 U.S.C.A. §§ 1331–46, which provided for the jurisdiction of the United States over the "outer Continental Shelf" (defined as areas seaward of those relinquished to the states by the Submerged Lands Act) and authorized the Secretary of the Interior to lease such areas for exploitation purposes. In United States v. States of Louisiana, Texas, Mississippi, Alabama and Florida, 363 U.S. 1, 80 S.Ct. 961, 4 L.Ed.2d 1025 (1960), the United States sought a declaration that it was entitled to full dominion and power over the undersea areas underlying the Gulf of Mexico that were more than three geographic miles seaward from the coast, and extending to the edge of the continental shelf. The State Department took the position that it could not accept an interpretation of the Submerged Lands Act that would result in recognition of state claims to "marginal seas of a greater breadth than 3 marine miles." 4 Whiteman at 62. The Court held that the Government's contention that state claims to historic seaward boundaries of more than three miles conflicted with national policy on the three-mile limit rested "on an oversimplification of the problem" inasmuch as the Submerged Lands Act allowed state claims of up to three marine leagues for "purely domestic purposes." 363 U.S. at 33, 80 S.Ct. at 980. Turning to the historic claims of the coastal states, the Court concluded that Texas was entitled, as against the United States, to the areas underlying the Gulf of Mexico to a distance of three leagues from her coast. Id. at 64. Florida was also held, on other grounds, to be entitled to a three-marine-league belt of land under the Gulf of Mexico, seaward from its coast. United States v. Florida, et al., 363 U.S. 121, 129, 80 S.Ct. 961, 4 L.Ed.2d 1025 (1960). The other Gulf states were held not to be entitled to rights in submerged lands lying beyond three geographic miles from their respective coasts. 363 U.S. at 79, 82, 80 S.Ct. at ——, ——. See further United States v. Louisiana, 394 U.S. 1, 11, 89 S.Ct. 768, 773, 22 L.Ed.2d 36, 44 (1969); 420 U.S. 529, 95 S.Ct. 1180, 43 L.Ed.2d 373 (1975) (Special Masters Report accepted and decree issued); 422 U.S. 13, 95 S.Ct. 2022, 44 L.Ed.2d 652 (1975) (supplemental decision). See also United States v. California, 381 U.S. 139, 85 S.Ct. 1401, 14 L.Ed.2d 296 (1965) discussed at p. 1253, note 4.

In United States v. Maine, 420 U.S. 515, 95 S.Ct. 1155, 43 L.Ed.2d 363 (1975), the Supreme Court held that the right to explore and exploit the sea bed beyond 3 miles belonged to the federal government, not to the defendants, the original states of the Union that had claimed these rights by succession to Great Britain.

3. In United States v. Ray, 423 F.2d 16 (5th Cir.1970), the Court of Appeals for the Fifth Circuit granted the United States a decree enjoining private persons, American citizens, from establishing a "new sovereign country" on two canal reefs on the continental shelf of the United States (outside its claimed territorial sea) without finding that these reefs were the property of the United States. The Court held that the structures interfered with the exclusive rights of the United States to exploit the reefs under the Geneva Convention on the Continental Shelf and the Outer Continental Shelf Lands Act.

But in Treasure Salvors, Inc. v. Unidentified Wrecked and Abandoned Sailing Vessel, etc., 569 F.2d 330 (5th Cir.1978), the Court of Appeals denied the United States sovereign rights to an abandoned vessel found by a private person on the Continental Shelf, since United States interests in the shelf were only for the purpose of exploring it and exploiting its natural resources (Id. at 339).

Compare the 1982 Convention, Article 73, on coastal state jurisdiction in the exclusive economic zone p. 1292 infra. For the right of "hot pursuit" as applied to violation of the continental shelf, see the 1982 Convention, Article 111(2), p. 1291 infra. See Feldman and Colson, The Maritime Boundaries of the United States, 75 A.J.I.L. 729 (1981).

# THE CONTINENTAL SHELF AND THE RIGHTS OF COASTAL STATES

*U.N. CONVENTION ON THE LAW OF THE SEA (1982)*

U.N.Doc. A/CONF. 62/122; 21 I.L.M. 1261 (1982).

ARTICLE 77

*Rights of the Coastal State in the Continental Shelf*

1. The coastal State exercises over the continental shelf sovereign rights for the purpose of exploring it and exploiting its natural resources.

2. The rights referred to in paragraph 1 are exclusive in the sense that if the coastal State does not explore the continental shelf or exploit its natural resources, no one may undertake these activities without the express consent of the coastal State.

3. The rights of the coastal State over the continental shelf do not depend on occupation, effective or notional, or on any express proclamation.

4. The natural resources referred to in this Part consist of the mineral and other non-living resources of the sea-bed and subsoil together with living organisms belonging to sedentary species, that is to say, organisms which, at the harvestable stage, either are immobile on or under the sea-bed or are unable to move except in constant physical contact with the sea-bed or the subsoil.

ARTICLE 78

*Legal Status of the Superjacent Waters and Airspace and the Rights and Freedoms of Other States*

1. The rights of the coastal State over the continental shelf do not affect the legal status of the superjacent waters or of the air space above those waters.

2. The exercise of the rights of the coastal State over the continental shelf must not infringe, or result in any unjustifiable interference with navigation and other rights and freedoms of other States as provided for in this Convention.

### *Notes*

1. Articles 77 and 78 are essentially the same as Articles 2 and 3 of the 1958 Convention on the Continental Shelf, except that the latter identified the waters above the shelf as "high seas". Compare the Exclusive Economic Zone, p. 1291 infra. Article 78(2) covers in part what is in Article 5(1) of the 1958 Convention.

2. Restatement (Third) § 511, Comment *b,* states:

> *"Sovereignty" and "sovereign rights."* A state has complete sovereignty over the territorial sea, analogous to that which it possesses over its land territory, internal waters, and archipelagic waters. See § 512; LOS Convention, Article 2(1). See also the 1958 Convention on the Territorial Sea and the Contiguous Zone, Article 1(1). The sovereignty over the territorial sea is subject, however, to the right of innocent passage for foreign vessels (*id.*

Articles 1(2) and 14(1); LOS Convention, Articles 2(3) and 17; see § 513(1) and (2)). The territorial sea within a strait or adjacent to archipelagic waters is also subject to the right of transit passage or archipelagic sea lanes passage (LOS Convention, Articles 38 and 53(1); see § 513(3) and (4)).

"Sovereign rights," which a coastal state enjoys in its exclusive economic zone and on its continental shelf, are functional in character, limited to specified activities. In the continental shelf, the coastal state exercises sovereign rights only "for the purpose of exploring it and exploiting its natural resources," both living and nonliving. See § 515; 1958 Convention on the Continental Shelf, Article 2; LOS Convention, Article 77. In the exclusive economic zone, a coastal state has sovereign rights "for the purpose of exploring and exploiting, conserving and managing the natural resources, whether living or nonliving, of the waters superjacent to the seabed and its subsoil," as well as "with regard to other activities for the economic exploitation and exploration of the zone, such as the production of energy from the water, currents and winds." See § 514; LOS Convention, Article 56(1)(a). In addition, international law confers on the coastal state limited jurisdiction in that zone for some other purposes, *e.g.*, with respect to marine scientific research and the protection and preservation of the marine environment, and artificial islands and certain installations and structures. *Id.* Articles 56(1)(b) and 60.

3. The question of scientific research was also covered in Article 5(1) and in 5(8) of the 1958 Convention, but despite the provision in the latter that "the coastal state shall not normally withhold its consent" to bona fide scientific research, such consent has not been forthcoming and scientific research on the continental shelves of the world by foreign scientists has been virtually nonexistent. At the Third Law of the Sea Conference, scientific research was the subject of intense negotiation, with the United States taking the lead in challenging coastal state control both on the continental shelf and in the exclusive economic zone. See 1982 Convention, Part XIII.

Article 79 of the 1982 Convention, like Article 4 of the 1958 Convention, recognizes the rights of other states to lay and maintain cables and pipelines subject to reasonable measures of the coastal state for the exploration of the Continental Shelf. The 1982 Convention provision also permits the coastal state to take reasonable measures to control pollution from pipelines, and requires the consent of the coastal state to the delineation of the course for laying pipelines. States laying pipelines shall pay due regard to cables or pipelines already in position.

### *2. The Exclusive Economic Zone*

## EXCLUSIVE ECONOMIC ZONE: ANTECEDENTS

Long before the law of the sea conventions, coastal states claimed exception to the rule of *mare liberum.* Coastal state claims that led to the development of the territorial sea, see p. 1240, were inspired in significant part by the desire for exclusive rights in the resources of that part of the sea, principally its fish. Coastal states also asserted a right to enforce measures of conservation outside their territorial sea designed to maintain the supply of fish for the benefit of national fisheries. See 3 Gidel, Le Droit International Public de la Mer 465 (1934).

A series of new claims by coastal states arose between 1945 and 1958, some to wide fishing zones, some to territorial sea (although these, too, may have been designed principally as a way to claim more fish and sea-bed resources). Considering the economic importance to many states of offshore fishing resources, it was not surprising that these countries early began to invoke the customs laws of the United States and other states as justifying, by analogy, attempts to exercise jurisdiction over fishing areas adjacent to territorial waters. Indeed, the parallel was invoked, although not without criticism, in the United States Congress as early as 1937 to justify proposals for a far-reaching appropriation of certain high seas fisheries. The Truman Proclamation asserting the exclusive jurisdiction of the coastal state to the mineral resources of the continental shelf beyond the territorial sea inevitably encouraged other coastal states to claim exclusive rights to fish in waters beyond the territorial sea.

Iceland's attempt to extend its fisheries jurisdiction from 12 to 50 miles was opposed in the International Court of Justice by the United Kingdom, whose vessels had fished off the Icelandic coast for centuries. In the *Fisheries Jurisdiction Case,* 1974 I.C.J. 3, the Court acknowledged an increasing and widespread acceptance of preferential fishing rights for coastal states. The Court said, however, that such rights are not absolute and could not imply the extinction of the concurrent rights of other states, particularly states that had historic claims to fish in particular waters. The Court concluded that Iceland could not unilaterally exclude the United Kingdom from its historic fishing grounds. The Court declared also that the two countries had an obligation to resolve their dispute by negotiation.

For years the United States resisted claims by other coastal states to large exclusive fishing zones, and strenuously supported claims by its nationals to fish in distant waters outside the territory of other states. For its part as a coastal state, the United States itself claimed only a limited conservation zone.

To deal with the problems of conservation and disputes arising from unilateral claims, the Geneva Conference of 1958 adopted a Convention on Fishing and Conservation of the Living Resources of the High Seas, 17 U.S.T. 138, T.I.A.S. 5960, 559 U.N.T.S. 285. The Convention provides in Article 6 that a coastal state has a "special interest in the maintenance of the productivity of the living resources in any area of the high seas adjacent to its territorial sea," and may thus take the initiative in prescribing measures of conservation (which must be non-discriminatory and based on "appropriate" scientific findings, and the need for which must be "urgent"). See generally 4 Whiteman at 768–77; Bishop, The 1958 Geneva Convention on Fishing and Conservation of the Living Resources of the High Seas, 62 Colum.L.Rev. 1202 (1962). On September 28, 1945, President Truman issued a proclamation asserting that the United States would consider it proper "to establish conservation zones in those areas of the high seas contiguous to the coasts of the United States." The United States would regulate fishing activities of its own nationals unilaterally, and those of foreign nationals by agreement with their states. 10 Fed.Reg. 12304 (1945), 4 Whiteman 945–62.

In time, however, in response to pressure from other coastal states and its own fishing interests, the U.S. began to assert fishing zones of its own. In

1966, Congress established a "Contiguous Fishery Zone" of 12 miles (9 miles beyond its territorial sea). Pub.L. 89–658, Oct. 14, 1966, 80 Stat. 908, 16 U.S.C.A. § 1091.

## *FISHERY CONSERVATION AND MANAGEMENT ACT OF 1976*

16 U.S.C.A. § 1801.

### Title I—Fishery Management Authority of the United States

#### *Sec. 101. Fishery Conservation Zone*

There is established a zone contiguous to the territorial sea of the United States to be known as the fishery conservation zone. The inner boundary of the fishery conservation zone is a line coterminous with the seaward boundary of each of the coastal States, and the outer boundary of such zone is a line drawn in such manner that each point on it is 200 nautical miles from the baseline from which the territorial sea is measured.

#### *Sec. 102. Exclusive Fishery Management Authority*

The United States shall exercise exclusive fishery management authority, in the manner provided for in this Act, over the following:

(1) All fish within the fishery conservation zone.

(2) All anadromous species throughout the migratory range of each such species beyond the fishery conservation zone; except that such management authority shall not extend to such species during the time they are found within any foreign nation's territorial sea or fishery conservation zone (or the equivalent), to the extent that such sea or zone is recognized by the United States.

(3) All Continental Shelf fishery resources beyond the fishery conservation zone.

#### *Sec. 103. Highly Migratory Species*

The exclusive fishery management authority of the United States shall not include, nor shall it be construed to extend to, highly migratory species of fish.

* * *

### Title IV—Miscellaneous Provisions

#### *Sec. 401. Effect on Law of the Sea Treaty*

If the United States ratifies a comprehensive treaty, which includes provisions with respect to fishery conservation and management jurisdiction, resulting from any United Nations Conference on the Law of the Sea, the Secretary, after consultation with the Secretary of State, may promulgate any amendment to the regulations promulgated under this Act if such amendment is necessary and appropriate to conform such regulations to the provisions of such treaty, in anticipation of the date when such treaty shall come into force and effect for, or otherwise be applicable to, the United States.

### *Notes*

1. In Title II, the Fishery Conservation and Management Act provides for foreign fishing pursuant to existing or future agreements, essentially on the basis of reciprocity.

2. In United States v. F/V Taiyo Maru, 395 F.Supp. 413 (D.Maine 1975), the U.S. District Court upheld the right of hot pursuit from the contiguous fisheries zone (note 2 supra). The court held that Articles 23 and 24 of the 1958 Convention on the High Seas do not forbid a coastal state to establish a contiguous fisheries zone (up to 12 miles) or to conduct hot pursuit from such a zone. For a critical comment, see Ciobanu, Hot Pursuit From a Fisheries Zone: A Further Comment on United States v. Fishing Vessel Taiyo Maru No. 28; United States v. Kawaguchi, 70 A.J.I.L. 549 (1976); Ridell, Hot Pursuit from a Fisheries Zone, 70 A.J.I.L. 95 (1976).

On hot pursuit from the exclusive economic zone, see p. 1296 infra.

3. Henkin writes:

> Developed maritime states early resisted coastal-state expansion. As distant fishing states, they rejected the notion that a coastal state might exclude them from wide coastal zones in which they had long fished. They feared, too, "creeping jurisdiction." Already they had seen how exclusive mining rights for coastal states on the continental shelf (beyond their territorial sea) had created pressures for exclusive fishing rights for coastal states in wide zones beyond the territorial sea. Developed maritime states feared that if the coastal state acquired exclusive fishing rights, its jurisdiction would continue to expand to other uses and would interfere also with navigation, scientific research, and military uses in wide coastal zones.
>
> But developed maritime states are also coastal states and have important national interests that stood to gain from coastal-state expansion. They had some sympathy with the economic needs of poor coastal states. They were reluctant to confront developing coastal states (supported by the rest of the Third World), especially since the latter had effective "possession" of the coastal areas and could seize them (or threaten to seize them) unilaterally. Pressed from without and by national interests from within, they acquiesced in the concept of an exclusive economic zone. (This, in fact, unleashed domestic forces that pressed unilateral expansion. While the conference was in process, the United States Congress declared a 200–mile fishing zone for the United States.)

Henkin, How Nations Behave 217 (2d ed. 1979) (footnotes omitted).

## THE EXCLUSIVE ECONOMIC ZONE IN THE 1982 CONVENTION

Extensive pressure from states with varying interests at stake led the Law of the Sea Convention to adopt the exclusive economic zone:

> The drive to extend coastal-state jurisdiction has come particularly from Latin–American states. Those rich in off-shore minerals have been reasonably content with their rights under the Convention of the Continental Shelf, especially with extravagant interpretations that would give them the resources of the entire submerged landmass out to

the ocean abyss. Some states, having little continental margin, have asked "compensation" in the form of rights in the deep sea-bed for many miles from their shores. Principally, however, fishing states have pressed for monopoly over fish equivalent to that enjoyed by their neighbors over coastal minerals. Within the general campaign of the poorer states for change in the international economic system and its law, and the general reexamination of the law of the sea that has followed upon Malta's initiative, mining and fishing states in Latin America have joined to propose a "patrimonial sea" of 200 miles in which the coastal state would have exclusive rights to all resources. A group of African states has also proposed such an "exclusive economic zone."

Henkin, Politics and the Changing Law of the Sea, 89 Pol.Sci.Q. 56–57 (1974).*

See generally Vicuña, The Exclusive Economic Zone: Regime and Legal Nature under International Law (1989); Kwiatkowska, The 200 Mile Exclusive Economic Zone in the New Law of the Sea (1989); Attard, The Exclusive Economic Zone in International Law (1987); Charney, The Exclusive Economic Zone and Public International Law, 15 Ocean Dev. & Int'l L. 233 (1985); Hollick, The Origins of 200–Mile Offshore Zones, 71 A.J.I.L. (1977).

### *U.N. CONVENTION ON THE LAW OF THE SEA (1982)*

U.N.Doc. A/CONF. 62/122; 21 I.L.M. 1261 (1982).

#### ARTICLE 55

*Specific Legal Regime of the Exclusive Economic Zone*

The exclusive economic zone is an area beyond and adjacent to the territorial sea, subject to the specific legal régime established in this Part, under which the rights and jurisdictions of the coastal State and the rights and freedoms of other States are governed by the relevant provisions of this Convention.

#### ARTICLE 56

*Rights, Jurisdiction and Duties of the Coastal State in the Exclusive Economic Zone*

1. In the exclusive economic zone, the coastal State has:

(a) sovereign rights for the purpose of exploring and exploiting, conserving and managing the natural resources, whether living or non-living, of the sea-bed and subsoil and the superjacent waters, and with regard to other activities for the economic exploitation and exploration of the zone, such as the production of energy from the water, currents and winds;

(b) jurisdiction as provided for in the relevant provisions of this Convention with regard to:

(i) the establishment and use of artificial islands, installations and structures;

(ii) marine scientific research;

(iii) the protection and preservation of the marine environment;

(c) other rights and duties provided for in this Convention.

2. In exercising its rights and performing its duties under this Convention in the exclusive economic zone, the coastal state shall have due regard to the rights and duties of other States and shall act in a manner compatible with the provisions of this Convention.

3. The rights set out in this article with respect to the sea-bed and subsoil shall be exercised in accordance with Part VI.

ARTICLE 57

*Breadth of the Exclusive Economic Zone*

The exclusive economic zone shall not extend beyond 200 nautical miles from the baselines from which the breadth of the territorial sea is measured.

ARTICLE 58

*Rights and Duties of Other States in the Exclusive Economic Zone*

1. In the exclusive economic zone, all States, whether coastal or land-locked, enjoy, subject to the relevant provisions of this Convention, the freedoms referred to in article 87 of navigation and overflight and of the laying of submarine cables and pipelines, and other internationally lawful uses of the sea related to these freedoms, such as those associated with the operation of ships, aircraft and submarine cables and pipelines, and compatible with the other provisions of this Convention.

2. Articles 88 to 115 and other pertinent rules of international law apply to the exclusive economic zone in so far as they are not incompatible with this Part.

3. In exercising their rights and performing their duties under this Convention in the exclusive economic zone, States shall have due regard to the rights and duties of the coastal State and shall comply with the laws and regulations adopted by the coastal State in accordance with the provisions of this Convention and other rules of international law in so far as they are not incompatible with this Part.

### *Notes*

1. In 1983, President Reagan established an exclusive economic zone for the United States by proclamation, asserting rights over living and nonliving resources in accordance with the 1982 Convention. 19 Weekly Compilation of Presidential Documents 383 (1983), 83 Dep't State Bull. No. 2075 at 70–71 (1983), 22 I.L.M. 464 (1983). See p. 1232 above. For the conclusion that the EEZ is now customary law, see Restatement (Third) § 514, Comment *a*. If the Exclusive Economic Zone is customary law, does it supersede the 1976 Act of Congress, p. 1290 above as law of the United States? See Chapter 3, p. 167 above.

2. Article 74 of the 1982 Convention, dealing with delimitation of exclusive economic zones between states with opposite or adjacent coasts, is identical with Article 83 which deals with delimitation of the continental shelf. See p. 1282

above. Delimitation problems in the exclusive economic zone and the shelf are generally the same, and are sometimes considered together.

3. The Restatement (Third) § 514, Comment *c*, states:

> *Rights of coastal state in exclusive economic zone*. The coastal state does not have sovereignty over the exclusive economic zone but only "sovereign rights" for a specific purpose—the management of natural resources and other economic activities. See § 511, Comment *b*. The coastal state's authority (called "jurisdiction" in the LOS Convention) is even more limited with respect to artificial islands in the exclusive economic zone and such installations and structures as may be required for economic purposes, and with respect to marine scientific research and the protection of the marine environment. See Comments *g-i*. These grants of power are further circumscribed by rules contained in Parts V, XII, and XIII of the Convention, which in large part have already become law by custom and tacit agreement. Among these are rules requiring coastal states to ensure that their laws and regulations for the prevention, reduction, and control of pollution from vessels conform and give effect to generally accepted international rules and standards, to adjust their enforcement measures to the gravity of the violation, and to impose only monetary penalties.
>
> While there is no provision in the Law of the Sea Convention with respect to salvage activities in the exclusive economic zone, the implication in Article 303 of that Convention seems to be that the coastal state may regulate such activities only in the 24–mile contiguous zone. See § 521, Reporters' Note 6.

4. Tuna, a commercially valuable fish, is found both on the high seas and in the exclusive economic zones of many states. As a "highly migratory species," it is covered by article 64 of the 1982 Convention (See Annex 1 to the Convention). The United States maintains that under this article, and under customary law, a coastal state does not have exclusive rights over tuna in its exclusive economic zones. The United States Fishery Conservation and Management Act of 1976, extending U.S. exclusive authority over fish within the 200–mile zone, excludes tuna, though not other migratory species. However, other coastal states have asserted exclusive authority over tuna within their EEZ and have seized U.S. vessels fishing for tuna within their zones without their authorization. In retaliation the United States has imposed embargos on the import of fish from these countries. Several South Pacific island states and Mexico have been seriously affected.

Is it plausible to regard tuna and other highly migratory species as "nonresidents" and therefore not a resource of the EEZ? Is the United States correct in construing the obligation to cooperate in article 64 of the LOS Convention as precluding exclusive rights of the coastal state in respect of highly migratory species? See Hey, The Regime for the Exploitation of Transboundary Marine Fisheries Resources (1989); Munro, Extended Jurisdiction and the Management of Pacific Highly Migratory Species, 21 Ocean Dev. & Int'l L. 289 (1990); Weld, Critical Evaluation of Existing Mechanisms for Managing Migratory Pelagic Species in the Atlantic Ocean, 20 Ocean Dev. & Int'l L. 285 (1989); Kelly, The Law of the Sea: The Jurisdictional Dispute Over Highly Migratory Species of Tuna, 26 Colum.J.Transnat'l L. 475 (1988); Burke, Highly Migratory Species in the New Law of the Sea, 14 Ocean Dev. and Int.L.J. 273 (1983); Oda, Fisheries Under the United Nations Conventions on the Law of the Sea, 77 A.J.I.L. 739

(1984); Note, The Tuna War: Fishery Jurisdiction in International Law, 16 U.Ill.L.Rev. 755 (1981).

Assuming that the law recognizes an exclusive right to tuna in the EEZ, is the United States a "persistent dissenter" entitled to an exception from that principle? See Chapter 2, p. 87. Is it relevant that the United States has not asserted an exception in its law for highly migratory species other than tuna?

5. In the exclusive economic zone, the coastal state is given exclusive rights with regard to artificial islands, installations and structures (Art. 60). It is responsible for conservation of living resources (Art. 61). Article 62 establishes the objective of "optimum utilization." See also the special provisions for stocks occurring within two or more economic zones (Art. 63); highly migratory species (Art. 64), anadromous stocks (Art. 66) and catadromous species (Art. 67). Exploitation of marine mammals is left to regulation by the coastal state (or an international organization) (Art. 65). Sedentary species are governed by the regime of the Continental Shelf (Art. 77(4).

If the coastal state does not have the capacity to harvest the entire allowable catch, it shall give access to other states taking into account "the need to minimize economic dislocation in States whose nationals have habitually fished in the zone or which have made substantial efforts in research and identification of stocks" (Art. 62(3)). In particular, there is a right to participate by land-locked states in the region (Art. 69), and states with "special geographical characteristics," having no zone of their own or one unable to supply the needs of their population (Art. 70). But developed land-locked states are entitled to participate only in the economic zones of developed coastal states of the region (Arts. 69(4), 70(5)). Articles 69–70 do not apply when the coastal state's economy is "overwhelmingly dependent" on the exploitation of the living resources of its exclusive economic zone (Art. 71).

Article 73 provides:

1. The coastal State may, in the exercise of its sovereign rights to explore, exploit, conserve and manage the living resources in the exclusive economic zone, take such measures, including boarding, inspection, arrest and judicial proceedings, as may be necessary to ensure compliance with the laws and regulations enacted by it in conformity with this Convention.

2. Arrested vessels and their crews shall be promptly released upon the posting of reasonable bond or other security.

3. Coastal State penalties for violations of fisheries regulations in the exclusive economic zone may not include imprisonment, in the absence of agreements to the contrary by the States concerned, or any other form of corporal punishment.

4. In cases of arrest or detention of foreign vessels the coastal State shall promptly notify, through appropriate channels, the flag State of the action taken and of any penalties subsequently imposed.

6. Is the exclusive economic zone "high seas"? Does it matter? See Article 55 and 58 supra; also Article 86, p. 1297 below. Compare Article 3 of the 1958 Convention on the Continental Shelf: "The rights of the coastal State over the continental shelf do not affect the legal status of the superjacent waters as high seas, or that of the airspace above those waters."

The Restatement (Third) § 514, Comments *b, d* and *e* state:

*b. Relation of exclusive economic zone to high seas.* The LOS Convention does not explicitly designate the exclusive economic zone as part of the high seas. See § 521, Comment *a.* According to the United States and other maritime states, however, the Convention reflects the general understanding that, as a matter of customary law as well as under the Convention, the rights and freedoms of other states in the zone, set forth in Subsection (2), are the same as on the high seas. See Comment *e.* As to matters not expressly covered by this section, any conflict that might arise between the interests of a coastal state and those of any other state concerning their respective rights and duties in the exclusive economic zone should be resolved "on the basis of equity and in the light of all the relevant circumstances, taking into account the respective importance of the interests involved to the parties as well as to the international community." LOS Convention, Article 59. Special procedures for settling such disputes are provided in the Convention, but will not apply to states not parties. Id. Article 297(1).

* * *

*d. Rights of other states in exclusive economic zone.* In the exclusive economic zone of any state, all other states may exercise most high seas freedoms, such as those of navigation, overflight, and laying of submarine cables and pipelines (§ 521), but their right to participate in fishing is subject to the special rights of the coastal state under Subsection (1). The rights of other states with respect to operation of ships, aircraft, and submarine cables and pipelines are both qualitatively and quantitatively the same as the rights recognized by international law for all states on the high seas. See Subsection 2.

*e. Due regard to rights and duties of other states.* The Convention explicitly applies to the exclusive economic zone the principle of customary international law that in exercising its rights a state must do so with due regard to the rights of other states. The coastal state must exercise its rights and perform its duties under Subsection (1) with due regard to the rights and duties of other states under Subsection (2). LOS Convention, Article 56(2). Other states must exercise their rights and perform their duties under Subsection (2) with due regard to the rights of the coastal state under Subsection (1). Id. Article 58(3).

7. On the right of hot pursuit from the EEZ, the 1982 Convention Art. 111(2) provides:

> The right of hot pursuit shall apply *mutatis mutandis* to violations in the exclusive economic zone or on the continental shelf, including safety zones around continental shelf installations, of the laws and regulations of the coastal State applicable in accordance with this Convention to the exclusive economic zone or the continental shelf, including such safety zones.

See generally, Korolera, The Right to Hot Pursuit from the Exclusive Economic Zone, 14 Marine Pol'y 137 (1990).

8. On the protection of the marine environment, including protection of the environment of the EEZ, see Section 4, p. 1321 infra. On marine scientific research, including research in the EEZ, see Section 5, p. 1324 infra.

# SECTION 3. THE REGIME OF THE HIGH SEAS

Once, all the seas were governed by a regime characterized by principles of commonage and freedom. See p. 1236 supra. The emergence of the concept of the territorial sea, followed by other special zones and privileges for coastal states, reduced the areas subject to that regime (now distinctively called the "high seas") and created additional exceptions to its principles of commonage and freedom. Under the law emerging from the Third U.N. Law of the Sea Conference, the extent of the "high seas" is reduced by further concessions to coastal states—by a wider territorial sea and recognition of archipelagic states, and the special status of the Exclusive Economic Zone. Even the high seas as thus reduced are subject to additional rights for coastal states, as in the special-purpose zones described above, the coastal state's rights in its continental shelf where it is under the "high seas" because it extends beyond the 200 mile economic zone, and new regimes for pollution control and scientific research.

Subject to these limitations the regime of the high seas continues to be characterized by commonage and freedom, but commonage does not necessarily mean, as it used to, that all states are free to take the resources of the sea and the sea-bed, and freedom is subject to increasing international regulation.

## DEFINITION OF "HIGH SEAS"

*U.N. CONVENTION ON THE LAW OF THE SEA (1982)*

U.N.Doc. A/CONF. 62/122; 21 I.L.M. 1261 (1982).

Article 86

The provisions of this Part apply to all parts of the sea that are not included in the exclusive economic zone, in the territorial sea or in the internal waters of a State, or in the archipelagic waters of an archipelagic State. This article does not entail any abridgement of the freedoms enjoyed by all States in the exclusive economic zone in accordance with article 58.

***Note***

Compare Article 1 of the 1958 Convention on the High Seas which defined "high seas" as "all parts of the sea that are not included in the territorial sea or in the internal waters of a State." For the status of the EEZ under the 1982 Convention, see p. 1291 above.

## A. THE PRINCIPLE OF FREEDOM

*U.N. CONVENTION ON THE LAW OF THE SEA (1982)*

U.N.Doc. A/CONF. 62/122; 21 I.L.M. 1261 (1982).

Article 87

*Freedom of the High Seas*

1. The high seas are open to all States, whether coastal or land-locked. Freedom of the high seas is exercised under the conditions laid down by this

Convention and by other rules of international law. It comprises, *inter alia*, both for coastal and land-locked States:

(a) Freedom of navigation;

(b) Freedom of overflight;

(c) Freedom to lay submarine cables and pipelines, subject to Part VI;

(d) Freedom to construct artificial islands and other installations permitted under international law, subject to Part VI;

(e) Freedom of fishing, subject to the conditions laid down in section 2;

(f) Freedom of scientific research, subject to Parts VI and XIII.

2. These freedoms shall be exercised by all States, with due consideration for the interests of other States in their exercise of the freedom of the high seas, and also with due consideration for the rights under this Convention with respect to activities in the Area.

ARTICLE 88

*Reservation of the High Seas for Peaceful Purposes*

The High Seas Shall be Reserved for Peaceful Purposes.

ARTICLE 89

*Invalidity of Claims of Sovereignty Over the High Seas*

No State may validly purport to subject any part of the high seas to its sovereignty.

ARTICLE 90

*Right of Navigation*

Every State, whether coastal or land-locked, has the right to sail ships under its flag on the high seas.

***Notes***

1. Articles 87–90 of the 1982 Convention essentially repeat Articles 2 and 4 of the 1958 Convention, subject to exceptions consequent upon recognition of a wide continental shelf (Part VI), and the provisions relating to scientific research (Part XIII).

2. Warships and other vessels owned or operated by a government in "non-commercial service" on the high seas have complete immunity from the jurisdiction of any other state. 1982 Convention Arts. 95, 96. Is the same rule applicable to aircraft? Compare Chapter 12, p. 1068 above.

3. All states, including land-locked states, have the right to freedom of navigation. Article 3 of the 1958 Convention gave states without seacoast free access to the sea, pursuant to agreement, by transit through the territory of the coastal state and access to its ports. The 1982 Convention extends and expands such rights in Part X, Articles 124–32.

## B. LIMITATIONS ON FREEDOM

### *HENKIN, CHANGING LAW FOR THE CHANGING SEAS*

Uses of the Seas 69, 72, 74–75 (Gullion ed. 1968).*

Like all law, the various laws of the seas may be seen as derogations from the principle of freedom. The freedom of the sea is, of course, subject to general law that applies at sea as elsewhere, for example rules protecting persons and property, or the law of the U.N. Charter outlawing war and other uses of force. There are limitations in special laws and agreements that have applied only, or especially, at sea—for example, those against piracy or slave-running, or wartime limitations on trade between neutrals and belligerents.

For our purposes, there is a limitation on freedom in the view that law excludes other nations from excavating where one nation has staked out a claim. There are different limitations in the other view—that no nation may seize the resources of the ocean bed. I stress also two special orders of limitation. The law has recognized special rights for coastal nations in coastal areas, limiting the freedom of other nations in those areas. (Other nations have acquired special rights, usually through long usage, to carry on particular activities in particular parts of the sea, e.g., "historic" fishing rights.) There are inevitable limitations on freedom when different nations compete to use the same areas for the same or different purposes, and the law regulates this competition.

* * *

*The Law of "Conflicting Uses"*

Freedom of the seas for all has meant of course that no state was free to exclude others. From the beginning, too, freedom had to give way to "conflicting uses"—if only between two vessels seeking to ply the same waters, or nations competing to fish in the same area. As uses of the sea grew, the possibilities of conflict grew. Even navigation and fishing had to accommodate each other. Later, ships had to watch out for cables, and recently for oil derricks, sea mounts, scientific buoys; submarines might run afoul of diving gear, installations on the seabed or military detection equipment. Nuclear tests prevented all other uses in large areas of seas for short periods. Other military uses, operations and pollutions might bar other uses for long times.

Early, as freedom led to conflict, conflict led to some regulation. Friendly nations began to leave each other alone, to develop navigation lanes, rules of navigation, laws about collisions and other mishaps at sea. General recognition of the special rights of coastal states helped to reduce conflict. As regards fishing, in particular, in some areas and for some species, there grew a network of international agreements designed to accommodate the claims of coastal states and of others, of states with historical rights and of newcomers, and to make some provision for conservation. Infrequently, nations also entered agreements determining their respective rights in other

* Reprinted by permission of The American Assembly.

resources, for example, the 1942 agreement between Great Britain and Venezuela with respect to mineral resources in the Gulf of Paria.

Some law grew also to regulate conflicts between different uses. The law developed principles of priority and some general standards of conduct. Traditionally, navigation has been a preferred use, and interferences with navigation (in time of peace) have been strongly resisted. (That nuclear tests at sea interfered with navigation, albeit temporarily, was a principal argument of those who considered them illegal.) "Reasonableness" has frequently been invoked as the standard of behavior: There may be "reasonable" interferences with some uses to promote others; when uses conflict there must be a "reasonable" balancing of interests to determine which use is to be preferred.

Conflicting uses are also the subject of agreement. In the nineteenth century agreements provided for the protection of oceanic cables. The 1958 Geneva conventions on the law of the sea, while codifying the principle of freedom, also included basic provisions to regulate conflicting uses. The Convention on the Continental Shelf, for example, provides that, subject to its right to take "reasonable measures" to explore the shelf and exploit its mineral resources, the coastal state may not interfere with laying cables or pipelines. Mining "must not result in any unjustifiable interferences with navigation, fishing or the conservation of the living resources of the sea." Installations and safety-zones around them must not interfere with "recognized sea lanes essential to international navigation." Mining must not "result in any interference with fundamental oceanographic or other scientific research carried out with the intention of open publication." And research on and concerning the continental shelf requires the consent of the coastal state but such consent shall be normally granted.

### *Notes*

1. For an examination of the law of navigation and its relation to other uses, see Bouchez, Ocean Navigation: International Legal Aspects, International Law Association, Report of the 56th Conference, New Delhi, 330 (1976).

2. See generally Krueger, Artificial Islands and Offshore Installations, International Law Association, Report of the 57th Conference, Madrid, 396 (1978). See also Pontavice, Rapport Concernant les Aspects Juridiques de l'Exploitation des Maisons sous la Mer, International Law Association, Report of the 57th Conference, Madrid, 343 (1978).

## PROHIBITED ACTIVITIES

### *a. Slave Transport*

### *U.N. CONVENTION ON THE LAW OF THE SEA (1982)*

U.N.Doc. A/CONF. 62/122; 21 I.L.M. 1261 (1982).

#### Article 99

#### *Prohibition of the Transport of Slaves*

Every State shall adopt effective measures to prevent and punish the transport of slaves in ships authorized to fly its flag and to prevent the unlawful use of its flag for that purpose. Any slave taking refuge on board any ship, whatever its flag, shall *ipso facto* be free.

### *Note*

There are a number of conventions outlawing slavery and slave trade. It has been urged that these are also violations of customary law and indeed international crimes. See Chapter 8, p. 595 above.

#### *b. Piracy*

### *U.N. CONVENTION ON THE LAW OF THE SEA (1982)*

U.N.Doc. A/CONF. 62/122; 21 I.L.M. 1261 (1982).

#### ARTICLE 100

*Duty to Co-operate in the Repression of Piracy*

All States shall co-operate to the fullest possible extent in the repression of piracy on the high seas or in any other place outside the jurisdiction of any State.

#### ARTICLE 101

*Definition of Piracy*

Piracy consists of any of the following acts:

(a) Any illegal acts of violence, detention or any act of depredation, committed for private ends by the crew or the passengers of a private ship or a private aircraft, and directed:

(i) On the high seas, against another ship or aircraft, or against persons or property on board such ship or aircraft;

(ii) Against a ship, aircraft, persons or property in a place outside the jurisdiction of any State;

(b) Any act of voluntary participation in the operation of a ship or of an aircraft with knowledge of facts making it a pirate ship or aircraft;

(c) Any act of inciting or of intentionally facilitating an act described in subparagraphs (a) and (b).

#### ARTICLE 105

*Seizure of a Pirate Ship or Aircraft*

On the high seas, or in any other place outside the jurisdiction of any State, every State may seize a pirate ship or aircraft, or a ship taken by piracy and under the control of pirates, and arrest the persons and seize the property on board. The courts of the State which carried out the seizure may decide upon the penalties to be imposed, and may also determine the action to be taken with regard to the ships, aircraft or property, subject to the rights of third parties acting in good faith.

### *Notes*

1. The 1982 Convention Articles 100, 101 and 105 repeat Articles 14, 15, and 19 of the 1958 Convention on the High Seas.

2. "It has long been recognized and well settled that persons and vessels engaged in piratical operations on the high seas are entitled to the protection of no nation and may be punished by any nation that may apprehend or capture them. This stern rule of international law refers to piracy in its international-law sense and not to a variety of lesser maritime offenses so designated by municipal law." 2 Hackworth at 681.

3. An increasing number of cases of piracy have been reported in recent years, especially in the waters of Southeast Asia (e.g., the Gulf of Thailand, the Malacca Straits, and the Sulu and Celebes Seas). See Rubin, The Law of Piracy 377–45 (1988); Dzurek, Piracy in Southeast Asia, 32 Oceanus 65–70 (Winter 1989–90).

4. On piracy, see generally Dubner, The Law of International Sea Piracy (1980); Boulton, The Modern International Law of Piracy: Content and Contemporary Relevance, 7 Int'l Relations 2493 (1981–83); Restatement (Third) § 522, Comment *c*, Reporters' Note 2. For earlier writings, see Harvard Research in International Law, Piracy, 26 A.J.I.L.Supp. 739 (1932); 2 Moore, Digest of International Law 951–79 (1906); 2 Hackworth at 681–95; Dickinson, Is the Crime of Piracy Obsolete?, 38 Harv.L.Rev. 334 (1925); Lenoir, Piracy Cases in the Supreme Court, 25 J.Crim.L. & Crim'y 532 (1934); Johnson, Piracy in Modern International Law, 43 Trans.Grot.Soc'y 63 (1957). See also In re Piracy Jure Gentium, [1934] A.C. 586 (attempt to commit a "piratical robbery" is equivalent to piracy under the law of nations). The municipal law of a number of states provides for the punishment of so-called *delicta juris gentium* other than piracy on the same basis as the latter. See Harvard Research in International Law, Jurisdiction with Respect to Crime, 29 A.J.I.L.Supp. 435, 569–72 (1935).

5. The 1982 Convention defines piracy to include acts against aircraft, but covers only acts by the crew or the passengers of a private aircraft, committed for "private" ends. For acts by others, see the Convention for the Suppression of Unlawful Seizure of Aircraft, p. 1073, the Anti–Hijacking Act of 1974, p. 1077 and the Hostage–Taking Act of 1984, p. 1078.

### *c. Uses Impinging on Coastal State Interests: Offshore "Pirate" Broadcasting*

In the late 1950's, a number of unauthorized radio and television stations operated in international waters in the North, Baltic, and Irish Seas. These stations, situated on fixed platforms or on ships flying foreign "flags of convenience," were a multiple source of irritation to the governments of the coastal states to which their broadcasts were directed: they used unauthorized wave lengths, evaded the payment of royalties due to holders of copyright on the material used (largely popular music), evaded income and other taxes, and either broke the monopoly of the coastal state's government on broadcasting or violated its prohibition of commercial broadcasting. In 1962, Belgium and the four continental Scandinavian countries enacted legislation directed at nationals of those states engaged in, or assisting, offshore broadcasting. See Hunnings, Pirate Broadcasting in European Waters, 14 I.C.L.Q. 410, 417–21 (1965). In view of the insufficiency of such laws to deal with stations owned and manned by foreigners, and because of the reluctance of some states to take direct unilateral action against stations operating off their shores, the Council of Europe opened for signature in early 1965 a convention intended to deal with the problem.

Briefly, the European Agreement for the Prevention of Broadcasts Transmitted from Stations Outside National Territories requires contracting states to make punishable under domestic law the operation of, or collaboration with, unauthorized broadcasting stations located outside national territories, and to apply such legislation to nationals and to foreigners otherwise within their jurisdiction. The Agreement applies only to stations situated "on board ships, aircraft, or any other floating or airborne objects" and thus does not cover stations installed on fixed platforms; it expressly provided, however, that nothing in the agreement prevents a party from applying the provisions thereof to such platforms. In December 1964, the Netherlands enacted the North Seas Installations Act and took action thereunder to silence a radio-television station operated from an artificial structure by individuals of undisclosed nationality and identity. Van Panhuys & van Emde Boas, Legal Aspects of Pirate Broadcasting: A Dutch Approach, 60 A.J.I.L. 303, 303–04 (1966). In 1967 the United Kingdom also enacted legislation to prohibit and punish "pirate" broadcasting. The Marine, & c., Broadcasting (Offences) Act, 1967, 1967 Ch. 41, enacted July 14, 1967, makes it unlawful to broadcast from a ship, aircraft or structure registered in the United Kingdom or located in United Kingdom tidal or "external" waters (defined as the "whole of the sea adjacent to the United Kingdom which is within the seaward limits of territorial waters adjacent thereto"). The statute makes the owner, master, operator, or one who procures the act of broadcasting (including supplying of equipment, food or advertising) liable to punishment of three months' imprisonment and/or fine of 400 pounds. The statute bases jurisdiction to prescribe and punish on territorial jurisdiction over the territorial waters or on citizenship of the persons responsible for the broadcast.

Unauthorized broadcasting from the high seas is dealt with in the 1982 Convention, Art. 109:

> 1. All States shall co-operate in the suppression of unauthorized broadcasting from the high seas.
>
> 2. For the purposes of this Convention, "unauthorized broadcasting" means the transmission of sound radio or television broadcasts from a ship or installation on the high seas intended for reception by the general public contrary to international regulations, but excluding the transmission of distress calls.
>
> 3. Any person engaged in unauthorized broadcasting may be prosecuted before the court of:
>
> (a) the flag State of the ship;
>
> (b) the State of registry of the installation;
>
> (c) the State of which the person is a national;
>
> (d) any State where the transmissions can be received; or
>
> (e) any State where authorized radio communication is suffering interference.
>
> 4. On the high seas, a State having jurisdiction in accordance with paragraph 3 may, in conformity with article 110, arrest any person or

ship engaged in unauthorized broadcasting and seize the broadcasting apparatus.

What of unauthorized broadcasting from the exclusive economic zone—to the territory of the state whose zone it is? to other territories? See generally Robertson, The Suppression of Pirate Radio Broadcasting: A Test Case for Control of International Activities Outside National Territory, 45 L. & Contemp.Probs. 71 (1982).

All the special rights claimed by coastal states in the high seas, e.g., the contiguous zone, customs and security zones, the right of hot pursuit, are, of course, limitations on the freedom of seas.

## ACTION TO PROTECT AGAINST FORBIDDEN ACTIVITIES

International law permits all states to protect the common interests in the high seas against unlawful activities. The law authorizes some measures by coastal states for example to protect against pirate broadcasting.

### *U.N. CONVENTION ON THE LAW OF THE SEA (1982)*

U.N.Doc. A/CONF. 62/122; 21 I.L.M. 1261 (1982).

#### Article 110

1. Except where acts of interference derive from powers conferred by treaty, a warship which encounters on the high seas a foreign ship, other than a ship entitled to complete immunity in accordance with articles 95 and 96, is not justified in boarding her unless there is reasonable ground for suspecting:

(a) That the ship is engaged in piracy;

(b) That the ship is engaged in the slave trade;

(c) That the ship is engaged in unauthorized broadcasting and the warship has jurisdiction under article 109;

(d) That the ship is without nationality; or

(e) That, though flying a foreign flag or refusing to show its flag, the ship is, in reality, of the same nationality as the warship.

2. In the cases provided for in paragraph 1, the warship may proceed to verify the ship's right to fly its flag. To this end, it may send a boat, under the command of an officer, to the suspected ship. If suspicion remains after the documents have been checked, it may proceed to a further examination on board the ship, which must be carried out with all possible consideration.

3. If the suspicions prove to be unfounded, and provided that the ship boarded has not committed any act justifying them, it shall be compensated for any loss or damage that may have been sustained.

4. These provisions shall apply mutatis mutandis to military aircraft.

5. These provisions shall also apply to any other duly authorized ships or aircraft clearly marked and identifiable as being on government service.

### *Notes*

1. This article duplicates Article 22 of the 1958 Convention, but adds the clauses on unauthorized broadcasting, vessels without nationality, and paragraphs 4 and 5.

2. In 1981, President Reagan issued a proclamation addressing "the continuing problem of migrants coming to the United States, by sea, without necessary entry documents * * *." The Proclamation instructed the Secretary of State "to enter into, on behalf of the United States, cooperative arrangements with appropriate foreign governments for the purpose of preventing illegal migration to the United States by sea." The Coast Guard was to be instructed to "enforce the suspension of the entry of undocumented aliens and the interdiction of any defined vessel carrying such territorial waters of the United States." The order applied to vessels of the United States, vessels without nationality, and vessels of foreign nations with whom the United States has entered into arrangements authorizing the United States to stop and board such vessels. The Attorney General, in consultation with other departments, was instructed to "take whatever steps are necessary to ensure the fair enforcement of our laws relating to immigration" and "the strict observance of our international obligations concerning those who genuinely flee persecution in their homeland." See Presidential Proclamation No. 4865, 46 Fed.Reg. 48, 107 (29 Sept. 1981), reprinted at, 8 U.S.C. § 1182.

By an exchange of letters the week before the proclamation issued, the United States entered into a cooperative arrangement with the government of Haiti. In effect, the parties agreed that the United States may do what the President's Proclamation instructed the Coast Guard to do, including the boarding of Haitian vessels, investigation, detention of a vessel and the persons aboard it, and return of the vessel and the persons aboard it to Haiti.

Challenges to the program on the ground that it violated the obligations of the United States under the Protocol to the Refugee Convention and the rights of individuals under the U.S. Constitution and laws were rejected in Haitian Refugee Center, Inc. v. Gracey, 600 F.Supp. 1396 (D.D.C.1985), aff'd, 809 F.2d 794 (D.C.Cir.1987).

The United States policy of interdiction on the high seas was continued in 1992 after the Haitian government was overthrown by military coup and a large number of Haitians attempted to seek asylum in the United States. On May 24, 1992, President Bush issued Executive Order 12807 which requires the Coast Guard to "enforce the suspension of entry of undocumented aliens by sea and the interdiction of any * * * vessel carrying such aliens" in waters "beyond the territorial sea of the United States." Ex. Order 12807, §§ 2(a) and 2(d), 57 Fed.Reg. 23, 133 (24 May 1992). Pursuant to that order, the Coast Guard intercepted boatloads of Haitian asylum seekers and returned them to Haiti without making a determination as to whether they were refugees, as required by Article 33 of the Refugee Convention and § 243(h) of the Immigration and Nationality Act. See Chapter 8 supra. In Haitian Centers Council, Inc. v. McNary, 969 F.2d 1350 (2d Cir.1992), the Court of Appeals found that Haitians intercepted in international waters fell within § 243(h)(1) of a 1980 amendment to the Immigration and Nationality Act. The Supreme Court granted certiorari in *McNary*, ___ U.S. ___, 113 S.Ct. 52, 121 L.Ed.2d 22 (1992), to resolve a conflict with a contrary decision reached by the Eleventh Circuit in Haitian Refugee Center, Inc. v. Baker, 953 F.2d 1498 (11th Cir.1992), cert. denied, ___ U.S. ___,

112 S.Ct. 1245, 117 L.Ed.2d 477 (1992). See p. 631 above for a discussion of the result in *McNary*.

Does international law permit the United States to protect against illegal immigration by boarding vessels on the high seas? Does the consent of the flag state matter? Can the United States establish a ring of military vessels on the high seas to keep vessels suspected of carrying asylum seekers from leaving their home state's territorial waters or from entering U.S. territorial waters?

## C. MILITARY USES OF THE HIGH SEAS

### *HENKIN, CHANGING LAW FOR THE CHANGING SEAS*

Uses of the Seas 69, 84–86 (Gullion ed. 1968).*

The law governing military uses at sea can be importantly affected by changes in law of general applicability, for example by agreements eliminating or controlling the use of some weapon. In a different way new agreement on a wider territorial sea may effectively bar military vessels and equipment from additional areas of sea, and even a wider continental shelf will tend to discourage military uses there. In deep sea, too, a general law aimed at other uses can affect military uses as well, as in the proposals to give the U.N. sovereignty or other rights in the seabed. * * *

Suggestions for new law about the military uses in particular take different forms and have different goals. Some have written about the need to protect, even promote, military uses, at least "defensive" ones: for example, law could expressly permit, and protect against violation by others, national "hardened" submarine rocket installations, fixed submarine maintenance facilities, research and communications stations, storage depots, repair works, or other submarine "strategic areas." Similarly, some foresee the need for regulating "traffic" in submarine military vehicles as they increase in quantity and mobility.

Usually, suggestions for regulating military uses propose various forms of disarmament or arms control in the sea. (Suggestions for protecting submarine military installations would also have some arms control qualities since they would require identification and disclosure of the installations.) Arms control proposals take different forms. One kind is typified by a proposal to establish a sea-wide network of buoys and equipment for detecting and tracking submarines. The network might be operated by some international authority. Most proposals would demilitarize or exclude particular weapons from all or parts of the sea. Recently attention has focused in particular on the seabed: some have proposed that it be wholly demilitarized, while others would at least exclude weapons of mass destruction. Supporters of such proposals usually invoke the precedent of outer space, where by U.N. resolution and subsequent treaty, nations agreed not to place weapons of mass destruction in orbit around the earth, on celestial bodies, or anywhere in space. (Antarctica, too, has been reserved by treaty for peaceful purposes only and nuclear explosions have been barred there for any purposes. The Spitsbergen Treaty of 1920 also barred militarization of that area.) But, again, in these and other cases, nations forewent what they did not yet have, had never relied on, perhaps could not appreciate. In the sea, military vessels and weapons are an integral and dominant element of national defense, for many nations; submarine-based missiles, indeed, are key weapons in global strategy, on which deterrence, security and perhaps world peace depend. Precedents and analogies apart, the United States surely will not give up its Navy and its submarine-based missiles, except—theoretically—in some final stage of general and complete disarmament.

On the other hand, it is not out of the question to consider the demilitarization of some parts of the sea, the elimination or control of some weapons or some uses. (Nuclear-testing underwater and in the atmosphere—including the air space above the seas—is forbidden by the Nuclear Test Ban of 1963.) While demilitarizing the seabed without demilitarizing the sea might contribute little to peace and military stability, it might forestall fixed military complexes and atomic "caches" that would be more difficult to eliminate or control later; it might also serve as another small step to slow down the arms race. Whether such proposals are feasible and acceptable is not clear. The ambiguous content of the term "demilitarization" would be especially discouraging. There is no indication that nations have already stationed weapons of mass destruction on the seabed or that the right to do so looms large in future plans for national deterrence systems. On the other hand, the United States, and probably the Soviet Union, apparently have considerable, sophisticated "military equipment" on the seabed, e.g., submarine detection devices. It is unlikely that the United States would agree to sacrifice them, and it is not clear that any agreement to that end could be effectively monitored. Proposals that would bar the seabed to weapons of mass destruction might also entail inspection problems, and a system to verify a ban on such weapons might interfere with submarine detection systems and perhaps other uses of the seabed. For these and other reasons some believe that, unlike outer space, proposals for controlling arms in the sea or on the seabed cannot be simple, and would hold more promise in a context of negotiation about disarmament rather than about the law of the sea.

It seems unlikely, then, that the United States would agree to a U.N. resolution "demilitarizing" the seabed; it might also be reluctant to agree to exclude weapons of mass destruction. Surely, it is not likely to accept a resolution granting to the U.N. complete sovereignty over the seabed, since such unqualified sovereignty would presumably subject all military uses of the seabed to the control of majority votes in the General Assembly.

### *Notes*

1. The testing of nuclear weapons on the high seas gave rise to substantial debate. See p. 1021 above. In 1963, the United States, Britain, and the Soviet Union adhered to the Treaty Banning Nuclear Weapons Tests in the Atmosphere, In Outer Space and Under Water, 480 U.N.T.S. 43. See also the Treaty on the Prohibition of the Emplacement of Nuclear Weapons and Other Weapons of Mass Destruction on the Seabed and the Ocean Floor and in the Subsoil Thereof, 23 U.S.T. 701, T.I.A.S. No. 3337. In the absence of a treaty provision prohibiting it, may states test nuclear weapons on the high seas? The 1982 Convention limits the use of the high seas to "peaceful purposes." (Article 88). Does weapons testing of any sort on the high seas violate this provision?

2. Regarding war and neutrality and their relation to the law of the sea, see Chapter 11, p. 1033.

3. See Treves, Military Installations, Structure, and Devices on the Seabed, 74 A.J.I.L. 808 (1980); Treves, La notion d'utilisation des espaces marins a des fins pacifiques dans le noveau droit de la mer, 1980 Annuaire Français 687; Truver, The Law of the Sea and the Military Use of the Oceans in 2010, 45 La.L.Rev. 1221 (1985). On the laws of war generally, see Chapter 11, supra.

## D. EXPLOITATION OF RESOURCES BEYOND NATIONAL JURISDICTION

### 1. *Mineral Resources of the Seabed*

#### *HENKIN, LAW FOR THE SEA'S MINERAL RESOURCES*

49–51, 58–59 (1968).*

However the continental shelf is defined, exploitation of mineral resources is or will soon be possible in the sea beyond. The major legal issue that is developing is who is—or should be—entitled to exploit these resources, on what basis, under what limitations. In general terms, the issue is between *laissez-faire* for interested states (subject to any "ground rules" they may agree on) and control by the international community. * * *

* * *

Two general attitudes are already in evidence. One insists that the sea's resources have always been "for the taking" and there is no reason why those who can take them should give up their right. In the long run, moreover—and in the less long run too—all of mankind will benefit if the sea's mineral resources are extracted as quickly, as efficiently, as economically as possible. What is called for, then, is law that will induce the technologically-advanced nations and their nationals to explore the ocean bed energetically and to begin to extract its minerals. This means law that imposes few limitations on national initiative, that assures to enterprising nations the fruits of their labor (as is just and reasonable), that affords them protection against encroachment and unfair competition. To achieve such law one need only reaffirm traditional legal concepts in favor of those who proceed to dig against any who come later. One could also adapt much of the law that protects sea-going vessels, giving to any installation the protection of the "flag it flies." [In time, as meaningful competition develops, as mining begins to conflict with other uses of the sea, the nations directly involved will wish to define and refine "ground rules" for peaceful and orderly competition and to accommodate conflicting uses.] * * *

* * *

The opposing view would argue that now is the time to lay down the basic principles that will shape the law of the future. As in regard to outer space, now is the time for "preventive law" to avoid certain evils. As mankind stands at the threshold of a new environment, before egotistic national interests form and vest, it is important to accept legal principles and establish international machinery to assure that there will not be an

* Footnotes omitted. Reprinted by permission of the Institute for the Study of Science in Human Affairs of Columbia University.

international "race" or conflict for the sea's wealth; that the resources that belong to all will not be grabbed for the selfish profit of a few; that the new environment will serve to reduce rather than widen the gulf between rich nations and poor.

* * *

* * * The essential character—and the ultimate acceptability—of an international body will depend, of course, on how such a body is organized, what powers it has, what functions it performs. The functions entrusted to an international body can vary from all to almost nothing, and there can be innumerable possible combinations of functions. An international body could be given exclusive authority to exploit the sea's resources, with all the powers and functions that implies, from preliminary explorations of the sea-bed to marketing minerals extracted and disposing of the proceeds. Others envisage a body that would control exploitation by others, for example through licensing and policing operations by states or private entrepreneurs. The powers of such an organization might include authority to promulgate the terms of such licenses and the regulations under which exploitation would be carried out. Presumably, it would have authority to dispose of any fees collected and allocate them to prescribed purposes.

Or, an international organization might be primarily policeman or umpire, authorized to inspect for compliance with rules adopted by the states, to prevent and settle disputes, to collect any agreed fees. An international body might, for example, operate a registry, pursuant to international agreement that no national claim is valid unless registered and that the first claim registered will prevail. * * * In addition—or instead—the international body might be designed for settling disputes, by adjudication or arbitration.

The powers and functions of an international body will largely determine its essential organization. Nations will be more willing to grant power to a body whose decisions they can essentially control (or veto). They will care less about the organizational framework of a body whose functions do not impinge on their important interests. Organization will also reflect considerations of politics and prestige. In a body with substantial functions related to the resources of the sea, the principle of organization will have to accommodate the desire of the many to see the community represented (probably on the basis of geographical distribution) and the interests of the few principal entrepreneurs—the technically-advanced nations. States with special mining interests—say, oil-producing nations—might also claim special representation.

* * *

Those who favor substantial *laissez-faire* (principally the technologically-advanced nations) will not be eager to have a strong international organization with substantial authority. If they feel compelled to accept some international body in principle they will seek to assure that its organization and its powers and functions leave maximum autonomy to individual states. Most nations, on the other hand, will not see themselves as major entrepreneurs in the sea and will seek an organization with as much control as possible over the activities of the states that will be the principal "miners."

Probably they would settle for a regime that includes some international organization reflecting some international authority and provides some revenue for international purposes.

### *MORATORIUM ON EXPLOITATION OF RESOURCES OF THE DEEP SEA-BED*

G.A.Res. 2574D (XXIV) (1969).

The General Assembly * * * (d)eclares that, pending the establishment of the aforementioned international régime:

(a) States and persons, physical or juridical, are bound to refrain from all activities of exploitation of the resources of the area of the sea-bed and ocean floor, and the subsoil thereof, beyond the limits of national jurisdiction;

(b) No claim to any part of that area or its resources shall be recognized.

The vote on the moratorium Resolution was 62–28–28; the United States challenged the statement of international law reflected in the resolution and the authority of the Assembly to declare a "moratorium."

### *DECLARATION OF PRINCIPLES GOVERNING THE SEA-BED AND THE OCEAN FLOOR, AND SUBSOIL THEREOF, BEYOND THE LIMITS OF NATIONAL JURISDICTION*

G.A.Res. 2749 (XXV) (1970).

*The General Assembly,*

*Recalling* its resolutions 2340 (XXII) of 18 December 1967, 2467 (XXIII) of 21 December 1968 and 2574 (XXIV) of 15 December 1969, concerning the area to which the title of the item refers,

*Affirming* that there is an area of the sea-bed and the ocean floor, and the subsoil thereof, beyond the limits of national jurisdiction, the precise limits of which are yet to be determined,

*Recognizing* that the existing legal régime of the high seas does not provide substantive rules for regulating the exploration of the aforesaid area and the exploitation of its resources,

*Convinced* that the area shall be reserved exclusively for peaceful purposes and that the exploration of the area and the exploitation of its resources shall be carried out for the benefit of mankind as a whole,

*Believing it essential* that an international régime applying to the area and its resources and including appropriate international machinery should be established as soon as possible,

*Bearing in mind* that the development and use of the area and its resources shall be undertaken in such a manner as to foster healthy development of the world economy and balanced growth of international trade, and to minimize any adverse economic effects caused by fluctuation of prices of raw materials resulting from such activities,

*Solemnly declares* that:

1. The sea-bed and ocean floor, and the subsoil thereof, beyond the limits of national jurisdiction (hereinafter referred to as the area), as well as the resources of the area, are the common heritage of mankind.

2. The area shall not be subject to appropriation by any means by States or persons, natural or juridical, and no State shall claim or exercise sovereignty or sovereign rights over any part thereof.

3. No State or person, natural or juridical, shall claim, exercise or acquire rights with respect to the area or its resources incompatible with the international régime to be established and the principles of this Declaration.

4. All activities regarding the exploration and exploitation of the resources of the area and other related activities shall be governed by the international régime to be established.

* * *

## *Notes*

1. The concept of the "common heritage of mankind" adopted in the Declaration (and later confirmed in Article 136 of the 1982 Convention) is usually attributed to Ambassador Pardo of Malta, who proposed the subject of sea-bed mining for consideration by the General Assembly. See U.N.Doc. A/6695 (1967). See also de Marffy, The Pardo Declaration and the Six Years of the Sea-Bed Committee, in 1 A Handbook on the New Law of the Sea 141 (Dupuy, ed. 1991). The concept was expressed earlier, including a statement by President Johnson: "We must ensure that the deep seas and the ocean bottoms are, and remain, the legacy of all human beings." 2 Weekly Compilation of Presidential Documents 930, 931 (1966).

On the common heritage of mankind generally, see Postyshev, The Concept of the Common Heritage of Mankind: From New Thinking to New Practice (Chalyan, trans. 1990); Kiss, Conserving the Common Heritage of Mankind, 59 Revista Juridica de la Universidad de Puerto Rico 773 (1990); Joyner, Legal Implications of the Concept of the Common Heritage of Mankind, 35 Int'l & Comp.L.Q. 191 (1986); Shraga, The Common Heritage of Mankind: The Concept and Its Application, 15 Annales d'Etudes Internationales 45 (1986); Van Hoof, Legal Status of the Common Heritage of Mankind, 7 Grotiana 49 (1986).

2. Restatement (Third) § 523, Reporters' Note 2 states:

> Even before the development of the doctrine of the continental shelf and of the concept of the exclusive economic zone (§§ 514–15), there was disagreement, then largely theoretical, as to who owns the sea-bed beyond a state's territorial sea, whether any state could acquire sovereignty or title therein, and whether a state or private person could lawfully exploit the resources of that sea-bed or subsoil and appropriate them to its own use. Discovery in the 1960s of vast mineral resources ("manganese nodules," containing also nickel, copper and cobalt) on the floor of the deep ocean beyond the continental shelves, and the development of technology for obtaining access to these resources, led to three different views as to the applicable law. It was generally agreed that these minerals are the common heritage of mankind (Declaration of Principles Governing the Sea–Bed and the Ocean Floor, and the Subsoil Thereof, Beyond the Limits of National Jurisdiction, adopted by G.A.Res. 2749 (XXV) 25 U.N. GAOR Supp. No. 28,

at 24, paras. 1–4, 9 (1970)), but there was disagreement on the application of this concept. Some considered that these minerals could be exploited only by or on behalf of mankind, not by any state or person for its own account; under this view, exploitation would be lawful only pursuant to a generally accepted international agreement. Others argued that, unless a state has agreed otherwise, it may exploit the resources of the sea-bed freely, and the first claimant in any area is entitled to exclude all others from mining there. See, *e.g.,* Ely, "The Law Governing the Development of Undersea Mineral Resources," 1 Offshore Technology Conference Proc. 19–42 (1969). A third view, which has been accepted by this Restatement, is that like the fish of the high seas the minerals of the deep sea-bed are open to anyone to take. Consequently, any state is entitled to extract and keep them. But no state may conduct or authorize mining operations on an exclusive basis or in such a way as effectively to appropriate large areas of the sea-bed in violation of Subsection (1)(a). See Subsection 1(b)(i). It would therefore not be permissible for any mining enterprise to reserve for itself an area of some 25,000 square miles (equal to the area of Belgium and the Netherlands combined) or more, as some enterprises have suggested.

An analogy may be made also to the law of finds as applied to shipwrecks, the finder having the exclusive right to bring up the find, and others being obliged to stay a reasonable distance away. See, *e.g.,* Hener v. United States, 525 F.Supp. 350, 354 (S.D.N.Y.1981).

3. Beginning in 1972, bills were introduced in the United States Congress which would authorize the licensing of United States nationals to mine the deep seabed in areas beyond national jurisdiction, and recognize the rights of other nationals on the basis of reciprocity. Initially, the executive branch opposed passage of such legislation on the ground that it would prejudice the negotiation of an international regime at the Law of the Sea Conference. However, as the Conference dragged on, the Administration, in 1977, endorsed passage of interim legislation which would authorize licensing pending the conclusion of a comprehensive law of the sea treaty.

The Deep Seabed Hard Mineral Resources Act, Pub.L. No. 96–283, 94 Stat. 553, passed in 1980, explicitly adopted the United States position that in the absence of a supervening treaty, states had the right to mine the seabed as an aspect of the freedom of the seas, and that national licensing would not be an assertion of sovereignty or ownership over any part of the seabed. The Act recognizes the character of seabed resources as the common heritage of mankind, and provides for the establishment of an international revenue-sharing fund. Congress' declared purpose in adopting the Act was to provide "assured and nondiscriminatory access" as well as "security of tenure" to U.S. nationals seeking to exploit deep seabed resources. While the Act was declared to be transitional pending U.S. adoption of an agreement resulting from the Law of the Sea Conference or any other multilateral treaty concerning the deep seabed, it establishes that any regulation issuing as a result of its passage not inconsistent with subsequent treaties shall remain valid.

Other states have enacted similar interim legislation, and the Provisional Understanding Regarding Deep Seabed Mining, signed by the United States and seven other parties in 1984, adopted a preliminary scheme for resolving overlapping claims to deep seabed mining areas.

The legality of unilateral legislation, "interim" or otherwise, was challenged by the Group of 77 essentially on the legal grounds reflected in the majority vote on the Moratorium Resolution. See Letter dated 23 April 1979 from the Group of Legal Experts on the Question of Unilateral Legislation Addressed to the Chairman of the Group of 77, (U.N.Doc. A/CONF. 62/77). See also Vicuña, National Laws on Seabed Exploitation (1979).

4. The dispute over the Moratorium Resolution reflected deeper and larger controversy over the character of the régime that is to govern seabed mining; the Moratorium Resolution was an early staking-out of legal positions to support bargaining in the negotiations to come at the Third UN Law of the Sea Conference. While all states had agreed that the resources of the seabed were the common heritage of mankind, they disagreed sharply as to how mankind was to keep the benefits of that heritage, consequently also on the principles that should govern exploitation, and the organization and role of any international seabed authority. The developed states sought essentially an international licensing system: an international authority would issue licenses to governments (or to their nationals), collecting fees or royalties that might go to international development purposes. The international authority would be organized to reflect the dominant interests of the states that had the capital, and the technology necessary to support exploitation, and to assure its limited function. The developing states, represented by the "Group of 77" (which actually includes more than 100 developing states), sought a régime whereby the exclusive right to mine the seabed beyond national jurisdiction would be vested in the International Sea–Bed Authority which would establish an Enterprise for that purpose. They wished an authority organized principally on the basis of majority-rule by states of equal voting authority. Some developing states sought to assure that seabed minerals would not compete with land-based minerals which they produced and exported.

In 1976, a compromise was proposed which would establish a "parallel" system, one set of mining sites to be exploited by states (or their corporations), the other by an operating arm of the Authority—the Enterprise. The developed states would also provide the Enterprise with capital and technology to enable the Enterprise to carry out its first exploitation. Differences continued, however, as to the organization of the Sea–Bed Authority. There was agreement in principle on a Council (with weighted representation) and an Assembly (with equal representation), as in the United Nations. The developed states, however, insisting on "assured access" to their part of the system, wished to distribute authority to make certain that the Assembly, which they could not control, could not interfere with such access. The developing states continued to press for effective control by the majority through the Assembly.

In 1980, a compromise was reached on the decision-making powers of the organs of the Authority, methods for insuring, and the terms for, transfer of capital and technology to the Enterprise, the criteria for licensing and taxing of state-owned and private mining companies, and limitations on seabed mining to protect land-based sources. Review of the system in 15–25 years was agreed to. Article 155(4) of the 1982 Convention provides that the Review Conference may, by three-quarters vote of the states parties, submit amendments to the existing system; the amendments shall go into force for all parties after they are accepted by three-quarters of the states parties.

By 1981 the new Convention was all but complete, and a vote on the final version was scheduled for April 1982. In 1981 the Reagan Administration said it wanted major changes in the treaty before it would sign it, but though some changes were made, the controversial sea mining provisions were largely retained. The Reagan Administration announced that it would not sign the Convention. See p. 1232 above. As of 1993, there has been no major activity by the United States or its nationals in the Area, nor does the Law of the Sea organization projected by the 1982 Convention appear likely to begin exploitation of the seabed mineral in the near future.

The deep seabed regime is set forth in the 1982 Convention in Part XI, Arts. 133–85, and in Annexes III and IV.

For a history and analysis of the negotiations at the Third UN Law of the Sea Conference, see generally Oxman, The Third United Nations Conference on the Law of the Sea, in 1 A Handbook on the New Law of the Sea 163 (Dupuy, ed. 1991); Stevenson & Oxman, The Preparations for the Law of the Sea Conference, 68 A.J.I.L. 1 (1974);—The Third United Nations Conference on the Law of the Sea: The 1974 Caracas Session, 69 A.J.I.L. 1 (1975);—The 1975 Geneva Session, 69 A.J.I.L. 763 (1975); and Oxman, The Third United Nations Conference on the Law of the Sea: The 1976 New York Sessions, 71 A.J.I.L. 247 (1977);—The 1977 New York Sessions, 72 A.J.I.L. 57 (1978);—The Seventh Session (1978), 73 A.J.I.L. 1 (1979);—The Eighth Session (1979), 74 A.J.I.L. 1 (1980);—The Ninth Session (1980), 75 A.J.I.L. 211 (1981);—The Tenth Session (1981), 76 A.J.I.L. 1 (1982).

## CUSTOMARY LAW OF THE SEABED

### *RESTATEMENT (THIRD) § 523*

(1) Under international law,

(a) no state may claim or exercise sovereignty or sovereign or exclusive rights over any part of the sea-bed and subsoil beyond the limits of national jurisdiction, or over its mineral resources, and no state or person may appropriate any part of that area;

(b) unless prohibited by international agreement, a state may engage, or authorize any person to engage, in activities of exploration for and exploitation of the mineral resources of that area, provided that such activities are conducted

(i) without claiming or exercising sovereignty or sovereign or exclusive rights in any part of that area, and

(ii) with reasonable regard for the right of other states or persons to engage in similar activities and to exercise the freedoms of the high seas;

(c) minerals extracted in accordance with paragraph (b) become the property of the mining state or person.

(2) Under the law of the United States, a citizen of the United States may engage in activities or exploration for, or exploitation of, the mineral resources of the area of the sea-bed and subsoil beyond the limits of national jurisdiction only in accordance with a license issued by the Federal Government pursuant to law or international agreement.

### *Notes*

1. The Restatement "restates the customary international law that applies before the Convention goes into effect, and would apply thereafter to non-

parties." Restatement (Third) Introductory Note to Part V. But compare the moratorium resolution, p. 1310 above, and the views of Third World states, p. 1308 above.

2. The Restatement analogizes mining in the deep seabed to fishing in high-seas waters. See § 523, Comment *b.* How large an area may a would-be miner preempt, for how long? What constitutes a mining activity and what constitutes its beginning?

3. The Restatement (Third) § 523, Comment *c* states:

> *c. Mining by persons.* Under customary international law, any person, natural or juridical, engaged in activities on the high seas is normally subject to the jurisdiction of the flag state of the ship used for such activity or of the state of which such person is a national. See, e.g., LOS Convention, Article 97 (jurisdiction in collisions on the high seas). A private person may engage in the activities indicated in Subsection (1)(b) only when properly licensed by a state. A state issuing such licenses is obligated to assure that the person licensed respects the rules set forth in this section and is responsible for any violation by such person.

4. On the law governing the seabed of the high seas generally, see Lévy, The International Sea–Bed Area; and Vicuña, The Régime for the Exploration and Exploitation of Sea–Bed Mineral Resources, both in A New Handbook on the Law of the Sea 587 and 635 respectively (Dupuy ed. 1991); Oxman, The High Seas and the International Seabed Area, 10 Mich.J.Int'l L. 526 (1989); 1 O'Connell, The International Law of the Sea 457–64 (Shearer, ed. 1982).

## SEA–BED MINING UNDER THE 1982 CONVENTION

### *U.N. CONVENTION ON THE LAW OF THE SEA (1982)*

U.N.Doc. A/CONF. 62/122; 21 I.L.M. 1261 (1982).

#### Article 136

*Common Heritage of Mankind*

The Area and its resources are the common heritage of mankind.

#### Article 137

*Legal Status of the Area and Its Resources*

1. No State shall claim or exercise sovereignty or sovereign rights over any part of the Area or its resources, nor shall any State or natural or juridical person appropriate any part thereof. No such claim or exercise of sovereignty or sovereign rights nor such appropriation shall be recognized.

2. All rights in the resources of the Area are vested in mankind as a whole, on whose behalf the Authority shall act. These resources are not subject to alienation. The minerals recovered from the Area, however, may only be alienated in accordance with this Part and the rules, regulations and procedures of the Authority.

3. No State or natural or juridical person shall claim, acquire or exercise rights with respect to the minerals recovered from the Area except in accordance with this Part. Otherwise, no such claim, acquisition or exercise of such rights shall be recognized.

ARTICLE 138

*General Conduct of States in Relation to the Area*

The general conduct of States in relation to the Area shall be in accordance with the provisions of this Part, the principles embodied in the Charter of the United Nations and other rules of international law in the interests of maintaining peace and security and promoting international co-operation and mutual understanding.

ARTICLE 139

*Responsibility to Ensure Compliance and Liability for Damage*

1. States Parties shall have the responsibility to ensure that activities in the Area, whether carried out by States Parties, or state enterprises or natural or juridical persons which possess the nationality of States Parties or are effectively controlled by them or their nationals, shall be carried out in conformity with this Part. The same responsibility applies to international organizations for activities in the Area carried out by such organizations.

2. Without prejudice to the rules of international law and Annex III, article 22, damage caused by the failure of a State Party or international organization to carry out its responsibilities under this Part shall entail liability; States Parties or international organizations acting together shall bear joint and several liability. A State Party shall not however be liable for damage caused by any failure to comply with this Part by a person whom it has sponsored under article 153, paragraph 2(b), if the State Party has taken all necessary and appropriate measures to secure effective compliance under article 153, paragraph 4, and Annex III, article 4, paragraph 4.

3. States Parties that are members of international organizations shall take appropriate measures to ensure the implementation of this article with respect to such organizations.

ARTICLE 140

*Benefit of Mankind*

1. Activities in the Area shall, as specifically provided for in this Part, be carried out for the benefit of mankind as a whole, irrespective of the geographical location of States, whether coastal or land-locked, and taking into particular consideration the interests and needs of developing States and of peoples who have not attained full independence or other self-governing status recognized by the United Nations in accordance with General Assembly resolution 1514(XV) and other relevant General Assembly resolutions.

2. The Authority shall provide for the equitable sharing of financial and other economic benefits derived from activities in the Area through any appropriate mechanism, on a non-discriminatory basis, in accordance with article 160, paragraph 2(f)(i).

***Note***

The Restatement (Third) § 523, Reporters' Note 4, states:

> *United States objections to Convention regime.* When the Third United Nations Conference on the Law of the Sea approved the Convention, the United States cast a negative vote (Introductory Note to this Part). In

explaining that vote, a spokesman for the United States said that the text was unacceptable as it would deter future development of deep sea-bed mineral resources, because of lack of certainty with regard to the granting of mining contracts, the artificial limitations on sea-bed mineral production, and the imposition of burdensome financial requirements; would not give the United States an adequate role in the decision-making process; would allow amendments to the Convention to enter into force for the United States without its approval; would provide for mandatory transfer of private technology related to sea-bed mining; and would allow the transfer of a portion of funds received from the miners by the International Sea–Bed Authority to national liberation movements. Statements by President Reagan and Ambassador Malone on July 9 and August 12, 1982, respectively, 18 Weekly Comp. of Pres. Docs. 887 (1982), U.S. Dep't of State, Current Policy No. 416 (1982). In a later statement the White House characterized the deep sea-bed mining regime of the Convention as "hopelessly flawed," and announced that the United States would not participate in the work of the Preparatory Commission established by the Conference to draft regulations for sea-bed mining. The Law of the Sea Convention, White House Office of Policy Information, Issue Update No. 10 (April 15, 1983), at 8.

### 2. *Living Resources*

## FISHING ON THE HIGH SEAS

The freedom to fish is the oldest freedom of the sea and remains an essential freedom in the regime of the high seas. The 1982 Convention confirms the "freedom of fishing" for all states and their nationals, but also recognizes the need to regulate and conserve living marine resources, including fish.

### *U.N. CONVENTION ON THE LAW OF THE SEA (1982)*

U.N.Doc. A/CONF. 62/122; 21 I.L.M. 1261 (1982).

#### Article 116

*Right to Fish on the High Seas*

All States have the right for their nationals to engage in fishing on the high seas subject to:

(a) their treaty obligations;

(b) the rights and duties as well as the interests of coastal States provided for, inter alia, in article 63, paragraph 2, and articles 64 to 67; and

(c) the provisions of this section.

#### Article 117

*Duty of States to Adopt With Respect to Their Nationals Measures for the Conservation of the Living Resources of the High Seas*

All States have the duty to take, or to co-operate with other States in taking, such measures for their respective nationals as may be necessary for the conservation of the living resources of the high seas.

ARTICLE 118

*Co-operation of States in the Conservation and Management of Living Resources*

States shall co-operate with each other in the conservation and management of living resources in the areas of the high seas. States whose nationals exploit identical living resources, or different living resources in the same area, shall enter into negotiations with a view to taking the measures necessary for the conservation of the living resources concerned. They shall, as appropriate, co-operate to establish subregional or regional fisheries organizations to this end.

### *Note*

In the late 1980's, the use of "driftnets" by some East Asian countries, such as Japan and the Republic of Korea, caused controversy. (Driftnets are gillnets or other combinations of nets over 2.5 kilometers in length and sometimes stretching up to 40 kilometers). Many states charged that the use of drift nets seriously depletes stocks of commercial fish and indiscriminately traps and kills porpoises, seabirds and a wide variety of fish not sought by fishermen. International efforts to ban the use of driftnets in fishing resulted in the 1989 Convention for the Prohibition of Fishing with Long Driftnets in the South Pacific and United Nations General Assembly Resolution 44/225, which recommends that "[i]mmediate action should be taken to reduce progressively large-scale pelagic driftnet fishing activities. * * * " In July 1990, it was reported that Japan and China would suspend and ban driftnet fishing. See Johnson, The Driftnetting Problem in the Pacific Ocean: Legal Consideration and Diplomatic Options, 21 Ocean Dev. & Int'l L. 5 (1990).

### *DAVIS, INTERNATIONAL MANAGEMENT OF CETACEANS UNDER THE NEW LAW OF THE SEA CONVENTION*

3 Bost.U.Int'l L.J. 484–88 (1985).*

During the 1960's the vast majority of IWC [International Whaling Commission] members were whaling nations. By the mid–1970's, however, many of the traditional whaling nations discontinued their whaling operations with the result that by 1977 fewer than half of all IWC members carried on commercial whaling. Also, in recent years many non-whaling states have joined the IWC, further diminishing the dominance of whaling states. This change in membership and an increased international concern with conservation of cetaceans has led the IWC to promulgate increasingly stringent regulations. These regulations have included prohibitions on the taking of the most endangered species of cetaceans, reduced catch quotas for less endangered species, and in 1982, the adoption by the IWC of an amendment to the Schedule of regulations providing for a complete moratorium on commercial whaling to become effective during the 1985/86 pelagic whaling season.

Conservationists have applauded the efforts of the IWC to increase protection for cetaceans. The IWC is, however, institutionally ill-equipped to gain compliance with truly effective regulations. Whaling nations have threatened to withdraw from the ICRW because their interests are no longer

* Reprinted with permission from the Boston University International Law Journal.

adequately represented in the IWC. Also, the right to object to amendments to the Schedule has been invoked with increasing frequency over the past several years. In particular objections have been lodged against the commercial whaling moratorium as well as the ban on sperm whaling passed at the 1981 meeting of the IWC. Concern has been voiced within the IWC that the ability of the IWC to regulate effectively is weakened by such objections.

The nullifying effect of the freedom to object to IWC regulatory action on the IWC's ability to regulate is mitigated somewhat by the influence exerted by member states on whaling nations. Notably, the United States has threatened to invoke sanctions (and on occasion has actually done so) authorized by domestic legislation against nations which have not complied with IWC regulations. Sanctions are authorized by the Packwood–Magnuson Amendment to the Magnuson Fishery Conservation and Management Act of 1976. This Amendment requires reduction by at least fifty percent of the fishing allocation within the United States 200–mile exclusive economic zone (EEZ) of any nation whose fishing operations "diminish the effectiveness" of the ICRW. Additional sanctions are provided by the Pelly Amendment to the Fishermen's Protective Act of 1967, which prescribes the prohibition of importation of fish products from any nation whose actions similarly "diminish the effectiveness" of the ICRW.

In practice, the administrative bodies responsible for invoking these sanctions, the Commerce Department and the State Department, have been reluctant to do so, preferring instead to slowly negotiate reduced quotas using the threat of sanctions as leverage. However, in *American Cetacean Society v. Baldrige,* a group of conservation organizations successfully argued in the United States District Court for the District of Columbia that application of sanctions under the Pelly and Packwood–Magnuson Amendments is mandatory and non-discretionary. This decision was upheld on appeal. Under this ruling the Secretary of State and the Secretary of Commerce must certify Japan under these statutes for failure to comply with IWC quotas. This decision may have the effect of forcing Japan, the leading hunter of whales for commercial purposes, into compliance with IWC regulations, particularly the commercial whaling moratorium which becomes effective during the coming pelagic whaling season. It should be noted, however, that this outcome is not certain and that the *American Cetacean Society* decision has the effect of scuttling an agreement between the United States and Japan to end Japanese whaling in 1988.

Even if, as a result of the imposition of sanctions, Japan complies with IWC quotas, uniform regulation of whaling activities is not assured under the auspices of the ICRW. Nations against whom invocation of such sanctions are ineffective remain free to lodge objections to regulations or withdraw from or remain outside of the IWC. To illustrate, the United States threatened to sanction the USSR under the Packwood–Magnuson Amendment for non-compliance with the IWC catch quota of 1,941 southern hemisphere minke whales for the 1984/85 harvest. However, unlike Japan, the USSR did not depend heavily on United States waters for its fish catch. Consequently, the threat of reduced fishing allocation was ineffective and the Soviet whaling fleet exceeded its quota of minke whales by about five hundred animals.

### Notes

1. In June 1991, the Antarctic Treaty Consultative Parties adopted the Protocol on Environmental Protection to the Antarctic Treaty (The Madrid Protocol) and it was open for signature on October 4, 1991. It has been called "the most comprehensive multilateral document ever adopted on the international protection of the environment." Blay, New Trends in the Protection of the Antarctic Environment: The 1991 Madrid Protocol, 86 A.J.I.L. 377 (1992). The Madrid Protocol contains, *inter alia,* comprehensive provisions for the conservation of Antarctic marine living resources. See 11th Antarctic Treaty Special Consultative Meeting, June 22, 1991, Doc. XI ATSCM/2, text of Final Act, reprinted in 30 I.L.M. 1455 (1991).

2. On May 19, 1992, the President transmitted to the Senate for advice and consent to ratification the Convention for the Conservation of Anadromous Stocks in the North Pacific Ocean. See Convention for the Conservation of Anadromous Stocks in the North Pacific Ocean, (U.S. *Digest,* Ch. 7, § 4), reprinted in 86 A.J.I.L. 792 (1992). The Convention is intended to establish an organization to coordinate the conservation of Pacific salmon and ecologically related species and discourage fishing activities of others that may adversely affect such conservations.

3. On conservation and protection of highly migratory species and marine mammals generally, see Lones, The Marine Mammal Protection Act and the International Protection of Cetaceans: A Unilateral Attempt to Effectuate Transnational Conservation, 22 Vand.J.Transnat'l L. 997 (1989); Kindt & Wintheiser, The Conservation and Protection of Maritime Mammals, 7 U.Hawaii L.Rev. 301 (1985); Nafziger, Global Conservation and Management of Marine Mammals, 17 San Diego L.Rev. 591 (1980). See also p. 1294 for discussion of highly migratory species in relation to the Exclusive Economic Zone.

### *KOERS, INTERNATIONAL REGULATION OF MARINE FISHERIES*

18–20 (1973).*

There are non-territorial restrictions on the freedom of fishing. Article 2 of the Convention on the High Seas of Geneva 1958 outlines the general basis for such limitations: it provides that States must exercise the freedom of fishing with reasonable regard for the interests of other States. Most restrictions in this category can be found in special international fisheries agreements concerned with questions of overfishing and with the protection of stocks of fish in general. These treaty-based limitations alter the freedom of fishing on the high seas. However, they do not yet materially affect the most essential characteristics of this concept. Of these characteristics, four are of special relevance. These are: (1) that all States have the right to engage in fishing operations on the high seas; (2) that States, in order to share in these resources and in their wealth, must actually engage in such fishing operations; (3) that the living resources of the high seas are not subject to formal ownership until they are captured; and (4) that fishing operations on the high seas are subject to a minimum of regulation. Inter-

* Footnotes omitted. Reprinted by permission of Fishing News (Books) Ltd., West Byfleet, England.

national fisheries agreements have not substantially modified these four elements of the freedom of fishing. The fact that States have, for the most part, an unrestricted right of access to the living resources of the high seas, and must exercise this right in order to share in these resources, is at the root of many of the problems faced by the international law of marine fisheries.

* * *

The freedom of fishing on the high seas and its limitations are in continuous interaction with each other. The mechanisms of this process are extremely varied and include virtually all techniques developed in centuries of international relations. They range from unilateral action by a single State to decisions of international organizations. Territorial restrictions are primarily based upon unilateral assertions by coastal States. The international legal validity of such claims will depend to a large extent upon the response of the community of States. Non-territorial restrictions, on the other hand, are largely the outcome of international agreements and the actions of international fisheries organizations. The present study will focus on the role of international fisheries organizations in the interaction between the freedom of fishing on the high seas and the non-territorial limitations applicable to this principle. These international fisheries organizations differ greatly from each other—in their terms of reference, their powers and their accomplishments, if any. For that reason, generalizations risk becoming oversimplifications. However, international fisheries organizations have in common that they are functional international organizations: they are designed to perform specific tasks. Moreover, the majority of these international fisheries organizations operate on a regional, rather than global, level. Consequently, as a group they can be characterized as examples of functional international cooperation of a regional scope.

### *Notes*

1. Koers discusses the functions and regulations of such organizations as the International Whaling Commission, the North–East Atlantic Fisheries Commission, the International North Pacific Fisheries Commission, the Permanent Commission of the Conference on the Use and Conservation of the Marine Resources of the South Pacific and the Japan–Soviet Fisheries Commission for the Northwest Pacific, in Chapter 2 of his book.

2. International regulation of marine fish beyond national jurisdiction must of course take account of national regulation in exclusive zones which reaches highly migratory species and anadromous and catadromous species. See p. 1294 supra. See also Oda, International Law of the Resources of the Sea (1979).

## SECTION 4. LAW OF THE SEA AND THE MARINE ENVIRONMENT

The protection of the marine environment has been addressed as part of the law of the sea as well as in the context of environmental protection generally. Problems of pollution by ships have been treated specially by the International Maritime Consultative Organization (IMCO) now the International Maritime Organization (IMO).

The Third UN Law of the Sea Conference concentrated on rules governing land-based sources of marine pollution, pollution from continental shelf activities and from deep sea-bed mining, and dumping. Most significantly, the 1982 Convention on the Law of the Sea gave coastal States, particularly port states, power to enforce international rules and to do so against foreign vessels, but made special provision for the settlement of disputes that might result. See p. 1326 below.

The provisions of the 1982 Convention on the marine environment are considered with other international agreements on marine pollution and other international actions for the protection of the environment generally, in Chapter 16 on the Environment.

### *DUPUY & RÉMOND–GOUILLOUD, THE PRESERVATION OF THE MARINE ENVIRONMENT*

2 A Handbook on the New Law of the Sea 1151–52 (Dupuy, ed. 1991) (footnotes omitted).

The preservation of the marine environment is regarded today as an important area of the new law of the sea. Although the 1958 and 1960 Conventions devoted only very scanty provisions, with a very general content, to this subject, the 1982 Convention, which was the result of prolonged work at the Third United Nations Conference on the Law of the Sea, devotes to it all of its Part XII, and Part V is also directly concerned with it. In the meantime some highly spectacular accidents, such as that of the *Torrey Canyon* in 1967 or those of the Ixtoc–I drilling platform in the Gulf of Mexico and the *Amoco Cadiz* off the Breton coast, revealed to the public 10 years later the magnitude of the disasters that threatened not only the coasts but also large portions of maritime spaces, together with their living resources. In the preparatory work and the sessions of the Stockholm Conference, held in 1972 under the auspices of the United Nations and relating to the human environment as a whole, the debates and principles devoted to the preservation of the marine environment occupied a prominent place.

For a long time, oil pollution was the only kind of pollution that attracted attention, even though about 60 per cent of all pollution originates on land. It is still true today, particularly in enclosed or semi-enclosed seas, such as the Mediterranean or the Caribbean, the English Channel or the Persian Gulf area, or along the major maritime navigation routes, that oil and its by-products are significant as clearly identifiable sources of pollution, present in still alarmingly large quantities. The other sources of pollution, apart from the marine dumping of wastes, such as the red muds dumped by the Société Montedison off the coast of Corsica, come from land areas, through natural intermediaries, such as rivers and their tributaries, or through artificial intermediaries. They are often more difficult to identify, since their origins are so diverse.

In the face of the growing dangers resulting from oil spills and from pollution originating on land but drained towards the coastal zones, international law and maritime law, as recently as 20 years ago, remained powerless or mute. Even today they remain incomplete. Some of the laws and regulations which have been established are still being made ineffective by the complaisance of flags of convenience States and coastal States.

Nevertheless, there are now substantial provisions of both kinds, and they give reason to hope for definite advances. They were set up in successive waves. Initially the approach was sectoral: there was concern about pollution caused by oil, then about the dangers posed by marine dumping, and then about land-originated pollution. Consideration was given first to punishing unlawful discharges, then to compensating victims, before the task of defining the preventive obligations incumbent on States and on the various users of the sea whom they control was undertaken. Eventually, the work of the Third United Nations Conference on the Law of the Sea made it possible, without reviewing the often technical details of the provisions adopted in special conventions, to take a global view of all the legal problems posed by the preservation of the marine environment, co-ordinating the jurisdiction and duties of all the States concerned.

## THE EEZ AND THE ENVIRONMENT

### *RESTATEMENT (THIRD) § 514, COMMENT i*

With respect to its exclusive economic zone, a coastal state has jurisdiction to adopt laws and regulations for the enforcement of "generally acceptable international rules and standards established through the competent international organization or general diplomatic conference" for the prevention, reduction, and control of pollution from ships of other states. A coastal state can also enforce its own laws and regulations adopted in accordance with applicable international rules and standards, with respect to a violation occurring within its territorial sea or exclusive economic zone. LOS Convention, Articles 211(5) and 220(1). Ordinarily, such enforcement takes place when the ship accused of the violation is voluntarily within a port or at an offshore terminal of the state concerned.

If the coastal state has clear grounds for believing that a foreign ship has violated applicable international rules, or the supplementary laws or regulations of the coastal state, in the exclusive economic zone, and the ship is not in port but is navigating in the exclusive economic zone or territorial sea of the coastal state, that state may require the ship to give information regarding its identity and its port of registry, its last and next port of call, and other relevant information required to establish whether a violation has occurred. If a violation has resulted in a substantial discharge causing significant pollution of the marine environment, and the ship has refused to give information or the information supplied is manifestly at variance with the evident factual situation, the coastal state may undertake physical inspection of the ship for matters relating to the violation. If the discharge causes or threatens to cause major damage to the coastline or related interests of the coastal state, or to any resources of its territorial sea or exclusive economic zone, the coastal state may, if the evidence warrants it, institute proceedings including detention of the ship in accordance with its laws. But the ship must be allowed to proceed on its journey as soon as it has furnished appropriate bond or other financial security. *Id.* Article 220(2)–(7).

Alternatively, in case of a discharge from a ship in violation of generally applicable international rules and standards, the flag state, the coastal state in whose coastal waters the discharge occurred, or the state damaged or threatened by the discharge, may request another state, in whose port or offshore terminal the ship has voluntarily stopped, to undertake investigations and, where warranted by the evidence, to impose penalties on the violators. If the aggrieved state requests it, the port state must transfer the records of the investigation to the coastal state and terminate its proceedings. In addition, any port state proceedings to impose penalties must be suspended if the flag state decides to institute proceedings against the ship in its own courts; but the coastal or port state that has instituted the original proceedings need not suspend them if they relate to an event involving major damage to the coastal state or if the flag state in question "has repeatedly disregarded its obligations to enforce effectively the applicable international rules and standards in respect of violations committed by its vessels." *Id.* Articles 218 and 228. See also § 512, Reporters' Note 7; § 604, Comments *d* and *e*.

## SECTION 5. MARINE SCIENTIFIC RESEARCH

Under the 1958 Conventions, marine scientific research was unrestricted on the high seas but subject to the control of the coastal state in its territorial sea. Research on the continental shelf also required coastal state consent but the 1958 Convention on the Continental Shelf provided that consent should not normally be withheld. In practice, coastal states have withheld their consent and since 1958 virtually no research has been done on any state's continental shelf by foreign scientists. Some states further restricted research by applying the consent requirement to the superjacent waters as well.

The 1982 Convention would not change the status of research in the territorial sea or on the high seas. (See Part XIII, especially Arts. 143, 245, 256, 257). As to the EEZ, the U.S. sought in the negotiations a regime that would not subject research to coastal state constraints. The developing countries, however, viewed control of scientific research as crucial for protecting their interests in the resources of the economic zone and the continental shelf. The views of the developing states prevailed. Coastal state consent is required for research in the exclusive economic zone and on the continental shelf (Art. 246). The coastal state shall normally grant consent unless the research falls into certain categories, e.g., is related to resource use (Art. 246(5)). See also Art. 296(2), whereby the coastal state is not obliged to submit to settlement under Part XV, section 2, disputes arising out of the exercise by the coastal state of its discretion under Article 246 or of its right to suspend research under Article 253. Compare also Article 297(2)(b), providing for conciliation in these two cases.

## *U.N. CONVENTION ON THE LAW OF THE SEA (1982)*

U.N.Doc. A/CONF. 62/122; 21 I.L.M. 1261 (1982).

### Article 245

#### *Marine Scientific Research in the Territorial Sea*

Coastal States, in the exercise of their sovereignty, have the exclusive right to regulate, authorize and conduct marine scientific research in their territorial sea. Marine scientific research therein shall be conducted only with the express consent of and under the conditions set forth by the coastal State.

### Article 246

#### *Marine Scientific Research in the Exclusive Economic Zone and on the Continental Shelf*

1. Coastal States, in the exercise of their jurisdiction, have the right to regulate, authorize and conduct marine scientific research in their exclusive economic zone and on their continental shelf in accordance with the relevant provisions of this Convention.

2. Marine scientific research in the exclusive economic zone and on the continental shelf shall be conducted with the consent of the coastal State.

3. Coastal States shall, in normal circumstances, grant their consent for marine scientific research projects by other States or competent international organizations in their exclusive economic zone or on their continental shelf to be carried out in accordance with this Convention exclusively for peaceful purposes and in order to increase scientific knowledge of the marine environment for the benefit of all mankind. To this end, coastal States shall establish rules and procedures ensuring that such consent will not be delayed or denied unreasonably.

4. For the purposes of applying paragraph 3, normal circumstances may exist in spite of the absence of diplomatic relations between the coastal State and the researching State.

5. Coastal States may however in their discretion withhold their consent to the conduct of a marine scientific research project of another State or competent international organization in the exclusive economic zone or on the continental shelf of the coastal State if that project:

(a) is of direct significance for the exploration and exploitation of natural resources, whether living or non-living;

(b) involves drilling into the continental shelf, the use of explosives or the introduction of harmful substances into the marine environment;

(c) involves the construction, operation or use of artificial islands, installations and structures referred to in articles 60 and 80;

(d) contains information communicated pursuant to article 248 regarding the nature and objectives of the project which is inaccurate or if the researching State or competent international organization has outstanding obligations to the coastal State from a prior research project.

6. Notwithstanding the provisions of paragraph 5, coastal States may not exercise their discretion to withhold consent under subparagraph (a) of that paragraph in respect of marine scientific research projects to be undertaken in accordance with the provisions of this Part on the continental shelf, beyond 200 nautical miles from the baselines from which the breadth of the territorial sea is measured, outside those specific areas which coastal States may at any time publicly designate as areas in which exploitation or detailed exploratory operations focused on those areas are occurring or will occur within a reasonable period of time. Coastal States shall give reasonable notice of the designation of such areas, as well as any modifications thereto, but shall not be obliged to give details of the operations therein.

7. The provisions of paragraph 6 are without prejudice to the rights of coastal States over the continental shelf as established in article 77.

8. Marine scientific research activities referred to in this article shall not unjustifiably interfere with activities undertaken by coastal States in the exercise of their sovereign rights and jurisdiction provided for in this Convention.

### *RESTATEMENT (THIRD) § 521, REPORTERS' NOTE 6*

*United States policy concerning scientific research.* In the oceans policy statement accompanying the 1983 proclamation on the exclusive economic zone (Reporters' Note 5 and § 511, Reporters' Note 7), President Reagan announced that the United States elected not to assert the right, recognized by international law, of "jurisdiction over marine scientific research within such a zone," in view of "the United States interest in encouraging marine scientific research and avoiding any unnecessary burdens." Nevertheless, the United States will recognize the right of other coastal states over marine scientific research within their exclusive economic zones "if that jurisdiction is exercised reasonably in a manner consistent with international law." See, Introductory Note to this Part.

## SECTION 6. SETTLEMENT OF SEA DISPUTES

The 1982 Convention includes a complex of provisions for resolving various disputes under the Convention. In several instances, agreement on a means of resolving disputes was indispensable to achieving agreement on the underlying substantive principles.

### *REPORT BY THE COMPTROLLER GENERAL OF THE UNITED STATES, LAW OF THE SEA CONFERENCE—STATUS OF THE ISSUES, 1978*

U.S.G.A.O. March 9, 1979.

#### DISPUTE SETTLEMENT

Under the ICNT, disputes about interpretation or applicability of treaty provisions could be settled by any peaceful means. [Art. 279–80] In addition to referral to the International Court of Justice for disputes between states, three other methods of settling disputes would be established—a Law of the Sea Tribunal, including a Seabed Disputes Chamber, an arbitration tribunal and a special arbitral tribunal composed of experts for particular dispute categories. [Art. 287]. Conciliation procedures may also be used if agreed to by both parties. [Art. 284]. The parties to a dispute are obligated to seek some peaceful means for dispute settlement, but the method selected depends on both the type of judicial issue involved and the preference of the parties.

— *Law of the Sea Tribunal.* Composed of 21 members elected for 9-year terms by secret ballot of parties to the treaty, the Law of the Sea Tribunal would have jurisdiction over all disputes submitted to it either under the treaty or by other international agreements giving it jurisdiction. [Annex VI] * * *

— *Arbitration procedures.* If both parties have not accepted the same settlement procedure, disputes must be submitted to arbitration unless the parties agree to some other procedure. [Annex VII] * * *

— *Special arbitration procedures.* These can be used in cases of disputes relating to application of treaty provisions to fisheries; protection of the marine environment; marine scientific research; and navigation including pollution from vessels. [Annex VIII] * * *

These dispute settlement procedures would be more limited in cases related to exercise by coastal states of their sovereign rights. In such cases, the aggrieved party would first have to establish that the claim is "well-founded" and not "frivolous or vexatious" and the other party would have to be notified. If these conditions are fulfilled, the court or tribunal would have jurisdiction over allegations that the coastal state exceeded its discretion and contravened (1) treaty provisions on freedom and rights of navigation, overflight, or laying of submarine cables, (2) other treaty provisions, national law or international law, or (3) specified international rules related to preservation of the marine environment. In addition, dispute settlement procedures would be applied to disputes related to use of living resources or marine scientific research in the economic zone or continental shelf area only under very limited circumstances. [Art. 296] * * *

### Seabed Disputes Chamber

To handle seabed mining disputes, the ICNT would establish the Seabed Disputes Chamber [Art. 186] * * *

This Chamber would have jurisdiction over disputes between the Authority and states parties or private miners involving (1) disputes relating to the conduct of activities or the granting of a contract to undertake any mining operations in the internationally governed area, (2) allegations that decisions made by the Assembly or the Council, or its organs, violated the treaty regulations or represented a misuse of its power, (3) interpretation or application of contracts concerning activities in the internationally governed area, (4) alleged violations by states of treaty provisions, (5) suspension of states for alleged gross violations of treaty provisions, and (6) alleged revelation of proprietary information by members of the international Secretariat. [Art. 187].

* * * The Chamber would handle all disputes with the Authority unless the parties agree to refer the case to binding arbitration. In disputes between states parties and/or private miners where the Authority is not involved, however, any party could require binding arbitration rather than a ruling of the Chamber. [Art. 188] * * *

Although the Seabed Disputes Chamber appears to provide a system of judicial review and dispute settlement, its powers would be limited by an ICNT article [190] providing that it could not challenge "legislative" and discretionary acts of the Assembly or Council and could not determine whether Assembly rules, regulations, or procedures conform to treaty provisions. The Chamber would, however, have jurisdiction over individual complaints that Assembly organs abused their powers or violated treaty regulations in particular cases and could refuse to give them effect. * * *

Still to be resolved are several major issues—(1) whether the Seabed Disputes Chamber or an arbitral tribunal would be entitled to review any abuse of regulatory or discretionary powers exercised by the Authority, (2) whether commercial arbitration would be available as an alternative method for handling disputes arising from contracts with the Authority in cases where the parties did not agree on another method, and (3) how that Chamber would be constituted. * * *

### *Notes*

1. The issues still open when the Comptroller General's report issued were resolved when the 1982 Convention was concluded. See Annex VI and Articles 279–99 of the Convention.

2. Restatement (Third), Introductory Note to Part V at n. 6, states:

> The provisions of the LOS Convention establishing new institutions and a system for the settlement of disputes arising under the Convention are not customary international law and will not become law for the United States unless the United States becomes a party to the Convention. See, *e.g.*:
>
> Section 502, Comment *f.* Where a state suffers a loss due to the failure of the flag state to exercise proper control, a special dispute settlement mechanism is provided in Part XV of the Convention.
>
> Section 511, Reporters' Note 8. A special procedure to resolve continental shelf issues is to be established. (Art. 76(8).)
>
> Section 514, Comments *b, j,* and Reporters' Note 2; § 515, Reporters' Note 2. Under the Convention there will be a special procedure for settling certain disputes between coastal and other states as to their respective rights and duties in the exclusive economic zone. (Art. 297.)
>
> Section 517, Comment *e,* and Reporters' Note 3. The Convention provides for submission of certain maritime boundary disputes to a conciliation commission. (Art. 298(1)(a).)
>
> In addition to effecting changes in the substantive rules governing mining in the deep sea-bed, the Convention would establish institutions and procedures that are binding only on parties to the Convention. See § 523, Comment *e,* and Reporters' Note 3.

3. If the 1982 Convention, including Part XI on the seabed, enters into force, there will inevitably be disputes between states party to the Convention

and any state not a party that proceeds to exploit resources of the deep seabed, or issues permits to private companies to do so. The Convention provides for the settlement of disputes between parties (Articles 187(a) and 188(1)), and Resolution II, para. 5(c), but makes no provision for disputes with non-parties. It has been suggested that the General Assembly might be asked to submit that question to the International Court of Justice for an advisory opinion. See Restatement (Third) § 523, Reporters' Note 2.

4. On the settlement of sea disputes generally, see Adede, The System for Settlement of Disputes under the United Nations Convention on the Law of the Sea[:] A Drafting History and Commentary (1987); Also, Expert Panel on the Law of Ocean Uses, U.S. Policy on the Settlement of Disputes in the Law of the Sea, 81 A.J.I.L. 438 (1987); Hakapaa, Some Observations on the Settlement of Disputes in the New Law of the Sea, in Essays on International Law 57 (Finnish Branch of the ILA, 1987); Oda, Some Reflections on the Dispute Clauses in the United Nations Convention on the Law of the Sea, in Essays in Honor of Judge Manfred Lachs 645 (Makarcyzyk, ed. 1984). See also Janis, The Law of the Sea Tribunal and the ICJ[:] Some Notions about Utility, 16 Marine Pol'y 102 (1992).

## SECTION 7. THE LAW OF OCEAN VESSELS

The principal uses of the sea have required vessels. Small vessels were individual property but larger vessels tended to be the property of the sovereign and enjoyed sovereign privileges and immunities. See Chapter 13. In time, all vessels that plied the seas came to enjoy the protection of the sovereign and vessels acquired "nationality," usually reflected in documents of registration and the right to fly the sovereign flag. Both the 1958 and 1982 Conventions place the law as to ships in the context of the law governing the high seas. The nationality and status of ships and the rights and duties of the flag state, however, have application as well in places other than the high seas.

### A. THE NATIONALITY OF VESSELS

*U.N. CONVENTION ON THE LAW OF THE SEA (1982)*

U.N.Doc. A/CONF. 62/122; 21 I.L.M. 1261 (1982).

ARTICLE 90

*Right of Navigation*

Every State, whether coastal or land-locked, has the right to sail ships flying its flag on the high seas.

ARTICLE 91

*Nationality of Ships*

1. Every State shall fix the conditions for the grant of its nationality to ships, for the registration of ships in its territory, and for the right to fly its flag. Ships have the nationality of the State whose flag they are entitled to fly. There must exist a genuine link between the State and the ship.

2. Every State shall issue to ships to which it has granted the right to fly its flag documents to that effect.

### ARTICLE 92

*Status of Ships*

1. Ships shall sail under the flag of one State only and, save in exceptional cases expressly provided for in international treaties or in this Convention, shall be subject to its exclusive jurisdiction on the high seas. A ship may not change its flag during a voyage or while in a port of call, save in the case of a real transfer of ownership or change of registry.

2. A ship which sails under the flags of two or more States, using them according to convenience, may not claim any of the nationalities in question with respect to any other State, and may be assimilated to a ship without nationality.

See also Restatement (Third) § 501.

### *Notes*

1. Convention Articles 90–92 are essentially the same as Articles 4–6 of the 1958 Convention on the High Seas. In the 1958 Convention (Art. 5), however, to the "genuine link" requirement was added: "in particular, the State must effectively exercise its jurisdiction and control in administrative, technical and social matters over ships flying its flag." In the 1982 Convention that clause is no longer attached to the "genuine link" requirement, but is included among the duties of the flag state (Article 94). That article includes also the duty to ensure safety at sea, extending and giving greater specificity to what is provided in Article 10 of the 1958 Convention. *Inter alia,* Article 94 provides for enquiry into "every marine casualty or incident of navigation * * * causing loss of life or serious injury to nationals of another State or serious damage to shipping or installations of another State or to the marine environment."

2. The requirement of a "genuine link" between the flag state and the ship has been a source of uncertainty. The report of the Senate Committee on Foreign Relations explaining the same clause in the 1958 Convention said:

> The International Law Commission did not decide upon a definition of the term "genuine link." This article as originally drafted by the Commission would have authorized other states to determine whether there was a "genuine link" between a ship and the flag state for purposes of recognition of the nationality of the ship.
>
> It was felt by some states attending the Conference on the Law of the Sea that the term "genuine link" could, depending upon how it was defined, limit the discretion of a state to decide which ships it would permit to fly its flag. Some states, which felt their flag vessels were at a competitive disadvantage with vessels sailing under the flags of other states, such as Panama and Liberia, were anxious to adopt a definition which states like Panama and Liberia could not meet.
>
> By a vote of 30 states, including the United States, against 15 states for, and 17 states abstaining, the provision was eliminated which would have enabled states other than the flag state to withhold recognition of the national character of a ship if they considered that there was no "genuine link" between the state and the ship.
>
> Thus, under the Convention on the High Seas, it is for each state to determine how it shall exercise jurisdiction and control in administrative, technical and social matters over ships flying its flag. The "genuine link" requirement need not have any effect upon the practice of registering

> American built or owned vessels in such countries as Panama or Liberia. The existence of a "genuine link" between the state and the ship is not a condition of recognition of the nationality of a ship; that is, no state can claim the right to determine unilaterally that no genuine link exists between a ship and the flag state. Nevertheless, there is a possibility that a state, with respect to a particular ship, may assert before an agreed tribunal, such as the International Court of Justice, that no genuine link exists. In such event, it would be for the Court to decide whether or not a "genuine link" existed.

Executive Report No. 5—Law of the Sea Conventions, 106 Cong.Rec. 11189, 11190 (86th Cong., 2d Sess., May 26, 1960). See generally McDougal & Burke, The Public Order of the Oceans 1013–15, 1033–35, 1073–75, 1080–82, 1087–88, 1137–39 (1962). Compare Boczek, Flags of Convenience 276–83 (1962). See also Flags of Convenience—Study by the Maritime Transport Committee of OECD, reproduced in ILO Doc. JMC/21/4, Joint Maritime Commission 21st session, Nov.–Dec. 1972; UNCTAD Secretariat, Economic Consequences of the Existence or Lack of a Genuine Link between Vessel and Flag of Registry, UNCTAD Doc. TB/B/C. 4/168 (1977); also, generally, Osieke, Flags of Convenience Vessels: Recent Developments, 73 A.J.I.L. 604 (1979).

3. What is a "genuine link"? Is a ship owned by a national or domiciliary of the flag state bound to the flag state by a "genuine link"? What if the shipowner is a corporation created under the law of the state of registry, the shares of which are held by foreign interests, or if the ship is owned in part by foreign interests and in part by domestic interests? Is a ship that is required by the law of the state of registry to carry a crew made up in whole or in part of nationals of that state connected to the latter by a "genuine link"? If only the officers are required to be nationals? For a summary and discussion of legislation regulating the nationality of ships, see Boczek, Flags of Convenience 39–53 (1962). Is there anything in the *Nottebohm Case,* p. 397 that helps to explain the application of the "genuine link" requirement to the nationality of vessels? To what extent do the criteria specified by the Court as relevant to the existence of a "genuine link" between an individual and a state also apply to the existence of a "genuine link" between a vessel and a state? What different policy considerations may be applicable? See McDougal & Burke at 1029–33; Boczek at 119–24.

The Restatement (Revised) § 501, Comment *b,* states:

> In general, a state has a "genuine link" entitling it to register a ship and to authorize the ship to use its flag if the ship is owned by nationals of the state, whether natural or juridical persons, and the state exercises effective control over the ship. In most cases a ship is owned by a corporation created by the state of registry. However, in determining whether a "genuine link" with the state of registry exists, the following additional factors are to be taken into account: whether the company owning the ship is owned by nationals of the state; whether the officers and crew of the ship are nationals of the state; how often the ship stops in the ports of the state; and how extensive and effective is the control that the state exercises over the ship.
>
> Although international law requires a genuine link between the ship and the registering state, the lack of a genuine link does not justify another state in refusing to recognize the flag or in interfering with the ship. A state may, however, reject diplomatic protection by the flag state when the

flag state has no genuine link with the ship. If another state doubts the existence of a genuine link, for instance, because there is evidence that the flag state has not been exercising its duties to control and regulate the ship (see § 502), it may request that the flag state "investigate the matter and, if appropriate, take any action necessary to remedy the situation." LOS Convention, Article 94(6); § 502, Comment *f.*

See also McConnell, Darkening Confusion Mounted Upon Darkening Confusion: The Search for the Elusive Genuine Link, 16 J.Mar.L. & Comm. 365 (1985).

4. For a comprehensive discussion of the effect of the rise of "flag of convenience" shipping (i.e., the registration for economic reasons of foreign-owned vessels in countries such as Panama, Liberia, and Honduras—sometimes referred to as the "Panlibhon" group) on the traditional rule that only the state of registration could set the requirements for and subsequently question a ship's right to its registry and flag, see Boczek, supra, passim. See also McDougal & Burke, supra, ch. 8, passim. See also Constitution of the Maritime Safety Committee of the Inter–Governmental Maritime Consultative Organization (Advisory Opinion), [1960] I.C.J. 150; Osieke, Flags of Convenience Vessels: Recent Developments, 73 A.J.I.L. 604 (1979); Resolution of UNCTAD Committee on Shipping. TD/B/C.4 (S–III) Misc. 2 at 23, 31 (1981); Juda, World Shipping, UNCTAD and the New International Economic Order, 35 Int'l Org. 493 (1981); Goldie, Environmental Catastrophes and Flags of Convenience—Does the Present Law Pose Special Liability Issues, 3 Pace Y.B.Int'l L. (1991); Momtaz, The High Seas, in 1 A Handbook on the New Law of the Sea 402–06 (Dupuy, ed. 1991); Egiyan, "Flag of Convenience" or "Open Registration" of Ships, 14 Marine Pol'y 106 (1990); Bergstrand & Doganis, The Impact of Flags of Convenience (Open Registries), in The Law of the Sea and International Shipping: Anglo–Soviet Post UNCLOS Perspectives 413 (Butler, ed. 1985). Restatement (Third) § 501, Reporters' Note 7.

5. Numerous bilateral commercial treaties provide, *inter alia,* that the nationality of a vessel is to be determined in accordance with the law of the state under whose flag it sails. The United States has treaties containing such a provision with Honduras (Dec. 7, 1927, 45 Stat. 2618, T.S. 764) and Liberia (Aug. 8, 1938, 54 Stat. 1739, T.S. 956), two states having large flag-of-convenience fleets. For a discussion of comparable treaty provisions, see Boczek, Flags of Convenience at 95–100. Could the United States refuse to recognize a Liberian-flag vessel as entitled to various privileges specified in the United States–Liberia treaty of commerce on the ground that the ship had no "genuine link" with Liberia?

## B. JURISDICTION OVER VESSELS

### *1. Requisition and Control of National Vessels*

In 1917, the British Government informed the Netherlands that it intended to requisition a number of vessels which, although owned by Dutch corporations and registered in the Netherlands, were "in reality British" because of the fact that British nationals owned the shares of the controlling corporations. The Netherlands Government delivered a strong protest, asserting that it alone had the right to requisition vessels flying the Dutch flag. In reply, the British Government changed its position, noting that it did not seek to rely upon the fact of British ownership or control but upon the recognized right of a belligerent to requisition neutral ships present in its territory. 111 Brit. & For.St.Pap. 465–69 (1917–18). The British–Dutch exchange is often cited as support for the general proposition that under international law, the right to requisition ships rests with the state of registry. Rienow, The Test of the Nationality of a Merchant Vessel 100–102 (1937); Boczek, Flags of Convenience 195–97 (1962). It is also admitted, however, that a state of "ultimate ownership" is entitled to requisition foreign-flag vessels with the consent or acquiescence of the country of registry, and the United States apparently expects that those states under whose "flags of convenience" many United States-owned vessels sail will acquiesce in the vessels' transfer to United States control and registry, either or both, in the event of an emergency requiring such transfer. See generally Boczek, supra at 188–208. If the state of registry should resist the transfer of its vessels to the control of another state, the latter could still requisition these or other vessels, whether or not owned by its nationals, which it finds *within its territory.* See generally, on the "right of angary," 6 Hackworth at 638–55. Boczek suggests that requisition by a state of national-owned vessels found on the high seas or in foreign ports might be justified, even without the consent of the flag state, on the ground that the latter is unable to afford the vessels adequate protection against the dangers of hostilities. Boczek, supra at 207. See 49 Stat. 2015, as amended, 46 U.S.C.A. § 1242, providing for the requisition of vessels owned by United States citizens.

### *U.S. DEP'T OF COMMERCE, TRANSPORTATION ORDER T–2 (AMENDED)*

November 25, 1972, 37 Fed.Reg. 25040, redesignated at 45 Fed.Reg. 44574 (1980), 44 C.F.R. 403 (1991).

Section 1. Prohibition of movement of American carriers to North Korea or to the Communist-controlled area of Viet Nam.

No person shall sail, fly, navigate, or otherwise take any ship documented under the laws of the United States or any aircraft registered under the laws of the United States to North Korea or to the Communist-controlled area of Viet Nam.

Sec. 2. Prohibition on transportation of goods destined for North Korea or the Communist-controlled area of Viet Nam.

No person shall transport, in any ship documented under the laws of the United States, or in any aircraft registered under the laws of the United States, to North Korea or to the Communist-controlled area of Viet Nam, any material commodity, or cargo of any kind. * * *

### *Note*

It has been stated that it is "unquestioned practice that the state which is responsible for a ship's conformity with international law has a competence equal to its responsibility and may control the movement and activities of its ships as its interpretation of community obligations and its national policies require." McDougal & Burke, The Public Order of the Oceans 1066 (1962). What is the significance in this context of national ownership? Could a state enforce penalties against a foreign-flag vessel found within its territory on the ground that the owner was one of its nationals and had failed to exercise control over the vessel in accordance with applicable legislation?

### 2. *Jurisdiction Over Acts Committed on National Vessels*

## RIGHTS AND DUTIES OF THE FLAG STATE

### *RESTATEMENT (THIRD) § 502*

(1) The flag state is required

(a) to exercise effective authority and control over the ship in administrative, technical, and labor matters; and

(b) (i) to take such measures as are necessary to ensure safety at sea, avoid collisions, and prevent, reduce, and control pollution of the marine environment, and

(ii) to adopt laws and regulations and take such other steps as are needed to conform these measures to generally accepted international standards, regulations, procedures, and practices, and to secure their implementation and observance.

(2) The flag state may exercise jurisdiction to prescribe, to adjudicate, and to enforce, with respect to the ship or any conduct that takes place on the ship.

### *Notes*

1. Compare the extent of United States jurisdiction asserted in 18 U.S.C.A. § 7(1), providing that the "special maritime and territorial jurisdiction of the United States" includes:

> The high seas, any other waters within the admiralty and maritime jurisdiction of the United States and out of the jurisdiction of any particular State, and any vessel belonging in whole or in part to the United States or any citizen thereof, or to any corporation created by or under the laws of the United States, or of any State, Territory, District, or possession thereof, when such vessel is within the admiralty and maritime jurisdiction of the United States and out of the jurisdiction of any particular State.

Does 18 U.S.C.A. § 7(1) purport to assert United States jurisdiction over crimes committed on foreign-flag vessels owned in whole or in part by a citizen of the United States? See Rienow, The Test of the Nationality of a Merchant Vessel 193–213 (1937); Restatement (Third) § 403, Reporters' Note 9; § 502, Reporters' Note 4. In United States v. Keller, 451 F.Supp. 631 (D.C.Puerto Rico 1978), the court stated that the determination of the citizenship of the owner of a vessel is a mixed question of law and fact, but did not indicate which considerations were legal and which factual.

A 1984 Amendment extended this jurisdiction to space vehicles, and to "Any place outside the jurisdiction of any nation with respect to an offense by or against a national of the United States." See Pub.L. 98–473, Title II, § 1210, 98 Stat. 2164 (1984). Chapter 12, p. 1068.

2. Article 97 of the 1982 Convention provides:

1. In the event of a collision or any other incident of navigation concerning a ship on the high seas, involving the penal or disciplinary responsibility of the master or of any other person in the service of the ship, no penal or disciplinary proceedings may be instituted against such person except before the judicial or administrative authorities either of the flag State or of the State of which such person is a national.

2. In disciplinary matters, the State which has issued a master's certificate or a certificate of competence or license shall alone be competent, after due legal process, to pronounce the withdrawal of such certificates, even if the holder is not a national of the State which issued them.

3. No arrest or detention of the ship, even as a measure of investigation, shall be ordered by any authorities other than those of the flag State.

Article 97 of the 1982 Convention is identical to Art. 11 of the 1958 Convention on the High Seas. The effect of this article is to overrule in part the holding of the Permanent Court of International Justice in the *Lotus Case*, p. 63 supra. To some extent, this result had already been achieved by the parties to the International Convention for the Unification of Certain Rules Relating to Penal Jurisdiction in Matters of Collisions and Other Incidents of Navigation, signed at Brussels on May 10, 1952. 439 U.N.T.S. 233 (entered into force Nov. 20, 1955). See [1956] II Yb.I.L.C. 281.

3. In October 1985, terrorists captured an Italian cruise ship in the Mediterranean Sea near Egypt, held its passengers hostage and killed an American on board before surrendering to Egypt. See 85 Dep't State Bull. 74 (Dec.1985). Italy asserted jurisdiction over the hijackers because the offenses took place on an Italian ship. The United States asserted jurisdiction based on 18 U.S.C.A. § 1203, the section of the U.S. Criminal Code that implements the Convention Against the Taking of Hostages, a treaty negotiated in 1979 and effective for the United States in 1985. The Convention authorizes a state to assert jurisdiction over hostage-takers on three bases, in addition to the normal territorial jurisdiction: (1) if it is the state of nationality or residence of the hijackers; (2) if it is the state whose activity was sought to be coerced; or (3) if it is the state of the nationality of the hostages. Pursuant to 18 U.S.C.A. § 1203, which adopts the bases of jurisdiction authorized by the Convention, the United States asserted jurisdiction on the basis that a number of the hostages—including the one killed—were U.S. nationals.

Since the United States had no statute that would make it a crime to murder a United States national on the high seas, could the United States have prosecuted the hostage-takers for murder had Italy transferred them to United States control?

For other issues raised by the incident see McGinley, The Achille Lauro Affair, 52 Tenn.L.Rev. 691 (1986); Schachter, In Defense of International Rules on the Use of Force, 53 U.Chi.L.Rev. 113, 138–41 (1986). And see Chapter 12, p. 1077.

4. Regina v. Leslie, 8 Cox Crim.Cas. 269 (Ct.Crim.App.1860), involved the question whether a conviction for false imprisonment could be sustained against the master of an English merchant ship who, under contract with the Chilean Government, transported to England a group of persons who had been banished from Chile and who were placed aboard the ship by Chilean Government officials while the ship was in Chilean waters. After indicating that the conviction could not be sustained for what was done in Chilean waters because the Chilean

Government could "justify all that it did within its own territory" and the defendant merely acted as its agent, the Court sustained the conviction for acts committed on the high seas, stating:

> * * * It is clear that an English ship on the high seas, out of any foreign territory, is subject to the laws of England, and persons, whether foreign or English, on board such ship are as much amenable to international straits apply, with such modifications as may be necessary, to archipelagic sea lanes passage. See LOS Convention, Articles 46–54.

***3. Jurisdiction Over Acts Committed on Foreign Vessels in the Territorial Sea***

*a. Jurisdiction of the Coastal State*

(1) Vessels in Innocent Passage

## THE DAVID

United States–Panama Claims Commission, 1933.
[1933–1934] Ann.Dig. 137.

The Facts.—On May 11, 1923, the steamer *Yorba Linda,* belonging to the General Petroleum Corporation, an American corporation, collided with the steamer *David,* belonging to the Compañía de Navegación Nacional, Panama. The latter Company started an action in the Court of Panama in respect of the alleged negligence of *The Yorba Linda* and obtained judgment for 27,103.50 balboas. This action was not begun by personal service but by service through publication, as permitted by Articles 470–473 of the Judicial Code of Panama. The Petroleum Company never appeared, but was represented by an attorney designated by the Court who offered no evidence. The judgment remained unsatisfied. Fifteen days after its confirmation by the Supreme Court of Panama the Petroleum Company issued a writ *in rem* of the United States District Court of the Canal Zone against *The David* and her owners, alleging that the collision had taken place in territorial waters of the United States and that it had been caused by the negligence of *The David.* The Marshal of the District Court thereupon arrested *The David* within a few hundred yards of Flamenco Island, and between that island and the San José Rock, which lies off the Pacific entrance to the Panama Canal. The judge of the District Court held the arrest to be valid, and the parties promptly settled the action. The terms of the settlement were that the Petroleum Company should pay to the Navegación Company the sum of $16,250, that the writ against *The David* should be discharged, and that the Panamanian judgment be cancelled.

Before the Commission it was alleged that the arrest of *The David* had been illegal as, first, it had taken place outside the territorial waters of the Canal Zone and, secondly, the vessel had been in innocent passage at the time and therefore immune from arrest even if within territorial waters. Damages were claimed in respect of the loss occasioned by the settlement and for the injury to the standing of the Navegación Company which the proceedings in the District Court had occasioned.

*Held* (by the majority): that the claim must be disallowed as the arrest had been made within territorial waters. The fact that the vessel had been in innocent passage did not confer on her any immunity.

I. *Jurisdiction over Ships in Innocent Passage.*—The question whether or not the arrest was lawful even if within the territorial waters of the Canal Zone was argued at great length by the parties. Upon this question the Commission said:

> The general rule of the extension of sovereignty over the three-mile zone is clearly established. Exceptions to the completeness of this sovereignty should be supported by clear authority. There is a clear preponderance of authority to the effect that this sovereignty is qualified by what is known as the right of innocent passage, and that this qualification forbids the sovereign actually to prohibit the innocent passage of alien merchant vessels through its territorial waters.
>
> There is no clear preponderance of authority to the effect that such vessels when passing through territorial waters are exempt from civil arrest. In the absence of such authority, the Commission cannot say that a country may not, under the rules of international law, assert the right to arrest on civil process merchant ships passing through its territorial waters.

## *U.N. CONVENTION ON THE LAW OF THE SEA (1982)*

U.N.Doc. A/CONF. 62/122; 21 I.L.M. 1261 (1982).

### Article 27

*Criminal Jurisdiction on Board a Foreign Ship*

1. The criminal jurisdiction of the coastal State should not be exercised on board a foreign ship passing through the territorial sea to arrest any person or to conduct any investigation in connection with any crime committed on board the ship during its passage, save only in the following cases:

(a) if the consequences of the crime extend to the coastal State;

(b) if the crime is of a kind to disturb the peace of the country or the good order of the territorial sea;

(c) if the assistance of the local authorities has been requested by the master of the ship or by a diplomatic agent or consular officer of the flag State; or

(d) if such measures are necessary for the suppression of illicit traffic in narcotic drugs or psychotropic substances.

2. The above provisions do not affect the right of the coastal State to take any steps authorized by its laws for the purpose of an arrest or investigation on board a foreign ship passing through the territorial sea after leaving internal waters.

3. In the cases provided for in paragraphs 1 and 2, the coastal State shall, if the master so requests, notify a diplomatic agent or consular officer of the flag State before taking any steps, and shall facilitate contact between such agent or officer and the ship's crew. In cases of emergency this notification may be communicated while the measures are being taken.

4. In considering whether or in what manner an arrest should be made, the local authorities shall have due regard to the interests of navigation.

5. Except as provided in Part XII or with respect to violations of laws and regulations adopted in accordance with Part V, the coastal State may not take any steps on board a foreign ship passing through the territorial sea to arrest any person or to conduct any investigation in connection with any crime committed before the ship entered the territorial sea, if the ship, proceeding from a foreign port, is only passing through the territorial sea without entering internal waters.

ARTICLE 28

*Civil Jurisdiction in Relation to Foreign Ships*

1. The coastal State should not stop or divert a foreign ship passing through the territorial sea for the purpose of exercising civil jurisdiction in relation to a person on board the ship.

2. The coastal State may not levy execution against or arrest the ship for the purpose of any civil proceedings, save only in respect of obligations or liabilities assumed or incurred by the ship itself in the course or for the purpose of its voyage through the waters of the coastal State.

3. Paragraph 2 is without prejudice to the right of the coastal State, in accordance with its laws, to levy execution against or to arrest, for the purpose of any civil proceedings, a foreign ship lying in the territorial sea or passing through the territorial sea after leaving internal waters.

***Notes***

1. The 1982 Convention, Articles 27–28, essentially duplicate Articles 19–20 of the 1958 Convention, but add the introductory clause to Section 5 referring to laws against pollution (Part XII of the 1982 Convention) and those protecting the Exclusive Economic Zone (Part V).

Like Article 20(1) of the 1958 Convention, Article 28 of the 1982 Convention provides: "The Coastal state should not stop * * *" The International Law Commission's final draft of the predecessor to Article 20(1) began as follows: "A coastal State may not arrest." At the 1958 Conference, the United States delegation proposed that the Commission's phrase should be replaced by "should, generally, not stop." "Stop" was clearly a better translation of the French word used by the Commission; the inclusion of "should, generally," was justified, the United States delegate explained, because the Commission's limitation of the coastal state's jurisdiction was not an established rule of international law. It was necessary to preserve the principle that "the coastal State's civil jurisdiction extended to the limits of its territorial sea." 3 U.N.Conf. on the Law of the Sea, Off.Rec. 82 (1958). Norway contended in reply, however, that the Commission's wording conformed to existing international law, and that the latitude left to coastal states by the United States proposal "would give no assurance of any kind." at 119. Denmark, Sweden, and the U.S.S.R. objected only to the word "generally" in the United States proposal, on the ground that the inclusion of this word weakened the principle "that a coastal State could not stop a ship for the purpose of exercising its civil jurisdiction in respect of an individual on board." The word "generally" was rejected, but the rest of the amendment was adopted. at 125. Did the supporters of the principle advanced by Denmark,

Sweden, and the U.S.S.R. win their point by omitting the word "generally"? Compare the French text of Article 20(1): "L'Etat riverain ne devrait ni arrêter ni dérouter un navire étranger passant dans la mer territoriale pour l'exercise de la jurisdiction civile à l'égard d'une personne se trouvant à bord." 516 U.N.T.S. at 219. Article 32 of the Convention provides that all texts are equally authentic.

Article 19 of the 1958 Convention (Art. 27, 1982 Convention), dealing with criminal jurisdiction, had a similar history. The United States proposed the substitution of "should, generally, not be exercised" for the Commission's "may not" and justified the change for substantially the same reasons advanced to support its amendment to Article 20. 3 U.N.Conf. on the Law of the Sea, Off.Rec. 221 (1958). The First Committee adopted the proposal, but the word "generally" was removed by the Plenary Meeting. 2 U.N.Conf. on the Law of the Sea, Off.Rec. 66 (1958).

2. The extent to which foreign government-owned vessels used for commercial purposes should be subject to the coastal state's civil and criminal jurisdiction while in innocent passage was a question which caused difficulties in the International Law Commission and in the First Law of the Sea Conference. The Commission had expressly adopted the restrictive principle of the Brussels Convention of 1926 concerning the immunity of such ships. See p. 1282 infra. The U.S.S.R. and Czechoslovakian members opposed this decision. [1956] 2 Yb.I.L.C. 276. In the First Committee, a Rumanian amendment which would have preserved the immunities of state-owned commercial ships from coastal state civil jurisdiction was defeated. 3 U.N.Conf. on the Law of the Sea, Off.Rec. 132 (1958). The Commission draft was overwhelmingly approved by the Plenary Meeting of the Conference (62–9–4). Four delegations of the Soviet bloc based their negative votes on the absolute theory of state immunity. 2 id. at 66. Reservations to the 1958 Convention have been entered by the Communist states to the articles permitting coastal states to exercise civil jurisdiction over state trading vessels. Articles 27–28, of the 1982 Convention however, appear under the subheading: "Rules Applicable to Merchant Ships and Government Ships Operated for Commercial Purposes."

(2) Vessels in Port

Restatement (Third) § 512, Reporters' Note 3 provides:

*Access to ports.* It has been said that, as no civilized state has "the right to isolate itself wholly from the outside world," there is "a corresponding obligation imposed upon each maritime power not to deprive foreign vessels of commerce of access to all of its ports." 1 Hyde, International Law Chiefly as Interpreted and Applied by the United States 581 (2d ed. 1945). The LOS Convention does not mention a right of access of ships to foreign ports, but the customary law on the subject, as reflected in a number of international agreements, has been confirmed by at least one international decision. Thus, the Statute on the International Regime of Maritime Ports of 1923, confirmed the freedom of access to maritime ports by foreign vessels on condition of reciprocity; but it allows the coastal state "in exceptional cases, and for as short a period as possible," to deviate from this provision by measures which that state "is obliged to take in case of an emergency affecting the safety of the state or the vital interest of the country." 58 L.N.T.S. 285, 301, 305; 2 Hudson, International Legislation 1162 (1931). Although this Statute has been ratified by less than 30 states and the United States is not a party to it, the Statute has been accepted as reflecting a customary rule of international law. An arbitral tribunal, relying on this Statute, stated that "[a]ccording to a great principle of international law, ports of every State must be open to foreign merchant vessels and can only be closed when the vital interests of a State so require." Saudi Arabia v. Arabian American Oil Company (ARAMCO), Award of August 23, 1958, 27 Int'l L.Rep. 117, 212 (1963).

The Institute of International Law has considered this issue in 1898, 1928, and 1957, and each time, after a heated discussion, it affirmed the right of access to ports, subject to various conditions. In 1898, the Institute agreed that, as a general rule, access to ports "is presumed to be free to foreign ships," except when a state, "for reasons of which it is sole judge," declares its ports, or some of them, closed "when the safety of the State or the interest of the public health justifies the order," or when it refuses entrance to ships of a particular nation "as an act of just reprisal." Resolutions of the Institute of International Law 144 (J. Scott ed. 1916). In 1928, the Institute stated that, as a general rule, access to ports "is open to foreign vessels," but, as an exception and for a term as limited as possible, "a state may suspend this access by particular or general measures which it is obliged to take in case of serious events touching the safety of the state or the public health"; it also confirmed the exception in case of reprisals. Institut de Droit International, Tableau Général des Résolutions, 1873–1956, at 102 (Wehberg ed. 1957); 22 Am.J.Int'l L. 844, 847 (1928). In 1957, the Institute distinguished between internal waters and ports, and pointed out that a coastal state may deny access to internal waters, "[s]ubject to the rights of passage sanctioned either by usage or by treaty," but should abstain from denying such access to foreign commercial vessels "save where in exceptional cases this denial of access is imposed by imperative reasons." On the other hand, the Institute declared that "it is consistent with general practice of States to permit free access to ports and harbors by such vessels." [1957] 2 Annuaire de l'Institut de Droit International 485–86. For discussion, see *id.* 171, 180, 194–98, 202–09, 212–22, 253–67; for the text of the 1957 resolution, see also 52 Am.J.Int'l L. 103 (1958).

It seems, therefore, that it is now generally accepted that "in time of peace, commercial ports must be left open to international traffic," and that the "liberty of access to ports granted to foreign vessels implies their right to load and unload their cargoes; embark and disembark their passengers." Colombos, The International Law of the Sea 176 (6th ed. 1967). But see Khedivial Line, S.A.E. v. Seafarers' International Union, 278 F.2d 49, 52 (2d Cir.1960) (plaintiff presented no precedents showing that "the law of nations accords an unrestricted right of access to harbors by vessels of all nations"); Lowe, "The Right of Entry into Maritime Ports in International Law," 14 San Diego L.Rev. 597, 622 (1977) ("the ports of a State which are designated for international trade are, in the absence of express provisions to the contrary made by a port State, presumed to be open to the merchant ships of all States," and they "should not be closed to foreign merchant ships except when the peace, good order, or security of the coastal State necessitates closure").

* * *

States may impose, however, special restrictions on certain categories of ships. For instance, the Convention on the Liability of Operators of Nuclear–Powered Ships, Brussels, 1962, provides that nothing in that Convention "shall affect any right which a Contracting State may have under international law to deny access to its waters and harbours to nuclear ships licensed by another Contracting State, even when it has formally complied with all the provisions" of that Convention. Art. XVII, 57 Am.J.Int'l L. 268 (1963). See also Reporters' Note 1. In 1985, New Zealand denied to United States nuclear ships access to its ports. See 21 Weekly Comp.Pres.Docs. 147 (1985). A directive of the Council of the European Economic Community regulates the entry into Community ports of oil, gas, and chemical tankers, Dec. 21, 1978, 22 O.J. Eur.Comm. (No. L. 33) 33 (1979); amended Dec. 11, 1979, *id.* (No. L. 315) 16 (1979). Access to ports by other categories of vessels (*e.g.,* fishing vessels) may also be subject to various restrictions.

A coastal state can condition the entry of foreign ships into its ports on compliance with specified laws and regulations.

* * *

The principles governing international aviation differ from those governing shipping; landing rights as well as overflight rights have to be specifically conferred. See § 513, Comment *i.*

On access to U.S. coastal waters and ports, see Restatement (Third) § 512, Reporters' Note 4.

## WILDENHUS' CASE

Supreme Court of the United States, 1887.
120 U.S. 1, 7 S.Ct. 385, 30 L.Ed. 565.

[Wildenhus, a Belgian national, killed another Belgian national below the deck of the Belgian vessel of which they were both crew members, which was at the time of the slaying moored to a dock in Jersey City. The local police authorities arrested Wildenhus, charging him with the killing, and held two other crew members as witnesses. The Belgian consul applied for a writ of habeas corpus, citing Article 11 of the treaty of March 9, 1880 (21 Stat. 776) between Belgium and the United States, which provided: "The respective consuls-general, consuls, vice-consuls and consular agents shall have exclusive charge of the internal order of the merchant vessels of their nation, and shall alone take cognizance of all differences which may arise, either at sea or in port, between the captains, officers and crews, without exception, particularly with reference to the adjustment of wages and the execution of contracts. The local authorities shall not interfere except when the disorder that has arisen is of such a nature as to disturb tranquillity and public order on shore, or in the port, or when a person of the country or not belonging to the crew shall be concerned therein." The Circuit Court refused to order the release of the prisoners, and the consul appealed to the Supreme Court.]

WAITE, C.J. * * * By sections 751 and 753 of the Revised Statutes the courts of the United States have power to issue writs of *habeas corpus* which shall extend to prisoners in jail when they are in "custody in violation of the constitution or a law or treaty of the United States," and the question we have to consider is whether these prisoners are held in violation of the provisions of the existing treaty between the United States and Belgium.

It is part of the law of civilized nations that, when a merchant vessel of one country enters the ports of another for the purposes of trade, it subjects itself to the law of the place to which it goes, unless, by treaty or otherwise, the two countries have come to some different understanding or agreement; for, as was said by Chief Justice Marshall in The Exchange, 7 Cranch, 144: "It would be obviously inconvenient and dangerous to society, and would subject the laws to continual infraction, and the government to degradation, if such * * * merchants did not owe temporary and local allegiance, and were not amenable to the jurisdiction of the country." * * * And the English judges have uniformly recognized the rights of the courts of the country of which the port is part to punish crimes committed by one foreigner on another in a foreign merchant ship. Regina v. Cunningham, Bell, Cr.Cas. 72; S.C. 8 Cox, Crim.Cas. 104; Regina v. Anderson, 11 Cox, Crim.Cas. 198, 204; S.C.L.R. 1 Cr.Cas. 161, 165; Regina v. Keyn, 13 Cox, Crim.Cas. 403, 486, 525; S.C. 2 Exch.Div. 63, 161, 213. As the owner has voluntarily taken his vessel, for his own private purposes, to a place within the dominion of a government other than his own, and from which he seeks protection during his stay, he owes that government such allegiance, for the time being, as is due for the protection to which he becomes entitled.

From experience, however, it was found long ago that it would be beneficial to commerce if the local government would abstain from interfering with the internal discipline of the ship, and the general regulation of the rights and duties of the officers and crew towards the vessel, or among themselves. And so by comity it came to be generally understood among civilized nations that all matters of discipline, and all things done on board, which affected only the vessel, or those belonging to her, and did not involve the peace or dignity of the country, or the tranquillity of the port, should be left by the local government to be dealt with by the authorities of the nation to which the vessel belonged as the laws of that nation, or the interests of its commerce should require. But, if crimes are committed on board of a character to disturb the peace and tranquillity of the country to which the vessel has been brought, the offenders have never, by comity or usage, been entitled to any exemption from the operation of the local laws for their punishment, if the local tribunals see fit to assert their authority. Such being the general public law on this subject, treaties and conventions have been entered into by nations having commercial intercourse, the purpose of which was to settle and define the rights and duties of the contracting parties with respect to each other in these particulars, and thus prevent the inconvenience that might arise from attempts to exercise conflicting jurisdictions.

The first of these conventions entered into by the United States after the adoption of the constitution was with France, on the fourteenth of November, 1788, (8 St. 106), * * * article 8 of which is as follows: "The consuls or vice-consuls shall exercise police over all the vessels of their respective nations, and shall have on board the said vessels all power and jurisdiction in civil matters in all the disputes which may there arise. They shall have entire inspection over the said vessels, their crew, and the changes and substitutions there to be made, for which purpose they may go on board the said vessels whenever they may judge it necessary. Well understood that the functions hereby allowed shall be confined to the interior of the vessels, and that they shall not take place in any case which shall have any interference with the police of the ports where the said vessels shall be."

It was when this convention was in force that the cases of *The Sally* and *The Newton* arose * * *. The Sally was an American merchant vessel in the port of Marseilles, and the Newton a vessel of a similar character in the port of Antwerp, then under the dominion of France. In the case of *The Sally,* the mate, in the alleged exercise of discipline over the crew, had inflicted a severe wound on one of the seamen, and, in that of *The Newton,* one seaman had made an assault on another seaman in the vessel's boat. In each case the proper consul of the United States claimed exclusive jurisdiction of the offense, and so did the local authorities of the port; but the council of state, a branch of the political department of the government of France to which the matter was referred, pronounced against the local tribunals, "considering that one of these cases was that of an assault committed in the boat of the American ship Newton by one of the crew upon another, and the other was that of a severe wound inflicted by the mate of the American ship Sally upon one of the seamen for having made use of the boat without leave." This was clearly because the things done were not such as to disturb "the peace or tranquillity of the port." Wheat.Elem. (3d Ed.) 154. The case of *The Sally* was simply a quarrel between certain of the crew while constructively on board the vessel, and that of *The Newton* grew out of a punishment inflicted by an officer on one of the crew for disobedience of orders. Both were evidently of a character to affect only the police of the vessel, and thus within the authority expressly granted to the consul by the treaty.

[The Court then analyzed a number of treaties subsequently entered into by the United States, and concluded that these treaties either impliedly, or as in the case of the Belgian treaty under consideration explicitly] gave the consuls authority to cause proper order to be maintained on board, and to decide disputes between the officers and crew, but allowed the local authorities to interfere if the disorders taking place on board were of such a nature as to disturb the public tranquillity, and that is substantially all there is in the convention with Belgium which we have now to consider. This treaty is the law which now governs the conduct of the United States and Belgium towards each other in this particular. Each nation has granted to the other such local jurisdiction within its own dominion as may be necessary to maintain order on board a merchant vessel, but has reserved to itself the right to interfere if the disorder on board is of a nature to disturb the public tranquillity.

* * * [T]he only important question left for our determination is whether the thing which has been done—the disorder that has arisen—on board

this vessel is of a nature to disturb the public peace, or, as some writers term it, the "public repose," of the people who look to the state of New Jersey for their protection. If the thing done—"the disorder," as it is called in the treaty—is of a character to affect those on shore or in the port when it becomes known, the fact that only those on the ship saw it when it was done, is a matter of no moment. Those who are not on the vessel pay no special attention to the mere disputes or quarrels of the seamen while on board, whether they occur under deck or above. Neither do they, as a rule, care for anything done on board which relates only to the discipline of the ship, or to the preservation of order and authority. Not so, however, with crimes which from their gravity awaken a public interest as soon as they become known, and especially those of a character which every civilized nation considers itself bound to provide a severe punishment for when committed within its own jurisdiction. In such cases inquiry is certain to be instituted at once to ascertain how or why the thing was done, and the popular excitement rises or falls as the news spreads, and the facts become known. It is not alone the publicity of the act, or the noise and clamor which attends it, that fixes the nature of the crime, but the act, itself. If that is of a character to awaken public interest when it becomes known, it is a "disorder," the nature of which is to affect the community at large, and consequently to invoke the power of the local government whose people have been disturbed by what was done. The very nature of such an act is to disturb the quiet of a peaceful community, and to create, in the language of the treaty, a "disorder" which will "disturb tranquillity and public order on shore or in the port." The principle which governs the whole matter is this: Disorders which disturb only the peace of the ship or those on board are to be dealt with exclusively by the sovereignty of the home of the ship, but those which disturb the public peace may be suppressed, and, if need be, the offenders punished, by the proper authorities of the local jurisdiction. It may not be easy at all times to determine to which of the two jurisdictions a particular act of disorder belongs. Much will undoubtedly depend on the attending circumstances of the particular case, but all must concede that felonious homicide is a subject for the local jurisdiction; and that, if the proper authorities are proceeding with the case in a regular way the consul has no right to interfere to prevent it. * * *

The judgment of the circuit court is affirmed.

### *Notes*

1. If the local police and judicial authorities may decide for themselves whether a particular incident disturbs the peace of the port, even though there is no actual disturbance, can it be said that the "peace of the port" doctrine ever allows the foreign vessel to claim immunity as of right? The British view is that "the subjection of the ship to the local criminal jurisdiction is * * * complete and that any derogation from it is a matter of comity in the discretion of the coastal state." Brierly, The Law of Nations 223 (6th ed. Waldock 1963). When the United States prohibition laws were held in Cunard S.S. Co. v. Mellon, 262 U.S. 100, 43 S.Ct. 504, 67 L.Ed. 894 (1923) to be applicable to foreign vessels temporarily in United States ports, the protests of foreign governments were based almost entirely on appeals to comity. Jessup, The Law of Territorial Waters and Maritime Jurisdiction 221–28 (1927). For general discussions of criminal jurisdiction over visiting foreign vessels, see id. at 144–94; Stanger,

Criminal Jurisdiction over Visiting Armed Forces 43–54 (Naval War College International Law Studies 1957–1958) (1965).

2. As the Chief Justice indicates in *Wildenhus' Case,* states customarily resort to international agreements in order to reconcile potential conflicts of jurisdiction that might arise from the presence of merchantmen in foreign ports. The Consular Convention of 1951 between the United States and the United Kingdom (3 U.S.T. 3426, T.I.A.S. No. 2494, 165 U.N.T.S. 121) provides in Article 22(2):

> Without prejudice to the right of the administrative and judicial authorities of the territory to take cognizance of crimes or offenses committed on board the vessel when she is in the ports or in the territorial waters of the territory and which are cognizable under the local law or to enforce local laws applicable to vessels in ports and territorial waters or persons and property thereon, it is the common intention of the High Contracting Parties that the administrative and police authorities of the territory should not, except at the request or with the consent of the consular officer,
>
> (a) concern themselves with any matter taking place on board the vessel unless for the preservation of peace and order or in the interests of public health or safety, or
>
> (b) institute prosecutions in respect of crimes or offenses committed on board the vessel unless they are of a serious character or involve the tranquillity of the port or unless they are committed by or against persons other than the crew.

Compare The 1982 Convention Article 27.

3. "It may be doubted whether in the absence of a concession by treaty, the territorial sovereign is deterred by the operation of any rule of international law from exercising through its local courts jurisdiction over civil controversies between masters and members of a crew, when the judicial aid of its tribunals is invoked by the latter, and notably when a libel *in rem* is filed against the ship. It is to be observed, however, that American courts exercise discretion in taking or withholding jurisdiction according to the circumstances of the particular case. Their action in so doing is not to be regarded as indicative of any requirement of public international law." Hyde at 742–43. On the application of the doctrine of *forum non conveniens* in litigation involving foreign merchant vessels and seamen, see The Ester, 190 Fed. 216 (E.D.S.C.1911) (summary of United States practice); Bickel, The Doctrine of Forum Non Conveniens as Applied in the Federal Courts in Matters of Admiralty, 35 Cornell L.Q. 12 (1949).

After the court has decided to retain a case for decision, whether in the exercise of its sound discretion or in compliance with legislative mandate, it must decide whether the forum's jurisdiction to prescribe shall be deemed to have been exercised so that United States law applies to the issue presented. See, e.g., McCulloch v. Sociedad Nacional de Marineros de Honduras, 372 U.S. 10, 83 S.Ct. 671, 9 L.Ed.2d 547 (1963); Lauritzen v. Larsen, 345 U.S. 571, 73 S.Ct. 921, 97 L.Ed. 1254 (1953).

The United States has not ordinarily applied its law to events and transactions aboard foreign vessels. In Lauritzen v. Larsen, the U.S. Supreme Court rejected the applicability to a foreign vessel of the Jones Act, providing for compensation to seamen for injury suffered in the course of their employment. "By usage as old as the Nation, such statutes have been construed to apply only to areas and transactions in which American law would be considered operative under prevalent doctrines of international law." Lauritzen v. Larsen, 345 U.S. 571, 577, 73 S.Ct. 921, 926, 97 L.Ed. 1254, 1265 (1953):

> International or maritime law in such matters as this does not seek uniformity and does not purport to restrict any nation from making and altering its laws to govern its own shipping and territory. However, it aims at stability and order through usages which considerations of comity, reciprocity and long-range interest have developed to define the domain which each nation will claim as its own. Maritime law, like our municipal law, has attempted to avoid or resolve conflicts between competing laws by ascertaining and valuing points of contact between the transaction and the states or governments whose competing laws are involved. The criteria, in general, appear to be arrived at from weighing of the significance of one or more connecting factors between the shipping transaction regulated and the national interest served by the assertion of authority. It would not be candid to claim that our courts have arrived at satisfactory standards or apply those that they profess with perfect consistency. But in dealing with international commerce we cannot be unmindful of the necessity for mutual forbearance if retaliations are to be avoided; nor should we forget that any contact which we hold sufficient to warrant application of our law to a foreign transaction will logically be as strong a warrant for a foreign country to apply its law to an American transaction.

Id. at 582, 73 S.Ct. at 928, 97 L.Ed. at 1267–68.

In listing and weighing the various factors connecting a particular incident to different states, the Court said: "[I]t is significant to us here that the weight given to the ensign overbears most other connecting events in determining applicable law. * * * [The law of the flag] must prevail unless some heavy counterweight appears." Id. at 585–86, 73 S.Ct. at 930, 97 L.Ed. at 1269–70.

But a tendency to find a "heavy counterweight" in Jones Act cases has become apparent. Hellenic Lines Ltd. v. Rhoditis involved injury to a Greek seaman on a ship flying the Greek flag, registered in Greece, and owned by a Panamanian corporation which was a subsidiary of a Greek corporation. But the Greek corporation had its principal offices in the United States and 95 percent of its shares were owned by a Greek citizen who was a permanent resident of the United States. The Court of Appeals said: "The Hero's flag is more symbolic than real * * *. Courts need not elevate symbols over reality. We therefore pierce the corporate veil and conclude that the Hero's flag is merely one of convenience." 412 F.2d 919, 923 (5th Cir.1969). The U.S. Supreme Court affirmed, 398 U.S. 306, 90 S.Ct. 1731, 26 L.Ed.2d 252 (1970), three justices dissenting.

In *Rhoditis,* the injury took place while the vessel was in an American port, although that factor did not appear to weigh heavily in the court's conclusion. In Antypas v. Cia. Maritima San Basilio, SA, 541 F.2d 307 (2d Cir.1976), cert. denied, 429 U.S. 1098, 97 S.Ct. 1116, 51 L.Ed.2d 545 (1977), where the injury took place on the high seas, the court applied the Jones Act on the basis of substantial contacts with the United States. But see De Oliveira v. Delta Marine Drilling Co., 707 F.2d 843 (5th Cir.1983), reh'g denied, 715 F.2d 577; Perez & Compania (Cataluna), S.A. v. Triton Pacific Maritime Corp., 826 F.2d 1449 (5th Cir.1987).

4. Vessels in distress that enter the territorial waters of a state in search of refuge or as a result of *force majeure* or other necessity are generally exempt from the jurisdiction of the port state. See Kate A. Hoff Claim (United States v. Mexico, 1929), 4 U.N.R.I.A.A. 444 (1951). However, "if the vessel or those on

board commit an offense against the local law subsequent to the entry in distress, the littoral state's power to punish is undiminished." Harvard Research in International Law, Draft Convention on the Law of Territorial Waters, 23 A.J.I.L.Spec.Supp. 241, 299 (1929). On the right of entry in distress, see generally Jessup, The Law of Territorial Waters and Maritime Jurisdiction 194–208 (1927); 2 Hackworth at 277–82; 2 O'Connell at 685–87. On the right of entry into ports in general, see Lowe, The Right of Entry into Maritime Ports in International Law, 14 San Diego L.Rev. 597 (1977). See also Restatement (Third) § 512, Comment *c,* Reporters' Note 3.

5. Restatement (Third) § 512, Reporters' Notes 5 and 6 state:

> 5. *Jurisdiction over foreign vessels in port.* Once a commercial ship voluntarily enters a port, it becomes subject to the jurisdiction of the coastal state. Cunard S.S. Co. v. Mellon, 262 U.S. 100, 124, 43 S.Ct. 504, 507, 67 L.Ed. 894 (1923); Benz v. Compania Naviera Hidalgo, S.A., 353 U.S. 138, 142, 77 S.Ct. 699, 1 L.Ed.2d 709 (1957). See § 502, Comment *d.*
>
> The coastal state "may out of considerations of public policy choose to forego the exertion of its jurisdiction or to exert the same in only a limited way, but this is a matter resting solely within its discretion." Cunard S.S. Co. v. Mellon, supra, at 124, 43 S.Ct. at 507.
>
> * * *
>
> Jurisdiction over foreign vessels in port is frequently limited by bilateral agreement. See, *e.g.,* United States–United Kingdom Consular Convention, 1951, Art. 22, 3 U.S.T. 3426, T.I.A.S. No. 2494, 165 U.N.T.S. 121.
>
> The authority of the coastal state generally applies to ships "voluntarily in port," not to ships driven to take refuge in a port by *force majeure* or other necessity. See Kate A. Hoff Claim (United States v. Mexico, 1929), 4 R.Int'l Arb. Awards 444 (1951); but see Cushin and Lewis v. The King, [1935] Can.Exch. 103, [1933–34] Ann.Dig. 207 ("putting into port under constraint does not carry any legal right to exemption from local law or local jurisdiction"). See also statement by Secretary Webster, August 1, 1842, 2 Moore, Digest of International Law 353, 354 (1906).
>
> For a study of the treatment by different states of foreign merchant vessels in port, see reports by the UNCTAD Secretariat, U.N.Docs. TD/B/C.4/136 (1975) and TD/B/C.4/158 (1977).
>
> 6. *Warships and other government ships operated for noncommercial purposes.* A warship (§ 501, Reporters' Note 1) in a foreign port must comply with the laws and regulations of the coastal state relating to navigation and safety. See LOS Convention, Art. 21(1) and (4); see also Harvard Research in International Law, The Law of Territorial Waters, 23 Am.J.Int'l L.Spec.Supp. 328 (1929). For an example of such legislation, see the Spanish order of March 23, 1958, Art. 6, U.N. Legislative Series, National Legislation and Treaties Relating to the Law of the Sea 145, 148 (U.N.Pub. ST/LEG/SER.B/19) (1980). If any such ship does not comply with port regulations, the flag state is internationally responsible for any damage caused, and the ship may be required to leave the port. See LOS Convention, Arts. 30–31.
>
> The coastal state has no jurisdiction over offenses committed on board foreign warships or other government ships operated for non-commercial purposes. See Bustamante Code of Private International Law, Havana,

1928, Art. 300, 86 L.N.T.S. 111, 4 Hudson, International Legislation 2279, 2323 (1931). (The United States is not a party to this instrument.) Under international law, government-owned vessels not used for commercial purposes enjoy immunity from arrest, attachment, or execution. See § 457, Reporters' Note 7. But there is no immunity for a foreign public vessel from a maritime lien based upon a commercial activity of the foreign state. See § 455(4) and Reporters' Note 3 thereto.

*b. Jurisdiction of the Flag State*

## UNITED STATES v. FLORES

Supreme Court of the United States, 1933.
289 U.S. 137, 53 S.Ct. 580, 77 L.Ed. 1086.

JUSTICE STONE: By indictment found in the District Court for Eastern Pennsylvania it was charged that appellee, a citizen of the United States, murdered another citizen of the United States upon the Steamship Padnsay, an American vessel, while at anchor in the Port of Matadi, in the Belgian Congo, a place subject to the sovereignty of the Kingdom of Belgium, and that appellee, after the commission of the crime, was first brought into the Port of Philadelphia, a place within the territorial jurisdiction of the District Court. * * * [T]he Padnsay, at the time of the offense charged, was unloading, being attached to the shore by cables, at a point 250 miles inland from the mouth of the Congo river.

The District Court * * * sustained a demurrer to the indictment and discharged the prisoner on the ground that the court was without jurisdiction to try the offense charged. 3 F.Supp. 134. The case comes here by direct appeal * * *.

Sections 273 and 275 of the Criminal Code, 18 U.S.C. §§ 452, 454 (18 U.S.C.A. §§ 452, 454), define murder and fix its punishment. Section 272, upon the construction of which the court below rested its decision, makes punishable offenses defined by other sections of the Criminal Code, among other cases, "when committed within the admiralty and maritime jurisdiction of the United States and out of the jurisdiction of any particular State on board any vessel belonging in whole or in part to the United States" or any of its nationals. And by section 41 of the Judicial Code, 28 U.S.C. § 102 (28 U.S.C.A. § 102), venue to try offenses "committed upon the high seas, or elsewhere out of the jurisdiction of any particular State or district," is "in the district where the offender is found, or into which he is first brought." As the offense charged here was committed on board a vessel lying outside the territorial jurisdiction of a state * * *, and within that of a foreign sovereignty, the court below was without jurisdiction to try and punish the offense unless it was within the admiralty and maritime jurisdiction of the United States.

Two questions are presented on this appeal, first, whether the extension of the judicial power of the federal government "to all Cases of admiralty and maritime Jurisdiction," by article 3, § 2, of the Constitution confers on Congress power to define and punish offenses perpetrated by a citizen of the United States on board one of its merchant vessels lying in navigable waters within the territorial limits of another sovereignty; and second, whether

Congress has exercised that power by the enactment of section 272 of the Criminal Code under which the indictment was found.

[The Court held that Congress had the constitutional power to define and punish crimes on American vessels in foreign waters, and that the language of the statute making it applicable to offenses committed on an American vessel outside the jurisdiction of a state "within the admiralty and maritime jurisdiction of the United States" was broad enough to include crimes in the "territorial waters" of a foreign country. Mr. Justice Stone continued:]

It is true that the criminal jurisdiction of the United States is in general based on the territorial principle, and criminal statutes of the United States are not by implication given an extraterritorial effect. United States v. Bowman, 260 U.S. 94, 98, 43 S.Ct. 39, 67 L.Ed. 149; compare Blackmer v. United States, 284 U.S. 421, 52 S.Ct. 252, 76 L.Ed. 375. But that principle has never been thought to be applicable to a merchant vessel which, for purposes of the jurisdiction of the courts of the sovereignty whose flag it flies to punish crimes committed upon it, is deemed to be a part of the territory of that sovereignty, and not to lose that character when in navigable waters within the territorial limits of another sovereignty. * * * Subject to the right of the territorial sovereignty to assert jurisdiction over offenses disturbing the peace of the port, it has been supported by writers on international law, and has been recognized by France, Belgium, and other continental countries, as well as by England and the United States. * * *

A related but different question, not presented here, may arise when jurisdiction over an offense committed on a foreign vessel is asserted by the sovereignty in whose waters it was lying at the time of its commission, since for some purposes, the jurisdiction may be regarded as concurrent, in that the courts of either sovereignty may try the offense.

There is not entire agreement among nations or the writers on international law as to which sovereignty should yield to the other when the jurisdiction is asserted by both. See Jessup, the Law of Territorial Waters, 144–193. The position of the United States exemplified in Wildenhus's Case, 120 U.S. 1, 7 S.Ct. 385, 30 L.Ed. 565, has been that at least in the case of major crimes, affecting the peace and tranquillity of the port, the jurisdiction asserted by the sovereignty of the port must prevail over that of the vessel. * * *

This doctrine does not impinge on that laid down in United States v. Rodgers [150 U.S. 249, 14 S.Ct. 109, 37 L.Ed. 1071 (1893)], that the United States may define and punish offenses committed by its own citizens on its own vessels while within foreign waters where the local sovereign has not asserted its jurisdiction. In the absence of any controlling treaty provision, and any assertion of jurisdiction by the territorial sovereign, it is the duty of the courts of the United States to apply to offenses committed by its citizens on vessels flying its flag, its own statutes, interpreted in the light of recognized principles of international law. So applied the indictment here sufficiently charges an offense within the admiralty and maritime jurisdiction of the United States and the judgment below must be reversed.

### *Notes*

1. Compare the 1982 Convention, Art. 94 (duties of the flag state) and Art. 97 (penal jurisdiction in matters of collision), p. 1335 supra, with Restatement (Third) § 502 (rights and duties of flag state), p. 1334 supra.

2. See the 1982 Convention, Art. 27 (criminal jurisdiction on board a foreign ship) and Art. 28 (civil jurisdiction in relation to foreign ships), p. 1337 and p. 1338, supra.

3. Would the Court have reached the same result if the defendant had not been a United States national? In Regina v. James Anderson, 11 Cox Crim.Cas. 198 (Ct.Crim.App.1868), an American crewman serving on a British vessel had been convicted of murder committed on board the vessel while the latter was in the Garonne River in France, about forty-five miles from the sea and about 300 yards from the nearest bank. The court upheld the conviction despite defendant's argument that the court had no jurisdiction, pointing out that although "the prisoner was subject to the American jurisprudence as an American citizen, and to the law of France as having committed an offense within the territory of France, yet he must also be considered as subject to the jurisdiction of British law, which extends to the protection of British vessels, though in ports belonging to another country." Id. at 204 (Bovill, C.J.)

4. In United States v. Reagan, 453 F.2d 165 (6th Cir.1971), the defendant was accused of killing a fellow seaman on an American vessel in a German harbor. The Court said in part:

> Since there is no "controlling treaty provision" the resolution of the question before us turns upon whether there has been "any assertion of jurisdiction by the territorial sovereign." It is our view that there was no "assertion of jurisdiction" by Germany and, therefore, that the district court was not without jurisdiction.
>
> The record shows that Reagan was taken into custody by German authorities on December 16, 1966, and judicially committed to a German mental institution on December 17, 1966, when his ship went to sea. He was subsequently released (after the return of the *SS Thunderbird* to port) and on April 5, 1967 the appropriate local court refused to issue a warrant for Reagan's arrest requested by the local prosecutor, finding that there was no probable cause for the issuance of such a warrant. The German court had before it the results of a rather extensive police investigation.
>
> * * * We do not believe that this preliminary proceeding constituted an "assertion of jurisdiction" by the local sovereign which would operate to oust the jurisdiction of the flag sovereign. It would appear that for whatever its reasons, the German court declined to "assert jurisdiction" within the meaning of *Flores,* supra. The application of the doctrine of "concurrent jurisdiction" is based on principles of comity. Assertion by the court below of its own jurisdiction in no way infringed upon the jurisdiction of the German court. The appropriate German authorities carefully scrutinized the matter and no formal charges were ever brought. There was no determination of Reagan's guilt or innocence. A different case would be presented if Reagan had been brought to trial in Germany or perhaps even if he had been indicted in Germany. We hold that the district court did have proper subject matter jurisdiction.

Id. at 171.

5. In March 1920, Charles Vincenti, a citizen of the United States, was arrested while on an American motorboat in British territorial waters off Bimini, Bahama Islands, British West Indies, by a special officer of the Department of Justice and by two internal-revenue agents holding a warrant against him for unlawful sale of liquor in Maryland and was taken back to the United States, although the motorboat was fired upon and pursued by British officials. Subsequently, the Department of State informed the British Ambassador that—

> * * * you will observe that the persons who arrested Vincenti and forcibly removed him from the Biminis Islands, acted on their own initiative and without the knowledge or approval of this Government in any way, and have been reprimanded and indefinitely suspended for their participation in the affair. Furthermore, it appears that Vincenti's bail has been exonerated and all proceedings subsequent to his unlawful arrest have been revoked. The incident is greatly regretted by this Government and I trust that the steps taken to make amends for it are entirely satisfactory to your Government.

The Ambassador replied that the action taken by the Government was satisfactory.

1 Hackworth 624 (1940).

What circumstances distinguish the jurisdiction exercised by the United States in the Vincenti affair from that exercised in United States v. Flores, supra?

In United States v. Conroy, 589 F.2d 1258 (5th Cir.1979), cert. denied, 444 U.S. 831, 100 S.Ct. 60, 62 L.Ed.2d 40, the court held that the United States Coast Guard had the authority to search an American vessel in foreign territorial waters. In that case the local government had agreed to the search but the court suggested that permission of the local government was not required. Id. at 1268. See also p. 1256, Note 3 supra.

For the application of U.S. Constitutional principles to searches and seizures at sea, and the relation of Constitutional principles to applicable principles of the international law of the sea, see Henkin, The Constitution at Sea, 36 Maine L.Rev. 201 (1984). Compare the *Alvarez–Machain* and *Verdugo* cases p. 177 infra.

# Chapter 15

# INTERNATIONAL WATERWAYS AND OTHER COMMON AREAS

## SECTION 1. INTRODUCTION

There are a number of areas in the world that have not been brought under the authority of any state. Some of these are uninhabited islands, many of which have emerged in recent times. See Note, Eruptions in International Law: Emerging Volcanic Islands and the Law of Territorial Acquisition, 11 Cornell I.L.J. 121 (1978); Note, Legal Claims to Newly Emerged Islands, 15 San Diego L.Rev. 525 (1978). See also Comment, To Be Or Not To Be: The Republic of Minerva—Nation Founding Individuals, 12 Colum.J.Trans.L. 520 (1973), describing the efforts of private individuals to proclaim a republic on an artificially created island in the Pacific Ocean.

The high seas, although steadily shrinking before the ever broadening claims of coastal states, have also remained free from claims of exclusive sovereignty by states. On their status and the impact of the 1982 Law of the Sea Convention, see Chapter 15.

Some parts of the universe have become accessible only in recent times. Among these are the polar regions, the moon and outer space. In regard to those areas, the question has arisen to what extent they are subject to claims of territorial sovereignty. Over some of these areas, notably the Arctic areas, claims of territorial sovereignty have been made, based in part on contiguity, in part on attenuated occupation, and in part on the so-called sector principle. See Section 3. But in regard to other such areas, in particular the moon and outer space, claims of territorial sovereignty have not been made and in regard to others, namely the Antarctic regions, such claims have been maintained, but, at least temporarily, have been frozen. See Sections 3 and 4.

In a special position are international rivers and other waters that are on or straddle national boundaries. The claims of multiple sovereigns related originally to the navigation of such waters. In more recent times, claims to their use and to be safeguarded from pollution have taken on equal importance. These common rights and areas are considered in greater detail in the materials that follow.

# SECTION 2. INTERNATIONAL WATERCOURSES

## A. CONCEPT AND SCOPE

Unlike the oceans, rivers and other inland waters such as lakes and canals are within the jurisdiction of national states. However, when they constitute boundary waters (e.g., contiguous rivers), they are often the subject of treaties providing for shared use. Because of the "dual sovereignty" over such waters, limits on unilateral action affecting use by other riparians are generally recognized. Rivers which traverse two or more states (i.e., successive rivers) have also been the subject of international agreement by the riparian states, though the legal limitations on unilateral action under customary law are not as clear as in the case of contiguous waters. For example, the Declaration of Asuncion of 1971 relating to the River Plate requires bilateral agreement before use can be made of boundary rivers, but allows use of successive rivers "provided it causes no appreciable damage to other states." However, both contiguous and successive rivers are generally regarded as international in the sense that there are some customary law obligations of the riparian states. In the 18th and 19th centuries, these obligations related mainly to navigation. The Congress of Vienna, in its Final Act of 1815, recognized that the riparian states had equal rights of navigation on rivers which separate or traverse two or more states. Although such rights of navigation were contained in treaties for particular rivers, the Permanent Court of International Justice concluded that riparian states shared a "natural community of interest" and therefore a "common legal right" in the equal use of both contiguous and successive rivers. Case concerning the International Commission of the River Oder, P.C.I.J. Ser. A, No. 23, p. 27 (1929).

In recent years, the problems of shared use have shifted from navigation to other uses, notably for irrigation, power, flood control, industry, waste disposal, and domestic purposes. Moreover, reductions in the water supply in many parts of the world and the general impairment of the quality of water have intensified the demands and conflicts among states sharing the waters. An important effect has been recognition of the physical linkages of a river basin or "system." Tributaries, even when distant from the international river, affect the quantity and quality of the waters. So do underground waters which are estimated to constitute 90% of fresh water resources. As there are about 170 international drainage basins in the world (according to a United Nations study), the significance of the "basin" as the unit for international agreement has been widely recognized in treaties and in official and unofficial declarations. (See resolutions of the International Law Association and of the Institut de Droit International below). However, many states object to the concept of "basin" as the unit for imposing customary law obligations. They maintain it would impair their sovereign rights over their natural resources, that it is too vague to apply, and that its wider scope would make agreement more difficult to achieve.

These conflicting views have been evident in the effort of the International Law Commission to codify the principles of "the law of non-navigational uses of international watercourses." See Yearbooks of International Law Commission, beginning with 1974. Unless states are given an unlimited right to use water in their territory irrespective of effects on others—a position now largely repudiated—, it is difficult to avoid placing on such states responsibility in respect of actions in their territory which materially affect the flow or quality of water reaching other states. One cannot, in the light of present knowledge, limit such responsibility only to the particular rivers and lakes which divide or cross two or more states. It is necessary to include waters which flow into such rivers, whatever term is used to designate those waters. This is recognized in the Draft Articles submitted by Special Rapporteur Stephen C. McCaffrey at the forty-third session of the International Law Commission which, in Article 2, define an international "watercourse" as "a system of surface and underground waters constituting by virtue of their physical relationship a unitary whole and flowing into a common terminus." U.N.Gen.Ass. 46th Sess., Suppl. No. 10 (A/46/10), at p. 173 (1991). The resolutions adopted by the unofficial international legal bodies—the Institut de Droit International and the International Law Association—are in accord with that conclusion. While the specific rules of customary law are still subject to some debate, there is reason to believe that the principles adopted by these unofficial bodies will increasingly be used as the bases of agreement by the states concerned.

For a survey of existing treaties and state practice, see Report of U.N. Secretary-General, Legal Problems relating to the Utilization of International Rivers, in [1974] 2 Y.B.Int'l L.Comm'n 194. The experience in respect of particular river basins is examined in The Law of International Drainage Basins (Garretson, Hayton & Olmstead eds. 1967). See also Berber, Rivers in International Law (1959); Chauhan, Settlement of International Water Law Disputes in International Drainage Basins (1981); Zacklin, The Legal Regime of International Rivers and Lakes (1981); Godana, Africa's Shared Water Resources: Legal and Institutional Aspects of the Nile, Niger and Senegal River Systems (1985).

## B. USE AND DIVERSION

### *INTERNATIONAL LAW COMMISSION*

Report on Work of its 31st Session, 1979.
GAOR 34th Sess.Supp. No. 10 (A/34/10).
Paragraph 130, pp. 459–460.

A number of Commission members emphasized that the drafting of general principles on the law of the non-navigational uses of international watercourses must of necessity be carried out bearing in mind the existing rules of general customary international law applicable to the subject-matter. The many treaties on navigation, pollution and power production should be studied with a view to deducing such rules. Experience had shown that the regulation of a particular international watercourse could be settled under general international law. The general rules to be formulated by the Commission should be more than residual rules, since they would be founded on customary law. It was said to be generally recognized that under modern international law, a State did not enjoy complete freedom in determining the use of the water of international watercourses within its territory. It would clearly not be the purpose of drafting general rules on the subject to iron out the natural inequalities in resources between States, or to depreciate the importance of the principle of national sovereignty over natural resources. But it was equally clear that there had always been in international law perceptions of a duty owed to neighbours regarding the way in which the natural resources of a territory were used. This was particularly compelling in regard to the uses of an international watercourse, as water constituted a *shared* natural resource. Another cardinal principle was the reasonable and equitable use of the water of an international watercourse. It was unthinkable that a nation which lived on the banks of a river should lose that river entirely, as a result of the application of modern technology in the interests of a higher riparian State. It was equally unthinkable that a lower riparian State should refuse to receive a natural flow of water by erecting a dam for the benefit of its own hydroelectric resources, thereby causing that water to flood valuable land in a neighbouring State. Both upper and lower riparians were obliged to take due account of the interests of the other.

## LAKE LANOUX CASE

Arbitration between France and Spain.
Int.Law Reports 101 (1957).

[The case arose out of a treaty between France and Spain of 1866 relating to the flow of boundary water which safeguarded the right of Spain to the natural flow of water into the River Carol, an outlet of Lake Lanoux. A French proposal to use the lake waters for hydroelectric generation was objected to by Spain, because it would change the natural flow. The arbitral tribunal found that the treaty would not be violated by France, since it would provide the previous quantity of water. The parties also argued on the basis of customary law and the tribunal acknowledged that the treaty should be interpreted by taking into account "international common law." The opinion of the tribunal on legal principles in the absence of agreement includes the following passages relating to the duty to negotiate]:

In effect, in order to appreciate in its essence the necessity for prior agreement, one must envisage the hypothesis in which the interested States cannot reach agreement. In such case, it must be admitted that the State which is normally competent has lost its right to act alone as a result of the unconditional and arbitrary opposition of another State. This amounts to admitting a "right of assent," a "right of veto," which at the discretion of one State paralyzes the exercise of the territorial jurisdiction of another.

That is why international practice prefers to resort to less extreme solutions by confining itself to obliging the States to seek, by preliminary negotiations, terms for an agreement, without subordinating the exercise of their competences to the conclusion of such an agreement. Thus, one speaks, although often inaccurately, of the "obligation of negotiating an agreement." In reality the engagements thus undertaken by states take very diverse forms and have a scope which varies according to the procedures intended for their execution; but the reality of the obligations thus undertaken is incontestable and sanctions can be applied in the event, for example, of an unjustified breaking off of the discussions, abnormal delays, disregard of the agreed procedures, systematic refusals to take into consideration adverse proposals or interests, and, more generally, in cases of violation of good faith.

* * * International practice reflects the conviction that States ought to strive to conclude such agreements: there would thus appear to be an obligation to accept in good faith all communications and contacts which could, by a broad comparison of interests and good will, provide States with the best conditions for concluding agreements. * * *

But international practice does not so far permit more than the following conclusions: the rule that States may utilize the hydraulic power of international watercourses only on condition of a prior agreement between the interested States cannot be established as a custom, even less as a general principle of law.

* * *

As a matter of form, the upstream State has, procedurally, a right of initiative; it is not obliged to associate the downstream State in the elaboration of its schemes. If, in the course of discussions, the downstream State submits schemes to it, the upstream State must examine them, but it has the right to give preference to the solution contained in its own scheme provided it takes into consideration in a reasonable manner the interests of a downstream State.

## *HELSINKI RULES ON THE USES OF THE WATERS OF INTERNATIONAL RIVERS*

International Law Association, Report of the Fifty–Second Conference, Helsinki 477 (1966).

Art. 1. The general rules of international law as set forth in these chapters are applicable to the use of the waters of an international drainage basin except as may be provided otherwise by convention, agreement or binding custom among the basin States.

Art. 2. An international drainage basin is a geographical area extending over two or more States determined by the watershed limits of the system of waters, including surface and underground waters, flowing into a common terminus.

COMMENT:

*(a) General.* Historically, the concern regarding use of an international river was almost completely for navigation, and there was little necessity for dealing with any portion of an international drainage basin other than the navigable channel of the stream.

With the relatively recent multi-use development of international rivers, the concern is no longer limited to the navigable portion of the international river, but rather encompasses all waters included in the entire system comprising the international drainage basin.

The drainage basin is an indivisible hydrologic unit which requires comprehensive consideration in order to effect maximum utilization and development of any portion of its waters. This conclusion is particularly significant when it is recognized that a state, although not riparian to the principal stream of the basin, may nevertheless supply substantial quantities of water to that stream; such a state thus is in a position to interfere with the supply of water through action with respect to the water flowing within its own territory.

Therefore, in order to accommodate potential or existing conflicts in instances of multi-use development and to provide the optimum rational development of a common resource for the benefit of each State in whose territory a portion of the system lies, the drainage basin approach has become a necessity.

Art. 3. A "basin State" is a State the territory of which includes a portion of an international drainage basin.

Art. 4. Each basin State is entitled, within its territory, to a reasonable and equitable share in the beneficial uses of the waters of an international drainage basin.

COMMENT:

*(a) General.* This Article reflects the key principle of international law in this area that every basin State in an international drainage basin has the right to the reasonable use of the waters of the drainage basin. It rejects the unlimited sovereignty position, exemplified by the "Harmon Doctrine," which has been cited as supporting the proposition that a State has the unqualified right to utilise and dispose of the waters of an international river flowing through its territory; such a position imports its logical corollary, that a State has no right to demand continued flow from co-basin States.

The Harmon Doctrine has never had a wide following among States and has been rejected by virtually all States which have had occasion to speak out on the point. It is noteworthy that, in the recent international rivers dispute between Bolivia and Chile over the Lauca River, Chile, the upper basin State, despite the heat of the controversy, did not assert the Harmon Doctrine in an attempt to justify its conduct; on the contrary it recognized that Bolivia has certain rights in the waters. See note from Bolivian Ambassador to the Chairman of the Council of the O.A.S., OEA/Ser.B/VI, April 15th, 1962. Similarly in the Jordan Basin dispute between Israel and certain Arab States both sides have adhered to the position that each is entitled to a reasonable share of the basin waters. 31 Dept. State Bull. 132 (1954); See U.S. Security Council Off.Rec., Supp. January–March, 1962, at 87–88 (S/5084) (1962). * * *

Art. 5. (1) What is a reasonable and equitable share within the meaning of Article 4 is to be determined in the light of all the relevant factors in each particular case.

(2) Relevant factors which are to be considered include, but are not limited to:

(a) the geography of the basin, including in particular the extent of the drainage area in the territory of each basin State;

(b) the hydrology of the basin, including in particular the contribution of water by each basin State;

(c) the climate affecting the basin;

(d) the past utilization of the waters of the basin, including in particular existing utilization;

(e) the economic and social needs of each basin State;

(f) the population dependent on the waters of the basin in each basin State;

(g) the comparative costs of alternative means of satisfying the economic and social needs of each basin State;

(h) the availability of other resources;

(i) the avoidance of unnecessary waste in the utilization of waters of the basin;

(j) the practicability of compensation to one or more of the co-basin States as a means of adjusting conflicts among uses; and

(k) the degree to which the needs of a basin State may be satisfied, without causing substantial injury to a co-basin State.

(3) The weight to be given to each factor is to be determined by its importance in comparison with that of other relevant factors. In determining what is a reasonable and equitable share, all relevant factors are to be considered together and a conclusion reached on the basis of the whole.

Art. 6. A use or category of uses is not entitled to any inherent preference over any other use or category of uses.

Art. 7. A basin State may not be denied the present reasonable use of the waters of an international drainage basin to reserve for a co-basin State a future use of such waters.

Art. 8. (1) An existing reasonable use may continue in operation unless the factors justifying its continuance are outweighed by other factors leading to the conclusion that it be modified or terminated so as to accommodate a competing incompatible use.

(2)(a) A use that is in fact operational is deemed to have been an existing use from the time of the initiation of construction directly related to the use or, where such construction is not required, the undertaking of comparable acts of actual implementation.

(b) Such a use continues to be an existing use until such time as it is discontinued with the intention that it be abandoned.

(3) A use will not be deemed an existing use if at the time of becoming operational it is incompatible with an already existing reasonable use.

* * *

## *Notes*

1. In 1951, the United States proposed a plan for building a dam on one of the tributaries of the Columbia River for flood control and power generation for the benefit of both the United States and Canada. The project would have created a lake some 100 miles long, of which 42 miles would have been in

Canada. The two Governments disagreed on the desirability of the project and on the compensation to be paid to Canadian interests affected, and in 1956 decided to undertake a study of the waters that flow across the international boundary. In 1959, the International Joint Commission established by the two Governments submitted a report on "principles for determining and apportioning benefits from cooperative use of storage of waters and electrical interconnection within the Columbia River System." In formulating the principles, the Commission "was guided by the basic concept that the principles * * * should result in an equitable sharing of the benefits attributable to their cooperative undertakings and that these should result in an advantage to each country as compared with alternatives available to that country. * * *" 3 Whiteman 986. Thereafter, the two Governments entered into negotiations which resulted in a Treaty between the United States and Canada Relating to the Cooperative Development of Water Resources of the Columbia River Basin, January 17, 1961, 15 U.S.T. 1555, T.I.A.S. No. 5638. The agreement entered into force in 1964. See also Agreement with Canada Concerning a Permanent Engineering Board for the Columbia River Basin, October 4, 1965, 16 U.S.T. 1263, T.I.A.S. No. 5877. See Austin, Canadian–United States Practice and Theory Respecting the International Law of International Rivers: A Study of the History and Influence of the Harmon Doctrine, 37 Can.B.Rev. 393 (1959); Cohen, Some Legal and Policy Aspects of the Columbia River Dispute, 36 Can.B.Rev. 25 (1958); Bourne, The Columbia River Controversy, 37 Can.B.Rev. 444 (1959).

2. Utilization of the Indus River, a major river system of the Indian subcontinent, has been a source of intense friction between India and Pakistan. The Indus, which rises in the Himalayas, had been used for irrigation from the beginning of civilization in the area. When the Indian subcontinent was partitioned between India and Pakistan in 1947, and those states gained their independence, the boundary was drawn across the Punjab in such a way that the headwaters of many tributaries were in India, while the Indus itself, and several tributaries were in Pakistan. The boundary also cut across the irrigation canal system leaving the control works in several cases in India. At the time of independence and partition, the Indian Independence Act, the Boundary Commission and the Arbitral Tribunal established to resolve questions arising out of partition did not deal specifically with the distribution of the water resources, but the Arbitral Tribunal handed down decisions predicated on continued supplies of water for irrigation. Disputes continued to arise after the Arbitral Tribunal finished its work, and several attempts at a permanent solution, including an effort to refer the matter to the International Court of Justice, failed. Between 1952 and 1954, Indian, Pakistani, and World Bank engineers conducted technical studies of the river resources. Negotiations continued from 1954 to 1960, and on September 19, 1960, India and Pakistan signed the Indus Waters Treaty, 419 U.N.T.S. 125. The International Bank for Reconstruction and Development, which had been a moving force in the negotiations, also signed in view of the fact that the treaty and annexes conferred certain functions on the Bank. The treaty provides generally for Indian use of the eastern rivers and, during a transition period, requires India to limit her withdrawals for agricultural use and for storage and to make deliveries to Pakistan. Western rivers are allocated to Pakistan, and India is required not to interfere with their flow except for withdrawals for domestic and non-consumptive uses, certain quantities for agricultural use and for generation of power. Also a Permanent Indus Commission was established to serve as a channel of communication and to promote cooperation in development of the water resources of the Indus and its

tributaries. On the day the treaty was signed, Australia, Canada, the Federal Republic of Germany, New Zealand, Pakistan, the United Kingdom, the United States, and the World Bank signed the Indus Basin Development Fund Agreement, Sept. 16, 1960, 12 U.S.T. 19, T.I.A.S. No. 4671, 444 U.N.T.S. 259, which provides financing for development of the river resources. The case is particularly noteworthy as an illustration of the potential role of international financing organizations, which are able to mobilize expertise and international financial resources for development. See 3 Whiteman 1022–31.

3. As in the case of the Indus dispute, the dispute between Israel and Syria, Jordan and Lebanon over the Jordan River is but one aspect of a more general atmosphere of tension between Israel and its Arab neighbors. The Jordan River headwaters lie in Lebanon, Syria and Israel, and its extreme lower course lies within Jordan. Both the Arab states and Israel have separately proposed plans for utilization of the waters of the Jordan. The Arab plan has not been implemented due to inability of the Arab states concerned to agree on a concrete project or plan.

4. In the absence of hard and precise rules for equitable sharing, procedural requirements for advance notice, information, and consultation become more important. See U.N.G.A.Res. 3129 (XXVIII 1973). Such procedural requirements need to be specific in order to be effective. For discussion of problems and of the role of mixed commissions, see Schachter, Sharing the World's Resources 69–74 (1977).

5. On pollution of rivers and lakes, see Chapter 16, Section 2.

## C. NAVIGATION

There probably exists no customary right of freedom of navigation in rivers passing through more than one state; any state controlling both banks of a river can, in the absence of treaty obligations to the contrary, effectively regulate and even block shipping to and from upper and lower riparian states. Beginning in 1815, however, when the Congress of Vienna proclaimed a general freedom of navigation for riparian states on the international rivers of Europe, a number of agreements have established regimes for such waterways. Navigation on the Rhine was regulated by the Treaty of Mainz of 1831 and the Treaty of Mannheim of 1868. The Treaty of Paris of 1856 extended the application of the principles of the Congress of Vienna to the Danube and its mouths, and an international commission charged with the improvement of navigational conditions was later created. The peace treaties that followed World War I extended the internationalization of the Danube and provided for future regulation of other rivers. In the Barcelona Convention of 1921 (7 L.N.T.S. 36), the contracting states agreed to accord to one another equality of treatment and freedom of navigation on "navigable waterways" under their sovereignty or authority; this Convention has, however, probably been of more theoretical than practical interest. The advent of World War II destroyed much of the progress that had been made in the interim, and in 1948 the Soviet-dominated Danube states concluded a Convention that rejected the principle of international control and set up a system of riparian regulation. See 1 Hackworth 596–610; 3 Whiteman 872–918; 1 O'Connell 625–39; 1 Oppenheim 575–78; Baxter, The Law of International Waterways 149–59 (1964).

# SECTION 3. THE POLAR REGIONS

*HACKWORTH, DIGEST OF INTERNATIONAL LAW*

Vol. 1, p. 456–58 (1940).

On January 29, 1934 the British Ambassador in Washington addressed a note to the Secretary of State, reading in part as follows:

> The United States Government will doubtless be aware that an expedition to the Antarctic led by Admiral Byrd left New Zealand on December 12th for a base in Ross dependency which was established on his previous expedition in 1928–1929. * * *
>
> His Majesty's Government in New Zealand understand that the expedition has the official backing of the United States Government and in these circumstances they feel it necessary to state that their attention has been drawn to articles in certain newspapers reporting that it is intended to establish a post office at Admiral Byrd's base in Ross dependency and that certain members of the expedition were before leaving the United States formally sworn in before the Postmaster General of the United States with the object of acting as postmasters at this post office. It is also understood that special stamps in connection with the expedition have been issued by the United States Government, and it has been reported that these will be used to frank letters posted at the expedition's base. While His Majesty's Government in New Zealand recognise that some allowance must be made for the absence of ordinary postal facilities in Ross dependency, they would point out that if a United States post office were to be officially established in the dependency, or if the United States Government were to sanction the use of United States postage stamps there without permission from the sovereign Power, such acts could not be regarded otherwise than as infringing the British sovereignty and New Zealand administrative rights in the dependency as well as the laws there in force.
>
> Although it is understood that the expedition is operating a wireless station in Ross dependency, no license for such a station was applied for, and similarly although it is understood that United States aircraft are being imported into the dependency for the purpose of making flights in or over its territory, the competent authorities received no application for permission for such flights. Since on his previous expedition Admiral Byrd established a wireless station at his base and carried aircraft to the dependency, and was not then required to obtain a license or formal permission he may have thought it unnecessary to do so on this occasion. His Majesty's Government in New Zealand are indeed willing to regard their offer of facilities as covering now, as on the previous expedition, permission both for the wireless station and for the flights over the dependency, but they would nevertheless point out that they would have preferred prior application to have been made to the competent authority by or on behalf of the expedition in accordance with the relevant legislation applicable. * * *

[On February 24, 1934, the State Department replied, indicating it was unnecessary to discuss the "interesting questions" contained in the British note and reserving "all rights which the United States or its citizens may have with respect to this matter." On November 14, 1934 the following was stated in an informal note to the British Ambassador:]

> It is understood that His Majesty's Government in New Zealand bases its claim of sovereignty on the discovery of a portion of the region in question. While it is unnecessary to enter into any detailed discussion of the subject at this time, nevertheless, in order to avoid misapprehension, it is proper for me to say, in the light of long established principles of international law, that I can not admit that sovereignty accrues from mere discovery unaccompanied by occupancy and use.

In reply, the following note, dated December 27, was handed to the Secretary of State by the British Ambassador on December 29:

> With reference to the letter which you were so good as to address to me on November 14th last, I have the honour, under instructions from His Majesty's Principal Secretary of State for Foreign Affairs, at the instance of His Majesty's Government in New Zealand to inform you that the supposition that the British claim to sovereignty over the Ross Dependency is based on discovery alone, and, moreover, on the discovery of only a portion of the region, is based on a misapprehension of the facts of the situation.
>
> 2. The Dependency was established and placed under New Zealand Administration by an Order in Council of 1923 in which the Dependency's geographical limits were precisely defined. Regulations have been made by the Governor General of New Zealand in respect of the Dependency and the British title has been kept up by the exercise in respect of the Dependency of administrative and governmental powers, e.g., as regards the issue of whaling licenses and the appointment of a special officer to act as magistrate for the Dependency.
>
> 3. * * * As regards Mr. Anderson's present mission, they understand that he is carrying letters to which are, or will be, affixed special stamps printed in the United States and that these stamps are to be cancelled and date-stamped on board the Expedition's vessel. They also understand that these stamps are intended to be commemorative of the Byrd Expedition and have been issued as a matter of philatelic interest.
>
> 4. In the above circumstances His Majesty's Government in New Zealand have no objection to the proposed visit of Mr. Anderson. They must, however, place it on record that, had his mission appeared to them to be designed as an assertion of United States sovereignty over any part of the Ross Dependency or as a challenge to British sovereignty therein, they would have been compelled to make a protest.

### *WHITEMAN, DIGEST OF INTERNATIONAL LAW*

Vol. 2, p. 1250–53 (1963).

In a note dated June 16, 1955, to the Secretary of State, the Australian Ambassador at Washington stated:

> I have the honour to refer to my letter of 11th March, 1949, depositing with the Government of the United States the Australian

Instrument of Ratification of the Convention of the World Meteorological Organization signed at Washington, D.C. on 11th October, 1947.

I wish to inform you that the Australian Government has now decided, by virtue of its membership of the World Meteorological Organization, to apply the Convention to the Australian Antarctic Territory which does not maintain its own meteorological service.

In his reply dated January 30, 1956, the Secretary of State, after acknowledging receipt of the Australian Ambassador's note and summarizing its contents, stated:

My Government wishes to point out, as it has on previous occasions, that it does not recognize any claims so far advanced in the Antarctic and reserves all rights accruing to the United States out of activities of nationals of the United States in the area. * * *

[The American Embassy in Santiago delivered the following aide memoire to the Foreign Minister of Chile on August 2, 1955:]

The Government of the United States of America notes Chilean law 11,846 was promulgated on June 17, 1955. That law purports to incorporate into Chilean provincial administration those areas claimed by Chile in the Antarctic. The Government of the United States wishes to reiterate that it has recognized no claims advanced with respect to the Antarctic by other countries and that it reserves all rights of the United States with respect to the area.

[The Department of State replied in like manner on November 5, 1956, to a Chilean memorandum transmitting a copy of a Decree implementing the above law.]

[On May 14, 1958, the Legal Adviser of the Department of State, Loftus Becker, said in the course of testimony before the Special Committee on Space and Astronautics of the United States Senate:]

* * * There [in Antarctica], for many, many years, the United States has been engaged in activities which under established principles of international law, without any question whatsoever, created rights upon which the United States would be justified in asserting territorial claims. I mean by that, claims to sovereignty over one or more areas of the Antarctic.

Notwithstanding this fact, the United States has not asserted any claim of sovereignty over any portion of Antarctica, although the United States has, at the same time, made it perfectly plain that it did not recognize any such claims made by other States.

Nonetheless, the United States has been consistent in asserting that under international law and practice, its activities in the Antarctic Continent have entitled it to rights in that area which it has at all times expressly reserved.

It is the position of the United States Government, and one well founded in international law, that the fact that the United States has not based a claim of sovereignty over one or more areas of Antarctica, upon the basis of the activities it has engaged in there, in no way derogates from the rights that were established by its activities.

## A. THE "SECTOR THEORY" AS APPLIED IN POLAR REGIONS

### *LAUTERPACHT, SOVEREIGNTY OVER SUBMARINE AREAS*

1950 Brit.Y.B.Int'l L. 376, 427.*

Some aspects of the doctrine of contiguity also underlie the claims to Arctic and Antarctic regions put forward by a number of states—such as Great Britain, Canada, New Zealand, France, Russia, and Norway—in so far as it is based on the so-called sector principle. By virtue of that principle areas have been claimed which are embraced by the projection northwards or southwards, as the case may be, of the areas bordering the respective maritime territories. While with regard to the Arctic these areas are, in a sense, contiguous to the territories of the states concerned, in the case of the Antarctic the contiguity is distinctly symbolic. In some cases an element of uncertainty is added to the situation by the fact that the territory claimed as the base of the sector is claimed by virtue of discovery. This applies, for instance, to Adélie Land claimed by France. While New Zealand has dissented from the suggestion that the Ross Dependency is claimed by virtue of discovery alone, the "effective settlement" of it has taken place largely by "display of State activity" in the wider sense such as issuing licenses and appointment of magistrates. Essentially, notwithstanding the controversial differences of the geographical features of the Arctic and Antarctic in relation to the mainland from which they project, the claims to them are based—in so far as they are based on legal grounds—on some as yet undefined kind of contiguity, variously referred to also as proximity, region of attraction, and continuity. It is of interest to note that when the Russian claim to Arctic islands was first put forward in 1916 it referred to them as constituting "an extension northward of the continental tableland [shelf] of Siberia."

### *ACADEMY OF SCIENCES OF THE U.S.S.R., INTERNATIONAL LAW*

190–93 (1961).

*Status of the Arctic.* The state territory of countries adjacent to the Arctic and having polar sectors in the Arctic includes all lands and islands lying within these sectors.

The term "polar sector of a State adjacent to the Arctic" means the expanse of which the base line is the coast of the given State, the apex the North Pole and the limits to either side the meridians from the North Pole to the eastern and western frontiers of the State.

It is in theory and practice recognized that all lands and islands discovered, as well as those which may be discovered in the future within the polar sector adjacent to the coast of a given State constitute part of that State's state territory. * * *

The status of the Soviet sector was determined by a Decree of the Central Executive Committee and the Council of People's Commissars of the

* Footnotes omitted. Reprinted by permission from the British Yearbook of International Law. Published by the Oxford University Press for the Royal Institute of International Affairs.

Soviet Union, dated April 15, 1926. This laid down that all lands and islands discovered, as well as those which may be discovered in the future, lying between the Arctic coast of the Soviet Union, the North Pole and the meridians 32°4′35″ East and 168°49′30″ West, are Soviet territory. An exception was made for islands which on April 15, 1926 the Soviet Union recognized as foreign state territory (that is, the eastern islands of the Spitzbergen Archipelago lying between 32° and 35° East and which are under the jurisdiction of Norway).

There are many reasons for the division of Arctic territories into sectors.

The States which have sectors in the Arctic are linked with the North Pole by an almost uninterrupted chain of islands or by a cap of almost unbroken ice which creates continuity between their mainland territory and their polar sectors.

The Arctic polar regions are sources of livelihood for the inhabitants of the coastal areas and are of exceptional economic importance to the State concerned. In the case of the Soviet Union, the Arctic regions are also of great importance from the point of view of defense, owing to their proximity to important centres.

The Arctic polar sectors have been substantially developed by the countries concerned and are partially settled. The Soviet people have played a particularly important part in the development of the Arctic. The study of the Arctic, including many areas lying outside the Soviet sector, has been a result of many centuries of consistent effort by Russian navigators and scientists, and of hard work and considerable material expenditure by the Soviet State and people.

*Status of Antarctica.* Interest in Antarctica began to develop at the end of the 19th century * * *.

The division of Antarctica into sectors gave rise to a prolonged conflict between Britain on the one hand and Argentina and Chile on the other.

The struggle of the capitalist States to partition Antarctica shows that the unilateral absorption of Antarctic territories is not an acceptable solution to the problem of the Antarctic regime. The problem of Antarctica can be justly solved only on an international basis, in a manner taking account of the special characteristics of its position.

Unlike those in the Arctic, sectors in Antarctica have no base lines, that is, the coast of the States claiming sectors. The mainland of Antarctica is thousands of miles away from other continents. Antarctica is of great importance to all countries, including the Soviet Union. From its waters come more than 90 per cent of the world's whale catch. * * *

The shortest intercontinental air routes may in the future lie across Antarctica. Finally, Antarctica is of interest to all countries including the Soviet Union, as a centre for important scientific research and observations. * * *

### *Notes*

1. The Norwegian Government in 1930 expressed its disapproval of the sector theory. The U.S. Minister to Norway informed the Department of State, in connection with a Norwegian expedition in the Antarctic:

> The Minister for Foreign Affairs told me the other day that Norway has no intention of annexing territory charted by the *Norvegia* but that it would object to applying the sector principle to the south polar regions * * *.

1 Hackworth 463.

Subsequently, the American Legation at Oslo advised the Department of State that, by a note of Nov. 5, 1930, the Norwegian Government had recognized the sovereignty of Canada over the Arctic islands known as "Sverdrup's Islands". The Minister added that Norway did not thereby acknowledge the so-called sector principle "which means the direct extension of Canada's borders converging to the North Pole." Id. at 465.

2. On June 14, 1991, the Arctic States (Canada, Denmark, Finland, Norway, Sweden, the U.S.S.R., and the United States) adapted the Arctic Environmental Protection Strategy. The objectives of this Strategy are to protect the Arctic environment and the indigenous peoples. The participating states commit themselves to meet periodically and to co-operate in achieving the Strategy's objectives.

3. See generally Legal Regimes of the Arctic: A Panel, 82 A.S.I.L.Proc. 315 (1988); Nature Protection in the Arctic: Recent Soviet Legislation, 41 Int'l & Comp. L.Q. 366 (1992).

## B. ANTARCTIC

Influenced perhaps by the momentum generated during the International Geophysical Year of 1957–58, during which scientific expeditions from many countries conducted research and experiments in Antarctica without regard to questions of territorial sovereignty, a conference called by the United States of those states having substantial interests in that continent succeeded in producing the Antarctic Treaty, signed on December 1, 1959, 12 U.S.T. 794, 402 U.N.T.S. 71. The most important provision of the treaty states that Antarctica "shall be used for peaceful purposes only" (Art. I), and, to that end, the treaty prohibits military installations, maneuvers, and weapons tests, including nuclear explosions of all kinds. The free exchange of scientific information and personnel is provided for (Art. III), and provision is made for the meeting at suitable intervals of representatives of contracting states in order to formulate and recommend measures in furtherance of the objectives of the treaty (Art. IX). In addition to other articles dealing with mutual inspection of Antarctic activities and installations by the contracting parties and with the exercise of jurisdiction over certain Antarctic personnel, the treaty provides in Article IV:

> 1. Nothing contained in the present Treaty shall be interpreted as:
>
> (a) a renunciation by any Contracting Party of previously asserted rights of or claims to territorial sovereignty in Antarctica;
>
> (b) a renunciation or diminution by any Contracting Party of any basis of claim to territorial sovereignty in Antarctica which it may have whether as a result of its activities or those of its nationals in Antarctica, or otherwise;
>
> (c) prejudicing the position of any Contracting Party as regards its recognition or non-recognition of any other State's right or claim or basis of claim to territorial sovereignty in Antarctica.

2. No acts or activities taking place while the present Treaty is in force shall constitute a basis for asserting, supporting or denying a claim to territorial sovereignty in Antarctica or create any rights of sovereignty in Antarctica. No new claim, or enlargement of an existing claim, to territorial sovereignty in Antarctica shall be asserted while the present Treaty is in force.

The Treaty contains no general provision governing jurisdiction over persons in Antarctica. It entered into force on June 23, 1961. As of January 1, 1992, the Treaty was in force for 41 states, including the United States. The Treaty may be amended at any time by unanimous vote of the contracting parties. At the expiration of thirty years from the date of entry into force, any of the original contracting parties may call for a conference of all contracting parties. The conference may amend the Treaty by majority vote. Failure to ratify any amendment constitutes withdrawal from the Treaty.

In 1980, the Convention on the Conservation of Antarctic Marine Living Resources, which came into force in 1982, was adopted. This Convention prescribes rather rigorous guidelines for the harvesting of any species. The target species is krill, a crustacean of about two inches that is the principal food of great whales and was thought, because of its being rich in protein and minerals, to be able to provide a major source of food for man and domestic animals. More recently, the interest in krill has abated.

Following adoption of the Convention on the Law of the Sea, the status of Antarctica was placed on the agenda of the 1983 General Assembly by some Third World nations. The question raised was whether Antarctica should be under the control of the parties to the Antarctica Treaty System or be part of the common heritage of mankind to be developed for the benefit of all nations. The parties to the ATS responded by inviting India and Brazil to become Consultative Parties and subsequently accepted China and Uruguay. They also invited all states that had acceded to the Treaty to send observers to their meetings and to participate in the discussions, but successfully resisted the creation of a U.N. Committee on Antarctica.

In June 1991, the Antarctic Treaty states approved the Protocol on Environmental Protection to the Antarctic Treaty. The Protocol is the most comprehensive multilateral agreement on the international protection of the environment. One of its most important features is the imposition of a moratorium on mining. On this Protocol, see Blay, New Trends in the Protection of the Antarctic Environment: The 1991 Madrid Protocol, 86 A.J.I.L. 377 (1992). This Protocol had been preceded by the Final Act and Convention on The Regulation of Antarctic Mineral Resource Activities, of June 2, 1988, 27 I.L.M. 859 (1988), by which the contracting states imposed substantial limitations on mineral resource activities in Antarctica.

### *Notes*

1. See generally Bernhardt, Sovereignty in Antarctica, 5 Calif.W.Int'l L.J. 297 (1975); Note, Sovereignty in Antarctica: The Anglo–Argentine Dispute, 5 Syr.J.Int'l L. & Comm. 119 (1977); Note, Quick Before It Melts: Toward a Resolution of the Jurisdictional Morass in Antarctica, 10 Cornell Int'l L.J. 173 (1976); Chopra, Antarctica in the United Nations: Rethinking the Problems and Prospects, 80 A.S.I.L. proc. 269 (1986); Joyner, The United States and Antarc-

tica: Rethinking the Interplay of Law and Interests, 20 Cornell Int'l L.J. 65 (1987); Scott, Protecting United States Interest in Antarctica, 26 San Diego L.Rev. 575 (1989); Hinkley, Protecting American Interests in Antarctica: The Territorial Claims Dilemma, 39 Naval L.Rev. 43 (1990).

2. The Antarctic Treaty also prohibits, in Article 5, the disposal of radioactive waste in Antarctica.

3. For additional measures seeking to protect the Antarctic environment, see Convention for the Conservation of Antarctic Seals, London, June 1, 1972, 29 U.S.T. 441, T.I.A.S. No. 8826, which, as of January 1, 1992, was in effect for 15 states, including the United States; and the Convention on the Conservation of Antarctic Marine Living Resources, Canberra, May 20, 1980, T.I.A.S. No. 10240, which, as of January 1, 1992, was in force for 28 states, including the United States.

4. For recent writings on Antarctica, see, e.g. Blay et al., Antarctica After 1991 (1989); Trofimov, Legal Status of Antarctica (1990); Suter, Antarctica: Private Property or Public Heritage? (1991); Sahurier, The International Law of Antarctica (1991); Redgwell, Antarctica, 39 Int'l & Comp.L.Q. 474 (1990); Bentham, Antarctica: A Minerals Regime, 8 J. Energy & Nat. Resources L. 120 (1990); Shepherd, The United States' Actions in Antarctica: The Legality, Practicality, and Morality of Applying the National Environmental Policy Act, 14 Geo. Mason U.L. Rev. 373 (1991); Bondareff, The Congress Acts to Protect Antarctica, 1 Terr.Sea J. 223 (1991); Deihl, Antarctica: An International Laboratory, 18 B.C.Envtl.Aff.L.Rev. 423 (1991); Redgwell, Antarctica, 40 Int'l & Comp. L.Q. 976 (1991); Herber, Mining or World Park? A Politico–Economic Analysis of Alternative Land Use Regimes in Antarctica, 31 Nat. Resources J. 839 (1991); Poole, Liability For Environmental Damage in Antarctica, 10 J. Energy & Nat. Resources 246 (1992).

## SECTION 4. THE MOON, OTHER CELESTIAL BODIES AND OUTER SPACE

### *TREATY ON PRINCIPLES GOVERNING THE ACTIVITIES OF STATES IN THE EXPLORATION AND USE OF OUTER SPACE, INCLUDING THE MOON AND OTHER CELESTIAL BODIES*

Done at London, Moscow, and Washington, January 27, 1967.

18 U.S.T. 2410, T.I.A.S. No. 6347, 610 U.N.T.S. 205.

Art. 1. The exploration and use of outer space, including the moon and other celestial bodies, shall be carried out for the benefit and in the interests of all countries, irrespective of their degree of economic or scientific development, and shall be the province of all mankind.

Outer space, including the moon and other celestial bodies, shall be free for exploration and use by all States without discrimination of any kind, on a basis of equality and in accordance with international law, and there shall be free access to all areas of celestial bodies.

There shall be freedom of scientific investigation in outer space, including the moon and other celestial bodies, and States shall facilitate and encourage international co-operation in such investigation.

Art. 2. Outer space, including the moon and other celestial bodies, is not subject to national appropriation by claim of sovereignty, by means of use or occupation, or by any other means.

* * *

[See Articles 3–13]

### *Notes*

1. As of January 1, 1992, this Treaty was in force for 98 states, including the United States.

2. The Treaty incorporates the principles enunciated in the Declaration of Legal Principles Governing the Activities of States in the Exploration and Uses of Outer Space, G.A.Res.1962 (XVII 1963) at 15. The major difference between the Treaty and the Declaration is the inclusion in the Treaty of articles concerning the military uses of space and providing for mutual inspection of facilities on the moon and other celestial bodies. See generally Dembling & Arons, The Evolution of the Outer Space Treaty, 33 J.Air.L. & Com. 419 (1967); Goedhuis, An Evaluation of the Leading Principles of the Treaty on Outer Space of 27th January, 1967, 15 Netherlands Int'l L.Rev. 17 (1968); Cheng, The 1967 Space Treaty, 95 J. du Droit International 532 (1968); 2 Whiteman 1312–14. Baker, Protection of the Outer Space Environment: History and Analysis of Article IX of the Outer Space Treaty, 12 Annals Air & Space L. 143 (1987). For a general discussion of cooperative efforts in outer space, see Gardner, Blueprint for Peace 246 (1966); Danilenko, Outer Space and the Multilateral Treaty–Making Process, 4 High Tech.L.J. 217 (1989); Jasentuliyana, Treaty Law and Outer Space: Can the United Nations Play an Effective Role?, 11 Annals Air & Space L. 219 (1986); Treaty Law and Outer Space: The Role of the United Nations: A Panel, 80 A.S.I.L.Proc. 368 (1986).

3. It is disputed where outer space begins. See generally Schachter, Who Owns the Universe, in Across the Space Frontier (Ryan ed. 1952). Many argue that the boundary should be near the lowest altitude (perigee) at which artificial earth satellites can remain in orbit without being destroyed by friction with the air (roughly 90 km above the surface of the earth). See Perek, Scientific Criteria for the Delimitation of Outer Space, 5 J.Space L. 111, 118 (1977). In 1968, the International Law Association adopted a resolution stating that the term "outer space" as used in the 1967 Treaty on Outer Space, supra, "includes all space at and above the lowest perigee achieved by * * * 27 January 1967, when the treaty was opened for signature, by any satellite put into orbit, without prejudice to the question whether it may or may not later be determined to include any part of space below such perigee." International Law Association, Report of the Fifty–Third Conference, xxii (Buenos Aires 1968). However, a study by COSPAR, U.N.Doc. A/AC. 105/164 (1976), indicates that it would be possible to build satellites with a high mass to area ratio which could survive even below 90 km. Should the boundary depend on a disintegration point that may vary depending on the type of satellite involved?

4. The reciprocal approach based on the theoretical limit of airflight calls for a boundary at about 84 km. See Haley, Space Law and Government 97 (1963). Critics note that this boundary would vary according to the configuration of the earth. Furthermore, technological progress has already made it possible for aircraft to exceed this limit by using rockets for part of their flight.

See Matte, Introductory Comments on the Aerospace Medium, in Proceedings of the Twentieth Colloquium on Outer Space 47, 48 (1978).

5. Some challenge the efforts to define the limits of outer space as unnecessary and possibly harmful and have advocated a "functional approach" which would base legal regimes governing space activities not on a boundary line, but on the nature of the activities. See McDougal, Lasswell & Vlasic, Law and Public Order in Space, 349–55 (1963); Matte, Aerospace Law 51 (1969); Matte, Introductory Comments on the Aerospace Medium, supra.

6. Is it possible to combine and reconcile these approaches? For an attempt, see Haanappel, Definition of Outer Space and Outer Space Activities, in Proceedings of the Twentieth Colloquium on the Law of Outer Space 53 (1978).

7. On July 13, 1976, the Soviet Union, Mongolia, Cuba, and the socialist states of Eastern Europe signed an agreement on the exploration and use of outer space for peaceful purposes. See 16 I.L.M. 1 (1977). The pact is a general pledge of mutual cooperation between states participating in the "Intercosmos" program.

8. On pollution of outer space, see Matter: Back Contamination Procedures and International Quarantine Regulations, 15 Colum.J.Transn.L. 17 (1976); Christol, The Modern International Law of Outer Space 129–51 (1982); Reijnen & Graaff, The Pollution of Outer Space, In Particular of the Geostationary Orbit: Scientific, Policy, and Legal Aspects (1989). On the use of nuclear power sources (NPS) in outer space, see id. at 765–810.

9. On space transportation systems (STS), see id. at 811–40.

10. On April 15, 1987, the United States and the U.S.S.R. concluded an Agreement on Cooperation in the Exploration and Use of Outer Space for Peaceful Purposes, 26 I.L.M. 622 (1987), by which the parties agreed to co-operate in space science, solar system exploration, space astronomy and astrophysics, earth science, solar-terrestrial physics, and space biology and medicine.

## THE GEOSTATIONARY ORBIT

The question of delimitation between air space and outer space was raised in 1976 when eight "equatorial" states (i.e., states with territory on the equator) claimed sovereign rights over that segment of the "geostationary orbit" above their territories. The geostationary orbit is a circular orbit of approximately 22,300 miles, above the earth's equator. A satellite placed in that orbit lies above the equator and turns on the polar axis of the earth in the same direction and at the same speed as the earth so that it appears stationary in relation to the underlying point. This orbit is used by satellites for telecommunication, broadcasting, meteorological services. For that reason, it is the most valuable and most utilized segment of outer space. Hundreds of geostationary satellites are in operation and billions of dollars have been invested in them.

The equatorial states asserted in the Bogota Declaration of 1976 that the segment of the geostationary orbit above their territory was part of their territory and that devices placed permanently in that segment require prior express authorization by the territorial state. One argument advanced by these states was that there was no agreed definition of outer space and hence no prohibition of an exercise of sovereign rights in space related to the underlying territory. They contended that the satellite was maintained in a stationary position by its relation to the territory beneath it and the gravitational "pull" of that area. The fact that the area was uniquely valuable and a limited resource distinguished it from the other areas of space that could be freely used by all. See Gorove, The Geostationary Orbit: Issues of Law and Policy, 73 A.J.I.L. 444 (1979).

The United States and a number of other countries rejected the claims of the equatorial states. They continued to place communication satellites in the geostationary zone. The International Telecommunications Union (ITU) also continued to allocate radio frequencies to states that requested them for the satellites, on a first-come, first-served, basis. While the ITU does not have any authority over orbital positions, it controls the allocations, because radio frequency is essential to the satellite's function. The allocations made by the ITU through the World Administrative Radio Conference for Space Telecommunications (WARC–ST) disregarded the claims of the equatorial states. Similarly, the U.N. Committee on the Peaceful Uses of Outer Space also rejected the claims of sovereign rights of the equatorial states. As of 1986, it appears that the issue is no longer pressed by the equatorial states, though they have not abandoned their claims.

A more complicated and controversial issue relating to the geostationary orbit concerns the allocation of frequencies on a first come, first served, basis. Many states have objected to that policy on the ground that permanent "slots" in the orbit spectrum will deny to late-comers the opportunity to utilize that valuable part of outer space in accordance with the principles of Article 1 of the 1967 treaty. One contention is that frequencies should be reserved and not presently allocated; another is that the frequency allocations should be made for a relatively short period so that the countries that later desire such use would have desirable frequencies allocated to them. The fact that the orbit-spectrum slots vary in value adds to the concern that the late-comers will be deprived of "equal rights." In opposition, it is argued that the most efficient use of the geostationary orbit is served by allocation to those states that can presently use it and that it is premature to make reservations for states that have no present need or capability. Improvements in technology may eventually allow all who require space satellites to receive allocations or alternatively to be granted rights to the use of existing satellites. The issues have been debated in the United Nations and the ITU without a final resolution. All states, however, tend to accept the treaty principle that the geostationary orbit should be used "for the benefit of and in the interests of all countries, irrespective of their degree of economic or scientific development." See generally Rothblatt, New Satellite Technology, Allocation of Global Resources and the International Telecommunication Union, 24 Colum.J.Transn.L. 37 (1986); Rutkowski, the World Administrative Radio Conference on the Use of Geostationary–Satellite Orbit, 24 Colum.J.Transn.L. 51 (1986); Note, Limited Space: Allocating the Geostationary Orbit, 7 Nw.J.Int'l L. & Bus. 788 (1986); Abdurrasyid, The Outer Space Treaty and the Geostationary Orbit, 12 Annals Air & Space L. 131 (1987); Doyle, Regulating the Geostationary Orbit: ITU's WARC–ORB 85–88, 15 J.Space L. 1 (1987); Doyle, Space Law and the Geostationary Orbit: The ITU's WARC–ORB 85–88 Concluded, 17 J.Space L. 13 (1989); Smith, Space

Law/Space WARC: An Analysis of the Space Law Issues Raised At the 1985 ITU World Administrative Radio Conference on the Geostationary Orbit, 8 Hous.J.Int'l L. 227 (1986); Straubel, Telecommunications Satellites and Market Forces: How Should the Geostationary Orbit Be Regulated by the FCC?, 17 N.C.J.Int'l L. & Com.Reg. 205 (1992).

## THE MOON TREATY

The Agreement Governing the Activities of States on the Moon and Other Celestial Bodies (generally known as the Moon Treaty) was adopted by the General Assembly in 1979. It entered into force on July 11, 1984, when the fifth state ratified it.

Unlike the 1967 Treaty on Principles or other agreements in outer space, the Moon Treaty did not require acceptance by the United States, the USSR, and the United Kingdom to enter into force. Also, in contrast to the Treaty on Principles and most other agreements on outer space, the Moon Treaty had only a small number of parties; as of December 31, 1991, only 8 states had accepted or acceded to it.

Opponents of ratification of the Moon Treaty in the United States have objected to the provision in Article 11 of the treaty which states that "the moon and its natural resources are the common heritage of mankind which finds expression in the provisions of this Agreement and in particular in paragraph 5 of this Article". Paragraphs 5 of Article 11 and Article 18 authorize the states parties to establish an international regime "* * * to govern the exploitation of the natural resources of the moon as such exploitation is about to become feasible." Article 11 also calls for an "equitable sharing by all States Parties" in the benefits derived from the resources of the moon.

### *Notes*

1. Is the "common heritage" provision in the Moon Treaty consistent with Article 1 of the 1967 Treaty on Principles, which provides that outer space, the moon and celestial bodies are free for use, with free access to all areas of celestial bodies? Would the "common heritage" principle preclude property rights in a moon-based resource that was taken from the moon? See Christol, The American Bar Association and the Moon Treaty, 9 J.Space L. 77 (1981); Senate Hearings on the Moon Treaty: Hearings before the Subcommittee on Science, Technology and Space, 96th Cong.2d Sess. (1980); Griffin, Americans and the Moon Treaty, 46 J.Air L.Comm. 729 (1981).

2. A critical view of the common heritage provision has also been expressed by Soviet lawyers. See Vereshchetin and Danilenko, Custom as a Source of International Law of Outer Space, 13 J.Space L. 22 (1985).

## MILITARY USES OF SPACE

By the 1967 Treaty on Principles (Article IV), the states that are parties have undertaken not to place in orbit any objects carrying nuclear weapons or other weapons of mass destruction or station such weapons in outer space in any other manner. The Treaty also requires that the moon and other celestial bodies be used exclusively for peaceful purposes.

Military activities in space involving surveillance by satellites and military communications have been generally recognized as consistent with the 1967 Treaty. See Dove, International Law and the Reservation of the Ocean Space and Outer Space as Zones of Peace, 15 Cornell I.L.J. 13 (1982). However, use of space for "defensive weapons" or for targeting and command and control activities present fresh questions concerning the principle that space is to be used exclusively for peaceful purposes. See Note, The Legality of President Reagan's Proposed Space–Based BMD System, 14 Georgia J.Int. & Comp.L. 329 (1984); Stojak, Current Proposals for the Future Control of Outer Space Weaponization, 10 Annals of Air and Space Law 453 (1985); Russell, Military Activities in Outer Space: Soviet Legal Views, 25 Harv.I.L.J. 153 (1984); Jasentuliyana, Civilian and Military Space Activities: A Third World Perspective, 12 Annals Air & Space L. 247 (1987); Johnson, The Impact of International Law and Treaty Obligations on United States Military Activities in Space, 3 High Tech.L.J. 33 (1988).

## REMOTE SENSING FROM OUTER SPACE

Controversy arising out of outer space activities has also arisen in respect of remote sensing satellites. One issue has been whether the free use of outer space under the treaty should include the right to obtain data concerning the resources and activities in a sensed state without the prior consent of that state. A second issue is whether the data so obtained could be made freely available by the sensing state without authorization of the sensed state. Still another issue is whether the sensing state has an obligation to give the sensed state the primary data (unanalyzed) and the analyzed data. Proposals for restricting the rights of sensing states and for according special rights to sensed states were made by the developing states. The United States sharply resisted attempts to restrict its freedom to sense and to disseminate the data at its discretion.

In 1985, the United Nations Commission on Peaceful Uses of Outer Space issued a report setting forth the U.N. Principles Relating to Remote Sensing of the Earth from Space, U.N.Doc. A/40/20 (1985). These Principles include the following:

— The sensed state has the right of access to primary and processed data, as well as analyzed information, concerning its territory as soon as such data are produced.

— The sensing state has the duty to disclose identified information that is capable of averting harm to the environment.

— There is no restriction on the right of the sensing state to disseminate information to third parties.

On remote sensing, see Schnapf, Explorations in Space Law, 29 N.Y.L.Sch. L.Rev. 687 (1985); Diedriks—Verschoor, Current Issues in Remote Sensing, 1984 Mich.Yb.I.L.Stud. 304; Ambrosetti, Remote Sensing from Outer Space, 17 N.Y.U.J.I.L. & Pol. 1 (1984); Hahn, Developments Towards A Regime for Control of Remote Sensing From Outer Space, 12 J.I.L. & Econ. 421 (1978);

Reimer, New Gathering From Space: Land Remote–Sensing and the First Amendment, 40 Fed.Comm.L.J. 321 (1988); Christol, Remote Sensing and International Space Law, 16 J.Space L. 21 (1988).

## BROADCASTING FROM OUTER SPACE

Space technology now makes it possible to broadcast television programs through space satellites to receivers in foreign countries. A number of states contend that such direct broadcasts (DTBS) require the prior consent of the receiving state.

A resolution adopted by the UN General Assembly in 1982 by a vote of 108 to 13, with 13 abstentions, states that prior consultation and agreement between transmitting and receiving states is legally required. The resolution also required that direct television broadcasting respect the "cultural and political integrity" of all states. See U.N. Resolution on Principles Governing the Use by States of Artificial Earth Satellites for International Direct Television Broadcasting, U.N.Res. 37/92 (1982).

The United States and Western European states opposed the resolution, citing, *inter alia,* Article 19 of the Universal Declaration of Human Rights on the right to seek, receive, and impart information and ideas through any media.

May, in view of the objections by the dissenting states, the resolution be regarded as evidence of customary law? Are the states that voted for the resolution (e.g., USSR) estopped from direct satellite broadcasting in the absence of prior consent by a state in which their broadcasts are received? In view of the widespread occurrence of DTBS and the absence of protests, does customary law now allow direct broadcasting across national frontiers? Which, if any, consideration should be given by international legal rules to the interest of states in preserving their cultural and social identity against intrusive foreign television broadcasts? See generally Christol, The Modern International Law of Outer Space 605–719 (1982).

# Chapter 16

# THE ENVIRONMENT

## SECTION 1. THE EMERGING INTERNATIONAL LAW OF THE ENVIRONMENT

The immense growth of industrialization, all forms of transportation, and the use of highly noxious materials that have characterized the post World War II era have greatly exacerbated harm to the environment. This has led to adoption in the vast majority of states of laws seeking to protect the environment. For an enumeration of United States statutes, see, e.g., Restatement (Third) § 601, Reporters' Note 8 and § 603, Reporters' Note 7.

Harm to the environment may take many forms. It can take the form of pollution of the atmosphere or of water resources. It may consist in an alteration of weather conditions, erosion caused by a change in the flow of a river, or any other man-made change in the environment.

Many forms of environmental harm cross national borders without a state's being able to protect its environment by effective barriers at its borders. Air and water pollution are obvious examples. In addition, disposal regulations and prohibitions imposed by municipal legislation designed to protect the domestic environment have led to disposal of noxious waste in areas not subject to national authority, particularly the high seas. As a consequence, the heightened concern for the environment has also manifested itself in international relations and international law.

The international concern for the environment is particularly acute in the case of common areas—such as the high seas, Antarctic areas, and outer space—and shared coastal areas and common water resources. It has led to the earliest formulations of international rules designed to protect the environment. See Chapter 14, Section 4 and Chapter 15, Section 1.

However, international law has gone beyond these cases and developed rules of more general scope. The main thrust in this development has come from the Conference on the Human Environment, held in Stockholm in 1972, which adopted the Stockholm Declaration on the Human Environment and an Action Plan. This led, in turn, to establishment by the United

Nations General Assembly of a United Nations Environment Program, with an Intergovernmental Governing Council and an Environmental Fund. U.N.Doc. A/CONF. 48/14/Rev. 1 (U.N.Pub.E.73.II.A.14) (1973). These programs have been implemented in a number of respects by multilateral international conventions referred to below.

Twenty years later, at the Rio Earth Summit held in June 1992 in Rio de Janeiro, the environmental agenda had grown to encompass a great many subjects of international concern. The international law of the environment, rather obviously, relates to transborder pollution, marine pollution, weather modification, contamination of outer space, polar areas, and common water resources. The United Nations Conference on Environment and Development (UNCED) recognized that the environment and development must be addressed in their mutual relationship and that many internal developments may affect the international environment. Population growth, the depletion of the ozone layer, deforestation, desertification, and preservation of biological diversity provide ready examples. If these subjects are to be addressed internationally, a proper legal, institutional, and financial framework must be created. At the Rio Earth Summit, all of these questions were addressed.

The Earth Summit approved three documents: the Rio Declaration on Environment and Development (27 non-binding principles); a Non-legally Binding Authoritative Statement of Principles for a Global Consensus on the Management, Conservation and Sustainable Development of all Types of Forests; and Agenda 21, an action plan on sustainable development to guide the policies of governments for the remainder of this century and the next. The Earth Summit also witnessed the signing of two treaties: the United Nations Framework Convention on Climate Change and the Convention on Biological Diversity, which the United States did not sign.

It was recognized at the Earth Summit that, if developing countries were to carry out their obligations under Agenda 21, they would need official development assistance (ODA). As was to be expected, the developed countries were not eager to provide the needed resources. However, the President of the World Bank Group stated that it would develop an environmental action plan to carry forward the UNCED agenda. It remains to be seen if the developed countries will join this effort.

In order to provide a proper institutional structure for carrying Agenda 21 forward, the Earth Summit agreed upon the creation of a Commission on Sustainable Development under the aegis of the Economic and Social Council.

On the Earth Summit and the preparatory work that preceded it, see Robinson (ed.), Agenda 21 & UNCED Proceedings (1922); Gardner, Negotiating Survival: The Road from Rio (1992); Adede, International Environmental Law from Stockholm to Rio—An Overview of Past Lessons and Future Challenges, 22 Envt'l Pol'y & L. 88 (1922); Biggs, Latin American Perspectives on UNCED 2 Y.B.Int'l Envt'l L. 431 (1991); Adams & Martinez–Aragon, Setting the Stage for the Earth–Summit: Brazil 1922, 22 Env'l L.Rept. (BNA) 10, 190 (1922); Kindall, UNCED and the Evolution of Principles of International Environmental Law, 25 John Marshall L.Rev. 19 (1991); Nitze, The Road Starts at Rio, 9 Envt'l Forum 10 (No. 3, 1992); Sand,

International Law on the Agenda of the 1922 "Earth Summit," 3 Colo.J.Int'l Envt'l L. & Pol'y 343 (1992); Speth, A Post–Rio Compact, 88 Foreign Policy 145 (Fall 1992); Strong, The Passage From Rio, 20 Development Forum 3 (No. 4, 1992); and the 1992 A.S.I.L.Proc.

### *O. SCHACHTER, THE EMERGENCE OF INTERNATIONAL ENVIRONMENTAL LAW*

J.Int'l Aff. 457 (1990) *

It has long been evident that international legal restraints and obligations were necessary to cope with environmental damage that transcended national boundaries. Governments have responded largely through agreements—multinational and bilateral—addressed to particular situations. General legal principles have also emerged in international forums, lawyers' commentary and in judicial and arbitral cases. Much of the impetus for international legal restraints has come from outside national governments—from scientific communities, concerned publics and international organizations.

As a result, a body of international environmental law has now come into being, though it is still partial and uneven. Most governments hesitate to give up sovereign rights over activities within their jurisdictions, while uncertainties as to causes and effects impede action. Most serious, perhaps, is the resistance to restraints that might reduce economic growth and well-being. The law that has evolved is in large part "soft"—composed of principles and standards of conduct not clearly accepted as obligatory and uncertain in application. On the other hand, in some areas, states have accepted the rules and decision procedures that have evolved as binding and comply with them in practice. With the great diversity of threats and the uneven character of responses to them, we can be sure that the law that evolves will be many-sided and complex.

* * *

* * * To say that a state has no right to injure the environment of another seems quixotic in the face of the great variety of transborder environmental harms that occur every day. Many result from ordinary economic and social activity; others occur by accident, often unrelated to fault. No one expects that all these injurious activities can be eliminated by general legal fiat, but there is little doubt that international legal restraints can be an important part of the response.

#### Defining Environmental Harm and Risk

Harm and risk, key concepts in international environmental law, do not lend themselves to simple, precise definitions. A wide and very diverse range of situations has been identified as constituting environmental harm, but no single general definition has emerged as authoritative. Arguably, no such general definition is required since specific examples of harm can be identified for purposes of international regulation and responsibility. However, a general conception of environmental harm is implicit in the basic

* [Footnotes omitted.]

principles of the Stockholm declaration and in the proposals for international action. The world tends more and more to perceive environmental harm as a single, aggregate problem.

One approach to a definition is to consider what kinds of transboundary environmental damage are, or should be, outside the definition of international law. It seems safe to say that not every detrimental effect resulting from environmental factors—in the broad sense—should fall within the concept. At least four conditions appear to be necessary. First, the harm must result from human activity. * * *

A second condition is that the harm must result from a physical consequence of the causal human activity. * * *

A third condition applicable to international environmental law is that the physical effects cross national boundaries. * * *

A fourth condition, rather less precise, is that the harm must be significant or substantial. * * *

The foregoing limitations on the meaning of environmental harm still leave a vast area of harmful situations to be covered by international law. Some of the practical problems of regulation can be discerned by considering the categories of harm that may be dealt with by international rules. Three major kinds of harm can be distinguished.

The first and most prominent category comprises situations in which human life-support systems are harmed by substances in the environment that result from human activity. * * *

The second broad category includes cases in which natural resources or artifacts of value to human beings are injured or depleted by environmental interferences caused by human conduct. * * *

A third category presents some unresolved issues of policy. It moves beyond a standard based on human health and well-being to the much wider criterion of preservation of the natural order. * * *

Defining environmental harm leads to the related concept of risk. Regulation should be directed toward action to avert or minimize risks before harm occurs. Risk is a probabilistic concept that takes account of the uncertainties of future events as well as the variations in severity of effects. A duty to prevent and minimize risk is legally distinct from a duty to act to contain and minimize harmful effects that have already occurred. In the former, the objective requires identifying situations in terms of degree of danger and adopting rules of conduct to reduce that danger.

* * *

### The Duty to Inform, Assess and Consult

The duty of a source state to inform others of impending harm to them or of significant risk of such harm is an obvious corollary of the general obligation to prevent and minimize transboundary harm. Notification would surely be an appropriate measure when a state has reason to believe that an activity or event in its jurisdiction may cause a significant risk of transboundary harm. After the Chernobyl nuclear disaster in 1986, the Soviet government was strongly criticized by other governments for its failure to give timely notice of the accident and the transborder injuries likely to occur. The Soviet leaders subsequently declared that they should have supplied such information. The International Atomic Energy Agency (IAEA), the competent international organization, called on states to give timely warning of accidents or operational difficulties in nuclear facilities that threaten transborder environmental damage.

* * *

LIABILITY AND COMPENSATION

International liability is an essential, though troubling, concept in regard to transborder environmental injury. * * *

* * *

There is no doubt that in principle, a state that violates a rule of international law by an activity involving transborder injury is liable to make reparation and to compensate the injured state. There is no dispute about this. The main controversy is whether liability should be imposed for lawful acts, that is, in the ILC's terminology, for the injurious consequences of acts not prohibited by international law.

## *RESTATEMENT (THIRD)*

### § 601. State Obligations with Respect to Environment of Other States and the Common Environment

(1) A state is obligated to take such measures as may be necessary, to the extent practicable under the circumstances, to ensure that activities within its jurisdiction or control

(a) conform to generally accepted international rules and standards for the prevention, reduction, and control of injury to the environment of another state or of areas beyond the limits of national jurisdiction; and

(b) are conducted so as not to cause significant injury to the environment of another state or of areas beyond the limits of national jurisdiction.

(2) A state is responsible to all other states

(a) for any violation of its obligations under Subsection (1)(a), and

(b) for any significant injury, resulting from such violation, to the environment of areas beyond the limits of national jurisdiction.

(3) A state is responsible for any significant injury, resulting from a violation of its obligations under Subsection (1), to the environment of another state or to its property, or to persons or property within that state's territory or under its jurisdiction or control.

### *Notes*

1. The obligations stated in this Section attach only if the state has failed to take measures "to the extent practicable under the circumstances" and "significant injury" results. In addition, the state's conduct must have failed to

"conform to generally accepted international rules and standards." The latter phrase includes rules of customary international law and international agreements. To what extent does it include rules adopted by international organizations, when the state involved is not a member of the organization or voted against the rule? Assuming a generally accepted standard can be found, would it be binding upon a state that has consistently rejected it? Can a standard be generally accepted if it is not accepted by an important state, such as the United States? To what extent is a state under an obligation to permit an injured state to investigate whether there has been compliance with generally accepted rules or standards?

2. Is the requirement of "significant" injury appropriate? Restatement (Third) § 601, Comment c, states that the word "significant" is intended to exclude minor incidents causing minimal damages.

3. The International Law Commission has been studying the problems of environmental harm under the rubric of "international liability for injurious consequences arising out of acts not prohibited by international law." See 1991 I.L.Rep. p. 277–304. It has provisionally considered whether a state's obligation in connection with transboundary injury to other states should include a duty to prevent, to inform, to negotiate and to repair. Thus far, it has concluded that only the failure to "repair" the injurious consequences would result in international liability. In regard to prevention, a majority of the Commission is of the view that its proposals should be recommendatory only, and that the Commission should in fact produce two separate instruments of different legal characters. The Commission also agreed that prior consent of the potentially affected state would not be required before an activity would be authorized. With regard to compensation, the Commission concluded that there should be a combined liability of the private operator and of the state, in which the former carried primary liability and the latter residual liability.

Critics of the Commission's approach have argued against liability for lawful activities. In their view liability should arise only for noncompliance with "primary rules" of conduct specifying the action (or lack of action) that would be internationally required. Such primary rules might include a duty to compensate for all transboundary harm resulting from specified extra-hazardous activities. See Brownlie, System of the Law of Nations: State Responsibility (Part I) 50 (1983); Magraw, Transboundary Harm: The International Law Commission Study of "International Liability", 80 A.J.I.L. 305 (1986). For an evaluation of the International Law Commission's work and an argument in favor of strict liability when there is actual transnational environmental damage, see O'Keefe, Transboundary Pollution and the Strict Liability Issue: The Work of the International Law Commission on the Topic of International Liability for Injurious Consequences Arising Out of Acts Not Prohibited by International Law, 18 Denv.J.Int'l L. & Poly 145 (1990).

4. The problem of attaching liability to conduct that constitutes an exercise of rights also appears in national laws. It has produced two doctrines that address that situation: the doctrine of abuse of rights (*sic utere tuo ut alienum non laedas* ), of which the spite fence is the much cited example, and the doctrine that makes an otherwise proper exercise of one's property rights wrongful unless the use compensates the person who is injured by the use. As might have been expected, both doctrines have been argued to be applicable also in the international context, particularly in the area of environmental law. It may be questioned whether this attempted transplantation is appropriate. The doctrine

of abuse of rights applies typically when an owner makes use of his property solely to harm another person. This is usually not the case in the situations of environmental harm, because the person causing the environmental harm normally is not moved solely by the desire to harm the persons injured. The approach that makes conduct wrongful only if appropriate compensation is not paid for the injury it causes others is a construction that may be needed in a municipal law system that prescribes injunctive relief for all wrongful conduct. When a court finds that the person causing the harm should be permitted to continue his activities, that injunctive relief is therefore improper, and that only damages should be awarded, this construction may be needed to obviate the possibility of an award of injunctive relief. For this situation under domestic law, see Boomer v. The Atlantic Cement Co., Inc., 26 N.Y.2d 219, 309 N.Y.S.2d 312, 257 N.E.2d 870 (1970). Under international law, which regards compensation as the principal form of relief and an absolute right to injunctive relief as questionable (see Chapter 7), such a construction may not be necessary.

5. For general works on international environmental law, see Kay & Jacobson, Environmental Protection—The International Dimension (1983); Schneider, World Public Order of the Environment (1979); Levin, Protection of the Human Environment (UNITAR 1977); Schachter, Sharing the World's Resources 74–83 (1977); Law, Institutions and the Global Environment (Hargrove ed. 1972); Dupuy, La Responsabilité des Etats pour les Dommages d'Origine Technologique et Industrielle (1976); Sand, The Effectiveness of International Environmental Agreements: A Survey of Existing Legal Instruments (1992); Kiss, International Environmental Law (1991); Caldwell, International Environmental Policy: Emergence and Dimensions (2nd ed. 1990); Magraw, International Law and Pollution (1991); Gardner, Negotiating Survival: Four Priorities After Rio (1992); Lang et al., Environmental Protection and International Law (1991).

# SECTION 2. TRANSBORDER POLLUTION

## TRAIL SMELTER CASE

## (U.S. v. CANADA)

3 U.N.Rep.Int.Arb.Awards 1911 (1941).

[The case was decided by a Special Arbitral Tribunal under a convention which required the application of the "law and practice followed in dealing with cognate questions in the United States of America as well as international law and practice." 3 U.N.Rep.Int'l Arb.Awards 1905, 1908. The arbitration grew out of air pollution from sulphur dioxide fumes emitted by a smelter plant at Trail, British Columbia, owned by a Canadian corporation. In a previous decision the Special Arbitral Tribunal had found that the fumes caused damage in the State of Washington during the period from 1925 to 1937. In holding Canada responsible and directing injunctive relief and payment of an indemnity, the Tribunal stated, id. at 1963–64:]

As Professor Eagleton puts it (Responsibility of States in International Law, 1928, p. 80): "A State owes at all times a duty to protect other States against injurious acts by individuals from within its jurisdiction." * * * These and many others have been carefully examined. International decisions, in various matters, from the Alabama case onward, and also earlier ones, are based on the same general principle, and, indeed, this principle, as such, has not been questioned by Canada. But the real difficulty often arises rather when it comes to determine what, *pro subjecta materie,* is deemed to constitute an injurious act.

* * *

No case of air pollution dealt with by an international tribunal has been brought to the attention of the Tribunal nor does the Tribunal know of any such case. The nearest analogy is that of water pollution. But, here also, no decision of an international tribunal has been cited or has been found.

There are, however, as regards both air pollution and water pollution, certain decisions of the Supreme Court of the United States which may legitimately be taken as a guide in this field of international law, for it is reasonable to follow by analogy, in international cases, precedents established by that court in dealing with controversies between States of the Union or with other controversies concerning the quasi-sovereign rights of such States, where no contrary rule prevails in international law and no reason for rejecting such precedents can be adduced from the limitations of sovereignty inherent in the Constitution of the United States.

[The Tribunal then discussed Missouri v. Illinois, 200 U.S. 496, 26 S.Ct. 268, 50 L.Ed. 572 (1906), New York v. New Jersey, 256 U.S. 296, 41 S.Ct. 492, 65 L.Ed. 937 (1921), and New Jersey v. New York, 283 U.S. 473, 51 S.Ct. 519, 75 L.Ed. 1176 (1931), dealing with water pollution, and Georgia v. Tennessee Copper Company, 206 U.S. 230, 27 S.Ct. 618, 51 L.Ed. 1038 (1907) and Georgia v. Tennessee Copper Company, 237 U.S. 474, 35 S.Ct. 631, 59 L.Ed. 1054 (1915), dealing with air pollution, and concluded: "[U]nder the principles of international law, as well as of the law of the United States, no State has the right to use or permit the use of its territory in such a manner as to cause injury by fumes in or to the territory of another or the properties or persons therein, when the case is of serious consequence and the injury is established by clear and convincing evidence." Id. at 1965. The Tribunal described in detail the measures of control to be imposed upon the Trail Smelter. These measures included the maintenance of meteorological and sulphur emission records and the specification of maximum hourly emission of sulphur dioxide under various conditions.]

## *Notes*

1. This landmark decision is frequently cited as laying down basic principles. For other decisions to the same effect, see the many claims submitted to the Foreign Claims Settlement Commission and settled by the arbitral tribunal created by the United States and Canada. 8 I.L.M. 118, 133–42 (1969). See also Re, The Foreign Claims Settlement Commission and the Lake Ontario Claims Program, 4 I.L.M. 473 (1965).

2. Does the principal case endorse a standard of strict liability? Compare the language of this decision with that of the Restatement (Third) § 601, reproduced above.

3. To prevent further injuries, the Tribunal in the principal case provided for control over emission of sulphur dioxide fumes at a cost of $20 million. On this regime, see Read, The Trail Smelter Dispute, 1 Can.Yb.I.L. 213 (1963). On further measures taken, see 3 U.N.Rep.Int.Arb.Awards 1911 (1978).

4. A Convention on Long–Range Transboundary Air Pollution was adopted in Geneva on November 13, 1979, T.I.A.S. No. 10541, 18 I.L.M. 1442 (1979). The purpose of the Convention is "to limit, and, as far as possible, gradually reduce and prevent air pollution including long-range air pollution." The principal means provided for are research and exchange of information. As of December 31, 1991, this Convention was in force for 33 states, including the United States. A 1984 Protocol provides for more adequate financing of the program. 24 I.L.M. 484 (1985). The OECD has also been active in this area. See OECD, Recommendation of the Council for the Implementation of a Regime of Equal Right of Access and Non–Discrimination in Relation to Transfrontier Pollution, May 17, 1977, OECD Doc. C (77) 28 (Final), 16 I.L.M. 977 (1977); OECD, Non–Discrimination in Transfrontier Pollution: Leading OECD Documents 35 (1978), 14 I.L.M. 242 (1978).

5. The principal United States statutes dealing with transfrontier pollution are the Clean Water Act, 334 U.S.C.A. §§ 1254–1376 (1977), and the Clean Air Act, 42 U.S.C.A. §§ 7401–42 (1977). The former Act applies to transfrontier pollution on condition of reciprocity. The Clean Air Act has similar provisions. In 1980, Canada revised its Clean Air Act of 1971 to create the reciprocity required by its United States counterpart. Can.Stat., ch. 45, § 21.1(19) (1980–81). For actions taken under these Acts, the Acid Precipitation Act of 1980 (42 U.S.C.A. §§ 8901–05, 8911–12), and other measures dealing with transborder pollution, see Restatement (Third) § 601, Reporters' Note 8.

## THE CHERNOBYL NUCLEAR PLANT EXPLOSION

On April 26, 1986, an explosion occurred at the Chernobyl atomic power plant near Kiev in the U.S.S.R. The explosion caused radioactive substances to be released into the atmosphere. It was not until three days later, when significantly higher levels of radioactivity were found in Scandinavian countries, that the U.S.S.R. acknowledged that an explosion had occurred. However, it failed to disclose any particulars as to the nature of the occurrence and the extent of the release of radioactive substances. It was not until eleven days later, when increased levels of radioactivity attributed to the Chernobyl explosion were found as far away as Japan, that Pravda published an official account. This account acknowledged that the release of radioactive substances continued, but "avoided discussion of the amount of radioactivity released, its potential effects, the doses that residents may have been exposed to in the hours or days before they were evacuated, or the dangers posed by the accident." N.Y. Times, May 6, 1986, § A, at 1, col. 6, at 6, col. 1. Many foreign countries filed protests with the U.S.S.R., complaining that it had failed properly to inform them of the accident. Did the U.S.S.R. have an international obligation to inform potentially affected countries of the occurrence of the accident and its potential effects? Compare Art. 198 of the Law of the Sea Convention (1982) which provides that a State, damaged or in imminent danger of being damaged by pollution, "shall immediately notify other States it deems likely to be affected by such damage, as well as the competent international organizations." See also Arts. 204–06 of the Convention requiring monitoring of, and reporting on, activities likely to pollute the marine environment. Are these provisions applicable by analogy? If the United States learned of the explosion by remote sensing, was it under an international obligation to notify potentially affected states of dangers created by the incident, as soon as it obtained the information? See Chapter 16, Section 3. Is the U.S.S.R. internationally liable for the injuries that may be suffered in other States as a result of the explosion? [Would the destruction of contaminated vegetables and milk by public officials in affected States be "significant injury"?] Would the U.S.S.R. be liable, if the injuries suffered as a result of the explosion were to manifest themselves only many years later? Is the U.S.S.R. under an international obligation to discontinue the practices that led to the accident and to adopt measures to avoid its reoccurrence? Would the United States, in a similar situation, be under any such obligations, if the nuclear plant were privately owned? See generally Sands, Chernobyl: Law and Communication: Transboundary Nuclear Air Pollution: The Legal Materials (1988); Malone, The Chernobyl Accident: A Case Study in International Law Regulating State Responsibility For Transboundary Nuclear Pollution, 12 Colum.J.Envtl.L. 203 (1987), Note, After Chernobyl: Liability For Nuclear Accidents Under International Law, 25 Colum.J.Transnat'l L. 647 (1987); The Report to the Congress from the Presidential Commission on Catastrophic Nuclear Accidents, August 1990.

## *INSTITUT DE DROIT INTERNATIONAL, RESOLUTION ON POLLUTION OF RIVERS AND LAKES*

Adopted at Athens Session, 1979.
58 Annuaire Inst.Droit Int. 196.

### Article I

1. For the purpose of this Resolution, "pollution" means any physical, chemical or biological alteration in the composition or quality of waters which results directly or indirectly from human action and affects the legitimate uses of such waters, thereby causing injury.

2. In specific cases, the existence of pollution and the characteristics thereof shall, to the extent possible, be determined by referring to environmental norms established through agreements or by the competent international organizations and commissions.

3. This Resolution shall apply to international rivers and lakes and to their basins.

### Article II

In the exercise of their sovereign right to exploit their own resources pursuant to their own environmental policies, and without prejudice to their contractual obligations, States shall be under a duty to ensure that their activities or those conducted within their jurisdiction or under their control cause no pollution in the waters of international rivers and lakes beyond their boundaries.

* * *

### Article V

States shall incur international liability under international law for any breach of their international obligations with respect to pollution of rivers and lakes.

ARTICLE VI

With a view to ensuring an effective system of prevention and of compensation for victims of transboundary pollution, States should conclude international conventions concerning in particular:

(a) the jurisdiction of courts, the applicable law and the enforcement of judgments;

(b) the procedure for special arrangements providing in particular for objective liability systems and compensation funds with regard to pollution brought about by ultrahazardous activities.

ARTICLE VII

1. In carrying out their duty to co-operate, States bordering the same hydrographic basin shall, as far as practicable, especially through agreements, resort to the following ways of co-operation:

(a) inform co-riparian States regularly of all appropriate data on the pollution of the basin, its causes, its nature, the damage resulting from it and the preventive procedures;

(b) notify the States concerned in due time of any activities envisaged in their own territories which may involve the basin in a significant threat of transboundary pollution;

(c) promptly inform States that might be affected by a sudden increase in the level of transboundary pollution in the basin and take all appropriate steps to reduce the effects of any such increase;

(d) consult with each other on actual or potential problems of transboundary pollution of the basin so as to reach, by methods of their own choice, a solution consistent with the interests of the States concerned and with the protection of the environment;

(e) co-ordinate or pool their scientific and technical research programmes to combat pollution of the basin;

(f) establish by common agreement environmental norms, in particular quality norms for the whole or part of the basin;

(g) set up international commissions with the largest terms of reference for the entire basin, providing for the participation of local authorities if this proves useful, or strengthen the powers or co-ordination of existing institutions;

(h) establish harmonized, co-ordinated or unified networks for permanent observation and pollution control;

(i) develop safeguards for individuals who may be affected by polluting activities, both at the stages of prevention and compensation, by granting on a non-discriminatory basis the greatest access to judicial and administrative procedures in States in which such activities originate and by setting up compensation funds for ecological damage the origin of which cannot be clearly determined or which is of exceptional magnitude.

### Notes

1. Irrigation may degrade the quality of water, especially by increasing its salinity. This occurred in respect of the Colorado River as a result of drainage and irrigation in the United States that increased the salt content of the water reaching Mexico with disastrous consequences to farming in Mexico. The United States maintained that its treaty obligation related only to the quantum, not the quality, of water. After some years of political pressure by Mexico, the United States agreed that Mexico was entitled to usable water. It undertook to reduce salinity and to deliver water not inferior to that received when the 1944 treaty was made. See Brownell & Eaton, The Colorado River Salinity Problem with Mexico, 69 A.J.I.L. 255 (1975).

2. Complex pollution problems which exist in the Great Lakes have been dealt with by the International Joint Commission of Canada and the United States. See Bilder, Controlling Great Lakes Pollution, in Law, Institutions and the Global Environment 294–380 (Hargrove ed. 1972); Cohen, The Regime of Boundary Waters, 146 Rec. des Cours 219 (1975–III); Vigod, Global Environmental Problems: A Legal Perspective on Great Lakes Toxic Pollution: U.S.–Canadian Strategies For a Solution, 12 Syracuse J.Int'l L. & Com. 315 (1985).

3. On state responsibility for river pollution generally, see OECD Secretariat, The International Responsibility of States in Relation to Transfrontier Pollution, OECD Doc. ENV (76) 3 (1976); Levin, Protecting the Human Environment (UNITAR 1977); Lester, Pollution in the Law of International Drainage Basins 89–123 (Garretson, Hayton & Olmstead eds. 1967); Note, The New River: The Possibility of Criminal Liability for Transnational Pollution, 10 Crim.Just.J. 99 (1987); Dunne (ed.), Transboundary Pollution and Liability: The Case of the River Rhine (1991).

## SECTION 3. MARINE POLLUTION

Marine pollution has received special attention from international law. This is readily understandable, since pollution of the marine environment, and especially the oceans, affects all states that use it.

The rapid growth of maritime traffic in recent years has enhanced pollution of the marine environment. In addition, dumping of noxious and harmful substances, including radioactive materials, oil spills from wells in maritime areas, and tanker disasters have added substantially to marine pollution. All of these developments have enhanced concern for the marine environment and produced international and national measures for its protection.

The 1958 Convention on the High Seas contains a number of provisions seeking to ensure safety at sea and to prevent pollution by discharges of oil and radioactive waste. 13 U.S.T. 2312, T.I.A.S. No. 5200, 450 U.N.T.S. 82 (Art. 10, 24–25).

Maritime disasters that occurred in subsequent years moved the drafters of the 1982 Law of the Sea Convention (see Chapter 15) to include provisions that deal not only with the types of pollution addressed in the 1958 Convention, but also with pollution from land-based sources and pollution through the atmosphere. The LOS Convention also provides for compulsory dispute settlement (see Art. 297(1)(c)), but, although the substantive provisions on pollution are accepted as customary law, its provisions on dispute settlement are binding only on states that are parties to the Convention.

## THE LAW OF THE SEA CONVENTION AND MARINE POLLUTION

### *U.N. CONVENTION ON THE LAW OF THE SEA*

#### Article 194

#### *Measures to Prevent, Reduce and Control Pollution of the Marine Environment*

1. States shall take all necessary measures consistent with this Convention to prevent, reduce and control pollution of the marine environment from any source using for this purpose the best practicable means at their disposal and in accordance with their capabilities, individually or jointly as appropriate, and they shall endeavour to harmonize their policies in this connection.

2. States shall take all necessary measures to ensure that activities under their jurisdiction or control are so conducted that they do not cause damage by pollution to other States and their environment, and that pollution arising from incidents or activities under their jurisdiction or control does not spread beyond the areas where they exercise sovereign rights in accordance with this Convention.

3. The measures taken pursuant to this Part shall deal with all sources of pollution of the marine environment. These measures shall include, *inter alia,* those designed to minimize to the fullest possible extent:

(a) Release of toxic, harmful and noxious substances, especially those which are persistent, from land-based sources, from or through the atmosphere or by dumping;

(b) Pollution from vessels, in particular measures for preventing accidents and dealing with emergencies, ensuring the safety of operations at sea, preventing intentional and unintentional discharges, and regulating the design, construction, equipment, operation and manning of vessels;

(c) Pollution from installations and devices used in exploration or exploitation of the natural resources of the sea-bed and subsoil, in particular measures for preventing accidents and dealing with emergencies, ensuring the safety of operations at sea, and regulating the design, construction, equipment, operation and manning of such installations or devices;

(d) Pollution from other installations and devices operating in the marine environment, in particular measures for preventing accidents and dealing with emergencies, ensuring the safety of operations at sea, and regulating the design, construction, equipment, operation and manning of such installations or devices.

4. In taking measures to prevent, reduce or control pollution of the marine environment, States shall refrain from unjustifiable interference

with activities carried out by other States in the exercise of their rights and in pursuance of their duties in conformity with this Convention.

5. The measures taken in accordance with this Part shall include those necessary to protect and preserve rare or fragile ecosystems as well as the habitat of depleted, threatened or endangered species and other forms of marine life.

### *Notes*

1. Article 220 provides for coastal state enforcement of international standards. A port state may act against vessels that have violated national laws which accord with the Convention or other international standards, while passing through the territorial sea or exclusive economic zone. When there are "clear grounds for believing" that a vessel navigating the territorial sea has committed a violation in the territorial sea, the coastal state may inspect the vessel and arrest it. When there is clear ground for believing that a vessel navigating in the territorial sea or the exclusive economic zone committed a violation in the economic zone, the coastal state may require the vessel to give relevant information; if the information is refused or if the information given is "manifestly at variance" with the facts and there has been substantial discharge and significant pollution of the environment, the coastal state may physically inspect the vessel; if the violation has resulted in major damage or threat of damage to the coastal state's interest, the state may cause proceedings to be taken in accordance with its laws.

2. Other articles of the 1982 Convention require states not to transfer damage from one area to another, or transform one type of pollution into another (Art. 195); to control pollution from the use of technologies or the introduction of alien or new species (Art. 196). Article 197 requires states to cooperate on a global or regional basis to elaborate international standards consistent with this Convention. States must immediately notify other states likely to be affected, and appropriate international organizations, of any pollution or imminent danger of pollution (Art. 198).

Later sections provide that states are liable under international law for failure to fulfil their obligations to protect the marine environment, and must assure recourse under their legal systems for prompt and adequate compensation and other relief for pollution by persons under their jurisdiction (Art. 235). The provisions of the Convention dealing with the environment do not apply to state-owned or state-operated vessels or aircraft used on noncommercial service (Art. 236).

This part of the Convention shall be without prejudice to obligations assumed under other agreements and to later agreements in furtherance of the principles of the Convention (Art. 237).

3. In addition to the Law of the Sea Convention, there are many international conventions dealing with particular forms of marine pollution. For an enumeration, see Waldichuk, Control of Marine Pollution, 4 Ocean Dev. 6 I.L.J. 269, 287–91, Table 1 (1977). See also the conventions discussed in Notes 2–6, p. 1389 infra.

*RESTATEMENT (THIRD)*

### § 603. Responsibility for Marine Pollution

(1) A state is obligated

(a) to adopt laws and regulations to prevent, reduce and control any significant pollution of the marine environment that are no less effective than generally accepted international rules and standards; and

(b) to ensure compliance with the laws and regulations adopted pursuant to clause (a) by ships flying its flag, and, in case of a violation, to impose adequate penalties on the owner or captain of the ship.

(2) A state is obligated to take, individually and jointly with other states, such measures as may be necessary, to the extent practicable under the circumstances, to prevent, reduce, and control pollution causing or threatening to cause significant injury to the marine environment.

#### *Notes*

1. This Section, which is based on the provisions of the LOS Convention, Arts. 194, 207–12, 217 and 220, applies the principles of Section 601 of the Restatement (Third) to marine pollution.

2. In using "the best practicable means at their disposal," states must regulate pollution not only from land-based sources, but also from vessels. The latter regulation includes proper regulation of design, construction, and equipment of vessels flying the state's flag, as well as navigational routing. See Art. 194(3)(b) and 211 of the LOS Convention. States must also adopt proper measures to protect the marine environment from pollution caused by deep seabed mining (Arts. 194(3)(c) and (d) and 208) and from noxious emissions by aircraft (Art. 212).

3. Collisions involving large tankers have led to revisions in 1960 and 1974 of international conventions dealing with safety at sea. The International Convention for the Safety of Life at Sea (SOLAS), London, June 17, 1960, 16 U.S.T. 185, T.I.A.S. No. 5780, 536 U.N.T.S. 27; London, November 1, 1974, 32 U.S.T. 47, T.I.A.S. No. 9700. See further Restatement (Third) § 603, Reporters' Note 2. The Convention was in force, as of January 1, 1992, for 117 states, including the United States and a 1978 Protocol for 77 states, including the United States.

4. The Torrey Canyon disaster, in which the United Kingdom destroyed a tanker without the consent of the flag state, prompted adoption of the International Convention Relating to Intervention on the High Seas in Cases of Oil Pollution Casualties, 1969, 26 U.S.T. 765, T.I.A.S. No. 8068. In 1973, the Convention was broadened to extend coverage to specified substances other than oil. As of January 1, 1992, the Convention was in force for 58 states and the Protocol for 26 states, including the United States.

5. Oil pollution of the seas is regulated by the International Convention for the Prevention of Pollution of the Sea by Oil, London, May 12, 1954, 12 U.S.T. 2989, T.I.A.S. No. 4900, 327 U.N.T.S. 3. As of January 1, 1992, it was in force for 70 states, including the United States. It was amended in 1962 and 1969, 17 U.S.T. 1523, T.I.A.S. No. 6109, 600 U.N.T.S. 332; 28 U.S.T. 1205, T.I.A.S. No. 8505. This Convention is superseded by the 1978 Protocol Relating to the International Convention for the Prevention of Pollution from Ships As Between

Parties to that Protocol. Done at London February 17, 1978; entered into force October 2, 1983. As of January 1, 1992 it was in force for 71 states including the United States.

6. The Convention on the Prevention of Marine Pollution by Dumping of Wastes and Other Matter, of December 29, 1972, 26 U.S.T. 2403, T.I.A.S. No. 8165, 1046 U.N.T.S. 120, prohibits dumping of high level radioactive waste and makes dumping of other radioactive wastes subject to special permit by national authorities. As of January 1, 1992, this Convention was in force for 70 states, including the United States. On this Convention see also Finn, Ocean Disposal of Radioactive Wastes: The Obligation of International Cooperation to Protect the Marine Environment, 21 Va.J.Int'l L. 621 (1981); Duncan, The 1972 Convention on the Prevention of Marine Pollution by Dumping of Wastes at Sea, 5 J.Mar.L. & Com. 299 (1973–74). Discharges other than dumping are the subject of the International Convention for the Prevention of Pollution from Ships (MARPOL), London November 2, 1973, 12 I.L.M. 1319 (1973). Annex V to the International Convention for the Prevention of Pollution from Ships, 1973, Regulations for the Prevention of Pollution by Garbage from Ships, entered into force December 31, 1988. As of January 1, 1992 it was in force in 51 states. The Protocol of 1978 relating to the International Convention for the Prevention of Pollution from Ships, 1973, with Annexes and Protocols, incorporates with modifications the provisions of the International Convention for the Prevention of Pollution from Ships, including its annexes and protocol. The 1973 Convention is not intended to enter into force and be applied on its own. Accordingly, as of October 2, 1983, the regime to be applied by the states parties to the 1978 Protocol will be that contained in the 1973 Convention, as modified by the 1978 Protocol. As of January 1, 1992, it was in force for 71 states including the United States. In addition, there are a number of special and regional conventions applicable to special areas. On these conventions, see Kay & Jacobson, Environmental Protections: The International Dimension (1983); Hakappaa, Marine Pollution in International Law 75 (1981); Trinagenis, International Control of Marine Pollution (1980); Restatement (Third) § 603, Reporters' Note 5.

7. On United States legislation on marine pollution, see Restatement (Third) § 603, Reporters' Note 7.

8. On marine pollution generally, see Hakappaa, Marine Pollution in International Law (1981); M'Gonigle & Zacher, Pollution, Politics and International Law–Tankers at Sea (1979); Tonczak, Defining Marine Pollution, 8 Marine Policy 311 (1984); Brown, Maritime Oil Pollution Literature: An Annotated Bibliography, 13 J.Mar.L. & Com. 373 (1982); Tharpes, International Environmental Law: Turning the Tide on Marine Pollution, 20 U.Miami Inter–Am. L.Rev. 579 (1989); M'Gonigle, "Developing Sustainability" and the Emerging Norms of International Environmental Law: The Case of Land–Based Marine Pollution Control, 28 Canadian Y.B.Int'l L. 169 (1990); Shaw et al., The Global Environment: A Proposal to Eliminate Marine Oil Pollution, 27 Nat.Resources J. 157 (1987); Gold, Marine Pollution Liability After "Exxon Valdez": The U.S. "All-or-Nothing" Lottery!, 22 J.Mar.L. & Com. 423 (1991); Boyle, Marine Pollution Under the Law of the Sea Convention, 79 A.J.I.L. 347 (1985); Kindt, Marine Pollution and the Law of the Sea (4 vol. with supplements, loose-leaf, first published in 1986).

# SECTION 4. WEATHER MODIFICATION AND CLIMATE CHANGE

Principles of international law relating to weather modification are in a state of development. The 1977 Convention on the Prohibition of Military or Any Other Hostile Use of Environmental Modification Techniques prohibits the "military or any other use of environmental modification techniques having widespread, long-lasting or severe effects" in order to inflict injury on another state. 31 U.S.T. 333, T.I.A.S. No. 9614, Art. 1. In April 1978, The World Meteorological Organization and the United Nations Environmental Program, at an Informal Meeting on Legal Aspects of Weather Modification, prepared Draft Principles relating to weather modification. 1978 Dig. U.S.Pract.Int.Law 1204. See also the United States—Canada Agreement relating to the Exchange of Information on Weather Modification Activities, 26 U.S.T. 540, T.I.A.S. No. 8056. On weather modification, see also Weiss, Who Pays for Weather Modification Damage, 4 Envir.Pol. & Law 22 (1978); Weiss, International Responsibility for Weather Modification, 29 Int.Org. (1975); Stewart & Wiener, The Comprehensive Approach To Global Climate Policy: Issues of Design and Practicality, 9 Ariz.J.Int'l & Comp.L. 83 (1992); Note, Weather Modification: The Continuing Search For Rights and Liabilities, 1991 B.Y.U.L.Rev. 1163 (1991).

In recent years, large-scale climatic changes, such as depletion of the stratospheric ozone layer protecting the earth from radiation and the possible melting of polar ice, have become the focus of attention. On stratospheric ozone depletion and the Vienna Convention for the Protection of the Ozone Layer, see Benedick, International Cooperation to Protect the Ozone Layer, U.S. Dep't of State, Bur. of Pub. Aff., Current Policy No. 808 (1986); Zanger, Carbon Dioxide's Threat to Global Climate: An International Solution, 17 Stanford J.Int.L. 389 (1981); Tambenfeld, The Atmosphere: Change, Policy and World Law, 10 Denver J.I.L. & Pol. 523 (1981); Kerr, Carbon Dioxide and A Changing Climate, Science 491 (Nov. 4, 1983); David, Two Views on Whether More Means Doom, Nature 751 (Oct. 27, 1983); Nanda, Global Climate Change and International Law, 32 Impact of Science on Society 365 (1962).

When the Vienna Convention appeared inadequate to deal with the progressive depletion of the ozone layer, the Montreal Protocol on Substances that Deplete the Ozone Layer was adopted. This Protocol was amended in 1990, which was, in turn, followed by the United Nations Framework Convention on Climate Change signed at the Rio Earth Summit. On these pioneering conventions, see Benedick, Ozone Diplomacy: New Directions in Safeguarding the Planet (1991); Brumnee, Acid Rain and Ozone Layer Depletion: International Law and Regulation (1988); Riaczyk, Montreal Protocol on Substances that Deplete the Ozone Layer: Conference Calling for Accelerated Phase–Out of Ozone–Depleting Chemicals is Planned for 1992, 5 Temp.Int'l & Comp.L.J. 363 (1991); Stewart, Stratospheric Ozone Protection: Changes Over Two Decades of Regulation, 7 Nat.Resources & Env't 24 (1992); Lawrence, Technology Transfer Funds and the Law—Recent Amendments to the Montreal Protocol on Substances that Deplete the Ozone Layer, 4 J.Envtl.L. 15 (1992); Note, The Montreal Protocol and Recent Developments to Protect the Ozone Layer, 15 Harv.Envtl.L.Rev. 275 (1991);

Note, Progress Toward a Healthy Sky: An Assessment of the London Amendments to the Montreal Protocol on Substances that Deplete the Ozone Layer, 16 Yale J.Int'l L. 571 (1991).

## SECTION 5. ENVIRONMENT AND TRADE

It is increasingly recognized that the environment and trade are necessarily linked. Specifically, environmentalists are claiming that free trade will encourage polluting industries to move to countries with no or lax environmental regulation and that countries with inadequate environmental regulation enjoy an improper trade advantage over countries that do provide proper protection of the environment. This has led to efforts to extend national environmental legislation to international trade. See Barber, Bridging the Environmental Gap: The Application of NEPA to the Mexico–United States Bilateral Trade Agreement, 5 Tul.Envtl.L.J. 429 (1992). It also has prompted proposals in Congress to use trade incentives and sanctions in order to force environmental reform in other countries. See Obey, Trade Incentives and Environmental Reform: The Search for a Suitable Incentive, 4 Geo.Int'l Envtl.L.Rev. 421 (1992). For the view that free trade need not detrimentally affect the environment, see Schoenbaum, Free International Trade and Protection of the Environment: Irreconcilable Conflict?, 86 A.J.I.L. 700 (1992); Weiss, Environment and Trade As Partners in Sustainable Development: A Commentary, 86 A.J.I.L. 728 (1992). The Single European Act of 1986, amending the EEC Treaty (see p. 1502 infra), contains a separate Part VII on the Environment. And the EEC has developed a Draft Charter on Environmental Rights and Obligations (December 1990), reprinted in 21 Ent'l Pol'y & L. 81 (1991). The recently signed NAFTA Treaty, see p. 1546 infra, has been criticized for taking insufficient account of environmental concerns, and the Clinton administration has indicated an intention to seek renegotiation on this issue.

In the Tuna dispute, the United States banned the import of tuna caught by Mexican fisherman without proper regard for dolphins. This ban was ruled incompatible with the G.A.T.T. See Dispute Settlement Panel Report on United States Restrictions on Imports of Tuna, 4 World Trade Materials 20 (1992), 30 I.L.M. 1594 (1991). For other materials on trade and environment, see Environment and International Trade (Report of the Secretary–General of UNCTAD), U.N. Doc. A/CONF.151/PC/48 (12 July 1991); Trade and Environment, GATT Doc. 1529, reprinted in 4 World Trade Materials 37 (1992); U.S. House Committee on Energy and Commerce, GATT: Implications on Environmental Laws, 102nd Cong., 1st Sess. (1992). See, generally, Arden–Clark, The General Agreement on Tariffs and Trade, Environmental Protection and Sustainable Development (1991); Sorsa, Environment—A New Challenge to the GATT? (1992); Adcock & Kildow, Environment and the Trading System, 16 Fletcher Forum of World Aff. 55 (1992); Cameron & Robinson, The Use of Trade Provisions in International Environmental Agreements and Their Compatibility With GATT, 2 Y.B. Int'l Envt'l L. 3 (1991); Charnovitz, Exploring the Environmental Exceptions in GATT: Article XX, 25 J. World Trade L. 37 (1991); Cheyne, Environmental Protection Treaties and the GATT, 1 Rev.Eur.Comm.Int'l Envt'l L. (1992); Kisiri,

International Trade and Environment—An Additional Non-Tariff Barrier Against Developing Countries' Trade?, 15 World Competition 75 (1992).

## SECTION 6. ENVIRONMENT AND HUMAN RIGHTS

There is a growing movement towards recognition of a basic human right to a safe environment. National constitutions may also grant protection of environmental rights. For a compilation, see Weiss, in Fairness to Future Generations: International Law, Common Patrimony and Intergenerational Equity, Appendix B (1989).

For general discussion see, e.g., Ksentini, Preliminary Report on Human Rights and the Environment, U.N.Doc. E/CN.4/Sub. 2/1991/8 (2 August 1991); Giagnocavo & Goldstein, Law Reform or World Reform: The Problem of Environmental Rights, 35 McGill L.J. 345 (1990); Gibson, The Right to a Clean Environment, 54 Saskatchewan L.Rev. 1 (1990); Glavovic, Human Rights and Environmental Law: The Case for a Conservation Bill of Rights, 21 Comp. & Int'l L.J. South Africa 52 (1988); Gormley, The Legal Obligation of the International Community to Guarantee a Pure and Decent Environment: The Expansions of Human Rights Norms, 3 Georgetown Int'l Envt'l L.Rev. 85 (1990); Gormley, The Right to a Safe and Decent Environment, 28 Indian J.Int'l L. 90 (1974); Ho, United Nations Recognition of the Human Right to Environmental Protection, 2 Earth L.J. 225 (1976); Hodkova, Is There a Right to a Healthy Environment in the International Legal Order?, 7 Conn.J.Int'l L. 65 (1991); Hondius, Environment and Human Rights, 41 Y.B. A.A.A. (Hague Academy of International Law) 68 (1971); Roberts, The Right to a Decent Environment: A Premature Construct, 12 Envt'l Pol'y & L. 185 (1986); Shelton, Human Rights, Environmental Rights & the Right to Environment, 28 Stan.J.Int'l L. 103 (1991); Shutkin, International Human Rights Law and the Earth: The Protection of Indigenous Peoples and the Environment, 31 Virg.J.Int'l L. 479 (1991); Singh, Right to Environment and Sustainable Development as a Principle of International Law, 29 J.Indian L.Inst. 289 (1987); Symonides, The Human Right to a Clean, Balanced, and Protected Environment, in Dritti Dell'uomo e Abiente: La Partecipazione dei Dittadini alle Decisioni sulla Tutela Dell'ambiente 239 (1990); Throme, Establishing Environment as a Human Right, 19 Den.J.Int'l L. & Pol'y 129 (1991); Uibopuu, The Internationally Guaranteed Right of an Individual to a Clean Environment, 1 Comp.L.Y.B. 101 (1977); Vukasovic, Protection of Environment: One of the Key Issues in the Field of Human Rights, 59 Revista Juridica Universidad de Puerto Rico 889 (1990).

# Chapter 17

# INTERNATIONAL ECONOMIC LAW AND ORGANIZATIONS

## INTRODUCTION

International economic law has been defined as "all the international law and international agreements governing economic transactions that cross state boundaries or otherwise have implications for more than one state, such as those involving movement of goods, funds, persons, intangibles, technology, vessels or aircraft." Restatement (Third) Part VIII, Introductory Note. While this definition would be broad enough to encompass international law and agreements affecting private parties in their commercial, financial and economic dealings, this Chapter will focus on the international law and agreements that apply principally or exclusively to states.

The principal role of the aspects of international economic law here discussed is to restrict or regulate the actions states may take that may affect other states' interests or the interests of their nationals. A broad range of actions may fall within this area. Illustrations would include a state's imposition of taxes, exchange controls, tariffs, import quotas, export subsidies, environmental controls or safety regulations.

This is an area dominated by international agreements; little customary law affecting economic relations has developed beyond the customary law related to state responsibility for injury to the economic interests of aliens examined in Chapter 9. The broad areas principally affected by these international agreements are international trade, international monetary affairs and international investment. Of these, trade and monetary relations have been subjected to substantial regulation by multilateral agreements, the most important of which are the General Agreement on Tariffs and Trade (GATT) and the Articles of Agreement of the International Monetary Fund (IMF). International investment has been the subject of a network of bilateral agreements, such as bilateral treaties of friendship, commerce and navigation and bilateral investment treaties for the encouragement and protection of foreign investment, under which specified legal protection is accorded to property and contractual interests of foreign investors, and bilateral investment guaranty arrangements, which are related to national programs providing insurance for investments against noncommercial risks. See infra.

The International Center for the Settlement of Investment Disputes was created by multilateral agreement to encourage investment in developing countries by providing arrangements for conciliation or arbitration of disputes between foreign investors and states in which investments are made. See p. 1459 infra.

There have been a number of unsuccessful efforts to develop multilateral investment codes regulating the treatment of foreign investments by capital-importing states. See p. 1453 infra. More recently the U.N. Commission and Centre on Transnational Corporations have attempted to develop a draft Code of Conduct on Transnational Corporations. See p. 1454 infra. Efforts over many years to develop a multilateral investment guaranty program culminated in the Convention sponsored by the World Bank establishing the Multilateral Investment Guarantee Agency, which commenced operations in 1988. See p. 1460 infra. The only important multilateral agreements now in force that regulate international investment as such have been those establishing economic communities, such as the European Economic Community, which are discussed in Chapter 19 at p. 1499 infra.

Other multilateral agreements establish a variety of international banking and finance institutions, such as the World Bank (and its affiliates, the International Development Association and the International Finance Corporation) and regional development banks, which support international private investment either by providing loans to developing countries themselves or providing part of the financing for projects that involve an investment of private capital from abroad.

In addition to the network of multilateral and bilateral agreements and multilateral institutions, informal groupings of states have played a growing role in international economic relations. The two most prominent have been the Group of 77 and the Group of Seven.

The Group of 77 is a grouping that now exceeds 120 of the developing countries of Africa, Asia and Latin America. The Group of 77 functions as a kind of caucus for its participants with respect to their common economic and political concerns. Many of the concerns of the Group of 77 were reflected in the formulation of the so-called New International Economic Order (NIEO), which advocated, among other things, a state's right to expropriate without an obligation under international law to pay compensation, greater support for commodity prices, and tariff preferences for the products exported by developing countries. The NIEO was embodied in the U.N. Charter of Economic Rights and Duties of States, U.N.Doc. A/Res./3281 (XXIX), which was adopted by the U.N. General Assembly over the objection of the United States and other industrialized states. See p. 688 supra.

The Group of 77 has often voted as a bloc in U.N. institutions. The Group's impact has been particularly pronounced in the proceedings of UNCTAD. See p. 1415 infra. The influence of the Group of 77, which was relatively powerful in the 1960s and 1970s, has waned in recent years. Severe economic problems in the developing countries, including the Third World debt crisis and declines in commodity prices, have diminished the collective impact of the Group's efforts to foster reform of the world's economic arrangements in favor of the developing world. Competition for capital from Eastern European countries and the republics of the former Soviet Union have further eroded the capacity of the developing countries to achieve enhancement of their economic development through collective action. In part because of the unwieldy size of the Group of 77, an inner circle, called the G–24, currently conducts many negotiations on behalf of developing countries at the United Nations.

The Group of Seven (G–7) is an informal grouping of seven major industrialized countries which include Canada, France, Germany, Italy, Japan, the United Kingdom and the United States. The heads of state of these countries come together with the head of the European Community in annual summit meetings to discuss issues of common concern, principally in the economic and environmental spheres, and to develop cooperative approaches. The finance ministers and central bank governors of the G–7 countries also meet on a regular basis to discuss and coordinate economic policies, including policies affecting interest rates and exchange rates. In 1986–87, the group entered into important agreements relating to interest rates and exchange rates which resulted in a substantial reduction in the value of the dollar, thereby improving the terms of trade for U.S. exports. The role of the Group of Seven is discussed in Funabashi, Managing the Dollar: From the Plaza to the Louvre (2d ed. 1989) and Destler & Heming, Dollar Politics: Exchange Rate Policy Making in the United States (1989).

## SECTION 1. INTERNATIONAL TRADE

### A. THE GENERAL AGREEMENT ON TARIFFS AND TRADE (GATT)

The United States' dominant economic position immediately after World War II gave it the power to lead a restructuring of post-war world trade aimed at eliminating the crippling protectionist measures of the inter-war period. Its position was that a liberalized system of international trade based on non-discrimination and elimination of trade barriers was essential to world economic well-being. The rules governing world trade were to be developed and enforced by an international trade organization, one part of a system of economic cooperation through international institutions, which was to include the World Bank and the International Monetary Fund.

It was evident, looking back at the inter-war period, that protectionism and balance of payments problems could have disastrous effects on domestic economies. This factor was borne in mind in the planning for the new international trade system which was to develop after the Second World War. It seemed necessary to build in safeguards to ensure that a return to a system of free trade would not produce phenomena similar to those of the early 1930s.

To achieve a rational re-ordering of world trade mechanisms, an international conference on trade and employment was held at Havana in the winter of 1947–1948. The Conference approved the Charter of an International Trade Organization (ITO) which included agreements on six topics: commercial policy; restrictive business practices; commodity agreements; employment; economic development and international investment; and a constitution for a new United Nations agency in the field of international trade. The Charter represented the first attempt to state and apply uniform principles of fair dealing to both private and state enterprises involved in international trade. Significantly, the Charter recognized the special position of developing countries by permitting them to impose restrictions on trade in the form of preferences and import quotas to protect "infant industries." The ITO Charter, however, never came into existence, as a result mainly of American and British opposition. In the United States, the reasons for failure to approve the Charter were manifold, and included the general "cold war" disenchantment with international institutions, the revival of protectionist sentiment, and the disaffection of the business community. See Gardner, Sterling Dollar Diplomacy 423 (1956).

The demise of the ITO did not create a complete void in the area of international trade relations. Shortly before the Havana Conference, negotiations had been completed for a General Agreement on Tariffs and Trade (GATT). The GATT represented the first global commercial agreement in history. It had originally been conceived of as a temporary device, to remain in effect until the ITO Charter had been ratified.

The GATT incorporates the code of commercial policy that was to have been part of the ITO structure. In pursuance of its principal purpose of reducing tariffs and other barriers to world trade, the GATT combines the bilateral approach to trade negotiations with the unconditional most-favored nation principle (according to which the most favorable benefits accorded by one nation to another are available to all other nations), which multilateralizes any concessions contained in bilateral agreements by making them available to all members of the GATT. A significant modification of this principle is the agreement on unilateral preferences for less developed countries embodied in Articles XXXVI–XXXVIII. See generally Curzon, Multilateral Commercial Diplomacy (1965).

The GATT itself has never entered into force. Instead, it has been applied pursuant to, and to the extent prescribed by, a Protocol of Provisional Application of Oct. 30, 1947, 61 Stat. pts. 5, 6, T.I.A.S. No. 1700, 55 U.N.T.S. 308, which became effective on January 1, 1948. This Protocol was concluded because it was desired to have the GATT in force as soon as possible, and the delay attendant upon the necessary parliamentary action in participating states made provisional application desirable. When the ITO, and the subsequently proposed Organization for Trade Co-operation (OTC), did not come into existence, the GATT, applied through the Protocol, became the principal instrument for regulating international trade.

The GATT has been the sponsor of eight major tariff and trade negotiations. The sixth, the so-called Kennedy Round, affected some $40 billion in trade and involved 48 participating countries. It achieved tariff reductions of 50 percent on a broad range of products, an anti-dumping code, and special exceptions for less developed countries. The seventh round, the Tokyo Round, which began in Geneva in 1973, involving over 100 countries, was concluded in 1979. In this Round, the focus was shifted to non-tariff barriers and nine agreements were adopted, including codes covering such matters as subsidies, unification of anti-dumping rules, customs valuation, discrimination against foreign goods in government purchasing, countervailing duties and quality specifications that operate to burden foreign imports. See Agreements Reached in the Tokyo Round of Multilateral Trade Negotiations, H.D. 96–153, 96th Cong., 1st Sess. (1979).

Negotiations in the eighth round of trade agreement negotiations under the auspices of the GATT, the so-called Uruguay Round, began in 1986 and have yet to be completed. The Ministerial Declaration established the general objectives and framework for the negotiations. 25 I.L.M. 1623 (1986). The parties agreed not to take any trade-restricting or distorting measures and to dismantle such measures inconsistent with the GATT during the negotiations. Although the negotiations, which involve more than 100 states, have addressed a broad range of matters, they have focused on four main issues: liberalization of trade in services, reduction of agricultural subsidies, increase in foreign protection of intellectual property rights, and improvements in GATT dispute resolution. The negotiators have reached provisional agreement on dispute resolution procedures to apply pending completion of the negotiations. See p. 1414 infra.

As of December 1992, the negotiators had not reached an overall agreement. Particularly intractable has been the issue of negotiating reductions in agricultural subsidies. The European Community (some of the members of which, particularly France, utilize agricultural subsidies heavily), the United States and the agricultural exporting nations repeatedly failed to end the impasse on agricultural subsidies in the negotiations. As this volume goes to press, a settlement of the agricultural subsidy issue between the United States and the European Community has been announced (over the opposition of the French Government) and the Uruguay Round negotiations have resumed. Negotiations were not successfully completed by March 1, 1993, in time to be submitted to Congress for its approval before the expiration of its "fast-track" procedure on June 1, 1993. Under this procedure Congress must approve or not without the possibility of amendments. If the fast-track legislation expires before Congress takes action to extend it, Congressional approval could be a lengthy process involving amendments that would require renegotiation with the other GATT members. It has been estimated that successful completion of the Uruguay Round will increase the volume of world trade by $200 billion by 2002. New York Times, Cl, Col. 6, Nov. 27, 1992.

The GATT lacks a permanent administrative structure found in some international organizations. The GATT refers only to action by the contracting states, of which as of 1992 there were 103, including all major industrial states other than Russia and the People's Republic of China. The action has generally been restricted to fact-finding and mediation. "Over its history, however, the GATT has evolved procedures and institutional practices, and a web of obligations requiring states to submit their actions in respect of trade to international scrutiny, to negotiate about them, and to consider the likely reactions of other states. While some GATT obligations have not been meticulously observed at the margin, overall the Agreement constitutes the prevailing norm of international trade among member states." Restatement (Third) Part VIII, Chapter 1, Introductory Note.

## 1. *Outline of the GATT Agreement*

*JACKSON AND DAVEY, LEGAL PROBLEMS OF INTERNATIONAL ECONOMIC RELATIONS*

296–298 (Second Edition 1986).*

The GATT agreement, including the remarkably detailed commitments on tariffs that comprise the "Tariff Schedules," fills many volumes of treaty text. The "General Articles" of GATT comprise the basic trade policy commitments of the contracting parties. These articles, now numbering thirty-eight and covering eighty or ninety pages of text * * * contain a number of detailed rules and obligations designed generally to prevent nations from pursuing "beggar-thy-neighbor" trade policies which would be self-defeating if emulated by other nations. * * *

GATT is not a single agreement, but is a series of over one hundred agreements, protocols, procés-verbaux, etc. Some of these protocols are amendments to the text of the general articles of GATT, while many are corrections or revisions (in the light of renegotiations) of the tariff schedules. Special "side agreements" have been completed in the context of GATT, which fill out details of obligations on certain subjects, but these apply only to the signatories of the side agreements.

The beginning point for understanding the GATT obligations is Article II, relating to the tariff schedules themselves. The detailed commitments by each country to limit tariffs on particular items by the amount negotiated and specified in its tariff schedule, is the central core of the GATT system of international obligations. The obligations relating to the tariff schedules are contained in Article II of GATT, which makes the schedules an integral part of GATT and its treaty commitments. Basically, for each commodity listed on a country's schedule, that country agrees to charge a tariff which will not exceed an amount specified in that schedule; it can, if it wishes, charge a lower tariff, however.

To a certain extent, the remaining obligations of GATT are designed to reinforce the basic tariff obligation; i.e., to prevent evasion of the tariff obligation by the use of other nontariff barriers, which would inhibit imports. Perhaps the principal exception to this statement is the important obligation contained in Article I, the "Most Favored Nation" clause (MFN). This clause makes a central feature of the GATT obligation system, the non-discrimination principle which had theretofore been contained in a number of bilateral treaties. Under this clause, each member of GATT is obligated to treat other GATT members at least as well as it treats any other country with regard to imports or exports.

A third important obligation of GATT is contained in Article III—the national treatment obligation. While MFN provides a non-discriminatory principle for the treatment of imports from foreign nations, the national treatment obligation specifies that imports shall be treated no worse than domestically produced goods, under internal taxation or regulatory measures.

 Footnotes omitted.

A number of other clauses of GATT limit the type of governmental actions that can be taken to affect imports or exports. Some analyses of international trade policy suggest that there are four basic ways of affecting imports: tariffs, quotas, subsidies and state trading mechanisms. Tariffs in GATT are permitted, but are limited by Article II as discussed above. Quotas, however, are prohibited by Article XI, unless one of the detailed exceptions applies.

Subsidies in GATT are regulated by Article XVI, which, however, does not provide much restraint on what a nation can do. Article VI allows a government unilaterally to use countervailing duties to offset foreign subsidies on goods. * * *

State trading refers to a system of regulating imports by requiring that all imports be made by a government agency or corporation, or by a private corporation to which has been given the monopoly of imports on a commodity. Article XVII of GATT contains some rather general and fairly loose obligations pertaining to state trading. * * *

In addition to the major obligations outlined above, GATT contains a number of obligations relating to the application of tariffs through customs procedure. These obligations limit systems of valuation for customs purposes (Article VII), the types of fees and formalities that can be utilized in connection with importation or exportation (Article VIII), the types of marks of origin that can be required (Article IX), and provide a requirement for publication and fair administration of trade regulations (Article X).

In addition to *obligations,* however, GATT contains a large number of exceptions. * * * It has been said that the GATT is "riddled with exceptions", and that "a lawyer could drive a four-horse team through any obligation that anybody had." Nevertheless, exceptions may be necessary to allow an agreement to be viable, giving it sufficient flexibility so that wholesale derogation from its obligations will not occur.

The most important exception to GATT is also its most general, namely the waiver authority of Article XXV. The CONTRACTING PARTIES, acting jointly can, by a specified vote, waive any obligation of GATT.

A second important exception to GATT is the escape clause of Article XIX, providing for the use of temporary restraints on imports in cases where imports are causing serious injury to domestic industry.

Important exceptions to GATT obligations are contained in Articles XII–XIV relating to trade policy in the event of a balance of payments crisis. Basically, these articles allow the use of quotas (despite the prohibition of Article XI) in such cases.

Customs unions and free trade areas are, under Article XXIV, allowed to deviate from the MFN principle so as to give certain preferred status to the trade of members of the customs union or free trade area.

Article XX and Article XXI contain some important general exceptions which allow deviation from GATT obligations for purposes of implementing national health and safety regulations, and national security.

### *Notes*

1. On the GATT generally, see Dam, The GATT: Law and International Economic Organization (1970); Hudec, The GATT Legal System and World Trade Diplomacy (2d ed.1990); A. Lowenfeld, Public Controls on International Trade (2d ed.1983); Jackson and Davey, Legal Problems of International Economic Relations 293–823 (2d ed. 1986 and 1992 Supp.); Long, Law and its Limitations in the GATT Multilateral Trade System (1985); Jackson, The World Trading System: Law and Policy of International Economic Relations (1989); and Jackson, Restructuring GATT (1990).

2. The GATT has not been a direct source of rights for private parties. See § 3(f) of the Trade Agreements Act of 1979, 19 U.S.C.A. § 2504(d). However, many provisions of United States legislation mirror international obligations contained in the GATT or its related codes and confer rights on private parties affected by imports. United States exporters, however, must seek intercession by the United States Trade Representative to obtain benefits of the GATT with respect to import restraints imposed by foreign states. See § 301 of the Trade Act of 1974, 19 U.S.C.A. § 2411.

3. GATT Article XXIV(12) binds each party to take "reasonable measures" to ensure observance of the GATT by regional and local governments. In the United States, prior state legislation has been held to be superseded by the GATT to the extent inconsistent with it. See, e.g., Bethlehem Steel Corp. v. Board of Comm'rs, 276 Cal.App.2d 221, 80 Cal.Rptr. 800 (1969).

4. The effective tariff burden on imported goods is determined not only by the tariff rate, but also by other factors, such as customs classification and valuation for customs purposes. For example, in Western Stamping Corp. v. United States, 417 F.2d 316 (C.C.P.A.1969), the issue was whether a toy typewriter was to be classified as a typewriter, which was duty-free, or as a toy, subject to 35 percent ad valorem duty, with the court upholding its classification as a typewriter.

In an effort to eliminate disparate treatment as a result of classification differences, a European Customs Union Study Group developed after World War II a Nomenclature for the Classification of Goods in Customs Tariffs, the so-called Brussels Tariff Nomenclature (BTN). A Convention on Nomenclature and a Convention to Establish a Customs Cooperation Council (CCC) were opened for signature on December 15, 1950. The CCC, whose task it is to supervise the application and interpretation of the Nomenclature, published a revised BTN with explanatory notes in 1955. Customs Cooperation Council, Nomenclature for the Classification of Goods in Customs Tariffs (4th ed. 1972). All major developed trading nations of the GATT, with the exception of the United States and Canada, have made the Nomenclature the basis of their customs tariffs. In 1970, the United States began participating in the CCC, and the United States International Trade Commission (formerly Tariff Commission) has published a series of draft schedules which would conform the Tariff Schedules of the United States (TSUS) to the BTN. However, resistance to the BTN developed in Congress on the ground that a more modern system should be established. In the meantime, work began in the CCC on a universal commodity code classification system, based on the BTN and on the "Standard International Trade Classification" (SITC) used by the United Nations in reporting trade statistics. In June, 1984, the Harmonized Commodity Description and Coding System, also called the "Harmonized System" was opened for signature. Since that time, 40 countries, including the United States, have adopted the system.

The GATT provides that the basic standard for determining value for customs purposes should be the price at which the imported or like goods are sold under fully competitive conditions. Under United States law, the valuation basis is in certain circumstances the American selling price (ASP), which is the wholesale price at which like articles manufactured in the United States are offered for sale. This valuation standard often has the net effect of increasing the duty and is therefore objectionable to exporting countries. Although the ASP standard violates Article VII of the GATT, it remains in effect by virtue of the grandfather clause of the Protocol of Provisional Application. Efforts to eliminate the ASP have thus far been unsuccessful.

On these problems, see also Jackson and Davey, Legal Problems of International Economic Relations 371–385 (2d ed.1986 and 1992 Supp.).

### 2. *Tariffs*

By virtue of Article I of the GATT, under which each member state undertakes to grant most-favored-nation (MFN) treatment, and Article II, under which each agrees to adhere to the tariffs listed in the schedules it has negotiated under the GATT, tariff reduction negotiations have, as noted above, been multilateralized through a series of seven negotiating rounds, in which states balance the concessions they make against all concessions they receive from whatever party grants them. An eighth, the Uruguay Round, has not yet been completed. See p. 1398 supra. The Article III national treatment obligation that imports shall be treated no worse than domestically-produced goods under internal tax or regulatory regimes applies domestically the non-discriminatory principle reflected in MFN treatment.

In addition to the most-favored-nation obligation of Article I, the GATT also imposes most-favored-nation treatment with respect to such matters as marks of origin (Art. IX(1)), quantitative restrictions (Art. XIII(1)), and export controls on goods in short supply (Art. XX(j)). There are certain specific exceptions to these MFN obligations, including preferences for developing countries and customs unions and free trade areas under specified circumstances.

#### *Notes*

1. A party to the GATT is obligated not to increase a tariff to a level above the rate to which it is committed by the tariff's inclusion in a schedule to which the party is committed. A tariff is "bound" when a state has filed with the GATT a commitment not to increase it or to lower it. The binding process occurs principally at the negotiating rounds conducted by the parties. A state may withdraw a "binding" if it negotiates substantially similar equivalent concessions on other products of interest to the principal beneficiaries of the original binding. Art. XXVIII. See Restatement (Third) § 803. Article XXVIII provides that periodically a state may modify or withdraw any concession by agreement with the contracting party with which it was originally negotiated and with any other party determined to have "a principal supplying interest." This is a party that "had, over a reasonable period of time prior to the negotiations, a larger share in the market of the applicant contracting party than a contracting party with which the concession was initially negotiated." Art. XXVIII, Note 4. This test can also be deemed to be met if discriminatory restrictions prevent a party from achieving such a share. According to the Restatement (Third) § 803, Reporters' Note 2:

* * * The United States was in such a situation vis-a-vis the Federal Republic of Germany, with respect to poultry following the creation of the European Economic Community. Germany had become bound as a result of negotiations with Denmark. In 1958, the United States had sold only one-third as much poultry to Germany as did Denmark; it had moved to approximate equality with Denmark in 1959, and exceeded it in 1960. Thereafter, import restraints pursuant to the Common Agricultural Policy led to a sharp decline in imports of poultry into the EEC, and the United States filed a formal complaint with the GATT. A GATT panel subsequently ruled on the amount of compensation due to the United States, assuming (without formally deciding) that the United States had standing under Article XXVIII as a principal supplier, although the concession was originally granted to Denmark. See Report of Panel on Poultry. GATT Doc. No. L/2088 (Nov. 21, 1963), repr. 3 Int'l Leg.Mat. 116 (1964); Walker, "Dispute Settlement: The Chicken War," 58 Am.J.Int'l L. 671 (1964); 1 Chayes, Ehrlich and Lowenfeld, International Legal Process 249–305 (1968). The United States withdrew concessions in an amount equal to that found by the GATT panel, selecting products of which the EEC was a principal supplier, but generalizing the increased duties to all suppliers of those products. See United States v. Star Industries, Inc., 462 F.2d 557 (C.C.P.A.), cert. denied, 409 U.S. 1076, 93 S.Ct. 678, 34 L.Ed.2d 663 (1972); Lowenfeld, "Doing Unto Others, The Chicken War Ten Years After," 4 J.Mar.L. & C. 599 (1973).

2. The MFN principle is stated in § 126 of the Trade Act of 1974, 19 U.S.C.A. § 2136(a). Sections 401–10 of the Act, 19 U.S.C.A. §§ 2431–2441, deny MFN treatment to Communist states unless a commercial agreement is in effect and limit the authority of the President to enter into such agreements. MFN treatment has been extended by the United States by bilateral agreement to the People's Republic of China. Restatement (Third) § 802, Reporters' Note 2.

3. The national treatment obligation of Article III, which is also found in most United States bilateral investment treaties and bilateral friendship, commerce and navigation (FCN) treaties, discussed at pp. 759–769 supra, forbids discrimination against imported goods once they have passed tariff and other similar barriers. Problems in this area arise typically when the more favorable treatment of domestically-produced goods results from domestic measures, such as labeling requirements, technical standards requirements, and anti-pollution rules, that may be regarded as not seeking to grant domestic producers a competitive advantage but instead as pursuing other domestic policies. Article XX of the GATT, in an effort to permit fair accommodation of competing interests, provides for potentially broad exceptions from national treatment. However, since the legislative motive is not always apparent, ambiguous situations can easily arise. See, e.g., the Federal Trade Commission ruling of April 1979, requiring animals formerly designated as "Minks, Japanese" to be designated in the future as "Japanese Weasel." On national treatment generally, see Jackson, World Trade and the Law of GATT c. 12 (1969).

### 3. *Quantitative Restrictions*

Quantitative restrictions on imports (quotas) are prohibited by Article XI of the GATT, subject to some important exceptions. Under Article XI(2)(c) import restrictions are permitted in the case of "any agricultural or fisheries product" in support of programs that attempt to restrict domestic output of the product in question or of some closely related product, provided that such programs do not alter the proportion of imports to domestic production that would otherwise obtain.

Quantitative restrictions are also permitted for certain law enforcement purposes, such as prevention of deceptive practices, protection of public morals, national treasures or human or animal health. Art. XX. Quantitative restrictions may also be imposed in escape clause cases, but not in countervailing duty or anti-dumping cases.

No quantitative restriction may be applied to imports of one party unless it is similarly applied to all third countries, and quotas must be allocated among supplying states so as to preserve the shares of imports they might be expected to have but for the restrictions. Art. XIII. See Restatement (Third) § 804, Comment *a*.

### *Notes*

1. Textile imports from low-wage and developing states led first to formal and informal quantitative restraints in developed states and eventually to a series of multilateral agreements, including the Multifiber Arrangement (MFA), renegotiated and renewed in 1986, under which importing and exporting states may negotiate bilateral pacts on actual trade levels for wool, cotton, ramie and synthetic fibers and blends. The Multifiber Arrangement expired in 1991, but was extended to December 31, 1992. As part of the negotiations in the Uruguay Round, member countries have discussed the creation of a substitute system to replace the MFA. The negotiators have agreed upon a 10–year period during which all existing bilateral agreements under the MFA must be eliminated. Finalization of these textile negotiations, however, may depend on the success of the negotiations on other open issues. For a discussion of these agreements and their relation to the GATT, see Jackson and Davey, Legal Problems of International Economic Relations 638–643 (2d ed. 1986 and 1992 Supp.).

2. Some controversies over excessive imports of certain products have been settled by voluntary quantitative limits on exports. Such quotas have not been regarded as violative of Article XI of the GATT because the exporting country has consented. Restatement (Third) § 804, Reporters' Note 4.

3. Quantitative restrictions are authorized by Article XII (or by Article XVIII with respect to developing states) for states in balance of payments difficulties.

## *4. Indirect Barriers to Imports*

The GATT also prohibits indirect restraints on imports. Article II states that "internal taxes and other regulations and requirements affecting local sale * * * purchase, transportation, distribution or use of products * * * should not be applied * * * so as to afford protection to domestic production." Parties are called upon to minimize the burden of import formalities. As noted above, this obligation has been implemented in a series of codes on such matters as technical standards, customs procedures and formalities, and government procurement.

### *Note*

State trading enterprises are enjoined to act in connection with imports and exports solely in accordance with non-discriminatory commercial considerations. Art. XVII. With respect to imports to be used by the government itself, however, only "fair and equitable treatment" for products of other states is required, and non-commercial government purchases are exempt from the national treatment principle of Article III.

### *5. Subsidies and Countervailing Duties*

The GATT prohibits a party other than a developing country from granting subsidies to exports of any products except specified primary products if the result is an export price lower than the comparable domestic price. The Subsidies Code proscribes export subsidies by any country (other than a developing country) for products (other than certain primary products) without regard to whether there is a differential in prices. Agreement on Interpretation and Application of Articles VI, XVI and XXIII of the General Agreement on Tariffs and Trade (Subsidies Code 1979), 31 U.S.T. 405, T.I.A.S. No. 9619.

Countervailing duties on imports that have benefitted from an export subsidy are authorized by Article VI(6) of the GATT, provided that the effect of the subsidization is "such as to cause or threaten material injury" to or "to retard materially the establishment of a domestic industry." "Injury" and "domestic industry" are elaborated in Article 6 of the Subsidies Code. The countervailing duty may not exceed the amount of the subsidy.

#### *Notes*

1. Difficult problems have arisen in determining what are forbidden subsidies. See e.g., Marks & Malmgren, Negotiating Non-tariff Distortions to Trade, 7 L. & Policy in Int'l Bus. 327 (1975).

2. Neither the GATT nor the Subsidies Code prohibits domestic production subsidies, such as property or income tax subsidies to encourage investment in productive facilities, even though such subsidies may permit lower export prices than would otherwise be applicable.

3. If subsidies are granted with respect to exports of primary products, they "shall not be applied in a manner which results in [the granting state] having more than an equitable share of world export trade in the product concerned." Art. XVI. This standard is elaborated in Article 10 of the Subsidies Code. A controversy developed from the agricultural policy of the European Economic Community, which has used import levies to maintain artificially high prices in the Community and has used a portion thereof to reduce the prices of surpluses sold abroad. See Bolger, The United States–European Community Agricultural Export Subsidies Dispute, 16 L. & Policy in Int'l Bus. 173 (1984).

4. Article 4 of the Subsidies Code provides that no countervailing duty shall exceed the amount of the subsidy and that it is desirable that it be smaller if it would be adequate to remove the injury. See Barcelo, Subsidies, Countervailing Duties and Antidumping after the Tokyo Round, 13 Cornell Int'l L.J. 257 (1980).

5. Another controversy involving the prohibition on export subsidies focused on provisions of the United States Internal Revenue Code that permitted deferral of United States tax on certain export-related income of a United States corporation that qualified as a domestic international sales corporation (DISC). A GATT panel found that the DISC provisions created a subsidy not permitted by the GATT and the report was adopted by the GATT Council in 1981. 16 J. World Trade L. 361–62 (1982). The issue was defused in 1984 when the DISC provisions were largely but not entirely supplanted by provisions granting tax

benefits to the export-related income of a foreign sales corporation (FSC) that is organized under foreign law and has substantial foreign activities. 26 U.S.C.A. §§ 921–927. See Jackson, The Jurisprudence of International Trade: The DISC Case in GATT, 72 A.J.I.L. (1978).

### 6. *Dumping and Anti–Dumping Duties*

Article VI(1) of the GATT defines "dumping" as sales below "normal value." Normal value means the price of the same product when destined for consumption in the producing state. In the absence of such a price, it means the price charged with respect to exports to third countries or the cost of production whichever is higher.

The GATT authorizes the imposition by the importing state of an anti-dumping duty to equal the full amount of the margin of dumping, but Article 8(1) of the Anti–Dumping Code, to which the United States is a party, states that it is desirable that the duty be lower if adequate to remove the injury. Agreement on the Implementation of the General Agreement on Tariffs and Trade (Anti–Dumping Code 1979), 31 U.S.T. 4919, T.I.A.S. No. 9650.

#### *Note*

Especially in the case of state trading countries and enterprises owned by the government, the same product may benefit from an export subsidy and may be sold at a price falling within the dumping definition. Both countervailing duties and anti-dumping duties may be imposed in respect of the same product, but not in such a way as to provide a duplicate response to a single effect of a foreign practice. Restatement (Third) § 806, Comment *a*.

### 7. *Emergency Action to Protect Domestic Producers*

Article XIX—the escape clause—of the GATT provides that a party may suspend its obligation or withdraw a concession with respect to a product if it finds that, as a result of unforeseen developments and of concessions given, the product is being imported into its territory in such increased quantities and under such conditions as to cause or threaten serious injury to its domestic producers. Such suspension or withdrawal may be taken only in case of emergency and only for so long as necessary to deal with it. A party must give advance notice to other parties and to states having a substantial interest as exporters and, except in critical circumstances, is required to consult with the parties primarily affected before taking action. Art. XIX(2). Any party injured by the action may respond by suspending substantially equivalent concessions on imports from the state resorting to the escape clause action.

#### *Note*

The GATT provides a number of alternatives to invoking the escape clause mechanism. Tariff concessions may be renegotiated at specified intervals under Article XXVIII. Exporting and importing parties may enter into an orderly marketing agreement so long as third parties are not adversely affected. Under Article XVII(4)(a) developing states may restrict imports temporarily to aid domestic industries.

### 8. *Customs Unions and Free Trade Areas*

Under Article XXIV of the GATT, two or more parties may form a customs union or a free trade area, provided that (i) the resulting tariffs and other restrictions on trade with other states are not on the whole higher or more restrictive than the general incidence of duties and restrictions previously applicable in the territory of the customs union or free trade area and (ii) duties and other restrictions on substantially all trade within the territory of the union or area are eliminated. Participating states must follow procedures specified in Article XXIV for notifying the GATT, consultation with the contracting states and negotiation with particularly affected states.

#### *Notes*

1. A customs union is a grouping of states in which duties and trade restrictions are eliminated with respect to internal trade while the same duties and trade restrictions are applied by all members of the union to imports from all other states (the common external tariff). The European Economic Community is the leading example. See p. 1499 infra. Other examples include the Andean Common Market (ANCOM), p. 1550 infra, and the Central American Common Market (CACM), p. 1549 infra. A free trade area also involves eliminating duties and restrictions on trade within the area, but each member is free to determine its own duties and restrictions with respect to trade with nonmembers. Examples include the European Free Trade Association (EFTA), p. 1545 infra and the Latin American Free Trade Association (LAFTA), p. 1549 infra. Those involving the United States are discussed in paragraphs 2 through 5 infra. At the signing of the North American Free Trade Agreement with Canada and Mexico on December 17, 1992, President Bush expressed the hope that the Agreement would eventually encompass all of the Western Hemisphere. In the meantime, efforts to establish free trade areas seem to be progressing in Latin America on other fronts under the auspices of the Andean Pact Organization and MERCOSUR (Argentina, Bolivia, Chile and Uruguay), which plan to establish customs unions by the mid–1990s. The Central American Common Market (CACM) and the Caribbean Community (CARICOM) seem to be moving forward again after a period of relative inactivity. Moreover, the Treaty Establishing the African Economic Community, signed on June 3, 1991, 30 I.L.M. 1241 (1991), involving the 51 member states of the Organization of African Unity calls for creation of a free trade area within 10 years. Similar developments have occurred in Southeast Asia with Japan and the United States indicating interest in participating in arrangements that would eventually include all Pacific Rim countries. The Association of Southeast Asian Nations (ASEAN) including Brunei Darussalam, Indonesia, Malaysia, Philippines, Singapore, and Thailand entered into agreements on January 28, 1992 agreeing to establish and participate in an ASEAN Free Trade Area (AFTA) within 15 years. The centerpiece is a common effective preferential tariff applicable to goods originating in ASEAN member states. 31 I.L.M. 506 (1992).

Problems have arisen as to whether the various free trade areas and customs unions that have come into existence fall within the terms of the exceptions specified in Article XXIV. See, e.g., Lortie, Economic Integration and the Law of GATT 13–39 (1975) (concluding that all ten regional economic cooperation agreements considered violate the requirements of Article XXIV).

2. In 1985, the United States and Israel entered into an agreement establishing a bilateral free trade area. Under the agreement all duties will be

eliminated in four stages by January 1, 1995. Agreement on the Establishment of a Free Trade Area Between the Government of the United States and the Government of Israel, signed April 22, 1985.

3. The Canada–United States Free Trade Agreement became effective on January 1, 1989. 27 I.L.M. 281 (1988). With this agreement, the United States and Canada have created a free trade area involving the largest volume of trade between any two nations. During the first year of the agreement, trade between the two countries increased by $30 billion. See Baker, The Canada–United States Free Trade Agreement, 23 Int'l Law. 37 (1989). The United States has implemented the Agreement in the United States–Canada Free Trade Agreement Implementation Act of 1988, Pub.L. No. 100–449, 102 Stat. 1851 (1988).

The principal goal of the Canada–United States agreement is the elimination of tariffs and other barriers to free trade between the two countries. More specifically, the agreement expands some of the parties' basic obligations under the GATT, creates new obligations with respect to trade in services, and establishes new dispute-resolution mechanisms.

With respect to the elimination of tariffs, the agreement has two main thrusts. First, it prohibits either party from increasing any existing duties on goods originating in the other country. Second, it calls for a progressive elimination of duties on designated goods by January 1, 1998, and for the acceleration of this process by consultation and agreement with respect to specific goods.

The agreement also extends the parties' obligations under the GATT with respect to prohibitions or restrictions on trade. For example, the agreement prohibits most restrictions with respect to energy. It eliminates import restrictions and minimum import requirements for oil, gas, coal, electricity, uranium and other related energy products, while also eliminating export taxes, minimum export price requirements and volume restraints.

The agreement establishes the first comprehensive arrangement with respect to trade in services. National treatment is required for most commercial services, except for transportation, telecommunications, child care, government-provided services, and services rendered by lawyers, doctors, and dentists.

Finally, the agreement creates two general dispute-resolution mechanisms. The first is the "institutional provisions" that apply to all disputes involving the application and interpretation of the agreement. To settle disputes, the parties may use one or more of the following four methods: (1) consultation, (2) the United States–Canada Trade Commission, (3) arbitration and (4) panel procedures. The second mechanism is the binational panel for dispute settlement in anti-dumping and countervailing duties cases. Under this arrangement, each party may request a binational panel to consider whether the other party's amendments to its anti-dumping and countervailing duties laws comply with the GATT and the Free Trade Agreement. In addition, a Working Group is created to develop a substitute system of rules to replace the current anti-dumping and countervailing duties laws of each country.

4. Pursuant to special authorization by Congress, a North American Free Trade Agreement between Canada, Mexico and the United States has been negotiated and signed and now awaits action by Congress. The Fact Sheet issued by the White House on August 12, 1992, states, in part, as follows:

> The President today announced that the United States, Mexico, and Canada have completed negotiation of a North American Free Trade Agree-

ment (NAFTA). The NAFTA will phase out barriers to trade in goods and services in North America, eliminate barriers to investment, and strengthen the protection of intellectual property rights. As tariffs and other trade barriers are eliminated, the NAFTA will create a massive open market—over 360 million people and over $6 trillion in annual output.

* * *

The NAFTA will create a free trade area (FTA) comprising the U.S., Canada, and Mexico. Consistent with GATT rules, all tariffs will be eliminated within the FTA over a transition period. The NAFTA involves an ambitious effort to eliminate barriers to agricultural, manufacturing, and services trade, to remove investment restrictions, and to protect effectively intellectual property rights. In addition, the NAFTA marks the first time in the history of U.S. trade policy that environmental concerns have been directly addressed in a comprehensive trade agreement. Highlights of the NAFTA include:

**Tariff Elimination.** Approximately 65 percent of U.S. industrial and agricultural exports to Mexico will be eligible for duty-free treatment either immediately or within five years. Mexico's tariffs currently average 10 percent, which is two-and-a-half times the average U.S. tariff.

**Reduction of Motor Vehicle and Parts Tariffs.** U.S. autos and light trucks will enjoy greater access to Mexico, which has the fastest growing major auto market in the world. With NAFTA, Mexican tariffs on vehicles and light trucks will immediately be cut in half. Within five years, duties on three-quarters of U.S. parts exports to Mexico will be eliminated, and Mexican "trade balancing" and "local content requirements" will be phased out over 10 years.

**Auto Rule of Origin.** Only vehicles with substantial North American parts and labor content will benefit from tariff cuts under NAFTA's strict rule of origin. NAFTA will require that autos contain 62.5 percent North American content, considerably more than the 50 percent required by the U.S.–Canada Free Trade Agreement. NAFTA contains tracing requirements so that individual parts can be identified to determine the North American content of major components and subassemblies, *e.g.* engines. This strict rule of origin is important in ensuring that the benefits of the NAFTA flow to firms that produce in North America.

**Expanded Telecommunications Trade.** NAFTA opens Mexico's $6 billion market for telecommunications equipment and services. It gives U.S. providers of voice mail or packet-switched services nondiscriminatory access to the Mexican public telephone network and eliminates all investment restrictions by July 1995.

**Reduced Textiles and Apparel Barriers.** Barriers to trade on $250 million (over 20 percent) of U.S. exports of textiles and apparel to Mexico will be eliminated immediately, with another $700 million freed from restrictions within 6 years. All North American trade restrictions will be eliminated within 10 years and tough rules of origin will ensure that benefits of trade liberalization accrue to North American producers.

**Increased Trade in Agriculture.** Mexico imported $3 billion worth of U.S. agricultural goods last year, making it our third-largest market. NAFTA will immediately eliminate Mexican import licenses, which covered 25 percent of U.S. agricultural exports last year, and will phase out remaining Mexican tariffs within 10–15 years.

**Expanded Trade in Financial Services.** Mexico's closed financial services markets will be opened and U.S. banks and securities firms will be allowed to establish wholly owned subsidiaries. Transitional restrictions will be phased out by January 1, 2000.

**New Opportunities in Insurance.** U.S. firms will gain major new opportunities in the Mexican market; firms with existing joint ventures will be permitted to obtain 100 percent ownership by 1996 and new entrants to the market can obtain a majority stake in Mexican firms by 1998. By the year 2000, all equity and market share restrictions will be eliminated, opening up completely what is now a $3.5 billion market.

**Increased Investment.** Mexican "domestic content" rules will be eliminated, permitting additional sourcing of U.S. inputs and, for the first time, U.S. firms operating in Mexico will receive the same treatment as Mexican-owned firms. Mexico has agreed to drop export performance requirements, which presently force companies to export as a condition of being allowed to invest.

**Land Transportation.** More than 90 percent of U.S. trade with Mexico is shipped by land, but U.S. truckers currently are denied the right to carry cargo or set up subsidiaries in Mexico, forcing them to "hand off" trailers to Mexican drivers and return home empty. NAFTA will permit U.S. trucking companies to carry international cargo to the Mexican states contiguous to the U.S. by 1995, and gives them cross-border access to all of Mexico by the end of 1999. U.S. railroads will be able to provide their services in Mexico, and U.S. companies can invest in and operate land-side port services. The combination of truck, rail, and port breakthroughs will help create an efficient, intermodal North American transport system.

**Protection of Intellectual Property Rights.** NAFTA will provide a higher level of protection for intellectual property rights than any other bilateral or multilateral agreement. U.S. high technology, entertainment, and consumer goods producers that rely heavily on protection for their patents, copyrights, and trademarks will realize substantial gains under NAFTA. The agreement will also limit compulsory licensing, resolving an important concern with Canada.

The objective of NAFTA is to open markets. It is not designed to create a closed regional trading bloc, and does not erect new barriers to non-participants. The NAFTA is fully consistent with GATT criteria for free trade agreements, and with U.S. support for strengthening the multilateral trading system in the Uruguay Round.

BNA Int'l Trade Rep. 1451–52 (Aug. 8, 1992). Under the fast-track procedures currently in place, the NAFTA will not go into effect until Congress has approved the implementing legislation on an up-or-down vote with no opportunity for amendments. However, it is anticipated that the Clinton Administration will seek to renegotiate or enter into supplemental agreements concerning some aspects of the agreement, and it is unclear whether Congress will ultimately approve on a fast-track basis or under the usual rules applying to trade legislation under which amendments would be permitted.

5. An Automotive Products Agreement was entered into between the United States and Canada in 1966, 17 U.S.T. 1372, T.I.A.S. No. 6093, which generally provided for the free movement of automobiles and parts between the two countries. It was determined by a GATT working party that the United States was in violation of the MFN treatment requirement of Article I of the GATT Agreement because duty-free treatment was not extended to vehicles and parts imported from other states. Moreover, the U.S.–Canadian agreement did not come within the definition of a customs union. The parties to the GATT eventually granted a waiver to the United States. BISD 14th Supp. 37, 20 Dec. 1969. See 1 Chayes, Ehrlich and Lowenfeld, International Legal Process 307–83 (1968). The Automotive Products Agreement was modified by Chapter 10 of the Canada–United States Free Trade Agreement. 27 I.L.M. 281 (1988).

### 9. *Special Treatment of Developing States*

Article XVII of the GATT allows states with "low standards of living" and in "the early stages of development" to depart from their obligations under the GATT by imposing tariffs or quotas, granting subsidies or by taking other measures to protect domestic industries or their balance of payments. Moreover, in 1971, the parties to the GATT granted a general waiver to permit developed countries to make tariff concessions to developing states that they did not grant to other states. BISD, 18th Supp. p. 24 (1972).

#### *Notes*

1. It is the position of the United States that it is contrary to the GATT for a developing state to grant a preference to a developed state in return for a preference granted to it. It also seems contrary to the GATT for a developed state to grant a preference to one developing state but not to others. Restatement (Third) § 810, Comment *b*.

2. Restatement (Third) § 810, Comment *c* states:

> Title V of the Trade Act of 1974 authorizes a Generalized System of Preferences, adopted in response to the GATT waiver of 1971. That legislation, renewed in 1984, authorizes the President to designate states as eligible to introduce eligible goods free of duty or subject to reduced duties. GSP treatment is not available, however, for products of Communist countries not entitled to MFN treatment (§ 802, Reporters' Note 2). Further, products of the following categories of states are ineligible for GSP treatment: members of the Organization of Petroleum Exporting Countries and similar cartel arrangements; states affording trade preferences to developed states other than the United States; states refusing to cooperate with the United States in narcotics control; states refusing to honor awards resulting from arbitrations with United States citizens; states that have expropriated investments or otherwise impaired the rights of United States investors in violation of international law, as defined in the Hickenlooper Amendment (§ 712, Reporters' Note 2), unless the President determines that designation of the state will be in the national economic interest of the United States. Products likely to damage domestic industries, including textile and apparel articles, watches, and import-sensitive steel and electronic articles, are ineligible for GSP benefits. The goods that may be exempt from duty are

limited to a fixed amount per year per country for any product category, adjusted for changes in the gross national product of the United States. In addition, if imports of any product from any country reach or exceed 50 percent of all imports of that product, then (subject to stated exceptions) duty-free imports of that product shall cease.

3. Developing countries have contended that the GATT's basic structure disfavors them and tends to keep in place tariff protection that is biased against imports of manufactured products from developing countries. In addition, they have argued that developed countries have increased non-tariff barriers against manufactured goods from developing countries. These complaints led developing nations to sponsor the creation of the United Nations Conference on Trade and Development (UNCTAD), which first met in 1964 and since has become a permanent institution affiliated with the U.N. General Assembly. See p. 1415 infra. See Pestieau & Henry, Non–Tariff Barriers as a Problem in International Development 39–96 (The Canadian Economic Policy Committee, Montreal 1972). Trade issues are discussed both in the GATT and UNCTAD, and the existence of the latter has made the GATT more responsive to the needs of the developing countries.

### *10. Commodity Agreements*

One of the most significant factors in the economic development of developing countries is the extent to which they depend on income from exports of primary commodities. Apart from making long-term attempts to diversify their economies, developing countries have therefore sought to stabilize commodity prices, through bilateral or multilateral commodity agreements.

There are three types of commodity agreements. The first of these—exemplified by the International Wheat Agreement—obligates importers and exporters to buy or sell certain guaranteed quantities at a price fluctuating between stipulated maximum and minimum prices. The second type—of which an example is the International Natural Rubber Agreement—establishes an international buffer stock administered by an authority which seeks to stabilize prices by buying the commodity whenever the price falls below a certain minimum and selling when it rises above it. The third type—exemplified by the International Coffee Agreement—seeks to assure equitable export shares between competing producers of a commodity in surplus production, by allocating export quotas and obligating the participating importers to limit their imports from non-participants.

Article XX(h) of the GATT permits parties to enter into commodity agreements, provided that they are open to participation by both exporting and importing states and are designed to assure the availability of supplies adequate to meet demand at stable prices. See Art. XXXVIII(2)(a).

### *Notes*

1. The United States as of 1991 was party to commodity agreements relating to coffee, cotton, jute, natural rubber, sugar, tropical timber, wheat and wine. Other states are parties to agreements relating to olive oil and cocoa. See Restatement (Third) § 811, Reporters' Note 2 and Khan, The Law and Organization of International Commodity Agreements (1982). In October 1985, the International Tin Council (ITC), the operating arm of the International Tin

Agreement, became insolvent and ceased its stabilizing efforts. Its member states denied liability to the ITC's creditors and their claims were eventually settled for a fraction of the amounts claimed. The Tin Agreement expired in 1989 and was not renewed. Mallory, Conduct Unbecoming: The Collapse of the International Tin Agreement, 5 Am.U.J.Int'l.L. & Pol'y 835, 836, 888 (1990). The Cocoa Agreement collapsed in 1988. The Coffee Agreement collapsed in 1989, but was extended to September 1992 without export quotas or other price support mechanism. The resulting free market produced a sharp drop in coffee prices. Negotiations are in progress to extend the agreement with a reintroduction of export quotas to support prices.

2. Under commodity agreements decisions are usually taken by weighted voting. Under the Coffee Agreement, for example, the exporting members as a group and importing members as a group each held 1,000 votes. Each member had five basic votes, and the remaining votes were allocated in accord with a member's export quotas or historic imports of coffee. Restatement (Third) § 811, Comment *a*.

3. There has been considerable pressure from developing countries for protection against commodity price fluctuations. See, e.g., Kreinin & Finger, A Critical Survey of the New International Economic Order, 10 J. World Trade L. 493 (1976). One consequence has been the establishment of a Compensatory Finance Facility under the International Monetary Fund (IMF) upon which developing states may draw by showing the impact on their economy of price fluctuations and expressing willingness to accept the IMF's conditions. See p. 1426 infra and Finger & Derose, The Compensatory Finance Facility and Export Instability, 14 J. World Trade L. 14 (1980).

### *11. Export Controls*

A party to the GATT is not permitted to impose restrictions on exports to achieve economic advantage for its products. Articles XI, XIII, XX, XXI. Other export controls, even if discriminatory, do not generally violate the GATT. Moreover, controls to prevent "critical shortages" of foodstuffs or other essential products (Art. XI) or controls essential to the acquisition or distribution of products in short supply (Art. XX(j)) are specifically envisaged.

Article XXI of the GATT provides a general exception to all GATT obligations for measures taken by a state that are "necessary for the protection of its essential security interests. * * * " Under the protection of this provision, the United States has operated a system for controlling exports of strategic materials (and technology) to potential adversaries. See generally Jackson and Davey, Legal Problems of International Economic Relations c. 13 (2d ed. 1986). The United States has also used export controls to deter conduct by foreign states deemed inimical to U.S. interests. See p. 1063 supra.

### *Notes*

1. Most of the OPEC states participating in the oil embargo imposed against the United States and the Netherlands in 1973 were not parties to the GATT.

2. Could export controls implemented by the United States alone or collectively with other states violate principles of international law other than those

contained in the GATT? Can they violate the provisions of bilateral treaties of friendship, commerce and navigation treaties to which the United States is party? See p. 759 supra. Can a state injured by a violation of international law by another state lawfully resort to a boycott? See Restatement (Third) § 812, Reporters' Note 1. Collective export controls sanctioned by the U.N. Security Council are lawful. See Diggs v. Shultz, 470 F.2d 461 (D.C.Cir.1972), cert. denied, 411 U.S. 931, 93 S.Ct. 1897, 36 L.Ed.2d 390 (1973).

### *12. Dispute Resolution*

The GATT contains several articles establishing dispute resolution procedures. Of these articles, Articles XXII and XXIII are the most important. The first step in the process is consultation. Under Article XXII, a complaining party may seek consultations "with respect to any matter affecting the operation of this Agreement." Under Article XXIII, a contracting party may seek consultations "when it considers that any benefit accruing to it directly or indirectly under the GATT is being nullified or impaired."

If consultation fails to achieve a resolution, the complaining party may request the Council of the GATT to appoint a panel. The panel investigates the dispute, hears arguments from the contracting parties and writes a report on its findings. If the disputing parties have not reached a settlement before the completion of the panel's report, the panel submits the report to the Council for adoption. Adoption of the report is effected by consensus of the Council. If, after adoption of the report, the disputing parties have not implemented the report's recommendations within a reasonable time, the complaining party may take retaliatory action against the offending party with the Council's authorization. (Article XXIII). See generally Davey, Handbook of GATT Dispute Settlement (1991).

During the period between 1948 and 1986, only 104 complaints were made invoking Article XXIII. Most disputes regarding the interpretation or implementation of the GATT are settled through consultations and do not involve other GATT parties. Of the 104 complaints, 52 were submitted to a panel for a report; of these 52, 50 of the reports were adopted or provided satisfactory solutions to the disputes. More recently, the parties have increased the submissions of disputes to panels; seven panels were established in 1987, and 14 were established in 1988.

In April 1989, the GATT members adopted a provisional set of rules and procedures that would govern dispute resolution until the end of the Uruguay Round negotiations. The improvements limit the amount of time permitted in the preliminary phases of the process and until the adoption of the panel report and standardize the procedures for panels. Under the revised rules, the Council should normally adopt the report of the panel within 15 months of the lodging of the initial complaint under Article XXIII. Also, alternative means have been provided by which to settle disputes; these include good offices, mediation, conciliation and arbitration. See Bello and Holmer, GATT Dispute Settlement Agreement: Internationalization or Elimination of Section 301?, 26 Int'l Law. 795 (1992), Forgues and Ostrihansky, New Developments in GATT Dispute Settlement Procedures, 24 Journal of World Trade 67 (April 1990), and Castel, The Uruguay Round and the Improvements to the GATT Dispute Settlement Rules and Procedures, 38 International and Comparative Law Quarterly 834 (Oct. 1989).

## B. UNITED NATIONS CONFERENCE ON TRADE AND DEVELOPMENT (UNCTAD)

The need for economic development policy on a world-wide basis was recognized in the late 1950's. The secular decline in the "terms of trade" between the primary products of developing nations and the manufactured products of the developed nations meant that the trade gap between the two classes of countries would continue to increase. See, e.g., Atallah, The Long–Term Movement of the Terms of Trade Between Agricultural and Industrial Products 3 (1958); Balassa, Trade Prospects for Developing Countries vii (1964). This would mean that developing countries would be unable to import the necessary capital goods to achieve their development goals. The attainment of an annual five percent growth rate, stated as the goal for the United Nations "Development Decade," was viewed as impossible, unless there were a radical reorganization of international trade.

As a prelude to this reorganization, the developing countries, surmounting the opposition of the developed countries, were successful in the United Nations in convening a Conference on Trade and Development, held in Geneva from March 23 to June 16, 1964. G.A.Res. 1785, 17 GAOR Supp. No. 17 (A/5217), at 14 (1964).

The Conference's tone was set by a report of its Secretary–General, Raul Prebisch, an Argentine economist, who had been one of the main proponents of the declining terms of trade thesis. See, e.g., Prebisch, Commercial Policy in the Underdeveloped Countries, 49 Am.Econ.Rev. 251 (1959). The report pointed out that the developing nations faced serious economic difficulties due to the declining terms of trade and the inability of these countries to gain access to developed countries' markets for manufactured and semi-manufactured products. The Final Act of the Conference reflected the theories of Dr. Prebisch and proposed solutions to the problems as perceived by the representatives of the underdeveloped nations.

One of the most significant features of the Conference was the establishment of a voting procedure similar to that of the United Nations General Assembly, i.e., one vote for each member (distinguishing UNCTAD from the other important economic agencies, such as the IMF and IBRD), and the frank recognition of the divergent interests of the developed and less developed states. This latter characteristic was apparent in the discussions of the Conference, at which the developed countries of both East and West took similar positions in opposition to proposals of developing nations. On the work of the Conference itself, see Kasdan, Toward a Reorganization of International Trade—United Nations Conference on Trade & Development, 19 Record of N.Y.C.B.A. 525, 532–539 (1964).

As a result of the 1964 Conference, the United Nations General Assembly voted to transform UNCTAD into a permanent organ of the General Assembly called the United Nations Conference on Trade and Development. The objective of UNCTAD is to promote international trade, particularly that of developing countries, with a view to accelerating economic development. To that end, it was called upon to formulate principles and policies, to make proposals for putting them into effect and, generally, to review and facilitate the co-ordination of activities of other institutions within the

United Nations in the areas of international trade and economic cooperation and development.

Policy guidelines are adopted at sessions of the Conference which take place every four years (most recently in 1992). Each state represented at the Conference has one vote; as in General Assembly votes on "important questions," decisions are taken by two thirds vote on substantive matters and by simple majority on procedural matters. UNCTAD has a Secretary General and a permanent secretariat. Ongoing activities are supervised by the Trade and Development Board, which has seven intergovernmental functional Committees, namely, Committees on Commodities, Manufacturers, Invisibles and Financing Related to Trade, Shipping, Transfer of Technology, Economic Cooperation among Developing Countries, and Preferences. Voting power in the Trade and Development Board is distributed partly on the basis of geography and partly on the basis of stage of economic development. The executive body of UNCTAD, the Trade and Development Board, holds its annual session in two parts. During the first part (September/October), the Board reviews topics related to "interdependence" and the debt problems of developing countries; during the second part (March/April), it focuses on international trade issues, such as protectionism, the role of services in development and the progress of multilateral trade negotiations. In addition, the Board reviews reports submitted by the intergovernmental committees, which include the seven listed above plus an intergovernmental group on restrictive business practices and an intergovernmental group on the least developed countries.

UNCTAD has been involved in a number of aspects of international trade and development. One of its early projects was development of a United Nations Charter of Economic Rights and Duties of States, which purported to establish a New International Economic Order (NIEO), but the United States and the overwhelming majority of non-Communist industrialized countries voted against, or abstained from voting on, the General Assembly resolution adopting the Charter. U.N.Doc.A/Res./3281 (XXIX). On this Charter generally, see Brower and Tepe, The Charter of Economic Rights and Duties of States: A Reflection or Rejection of International Law? 9 Int'l Lawyer 295 (1975); Rothstein, Global Bargaining—UNCTAD and the Quest for a New International Economic Order (1979).

UNCTAD has focused generally on the need for developed countries to adopt policies to open their markets to an expansion of exports from developing countries and on the need to enhance the export capacity of developing countries through the strengthening of technological capabilities and promoting appropriate national trade and transport policies.

In addition, one of UNCTAD's major activities has been the improvement of conditions in world markets for a wide range of primary products exported by developing countries. Among its objectives have been price stabilization and increased participation by developing countries in the marketing and processing of their commodities. A notable step was the adoption in June 1980 of the Articles of Agreement of the Common Fund for Commodities. The primary task of the Common Fund is to finance buffer stocks established by international commodity agreements.

UNCTAD was involved in the development of the Generalized System of Preferences (GSP), under which manufacturers exported by developing countries are given preferential tariff treatment by developed countries. See p. 1411 supra. UNCTAD's Committee on Preferences continues to keep under review, and seeks to improve, the GSP.

UNCTAD has also been heavily involved in dealing with the problems for the developing countries created by their heavy burden of public debt, by their balance of payments deficits and by inflation. UNCTAD also assists governments of developing countries individually and collectively in their developmental efforts through technical cooperation involving advisory services, training, research and analysis, and provides support for negotiations at the inter-governmental level aimed at the restructuring of international economic relations.

### *Note*

In the most recent UNCTAD conference, UNCTAD VIII, completed in February 1992, the member countries focused on the revitalization and restructuring of the UNCTAD machinery and operations. To this end, the member countries agreed to aim for developing a greater substantive and technical basis for policy discussion and decisions, increased effectiveness in addressing development issues, and greater participation of officials responsible for policy formulation at the national level. The other issues addressed included resources for development, international trade, technology, services, and commodities.

# SECTION 2. INTERNATIONAL MONETARY LAW

## A. THE INTERNATIONAL MONETARY SYSTEM: THE BRETTON WOODS INSTITUTIONS

With the 1920's came the desire to restore the gold-standard-based monetary system that had existed before World War I. However, the exchange rates established did not take account of the divergence between price of goods and production costs that had occurred since 1913, and the effort failed due to Great Britain's departure from the gold standard in 1931 and the Great Depression in the United States in the 1930's. The depression of the next decade caused low economic activity in the major industrial countries, resulting in a drop in imports, the collapse of commodity prices, and a decline in international trade. To counter the reduced ability to buy foreign goods in exchange for exports, many countries reduced their reserves of gold and international currencies to a low level. To protect these reserves, countries imposed restrictions on citizens' freedom to buy abroad, devised multiple currency systems with more favorable rates for preferred transactions and less favorable for others, held down market values by official purchases and unilaterally devalued their currencies to secure competitive advantages. Exchange rates were chaotic as each country freely modified its currency's rate to stimulate its own exports and protect its own import-substitutive industries in the dominant "beggar-thy-neighbor" policy of the time.

To avoid a post-World War II slump, the United States and Great Britain conceived of the idea for a conference on international monetary cooperation in the early 1940's. This culminated in a multinational Conference held in Bretton Woods, New Hampshire in 1944, at which two international institutions were created, the International Monetary Fund (IMF or the Fund) and the International Bank for Reconstruction and Development (IBRD or World Bank). The purposes of the IMF were to establish a framework for a multilateral system of payments and a mechanism to prevent significant fluctuations in currency exchange rates, to provide short- or medium-term funds for states needing reserves, to develop and administer a code of conduct for states in international monetary matters and to serve as a forum for discussion and resolution of international financial and monetary issues. The purpose of the IBRD was to mobilize economic resources for long-term economic development. See p. 1437 infra.

Another goal of the Bretton Woods institutions was the promotion of orderly change through expansion of trade, high levels of employment and income, and development of the resources of each member. The Fund and IBRD could be consulted on problems and give technical assistance with respect to monetary, financial and development issues. The immediate consequences of the Conference were the elimination of wartime restrictions and discriminatory practices and the stimulation of post-war trade expansion.

## B. THE INTERNATIONAL MONETARY FUND

### 1. *Introduction*

One of the principal purposes of the IMF was to provide financing to countries for redress of temporary balance of payments problems under appropriate conditions. Resort to previously utilized methods of exchange and payments restrictions, restrictive trade measures, export subsidies or competitive rate practices was outlawed. The Articles of Agreement of the Fund provided the formal rules for an international monetary system. Member quotas supplied the resources for the Fund from which members could borrow; exchange controls on international payments were prohibited except on capital payments needed to ease balance of payments burdens; exchange rates were pegged to a "par value" in gold; and national gold and currency reserves were augmented so that short run deficits would not end in domestic deflation and unemployment. As of May 1, 1992, 157 states were members of the Fund. Nonmembers included the Peoples Republic of China and certain other communist states. Among recently added members are most of the republics of the former U.S.S.R., Switzerland, and the Republics of Croatia, Slovenia and Bosnia–Herzegovina.

Since its founding the IMF has been a leading forum for the discussion of international financial and monetary matters, and it has served as a source of reserves made available to members to enable them to correct international payment imbalances without resorting to measures that might adversely affect other members, subject to conditions imposed by the Fund that have affected economic and monetary policies of the states assisted in important ways. The code of conduct embodied in the Bretton Woods Agreement lasted for about 25 years, but was fundamentally altered in 1971, when the United States announced that it would no longer assure the convertibility of the U.S. dollar into gold (at $35 per ounce) or other reserve assets.

Article IV of the Bretton Woods Agreement created a system of fixed par values for the currencies of member states, which could be changed only with the concurrence of the Fund and only under conditions of "fundamental disequilibrium." All currency values were fixed in terms of gold and member states undertook through intervention in exchange markets to maintain the value of their currencies within one percent of parity. After the United States abandoned convertibility of the U.S. dollar into gold or other reserve assets and after some efforts to retain a par value system based on realigned exchange rates, the international monetary system shifted in early 1973 to a system of floating exchange rates in which major states no longer undertook to maintain any specific exchange rate with other currencies or gold.

During the period from 1971 to 1976, the institutional arrangements of the Bretton Woods Agreement were basically retained, as were many aspects of the code of conduct, including the provisions related to exchange controls, p. 1423 infra. In January 1976 an agreement was reached amending the Articles of the IMF principally to amend Article IV to accommodate and reflect the floating exchange rate system.

The principal source of financial resources for the Fund is the capital subscriptions or quotas of its members. These quotas are now expressed in Special Drawing Rights, called SDRs, which were created by the Fund as a supplement to existing international reserve assets.

The financial assistance provided by the Fund to its members is accomplished through purchases of currency. In drawing from the Fund, a member buys freely convertible currencies of other members with its own currency. Upon repayment (usually within three to five years) the member repurchases its own currency with currencies acceptable to the Fund. During the year ending April 30, 1992, the purchases from the Fund totalled about 5.3 billion in Special Drawing Rights (SDRs), which are defined at p. 1429 infra, and repurchases totalled about SDR 4.8 billion. The total Fund credit outstanding was about SDR 26.7 billion. The arrangements through which currencies are purchased by member states and subsequently repurchased by them involve what are called regular and special facilities described at p. 1425 infra.

During the period from 1979 through 1985, the Fund was heavily involved in assisting developing country members deal with problems resulting from dramatic increases in international debt, oil prices and interest rates. Between mid–1982 and the end of 1984, the Fund lent SDR 22 billion in support of adjustment programs in 70 member countries. In addition, it helped arrange financial packages for debtor members from governments, commercial banks and other financial institutions. On occasion the Fund would request commercial banks to commit new loans before the Fund approved adjustment programs and provided financing for debtor countries from its own resources. Each dollar of Fund financing has been estimated to "unlock" from four to seven dollars of new loans and refinancing from governments and commercial banks. By April 1985, 21 Fund members had agreed with commercial banks to restructure $150 billion (20 percent) of the bank debt of developing countries. The willingness of commercial banks to accept lower spreads, longer repayment periods and grace periods under these rescheduling arrangements was materially enhanced by the effectiveness of adjustment efforts undertaken by debtor states with support from the resources of the Fund.

During the early 1990's, the IMF has committed its resources to three principal areas. First, it has assisted those member countries whose economies were disrupted by the invasion of Kuwait and the Gulf War in adjusting the resulting payments imbalances. Second, it is providing both financial and technical assistance to the Eastern European countries in transition from centrally planned to market-based economies. In particular, it is supplying policy advice, technical assistance, and balance of payments financing in support of macroeconomic and structural reform programs in these countries. Third, it is continuing its efforts to assist its poorest members in achieving economic growth.

### *Note*

For discussion of the development and functioning of the IMF, see, e.g., Gwin and Feinberg, The International Monetary Fund in a Multipolar World: Pulling Together (1989); de Vries, Balance of Payments Adjustments, 1945 to 1986: The IMF Experience (1987); Gold, Developments in the International Monetary System, the International Monetary Fund and International Monetary Law since 1971, 174 Recueil des Cours 107 (1982) and Legal and Institutional Aspects of the International Monetary System: Selected Essays, Vol. I (1979), Vol. II (1985); de Vries, The International Monetary Fund, 1972–1982: Cooperation on Trial (1985); Dam, The Rules of the Game: Reform and Evolution in the International Monetary System (1982); Edwards, International Monetary Collaboration (1985); A. Lowenfeld, The International Monetary System (2d ed. 1984); Mann, The Legal Aspect of Money (4th ed. 1982). Reviews of the Fund's operations are contained in the Fund's annual reports. Official actions by the Fund (including decisions of the Board of Governors and Executive Directors) are published in Selected Decisions of the International Monetary Fund.

### 2. *The Main Features of the IMF Articles*

Under the Articles, each member of the Fund is assigned a quota, which reflects its relative position in the world's economy. One quarter of the quota (including any increases) had generally to be paid in gold (under the original Articles) or must (under the amended Articles) be paid in SDRs or convertible currencies specified by the Fund. The other three quarters may be paid in the member's own currency. Quotas may be changed with the member's consent and overall quotas are reviewed at intervals of not more than five years.

At the Ninth General Review of Quotas in 1990, the Fund's Board of Governors approved an increase in IMF quotas of 50 percent from SDR 90.1 billion to SDR 135.2 billion. The Interim Committee recommended that this quota increase be distributed in a way consistent with any changes in the members' relative economic position while maintaining a balance between different groups of countries. As a result, 60 percent of the increase has been distributed among all members in proportion to their current quotas;

40 percent has been distributed in proportion to members' shares in the total of "calculated quotas", which are intended to reflect changes in their relative economic positions. Each member was required to pay 25 percent of its increase in SDRs or in currencies of other members acceptable to the IMF and 75 percent in its own currency. The United States remains the largest quota holder in the Fund, with 19.62 percent of total quotas.

The member's required contribution to the resources of the Fund, the amounts of its drawing rights and its voting power are geared to its quota. The bulk of IMF resources is provided by these quota subscriptions, but the IMF may borrow in order to supplement its reserves.

The first amendment to the Articles in 1969 gave the Fund the authority to issue Special Drawing Rights (SDRs), the first international reserve asset to be created by a decision of the international community. See p. 1429 infra. The SDRs are allocated to particular members by the Board of Governors in order to supplement existing reserve assets. Parties can engage in SDR transactions when one member needs currency for balance of payments outflows only with the Fund's approval and its designation of a member to receive SDRs in exchange for currency.

Training and technical assistance to members are available in various forms, and are directed largely to developing countries. The IMF Institute provides training facilities to officials of member governments. Technical advisory assistance aimed at establishing or strengthening national monetary systems is provided by experts, upon request by member countries, through the activities of the Central Banking Service. Experts are generally assigned for periods of one year and are responsible solely to the institution to which they are assigned. The IMF Fiscal Affairs Department provides technical assistance in tax policy. With the aid provided by the Fund staff and experts, member countries can establish policies aimed at rectifying their balance of payments problems.

### 3. *Structural Framework*

#### a. *Organization*

The Fund is composed of the Board of Governors, the Executive Directors, and the Managing Director and staff. Nearly all powers originally vested in the Board have now been delegated to the Executive Directors. The Board meets once a year in conjunction with the annual meeting of the World Bank, with each country represented by a Governor (usually the Minister of Finance or President of the Central Bank) and an alternate.

The Executive Directors supervise the day-to-day management of the Fund. There are 22 Executive Directors, six of whom are appointed by the six countries having the largest quotas (United States, United Kingdom, Germany, France, Japan and Saudi Arabia) and 16 elected at two-year intervals by the remaining members through the formation of "constituencies." The Articles provide for two Executive Directors to be elected by the American Republics not entitled to appoint (XII(3)(b)(iv)), but since 1956 an additional Director has been elected by them. No provision is made for representation of other regional groups, but in practice countries with homogeneous interests have combined to form fairly stable combinations in order to muster the prescribed minimum number of votes necessary to elect an Executive Director. In addition, the number of appointed Directors may be augmented by one or two if during the two years preceding an election the six member countries with the largest quotas do not include the two members that have provided the largest absolute amounts of currency used by the Fund in its activities (Art. XII(3)(c)). Saudi Arabia, a large creditor of the Fund in the early 1980's, was entitled to appoint an additional Director.

The Managing Director of the Fund is selected by the Executive Directors for an initial term of five years. He is Chairman of the Executive Directors and participates in meetings of the Board of Governors, is chief of the Fund's operating staff and, under the direction of the Executive Directors, manages the ordinary business of the Fund.

*b. Voting*

The IMF was one of the first post-war international organizations to provide for unequal voting power. Each member is allotted the same basic number of votes (250) in recognition of the equality of states and to give adequate voice to all members. Additional votes are allocated in proportion to a country's quota, expressed since 1972 in SDRs (one vote for each SDR 100,000 of quota). As of April 1992, there were a total of 951,465 votes, the largest allotment being 179,433 votes allotted to the United States (18.86 percent of the total) and the smallest being 270 allotted to the Maldives.

The voting scheme applies to the Board of Governors and the Executive Directors. The Articles are silent on the relationship between the Executive Directors and the group of members which they represent. The degree to which the Executive Directors wish to adhere to the advice of members is left to their discretion. Votes are cast as a unit by the Executive Director concerned.

The idea of weighted voting was accepted in the early days of negotiating the Articles. The assumption was that a country's voice in an international financial organization should be related to its contributions to the organization's resources. Most decisions taken by the Board of Governors or the Executive Directors are adopted by a simple majority of the votes cast. However, for more important decisions, a larger majority is required. Broadly, a 70 percent majority of the total voting power is needed to resolve such operational issues as rates of charges on the use of the Fund's resources and the rate of interest on holdings of SDRs. An 85 percent majority (often referred to as a "high" majority) is required to decide matters concerned with, for example, the structure of the Fund, changes in quotas, the allocation of SDRs, and the disposition of the Fund's gold. The United States alone, or the members of the European Community or the group of developing countries voting together, can veto proposals subject to a high majority. In practice, formal votes are rarely taken by the Executive Directors. In most cases, decisions are taken by the Executive Directors by consensus; however, these decisions usually take cognizance of the distribution of voting power.

## Notes

1. In response to claims by developing countries that they had inadequate voting power, the size of the Board of Executive Directors was increased in order to give them greater representation, and increased emphasis has been laid on the

involvement of all members in Fund decisions. The Fund has adopted rules that permit members to abstain at various stages of an election and not have their votes count toward the election of any Executive Director and has made it easier for members to prevent the inclusion of their allotted number of votes in the unit cast by the Executive Director.

2. Weighted voting is not expressly provided for in the committees which the Board is empowered to establish. Does the Board have an implied authority to prescribe weighted voting? See Gold, Weighted Voting Power: Some Limits and Problems, 68 A.J.I.L. 687 (1972).

### 4. *The Shift From Fixed to Floating Exchange Rates*

Under the original agreement, each nation undertook the maintenance of a "par value" in gold for its currency and the obligation to convert foreign official holdings of its currency into gold or the currency of the holder. Spot transactions of exchange had to take place within a prescribed margin of parity relationships, and governments intervened in the exchange markets to maintain the par values of their currencies. Changes in par values were allowed only when "fundamental disequilibria" in balance of payments made it necessary.

Gold was the main reserve asset of the system. But gold convertibility turned out to be inadequate. The supply needed for monetary purposes was not available due to the limited production of gold and the growth of individual and commercial uses. Differences between the official and private market led to official sales in private markets, speculation, and pressure for change in official prices. Countries purchased dollars in order to finance transactions, since the growth in capital transactions was not satisfied by the gold reserves alone. Finally, par values no longer reflected the changes that had occurred in the relations among countries, as the rapid growth of Japan and Europe created imbalances in payments.

At the time of the Bretton Woods Conference, the dollar was the most widely used currency. To obtain additional liquidity in the system, countries maintained their par values through intervention of the dollar since the United States was willing to buy and sell gold for officially held dollars. The dollar became overvalued as other countries did not make needed adjustments, and the United States accumulated short term debt abroad. Dependence on the dollar led to a balance of payments deficit that in 1971 was three times the value of United States gold holdings.

The late 1960's saw the revaluation or devaluation of a number of widely used currencies, such as the pound sterling, French franc, and Deutsche mark. In May, 1971, the mark and Netherlands guilder were allowed to float without government intervention to maintain stable rates. In August, 1971, the United States suspended the convertibility of the dollar into gold or other reserve assets. This act was followed by the decision of several other countries to allow their currencies to float.

The Articles did not provide for floating, and floating was in fact a violation of the obligation to keep transactions within a prescribed margin (Art. XV, sec. 2), unless it was part of multiple currency practices approved by the Fund (Art. VIII, sec. 3). However, the Fund tolerated floating rates beginning with the 12 year float of Canada in 1950. At first, the Fund merely refrained from voicing formal objection, but thereafter it allowed access to its resources by those members permitting floating rates. Floating came to be viewed as the best remedy for inflation that could not be controlled in the short run and useful in accomplishing the transition to different parity levels.

In reacting to the chain of events in the early 1970's, the Fund merely noted the circumstances accounting for the actions of the members, emphasized their obligation to collaborate with the Fund to promote exchange stability, welcomed the expressed intent of the members to resume compliance with their obligations as soon as circumstances permitted, and stated that the Fund would remain in close consultation with them. No sanction was brought to bear on the members; instead, attention was turned to reform of the system to adapt it to the needs of a changed world situation. Recognition that governments could not maintain stable rates due to hostilities in the Middle East, petroleum price increases, labor unemployment and inflation led to the adoption by the Executive Directors of guidelines for the management of floating rates. ED Doc. No. 4232 (74/67) (June 13, 1974).

### 5. *Revision of the System*

A new exchange rate structure was agreed upon by the Group of Ten in the Smithsonian agreement in 1971 and approved by the Fund. The United States declared a new par value in 1972. Par Value Modification Act, Pub.L. No. 92–268, March 31, 1972. However, it was realized that fundamental reform of the system was needed. An Interim Committee established in 1974 to devise a new monetary system proposed amendments in the Jamaican Agreement of 1976. These were approved by the Board of Governors and submitted to the legislative bodies of member countries.

The amendments provide for elimination of the central role of gold by abolishing its official price, eliminating all requirements for its use in Fund transactions, and empowering the Fund to dispose of its holdings. The Group of Ten agreed to these arrangements as well as to submitting semiannual reports on their gold activity.

Quotas were expanded, and the required "high" majority of 85 percent for decisions of major policy significance in the Fund was established. This was intended to ensure wide support for such decisions and protect the concerns of the major industrial countries. Further expansion of the Fund's financing ability was provided for by a temporary 45 percent expansion of access to regular facilities, liberalization of the Compensatory Finance Facility, and expansion of SDR uses.

New exchange rate provisions replaced the par value system, legalizing such practices as floating and allowing members to choose their own exchange arrangements. A general obligation was imposed on members to collaborate with the Fund and each other to assure orderly exchange arrangements and promote a stable exchange rate system. The Fund was given authority for surveillance over the policies of members and the adoption of principles of guidance for such policies.

### *Notes*

1. The revised Articles of Agreement of the International Monetary Fund, Second Amendment, April 30, 1976, 29 U.S.T. 2203, T.I.A.S. No. 8937 entered in force for the United States on April 1, 1978.

2. On the interpretation of the Articles of Agreement by the Executive Directors, see Gold, Interpretation by the Fund (International Monetary Fund Pamphlet Series II, 1968); Mann, Interpretation of the Constitutions of International Financial Organizations, 43 Brit.Yb.I.L. 1 (1968–69).

### 6. *Use of IMF Resources by Member States*

Members of the Fund may apply to use the resources of the Fund to assist in dealing with balance of payments problems. Freely convertible funds, for example U.S. dollars, pounds sterling, or yen, are sold to the member state for its own currency subject to the member's agreement to repurchase the convertible funds within a stated period (normally three to five years) for other currencies acceptable to the Fund and subject to conditions negotiated with the Fund concerning the economic policies to be pursued by the member during that period.

Drawings on the resources of the IMF are usually made in "tranches" representing one quarter of the drawing member's quota. The Fund's credit under its so-called regular facilities is made available in four segments or tranches of 25 percent of the member's quota each. A drawing that raises the Fund's holdings of the member's currency by 25 percent of its quota is a first credit tranche purchase, from 25 to 50 percent is a second credit tranche purchase, and so on through the fourth credit tranche. Since one quarter of the member's quota was actually contributed by it in gold or reserve assets, a drawing of the first credit tranche ("reserve tranche") is in effect a drawing against the assets it has contributed. A drawing of the first credit tranche requires only that a member demonstrate reasonable efforts to overcome its balance of payments difficulties. Performance criteria and charges are not applied and repurchases are normally required in 3¼ to 5 years, while drawings under subsequent credit tranches are subject to charges and conditions that are usually increasingly restrictive for each successive tranche.

Conditions for drawings in excess of the first credit or reserve tranche may be negotiated at the time of an actual drawing or, as is frequently the case, in advance, in connection with a stand-by arrangement. A stand-by is an arrangement under which the member is assured that it will be able to draw on the resources of the IMF up to a stated amount within a stated period of up to three years on the basis of conditions and understandings negotiated with the Fund at the time the stand-by arrangement is effected. Stand-by arrangements focus on macroeconomic policies—such as fiscal, monetary, and exchange rate policies—aimed at overcoming balance of payments difficulties. Performance criteria to assess policy implementation, such as budgetary and credit ceilings, reserve and external debt targets, and avoidance of restrictions on current payments and transfers, are applied during the period of the arrangement, and purchases (or drawings) are made in installments. Repurchases are made in 3¼ to 5 years, except in the case of purchases made with resources borrowed by the Fund under the enlarged access policy.

Under extended arrangements, the Fund supports medium-term programs that generally run for three years (up to four years in exceptional circumstances) and that are aimed at overcoming balance of payments difficulties stemming from macroeconomic and structural problems. Typically, a program states the general objectives for the three-year period and the policies for the first year; policies for subsequent years are spelled out in annual reviews. Performance criteria are applied, and repurchases are made in 4½ to 10 years, except in the case of purchases made with resources borrowed under the enlarged access policy.

Introduced as a temporary policy, the enlarged access policy is used to increase the resources available under stand-by or extended arrangements for programs that need substantial Fund support. Since 1986, access to the Fund's general resources under the enlarged access policy has been subject to annual limits of 90 percent or 110 percent of quota; three-year limits of 270 percent or 330 percent of quota; and cumulative limits, net of repurchases, of 400 percent or 440 percent of quota, depending on the seriousness of a member's balance of payments need and the strength of its adjustment effort. In November 1990, the Fund suspended temporarily (until the end of 1991) the lower annual, three-year, and cumulative limits. The Fund borrowed to help finance purchases under the enlarged access policy, and repurchases of purchases financed with borrowed resources are made in 3½ to 7 years.

The Fund also provides funding for special purposes through so-called special facilities. The resources of these facilities are not part of the Fund's general resources but are administered by the Fund as a service to members. For that reason, the constraints that the Articles place on nondiscriminatory use of the Fund's resources do not apply to these facilities. A variety of special facilities have been created, some of which have been terminated or permitted to lapse after their particular purposes have been served. In the mid-1970s the Fund created two such facilities—the Oil Facility Subsidy Account and the Trust Fund—and in 1980 set up the Supplementary Financing Facility Subsidy Account. The Oil Facility Subsidy Accounts assisted Fund members most seriously affected by oil price increases.

*Compensatory and contingency financing facility* (CCFF). The purpose of this facility established in 1988 is twofold. The compensatory element provides resources to members to cover shortfalls in export earnings and services receipts and excesses in cereal import costs that are temporary and arise from events beyond their control. The contingency element helps members with Fund arrangements to maintain the momentum of reforms when faced with a broad range of unforeseen adverse external shocks, such as declines in export prices, increases in import prices, fluctuations in interest rates, and natural disasters by providing assurances of protection against such shocks in advance. Repurchases are made in 3¼ to 5 years. In November 1990, the Fund introduced a temporary oil import element in the CCFF—which lapsed at the end of 1991—to compensate members for sharp increases in import costs for crude petroleum, petroleum products, and natural gas.

*Buffer stock financing facility.* Under this facility the Fund provides resources to help finance members' contributions to approved buffer stocks. Repayments are made within 3¼ to 5 years, or earlier.

In addition to balance of payments assistance under its tranche policies and special facilities, the Fund provides emergency assistance in the form of purchases to help members meet payments problems arising from sudden and unforeseeable natural disasters. Such purchases do not involve performance criteria or the phasing of disbursements, and must be repurchased in $3\frac{1}{4}$ to 5 years. See Gold, Natural Disasters and Other Emergencies Beyond Control: Assistance by the IMF, 24 Int'l Law. 621 (1990).

Special facilities have also been established to help deal with protracted balance of payments problems of low-income countries.

*Structural adjustment facility* (SAF) arrangements. This facility set up in 1986 enables the Fund to provide resources on concessional terms to support medium-term macroeconomic adjustment and structural reforms in low-income countries facing protracted balance of payments problems. The member develops and updates a medium-term policy framework for a three-year period. Within this framework, detailed yearly policy programs are formulated and are supported by SAF arrangements, under which annual loan disbursements are made. The programs include quarterly benchmarks to assess performance. The rate of interest on SAF loans is 0.5 percent, and repayments are made in $5\frac{1}{2}$ to 10 years.

*Enhanced structural adjustment facility* (ESAF) arrangements. The objectives, conditions for eligibility, and program features under these arrangements established in 1987 are similar to those under SAF arrangements. However, ESAF arrangements differ in the scope and strength of structural policies, and in terms of access levels, monitoring procedures, and sources of funding. In November 1990, the Board endorsed the possibility of an additional one-year ESAF arrangement for members that have already completed a three-year ESAF arrangement, provided the fourth arrangement is approved before the end of November 1992, and so long as resources are available.

Under the SAF and ESAF programs, the member country must submit a policy framework paper (PFP), a paper prepared by the members' national authorities, the World Bank and the Fund. The PFP outlines the member's economic and structural objectives, the strategy to achieve these objectives and the proposed financing to support the strategy. Because the PFP requires more formal coordination between the World Bank and the Fund, it incorporates strategies both to alleviate payments imbalances and to address long-term issues of structural adjustment and sector policies as well as analyses of the social impact of the strategies.

### *Notes*

1. "Conditionality" refers to the policies members are expected to follow when they use Fund resources to assist in dealing with balance of payments deficits. See Guitian, Fund Conditionality, IMF Pamphlet Series, No. 38 (Washington 1981) Note, International Monetary Fund Conditionality and Options for Aggrieved Fund Members, 20 Vand.J.Transnat'l L. 665 (1987). The basic concept has been described as follows:

> Balance of payments adjustment for a member does not necessarily mean that it moves to a position of balance or surplus in its current account. For many developing countries, and especially for the poorer ones, it is often appropriate to maintain a deficit in the current account in order to finance investment with foreign borrowing as well as with domestically mobilized savings. Adjustment does mean, however, that the member attains a position where any deficit on current account transactions can be financed by sustainable flows of capital and maintained without restrictions.

> The Fund attaches to the use of its resources a degree of conditionality sufficient to provide confidence that the borrowing member will overcome its balance of payments difficulties and be able to repurchase its currency from the Fund without undue strain during the specified period. The degree of conditionality thus depends largely on the character of the member's balance of payments problem. If the problem results from temporary factors, such as a cyclical decline in export earnings, the member need only continue its existing policies until the situation returns to normal. On the other hand, if the difficulty is caused by deep-seated factors, such as a persistent deterioration in the terms of trade, excessive domestic demand, cost-price distortions, including overvaluation of the domestic currency, or a permanent decline in net capital inflows, the member's policies need to be changed.
>
> The member describes in a letter of intent the policies it intends to implement in order to have access to the Fund's resources under [drawing or] stand-by * * * arrangements. This letter normally contains a summary of the member's policy objectives with respect to its balance of payments, economic growth, and movements in the general price level, as well as an outline of measures being adopted to achieve these objectives.

The Role and Function of the International Monetary Fund 47–49 (Washington 1985).

Recently, with the increased cooperation between the World Bank and the IMF, members applying for assistance have faced the challenge of cross-conditionality. Cross-conditionality refers to the arrangement under which a borrowing country is required to accept conditions of one financial institution as a precondition for financial support of the other. Although the cross-conditions do not appear as explicit preconditions, they have become a regular practice resulting from increased collaboration between the World Bank and the IMF. See note 7 infra. The cross-conditionality arrangements, however, may involve a variety of financial institutions in addition to the IBRD and the IMF, including commercial banks and export credit agencies. For example, a commercial bank may condition its loan on the borrower's ability to draw under a stand-by arrangement from the IMF. See Feinberg, The Changing Relationship Between the World Bank and the International Monetary Fund, 42 Int'l Org. 551, 556 (1988) and Kremmydas, The Cross–Conditionality Phenomenon—Some Legal Aspects, 23 Int'l Law. 651, 654 (1989).

2. Comment *e* to Restatement (Third) § 821 states

> The basic condition for use of the Fund's resources is that they must be used in a manner consistent with the Articles of Agreement. Except for drawings within the member's reserve tranche position * * * and drawings under certain special facilities, the Fund will examine the economic situation and policies of a member state prior to approval of a drawing or stand-by. The Fund may negotiate arrangements with the state's authorities with respect to economic policies to be pursued by the state during the period the drawing or stand-by is outstanding. Such arrangements are not international agreements in the sense that non-compliance is a breach of an international obligation * * *. However, an unjustified failure to live up to an arrangement with the Fund in connection with a drawing or stand-by may be a basis for non-renewal of a stand-by or for limitations on future drawings, and failure to achieve performance criteria in a stand-by arrangement may interrupt the right to make further drawings thereunder.

3. SDRs are reserve assets created from time to time by decision of the Fund and allocated to member states that participate in the Special Drawing Rights Department in proportion to their quotas. SDRs were created in response to an anticipated shortage of world reserves and were intended to be a supplemental source of reserves independent of the production of gold or of balance of payments deficits of reserve currency states, especially the United States. The shortage of reserves did not develop and as of March 1992 SDRs constituted about 2.2 percent of all reserves, but SDRs have been used not only as an asset that Fund members can use to comply with their reserve asset subscription obligations, but also to settle official balances among states.

Under the original Bretton Woods regime under which the U.S. dollar was pegged at 35 U.S. dollars to the ounce of gold, an SDR equalled one U.S. dollar. Since the advent of floating exchange rates, the SDR has been calculated daily with reference to the market exchange rates of the currencies of the five member states (France, Germany, Japan, United States and United Kingdom) with the largest exports of goods and services during the period 1985–1989. The use of the SDR has grown not only in transactions involving the IMF and in official intergovernmental settlements but also as a unit of account in many other international state and private agreements, including loans, construction and mining agreements and limitations on the liability of owners of ships, aircraft and other carriers. See Gold, The SDR in Treaty Practice: A checklist, 22 I.L.M. 209 (1983).

### 7. *Obligations of Member States*

#### a. *Exchange Arrangements*

Article IV specifies the members' obligations with respect to exchange arrangements. There is a general obligation on each member to collaborate with the Fund and with other members to promote orderly exchange arrangements and a stable system of exchange rates. Members are also obligated to pursue economic and financial policies that promote orderly economic growth with reasonable price stability and to foster orderly underlying economic and financial conditions. In addition, they are required to avoid exchange rate and other policies that prevent effective balance of payments adjustment or provide an unfair competitive advantage over other members.

Under the amended IMF Articles member states may adopt any exchange arrangement consistent with orderly economic growth and reasonable price stability, provided that it is not linked to gold and does not involve multiple currency practices or discriminate against the currency of any other member state without the approval of the Fund.

Members may peg the value of their currency to that of another currency or to the SDR or some other composite measure or they may enter into cooperative arrangements, under which they maintain the value of their currency in relation to the value of the currency or currencies of other members within the same group, or adopt other exchange arrangements. Members must notify the Fund promptly of any change in their exchange arrangements.

Many members have pegged their currencies to the currency of a major trading and financial partner because of the convenience and certainty that pegging offers to those involved in international transactions and in international planning. A second group have pegged their currency to various composites of currencies, such as the SDR or the currencies of the eight members of the European Monetary System (EMS). These tend to be countries with diversified trade patterns which find that the composites reduce the effect of fluctuations among the values of the major currencies on the prices of imports and exports. A third group maintains the value of their individual currencies within a predetermined range of other currencies in the group. Most of the remaining members use a managed floating system which permits smoother and more rapid adjustments to payments imbalances.

For a discussion of the amendments to and the functioning of Article IV, see Gold, Strengthening the Soft International Law of Exchange Arrangements, 77 A.J.I.L. 443–489 (1983).

### *Notes*

1. Comment *a* to Restatement (Third) § 821(1) states, in part:

> While the provisions of the original Articles of Agreement requiring members to maintain a par value for their currencies have been eliminated from the amended Articles * * *, the principle that exchange rates are a subject of international concern is maintained, and is the basis of the obligations stated in Subsection (2). Under Article IV(2) of the amended Articles, each member state must notify the Fund of the exchange arrangements it intends to apply and of any changes in those arrangements. Notification need not be given in advance of their implementation, but must be given promptly thereafter. Members are expected to respond to questions from the Fund and, on request, to consult with the Fund on these arrangements and on the effect they may have on other member states or on the international economy as a whole.

2. Prohibited discriminatory arrangements would include, for example, permitting foreign currency operations to be undertaken for transactions in some currencies but not in others. Prohibited multiple exchange practices include official action causing exchange rate spreads and cross-rate quotations to differ unnecessarily from those that arise in the marketplace.

#### *b. Consultation and Cooperation*

Article IV(3)(b) of the amended Articles requires the Fund to exercise "firm surveillance over the exchange rate policies of members" and to adopt "specific principles for the guidance of all members with respect to those policies."

Each member is required to furnish relevant information and to consult with the Fund periodically (usually every 12 months) with respect to its exchange rate policies. The results are reported to the Executive Board by the Managing Director. The Managing Director may initiate further discussions with a member state if so directed by the Executive Board or on his or her own initiative.

"Exchange rate policies" with respect to which the member states must inform and consult with the Fund clearly extend beyond the "exchange arrangements" provided for in Article IV(2), supra p. 1429, and include, for example, member states' intervention (or not) in foreign exchange markets, the level of government borrowing or lending for balance of payments purposes, and restrictions on or incentives to current transactions or capital transfers.

Other obligations to consult relate to specific matters, such as drawings, exchange restrictions and use of SDRs. In addition to its regular consultations, the Fund holds special consultations as necessary with those countries whose policies have a major influence on the world's economy.

### *Notes*

1. Article IV(1) of the amended Articles refers to "the orderly underlying conditions that are necessary for financial and economic stability," and the 1977 Decision on Surveillance, Ex. Bd. Decision No. 5392 (77/63), April 29, 1977, Selected Decisions of the IMF 10, 13 (10th issue 1983), states that the Fund's appraisal of a member's exchange rate policies "shall be made within the framework of a comprehensive analysis of the * * * economic policy strategy of the member, and shall recognize that domestic as well as external policies can contribute to timely adjustment of the balance of payments."

2. The 1977 Decision on Surveillance also states that members (i) shall avoid manipulating exchange rates in order to prevent effective balance of payments adjustments (an obligation contained in Article IV(1) of the Amended Articles); (ii) should intervene in the exchange market if necessary to counter disorderly conditions in the exchange value of their currency; and (iii) should take into account in their intervention policies the interests of other member states. It is unclear to what extent items (ii) and (iii) are obligatory, but compliance can at least be the subject of consultations and negotiations with respect to drawing on the Fund's resources.

### c. *Exchange Restrictions: Current and Capital Transactions*

Under Article VI(3) of the Articles, members are permitted to exercise such controls as are necessary to regulate international movements of capital (e.g. investments in and repatriation of equity capital and making and repayment of long-term loans), but not in a manner that will restrict payments for current transactions. Article VIII provides that member states that agree to accept its provisions are not permitted to restrict payments for current transactions (e.g. payment of the sales price for imported products or services, royalties for the licensing of patents, interest on debt obligations, and dividends on corporate stock) without prior approval of the Fund.

### *Notes*

1. Article XIV of the Articles of Agreement permits a member state when it joins the Fund to declare that it intends to maintain restrictions on current transactions for a transitional period (with no limit on the duration thereof). Such a member is obligated to endeavor to withdraw the restrictions on current payments as soon as conditions permit and to consult with the Fund periodically to that end. Imposition of new restrictions, reimposition of a previously-terminated restriction, and a decision of a state no longer to accept the obligations of Article VIII, require prior approval of the Fund.

2. For a case holding that approval by the Fund of restrictions on current payments after their imposition is sufficient compliance with the approval requirement of Article VIII, see Callejo v. Bancomer, S.A., 764 F.2d 1101 (5th

Cir.1985) (act of state doctrine applied because Mexican exchange controls did not violate IMF Articles).

*d. Sanctions*

A variety of sanctions is provided for in the Articles. The Fund's primary method of securing compliance with member's obligations under the Articles is through consultations with officials of the offending state. The Fund can informally communicate its views or present a report to a member. Art. XII, sec. 8; Art. V, sec. 5. A report can be published about a member's condition, Art. XII, sec. 8, or a "general scarcity" of the currency of a country in surplus can be declared, Art. VII, sec. 1. Punitive rates may be imposed when the use of resources rises to an excessive level. Art. V, sec. 8(c) and (d). A member may be declared ineligible to use new resources, SDR rights may be suspended, or the member's withdrawal compelled. See Article XXVI, sec. 2(a); Article V, sec. 5; Article VI, sec. 1; Article XIV, sec. 3; Article XXVI, sec. 2(c). A Third Amendment of the Articles of Agreement, effective on November 11, 1992, adopted Article XXVI, sec. 2(b), which added a sanction short of compulsory withdrawal. It permits suspension of a member's voting and related rights by a decision taken by a 70 percent majority of the total weighted voting power, if a member, having previously been held ineligible to use the resources of the Fund, continues to fail to comply with its obligations under the Articles. The IMF has used its powers to impose sanctions cautiously. This has led to claims that the IMF lacks sufficient effective influence over its members and has led to suggestions for additional more flexible sanctions.

*e. Enforceability of Agreements Violating Lawful Exchange Controls*

Art. VIII(2)(b) provides that "exchange contracts which involve the currency of any member and which are contrary to the exchange control regulations of that member maintained or imposed consistently with this agreement should be unenforced in the territories of any member." This clause has been interpreted by the Fund to prohibit disregard of such regulations on traditional conflict of law grounds or grounds of public policy (*ordre public*). Controversy exists as to whether these interpretations are binding on member courts. See Williams, Extraterritorial Enforcement of Exchange Control Regulations under IMF Agreement, 15 Va.J.Int'l.L. 319 (1975). Judicial interpretations also differ as to the content of the key terms used in the clause, such as "exchange contract," "involve," "exchange control regulations." The European courts have given these words broad scope, while the United States courts generally have not. See French v. Banco Nacional de Cuba, 23 N.Y.2d 46, 295 N.Y.S.2d 433, 242 N.E.2d 704 (1968), where the act of state doctrine was applied rather than Art. VIII, with the effect that the regulations of a nonmember country inconsistent with the Fund agreement were enforced in a member court. But in Banco Frances e Brasileiro SA v. Doe, 36 N.Y.2d 592, 370 N.Y.S.2d 534, 331 N.E.2d 502 (1975), the New York Court of Appeals embraced an expansive application of the Article based upon a perceived policy of broad co-operation embodied in the IMF Agreement. The Court held it would entertain an action for rescission of currency exchange contracts and damages in tortious fraud and deceit arising from alleged violations of Brazil's exchange control regulations. A month later, the same court concluded that New York substantive law controlled due to New York's "paramount interest in the outcome" as the "financial capital of the world," and then stated that Art. VIII did not encompass a claim dealing with a letter of credit which was held not to constitute an "exchange contract". J. Zeevi & Sons, Ltd. v. Grindlays Bank (Uganda) Ltd., 37 N.Y.2d 220, 229, 371 N.Y.S.2d 892, 898, 333 N.E.2d 168, 174 (1975), cert. denied, 423 U.S. 866, 96 S.Ct. 126, 46 L.Ed.2d 95 (1975). Moreover, loan agreements have been held not to constitute "exchange contracts" covered by Article VIII(2)(b), see, e.g., Libra Bank Ltd. v. Banco Nacional De Costa Rica, 570 F.Supp. 870, 900 (S.D.N.Y. 1983). See Note, The IMF and New York Courts, 9 Vand.J.Trans.L. 199 (1976); Note, Enforcement of Foreign Exchange Control Regulations in Domestic Courts, 70 A.J.I.L. 101 (1976). With respect to the meaning of "exchange contracts" and other key terms of Article VIII(2)(b), see Gold, The Fund Agreement in the Courts, Vol. II 393–427 (1982).

Some of the principal United States, English and German cases and the perceived inconsistency between the governmental recognition of the economic cooperation objectives of the IMF and the judicial disregard of them by the courts of a number of members, including the United States and the United Kingdom, are discussed in Ebke, Article VIII, Section 2(b), International Monetary Cooperation, and the Courts, 23 Int'l Law. 677 (1989). See also Gold, Exchange Controls and External Indebtedness: Are the Bretton Woods Concepts Still Workable?, 7 Hous.J.Int'l L. 1 (1984).

## SECTION 3. INTERNATIONAL DEVELOPMENT

### A. INTRODUCTION

One of the principal objectives of international economic development is to facilitate the transfer of capital and managerial and technical knowhow to the developing countries in order to promote the development of their economies and thereby enhance the well-being of their populations.

Encouraging sustainable economic development involves a complex amalgam of institutions, mechanisms and processes which continue to evolve as international economic conditions change and environmental concerns increase. See generally Garcia–Amador, The Emerging International Law of Development (1990). As noted in Sections 1 and 2, international trade and international monetary institutions and rules are involved to a significant extent. In the trade sphere, for example, special arrangements are designed to stabilize the international prices of various primary commodities on which foreign currency earnings of many developing countries are dependent, and special trade preferences are granted by industrialized countries for products of developing countries. In the monetary sphere, the IMF extends special financing to developing countries to assist their efforts to stabilize the value of their currencies and deal with their balance of payment difficulties.

Major international lending institutions, such as the International Bank for Reconstruction and Development (the World Bank) (and its affiliates, the International Development Association and the International Finance Corporation), regional banks, such as the Asian, European and Inter–American

Development Banks, and national development banks in the developing countries have, as their principal purpose, the encouragement of the economic development of the developing countries by providing capital for infrastructure or productive projects on a loan or grant basis.

Investment by multinational, or as they are frequently called, transnational corporations (TNCs), in developing countries also has an important role to play in the economic development process. Private investment brings not only capital, but more importantly, technological and managerial knowhow to the developing country. Capital is often available from international and national lending institutions but sophisticated technical and management knowhow often is not.

During much of the Post–War period, many developing countries displayed considerable suspicion of, and hostility toward, TNCs, the far-flung activities of which seemed beyond the capability of most developing countries to regulate. See Bondzi–Simpson, Legal Relationships Between Transnational Corporations and Host States 25–46 (1990). The first phase of the post-colonial period was marked by the assertion by the developing countries of permanent sovereignty over natural resources and nationalization of the natural resource properties owned by TNCs. During and following this phase, many developing states attempted to achieve development goals without a significant involvement by TNCs. The developing countries formed the Group of 77 to further their interests, particularly in the institutions of the United Nations, and the Group of 77 successfully engineered the adoption by the General Assembly of resolutions supportive of their position on economic issues, including the Declaration on the Establishment of a New Economic Order, G.A.Res. 3201 (S–IV 1974) and Resolution 3281, the Charter of Economic Rights and Duties of States (XXIX 1974). See p. 689 supra. A U.N. Commission and a Centre on Transnational Corporations were established in 1984 to study TNCs, with the objective of increasing the contributions of TNCs to economic development, regulating their conduct and enhancing the capacity of developing countries to negotiate effectively with them.

In recent years, however, the realization has grown that the best prospects for achieving economic development lie in moving away from centrally managed economies and state-owned enterprises toward freer economies and privatization. As noted in the 1992 International Finance Corporation Annual Report at pp. 11–12 *:

> Transferring ownership of manufacturing or service-providing enterprises from governments to private parties—the process of privatization—has become one of the most pervasive global phenomena of the last decade. According to a recent study by the IBRD, approximately 80 countries have moved privatization to the top of their public policy agenda in recent years * * *.

* * *

Privatization is the *sine qua non* of the conversion of the centrally planned East European and CIS economies to market economies. In the former Soviet-bloc countries, privatization is not simply a matter of transferring assets of a few state-owned companies to private investors; it is fundamental to the transformation of an entire political and economic system. The task is enormous, as hundreds of thousands of state enterprises, from small retail stores to huge industrial complexes, have been, or will be, transferred to private ownership over the next few years.

The trend toward privatization is by no means confined to the former Soviet-bloc countries. Privatizations are occurring, with varying speed, in countries in Latin America, South Asia, East Asia, the Middle East, and Africa. * * *

A variety of reasons can be cited for the worldwide trend toward privatization. The root cause, particularly in Eastern Europe and in Latin America, is the realization by governments that state enterprises are generally much less efficient than private companies in making products and providing services. Even in utility sectors that are so-called "natural monopolies," where regulation is important, it has been demonstrated that companies with private ownership deliver services more efficiently.

State enterprises are often less efficient because they are not given appropriate profit incentives and are rarely held accountable for performance. The most critical performance indicator for a private company is profit. Managers of government-owned companies, however, often have multiple noncommercial and political objectives and may have restricted decision-making powers. They may, for example, be expected to increase employment, irrespective of the cost of efficiency of doing so. Or they may be required to sell goods at artificially low prices. Consequently, it is difficult to hold these managers accountable for financial results or failures to improve efficiency. They can always provide plausible explanations for unprofitable operations, and there is usually no effective penalty for financial failure. At best, there is little incentive to risk changes that might improve operations. At worst, the lack of accountability and of transparent performance criteria may encourage corruption.

State enterprises may also undermine competition in the marketplace. They face no credible bankruptcy threat, as experience shows that governments usually bail them out when losses multiply. Frequently, where government-owned companies compete in markets with private firms, the former survive only because governments have been willing to provide protection or subsidies or both.

* * *

As a result of these changes over the past decade, there are few policymakers who doubt that free competitive markets and a prominent role for private enterprise are essential components of a successful economic development strategy.

Related to the trend toward freer economies and privatization is the growing realization that TNCs have an important, if not an essential, contribution to make to economic development of the developing countries. With respect to sophisticated technology controlled by TNCs, the contribution could be irreplaceable. To encourage investment by TNCs in the developing world, and the flow of technology and management expertise that accompanies such investment, it became increasingly obvious that the legal climate for foreign investment had to be improved and, more specifically, ways had to be found to improve the level of legal security of investment by TNCs in developing countries.

As discussed in Section 1, there is in existence today a large body of international trade law embodied principally in the General Agreement on Tariffs and Trade (GATT) and the trade agreements entered into under the aegis of the GATT. There is also a significant body of international monetary law embodied in the Articles of Agreement of the International Monetary Fund (IMF). There is at present no comparable body of international law governing international investment or development. Efforts to develop multilateral investment codes regulating the treatment of foreign investment and a code of conduct for TNCs have not been crowned with success.

The gaps in the legal regulation and protection of foreign investment resulting from the failure to produce substantive rules governing international investment by TNCs on a multilateral basis have been filled, in part, over the last 25 years or so by a variety of national and international arrangements, both substantive and procedural, aimed at improving the regulation of investments in developing countries and their legal protection against noncommercial risks. These have included national programs adopted in capital-exporting states to insure investments by their nationals in developing countries against noncommercial risks. See p. 1448 infra. They have also included, more recently, a proliferation of bilateral investment treaties between industrialized and developing countries aimed at protecting investments made by a national of one contracting party in the other from specified noncommercial risks, and in many cases, at improving access of foreign investment to developing countries. See p. 764 supra. And, importantly, there have been two multilateral conventions that make a substantial contribution to the legal security of international investment—the International Convention on the Settlement of Investment Disputes between States and Nationals of Other States, p. 1459 supra, and the Convention establishing the Multilateral Investment Guarantee Agency, p. 1460 infra. These multilateral conventions and the growing network of bilateral investment treaties constitute the beginnings of what may well evolve into a substantial body of international law regulating, and providing increased legal protection for, international investment.

This section will provide an introduction to some of the major institutions involved in financing international development. Section 4 will discuss the regulation and legal protection of international investment.

## B. INTERNATIONAL BANK FOR RECONSTRUCTION AND DEVELOPMENT (IBRD), INTERNATIONAL DEVELOPMENT ASSOCIATION (IDA) AND THE INTERNATIONAL FINANCE CORPORATION (IFC)

### THE WORLD BANK ANNUAL REPORT 1992

4–5, 105–106 *

The World Bank * * * refers to the International Bank for Reconstruction and Development (IBRD) and its affiliate, the International Development Association (IDA). The IBRD's other two affiliates are the International Finance Corporation (IFC) [discussed at p. 1438 infra] and the Multilateral Investment Guaranty Agency (MIGA) [discussed at p. 1460 infra]. The Bank, the IFC, and MIGA are sometimes referred to as the "World Bank Group."

The common objective of these institutions is to help raise standards of living in developing countries by channeling financial resources to them from developed countries.

The IBRD, established in 1945, is owned by the governments of 160 countries. The IBRD, whose capital is subscribed by its member countries, finances its lending operations primarily from its own borrowings in the world capital markets. A substantial contribution to the IBRD's resources also comes from its retained earnings and the flow of repayments on its loans. IBRD loans generally have a grace period of five years and are repayable over fifteen to twenty years. They are directed toward developing countries at more advanced stages of economic and social growth. The interest rate the IBRD charges on its loans is calculated in accordance with a guideline related to its cost of borrowing.

The IBRD's charter spells out certain basic rules that govern its operations. It must lend only for productive purposes and must stimulate economic growth in the developing countries in which it lends. It must pay due regard to the prospects of repayment. Each loan is made to a government or must be guaranteed by the government concerned. The use of loans cannot be restricted to purchases in any particular member country. And the IBRD's decisions to lend must be based on economic considerations alone.

The International Development Association was established in 1960 to provide assistance for the same purposes as the IBRD, but primarily in the poorer developing countries and on terms that would bear less heavily on their balance of payments than would IBRD loans. IDA's assistance, therefore, is concentrated on the very poor countries—those with an annual per capita gross national product of $610 or less (in 1990 dollars). More than forty countries are eligible under this criterion.

Membership in IDA is open to all members of the IBRD, and 142 of them have joined to date. The funds used by IDA, called credits to distinguish them from IBRD loans, come mostly in the form of subscriptions, general replenishments from IDA's more industrialized and developed members, and transfers from the net earnings of the IBRD. The terms of IDA credits, which are traditionally made only to governments, are ten-year grace periods, thirty-five- or forty-year maturities, and no interest.

* * *

While the World Bank has traditionally financed all kinds of capital infrastructure, such as roads and railways, telecommunications, and port and power facilities, the centerpiece of its development strategy emphasizes investments that can directly affect the well-being of the masses of poor people of developing countries by making them more productive and by integrating them as active partners in the development process.

The Bank's efforts to reduce poverty cut across sectoral lines and include investments to improve education, ensure environmental sustainability, expand economic opportunities for women, strengthen population-planning, health, and nutrition services, and develop the private sector. The Bank's support of economic restructuring in many of its borrowing member countries is based on the knowledge that the precondition for restoring economic growth—the cornerstone of successful development and poverty reduction—is structural adjustment.

## THE INTERNATIONAL FINANCE CORPORATION ANNUAL REPORT 1992 *

### Preface

The International Finance Corporation (IFC), a multilateral institution, was established in 1956 with a mandate to foster economic growth by promoting private sector investment in its developing member countries. Although IFC's activities are closely coordinated with, and complement, the overall development objectives of the other World Bank Group institutions, IFC is legally and financially independent, with its own Articles of Agreement, shareholders, financial structure, management, and staff.

IFC combines the characteristics of a multilateral development bank and a private merchant bank. Its share capital is provided by its 147 developed and developing member countries, which collectively determine its policies and activities. IFC's profitability, strong shareholder support, and substantial paid-in capital base have allowed it to raise most of the funds for its lending activities through its triple-A rated bond issues in the international financial markets. Equity investments are financed from the capital base and retained earnings.

In its project financing role IFC provides loans and makes equity investments. Unlike most multilateral institutions, IFC does not require government guarantees for its financing. Like a private financial institution, the Corporation prices its finance and services in line with the market and seeks profitable returns. IFC shares full project risks with its partners.

IFC's experience in doing business in developing countries as well as its risk-management skills and thorough project appraisals all contribute to the success of the private sector projects it supports. These qualities also enable IFC to play an important catalytic role in mobilizing additional project funding from other investors and lenders, either in the form of cofinancing or through loan syndications, the underwriting of debt and securities issues, and guarantees. In addition to project finance and resource mobilization, IFC offers a full array of advisory services and technical assistance, helping private businesses in the developing world to increase their chances of success and advising governments on creating an environment that encourages private investment.

In its 36 years of operation, IFC has provided nearly $11 billion in financing for more than 1,000 companies in 98 developing countries. Today IFC is the largest source of direct financing for private sector projects in developing countries. IFC has a vital role to play in helping developing countries to make the transition to open, market-oriented economies and to build strong private sectors. As more and more developing countries adopt market-based policies, demand for IFC's services—loans, equity investments, resource mobilization, and advice—continues to grow.

### *Notes*

1. The IBRD issues an annual World Development Report. The 1992 report focuses on environmental issues, analyzing key linkages between the natural environment and economic growth, population, and poverty. It concludes that within the current environmental debate too little attention is often paid to key local problems of inadequate sanitation and clean water, urban air pollution, indoor air pollution, and severe land degradation, and that continuing undervaluation of the environment has damaged human health, reduced productivity, and undermined future development prospects. The report also asserts that continued, and even accelerated, economic and human development is sustainable, and can even be consistent with *improving* environmental conditions, but that this will require major shifts in policies, programs, and institutions.

The report deals with the significance for environmental quality of population programs, female education, agricultural extension and research, sanitation and clean water, and the removal of policies that encourage overuse of natural resources and discourage technological transfer. It calls for the establishment of policies and institutions that force decisionmakers to adopt behavior less damaging to the environment. In addition, the report offers a detailed strategy for financing proposed reforms.

2. The IBRD, IDA and IFC are owned and controlled by the member states. Although each has some distinctive features, the structure of the IBRD illustrates the pattern. Each member subscribes to shares in numbers roughly proportional to its economic strength. Each has 250 votes plus one vote for each share of stock, which has the effect of increasing the relative voting power of poorer countries. While the United States has provided over 17.9 percent of the subscribed capital, it holds only about 17.37 percent of the vote, while Malawi which has provided 0.05 of the total capital has about 0.07 percent of the vote.

Management of the IBRD is exercised ultimately by a Board of Governors, consisting of one Governor for each member state. Most responsibilities of the Governors, including making policy, have been delegated to the 22 full-time Executive Directors who meet at least once a week. All loans must be approved by the Executive Directors and they select the President who is responsible for conduct of the IBRD's regular business and its organization and staff. Five of the Executive Directors are appointed by the largest shareholders (United States, United Kingdom, France, the Federal Republic of Germany and Japan) while the rest are elected by the Governors representing the other member countries. All votes of an elected Executive Director are cast as a unit, but in practice, as in the case of the International Monetary Fund, most decisions are made by consensus, rather than by formal vote. The Governors meet once a year in conjunction with the annual meeting of the International Monetary Fund to review operations and basic policies.

The IBRD and IDA share the same staff. While IFC has its own operating and legal staff, it shares certain administrative and other services with the IBRD. The same person is President of all three institutions.

3. Whereas assistance to large-scale industrial projects is provided directly through IBRD loans, support for medium-sized and small-scale productive enterprises—now running at more than $1 billion per year—is largely channeled through local development finance companies (DFCs). Some of these are privately controlled, while others are government-owned. DFCs are financial institutions whose major activity is to mobilize medium-term and long-term resources to finance investment projects of productive enterprises. Most DFCs lend to manufacturing enterprises, though some also specialize in particular sectors or activities, such as agricultural industries, tourism, and small-scale enterprise.

While common in most developing countries, small-scale enterprises (those with assets of less than $250,000) generally find it more difficult to raise capital than do larger enterprises. The IBRD uses DFCs to help small enterprises, but it also looks to a wider range of institutions such as commercial banks, investment companies, and cooperatives to promote their development. IFC's investments in development finance companies sometimes complement the IBRD's involvement in that the IFC invests in equity to provide a base for borrowing by the DFC of IBRD funds. In other cases, IFC makes its own direct loans to DFCs.

4. Effective July 1, 1982, the IBRD shifted from making fixed interest rate loans to a system of loans with interest at floating rates, representing the IBRD's cost of funds plus a 50–basis–point (0.5%) spread, adjusted at six-month intervals.

5. Because of the adverse trends in the world economy of the 1980's, the IBRD has attempted to play a more centralized role in coordinating support from all sources of finance. First, multilateral and bilateral donors have acted in concert through the Paris Club, country consultative groups and consortia, and regional groups. These groups provide the necessary funding to support adjustment programs and assure that adequate funds flow to development priorities.

Second, the IDA established the Special Facility for Africa (SFA) in 1985 and the Special Program of Assistance (SPA) to sub-Saharan countries in 1987. The SFA helps finance structural adjustment programs and rehabilitation projects in low-income African countries by direct contributions of donor countries, by joint financing through Special Joint Financing (SJF), and by cofinancing of adjustment programs. The SPA provides assistance for low-income, debt-distressed countries of sub-Saharan Africa undertaking adjustment. Through cofinancing of adjustment credits, SPA can mobilize the necessary resources needed for funding.

Third, the IDA uses the Policy Framework Paper (PFP) to coordinate efforts of the IBRD, IMF, and recipient governments in assessing the financial needs of the member country. Before giving its final approval to a funding program, a PFP is prepared by the recipient government, the IBRD and the IMF. In addition, the PFPs provide a framework in which other lenders may commit their resources.

During the early 1980's, the IBRD recognized two areas, status of women and the environment, which needed to be addressed in order to improve its development programs. IBRD reports and research indicated that the disadvantaged status of women in such areas, for example, as access to education and health facilities had an adverse effect on the progress of its development programs. In response, the IBRD established the Women in Development Division to aid and advise member governments in including women in their programs for economic and social development.

In addition, the IBRD has placed more emphasis on environmental considerations and, in 1988, established an internal structure and process for dealing with these issues. As part of the project approval process, the IBRD performs a mandatory review of environmental issues and prepares reports on these issues with its proposed strategy to address them. In 1991 the Global Environment Facility (GEF) was established as a pilot program under which grants or concessional loans are provided to developing countries to help them implement programs that protect the global environment. The program is targeted to focus on four areas: protection of the ozone layer; limiting emissions of greenhouse gases; protection of biodiversity; and protection of international waters. The program will be implemented by UNEP, UNDP, and the IBRD.

6. In recent years, the IBRD has helped to meet the growing needs of its borrowing member countries by becoming increasingly active in stimulating the flow to them of external capital. Cofinancing, one of the most important ways by which these flows can be tapped, directly associates IBRD funds with those provided by other sources in financing specific projects or programs in developing countries. Cofinancing has become a regular feature of the IBRD's activity. See Silkenat, The Role of International Development Institutions in International Project Financing: IBRD, IFC and Cofinancing Techniques, 17 Int'l Law. 615, 621–23 (1983). In fiscal 1992 about 52 percent of all Bank-assisted projects and programs involved some form of cofinancing.

The three main categories of cofinancing partners are (a) official sources, which include governments, their agencies, and bilateral and multilateral development institutions; (b) export credit institutions, which are directly associated with financing the procurement of certain goods and services from a particular country; and (c) private financial institutions. This last category consists primarily of commercial banks, but it may also include insurance companies, pension funds, and other private sources.

In structuring cofinancing for large infrastructure projects, emphasis is placed on combining private-sector capital and finance with support from governments and the IBRD. One vehicle for project financing is the Expanded Cofinancing Operations (ECO) program, which, by providing partial IBRD guarantees, is intended to support eligible IBRD borrowers seeking to gain or improve access to syndicated commercial-bank loans or international capital markets.

7. Technical assistance financed and administered by the IBRD consists of two broad categories of services: (a) engineering-related, such as feasibility studies, engineering design, and construction supervision and (b) institution-related, such as diagnostic policy and institutional studies, management support, and training.

In earlier years, the IBRD was primarily involved with the first type of activities to ensure the technical quality of projects. More recently, there has been a greater emphasis on institutional improvements, project-related training, and policy studies. Lately, IBRD-financed technical assistance has also focused on improving national economic management within the framework of structural-adjustment loans.

8. There is a multiplicity of donors, lenders and providers of technical assistance involved in assisting the flow of capital and know-how to the developing countries. Solely in the public sphere, at least a dozen international institutions and about 30 national organizations are involved in some way.

The IBRD has almost continuous contact and close working relations with U.N. agencies and commissions, regional development banks, the Organization for Economic Co-operation and Development (OECD), regional organizations such as the European Communities and the Permanent Executive Committee of the Inter–American Economic and Social Council of the Organization of American States, and most of the national agencies that provide development finance and technical assistance. In addition, closer links have been forged with many nongovernmental organizations engaged in development activities.

The IBRD plays a leading role in efforts to coordinate assistance from a variety of sources to individual countries. For this purpose, it has organized and served as chairman of a number of coordinating groups of national and international organizations. See Oliver, International Economic Cooperation and the World Bank (1975).

9. It has been suggested that the distinctions between the responsibilities of the IBRD and the International Monetary Fund are becoming blurred, especially in the area of renegotiations of the external debt of debtor states and that the synergism between the two institutions is salutary. Gold, Relationship between the International Monetary Fund and the World Bank, 15 Creighton L.Rev. 499 (1981–82).

The blurring of roles has resulted in part from reforms instituted by the IBRD and the Fund to address the economic conditions of the 1980's and 1990's. For example, the IBRD has expanded its scope of operations to include structural and adjustment loans, while the Fund has established facilities to provide greater financial assistance over longer loan periods. With the common objective of structural reform in member states, the staffs of the two institutions have collaborated and shared information. In addition, the IBRD and the Fund have formalized their collaboration through the Fund's Structural Adjustment Facility (SAF) established in 1986.

One significant aspect of increased cooperation is the imposition of cross-conditionality on requests for assistance by member countries. Cross-conditionality may be imposed in several forms but most noticeably in the form of "consultative cross-conditionality" and "indirect financial cross-conditionality." Under both of these forms, a loan from one institution is preconditioned on the existence of an arrangement with another institution. For example, the IBRD requires that a member have previously undertaken an IMF program before it approves an application for a Structural Adjustment Loan. In addition, commercial banks may condition their loans on the fulfillment of the Fund's target goals. In the event of nonfulfillment of target goals, the commercial banks may cease disbursements on the loans. See Nicholas Kremmydas, The Cross–Conditionality Phenomenon—Some Legal Aspects, 23 Int'l Law. 651 (1989), and

Richard E. Feinberg, The Changing Relationship Between World Bank and the International Monetary Fund, 42 Int'l Org. 551 (1988).

10. By participating in development projects, the IFC encourages and promotes contributions from other sources. In fact in 1990, for every dollar invested by the IFC, other lenders or investors supplied an average of $5.20. Loan syndication has proven to be one of the IFC's most effective catalytic functions.

In 1990, the IFC established the Multi–Country Loan Facility (MLF) to increase its assistance to small and medium-sized projects. Through this facility, the IFC can provide funds to developmentally valuable projects which, because of their size, would not otherwise qualify for IFC support and can mobilize foreign exchange lending for international commercial banks. Under the facility, the IFC and these commercial banks agree to provide matching amounts of finance to the selected projects. The commercial bank acts as project appraiser and loan supervisor while the IFC acts as lender of record.

As one of its services, the IFC provides both financial and technical assistance to developing countries. For several years, the Foreign Investment Advisory Service (FIAS), has operated in conjunction with the IFC and the Multilateral Investment Guaranty Agency (MIGA), see p. 1460, to assist member countries in developing policies and programs to attract direct foreign investment. Although the FIAS has concentrated its efforts primarily in Asia and sub-Saharan Africa, it recently has expanded its scope to accommodate the countries of Eastern Europe which have opened the doors for foreign investment and privatization. In addition, the IFC provides advisory services through Corporate Finance Services (CFS) which was established in 1989. The CFS focuses its attention on corporate structure and provides assistance primarily for financial restructuring and privatization. Both the FIAS and CFS supplement assistance and services provided by the IFC's Technical Assistance (TA) Trust Funds Program.

The IFC has established several initiatives in recent years in response to concerns specific to various geographic regions. In Africa, the IFC created three facilities: the African Project Development Facility (APDF), the African Enterprise Fund (AEF), and the African Management Services Company (AMSCo). The APDF helps African entrepreneurs prepare viable projects for the creation of new businesses or the expansion, privatization, or diversification of old ones. The AEF finances small and medium sized projects (projects too small for IFC support) in sub-Saharan countries. AMSCo provides management training for African nationals by placing executives from its shareholders (e.g., the IFC and other financial institutions) in senior positions of the African company. These executives manage the company and train African nationals, who eventually replace the executives. In Asia, the IFC established the South Pacific Project Facility (SPPF) to assist small island entrepreneurs in preparing development projects and to provide funding. In Eastern Europe, the IFC created the Polish Business Advisory Service (PBAS) to provide financial and technical assistance to emerging businesses and entrepreneurs in Poland. In the Caribbean, the IFC created the Caribbean Project Development Facility (CPDF) to assist entrepreneurs in 27 countries in securing financing for the creation or expansion of businesses.

11. In response to changes in the world economy, the IDA has shifted the allocation of its resources to emphasize its four main goals: expansion of macroeconomic and structural adjustment programs; enhancement of response

by public and private sectors to incentives; restructuring of public investment programs; and increased support of human resource development (e.g., population nutrition and education). The IDA has reduced the proportion of lending directly supporting agriculture, industry, energy and power and has increased the proportion supporting health, education, water supply and urban development.

## SECTION 4. INTERNATIONAL INVESTMENT

### A. INTRODUCTION

Private foreign direct investment in developing countries brings in capital, generates employment, and is an important means of facilitating technical and managerial knowhow transfers and foreign market access. Through training of local staff, foreign direct investment helps to transfer product and process technologies and contributes to the development of local management and marketing skills. Thus, flows of privately owned investment resources into developing countries are a powerful fuel for economic growth and development.

The sea change in the area of economic development that is now in progress is the recognition throughout much of the developing world that economic development can proceed much more vigorously in a private-enterprise-free-market environment than in an environment dominated by state-owned enterprises and central planning. As a consequence, developing countries are increasingly recognizing the myriad benefits of private foreign direct investment and are taking steps to promote it.

In recent years private foreign direct investment has outpaced other forms of foreign capital inflows to developing countries. In 1991 it was estimated to have reached $24.8 billion (on a cash flow basis) in developing countries—about three times its size in 1986. 1992 MIGA Annual Report at p. 6. Some further perspective on the importance of foreign direct investment is contained in the following excerpt from the 1992 Annual Report of the International Finance Corporation at pp. 7–8*:

> Since 1986, new private investment in developing countries has grown from 10 percent to nearly 12 percent of GDP [gross domestic product] in 1991—the highest level since the 1970s. However, in the 1970s much investment was made in response to widespread protectionist policies and was therefore inefficient on an international scale; today private investment is likely to have a greater developmental impact, since it tends to be concentrated in countries that are liberalizing their economies and seeking closer links with international markets.
>
> Foreign direct investment (FDI) has been growing rapidly, and, although unevenly spread, is now an important source of development financing in many countries. In 1990 FDI accounted for more than 10 percent of private investment in developing countries, compared with an

average of about 6 percent during the period 1978–88. FDI accounted for almost one-third of net long-term resource flows to the developing world in 1991, a proportion that has doubled since 1985.

Governments throughout the developing world recognize the increasing importance of private investment—particularly FDI—both in overall capital formation and in gaining access to technology, managerial expertise, and international distribution channels. This recognition, as well as the scarcity of alternative sources of funding and the poor performance of state enterprises, are the driving forces behind the movement toward private sector development seen throughout the developing world.

* * *

Regional patterns of FDI flows are very varied. New investment flows to East Asia and Latin America are growing rapidly and are much larger than flows to other regions—the value of investment in each of the two regions tripled over the past five years. Together, these regions have consistently accounted for over three-quarters of total FDI flows to developing countries in recent years. FDI to Eastern Europe is also growing briskly, although from a much smaller base, and now accounts for 10 percent of total FDI flows to developing countries. FDI is expanding less rapidly in South Asia, the Middle East and North Africa, and sub-Saharan Africa.

Compared with FDI, the other forms of private financial flows to developing countries are quite small. Commercial bank lending, for example, remains far below the levels of the early 1980s and earlier, despite a slight increase over the past few years. International banks have re-entered countries such as Argentina, Chile, and Mexico, which have adopted market-based policies with some success, but generally in the capacity of intermediaries for other lenders.

Unlike international trade relations, which are subject to an international legal regime under the General Agreement on Tariffs and Trade, discussed at p. 1396 supra, and international monetary relations, which are subject to a legal regime administered principally by the International Monetary Fund, discussed at p. 1418 supra, international investment is not regulated by a cohesive international legal regime.

There is a wide range of topics that may be subsumed under the heading of regulation of international investment. One is regulating the access of foreign investment to the markets of the host country. This is often referred to as regulation of the right of establishment. It encompasses both the host state's right to restrict the access of foreign investors to certain spheres of economic activity and its duty to ensure access to others. Another aspect of the right of establishment involves ensuring fair and equitable treatment of foreign investment, one aspect of which may involve according national or most-favored-nation treatment, subject only to carefully circumscribed exceptions. Another topic is the regulation of the conduct of multinational or transnational enterprises and their relations with home and host countries. International accounting standards, regulation of anti-competitive or corrupt practices and labor standards, and labor-management relations are included among the aspects of transnational corporation conduct that have been of concern. Regulation of international tax matters, such as transfer pricing within a multinational enterprise, which can result in artificial shifting of income to reduce international tax burdens and to deprive the host state of its rightful share of tax revenues, has also been on the transnational enterprise agenda. A matter of particular concern to the investor is the extent of legal protection accorded to the foreign investment under the laws of the host government and under international law.

Many bilateral and multilateral international agreements have significant impact on international investment. The most important multilateral agreements, albeit regional in scope, are the agreements establishing the European Community, which involve extensive regulation of cross border investments within the Community. They encompass such matters as the right of establishment, regulation of transfers of capital, technology and services, cross-border mergers, and regulation of competition. Significant multilateral efforts focused more specifically on regulation of investment flows from developed to developing countries have not as yet enjoyed success. The efforts that have failed have included attempts to formulate multilateral codes for the regulation and protection of private investment abroad, discussed at p. 1453 infra, and for the regulation of transnational corporations, discussed at p. 1455 infra. There have been a number of regional multilateral agreements governing the legal protection of foreign investment, discussed at p. 1454 infra, which have not yet had a significant impact.

The principal device that has been utilized in recent years to embody an international legal regime aimed at promoting and providing protection to foreign investment is the network of bilateral investment treaties, which are discussed at p. 764 supra. These are designed to provide specific legal protection against the noncommercial risks that often accompany an investment made by a private investor in a foreign country, particularly in a country in which economic or political instability may be present. Many of these treaties, including, in particular, those entered into by the United States, also seek to ensure broadened access to local markets for foreign investment. The principal contribution of these treaties to enhancing the legal protection of the foreign investor has been to provide substantive rules regarding such matters as the capital-importing state's obligation to provide nondiscriminatory and national, and often most-favored-nation, treatment to foreign investments and to pay full compensation in the event of expropriation. Many of the treaties have also contained procedural protection in the form of mandatory submission of disputes between the investor and the capital-importing state to binding international arbitration.

It may be that these bilateral investment treaties and the small number of regional multilateral investment treaties will eventually evolve over time into broadly based multilateral arrangements for the regulation and protection of international investment or possibly some of the norms expressed in bilateral and regional agreements will evolve into norms of customary international law. Such evolution is likely to extend over a period of years, but there is evidence that the pace of efforts to regulate and improve the legal security of international investment is quickening, spurred by the compelling need to attract private capital and knowhow from abroad on the part of developing countries of the Third World and the countries in Eastern

Europe and the former Soviet Union that are moving from communism and managed economies toward freer economies and privatization.

In addition to bilateral treaties and the occasional multilateral agreement regulating aspects of international investment and the as-yet unsuccessful efforts to produce multilateral codes regulating and providing legal protection for international investment there have been efforts to develop guidelines for the conduct and treatment of international investment. Although not intended to articulate binding norms, such guidelines may nonetheless prove to be building blocks for the eventual development of regulatory schemes. One significant effort in this regard has been the Guidelines for Multinational Enterprises promulgated by the Governments of the OECD Member States. These Governments jointly recommend to multinational enterprises operating in their territories the observance of the Guidelines. The basic premise of the Guidelines is that multinational enterprises can bring substantial benefits to the economies of home and host countries but their transnational activities, organization and financial resources transcend the capacity of individual states to regulate and may lead to abuses of economic power and conflicts with national policy objectives. The Guidelines, which are set forth in the Document Supplement, relate to such matters as contributing positively to the economic and social policies of home and host countries, timely disclosure of meaningful information concerning their operations and finances, avoidance of anti-competitive activities, respect for national employment and industrial relations laws and policies and environmental protection regimes. OECD Member States are to cooperate concerning national treatment of foreign-controlled enterprises, conflicting requirements imposed on multinational enterprises by governments in different countries and international investment incentives and disincentives. See The OECD Declaration and Decisions on International Investment and Multinational Enterprises: 1991 Review (1992).

An important straw in the wind is the 1992 Report to the Development Committee of the World Bank Group and the IMF entitled Legal Framework for the Treatment of Foreign Investment, which includes a set of Guidelines on the Treatment of Foreign Direct Investment. The Report and Guidelines were published by the World Bank Group on September 25, 1992. The Guidelines suggest the appropriateness of providing broad legal protection for direct foreign investment against non-commercial risks. In publishing the Report and Guidelines, the President of the World Bank Group stated that the Guidelines would be relevant to the "continuous efforts in our member countries to improve investment climates and facilitate greater investment flows." 31 I.L.M. 1366 (1992). The fact that the Guidelines have been developed and published by the World Bank Group and the IMF, the principal institutions enjoying virtually universal membership that are centrally involved in international development, implies that the Guidelines have the potential to influence significantly the progressive development of international law in this area. The Guidelines are discussed at p. 1459 infra.

Agreement between the state of the private investor's nationality and the host state on substantive principles of customary international law relating to protection of foreign investment has often not been attainable because of basic doctrinal differences on the applicable rules. See p. 687 supra. Even when this has been the case, host governments have increasingly been willing to accept the procedural device of submitting investment disputes to binding international arbitration, and to this end many developing states have become parties to the Convention on the Settlement of Investment Disputes Between States and Nationals of Other States, p. 1459 infra. In the frequent cases in which compulsory international arbitration of investment disputes between investors and host governments is not mandated by a treaty, binding arbitration may be available because the host state and the investor have agreed on an *ad hoc* basis to arbitration of such disputes under the rules of the International Centre for the Settlement of Investment Disputes (ICSID), UNCITRAL, the International Chamber of Commerce, or some other international arbitral regime.

One widely used technique for closing the gaps that remain in the substantive and procedural protection that the foreign investor enjoys against noncommercial risks is the bilateral investment insurance schemes that have been provided by many developed states with respect to certain investments made by their nationals in selected developing countries. The United States foreign investment insurance program, which is administered by the Overseas Private Investment Corporation (OPIC), is discussed in the following section.

In addition to bilateral arrangements intended to enhance the legal security of foreign investors, there have been a variety of multilateral efforts toward this end. The most successful of these to date has been the Multilateral Investment Guarantee Agency (MIGA), discussed at p. 1460 infra, established under the auspices of the World Bank with extensive participation by developing as well as developed states, which has begun to operate successfully. See generally the 1992 MIGA Annual Report.

## B. OPIC AND EXIMBANK INVESTMENT GUARANTIES

### *1. The Overseas Private Investment Corporation*

The Overseas Private Investment Corporation (OPIC) administers a program of insurance and guaranties for United States private investments in less developed countries against certain non-commercial risks. OPIC, a self-supporting corporation wholly-owned by the United States Government, was created in 1969 to take over the functions of the Investment Guaranty Program of the Agency for International Development (AID). 22 U.S.C.A. §§ 2191–200.

The OPIC investment insurance program provides insurance protection against three specific types of non-commercial risk: inconvertibility of foreign currency into dollars, expropriation of investment by the host government, and war, revolution, insurrection and civil strife. The loan guaranty program is broader, offering protection against any default, whether for commercial or political reasons. In addition to these two main activities OPIC operates a special program that insures United States construction and service contractors against both political and some commercial risks.

OPIC's investment insurance is available to United States citizens; to corporations, partnerships or other associations created under the laws of the United States or of any state or territory which are substantially beneficially owned by United States citizens; and to foreign businesses that are wholly-owned[1] by any of the above. A United States corporation qualifies as "substantially beneficially owned" if a majority of each class of its issued and outstanding stock is beneficially owned by United States citizens.

Only investments in "less developed friendly countries" are eligible for insurance, and insurance will not be granted unless the United States and the host government have previously entered into an agreement for the institution of the program. The purpose of these agreements is to provide, in advance, orderly procedures for the handling of claims, the transfer of foreign currencies and other issues that are likely to arise between the two governments. The agreements generally provide that OPIC may offer insurance coverage to eligible investors in projects that are approved by the foreign host government, that the rights of the United States as assignee and subrogee will be recognized and that any disputes arising from the agreement or the guaranty program will be resolved by negotiation or, eventually, by impartial international arbitration. The agreements are generally implemented by an exchange of diplomatic notes.

The investment must be new, or must constitute a significant expansion, modernization or development of an existing enterprise. No fixed form of eligible investment is prescribed; for example, eligible investments may be in the form of conventional debt or equity, contribution of goods or services, licensing agreements, certain technical assistance and construction contracts, or special arrangements such as contractual joint ventures. OPIC insurance covers both initial investment and rights under related securities or contracts, and may usually be obtained for retained earnings or accrued interest, to a dollar limit equal to the insurance coverage on the initial investment.

OPIC may not issue insurance for investments that are likely to cause the investor to reduce the number of employees in the United States because United States production is being replaced by production of the foreign investment of the same product for the same market as the investor's United States production ("runaway shops"). Investments need not be tied to United States procurement, but substantial procurement in other developed countries may jeopardize eligibility for coverage. The developmental benefit to the host country is also a factor in determining eligibility, as is the extent to which the host government fosters private economic activity. Finally, preference is given to investments by smaller United States firms, and to investments in the poorest of developing countries.

The insured is required to bear at least 10 percent of the total risk of loss; thus, all OPIC insurance is limited to 90 percent of a proposed investment (plus 90 percent of any exposed retained earnings or interest, up to the amount of the original investment). For certain investments, OPIC has chosen to limit coverage even further. Insurance for large equity investments, particularly in extractive industries, is typically limited to 75 percent of the total equity investment, but may be reduced to as low as 50

1. In the case of foreign corporations, only 95 percent United States ownership is required.

percent. Parent-to-subsidiary loans may usually be insured only for 85 percent of their value, although exceptions are made for small business.

Insurance contracts are written for a maximum of 20 years with premiums payable annually. The premium rates charged by OPIC vary with the nature of the investment and the coverage but do not vary depending on the country in which the investment is made, whatever the level of political risk may be.

When an investor makes a claim, OPIC determines its validity and the amount that is due the investor; disputes between OPIC and the investor are submitted to binding arbitration. As a result of one such arbitration OPIC was found liable to International Telephone & Telegraph Corporation, Sud America, for cash payments and note guarantees totalling $95 million in connection with the nationalization of I.T.T. property by the Chilean government.

See generally Stillwell, Encouraging Investment in LDC's: The United States Investment Guaranty Program, 8 Brooklyn J.Int'l L. 365 (1982); T. Meron, OPIC Investment Insurance Is Alive and Well, 73 A.J.I.L. 104–111 (1978); and T. Meron, Investment Insurance in International Law (1976).

*a. Inconvertibility Coverage*

In essence, OPIC's convertibility insurance assures the investor that any rights or guarantees with respect to convertibility and repatriation of earnings and capital which the investor enjoys at the time of the original investment will continue for the life of the contract.

The convertibility guaranty for earnings on the investment or for the return of the investment may be invoked in three situations:

(a) when the investor is prevented from converting his local currency into United States dollars for a period of thirty days by direct operation of law, decree, regulation, or affirmative administrative determination (i.e., outright blockage);

(b) when the investor is prevented from converting his local currency into United States dollars by the failure for 60 days of the applicable government authorities to grant a duly submitted application for transfer (i.e., passive blockage achieved through governmental inaction);

(c) when the investor is permitted to convert his local currency into United States dollars, but only at a discriminatory rate of exchange which is less than 99 percent of the reference rate, which is generally the official exchange rate for the type of transfer involved (e.g., dividend remittance).

In these situations, OPIC will pay the investor in dollars a sum equal to 99 percent of the dollar equivalent of his inconvertible local currency.

The insurance affords no protection against the effects of currency devaluation or inflation. Local currency held by the investor for more than 18 months is not eligible for reimbursement. In addition, the investor cannot invoke the guaranty to alleviate the effect of any exchange regulation or practice that was in effect when the contract was executed.[2]

2. Payment of claims under convertibility insurance is made by OPIC in dollars against delivery to it of the local currency. The exchange rate used to determine payment is the

Inconvertibility coverage is available both for debt and equity; however, some debt insurance incorporates a 10 percent or 15 percent first loss deductible.

*b. Expropriation Coverage*

OPIC's expropriation coverage provides compensation in dollars to the United States investor if the host government subjects his property to "expropriatory action" with or without compensation. "Expropriatory action" is defined to include not only outright nationalization, but also less drastic actions sometimes termed "creeping expropriation." The OPIC Contract of Insurance (OPIC Form 234 KGT 12–70) (Second Revision) defines expropriatory action as:

> any action which is taken, authorized, ratified or condoned by the Government of the Project Country, commencing during the Insurance Period, with or without compensation therefor, and which for a period of one year directly results in preventing:
>
> (a) the Investor from receiving payment when due in the currency specified of amounts which the Foreign Enterprise owes the Investor on or in respect of the Securities; or
>
> (b) the Investor from effectively exercising its fundamental rights with respect to the Foreign Enterprise either as shareholder or as creditor, as the case may be, acquired as a result of the Investment; provided, however, that rights acquired solely as a result of any undertaking by or agreement with the Government of the Project Country shall not be considered fundamental rights merely because they are acquired from such undertaking or agreement; or
>
> (c) the Investor from disposing of the Securities or any rights accruing therefrom; or
>
> (d) the Foreign Enterprise from exercising effective control over the use or disposition of a substantial portion of its property or from constructing the Project or operating the same; or
>
> (e) the Investor from repatriating, and from exercising effective control in the Project Country over, amounts received in respect of the Securities as Investment Earnings or Return of Capital, which action commences within the eighteen (18) months immediately succeeding such receipt. * * *

Under this broad definition, the investor enjoys significant protection against foreign government interference with its property rights that falls short of an outright and permanent taking. The Contract treats a partial loss under sections (a) to (d) as a total loss and provides that the investor must assign all its property rights in the investment and any claims or causes of action connected therewith to OPIC before receiving compensation.

effective free market rate of exchange, or, if no effective market exists, the rate at which other U.S. investors convert local currency into dollars for remittance of earnings. If neither of these methods can be used, the rate used is the most depreciated rate of exchange recognized by the central bank of the host country for sales to its residents of U.S. dollars that is applicable to at least 10 percent of such transactions.

If a loss occurs under section (e), the investor is compensated only to the extent of the loss—not for its total investment.

The investor and the foreign enterprise must take all reasonable measures, including administrative and judicial proceedings in the host country, to prevent or contest the expropriatory action. An offer by the host government to pay compensation will not prevent the operation of the guaranty. On the other hand, an investor may not invoke the guaranty when subjected to a non-discriminatory increase in taxation, or to a non-discriminatory regulatory measure that is reasonably related to a valid regulatory purpose, despite any adverse effect upon the investor's profits.

*c. War, Revolution, Insurrection And Civil Strife Coverage*

This basic coverage provides compensation for the loss of an investor's interest in the tangible property of the foreign enterprise if the loss is directly caused by war, revolution or insurrection. In addition, coverage is available for civil strife, terrorism and sabotage. The Contract covers hostile acts of any national or international organized force, and acts of any organized revolutionary or insurrectionary forces, including acts of sabotage. The Contract also covers damage which is a direct result of actions taken to combat or defend against an actual or anticipated act of war, revolution, insurrection, civil strife, terrorism or sabotage.

Compensation under insurance for equity investment, certain debt, and construction service contracts is measured by the depreciated book value of the covered property, but is limited to the lesser of (a) the repair or replacement cost of the property or (b) the diminution in fair market value of the property. Some loan insurance contracts cover the obligation itself, rather than underlying property, and compensate the lender for the amount of any defaulted installments of principal or interest. These contracts are limited, however, by a first-loss deductible borne by the insured.

### Notes

1. In general, the annual fee charged by OPIC for investment insurance is 0.4–0.9 percent for expropriation, 0.3–0.5 percent for inconvertibility, 0.4–0.9 percent for war, revolution, and insurrection, and 1.3–2.3 percent for combined coverage. These rates may be increased or decreased by up to one third depending on the risk profile of the specific project. The rates for natural resource and hydrocarbon projects or large projects ($50 million of total project costs or $25 million of insured investment) may vary by more than one third of the base rates.

2. The model OPIC investment guaranty agreement, on which the actual agreements are closely patterned, is set forth in the Document Supplement.

### 2. Export Credit Insurance Programs

In order to stimulate the financing necessary to promote exports, particularly to areas where noncommercial as well as commercial risks are most serious, many of the industrialized countries have instituted programs of export credit insurance covering short- and medium-term credits.

The United States has two programs. Under one program, the exporter can obtain insurance coverage with respect to political and commercial risks for export transactions involving short-term and medium-term credit. The insurance is available through the Export–Import Bank of Washington (Eximbank), an instrumentality of the United States Government, in partnership with the Foreign Credit Insurance Association (FCIA), an association of private insurance companies. This program is administered by the FCIA, which acts as an agent for the member insurance companies and for Eximbank. The private insurance companies underwrite the commercial credit risks, while the Eximbank covers the political risks and reinsures the commercial risks. Normally, 90 percent of a commercial loss and 100 percent of a political loss are covered. Eximbank also administers a separate program under which the exporter may secure nonrecourse financing from his commercial bank for medium-term credits. Eximbank will either grant a commercial and political risk guaranty to the commercial bank or participate directly in the financing of the transaction.

## C. MULTILATERAL EFFORTS TO PRODUCE INVESTMENT CODES

In view of the wide gulf between the positions adopted by various groups of states in the post-World War II period, and particularly between the developed and the developing countries, it is not surprising that efforts to codify the law of state responsibility for injury to the economic interests of aliens have been fruitless. As noted above, p. 684, the International Law Commission after debating the issues for years, failed to reach agreement on a draft codification.

The OECD prepared a Draft Convention on the Protection of Foreign Property. The Draft Convention was adopted on October 12, 1967, by the Council of the OECD, with Spain and Turkey abstaining. In the Resolution adopting the Draft Convention, the Council stated that it considered the Draft Convention to embody "recognized principles relating to the protection of foreign property, combined with rules to render [them] more effective," and that it commended the Draft Convention "as a basis for furthering and rendering more effective the application of these principles." Among the provisions were the following:

> Art. 2. Each Party shall at all times ensure the observance of undertakings given by it in relation to property of nationals of any other Party.
>
> Art. 3. No Party shall take any measures depriving, directly or indirectly, of his property a national of another Party unless the following conditions are complied with: (i) The measures are taken in the public interest and under due process of law; (ii) The measures are not discriminatory; and (iii) The measures are accompanied by provision for the payment of just compensation. Such compensation shall represent the genuine value of the property affected, shall be paid without undue delay, and shall be transferable to the extent necessary to make it effective for the national entitled thereto.

In view of these provisions, it is hardly surprising that the Convention did not attract support in the developing countries in 1967. See pp. 679 to 691 supra.

In 1976, the OECD adopted a Declaration on International Investment and Multinational Enterprises, to which were annexed Guidelines for Multinational Enterprises. The Guidelines, which as amended in 1979, 1984 and 1991 are contained in the Document Supplement, set forth the expectations of the OECD members with respect to the behavior within their territories of multinational enterprises. See generally The OECD Guidelines for Multinational Enterprises (1986) and The OECD Declaration and Decisions on International Investment and Multinational Enterprises, 1991 Review, 37–55 (1992). There have also been a number of regional efforts to develop multilateral investment regimes. The most important is the regime established for the European Community discussed in Chapter 1499. Another example is the Uniform Code on Andean Multinational Enterprises. 30 I.L.M. 1296 (1991).

The most significant steps toward development of multilateral investment codes in recent years have been the work on the Code of Conduct on Transnational Corporations, which is discussed in the following section, and the Guidelines on the Treatment of Foreign Direct Investment published by the World Bank Group in 1992, which is discussed at p. 1459 infra.

There has, however, been an extensive proliferation of bilateral investment agreements providing protection for private investment in developing countries. These are discussed at p. 764 supra.

Broadly based multilateral efforts have been channelled into avenues with more immediate productive potential than investment codes. The leading examples are the Convention on the Settlement of Investment Disputes Between States and Nationals of Other States, discussed at p. 1459 infra, and the Convention Establishing the Multilateral Investment Guarantee Agency, discussed at p. 1460 infra.

## D. U.N. COMMISSION AND CENTRE ON TRANSNATIONAL CORPORATIONS

A noteworthy multilateral effort to develop principles intended, among other things, to regulate international investment and to deal with legal protections against certain non-commercial risks has occurred under the auspices of the U.N. Commission and Centre on Transnational Corporations. The principal focus of their efforts was on the activities of multinational corporations and on developing a Code of Conduct on Transnational Corporations.

The Commission (consisting of 48 members) and the Centre were established by the U.N. Economic and Social Council in November of 1974. The Centre, an autonomous body within the U.N. Secretariat, has served as a focal point for all matters related to transnational corporations and acted as secretariat to the Commission. The broad objectives of the Centre's activities are to further the understanding of the nature of transnational corporations and of their political, legal, economic and social effects on home and host countries and in international relations, particularly between developed and developing countries; to secure effective international arrangements aimed at enhancing the contribution of transnational corporations to national development goals and world economic growth, while controlling and eliminating their negative effects; and to strengthen the negotiating capacity of host countries.

In 1975 the Centre began work on the Code of Conduct and shortly thereafter initiated a project on establishment of international standards of accounting and reporting by transnational corporations. The Centre has also prepared numerous studies of the role of transnational corporations and their impact on economic development and international trade and finance. See, e.g., Transnational Corporations in World Development, Third Survey, E/C. 10/1984/2, and Transnational Corporations in South Africa and Namibia, E/C. 10/1984/10. The Centre also attempts to assist and enhance through its research activities and technical assistance, the negotiating capabilities of developing countries in their dealings with transnational corporations. See Measures Strengthening the Negotiating Capacity of Governments in their Relations with Transnational Corporations. Joint Ventures among Firms in Latin America, E/C. 10/1982/15.

The basis for the conclusion that there was a need for a Code of Conduct on Transnational Corporations was summarized as follows in the 1985 Report of the Centre on Transnational Corporations on Work on the Formulation of the United Nations Code of Conduct on Transnational Corporations, E/C. 10/1985/s/2 at pp. 6–7 (hereinafter cited as "1985 Report on Code of Conduct"):

* * *

4. It is essential at the outset to restate basic arguments that have established the need for the code. Broadly speaking, this need rests on the evolutionary nature of international norms, the desire to minimize the negative effects of the operations of transnational corporations and the desire to maximize their positive contributions to economic growth and development in the context of an interdependent world. Together, these three considerations establish a commonality of interest among all States in adopting a code of conduct which, in a balanced manner, sets out the rights and expectations of the international community with regard to transnational corporations.

5. First, sections of the international community have traditionally held the position that there are certain standards at the international level concerning the treatment of foreign investors by which host countries must abide. The traditional concept of State responsibility in international law embodies the bulk of those standards. However, an assessment of the status of the various concepts of State responsibility and the complex interplay between State practice, official positions and political and economic developments indicates that the development of international norms is essentially an evolutionary process. International norms are not immutable or static. They are influenced and shaped by the changing needs and realities of the international community; therefore, the participation of all countries is required in the formulation of such norms. Without the code, the instability and uncertainty arising from disputes over the traditional concept of State responsibility are likely to continue and probably to worsen. A code of conduct would contribute greatly to the resolution of those disputes, not only by allowing the participation of all countries in the formulation of generally accepted norms of State responsibility, but also by reformulating

traditional international law by setting out the rights and responsibilities of States as well as transnational corporations.

6. Second, instances of corporate misconduct during the 1970s in such areas as interference in the internal affairs of States, illicit payments, and marketing practices led to a widespread demand for some form of international regulation, or the formulation of international standards of behaviour for transnational corporations. It became clear that the national legislation of any one State was inherently incapable of coping with the international dimension of some of the issues raised by the activities of transnational corporations. This led the General Assembly, in 1974, to call for a code of conduct that would seek, *inter alia,* to regulate the activities of transnational corporations in host countries, to eliminate restrictive business practices and to conform the activities of transnational corporations to the national development plans and objectives of developing countries, and in this context to facilitate, as necessary, the review and revision of previously concluded arrangements. (General Assembly resolution 3202 (S–VI), sect. V).
* * *

7. Third, the important role of transnational corporations in the global economy emphasizes the need for a stable multilateral framework that would help to promote their positive contributions to economic growth and development, as recognized by the General Assembly in adopting the International Development Strategy for the Third United Nations Development Decade. This shared desire for economic growth is not only based on the recognition that a growing world economy facilitates conscious efforts to obtain a more equitable sharing of benefits of this growth, especially between developed and developing countries. In addition, economic growth facilitates structural change in the world economy in the interest of a more efficient international division of labour and a better harnessing of the economic and human resources of all countries. As one of the leading actors in the world economy, transnational corporations can be important agents of economic growth and structural change. But, while transnational corporations influence the performance of the world economy, they are themselves influenced by the public policy framework set by governments for their activities. As illustrated by the experience of the General Agreement on Tariffs and Trade (GATT) and the International Monetary Fund (IMF), the establishment of a multilateral policy and institutional framework provides the stability and predictability that facilitates international economic co-operation. The need for the creation of such a framework for foreign direct investment and transnational corporations is today further reinforced by the adverse economic conditions faced by most countries, particularly the developing countries, and by the acknowledged difficulties in the implementation of the International Development Strategy for the Third United Nations Development Decade.

8. Thus, a broad commonality of interests exists in establishing standards of behaviour, and in encouraging the observance of those standards, through which frictions and conflicts disruptive and costly for all parties involved can be reduced. Naturally, a framework which is based on and promotes that convergence of interests in an interdepen-

> dent world cannot be established unilaterally or bilaterally. Rather, it has to be negotiated on a multilateral basis, taking into account the interests of all parties concerned.

While agreement was eventually reached within the Commission on Transnational Corporations in 1990 on a draft Code of Conduct, agreement was possible only by papering over basic disputed issues through adoption of language that is broad and abstract enough to accommodate the competing positions without resolving the underlying differences. The President of the forty-sixth session of the General Assembly convened a round of informal consultations on the Code on July 21–23, 1992. The conclusion reached was that no consensus was possible on the draft Code. Delegations felt that the changed international economic environment and the importance attached to encouraging foreign investment required that a fresh approach, which might include the preparation of guidelines or other instrument on foreign investment, should be examined at the next meeting of the Commission on Transnational Corporations.

The completion of the Code in a satisfactory manner was frustrated by disagreements on a number of fundamental issues. Perhaps the most basic was the relevance of customary international law to the norms to be established under the Code. The 1985 Report on the Code of Conduct commented as follows on this issue, at pp. 12–13:

> 25. There are at least two different schools of thought on this matter. The first maintains that the code should allow for the applicability of customary international legal principles in relevant areas to amplify or qualify the broad standards enunciated in the code. According to this view, the applicability of international law to the relations between States and transnational corporations is not limited to international obligations expressly founded on conventions, treaties or other international agreements. In addition, customary international law is seen as prescribing principles and rules with respect to such matters as jurisdiction over transnational corporations, permanent sovereignty of States over their natural wealth and resources, renegotiation of State contracts, nationalization and compensation, non-discriminatory treatment of transnational corporations, diplomatic protection of aliens and alien property, and procedures for the settlement of disputes between Governments and transnational corporations. It follows that the provisions of the code would not derogate from the application of those customary principles of international law, subject of course to the express undertakings of the States concerned under conventions, treaties and other international agreements concluded by such States. The proponents of this view accordingly maintain that the code ought to take into account the relevance of international law by incorporating stipulations with respect to its applicability to the relations between Governments and transnational corporations.
>
> 26. The second school of thought questions the existence of universally recognized principles of customary international law governing the treatment of transnational corporations or foreign investors. Adherents to that school maintain that this area falls primarily within the purview of national law, subject to international legal norms and specific under-

takings and obligations expressly stipulated in international instruments, such as codes of conduct and conventions, treaties and other international agreements, to which the States concerned have freely subscribed. A view closely associated with the foregoing position is that, if universally recognized principles of international law were to be adopted to govern the relations between States and transnational corporations, they would not necessarily be congruent with customary international law, but would take into account developments in the international community in the twentieth century, in particular the second half of the century. Among those developments are the emergence of the socialist countries of Eastern Europe, the emergence of developing countries from colonialism, and the quest for a new international economic order and its implications for a more equitable and balanced international legal order.

Another difficult issue was to what extent, if at all, preferential treatment for developing countries should be reflected in exceptions to the general requirement that foreign investors be accorded at least national treatment, for example, to permit developing countries to grant special incentives to the development of domestic industries.

Other issues related to the extent to which transnational corporations and developing states should be free in their contractual relationships to make an unrestricted choice of governing law and of the forum for the settlement of disputes. Another source of controversy was whether, in the event of expropriation, the expropriating state is obligated to pay compensation under international law. Paragraph 57 of the 1990 draft Code of Conduct states unhelpfully that "compensation is to be paid by the State concerned, in accordance with the applicable legal rules and principles." With respect to the transfer of payments relating to investments, many developing country delegations objected to inclusion of a provision, supported by various developed countries, stating that transnational corporations should generally be permitted to transfer without restriction all payments related to their investments, including repatriation of capital, remittance of dividends, and payment of royalties under licensing arrangements and technical assistance fees. Many developing countries objected to the "without restriction" formulation, noting that transfer of payments should explicitly be made subject to host country exchange control laws and regulations. See 1985 Report on Code of Conduct at pp. 12–33. The 1990 draft does not restrict the imposition of exchange controls by host countries.

In the 1990 draft of the Code of Conduct a number of key provisions, such as paragraph 57 referred to above, incorporate vague formulations that reflect rather than resolve disagreements between groups of governments on basic issues. See letter dated 31 May 1990 from the Chairman of the reconvened special session of the Commission on Transnational Corporations to the President of the Economic and Social Council. E/1990/94 12 June 1990. The 1990 draft is contained in the Document Supplement. In general, the provisions deal with standards rather than regulatory rules and are quite abstract. Efforts to complete the Code for submission to the General Assembly seem dead at least for the time being. The Centre on Transnational Corporations has been made part of the Transnational Corporations and Management Division of the Division of Economic and Social Development (DESD) of ECOSOC.

### *Note*

Consider the extent to which the provisions of the 1990 draft, if they ever became effective, would be capable of providing meaningful regulation of the conduct of transnational corporations or protection of the rights and interests of transnational corporation investors.

## E. WORLD BANK GUIDELINES FOR THE TREATMENT OF FOREIGN INVESTMENT

## REPORT TO THE DEVELOPMENT COMMITTEE [OF THE WORLD BANK GROUP AND THE IMF] ON THE LEGAL FRAMEWORK FOR THE TREATMENT OF FOREIGN INVESTMENT

[See Report and Guidelines I through VI]

### *Note*

The Report to the Development Committee of the World Bank Group (IBRD, IFC, ICSID and MIGA) and the IMF and the Guidelines on the Treatment of Foreign Direct Investment were approved and published by the Committee on September 25, 1992. The Committee agreed "without reservation" to call the Guidelines to the attention of the member states of the institutions involved. In publishing the Report and Guidelines, the President of the World Bank Group stated that they "should be of great relevance to the continuous efforts in our member countries to improve investment climates and facilitate greater investment flows." In addition, they "may also assist in the progressive development of international law in this important area." 31 I.L.M. 1366 (1992). The dramatically changed attitude of many developing countries toward legal protection for foreign private direct investment is reflected in some of the differences between the 1990 Draft Code of Conduct for Transnational Corporations, discussed at p. 1454 supra, and the 1992 Guidelines on the Treatment of Foreign Direct Investment. The Report and Guidelines are included in the Document Supplement.

## F. MACHINERY FOR SETTLEMENT OF INVESTMENT DISPUTES

### *CONVENTION ON THE SETTLEMENT OF INVESTMENT DISPUTES BETWEEN STATES AND NATIONALS OF OTHER STATES*

Washington, March 18, 1965.
17 U.S.T. 1270, T.I.A.S. No. 6090, 575 U.N.T.S. 159.

[Articles 25–55]

### *Notes*

1. The International Centre for Settlement of Investment Disputes (ICSID) was established on October 14, 1966, by the entry into force of the Convention on

the Settlement of Investment Disputes between States and Nationals of Other States. 17 U.S.T. 1270, T.I.A.S. No. 6090, 575 U.N.T.S. 159. As of June 30, 1992, the Convention had been signed by 113 countries and ratified or acceded to by 100, including many developing countries. The Convention is set forth in the Document Supplement. For a brief description of the Convention, see Broches, The Convention on the Settlement of Investment Disputes: Some Observations on Jurisdiction, 5 Colum.J.Transnat'l L. 263 (1966). See also Boskey & Sella, Settling Investment Disputes, [1965] 3 Finance and Development (The Fund and Bank Review) 129; Report of the Committee on International Law, Association of the Bar of the City of New York, 20 Record 400–09 (1965). For the United States implementing legislation, see Convention on the Settlement of Investment Disputes Act of 1966, 80 Stat. 344 (1966).

2. ICSID provides facilities for the conciliation and arbitration of investment disputes between Contracting States and Nationals of other Contracting States. As of June 30, 1992, twenty-seven such disputes, two of them involving conciliation and the remaining twenty-five arbitration, had been resolved under the Convention. Both of the conciliation proceedings were closed following settlements agreed between the parties, one prior to the constitution of a conciliation commission. Of the arbitration cases, twelve were settled by the parties. Arbitral awards were rendered in eleven cases. In four of them, there were annulment and resubmission proceedings under Article 52 of the Convention. The cases have concerned a variety of different kinds of investment in the agriculture, banking, construction, energy, health, industrial, mining and tourism sectors. See ICSID Cases. Doc. ICSID/16/Rev. 2 Introduction (November 15, 1991).

3. What advantages do you perceive from the point of view of the capital-exporting and the capital-importing states to this approach to the problem of providing legal security for international investments as compared with the other alternatives? The problem of determining the substantive rights and duties of the parties (by-passed in the Convention) remains. Is the Convention likely to facilitate the resolution of this problem in specific cases? What advantages are gained by providing for compulsory arbitration through a multilateral convention? See Fatouros, Government Guarantees to Foreign Investors 351–55 (1962).

## G. MULTILATERAL INVESTMENT INSURANCE

A third approach to multilateral protection of foreign investments has been directed toward creation of an international agency to insure investments in the less developed countries against noncommercial risks and to provide advisory services to assist member countries in creating a more attractive climate for private foreign investment. See International Bank for Reconstruction and Development, Multilateral Investment Insurance (March, 1962) [hereinafter cited as "World Bank Report"]. After more than two decades of effort, in October 1985, the Board of Governors of the World Bank opened for signature a Convention Establishing the Multilateral Investment Guarantee Agency (MIGA). The structure and operations of MIGA are described in MIGA Annual Report 1992 (Sept. 1992).

Generally, the proposals previously made contemplated a multilateral agreement between both capital-exporting and capital-importing states to establish an agency that would insure investments by the nationals of one or more contracting states in other contracting states. The scope of the protection was limited to the political risks of expropriation, inability to convert local currencies, and armed conflict. Losses were to be covered by the premiums paid by investors and, if necessary, by the contributions or pledged reserves of the member states.

Many of the problems inherent in the investment code approach also burdened the insurance proposals. In fact, some of the proposals called for incorporation of an investment code as an integral part of the insurance plan. One major problem was the definition of the risks to be covered. Too broad a definition might result in a high rate of successful claims and impair the financial stability of the agency. On the other hand, a broad definition might be considered by the capital-importing states as an unwarranted infringement of their freedom of action. Too narrow a definition could make the insurance unattractive to investors able to take advantage of the various national insurance programs.

Almost all the proposals took the position that only new investments could be insured since insuring existing investments would require huge capital commitments and obligations. Some of the proposals would have vested the administering agency with discretion to decide which applications for coverage would be granted and to suspend the operation of the program in particular countries—thus raising the possibility of difficult political problems. World Bank Report at 30–31.

The scope of membership and of liability for losses also raised difficult questions. Participation by both capital-importing and capital-exporting countries was favored over participation by the latter alone. Many of the proposals called for the capital-importing countries to share in the capital contributions and consequently in any losses not covered by premium income. Presumably, the fact that the capital-importing states would participate in risks would induce them to avoid acts against foreign investments. However, as a practical matter they would frequently have little or no control over convertibility and war risks. In addition, there would be little incentive for the capital-importing states to participate in such a program since they could derive the same benefits from the existing national programs without sharing the risks. World Bank Report at 20–22.

Under the national insurance programs, the insuring government, subrogated to the rights of an investor whose claim has been paid, can engage in negotiations and employ the entire range of its diplomatic power to recover from the host government. Additionally, the insuring government can settle the dispute on a basis other than a purely monetary settlement. On the other hand, a multilateral agency whose sole function is to administer the program could not agree to other than a monetary settlement. If a host government proved unwilling to negotiate a settlement or to submit to arbitration, the agency's only sanction would be publicity or a refusal to write further insurance in that country.

The 1962 World Bank Report assessed the various proposals, analyzed the advantages and disadvantages of multilateral insurance and pointed out the substantial difficulties involved. Soon after the Report was issued in 1962, the OECD began work on a draft convention. In its final act, the UNCTAD Conference of 1964 (dominated by the capital-importing countries) affirmed the need for private investment in the developing countries and requested the World Bank to expedite its studies of multilateral investment insurance. Final Act and Report of the United Nations Conference on Trade and Development, U.N.Doc.E/CONF. 46/141, Vol. 1 at 49–50 (1964). In June, 1965, the OECD transmitted a report and draft articles for an International Investment Guarantee Corporation to the World Bank for consideration. See 8 Harv.Int'l L.J. 328 (1967) for a partial text of the OECD draft. The accompanying report is summarized at 5 I.L.M. 96 (1966).

Building on the OECD draft and report, the Staff of the World Bank began drafting an Agreement for an International Investment Insurance Agency. See Martin, Multilateral Investment Insurance: The OECD Proposal, 8 Harv.Int'l L.J. 280 (1967). Draft articles of agreement were prepared in 1966, 1968 and in 1972. The 1972 draft and a Staff Memorandum on Principal Outstanding Issues were circulated to the Executive Directors of the Bank on April 16, 1973. There was, however, insufficient support among developed and developing states to enable the proposal to go forward. See Meron, Investment Insurance in International Law 30–37 (1976).

In 1974, the Inter–Arab Investment Guarantee Corporation was established and has since been operating successfully. See Shihata, Arab Investment Guarantee Corporation—A Regional Investment Insurance Guarantee Corporation, 6 J. World Trade L. 185 (1972).

The Convention Establishing the Multilateral Investment Guarantee Agency is designed to encourage the flow of investment to and between developing countries by issuing guarantees against non-commercial risks and carrying out various investment promotional and advisory activities. The Convention became effective upon ratification by at least five Category One countries (developed countries) and at least fifteen Category Two countries (developing countries), subscribing to at least one third (about $360 million) of MIGA's capital. In April 1988, MIGA was formally constituted and became the newest member of the World Bank Group (along with the Bank, IDA, IFC and ICSID). As of June 30, 1992, 115 states had signed the Convention, 85 states had become full members, the subscribed capital of MIGA exceeded $844 million, and the Agency was operating profitably. It began operations and providing insurance coverage in 1990. For a discussion of the background and purposes of the Convention, see Shihata, The Multilateral Investment Guarantee Agency, 20 Int'l Law. 485 (1986). See also Shihata, MIGA: A Fresh Investment for Cooperation, 26 EFTA Bull. 6–7 (1985). In addition, the World Bank has published an extensive commentary (approved by the Bank's Executive Directors) on the Convention in a single volume with the Convention (hereafter cited as the "Commentary").

The MIGA Convention differs from earlier proposals in a number of respects:

(1) MIGA provides a broader framework, going beyond investment insurance, for international economic policy coordination between capital-importing countries, capital-exporting countries and foreign investors;

(2) While earlier proposals were focussed on investment flows from developed to developing countries, MIGA is also expected to promote investment flows between developing countries;

(3) Political oversight of, and financial responsibility for, MIGA will be shared by both home and host countries; and

(4) There are a number of safeguards to ensure the host governments' control over investment activities in their territories and provisions requiring MIGA to work toward improving investment conditions through agreements with those countries.

Thus, in pursuance of its overall objective of encouraging flows of investments for productive purposes to developing countries, MIGA is charged with promoting "mutual understanding and confidence between host governments and foreign investors, heighten awareness of investment opportunities and increase information, knowledge and expertise related to the investment process. More particularly, MIGA will insure eligible investments against losses resulting from non-commercial risks and carry out various research and promotional activities." Commentary at p. 6.

MIGA provides four basic types of investment guarantees against non-commercial risks. First, an investor may insure against currency transfer restrictions. This guarantee covers: "(a) any action by the Host Government that prevents the Guarantee Holder * * * from directly or indirectly (i) converting dividends, profits or other monetary benefits from or proceeds from the disposal of, the Guaranteed Investment in Local Currency into Guarantee Currency * * *, or (ii) transferring outside the Host Country the Guarantee Currency into which the Local Currency was converted; and (b) failure by the Host Government to grant an application by or on behalf of the Guarantee Holder for such conversion and/or transfer * * *." Second, an investor may obtain coverage against losses due to expropriation. This guarantee covers both direct and creeping expropriation by the Host Government. Third, an investor may insure against repudiation or breach of contract by the Host Government. Under this guarantee, the Guarantee Holder must be "(a) * * * denied for no fault or negligence on its part access to a judicial or arbitral forum which * * * is independent from the executive branch * * *, observes reasonable standards of due process and is authorized to determine the claim of repudiation or breach; or (b) * * * unable to obtain a final and binding decision on the claim of repudiation or breach within the period specified in the [Guarantee] Contract * * *; or (c) * * * unable to obtain enforcement of such a final and binding decision * * *." Fourth, an investor may obtain coverage against losses caused by war, revolution and civil disturbance. This guarantee covers destruction or damage to tangible assets and interruption of essential business operations. Sections 7, 9, MIGA General Conditions of Guarantee for Equity Investments, January 25, 1989.

MIGA can insure new investment or investments for expansion, modernization or restructuring of existing enterprises. The investment, however, must involve nationals of member countries and must be located in a developing country.

Typically, MIGA issues a guarantee for a maximum of 15 years at a rate of premium between 0.3 and 1.5 percent of the guaranteed amount per year. MIGA can cover up to 90 percent of the amount of an eligible investment with a maximum coverage limit of $50 million. MIGA is enjoined to cooperate with and seek to complement the activities of other investment insurers. To this end, MIGA has the authority to enter into reinsurance and coinsurance agreements for eligible investments with both private and public investment insurers.

The Commentary elaborates upon the basic insurance coverages offered by MIGA as follows:

> 13. The currency transfer risk is broadly defined in Article 11(a)(i). It is intended to encompass all forms of new direct restrictions, including additions to existing restrictions, as well as indirect or disguised restrictions, whether such restrictions are imposed by law or in fact. The restriction must be "attributable to the host government;" restrictions imposed by public agencies and other public organs of the host country are intended to be covered by this language. The provision is also intended to include the failure of the host government to act within "a reasonable period of time" on a transfer application. ...
>
> 14. Article 11(a)(ii) defines the expropriation risk. It would encompass measures attributable to the host government such as nationalization, confiscation, sequestration, seizure, attachment and freezing of assets. The phrase "any legislative or administrative action" in the provision includes measures by the executive, but not measures taken by judicial bodies in the exercise of their functions. Measures normally taken by governments to regulate their economic activities such as taxation, environmental and labor legislation as well as normal measures for the maintenance of public safety, are not intended to be covered by this provision unless they discriminate against the holder of the guarantee. In defining these measures, the Agency's practice would not be meant to prejudice the rights of a member country or of investors under bilateral investment treaties, other treaties and international law.
>
> 15. The breach of contract risk is contained in Article 11(a)(iii). Indemnification is available only when an investor has no forum to pursue the contractual claim against the government or when recourse to such a forum is hampered by an unreasonable delay as defined in the guarantee contract or when, after obtaining a final decision in his favor, the investor is unable to enforce it.
>
> 16. Article 11(a)(iv) encompasses the risk of war and civil disturbance. It is intended to include revolutions, insurrections, coups d'état and similar political events which are typically outside the control of the host government. Acts of terrorists and similar activities which are specifically directed against the holder of the guarantee are, however, not intended to be covered by this provision but may be covered under Article 11(b), which is discussed below.
>
> 17. The Convention provides additional flexibility by allowing the coverage of other specific non-commercial risks, but only at the joint request of the investor and the host country and with approval of the Board [of Directors of MIGA] by special majority (Article 11(b)). Such approval may be issued on a case by case basis or in the form of regulations specifying the cases to be covered under this provision.
>
> 18. Events occurring before the conclusion of the contract of guarantee, governmental action to which the holder of the guarantee has

agreed or for which he is responsible, and losses resulting from currency devaluation and depreciation are specifically excluded by Article 11(b) and (c).

Commentary at 5–7.

Eligible investments are described in the Commentary as follows:

19. Article 12 defines the type of investments eligible for coverage by the Agency. This provision endeavors to strike a balance between the need to preserve the Agency's scarce capital to promote flows of direct investment and the need to assure future flexibility by allowing the Board to extend coverage to other types of investment. It is envisaged that the Agency will focus on guaranteeing investments eligible under Article 12(a), i.e. equity investment, different forms of direct investment, and medium- or long-term loans made or guaranteed by owners of equity in the enterprise concerned (so-called equity-type or sponsored loans). The term "direct investment" is a generic term whose precise scope will have to be determined by the Board. The Board is expected to be guided by the International Monetary Fund's definition of foreign direct investment as an "investment that is made to acquire a lasting interest in an enterprise operating in an economy other than that of the investor, the investor's purpose being to have an effective voice in the management of the enterprise." The Board may consider as direct investment such new forms of investment as service and management contracts as well as franchising, licensing, leasing, and production-sharing agreements where the investor's return depends on the performance of the enterprise. In any case, it is immaterial whether the investment is made in monetary form or in kind such as the contribution of machinery, services, technical processes and technology.

20. Article 12(b) gives the Board flexibility, in the future, to extend the Agency's coverage to other forms of investment. It authorizes the Board, by special majority, to extend coverage to any medium- or long-term form of investment except loans which are not related to a specific investment covered or to be covered by the Agency. To conserve the Agency's scarce resources, the Agency would not guarantee or reinsure any export credit, regardless of its form, which is provided, guaranteed or reinsured by a government or an official export credit agency. Because the coverage of the Agency is restricted to investments, exports will be covered (within the limits of the preceding sentence) only to the extent that they represent a contribution to a specific investment. * * *

21. To serve its objective without undermining its financial viability, the Agency will limit its guarantees to sound investments. It should satisfy itself that the investment concerned will contribute to the economic and social development of the host country, comply with the laws and regulations of that country, and be consistent with the country's declared development objectives. It should also be satisfied that appropriate investment conditions, including the availability of fair and equitable treatment and legal protection, will apply to the investment concerned (Article 12(d)). In case no such protection is assured under the laws of the host country or under bilateral investment treaties, the

Agency will issue the guarantee only after it reaches agreement with the host country pursuant to Article 23(b)(ii) or otherwise on the treatment to be extended to the investments covered by the Agency. Investments guaranteed by the Agency should also be new, that is implemented subsequent to the registration of the application for the guarantee by the Agency (Article 12(c)). The exclusion of preexisting investments would not bar the Agency from covering investments made to develop an existing investment or from covering the reinvestment earnings which could otherwise be transferred outside the host country. The term "earnings" in Article 12(c)(ii) is intended to include royalties and license fees.

22. To qualify for a guarantee, investors who are natural persons must be nationals of members other than the host country. If investors are juridical persons, they must be incorporated and have their principal place of business in a member country other than the host country or have the majority of their capital owned by a member country or its nationals, other than the host country or its nationals. Privately and publicly owned investments are eligible as long as they are operated on a commercial basis (Article 13(a)(iii)). It is expected, however, that the bulk of guaranteed investments will be privately owned.

Id. at 6–8.

With respect to Host Country Approval and Subrogation, the Commentary states:

25. Article 15 provides that the Agency will not conclude any contract of guarantee before "the host government has approved the issuance of the guarantee by the Agency against the risks designated for cover." Any host government may withhold its approval. This enables the host country to evaluate a proposed investment before giving its consent. The Agency is expected to establish procedures for obtaining consents under this provision. These may include requesting approvals on a no objection basis (Article 38(b)). Although the approval of the home country of the investor is not required, it would not be appropriate for the Agency to cover an investment if informed by the investor's home country that it would be financed with funds transferred outside such country in violation of its laws.

26. Article 18(a) provides that where the Agency compensates or agrees to compensate an investor under a contract of guarantee, it assumes the rights that the investor acquired against the host country as a result of the event giving rise to the claim against the Agency. Subrogation is an accepted principle of insurance law. It provides for the assignment of an existing claim from the guaranteed investor to the Agency and the Agency as subrogee acquires the same rights as the investor had. The contracts of guarantee will define the terms and conditions of subrogation. These terms and conditions are of special significance for the investor in view of the fact that the Agency will compensate investors only for part of their losses (Article 16). Article 18(b) provides for the recognition of the Agency's right of subrogation by all members.

27. Under Article 18(c), the Agency has the right to treatment as favorable as would be given the holder of the guarantee with respect to the use and transfer of local currencies of host countries received by the Agency as subrogee. In addition, the Agency is authorized to use these currencies for the payment of its administrative expenditures or other costs and is directed to seek to enter into agreements with host countries on other uses of these currencies if they are not freely usable. * * *

Id. at 8–9.

MIGA has international juridical personality and functions autonomously with a Council of Governors (one from each member), a Board of Directors elected by the Council and a President elected by the Board. The voting arrangements involve parity between Category One (developed) and Category Two (developing) states on the assumption that all members of the World Bank eventually become members of MIGA.

MIGA is expected to meet its liabilities from premium income and other income, including return on investments. In addition to relying on the capital subscriptions of member states, MIGA is authorized to underwrite investments sponsored by member countries on the basis of a special "Sponsorship Trust Fund" kept apart from MIGA's own funds and sustained by states electing to serve as sponsoring countries. This "sponsorship window" is a particularly interesting innovation because it has no financial ceiling and it permits coverage in countries other than Category Two developing countries.

Shihata has summed up the role of MIGA as follows (footnotes omitted):

MIGA is not envisaged as only an insurance mechanism. MIGA will also seek to stabilize and improve investment climates in its developing member countries and thus stimulate investment flows to these countries. This mandate is reflected in a number of the provisions of the Convention. It is reinforced by MIGA's institutional structure and internal dynamics.

In the past, the need for fair and stable investment conditions has been emphasized from the point of view of investors and their home countries. However, host countries clearly serve their national interests by providing sound investment conditions. Their ability to attract badly needed resources and to bargain for better terms and conditions is obviously strengthened by the availability of better investment climates in their territories. The establishment of an international development institution, financed and controlled jointly by developed and developing countries, manifests the common interest in creating a favorable investment climate in the latter countries.

Frequently, issues related to foreign investment have also become intermingled with the political interests of home and host countries. As a result, investment disputes often became highly politicized. MIGA seeks to remove the disputes from the political arena and ensure that they will be resolved only on the basis of legal and economic criteria. It is explicitly prohibited from interfering in the political affairs of its members. Moreover, MIGA's internal dynamics will result in its playing an important role as an intermediary between investors and host countries. To attract business and generate revenues, it must offer effective guarantee protection and pay claims which are justified. To minimize underwriting losses, it must avoid claims and, where they do occur, secure recovery from the host country whenever possible. Recovery procedures could jeopardize MIGA's good relations with developing member countries which could easily curtail MIGA's operations by denying their approval for further guarantees. Therefore MIGA must ensure that the goodwill of member countries is not lost and that their common interest in the Agency's functioning prevails over the conflicting interests in a particular dispute.

The competing pressures will force MIGA to cover risks that are unlikely to invite adverse host governmental action which could give rise to claims. At the same time, MIGA will have to ensure that these investments are accorded stable and predictable treatment. * * *

Where disputes nevertheless arise between investors and host countries, MIGA will become involved in the process of conflict resolution in a way that will place it in a unique position to facilitate an amicable settlement. The Convention indeed directs MIGA to encourage such settlements. In the case of disputes, MIGA's assessment, based on the broad information available to it, together with its worldwide experience, is likely to moderate the conflicting claims of an investor and a host country and increase the likelihood of a settlement.

Another way in which MIGA may encourage host governments and investors to arrive at amicable settlements is to reduce the financial burden of any settlements by accepting the local currency of the host country on a temporary basis and paying the investor out of its own funds in freely usable currency. MIGA might then, under an agreement with the host country, sell the local currency to the World Bank, other international institutions, companies importing goods from the host country, or to the host government itself over a period of time and restore its financial position accordingly. MIGA might also facilitate the settlement by paying the investor in cash and accepting debt instruments from the government as reimbursement. As a variant of this approach, MIGA could persuade the investor to accept installments rather than insisting on a cash payment by backing the government's commitments with its guarantee. In view of its developmental mandate and policy interests, MIGA can be anticipated to facilitate settlements amicably at least as successfully as some of the national agencies have done. In this, as well as in all its other activities, MIGA will be serving its broad mandate of encouraging additional investment flows among its members and to developing countries in particular.

Shihata, The Multilateral Investment Guaranty Agency, supra at 495–97.*

## *Notes*

1. During its fiscal year ended June 30, 1992, the Agency issued 21 guarantee contracts, involving eight host countries and seven investor countries. The total insurance coverage was $313 million with respect to more than $1 billion in direct foreign investment. Reinsurance contracts were issued for three

* Footnotes omitted. Reprinted by permission of the International Lawyer.

projects with two national investment insurance agencies and one private company. In addition, twenty-four advisory projects were completed through the Foreign Investment Advisory Service (FIAS), a jointly sponsored program of MIGA, the IFC, and the World Bank, which advises developing countries on improving policies, regulations, and procedures to attract foreign investment. Either directly or through participation in the work of FIAS or other units of the World Bank Group, MIGA has worked with a number of countries to liberalize laws and regulations applying to foreign investments. Several developing member countries have amended their laws to facilitate recourse to international arbitration as the means of settling investment disputes or have enacted new statutes for this purpose. Many have entered into bilateral treaties for the promotion and protection of foreign investments. MIGA also concluded legal protection agreements with six member countries.

2. Where, in MIGA's opinion, appropriate investment conditions do not exist, it seeks to enter into a legal protection agreement with the potential host country on the treatment of investments guaranteed by it. Shihata, The Multilateral Investment Guarantee Agency supra, at 491. Article 23(b)(ii) of the Convention states that such agreements "will assure that the Agency * * * has treatment at least as favorable as that guaranteed by the member concerned for the most favored investment guarantee agency or State in an agreement related to investment." When an investment covered by MIGA is located in a country that has concluded a legal protection agreement with the agency, the provisions of any bilateral or multilateral investment treaty to which the host country is a party apply to the insured investment, even if the country from which the investment originates has not concluded an investment treaty with the host country. Although MIGA—not the investor—is the beneficiary of the most favorable treatment, the investor benefits indirectly from the protection granted MIGA. Furthermore, since the legal protection agreement enhances the overall investment climate in a developing host country, it also serves the host country's interests.

3. MIGA carries out promotional activities such as conducting research, providing information, policy advice and technical assistance to member governments, including, for example, advice on drafting of investment codes and reviewing investment incentive programs. Convention Art. 23(a).

4. MIGA's objective is to complement national and regional programs rather than compete with them. It therefore focuses on guaranteeing investments from members without an investment guaranty program, co-guaranteeing investments with national and regional agencies, providing reinsurance for national and regional agencies, guaranteeing investments that fail eligibility tests of the national and regional program concerned and guaranteeing investments financed by investors from different member countries. It also participates in arrangements for reinsurance with private insurers in member states.

5. The voting arrangements in the MIGA are unique and are described as follows in the Commentary:

> 63. The voting structure of the Agency reflects the view that Category One and Category Two countries have an equal stake in foreign investment, that cooperation between them is essential, and that both groups of countries should, when all eligible countries become members, have equal voting power (50/50). It is also recognized that a member's voting power should reflect its relative capital subscription. The Convention, therefore, provides that each member is to have 177 membership votes plus one subscription

> vote for each share of stock held by it (Article 39(a)). The number of membership votes is computed so as to ensure that if all [World] Bank members joined the Agency, developing countries as a group would have the same voting power as developed countries as a group. * * *

Commentary at p. 18.

## H. UNITED NATIONS INDUSTRIAL DEVELOPMENT ORGANIZATION (UNIDO)

UNIDO was established in 1966 as an executing agency for the United Nations Development Program (UNDP), from which it received a large portion of its funding. In 1975, the General Assembly endorsed a recommendation to make the organization a specialized agency with more autonomy, expanded functions and a separate industrial development fund. A constitution was drawn up in 1979, to become effective upon ratification by 80 states. These were received by June 1985, and the first General Conference of 120 members was held in August 1985. Upon approval by the General Assembly in early 1986, UNIDO formally became a specialized agency.

UNIDO's purpose is to promote and accelerate industrial development in the developing countries and to strengthen cooperation in and coordination of all U.N. activities in this field. Its new constitution also states as its goal facilitating the establishment of a new international economic order.

UNIDO has a support program that includes research, symposia and training courses to improve technological and management skills in, and impart technological advances to, developing countries. To promote links between investors and developing country enterprises, it maintains investment promotion offices in Cologne, Paris, Seoul, Tokyo, Vienna, Washington, Warsaw and Zurich and prepares portfolios of prospective opportunities. It sponsors field projects and provides technical assistance in the form of expert services, equipment and training fellowships.

The General Conference, consisting of representatives from all member states, elects an industrial development board (IDB), consisting of 33 members from developing countries, 15 from industrialized countries and five from centrally planned economy countries, to serve for four-year terms. The IDB meets annually, the General Conference biannually. UNIDO's Director–General is appointed by the General Conference for a four-year term.

Under the Director–General, there are five departments: (1) Programme and Project Development, (2) Industrial Operations, (3) Industrial Promotion, Consultations and Technology, (4) External Relations, Public Information, Language and Documentation Services, and (5) Administration.

To finance costs of administration and research, UNIDO uses resources created by contributions of its member countries. UNIDO, however, finances its technical assistance projects through four principal means. First, the United Nations Development Program (UNDP) acts as the primary funding source for financing-related activities. Second, enterprises of developing countries may create self-financing trust funds. Third, the Industrial Development Fund (IDF), created by contributions from governments, non-governmental organizations and intergovernmental organizations, supplements funds provided by UNDP. Fourth, certain third party trust funds, established by government and non-governmental organization contributions, are available.

In addition to its assistance in individual projects, UNIDO has taken steps to develop specific sectors vital to the industrial development process. One such step is the creation of the System of Consultations which provides a forum for the exchange of information on particular areas of industry. Through this forum, governments, industry and labor discuss problems from various points of view. UNIDO has also established an International Centre for Genetic Engineering and Biotechnology to address problems of starvation, illness and energy shortage and has outlined a project to establish an International Centre for Science and High Technology to promote research and training in vital scientific areas.

# Chapter 18

# INTERNATIONAL ORGANIZATIONS FOR TECHNICAL, SOCIAL, AND CULTURAL COOPERATION

## SECTION 1. INTRODUCTION

Many international organizations are concerned both with the maintenance of international peace and with technical, social, and cultural cooperation. The United Nations and various regional organizations provide prominent examples. The operations of international organizations in the maintenance of international peace are discussed in Chapter 11 and their operations in the field of trade and development in Chapter 17. The legal status and structure of these organizations is treated in Chapter 5.

All of the international organizations for technical, social, and cultural cooperation maintain working relationships with the United Nations. Many of them are specialized agencies within the terms of Chapter IX of the United Nations Charter and report annually to the Economic and Social Council under Article 64 of the Charter. All of these organizations have their own structure, including legislative and executive bodies as well as a secretariat, and their own budgets. The organizations include the following:

FAO: Food and Agriculture Organization
IAEA: International Atomic Energy Agency
ICAO: International Civil Aviation Organization
IFAD: International Fund for Agricultural Development
ILO: International Labour Organization
IMO: International Maritime Organization
ITU: International Telecommunication Union
UNESCO: UN Educational, Scientific and Cultural Organization
UPOV: International Union for the Protection of New Varieties of Plants
UPU: Universal Postal Union
WHO: World Health Organization
WIPO: World Intellectual Property Organization
WMO: World Meteorological Organization
WTO: World Tourism Organization

# SECTION 2. EDUCATION, SCIENCE AND CULTURE

## A. UNITED NATIONS EDUCATIONAL, SCIENTIFIC AND CULTURAL ORGANIZATION (UNESCO)

UNESCO came into being on November 16, 1946. Its purpose is to promote collaboration among nations in education, science, and culture in order to advance the objectives of international peace and the common welfare of mankind.

In the field of education, UNESCO stresses literacy programs and efforts to make primary education universal. It encourages the spread of the scientific attitude necessary for technological advance and the opening to women of careers traditionally reserved for men.

In the natural sciences, UNESCO seeks to promote international scientific cooperation, such as the ongoing Man and the Biosphere Programme, begun in 1971, which sponsors projects to solve practical problems of environmental resource management.

UNESCO's programs in mass communication attempt to foster a free and balanced flow of information, and to increase the scope and quality of press, film and radio services throughout the world. In 1980, UNESCO approved a "New World Information and Communication Order" (NWICO) which included plans for an international code of ethics and a licensing system for journalists. Western members objected to NWICO on the grounds that it would restrict the free flow of information. NWICO is presently only a set of general objectives and has not been implemented.

The organs of UNESCO are a General Conference (composed of representatives from each member state), an Executive Board (consisting of 51 government representatives elected by the General Conference) and a Secretariat.

National commissions act as liaison groups between UNESCO and the educational, scientific and cultural life of the member states.

Alleging increased politicization, improper management, and a bias unfavorable to the West, the U.S. withdrew from UNESCO in December 1984. The United Kingdom and Singapore followed suit one year later. [As of July 15, 1992, neither the United States, nor the United Kingdom, nor Singapore had rejoined.] See 24 I.L.M. 489 (1985), 23 I.L.M. 218 (1984). See also Comment: Conflicts Over Government Control of Information—The United States and UNESCO, 59 Tul.L.Rev. 1071 (1985). On UNESCO generally, see Lawes & Thomson, UNESCO (1957). On the UNESCO World Heritage Convention, see Suter, The UNESCO World Heritage Convention, 8 Envtl. & Plan.L.J. 4 (1991). On UNESCO's role in settling international art theft disputes, see Note, International Art Theft Disputes: Harmonizing Common Law Principles With Article 7(b) of the UNESCO Convention, 15 Fordham Int'l.L.J. 129 (1991/92).

## B. WORLD INTELLECTUAL PROPERTY ORGANIZATION (WIPO)

Established by a multi-lateral convention in 1967, WIPO became a specialized agency of the U.N. in 1974. It originated from two previously existing organizations: the International Union for the Protection of Industrial Property, which was established by the Paris Convention of 1883, and the International Union for the Protection of Literary and Artistic Works, established by the Berne Convention of 1886. It now administers the following Unions:

*Paris Union* (for the protection of industrial property);

*Madrid Union* (for the international registration of marks);

*Nice Union* (for the international classification of goods and services for the purposes of the registration of marks);

*Lisbon Union* (for the protection of appellations of origin and their international registration);

*Locarno Union* (establishing an international classification for industrial designs);

*IPC Union* (for the establishment of worldwide uniformity of patent classification);

*PCT Union, Patent Cooperation Treaty (PCT)* (for cooperation in the filing, searching and examination of international applications for the protection of inventions where that protection is sought in several countries);

*TRT Union* (for the filing of an 'international application' where protection is sought for a trademark in several countries);

*Budapest Treaty* (which provides for the international recognition of the deposit of microorganisms for the purposes of patent procedure);

*Berne Union* (for the protection of literary and artistic works);

*Rome Convention* (for the protection of performers, producers of phonograms and broadcasting organizations);

*Geneva Convention* (for the protection of producers of phonograms against unauthorized duplication of their phonograms);

*Brussels Convention* (relating to the distribution of programme-carrying signals transmitted by satellite) and

*International Union for the Protection of New Varieties of Plants* (Union internationale pour la protection des obtentions vegetales (UPOV).

Once the treaties enumerated hereinafter come into effect, "Unions" will also mean:

the two *Vienna Agreements* (which provide, respectively, for the establishing of an international classification of the figurative elements of marks, and the protection of type faces and their international deposit);

*Geneva Treaty* (on the international recording of scientific discoveries);

*Madrid Multilateral Convention* (on double taxation of copyright royalties).

WIPO's aim is to promote, through cooperation among States, the protection of intellectual property throughout the world. It also promotes administrative cooperation among the various Unions. The Union treaties generally require that member states accord foreign nationals and residents the same advantages regarding the protection of trademarks, inventions, designs (Paris Convention), and copyrights (Berne Convention) that may extend to their own nationals. They also provide for minimum standards of protection.

WIPO proposes revisions of old, and encourages the conclusion of new, treaties that extend and strengthen protection of scientific, industrial and artistic work. It collects and distributes information and maintains services for international registration. WIPO also has a program for developing countries which includes training of specialists, creating and modernizing domestic legislation and institutions, stimulating inventive activity and facilitating the transfer of technology.

The WIPO Permanent Committees for Development Co-operation Related to Industrial Property and Related to Copyright and Neighboring Rights plan and review activities in these fields. The WIPO Permanent Committee on Industrial Property Information is responsible for intergovernmental co-operation in industrial property documentation and information matters, such as the standardization and exchange of patent documents.

In 1989, three diplomatic conferences were held: (1) the Diplomatic Conference for the Conclusion of a Treaty on the International Registration of Audiovisual Works held at WIPO headquarters, which resulted in the unanimous adoption of a Treaty on the International Registration of Audiovisual Works, that entered into effect in February, 1991; (2) the Diplomatic Conference for the Conclusion of a Treaty on the Protection of Intellectual Property in Respect of Integrated Circuits held in Washington, D.C. produced, on May 26, 1989, a treaty on Intellectual Property in Respect of Integrated Circuits, see Correa, Legal Protection of the Layout Designs of Integrated Circuits: The WIPO Treaty, 12 Eur.Intell.Prop.Rev. 186 (1990); and (3) the Diplomatic Conference for the Conclusion of a Protocol Relating to the Madrid Agreement Concerning the International Registration of Marks held in Madrid, led to unanimous adoption, on June 27, 1989, of the Protocol Relating to the Madrid Agreement Concerning the International Registration of Marks.

Also, since 1985, a WIPO Committee of Experts has been working on developing a treaty to harmonize patent laws throughout the world. In 1990, WIPO completed a draft "Basic Proposal," which is in the form of a draft treaty for harmonizing patent laws throughout the world. It has not yet entered into force. See Pagenberg, The WIPO Patent Harmonization Treaty, 19 AIPLA Q.J. 1 (1991); Fiorito, The WIPO "Basic Proposal" For Harmonization of Patent Laws Viewed From the U.S. Practitioners Point of View, 19 AIPLA Q.J. 24 (1991); Fiorito, The "Basic Proposal" for Harmonization of U.S. and Worldwide Patent Laws Submitted by WIPO, 73 J.Pat. [ & Trademark] Off. Socy. 83 (1991). On WIPO's role in settling intellectual property disputes, see Catemerio, WIPO: Settlement of Intellectual Property Disputes Between States, 51 Trademark World 33 (1992).

WIPO includes 129 members, some of which belong to one or both of its constituent unions. A General Assembly meets biannually. The Paris and Berne unions each elect executive committees; the joint membership of the two committees forms WIPO's Coordination Committee, which meets annually. The International Bureau serves as secretariat, both for the unions and for WIPO. Headquarters are in Geneva.

### C. WORLD TOURISM ORGANIZATION (WTO)

WTO was established as an intergovernmental agency in 1975 upon ratification by 51 countries of statutes adopted in 1970. It replaced the International Union of Official Travel Organizations (IUOTO), which was formed in 1925. Its relationship with the U.N. is governed by an Agreement made in 1977.

WTO's purpose is to promote and develop tourism as a means of advancing economic expansion, international understanding, and peace.

The organization collects and distributes information on international tourism, including data, regulations, facilities and events. It encourages international cooperation through technical meetings and shared projects. It offers an international program of vocational training through the International Center for Advanced Studies in Tourism (CIEST) in Mexico.

WTO is comprised of 109 full member states, 4 associate members (territories), and 163 affiliate members, which are governmental and non-governmental bodies and associations. Its General Assembly meets every two years. The Executive Council meets at least twice a year. It consists of representatives elected by the full members on the basis of equal geographical distribution, and two non-voting representatives of the associate and affiliate members. WTO's headquarters are in Madrid.

## SECTION 3. AVIATION

### A. INTERNATIONAL CIVIL AVIATION ORGANIZATION (ICAO)

Seven years after the first airplane flight in 1903, an unsuccessful attempt was made by 19 European nations to regulate the international aspects of air navigation. However, in 1919, the Versailles Peace Conference did produce a Convention on the Regulation of Aerial Navigation. This Convention, in addition to dealing with aspects of international air navigation, created a supervisory organization, the International Commission for Air Navigation (ICAN). The Convention had limited impact, due to the still primarily regional use of the airplane. The same was true of the Pan American Convention of 1928 on Commercial Aviation.

The second world war brought drastic change. The airplane became a principal carrier of passengers and freight. Regulation was needed of the legal problems incident upon flights into and over foreign territories and the maintenance of navigational facilities. A conference to deal with these problems was convened in Chicago in 1944, with 52 states in attendance.

This conference resulted in the Convention on International Civil Aviation, concluded at Chicago on December 7, 1944, 61 Stat. 1180, T.I.A.S. No. 1591, 15 U.N.T.S. 295, which became effective on April 4, 1947, upon the ratification by the 26th state. This Convention supersedes the earlier Paris and Pan American Conventions. The Chicago Convention regulates the rights and obligations of contracting states, provides for the adoption of uniform regulations and standards of air navigational practices and international recognition of certificates of airworthiness, requires installation of navigational facilities by members, and calls for reduction of customs and immigration formalities.

The basic principle underlying the Convention is that every state has complete and exclusive sovereignty over the airspace above its territory and that, therefore, the consent of a contracting state is required for air navigation over or into its territory. Since multilateral agreement on the rights in commercial civil aviation could not be reached by all parties at the conference, two supplementary agreements were concluded. The International Air Service's Transit Agreement, 59 Stat. 1693, 84 U.N.T.S. 389, allows aircraft of a signatory state to fly over, or land for technical reasons in, the territory of any other signatory state. The International Air Transport Agreement, 59 Stat. 1701, 3 Bevans 992, regulates the carriage of freight between a signatory state and the state of the aircraft's registration. Other commercial air rights and obligations are determined essentially by bilateral agreements.

These multilateral and bilateral agreements have been supplemented by conventions on related subjects. The Geneva Convention of 1948, T.I.A.S. No. 2847, 310 U.N.T.S. 151, deals with international recognition of property and other rights in aircraft on flights crossing different territories. The Rome Convention of 1952, 310 U.N.T.S. 181, deals with damage caused by foreign aircraft to third parties on the surface. The Warsaw Convention of 1929, 49 Stat. 3000, 2 Bevans 983, which both regulates the liability of the air carrier to passengers and consignors and establishes limits to this liability, was amended by several protocols. The Hague Protocol in 1955, 478 U.N.T.S. 371, doubled the limits of liability. The Guatemala City Protocol (1971), which is not yet in force, provides for absolute liability of the air carrier and a liability limit of U.S. $100,000, unless the carrier was reckless or grossly negligent. The conference at Montreal in 1975 adopted 4 protocols, suggesting replacement of the definition of the amount of liability in terms of gold for that of the IMF Special Drawing Rights and the notion of the carrier's strict liability, with limited defenses, for cargo and mail.

The ICAO became a specialized agency of the United Nations in October of 1947. Its highest organ is the Assembly, which meets every 3 years. The Assembly elects delegates for 3–year terms to the Council, the governing body which is responsible to the Assembly. In order to ensure adequate geographical representation, delegates are taken from both states with important roles in air transport and navigational facilities and others. The Council adopts international standards and recommends practices, incorporating these into the Convention through Annexes, acts as arbiter between member states with regard to implementation of the Convention, and investigates situations posing obstacles to the proper development of air navigation. As of June 12, 1992 the ICAO membership totalled 168.

Regional air navigation meetings are held to deal with the requirements of particular areas. Every state is responsible for providing the recommended facilities within its own territories, and the ICAO oversees the implementation of the regional plans. In addition, three regional bodies have been established. The European Civil Aviation Conference (ECAC) was established in 1956. The African Civil Aviation Commission (AFCAC), formed in 1969, comprises members of the OAU and the Economic Commission for Africa. The Latin American Civil Aviation Commission, created in 1973, consists of states in Central and South America and the Carribean. These bodies work in close liaison with the ICAO. The ICAO has also been active in promoting codification and development of international (public and private) air law.

For a detailed look at some of the ICAO's activities, see Abeyratne, Facilitation And The ICAO Role—A Prologue For The Nineties, 15 Annals of Air & Space L. 3 (1990); Sochor, From The DC–3 To Hypersonic Flight: ICAO In A Changing Environment, 55 J.Air L. & Com. 407 (1989); Getler, ICAO And Bilateralism: The Case Of Standard Bilateral Clauses, 16 Annals of Air & Space L. 57 (1991); Kirsch, The 1988 ICAO And IMO Conferences: And International Consensus Against Terrorism, 12 Dalhousie L.J. 5 (1989); Milde, The Role Of ICAO In The Suppression Of Drug Abuse And Illicit Trafficking, 13 Annals of Air & Space L. 133 (1988); Kotaite, ICAO Policy And Programmes In The Field Of Aviation Security, 10 Annals of Air & Space L. 83 (1985); Fitzgerald, ICAO And The Joint Financing Of Certain Air Navigation Services, 11 Annals of Air & Space L. 17 (1986).

### *Notes*

1. On the role of ICAO in dealing with the financial and economic aspects of air transport, see Binaghi, The Role of ICAO, in McWhinney & Bradley, The Freedom of the Air 17 (1968).

2. On ICAO generally, See Buergenthal, Law–Making in the International Civil Organization (1969). For the decision rendered by the International Court of Justice on the claim by India that Pakistan's breach of the Chicago Convention had terminated the provision providing for adjudication of disputes by the Court, see p. 488 supra.

3. ICAO also prepared the Hague, Montreal, and Tokyo Conventions on hijacking and related offenses. See Chapter 12.

# SECTION 4. COMMUNICATIONS

## A. INTERNATIONAL TELECOMMUNICATION UNION (ITU)

The Convention of the International Telecommunication Union was signed on November 12, 1965, and entered into force, in accordance with its Article 52, on January 1, 1967, 18 U.S.T. 575, T.I.A.S. No. 6267.

The first International Telegraph Union Convention was signed in Paris on May 18, 1865. In 1885, at Berlin, the first regulations relating to international telephone services were inserted in the Telegraph Regulations annexed to the 1865 Convention. The first International Radiotelegraphic Convention was signed at Berlin on November 3, 1906. The first International Telecommunication Convention was signed at Madrid on December 3, 1932, and entered into force on January 1, 1934. This last-mentioned convention replaced the earlier radiotelegraph and telegraph conventions, and established the ITU to replace the Bureau of the International Telegraph Union, which had been established in 1865. The Madrid Convention was revised at Atlantic City, New Jersey, in 1947, at Buenos Aires in 1952, and again at Geneva in 1959. The structure and administration of the ITV are regulated by a Convention adopted at Nice, on June 30, 1989. (This Convention replaced an earlier convention adopted on November 6, 1982).

The purposes of ITU, whose membership totals 167, are to maintain and extend international cooperation for the improvement and rational use of telecommunication, to promote the development and efficient operation of technical facilities, and to harmonize the actions of nations in the attainment of these ends (Article 4, section 1).

The ITU has six main functions: to effect the allocation of the radio-frequency spectrum and register radio-frequency assignments to avoid harmful interference between radio stations of different countries; to coordinate efforts to eliminate harmful interference; to foster collaboration among its members in order to lower rates for telecommunications; to foster the development and improvement of telecommunication equipment and networks; to promote the adoption of measures for ensuring the safety of life through the cooperation of telecommunication services; and to undertake studies, formulate recommendations and opinions, and collect and publish information (Article 4, section 2).

The ITU's organs consist of: a Plenipotentiary Conference, which is the supreme organ of ITU (Articles 5 and 6); Administrative Conferences (Articles 5 and 7); an Administrative Council composed of forty-three members of the organization and elected by the Plenipotentiary Conference (Articles 2, 5 and 9); a General Secretariat, with a Secretary–General elected by the Plenipotentiary Conference (Articles 5, 6 and 10); the International Frequency Registration Board (IFRB), composed of independent members elected by the Administrative Conference (Articles 5, 7 and 13); an International Radio Consultative Committee (CCIR); an International Telegraph and Telephone Consultative Committee (CCITT) composed of the telecommunications administrative officials of members and certain private operating agencies (Article 14) and a newly created Telecommunications Development Bureau (BDT). The Plenipotentiary Conference determines general policies, considers reports, and determines the general outline of the budget. The Administrative Conferences revise the regulations governing each form of telecommunication (Article 7, section 3(1)). Administrative conferences (Radio and Telegraph/Telephone) adopt regulations which bind all Members of the Union. The present Radio Regulations were adopted in 1979 and entered into force on January 1, 1982. They were subsequently revised in many specialized radio conferences. The Telecommunications Regulations were adopted in Melbourne on December 9, 1988 and entered into force on July 1, 1990. The Administrative Council supervises ITU's administrative functions between sessions of the Plenipotentiary Conference, reviews and approves the budget, and coordinates ITU's activities with other international organizations (Article 9). On the newly created Telecommunications Development Bureau, see Harris, The New Telecommunications Development: Bureau of the International Telecommunication Union, 7 Am.U.J.Int'l L. & Pol'y 83 (1991).

On the role of the ITU's World Administrative Radio Conference (WARC) with respect to global regulation of satellite communications, see Rothblatt, New Satellite Technology, Allocation of Global Resources and the International Telecommunications Union, 24 Colum.J.Transnat'l L. 37 (1985). See also Rutkowski, The World Administrative Radio Conference on Use of the Geostationary Satellite Orbit: Airing the Views of U.S. Regulators and Users, 24 Colum.J.Transnat'l L. 51 (1985); Smith, Space Law/Space WARC: An Analysis Of The Space Law Issues Raised The 1985 ITU World Administrative Radio Conference On The Geostationary Orbit, 8 Hous.J.Int'l L. 227 (1986).

## B. INTERNATIONAL TELECOMMUNICATIONS SATELLITE ORGANIZATION (INTELSAT)

Comsat, a private United States corporation, the shares of which are traded on several United States stock exchanges, was created by the Satellite Act of 1962, 47 U.S.C.A. § 731 (1982), for the express purpose of planning and constructing an international communications satellite system. Although Congress gave Comsat the initial responsibility of establishing the system, it intended that a number of nations would operate the system on a cooperative basis. ITT World Communications, Inc. v. FCC, 725 F.2d 732, 736 n. 4 (D.C.Cir.1984).

On August 20, 1964, an Executive Agreement Establishing Interim Arrangements for a Global Communications System, 15 U.S.T. 1705, T.I.A.S. No. 5646, was signed by the United States and ten other nations. It established the International Telecommunications Satellite Consortium (INTELSAT), which acquired the system created by Comsat. Comsat became the United States representative to INTELSAT and the manager of the system.

Comsat serves not only as the sole United States representative to INTELSAT, but also as the exclusive lessor to U.S. domestic "common carriers," such as A.T. & T., of capacity ("space segment") in INTELSAT facilities. Comsat is in effect a "carrier's carrier." 47 U.S.C.A. § 741 (1982) 47 U.S.C.A. § 153(h) (1982) (definition of "common carrier"); see also Matter of Satellite Business Systems, 91 F.C.C.2d 940 (1982). Comsat is not foreclosed, however, from retailing as well as wholesaling satellite circuits. Modification of Authorized User Policy, 90 F.C.C.2d 1394 (1982). Although the United States opted against establishing a state-owned corporation, it ensured representation of the public interest by, *inter alia,* giving the President the right to appoint three of the fifteen members of Comsat's Board of Directors. 47 U.S.C.A. § 733 (1982) (private common carriers owning stock in Comsat elect six directors; the remaining directors are elected by other stockholders). See also 47 U.S.C.A. § 721(a) and (c) (1982) (implementation of policy).

The Department of State must be notified when Comsat enters into negotiations with foreign entities. 47 U.S.C.A. § 742 (1982). Comsat and the State Department also coordinate U.S. positions in INTELSAT (Hearing on Government Use of Satellite Communications, Hearing of the Committee on Government Operations of the House of Representatives, 89th Congress, 2nd Session, 1966, p. 406–07). The great majority of the other parties to

INTELSAT are represented either by their governments or by publicly controlled postal or other telecommunications organizations directly responsible to their governments.

The most important organizational features of INTELSAT are the following:

1. The subject matter of the agreements is the "space segment of INTELSAT," defined by Article I(h) to include the telecommunications satellites themselves, as well as the tracking, telemetric control, command, monitoring and related facilities and equipment required to operate the satellite system. The earth stations which utilize the satellites are owned and operated not by INTELSAT, but by the participating telecommunication entities, in accordance with the national laws to which they are subject. The United States earth stations used to access INTELSAT by Comsat are operated by the Earth Station Ownership Committee, a joint venture of Comsat and other United States common carriers.

2. The prime objective of INTELSAT is the provision, on a commercial non-discriminatory basis, of a space segment for "international public telecommunications services," defined by Article I(k) of the Agreement, in part, as "fixed or mobile telecommunications services which can be provided by Satellite and which are available for use by the public."

3. Membership in INTELSAT is open to the government of any state which is a member of the ITU. But, as stated in both the Preamble and Article XIX(a) of the Agreement, it is intended that access to the system be available to all nations of the world.

4. Investment and use are correlated. INTELSAT members participate by way of investment shares which, according to Article V(b), are determined by the percentage of utilization of the INTELSAT space segment. The INTELSAT space segment is owned by INTELSAT under Article V of the Agreement. No signatory may have an investment share of less than 0.05%. There is no guaranteed minimum investment quota.

5. The organizational structure of INTELSAT includes an Assembly of Parties, a Board of Governors, an executive organ responsible to the Board of Governors, and a Meeting of Signatories. The function of the Assembly of Parties is "to give consideration to those aspects of INTELSAT which are primarily of interest to the parties as sovereign states" (Article VII). The Meeting of Signatories is concerned principally with financial and operational matters and establishes the minimum investment share required for membership on the Board of Governors. At the Board level, voting power is adjusted so as to prevent any one signatory from having majority control. Although in principle each governor on the Board has a vote equal to the part of the investment share which he represents, no governor may cast more than 40% of the total votes. Moreover, decisions on substantive matters require either (a) the support of at least four governors representing at least two-thirds of the investment shares, or (b) the support of all but three governors, regardless of the total investment share they may represent.

6. As an organization with juridical personality, INTELSAT has the power to conclude agreements with states or other international organiza-

tions and the capacity to contract, acquire and dispose of property, and to be a party to legal proceedings.

In 1973, INTELSAT changed its *modus operandi.* This marked a decline in the role of Comsat as manager of INTELSAT operations in favor of a more competitive-based services procurement policy. Under the Definitive Agreements concluded August 20, 1971, ("Agreement Relating to the International Telecommunications Satellite Organization 'INTELSAT,'" an agreement with four annexes, 23 U.S.T. 3813, T.I.A.S. No. 7532; and "Operating Agreement Relating to the International Telecommunications Satellite Organization 'INTELSAT,'" with one annex, 23 U.S.T. 4091, T.I.A.S. No. 7532), a Director–General, responsible to, and acting in accordance with, the policies and directive of the Board of Governors for all management services, replaced the Board of Governors as the INTELSAT organ responsible for technical and operational as well as for administrative and financial services. The Director–General may contract with outside entities for services of a technical and operational nature "to the maximum extent practicable with due regard to cost and consistent with competence, effectiveness and efficiency" (Article XI(c)(ii) of the Agreement).

Technological advances in the late 1970's and early 1980's also prompted two United States corporations to petition the Federal Communications Commission (FCC) for authorization to establish separate private satellite systems that, for the first time, would compete directly with INTELSAT for transatlantic communications traffic. Application of Orion Satellite Corp., File No. C55–83–002–P (March 11, 1985); Application of International Satellite Inc., File Nos. C55–83–044–PPPPP(LA), I–P–C–83–073 (August 12, 1983). The FCC granted provisional authorization pursuant to an Executive policy of fostering free market principles in a limited area of satellite communications (long-term leasing of "transponders") and an Executive determination that the proposed satellite systems were "required in the national interest." Satellite Communications Act, 47 U.S.C.A. 701(d) (1982). The United States move has met with opposition from the Director–General of INTELSAT and from other member states, who argue that the signatories to the Definitive Agreements intended to achieve "a single global commercial telecommunications satellite system" (Preamble). This purpose, it is argued, is evident from the pricing structure mandated by the INTELSAT agreements, which establishes an inflexible non-discriminatory pricing system designed to subsidize "thin" use by the third world and developing countries with "heavy" use by the industrialized nations.

These agreements must be evaluated in the light of provisions in the Definitive Agreements that contemplate explicitly the creation of satellite facilities outside of INTELSAT. Article XIV(d) of the Definitive Agreements, governing use of non-INTELSAT satellite facilities for "international public telecommunications services," requires a signatory, party or person within the jurisdiction of a party, prior to construction and implementation of a separate system, to furnish all relevant information and to consult with INTELSAT (1) to ensure technical compatibility with INTELSAT's system and (2) to avoid "significant economic harm" to the global system of INTELSAT. Neither Article XIV(d) itself nor any other provision of the INTELSAT agreements provides that an adverse recommendation made pursuant to an Article XIV(d) procedure shall preclude a party from authorizing the establishment of a separate satellite system. To date, Article XIV(d) procedures have not produced recommendations at odds with a state's intention to authorize a separate satellite system. Rather, they have resulted in more than fifty separate systems found to be compatible with the INTELSAT system.

In 1985, the United States Congress made a declaration of policy "to authorize use and operation of any additional space segment facilities only if the obligations of the United States under Article XIV(d) have been met." Foreign Relations Authorization Act, Fiscal Years 1986 and 1987 Pub.L. No. 99–93, § 146, 99 Stat. 404, 425 (to be codified at 22 U.S.C.A. § 265 (1985)). It remains open to question whether the U.S. may conclude a bilateral agreement with another nation consistent with the 1985 Authorization Act, but at odds with an Article XIV(d) finding that such a system would cause INTELSAT "significant economic harm." It is equally uncertain whether the United States may unilaterally authorize such a separate system, notwithstanding the 1985 Authorization Act. Resolution of these questions may have a profound effect on the future of INTELSAT as a "global" satellite communications system.

On these questions, see also Colino, The Possible Introduction of Separate Satellite Systems: International Satellite Communications at a Crossroad, 24 Colum.J.Trans.L. 13 (1985) (argument by Director–General of INTELSAT against the proposed separate systems); Emerging Competitive Forces in International Communications Satellite and Cable, Panel Discussion, 54 Antitrust L.J. 235 (1985) (arguments in favor of competition); Godwin, The Proposed Orion and ISI Transatlantic Satellite Systems: A Challenge to the Status Quo, 24 Jurimetrics J. 297 (1984); Rein & Frank, The Legal Commitment Of The United States To The INTELSAT System, 14 N.C.S. Int'l L. & Com.Reg. 219 (1989); Note, INTELSAT: Greater Price Flexibility To Preserve The System, 3 Am.U.J.Int'l L. & Pol'y 383 (1988); Note, Pirates or Pioneers In Orbit? Private International Communications Satellite Systems And Article XIV(d) Of The INTELSAT Agreements, 9 B.C. Int'l & Comp.L.Rev. 199 (1986).

On related questions of extraterritorial application of U.S. antitrust laws to INTELSAT, notably to the arguably anti-competitive practices of INTELSAT under its procurement policy, see Chapter 10, Section 2. See also Note, A Search in the Heavens: Should INTELSAT be Subject to U.S. Antitrust Laws?, 24 Colum.J.Trans.L. 133 (1985); Butler, The Antitrust Liability Of COMSAT In Its Role As Representative To INTELSAT, 17 N.C.J.Int'l L. & Com.Reg. 547 (1992).

## C. UNIVERSAL POSTAL UNION (UPU)

The perceived need to replace the complex system of bilateral agreements regulating the movement of mail between countries led to the first attempt to conclude a universal postal agreement at the International Postal Conference in Paris in 1863. In 1874, an International Postal Conference meeting in Bern adopted the Treaty Concerning the Establishment of a General Postal Union and an International Bureau for distribution of information. A multilateral Convention governing international postal service came into force on July 1, 1875. The name of the organization was changed to the Universal Postal Union at a Congress in Paris in 1878. The Constitution of the UPU and the Convention signed on July 10, 1964 (16 U.S.T. 1291, T.I.A.S. No. 5881) are direct successors of the earlier agreements. The aim of the organization is to ensure the organization and improvement of the postal services and to promote the development of international cooperation in this field.

The Constitution regulates the organization's structure. The Congress is composed of representatives of member states, each member having one vote (Arts. 14, 101). Since the organization deals with technical matters and does not anticipate political problems, plenary meetings are comparatively infrequent (every five years). The provisions at present in force are those adopted at the Washington Congress of 1989, which came into effect on January 1, 1991. To assure continuity between sessions of Congress, there is an Executive Council composed of forty members appointed by the Congress on the basis of equitable geographic distribution (Arts. 17, 102). A Consultative Council for Postal Studies (CCPS), composed of 35 members elected by the Congress, operates through a Management Council. It is similar to the special consultative committees which exist within such other technical agencies as the ITU, and organizes studies of major problems affecting postal administration. The Congress also appoints Administrative Conferences and Special Committees to promote studies and conferences (Arts. 16, 19). The International Bureau has been retained (Art. 20) and is responsible for the dissemination of information about international postal service.

Upon its agreement to become a U.N. specialized agency (concluded in 1947, in force July 1, 1948), the UPU ceased to be an "open union." Admission of new members depended on the decision of a two-thirds majority of member countries, and membership was restricted to sovereign states. At the Vienna Congress in 1964, a new admission procedure was adopted which exempts U.N. members from this procedure, allowing them to become members by submitting a unilateral declaration of adhesion to the organization. As of January 1, 1992 there were 168 members. Another result of UPU cooperation with the U.N. was its participation in the U.N. Development Program (UNDP), which provides funds for stimulating the administration of postal projects in member countries.

UPU regulations are binding only upon members acceding to them. In the event of disputes between the postal administrations of members, the Constitution provides for compulsory arbitration (Art. 32). Of particular interest is Article 2 of the Convention which provides that, when a member state fails to observe the provisions of the Constitution or the Convention, other member states are free to discontinue postal service with that state after having given prior notice by telegram to the administrations concerned. Complaints had been made about disruption of mail service by the former U.S.S.R. See Comm. on Post Office and Civil Service, Subcommittee on Postal Operations and Service, H.R., 98th Cong., 1st Sess. Serial No. 98–20 (Oct. 4, 1983).

The Convention, supported by Detailed Regulations, governs the postal regulations of the organization's members. Letter mail service is regulated, as are basic charges, weight limits, and dimensions for articles and correspondence.

On the Universal Postal Union generally, see Codding, the Universal Postal Union (1964); The UN and the UPU, Union Postale No. 10/1970; Memorandum on the Rule of the Post as a Factor in Economic, Social and Cultural Development (1974 publication of UPU); Note, International Agreement—Liability Limitations Under The Universal Postal Union Convention Apply To Air Carriers Acting As Agents Of The United States Postal Service, 52 J.Air.L. & Com. 711 (1987).

## SECTION 5. SHIPPING

### A. INTERNATIONAL MARITIME ORGANIZATION (IMO)

A specialized agency of the U.N., the International Maritime Consultative Organization (IMCO) was established by a Convention approved at a United Nations maritime conference in 1948. The Convention entered into force on March 28, 1958, upon ratification by the required 21 states, 17 of which had to possess a total tonnage of not less than 1 million gross tons of shipping. 9 U.S.T. 621, T.I.A.S. No. 4044, 289 U.N.T.S. 48 amended Sept. 15, 1964, 18 U.S.T. 1299, T.I.A.S. No. 6285, and Sept. 28, 1965, T.I.A.S. No. 6490. The delay was due to the judgment of some shipping states that IMCO should confine itself to technical questions and not concern itself with commercial matters. During the 9th regular session of the IMCO Assembly, an amendment to change the organization's name to the International Maritime Organization (IMO) was adopted (IMCO Res. A 358 (IX) (1975)).

The IMO's purposes are to provide machinery for cooperation in the areas of governmental regulation, practices and technical matters of all kinds affecting shipping in international trade, to encourage the adoption of the highest standards of maritime safety and efficiency, and to encourage abolition of discrimination and unnecessary restrictions so as to increase the availability of shipping for international commerce (Art. 1). IMO has a special responsibility for the safety of life at sea and for the protection of the marine environment through prevention of pollution of the sea caused by ships and other craft. IMO also deals with legal aspects of international shipping and with facilitation of international maritime traffic. It is also responsible for providing technical assistance in maritime matters to developing countries. IMO has helped to establish and develop maritime training establishments around the world. The most important of these are the World Maritime University, which was opened in 1983 in Malmö, Sweden, the IMO International Maritime Agency in Trieste, Italy, and the IMO International Maritime Law Institute in Malta.

It is a consultative and advisory body (Art. 2), whose functions are to make recommendations, to provide for the drafting of conventions and the convening of conferences, and to provide machinery for consultation.

The plenary body, composed of all members, is the Assembly, meeting every two years to formulate rules of procedure and to make budgetary decisions. Thirty-two Council members are elected by the Assembly, with numerical representation given to governments with the largest interests in providing international shipping services (eight members), governments of other nations with the largest interest in seaborne trade (eight members), and other governments with a special interest in maritime transportation or navigation (sixteen members) (Articles 17–18). The Council takes effective action by making recommendations on the drafting of conventions, matters connected to the purposes declared in Article 1, and the convening of conferences. The Maritime Safety Committee makes recommendations to the Assembly, and was originally composed of 16 members elected by the Assembly with at least 8 representing the largest ship-owning nations (Art. 28). At its ninth regular session, the Assembly adopted an amendment making the Committee open to all members (IMCO Ass.Res.A. 315 (E.S.V.) 1975). A large role is assigned to the Council and the Committee. In addition, there is a secretariat (Art. 33), and a Legal Committee (established as a principal organ by amendment in 1975, IMCO Ass.Res.A. 358 (IX) 1975).

Lengthy delays have occurred in the entry into force of amendments to technical provisions of conventions for which the IMO is depositary. These have been occasioned in part by constitutional requirements of member states. To avoid these delays, the IMO adopted a new procedure to replace the traditional "explicit acceptance" approach (IMCO Res.A. 293 (VIII) 1973). Through a "tacit acceptance" procedure, an amendment is considered effective for all contracting states, after adoption by the appropriate IMO body, unless a specified minority objects by a certain date, or other requirements, varying with each convention, are met. This approach raises problems for states that might be bound by default, and for the LDC's which have to make assessments of technical amendments in a short span of time. See Adede, Amendment Procedures for Conventions with Technical Annexes: The IMCO Experience, 17 Virginia J.I.L. 201 (1977).

### *Notes*

1. On the IMO, see also Johnson, IMCO—The First Four Years, 12 I.C.L.Q. 31 (1963); Note, IMCO Convention, 5 UCLA L.Rev. 353 (1976).

2. On anti-pollution conventions developed under the auspices of IMO, see Note, Environmental Law—A Survey of International Maritime Controls: Prelude to Geneva, 8 Vand.L.Transn.L. 477 (1975). On the IMO's work on pollution, see Boyle, Marine Pollution Under the Law of the Sea Convention, 79 A.J.I.L. 347 (1985).

3. The IMO has also played an active role in combatting terrorism on the high seas. On March 10, 1988, in response to concern about maritime terrorism, an international diplomatic conference held in Rome adopted the Convention For The Suppression Of Unlawful Acts Against The Safety Of Maritime Navigation, IMO Doc. SUA/CON/IS (1988), and a related Protocol For The Suppression Of Unlawful Acts Against The Safety Of Fixed Platforms Located On The Continental Shelf, IMO Doc SUA/CON/16/Rev. 1 (1988). Both the Convention and the Protocol supplement other international conventions aimed at terrorism. The Convention and the Protocol entered into force on January 3, 1992, but as of April 1, 1992, neither had been ratified by the United States. For further reading on the Convention, see Halberstam, Terrorism On The High Seas: The Achille Lauro, Piracy And The IMO Convention on Maritime Safety, 92 A.J.I.L. 269 (1988); Kirsch, The 1988 ICAO And IMO Conferences: An International Consensus Against Terrorism, 12 Dalhousie L.J. 5 (1989).

## B. INTERNATIONAL MARITIME SATELLITE SYSTEM (INMARSAT)

The burgeoning maritime traffic and consequent danger of accidents and pollution has greatly increased the need for effective communication. The forecast of congestion of high frequency transmission facilities, insufficient geographical coverage, poor quality and delay in medium frequency broadcasts, inability to expand facilities and unfavorable prospects for improvement moved the IMO to seek an alternate solution for meeting this need. IMO, Doc. MACSAT/CONF. 3 (30 Oct. 1974), pp. 3–6. Recognizing that the development of an effective communications system is possible through space technology, providing 24–hour service for all maritime regions, an International Diplomatic Conference of Governments in London in 1975–76, under the auspices of IMO, approved in 1976 a Convention on the International Maritime Satellite System (15 I.L.M. 233), which was opened for signature on Sept. 13, 1976.

The Convention has created an international intergovernmental organization to manage this system. Its purpose is to provide a space segment in a satellite system for maritime communication. Each member state may designate any type of entity, including a private entity, to fulfill the obligation of the Convention (Art. 4).

The Assembly is composed of all members, each with one vote. It determines the broad policy of the organization and expresses views on the reports of the Council. The latter is a technical body, composed of 22 members, 18 of which represent members with the general investment shares and 4 being chosen by the Assembly to ensure geographical representation (Art. 14). The Council prepares the work programs and administrative regulations. The votes are weighted in proportion to the investment share of each member, in accordance with the organization's principle of operation on an economic basis (Art. 5). The Directorate is the executive organ.

Investment shares are based on the proportion of space segment used by each member in relation to all other members. (Operating Agreement Art. V, IMCO MARSAT/CONF/29 (Feb. 28, 1976)). Allocation is based on two factors, a ship and a land part (Art. V(2)). The Annex provides a list of investment shares prior to a first determination on the basis of utilization. The U.S. has 17, the UK has 12, and the USSR has 11 shares. 15 I.L.M. 246 (1976).

Procurement policy is based on the award of contracts on international bidding, determined by the criteria of price, quality, and most favorable delivery (Art. 20).

### *Note*

On INMARSAT, see Inmarsat, 8 J.Mar.L. 95 (1976).

# SECTION 6. LABOR

## A. INTERNATIONAL LABOUR ORGANIZATION (ILO)

### 1. *History*

The ILO antedates most of the other specialized agencies by twenty-five years, the original constitution being embodied in the peace treaties concluding World War I (Part XIII of the Treaty of Versailles of June 28, 1919, of the Treaty of Saint Germain of Sept. 10, 1919, and of the Treaty of Trianon of June 4, 1920, and Part XII of the Treaty of Neuilly of Nov. 27, 1919). During the first twenty-five years, the ILO functioned as an official intergovernmental organization, autonomously associated with the League. The bulk of its work consisted of elaborating international conventions regulating such conditions as working hours, female labor, industrial injury, and unemployment compensation, and of providing advice on labor questions.

In 1944, on the threshold of the Organization's post-war expansion, a conference held in Philadelphia adopted a Declaration (Declaration concluding the Aims and Purposes of the ILO, adopted 5/10/44, 3554, T.I.A.S. No. 1868 at 80, 5 U.N.T.S. 104) which redefined the aims and purposes of the ILO. Emphasis was laid upon the social, spiritual, and economic welfare of people. The guiding principles established were that (1) labor is not a commodity, (2) freedom of expression and association is essential to sustained progress, and (3) all human beings have a right to pursue their material and spiritual well-being in conditions of freedom, dignity, and equal opportunity.

The dissolution of the League necessitated articulation of a new relationship with the U.N. through the adoption of instruments of amendment in 1945 and 1946. The ILO became the first international organization to be linked to the U.N. as a "special agency" through a Special Agreement between the U.N. and ILO, effective Dec. 16, 1946.

The ILO Constitution was then revised, with the Philadelphia Charter appended in an Annex. ILO practice shows that these two instruments are treated as an organic whole. Another post-war change in the Organization was in the attention given to technical assistance.

### 2. *Organization*

#### STRUCTURE

In 1919, the European countries wanted a labor organization which would develop rules regulating working conditions and persuade governments to adopt these, while the United States pushed for an organization that would aid the development of independent labor movements. The compromise reached established a structure unique to the ILO: a tripartite system of representation. Each member was given the right to send four delegates to a Conference, two of them government representatives and one delegate each representing workers' and employers' organizations (Art. 3(5)). The latter delegates were to speak and vote independently, being elected by the most "representative organizations" of workers and employers in each country. Difficult questions have arisen in the implementation of these provisions. For example, how are delegates to be selected when there are no organizations in a member country of the prescribed categories? What criteria determine whether the organizations are "most representative"? If not by numbers, are they to be subjectively chosen in terms of "ruling groups"? See Beguin, ILO and the Tripartite System, International Conciliation 523 (1959). So that the importance of labor representation would not undercut the ultimate responsibility of governments to enforce the adopted legislation, the ratio of two government delegates for every worker and employer delegate was established.

The principal organ of the ILO is the International Labour Conference, which meets annually. Workers' and employers' representatives have an equal voice with those of governments. The ILO's Governing Body is its executive body. It now has 56 regular members. Of the 28 government representatives, ten hold non-elective seats representing member states of "chief industrial importance" and 18 represent members elected by the conference. In 1986, the conference adopted amendments to the constitution relating to the membership of the Governing Body. Under the new provisions, the regular membership will be increased to 56 government members and 28 employers' and workers' members respectively. The category of states of "chief industrial importance" will disappear. The amendments will not come into force, however, until instruments of acceptance have been deposited by two-thirds of member states, including five of the ten states of chief industrial importance.

## LEGISLATION

Conventions and Recommendations which set international labor standards are adopted at meetings of the International Labor Conference which are held annually (Art. 19). Conventions, ratified by member states, create binding obligations, while Recommendations are guidelines on policy, legislation, and practice.

Between 1919 and 1990, 169 Conventions and 176 Recommendations were adopted, covering a range of matters such as certain basic human rights (freedom of association, abolition of forced labor, elimination of discrimination in employment), labor administration, industrial relations, employment policy, working conditions, social security, occupational safety and health, and employment of women and children and special categories of workers (migrants and seafarers). The body of basic principles thus developed was compiled into an International Labor Code issued in 1939 and 1951. For the 1951 Code, see International Labour Office, The International Labour Code, 1951 (1952).

Each member state is required to submit all Conventions and Recommendations adopted by the Conference to its competent national authority in order to give effect to the provisions. The procedure of adoption at Conferences, established instead of the more conventional method of signing by plenipotentiaries, gives the Conventions their hybrid nature of legal and contractual characteristics.

A supervisory procedure has been established to monitor the implementation and application of Conventions by ratifying states. Each member must submit reports every two years (Arts. 19, 22), and copies of these reports must be sent to the member's, workers' and employers' organizations (Art. 23). A committee of independent experts evaluate these reports, and tripartite bodies examine individual cases of compliance.

The enforcement of obligations can be achieved through contentious proceedings as well. Individual associations of workers and employers may submit reports to the International Labour Office on the failure of their government to observe a Convention (Art. 24). Members who have ratified a Convention and are dissatisfied with the adherence of other ratifying members may file a complaint. A Commission of Inquiry investigates the charges and files a report with findings of facts and recommendations on steps to be taken. The members can accept the report or refer the matter to the ICJ, whose decision is final (Arts. 26–29, 31–34). Complaints have been infrequent, and thus far all members have accepted the Commission's suggestions.

### *3. Problems in a Changing World*

The ILO was created at a time when its constituency of democratic countries were at the same stage of development. Its two goals of universal membership and pure tripartite representation posed no conflicts. The emergence of communist and socialist countries, as well as the increased degree of governmental control over employer and worker groups in both democratic and developing countries, has put a strain upon adherence to the organization's original ideals. Noncompliance with the requirement of equal and independent representation was first raised in the 1920's when the credentials of Italy's worker delegates were challenged, was brought up again in 1946 with the ILO's invitation to the USSR to rejoin the organization, and remained a problem throughout the Cold War as non-Communist member states challenged the seating of worker and employer delegates from several Communist countries (e.g., Hungary, Czechoslovakia) on the ground that these delegates were not really independent of their governments.

In 1970, the United States cut off its ILO assessments, comprising 21% of all contributions to the ILO fund, in order to exert pressure against the appointment of a Soviet delegate as assistant Director–General and to indicate dissatisfaction with the use of the ILO by members as a forum for political issues. Since the validity of the assessments was not challenged, which was the case in 1962 with regard to the contributions of other countries to the U.N. (ICJ, On Certain Expenses of the U.N., ICJ Rep. 158 (1962)), did this action constitute a violation of an international obligation? On November 5, 1975, the United States gave notice of its intent to withdraw from the ILO (14 ILM 1582–4 (1975)). Four reasons were given: (1) the system of tripartite representation had eroded due to the admission of non-democratic members, (2) the usual procedures for prosecuting member violations of obligations had been bypassed in recent years, as Conferences passed resolutions on member states' actions without prior referral to the appropriate investigating commission, (3) the organization ignored the alleged violation of rights in all but a handful of states, thus expressing only a selective concern for human rights, and (4) the organization had become increasingly politicized and heedless of its goal of promoting social welfare.

Before a member's withdrawal is effective, two years notice must be given and all financial obligations must be met (Art. 1(5)). The United States did not pay its financial obligations, but permitted the two years to elapse and declared its membership in the ILO terminated. United States withdrawal did not affect practice in the United States, since 6 out of the 7 Conventions it has ratified pertain to technical maritime matters.

In February, 1980, President Carter issued a statement to the effect that a majority of the members of the ILO had successfully joined together to return the ILO to its original purposes and that "[I] have decided, therefore, that the United States should now rejoin the ILO. * * *" 80 State Dep't Bull. No. 2037, p. 65 (1980). On the United States' current role in the ILO, see Schlossberg, United States' Participation In The ILO: Redefining The Role, 11 Comp.Lab.L.J. 48 (1989); Moy, The U.S. Legal Role In International Labor Organization Conventions And Recommendations, 22 Int'l Law 767 (1988). On the relationship between the ILO and British labor law, see Ewing, British Labour Law And The ILO, 139 New L.J. 1680 (1989).

### *Notes*

1. The ILO Constitution emphasizes the necessity of cooperation between federal and state governments in the enforcement of Conventions which relate to matters falling within the domain of a constituent state. Federalist countries must report on the laws of their constituent states as well as those of the federal government. Ratification of Conventions is more difficult in federations, but the United States' record is worse than that of Canada, Australia, or Switzerland: it has ratified only 7 of 143 Conventions, declaring the remainder to be within the domain of its states.

2. The ILO does not allow reservations to Conventions to be made when member states ratify them, since this would hamper the goal of a uniform system of obligations, which must be reciprocally assumed. Other methods have been provided to allow ratifying developing countries some flexibility in the assumption of obligations. See Gormley, Modification of Multilateral Conventions by "Negotiating Reservations" and Alternatives: Comparative Study of the ILO and the Council of Europe, 39 Fordham L.Rev. 59 (1970).

3. On the ILO generally, see Alcock, History of the ILO (1971). On the United States withdrawal, see Note, U.S. Assaults ILO, 65 Am.J.Int.L. 136 (1971); Note, Prospective U.S. Withdrawal from ILO, 17 Harv.Int.L.J. 623 (1976). Osieke, Constitutional Law and Practice in the International Labour Organization (1985); Leary, International Labour Convention and National Law (1982); Kruglak, The Politics of United States Decision–Making in United Nations Specialized Agencies: The Case of the International Labour Organization (1980); Galenson, The International Labour Organization: An American View (1981). On ILO activities in regard to Multinational Enterprise, 10 J.Int.L. & Econ. 267 (1975); Note; Multinational Collective Bargaining, 9 Vand.J.Transn.L. 101 (1974). On the role of the ILO with respect to the labor crisis in Poland provoked by Poland's efforts to suppress the independent labor union Solidarity, see Note, the International Labour Organization and the Polish Independent Labor Movement, 22 Va.J.I.L. 555 (1982). On the role of the ILO in the evolving market economics of Eastern European countries, see Engels, Who Is Who In The Eastern European Industrial Relations Landscape: Identifying Proper Collective Bargaining Partners In Reforming Socialist Systems Through The Application Of ILO Convention Nos. 87 and 88, 13 Comp.Lab.L.J. 167 (1992). On the ILO and indigenous peoples, see Barah, Revision Of ILO Convention No. 107, 81 A.J.I.L. 756 (1987); Swepsten, A New Step In The International Law On Indigenous And Tribal Peoples: ILO Convention No. 169 of 1989, 15 Okla. City U.L.Rev. 677 (1990).

# SECTION 7. AGRICULTURE

## A. FOOD AND AGRICULTURE ORGANIZATION (FAO)

The creation of the FAO was recommended by a Conference on Food and Agriculture held in 1943. In October 1945, delegates of 42 countries met in Quebec, Canada, and founded the organization. Representatives of the 164 member states meet every two years to approve a budget and program of work (Art. 3). Each member has one vote. Forty-nine members are elected to a Council which serves as intermediate governing body, meeting at least three times between conferences (Art. 5). Committees of the Council concern themselves with specialized areas (Art. 6). A Director–General and professional staff compose the Secretariat (Art. 7).

The FAO was established to provide international backing for national programs in the development of agriculture, forestry, and fisheries. Its aim is to raise nutritional levels and standards of living, improve the efficiency of the production and distribution of food and other agricultural products, better the conditions of rural populations, and thus contribute to an expanding world economy (Preamble to the Constitution).

In furtherance of these goals, the FAO provides information on production, trade, and consumption of agricultural products through an information servicing network. At the end of 1976, 85 FAO members, the EEC Commission, and the Central American Economic Integration Secretariat joined the FAO's Global Information and Early Warning System, which watches world food projects on a continuing basis. It oversees ongoing studies that aid member countries in the development of policy guidelines for the future. Advice is given to developing countries on how to increase foreign exchange and expand employment opportunities. The Food Security Assistance Scheme, established in 1976, assists these countries in formulating national food security policies. Contributions to international policy-making are made through such permanent commissions as the Committee on Commodity Problems, the Consultative Group on International Research, and the Codex Alimentarius Commission (which draws up standards of quality for foodstuffs in international trade jointly with WHO). Through the Organization's Investment Centre, financing for investment in agriculture in developing countries is found. The Technical Cooperation Programme (TCP), established in 1976, promises third world developing countries quick technical and material aid for small scale but urgent projects.

Since 1961, the FAO has co-sponsored with the U.N. the World Food Program, a multilateral agency which uses food aid in support of development and for emergency situations. To enlarge the public consciousness on the extent and causes of world hunger through the involvement of non-governmental groups in the work of the FAO, the Freedom from Hunger Campaign Action for Development was begun in 1960.

The largest source of funds for financing the field activities of FAO is the U.N. Development Program (UNDP). A U.N. World Food Conference held in 1976 adopted an Agreement Establishing the International Fund for Agricultural Development (on June 13, 1976) which, mobilized additional resources for agricultural development in developing member states (Art. 2) within the framework of a specialized U.N. agency structure (Art. 8) (A/Conf. 73/15 (1976); 15 I.L.M. 922 (1976)). 28 U.S.T. 8435; T.I.A.S. No. 8765.

On FAO generally, see Hambidge, The Story of FAO (1955). On the world food situation, see Gardner, World Food and Energy Crisis, A Report (1974); Willet, World Food Situation: Problems and Prospects to 1985 (1975).

### B. INTERNATIONAL FUND FOR AGRICULTURAL DEVELOPMENT (IFAD)

IFAD was established in 1976, following a proposal by the 1974 U.N. World Food Conference. It began operating in December 1977.

IFAD's objective is to mobilize financial resources for increasing food production and to improve the nutritional level of the poorest populations in the developing countries.

The Fund makes resources available for agricultural development in the form of grants and loans. It funds projects to expand food production systems and to strengthen related national policy and institutions. Through investment in irrigation, seeds and fertilizer, and improvements in research and marketing, the projects have led to increased production in countries such as Benin, Zaire, and Bangladesh. IFAD also makes money available to rural landless populations to acquire income-generating assets.

IFAD has 148 members which are represented on the Governing Council in three categories: industrialized, OPEC, and recipient developing countries. The Executive Board consists of 18 members elected by the Governing Council, one-third by each category. The organization's headquarters are in Rome. On IFAD, see King, The International Fund for Agricultural Development: The First Six Years, 3 Dev.Pul.Rev. (1985).

## SECTION 8. WEATHER

### A. WORLD METEOROLOGICAL ORGANIZATION (WMO)

The Convention on WMO was drafted on October 11, 1947 by the Directors of the International Meteorological Organization, WMO's predecessor, which was established in 1878, and entered into force on March 23, 1950. 1 U.S.T. 281, T.I.A.S. No. 2052, 77 U.N.T.S. 143; amended, April 11 and 27, 1963, 16 U.S.T. 2069, 2073, T.I.A.S. No. 5947; April 11, 26 and 27, 1967, 18 U.S.T. 2795, 2800, T.I.A.S. No. 6364.

WMO was created to facilitate cooperation in the establishment of facilities for meteorological and other geophysical observations related to meteorology; to promote the exchange of weather information; to promote standardization of meteorological observations and to ensure uniform publication of observations and statistics; to further the application of meteorology to aviation, shipping, agriculture and other activities; and to encourage research and training (Article 2).

WMO's structure is somewhat different from that of other technical organizations. The plenary body is the World Meteorological Congress, [it meets every four years and is] composed of delegates representing all members, each member having one vote (Articles 7, 11). The Executive Committee is composed of the President and Vice-Presidents of the Organization, the Presidents of Regional Associations, and Directors of meteorological services of member governments. Each member has one vote (Articles 13, 16). There are Regional Associations of members, whose meteorological networks extend into the geographical region (Article 18). The Congress may establish Technical Commissions (Article 19). The Secretariat is headed by a Secretary-General appointed by the Congress (Articles 20, 21). Expenses of WMO are borne by the members, as apportioned by the Congress (Article 24).

### *Notes*

On the program to create a World Weather Watch, see Gardner, Blueprint for Peace 327–328 (1966). On WMO's accomplishments and plans for the future, see Leese, World Meteorological Organization—Demonstrated Accomplishments And Strong Plans For The Future In Applying Space Technology, 14 J.Space L. 140 (1986).

## SECTION 9. HEALTH

### A. WORLD HEALTH ORGANIZATION (WHO)

WHO has a Constitution which was signed at the International Health Conference in New York on July 22, 1946, and which came into force on April 7, 1948. 62 Stat. 2679, T.I.A.S. No. 1808, 14 U.N.T.S. 185; amended October 25, 1960, World Health Assembly Resolution 12.43, 11 U.S.T. 2553, T.I.A.S. No. 4643, 377 U.N.T.S. 380. Membership in WHO is open to all States (Article 3).

The objective of WHO is "the attainment by all peoples of the highest possible level of health" (Article 1). WHO accordingly has a wide range of functions including: to act as the directing and coordinating authority on international health work; to stimulate and advance work to eradicate epidemic, endemic and other diseases; to promote improved standards of teaching and training; to establish international standards with respect to biological and pharmaceutical products; to standardize diagnostic procedures; to foster activities in the field of mental health; to provide administrative and technical services; to promote professional cooperation in the field of health; to provide information; and to propose conventions, agreements, and regulations and make recommendations with respect to international health matters (Article 1).

The main organs of WHO are the World Health Assembly (WHA), the Executive Board, and the Secretariat (Article 9). The World Health Assembly, the supreme governing body, meets annually (Article 13) and is composed of delegates representing all member states (Article 10). WHA determines policies and programs of WHO and votes the budget (Article 18). WHA has some quasi-legislative power; it has the authority to adopt, by two-thirds vote, conventions or agreements with respect to matters within the competence of WHO (Article 19). It also has the authority to adopt regulations relating to sanitary and quarantine requirements; medical nomenclature; international diagnostic standards; safety, purity, and potency of biological and pharmaceutical products moving in international commerce; and advertising and labelling of such products (Article 21). The Assembly's quasi-legislative power derives from the provision that regulations adopted pursuant to Article 21 become binding on all members of WHO after due notice of their adoption, except that those members who notify the Director–General of their rejection are not bound (Article 22). Members may also accept regulations subject to reservations.

The Executive Board, a technical and non-political organ, is composed of 31 persons designated by members of WHO selected by the Assembly (Article 24). The Board meets twice a year (Article 26), and its functions are to give effect to decisions of WHA, to act as the executive organ of the Assembly, to advise the Assembly, and to take emergency measures to deal with events requiring immediate action (Article 28). The Secretariat, under the direction of a Director–General, comprises the technical and administrative staff (Article 30).

The main thrust of WHO's recent activities has been towards promoting national, regional, and global strategies for the attainment of "Health for All by the Year 2000," and the attainment of a level of health that will permit a socially and economically productive life. WHO has also focused its resources on a global AIDS strategy. See Note, The AIDS Pandemic: International Travel And Immigration Restrictions And The World Health Organization's Response, 28 Va.J.Int'l.L. 1043 (1988); Note, The World Health Organization's Resolution Condemning AIDS–Related Discrimination And Ongoing United States Noncompliance At The Border, 12 N.Y.L.Sch.J.Int'l & Comp.L. 151 (1991).

### *Notes*

1. WHO publishes annual reports, entitled "The Work of WHO," on its activities.

2. In 1980, dissatisfied with the Camp David accords between Egypt and Israel, members of the Eastern Mediterranean Region of WHO sought to transfer the site of the organization's Eastern Mediterranean Regional Office from Alexandria, Egypt, to Amram, Jordan. The I.C.J. ruled in its Advisory Opinion on the Interpretation of the Agreement of 25 March 1951 between the WHO and Egypt, 1980 I.C.J. 73, reprinted in 20 I.L.M. 88 (1980), that WHO was required to give Egypt reasonable notice of the transfer and to negotiate in good faith so that the transfer would be effected with minimal damage to Egypt's interests. See 1980 I.C.J. Pleadings No. 65. See also Note, I.C.J. Advisory Opinion on WHO–Egypt Agreement of 1951, 10 Den.J.I.L. & Pol. 561 (1980).

## SECTION 10. ATOMIC ENERGY

### A. INTERNATIONAL ATOMIC ENERGY AGENCY (IAEA)

IAEA is an autonomous organization under the aegis of the United Nations; it is not a "specialized agency." IAEA was constituted by a Statute (entered into force July 29, 1957, 8 U.S.T. 1093, T.I.A.S. No. 3873, 276

U.N.T.S. 3; amended October 4, 1961, 14 U.S.T. 135, T.I.A.S. No. 5284, 471 U.N.T.S. 334). Among the parties are most of the important producers of atomic power or materials (i.e., Canada, France, the U.S.S.R., United Kingdom, and United States).

IAEA was established to promote the peaceful and safe uses of atomic energy (Article 2). To these ends, the Agency is authorized to encourage research, promote the development and practical application of atomic energy for peaceful uses, provide materials and facilities for this purpose, foster the exchange of scientific information, establish and administer safeguards against the military use of materials, services and facilities the Agency distributes, and establish safety standards to protect health and property (Article 3). IAEA acquires its atomic materials through voluntary contributions of members. (Article 11, section E). IAEA is empowered to establish a staff of inspectors (Article 12, section B) and has the right to send them into the territory of recipient states with complete access to facilities, data, and persons involved in IAEA-aided projects (Article 12, section A(6)). IAEA may, at the request of parties, apply its safeguards to bilateral or multilateral agreements for the development and use of atomic energy, or to a state's own activities at the request of that state (Article 3, section A(5), 6)). The United States has requested IAEA safeguards in some of its bilateral arrangements (e.g., Agreement Between the International Atomic Energy Agency, Japan and the United States for the Application of Safeguards, July 10, 1968, T.I.A.S. No. 6520). The United States has also entered into an agreement with IAEA for the application of IAEA safeguards, including inspection, to several civil atomic energy power plants in the United States (June 15, 1964, 15 U.S.T. 1456, T.I.A.S. No. 5621, 525 U.N.T.S. 3). IAEA's inspection power is an example of a potentially strong executive function; it has thus far been limited in scope by the reluctance of states to submit installations of such strategic importance to international scrutiny.

The organizational structure of the Agency includes a General Conference of representatives of all members meeting in annual session (Article 5, section A); a thirty-five member Board of Governors, which is partially self-perpetuating through its power to appoint nine members of the new Board, including the "five members most advanced in the technology of atomic energy, including the production of source materials" (Article 6, section A(1)); a Director–General heads the staff of the Agency (Article 7).

Administrative expenses of IAEA are contributed by members, according to a scale based on the United Nations apportionment of expenses. (Article 14, section D). The Agency charges for materials, services, equipment, and facilities provided by it, in accordance with rates fixed by the Board of Governors (Article 14, section E).

### *Notes*

1. As stated by the principal commentator on IAEA, "[T]he actual pattern of operations during the Agency's first decade differed considerably from the expectations of the principal authors of the Statute." Szasz, The Law and Practice of the International Atomic Energy Agency 359 (1970). In the main, the Agency has concentrated on providing technical and research assistance, the development of health and safety standards, and the development of atomic

energy law, through conventions or other instruments, on such subjects as civil liability for nuclear damage, waste disposal, emergency assistance, and the like.

2. In 1985, the U.S.S.R. concluded an agreement with IAEA by which the organization will monitor safety standards at certain "peaceful nuclear facilities" designated by the U.S.S.R. Agreement Between the Union of Soviet Socialist Republics and the International Atomic Energy Agency for the Application of Safeguards in the Union of Soviet Socialist Republics, done at Vienna, February 21, 1985, entered into force June 10, 1985, reprinted in 24 I.L.M. 1411 (1985). On recent developments, see also Lamm, The Utilization of Atomic Energy and International Law (1984).

3. In 1986, in the aftermath of the Chernobyl nuclear power station accident, the IAEA took swift action to promote ratification of two conventions related to nuclear safety. The first was the Convention On Early Notification Of A Nuclear Accident, which entered into force on October 27, 1986. The second was the Convention On Assistance In The Case Of A Nuclear Accident Or Radiological Emergency, which entered into force on February 26, 1987. These conventions reflect growing international concern about the environmental dangers resulting from industrial development and constitute important steps toward multilateral efforts to mitigate the consequences of transboundary releases of contaminants in the atmosphere. However, the effectiveness of the procedures established by these conventions is limited by the exclusion of military nuclear accidents from the category of notifiable events, the discretionary nature of the assistance for which they provide, and the reservation to the conventions' dispute-resolution procedures made by many signatories. See Note, Nuclear Energy Safety, 28 Harv.Int'l L.J. 558 (1987); Note, Chernobyl Fallout: Recent IAEA Conventions Expand Transboundary Nuclear Pollution Law, 23 Stan.J.Int'l L. 651 (1987); Note, The International Atomic Energy Agency: An Expanding Role In The Post–Chernobyl World, 12 N.C.J.Int'l L. & Com.Reg. 269 (1987).

4. On the IAEA's assistance to the Commonwealth of Independent States in preventing the proliferation of nuclear weapons, see Levin, Where Have All The Weapons Gone? The Commonwealth of Independent States' Struggle To Stop The Proliferation Of Nuclear Weapons And The New Role Of The International Atomic Energy Agency, 24 N.Y.U.J.Int'l L. & Pol. 957 (1992).

## SECTION 11. OTHER ORGANIZATIONS

It is impossible, within the limits of available space, to describe in any detail the organization and functions of the many other international organizations active in the fields of technical, social, and informational cooperation that are not related to the United Nations. An example is the International Bureau for the Protection of Industrial Property, which functions in connection with the Paris Convention for the Protection of Industrial Property and the Madrid Arrangement for the Registration of Trademarks.

The United Nations itself, through the Secretariat and the Economic and Social Council, performs many important tasks of coordination, technical assistance, and information gathering and dissemination. It administers the international system of control of traffic in narcotic drugs. The regional economic commissions (Economic Commission for Europe, Economic Commission for Latin America, Economic Commission for Asia and the Far East,

Economic Commission for Africa) provide important statistical services. The Secretariat publishes the World Economic Survey, the Statistical Yearbook, and the Demographic Yearbook. The United Nations Institute for Training and Research (UNITAR) was created to provide training and research facilities, primarily for developing countries.

The significance of the proliferation of these agencies lies in the gradual weaving together of the world, on a functional basis, into a web that creates interdependence, cooperation, and a common approach to many problems.

For additional information on international organizations, see New Zealand Ministry of External Relations and Trade, 1992 United Nations Handbook (1992); Rengger (ed.), Treaties and Alliances of the World (1990); Taylor & Groom (ed.), Global Issues in the United Nations' Framework (1989); Harrod & Schrijver, The UN Under Attack (1988); Karns & Mingst (ed.), The United States and Multilateral Institutions (1990); Wells (ed.), Peace by Pieces (1991); Kaufmann (ed.), Effective Negotiation: Case Studies in Conference Diplomacy (1989); Taylor & Groom (ed.), International Institutions at Work (1988).

# Chapter 19

# REGIONAL ECONOMIC COMMUNITIES

## SECTION 1. INTRODUCTION

Most international organizations facilitate primarily intergovernmental cooperation. Their institutions are normally given only most limited transnational jurisdiction. When such jurisdiction is granted, it frequently can be exercised only by unanimous action. The European Communities, whose examples have been emulated in other parts of the globe, form remarkable exceptions. Not only are they organizations whose purposes extend to economic life in considerable breadth rather than to particular sectors only, their institutions have large measures of truly transnational authority, displacing sovereign powers theretofore possessed by the constituent states. They are therefore in a true sense transnational organizations possessing sovereign powers in broad areas of human endeavor.

As might have been anticipated, in their exercise of these transnational powers these organizations have had to cope with the resistance of constituent states loath to relinquish their claims to sovereign powers. The relative success of the European Communities, and especially the EEC, in dealing with, and in most instances overcoming, this resistance renders them of particular interest also to students of international law who are not primarily interested in regional approaches towards problems of economic life. For the European Communities form a telling example of how truly transnational organizations can work in dealing with matters of great political significance in the member states.

## SECTION 2. THE EUROPEAN COMMUNITIES

### A. EUROPEAN ECONOMIC COMMUNITY (EEC)

#### 1. *Developments Leading to Its Creation*

*a. Introduction*

The Second World War brought to many Europeans the realization that political and economic integration would contribute substantially to the maintenance of post-war peace and to the healthy economic development of the European continent. More energetically than ever before, the protagonists of European integration attempted to move the countries of Europe towards cooperating in the establishment of a politically and economically united Europe. The United States, which had won the war with overwhelming economic might, formed a shining example of the many advantages afforded by a large politically and economically integrated unit. It was realized by many that only a cooperative effort would enable Europe to recapture a leading position in world affairs. However, the proponents of European integration infrequently acted in unison. Many movements favoring various forms of integration have come into being, but only a few have achieved concrete results.

*b. The Benelux*

As early as 1944, when their countries were still occupied by the German armies, the governments-in-exile of the Netherlands, Belgium, and Luxembourg signed in London the first of the conventions that led eventually to the establishment of the so-called "Benelux" customs union. It was agreed that the customs union should become effective as soon as the occupying forces had been driven away and the policies of the three countries had been sufficiently coordinated. In 1948, in pursuance of this initial agreement, all customs duties were abolished between the Netherlands and the Belgium–Luxembourg Economic Union, which had been initiated as early as 1921, and a common tariff on foreign goods was instituted. In 1949, the progressive elimination of quantitative restrictions was provided for. A treaty of February 3, 1958, which became effective on November 1, 1961, provided for close co-operation in a number of additional areas.

*c. The Stillborn French–Italian Customs Union*

In 1947, France and Italy, inspired by the Benelux example, commenced negotiations that led to the signing in 1949 of a customs union agreement. However, the agreement was never ratified. The policies of the two countries appeared insufficiently coordinated to permit even this limited an economic merger.

*d. OEEC and the OECD*

The Organization for European Economic Cooperation was organized in 1948 following General Marshall's historic call for aid to Europe and his simultaneous statement that such aid could be effective only if accompanied by closer economic cooperation between the countries of Europe. In addition to distributing foreign aid, the OEEC was to work out a rational development plan for the economies of the participating countries.

However, the profound differences between the conditions prevailing in the participating countries, the intergovernmental structure of the controlling bodies, and the requirement of unanimity of decisions largely prevented effective coordination of social and economic policies. Nevertheless, the OEEC did play a large part in promoting trade by substantially reducing quantitative restrictions and by cooperating in the establishment, in 1950, of the European Payments Union, and multilateral financial clearings, including the extension of credit to debtor countries.

In 1961, the OEEC was reconstituted as the Organization for Economic Cooperation and Development. The United States and Canada, which had been only associate members of the OEEC, became full members of the OECD, which provides an institutional framework for cooperation in the solution of the economic problems of the Atlantic Community and for coordination of programs of aid to underdeveloped countries.

*e. Council of Europe*

The formation of the OEEC provided further stimulus to those striving for the unification of Europe. Responding to the urgings of such leading political figures as Sir Winston Churchill and Paul–Henri Spaak, a large number of European nations, on May 5, 1949, signed the Statute of the Council of Europe. On the Council, see Chapter 15.

*f. European Coal and Steel Community (ECSC)*

The experience with the OEEC and the Council of Europe taught that effective economic coordination and integration could be achieved only by the creation of a structure within which effective policies could be evolved by institutions with a large degree of independence. Realizing that projects involving the creation of supra-national bodies and the surrender of at least parts of the sovereignty of participating nations are frequently viewed with suspicion and ordinarily endorsed with reluctance, the protagonists of European integration resolved to advance their proposals gradually. On May 9, 1950, Robert Schuman launched his famous call for the establishment of the European Coal and Steel Community. The responses to the "Schuman Plan" were extremely favorable, and the treaty establishing the ECSC was signed by France, Germany, Italy, and the three Benelux countries on April 18, 1951, and became effective on July 23, 1952.

The ECSC treaty, which provides for the establishment of a common market, comprising a customs union, in coal and crude steel, created an institutional structure that was to be an example to the draftsmen of the later common market treaties. The ECSC was administered by a High Authority, an independent executive whose members were appointed for six years, and the Council, to which each of the six countries appointed one member. By the Treaty of April 8, 1965 (effective July 1, 1967), the so-called Merger Treaty, the High Authority and the Council of the ECSC were amalgamated with the Commissions and Councils of the EEC and Euratom into one Commission and one Council for the three communities. The Court of Justice and the Assembly were common to the three communities and continue to be so.

*g. The Ill–Fated European Defense Community*

The favorable reception accorded to the Schuman plan stimulated other proposals for partial economic integration, such as that providing for the so-called "green pool," none of which were accepted. It also encouraged further steps in the direction of political integration. A treaty providing for a European Defense Community was drafted and signed on May 27, 1952.

However, attempts at political integration of Europe suffered a severe setback when the French parliament, concerned about German re-armament, rejected the treaty in 1954.

*h. The Preparation, Signing, and Ratification of the Treaties of Rome*

Undaunted by this defeat, the proponents of European unification decided to concentrate their efforts on economic integration and to limit their efforts, at least initially, to the six countries that were members of the ECSC. In June 1955, at the urging of the Benelux countries, the foreign ministers of the six countries met at Messina, Sicily, and resolved that it was desirable "to achieve a united Europe through the development of common institutions, the progressive amalgamation of national economies, the creation of a common market and the gradual harmonization of their social policies." A committee of government representatives under the chairmanship of Paul–Henri Spaak was appointed and charged with the preparation of a preliminary report on the treaties that were needed. This report was issued on April 21, 1956, and approved at a conference held in Venice on May 29 and 30, 1956. It provided the general outlines for the treaties that were to establish the European Economic Community and the European Atomic Energy Community. Approval of the report was followed by extensive negotiations, which resulted in the signing of the two treaties by the six participating countries in Rome, on March 25, 1957. Both treaties were ratified in the second half of 1957 and became effective on January 1, 1958.

*i. The Accession of New Members*

On January 1, 1973, three new members, to wit, the United Kingdom, Ireland and Denmark, joined the EEC. This necessitated rather elaborate arrangements dealing with transitional problems and adjustments in the composition of the institutions. On these arrangements, see 5 Smit & Herzog, The Law of the European Economic Community, App. On January 1, 1986, Greece, Portugal, and Spain joined the EEC under similar arrangements. See Schloh, The Accession of Greece to the European Communities, 10 Georgia J.I. & C.L. 385 (1980). Many of the remaining European states are now seeking accession. Norway, Sweden, Finland, and Austria are now in the waiting line. Former East European bloc countries have also indicated their desire to join.

*j. Treaty Revisions*

In 1986, for the first time in nearly thirty years, the EEC Treaty underwent a substantial revision. The European Council started the movement at its Milan Session in June 1985. An Intergovernmental Conference met from September 1985 to February 1986. On February 17 and 28, 1986, a "SINGLE EUROPEAN ACT" was signed (now published as Supp. 2/86 to the Bulletin of the EC). Its name reflects the belief that the political cooperation practiced by the member states since 1970, independently from the European Communities, should be put in the form of a treaty and be regulated by the same "single" text that also contains important revisions of the EEC Treaty.

The Treaty revisions are important in many respects. They add subjects such as research, technological development and environment. They change unanimity requirements on decision-making into requirements of majority. They introduce a set of "safeguards" in favor of the minority and a new procedure of cooperation by the Council with the European Parliament, and they add provisions for progressively establishing the internal market over a period expiring on 31 December 1992. The Single European Act was ratified by the member states in accordance with their respective constitutional requirements. On this Act, see Lodge, The Single European Act: Towards a New Euro–Dynamism?, 3 J.Comm.Mar.St. 203 (1986); Bermann, The Single European Act: A New Constitution for the Community?, 27 Colum.J.Transnat'l L. 529 (1989); Note, Institutional Reform Under the Single European Act, 3 Am.U.J.Int'l L. & Pol'y 299 (1988); Kapteyn, Introduction To The Law of the European Communities After the Coming Into Force of the Single European Act (2nd ed. 1989); Swann, The Single European Market and Beyond: A Study of the Wider Implications of the Single European Act (1992).

The progress made under the Single European Act encouraged the Member States to make the next step towards a political union. In December 1991, they signed the European Union Treaty at Maastricht. This Treaty substantially amends the EC Treaties to provide for significant political integration; it also provides for European Community citizenship, and commits the Member States to establish a common European currency by 1999. These efforts suffered a significant setback when Denmark failed to ratify the Treaty and France voted for ratification with only a slight majority. While the January 1, 1993, target date for ratification of the Union Treaty was not met, it would appear that, after some modifications, it will be ratified. In fact, on May 18, 1993, Denmark did ratify the Maastricht Treaty, although with significant reservations about the single currency, common defense, European citizenship, and combined police.

*k. Bibliography*

The literature on the EEC is abundant. The most comprehensive commentary in English is Smit & Herzog, The Law of the European Economic Community (6 vol. with supplements, loose-leaf, first published in 1976). The leading European commentaries are Megret, Le droit de la Communauté économique européenne (1970); Von der Groeben, Boeckle & Thiesing, Handbuch für europäische Wirtschaft (3d ed. 1983); Quadri, Monaco & Trabucchi, Trattato institutivo della Communitá Economica (4 vol. 1965).

The veritable flood of books, law reviews, and articles on European Communities law shows no sign of abating. The Smit & Herzog Commentary provides a detailed bibliography for each article of the Treaty. The CCH Common Market Reporter contains many current items and court decisions of interest to practitioners.

### *2. The Structure, Goals, and Administration of the Treaty*

*a. The General Structure of the Treaty*

The Treaty is divided into six parts. Part I is entitled Principles and sets forth the general aims of the EEC and the means by which these aims are to be achieved. It also contains Article 8 providing for the gradual creation of the Common Market in a transitional period of twelve years.

Part II, entitled *Bases of the Community,* deals in Title I with the *Free Movement of Goods,* in Title II with *Agriculture,* in Title III with the *Free Movement of Persons, Services, and Capital,* and in Title IV with *Transport.*

*Policy of the Community* is the heading of Part III. Title I, entitled *Common Rules,* deals with rules governing competition, dumping practices, state subsidies, fiscal problems, and harmonization of laws of member states. Title II, entitled *Economic Policy,* contains provisions relating to economic policy, balance of payments, and commercial policy. Title III on *Social Policy* relates to social provisions and the European Social Fund. Title IV provides for the establishment of The European Investment Bank.

The heading of Part IV is *The Association of Overseas Countries and Territories.* Since most of the countries and territories to which it applies have gained independence, this part has lost most of its significance.

Part V, entitled *Institutions of the Community,* regulates the composition and functions of the various institutions of the Community, including the Assembly, the Council, the Commission, the Court of Justice, and the Economic and Social Committee. It also contains provisions concerning the finances of the Community.

Part VI, finally, contains *General and Final Provisions,* including provisions relating to internal housekeeping and to relations with nonmember states.

Annexed to the Treaty are a number of appendices, protocols, and conventions elaborating on, or supplementing, provisions in the Treaty.

### *b. The Objectives of the EEC*

The Treaty goes far beyond the establishment of merely a customs union providing for the gradual elimination of internal customs duties and the eventual institution of a common tariff on goods imported from non-member states. Of potentially far greater importance are the other objectives set forth in the preamble and Article 2, as well as the means to be used in attaining these objectives described in Article 3 of the Treaty.

Importantly, the very first clause of the preamble, by explicitly recognizing that the Treaty will serve "to establish the foundations of an ever closer union among the European peoples," makes clear that the goal of political, as distinguished from economic, integration has not been abandoned.

Further, Article 2 of the Treaty, in setting forth in general terms the aims of the EEC, makes clear that pervasive economic integration is the final goal.

### *c. The Means for Attaining the Objectives*

The aims of the EEC are to be achieved by resort to measures that are specified succinctly in Article 3 and accorded more elaborate treatment in subsequent provisions. Article 3 provides:

> For the purposes set out in the preceding Article, the activities of the Community shall include, under the conditions and with the timing provided for in this Treaty:
>
> (a) the elimination, as between Member States, of customs duties and of quantitative restrictions in regard to the importation

and exportation of goods, as well as of all other measures with equivalent effect;

(b) the establishment of a common customs tariff and a common commercial policy towards third countries;

(c) the abolition, as between Member States, of the obstacles to the free movement of persons, services and capital;

(d) the inauguration of a common agricultural policy;

(e) the inauguration of a common transport policy;

(f) the establishment of a system ensuring that competition shall not be distorted in the Common Market;

(g) the application of procedures which shall make it possible to co-ordinate the economic policies of Member States and to remedy disequilibria in their balances of payments;

(h) the approximation of their respective municipal law to the extent necessary for the functioning of the Common Market;

(i) the creation of a European Social Fund in order to improve the possibilities of employment for workers and to contribute to the raising of their standard of living;

(j) the establishment of a European Investment Bank intended to facilitate the economic expansion of the Community through the creation of new resources; and

(k) the association of overseas countries and territories with the Community with a view to increasing trade and to pursuing jointly their effort towards economic and social development.

Of further and pivotal importance to the scheme of the Treaty is Article 7 prohibiting any discrimination on the ground of nationality. Indeed, many of the provisions in the Treaty are elaborations on this principal theme.

### d. *The Time–Tables*

The drafters of the Treaty understood that a complex supra-national structure of the nature contemplated could not be instituted all at once. They therefore provided in Article 8 of the Treaty for a transitional period of twelve years, consisting of three stages of four years each, during which the Common Market was to be gradually established.

The Accession Treaty, providing for the accession of the United Kingdom, Ireland and Denmark, provided for a new transitional period of five years, which began on January 1, 1973. During this period, the new members had to take the necessary measures to reach the level of integration achieved by the old members. Similar arrangements regulate[d] the accession of Greece, Portugal, and Spain.

### e. *The Institutions of the EEC*

To ensure proper observance and implementation of its provisions, the Treaty has created its own institutions. Indeed, insofar as it relies for the application and implementation of the Treaty on its own institutions rather than on those of its member states, the EEC bears a distinct supra-national character. It should be noted, however, that the Treaty's reliance on its own institutions is not exclusive. Proper observance of the Treaty and of implementing measures remains in large measure the concern of the national authorities.

The principal institutions of the EEC are the Assembly, the Council, the Commission, and the Court of Justice. In addition, there are a number of what may be called specialized agencies which are given advisory or executive tasks in special areas. A somewhat intermediate position is taken by the Economic and Social Committee, a body with broad advisory functions that may, and in some matters must, be consulted by the Council or the Commission.

Initially, the EEC and Euratom shared with the ECSC only the Assembly and the Court of Justice. The identical bodies functioned in all three communities. An agreement, signed by the governments of the member states on April 8, 1965, which became effective on July 1, 1967, merged the executives of the three communities into one Council and one Commission. One Economic and Social Committee had already been provided for by Article 5 of The Convention of 1957.

The negotiations leading to the adoption of this agreement required considerable time and effort. A major difficulty was to determine where the various institutions should have their provisional headquarters. The agreement represents a compromise designed to compensate Luxembourg for the loss of the headquarters of the ECSC executives.

The Court of Justice's permanent seat has remained in Luxembourg, while the Commission maintains its headquarters in Brussels. The Council, which averages more than 80 meetings a year, usually convenes in Brussels. However, the European Parliament still does not have a permanent seat. It holds its plenary sessions in Strasbourg and its committee meetings in Brussels, while its Secretariat is based in Luxembourg.

On the merger agreement, see also EEC Commission, Eighth General Report on the Activities of the Community c. 1 (1965); Houben, The Merger of the Executives of the European Communities, 3 Common Market L.Rev. (1965).

The following is a synopsis of the provisions of the Treaty and the merger agreement relating to the institutions.

(1) The European Parliament

The Treaty of Rome uses the term "Assembly". Although, in 1962, the Assembly decided to name itself the "European Parliament", some member states did not accept this appellation. The Single European Act now always uses "European Parliament". Members of the Parliament were originally national parliamentarians delegated from the national parliaments to sit as members of the European Parliament. On September 20, 1976, pursuant to Article 138 of the Treaty, the Council drew up an "Act concerning the election of the representatives of the Assembly by direct universal suffrage," Off.Journ. 1976 No. L 278 p. 1, which entered into force after approval by the member states. There have been direct elections in 1979 and, after expiry of the first five-year-term, in 1984, and again in 1989, in each case according to the election laws of the member states. Therefore, the Community still has no uniform electoral procedure, even though Article 138 calls for one. In 1982, the European Parliament proposed a proportional representation system, but the United Kingdom, which has a district constituency system, blocked it at the Council of Ministers level. Electoral methods still vary among the Member States, but all except the United Kingdom use proportional representation in some form.

The Parliament has 518 members. It has no legislative authority, but usually is, and sometimes must be, heard in an advisory capacity. By a two-thirds majority of votes representing a majority of its members, it may vote the members of the Commission out of office.

(2) The Council

The Council, to which each of the twelve countries appoints one member, has both legislative and executive powers. In cases in which the Treaty requires a qualified majority, the votes of the members are weighted in order to prevent, at least when no previous proposal by the Commission is required, that the large countries voting as a bloc outvote the small ones. Fifty-four votes are required for a qualified majority.

(3) The Commission

The Commission is the principal executive organ; it may also exercise legislative power delegated by the Council. The 17 members of the Commission are appointed by the twelve countries "in common agreement." They serve for a period of four years and may be reappointed. The Treaty provides that they shall act "in complete independence" and shall not seek or accept any instructions from any government or other body. The Commission acts by a majority of its members.

(4) The Court of Justice

The Court of Justice is presently composed of thirteen-members. They are appointed for a term of six years by the twelve countries "acting in common agreement." It is assisted by six advocates-general who deliver advisory opinions in every case submitted to the Court. Every three years, the term of office of half of the judges and advocates-general, who are eligible for reappointment, terminates. Both the number of judges and of advocates-general may be increased by unanimous vote of the Council.

The task of the Court is described in broad terms: It shall ensure the observance of the law in the interpretation and application of the treaty. In 1989, the Treaties were revised to provide for a Court of First Instance, to which special categories of cases are to be submitted first. At present, employee and competition cases are within the competence of this Court.

### (i) *SUBMISSION BY EEC INSTITUTIONS*

According to Article 169, if the Commission finds that a member state has failed to comply with its obligations under the Treaty, it may render a reasoned opinion requiring the state to conform within a stated period. If the member state fails to do so, the Commission may submit the dispute to the Court.

Under Article 173, the Council or the Commission may demand that the Court review acts of the Council and Commission other than recommendations or opinions (on these categories, see p. 1511 infra) on the grounds of (1) lack of competence, (2) error of substantial form, (3) violation of the Treaty or any legal provision relating to its application, or (4) abuse of power. The grounds specified, all of which refer to concepts that, although not always sharply defined, are familiar to European lawyers, purport to be exhaustive. Whatever other defects may inhere in the acts attacked, they may not form the basis of review under Article 173. The litigation must be initiated within two months after publication of the act or its notification to the plaintiff, or, in the absence of either, after the plaintiff obtained knowledge of the act. If the Court finds the attack well-founded, it must declare the act null and void; regulations may be declared partially void.

When the Council or Commission fails to act in compliance with the Treaty, under Article 175, the other institutions may request appropriate action and, if no such action is forthcoming within two months thereafter, submit the matter to the Court.

The Community itself may, under Article 179, be a party in proceedings before the Court relating to disputes between it and its employees.

Finally, the Commission may institute proceedings before the Court relating to resolutions of the Board of Directors of the European Investment Bank (Article 180(b) and (c)) while the Community itself may be a party to proceedings brought under an arbitration clause (Article 181).

### (ii) *SUBMISSION BY MEMBER STATES*

Under Article 170, a member state may complain before the Court of any failure by another member state to live up to its Treaty obligations. The dispute must be submitted preliminarily to the Commission which must give a reasoned opinion, but the Court may proceed if the Commission has failed to issue such an opinion within three months after the dispute's submission.

A member state may also elicit review under the conditions and on the grounds specified in Article 170 and complaint pursuant to Article 175 of the Council's or Commission's failure to act. Finally, a member state has the same standing as the Commission to complain under Article 180 of resolutions of the Board of Directors of the European Investment Bank and may submit a dispute to the Court pursuant to a compromise concluded with another member state (Article 182).

In addition, while the Court has tended to limit the scope of the questions it can determine under Article 177, it is not technical about the manner in which such questions must be submitted. If the submission is unduly broad and comprises questions of application of community law in relation to facts or to national law, the Court will cull from the submission the issues it can properly decide. Another manifestation of the Court's disinclination to get involved in law application as distinguished from law determination is its refusal to consider whether the submission by the national tribunal was necessary. All the Court professes to do is to decide the questions of community law that are referred to without considering the relevance of these questions in the context of the national litigation. But see *Simmenthal*, infra at 1527.

Whether the Court will persist in limiting its task to abstract law finding remains to be seen. It would seem that uniformity of interpretation of community law can be promoted more effectively by a more flexible approach, including a willingness to apply the law to facts stated.

### (iii) *SUBMISSION BY NATIONAL TRIBUNALS*

Many of the provisions of the Treaty and of implementing measures must be applied directly by national tribunals. In an effort to promote uniformity of interpretation, Article 177 of the Treaty makes the Court competent to render preliminary decisions on issues of community law that arise in litigation conducted before national tribunals. Under Article 177, the issues of community law on which a preliminary decision may be sought must concern (a) the interpretation of the Treaty, (b) the validity and interpretation of acts of institutions of the Community, or (c) if prescribed by the statutes of any bodies created by the Council, the interpretation of such statutes. When any such issue arises in national litigation, the national tribunal may, and if no appeal lies from its judgment must, request a ruling from the Court. Although the language of Article 177, in prescribing the conduct of national courts confronted with an issue of community law, raises problems of interpretation, this seems to be its fair construction.

Thus far, the Court, in deciding cases brought before it under Article 177, has tended to have a somewhat limited conception of its task: It states merely the proper interpretation of the legal provision involved without applying the provision to the facts in the case before it. However, the Court has given itself a measure of leeway by, if need be, interpreting questions submitted broadly and in some instances by answering questions that had not been asked, but had to be resolved in deciding the controversy before the national tribunal.

### (iv) *SUBMISSION BY PRIVATE PERSONS*

Under the Treaty, a natural or legal person may complain to the Court of either action or inaction by EEC institutions. In the circumstances defined in Article 173, a person may seek review of a decision addressed to him or a decision [of the Council or Commission] that, "although in the form of a regulation or a decision addressed to another person, is of direct and specific concern to him." Article 175 authorizes a private person to complain to the Court that one of the institutions of the Community, although afforded a two months' period of grace, "has failed to address to him an act other than a recommendation or an opinion." Employees of the Community may sue it before the Court under the conditions specified in Article 179. Article 181 renders the Court competent to act upon an arbitration clause in a contract concluded by or on behalf of the Community and private persons.

The Treaty does not authorize private persons to complain before the Court of acts performed or failures to act by member states in violation of the Treaty. However, Article 177 indicates the manner in which such complaints can eventually be channeled to the Court for a preliminary ruling. Furthermore, a private person can request the appropriate EEC institutions or his own state to submit a complaint of Treaty violation.

### (v) *GENERAL PROVISIONS*

Most of the provisions that define the questions the Court may decide prescribe specifically or by clear implication by whom such questions may be submitted. However, there are a few provisions that are formulated more broadly. Article 172 authorizes the Council to confer on the Court full competence in all matters relating to penalties prescribed in its regulations. Regulation 17, implementing Articles 85 and 86 of the Treaty, forms an important example of a case in which the Council has exercised this authority. Furthermore, Article 178 grants the Court full competence to adjudicate claims against the Community grounded in principles of noncontractual liability.

The initiation of proceedings before the Court does not occasion a stay of the effectiveness of the acts complained of. However, Article 185, while stating this general rule, provides that the Court may order a stay. Of great importance is Article 187 which makes judgments of the Court enforceable in the member states under the conditions specified in Article 192. This Article declares decisions of the Council or Commission imposing a pecuniary obligation enforceable in member states in accordance with the rules regulating execution upon domestic judgments.

Pursuant to Article 188, the Court has formulated itself the rules governing proceedings before it.

### (5) The Economic and Social Committee

The 109 members of this Committee are appointed by the Council for a renewable term of four years. According to Article 193, the Committee's members shall come from varied walks of economic and social life, including industry, trade, labor, and the general public. In many instances, its advice must be sought before the Council or Commission may proceed. The Committee is divided into sections whose fields of interest relate to the various areas covered in the Treaty, including specifically agriculture and transport.

### (6) The European Social Fund

The European Social Fund is assigned the general task of increasing the availability of employment and the geographical and occupational mobility of workers within the Community. Administered by the Commission, which is assisted for that purpose by a special committee, the Fund provides financial assistance to public programs of occupational retraining, resettlement, and temporary aid to employees of enterprises that change to other production. In an elaborate Regulation, the Council has specified the functions of the special committee and the conditions under which the Fund disburses its financial aid.

### (7) The European Investment Bank

The European Investment Bank has as its principal task, by granting loans and guarantees, to help the development of less developed regions and to facilitate modernization of enterprises and the undertaking of projects of common interest to member states. A separate Protocol regulates the contributions of the member states to the Bank's capital and contains provisions as to administration of the Bank.

(8) Other Advisory Committees

The Treaty provides for the creation of a number of advisory committees in addition to the Economic and Social Committee. These are generally intended to be rather small bodies of experts, who assist the Commission in carrying out its more specialized tasks, and include the Committee on Transport, the Monetary Committee, and others. See, e.g., Articles 83, 105, 111, 113, and 124.

*f. Means of Implementation of Treaty Provisions*

The Treaty provides for five kinds of measures that may be taken by the Council and the Commission whenever the Treaty bestows powers of implementation: Regulations, directives, decisions, and recommendations or opinions (Article 189). However, when the Treaty specifically provides for the use of a particular measure, only that measure may be employed. See, e.g., Articles 43, 54(2), 63(2), 87, and 94. It has further been argued that in some instances the Treaty grants implementing powers *sui generis* that cannot be rubricated within the categories of Article 189. See, e.g., Article 14(7).

(1) Regulations

Regulations are legislative measures that are directly binding in all member states. They must state the reasons that moved their adoption and refer to the proposals and comments required by the Treaty (Article 190). They must be promulgated in the Official Journal and become effective on the date specified in the regulation or on the twentieth day after their promulgation (Article 191).

(2) Directives

Directives are binding orders addressed to member states requiring them to accomplish a stated purpose, while leaving them freedom in the selection of the form in which, and the means by which, that purpose is to be achieved (Article 189). In certain circumstances, directives, such as directives prohibiting state action, may create directly enforceable rights for the citizens. Directives must also state the grounds for their adoption and refer to comments received from bodies whose consultation is required, but need not be promulgated in the Official Journal (Articles 190 and 191). They are communicated to the member states by means not specified in the Treaty.

(3) Decisions

Decisions are determinations binding only upon the states or persons to whom they are addressed. The provisions of Article 190 also apply to decisions, which need not be promulgated. The means by which they are communicated are not prescribed by the Treaty.

(4) Recommendations or Opinions

The nature of recommendations or opinions is indicated by their name. As Article 189(4) prescribes, they have no binding force.

*g. Financial Affairs*

The financial affairs of the Community are regulated in Articles 199 through 209 of the Treaty, as amended by the Merger Treaty, the Luxembourg Treaty of April 22, 1970, the Treaty of 1975, and the Treaties of

Accession. The financial year runs from January 1 through December 31. Each of the institutions draws up its own budget which it submits to the Commission. The Commission combines these budgets into a preliminary draft budget. This preliminary draft, together with its views on, and suggested changes in, the component parts, the Commission submits to the Council on or before September 30 of the year preceding that covered by the budget. The Council, after consultation with the institutions whose proposed budgets it wishes to change, draws up the draft budget by a qualified majority vote and transmits it to the Assembly on or before October 31. The European Parliament may propose, and as to discretionary expenditures make, amendments. If it does not do so within one month, the budget is approved. If the Assembly does recommend or make timely amendments, the draft is returned to the Council, which, after discussion with the Commission and other appropriate institutions, approves the budget of its liking by qualified majority vote. As to discretionary expenditures, this vote may again be overridden by Parliament by majority vote representing 60% of those voting.

Each member state must contribute to the budget in accordance with scales. Other scales determine the proportion of contributions to the European Investment Bank and to the Development Fund for the Overseas Countries and Territories. The adjustments made in the scale of contributions to the expenses of the European Social Fund are also reflected in the scale according to which the votes of the members of the Council are weighted when the Council determines the budget of the Fund. See Article 203(5).

Article 201 contemplates the replacement of financial contributions of member states by the "Community's own resources." This has come to pass. A Decision of 21 April 1970, on the replacement of financial contributions from member states by the Communities' own resources, Off.Journ.1970, No. L 94 p. 19, provides that the Communities receive directly the Common Customs Tariff duties and the agricultural levies levied at the border of the Communities by national customs officials and, in addition, as the budget may require, up to 1% of the member states' value added tax. The maximum VAT rate has been raised from 1 to 1.4% by Decision of May 7, 1985, Off.Jour.1985, No. L 128 p. 15, in the context of the accession of Spain and Portugal. This decision entered into force on January 1, 1986, and replaces the Decision of 1970.

### h. *Admission to, and Agreements with, the Community*

The Treaty mentions two kinds of international agreements that may be concluded by the Community: (1) agreements establishing an association with the Community (Article 238), and (2) agreements relating to tariffs and commercial policy (Article 113). The procedure to be followed in negotiating and concluding such agreements is specified in the Treaty. As a general rule, the Commission negotiates and the Council concludes agreements between the Community and another state or international organization. See Article 228. The Community, in addition to the powers to negotiate and conclude international agreements specified in the Treaty, has implied authority to conclude international agreements in other areas of its concern. See 5 Smit & Herzog Prelim. Obs. on Arts. 189–192, No. 7.

(1) Admission to Membership

According to Article 237, every European state—and the term European is to be taken in a broad sense—may address an application for membership to the Council, which must solicit the views of the Commission and may rule favorably on the application only by unanimous vote. The conditions for membership and the necessary amendments to the Treaty are to be incorporated in an agreement between the old member states and the applicant, which must be ratified by all signatories in accordance with their constitutional laws. Application of the United Kingdom, Ireland, and Denmark led to admission on January 1, 1973; those of Greece, Portugal and Spain to admission on January 1, 1986.

(2) Agreements of Association

Association agreements may be concluded with any state, union of states, or international organization. The only requirements imposed by the Treaty as to their contents is that they must create "an association embodying reciprocal rights and obligations, joint actions and special procedures." The Community has established a network of trading agreements with countries on all continents in the form of association agreements, free trade agreements, and cooperation agreements.

(i) *ASSOCIATION WITH TURKEY*

The Agreement of Association with Turkey became effective on December 1, 1964. It provides for a preparatory stage of 5 years, which may be and has been extended during which Turkey, with the help of the Community, will prepare itself for the introduction of a program leading to a customs union. The assistance to be given by the Community during this stage consisted of annual tariff quotas for Turkish products and of financial aid in the form of loans for economic development.

During the transitional stage, which was to last for 12 years, Turkey was to make the gradual adjustments that will lead to a complete customs union and to harmonization of economic policies by the end of the stage. The timetables and other details relating to the transitional period are regulated in a separate protocol signed in 1970.

An Association Council, which acts by unanimous vote and is composed of representatives of the member states, Turkey, and the Community, is to take the necessary implementing measures. Disputes may be submitted to the Court or be settled by arbitration or other appropriate procedures.

(ii) *ASSOCIATION OF OVERSEAS COUNTRIES AND TERRITORIES*

Part IV of the Treaty, encompassing Articles 131 through 136, concerns the relations of the Community to the non-European countries and territories that, at the time the Treaty was negotiated, were in some way under the dominion of the member states. Annexed to the Treaty, at the time it went into effect, was an Association Convention concluded with such states in Africa. A new convention was signed with 18 African states and Malagasy on July 20, 1963, and went into effect on June 1, 1964. This so-called Yaounde Convention was renewed by the signing of a new Convention on July 29, 1969, and upon the latter's expiration, was followed by the Lomé Convention, infra. Part IV continues to apply to St. Pierre and Miquelon, the Comoro Archipelago, the French Somali Coast, New Caledonia, the French settlements in Oceania, Surinam, and the Southern and Antarctic Territories. Furthermore, pursuant to a special convention between the member states, which became effective on October 1, 1964, the Netherlands Antilles were added to the countries that come under the regime of Part IV. See Official Gazette No. 150, Oct. 1, 1964, p. 2413.

The association with these dependent territories is governed both by the Treaty and by provisions adopted by the Council pursuant to Article 136(2). See Official Gazette No. 93, June 11, 1964, p. 1472. The Council's provisions relating to trade and aid follow in essence the parallel provisions in the Yaounde Convention, concluded with the 19 newly independent African states.

On February 28, 1975, the EEC concluded in Lomé an association agreement with a large number of African, Pacific, and Caribbean (APC) countries. The Lomé Convention follows in broad lines and supersedes the Yaounde Convention, the Arusha Convention (which had been concluded with Eastern African States), and other association agreements concluded with non-European States.

(3) Tariff and Commercial Agreements

The Treaty aims for a co-ordinated economic policy in regard to outsiders and provides for the conclusion by the Community of international tariff and commercial agreements with other states. The Treaty designates the Commission as the institution that is to conduct the negotiations in consultation with a Special Committee appointed by the Council. However, the Commission may open negotiations only upon authorization by the Council. Agreements negotiated by the Commission are concluded on behalf of the Community by the Council. In all these matters, the Council, after the end of the second stage, acts by a qualified majority vote.

On the basis of these provisions, the Community has concluded a number of trade agreements. These provisions also form the legal basis on which the Commission has participated in the so-called Dillon, Kennedy, Tokyo and Uruguay Rounds of negotiations with the countries that are parties to the General Agreement on Tariffs and Trade (GATT).

*i. Miscellaneous*

The sixth and final part of the Treaty, while harboring provisions of assorted plumage, deals principally with the status of the Community in regard to outsiders, including both sovereign states and private persons, as well as insiders, the latter category embracing both officials and employees of the Community.

According to Article 210, the Community has legal personality. Article 211 bestows upon it in each member state the most extensive legal capacity accorded by the municipal law of that state.

The Council is entrusted by Article 24 of the Merger Treaty with the task of prescribing the conditions of service of Community officials and employees.

Article 213 authorizes the Commission to collect information under conditions specified by the Council. Member states may refuse to supply information, however, if the conditions specified in Article 223 are met.

A duty not to disclose information in the nature of a professional secret is imposed on all Community officials and employees by Article 214.

Article 215 contains most interesting provisions as to the contractual and non-contractual liability of the Community. The contractual liability of the Community is governed by "the law applying to the contract concerned;" its non-contractual liability shall be determined "in accordance with the general principles common to the laws of Member States." The giving of more concrete contents to these rather indeterminate provisions will undoubtedly prove an intellectually challenging task. See Bayerische HNL, Cases No. 83 and 94/76, 4, 15 and 40/77, 197 & SECR 1209.

By Regulation 1, issued pursuant to Article 217, the official and working languages of the Community are German, French, Italian, Dutch, English and Danish. Separate rules regulate the use of language in the Court of Justice.

Article 235 grants the Council general authority, by unanimous vote on a proposal of the Commission and after consultation with the Assembly, to enact provisions granting the powers necessary to further the aims of the Community.

Article 240, finally, provides that the Treaty is concluded for an unlimited period.

### *3. Implementation of the Common Market: Treaty Provisions and Developments to Date*

Elaborating upon the enumeration provided in Article 3, the Treaty accords detailed treatment to the various means to be employed in achieving the Common Market. The following summary deals with some of the principal provisions and describes developments that have occurred since the Treaty became effective. It does not discuss the gradual adjustments to be made by the new members.

#### *a. Rules Dealing With Specific Aspects of Economic Life*

(1) Free Movement of Goods

##### (i) *ELIMINATION OF INTERNAL CUSTOMS DUTIES AND EQUIVALENT LEVIES*

The manner in which internal import and export duties are to be eliminated is regulated in Articles 12 through 17 of the Treaty. Member states may neither create new duties and equivalent levies nor increase existing ones. Existing import duties and equivalent charges had to be abolished within the transitional period which ended on January 1, 1970. The timing and percentages of the periodic reductions of customs duties are prescribed in the Treaty. However, in accordance with Article 14(7), the Council of Ministers, by unanimous vote, has from time to time accelerated reductions, so that, as of July 1, 1968, the duties on industrial goods had been eliminated. As a complement to this, the common external tariff was instituted on the same date. The Commission has taken the necessary measures to ensure observance by member states of their obligations in this area.

According to Article 16, export duties and equivalent levies were to be abolished at the end of the first stage, on January 1, 1962.

Considerable progress has also been made in the abolition of internal levies equivalent to customs duties. The Commission has studied hundreds of charges, many of which have been disposed of.

As a general rule, the provisions relating to the gradual elimination of internal duties—as all other provisions prescribing the establishment of the Common Market—also apply to agricultural products. Article 38, paragraph 2, specifically so provides. However, in the field of agriculture, which was a matter of special concern to the drafters of the Treaty and is the subject of detailed regulation in Articles 38 through 47 of the Treaty, exceptions may be made within the framework of measures authorized by these provisions. The products to which special measures may be made applicable are listed in Annex II to the Treaty, to which the Council, pursuant to Article 38(3), made the last possible additions by Regulation 7a, Dec. 18, 1959, 1961 O.J. 71.

Since the Treaty became effective, the Council and the Commission have adopted a large number of regulations designed to establish common market organizations for specified agricultural products. Virtually all of the Community's agricultural output has been brought under the coverage of EEC regulation. Broadly speaking, the numerous regulations issued in regard to these agricultural products establish regimes of variable levies on imports and of variable refunds on exports designed to bridge the gap between the local price and the foreign price of the product. To the extent that they are not the subject of common market organizations, agricultural products remain under the general regime of Articles 12 through 17.

(ii) *ELIMINATION OF INTERNAL QUANTITATIVE RESTRICTIONS*

This subject is treated in Articles 30 through 37 of the Treaty. Quotas on imports in internal trade more restrictive than those in effect on January 1, 1958, may not be imposed. Furthermore, all internal quotas on imports had to be abolished at the latest by January 1, 1970. Export quotas in internal trade are prohibited; those on trade with non-member countries had to be eliminated by the end of the first stage. Measures equivalent in effect to import and export quotas are subject to the same provisions. However, prohibitions or restrictions in regard to import, export or transit may be imposed when justified on grounds of public safety, the protection of national treasures, or for similar reasons. Article 33 of the Treaty contains detailed provisions regulating the gradual elimination of import quotas, which, however, have lost most of their importance because of the quicker pace with which the member states have proceeded toward abolition of all quotas. Indeed, there remain only few products for which quotas determined in accordance with Article 33 still exist. The Commission nevertheless remains intent upon further elimination of quotas.

While quotas are largely abolished, much remains to be done towards elimination of measures equivalent to quantitative restrictions and of administrative formalities. The Commission has been working on various measures designed to eliminate provisions that are equivalent to quantitative restrictions and all but a few formalities regarding imports and exports. It also expects that the harmonization of legislation of member states will remove many obstacles that are equivalent in their effect to quantitative restrictions.

Within the context of provisions regulating the elimination of internal quantitative restrictions, Article 37 requires the gradual adjustment of state monopolies so as to ensure, at the expiration of the transitional period, the elimination of "all discrimination between nationals of member states in regard to conditions of supply or marketing." As long as this elimination has not been effectuated, the Commission may authorize other member states to apply protective measures.

The Commission has addressed recommendations on desirable adjustments to member states pursuant to Article 37, paragraph 6, of the Treaty.

### (iii) *CREATION OF A COMMON EXTERNAL TARIFF*

The aim of Articles 18 through 20 of the Treaty is the gradual establishment within the transitional period of a tariff on goods imported from non-member states that is the same in all member states. According to Article 19, as a general rule, this common tariff shall be the arithmetical average of the tariffs levied in the four customs territories on January 1, 1957. This general rule is subject to a number of exceptions. Under some, tariffs on goods listed on specified lists may not exceed percentages enumerated in the Treaty. Some tariffs are fixed in a list appended to the Treaty. Still others are to be subject to tariffs to be determined by negotiations among the member states or, in case no agreement can be reached, by the Council. Further, depending on the product involved, the Council or the Commission, may, in case of threatening short supply, grant tariff quotas at a reduced rate. The Commission also has general authority to authorize a member state "encountering special difficulties" to postpone, subject to specified limitations, the lowering or raising of the duties on certain headings of its tariff.

Member states must, to the extent necessary, harmonize their customs legislation and administration. Changes in the common tariff may be made by unanimous vote of the Council and, after January 1, 1970, if the changes are limited in time and scope as provided in the Treaty, by qualified majority vote of the Council.

Ahead of the schedule prescribed by the Treaty, the Council, by Regulation No. 950/68 of June 28, 1968, provided that the common external tariff be in effect as of July 1, 1968. However, exceptions have been made with regard to particular products. A number of duties have been temporarily suspended or reduced by the Council pursuant to Article 28. Also, although representing only a very small percentage of the total Community imports from non-member states, a fair number of tariff quotas, authorizing reduced tariffs for specified quantities of particular products, have been granted under Article 25. Further, in pursuance of the Council's important decision of April 4, 1962, in the agricultural sector the Commission has authorized the imposition of countervailing charges, designed to adjust the price of the imported to that of the domestic product, on imports of certain goods processed from agricultural products.

Acting in the spirit of Article 27, the Commission has formulated a program for common customs legislation concerning such matters as nomenclature, customs valuation, a common list of exceptions on economic grounds, a definition of origin, temporary admission, customs clearance, dumping practices, bonded warehouses, free ports, and the elimination of formalities. This program is inspired not only by the desire to promote internal as well as external trade, but also by the necessity to implement the customs union and to develop uniform regulation in all member states eliminating barriers and aids that distort the free flow of trade into and within the Community. It has led to adoption by the Council of regulations concerning nomenclature, customs valuation, the origin of goods, and transit of goods.

### (iv) *PROTECTIVE MEASURES*

The Treaty, in addition to creating possibilities for mostly limited escape from each of the three sets of provisions requiring elimination of internal duties, abolition of quantitative restrictions, and creation of a common outer tariff, enables resort to protective measures that may cut across all of the provisions of Title I of Part II. Article 115 permits the Commission to authorize states to take protective measures in order to avoid diversion of trade or economic difficulties occasioned by the common commercial policy. In case of emergency during the transitional period, a state may even adopt such measures without prior authorization by the Commission, which may, however, subsequently order that such measures be modified or revoked. Article 226 goes even further and generally permits the Commission to authorize a state to take protective measures that involve deviations "from the provisions of this Treaty." However, these measures may be taken only during the transitional period and under prescribed conditions which include "difficulties which may seriously impair the economic situation in any region."

Protective measures under Article 115 or Article 226 have been taken in a not inconsiderable number of cases.

### (2) Common Agricultural Policy

Because the field of agriculture provides fertile soil for an abundant harvest of complex problems, it was proposed at the negotiations that led to the signing of the Treaty to exclude agriculture from its coverage. However, the proponents of inclusion prevailed, and Articles 38 through 47 of the Treaty provide the basic rules under which a common market in agricultural products is to be achieved. As was expected, implementation of these rules has created grave difficulties which, both in 1962 and 1964, threatened the very existence of the EEC. Both times, however, the differing views of the member states were reconciled and important regulations adopted.

Traditionally, agriculture has been the beneficiary of protective measures. Its dependence on unpredictable climatic conditions frequently occasioned hardships: Good conditions led to oversupply; bad ones to loss of crops or poor harvests. In time, the farmer came to look to the state to protect him from such hardships by keeping prices at a level that guaranteed him a reasonable return. Furthermore, a desire to maintain a certain level of national self-sufficiency in agricultural production also promoted adoption of protectionist measures. Usually, these protectionist measures consist of high tariffs, if necessary qualified by tariff quotas, of quantitative restrictions, and of price supports.

The Treaty anticipates the reluctance of member states to jettison these protectionist schemes altogether. In principle, the Treaty is based on the idea that intra-Community trade should be subject to the untrammeled forces of free competition and that regulation is needed only to remove barriers that interfere with the free play of competition. However, as to agricultural products, the Treaty provides the Community with the choice of either free competition or a regulated economy. In numerous measures, the Community, proceeding under the exceptional provisions of Articles 39 through 46, has opted for the second alternative as to most of its agricultural production.

The principal thrust of the Community regulation is to substitute Community market organizations for national market organizations. Community regulation is on a product-by-product basis: For each product, although usually similar in essentials, it is frequently different as to details.

The market organization for the various agricultural products have been put in effect by hundreds of Council and Commission regulations and decisions. Indeed, the pressures that have led to differentiating treatment of the various products have produced rather complicated sets of rules whose import can here be sketched only with a broad brush.

Community regulation generally follows the basic pattern laid down in Regulation No. 120/67, which creates a common market organization for most grain products (for simplicity's sake, called cereals). This market organization has a triple aspect. First, it eliminates tariffs on intra-Community commerce; second, it protects the internal price structure against cheaper imports from third states; and third, it assists the exporter in exporting his products to lower-price states.

In order to regulate the internal price, the Community must set a target price. This is the price that the Community considers the appropriate minimum wholesale price for the product involved in the market in which there is the greatest deficiency in the supply of the product (for cereals, Duisburg). A target price must be protected by an intervention price, which is the price at which the intervention agency of a member state must enter the market to prevent the product from dropping unduly below the target price.

It is clear that by purchasing all products offered for sale at or below the intervention price, the Community can effectively maintain an internal price close to the target price level. However, if imports of cheaper products were freely permitted, the Community's purchasing power might be sorely tested. Therefore, provision is made for the imposition of levies on imports from third states that are designed to increase the price of the imported product to the level of the target price. Conversely, in order to permit export of agricultural products to non-member states, member states are authorized to grant their exporters a refund or subsidy that will decrease the export price to the level prevailing in the country to which the export is made. Since the prices on foreign markets fluctuate, the levies and refunds are adjusted constantly and are therefore called variable.

The appropriate levy is computed by reference to the threshold price and the c.i.f. price. The threshold price is the price that would have to be charged for the product at the border point of entry in order for it to bring the target price in the market area in which there exists the greatest deficiency in supply. The c.i.f. price is determined by the Commission on the basis of the most favorable price on the world market for delivery c.i.f. to the border crossing point (Rotterdam, for cereals). The proper levy on imports from a non-member state is the difference between the c.i.f. price and the threshold price.

The refund or export subsidy that may be granted on exports from a high-price member state to a low-price non-member state is determined periodically by the Council.

The target prices have been set at a level that does not guarantee a reasonable return in the markets of at least some member states. Provision is therefore made for paying compensation for losses suffered by producers in such markets. This compensation is scheduled to decrease as time progresses, so that producers will be encouraged to phase out their production gradually.

For the purpose of financing the operation of Community-wide market organizations, the Council has set up a separate fund, called the European Agricultural Guidance and Guarantee Fund (EAGGF). The function of the Fund is to finance refunds on exports, intervention prices, and compensation paid to producers harmed by introduction of the single-price system. The revenues of the Fund consist primarily of contributions made by member states.

As these market organizations were created and implemented, serious problems developed. First, the fear of many that support prices would be maintained at too high a level were realized to a not inconsiderable extent. This, coupled with steady technological improvement of production methods resulting in higher yields, led to mounting surpluses, especially of butter, milk powder, wheat, and sugar. Second, in 1969 France devaluated, and Germany revaluated, its currency. These prompted both countries to take special measures to avoid disruption of their agricultural markets caused by a sudden increase in support prices (set in units of account that would not reflect the devaluation) in France and a sudden decrease in support prices and, at least initially, higher market prices for importers in Germany. Third, the financial arrangements for the various market organizations which left considerable authority in the member states proved increasingly awkward.

These problems prompted the Commission in December 1968 to submit a Memorandum on the Reform of Agriculture in the EEC urging a Community price policy in the various market organizations and concentration of the financial arrangements in the hands of the Community. In the marathon session, held towards the end of December 1969, the proposed financial arrangements were approved by the Council. The ultimate goal of the price supports is to accommodate Community prices to those prevailing on world markets. However, thus far it has proved politically impossible to reach that goal. In the most recent Uruguay Round under the GATT, the United States has insisted that the Community substantially reduce its price supports. Agreement was reached in December 1992. France protested, but acknowledged that it could not veto the Community's agreement.

(3) Free Movement of Persons, Services, and Capital

The Treaty seeks to eliminate not only impediments to the free flow of goods, but also barriers to free movement of persons (Articles 48–58), services (Articles 59–66), and capital (Articles 67–73). The thrust of the provisions in all three areas, which together constitute Title III of Part II of the Treaty, is that the restrictions with which they deal must be eliminated within the transitional period, that no new restrictions may be introduced, and that only restrictions designed to serve the public order, safety, and health may be maintained or imposed. As of January 1, 1993, all border controls between Member States have been abolished.

(i) *WORKERS*

Chapter I of Title III contains provisions that regulate the elimination of discrimination based on nationality in all matters relating to employment of workers, a broad term that encompasses all persons working for wages or salary, including professional athletes. Free movement of workers, within the meaning of Articles 48 and 49, was achieved by Regulation No. 1612/68 and Directive No. 68/360.

(ii) *RIGHT OF ESTABLISHMENT*

Chapter II of Title III deals with the right of establishment. It provides for abolition in the course of the transitional period of restrictions on the freedom of establishment. The term nationals includes both natural persons and companies established under the laws of, and having their registered office, central administration, or principal place of business in, a member state. In contradistinction to the provisions on the movement of workers, the provisions on freedom of establishment, like those relating to free movement of services, in terms go beyond requiring merely abolition of discrimination based on nationality: they provide for abolition of all restrictions for nationals of member states. The right of free establishment accorded by the Treaty accrues to anyone who carries on non-wage-earning activities through an establishment.

An important part of the Council's task in this area consists of the issuance of directives concerning the recognition of diplomas, certificates, and other qualifications. Pursuant to Article 54, the Council has formulated a General Program for the Abolition of Restrictions on Freedom of Establishment, which indicates in detail and by reference to particular economic activities how the Treaty goals are to be achieved. See Official Gazette No. 2, Jan. 15, 1962, p. 36. Many directives addressed to particular forms of establishments and services have been adopted.

(iii) *SERVICES*

Chapter III, dealing with free movement of services, complements Chapters I and II. Providing for abolition of all restrictions on nationals of member states in the rendition of services within the Community, it covers activities that are neither wage- nor salary-earning activities nor activities conducted through an establishment.

Pursuant to Article 63(1), the Council, on December 18, 1961, issued a General Program for the Abolition of Restrictions on the Freedom to Render Services, which particularizes the manner and time within which the rendition of specified services was to be liberalized. See Official Gazette No. 2, Jan. 15, 1962, p. 32.

(iv) *CAPITAL*

Chapter IV, relating to the free movement of capital, in one respect is of more limited ambition than its three predecessors: It prescribes abolition of restrictions only "to the extent necessary for the proper functioning of the Common Market." However, the benefit of its provisions accrues to all persons resident in member states regardless of their nationality, and it explicitly proscribes discrimination based either on nationality or place of residence or on the place in which the capital is to be invested. Member states are exhorted to be nondiscriminatory and as liberal as possible in the granting of foreign exchange licenses. The introduction of a common currency by 1999 contemplated by the Union Treaty will, of course, displace the EC Treaty provisions.

(4) Transportation

Surface transportation in the member states is the subject of encompassing national regulation. In addition, all railway transportation is, either directly or indirectly, in the hands of the national governments. These circumstances required that the Treaty devote special attention to transportation and provide the means for adjusting national regulation and practices to a Community-wide transportation system. Articles 74 through 84, constituting Title IV, which concludes Part II of the Treaty, seek to provide these means and require the evolution of a common policy in regard to transportation within the transitional period. The Treaty provisions apply to transportation by rail, on the road, and on inland waterways. The Council is given the power, by unanimous vote, to adopt rules regulating maritime and air transportation. The Council has taken significant steps towards replacing state regulation of air transportation by competition.

In addition to requiring development of a common transportation policy, the Treaty, in Article 76, commands member states to refrain from applying national provisions in a manner that results in discrimination on the basis of nationality. Discrimination in transportation rates and conditions on the basis of country of origin or destination of the goods carried is outlawed by Article 79(1) and Regulation No. 11 of June 27, 1960, Official Gazette No. 52, Aug. 16, 1960, p. 1121. Favoring particular enterprises by prescribing special rates and conditions is also prohibited, but aid needed to coordinate transportation or to sustain operations partaking of the nature of a public utility is permitted. Charges collected for frontier crossings may not exceed a reasonable level.

The Commission has submitted to the Council action programs for implementation of the Treaty provisions on transportation. In pursuit of these programs, the Council has adopted a number of the Commission's proposals.

The greatest progress has been made in regard to road transportation. A system of Community licenses (quotas) has been created, a standard rate system has been introduced, and social measures have been harmonized.

Rail transportation and transportation by inland waterways have been affected to a lesser extent by Community measures, but here again the Commission keeps pressing for greater activity by the Council.

No agreement has yet been reached on how to apply the Treaty provisions and Regulation No. 11 to Rhine shipping. Pipeline transportation is also still an object of study.

The Commission is continuing the very detailed study of transportation and its national regulation that it commenced right after the Treaty became effective and that forms the basis for all of its proposals in this area.

*b. General Policies*

(1) Antitrust Policy

Articles 85 through 94, the first in Part III, entitled Policy of the Community, contain the basic rules governing competition in the Community. Their brevity stands in inverse proportion both to their present and to their potential importance. They evidence one of the most basic decisions taken in devising the structure of the Common Market, namely, that the Community shall be based on a regime of free competition rather than of extensive official regulation. In the countries of the EEC in which antitrust laws and, more importantly, antitrust enforcement had thus far played only a limited role, these provisions mark the beginning of a new era in which anticompetitive protective measures, both of an official and a private nature, will have to give way to freer forces of competition.

The interpretation and implementation of Articles 85 and 86, outlawing what may broadly be called agreements in restraint of trade and improper monopolistic practices, have already generated much dispute and controversy. Implementing regulations requiring registration of anticompetitive agreements have brought forth a deluge of registrations.

The Council has authorized the Commission to grant group exemptions to certain categories of agreements, including distribution and licensing agreements. The Commission has issued group exemptions for all of these categories.

Under the general heading of Rules Governing Competition, the Treaty also deals with dumping practices (Article 91) and government subsidies (Articles 92 through 94). On March 11, 1960, the Commission issued Regulation No. 8/60, implementing Article 91(2) of the Treaty, the so-called "boomerang" provision. Under this provision, all dumped goods may be re-exported to the dumping country free of all charges. Article 92 declares subsidies disturbing competition incompatible with the Common Market. Certain kinds of subsidies are specifically characterized in the Treaty as being compatible or not compatible with the Common Market.

(2) Tax Policy

The provisions of Articles 95 through 99 of the Treaty are designed to lead to proper modification of provisions of national tax laws that stand in the way of achievement of the Community's goals. Of great importance is Article 99 which requires the Council, upon proposal of the Commission and by unanimous vote, to take the necessary measures to harmonize all forms of indirect taxation in the member states. Acting on the basis of the well-known Neumark Report, a report of the Fiscal and Financial Committee on Tax Harmonization in the Common Market under the chairmanship of Professor Fritz Neumark, the Commission, on November 5, 1962, laid before the Council the first draft directive to harmonize legislation on turnover taxes. After the Economic and Social Committee and the European Parliament had issued their opinion on this draft, the Commission submitted a revised draft to the Council on June 9, 1964. It took three more years before the Council finally acted on these proposals and adopted a number of directives to carry them out. The brunt of these directives was the requirement that the member states replace, by the latest on January 1, 1970, their systems of turnover taxes by a system of taxation on added value, under which a turnover tax imposed on a product that passes through various stages on the way from manufacturer to consumer is calculated only on the basis of the value added in the stage at which the tax is imposed. France, Holland, Germany, and Luxembourg complied with these directives and introduced an added-value tax. Belgium and Italy declared they needed more time to make the necessary adjustments. In view of these developments, the Council postponed until January 1, 1973, the ultimate date on which the member states had to have introduced an added value type tax. Italy met the deadline on the last day.

The Council has adopted a directive requiring harmonization of taxes on accumulations of capital and abolition of stamp duties on the sale of securities and is working on various other projects in this area.

The implementation of the VAT directives has been plagued with problems. The Council has been forced to carve out numerous temporary exemptions to meet the exigencies of particular national policies and defer the introduction of the VAT system to less industrialized countries such as Greece. At the same time, it has also vigorously prosecuted countries which violate the various taxation directives. Numerous proposals for development and furthering of a uniform European VAT system are pending, and the process of harmonization of the tax law is proceeding slowly.

(3) Harmonization of Laws

In addition to providing for harmonization or approximation of laws in specially indicated areas (see, e.g., Articles 27 and 99), the Treaty, in Articles 100 through 102, empowers the Council—in some cases the Commission—to issue directives or recommendations for approximation of laws that have a direct bearing on the establishment and functioning of the Common Market. Further, Article 220 of the Treaty exhorts the member states to conclude, if necessary, treaties on designated subjects.

Exercising the authority bestowed by Article 100, the Council has issued a great many directives.

Treaties designed to promote uniformity of law have been proposed or made in regard to patents, companies, the recognition accorded to foreign judgments, and choice of law.

In the fall of 1962, a Committee designated by the EEC, published a draft patent convention of 217 articles. The draft was to be reviewed by governments, trade associations, and professional groups. After revision in the light of the comments received, it was to be presented for approval and ratification by the member states. However, these developments did not occur, and nothing of substance happened until 1969. In March of 1969, the Council decided that the European patent was to be regulated in two conventions, the first dealing with the procedure for obtaining a patent and the second providing for uniform protection of such patents in the member states. Two Conventions on these subjects were concluded in 1973 and 1975.

Of the various proposals for the creation of a European corporation or "société commerciale de type européen," none have as yet received official EEC sanction. See, e.g., Sanders, Naar een Europese N.V. (1959); Rault, Pour la Création d'une société commerciale de type européen, 13 Revue trimestrielle de droit commerciale 741 (1960); Note, 2 Common Market L.Rev. 244–45 (1964). However, the Council has promulgated a number of directives in particular areas of corporate law and practice.

A committee of experts designated by the EEC developed a draft treaty on recognition of foreign judgments. On this draft, see Weser, Bases of Judicial Jurisdiction in the Common Market Countries, 10 Am.J.Comp.L. 323, 339–40 (1961). For criticism of the draft, see Nadelmann, Common Market Assimilation of Laws and the Outer World, 58 A.J.I.L. 724 (1964). An Agreement on this subject was signed and ratified and became effective on February 1, 1973.

In 1982, the Rome Convention on the Law Applicable to Contractual Obligations came into effect. O.J.L. 266, 9.10.1980. To ensure complete harmonization of the various national laws, Article 18 states that it is to be interpreted and applied uniformly.

In addition to being stimulated by these various measures and proposals, harmonization of national laws is or will be effectuated or promoted by measures institutions of the EEC have taken and will in the future take in areas in which they may act legislatively.

(4) Policy in Regard to Business Cycles

Article 103 of the Treaty prescribes a common policy in regard to business cycles; it gives the Council power to adopt, by unanimous vote, whatever measures may be appropriate and to implement these measures by directives adopted by qualified majority vote.

(5) Balance of Payments Policy

Articles 104 through 109 of the Treaty concern policies to be pursued in regard to the balance of payments of the member states. Equilibrium in the balance of payments in regard to both member and non-member states is to be the basic goal. Member states must coordinate their policies to achieve this objective. The Council may issue pertinent recommendations. A Monetary Committee, with consultative status, is assigned specified tasks in this area.

Balance of payments difficulties may generate investigation and recommendations by the Commission and, if necessary, specified action by the Council. Article 108 so provides. In addition, in case of a sudden crisis, a member state may provisionally take protective measures under Article 109. The Council may modify, suspend, or abolish such measures.

(6) Common Commercial Policy

Articles 110 through 116 of the Treaty contain provisions that are designed to lead gradually to, and to govern the pursuit of, a common commercial policy. Of great importance is Article 111, which, in addition to prescribing the development within the transitional period of a common policy in regard to trade with non-member states, charges the Commission with the duty of submitting proposals for appropriate action to the Council and of presenting to the Council recommendations on tariff negotiations with non-member states concerning the common customs tariff. These negotiations are to be conducted by the Commission upon authorization from, and in consultation with a special Committee appointed by, the Council. In pursuance of these provisions, the Commission, assisted by the Special 111 Committee, has conducted the Kennedy, Dillon, Tokyo, and Uruguay Rounds on negotiations on tariff reductions with adherents to the General Agreement on Tariffs and Trade (GATT).

In addition to negotiating on a multilateral scale, the Community has concluded a number of bilateral trade agreements.

The Treaty, in Article 113, requires harmonization within the transitional period of measures of export aids on goods exported to non-member states. Articles 113 and 114 provide that the common commercial policy shall be based on uniform principles and that the common commercial policy shall be based on uniform principles and that agreements with non-member states shall be negotiated by the Commission upon authorization from, and in consultation with a special Committee appointed by, the Council. Article 115 permits, in specified exceptional circumstances, protective measures, and Article 116, of fundamental importance within the scheme of the Treaty, provides that after the transitional period the Council, by qualified majority vote, may act for the member states with respect to matters arising within the framework of any international organization of an economic character. The latter category clearly encompasses such organizations as GATT, OECD, the World Bank, the International Monetary Fund, and similar organizations.

An important development is the Arrangement on Guidelines for Officially Supported Export Credits, which entered into effect in October 1983. Before ratification of the Guidelines, countries would compete for export business by attempting to offer the lowest interest rates on long term loans to foreign buyers. The purpose of the Guidelines is to eliminate this competition, enabling signatories to compete with each other on the basis of the quality of their products rather than on the amount of government subsidy.

(7) Social Policy

Articles 117 through 122 lay the basis for close cooperation and harmonization of laws in the field of social provisions, including such matters as labor legislation, social security, trade union regulation, workmen's compensation, equal pay for men and women doing equal work, paid vacation, and similar subjects. The Council has issued a number of regulations prescribing the collection of data concerning wages and other employers' costs in designated areas of economic endeavor. It has also negotiated an agreement with the International Labour Organization providing for collaboration in the improvement of living and working conditions of workers and issued a number of recommendations relating to such subjects as a uniform list of occupational diseases, social services for migrant workers, and equal pay for men and women.

Because of the depressed state of the European economy in the early 1980's, a major social policy goal was the protection and retraining of workers in declining industries. Many programs in pursuit of this goal have been adopted.

### 4. *The Transnational Character of the EEC*

## ITALIAN FINANCE ADMINISTRATION v. SIMMENTHAL S.p.A.

Court of Justice of the European Communities, Case No. 106/77.
March 8, 1978, 1978 E.C.R. 629, CCH C.M.R. ¶ 8476.

* * *

OPINION

In an order of July 28, 1977 received at the Court on August 29, 1977, the Pretore of Susa referred to the Court of Justice for a ruling pursuant to Article 177 of the EEC Treaty, two questions relating to the principle of the direct applicability of Community law as set out in Article 189 of the Treaty for the purpose of determining the effects of that principle when a rule of Community law conflicts with a subsequent provision of national law.

It is appropriate to draw attention to the fact that at a previous stage of the proceedings the Pretore referred to the Court of Justice for a preliminary ruling questions designed to enable him to decide whether veterinary and public health control fees levied on imports of beef and veal under the consolidated text of the Italian veterinary and public health laws, the rate of which was last fixed in the scale annexed to Law No. 1239 of December 30, 1970 (Gazzetta Ufficiale No. 26 of February 1, 1971), were compatible with the Treaty and with certain regulations—in particular Council Regulation (EEC) No. 805/68 of June 27, 1968, on the common organization of the market in beef and veal (Official Journal, English Special Edition 1968 (I), page 187). Having regard to the answers given by the Court in its judgment of December 15, 1976, in Case No. 35/76 (Simmenthal S.p.A. v. Italian Minister for Finance [1976] E.C.R. 1871), the Pretore held that the levying of the fees in question was incompatible with the provisions of Community law and ordered the Amministrazione delle Finanze dello Stato (Italian Finance Administration) to repay the fees unlawfully charged, together with interest.

The Amministrazione appealed against that order.

The Pretore, taking into account the arguments put forward by the parties during the proceedings arising out of this appeal, held that the issue before him involved a conflict between certain rules of Community law and a subsequent national law, namely the said Law No. 1239/70. He pointed out that in order to resolve an issue of this kind, according to recently decided cases of the Italian Constitutional Court (Judgments No. 232/75 and No. 205/76 and Order No. 206/76), the question of whether the law in question was unconstitutional under Article 11 of the Constitution must be referred to the Constitutional Court itself.

The Pretore, having regard, on the one hand, to the well-established case law of the Court of Justice relating to the applicability of Community law in the legal systems of the Member States and, on the other hand, to the disadvantages that might arise if the national court, instead of declaring of its own motion that a law impeding the full force and effect of Community law was inapplicable, were required to raise the issue of constitutionality, referred to the Court two questions framed as follows:

"(a) Since, in accordance with Article 189 of the EEC Treaty and the established case law of the Court of Justice of the European Communities, directly applicable Community provisions must, notwithstanding any internal rule or practice whatsoever of the Member States, have full, complete and uniform effect in their legal systems in order to protect subjective legal rights created in favor of individuals, is the scope of the said provisions to be interpreted to the effect that any subsequent national measures which conflict with those provisions must be directly disregarded without waiting until those measures have been eliminated by action on the part of the national legislature concerned (repeal) or of other constitutional authorities (declaration that they are unconstitutional) especially, in the case of the latter alternative, where, since the national law continues to be fully effective pending such declaration, it is impossible to apply the Community provisions and, in consequence, to ensure that they are fully, completely and uniformly applied and to protect the legal rights created in favor of individuals?

"(b) Arising out of the previous question, in circumstances where Community law recognizes that the protection of subjective legal rights created as a result of 'directly applicable' Community provisions may be suspended until any conflicting national measures are actually repealed by the competent national authorities, is such repeal in all cases to have a wholly retroactive effect so as to avoid any adverse effects on those subjective legal rights?"

* * *

THE SUBSTANCE OF THE CASE

The main purpose of the *first question* is to ascertain what consequences flow from the direct applicability of a provision of Community law in the event of incompatibility with a subsequent legislative provision of a Member State.

Direct applicability in such circumstances means that the provisions of Community law must be fully and uniformly applied in all the Member States from the date of their entry into force and for so long as they continue in force. These provisions are therefore a direct source of rights and duties for all those affected thereby, whether Member States or individuals, who are parties to legal relationships under Community law. This consequence also concerns any national court whose task it is as an organ of a Member State to protect, in a case within its jurisdiction, the rights conferred upon individuals by Community law.

Furthermore, in accordance with the principle of the precedence of Community law, the relationship between provisions of the Treaty and directly applicable measures of the institutions on the one hand and the national law of the Member States on the other is such that those provisions and measures not only by their entry into force render automatically inapplicable any conflicting provision of current national law but—in so far as they are an integral part of, and take precedence in, the legal order applicable in the territory of each of the Member States—also preclude the valid adoption of new national legislative measures to the extent to which they would be incompatible with Community provisions. Indeed, any recognition that national legislative measures which encroach upon the field within which the Community exercises its legislative power or which are otherwise incompatible with the provisions of Community law had any legal effect would amount to a corresponding denial of the effectiveness of obligations undertaken unconditionally and irrevocably by the Member States pursuant to the Treaty and would thus imperil the very foundations of the Community.

The same conclusion emerges from the meaning and purpose of Article 177 of the Treaty, which provides that any court or tribunal of a Member State is entitled to make a referral to the Court of Justice whenever it considers that a preliminary ruling on a question of interpretation or validity relating to Community law is necessary to enable it to give judgment. The effectiveness of that provision would be impaired if the national court were prevented from directly applying Community law in accordance with the decision or the case law of the Court of Justice.

It follows from the foregoing that every national court must, in a case within its jurisdiction, apply Community law in its entirety and protect rights which it confers on individuals and must accordingly set aside any provision of national law which may conflict with it, whether prior or subsequent to the Community rule. Accordingly any provision of a national legal system and any legislative, administrative or judicial practice which might impair the effectiveness of Community law by withholding from the national court having jurisdiction to apply such law the power to do everything necessary at the moment of its application to set aside national legislative provisions which might prevent Community rules from having full force and effect are incompatible with those requirements which are the very essence of Community law. This would be the case in the event of a conflict between a provision of Community law and a subsequent national law if the solution to the conflict were to be reserved for an authority with a discretion of its own, other than the court called upon to apply Community law, even if such an impediment to the full effectiveness of Community law were only temporary.

The first question should therefore be answered to the effect that a national court which is called upon, within the limits of its jurisdiction, to apply provisions of Community law is under a duty to give full effect to those provisions, if necessary refusing of its own motion to apply any conflicting provision of national legislation, even if adopted subsequently, and it is not necessary for the court to request or await the prior setting aside of such provision by legislative or other constitutional means.

The essential point of the *second question* is whether—assuming it to be accepted that the protection of rights conferred by provisions of Community law can be suspended until any national provisions which might conflict with them have in fact been set aside by the competent national authorities—such setting aside must in every case have unrestricted retroactive effect so as to prevent the rights in question from being in any way adversely affected.

It follows from the answer to the first question that the national courts must protect rights conferred by provisions of the Community legal order and that it is not necessary for such courts to request or await the actual setting aside by the national authorities empowered so to act of any national measures which might impede the direct and immediate application of Community rules.

The second question therefore appears to have no purpose.

### Costs

The costs incurred by the Government of the Italian Republic and by the Commission of the European Communities, which submitted observations to the Court, are not recoverable. Since these proceedings are, for the parties to the main action, in the nature of a step in the action pending before the Pretore of Susa, the decision on costs is a matter for that court.

For these reasons, the Court of Justice, in answer to the questions referred to it by the Pretore of Susa in an order of July 28, 1977, hereby rules:

> A national court which is called upon, within the limits of its jurisdiction, to apply provisions of Community law is under a duty to give full effect to those provisions, if necessary refusing of its own motion to apply any conflicting provision of national legislation, even if adopted subsequently, and it is not necessary for the court to request or await the prior setting aside of such provisions by legislative or other constitutional means.

## *OPINION OF ADVOCATE GENERAL GERHARD REISCHL*

* * *

1. In my view, it would be appropriate to start the observations which have to be made in this matter with a comprehensive account of the relevant decided cases of the Court on the nature of Community law and on its effectiveness for citizens of the Common Market as well as on the relationship between Community and national law. I think it right to remind the Court of this case law not only because this will make apparent the spirit and basic attitude adopted by the Court in dealing with such problems, but also because the cases hitherto decided give a definite indication of the solution of the problem before us.

In the first place, emphasis must be laid on a ruling of a fundamental nature which was to some extent made in a very early case. This is that the Community constitutes a new legal order of international law and that Community law is independent of the legislation of Member States (Case No. 26/62, judgment of February 5, 1963, in N.V. Algemene Transport-en Expedite Onderneming Van Gend & Loos v. Nederlandse Administratie der Belastingen (Netherlands Inland Revenue Administration) [1963] E.C.R. 12). Similarly, in Case No. 6/64 (judgment of July 15, 1964, in Flaminio Costa v. ENEL [1964] E.C.R. 593) it is stated that the EEC Treaty has created its own legal system which, on the entry into force of the Treaty, became an integral part of the legal systems of the Member States, and in Case No. 11/70 (judgment of December 17, 1970, Internationale Handelsgesellschaft mbH v. Einfuhr and Vorratsstelle für Getreide und Futtermittel [1970] E.C.R. 1134) it is stated that the law stemming from the Treaty is an independent source of law.

It is of the essence of these findings that the Member States have limited their sovereign rights, albeit within limited fields (Case No. 26/62) or—as is stated in Case No. 6/64—that the Member States' sovereign powers have been transferred to the Community. The judgment in Case No. 48/71 (judgment of July 13, 1972, in Commission of the European Communities v. Italian Republic [1972] E.C.R. 527) indeed mentions a definitive limitation of their sovereign rights—an idea which incidentally is also to be found in the case law of the Italian Constitutional Court (judgment No. 183) with reference to Article 11 of the Italian constitution.

Furthermore, an important feature of Community law is that the subjects of this law include the nationals of the Member States (Case No. 26/62). A whole host of provisions of Community law—there is an extensive case law on this point—have direct effect in the national law of all the Member States (Case No. 48/71), that is to say, that they confer upon individuals rights which they may invoke before their national courts (Case No. 26/62) and which national courts are bound to apply (Case No. 6/64).

As far as the relationship between Community law and national law in general is concerned, the findings of the Court—for example, in Case No. 6/164 ( [1964] E.C.R. at page 594) and in Case No. 167/73 (judgment of April 4, 1974, in Commission of the European Communities v. French Republic [1974] E.C.R. 371) mean that Community law takes precedence over national provisions. In other cases, these findings are defined as meaning that this precedence applies as against national provisions of every kind (Case No. 48/71 and judgment of July 7, 1976, in Case No. 118/75, Lynne Watson and Alessandro Belmann [1976] E.C.R. at page 1198 [¶ 8368] ); in this connection later legislative measures (Case No. 6/64 and judgment of December 14, 1971, in Case No. 43/71, Politi S.A.S. v. Ministry for Finance of the Italian Republic [1971] E.C.R. 1039), as well as constitutional law (Case No. 11/70) are expressly mentioned. Accordingly—as is stated in Case No. 167/73 [1974] ECR at page 371—"all contrary provisions of internal law are rendered inapplicable," they "cannot therefore be inconsistent" with the Community legal system (Case No. 6/64 at page 594) and cannot therefore be invoked against Community law (Cases Nos. 48/71 and 118/75).

Moreover, in this connection the arguments for a uniform application of Community law (for example, in Case No. 11/70) must be borne in mind. In the judgment in Case No. 6/64 (at page 594) the Court held on this point that "the executive force of Community law cannot vary from one State to another in deference to subsequent domestic laws"; in an order in Case No. 9/65 of June 22, 1965 (Acciaierie San Michele S.p.A. (in liquidation) v. High Authority of the ECSC, published with the judgment of March 2, 1967, in Joined Cases Nos. 9 and 58/65 [1967] E.C.R. at page 30), the Court stressed that the Treaty cannot have different legal consequences varying with the Member State concerned; the complete and uniform application of the Treaty is imperative. In other parts of the case law—for instance, in Case No. 48/71 [1972] E.C.R. 532—the Court lays general emphasis on the proposition that the rules of Community law must be fully applied at the same time and with identical effects over the whole territory of the Community.

Finally other passages from the last-mentioned case which have particular relevance to this case must be cited. Thus it is stated in that case ( [1972] E.C.R. at page 532) that in the case of a directly applicable Community rule "the argument that its infringement can be terminated only by the adoption of measures constitutionally appropriate to repeal the provision establishing the tax would amount to saying that the application of the Community rule is subject to the law of each Member State and more precisely that this application is impossible where it is contrary to a national law." These passages also stress that an automatic consequence of the validity of Community law is that the competent national authorities are prohibited from applying a national rule declared to be incompatible with the Treaty and Member States cannot place any obstacle in the way of any such prohibition.

2. Against the background of this case law, the only possible answer to the first question is that, in the case of directly applicable Community provisions, conflicting national provisions which were adopted subsequently may no longer be applied; this position applies with immediate effect and it is not necessary to await repeal by the legislature or a declaration by a constitutional court that they are unconstitutional.

### *Notes*

1. The principal case demonstrates the supremacy of Community law. For earlier decisions, see the opinion of Advocate–General Reischl.

2. Since Community law prevails even over inconsistent constitutional law of the member states, the question arises to what extent Community law can override basic freedoms guaranteed by member state constitutions. In Internationale Handelsgesellschaft mbH v. Einfuhr und Vorratsstelle für Getreide und Futtermittel, Case No. 11/70, Dec. 17, 1970, 16 Rec. 1125 (1970), CCH C.M.R. ¶ 8126, 11 C.M.L.R. 255 (1972), the Court stated (at 16 Rec. 1135): "[T]he validity of a Community instrument or its effect within a Member State cannot be affected by allegations that it strikes at either the fundamental rights as formulated in that State's constitution or the principles of a national constitutional structure." However, in that same decision, the Court ruled that fundamental rights form an integral part of the general principles of law of which the Court of Justice ensures observance. The German Constitutional Court has taken the position that Community law cannot override basic civil liberties provisions in the German Constitution. Decision of May 29, 1974, 27 N.J.W.

1697 (1974) (with an annotation by G. Meier); Decision of June 8, 1977, Case 2 BrR 499/74, 1042/75, 30 N.J.W. 2024 (1977).

## OPINION OF THE COURT GIVEN PURSUANT TO ARTICLE 228 OF THE EEC TREATY

Opinion 1/75, 1975 E.C.R. 1355 (1975), CCH C.M.R. ¶ 8365, 17 C.M.L.R. 85 (1976).

On 14 July 1975 the Court of Justice received a request for an opinion submitted by the Commission of the European Communities pursuant to the second subparagraph of Article 228(1) of The Treaty establishing the EEC, according to which:

> The Council, the Commission or a Member State may obtain beforehand the opinion of the Court of Justice as to whether an agreement envisaged is compatible with the provisions of this Treaty. Where the opinion of the Court of Justice is adverse, the agreement may enter into force only in accordance with Article 236.

STATEMENT OF THE QUESTION

The object of this request is to obtain the opinion of the Court on the compatibility with the EEC Treaty of a draft "Understanding on a Local Cost Standard" drawn up under the auspices of the OECD, and more particularly on the question whether the Community has the power to conclude the said Understanding and, if so, whether that power is exclusive.

* * *

DISCUSSION

The question arising from the request for an opinion prompts the following considerations:

**A—Admissibility of the request for an opinion**

The second subparagraph of Article 228(1) lays down that the Council, the Commission or a Member State may request the Court for an opinion as to the compatibility with the provisions of the Treaty of an agreement to be concluded with one or more third countries or with an international organization.

The formal designation of the agreement envisaged under international law is not of decisive importance in connexion with the admissibility of the request. In its reference to an "agreement," the second subparagraph of Article 228(1) of the Treaty uses the expression in a general sense to indicate any undertaking entered into by entities subject to international law which has binding force, whatever its formal designation.

The Understanding in question fulfills these conditions. It contains a "standard," that is to say a rule of conduct, covering a specific field, determined by precise provisions, which is binding upon the participants. The very fact that the standard expressly provides that derogations shall take place only in exceptional cases and under strict conditions is sufficient evidence that the Understanding is such as to bind the contracting parties and therefore fulfils the conditions of the second subparagraph of Article 228(1) of the Treaty.

Moreover, discussions concerning the substance of the agreement are at an end and the conclusion of the Understanding in the form of a resolution of the Council of the OECD is now envisaged.

At the same time, the "draft Report to the Council of the OECD concerning the Understanding on a Local Cost Standard" states that there only remains to be clarified "the form of the participation in the Understanding by the European Economic Community, whose decision on the subject is to be made very soon."

In view of these factors and bearing in mind the recommendation of the Commission concerning the "form" of the Community's participation in the Understanding in question, it cannot be doubted that the draft Understanding constitutes an agreement "envisaged" within the meaning of the second subparagraph of Article 228(1) of the Treaty.

Moreover, the fact that the Commission raised the problem of the compatibility of this agreement with the provisions of the Treaty for the purpose of obtaining the opinion of the Court of Justice on the extent of the Community's powers to conclude the agreement envisaged cannot be sufficient of itself to render the request inadmissible with respect to the second subparagraph of Article 228(1) aforementioned.

The compatibility of an agreement with the provisions of the Treaty must be assessed in the light of all the rules of the Treaty, that is to say, both those rules which determine the extent of the powers of the institutions of the Community and the substantive rules.

It is the purpose of the second subparagraph of Article 228(1) to forestall complications which would result from legal disputes concerning the compatibility with the Treaty of international agreements binding upon the Community. In fact, a possible decision of the Court to the effect that such an agreement is, either by reason of its content or of the procedure adopted for its conclusion, incompatible with the provisions of the Treaty could not fail to provoke, not only in a Community context but also in that of international relations, serious difficulties and might give rise to adverse consequences for all interested parties, including third countries.

For the purpose of avoiding such complications the Treaty had recourse to the exceptional procedure of a prior reference to the Court of Justice for the purpose of elucidating, before the conclusion of the agreement, whether the latter is compatible with the Treaty. This procedure must therefore be open for all questions capable of submission for judicial consideration, either by the Court of Justice or possibly by national courts, in so far as such questions give rise to doubt either as to the substantive or formal validity of the agreement with regard to the Treaty.

The question whether the conclusion of a given agreement is within the power of the Community and whether, in a given case, such power has been exercised in conformity with the provisions of the Treaty is, in principle, a question which may be submitted to the Court of Justice, either directly, under Article 169 or Article 173 of the Treaty, or in accordance with the preliminary procedure, and it must therefore be admitted that the matter may be referred to the Court in accordance with the preliminary procedure of Article 228.

Similarly, the fact that discussions concerning the substance of the Understanding in question are now at an end cannot constitute a valid argument on which to base a finding that the request for an opinion is out of time, since the Treaty, by reason of the non-contentious character of the procedure contained in the second subparagraph of Article 228(1), does not lay down a time-limit for the submission of such a request.

There is therefore no reason why the request for an opinion should not be admitted.

**B—The reply to be given to the questions submitted**

*1. The Existence of a Community Power to Conclude the OECD Understanding on a Local Cost Standard*

Articles 112 and 113 of the Treaty must be borne in mind in formulating a reply to this question.

The first of these provisions provides that:

> * * * Member States shall, before the end of the transitional period, progressively harmonize the systems whereby they grant aid for exports to third countries, to the extent necessary to ensure that competition between undertakings of the Community is not distorted.

Since there is no doubt that the grant of export credits falls within the system of aids granted by Member States for exports, it is already clear from Article 112 that the subject-matter of the standard laid down in the Understanding in question relates to a field in which the provisions of the Treaty recognize a Community power.

Furthermore, Article 113 of the Treaty lays down, in paragraphs (1) and (2), that:

> * * * the common commercial policy shall be based on uniform principles, particularly in regard to * * * export policy * * *.

The field of the common commercial policy, and more particularly that of export policy, necessarily covers systems of aid for exports and more particularly measures concerning credits for the financing of local costs linked to export operations. In fact, such measures constitute an important element of commercial policy, that concept having the same content whether it is applied in the context of the international action of a State or to that of the Community.

Directives concerning credit insurance, adopted by the Council towards the end of 1970 and the beginning of 1971 expressly recognize the important role played by export credits in international trade, as a factor of commercial policy.

For these reasons the subject-matter covered by the standard contained in the Understanding in question, since it forms part not only of the sphere of the system of aids for exports laid down at Article 112 of the Treaty but also, in a more general way, of export policy and, by reason of that fact, of the sphere of the common commercial policy defined in Article 113 of the Treaty, falls within the ambit of the Community's powers.

In the course of the measures necessary to implement the principles laid down in the above-mentioned provisions, particularly those covered by Article 113 of the Treaty, concerning the common commercial policy, the Community is empowered, pursuant to the powers which it possesses, not only to adopt internal rules of Community law, but also to conclude agreements with third countries pursuant to Article 113(2) and Article 114 of the Treaty.

A commercial policy is in fact made up by the combination and interaction of internal and external measures, without priority being taken by one over the others. Sometimes agreements are concluded in execution of a policy fixed in advance, sometimes that policy is defined by the agreements themselves.

Such agreements may be outline agreements, the purpose of which is to lay down uniform principles. Such is the case with the Understanding on local costs: it does not have a specific content adapted to particular export credit transactions; it merely lays down a standard, sets out certain exceptions, provides, in exceptional circumstances, for derogations and, finally, lays down general provisions. Furthermore, the implementation of the export policy to be pursued within the framework of a common commercial policy does not necessarily find expression in the adoption of general and abstract rules of internal or Community law. The common commercial policy is above all the outcome of a progressive development based upon specific measures which may refer without distinction to "autonomous" and external aspects of that policy and which do not necessarily presuppose, by the fact that they are linked to the field of the common commercial policy, the existence of a large body of rules, but combine gradually to form that body.

### 2. *The Exclusive Nature of the Community's Powers*

The reply to this question depends, on the one hand, on the objective of the Understanding in question and, on the other hand, on the manner in which the common commercial policy is conceived in the Treaty.

At Nos. I and II the Understanding itself defines the transactions to which the common standard applies, and those which, on the other hand, are excluded from its field of application because they are directed to specifically military ends or because they have been entered into with developing countries.

It is to be understood from this definition that the subject-matter of the standard, and therefore of the Understanding, is one of those measures belonging to the common commercial policy prescribed by Article 113 of the Treaty.

Such a policy is conceived in that article in the context of the operation of the Common Market, for the defence of the common interests of the Community, within which the particular interests of the Member States must endeavour to adapt to each other.

Quite clearly, however, this conception is incompatible with the freedom to which the Member States could lay claim by invoking a concurrent power, so as to ensure that their own interests were separately satisfied in external relations, at the risk of compromising the effective defence of the common interests of the Community.

In fact any unilateral action on the part of the Member States would lead to disparities in the conditions for the grant of export credits, calculated to distort competition between undertakings of the various Member States in external markets. Such distortion can be eliminated only by means of a strict uniformity of credit conditions granted to undertakings in the Community, whatever their nationality.

It cannot therefore be accepted that, in a field such as that governed by the Understanding in question, which is covered by export policy and more generally by the common commercial policy, the Member States should exercise a power concurrent to that of the Community, in the Community sphere and in the international sphere. The provisions of Articles 113 and 114 concerning the conditions under which, according to the Treaty, agreements on commercial policy must be concluded show clearly that the exercise of concurrent powers by the Member States and the Community in this matter is impossible.

To accept that the contrary were true would amount to recognizing that, in relations with third countries, Member States may adopt positions which differ from those which the Community intends to adopt, and would thereby distort the institutional framework, call into question the mutual trust within the Community and prevent the latter from fulfilling its task in the defence of the common interest.

It is of little importance that the obligations and financial burdens inherent in the execution of the agreement envisaged are borne directly by the Member States. The "internal" and "external" measures adopted by the Community within the framework of the common commercial policy do not necessarily involve, in order to ensure their compatibility with the Treaty, a transfer to the institutions of the Community of the obligations and financial burdens which they may involve: such measures are solely concerned to substitute for the unilateral action of the Member States, in the field under consideration, a common action based upon uniform principles on behalf of the whole of the Community.

Similarly, in relation to products subject to the ECSC Treaty, it is of little importance to note that the power of the Member States to conclude the Understanding envisaged is safeguarded by Article 71 of that Treaty, according to which:

> The powers of the Governments of Member States in matters of commercial policy shall not be affected by this Treaty * * *.

The matter under discussion has been referred to the Court pursuant to the second subparagraph of Article 228(1) of the EEC Treaty. The opinion which it has been called upon to give therefore bears upon the problem of the compatibility of the agreement envisaged with the provisions of the EEC Treaty and will define the power of the Community to conclude that agreement solely in relation to those provisions.

Independently of the question whether, in view of the necessity of ensuring that international transactions to which the Communities are party should have as uniform a character as possible, Article 71 of the ECSC Treaty retains its former force following the entry into force of the EEC Treaty, that provision cannot in any event render inoperative Articles 113 and 114 of the EEC Treaty and affect the vesting of power in the Community for the negotiation and conclusion of international agreements in the realm of common commercial policy.

Accordingly,

THE COURT

gives the following opinion:

> The Community has exclusive power to participate in the Understanding on a Local Cost Standard referred to in the request for an opinion.

### *Notes*

1. In Commission v. Council, Case No. 22/70, March 31, 1971, 17 Rec. 263 (1971), CCH C.M.R. ¶ 8134, 10 C.M.L.R. 335 (1971), the Commission attacked a Council decision permitting the Member States to continue negotiations concerning the European Road Transport Agreement on the ground that the conduct of these negotiations was within the exclusive competence of the Community. The Court ruled that the Community's treaty-making power was not limited to the instances in which the Treaty specifically authorizes the Community to enter into international agreements, but extended to all subjects within the Community's concern. On this decision, see also Smit & Herzog, The Law of the European Economic Community ¶ 228.04.

2. The breadth of the Court's rulings would appear to confirm that the EEC also has exclusive power to participate in conventions that relate to commercial policy in regard to the territorial seas, continental shelves, and other segments of the seas. On this aspect, see Officer van Justitie v. Kramer, Cases Nos. 3, 4 & 6/76, July 14, 1976, 1976 E.C.R. 1279, CCH C.M.R. ¶ 8372, 18 C.M.L.R. 440 (1976), in which the Court ruled that, concomitantly with the development of a common fisheries policy, the EEC acquired the power to enter into international agreements dealing with fisheries. See further Smit & Herzog, The Law of the European Economic Community 1.05 (1978 Supp.).

## DEFRENNE v. SABENA

Court of Justice of the European Communities, Case No. 43/75, April 8, 1976.
1976 E.C.R. 455, CCH C.M.R. ¶ 8346, 18 C.M.L.R. 98 (1976).

By a judgment of 23 April 1975, received at the Court Registry on 2 May 1975, the Cour du travail, Brussels, referred to the Court under Article 177 of the EEC Treaty two questions concerning the effect and implementation of Article 119 of the Treaty regarding the principle that men and women should receive equal pay for equal work.

These questions arose within the context of an action between an air hostess and her employer, Sabena S.A., concerning compensation claimed by the applicant in the main action on the ground that, between 15 February 1963 and 1 February 1966, she suffered as a female worker discrimination in terms of pay as compared with male colleagues who were doing the same work as "cabin steward."

According to the judgment containing the reference, the parties agree that the work of an air hostess is identical to that of a cabin steward and in these circumstances the existence of discrimination in pay to the detriment of the air hostess during the period in question is not disputed.

THE FIRST QUESTION (DIRECT EFFECT OF ARTICLE 119)

The first question asks whether Article 119 of the Treaty introduces "directly into the national law of each Member State of the European Community the principle that men and women should receive equal pay for equal work and does it therefore, independently of any national provision, entitle workers to institute proceedings before national courts in order to ensure its observance?"

[Article 119, reads as follows:

Each Member State shall during the first stage ensure and subsequently maintain the application of the principle that men and women should receive equal pay for equal work.

For the purpose of this Article, "pay" mean the ordinary basic or minimum wage or salary and any other consideration, whether in cash or in kind, which the worker receives, directly or indirectly, in respect of his employment from his employer.

Equal pay without discrimination based on sex means:

(a) that pay for the same work at piece rates shall be calculated on the basis of the same unit of measurement;

(b) that pay for work at time rates shall be the same for the same job.]

If the answer to this question is in the affirmative, the question further enquires as from what date this effect must be recognized.

The reply to the final part of the first question will therefore be given with the reply to the second question.

The question of the direct effect of Article 119 must be considered in the light of the nature of the principle of equal pay, the aim of this provision and its place in the scheme of the Treaty.

Article 119 pursues a double aim.

First, in the light of the different stages of the development of social legislation in the various Member States, the aim of Article 119 is to avoid a situation in which undertakings established in States which have actually implemented the principle of equal pay suffer a competitive disadvantage in intra-Community competition as compared with undertakings established in States which have not yet eliminated discrimination against women workers as regards pay.

Secondly, this provision forms part of the social objectives of the Community, which is not merely an economic union, but is at the same time intended, by common action, to ensure social progress and seek the constant improvement of the living and working conditions of their peoples, as is emphasized by the Preamble to the Treaty.

This aim is accentuated by the insertion of Article 119 into the body of a chapter devoted to social policy whose preliminary provision, Article 117, marks "the need to promote improved working conditions and an improved standard of living for workers, so as to make possible their harmonization while the improvement is being maintained."

This double aim, which is at once economic and social, shows that the principle of equal pay forms part of the foundations of the Community.

Furthermore, this explains why the Treaty has provided for the complete implementation of this principle by the end of the first stage of the transitional period.

Therefore, in interpreting this provision, it is impossible to base any argument on the dilatoriness and resistance which have delayed the actual implementation of this basic principle in certain Member States.

In particular, since Article 119 appears in the context of the harmonization of working conditions while the improvement is being maintained, the objection that the terms of this article may be observed in other ways than by raising the lowest salaries may be set aside.

Under the terms of the first paragraph of Article 119, the Member States are bound to ensure and maintain "the application of the principle that men and women should receive equal pay for equal work."

The second and third paragraphs of the same article add a certain number of details concerning the concepts of pay and work referred to in the first paragraph.

For the purposes of the implementation of these provisions a distinction must be drawn within the whole area of application of Article 119 between, first, direct and overt discrimination which may be identified solely with the aid of the criteria based on equal work and equal pay referred to by the article in question and, secondly, indirect and disguised discrimination which can only be identified by reference to more explicit implementing provisions of a Community or national character.

It is impossible not to recognize that the complete implementation of the aim pursued by Article 119, by means of the elimination of all discrimination, direct or indirect, between men and women workers, not only as regards individual undertakings but also entire branches of industry and even of the economic system as a whole, may in certain cases involve the elaboration of criteria whose implementation necessitates the taking of appropriate measures at Community and national level.

This view is all the more essential in the light of the fact that the Community measures on this question, to which reference will be made in answer to the second question, implement Article 119 from the point of view of extending the narrow criterion of "equal work," in accordance in particular with the provisions of Convention No. 100 on equal pay concluded by the International Labour Organization in 1951, Article 2 of which establishes the principle of equal pay for work "of equal value."

Among the forms of direct discrimination which may be identified solely by reference to the criteria laid down by Article 119 must be included in particular those which have their origin in legislative provisions or in collective labour agreements and which may be detected on the basis of a purely legal analysis of the situation.

This applies even more in cases where men and women receive unequal pay for equal work carried out in the same establishment or service, whether public or private.

As is shown by the very findings of the judgment making the reference, in such a situation the court is in a position to establish all the facts which enable it to decide whether a woman worker is receiving lower pay than a male worker performing the same tasks.

In such situation, at least, Article 119 is directly applicable and may thus give rise to individual rights which the courts must protect. * * *

THE TEMPORAL EFFECT OF THIS JUDGMENT

The Governments of Ireland and the United Kingdom have drawn the Court's attention to the possible economic consequences of attributing direct effect to the provisions of Article 119, on the ground that such a decision might, in many branches of economic life, result in the introduction of claims dating back to the time at which such effect came into existence.

In view of the large number of people concerned such claims, which undertakings could not have foreseen, might seriously affect the financial situation of such undertakings and even drive some of them to bankruptcy.

Although the practical consequences of any judicial decision must be carefully taken into account, it would be impossible to go so far as to diminish the objectivity of the law and compromise its future application on the ground of the possible repercussions which might result, as regards the past, from such a judicial decision.

However, in the light of the conduct of several of the Member States and the views adopted by the Commission and repeatedly brought to the notice of the circles concerned, it is appropriate to take exceptionally into account the fact that, over a prolonged period, the parties concerned have been led to continue with practices which were contrary to Article 119, although not yet prohibited under their national law.

The fact that, in spite of the warnings given, the Commission did not initiate proceedings under Article 169 against the Member States concerned on grounds of failure to fulfil an obligation was likely to consolidate the incorrect impression as to the effects of Article 119.

In these circumstances, it is appropriate to determine that, as the general level at which pay would have been fixed cannot be known, important considerations of legal certainty affecting all the interests involved, both public and private, make it impossible in principle to reopen the question as regards to past.

Therefore, the direct effect of Article 119 cannot be relied on in order to support claims concerning pay periods prior to the date of this judgment, except as regards those workers who have already brought legal proceedings or made an equivalent claim.

* * *

On those grounds,

THE COURT

in answer to the questions referred to it by the Cour du travail, Brussels, by judgment dated 23 April 1975 hereby rules:

1. The principle that men and women should receive equal pay, which is laid down by Article 119, may be relied on before the national courts. These courts have a duty to ensure the protection of the rights which that provision vests in individuals, in particular in the case of those forms of discrimination which have their origin in legislative provisions or collective labour agreements, as well as where men and women receive unequal pay for equal work which is carried out in the same establishment or service, whether private or public.

2. The application of Article 119 was to have been fully secured by the original Member States as from 1 January 1962, the beginning of the second stage of the transitional period, and by the new Member States as from 1 January 1973, the date of entry into force of the Accession Treaty. The first of these time-limits was not modified by the Resolution of the Member States of 30 December 1961.

3. Council Directive No 75/117 does not prejudice the direct effect of Article 119 and the period fixed by that Directive for compliance therewith does not affect the time-limits laid down by Article 119 of the EEC Treaty and the Accession Treaty.

4. Even in the areas in which Article 119 has no direct effect, that provision cannot be interpreted as reserving to the national legislature exclusive power to implement the principle of equal pay since, to the extent to which such implementation is necessary, it may be achieved by a combination of Community and national provisions.

5. Except as regards those workers who have already brought legal proceedings or made an equivalent claim, the direct effect of Article 119 cannot be relied on in order to support claims concerning pay periods prior to the date of this judgment.

### *Notes*

1. The principal case provides a striking illustration both of the extent to which the EEC Treaty affects basic societal relations and what an international court with compulsory competence can achieve. To what extent does the Court's decision in effect import the equivalent of a limited Equal Rights Amendment into the laws of the Member States? See also Note 2 on the Simmenthal Case, p. 1532 supra.

2. What is the legal basis for the Court's giving its ruling prospective effect only?

## B. EUROPEAN COAL AND STEEL COMMUNITY (ECSC)

On May 9, 1950, Robert Schuman, then Foreign Minister of France, proposed the establishment of a Coal and Steel Community between France, West Germany, Italy, the Netherlands, Belgium, and Luxembourg. The response to the "Schuman Plan" was favorable, and the European Coal and Steel Community (ECSC) was established by a treaty signed at Paris on April 18, 1951, which became effective on July 23, 1952, 261 U.N.T.S. 140, 1 Europ.Y.B. 359.

The treaty establishes among the parties a common market, based on a customs union, and predicated on common policies and objectives. These objectives include the assurance of adequate supplies of coal and steel, establishment of the lowest economic prices, the equalization of access to coal and steel by all consumers within the customs union, the regulation of the industries to insure rational utilization of resources, the expansion of production and international trade, and the improvement of the living and working conditions of the work force of the industries (Article 3). The basic principles of regulation entail the abolition of import and export duties within the Community, the prohibition of discriminatory practices by governments or by enterprises, the prohibition of state subsidies, and the elimination of other restrictive practices (Article 4).

In order to implement the broad policies of the Community, and in order to enforce the more detailed provisions for regulating the affected industries, the treaty established several institutions. The Commission (formerly the High Authority), the executive arm of the Community, which has since been merged with the counterpart institution of the European Economic Community and the European Atomic Energy Community, is composed of members who are not to receive or accept instructions from any government or other organization and who, therefore, are servants of the supra-national Community, not of the constituent states of the Community. The Commission is empowered to raise funds by borrowing and by placing levies on the production of the coal and steel industries (Article 49); these levies are intended to cover administrative expenses and disbursements for certain assistance rendered (Article 50). These provisions on financing enable the Commission to exercise its functions without regard to national governmental policies and without dependence on financial contributions.

The substantive competence of the Commission is both extensive and intensive. It has important regulatory powers regarding levels of production and quotas for production (Article 58); it may regulate prices and pricing practices (Articles 60, 61); it may establish regulations to eliminate discriminatory practices (Article 63); it must also approve any action by a member state that may impair the conditions of competition, or that may distort the market in the coal and steel industries (Chapter VII).

The Council of Ministers of ECSC, which has also been merged with its counterpart in the other European Communities, is both a policy-making organ and an executive organ of the Community. The Council and the Commission are to consult together on matters affecting the policies of the Community (Article 26). The Council is composed of representatives of the member governments (Article 27).

The Assembly, which is shared with the other Communities, is composed of representatives of the peoples of the member states; membership is distributed according to the population of the member states. Representatives in the Assembly are elected by a system of direct universal suffrage. The Assembly's powers are consultative; the Assembly may discuss any matter related to the treaty and its application to member states, and it exercises general supervisory powers (Article 20).

The Court of Justice functions for all three European Communities and among its responsibilities are the interpretation and application of the provisions of the ECSC Treaty and the regulations issued by the Commission (Article 31). The Court hears appeals by member states for annulment of decisions and recommendations of the Commission; the Court may not, however, review the substantive bases of decisions or recommendations of the Commission, except when the Commission is alleged to have clearly misconstrued the provisions of the treaty (Article 33). Enterprises and associations also have the right of appeal to the Court, against recommendations and decisions of the Commission (Article 33). The Court may also hear petitions of member states and enterprises based on the failure of the Commission to implement provisions of the treaty (Article 35).

### *Note*

On the ECSC generally, see Mason, The European Coal and Steel Community (1955).

## C. EUROPEAN ATOMIC ENERGY COMMUNITY (EURATOM)

Euratom was established by a treaty signed at Rome on March 25, 1957, 298 U.N.T.S. 167, 5 Europ.Y.B. 455. Euratom is closely related to the other two European Communities and shares their institutions.

The aims of Euratom are to develop research (Articles 4–11); to disseminate information (Articles 12–29); to enforce uniform safety standards (Articles 30–39); to facilitate investment (Articles 40–51); to ensure regular and equitable distribution of supplies of nuclear material (Articles 52–76); to guarantee that nuclear materials are not diverted from their designated uses (Articles 77–85); to exercise certain property rights in respect of such materials (Articles 86–91); to create a common market for the free movement of capital for investment and personnel for nuclear industries (Articles 92–100); and to promote the peaceful uses of atomic energy (Articles 101–106).

The organs of Euratom are an Assembly, common to the EEC and the ECSC as well (Articles 107–114), a Council (Articles 115–123) which has been merged with those of the EEC and the ECSC, a Commission (Articles 126–127), which has also been merged with those of the EEC and the ECSC, a Court of Justice (Articles 136–160) common to Euratom and the other two Communities, and an Economic and Social Committee (Articles 165–170), shared with the EEC. Euratom, through the Commission, was to have a right of option on all ore, source material and special fissionable material produced in member states, and was to have had the exclusive right of contracting with regard to supplies of such materials from inside or outside Euratom (Article 52). These features of Euratom, the most truly "supranational" provisions of any of the European Communities, have not been implemented as a result of the reluctance on the part of the member states to relinquish control of so vital a sector of the national economy and strategic capability.

Inspectors of Euratom are to have access to places, persons and data in order to ensure that nuclear materials are not diverted and to ensure that provisions regarding supplies and controls are observed (Article 81). Euratom is empowered to establish joint enterprises for the execution of undertakings of great importance (Articles 45–46). Member states are required to abolish import and export charges and quantitative restrictions on products listed in the Treaty (Article 94). See generally Mathijsen, Problems Connected With the Creation of Euratom, 26 Law & Contemp.Prob. 438 (1961); Gaudet, Euratom, Progress in Nuclear Energy, in Law and Administration 140 (Marks ed. 1959); Burholt, The Regulatory Framework for Storage and Disposal of Radioactive Waste in the Member States of the European Community (1988).

## D. EUROPEAN FREE TRADE ASSOCIATION (EFTA)

EFTA was created by a convention signed at Stockholm which entered into force May 3, 1960, upon ratification of all signatory states. 370 U.N.T.S. 3.

EFTA was an outgrowth of the inability of other members of the Organization for European Economic Cooperation (established in 1948 to implement the European recovery program) to agree with the six members of EEC on a plan for a broader economic community. The members of EFTA, known popularly as the "Outer Seven", included Austria, Denmark, Norway, Portugal, Sweden, Switzerland, and the United Kingdom. The United Kingdom and Denmark relinquished their memberships when they acceded to the EEC.

The purposes of EFTA are similar to those of the EEC, that is, sustained expansion of economic activity, full employment, increased productivity and rational use of resources, financial stability, improved living standards, trade under a regime of fair competition, and the harmonious development and expansion of world trade and progressive removal of barriers to trade (Article 2). The Convention provides for the reduction and eventual (by 1970) elimination of import duties within the Association (Article 3). Export duties were eliminated by the end of 1962 (Article 8). The Convention provides for cooperation in customs administration (Article 9). Quantitative restrictions were eliminated by 1969 (Article 10). There are also provisions relating to government aid (Article 13), discriminatory practices (Article 13), restrictive trade practices (Article 15) and dumping (Article 17). Agricultural products and fish are exempted from provisions of the Convention, although general objectives are established with regard to such products (Articles 21–28).

The organs of EFTA are: a Council composed of representatives of members, each member having one vote (Article 32); examining committees appointed by the Council and serving EFTA directly (Articles 31, 33), and serving under conditions similar to those prescribed for the EEC Commission; a Secretariat (Article 34); and committees as may be established by the Council (Article 32(3)).

EFTA differs fundamentally from the EEC in a number of respects. The organs of EFTA do not have the extensive supranational powers (for example, in connection with the harmonization of national laws and the implementation of common agricultural and transport policies) held by the Commission and the Council of the EEC. EFTA has no judicial organ. While internal tariff barriers are to be removed, no provision is made for creation of a common external tariff.

### E. THE EUROPEAN ECONOMIC AREA

As the January 1, 1993, date for the elimination of all remaining obstacles to trade within the European Economic Community approached, the EFTA countries became concerned about being shut out of the expected increase in trade and sought association with the "1992" program. An agreement was reached in Luxembourg on October 22, 1991, which created the "European Economic Area." With few exceptions (including agricultural products), goods, persons, services, and capital are to move freely between all the constituent countries, but the EFTA countries must accept the EEC rules on product standards, banking supervision, and the like. A joint EFTA–EEC Council of Ministers will implement the agreement. If ratified, the agreement will create a trading bloc encompassing 19 countries (in addition to the 12 EEC members, Ireland, Iceland, Norway, Sweden, Finland, Switzerland, Liechtenstein and Austria) with a population of over 380 million people.

### F. COUNCIL FOR MUTUAL ECONOMIC ASSISTANCE (CMEA)

The Council for Mutual Economic Assistance (COMECON, also CMEA) is the East European counterpart to the European Community and OECD. It was established in 1949 on the initiative of the Soviet Union to promote economic and technical cooperation among its members.

#### *Note*

On CMEA, see also Ustor, Decision–Making in the Council for Mutual Economic Assistance, 134 Rec. des Cours 163 (1971–III); Szasz, The Legal Mechanism of CMEA Integration, 2 Questions of International Law 191 (1981); Hoya, East–West Trade: Comecon Law, American–Soviet Trade (1984).

## SECTION 3. THE NORTH AMERICAN FREE TRADE AGREEMENT (NAFTA)

In 1965, the United States and Canada entered into an agreement, under which automobiles and automobile parts could move freely from country to country without being subject to import duties at the border. 17 U.S.T. 1372, T.I.A.S. 6093. At the time this so-called Auto–Pact was negotiated, both sides drew significant advantages from the arrangement. Because all Canadian automobile manufacturers were subsidiaries of their American counterparts, American manufacturers did not fear Canadian competition. One of them has been reported as stating, somewhat less than prophetically, that Americans would always prefer American-made cars over all others.

When the EEC Treaty proved to be a success, more and more voices were heard urging further integration of U.S.–Canadian trade. Various efforts were made to stimulate further sectoral integration. The sectors considered were subway cars (many of New York's subway cars are manufactured in Canada), computers, and lumber. Some, however, urged a more radical approach and advocated wholesale integration. See Smit, The Relevance of the EEC Experience to Additional Prospective Sectoral Integration Between Canada and the United States, 10 Canada–U.S. L.J. 53 (1985).

In the nineteen-eighties, these efforts bore fruit. In March, 1985, President Reagan and Prime Minister Mulroney asked their trade officials to explore ways to eliminate barriers to trade and investment between the United States and Canada. Under Congressionally granted "fast track" authority, negotiations began in 1986. The United States and Canada reached an agreement on the framework of a free trade area in 1987. And on January 1, 1989, the Canada–United States Free Trade Agreement came into effect. 27 I.L.M. 293 (1988). The agreement created the world's largest free trade area, affecting trade of roughly $125 billion. It establishes a free trade area, in which goods originating in the member states are to move freely across national borders. It differs from the EC Treaties, which, among other things, also provide for a common external tariff. A significant feature of the Canada–United States Free Trade Agreement is that it provides elaborate dispute settlement mechanisms for resolving disputes. These mechanisms, providing for ad hoc tribunals and therefore a far cry from the European Court of Justice, have already produced important decisions. On the dispute settlement devices, see Sohn, Dispute Resolution Under A North American Free Trade Agreement, 12 Canada–U.S. L.J. 319 (1987); Lowenfeld, Binational Dispute Settlement Under Chapter 19 of the Canada–United States Free Trade Agreement: An Interim Appraisal, 24 N.Y.U.J.Int'l L. & Pol. 269 (1991); Cannon, Binational Panel Dispute Settlement Under Article 1904 of the United States–Canada Free Trade Agreement: A Procedural Comparison with the United States Court of International Trade, 22 L. & Pol'y Int'l Bus. 689 (1991); Graham, Dispute Resolution in the Canada–United States Free Trade Agreement: One Element of a Complex Relationship, 37 McGill L.J. 544 (1992); Cluchey, Dispute Resolution Provisions of the Canada–United States Free Trade Agreement, 40 Me.L.Rev. 335 (1988); Rugman & Anderson, The Dispute Settlement Mechanisms' Cases in the Canada–United States Free Trade Agreement: An Economic Evaluation, 24 Geo.Wash.J.Int'l L. & Econ. 1 (1990); Hage, Dispute Settlement Under the Canada–United States Free Trade Agreement, 28 Canadian Y.B.Int'l L. 361 (1990); Boddez & Rugman, Red Raspberries: Effective Dispute Settlement in the Canada–United States Free Trade Agreement, 11 Nw.J.Int'l L. & Bus. 621 (1991); Castel, The Settlement of Disputes Under the 1988 Canada–United States Free Trade Agreement, 83 A.J.I.L. 118 (1989). On the Canada–United States Free Trade Agreement generally, see Rosenthal, Antitrust Implications of the Canada–United States Free Trade Agreement, 57 Antitrust L.J. 485 (1988); Baker & Battram, The Canada–United States Free Trade Agreement, 23 Int'l L. 37 (1989); Feltham et al., Competition (Antitrust) and Antidumping Laws in the Context of the Canada–United States Free Trade Agreement, 17 Canada–U.S. L.J. 71 (1991); Cattanach & O'Connor, Environmental Concerns Raised by the Canada–United States Free Trade Agreement, 18 Wm.Mitchell L.Rev. 461 (1992); Tocco, United States–Canada Free Trade Agreement, 12 Hamline L.Rev. 479 (1989); Nafziger & Rooklidge, The United States–Canada Free Trade Agreement: Exporting Art by the Numbers, 18 Pepp.L.Rev. 449 (1991).

The favorable reception accorded the Canada–United States Free Trade Agreement moved the member states to open negotiations with Mexico with the aim of bringing about a North American Free Trade Agreement. These negotiations led to a signing of an agreement with Mexico at the end of 1992.

___ U.S.T. ___, T.I.A.S. ___. The principal features of the NAFTA are the following: elimination of all tariffs between the treaty parties, some immediately and some over a period as long as ten years; restrictions on indirect trade barriers, such as technical and safety standards; limitations on "buy national" and government procurement policies favoring national purveyors; national treatment of foreign investors; liberalization of cross-border flows of services, including telecommunications, financial services, and the like; limitation of protective measures; and limitations on rules of origin. The Clinton administration has indicated that it wishes to take a close look at the environmental implications of NAFTA. On the dispute settlement devices, see Smith & Whitney, The Dispute Settlement Mechanism of the NAFTA and Agriculture, 68 N.D.L.Rev. 567 (1992); Note, Dispute Settlement Under the North American Free Trade Agreement: Will the Political, Cultural and Legal Differences Between the United States and Mexico Inhibit the Establishment of Fair Dispute Settlement Procedures?, 22 Cal.W.Int'l L.J. 353 (1991/92). On the NAFTA generally, see Alexander, The North American Free Trade Area: Potential Framework of an Agreement, 14 Hous.J.Int'l L. 85 (1991); Ansley, The North American Free Trade Agreement: The Public Debate, 22 Ga.J.Int'l & Comp.L. 329 (1992); Murphy, The Dilemma of Hydrocarbon Investment in Mexico's Accession to the North American Free Trade Agreement, 9 J.Energy & Nat.Resources L. 261 (1991); Wilburn, The North American Free Trade Agreement: Sending U.S. Jobs South of the Border, 17 N.C.J.Int'l & Comp.L. 489 (1992); Luney, The Japanese View Toward NAFTA and Regional Trade Zones, 2 Duke J.Comp. & Int'l L. 297 (1992); McKellar, NAFTA and the GATT: A Regional Perspective on the Uruguay Round, 18 Brooklyn J.Int'l L. 87 (1992); Note, The North American Free Trade Agreement: In Whose Best Interest?, 12 Nw.J.Int'l L. & Bus. 536 (1992).

No doubt, other Latin American countries will press for membership in, or association with, NAFTA. Whatever the fate of these efforts, NAFTA will, with the European Communities, cover a major part of world trade. The developments of regional economic associations has an important impact on GATT. The associations may facilitate further liberation of world trade, but they may also lead to insulation of trading blocs. See Trading Blocs Are Taking Over, J. of Commerce, April 6, 1992, at 10A.

## SECTION 4. LATIN AMERICAN REGIONAL ORGANIZATIONS

### A. INTRODUCTION

There are a number of regional international organizations in Latin America. Among them are the Caribbean Community (CARICOM), the Andean Pact Organization, the Latin American Integration Association (LAIA), the Central American Common Market, and more than thirty specialized organizations. They all face the difficult task of reconciling the needs of member countries of vastly different levels of economic development, while dealing as a community with the outside world. At least one of the organizations, CARICOM, must also make provision for the vestiges of the colonial relationship that existed between several of its members and the United Kingdom, and relationship with the European Communities that comes along with this status. Latin American regional organizations have met these problems by creating various forms of subregional organization that are given preferential treatment.

## B. LATIN AMERICAN FREE TRADE ASSOCIATION (LAFTA)

The Latin American Free Trade Association was created in 1960 by the Montevideo Treaty, ratified at that time by seven members, Argentina, Brasil, Chile, Mexico, Paraguay, Peru, and Uruguay and by Colombia and Ecuador in 1961, Venezuela in 1966, and Bolivia in 1967. The objective of LAFTA was to establish a free-trade area within a 12–year transitional period.

### *Note*

On LAFTA, see Lortie, Economic Integration and the Law of GATT (1975).

## C. LATIN AMERICAN INTEGRATION ASSOCIATION (LAIA)

With the adoption of the Montevideo Treaty of 1980, LAFTA was replaced by the Latin American Integration Association (LAIA). This Treaty has been ratified by Argentina, Bolivia, Brazil, Chile, Colombia, Ecuador, Mexico, Paraguay, Uruguay, and Venezuela.

The Treaty states that "[t]he long-term objective of * * * [LAIA] shall be the gradual and progressive establishment of a Latin American common market" (Art. 1).

Since little progress was made under this treaty, Argentina and Brazil decided to pursue integration by a process of sectoral integration. The steps taken in this direction resulted in the signing, on March 26, 1991, of a Treaty Establishing a Common Market between Argentina, Brazil, Paraguay and Uruguay which created the "common market of the southern cone" (MERCOSUR), 30 I.L.M. 1041 (1991). This Treaty, inspired by the EC Treaty, will have an institutional structure to be created at a special meeting in 1994, before the end of the transitional period. Concurrent with the signing of this Treaty, the United States signed an agreement with the members of MERCOSUR establishing a Council on Trade and Development, 30 I.L.M. 1034 (1991). The purpose of this Council is to conduct periodic consultations on trade and investment and to carry out an Immediate Action Program as defined in the Treaty, including co-operation in the Uruguay Round, access to technology, trade aspects of intellectual property rights, export subsidies, and the like.

## D. CENTRAL AMERICAN COMMON MARKET (CACM)

### *LORTIE, ECONOMIC INTEGRATION AND THE LAW OF GATT*

36–37 (1975).*

The first attempts to bring about some degree of economic cooperation among the five Central American republics were at the beginning of the

* Reprinted with permission of the author.
Footnotes omitted.

1950s. During the 1950s several schemes were proposed or experienced; the Nicaragua–El Salvador free-trade area discussed earlier is a case in point. The most important step in the formation of a customs-union in this area was provided by the signing by Guatemala, El Salvador, Honduras, and Nicaragua of the General Treaty on Central American Integration in December 1960 in Managua. Later, in July 1962, Costa Rica joined the union.

This new and broader treaty committed the Contracting Parties, in principle, to free all regional trade and establish a common market by mid–1966. A relatively brief list of exceptions was annexed to the Managua Treaty. It comprised those products whose immediate liberation from trade restraints, whether customs duties or quantitative restrictions, might seriously affect already existing productive activities or occasion substantial losses in fiscal revenue. Four different kinds of special treatment were reserved for goods appearing on the list of exceptions. * * *

It must be said in defense of the Treaty that duties were eliminated on about three-quarters of the items in the tariff schedule as soon as the agreement went into effect and on an additional 20 percent during the following years. By 1967 about 98 percent of the tariffs on items in intra-Central American trade had been eliminated, and uniform customs duties against the rest of the world had been introduced for more than 80 percent of the national-import tariff items. The levels of tariffs to the outside world were increased * * *. Resorting to the effective rate of protection method, it has been shown that protection had increased for the region as a whole by about 40 percent.

The integration scheme was not fully reviewed by the Contracting Parties because only Nicaragua was a member of GATT. Thus, the legal problem was the one caused by the raising of some "bound" tariffs in order to achieve the common external tariff. The problem was simplified, however, by two considerations. The first one was that Nicaragua was so small that no damage would be caused to third parties. The second consideration, which was highly important, was that the International Monetary Fund (IMF) had agreed that the raising of some tariffs was necessary in view of Nicaragua's balance-of-payment problems. Thus, Nicaragua was given permission to participate in the harmonization of the Central American Common Market (CACM) external tariff.

ANCOM's most important achievement is the development of a common system for the treatment of foreign capital. It is implemented through the provisions of Decision 24, the Common Code for the Treatment of Foreign Investment. According to Decision 24, foreign owned or foreign controlled enterprises are gradually required to divest majority ownership and control over a 15 to 20–year period, the purpose being to transfer to local majority ownership and majority control all foreign investment within a member state. Along with imposing other restrictions on the use of foreign capital, Decision 24 limits the amount of profit a foreign investor may repatriate, denies foreign investors access to short term local credit, and prohibits a corporation domiciled in a foreign country from loaning funds to a subsidiary organized and operating in an ANCOM-member country at an interest rate in excess of three percentage points above the prime rate in the country of origin.

On May 28, 1979, the foreign ministers of the five member states of ANCOM signed the Treaty Creating the Court of Justice of the Cartagena Agreement. The Treaty entered into force on May 7, 1983. It provides for a court of five justices selected from a list of candidates supplied by the individual members states. The Andean Court's central role is to interpret the norms of the legal order created by the Cartagena Agreement. The Court has competence in three areas. First, the Court may revise Commission Decisions and Junta Resolutions on compliance with the norms of the Cartagena Agreement. Second, the Court may pass upon complaints by the Junta or a member state that another member state is not complying with the Agreement. Finally, the Court may render advisory opinions.

The Treaty which created the Andean Court of Justice also provides for the binding force of Decisions of the Commission; these Decisions bind member states as of the date of their approval and are directly applicable in the member states from the date of their publication without the need of an expressed act of incorporation into domestic law. The decisions of the Andean Court are also directly applicable within the member states without the need of further transformation or exequatur.

The Cartagena Agreement was modified on a number of occasions. The most substantial changes were made by the Quito Protocol, bringing the Andean integration process more in line with that of the European Communities. See 28 I.L.M. 1165 (1989).

At a Summit Meeting on May 26, 1989, the member states issued a Manifest of Cartagena de Indias by which they committed themselves to take a number of specified measures towards implementing the Andean Common Market. 28 I.L.M. 1282 (1989).

### *Note*

On ANCOM, see Garcia Amador, The Andean Legal Order (1978); Morawetz, The Andean Group: A Case Study in Economic Integration Among Developing Countries (1974).

## SECTION 5. AFRICAN REGIONAL ORGANIZATIONS

### A. INTRODUCTION

Regional international organizations in Africa present a complex and constantly changing picture. For example, West Africa has seen at least sixteen purely economic organizations since 1958. The East African Community (EAC), which included a common market composed of Kenya, Uganda, and Tanzania, was long considered one of the most successful regional organizations on the continent, but it disintegrated due to internal strife in 1977. In the southern portion of the continent, the South African Development Coordination Conference (SADCC) came into being in 1980, but the main common denominator among its members is a shared animosity towards, and dependence on, South Africa. It is unclear what the future holds for any African regional organization.

Tribalism, nationalism, the linguistic and cultural schisms between the elites in the former French and British colonies, the competition for foreign trade and investment, the minimal incentives for trade between primary producer economies, and conflicting ideological leanings that span the entire spectrum are the major factors that have rendered African regional organizations unstable. The perception that a bloc of nations speaking together wield more political and economic clout than a single nation, similar histories of dependence on strong economic sources such as South Africa, France, and multinational corporations, and similar patterns of transition from colonialism are the primary forces leading to regional organizations. Although the actual achievements of African multinational organizations have been limited, they continue to provide a forum for communication, deliberation, consultation and concerted action.

The following provides a brief outline of the major regional economic organizations in existence today: UDEAC, ECOWAS, and SADCC. For further information, see African Regional Organizations (Mazzeo ed. 1984); Akintan, The Law of International Economic Institutions in Africa (1977).

## B. CENTRAL AFRICAN ECONOMIC AND CUSTOMS UNION (UDEAC)

### *AKINTAN, THE LAW OF INTERNATIONAL ECONOMIC INSTITUTIONS IN AFRICA*

167–169, 175 (1977).*

#### 1. History

There have been various forms of economic co-operation among the French-speaking States in Central Africa. This is just a follow up of the very close economic ties among the States making up the area which started during the Colonial days. One of the earliest institutions in this field is the Union Douaniere Equatoriale (UDE) which was based on the Treaties of 1959 and 1960. Members of UDE were Central African Republic, Congo (Brazzaville), Gabon and Chad. Cameroon became a member in 1961 and it finally developed into UDEAC in 1964. Both Chad and Central African Republic left UDEAC in 1968 to form yet a new Union known as Union Economique de l'Afrique Central (UEAC) together with Zaire Republic (formerly known as Congo Kinshasa). In December 1968, Central African Republic left UEAC and rejoined UDEAC.

The objectives of both UDEAC, UDE and UEAC are the same but there seem to be some differences in the approach adopted in each case. Only UDEAC seems to be still effectively functioning and as such a more detailed examination of the Treaty establishing it which was signed in Geneva, Switzerland on December 8, 1964 will be made.

#### 2. Objectives

The objectives of UDEAC are set out in the preamble to the Treaty. They include the extension of the national markets of member states through the removal of barriers to interregional trade, the adoption of a

* Reprinted with permission of A.W. Sijthoff & Nordhoff International. Footnotes omitted.

procedure of equitable distribution of industrialization projects and the co-ordination of development programmes for the various production sectors.

According to our classification of economic unions, it is clear that the founders of UDEAC intended the activities of the organization to extend beyond that envisaged by a free trade area. This is clear from the fact that the union is required to adopt, inter alia, a procedure for equitable distribution of industrialisation projects and to co-ordinate the development programmes for the various production sectors. These two functions are not usually included in the activities of a free trade area. The union cannot, however, be said to be a common market because the objectives are not comprehensive enough as required of a common market. In practice UDEAC can be said to be a customs union. The reasons for coming to this conclusion are based on the provisions of Articles 27 to 46 of the Treaty which are discussed more fully below.

### 3. Membership

Membership in the Union is open to "any independent and sovereign African State requesting admission". Despite the open policy regarding qualification for membership, it is not likely or feasible under the present arrangements that more members, particularly from the non-French speaking area of Africa would join. This is because the arrangements and facilities provided by the Union are in most cases just a continuation of the pre-independence arrangements in the area which may not interest non-French speaking countries. The original members are Cameroon, Central African Republic, Congo (Brazzaville), Gabon and Chad. A new State can only be admitted to membership on the unanimous consent of the members.

Taken together, the five countries have a total area of nearly 1,200,000 square miles, as large as the whole of Western Europe or India. Its total population as of 1963 was estimated at about ten million which was an average of about nine persons per square mile, ranging from 24 in Cameroon to five in Central African Republic and Gabon. The whole area is poorly provided with transport facilities. Railways are few and the road system both within the countries and between them is bad. These factors constitute a great obstacle in the way of close economic cooperation.

### 4. Organs

Unlike in the East African Community where supranational institutions have been established, with many decision-making and legislative powers delegated to many institutions, the position is different in UDEAC. Article 2 of UDEAC Treaty establishes three organs for the Union; viz. the Council of Heads of State, the Management Committee, and the General Secretariat.

#### *(I) Council of Heads of State*

This is made up of the Heads of State of the member States, or their representatives where they cannot personally attend a meeting of the Council. The Council is the principal organ of the Union and it is the only organ vested with decision-making power. Chairmanship of the Council is rotated annually among the Heads of State according to alphabetical order of the States unless otherwise agreed by the Council.

The powers of the Council include power to (a) determine and co-ordinate the customs and economic policy of member States; (b) supervise the Management Committee; and (c) take all important decisions, including the appointment of the Secretary–General of the Union, choice of the headquarters of the Union, drawing up of the budget and apportioning member's annual contributions, decide on tariff negotiations with non-member Countries and arbitrate in disputes arising between member States concerning the application of the Treaty. It is further provided that "decisions of the Council concerning economic, customs and fiscal legislation shall be taken by the delegation of the powers of the national legislative assemblies in accordance with the institutional rules of each State." This means that the Council is in fact incapable of taking any decision in this field that would be binding on member States without this provision which has in a way conferred on the Council a sort of legislative power of the national legislative assemblies.

* * *

### 7. Conclusion

UDEAC Treaty can be regarded as providing for the loosest form of economic co-operation. The major defect of the Treaty is the concentration of the most important decision-making powers in the Council of Heads of State. The usual and more progressive attitude nowadays is to delegate most of the major powers to organs lower than the Council of Heads of State, thereby creating a cadre of officials devoted to the cause of the institution. Not much progress towards further union can be made unless the present Treaty is drastically amended to give both legislative and executive powers to an institution falling below the Council of Heads of State.

#### *Note*

On UDEAC, see also Nowzad, Economic Integration in Central and West Africa, in Tharp, Regional International Organizations 201 (1971).

## C. ECONOMIC COMMUNITY OF WEST AFRICAN STATES (ECOWAS)

While there have been many attempts towards creating economic unions in West Africa, actual progress has been very slow. A West–African Customs Union created in 1959 failed because of the member states' inability to agree on the distribution of revenues collected on imports. A first step towards creating an economic community was made when twelve West–African states, including the two language groups of West Africa, adopted Articles of Association for the Establishment of an Economic Community in May of 1967. In time, this led to the signing, on March 28, 1975, in Lagos of the Treaty of the Economic Community of West Africa (ECOWAS) by fifteen countries in the West African region. Since then, however, very little further progress has been made.

#### *Note*

On ECOWAS, see also Akintan, The Law of International Economic Institutions in Africa 178–93 (1977); ECOWAS, Economic Community of West African

States (1981); Ezenwe, ECOWAS and the Economic Integration of West Africa (1983); Munu, The Future of ECOWAS (1989).

## D. SOUTHERN AFRICAN DEVELOPMENT COORDINATION CONFERENCE (SADCC)

The Southern African Development Coordination Conference (SADCC) was established in 1980 by nine countries opposed to the apartheid regime in South Africa and its economic domination of the region. According to a joint communique issued upon its founding by the member governments, its purposes are:

1. the reduction of economic dependence, particularly, but not only, on the Republic of South Africa;

2. the forging of links to create a genuine and equitable regional integration;

3. the mobilization of resources to promote the implementation of national, interstate and regional policies;

4. concerted action to secure international cooperation within the framework of our strategy for economic liberation.

Unlike many African regional organizations, SADCC has achieved many concrete benefits. It has begun a massive program of rehabilitating and upgrading the communications and transportation infrastructure of the member countries with most of the funding provided by the African Development Bank and Western nations. Its next major goal, although so far unachieved, is to insure an adequate food supply and distribution system for the region. See generally Meyns, The Southern African Development Coordination Conference (SADCC) and Regional Cooperation in Southern Africa, in African Regional Organizations 208–9 (Mazzeo ed. 1984).

The SADCC's principal focus on transportation and communications projects represents a novel initiative in regional cooperation among Third World countries. Decisions are taken essentially at the political level rather than by technocrats appointed at the administrative level. Given the basic agreement on common interests, decisions can be based on the principle of consensus.

The supreme body of SADCC is the Summit Meeting. It is "responsible for the general direction and control of the performance of the functions of SADCC and the achievement of its objectives." It meets at least once a year. The body charged with overall execution of SADCC policies is the Council of Ministers, which also meets at least once a year. It is responsible "for the overall policy of the SADCC, its general coordination, the supervision of its institutions and the supervision of the execution of its programmes." Commissions for sectoral areas and the Executive Secretary, established by the Summit Meeting, report to the Council. The Council of Ministers may, if the need arises, appoint *ad hoc* committees of ministers for particular program areas. The Council has a Standing Committee of Officials to assist it in its business, and may appoint Sub–Committees of officials for particular program areas, if the need arises. The Council also convenes the annual consultative conference with SADCC's international development coordination partners. Decisions taken by the Council of Ministers are subject to approval by the Summit Meeting. The chairmanship of the Summit Meeting and the Council of Ministers rotates among members.

The main technical bodies of SADCC are the commissions for sectoral areas. By the end of 1981, only one such commission, the Southern African Transport and Communications Commission (SATCC), based in Maputo, had been established. Not every area of cooperation SADCC has embarked upon may need such a commission. The Summit Meeting will decide, according to practical requirements, on the establishment of further commissions. SADCC Commissions are governed by separate conventions approved by the SADCC Council of Ministers and ratified by member countries. The supreme body of SATCC is the Council of Ministers; its executive body is the Coordinating Committee supported by a Technical Unit. SATCC's objectives are to contribute to the fulfillment of SADCC's four-point strategy by promoting rational and integrated utilization of the transport and communications systems existing in the region; by promoting new development programs and projects, and the modernization of existing systems; and by seeking participation of the independent states in the region.

The SADCC Secretariat is a purely administrative body established "for the general servicing of the SADCC and for liaison with its specialized institutions." As SADCC activities expand to cover more specific areas of cooperation, the Secretariat can ensure the smooth functioning of the organization by providing the Council of Ministers with administrative support.

### E. THE AFRICAN ECONOMIC COMMUNITY

On June 3, 1991, 51 African heads of state convened at Abuja, Nigeria, and signed the Treaty Establishing the African Economic Community, 30 I.L.M. 1241 (1991). The Treaty provides for establishment of a common market in 6 stages of variable lengths over a transitional period of 34 years. The Community's aims are quite ambitious and contemplate the eventual integration of all sectors and the adoption of a single African currency. The institutional framework is strongly inspired by that of the European Communities.

## SECTION 6. THE MID–EAST: ARAB ECONOMIC UNION

The Convention of Arab Economic Union Between Members of the League of Arab States was adopted by the Arab Economic Council, an organ of the League of Arab States, in 1957. By 1964, seven states had signed the Convention, but only five (Kuwait, Egypt, Iraq, Syria and Jordan) had ratified it. As among the latter five, the Convention became effective on April 30, 1964. The Arab Economic Union Council, a body created under the Convention, decided on August 13, 1964, to establish an Arab Common Market. This decision has been ratified by all members of the Union except Kuwait. Since then, little progress has been made.

### *Note*

On the Arab Common Market generally, see Diab, The Arab Common Market, 4 J.Com.Mar.St. 238 (1965). Also see McKeon, The Arab Maghreb

Union: Possibilities of Maghrebine Political and Economic Unity, and Enhanced Trade in the World Community, 10 Dick.J.Int'l L. 263 (1992).

*

# Index

**References are to Pages**

## A

# H

References are to Pages

## L



## M

## P

# S

References are to Pages



## T

## U

## V



## W



## Y



## Z



†

0-314-02272-4
90000
9 780314 022721